*International Directory of*

# COMPANY HISTORIES

# *International Directory of* COMPANY HISTORIES

## VOLUME 48

*Editor*
Tina Grant

St J
ST. JAMES PRESS®

THOMSON
GALE™

Detroit • New York • San Diego • San Francisco • Cleveland • New Haven, Conn. • Waterville, Maine • London • Munich

THOMSON
GALE

# International Directory of Company Histories, Volume 48

Tina Grant, Editor

**Project Editor**
Miranda H. Ferrara

**Editorial**
Erin Bealmear, Joann Cerrito, Jim Craddock, Stephen Cusack, Peter M. Gareffa, Kristin Hart, Melissa Hill, Margaret Mazurkiewicz, Carol A. Schwartz, Christine Tomassini, Michael J. Tyrkus

**Imaging and Multimedia**
Randy Bassett, Robert Duncan, Lezlie Light

**Manufacturing**
Rhonda Williams



*For more information contact*
St. James Press
27500 Drake Rd.
Farmington Hills, MI 48331-3535
Or you can visit our Internet site at http://www.gale.com/stjames



**LIBRARY OF CONGRESS CATALOG NUMBER 89-190943**

ISBN: 1-55862-466-X

**BRITISH LIBRARY CATALOGUING IN PUBLICATION DATA**

International directory of company histories. Vol. 48
I. Tina Grant
33.87409

Printed in the United States of America
10 9 8 7 6 5 4 3 2 1

# CONTENTS

Preface . . . . . . . . . . . . . . . . . . . . . . . . . . . . . . . . page vii
List of Abbreviations . . . . . . . . . . . . . . . . . . . . . . . . . . . ix

## Company Histories

Aisin Seiki Co., Ltd. . . . . . . . . . . . . . . . . . . . 3
American Financial Group Inc. . . . . . . . . . . . 6
American Lung Association . . . . . . . . . . . . 11
AmSouth Bancorporation . . . . . . . . . . . . . 15
Amstrad plc . . . . . . . . . . . . . . . . . . . . . . . 19
AmSurg Corporation . . . . . . . . . . . . . . . . 24
Applied Films Corporation . . . . . . . . . . . . 28
Ariens Company . . . . . . . . . . . . . . . . . . . 32
Arla Foods amba . . . . . . . . . . . . . . . . . . . 35
Asahi Glass Company, Ltd. . . . . . . . . . . . . 39
Associated Milk Producers, Inc. . . . . . . . . . . 43
Banco Bilbao Vizcaya Argentaria S.A. . . . . . 47
Blonder Tongue Laboratories, Inc. . . . . . . . . 52
Blount International, Inc. . . . . . . . . . . . . . 56
Bon Appetit Holding AG . . . . . . . . . . . . . 61
Boston Market Corporation . . . . . . . . . . . . 64
Brannock Device Company . . . . . . . . . . . . 68
Buck Knives Inc. . . . . . . . . . . . . . . . . . . 71
Cadence Design Systems, Inc. . . . . . . . . . . 75
CAE USA Inc. . . . . . . . . . . . . . . . . . . . . 80
Cambridge SoundWorks, Inc. . . . . . . . . . . 83
Candela Corporation . . . . . . . . . . . . . . . . 87
Cirrus Logic, Inc. . . . . . . . . . . . . . . . . . . 90
Clearly Canadian Beverage Corporation . . . . 94
Collectors Universe, Inc. . . . . . . . . . . . . . . 98
Colorado MEDtech, Inc. . . . . . . . . . . . . . 101
Compagnie des Alpes . . . . . . . . . . . . . . . 106
Consolidated Freightways Corporation . . . . . 109
Coop Schweiz Genossenschaftsverband . . . . 114
Corticeira Amorim, Sociedade Gestora de Participaço es Sociais, S.A. . . . . . . . . . 117
Creo Inc. . . . . . . . . . . . . . . . . . . . . . . . 121
Cypress Semiconductor Corporation . . . . . . 125
Deutsche Telekom AG . . . . . . . . . . . . . . 130
Dewey Ballantine LLP . . . . . . . . . . . . . . . 136
The Eastern Company . . . . . . . . . . . . . . . 140
Educational Broadcasting Corporation . . . . . 144
Elsinore Corporation . . . . . . . . . . . . . . . . 148
Esselte Leitz GmbH & Co. KG . . . . . . . . . 152
Exelon Corporation . . . . . . . . . . . . . . . . . 156
Expand SA . . . . . . . . . . . . . . . . . . . . . . 164
Fairchild Dornier GmbH . . . . . . . . . . . . . . 167
Farmland Industries, Inc. . . . . . . . . . . . . . . 172
First Tennessee National Corporation . . . . . 176
Fuji Electric Co., Ltd. . . . . . . . . . . . . . . . . 180
geobra Brandstätter GmbH & Co. KG . . . . . 183
GlobalSantaFe Corporation . . . . . . . . . . . . 187
GoodTimes Entertainment Ltd. . . . . . . . . . . 193
Groupe Partouche SA . . . . . . . . . . . . . . . 196
Grupo Aeropuerto del Sureste, S.A. de C.V. . 200
HDR Inc. . . . . . . . . . . . . . . . . . . . . . . . 203
Hugo Boss AG . . . . . . . . . . . . . . . . . . . 206
Indian Oil Corporation Ltd. . . . . . . . . . . . . 210
Infinity Broadcasting Corporation . . . . . . . . 214
International Lease Finance Corporation . . . 218
Ipsos SA . . . . . . . . . . . . . . . . . . . . . . . 221
The Island ECN, Inc. . . . . . . . . . . . . . . . . 225
J. D'Addario & Company, Inc. . . . . . . . . . . 230
Jackson Hewitt, Inc. . . . . . . . . . . . . . . . . 234
John W. Danforth Company . . . . . . . . . . . 237
Kettle Foods Inc. . . . . . . . . . . . . . . . . . . 240
Kimball International, Inc. . . . . . . . . . . . . . 243
Kyowa Hakko Kogyo Co., Ltd. . . . . . . . . . 248
L-3 Communications Holdings, Inc. . . . . . . 251
LabOne, Inc. . . . . . . . . . . . . . . . . . . . . . 254
Lauda Air Luftfahrt AG . . . . . . . . . . . . . . 258
The Legal Aid Society . . . . . . . . . . . . . . . 261
Leggett & Platt, Inc. . . . . . . . . . . . . . . . . 265

LoJack Corporation . . . . . . . . . . . . . . . . . 269
Magellan Aerospace Corporation . . . . . . . . 274
Maus Frères SA . . . . . . . . . . . . . . . . . . . 277
McCarthy Building Companies, Inc. . . . . . . 280
The Men's Wearhouse, Inc. . . . . . . . . . . . . 283
Mouvement des Caisses Desjardins . . . . . . . 288
Nikon Corporation . . . . . . . . . . . . . . . . . . 292
Nordson Corporation . . . . . . . . . . . . . . . . 296
JSC MMC Norilsk Nickel . . . . . . . . . . . . . 300
Northeast Utilities . . . . . . . . . . . . . . . . . . 303
Option Care Inc. . . . . . . . . . . . . . . . . . . . 307
Pan-American Life Insurance Company . . . . 311
Pierre & Vacances SA . . . . . . . . . . . . . . . 314
The Port Authority of New York and New Jersey . . . . . . . . . . . . . . . . . . . 317
Praxair, Inc. . . . . . . . . . . . . . . . . . . . . . . 321
Prudential plc . . . . . . . . . . . . . . . . . . . . . 325
Pumpkin Masters, Inc. . . . . . . . . . . . . . . . 330
PW Eagle, Inc. . . . . . . . . . . . . . . . . . . . . 333
Quality Chekd Dairies, Inc. . . . . . . . . . . . . 337
Riverwood International Corporation . . . . . . 340
Roularta Media Group NV . . . . . . . . . . . . 345
Sabaté Diosos SA . . . . . . . . . . . . . . . . . . 348
St. Louis Music, Inc. . . . . . . . . . . . . . . . . 351
Segway LLC . . . . . . . . . . . . . . . . . . . . . . 355
SLI, Inc. . . . . . . . . . . . . . . . . . . . . . . . . 358
Snow Brand Milk Products Company, Ltd. . . 362
Solectron Corporation . . . . . . . . . . . . . . . . 366
Standard Chartered plc . . . . . . . . . . . . . . . 371
OAO Surgutneftegaz . . . . . . . . . . . . . . . . 375
Swiss International Air Lines Ltd. . . . . . . . . 379
TA Triumph-Adler AG . . . . . . . . . . . . . . . 382
Taylor Guitars . . . . . . . . . . . . . . . . . . . . . 386
The Terlato Wine Group . . . . . . . . . . . . . . 390
Terumo Corporation . . . . . . . . . . . . . . . . . 393
Tiscali SpA . . . . . . . . . . . . . . . . . . . . . . . 396
Transiciel SA . . . . . . . . . . . . . . . . . . . . . 400
Universal Corporation . . . . . . . . . . . . . . . . 403
Varian, Inc. . . . . . . . . . . . . . . . . . . . . . . 407
VICORP Restaurants, Inc. . . . . . . . . . . . . . 412
AO VimpelCom . . . . . . . . . . . . . . . . . . . 416
Wella AG . . . . . . . . . . . . . . . . . . . . . . . 420
Westpac Banking Corporation . . . . . . . . . . 424
White Mountains Insurance Group, Ltd. . . . . 428
Whittaker Corporation . . . . . . . . . . . . . . . 432
OJSC Wimm-Bill-Dann Foods . . . . . . . . . . 436
WPP Group plc . . . . . . . . . . . . . . . . . . . . 440
X-Rite, Inc. . . . . . . . . . . . . . . . . . . . . . . 443
ZF Friedrichshafen AG . . . . . . . . . . . . . . . 447

Index to Companies . . . . . . . . . . . . . . . . . . . . . . . . 453
Index to Industries . . . . . . . . . . . . . . . . . . . . . . . . 647
Geographic Index . . . . . . . . . . . . . . . . . . . . . . . . 683
Notes on Contributors . . . . . . . . . . . . . . . . . . . . . . 715

# PREFACE

The St. James Press series *The International Directory of Company Histories (IDCH)* is intended for reference use by students, business people, librarians, historians, economists, investors, job candidates, and others who seek to learn more about the historical development of the world's most important companies. To date, *IDCH* has covered over 5,625 companies in 48 volumes.

## Inclusion Criteria

Most companies chosen for inclusion in *IDCH* have achieved a minimum of US$25 million in annual sales and are leading influences in their industries or geographical locations. Companies may be publicly held, private, or nonprofit. State-owned companies that are important in their industries and that may operate much like public or private companies also are included. Wholly owned subsidiaries and divisions are profiled if they meet the requirements for inclusion. Entries on companies that have had major changes since they were last profiled may be selected for updating.

The *IDCH* series highlights 10% private and nonprofit companies, and features updated entries on approximately 45 companies per volume.

## Entry Format

Each entry begins with the company's legal name, the address of its headquarters, its telephone, toll-free, and fax numbers, and its web site. A statement of public, private, state, or parent ownership follows. A company with a legal name in both English and the language of its headquarters country is listed by the English name, with the native-language name in parentheses.

The company's founding or earliest incorporation date, the number of employees, and the most recent available sales figures follow. Sales figures are given in local currencies with equivalents in U.S. dollars. For some private companies, sales figures are estimates and indicated by the abbreviation *est.* The entry lists the exchanges on which a company's stock is traded and its ticker symbol, as well as the company's NAIC codes.

Entries generally contain a *Company Perspectives* box which provides a short summary of the company's mission, goals, and ideals, a *Key Dates* box highlighting milestones in the company's history, lists of *Principal Subsidiaries, Principal Divisions, Principal Operating Units, Principal Competitors,* and articles for *Further Reading.*

American spelling is used throughout *IDCH,* and the word ''billion'' is used in its U.S. sense of one thousand million.

## Sources

Entries have been compiled from publicly accessible sources both in print and on the Internet such as general and academic periodicals, books, annual reports, and material supplied by the companies themselves.

## Cumulative Indexes

*IDCH* contains three indexes: the **Index to Companies**, which provides an alphabetical index to companies discussed in the text as well as to companies profiled, the **Index to Industries**, which allows researchers to locate companies by their principal industry, and the **Geographic Index**, which lists companies alphabetically by the country of their headquarters. The indexes are cumulative and specific instructions for using them are found immediately preceding each index.

## Suggestions Welcome

Comments and suggestions from users of *IDCH* on any aspect of the product as well as suggestions for companies to be included or updated are cordially invited. Please write:

The Editor
*International Directory of Company Histories*
St. James Press
27500 Drake Rd.
Farmington Hills, Michigan 48331-3535

## *ABBREVIATIONS FOR FORMS OF COMPANY INCORPORATION*

| | |
|---|---|
| A.B. | Aktiebolaget (Sweden) |
| A.G. | Aktiengesellschaft (Germany, Switzerland) |
| A.S. | Aksjeselskap (Denmark, Norway) |
| A.S. | Atieselskab (Denmark) |
| A.Ş. | Anomin Şirket (Turkey) |
| B.V. | Besloten Vennootschap met beperkte, Aansprakelijkheid (The Netherlands) |
| Co. | Company (United Kingdom, United States) |
| Corp. | Corporation (United States) |
| G.I.E. | Groupement d'Intérêt Economique (France) |
| GmbH | Gesellschaft mit beschränkter Haftung (Germany) |
| H.B. | Handelsbolaget (Sweden) |
| Inc. | Incorporated (United States) |
| KGaA | Kommanditgesellschaft auf Aktien (Germany) |
| K.K. | Kabushiki Kaisha (Japan) |
| LLC | Limited Liability Company (Middle East) |
| Ltd. | Limited (Canada, Japan, United Kingdom, United States) |
| N.V. | Naamloze Vennootschap (The Netherlands) |
| OY | Osakeyhtiöt (Finland) |
| OAO | Otkrytoe Aktsionernoe Obshchestve (Russia) |
| OOO | Obshchestvo s Ogranichennoi Otvetstvennostiu (Russia) |
| PLC | Public Limited Company (United Kingdom) |
| PTY. | Proprietary (Australia, Hong Kong, South Africa) |
| S.A. | Société Anonyme (Belgium, France, Switzerland) |
| SpA | Società per Azioni (Italy) |
| ZAO | Zakrytoe Aktsionernoe Obshchestve (Russia) |

## *ABBREVIATIONS FOR CURRENCY*

| | |
|---|---|
| $ | United States dollar |
| £ | United Kingdom pound |
| ¥ | Japanese yen |
| A$ | Australian dollar |
| AED | United Arab Emirates dirham |
| B | Thai baht |
| B | Venezuelan bolivar |
| BFr | Belgian franc |
| C$ | Canadian dollar |
| CHF | Switzerland franc |
| COL | Colombian peso |
| Cr | Brazilian cruzado |
| CZK | Czech Republic koruny |
| DA | Algerian dinar |
| Dfl | Netherlands florin |
| DKr | Danish krone |
| DM | German mark |
| E£ | Egyptian pound |
| Esc | Portuguese escudo |
| EUR | Euro dollars |
| FFr | French franc |
| Fmk | Finnish markka |
| GRD | Greek drachma |
| HK$ | Hong Kong dollar |
| HUF | Hungarian forint |
| IR£ | Irish pound |
| K | Zambian kwacha |
| KD | Kuwaiti dinar |
| L | Italian lira |
| LuxFr | Luxembourgian franc |
| M$ | Malaysian ringgit |
| N | Nigerian naira |
| Nfl | Netherlands florin |
| NIS | Israeli new shekel |
| NKr | Norwegian krone |
| NT$ | Taiwanese dollar |
| NZ$ | New Zealand dollar |
| P | Philippine peso |
| PLN | Polish zloty |
| PkR | Pakistan Rupee |
| Pta | Spanish peseta |
| R | Brazilian real |
| R | South African rand |
| RMB | Chinese renminbi |
| RO | Omani rial |
| Rp | Indonesian rupiah |
| Rs | Indian rupee |
| Ru | Russian ruble |
| S$ | Singapore dollar |
| Sch | Austrian schilling |
| SFr | Swiss franc |
| SKr | Swedish krona |
| SRls | Saudi Arabian riyal |
| TD | Tunisian dinar |
| W | Korean won |

*International Directory of*

# COMPANY HISTORIES

# AISIN

## Aisin Seiki Co., Ltd.

**2-1, Asahi-machi**
**Kariya, Aichi 448-8560**
**Japan**
**Telephone: (81) 566-24-8239**
**Fax: (81) 566-24-8003**
**Web site: http://www.aisin.co.jp**

*Public Company*
*Incorporated:* 1943 as Tokai Aircraft Co., Ltd.
*Employees:* 36,434
*Sales:* ¥1,128.5 billion ($8.93 billion) (2001)
*Stock Exchanges:* Tokyo
*NAIC:* 336111 Automobile Manufacturing; 336322 Other Motor Vehicle Electrical and Electronic Equipment Manufacturing; 33633 Motor Vehicle Steering and Suspension Components (Except Spring) Manufacturing; 336340 Motor Vehicle Brake System Manufacturing; 336350 Motor Vehicle Transmission and Power Train Parts Manufacturing; 336399 All Other Motor Vehicle Parts Manufacturing

Aisin Seiki Co., Ltd. is a leading international manufacturer and supplier of engine-related products, drivetrain-related products, brake and chassis-related products, and various other automotive parts. The company also manufacturers environmentally friendly vacuum pumps and industrial cooling systems. Through its Creative Lifestyle Products division, Aisin sells beds, furniture, fabrics, medical instruments, gas engine drive heat-pump air conditioners, and housing equipment such as microcomputer controlled shutters and high-tech toilet seats. Overall, the company has over 100 subsidiaries that operate in North and South America, Europe, Asia, and Oceania. Aisin's automotive segment accounts for nearly 95 percent of company sales, while its creative lifestyle and energy and environment products make up the rest. Toyota owns approximately 27 percent of the firm.

### *1940s Origins*

In 1943, Aisin was founded as Tokai Aircraft Company by Kiichiro Toyoda, the founder of the Toyota Group. Tokai Aircraft was founded to manufacture engine parts for World War II aircraft. In 1945, at the close of the war, Tokai Aircraft switched its production to sewing machines and automotive parts, both products that had been in short supply during the war. In 1949, Tokai Aircraft Company changed its name to Aichi Kogyo Company. This company then merged with Shinkawa Kogyo Co. Ltd. in 1965 to form Aisin Seiki Co. Ltd.

### *International Growth Begins: 1969*

In the 1950s and 1960s, Aisin's operations were confined to Japan. As part of the Toyota Group, Aisin grew steadily, supplying parts to its parent automotive company and continuing to produce sewing machines. During the year 1969 and throughout the 1970s, however, the company pursued aggressive international growth. In 1969, Aisin reached a technical agreement for power-steering gears with Zahnradfabrik Friedrichshafen of West Germany. Aisin-Warner Limited was also established as a joint venture in 1969.

Aisin U.S.A. was formed in 1970, and in 1971 Aisin Europe was established in Belgium. A technical agreement for bumper shock-isolators was concluded with Menasco Manufacturing Company in the United States in 1972. The formation of Aisin (U.K.) Ltd. and Aisin (Australia) Pty. Ltd. also took place in 1972. The Liberty Mexicana subsidiary was formed in Mexico in 1973, and Aisin do Brasil was established in Brazil in 1974. The year 1977 saw the formation of Aisin Asia in Singapore, and in 1978 Aisin Deutschland was established in West Germany. Finally, in 1979, the Elite Sewing Machine Manufacturing Company was established in Taiwan as a joint venture.

Aisin U.S.A. was established to import aftermarket auto parts for imported cars—mostly Toyotas—in the United States and also to import specially prepared aftermarket parts for U.S.-made automobiles. In 1990, Aisin U.S.A. imported twice as many parts for American cars as for imported cars. At the same

### Company Perspectives:

*At the core of diversified operations at Aisin Group, Aisin Seiki strives for a creative evolution of new businesses for a global company. Capitalizing on its established excellence in technological development, quality assurance, and manufacturing, Aisin Seiki is perpetually evolving and expanding into new business areas. With dynamism, innovation, and creativity, which are also at the core of the Aisin management philosophy, we strive to grow as a global company, a company that interconnects with various communities and is actively involved in environmental preservation.*

time, Aisin Seiki Company supplied a wide range of products worldwide through its network of 14 overseas subsidiaries and its branches in North America, Europe, Southeast Asia, and throughout the Pacific. In 1989, only five percent of Aisin's sales had been to export markets.

After World War II, the Japanese economy grew steadily. The increase in individual consumption brought about a sharp rise in domestic demand and business expanded. Aisin answered the increased demand for consumer production and worked consistently to improve efficiency in its factories, increase sales, and cut costs through rationalization.

Managers of the automotive sector worked during the late 1980s to increase sales of automotive-body products such as seat components, sun-roofs, and electronic control equipment for automatic transmissions. This increase contributed to an almost ten percent sales growth in 1989. At the time, automotive-body products were the largest single group of products Aisin Seiki offered, comprising about 25 percent of sales.

By 1990, Aisin's home and industrial and the new business sectors were still very small in scale but growing rapidly. Through expanded sales of gas heat-pump air conditioners and beds, sales increased 14.2 percent in 1989. Into the 1990s, intensive research and development continued in new products such as cryocoolers, Stirling engines, and a supplemental drive unit for artificial human hearts.

### *Continued Growth: Late 1980s–90s*

During 1988, Aisin made efforts to strengthen project development in the United States by separating the manufacturing division from Aisin U.S.A. and creating a new subsidiary, Aisin U.S.A. Manufacturing Company. Aisin America, Inc. was also established to control jointly both the manufacturing and sales divisions. Then, in 1992, Aisin U.S.A. was merged with Aisin America to form Aisin World Corp. of America.

During the majority of the 1990s, Aisin continued its growth strategy and expanded internationally as it had during the previous decade. Subsidiaries were created in Indonesia and Mexico, along with a brake system research and development center. Disaster struck in 1997, however, when a fire destroyed an Aisin brake factory in Japan. The plant supplied Toyota with

### Key Dates:

**1943:** Kiichiro Toyoda establishes the Tokai Aircraft Company.
**1945:** Tokai begins manufacturing sewing machines and automotive parts.
**1949:** The firm changes its name to Aichi Kogyo Company.
**1965:** The company merges with Shinkawa Kogyo Co. Ltd. to form Aisin Seiki Co. Ltd.
**1970:** Aisin U.S.A. is formed.
**1979:** The Elite Sewing Machine Manufacturing Company is established in Taiwan.
**1988:** Aisin U.S.A. Manufacturing Inc. and Aisin America Inc. are created to strengthen U.S. operations.
**1992:** Aisin America merges with Aisin U.S.A. to create Aisin World Corp. of America.
**1997:** A fire destroys an Aisin brake plant in Japan.
**2001:** Advics Co. Ltd. is established to oversee worldwide brake systems sales.

almost 90 percent of its major brake parts that were used in nearly all Toyota models. Overall, the fire cost Toyota $195 million and forced the car maker to shut its 18 assembly factories in Japan for almost a week due to lack of parts.

The fire also threatened Aisin's supplier relationship with Toyota. In the case of Aisin, Toyota had been going against its policy of double-sourcing materials, in which the firm typically chose two suppliers to split orders evenly. A Toyota spokesman commented in a March 1997 *Automotive News* article, "Do we really source from them because of economic or technical features, or are there other reasons, like relying on our long history?" In the long run, the fire did not change the company's alliance and Aisin proved its commitment to safety and quality when later that year, its plants became QS9000 and ISO9001 certified.

Just after the fire, the economy in Japan began to falter, decreasing demand in Aisin's home country. Domestic sales in 1999 fell to ¥747 billion, down from ¥766 billion in 1998. Aisin responded by cutting costs, restructuring various operations, and expanding into growth markets. Domestic sales rebounded in 2000, growing to ¥847 billion, and then again in 2001 to ¥904 billion. That year, total net sales climbed to ¥1,128 billion.

Aisin proved its relationship with Toyota stood strong when in 2001 it formed a partnership with Toyota Motor Corp. along with Sumitomo Electric Industries Ltd. and Denso Corp. to form Advics Co. Ltd. The new company was positioned to become the second-largest supplier of brake systems in the industry behind Robert Bosch GmbH, with projected global sales reaching $2 billion by 2005. Toyota, of course, was the new firm's largest customer.

Aisin management's long-term strategy included strengthening its auto parts business along with finding new opportunities for its creative lifestyle segment. The company also focused on increasing its production efforts in North America, Europe, and Asia. Looking to globalization and technological developments as key to its future success, Aisin appeared to be well on track to maintain its strong position in the automotive sector.

### *Principal Subsidiaries*

Aisin Holdings of America Inc. (U.S.); Aisin Personnel Service Inc. (U.S.); Aisin World Corp. of America (U.S.); Aisin U.S.A. Mfg. Inc.; Aisin Electronics Inc. (U.S.); Aisin Drivetrain Inc. (U.S.); Aisin Automotive Casting Inc. (U.S.); IMRA America Inc. (U.S.); Intat Precision Inc. (U.S.); ATTC Manufacturing Inc. (U.S.); AW North Carolina Inc. (U.S.); Liberty Mexicana S.A. de C.V.; Aisin do Brasil Ltda.; Aisin Europe S.A. (Belgium); Aisin Asia Pte. Ltd. (Singapore); Siam Aisin Co. Ltd. (Thailand); Aisin Hongda Automobile Parts Co. Ltd. (China); Elite Sewing Machine Mfg. Co. Ltd. (Taiwan); Aisin Takaoka Co. Ltd.; Aisin Chemical Co. Ltd.; Aisin AW Co. Ltd.; Aisin Development Co. Ltd. Advics Co. Ltd.

### *Principal Competitors*

Delphi Automotive Systems Corporation; Continental AG; TRW Inc.; Robert Bosch GmbH.

### *Further Reading*

"Japan's Aisin Forms Autoparts Joint Venture in India," *AsiaPulse News*, July 19, 1999.

"Japan's Aisin Seiki, Hitachi Air Tie Up in Gas Heat Pump Equipment," *AsiaPulse News*, October 4, 2000.

Treece, James B., "Just too Much Single-Sourcing Spurs Toyota Purchasing Review," *Automotive News*, March 3, 1997, p. 3.

Wilson, Amy, "Japan Venture's Goal: Big 3 Brake Systems," *Automotive News*, March 18, 2002, p. 16.

—Joan Harpham
—update: Christina M. Stansell

# American Financial Group Inc.

**One East Fourth Street**
**Cincinnati, Ohio 45202**
**U.S.A.**
**Telephone: (513) 579-6739**
**Fax: (513) 579-2113**

*Public Company*
*Incorporated:* 1955 as Henthy Realty Company
*Employees:* 7,300
*Total Assets:* $3.9 billion (2001)
*Stock Exchanges:* New York
*Ticker Symbol:* AFG
*NAIC:* 524113 Direct Life Insurance Carriers; 524126 Direct Property and Casualty Insurance Carriers

American Financial Group Inc. (AFG)—formerly known as American Financial Corp.—is a diversified holding company with subsidiaries that offer private passenger automobile and specialty property and casualty insurance as well as retirement annuities, life, and supplemental health and long-term care insurance products. AFG operates with three main insurance segments—Personal, Specialty, and Annuity and Life—and has interests in United States, Puerto Rico, Canada, Mexico, Europe, and Asia. The Lindner family owns nearly 45 percent of AFG.

## *Origins*

AFG's principal founders were chairman and president, Carl H. Lindner, and his younger brothers, Robert D. and Richard E. Lindner. The Lindner brothers, born and raised in Ohio, started in business without the benefit of formal education, business connections, or family money. Carl Henry Lindner, born April 22, 1919, and his brothers left high school before graduating to help with the family's small dairy business. The business finally succeeded in the 1940s under Carl Lindner's leadership, with an entrepreneurial concept credited to their father. The Lindners' United Dairy Farmers outlets, stores where purchasers could save on the cost of milk by direct purchase instead of home delivery, were spread through the Cincinnati area. The success of the outlets spurred the Lindner brothers into further business ventures.

On November 15, 1955, Henthy Realty Company was incorporated in Ohio by the Lindners. By 1959, the company owned three small savings and loan associations in Ohio and recorded assets of $17.7 million.

## *AFC Expands into Insurance: 1960s*

In September 1960, the company adopted the name, American Financial Corporation (AFC). Through its subsidiaries, this financial holding company owned office buildings in Cincinnati, Norwood, and Loveland, Ohio; leased motor vehicles; and developed commercial properties.

In 1962, American Financial Corporation obtained property and casualty insurance business with the acquisition of Dempsey & Siders Agency. In 1963, AFC undertook life insurance business by acquiring United Liberty Life. The same year AFC acquired 98 percent of the outstanding shares of Athens National Bank in Ohio. The stock purchase totaled $2.3 million in cash and assumption of seller debt.

During the 1960s, American Financial Corporation acquired large stock positions in a number of companies, including the Insurance Company of North America, Chubb & Son, and Ohio Casualty. From 1968 to 1972, AFC pursued several companies, acquiring or gaining control of 16 concerns and their subsidiaries, seven of which were insurance related.

AFC remained active in the financial arena, and in 1966 sold its interest in Athens National Bank before acquiring a 92 percent share of The Provident Bank in Ohio. According to *Barron's*, July 4,1988, the management of Provident Bank resisted the takeover bid. AFC triumphed and its assets increased to nearly $350 million.

In February 1971, AFC pursued a new venture—*The Cincinnati Enquirer*. AFC acquired 95.5 percent of the daily newspaper, beating out such competitors as the Knight-Ridder chain and Omaha investor Warren Buffett. At the close of 1971,

**Company Perspectives:**

*American Financial Group strives to deliver financial solutions that fulfill today's needs and tomorrow's dreams—to be a trusted partner delivering long-term value to our customers, employees, and investors. Our purpose is to enable individuals and businesses to manage financial risk. We provide insurance products and services tailored to meet the specific and ever-changing financial risk exposures facing our customers. We build value for our investors through the strength of our customers' satisfaction and by consistently producing superior operating results.*

AFC's stockholders numbered more than 14,000 and its assets stood at over $538 million.

### *National General Corporation Is Acquired: 1974*

By late 1973, AFC had amassed approximately 96 percent of common stock and 85 percent of the warrants and had gained financial control of a West Coast conglomerate, National General Corporation. The merger was completed in March 1974.

National General Corporation, incorporated in Delaware in 1952 as National Theatres, Inc., was involved in the operation of motion picture theaters in the United States and abroad, motion picture production and distribution, and cable and closed-circuit television. However, 70 percent of National General Corporation's (NGC) assets were in insurance and publishing.

NGC's holdings included the publishers Grosset & Dunlap, Inc., and Bantam Books, Inc.; the Great American Life Insurance Company of East Orange, New Jersey, procured in 1968; and its parent sponsor, the Great American Insurance Company.

Great American Life Insurance Company (GALIC) was originally located in East Orange, New Jersey. The company was sponsored by Great American Insurance Company, and initial resources were generated by the purchase of 100,000 shares of common stock. GALIC was incorporated and licensed in 1959. In 1962, GALIC sold an additional 100,000 shares of common stock to its sponsor for nearly $1.3 million. At that time, GALIC, licensed in all states except Kansas and New York, wrote nonparticipating life, accident, and health insurance.

The Great American Insurance Company (GAIC) was incorporated in New York on March 6, 1872, and began business in New York City the following day with $1 million in authorized capital. The company remained at this status until 1903, when it received additional capital of $500,000 and was paid surplus funds of over $913,000. Eight years later, in May 1911, The Rochester German Insurance Company, located in Rochester, New York, merged with GAIC.

Starting in 1918, Great American Insurance Company began steadily to increase its capital from the $2 million gained in 1911 from the merger. GAIC created a holding company in 1929 that was dissolved in 1953. The increases in capital were facilitated by the trading of shares in a number of other insurance companies, including the Detroit Fire & Marine Insurance Company, the American Alliance Company, Great American Indemnity Company, and the Rochester American Insurance Company.

In May 1948, GAIC's corporate structure was simplified. Its wholly-owned subsidiary, County Fire Insurance Company, in Philadelphia, was dissolved, the outstanding capital stock canceled, and its assets and liabilities transferred to GAIC. In 1953, the group was simplified further by dissolution of the affiliate, Great American Corporation, and a merger with the affiliate, American Alliance Insurance Company.

First Insurance Company of Hawaii was acquired by GAIC in 1963. Another acquisition, that of Constellation Insurance Company, renamed in 1975 Constellation Reinsurance Company, was completed two years later. By 1966, GAIC's assets had grown to $15.6 million.

In 1967, control of Great American Insurance Company was taken by the newly formed Great American Holding Corporation. The following year this holding company became a subsidiary of National General Corporation and then was merged with that organization less than four months later. The administrative offices of Great American Insurance Company were moved to the National General Corporation's headquarters in Los Angeles, California, in 1970.

The offices were again moved after the merger of National General Corporation and American Financial Corporation, this time to Cincinnati, Ohio, AFC's headquarters. AFC had already gained control of GAIC in December 1971. AFC's 1974 merger with National General Corporation gave AFC direct ownership and all outstanding capital stock in GAIC, whose assets totaled $566 million. According to *Barron's*, July 4, 1988, "What attracted [Carl] Lindner to the company [National General Corporation] was its giant property and casualty operation, Great American Insurance Co." With the NGC merger and the acquisition of Great American Insurance Company and GALIC, AFC's assets escalated to over $2 billion. The merger also launched American Financial Corporation as one of the country's major international insurance concerns.

Great American Insurance Company and its subsidiaries were writing practically all forms of insurance in every state and territory, as well as in Canada and in other countries. There were approximately 5,600 agents and brokers representing the company worldwide, with regional offices in 18 U.S. cities.

While Carl Lindner remained in active control as chairman, GAIC administration was directed by Stanley R. Zax, president since December 1973. GALIC was led by Jovite LaBonte, who had been appointed president and director in 1972.

Under LaBonte's direction, GALIC stopped writing group life coverage and individual and group accident and health policies in 1974. The company's business—produced through managing general agents, agents, and brokers—included nonparticipating ordinary life and term contracts. In 1975, GALIC introduced a new product line—tax sheltered and single-premium annuity contracts. By 1980 these contracts produced 97 percent of all premium income.

**Key Dates:**

**1955:** The Lindner brothers establish the Henthy Realty Company.
**1960:** The company adopts the name American Financial Corporation (AFC).
**1962:** AFC acquires Dempsey & Siders Agency, a property and casualty business.
**1963:** The firm branches out into life insurance with the purchase of United Liberty Life.
**1971:** AFC gains control of The Great American Insurance Company (GAIC).
**1974:** National General Corporation is acquired.
**1976:** All AFC insurance operations are consolidated under GAIC.
**1984:** AFC acquires a 49.9 percent interest in the MIC group.
**1989:** The firm launches a new group of specialty product lines.
**1995:** American Premier Underwriters merges with AFC, creating a new company entitled American Financial Group Inc.
**1999:** Worldwide Insurance Co. is purchased.
**2001:** GAIC sells its Japanese division.

## *Financial Problems Bring Change: Mid- to Late 1970s*

Although the property and casualty insurance industry experienced some difficulty at the time of NGC's merger, AFC had now moved decisively into the insurance industry. *The National Underwriter*, October 24, 1975, reported that, according to Charles Keating, who was AFC's executive vice-president from 1973 to 1977, "the management of AF[C] has been intentionally evolving toward the insurance business ever since it was formed." An estimated 60 percent of AFC's revenues in 1975 were being generated from property and casualty insurance, mostly from Great American Insurance Company.

The stock market collapse in 1973–74 lessened the values AFC was able to realize from the sale of Bantam Books, Grosset & Dunlap, and the various theater units gained from the NGC merger. Inflation caused insurance claims and expenses to soar above premium income. Housing starts plummeted during the 1974–75 recession. The merger was costly—more than $500 million in cash, security, and debt assumption.

By early 1975, American Financial Corporation was facing a serious crisis—the maturity of an $85 million debt issue without cash or bank lines for payment. This situation existed in spite of the fact that, at the close of 1974, GAIC's new premiums written exceeded $387 million and consolidated policyholders' surplus funds totaled $112 million. To cover the debt, AFC sold several small insurance operations. American Empire Insurance Company and Constellation Reinsurance Company were sold to and absorbed by Great American Insurance Company. AFC also sold *The Cincinnati Enquirer*, the price in excess of $50 million, providing a $10.6 million profit for AFC. In addition, GAIC increased premiums for commercial lines and shortened auto policies to six months. AFC was soon back on solid ground.

AFC's insurance divisions underwent considerable structural change in 1976. AFC sold its 68 percent interest in United Liberty Life Insurance Company to GAIC for consolidation purposes. Great American Insurance Company in Cincinnati was incorporated as the result of the merger of Great American Insurance Company in New York with American Continental Insurance Company of Ohio. The latter had been incorporated in October 1942 as Manufacturers & Merchants Indemnity Company and had undergone several name changes, from Selective Insurance Company in 1956 to American Continental Insurance Company in 1972. In October 1976, all AFC's insurance operations were consolidated under Great American Insurance Company.

At the close of 1976, GAIC had 4,320 employees and had written $578 million in net premiums. Its subsidiaries included Agricultural Insurance Company, American National Fire Insurance Company, Great American Life Insurance Company, Republic Indemnity Company of America, American Alliance Insurance Company, Fidelity National Life Insurance Company, American Insurance Agency, American-Financial Insurance Group, and the Constellation Reinsurance Company. In 1977, the latter was reorganized and sold.

From 1977 to 1979, AFC and GAIC pursued a number of stock and acquisition interests. In 1977, AFC purchased the Stonewall Insurance Company, which included two property-casualty insurance and two life-health subsidiary companies. GAIC purchased the outstanding stock in these enterprises but later sold the two life insurance divisions.

In 1978, GAIC acquired K.C.C. Holding Company and purchased all outstanding stock in American Continental Insurance Company and its two affiliate insurance companies. In late 1979, the outstanding capital stock was acquired in Transport Management Company in Dallas.

Ronald F. Walker, GAIC's executive vice-president since 1972, took over its presidency in 1980. During Walker's first year in office, Great American Insurance Company sold two of its life insurance subsidiaries to Great American Life Insurance Company: United Liberty Life Insurance Company and FN Life Insurance Company. The latter was absorbed by GALIC, now located in Ohio, by a merger in 1982. Carl Lindner continued to serve actively as chairman and CEO.

In 1981, Lindner made the company private. He and his immediate family owned nearly 90 percent of AFC and the majority of its subsidiaries, including Great American Insurance Company and Great American Life Insurance Company.

## *Finding Opportunity in the Insurance Industry: 1980s*

Lindner had long established a reputation for insurance company acquisitions. During the 1980s, AFC made major stock purchases in Mission Insurance Company (MIC), a property-casualty insurance concern in California, which concentrated on workers' compensation insurance. The insurance industry was beginning to emerge from the past decade's recession years, and by early 1984 Lindner had acquired a 49.9 percent interest in the MIC group.

Mission Insurance Company's financial troubles soon came to light—a situation blamed on poor underwriting and the company's reinsurance business. Final reports in 1983 showed a loss of $37.3 million. Stock plunged from $41 to $6.38 a share; a loss of $198 million was recorded in 1984, leaving a net worth of $43 million to support the $400 million of premiums in force.

In March 1985, AFC initiated a recapitalization program for MIC. Shares of the Transport Indemnity Company, a trucking insurance company acquired by GAIC in 1981 that had been losing money, were added to MIC's capital and surplus. However, AFC's efforts did not solve the failing concern's problem. In October 1985, the California Insurance Commissioner declared MIC insolvent and placed it under conservatorship. For the first nine months of the year, AFC was $31 million in the red. According to *Barron's*, July 4, 1988, "Lindner's American Financial took a loss of $162 million, writing off the entire value of its stock interest and Mission loans."

During AFC's harried involvement with MIC, Great American Insurance Company, then ranked number 24 among casualty insurers, was operating as the company's core insurance operation and generating enormous cash revenues. In mid-1984, about the same time MIC's flaws had surfaced, GAIC implemented significant price increases.

By 1986, the property and casualty insurance industry had rebounded from its crisis era. AFC added several new product lines, including life insurance. Great American Life Insurance Company's activity had by then become focused predominantly on individual tax-sheltered annuities, which accounted for almost all premium income in 1986.

American Financial Corporation's annual report for 1987 showed that property and casualty insurance represented 27 percent of its revenues, with life insurance and annuities at eight percent. While ranked as the second-largest contributor of revenues, property and casualty insurance was AFC's highest source of assets, with life insurance and annuities second at 26 percent and 21 percent, respectively. That year, Great American Insurance Company showed net earnings of $200 million. The years 1988 and 1989 saw slightly smaller net earnings of $188 and $102 million, respectively.

Nearly all of the 1987 premiums of AFC's annuity and life insurance business were related to annuities, sold primarily to teachers. These annuity premiums increased 26 percent from 1985 to 1986, and decreased by 11 percent from 1986 to 1987. The decline was attributed to a reduced demand for IRA's due to new tax regulations.

By the late 1980s, AFC had grown from a small company with $17.7 million in assets and 50 employees to a conglomerate with 53,000 employees and $12 billion in assets. American Financial's primary insurance business in 1990 was in multi-line property and casualty insurance, headed by its wholly-owned subsidiary, Great American Insurance Company. Continually evolving to capture long-term success, in 1989 the company introduced a new group of specialty product lines, including animal mortality and a broad range of individually tailored insurance programs. In January 1989, GALIC stopped writing additional life insurance policies and Great American Life Insurance Company's business remained almost exclusively in tax-sheltered annuities.

### *The Formation of American Financial Group: 1995*

AFC underwent several changes during the 1990s, the most significant being the 1995 merger with American Premier Underwriters, an insurance company partially owned by the Lindner family. Under the terms of the deal, a new holding company entitled American Financial Group Inc. (AFG) was created. Then, in 1997, AFG began a restructuring effort in order to cut back on expenses and merged with two of its subsidiaries, AFC and American Financial Enterprises Inc. It also began selling off unprofitable businesses and, in 1998, GAIC sold the majority of its Commercial Lines Division to Ohio Casualty Insurance Company.

Despite the changes in its operating structure, Carl Lindner remained in control of AFG. As chairman and CEO, Lindner continued to eye expansion in the insurance sector as key to future growth for the company. As such, AFG acquired Worldwide Insurance Co. in 1999 from an Aegon USA subsidiary. The deal bolstered AFG's auto insurance business.

Meanwhile, AFG's property and casualty business was suffering due to a weakening underwriting market, intense competition, and lower premium rates. During 1999, AFG's stock fell by as much as 35 percent. Feeling that the company was undervalued, Lindner purchased approximately 560,000 AFG shares for over $11.6 million on the open market in March 2000.

During the first year of the new millennium, AFG was focused on strengthening its internal technology platform and set plans in motion to offer automobile insurance quotes on the Web. The firm also began cross selling its property and casualty products with its life insurance and annuity products. In February 2000, GALIC launched its long-term care insurance product line as part of AFG's strategy to build the Great American brand name. It also announced the sale of GAIC's Japanese property and casualty division to Mitsui Marine and Fire Insurance Company of America.

The firm posted a net loss of $56 million in 2000, due in part to a $91.4 million write down of its stake in Chiquita Brands International, a food concern whose finances were plagued by a trade dispute between the United States and the European Union related to banana imports. After the loss, AFG began to implement rate increases to secure future profits. Lindner commented on AFG's strategy in a 2001 company press release, stating that "we will continue to maintain a strong reserve position. We expect improvement in our personal groups' combined ratio, we expect continued growth through new product development in life and annuities, and we will continue to look for ways to use e-commerce to expand business opportunities." Lindner also claimed that "we will sacrifice market share to achieve profitability."

As the insurance industry as a whole began to recover from downward trends of the 1990s, AFG's rate increases began to show signs of success. Net earnings increased to $105.7 million and the firm reported a loss of $14.8 million—down from the

$56 million loss reported in 2000. AFG management felt confident that the company was headed in the right direction and expected significant improvement in its financial results in 2002 and the years to come.

## *Principal Subsidiaries*

AFC Holding Company; American Financial Capital Trust I; American Financial Corporation; American Money Management Corporation; American Premier Underwriters, Inc.; Pennsylvania Company; Atlanta Casualty Company; Infinity Insurance Company; Infinity National Insurance Company; Infinity Select Insurance Company; Leader Insurance Company; Leader Specialty Insurance Company; TICO Insurance Company; Republic Indemnity Company of America; Republic Indemnity Company of California; Windsor Insurance Company; Regal Insurance Company; Premier Lease & Loan Services Insurance Agency, Inc.; Premier Lease & Loan Services of Canada, Inc.; Great American Insurance Company; American Empire Surplus Lines Insurance Company; American Empire Insurance Company; Fidelity Excess and Surplus Insurance Company; Great American Alliance Insurance Company; Great American Assurance Company; Great American Contemporary Insurance Company; Great American Custom Insurance Services, Inc.; Great American E&S Insurance Company; Great American Fidelity Insurance Company; Great American Financial Resources, Inc.; AAG Holding Company, Inc.; Great American Life Insurance Company; Annuity Investors Life Insurance Company; Loyal American Life Insurance Company; United Teacher Associates Insurance Company; Great American Life Assurance Company of Puerto Rico, Inc.; Great American Insurance Company of New York; Great American Management Services, Inc.; Great American Protection Insurance Company; Great American Security Insurance Company; Great American Spirit Insurance Company; Mid-Continent Casualty Company; Oklahoma Surety Company; National Interstate Corporation; Transport Insurance Company; Worldwide Insurance Company.

## *Principal Competitors*

The Allstate Corporation; The Progressive Corporation; State Farm Insurance Companies.

## *Further Reading*

''American Financial Group Restructures Operations,'' *Best's Review—Life-Health Insurance Edition*, September 1997, p. 97.

''Carl Lindner Wields His Clout in the Boardroom,'' *Business Week*, July 2, 1984.

''Investments Cause American Financial to Take a Loss,'' *A.M. Best Newswire*, February 12, 2001.

Lombaerde, Geert De, ''American Financial Diversifies, Heads Onto Web,'' *Business Courier Serving Cincinnati*, May 12, 2000, p. 31.

——, ''American Financial's Charm Cast Spell on Another Analyst,'' *Business Courier Serving Cincinnati*, December 29, 2000, p. 19.

Norris, Floyd, ''Rescue Mission: Saving Carl Lindner's Ailing Insurer Won't Be Easy,'' *Barron's*, October 14, 1985.

—Janie Pritchett
—update: Christina M. Stansell

# American Lung Association

1740 Broadway
New York, New York 10019
U.S.A.
Telephone: (212) 315-8700
Toll Free: (800) 586-4872
Fax: (212) 765-7876
Web site: http://www.lungusa.org

*Non-Profit Organization*
*Founded:* 1904 as the National Association for the Study and Prevention of Tuberculosis
*Employees:* 200
*Sales:* $23 million (2000)
*NAIC:* 813211 Grantmaking Foundations; 813212 Voluntary Health Organizations

The American Lung Association (ALA) is a non-profit organization dedicated to fighting lung disease. The group's original goal was to combat tuberculosis, an often-fatal respiratory disease that was widespread in the early 20th century. When the severity of the tuberculosis epidemic eased by the 1950s, the organization took on broader goals, working to study and prevent other lung diseases, to combat air pollution, and educate the public about the dangers of cigarette smoking. The ALA operates a national office in New York City and has close to 80 state and local affiliates. The ALA funds research on lung disease and runs public awareness and education campaigns on issues related to lung health. The organization also maintains an office in Washington, D.C., to advocate ALA positions with legislators. The ALA is funded through grants and donations, membership dues, and corporate contributions. It has run a Christmas Seal campaign since 1907, raising money through the sale of special stamps. Contributions to the ALA through the Christmas Seal, Chanukah Seal, and other direct mail campaigns amounted to over $51 million in 2000. The organization is run by a board of directors that coordinates activities at a national level. Staff at the national office coordinate media outreach and public awareness, provide epidemiological data of interest to the medical community, train volunteers, and oversee the group's research funding.

### *Fighting Tuberculosis in the Early 20th Century*

Tuberculosis is a virulent disease of the lungs. It had long been known and studied in Europe, where it went by several names, including phthisis, consumption, and "the white plague." Though it affected people of all ages and social classes, it became a leading killer of the urban poor, particularly after the 1850s. In 1882, the German physician Robert Koch isolated the tubercle bacillus. Until that time, the disease was generally thought to be inherited. Doctors offered little hope to patients diagnosed with tuberculosis. It was often fatal, and the most effective treatment, until drugs were developed in the 1940s, was rest, fresh air, and a change of climate.

In the United States at the end of the 19th century, tuberculosis patients were treated at sanatoriums which were often located in the mountains. Many sanatoriums were private or church supported. The first sanatorium for the poor was opened in 1884 in Saranac Lake, New York, and the state of Massachusetts opened the first state sanatorium in 1898. By 1904, when the organization that became the American Lung Association was founded, tuberculosis was the leading cause of death in the United States, and despite the growth of sanatoriums, treatment was limited and the disease considered incurable. Several organizations had already come together to do something about tuberculosis. There were some two dozen voluntary societies, and influential doctors such as Edward Trudeau, who had founded the Saranac Lake sanatorium, were interested in uniting on a national level for a concerted campaign against the disease.

After several preliminary meetings, a group with over 200 members, almost all of them doctors, formed the National Association for the Study and Prevention of Tuberculosis (NASPT) on June 6, 1904. The group raised money through membership dues as well as donations. The popular cause brought in gifts from the likes of John D. Rockefeller, and by 1905 the group was able to pay its Executive Secretary a $5,000 salary to head the association from New York. The NASPT was the first group of its kind in the United States in that it was made up of volunteers dedicated to fighting one specific disease.

**Company Perspectives:**

*The American Lung Association's mission is to prevent lung disease and promote lung health.*

The NASPT affiliated with state and local organizations across the country, at first primarily building awareness of tuberculosis as a contagious disease. The idea that tuberculosis was hereditary still lingered. Another common myth about the disease was that it was incurable, and thus it was a waste to spend money on treatment. The NASPT tried to convince legislators and public health departments to fund sanatoriums so that infected patients could be removed from the community before they spread the disease. In this era, drugs to fight tuberculosis had not yet been developed. The NASPT sponsored programs to educate the public about the disease, as early detection offered patients the best hope of survival. The group also raised money for medical care of indigent patients, as there was no national health insurance system.

The NASPT had broad aims, but it needed more money to fund its programs. It began raising money through its Christmas Seals program in 1907. Emily P. Bissell was responsible for the first successful Christmas Seals campaign. Bissell was the cousin of a doctor in Wilmington, Delaware, who ran an open-air shelter for tubercular patients. She was also the secretary for the Delaware Red Cross. Bissell had heard of a successful project in Denmark to raise money for the care of tubercular children through the sale of special stamps. She took it on herself to raise money for her cousin's shelter, which was doomed to close if it could not come up with $300. With the permission of the Red Cross and the NASPT, Bissell herself drew the stamp, borrowed money to have 50,000 printed, and began selling them in Wilmington's main post office. The idea was for people to buy the special stamp and put it on their Christmas cards. It was not U.S. postage but a means of raising money and also awareness. The fund-raising campaign brought in only around $25 on their first day, and Bissell doubted they would make the $300 needed to keep the tuberculosis shelter open. So Bissell journeyed to Philadelphia for an interview with the editor of the influential *North American*, the city's leading paper. The editor was politely uninterested in the Christmas Seals, but Bissell next ran into a columnist for the paper, who thought she had a great idea. The columnist asked her to send the paper all 50,000 stamps, and within a few weeks they were all sold. Bissell's campaign raised about $3,000, enough money to preserve the tuberculosis shelter and to buy land for another, more modern tuberculosis hospital. The next year, the Red Cross sponsored a nationwide sale of Christmas Seals with a stamp designed by the renowned illustrator Howard Pyle. That sale brought in $135,000. The NASPT took over the Christmas Seal sale from the Red Cross in 1910 and in 1919 began using as the seal's symbol the double-barred cross. The NASPT changed its name in 1918 to the National Tuberculosis Association (NTA), and in 1920 the group registered the double-barred cross as its trademark.

By 1920, the NTA had enough financial backing that it could fund research. The NTA backed research that led to improvements in the tuberculin skin test and in the chest x-ray. The association continued to sponsor public health campaigns, for instance going into schools to promote good nutrition, a key to resisting infection. The NTA also had a medical arm, first called the American Sanatorium Association, and in 1939 taking the name the American Trudeau Society (after Dr. Edward Livingston Trudeau). The medical branch supported a variety of research into tuberculosis, set standards for treatment, and met annually to discuss new developments. The prospects for tubercular patients were much better in the 1930s and 1940s. Improved diagnostic techniques meant more people were caught at an earlier stage of the disease. Drugs to fight tuberculosis were developed in the 1940s. The antibiotic streptomycin was developed in 1943, and para-aminosalicyclic acid (PAS) was in clinical trials beginning in 1945. In 1948, the NTA began funding individual physicians and medical students to do research on tuberculosis. Another powerful anti-tubercular drug, isoniazid, debuted in 1952. By 1954, the death rate from tuberculosis in the United States had fallen to one-fiftieth of what it had been when the NTA began in 1904.

### *Finding a New Mission in the 1950s*

By the mid-1950s, the NTA had grown to encompass close to 3,000 state and local affiliates. The NTA's annual income had risen to almost $24 million through fund-raising, donations, and membership. The NTA had had wide influence in getting tuberculosis hospitals and sanatoriums built and in getting hospitals to set aside beds in tuberculosis wards. It had sponsored mass tuberculosis screenings in schools and factories, using portable x-ray machines and chemical tests. The disease was no longer the feared killer it had been at the beginning of the century. It still disproportionately affected the poor, especially people living in hospitals and prisons. However, the worst of the ''white plague'' seemed to have passed, and the National Tuberculosis Association considered whether it should have a different mission.

The NTA considered a variety of options in the early 1950s. Some members wanted to continue to focus exclusively on tuberculosis, as the disease had not yet been eradicated and in some areas of the country it was still a pressing problem. Other proposals were to merge with the American Heart Association, to disband the organization, or to become a group dedicated to general public health issues. In 1956, the group decided that its best option was to continue to fight tuberculosis, while also funding research and prevention of other lung diseases. Other lung diseases included respiratory infections, asthma, diseases due to air pollution, and respiratory allergies. The association moved slowly into its broadened mission, for example giving grants to doctors and researchers who studied these other lung ailments.

By the early 1960s, the NTA was a major voice in public policy debates on the issues of smoking and air pollution. The NTA board of directors issued a policy statement in 1960 declaring cigarette smoking a major cause of lung cancer, and then prompted President Kennedy to appoint an advisory committee on smoking and health. The NTA began its first public education campaign on the dangers of smoking in 1964, producing an award-winning film. The NTA was a strong anti-smoking lobbyist in Washington, weighing in on issues like cigarette advertising, the Department of Agriculture's support for the tobacco industry, and provisions for warning labels on cigarette packages. The NTA also approached air pollution as a public health issue.

**Key Dates:**

**1904:** National Association for the Study and Prevention of Tuberculosis is founded.
**1907:** Emily Bissell organizes the first Christmas Seal campaign.
**1918:** The organization's name is changed to National Tuberculosis Association.
**1956:** The Association adopts a broader mission to combat all respiratory diseases.
**1960:** The Association issues its first policy statement on the dangers of cigarette smoking.
**1973:** The organization's name is changed to American Lung Association.
**1981:** The ALA begins a broad asthma initiative.
**1987:** The first in-flight smoking ban is adopted with ALA backing.
**1990:** The ALA successfully lobbies for amendments to the Clean Air Act.
**2000:** The ALA issues its first annual "State of the Air" report.

Its January 1965 *NTA Bulletin* was completely devoted to the health effects of air pollution. The NTA began promoting "Cleaner Air Week" in 1961, an event founded in 1949 by another advocacy group, the Air Pollution Control Association (APCA). The event came to be called "Clean Air Week," and the NTA took it over from the APCA altogether in 1975.

### *Changes in the 1970s*

By the late 1960s, the National Tuberculosis Association was strongly associated with anti-smoking and anti-pollution campaigns. The group seemed to have made a successful transition from an organization focused on one disease to a broader advocacy group for lung health. In 1967, the board of directors voted to change the name of the group to better reflect its new aims. That year the group became the National Tuberculosis and Respiratory Disease Association (NTRDA). This name was a mouthful, and affiliates at the local level continued under many different names. In 1973, the national board again voted to change the name, this time to the more succinct American Lung Association.

The organization continued to rely on the annual Christmas Seals campaign as its core fund raiser. By the late 1960s, however, the campaign was less able to meet the organization's expenses. National mailings of the stamps were still done manually, and it was a cumbersome job. Some regional affiliates began computerizing their Christmas Seal mailing lists in the early 1970s. The group began considering other ways to raise funds. The ALA had income of $50 million in 1977, and the next year an executive committee set a goal of doubling the group's income by 1983. The percentage of revenue paid to the national organization by local affiliates was increased several times over the 1970s.

The ALA continued to focus on smoking-related issues in the 1970s. It began its first "Kick the Habit" campaign in 1970, encouraging smokers to quit. It also began publicizing the issue of second-hand smoke. Tuberculosis was a highly treatable disease by the early 1970s. A new drug, rifampin, which came out in 1971, could rapidly treat tuberculosis symptoms. Patients could now be cured in weeks, whereas earlier treatments had taken months. At this time, special hospitals for tubercular patients were closed and physicians began to treat tubercular patients in general hospitals.

### *Focus on New Problems in the 1980s–90s*

Combatting smoking continued to be a core mission of the ALA in the 1980s. Throughout that decade, the group put out a range of materials designed to help people quit smoking and alerting women to the dangers of smoking during pregnancy. In 1981, the ALA worked with the American Cancer Society and the American Heart Association to approach the dangers of smoking from a broader perspective. The ALA opened a new office in Washington, D.C., in the early 1980s. Its Government Relations office put it in closer touch with lawmakers and government officials, whose support was key for the ALA's public health initiatives. ALA lobbying brought about some significant changes in the 1980s, including the first ban on smoking on domestic air flights in 1987. This law banned smoking on flights of less than two hours. In 1989, the ALA helped strengthen the law so that smoking was banned on all flights under six hours, which included 99 percent of domestic flights.

Asthma became a principal focus of the ALA during the 1980s. By 1984, some 5.5 million Americans were estimated to have asthma, and the ALA put out its first public information handbook addressing the disease. Asthma became even more prevalent during the 1990s, and it was a growing health issue for children. The ALA began a program called Open Airways for Schools in 1991 that taught elementary school children how to manage their asthma. Over the 1990s, this program reached over 25 percent of elementary schools in the United States. The ALA also continued its work on other diseases of the lungs. The group adopted guidelines for dealing with occupational lung diseases in the early 1980s, and in 1988 the ALA explored issues related to lung disease and AIDS. The ALA was also instrumental in pushing amendments to the Clean Air Act in 1990. The amendments marked the first major changes in air pollution laws in over a decade. Lawsuits filed by the ALA in 1991 and 1993 eventually led to new air quality regulations in 1997.

Going into the 21st century, the ALA found itself faced with many of the same problems it had dealt with in the previous decades: the ever-growing incidence of asthma, a global resurgence of tuberculosis, and the continuing need to educate people about the dangers of smoking and air pollution. Many of these problems disproportionately affected poor and minority communities. Low-income neighborhoods were more prone to indoor air pollutants because of sub-standard housing, and poor indoor air could trigger asthma and allergy attacks. In 2000, ALA affiliates carried out a variety of programs across the country which addressed the particular problems of low-income communities. The ALA began a collaborative effort in 2000 with a group representing the nation's 118 historically African American colleges to help train volunteers and interns for programs on asthma control, tobacco risks, community organizing against environmental hazards, and other outreach efforts.

Approaching the 100-year anniversary of the ALA's founding, the group still found lung disease a formidable foe. The number of asthma cases in the United States had grown to around 26 million by 2000, and this number was expected to grow over the next 20 years. Despite the ALA's many victories in anti-smoking legislation since the 1960s, smoking remained the leading preventable cause of death. The ALA continued to evaluate the nation's air quality. It began an annual "State of the Air" report in 2000 giving data on air quality in communities across the United States. This first report found that the health of some 133 million people was at risk because of poor air quality, as over 120 major metropolitan areas got a failing grade for controlling smog. The organization had grown beyond its original focus on one deadly disease, but still faced a myriad of lung conditions that threatened the nation's well-being.

### *Further Reading*

Bissell, Emily P., "The Story of the Christmas Seal," National Tuberculosis Association, 1946.

"Many Metropolitan Areas Given an 'F' for Air Quality," *Nation's Health*, July 2000, p. 6.

Ogasawara, Frances R., *History of the American Lung Association*, New York: American Lung Association, 1994.

Shryock, Richard Harrison, *National Tuberculosis Association, 1904–1954*. New York: National Tuberculosis Association, 1957.

—A. Woodward

# AmSouth Bancorporation

AmSouth Center
**1900 Fifth Avenue North**
**Birmingham, Alabama 35203**
**U.S.A.**
**Telephone: (205) 320-7151**
**Fax: (205) 581-7755**
**Web site: http://www.amsouth.com**

*Public Company*
*Incorporated:* 1972
*Employees:* 12,296
*Total Assets:* $38.6 billion (2001)
*Stock Exchanges:* New York
*Ticker Symbol:* ASO
*NAIC:* 522110 Commercial Banking; 551111 Offices of Bank Holding Companies

AmSouth Bancorporation is a regional bank holding company with interests in consumer banking, commercial banking, and wealth management. Through subsidiary AmSouth Bank, the firm operates approximately 600 branch offices and 1,200 ATMs in Alabama, Florida, Tennessee, Mississippi, Louisiana, and Georgia.

AmSouth Bancorporation was incorporated in 1972 to take advantage of new state and federal laws related to the banking industry. Indeed, during the early 1970s Alabama began to deregulate its banking sector, making it easier for holding companies to merge with or acquire other banks. Similarly, during the mid-1960s and early 1970s, Congress had eliminated several federal banking industry restrictions and created a variety of favorable tax incentives for specific banking activities. By moving to a holding company format, companies like the newly formed AmSouth Bancorporation were able to take advantage of deregulation and to participate in a number of non-banking-related financial markets.

Because of regulatory changes, several holding companies were formed in Alabama during the 1970s. The owners and managers of most of those holding companies hoped to establish regional or state-wide dominance by adding new banks to their portfolios. Specifically, many of them hoped to improve the performance of the institutions that they acquired and also benefit from various economies of scale. AmSouth Bancorporation, like other holding companies formed at the time, was structured as a corporation with its founding bank (Birmingham-based AmSouth) as its major subsidiary. Throughout the 1970s, AmSouth engaged in an aggressive growth and acquisition campaign that would make it the largest bank in Alabama by the end of the decade.

### *AmSouth Expansion: 1970s–80s*

The man chosen to direct AmSouth's rampant expansion during the 1970s, which would continue into the 1990s, was John W. Woods. Woods was born in 1931 into a military family, and in the 1950s he tried to join the Marines but was rejected because he was color blind. He did, however, pass the entrance test for the Air Force, where he served as a pilot for two years. Woods credited his military experience with giving him the confidence and personal strength that later helped him to build one of the most successful banks in the United States. "There are tough moments in everybody's career," Woods related in the November 13, 1991 issue of *American Banker*, "and every time there's been a tough moment, I think about that Air Force training and think, by golly, I can whip this, too."

Immediately after leaving the service, Woods accepted an entry level position at New York-based Chemical Bank, where he had a successful career and eventually earned the title of vice-president in charge of Chemical's southern division. Woods spent several years traveling to banks throughout the Southeast, selling correspondent banking and loan syndication services. AmSouth hired Woods away from Chemical in 1969, and although he had only 12 years in the banking industry, he was named president of AmSouth's lead Birmingham bank. Three years later Woods was chosen to lead the newly formed holding company, AmSouth Bancorporation.

Under Woods' direction, AmSouth expanded rapidly during the 1970s and early 1980s by purchasing competitors and integrating their assets and branches into the AmSouth banking

### Company Perspectives:

*To succeed as a bank, we give you a quality of service you won't find anywhere else—a relationship that is unparalleled. That extra level of service begins, we believe, with six basic values that we practice at AmSouth every day: do more that is expected; if something's wrong, make it right; make time for people; improve someone's life; make a difference; and do the right thing.*

chain. By the early 1980s, AmSouth had become the largest banking chain in Alabama, with nearly 20 percent of all state bank deposits. Besides simply increasing AmSouth's asset base, Woods and his fellow executives achieved success by improving the financial performance of their acquisitions. Not only did the banks that they purchased benefit from improved management, they profited from having AmSouth's well-known and respected name attached to their branches. In fact, an integral aspect of Woods strategy was to focus on expanding into areas where the AmSouth name was already established. Finally, the bought-out banks enjoyed access to a larger base of lending capital, as well as centralized, efficient administrative operations.

Although AmSouth Bancorporation was created in 1972, the history of its banking chain actually dates back long before the start of the 19th century. AmSouth's immediate predecessor, the First National Bank of Alabama, was founded in the late 1800s, and AmSouth eventually acquired a patchwork of Alabama financial institutions with similarly rich histories. In 1983, AmSouth absorbed the Commercial National Bank (CNB) of Anniston. E. Guice Potter, CNB's president, stayed with AmSouth, assuming the title of president of the newly named AmSouth Bank in Anniston. Potter's father had gone to work at CNB in 1926, just six years after it was established. Potter, who had succeeded his father as president of CNB in 1974, stayed with AmSouth until his retirement in 1994.

As AmSouth continued to purchase Alabama banks and to increase its existing operations, the holding company flourished. Although Woods was at the helm of the swelling operation, the company's success was also attributable to savvy AmSouth executives like William L. Marks. Marks joined AmSouth's acquisition and turn-around team in 1977. The 33-year-old Marks was hired away from Wachovia Bank and Trust Co. and named president of AmSouth's new American National Bank subsidiary. Similar to other AmSouth acquisitions, the bank suffered from a troubled loan portfolio, poor marketing strategy, and generally weak management. However, it had a lot of potential.

Marks went to work revitalizing the bank and integrating it into the AmSouth empire. Within three years, the subsidiary made more money than it had in its entire 16-year history. "We decided what needed to be done and turned it around," recalled Marks in the March 12, 1990 issue of *New Orleans City Business.* During the next 13 years, Marks would be moved around to several other new AmSouth banks. He consistently boosted productivity and profits at his posts, and, like his fellow regional managers, contributed significantly to the holding company's success. Marks was hired away in the early 1990s by Whitney National Bank, a struggling New Orleans institution. Interestingly, the 107-year-old Whitney had hired its first out-of-state chief executive from AmSouth Bancorporation's predecessor in 1930.

### *Moving into the Florida Market: 1987*

By 1984, AmSouth had blossomed into a dominant Alabama financial institution with nearly $5 billion in assets and more than $45 million in annual net income. Although that growth was impressive, it turned out to be mere preparation for the explosive expansion that AmSouth would conduct during the next decade. In fact, a turn of events in 1985 set the stage for what would become a major evolution in the banking industry. In that year, Congress effectively gave the okay for holding companies to engage in interstate banking. That meant that AmSouth could begin expanding outside of Alabama (and that AmSouth could potentially become a takeover target for larger out-of-state holding companies).

By increasing its Alabama holdings, AmSouth managed to swell its total asset base to nearly $7 billion by the end of 1986. Then, in 1987, AmSouth launched a major expansion into the Florida panhandle with its purchase of First Mutual Savings Association, a major regional thrift institution. Within the year, AmSouth had assembled a subsidiary bank with nearly $1 billion in assets. Unfortunately, that investment soon soured when the Florida real estate market collapsed, and AmSouth's Florida subsidiary was devastated as more than 40 percent of its total loans were eventually classified as nonperforming.

Although AmSouth also ventured into Tennessee in the late 1980s and considered other investment opportunities in Florida and Georgia, the company slowed its growth plans and focused on weathering a severe banking industry downturn. Indeed, in the late 1980s, the U.S. banking industry was trounced by the collapse of real estate and construction markets, as well as a general economic malaise in the United States during that time. As the number of nonperforming bank loans soared, many banks and thrifts were forced into bankruptcy. Although AmSouth was pressured, its tradition of sound management and making high quality loans paid off, allowing it to sustain meager profit growth during the late 1980s and early 1990s.

One of AmSouth's investments in Alabama that did not fare as well as others during the late 1980s was its loan to the Birmingham Turf Club, a venture initiated for the purpose of bringing horse racing to Birmingham. AmSouth had loaned $17 million to the organization and was eventually forced to write off the entire amount. Marks defended the loan decision on the basis that the venture would have brought more than 1,000 jobs to the Birmingham area. Nevertheless, AmSouth's local image was tarnished by the whole affair. Moreover, a string of fiscal problems and executive turmoil punctuated the AmSouth story between 1987 and 1992, before the banking industry in general began to recover.

Despite its losses in the 1987 Florida debacle, that acquisition boosted AmSouth's holdings to nearly $9 billion by 1989. Over the following three years, AmSouth's portfolio grew to about $10 billion. AmSouth's profit growth slowed during the

**Key Dates:**

**1972:** AmSouth Bancorporation is created to take advantage of new state and federal banking laws.
**1983:** The company absorbs the Commercial National Bank of Anniston.
**1985:** Congress allows holding companies to engage in interstate banking.
**1987:** AmSouth expands into Florida with the purchase of First Mutual Savings Association.
**1991:** The firm launches a three-year restructuring program.
**1993:** AmSouth's assets rise to $12.5 billion.
**1996:** C. Dowd Ritter is named chairman and CEO.
**1999:** AmSouth acquires First American Corp.
**2001:** The firm focuses on Florida expansion.

period. Net income actually declined from $73 million in 1986 to $66 million in 1987, and then buoyed up around the $80 million mark until 1991. Spurred by recovering markets and improving loan portfolios in 1992, AmSouth enjoyed a net income surge to $108 million. Encouraged by improving margins and markets, AmSouth regained its vigor for growth and renewed its aggressive expansion strategy. Simultaneously, AmSouth was undergoing a three-year restructuring that it began in 1991. The intent was to slash operating costs by developing scrupulous performance standards for all of its subsidiaries and branches.

### *Growth Through Acquisition: Early 1990s*

AmSouth elected to focus on the central and west Florida banking markets for expansion during the early 1990s. It started by acquiring First National Bank of Clearwater for about $90 million, and then snapped up an Orlando entity, Orange Bank, for about $50 million. Orange was the largest independent bank in the county, with 20 branches and $376 million in assets. AmSouth soon added nearby Mid-State Federal Savings Bank for about $100 million. After tagging St. Petersburg First Federal to its portfolio, AmSouth's Florida assets had suddenly surged to nearly $2 billion. During the same period, AmSouth boosted its holdings in Tennessee, where it would have 21 offices by 1994, and Georgia, where it would operate seven.

AmSouth's growth during the early 1990s was representative of a dynamic trend of consolidation within the U.S. banking industry that had been occurring since interstate banking began in the 1980s. Indeed, as smaller banks continued to face greater competitive pressures from less-regulated, non-bank financial institutions, the percentage of U.S. assets held by commercial banks had dropped from about 37 percent in the late 1970s to 25 percent by the early 1990s. To combat competitive threats, banks began merging to achieve economies of scale. The number of independent banking entities in the United States plunged from about 13,000 in 1983 to less than 10,000 by 1990. Meanwhile, the number of multi-bank holding companies grew from about 300 to around 1,000. Augmenting the consolidation trend was the fact that computers and electronic banking devices were increasingly making it easier for banks to operate across broad regions.

As a result of its acquisition activity, AmSouth's assets and income surged in 1993 to a $12.5 billion and $147 million, respectively. Furthermore, it was acquiring new banks and expanding existing subsidiaries at a rapid pace. Importantly, in 1993, AmSouth announced an agreement to purchase Fortune Bancorp. of Clearwater Florida. With 46 offices, Fortune was a major-league financial institution and gave AmSouth a commanding presence in central Florida.

By 1994, AmSouth would have at least 125 banking offices in Florida and more than $6 billion in assets. With its other operations, including about 150 Alabama offices, its total asset base would rise past the $17 billion mark by early 1995. Furthermore, the company's profits continued to be augmented by its emphasis on fee-based income activities, particularly trust services, mutual funds, and mortgage retail services. In a 1993 article for the *Orlando Business Journal*, banking analyst Sam Beebe suggested that AmSouth was ''going to be very competitive'' well into the 1990s.

After nearly 25 years of service at AmSouth, Woods was formulating plans for his retirement in 1995. Reminiscent of his early years in the armed services, Woods was an avid military history buff and was looking forward to doing a lot more reading in that area. In addition, he planned to spend more time at his 700-acre cattle-breeding farm near Birmingham. ''Its kind of my entrepreneurial outlet,'' Woods explained in the November 13, 1991 issue of *American Banker*, noting that ''on the farm, if I make a bad decision I pay for it pretty quickly.'' In 1996, C. Dowd Ritter was named to take over as chairman and CEO of the firm.

### *Internal Operations and Restructuring: Late 1990s and Beyond*

Ritter, the firm's chief operating officer and president since 1994, found himself at the helm of a company in which many analysts felt was facing possible takeover attempts by 1997. At the time, the banking industry as a whole was undergoing major consolidation, especially in the South. Strong regional players including AmSouth were becoming increasingly attractive to larger competitors such as Wachovia Bank Corp. and SunTrust Corp. AmSouth had also been struggling for the past several years due to poor integration of its previous Florida acquisitions. Then, in early 1999, it lost $14 billion in trust assets when Chase Manhattan Bank was awarded custody of Alabama's retirement systems account.

AmSouth, however, remained intact and spent the next several years focused on strengthening its internal operations. In 1998, AmSouth sold off its bond administration and stock transfer businesses and also began divesting portions of its credit card portfolio. A 1999 *American Banker* article reported that Ritter had spent the ''past five years cleaning up a troubled Florida operation, paring back inefficient staff and business units, and reviving revenues.'' Confident that his restructuring program had paid off, Ritter announced the $6.3 billion acquisition of First American Corp. in the spring of 1999. The deal with the Tennessee-based financial services concern was the first AmSouth purchase since its buying spree of the early 1990s.

During 2000, AmSouth once again restructured. This time, rising short-term interest rates and credit quality problems were taking their toll on the firm's bottom line. While industry analysts pointed to the First American Corp. purchase as the culprit in AmSouth's faltering earnings, the company claimed the acquisition integration was going smoothly and continued to eye expansion as key to future profit growth. During 2001, the company once again began to focus on the Florida region, especially in the Naples, Tampa, Orlando, and Jacksonville markets. At the time, Florida accounted for nearly 20 percent of company deposits and the firm believed that number could be pushed even higher due to Florida's population growth rates.

In 2001, AmSouth's net income surged to $536.3 million, an increase of 63 percent over the previous year's figures. As the banking industry remained highly competitive, Ritter announced a six-part strategy designed to ensure AmSouth's future success. These initiatives included: doubling the company's business banking segment; doubling the contribution of its wealth management business; expansion in the high-growth Florida markets; aggressive growth in the firm's consumer banking segment; increasing sales productivity and service quality; and utilizing the Internet in all business segments.

### *Principal Subsidiaries*

AmSouth Bank; AmSouth Capital Corporation; AmSouth Investment Services, Inc.; OakBrook Investments, LLC; Rockhaven Asset Management, LLC; Sawgrass Asset Management, LLC.

### *Principal Competitors*

Bank of America Corp.; Regions Financial Corporation; SouthTrust Corporation.

### *Further Reading*


Ackermann, Matt, ''AmSouth's Effort to Rebuild Trust Biz Enters New Phase,'' *American Banker*, January 8, 2002, p. 1.

Beall, Pat, ''The New Bank on the Block: AmSouth Pick Orange Bank and Breaks with Age-Old Tradition,'' *Orlando Business Journal*, April 30, 1993, p. 13.

Boraks, David, ''AmSouth Sets Sights on Florida Expansion,'' *American Banker*, May 9, 2001, p. 1.

Burger, Frederick, ''AmSouth's Potter Will Retire January 1,'' *Anniston Star*, December 24, 1993, p. 1.

Campbell, Harvey E., ''AmSouth Bancorporation to Acquire Fortune Bancorp,'' *PR Newswire*, September 13, 1993.

Cline, Kenneth, ''AmSouth's John Woods Sees Smooth Flying Ahead,'' *American Banker*, November 13, 1991, p. 1.

Finn, Kathy, ''CEO Aims High,'' *New Orleans City Business*, March 12, 1990, p. 1.

Moyer, Liz, ''After Putting House in Order, AmSouth Chief Now Looking Outward,'' *American Banker*, June 2, 1999, p. 6.

——, ''AmSouth, in Takeover Spotlight, Has New Chief Financial Officer,'' *American Banker*, October 28, 1997, p. 7.

Silvestri, Scott, ''AmSouth: Merger Not the Culprit,'' *American Banker*, September 25, 2000, p. 1.

Underwood, Jim, ''C. Dowd Ritter Elected President and COO of AmSouth,'' *PR Newswire*, August 18, 1994.

——, ''Dan L. Hendley to Resign as President and Chief Operating Officer of AmSouth Bank N.A.,'' *Business Wire*, August 10, 1990.

Weaver, Danielle, ''AmSouth Wins Fortune, May Stop Now,'' *Orlando Business Journal*, September 17, 1993, p. 6.

Weil, Dan, ''Analysts and Investors Cheer AmSouth's Deal for First American,'' *American Banker*, September 20, 1999, p. 5.

Werner, Lisa, ''AmSouth to Expand into Central Florida with December 9 Merger of Mid-State Federal Savings Bank,'' *PR Newswire*, December 8, 1993.


—Dave Mote
—update: Christina M. Stansell

# Amstrad plc

**Brentwood House**
**169 King's Road**
**Brentwood, Essex CM14 4EF**
**United Kingdom**
**Telephone: (0277) 228-888**
**Fax: (0277) 211-350**
**Web site: http://www.amstrad.com**

*Public Company*
*Incorporated:* 1968 as AMS Trading Company
*Employees:* 63
*Sales:* £60.9 million ($193.2 million) (2001)
*Stock Exchanges:* London
*Ticker Symbol:* AMT
*NAIC:* 334220 Radio and Television Broadcasting and Wireless Communications Equipment Manufacturing; 334290 Other Communications Equipment Manufacturing; 334210 Telephone Apparatus Manufacturing

Amstrad plc, previously known as a consumer-electronics and computers manufacturer, achieved a name for itself by turning electronic products—television, video cassette recorders, word processors, personal computers, camcorders, and satellite dishes—into affordable goods found in homes and businesses throughout Europe, North America, and Australasia during the 1980s. After experiencing a wave of difficulties during the 1990s, Amstrad and its subsidiaries now offer the e-m@iler, a digital telephone answering machine that allows customers to send and receive email, browse the Internet, and play Sinclair ZX Spectrum games. Amstrad also supplies digital satellite decoders to British Sky Broadcasting (BSkyB), and through its Hong Kong operations, sells audio equipment across the globe. Sir Alan Sugar, the company's creator, owns nearly 30 percent of Amstrad.

## *Origins and Growth Through the 1970s*

For many people, Amstrad is synonymous with Alan Sugar, the founder and marketing genius behind the company. In 1965, at 17 years of age, Sugar began selling reconditioned television sets from his home in Hackney, north London. After working as a salesman for several local electrical shops, Sugar, the son of a London East End garment maker, started his own company in 1968. AMS Trading Company, later abbreviated to Amstrad, began business as a buyer and seller of electrical goods. Originally, these goods were not manufactured by Sugar's company. Its first products included cigarette lighters and home intercoms. In the next few years, Amstrad broadened its product range to include hi-fi amplifiers, tuners, car radios, aerials, and transistor radios.

In 1969, Sugar opened Global Audio, his first retail venture. By 1970, he already had tired of mere retailing and sought a new avenue of expansion. He decided to manufacture plastic turntable covers at £2.95 each. He found a way to reduce radically the cost of production, as a result achieving high sales volumes and margins, along with low retail prices.

A year later, in 1971, Sugar expanded his manufacturing capacity by appointing four Far Eastern contractors for his electrical components. By 1974, most of Amstrad's products were being manufactured in the Far East.

As a measure of its early growth, Amstrad's sales reached a total of £207,534 in 1971 with profits of £24,242. In 1972, sales and profits tripled. By 1973, profits rose to £194,063 on sales of £1.32 million.

In 1978, Sugar declined Audiotronic Holdings's offer to purchase a 78% stake in Amstrad for £2 million. He chose instead to list his company on the stock market. By then, sales of his products were soaring. Volume sales of car radio-cassette players, for example, were 276,000 in 1976, rising to 418,000 a year later, and reaching 588,000 units in 1978.

Sales touched one million units in 1979. Finally, in 1980, when a host of U.K. consumer-electronics manufacturers were going to the wall in the face of persistent competition from U.S. and Far Eastern manufacturers, Sugar brought Amstrad to the London Stock Exchange. At the time the company's 1980 turnover was £8.8 million, and profits stood at £1.4 million.

Amstrad's fortunes grew steadily during the early 1980s. Between 1980 and 1983, compound profit growth for the com-

## Company Perspectives:

*The future of Amstrad lies in understanding the latest technology and then creating and developing products using that technology. At Amstrad, we are "Always Innovating."*

pany averaged 56 percent. Hong Kong eventually became Amstrad's manufacturing base when a subsidiary, Amstrad International (Hong Kong), was established there in 1982. Sugar chose as a top executive in the Far East a Hong Kong woman, Callen So. She became marketing and sales director in 1982, having joined the group in 1971 as a secretary at the age of 19 years. So's appointment was evidence that Alan Sugar never insisted on formal qualifications when hiring his senior managerial staff.

Sugar was responsible for Amstrad's renowned agility in product development and marketing, allowing the company to jump in and out of markets at will. At the height of the 1982 recession, for example, Sugar took Amstrad out of the depressed car-radio cassette-player market. This move was not difficult to achieve because the manufacture of these products had always been placed with subcontractors in South Korea. Sugar had no directly employed workers to lay off as he left one market and leaped into another.

More importantly, Sugar displayed no emotional or technical commitment to retaining products whose markets have fallen away. In 1984, Amstrad dropped out of selling video cassette recorders not long after entering the market, again owing to a depression in that particular area. However, the company just as quickly returned to the same market a year later, having changed its supplier in Japan to help improve margins.

### *Opportunity in the PC Market: Mid- to Late 1980s*

Amstrad doubled in size each year during the early 1980s. By 1983, Sugar had identified the potential for large profits to be made from the expanding personal computer (PC) market. In 1984, Amstrad launched a new home computer, the CPC464, known as Arnold. The 64k-memory personal computer was introduced as a direct competitor of the 64k computer put on the market by Commodore Computers. Having had the CPC464 assembled in South Korea, Amstrad used popular retail outlets such as Comet, Dixons, and Rumbelows to sell its units. The machines, operating on cassette programs, were aimed at the beginner computer market.

Also in 1984, Amstrad augmented its U.K. manufacturing capacity by building a new 160,000-square-foot factory at Shoeburyness, at a cost of £2.5 million. The new factory began manufacturing consumer products, such as medium-sized color television sets and VHS video recorders. It also produced audio equipment, including remote-control hi-fi units. Indeed, after Amstrad achieved in two years a 40 percent share of the U.K. audio market on the strength of its Tower music systems, Sugar, at the age of 37, won the Guardian Young Businessman of the Year Award in 1984.

Part of Sugar's success has come from Amstrad's no-frills policy in developing new product lines. Sugar believes strongly in giving customers what they want, and nothing more. As he told his 1985 annual general meeting: "We produce what the mass market customer wants and not a boffin's ego trip."

Later that year, Amstrad eclipsed its early success in the personal computer market when it introduced the PCW8256 word processor, pitched at those looking for nothing more than a sophisticated typewriter and incorporating the latest in word-processing software. The PCW8256 was typical of Amstrad products in that its market included people who had never yet bought a word processing unit because of the high price. By paying close attention to component costs, quality control, and packaging, Amstrad succeeded with the PCW8256, as with its other products, in delivering a particular product to a particular market at just the price the mass-market customer could afford.

The one problem with the PCW8256 was its incompatibility with IBM software. Amstrad remedied this difficulty in 1986 by introducing its new PC1512 computer line. The IBM-compatible personal computer took on IBM on the U.S. computer giant's home ground. Here was a personal computer with word-processing software, complete with a monitor, disc drive, and printer, that was both relatively inexpensive and simple to use.

Amstrad's expansionist phase included paying $7.7 million, in 1986, for the name and right to market the products of Sinclair Research Ltd., the troubled computer company founded by U.K. inventor Sir Clive Sinclair. Backed by Malcolm Miller, Amstrad's marketing and sales director, the Sinclair acquisition gave the company access to a significant slice of the leisure end of the U.K. computer market.

Continuing from strength to strength, in 1987 Amstrad was listed on the FTSE-100 in London, the market index of the United Kingdom's top 100 companies, a mere seven years after the company first came onto the market. Building on the success of the PC1512 computer line, Amstrad brought to the market its upgraded PC1640 model. The PC1512, with its powerful color system, appeared a perfect fit for the home-computer market. The PC1640, on the other hand, with its enhanced graphics facility, was ideal for the expanding business-computer market.

By now, Sugar and his marketing team had perfected their product-development formula: catch sight of a rising product, study it, copy it, amend it to include a few user-friendly gadgets, and then farm out its production to a Far Eastern or Scottish manufacturer. Then, after fixing a retail price with two nines in it that was lower the competition's, Amstrad would introduce the consumer product to those who previously had been unable to afford such an item. Finally, Amstrad would bombard its market with blanket advertising.

In late 1987, Amstrad launched the successor to its successful PCW8256 word processor, the PCW9512. The enhanced word processor, fitted with a letter-quality, daisy-wheel printer, put yet another nail in the coffin of the office and home typewriter, much as Alan Sugar had intended.

As a measure of Sugar's success, his own share stake in Amstrad grew in value at one point to £590 million. However, problems began for the company in 1988. In that year, Funai-

## Key Dates:

**1965:** Seventeen-year-old Alan Sugar begins selling reconditioned television sets from his home in London.
**1968:** Sugar establishes AMS Trading Company, later abbreviated as Amstrad.
**1971:** The firm expands its manufacturing capacity to the Far East.
**1979:** Sales reach one million units.
**1980:** Amstrad lists on the London Stock Exchange.
**1982:** A subsidiary is established in Hong Kong.
**1984:** The firm launches the CPC464, or Arnold, a home computer.
**1986:** Amstrad purchases the rights to market the products of Sinclair Research Ltd.
**1989:** After twenty years of growth, profits falter.
**1992:** The firm acquires a 71.3 percent stake in Betacom plc.
**1994:** Amstrad purchases Viglen computers.
**1997:** The company sells its consumer electronics and satellite business to Betacom; Betacom changes its name to Amstrad plc.
**2000:** The e-m@iler is launched and Amserve is established to oversee the retail and distribution of the product.
**2002:** Amstrad develops the e-m@ilerplus, which offers Internet access and allows customers to play Spectrum games.

Amstrad, of which Amstrad was a 49 percent stake holder and a top customer, began production of video cassette recorders (VCR's) in the United Kingdom. Shifting the VCR manufacturing base from the Far East to the United Kingdom was intended to help Amstrad escape the effect of a rising yen and anticipated sanctions from the European Commission on electronic goods manufactured overseas.

As Amstrad grew, flexibility suffered as Sugar struggled to maintain direct control of his company. In 1988, he spent much of the year establishing further subsidiaries in Italy, West Germany, the Netherlands, and Belgium. The company work force doubled to 1,600 people. Sugar reacted to this expansion by delegating more and more responsibility to his lieutenants in the field, while previously he had been able to bark orders across his headquarters' open-plan offices, so near was his senior management team.

### *A Disastrous Year: 1989*

After 20 years of solid growth, Amstrad revealed a profit slump from £160 million a year earlier to £76 million in 1989, on static turnover. City analysts were both stunned and satisfied that the skepticism many had long exhibited towards the company had proved warranted. With his customary candor, Sugar acknowledged that 1989 had been a disastrous year for Amstrad.

The consensus is that during the late 1980s Sugar's management team had extended itself too far as the company grew too rapidly. Sugar had not been able to keep his eye on his company when it mattered most. As one rival told a national newspaper in 1989, ''Amstrad has always been a company that Alan could put his arms round. And now it's growing too big for that.'' Technical and managerial difficulties at Amstrad appeared to be the causes of Sugar's troubles in 1989. When he ought to have supported his management team, Sugar did not. Instead, he displayed his long-standing distaste for bureaucracy. Amstrad has never had more than four layers of management, and Sugar could always reach any one layer with speed.

A management stretched to the limit of its capabilities was going to make mistakes, and Amstrad's did. In 1988, a sophisticated component used in the new PC2000 computer was found to be faulty, delaying the launch of the line. The fault was not detected at an early stage, but was found after the computers had been manufactured and distributed, requiring them to be recalled. The screening and repair of other products in Amstrad's PC2000 line, including the PC2286 and PC2386, forced a slowdown in supply to the company's distributors. A £325 million build-up in inventory followed, which Sugar swore at the time would not be cleared by resorting to fire sales. Instead, he promised an orderly reduction in inventory through an aggressive marketing campaign.

Worse was to follow. A decision by Amstrad to take personal responsibility for the PC2000's distribution in West Germany led its former distributor, the Schneider Company, to depress demand for the new products by dumping its existing stock at bargain prices. Elsewhere, a labor shortage in Taiwan led one audio subcontractor to delay delivery of its order. In the United Kingdom, Funai-Amstrad failed to meet VCR production targets. This delay led to lower than anticipated VCR sales in the United Kingdom during the Christmas season in late 1988.

Then a global shortage of computer microchips led to soaring prices for the components and higher production costs for the PC2000 line. To secure a steady supply of microchips, Amstrad bought into, but lost money on, a U.S. microchip supplier, Micron Technology. The value of the holding fell from £45 million to £30 million before the supply of memory chips improved, and this decline was reflected in Amstrad's poor 1989 profits.

The launch of the television satellite Sky heralded a major new market for Amstrad, the supply of Astra satellite dishes and receiving equipment. In the financial year ended June 30, Amstrad sold £107 million worth of Sky equipment in the United Kingdom, the Netherlands, and Germany, and saw satellite as being an important part of the group's product range. The subsequent merger between Sky and BSB (British Satellite Broadcasting), resulting in Astra's becoming the preferred system, further enhanced Amstrad's already dominant position in this market.

In 1989, Sugar brought Callen So from Hong Kong to his Brentwood headquarters to play a role in components sourcing. From her new base she supported efforts to relocate Amstrad's manufacturing base in Europe, in part because the cost advantage of using Far East suppliers had been reduced, but also to avoid anti-dumping measures against Amstrad threatened by the European Commission in Brussels after 1992. Sugar also recruited a team of managerial experts. Prominent among the new recruits was Peter Thoms from Gillette, who became the new finance director, freeing Ken Ashcroft to deal with inventory control and City relationships, and John Benjamin from Mars Inc., who became the new manufacturing director.

During a troubled 1989, Sugar saw his personal stake in Amstrad fall sharply by £1 million a day to settle, at one point, at £118 million. This still left Alan Sugar the 70th-wealthiest man in the United Kingdom, according to the *Sunday Times*. During this period, Amstrad fell to third place in the league table of U.K. business microcomputer suppliers, behind Compaq with a 13.3 percent market share, and IBM, leading with a 26.1 percent share. Amstrad's own 11.3 percent share kept it ahead of Apple, the U.S. computer maker, which trailed with a 5.8 percent share.

In late 1989, Sugar announced that his company was abandoning the audio and music-systems market. Long adept at pinpointing the needs of the audio market, Amstrad had decided that the margins available from the market no longer warranted the effort. As Sugar told *Financial Weekly* on November 10, 1989, "Our success is at the bottom and calls for a disproportionate amount of management effort when compared with sales and net margins generated."

The abandonment of the audio market was significant because it signaled a marked change in the company's strategy. Until 1989, Sugar had maintained that he was interested in products that sold a minimum 100,000 units a year, but now the criterion for participation was colored by talk of profit contribution rather than volume.

Sugar was suggesting unwittingly that Amstrad was reaching maturity. He continued: "Until recently, most of our products have been relatively low-ticket items, requiring mass sales to provide budgeted profits." As products increased in price, particularly for the business market, the profit margin had allowed Amstrad to sell fewer units while maintaining the company's overall targets. In other words, volume was no longer to be considered the sole source of the company's profits.

In 1990, Alan Sugar insisted that Amstrad's problems of recent years were behind it. The company's share price began to climb from a five-year low reached in 1989, after Sugar threatened to privatize Amstrad once again if investors did not look upon it more favorably.

Defying its critics, who insisted that Amstrad's problems would prove fatal, in April 1990 the company unveiled plans for a combined telephone, facsimile, and answering machine in a bid to return to financial health. Sugar announced at the time that his company would introduce one product every month. Recognizing the potential for growth in laptop computers, Amstrad launched its new and highly regarded ALT range in early 1990, followed by a totally redesigned range of desktop PC's, the Generation-3 range. Reporting the year's results in October 1990, Sugar was able to confirm that inventory had been reduced from a peak of £325 million to a manageable £180 million, and that the company was once again cash-positive.

### *Tough Times: 1990s*

Returning Amstrad to its former glory proved to be out of Sugar's reach during the 1990s. In 1992, he tried to take the company private; however, shareholders voted against the move. Sugar then spent the majority of the decade looking for new opportunities that would match the good fortune of the mid-1980s. The company's efforts included venturing into the telecommunications market. In 1992, Amstrad purchased a 71.3 percent interest in Betacom plc, a United Kingdom-based telephone supplier. The following year, Dancall Telecom, a Danish mobile phone company, was purchased. This company was later sold in 1997.

Viglen, the largest mail order supplier of personal computers in the United Kingdom, was acquired in 1994, followed by the purchase of modem specialist Dataflex Design Communications in 1995. During this time period, Amstrad launched new personal digital assistants (PDA's), various satellite receivers, and mobile phones, but was unable to bring a product to market that had significant sales results.

By 1997, rumors surrounded the company concerning the uncertainty of its future. In a restructuring effort, Amstrad broke up later that year. Its consumer electronics and satellite business was sold to Betacom and Amstrad delisted from the London exchange. Shareholders received shares in Viglen Technology plc, a newly-listed company, and Betacom plc, who had previously named Sugar as chairman. Then in November, Betacom changed its name back to Amstrad plc. In 1999, Amstrad sold the original Betacom business to Alba PLC along with the Answercall and Cable & Wireless branded telecommunications businesses.

Amstrad, a mere shadow of the company it was in the 1980s, entered the new millennium determined to stay afloat. Its employee count had dwindled to 71, down from 1,600 employees in 1988. A May 2000 *Marketing* article claimed that "Sugar would dearly love to recover the former glory of two decades ago when Amstrad was a pioneer in the low-cost electronics market, and every home seemed to have one of its branded hi-fi's or computers." Indeed, the company's main strategy continued to focus on developing cutting edge products that were affordable.

### *The e-m@iler Launch: 2000*

The company appeared to have a breakthrough in 2000 when the firm launched its e-m@iler, a telephone device with an LCD screen and keyboard that allowed a consumer to read and write email and browse the Web. The product also allowed advertisers to promote their brands to e-m@iler customers, a facet that Sugar hoped to cash in on. While analysts gave the product a lukewarm reception reflected in a 17 percent drop in Amstrad's share price, Sugar pursued the new product with a strong belief that it had the potential to secure huge revenues. As such, Amserve Ltd. was created as a subsidiary to oversee the advertising, retail and distribution of the e-m@iler. In June 2000, Dixons Group plc purchased a 20 percent stake in Amserve for £15 million.

By now, Amstrad's focus was on its satellite set top boxes or receivers, its Hong Kong audio products manufacturing operations, and its e-m@iler technology. In 2000, sales related to its satellites peaked due to a BSkyB marketing promotion in which it offered its customer's free satellite equipment. Total group sales for the firm reached £126.6 million but fell to £60.9 million in 2001, due to the decrease in demand from BSkyB after it ended the free receiver promotion.

During 2002, the company developed the e-m@ilerplus, a product that offered enhanced Internet access and allowed the customer to download and play Sinclair ZX Spectrum games. By June 2001, there were 92,000 registered e-m@ilers. In 2002, the company's advertising budget related to this product reached £8 million. While Amstrad was a long way from the success of the 1980s, Sugar and his management team were confident that demand for the e-m@iler would continue to grow. Whether or not Amstrad would remain an independent, healthy company, however, remained to be seen.

### *Principal Subsidiaries*

Amserve Ltd. (80.1%); Amstrad Consumer Products Ltd.; Amstrad Satellite Products Ltd.; Amstrad International Ltd. (Hong Kong).

### *Principal Competitors*

LM Ericcson; Pace Micro Technology plc; Sony United Kingdom.

### *Further Reading*

''Amstrad Flies the Flag with E-mailer Plus TV Campaign,'' *Electronics Weekly*, March 6, 2002, p. 14.

''Amstrad Pays the Price of Sugar,'' *Investors Chronicle*, February 21, 1997, p. 52.

Dignam, Conor, ''Sugar and Spice,'' *Marketing*, May 25, 2000, p. 32.

''Dixons Buys 20 Percent of Amstrad e-m@iler Arm,'' *Electronics Weekly*, May 25, 2000, p. 32.

Druce, Chris, ''Amstrad's Subsidies on E-mailer Continue to Eat Profits,'' *Electronics Weekly*, October 3, 2001, p. 1.

Lloyd, Tom, ''A One Man Band? If It Is, It's a Big One,'' *Financial Weekly*, October 7, 1987.

Skapinker, Michael, ''The London Street Trader Who Would Like to Be as Big as Sony,'' *International Management*, September 1986.

''Sugar Lumps It,'' *Economist* (U.S.), June 7, 1997, p. 70.

Vlessing, Etan, ''Amstrad's Sugar Goes Back to School,'' *Financial Weekly*, November 10, 1989.

Thomas, David, *Alan Sugar: The Amstrad Story*, Random, Century, 1990.

—Etan Vlessing
—update: Christina M. Stansell

# AMSURG

# AmSurg Corporation

**20 Buxton Hills Boulevard**
**Nashville, Tennessee**
**U.S.A.**
**Telephone: (615) 665-1283**
**Toll Free: (800) 945-2301**
**Fax: (615) 665-0755**
**Web site: http://www.amsurg.com**

*Public Company*
*Incorporated:* 1992
*Employees:* 614
*Sales:* $202.31 million (2001)
*Stock Exchanges:* NASDAQ
*Ticker Symbol:* AMSG
*NAIC:* 621493 Freestanding Ambulatory Surgical and Emergency Centers

AmSurg Corporation is the nation's leader of practice-based, single-specialty ambulatory surgery centers and the second-largest ASC owner-operator company in the United States. Through its subsidiaries, AmSurg develops, acquires, and operates practice-based ASCs and specialty physician networks in partnership with surgical and other group practices. The company's licensed outpatient ASCs are usually equipped and staffed for a single medical specialty and are typically located in, or adjacent to, a physician group practice. AmSurg targets ownership in centers that perform gastroenterology, ophthalmology, orthopedics, otolaryngology (ear, nose, and throat) and urology procedures. These medical specialties usually require a high volume of lower-risk procedures that can be performed in an outpatient setting on a safe and cost-effective basis. The company, owner of a majority interest in 95 ASCs in 27 states and the District of Columbia, also has five additional centers scheduled for development during 2002. In 2001, AmSurg ranked fourth on the June *Investor's Business Daily's* list of ''Top Medical Companies'' and seventh in the accompanying ''Profit Diagnosis'' list of medical companies with relative price strengths ratings of 90 or higher. In the July-August 2001 issue of *FSB: Fortune Small Business,* AmSurg was cited for a second year and ranked 12th on the *FSB* 100 list of ''America's Fastest Growing Small Companies.'' AmSurg was also included in the October issue of *Forbes* list of the ''200 Best Small Companies in America.'' AmSurg ranked 139th on the *Forbes* list in 2000 but improved its ranking to 79th in 2001.

## *1970–97: Evolution of Cost-Contained Patient Care*

In 1970, according to The Federated Ambulatory Surgery Association (FASA), several Phoenix, Arizona-based anesthesiologists opened the first ASC and pioneered a way of providing high-quality, cost-effective health care for surgeries that did not require hospital admission. Some surgeons opened surgical facilities in their offices. For many years, private insurance companies, managed-care organizations, and self-insured employers implemented various cost-containment measures to limit the growth of health-care expenditures. However, as changes in technologies and techniques enabled doctors to perform an increasing number of surgeries in hospitals, physicians treated more patients and received less income from patient visits. In a February 4, 2002 interview for the *Wall Street Transcript*, AmSurg president and CEO Ken P. McDonald told newswriter Michael Smith that ''in the beginning doctors built ASCs to tap the facility-fee side of the income in the surgical process.'' By law, surgeons who performed a surgery in a hospital did not receive any of the hospital's facility fee. Hence, physicians looked to ASCs as ''an opportunity . . . to recoup their lost income,'' McDonald explained.

FASA was formed as a non-profit association to represent the interests of the entire ASC industry, including physicians, nurses, administrative staff, and owners. The Association advocated for ASCs before the media, Congress, state legislatures, and regulatory bodies. FASA emphasized the need for insurance coverage by Medicare and private payers, quality standards, and reasonable conditions of coverage. The association also played a significant role for the formation of the ASC accrediting body known as the Accreditation Association for Ambulatory Health Care (AAAHC), which required that all facility members be accredited, licensed, or certified by Medicare.

In 1978, another organization—the Society for Office Based Surgery (SOBS)—was formed to represent the regulatory and

**Company Perspectives:**

*Our strategy focuses on providing high volume, lower-risk ambulatory surgery services in single specialty settings, which we believe results in lower costs, improved operating efficiencies and greater convenience and appeal to patients, physicians, private and governmental payers, and managed care organizations. In addition, our center operations are designed to enhance physician productivity and maximize efficient use of the centers. We intend to continue to grow through the acquisition of surgery centers, the development of new surgery centers, and through same-center revenue growth.*

legislative interests of ASC surgeons and anesthesiologists. SOBS provided them with a forum for sharing information about developing their own facilities. Initially, only board-certified surgeons and anesthesiologists were admitted in the Society. These professionals realized that ASCs were a cost-effective alternative that offered them maximum efficiency for patient care and an environment that was more convenient and less stressful than could be found in hospitals.

The success of office-based surgical suites triggered the development of single and multi-specialty centers. As an advocate for ASC development, in the mid-1980s, SOBS changed its name to the American Association of Ambulatory Surgery Centers (AAASC), and defined itself as a physician-led organization dedicated to advocacy for the ambulatory surgery industry. Among the association's early lobbying successes was the part it played in 1982 for the creation of the Medicare ASC facility-fee benefit. This achievement contributed substantially to the growth of Medicare-certified ASCs.

Meanwhile, in 1981, five former executives from Hospital Affiliates International founded American Healthcorp Inc. in order to own and manage hospitals. Nashville, Tennessee-based Healthcorp diversified by providing hospital-based treatment centers for diabetics and by offering medical-management services to managed-care organizations and third-party administrators. Healthcorp's physicians frequently spoke about their desire for a company that would be a business partner, a risk partner, and a financial partner for setting up ASCs. These discussions led to Healthcorp's November 1992 acquisition of AmSurg, a private company formed in April 1992 to develop, own, and manage practice-based surgery centers in partnership with surgical and other group practices. Healthcorp and a group of private Nashville investors funded the purchase of AmSurg, which became a 59 percent-owned Healthcorp subsidiary and consistently produced substantial revenues and profits. By the end of fiscal 1995, the subsidiary had 18 centers in operation and was developing or negotiating for 11 more.

## *1997–99: Establishing Market Leadership*

On March 11, 1997, Healthcorp spun off AmSurg and distributed its common stock to Healthcorp shareholders. Healthcorp chairman and chief executive officer Thomas G. Cigarran believed that if both companies functioned independently as public companies they could more effectively finance the expansion of their businesses and provide greater value to stockholders. AmSurg filed plans with the Securities and Exchange Commission, went public December 3, 1997, and was traded on the NASDAQ Stock Exchange.

AmSurg senior vice-president Rodney Lunn, during a March 24, 1997, interview for Crain Communications, Inc., told newswriter Raquel Santiago that the company was already developing surgery centers in three Ohio cities—Cleveland, Lorain, and Willoughby. He pointed out that AmSurg helped physicians to ''develop a lower-cost alternative to other outpatient settings by having smaller, focused, and efficient centers'' that specialized in certain procedures. The Willoughby ASC, opened in June, housed three gastroenterologists; in late 1997, the Lorain ASC also offered gastroenterology procedures while the Cleveland venue provided ophthalmology care.

By year end 1997, AmSurg managed 39 ASCs and had an additional eight centers under development. Revenues increased 65 percent to $57.4 million from $34.9 million for 1996; net income grew 70 percent to $2.5 million from $1.5 million. The company attributed its growth to the value it created for its three constituencies: the patient, the physician, and the payer. As reported in the company's *1997 Annual Report*, through surveys conducted among its patients, AmSurg found that over and above high-quality care and lower costs, patients thought that the company's ASCs were ''less intimidating than either hospitals or traditional stand-alone surgery centers.'' Patients were also complimentary about ease of scheduling, access to the facility, uncomplicated admissions and discharge, the convenience of venue location, and the patient-friendly atmosphere at an AmSurg Center.

Physicians working with AmSurg reported multiple benefits that allowed them to dominate the market for their specialties. Patients expressed great satisfaction for the high-quality care they received from physicians focused on one specialty only. The ASCs, usually adjacent to, or within walking distance of the physicians' offices, gave doctors greater flexibility for scheduling appointments and allowed them to create partnerships within their specialties.

AmSurg contributed the expertise needed for dealing with constant changes in delivering and marketing health-care, namely, the design, building, staffing, equipment, and general operation of the facilities as well as risk management, quality accreditation, and business development. In comparison to the operation of other free-standing ambulatory surgery centers, AmSurg's emphasis on the specific needs of a single-specialty practice group of physicians allowed the company to significantly decrease the size of its ASCs, the number of personnel, and the amount of equipment. Thus, AmSurg created value by meeting payers' criteria for high-quality care in the lowest cost venue for a given surgical procedure. ASCs administered by AmSurg were not the same as rural health clinics, urgent care centers, or any other ambulatory-care centers that provided diagnostic or primary health care. The only patients admitted to AmSurg ASCs were those who had seen a health-care provider who recommended surgery as an appropriate treatment.

After six years of developing and managing the daily operations of practice-based surgery centers, by year end 1998

## Key Dates:

**1970:** Several anesthesiologists open an outpatient surgicenter in Phoenix, Arizona.
**1982:** Medicare approves payment of facility-fee benefits to ambulatory surgical centers (ASCs), also known as surgicenters.
**1992:** AmSurg is formed as a private company and pioneers the development of Medicare-certified and licensed physician practice-based ASCs.
**1992:** American Healthcorp, Inc. acquires AmSurg.
**1997:** Healthcorp spins off AmSurg, which becomes a public company and increases marketing of its business model for the operation of ASCs.
**1999:** AmSurg posts double-digit increases in same-center revenues.
**2001:** AmSurg completes a stock offering that nets $66.3 million.

AmSurg was a leader in its industry segment. Centers in operation increased to 52, compared to 39 in the previous year; the development of three new specialty networks brought the total number of ASC networks to seven; and the Joint Commission on Accreditation of Health-care Organizations (JCAHO) enhanced the company's leadership position by granting initial or renewed three-year accreditation for 22 centers. According to the *AmSurg 1998 Annual Report*, several structural strengths supported the company's consistent growth: newly established ASCs usually reached break-even point within 90 days of opening and typically met their goals for annualized performance within a year. Furthermore, because surgeons sharpened their skills by performing a large number of specific procedures, the increased volume of procedures resulted in rapid revenue growth while providing high-quality care and patient satisfaction at lower costs.

For both 1998 and 1999, AmSurg posted double-digit increases in same-center revenues; by year-end 1999 the company had 63 ASCs in operation, 12 others under development, and eight newly-established partnerships. The company, with 208,000 surgical procedures performed in its ASCs during 1999 (a growth of 33 percent), emerged as a clear leader of the rapidly expanding practice-based surgery center segment. Health-care analysts estimated that on an annual basis, approximately six million surgeries were performed in ASCs, that is, more than half of all the surgical procedures performed each year in the United States. AmSurg was a significant player in an industry expected to grow annually at approximately 8 percent because of continuing health-care trends, including steadily improving technology that enabled an increasing variety of surgical procedures to be conducted outside the high-sensitivity surgical facilities of hospitals.

### *2000 and Beyond*

In January 2000, AmSurg signed an agreement with Physicians Resource Group, Inc. to purchase PRG's ownership position in a number of its single-specialty ophthalmology surgery centers. This acquisition, combined with AmSurg's own ophthalmology centers, gave the company the largest industry presence in practice-based ophthalmology ASCs, thereby joining the company's dominant market position in gastroenterology surgery centers. Continuing substantial cash flow from operations—which was more than double diluted earnings per share—enabled the company to fund internally the major portion of its center acquisitions and developments.

In May 2001, AmSurg completed a stock offering that netted the company $66.3 million. According to Cheryl Jackson's article in the May issue of *American Medical News*, Charles Lynch, analyst at CIBC World Markets, commented that AmSurg was "in great shape operationally. They're kind of peeling out this low-end surgery from the hospital industry . . . The physicians are happier. The patients are happier. The HMO's are happier." As Jackson stated in her article, "AmSurg usually focused on markets where it would not be in head-to-head competition with hospitals."

By mid-2001, the typical surgeries performed at AmSurg centers within each specialty included gastroenterology (colonoscopy and other endoscopy procedures), ophthalmology (cataracts and retinal laser surgery), orthopedics (knee arthroscopy and carpal tunnel repair), otolaryngology (ear, nose, and throat procedures), and urology (cystoscopy and biopsy). AmSurg marketed directly to third-party payers, including health maintenance organizations (HMOs), preferred provider organizations (PPOs), and other managed-care organizations and employers. The company worked consistently at having its ASCs obtain and maintain three-year certification from JCAHO or AAAHC.

Because of its strategy for the design of ASCs, AmSurg could charge facility fees lower than those of hospitals and free-standing, multi-specialty outpatient surgery centers. Furthermore, more efficient staffing, better utilization of space, and a specialized operating environment focused on cost containment contributed a cost-effective alternative to other surgery venues. Each ASC had two or three operating or procedure rooms as well as areas for reception, preparation, recovery, and administration and could provide for 2,500 or more procedures annually.

In September 2001, AmSurg opened a new ASC that offered two different types of surgical treatments in the same building, according to freelance writer Trent D. McNeeley's story in the July 11, 2001 issue of the *Nashville Business Journal*. The first suite, the Louisville Endoscopy Center, offered treatments from the physicians of Louisville Gastroenterology Associates; the other suite, tentatively named the Bluegrass Surgery and Laser Center, offered surgical eye treatments by Dr. Donald W. Bennett of Bennett & Bloom Eye Centers. The doctors formed a partnership for the funds needed to buy the land, build the center, and acquire the equipment needed for each suite. AmSurg managed the entire facility.

Despite the destruction of New York City's World Trade Center on September 11, 2001, as well as a turbulent economy, the health-care industry continued to enjoy high growth and robust profit margins, Molly Cate wrote in the December 3, 2001 issue of the *Nashville Business Journal*. She pointed out several reasons for what she called a rush "to enter the [ASC] business: the baby-boomer bubble, advances in technology, and the push from all sides toward outpatient treatment. About 70 to 80 percent of surgical procedures are now performed on an outpatient basis. That compares to only 15 percent in 1980.'' Cate quoted industry analyst Darren Lehrich's statement about the possibility of continuing growth of the ASC business: ''There are about 3,200 ambulatory surgery centers in the country. Two-thirds of those facilities are still controlled by physicians or independent partnerships. And there's still a lot of growth yet to come.'' Lehrich, who rated AmSurg at ''outperform,'' estimated that AmSurg had a 3 percent market share of the ASC sector.

Revenues for 2001 increased 41 percent to $202.31 million from $143.26 million for 2000. Net earnings were $14.9 million, up 64 percent from $9.1 million; earnings per diluted share rose 30 percent to 78 cents for 2001, compared to 60 cents for 2000. AmSurg set new records in revenues, net earnings, and same-center revenues for each of the four years since it became a public company.

Thus, in a relatively short time, AmSurg proved the strength of its business model, established itself as the nation's leading practice-based, single-specialty surgery center company, and was in a sound financial position to penetrate a larger portion of the potential market for its services.

### *Principal Competitors*

HCA, Inc.; HealthSouth Corporation; Laser Vision Centers, Inc.; Opticare Health Systems, Inc.; United Surgical Partners International, Inc.

### *Further Reading*

Cate, Molly, ''Partnership With Physicians Key to AmSurg's Business Model, Success,'' *Nashville Business Journal,* January 1, 2001.

——, ''Surgery Centers Gain Luster as Population Ages, Economic Forces Encourage Outpatient Procedures,'' *Nashville Business Journal,* December 3, 2001.

Jackson, Cheryl, ''Surgery Center Firm Completes Stock Offering,'' *American Medical News,* May 7, 2001.

McNeeley, Trent D., ''AmSurg Tenants Will Offer Endoscopy, Eye Treatments,'' *Nashville Business Journal*, July 11, 2001.

Santiago, Raquel, ''Operation Expansion: AmSurg Forming Surgery Center Network,'' *Cain's Cleveland Business*, March 24, 1997.

Smith, Michael L., ''CEO Reports on the Single Biggest Near-Term Opportunity for AmSurg,'' *Wall Street Transcript*, February 4, 2002.

''Surgery Center Marketing Targets Patient Flow to Practices,'' *Physician Compensation Report*, June 2001.

—Gloria A. Lemieux

Applied Films

# Applied Films Corporation

**9586 I-25 Frontage Road**
**Longmont, Colorado 80504**
**U.S.A.**
**Telephone: (303) 774-3200**
**Fax: (303) 678-9275**
**Web site: http://www.appliedfilms.com**

*Pubic Company*
*Incorporated:* 1976 as Applied Films Laboratory Inc.
*Employees:* 642
*Sales:* $112.7 million (2001)
*Stock Exchanges:* NASDAQ
*Ticker Symbol:* AFCO
*NAIC:* 334413 Semiconductor and Related Device Manufacturing

Applied Films Corporation is a leading provider of thin film deposition equipment to the Flat Panel Display (FPD) market, the architectural and automotive glass industry, and the web packaging industry. In addition, the company is pursuing the market for coatings on polyethylene terephthalate bottles. These deposition systems are used to deposit thin films that improve the material properties of the base substrate. The thin films offer electronic, reflective, filter, protective, and other properties that provide critical elements in the composition of commercial and industrial products. Applied Films also markets glass substrates to the FPD industry, which are used as a component in the production of black and white liquid crystal displays (LCD). Flat panel displays are used in a wide variety of consumer and industrial products, including cellular telephones, personal digital assistants, calculators, laptop computers, scientific instruments, televisions, desktop monitors, video games, gasoline pumps, automotive instruments, and other electronic devices. Demand for FPD's is rapidly growing due primarily to market and technological forces concerning wireless and portable communication devices and the emergence of flat panel computer monitors and flat panel televisions. The company's web-coated products are increasingly used for decorative packaging to enhance consumer appeal in various products. Web coaters apply a thin film to paper, plastic, or foil that also creates a protective barrier and prolongs product shelf-life. In addition, the company's large glass systems serve the architectural, automotive, and solar glass markets, which are driven by the demand for energy conservation and alternative energy sources. Applied Films operates its Large Area Coatings division as a wholly owned subsidiary with manufacturing in Alzenau, Germany.

### *1970s Origins*

Applied Films Corporation was originally founded on March 2, 1976 as Applied Films Laboratory, Inc. to produce and provide thin-film coatings and coating systems based on planar magnetron sputtering technology and high-speed, inline deposition techniques. These enabling technologies were developed by two of the company's cofounders, John Chapin and Richard Condon. Chapin invented the planar magnetron, which enabled producers of thin film coated glass and semiconductor chips to deposit sputtered thin film coatings at low cost. Condon innovated the in-line sputtering systems, which were widely adopted by the industry. With these early technological innovations, Chapin and Condon formed Applied Films Labs, Inc. in Colorado with another cofounder, Cecil Van Alsburg, who served as the company's president and chief executive officer from 1976 to 1998. Chapin served as vice-president of research and Condon as vice-president of engineering.

### *1990s Merger with Donnelly*

Since its inception, Applied Films pursued both thin films research and development and limited thin films production. A large portion of the company's early business focused on coating monitor screens for IBM laptops. On May 1, 1992, the company merged with the Donnelly Coated Corporation, a wholly owned subsidiary of the Donnelly Coporation of Holland, Michigan, which primarily manufactured and sold fabricated, molded, and thin coated glass for the automotive and electronic industries. As a result of the merger, Donnelly purchased 50 percent of the Applied Film's outstanding common stock, with the remaining 50 percent owned by the former shareholders of Applied Films. The new company, named Donnelly Applied Films Corporation, operated manufacturing facil-

**Company Perspectives:**

*Applied Films is a leading supplier of thin film coated glass and physical vapor deposition equipment to the information technology industry, particularly flat panel displays (FPD), roll coaters for use in the deposition of capacitor and barrier films, and large glass coaters for the production of thin films used in the architectural and automotive industries. Flat panel displays are found in a wide variety of consumer and industrial products, including cellular telephones, calculators, pagers, video games, office products, and laptop computers. FPDs have also been identified as a potential replacement for the CRT in televisions and computer monitors.*

ities in both Boulder, Colorado, and Michigan until the end of 1993, when it consolidated all its manufacturing operations in Boulder.

In November 1997, the company announced its initial public offering of 1.9 million shares of common stock at the price of $8.50 per share. In connection with the offering, Donnelly sold its 50 percent interest in the company, comprising 1.4 million shares, and Applied Films issued the remaining 500,000 shares. In December 1997, an additional 176,439 shares were issued in connection with the completion of the initial offering. Applied Films planned to use the net proceeds from the offering to repay the debt incurred by investment in new production capacity and working capital. With the divestiture of the Donnelly shares, the company became known as Applied Films Corporation.

### *Late 1990s: New Ventures*

In 1997, Applied Films began marketing thin film coating equipment to FPD manufacturers, netting $2.8 million in sales. In 1998, net sales of thin coating equipment rose significantly to $13.9 million, proving that the company had found a profitable niche. At the same time, the company began relocating its thin film production coaters from Boulder to its new Longmont, Colorado, facility to improve operating efficiencies and its competitive position. The company believed that its dual capability in thin film coatings and thin film equipment provided the foundation for significant future growth.

In May 1998, the board of directors of Applied Films elected Thomas T. Edman as president and CEO. The former president and CEO, Cecil Van Alsburg, continued with the company as chairman of the board. Edman previously joined the company in 1996, serving first as vice-president of market development and then as executive vice-president and chief operating officer. Before joining Applied Films, he had been the general manger of the High Performance Materials Division at Marubeni Specialty Chemicals, Inc., a large Japanese trading corporation. With a new CEO in place, the company intended to pursue continued growth of its coated glass business in three ways: (1) attempting to be a low- cost producer through the building of its own coating systems and achieving production efficiencies by means of technology; (2) leveraging and strengthening its key relationships with many of the world's leading FPD customers; and (3) seeking strategic business partnerships to increase its customer base and manufacturing capacity.

In June 1998, Applied Films entered into a 50/50 joint venture in China with the Japanese firm Nippon Sheet Glass Company, Ltd., the world's largest supplier of substrate glass for flat panel displays, to produce thin film coated glass for LCD displays. The benefit of this agreement for Applied Films lay in facilitating greater access to its key customer base in Southeast Asia, where 90 percent of the FPD finished goods manufacturing was located. The agreement stipulated that the joint venture would operate in Suzhou, China, where Nippon operated a plant that manufactured LCD substrate glass and provided thin coating services. The strategic partnership was expected to improve customer service through just-in-time delivery and to reduce labor and transportation costs. Under the agreement, Nippon would contribute its Suzhou coating line to the joint venture, while Applied Films would provide one of its thin coating systems. The financing of the joint venture totaled $6.4 million with each of the partners contributing 50 percent of the capital. Applied Films anticipated that the venture would give it a manufacturing foothold in Asia from which it could expand operations.

The new company, Suzhou NSG-AFC Thin Film Electronics Co. Ltd., represented a new step in forging stronger ties between the two companies. Previously, Applied Films had entered into a relationship with Nippon to provide much of the coated glass needs of Nippon's customers. Applied Films was a major international supplier of thin film coated glass for low-information-content liquid crystal displays (TN LCDs), which could be found in watches, calculators, video games, toys, and other electronic products. The company also supplied thin film coated glass for higher information content black and white STN LCD's, which are typically used in cellular telephones, pagers, and digital personal assistants. This three-year arrangement provided a basis for Applied Films to sell its coated-glass products with the help of Nippon's marketing power. This initial arrangement was particularly important in assisting Applied Films to expand its capacity in the STN market, which had more challenging quality requirements.

At the same time, the company began entering new markets with its coating equipment technology. Applied Films saw the emerging plasma display panel (PDP) industry, which represented one of the fastest growing segments of the FPD market, as particularly important. PDP's were more sophisticated and technologically advanced in providing high information content. It appeared to provide the means to produce the large thin high-definition television screens that the industry had so long anticipated. Because the PDP industry anticipated that between four and eight billion dollars would be invested in PDP production facilities during the following five years, Applied Films aimed to become a major supplier of thin film coating equipment to this emerging market. Overall, Applied Films appeared to be well positioned in a high-growth market. Flat panel displays were abundant in numerous commercial products and were expanding with the emergence of flat panel, high-definition TV's and computer terminals. In addition, the market for higher resolution FPD's was expected to expand to such applications as on-board navigation devices for automobiles and commercial airplanes, instrumentation, medical electronics, personal digital assistants, and other products.

**Key Dates:**

**1976:** The company is incorporated in Colorado as Applied Films Lab, Inc.
**1992:** The company reincorporates in Michigan as Applied Films Corporation and merges with Donnelly Coated Corporation of Holland, Michigan, becoming Donnelly Applied Films Corporation.
**1994:** The company ceases operations in Holland, Michigan, consolidating all operations in Boulder, Colorado.
**1995:** The company reincorporates as a Colorado corporation.
**1997:** The company makes its initial public offering of 1.9 million shares of common stock.
**1998:** The company forms joint venture in China with Nippon Sheet Glass Co., Ltd.
**2001:** The company acquires the Large Area Coatings division of Unaxis Holding Ltd for $60 million in cash and 673,353 shares of Applied Films' common stock.

By the end of the 1998 fiscal year, the company's net sales rose by 55.8 percent to a record of $53 million compared with $34 million in 1997. This sales and earnings growth stemmed largely from increased sales of thin film coated glass and continuing significant growth in sales of thin film coating equipment. Nevertheless, despite this impressive growth, the company anticipated slower growth for 1999 due to adverse economic conditions in Asia, where the majority of its customer base was located. Indeed, from 1997 through 1999, sales to international customers ranged between 78 and 85 percent of the company's gross sales. The company's primary markets were China (including Hong Kong), Korea, Japan, Taiwan, and Malaysia.

### *Restructuring for a New Millennium*

In response to the Asian banking and currency crisis, Applied Films unveiled a restructuring plan in August 1998 to reduce costs and improve operating efficiencies stemming from lower sales in Asia. The company's cost containment measures included closing one of its five thin film production lines, laying off 27 production workers, cutting back production of thin film coated glass to five days a week with no overtime, and reducing executive management pay by 10 percent. At the time of the restructuring, Applied Films had 275 employees. The company had begun to see the sales slowdown during its last quarter of 1998 and Wall Street analysts expected the company to fare worse in the coming months. By late January 1999, few companies had been hit harder by the Asian financial crisis than Applied Films. The company reported that its second quarter sales had plummeted by more than 50 percent from the previous year, recording a net loss for the quarter. The company had recorded sales of $6.2 million for the quarter compared to sales of $13.2 million for the second quarter of 1998. As a result of the continuing slowdown in sales, the company cut another 20 workers and reduced its production levels.

Nevertheless, by the fourth quarter sales began to improve due primarily to the company's joint venture with Nippon in Suzhou, China. The joint venture instituted a 24-hour-a-day, seven-days-a week operation late in the fourth quarter of fiscal 1999, its first quarter of operation. In August 1999, the company forged another strategic partnership when it signed an exclusive agreement with Information Products Inc. (IP) to provide it with coated glass for the rapidly growing touch screen market. In return, the agreement stipulated that IP would sell its coated glass products exclusively through Applied Films' distribution network in China and Hong Kong. The market for touch screens had been experiencing explosive growth, primarily driven by demand for Personal Digital Assistants. The global market for Personal Digital Assistants was estimated to be about $400 million and was expected to grow at an annual compounded rate of 21 percent. The strategic partnership with IP enabled Applied Films to enter the high-growth touch screen market, a new growth area for the company.

In December 1999, the company announced that it had executed its first multi-million dollar contract with a Taiwanese company to produce an ATX-700 Sputtering System, its latest development in equipment platforms for the FPD and PDP markets. The ATX-700 system represented a design innovation with its ease of automation, lower particulate levels, and lower cost of ownership to plasma display panel manufacturers.

On March 9, 2000, Applied Films offered 3,066,500 shares of common stock at $23.50 per share. The proceeds from the sale were anticipated to raise $55.1 million, which the company intended to use for working capital, including the production and sale of coating equipment, expansion of production capacity, debt reduction, financing of research and development, and funding of potential acquisitions. The issuing of new shares of stock signaled growing confidence by the company concerning its prospects for future growth. This confidence was bolstered by a significant increase in the company's fiscal 2000 third quarter net income which rose by 464 percent to $1.6 million compared to a net loss of ($386,000) for the same period in fiscal 1999. The company attributed the strong earnings to increased demand for its thin film coated glass products driven by growth of applications in wireless communication devices.

In October 2000, Applied Films announced that it had entered into a definitive agreement to acquire Large Area Coating (LAC), a division of Unaxis Holding Ltd of Zurich, Switzerland. Applied Films, which purchased the division for $60 million in cash and 673,353 shares of its common stock, completed the acquisition in January 2001. The company planned to operate LAC, located in Alzenau, Germany, as a wholly owned subsidiary. LAC included the former Display Coatings division of Balzers Process Systems GmbH and the Web Coatings, Architectural, and Container Barrier Coatings groups of Leybold GmbH. Both Applied Films and LAC produced physical vapor deposition equipment for the flat panel display industry. In addition, LAC provided roll coaters for depositing capacitor and barrier films and large glass coaters for the production of thin films used in the architectural and automotive industries. These specialized coating films were designed for application on windows and windshields to help stabilize hot and cool temperatures in offices and automobiles. The acquisition brought Applied Films a staff of 110 technical staff, access to more than 200 patents, a large backlog of orders for equipment, and greater opportunities in the web coater, barrier coating, and glass coating equipment markets. Also of importance was

LAC's strength in the coating of color filters, which served to enhance Applied Film's position in the plasma display market for flat-screen TV's. LAC also offered coating technology equipment that put a protective film coating on such products as plastic soda and beer bottles and potato chip bags to lengthen their shelf life. The purchase of LAC helped Applied Films in building diversification in geography and products, more than doubling its market share in the display market to 45 percent.

As a result, the acquisition of LAC considerably altered the amount and nature of Applied Films' revenues. The majority of revenues stemmed from the sale of thin film coating equipment to producers in the display, architectural glass, and packaging markets. The company sold its equipment to manufacturers of flat panel displays, which were used in the production of laptop and desktop monitors and to producers of plasma display panels, which were incorporated into hang on the wall televisions. The equipment sold to the architectural glass industry was used to produce large glass panels for the construction of commercial buildings, skyscrapers, and automobiles, and for the generation of solar energy utilizing sunlight. The company also sold equipment to the web-packing industry for the manufacture of rolled films, which comprised plastic or thin foil requiring a thin film layer application to enhance the protective barrier of the package in order to extend the shelf life of perishable foods. The marketing of equipment to the bottling industry that extended the shelf life for beverages in plastic bottles also substantially contributed to revenues.

Despite the stock market's precipitous decline in 2001, which hit technology stocks particularly hard, the company's net revenues for the year rose to $112.7 million, a 167 percent increase in revenue over the previous year. The revenue increase resulted from equipment sales stemming from the acquisition of LAC, renamed Applied Films Germany. The company projected that its long-term growth would be driven by its ability to provide thin film process technology and equipment for emerging technologies in the flat panel display and bottling industries. Until 1997, the company had focused primarily on the sale of thin film coated glass. Subsequently, Applied Films devoted substantial resources to the development and sale of equipment for thin film coating, which appeared to offer the most significant opportunities for growth. Although the acquisition of the Large Area Coating business provided additional expertise and diversified products, the company operated within a highly competitive industry. Most of Applied Films' competitors had substantially greater financial, technical, marketing, and sales resources. Nevertheless, Applied Films had positioned itself well for future growth with a diversified range of products, an aggressive research and development program, and operations in Alzenau and Hanau, Germany; Brussels, Belgium; Hong Kong and Shanghai, China; Seoul, Korea; Tokyo and Osaka, Japan; and Taipai, Taiwan.

### *Principal Divisions*

Applied Films Germany.

### *Principal Competitors*

Ulvac Japan, Ltd; Anelva Ltd.; Samsung/Corning; Merck Display Technology; Wellite; General Vacuum; Von Ardenne; British Oxygen Coating Technologies Corporation; Tetra-Pak.

### *Further Reading*

Benjamin, Jeff, "Streetwise: A Big Bulge in Flat Screens," *Investment News*, December 18, 2000.

"Donnelly Corporation Forms Joint Venture With Applied Films Laboratory, Inc.," *Financial News*, February 24, 1992.

Draper, Heather, "Applied Films Corp.," *Denver Rocky Mountain News*, January 7, 2001.

Hudson, Kris, "Effects of Asian Crisis Lead Two Boulder, Colo., Firms to Cut Jobs," *Daily Camera*, August 8, 1998.

——, "Longmont, Colo.-Based Maker of Film-Coated Glass Lays Off 20 Workers," *Daily Camera*, January 29, 1999.

"Top 100/Applied Films Co. Diversity of Uses Drives Success Coating Graces Goods," *Denver Post*, August 12, 2001.

"U.S. Display Consortium and Donnelly," *Business Wire*, May 31, 1994.

—Bruce P. Montgomery

# Ariens Company

**655 West Ryan Street**
**P.O. Box 157**
**Brillion, Wisconsin 54110**
**U.S.A.**
**Telephone: (920) 756-2141**
**Toll Free: (800) 678-5443**
**Fax: (920) 756-2407**
**Web site: http://www.ariens.com**

*Private Company*
*Incorporated:* 1933
*Employees:* 900
*Sales:* $130 million (2001)
*NAIC:* 333112 Lawn and Garden Tractor and Home Lawn and Garden Equipment Manufacturing

Ariens Company is a leading manufacturer of lawn mowers, garden tractors and tillers, and snow blowers. The company manufacturers lawn mowers and snow blowers under its Ariens brand. It also manufactures a line of lawn care equipment geared for a commercial market under the Gravely brand. Ariens operates a subsidiary company, Stens Corporation, which produces a full line of small engine and outdoor equipment replacement parts. Stens is headquartered in Jasper, Indiana. It maintains distribution centers in eight states and sells to customers in 50 countries. Gravely and Ariens products are made at the company's extensive plant in Brillion, Wisconsin, and sold through a dealership network extending throughout North America and more than 35 other countries. The company began as an iron works, made farm equipment in the 1930s, and began serving a consumer market in the 1950s. Ariens is still owned and managed by members of the Ariens family.

## *Early Years*

The company that became today's Ariens began as a family business. Henry and Christine Ariens came to the small town of Brillion, Wisconsin, in 1893. There, they began operating an iron foundry from the garage behind their house. The home business evidently went well, and by 1897 they had built a factory, the first heavy industry to open in Brillion. The foundry was called Brillion Iron Works. The company flourished for 30 years, but it was hard hit at the very beginning of the Great Depression. Brillion Iron Works declared bankruptcy in 1929. Though the foundry was insolvent, it did not cease operating completely. In the same year as the bankruptcy, the company invented the first viable rotary tiller in the United States. The rotary tiller was a powerful farm implement that used rotating metal blades to lift and turn soil to prepare it for planting. Other inventors had come up with similar machines, but it had always been difficult to harness an adequate power source. The company put out various models in the early 1930s, and then in 1933 brought out the Ariens Rotary Tiller, powered by a four-cylinder, 14-horsepower engine.

At this juncture, the company that Henry and Christine Ariens had founded split into two separate entities. The Brillion Iron Works continued, now run by the oldest of the Ariens' sons, Steve. Steve Ariens also headed an ancillary company, established in 1933 as the Ariens Company. The Iron Works became a leader in ductile iron casting and remained a privately held corporation until the 1970s, when it was sold to Beatrice Foods. The Ariens Company concentrated on tillers and other farm implements. Two other brothers, Leon and Francis, also managed the new firm. The company put out a range of tillers in the 1930s and 1940s.

## *Producing Consumer Goods in the 1950s–60s*

During World War II, the Ariens factory was converted to production of tools and materials for the benefit of the military. After the war, the company went back to producing tillers. The company had a line of tillers of different sizes and motor strengths for farm use. However, new technology led to the development of better and smaller horsepower motors, and in 1950 Ariens began producing small machines for the backyard gardener. Its first products of this type were the Jet Tiller and the Imperial Riding Mower. Ariens was able to tap the growing legions of suburbanites for its new line. Its high-end equipment appealed to wealthier property owners. The riding mower was an attractive alternative to the back-straining work of the old-

### Company Perspectives:

*Ariens' Vision Statement is "Passionate People! Astounded Customers!" That vision, in conjunction with the company's Core Values, encapsulates the way Ariens does business. Core Values: Be honest. Be fair. Keep commitments. Respect the individual. Encourage intellectual curiosity.*

fashioned push mower, especially for those with extensive grounds.

Ariens was still producing agricultural equipment. In 1954, the company revamped its entire line of tillers and also brought out a new and improved tiller called the Trans-A-Matic. However, the company increasingly leaned toward the consumer end of the market. Beginning in 1955, Ariens dedicated a team of engineers to develop new products. It hoped to reduce the lag time, then one to two years, between an initial design and when a product came on the market. In 1960, the company brought out one of its best known products, the Ariens Sno-Thro, a self-propelled snow thrower. As the riding mower was a welcome alternative for some to the laborious push mower, the snow thrower offered consumers a cure for the dreaded snow shovel. Ariens was able to put a powerful motor in a relatively small machine, and it believed it had a market that would stretch from New England to Montana. That year the company also produced the first rear-tine tiller designed for consumers.

The firm did well, and expanded both its plant and its offices in Brillion. In 1963, the company built a new factory of 23,000 square feet. Ariens began to sell its products in Canada and in several other foreign countries. It had a thriving domestic market and soon became the leading snow thrower manufacturer in the United States.

## *Acquisitions in the 1970s–80s*

In 1969, a new generation of the family led the company, as Michael Ariens became president and Steve Ariens moved up to chairman of the board. Ariens entered an era of acquisition and expansion around this time. By the mid-1970s, the company employed over 400 people, and it sold its goods through as many as 6,000 dealers across the country. Ariens had built a national reputation with its riding mowers and snow throwers, as well as its line of rotary tillers. The firm's first big acquisition occurred in 1974, when Ariens bought up the New Holland division of the Sperry Rand corporation. New Holland, of Belleville, Pennsylvania, made a line of lawn and garden tractors, sold through a network of some 1,000 dealers. Ariens discontinued its own small selection of lawn tractors and moved the New Holland plant into expanded quarters in Brillion. The purchase of New Holland gave Ariens a more complete offering for the backyard gardener. Two years after the New Holland acquisition, the company announced plans to expand its manufacturing facilities yet again. It had added some 100,000 square feet when it bought New Holland. In 1976, the company began work on a new plant on 57 acres of land. When completed, Ariens' buildings occupied about 485,000 square feet, which the company proudly compared to the cramped garage in which Henry and Christine Ariens had started their business. The expansion cost an estimated $1.5 million.

Next, Ariens made another purchase, adding another brand name to its line of products. In 1982, the firm bought North Carolina-based Gravely Co. from its parent McGraw-Edison. Gravely was known primarily on the East Coast as a maker of lawn and garden power equipment. It had a long history, putting out its first tractor in 1916. The firm had gone through several owners, and by the 1980s was known as a high-end maker of home lawn and garden equipment, as well as equipment for commercial landscapers. Gravely continued to manufacture its line out of its Clemmons, North Carolina, plant for ten years after the merger. In 1985, subsidiary Gravely itself made an acquisition. It picked up a manufacturer of commercial chippers and vacuums called Promark.

## *New Products in the 1990s and After*

The company went through several changes of management in the 1990s. In 1992, Michael Ariens, grandson of founder Henry Ariens, took the position of chairman of the board, and for the first time a non-family member led the company. David Vander Zander took over as president of Ariens, though he held the post only briefly. In 1995, Henry and Christine Ariens' great-grandson Dan Ariens took over the presidency of a new subsidiary company. After three years in that post, Dan came back to head Ariens. Entering the 21st century, the company was still controlled by the founding family, now in the fourth generation.

Ariens expanded its line of lawn mowers and snow throwers in the 1990s. It made walk-behind mowers, riding mowers, and machines sold as "zero-turn" mowers for their low turning radius. Most mowers were gas-powered, but the company also developed battery-powered mowers in the mid-1990s. Battery-powered mowers were considered more convenient to use and environmentally sound than those powered by gas, and consumer interest in the machines was rising. Ariens teamed up with an Ohio firm, Lucerne Products Inc., to come up with a reliable and compact power source for the new model. By 1996, the company had developed a competitively priced battery-powered machine with all electronic controls. Ariens also made snow throwers in a variety of sizes and types. Some were small machines geared to consumers, while others were heavy-duty professional models.

Ariens continued to upgrade its plant and equipment in the 1990s. In 1992, the company decided to shut the North Carolina plant where the Gravely line was manufactured. Gravely products were then made out of Brillion. The brand had been principally marketed on the east coast, and sales and marketing operations for Gravely remained in North Carolina for another five years. In 1997, the company consolidated all the Gravely offices into its Brillion facilities. Soon after, Ariens invested some $1.5 million to renovate its powder-coating operations. Powder coating is a metal finishing process that is critical to the look and durability of the finished machine. Ariens needed a high quality coating system, even more rugged than that used in the automotive industry, because its products were subjected to constant stress from salty snow, muddy grass, lawn chemicals, and the like. Ariens replaced its outdated coating system, which

**Key Dates:**

**1893:** Henry and Christine Ariens settle in Brillion and begin operating a foundry in a garage.
**1897:** Brillion Iron Works is founded.
**1933:** Ariens Co. is founded to market roto-tillers.
**1950:** The company debuts its riding mower.
**1960:** Ariens first markets a snow thrower.
**1982:** The company acquires Gravely.
**1995:** Stens Corp. is acquired.

had been originally designed to handle only two colors, adding four powder-coating booths as well as new equipment such as conveyors and curing ovens which finished off the coating process. The new equipment gave the company increased flexibility in its manufacturing process, allowing for quick color changes and more refined quality control.

Ariens made another significant acquisition in the mid-1990s. The company bought Jasper, Indiana-based Stens Corporation in 1995. Stens made replacement parts for a variety of outdoor power tools. It had dealers and distributors across the United States and in over 50 countries abroad. Stens continued to make and market its products under its own name, but management of the company passed to Dan Ariens. When he became president of Ariens Co. in 1998, presidency of Stens Corp. passed to his brother Peter.

The company embraced the Internet in the late 1990s, selling a few of its top models on-line beginning in 1999. By the late 1990s, Ariens was manufacturing not only its own line, but putting out mowers under the brand names Scotts and Husquvarna. It also manufactured snowblowers for Lesco. Ariens brought out new models in all its lines for 2001. A new Ariens mower model ZOOM 2050 was touted as cutting mowing time in half; the Gravely line offered models with enhanced features; and the Stens line of replacement parts included new and improved products. Ariens continued to work on building dealership loyalty to its brands, aiming for them to handle all three lines.

### *Principal Subsidiaries*

Stens Corporation.

### *Principal Competitors*

Deere & Co.; The Toro Co.; Honda Motor Co., Ltd.

### *Further Reading*

"Ariens Co. Adds Work in Brillion," *Wisconsin State Journal*, July 25, 1992.
"Ariens Co. Recalls 40,000 Lawn Mowers," *Capital Times* (Madison, Wis.), March 15, 2001.
"Ariens Co. to Expand at Brillion," *Milwaukee Journal*, August 13, 1976.
Babyak, Richard J., "Rewarding Renewal," *Appliance Manufacturer*, April 2000, pp. 51–2.
"Gravely to Move Unit to Wisconsin," *Wisconsin State Journal*, January 22, 1997.
Remich, Norman C., Jr., "With Solid-State Relay, the Grass Is Greener," *Appliance Manufacturer*, October 1996, p. 60.
"Sears, Ariens Pursue Online Appliance Sales," *Appliance Manufacturer*, April 1999, p. 17.
"Tractor Line Added by Ariens Acquisition," *Milwaukee Journal*, July 6, 1973.

—A. Woodward

ARLA FOODS

# Arla Foods amba

**Skanderborgvej 277**
**DK-8260 Viby J.**
**Denmark**
**Telephone: (+45) 89 38 10 00**
**Fax: (+45) 86 28 16 91**
**Web site: http://www.arlafoods.com**

*Cooperative*
*Founded:* 1869 as Arla ek. for.
*Employees:* 18,200
*Sales:* DKr 38.13 billion ($4.66 billion)
*NAIC:* 311512 Creamery Butter Manufacturing; 311225 Fats and Oils Refining and Blending; 311511 Fluid Milk Manufacturing; 311513 Cheese Manufacturing; 311514 Dry, Condensed, and Evaporated Dairy Product Manufacturing; 312111 Soft Drink Manufacturing

Arla Foods amba is a cooperative formed by the 2000 merger between Sweden's Arla and Denmark's MD Foods. The company controls 95 percent and 65 percent of the dairy production markets in Denmark and Sweden, respectively. Yet these countries represent only half of Arla Foods's Dkr 38 billion ($4.66 billion) in annual sales. The United Kingdom is the company's third-largest market, accounting for 16.8 percent of sales; Germany and the rest of Europe add 18 percent of sales; while the company is also active in the Middle East and Asia, which together provide more than 11.5 percent of sales. Fresh milk products are the company's largest product segment, with more than 40 percent of sales. Cheese, including the international brand success Rosenborg, provides 28 percent of sales. Arla Foods is also one of the world's leading suppliers of powdered milk products, which add 15 percent of sales, and a strong player in the butter market, particularly under its 100-year-old Lurpak brand. Butter and spreadables generate 11 percent of sales. The merger between Arla and MD Foods represented a major step forward in what many observers consider the necessary consolidation of the European dairy industry as it braced itself for competition on a global scale. At the beginning of 2002, Arla Foods revealed that it had been holding merger talks with one of the United Kingdom's largest dairies, Express Dairies. Concern that such a merger would not pass the review of monopolies and merger commissions forced the two sides to abandon talks, however.

### *Cooperative Origins in the 19th Century*

The merger of Swedish dairy cooperative Arla with its Danish counterpart, MD Foods, created Europe's leading dairy products company in 2000. Both companies had their roots in the cooperative movements of the late 19th century. The world's first cooperative appeared in Rochdale, England, in 1844, establishing a set of principles that were to be adopted throughout the world. The cooperative movement reached Sweden by the 1860s; at the end of that decade, a new cooperative was formed among dairy producers that was to form the basis of the later Arla ek. for. group. As with other countries, dairy cooperatives operated at first on a largely local level. As production methods improved, and as transporting raw milk and dairy products became easier, local cooperatives began to group together into a smaller number of larger cooperatives.

Over the following decades, the number of dairy cooperatives in Sweden continued to shrink. By the early 1970s, the consolidation of the Swedish dairy industry gathered still greater force, leading to the creation of the Arla economic cooperative in 1975. By then, Arla had already proved itself as one of Sweden's most innovative cooperatives as well. In 1974, Arla developed a means of binding water and fat into a smooth emulsion—producing what was to become known as ''spreadable'' butter. Meanwhile, Arla's symbol, the Arla cow, was to become one of Sweden's most-recognized trademarks. By the 1990s, Arla had grown to become Sweden's largest dairy producer, with some 65 percent of its domestic market. Yet exports still represented only a tiny fraction of the company's sales.

Over in Denmark, Arla's counterpart was also building a successful business, including a thriving export trade based on its butter products. Although founded in 1970, Mejeriselskabet Danmark was to grow to become that country's dominant dairy products group, capturing some 95 percent of the domestic

**Company Perspectives:**

*Arla Foods' objective is to be the consumers' and customers' preferred dairy. In Northern Europe—with a wide range of dairy products. In Southern Europe—with selected ranges of cheese and butter. Outside Europe—with a product range adapted to the individual markets. Moreover, Arla Foods intends to maintain and develop its position as an innovative global supplier of added value, milk-based ingredients for leading food producers throughout the world. With Northern Europe as its natural domestic market, Arla Foods is dedicated to providing consumers with a broad range of high-class dairy products. From a solid base in Denmark and Sweden, where the Group has its roots, Arla Foods aims at maintaining close links with customers in all key export markets through a network of sales companies. In addition, through Arla Foods Ingredients, the Group is one of the world's leading global suppliers of added-value, milk-based ingredients to selected sectors of the food industry. Arla Foods's nearly 15,000 dairy farmer owners have helped make it one of the world's leading dairy products manufacturers and the leading dairy group in Europe.*

market by the end of the 1990s. Yet Denmark itself represented only approximately 10 percent of the cooperative's sales.

Mejeriselskabet (''Dairy Company'') Danmark started out as a cooperative among four small Danish dairies, which grouped together in 1970 in order to confront an increasingly competitive market for dairy products. Over the following two decades, MD Foods, as the cooperative came to be known in 1988, grew by absorbing other dairy members and merging with other Danish dairy cooperatives. From the start, exports, especially to the nearby United Kingdom, represented a significant share of the group's sales.

Much of MD Foods' international success came from its butter exports. In the early 19th century, however, Danish butter was considered to be inferior in quality to that of its European neighbors, who often referred to it as ''mast butter'', that is, its best use was for greasing the masts on sailing ships. Yet by the mid-19th century, Danish dairies had made steady improvements in the butter recipes, and by the 1860s, a number of British shopkeepers had begun to promote Danish butter. Among these was one John Sainsbury, whose name was later to become synonymous with supermarkets in the United Kingdom.

A turning point for Danish butter in the United Kingdom came in 1879 when it was awarded first prize for its category (lactic butter) at the Royal Agricultural Society's International Exhibition. Having found a market, Danish dairies began shipping larger quantities of butter overseas—reaching shipping 12,000 tons to England by 1882, a figure that multiplied by more than six times by the end of the century. The opening of this market, and the appearance of new machinery, notably the invention of the continuous cream separator, encouraged the appearance of cooperative dairies based on the Rochdale model. The first cooperative, established in 1882, was quickly followed by others: by 1890, more than 200 cooperatives were operating in Denmark, a number that was to top 1,400 between the two world wars.

By the turn of the century, Danish butter had become so popular that it had inspired a crowd of imitators. In order to protect the reputation of Danish butter, granting a level of quality assurance, the Danish Ministry of Agriculture defined new quality standards and established an official seal, the Lur Mark, to guarantee its butter. Only qualifying dairies were allowed to use the market—and Lur-branded butter quickly became the trademark for Danish butter exports.

Lur butter was to achieve a strong degree of consistency both in flavor and quality throughout the Danish dairy industry. Its success encouraged the appearance of a large number of export groups—both local and regional cooperatives and associations and private export companies. The resulting competition served to keep the price of Danish butter on the international market low, which, in turn, kept sales high—by the early 1930s, the United Kingdom alone was importing more than 130,000 tons of Danish butter per year.

Denmark's dairy industry was hit hard first by the Great Depression, then by the Nazi occupation of Denmark during World War II. Recovering from the war years, the country's dairies once again returned to exporting Lur butter to overseas markets, particularly to the United Kingdom, which remained the Danish dairy industry's single-largest foreign market. Indeed, the relationship between the two countries was such that, in 1949, the British and Danish governments put into place a butter agreement placing quotas on Danish butter imports and restricting the prices that could be charged.

The end of the butter agreement in 1955 opened the way for renewed competition among the various dairy cooperatives and export companies. Instead, however, the Danish dairy industry decided to band together. In 1955, nine of the country's largest export dairy cooperatives joined to create a new sales and marketing group for the United Kingdom, known as Butterdane (or *Andelssmor* in Danish). The new group helped forestall a price war, guaranteeing strong prices for Danish butter exports.

The advent of new machinery, particularly the development of the continuous butter making machine and the invention of a butter packaging machine, was also transforming the Danish butter industry. An immediate result of the butter packaging machine was a new marketing opportunity. Until the late 1950s, Danish butter imports had arrived in the United Kingdom in large, 112-pound wooden barrels. The butter packaging machine, capable of packing butter into small, foil-wrapped portions—which, in addition to providing greater hygiene, was also more suited to the rising number of self-service supermarkets—encouraged the Danish Dairy Board to adopt a new brand name, Lurpak, not only for its butter exports, but for butter sold on the domestic market as well. Backed by a strong advertising campaign, Lurpak proved an instant success in the United Kingdom, with sales quadrupling by the 1960s.

### *Merging for the 21st Century Global Market*

The creation of the European Common Market created a new competitive climate for the European dairy industry during the 1960s, leading the Danish dairy industry into a consolidation

**Key Dates:**

**1869:** The oldest predecessor cooperative, Arla ek. for., is founded in Sweden.
**1970:** Mejeriselskabet Danmark is formed by four Danish dairies.
**1975:** Arla is formed to consolidate Swedish dairy cooperatives.
**1988:** Mejeriselskabet Danmark changes its name to MD Foods and prepares for international expansion.
**1989:** MD Foods forms MD Foods International A/S to promote its international growth.
**1990:** MD Foods launches its U.K. expansion with the acquisition of Associated Fresh Foods.
**1995:** Arla opens a subsidiary in the United Kingdom.
**1999:** MD Foods acquires Klover Melk, the second-largest dairy cooperative in Denmark, gaining control of 90 percent of the Danish dairy market.
**2001:** MD Foods and Arla merge to form Arla Foods amba, the largest dairy products group in Europe.

phase that resulted in the formation of a small number of dominant dairy groups, MD Foods and Klover Melk, which together accounted for more than 90 percent of the Danish dairy market.

With little room left to maneuver at home, MD Foods began concentrating on its international position. In 1989, the group created a new subsidiary, MD International, charged with the group's global expansion, particularly through the acquisition of existing dairy products manufacturing operations in targeted countries. In that same year, MD Foods set up a U.S. import branch, MD Foods USA, which started up manufacturing operations in that country some ten years later, with a Havarti cheese-making plant opened in Wisconsin.

MD Foods' primary expansion target remained the United Kingdom, however. In 1990, MD Foods acquired its first production facilities in that country, buying up Associated Fresh Foods, based in Leeds, then the fifth-largest dairy in the United Kingdom. Two years later, MD Foods added Oakthorpe Dairy, in north London, and two other dairies which formerly comprised the dairy operations of Consolidated Retail Services. That same year, MD Foods bought another dairy, Sunderland & District Creamery, moving its operations to Newcastle. In 1993, the group acquired Bamber Bridge dairy, located in England's northwest region. Further U.K. expansion came in 1996 with the acquisition of a dairy at Hatfield Peverel. These acquisitions enabled MD Foods to diversify its product offerings in the United Kingdom, adding a significant fresh milk component of nearly one million kilos of milk per year. Meanwhile, the company continued to make inroads in other areas of the U.K. dairy market, particularly with the highly successful 1997 launch of its Lurpak spreadable product line.

By then, Sweden's entry into the European Union had encouraged Arla to step up its efforts to expand internationally. In 1993, Arla had created a new export department, then began a review of potential markets before setting its targets on the United Kingdom, Germany, and the other northern European and Scandinavian countries. Arla's export effort featured a different product mix than its Danish competitor, with an emphasis on fresh cheeses and spreads—which remained something of an Arla speciality—as well as powdered milk products. Arla's strength in innovative products gave it an edge in this latter category, as the company's range boasted some 60 different powered milk products, many of which were geared toward the baby foods segment. In 1995, Arla set up a new subsidiary, Arla UK.

By the end of the decade, Arla had succeeded in boosting its international sales to 12 percent of its total annual sales. Yet the company recognized that this percentage, combined with its restricted growth opportunities within Sweden itself, was not enough to enable it to compete in the increasingly competitive European market, which by then was heading toward the introduction of a single currency.

MD Foods found itself in a similar position following its absorption in 1999 of its largest domestic rival, Klover Melk, which gave it more than 90 percent of the Danish dairy products market. Following that acqusition, MD Foods and Arla began talks, signing a merger agreement in 1999.

The merger itself was carried out in April 2001, creating Arla Foods, the largest dairy products group in Europe and one of the largest in the world, with a total milk volume of more than 6.2 billion liters per year. Arla Foods immediately revealed its commitment to maintaining its leadership in Europe while pursuing its expansion into other markets. Soon after the merger, the group entered a partnership with SanCor, the largest dairy company in Argentina, to build and operate a whey processing facility. At the same time, Arla Foods formed a new subsidiary in the United Arab Emirates to promote its products throughout the Persian Gulf region. Later that year, Arla Foods traveled to New Zealand, forming a joint-venture marketing partnership with that country's Fonterra dairy group.

Despite its interest elsewhere in the world, the United Kingdom remained Arla Foods primary export market, which, accounting for nearly 17 percent of the group's sales, trailed only its operations in Denmark and Sweden. In February 2002, Arla revealed that it had entered talks to acquire one of the United Kingdom's largest dairies, Express Dairies. When it became certain, however, that such a link-up would run up against monopoly concerns, the two sides abandoned the talks. Nonetheless, as the European dairy market moved toward consolidation—particularly in the face of growing competition from non-European companies—Arla Foods appeared certain to seek other acquisition targets in the near future.

### *Principal Subsidiaries*

Arla Foods Holding A/S; Medani A/S; Kingdom Food Products ApS; Arla Foods Leasing A/S; Rynkeby Foods A/S (50%); Kinmaco ApS, GB Finans A/S; Arla Insurance Co. Ltd; Arla Foods Fastighetsförvaltning AB (Sweden); De Danske Mejeriers Fællesindkøb Amba; Dairy Fruit A/S; A/S Crispy Food International; IFEG International ApS; Ejendomsselskabet Østre Gjesingvej 19 A/S; Danapak A.m.b.a.; Danapak A/S; Danapak Flexibel A/S; Danapak Kartonnage A/S; Danapak Plast A/S; Tölkki OY (Finland); Norsk Danapak A/S (Norway); Danapak Faltschachtelsysteme GmbH (Germany);

Danapak Cartons Ltd. (England); Danapak R&D Center A/S; Danapak leasing ApS; Dana-Green 2000 A/S (51%); Medipharm USA; Arla Foods Ingredients S.A. (Argentina); Arla Foods Hellas S.A. (Greece); JO-Bolaget Fruktprodukter HB (Sweden); Synbiotics AB (Sweden); Biolac GmbH (Germany); Dan Vigor Ltd. (Brazil); Semper Holding AB (Sweden); Delimo A/S.

### *Principal Competitors*

Nestlé S.A.; Dairy Farmers of America Inc; Groupe Danone (DA); Snow Brand Milk Products Co Ltd; Prairie Farms Dairy Inc; Land O'Lakes Inc.; Meiji Milk Products Co Ltd; Lactalis; Morinaga Milk Industry Co Ltd; Royal Numico NV; Friesland Coberco Dairy Foods Holding NV; Uniq Plc.

### *Further Reading*

"Arla Targets Flavoured Milk at Adults Too," *Grocer*, March 23, 2002, p. 2.

"Arla: The Vikings Are Coming," *Grocer*, July 1, 2000, p. S9.

"Arla to Become Dominant in Milk Powder Products," *Eurofood*, July 5, 2001, p. 3.

Bedington, Ed, "It's Time for the Big Bucks and Big Ideas," *Grocer*, September 1, 2001, p. S16.

——, "Packing It in at Home and Abroad," *Grocer*, June 16, 2001, p. S10.

"Express and Arla Talks End," *Eurofood*, February 28, 2002, p. 2.

Friend, John, "Arla in Front Line as Sweden Bids for EU Business," *Grocer*, July 8, 1995, p. 58.

—M.L. Cohen

# Asahi Glass Company, Ltd.

**21-1, Yurakucho 1-chome**
**Chiyoda-ku, Tokyo 100-8405**
**Japan**
**Telephone: (81) 3-3218-5555**
**Fax: (81) 3-3287-0772**
**Web site: http://www.agc.co.jp**

*Public Company*
*Incorporated:* 1907
*Employees:* 48,809
*Sales:* ¥1.31 trillion ($10.5 billion)
*Stock Exchanges:* Tokyo Osaka Nagoya Fukuoka Sapporo
*Ticker Symbol:* ASGLY
*NAIC:* 327211 Flat Glass Manufacturing; 327215 Glass Product Manufacturing Made of Purchased Glass; 325181 Alkalis and Chlorine Manufacturing; 325188 All Other Basic Inorganic Chemical Manufacturing

Asahi Glass Company, Ltd. operates as the leading glass manufacturer in Japan and is also one of the largest glass manufacturers in the world. The firm's flat glass and fabricated glass segment secured 45.3 percent of sales in 2001. This unit manufactures products such as windshields for the automotive industry and glass used in construction. Overall, Asahi controls nearly 20 percent of the global flat glass industry. The company's electronics and display operations business segment also manufacturers glass bulbs, cathode ray tubes, and glass substrates used in television, computer monitors, and liquid crystal displays. Through its chemical operations segment, Asahi produces chlor-alkalis, fluorochemicals, and urethanes. Asahi has over 200 subsidiaries, with the majority of sales, in order of volume, stemming from Japan, Asia, Europe, and the Americas.

## *Origins*

Asahi's founder, Toshiya Iwasaki, was born into Japan's most formidable industrial family in 1881, and he decided early in life to build his country's first successful glass company. A nephew of Mitsubishi founder Yataro Iwasaki, he studied applied chemistry at the University of London before returning to fight in the Russo-Japanese War of 1904 to 1905. As a member of the Imperial Cavalry, Iwasaki realized the importance of increasing Japan's native industrial base. Drawing upon his chemical studies, he decided to make glass his area of specialization.

Japan had been unable to support even a single glass-making facility until 1907, although the Meiji government had tried to establish sheet glass manufacturing. The country had just emerged from 200 years of isolation, and in the last half of the 19th century Japanese businessmen scrambled to compress centuries of technological progress into a few decades of growth. They had succeeded in most areas by the turn of the century, but the glass-making field remained open until Iwasaki founded Asahi Glass in 1907 with a factory in Kansai. Iwasaki was able to draw upon his family's powerful banking and political allies, and from the beginning he planned to build a world-class organization. Instead of merely importing technology from Belgium, then the world leader in flat glass production, he brought over Belgian glass-blowers to get his company started properly. By 1909, these craftsmen had succeeded in producing Japan's first flat glass, giving Asahi a national lead it has never relinquished.

Because the Japanese industrial economy remained primitive, Asahi was forced to engineer its own equipment and to produce its own raw materials. This situation led to the 1916 construction of an addition to the Kansai factory, where the company began making its own fire bricks for use in its glass furnaces, and in 1917 to the production of soda ash, required in glass manufacture, at a separate facility in Kita-Kyushu. Asahi thus got its start not only in glass but also in ceramics and in alkali-chlorine-based chemistry, which have remained the firm's three main concerns. With a concerted marketing effort and the economic boom afforded by World War I, Asahi was soon profitable and grew rapidly. The company faced a temporary setback in the early 1920s, when large quantities of natural soda ash were imported from Kenya and dumped on the Japanese market at artificially depressed prices, undercutting Asahi's position as the country's leading supplier of that commodity. In the ensuing political battle Japan adopted its first anti-dumping legislation, and Asahi recovered by 1924.

## Company Perspectives:

*"Look Beyond" is the slogan of the AGC Group, and it is the title of the AGC Group Vision as well. "Look Beyond" captures and expresses this vision. It inspires the Group's mission and shared values to which every member of the Group must subscribe. As a global materials and components supplier based on our core technologies in glass, fluorine chemistry, and their related fields, we will continue to: Look Beyond . . . Anticipate and envision the future; Look Beyond . . . Have perspectives beyond our own fields of expertise; and Look Beyond . . . Pursue innovations, not becoming complacent with the status quo. By "Looking Beyond," we will continue to create value worldwide, demonstrating the vast potential of the Group's entire organization.*

Along with the rest of Japanese industry, Asahi found excellent markets and a convenient labor pool in neighboring China. As the two countries edged toward war in the 1930s, Asahi shifted a good part of its growing glass and chemical business from Japan to 17 small Chinese plants. With the onset of World War II, Asahi found itself with four times as many overseas as domestic plants. The company was caught up in Japan's mammoth war effort, and in 1944 the government merged Asahi with another chemical firm to form Mitsubishi Chemical Industries Limited. The new name was an indication of Asahi's close ties with the Mitsubishi group, which today remains among Asahi's largest stockholders. This belated effort at rationalizing Japan's chemical industry was little help, however, and by the following year Japan was totally defeated. Asahi lost its 17 Chinese factories.

### *Finding Postwar Opportunity*

The postwar years were grim. Allied occupation forces took control of the Japanese economy and directed its every move, initially in the hopes of dismantling the great trading companies, or *zaibatsu*. As Mitsubishi was one of the most important *zaibatsu*, the recently formed Mitsubishi Chemical Industries was again broken into its constituent pieces, and a new Asahi Glass was incorporated in 1950. The reborn Asahi faced formidable problems but equally vast were the opportunities for growth. The company's four domestic plants had survived the war in relatively good condition, and the rebuilding of Japan would require a great number of new glass products. In addition, two inventions still largely unknown in Japan would soon play a dominant role in its development into economic maturity—the automobile and television. As Japan's young auto industry got off the ground in the 1950s, it sparked a huge increase in the demand for windshield glass, which Asahi met with the 1956 creation of Asahi Processed Glass. Similarly, after the 1953 inauguration of Japanese television broadcasts, Asahi established Asahi Special Glass for the manufacture of cathode-ray tubes. As the subsequent history of Japanese industry made clear, Asahi had established strongholds in what became two of Japan's most important industries, ensuring the company's rapid growth into an international power.

Postwar domestic demand for glass kept Asahi busy for the next two decades, when corporate profits averaged three times those of the rest of Japanese industry. At the same time, Asahi's chemical business continued its evolution from a producer of strictly inorganic substances to a diversified supplier of both organic and inorganic compounds. To its traditional strength in caustic soda and soda ash, Asahi added production facilities for chloromethane, propylene glycol, and eventually fluorine compounds.

### *Overseas Expansion: Late 1950s–80s*

Perhaps of greater significance in the long run was Asahi's decision to renew its foreign operations in both glass and chemicals. Beginning with the 1956 construction of Indo-Asahi Glass in Calcutta, India, Asahi committed itself to a program of overseas expansion unusual for a Japanese materials-manufacturing concern. The focus of this expansion was Southeast Asia, where Asahi established dominant positions in Thailand, Indonesia, and the Philippines and maintained a significant presence in many other countries. European and U.S. operations, on the other hand, had to wait until the 1980s. Asahi entered the European market in a major way with its 1981 acquisition of Belgium's Glaverbel S.A. and the Dutch company, MaasGlas B.V., giving Asahi approximately 10 percent of the European flat glass market. U.S. investments were restricted to the automobile industry: during the 1980s Asahi supplied window glass to the U.S. plants of Honda and Toyota from its own factories in Ohio and Kentucky. Finally, to round out its foreign operations, Asahi also manufactured television tubes from plants in Taiwan and Singapore and Corning-Asahi Video products as part of a 1988 U.S. joint venture with Corning Glass.

Such overseas expansion became especially important after the 1965 worldwide introduction of the float process method of flat glass production. Developed in England but soon licensed around the world, the float process had made it possible for anyone to produce excellent flat glass at low cost and without extensive technological experience. It thus became necessary for Asahi, which for years had exported flat glass throughout Asia, to enter into cooperative ventures with local manufacturing concerns in its various national markets or suffer a sharp reduction in its overall sales. With domestic Japanese demand leveling off after the boom years of 1950 to 1970, Asahi was forced to rely more heavily on foreign joint ventures.

As the 1980s began, the fundamental problem of shrinking domestic demand and increasingly standardized production techniques remained a real threat to Asahi's continued growth. In response, the company at first favored a program of diversification outside the glass industry by expanding its already substantial chemical business. Asahi entered into joint ventures with Olin, PPG Industries, and Britain's ICI to produce a wider variety of compounds, including fluorochemicals and plastics, and pioneered the new ion-exchange membrane technique for its manufacture of caustic soda. A company plan developed in the early 1980s called for reducing glass sales to less than 40 percent of total Asahi revenue by the year 2000.

However, this plan changed in the late 1980s under the leadership of Jiro Furumoto, president and chief executive officer from 1987 to 1998. Technological developments opened up a range of innovative glass products for Asahi, promoting

## Key Dates:

**1907:** Toshiya Iwasaki establishes Asahi Glass.
**1909:** Asahi craftsmen produce Japan's first flat glass.
**1944:** The Japanese government merges Asahi with a chemical firm to form Mitsubishi Chemical Industries Ltd.
**1950:** Mitsubishi Chemical Industries breaks up and Asahi Glass incorporates.
**1956:** Asahi Processed Glass is created to meet demand for windshield glass.
**1965:** The float process method of flat glass production is introduced in England.
**1981:** The firm acquires Glaverbel S.A. and MassGlas B.V.
**1992:** Floatglass India Ltd. is established.
**1995:** Asahi enters the automotive glass industry in China.
**1999:** The firm launches its "Shrink to Grow" management plan.
**2001:** Asahi consolidates all of its India-based operations into Asahi India, creating the largest glass company in the region.

Furumoto to design what he called "AGC Vision 21." This corporate forecast called for Asahi sales in the year 2000 of ¥2.4 trillion split evenly between glass and non-glass operations. The key point of Furumoto's plan was to reach ¥800 billion annually in new products, including "new glass," the various applications for glass made possible by technological changes. New-glass uses included reflective building glass, glass-reinforced concrete, flat screens for high-definition televisions, and glass hard discs for personal computers.

Asahi thus planned to maintain and expand its position in the growing field of glass manufacturing. Its strategy of the late 1980s included the employment of its highly automated domestic plants for high-tech, value-added production, while farming out to its foreign subsidiaries the production of standard flat and automobile glass. The other half of Asahi sales were expected to come from chemical products, including old standbys like soda ash and new environmentally safe replacements. At the time, the company continued a small business in refractory products—3 percent of sales—and also pursued its growing segment of the electronics industry—at 4 percent of sales.

### *Continued Growth: 1990s*

Asahi spent the majority of the 1990s expanding internationally. In 1991, Dalian Float Glass Co. was established in China, and the following year Floatglass India Ltd. was created. Growth continued with the 1993 purchase of U.S.-based AFG Industries Inc. The firm also launched Asahi Allglass Pte. Ltd. in Singapore and Beijing Asahi Glass Electronics Co. Ltd. in China.

Asahi continued to focus on China in 1995. It entered the automotive glass industry in the region and also purchased an interest in Qinhuangdao Haiyan Safety Glass Co. Ltd. The company also developed new products as technological advancements in both the television and communications industry continued at breakneck speed. The company began manufacturing fluoro-resin plastic optical fibers that had gigabit communication data throughput capabilities and developed its PD200 glass used in plasma display panels. In 1996, the firm established subsidiary P.T. Video Display Glass Indonesia. In 1998, Video Monitores de Mexico, S.A. de C.V. was also created.

### *The "Shrink to Grow" Management Plan: 1999 and Beyond*

Furumoto retired in June 1998, leaving Shinya Ishizu as president and Hiromichi Seya as chairman. The pair were almost immediately faced with challenges as the Japanese economy faltered. Japan accounted for nearly 70 percent of the company's sales, and when the region experienced a financial crisis, Asahi's earnings plunged. During 1999, the company's net income fell to ¥5.09 trillion, down from ¥20.36 trillion reported in 1998.

As such, the new management team implemented a new business plan they called "Shrink to Grow." The three-year plan was developed with a focus on maintaining profitability and growth. As part of the company's 2000 shrink plan, it reduced overall fixed costs by ¥2.6 billion, closed its float glass line at its Keihin factory, shutdown Chiba Vinyl Chloride Monomer Co. Ltd., and cut 900 jobs. As part of its 2000 growth strategy, Asahi acquired Hankuk Electric Glass Co. Ltd., purchased Imperial Chemical Industries' fluoropolymer operations, and opened a float glass plant in Spain. During that year, net income increased to ¥13,164 million.

In 2001, the firm continued its Shrink to Grow efforts. It sold its interest in Nippon Dry-Chemical Co. Ltd., divested Asahi Komag Co. Ltd., and also stopped production of synthetic soda ash. The company also created three new Thai subsidiaries, and consolidated its India operations to create a single company—the largest glass concern in India.

As part of the overall Shrink to Grow plan, Asahi management expected to raise return on equity (ROE) to 10 percent per year by 2004. During 1999, ROE was .8 percent but climbed to 2.2 percent in 2000. By 2001, it reached 4.1 percent. The company's long term goals included: restructuring its low-profit businesses, which included the planned spin-off of its ceramics operations; expanding its displays business along with its electronics and optical-related materials business; increasing its focus on its fluorochemicals operations that were involved with the development of fluorinated resin optical fibers used in the life sciences and electronics industries; and developing new business opportunities. Overall, Asahi aimed to become the leading corporate group in terms of growth and profitability in both the glass and fluorochemicals markets.

While competition remained fierce in the early years of the new millennium, Asahi management felt its new business strategy left it well positioned in each of its business segments. Situated among the leading glass-makers in the world, Asahi appeared to be on track for future success.

### *Principal Subsidiaries*

Asahi Fiber Glass Co., Ltd.; Ise Chemicals Corp. (52.4%); Optrex Corporation (60%); Seimi Chemical Co. Ltd.; Tokai Kogyo Co. Ltd.; A.G. Finance Co. Ltd.; Asahi Glass Fine Techno Co. Ltd.; Glaverbel S.A. (Belgium; 60.9%); Asahi TV Glass Pte. Ltd. (Singapore); Pacific Glass Corporation (Taiwan); Asahi Glass America Inc. (U.S.); Asahi Glass Engineering Co. Ltd.; Asahi Techno Glass Corp. (54.7%); Asahi Techno Vision Pte. Ltd. (Singapore); AFG Industries Inc. (U.S.).

### *Principal Operating Units*

Glass and Related Operations; Electronics and Display Operations; Chemicals Operations; Ceramics.

### *Principal Competitors*

Nippon Sheet Glass Company Limited; PPG Industries Inc.; Compagnie de Saint-Gobain SA.

### *Further Reading*

''Asahi to Consolidate India Operations,'' *Hindu*, September 24, 2001.

''Asahi Glass Company Ltd.,'' *Strategic Finance*, March 2001, p. 64.

''Asahi Glass Targets $12.7 Bln Sales, Higher Gains by 2001,'' *AsiaPulse News*, June 18, 1999.

''Japan Chemical Week: Asahi Glass Seeking Top World Place in Fluorine-based Water/Oil Repellents,'' *Chemical Business Newsbase*, August 1, 2001.

Mushakoji, Kinhisa, *The Process of Internationalization: Asahi Glass Company, Ltd.*, Tokyo Institute of Comparative Culture Business Series #99, 1985.

Savage, Eleanor Van, ''Asahi Focuses on Expanding Key Markets As Part of its Management Plan,'' *Chemical Market Reporter*, February 21, 2000, p. 20.

Wray, William D., *Mitsubishi and the N.Y.K., 1870–1914: Business Strategy in the Japanese Shipping Industry*, Cambridge, Mass.: Harvard University Press, 1984.

—Jonathan Martin
—update: Christina M. Stansell

# Associated Milk Producers, Inc.

**315 North Broadway**
**New Ulm, Minnesota 56073**
**U.S.A.**
**Telephone: (507) 354-8295**
**Fax: (507) 359-8651**
**Web site: http://www.ampi.com**

*Private Company*
*Incorporated:* 1969
*Employees:* 1,600
*Sales:* $1.2 billion (2001 est.)
*NAIC:* 422430 Dairy Products (Except Dried or Canned) Wholesalers; 311511 Fluid Milk Manufacturing; 311512 Creamery Butter Manufacturing; 311513 Cheese Manufacturing; 311514 Dry, Condensed, and Evaporated Dairy Product Manufacturing

Associated Milk Producers, Inc. (AMPI) is one of the ten largest dairy cooperatives in the United States with 4,600 members that market over five billion pounds of milk per year. The co-op runs one of the largest butter packaging plants in the country, is one of the largest cheddar manufacturers in the United States, packages nearly 60 percent of the instant milk consumed in the country, and operates 14 manufacturing facilities. Before 1998, AMPI's operations were divided geographically into three semi-autonomous divisions. The North Central Region, which included western Wisconsin, Minnesota, Missouri, Iowa, Nebraska, and South Dakota, processed most of its milk into cheese and other products that are marketed under the name State Brand and numerous other private labels. The Morning Glory Farms Region was comprised of member farms located in eastern Wisconsin, Illinois, Indiana, Ohio, and Michigan. AMPI's Southern Region supplied mainly Grade A drinking milk. Farms in Arkansas, New Mexico, Oklahoma, Texas, and several other states were also part of this region. In January 1998, AMPI's Southern Region operations joined with three other co-ops to form Dairy Farmers of America Inc. AMPI's North Central Region remained intact and continued to operate under the AMPI name.

### *Origins*

Agricultural cooperatives emerged in the United States after the 1922 enactment of the Capper-Volstead Act, which gave small farmers the right to join forces, thereby obtaining greater control over the supply and price of their products. However, with the decline of both milk consumption and dairy farm income in the late 1960s, dairy co-ops began to band together into larger and larger entities. Six dairy cooperatives in Kansas, Texas, Arkansas, and Oklahoma merged in 1967 to form Milk Producers, Inc. (MPI). MPI acquired eight more southwestern co-ops in its first year. By 1969, MPI had expanded north, with member farms located in South Dakota and Minnesota. That year, MPI merged with 14 smaller co-ops in the Chicago area to form AMPI.

Harold Nelson had organized the consolidation. Nelson had been manager of the Texas Milk Producers Federation and the general manager of MPI before he became AMPI's first general manager. John Butterbrodt, a member from a Wisconsin cooperative, was elected president. AMPI set up headquarters in San Antonio, Texas. Two other large dairy cooperatives, Mid-American Dairymen, Inc. and Dairymen, Inc., were formed around the same time as AMPI through similar consolidation processes.

Because of economic pressures, smaller dairy cooperatives throughout the central part of the United States were eager to join the growing AMPI. Before it was two years old, AMPI was the biggest dairy cooperative in the country. By 1971, AMPI had 45,000 members, thanks in part to a merger that year with Pure Milk Products Cooperative, a fairly large Wisconsin organization.

Many of the largest markets in the central United States, including Chicago, Madison, Indianapolis, Houston, Dallas, San Antonio, and Memphis, were getting at least three-fourths of their raw milk supply from AMPI by the middle of 1972.

### *Legal Troubles: 1970s*

Despite its economic success, AMPI spent much of the next few years embroiled in a series of legal controversies. Shortly after AMPI was formed, the company established a political

**Company Perspectives:**

*AMPI actively seeks to develop a comprehensive national agricultural policy, initiating discussion on farm policy issues whenever feasible and possible to achieve an effective farm bill that enhances farmer and rancher profitability while addressing key agricultural trade issues, environmental stewardship concerns, and other key problems impacting agriculture.*

trust called TAPE, an acronym for Trust for Agricultural Political Education, which later became C-TAPE. In 1972, consumer advocate Ralph Nader began to argue that recent increases in federal price supports for dairy products (a reversal of a previous decision) were the result of illegal contributions by TAPE and the political arms of the other large diary co-ops to President Nixon's re-election campaign. Suits were filed against the Commodity Credit Corporation and Agriculture Secretary Earl Butz, asking for a rollback of the increases on the grounds that they were illegal because they were made on the basis of political rather than economic considerations. A month later, a civil antitrust suit was filed in federal court charging AMPI with a number of monopolistic practices. The suit alleged that AMPI had, among other things, manipulated the milk supply to control prices and conspired with milk haulers and processors against independent competitors.

AMPI's situation got much worse; its political operations were soon tied in with the Watergate investigation. In 1974, two high-ranking AMPI officials pleaded guilty to a range of charges concerning campaign contributions. First, David Parr, special counsel to AMPI, admitted that he had authorized illegal contributions to Hubert Humphrey's unsuccessful 1968 presidential campaign. Parr also admitted authorizing payments to several other lesser campaigns, as well as allowing co-op employees to work on these campaigns while on the AMPI payroll. Nelson pleaded guilty to a series of campaign-fund violations shortly thereafter. While the company's legal entanglements were unfolding, Nelson was succeeded as general manager of AMPI in 1972 by George L. Mehren, a former assistant secretary of agriculture under President Lyndon Johnson.

The most widely-publicized episode of this period was the charge that representatives of AMPI, specifically attorney Jake Jacobsen, had bribed Treasury Secretary John Connally. The charges against Connally and Jacobsen alleged that AMPI had paid Connally in return for special consideration in dairy price support issues. Litigation involving AMPI eventually forced the co-op's top managers to spend as much as a quarter of their time in hearings and depositions. By 1975, Connally was acquitted of the bribery charges. Ironically, Jacobsen, the chief witness against him, was convicted by a different jury of paying the bribe. As a result of the scandal, AMPI owed over $16 million in unpaid taxes and fraud penalties from 1972 and 1973.

AMPI was damaged by the scandal's negative publicity as well as by an industry slump but remained a leading force in the American economy. Between 1971 and 1974, AMPI lost about 12 percent of its members, some leaving in response to the company's political complications. Eighteen percent of all dairy farms folded over the same period, victims of a periodic slump in the industry. Nevertheless, by 1974 AMPI ranked 155th on *Fortune* magazine's list of America's largest industrial corporations. The company was supplying 12.5 percent of the nation's wholesale raw milk and was running the largest cheese-processing plant in the country. C-TAPE, despite a drop in contributions in the wake of Watergate, was the second richest special-interest lobbying group in the United States, just behind an American Medical Association-headed coalition.

During the late 1970s, AMPI worked to revive its image. The company reorganized its corporate structure, establishing a system of semi-autonomous regional groups under separate management teams. In spite of all the scandals and convictions, C-TAPE continued to operate successfully and was instrumental in winning further price supports for milk as soon after the turmoil as 1976.

By the early 1980s, AMPI appeared to be back on track. The co-op had about 32,000 members in 20 states and Canada by 1981, and its annual sales had reached $2.4 billion. In 1982, the suit for monopolistic practices originally filed in 1971 finally made it into the federal courts. The case, which had been initiated by the National Farmers' Organization, was decided in favor of AMPI and two fellow cooperatives. However, within months, an appeals court ruled that AMPI and the others had conspired to eliminate competition, and the decision was reversed. The U.S. Supreme Court later upheld the appeals court ruling in 1989. The case did not harm AMPI's ability to sway the industry, however. In 1983, C-TAPE helped in the defeat of a bill in Congress that would have cut price supports for dairy farms.

### *Mergers and Acquisitions: Mid- to Late 1980s*

AMPI dropped in membership by 1985, but its revenues remained about the same. AMPI's 23,300 member farms were delivering about 15.7 billion pounds of milk by 1985, and the company's revenue remained around $2.4 billion. Growth for the co-op came through mergers and acquisitions. In 1986, AMPI strengthened its position in the Great Lakes area by merging its Mid-States Region with the Morning Glory Farms Cooperative, a 2,200-member group based in Shawano, Wisconsin. The combined unit was dubbed the Morning Glory Farms Region. In September of 1986, AMPI's North Central region acquired the largest cheese plant in the country, Falls Dairy in Jim Falls, Wisconsin. The plant had an annual cheese output of 84 million pounds, mainly for Kraft, processed from about a billion pounds of milk. Together, AMPI's plants in all three regions produced 126 million pounds of butter (ten percent of the U.S. output), 218 million pounds of nonfat dry milk (17 percent), 334 million pounds of American cheese (12 percent), and 160 million pounds of dry whey (16 percent) in 1986. By 1988, the co-op marketed well over 17 billion pounds of milk, compared with 7.5 billion pounds for its closest rival, Mid-America Dairymen.

Under general manager Ira Rutherford, the co-op earned over $12 million in 1989, triple the previous year's figure, on sales of just under $3 billion. A total of $42 million was invested in new property, facilities, and equipment during the year, much of it at the new Stephenville, Texas, plant, a 96,000-

**Key Dates:**

**1967:** Six dairy cooperatives merge to form Milk Producers Inc. (MPI).
**1969:** MPI joins with 14 co-ops to form Associated Milk Producers Inc. (AMPI).
**1971:** By now, AMPI has 45,000 members.
**1974:** Two high-ranking AMPI officials plead guilty to charges related to campaign contributions.
**1986:** AMPI's merges its Mid-States Region with Morning Glory Farms Cooperative and acquires Falls Dairy of Wisconsin.
**1990:** AMPI records its first net loss when farm milk prices fall by 25 percent.
**1998:** Four co-ops, including the southern region of AMPI, form Diary Farmers of America Inc.
**2001:** Earnings reach $10.8 million on sales of $1.2 billion.

square-foot facility capable of making cheese and whey from 1.4 million pounds of milk a day.

As the 1990s began, things took a turn for the worse at AMPI. In 1990, farm milk prices took a 25 percent plunge. AMPI lost $27 million for the year, its first net loss. Attrition of dairy farms continued to erode AMPI's membership numbers, and this decline accelerated during the early 1990s. Furthermore, AMPI's total milk deliveries began to shrink year by year. Although the company managed to record sales of $3.06 billion for 1990, the outlook was bleak. In 1991, Ira Rutherford resigned as general manager, a post he had held for 12 years. He was replaced by Noble Anderson, head of the company's Southern Region. That year AMPI managed to turn a modest profit ($698,000), although membership and deliveries continued to decline.

In 1992, AMPI recorded its second largest loss in three years. Most of the damage resulted from the bankruptcy of Hawthorn-Mellody, a major customer to whom AMPI had extended a great deal of credit over the years. For the year, the company posted a loss of $12.6 million, absorbed mostly by the Morning Glory Farms Region. In spite of the problems, AMPI managed to devote $31 million to the purchase of new property and equipment. In the summer of 1992, the company opened a new cheese plant south of Roswell, New Mexico. The plant, able to produce 190,000 pounds of cheese a day, was to become the largest in the AMPI system.

By 1993, the finances of AMPI had improved but membership had dropped. AMPI member farms numbered 13,400, nearly a 50 percent decrease over ten years. However, the company had improved its results dramatically over the previous year, posting a net margin of $10.8 million on sales of $2.7 billion. In an effort to keep costs in check, a number of plants were closed, sold, or leased, as the company concentrated on cash management policies.

### *The Formation of Dairy Farmers of America: 1998*

Into the mid-1990s, the trend toward fewer and larger dairy farms continued and was reflected in AMPI's membership figures. While AMPI's dominant position among dairy suppliers remained intact, the co-op soon began merger talks with three other large dairy concerns. By the end of 1997, AMPI's Southern Region operations, along with Mid-America Dairymen Inc., Milk Marketing Inc., and Western Dairymen Cooperative Inc., decided that joining forces was perhaps the best option for future growth. An October 1997 *Denver Business Journal* article commented on the reasoning behind the deal, suggesting that "the relaxation of international trade barriers on dairy products has given the co-ops an opportunity to take advantage of world milk markets, and the end of the dairy price support program forced the groups to realize how many services and service territories they duplicate." The article went on to claim that "by combining resources and assets under one name and one vision, they could build better, more efficient and dynamic opportunities for members." The deal was approved, and in January 1998 Dairy Farmers of America Inc., the largest milk marketing cooperative in the United States, was formed from the merger of the aforementioned dairy concerns.

After the deal, AMPI's operations included that of its North Central Region, which manufactured value-added products. While the co-op produced nearly five billion pounds of milk per year, nearly 85 percent was used for manufactured products such as cheese, butter, and powdered milk. This diversification protected it from price fluctuations and allowed its plants to shift focus to higher profit products when necessary. AMPI's sales in 1998 were $964 million.

A smaller, leaner AMPI entered the new millennium as one of the top ten dairy co-ops in the United States. Its 93,000-square-foot New Ulm butter factory was one of the largest butter facilities in the region, producing approximately 20,000 pounds of butter per hour. AMPI was well positioned to capitalize on increased demand for butter products. In fact, butter was an expanding market with per capita consumption growing from 3.6 pounds in 1989 to over four pounds in 2000, according to industry magazine *Dairy Foods.*

During 2002, Paul Toft was elected to serve a second term as president of the co-op while Mark Furth remained its general manager. During the group's annual two-day delegate meeting in March 2002, Furth reported that AMPI's earnings, sales, and return on equity had surpassed 2000 figures and claimed that AMPI's promising results were directly related to the success of its consumer-packaged dairy products, which accounted for over half of its $1.2 billion sales in 2001.

AMPI's strategy at this time continued to revolve around remaining competitive in the ever-changing dairy industry. Through the AMPI Political Action Committee (AMPI PAC), the group communicated with the federal government on issues related to the dairy industry. It also supported the Midwest Dairy Coalition and encouraged its members to be actively involved in agricultural campaigns. Having overcome the financial problems of the 1990s, AMPI appeared to be on track for future success in the dairy industry.

### *Principal Competitors*

Dairy Farmers of America Inc.; Foremost Farms USA Cooperative; Land O'Lakes Inc.

### *Further Reading*

''Associated Milk Charged with Monopoly in 14-State Area by Justice Department,'' *Wall Street Journal*, February 2, 1972, p. 6.

''Associated Milk Offers to Settle U.S. Antitrust Suit,'' *Wall Street Journal*, June 21, 1974, p. 2.

Aven, Paula, ''Dairy Cooperatives Will Vote in Nov. on Merger,'' *Denver Business Journal*, October 17, 1997, p. 7A.

Blair, Jess F., ''New Mexico Dairy Plant to Open Soon,'' *Feedstuffs*, June 29, 1992, p. 11.

Clark, Edward, ''AMPI Shows $12 Million Loss in 1992,'' *Feedstuffs*, April 12, 1993, p. 7.

Demetrakakes, Pan, ''Buttering Up,'' *Food Processing*, July 1999, p. 75.

''Ex-Dairy Co Op Aide Admits Conspiracy to Bribe Connally in Milk-Price Matter,'' *Wall Street Journal,* August 1, 1974, p. 3.

Falk, Carol H., ''Connally Is Acquitted of Bribery Charge and Indicates He May Return to Politics,'' *Wall Street Journal*, April 18, 1975, p. 5.

Fusaro, Dave, ''Bigger, Smarter, More Global,'' *Dairy Foods*, July 1999.

''Large Milk Co Op Assessed by I.R.S.,'' *New York Times*, April 14, 1976, p. 59.

Mans, Jack, ''Around-the-Clock Butter,'' *Dairy Foods*, February 2000, p. 38.

Markgraf, Sue, ''Dairy Farmers of America,'' *Dairy Foods*, April 1998, p. 69.

McMenamin, Michael, and Walter McNamara, *Milking the Public*, Chicago: Nelson-Hall, 1980.

''Milk Co Op Aide Pleads Guilty to Clearing Campaign Gifts to Humphrey and Others,'' *Wall Street Journal*, July 24, 1974, p. 8.

Naughton, James M., ''Connally Acquitted of Bribery Charge; Hints He May Resume Political Career,'' *New York Times*, April 18, 1975, p. 1.

Otto, Alison, and Jerry Dryer, ''Movers and Shakers,'' *Dairy Foods*, April 1987, p. 41.

Shaffer, Richard A., ''How a Big Dairy Co Op Helps Farmers Despite Legal Woes and Industry Slump,'' *Wall Street Journal*, November 5, 1974, p. 32.

—Robert R. Jacobson
—update: Christina M. Stansell

# Banco Bilbao Vizcaya Argentaria S.A.

**Gran Via 1**
**Bilbao, Vizcaya 48001**
**Spain**
**Telephone: (34) 94 487 55 55**
**Fax: (34) 94 487 61 61**
**Web site: http://www.bbva.com**

*Public Company*
*Incorporated:* 1988
*Employees:* 108,082
*Total Assets:* Pta 54.45 trillion ($272.53 billion) (2001)
*Stock Exchanges:* Madrid New York
*Ticker Symbol:* BBV
*NAIC:* 522110 Commercial Banking; 233110 Land Subdivision and Land Development; 522298 All Other Non-Depository Credit Intermediation; 523930 Investment Advice; 524128 Other Direct Insurance (Except Life, Health, and Medical) Carriers; 524210 Insurance Agencies and Brokerages

Banco Bilbao Vizcaya Argentaria S.A. (BBVA) was formed from the merger of Banco Bilbao Vizcaya S.A. and Argentaria Caja Postal y Banco Hipotecario S.A. Completed in early 2000, the deal created the second-largest financial institution in Spain and Latin America. BBVA operates in 11 Latin American countries with interests in retail banking, wholesale banking, investment banking, and asset management and private banking, real estate, insurance, and e-business. During 2000, the firm strengthened its market share in Mexico with the purchase of that country's second largest bank, Bancomer S.A.

Originally operating independently, Banco de Bilbao and Banco de Vizcaya shocked the financial world by merging in January 1988 to become one of Spain's largest banks, Banco Bilbao Vizcaya S.A. (BBV). Both banks had grown from their bases in Bilbao, where they financed the railroad, mining, steel, and shipping industries. And both banks had weathered Spain's repeated financial crises and the major economic disruptions of its brutal civil war to emerge as strong, well-managed financial institutions.

When the two banks merged in 1988, they did so to assure continued profitability after the integration of the European Economic Community, or European Union, in 1993. The merger positioned BBV to compete effectively, both domestically and internationally, under the new banking rules that went with EEC membership.

### *History of Banco de Bilbao*

Banco de Bilbao was the older of the two banks. After laws were passed in 1856 allowing the creation of banks and thrift institutions, the Trade Association of Bilbao, a group of businessmen in the developing Basque area, established an office on the Calle de la Estufa in Bilbao to provide financial assistance to businesses. The new bank took over functions formerly filled by the Bilbao consular office, which closed. The Trade Association was also authorized to issue bank notes.

The Trade Association of Bilbao, soon known as Banco de Bilbao, continued to issue notes and business loans until 1878, when the Bank of Spain was named the sole issuer of bank notes for the country. Banco de Bilbao did not acquiesce quietly, but its lobbying efforts against the change failed. As a result, the bank reorganized. Banco de Bilbao continued to specialize in business loans, but in a step unique to Spanish banking, it also established the first savings bank in Spain, the savings association Sociedad Bilbaina General de Credito.

Those new financial activities made Banco de Bilbao a major backer of the industrial development in the north, which turned Bilbao and the neighboring Vizcaya into Spain's industrial center in the last decades of the 19th century and produced the highest per capita income in the country. Banco de Bilbao helped finance the construction of the Port of Bilbao as well as the development of railroad transport and the mining and steel industries.

Banco de Bilbao was able to become involved in these projects because it was virtually the only game in town until the end of the century. Branches of the Bank of Spain, the Caja

## Company Perspectives:

*At BBVA, quality is not an element of mere improvement, but rather a factor which contributes towards consolidating sustainable competitive advantages. It is not an objective in itself, but rather a commitment to the Group's growth to international expansion and to technological development.*

General de Depositos, and the Banco de Castilla were established in Bilbao, but as the only independent local financial entity, Banco de Bilbao was able to take a leading position in financing heavy industry.

Because of this role in industry, the bank was able not only to weather financial storms that shook Spain in the last half of the 19th century, including the panic of 1896 that caused much of the Spanish banking system to fail, but even to remain profitable.

Banco de Bilbao built on its position of strength with a two-part strategy of expansion—domestic and international—as the new century opened. The bank began its international expansion by establishing a Paris branch in 1902, becoming the first Spanish bank to have a foreign presence. At home, Banco de Bilbao merged with the Banco de Comercio to extend its industrial financing activities.

World War I meant disruption for the Spanish economy and operating problems for Banco de Bilbao's branches in other European centers such as Paris and London. However, because of Banco de Bilbao's continued investments in emerging industries and capital improvements, the war in fact promoted the bank's expansion. It formed subsidiary companies and entered into joint ventures to finance major industrialization projects. The institution was not alone in this enviable financial situation; Banco de Vizcaya and Banco de Bilbao worked together in these years, promoting and financing industrial ventures. Other banks in the north that financed industrialization also emerged from the war in good shape.

The postwar years were marked by economic nationalism in Spain, a policy entrenched under the Second Republic. Under that policy Banco de Bilbao's emphasis on underwriting nascent industrialization again led to profits. However, the stock market crash of 1929 had a major impact in Spain. The financial crisis led to insolvency for such major Spanish financial institutions as Banco de Barcelona and Credito de la Union Minera.

On the heels of the Depression came the Spanish Civil War. The ideological battle between the Loyalists, who were faithful to the liberal constitution of the republic that replaced the monarchy in 1931, and the Nationalists, who campaigned for Spain's identification as a Catholic nation, devastated a country that was still considered underdeveloped and even backward by the standards of the rest of Europe. When Francisco Franco came to power in 1939, the country faced huge material losses at home. Land, neglected during the conflict, was not immediately productive again. Industries found it difficult to obtain raw materials, equipment, and fuel. Then came the isolation imposed by the Allies during World War II. Spaniards called the 1940s ''the years of hunger.''

Franco's government attempted to meet these economic problems with tight new regulations on banking. Franco's Ministerial Order of May 17, 1940 established a policy of adhering to the banking status quo. To meet this new form of government intervention, Banco de Bilbao expanded into other parts of Spain through acquisition—between 1941 and 1943, it acquired 16 banks—reorganized its internal structure to operate effectively at a national level, and expanded its international presence. The bank gave its London and Paris offices a greater role in company operations, and in 1945 it established a branch specifically to form contacts for cooperative ventures in the United States and South America. While the bank continued to emphasize industrial development, more important after World War II than ever, it also developed commercial activities and provided personal financial services.

The first centennial of the Banco de Bilbao in 1957 coincided with another event that would have a major impact on its future. That was the year the European Economic Community was formed, the first step toward an international economy. While not immediately ready to integrate its economy into the European economy, Spain became a member of the International Monetary Fund, the International Bank for Reconstruction and Development, and the Organization for European Economic Cooperation (OEEC) in 1958 and 1959.

Spain's immediate task was to halt the country's financial decline. Toward this end, Franco's government passed a stabilization plan in 1959 that devalued the peseta, placed a ceiling on government spending and on credit for government agencies (which had been fueling inflation), limited private credit expansion, improved tax collection, abolished price controls, froze wages, established higher bank rates, and encouraged foreign investment. With the stabilization plan and full membership in the OEEC came foreign assistance in redevelopment. The U.S. government, a group of U.S. banks, the OEEC, and the International Monetary Fund jointly pledged $5.75 million in assistance, with promises of more to come.

By 1962, a new government department was created to plan and coordinate economic development, and the Law of Banking and Credit institutionalized the preeminent position of the major Spanish banks. As a result of the changes, Banco de Bilbao reorganized again, becoming a multi-purpose bank at home and creating a subsidiary, the Banco Industrial de Bilbao, to continue its emphasis on developing new industrial companies.

By the end of the 1960s, analysts were talking of a Spanish economic miracle. Centers of industrialization such as Bilbao experienced relative prosperity as factories created jobs and acceptable standards of living for the working class, produced opportunities for commerce for the middle class, and increased the wealth of the owners. The so-called miracle was again profitable for Banco de Bilbao.

In the 1970s, Banco de Bilbao continued to develop into a diversified financial group and into a consumer bank as well. In 1970, the bank began a campaign to attract female customers; in 1971 it began to issue credit cards; and in 1972 it offered ''instant credit'' to attract customers.

## Key Dates:

**1856:** The Trade Association of Bilbao is formed after laws are passed that allow for the creation of banks.
**1878:** The Bank of Spain is named the sole issuer of bank notes.
**1896:** A panic causes much of the Spanish banking system to fail.
**1901:** Banco de Vizcaya is formed.
**1902:** Banco de Bilbao opens a branch in Paris, France.
**1918:** Banco de Vizcaya expands into Madrid and acquires Banca Luis Roy Sobrino.
**1935:** By now, Banco de Vizcaya operates 200 offices.
**1940:** Franco establishes the Ministerial Order that forces banks to adhere to the banking status quo.
**1941:** Banco de Bilbao begins an aggressive acquisition spree.
**1959:** Franco devalues the peseta to halt the country's financial decline; Spain joins the Organization for European Economic Cooperation.
**1964:** Banco de Vizcaya establishes Induban as its industrial-banking arm.
**1971:** Banco de Bilbao begins to issue credit cards; Banco de Vizcaya creates Liscaya as a leasing company for major corporations.
**1986:** Spain enters the European Economic Community.
**1988:** Banco de Bilbao and Banco de Vizcaya merge, forming Banco Bilbao Vizcaya (BBV).
**1991:** Argentaria Caja Postal y Banco Hipotecario S.A. is formed.
**1993:** Spain becomes part of the European Union.
**1994:** The company begins reorganizing under its "1,000 Day Program."
**1997:** BBV acquires Argentina-based firms Banco Credito Argentina and Banco Frances.
**1999:** BBV announces its merger with Argentaria, forming Banco Bilbao Vizcaya Argentaria (BBVA).
**2000:** BBVA acquires Bancomer S.A.

The inflationary pressures of the decade, due especially to skyrocketing oil costs, led to laws that again strengthened the position of the big Spanish banks. A program to combat inflation adopted in 1974 raised the bank rate one percent to make it comparable to international rates. The program also extended access to credit, making business investments easier. And it allowed banks more flexibility by eliminating differences between industrial and commercial banks. The revamping of the banking system encouraged Banco de Bilbao's development into commercial services. The bank was also able to absorb six Spanish banks that were not able to adapt as successfully.

Diversification and expansion continued into the 1980s after Franco's death and the return of the monarchy. By this time, Banco de Bilbao had become a major financial group with 16 banks in Spain and abroad and 50 companies providing banking-related financial services.

Spain's entry into the European Economic Community (EEC) in 1986, with its promise of full integration into the European economy by 1993, and fewer restrictions on competition throughout the European market, prompted Banco de Bilbao to look for the opportunity to grow still larger. Despite the long-term trend toward aggregation of financial services, Spain still had more banks per capita than other European countries, and analysts suggested that the Spanish banking system would be more competitive if it had fewer stronger banks.

To remain competitive by becoming larger, Banco de Bilbao took an unprecedented step in 1987 when it made a hostile takeover bid for its rival, Banco Español de Credito, known as Banesto. Banesto was ranked as Spain's number-two bank while Banco de Bilbao was ranked number three, but a tradition of feuding among the families on Banesto's board made it a takeover target. Banco de Bilbao had to drop its bid when three of the four Spanish stock exchanges that must approve such actions announced they would not allow the takeover—only the Bilbao Exchange had been in favor of Banco de Bilbao's bid. José Angel Sanchez Asiain, the bank's chairman, told the *New York Times*, "One day someone will have the answer for this historic failure, which halts the modernization of Spain."

Despite the failure of its bid for Banesto, Banco de Bilbao still wanted to grow to meet the new economic realities. On January 27, 1988, Banco de Bilbao merged with its local rival, Banco de Vizcaya. Both banks were considered well-managed organizations in very much the same market. It was "the concern by both banks for efficiency and the capacity to generate income, which made it possible to easily overcome the resistance to losing one's individuality," Asiain said of the merger.

In a speech on the merger, Banco de Vizcaya's chairman, Pedro Toledo Ugarte, alluded to the historical tendency of businessmen in Bilbao to unite to form larger corporations in order to face changes they could not face with their own resources. He saw Spain's entry into the EEC as one of those challenges. "Given the importance of the financial sector, every country wants some of the institutions which compete worldwide to be made up of and managed by its own people," he said. "We all know that this requires management, technologies and, without doubt, a minimum size."

### *History of Banco de Vizcaya*

Banco de Vizcaya had a history very similar to that of its new partner. Founded in 1901 to serve Bilbao merchants, Banco de Vizcaya made commercial loans and took business deposits. From this start, the bank expanded throughout the Basque country and then into the rest of Spain.

Banco de Vizcaya began its expansion by absorbing Banco Vascongado in 1903 and Banca Jacquet e Hijos in 1915. In 1918, it earned a national presence when it absorbed the Banca Luis Roy Sobrino in Madrid and made it into Banco de Vizcaya's first branch in the capital. By the 1920s, its expansion policy had resulted in new branches in San Sebastian, Barcelona, and Valencia. The end of the decade saw a strong network of Banco de Vizcaya branches throughout Spain and the beginnings of a presence in France, with its investment in the Banque Française et Espagnol en Paris.

With such a network in place, Banco de Vizcaya became involved in the same sort of industrial financing in which Banco de Bilbao was specializing at the same time. This emphasis meant that even when the crash of 1929 hit the Spanish economy hard, Banco de Vizcaya generated profits and was still able to pay its shareholders dividends.

By 1935, the bank had 200 offices. Despite the 1940 restrictions on banking, Banco de Vizcaya continued to grow, primarily through acquisitions of banks that were in weaker positions. The bank aggressively promoted business through the next 20 years, especially chemicals, textiles, paper, construction, and real estate.

Besides expanding through absorptions and new branches, Banco de Vizcaya became a more diversified financial-services group in the 1960s. It founded Induban in 1964 as its industrial-banking arm, Finsa in 1965 as its real estate-property investment company, Gesbancaya in 1970 as a personal-investment management company, and Liscaya in 1971 as a leasing company for major corporations. Banco de Vizcaya also developed an insurance company when it became part of Plus-Ultra in 1972. At the same time, the bank expanded internationally into Mexico City, New York, Amsterdam, and London, and became heavily involved in the Eurocurrency markets. In addition, the bank rationalized its own operations by completely automating its services. In 1967, the bank set up regional administration centers with direct links to a central electronic data-processing center.

In 1970, Banco de Vizcaya also began to move in another direction, consumer services. The bank was a pioneer in the introduction of credit cards, automated teller machines, gasoline checks, and other consumer products.

The liberalization of banking regulations in 1974 led to further expansion for Banco de Vizcaya. The bank's 305 offices in 1970 had grown to 904 offices by 1980. In 1979, managers took a step that was not yet common among Spanish banks: calling upon an independent auditing firm to publicly document its position, a move that has had an impact upon Spanish banking ever since.

### *Banco Bilbao Vizcaya: 1990s*

Banco de Bilbao and Banco Vizcaya were both established to serve business; both financed industrial development in Spain; both weathered changing economic conditions by being adaptable to new ways of doing business; and both took every opportunity to expand. The two banks were profitable. Together, they had the scale to continue that profitability in an economic climate that went through dramatic changes when Spain was incorporated into the European Economic Community, or European Union, in 1993.

One key development of the European Union that affected BBV was the implementation of the European Monetary Institute, which was created to help aid in the development of the European Central Bank (ECB). Eventually established in 1998, the ECB created a single monetary policy and interest rate for those participating in the Union. That year, Spain, along with Austria, Belgium, Finland, France, Germany, Ireland, Italy, Luxembourg, the Netherlands, and Portugal cut interest rates in order to promote growth and pave the way for a unified currency. This new currency, the euro, was adopted in 1999 by the aforementioned countries and used for foreign exchange and electronic payments.

After Spain entered the European Union, BBV set it sights on becoming an international leading financial institution. The firm began a new strategy in 1994 entitled the ''1,000 Day Program,'' which was set in place to develop the company as the preferred financial provider not only in Spain but in Latin America as well.

BBV spent the greater part of the 1990s intent on its growth-through-acquisition policy. In 1995, the firm purchased Banco Continental in Peru and increased its holding to 70 percent in Groupo Financiero Probursa in Mexico. The company also acquired Banca Cremi and Banco de Oriento from the Mexican government. In August 1996, it took a 40 percent stake in Banco Ganadero, the largest bank in Columbia.

The following year, BBV began its takeover of the Argentine market with the acquisition of both Banco Credito Argentina and Banco Frances. By this time, BBV had $120 billion in assets and was closing in on its rival Banco Santander, a company that laid claim to $137 billion in assets. Both firms were in fierce competition in Latin America, each vying for the leading position in the industry. Together, both BBV and Santander had spent over $5 billion in acquisitions since 1991 and remained focused on additional purchases. A 1997 *Business Week* article commented on the recent spending spree of the two companies, claiming that what was driving the Spanish firms were ''falling margins at home and the lure of 20 percent return on equity in some Latin countries.'' The article went on the state that ''throughout the region, their rivalry is shaking up banking—nowhere more dramatically that in Argentina.''

### *The Argentaria Merger: 1998*

Continuing with its expansion in Argentina, BBV took control of the top Argentine pension fund, Consolidar, in 1999. Later that year, the firm announced that it would merge with Argentaria Caja Postal y Banco Hipotecario S.A., which was formed in 1991 to focus on corporate banking. The new company, entitled Banco Bilbao Vizcaya Argentaria S.A. (BBVA), operated as the second largest financial institution in both Spain and Latin America. Its size gave it considerable means to expand further in Latin America and also laid the groundwork for management's plans to extend its reach into other countries, including France, Italy, and Portugal.

Having purchased banks in ten different countries over the past decade, BBVA made yet another strategic move in 2000 when it made a $2.4 billion purchase of Bancomer S.A., Mexico's second-largest bank. Entitled BBVA-Bancomer, the newly-acquired company controlled nearly 30 percent of Mexico's banking assets with over 2,000 branches. Meanwhile, competitor Santander had purchased Mexico's third-largest bank, Banca Serfin.

Competition in the global banking industry continued in 2001. BBVA focused on developing new technology, and while its e-banking venture, Uno-E, lost money, the company continued to eye the Internet as a potentially lucrative banking avenue. The company also continued with plans to increase its share in Brazil—in 2001, it controlled just one percent of that market.

The Argentine market became increasingly volatile during 2001 because of a monetary crisis, and BBVA stood to register losses due to its strong involvement in Argentina's banking industry. Nevertheless, the company continued to look to the future, determined to increase its market share. Having grown dramatically since its 1988 merger, BBVA appeared to be well positioned for future prosperity.

### *Principal Subsidiaries*

BBVA Group Central Services; Banco de Credito Local; BBVA Finanzia; BBVA Privanza; Uno-e Bank; Banc Internacional d'Andorra-Banca Mora; BBVA Banco Frances (Argentina); BBVA Brazil; BBVA Banco Ganadero (Columbia); BBVA Privanza Bank Jersey Ltd. (Channel Islands); BBVA Banco BHIF (Chile); BBVA Privanza International Gibralter Ltd.; BBVA Maroc (Morocco); BBVA Bancomer (Mexico); BBVA Panama; BBVA Paraguay; BBVA Continental (Peru); BBVA Portugual; BBVA Puerto Rico; BBVA Privanza Bank (Switzerland); BBVA Banco Uruguay; BBVA Banco Provincial (Venezuela).

### *Principal Competitors*

Santander Central Hispano S.A.; Banco Popular Español S.A.; Grupo Financiero Banamex, S.A. de C.V.

### *Further Reading*

''Argentina: BBV Acquires Consolidar, Reinforces Position,'' *South American Business Information*, June 1, 1999.

''Argentina: Consequences of the Merger,'' *South American Business Information*, October 21, 1999.

''Banco Bilbao Vizcaya,'' Bilbao: Banco Bilbao Vizcaya, 1988.

''Banco Bilbao Vizcaya (BBV),'' *Privatization International*, October 1999.

''Banks Could Lose US$20Bil in Argentina,'' *South American Business Information*, January 18, 2002.

''BBV, Argentaria Conclude Merger,'' *Wall Street Journal*, October 20, 1999, p. 15.

''BBVA to Grow in 2002,'' *South American Business Information*, January 2, 2002.

''A Latin Union,'' *LatinFinance*, February 2000, p. 31.

''Mergers Swallow Up Top Two,'' *Banker*, July 2001, p. 151.

''The New Conquistadors in Latin America,'' *Business Week International Edition*, June 16, 1997.

''A New Superpower in Mexican Banking,'' *Business Week*, June 16, 2000.

''Q&A with BBVA's Ybarra and Gonzalez,'' *Business Week Online*, April 23, 2001.

Warner, Alison, ''New World Ventures,'' *Banker*, October 1996, p. 51.

—update: Christina M. Stansell

Billabong
International
Limited

# Blonder Tongue Laboratories, Inc.

**One Jake Brown Road**
**Old Bridge, New Jersey 08857-1000**
**U.S.A.**
**Telephone: (732) 679-4000**
**Fax: (732) 679-4353**
**Web site: http://www.blondertongue.com**

*Public Company*
*Incorporated:* 1950
*Employees:* 437
*Sales:* $53.6 million
*Stock Exchanges:* American
*Ticker Symbol:* BDR
*NAIC:* 33431 Audio and Video Equipment Manufacturing

Blonder Tongue Laboratories, Inc., located in Old Bridge, New Jersey, manufacturers a comprehensive line of electronic equipment intended primarily for the private cable television industry. Its customers include multiple dwelling units (MDUs), the lodging industry, and institutions such as hospitals, schools, and prisons. Following a one-stop shopping approach, Blonder Tongue offers all the electronic equipment required to create a cable TV or security system, ranging from products that acquire and distribute signals to ones that offer interdiction in order to prevent signal piracy. Interdiction products are also sold to cable giant Cablevision, which account for 30 percent of the company's annual sales. In addition to traditional analog cable TV, Blonder Tongue is heavily involved in the development and sale of products geared toward the emerging broadband technologies, including digital satellite receivers and cable modems.

## *Ike Blonder and Ben Tongue Meet During World War II*

Isaac ''Ike'' Blonder, one of the founders of Blonder Tongue, was born in New York City in 1916. At the age of six he moved to rural Connecticut, where he developed a passion for the new radio technology. As a teenager he helped out in his father's auto repair garage, repairing early car radios, in addition to working on his neighbor's home sets. After earning a B.S. in Physics from the University of Connecticut and an M.S. in Physics from Cornell University, in 1941 Blonder worked for a brief period as a troubleshooter in a General Electric radio factory. He then accepted a one-year commission in the U.S. Army in order to be involved in military research. Pearl Harbor soon followed, however, placing the United States on a war footing, and Blonder found himself shipped to England to serve as a radar officer in the British Army. While in the service, he became friends with another radar officer, Robert Rines, whose father was a patent attorney in the radio business. When the war was over, Blonder began to search for a job after he was decommissioned. It was Rines' father who suggested that Blonder visit Panoramic Radio Corporation, located in Manhattan. Still dressed in his army uniform, he observed a young man working on a band pass amplifier, and the two fell into conversation. The young man was Ben Tongue, and this chance meeting would lead to the eventual creation of Blonder Tongue Laboratories. Robert Rines also played an important role in the company's development. (Decades later Rines became better known to the general public as one of the most prominent hunters of the Loch Ness Monster, an interest he shared with Blonder.)

Designated 4F by his draft board, Tongue attended Northeastern University from 1942 to 1945, earning an electrical engineering degree. He had only been working at Panoramic for a short time before meeting Blonder, who soon joined him at the company, which was involved in the manufacture of spectrum analyzers, used in radio tuners. The two men became roommates for a period of time, sharing a Brooklyn basement apartment large enough to accommodate their accumulation of electronic equipment. Blonder stayed with Panoramic less than two years, opting to teach physics at City College in New York. Because it had been heavily dependent on government contracts that were terminated after the war, Panoramic was forced to radically downsize. Staffing levels fell from 150 employees to just seven, resulting in Tongue being named chief engineer at the age of 27. Blonder in the meantime grew bored with teaching and in 1948 took an engineering position at TeleKing Corporation, a New York television manufacturer. Not only did he become involved in television, he gained his first experience

**Company Perspectives:**

*Blonder Tongue's focus has always been and continues to be customer driven. To this end, we have adopted a philosophy of Quality, as defined by the customer. This philosophy is exemplified by our company slogan, "The Standard Of Quality In TV Signal Distribution."*

with a master antenna system. Because several TeleKing lab engineers needed access to the one television antenna on the roof of the building, Blonder developed a splitter and amplifier system so that several televisions could share a single feed.

Although no longer roommates, both Blonder and Tongue were living north of New York City when they began exploring the possibility of starting their own business. Deciding to take advantage of the mounting interest in television, in 1949 they conceived of a device to improve television reception for outlying areas, a tricky proposition at the time because tuning a channel also required adjusting a booster. A prototype of a device to allow viewers to simultaneous adjust the tuner and booster was built, although it never went into production. Despite lacking a product, however, Blonder and Tongue pooled their money, some $5,000, and started up a business in early 1950, calling it Blonder Tongue Laboratories. They rented an old dance hall in Yonkers, New York, which had formerly housed an illegal gambling operation that took bets on horse races from the nearby track. Within days, Blonder Tongue was raided by the local police, who suspected that two engineers were actually bookies attempting to again set up shop.

In the beginning, Blonder and Tongue earned money by installing high-end televisions for wealthy Westchester homeowners while developing their first marketable product, a broadband booster that allowed for the amplification of all 12 channels (2 through 13) rather than just one at a time. Blonder turned to a pair of friends, Dave Gelass and Harold Baker, who were sales representatives for Centralab Corporation and as a favor took the Blonder Tongue booster, the HA-1, to the May 1950 Chicago Parts Show. Because it was the only product on the market that was an automatic tuner, a number of sales reps at the show expressed an interest in representing Blonder Tongue. Very quickly the new company had orders for the HA-1, which was initially listed at $49.50 and sold to distributors for $20. Some fifty people were hired to produce the product at the Yonkers facility, and demand was so high that many customers simply maintained standing orders for the HA-1, so that once an order was completed another automatically opened. By year's end, Blonder Tongue generated nearly $33,000 in sales, resulting in a profit of more than $5,400.

### *Incorporation in 1950*

The company incorporated in 1950, with Blonder becoming chairman and Tongue the president of the organization. Rines, also given a stake, made a valuable contribution to the business as a patent attorney and adviser. Over the years, Tongue received 30 patents and Blonder 39. Early in 1951, Blonder Tongue, needing more space, moved to a larger facility in Mount Vernon, New York, where it soon began to produce a new product. Having learned that their HA-1 was being used as part of master antenna systems for apartment buildings, Blonder and Tongue developed a device more suited to the purpose, a high-gain, higher power broadband amplifier, the CA-41-M. They followed up with similar broadband amplifiers, much of the technology subsequently copied by others. Blonder Tongue made products that could have established it as a major player in the cable television industry, which was just starting to develop in mountainous areas of the country where television reception was poor or non-existent. The reason Blonder Tongue did not aggressively pursue the cable business was purely financial. Cable operators were struggling and often took as long as a year to pay their bills. Also operating on a shoestring, Blonder Tongue had no choice but to sell their products to distributors who could pay immediately. They in turn sold the equipment for television installations in homes and apartment buildings. Although Blonder Tongue did develop a line of cable quality equipment, it simply could not afford to finance the early cable operators, as a result opting to focus on products geared toward individuals or small master antenna systems.

Another successful product developed and sold by Blonder Tongue in the 1950s was a UHF converter, which was sold both under the Sears Roebuck and Radio Shack labels. To keep up with the demand for its products, the company was forced to continually relocate to larger facilities. After only a year of operating out of the Yonkers dance hall, Blonder Tongue moved to Mount Vernon, New York, but soon outgrew that space as well. Deciding that New Jersey offered a better business climate, in 1952 Blonder and Tongue moved their company to Westfield, New Jersey, where they began to manufacture a number of products for master antenna systems. In 1955, the business relocated again, virtually overnight, in response to a renegade union's attempt to organize its workers. According to Tongue, the union organizer "turned out to be an infiltrator from the FBI, gathering information on the UE [an alleged communist union]. So he was sort of a two-faced fellow." Established now in Newark, New Jersey, Blonder Tongue was soon back in business and another union stepped in to represent the workers.

Over the next several years, Blonder Tongue spread its operations to a number of locations in Newark, as the company developed a line of products for closed-circuit television, including monitors and cameras. The company had particular success with its Vidicon industrial camera. However, around 1960 Japanese competitors introduced an inexpensive camera that forced Blonder Tongue out of the business. The company then entered the audio market, producing radios, tuners, a graphic equalizer, amplifiers, and speakers. Although these products sold well for a time, they were all based on monaural technology, and when stereo became popular the company elected not to invest in the new technology and left the field. To this point, Blonder and Tongue, although the top officers of the company, concentrated on engineering and product development, leaving day-to-day operations to a manager. They were shocked to learn in the mid-1960s that the company was in such severe financial trouble that it was on the verge of failure. Taking immediate action, they fired the manager, cut staff, consolidated operations, and assumed more active roles in the running of the business. Tongue relinquished his position as

**Dates:**

**1950:** Ike Blonder and Ben Tongue establish a company in Yonkers, New York.
**1952:** The company moves to Westfield, New Jersey.
**1955:** The company moves to Newark, New Jersey.
**1970:** The company moves to Old Bridge, New Jersey.
**1989:** Blonder and Tongue sell the company.
**1995:** Blonder Tongue goes public.

chief engineer and became the CEO. The business soon stabilized and returned to profitability.

During the 1960s, Blonder Tongue products made inroads with cable television, but mostly with smaller operations and generally through word of mouth rather than as the result of active promotion. For several years, Blonder became personally involved in the cable business, serving as the president of a small system in Sonoma County, California, while continuing to fulfill his duties in New Jersey. He and Tongue also became involved in other television ventures. In 1964, they launched a Patterson, New Jersey, UHF television station broadcasting into the New York City market, channel 47. Searching for a paying niche, they turned to foreign-language programming, trying several languages before discovering a large untapped Spanish market. Channel 47 became the first successful Spanish-speaking station in the country. After Blonder Tongue moved out of rapidly deteriorating Newark in 1970, relocating to Old Bridge, New Jersey, the company became involved in the first successful subscription television station, channel 68 in Newark, New Jersey. Its system for scrambling signals in order to create subscription television (STV) had been approved by the FCC in 1971 and applied to channel 68 in 1974. The venture soon ran out of funds, but Wometco Broadcasting acquired the station and contracted with Blonder Tongue for STV decoders. The technology was then applied to other pay-per-view stations around the country. However, the business ultimately dried up because Canadian companies had been selling decoders and, more importantly, STV was only capable of scrambling a single station and was therefore unable to compete with the emerging cable systems that began to offer a multitude of channels. Blonder Tongue then designed a pay-per-view system for cable called Guardsman, which was introduced in 1985.

### *Blonder and Tongue Sell Business in 1989*

In 1989, after almost four decades in business together, Blonder and Tongue decided it was time to step down. They sold the business to two electrical engineers, James Luksch and Robert Palle, who had experience with cable television equipment manufacturer Texscan. Luksch teamed with Carl Pehlke to form Texscan in 1965 and ultimately became president of the company. Palle worked at Texscan from 1976 to 1985, serving in a number of positions. When they acquired Blonder Tongue the business was generating around $10 million in annual sales and essentially breaking even. Electing to retain the Blonder Tongue name, Luksch took over as chairman and Palle became chief operating officer. When the FCC in 1991 permitted private cable operators to transmit signals via microwaves over allocated frequency bands, they positioned the company to take advantage of the resulting boom in the private-cable industry. In 1993, Blonder Tongue acquired MAR Associates, a California maker of microwave amplifiers, transmitters, receivers, and accessories. A year later, the company introduced a line of private cable products geared toward smaller system operators. In 1995, Blonder Tongue gained access to Philips Electronics' interdiction technology in order to provide signal protection for the private cable industry. As a result of these efforts, the company saw its revenues grow from $22.7 million in 1992 to nearly $52 million in 1995, with net earnings increasing from $1.3 million to more than $6.4 million during this period.

In December 1995, Blonder Tongue went public, netting over $14 million, money used to reduce bank debt and acquire the company's Old Bridge facilities. The Telecommunications Act of 1996 appeared to offer even greater opportunity for the company, with long-distance telephone companies now allowed to compete in the cable television business and likely in the market for new equipment. By now, close to 80 percent of Blonder Tongue's sales were to private cable operators, serving MDUs, hotels, schools, and prisons. In 1996, the company lost one of these major customers, Interactive Cable Systems, which caused a temporary dip in revenues. During the same year, it entered into a license agreement with a subsidiary of EchoStar to manufacture commercial satellite receivers for private cable operators. In 1999, Blonder Tongue, drawing on its STV legacy, signed a major deal with a major cable operator, Cablevision, which agreed to order 100,000 interdiction subscriber management units, a contract worth over $800 million. Not only would the devices scramble pay-per-view channels, they allowed Cablevision to better manage their changing channel lineups and programming packages.

In the early years of the new century, Blonder Tongue experienced falling revenues, although it remained a profitable business. Management took steps to better position the company for the future, one that was becoming increasingly digital. Blonder Tongue's less-expensive analog products remained viable with many of its customers, yet the company began to actively develop digital products. It also tried to attract more business from major cable companies, while maintaining its dominance in private cable and small franchise cable operators. The company's QQQT product line provided an inexpensive digital upgrade to some 8,000 small U.S. cable systems. In 2002, Blonder Tongue signed an exclusive agreement to distribute products from Third Millennium Technologies to provide low-cost broadband Internet capabilities to multiple dwelling unit cable providers. The company also looked to expanded its interdiction products to capture more sales from the larger franchise cable market, which held the greatest potential for sustained growth. With a solid reputation for producing quality electronics, Blonder Tongue was likely to enjoy continued success in a digital world.

### *Principal Subsidiaries*

Blonder Tongue International, Inc.; Blonder Tongue Investment Company; Vu-Tech Communications, Inc.

### *Principal Competitors*

ARRIS; Lucent Technologies Inc.; Scientific-Atlanta, Inc.

### *Further Reading*

Brown, Karen, ''Blonder Tongue Labs Snags $16M Contract with Cablevision,'' *Cable World,* September 20, 1999, p. 26.

Coughlin, Kevin, ''Jersey Inventors Join Hall of Fame,'' *Star-Ledger,* February 22, 2002.

Lockwood, Lawrence, ''Ben Tongue, An Oral History,'' CableCenter.org, October 1992.

Taylor, Archer S., *History Between Their Ears: Recollections of Pioneer CATV Engineers*, Denver, Colo.: Cable Center, 2000, pp. 187–202.

Thomas, Myra A., ''Getting Ahead,'' *Business News New Jersey,* September 22, 1997, p. 14.

—Ed Dinger

# Blount International, Inc.

**4520 Executive Park Drive**
**Montgomery, Alabama 36116-1602**
**U.S.A.**
**Telephone: (334) 244-4000**
**Fax: (334) 271-8150**
**Web site: http://www.blount.com/**

*Public Company*
*Incorporated:* 1949 as Blount Brothers Construction Company
*Employees:* 3,200
*Sales:* $468.7 million (2001)
*Stock Exchanges:* New York
*Ticker Symbol:* BLT
*NAIC:* 332213 Saw Blade and Handsaw Manufacturing; 33251 Hardware Manufacturing; 332991 Ball and Roller Bearing Manufacturing; 332992 Small Arms Ammunition Manufacturing; 332993 Ammunition (Except Small Arms) Manufacturing; 333120 Construction Machinery Manufacturing; 333613 Mechanical Power Transmission Equipment Manufacturing; 421460 Ophthalmic Goods Wholesalers; 551112 Offices of Other Holding Companies

Blount International, Inc. is a diversified manufacturing and distributing business. The company's three main businesses include outdoor products, industrial and power equipment, and sporting equipment. Its product line ranges from specialty riding mowers to log loading machinery.

Blount's manufacturing facilities are spread throughout the United States, Canada, and Brazil. Its distribution network is active in more than 100 countries. The company makes chain saw accessories and concrete cutting system through its Oregon Cutting Systems Division, which accounts for three-quarters of Outdoor Products sales. It produces lawn mowers through Dixon Industries, Inc. The Industrial and Power Equipment segment supplies timber harvesting equipment, industrial tractors, and components for the gear industry.

## *Origins*

By the time Winton Blount, a former B-29 pilot, and his brother Houston returned to their hometown of Union Springs, Alabama, after World War II, the family sand and gravel business had almost completely deteriorated. Winton and Houston's father had died during the war, and along with him the driving force behind the company. The two brothers, however, were determined to rebuild it, and within a few weeks they had purchased U.S. Army surplus equipment to use for sand and gravel projects. Winton, ever on the lookout for opportunities and bargains, decided rather impulsively to purchase four D-7 Caterpillar tractors a short time later. When Houston asked his brother why he had purchased the tractor's, Winton replied that they were going into the contracting business.

The first contracts the brothers landed were for constructing fish ponds in and around Union Springs. By the summer of 1946, the two siblings were doing subcontract work for the Alabama Highway. Although neither Winton nor Houston had any prior experience in constructing highways, they worked on numerous highways, roads, and bridges throughout Mississippi and Alabama during the late 1940s. Their first big break came in 1949 with a $1 million contract to build the superstructure for a viaduct in Birmingham, Alabama.

By 1951, the brothers had constructed their first building, followed shortly by a few gymnasiums. In the same year, the company, known as Blount Brothers Construction Company, procured a very lucrative contract to build a 500,000-square-foot plant used by Sperry to manufacture missile components for the U.S. Navy. In 1952, the company won a contract that significantly altered the way it conducted business. A highly technical project, the contract was for building segments of a wind tunnel for the U.S. Air Force at the Arnold Engineering Development Center, near Tullahoma, Tennessee. Winton and Houston soon discovered that highly technical projects were not only more profitable, but that there was less competition for such contracts. As a result, they started to concentrate on

### Company Perspectives:

*We want to create within the Blount organization a place where people can and will want to come and devote their lives toward building a more successful enterprise. To do so, we seek to create a climate where individuals can develop to their maximum potential. It is our belief that if people are set free to express themselves to the fullest, their accomplishments will be far beyond their dreams, and they will not only contribute to the growth of the company, but will also be more useful citizens and contribute to the larger society. We hold a deep and abiding faith in the American Enterprise System. We understand and have tolerance for a wide range of individual interpretations of this system, but we brook no adherence to any other way of life. We believe in a person's responsibility and duty as a citizen to look beyond the office, and we encourage participation in civic, cultural, religious, and political affairs of our country. We do not Seek Conformity; We do Seek Participation. We believe we have no greater responsibility to the American Enterprise System than to ensure that our business operates at a reasonable profit. There is no way to provide opportunity for growth or job security other than to make profits. To accomplish this on a continuing basis, we believe it is necessary to grow. We believe growth is necessary to provide opportunities on an ever increasing scale for our people to make their mark. Therefore, we are dedicated to growth—growth as a company, growth as an organization, and growth as individuals. This is what we stand for. This is what we are about.*

complex construction-type projects, some of which were one-of-a-kind buildings. Soon after the U.S. Air Force project, the company constructed an atomic energy facility at Oak Ridge, Tennessee, and took on other increasingly complex projects.

By the middle of the decade, the Blount brothers were not only deeply involved in the construction industry, but also in the materials business, including gravel and sand, as well as asphalt and concrete pipe production. At this time, Houston Blount decided that he wanted to devote his attention exclusively to the materials operation. Thus, the two brothers organized all their plants in the materials business and formed the Vulcan Materials Company. Houston resigned from Blount Brothers Construction to become president and chief executive officer of the new firm.

### *Explosive Growth in the 1950s and 1960s*

Under Winton's strong leadership, Blount Brothers Construction continued to grow. The company was awarded major contracts by the U.S. Air Force to build Bomark and Nike nuclear missile bases in California, Massachusetts, Michigan, and Minnesota. In 1958, Blount Brothers constructed the first intercontinental missile facility in Wyoming. It was the first time the firm was asked to build a site under the ''principle of concurrency,'' meaning that the design and testing of the missile was carried out as the facility itself was being designed and constructed; each testing of the missile resulted in a change of building specifications on the job site. Shortly afterwards, the company was contracted by the U.S. Navy to build an ''indoor ocean'' so that ship models could be tested under the most stringent conditions. The company also constructed the launching facilities at Cape Canaveral for the Mercury, Gemini, and Apollo space programs, as well as the world's biggest rocket test silo. Other projects during the late 1950s involved the construction of nuclear reactors, a cyclotron, the Atlanta airport, and numerous dams and river locks.

By 1962, Blount Brothers was growing so rapidly that it passed the $100 million mark for construction contracts. In the same year, the construction industry's trade publication, *Engineering News-Record,* ranked Blount as the thirty-third largest construction company in the United States. However, although Blount benefited from the federal government's practice of awarding lump-sum contracts to the lowest bidder that could provide high-quality work, another government policy of using public work funds to regulate the economy began to create extreme cycles within the construction industry as a whole. As a consequence of this latter policy, management at Blount decided to decrease its reliance on government contracts and seek more work in the private or corporate sector.

In order to capture a significant share of the contracts in private industry, the company started a business development department and opened satellite offices in Boston, Chicago, and Houston. Initially, Blount was forced to accept small jobs, but these soon grew into larger and larger contracts. In 1967, management decided to embark upon an aggressive acquisitions program to accelerate its entry into private sector construction. The first acquisition was the Benjamin F. Shaw Company, a leader in the manufacture and installation of piping for chemical, paper, and power plants, as well as for oil refineries.

### *Company President Turns Postmaster in 1968*

Winton Blount resigned from his position as president and chairperson in 1968 to accept a nomination as Postmaster General of the United States in Richard Nixon's new cabinet. During his leave of absence, Austin Paddock, the administrative vice-president of United States Steel Company, was chosen to replace Winton. When Winton Blount left the company, he insisted that it no longer bid for government contracts while he was postmaster. Since over 50 percent of the company's construction contracts were still with the government, this meant the elimination of a huge amount of business at one stroke; at the same time, it also meant that the firm would devote itself to getting all of its contracts from private industry.

To compensate for the elimination of federal contracts, Blount continued its acquisition program. The most important acquisition during this time involved the purchase of J.P. Burroughs & Sons, an agribusiness firm based in Saginaw, Michigan. Buying Burroughs, a public company listed on the American Stock Exchange, allowed privately owned Blount to acquire all of the Burroughs shareholders. This move had been anticipated for years by management and led to Blount's listing on the American Stock Exchange in July 1972. In addition, the acquisition introduced the company, now known as Blount, Inc., to the field of agribusiness, which involved the manufacture of seed cleaners, roller mills, grain dryers, and bucket elevators.

**Key Dates:**

**1946:** Blount Brothers go into the contracting business.
**1951:** The Blounts begin to land more complex military construction projects.
**1968:** Co-founder Winton Blount is named U.S. Postmaster General.
**1971:** Blount becomes a Delaware corporation.
**1972:** Blount, Inc. goes public after acquiring J.P. Burroughs & Sons.
**1985:** Blount acquires Omark Industries of Portland, Oregon.
**1994:** Blount exits the construction business to focus on manufacturing.
**1997:** Federal Cartridge is acquired.
**1999:** Lehman Brothers acquires Blount in a leveraged buy-out (LBO).
**2001:** Federal Cartridge sold to Alliant Techsystems (ATK).

## *Growing Agribusiness in the 1970s*

When Winton Blount returned to the company in 1974 and assumed his former position as president and chairperson, he decided that it was time to determine the future direction of the firm. Taking advice from both Blount management and his brother Houston, Winton decided that the company would not become a conglomerate with operations in a variety of unrelated fields but rather focus solely on the construction and agribusiness industries. Since the company was already well established in the construction industry, Winton immediately turned his attention to expanding its agribusiness operations. In 1976, Blount, Inc. purchased Modern Farm Systems, a manufacturer and distributor of grain bins and metal farm buildings. With facilities in Iowa, Indiana, Mississippi, Nebraska, and Pennsylvania, the acquisition enabled Blount, Inc. to quickly set up a comprehensive system to process, handle, and store grain.

In order to develop its agribusiness operations, Blount Inc. purchased York Foundry & Engine Work in 1977. Located in York, Nebraska, the company manufactured and distributed such items as bucket elevators and belt conveyors used to handle feeds, fertilizers, grains, and various other bulk materials. A further acquisition during the same year involved Redex Industries of Elm Creek, Nebraska, another manufacturer of materials handling equipment. The third purchase of that year was Mix-Mill Manufacturing Company of Bluffton, Indiana, a maker of different types of farm equipment used to process feed for cattle, poultry, and hogs. These acquisitions, in combination with increased grain production during the mid-1970s, led to record sales for the company; by 1979, Blount's agribusiness operations made up 45 percent of its operating income.

While Blount's agribusiness revenues were beginning to rise, management decided to expand its construction operations overseas due to a decline in the U.S. market. Offices were opened in the Middle East, and within a short period Blount had secured major contracts with Saudi Arabia and Iran. Two of the largest contracts were a $150 million agreement for construction in Tabuk, Saudi Arabia, and a collaborative effort with the French firm Bouygues involving a $3.5 billion contract for constructing the University of Riyadh in Saudi Arabia. On the domestic front, Blount purchased Fred J. Early Jr. Company, a prominent contracting firm located in San Francisco, in order to extend its operations west of the Rocky Mountains. Additional acquisitions such as the R.S. Noonan Company, a process engineering firm, and Hoad Engineers, which provided consulting engineering services, gave Blount the opportunity to enter the utility, paper, chemical, cement, and petrochemical fields. In a risky undertaking, for $61 million the company's management also decided to acquire the Washington Steel Company, a manufacturer of specialty steels. This purchase added a third major product line to Blount's well-established construction and agribusiness operations.

## *Changing the Mix in the 1980s*

In 1980, Blount reported revenues of just over $554 million; by the end of fiscal 1982 revenues had increased dramatically to $788 million. The cash flow from the construction project in Saudi Arabia was a boon for the company, as was the performance of Washington Steel and the success of its agribusiness expansion into such countries as Mexico, West Germany, China, Venezuela, Nigeria, and Egypt. Revenues for 1984 were a hefty $847 million and earnings a record $24.3 million. Yet at the pinnacle of its success, trouble started to brew. Blount's foreign construction contracts began to decrease, and the farm machine business market suddenly tumbled into a worldwide depression. Anticipating these difficulties, Winton Blount began to implement a diversification strategy. Slowly beginning to sell off all the company's agribusiness holdings, in 1985 he purchased Omark Industries, a chainsaw and materials handling equipment manufacturer for the pulpwood and timber industry and a leading producer of gun care equipment. In addition, Blount also bought W&E Environmental Systems, a Swiss-based resources recovery firm specializing in turning garbage into energy. These acquisitions, and the continued success of its projects in Saudi Arabia, helped push revenues past the $1 billion mark in 1986.

In 1987, although he remained the board's chairperson, Winton Blount decided to decrease the time he spent in managing the day-to-day operations of the company. He promoted his son, Winton Blount III, to the position of vice-chairperson and gave him the primary responsibility of supervising the company's construction business. Having previously been the head of Blount's international construction operations, Winton Blount III seemed a natural choice. Yet from the very beginning of the younger Blount's tenure, the company's performance began to suffer. Washington Steel Corporation was sold off, in spite of its turning a profit during one of the most difficult periods in the steel industry. A $100 million, 80 megawatts cogeneration project located in Pennsylvania landed in court following a dispute between Blount and Schuykill Energy Resources. Problems with the company's handling of a $150 million office complex for AT&T in Chicago also gave rise to litigation. Other construction projects in which the company lost control or entered into contract terms that were unfavorable led to declining revenues and profitability. The younger Blount was asked to vacate his position as vice-chairperson, and his father returned to turn the company around. By the end of fiscal

1990, however, revenues had dropped from over $1 billion to $683 million; revenues for the construction operations alone declined from over $600 million to $348 million.

The early 1990s were a period of disruption and realignment for the company. William R. Van Sant, president and chief executive officer of Blount from December 1990 to October 1992, suddenly resigned, creating a large gap in management. Van Sant had helped the company shift its focus to a more diversified mixture of manufacturing equipment and construction operations. John M. Panettiere, a management expert with considerable experience in the auto industry, was appointed president and chief operating officer, and he immediately began to help Winton Blount iron out the company's problems. One of their first decisions was to sell the resource recovery operation and not seek any additional contracts in the waste-to-energy business. Their second decision involved a stronger commitment to manufacturing, including outdoor products, such as saw chains and specialty riding mowers; industrial and power equipment, such as industrial tractors and equipment for timber harvesting and loading; and sporting equipment, such as small arms ammunition, gun scopes, and gun care equipment. The company's overall realignment worked. In 1993, revenues increased to over $691 million from a 1992 figure of $637 million.

## *Exiting Construction in 1994*

In early 1994, management decided to sell almost all of its construction business to Montgomery's Caddell Construction Company, headed by one of Blount's former employees. This decision opened the way for the company to eliminate the substantial operating losses its construction business experienced in the late 1980s and early 1990s. Although revenues dropped sharply as a result of this move, Blount was able to focus entirely on its three remaining divisions of outdoor products, sports equipment, and industrial equipment. Finally rid of the lingering effects of a worldwide slowdown in the construction industry, Blount's prospects for the future appeared much brighter.

Blount announced agreements to acquire Simmons Outdoor in late 1995, and Frederick Manufacturing and Orbex in late 1996. Frederick was a Kansas City maker of lawn mower accessories. Orbex made a variety of outdoor products and Simmons, sporting optics. These acquisitions were soon consolidated into the new Sporting Equipment Group.

Blount ended 1996 with 4,400 employees and earnings of $55.2 million on revenues of $649.3 million. Blount's Sporting Equipment Group accounted for $147.1 million of sales in 1996, producing operating income of $19.8 million. Group sales were doubled by the $112 million purchase of Federal Cartridge Company from St. Paul, Minnesota-based Pentair, Inc. in November 1997. Blount picked up the ammo manufacturer as part of a strategy to round out its sporting equipment brand offerings, which then included Simmons, RCBS, CCI, Speer, Ram-Line, Weaver, and Orbex. Pentair was unloading the munitions business to gain money for acquisitions related to its core businesses: electrical and electronic enclosures, professional tools and equipment, and water products. Operating profit at Federal Cartridge had fallen from $20 million to less than $2 million in 1995—the results of a stockpiling effort the year before among gun users fearful of new gun control regulations. Federal Cartridge employed 900 workers and had sales of $130 million in 1995.

Blount's long-term prospects prompted the Fort Worth, Texas-based Bass group to acquire a 5.3 percent stake in the company in the summer of 1996. This was soon raised to 8.2 percent. In April 1999, the company agreed to be acquired by a unit of Lehman Brothers Holdings Inc. for $1.16 billion. Blount issued $825 million in debt, including $325 million in junk bonds, to finance the leveraged buyout. Lehman and Blount's existing management owned 90 percent of shares after the transaction, with existing shareholders holding the rest. The Blount family owned 63 percent of shares before the deal. Blount executives had discussed selling the company to a number of bidders, but few other than Lehman were interested acquiring all of Blount's operations.

There was speculation that Lehman, as a financial buyer, would divide Blount's operations, and this was soon realized. In December 2001, Minneapolis-based aerospace and defense company Alliant Techsystems Inc. (ATK) bought Blount's Sporting Equipment Group for $235 million in stock. The "top prize" of the deal was Federal Cartridge. This operation of 1,700 employees made small-caliber ammunition and was a leader in the law enforcement market. ATK already dominated the U.S. military munitions market. Also included in the sale were Estate Cartridge, Inc., a maker of sporting shotgun shells acquired in October 2000, Simmons Outdoor Corporation, and other assets of the Sporting Equipment Division.

Blount acquired Fabtek Inc., a $21 million-a-year timber harvesting equipment business, in September 2000, making it part of the Industrial and Power Equipment Group. Blount bought Windsor Forestry Tools, Inc. from Snap-On Incorporated in October 2000. Windsor made cutting chain and guide bars for chain saws and timber harvesting equipment.

Harold E. Layman, president and COO since 2000, succeeded John M. Panettiere as CEO in April 2001. The company had a net loss of $43.6 million on sales of $469 million for the year.

## *Principal Subsidiaries*

Blount, Inc.; Blount Holdings, Ltd. (Canada); Dixon Industries, Inc.; Gear Products, Inc.; Frederick Manufacturing Corporation.

## *Principal Operating Units*

Outdoor Products Group; Industrial & Power Equipment Group.

## *Principal Competitors*

Caterpillar Inc.; Deere & Company; MTD Products Inc.

## *Further Reading*

Agoglia, John, "Blount Fired Up for Acquisition Mode," *Sporting Goods Business* (San Francisco), July 21, 1997, p. 13.

''Alliant to Purchase Ammunition Business from Blount,'' *New York Times,* November 14, 2001, p. C4.

''Bass Group Purchases 5.3% Stake in Blount, May Buy Up to 15%,'' *Wall Street Journal,* August 13, 1996, p. B2.

''Blount Reaps $325M in Junk Bond Deal,'' *Corporate Financing Week,* August 30, 1999, p. 5.

''Blount Sells Construction Units to Caddell Construction,'' *Engineering News Record,* February 7, 1994, p. 13.

Blount, Winton M., *The Blount Story: American Enterprise at Its Best,* New York: Newcomen Society in North America, 1980.

Blount, Winton M., and Richard Blodgett, *Doing It My Way,* Lyme, CT: Greenwich Publishing Group, 1996.

Brook, Rick, ''Blount Agrees to Be Acquired by Unit of Lehman Brothers for $1.16 Billion,'' *Wall Street Journal,* April 20, 1999, p. A4.

Cook, James, ''Moving the Mail,'' *Forbes*, September 9, 1985, pp. 62–3.

Hinds, Gary, ''Minnesota-Based Propulsion-System Maker Acquires Ammunition Business,'' *Standard-Examiner* (Ogden, Utah), December 11, 2001.

Hussey, Allan F., ''Profit Builder,'' *Barrons*, May 16, 1983, pp. 61–2.

Kempfer, Lisa, ''Building a New Vision,'' *Computer-Aided Engineering* (Cleveland), November 1997, p. 12.

Levy, Melissa, ''Pentair Inc. to Sell Federal Cartridge Unit; Business Is Being Sold to Blount International Inc. of Montgomery, Ala. for an Undisclosed Amount,'' *Star Tribune* (Minneapolis), June 17, 1997, p. 1D.

*Montgomery Advertiser,* ''Winton 'Red' Blount: Friendships and Harmony,'' http://www.montgomeryadvertiser.com/1news/ specialreports/blount/

Peterson, Susan E., ''Alliant Techsystems Completes Acquisition of Blount Business; Federal Cartridge Is Deal's Top Prize,'' *Star Tribune* (Minneapolis), December 11, 2001, p. 3D.

Peterson, Susan E., and Patrick Kennedy, ''Alliant to Acquire Blount's Munitions; $250 Million Deal Seen as a Good Fit,'' *Star Tribune* (Minneapolis), November 14, 2001, p. 1D.

Thurman, Russ, ''Blount Signs Agreement to Sell Sporting Equipment Group,'' *Shooting Industry,* December 2001, p. 16.

''Woodn't You Know!,'' *Managing Intellectual Property,* April 1999.

—Thomas Derdak
—update: Frederick C. Ingram

# Bon Appetit Holding AG

**Lochackerweg 5**
**3302 Moosseedorf**
**Switzerland**
**Telephone: (+41) 31 858 48 48**
**Fax: (+41) 31 858 48 95**
**Web site: http://www.bon-appetit.ch**

*Public Company*
*Incorporated:* 1986 as Prodega AG
*Employees:* 5,051
*Sales:* CHF 3.19 billion ($2.02 billion)(2001)
*Stock Exchanges:* Zurich
*Ticker Symbol:* BOAN
*NAIC:* 445299 All Other Specialty Food Stores; 551112 Offices of Other Holding Companies

Bon Appetit Holding AG is the leading publicly listed food trade company in Switzerland. Bon Appetit acts as a holding company active in three primary areas: Retail Services; Logistics Services; and Catering Services. Bon Appetit operates as a retailer with supermarket and hypermarket group Magro, which operates in French-speaking Switzerland with eight hypermarkets and five supermarkets; Pick Pay, a network of brand-name discount stores; and Frimago, which markets and franchises a network of more than 2,000 convenience stores under brands Visavis and Primo. Retail services accounted for 37 percent of the group's sales of CHF 3.2 billion ($2 billion) in 2001. Catering Services represented 40 percent of sales and operates as two primary divisions: Cash and Carry and Wholesale Catering Services and Wholesale Catering Supplies. Subsidiaries in these divisions include Prodega Ltd., which operates 16 cash and carry stores under the Prodega name and three stores under the Growa name. Prodega also oversees the catering supplies operations under the Howeg and Hugo Dubno brand names. Since 2001, the company has extended its catering supplies activities to France through the Aldis Service Plus joint-venture with German retailing giant Metro. Logistics Services, contributing 40 percent of Bon Appetit's revenues, is carried out by subsidiary Usego, Switzerland's leading provider of logistics and distribution services for food and "near-food" products for more than 4,200 retailers, including members of the Bon Appetit network and third-party retailers, in Switzerland. Formed through a series of mergers, Bon Appetit Group expects to top CHF 5 billion in sales by 2003. The company is led by CEO Beat Curti and chairman Mario Fontana and is listed on the Swiss Stock Exchange.

### *Wholesale Food Innovators in the 1960s*

The origins of Bon Appetit Holdings lay in the mid-1960s, when Hans-Edi Curti and Pierre Grandjean, both operators of wholesale food businesses, joined with Heinz Wehrli, a wine and spirits wholesaler, to found Pro Detailhandel und Gastgewerbe (Pro Retail Trade and Catering)—or Prodega, in 1965. Prodega started out as an innovator, introducing the "cash and carry" concept to the Swiss bulk products marketplace. Prodega opened its first store in a rented building in Schönbuhl that year, targeting small and mid-sized catering and retail branch customers. By 1968, the company moved to a new, self-built store in Moosseedorf, which also became the location for the company's headquarters.

The success of the cash and carry formula quickly attracted others. In 1970, a new store opened in Langenthal, near Berne, under the name Cash + Carry, owned by wholesaler group Growa Lebensmittel AG, itself founded in 1967 to supply the VeGe supermarket chain. Another company, Gromerco, itself part of the Usego wholesale group, had started up a similarly named chain of stores, Cash & Carry. By then, the Curti family had launched a new store and company under the name C-C Legromarkt.

In 1979, Prodega, Gromerco and the C-C Legromarkt merged to form Prodega Cash & Carry. Into the early 1980s, the newly enlarged group's five stores were reorganized under a single, unified management, which then carried out an extensive modernization program, including renovating the stores and redefining its operations. Prodega Cash & Carry then began opening new stores, in Dübendorf, Heimberg, and Chur. With eight stores in operation by the mid-1980s, and a 30 percent market share, Prodega Cash & Carry was able to claim market leadership of this segment in Switzerland.

## Company Perspectives:

*From warehouse to brainhouse. We are changing from a products-oriented to a service-oriented and Internet-supported food-trading company and are gearing our services systematically to our customers. We work consistently on improving the efficiency of our processes and on developing and exchanging know-how. We see ourselves as a learning organization. Partnership is our business. Partnership exists if all those involved in a transaction can derive a concrete benefit from it. This attitude characterizes both cooperation with our employees, customers, suppliers, and shareholders as well as our resolve to enter into alliances and to cultivate them—at both the local and international level—regardless of size.*

Building on this position, Prodega Cash & Carry went public in 1986. The company acquired a new cash and carry business, CC Market Liga, operating in Basel that same year. The company's network now covered much of German-speaking Switzerland. In 1989, Prodega grew again when it acquired Growa Lebensmittel AG, which by then had added two more stores, in Bellach and Emmenmatt. Under Prodega, the new subsidiary was renamed Growa Ltd. and converted into a wholesales supplies business. The three Growa stores were then placed under the oversight of the Prodega Cash & Carry network stores. The Growa stores were later developed into a separate brand concept, offering a more limited range and smaller stores than the Prodega stores.

### *Expansion in the 1990s*

Prodega began redeveloping its store format at the beginning of the 1990s, introducing design concepts borrowed from the traditional supermarket circuit to enhance the appeal of its stores to its customers. The company opened two new stores featuring the new store design in 1990 in Biel and Rotkreuz before refitting the rest of the Prodega chain. The Rotkreuz chain had replaced the company's store at Hünenberg; in 1992, Prodega replaced another of its smaller, older stores, at Emmenbrücke, with a larger facility in Kriens. That year the company opened another Prodega market, in Reinach. At the same time, its Growa network expanded with a new and larger store at Rupperswil. Then, in 1993, the company moved into western Switzerland with the opening of a Prodega market in the Givisiez.

Not content with merely adding to its network of stores, Prodega began looking for other expansion opportunities in the early 1990s. The first of these came in 1993 when the company acquired two wholesale supply businesses, Howeg-Planteurs Réunis in Switzerland (majority owned by another Curti family business, Hofer & Curti), which soon after became Usego-Hofer-Curti or UHC), and Ewoco, based in France, which also operated its own cash and carry markets. This move enabled Prodega to diversify its offering, adding the wholesale supply delivery and logistics to its cash and carry operations. Ewoco also gave the company its first international operations.

Prodega added new stores in the mid-1990s. In 1995, the company transferred the Rupperswil store to the Prodega brand as it redeveloped the Growa brand to focus on smaller stores and a more limited range than the 15,000 items typically found in a Prodega market. In 1996, a new Prodega opened in Rüschlikon and the following year the company added its seventeenth store, a Prodega market, in Dietikon. The company continued its remodeling program as well as adding new technology. The Dietikon store, for example, claimed to be the first store in Europe to offer self-scanning bays.

In 1998, Prodega added a new market, in Crissier, near Lausanne, making the company the dominant player in French-speaking Switzerland's retail and catering supply market. Prodega then acquired Schweizerische Speisewagen-Gesellschaft (SSG), giving the company a new area of operations. SSG was founded in 1902 and had grown into Switzerland's leading transport catering company, providing mini-bar and dining services for railroad cars and stations, roadside service stations, airports, shopping malls, and cruise and tourist ships. This acquisition prompted Prodega to change its name, and in 1998, the company became Bon Appetit Holding AG.

### *Merging for Leadership in the 21st Century*

Prodega was not the only business interest of the Curti family. In 1982, the Curti families and Hofer families, linked together as Hofer & Curti AG, acquired rising retail group Pick Pay, which had been launched in the Zurich area in 1968 and had grown into a network of 20 shops in Basel, St-Gall, and Zurich by the early 1980s. Under Hofer & Curti, Pick Pay went public in 1986, then moved into French-speaking Switzerland under the Soroma SA name.

By 1995, the Curti and Hofer families had built Pick Pay into a chain of 100 retail stores. At that time, Hofer & Curti had also begun acquiring a stake in another group, Usego-Trimerco Holding, a company which traced its origins to the cooperative movement of the turn of the 20th century. In 1907, a new cooperative was founded in Lucerne, then three years later moved to the town of Olten and changed its name to Usego (Union Schweizerische Einkaufs-Gesellschaft Olten). After expanding into several other towns through the mid-1960s, Usego changed its status, from cooperative to limited liability company in 1969. Two years later, Usego merged with another company, Waro AG, and changed its name to UTH (Usego Trimerco Holding).

Reorganized in 1977, UTH now separated its operations into two main bodies: Usego, which became the company's wholesale division, and Waro, which operated UTH's retail division. UTH went public in 1984, fought off a hostile takeover in 1985, but finally was forced to open its shareholding to new investors, including Hofer & Curti by 1990. In 1992, UTH inaugurated two new marketing franchises, Primo and Visavis, offering wholesale services to the convenience foods sector. These brand names took over for several networks of independently operated stores, including the Usego, Monamigo, and Famila franchise networks.

Hofer & Curti meanwhile gained control of UTH. This occurred following a transaction in 1994 that exchanged

**Key Dates:**

**1965:** Prodega AG (Pro Detailhandel und Gastgewerbe) is founded as a cash and carry store.
**1986:** Prodega goes public and acquires CC Markt Liga.
**1989:** The company acquires Growa Levensmittel AG.
**1998:** Prodega acquires Schweizerische Speisewagen-Gesellschaft (SSG), bringing the company into the transport catering market; Prodega changes its name to Bon Appetit Holdings AG.
**2001:** The company opens the first Starbucks coffee shops in Switzerland and Austria as part of a franchise license agreement.

another company's shares in UTH for UTH's Waro AG division. Afterward, UTH focused on the wholesale trade. UTH was then merged with Pick Pay and changed its name to UHC (Usego Hofer Curti) in 1996.

The Curti family had become the majority shareholder of UHC and began preparing to merge its two businesses, Bon Appetit and UHC. The Hofer family at last agreed to back the merger in 1999, and UHC was brought under the Bon Appetit group, creating a company with revenues of more than CHF 3.3 billion and nearly 7,000 employees. Usego became the group's wholesale supplies business, while Bon Appetit took over its expanded retail section. Although still small in comparison with Swiss retail giants Migros and Coop—neither publicly listed—Bon Appetit nonetheless was able to claim the position of the country's leading publicly listed food services group.

The enlarged group now turned its focus to the future, adopting a new strategy aimed to transform itself from a product-oriented group to a group providing services to its key target markets as reflected in Bon Appetit's new motto: "From warehouse to brainhouse." The company also added e-commerce initiatives, notably taking a stake in leading online retailer LeShop.ch as well as forming a partnership with net-tissimo.com. At the same time, Bon Appetit continued to expand its store network, opening a new Prodega store in St.-Blaise, in the Neufchatel canton, at the beginning of 2000. Meanwhile, in France, the company formed the Aldis Service Plus 50–50 joint-venture with Germany's Metro AG, which took over the former Ewoco operations in that country.

In 2001, Bon Appetit expanded again, forming a partnership with Starbucks Inc. to acquire the exclusive franchise in Switzerland and Austria to develop the Starbucks coffeehouse chain in those countries. The first Starbucks opened in Switzerland in July 2001, and that highly successful opening quickly led the network to expanding to five outlets by the end of the year. In December 2001, Bon Appetit opened its first Starbucks in Austria, in the city of Vienna. With the prospect of further Starbucks openings—and the possibility of extending its license elsewhere in Europe—Bon Appetit was able to forecast a nearly doubling of its revenues, to CHF 5 billion, by 2005.

### *Principal Subsidiaries*

Prodega Ltd.; Austrian Star Gastronomie GmbH; Magro; Pick Pay; Swiss-Star Ltd. (50%); Aldis Services Plus (50%); Usego AG.

### *Principal Divisions*

Retail Services; Catering Services; Logistics Services.

### *Principal Competitors*

Metro Holding AG; Migros-Genossenschafts-Bund; Coop Schweiz Genossenschaftsverband.

### *Further Reading*

"Bon Appetit Reveals Above-Average Growth," *Eurofood*, February 14, 2002.

Burgi, Katrin, "Koffeinhaltiger Appetizer," *Cash Invest*, October 26, 2001, p. 84.

Ratcliffe, Alice, "Starbucks Takes Swiss Route to European Continent," *Reuters*, July 3, 2001.

Voigt, Birgit, "Curti rüstet sich für die Zukunft," *Tages-Anzeiger-Wirtschaft* May 19, 1999.

—M.L. Cohen

Boston Market®

# Boston Market Corporation

**14103 Denver West Parkway**
**Golden, Colorado 80401-4086**
**U.S.A.**
**Telephone: (303) 278-9500**
**Toll Free: (800) 365-7000**
**Fax: (303) 216-5339**
**Web site: http://www.bostonmarket.com**

*Wholly Owned Subsidiary of McDonald's Corporation*
*Incorporated:* 1985
*Employees:* 15,000
*Sales:* $700 million (2001 est.)
*NAIC:* 722211 Limited-Service Restaurants; 722320 Caterers

Boston Market Corporation—formerly Boston Chicken Inc.—grew rapidly after its start in 1985. The quick expansion, however, proved to be the demise of the firm, and in 1998 Boston Market was forced to declare bankruptcy. McDonald's Corporation purchased the struggling chain of restaurants in 2000 and implemented a turnaround strategy designed to rebuild the Boston Market brand. In 2002, the company operated 650 company-owned restaurants in 28 states that offered home-style entrees, fresh vegetables, sandwiches, salads, soups, side dishes, and desserts. Boston Market also offers catering services along with frozen meals available in supermarkets through a partnership with HJ Heinz Company.

## *Background*

Boston Chicken was started in 1985 by two young friends eager to launch their own enterprise. Arthur Cores was a 33-year-old graduate of Northeastern University. With a degree in business, he had worked for several years as the manager of a gourmet grocery store and as a manager for top-notch catering companies. Cores' friend, Steven (Kip) Kolow, was 29 years old and had experience working in real estate. One day in 1985, they decided to come up with a simple business plan.

Cores' experience in the gourmet food industry led him to believe that a market existed for fast, high-quality, home-style food. ''I saw the trend in gourmet shops that people wanted to buy plain, simple, everyday foods,'' Cores recalled in the August 6, 1990 issue of *Boston Business Journal*. Building from that insight, the two devised a plan for a restaurant called Boston Chicken. Their concept was simple: provide consumers with an alternative to both the existing fast food offerings and the hassle of having to go home and prepare a fresh meal.

## *Boston Chicken Opens its Doors: 1985*

Cores and Kolow borrowed recipes for chicken soup and oatmeal cookies from their grandmothers, and Cores also concocted some of his own dishes based on traditional side dishes such as mashed potatoes and squash. To their array of vegetable and salad sides they added sweet corn bread. Their various side dishes would complement the centerpiece of every meal—marinated chicken roasted in brick-fired rotisseries. The two men rented a small, vacated store in Newton, Massachusetts, and opened their doors to business in December 1985.

Not long after it opened, Boston Chicken was a smash. Customers began flocking to the take-out chicken store and telling their friends about their discovery. Soon, people were lined up at the small store waiting for their orders. During the late 1980s, articles appearing in the *Boston Globe* raved about Boston Chicken, attracting customers from all over the Boston area. Growing sales kept Cores and Kolow busy between 1986 and 1989. In fact, they had several offers from individuals in the business community interested either in buying the store or partnering with the two entrepreneurs to expand the concept.

Then, the founders of Boston Chicken were approached by George Naddaff, a local businessman with a knack for growing start-up businesses. Naddaff had opened the first Kentucky Fried Chicken stores in the Boston area and had increased his holdings of that franchise to 19 stores within three years. He had also started his own chain of child care centers, which he eventually took public, and had founded a chain of business brokerage offices. Naddaff headed a venture capital company,

## Company Perspectives:

*Boston Market Corporation recognizes that in an increasingly fast-paced world, more and more people are pressed for time and looking for ways to make their lives easier. Many consumers want an alternative to cooking that allows them to slow down and spend more time with their family and loved ones. Boston Market restaurants offer fresh, delicious, home-style meals just like you would prepare and serve at home if you had the time—without the hassle of preparation and clean-up.*

Business Expansion Capital Corp., that found resources for start-up companies that could be replicated—companies like Boston Chicken.

One evening early in 1989, Naddaff's wife sent him to the Boston Chicken take-out store in Newtonville to pick up dinner. When he saw the long line stretching outside the restaurant, he became fascinated. Naddaff bought dinner and left, but he kept coming back for weeks to watch Kolow and Cores feed the non-stop dinner crowds. Finally, he approached the owners one night and asked them if they would be interested in selling their concept, recipes, and methods of operation. ''I'd been watching them for several weeks and they were right on the money,'' Naddaff declared in the *Boston Business Journal* article.

### *Cores and Kolow Partner with Naddaff: 1989*

Cores and Kolow had turned down previous suitors because they were concerned about losing control of their creation to someone who might inadvertently destroy it. However, they trusted Naddaff and believed that he could help Boston Chicken successfully flower into a chain. They eventually cut a deal with Naddaff, and New Boston Chicken Inc. was established in March 1989. Cores and Kolow effectively sold their rights to Boston Chicken but retained ownership of the original restaurant. Kolow continued to manage the restaurant, while Cores joined the newly formed corporation as head of product development.

To make sure that the Boston Chicken concept could be successfully replicated, Naddaff got a group of private investors to contribute $1.1 million for two new stores. Both were immediate hits, and Naddaff quickly began gathering more capital. By the middle of 1990, he had expanded the New Boston Chicken chain to a total of 13 restaurants, ten of which had been opened after the start of the year. Furthermore, an additional 15 or more stores were expected to open by the beginning of 1991 in Massachusetts, Connecticut, and New York. Naddaff expected the combined sales to top $7 million annually in 1990. But sales topped projections, jumping past $8.2 million and then rising to nearly $21 million in 1991.

By 1991, individual stores were bringing in $800,000 annually, on average, about 80 percent of which was attributable to take-out business. A major appeal was price. For $5 to $7, a person could buy a relatively healthy, freshly cooked, home-style meal. The same plate would cost $10 to $15 in a nice sit-down restaurant and would take more than one hour to prepare at home. Although growth capital was scarce, New Boston Chicken planned to expand the popular concept internationally to more than 400 stores within four years. Naddaff was even working to have a chicken bred specifically for his chain.

However, in 1991, Boston Chicken caught the eye of another chain-store capitalist—Saad J. Nadhir. Nadhir was an executive with Blockbuster Video at the time. He was driving around Newton, Massachusetts, when he, just like Naddaff a few years earlier, noticed a long line of customers waiting outside of a Boston Chicken outlet. Nadhir brought his colleague, Scott Beck, over to take a look at the restaurant and both were intrigued. They checked out Naddaff and the chain and determined that it had potential. They also believed that they had a better chance than Naddaff to exploit that potential.

Beck, in particular, was in a better position to grow the Boston Chicken chain. Although he was in his early thirties at the time, he had already established himself as a savvy corporate contender. While in his twenties, Beck had talked his father and a family friend into buying several Blockbuster Video stores, and he had spent the next several years whipping the outlets into shape and opening a string of new stores. By the late 1980s, Beck, with the help of his partner Nadhir, had increased his 106-store, Midwest operation into the largest Blockbuster chain in the United States. He cashed out in 1989, at the age of 31, selling his stake to Blockbuster for $120 million.

### *Beck and Nadhir: Early to Mid-1990s*

Beck and Nadhir bought a controlling interest in Boston Chicken from Naddaff in March 1992. They shortened the chain's name to Boston Chicken, Inc., moved the headquarters to Beck's native suburban Chicago, and immediately began assembling a staff comprised largely of young executives formerly of Blockbuster. Importantly, they hired 43-year-old Jeff Shearer as a key strategist. Shearer had served as a partner in their Blockbuster franchise and had been a general manager with the Bennigan's restaurant organization in the early 1980s. They also recruited restaurant veterans Alan Palmieri, Warren Ellish, and Eddie Palms.

Six months after taking control of Boston Chicken, Beck and company were overseeing a chain of 53 restaurants in ten states. They were planning to open at least 30 in the Chicago area over the next 12 months. Planning to retain Boston Chicken's basic strategy of providing fast, fresh, high-quality food, they also made several operational and organizational changes. As they had done at Blockbuster, they would target key markets and try to take advantage of name recognition rather than spreading their resources too thinly over large regions. Beginning by establishing a national buying and distribution network designed to complement their ambitious expansion plans, Beck and his team meticulously tweaked in-store operational elements, such as food display techniques.

By the end of 1992, Boston Chicken had 83 stores operating in its chain and several new outlets under construction. Total restaurant sales rose to nearly $43 million that year as Boston Chicken, Inc.'s revenue from its franchised and owned outlets increased to about $8.3 million. The company's basic strategy

**Key Dates:**

**1985:** Boston Chicken is established by Arthur Cores and Steven Kolow.
**1989:** Cores and Kolow partner with George Naddaff to create New Boston Chicken Inc.
**1991:** Sales rise to nearly $21 million.
**1992:** Saad J. Nadhir and Scott Beck buy a controlling interest in the company and shorten the firm's name to Boston Chicken Inc.
**1993:** Boston Chicken goes public; the chain nearly triples in size to 217 stores.
**1995:** The restaurant's name is changed to Boston Market.
**1997:** The company begins a restructuring effort as sales and stock price begin to falter.
**1998:** The firm files for Chapter 11 Bankruptcy.
**2000:** McDonald's Corporation purchases the Boston Market chain.

for growth in 1992 and into 1993 was to find well-heeled, experienced restaurateurs in key regional markets who were willing to expand the chain in their area. The degree of financing provided by Boston Chicken varied among the developers. The overall expansion effort would be directed from a centralized, streamlined headquarters office where Beck and his team were based.

Representative of the ''area developers'' that Boston Chicken recruited to expand its chain was New York's Donald Cepiel. Cepiel started his fast-food industry career at the age of 16 peeling potatoes at a McDonald's restaurant. By 1993, the 43-year-old entrepreneur owned 21 Burger King outlets, among other holdings. He purchased the rights to Boston Chicken in 1991 and had three outlets built by mid-1993. Interestingly, in October 1993, Cepiel purchased the same site on which the McDonald's that first employed him had once stood. He began building a new Boston Chicken there and planned to open two more in the area during 1994.

Although Boston Chicken experienced surprisingly strong growth during 1991 and 1992, that expansion was a mere prelude to the explosive gains that Beck and team would achieve in 1993 and 1994. During 1993, in fact, the chain nearly tripled in size to 217 stores. Aggregate restaurant sales rose to $154 million, and Boston Chicken, Inc.'s revenues jumped five-fold to $43 million. To accumulate capital for even more growth, Boston Chicken went public in November 1993. Enthusiastic investors bought heavily as Boston Chicken's stock price soared.

While Boston Chicken's rampant growth was largely the result of the ingenious concept devised in 1985 by Cores and Kolow, it was also the result of the savvy operational strategy created by Beck and his experienced management team. Indeed, they had carefully engineered systems for all aspects of the company's activities, from selecting real estate and constructing stores to tracking customer preferences and preparing food. For example, the company had developed a system by which a store could be completely built and operational within less than 75 days after the start of construction.

One of the chain's most impressive elements was its advanced computer systems. During the early 1990s, the company developed its own software at a cost of about $10 million. The software was used to drive a company-wide system that integrated all of Boston Chicken's operations, gathering and processing reams of data. For example, the system would alert store managers to put out more of a certain side dish based on how many had been rung up at the register—the system would even alter its advice according to the seasons and the established preferences of that store's customer base. Boston Chicken's store computers could also make up worker schedules, automatically reorder food and supplies from vendors, and update the store's financial results on an hourly basis. ''I've never seen systems as impressive and sophisticated as Boston Chicken has,'' said stock analyst Michael Moe in the October 9, 1994 *Denver Post.*

Boston Chicken continued to use its advanced processes and systems to grow during 1994. By mid-1994, in fact, the company was employing 16,500 workers and operating a total of 330 stores, and the chain was expanding at a rate of one new store every business day. As its operations expanded, the company began looking for a new facility to house its burgeoning headquarters. Not surprisingly, Boston Chicken moved its offices to Golden, Colorado, in August 1994, where Beck had moved his family a few years earlier in an effort to improve their quality of life. There, the company opened a 42,000-square-foot, $10 million ''support center'' designed to accommodate future growth. The center housed about 140 employees when it opened.

Boston Chicken posted huge gains during the remainder of 1994, ending the year with 534 stores in its chain and continuing to add about one store each day and to hire 100 new workers every week. As annual restaurant sales rose past the $100 million mark in 1994, and the company posted strong earnings, Boston Chicken continued to seek new funds for expansion into the mid-1990s. In fact, management announced its intent to grow the chain at a rate of more than 325 stores annually at least through the end of the decade; the organization already had about 1,000 non-refundable commitments from potential outlet operators who wanted a piece of the action. ''They have the most aggressive expansion program ever undertaken in the restaurant industry,'' surmised analyst Mike Mueller in the April 10, 1994 issue of *Restaurant Business.*

### *Boston Market Declares Bankruptcy: 1998*

That aggressive expansion program however would prove to be the root cause of the company's financial demise. Boston Market—the firm's name was changed in 1995 to better reflect its growing menu—had indeed seen stellar growth through early 1997, when the firm had over 1,100 restaurants in operation and over $1 billion in sales. In February of that year, the company formed Boston Market International and Progressive Food Concepts to oversee expansion in international markets as well as in new areas such as offering Boston Market food in supermarkets.

Meanwhile, problems surfaced during the summer of 1997. Poor employee training, high operating expenses, and its lending policy to developer-franchisees had started to take their toll on company finances. Slowing sales, brought on by changing consumer demand, forced Boston Market's stock to plummet from $41.50 per share in December 1996 to approximately $17 per share by May 1997. The restaurants also began to lose customers due to slow service. A 1997 *Nation's Restaurant News* article wrote that Beck claimed that the sluggish sales were a result of consumers avoiding "the more profitable dinner purchases in favor of heavily promoted and heavily couponed lunchtime sandwiches." During the first three months of 1998, Boston Market posted losses of $312.6 million and company auditors made public the fact that the company was close to financial ruin.

During 1998, J. Michael Jenkins was named chairman and CEO of the firm as both Nadhir and Beck resigned. The company looked to his restaurant experience—Jenkins was the former CEO of Vicorp Restaurants Inc.—as crucial to getting Boston Market back on its feet. Nevertheless, stores sales continued to falter, and by July losses had reached $437.1 million. On October 5, 1998, the firm declared Chapter 11 bankruptcy. Boston Market closed nearly 400 restaurants as part of its reorganization plan. In December 1999, McDonald's Corporation announced that it intended to purchase the Boston Market chain.

### *The McDonald's Purchase: 2000*

A Boston Market executive commented in a 2000 *Business Journal* article that "when McDonald's agreed to purchase our assets it was a really big win for the company. Basically it enables us to emerge from Chapter 11 in the fastest way possible." For McDonald's, the $173 million deal—completed in May 2000—was a fairly inexpensive method of diversification, a strategy that the world's largest food service company had been focusing on.

Under new ownership, Boston Market began retooling its business operations. Jeffrey Kindler replaced Jenkins as chairman of the new McDonald's subsidiary, and in 2001 Michael Andres took over the CEO post. During 2000, the company launched its line of frozen meals in supermarkets through a partnership with HJ Heinz Company. While McDonald's had originally planned to convert most of the Boston Market restaurants into a McDonald's location or one of its other brands, including Chipotle Mexican Grill or Donatos Pizza, the parent company instead decided to slowly rebuild the Boston Market brand and planned for expansion during 2002. In fact, during that year the firm planned to open a Boston Market restaurant in Australia.

McDonald's reported that Boston Market sales had improved by eight percent from 2000 to 2001, and a 2002 Food Institute reported that Boston Market topped its list of leading quick casual chains based on sales and store count. While Boston Market had barely escaped financial disaster, operations under its new parent appeared to be heading in the right direction. Whether or not the brand would be able to regain the momentum of the early 1990s however, remained to be seen.

### *Principal Competitors*

Buffets Inc.; Luby's Inc.; KFC Corporation.

### *Further Reading*

"Boston Chicken Needs to Keep Its Ducks in a Row As it Takes Flight," *Nation's Restaurant News*, February 24, 1997, p. 31.
"Boston Market Is Nation's Top Quick Casual Chain," *Food Institute Report*, February 4, 2002, p. 3.
Conner, Chance, and Jeffrey Leib, "Ruffling the Competition: New Blockbuster Boston Chicken Sets High Goals," *Denver Post*, May 29, 1994, p. G1.
Davis, Jessica, "Boston Chicken Hatches Its Expansion Strategy," *Philadelphia Business Journal*, November 11, 1994, p. 7.
Romeo, Peter, "What's So Special About Boston Chicken?" *Restaurant Business*, April 10, 1994, p. 92.
Heimlich, Cheryl Kane, "Chicken Wars: One Down, but Another Far From Out," *South Florida Business Journal*, July 29, 1994, p. A1.
Kane, Tim, "Region's Burger King Back to Site Where He Started," *Capital District Business Review*, October 4, 1993, p. 4.
Kramer, Louise, "Larry Zwain: Keeping a Positive Outlook," *Nation's Restaurant News*, January 1997, p. 228.
Landwehr, Rebecca, "Boston Chicken Gets a Break," *Business Journal*, February 18, 2000, p. 32B.
Papiernik, Richard L., "Boston Chicken Execs Shuffled in Shakeup," *Nation's Restaurant News*, June 9, 1997, p. 23.
——, "Boston Chicken Files for Ch. 11, Shutters 178 Units," *Nation's Restaurant News*, October 12, 1998, p. 1.
——, "Did Somebody Say McRescue?," *Nation's Restaurant News*, December 13, 1999, p. 1.
Parker, Penny, "Chicken Goes High-Tech: Restaurant Chain's Goal: Roast Competition with On-Line Help," *Denver Post*, October 9, 1994, p. H1.
Pearlstein, Steven, "Boston Chicken: Hot Stuff," *Washington Post*, July 4, 1994, p. A9.
Smith, Rod, "McDonald's Plans to Begin Expansion of Boston Market," *Feedstuffs*, June 5, 2000, p. 8.
Warner, Fara, "America, Meet the New Age Chicken," *Adweek's Marketing Week*, May 13, 1991, p. 22.
Waters, Jennifer, "Boston Chicken: Flying on Broken Wings," *Restaurants & Institutions*, June 15, 1998, p. 47.
Witt, Louise, "Investors Flock to Boston Chicken," *Boston Business Journal*, August 6, 1990, p. 1.
Zuber, Amy, "Boston Market 1 Year Later," *Nation's Restaurant News*, June 4, 2001, p. 1.

—Dave Mote
—update: Christina M. Stansell

# Genuine Brannock Device®

# Brannock Device Company

**116 Luther Avenue**
**Liverpool, New York 13088**
**U.S.A.**
**Telephone: (315) 475-9862**
**Fax: (315) 475-2723**
**Web site: http://www.brannock.com**

*Private Company*
*Founded:* 1927
*Employees:* 20
*Sales:* $1.5 million (2001 est.)
*NAIC:* 334510 Navigational, Measuring, Electromedical, and Control Instruments Manufacturing

Designed in 1927, the Brannock Device quickly became a ubiquitous but publicly unheralded product. Despite a publicity shy owner, the device remained the retail shoe industry's standard foot-measuring tool more than 75 years later with virtually no changes and sales topping well over a million units. It was also one of the very few products produced by the Brannock Device Company. Its measuring accuracy, quality construction, and simple but functional design kept it dominating the market with at least a 90 percent market share into the 21st century.

### *Intrigued By Foot Measuring Problem*

In 1906, Otis Brannock partnered with Ernest Parks to establish the Park-Brannock Shoe Company in a small storefront at 321 South Salina Street, Syracuse, New York. The store, catering mostly to women at first, quickly grew successful. In the early 1920s, when Charles Brannock, the son of Otis, worked at the store during college vacations, he noticed a problem. Shoe stores at that time used an over-sized ruler-type device to measure a customer for her shoe size. This crude block of wood measured the length of the foot but not the width. People with wide feet, long arches, or unusual foot sizes frequently ended up with the wrong size shoes.

The shoe industry lacked a tool that could calculate shoe size accurately enough to allow room for comfort and prevent foot problems. Charles Brannock became so fascinated by this problem that he had trouble sleeping. In Brannock's words, "The shoe salesman, like a doctor, has a distinct responsibility to his customers, because a mistake in the fitting of a shoe, particularly a child's shoe, can definitely endanger the health." Charles Brannock often woke up at night in the Delta Kappa Epsilon fraternity house at Syracuse University to scribble notes and make sketches of a device that would measure the foot in three ways at the same time. He wanted to measure heel to toe length, arch length, and foot width.

It took two years to perfect a device that would provide the three measurements at once without repositioning. Brannock built the first prototype from his childhood Erector Set. Then, he carefully studied shoe and foot sizes. He created the next working model out of cardboard and included calibrations. After a third prototype, production began with hand assembly of aluminum parts.

At the time, Brannock was thinking only of his father's store. He failed to see the global marketing potential of his invention. The device immediately saved the store's salespeople time while providing more accurate and complete measurement of its customers shoe sizes. Word traveled quickly throughout Syracuse that no store could fit a person with shoes as well as Park-Brannock. The store began stocking shoes for customers with unusually sized feet. After a national shoe representative visited the store, orders for the device quickly followed.

### *Device Company Founded in 1927*

By 1926, Charles Brannock began offering his device to shoe retailers on a rental basis. That soon changed to an operation with a sales force scattered across the country. In 1927, the Brannock Device Company was founded. A year later, on August 28, Brannock received a patent on his invention. By 1929, Brannock began phasing out the sales force. Instead, he provided deep discounts to shoe companies that distributed the devices to their stores, an arrangement that cost less than selling the device directly to shoe stores.

The device frequently earned enthusiastic new customers. A captain in the United States Navy asked a shoe salesman in 1933

**Company Perspectives:**

*The Brannock Device Company strives to follow the philosophy and passion of the company founder, Charles Brannock. The company believes there are a lot of ways to make the Brannock foot measuring device better, but not cheaper. Its goal is not to redesign or re-invent but to improve the process by which the device is made.*

to study why so many sailors' suffered from foot problems. The salesman used the Brannock Device to determine that the problem was not the Navy shoe but improper foot measurements. The navy captain responded by writing an article in the July 1933 issue of *United States Naval Institute Proceedings* detailing how the Brannock Device eliminated foot problems aboard his ship.

### *Sales Reach 33,000 Before 1940*

By 1939, some 33,000 Brannock devices were in use around the world. The first non-U.S. sales came in 1929 through I. Singer of London, England. Seven years later, the distribution rights went to Henry Maitland Marler of Feature Shoes Limited, an affiliate of the Selby Shoe Company. Global sales reached into Canada, South America, Great Britain, Norway, Sweden, Belgium, South Africa, Palestine, Australia, New Zealand, and the Malay states. Selby absorbed the high costs of the trademarks, patents, and designs required for international sales and had exclusive rights to distribute the device in South America, South Africa, and other regions.

While the Brannock Device developed, so did the Park-Brannock Shoe Company. By February of 1937, the store's growth required a move to a three-story building at 427 South Salina Street. In 1946, Park-Brannock built a six-story, state-of-the-art store at 473–475 South Salina with individual floors for different types of shoes. The partners had also expanded into other lines, including hats, women's hosiery and purses, and children's shoes. To entertain children while their parents shopped, the store boasted several merry-go-rounds. Its design caused several shoe magazines to write positive reviews. An example of the store's innovations was the men's department, which was created to look like a great room inside a ship. At least one of the Park-Brannock Shoe Store advertisement's declared the store ''one of America's finest shoe stores.''

### *1941: War Helps Push Sales*

Brannock built upon the successful publicity the Navy captain generated in 1933. He sent the captain's article to other ships and soon had his device in use by several branches of the U.S. armed services. World War II gave the device another sales push. In 1941, the U.S. Army hired Brannock to ensure its soldiers were properly fitted for shoes and boots. Brannock spent several weeks at army camps studying their shoe fitting problems and testing various models of his device geared specifically toward fitting the regulation army shoe. To dramatically save time, Brannock created a version of the device that measured both feet at once and was calibrated specifically for standard army shoe sizes.

By 1947, high demand forced Brannock to move his device company out of the Park-Brannock Shoe Store and into a small machine shop at 509 East Fayette Street. It remained there for 50 years. Brannock walked between the two locales to supervise both the shoe store and the device company.

Brannock took on marketing the device with aplomb. He advertised both the store and the device in local newspapers and in trade journals like *Boot and Shoe Recorder*. He gave other stores the idea of using the device in their own advertising. Its popularity led it to be shown in advertisements for a wide array of other products, including insurance, magazines, carpets, floorings, and die castings. For several years the Proctor and Collier Advertising Agency handled the advertising.

### *Never A Serious Competitor*

From 1938 to 1968, Brannock attended the annual National Shoe Fair in Chicago to increase awareness of his device. Throughout the 20th and into the 21st century, the Brannock device never faced serious competitors. Year after year, it commanded at least 90 percent of the market. The Brannock Device seemed foolproof and never wore out. Many shoe stores used the same device for 30 or 40 years. ''They're almost impossible to break, unless maybe you run over one with a truck,'' said Tim Follett, the company's vice-president in 2002. The biggest concern seemed to be the numbers wearing off. In addition, competitors had trouble finding any way to distinguish their own product.

In 1962, both Otis Brannock and Ernest Park died, leaving Charles to head the Park-Brannock Shoe Store. Nineteen years later, in 1981, the Hotel Syracuse purchased the shoe store site for its new Hilton Tower. Rather than consider another site, Brannock chose to let the store permanently close its doors. It was a time when many downtown retailers had or were moving to suburban malls or to the city's outskirts. Brannock seemed shocked by the steep decline in downtown shopping. He took a tour of other New York cities to do an informal study on the health of downtown areas. The tour convinced him not to attempt to re-open the store downtown, and no other site pleased him. Throughout the 1980s, when Brannock was in his 80s, he still came to work every day. Total sales of his device topped 900,000 by 1983.

### *Device Unchanged 75 Years Later*

Even 75 years after its invention, the Brannock Device remained essentially unchanged. However, Brannock had developed many different models of the device. There were models designed especially for women, men, juniors, growing girls, athletes, ski-boots, and the military. The latest model, developed in 1996, was the Pro Series designed to fit customers with feet from size ten to 25. Basketball players from the Chicago Bulls and Atlanta Hawks field tested the model. Nevertheless, all the models worked and looked the same. Each had four basic parts: the base plate, the width bar, a length pointer made of cast aluminum, and a length-width scale. All were made of aluminum in the same cross-like shape, with the same two sliding attachments and the same graduated calibration markings. Most still had the traditional black and chrome colors but some did come in green, purple, or red. The cost in the early 1990s for a single Brannock Device was about $56.

### Key Dates:

**1925:** Charles Brannock invents the Brannock Device.
**1927:** The Brannock Device Company is founded.
**1928:** The Brannock Device is patented on August 28.
**1939:** 33,000 Brannock Devices are in use worldwide.
**1983:** Total sales of the device top 900,000 units.
**1992:** Charles Brannock dies on November 22.
**1993:** Salvatore Leonardi buys the company.
**1998:** National Museum of American History accepts company records into its technology and invention collection.

Beyond its great functionality, Brannock's device has also been hailed as an example of great design. ''Like most superior examples of industrial design, it feels utterly modern, as if it had been created yesterday. Best of all is its spectacular functional specificity—simply put, it's a perfect execution of what it was meant to be,'' wrote Paul Lukas in the September 2001 edition of *Fortune Small Business*. ''It shows incredible ingenuity and no one has ever been able to beat it. I doubt if anyone ever will, even if we get to the stars, or find out everything there is to find out about black holes,'' remarked Manhattan graphic and industrial designer Tibor Kalman.

With a dominant market share, a unique product, and worldwide sales, the company could have become widely renowned. However, Charles Brannock, a very private person, kept his company out of the spotlight. He hated publicity and would not talk to reporters. Very little was written about him or the company. Longtime friend Gus Charles stated that Charles Brannock expressed deep pride in his device and was devoted to his work. Two of Brannock's passions outside of work were downhill skiing and Syracuse University sports.

### *Brannock's Death in 1992*

Brannock deliberately kept his business small. Every Brannock Device Company employee received the same quiet courtesy from the company owner. Although he ran the firm until shortly before his death, Brannock gave employees input into major decisions. He believed in hard work. In fact, he was actively working until about six months before his death at age 89 on November 22, 1992.

After Brannock's death, the company became part of the Brannock Estate. A close friend of Brannock and the company's accountant, Gus Charles, was executor. During this time, the company ran much as it had in the past. Gus Charles wanted to continue Brannock's philosophy and way of doing business. For that reason, all potential buyers were interviewed and were only considered if they agreed not to change or cheapen the product.

### *Leonardi Buys the Company in 1993*

In November 1993, Salvatore Leonardi bought the Brannock Device Company from the Brannock Estate. A graduate of the University of Miami, Leonardi held a series of jobs until 1972, when he joined the family business, Leonardi Manufacturing, a factory that made women's handbag frames and later became a job shop. Leonardi spent 21 years at the factory until his brother's sons were ready to take the reins; subsequently, he began to look for a product-line business.

When Leonardi took over Brannock, the company had no computer-based accounting system or manufacturing capabilities. The company outsourced most production steps and handled just the final assembly of the device. To increase efficiency and control, Leonardi wanted to bring more of the manufacturing inside the company.

In 1995, Leonardi moved the company from its cramped headquarters in Syracuse to a larger facility just outside the city in Liverpool. The new facility provided room to install machinery and expand manufacturing on site. Leonardi drew on his knowledge of high-end machining tools and production work to install computer-controlled machinery for some manufacturing steps. He also installed a robotic sanding machine station and upgraded the company's accounting process.

As a result, the company virtually eliminated the normal 12 week waiting period for orders. It also began custom work, putting a company's name, logo, colors, and calibrations onto the Brannock Device. In 2001, as much as 40 percent of the company's business came from custom work done for Foot Locker (Europe), Nike, New Balance, Lang Ski Boots, and others. ''We've brought a lot of processes in house that were previously done by other people. This has given us better control, better quality, and reduced the cost to us,'' explained vice-president Tim Follett. ''Shipping, accounting, billing—all have been computerized and updated to run in the 21st century.''

The device attained even greater renown after Brannock's death. The Smithsonian's National Museum of American History deemed both the Park-Brannock Shoe Store and the Brannock Device Company historically important, accepting 12 cubic feet of company records into its Archives Center in November 1998.

### *Principal Competitors*

Woodrow Engineering (Ritz Stick).

### *Further Reading*

Craig, Barry, ''Why the Shoe Fits,'' *Technology and Innovations*, Summer 2000.
Davidson, Martha, ''A Fitting Place for the Brannock Device Company Records,'' *Lemelson Center News*, Fall 2001.
Lukas, Paul, ''Sole Proprietorship,'' *Fortune Small Business*, September 2001.
Watia, Amy K., ''Brannock Device Company Records: 1925–1998,'' *Archives Center*, Washington, D.C.: National Museum of American History, Fall 1991.

—Chris Amorosino

# Buck Knives Inc.

**1900 Weld Boulevard**
**El Cajon, California 92020**
**U.S.A.**
**Telephone: (619) 449-1100**
**Toll Free: (800) 215-2825**
**Fax: (619) 562-5774**
**Web site: http://www.buckknives.com**

*Private Company*
*Incorporated:* 1961
*Employees:* 300
*Sales:* $56.6 million (2000 est.)
*NAIC:* 339920 Sporting and Athletic Goods Manufacturing

Buck Knives Inc. is one of America's best known manufacturers of quality knives used for hunting and fishing. Operating near San Diego, California, the company is run by the fourth generation of the Buck family, which is deeply religious and prides itself on quality workmanship. Buck Knives is also known for its innovations over the years. In the beginning its tempering process set it apart from the competition. Later on, superior knife design was important in establishing the brand. The introduction of a folding hunting knife in the 1960s was a key factor in the company's growth, as was the MP bayonet developed for the military in the 1980s, as well as the Crosslock Series of knives, named knife of the year in 1994, and the more recent BuckTool, a popular multi-tool utensil. In all, Buck Knives offers hundreds of knife styles, most of which are produced at the company's 4.5 acre El Cajon, California, manufacturing facility. It also crafts expensive limited-edition commemorative knives that are highly valued by collectors. More recently Buck Knives has begun to extend its brand to a wide range of outdoor products via licensing agreements.

### *Hoyt Buck Begins Making Knives in Early 1900s*

The roots of the Buck family involvement in knifemaking reach back four generations to Hoyt Buck, born in 1889 near Leavenworth, Kansas. With his formal schooling limited to the fourth grade, he became an apprentice to a Leavenworth blacksmith at the of 13. One of his jobs was to sharpen reapers and hoes for local farmers, and he soon realized that the metal of these tools did not hold an edge, resulting in frequent return visits and the need for him to constantly work the smithy's grindstone. Through trial and error the youngster developed a method to temper the metal of these tools so they would remain sharp for longer periods of time. Using discarded rasps, he then applied this technique to making knife blades that could hold an edge. Many years passed, however, before Hoyt Buck turned his discovery to commercial use. He quit the blacksmith trade at the age of 18 and moved to the Pacific Northwest. There he married and started a family, which he supported primarily through hard labor in the sawmills of the Northwest, working as a resawyer, trimming rough lumber into finished planks. It was not until America's entry into World War II, when the government called for donations of fixed-blade knives, that Hoyt Buck again put his knifemaking skills to use. He set up a small blacksmith shop in the basement of the Idaho church where he served as a lay pastor and turned out knives for the military. He earned such a high reputation for quality that by the end of the war there was a long waiting list of servicemen desiring a handcrafted Buck knife.

With the war over, in 1946 Hoyt and his wife moved to San Diego, where their son Al lived with his family. Hoping to start a knife company with his son, he set up his forge, anvil, and grinder in a lean-to next to Al's garage and began turning out knives in the afternoons. Mornings were spent drumming up orders by visiting potential customers in the area, such as butcher shops, restaurants, and sporting goods stores. For raw material he used discarded metal file blades (purchased for a penny a piece from the nearby Consolidated Vultee airplane plant), rosewood scraps for the handles, and leather scraps for the sheaths. While establishing the small business, Hoyt also lobbied his son, who was content to work as a bus driver and skeptical about his chances of earning a living making knives. Finally, in 1947, Al agreed to join his father and they established a business, H.H. Buck & Son. It would be a brief partnership, however, because a year later Hoyt was diagnosed with cancer. He spent the final months of his life making sure that Al possessed the grinding skills required to produce a knife worthy of the Buck name. Once satisfied, he moved back to the Northwest and died at the age of 59.

## Company Perspectives:

*For nearly a century, we've been making knives that are so distinctive that they've been handed down from generation to generation. With that kind of responsibility you can't cost. Clearly, our mission is to take our best and make it better.*

### *Buck Knives Close to Bankruptcy by 1960*

When Al took over, he could only produce around 25 handmade knives a week, and to make ends meet he had to sharpen lawnmowers and saws. His wife Ida chipped in, doing the books, and their son, Charles "Chuck" Buck, began to help out as soon as he was old enough. To sell Buck knives beyond San Diego, Al turned to mail order, running small ads in outdoor magazines. Even this effort was slow in paying off, and at one point his advertising consultant refused to continue placing ads until Al caught up on the account. Although the product was gaining a sterling reputation by word of mouth, the family company was on the verge of bankruptcy by 1960.

The pastor of the family's church, Robert Wilson, intervened and convinced a quality control manager at Ryan Aeronautics, Howard Craig, to help. Craig and Al Buck, in fact, sat next to each other in the church choir. Moreover, Craig was knowledgeable about metals and part-owner of a small business that performed custom welding for airplane parts. Wilson convinced Al to incorporate in order to raise the funds necessary to set up a factory capable of mass-producing knives. Craig was so enthusiastic about the idea that he enlisted a number of business associates, who then joined Al to create Buck Knives, Inc. On April 7, 1961, the articles of incorporation were filed, and a month later Al Buck was named president and chairman of the board. To ensure that he retained control of the corporation only a limited number of shares were offered for sale. Although there was little interest in the company from outside investors, Buck Knives managed to raise $35,000, which was used to establish a new San Diego production facility—in reality a 3200-square-foot Quonset hut.

Buck Knives started out with a line of six fixed-blade hunting knives employing a new, rust-resistant steel alloy. The price, much higher than other sport knives, caused some resistance from dealers. To drum up interest among retailers, Al and Ida traveled around the country in a camper for two months in 1962. Using local phone books to find addresses, the couple visited sporting goods stores to convince the owners to offer Buck knives. If the price was a cause for concern, Al offered to take back any merchandise that did not sell; however, knife buyers proved willing to pay more for a higher quality product, making the issue of price moot. Once a store took on a consignment of Buck knives, it soon placed a reorder. Of the 250 stores the couple contacted, they took home orders from 100 of them.

Al Buck proved to be a maverick in a staid knife industry. Charging far more for a knife than his competition, he was initially laughed off as a businessman soon destined to fail. Once he proved that sportsmen accepted a higher price for quality merchandise, he upset the status quo even further by launching a national ad campaign (at least by the standards of the day) to boast of the workmanship of Buck knives and explain why they were worth the high price. Moreover, he offered an unprecedented lifetime guarantee. Despite these efforts, the company struggled during the first two years following incorporation, and at one point was unable to meet payroll for three weeks. Al Buck and his son took some college courses to become more sophisticated in their understanding of business and finances, and received a $20,000 loan from the Southern California National Bank in San Diego to regain stability. In addition, a further sale of stock raised $50,000 in much need funding. As important as these factors were, however, Buck Knives truly established itself as both a viable business and a major force in the knife industry when in 1964 it introduced a folding lockblade knife, the revolutionary Model 110 Folding Hunter. Rival companies were already selling folding hunting knives featuring locking mechanisms that prevented the blade from closing on the user's hand. After taking apart and studying these knives, the company developed a much improved lockblade folding knife that became so popular that the product almost overnight made Buck Knives a world leader in sport knives.

During the rest of the 1960s, Buck Knives struggled to keep up with the demand for its products. The company turned to an outside manufacturer in order to enter the lucrative basic pocket knife market, but because of its high standards rejected so many of the knives that it eventually bought out the supplier at a dollar a knife. Even after moving operations to a 15,000-square-foot manufacturing plant in 1968, Buck Knives was soon running two shifts to simply make a dent in backorders. A year later, the company moved again, this time to a 30,000-square-foot facility in El Cajon, but the sales force was held back until the plant was fully operational. Once allowed to fully tap the marketplace, the reps were generating as many orders in a single day as they had in an entire month just five years earlier. In order to meet the rising demand for Buck knives during the 1970s, the company refined its production process. Nevertheless, Buck Knives was forced to branch out to six other sites during this period. By the end of the decade, work began on a new manufacturing plant and corporate headquarters, encompassing some 200,000 square feet under one roof, located on more than ten acres of land. Buck Knives completed the move into its new home in August 1980.

A year earlier, in June 1979, 69-year-old Al Buck stepped down from the presidency in favor of 43-year-old Chuck Buck, a move almost five years in the making. Rather than attempt to simply maintain the success achieved by his father, Chuck was determined to make his own mark and take the business to even greater heights. Accounting and ordering were computerized, and he also brought in a new marketing and sales team. The recession of 1982, which severely affected consumer spending, set back his plans, hurting business so much that the company cut its work force from 600 to just 280. The downturn in the economy forced the company to face some crucial issues. In order to begin doing business with mass merchandisers, Buck Knives altered its cash-up-front credit policy, introducing discounts and extended terms for all purchasers. In August 1982, the company completed an agreement with Kmart to stock its 2,000 stores, which led to Buck knives becoming available to the other major chains within the next few years. In addition, the company looked to new markets. In the beginning of the 1980s, almost all Buck knives were sold in the United States; by 1990, foreign sales accounted for 11 percent of the company's total revenues. Chuck Buck also learned

### Key Dates:

**1902:** Hoyt Buck learns to temper steel and make knives as a 13-year-old blacksmith apprentice.
**1942:** Buck returns to knifemaking to support the war effort.
**1946:** Buck joins his son in San Diego to start a knife business.
**1961:** Al Buck incorporates the business as Buck Knives Inc.
**1964:** The Model 110 Folding Hunter is introduced.
**1979:** Chuck Buck takes over as chief executive.
**1999:** C.J. Buck becomes the fourth generation to head the business.

through the sales force that the company was losing its reputation as an innovator. As a result, Buck Knives began to expand its product mix, which numbered 40 knives in 1982—many of which were undercut by cheaper imitations—but would grow to 200 ten years later. The company came out with three fixed-blade fish fillet knives with Kraton handles that became tacky when wet. It also launched the BuckLites series of lockblade knives that were half the weight of the company's Folding Hunter and much less expensive.

## *Big Knives Fuel 1980s Growth*

Buck Knives received a major boost in the mid-1980s when it introduced the BuckMaster, a big knife geared for survival, with a hollow-handle for storage and a saw on the back edge of the seven-and-a-half inch blade. It also gained immeasurable help from Sylvester Stallone's film *First Blood*, whose main character, Rambo, carried a similar big knife. The product was the result of a partnership between Buck Knives and Probis III Ltd., founded in 1982 by Charles Finn to develop survival tools and weapons. After the success of the BuckMaster, the company manufactured a high-tech folding knife designed by Finn, followed by another multipurpose big knife, the M9 bayonet, for which the U.S. Army contracted for more than 300,000 units. With Buck Knives acting as the subcontractor, the two partners fell out over pricing. Although the Army received its bayonets at the agreed price, Probis and Buck Knives went to court over their differences, the matter not settled until April 1991 when Buck Knives agreed to buy the patents to the three knives developed with Finn.

The public fascination with big knives faded in the early 1990s, although the desire for a multipurpose tool remained high. Buck Knives teamed with Wenger of Switzerland to create the SwissBuck Line, in the tradition of the Swiss Army knife. To compete in the inexpensive knife market, the company began distributing a foreign line called Ultrablade, although it chose not to apply the Buck label. The company also came out with a line of knives intended for women, small enough to fit in a purse and featuring designer colors. It soon became clear, however, that a woman in the market for a knife was, like her male counterpart, more interested in the quality of the product than in making a fashion statement.

In 1991, Al Buck died. Family members continued to own 60 percent of the company. While they were regularly approached by suitors interested in buying the business, they gave little consideration to offers. Instead, Chuck initiated a long-term succession plan, which allowed his 31-year-old son, C.J., time to prepare to take over. As executive vice-president, C.J. took on most of the day-to-day responsibilities. With a fourth generation of the Buck family easing into a leadership capacity, Buck Knives looked to continue moving forward, rather than regress like so many family-run companies. In 1994, Buck Knives topped the $50 million mark in annual revenues for the first time, fueled in large part by the success of its "CrossLock" series developed for law enforcement and paramedic crews and named by *Blade* magazine as its Knife of the Year. Overseas sales also continued to grow, now accounting for 17 percent of total revenues. Moreover, the company took steps to diversify beyond knives, entering the flashlight market with Buck Lights. For several years management considered licensing, hesitant about putting its name on anything but knives, but consumer research revealed that Buck Knives had tremendous brand awareness and offered a major growth engine for the future. In early 1998, Buck Knives signed an exclusive agreement with Compass Licensing to pursue the kind of outdoor products a Buck knife consumer would use. They would ultimately be placed under an umbrella brand, Buck Knives Outdoor Products. As part of the deal, the company retained the right to reject any products that did not meet its quality standards. By the end of the year, Compass lined up five acceptable licensees: Berlin Gloves, Champion Bow Company, Chippewa Boots, The Mad Bomber Company, and Trivantage Apparel. All of the products were intended to find initial distribution in sporting goods chains as well as independent retailers.

In February 1999, C.J. Buck took over as president and CEO of Buck Knives, with his father retaining the chairmanship. The passing of the torch to a new generation was reinforced the following year when Ida Buck died at the age of 90. The days of driving with her husband across the country in a camper, hoping to convince small-town shopkeepers to take a handful of knives to sell, were long past. Buck knives were now marketed around the world, a brand that was only now just beginning to realize its full potential. As one era passed, a new one was beginning to dawn. The company that started out in a lean-to next to the family garage in San Diego, in 2002 began to consider moving its headquarters and manufacturing plant to a lower cost part of the country. The towns of Post Falls, Idaho, and Bend, Oregon, appeared to be the leading candidates. No matter where Buck Knives chose to conduct business, however, there was no doubt that family commitment to producing the highest quality products would remain unchanged.

## *Principal Subsidiaries*

Buck Knives Outdoor Products.

## *Principal Competitors*

Alcas Corporation; Swiss Army Brands Inc.; W.R. Case & Sons Cutlery Company; Leatherman Tool Group Inc.; Colonial Knife Company Inc.

### *Further Reading*

Biberman, Thor Kamban, " 'Rambo' Sharpens Company Profits," *San Diego Business Journal,* January 6, 1986, p. 2.

Buck, Al, *The Story of Buck Knives,* El Cajon, Calif.: Buck Knives Inc, 1991.

Farrell, Scott, "Buck on Buck," *Shooting Industry,* November 1, 1991, p. 20.

Kowsky, Kim, "Patent Dispute Over Knife Has Bitter Edge," *Los Angeles Times,* December 20, 1989, p. 2.

Roberts, Rich, "Still on the Cutting Edge," *Los Angeles Times,* December 23, 1992, p. 6.

Siedsma, Andrea, "This Is One Company On the Cutting Edge," *San Diego Business Journal,* September 22, 1997, p. 1.

—Ed Dinger

how big can you dream?™

# Cadence Design Systems, Inc.

**2655 Seely Avenue**
**San Jose, California 95134**
**U.S.A.**
**Telephone: (408) 943-1234**
**Fax: (408) 943-0513**
**Web site: http://www.cadence.com**

*Public Company*
*Incorporated:* 1988
*Employees:* 5,600
*Sales:* $1.4 billion (2001)
*Stock Exchanges:* New York
*Ticker Symbol:* CDN
*NAIC:* 511210 Software Publishers

With revenues of $1.43 billion in 2001, Cadence Design Systems, Inc. is the world's leading developer of electronic design automation (EDA) products and services. EDA software is a form of computer-aided design and engineering (CAD/CAE) software specifically geared towards automating the design of electronic systems and integrated circuits (IC's). The company's products and services are used by companies in the computer, communication, and consumer electronics industries to design and develop IC's and electronic systems, including semiconductors, computer systems and peripherals, telecommunications and networking equipment, wireless products, automotive electronics, and various other electronic products. Cadence has operations in North America, Europe, Japan, and the Asia Pacific region.

Cadence Design Systems Inc. was incorporated in June 1988 as the new company resulting from the merger of CAD software companies, ECAD Inc. and SDA Systems Inc. Computer-aided design of IC's was a rapidly growing field when Cadence started operations. As chip manufacturers tried to fit increasingly more tiny transistors on each chip, the complex layout of the chip's design and its verification came to depend on design automation software.

ECAD, based in Santa Clara, California, developed and sold CAD/CAE software to accelerate the design of IC's, including both the schematic design and the testing phases. The company's specialty was design-verification software, in which it was a technology leader. The company's largest clients were Digital Equipment, NCR, Data General, National Semiconductor, and Advanced Micro Devices.

### *ECAD History*

ECAD was founded in August 1982 by Glen M. Antle, who held the posts of chairperson and chief executive officer until the SDA merger. Antle had worked on IC's and semiconductors since 1959 at Texas Instruments, ITT, Teledyne, and Data General. Until founding ECAD, Antle had headed the microelectronics products division of Systems Engineering Laboratories (SEL) in Sunnyvale, California. When SEL began developing a 32-bit computer, the company's CAD team devised an extremely fast algorithm for testing the new design. This new CAD testing technology would become the basis of ECAD's software products.

In 1982, SEL was acquired by Gould Inc., and the Sunnyvale facility was shut down. Gould/SEL granted Antle the marketing rights to the CAD technology plus $25,000 in funding for the new software technology, in exchange for completing some unfinished work on an operating system on which Antle and his team were working. Thus, Antle incorporated his own company, ECAD Inc., and operations began in January 1983.

ECAD began selling its first CAD integrated software package, Dracula, in April 1983. Dracula was a set of programs for integrated-circuit layout verification, which ran many times faster than the software of its competition. The package included a design-rule checker, an electrical rule checker, and a layout-versus-schematic consistency checker among other programs. In April 1984, ECAD acquired Simon Software, which produced the Simon Simulator, the only circuit-simulation program on the market developed especially for the MOS (metal oxide semiconductor) technique of chip design. ECAD's second major product family, SYMBAD, provided the automation of layout design of ICs. In August 1987, ECAD entered the printed circuit board design and layout market with its acquisition of the product line of Omnicad Corporation.

### Company Perspectives:

*At Cadence, we've pledged ourselves to total customer satisfaction. In fact, commitment to customer success is one of our core company values. In support of this promise, Cadence president and CEO Ray Bingham created the Worldwide Customer Advocacy (WCA) organization. To ensure that every customer is satisfied with the Cadence experience, WCA was recently expanded to include Education Services and Customer Support. These changes allow WCA to focus on the primary mission of establishing a customer-centric corporate culture—one that fosters a universal commitment to customer needs, stronger customer relationships, and superior business value.*

Unlike most other CAD companies, ECAD provided only software, and its software was designed in versions to run on different kinds of hardware. ECAD's software was made available for computers manufactured by IBM, Sun Microsystems, Apollo, Gould, Ridge, and Elxsi. ECAD also had original equipment manufacturer (OEM) contracts to sell its software as part of the CAD/CAE systems supplied by Daisy Systems, Control Data, and VIA systems.

ECAD had made a profit every year since 1983, and its sales and profits increased steadily. Its 1986 revenues were $16.59 million, and profits were $1.5 million. The following year, sales rose to $23.90 million, and profits more than doubled to $3.16 million. The company went public on June 10, 1987 with a sale of 1.5 million shares of common stock, raising $11.3 million in capital. Moreover, ECAD had begun marketing overseas, targeting Taiwan, Hong Kong, and western Europe. By 1987, the company had subsidiaries in France, West Germany, the United Kingdom, and Hong Kong; a research and development center in Taiwan; and a licensed distributor in Japan.

### *SDA History*

SDA Systems Inc., located in San Jose, California, developed and sold computer-aided engineering software for the physical design of semiconductor chips. SDA was founded in 1983 by James Solomon, a product manager at National Semiconductor Corporation. Solomon started his own company, with National Semiconductor's support, in order to attract the specific engineering talent needed for developing design software.

SDA received start-up financing from National Semiconductor and General Electric Co., of $1.5 million each, by establishing special corporate sponsor/client partnerships with these companies. Similar sponsorship relationships were subsequently established with Harris Corporation and L.M. Ericsson Telephone Co., also yielding contributions of $1.5 million each. In April 1987, SDA signed similar technology partnerships with Toshiba Ltd. of Japan and SGS Corporation of Italy. These types of alliances yielded more financing for less equity than funding from venture capital firms, yet, unlike straight sales contracts, they also brought in up-front cash. Although they owned equity, none of the corporate sponsors had any direct control of SDA. SDA did not mind having to share its technology, because the close relationship with its clients helped the company provide better products to serve its clients' needs.

SDA's primary technological innovation was its design framework architecture, which permitted designers to link software tools from various vendors in a common user interface and database. In 1985, SDA was the first software company to commercially introduce such a framework product. Like ECAD, SDA also distinguished itself from its competitors at the time by providing versions of its software that could run on different computer hardware platforms, such as workstations from Sun Micrososytems, Digital Equipment, and Apollo Computer.

In 1984, 33-year-old Joseph B. Costello joined SDA as vice-president of customer service. He held a number of positions, and in March of 1987 became SDA's president and chief operating officer. Costello had received an M.A. in physics from Yale University and had begun Ph.D. studies at the University of California at Berkeley before becoming a research and development manager at National Semiconductor. Upon Costello's appointment, Solomon retained the posts of chairperson and chief executive.

In 1986, SDA had about $6 million in sales, which jumped to $18 million the following year, allowing the company to turn a profit. Having raised an additional $8.3 million in the sale of preferred stock, the company filed for an initial public stock offering of 3.4 million shares at $7.50 to $9 per share in September 1987. However, the October 19, 1987 stock market collapse caused those plans to be canceled.

### *Cadence is Established: 1988*

In February 1988, an agreement was reached for ECAD Inc. to acquire SDA Systems Inc. for a stock swap of $72 million. At the time, ECAD had 197 employees and SDA had 161. The merger was completed on May 31, and a new company, Cadence Design Systems, Inc., was incorporated on June 1. Although Antle was originally to become co-chair and chief executive officer of the merged company, he did not stay after the merger. Similarly, ECAD's president and chief operating officer, James Hill, had resigned following the decision to merge in February. Thus, Costello became Cadence's chief executive officer as well as president. Costello was credited with helping to facilitate the merger through his communication efforts among all the employees.

For the year ending December 31, 1988, Cadence's sales were $78.61 million, net income was $15.96 million, and the company had 433 employees. In August 1989, Cadence raised $1.6 million in an additional stock offering, increasing the public share of Cadence's stock. Until that time, corporate sponsors of former SDA still owned sizable stakes in the company, such as Harris Corporation with 10 percent.

Cadence continued its strategy of offering software for multiple computer platforms. In addition to versions for Sun Microsystems, Digital Equipment, and Apollo computers, Cadence began making software available for Hewlett-Packard, Sony, and NEC computers in 1989 and 1990. Meanwhile, its competitors, Mentor Graphics Corporation, Daisy Systems Corporation, and Valid Logic Systems Inc., continued to bundle software with computer hardware for turnkey systems. Software porta-

**Key Dates:**

**1982:** ECAD Inc. is established.
**1983:** SDA Systems Inc. is founded by James Solomon.
**1984:** Joseph Costello joins SDA.
**1987:** ECAD goes public with sales of nearly $24 million.
**1988:** ECAD acquires SDA and forms Cadence Design Systems; Costello is named CEO and president of the new firm.
**1989:** Cadence establishes a subsidiary in Tokyo.
**1991:** The company acquires Valid Logic Systems Inc. and becomes the leading EDA supplier.
**1993:** Comdisco Systems Inc. is purchased.
**1997:** Cooper & Chyan Technology Inc. and High Level Design Systems are acquired; Costello leaves the firm to head up Knowledge Universe LLC.
**2000:** Cadence creates the subsidiary Tality Corporation.
**2001:** Avant! pleads guilty to stealing source code from Cadence.

bility was already common for various applications, but it did not become common for CAD software until the early 1990s.

Cadence soon became the world's leading supplier of IC, or chip, design software. In 1989, Cadence had a 15.4 percent market share, ahead of Seiko Instrument and Electronics with 11.5 percent (mostly in Japan), and Mentor Graphics Corporation with 8.4 percent, according to the market research firm Dataquest Inc. A year later, Dataquest put Cadence's market share at 44.2 percent.

Cadence was able to hold the largest share of the international IC design software market by becoming a dominant supplier to the large Japanese market. In 1989, Japan was producing 40 percent of the world's semiconductors, and Cadence was serving nine of the top ten Japanese chip makers, earning 30 percent of its 1989 revenues from Japan. Cadence attained its success in the Japanese market in part by implementing its predecessor SDA's practice of partnering with firms instead of merely contracting distributors. In April 1989, a subsidiary, Cadence Design Systems K.K., was established in Tokyo. This subsidiary served as more than just a sales office by also handling marketing, finance, and research and development.

### *New Product Strategies and Expansion: Late 1980s to Early 1990s*

Cadence began implementing a new product strategy in 1989, expanding into systems design software, used for the overall design of an electronic product such as a computer, instead of merely IC chip design. This involved providing software that could handle mechanical design, computer-aided manufacturing, and documentation, among other tasks. Although Cadence was the leading chip CAD provider, the chip design market in 1989 was only $179 million, compared to the $880 million systems-design market, which was the largest component of the overall $1.05 billion EDA market. In 1989, the EDA software industry was growing at 25 percent annually. Costello aspired to make Cadence into the leading EDA company by 1992, up from fourth place in 1989, and was determined that the company would first have to become at least the second-largest supplier of system-design tools.

To this end, Cadence acquired three other CAD companies with complementary technologies. In March 1989, Cadence acquired Tangent Systems Corporation, a subsidiary of Intergraph Inc. based in Santa Clara, California. Tangent supplied gate-array products, integrated circuit layout design software. In November 1989, Cadence acquired Gateway Design Automation Corporation of Lowell, Massachusetts. Gateway's strength was in simulation software, and the company's main product was the Verilog line of logical simulation software. In April 1990, Cadence acquired Automated Systems Inc., a supplier of printed circuit board design software and fabrication services located in Milwaukee, Wisconsin.

Cadence also invested heavily in research and development at the unusually high ratio of 21 percent of revenues, or $29 million, in 1989. To focus on the systems design market, the company formed new divisions devoted to systems design and analog design. Cadence introduced a full systems-design software package, Amadeus, in September 1990.

At the end of 1989, Cadence's sales had nearly doubled from $78.61 million in 1988 to $142.84 million, while net income jumped from $15.96 million to $27.78 million. Moreover the company's work force increased from 433 to 978 within the year. The following year, sales reached $231.4 million, and Cadence became the second leading EDA supplier, following Mentor Graphics Corporation.

By late 1990, Cadence was developing CAD software based on a new systems-design methodology, which enabled designers to portray their ideas in a high-level hardware description language (HDL), instead of in gate-level engineering, in what was known as a ''top-down'' approach to systems design, the latest trend.

Cadence's Verilog-XL simulator software, that of acquired Gateway Design Automation, already used an HDL of its own. In May 1990, Cadence announced its intention to make the HDL of Verilog available in the public domain for custom and third-party software development. Cadence subsequently sponsored the formation of the Open Verilog International committee to oversee file compatibility with Verilog's HDL and to promote the adoption of Verilog HDL as a standard by the Institute of Electronics and Electrical Engineers. While Cadence gained some backers from among its competitors for Verilog HDL, others in the industry preferred the existing VHDL standard. In May 1992, Cadence called for the interoperability of Verilog HDL and VHDL. Finally, by 1993, Cadence introduced a product based on the VHDL industry standard, a simulator called Leapfrog.

In December 1991, Cadence acquired and merged with Valid Logic Systems Inc., the third-ranking EDA supplier, in exchange for $200 million in stock. Valid president and chief operating officer L. George Klaus was made executive vice-president and chief operating officer of Cadence, and Valid chairperson and CEO W. Douglas Hajjar became vice-chairperson. Valid was a developer of EDA software especially for electronic systems and printed circuit boards, and its product lines were merged into those of Cadence's over the course of 1992. Thus Cadence entered 1992 as the leading EDA supplier, surpassing Mentor Graphics, with a 24 percent market share.

Although Cadence's revenue was slightly higher in 1991 over 1990, the company recorded a net loss of $22.4 million, largely due to $49.9 in million restructuring costs and $1.7 in merger costs associated with the merger with Valid Logic Systems. In the months following the merger, 10 percent of Cadence's employees were laid off in an effort to eliminate redundancies. Sales growth also slowed in the first half of 1991 due to a weaker economy.

In July 1993, Cadence acquired Comdisco Systems Inc., a subsidiary of Comdisco, Inc., for $13 million in stock. Comdisco Systems was the leader in design software for digital signal processing and communications applications, with an estimated 70 percent market share. Comdisco's technology had brought design to a higher level of abstraction than currently available. The company had pioneered system-level design in 1988 with the introduction of its signal processing worksystem. Cadence thus gained the leading position in the growing markets of block-diagram digital signal processing design tools and in network analysis tools. The unit was renamed the Alta Group in June 1994 with the acquisition of Redwood Design Automation.

After record revenue and profits in fourth quarter 1992, the company experienced a decline in revenue of 35 percent and an operating loss in first quarter 1993. Lower sales were attributed to a change in product strategy that confused customers and to poor economic conditions, especially in the Japanese market.

In response to the surprisingly lower sales, Cadence introduced a re-engineering plan in April 1993. This involved focusing on improving financial results, the hiring of new managers, including a new chief operating officer and a new chief financial officer, and the strengthening of international sales operations. The restructuring yielded immediate positive results, as revenues increased each quarter of 1993, and there were no operating losses in the succeeding quarters. The year still ended in a net loss of $12.78 million, due to $13.5 million in restructuring costs.

Lower revenues in 1993 were also seen as part of an industry trend confronting both of the larger EDA companies, Cadence and Mentor. In addition to financial losses, both companies also suffered defections of engineers and executives to start-up firms. A perception had emerged that the broad-line suppliers of EDA software were no longer on the cutting edge of technology in the fields of electronics systems design and high-level design automation. Furthermore, the EDA market had matured and was nearing saturation at the higher end, according to some industry observers.

One area in which Cadence did have an advantage over smaller start-ups was in its ability to provide a full array of support and consulting services. In 1991, Cadence formed a consulting services group as part of its new systems division. The group advised EDA users on selecting and developing tools for their design environments. In 1993, Cadence established its Spectrum Services consulting group, which soon began to be used by some of Cadence's largest software customers. Although income from sales of products declined in 1993, revenue from maintenance services increased by $23.9 million that year. In December 1993, Cadence sold its Automated Systems division, manufacturer of complex printed circuit boards, which the company had acquired in 1990.

By early 1994, Cadence appeared on its way back to recovery after the slump in 1993. With sales of IC design software once again growing, sales of systems design also began to show life after falling from $100 million in 1990 to between $35 and $40 million in 1993. During this time period however, Cadence continued to rely on its design services as the EDA industry as a whole experienced weakening demand.

### *Changes in Management: Late 1990s*

Cadence experienced significant changes in the latter half of the 1990s and found itself in industry headlines for the remainder of the decade and into 2000. In 1997, the company acquired High Level Design Systems and Cooper & Chyan Technology Inc. Costello, credited with transforming Cadence into an industry leader, shocked analysts when, later that year, he resigned his post to become an executive at Knowledge Universe LLC. Jack Harding, the CEO and president of Cooper & Chyan, was named his predecessor. Harding commented on his new position in an October 1997 *Electronic News* article claiming "I am not Joe Costello and I am not going to try to be. Joe brought this company to a billion dollars largely on his back. I plan to take it to four billion with a team."

Harding's plans, however, never reached fruition. By 1999, company sales were faltering and stock price had plummeted. In the spring of that year, Harding was ousted and Ray Bingham, Cadence's chief financial officer, was named CEO. Having worked closely with Costello, industry analysts believed that Bingham would lead Cadence back to financial health.

While making headlines for its management changes, Cadence also came under fire in March 2000 for its role in an executive payoff related to its 1999 purchase of OrCAD Inc. The class action suit claimed that the company had paid five OrCAD executives to support the acquisition. The claim was settled later that year. On a more positive note for the company, a longstanding court case with Avant! Corporation came to a resolution in 2001. In July of that year, Avant! was found guilty by the Superior Court of California of stealing several of Cadence's trade secrets in the mid-1990s. After pleading no contest to the charges, Avant! was ordered to pay $194.6 million in criminal restitution.

Meanwhile, Bingham had been focusing on creating strategic partnerships to revitalize Cadence's position in the industry. During 2001, the company partnered with Agilent Technologies, IBM, and Sun Microsystems to develop radio-frequency design for wireless and wireline communications and various other cutting-edge technologies. It also acquired Silicon Perspective Corporation, a design technology firm, and CadMOS Design Technology Inc., a design tools firm. The company also sought expansion in China, which was projected to become the largest Asian EDA market by 2004.

As worldwide economies began to slow during 2000, Cadence's design services segment was negatively affected. As such, the company reorganized its electronics design services businesses into Tality Corporation. While the subsidiary was originally scheduled for an initial public offering, Cadence was forced to change its plans as market conditions worsened. Cadence continued to restructure this subsidiary during 2002, making a series of job cuts and closing several design centers.

Under the leadership of Bingham, Cadence secured record level sales in 2001 despite the challenging economy. In fact, net income soared to $141.3 million, an increase of 182.6 percent over 2000 figures. It appeared as though Cadence's shift in focus from design services back to design tools and new product development in both analog and digital design had begun to pay off. As technology continued to change at breakneck speed in the early years of the new millennium, Cadence management was confident that the company would continue to lead the EDA industry.

### *Principal Subsidiaries*

1Chip Silicon Systems, Inc.; 849 College Ave, Inc.; Ambit Design Systems, Inc.; Arkos Design Systems, Inc.; Beijing Cadence Electronics Technology Co., Ltd. (China); Cadence China Ltd.; Cadence Design Service Y.K. (Japan); Cadence Design Systems (Canada) Limited; Cadence Design Systems (Cyprus) Limited; Cadence Design Systems (India) Private Ltd.; Cadence Design Systems (Ireland) Limited; Cadence Design Systems (Israel) Limited; Cadence Design Systems (Japan) B.V.; Cadence Design Systems (Taiwan) B.V.; Cadence Design Systems AB (Sweden); Cadence Design Systems Asia Ltd. (Hong Kong); Cadence Design Systems B.V. (Netherlands); Cadence Design Systems GmbH (Germany); Cadence Design Systems S.A.S. (France); Cadence Design Systems S.r.l. (Italy); Cadence Design Systems, Ltd. (U.K.); Cadence Korea Ltd.; Cadence Taiwan, Inc.; Cadence Technology Inc.; Cadence Technology Limited (Ireland); CadMOS Design Technology, Inc.; Cooper & Chyan Technology GmbH (Germany); Cooper & Chyan Technology, Inc.; Design Acceleration, Inc.; Detente Technology, Inc.; Diablo Lighting, Inc.; Diablo Research Company LLC (Canada); DSM Technologies, Inc.; Orcad Europe S.A.R.L. (France); Quickturn Design Systems International, Inc.; Silicon Perspective Corporation; Symbionics Group Limited (U.K.); Tality Corporation.

### *Principal Competitors*

Avant! Corporation; Mentor Graphics Corporation; Synopsis Inc.

### *Further Reading*

Ball, Richard, ''Avant! Guilty of Stealing Source Code Off Cadence,'' *Electronics Weekly*, May 30, 2001, p. 3.

Burrows, Peter, ''Cadence Shoots for the Top,'' *Electronic Business*, October 29, 1990, pp. 36–40.

Card, David, ''SDA Says It's Not Just Another CAE Start-Up,'' *Electronic Business*, May 1, 1987, p. 124.

Caruso, Denise, ''Startup ECAD Thinks Big in CAD/CAE Marketplace,''

Dorsch, Jeff, ''Surviving CAE Evolution,'' *Electronic News*, June 14, 1993, p. 1.

''ECAD to Buy SDA Systems in $72M Deal,'' *Electronic News*, February 29, 1988, pp. 1, 30.

Fasca, Chad, ''New Cadence Chief Talks Teamwork,'' *Electronic News*, October 27, 1997, p. 1.

Goering, Richard, ''Cadence Acquires Comdisco Systems,'' *Electronic Engineering Times*, July 12, 1993, p. 1.

Hof, Robert D., ''Sure, He's Wild and Crazy—Like a Fox,'' *Business Week*, October 30, 1989, p. 132.

Holden, Daniel, ''Cadence Snubs VHDL International, Pushes Verilog for ASIC Design,'' *Electronic News*, June 15, 1992, p. 13.

Jones, Stephen, ''High-Tech Firms ECAD and Impact Systems Seek Public Money,'' *San Jose Business Journal*, May 18, 1994, p. 6.

Jones, Stephen, ''SDA Systems Inks Alliances with a Japanese and Italian Firm,'' *San Jose Business Journal*, May 4, 1987, p.13.

Kerr, John, ''Breaking into Japan: Small U.S. Companies Show How It's Done,'' *Electronic Business*, November 13, 1989, pp. 72–6.

McLeod, Jonah, ''Going the Distance with Mergers, Acquisitions,'' *Electronics*, December 1989, p. 86.

——, ''Why Cadence Is the Top Dog in the IC Design Pack,'' *Electronics*, June 1989, pp. 121–22.

Morrison, Gale, ''Cadence Looks t Regain Physical Share,'' *Electronic News*, October 23, 2000, p. 14.

——, ''Cadence Suffers Loss,'' *Electronic News*, April 24, 2000, p. 1.

Ricciuti, Mike, ''Cadence Design Systems Inc.,'' *Datamation*, June 15, 1992, p. 142.

Steffora, Ann, ''A New Deal at Cadence,'' *Electronic News*, May 3, 1999, p. 1.

——, ''Services Fuel Cadence's Growth,'' *Electronic News*, April 27, 1998, p. 48.

Stitt, Wendy, ''And in This Corner . . . : Cadence Design Systems Continues to Trade 'Friendly' Punches with Mentor Graphics,'' *San Jose Business Journal*, March 18, 1991, p. S12.

Wiegner, Kathleen K., ''The Hot Box Syndrome,'' *Forbes*, April 17, 1989, pp. 178–80.

—Heather Behn Hedden
—update: Christina M. Stansell

# CAE USA Inc.

**4908 Tampa West Boulevard**
**Tampa, Florida 33634-2411**
**P.O. Box 15000**
**Tampa, Florida 33684-5000**
**U.S.A.**
**Telephone: (813) 885-7481**
**Fax: (813) 887-1419**
**Web site: http://www.cae.com**

*Wholly Owned Subsidiary of CAE Inc.*
*Incorporated:* 1935
*Employees:* 800
*Sales:* $80 million (2000)
*NAIC:* 334511 Search, Detection, Navigation, Guidance, Aeronautical, and Nautical System and Instrument Manufacturing

CAE USA Inc., formerly known as Reflectone, is one of the few remaining producers of full-fledged flight simulators for military and civil planes. This subsidiary of CAE Inc. was created when the Canadian defense giant acquired the Tampa-based flight simulator business known as Reflectone from BABE Systems.

### *Inventive Origins*

Luther G. Simjian, a Turk of Armenian descent, arrived in the United States in 1921 at the age of 16. Simjian went on to study in the Middle East and France before finishing his secondary education in New Haven, Connecticut. A stint at the Yale University Medical School's photo lab steered him away from a planned career as a doctor; instead he became director of the school's new photography department in 1928.

Simjian then started on the 200 inventions he would patent during his lifetime. The first was the self-focusing camera, in 1932; a color X-ray machine followed two years later. The deaths of friends in World War II led him to create a simulator for training pilots and gunners known as the Optical Range Estimation Trainer.

Simjian learned early, as he wrote in a privately published autobiography, that ''I can't stick with just one idea for too long.'' Subsequent inventions included a remote-controlled postage meter, an ultrasonic device for medical exploration, a computerized indoor golf practice range, and the foundations of the automated teller machine (ATM). Most of his patents, though, dealt with electronics or optics.

Inventor Luther Simjian founded Reflectone in 1935 in Stamford, Connecticut. An early product, called ''Reflect One,'' was a boudoir chair equipped with mirrors that allowed the view of one's hair from four different angles. Mirrors figured in a few of the company's early offerings.

During World War II Reflectone developed technologies to train Allied military personnel. In the 1950s, Reflectone took a leading role in electronic countermeasures simulation for the B-52 bomber.

Reflectone merged with the Universal Match Company in the early 1960s. The use of flight simulators increased dramatically during the decade. Reflectone built the first helicopter simulator in 1971, for the U.S. Coast Guard.

### *A Move to Florida in 1979*

Needing more space to complete contracts related to the U.S. Air Force's A-10 antitank aircraft, Reflectone relocated its facilities from Stamford, Connecticut to Tampa, Florida in 1979. It employed a technical staff of 135 at the time. That figure would more than quadruple in the next seven years.

Tallahassee investor John Mowell took over the company in 1981, becoming its chairman and CEO. He would hire a succession of four presidents to handle day-to-day management of the company in the next eight years.

Reflectone In-Flight Systems, Inc. was formed in 1984 to enter the market for in-flight entertainment (IFE) systems on commercial airliners. This unit found a shortage of airlines willing to invest in new IFE systems, and it was dissolved in May 1986.

## Key Dates:

**1935:** Inventor Simjian starts Reflectone in Stamford, Connecticut.
**1971:** Reflectone builds the first helicopter simulator.
**1979:** Company relocates to Tampa, Florida.
**1989:** British Aerospace acquires a controlling interest.
**1997:** BABE Systems buys remainder of shares; renames company.
**2001:** Simulator giant CAE Inc. buys Reflectone business from BABE Systems.

Reflectone continued to focus on military training systems, even after losing one of its biggest awards in 1986. The company had been awarded a contract to build 24 simulators for the Fairchild Republic T-46A trainer before this program was canceled by Congress. The company had simulators for several other types of military aircraft in development or in production. In fact, military training made up 95 percent of Reflectone's business, according to one executive. The company was looking to expand its negligible overseas business and had a few civil projects under way. Reflectone International Training Academies, Inc. trained civil airline pilots on three simulators in Tampa. The Reflectone Media Systems subsidiary produced interactive video disks for vocational training and other uses.

As the U.S. military continued to encourage high levels of competition in its procurement contracts, major aircraft manufacturers were vying for a piece of the growing military training market, altogether worth between $8 and $10 billion in the mid-1980s. Unfortunately, Reflectone had a chronic problem of falling behind schedule on its military work, such as producing trainers for the Navy's EA-6 communications aircraft and the Air Force's C-141 tankers. Ultimately, this produced losses of $11 million between 1987 and 1989. The company's new president Charles J. Cunningham, Jr., a retired Air Force three-star general, believed that Reflectone had taken on contracts that carried too much risk. It sought $1 million in reimbursement from the Department of Defense over problems with the design database and government-furnished equipment that hindered one Marine Corps training program.

Reflectone signed about $50 million in new contracts in fiscal 1989, half of it commercial business for British Aerospace, which acquired a 38 percent shareholding in Reflectone's voting stock. In July of that year, Cunningham resigned, after little more than a year as president. (He went on to teach business ethics at the University of Tampa.) At the time, the commercial contracts had brought in little cash, and the Navy was behind on $4 million in payments. Reflectone lost about $13.6 million in fiscal 1989; it was late filing its annual reports and in violation of loan covenants.

According to the *St. Petersburg Times,* a petty dispute between two government agencies was the final straw for Reflectone's shaky independence. While the Navy and the Federal Aviation Administration argued over who should inspect safety manuals for modified Boeing 707s, Reflectone missed a critical deadline and lost the $48 million contract. It was out-of-pocket $7 million.

### *BABE-Controlled in the 1990s*

British Aerospace (BABE) agreed to buy a controlling (52 percent) interest in the summer of 1989, increasing its capital by $3.6 million. BABE also loaned Reflectone $4.1 million to keep going.

Richard G. Snyder, formerly president of Toronto-based CAE Industries Ltd.'s Link Tactical Simulation Division, was named Reflectone president and CEO in January 1990. Employment at Reflectone would fall to 400 in the next two years. A new chairwoman, Tampa lawyer Stella Ferguson Thayer, was elected in June 1992.

Under BABE control, Reflectone sought more commercial work. BABE's own British Aerospace Simulation Ltd. subsidiary was able to direct more business to Reflectone, which soon landed new contracts with Ansett Airlines of Australia and a handful of U.S.-based regional airlines. Reflectone also began installing amusement park rides, including three at Sea World in Orlando.

The company narrowed its losses to just $3.3 million in fiscal 1990 as sales grew 20 percent to $49.7 million. Reflectone was finally able to post a profit, $122,000, in the final quarter of an abbreviated fiscal year ending December 31, 1990, although it lost $1.3 million for the year. It did post net income of $1.4 million in 1991. Revenues reached $54 million in 1992.

Reflectone bought the assets of a once-leading commercial flight simulator manufacturer for $4 million in January 1994. AAI-Microflite Simulation International Corp. had once been a division of The Singer Co. and lead the simulator market between 1975 and 1985. By the end of 1994, consolidation in the shrinking industry had reduced the number of large jet airliner simulators to four: CAE Electronics, Thomson Training & Simulation, FlightSafety International, and Reflectone. Less than 10 percent of Reflectone's 1993 revenues of $63 million were for civil airliner simulators, however.

The company lost $3.8 million in 1994, although things would soon be looking up. Reflectone received the largest contract in its history in July 1995, a $77 million order to build flight simulators for Lockheed Martin Aeronautical Systems. The company posted a profit of $4.5 million for the year on record sales of $170.5 million.

British Aerospace Holdings Inc. bought Reflectone's remaining shares for $39 million in early 1997. BABE then installed John Pitts, a West Point graduate, as CEO. At the time, Reflectone had 950 employees in the United States, half of them in Tampa, and another 80 at a subsidiary in England. Pitts installed a new top management team. This changing of the guard was accompanied by the passing of company founder Luther Simjian, who died at his Fort Lauderdale home on October 23, 1997.

Pitts sought to make the company more proactive in customer dealings—anticipating needs rather than putting out fires. According to the *Tampa Tribune,* he also urged managers to see themselves as part of a larger organization. Indeed, its parent was about to become larger still: BABE merged with Marconi Electronics Systems in November 1999, creating BABE Systems, the world's second largest defense contractor, a $20 billion enterprise. Reflectone was renamed BABE Systems Flight Simulation and Training, Inc. (BABE Systems FS&T) after the merger.

### *A New Owner in 2001*

In February 2001, BABE Systems sold off the simulation and training business formerly known as Reflectone. CAE Inc. of Canada won a bidding war with rival L-3 Communications and paid $80 million for the unit, which became the company's U.S. subsidiary, known as CAE USA Inc. The purchase brought the Canadian firm more into the U.S. military market.

John Lenyo was named president of CAE USA in June 2001, replacing John Pitts. Lenyo had a long history of working in the simulator industry and had joined BABE Systems FS&T in January 1999 as vice-president of Marketing and Business Development.

### *Principal Competitors*

Bombardier Inc.; L-3 Communications Holdings, Inc.; Logicon, Inc.

### *Further Reading*

''A Day in the Life of Florida Business,'' *Florida Trend,* June 1988, p. 36.

Gilpin, Kenneth N., ''Luther Simjian Is Dead at 92; Held More Than 200 Patents,'' *New York Times,* November 2, 1997, p. 45.

Goldstein, Alan, ''After Three Years, Reflectone Back in the Black,'' *St. Petersburg Times,* Bus. Sec., February 15, 1991, p. 1E.

——, ''Maker of Flight Trainers Rebounds,'' *St. Petersburg Times,* Bus. Sec., September 15, 1990, p. 15A.

Greiff, James, ''Stock Deal Key to Reflectone's Survival,'' *St. Petersburg Times,* Bus. Sec., October 18, 1989, p. 2E.

Holding, Ren, ''The Mission: Defend Ethics; Ex-General Now Fights Barbarianism in Business,'' *St. Petersburg Times,* Bus. Sec., February 12, 1990, p. 6.

Hundley, Kris, ''Company Buys Reflectone Inc.,'' *St. Petersburg Times,* Bus. Sec., February 14, 1997, p. 1E.

Huntley, Helen, ''Reflectone Inc. Chooses Lawyer as Chairwoman,'' *St. Petersburg Times,* Bus. Sec., June 13, 1992, p. 13A.

Jackovics, Ted, ''Tampa, Fla. Flight-Simulator Maker Must Adjust as Industry Changes,'' *Tampa Tribune,* April 24, 2000.

Liebowitz, David S., ''Of Food and Flight Simulators,'' *Financial World,* April 13, 1993, p. 87.

Nelms, Douglas W., ''And Then, There Were Four,'' *Air Transport World,* November 1994, p. 99.

Norris, Kim, ''Reflectone Aims to Diversify Through Deal,'' *St. Petersburg Times,* Bus. Sec., January 25, 1994, p. 1E.

''Reflectone Focuses Marketing Strategy on Military Training,'' *Aviation Week & Space Technology,* September 1, 1986, p. 250.

Simjian, Luther, ''ATM Inventor Dies at 92,'' *Ottawa Citizen,* Bus. Sec., November 5, 1997, p. D1.

Sokol, Marlene, ''Defense Contractor Loses Its President,'' *St. Petersburg Times,* Bus. Sec., July 1, 1989, p. 12A.

——, ''On the Defensive: Reflectone Fights History of Slowness on Military Work,'' *St. Petersburg Times,* Bus. Sec., May 1, 1989, p. 7.

——, ''Small Business Losing Defense: Big Corporations Win Military-Contract Game,'' *St. Petersburg Times,* Bus. Sec., October 9, 1989, p. 12.

Stengle, Bernice, ''Seeing Success Without Mirrors,'' *St. Petersburg Times,* Bus. Sec., May 16, 1992, p. 13A.

Trigaux, Robert, ''Big Contract Lifts Reflectone,'' *St. Petersburg Times,* Bus. Sec., July 27, 1995, p. 6E.

Ward, J.T., ''Simulator Company Is Healthy and Happy,'' *St. Petersburg Times,* Bus. Sec., June 4, 1996, p. 1E.

—Frederick C. Ingram

# Cambridge SoundWorks, Inc.

**100 Brickstone Square**
**Andover, Massachusetts 01810**
**U.S.A.**
**Telephone: (978) 475-3608**
**Toll Free: (877) 937-4434**
**Fax: (978) 475-7265**
**Web site: http://www.cambridgesoundworks.com**

*Wholly Owned Subsidiary of Creative Technology, Inc.*
*Incorporated:* 1988
*Employees:* 250 (est.)
*Sales:* $50 million (1997)
*NAIC:* 334310 Audio and Video Equipment Manufacturing

Located outside of Boston, Massachusetts, Cambridge SoundWorks, Inc. is a subsidiary of Creative Technology and manufactures a wide range of speaker systems for home stereo, home theater, car audio, and personal computers. Products are sold through 24 retail locations, with 12 located in Massachusetts, seven in California, three in New Hampshire, and two in Maine. Cambridge SoundWorks sells to the New York market through an exclusive distribution deal with J&R Music and Computer World, a major electronic retailer in the city. In addition, the company sells through its own catalog and a sister Web site, hifi.com, and Creative Labs distributes its multimedia speakers around the world.

## *Early Life and Career of Henry Kloss*

Legendary audio engineer Henry Kloss was born in Altoona, Pennsylvania, in 1929 and raised in the area. As a boy, he was a precocious builder, adding rooms and bathroom fixtures to the cabin he shared with his mother and two sisters. To support his studies at the Massachusetts Institute of Technology (MIT), which he entered in 1948, Kloss worked part-time for a contractor. He purchased woodworking tools in order to make furniture for his apartment, but instead became involved in audio, building enclosures for a speaker system designed by an MIT professor and his student to improve the sound of live FM broadcasts of the Boston Symphony Orchestra. Drafted into the service during the Korean War, Kloss dropped out of MIT and would never complete his degree. While stationed in New Jersey, however, he a took a night course in high fidelity at New York University. His teacher, Edgar Villchur, had an idea for a new loudspeaker, and after Kloss was discharged from the service he teamed up with Villchur in 1953 to found Acoustic Research to develop and manufacture it. Two other partners, Malcolm Lowe and J. Anton Hoffman, provided $5,000 in seed money, and Kloss supplied the facility, an abandoned furniture factory in East Cambridge where he was already operating a cabinet and speaker-assembly shop.

Developing Villchur's idea, Kloss designed the first acoustic-suspension loudspeaker, the AR-1, which used air in a sealed cabinet to better produce sound than any product before it. The system was exceptionally good with low frequency sounds, which were crucial in the reproduction of classical music, yet it did not sacrifice quality in the rest of the frequency range. Until that time, in order to realize good-sounding bass, audio designers would have had to resort to building speakers the size of a refrigerator. The AR-1 was so far ahead of its time that early demonstrations to retailers were met with suspicion. Surely some kind of trickery was involved, because everyone knew that good bass could never emerge from such small, bookshelf speakers. Once the dealers became believers, the AR-1 forever changed the hi-fi industry.

Although Kloss was a gifted designer, much of his success was a triumph of perspiration over inspiration. What truly separated him from others, however, was his ear. Kloss simply knew what sounded good. Unconcerned with a strict adherence to accepted design specifications, he was committed to producing a broad, smooth, clean sound that would become recognized by audiophiles as the ''Boston sound.'' Moreover, he was devoted to producing affordable products, more interested in making quality audio components available to ordinary people than in amassing wealth. Like an artist, or perhaps a prophet, Kloss began to develop a cult-like following for his work.

After three years with Acoustic Research, Kloss was frustrated with Villchur, who continued to live in Woodstock, New York, and contributed little to the running of the business. In 1957, Kloss, Lowe, and Hoffman started a new company, KLH,

### Company Perspectives:

*We believe in every product we sell. In fact, we don't sell anything we wouldn't recommend to our very best friends or own ourselves.*

which took its name from the first letter of their last names. Not only did Kloss design more speakers, he made other important contributions to the audio industry, especially in his pioneering use of the transistor. In 1960, he introduced the Model Eight, the first high-end tabletop FM radio (and now a valuable collector's item). Although monaural, it produced a quality sound and was marked by its ''high selectivity,'' the ability to tune in a station from a crowded bandwidth. In 1961, KLH brought out the Model Eleven, the first mass-produced portable stereo system. Essentially contained in a suitcase, the Model Eleven was perfect for dormitories and small apartments and was a key factor in the rapid rise of rock music.

## *Kloss Founds Advent in 1967*

Kloss left KLH in 1967, after the business was sold to Singer for $4 million, to found yet another company, Advent. He not only produced one of the most popular speakers of the era, he made a number of other contributions during his decade with the company. He was instrumental in convincing Ray Dolby to adapt his noise reduction technology for audio tape to consumer products. In 1968, Kloss produced the first tape recorder, Model 40, with Dolby B noise reduction. He then added the chromium dioxide cassette to the mix, which, combined with the Dolby system, transformed tape into a medium suitable for music. In 1971, Kloss introduced the Advent 200/201, the first high-fidelity cassette deck.

It was also during his years at Advent that Kloss became a pioneer in television, developing a passion that would all but ruin him financially yet ultimately lead to his comeback with the creation of Cambridge SoundWorks. Despite his general distaste for television, which at one point he denounced as ''that demeaning little box,'' he enjoyed movies. Decades before the commercialization of the home theater idea, Kloss decided to replicate the movie theater experience in the living room. Reportedly, he claimed to have never watched television before deciding to build one. He combined known technologies to produce the first large screen, projection color television, the Advent VideoBeam 1000, launched in 1972. Convinced that the projection television market was on the verge of tremendous growth, he invested heavily in its development, while paying scant attention to the stereo business. Although the demand for Advent speakers was tremendously high, Kloss kept the price so low that the company enjoyed little benefit from its success. By 1975, Advent had invested $2 million into projection television but had only managed to sell a limited number of the expensive sets, which were generally bought by bars and bowling alleys to show sporting events rather than by consumers to watch movies at home. The result was that Advent posted a loss in 1975, and the company's lenders along with the chairman of the board excluded Kloss from future decisions on product determination.

While Advent struggled to right itself, Kloss left in 1977 to co-found Kloss Video Corp. to continue pursuing his dream for big screen television combined with high-quality sound. He soon achieved a breakthrough, one that elicited a proud response to the press: ''For the first time in my life, I had an *invention.*'' That invention was the Novatron projection tube, which used mirror optics to create a brighter picture while also significantly lowering manufacturing costs. For an entire decade, Kloss sought to make a success of his projection television, but in the end he lost out to Japanese competitors. Unlike his system, which employed a projector and a separate screen, the Japanese units were self-contained and less expensive. By 1988, Kloss was forced to sell the business and was in such poor straits financially that according to *Fortune* he could not pay his own living expenses.

## *Cambridge SoundWorks: 1988 Comeback Bid*

Kloss decided to return his attention to audio equipment, and in order to fund a new venture he appealed to an old friend, Henry Morgan, who had made money investing in earlier Kloss ventures. Morgan instantly cut a check for $250,000 in a handshake deal. Kloss and Tom DeVesto, who held senior management positions at both Advent and Kloss Video, then co-founded Cambridge SoundWorks in 1988. A year later they had a product to sell, Ensemble, and Kloss had yet another notable achievement: the first dial-subwoofer/satellite speaker system. The surround sound system used two sub-woofer suitcase-size boxes, which could be hidden under the couch or behind drapes because the human ear is generally incapable of detecting the location of very low frequency sounds, combined with two book-size satellite speakers. Aside from the technical achievement, Ensemble was also noteworthy because of the manner in which Kloss and DeVesto chose to sell the product. Kloss had always insisted that his stereo equipment be sold through reputable dealers so that customers would receive any necessary technical support. Because the marketplace was so crowded, with hundreds of speaker companies offering entire lines, retailers opted to focus on three or four manufacturers. Narrowing the choices for consumers not only eliminated confusion, it lowered inventory costs. Although Kloss' reputation would be useful in establishing the Cambridge SoundWorks brand with retailers, Kloss and DeVesto elected to leverage the Kloss name in a direct marketing effort, based on the belief that customers would be willing to buy Kloss-designed speakers without hearing them first, provided they were given a liberal return policy. Selling direct had other advantages as well. By cutting out the middleman, Cambridge SoundWorks could maintain lower prices, which had always been a prime consideration for Kloss, and also provided a competitive edge. Moreover, the company would be paid immediately, eliminating the need for a credit department or sales reps in the field, as well as the expense of courting dealers at trade shows. In turn, cash was freed up for marketing and product development. Advertising in both national publications and local media, the company was able to sell 8,000 sets of speakers and turn a profit of $4 million in its first year.

In 1990, Cambridge SoundWorks introduced a more compact version of Ensemble, which it called Model Eleven, a tribute to Kloss's portable stereo system of the 1960s. Also in

## Key Dates:

**1953:** Henry Kloss co-founds Acoustic Research.
**1957:** Kloss and two partners start KLH.
**1967:** Kloss founds Advent.
**1977:** Kloss co-founds Kloss Video Corp.
**1988:** Kloss and Thomas DeVesto start Cambridge SoundWorks.
**1996:** Kloss retires from Cambridge SoundWorks.
**1997:** Creative Technology buys the company.
**1998:** DeVesto resigns.
**2002:** Henry Kloss dies at the age of 72.

1990, the company began to sell high-end audio products from other companies that would be compatible with its speaker systems and opened a factory outlet store in West Newton, Massachusetts. A year later, Cambridge SoundWorks launched a catalog to supplement its advertising efforts. By the end of 1993, the company was generating more than $14 million in annual sales, 40 percent of which came from the factory outlet. In order to expand its retail operations, in both New England and northern California, where sales were particularly strong, the company decided to raise money through an initial public offering (IPO) in 1994. After conducting an expensive and grueling road show of breakfast and lunch meetings with prospective investors, DeVesto and the IPO team were faced with a suddenly skittish stock market. Already a high number of initial offerings had been cancelled because of the poor economic climate. Cambridge SoundWorks had hoped to price its shares at $10 but in the end had to settle for $8, in the process netting almost $10 million. With the proceeds, the company opened seven stores in New England and six in California in 1994. The following year, it opened seven more in New England and two in California, followed in 1996 by an additional three units in New England and two in California. Moreover, the company began selling a small volume of products internationally through distributors, mostly in the Far East. Of more importance was an agreement struck in 1995 with the Best Buy retail chain to sell Cambridge SoundWorks products in its 220 stores.

In 1994, Cambridge SoundWorks became involved in a flap with another Boston-area audio company, Bose, which sued it, claiming patent infringement and false advertising. The company claimed that the subwoofers in the Ensemble systems employed technology protected by patents issued to Bose. It also objected to newspaper ads that maintained Ensemble was ''Better than Bose at Half the Price.'' Cambridge SoundWorks countersued, but only a few months later the two parties decided to abandon the fight and came to a non-monetary settlement. Although Cambridge SoundWorks was allowed to continue to use its advertising claim, it chose not to continue the campaign.

In December 1995, Cambridge SoundWorks created a multimedia division in order to market SoundWorks, a speaker system for the personal computer that had received strong reviews and was set to be shown at the important Consumer Electronics Show in Las Vegas early in 1996. As with Ensemble, SoundWorks relied on a subwoofer and satellite speaker system. Despite a number of successes, especially in the critical acceptance of its products, Cambridge SoundWorks was not doing particularly well financially. Profits fell to little more than $200,000 in 1994, followed by a loss of more than $771,000 in 1995, and the price of its stock languished in the $4 range. In April 1996, Kloss retired as director of product development, although he announced that he would remain as a consultant to the company and continue to serve on the board. Several months later, Kloss decided to resign from the board of directors and the *Boston Herald* reported that his departure from the company was not without some bitterness. According to a source, ''Henry's ego was bruised and there were some hard feelings, but he didn't put up a big fight to stay. He and Tom weren't getting along for a couple of years, which is one reason why Henry kept his office on California street when Tom moved to the new headquarters on Needham street.'' In addition, other senior and mid-level managers were terminated, which another source described as housecleaning intended to ''purge the company of the last guard of the Kloss era.''

DeVesto introduced a number of changes to help improve the fortunes of Cambridge SoundWorks. He decided to move a number of retail stores located in strip malls to higher-end shopping malls. He also signed a development deal with another well-know loudspeaker designer, Roy Allison, to add even more luster to the Cambridge SoundWorks product lines. In 1997, Creative Technology, a Singapore-based maker of popular computer Sound Blaster sound card and other multimedia computer products, agreed to purchase a 20 percent stake in Cambridge SoundWorks, which would develop a line of multimedia speakers for exclusive distribution by Creative Technology. Within months, Creative Technology was pleased enough with the arrangement that it made a tender offer for the company. In late October 1997, a price of $10.68 per share was settled upon, and on October 30 the merger agreement was executed. For Cambridge SoundWorks, life under Creative Technology promised greater opportunities for expansion. For the parent corporation, the acquisition was to some extent a way to hedge its bets because the future of internal sound cards was uncertain, as audio device manufacturers might opt to take advantage of the external Universal Serial Bus (USB) that was becoming available on home computers.

Cambridge SoundWork's connection to its founders came to an end in May 1998 when DeVesto resigned, the result of what observers characterized as a clash of cultures. He and Kloss agreed to work together again in 2000 when Kloss produced a new radio for DeVesto's company, Tivoli Audio. In February 2002, at the age of 72, Kloss died of natural causes. In the meantime, Cambridge SoundWorks, the last of the companies that he helped to found, expanded its product lines and broadened its distribution channels. Although under the auspices of a large corporate parent, many of the products manufactured by Cambridge SoundWorks continued to be a testament to a man who made some of the most significant contributions to the audio industry in the second half of the 20th century.

### *Principal Competitors*

Bose Corporation; Boston Acoustics, Inc.; Polk Audio, Inc.

### *Further Reading*


Baker, Thomas, ''Self-Inflicted Wounds,'' *Forbes*, August 31, 1981, p. 100.

''Creative May Be Eyeing Home Theater Market with Cambridge Acquisition,'' *Multimedia Week,* November 10, 1997.

''Henry Kloss, 72, Industry Legend, Innovator, Dies,'' *Twice,* February 22, 2002, p. 3.

''Henry Kloss, 72, Pioneer in Stereo, Television Industry,'' *The Boston Globe,* February 5, 2002, p. B7.

Lander, David, ''Henry Kloss, Dead at 72,'' *Stereophile.com,* February 11, 2002.

Rosenberg, Ronald, ''A Sound Reputation At Cambridge SoundWorks, An Audio Legend is Back,'' *Boston Globe,* May 25, 1994, p. 43.

Welles, Edward O., ''What Becomes a Legend,'' *INC.,* June 1989, p. 21.


—Ed Dinger

# Candela Corporation

**530 Boston Post Road**
**Wayland, Massachusetts 01778**
**U.S.A.**
**Telephone: (508) 358-7400**
**Toll Free: (800) 773-8550**
**Fax: (508) 358-5569**
**Web site: http://www.clzr.com**

*Public Company*
*Incorporated:* 1970
*Employees:* 315
*Sales:* $64.8 million (2001)
*Stock Exchanges:* NASDAQ
*Ticker Symbol:* CLZR
*NAIC:* 334510 Electromedical and Electrotherapeutic Apparatus Manufacturing

Candela Corporation, located in Wayland, Massachusetts, designs, manufactures, and markets laser systems for use in a wide range of medical applications: hair removal; vascular lesion treatment, including spider veins, leg veins, rosacea, scars, warts, and port wine stains; removal of age spots, tattoos, and other benign pigmented lesions; microdermabrasion for skin exfoliation; psoriasis; and other skin treatments. The lasers are sold to both physicians and personal care practitioners. Since entering the medical market in the mid-1980s, Candela has installed over 5,000 of its systems in some 55 countries.

## *Candela Formed in 1970*

Candela's co-founder and first chief executive, Horace W. Furumoto, was a Japanese-American who was born and raised in Hawaii. He studied physics at the California Institute of Technology then earned a Ph.D. in the subject from Ohio State University. He moved to the Boston area with his wife, who elected to attend Harvard University to complete her doctorate in physics. Furumoto worked for both NASA's electronic research laboratory in Cambridge and for defense contractor Avco, where in the early 1960s he became involved in the development of the world's first high-energy dye laser. The first working laser, using a rod of ruby to emit photons of light, had been created in 1960 by T.H. Maiman. Dye lasers employed organic dyes as the lasing medium, taking advantage of the fact that different colors produced a wide range of radiating frequencies. In effect, changing colors allowed the laser to be tuned to a particular frequency, giving it much greater versatility, especially in industrial applications. When the Avco research laboratory was moved to the West Coast, Furumoto decided to stay in the Boston area. Along with physicist Harry Ceccon, a colleague from his time at NASA, he started a business in 1970 to supply the scientific community with custom lasers as well as the flashlamp components used to control the length of a pulse in dye lasers. Taking his wife's suggestion, Furumoto named the company after the scientific term describing a unit of light: candela.

For more than decade, Candela Corporation served a narrow scientific and industrial market. It was not until 1981 that the company entered into the medical arena. Furumoto began to collaborate with Dr. John A. Parrish, the newly appointed chairman of the department of dermatology at Harvard Medical School. He was also the chief of dermatology services at Massachusetts General Hospital, where the two men worked in the photo medicine lab to develop a working dermatology laser. Furumoto was soon working on a second medical application for the tunable dye laser when a British physician named Graham Watson, a man interested in smashing kidney stones without invasive surgery, came upon one of Candela's systems at MIT that was being used to inspect the inside of an engine. Watson tested the laser on some loose kidney stones, with no effect; nevertheless, he contacted Furumoto and encouraged him to research the possibility of using lasers for urology purposes. By the end of 1985, Candela was on the verge of perfecting both of these lasers for medical applications, which promised far more commercial potential than the company's traditional products. To fund the necessary expansion, the company, after changing its name to Candela Laser Corporation, went public in June 1986 at $3 a share, raising almost $5 million.

While its urology laser entered the initial testing phase, Candela built up its marketing and sales operations. Since its foundation, the company had been driven by a devotion to

**Company Perspectives:**

*We maintain our success through our visionary solutions and by utilizing the simple formula of combining efficacy and economics to help our customers succeed. In the years ahead, our industry leadership will only grow, guided by our clinical and academic collaborations, and driven, as always, by the needs of the customers we serve.*

technology, which was a suitable stance because of its specialized customers. Now that it was making lasers that were more commercial, it had to become far more sophisticated about its marketing. After gaining Food and Drug Administration clearance on its urology laser and shipping the first 12 units in June 1987, Candela turned to an advertising agency for a corporate identity makeover and a new logo. To launch its dermatology laser, the company also raised another $5 million in a private offering. Furthermore, in early 1988 it entered into a joint venture with the major Japanese international trading company, Mitsui & Co., in order to form Candela International Corporation. With nearly half of its sales expected overseas, gaining access to Mitsui offices in some 90 countries was seen as a key to future growth. With the company's balance sheet already benefiting from the sale of its two medical lasers, Candela was well on its way to delivering a laser that could be used in breaking up gallstones. Moreover, it was already working on a product that could treat certain eye disorders, and researchers were contemplating the use of a laser in the removal of plaque from clogged coronary arteries.

Candela's momentum was stalled, however, when in November 1988 the company's auditor withdrew its opinion on the results for that fiscal year which had ended on June 1988. At issue, according to the company, was the point in time at which revenues on sales to distributors were recognized. Of Candela's revenues of $15.8 million in 1988, $3.8 million came from the distributors, who did not actually pay for the units until they were in turn paid by their customers. Although the sales cycle had in some cases been longer than anticipated, the company argued that there was never any doubt that the units had been sold to the distributors, and that in fact the company had been consistently booking sales in this manner for years. Management also maintained that there were no accusations that the company was attempting to inflate its numbers, despite preparing for yet another secondary offering of stock intended to fund the launch of the gallstone laser. Nevertheless, the controversy had an adverse effect on Candela. A secondary offering was cancelled and the price of the company's stock began to slide, although Candela was still able to raise $7 million through a private placement of stock, selling 1 million shares to Singatronics Asset Holdings Private Ltd. of Singapore. Matters would worsen, however, when the restated results were finally released in March 1989. Instead of reporting a profit of $727,830 on revenues of $15.8 million, Candela now posted a $3.7 million loss on $11.5 million in revenues. According to management, the restatement reflected not only changes in the way sales to distributors were handled but also revenues from extended warranties and the way the company carried value and classified certain assets. As a result, Candela's stock took a hit and the company was forced to cut staff and turn its attention from expansion to improving profitability.

### *Furumoto Forced Out in 1990*

By 1990, according to press reports, serious friction developed between Furumoto and the man he hired as his chief financial officer, Gerard Puorro. Furumoto was seen by Puorro and others on the board as an out-of-touch scientist who simply lacked the skills required to revive the business. Quoted in a 1993 *Boston Globe* article, Puorro maintained, "We were doing well, but we needed to be focused and instead we were doing an astronomy laser project—an esoteric project that had no relation to our main business. We had too many people, too many projects and in 1991 we were like the guy going down a fast-moving river who sees the waterfalls and tries to go back." The two men were unable to come to terms and Furumoto told the board that one of them would have to go. In the end, the board backed Puorro and ousted Furumoto. According to the *Globe,* "Furumoto insists he was kicked out because he wanted to do unpopular things: lower operating costs through layoffs, slash some unpromising research and development programs, and restructure the company." When Furumoto resigned as chief executive and chairman, he purchased the non-medical laser business for $1.3 million in Candela stock, a unit which accounted for only 4 percent of annual revenues, and agreed not to compete in the medical laser field for one year. John Pavlic took over as president of Candela, but he was soon replaced by Puorro.

The prospects for Candela actually appeared to be improving even as Furumoto departed. The company announced that it had established a European operation, headquartered in Holland. With the launch of its SPTL Vascular Lesion Laser, Candela in 1991 introduced its first marketing kits for use by private practice physicians who purchased a laser. Over the years, the program would be expanded to other laser lines, and physicians were provided with sample press releases and advertisements, broadcast quality video of laser treatments, informational videos, and patient pamphlets. Candela eventually created a Partnership Program to provide marketing services to physicians. For 1991, the company reported revenues of $36.5 million and net income of nearly $2 million. Although revenues fell to $35.4 million for 1992, profits improved, topping $3.8 million.

Despite these positive results, however, Candela began to experience some problems, the result of increased competition in the marketplace and some decisions that failed to pan out. Management was also distracted in the summer of 1992 by a takeover bid by a pair of investor brothers, Kirk Terry Dornbush and Robert Earl Dornbush, who claimed to own 7.9 percent of the company's stock. Their offer was rejected and a poison-pill provision—designed to limit the amount of stock that could be purchased without management approval—was adopted by Candela's board, which denied that the move was connected to the Dornbush initiative. Perhaps of more concern to the company was the emergence of Furumoto as a competitor in the medical laser field. After abiding by the one-year ban, Furumoto's new company, Cynosure, introduced a dermatological laser that was half the price of Candela systems. One month later Candela sued Furumoto and Cynosure, claiming patent infringement. Although owned by Candela, the patent had originally been Furumoto's, so that he was keenly aware of every

**Key Dates:**

**1970:** Horace Furumoto and Harry Ceccon found Candela.
**1981:** The company begins work on medical lasers.
**1986:** Candela goes public.
**1991:** Furumoto resigns as president and chairman.
**1994:** A patent suit is resolved in Furumoto's favor.
**2000:** The company's revenues top $75 million.

feature of the laser in question. His new device, he insisted, was based on non-patentable ideas which had been circulating since 1959. While Candela's laser relied on a continuous wave of light, the Cynosure laser employed short pulses of light. Aside from being much less expensive, it prevented damage to surrounding tissue. While the matter made its way through the courts, Candela sales were severely undercut. Moreover, the company was forced to take writedowns on an obsolete dermatological laser as well as related expenses. As a result of these factors, Candela saw its fiscal 1993 revenues fall to $33.2 million while posting a $9.2 million loss.

In December 1993, with Candela's stock price falling below $4, the Dornbush brothers expressed their displeasure about the financial performance of the company, demanding access to a list of shareholders in order to force a merger or outright sale. They also insisted the board be expanded from four to six months and that they be given control of the extra seats. It was not until January 1995, when Candela's stock traded below the $2 mark, that the two sides agreed to an accommodation and Robert Earl Dornbush was named to the board, a position he held until he sold his stake in the company in 1999.

### *Patent Suit Settled in 1994*

In 1994, the patent suit against Furumoto was finally settled in favor of Candela's founder. Revenues continued to erode, falling to $28.2 million in fiscal 1995, along with a net loss of $1.6 million, before rebounding in 1996. The company began to focus its efforts on the aging baby boom generation, developing lasers capable of removing tattoos, treating pigmented lesions (such as freckles and age and sun spots), as well as a laser system to treat leg veins. The advent of scanners, computer-driven beam delivery systems that ushered in a new generation of aesthetic and cosmetic lasers, also opened up new markets for Candela. Instead of appealing to the 15,000 dermatologists and plastic surgeons practicing in the United States, the company began to market products that appealed to a much larger pool of physicians, numbering some 110,000, involved in a variety of disciplines. Moreover, Candela decided to directly tap into the baby boom market, forming a subsidiary called Candela Skin Care Centers, Inc. to order to provide cosmetic laser procedures. To reflect this diversification strategy, in January 1996 the company changed its name from Candela Laser Corporation back to Candela Corporation. In March 1997, the subsidiary launched what it intended to be a chain of clinics called LaserSpas, the first debuting in the resort town of Scottsdale, Arizona. The company then purchased a Boston health club and beauty salon to serve as a second location. In addition to laser procedures to address wrinkles, stretch marks, spider veins, and other skin conditions, the spas also offered more traditional massages, facials, and fitness programs. Although Candela was now in competition with doctors who had purchased laser equipment from them, management believed that the market of potential baby boom customers was large enough to accommodate everyone. The venture was short-lived, however, and by the end of 1997 the Arizona facility was shuttered; a year later, the Boston unit ceased offering laser procedures, and a buyer of the spa was sought. Management announced it would now focus all of its attention on manufacture.

Adopting a philosophy designed to "drive technologies and expand markets," Candela began to make strides at the end of the 1990s. It introduced important enhancements to existing product lines and launched a skin exfoliation system called GentlePeel. Moreover, the company enjoyed success overseas. After reporting $37 million in revenues and a loss of $4.5 million in 1998, Candela's sales improved to $58.6 million in 1999, when the company posted net income of nearly $7.5 million. The year 2000 would bring even stronger results, with revenues growing to $75.4 million and profits improving to more than $14.5 million. With a sluggish U.S. economy in 2001, Candela's momentum was stunted, as sales fell to $64.8 million and net income to $2.5 million. Nevertheless, management remained optimistic and was further encouraged by the April 2002 FDA clearance for its new Vbeam laser to be used in treating periorbital wrinkles. More importantly, the demographics continued to favor Candela: baby boomers were likely to spend an increasing portion of their disposable income on laser procedures that promised to reverse the effects of aging.

### *Principal Subsidiaries*

Candela Iberica, S.A. (Spain); Candela France SARL; Candela KK (Japan); Candela Laser (Deutschland) GmbH (Germany); Candela Bangkok; Candela Skin Care Centers, Inc.

### *Principal Competitors*

Cynosure, Inc.; Laserscope; Lumenis Ltd.; Palomar Medical Technologies Inc.

### *Further Reading*

Hower, Wendy, "Candela Laser Sues Founder on Patent," *Boston Business Journal,* November 16, 1992, p. 1.
Reidy, Chris, "A Workout, Massage and Laser Treatment: Candela Tries New Wrinkle in Back Bay," *Boston Globe,* May 6, 1997, p. C3.
Rosenberg, Ronald, "High-Tech Patent Fight," *Boston Globe,* July 18, 1993, p. 64.
——, "Laser Fight: Candela v. Cynosure Involves Patents, Profits, Personalities," *Boston Globe,* November 17, 1993, p. 49.
Simon, Jane Fitz, "Audit Problem Stops Candela's Public Offering," *Boston Globe,* November 2, 1988, p. 71.
——, "Lasers Glow Like Gold At Candela," *Boston Globe,* May 10, 1988, p. 33.
Veronia, Nicholas, "At Candela, Ghost of Endo-Lase Is Fading Slowly," *Boston Business Journal,* February 27, 1989, p. 6.

—Ed Dinger

# Cirrus Logic, Inc.

**4210 South Industrial Drive**
**Austin, Texas 78744**
**U.S.A.**
**Telephone: (512) 445-7222**
**Toll Free: (800) 888-5016**
**Fax: (512) 445-7581**
**Web site: http://www.cirrus.com**

*Public Company*
*Incorporated:* 1984
*Employees:* 1,356
*Sales:* $778.7 million (2001)
*Stock Exchanges:* NASDAQ
*Ticker Symbol:* CRUS
*NAIC:* 334413 Semiconductor and Related Device Manufacturing; 334310 Audio and Video Equipment Manufacturing

Cirrus Logic, Inc. is a leading manufacturer of audio chips used in consumer entertainment electronics, including audio/video receivers, DVD-based products, game boxes, and personal video recorders. The firm sells over 200 products to 3,000 customers such as Apple, Bose, Creative Technologies, Dell, IBM, Panasonic, and Sony. During the latter half of the 1990s, Cirrus restructured operations and eventually exited the magnetic storage integrated circuit (IC) market in order to focus on higher margin analog technologies that are used in the audio, communications, and data acquisition markets. The company also develops digital signal processing (DSP) technologies used for Internet-related applications.

### *Beginnings*

Cirrus Logic traces its origins to a small company called Patil Systems, which was founded in Utah in 1981 by Suhas Patil, a former Massachusetts Institute of Technology (MIT) professor then teaching at the University of Utah. While at MIT, Patil had developed a microchip-level software system for controlling computer hard disk drives that he called Strategic/Logic Array (S/LA). The S/LA system represented a substantial improvement in the management of hard drive functions since it behaved more consistently and was easier to design than existing systems. Patil gathered together several associates and formed Patil Systems to market his new product.

Over the next three years, however, the company's efforts produced little commercial success. ''I made the rounds and couldn't give it away,'' Patil would later recall in Upside. For help with the marketing and management of his tiny, eleven-employee company, Patil contacted Michael Hackworth, a former marketing executive for Fairchild Industries and Motorola who was senior vice-president of Signetics, the Sunnyvale, California-based semiconductor subsidiary of North American Philips, in 1984.

The prospect of working with Patil sparked Hackworth's interest. Although a prominent executive at Signetics, he was unhappy with the way the company operated and especially with the inefficiency with which it introduced new products. When Patil first contacted him, Hackworth thought that S/LA software might be of use to Signetics. However, as he later remarked in Upside, ''When I got in and met the people and understood what they had, it hit me like a ton of bricks that this could be the basis for a new kind of chip company.'' Hackworth perceived that Patil's S/LA system could be used to develop a wide range of highly specialized semiconductors in a relatively short time. All the development process would require was a systems engineer who could program and arrange the chips to facilitate whatever function the product was supposed to carry out.

Instead of absorbing Patil Systems into Signetics, Hackworth left Signetics to join Patil Systems. He became president and CEO, while Patil assumed the posts of chairman and executive vice-president of products and technology. The company reincorporated in California in 1984 under the name Cirrus Logic, Incorporated, and moved its headquarters to Fremont, in the northern half of the state. The company's new name came about when Hackworth decided that Patil Systems needed a new name, but one that did not dip into the alphabet soup of Greek prefixes and suffixes in which the Silicon Valley seemed to swim. One of his daughters came up the idea of renaming the company after cirrus clouds, the highest clouds in

## Company Perspectives:

*An exciting revolution is taking place in digital entertainment electronics. And it's sweeping across 650 million households worldwide as living rooms magically transform into thrilling home theaters. The market opportunity is enormous for DVD-based systems as well as Audio/Video Receivers, Game Boxes, Personal Video Recorders, Set-top Boxes, MP3/CD Players, and Wireless Residential Gateways. Winning in these growth markets will require powerful IC-plus-software solutions that deliver the state-of-the-art features that consumers demand. One semiconductor company is exceptionally well positioned to provide such solutions. A company that stands ready to offer the worldwide support and digital entertainment focus needed to capitalize on this timely window of opportunity. A company that offers Total Entertainment OEM solutions in every room and every corner, enabling consumers to experience extreme entertainment from digital content like never before. This company is Cirrus.*

the sky, as a way of expressing the elevated complexity of its products.

### *Opportunity in the Burgeoning PC Market: 1980s*

Under Hackworth, Cirrus Logic pursued a strategy that emphasized developing peripheral devices in which the company's semiconductors were used. This emphasis stemmed in part from Hackworth's experience at Signetics, which had developed a 2650 microprocessor only to see it fail because its application in peripheral devices had not been taken into account during the design process. Under this plan, Cirrus Logic would use the versatility of the S/LA system in an opportunistic manner, jumping into new peripheral markets as they emerged. The company bought raw microchips from outside foundries to avoid the burden of running its own fabrication operations.

When major opportunities presented themselves, Cirrus Logic did not ignore them. Originally, Hackworth's master plan had envisioned the company developing products for microcomputers, but not the microcomputers themselves. But in the mid-1980s, the boom in personal computers began. Cirrus Logic responded with a neat product development sidestep, simply applying the concepts it had intended for peripherals to the emerging PC market instead.

The company's first major effort in marketing its hard drive controller resulted in its first major success. Though it faced daunting competition from more established companies such as Adaptec and Western Digital, Cirrus Logic had an advantage: it had developed the first controller chip that could be mounted inside the drive mechanism rather than on a card outside it. This innovation would eventually lead to more compact hard drives. At first, Cirrus Logic's product was too advanced to sell easily; an official from prominent hard drive manufacturer Seagate Technology told Hackworth that the Cirrus Logic controller was five years ahead of what his company wanted. Cirrus Logic modified the chip to fit Seagate's needs and received a contract from them. Conner Peripherals, which made hard drives for Compaq Computer PCs, soon followed with orders of their own.

Cirrus Logic's successful entry into the PC hard drive market paved the way for future successes. While its hard drive controller chip drove sales, accounting for as much as 80 percent of total revenues, the company developed new graphics and communications-related products. In 1987, IBM unveiled Video Graphics Array (VGA), its new technology standard for graphics display. This started a scramble among chipmakers to develop products to conform to the new standard, a competition that Cirrus Logic won, producing the first fully compatible VGA controller microchip. In 1989, the company developed a VGA controller for flat-panel liquid crystal diode (LCD) displays, barely anticipating the boom in notebook computers, which used such displays.

### *Cirrus Goes Public: 1989*

Cirrus Logic went public in 1989. It used the cash raised by the initial public offering (IPO) to finance a series of acquisitions that broadened its technological expertise. In 1990, it acquired Data Systems Technology, which specialized in data compression and error-correction algorithms for modems. The next year, it purchased a controlling interest in Pixel Semiconductor, a video-imaging technology firm with expertise in the multimedia field, from Visual Information Technologies. It later absorbed Pixel Semiconductor's operations into its own. In 1992, it acquired R. Scott Associates, a modem software company, and Acumos, which specialized in high-integration desktop graphics. In 1993, it acquired Pacific Communication Sciences, a leading developer of Cellular Digital Packet Data communications technology. Also in 1993, Cirrus Logic announced that it would produce custom microchips for companies licensed by Apple Computer to manufacture Apple's Newton personal digital assistant.

In its first 15 years, Cirrus Logic grew from a tiny company struggling to raise a few million dollars in capital to an important presence in the microchip industry with well over $500 million in annual sales. At the same time that its sales skyrocketed, it broadened its technological expertise with similar rapidity. But its rapid growth brought problems as well as benefits, and in the wake of its rapid string of acquisitions in the early 1990s problems in incorporating these new subsidiaries became apparent. Difficulties in communication sometimes produced delays in developing and delivering new products. Consequently, the company embarked on a reorganization in 1993 designed to decentralize and streamline operations at the same time.

Cirrus Logic's growing importance as a supplier of semiconductors also increased concern over continued access to sufficient quantities of raw chips. Cirrus Logic had not only taken pride in its ''fablessness,'' its lack of chip fabrication operations and consequent need to rely on outside foundries, but considered it a necessity. ''We will never eliminate the fabless approach,'' Michael Hackworth declared in 1993. ''The foundry thing has provided us with enormous flexibility that we would never ever have if we had to drag our own clean room for fabricating raw chips around with us. The chances of us doing a [brand-new] clean room on our own are zero or none.'' However, the production glut in raw chips that had made life easy for

### Key Dates:

**1981:** Patil Systems is founded in Utah by Suhas Patil.
**1984:** The firm reincorporates as Cirrus Logic; Michael Hackworth is named president and CEO.
**1989:** Cirrus goes public and develops a VGA controller for flat panel liquid crystal diode displays.
**1990:** The firm acquires Data Systems Technology.
**1994:** Cirrus enters into its first joint fabrication venture with IBM.
**1995:** The firm begins its second joint fabrication venture with Lucent Technologies Inc.
**2001:** The company exits the magnetic storage IC market to focus on consumer electronics.

Cirrus Logic and similar fabless chipmakers began to dry up in the 1990s at the same time that demand for the company's products began to pick up from levels that were already quite high. In 1993, Cirrus Logic signed agreements with its suppliers to buy a set number of chips over three years in return for guarantees of foundry capacity, but even this did not prove entirely satisfactory.

Fortunately, Hackworth had not ruled out a joint fabrication venture with another semiconductor company with which it was not in direct competition. Thus, in 1994, Cirrus Logic took a first tentative step toward fabrication by signing a joint venture with IBM. Under the terms of the agreement, the two companies would refurbish an under-used IBM plant in East Fishkill, New York, that once manufactured chips for mainframe computers. Even with IBM's help, Cirrus Logic estimated that the venture, which was named MiCRUS, would cost it tens of millions of dollars. In 1995, Cirrus Logic took a second step into the fabrication scene by partnering with Lucent Technologies Inc. in another joint fabrication venture entitled Cirent Semiconductor.

## *Major Restructuring Efforts: Late 1990s and Beyond*

These two fabrication efforts, however, would eventually prove to be both costly and strategically ineffective. In fact, Cirrus was plagued with problems during the latter half of the 1990s that resulted from poor investments and slow product development as well as overcapacity in both of its fabrication ventures. The firm began to reorganize in 1996 and, due to restructuring charges, the company posted a loss of $46.2 million on revenues on $917.2 million for the year. In early 1997, the company announced it would cut 400 jobs.

As the semiconductor industry became increasingly competitive, problems continued for Cirrus Logic. In 1998, the firm was forced to cut its workforce once again, and it also announced it would divest its graphics, modems, and advanced systems products businesses. An analyst with market research firm In-Stat Group remarked in a 1998 *Electronic News* article that ''it's interesting how things change and how companies who were on top at one point are struggling; it really tells you how tough the semiconductor market is.'' The analyst continued that ''it paints a pretty bad picture as far as chip companies go that are related to PC's. . . . [A] lot of this is being driven from the low cost PC's and people having to figure out how to make money in this new environment.''

In 1999, Hackworth stepped down from the CEO post—he remained chairman—and Cirrus Logic turned to David French, hired one year earlier as president and chief operating officer, to turn the company around. As CEO, French continued to reposition Cirrus Logic by making a series of significant moves. During the year, the company ended its fabrication partnerships with both IBM and Lucent. While forced to take a $127.7 million restructuring charge as a result, management expected the move back to a fabless business model would pay off in the long run. Cirrus Logic also acquired AudioLogic Inc., an audio technology firm. The purchase bolstered the company's audio IC division, which accounted for nearly 55 percent of sales by the end of 1999. The company's two other main business segments included storage IC's and data acquisition technology used for communication and industrial applications.

As Cirrus Logic entered the new millennium, changes continued. Company headquarters were moved from California to Austin, Texas, in an effort to cut costs. The early years of the new century were also marked by weakening global economies and faltering conditions in the worldwide semiconductor industry. In response, Cirrus Logic exited the magnetic storage IC market in order to focus on the cutting edge digital entertainment industry. As part of this new strategy, the company acquired four companies: LuxSonor Semiconductor Inc., a DVD decoder specialist; Stream Machine Co., an encoder firm; ShareWave Inc., a wireless home-networking company; and Peak Audio Inc., a Colorado-based audio networking concern.

French believed this new focus would pay off handsomely, especially since new consumer electronics products were based on digital audio and video technologies rather than on analog components. Consumer electronic products such as DVD players, MP3 players, and surround-sound audio equipment utilized digital semiconductor technology including decoders, optical-drive controllers, DSP's, and digital-to-analog converters, all of which Cirrus specialized in. Cirrus Logic eyed increased demand for this technology as key to its return to profitability. Having undergone significant restructuring over the past five years, Cirrus Logic management felt confident that with its new strategy, the company would emerge successful in the years to come.

### *Principal Subsidiaries*

Cirrus Logic International Ltd. (Bermuda); Cirrus Logic KK (Japan); Cirrus Logic GmbH (Germany); Cirrus Logic Korea Co. Ltd. (Korea); Cirrus Logic (UK) Ltd.; Cirrus Logic International SARL (France); Cirrus Logic software India, Pvt. Ltd.; EAudio, Inc.; EMicro Corporation; Crystal Semiconductor Corporation; Pacific Communication Sciences, Inc.

### *Principal Competitors*

LSI Logic Corporation; STMicroelectronics N.V.; Texas Instruments Inc.

### *Further Reading*

Arnold, Bill, ''Cirrus Takes the PC Market By Storm,'' *Upside*, August 1993.

Ascierto, Jerry, ''Cirrus Logic Bows Out of Cirent,'' *Electronic News*, July 5, 1999, p. 21.

Brown, Peter, ''Cirrus Slashes Again,'' *Electronic News*, September 28, 1998, p. 1.

——, ''Hackworth Steps Down at Cirrus,'' *Electronic News*, February 15, 1999, p. 1.

''Cirrus Logic Acquires AudioLogic,'' *EDGE: Work-Group Computing Report*, August 2, 1999.

Hof, Robert D., ''Real Men Have Fabs,'' *Business Week*, April 11, 1994.

Lammers, David, ''Cirrus' Digital Entertainment Bet May Pay Off,'' *Electronic Engineering Times*, March 18, 2002, p. 8.

Ohr, Stephan, ''CEO French Targets Internet Audio, Storage Markets,'' *Electronic Engineering Times*, November 29, 1999, p. 4.

Wilson, Ron, ''In the Red, Cirrus Lays Off 400 and Restructures,'' *Electronic Engineering Times*, April 28, 1997, p. 4.

—Douglas Sun
—update: Christina M. Stansell

# Clearly Canadian Beverage Corporation

**2489 Bellevue Avenue**
**West Vancouver**
**British Columbia V7V 1E1**
**Canada**
**Telephone: (604) 683-0312**
**Toll Free: (800) 663-0227 (Canada) (800) 663-5658 (U.S.)**
**Fax: (604) 683-2256**
**Web site: http://www.clearly.ca**

*Public Company*
*Incorporated:* 1987 as International Beverage Corporation
*Employees:* 119
*Sales:* $23.26 million (2001)
*Stock Exchanges:* Toronto
*Ticker Symbols:* CLV
*NAIC:* 312111 Soft Drink Manufacturing; 312112 Bottled Water Manufacturing

Clearly Canadian Beverage Corporation is a British Columbia-based maker of so-called ''new age'' or ''alternative'' beverages that include flavored sparkling water and fitness drinks. The company's original Clearly Canadian brand has been joined in recent years by Reebok Fitness Water Beverages, vitamin-enhanced drinks made under license from the shoe manufacturer; Tre Limone, a beverage flavored with a blend of lemon, ginger, and spices; and Clearly Canadian O + 2, bottled water that has several times the amount of oxygen found in plain water. The company's products are sold throughout Canada and the United States and in select overseas markets. Spectacularly successful during its early years, the company has been struggling to adapt to a highly competitive marketplace since the mid-1990s.

### *1980s Beginnings*

Clearly Canadian was founded by Donald Mason in Vancouver, British Columbia, Canada. Mason had worked for 15 years in the grocery business before finding success as a stock investor and promoter. His first beverage venture was launched in the mid-1980s when he acquired the Canadian rights to distribute Jolt, a highly caffeinated cola drink. Coke and Pepsi had a tight hold on the cola market, however, and once its novelty value had worn off, Jolt quickly fizzled. Needing a new product, Mason decided to try the opposite side of the soft drink spectrum and create a beverage for health-conscious consumers. He renamed his existing publicly traded company International Beverage Corporation and began to produce Clearly Canadian, which was made from spring water flavored with natural ingredients and less sugar than typical soft drinks. Funding for the launch of Clearly Canadian was obtained in part from beverage distributor Camfrey Resources, Ltd., which was granted a royalty on every case sold in certain territories outside Canada. The new drink, which was distinguished by its clear color and blue-tinted bottles, began shipping in January 1988. Along with an unflavored version, the premium-priced soda was offered in Mountain Blackberry, Country Raspberry, and Orchard Peach varieties.

Having virtually invented the category which became known as ''alternative'' or ''new age'' soft drinks, Clearly Canadian quickly found favor with the public, particularly in California. Over the next several years, International Beverage undertook a rapid expansion of its distribution area, gaining full penetration of Canada and the United States and also reaching Japan and England. Sales, which had totaled 800,000 cases in 1989, jumped to 2.5 million in 1990, and revenues took a similar leap, going from under $5 million to $17 million.

In May 1990, the company changed its name to Clearly Canadian Beverage Corporation, reflecting its now exclusive focus on the natural soft drink. At the same time a 3.5 to 1 reverse stock split was effected to boost the share price. The stock was being traded on both the Vancouver and NASDAQ exchanges.

Despite its rapid growth, Clearly Canadian had just 34 employees, and owned only the wells, the trade style, and the formulas of its flavors. The firm's rapid expansion was facilitated by a strategy of contracting out most of its functions. Of major importance was the company's network of regional distributors,

**Company Perspectives:**

*We will continue in the pioneer spirit, moving forward and blazing new trails to growth in the Alternative Beverage industry.*

many of whom normally handled alcoholic beverages. Each one was asked to invest in the company, which gave them greater incentive to promote the drinks. Production was also contracted out, with spring water trucked to a handful of regional bottlers from the company's wells in eastern and western Canada. Though it had originally used little advertising, by this time a campaign featuring the slogan "Get Wild—Naturally" was in place, which helped spur the company's astronomical growth rate. Fiscal 1991 saw revenues nearly quadruple, to $61.2 million, and a first-ever profit of $5.9 million was recorded.

### *Competition in the Early 1990s*

The company's growth was drawing the attention of investors, who boosted the share price almost six-fold by the end of 1991. The competition was heating up, however, and soon similar products were being marketed by giants like PepsiCo, Coca-Cola, Seagrams, and Perrier Group. Clearly Canadian sent a letter to the latter firm in July 1992 demanding that it cease production of Ice Mountain, a similarly packaged drink. Perrier subsequently filed suit, which was met by a countersuit from Clearly Canadian. The dispute was later settled out of court. Despite the tightening market, sales for fiscal 1992 continued to grow by leaps and bounds, hitting a record $155.2 million, with profits of $14 million.

The agreement that had been signed early on with distributor Camfrey Resources, which guaranteed Camfrey 25 cents per case sold outside Canada in exchange for a $1.6 million loan, was proving to be an albatross around the company's neck as its rapid revenue growth forced it to pay out millions in royalties. In early 1993, Clearly Canadian made a deal to pay Camfrey C$22.9 million to terminate the agreement and buy up its options to distribution rights in the United States, Europe, and Australia.

By mid-1993, the fierce competition from rivals such as Coca-Cola's Fruitopia and other types of alternative beverages like bottled teas had begun to take its toll, and Clearly Canadian's revenues and high-flying stock price began to wither. The company soon cancelled plans for a $40 million European stock offering and relied on other funding to pay the settlement with Camfrey.

Nonetheless, Clearly Canadian was still the alternative beverage leader with an 18 percent share of the market, and it was continuing to focus on growth abroad. Deals were inked with companies in Poland and the Middle East and expansion was ongoing in Mexico, where distribution had commenced the previous fall through Natural Beverage of Tucson, Arizona. The United States remained the firm's major source of revenue, accounting for 90 percent of sales. The company was by now marketing seven different flavors and had added six-ounce bottles to its standard 11-ounce size to help generate sales in hotel bars and restaurants.

The intensity of the company's competition was dramatically revealed in its results for fiscal 1993, which showed revenues of $90.9 million, a decline of more than a third, and earnings of just $293,000. At the start of 1994, the company announced it was taking several measures to boost market share, including the creation of two new drinks: "Clearly Two," a 2-calorie diet variety, and "Clearly Tea," a lightly carbonated iced tea drink. New flavor and packaging options were also added to the Clearly Canadian line, and an aggressive $10 million ad campaign was planned. In addition to seeking new customers, the company was cutting costs by consolidating production capacity and inventories. A wage freeze and a reduction in executive salaries of 10 percent were instituted as well.

### *Writedowns and Legal Troubles in 1995*

In early 1995, Clearly Canadian scrapped the national rollout of Clearly Tea and ceased its operations in Mexico, resulting in a combined write-off of C$4.2 million. In May, a judge ruled that the company would have to pay C$5.9 million to Blue Mountain Springs Ltd. for breach of contract. In 1988, Clearly Canadian had arranged with Blue Mountain to buy up to 100,000 gallons of water a day for 99 years at 10 to 20 cents per gallon. However, the company had soon thereafter found a different source and had not used any water from Blue Mountain, which later sued for $75 million. Later, in November, several investor-initiated class action suits were settled for $2.5 million. Other controversy erupted during the year among shareholders over the company's generous compensation of its executives, which included a plush retirement package.

The year 1995 also saw Clearly Canadian begin a campaign to buy back distribution rights from its U.S. and Canadian distribution network, a move that was expected to help boost the beverages' presence on store shelves. Over the next two years the company spent $10 million to recover more than three-fourths of this territory. Twenty-one employees were hired to promote the firm's drinks, replacing the outside contractors previously utilized. Revenues continued to drop, hitting $48.2 million for the year with a loss of $4 million.

In 1996, the company again sought to make an impact with new products, this time introducing fruit-flavored, non-carbonated "Orbitz," which featured floating, flavored gel globules, and "Quencher," a lightly carbonated fruit juice sold only in California. During the summer a bid was made to purchase beverage and snack food producer Sun-Rype Products, many of whose shares were owned by fruit growers in British Columbia. Sun-Rype management opposed Clearly Canadian's offer, labeling it hostile, and the $40 million stock swap wound up in front of the British Columbia Securities Commission before it was rejected by nearly 90 percent of Sun-Rype shareholders.

While this drama was unfolding, Clearly Canadian arranged to buy Blue Mountain Springs Ltd. for C$4.5 million, eliminating paying the C$5.9 million judgment, which had been under appeal. The purchase involved just the Blue Mountain name, as well as 44 acres of land adjacent to its spring, but not the actual source or a nearby bottling plant.

In the months following its introduction, the company's Orbitz beverage had proven to be a hit, and its availability was

**Key Dates:**

**1988:** Clearly Canadian flavored sparkling water is introduced.
**1992:** Annual sales for the beverage company hit a peak of $155.2 million.
**1993:** A royalty agreement with Camfrey Resources is terminated for $22.9 million.
**1994:** Clearly Tea and Clearly Two beverages are test-marketed.
**1996:** Orbitz, with free-floating gel spheres, debuts.
**1997:** Cascade Clear Water Co. of Burlington, Washington, is purchased.
**1998:** Clearly Canadian O+2, Battery, and REfresher drinks are introduced.
**2000:** Packaging of flagship line is redesigned and diet flavors are added.

expanded across the United States, with new flavors and color combinations added during the year. The premium-priced drink, which cost as much as 50 percent more than regular sodas, found favor with younger, novelty-seeking consumers. Quencher, which had been launched at the same time, was soon shelved, however. Sales results for 1996 showed a slight improvement, hitting $50.1 million, with earnings back in the black, at $450,000.

### *Cascade Clear Purchased in 1997*

In fall 1997, the company acquired Cascade Clear Water Co. of Burlington, Washington. The $15 million deal gave Clearly Canadian a bottler of non-carbonated water under its own and other labels, as well as a home and office bottled water delivery service. Early 1998 saw the company expanding its imports to Europe and launching a new beverage brand, REfresher, produced at the Washington plant, which was located close to British Columbia along the United States-Canadian border. The noncarbonated, vitamin-enriched sports drink was aimed at 15–30 year olds and came in four fruit flavors.

In May, a lawsuit with Bush Boake Allen (BBA) was settled. BBA had charged Clearly Canadian with infringement of a patent in its manufacturing of the Orbitz beverage, for which BBA had previously supplied raw materials. The company agreed to pay BBA a licensing fee as part of the settlement. In June, Clearly Canadian bought back the rights to distribute its beverages in several key Mid-Atlantic U.S. states, completing the process of taking full control of North American distribution.

In September 1998, another new beverage, Battery, was introduced. The caffeine-enhanced, berry-flavored energy drink was licensed for sale in the United States and Canada from Oy Sinebrychoff Ab of Finland, which had successfully marketed it in Europe. The fall also saw introduction of Clearly Canadian O+2, a water-based drink that was enhanced with up to 10 times the normal level of oxygen. Available in fruit flavors or unflavored, it was marketed to athletes.

In early 1999, the company announced plans to expand its Washington State facility, adding 9,000 square feet of office space and a new production line for carbonated beverages. Many of Clearly Canadian's administrative operations were subsequently transferred to the new site. The move was made to reduce corporate taxes, which were higher in Canada, and CEO Mason announced that future acquisitions would be made through the company's U.S. subsidiary. Most production would take place in the United States now as well, using water trucked from Canada.

In the fall of the year, Clearly Canadian won a lawsuit against an insurance company for C$1.8 million to cover some of its losses from an earlier legal settlement, and sold its 10 percent stake in Sun-Rype Products for C$3.6 million. The sale of 30 percent of Clearly Canadian to a South African investment firm fell through when the latter failed to secure financing, however, and sales of Orbitz were suspended due to dwindling sales, resulting in a significant writedown. A restructuring was completed that eliminated some leased properties and reduced staffing during the year as well.

### *A New Look in 2000*

In March 2000, the company relaunched its flagship brand with enhanced flavors and redesigned packaging, which resulted in writedowns on now-unusable bottling materials. The size of single-serving bottles was increased from 11 to 14 ounces, though the price was not changed, and a new line of diet flavors was added. The company had also begun distributing a licensed coffee-flavored beverage, Jamaican Gold, and had added to its home and office water delivery operation with the acquisition of Home Service Networks, Inc. of Washington state.

Another new beverage was launched in April 2000 when the company introduced Tre Limone, a carbonated lemon-ginger drink. The premium-priced, "European style" Tre Limone shared the new packaging approach of Clearly Canadian, a shrink-sleeve plastic covering over a glass bottle. The new product, along with the flagship brand's packaging changes, were gaining notice at the retail level, and the company announced it was gaining listings with a number of major retail chains.

In the latter half of 2000, reports surfaced that CEO Mason was being investigated by the British Columbia Securities Commission for failing to report insider stock trades that had been made through offshore companies. He vowed a vigorous defense of the allegations. Later in the year, Clearly Canadian hired McDonald Investments, Inc. of Cleveland to advise it on strategic options, including the potential sale of the company. The firm suffered another blow in early 2001 when its stock on the NASDAQ exchange dropped below $1 and was delisted, subsequently moving to the Over-the-Counter bulletin board.

In the spring, another new product was announced as part of a three year licensing deal with Reebok International Ltd. Reebok Fitness Water contained a blend of vitamins and minerals and was available in 24-ounce bottles in one unflavored and two low-calorie varieties. It was first marketed in April in select locations around the United States. Seeking capital to promote the new product, in May Clearly Canadian's U.S. subsidiary sold its home and office water business to Cullyspring Water Co., Inc. for $4.8 million. The following February the company also sold its Burlington, Washington, production facility and the

Cascade Clear and private label water businesses to Advanced H2O, Inc. for a total of $6.3 million plus future royalty payments. Advanced also agreed to provide Clearly Canadian with at-cost bottling services for ten years. The numbers for fiscal 2001 continued to prove disappointing, with revenues of $23.26 million and losses of $7.2 million reported.

In the decade following its peak year of 1992, Clearly Canadian had experienced a series of strategic missteps and legal troubles, as well as shrinking revenues due to increased competition in the marketplace. Struggling to regain its footing in the $10 billion alternative beverage market, which it had more or less started, the company was now shedding unprofitable lines and refocusing on its core brand along with the new Reebok-licensed sport water.

### *Principal Subsidiaries*

CC Beverage Corporation (U.S.); Clearly Canadian Beverage (International) Corporation (Barbados); 546274 Alberta Ltd.; Blue Mountain Springs Ltd.

### *Principal Competitors*

Cadbury Schweppes Beverage Unit; Coca-Cola Company; PepsiCo Inc.; Quaker Oats Company; Laurent-Perrier U.S.; Great Brands of Europe; Hansen Natural Corporation; Ferolito Vultaggio & Sons; Odwalla Inc.

### *Further Reading*

''Clearly Canadian Sells U.S. Cascade Clear Brand, Bottling Plant for $6.3M US,'' *Canadian Press*, February 27, 2002.

Damsell, Keith, ''Douglas Mason Can See Clearly Now,'' *Financial Post*, July 27, 1996, p. 12.

——, ''Investors Left Flat by Beverage Saga,'' *Financial Post*, August 29, 1997, p. 17.

Fletcher, Anne, ''Beverage Firm Turns Away From Cola Wars to Healthy '90s Niche,'' *Financial Post*, October 10, 1989, p. 15.

Francis, Diane, ''Another Casualty of Revenue Canada: Moving South Has Helped to Slash the Tax Bill for Clearly Canadian,'' *National Post*, March 6, 1999, p. D3.

Hasselback, Drew, ''Clearly Canadian Erects For Sale Sign,'' *National Post*, November 30, 2000, p. C6.

——, ''New Look and Taste for Clearly Canadian,'' *National Post*, February 10, 2000, p. C3.

——, ''Running On Empty,'' *National Post*, April 16, 2001, p. C4.

Ingram, Mathew, ''Court Orders Clearly Canadian to Pay Up,'' *Globe and Mail*, May 26, 1995, p. B7.

Lush, Patricia, ''Beverage Firm Expanding,'' *Globe and Mail*, June 17, 1992, p. B12.

——, ''Clearly Canadian Boosts Advertising—Beverage Maker Predicts Profit,'' *Globe and Mail*, June 25, 1994, p. B18.

——, ''Toast of Howe Street Is Clearly Canadian,'' *Globe and Mail*, August 6, 1991, p. B1.

McClearn, Matthew, ''Gone Flat,'' *Canadian Business*, February 5, 2001, pp. 16–18.

McCullough, Michael, ''Just Add Hype,'' *Canadian Business*, December 1, 1996, p. 130.

Mudry, Brent, ''B.C. Securities Commission—BSCS Wins Key Mason-Related Offshore Documents,'' *Canada Stockwatch*, July 5, 2001.

——, ''SWI Steelworks Inc - Clearly Canadian's Doug Mason Under Formal Investigation,'' *Canadian Stockwatch*, July 12, 2000.

Rojo, Oscar, ''Beverage Firm Uses NAFTA to Compete Against Giants,'' *Toronto Star*, February 5, 1996, p. D3.

Schreiner, John, ''Contents Under Pressure,'' *Financial Post*, June 23, 2000, p. C7.

——, ''Lawsuit Latest to Clearly Canadian Loss,'' *Financial Post*, May 27, 1995, p. 42.

——,, ''Waters Get Clearly Competitive,'' *Financial Post*, August 3, 1992, p. 21.

Williamson, Robert, ''Drink Guru Sees Next Wave Clearly,'' *Globe and Mail*, June 26, 1993, p. B20.

Willis, Gerri, ''Beverage Firm's Plan to End Royalty Agreement Applauded,'' *The Globe and Mail*, August 5, 1992, p. B15.

—Frank Uhle

# Collectors Universe, Inc.

**1936 East Deere Avenue**
**Santa Ana, California 92705**
**U.S.A.**
**Telephone: (949) 567-1234**
**Toll Free: (800) 325-1121**
**Fax: (949) 553-1202**
**Web site: http://www.collectors.com**

*Public Company*
*Incorporated:* 1999
*Employees:* 251
*Sales:* $52.4 million (2001)
*Stock Exchanges:* NASDAQ
*Ticker Symbol:* CLCT
*NAIC:* 453998 Auction Houses; 812990 All Other Personal Services

Collectors Universe, Inc. is a collectibles company engaged in the grading, auctioning, selling, and authentication of collectible coins, sports cards, currency, stamps, sports and entertainment memorabilia, autographs, and other collectibles. Trademarks include Collectors Universe, Professional Coin Grading Service, Professional Sports Authenticators, Bowers and Merena, and Lyn Knight Currency Auctions. The company conducts multi-venue auctions at which dealer and collectors buy and sell high-end collectibles and operates an online collectibles marketplace where it publishes information about items for auction. It also operates co-branded Web sites with ebay and Yahoo!.

## *1986–90: Standardized Coin Grading*

Early in 1986, an increase in public awareness and interest in the investment market for coins—in part caused by a sharp rise in gold prices—led a group of leading coin dealers to agree to abide by the opinion of a trio of California-based coin dealers in assessing the value of traded coins. These 32 dealers formed Professional Coin Grading Service (PCGS) to standardize grading and make it possible for dealers to buy and sell coins sight unseen. By year's end, 50 dealers nationwide agreed to recognize PCGS's grading standards.

Reliable grading is critical to the coin-trading industry because, along with rarity and demand, it determines a coin's price. Prior to the 1950s, dealers employed a system of descriptive terms, such as ''uncirculated,'' ''brilliant uncirculated,'' or ''gem brilliant uncirculated'' to convey aspects of the coin's appearance which determine its level of preservation. Then in 1949, Dr. William Sheldon devised a 70-point system, now widely accepted on this continent, which assigns a coin in poorest condition the grade of 1, while a perfect or uncirculated coin received the grade of Mint State (MS) 70.

Dealers had traditionally graded coins themselves, creating a potential conflict of interest. In addition, their grade was often not honored by other dealers. In the early 1980s, scams and inconsistencies became so rampant that state and federal regulators considered regulating coins as securities. It was in response to this state of affairs that David G. Hall, a native Californian and a rare coin enthusiast from an early age, came up with the idea for Professional Coin Grading Service.

Coins graded by PCGS graders were sealed after being graded, offering not just an opinion, but a guarantee of the grade assigned. PCGS's rating made use of Dr. Sheldon's scale, using various criteria for selecting a grade, such as wear and tear, scratches, nicks, marks, luster, and color. The service guaranteed to pay the difference in market price for any PCGS-graded coin later determined to be of a lower grade than originally assigned.

The possibility of rating coins using a precise, universally accepted numerical grading system did not win advocates in every corner, however. ''Grading is primarily a subjective art,'' according to Harvey Stack of Stack's Coin Company, as quoted in the *New York Times* of October 18, 1986. ''Adjectival language has a bit more elasticity and can cover a broader horizon.'' However, by 1989 nearly all 500 major dealers nationwide belonged to PCGS, making it the largest coin grading operation in the nation. PCGS's system had become the industry standard. The company slabbed 70,000 to 90,000 coins a month, up from 8,000 when it started three years earlier. The

**Company Perspectives:**

*We believe that, over time, the high-end collectibles market will continue to grow as a result of increased nostalgia for memorabilia, an increase in leisure and disposable income, the desirability of owning collectibles, and investor confidence that collectibles will appreciate in value. We also believe that the convenience and efficiency of the Internet will stimulate further growth in the high-end collectibles market. It is also our view that this growth is dependent upon the availability of reliable authentication and grading services, authoritative information necessary to value collectibles, and trading forums or venues that enable buyers and sellers of collectibles to maximize the value of their collectibles. As a provider of these services to the collectibles markets, we have the opportunity to benefit directly from such growth in terms of increased demand for our services.*

company has also established a computerized exchange, the American Numismatic Information Exchange (ANIE), through which selected dealer-members entered daily bids and asking prices for as many as 200,000 coins.

In 1990, PCGS changed the industry again, introducing the ultimate grader: a computer called The Expert that was used in tandem with human graders. The Expert used a camera system to "see" each coin as a whole and to scan and scrutinize its surface section by section, noting flaws, nicks, and other signs of wear. It also looked at "light flow," or "reflective analysis," to measure the coin's depth of mirror and luster and its overall "mood." In all, the computer made about 2.2 billion calculations per coin before completing its "digital fingerprint"—storing its data on an optical disk for later use in tracking in the event it was lost or stolen.

In response to The Expert's introduction, the American Numismatic Association sold its own human grading system, opting to independently monitor grading services and set standards without conflicts of interest. In fact, initial faith in The Expert's capabilities led PCGS to make some advertised statements about it that came under scrutiny by the Federal Trade Commission (FTC). Hall conceded that the company's claims about its grading accuracy were overstated and, in 1990, agreed to submit its advertising to the FTC for review for the next five years.

### *1991–99: Growth of a Professional Sports Authenticator*

The following year, convinced that sports card hobbyists needed a way to be sure that the vintage cards they were buying were real and had not been re-glossed or re-cut, Hall founded Professional Sports Authenticator (PSA). Convincing dealers to come on board this time, however, was not easy: they were afraid the grading service would diminish the price of their wares, and for its first three years, PSA lost an average of $10,000 a month and stayed afloat only through infusions from PCGS. Then, as more card buyers demanded it, dealers began to submit cards to PSA. By 1996, PSA was grading almost 10,000 cards a month. When sports card trading on the Internet exploded in 1999, PSA, with 90 percent of the card-grading market, increased its business almost fivefold to roughly 80,000 per month. It had become the largest and most respected sports card grading service in the nation.

### *1999–2001: Growth Through Acquisition*

The Internet created new opportunities for trading in the site-unseen collectibles market. In February 1999, Hall combined PSA and PCGS along with three other companies in the collectibles and auction industry and formed Collectors Universe, Inc. For its first fiscal year ending that June, Collectors Universe totaled more than $20 million in sales. However, the company's initial public offering (IPO) that year raised only a lackluster $24 million.

Collectors Universe opened a new auction site, Sports Collectors Universe, selling items on consignment via the Internet. Conducting online auctions proved to be the company's fastest growing revenue stream; however, the bulk of its sales—more than 78 percent—continued to come from its authentication and grading services. The company also launched a PSA spin-off service in 1999—PSA/DNA, Guaranteed Authentic—allowing collectors to mark their memorabilia with a unique strand of synthetic DNA contained in an invisible ink compound. It later branched out to include sports autograph verification, relying upon four specialists who independently compared autographs in question to images of authentic autographs in PSA's computers. In a much publicized event in 1999, PSA/DNA DNA-stamped Mark McGwire's 70th home run ball and 900 Sammy Sosa autographs. In 2000, PSA/DNA was selected by the NFL and National Football League Players Incorporated to authenticate all player-related merchandise for the new NFL Auction on ebay. Ebay also partnered with Collectors Universe to feature its authentication and quality verification services online.

Collectors Universe also began to grow through acquisitions. In late 1999, Professional Stamp Experts joined Collectors Universe and began service on the Internet in January 2000. In 2000, Collectors Universe acquired the assets of three companies owned by the renowned coin dealer Q. David Bowers and his business partner, Raymond N. Merena: Auctions by Bowers and Merena Inc., Bowers and Merena Galleries Inc., and Bowers and Merena Research Inc. Of the ten highest prices for U.S. coins sold at auction, Bowers and Merena had been responsible for seven, including the highest seller, the 1804 Childs Silver dollar, auctioned in 1999 for $4,100,000. The combined revenue for the Bowers and Merena companies in 1999 was $13 million. Bowers continued to head the trio of companies as a division of Collectors Universe, and Merena joined the Collectors Universe board of directors.

In 2000, Collectors Universe acquired the privately held Odyssey Publications Inc., which published *Autograph Collectors Magazine* and other periodicals and price guides for celebrity autograph collectors. The company expanded Odyssey's operations to include the sale of celebrity and historical autographs and memorabilia and transferred publication of its *Sports Market Report* to Odyssey. In April 2001, *Sports Market Report*, formerly distributed to members of PSA's Collectors Club only, became a magazine with national distribution. Collectors

## Key Dates:

**1986:** David G. Hall forms Professional Coin Grading Service (PCGS).
**1990:** PCGS introduces computerized coin grading.
**1991:** Hall founds Professional Sports Authenticator (PSA).
**1999:** Hall founds Collectors Universe; Professional Stamp Experts joins Collectors Universe.
**2000:** The company acquires Bowers and Merena, Odyssey Publications Inc., and James Spence Autographs.

Universe also purchased James Spence Autographs, one of the foremost sports autographs authorities in the United States in 2000. This acquisition enabled the company to increase its authentication services for sports autographs and memorabilia, a service in demand since the sports card market had not long before come under scrutiny by the FBI for its widespread misrepresentation.

Business was booming. In 2000, Record revenues of $42 million for the company as a whole were up about 88 percent from the prior year. PCGS became the official grading and authentication service for the gold treasure of pre-1858 coins recovered in 1989 from the *SS Central America*. Collectors Universe entered into partnerships in 2000 with Yahoo! Inc. and Shop At Home Inc. In 2001, Collectors Universe began a three-year agreement with The Topps Company, Inc. to grade selected limited quantity sports cards prior to sale. Inter@ctive Week, a weekly Internet trade magazine, listed Collectors Universe as the highest-ranking Internet company in the collectibles category of e-commerce companies. *PC Magazine* called it the top coin auction site, and *Yahoo! Life* named it the top collector's site.

However, 2001 brought concern that the slowing economy and lower stock market prices would dampen collectibles prices. In 2000, in fact, the company had discontinued its weekly Internet auctions due to sizeable losses. However, at Collectors Universe the view was that the market for collectibles had begun to stabilize in the new millennium. The company underwent a change of guard when Roger W. Johnson succeeded David G. Hall as CEO but remained focused on its strategy of consolidating the major collectibles markets and maintaining the number one position in each important market.

### *Principal Subsidiaries*

Lyn Knight Currency Auctions, Inc.

### *Principal Competitors*

Certified Sports Authentication; Sportscard Guaranty Co.; ebay Inc.; Yahoo Inc.; Sotheby's Inc.; Christie's Inc.

### *Further Reading*

Aaron, Robert, "Computer Judges 'Eye Appeal,' Wear and Tear," *Toronto Star*, August 4, 1990, p. 14.

Henricks, Mark, "What's New In the Coin Trade: As Trading and Con Games Increase, So Does 'Slabbing'," *New York Times*, September 17, 1989, p. 15.

Mitchell, Richard, "The Battle to Authenticate Sports Autographs," *ID World*, March 2000, p. 48.

"Should You Invest in Coins?," *Consumer Reports*, July 1991, p. 483.

—Carrie Rothburd

# Colorado MEDtech, Inc.

**6176 Longbow Drive**
**Boulder, Colorado 80301**
**U.S.A.**
**Telephone: (303) 530-2660**
**Fax: 303) 581-1010**
**Web site: http//www.cmed.com**

*Public Company*
*Incorporated:* 1977 as Cybermedic Inc.
*Employees:* 535
*Sales:* $77.2 million (2001)
*Stock Exchanges:* NASDAQ
*Ticker Symbol:* CMED
*NAIC:* 334510 Electromedical and Electrotherapeutic Apparatus Manufacturing; 339112 Surgical and Medical Instrument Manufacturing

Colorado MEDtech, Inc. (CMED) is a leading full-service provider of advanced medical products and comprehensive outsourcing services. CMED operates three core operating units, including the RELA division, the Imaging and Power Systems division (IPS), and CIVCO Medical Instruments Co., Inc, a wholly owned subsidiary of Colorado MEDtech. The RELA division provides custom product development and outsourcing services, specializing in the design and development of diagnostic, biotechnology, and therapeutic medical devices, medical software systems, and medical device connectivity. RELA also provides manufacturing services for electronic and electromechanical medical devices and instrumentation systems assembly for major manufacturers. The IPS division designs, develops, and produces imaging system hardware and software, including advanced magnetic resonance imaging (MRI) systems and application software, high-performance radio frequency amplifiers for MRI systems and high-voltage x-ray generator subsystems for computed tomography scanners. The CIVCO subsidiary designs, develops, manufactures, and distributes specialized medical accessories and supplies for imaging equipment and for minimally invasive surgical equipment.

## *Founding of Company*

Colorado MEDtech was founded on October 19, 1992 when Cybermedic Inc., a publicly traded company, and RELA Inc., a privately held company, signed a definitive agreement to merge. Under the agreement, Cybermedic, the parent company in the merger, adopted the trade name ''Colorado MEDtech.'' The agreement called for approximately three million shares of Cybermedic common stock to be issued to RELA's shareholders, resulting in five million Cybermedic shares outstanding after the merger. The company's stock would continue to be traded on the NASDAQ system under Cybermedic's symbol CMED. The agreement also stipulated that Cybermedic and RELA would operate as separate divisions of CMED. Cybermedic developed, manufactured, and marketed non-invasive cardiopulmonary diagnostic instruments, and RELA specialized in the design and development of medical products and software systems. Management anticipated the merger to improve the financial strength of the two companies and to produce operating efficiencies that would make CMED a leader in the health care equipment industry.

Following the merger, the annualized sales of both companies totaled $15 million with combined assets of more than $7 million and $2 million in shareholders' equity. Dean Leffingwell, founder of RELA and newly appointed chairman of the board, announced the appointment of John Greenbaum, formerly of Eli Lily Corp. as CMED's president and chief executive officer. Greenbaum also was to continue in his position as president of RELA. Lockett Wood, founder of Cybermedic, became president of CMED's Cybermedic's division.

## *Facing a New Health Care Climate in the Early 1990s*

With the merger and the changing climate of the health care industry under President Clinton's proposed health-reform plan, CMED confronted new opportunities along with the challenge of maintaining its markets. Clinton's health-care reform plan prompted enormous national and Congressional debate on the future of the country's health care industry. The President's proposal had also ignited the introduction of numerous other proposals that offered alternative insurance reforms, financial

## Company Perspectives:

*Colorado MEDtech, Inc. is a medical device outsourcing and critical components company, providing advanced engineering, scientific and medical expertise for the research and development, design and manufacturing needs of its clients. This encompasses designing new medical devices and instruments, applying advanced technologies to improve existing products and providing contract manufacturing services. Clients include major medical device, biotechnology, and pharmaceutical companies. The Company also manufactures and markets proprietary critical components, including high-performance frequency amplifiers for MRI systems, high-voltage x-ray generator sub-systems for computed tomography (CT) scanners, specialized medical imaging accessories and minimally invasive surgical equipment.*

schemes, and payment options. In this uncertain environment, CMED's combined capabilities appeared to position it well as a medical technology management company with a proven product line, centralized manufacturing, and improved research and development resources. The challenge not only was to ensure that the merger proceeded smoothly, but also to steer the company toward profitability in a changing marketplace that appeared to be headed toward more managed patient care.

In June 1993, John V. Atanasoff II was appointed as the company's president, CEO and chairman. Atanasoff's experience had been in various segments of the high technology industry, including as president and CEO of Cybernetics, which developed and manufactured specialized equipment for the electronics and computer graphics markets. Under Atanasoff's direction, CMED down-sized operations to eliminate redundancies and effect administrative changes. Atanasoff's vision included designing a leaner company that focused on core business operations in diagnostics and device and pharmaceutical manufacturing. By doing so, the company could better pursue opportunities in the medical instruments industry, which then represented approximately $68 billion and was growing at a rate of about 8 percent per year. In 1993, the U.S. market alone totaled $31 billion.

CMED was also committed to developing new product technologies for the health care industry, including non-invasive cardiac output monitoring. In 1993, current technology required the use of an invasive catheter that could result in life-threatening complications. As a result, the company began developing and manufacturing non-invasive technologies through its RELA division. The company also looked to capitalize on new market opportunities in managed care given the rapidly changing nature of the health care industry from traditional care providers, such as hospitals and physicians, to managed care. CMED's greatest challenge was to establish plans and profits that would see it through the dramatic changes underway in the health care industry and help it grow from a small high technology company to a medium-sized product-oriented growth company.

### *Mid-1990s: A Time of Growth*

Atanasoff's plans for profitability began to pay off as the company announced results for its year ended June 30, 1994. Sales increased to $20.6 million compared to $17.5 million in 1993. In addition, the company reported net income of $800,000, or 15 cents per share, compared to a net loss of $1.1 million, or 25 cents per share in the pervious year. Atanasoff had achieved his initial goal of making CMED's core businesses profitable, but to keep the momentum going the company had to begin focusing on investments in product development and business expansion through acquisitions and licensing of synergistic products and services.

By December 1994, the company was continuing to make important progress in expanding its base businesses and pursuing new market opportunities. The company had increased its revenue by 18 percent, retired its bank debt, and secured a significant line of credit for future product development. In addition, CMED established an alliance with Eric Jaeger Co., a German company, to distribute that company's respiratory care products in the United States. This alliance also provided a European distribution channel for CMED's future products. The company developed a new product for the respiratory care market, the Heat-Moisture-Exchange Filter, otherwise known as VenShield or the ''artificial nose,'' which received Food and Drug Administration (FDA) approval for production. CMED developed the filter jointly with Vencor Inc., a Louisville, Kentucky Fortune 500 operator of acute-care hospitals and nursing homes, which not only provided investment funds, but also insight into the needs of the managed care and home care markets. Vencor had taken an initial interest in CMED on December 6, 1993 when it purchased 500,000 shares or about 9 percent of the company's common stock. In 1994, Vencor purchased another 13 percent, increasing its interest in CMED to 22 percent, making it the company's largest shareholder. The price of the shares, which were purchased directly from the company, was not disclosed. The deal with Vencor, a rapidly growing $300 million company, provided CMED with enough capital to produce high-usage disposable respiratory filtration products at a lower cost than was currently available on the market.

Based on these successes, the company planned to take advantage of its research and manufacturing capabilities and to continue to develop and produce mass numbers of low-end, disposable diagnostic and therapeutic products such as the VenShield. CMED also entered another market niche including the production of diagnostic equipment for food inspection utilizing DNA sampling. As a result, two years later in April 1996, the company signed a $1.3 million contract to supply its new ''RiboPrinter'' product—a testing instrument for food-borne bacteria—to Wilmington, Delaware-based Qualicon LLC, a venture of DuPont and TBK of Japan. The RiboPrinter was designed to detect E. Coli bacteria using DNA analysis. The product had the advantage of employing a much faster detection system than other current laboratory processes, which was important to food manufacturers. With the production of this microbial or bacteria detector, the company began a significant shift from being a design/development company to becoming a products-oriented firm. Although a relatively small firm with only 160 employees, by 1994 the company seemed to have found its competitive niche. It devoted fully half of its 52,000 square-foot facility to research, development, and administration and the other half to manufacturing.

**Key Dates:**

**1977:** Precursor company, Cybermedic Inc., Inc. in Colorado.
**1992:** Cybermedic Inc. merges with Rela Inc. to form Colorado MEDtech, Inc.
**1993:** Colorado MEDtech sells 500,000 shares or 9 percent of company stock to Vencor, Inc.
**1994:** Company sells additional 13 percent of company stock to Vencor, Inc., increasing Vencor's ownership interest to 22%.
**1995:** Company sells its cardiopulmonary product lines to Warren E. Collins, Inc.
**1997:** Company acquires Novel Biomedical, Co. and the operating assets of Erbtec Engineering, Inc.
**1998:** Company acquires the operating assets of Eclipse Automation Corporation.
**1999:** Company acquires the assets of Creos Technologies LLC and CIVCO Medical Instruments Co. Inc.
**2000:** Company resists hostile takeover attempt.

In March 1995, CMED announced that it had won a $3 million contract from New Jersey-based Ohmeda Inc, a large medical company with about $800 million a year in revenue and a subsidiary of the $5.2 billion industrial conglomerate BOC Group based in the United Kingdom. The agreement called for CMED to produce heart monitors and to help Ohmeda develop a system for managing infusions.

On August 16, 1995, the company sold its money-losing cardiopulmonary product lines to Warren E. Collins, Inc. The sale included all inventories, intangible property rights, customer lists, and tooling associated with the cardiopulmonary product lines as well as the trade name Cybermedic. In addition, despite its repeated successes, in September 1995 the company announced that it was recalling its bacterial filter product VenShield and halting production until tests and improvements could be made. In June, the company had shipped initial orders of the filter to several hospitals, which first identified the undisclosed problems. Nevertheless, because the filter was in the early stages of production, it represented less than 3 percent of the company's revenues.

In 1997, the company experienced several important developments. The producer of diagnostic and therapeutic medical devices and software saw its sales jump dramatically. Revenues rose 74 percent and an increase in earnings per share of 38 percent pushed CMED to the number one position among publicly held health care, biotechnology, and pharmaceutical companies in the Denver Post/Bloomberg 100. Overall the company ranked 15th. The company attributed its growth to a significant expanding market in diagnostic systems, minimally invasive catheters and software.

Strong sales, however, did not account for all of the growth. In February 1997, the company completed a $1.9 million acquisition of Novel Biomedical Inc. of Plymouth, Minnesota. The acquisition was completed with cash, stock, and stock options. Novel Biomedical specialized in developing, designing, and producing disposable medical devices, primarily catheters used in angioplasty and other procedures. In October, CMED also acquired the operating assets of Erbtec Engineering Inc. for $5,350,000 cash and issuance of 88,708 of common stock, resulting in a total purchase value of about $6,100,000. Erbtec produced advanced radio frequency subsystems used in MRI systems. By the end of 1997, CMED's impressive growth led it to be moved from Nasdaq's Small Cap exchange to its National Market System. With these two acquisitions, CMED had increased its workforce to 400 in four facilities.

The company's rapid growth and success was recognized in October 1998 when *Forbes* magazine selected CMED as one of America's best 200 companies. The company's RELA subsidiary also signed a five-year manufacturing agreement to develop an HIV and Hepatitis C blood detection system for Gen-Probe Inc. of San Diego, California. The system, called TIGRIS, was intended for use in American blood banks. Gen-Probe initially approached CMED in 1996 with the idea of developing a DNA probe to detect HIV in blood. The company's engineers under the RELA division then designed a prototype and built several systems that underwent rigorous testing before determining its efficacy. As a result of this success, Gen-Probe entered into a five-year contract valued at $20 million to have CMED produce the TIGRIS system under the Gen-Probe brand name. At the same time, the company was producing a new proprietary product called FreshAir, designed to convert air from the atmosphere into high-grade oxygen in order to assist seriously ill patients dependent on oxygen.

In addition, in April 1998 CMED signed a licensing agreement with TAVA Technologies for TAVA's Plant Y2KOne products for year 2000 compliance. Under the licensing agreement, CMED would modify TAVA's product software to tailor it specifically to the needs of the health care market. The modified system provided a combination of tools and services to support health care institutions' efforts to conform with year 2000 compliance for their biomedical devices. To provide these services and software system, CMED formed a new subsidiary operation under BioMed Y2, Inc. By the end of 1998, BioMed had already received orders totaling more than $1.5 million from health care providers to assist them in evaluating medical devices for Year 2000 compliance.

On November 6, 1998, Vencor announced that it had sold its entire stake in CMED for $22 million to repay debt. The sale included 3 million shares at $6.38 each to 25 institutional accounts, including CMED, which repurchased 655,000 of its own shares. Three days later on November 9, the company announced that net income for the first quarter rose to $1,3185,905, an increase of 99 percent compared to $663,709 in the same quarter in the previous year. Sales totaled $13,408,421, an increase of 85 percent, compared to $7,260,230 in the same period in 1997. In addition, in December the company's board of directors announced that it had adopted a Shareholder Rights Plan. The rights plan was aimed at providing protection against coercive or hostile takeover tactics, and to ensure that anyone seeking to take over the company would first need to negotiate with the company's board of directors.

In 1999, the company achieved several strategic developments. In February, it acquired selected operating assets of

Eclipse Automation Corporation, which became CMED's Automation division. In August, CMED acquired certain operating assets of Creos Technologies LLC, a developer and producer of high voltage x-ray generator systems for computed tomography scanners. CMED also announced that it was expanding its injection molding capability through the acquisition of CIVCO Medical Instruments Co. Inc. of Kalona, Iowa, a producer of ultrasound imaging equipment and minimally invasive surgical products. CMED completed the acquisition on November 15, 1999 by exchanging 736,324 of its own shares for all the outstanding shares of CIVCO and related estate. The company operated CIVCO as a subsidiary of CMED.

### *Late 1990s and Beyond: Corporate Troubles and Restructuring*

By the end of 1999, however, the company began experiencing difficulties. Shares in the company plummeted when the company announced that earnings for the second quarter ending December 31 would not meet expectations. Despite winning accolades in business magazines and local newspapers, its shares dropped 40% to $8. CEO John Atanasoff said the company was having difficulty meeting development deadlines for several clients. To maintain good relations and compensate clients for production delays, Atanasoff offered discounts totaling just under $1 million. Another problem stemmed from higher than expected costs of consolidating three manufacturing plants into one in Longmont, Colorado. This downturn came after the company had recorded 26 straight profitable quarters, 50 percent annual sales growth over the previous three years, and had increased its workforce to 600. A major product development problem involved software code that had to be rewritten. Nevertheless, on December 23, 1999, Ken Trbovich, an analyst with Bigelow & Co., a Denver investment bank, said in the *Denver Post* that the company's units that made "x-ray machines and power systems for x-ray machines were in fine shape." He stated that the problems were in the RELA subsidiary, which produced equipment under contract to other companies. "The difficulties there," he stated, "are swamping the positive developments that are taking place in other parts of the business." Trbovich nevertheless criticized the company for not addressing the problems quickly and noted that it was adversely affecting the company from a fundamental earnings perspective.

The company's troubles continued into 2000 when analysts criticized the medical technology firm's management team for withholding information about a backlog of contracts and slower than expected growth in the company's engineering consulting division. By mid-2000, a new executive team had taken over. John Atanasoff resigned as chief executive officer and was replaced by Stephen Onody. Greg Gould was promoted to chief financial officer, and Bill Wood, product development and technology officer and a key leader in the company's early years, returned to the firm. Upon taking over the new management discovered quality control problems and immediately sought not only to address quality issues, but also to invest heavily in staff, consultants, and other improvements.

More trouble came in October when the company's weakened financial position invited a takeover attempt by Anthony Fant, CEO of Minneapolis-based HEI Inc. and self-described turnaround artist. On August 31, 2000, in a filing with the SEC, Fant disclosed that he had been acquiring CMED stock since early May and had accumulated 1,214,300 shares, or about 9.9 percent of the total shares outstanding. On September 11, Fant sent a letter to CMED's board of directors proposing a transaction in which HEI would acquire the company for HEI common stock having a value of $12 per CMED share. HEI's offer limited the number of HRI shares that would be issued to 8.5 million. On the same day that he made this proposal to the company, Fant filed suit against the company and its board in U.S. District Court alleging that certain provisions of the company's bylaws and its shareholders' rights plan violated the rights of shareholders to hold a special meeting to elect directors. Fant said he intended to demand a special meeting of shareholders to replace the company's board of directors. In a letter to shareholders, however, CEO Stephen Onody stated that the company's new management team had initiated a renewed focus on core business operations, which had already helped the company expand contracts with major corporate clients, including General Electric Medical Systems and Hitachi Medical Group, and land new contracts for development of medical imaging machines during the first quarter ended September 30. Part of this restructuring plan had included selling CMED's Catheter and Disposables Technology, Inc. subsidiary in April and acquiring certain operating assets of the ultrasound accessories and supplies business of ATL Ultrasound for $4,384,000. With the acquisition of ATL's imaging assets, CMED had formed a new Imaging and Power Systems division. Because of these developments, CMED's management successfully resisted Fant's efforts to put his offer to a vote by investors. As a result, in October Fant announced that he would no longer pursue his acquisition offer and dismissed the lawsuit.

On January 25, 2001, the company received more bad news when the Food and Drug Administration (FDA) received a letter warning CMED that certain areas of its Longmont medical device manufacturing plant was not compliant with federal quality standards. According to the company's general counsel, Peter Jensen, the FDA warning dealt primarily with administrative processes and did not stem from product defects. Despite the company's hope for a quick resolution, it was not until nine months later in October when the company received FDA clearance allowing the Longmont facility to resume manufacturing operations. The company announced that it had spent $2 million to correct the problems, which adversely affected revenues at a cost of approximately the same amount.

During 2001, the company also continued to restructure operations to focus on its core markets of medical technology, software services, and medical imaging products and services. As a result of this effort, CMED phased out two business divisions, CMED Automation and BioMed Y2K, Inc. In addition, the company integrated its CMED Manufacturing division into RELA. As a result of these developments, the company organized its core operations around three primary operating divisions, including RELA, Imaging and Power Systems, and CIVCO.

As a result of this restructuring and the resolution of the FDA problem, the company believed that it could return to profitability. Nevertheless, for fiscal year 2001 revenue had increased just 4 percent to $77.2 million from $74 million in fiscal year 2000. The deficiencies sited by the FDA had clearly adversely affected both product development and manufacturing outsource revenue. With resolution of the FDA issue, the company could return to the manufacture and distribution of medical devices. This development appeared to bode well for a company that, even during its difficult times, continued to increase substantially its investment in research and development to improve or produce new products and technology.

### Principal Subsidiaries

CIVCO Medical Instruments Co., Inc.

### Principal Divisions

RELA; Imaging and Power Systems.

### Principal Competitors

Plexus Corporation; Relys International, Inc., Analogic Corporation, ACT Manufacturing, Inc.; KMC Systems, Inc.; UMM Electronics Inc.; Spartorn Corporation.

### Further Reading

Austin, Marsha, "Medtech CEO Resists Buyout Offer: Investor Goes to Court to Block 'Poison Pill'," *Denver Post*, October 11, 2000.

——, "Colorado Medtech Plant Fails to Meet Federal Standards," *Denver Post*, February 1, 2001.

Branaugh, Matt, "Medtech Gets FDA Clearance," *Daily Camera*, October 16, 2001.

"Colorado MEDtech Acquires Minn. Firm," *Denver Post*, March 4, 1997.

"Colorado MEDtech, Inc. Named One of Forbes 200 Best Small Companies," *Business Wire*, October 29, 1998.

"Colorado's MEDtech Expects High Returns In Future," *Daily Camera*, December 17, 1996.

"Cybermedic and RELA Merger Completed, Creating Colorado MEDtech," *Business Wire*, October 12, 1992.

DiBattista, Laurie, "Healthy Growth Pushes Colorado Medtech to Top," *Denver Post*, July 12, 1998.

DuBow, Wendy, "Boulder County's Public Companies: Top 10 Return on Equity—Colorado MEDtech Turnaround Complete," *Boulder County Business Report*, June 1995.

Gellici, Janet, and Arthur Harrison, "Med Supplier Faces Culture Change," *Denver Post*, November 15, 1993.

——, "Slow Road to Success," *Denver Post*, December 19, 1994.

"Gunbarrel, Colo., Medical Equipment Developer Enjoys Rapid Growth," *Daily Camera*, July 14, 1998.

Huber, Eric, "Woes Stunt MEDtech's Growth," *Denver Post*, December 23, 1999.

Reiner, Eric, "A Tale of Three Stocks," *Colorado Business Magazine*, March 1998.

Sommars, Jack, "The Magnificent Seven," *Colorado Business Magazine*, June 1998.

"Vencor To Increase Its Stake In Colorado Medtech," *Daily Camera*, May 29, 1997.

—Bruce P. Montgomery

# Compagnie des Alpes

**6, Place Abel Gance**
**92100 Boulogne-Billancourt**
**France**
**Telephone: (+33) 1-46-94-44-49**
**Fax: (+33) 1-46-94-46-99**
**Web site: http://www.compagniedesalpes.com**

*Public Company*
*Incorporated:* 1989
*Employees:* 1,399
*Sales:* EUR 220.99 million ($189.4 million)
*Stock Exchanges:* Euronext Paris
*Ticker Symbol:* CDA
*NAIC:* 713920 Skiing Facilities

Compagnie des Alpes is the world's leading ski lift operator, a specialty which includes not only the construction and operation of ski lifts but also the maintenance—and generation of snow—of ski areas under the company's control. Compagnie des Alpes recorded over 13 million ''skier days'' and 135 skier passages in the 2000–2001 season. Long considered a subsidiary of the French government's Caisse des Dépots (C3D), which continues to hold 44 percent of its stock, CDA concentrates its operation and management of ski areas on larger, high-altitude resort areas. The higher-altitude locations guarantee the company greater snow cover and operations spanning the full four-month European ski season. CDA already holds a 25 percent share of the French ski market, the world's largest, including sites at Les Arcs, Tignes, Meribel, Chamonix, and other prestigious resort areas. CDA has also begun to explore geographic expansion, notably in Switzerland and Italy. The company has also entered a cooperation agreement with Canada's Intrawest, including an exchange of shares, designed to help CDA enter the North American ski market. At the same time, the company has begun to diversify, moving into the operation of a chain of boutiques, Le Ski Shop, offering sales and rentals of ski and related clothing and equipment. The company has also begun land development activities, building up a portfolio of more than 150,000 square meters of building rights in the Les Arcs, Les Menuires, La Plagne, and Flaine resort areas. Nonetheless, ski lift ticket sales remain the primary source of CDA's revenues, at more than 90 percent of the company's EUR 221 million in sales in 2000–2001. Led by chairman and CEO Jean-Pierre Sonois, the company expects to break the EUR 300 million mark by 2005.

### *Lifting the Ski Lift Industry in the 1990s*

The French ski industry boomed in the second half of the 20th century as skiing became one of the country's most popular sports. The development of the country's vast, ski-able region in the Alpes and elsewhere saw the creation of a large number of resorts and resort communities. If ski resorts in Austria and Switzerland, and in Italy as well, had become primary destinations for the international skiing community, France's slopes typically attracted primarily French skiers. French slopes were considered a public treasure and remained under control of their local municipalities.

The growing numbers of ski slopes and resorts, building international competition (with the North American ski industry convincing growing numbers of skiers to holiday closer to home), and domestic competition from resorts in the Pyrenees mountains on the border between France and Spain forced communities in the Alpes ski region to make continuous improvements to their ski trails and equipment, especially ski lifts and snowmaking equipment. While ski lifts were necessary for getting the growing number of skiers up to the top of slopes, snowmaking equipment became increasingly necessary to guarantee sufficient coverage. Both presented enormous and constant investment costs that proved too onerous for most communities to bear alone. Communities were also responsible for repairing slopes damaged by avalanches and weather conditions.

Over time, a number of communities turned to the government-owned Caisse des Dépôts et Consignations for help in meeting the heavy investment costs needed to maintain the quality of their slopes and infrastructure, including ski lifts. C3D soon built up a portfolio of mountain resorts under its guidance. Among these was Les Arcs, which had been placed under the direction of Jean-Pierre Sonois in the late 1970s.

### Company Perspectives:

*Our Commitment: Continue to follow the same strategic path which has made the Compagnie des Alpes the world's leader in ski area management, especially: maintain sustained growth for the Group, both in terms of activity and earnings, and thereby create value for our shareholders; stimulate the Group's organization by enhancing its industrial dimension and capitalizing on synergies and by introducing operating standards and reducing costs, especially purchasing costs; improve our financial communications, especially by strengthening our operations aimed at individual shareholders.*

*Our Goal For 2005: to break the EUR 320 million sales barrier. This represents average annual growth of at least ten percent for the Group. Half of this growth will be organic and the other half external.*

During the 1980s, the spiraling costs of maintaining the integrity of their slopes and equipment were bringing communities under increasing financial pressure. Toward the end of the decade, Sonois proposed grouping a number of ski resorts into a single network. Such a network would be able to cut costs. With the failing economy at the end of the 1980s, a number of communities were eager to turn over the operations of their ski lifts and slopes to a third party.

In 1989, Caisse des Dépôts et Consignations, through its investment wing Caisse des Dépôts—Développement (C3D), agreed to take over operations in a number of the region's most prominent ski areas. In that year, C3D created a new publicly-operated subsidiary, Compagnie des Alpes, which was given as a charter to act as a specialist in ski area management, with a focus on the more profitable high-altitude areas. Sonois was placed at the head of the new company as chairman and CEO. C3D remained the company's primary shareholder.

CDA quickly built up its network of ski areas and by 1991 had built up a strong position in the sector. The company took an initial share in SATAL (Société pour l'Aménagement Touristique Argentière Lognan), giving it access to that company's operations in the Grand Montets resort area in the Chamonix Valley. CDA gained majority control of SATAL soon after. The company also moved into Tignes, taking over STGM (Société d'exploitation des Téléphériques de la Grande Motte). CDA also negotiated the concessions for several other communities, forming separate subsidiaries for these operations, such as of STAG (Société d'exploitation des Téléphériques de l'Aiguille Grive), placing the company in the Peisey-Nancroix/Vallandry ski area, and SEVABEL (Société d'Exploitation de la Vallée des Belleville), which took over the ski lift and slope maintenance operation of the Les Menuires and Saint-Martin-de-Belleville ski resort areas.

For ski communities hard hit by the slump in the French ski industry at the beginning of the 1990s, the arrival of CDA offered a way out of the continual and expensive investments needed to maintain their slopes and equipment. CDA was able to continue its rapid growth into the mid-1990s. After taking majority control of SATAL, the company moved into the La Plagne ski region through a majority shareholding position in SAP. The acquisition of STAR strengthened CDA's position in Les Arcs.

In 1995, CDA made one of its largest acquisitions to date, buying up nearly all of the shares in CIEL (Centre Investissements et Loisirs), which held a 36 percent stake in Meribel Alpina. That company held the concessions for the Meribel ski slopes in the Allues valley region, one of France's most prestigious ski ranges. The following year, CDA's acquisition of SMA (Société les Montagnes de l'Arc) gave it full control of STAR and the Les Arcs concession. In 1997, the company, through its position in Meribel Alpina, entered four more communities—Flaine, Samoëns, Morillon and Sixt—when Meribel Alpina acquired Grand Massif Développement, concentrated on the Haute Savoie region. CDA was meanwhile building up its own position with Meribel Alpina. By 1998, CDA held some 43 percent of Meribel Alpina's shares.

## *International Growth and Diversification for the New Century*

CDA had grown rapidly during the early 1990s and by mid-decade had taken control of more than 20 percent of the French market. The company's concentration on only high-altitude, high-prestige locations gave it a dominant position among the market's most active ski areas. Yet the CDA was finding domestic growth more and more difficult to come by and the region began to balk at the appearance of a dominant—and even monopolistic—player in the sector. CDA, at the same time, was leery of remaining a single- product, single-market company.

In the late 1990s, Sonois led the company in a new strategy designed to diversify the company both geographically and into other business areas. The acquisition of STAR had given the company a number of boutiques. CDA decided to build on this opportunity, launching its chain of Le Ski Shop stores, which offered sales and rentals of ski and related clothing and equipment. CDA also moved into property development, putting together up a portfolio of building rights for properties in its ski resort areas.

Geographically, CDA looked both toward its neighbors and overseas for growth. In 1996, the company made its first foreign acquisition, taking over ski lift operator CMBF (Courmayeur Mont-Blanc Funivie SpA) in conjunction with the Val d'Oste regional authority. The acquisition gave CDA an important foothold in the as yet highly fragmented Italian market.

CDA's next stop was North America. In 1998, the company signed a cooperation agreement with Intrawest, based in Canada, the leading North American ski resorts property developer and operator. The agreement, which included a shares swap that made Intrawest CDA's second-largest shareholder after C3D, was expected to enable CDA to enter the North American market with an eye on entering the Vail and Aspen ski areas. At the same time, Intrawest was able to begin preparations to begin property developments in France, notably through acquisitions of parts of CDA's building rights portfolio.

## Key Dates:

**1989:** C3D, an investment arm of the government-run Caisse des Dépôts et Consignations, launches Compagnie des Alpes to group its portfolio of ski resorts operations.
**1991:** CDA's portfolio expands to include the acquisition of a stake in SATAL and majority control of STGM, as well as the launch of STAG and SEVABEL.
**1994:** CDA takes a majority stake in SATAL as well as in SAP and STAR.
**1996:** CDA moves into Italy with a majority shareholding in Courmayeur Mont-Blanc Funivie SpA.
**1998:** CDA signs a cooperation agreement with Canada's Intrawest.
**2000:** CDA purchases 90 percent of Meribel Alpina and a 22 percent share of Télé-Verbier, marking company's first move into Switzerland.
**2001:** CDA acquires 35 percent of Saas-Fee Bergbahnen to expand company's operations in Switzerland.

In 2000, CDA stepped up its shareholding position in Meribel Alpina to 90 percent. In exchange for approval of the transaction by the mergers and monopolies commission, CDA had to agree not to seek further expansion in the French Alps. The acquisition also removed Meribel from its over-the-counter (OTC) listing on the Paris stock exchange.

That year, CDA turned its expansion interest to Switzerland. In 2000, the company acquired a nearly 22 percent stake in Télé-Verbier, which provided ski lift operations in the vast Quatre Vallées area. Although somewhat contested by Swiss protectionists, that CDA acquisition was soon followed by a new move into Switzerland. In February 2001, CDA acquired a 35 percent share of Saas-Fee Bergbahnen, giving it a foothold in the canton of Valais.

As CDA continued to look for new acquisition opportunities—including in the remaining major European ski destination, Austria—the company began to see the first fruits of its partnership with Intrawest. In December 2001, the company agreed to sell its partner a nine hectare area in Les Arcs as the site for Intrawest's proposed new ski village development. In exchange, CDA was given the concession for constructing and building the new ski lifts needed for the site as well as space for the opening of a Le Ski Shop boutique. Under Sonois' guidance, CDA had grown to become the world's leading ski lift operator in just ten years. The company's commitment to new acquisitions, and its target of revenues of more than EUR 300 million by 2005, gave it confidence that it would continue to occupy the summits of its industry in the new century.

### *Principal Subsidiaries*

CMBF (57.12%; Italy); FDA (51.00%; Italy); STGM (77.72%); SATAL (80.53%); STAG (99.99%); SAP (84.45%); SEVABEL (81.62%); SCIVABEL (99.94%); CIEL (99.98%);SMA (96.01%); SKI SHOP (99.98%); MERIBEL-ALPINA (90.00%); GMD (80.95%); DSF (ex SEPAD) (99.99%); SERM (99.86%); LRMS (99.96%); SIXT DÉVELOPPEMENT (99.80%); SAG (99.99%); TELEVERBIER (21.80%; Switzerland).

### *Principal Competitors*

Intrawest Inc.; Titlisbahnen-Bergbahnen Engelberg-Trubse AG; Rothornbahn und Scalottas AG; Skistar AB.

### *Further Reading*

Sullivan, Aline, "For Investors Unafraid of Heights, Ski-Resort Stocks Provide a Way to Plunge," *International Herald Tribune*, December 6, 1997
Elliott, Robert, "French Ski Stocks to Carve Gains from Travel Slump," *Reuters*, December 11, 2001.
Couvelaire, Anne-Louise, "Compagnie des Alpes: le canon de la neige," *Nouvel Observateur*, December 2000.
Marquetty, Fabio, "Trois questions à Jean-Pierre Sonois, Président du directoire de la Compagnie des Alpes," *Le Journal Des Finances*, December 1, 2001, p. 18.
Chevallard, Lucile, "La Compagnie des Alpes cherche à augmenter le nombre de ses clients," *Les Echos*, September 13, 2001 p. 32.
Dupuy, Héléna, "Ces entreprises qui managent aux sommets," *La Tribune*, February 21, 2001.

—M.L. Cohen

# Consolidated Freightways Corporation

**16400 S.E. CF Way**
**Vancouver, Washington 98683**
**U.S.A.**
**Telephone: (360) 448-4000**
**Fax: (360) 448-4308**
**Web site: http://www.cf.com**

*Public Company*
*Founded:* 1929 as Consolidated Freightways, Inc.
*Employees:* 18,100
*Sales:* $2.24 billion (2001)
*Stock Exchanges:* NASDAQ
*Ticker Symbol:* CFWY
*NAIC:* 484121 General Freight Trucking, Long-Distance, Truckload; 551112 Offices of Other Holding Companies

Consolidated Freightways Corporation ranks third among North America's leading long-haul, less-than-truckload (LTL) freight companies, which carry shipments for several customers in one vehicle. With a system of over 300 terminals, the company provides service across the United States, while its subsidiaries in Canada and Mexico are leading carriers in those countries. In addition to its continental services, the company offers international delivery to over 80 nations around the world. Consolidated Freightways Corporation was formed through the December 1996 spinoff of CF MotorFreight and four related companies from Consolidated Freightways, Inc. The old parent was renamed CNF Transportation, and the ''new'' firm carried on with a clarified focus on the LTL long-haul market segment. In a competitive, mature industry, CF is trying to stay a step ahead by offering premium services such as time and date specific delivery and satellite tracking of shipments. The firm's Redwood Systems subsidiary provides logistics services such as warehousing, contract hauling, and inventory management.

### *Depression-Era Foundations*

Consolidated Freightways was created in 1929 by Leland James, a 36-year-old entrepreneur who merged four Portland, Oregon, short-haul trucking companies into a single firm and began expanding the range of its operations. The trucking industry at that time was far from the dominating force it has since become; particularly in the West, a shortage of well-paved roads had retarded its growth until after World War I. The long-haul trucking business would require the eventual construction of a national system of interstate highways. Leland James's new trucking firm, therefore, concentrated on establishing its presence in Portland and the immediate surroundings, but meeting with considerable success it lengthened its routes and was soon carrying freight between many of the widely scattered cities of Oregon and Washington.

The onset of the Great Depression sparked a series of ferocious rate wars among truckers across the country. With a drop-off in tonnage and sharp downward pressure on rates, competition stiffened among the scores of trucking companies in the Pacific Northwest, many of which consisted of little more than a single vehicle and its hard-pressed owner. It was on these marginal competitors that the downturn weighed most heavily, while more substantial firms such as Consolidated were able to wait out the lean times and in some cases pick up additional business from customers in need of more reliable and efficient delivery than was offered by the railroads. Indeed, the real struggle shaping up in transportation was between the older railroads, whose strength lay in the long distance shipment of bulk goods to a limited number of destinations, and the nascent trucking companies, which could provide pinpoint delivery of smaller items wherever permitted by paved roads. As the latter were rapidly filling in to accommodate America's growing love of the automobile, truckers such as Consolidated had time on their side in the protracted battle with the railroads.

In 1935, the federal government stepped into the rather chaotic competition among truckers, placing interstate carriers under the general jurisdiction of the Interstate Commerce Commission (ICC), which for years had regulated the railroads. The Motor Carrier Act was indicative of the trucking industry's

### Company Perspectives:

*We have a well-tuned strategy, backed by a seasoned management team, and we're making measurable progress in attracting quality customers, reducing costs, and adjusting freight mix. Cost control has become a way of life at CF. The "Pride" program is the centerpiece and cost management extends throughout every part of our business. Effective cross-functional problem-solving teams are in place throughout CF. They will continue to analyze every aspect of planning and execution necessary to boost our revenues and yields. CF has faced difficult times in the past and emerged as a stronger company. In 1997 and 1998, we were the leading national LTL carrier in terms of profitability, and our plan is to return to that position again. While improving our performance, we are dedicated to meeting customer needs through superior service. The entire company shares in this commitment, from the CEO and president to our experienced teams of employees throughout CF's North American network.*

rapid growth, as the major firms now regularly transported goods across state lines and soon would be taking them across the entire country. Consolidated had already established itself as one of the leading truckers in the Northwest, with routes crisscrossing Washington, Oregon, and reaching down to the prosperous cities of California as well. It was not until the advent of World War II, however, that Consolidated enjoyed the remarkable growth that would characterize its history for the coming decades. With the major railroads overburdened by the demand for war material and personnel, truckers became a more vital part of the country's freight systems. Consolidated added dozens of new terminals throughout much of the western United States and by the war's end had extended its service as far east as Chicago, the nation's transport hub.

### *Postwar Era Brings Rapid Growth*

On the eve of the greatest expansion in the history of U.S. trucking, Consolidated's 1950 revenue stood at $24 million and its net income at $700,000, with the company operating 1,600 pieces of freight equipment. Leland James remained chairman of the company he had created, then one of the largest trucking firms in the western United States. True to its name, Consolidated had achieved much of its growth by means of acquisitions and mergers, a trend that would greatly accelerate as the trucking industry matured during the 1950s. In one respect, at least, the business was already mature, as the figures for Consolidated's 1950 income indicate. Trucking has always been a highly competitive, service-oriented industry, and despite the general rate regulation of the ICC, margins tend to remain very thin and net income stays low. The resulting premium on efficiency has tended to encourage the kind of horizontal combination that Consolidated pursued during the 1950s, by the end of which time the company had annexed 53 of its former competitors.

The majority of those acquisitions were made after 1955, when Leland James named Jack Snead president of Consolidated. Snead oversaw the rise of Consolidated from regional power to national leadership, not only extending the company's reach to the Atlantic Ocean but intensively building local service networks in each of the cities along Consolidated's routes. In addition, Consolidated adopted the trucking industry's more cooperative attitude toward the railroads, as the two modes of transport each specialized in those areas of the freight business for which they were best suited. Increasingly during the 1950s, truckers and railroads joined forces by means of the piggyback system, in which a standard-sized container was moved from truck to rail and back to truck for final delivery. Jack Snead led Consolidated into the piggyback business, and, less successfully, into fishyback, or truck-ship combinations. A sizable investment in Hawaiian Marine Freightways was abandoned within 24 months, but Consolidated nevertheless succeeded in establishing the beginnings of a sea link to complement its growing truck and truck-rail service.

### *Diversification into Manufacturing in the 1950s*

Consolidated also enjoyed the security of operating as its own builder of trucks and related equipment. Immediately after World War II, Leland James started Freightliner Corporation in Portland to supply Consolidated with the larger, lighter, and more sophisticated trucks and trailers increasingly needed to complete in the maturing freight industry. Freightliner originally built only for its parent company, but in 1951 it signed an agreement with White Motor Corporation of Ohio under which White would retail Freightliner trucks through its chain of dealerships across the country. The partnership proved successful for the next 25 years, with sales made at White dealerships returning a profit to Freightliner while allowing it to operate at a volume large enough to provide the economies of scale. Consolidated still had ready access to new trucks at the lowest possible cost.

To the established business at Freightliner, Jack Snead added other manufacturing concerns: Transicold Corporation (railway components) and Techni-Glas Corporation (glass-fiber products). Between its expanded truck lines and the newly acquired manufacturing subsidiaries, Consolidated's sales more than doubled during Snead's five-year tenure, hitting $146 million in 1959 and making Consolidated easily the largest common carrier in the United States. In order to oversee this suddenly complex organization, in 1956 Snead had moved corporate headquarters from Portland to Menlo Park, California, a San Francisco suburb, where company executives were close to Consolidated's bankers and underwriters. The company then employed nearly 11,000 people, operated 13,800 pieces of equipment in 34 states and Canada, and had made a name for itself as one of the most aggressive young firms in the transportation industry. It was also, as later developments revealed, in serious trouble.

### *Emphasis on LTL Emerges in the 1960s*

In 1960, a combination of recession and the inadequate integration of Consolidated's many businesses led to a $2.7 million year-end loss and the suspension of dividend payments. Jack Snead was asked to resign and in his place William G. White was named president and also chairman of Consolidated. White found that Consolidated's many acquisitions had been only rudimentarily integrated, with as many as five different

**Key Dates:**

**1929:** Consolidated Freightways, Inc. is founded by Leland James in Portland, Oregon.
**1935:** The federal government begins regulating interstate truckers.
**1955:** Jack Snead becomes president of Consolidated Freightways, Inc., beginning a period of acquisitions.
**1960:** William White replaces Snead and integrates the firm's loosely connected units.
**1981:** Consolidated sells its Freightliner manufacturing subsidiary.
**1989:** Consolidated acquires Emery Air Freight.
**1996:** CF MotorFreight and four other subsidiaries of Consolidated Freightways, Inc. are spun off as Consolidated Freightways Corporation.
**1998:** CF opens a joint venture in Mexico.

terminals serving a single city, and that several of the nontrucking businesses were performing poorly. The new chief executive began a drastic program aimed at correcting both problems, beginning with a new emphasis on coordinated control from the Menlo Park headquarters—no small feat for a nationwide company in the precomputer age. Traffic routes were better defined, terminals consolidated, and new financial controls elaborated for the far-flung enterprise. Most decisive of all, White committed his company to becoming a specialist in LTL shipment. LTL is generally more difficult than truckload shipping, requiring a higher level of coordination and efficiency from both staff and equipment, but Consolidated had already established a reputation in the field, and White decided to make LTL the company's own niche.

Along with these changes in the trucking business, White sold off a number of Consolidated's manufacturing and peripheral companies. Transicold and Youngstown Steel Car were both eventually sold, along with a household moving service, a piggyback leasing company, and a fledgling package division unable to sustain direct competition from United Parcel Service. The combined effect of these steps was outstanding: Consolidated's revenue increased about 15 percent per year during the 1960s and operating profits remained consistently above industry norm. Sales for 1969 reached $451 million, and Freightliner maintained its tradition of manufacturing excellence. At this point, White added two new wrinkles to the company's generally solid core in trucking: in 1969, Consolidated again ventured into the sea-borne container business, this time paying $25 million for 51 percent of Pacific Far East Line Inc., one of the pioneers in Pacific container shipping; the following year it entered the new field of air freight, forming CF AirFreight with initial service between three cities. Consolidated thus became one of the first companies to offer the beginnings of a true intermodal system that was able to transport containers by truck, rail, air, or sea.

The Pacific Far East Line investment was short-lived, however. A scant five years after buying into the company, Consolidated wrote off its investment, taking a $14 million charge at the bottom line for 1973. By that time, the trucking industry was plunged into the turmoil created by the Middle East oil embargo, when soaring gas and diesel prices threatened to ruin the large trucking firms. Fortunately the ICC responded with quick rate relief and the only net effect was to swell Consolidated's revenues to $800 million in 1974 and inaugurate a trend toward lighter, more fuel-efficient tractors and trucks at Freightliner. The latter was about to enter a tumultuous period in its own history. Not only did it have to contend with the new emphasis on fuel efficiency, the truck manufacturer also endured a rollercoaster sales cycle in 1974 and 1975, when a new federal law mandating an expensive brake system set off a rush of orders in 1974 and a near drought the following year. Freightliner became increasingly dissatisfied with the sales effort it was receiving from the White Motor dealerships, and in 1977 it severed the 25-year-old relationship and began to build a network of its own dealers and agents. With about ten percent of the U.S. market, Freightliner was known as a builder of relatively expensive, premium trucks, and apparently could not handle competition from the likes of International Harvester and Mack. In 1981, Consolidated announced the sale of Freightliner and its few other remaining manufacturing subsidiaries to Daimler-Benz for about $300 million. Daimler-Benz was already the number-one truck maker in the world and viewed the purchase of Freightliner as the easiest means of entry into the big U.S. market.

### *Trucking Deregulation in the 1980s*

There may well have been other considerations behind Consolidated's decision to sell its manufacturing assets. In 1980, the trucking industry was largely deregulated by U.S. president Jimmy Carter's administration; for the first time since 1935, truckers were free to set rates as they pleased, and most analysts predicted another round of frantic mergers and takeovers as the price competition took its toll. Ray O'Brien, new chief executive at Consolidated, took seriously the prospect of renewed rate wars and made a decision to strengthen his hand in trucking while abandoning the manufacturing business, in which Consolidated would never become a leader. The air freight business had grown, and by 1980 CF AirFreight had developed from a small forwarder into the number-three heavy air freight carrier in North America, with $100 million in annual revenues and an expanding service network.

Consolidated was able to create four regional trucking companies to specialize in overnight delivery. These Con-Way companies were doing $600 million in sales in the early 1990s and appeared to be well-positioned in regional markets, as did CF MotorFreight in its long-haul trucking business. Deregulation did indeed usher in an era of bitter competition in trucking, with some 54 percent of the players out of business within eight years, but Consolidated prospered mightily, due in part to its size and in part to the decision to concentrate most of its energies on trucking. Although freight rates were lower at decade's end than at the time of deregulation in 1980, Consolidated had doubled its long-haul business and firmed its hold on the trucking industry's top position.

### *Losses in the Early 1990s*

This prosperity was not long lived. In April 1989, Consolidated made an acquisition that performed poorly. Lary Scott, who had been promoted to president and CEO in 1988, decided to catapult his company to the top of the air freight ranks via the $458 million acquisition of Emery Air Freight Corporation. An industry leader doing about $1.2 billion in revenue, Emery's strengths in overseas transport were expected to compensate for CF AirFreight's weaknesses.

However, Emery had deficiencies of its own: its $306 million takeover of Purolator Courier Corporation in 1987 left it heavily laden with debt, and by 1990 the company was losing nearly $1 million a day, leaving Consolidated with a $41 million net loss and $684 million in debt. At the same time, Chemical Bank was clamoring for an up-front payment of $85 million on a $900 million loan it had arranged. Scott was asked to leave and Chairman Ray O'Brien asked Donald E. Moffitt, a former Consolidated executive, to come out of early retirement and replace his former rival as president and CEO. As Moffitt would later recall, Consolidated's predicament was ''god-awful.'' He suspended the corporation's common stock dividend payments, declined the Chemical Bank loan, and secured a scaled-back credit facility.

Together with Emery CEO Roger Curry, who was hired in 1991, they set out to reduce overhead and increase shipping volumes. Instead of duking it out with Federal Express, UPS, and others, Emery shifted its focus to overnight delivery of packages weighing more than 70 pounds. Layoffs reduced the operation's payroll by 2,000, slashing $200 million from overhead. Known as a morale-booster, Curry launched a profit-sharing program for management and nonunion workers that promised what Moffitt called ''a piece of the action.'' There was $17 million in net income to share by 1993. In 1994, the shaped-up shipper won a 10-year, $880 million contract with the U.S. Postal Service. An air freight boom cemented the turnaround, allowing Emery to boost its rates by more than 7 percent that year. By 1995, Emery had captured nearly one-fourth of the over-70-pound segment and was the air freight industry's most profitable firm.

In the meantime, Consolidated Freightways had encountered major challenges as well. Price wars and other pressures had shaved profit margins at the long-haul-trucking operation from 6.5 percent in 1988 to 1.5 percent in 1993, and a 24-day Teamsters strike pushed it $46 million into the red in 1994. However, the new labor agreement that came out of the strike did have one major concession: the union increased Consolidated's rail-freight allowance from 8 percent to 28 percent, thereby permitting the shipper to cut some of its costs by sending some parcels by train.

Some analysts questioned the future viability of the LTL industry as a whole, noting its mature two to three percent annual growth rate, a suicidal price war, and increasing competition from nonunion, regional upstarts. Industry observer Paul Schlesinger told *Financial World*'s Jennifer Reingold that ''long-haul carriers are the mainframes of the 1980s,'' destined to remain in existence, but in a much smaller role than they once knew. Moffitt blamed many of the industry's problems on discounting, calling it ''a cancer'' that ''spreads and feeds on itself.''

The disease took a heavy toll on Consolidated's long-haul business, which lost more than $125 million from 1992 through 1996, achieving profitability only once during that period. Moffitt transferred Curry to the trucking division in July 1994, joking to *Forbes*'s Kate Bohner Lewis that it was Curry's ''reward for fixing up Emery.'' In late 1996, the parent company elected to spin off CF MotorFreight and four other long-haul subsidiaries as Consolidated Freightways Corporation. The ''old'' Consolidated Freightways, Inc.—which retained its Con-Way Transportation Services, Emery Worldwide, and Menlo Logistics operations—was renamed CNF Transportation. The two companies began operating independently on December 3, 1996.

### *CF Begins Independent Operations: 1996–2002*

Bolstered by a cash infusion from a stock offering, the ''new'' Consolidated Freightways, or CF, emerged with little debt and an improved capital structure. Curry took on the task of turning CF's LTL infrastructure and expertise into a profit-generating enterprise. Success came quickly, as the company announced a $3.3 million profit in its first quarter of independent operation. Along with productivity improvements and cost-cutting, Curry relied on a teamwork-building program to improve CF's performance. In an effort to generate high employee morale, he introduced a stock grant program designed to make all eligible employees shareholders in the company.

CF recognized that only by offering innovative services with an exceptional focus on customer satisfaction could it hold its own in a fiercely competitive industry. In January 1997, Redwood Systems was formed as a third-party logistics management company offering complete supply-chain management. The new subsidiary would give CF the opportunity to better understand its customers' operations. Later in the year, the company introduced CF PrimeTime Air, a service specializing in time-definite deliveries. The company appeared well-positioned at year's end to be a profitable leader in its industry. CF reported a net income of $20.4 million on sales of $2.30 billion for 1997.

The profitable period continued into 1998, when the company reported a net income of $26.3 million. CF's reliability was given a boost in February of that year, when the company signed a five-year contract with the Teamsters union that put a moderate wage increase in place. The agreement stopped the flight of customers to CF's nonunion competitors, as worries about a repeat of the 1994 Teamsters strike subsided. CF also enhanced its service to Mexico in 1998 with the formation of a joint venture with the Mexican holding company Alfri Loder. The agreement made CF the first U.S. trucking company to own and operate a subsidiary in Mexico under the investment provisions of the North American Free Trade Agreement. In the past, freight had been handed off to a connection carrier at the Mexican border. This arrangement would be continued, but CF would now be a 49 percent owner of the Mexican carrier, greatly increasing the reliability of its LTL shipping in Mexico.

Ill-advised decisions in 1999 inaugurated a period of poor financial performance at CF. The company suffered that year from a decision to take on marginal freight, including freight from carriers that had gone out of business. In addition, the switch to a new outsourced information technology system required a large investment. As a result, net income for 1999 was $2.7 million on sales of $2.38 billion.

CF hoped to put its performance back on track in 2000. Roger Curry retired in January of that year, and a new management team met in June of that year to develop a profitable strategy. The new CEO was Patrick Blake, a 30-year CF employee whose had first begun loading and driving for the company in 1971. As part of its turnaround strategy, CF sold its Menlo Park headquarters in August 2000 and moved to new offices in Vancouver, Washington. The company also bought FirstAir Inc.,a Minnesota-based air freight forwarder, in an acquisition designed to improve CF's position in the expedited-transportation market. The new air division was renamed CF AirFreight, recalling the company that had operated before the 1989 acquisition of Emery. In addition, CF brought in outside experts to help it use its terminals more efficiently. Still, Blake emphasized that a turnaround would take some time. The company reported a net loss of $7.6 million for 2000.

Unfortunately, CF's performance only worsened in 2001 as a declining economy and the impact of the September terrorist attacks in New York pushed the company's net loss to $104.3 million for the year. The company's administrative staff was cut from 900 to 800 in June of that year, and hundreds of other employees were laid off at sites across North America. The loss of a major account late in 2001 contributed to a net loss of $36.5 million for the first quarter of 2002. Nevertheless, Blake found reason for optimism as the company secured a $45 million loan early in 2002. The company showed it was still committed to long-term growth as it entered into an agreement to acquire all of its Mexican joint venture. Blake continued to stress basic cost-cutting and productivity-increasing strategies and he looked for profit in the long term.

### *Principal Subsidiaries*

Canadian Freightways, Ltd. (Canada); Epic Express (Canada); Milne & Craighead (Canada); Redwood Systems; CF Mexico; CF AirFreight.

### *Principal Competitors*

Yellow Corporation; Roadway Express.

### *Further Reading*


Armbruster, William, ''CF to Buy Air Freight Forwarder,'' *Journal of Commerce*, May 16, 2000, p. 13.

Gardner, Steven, ''Slow Economy Slams Vancouver, Wast-Based Consolidated Freightways,'' *Knight-Ridder/Tribune Business News*, September 4, 2001.

Hall, Kevin G., ''Trucking Company Puts Nafta Theory into Trade Practice,'' *Journal of Commerce*, October 16, 1998, p. 1A.

Heaster, Randolph, ''Black Ink Is Back At Consolidated Freightways,'' *Kansas City Star*, June 23, 1997.

Isidore, Chris, ''Analysts Speculate: Roadway's Move Cold Spur LTL Merger,'' *Journal of Commerce and Commercial*, August 25, 1995, p. 2B.

——, ''A Turnaround at Consolidated,'' *Journal of Commerce*, April 24, 1997, p. 8B.

Johnson, Gregory S., ''Teamsters, Truck Lines Agree on Tentative Pact,'' *Journal of Commerce*, February 10, 1998, p. 1A.

Lewis, Kate Bohner, ''Full Circle,'' *Forbes*, March 27, 1995, pp. 56–7.

Mathews, Anna Wilde, ''Trucking Firms Hauling Small Loads See Smoother Ride,'' *Wall Street Journal*, September 26, 1996, p. B9.

Reingold, Jennifer, ''Halftime Hubris,'' *Financial World*, March 1, 1994, pp. 24–7.


—Jonathan Martin
—updates: April Dougal Gasbarre and Sarah Ruth Lorenz

# Coop Schweiz Genossenschaftsverband

**Thiersteinerallee 12**
**Postfach 2550**
**CH-4002 Basel**
**Switzerland**
**Telephone: (+41) 61-336-66-66**
**Fax: (+41) 61-336-60-40**
**Web site: http://www.coop.ch**

*Cooperative*
*Incorporated:* 1890 as Union Suisse des Sociétés de Consommation
*Employees:* 46,197
*Sales:* CHF 13.6 billion ($8.2 billion)(2001)
*NAIC:* 445110 Supermarkets and Other Grocery (Except Convenience) Stores; 445120 Convenience Stores; 447110 Gasoline Stations with Convenience Stores; 522110 Commercial Banking; 522120 Savings Institutions

Coop Schweiz Genossenschaftsverband is Switzerland's second-largest food products retailer, behind fellow cooperative Migros. Coop is also the country's leading electronics and appliance retailer through subsidiary Interdiscount/Radio TV Steiner. Together the Coop retail empire consists of nearly 1,600 convenience stores (including many with filling stations), supermarkets, superstores, and other retail formats, such as hardware stores and the Vitality health and beauty products chain, for a total sales surface area of nearly 1.2 million square meters. Although much of the group's sales are made through major brand products, one of Coop's chief selling points is its range of environmentally and socially conscious labels, including Coop Naturaplan, a range of organic food products; the textiles and cosmetics line Coop Naturaline; appliance and other products under Coop Oecoplan; and the socially conscious brand of Cooperacion/Max Havelaar import products. The cooperative group manufactures many of the products sold under its brand names. Together these products generated more than CHF 1 billion in 2001, out of group total sales of CHF 13.6 billion. The year 2001 also reflected the first year of the ''new'' Coop when in April the group, which then consisted of the Coop and 14 regionally operating cooperating societies, merged together to form the single Coop business. Coop has also redirected its focus on its food products and other retail products, selling off its majority shareholding in banking group Coop Bank and selling its agricultural subsidiary in 2000.

### *Swiss Cooperative Force at the Turn of the 20th Century*

The cooperative movement spread throughout Europe during the mid-19th century when the developing urban working class, cut off from traditional agrarian food sources, began grouping together in order to assure themselves of quality foods at fair prices. The first cooperative was founded in Rochdale, England, in 1844; its principles of honesty and democracy were soon adopted by societies in other European countries and around the world. As the cooperative movement developed, many cooperative societies began to band together to found intermediate wholesale societies in order to negotiate bulk purchases at lower prices. These wholesale societies soon entered manufacturing as well, supplying goods to their member societies.

In Switzerland, various attempts were made in the second half of the 19th century to group together the rapidly growing numbers of cooperative societies, most often called consumer societies until the codification of the cooperative society under Swiss legislation in 1883. In 1890, a group of 27 cooperative societies met to form a new group, the Union Suisse des Sociétés de Consommation (USC). By the end of that year, USC had grown to include 43 member societies. Two years later, USC had grown sufficiently to open a central bulk products storage and distribution center. The following year, USC officially adopted its status as a cooperative society, and in 1897 USC joined the International Cooperative Alliance.

USC began publishing a newsletter for its members that same year. This newsletter was replaced in 1902 by the cooperative's own newspaper, the *Genossenschaftliches Volksblatt*, later to be renamed the *Coop Zeitung*. A French-language edition, *Cooperation*, followed in 1904; in 1906, the cooperative

**Company Perspectives:**

*Coop's ambition is to be the best large retailer in Switzerland and the closest to its clients. That is why Coop responds to the leading consumer trends in dynamic quality of life, freshness, health and convenience.*

launched an Italian-language edition as well. By then, USC had purchased a new warehouse, in Wülfingen, bought in 1900. In 1905, the cooperative group added a new chemical laboratory in order to provide testing and control procedures for its food products. Two years later, USC built a new warehouse site in Pratteln, which included coffee-roasting, milling, and other facilities.

USC followed the international cooperative movement in adding new services for its members, including an insurance component, later to be renamed Coop Assurance, in 1909. The following year, USC opened its own printing facility in order to support the growing number of subscribers to its newspapers. Then in 1912, USC entered production of footwear with the construction of its own factory. That same year, USC began offering banking services. The group also acquired the Zürcher Satdtmühle, then the country's largest grain mill.

After forming the Bell S.A. alliance for distributing meats to its member societies in 1914, USC entered dairy production in 1916 with the creation of the Coopérative Laitière des Sociétés Suisses de Consommation. The company also entered farming, acquiring a number of farms, then founded the Coopérative Suisse pour la Culture Maraichère (SGG) in 1918 for its vegetable growing activity. The following year, USC began producing furniture as well.

USC's expansion continued in the 1920s with the founding of a the cooperative's own vacation colony in 1921 and the creation of a training academy in 1923. In 1927, USC formalized its banking services, creating a new subsidiary, the Banque Centrale Cooperative. In 1935, USC changed its name to Union Suisse des Coopératives de Consommation. At that time, also the group began promoting its own branded products under the Coop name.

World War II interrupted USC's growth. The years following the war, however, were a time of brisk economic growth and vast changes in the retail sector. One of the most important of these was the widespread adoption of the so-called American supermarket style of self-service stores. The first of USC's coop members opened a self-service supermarket in Zurich in 1948. Before long, the concept had conquered nearly all of the Swiss grocery market.

### *Streamlining in the 1970s*

By 1950, USC's membership numbered more than 570 individual cooperative societies. This was to prove to be the highest number in the group's existence as in ensuing years the group moved toward encouraging mergers among its member societies as well as absorbing a large number of societies into the USC structure itself. USC also began to reorganize its distribution network, creating 30 regional warehouses and distribution centers throughout Switzerland in 1954. At the same time, the group moved to standardizing other practices among its member societies, such as the creation of a single system of member rebates offered throughout its network of stores, which topped 3,200 in 1960. The group also adopted a single logo in 1960, placing its members' stores under the Coop brand.

By 1965, USC had begun to develop its first national sales strategy and rolled out its first television advertising campaigns. Yet by then, USC's dominance in the Swiss retail food market had been challenged by fast-rising Migros, which became the country's leading retailer in the mid-1960s. USC responded by reorganizing its member base, encouraging a wider scale of mergers. By the end of the decade, the number of member societies had already been scaled back to 400, but in 1969 USC went still further to adopt a plan that called for the number of its member societies to be reduced to just 40 by the middle of the 1970s.

An important part of the group's strategy, which included a continued reorganization of its distribution and purchasing operations into a centralized structure, came with the adoption of a new name, Coop Schweiz (alternatively Coop Suisse). Meanwhile, while merging its member societies, Coop continued to expand into other areas, such as opening a new cheese-making facility in Kirchberg and launching a new subsidiary, Coop City SA, to govern the group's move into larger, department-store formats.

By 1979, Coop had succeeded in reducing its membership ranks to just 67 societies. The group then launched the second phase of its consolidation drive, pledging to scale back its number of member societies to just 40, supported by 18 distribution centers, by 1982—a goal the group was to meet by 1983. By then, Coop had branched out into a new product area when the 1980 acquisition of Radio TV Steiner took it into the home electronics market. The following year, Coop added a travel component as well, taking a 40 percent stake in Popularis Tours (subsequently sold to Swiss travel leader Kuoni in 1990).

Coop moved into other new areas in the 1980s, such as hardware stores, with the formation of Baticentre Coop in 1984, and florist shops, with the launch of Centre de Fleurs Coop in 1985. The group once again returned to its drive to merge its member societies, beginning a new plan which called for the reduction of the number of member societies to just 18, based around its 18 regionally operating warehouse and distribution centers.

### *Restructuring for the New Century*

At the end of the 1980s, Coop launched a new label, Coop Oecoplan, for its paper goods and appliances range. This was to be the first of the company's environmentally and socially conscious brands—which became the thrust of the group's own-label products in the 1990s. That brand was joined in 1992 by the Max Havelaar/Cooperación label, which promoted social and environmental responsibility among the group's import products. Two more labels appeared in 1994, the organic foods brand Coop Naturaplan and the textiles and cosmetics range Coop Naturaline.

## Key Dates:

**1890:** Founding of the Union Suisse des Sociétés de Consommation (USC), which grouped 43 cooperative society members by the end of the year.
**1893:** The group formally adopts its status as a cooperative society.
**1909:** The co-op begins offering insurance services to members.
**1912:** USC offers banking services to its members, forming the basis of the future Coop Bank.
**1935:** The group changes name to Union Suisse des Coopératives de Consommation.
**1948:** The first member store adopts American-style self-service supermarket format.
**1969:** The co-op launches its first merger plan in order to reduce the number of member societies and changes its name to Coop Schweiz.
**1980:** The group acquires Radio TV Steiner to enter retail consumer electronics market.
**1989:** Coop Schweiz launches the first of its environmentally and socially conscious labels, Coop Oecoplan.
**1992:** The launch of Max Havelaar/Cooperación import products brand.
**1993:** Coop Naturaplan organic foods label and Naturaline textiles and appliances brand are launched.
**1994:** The group acquires IMPO Import Parfumieren and furniture store chain TopTip.
**1996:** Coop acquires Interdiscount to become Switzerland's leading home electronics retailer.
**2001:** "CoopForte" streamlining initiative results in a centralized board of directors, a focus on retailing, and the Coop name for all co-op members.

Toward the mid-1990s, Coop had already taken on the aspects of a unified company rather than a grouping of independent societies. In 1994, the group began a series of acquisitions, including those of IMPO Import Parfumerien and TopTip, a chain of furniture stores. The following year, Coop bought up Steinfels, a manufacturer of detergents and cleaners for the industrial and public sectors. Then in 1996, Coop added the K3000 chain of supermarkets. That same year, the company acquired the Swiss operations of the Interdiscount consumer electronics retail group, merging that with its Radio TV Steiner stores to create the Swiss home electronics leader.

By then, Coop was moving toward transforming itself into a single, centrally operated entity. The group adopted a new management structure, grouping its management under a central board of directors, which was then given decision-making stature. Then, in 1997, Coop launched a new merger plan, called "Regioforte," that called for a reduction of its member societies, by then just 14, to a maximum of eight. Yet resistance from a number of the group's members forced the group to abandon that plan. Instead, a new plan, called "CoopForte," was put into place in 1998 that called for the reduction of the entire group to just a single entity by 2001. As part of that restructuring, the group also began shedding a number of activities in order to focus on its core business of retailing. As such, Coop sold off its cheese-making facility in 1998, then sold its controlling share of Coop Banque to Banque Cantonale de Bâle in 2000. At the same time, Coop ended its farming activity.

The new, streamlined Coop celebrated its first year with rising sales, topping CHF 13.6 billion for the year. A significant portion of those sales by then came from its own-brand labels, which topped CHF 1 billion in sales, beating the group's sales forecasts by two years. At the same time, the group celebrated its two-millionth member. In August 2001, Coop launched its own Internet-based home delivery service. Meanwhile, Coop then debuted its newest store concept, the large-scale Mégastore Coop, the first of which opened in Crissier, near Lausanne, in October 2001. The group also reinforced its printing and publishing wing with the acquisition of a 50 percent share in Betty Bossy Verlags AG, the leader publisher of cookbooks and cooking magazines in Switzerland. Coop was prepared to greet the 21st century as a streamlined retailing powerhouse, while remaining committed to its founders' cooperative ideals.

### *Principal Subsidiaries*

Bell Holding AG; Argo AG; Coop Mineralöl AG; CWK AG; Chocolats Halba AG; Impo AG; Interdiscount/Radio TV Steiner AG; Nutrex AG; Pasta Gala SA; Reismühle Brunnen AG; Steinfels Cleaning Systems AG; Swissmill; SILAG; Rhein Terminal AG; TopTip AG; Betty Bossy Verlags AG (50%).

### *Principal Competitors*

Metro Holding AG; Maus Freres SA; Migros-Genossenschafts-Bund.

### *Further Reading*

"Avec l'arrivée de Coop, la concurrence dans la distribution alimentaire sur Internet se durcit," *Le Temps*, August 30, 2001.
"Coop beteiligt sich an Betty Bossy," *Neue Zurcher Zeitung*, November 24, 2001.
"Les deux géants Migros et Coop ont encore accru leur domination sur le marche du commerce de detail l'année dernière," *Agefi Suisse*, July 4, 2001.

—M.L. Cohen

# AMORIM

# Corticeira Amorim, Sociedade Gestora de Participaço es Sociais, S.A.

**Edificio Amorim**
**Rua de Meladas 380**
**Apartado 20**
**4536-902 Mozelos VFR Codex**
**Portugal**
**Telephone: (+351) 22 747 5400**
**Fax: (+351) 22 747 5410**
**Web site: http://www.amorim.com**

*Public Company*
*Incorporated:* 1922 as Amorim e Irmãos Lda.
*Employees:* 4,190
*Sales:* EUR 481.8 million ($385.44 million) (2000)
*Stock Exchanges:* Lisbon
*Ticker Symbol:* COR
*NAIC:* 321999 All Other Miscellaneous Wood Product Manufacturing

Corticeira Amorim, Sociedade Gestora de Participaço es Sociais, S.A. is the world's leading producer of cork and cork products, including corks and stoppers for wine, port, champagne, and other alcoholic beverages; wall coverings and floor coverings; and other products, such as cork gaskets for the automotive industry. Corks and stoppers nonetheless represent the largest part of the company's production, which tops 3.5 billion corks produced each year and distributed through a worldwide distribution network in 19 countries. Corticeira Amorim is vertically integrated, controlling production from the raw material to the finished product. The company has grown in large part because of its ability to achieve economies of scale—using scrap and non-bottle graded cork as the basis of its diversified cork products range. The company produces some 75 percent of Portugal's cork and holds a 15 percent share of the worldwide market. Beyond cork, the Amorim Group, under holding company Amorim Investimentos e Participaço es (AIP), has expanded strongly since the 1990s, diversifying into such areas as tourism (the company owns more than 25 hotels), real estate, insurance, textiles, banking, temporary employment services, telecommunications (through Telecel), and even the oil industry, through its shareholding in GALP, Portugal's leading oil company. Corticeira Amorim is one of the six chief subholdings under AIP and its largest revenue producer, with revenues of nearly EUR 500 million per year. Listed on the Lisbon stock exchange, Corticeira Amorim remains nonetheless controlled by the founding Amorim family. Américo Amorim, longtime chairman and chief architect of Corticeira Amorim's growth in the second half of the 20th century, retired in 2001 and was replaced by Antonio Amorim, representing the fourth generation of Amorims to lead the cork company.

## *Stopping Starts in the 19th Century*

French monk Dom Perignon was credited with being the first to use cork to seal his bottles of sparkling wine in the 17th century, yet cork had been used as long ago as pre-common era Egypt for its airtight, water-tight properties. Cork was derived from the bark of a species of oak tree specific to the Mediterranean basin, and especially concentrated in Portugal and to a lesser extent in Spain. The first cork factories developed in the late 18th century, but the cork stopper industry grew strongly during the 19th century in parallel with the wine and port industries. Although cork remained useful for a variety of other products and applications—ranging from fishing bobbers to flooring—it came into widest use as the material for bottle stoppers.

Despite its position as primary source of raw cork, Portugal's lack of industrial infrastructure meant that nearly 80 percent of its raw cork was shipped overseas for transformation, a situation that was to last until well into the 20th century. Nonetheless, the production of Portugal's alcoholic beverage specialty, port, stimulated a cottage industry of small cork producers by the middle of the 19th century.

One of the new cork makers was Antonio Alves Amorim, who opened a cork stopper factory in Lisbon in 1870. While

**Company Perspectives:**

*In the threshold of a new millennium, the major concern of the Amorim Group is the deepening of some of its current priorities: to extend and reinforce the Group both in the national and the international contexts; to ensure the training and motivation of its staff; the respect for Ecology and the Environment.*

Amorim, and three workers, provided the manpower, financial backing came from one of the region's wealthy and politically powerful families. After 30 years at the factory, Amorim and his backers became embroiled in a legal dispute over the sharing of profits—a dispute that Amorim lost. Amorim then retired, at the age of 78, to the village of Lamas.

Yet Amorim's wife, 33 years his junior, was determined to rebuild the family business. In 1908, she constructed a shed at the back of their house and installed two cork stopper machines. Joined by her sons, the Amorim family grew quickly—by 1914 the company operated 17 stopper machines. The family business continued to grow and by 1922 production was moved to a new purpose-built factory. At that time the company officially incorporated as Amorim e Irmãos Lda. The company counted nine shareholders, all Amorim brothers. In that year, family patriarch Antonio Amorim died.

Civil wars in Algeria and Spain, meanwhile, were devastating those countries' cork oak forests. The cork oak was in fact a somewhat fragile resource—it took 40 years for a cork oak to reach maturity, then another nine years before it was able to yield its first cork harvest. The destruction of its neighbors' cork oak forests made Portugal the center of the world's cork production.

The Amorim brothers—only five of whom were directly active in the company—were quick to seize on this new opportunity. By the 1930s the company had grown to become one of Portugal's largest stopper producers. In 1935, the company was able to build a new and larger factory, this time in Rossio, at the heart of Portugal's cork oak plantation. Much of the country's raw cork harvest had by then come under control of foreign companies, which exported the raw cork. By moving close to the cork oak forests, Amorim was able to cut out its reliance on middlemen and purchase raw cork directly from local producers.

Yet Amorim e Irmãos was nearly wiped out as a fire completely destroyed its warehouse and factory in March 1944. The Amorim brothers—José, Henrique, Américo, Ana, and Rosa—quickly rebuilt, however, and production resumed before the end of that year.

## *King of Cork in the 1980s*

The next generation of the Amorim family, brothers José, Antonio, Joaquim, and especially Américo, entered the business in 1950. The new generation of Amorims were to transform the country and the Portuguese cork industry over the next 40 years. Led by Américo, who was later to be dubbed "the King of Cork," the company stepped up its production to meet the postwar era's boom in demand. An important part of the company's success came with its increasing vertical integration—before long the company controlled not only its production and distribution, but also had acquired the harvesting rights to a growing area of cork oak forests and plantations.

Yet Amorim's biggest innovation at the time came with the diversification of the company's operations. Manufacturing of cork stoppers produced a great deal of scrap cork—as much as 75 percent of the raw crop. Much of the waste cork was made up of dark cork considered unsuitable for stopper use. As Amorim's business grew in the 1950s, it found itself confronted with growing levels of scrap cork. The company began to look for ways to make use of its scrap cork.

In 1963, Amorim inaugurated a new factory for the production of cork agglomerates and other crushed cork products, including flooring and insulation, as well as gaskets and other anti-vibration products for the automotive industry. The company then incorporated this new subsidiary as Corticeira Amorim SA. In 1966, the company built a new factory dedicated to the production of thermal and acoustic insulation products, which made use especially of agglomerates made from dark cork.

The 1960s also saw Amorim's first moves to establish international operations. In 1960, the company opened a trading office in Brazil as it sought entry into the South American market. In 1968, Amorim opened a warehouse and formed a partnership with a local company in Vienna, Austria, and began exporting its cork products to the Eastern Bloc countries. This partnership was followed in the same year by the creation of a joint venture in Hungary, Hungarokork Amorim Rt.

In the 1970s, Amorim began to look beyond Portugal for its raw cork needs. In 1972 the company acquired Comatral (Compagnie Marocaine de Transformation du Liége) in Morocco. By then Amorim had succeeded in transforming the Portuguese cork industry—by the early 1970s, half of the country's cork exports were now industrial products, rather than the raw cork itself.

Amorim was spared by the Portuguese revolution of 1974 that ended the Salazar dictatorship. Despite the nationalization of most of the country's industries, the relatively small cork industry was left untouched. Previously the company's expansion had been hampered by government restrictions. With the installation of a new regime, the company now was able to step up its industrial and international expansion.

In 1976 Amorim moved into Spain, acquiring Seville-based Samec. Then, in 1979, the company launched a new subsidiary, Ipocork, later renamed Amorim Revestimentos, which began producing cork-based paving and covering products. By then Amorim had become one of the world's leading producers of cork stoppers for wine and port and other products. In 1983, the company added the champagne category with the inauguration of a new subsidiary, Champcork—Rolhas de Champanhe SA.

## *Diversified and International for the 21st Century*

Amorim's diversification slowly began to expand beyond its core cork business. In 1979, the Amorim family entered the insurance world, setting up Albertina Ferreira de Amorim. That

## Key Dates:

**1870:** Antonio Alves Amorim establishes a cork stopper production factory for the Lisbon port wine industry.
**1908:** Amorim's wife and children launch a new cork stopper business in Lamas.
**1922:** The company is incorporated as Amorim e Irmãos Lda. with the nine Amorim brothers as shareholders.
**1935:** A new factory is established in Rossio, placing the company in the heart of the cork oak growing region.
**1960:** A marketing and distribution subsidiary is opened in Brazil to enter the South American market.
**1963:** The company establishes Corticeira Amorim for production of diversified cork-based products.
**1968:** The company opens a warehouse in Vienna, Austria, and a joint venture in Hungary to enter Eastern Bloc countries.
**1972:** The company acquires Comatral of Morocco to tap into the cork production industry in that country.
**1976:** Samec, based in Seville, Spain, is acquired, adding cork production facilities in the second largest cork production market.
**1979:** The company launches Ipocork cork paving subsidiary.
**1983:** The company launches a champagne stopper subsidiary, Champcork.
**1988:** Amorim forms a new holding company, Amorim Investimentos, regrouping its cork operations under Corticeira Amorim.
**1989:** The company acquires cork-flooring producer Wicanders Group, based in Sweden.
**1992:** The company acquires Carl Ed. Meyer of Germany and begins a program of acquiring cork distributors and producers in 30 countries.
**1996:** A code of practice designed to eliminate TCA tainting is adopted.
**1998:** The company acquires Inter Champagne and General Cork, boosting its champagne and technical stoppers production.
**2000:** The company inaugurates a new state-of-the-art production facility that claims to enable TCA-free cork production.

business was followed in 1981 by a major shareholding in Sociedade Portuguesa de Investimento. In 1983, the company formed a trade subsidiary, Comércio de Importa ça o. The privatization of Portugal's banking industry in the mid-1980s led the company to establish Banco Comercial Português.

Amorim's increasingly diverse holdings led the family to restructure the company in 1988. In that year, a new holding company was put into place—Amorim Investimentos e Participaço es. The companies comprising Amorim's cork and cork-based production were placed under Corticeira Amorim. That division grew in 1989 with the acquisition of Sweden's Wicanders Group, a maker of cork flooring products. In 1992, Amorim began a policy of buying up other cork producers and distributors, beginning with Carl Ed. Meyer GmbH in Germany. That acquisition program was to place Amorim in more than 30 countries by mid-decade.

The Amorim holding company meanwhile accelerated its diversification moves, entering the real estate world in 1989 and launching a tourism division with the construction of its first hotel in that same year, followed by the acquisition of a casino one year later. The company also had purchased shares in two textile producers, Veldec and Velpor. Other investments included the launch of Telece—Telecomunicaço es Pessoais, Portugal's first private cellular phone company, in 1991, and the purchase of a share of Portuguese petroleum leader GALP in 1992.

Cork remained at the center of the Amorim empire, however. By the end of the 1990s, the company was not only the world's largest maker of corks and cork stoppers, it also had captured 75 percent of the world's cork flooring market and 95 percent of the market for cork gaskets. Yet corks and stoppers remained its chief revenue generator. In 1993, the company began development of a new system for cleaning and producing cork that aimed at eliminating the chemical TCA (2–4–6 Trichloroanisole), which had long plagued the wine industry—minute amounts of TCA were enough to taint wine and destroy its flavor. An estimated one in 12 bottles of wine was said to be "corked" by TCA.

The TCA problem came to a head in the late 1990s as the wine industry—led by the large supermarket chains—began looking for alternatives to the traditional cork-based stopper. The introduction of new cork type based on synthetic materials presented an immediate challenge to Amorim. While producers and purchasers of high-end wines and champagnes continued to insist on traditional cork stoppers, a growing number of wine growers, bottlers, and distributors—especially in the "new" wine markets of California, Chile, Australia, and elsewhere—were adopting synthetic stoppers, and even screw-caps (which were acknowledged as the best way to seal a bottle of wine). This development was aided by widespread consumer indifference—the majority of consumers barely noticed whether a stopper was cork or synthetic. Many wine drinkers were barely able to recognize the taste of corked wine. Meanwhile, for wines meant to be drunk young, which accounted for the vast majority of the world's wine production, synthetic stoppers were considered a perfectly acceptable means of sealing bottles. Nonetheless, natural cork continued to be considered a requirement for wines expected to age in their bottles for many years.

Amorim fought back, leading research efforts to understand TCA and to develop means of eliminating the chemical from its corks. In 2000 the company opened a new state-of-the-art production facility that the company claimed was able to eliminate TCA entirely. The company also continued to boost its position as market leader, through such acquisitions as Inter Champagne—Fabricante de Rolhas de Champanhe and General Cork, both acquired in 1998.

"King of Cork" Américo Amorim stepped down from the chairmanship of Corticeira Amorim in 2001, although he remained chairman of the parent holding company. Antonio Amorim, who had been in charge of the company's Amorim & Irmãos subsidiary and who represented the fourth generation of the Amorim family to enter the business, took over as chairman of Corticeira Amorim. With worldwide production and consumption of wine rising steadily at the turn of the century, Amorim expected to remain an industry fixture.

### Principal Subsidiaries

Alcorex - Sociedade Tecnica de Corticas, Lda; Amorim & Irmäos (Madeira) Inv. E. Part. Fin. S.A.; Amorim & Irmäos II, Ind. e Comercio de Cortica, S.A.; Amorim & Irmäos, S.A.; Amorim & Irmäos SGPS, S.A.; Amorim & Irmäos Servicos, S.A.; Amorim & Irmäos-IV, S.A.; Amorim & Irmäos-V, S.A.; Amorim (U.K.) Ltd.; Amorim Argentina, SA; Amorim Benelux BV; Amorim Cork Australia, Pty. Ltd.; Amorim Cork Deutschland GmbH & Co. KG; Amorim Cork Distribution Netherlands, BV; Amorim Cork Internacional S.A.; Amorim Cork Italia, Spa.; Amorim Cork, GmbH; Amorim Corks America; Amorim Deutschland, GMBH; Amorim Flooring (Switzerland) AG; Amorim Flooring Austria GesmbH; Amorim Flooring Denmark A/S; Amorim Florestal - Comercio e Exploracao, SA; Amorim Florestal Espanha, SA; Amorim France S.A.; Amorim Iberica Decoracao, SA; Amorim Industrial Solutions - Industria de Cortica e Borracha I, S.A.; Amorim Industrial Solutions - Industria de Cortica e Borracha II, S.A.; Amorim Industrial Solutions Inc.; Amorim Industrial Solutions, SGPS, SA; Amorim Isolamentos S.A.; Amorim Plus- Aglomerados de Cortica S.A.; Amorim Revestimentos, SA; Amorim Sverige AB; Amorim Wood Supplies, GmbH; Amorona-Sociedade de Investimentos, SA; Aplifin-Aplicacoes Financeiras, SA; Auscork Holding, GMBH; C.D.M.-Composite Damping Material, SA; Carl Ed. Meyer Korken GmbH & Co.; Champcork S.A.- Rolhas de Champanhe, SA; Comatral-C. Marocaine de Trasnf. du Liege, SA; Cork International; Cork Producers, Suppliers & Co., Ltd.; Corkline Services, AG; Cortam - Corticeira Amorim Maroc, SA; Corticeira Amorim Algarve Lda.; Corticeira Amorim Industria S.A.; Cortrade Cork Trading, AG; Drauvil Europea, SL; F.P. Cork; Ginpar S.A.; Goma Cork Trading, AG; Hungarocork Amorim, RT; Industria Corchera, S.A.; Infocork - Comercio e Servicos, Lda.; Infocork USA, Inc.; Inter Champanhe-Fab. de Rolhas de Champanhe, S.A.; International Cork Services, AG; Irmorim Imobiliaria, SA; Itexcork-Ind. de Transf. e Exportacao de Cortica Lda.; KHB Kork Handels Beteiligung GmbH; Korken Schiesser GMBH; Labcork-Laboratorio Central do Grupo Amorim, SA; Lusoliege SARL; Manuel Pereira de Sousa; Moraga-Comercio e Servicos, SA; Ofequipa-Manuntecao e Equip. Industrias, Lda.; Osi-Organizacao e Sistemas Informaticos Lda.; Portocork America, Inc.; Portocork Internacional S.A.; Portocork South Africa, Ltd.; Praemium Cork Holding, GMBH; Prataplas-Industria de Plasticos, Lda.; Proli SARL; Raro-Industrias e Comercializacao de Cortica, SA; Real Cork Trading, AG; S.A. Maison Pairot; S.A.M. Clignet; S.C.I. Friedland; Salco Industrial Corchera, SL; Societe Fabrique Liege de Tabarka; Sopac - Soc. Portuguesa de Alom. de Cortica, Lda; Vasconcelos & Lyncke Australia Pty, Ltd.; Vasconcelos & Lyncke Lda.; Victor Y Amorim, SRL.

### Principal Competitors

Sabate Diosos SA; Supreme Corq Inc.; Cortex AS.

### Further Reading

"Family Values: Portuguese Business," *Economist,* June 3, 1995, p. 60.

"It Grows on Trees," *Economist,* May 4, 1996, p. 64.

Reid, T.R., "Cork Growers Hope Incomes Don't Crumble with Advent of Plastic Stoppers," *Dallas Morning News,* December 12, 1999, p. 28A.

Roberts, Martin, "Plastic Inflow Threatens to Seal Fate of Cork," *Birmingham Post,* August 28, 2000, p. 10.

—M.L. Cohen

# Creo Inc.

**3700 Gilmore Way**
**Burnaby, British Columbia**
**V5G 4M1**
**Canada**
**Telephone: (604) 451-2700**
**Fax: (604) 437-9891**
**Web site: http://www.creo.com**

*Public Company*
*Incorporated:* 1983
*Employees:* 4,000
*Sales:* $656.5 million (2001)
*Stock Exchanges:* NASDAQ Toronto
*Ticker Symbols:* CREO; CRE
*NAIC:* 334610 Manufacturing Magnetic and Optical Recording Media; 511210 Software Publishers; 334410 Semiconductor and Other Electronic Components Manufacturing

Creo Inc. and its principal operating division, CreoScitex, is a world leader in creating solutions for the graphic arts industry. CreoScitex manufactures more than 300 products. Its offerings include professional digital cameras; inkjet proofers; thermal imaging devices for film, plates, and proofs; color and copydot scanning systems; and prepress workflow software. CreoScitex is also a supplier of on-press imaging technology and components for digital offset presses. CreoScitex products are available through direct and indirect sales channels managed by distribution units in the U.S., Belgium, Hong Kong, and Japan.

### *Beginnings in the 1980s*

In 1983, Creo was incorporated in British Columbia. The name was derived from the Latin word meaning, "I create." Creo was situated in Burnaby's Discovery Park, an area that the *Vancouver Sun* described as, "a nesting ground for high-tech companies that have ideas, expertise and enthusiasm but lack capital or marketing experience."

Creo was founded by Dan Gelbart and Ken Spencer. Spencer was an electrical engineer born and raised in Greater Vancouver. He obtained an MBA before settling in to work for high tech companies, including MacDonald Dettwiler and Associates in Richmond, British Columbia. Gelbart, also an electrical engineer, emigrated from Israel in 1973. Gelbart met Spencer when he was working for a branch of MacDonald Dettwiler. According to the *Vancouver Sun,* Spencer described British Columbia's high tech industries as "incestuous," saying, "We've all worked for one another at one time or another." Spencer and Gelbart laid the foundations for a company that has shown steady and impressive growth over the years.

In the early years, Creo started out as a small electro-optical developer. For the first few years, Spencer and Gelbart dabbled in several projects, many of which were profitable. In it's first year, Creo received funds from grants from the Science Council of B.C., the National Research Council and a $2.4 million contract under Supply and Service's, Canada's unsolicited proposals program.

Before long, Creo honed in on developing an optical tape recorder. Following three years of Research and Development, the product's prototype was ready for unveiling. The optical tape storage system was able to store a terabyte or one trillion bytes of information in a single reel. That amount is loosely the equivalent of two million 500-page books or 5,000 magnetic computer tapes. Creo anticipated that their typical customer would be companies, libraries, and hospitals—in other words, entities that collect and store huge amounts of data.

The recorder required 1,200 working hours to build and resembled a compact storage box. It used two lasers to blast data onto a reel of 35-mm optical tape that was roughly a kilometer long. The data could be accessed in seconds. At that point, no one else in the world was thought to be doing the type of work that Creo was doing. Their product was the only one of its kind.

In March 1988, the federal government allocated a $325,000 grant to Creo to purchase computer-related design equipment for production and testing of the optical tape recorders. Creo anticipated going into production in mid-1989. The aim was 200 units a year, selling at about $200,000 per unit. Sales were

## Company Perspectives:

*It is important to us that Creo be a place where strong values and solid management philosophies hold true. The innovative technology of Creo is supported by the company's unique business philosophy. Several simple principles guide Creo employees around the world: Our priority is to provide unique and sustainable value to our customers. 1. All decisions must be based on sound economics. 2. Key decisions are made in consensus, with full team agreement to accept and implement the decision. 3. We believe that people are most effective when self-managed. 4. Compensation is based on contribution, gauged largely by an annual peer review. 5. All employees share the wealth created by their hard work and innovation.*

to be concentrated in the U.S. The *Vancouver Sun* quoted Spencer as saying, "We're the only company in North America going after the big market. With those years of R&D behind, and with a handful of patents on their product, we're not overly worried about competition."

In 1989, Creo received its first award—the Electronic Manufacturer's Association of B.C.'s "Most Innovative Product" award for another one of its projects—the *32-Beam Laser Photoplotter.* In 1991, Creo again won this award for its Optical Tape Recorder. It was also listed in *R&D*'s "Top 100 Most Innovative Products." In 1992, the Optical Tape Recorder won the Science Council of B.C.'s Gold Medal for "Most Innovative Product." In the years to come, Creo products were to receive many more awards from various organizations and in various categories.

In January 2, 1990, the North American Free Trade Agreement, with its proposal to remove tariffs on computers and equipment, proved a boon to Creo. Spencer said that the agreement provided his company better access to a market ten times the size of the Canadian market. He predicted that the agreement would either allow Creo to lower its prices or to retain the tariff price and earn more profits. The anticipated result would be either increased sales volume or company growth—with a corresponding need to hire more employees in both cases.

By 1992, Creo employed 100 persons. In that same year, they signed a major contract with the billion-dollar Japanese firm Dainippon Screen Manufacturing Co. Ltd. The $8 million dollar contract covered research and development and first year's production to manufacture a plotter engine. Dainippon built products for graphic arts and semiconductor industries. They used a plotter, costing $300,000, to create a printing plate from a piece of film. Under the contract, Creo produced the "guts" of the plotter—the engine. It took a few hundred hours to make each unit.

This established Creo with two major products: the optical tape recorder and the plotter engine. By now, the recorder was being sold to U.S. defense and intelligence markets, the European Space Agency, and the Canada Centre for Remote Sensing. The company also attained annual sales of $10 million and had been profitable since receiving grants in its first year. Majority ownership rested with Creo's employees and management, with the Federal Business Development Bank owning 12 percent of company shares.

### *1993: A Change of Focus*

In 1993, Creo focused its efforts and technological innovations on the multi-billion dollar graphic arts industry. According to the company web site, "Precision mechanics, electronics, and optics specialists developed hardware that used laser technology to reproduce high-resolution images on film." This film was then used to expose printing plates. With these early hardware innovations, Creo gained a reputation for high-quality workmanship and reliable equipment.

In 1994, Webcom Ltd., the big Canadian book manufacturer announced its intent to use a digitized computer-to-plate system developed by Creo Products Inc. The Creo 3244 Platesetter was capable of creating a full-sized aluminum plate in three minutes from PostScript digital files, at a dpi (Dots Per Inch) of 2,400. The time increased to four minutes at a dpi of 3,200. (PostScript is a page description language developed by Adobe Systems Inc. It is used in many printers, pagesetters, and display systems.)

The Creo 3244 was designed to be operated unattended in full daylight and could function in either the prepress area or adjacent to the press. This allowed for just-in-time plate making and quick plate remakes controlled by the press operator. Webcom found that once a book was published in hard cover, it was much easier and cheaper to reformat the book for publication in soft cover after they had moved to a digital format. Furthermore, once digitized, a book could be moved readily to another storage medium, such as a compact disc. The *Vancouver Sun* quoted Webcom President Warren Wilkins as saying, "Creo offers a system that now works and works better than other systems in the market. This machine allows us to store 50,000 plates online and you might need 12 plates for a book."

Creo anticipated that sales of its large-format Platesetters, selling for under $1 million, would triple in 1995 from $15 million to $45 million. Employment had risen to 270 people and was expected to reach 350 in the coming year. The Platesetter was being marketed in the U.S. and in Europe. When R.R. Donnelly & Sons co. in Chicago began ordering substantial numbers of the product, Creo became the leading supplier of computer-to-plate systems.

Next, Creo attempted to make the prepress process better and faster. (Prepress refers to the preparation and assembly of text and pictures). They wanted to reduce the time involved in the cycle and eliminate inconsistencies associated with film work.

Creo's first Computer-to-Plate (CTP) technology was based on visible light technology. In 1995, the company introduced a new thermal imaging technology that used heat rather than light to image infrared-sensitive materials such as proofing media and thermal plates. With this technology, they were able to offer higher resolutions and eliminate the challenges associated with working with light sensitive plates. Printers had additional process control in presswork and could produce consistent, high quality output while reducing prepress costs. The product was thought to be environmentally friendly, given that it uses no

**Key Dates:**

**1983:** Creo is incorporated.
**1989:** The company wins Electronic Manufacturers' Association of British Columbia's Most Innovative Product Award.
**1990:** Creo develops first large-format Postscript imagesetter engine.
**1993:** Creo redirects its focus to automating the prepress phase of the printing industry.
**1994:** The first true production Computer-to-Plate (CTP) system is delivered to customers in the United States.
**1995:** The first thermal system is introduced at the trade fair DRUPA 95; the first CTP system installed in Asia.
**1999:** Creo goes public on the Toronto and NASDAQ exchanges.
**2000:** Creo acquires the assets of the digital prepress business of Scitex Corporation Ltd. and forms CreoScitex.
**2002:** Creo Products shortens its name to Creo Inc.

film and therefore has no metal contaminants. Creo's web site reports that, ''Creo's innovations have secured patents and won awards, but most importantly they have helped printers worldwide succeed and meet their daily business objectives.''

The *Vancouver Sun* reported, ''If you read mass-market U.S. magazines such as *Sports Illustrated, Glamour* or *Scientific American*, chances are you've already seen the end-product of Creo's CTP technology.'' By August 1998, Creo's workforce hit 1,023. Vice-President and CEO Mark Dance anticipated a continued growth of 25 to 30 percent per year.

In 1999, Creo reported that eight out of ten of the largest North American commercial printers used its products. Under the terms of a joint venture with the German printing press maker, Heidelberger Druckmaschinen AG, Creo's technology was being distributed worldwide. However, Creo was not well-known. ''Creo has a puny public profile,'' wrote the *Vancouver Sun,* ''largely because it is privately owned.'' At that time, employees and founders owned more than 50 percent of the firm, and Goldman Sachs owned 13 percent, thanks to a $27 million investment in Creo in late 1995.

In July of that same year, Creo filed for an initial public offering (IPO) of five million shares. At that time it had an implied market value of C$666 million. The Company planned to use the monies raised from the IPO for working capital and for other general corporate purposes. Sales in the last quarter of 1999 were the best in Company history. Shares hit a new high. In the meantime, the company continued to pursue its stated objectives: to expand its sales base and product line, while pouring millions of dollars in research and development.

### *Formation of CreoScitex: 2000 and Beyond*

During the first quarter of 2000, Creo's shareholders approved the acquisition of a major competitor, the Israel-based Scitex Corporation Ltd.'s preprint division. The share transaction was valued at just over $500 million. This made Scitex the largest single Creo shareholder with a 27 percent stake. The acquisition gave the Creo and Scitex combination as much as 20 percent market share for preprint equipment. Analysts reported that nine out of ten of the largest commercial printers in North America had adapted Creo systems by then, and the company had twice the number of installed systems of any of its competitors. The *Vancouver Sun* quoted Tobias Fischbein, an analyst at Ilanot Batucha Investment Ltd., as saying, ''The transaction seems like a good one for both sides. It creates an absolute leader in the area of digital prepress and cancels competition that was very intense in recent quarters.''

In April 2000, the print-on-demand initiatives of Creo Products Inc. and Scitex were united to form CreoScitex. CreoScitex became the principal division of Creo Products. Revenue in the second quarter grew by 50 percent and net earnings increased by 66 percent. Because of the acquisition, Creo ended its long-time joint venture with Heidelberger Druckmaschinen AG. When the two companies were unable to agree on modifications to the joint venture contract, Creo opted out and instead negotiated a original equipment manufacturer (OEM) agreement with Heidelberger.

In June 2000, Creo Products paid $24 million in cash and stocks for Intense Software. Also based in Vancouver, Intense Software developed software for graphic designers, business users and printing professionals. It also custom engineered software under contract. The acquisition gave Creo exclusive rights to technologies and products that complemented CreoScitex, as well as giving the Company access to Intense Software's network of 50 software distributors and resellers in North America, Europe, Asia, Japan, and Latin America.

By this time, Creo had 4,000 employees worldwide, had expanded its product line, and extended its global reach. It had three research and development and manufacturing centers: one in Vancouver, one in Israel, and one in the United States. In November 2000, despite a healthy period of growth, Creo shares dropped $7 a share to $38 in one day. The *Province* reported it as ''a day of high tech bloodletting in the North American markets.''

In January 2001, Creo increased its share of Nihon CreoScitex to 81 percent. This subsidiary had been minority owned. The increase was expected to allow Creo to further penetrate the Graphic Arts Industry in Japan.

In February 2001, Creo was named one of the best ethical stocks for Canadians. The first quarter of 2001 was positive. Creo's adjusted earnings were $10 million, compared to $5 million in the first quarter of 2000.

In 2002 Creo appeared poised for a continued period of profitability and growth. In addition to its core product lines described earlier, CreoScitex is also an OEM supplier of imaging technology for on-press imaging equipment, while a global network of sales and service offices, dealers, resellers, and OEM partners offer international sales and customer support.

## Principal Subsidiaries

Nihon Creoscitex (Japan; 81%); CreoScitex Europe S.A. (Europe); CreoScitex Corporation Ltd. (Israel), CreoScitex Asia Pacific (H.K.) Ltd. (Hong Kong); CreoScitex America, Inc. (U.S.); CreoScitex Middle-East-Africa; Printcafe Software Inc. (U.S.; 30%).

## Principal Operating Units

CreoScitex.

## Principal Competitors

Agfa-Gevaert NV; Barco NV; Scitex Corporation; AB Dick Co.

## Further Reading


Boei, William, ''Acquisition Leads to End of Joint Venture,'' *Vancouver Sun*, April 6, 2000.

——, ''Burnaby Printing-Technology Firm Hits a New High with First Year-End,'' *Vancouver Sun*, 1999, P.D4.

——, ''C.-Bred Creo Keeps Growing,'' *Vancouver Sun*, August 18, 1998.

——, ''Creo CEO Beams after Graphics Firm Turns Record Profit,'' *Vancouver Sun*, May 6, 2000, p. E4.

——, ''Creo Products to Pay $24 million in Cash, Stocks for Intense Software,'' *Vancouver Sun*, June 1, 2000.

——, ''First Quarter Best So Far, Burnaby's Creo Reports,'' *Vancouver Sun*, January 25, 2000.

''Burnaby Printing-Tech Company Poised to Float $83-Million IPO'', *Vancouver Sun*, May 20, 1999.

''Creo Buying Israel-Based Preprinting Division'', *Vancouver Sun*, Jan 19, 2000.

''Creo's Upward Trend Continues,'' *Province*, April 26, 2000.

Ford, Ashley, ''Creo Slips Despite 'Remarkable Growth Year',''*Province*, November 12, 2000.

''High Tech Entrepreneur Says: Roll Out the Carpet!,'' *Vancouver Sun*, March 17, 1989.

Lamphier, Gary, ''Creo Set to Take Business Public,'' *Vancouver Sun*, February 5, 1997.

Nutt, Rod,'' Creo Snatches Scitex Corp. in $500-Million Share Deal,'' *Vancouver Sun*, March 31, 2000.

Smith, David, ''Creators Ready to Unveil Super Tape,'' *Vancouver Sun*, April 6, 1988.

——, ''Creo Becomes Top Supplier of Plate Systems,'' *Vancouver Sun*, October 30, 1999, p. C13.

——, ''Creo Expects Plate-Setter to Be a Trend-Setter,'' *Vancouver Sun*, November 22, 1994.

Spencer, Ken, ''Burnaby Company Lands Big Japanese Contract,'' *Vancouver Sun*, March 12, 1992.

Wanless, Tony, ''Creo Believes in Innovating,'' *Province*, May 3, 1992.


—June Campbell

CYPRESS

Driving the Communications Revolution™

# Cypress Semiconductor Corporation

**3901 North First Street**
**San Jose, California 95134-1599**
**U.S.A.**
**Telephone: (408) 943-2600**
**Fax: (408) 943-2796**
**Web site: http://www.cypress.com/**

*Public Company*
*Incorporated:* 1982
*Employees:* 4,160
*Sales:* $819.2 million (2001)
*Stock Exchanges:* New York
*Ticker Symbol:* CY
*NAIC:* 334413 Semiconductor and Related Device Manufacturing; 334210 Telephone Apparatus Manufacturing

Cypress Semiconductor Corporation designs, manufactures, and distributes a range of integrated circuits for the worldwide data communications, telecommunications, personal computer, and military systems markets. After starting up as a producer for the niche semiconductor products markets, Cypress turned its focus to mainstream chip markets in the 1990s. After its profitable SRAM memory chips became commodities in the mid- to late 1990s, Cypress turned its considerable research and development efforts to chips for mobile phones, wireless networks, and USB ports. Cypress prides itself on its entrepreneurial atmosphere. Its outspoken founder, president, and CEO, Thurman John (T.J.) Rodgers, is known as a tough boss of the ''No Excuses Management'' school—in fact, he co-wrote the book of the same name.

### *The General Patton of the Semiconductor Industry*

Company founder T.J. Rodgers, who was named ''America's Toughest Boss'' by *Fortune* magazine in 1993, gained a reputation in the semiconductor industry for his visionary management, entrepreneurial and manufacturing techniques, and outspoken criticism of the U.S. semiconductor industry. Born and raised in Oshkosh, Wisconsin, his father a car salesman, his mother a schoolteacher, Rodgers displayed a talent for entrepreneurship at an early age. As a child, Rodgers learned electronics from his mother, who had taught basic electronics during World War II. In his high school chemistry lab, Rodgers created his first ''product,'' a smoke bomb dubbed the ''Thurm-O-Flare,'' a project which ended when Rodgers blew up the lab and put himself in the hospital. Rodgers was recruited to play football at Dartmouth University, where he earned bachelors degrees in physics and chemistry, graduating second in his class, and first in both majors. Accepted into Stanford University's physics program, Rodgers instead decided to study electrical engineering—despite having taken only a single semester of electrical engineering at Dartmouth—earning his masters and doctoral degree by 1975.

At Stanford, Rodgers studied under William B. Shockley, whose Shockley Electronics became the breeding ground of the famed Fairfield Eight (including Robert Noyce and Gordon Moore of Intel Corp.). While at Stanford, Rodgers invented a wafer etching technology called VMOS; he patented the technology, then sold it for cash and royalties to American Microsystems, Inc. (AMI), where he worked until he was fired—when the VMOS process was eclipsed by new technology—in 1979. In that year, the 31-year-old Rodgers attempted to start his own company—a goal he had set himself to achieve by age 35—but was unable to find financial backing. Instead, he accepted a position with Advanced Micro Devices (AMD), where he worked until leaving to found Cypress in November 1982.

Rodgers faced the daunting task of starting up—and arranging venture capital for—a new company during the recession of the early 1980s. Nonetheless, Rodgers attracted the interest of L.J. Sevin, founder of Mostek Inc., during the 1970s. After preparing a business plan for his proposed company, Rodgers, with Sevin's backing, began raising the $7.5 million in start-up funds envisaged in his business plan. Rodgers quickly found offers totalling $13.5 million, enabling him to choose his investors. As he told *Santa Clara County Business:* ''We were therefore in the position of picking backers as opposed to begging for backers. Only the best! We picked backers that had 'value-added.' '' Initial backers included Sevin, Sequoia's Don

### Company Perspectives:

*CYPRESS CORE VALUES . . . Core Value #1:* Cypress is about winning. *We will not tolerate losing. We thrive on competing against the world's best. Individuals can choose to compete and win in business at Cypress. Core Value #2:* Cypress people are ''Only the Best.'' *We are smart, tough, and work hard. We tell the truth. We make no excuses. We value knowledge, logic, and reason. We deplore politicians. We are aggressive problem solvers who take ownership and get results quickly. Core Value #3:* We ''do what's right for Cypress.'' *We are company owners. We choose ''Cypress wins'' over ''looking good.'' We reward personal initiative. We are loyal and fair to our people. We follow the spec or change it. We keep commitments to customers. Core Value #4:* We make our numbers. *We gain market share, while we make excellent profit. We each set aggressive, quantitative goals—and we achieve them. We constantly improve. We do not tolerate waste. Core Value #5:* We invent and build state-of-the-art products. *Our technology challenges the world's-best head on, and we spend a fraction of what they do. Our first silicon always works on schedule. We manufacture at the world's lowest cost. We manufacture with excellent quality.*

Valentine and Pierre Lamond, J.H. Whitney of New York, and Kleiner, Perkins, Caulfield, and Byers. In exchange for this backing of Cypress, Rodgers gave up 75 percent of control over the company. Cypress continued to attract venture capital, raising some $48 million in the years leading to its initial public offering in 1986. Cypress was underway by April 1983.

Cypress debuted its first product, a CMOS (complementary metal oxide silicon) memory chip, by the beginning of 1984. The chip contained the world's smallest and fastest CMOS transistors, which were 1.2 microns wide (compared to a human hair at approximately 100 microns wide) and operated three times faster than competing semiconductors while using 80 percent less energy. The company immediately set to work on a new round of CMOS transistors, shrinking them to 0.9 microns. By 1985, the company was profitable and posting revenues of $17 million. Following Rodgers original business plan—and hitting the targets envisaged therein—the company sought to operate solely within niche markets, those with sales of no more than $40 million. In this way, the company could avoid head-on competition with the semiconductor industry's U.S. and Japanese giants, which had neither the flexibility nor the interest in producing for such small markets. By 1987, the company was producing more than 70 types of chips, all targeted at high-end, sophisticated markets. Sales had already tripled to $55 million in 1986. Also in that year, the company's initial public offering raised $73 million, one of the largest public debuts for the time. By then, the company had added a second wafer fab, in Round Rock, Texas.

Cypress's extraordinary growth—by 1990 sales would reach $225 million, and net earnings of $33 million—was credited to an unusually intense corporate culture, beginning with its hiring process, a daunting marathon of some ten interviews. Rodgers quickly earned a reputation as the ''General Patton'' of the semiconductor industry, demanding that employees create weekly task lists, and putting into place a computerized system for tracking completion of the tasks employees set for themselves—and those who did not meet their targets could expect a withering dressing down from Rodgers. The company's manufacturing processes were equally as strict, enabling the company the flexibility to turn production quickly from one product to the next. As Rodgers explained to *Business Month:* ''A semiconductor is a very unforgiving entity. If it takes 1,000 tasks to make one and you do 999 right but then forget one or do one wrong, the semiconductor won't work. Our system forces management to stick its nose in a big book every single week and find out what is going on. We can't afford surprises.'' In exchange for the high-pressure environment, Cypress employees received stock in the company. Rodgers, unlike many high-flying Silicon Valley CEO's, gave himself the same benefits—and imposed upon himself the same demands—as every other Cypress employee.

As Cypress grew, Rodgers also blossomed as an outspoken critic of the U.S. semiconductor, and particularly its quest, through Sematech and U.S. Memories, for U.S. government backing and intervention to help it compete against the rising Japanese power in the industry. Rodgers, a self-described Libertarian, instead demanded that the industry remain true to free market principles, a position that earned him little love among CEO's of his industry. Critics at the time pointed out that Cypress's focus on the niche markets—by 1990 the company was producing 159 products, generating as little as $1.6 million in sales each—enabled it to avoid the bruising head-to-head competition of the mainstream commodity markets. Nonetheless, Rodgers could hardly be faulted for the company's strong growth and its industry-leading productivity and profitability. At the end of 1990, the company bought its Bloomington, Minnesota, wafer fab from Control Data VTC, paying just $14.7 million. The company also opened the first two of its design centers, in Mississippi and Texas.

### *A Mid-Life Crisis in the 1990s*

Static RAM chips (SRAM's) provided the bulk of Cypress's revenues. Still, the company began branching out into other territories, including PROM's and RISC processors, featured in, among others, Sparc processors for Sun workstations—a market that Rodgers predicted would eclipse the Intel-dominated personal computer market. As Cypress grew during the 1980s, Rodgers fought hard to maintain its entrepreneurial spirit. Rather than creating subsidiaries, Cypress instead began acting as a venture capitalist, spinning off divisions into separate start-up companies, wholly owned by Cypress, each with its own CEO and administrative and financial departments. Cypress's three subsidiary companies, which included Ross Technologies, created to produce high-performance RISC processors, contributed 10 percent of Cypress's sales by 1990; by 1991, these subsidiaries accounted for 28 percent of the company's revenues.

As sales continued to rise, reaching $286 million and record profits of $34 million in 1991, Rodgers strove to maintain the company's entrepreneurial origins. However, the company was headed for trouble: the SRAM markets had developed enough to attract the interest of the larger semiconductor companies,

**Key Dates:**

**1982:** T.J. Rodgers forms Cypress Semiconductor.
**1984:** Debut of the company's first product—a CMOS chip.
**1986:** The company's IPO raises $73 million.
**1988:** Cypress lists on the New York Stock Exchange.
**1990:** A plant in Bloomington, Minnesota, is acquired.
**1992:** The company's first annual loss prompts restructuring.
**1996:** Memory chip production is moved from San Jose headquarters.
**1999:** Acquisitions and licensing deals bring Cypress into leadership of booming USB chip market.
**2000:** The company's sales pass $1 billion.

including Motorola, Micron Technology, Toshiba, Fujitsu, and Hitachi, sparking a price war that saw prices for SRAM's cut in half. With SRAM's moving into the mainstream, prices falling with the increasing supply, and a shrinking market facing a worldwide recession, Cypress stumbled into a mid-life crisis. Adding to its woes, Cypress had hitched its wagon to Sun's workstations. However, that market never developed into the Intel-killer Rodgers had hoped; worse, in 1992, Sun began reducing its inventories, cutting back on its orders to Cypress. Meanwhile, Cypress's Ross Technologies subsidiary was developing a new Sparc processor, with no guarantees that Sun would purchase it. Indeed, when Ross was late in delivering the new chip, Sun turned to Texas Instruments for supplies instead. Meanwhile, the personal computer market was moving into a new explosion in growth, and Cypress found itself on the outside of this crucial market. Rodgers's style of micromanagement was also criticized, particularly as the company was late with another important product, a one-megabyte SRAM chip, allowing his competitors to beat Cypress to the market. On top of all of this, Rodgers insisted on maintaining the company's assembling and testing facilities at its San Jose plant, despite the fact that keeping these activities in the United States cost the company some $17 million per year over what it would cost to move them overseas.

In 1992—to the delight of Rodgers's enemies, who had long chafed under his criticism—Cypress tripped up. Revenues shrunk to $272 million and the company posted its first loss in its history as a public company to the tune of $21 million. Chastened, Rodgers was forced to reorganize the company and adapt himself to Cypress's new conditions. Long pressured by his board of directors to move the testing and assembly facilities to Asia (although actual manufacturing would remain in the United States), Rodgers agreed, slashing some 700 jobs. It took Cypress only three weeks to move these operations. Rodgers also agreed to tone down his micromanagement of the company's activities in order to focus instead on its long-term growth. As part of the reorganization, Cypress brought its subsidiaries back into the company as divisions, while selling off the Ross subsidiary to Fujitsu for $23 million in 1993.

The glee with which Rodgers's detractors greeted the company's difficulties proved short lived. By 1993, the company was back on course, raising revenues to nearly $305 million and regaining profitability, with net earnings of $8 million. The following year, with an aggressive push into new product territories, including the personal computer market, Rodgers—who had taken the lessons learned over the last years to heart—once again led the company to new heights.

For the year ended 1994, Cypress posted sales of $406 million, and a net profit of $50.5 million. Aiding the companies return to growth were a series of acquisitions made between 1993 and 1994. The first, of IC Designs, Inc. for $16 million, brought that company's programmable clock oscillators for the personal computers; next, the company acquired Performance Semiconductor Corp.'s line of FCT-T high-speed logic chips, paying $5 million. In 1994, Cypress also acquired CONTAQ Microsystems Inc., and its line of personal computer chipsets, for $1.7 million.

Cypress arrived in the personal computer market to ride the surge in PC sales of the mid-1990s, spurred in particular by the introduction of the new Pentium processor, the first new PC chip since the introduction of the 486 at the beginning of the decade. The new computer market presented a double opportunity for Cypress—which began designing chipsets for the Pentiums—as the high-performance nature of the emerging technology opened a fresh demand for Cypress's core SRAM products. Where only 40 percent of personal computers contained SRAM in 1993, it was estimated that 80 percent would contain SRAM by 1997. Yet the company saw even greater benefits from the booming networking and telecommunications industries. By the end of 1995, revenues neared $600 million, and Cypress began making plans to become a $1 billion company, joining the industry's top ten, by the end of 1997.

In April 1996, the company began building a second wafer fab in Round Rock to meet the surge in demand. That project was delayed as the industry went through a worldwide slump in memory sales. Meanwhile, Rodgers's writing talents—he had also published a book, called *No Excuses Management* outlining his management philosophy in 1992—made the headlines in the summer of 1996. After receiving a form letter from a Catholic nun criticizing Cypress for not having any women or minorities on its board of directors, Rodgers wrote a six-page letter attacking such "political correctness" and the election-year hot potato of corporate responsibility and asserting that hiring on the basis of race or gender was immoral and "a lousy way to run a company." For this position, Rodgers was widely applauded among the executive and investor communities. Ever outspoken, in June 1997 Rodgers testified before a U.S. Senate subcommittee against "corporate welfare."

In October 1996, Cypress shut down its manufacturing facilities at its San Jose headquarters, converting the facility solely to research and development activities. Picking up the production was a second Minnesota wafer fab, and the start of construction on the new wafer fab in Round Rock, expected to be completed by 1998. At the end of 1996, however, Cypress found that its revenues had slipped back to $528 million in the face of the industry-wide slowdown. Though the company was planning to become a $1 billion company as early as 1997, it would not reach this goal until 2000.

### *Focusing on USB and Data Communications in the Late 1990s*

Cypress restructured its manufacturing operations in the spring of 1998 to reduce its exposure to the volatile SRAM market. It stopped making memory chips at its plants in Round Rock, Texas and Bloomington, Minnesota, and also moved test operations from Thailand to the Philippines. SRAM production would continue at a second site called Fab 4 in Minnesota, where it was developing a 0.35-micron process. SRAM sales accounted for about 42 percent of revenues at the beginning of the year. Cypress was reluctant to exit the SRAM business altogether; it had over the years accounted for about 60 percent of the company's profits.

Sales slipped to $555 million in 1998, producing $111.2 million worth of red ink (after a $92.4 million restructuring charge). SRAM had become a commodity, and the Asian financial flu depressed sales in an important market. The semiconductor market, depressed for five years, began to show an upswing in late 1999. Nevertheless, turning its attention from the maturing PC market to data-communications applications proved the key to Cypress's recovery, noted *Electronic Buyers' News.*

Universal serial bus (USB) chips were another particularly exciting growth prospect. This technology made it much easier to connect personal computers with a variety of peripherals, from printers to joysticks. It also provided a much faster connection than parallel and serial ports.

After the Windows 98 operating system, which supported USB, was released, the market exploded beyond the expectations of all but the most astute industry observers. In May 1999, Cypress bought USB specialist Anchor Chips Inc. for $15 million and in September, it licensed advanced USB technology from rival Intel Corp., allowing it to enter the higher end of the market; Cypress already dominated the low end, with 20 million USB chips shipped. Cypress bought another USB chipmaker, Massachusetts-based ScanLogic Corp., in May 2001.

In March 2000, Cypress launched a new startup, Cypress MicroSystems Inc., to develop and market systems-on-a-chip (SOCs) for the eight-bit microcontroller market. SOCs were used in advanced data communications applications.

Cypress had sales of $1.29 billion for 2000, producing a net $277.3 million profit. The next year, sales slipped to $819.2 million and Cypress stomached a massive $407.4 million loss. Cypress made more than a dozen acquisitions in 2000 and 2001 as it focused on the fast-growing data communications business. By the end of 2001, Cypress's SRAM business accounted for less than half of total revenues, which were half of what they had been two years earlier. Nevertheless, the company laid off 14 percent of its workforce, or 650 employees, in mid-2001 due to a decline in orders. Most of the job cuts were in its Philippines fabrication operation, though 150 administrative jobs, mostly at the San Jose headquarters, were also shed.

As the company diversified, it reorganized into divisions based on market sectors rather than product offerings. In 2001, Cypress had four autonomous profit centers: memory, data communications, interface (USB), and timing technology. Four others were in the making: wide area networks (WANs), storage networks, wireless terminals (PDA's and mobile phones), and wireless infrastructures (base stations). By the end of 2001, Cypress had four divisions and 13 business units.

Entering 2002, Cypress's main focus in the datacom business was developing components for the latest generations of mobile phones. Next was supporting the Bluetooth wireless networking system.

Cypress created a new subsidiary, Silicon Magnetic Systems, in May 2002 to develop magnetic RAM (MRAM) chips using technology licensed from Minnesota start-up NVE Corp. Due to their small cell size, MRAM's promised to be powerful, inexpensive to build, fast, and durable.

### *Principal Subsidiaries*

Cypress MicroSystems; Cypress Semiconductor (Minnesota) Inc.; Cypress Semiconductor (Texas) Inc.; Cypress Semiconductor Technology, Ltd. (Cayman Islands); Cypress Semiconductor Philippines Inc.; Silicon Light Machines Corporation; Silicon Magnetic Systems.

### *Principal Divisions*

Memory Products; Data Communications; Timing Technology; Personal Communications.

### *Principal Operating Units*

WAN (Wide Area Network); SAN (Storage Area Network); WIT (Wireless Terminals); WIN (Wireless Infrastructure).

### *Principal Competitors*

Advanced Micro Devices Inc.; Integrated Device Technology, Inc.; Samsung Electronics Co., Ltd.; STMicroelectronics N.V.; Xilinx, Inc.

### *Further Reading*


Bottoms, David, "Roaring Back," *Industry Week,* November 4, 1996, p. 20.

Bradley, Gale, "Cypress' T.J. Rodgers' Attack on 'Corporate Welfare' Supported," *Electronic News,* July 14, 1997, p. 12.

Brandt, Richard, "Humble Pie for T.J. Rodgers," Business Week, November 23, 1992, p. 81.

——, "The Bad Boy of Silicon Valley," *Business Week,* December 9, 1991, p. 64.

Braun, Alexander E., "Movers & Shakers: T.J. Rodgers, Cypress Semiconductor President and CEO," *Semiconductor International,* February 2001, pp. 20–32.

Cassell, Jonathan, "Diversity Proposal Fails at Cypress: Rodgers Prevails in Shareholder Fight with Nun," *Electronic News,* May 10, 1999, p. 10.

Daszko, Marcia, "Venture Upstart: A Conversation with T.J. Rodgers," *Santa Clara County Business,* June 1986, p. 22.

Delevett, Peter, " 'Check Your Oil, Mister?' Rodgers Asks," *Business Journal,* March 31, 2000, p. 4.

D'Souza, Dinesh, "A Capitalist Manifesto," *Forbes,* September 22, 1997, p. 126.

Evans, Jim, "Diversifying Pays Off for Cypress; Custom Devices Keep Company Afloat During Memory Slump," *Electronic Buyers' News,* June 16, 1997, pp. 1f.

Graham, Jeanne, ''Cypress Melds Many Into One—Collective Makeup Stokes Its Entrepreneurial Fire,'' *EBN,* Companies to Watch Sec., December 17, 2001, p. 30.

Jones, Stephen, ''T.J. Rodgers: A Patton-Like General Whose Weapon Is Cypress,'' *Business Journal—San Jose*, February 9, 1987, p. 12.

Kosseff, Jeffrey, ''Cypress Sees Its Future in Wireless, Expands Design Engineering, R&D,'' *Oregonian* (Portland), September 18, 2000, p. C1.

Lublin, Joann S., ''Roundtable—Setting the Tone: A CEO and a Professor Offer Their Insights on How to Keep the Troops Motivated,'' *Wall Street Journal,* April 8, 1999, p. R10.

MacLellan, Andrew, ''Cypress Cuts Back on SRAM's—Announces $85M Restructuring,'' *Electronic Buyers' News,* March 16, 1998, p. 1.

——, ''Thurman John Rodgers, Cypress Semi—After Rough Spell, He's Coaching Company Past $1B Mark,'' *Electronic Buyers' News,* December 20, 1999, p. 72.

Malone, Michael S., ''Been Here, Done This,'' *Forbes,* May 28, 2001, p. 47.

Murphy, Tom, ''Cypress Spins Off Microcontroller Company,'' *Electronic News,* March 13, 2000, p. 16.

O'Reilly, Charles III, and Jeffrey Pfeffer, ''Cypress Semiconductor: What's Missing?'' *Hidden Value: How Great Companies Achieve Extraordinary Results with Ordinary People,* Boston: Harvard Business School Press, 2000, pp. 201–30.

Pitta, Julie, ''Silicon Valley's (Profitable) Gadfly,'' *Forbes,* November 26, 1990, p. 56.

Rehfeld, Barry, ''Teeing Off on Corporate Welfare,'' *Institutional Investor,* August 1997, pp. 27+.

Reinhardt, Andy, ''The Sweet Smell of Semiconductors,'' *Business Week Online,* June 19, 2000.

Ristelhueber, Robert, ''Cypress Creates Magnetic RAM Subsidiary,'' *EBN,* May 6, 2002, p. 4.

——, ''Cypress vs. IDT,'' *Electronic Business,* June 1998, pp. 44ff.

Robertson, Jack, ''T.J. Picks Up Unexpected Assist,'' *Electronic Buyers' News,* September 18, 2000, p. 4.

Rodgers, T. J., William Taylor, and Rick Foreman, *No Excuses Management,* New York: Doubleday Currency, 1992.

Schniedawind, John, ''Cypress' All-American CEO Survives Tough Market,'' *USA Today,* July 14, 1993, p. 4B.

Schonfeld, Erick, ''Clos de la Tech: One Chipmaker's Stab at the Best Pinot Noir,'' *Fortune,* February 1, 1999, p. 12.

Sperling, Ed, ''Talking with T. J.,'' *Electronic News,* February 18, 2002, pp. 2f.

Spiegelman, Lisa, ''A Mea Culpa from Cypress' T.J. Rodgers,'' *Investor's Business Daily*, February 15, 1995, p. A4.

—M.L. Cohen
—update: Frederick C. Ingram

# Deutsche Telekom AG

**Friedrich-Ebert-Allee 140**
**53113 Bonn**
**Germany**
**Telephone: (49) (228) 181-0**
**Fax: (49) (228) 181-8872**
**Web site: http://www.telekom.de**

*Public Company*
*Incorporated:* 1989 as Deutsche Bundespost Telekom
*Employees:* 257,058
*Sales:* EUR 38.14 billion ($43.05 billion) (2001)
*Stock Exchanges:* New York Frankfurt
*Ticker Symbols:* DT; DTE
*NAIC:* 513310 Wired Telecommunications Carriers; 513322 Cellular and Other Wireless Telecommunications; 513340 Satellite Telecommunications; 513390 Other Telecommunications

Deutsche Telekom AG is the third largest telecommunications company in the world and number one in Europe. Headquartered in Bonn, Deutsche Telekom is Germany's leading provider of fixed-line telephone service. The company's T-Online International subsidiary is Europe's number one Internet Service Provider (ISP) with almost ten million subscribers. Deutsche Telekom offers a variety of mobile phone services to some 50 million customers in Europe, Asia, and the United States through its subsidiary T-Mobile International. The company has a broad range of international subsidiaries, including American mobile communication systems providers VoiceStream Wireless and Powertel, and a 59 percent share in Hungary's former telephone monopoly Magyar Távoközlési. After privatizing Germany's former telecommunication monopoly in 1995, the German government still owns about 43 percent of Deutsche Telekom.

### *1833–1933: The Telephone Conquers Germany*

The optical telegraph was first introduced in the German state of Prussia in 1833. Thirteen years later, the first telegraph line connected the two biggest cities of the state, Berlin and Potsdam. However, it took another 31 years until the human voice was first successfully transmitted over a wire in Germany. In 1877 the first postmaster of Germany's united postal system Deutsche Bundespost, Heinrich von Stephan, approved an experiment with two telephones built by American inventor Alexander Graham Bell. For the first time in Germany, voices were transmitted over a distance of more than two kilometers. Von Stephan realized the potential of the new medium and put telephone services under the control of his postal authority, the Bundespost.

By 1880, 16,000 German households subscribed to telephone services. In the following decades, the telephone won more and more acceptance in Germany and the technology was greatly improved. Beginning in 1881, telephone networks were being established in the country's largest cities such as Berlin, Hamburg, Frankfurt am Main, and Cologne. By 1898 the number of Berlin's telephone subscribers had climbed up to 46,000—more subscribers than in all of France. From 1912 on, Germany's telephone cables were laid underground in a constantly expanding cable network.

While in the early times of the telephone callers were connected with each other by a telephone operator, this system was eventually replaced in 1908, when the first automatic telephone connection in Germany was made. Automated systems started replacing operator-based telephony in the following decades. Advances in telecommunications technology made it possible to interconnect local networks and increase their capacity. The 1920s brought self-dialing, long distance, and mobile phone service to Germany. In 1926, for the first time, train passengers traveling between Berlin and Hamburg could call anywhere in the world. In 1933 public telex service was introduced between the two cities.

### *1933–49: Used by the Nazis and Destroyed by War*

After Adolf Hitler came to power in January 1933, the Bundespost became an instrument of the Nazi totalitarian state and, as such, its propaganda machine. Letters and telephone calls were routinely intercepted and used to identify Jews and dissidents. During World War II telephone services of the

## Company Perspectives:

*Deutsche Telekom is Europe's largest telecommunications company and one of the worldwide engines of innovation in the industry. Our products and services set standards not only in Germany, but also around the world. We make sure that our customers always have access to state-of-the-art solutions - from high-speed network access services to mobile Internet and beyond - and that they are the first to benefit from the fascinating prospects and possibilities of the communications revolution.*

Bundespost continued to function right up until Allied occupation in all areas of Germany. However, the service was in chaos by the time of Germany's surrender on May 7, 1945. Of the 3,420 buildings the Bundespost had owned before the war, 1,483 had been completely destroyed or damaged by bombing between 1940 and 1945, as well as during the fighting within Germany before its surrender. Many of its former personnel were dead or missing, and many telephone lines were cut.

As U.S., British, and Soviet forces assumed control of government, they also took over postal and telephone services. Between 1945 and 1947, political rifts and eventually the Cold War broke out between the Western allies and the Soviet Union. In 1947 the British and American occupation zones were merged for economic purposes, and administration began to be handed back to the Germans. The Soviets' refusal to participate in the currency reforms of June 1948 and the Berlin blockade meant that a unified postal structure for all occupation zones was doomed. Postal services in the eastern part of Germany were turned over to the new East German state established by the Soviets in 1949. An elected Parliamentary council from all three western zones met at Bonn on September 1, 1948 to draw up the West German constitution or Basic Law. In April 1949, U.S., British, and French governments guaranteed full powers of self-government to the new West German state. The Bundespost was reborn as a state body under the control of a cabinet ministry and assumed control over posts, telephones, and telegraphs in the new Federal Republic of Germany. The new constitution specifically forbade the privatization of posts and telecommunications.

### *1950–70: Rebuilding the Network*

During the 1950s the Bundespost had to rebuild its communications network and hundreds of post office buildings. Much of prewar Germany's communications had centered on east-west communication networks between Berlin and western industrial cities. The new West Germany was a long, narrow country in which many lines of communication now ran north-south. West Berlin had become an isolated city in an alien country. After the war, the division into different occupation zones had fragmented communications and delayed the formation of an integrated network.

The reconstruction of the telephone service was accomplished by the end of 1951, but installation of new private telephones was slow. By 1952, there were still only five telephones per 100 inhabitants in Germany, compared to 28 and 11 per 100 inhabitants in the United States and Britain, respectively. By the 1960s, however, Germany's communications network had been fully restored, and telephone subscribership was on a par with other industrial countries. As postwar Germany's prosperity rose, the demand for telecommunication services grew. The Bundespost invested in satellite communications; new transatlantic self-dialing facilities from Bonn, Frankfurt, and Munich became available in 1970.

### *1970–89: First Steps Towards Reform*

Attempts to free the Bundespost, including its telephone service, from political control date back to the 1920s. Around that time the government of the Weimar Republic was looking for a structure that would allow the Bundespost a measure of independence as a profit-making organization. In 1924, laws were passed allowing the Bundespost a considerable degree of financial autonomy from government control. The success of this reform, however, was restricted by interference from politicians and trade unions, and was finally reversed altogether by the Nazis.

The issue came up again when Germany experienced an unprecedented economic boom after World War II and many business and consumer groups began criticizing the post office monopoly for inefficiency. A 1970 law formally stated that the monopoly had been effectively superseded by a reservation that prevented the establishment of a rival undertaking, but little changed. In 1973 a further reform, the Postal Organization Act, limited government intervention in the Bundespost ''only to what is politically necessary and to facilitate post office management.'' Under the new structure, the Bundespost was headed by an executive committee assisted by a supervisory council. The committee, however, remained responsible to the government.

German business continued to complain that the Bundespost's phone network was inefficient and expensive and that German manufacturers might be disadvantaged by a backward telecommunications market. However, several powerful interest groups opposed change for fear of job losses and disappearance of preferential treatment under a more competitive system that included: the Social Democratic Party; the postal union Deutsche Postgewerkschaft; the Bavarian State Government; large contract suppliers to the Bundespost, including the German electronic giant Siemens AG; and the Bundespost's employees, who enjoyed the status of civil servants with considerable job security and pension benefits.

Pressures from both the European Community (EC) and the United States finally forced Bonn to make recommendations about the future of the Bundespost. Under Chancellor Kohl's Christian Democrat-dominated government, the so-called Witte Commission began to explore the possibility of privatization in 1985 and presented a report in September 1987. The commission recommended the opening of the telecommunications equipment and services market to outside bidders, a change that was likely to be required by EC competition law. The Bundespost would continue to operate in all its present fields, but some competition would be allowed in radio paging, mobile telephones, modems, videotext, and some satellite systems. However, the basic telephone monopoly, which earned 90 percent of the Bundespost's telecommunications income, would be

## Key Dates:

**1877:** Heinrich von Stephan puts telephone services under the control of his postal authority.
**1912:** Germany's telephone network is laid underground.
**1933:** The Nazis take over control of the Post Office.
**1949:** Deutsche Bundespost assumes control over posts, telephones, and telegraphs in the new Federal Republic of Germany.
**1989:** New legislation passes the German parliament, and Deutsche Bundespost Telekom is established.
**1990:** The telecommunications companies of former East and West Germany are merged.
**1994:** The Posts and Telecommunications Reorganization Act passes the governing bodies.
**1995:** Deutsche Bundespost Telekom becomes a public stock company and is renamed Deutsche Telekom AG.
**1996:** Deutsche Telekom shares are traded at the New York Stock Exchange for the first time.
**1997:** The telephone network in the eastern German states is fully digitized.
**1998:** The German fixed-network telephone market is opened to competition.
**2001:** Deutsche Telekom takes over American mobile phone service providers VoiceStream and Powertel.

retained. The commission also recommended that the Bundespost be divided into three businesses: Postdienst (postal services), Postbank (bank services), and Telekom (telecommunications), with a minimal level of political interference above the level of their respective management boards.

The report drew criticism from both sides; while liberals condemned it for not going far enough, opponents claimed it went too far. As a result, the original proposals were heavily altered before the new law passed the Bundestag, Germany's parliament, in 1989. Deutsche Bundespost, was divided into three separate companies: Deutsche Bundespost Postdienst, Deutsche Bundespost Postbank, and Deutsche Bundespost Telekom. Each company had its own board of management and separate accounts. However, a common directorate was added between the three businesses and a proposal for incentive-based pay was limited. The Ministry of Posts and Communication still had ultimate supervisory and regulatory authority in the public interest.

### *1990–94: The Telephone Reunification of Germany*

What the postal reformers could not foresee was the collapse of East Germany in November 1989 and Germany's reunification in October 1990. German reunification brought with it the integration of East Germany's own telecommunications monopoly, Deutsche Post, into the Bundespost. It soon became apparent that the necessary infrastructure investment was much larger than previously anticipated. Only 10 percent of East Germany's households had a telephone, compared to 98 percent of West Germany's. East Germans who applied for a telephone line often waited ten years and longer to get it. By 1989 the number of applications had risen to 1.3 million. More than 3,500 small East German towns were left without a public phone. Every call to West Germany was channeled through one of 15 connection centers to East Berlin's foreign connections office which was equipped with 111 lines to the West. Moreover, much of the existing East German telephone equipment predated World War II. Small wonder this bottleneck brought the quickly increasing telephone communication from East to West close to breakdown.

Within six months Deutsche Bundespost Telekom launched its ambitious Telekom 2000 program, a seven-year investment plan of DM 60 billion. The program not only aimed for bringing the telecommunications network of former East Germany up to Western standards, but also for installing a state-of-the-art infrastructure good enough to meet the demands of the year 2000 and beyond. Telekom emerged as one of the biggest employers in eastern Germany. The company took over almost all employees from Deutsche Post's Telekom division. Up to 4,000 of Deutsche Bundespost Telekom's employees were sent to eastern Germany to support their new colleagues.

To make telephone connections available quickly, Telekom made it a priority to establish a mobile telecommunication infrastructure in the eastern part of Germany. Its C- and the new digital D1-cell phone networks reached 80 percent of the population in the eastern German states by the end of 1991. Three years later former East Germany was covered by Telekom's digital mobile phone network. In August 1992 uniform area codes were introduced for the whole country. In mid-1991 Telekom established a digital overlay-network over the existing analog long-distance network. The first digital connection centers were set up in eight eastern German economic centers. From there the digital network was gradually expanded and by 1993 the number of telephone connections between East and West had grown from under 1,000 to 30,000.

In the final phase of the program Telekom technicians worked around the clock to finish the task. It took some 40,000 kilometers of optic fiber cable to build the new digital long-distance network and over ten million kilometers of copper cable to expand the 1,500 local networks. By 1997, Telekom 2000 had reached its goals. The telephone network in the eastern German states was fully digitized and the number of telephone connections had quadrupled since 1990. According to Deutsche Telekom, the former East Germany had the most modern and efficient telecommunications infrastructure in the world.

The enormous costs of updating the former East German telephone system caused many opposition politicians to drop their objections against privatizing Deutsche Bundespost. Privatization was increasingly regarded as a way to make profits and increase efficiency, and the support of the Social Democrats for the two-thirds majority vote in the Bundestag necessary to make changes in the constitution became more likely. In September 1991, the Social Democrat party said it would support privatization under certain circumstances. The negotiations that followed went slowly. Whenever a compromise was in sight, the party added new demands to its list.

Helmut Ricke, Telekom's CEO since 1990, and his management team decided to move ahead and completely reorganize Telekom. In September 1992 the company abandoned the government agency structure, and six months later Ricke presented a more customer-focused organization. Throughout the company he established separate divisions for private and business customers and a third one for key accounts. In mid-1993 Telekom spun off its mobile telecommunications business as a private company, Deutsche Telekom Mobilfunk GmbH (DeTeMobil), allowing it to better compete in the already liberalized market for mobile phone services. Meanwhile, the Christian Democrat Minister of Postal Services and Telecommunications, Christian Schwarz-Schilling, who had worked relentlessly for postal reform, resigned suddenly and was succeeded by Wolfgang Bötsch.

The final impulse for Telekom's privatization came from the EC. At a meeting in Brussels in May 1993 Bötsch and his European colleagues decided to open their markets for network-based telephone communication to competition by 1998. Six months later a new proposal for postal reform was presented in Bonn. The postal workers' union fought Telekom's privatization until the end and organized a major strike in late spring of 1994. However, in July 1994 the Posts and Telecommunications Reorganization Act passed the Bundestag and the Bundesrat, the German parliament's upper house. However, the law required the German government to be the majority shareholder in the former Bundespost companies for at least five more years and extended the monopolies for postal and phone services until the end of 1997. On January 1st, 1995, Deutsche Bundespost Telekom was transformed into a public stock company and renamed Deutsche Telekom AG.

Just a few weeks before Telekom's transformation into a public stock company, Helmut Ricke, who had put the reunited Deutsche Telekom on the track to privatization, resigned as CEO. Ex-Sony manager Ron Sommer became the company's new chairman, and his first big task was to attract investors who would buy Telekom shares at the company's initial public offering (IPO). As a monopolist, Deutsche Bundespost Telekom had been a profitable business with considerable yields for the German federal budget. However, its capital base had suffered badly in the early 1990s because of the necessary infrastructure investments. An additional burden was the cost for its civil servants for whom Telekom had to pay the difference between the retirement benefits they received from public funds and 75 percent of their final salary. In 1994, the company's budget for retirement benefits exceeded the budget for basic salaries by 50 percent.

Deutsche Telekom launched a huge image campaign to attract private German investors, including a new ''T'' logo and brand name. Telekom's top management courted the world's largest banks as well as other large institutional and private investors. In the United States alone, Telekom organized 17 ''road shows.'' Both measures were extremely successful. Within two years of its introduction, the pink ''T'' was recognized by nine out of ten Germans as Telekom's logo. Some 400,000 Germans bought Telekom shares which were termed T-Aktien or T-Shares. Some banks placed orders worth between DM 500 million and DM 1 billion.

On November 18th, 1996, the largest European IPO to date took place. After the first Telecom stock quote was announced at Germany's major stock exchange in Frankfurt am Main, the CEO, together with CFO Joachim Kröske, jetted to New York to be present at an IPO party at the Guggenheim Museum where Liza Minelli sang ''Money Makes the World Go Round'' under a dome of pink light. The heavily oversubscribed shares debuted at 19 percent over issue price on the first trading day. The more than 700 million T-shares sold to private investors accounted for about one-quarter of Deutsche Telekom's share capital. The rest was still held by the German government. An agreement guaranteed that the German government could only sell shares to third parties if Deutsche Telekom agreed.

While investors were told that new T-shares would not be issued in 1997 and 1998, a second batch was issued in mid-1999, raising EUR 15 billion for the company. The government's stake decreased to about two-thirds of the total share capital after that transaction. As in the IPO, Telekom was the beneficiary of the new stock offering, and the money was used to boost the company's capital base. In early March 2000 the T-shares reached an all-time high of seven times the initial issue price. Three months later the third issue was launched, this time to benefit Deutsche Telekom's major shareholder, the government, which had ''parked'' its shares at the Kreditanstalt für Wiederaufbau, a government-dominated development bank. The government's stake now stood at 60 percent.

### *1998: Market Liberalization Spurs New Strategy*

On January 1st, 1998, the German fixed-network telephone market was opened to competition. Almost immediately, the average cost for long-distance calls dropped by up to 30 percent. German consumers jumped at the opportunity—although with a healthy portion of skepticism. While they took advantage of ''call-to-call'' offers from Telekom's competitors for long-distance calls, they were hesitant to completely switch to a new provider.

From the beginning, Deutsche Telekom fought fiercely against its competitors—by any means available. For example, the company placed newspaper ads asking businesses with large phone systems, such as hotels, to make the use of alternative providers impossible. The company also warned customers that it would charge high ''compensation fees'' should they switch to other providers. Telekom's competitors, which mostly depended on the former monopolist's infrastructure, were not only charged for renting the phone lines but were also charged high ''takeover fees'' not always related to real cost when customers switched to a new phone company. When customers nonetheless decided to switch, Deutsche Telekom took a great deal of extra time to connect them with their new provider of choice, competitors complained. Finally, Deutsche Telekom challenged every directive made by the newly established regulation agency Regulierungsbehörde für Telekommunikation und Post in appeals court. About 250 such lawsuits were pending by mid-2001, and it was estimated that resolutions might take another three to five years.

Two years after the market was opened, about 50 companies competed with Deutsche Telekom. About two-thirds of all long-distance calls in 1999 were placed with an alternative ''call-by-call'' provider, saving customers up to 85 percent. However, Telekom recaptured about half of the competition's revenues through network usage fees. Thus, the company's long-distance market share in terms of revenues was around 90 percent.

Furthermore, roughly four-fifths of German customers preferred Deutsche Telekom as their basic phone company and did not plan to switch providers.

In the face of fundamental changes in the market for telecommunications, with mobile telephony and Internet-based applications on the rise, Deutsche Telekom decided to focus on four growth areas and do away with activities that were not in line with them. The new growth plan was given the acronym TIMES, identifying new markets as telecommunications, information technology, multimedia, entertainment, and security services. Deutsche Telekom announced that they would concentrate on mobile phone and Internet-based communication and data transfer, broadband network access, and systems applications software development. The company set up a subsidiary to sell a significant part of Deutsche Telekom's real estate and sold part of the shares the company held in German cable TV networks.

### *1990s: Rocky Road to International Growth*

In June 1995 Deutsche Telekom announced a strategic alliance with French carrier France Telecom and American phone company Sprint called Global One. However, five years later the alliance which ex-CEO Ricke had pushed through against strong resistance, fell apart. Another deal fell through in 1999 when Olivetti SpA—not Deutsche Telekom—took over Telecom Italia. Instead, Deutsche Telekom acquired French fixed-line carrier Siris SAS and British mobile phone company One-2-One.

In May 2001 Deutsche Telekom finalized the takeover of American mobile phone service providers VoiceStream Wireless Corporation and Powertel, Inc. The transaction was financed by issuing 1.12 billion ''T-Shares,'' a move that ultimately diminished the German government's stake in the company to about 43 percent. The new partnership enabled Deutsche Telekom to offer frequent travelers between Europe and the United States one phone number and one rate for voice and data services.

By mid-2000, the situation at the world's stock markets had become unfavorable. Share prices dropped in connection with the so-called burst of the Internet bubble, and Deutsche Telekom postponed the IPO of its subsidiary T-Mobile International AG, which the company had founded in the same year. The T-shares themselves came under pressure as investors lost their confidence in the stock market. In September 2001, five years after Deutsche Telekom's IPO, its shares were valued below the initial share price for institutional investors. Consequently, the company's plan to use its shares as an ''acquisition currency'' for international acquisitions came to a halt.

The company's IPO enabled Deutsche Telekom to get rid of about half of its DM 125 billion of debt. Although it did not seem as if Deutsche Telekom was seriously threatened by competitors in its home market, the company was struggling with self-made problems. Some 190,000 employees kept personnel costs high. In 1997 alone, the company had encountered DM 2 billion losses from bad investments in Malaysia and Indonesia, the Global One alliance, and from selling telephones and fax machines. In 1998 mobile phone services accounted for about one-fifth of Deutsche Telekom's revenues. Rival Vodafone-owned Mannesmann, however, had become Germany's mobile phone market leader and made handsome profits while Deutsche Telekom lost money, mainly through its foreign subsidiaries. In 1999 and 2000 Deutsche Telekom's profits dropped dramatically, due to decreasing revenues from fixed-line network business.

In late 1999 Deutsche Telekom's Internet service provider T-Online was reorganized as T-Online International AG. The company was profitable in 1999, but slipped into the red in 2000, due mainly to the flat rate the company introduced for unlimited Internet access. At a time when many dot-coms went bankrupt in the United States, T-Online was planning to push up online advertising revenues and to develop online content that users would be willing to pay for—a business model that in general had not been successful. To generate more e-commerce traffic, T-Online cooperated with auto maker Daimler-Chrysler and tourism companies TUI and C&N.

In the first quarter of 2001 Deutsche Telekom once again restructured its business organization. Corresponding with the company's new strategy, all activities were organized in four business divisions: T-Mobile, T-Online, T-Systems, and T-Com. In the new systems applications field, Deutsche Telekom took over software systems developer debis Systemhaus GmbH from DaimlerChrysler AG. In the area of network access the company focused on winning new customers for its high-speed digital ISDN and broadband T-DSL services. Deutsche Telekom was also working on T-NetCall, a new service for Internet-based phone calls between PCs and from PC to phone.

In 2001 a group of shareholders filed a lawsuit against Deutsche Telekom for undervaluing its real estate. The company had allegedly written down the balance-sheet value of its real estate by EUR 2 billion, which reduced profits for the year 2000 by EUR 1.5 billion—based on German accounting law. In September 2001, the federal administrative court ruled that some of Deutsche Telekom's ''interconnection-fees'' to its competitors were illegal. A month later another court ruling required Deutsche Telekom to make its local network accessible to competitors for much less than the company had charged. At the time Deutsche Telekom still owned 98 percent of all phone lines to households. Despite market liberalization and despite many difficulties, Deutsche Telekom was still Germany's number one phone company and a leading force in the world's evolving telecommunications market.

### *Principal Subsidiaries*

DeTeLine Deutsche Telekom Kommunikationsnetze GmbH; T-Mobile International AG; Deutsche Telekom Mobile Holdings Ltd. (U.K.); T-Online International AG (81.71%); DeTeSystem Deutsche Telekom Systemlösungen GmbH; debis Systemhaus GmbH; DeTeCSM Deutsche Telekom Computer Service Management GmbH; DeTeImmobilien Deutsche Telekom Immobilien und Service GmbH; T-Nova Deutsche Telekom Innovationsgesellschaft mbH; T-Data Gesellschaft für Datenkommunikation mbH; Kabel Deutschland GmbH; VoiceStream Wireless Corporation (U.S.); Powertel, Inc. (U.S.); One-2-One (U.K.); SIRIS S.A.S. (France); max.mobil Telekommunikation Service GmbH (Austria); MAT A V Magyar Távoközlési Rt. (Hungary; 59.49%); Slovenské Telekomunikácie a.s. (Slovakia; 51%); HAT-Hrvatske telekomunikacije d.d. (Croatia; 35%); MTS, OJSC Mobile TeleSystems (Russia; 36.2%).

## Principal Competitors

Arcor AG & Co.; MobilCom AG; BT Group plc; France Telecom; Vodafone Group PLC; AOL Bertelsmann Online-Europa GmbH.

## Further Reading


" 'Befreiungsanläufe' der deutschen Telekom; Gründung von Tochtergesellschaften," *Neue Zürcher Zeitung,* March 13, 1993, p. 32.

"Bund parkt Telekom-Aktien bei der KfW," *Frankfurter Allgemeine Zeitung*, June 26, 1997, p. 15.

Christ, Peter, "Darüber lache ich nur," *Die Woche,* February 6, 1998, p. 13.

Davis, Bernard, ed., *Federal Republic of Germany*, Philadelphia: National Philatelic Museum, 1952.

"Der Ärger in Brüssel über die Telekom wächst," *Frankfurter Allgemeine Zeitung*, January 21, 1998, p. 14.

*Die Deutsche Telekom - Schrittmacher für den Aufbau Ost,* Bonn, Germany: Deutsche Telekom AG, 1997, 19 p.

Franke, Michael, and Matthias Kietzmann, "Telefonieren; Günstig ins Ortsnetz," *Focus,* August 20, 2001, p. 172.

Goerth, Charles L., *The Postal System of Germany*, Valparaiso: Germany Philatelic Society, 1968.

Holzwart, Gerhard, "Vom Local Hero zum Global Player - Times soll es richten," *Computerwoche,* June 23, 2000, p. 9.

"Is the Price Right?," *Economist,* November 23, 1996, p. 87.

"Kurth: Gute Chance für Wettbewerb im Ortsnetz," *Frankfurter Allgemeine Zeitung*, July 20, 2001, p. 13.

Piller, Tobias, "Aus der Traum," *Frankfurter Allgemeine Zeitung*, May 25, 1999, p. 23.

Preissner, Anne, "Feine Gesellschaft," *manager magazin,* January 1, 2001, p. 18.

Reiermann, Christian, "Postreform; Vorwärts in die Vergangenheit," *Focus,* May 21, 1994, p. 50.

Stüwe, Heinz, "Gefährdeter Wettbewerb," *Frankfurter Allgemeine Zeitung*, December 28, 1999, p. 15.

Wild, Bernhard, "Die größte Aktienemission der Geschichte," *Süddeutsche Zeitung*, November 20, 1996.


—Clark Siewert
—update: Evelyn Hauser

# Dewey Ballantine LLP

**1301 Avenue of the Americas**
**New York, New York 10019-6092**
**U.S.A.**
**Telephone: (212) 259-8000**
**Fax: (212) 259-6333**
**Web site: http://www.deweyballantine.com**

*Partnership*
*Founded:* 1909 as Root, Clark & Bird
*Employees:* 1,300+
*Sales:* $306.5 million (2000)
*NAIC:* 54111 Offices of Lawyers

Dewey Ballantine LLP is one of the world's largest international law firms. Its 500 plus lawyers work out of offices in New York City, Los Angeles, London, Menlo Park, Hong Kong, Budapest, Prague, Warsaw, and Washington, D.C. Legal publications consistently rank Dewey Ballantine as one of the top law firms handling corporate mergers, acquisitions, and other complex legal and financial transactions. It is a full-service law firm with expertise in legal specialties ranging from litigation, real estate, tax, and intellectual property to antitrust, telecommunications, and bankruptcy. Small and large clients from North America, Europe, the Middle East, Asia, Africa, and Latin America use Dewey Ballantine lawyers for both domestic and international legal matters. Its recent clients include Blue Cross/Blue Shield, PG&E Corporation, Walt Disney, and the Mutual Life Insurance of New York. Dewey Ballantine's legacy features lawyers who made significant public policy and government contributions, including Elihu Root, Sr., Grenville Clark, and Thomas E. Dewey.

## *Origins and Early History*

After graduating from Harvard Law School in 1906, Elihu Root, Jr., and Grenville Clark worked for different law firms before forming their own firm in 1909. Joined by Francis W. Bird, another law school classmate, the firm of Root, Clark & Bird began at 31 Nassau Street in the financial district of lower Manhattan.

Soon Bird left the firm, but in 1913 Emory R. Buckner and Silas W. Howland, both also Harvard Law School graduates, became name partners. These young attorneys received a big boost when Elihu Root, Sr., joined the firm as ''of counsel'' in 1917. Root had a distinguished record of government experience, having served as secretary of both the War Department and the State Department and U.S. senator from New York. He also won the Nobel Peace Prize and was the subject of two biographies. The elder Root stayed with his son's law firm until his death in 1937.

After World War I, the young law firm gained a variety of new clients. For example, it represented the estates of Marshall Field and Andrew Carnegie and also served beer makers who contested the constitutionality of the Volstead Act and the Eighteenth Amendment that banned alcoholic beverages.

The Root Clark firm rapidly grew after World War I from just six lawyers at the start of 1919 to 39 in 1922, which made it one of the largest New York City firms. It also changed its name in 1925 from Root, Clark, Buckner & Howland to Root, Clark, Howland & Ballantine when Buckner left to become the U.S. Attorney for the Southern District of New York and Arthur A. Ballantine became a name partner. The first solicitor of what later was named the Internal Revenue Service, Ballantine headed the firm's growing tax practice.

During the 1920s, the Root Clark firm represented the American Bosch Magneto Corporation, the American subsidiary of Germany's Robert Bosch Magneto Company that had been seized by the American government during World War I. After the war, the German company regained control of American Bosch. The firm continued to serve American Bosch in the 1930s.

Also in the 1920s, the firm helped the plaintiff in Bibb Manufacturing Company v. Pope win a trial verdict that survived appeals. Root Clark received about $100,000 for helping Bibb, a very large fee at that time. Other clients in the 1920s included Beneficial, Dillon Read, and Guggenheim Brothers. Unlike most large law firms that at the time recruited mostly white Protestant males, Root Clark hired its first woman partner and its first Jewish lawyers in the 1920s. That emphasis on diversity remained a vital part of the firm in the decades to come.

**Company Perspectives:**

*Our lawyers share an aggressive commitment to unrivaled client service. From our most junior associate to our most senior partner, we never lose sight of the need to produce high-quality legal work in a responsive, cost-effective, and personalized manner. We believe that there is no substitute for ''battle-tested'' experience. We combine an exhaustive knowledge of the substantive legal areas with business savvy and an in-depth knowledge of our clients' businesses and industries. By understanding our clients' businesses, we can better assist them in solving and, more importantly, avoiding legal issues.*

In the early 1930s, Root Clark established an office in Paris, but it later was closed. About the same time, the firm developed expertise in representing various trade associations. The Textile Finishers Association became the first such association to engage Root Clark's services, then the Boiler Institute and also the Vinyl Fabrics and Sporting Arms associations soon hired Root Clark.

From 1932 to 1935 the firm did extensive work on the bankruptcy and reorganization of Paramount Pictures Corporation. The firm set up a special office in Paramount's headquarters, and its lawyers traveled to Hollywood and several theater subsidiary offices around the United States. Finally Paramount was successfully reorganized, and the demands of its creditors were met. The fact that Root Clark received the large fee of $450,000 for its Paramount work illustrated how some law firms prospered during the depression by helping clients facing bankruptcy and reorganization.

In the 1930s, the firm gained other work from helping clients deal with the many laws and regulations passed during the Roosevelt administration. Its international practice grew with work for Cuba's sugar business, the Havana Electric Company, and Chile's major nitrate producers.

The Root Clark firm served several other important clients before World War II. For example, it represented American Telephone & Telegraph Company (AT&T) and the New York Telephone Company in their rate matters and other dealings with the Federal Communications Commission. It also served several railroads in their bankruptcy and reorganization endeavors. Its real estate practice included helping its client Hart Schaffner and Marx of Chicago gain use of a New York building on Fifth Avenue and Forty-second Street.

In 1937, Grenville Clark played a crucial role in maintaining the constitutional separation of powers between the judicial, executive, and legislative branches of the federal government. President Franklin Roosevelt was frustrated when some of his New Deal laws, such as the Agricultural Adjustment Act, were found unconstitutional by the U.S. Supreme Court. Since the Constitution did not specify the number of court justices, Roosevelt tried to get Congress to add more justices that the president of course would have the power to appoint. Clark and others prevailed when the Senate rejected FDR's so-called ''court packing'' scheme.

Ferdinand Lundberg in 1939 listed Root, Clark, Buckner and Ballantine with 13 partners as one of the nation's ''law factories.'' The large law firms that served mostly corporations ''are organized on factory principles and grind out standardized legal advice, documents, and services as systematically as General Motors turns out automobiles,'' said Lundberg. None of the big New York law firms at that time revealed their clients, for that was considered a form of unprofessional advertising by the American Bar Association. Lundberg argued that the large American law firms were the ''brains of American capitalism'' that served as ''switchboards of social control to the dominant beneficiaries of the established social system. On behalf of their beneficiaries the law offices collect rents, advise on reinvestments, administer estates, suggest political attitudes, and give counsel on dealings with the villeins.''

In 1940, the Root Clark firm began representing Nathan W. Levin in his business and investment dealings for the family of deceased Julius Rosenwald, the major stockholder of Sears Roebuck & Co. At the same time the firm gained Salomon Brothers & Hutzler, later renamed Salomon Brothers, as a client.

In World War II the firm represented Brewster Aeronautical Corporation, a Long Island City-based manufacturer of airplanes for the British Air Force. The firm handled several war contract terminations, including Brewster's contract with the British. During the war, some of the firm's attorneys continued to be heavily involved in public policy issues, a good example being Grenville Clark's key role in creating the 1940 Selective Service Act.

### *Postwar Developments*

In 1945, the retirement of Grenville Clark led to a serious challenge for Root, Clark, Buckner & Ballantine. On January 1, 1946, partners George E. Cleary, Leo Gottlieb, Henry J. Friendly, and Melvin C. Steen left the firm to form their own general law partnership called Cleary, Gottlieb, Friendly & Cox. They also brought three associates with them from Root Clark.

The departing partners took with them considerable legal business for clients such as Pan American Airlines, Federated Department Stores, Salomon Brothers, and the estates of some members of the prominent Guggenheim and Lehman families. Root Clark also lost several tax clients such as Royal Typewriter Company, Food Machinery Corporation later renamed FMC, Eckert Corporation, Luckenbach Steamship Company, the construction engineering company of Amman & Whitney, and Chilean Nitrate & Iodine Sales Corporation.

Elihu Root, Jr., retired in 1952, and two years later John Marshall Harlan left when President Eisenhower appointed him to be a Second Circuit judge and then a U.S. Supreme Court justice. According to Paul Hoffman in his 1982 book, Harlan was Root Clark's ''leading litigator who had defended Du Pont in what was then the biggest antitrust suit ever brought by the U.S. Government.''

Also in 1954, the law firm faced the loss of the Bank of Manhattan, its main client that was being acquired by the Chase Bank. The firm then recruited Thomas E. Dewey to head its

## Key Dates

**1909:** Three Harvard Law School graduates start the firm of Root, Clark & Bird in New York.
**1913:** Two other Harvard Law graduates join to create Root, Clark, Buckner & Howland.
**1917:** Elihu Root, Sr., joins his son's firm during World War I.
**1933:** Arthur A. Ballantine rejoins the firm that becomes Root, Clark, Buckner & Ballantine.
**1955:** After completing his term as New York State governor, Thomas E. Dewey becomes the lead name partner of Dewey, Ballantine, Bushby, Palmer & Wood.
**1977:** The firm opens its Washington, D.C., office in response to increased federal regulations.
**1986:** The firm opens its Los Angeles office, its first on the West Coast.
**1990:** The firm moves its headquarters to New York City, adopts the new name of Dewey Ballantine, and expands its European practice with new offices in Prague, London, Budapest, and Warsaw.
**1994:** A Hong Kong office is opened, the firm's first office in Asia.

revival. Dewey was very well known as the former three-term governor of New York State who twice had run as the Republican candidate for president of the United States. He had made headlines in 1948 when newspapers wrongly proclaimed his victory over Harry Truman.

Dewey became the firm's leading name partner on January 1, 1955. By working full-time and avoiding politics and most other outside commitments, Dewey helped the firm gain new clients, including Turkey's government and the Japanese Trade Council. Dewey's expertise as a courtroom lawyer was evident when he represented Schenley Industries, New York State, and Eli Lilly and Company in various legal battles. The firm also received considerable work from the Chase Manhattan Bank, although New York's Milbank Tweed served as the merged bank's lead outside counsel. Other clients during the Dewey era included GTE, ADM, Continental Oil, Alpha, Dart Industries, and Equitable Life.

Meanwhile, the firm opened offices in Paris and Brussels and expanded its ranks of partners and associates. From 105 lawyers in 1958, Dewey, Ballantine, Bushby, Palmer & Wood grew to 147 lawyers in 1968 and 186 in 1973.

When Dewey died in 1971, his law firm was the second largest in New York City. However, it "went into a decade-long decline in 1971," according to Erwin Cherovsky in his book on New York law firms. The Brussels office was closed in 1972, and the Paris office also was shut down.

Dewey Ballantine opened a new office in Washington, D.C., in 1977. "The old school said that you could sit in New York and do everything, or maybe get on a plane and come down here for a day," said Felix Laughlin, the founder of the new office, in Hoffman's 1982 book. "But if you're here [in Washington, D.C.] full time, you're in almost daily contact with the regulatory agencies and you get things done a lot faster." Many other law firms also opened offices in the nation's capitol in response to many new laws such as the 1964 Civil Rights Act and several environmental protection laws passed a few years later. "Today every industry must move in lockstep with federal regulators–on everything from equal opportunity to occupational safety, from environmental protection to pension planning," said Paul Hoffman in 1982. "All this requires lawyers who know the regulations . . . and the regulators."

In 1981, Dewey Ballantine represented long-term client Conoco when several firms tried to take it over. Du Pont finally acquired Conoco, while Seagram and Mobil failed in their bids. AT&T, Dewey Ballantine's largest client at the time, in 1982 settled the federal government's antitrust lawsuit.

In 1983, Joseph Califano returned to Dewey Ballantine and became its managing partner. Well known as President Carter's secretary of the Department of Health, Education, and Welfare, Califano spearheaded the revival and growth of the firm. Dewey Ballantine went from 191 lawyers in 1986 to 278 in 1990. With the help of an increasing number of paralegals and other support staff, the firm's gross revenue grew from $71.5 million in 1986 to $139 million in 1989. Under Califano's leadership, the firm closed its Paris office in 1985 to reduce its costs and opened its Los Angeles office the same year when it hired the commercial litigation group of Lillick McHose & Charles. In the 1980s many big law firms grew rapidly as the nation added millions of new jobs, many from small business entrepreneurs and many from the growth of computer and other high-tech industries.

### *The 1990s and Beyond*

When the firm in September 1990 moved its New York headquarters to 1301 Avenue of the Americas, it also shortened its name to Dewey Ballantine. A 1990 alliance with the United Kingdom's Theodore Goddard led to the firm opening joint venture offices in Prague, Warsaw, and Budapest. Later Dewey Ballantine ended its ties to Theodore Goddard and gained full control of the three eastern European offices. It also opened its London office in 1990.

Erwin Cherowsky in 1991 reported that Dewey Ballantine represented corporate or institutional clients such as Prudential Bache, the Federal Savings and Loan Insurance Corporation (FDIC), Martin Marietta Corporation, E.F. Hutton, the General Electric Pension Fund, the Louis Dreyfus Group, and World Airways.

The firm continued its expansion with the 1994 opening of an office in Hong Kong to serve various clients in China and Southeast Asia. Dewey Ballantine in the 1990s remained one of the nation's top law firms engaged in corporate mergers and acquisitions. For example, it worked on five of the United States' ten largest mergers on acquisitions in 1997. In the first half of 2000 the firm was the leading merger/acquisition law firm, having worked on deals worth more than $38 billion that represented over 40 percent of that market.

Based on Dewey Ballantine's 2000 gross revenue of $306.5 million, *The American Lawyer* ranked the firm as the nation's forty-third largest law firm, down from number 36 in 1999. That continued the firm's declining rating, from number 31 in 1998 and number 25 in 1997. However, its gross revenues climbed from $227.5 million in 1997 to $250 million in 1998 and $277 million in 1999.

In 2001 Dewey Ballantine, along with three other outside law firms, represented PG&E Corporation when its subsidiary Pacific Gas and Electric Company entered Chapter 11 bankruptcy, the third largest corporate bankruptcy in history, according to *The American Lawyer* in June 2001. The firm also represented the Coalition for Fair Lumber Imports Executive Committee, a client since 1985, and other U.S. lumber interests when they complained that Canadian companies benefitted unfairly from Canadian government subsidies. According to a January 2001 fact sheet, the firm "recently completed the multi-tranche financing of Alliance Gas Pipeline, the largest project finance transaction ever consummated in North Africa."

These are just a few examples of Dewey Ballantine's work around the world. From the legal frontiers of intellectual property law dealing with computers and the Internet to helping former communist nations privatize their economies, the firm at the start of the new millennium continued its long history of noteworthy legal services.

### *Principal Operating Units*

Antitrust; Bankruptcy and Reorganizations; Capital Markets; Debt Finance; Emerging Markets; Employee Benefits and Compensation; Energy; Environmental; Insurance; Intellectual Property; International Legislative Reform; International Trade; Investment Management; Leasing; Legislative; Litigation; Mergers and Acquisitions; Private Equity; Privatizations; Project Finance; Real Estate; Securitization; Tax; Technology; Telecommunications; and Trusts and Estates.

### *Principal Competitors*

Fried, Frank; Harris, Shriver & Jacobson; Skadden, Arps, Slate, Meagher & Flom LLP; Willkie Farr & Gallagher.

### *Further Reading*

"Big Suits," *American Lawyer*, June 2001, pp. 57–58.

Cherovsky, Erwin, *The Guide to New York Law Firms,* New York, St. Martin's Press, 1991, pp. 79–83.

Cousins, Norman, and J. Garry Clifford, eds., *Memoirs of a Man: Grenville Clark,* collected by Mary Clark Dimond, NewYork: W.W. Norton & Company, Inc., 1975.

Dunne, Gerald T., *Grenville Clark: Public Citizen,* NewYork: Farrar Straus Giroux, 1986.

Gottlieb, Leo, *Cleary, Gottlieb, Steen & Hamilton: The First Thirty Years,* New York: Cleary, Gottlieb, Steen & Hamilton, 1983.

Hoffman, Paul, *Lions in the Street: The Inside Story of the Great Wall Street Law Firms,* New York: Signet/The New American Library, 1973.

——, *Lions of the Eighties: The Inside Story of the Powerhouse Law Firms,* Garden City, N.Y.: Doubleday & Company, Inc., 1982.

Jessup, Philip C., *Elihu Root,* 2 volumes, New York: Dodd, Mead, 1938.

Leopold, Richard W., *Elihu Root and the Conservative Tradition,* Boston: Little, Brown and Company, 1954.

Lundberg, Ferdinand, "The Law Factories: Brains of the Status Quo," *Harper's Magazine*, July 1939, pp. 180–92.

Smith, Richard Norton, *Thomas E. Dewey and His Times*, New York: Simon and Schuster, 1982, pp. 620–21.

—David M. Walden

# The Eastern Company

**112 Bridge Street**
**P.O. Box 460**
**Naugatuck, Connecticut 06770-0460**
**U.S.A.**
**Telephone: (203) 729-2255**
**Fax: (203) 723-8653**
**Web site: http://www.easterncompany.com**

*Public Company*
*Incorporated:* 1912
*Employees:* 634
*Sales:* $88 million (2001)
*Stock Exchanges:* American
*Ticker Symbol:* EML
*NAIC:* 332510 Hardware Manufacturing

Founded in 1858, the Eastern Company of Naugatuck, Connecticut, manufactures and sells industrial hardware, custom locks and other security products, and metal products from nine locations in the United States, Canada, Mexico, Taiwan, and China. The company's customers are mainly original equipment manufacturers, distributors, and locksmiths.

### *Tuttle and Whittemore Team Up in 1858*

Bronson Beecher Tuttle had a genius for making things. His friend John Howard Whittemore had a genius for figures. In the summer of 1858, when the hoe shop of Bronson's father Eben burned to the ground, Bronson talked his father into letting him start a malleable iron business on the site. Together, the younger Tuttle and Whittemore went into business on October 4, 1858, opening a small foundry. In a single small building with a handful of craftsmen, the co-owners pulled in annual salaries of $600, a fair income at the time.

They succeeded because they caught a wave. Their business—making malleable iron castings—was a relatively new process in the 19th century. Malleable iron vastly outperformed the more common material of the day-cast iron. Cast iron could not withstand a heavy blow and often broke when dropped on a hard surface. Malleable iron withstood enormous pressures, sustained severe and repeated shocks, resisted corrosion, and had great flexibility in comparison to cast iron. In the second half of the 19th century, the country's growth demanded huge quantities of metals for wagons, saddlery hardware, farm implements, railroads, guns, and hundreds of other products that were made with metal parts. In the company's early years, carriage irons and harness trimmings comprised nearly half the business. Iron farm implements were also a staple.

### *Production Boost from Civil War Needs*

The Civil War required new production peaks to meet the demands for war products—guns, wagons, gun-carriages, railroad train parts, and many other implements. After the war, the company made major sales in castings for ''steel-laid'' shears, a product that would remain its primary source of revenue for the next 50 years, and the Naugatuck foundry was soon supplying all the chief shear-makers in the United States.

By 1870, Tuttle and Whittemore's initial capital investment of $10,000 had tripled to $31,000, and the company's work force of 90 in 1870 more than quadrupled by 1883 to 368. The business expanded by buying malleable iron foundries in Troy, New York, and Bridgeport and New Britain, Connecticut. Later it held interests in plants in at least nine other cities, including one in Denver. By 1887, capitalization reached $100,000. The company name, The Naugatuck Malleable Iron Company, no longer fit its expanding operations. Tuttle and Whittemore renamed it The Eastern Malleable Iron Company.

Over the following decades, Eastern changed its product mix with the changes in the U.S. economy. When transportation shifted from the horse and wagon to the automobile at the turn of the 20th century, Eastern kept right on rolling. Metals that previously would have been crafted into buggies and railroad cars flowed into cars and trucks instead. Eastern produced hundreds of parts for an early car called the Maxwell.

### *Civic Contributions in the 1890s*

Whittemore was still remembered for major contributions to the center of the company's home town of Naugatuck 144 years

## Key Dates:

**1858:** B.B. Tuttle and J.H. Whittemore establish Tuttle & Whittemore iron works.
**1887:** Encompassing by now several iron works, the company is renamed Naugatauk Malleable Iron Company.
**1912:** The company is incorporated as Eastern Malleable Iron Company.
**1935:** Lewis A. Dibble becomes company president.
**1961:** Company is renamed The Eastern Company.
**1970:** Decade is characterized by acquisitions.
**1980:** Decade is characterized by sell-offs and reorganization.
**2000:** Company sales jump 63 percent to $88 million over a four-year period.

after Eastern's founding. He engaged a leading architectural firm to design many of Naugatuck's town buildings, including the Naugatuck National Bank (1893), Salem School (1894), the Whittemore Library (1894), the Congregational Church (1903), and Hillside School (1904), all of which were still in use nearly a hundred years later.

Shortly after the deaths of both owners (Tuttle in 1903; Whittemore in 1910) the company began to struggle. Competition increased greatly. The country's economy became much more complex. And the company had grown overly dependent on a limited product line.

### *Company Reforms in 1930s–40s*

In 1928, Eastern had several plants—three in Connecticut and one each in New York and Delaware. A survey the next year concluded that the company's plants produced similar products and were so close together that they competed with each other. Company management faced two other major problems. Many of the industries Eastern served had moved to the Midwest, where the company had no plants. As a consequence of these factors, sales at the foundries had dwindled.

Management did not unite behind the need for action until 1935. By then, the decision makers at Eastern agreed that drastic reforms were required as well as a strong leader to implement these changes. They wanted someone from outside the malleable iron industry, so he would not be bound by the iron industry's traditional methods of operating.

All the company's problems were not of its own doing. Hanging over Eastern and the entire country at this time was the Great Depression. Combined with company internal problems and industry-wide challenges, the Depression nearly brought Eastern down.

In 1935, Lewis A. Dibble took over the company reins. The company board found Dibble right in Naugatuck. He had been president of the Risdon Tool and Machine Company, an operation he had built into one of the country's leading producers of precision sheet brass and wire products. Dibble acted quickly. He eliminated four of Eastern's six plants, keeping only the Naugatuck and Wilmington, Delaware, facilities. Skilled workmen from the closed plants were offered jobs with the remaining operations—an unusual move in those days when the nation was still mired in an economic depression.

Dibble used savings from the plant closings to explore new market niches and make promising acquisitions. In February 1936, Eastern spent about $800,000 to buy Cleveland's Eberhard Manufacturing Company. Eberhard, formerly one of the strongest foundries in the Midwest, did malleable work, but it also boasted a strong line of proprietary transportation hardware products such as locks and hinges for truck doors. Eberhard had fallen on financial hard times. Dibble sent Charles Brust to Cleveland to turn the new subsidiary around.

In 1944, Eastern bought a company founded in 1845, the Frazer & Jones malleable iron works of Syracuse, New York. Frazer & Jones was one of the oldest foundries in the industry and served a special market niche—the railroad. Three years later Eastern made a third acquisition, the Eastern Castings Corporation of Newburgh, New York. The Newburgh facility made aluminum castings.

By eliminating four plants, then making these three strategic purchases, Dibble met the goal of diversifying operations and expanding the company geographically. These changes meant Eastern could become a leader in heavy malleable castings, light malleable castings, machined castings, steel castings, and aluminum castings. The Naugatuck plant continued to lead the company. It produced a wider variety of metals than any of the other four foundries, plus it housed the central research laboratory and an experimental foundry that all five plants used.

Dibble's business approach became the company's philosophy. Eastern sought to be a domineering factor in niche markets rather than one of many players in larger markets. Among his beliefs was the idea that "it is far better for a plant to be too small than to be too large."

### *1950s: A Move Into More Modern Markets*

Combined, the five foundries had about 2,000 employees and served some 2,800 customers. In the early 1950s, sales reached $15 million. Eastern was considered one of the nation's dominant firms in sheet metal production and precision wire products.

After World War II, Eastern began moving into more modern markets. Now the chairman of the board, Dibble, along with company president Charlie Brust, put the firm's future under the microscope again. Eastern was basically a casting company with five non-competing plants with very different capabilities. Its business was highly cyclical. Dibble and Brust led a company pursuit for products it could call its own and at the same time would help reduce its financial ups and downs.

Dibble and Brust studied one of Frazer & Jones's biggest customers—the Pattin Manufacturing Company of Marietta, Ohio. Pattin had a mine roof support product that largely replaced timbers as a means of preventing underground mine roof collapses. The Eastern executives liked the product. They purchased Pattin in 1955 to help assure Eastern's production stability and to secure a profitable product. At about the same time, Eastern decided to abandon the foundry jobbing business and become a manufacturer of proprietary products, primarily in the transportation hardware sector.

The company closed its large Wilmington foundry in 1961 because that facility had mainly served the railroad industry, a sector that was drying up. To emphasize the new focus, the company changed names again. Eastern Malleable Iron Company officially adopted the name The Eastern Company on February 22, 1961.

### *Acquisitions and Divestitures: 1960s–80s*

A second surge of acquisitions took place during the 1960s. In 1961, the company spent a total of $1,084,000 to buy Wilfrid O. White & Sons, Inc. of Boston and Thompson Materials Company of Belleville, New Jersey. Other acquisitions that decade included Illinois Lock Company of Wheeling, Illinois (1965); K-S Marine Products, Inc. (1966); and Local Steel & Supply Company of Mineola, New York (1968). Expansion into Canada came in 1968 when Eastern spent about $1 million to build the Eber-East Products, Ltd. plant as a subsidiary of Eberhard in Tillsonburg, Ontario.

In the 1960s, the company faced a major decision—should it upgrade or abandon its remaining foundries? The foundries were old and basically used 19th-century methods. Eastern had increasing difficulty finding workers interested in lugging heavy ladles of metal around from its coal-fired melting furnaces. Management also worried about pollution.

Studies showed a future in Eastern's specialized area of the foundry business. The company modernized its foundries in Syracuse and Naugatuck in the 1960s at a cost of more than $3 million. It automated operations, added labor-saving equipment, and switched to electric induction furnaces.

The 1970s brought two more additions. In May 1971, Eastern picked up the Digital Depth Indicator line from Lykes Brothers, Inc. of Clearwater, Florida. With 22,000 shares of common stock, Eastern bought Marion Mine Service, Inc. in Marion, Illinois.

While most companies were on buying sprees in the 1980s, Eastern slimmed down its operations. After buying Danforth Anchors in 1969, it sold the firm in 1983. Local Steel & Supply was sold in 1986. A year later, Eastern sold Pattin Manufacturing Division for $6 million. That same year it unloaded Marion Mine Service. From 1940 through approximately 1988, Eastern was one of only a few publicly-traded U.S. corporations to record an unbroken string of paying consecutive quarterly dividends.

### *1990s and Beyond*

By the 1990s, the company hardly resembled its early foundry-based operation. Then, in May 1990, the board approved a plan to discontinue its malleable iron business. A year and a half later, the board voted to end the company's high alloy stainless steel castings business. Eastern continued to evolve when it sold all the substantial assets of its construction segment in August 1995.

In 1997, sluggish performance caused a major shareholder, New York-based Millbrook Capital Management, to try to gain a foothold on the board of directors. The group also offered to buy the company for $15 per share in cash or $42 million in July of that year. Senior analyst Shirley Westcott, of the Institutional Shareholder Services, called the company's performance "pretty pathetic," claiming an investor would have gotten a higher return investing in U.S. Treasury notes. Eastern representatives claimed the company had made a financial turnaround and was far ahead of 1997 targets. Both the purchase and proxy attempts failed, but shortly afterwards the company chief executive left and was replaced by Leonard F. Leganza.

In 2001, Eastern had three major divisions: the industrial hardware group, security products, and metal products. The industrial hardware group supplied latches, locks and other security hardware to the industrial sector, especially transportation companies. This division's operations, headed up Eberhard, spanned Canada, the United States, and Mexico. Sesamee Mexicana also produced products for this division. Eberhard gear could be found in tractor-trailer trucks, moving vans, off-road construction and farming equipment, school buses, military vehicles, and recreational boats. The industrial hardware group's fasteners and closure devices were used on equipment such as metal cabinets, machinery housings, and electronic instruments. In 2000, about 39 percent of the company's sales and 49 percent of its earnings came from this division.

The security products group included the Illinois Lock Division, Greenwald Industries Division, CCL Security Products, World Lock Company, and World Security Industries. This group manufactured products to safeguard property and control access. Illinois Lock made keyed, electric switch, and high-security locks for original equipment manufacturers (OEM's). CCL Security products included brand-name keyless locks like Sesamee, Presto, and Huski. Business sectors using this group's products included the computer, electronic, vending, and gaming industries. Eastern's security products group also supplied product to the luggage, furniture, and laboratory equipment industries. A mid-2000 year addition to the fold, Greenwald Industries, produced coin accepters and metering systems used in self-service laundry facilities. Greenwald also offered Smart Cards for use in parking meters and laundry facilities. This group of Eastern's operations accounted for 36 percent of sales and 30 percent of earnings in 2000.

Frazer & Jones headed Eastern's metal products group. Its anchoring devices for supporting underground mine roofs had become an industry-accepted safety standard. The Canadian, Australian, and U.S. mining industries all used Frazer & Jones metal products. Eastern's metal products group also produced precision, small-size castings used by the construction and electrical industries. In 2000, the company derived 25 percent of its sales and 21 percent of its earnings from this group.

Based on sales, the company's new direction seemed to work. In 1996, sales were $56 million. Sales grew four consecutive years through 2000, reaching $88.19 million. The company focused on strengthening and expanding its industrial hardware and security product segments. Acquisition of Ashtabula Industrial Hardware Company, a designer and manufacturer of door control hardware for school and courtesy buses, gave Eastern a new market for products from its Canadian Eberhard operation. Eberhard's product line was expanded when Eastern acquired two latching products from Hansen International in 2000.

### *Principal Subsidiaries*

Eberhard Hardware Manufacturing Ltd. (Canada); Sesamee Mexicana (Mexico); World Lock Co. Ltd. (Taiwan); World Security Industries Co. Ltd. (Hong Kong).

### *Principal Divisions*

Frazer & Jones; CCL Security Products; Custom Locks Group; Illinois Lock; Eberhard Manufacturing.

### *Principal Operating Units*

Industrial Hardware; Security Products; Metal Products.

### *Principal Competitors*

Assa Abloy AB; The Stanley Works; Strattec Security Corporation.

### *Further Reading*

McMillen, Russell G., *The Eastern Company Since 1958: From Farm Tools to Yachting Instruments,* New York: Newcomen Society in North America, 1971.

Monagan, Charles, ''The Eastern Company,'' in *Greater Waterbury – A Region Reborn,* Chatsworth, Calif.: Windsor Publications, Inc., 1989.

Leuchars, William G., ''Eben Tuttle's Iron Foundry'' in *Naugatuck Stories and Legends,* Naugatuck, Conn.: Naugatuck Historical Society, 1969, pp. 63–7.

Weeks, Jack, *Yankee Iron: The Story of the Eastern Malleable Iron Company,* Naugatuck, Conn.: Eastern Malleable Iron Company, 1952.

—Chris Amorosino

# thirteen
WNET NEW YORK

# Educational Broadcasting Corporation

**356 West 58th Street**
**New York, New York 10019**
**U.S.A.**
**Telephone: (212) 560-2000**
**Fax: (212) 582-3297**

*Non-Profit Company*
*Incorporated:* 1961 as Educational Television for the Metropolitan Area, Inc.
*Employees:* 479
*Sales:* $171.6 million (2001)
*NAIC:* 513120 Television Broadcasting

Based in midtown Manhattan, Edcuational Broadcasting Corporation (EBC) is the corporate parent of Channel Thirteen/WNET, a New Jersey-based public television station serving the New York City metropolitan area. Thirteen/WNET is also an important contributor to the Public Broadcasting Service (PBS) network, providing a large portion of its programming, including the *Newshour with Jim Lehrer* as well as a wide variety of cultural and arts programming. Moreover, the six million viewers that Thirteen/WNET delivers each week is a key factor for other PBS producers when approaching corporate and private foundation underwriters. In addition to Thirteen/WNET, EBC now controls WLIW, a Long Island public television station, which was expected to complete a merger with Thirteen/WNET in 2002.

### *Public Television Origins in the 1950s*

WNET resulted from a 1970 merger of a public television station, WNDT, with a producing organization, NET (the National Educational Television and Radio Center). The roots of NET reach back to the end of 1952 when ''National'' was not part of its name and the newly incorporated Educational Television and Radio Center was simply known as the ''Center.'' Earlier that year the Federal Communications Commission (FCC) set aside 242 television stations for educational purposes. Unlike Europe, where a public television system was centralized and created from the top down, non-commercial television in America evolved in an almost haphazard manner. Demand for television frequencies from commercial interests following World War II had been so high that in 1948 the FCC initiated a four-year freeze on new licenses in order to decide how to make enough channels available. Advocates for reserving television bandwidth for educational/public purposes took advantage of the freeze to lobby the FCC. Many of these pioneers were affiliated with the college educational radio stations that had formed the National Association of Education Broadcasters (NAEB) and had been successful in their fight to reserve FM radio frequencies for educational purposes. NAEB and other educational organizations created the Joint Committee on Educational Television, which then received funding from the Ford Foundation in order to take on the powerful commercial forces that were poised to dominate television. Even after the FCC agreed to reserve stations for public use, a year passed before the first educational television station, located in Houston, was on the air. From the outset advocates of educational public television recognized that the new stations would need a program exchange service in order to fill their air time. It was for this purpose that the Center was created, funded by a $1.35 million grant from the Ford Foundation. In May 1954, the Center, operating out of Ann Arbor, Michigan, offered its first slate of educational fare, some five hours delivered by mail on kinescope film, including such programs as *Geography in Conflict, Understanding Your Child,* and *From Haydn to Hi-Fi.* At that point, however, only six public television stations were operational—and none in the New York City area.

By the end of the 1950s, New York still lacked a public television station. Nevertheless the Center moved to the city, added ''National'' to its name, and began billing itself as America's ''fourth network.'' Because all of the seven New York VHF channels that were available to most television sets of the day were already allocated to commercial interests, the FCC in 1952 was able to offer only a UHF channel for public use in New York City. Virtually no one could receive the frequency, so it was not activated, despite some efforts from a organization called the Metropolitan Educational Television Association (META), formed in the mid-1950s and comprised of representatives from area educational institutions and universities. META eventually turned its attention to production,

**Company Perspectives:**

*For four decades, Thirteen has been asking big questions. And in so doing, it has encouraged its viewers to ask illuminating questions of themselves and their world. This is the vision that drives the non-commercial, educational, inspiring public television that Thirteen provides.*

creating a few programs for the Center to distribute. Because the sponsoring organizations of META's board members all competed with it for funding, it was decided in 1959 to dissolve META and donate its broadcasting facility to New York University. Two years later, one of the area's seven VHF stations, channel 13, became available. The head of the Center, John White, was informed of this development by a broker, Howard Stark, who had been hired to secure a much needed New York station for the budding national network of public television stations.

### *The Early Years of Channel 13*

Channel 13 was the only one of the major New York metropolitan television stations located on the New Jersey side of the Hudson River. The FCC granted the license in 1946 to Bremer Broadcasting Corporation largely because of the company's New Jersey roots. The company's founder, Frank V. Bremer, was a radio pioneer who had been broadcasting in the state since the earliest days of the medium. Channel 13, using the call letters WATV, may have technically been a New Jersey station, but it was clearly intended to primarily serve New York City. Like the other area stations, its broadcasts emanated from the Empire State Building, although WATV continued to maintain its studios in Newark. In the beginning, it had actually attempted to transmit from New Jersey, only to discover that viewers in the state had their antennas directed towards Manhattan, making the move to the Empire State Building a virtual necessity. Still, WATV was the poor cousin among the city's television stations. In 1957, Bremer, now known as Atlantic Television Corporation, sold channel 13, plus AM and FM radio stations located in Newark, for $3 million to National Telefilm Associates, Inc. (NTA), which renamed the television station WNTA. NTA was established in 1951 as Ely Landau, Inc., a California television film distributor named after its founder, who three years later took on two partners and reorganized the business under the NTA name. WATV was intended to be a commercial outlet for NTA properties, but after the corporation lost $7 million in 1960, it began looking to unload its Newark media interests, pare down debt, and concentrate on its syndication business.

When White heard that channel 13 was about to become available, he assembled a group of influential New Yorkers, including businessmen and educators, to bid on the station and make it a non-commercial enterprise. The citizen's group made a $4 million cash offer, which was promptly rejected. Other interested parties soon emerged, including Landau, who resigned as chairman of NTA in order to form a company to bid on channel 13. David Susskind, in conjunction with Paramount Pictures, and 20th Century Fox were also reported to be in the running. White's group upped its bid to $5.5 million but fell far short of the $8 million reportedly offered by one of the commercial interests. Channel 13 would have likely remained a commercial station were it not for the newly appointed head of the FCC, Newton Minow, who very much wanted to see New York have an educational/public television outlet. By setting up hearings to discuss channel 13, he was able to determine its fate. Faced with a delay of at least a year, the commercial bidders withdrew, leaving the field open to the citizen's group, which in May 1961 was chartered as Educational Television for the Metropolitan Area (ETMA). Despite having a clear advantage, ETMA faced further hurdles in acquiring channel 13. For a time it appeared that NTA's fortunes might improve enough so that the corporation would retain the station. A deal for re-run rights to "Play of the Week" with WNEW-TV ultimately fell through, but the development boosted the final purchase price of WNTA. For a time, New Jersey Governor Robert Meyner also held up the transfer of his state's only VHF channel to ETMA, but at the eleventh hour backed off when the new owners agreed to schedule programming oriented specifically for a New Jersey audience. On December 22, 1961, the transfer was completed, with ETMA paying NTA $6.45 million, of which $1.25 million came from the six area commercial television stations which were happy to eliminate a competitor for local ad dollars.

In April 1962, ETMA, which sounded too much like the earlier META organization, changed its name to Education Broadcasting Corporation and a month later gained non-profit status. White hoped to make the new station into something of a subsidiary of the Center, but the Ford Foundation, the principal backer of both groups, vetoed the merger plan and forced White to sever his ties with the station. Free of the Center, channel 13, now known as WNDT (New Dimensions in Television), went on the air at 8:00 p.m. on September 16, 1962, introduced by legendary television news pioneer Edward R. Murrow, who stated, "Tonight you join me at the birth of a great adventure." Following this historic broadcast, however, the adventure would be delayed for two weeks, the result of a strike by the American Federation of Television and Radio Artists, which was concerned about the non-actors that would likely appear on educational television. Once WNDT returned to the air, it quickly faced a financial crunch. Within two years, the station was on the verge of failure, forcing White and the Center, now known by the acronym NET, to step in with a rescue effort. Ford once again squelched merger plans, giving the new EBC board a year to improve its fund-raising efforts. Because it succeeded, merger talks were again halted, although White tried once more two years later. WNDT may have been able to survive, but it fell far short of its potential in both fund raising and programming. Instead of taking advantage of its New York locale and becoming America's preeminent public television station, WNDT was merely an adequate operation.

### *NET and WNDT Merge in 1970*

Developments in Washington ultimately resulted in NET and WNDT joining forces. In 1967, the Corporation for Public Broadcasting (CPB) was created and funded by Congress in order to create programming for the loose system of educational television stations(now more commonly known as public television stations) spread across the country. Two years later, the

## Key Dates

**1946:** Bremer Broadcasting acquires a license to Channel 13 in Newark, New Jersey.
**1952:** Educational Television and Radio Center is established, later to be known as NET.
**1961:** Educational Television for the Metropolitan Area (ETMA) is formed to purchase Channel 13, WNTA, which is renamed WNDT.
**1962:** ETMA is renamed Educational Broadcasting Corporation (EBC).
**1970:** WNDT merges with NET to become WNET.
**2001:** WLIW-TV agrees to merge with WNET under EBC control.

Public Broadcasting Service (PBS) was established to distribute CPB programming as well as productions from local public stations. As a result of these changes, NET began to lose its place in the emerging public television landscape. While PBS began to assume the mantle of America's fourth television network, NET was turning into a fifth wheel, despite its solid reputation and strong organization. Now it was Ford that suggested NET and WNDT join forces, combining NET's producing resources with WNDT's broadcasting facilities to create what the country's public television system so desperately needed: a powerful flagship station located in the top media market. Because the two organizations were located in Manhattan, there was resistance from both sides. However, since the major benefactor of each party was Ford, a compromise was ultimately found and consummated on June 29, 1970. The chairman of WNDT was paired with the president of NET to run the new operation, renamed WNET (eventually becoming known as Thirteen/WNET), with EBC serving as the corporate parent.

To breathe life into Thirteen/WNET, a young publishing executive named John Jay Iselin was hired as general manager of the station. Under his leadership, Thirteen/WNET began to create exciting local programming as well as become a major producer of programming for PBS. In 1971, Thirteen/WNET launched *The Great American Dream Machine,* a critically acclaimed anthology show. In that same year journalist, Bill Moyers began to host *This Week,* a show devoted to news and commentary. Thirteen/WNET founded Television Laboratory in 1972 in order to make the work of independent filmmakers available to the general public. A year later, the station produced the controversial documentary series *An American Family.* Other programming highlights of the 1970s included the introduction of *Theatre in American* (1974)and *Dance in America* (1976), the critically acclaimed series *The Adams Chronicles* (1976), the launch of *The MacNeill/Lehrer Report* (1976), the premiere of *Live from Lincoln Center* (1976) and *Live From the Met* (1977), and *The Shakespeare Plays* (1979). Highlights of the 1980s included *Brideshead Revisited* (1982), *Nature* (1982), *American Playhouse* (1982), *The Brain* (1984), *Heritage: Civilization and the Jews* (1984), *American Masters* (1986), and *The Story of English* (1986).

By the mid-1980s, Thirteen/WNET had established itself as a producer of cultural programming that was now seen around the world. Despite a well-deserved reputation, the organization faced severe financial problems, which resulted in cutbacks in 1986. Iselin was replaced as president of Thirteen/WNET in 1987 by William Baker, who had considerable commercial television experience with Group W, as well as ties to public broadcasting. He was both a member of the board of Connecticut Public Television and served on the National Association of Broadcasters' Task Force. Improving Thirteen/WNET's finances while maintaining its ability to produce quality programming became Baker's primary concern. Even as a slumping economy forced another period of belt tightening at the station, he and chairman Henry R. Kravis launched a $65 million capital campaign in 1992. Of that amount, $35 million would be set aside for an endowment, $15 million would be used to upgrade facilities, and another $15 million would be set aside as a contingency fund. In fact, the fund-raising efforts of Thirteen/WNET were so successful that by 1997 the endowment fund grew to $70 million.

Thirteen/WNET was one of the few public television stations to enjoy the security of an endowment fund. Moreover, the station was able to finance the conversion from analog to digital transmission (at the cost of $30 million), as mandated by the FCC in the mid-1900s with a May 2003 deadline. Most public television stations were not so fortunate, including Long Island's WLIW-TV, channel 21, which lacked the $5 million to $10 million it needed to upgrade to digital technology, despite being the fourth most-watched public television station. Thirteen/WNET, on the other hand, was America's most watched public television station. In November 2000, Thirteen/WNET began discussing the possibility of taking over WLIW-TV, a decade-old idea, as well as WNSE-TV, channel 25, a Brooklyn-based, New York City Board of Education-owned station. By the summer of 2001, a deal was struck with WLIW-TV, calling for EBC to contribute $4.6 million to the station's digital conversion, $700,000 annually for five years in order to produce Long Island programming, and another $750,000 to be used to promote WLIW-TV and its programming. In exchange, EBC would hold the station's license and receive all of the station's future fund-raising efforts. In addition, all bequests, as were legally possible, would be transferred to Thirteen/WNET's corporate parent. Moreover, programming decisions for WLIW-TV would be made by a joint committee equally divided between the two stations. If necessary, a final decision rested with the president of EBC. The alliance between the two public stations, the audience of which greatly overlapped, also allowed for better coordination of fund-raising efforts. No longer during pledge weeks would both stations compete for the attention of the same viewers, sometimes with similar special programming.

On July 31, 2001, the Board of WLIW-TV agreed to the merger plan, which was forwarded for final review to the FCC. The WNSE-TV merger discussions continued with the New York City Board of Education, but this matter soon took a backseat to the events of September 11, 2001. When on that morning terrorists crashed two jetliners into the Twin Towers of the World Trade Center, Thirteen/WNET not only lost two analog transmitters and a digital transmitter and its antennae, it also suffered the tragedy of having one of its engineers killed. In an instant, it became a non-broadcaster, losing about a third of its viewers, with only cable television subscribers able to receive its programming. A temporary antenna located in New Jersey was used to provide analog-only transmission, which was low powered, and Thirteen/WNET was still unable to adequately reach all of its viewers. As the station developed a long-term solution, either using the Empire State Building or by building a new tower, it faced the possibility of decreased funding, the result of pledge drives appealing to a much smaller audience. Moreover, other PBS-producing stations faced problems with underwriters, who wanted to be assured that the full New York audience could be delivered before committing their money. In the 40 years since the Educational Broadcasting Corporation was formed to buy Channel 13 and the 30 years since the station merged with NET to form Thirteen/WNET, New York public television grew so important that its fiscal health now affected the entire PBS network.

### *Principal Subsidiaries*

Thirteen/WNET; WLIW-TV.

### *Principal Competitors*

WCBS; WNBC; WNYW; WABC; WWOR; WPIX.

### *Further Reading*

Block, Valerie, "WNET Winded From Lost Airtime," *Crain's New York Business,* November 5, 2001, p. 3.

Carter, Bill, "PBS Channels In New York Plan Merger," *New York Times,* August 1, 2001, p. B1.

——, "Record WNET Fund Drive," *New York Times,* April 9, 1992, p. 24.

Day, James, *The Vanishing Vision,* Berkeley, California: University of California Press, 1995, 443 p.

*Hudson Stoddard Report: Pre-History Through 1961–1970,* New York: WNET/Thirteen, 1987.

Odenwald, Dan, "New York's Ex-Rival Stations Merge Under Single License," *Current,* August 6, 2001.

Sikov, Ed, "Only the Best," New York: WNET/Thirteen, 1987.

—Ed Dinger

# Elsinore Corporation

**202 Fremont Street**
**Las Vegas, Nevada 89101**
**U.S.A.**
**Telephone: (702) 385-4011**
**Fax: (702) 387-5125**
**Web site: http://www.fourqueens.com**

*Public Company*
*Incorporated:* 1972
*Employees:* 889
Sales: $59.2 million (2001)
*Stock Exchanges:* Over-the-Counter Bulletin Board
*Ticker Symbol:* ELSO
*NAIC:* 721120 Casino Hotels

The Elsinore Corporation owns and operates the Four Queens Hotel and Casino in downtown Las Vegas. The Four Queens hotel provides accommodations in 690 rooms, including 45 suites, and houses 14,600 feet of meeting and convention space. The 30,000 square foot casino offers gaming with nearly 1100 slot machines, a keno lounge, a sport book, and over 25 gaming tables. The Four Queens also distributes a table game, Multiple Action blackjack, in Nevada and New Jersey. The Four Queens is part of the Freemont Street Experience, a covered pedestrian mall where special events and a nightly laser light show draw visitors downtown. The original owner of the Four Queens named the property for his four daughters. In 2002 Elsinore announced plans to sell the Four Queens, its main asset, to a Nevada-based gaming company called SummerGate Inc. Though this deal fell through in July 2002, the company's future plans remained unclear.

### *1970s Origins*

The Elsinore Corporation originated as a wholly owned subsidiary of the Hyatt Corporation; formed in 1972, Elsinore oversaw casino hotel operations in Nevada. The Four Queens Hotel and Casino in downtown Las Vegas, in operation since 1966, offered 316 hotel rooms and 20,000 square feet of gaming space with slot machines and table games with low to mid-level betting. The Hyatt Lake Tahoe, secluded on a private beach on the north shore of Lake Tahoe, offered 433 hotel rooms in an upscale setting, an 18,000 square foot gaming area, and convention and meeting facilities.

During the 1970s business and revenues grew at the Elsinore properties, particularly at the Four Queens, as a rise in available hotel accommodations in downtown Las Vegas drew more people to downtown casinos. In 1978 alone casino income increased 23 percent due to new business activity and a 6,000 square foot expansion of the Four Queens gaming area. Revenues at both hotels increased with higher occupancy rates and higher average room rates. Elsinore recorded casino revenues of $33.7 million in 1979, compared to $18 million in 1976, and hotel revenues climbed to $17.6 million compared to $9.5 million in 1976. The company reported net income of $5.5 million in 1979, compared to $682,000 in 1976.

Elsinore became an independent company in 1979 when the Pritzker family of Chicago took Hyatt private. Hyatt shareholders received 1.12 shares of Elsinore stock and $13.00 cash for each share of Hyatt common stock. Hyatt retained 27.5 percent interest in Elsinore and continued to manage the Lake Tahoe facility. In June, a public offering of stock raised $17.6 million, which Elsinore invested in a joint venture with Playboy Enterprises Inc. (PEI) to construct a hotel and casino in Atlantic City. A January offering of subordinated debentures raised $22.5 million. Elsinore applied those funds to refurbishment and expansion of the hotel at the Four Queens. The project involved the construction of an 18-story tower holding 400 guest rooms, twofold expansion of the three restaurants, and expansion of casino space to 33,000 square feet.

In 1980, Playboy/Elsinore Associates began construction on a $159 million hotel and casino in Atlantic City. The Playboy Hotel and Casino offered 500 hotel rooms and suites, 52,000 square feet of gaming space, 25,000 square feet of convention and meeting facilities, and a 1,000-seat entertainment lounge, the Playboy Cabaret. Elsinore and Playboy sought to attract the international, high roller market with a design modeled on European casinos and Playboy casinos in England. Spread over three floors in small rooms the Playboy provided an intimate setting for gaming, including European favorites such as Euro-

## Key Dates:

**1979:** Elsinore becomes an independent company when its parent, the Hyatt Corporation, becomes a private company.
**1981:** The Playboy Hotel and Casino opens in Atlantic City.
**1984:** After New Jersey Casino Commission forces Playboy Enterprises to sell its interest to Elsinore, Atlantic City property is renamed Atlantis Casino Hotel.
**1985:** While the Four Queens prospers, losses and debt at Atlantic City property leads to bankruptcy.
**1988:** To pay debt, Elsinore sells its Hyatt Lake Tahoe property and agrees to sell Atlantis.
**1994:** Joint ventures begin construction on two Native American casinos.
**1995:** Elsinore files Chapter 11 bankruptcy.
**1997:** Riviera Management begins to operate the Four Queens and changes its gaming format.
**2000:** Payment from former casino partner gives company a temporary reprieve from losses.
**2002:** Potential sale of Four Queens leaves Elsinore's future questionable.

pean Single O Roulette, American Double O Roulette, and Chemin de Fer, a game similar to baccarat. The Playboy Hotel and Casino in Atlantic City opened on April 14, 1981.

### *The 1980s: Problems at Playboy Hotel and Casino Lead to Bankruptcy*

While business at the Four Queens and Hyatt Lake Tahoe provided some financial stability for the company, the new hotel and casino venture in Atlantic City proved troublesome from the beginning. Within a few months of operation it became clear that the market for luxury, high stakes gaming was limited in Atlantic City. The high roller business proved to be barely profitable, with participants given free hotel accommodations, meals, and other incentives. Most local gaming business was being generated from bus groups and low stakes players. Also, while the 22-story tower was easily spotted from a distance, its narrow entrance in a bland section of town made the facility difficult to locate from the street. By August, Playboy and Elsinore began to direct its promotional efforts to the mass market.

In it's first full year in operation, in 1982, the Playboy Hotel and Casino lost $10.8 million. That year Robert Maxey, formerly president of Golden, Nugget, Inc., became president and CEO of Elsinore. Upon his first visit to the Playboy Hotel and Casino, Maxey immediately noticed basic problems with the casino, particularly that it was not located on the first floor for easy street access, and that the casino was not all on one, spacious floor. Maxey decided to change the company's marketing strategy to use the three-story casino to its best advantage. Maxey planned to redesign each floor of the casino to appeal to different income levels. The first level casino appealed to low stakes gamblers with an emphasis on slot machines, an expanded coffee shop, and easy access to the bus unloading and loading site. The second story offered more table games and a bar and restaurant for mid-level players. The third casino level was to be remodeled in luxury for high stakes gaming.

Meanwhile, in April 1982, after some questionable dealings by Hugh Hefner's other enterprises came to light, the New Jersey Casino Control Commission demanded that PEI sell its 45.7 percent interest in Playboy/Elsinore Associates. Though a buyout from Elsinore should have been based on the actual value of the property, a money-losing operation, the Commission allowed PEI to sell its stock for the amount of its initial investment of $51 million.

Elsinore completed its acquisition of PEI's interests in joint venture subsidiaries that operated the Playboy in Atlantic City in April 1984. Elsinore Shore Associates (ESA), formerly Playboy/Elsinore Associates, paid PEI $7.6 million in cash with the balance due according to the terms of a promissory note. Also, ESA owed PEI $5.6 million in management fees, due by April 1990. ESA owned 91.5 percent of the hotel-casino, with 8.5 percent owned by unaffiliated third parties.

Elsinore renamed the Atlantic City property Atlantis Casino Hotel, after the mythological civilization. The Riverboat Casino on the first level was completed in March 1984 and refurbishment of the second level, in an Asian, Shangri-la motif, began in December. In June the company launched an advertising campaign, using the monolithic appearance of the glass tower in a spoof on the movie *2001: A Space Odyssey*. With music from the title soundtrack and the tagline, "Civilization Comes to Atlantic City," the television commercials showed the hotel appear from under the ocean. Advertising media included newspapers, magazines, radio, and billboards.

With the consolidation of Atlantis revenues for the last three quarters of 1984, Elsinore recorded revenues of $77.5 million. Though The Playboy Hotel and Casino managed to earn a net profit of approximately $500,000 in 1983, by 1984 the facility operated at a loss of approximately $9 million, with revenues declining 19.4 percent, by $30 million, primarily in casino gaming. Lack of name recognition hurt the company's business while free food and alcohol and other expenses exceeded intake from a clientele of primarily low stakes gamblers. The Atlantis won $3,291 per square foot of gaming space compared to an overall average in Atlantic City of $4,594. Elsinore's Lake Tahoe property operated profitably with increased hotel and casino revenues; however, a strike by the Culinary Workers Union and Bartenders Union at the Four Queens (and several other Las Vegas hotels) resulted in a net loss of $233,000 at that property.

In 1984 the company recorded a net profit of $5.6 million due to the extinguishment of debt, but the refinancing of this debt pushed Elsinore into bankruptcy within the next year. Elsinore Finance Corporation (EFC) issued $115 million of senior mortgage bonds at 15.5 percent interest due November 1, 1999. Elsinore used the funds to refinance a $69.2 million first mortgage held by ESA, to pay other debt, and to pay PEI. Elsinore secured the new debt with a $25 million lien on the Hyatt Lake Tahoe and a $90 million mortgage on the Atlantis. The bonds increased the company's interest expense, however, as interest rates declined shortly afterward. Also, according to David Johnston in *Temples of Chance,* the Pritzker family's influence on the Elsinore board of directors led the Hyatt Lake Tahoe to loan $20 million to the Hyatt Corporation at 8.5 percent interest, though Elsinore paid 15.5 percent interest on the same money.

Elsinore's financial troubles became evident early in 1985. After making only one payment to PEI, Elsub, the financing subsidiary of the Atlantis, was unable to make a $400,000 payment in April. In November, Elsub missed a $7 million payment on interest due on the senior mortgage bonds and the Lake Tahoe property missed a $2 million payment. This situation led PEI to file an involuntary petition for reorganization under Chapter 11 Bankruptcy Code as well as a civil lawsuit. Elsinore subsidiaries followed with their own bankruptcy filings, prompting Maxey to resign; Jeanne Hood, president of the Four Queens since 1977, became president of Elsinore.

Under the plan of reorganization Elsinore planned to sell the Hyatt Tahoe to pay $20 million in accrued interest through June 30, 1986, while the balance due bondholders was to be paid in company stock. The company also planned to sell the Atlantis. Elsinore subsidiaries wrote down the value of assets at $37.9 million in 1985 and $42.4 million in 1986, resulting in net losses of $24.2 million in 1985 and $39.6 million at Elsinore in 1986. Despite the company's financial instability, the New Jersey Casino Control Commission renewed the Atlantis gaming license annually, allowing operations to continue.

An uneasy stability stemmed from a brisk business at the Four Queens. As poor management decisions by Hood drove high stakes gamblers from the Atlantis to competing casinos, Atlantis revenues declined 9.2 percent in 1985, to $181 million, primarily from a $10 million decline in casino revenues. Meanwhile, the culmination of marketing programs at the Four Queens resulted in increased hotel occupancy from 83 percent in 1985 to 94 percent in 1986. Overall revenues increased 13.2 percent in 1985 to $87.8 million, and 9.3 percent in 1986 to $95 million due to growth in its Las Vegas operation. Interest on income tax assessments led to a pretax loss of $2.4 million at the Four Queens in 1986, however.

Litigation between Atlantis and its creditors delayed final court approval of the Plan of Reorganization until 1988, costing the company $15 million in legal fees. Under the plan, Elsinore sold the Hyatt Lake Tahoe to the Hyatt Corporation for $45.3 million, $28.8 million in cash plus the assumption of debt. In June 1989, Elsinore finalized the sale of the Atlantis and its subsidiaries to Donald Trump. That year the company recorded $67.5 million in revenues and a loss of $11.6 million.

## *Early 1990s*

By 1990, the company had achieved a somewhat stable financial position on the strength of its Four Queens property. That first full year of operating a single hotel and casino, Elsinore recorded $68.3 million in revenues and net income of $2.2 million, despite competition from large, new casino hotels on the Las Vegas Strip. The recession of 1991 and 1992 negatively affected business, but the property did well compared to other downtown properties, attaining higher income and lower expenses. Also, the Four Queens created and patented a new game, Multiple Action Blackjack, which found immediate popularity at Four Queens, and the company licensed the game to casinos in New Jersey. Business rebounded in 1993, garnering $67 million in revenues; however, a $2 million income tax interest and assessment from 1980 to 1983 eroded $4 million in operating revenues for a net loss of $2.5 million.

With Thomas E. Martin as president of Elsinore, the company initiated several programs to enhance operations at the Four Queens. These involved cost reduction, improved employee relations, including a stock options program, and enhanced customer service. The Four Queens emphasized the smaller, welcoming ambiance of the property, as an advantage over new mega-resorts along the Las Vegas Strip, obtaining a high level of customer loyalty through repeat business. The Reel Winners program for frequent customers counted 38,000 members at this time. The company reorganized the layout of the casino to make better use of the space and to accommodate a new mix of games, such as the addition of Let-it-Ride and Caribbean Stud Poker table games, as well as electronic slot machines. Promotional programs focused on niche markets in the southwestern United States, especially southern California. Special package programs successfully attracted Hawaiians to the Four Queens, leading the company to open a Hawaiian style café in April 1994. In June, the Four Queens opened a moderately priced Italian restaurant. Hugo's Cellar, the casino hotel's fine dining restaurant, was named one of the best restaurants in Las Vegas in 1993.

Elsinore prepared for the redevelopment of downtown Las Vegas, in the vicinity of the Four Queens, contributing $3 million to the project. Meeting facilities were expanded to 15,000 square feet, double its existing capacity in 1993 and, in January 1994, the Four Queens began an 18-month refurbishment of its 704 hotel rooms in preparation for the grand unveiling of the Freemont Street Experience. Redevelopment of downtown Las Vegas at Freemont Street and Las Vegas Boulevard involved a covered pedestrian mall closed to motor vehicles, an area which included the entrance to the Four Queens. The company planned to renovate the exterior of the property at street-level and to open a new entryway on Freemont Street. The canopy covering the pedestrian mall was designed with special, reflective materials to maximize the effects of laser light shows choreographed to music.

In early 1994, Elsinore announced new joint ventures with Native American tribes. One proposal involved a Class II gaming facility on the land of the Twenty-nine Palms Band of Mission Indians near Palm Springs. Another project planned for a Las Vegas-style casino at Jamestown on S'Klallam tribal land on the Olympic peninsula northwest of Seattle. Both of these projects received regulatory approval from the National Indian Gaming Commission in August. The company funded its projects with a new financing and a public offering of stock. In autumn 1993, the company obtained $60 million in first mortgage notes to pay debt, refurbish the Four Queens, and to fund development of new casinos. An additional $3 million in short term mortgage notes provided funds to supplement working capital. In January 1995, Elsinore raised $4 million through a public offering of stock.

The Spotlight 29 Casino and the 7 Cedars Casino opened in January and February 1995, respectively. Spotlight 29, a $10 million project, involved a 74,000 square foot facility in a circular design. Gaming included off-track betting, bingo, pull tabs, poker, Asian card games, and other card games. The 7 Cedars offered blackjack, craps, roulette, poker, keno, bingo, pull-tabs, and other games in a 54,000 square foot gaming space. Initially, business at 7 Cedars exceeded expectations, returning a small profit when losses were expected during the slow, winter season. From the start Spotlight 29 lost money due to competition from Class III gaming at other tribal casino operations in California. To maintain cash flow at that casino Elsinore obtained $1.4 million in convertible subordinated notes in March.

### *1995 Bankruptcy Woes*

Disappointing results at the two Native American casinos and other problems inclined Elsinore to another bankruptcy in 1995. In March, the Twenty-nine Palms Band installed Class III, electronic slot machines at Spotlight 29 without a compact with the state of California. As the company believed this act to be in violation of Nevada gaming regulations and its management contract, Elsinore filed appropriate lawsuits to dissolve its partnership in the casino. Also, construction of the Freemont Street Experience, which opened in November, had a negative impact on casino revenues at the Four Queens. Elsinore filed for bankruptcy protection in October 1995, as it could not make its interest payment on the first mortgage notes. As a result Elsinore recorded a net loss of $45.8 million on $57 million in revenues in 1995.

The court approved a Plan of Reorganization in March 1996, at which time Elsinore issued common stock in return for a reduction of the claim on the first mortgage notes from $60 million to $30 million. The investment firm Morgens, Waterfall, Vintiadis & Company (MWV) obtained 99 percent ownership of the company, naming Bruce Waterfall as chairman and Jeffery T. Leeds as president and CEO. In August, Riviera Holding Corporation assumed management of the Four Queens as part of the bankruptcy reorganization.

The newly formed management company, Riviera Gaming Management-Elsinore (RGME), changed the gaming format of the Four Queens, believing slot machines to be the most profitable means of revenue support. RGME removed several table games, including some of the popular Caribbean Stud and Let-it-Ride games, and added more slot machines. In 1998, the Four Queens offered 26 game tables, compared to more than forty during the mid-1990s, and 1,068 slot machines, compared to fewer than 1,000 previously. The change in format changed the customer base at the Four Queens to a low stakes clientele.

These actions contributed to lower casino revenues, from $42.3 million in 1996 to $36.5 million in 1997. Overall revenues declined from $61.2 million in 1996, with a net loss of $1.6 million, to $53.8 million in 1997. The institution of new promotions for slot machine gaming facilitated a rebound in casino revenues to $39.4 million in 1998, though hotel and food and beverage revenues continued to decline. Total revenues of $55.9 million in 1998 included the first payment of $1.2 million from a settlement with Palm Springs East for Elsinore's investment in Spotlight 29. Royalties from Multiple Action blackjack accounted for $103,000 in revenues, down from $198,000 in 1996.

While attempts to find a buyer for the Four Queens failed, payments from Palm Springs East compensated for operating losses. Elsinore received $1.2 million in 1999 and $6.2 million in 2000, for a total settlement of $8.6 million. Also, Elsinore terminated its management agreement with RGME, saving more than $1 million in annual fees, and hired a new general manager for the Four Queens, Dual Cooper. In 2000, Elsinore recorded a net profit of $5.1 million on total revenues of $60.7 million. Management at Elsinore viewed this profitability as a temporary respite, however, as cash flow was not expected to handle the $8 million principal on notes payable in October 2003.

In May 2002 Elsinore announced that it had entered an agreement to sell Four Queens to SummerGate Inc. for around $22 million. With Four Queens representing the clear majority of Elsinore's assets, Elsinore planned to dissolve. By July of that year, however, the agreement had been dissolved and Elsinore's future was again unclear.

### *Principal Subsidiaries*

Four Queens, Inc.; Four Queens Experience Corporation; Elsinore Finance Corporation.

### *Principal Competitors*

Boyd Gaming Corporation; Harrah's Entertainment, Inc.; Las Vegas Sands, Inc.; MGM Mirage; Mandalay Resort Group Inc.; Park Place Entertainment Corporation.

### *Further Reading*

Cuff, Daniel F., "Elsinore, Which Owns Casinos, Picks President," *New York Times*, October 6, 1982, p. D2.

Dougherty, Philip H., "Advertising: Playboy Casino Campaign," *New York Times*, March 10, 1983, p. D16.

"Elsinore Files for Chapter 11 Protection; Flagship Property, Four Queens, Remains Fully Operational," *PR Newswire*, October 31, 1995.

"Four Queens Hotel and Casino Is Giving Las Vegas Back to the Adults," *PR Newswire*, November 1, 1995.

Greenhouse, Steven, "Playboy Petitions Over Casino's Debt," *New York Times*, November 14, 1985, p. D4.

Johnston, David, *Temples of Chance: How America Inc. Bought Out Murder Inc. to Win Control of the Casino Business*, New York: Doubleday, 1992.

"Palm Springs Meets Las Vegas on the Colorado River; Elsinore Corp. Announces Major Role in New Project," *Business Wire*, April 29, 1994.

"Riviera Assumes Management of Four Queens; 700-Room Hotel and 33,000 Square Foot Casino in Prime Location," *PR Newswire*, August 15, 1996.

"7 Cedars Casino Opens in Washington State; Elsinore Opens Second Native American Casino Project This Year," *Business Wire*, February 6, 1995.

—Mary Tradii

# Esselte Leitz GmbH & Co. KG

**Siemensstrasse 64**
**D-70469 Stuttgart**
**Germany**
**Telephone: (49) (711) 8103-0**
**Fax: (49) (711) 8103-486**
**Web site: http://www.leitz.de**

*Private Company*
*Incorporated:* 1871 as Werkstätte zur Herstellung von Metallteilen für Ordnungsmittel Louis Leitz
*Employees:* 1,650
*Sales:* $231 million (2000)
*NAIC:* 322233 Stationery, Tablet, and Related Product Manufacturing

Esselte Leitz GmbH & Co. KG is Germany's leading manufacturer of premium binders and other products for filing and archiving documents. The Leitz Ordner—the "Mercedes" of loose leaf binders which on average costs two and a half times as much as other binders—has a market share of about 40 percent in Germany. Roughly two out of three hole punches in Germany are made by Leitz, as well as one quarter of all report covers. The company also makes tab organizers, file folders, staplers, letter trays, filing systems, binding and laminating machines and supplies, and offers electronic archive system software. The Stuttgart-based company with an over 125-year-long tradition was acquired by Swedish office supplies maker Esselte in 1998. An essential part of Esselte's business strategy, the company markets the Leitz brand all over Europe.

## *Reinventing the German Office: 1871—1925*

The formation of the German Empire under Prussia's Wilhelm I—a unified German state that put an end to protectionism and bureaucracy among the four German kingdoms of Prussia, Bavaria, Saxony, and Württemberg, five grand duchies, 13 duchies and principalities, and three free cities—created a national economy of an unprecedented scope. This in turn spurred the imagination of bankers and entrepreneurs and triggered the unprecedented wave of economic activity that became known as the *Gründerzeit.* One of those new entrepreneurs was the mechanic Johann Ludwig Leitz, who in 1871 set up "a workshop for the manufacture of metal parts for office organizing materials" in a backyard in the German city of Stuttgart. Starting out with three workers, Leitz made *Biblorhaptes,* an early kind of binder which businesses used to file their correspondence and other documents. At the time, a French manufacturer dominated the market with a high quality product. However, within a few years, the Leitz *Biblorhapt* gained a reputation in Germany. The business even grew through the economic crisis that followed the *Gründerjahre* and Leitz moved to a bigger location.

Besides its first success in form of awards at regional trade shows, the company also had to overcome some tough challenges. A lot of time and money was spent on "patent and trademark wars." Then, in 1884, Leitz' production manager Bux left the company, set up his own shop, and started competing against his former employer with lower prices. For three years Leitz didn't make any profits for that reason—until Bux went bankrupt in 1887. The company started thriving again and by 1888 employed almost 20 people. Louis Leitz—the founder had changed his name—spent most of the 1890s improving his product. In 1892, the company introduced a hole punch and a year later the first binder-mechanism using a lever—a big improvement over the older models. Four years later, Leitz launched a further improved product with the lever placed outside the metal rings that held the paper sheets. This model became the prototype of the ring binders used in German offices for the next century, and the "Leitz Ordner" became synonymous with them.

In 1897, Louis Leitz decided to significantly expand the scope of the company. A year later Leitz' 60 employees moved to a newly built factory in the small town Feuerbach, which later became a part of Stuttgart. The new building remained the company's headquarters throughout the next century.

After the turn of the century, Leitz continued to create innovative products and more efficient technologies. In 1901, the company started making "quick binders," report folders with a simple metal fastener. Beginning in 1902, more and more production technologies were refined so that the covers of file boxes and binders were made in just one production step. In

### Company Perspectives:

*Esselte is* committed *to meeting the needs of the customer by delivering* quality products *that bring* innovation, efficiency, and style *to the way people work in the office and at home.*

1905, the first flexible hole punch, ''Komet,'' with two different widths was introduced, followed by an ''extra strong'' model. In 1908, the company started offering two different kinds of binders, one of higher quality, one more affordable. New back labels and the *Griffloch*—a metal-framed hole in the back of the binder that made it easier to pull them out of a shelf—were added. The company's first subsidiary was established in Berlin, and the capacity of the plant in Feuerbach greatly expanded. By 1913, Louis Leitz was Germany's largest manufacturer of binders and file boxes. In that year, the company led negotiations between seven German companies in the same business that resulted in an agreement among them to place certain price caps in order to ensure profitability for all of them.

## *Surviving Two World Wars: 1914–45*

In 1914, World War I began and Leitz had to face challenges such as scarcity of raw materials and fuel, government-imposed restrictions, and unreliable transportation. However, the main challenge was that many Leitz workers had to serve in the German Army—including Eberhard Leitz, one of the founder's sons. He came back when the war ended in November 1918, but the year of regained peace was a year of loss for the company: Louis Leitz died. His two sons, Eberhard and Ludwig, took over at a time of economic turmoil. The German Weimar Republic ever so slowly slipped into inflation that after five years exploded into hyperinflation. Leitz issued new list prices every month for the years 1919 and 1920 that increased 200 percent each time. After a short break in 1921, prices grew by rates in the 1,000 percent range and reached six- and seven-digit percent increases in July 1923. With concerted action, Leitz managed to expand even in those difficult times. In its 50th anniversary year, the company reported 250 employees on its payroll. In 1923, Leitz took over the Stuttgart-based binder-manufacturer Schukir. In the second half of the 1920s, the company introduced new products, such as a hole punch with a little arrow that helped center the paper, binders designed to stand rather than lay, a binder with an expanded capacity for documents, a much smaller than the usual binder model, and a little metal clamp that fit over the rings and kept the documents in place. In addition, Leitz launched a promotional newsletter for its retail partners with helpful tips on how to make their business thrive.

The late 1920s and early 1930s brought more political and economic turmoil to Germany. The worldwide economic depression was taking its toll on the country's export-oriented economy. Unemployment reached new highs, causing widespread poverty and political unrest. In January 1933, Adolf Hitler, leader of the right-wing National Socialist party, took over as Germany's new chancellor. It took him only a few years to eliminate many of his political opponents and to prepare the country for another war. Leitz, however, kept expanding its business. In 1933, the company acquired two Berlin-based competitors: Grünewald's Registrator & Co. and Regga Briefordner-Fabrik. Two years later Leitz introduced the fully automated production of quick-binders.

In 1935, Eberhard Leitz's 20-year-old son Manfred joined the family business. However, shortly after he had to leave for the two years of mandatory military service the Nazis—as the National Socialists were called—had introduced in the same year. By 1939, the Leitz catalogue offered some 300 products which were shipped to 84 countries around the world.

World War II began on September 1, 1939, when German troops invaded Poland. As a manufacturer of products with little importance for the German war economy, Leitz again had to cope with rationed supplies of necessities for running its business, including coal and electricity. The government required civil products to be simplified and made from less raw materials. Moreover, the following draft of men to serve in the army reduced the company's workforce by more than half. In 1943, they were partly replaced by slave workers from France. When the Allied forces flew air-attacks on Stuttgart, Leitz had to hand over part of its production facilities to the firm Bosch for the war effort. One day before the American army took over Stuttgart, the *Wehrmacht* took shelter at Leitz' headquarters. Because the city surrendered without much resistance, the buildings remained untouched.

## *From Binders to Office Systems: 1945–59*

A few weeks after Germany's unconditional surrender ended the war, Leitz resumed operations. In mid-July 1945, the company started out with 22 workers, a modest number compared to its pre-war staff of 750. The supply of gas and electricity—and consequently the production process—were frequently interrupted. In January 1947, the company even had to shut down operations completely for a week-long power-outage. In the same year, the company had to clear out its warehouse to be used by the military administration. The foundation of the Federal Republic of Germany in 1949, uniting the three zones occupied by the Western Allies, cleared the way for postwar reconstruction. In the same year, the first of the third generation of the Leitz family, Manfred Leitz, joined the company, which was transformed from Louis Leitz OHG into Louis Leitz KG. In 1950, when Martin Leitz and Dr. Herbert Klaiber joined the top management team, the company's output exceeded the pre-war figure for the first time. The year 1951 marked the beginning of the reconstruction and expansion of the company's buildings and facilities.

At the beginning of the 1950s, Leitz made a strategic decision: to expand its product range from binders and related products to all office systems for organizing and filing paper. In 1953, a brand-new production plant started operations in Düsseldorf and the facilities in Berlin were extended for a higher capacity. In the same year, Leitz started making different kinds of ''ALPHA'' hanging folders. However, the company got off to a bumpy start. Due to high fluctuations in the orders received, Leitz had to adjust output by introducing part-time work schemes and layoffs. In 1954, Ludwig Leitz died, and a year later his brother Eberhard also passed away. Their sons Martin and Conrad now took charge of the family business. By 1955, the number of Leitz employees had exceeded the 1,000

## Key Dates:

**1871:** The mechanic Johann Ludwig Leitz sets up a workshop in Stuttgart.
**1896:** The Leitz Ordner is introduced to the market.
**1913:** Louis Leitz is Germany's largest manufacturer of binders.
**1949:** Louis Leitz OHG becomes Louis Leitz KG.
**1956:** Leitz takes over office supplies manufacturer Herm. Herdegen GmbH.
**1971:** The company's first foreign subsidiary is established in the Netherlands.
**1992:** The company restructures its organization into a group of companies under the umbrella of Louis Leitz KG.
**1994:** Leitz takes over the Turkish market leader for office supplies, Mahir & Numan A.S.
**1998:** The Swedish conglomerate Esselte AB acquires Louis Leitz International GmbH.

mark. In 1956, Leitz took over office supplies manufacturer Herm. Herdegen GmbH. Three years later the company ventured into organizational consulting. As an added value to Leitz' customers, the organizational advisors analyzed the flow of information in a given company, calculated the time, space, and cost required for alternative filing and archiving solutions, and presented the optimal combination of Leitz filing systems to the customer.

### *Further Growth: 1960–93*

The 1960s and 1970s were years of unprecedented growth for Leitz. By 1971, the company's 100th anniversary year, Leitz shipped its products to 120 countries around the world. In addition, the company's first foreign subsidiary was established in the Netherlands. However, the company's main growth happened in Germany. Bernhard Klaiber replaced his father, Dr. Herbert Klaiber, who retired, in the top management team. A new production facility was built at the Feuerbach location. Another new plant for the manufacture of plastic foil sheet protectors was erected in record time in Münchingen near Stuttgart. By 1975, Leitz employed about 2,000 people at six locations, including Feuerbach, Münchingen, Düsseldorf, Berlin, Rangendingen, and Uelzen. In 1979, the company started making products from plastic.

The 1980s were a decade of significant growth, excellent profits, and more changes in management. Manfred Leitz was succeeded by Helmut Leitz, who took over responsibility for marketing and distribution. In 1988, Eberhard Leitz entered the business, followed by Joachim Leitz in 1990. That year marked the reunification of the two separate German states that World War II had created. The expanded market caused a significant boost in sales for Leitz. In 1990, the company's new state-of-the-art central warehouse in Heilbronn opened its doors. A new sales office was established in Leipzig. Due to high demand from the new eastern German states, sales for Leitz products peaked in 1992 at DM 524 million. The company's workforce had grown to 3,000. The production plant in Münchingen was greatly expanded. A novelty in Leitz' product range—small binding machines for the office—was introduced in 1992. It was also in 1992 that the company restructured its organization into a group of companies under the umbrella of Louis Leitz KG.

### *Buying and Being Bought: 1993–2000*

The growth period of the 1980s and early 1990s was followed by a period of consolidation due to a stagnating market. Three out of eleven domestic sales offices were closed down, as well as the plants in Rangendingen and Düsseldorf. With domestic markets shrinking, Leitz saw a possible solution in another effort to expand internationally. The company had set up a subsidiary in the United Kingdom—Leitz (UK) Ltd.—in 1998. In 1994, Leitz took over the Turkish market leader for office supplies, Mahir & Numan A.S., hoping for more business in the Middle East. In the same year, the company acquired a share in the French Centra, Mecarex, and Tarifold group, which competed in the low-price segment while the Leitz brand was positioned at the premium price level. In 1996, the company's 125th anniversary year, the Leitz Ordner—as the company's binder was called in German—turned 100. Leitz itself was Germany's largest manufacturer for office supplies and the 50 million Leitz Ordners that were shipped annually generated one-third of the company's sales. Four of the six top Leitz executives were great-grandsons of the company founder. The company's foreign subsidiaries and sales offices in the United Kingdom, France, Turkey, the Netherlands, Austria, Sweden, Singapore, and the United States generated almost one-third of the company's revenues. Leitz product catalogue had grown to more than 2,000 articles.

However, the market for office products had changed in the 1990s. A growing number of internationally operating office supply retail chains entered the German market and started competing for market share with lower prices. Overcapacities among office supplies manufacturers put further pressure on prices, a situation which in turn significantly lowered profits. On top of that, electronic data storage systems started competing with paper-based filing systems. To survive and secure the long-term future of the company in this environment, Leitz was looking for a solution to turn the family business into a "higher-class player" with at least one billion German marks in sales—almost double what the company was hitherto generating. Buying or being bought—those were the two options. However, the company's funds and possibilities for financing a larger deal were limited.

In 1998, the Swedish conglomerate Esselte AB acquired Louis Leitz International GmbH for an estimated DM 580 million. The holding company Louis Leitz GmbH & Co. KG remained as a financial holding company for the heirs of the Leitz family. The new parent took over Leitz's management team and placed the responsibility for export management, especially in Central Europe, in Stuttgart. Although the family business disappeared, the Leitz brand endured.

### *Principal Competitors*

Herlitz AG; Elba Bürosysteme GmbH; Avery Dennison Corporation; Smead Manufacturing Company.

### *Further Reading*

''Der Druck auf deutsche Büroartikelhersteller wächst weiter,'' *Frankfurter Allgemeine Zeitung*, August 19, 1998, p. 16.

Hein, Christoph, ''Es hiess zu lange: Leitz bleibt, wie es ist,'' *Frankfurter Allgemeine Zeitung*, September 30, 1999, p. 30.

Karle, Roland, ''Wenn Schwaben mit den Schweden,'' *HORIZONT*, May 10, 2001, p. 99.

''Leitz bündelt Ordnerfertigung in Stuttgart,'' *Frankfurter Allgemeine Zeitung*, July 3, 1996, p. 22.

*Leitz im Wandel der Zeit,* Stuttgart, Germany: Louis Leitz International GmbH & Co., 1996, 22 p.

Schindler, Holger, ''Leitz-ein Inbegriff deutschen Ordnungsdrangs,'' *Süddeutsche Zeitung*, August 4, 1998.

Spies, Felix, ''Esselte Leitz stärkt deutschen Standort,'' *Süddeutsche Zeitung*, October 9, 2001, p 31.

''Das Traditionsunternehmen Louis Leitz wird an Esselte verkauft,'' *Frankfurter Allgemeine Zeitung*, August 4, 1998, p. 14.

—Evelyn Hauser

# Exelon Corporation

10 South Dearborn Street, 37th Floor
Chicago, Illinois 60690-3005
U.S.A.
Telephone: (312) 394-7398
Fax: (630) 663-7599
Web site: http://www.exeloncorp.com

*Public Company*
*Incorporated:* 1902 as Philadelphia Electric Company (PECO) and 1907 as The Commonwealth Edison Co., Inc. (Unicom)
*Employees:* 29,200
*Sales:* $15.1 billion (2001)
*Stock Exchanges:* New York
*Ticker Symbol:* EXC
*NAIC:* 221122 Electric Power Distribution; 221113 Nuclear Electric Power Generation; 221112 Fossil Fuel Electric Power Generation; 551112 Offices of Other Holding Companies

Exelon Corporation was formed from the 2000 merger of PECO Energy Company and Unicom Corporation. The deal created one of the largest utilities in the United States, with over $15 billion in revenues. Exelon serves five million electric and natural gas customers and operates with three main business segments: energy generation, energy delivery, and unregulated enterprises. With headquarters in Chicago, the company provides electricity to customers in both Illinois and Pennsylvania and also distributes natural gas in Pennsylvania. Through Exelon Nuclear, the firm operates ten stations and 17 nuclear units, making it the largest nuclear fleet in the United States.

## *The History of PECO*

The Philadelphia Electric Company was incorporated in 1902 but finds it origins in The Brush Electric Light Company of Philadelphia, which was formed in 1881. In 1880, Thomas Dolan convinced ten of Philadelphia's wealthiest entrepreneurs to invest in a company in ''the business of manufacturing, procuring, owning and operating various apparatus used in producing light, heat, or power by electricity or used in lighting buildings.'' The new venture traded a 50 percent share, or $100,000, of its stock for a license of the Brush arc dynamo, an electric generator that was then considered the best way to generate power for lighting.

Electric utilities customarily focused on a particular product, such as street lighting or industrial applications, in the late 1800s. As its name implied, The Brush Electric Light Company was primarily involved in commercial and street lighting. The Brush Company's first president was Henry Lewis, a dry goods merchant who served until his death in 1886. Dolan, who had been treasurer, chairman of the executive committee, and de facto head of the company, assumed the presidency at that time. He deflected early criticism of Brush's poles and wires, oversaw the construction of its first permanent generating facility, and helped increase the company's capitalization to $1 million to finance construction and expansion.

Throughout this early stage in the history of electric utilities, competition and fragmentation characterized the industry. Within the same city, varying voltages, currents, and frequencies provided by a multitude of companies made it difficult to develop standardized products. Utilities began to consolidate near the end of the 19th century to end competition and coordinate service. Brush merged with its most powerful rival, The United States Electric Lighting Company of Pennsylvania, in 1885.

The merged companies secretly formed an ''Electric Trust,'' known more commonly today as a holding company, in 1886. Secrecy was required because of the mistrust in which the public and politicians held such combines. The Trust soon acquired or controlled four more small local utilities, issuing $3.5 million in bonds as financial backing. However, as its existence came to light in the early 1880s, public and media criticism of the ''monopoly'' intensified. The Trust's ''unpopularity stemmed from its very name. Its behind-doors management of the operating companies could never bring it goodwill,'' according to Nicholas B. Wainwright in his *History of The Philadelphia Electric Company, 1881–1961*.

## Company Perspectives:

*At Exelon, everything we do is guided by our four core values: 1) boldness in staking out a leadership role in tomorrow's energy markets; 2) creativity in improving the quality of life through energy; 3) accountability to our customers, shareholders, employees, and communities; 4) commitment in operating facilities safely, protecting the environment, and developing our businesses responsibly.*

Competition hurt Brush as well. Its competitor, the Edison Electric Light Company of Philadelphia, had grown to equal the Trust in profits by 1892. Around the same time, local entrepreneur Martin Maloney reentered the electric industry after a successful gas venture. Maloney hoped to eliminate wasteful competition by consolidating Philadelphia's electric companies and standardizing service. He chartered the Pennsylvania Heat, Light and Power Company in 1895 with a massive capitalization of $10 million and immediately began to acquire competitors, taking over Columbia Electric Light Company and courting the Philadelphia Edison Company. By March 1896, he had merged with Edison and earned a seat on its board of directors.

When Maloney's Pennsylvania Heat acquired the Electric Trust and all its subsidiaries later that year, Thomas Dolan joined its board of directors. Unlike the Electric Trust, Maloney's consolidation scheme proceeded relatively smoothly in part because of a good public perception of his goals, which he stated in his first annual report: "To secure that class of service that would enable the Company to furnish to its patrons electricity under such conditions that they could use it more generally and apply it in many ways that the high prices prevailing prevented, and to demonstrate to the citizens of Philadelphia that a corporation could work for the benefit of the public and its stockholders at the same time." Maloney did, in fact, cut residential rates to below the national metropolitan average.

In 1898, Maloney absorbed five of Philadelphia's eight remaining independent arc lighting companies. A threat to his progress arose the following year with the formation of the $25 million National Electric Company. This new entity immediately acquired the Southern Electric Light and Power Company, one of the few strong competitors remaining. Maloney negotiated a merger of the two big companies that year. The combination had assets of $19.9 million and net profits of $518,000. The companies incorporated as the Philadelphia Electric Company (PE) in 1902.

Maloney retired and was succeeded as president by 29-year-old Joseph B. McCall, who guided the company through the difficult period of legal, financial, and technical reorganization that ensued. Demand had risen rapidly, and by the turn of the century, it was clear that the utility would need a massive central generating station. When PE's Station A on the Schuylkill River was completed in 1903, it was the largest in the state, generating over 7,000 kilowatts (kW). Although PE standardized much of its service as alternating current, most of downtown Philadelphia, which was served by the Edison division, continued to operate on direct current until 1935 (reflecting Thomas Edison's conviction that alternating current was dangerous). PE moved to a new, larger headquarters at the corner of Tenth and Chestnut streets in Philadelphia in 1907. That location would remain the center of PE operations until 1973.

Many factors encouraged a dramatic expansion of the electric industry during the first two decades of the 20th century. Larger, more efficient equipment was developed and service areas were expanded to include rural areas. Company-sponsored sales departments promoted appliances like the electric washer, iron, refrigerator, and vacuum cleaner to encourage increased use of electricity. As new applications for electric power developed, demand increased significantly. PE raised its generating capacity to meet this ever-expanding demand: each of the 30,000- and 35,000-kW units installed in 1915 and 1916 had a higher capacity than the entire PE system of 1903 (at 20,000 kW).

After the United States entered World War I the following year, the manufacture of munitions, ships, and steel in the Philadelphia area kept PE operating at capacity throughout the era. The company was often challenged by coal shortages and government rationing during the conflict. A centennial history published by PE in 1981 quoted an employee of the time who affirmed "the sigh of relief" felt at Schuylkill Station on Armistice Day.

By 1918, PE had 103,000 customers, a figure that nearly tripled within five years to 306,000 in 1923. During that period, the electric utility added twelve generators with a total capacity of over 300,000 kW. Joseph B. McCall advanced to the chairmanship of the company in 1924, and was succeeded as president by Walter H. Johnson, who served for four years. Later that decade, PE completed its first hydroelectric project on the Conowingo River in northeast Maryland. The company obtained land and financing, met political and regulatory requirements, and overcame construction obstacles to complete the unit in 1928. With a generating capacity of 252,000 kW, the hydroelectric dam ranked second only to the one at Niagara Falls. That same year, William H. Taylor assumed PE's presidency.

PE recorded another influential event during the prosperous decade of the 1920s: the creation of the Pennsylvania-New Jersey Interconnection in 1927. This cooperative linked Public Service Electric and Gas Company of New Jersey (which had had a partnership with PE since 1923) and Pennsylvania Power & Light Company (of Allentown) with Philadelphia Electric. The organization took advantage of regular fluctuations in each utility's power requirements to achieve economies of scale. For example, Allentown experienced morning peaks in October due to its coal mining activities, while Newark and Philadelphia scored highs in the December holiday season. The three original members were joined by the General Public Utilities Corporation and the Baltimore Gas and Electric Company in 1956, when the cooperative's name was changed to the Pennsylvania-New Jersey-Maryland Interconnection (PJM). The Potomac Electric Power Company (PEPCO), serving metropolitan Washington, D.C., joined in 1965. The cooperative promoted savings and reliability.

In the early 20th century, Philadelphia Electric's service area was surrounded by three major electric and gas utility compa-

## Key Dates:

**1902:** The Philadelphia Electric Company (PE) is incorporated.
**1907:** Samuel Insull merges Commonwealth Electric Company and Chicago Edison Company to form Commonwealth Edison (ComEd).
**1927:** The Pennsylvania-New Jersey Interconnection is created.
**1929:** PE merges with United Gas Improvement Company.
**1932:** Banks take over Insull's MWU holding company; Insull is forced to resign amid fraud and embezzlement charges.
**1943:** PE becomes an independent company once again.
**1953:** The Public Service Company of Northern Illinois merges with ComEd.
**1960:** ComEd operates the nation's first privately financed commercial nuclear power station.
**1968:** Regulatory delays prevent the completion of PE nuclear power plants in Limerick.
**1974:** ComEd acquires Cotter Corporation.
**1980:** ComEd's earnings per share sink to their lowest level in 15 years.
**1987:** PE's earnings fall after the Public Utilities Commission refuses to allow a rate hike.
**1994:** PE adopts the name PECO Energy Company; ComEd becomes part of a new holding company, Unicom Corporation.
**2000:** PECO and Unicom merge to form Exelon Corporation.

nies under the aegis of United Gas Improvement Company (UGI) (which, coincidentally, had Thomas Dolan as a board member in common with PE). In spite of the general public's suspicion of monopolies, the financial community viewed the consolidation of UGI and PE as ultimately inevitable and beneficial. UGI acquired a controlling stake in Philadelphia Electric in February, 1928, and the two merged on October 31, 1929, adding 1,380 square miles, 88,000 electric customers and 112,000 gas customers, as well as 78,000 kW of electric generating capacity and three gas producing plants to Philadelphia Electric's operations. PE was reorganized into the Philadelphia and five suburban operating and commercial divisions.

The effect of the Depression on Philadelphia Electric was characterized by company historian Nicholas Wainwright as "harassing but not crippling." Net income actually increased in spite of a steady decline in residential and industrial customers. There were no large-scale layoffs; PE relied on attrition to shorten its payrolls. The company was surviving well enough, in fact, that during the depth of the Depression in 1932, it ordered one of the era's largest generating units. The 165,000 kW machine known as "Big Ben" was the first in the country to burn pulverized coal and employ electrostatic emissions reducers. It ran from 1935 to 1977. In 1938, Horace P. Liversidge, who had first been employed by PE in 1898 as a wiring inspector, advanced to the company's presidency. Liversidge has been credited with shaping the company's modern history.

The Depression also brought Franklin D. Roosevelt's New Deal and with it the Securities and Exchange Commission, which regulated the activities of holding companies, in 1935. Electric utilities had been regulated since the 1910s, but holding companies were not regulated early in the 20th century. Although some holding companies were legitimate structures created to coordinate associated industries, many were precarious "pyramids" of companies. The organizers of these corporate entities could use the combined value of subsidiaries to finance loans, then charge the subsidiaries outrageous rates for the redistributed funds. As the oldest public utility holding company in the world, UGI was reluctant to submit to a breakup order, but by 1943, Philadelphia Electric was once again an independent company. PE retained the suburban gas and electric utilities that had been merged into it in 1929.

World War II once again forced a concentration of manufacturing capacity on war production: Philadelphia produced ships, tanks, and armaments, and PE supplied the power to do so. Before the United States entered the war in December 1941, these preparations were made in addition to normal civilian production. Voluntary and mandatory restrictions on the use of power, as well as curtailment of civilian production, prevented a wartime power shortage.

The postwar era brought a new focus on PE's gas operations, especially after 1948, when the "Big Inch" and "Little Big Inch" interstate pipelines were converted from oil to natural gas transmission. Philadelphia Electric completed its conversion from manufacturing gas locally to purchasing gas produced in the Gulf states in 1964 and even undertook its own exploration and production efforts in the late 1970s.

R. George Rincliffe advanced through the executive ranks to PE's presidency in 1952. He assumed the company's chair and newly created chief executive office ten years later, holding those positions until his retirement in 1971. During his tenure, Rincliffe oversaw the unabated expansion of PE's capacity through a variety of methods, including traditional generators, hydroelectric plants, and nuclear power. The company brought its Eddystone plant, which featured the world's most efficient coal-fired generating unit, on line in 1960. A joint minemouth generation project among members of the PJM to create the Keystone plant in Indiana, Pennsylvania, was undertaken in 1962. Located at the fuel source, Keystone generated power and linked the PJM with other cooperative systems on the National Electric Reliability Council, a U.S./Canada grid that aided in the efficient supply of bulk power throughout North America. Keystone began running in 1967, the same year that Pennsylvania Electric's Muddy Run pumped-storage hydroelectric generating plant (the largest of its type) on the Susquehanna River began operation.

Philadelphia Electric first participated in studies on the feasibility of using nuclear energy to drive power plants as a member of the Atomic Power Development Associates, Inc., in 1952. Then, in 1958, the company joined over fifty other utilities to build a prototypical reactor dubbed Peach Bottom No. 1. It took almost a decade for the unit to go into production, but by that time, PE had committed itself to shares in four 1-million-kW nuclear units. The company regarded nuclear power generation as vital for two reasons. First, during the 1950s, demand for electricity rose sharply due to the advent of television, increased commercial and residential use of air conditioning, and industrial expansion. Second, the federal government established the first stringent emissions controls in 1960. The company reasoned that nuclear capabilities would enable it to maintain standards of service while conforming to clean air and water standards. PE's employment of nuclear energy seemed to be progressing well until 1968, when regulatory and other delays prevented completion of two wholly-owned nuclear power plants at Limerick, Pennsylvania, until the mid and late 1980s.

Robert F. Gilkeson assumed PE's helm in 1971 at the outset of a decade characterized by federal, state, and local regulation of virtually every aspect of its business, from employment to environmental practices. Economic fluctuations influenced decisions about capital investment and rate increases. Gilkeson launched a Corporate Communications Department in 1975 to act as a liaison between the utility and the media, government agencies, and the general public. J.L. Everett, III succeeded Gilkeson in 1978, just in time to see Philadelphia Electric's total assets exceed $5 billion for the first time.

PE was faced with another series of regulatory and financial hurdles in the 1980s. The utility suffered one of the most damaging and traumatic episodes in its history when inspectors from the Nuclear Regulatory Commission (NRC) found a control room employee ''inattentive to duty,'' or, as Amy Barrett of *Financial World* alleged in a May 1990 article, ''operators were found playing video games and having rubber band fights in the control rooms'' at the Peach Bottom nuclear facility. The plant was ordered closed within 24 hours and remained shut down for over two years. During that time, criticism from the NRC and the influential Institute of Nuclear Power and Operations poured in. Joseph F. Paquette, Jr., was called back to PE after a brief hiatus to accept the chair and chief executive office of the troubled company in 1988. He set out to transform the company by focusing on long-term strategic planning, human resource management, and downsizing.

Over the course of the 1980s and into the 1990s, the Pennsylvania Public Utilities Commission (PUC) executed several policy reversals with regard to Philadelphia Electric, its nuclear operations, and its rates. In 1982, the PUC refused to allow a rate hike to pay for the second phase of the plant and halted the project. Three years later, as Limerick's first phase was nearing completion, the Commission gave PE the green light on Limerick II, but set stringent time and financial limitations on the project. Although the plant came in almost $400 million under budget and nine months ahead of schedule, the PUC refused to increase rates to help cover capital costs, citing ''excess reserve power capacity'' and thereby implying that Limerick II was inherently wasteful. Earnings in the late 1980s and early 1990s reflected the rate ruling, as per share income plummeted from a high of almost $3 million in 1984 to $2.33 million in 1987 and $0.07 million in 1990. That year, CEO Paquette instituted cost-cutting measures that included an early retirement program, reduced advertising budget, and executive pay cuts of 2 percent to 10 percent. Paquette himself took his second salary cut that year.

These cost-cutting efforts bore fruit before the middle of the decade, as per share earnings recovered somewhat to $2.45 million in 1993 on year-to-year revenue and profit increases of 0.6 percent (to $3.99 billion) and 23 percent (to $590.6 million), respectively. The importance of nuclear generation to Philadelphia Electric's operations was reflected in the fact that the nuclear segment of the company's total electric power output was 60 percent in 1993. A reorganization undertaken that year created five strategic business units—Consumer Energy Services, Gas Services, Nuclear Generation, Power Generation, and Bulk Power Enterprises. During 1994, the utility changed its name to PECO Energy Company.

By the mid-1990s, PECO ranked among America's top 25 electric and gas utilities in terms of annual sales in 1994. With a service area of 2,475 square miles in southeastern Pennsylvania, including the city of Philadelphia, the company served over three million customers. Paquette retired in 1997 leaving Corbin A. McNeill, Jr., at the helm. Under his leadership, PECO prepared for deregulation by buying troubled nuclear power plants on the cheap, and then reorganizing the facilities to operate at a profit. Even as PECO faced increased competition, earnings per share during 1999 grew by 17 percent, which was more than double the industry average at the time.

### *The History of Unicom*

Samuel Insull helped make Commonwealth Edison an industry giant and in fact laid the foundations of the electrical power industry. Insull popularized mass production and selling at the lowest possible cost, developed modern public relations, and devised methods for marketing securities in a way that led to the large public corporations of the later 20th century.

At the age of 21, Insull possessed outstanding financial acumen and unwavering ambition to succeed in business. In the early 1880s, he traveled from his home in London to the United States to take his position as Thomas Edison's personal secretary. Insull gained from his employer vast financial responsibilities and decision-making power, while quadrupling sales at Edison Electric Light Company's main factory and selling central power plants to cities across the country.

Edison's company was renamed Edison General Electric Company in 1889, and soon thereafter it merged with Thomson-Houston Electric Company, forming General Electric Company. At the time, Insull was offered a $36,000-a-year executive position at General Electric (GE), but instead he took a $12,000-a-year position as president of Chicago Edison Company. The 32-year-old Insull borrowed $250,000 from the newspaper tycoon Marshall Field, purchased a large share of the company's stock, and then went to work selling electricity.

There were almost four dozen electric companies competing for Chicago's electricity business when Insull came on the scene. At the time, less than 1 percent of Chicago's homes used electric lamps. Insull's goal was to grow—exponentially. Expansion spelled greater volume, which meant lower unit costs of production, which meant greater profit. More income meant more investment, and more growth, and so on.

Insull formed a 25-person sales department and, according to Forrest McDonald's biography of Insull, told them to ''sell at the lowest possible price.'' Insull was not lowering prices to compete. He maintained that competition was ''economically wrong'' and was instead lowering prices in an attempt to wipe out competition all together. Insull quietly bought exclusive rights to electric equipment manufactured by General Electric and most other U.S. manufacturers to thwart competition. In his first 42 months in Chicago, Insull increased Chicago Edison's sales almost five times. He also expanded Chicago Edison by buying out competitors.

Local politicians soon caught wind of Edison's success. Accustomed to receiving kickbacks from companies doing business in Chicago, a group of politicians reportedly devised a plan to extort $1 million from Chicago Edison. They formed a dummy company, called Commonwealth Electric Company, and gave it a 50-year franchise to provide the city's electricity. The founders of Commonwealth planned to force Insull to buy their company for $1 million or be frozen out of the market. They did not realize, however, that Insull owned the rights to the equipment it would take to run this company. Insull therefore was able to buy Commonwealth with its 50-year electricity franchise for the city of Chicago for just $50,000.

In 1907, Insull merged Commonwealth Electric Company and Chicago Edison Company to form Commonwealth Edison, a company whose sales exceeded the combined sales of New York Edison, Brooklyn Edison, and Boston Edison. After the merger, Insull formed a holding company called Middle West Utilities (MWU) to own small interests in ComEd and other investor-owned utilities. MWU itself was also a publicly traded company. Insull controlled MWU, and by 1912 MWU, in turn, controlled utilities in 13 states through relatively small shareholdings. Insull wanted nothing less than a monopoly wherever he operated, and in order to achieve this, he was willing to sacrifice a degree of control. Therefore, Insull agreed that his exclusive franchises with municipalities should be regulated by a state commission.

In 1906, Insull's customers numbered 50,000; in 1909, that number had reached 100,000. ComEd's growth was both rapid and smart. Insull diversified customers, spreading the demand for power as much as possible. For instance, he obtained major contracts with Chicago electric streetcar companies, which drew the most power when residential customers were at work and not at home using electric lamps and appliances. He went after big industry, offering huge subsidies to induce these daytime users away from using small, private power stations. Insull termed this approach to business ''massing production'' and was succeeding at it before Henry Ford gained fame as a mass producer of the automobile.

Taking an idea he learned from the English electricity business, Insull charged a dual rate for power: a higher rate for the first several hours of electrical usage, and a progressively lower rate thereafter. This covered the costs of adding equipment for new customers and encouraged greater use. He also kept cutting rates. The company, from early on, regularly paid out an eight cent dividend to shareholders.

Insull approached generating electricity with the same zeal he showed for selling electricity. He ignored the apparent limits of the day's technology, pushing his engineers to build generators that were several times larger than any other generators in existence. Historical accounts suggest that Insull was progressive in his dealings with workers, not out of personal convictions but rather to ensure the effective and continuous operation of ComEd's facilities. Insull hired women and minorities, gave his employees relatively generous benefits, and maintained a cooperative relationship with labor leaders.

Insull was ahead of his time in yet another significant way—he was a master at public relations. He established an advertising department as early as 1901, and his rate cuts were well timed and well publicized. Moreover, he published and distributed a free tabloid, *Electric City*, which shaped a positive public opinion of electricity, and, of course, the electric company itself. Insull began publishing annual reports 15 years before they became standard.

During World War I, Insull was a fervent supporter of England. He personally spent $250,000 attempting to sway public opinion in favor of the U.S. entry into the war, after which Insull worked to raise money for the war effort. After World War I, Insull was able to capitalize on the high profile he had cultivated during the war to promote the interests of ComEd.

The postwar period was a time of immense growth in demand for the electric industry. In 1923, the year the electric refrigerator became available to residential customers, ComEd added over 75,000 new customers to its service area, its largest annual increase up to that time. ComEd proved to be the only major steam-power electric company in the nation that neither raised its rates nor cut its dividends during the postwar period, though money for expansion was scarce. Insull exploited an idea he got from Pacific Gas & Electric, launching a hugely successful customer ownership drive. From 1919 to 1921, the number of ComEd shareholders who lived in Illinois grew from 50,000 to 500,000. Insull's name was equated with trust by small investors.

The phenomenal control Insull had been able to exercise over his empire's destiny began to crumble around 1926; he made several less-than-wise, if not illegal, financial moves over the next few years. After the October 1929 stock market crash, Insull, who believed the Great Depression would be short, continued to spend great sums of money on both the company and his many philanthropic endeavors. During that time, he was perhaps most recognized for his contribution to the Chicago Civic Opera. ComEd continued to grow and its stock continued to rise.

Much of this growth, however, was deceptive. Assets and earnings were inflated, and in 1931 utility stock prices plunged. MWU's stock dropped from $570 to $1.25 per share. Insull had financed much of MWU's growth by using other utility properties as collateral. In 1932, banks took over MWU, and Insull was forced to resign, claiming a personal loss of nearly $15 million. Eventually he was tried for fraud and embezzlement. Though Insull was not found guilty, he had left the power industry for good.

ComEd itself, however, weathered the Depression relatively well, and business carried on. Modern conveniences such as the air conditioner and the electric water heater came on the scene in the 1930s and continued to stimulate increased demand for electricity.

During World War II, reserve capacity attracted war industries to the Chicago area; in 1943 about 40 percent of the company's yearly output was tied to war production. In 1947, the city of Chicago conducted a study of ComEd's service and found the company was significantly overcharging, especially residential and commercial customers. The utility's initial franchise with the city was soon to expire, and a battle involving politicians, the utility, and customers ensued.

As a utility overseen by a regulatory commission, ComEd was allowed a reasonable rate of return, but there was a great deal of debate over what ''reasonable'' meant. In comparing utilities in the nation's 23 largest cities, ComEd was found to spend twice as much on advertising as any other utility. Critics questioned whether customers should pay higher rates to support advertising of a monopoly. They also wondered if legal fees would be passed on to customers if the city were to take ComEd to court? Although these and other criticisms were addressed in the report, in the media, and by members of the city council, a powerful faction in the city council supported ComEd, and the city ultimately signed a 42-year franchise that did little to address these criticisms. Some observers believed that neither the franchise agreement nor the state regulatory body, the Illinois Commerce Commission (ICC), clearly defined ''reasonable rate of return.'' It was left up to ComEd, although the ICC did set a maximum rate.

ComEd's customers did not feel the sting of this arrangement until many years down the road, when Edison's nuclear program ran into decades of cost overruns. In the short term the company flourished, and customers benefited. By 1951, ComEd had assets of $1 billion. In 1953, the Public Service Company of Northern Illinois—which had been created in 1950 by the merger of Western United Gas & Electric Company and Illinois Northern Utilities Company—merged with ComEd. The following year, ComEd created the Northern Illinois Gas Company to own and operate its gas properties. In 1955, the company began using an electronic computer for billing, and by 1959 ComEd was reaching two million customers.

Rate reductions averaged more than $36 million a year between 1962 and 1967; the utility's operating revenues rose from $492 million in 1962 to $658.7 million in 1966. In 1966, ComEd absorbed the Central Illinois Electric and Gas Company, basically establishing an integrated electric system for all of northern Illinois and further capitalizing on economies of scale.

In 1960, ComEd began operating the nation's first privately financed commercial nuclear power station, a 200,000-kilowatt facility called Dresden I near Morris, Illinois. ComEd was leading the national charge toward nuclear power. J. Harris Ward became ComEd's chairman the next year. He linked the company's growth to nuclear power and committed large sums of capital investment to this program.

The utility's ambitious plans called for 40 percent of its entire generating capacity to be supplied by seven nuclear-fueled plants by 1973. By 1969, however, the company's nuclear program was experiencing technical difficulties, falling behind schedule, and suffering rapidly escalating costs. ComEd was forced to begin building a $160 million coal-fired unit at its Powerton plant in Pekin, Illinois. ''The delays forced us to double-build,'' Ward was quoted as stating in the September 15, 1969 issue of *Forbes*. This adjustment in ComEd's nuclear program was only one in a long line of costly setbacks.

The company's commitment to nuclear-generated power was due, in part, to nuclear power's potential as a cleaner fuel. The problems associated with burning fossil fuels came to a head in 1970 when the Chicago Department of Environmental Control named ComEd the worst polluter in Chicago, accusing the electric company's fossil-fuel plants of causing more sulfur pollution than all other companies in the city combined. Thomas G. Ayers, president of ComEd, began bringing in low-sulfur coal from Montana, cutting sulfur emissions by 60 percent by 1973. That same year, he was elected chairman and CEO of ComEd. By 1972, ComEd was using nuclear power to generate 22 percent of its capacity, more than any other investor-owned utility in the nation. In the interest of assuring a uranium supply, ComEd acquired Cotter Corporation, a uranium mining and milling company in 1974.

In 1971, planning began on a joint proposal with the Tennessee Valley Authority to build and operate the United States' first commercial fast breeder reactor. This kind of power plant would produce more fuel than it used. It would also produce more highly radioactive waste than its predecessors. The project was approved by the Atomic Energy Commission in 1972, and though that breeder reactor was completed and more followed, the problems of disposing of the high-level nuclear waste continued. Nevertheless, in 1973 the company, for the third time in its history, received the industry's Edison award for its leadership in the development of the breeder reactor.

During the 1970s, ComEd faced soaring operating and expansion costs, a situation that was exacerbated by problems of getting rate increases and plant construction clearances. The widely publicized nuclear accident at Three Mile Island, Pennsylvania, in 1979 heightened attention of both the public and regulators, and ComEd sent teams of nuclear experts to assist and study the situation. In 1980, in the middle of ComEd's $4.5 billion construction of six new nuclear plants, earnings per share sank to their lowest level since 1965. As heavy industry in the area stopped growing, ComEd's sales slowed drastically.

Into this bleak picture stepped ComEd's newly appointed CEO, James O'Connor. Beginning in 1980, the ICC granted the utility a series of large rate increases. ComEd began to rebound, and by December 1984 O'Connor was predicting that rates would increase about 2.5 percent a year for three years, level off in 1988, and then stabilize.

In 1986, as ComEd struggled to finance the $7.1 billion building program for the last three of 12 nuclear plants, problems with the company's Braidwood nuclear plant increased its construction cost more than 40 percent. This meant that ComEd would need a 4.8 percent annual increase for 11 years to cover the cost. Many observers felt that ComEd should have canceled or postponed some of its plants in the early 1980s due to underestimated construction costs and overestimated demand.

As a result of overbuilding in its nuclear program, ComEd's generating capacity exceeded average peak demand by 33 percent in 1990 (most utilities maintain a 15 percent surplus). Thus, while many major utilities around the nation were found to be spending $15 to $51 on conservation per customer, ComEd was spending 39 cents per customer, according to a study by a committee of the Chicago City Council.

In 1990, the company's net income fell to $128 million, or 22 cents per share, from the previous year's $693 million, or $2.83 per share, largely because of court-ordered refunds and rate rollbacks. Also in 1990, at a time when customers were growing increasingly unhappy with paying some of the nation's highest rates, the utility's franchise term with the city of Chicago was due to expire. A coalition of community and environmental groups had formed in 1988 to pressure the city to stir up public debate over the city's electricity options. These amounted to a renegotiated franchise or municipal acquisition. Meanwhile, ComEd waged an advertising campaign to tout the quality of its service.

In the summer of 1990, two major substation fires caused 60,000 customers to lose power for up to three days. The city postponed its decision on the franchise issue to allow more time to study the utility's reliability. Negotiations on a new franchise concluded in 1991, and ComEd was granted a 29-year contract.

The company's costs were still high, and with a series of lawsuits on the verge of settlement ComEd cut its dividend in 1992 by a whopping 47 percent. A year later, the company agreed to the biggest refund in utility industry history. Over the next 12 months, ComEd would pay back $1.34 billion to its customers, primarily because it had passed the costs of building unnecessary nuclear plants on to them. A rate reduction of $339 million was also effected.

In 1994, ComEd became part of a newly created holding company, Unicom Corporation. The company had recently been granted legislative approval to create an unregulated energy subsidiary, and the new corporate structure was intended to facilitate this. A subsidiary, Unicom Thermal, was also formed to develop new types of cooling systems to take advantage of laws mandating reductions in ozone-depleting cooling agents. Other subsidiaries would become involved in energy consulting and the manufacture of power generators, though revenues from these operations were small.

Troubles with the company's nuclear power plants continued to bring down profits, and in 1995 a 16 percent reduction in the work force was announced. Moreover, ComEd was being fined regularly by the Nuclear Regulatory Commission for incidents ranging from workers planting a small quantity of radioactive material in a coworker's pocket, to an employee being allowed to work while visibly drunk. By the mid-1990s only half of the company's reactors were typically online, with the Zion plant the most seriously troubled. Other problems arose when the company announced the possibility of "rolling blackouts" when peak energy demands exceeded production capacity. Critics pointed out that the company was still charging one of the highest rates for power in the country, yet was openly resisting buying extra electricity during the peak summer cooling season to keep its customers supplied with power.

In January 1998, ComEd finally moved to permanently close its Zion plant, and the following month CEO O'Connor stepped down. His successor was 52-year old John W. Rowe, former CEO of New England Electric System and a lawyer with a strong background in nuclear power issues. Rowe's challenge was not only to bring up the company's ailing bottom line but to develop a strategy for the impending power industry deregulation that Illinois legislators had enacted. This would finally open up the power marketplace to all comers, with business customers available in 1999 and residential users to follow in 2002. Rowe's strategy, which he had developed in his years with New England Electric, was to focus more on delivery of power than production, opening the door to purchasing energy from outside providers. To that end he sold 16 of ComEd's non-nuclear plants for $4.8 billion in early 1999, while the company also sought approval of a $3.4 billion bond issue. He also announced the company's intention to purchase more energy industry service companies, such as heating and air conditioning contractors. Perhaps his boldest gesture was to publicly admit that ComEd's long-time nuclear power strategy had been a mistake.

### *The 2000 Merger*

Both PECO and Unicom were facing challenges related to deregulation when they announced their merger in September 1999. For instance, *The Philadelphia Business Journal* reported in July 1999 that PECO had lost over 34 percent of its customer load since the market had opened for competition in January. Unicom's ComEd was also experiencing a rash of problems caused by its out-of-date wires, cables, and transformers in the Chicago area. The region experienced power outages from July through August and the firm was forced to spend $20 million to remedy the situation.

Management of both companies believed that in order to operate in the highly competitive environment, it was necessary to evolve from a stand-alone regional utility concern into a large, formidable industry player. As such, PECO and Unicom eyed the merger of equals as a unique opportunity to strengthen their foothold on the U.S. utilities industry. The proposed deal was met with some opposition—the two companies seemed like an odd fit due to PECO's strategy of acquiring nuclear power plants and Unicom's focus on electricity delivery rather than power generation. However, both Rowe and McNeill believed that together, the combined company would be a huge force in both generation and distribution. Rowe claimed in a 1999 *United Press International* article that the merger would create "a base from which we will build a leading energy delivery business and establish ourselves as a significant competitor in the emerging retail energy marketplace."

Indeed, the combined entity would operate as one of the largest utility firms in the United States, controlling nearly 20 percent of the country's nuclear generation market and serving approximately five million customers. The $31.8 billion merger was officially completed in October 2000. Operating under the new name Exelon Corporation, the company had three main business divisions, including Exelon Generation, which included its nuclear, fossil, and hydro fleet operations, as well as a wholesale marketing division; Exelon Energy Deliver, which included the electricity and gas retail operations of both ComEd and PECO Energy; and Exelon Enterprises, a unit that included the company's utility and energy services that catered to businesses.

Exelon's first year of operation proved to be rocky. The firm's aggressive expansion of its Enterprises business group—

a group that focused on forays into new ventures, especially in the telecommunications market—failed to pay off. The company laid off over 1,500 employees in that division as it reported losses through 2002. Then, in March 2002, co-CEO McNeill announced his resignation amid rumors that he was unable to see eye-to-eye with Rowe on the expansion direction of the company. McNeill, ready to pursue a large acquisition to bolster Exelon's generating capacity, was challenged by Rowe, who felt that a purchase of a mid-sized utility offering both generation and distribution would best fit Exelon's portfolio. In the end, McNeill stepped down as both an executive and director of the firm, leaving Rowe at the helm.

By February 2002, electricity prices were down nearly 30 percent and the power generation sector of the industry was experiencing an over supply. In fact, the power generation industry overall was faltering due to the public collapse of Enron Corporation, a disaster that left consumers leery of the competitive energy market. To make matters worse, Exelon was hit by a class action law suit in May 2002 by shareholders that claimed the company reported misleading statements regarding its financial position in April through September 2001. The suit claimed that Exelon failed to reveal significant information regarding the losses experienced by its Enterprises group. While the company claimed that it would meet its projected $4.50 per share earnings for 2001, it instead secured consolidated earnings of $4.43 per share.

Despite these challenges, Exelon management was confident that the company would continue to grow as a leading utility concern. With a long-standing history behind it, the newly formed entity was indeed prepared to handle the obstacles brought on by the changing marketplace. How the company chose to handle these obstacles however, remained to be seen.

### *Principal Subsidiaries*

Commonwealth Edison Company; PECO Energy Company

### *Principal Divisions*

Exelon Energy Delivery Company, LLC; Exelon Generation Company, LLC; Exelon Ventures Company, LLC.

### *Principal Competitors*

Ameren Corporation; Dynegy Inc.; PPL Corporation.

### *Further Reading*


Barrett, Amy, "The Luck of the Irish," *Financial World*, May 29, 1990, pp. 28–9.

Bleiberg, Robert M., "PECO's Woes," *Barron's*, May 28, 1990, p. 12.

Crown, Judith, "Why O'Connor is Turning Off the Lights: Faced with Nuclear Dereg Turmoil It Was Time to Exit," *Crain's Chicago Business*, October 13, 1998, p. 1.

Daniels, Steve, "After Shocking Summer, ComEd Strikes Deal," *Crain's Chicago Business*, December 20, 1999, p. 22.

——, "Cash in Hand, ComEd Gets Ready to Shop: Set to Buy Energy Service Providers in Growth Bid," *Crain's Chicago Business*, March 29, 1999, p. 4.

——, "Exelon Halts Campaign to Diversify," *Crain's Chicago Business*, August 27, 2001, p. 3.

——, "Exelon in Search of Powerful Deal," *Crain's Chicago Business*, February 18, 2002, p. 1.

——, "Exelon Power Struggle," *Crain's Chicago Business*, March 4, 2002, p. 1.

"Exelon: A Bright Light in Energy," *Business Week*, March 2002.

Feiler, Jeremy, "Exelon in Retrenchment," *Philadelphia Business Journal*, November 2, 2001, p. 1.

Knowles, Francine, "Shareholders OK Edison Restructuring," *Chicago Sun-Times*, May 11, 1994, p. 63.

Laabs, Jennifer J., "Plant Shutdown Forces Changes in Operations," *Personnel Journal*, v. 72, March 1993, pp. 112–22.

Lashinsky, Adam, "A ComEd Peace Treaty," *Crain's Chicago Business*, September 27, 1993, p. 1.

McDonald, Forrest, *Insull*, Chicago: University of Chicago Press, 1962.

Munson, Richard, *The Power Makers*, Emmaus, Pa.: Rodale Press, 1985.

Oloroso, Arsenio Jr., and Judith Crown, "Rowe's Strategy: Power Up ComEd—Rowe's Formula: Cost-Cutting, Asset Sales, Mini-Mergers," *Crain's Chicago Business*, June 15, 1998, p. 1.

*Philadelphia Electric Company, Milestones: Philadelphia Electric Company, 1881–1981*, Philadelphia: Philadelphia Electric Company, 1981.

Samuels, Gary, "Burying the Hatchet," *Forbes*, December 5, 1994, p. 56.

Snyder, David, "In a Sound Bite: A Cultural Revolution Begins at ComEd," *Crain's Chicago Business*, July 20, 1998, p. 11.

"Unicom, PECO to Merge in $31.8B Deal," *United Press International*, September 27, 1999.

Wainwright, Nicholas B., *History of The Philadelphia Electric Company, 1881–1961*, Philadelphia: The Philadelphia Electric Company, 1961.


—Carole Healy and April Dougal Gasbarre
—updates: Frank Uhle and Christina M. Stansell

# Expand SA

89, rue Escudier
92100 Boulogne-Billancourt Cedex
France
Telephone: (+33) 1-47-12-40-40
Fax: (+33) 1-47-12-40-94
Web site: http://www.expand.fr

*Public Company*
*Incorporated:* 1973
*Employees:* 733
*Sales:* EUR 189.33 million ($179.2 million)
*Stock Exchanges:* Euronext Paris
*Ticker Symbol:* EXP
*NAIC:* 512110 Motion Picture and Video Production

Expand SA has carved a place for itself as France's leading television programming production company and has become one of the top three European audiovisual production companies. The company has organized its operations around four primary divisions: Games and Entertainment; Fiction and TV Series; Animated and Children's Programming; and Magazine Programs and Documentaries. The company's games and entertainment division is its strongest and provides much of the short-term funding for its other, longer-cycle products. Featuring a strong palette of game show programs—Expand is the French leader of this segment—including the French version of "Who Wants to Be a Millionaire?," the most popular game show worldwide at the turn of the century, the company's "flux" programming (i.e., recurrent daily and/or weekly programming that combines low production costs with strong programming schedules to generate immediate profits) contributed more than half of its EUR 190 million in 2000 revenues. Expand also has been a leader in the so-called "adventure game" category, building on its long-running success with "Fort Boyard," in production since 1990 and the most exported French program of all time with the creation of "The Desert Forges." In France, the company has adapted the popular reality-type program "Survivor" for the French market. Expand's 1999 merger with Ellipse Programmes gave it a strong package of animated and children's programming, as well as boosting its second largest division, Fiction and TV Series. That division provides more than 30 percent of the company's revenues, through the production of more than 120 telefilms and series per year. Listed on the Euronext Paris stock exchange, Expand agreed to be acquired by film production company StudioCanal, itself a subsidiary of giant Vivendi Universal, which held more than 96 percent of Expand's stock by January 2002. The company continues to be led by cofounders and co-CEOs Philippe Poiret and Patrick Wallaert.

## *Medical Communications in the 1970s*

Expand existed as a small Paris-based communications firm specializing in the medical representation market at the beginning of the 1970s. In 1973, that company was taken over by partners Philippe Poiret and Patrick Wallaert, who began building it into one of France's leading healthcare communications companies. A major market for the company became the training of physicians and other medical personnel.

During the 1970s and early 1980s, Poiret and Wallaert diversified the company's activities. Expand entered the recruitment and training of medical sales representatives, primarily for pharmaceutical companies. Expand also began producing medical advertising, which led the company into the media buying field, placing print and other ads. Seeking fresh capital for growth in the second half of the 1980s, Expand listed its stock on the Paris stock exchange's secondary market in 1985.

A meeting with Dominique Ambiel in 1987 led the company into a new direction. Ambiel had been working under Francois Leotard, a French minister. Ambiel was placed in charge of a dossier governing film and television issues. At that time, French television was undergoing something of a revolution: for most of its history, French television had been a government-dominated affair limited to just three channels. The 1980s, however, had seen the emergence of the country's first privately owned stations, notably the privatized TF1, and the newly created Canal Plus, M6, and Arte. The new stations represented a far larger market for television production, and particularly, a new market for game show and other entertainment programming.

**Key Dates:**

**1973:** Philippe Poiret and Patrick Wallaert take over a small communications firm and diversify into recruitment, sales training, and educational seminars.
**1985:** Expand goes public on the Paris stock exchange secondary market.
**1988:** Expand creates Expand Images and enters audiovisual production for the television market.
**1990:** The launch of Fort Boyard gives Expand its biggest success; the program becomes the most exported of all French programs.
**1999:** Expand sells off its Expand Santé division and refocuses its operation around its audiovisual production.
**2000:** Company merges with Ellipse Programmes, then acquires DMD Productions.
**2001:** StudioCanal acquires majority shareholding of Expand.
**2002:** StudioCanal moves to take over full control of Expand, gaining 96 percent of shares by January 2002.

Expand decided to place its existing healthcare operations into a newly named Expand Santé division and to create an entirely new division, Expand Images, for its entry into audiovisual production in 1988. Ambiel was placed in charge of the new division and led the company on an acquisition spree that saw the absorption of some 20 companies specializing in audiovisual production. One of these companies belonged to Jacques Antoine, considered the father of French game show programming.

Expand Images had an international hit on its hand with the debut of ''Fort Boyard'' in 1990. This adventure game show, set in a former prison fortress located off the coast of La Rochelle, presented its group of contestants with a series of challenges—both physical and intellectual—and the opportunity to raise funds for a favorite charity. The show was an instant hit in France, remaining in position throughout the decade, with no signs of letting up at the turn of the century. By 2001, Expand had sold more than 150 programs to the French market.

Yet the success of ''Fort Boyard'' was achieved especially on the international level. The show's formula was quickly adopted by a variety of other countries. Part of the company's sales came from exports of its original French-language broadcasts to other countries, where episodes were then subtitled or dubbed into the local language. In this way, a long list of countries, including Finland, Ukraine, Poland, Portugal, and Venezuela, boosted the success of the program. Still greater success derived from attracting contracts for new, country-specific programming using Expand's ''Fort Boyard'' set. More than 14 countries developed their own versions of the ''Fort Boyard'' formula, and by the end of the 1990s Expand had produced more than 400 country-specific programs for markets such as Canada, The Netherlands, Israel, the United Kingdom, Norway, Denmark, Sweden, and others.

''Fort Boyard'' became the most exported French program of all time, with more than 1,000 programs sold around the world. At home, Expand continued to build up its portfolio of programming, becoming especially strong in the game show format but also as a maker of televised films and series. By the mid-1990s, the company had captured a leading position in the French market, fighting principal rival Ellipse Programmes for the largest share of the country's television viewing hours.

Expand Santé, meanwhile, kept pace with Expand Images' growth, firmly establishing itself as the French leader in its sector and one of the largest across Europe. During the 1990s, the company launched its own digital television network, Medicine Plus, targeting an international medical market. Another major initiative taken by the company was the launch of its Internet-based portal Club Medical, linking physicians across France.

## *Pure Player for the New Century*

By the late 1990s, the two divisions roughly equaled each other in terms of revenue generated for the parent, which topped the FFr 1 billion mark. Yet the company's stock remained somewhat undervalued compared with Expand Images' pure-play competitors. At the same time, future growth in the French market for Expand Images' categories seemed limited, since the company was already a dominant player—instead the company would have to look for continued growth on a European scale.

A downturn in Expand Santé's core pharmaceuticals market encouraged Poiret and Wallaert to consider its options. After considering a spin-off of one or the other of its divisions, Expand instead opted for a sell-off of its Expand Santé division, to Schroder Ventures for FFr 279 million. The company now determined to refocus itself as a pure-play audiovisual production company. As Dominique Ambiel told *La Tribune:* ''We concentrated the last ten years on becoming the leader in audiovisual production in France, and in the next 10 years we will become the leader in Europe.''

The company took two strong steps toward achieving this goal in 2000. The first came when Expand Images merged with rival Ellipse Programmes, itself a subsidiary of film production house StudioCanal, creating a new company, Expand SA. The merger proved highly complementary, combining Expand Images' expertise in games and entertainment programming with Ellipse's strength in animated and children's programming, creating a French powerhouse with programming depth across nearly all the major programming segments. A second step toward filling out the company's programming came with its acquisition of DMD Productions, owned by Michel Drucker, one of France's best-known television personalities.

These moves came with the company's announcement of its intention of more than doubling its revenues, topping EUR 450 million by 2003. Part of the company's new urgency was inspired by the entry of one of the European leaders, Endemol Productions, into its home territory; by the middle of 2001, Endemol and Expand were neck-and-neck for the French leadership.

By then, Expand had turned toward bigger pockets to fuel its international ambitions. The merger with Ellipse had brought in StudioCanal, itself a subsidiary of Vivendi Universal, as one of the company's major shareholders. In 2001, Poiret and Wallaert agreed to sell their own stake in the company, through financial investment company Finexpand, giving StudioCanal a majority share. At the end of 2001, StudioCanal exercised its option to make a takeover bid of the entire company, and by January 2002 had succeeded in gathering more than 96 percent of Expand's stock.

Expand, meanwhile, had continued to build on its success at home, gaining the French rights to develop the highly popular game show "Who Wants to Be a Millionaire?" for the French market, where the program met with similar success. The company also had garnered the rights for the U.S.-based "reality" game show, "Survivor," which was broadcast in the summer of 2001 to the French market as "Les Aventuriers de Koh-Lanta." At the same time, Expand had been developing a new program, based on the "Fort Boyard" concept, "The Desert Forges," which had been generating a good deal of international sales, even if its success in France remained somewhat limited. Expand appeared certain to continue its strong record of expansion in the new century.

## *Principal Subsidiaries*

Audiovisual Production: Expand Images SA; SCI Moreau Vauthier SCI. Games and Entertainment: The Desert Forges Productions (Jordan); Little Box Productions SNC; Zen Productions SA; DIEM SA; DMD Productions SA; Adventure Line Productions SA; Starling SARL (50%); Pegasus Télévision SAS (50%); Calt Production SARL (50%); Pro TV SA (49%). Catalogue Programs: Ellipse Distribution SNC; Ellipse Program USA; Ellipse Deutschland Société; Sirius Films Productions SA; Expand Droits Audiovisuels SA; Le Sabre SA; Elma Antilles SNC; Ellipse Animation SNC; Ellipse Réunion SNC; Mars International Productions SA; Point du Jour International SNC; Point du Jour Productions SA; Ellipse International SNC; Expand Interactive SA; Caudim SA; Expand Licensing SA; Anabase Productions SARL; Home Made Movies SA; Expand Drama (Mars International Fictions) SA; Osby Films SA; Elimca Productions SNC; Alizés Films SAS (80%); Expand Music (son et futur édition) SARL (69,93%); Elma Productions SA (67,34%); K'ien Productions SARL (60%); Alizés SARL (50%); Le Studio Ellipse SA (50%); Brigade Légère SA (49,97%).

## *Principal Competitors*

Antenña TV S.A.; Crown Media Holdings, Inc; Endemol Entertainment Holdings NV; HIT Entertainment PLC; The Television Corporation plc; EM.TV & Merchandising AG.

## *Further Reading*


Delarue, Emmanuel, "Expand profite de son recentrage sur l'audiovisuel," *La Tribune,* November 29, 1999.

Esquirou, Martine, "Interview: Le PDG du Groupe Expand," *Les Echos,* October 10, 1999, p. 19.

"Les ambitions d'Expand à l'international," *L'Expansion,* October 21, 1999, p. 14.

Riemer, Blanca, "Fusion Expand-Ellipse dans la production audiovisuelle," *La Tribune,* February 11, 2000.

——, "Le producteur Expand veut devenir un leader européen," *La Tribune,* July 7, 1999.

——, "StudioCanal prend le contrôle du groupe de production Expand," *La Tribune,* June 26, 2001.


—M.L. Cohen

# Fairchild Dornier GmbH

**P.O. Box 1103**
**82230 Wessling**
**Germany**
**Telephone: (49) 8153-30 0**
**Fax: (49) 8153-30 2007**
**Web site: http://www.fairchilddornier.com**

*Private Company*
*Incorporated:* 1936 as Fairchild Engine & Airplane Corporation
*Employees:* 4,400
*Sales:* $710 million (2001 est.)
*NAIC:* 336411 Aircraft Manufacturing; 336413 Other Aircraft Parts and Auxiliary Equipment Manufacturing; 541710 Research and Development in the Physical, Engineering, and Life Sciences

In 2001 Fairchild Dornier GmbH was the world's third-largest manufacturer of regional jets. Its two namesake predecessor companies produced some of aviation's most unique and effective military aircraft. After merging, both Fairchild and Dornier then set their sights on the hotly contested market for small regional airliners. In 2002, however, Fairchild Dornier filed for bankruptcy protection and shuttered its U.S. operations; the future of the company in Germany also remained uncertain.

### *Origins*

The original Fairchild company was established in 1936 as a holding company for the aircraft interests of Fairchild Camera founder Sherman Fairchild. While its Ranger Aircraft Engine subsidiary produced engines for the navy, Fairchild participated in the aviation market largely as a subcontractor during World War II. After the war, Fairchild sought new opportunities in the growing aircraft industry but was hampered by a lack of capital and engineering talent. Nonetheless, the company turned out a successful cargo design called the C-82. It sought to extend its work in this area by developing a second, larger design, the C-119 ''Flying Boxcar,'' but lost the manufacturing competition to the Kaiser-Frazier company. While Fairchild was awarded a subcontract for the C-119 and a subsequent design called the C-123, its employees' resentment for Kaiser was reflected in their work. Furious with Fairchild's performance, the air force virtually shunned the company.

Fairchild turned instead to commercial designs. It established an arrangement with the Dutch airplane builder Fokker to build versions of its popular F-27 airliner. The company also began development of its Goose guided missile system. Unable to sell either design, Fairchild fell into a deep crisis that lasted from 1958 through 1960. Sherman Fairchild returned from retirement to head the company briefly and was successful in repairing damaged relations with the government and returning financial discipline. He was replaced in 1961 by Edward G. Uhl, an engineer.

### *Acquisitions in the Mid-1960s*

Uhl's first actions as head of Fairchild were to fire several executives, slash costs, and switch the company from product diversification to technology diversification. Uhl was convinced that Fairchild's greatest weakness was its lack of engineering talent. Rather than spend years building a capable staff, Uhl began an acquisition campaign that included the Hiller Aircraft Company in 1964. The following year, Uhl found an opportunity to buy a financially distressed manufacturer with an army of good engineers. On September 30, Fairchild took control of the Republic Aviation Corporation, a military aircraft manufacturer based in Farmingdale, on New York's Long Island.

Republic Aviation was founded in 1931 by a Russian immigrant named Alexander P. Seversky. A graduate of the Russian naval academy and military aeronautics school, Seversky learned to fly and during World War I was Russia's leading fighter ace. In 1917, while Seversky was in Washington, D.C., to procure aircraft, the Bolsheviks seized power in Russia. Seversky and several in his delegation elected to stay in America.

Seversky worked as a consulting engineer and test pilot and developed a solid-fuel shore bombardment rocket for the navy. In 1922, he perfected a bomb sight device, which he sold to the U.S. government for $50,000, using the payment to establish

**Company Perspectives:**

*Customers Come First. Fairchild Dornier is a company that values action. We believe in listening to our customers and following through by delivering products that meet their needs. The 328JET, for example, was developed in recognition of the growing demand for jets to replace turboprops. The 728JET Family will provide a series of state-of-the-art, 55- to 110-seat aircraft that will give airline operators the flexibility they need to match their fleets to changing market needs. At Fairchild Dornier, we believe that we are in business for one reason: to serve our customers. If our customers succeed, then we will succeed. We embrace the concept of customer satisfaction—before, during, and after the sale.*

the Seversky Aero Corporation. Rather than building aircraft, Seversky concentrated on improved structures, landing gear, and air-to-air refueling systems.

The Great Depression took a heavier toll on the aviation industry than on others. Seversky's was one of hundreds of aeronautics firms that were forced into bankruptcy in 1931. The company was rescued by the financier Paul Moore, who reorganized the enterprise as Seversky Aircraft Corporation. Moore retained Seversky as president, and took on Alexander Kartveli—an associate of Seversky's and also a Soviet immigrant—as an engineer.

Seversky and Kartveli worked feverishly to perfect the concept of a single-skin all-metal aircraft. The result of their work was the SEV-3, a floatplane fitted with retractable wheels. This design failed to win a volume order but served as a necessary step in developing additional all-metal aircraft. Seversky succeeded in selling a subsequent trainer model, the BT-8, to the government. Lacking a factory, Seversky Aircraft was forced to subcontract its manufacturing business to the Kirkham Engineering Company in Farmingdale, New York.

In 1935, Seversky Aircraft was forced to terminate its manufacturing agreement with Kirkham Engineering when the Colombian government failed to pay an installment. Seversky collected his half-finished aircraft and completed assembling them at an abandoned warehouse nearby. At this site, Seversky began work on the P-35, another derivative of his original design. The P-35 won a government design competition against the Curtiss P-36 Hawk, bringing in a badly needed order for 77 aircraft. Seversky had difficulty overcoming several shortcomings in the P-35, including a jam-prone starter, leaky fuel tanks, and faulty landing gear. The company lost $70,000 on the order and the following year lost an order to Curtiss for 210 additional aircraft.

Seversky's overly enthusiastic drive to sell aircraft, his disdain for Curtiss, and his difficult personality caused his company to become increasingly alienated from the American military establishment. As Seversky's reputation grew, his company's business declined. He was forced to turn to a greater number of export customers, including the Soviet Union and Japan, which held tenuous regard for human rights and even proprietary aircraft designs.

Seversky converted the P-35 to a racer and struck up a relationship with the aviatrix Jacqueline Cochrane in an attempt to win recognition for the aircraft's performance. The design won several races but failed to win more sales. Most of the government's P-35s were stationed in the Philippines and were later destroyed during the Japanese invasion of that country.

Hoping to reduce his company's reliance on military sales, Seversky spent tremendous sums on the development of a large five-propeller passenger craft. By 1939, however, Paul Moore had had enough of Seversky. That year, while the founder was on a sales mission to England, the company's beleaguered board of directors voted to oust Seversky and install its own candidate, W. Wallace Kellett, as president of the firm. Seversky was given $80,000 and retired into a more distinguished career as a columnist.

Kellett slashed the payroll from 500 to 185 employees and later won a lucrative Swedish export order. With a $10 million backlog, the company was profitable for the first time. Hoping to rid the company of its bad name, the board voted to change the company's name to Republic Aviation.

### *Famous Fighters in World War II and the Cold War*

Alexander Kartveli remained with the firm and was instrumental in designing its next fighter, the P-47 Thunderbolt. A clear improvement over the lightly armed P-35, the P-47 was the first fighter capable of providing uninterrupted air cover for American bombers between Britain and Germany. As a result, the P-47 secured a leading role for Republic during World War II. Republic Aviation, still located in Farmingdale, grew to employ more than 32,000 workers, a great many of whom were women. By 1944, Republic was turning out 20 P-47s a day.

With the end of the war drawing near, the company began planning for much leaner times. Fearing the loss of its military contracts, Republic hoped to convert a new high-altitude reconnaissance craft it had developed into a civilian airliner. The four-engine RC-2 Rainbow was as sleek as a missile, and its speed was unrivaled, but the two launch customers, Pan American and American Airlines, lost interest after learning the airliner's cost. A second project for the civilian market was the RC-3 Seabee. Conceived of as a family sedan floatplane, the Seabee suffered from a collapse in public interest in private aviation. After only about 1,000 Seabees were built, Republic abandoned the civil aviation market.

British and American manufacturers quickly began development of jet aircraft after Germany's Me-262 fighter jet appeared during the final months of the war. Under Karveli's direction, Republic began work on its own jet design, the F-84 Thunderjet. Fitted with an Allison J-35 engine, the F-84 first flew in 1946. The Thunderjet was capable of air-to-air refueling and carrying nuclear bomb payloads. The design saw heavy action during the Korean War, and by 1953 more than 7,000 were turned out for the Air Force and several foreign air services.

While the F-84 proved to be a formidable fighter bomber, its development took a heavy toll on Republic. Costs were so high that the company only narrowly avoided bankruptcy. Nevertheless, having demonstrated its ability to build a great jet, Republic won further government funding for an experimental rocket-

### Key Dates:

**1931:** Republic Aviation is founded as Seversky Aircraft Corporation.
**1936:** Fairchild Aircraft is founded.
**1946:** After building thousands of P-47 fighters in WWII, Republic unveils its F-84 Thunderjet.
**1964:** Fairchild acquires Hiller Aircraft Company.
**1965:** Fairchild Hiller acquires Republic Aviation.
**1971:** Fairchild acquires Swearingen Aircraft Company.
**1972:** Fairchild wins bid to build A-10 Thunderbolt tank-killer aircraft.
**1990:** Former Wings West managers purchase Fairchild.
**1996:** Fairchild Aircraft acquires Dornier Luftfahrt, forming Fairchild Dornier.
**2002:** Fairchild Dornier files for bankruptcy and seeks a strategic partner.

powered version, the XF-91, and a successor to the F-84, the F-105 Thunderchief. The Thunderchief matched or outperformed all competing designs during the mid-1950s, including the North American F-86 and Lockheed F-104. The multi-role F-105 was the U.S. Air Force's standard fighter bomber throughout the 1950s, and more than 800 were built. During the late 1950s, the company began development of a ramjet-powered fighter called the XF-103. Capable of speeds in excess of 3,000 miles per hour, the titanium fighter was deemed too expensive by the Air Force and was canceled.

When President Kennedy took office, Defense Secretary Robert McNamara attempted to rein in aircraft development costs by ordering development of a fighter bomber suitable for use by both the Air Force and Navy. This strategy caught Republic by surprise. As Boeing Co., General Dynamics Corp., and Grumman Corp. scrambled to meet the call, Republic found itself simply unprepared to develop such a design. Like Martin Aircraft some years before, Republic elected to concentrate its resources on space projects. The company was chosen to make space suits and build satellites and rocket engines, but despite these efforts, Republic was unable to secure a lasting position in the space industry.

By the time production of the F-105 ended in 1965, Republic was left only with a few subcontracting arrangements, including building aft sections of McDonnell's F-4 Phantom. With all but 3,700 employees laid off and in dire need of financial backing, Republic was acquired by the new Fairchild-Hiller company. As a division of Fairchild-Hiller, Republic afforded its parent company a better relationship with the military. By 1966, Fairchild-Hiller's finances had become strong enough that it was able to bid for the acquisition of another distressed airplane builder, the Douglas Aircraft Co.

While Fairchild-Hiller lost out to McDonnell Aircraft on that bid, it retained a strong interest in commercial aircraft. As a result of its close relationship with Fokker, the company began negotiations to manufacture the Dutch company's new F-28 jetliner in the United States under license. However, the partnership was later terminated with a $30 million write-off when sales of the Fokker-Fairchild F-228 failed to materialize.

The Republic Aviation Division won valuable subcontracts to manufacture parts for Boeing Co.'s 747 and supersonic transport, or SST. Republic also won a design competition to develop a vertical take-off and landing fighter jet with the German company Entwicklundring Sud. Unfortunately, both the SST and the fighter were later canceled.

In a 1969 design competition with McDonnell-Douglas Corporation, Republic lost a highly profitable contract for the F-15. Many considered Republic's design to be vastly superior, but McDonnell-Douglas maintained an extremely competent lobbying organization. In addition, the Pentagon had just awarded the F-14 Tomcat to Grumman, located in Bethpage, a scant nine miles from Republic. In the world of political ''horse trading,'' two major contract awards for the same congressional district would never be tolerated.

### *Swearingen Aircraft Acquired 1971*

In 1971, the company had changed its name to Fairchild Industries and was looking to acquire another aircraft manufacturer with excess capacity—and located away from the east coast. In November of that year the search ended with the Swearingen Aircraft Company. At the time it was acquired by Fairchild, Swearingen was little more than a design shop with a small manufacturing facility located in San Antonio, Texas. The company was founded in 1959 by a talented aircraft designer named Ed Swearingen, Jr. Originally a one-man operation, the Swearingen Aircraft Company was established solely for the purpose of modifying twin-engine Queen Air business craft, built in Wichita by Beech Aircraft. Unlike other aircraft modifiers, Swearingen did not merely add new fixtures and controls. Instead, the company replaced the Queen Air's original fuselage with one of its own design. Swearingen marketed the rebuilt aircraft under the name Merlin.

During the 1960s, Swearingen incorporated further enhancements on the Queen Air, which were sold as the Merlin II and Merlin IIB. Swearingen sold a total of 115 Merlins. By 1970, the company had so radically altered the original Beech design that Ed Swearingen decided to build the craft from scratch. He called the new business craft the Merlin III but also developed a commuter airline version called the Metro.

While Swearingen went deeply into debt to finance production of the new craft, the project gained the attention of Fairchild. Seeing the opportunity to buy into a promising civilian craft at the earliest stage, Fairchild negotiated a deal to buy out Swearingen. The San Antonio facility remained in operation for several more years as Fairchild Swearingen until the founder's name was eventually dropped.

In 1972, Fairchild Republic won a competition to produce a new ground attack aircraft, the A-10 Thunderbolt. This unusual craft, called Warthog by the pilots who flew it, was designed not to fly against other aircraft but against tanks and artillery. Heavily armored, the A-10 carried a powerful 30mm rapid fire cannon that could destroy a tank in half a second. The A-10 was extremely maneuverable, able to snoop around trees and loiter at low altitudes for hours. The U.S. Air Force, addicted to flashy supersonic fighters, wanted no part of the project, but with no other anti-tank alternative, production of the A-10 began. The air force was obligated to maintain the craft. In battle, the A-10 would be under the direction of the army.

Hoping to remain a step ahead of cancellation, Fairchild immediately began searching for another civilian project in which to invest profits from the A-10. The company studied a number of designs with Sweden's Saab-Scania, settling on a 34-passenger twin-prop called the SF-340. Fairchild and Saab agreed to develop and manufacture the airliner jointly and to coordinate sales efforts.

In 1982, with A-10 production nearing the end of its cycle, Fairchild won a second contract to produce the T-46 jet trainer for the air force, but air force officials were so incensed by the presentation of a mock-up when a finished version was due that they requested a full review of the company. They found Fairchild unable to control costs or affect engineering discipline because the company's senior executives were waging a pitched battle for control of the company and driving it into complete disarray.

After Fairchild delivered the last of 700 A-10s in 1984, the company was unable to cover rising costs on the T-46. No longer able to support the SF-340 project, Fairchild bailed out after building only 96—half what was needed to break even. The divided management attempted to steer the company into the communications and space industries (the company built numerous space components, including the Space Shuttle's tail fins), but when the air force canceled the T-46 in 1987, it sounded the death knell for the Republic division. Republic's Farmingdale site was sold to a shopping mall developer in 1988, and many of its employees moved to Grumman.

### *1987 Restructuring*

In July 1987, Fairchild restructured its operations and sold its San Antonio operations to Los Angeles-based GMF Investments, headed by renegade board director Gene Morgan. Fairchild continued to collect small contracts for updated versions of the Metro from the air national guard and a handful of commuter airlines. After a while, its president and two other executives were fired for ''philosophical differences'' with Morgan. After a boardroom showdown in January of 1990, Fairchild declared bankruptcy. It remained under Chapter 11 supervision until August 15, when a former Fairchild customer named Carl Albert bid for the company.

Albert had purchased many Fairchild Metros during his career as head of the Wings West commuter airline. As a one-time customer, he knew how to sell them. When the AMR Corporation bought out Wings West, Albert had $42 million to spend. Later that year, Albert and a group of investors organized Fairchild Aircraft Incorporated and acquired the airplane builder for $66.4 million. They immediately laid plans to rebuild the company, riding their bets on a newer, more versatile Metro III.

Months later, the A-10 proved itself in battle in Kuwait, destroying 1,000 tanks, 1,200 artillery pieces, and 2,000 military vehicles. Some Warthogs returned from battle with as much as 20 feet of wing missing, tails shot off, and gaping holes in the fuselage. The effectiveness and incredible resilience of the craft forced many in the Pentagon to rethink their earlier treatment of Fairchild. The company sold its rights to the aircraft to Grumman before closing its Farmingdale plant.

Under Carl Albert, Fairchild emerged as a financially sound company—and the only consistently profitable small aircraft manufacturer. The company manufactured derivatives of its low-cost, successful new Metro 23, including passenger, cargo, military, and aerial surveillance versions. Fairchild had 1,000 employees and annual sales of $580 million at the beginning of the 1990s.

Several new contracts from the U.S. government and Aeromexico, among others, prompted Fairchild to double production and hire more employees for its San Antonio plant in 1991. The company was also looking abroad for low-cost manufacturing capability and design expertise.

Fairchild Aircraft Aircraft and LET Narodni Podnik, a Czech aircraft manufacturer, discussed producing a westernized version of the Let L610 40-seat turboprop airliner. However, talks stalled in early 1993 due to Let's inability to restructure its debt and raise financing to build a second prototype for U.S. certification. Nevertheless, in June of the year Fairchild announced plans to acquire a majority stake in Let via its quasi-governmental holding company, Aero. The Czech manufacturer employed between two and three thousand workers at its site in Kunovice.

Fairchild planned to invest $100 million in the company. Besides Let's L610, Fairchild would be marketing its unpressurized 19-seat L420 airliner and planned to subcontract Let some work on its own Metro 23 airliner. Fairchild was ultimately unsuccessful in its attempt to acquire Let, however.

Around the same time, a secret plot to acquire Fairchild emerged. Two years earlier, during Fairchild's bankruptcy proceedings, Israeli Aircraft Industries (IAI) had been contacted by company-restructuring specialist Quadrant Management about joining its bid for the company. In a 1993 lawsuit, IAI claimed Sanwa Bank, a Fairchild creditor, called off the talks due to an Arab boycott of Israel.

### *Fairchild Dornier Created in 1996*

Daimler-Benz Aerospace AG (DASA) sold Fairchild its financially troubled Dornier Luftfahrt GmbH regional aircraft unit in June 1996, thus creating Fairchild Dornier GmbH. Dornier had roots going back to 1914 and was a pioneer in all-metal aircraft construction. DASA acquired the company in 1985 but came to rue its involvement in the fiercely competitive regional airline business. Although its new Dornier 328 was faster and quieter than other turboprops, the marketplace was crowded and steering towards new regional jets. Dornier Lufthahrt lost $337 million (DM499 million) in 1995.

The 328JET, a 30-seat, jet-powered version of the 328 turboprop inherited from Dornier, began flight testing in January 1998. This type spawned a number of derivatives, including the 428JET, a 44-seat stretched version scheduled to begin deliveries in 2003. A freighter version was also under development.

Planned derivatives of another model, the 70-seat 728JET, included a shortened version, the 528JET, and a stretched version, the 928JET. Fairchild Aerospace was launching business aircraft versions of both the 328 JET and its 728JET, dubbed the Envoy 3 and the Envoy 7.

The 728JET claimed to offer regional airlines the first true 50/90-seat family of jets, noted *Flight International.* The project had the backing of the German government, which guaranteed $350 million worth of loans to help protect jobs at the Dornier factory near Munich. Lufthansa signed up as an early customer.

The 728JET family had projected development costs of $1 billion, making Fairchild scramble for additional capital. The company entered discussions with a number of North American aircraft manufacturers (including Boeing and Bombardier) as well as with the French-Italian ATR regional aircraft consortium. DASA still owned a fifth of Dornier but declined to invest any more money in it.

The search for a strategic partner in the 728JET program dragged on for years. U.S. venture capital group Clayton Dubilier & Rice took a 71 percent share in the company in April 2000. Chuck Pieper, one of its partners, became chairman of Fairchild Dornier. Allianz Capital Partners owned another 15 percent of the company. In October 2000, former McDonnell Douglas executive Louis F. Harrington was named CEO.

Though the pricey $29.5 million 728JET had landed 125 firm orders, several customers failed to complete purchases of nearly a dozen of the company's main product, the 328JET, after the September 11 terrorist attacks on the United States. In addition, the Chinese government did not grant an import license for the plane in time for a scheduled delivery to Hainan Airlines.

Fairchild Dornier filed for bankruptcy protection in Germany on April 3, 2002. The U.S. operations were shut down and more than 300 employees at San Antonio and a marketing office in Herndon, Virginia, were laid off without severance. The firm still employed 3,700 in Germany, whose salaries were secured by the government. The government-appointed administrator gave Fairchild Dornier three months to devise a rescue plan.

### *Principal Subsidiaries*

Fairchild Dornier Inc. (U.S.); Fairchild Gen Aero, Inc. dba Fairchild Aircraft Services (U.S.); Metro Support Services, Inc. (U.S.).

### *Principal Competitors*

ATR ''Integrated''; Bombardier Inc.; Embraer-Empresa Brasileira de Aeronáutica S.A.

### *Further Reading*

''A-10 Warthogs Damaged Heavily In Gulf War . . . ,'' *Aviation Week & Space Technology*, August 5, 1991, pp. 42–3.

Bredemeier, Kenneth, ''Fairchild Dornier Cuts Workforce,'' *Washington Post,* April 12, 2002, p. E3.

Bright, Charles D., *Jet Makers*, Lawrence, Kansas: Regents Press of Kansas, 1978.

Chuter, Andy, ''Fairchild Wraps Up 328JET Testing and Confirms Stretch Plans,'' *Flight International,* May 5, 1999, p. 16.

Egozi, Arie, ''IAI Plan for Fairchild Purchase was 'Foiled,' '' *Flight International,* June 9, 1993, p. 14.

Flottau, Jens, ''Ailing Fairchild Dornier Seeks to Buy Time,'' *Aviation Week & Space Technology,* April 8, 2002.

——, ''Berlin Air Show to Open Under Stormy Skies,'' *Aviation Week & Space Technology,* April 29, 2002, p. 76.

Hegmann, Gerhard, ''Jetmaker Faces Liquidity Crisis,'' *Financial Times* (London), Companies & Finance: The Americas, March 22, 2002, p. 28.

Jasper, Chris, ''Fairchild Seeks Partners to Meet 728JET Development Costs,'' *Flight International,* August 25, 1999, p. 5.

Lopez, Ramon, ''DASA Ready to Finalise Sale of Dornier Unit to Fairchild,'' *Flight International,* May 8, 1996, p. 6.

Moorman, Robert W., ''Fairchild Steals the Show,'' *Air Transport World,* June 1993, p. 206.

Moxon, Julian, ''Debts Hold Up Let Alliance Plans,'' *Flight International,* May 12, 1993.

North, David M., ''Manufacturers' Joint Work Cuts Costs,'' *Aviation Week & Space Technology,* May 30, 1983, p. 262.

Sparaco, Pierre, ''Fairchild Dornier Launches All-New Regional Twinjets,'' *Aviation Week & Space Technology,* May 25, 1998, p. 20.

Stoff, Joshua, *The Thunder Factory*, Osceola, Wisconsin: Motorbooks International, 1990.

Thornton, Chris, ''The Dimensions Debate,'' *Flight International,* June 9, 1999, p. 149.

Tieman, Ross, ''Fight to Get Dornier Flying Again,'' *The Business,* April 7, 2002, p. 15.

Warwick, Graham, ''Fairchild Considers New Wing for Metro 23,'' *Flight International,* August 5, 1992, p. 12.

Wells, Annabel, ''Head Start,'' *Flight International,* May 5, 1999, p. 3.

—John Simley
—update: Frederick C. Ingram

# Farmland Industries, Inc.

**12200 North Ambassador Drive**
**Kansas City, Missouri 64163-1244**
**U.S.A.**
**Telephone: (816) 713-7000**
**Fax: (816) 713-6323**
**Web site: http://www.farmland.com**

*Cooperative*
*Incorporated:* 1929 as Union Oil Company
*Employees:* 14,500
*Sales:* $11.8 billion
*NAIC:* 324110 Petroleum Refineries; 311611 Animal (Except Poultry) Slaughtering; 325311 Nitrogenous Fertilizer Manufacturing; 325312 Phosphatic Fertilizer Manufacturing

Operating out of Kansas City, Missouri, Farmland Industries, Inc. is North America's largest agricultural cooperative. It is owned by some 1,700 local co-ops, which represent approximately 600,000 agricultural producers. Embracing a farm-to-table mission, the co-op essentially divides its activities between ''inputs'' and ''outputs.'' On the input side, Farmland and its joint venture partners help farmers in their production efforts by providing such items as fertilizers, insecticides and herbicides, animal feeds, and petroleum products. On the output side, Farmland adds value to members' food and fiber products, and markets them throughout the world. In recent years, a major part of the output strategy is to enhance the Farmland name and its copyrighted phrase, ''Proud to be farmer-owned.'' The co-op also employs vertical integration as much as possible. With petroleum products, for instance, Farmland pumps crude from its own wells, refines it in its own facilities, and markets the resulting products through its Ampride service stations. With hogs and beef, the co-op is involved in the raising of the animals through feed, the slaughtering and packaging process, as well as marketing the meats under the Farmland label.

### *Farmland's Founder Active in Cooperative Movement in 1920s*

Farmland's founder, Howard A. Cowden, was born in 1893 on a southwestern Missouri farm settled by his grandfather. Unlike other farms in his native Polk County, which averaged less than 100 acres in size, the Cowden farm at 500 acres was one of the largest. Although his father was a progressive farmer who was hardworking, efficient, and put the latest ideas into practice, he struggled to prosper. Cowden became keenly aware that farmers were at an economic disadvantage in the marketplace: they faced high interest rates on mortgages, paid high transportation costs, and had virtually no leverage in the pricing of their commodities. All too often farmers were faced with a ''take it or leave it'' proposition.

Rather than becoming a farmer, Cowden became a school teacher, spending a year in a one-room schoolhouse before teaching intermediate grades at a school in Pleasant Hope, Missouri. There he became inspired by a novel, *The Brown Mouse* by Herbert Quick, the hero of which was a young farmer who became a teacher and helped his community by advancing the concepts of progressive agriculture and cooperatives. Cowden emulated the book and organized Farm Clubs in Polk County. Cowden quit his teaching position during World War I in favor of military training with the Student Army Training Corps, but the war soon ended and in early 1919 he was at a crossroads in his life. Uninterested in returning to the farm and dissatisfied with teaching, he accepted a job as secretary of the Polk County Farmers Association, which launched a lifelong career in the agricultural cooperative movement. Cowden owed his position in large part to William Hirth, publisher of *The Missouri Farmer and Breeder,* which promoted the formation of local Farm Clubs. County associations resulted and by 1917 a statewide organization was established, the Missouri Farmers Association (MFA), which allowed Farm Clubs to buy supplies in bulk and pass on the savings to their members. Hirth urged that county associations hire a paid secretary to better serve members and help push the Farm Clubs into becoming fully realized cooperatives. He recognized Cowden's potential when the young man had set up Farm Clubs in Polk County and wrote some columns for *The Missouri Farmer.* Hirth began an effort to enlist Cowden in the ''Farm Club fight.''

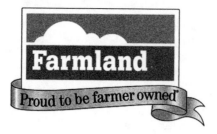

**Company Perspectives:**

*Farmland is committed to serving the needs of its member-owners and the consumers who buy their products. Indeed, it is our mission: To be a global, consumer-driven, producer-owned, "farm-to-table" cooperative system.*

Cowden was 26 years old when he became secretary of the Polk County Farmers Association as well as manager of the Polk County Farmers Exchange, a local cooperative. In addition to pooling orders for supplies, Cowden began selling eggs to Kansas City, securing better prices for farmers than they were able to get from local producers. Out of this effort he formed the Producers' Produce Company, which then purchased a cold storage facility to handle the eggs and cream of local farmers. When MFA expanded its statewide operations in 1920, the organization hired "fieldmen," and once again Hirth was instrumental in securing a post for Cowden, who now made connections throughout Missouri. He also became familiar with cooperative efforts in other states, in particular the Cottonwood Oil Company in Minnesota. With the rising importance of tractors and trucks to modern farming, the cost of fuel and lubricants was becoming an important factor to farmers. After visiting Cottonwood, Cowden urged MFA to buy petroleum products in bulk for its members, and as a result the association began contracting with Standard Oil and other major companies.

### *Union Oil Company Formed as a Cooperative in 1929*

As Cowden gained more prominence in MFA during the 1920s, his relationship with Hirth began to sour. By 1927, Hirth, who apparently felt his own power was being eclipsed by the younger man, actively campaigned for Cowden's dismissal. Rather than become involved in a nasty public spat, Cowden resigned, deciding to enter the wholesale oil business. Through a friendly executive committee he was able to secure the MFA oil contract held by Standard Oil, and as a result incorporated the Cowden Oil Company in January 1928. He was well aware, however, that his MFA contract would likely be short lived once Hirth succeeded in taking control of the association. Moreover, he faced statewide opposition from Hirth's many friends. After running the commercial venture for several months, Cowden took steps to transform the business into a regional wholesale petroleum cooperative. In January 1929, he dissolved Cowden Oil and transferred all assets to a new firm, Union Oil Company, which he organized as a cooperative under Missouri statutes. Although six farmer-own cooperatives formed the basis of Union Oil, he made sure that his control of the organization was absolute.

Since Union Oil was intended as a regional enterprise, Cowden elected to operate out of Kansas City. By the end of its first year of operation, Union Oil served 22 local cooperatives and was supplied by Kanotex Corporation. Cowden was also able to purchase a two-story structure in Kansas City and some old equipment from the Continental Oil Company in order to create different blends of oil. Union Oil became the first cooperative in the country to run an oil-compounding plant. The need to take additional steps in vertical integration became apparent in late 1932 when Union Oil's supplier, Conoco, terminated a five-year contract. Although major oil companies failed to crush cooperative upstarts, due to the intervention of President Roosevelt, it became apparent to Cowden that gaining control of basic supplies was essential, as was the need for a refinery.

In addition to petroleum products, Union Oil began offering a line of automobile accessories under the CO-OP brand, as well as a CO-OP paint and twine. With the organization becoming involved in a wide range of products, it was decided in February 1935 to change the name to Consumers Cooperative Association (CCA). By now the organization had 259 local cooperatives as members and was generating more than $2 million in annual revenues. CCA established a grocery division in 1935 and soon the CO-OP label was applied to over 200 products. Although operations prospered in some locations, overall the Grocery Department was not a very important part of CCA. It proved more useful as a public example of the power of cooperatives to meet consumer needs than as a significant profit center. Another enterprise that proved unsuccessful was the move to supply tractors. CCA fared better with the jobbing of lumber and building materials. Despite such diversification, however, the sale of petroleum products remained the co-op's major activity, accounting for 82 percent of all revenues in 1939. To support its petroleum business, CCA built a refinery in Phillipsburg, Kansas. When it became operational in 1939, the facility greatly increased the organization's income and led to a period of prosperity during the 1940s. CCA added producing wells to its business mix and emerged at the end of World War II as a significant independent oil company.

CCA became involved in a variety of other areas after the war, including the production of flour and feed, the manufacture of household and electrical appliances, and the development of insurance and finance associations. Of particular importance was the feed program, which in its first year generated more revenue than the grocery business did in its tenth year. (CCA ultimately closed the Grocery Department in 1953.) Another highly profitable business for CAA was fertilizer, which farmers began to use at an accelerated rate following the war. To meet the demand, as well as establish some verticality in the business, CCA decided to build a nitrogen plant in 1954, a very expensive endeavor that pushed the co-op to the brink of receivership. The organization was forced to make some difficult decisions, closing down some departments, but in the end CCA was better positioned for the future.

By 1958, CCA topped $100 million in annual revenues, ranked 327th among the *Fortune* 500, and was one of the largest co-ops in America. In many ways it was an industrial powerhouse, controlling a wide range of assets: oil wells, pipelines, refineries, grease and paint factories, feed mills, fertilizer works, warehouses, and a fleet of trucks. Petroleum products continued to dominate the co-op's business, accounting for 70 percent of revenues, but that percentage would dip below 50 percent over the next few years as fertilizer became an increasingly more important revenue stream. The emphasis of CCA was now clearly on the farm supply and service field, making the use of the word "consumer" in its title less appropriate. The organization also faced mounting pressure to better serve farmers by engaging in the marketing of agricultural products,

**Key Dates:**

**1928:** Howard Cowden forms Cowden Oil Co.
**1929:** Cowden Oil is dissolved to form a cooperative named Union Oil Company.
**1935:** Union Oil changes its name to Consumers Cooperative Association (CAA).
**1939:** An oil refinery in Phillipsburg, Kansas, opens.
**1961:** Cowden retires.
**1966:** CAA changes name to Farmland Industries, Inc.
**1982:** The company's first net loss is posted.
**1999:** Farmland's revenues top $10 billion.

an area which CCA had intentionally avoided. In 1958, the CCA Board finally agreed to become involved in marketing as opportunities might arise. A year later the co-op formed a subsidiary, Farmbest, Inc., to purchase the Crawford County Packing Company in Denison, Iowa, and entered the hog-processing business.

### *Cowden Retires in 1961*

In 1961, Cowden, who was 68 years old, resigned as CCA's chief executive but stayed on as chairman, a newly formed position. Dissatisfied with this diminished role, however, he soon relinquished the chairmanship as well, although he stayed on as a director-at-large until 1963. Replacing him was longtime CCA executive Homer Young, who had joined the co-op in 1931. It was during his tenure that the board decided to change the organization's name from ''Consumers Cooperative Association'' to something that better described its contemporary mission. After paring down the candidates, the board settled on two finalists: Farmbest Industries, Inc. and Farmland Industries, Inc. The latter was chosen at a meeting on May 25, 1966. Ties to the cooperative movement were retained by the continued use of the CO-OP trademark on all products. Aside from the change in name, Young was also instrumental in expanding Farmland's manufacturing capabilities, with a particular emphasis on the production of farm chemicals.

Not only was Young's replacement, Ernest T. Lindsey, not one of the organization's ''founding fathers,'' he came to the job with limited farm experience. Although born on a Texas farm, he grew up in small towns and earned a degree in chemistry before going to work for Humble Oil Corporation, which eventually became Exxon. Nevertheless, he endeavored to maintain Farmland's commitment to family farmers while at the same time making the tough business decisions expected of anyone at the helm of a major industrial operation. He oversaw the reorganization of the food-marketing business and in 1970 created Farmland Agriservices to purchase hogs, cattle, and poultry for Farmland Foods, Inc., which was formed to handle the co-op's meat business. Under Lindsay, Farmland eliminated an unprofitable cooperative trucking company, National Farm Lines, but branched into insurance. Young had earlier saved from failure the Farmers Elevator Mutual Insurance Company because it insured many of Farmland's member cooperatives. With control of one institution, Lindsay acquired the Farmers Life Insurance Company in 1967 and over the next several years expanded Farmland's line of insurance services. In 1974, all of the insurance enterprises were organized under Farmland Insurance Services. Lindsay was also in charge when Farmland merged with Far-Mar-Co, Inc., which had been formed in 1968 when four regional grain cooperatives combined operations. The merger of the country's largest farm supply cooperative and the largest grain-marketing cooperative was finalized in February 1977, resulting in Farmland topping $3 billion in annual revenues and moving up to 78th place on the *Fortune* 500 list.

For the most part, the 1970s were a bumper time for America's farmers, but overexpansion led to serious problems when the economy slumped in the early 1980s. Despite its size, Farmland was still dependent on the plight of farmers, and in 1982 it posted its first losing year in its history. In 1985 and 1986, Farmland lost $210 million and because of volatile price swings elected to stop marketing grains, selling off Far-Mor-Co. Lindsay was succeeded as CEO in 1986 by James Rainey, who, during his five years at the top, managed to return the organization to fiscal health. He also took steps to ensure its survival should another lean period in agriculture emerge. He was replaced in 1991 by Harry Cleberg, who had been raised on a South Dakota farm and by the age of 17 ran a local grain elevator. During the 1980s, he served as Farmland's troubleshooter and played an important role in fixing ailing units. He took a more aggressive stance than Rainey and returned Farmland to the grain marketing business through a number of purchases, including Union Equity Cooperative exchange, a transaction that brought Far-Mor-Co back into the cooperative fold. He also turned to international markets, contracting to sell wheat overseas and forming joint ventures with foreign partners. In 1993, he oversaw the purchase of British Petroleum's Tradigrain unit (an international grain trader with operations in six countries), as well as the acquisition of two major beef processing plants and a large refrigerated trucking line.

Cleberg's stated ambition for Farmland was to gain a presence in ''every sector of the global food chain.'' Instead of being a regional cooperative, in his eyes Farmland was now a North American cooperative, even an international cooperative, one that was ''a global, consumer-driven, producer-owned, farm-to-table'' operation. He also remained committed to the Farmland's original values, seeing the organization as taking the side of family farmers against corporate farming interests. Nevertheless, revenues grew steadily under Cleberg, increasing from $3.4 billion in fiscal 1992 to more than $10.7 billion in 1999.

Cleberg retired in 2000, replaced by Robert Honse, who had 27 years with Farmland and was well groomed for the top position. He took over during difficult economic conditions, which resulted in a loss of $29.25 million for fiscal 2000, despite revenues increasing to $12.2 billion. Honse instituted cost-cutting measures, eliminating hundreds of jobs and shedding assets. Although Farmland lost another $90 million in fiscal 2001, he succeeded in paring debt by $268 million and cutting administrative costs by close to $40 million. While Honse was eager to move Farmland more aggressively into branded case-ready and precooked pork and beef products, he shied away from the international grain trading business, in March 2002 announcing that the Tradigram operations would either be sold or closed. Farmland was also facing pressure from so-called new wave cooperatives. After more than 70 years in operation, Farmland faced a period of uncertainty, but throughout its history the organization had always proved flexible enough to meet any challenge.

### *Principal Subsidiaries*

Farmers Petroleum, Inc.; Farmland Foods, Inc.; Farmland Insurance Agency; Farmland National Beef Packing Co.; Pipeline Company; Farmland Securities Co.; Farmland Transportation, Inc.

### *Principal Competitors*

Agway, Inc.; Cargill, Inc.; Hormel Foods Corporation; Purina Mills, Inc.; Royal Dutch/Shell Group; Transammonia, Inc.

### *Further Reading*

Fite, Gilbert Courtland, *Beyond the Fence: A History Farmland Industries, Inc., 1929–1978,* Columbia, Mo.: University of Missouri Press, 1978, 404 p.

Gilmore, Casey, ''New Products, Markets Give Farmland Successful '93,'' *Kansas City Business Journal,* December 31, 1993, p. 3.

——, ''Pacesetter,'' *Kansas City Business Journal,* March 20, 1995, p. 3.

Gose, Joe, ''Farmland Considers 1992 Watershed Year,'' *Kansas City Business Journal,* November 13, 1992, p. 1.

Howie, Michael, ''Farmland Looking to Make Changes After 'Difficult Year',*'' Feedstuffs,* December 18, 2000, p. 6.

Nicolova, Rossitsa, ''Harry Is A World-Class Leader,'' *Business Journal Serving Metropolitan Kansas City,* June 23, 2000, p. 3.

Zganjar, Leslie, ''New Farmland CEO's Success Isn't In Attire—It's His Attitude,'' *Business Journal Serving Metropolitan Kansas City,* September 1, 2000, p. 24.

—Ed Dinger

FIRST TENNESSEE

*All Things Financial.*

# First Tennessee National Corporation

**165 Madison Avenue**
**Memphis, Tennessee 38103**
**U.S.A.**
**Telephone: (901) 523-4444**
**Toll Free: (800) 489-4040**
**Fax: (901) 523-4945**
**Web site: http://www.firsttennessee.com**

*Public Company*
*Incorporated:* 1864 as First National Bank of Memphis
*Employees:* 9,861
*Total Assets:* $19.2 billion (2001)
*Stock Exchanges:* New York
*Ticker Symbol:* FTN
*NAIC:* 522110 Commercial Banking; 551111 Offices of Bank Holding Companies

One of the 50 largest bank holding companies in the United States, First Tennessee National Corporation has provided banking services to Tennesseans since the Civil War, when the company's oldest and primary subsidiary, The First National Bank of Memphis, was organized. By 2000, the firm was operating as a national, diversified financial services firm with interests in retail and commercial banking, investment and trust products, credit card products, securities, transaction processing, and mortgage banking. First Tennessee has over 400 bank branches in Tennessee, Arkansas, and Mississippi through its Regional Banking Group business division. Subsidiary First Horizon Home Loans provides home loans and short-term finance products in 136 offices in 31 states. Overall, First Tennessee serves over 1.1 million customers and 90,000 businesses across the United States.

## *Early History: 1860s–1920s*

During the Civil War, many southern cities were negatively affected by the conflict. Once a bustling center of commerce, Memphis first suffered the destructive effects of war when in 1862 Union troops gained control of the city and placed it under military rule. Two years into this military occupation, a resident named Frank S. Davis decided to form a bank. Davis was convinced that Memphis would need additional banking and credit facilities once a national system of banks regulated by the federal government emerged, a prospect ensured by the passage of the National Banking Act of 1863. To that end, he organized a meeting to be convened on March 10, 1864 to discuss the possibilities of organizing a nationally chartered bank. That day, Davis and several other Memphis residents drafted the articles of association for such an enterprise and filed an application for a national charter. The charter was granted on March 25, 1864, marking the formal beginning of the city's new bank, The First National Bank of Memphis.

With Davis serving as the bank's president, and all of those who attended the first meeting selected as directors, First National began operations during the last year of the Civil War, operating initially out of one rented room, then moving, two months later, to larger space, for which the bank paid $75 in monthly rent. Despite the pernicious economic climate in which it emerged, the bank survived its first year, proving to be enough of a viable venture to merit the purchase of a two-story building in 1865.

The purchase of First National's new banking quarters coincided roughly with the end of the war and, it was hoped, a return to the economic vibrancy the city had once enjoyed. However, the resumption of a healthy business climate was slow in coming; Memphis reconstruction did not begin in earnest until the summer of 1866, when railroads leading in and out of the city were rebuilt and funding for public improvement programs was approved. During this time, many former Memphis residents returned home after relocating during the war. Thousands poured into the city over the next ten years, bringing the city's population to 45,000 and restoring economic prosperity to Memphis. First National, a fledgling banking concern, shared in the prosperity of the community it served. By the time Davis retired in 1882, after presiding over the bank for 18 years, the calamities engendered by war, and ensuing outbreaks of yellow fever, had come to an end, and the bank stood on solid ground.

Deposits at First National surpassed $1 million in 1897 by virtue of a rare acquisition completed that year, the purchase of

**Company Perspectives:**

*Our goal is to be the most efficient revenue growth company. We will never relinquish our focus on revenue growth, for that is the foundation for our future.*

the German Bank, which increased deposits from $700,000 to roughly $1.15 million. In 1913, the bank earned the distinction of being selected to execute the implementation of the Federal Reserve Act. Named as one of five banks in one of the 12 banking districts created by the Federal Reserve Act, First National assisted in the incorporation of the Federal Reserve Bank of St. Louis, of which the Federal Reserve Bank of Memphis was a branch.

In 1926, First National completed the first merger in its history, joining with one of Memphis' most respected banking institutions, the Central-State National Bank. According to the terms of the merger, First National would retain its name and charter, which by then had existed for 62 years, while the new bank's leadership would be drawn from Central-State. As a result, Central-State president S.E. Ragland became president of First National. The merger proved timely, occurring before the onset of the Great Depression, during which half of the nation's banks failed, and predating a period in which Memphis experienced a significant rise in population.

### *Postwar Expansion: 1950s–80s*

Better equipped after the merger to handle the increasing banking needs of a rapidly growing population, First National used its new financial resources to expand the scope of its operations. While America's entry into World War II forestalled First National's plans for significant expansion until the 1950s, some physical growth was recorded, such as the establishment of a suburban branch, the Crosstown Branch, in 1942. During the 1940s, Memphis continued to grow, entering the decade as the nation's 32nd largest city and ranking 26th by 1949, commensurately increasing the bank's need to expand. By 1952, First National operated seven branch offices in the region surrounding Memphis, and the bank's leadership began to look for a new site for First National's headquarters, which were in need of expansion.

In 1961, plans were announced for the construction of a 25-story bank and office building to replace existing accommodations. Three years later, the building was finished, and First National moved in, opening six additional branch offices at the same time. While First National remained largely a regional bank, its area of service was wide enough to warrant further expansion, making it, by 1967, the largest bank in the Mid-South. In 1969, as First National was evolving into a statewide banking concern, a one-bank holding company, First National Holding Company, was formed. Two years later, the structure of the holding company was changed, becoming a multi-bank holding company to enable the bank to acquire other banks throughout Tennessee. Concurrent with the structural change of First National's holding company, a name change was made, and First National Holding Company became First Tennessee National Corporation.

First Tennessee, with its principal subsidiary, First National Bank of Memphis, began acquiring Tennessee-based banks at a rapid pace. Five banks were purchased in 1972, with more to follow throughout the decade as First Tennessee extended its presence outside of Memphis and into other regions within the state. In 1974, First Tennessee's management selected a common name for the banks absorbed by the holding company, naming each First Tennessee Bank, a process concluded in 1977, when First National Bank of Memphis, the name selected by Frank S. Davis and other Memphis residents in 1864, became First Tennessee Bank.

First Tennessee continued to acquire Tennessee-based banks throughout the 1980s. As it solidified its presence in markets outside of Memphis, the bank also acquired several nonbanking financial institutions, gradually diversifying beyond its retail and commercial banking core. This diversification would become more important when First Tennessee made a strategic shift in the early 1990s toward a greater interest in bonds and mortgage lending, but by the early 1980s the holding company had already begun to invest its energies in business lines apart from retail and commercial banking. In 1981, First Tennessee established First Express, a nationwide check clearing service, and, the following year, First Tennessee became the first bank in the Southeast to offer discount brokerage services.

### *Focus on Bond and Mortgage Lending Business: 1990s*

As it entered the 1990s, after restructuring its banking organization in 1987 to give its regional departments more autonomy, First Tennessee's leadership decided a more profitable future could be realized in nontraditional banking areas. The holding company's retail and commercial banking operations would continue to provide substantial earnings, generating, along with its credit card, trust services, check clearing, and transaction processing businesses, approximately 80 percent of its annual pre-tax income during the early 1990s. However, as bank acquisitions became increasingly expensive and First Tennessee's market share throughout the state became more entrenched, it became apparent that a greater return on investments could be achieved by strengthening its bond and mortgage lending businesses.

Between 1990 and 1993, First Tennessee's bond division, involved in purchasing and selling fixed income securities, more than doubled its volume of business, jumping from $66 billion worth of securities bought and sold in 1990 to $147.8 billion by 1993. This rate of growth, 30.8 percent compounded annually, was eclipsed by First Tennessee's mortgage expansion, an increase primarily realized through two important acquisitions in 1993. That year, the holding company purchased Maryland National Mortgage Corporation and SNMC Management Corporation, which added more than $6 billion to First Tennessee's mortgage origination total and positioned the company as one of the ten largest mortgage originators in the nation. The addition of Maryland National and SNMC (raising First Tennessee's mortgage origination total from $700 million to $7.2 billion) enabled the holding company to record an annually compounded growth rate of 55.3 percent in mortgage originations between 1990 and 1993.

## Key Dates:

**1864:** The First National Bank of Memphis is formed.
**1897:** German Bank is acquired; First National's deposits exceed $1 million.
**1913:** First National is selected to execute the implementation of the Federal Reserve Act.
**1926:** The firm merges with Central-State National Bank.
**1952:** By now, First National operates seven branch offices.
**1969:** First National Holding Company is created.
**1971:** The holding company adopts the name First Tennessee National Corporation.
**1977:** First National Bank of Memphis changes its name to First Tennessee Bank.
**1982:** First Tennessee becomes the first bank in the Southeast to offer discount brokerage services.
**1993:** Maryland National Mortgage Corporation and SNMC Management Corporation are acquired.
**1995:** The company purchases Carl I. Brown and Company.
**1999:** First Tennessee adopts the tagline, "All Things Financial."

Increased activity in the bond and mortgage markets also meant increased activity at the national level. By 1993, the company's First Express business was operating in 43 states, and its bond division was serving customers in every state. Moreover, the company became a member of several national and international automated teller machine (ATM) service programs in more than 100,000 locations.

In the mid-1990s, First Tennessee was the dominant retail and commercial banking institution throughout much of Tennessee, ranking as the leader in deposit share in three of the state's five metropolitan areas. The holding company looked to expand beyond Tennessee's borders and beyond the traditional banking arena, striving to become a more diversified, nationally-oriented financial institution. In January 1995, First Tennessee announced that the company had acquired Carl I. Brown and Company, headquartered in Kansas City, Missouri. With the completion of this acquisition, First Tennessee ranked among the top ten retail and wholesale mortgage originators in the country, with mortgage offices in 25 states.

### *Continued Success: Late 1990s and Beyond*

As the company worked to position itself as a diversified financial services firm, First Tennessee watched—like most regional banking concerns—as large competitors grew even larger through takeovers and acquisitions. As the industry consolidated during the late 1990s, First Tennessee avoided entering the fray and instead focused on achieving revenue growth by manipulating existing operations. Indeed, from 1990 through 1998, the company had secured an average annual growth rate of 15.3 percent, which was higher than its regional counterparts. Ralph Horn, chairman of First Tennessee commented in a 1999 *American Banker* article that his goal was to achieve consistent, rather than flashy growth. "First Tennessee can increase market share without taking the risk of making a big acquisition and stubbing our toe," he stated.

During 1999, the company began to feel the negative effects of rising interest rates, which forced a slowdown in its mortgage business. Its capital markets division also faltered as a result of Y2K concerns. First Tennessee's regional banking group, on the other hand, experienced significant growth, recording revenue of $767.8 million, up from $678.7 million in 1998. That year the firm launched a new tagline—"All Things Financial"—to signal its shift from a traditional regional banking firm to a diversified financial services company.

As First Tennessee entered the new millennium, it failed to achieve the level of growth that it had been able to secure for the past ten years—between 12 and 15 percent. As such, the company made several strategic moves to strengthen its position in the industry. It sold its corporate and municipal trusts business, the MONEY BELT segment of its ATM business, and its co-branded and single-relationship credit card accounts. The firm's capital markets business segment acquired Midwest Research-Maxus Group Ltd., an equity research firm. First Tennessee's mortgage banking unit also adopted a single brand name—First Horizon Home Loans—in an effort to cross-sell a variety of First Tennessee products to existing customers.

The firm's repositioning efforts appeared to pay off, and in 2001 the company reported record earnings. During that year, the firm announced the acquisition of Synaxis Group Inc., a network of insurance agencies located in Georgia, Kentucky, and Tennessee, that would be integrated into its First Tennessee Bank subsidiary. First Tennessee's strategy for the future was focused on building and strengthening its regional banking, mortgage, capital markets, and transaction processing businesses. By 2002, First Tennessee had offered its shareholders over a century of consecutive quarterly dividends. With a longstanding history of success behind it, the holding company appeared to be well positioned to secure continued growth well into the future.

### *Principal Subsidiaries*

First National Bank of Springdale; FNBS Investment Advisory Corporation, Inc.; FNBS Investments, Inc.; First Tennessee Bank National Association; First Horizon Insurance Services, Inc.; First Horizon Merchant Services, Inc.; First Horizon Money Center, Inc.; First Horizon Strategic Alliances, Inc.; First Tennessee ABS, Inc.; First Tennessee Brokerage, Inc.; First Tennessee Capital Assets Corporation; First Tennessee Securities Corporation; FT Insurance Corporation; FT Mortgage Holding Corporation; First Horizon Home Loan Corporation; First Tennessee Mortgage Services, Inc.; First Horizon Asset Securities, Inc.; First Horizon Mortgage Loan Corporation; FH-FF Mortgage Services, L.P.; FT Real Estate Securities Company, Inc.; JPO, Inc.; TSMM Corporation; Synaxis Group, Inc.; Hickory Capital Corporation; Highland Capital Management Corp.; Tennessee Martin & Company, Inc.; Norlen Life Insurance Company.

### *Principal Divisions*

First Tennessee Regional Banking Group; First Horizon; FTN Financial; Transaction Processing.

### *Principal Competitors*

AmSouth Bancorporation; Bank of America Corp.; Union Planters Corporation.

### *Further Reading*


Bergquist, Erick, and Marc Hochstein, ''First Tennessee Unit, Not Keen on Horizon, Buys Itself Back,'' *American Banker*, May 4, 2000, p. 1.

''First Tennessee Completes Acquisition of Nashville-Based Insurance Broker,'' *Business Wire*, January 4, 2002.

*First Tennessee National Corporation —The First Hundred Years: A History of the First National Bank of Memphis*, Memphis: First Tennessee National Corp., n.d.

Gjertsen, Lee Ann, ''First Tennessee to Fill Commercial Lines Gap,'' *American Banker*, December 18, 2001, p. 8.

Keenan, Charles, ''First Tennessee Hungers for Pat on the Back,'' *American Banker*, September 16, 1999, p. 1.

Lacy, Sarah, ''First Tennessee Repositioning Yields Results,'' *Memphis Business Journal*, March 10, 2000, p. 1.

Ring, Niamh, ''First Tennessee Trying to Build a New Image,'' *American Banker*, January 15, 1999.

Roosevelt, Phil, ''First Tennessee Buying Its Way into the Industry's Big Leagues,'' *American Banker*, December 3, 1993, p. 10.

''Why 1st Tennessee Decided to Join the Big Leagues in Home Lending,'' *American Banker*, September 3, 1993, p. 10.

Yawn, David, ''First Tennessee Sees Growth in Bond, Trust Divisions,'' *Memphis Business Journal*, December 17, 1990, p. 43.


—Jeffrey L. Covell
—update: Christina M. Stansell

# Fuji Electric Co., Ltd.

**Gate City Ohsaki**
**East Tower 11-2**
**Osaki 1-chrome**
**Sinagawa-ku**
**Tokyo 141-0032**
**Japan**
**Telephone: (81) 3 5435-7206**
**Fax: (81) 3 5435-7486**
**Web site: http://www.fujielectric.co.jp**

*Public Company*
*Incorporated:* 1923
*Employees:* 27,103
*Sales:* ¥891 billion ($7.25 billion) (2001)
*Stock Exchanges:* Tokyo
*Ticker Symbol:* 6504
*NAIC:* 335313 Switchgear and Switchboard Apparatus Manufacturing; 333319 Other Commercial and Service Industry Machinery Manufacturing; 335314 Relay and Industrial Control Manufacturing; 334413 Semiconductor and Related Device Manufacturing; 335999 All Other Miscellaneous Electrical Equipment and Component Manufacturing; 345150 Instrument Manufacturing for Measuring and Testing Electricity and Electrical Signals; 334519 Other Measuring and Controlling Device Manufacturing

Fuji Electric Co., Ltd. is a manufacturer of measuring instruments, semiconductors, integrated circuits, drive components, open remote processing input/output (PIO) devices, and organic photo conductors for printers and copiers. The firm operates with four main business segments, including the Energy & Electric Systems Group, the Electronics Group, the ED&C Drive Systems Group, and the Retail Support Equipment & Systems Group. As part of its management plan, Fuji Electric is focused on expansion in business areas related to the environment, information systems, services, and components. While the company is international in scope, the majority of Fuji Electric's sales stem from its domestic operations.

### *1920s Origins*

Fuji Electric was founded in 1923 as a joint venture to facilitate technological cooperation between Furukawa Electric of Japan and Siemens of Germany. Nearly a year and a half after its founding, Fuji Electric began production at a new factory in Kawasaki, near Tokyo. The company manufactured a variety of electrical components as well as telephones. In 1930, Fuji began making mercury-arc rectifiers, and in 1933 it added porcelain expansion-type circuit breakers to its product line. As the joint research between Furukawa and Siemens led Fuji further into the heavy machinery sector, Fuji decided that its telephone division would be better off as a separate company, and in 1935 that division was incorporated as Fujitsu, Ltd.

A second technical agreement, between Fuji and the German company Voith, led to a production agreement for that company's 4850-horsepower Francis turbines. As electric power came into widespread use in Japan, particularly in industry, Fuji began production of small and industrial watt-hour meters and larger, more advanced circuit breakers.

As militarists consolidated their hold on the Japanese government during the 1930s, they promoted a rapid economic and military mobilization. As Japan marched toward World War II, Fuji came under a greater degree of central control, leading it to cooperate more closely with other manufacturing interests related to Furukawa Electric. As a result, new factories at Matsumoto, Fukiage, Tokyo, and Mie were completed between 1942 and 1944 and immediately brought on line to manufacture a variety of products for the war effort. These factories were heavily bombed in the last year of the war, effectively crippling the company.

When the war ended in 1945, Fuji Electric was placed in government custody until military investigations were carried out and the company could be rehabilitated. Fuji began production again in stages, as factories were repaired and markets recovered.

**Company Perspectives:**

*We, Fuji Electric, pledge as responsible corporate citizens in a global society to strengthen our trust with communities, customers, and partners. Our mission is to contribute to prosperity, encourage creativity, and seek harmony with the environment.*

### *Expansion: 1950s–70s*

In 1952, Fuji Electric helped to establish the heavy engine manufacturer Fuji Diesel, and the following year Fuji concluded another technical agreement, with the West German company Demag, to license technology for the production of magnetic motor starters, which it began to produce in 1954.

To a country so poor in natural resources, atomic power held tremendous potential in the 1950s. Accordingly, Fuji Electric joined the Daiichi Atomic Power Industry Group. Founded in 1956, this consortium of 22 companies built the first nuclear power plant in Japan through a combination of technology development and licensing. The 166-megawatt Tokai Nuclear Power plant went on line in 1960.

Fuji developed in two directions during the 1960s. It engineered larger and more powerful heavy machinery, such as transformers and propulsion equipment, and at the same time pioneered new diode and miniature circuit technologies. Fuji's strengths in research and development were greatly enhanced by the establishment in 1964 of its Central Research Laboratory.

During this period, Fuji built new factories in Chiba, Kobe, and Suzuka to manufacture heavy transformers, control systems, switchgears, and motors. The company also made a technical agreement with Seeburg of the United States to purchase vending machine technology. The machines, produced at the Mie factory, became very profitable. Fuji's manufacturing capacity was expanded further in 1968 when it took over the operations of its smaller rival, Kawasaki Denki Seizo.

By 1970, Fuji Electric began to recognize that its spectacular growth had left weaknesses in its organization. Rival manufacturers had emerged with stronger positions in several markets. The company took measures to strengthen the Furukawa group, but it also set up a second, more specialized 15-company group specifically for heavy industrial projects.

Fuji Electric opened its eighth factory, to manufacture circuit breakers and control systems, in Ohtawara in 1974. The company also introduced a variety of new products and processes, including large-capacity steel furnaces, process computers, and robots during the early 1970s.

Fuji survived the oil crisis of 1973 without great strain, and in the mid-1970s started to benefit from the dove-tailing of research efforts carried out with Fuji group members, primarily Fujitsu. This effort resulted in the development of several improved-technology items in control systems and computers, as well as more efficient generators and larger transformers.

By the late 1970s, Fuji had greatly strengthened its position as a leader in industrial electronics and had forged a close relationship with Fujitsu, which had emerged as Japan's leading computer software developer. Fuji made a major commitment to technology in 1980 when it established a special corporate research and development subsidiary to concentrate attention on new technologies, previously developed by different divisions, in one place.

### *Growth Continues: 1980s*

Fuji became involved in numerous foreign turnkey projects, many of them power plants. During 1980 and 1981, Fuji completed a geothermal power station and a 495-megawatt hydroelectric plant. Projects like these have given Fuji an international reputation for superior power-generating technology and engineering. This reputation for quality was established over many years, but was first achieved with smaller devices. Fuji's strength in this market continued into the 1980s and even led the company to expand its capacity by opening a ninth plant in Kobe in 1983.

By the late 1980s, the company was divided into five groups. The electric machinery group was responsible for plants and heavy machinery. The systems group covered instrumentation, information systems, and mechatronics, including robots and data processing equipment. The standard machinery and apparatus group manufactured programmable controllers, heavy motors, and magnetic devices. The electronics group produced large diodes, transistors and circuits, as well as computer components and measuring equipment. The vending machine and appliance group manufactured vending machines and large refrigerator display units like those found in grocery stores.

At the time, Fuji Electric was unique among Japanese electronics firms because it had no in-house computer development. Instead, it manufactured semiconductors, hard disks, and other components for its affiliate Fujitsu. Fuji Electric and Fujitsu maintained a substantial cross-ownership of stock.

Known for attracting some of the most talented engineers, and with hundreds of monuments to its accomplishments in Japan and abroad, Fuji Electric headed into the 1990s as a leading industrial electronics firm. Fuji was also in an excellent position, with its strong research organization, to develop leadership in new areas. The firm introduced a host of new products in 1990, including the 50kW on-site fuel cell, a general purpose inverter series that used 32-bit DSP, a slim 5.25-inch magneto-optical disk drive, and the Easy Access can vending machines.

### *Restructuring for the New Millennium*

In order to prepare itself for its entrance into the new millennium, Fuji Electric launched its ''New Vision 21 Plan'' in 1991. This management strategy divided the firm into eight different business groups. In its new formation, the company continued to develop new products including new magnetic disks, advanced water treatments systems, ink jet heads, various controllers for control systems, levitation melting technologies, and power transistors for use in space.

Fuji Electric also established several new subsidiary companies, including Scotland-based Fuji Electric Ltd. in 1991. Three

## Key Dates:

**1923:** Fuji Electric is founded as a joint venture between Furukawa Electric and Siemens.
**1935:** The company spins off its telephone division.
**1945:** Fuji Electric is placed under government custody after the war.
**1956:** The firm joins the Daiichi Atomic Power Industry Group.
**1964:** The Central Research Laboratory is established.
**1974:** The company's eighth factory is established.
**1980:** A subsidiary is created to focus on research and development in new technologies.
**1991:** The company reorganizes itself into eight business segments as part of the ''New Vision 21 Plan.''
**1999:** Fuji Electric restructures into four main divisions.
**2000:** The firm returns to profitability after three years of losses.

years later, the firm created Fuji Electric Dalian Co. Ltd., Fuji Electric Technology and Service Shenzhen Co. Ltd., and Suzhou Lanlian-Fuji Instruments Co. Ltd. The following year, Fuji/GE Taiwan Co. Ltd., P.T. Bukaka Fuji Electric, Fuji Electric Philippines Inc., Fuji Electric France S.A., and Fuji Electric Korea Co. Ltd. were established. The company continued to create new subsidiaries throughout the remainder of the 1990s throughout Asia and in Latin America. In 1999, Fuji Electric Imaging Device Co. Ltd. and Fuji Electric Storage Device Co. Ltd. were launched. That year the company also partnered with Hitachi Ltd. to form Fuji Hitachi Semiconductor Co.

Meanwhile, Fuji Electric's financial performance began to falter during this time period due to a weakening economy and fierce competition. The company's sales dropped off and in fiscal 1999, the company reported a net loss of ¥17.4 billion. That year the firm adopted a new company structure and also began to utilize an executive officer system. Under this new plan, Fuji Electric's operations fell into four operating segments including Energy & Electric Systems, Electronics, ED&C Drive Systems, and Retail Support Equipment & Systems. Company headquarters were moved to Gate City Ohsaki.

In June 2000, Fuji Electric announced the formation of its ''S21 Plan,'' which focused on satisfaction, speed, and sensibility. Under this plan, management looked to expansion in product areas related to the environment, information systems, services, and components. The company also eyed corporate alliances and constant restructuring as key to future success. In fiscal 2001, Fuji Electric returned to profitability for the first time in three years.

Several new companies were launched during this time period, including Japan Motor & Generator Co. Ltd., a joint venture between Fuji Electric, Hitachi Ltd., and Meidensha Corporation. The company also merged certain subsidiaries together to create Fuji Electric Power Engineering & Service Co. Ltd. and Fuji FKE Co. Ltd. In 2001, Fuji Semiconductor Inc. and Fuji Electric Systems Co. Ltd. were also established. In early 2002, Fuji Electric set plans in motion to purchase Sanyo Electric Co.'s vending machine business.

Even as Fuji Electric's operating environment remained challenging, company management was confident that the firm would prosper as a leading electronics concern in Japan. Focused on implementing the business strategies in its S21 Plan, Fuji Electric appeared to be on the right track for future growth and profits.

### *Principal Subsidiaries*

Fuji Electric Construction Co., Ltd.; Fuji Denki Sosetsu Co., Ltd.; FFC Limited Development; Fuji Electric Systems Co., Ltd.; Tochigi Fuji Co., Ltd.; Azumi Fuji Company; Fuji FKE Co., Ltd; Fuji Electric Excel Co., Ltd.; Fuji Gas Turbine Research; Center Co., Ltd.; Service Co., Ltd.; Fuji IT Co., Ltd.; Fuji Electric Instruments Co., Ltd.; Fuji Electric Chiba Tech. Co., Ltd.; Fuji Electric Technica Co., Ltd.; Chichibu Fuji Co., Ltd.; Fuji Denki Seiki Co., Ltd.; Fuji Electric Motor Co., Ltd.; Fuji Electric Hi-Tech Corp.; Fuji/GE Private Ltd.; Fuji/GE Taiwan Co., Ltd.; Fuji Electric Dalian Co., Ltd.; Ibaraki Fuji Co., Ltd.; Fuji Electric F-Tech Co., Ltd.; Fuji Electric Storage Device Co., Ltd.; Fuji Electric (Malaysia) Sdn. Bhd.; Fuji Electric Imaging Device Co., Ltd.; U.S. Fuji Electric Inc.; Hong Kong Fujidenki Co., Ltd.; Hokuriku Fuji Co., Ltd.; Iiyama Fuji Co., Ltd.; Omachi Fuji Co., Ltd.; Fuji Electric Philippines, Inc.; Fuji Electric (Scotland) Ltd.; Fuji Electric Taiwan Co., Ltd.; Fuji Denki Reiki Co., Ltd.; Fuji Denki Reiki Seizo Co., Ltd.; Fuji Electric V&C Altec Co., Ltd.; Shinshu-Fujidenki Co., Ltd.; Fuji Logistics Co., Ltd.; Fuji Life Corp.; Asahi Keiki Co., Ltd.; Fuji Almacs Co., Ltd.; Fuji ElC Co., Ltd.; Tokai Fuji Electric Co., Ltd.; Kansai Fuji Electric Co., Ltd.; Hoei Denki Co., Ltd.; Chubu Fuji Electric Co., Ltd.; Kyushu Fuji Electric Co., Ltd.; Hokkaido Fuji Electric Co., Ltd.; Tohoku Fuji Electric Co., Ltd.; Chugoku Fuji Electric Co., Ltd.; Shikoku Fuji Electric Co., Ltd.; Fuji Electric GmbH; Fuji Electric (Asia) Co., Ltd.; Fuji Electric Corporation of America; Fuji Electric Singapore Private Ltd.

### *Principal Competitors*

Hitachi Ltd.; Matsushita Electric Industrial Co., Ltd.; Toshiba Corporation.

### *Further Reading*

''Hitachi, Fuji Form High-Volt Venture,'' *Electronic Engineering Times*, September 6, 1999, p. 30.
''Japan's Fuji Electric Reduces Group Net Loss to US$67.95 Mln,'' *AsiaPulse News*, May 12, 2000.
''Japan's Fuji Electric Restructures Production to Cut Costs,'' *AsiaPulse News*, November 9, 2001.
''Japan's FTC Lets Fuji Electric Buy Sanyo Drink Machine Business,'' *AsiaPulse News*, March 25, 2002.
''Three Big Japanese Firms Create Motor Co.,'' *Manufacturing News*, June 13, 2000, p. 4.

—update: Christina M. Stansell

# geobra Brandstätter GmbH & Co. KG

**Brandstätterstrasse 2-10**
**D-90513 Zirndorf**
**Germany**
**Telephone: (49) (911) 9666-0**
**Fax: (49) (911) 9666-120**
**Web site: http://www.playmobil.com**

*Private Company*
*Incorporated:* 1876 as Andreas Brandstätter
*Employees:* 2,226
*Sales:* DM 534.3 million ($255.6 million) (2000)
*NAIC:* 339932 Game, Toy, and Children's Vehicle Manufacturing; 421920 Toy and Hobby Goods and Supplies Wholesalers

Geobra Brandstätter GmbH & Co. KG is Germany's number one toy maker. It's main product, the Playmobil series of plastic toys for children ages three to ten, accounts for almost 90 percent of the company's total sales, about 63 percent of which come from abroad. Besides geobra Brandstätter's production plant in Germany the company has production facilities on the island of Malta and in Spain, and maintains Playmobil sales offices in eight western European countries as well as in the United States and Canada. The geobra Brandstätter group also includes mold making specialist brandform and software company Hob electronic with subsidiaries in the United States, Austria, and Benelux. The company founder's great-grandson Horst Brandstätter controls and owns the company.

## *1876–1939: From Strong Box Locks to Piggy Banks*

In 1876, master locksmith Andreas Brandstätter founded his own workshop in the German town Fürth in Bavaria. Together with his six apprentices he started making metal ornamental fittings and locks for strong boxes. A quarter of a century later, in 1908, his son Georg took over the family business. He renamed the company Metallwarenfabrik Georg Brandstätter, moved the business to a new location in Fürth and started the industrial manufacturing of metal products. In 1921, the company moved to the neighboring town Zirndorf which remained its headquarters for the years to come. Five years later the company was officially registered as an "Offene Handelsgesellschaft," the legal form of a private company that traded goods. Its purpose was registered as "the manufacture of hardware and toys and the trade therewith." In 1927, three new owners entered the family business: Georg Brandstätter's two sons Karl and Richard and his son-in-law Karl Bauer. After Georg Brandstätter's death in 1935 his widow Kunigunde also became a co-owner.

In the 1930s the company started using the name geobra, an acronym derived from the owner's name—Geo-rg Bra-ndstätter. One of the company's product lines was toys made from sheet metal. A catalogue from 1939 offered a variety of miniature scales with tiny weights, cash registers, as well as wrapping paper and pencil holders—all the necessary items for children to play "store." The geobra toy line also included metal piggy banks in the form of cash boxes or cash registers, which automatically calculated money added to the box and was available in different currencies. Another line of toys included a variety of toy telephones and do-it-yourself construction sets for telephones, field telephones and a Morse code device with buzzers and flashing lights. Geobra also sold electrical tool boxes for do-it-yourself hobbyists for electric bell and light installations and additional accessories such as high and low-current electric motors and dynamo machines. The eclectic selection of geobra products also included electric irons, microscopes, globes, and model planes.

## *1940–69: From Hula Hoops to Water Skis*

After World War II, the fourth family generation moved into management positions. Dr. Karl Brandstätter was killed in World War II in 1940, leaving his seven-year old son Horst behind. After Karl Bauer's death his son Hubert became a personally liable co-owner of geobra Brandstätter in 1952. Horst Brandstätter joined the company in the same year at age 19. After his father had died, all that Horst Brandstätter had was a contract that he would become a co-owner of the company at age 21. At that time the company was managed by his uncles Richard Brandstätter and Karl Bauer and his cousin Hubert Bauer who were not interested in sharing the power with Horst. However, within a short time Horst Brandstätter managed to take on more

**Company Perspectives:**

*For all these years, the courage to take new paths has been part of the company's basic philosophy. This courage, together with the willingness to invest, are the keys for guaranteeing the employees' existence, a stable partnership with retailers and consumers as well as the company's general security for the years to come.*

and more responsibilities, simply by offering his help whenever he could. After Richard Brandstätter's death in 1964, his son Michael became a co-owner and managed geobra Brandstätter's fiberline subsidiary which manufactured motor boats and water skis, until he sold his share in 1975. After Hubert Bauer retired from geobra Brandstätter management in 1985, Horst Brandstätter became the company's sole Executive Director.

Horst Brandstätter, who had learned the mold-making craft as an apprentice, focused the company's production on a new material that started replacing metal in several areas—plastic. Beginning in 1958 geobra Brandstätter started working on its first major success when the hula hoop wave swept over to Europe from the United States. Horst Brandstätter, who besides his technical skills also had a healthy sense for business opportunities, worked day and night for two weeks on designing a machine that was able to make hoops out of plastic hoses. For the merely two years that the boom lasted, the company was showered with cash. The broadened capital base was used to expand the company's range of plastic products. Horst Brandstätter further developed the technology he had used to make the plastic hoops, where a plastic hose was heated up inside a machine and molded into a certain shape by using air pressure. Knowing how to make bottles, Brandstätter refined this process to make irregularly shaped things in a single production step. The company also started producing plastic toy racing cars and tractors with pedals on which kids could ride. Another trend of the reconstruction period was piggy banks, which were manufactured around the clock by an automated process. On Monday mornings, 100,000 piggy banks which had been produced solely by machines over the weekend, were ready for sale. Besides items made from plastic, the company also ventured into electronics such as turntables and intercoms. When competitors started copying geobra products and selling them for less, Horst Brandstätter decided to make larger plastic products. A new technology using a blowing agent that worked much like baking soda allowed the production of such products with thick walls, but without cavities. After considerable investments in new machinery geobra Brandstätter started making floor and ceiling tiles, children's desks and scooters, hockey sticks, tennis rackets and water skis as well as larger items such as sports boats and oil tanks—all made from plastic. In 1969, the company set up a state-of-the-art production facility and warehouse at a second location in Dietenhofen in Mittelfranken.

### *1970–76: From geobra to Playmobil*

At the onset of the 1970s, geobra Brandstätter was under attack by competitors in the Far East, Italy, and Yugoslavia, who copied the company's products and sold them at lower prices. In 1971, the company started establishing a new production facility on the Mediterranean island of Malta. According to the country's custom, the government set up a building and rented it to the company at a reasonable price. Wages on Malta were only one third of German wages, but most of all, Malta was just around the corner compared with the Far East. However, in addition to competitive pressure the first ''oil shock'' of the early 1970s pushed up prices for raw plastic significantly. Before the crisis hit the market, the company purchased its major raw material for about DM 0.80 per kilogram which rose to over DM 5 at its peak. Moreover, vendors were not able to deliver the high amounts of raw plastic needed to manufacture geobra products. As a result, the company slipped deeply into the red and was confronted with a situation that threatened its very existence.

However, the innovation that would save geobra Brandstätter was already in the works. In 1971, Horst Brandstätter had asked his master mold-maker and chief developer Hans Beck to create something new: a toy system, perhaps a series of vehicles, perhaps with some simple figurines sitting in them which might later be followed up with a matching garage. Beck, who showed a passion for designing toys early on, when he watched his brothers and sisters playing and started making toys for them, had been hired by Horst Brandstätter in 1958. Brandstätter's requirements for the new product line included the sparing use of plastic material, a small size so it would take up little space in production facilities and warehouses, and a basic idea that was expandable into a whole system in order to extend its life cycle. Beck came up with little plastic figurines, about three inches tall, with movable heads, arms and legs, and an irresistibly sympathetic smile and appeal. When the International Toy Fair approached at the beginning of 1974, Brandstätter asked Beck if he could pull off a model series in time for the upcoming trade show, which he did. However, when the first brightly colored model figurines branded Playmobil—plastic Indians, knights, and construction workers—were displayed at the Toy Fair, nobody seemed to be interested. The idea was too far out from what toy industry representatives had known and seen before.

The only exception was Hermann Simon, a Dutch businessman and the largest toy wholesaler in Europe. He foresaw the huge potential that Playmobil had and—one day before the trade show closed—placed an order worth DM 1 million. Horst Brandstätter used this opportunity to further stir up the demand. At the trade show's closing festivities he approached the director of Vedes Vereinigung der Spielwaren-Fachgeschäfte, Germany's largest wholesale organization for toys, told him about the DM 1 million deal and offered him the exclusive rights to sell Playmobil in Germany. Finally, he wrote letters to big German department stores and told them that Vedes had showed an interest in exclusively selling the newly developed toy system his company had developed. Soon after, orders from department stores that were concerned about missing a new trend started coming in.

The additional orders were a huge challenge since only the first order worth DM 1 million in Playmobil figurines was enough to occupy the company's complete production capacity. When during the year orders mounted up to three times that figure, and machine building companies needed more than a

**Key Dates:**

**1876:** Andreas Brandstätter sets up shop as a lockmaker.
**1908:** The founder's son Georg takes over the business.
**1921:** The company moves from Fürth to Zirndorf.
**1952:** Dr. Karl Brandstätter's son Horst enters the family business.
**1958:** The company has its first major success making hula hoops.
**1971:** A production facility is set up on Malta in the Mediterranean.
**1972:** The company changes its name to geobra Brandstätter GmbH & Co. KG.
**1974:** Playmobil toys are first introduced to the market.
**1980:** The company's first foreign sales office is established in the United Kingdom.
**1985:** Horst Brandstätter becomes the company's sole owner.
**1986:** Playmobil USA Inc. is established.
**1995:** A Playmobil theme park opens in Palm Beach, Florida.
**2000:** Consumers can order Playmobil products over the Internet.

year to deliver the desperately needed plastic molding machines, Horst Brandstätter started shopping around for used ones, picking them up wherever a company was willing to sell. Finally, the company managed to produce 3.5 million Playmobil figures worth about DM 3 million, but orders kept pouring in. In 1976, geobra Brandstätter made another big investment to boost production capacity. As a result, the company's net sales doubled again as they had the year before, from DM 24 million in 1974 to DM 44 million in 1975, reaching over DM 100 million in 1976. Within only a few years, geobra Brandstätter became Germany's largest toy manufacturer.

### *1977–2000: From Mini Skirts to Space Suits*

In the beginning, there were only male Playmobil figures. After two years the first female ones were introduced which—according to the fashion trend of the time—were wearing mini skirts. Unlike most other toys, the main focus of the Playmobil system were not so much things, but rather little plastic people. Their hands were designed so they could grab a tool or sword; their heads and arms could move; they were able to bend down, sit, or stand; and they could be equipped with various accessories such as hats or helmets, vests or coats. In 1981, Playmobil adults were joined by Playmobil kids and babies. Geobra Brandstätter's engineers put a great deal of energy into refining the plastic molding technology used to make the little figures. Pioneering the field, they made it possible to combine four different components of raw material in one production step. As a result, a brown monkey with a movable head, arms and legs and rosy cheeks could be made in a single step—no additional assembly necessary. Refined technologies made it possible to create even more sophisticated characters. In the beginning, the unmistakable Playmobil smile was printed onto the round heads. Later it became possible to mold them directly into the plastic. The first Playmobil figures' arms and hands were molded into one piece. From 1982 on, their tiny hands could be turned. Playmobil men grew bellies and beards; women switched from minis to long skirts and pants.

Around the figures, Playmobil developers and designers created whole worlds for them to dwell and move around in. The pirate ships and knight castles of the early years were soon followed by anything imaginable: medieval towns and fairy tale castles; jungle ruins and treasure caves; modern and farm houses; police station and dentists offices. Other popular themes included foreign countries, the circus, the zoo, railroads, and sports settings. By 1999, the Playmobil product line included figures in about 500 variations and more than 10,000 single parts. To limit the space needed at toy retailers, geobra Brandstätter eliminated as many models each year as were newly introduced. Many of the West German children who grew up with Playmobil later turned into eager collectors or introduced their own kids into the colorful plastic world. Furthermore, the figures with the irresistible smile made their way into doctor's offices, galleries, and museums.

During the 1980s geobra Brandstätter established sales offices abroad to more efficiently market Playmobil outside of Germany. Starting with the first two in the United Kingdom in 1980 and in France in 1981, they were followed by foreign subsidiaries in Benelux, Greece, the United States, and Canada. During the 1990s sales offices were also set up in Italy, Austria, and Switzerland. Although the company was able to grow significantly against the downwards industry trend, foreign sales, which accounted for roughly 60 percent of the total, fluctuated heavily during the 1990s. On the other hand, the refined technologies that made more detailed characters possible pushed production costs up.

The 1990s brought about some changes for geobra Brandstätter. Up until then, Horst Brandstätter did not think much of advertising campaigns, since Playmobil toys seemed to sell all by themselves. During the 1980s, the company had successfully prevented Playmobil from being copied by German competitors. However, with globalization shifting to a higher gear, foreign competitors with enormous advertising budgets were taking over market share. On top of that, when West and East Germany re-united in 1990, East German consumers did not buy as many Playmobil products as geobra Brandstätter expected. In response the company launched a DM 12 million advertising campaign which was expanded in the following years, but never reached the expenditures of other brand name toy manufacturers. When Playmobil started losing ground to computer-based games and licensed articles from Hollywood movies such as *Godzilla* or *Star Wars* and TV series like *The Simpsons*, geobra Brandstätter loosened its rigid product philosophy. Technical effects such as blinking lights, battery-powered functions, and sounds were not taboo anymore and the first Playmobil space station with astronauts was introduced in 1999. To reach its potential customers at the earliest age, the Playmobil line of baby toys for one to three year olds first introduced in 1990 was expanded. Another measure was the introduction of so called ''starter kits,'' figures and sets that were priced very modestly. While the company still refused to jump on every trend—such as the dinosaur wave—and to include any figures or worlds that featured violence, it did open up to interactive CD-ROMs and licensing the Playmobil brand to other manufacturers. To draw further attention to the Playmobil brand geobra Brandstätter opened so-called FunParks during the second half of the 1990s, two of them in Florida, and four in Europe, including Paris, Athens, Malta, and finally one in Zirndorf in 2000. In that year, the company also opened its Playmobil online shop.

For Horst Brandstätter the 1990s were the time to think about and prepare his company for the future. In 1990, he and his employees moved to the new headquarters after the business had outgrown the capacity of the old location. The brand-new futuristic building which also included a health club with two full-time fitness trainers was set up on a hill because the CEO thought it would boost his workforce's productivity if they were able to see the horizon. Brandstätter's main challenge was to strengthen the Playmobil brand in an increasingly difficult market: the number of potential customers was declining due to decreasing birth rates; the market for traditional toys was shrinking worldwide and becoming more dependent on short-term trends; the company's main customer group—boys up to age ten—were increasingly switching to electronic toys and computer-based games; and the mid-sized company was competing against a number of—mainly American and Japanese—global players. Horst Brandstätter's main hope was the American market—the biggest toy market in the world. A major breakthrough occurred when Playmobil was listed by American retail chain Target. Since the early 1990s, Horst Brandstätter tried to gradually withdraw from his job, spending half of each year in Florida while exchanging faxes daily with his German office. During his absence, the company was managed by two executives. After his disappointing experience implanting managers from outside the company, he appointed 42-year old Andrea Schauer one of the two executive directors. Schauer had joined the Playmobil marketing team in the early 1990s. Brandstätter's two sons had other plans. Klaus Brandstätter was managing his own company HOB Electronic which transitioned from manufacturing peripheral equipment for IBM computers to developing software for computer networks. Conny Brandstätter was working on an innovative product line of self-watering plastic planter pots in a separate geobra division. In 1996, Brandstätter established Stiftung Kinderförderung von Playmobil, a non-profit foundation with the goal to promote a violence-free childhood. The foundation had been named to inherit a major portion of the geobra Brandstätter shares.

### *Principal Subsidiaries*

PLAYMOBIL Malta Ltd.; PLAYMOBIL S.A. (Spain); PLAYMOBIL France S.A.R.L.; PLAYMOBIL Austria GmbH; PLAYMOBIL Swiss GmbH; PLAYMOBIL Benelux B.V. (99%); PLAYMOBIL U.K. Ltd.; PLAYMOBIL Italia S.R.L. (95%); PLAYMOBIL Hellas S.A. (Greece); PLAYMOBIL USA Inc.; PLAYMOBIL Canada Inc. (65%).

### *Principal Competitors*

Hasbro, Inc.; LEGO Company; Mattel, Inc.

### *Further Reading*

"25 Jahre Playmobil - Das bekannteste Lächeln seit Mona Lisa," *Spielzeugmarkt,* No. 2/99.

"Der Computer hat die Erfolgsserie von Playmobil unterbrochen," *Frankfurter Allgemeine Zeitung*, March 15, 2000, p. W1.

"Die bunte Spielfigur als Kunstwerk der Spritztechnik," *Frankfurter Allgemeine Zeitung*, December 23, 1997, Technik und Motor, p. 1.

Haacke, Brigitte V., "Kugelrunder Kopf," *Wirtschaftswoche,* June 21, 2001, p. 92.

"Horst Brandstätter: 'Wir bleiben unserer Linie treu,' " *Spielzeugmarkt,* No. 2/99.

"Playmobil fehlt ein zugkräftiges Babyprogramm," *Frankfurter Allgemeine Zeitung*, February 6, 1993, p. 15.

"Playmobil für die gewaltfreien Kinder der Welt," *Süddeutsche Zeitung*, November 17, 1998.

Zumbusch, Johannes, "Porträt: Playmobilhersteller Horst Brandstätter—Ein bisschen verspielt," *Wirtschaftswoche,* November 2, 1990, p. 106.

—Evelyn Hauser

GLOBALSANTAFE

# GlobalSantaFe Corporation

**777 North Eldridge Parkway Suite 1100**
**Houston, Texas 77079-4493**
**P.O. Box 4577**
**Houston, Texas 77210-4577**
**U.S.A.**
**Telephone: (281) 596-5100**
**Fax: (218) 531-1260**
**Web site: http://www.gsfdrill.com**

*Public Company*
*Incorporated:* 1946 as Santa Fe Drilling Company
*Employees:* 8,700
*Sales:* $1.35 billion (2001)
*Stock Exchanges:* New York
*Ticker Symbol:* GSF
*NAIC:* 213111 Drilling Oil and Gas Wells

GlobalSantaFe Corporation (GSF) is the world's second largest offshore drilling contractor. It was created by the 2001 merger of Global Marine and Santa Fe International, both companies that trace their earliest roots to the Union Oil Company. Kuwait Petroleum Corp. owns 18 percent of GlobalSantaFe. GSF is the world's second largest offshore driller after Transocean Inc. GSF operated 58 mobile offshore rigs and 31 land rigs after its formation. The company offers use of its rigs on a turnkey and dayrate basis. The latter provided a rig and crew priced at a daily rate, and accounted for more than 80 percent of GSF's operating cash flow. GSF also offers drilling management services.

### *Santa Fe International Formed 1946*

Crude oil production was at an all-time high during World War II when oil was needed to fuel the war. To meet the high demand for oil, most oil companies maintained their own drilling departments. However, when the war ended in 1945, the world had more oil than it needed. Many oil companies closed their drilling departments, which were extremely costly to maintain. They decided instead to outsource their drilling to independent contractors, drillers with equipment who could be paid on a per-day basis.

J.D. ''Joe'' Robinson, a drilling superintendent at Union Oil Company in Santa Fe, California, anticipated the company he worked for would follow suit and shut down its drilling department and outsource their drilling. Robinson planned to start his own drilling company and make an offer to purchase Union's rigs. He would then bid on Union's drilling. Robinson's plan succeeded.

On December 19, 1946, Santa Fe Drilling Company was incorporated. Robinson and 61 drillers he had worked with put up $250,000 of their own money and secured loans for another $600,000. They paid Union $753,000 for their eight rigs. Santa Fe had about $100,000 left over for operating expenses.

Santa Fe set up shop in Union's former drilling headquarters in Santa Fe, California, but later relocated to Dallas, Texas. During its first years in business, the company kept careful watch over its expenses. Included in the purchase of Union's equipment and office space was a warehouse that contained several gallons of orange paint. ''Not wanting to waste anything, the paint went on rigs, office windows, frames, awnings, signs, and anything else in need of paint.'' Santa Fe became known for its orange equipment.

In 1947 the company began drilling wells in California. The following year Santa Fe landed its first international job—drilling a well in Venezuela. A few years later, Santa Fe embarked on its first desert job in the neutral zone between Kuwait and Saudi Arabia. Teams of drillers were hired to work in Tunisia, Iran, and Kuwait. The company was in full swing.

### *Global Marine Founded 1953*

Global Marine was also related to the Union Oil Co. It grew out of the CUSS Group formed in 1946 by the Continental, Union, Shell and Superior oil companies to study the feasibility of drilling off the coast of California. This evolved into the Global Marine Drilling Co. within several years.

### Company Perspectives:

*CULTURE OF COMMITMENT. Our strength comes not only from our equipment but also from our culture. Our commitment to safety, operational excellence, innovation, and ethical business conduct will guide our effort to heighten GlobalSantaFe's leadership position in the industry. SAFETY in all operations is, and must always be, our top priority. It is a core value that is shared throughout the Company. Our total commitment to an injury-free workplace drives decisions at every level of the Company. Drilling rigs are environments where complacency and negligence cannot be tolerated. Safety requires the vigilance and participation of every member of the GlobalSantaFe family. Protection of human life and our environment is the primary responsibility of every individual throughout our company—on or off the job.*

The future of offshore drilling looked bright throughout the 1950s. War in the Middle East and new U.S. government import restrictions led to great need for domestic oil production, and petroleum firms were scouring the Gulf of Mexico. The situation changed dramatically in 1958 when the state of Louisiana and the federal government became embroiled in a dispute over the ownership of the tidelands where oil companies were drilling. During the fight lease sales dried up, and the number of drilling rigs in U.S. coastal waters fell from 120 to 40. By this time, Global's major shareholders were Aerojet-General Corp. and Union Oil Co. of California. With the offshore-drilling market tumbling, a group of employees led by engineers Robert F. Bauer and Almeron Field bought Union's share of the company.

Within a few years the tidelands dispute was settled, and market conditions changed for the better. Global grew rapidly, going public in 1962. By the mid-1960s it was one of the world's biggest offshore drilling firms, with rigs off the coasts of Alaska, Nigeria, Australia, Libya, California, and Louisiana and in the Persian Gulf and the North Sea. The firm was not an oil company and did not sell oil. Global rented its rigs and crews to oil companies for offshore drilling. By 1965 the firm's revenues reached $21.5 million, and all of its rigs were rented for two or more years in advance.

Offshore drilling had not existed until the late 1940s, and rig designs were rapidly becoming more sophisticated, able to work in deeper waters for longer periods, with greater comfort for the crew. While other firms worked on shallow-water platforms using a ''jack-up'' design, Global put its resources into building a fleet of self-propelled vessels that drilled though wells in their center. The firm believed these vessels had greater speed and flexibility.

### *Santa Fe Expands: 1950–81*

Throughout the next couple of decades, Santa Fe expanded its fleet and territory as quickly as possible, while striving to maintain a high safety record and offer its customers high-quality service. By 1954, Santa Fe had 21 land rigs operating in the United States, Europe, North Africa, South America, and the Middle East. Around the same time, the company began drilling offshore. Santa Fe won a contract in Trinidad to use a land rig hooked up to a jackup barge that would enable it to drill oil offshore.

Santa Fe realized that if it wanted to capitalize on offshore drilling, it needed to design rigs suited for this purpose. In 1957 the company unveiled Blue Water No. 1, its first semi-submersible rig. Blue Water No. 1 enabled the company to drill the first well ever drilled by a semi-submersible rig in the Gulf of Mexico. Two years later, Santa Fe landed a contract for Blue Water No. 2, an enhanced version of Blue Water No. 1. To increase its cash flow, in 1963 Santa Fe entered into a joint venture with the Kuwait Drilling Company.

Despite its ambitious expansion in the preceding decades, Santa Fe knew that the drilling business was precarious at best. The drilling industry was highly competitive and vulnerable to fluctuations in oil and natural gas prices, political turmoil and war in international countries, unfavorable weather conditions, and the extraordinarily high cost of repairing and replacing rigs. The company knew that consolidation was the key to its future success.

In 1981, Santa Fe was acquired by the Kuwait Petroleum Corporation (KPC). KPC was founded in 1980 to help manage Kuwait's growing oil endeavors and had quickly become a world leader in the oil industry. Its aim was to protect Kuwait's oil reserves and maximize its revenue.

### *Global Marine Branches Out in the 1970s*

With its core business also doing well, Global branched into related fields. Through its subsidiary Global Engineering Company it began training crews and inspecting ships for the U.S. Navy. It also installed a secret underwater testing site for the Navy's Polaris missiles. Through another subsidiary it engaged in long-range weather forecasting, usually for other companies involved in ocean exploration. It took core samples of the ocean floor for the National Science Foundation, raised shrimp in Hawaii, and mined for gold off Alaska. Along with other offshore oil companies, Global began to engage in its own oil exploration. It bought interests in the Canadian Arctic and North Sea, where some petroleum companies had found oil. It continued to build drilling vessels, owning 12 by the middle of the 1970s. Sales grew as its fleet expanded, reaching $89 million by 1974.

At about this time, worldwide publicity was briefly turned on Global Marine when it reportedly participated in a covert and controversial attempt to raise a Soviet submarine off the floor of the Pacific Ocean, along with the Central Intelligence Agency and Howard Hughes's Summa Corporation. The submarine broke in half as it was raised, reportedly spilling nuclear missiles onto the ocean floor.

### *To the Brink and Back: Global Marine in the 1980s*

Despite its growing sales and fleet, Global faced trouble because of its heavy reliance on self-propelled vessels, the wisdom of which some industry analysts questioned. The vessels were less stable than other types of rigs in rough seas, and

**Key Dates:**

**1946:** J.D. "Joe" Robinson founds Santa Fe Drilling Company to operate former Union Oil drilling operations.
**1953:** Global Marine founded by Aerojet-General Corp., Union Oil Co., et al.
**1957:** Santa Fe unveils Blue Water No. 1, its first semi-submersible rig.
**1962:** Global Marine goes public.
**1968:** Santa Fe is renamed Santa Fe International Corporation.
**1974:** Global Marine reportedly helps in failed attempt to recover crashed Soviet sub.
**1981:** Kuwait Petroleum Corporation (KPC) acquires Santa Fe.
**1986:** Global Marine files Chapter 11.
**1991:** Santa Fe receives Galaxy I, a large, harsh-environment jackup rig.
**1997:** Santa Fe launches IPO; Global Marine revenues are $1 billion.
**1998:** Glomar Explorer sets world drilling depth record of 7,718 feet.
**2001:** Global Marine merges with Santa Fe to form GlobalSantaFe.

since they cost more to build, they cost more to rent. Because other types of rigs were judged better suited to the North Sea and Gulf of Mexico, Global missed many of the jobs it might have won. As a result, it lost money in 1976 and 1977. Further, it owned one of the oldest fleets in its industry. Finally in 1979, with oil prices rising, Global ordered 17 jack-up rigs for $400 million, to better compete for jobs in shallow waters. To finance its expansion, Global borrowed heavily, leaving it with a 4-to-1 debt-to-equity ratio.

At first this seemed a wise plan. Global's revenues grew from $91 million in 1976 to $456 million in 1982. It paid off substantial amounts of its debt and ordered eight more rigs, to further modernize its fleet. However, oil prices collapsed in the following years, and with an oversupply of natural gas as well, rig rates plummeted by more than 50 percent between 1981 and 1983. In 1983 one of the firm's drillships, the *Glomar China Sea,* sank in a typhoon off the coast of China, killing its entire crew of 84. In 1984 Global had to make a $120 million interest payment on its new rigs, at a time when half of its rigs were leased under break-even contracts. President C. Russell Luigs slashed spending and cut exploratory drilling. The firm made stock and bond offerings to raise cash. Its debt-to-equity ratio nevertheless remained at two-to-one.

The market remained soft and Global lost $560 million between 1984 and 1986, forcing it to file for bankruptcy protection in 1986. Daily rates on its rigs had fallen from a peak of $50,000 during the early 1980s to $12,000 by 1986, while 75 percent of its drilling fleet stood idle. Sales dropped from $454 million in 1982 to $225 in 1986. Global's suspension of $20 million a month in interest payments prior to its bankruptcy essentially saved the company. Luigs gambled that Global's creditors would not foreclose. Global owed about $1.1 billion to a consortium of eight creditors, and many felt they would be more severely hurt by selling the firm's assets than by giving it a chance to recover.

Global's financial situation was extremely complicated because it had borrowed using specific company assets, usually drilling rigs, as collateral for specific loans. However, each rig was financed at different times by different creditors for different interest rates, and this lead to difficulty in coming up with a reorganization plan acceptable to enough of its creditors. The largest creditor was the U.S. Maritime Administration, which had guaranteed $200 million of Global's debt through federal programs geared toward reducing U.S. dependence on foreign oil.

Drilling picked up somewhat in 1987, but Global still had only about half of its rigs active, mostly in the Gulf of Mexico, while a worldwide oversupply of drilling rigs kept prices low. The firm continued to lose money ($155.6 million in 1988 alone) as it struggled to reorganize.

Global emerged from bankruptcy in early 1989. Ironically, it was again one of the strongest offshore drilling firms. Many of its competitors had also gone bankrupt and had not yet reorganized. Global had dealt with its financial problems, at least temporarily, and it now had one of the largest, most modern, and efficient fleets in the industry. It also had reduced its costs, cutting its workforce to 1,500 from over 3,000 in 1985, and hiring more lower-paid foreign workers. Its creditors traded two-thirds of the firm's debt for ownership of over 90 percent of the company. Over the next three years, Global only had to pay one year's interest on its remaining $446 million in debt. Meanwhile, the market had picked up somewhat. Nearly all of Global's rigs were at work, and the day rate had risen to about $26,000. Yet overall it remained a difficult time, alleviated only briefly in 1990 when oil prices rose in response to Iraq's invasion of Kuwait.

### *Global Marine: Setting Records in the 1990s*

Under these conditions, Global was able to cut its debt by another $60 million by the end of 1991, aided by the terms of its new debt service agreement. However, company officials felt that this would not be enough to avoid a fiscal crisis by 1995. They resolved to recapitalize Global and cut its debt further. The firm sold one of its smaller jackup rigs for $18 million, and used the money to lessen its debt. The firm's policy was to retire rigs that were becoming obsolete. It therefore retired the Glomar Biscay semi-submersible rig and the Glomar Atlantic drillship, reducing the average age of its fleet to about ten years. The Biscay was sold for scrap, while the Atlantic was purchased for use outside the drilling industry. Global sold 26 million shares of common stock and $225 million of senior secured notes. These moves decreased Global's total debt by $142 million.

These financial successes not withstanding, 1992 was another difficult year for Global Marine. The average utilization rate for its rigs declined from 86 percent in 1991 to 78 percent in 1992, while the average day rate fell to $27,600 from $29,300. The North Sea market became particularly weak. The natural gas market also softened, and sales at Challenger Minerals Inc., the firm's oil and gas subsidiary, fell to $19 million, down from $28 million in 1991. The firm sold an additional 3.9 million shares of stock in January 1993, raising another $7.8 million.

Global Marine trimmed its British North Sea workforce in the early 1990s, but by 1995 conditions there had improved and the company was refurbishing three new acquired jack-up rigs. After losing $27 million in 1993, Global Marine posted profits of $5 million in 1994 and $52 million in 1995.

Tales of Global Marine's spy sub adventures resurfaced in the 1990s. In 1993, Russia reported that the US sub, dubbed the *Glomar Explorer,* had in fact recovered two of its nuclear warheads. In 1996, Global Marine signed a 30-year lease with the US Navy and pulled the vessel from its 16-year retirement and converted it to a drilling rig to test prospective drill sites. In November 1998, the *Glomar Explorer* set a world depth record by drilling in 7,718 feet of water in the Gulf of Mexico.

World demand for oil was 71.6 million barrels per day in 1996, up 25 percent in ten years. Oil rigs capable of drilling in ultra-deep water were most in demand. With record day rates for its rigs and record utilization of them, the year 1996, with revenues of $681 million, was a record one for Global Marine—1997 was even better. Global's net earnings before special items were $270 million, on revenues were $1.07 billion in 1997. The company claimed it was the first offshore driller to post more than $1 billion in revenues in a year. About 40 percent of revenues came from deepwater drilling; the company was preparing to set up a rig at the deepest point ever in the Gulf of Mexico.

### *New Rigs and an IPO: Santa Fe 1991–2001*

Santa Fe believed it could find a niche in the drilling industry in which it would offer services in areas with extremely harsh weather conditions such as winds of up to 100 mph and waves as high as 38 feet. Meeting this demand, however, required the construction of rigs that could stand up to such fierce weather conditions and drill effectively in spite of them.

In 1991 Galaxy I, one of the largest harsh-environment jackup rigs in the world, was built for Santa Fe by Keppel Fels of Singapore. Galaxy II, a $150 million, enhanced version of Galaxy I, was delivered to Santa Fe in 1998 under a five-year contract. The heavy-duty rig earned Santa Fe approximately $130,000 a day.

Santa Fe went public in 1997, selling 35 million shares of common stock. The proceeds from the initial public offering went to KPC (which now held 69 percent of Santa Fe) to help finance its exploration and production in Kuwait. During the same year, Santa Fe announced an agreement with U.K.-based Amoco Exploration Company to provide a new heavy-duty, harsh-weather rig—Galaxy III—for drilling operations in the U.K. sector of the North Sea. Keppel Fels, the company that constructed Galaxy I and II, also constructed Galaxy III. "This is a momentous occasion for Santa Fe," said Steve Garber, Santa Fe's president and chief executive officer. "Building a new rig of this caliber is a powerful signal not only of our position in the marketplace, but of the strength of the demand in our industry. We are extremely pleased to expand our long-standing relationship with Amoco through this new addition to our rig fleet."

Galaxy III reached its destination in the North Sea on December 5, 1999. The new rig was transported from Keppel Fels in Singapore aboard the Transshelf, a heavy-lift ship. Moving such a large rig was not easy, and the journey took 61 days. With the addition of Galaxy III, Santa Fe operated six of the industry's 17 heavy-duty, harsh equipment jackup rigs.

Around the same time, Santa Fe also landed a three-year contract for a 3,000 horsepower land rig in Kuwait. The $19.5 million rig was larger than any other land rig operating in the Middle East. The rig was named Santa Fe Rig 180 and was equipped with three mud pumps and five diesel engines. Garber commented on the Rig 180 in a company press release: "The addition of Rig 180 to our fleet, coupled with the recent completion of four new land rigs in Venezuela, each with a term contract, reinforces Santa Fe's confidence in land drilling activities in the major international oil provinces. We have been engaged in land rig operations in the Middle East for forty-seven years and are one of the largest drillers in the area."

In mid-2000 Santa Fe completed its second public offering of 30 million shares via its immediate parent SFIC Holdings (Cayman) Inc, a wholly owned subsidiary of KPC. As with the first public offering, Santa Fe did not receive the proceeds from the offering; instead, KPC used the proceeds to fund other ventures. After the second public offering, SFIC owned about 44.5 million shares or 39 percent of Santa Fe's stock.

In 1999 the drilling industry—vulnerable to many uncontrollable factors, including the demand for oil and fluctuations in oil prices—suffered a downturn that affected Santa Fe. That year the company posted a net income of $149.8 million on revenues of $614.2 million, down from its 1998 net income of $287.1 million, posted on revenues of $811.3 million. The company attributed the slip in sales to a sluggish year for the drilling industry as a whole and the cost of new equipment.

In 2000, the company believed that if oil and gas prices remained at or around current levels, the offshore drilling market would improve somewhat in the near future. Santa Fe President and CEO Steve Garber indicated that in the future the company planned to solidify its niche as a harsh-weather driller and would focus on drilling in "deep, difficult, and remote" places. To reach this goal the company was designing a new, high-tech semisubmersible rig. "We are convinced that in the long-term demand for high quality rigs aimed at the deep water field development market will be strong and we intend to be in a good position to take advantage of that demand," said Garber. Also in 2000, Santa Fe had bid to construct and operate a new winterized rig on a man-made island in the northern Caspian region of Kazakhstan. In 2001, Santa Fe ordered two high-performance jackup rigs and two ultra-deepwater semi-submersible rigs from PPL Shipyard PTE, Ltd. of Singapore.

### *Global Marine in the Late 1990s*

Robert Rose, former CEO of rival Diamond Offshore Drilling, was named to head Global Marine in May 1998 after president and COO John Ryan retired. At the same time, chairman C. Russell Luigs relinquished the title of CEO to Rose, who had started his career at Global Marine in the 1960s.

The company was already being rumored as a takeover target by Santa Fe International. A 1998 downturn in oil prices helped make the company a ''sitting duck,'' according to *Business Week.* The two company's operations seemed to dovetail nicely. Santa Fe was active mostly outside the US, while Global Marine focused on the Gulf of Mexico. In December, Global Marine announced it was seeking merger partners. Consolidation in the energy industry had reduced the company's number of clients, who were pressuring the company to reduce rates in light of lower prices. In fact, Global Marine had ''stacked,'' or idled, a handful of its jack-up rigs by the end of the year.

A new drillship, the *Glomar Jack Ryan,* was rolled out by Global Marine in October 2000. Built over three years at the Harland & Wolff Shipyard in Northern Ireland, this $368 million ''elephant hunter'' and its predecessor, the *Glomar C.R. Luigs,* were designed to drill in water up to 12,000 feet. Global Marine was receiving a dayrate of $195,000 for the *Jack Ryan* under a three-year contract with ExxonMobil Inc.; it began drilling in Trinidad in December 2000. The *Glomar C.R. Luigs* had begun drilling in the Gulf of Mexico in April 2000 under contract from BHP Petroleum.

Although oil prices had risen again, Global Marine took several cost-cutting measures in 2000 when expected increases in exploration funds were not immediately forthcoming from the major oil companies. (Their exploration and production spending increased from $36 billion to $43 billion in 2001, however.) The company trimmed its IT (information technology) staff 30 percent, shut an operations office in the Netherlands, and cut some administrative positions.

## *A ''Merger of Equals'' in 2001*

Mirroring the consolidation among large energy firms, the oil field service business itself also underwent a wave of mergers, as firms combined to bolster their bargaining power. Transocean Sedco Forex agreed to buy R&B Falcon in August 2000 in a deal worth $8 billion. In May 2001, Pride International announced the $2 billion acquisition of Marine Drilling.

In September 2001, Global Marine and Santa Fe International agreed to merge in a $3 billion stock swap. Santa Fe, the nominal buyer in this merger of equals, also assumed $900 million in debt in the deal. On December 19, 2001, Global Marine became a subsidiary of Santa Fe International, which changed its name to GlobalSantaFe Corporation.

The union created the world's second largest offshore drilling contractor. The combined company had more than 100 rigs around the world, including 59 offshore rigs of all classes and 31 land-drilling rigs. It also performed drilling management services in the Gulf of Mexico and the North Sea.

The merger was expected to generate few savings in terms of merging redundant functions, and employment was actually expected to go up as GSF hired more employees to bolster its over tasked engineering departments. The merger did make the combined company more valuable to clients, in that it was able to offer them any type of rig anywhere in the world.

Stedman Garber, Jr., CEO at Santa Fe International, became president and CEO of the new company, while Global Marine's Robert Rose became chairman.

Headquartered, like Global Marine, in Houston, the new company was incorporated in the tax-friendly Cayman Islands. Santa Fe International had incorporated there in 1990.

GSF had to evacuate 84 crewmembers from one of its offshore drilling rigs in December 2001. The *Key Singapore* broke free from tugboats ferrying it to Egypt when it encountered a severe storm off the coast of Israel.

GlobalSantaFe reported revenues of $1.35 billion in 2001, including Santa Fe International's results only for the 42 days from the merger date. Net income was $198.8 million, up from $113.9 million the year before. GlobalSantaFe had 89 active rigs at the end of the year, compared to 33 at the end of 2000. The number of turnkey wells it drilled was down, from 122 to 97. Dayrate contract drilling services accounted for more than 80 percent of GSF's operating cash flow.

## *Principal Subsidiaries*

Applied Drilling Technology Inc.; Challenger Minerals Inc.; Entities Holdings, Inc.; Geothermal Royalty Holdings, Inc.; GlobalSantaFe Drilling (N.A.) N.V. (Netherlands Antilles); GlobalSantaFe Holding Company (North Sea) Ltd. (U.K.); GlobalSantaFe Operations (Barbados) Inc. (Cayman Islands); Platform Capital N.V. (Netherlands Antilles); Santa Fe Drilling (Nigeria) Limited (60%); Santa Fe Operations (Nigeria) Limited (60%); Santa Fe Drilling Operations, Inc. (Cayman Islands); Santa Fe International Services, Inc. (Panama); Sphere Supply, Inc.

## *Principal Divisions*

Contract Drilling; Engineering Services & Project Management; Turnkey Services; Geoscience Services.

## *Principal Competitors*

Diamond Offshore Drilling, Inc.; Nabors Industries, Inc.; Noble Corporation; Pride International, Inc.; Transocean Inc.

## *Further Reading*


Antosh, Nelson, ''5 Firms Answer Call of Islands; Houston Companies See Offshore Reincorporation as Way to Boost Profits, Despite Potential Backlash,'' *Houston Chronicle,* April 20, 2002, p. A1.

——, '' 'Elephant Hunter' Ready for Deep Water,'' *Houston Chronicle,* October 7, 2000, Bus. Sec., p. 2.

——, ''Gulf Provides Wave of Hope to Drillers; GlobalSantaFe Hopes Offshore Climate Will Equalize with Economy,'' *Houston Chronicle,* January 22, 2002, p. B2.

Banerjee, Neela, and Andrew Ross Sorkin, ''2 Big Mergers Are Reached as Oil Industry Consolidates,'' *New York Times,* September 4, 2001, p. C1.

Bray, Julian, ''Global to Cash In on Upswing,'' *Lloyd's List,* April 21, 1995, p. 2.

Chubb, Courtney, ''Santa Fe's Triumphant New York Offering Unlikely to Herald Wave of Similar Deals,'' *Oil Daily,* June 12, 1997.

''Contract Drillers Tap a Money Field,'' *Business Week,* March 13, 1965.

Davis, Michael, "Global Marine in the Market for Drilling Company," *Houston Chronicle,* January 19, 1999, p. 1.
——, "Global Marine's Year a Record-Setter," *Houston Chronicle,* January 16, 1998, p. 2.
"Fels Ships Oil Rig to the U.S.," *Straits Times,* August 27, 1998.
Field, Alan M., "Staying Afloat," *Forbes,* October 6, 1986.
Fowler, Tom, "Two Texas Drillers to Join Forces," *Houston Chronicle,* September 4, 2001, Bus. Sec., p. 1.
Gaddy, Dean E., and Jeannie Stell, "Jack Ryan Drillship to Use Retractable Thrusters, MUX Control Systems," *Oil & Gas Journal,* November 27, 2000, pp. 38–42.
"Global Marine Borrows, Slashes Rates—and Sticks Its Neck Out Further," *Business Week,* December 19, 1983.
"Global Marine Predicts Boom," *Lloyd's List,* June 30, 1995, p. 2.
"Global Splash," *Barron's,* April 25, 1966.
Ivanovich, David, "Offshore Rigs Finding Work; Global Marine Chief Cites Rising Energy Needs," *Houston Chronicle,* January 21, 1997, Bus. Sec., p. 3.
Ivey, Mark, "Global Marine: Pumped Up by Kuwait," *Business Week,* October 29, 1990.
Johnson, Maryfran, "On-Site at Global Marine: 'Everything Perfect'," *Computerworld,* January 10, 2000, p. 18.
King, Julia, "Global Marine Gives CIO a Shove," *Computerworld,* July 24, 2000, pp. 1, 16.
"Largest Oil Driller Seeking Merger; Firms Combine to Stay Profitable," *Times-Picayune,* December 5, 1998, p. C2.
Marcial, Gene G., "Drilling Hard at GlobalSantaFe," *Business Week,* December 17, 2001, p. 149.
——, "These Oil Rigs Are Sitting Ducks," *Business Week,* May 11, 1998, p. 85.
Moreno, Jenalia, "Global Marine Appoints New Chief Executive," *Houston Chronicle,* May 6, 1998, Bus. Sec., p. 1.
"Now All Global Marine Needs Is a Market," *Business Week,* March 13, 1989.
"Santa Fe International Corp. SDC," *Energy Alert,* August 1998.
"Santa Fe, Snyder Announce Merger," *Energy Daily,* January 15, 1999.
Stuart, Reginald, "Global Marine Searches World for Undersea Riches," *New York Times,* March 20, 1975.
Tirschwell, Peter, "Global Marine to Reactivate Ship Believed Built to Raise Soviet Sub," *Journal of Commerce,* August 19, 1996, p. 1B.
Toal, Brian A., "A Reunion of Global and Santa Fe," *Oil & Gas Investor,* March 2002, pp. 47+.
——, "A Tale of Two Turnarounds," *Oil & Gas Investor,* May 1993, p. 47.
Vogel, Todd, "Missing the Boat for the Ship," *Forbes,* November 15, 1975.
"A Wet 'N Wild Ride for Global Marine," *Kiplinger's Personal Finance Magazine,* October 1996, p. 28.
Wetuski, Jodi, "Global Marine: Offshore Driller Mergers Needed to Serve Monster Oil Firms," *Oil & Gas Investor,* March 1999, pp. 11–12.

—Scott M. Lewis
—updates: Tracey Vasil Biscontini and Frederick C. Ingram

# GoodTimes Entertainment Ltd.

**16 East 40th Street**
**New York, New York 10016**
**U.S.A.**
**Telephone: (212) 951-3000**
**Fax: (212) 213-9319**
**Web site: http://www.goodtimes.com**

*Private Company*
*Employees:* 500
*Sales:* $475 million (2000 est.)
*NAIC:* 512120 Motion Picture and Video Distribution

Operating out of New York, GoodTimes Entertainment Ltd. is primarily a video distributor, producing many of its own titles while also acquiring programming from third parties. Since its foundation in 1984, the company has constantly adapted to changing conditions: reliance on inexpensive public domain movies gave way to the development of fitness videos, then original animation and live action features, a foray into book publishing, and eventually a video game software distribution operation that resulted in the spin-off of GoodTimes Interactive. The company has also sought to branch out into a wide range of tie-in products connected to celebrities such as Richard Simmons and Naomi Judd. In recent years, GoodTimes has sought to find niche video markets, becoming heavily involved in Christian product as well as Broadway shows.

### *The Cayre Brothers in 1969*

The founders of GoodTimes are brothers Kenneth Cayre, Joseph Cayre, and Stanley Cayre, the offspring of Syrian immigrants. Their father was a small-time businessman, who during the 1940s sold whiskey and cigarettes on a Caribbean pleasure boat, then later owned a souvenir shop in Miami Beach. Rather than attend college, the Cayre brothers went into business together and moved to New York, where in 1969 they started a record label, SalSoul Records, which licensed and distributed Latin music. Because of their Miami background, the brothers had a better sense of the popularity of Latin music than the major record labels. Over the next several years, helped in large part by staging concerts of imported Latin stars, SalSoul gained a 70 percent share of the Latin record business, issuing eight to ten records each month and generating nearly $50 million in annual revenues. The majors eventually took notice and entered the market. That development, along with a general malaise in the record industry, led the Cayre brothers in 1979 to sell most of their catalog to their distributor, RCA, for $100 million.

Joe Cayre then began searching for a new business for the family, narrowing down the possibilities to cell phones and videos. The brothers chose the latter, since the video business was more in keeping with their experience in records. In the early 1980s, VCRs were just beginning to make serious inroads with consumers, and movies available for sale on video were priced extremely high, from $40 to $90. Visits to video stores revealed to the Cayres that customers would be attracted to a price point in the $10 range. The only way to satisfy that market was to turn to public domain titles, movies on which the copyright had lapsed and no royalties were due. In 1984, the Cayre brothers created GoodTimes Home Video with a list of 25 public domain movies to which they purchased the masters, then made copies. The company unveiled its titles at the Consumer Electronics Show in a prepack with each tape priced for consumers at $14.95. Retailers were so impressed that GoodTimes sold 5,000 prepacks. As important as this initial sale was, it would pale in comparison to a relationship GoodTimes forged with retail giant Wal-Mart when Joe Cayre visited its Arkansas headquarters in 1984. Wal-Mart buyers were impressed by the low-priced videos but skeptical about Caryre's claim that Wal-Mart would be able to sell $10 million of the product in the first year. To back up his claim, he offered to pay for shipping, including return freight on unsold product, as well as purchasing choice shelf space at the front of the store. Moreover, a wholesale price of $7 per tape meant that Wal-Mart stood to realize a healthy profit. In the end, Cayre left town with a $1 million order from Wal-Mart. With a steady customer in hand, GoodTimes then invested $18 million to create a tape duplicating plant in New Jersey, which would ultimately grow into an operation capable of producing 150,000 tapes a day, and double that amount if necessary. From the beginning, GoodTimes opted to control its tape duplication, rather than rely on third parties and take a chance of missing deadlines or providing

**Key Dates:**

**1984:** GoodTimes Home Video is formed.
**1986:** The company enters into a licensing deal with Hearst Corporation.
**1992:** The company begins production of original animation titles.
**1993:** The holding company GoodTimes Entertainment is created.
**1995:** GoodTimes Interactive is spun-off as a public company.
**2001:** Bethlehem label is created for Christian-oriented videos.

poor quality products to its customers. In addition, GoodTimes rejected poorer quality SLP, 6-hour mode taping, in favor of LP, 4-hour mode, and it even dubbed at SP, 2-hour mode, if customers requested it.

Wal-Mart sold $3 million worth of GoodTimes videos in its first year, far less than the $10 million Joseph Cayre projected, but still a healthy business. Revenues then soared in the second year of the relationship after a chance meeting between Cayre and Wal-Mart's Sam Walton. According to *Forbes,* Cayre was sitting in the waiting room when Walton entered and struck up a conversation. Learning that Cayre sold videos, Walton took the vendor on a tour of one of his stores in order to learn more about the video business. Cayre was then able to pitch a new video rack, one that would offer enough space to feature the face of the box rather than just the spine. Walton agreed to the idea, resulting in a second year jump to $30 million in sales.

With a steady income from Wal-Mart, GoodTimes was able to expand beyond public domain movies, acquiring the licenses to more recent titles, such as *Close Encounters of the Third Kind.* In addition, the company ventured into the creation of original material, investing $25,000 to produce the ''29 Minute Workout,'' starring Miss Connecticut of 1985, a tape that would go on to sell 1 million units. In 1986, GoodTimes established a licensing deal with the Hearst Corporation to produce exercise and diet titles with the Cosmopolitan label. The company also produced children's titles under the Good Housekeeping label. In 1989, GoodTimes tested the video magazine market with the production of two music-based products, one aimed at the audience for heavy metal and the other at consumers of rap music.

### *Great American Entertainment Established in 1990*

GoodTimes not only supplied video products to record stores and major retailers like Wal-Mart, it also made inroads in placing its products in book stores, toy stores, drug stores, and even clothing stores. Out of these efforts resulted the 1990 launch of a rackjobbing operation called Great American Entertainment. This was a natural progression in vertical integration for GoodTimes, which already had a major duplication facility. To support its distribution network, GoodTimes invested heavily in technology to create a state-of-the-art automatic replenishment program. The company not only knew what kind of videos sold well in particular areas and could then supply an appropriate mix of titles, it knew which titles were sold each day and was able to instruct the duplicating unit to create replacements, which they provided overnight to stores. The result was that retailers were able to maximize revenues while maintaining a minimum amount of inventory.

GoodTimes success with low-price videos was not lost on larger media companies, as well as smaller rivals that offered even cheaper public domain titles. To maintain its momentum, GoodTimes adapted to changing conditions in the early 1990s as it evolved into a diversified entertainment company. In 1993, it established GoodTimes Entertainment to serve as a holding company for GoodTimes Home Video as well as the company's new wide-ranging ventures. It also established a unit to sell B-movies to video stores for rental and created an international unit to distribute video overseas. GoodTimes looked to expand on its successful children's video business by teaming with toymaker Fisher Price to create a Fisher Price label to produce videos and movies, as well as to publish books.

To supply product for both its domestic and foreign distribution operations, GoodTimes decided in 1992 to invest more than $70 million in the production of nearly 30 animated features in the direct-to-video market. Relying on standard children's fare, GoodTimes was able to mirror Disney's releases, offering less expensive alternatives to such features as *Aladdin* and *Beauty and the Beast.* Disney sued, maintaining that GoodTimes infringed upon its ''trade dress,'' essentially the look of its packaging. Although GoodTimes was required to print its name at the top of the box, the court sided with GoodTimes and allowed it to continue to produce its Disney alternatives. GoodTimes' *Snow White* featured dwarfs named Sunbeam, Toadstool, Fawn, Hedgehog, Robin, Cricket, and Tadpole. Even when Disney released original material like *The Lion King,* GoodTimes had a product ready to take advantage of Disney's marketing efforts. Its *Leo The Lion, King of The Jungle* offered a main character with a Bronx accent. Both Disney and GoodTimes were major moneymakers for Wal-Mart, which may have led to the retailer's decision in 1994 to create a special video floor display that granted each rival 40 percent of the shelf space. Too large for the usual electronics department location, the units were positioned in main traffic aisles. In addition to Disney, GoodTimes conflicted with MPI Home Video over the release of the public-domain John Wayne feature *McLintock!* MPI's version, promoted as a producer's cut, was authorized by the estate of John Wayne. MPI sued GoodTimes, claiming that it held the rights to the music used in the film. The courts ultimately ruled that the music rights had been sold to United Artists, which in turn sold them to EMI, which had licensed them to GoodTimes, thereby making it possible for GoodTimes to sell its version of the movie.

One of GoodTimes' ventures in the early 1990s that proved to be especially successful was GT Interactive, a unit devoted to video and computer games. The concept behind the new business was simple but effective: use GoodTimes' reputation and infrastructure to acquire shelf space and provide distribution in order to become an attractive partner for the best game developers. GT Interactive quickly established itself as a viable business when in 1993 it was able to secure the rights to publish *Wolfenstein*, a three-year-old action game created by id Software. Even though sales were considered to be tapped out, GT

Interactive was able to sell 100,000 units. In short order, the unit was asked by Wal-Mart to take over its software display (a move echoed two years later by Target), and it also gained the rights to *Doom II,* the follow-up to the immensely popular shareware game *Doom*. Although the Cayre brothers were generally averse to making GoodTimes a public company, they elected to spin-off GT Interactive and take it public in order to raise the capital and provide the flexibility needed to acquire game developers. The initial public offering, held in December 1995, raised $150 million.

### *A Challenge in the 1990s*

In the mid-1990s GoodTimes was faced with a highly competitive video market. With public domain essentially a dead sector—as larger entertainment companies distributed low-price, newly released movies on their own—and with sales of fitness tapes falling off, GoodTimes had to scour for licensing opportunities. To develop its own material, in addition to animation, GoodTimes looked to produce some live action movies, although the Cayres were wary of becoming too involved in the expensive and risky business of movie production. A $5 million production of *Pocahontas: The Legend*, which offered a theatrical-release and direct-to-video family version, failed to produce the kind of results that warranted further investment in live-action features.

GoodTimes searched for other niche opportunities. It signed a ten-year deal for the rights to *Late Night with David Letterman.* In 1995, it created GoodTimes Publishing, a children's book division aimed at toddlers to eight year olds. The company also pursued licensing opportunities for one of the stars of its fitness videos, Richard Simmons, whose *Sweating To The Oldies* was a high selling title for GoodTimes. Special units such as GoodTimes Licensing and Merchandising and GoodTimes Foods sought to extend the Simmons brand to low-fat snack foods as well as fitness apparel and footwear. Just as it had vertically integrated its video business, GoodTimes hoped to do the same with celebrities that worked with the company. In this vein, country singer Naomi Judd was signed to a licensing and merchandising deal intended to take advantage of a talk show she was set to begin hosting in the fall of 1997. Again, GoodTimes contemplated a wide array of products under the Naomi Judd name, including cosmetics, skin-care products, apparel, and packaged foods. The talk show, however, proved unsuccessful.

These ventures outside of the video business failed to establish GoodTimes as a diversified entertainment company. In the late 1990s, the company struggled to find a suitable business mix for a changing environment. There was speculation that GoodTimes was preparing to go public in 1998, stoked by the implementation of cost-cutting measures that led observers to conclude the company was dressing its balance sheet in preparation of an offering. Because the video business had peaked years earlier, however, any attempt by GoodTimes to go public was never realized.

GoodTimes narrowed its focus and looked for profitable niches to exploit in the video industry. In 2000, GoodTimes became heavily involved in the Christian market, distributing the video of *The Omega Code*, a low-budget Christian film that in 1999 showed surprising strength at the box office. After grossing $14 million at the box office, it sold over one million units for GoodTimes in videotape. In 2001, GoodTimes signed a ten-year deal with the producers of *The Omega Code*, Gener8Xion Entertainment, to produce and distribute at least four movies a year. With a steady source of product in hand, GoodTimes then established the Bethlehem label for Christian-oriented videos. To serve as president and lead GoodTimes into a new era, the former president of PolyGram Video, Bill Sondheim, was hired. The company then entered another niche market when in the summer of 2001 it signed a five-year deal to distribute videos and DVD's with the Broadway Television Network, which had been created to produce pay-per-view broadcasts of popular Broadway shows. Because the broadcasts attracted relatively few viewers and were limited to a single showing, the upside for video sales appeared promising. GoodTimes planned to release four to five titles each year. Sondheim was already well familiar with this type of programming, having distributed *Cats*, *Lord of the Dance*, and *The Three Tenors* during his time at PolyGram. GoodTimes even used the Broadway connection with Richard Simmons, producing *Broadway Sweat/Tone-Up on Broadway*, while at the same time repackaging his earlier fitness titles. Whether the new niche businesses would prove profitable for GoodTimes remained an open question. What was certain, however, was that the company had the entrepreneurial spirit to continuously adapt and search out new niche opportunities.

### *Principal Competitors*

AOL Time Warner Inc.; Viacom Inc.; Walt Disney Company.

### *Further Reading*

Cella, Catherine, "It's a Family Affair: How the Cayre's Vertical Video Empire Grew Up and Out," *Billboard*, July 23, 1994, p. 62.

Eng, Paul M., "Lots of Doom But No Gloom," *Business Week*, September 2, 1996, p. 74.

Fitzpatrick, Eileen, "GoodTimes Links with Broadway TV Network to Distribute Live-Performance Event Videos," *Billboard*, July 14, 2001, p. 83.

Goldstein, Seth, "For the Good Times: A Talk with Joe Cayre," *Billboard,* July 23, 1994, p. 64.

——, "GoodTimes Gets More Gold From Disney Coattails," *Billboard,* April 23, 1994, p. 77.

Upbin, Bruce, "Scholars of Shelf Space," *Forbes*, October 21, 1996, p. 210.

—Ed Dinger

# Groupe Partouche SA

**141 bis, rue de Saussure**
**75017 Paris**
**France**
**Telephone: (+33) 1-47-64-33-45**
**Fax: (+33) 1-47-64-19-20**
**Web site: http://www.partouche.fr**

*Public Company*
*Incorporated:* 1973
*Employees:* 3,341
*Sales:* EUR 258.8 million ($214 million)
*Stock Exchanges:* Euronext Paris
*Ticker Symbol:* PAR
*NAIC:* 713210 Casinos (Except Casino Hotels)

Groupe Partouche SA is gambling on keeping its number one position in France's casino industry. The Paris-based group owns and operates 30 casinos, including 25 in France and five abroad. Casino operations make up some 80 percent of the company's turnover of nearly EUR 260 million in 2000—and slot machines account for nearly 90 percent of its casino revenues. Partouche also operates a number of restaurants, most of which serve the company's casinos in keeping with strict French regulations governing casino operations. The company's operations are focused on France, Belgium, and North Africa. Partouche also operates a number of hotels, including thermal and other spa resorts. The company, founded by Isidore Partouche, continues to be dominated by the Partouche family, despite its listing on the Euronext Paris stock exchange. Indeed, the Partouche family owns more than two-thirds of the company's stock and holds nearly all key positions in the company, including direct management of most of its casinos. Hubert Benhamou, nephew of Isidore Partouche, functions as chairman of the group, while Partouche's son, Patrick, is the company's managing director. Partouche himself, as head of the company's supervisory board, maintains a say in the company's development. This includes its ''Pasino'' concept, grouping under one complex a casino, shopping mall, a number of themed restaurants, a theater, and other amenities. In 2001, the company launched a Pasino in Aix-en-Provence, adding to a Pasino opened in Djerba, Tunisia. At the beginning of 2002, Partouche launched what many saw as a salvo in a coming takeover battle against aggressively growing Accor for control of rival Compagnie Européenne de Casinos. If successful, Accor's acquisition will place Partouche in second place in the French market.

### *A Start in the 1970s*

Isidore Partouche and family were members of the ''Pied Noir'' community of French citizens living in Algeria that were forced to repatriate to France after Algeria's declaration of independence at the beginning of the 1960s. Partouche had previously worked for Philips in Algeria. In 1965, Partouche decided to enter the French leisure market, operating go-cart tracks at first, then night clubs. In 1973, however, Partouche, with the financial support of his family, bought a failing spa resort and mineral water source, Saint-Amand-les-Eaux. The purchase also gave Partouche the spa's failing casino. Partouche soon returned the casino to profitability, yet his primary interest for the time being was in building up his interests in the bottling and distribution of mineral water. This was in part because of the strict French government regulations that hampered the growth of the casino industry in the country.

Gambling remained outlawed in France until the beginning of the 20th century. Legislation adopted in 1907 allowed casino gambling in the country, but only in the country's spa resorts and ocean side beach communities, with further legislation prohibiting the opening of casinos less than 100 kilometers from Paris. A number of other restrictions were placed on the profession, such as an insistence that casinos remain open only on a seasonal basis, with the year ending in October, and that casinos provide restaurants and entertainment. Casinos were also required to charge an entrance fee to its customers. An important limitation on French casinos was a ban on slot machines, which had been particularly responsible for the success of Las Vegas. Instead, France's casinos were limited to just a handful of games, including Baccarat, Blackjack, and Roulette. An immediate result of these restrictions was that France's casinos became strongly associated as playgrounds for the world's wealthy, as exemplified in several of the James Bond series of films. Yet by the 1970s, France's casino industry

## Company Perspectives:

*The future will involve the creation of major establishments, such as Le Pharaon in Lyon or the future Aix-en-Provence Pasino, which will be born with the new century. It will also involve continuous and general improvements to our casinos in order to meet, in the spirit of the Partouche Group, the expectations of our clients and friends. Our efforts abroad will be directed towards defending and illustrating our philosophy. Our way is the right one, even if it is not the easiest. We shall not deviate from it.*

remained a relatively small and fading sector dominated by the Groupe Barrière.

Partouche continued to develop his interests in mineral water, building up a portfolio of labels that included Amanda, Arline à Francoville, Eau d'Alet-les-Bains, Source Luceux, as well as a Belgian brand, Source Baudour. Expanding and supporting the company's bottling and distribution operations took up most of the company's finances and expansion of its casino holdings, hampered by legislation, remained on the backburner. Nonetheless, Partouche continued to pick up new casinos during the 1970s and 1980s.

In 1976, Partouche bought the Le Touquet's casino from the Barrière family, creating the subsidiary SA Le Touquet's. That subsidiary went on to build a new casino, in Calais, in 1982. In 1986, the company took over a casino of Forges-les-Eaux, which, at 110 kilometers from Paris, lay just outside the capital city's restricted zone. That same year, the company opened a new casino at Boulogne sur Mer. Two years later, Partouche added to his growing casino holdings with the purchase of a casino in Dieppe.

Joining Partouche in the business were members of his family, including son Patrick and nephew Hubert Benhamoun, who were later to take over the day-to-day operations of the company. By placing family members in charge of his company's casinos, and allowing them a good deal of discretion over their individual businesses, Partouche nonetheless retained tight control of the company's gambling operations. Yet the casino market during the 1980s was increasingly facing difficulties, with many of the country's primarily small operators facing financial ruin.

### *Leadership Slot in the 21st Century*

The French government promised changes in the legislation governing casino gambling in 1988 in order to shore up the struggling sector. Among the announced changes was the government's intention to legalize the placement of slot machines, although these were still to be separated from the classic gaming tables, where an entry fee continued to be required. The admittance of slot machines was expected to revolutionize the industry, attracting a far broader and different clientele from the industry's hitherto upscale players. Another component of the new legislation was also to enable casino operators to attract new markets, as casinos were now permitted for the first time to open in towns with populations of more than 500,000.

Isidore Partouche immediately recognized the potential of the proposed new legislation, and determined to lead the company into a new, more focused direction as a casino operator. In 1989, Partouche adopted a new strategic direction and began winding up its water bottling and distribution business. Proceeds from the sale of those operations were then used to begin buying up casinos around France, beginning with the acquisitions of casinos in Fécamp, Bagnoles-de-l'Orne, and Vichy. At the time, Partouche established a pattern of buying up smaller and more financially fragile competitors, building up a fast-growing empire that was to overtake long-time market leaders Groupe Barrière before the end of the decade.

By 1991, however, the government still had not delivered on its promise to enact the new casino industry rules. The legislation finally came that year, but only after Partouche threatened to take legal action against the government. Armed with its permits to install slot machines at its casinos, the company stepped up its expansion program. By the end of 1991, the company had acquired the Lyon-Vert casino, located at la Tour-de-Salvagny, as well as two subsidiary casinos located in Saint-Galmier and Juan-des-Pins. The following year, the company acquired the concession for the then-shuttered casino at Royat.

The company began eyeing entry into one of the larger urban markets authorized by the new casino legislation. In order to build capital for an investment—with Lyon as the company's primary target—Partouche sold off two of its earlier casino acquisitions, Fécamp and Bagnoles-de-l'Orne. The company once again turned acquisitive. In 1994, Partouche added a casino at Aix-en-Provence, which gave it access to the Marseilles market nearby. By the end of the year, the company had added two more casinos, at La Ciotat and Palavas. The following year, Partouche bought up a 50 percent share in a casino in Grasse with partner Group Boucau.

In 1995, Partouche decided to step up its expansion ambitions, and especially with an eye on expanding its holdings internationally. That year, the company took a listing on the Paris stock exchange's secondary board. By the end of 1995, the company had made its first international acquisition, of the casino at Belgium's resort town Knokke Le Zoute.

Partouche had gained quickly on rival Groupe Barrière. In 1996, the company moved in on its rival's territory, buying up a minority stake in Société Fermiere du Casino Municipale de Cannes, a subsidiary of Barriere which operated casinos and a hotel in that famed city. Yet Partouche's attempt to gain control of that money-losing operation was blocked by the Barrière family.

Partouche could be consoled in the knowledge that by then his company was well on its way toward becoming France's leading casino operator. The company continued to expand in 1996, opening a casino in Agadir, Morocco, in partnership with Club Méditerrané. In 1997, Partouche added a new dimension to the company's operations when it acquired a four-star hotel, part of the complex housing its Juan-les-Pins casino, which was subsequently renamed Le Méridien-Garden Beach. That year, the company also was granted a concession to open a casino in the city of Lyon.

The company made a new move internationally when it opened a casino in Djerba, Tunisia, in 1998. Dubbed a

## Key Dates:

**1973:** Isidore Partouche purchases thermal spa, mineral water, and casino complex at Saint-Amand-les-Eaux.
**1976:** The company buys a second casino at Touquet.
**1982:** Partouche acquires a casino at Forges-les-Eaux and opens a new casino at Boulogne sur Mer.
**1989:** Company begins selling off its bottled water operations.
**1991:** Partouche is granted a concession to install slot machines in its casinos.
**1995:** Groupe Partouche goes public on the Paris secondary market and opens its first foreign casino in Belgium.
**1996:** The company opens a casino in Morocco in partnership with Club Med.
**1999:** Partouche acquires 50 percent of Société Française de Casinos (SFC), which operates four casinos.
**2000:** The company takes a majority shareholding in SFC.

''Pasino,'' the complex combined a casino with other operations that included a shopping mall, themed restaurants, and a theater. The complex was to prove a money-loser, in part because Tunisian law prohibits Tunisians themselves from gambling, but remained among Partouche's favorites, in part because it represented his return of sorts to his North African roots.

Partouche joined the Parisian main board in 1998. The company then continued its quest to establish itself in the Cannes market. In that year, the company acquired the Carlton Casino Club from London Clubs International. Later that same year, Partouche acquired a 99 percent stake, from Groupe Vivendi, in the company Cannes Balnéaires, which owned the closed Palm Beach casino in Cannes. Partouche began preparing to reopen the Palm Beach, spending some FFr 50 million on its renovation. That structure opened again in 1999.

Partouche stepped up its expansion at the turn of the century. The company opened a new casino at San Roque, in Andalousia near Gibraltar, in July 1999. In November 1999, the company took a 50 percent share of Société Française de Casinos (SFC), which held three casino properties at La Barboule, Mont-Dore and Gruissan in Auxerre, and a fourth casino on the Narbonne coast. At the same time, the company opened, in partnership with Hilton, a casino at the company's Hotel Athénée Palace in Bucarest. That endeavor proved unsatisfactory for Partouche, which sold the Bucarest casino at the end of 2001.

The company increased its position in SFC to majority ownership in October 2000. By then the company had opened its casino in Lyon, the first large French city to authorize casino gambling. That casino opened as part of the Hilton hotel complex at La Cité Internationale. The company continued to make acquisitions in 2000, picking up a casino at Châtel-Guyon and a floating casino, the Lydia, moored at Port Barcarès, on the beach near Perpignan.

In December 2000, the company acquired the Hotel Parabella in Aix-en-Provence, then purchased an adjoining spa, and began preparing a conversion of the complex to the newest, and largest, ''Pasino,'' which opened its doors in July 2001. Meanwhile, Partouche began looking beyond casinos as it began diversifying its operations for the new century. In November 2001, the company bought the Hotel Savoy in Cannes, located close by the company's Carlton Casino in that city. Partouche also acquired and renovated a restaurant in the northern city Le Havre, which reopened in 2001 as La Villa. In December 2001, the company bought up the thermal spas at Contrexeville and Vittel, a purchase which also gave it control of a casino at Contrexeville.

These diversification moves nonetheless complemented the company's existing casino operations, allowing the company to expand the range of services it was able to offer its clientele. Over the past decade, Partouche had been one of the leaders in the consolidation of the French casino gambling sector—by the end of 2001, Partouche claimed 19 percent of the French market, ahead of both Group Barrière and Accor.

Yet in December 2001, Accor, already one of the world's leading hotel groups, stepped up its expansion into France's casino market when it announced an offer to acquire Compagnie Européenne de Casinos (CEC), a move that would make Accor undisputed leader in the French market (and one of the top casino groups in all of Europe). Yet Partouche struck back, acquiring nearly seven percent of CEC for a significantly higher share price, a move that for many observers signaled the start of a takeover battle. With its strong record of growth, Partouche was unlikely to let go of its leadership position without a good fight.

### *Principal Subsidiaries*

Sa Casino De Saint Amand; Sa Grand Casino De Cabourg; Sa Casino Du Grand Café; Sa Grand Casino De Beaulieu; Sa Forges Thermal; Sa Casino & Bains De Mer De Dieppe; Sa Jean Metz; Sa Le Touquet's; Sa Casinos Du Touquet; Sa Casinos De Vichy; Sa Numa; Sa Eck (Belgium); Sa Casino Le Mirage (Morocco); Sa Le Grand Casino De Djerba (Tunisia); Casino Nuevo De San Roque (Spain); Groupe Partouche Romania (Romania); Sa Sathel; Sa Casino Municipal De Royat; Sa Casino Le Lion Blanc; Sa Eden Beach Casino; Sa Casino Municipal D'aix Thermal; Sa Casino Des Flots Bleus; Sa Casino De Palavas; Sa Casino De Grasse; Sa Grand Casino De Lyon; Sa Lcl France & Cie (Casino Carlton); Sa Phoebus Casino Gruissan; Sa Casino Mondore; Sa Casino Bourboule; Sa Casino Chatel Guyon; Sa Elysee Palace Hotel; Sa Hotel International De Lyon; Snc Garden Beach Hotel; Snc Egh-La Part Dieu; Snc Hotel Du Golf; Sarl Aquabella; Hotel Casino Phoebus; Splendid Hotel; Sa Cannes Balneaires (Palm Beach); Sa C.H.M.; Sarl Societe Immobiliere De La Tour; Sa Baratem; Sa Holding Garden Pinede; Sci Hotel Garden Pinede; Sci Rue Royale; Elysée Palace Expansion; Elysée Palace Sa; Sa Groupe Partouche Belgique (Belgium); Sa Sikb (Belgium); Sprl Caskno (Belgium); Sprl Artmusic (Belgium); Sarl Sek; Sci De L'eden Beach Casino; Sci Palavas Investissement; Sc Du Casino De Grasse; Sa Lydia; Sci Lydia Investissement; Sci Les Thermes; Sarl Therm'park; Port La Nouvelle; Sa Gcjb; Sarl Sed; Sarl Sf2d; Sa Sfc; Sarl Sihct; Sci Montdore; Sci Phoebus; Sci Azt;

Sa Semcg; Sci Fonciere Grands Hotels; Cie Thermale; Café Carmen.

### *Principal Operating Units*

Casinos; Hotels; Spas.

### *Principal Competitors*

Groupe Barrière SA; Accor Casinos; Société des Bains de Mer et du Cercle des Étrangers à Monaco; Compagnie Européenne de Casinos; Groupe Tranchant; Groupe Moliflor; Groupe Emeraude SA; Hôtels et Casino de Deauville SA.

### *Further Reading*

Bovas, Michel, and Frédéric Dubessy, ''Les grands groupes verrouillent le marché des jeux,'' *La Tribune*, March 9, 2000.

Durieux, Isabelle, ''Partouche: casino royal,'' *L'Expansion,* November 6, 1997, p.164.

Graham, Robert, ''French Casinos Hit Jackpot with Low-Roller Machines,'' *Financial Times*, August 28, 1998.

''Groupe Partouche Buys Europeenne de Casinos Shares,'' *Reuters*, December 31, 2001.

''Isidore Partouche, l'as des casinos,'' *Les Echos,* March 4, 1999, p. 16.

Minder, Raphael, ''Accor May Have to Raise the Stakes in Casino Bid,'' *Financial Times*; January 4, 2002.

Tillier, Alan, ''Goodbye Baccarat, Hello Vegas,'' *European*, March 9, 1998.

—M.L. Cohen

# Grupo Aeropuerto del Sureste, S.A. de C.V.

**40 Boulevard Manuel Avila Camacho**
**11000 Mexico City, D.F.**
**Mexico**
**Telephone: (525) 284-0400**
**Fax: (525) 202-1911**
**Web site: http://www.asur.com.mx**

*Public Company*
*Incorporated:* 1998
*Employees:* 598
*Sales:* 2.81 billion pesos ($306.6 million) (2001)
*Stock Exchanges:* Mexico City
*Ticker Symbols:* ASUR
*NAIC:* 488112 Airport Operations, except Air Traffic Control; 531190 Lessors of Other Real Properties; 551112 Offices of Other Holding Companies

Grupo Aeroportuario del Sureste S.A. de C.V. (Asur) is a holding company that, through its subsidiaries, is engaged in the operation, maintenance, and development of nine airports in southeastern Mexico. As operator of these airports under a 50-year concession from the Mexican government, Asur charges fees to airlines, passengers, and others for the use of airport facilities. The company also derives rental and other income from commercial activities conducted at its airports, such as the leasing of space to restaurants and retailers. Asur's chief source of revenue is the airport at Cancun, Mexico's second-busiest in terms of passenger traffic. Like Cancun, the airports serving Cozumel and Huatulco mainly accommodate beach vacationers. Merida, Oaxaca, Veracruz, and Villahermosa draw, in addition to business travelers, tourists interested in the archeological sites and museums that display Mexico's indigenous past. Minantitlan, like Villahermosa, is close to the heart of Mexico's petroleum-extracting and petrochemical industries. Tapachula's airport is near the Pacific Ocean and the border with Guatemala.

## *Under Federal Administration: 1939–95*

Mexico's first airfield was built in 1910. This became the center of the nation's military training in aviation. During the 1920s more airfields were built by state and local governments and by the nascent commercial carriers. The secretariat of communications and public works constructed Mexico City's airport, inaugurated in 1939. During the 1940s, the federal government built a number of others with World War II aid from the United States. Those in Asur's future territory were in Campeche, Chetumal, Ciudad del Carmen, Cozumel, Itxtepec, Merida, and Veracruz. The state and municipal governments built the airport in Oaxaca.

Aeropuertos y Servicios Auxiliares (ASA) was established in 1965, after the introduction of jet airliners made larger facilities essential. A decentralized federal agency, it assumed administration of 33 airports. Among those that came under ASA's jurisdiction in this period were the airports serving Tapachula and Villahermosa. The airports in Cancun and Cozumel came under ASA jurisdiction between 1970 and 1976, and the one in Minatitlan was added between 1976 and 1982. In 1977 the ASA administered 47 airports, of which 28 were in the international category.

Interviewed for the Mexican business magazine *Expansion* at this time, director general Enrique M. Lodeza said, concerning the agency's finances, "Three years ago the enterprise was self-sufficient, but given the increased costs of operation without any rate increase, the increase in personnel to staff new airports and the effects of the [1976] devaluation [of the peso], our expenses have gone up so that now, we have an operating deficit of 70 million pesos [about $3 million]. We don't deny the necessity of a rational administrative effort, in order to be a self-supporting entity again. We hope to reach this point in 1980, based on a new financial as well as administrative organization." At this time, airport services—such as landing fees—were accounting for 72 percent of ASA's annual revenues of 550 million to 600 million pesos ($24 million to $26 million). The rest of its revenues came from such sources as rent received from airport shops and airport-located government facilities such as postal, telephone, and telex offices.

In 1988, the federal government began to seek investment by private capital in airport infrastructure. Hakim Grupo Industrial, a large construction firm, was put in charge of expanding Mexico City's Benito Juarez International Airport, and the privatization of the nation's airports was seen as the only solution for a

**Company Perspectives:**

*At ASUR, we are committed to the development of Mexico. We therefore want to contribute our experience in airport operations, and that of our Strategic Partner, to the growth of the air cargo industry. Our airports, mainly those at Cancúún, Veracruz and Méérida, have the potential to become major air cargo hubs, and to position themselves among the most important on the American continent.*

government with other financial priorities. In April 1991, ASA's director general, Jose Andres de Oteyza, told the federal district's assembly of representatives, ''Notwithstanding that our resources are very valuable and our investments are productive, our budget hasn't been augmented in a corresponding manner, because what we collect goes to the treasury to support the public finances.''

In 1991, the ASA administered 61 airports that served 36.1 million passengers, and it registered a profit of some 400 billion pesos (about $133 million). However, the agency's own budget came to only 148.29 billion pesos ($49.27 million), and both infrastructure and services were suffering. The ASA reserved for itself the construction and administration of runways, platforms, control towers, fuel, security, and basic operation, and its projects at this time included construction of the airport at Huatulco and the expansion of the Cancun and Merida airports. The agency was, however, seeking private investment for other infrastructure and commercial operations. Grupo Constructor Dicas, for example, had signed an agreement to build a satellite terminal at Cancun for international traffic. By the fall of 1995, 22 joint-venture projects had been carried out, representing investment of about $350 million in the nation's 14 largest airports.

### *The Privatization Process: 1995–2000*

At this time, ASA was administering the 68 most important airports in Mexico, but only seven were profitable. Only 32 of the 68 had computers. The number of computers averaged only 2.8 for each airport, and 49 percent were obsolete. Even so, ASA turned a profit of about $200 million that year, since the profitable airports accounted for 65 percent of all air traffic. With Mexico in recession following a new peso crisis, however, the nation's Congress in December 1995 approved a constitutional amendment authorizing privatization of the airports. The secretariat of communications and transport then divided 35 of Mexico's most valuable airports into four regions, each of which contained both profitable and unprofitable airports so that the holding companies for each group would receive an overall annual return on their investment that ASA officials calculated at about 15 percent. A New York investment banker later told Brian Caplen of *Euromoney*, ''These will be some of the first businesses in Mexico not to be controlled by a family or a single shareholder. The government doesn't desperately need the money from privatization but it wants to take them out of the public sector to improve the management and modernize them.''

The next stage of the privatization process authorized strategic partnerships between foreign and Mexican investors as official operating service providers. Groups interested in bidding for the concessions were screened to avoid the purchase of the airports by drug cartels. The investing partners were restricted to a 15 percent share of the holding company, with the remaining shares to be publicly sold later. They were required to hold at least 7.5 percent of the shares for ten years. Foreign investment was limited to 49 percent of the holding company. Bidders had to place a $10-million bond before being given access to data profiles of the airports. The process moved slowly because of the government's much-criticized and poorly executed ''rescue'' of the banking system and its failed conversion of public highways into privately operated toll roads.

Grupo Aeroportuario del Sureste (Asur) was incorporated as a wholly-owned entity of the federal government in 1998. The concession to operate its nine airports in southeastern Mexico was awarded to a consortium called Inversiones y Tecnicas Aeroportuarias (ITA), comprised of Copenhagen Airports A/S (majority-owned by the Danish government); the French construction firm Groupe GTM; the Mexican construction firm Triturados Basalticos y Derivados (Tribasa), S.A. de C.V.; and Cintra Concesiones de Infraestructura de Transporte, S.A., a subsidiary of the Spanish company Grupo Ferrovial SA. ITA paid 1.17 billion pesos ($120 million) for its 15-percent stake. The concession was for 50 years, with the possibility of extension for up to an aggregate of an additional 50 years. Under a technical-assistance agreement, ITA also assumed management and consulting services to Asur in exchange for a fee.

The Asur concession consisted of the airports serving Cancun, Cozumel, Huatulco, Merida, Minatitlan, Oaxaca, Tapachula, Veracruz, and Villahermosa. Only Cancun, Mexico's second-busiest in terms of passenger traffic, was profitable. Asur had revenues of $88.84 million in 1998 and $105.53 million in 1999. Net income came to $32.7 million in 1998 and $17.59 million in 1999. Another 74 percent of Asur's shares were sold to the public in 2000. Of the $335.8 million raised, 92 percent was placed outside Mexico in the form of American Depositary Receipts, with the buyers including institutional investors such as Morgan Stanley & Co.'s asset management group. No single investor was allowed to hold more than 10 percent of the company. ITA retained management responsibility but did not control the board of directors.

### *Asur in the New Century*

At the beginning of 2000, Asur began the process of receiving bids for concessions to operate shops at the airports of Cancun, Cozumel, and Merida for ten years. Commercial areas of the Cozumel and Merida airports began operations in late 2001. The company was investing $59 million in the remodeling and expansion of the Cancun airport, with new areas to include restaurants, bars, cafeterias, convenience stores, banks, and playgrounds. This project included a 13,777-square-foot shopping center, the installation of air conditioning, an integrated operational system to facilitate airline activities, and 239 monitors to enable passengers to check on the status of their flights.

Writing in the *Mexico City News* in 2000, Jose Antonio O'Farrill Avila offered an unflattering view of Asur's administration of the Cancun airport. He claimed that the company's officers were at odds with the car-rental companies and vendors in the commercial area and also with taxi drivers serving the airport. He also wrote that airport employees were extorting

## Key Dates:

**1965:** Aeropuertos y Servicios Auxiliares (ASA) assumes control of 33 Mexican airports.
**1995:** A constitutional amendment authorizes the privatization of the nation's airports.
**1998:** A consortium, Grupo Aeroportuario del Sureste S.A. de C.V. (Asur), wins the concession to run nine airports in southeastern Mexico.
**2001:** Asur's airports serve 11.24 million passengers.

space-rental fees for Asur from tourism service agencies and taking bribes from "the hotel time-share promoters who lobby in the airport. They are a constant plague for tourists soon off the planes. . . . Intolerance, inefficiency and bad administration are Asur's trade marks." The company was reported in 2002 to be sending all airport employees to three-day customer-service training programs.

Asur's revenues reached 1.16 billion pesos ($120.62 million) in 2000. Its net income was 209.58 million pesos ($21.81 million). Its nine airports accommodated 11.45 million passengers. The September 2001 World Trade Center took a heavy toll on the company's fourth quarter for that year, with passenger traffic dropping 12 percent compared to the same period in 2000. Nevertheless, revenues for 2001 reached a new high of 1.21 billion pesos (about $131.8 million), of which revenue from aeronautical services accounted for 85 percent. (Passenger charges collected by airlines accounted for 76 percent of aeronautical revenues in 2000.) Nonaeronautical services included leasing space in the airports to commercial tenants. Revenue from Cancun alone accounted for about two-thirds of the total. The company's airports served 11.24 million passengers during the year, of which Cancun accounted for about two-thirds. Fifty-nine percent of the passengers were on international flights.

Business was still slow in the first quarter of 2002, with passenger volume down by 9 percent and operating profits falling by 21 percent from the corresponding period in 2001. The remodeling of the Cancun airport and expansion of the Cozumel airport were scheduled to be completed in 2002. An Asur executive said the company expected no increase in the number of passengers before 2003 but predicted a small gain in revenues. He said that Asur had no debt and no plans to seek credit. The company intended to raise its revenue from airport businesses such as retailers, restaurants, and advertisers to 25 percent of the total by 2004 and was redrawing its rental agreements to achieve that goal.

### *Principal Subsidiaries*

Aeropuerto de Cancun, S.A. de C.V.; Aeropuerto de Cozumel, S.A. de C.V.; Aeropuerto de Huatulco, S.A. de C.V.; Aeropuerto de Merida, S.A. de C.V.; Aeropuerto de Minatitlan, S.A. de C.V.; Aeropuerto de Oaxaca, S.A. de C.V.; Aeropuerto de Tapachula, S.A. de C.V.; Aeropuerto de Veracruz, S.A. de C.V.; Aeropuerto de Villahermosa, S.A. de C.V.; Servicios Aeroportuarios del Suereste, S.A. de C.V.

### *Principal Competitors*

Aeroports de Montreal; Aeroports de Paris; British Airports Authority; Fraport AG.

### *Further Reading*

Amaro Gonzalez, Rodolfo, and Jose Aribal Habeica Villanueva, *Problema de informacion asimetrica en aeropuertos y servicios auxiliares,* Thesis, Mexico City: Instituto de Tecnologica Autonoma Mexicana, 1996.
"ASA: a vuelo de pajaro," *Expansion,* March 15, 1978, pp. 37–8.
Beard, Alison, "Mexican Airport Group Poised for Take-Off," *Financial Times,* May 20, 2002, p. 23.
Caplen, Brian, "Creating a Corporate Role Model," *Euromoney,* October 1998, p. 18.
Fritsch, Peter, "Investors to Get a Play on Cancun, Mexico's Fast Growth," *Wall Street Journal,* September 8, 2000, p. A15.
Javier Calderon, Lino, "Air Pressure," *Business Mexico,* September 1995, pp. 12, 14–15.
Monjaras Moreno, Jorge A., "Por no poder atenderlos," *Expansion,* October 28, 1992, pp. 55–7.
Nirdlinger, Dan, "In Flight," *Business Mexico,* April 1998, pp. 54–5.
O'Farrill Avila, Jose Antonio, "Serious Problems at Cancun's International Airport," *Mexico City News,* August 28, 2000.
"A Public Privatization Out of Mexico," *LatinFinance,* November 2000, p. 70.
Ruiz Romero, Manuel, *La aviacion civil en Mexico,* Mexico City: Universidad Nacional Autonoma de Mexico, 1999, pp. 40–8.

—Robert Halasz

# HDR Inc.

**8404 Indian Hills Drive**
**Omaha, Nebraska 68114-4049**
**U.S.A.**
**Telephone: (402) 399-1000**
**Toll Free: (800) 366-4411**
**Fax: (402) 399-1238**
**Web site: http://www.hdrinc.com**

*Private Company*
*Incorporated:* 1917 as the Henningson Engineering Company
*Employees:* 3,000
*Sales:* $450 million (2001 est.)
*NAIC:* 541310 Architectural Services; 541330 Engineering Services; 541710 Research and Development in the Physical, Engineering, and Life Sciences

HDR Inc. is America's leading hospital and prison design firm. The venerable company ranks among the 50 largest architecture and engineering (A/E) firms in the United States. HDR, which completed an employee buyout in 1996, is known for its innovative, entrepreneurial culture.

### *Origins*

Company founder H.H. Henningson was born in Jewell, Iowa. After sixth grade, he left school and worked as a cowboy in Montana. After a brief stint as a soldier during the Spanish-American War, he applied to Iowa State University. When his application was rejected, he successfully appealed to the governor of Iowa to allow him to attend the university based on his rights as a taxpayer. He graduated with a degree in electrical engineering in 1907.

Henningson then worked for Westinghouse for several years before taking a sales position with the Alamo Engine & Supply Company. In 1917, he established the Henningson Engineering Company in Omaha, Nebraska (at the corner of 12th and Harney Streets) to design municipal improvements to the rapidly evolving Midwest. Henningson also handled some of the construction of these facilities.

Henningson's business grew rapidly in the 1920s and the firm earned a reputation for delivering on time and within budgets. H.H. borrowed money during the Great Depression in order to pay his workers.

In the 1930s, programs resulting from the New Deal led to a mass of new work for the firm, then called Henningson Engineering Company. The Rural Electrification Act (REA) had Henningson designing power systems for many districts across the Nebraska prairies. In addition to the work supplied by the alphabet agencies (REA, WPA, etc.), Henningson had a contract to design a winter training camp in Montana for the Army. The firm employed 40 people by the end of the decade and moved into new office buildings in 1937 and 1940.

### *Postwar Growth*

Two employees became new partners in the firm after World War II. Willard A. Richardson, an electrical engineer, became secretary-treasurer, and Charles W. Durham was named vice-president, each taking a one-third interest in the company. The company was renamed Henningson, Durham & Richardson, Inc. in 1950. The same year, the company decided to build its own office building.

At the time, HDR employed 75 people and boasted annual revenues approaching $250,000. The company opened branch offices in Colorado Springs and Denver, where it was designing sewage systems, and in Phoenix, where it was designing the utilities for the Sun City community. An architectural department was established in 1955, and the company bought its first aircraft, to facilitate the long commute to Minot, North Dakota, where the firm had landed a contract to design an entire Air Force base. One significant postwar project was designing 500 miles of high-voltage power lines for the Northwest Missouri Electric Coop. The project was financed by an $18.5 million loan from the REA, the largest that agency had ever made.

By the end of the decade, HDR had already outgrown its new headquarters building. Its new home would be Kiewit

### Company Perspectives:

*MISSION—To be the preferred provider of a full range of superior professional architectural, engineering, planning, science and consulting services, to public and private clients. VISION—Shaping the future through creative solutions and visionary leadership.*

Plaza, one of Omaha's largest high-rises. HDR opened three more branch offices in the 1960s as employment rose to 200. The firm was then bringing in $3 million a year. A new office in Madrid, which specialized in irrigation projects, gave HDR an international presence. At home, the company built its first major medical facility, Omaha's Methodist Hospital.

Other major projects abroad included a $105 million aqueduct in Rio de Janeiro, as well as municipal planning in Sudan, Korea, Vietnam, Libya, and Iran. The U.S. Air Force had the firm designing more air bases in Newfoundland and Greenland, as well as an expansion of the U.S. Air Force Academy in Colorado Springs. The firm also began designing post office facilities.

By 1970, HDR had grown to 300 employees. The firm was becoming more corporate, with a new Lear jet (a first among architectural-engineering firms) and another new headquarters building completed in 1972. Major building projects included the medical school at King Abdulaziz University in Saudi Arabia. A separate division dedicated to designing judicial buildings was established, and the company ventured into environmental services, beating out 400 rivals to win a joint venture contract to plan the Trident Submarine Base Support Site in Bangor, Maine.

HDR also grew by acquisition. It bought the Seattle architectural firm Durham Anderson and Freed in 1974. Los Angeles-based Stanton Stockwell followed soon after. HDR acquired Minneapolis-based Pfeifer and Shultz, which specialized in power plant design, in 1976. Between 1973 and 1978, HDR grew from 350 to 850 employees; annual revenues increased from $10 million to $35 million.

### *Nouveau Owners in 1983*

Paris-based Bouygues S.A. (pronounced ''Bweege'') acquired HDR in 1983 for $60 million. The owner, the largest construction company in France, gave HDR access to state-of-the-art European technology. France, after all, boasted a 200–m.p.h. train system, the très grande vitesse or TGV. HDR soon designed such a system for the state of Texas, but the plans were scrapped. (Plans for a high-speed rail system linking Orlando, Tampa, and Miami in Florida proceeded throughout the mid-1990s, however.) In the 1980s, HDR expanded into waste and recycling services in the United States.

Annual revenues rose slightly to $182 million in 1994, though profits fell somewhat. HDR and Bouygues hoped to expand into providing waste disposal, transportation services, and water and power to some of the many communities across the country that were opening these functions up to private bidders.

Francis Jelensperger was named CEO of HDR in November 1994. He had first visited the United States in the 1960s, touring the country in a wood-sided station wagon. In 1967 he graduated from Hautes Etudes Commerciales in Paris. He returned in 1980 after working in France and Africa, and joined HDR in Omaha in 1987. A few months after becoming CEO, he moved to HDR's 156-person Dallas office to work more closely on business in the southern United States and Latin America.

In the mid-1990s, HDR had 1,600 employees in 60 offices across the country. Annual revenues reached $300 million. The Internet changed the way the company worked, allowing personnel from 11 offices to collaborate on the $350 million Boston Central Artery Tunnel. Transportation was the company's largest business sector; projects such as bridges and train and trolley lines accounted for $59 million of HDR's revenue in 1995.

### *1996 Employee Buyback*

An employee group bought HDR back from Bouygues in September 1996 for about $55 million. Even through more than a dozen years of French ownership, the independent, entrepreneurial company remained very much associated with Omaha. Yet, Bouygues had wanted to relocate HDR's corporate headquarters to a higher-profile city such as Dallas.

Under the buyback plan, eligible employees were given more than 50 percent of the private company's stock as the four Midwestern banks that financed the deal were paid off. Jelensperger was replaced as chairman by Richard Bell in August 1997.

The newly independent company's growth accelerated after it bought its freedom. HDR soon had plans to double the size of its headquarters. In the five years following the buyback, HDR would add 20 offices (bringing its total to 60) and increase employment by two-thirds to 3,000 people, noted Steve Jordon in the *Omaha World-Herald.* His sources told him that HDR had failed to thrive under Bouygues, which wanted to integrate HDR's own architecture and engineering services with the construction process. HDR was simply not strong enough in project management. Bouygues also failed to invest in HDR or fund acquisitions, said Chairman Richard Bell.

In 1999, HDR opened a London office to capitalize on the anticipated privatization of the British healthcare system by designing modernized facilities. The company also was growing in the United States. In 1999, its HDR Architecture subsidiary bought Ehrlich-Rominger of Los Altos, California, a firm specializing in microelectronics and biosciences architecture. Ehrlich-Rominger had been founded in 1968 and boasted 125 employees and branch offices in Sacramento, San Diego, Tucson, and Boise. The previous year (1998), HDR had acquired Simpson Group, an architectural and engineering firm based in San Antonio, Texas that had an 80-year history. Two other acquisitions were made in 2000: Edward Consulting Engineerings, Inc., served the electronic and heavy industrial manufacturing sectors, and selected assets of Braun Intertec Corporation related to environmental consulting.

## Key Dates:

**1917:** Henningson Engineering is founded to design infrastructure for Midwestern communities.
**1937:** Henningson survives Great Depression through REA work.
**1950:** The firm is renamed Henningson, Durham & Richardson after taking on two new partners.
**1983:** French construction company Bouygues S.A. buys HDR.
**1996:** Employees buy HDR back from Bouygues.
**1999:** HDR buys high-tech design firm Ehrlich-Rominger.

The purchase of Ehrlich-Rominger made that company's leader, Robert D. Cavigli, HDR's largest shareholder. In May 2000 Cavigli became president of the HDR Architecture subsidiary, which accounted for a quarter of the firm's total billings. The engineering unit accounted for the other three-fourths.

In early 2001, HDR cut 60 jobs from its science and technology areas, which had suffered from weakness in the national economy. The company's other divisions, however, continued their streak of uninterrupted growth begun after HDR's buyback from the French. Revenues were expected to reach $450 million in 2001.

### *Principal Subsidiaries*

HDR Architecture, Inc.; HDR Construction Control Corporation; HDR Design-Build, Inc.; HDR Engineering, Inc.

### *Principal Divisions*

Environmental and Resource Management Group; Healthcare Group; Interiors Group; Justice Division; Management Consulting Group; Planning and Development; Project Development; Science and Technology; Sustainable Design Group; Transportation Services; Water Group.

### *Principal Competitors*

CH2M Hill Inc.; HNTB Corp.; The Louis Berger Group; Parsons Brinckerhoff Inc.; Sargent & Lundy LLC; URS.

### *Further Reading*


De Zutter, Mary, ''HDR Built Revenue in '94,'' *Omaha World-Herald,* Bus. Sec., April 29, 1995, p. 38.

Durham, Charles W., and Robert F. Krohn, *Henningson, Durham & Richardson: Offering Professional Design Services Since 1917,* New York: Newcomen Society in North America, 1978.

Jordon, Steve, ''Engineering Firm Aims High; Workers' Buyback Energizes HDR Inc.,'' *Omaha World-Herald,* March 4, 2001, p. 1M.

——, ''HDR Buys California-Based Ehrlich-Rominger,'' *Omaha World-Herald,* Bus. Sec., August 4, 1999, p. 22.

——, ''Omaha, Neb. Architectural Firm Fetched $60 Million in 1983 Sale,'' *Omaha World-Herald,* December 15, 1998.

Kelley, Matt, ''HDR's Chief Executive to Move to Texas April 1,'' *Omaha World-Herald,* Bus. Sec., March 13, 1995, p. 12.

Korman, Richard, ''Salvage Blunders Prove Costly,'' *ENR,* June 30, 1997, p. 10.

Olson, Chris, ''HDR Inc. to Expand Headquarters,'' *Omaha World-Herald,* April 16, 1997, p. C3.

——, ''Omaha-Based HDR Celebrates Ending of Its French Ownership,'' *Omaha World-Herald,* September 6, 1996, p. B16.

——, ''Omaha Firm on Track with Transportation Projects,'' *Omaha World-Herald,* March 12, 1996, p. B16.

——, ''Workers to Return HDR Ownership to Omaha,'' *Omaha World-Herald,* April 3, 1996, p. B22.

Reilly, Bob, ed., *Lucky* (biography of Charles W. Durham), Omaha: Barnhart Press, 1998.

Taylor, John, ''Achieving a Goal of His Youth, a French Native Builds a Career at HDR, a Life in the USA,'' *Omaha World-Herald,* November 20, 1994, p. 1M.


—Frederick C. Ingram

# Hugo Boss AG

**Dieselstrasse 12**
**D-72555 Metzingen**
**Germany**
**Telephone: (49) (7123) 94-0**
**Fax: (49) (7123) 94-2014**
**Web site: http://www.hugoboss.com**

*Public Company*
*Incorporated:* 1985
*Employees:* 4,240
*Sales:* $969.7 million (2001)
*Stock Exchanges:* Frankfurt
*Ticker Symbol:* BOS
*NAIC:* 315220 Men's and Boys' Cut and Sew Apparel Manufacturing; 315234 Women's and Girls' Cut and Sew Suit, Coat, Tailored Jacket, and Skirt Manufacturing

Hugo Boss AG is Germany's largest manufacturer of men's and women's clothing and one of the world's leading design houses for men's fashion. The group consists of four major divisions: Hugo Boss AG (company headquarters); Switzerland-based Hugo Boss Industries (the group's second logistics and management center); Hugo Boss Textile Industry (the company's major production plant in Izmir, Turkey); and American subsidiary Hugo Boss USA. The Hugo Boss line of products includes the three main men's business wear brands—Boss, Hugo, and Baldessarini—as well as the more casual Boss Sports and Boss Golf lines. The company also designs and licenses accessories and fragrances and launched its first line of women's business wear in the late 1990s. Hugo Boss fashions are sold in more than 90 countries around the world through over 350 mono-brand franchise shops, as well as through upscale specialty stores and retail chains. About 65 percent of the company's sales derive from Europe; Germany is its biggest market and the United States its second biggest. The Italian textile group Marzotto owns a 50.7 percent share in Hugo Boss.

### *1923–45: The Dark Era*

In 1923, the year when post-World War I Germany was shaken by high unemployment and hyperinflation, German master tailor Hugo Boss set up shop in the small town of Metzingen, about 20 miles south of Stuttgart. Boss started out making protective suits for industrial workers and other work clothes for men. Other Boss specialties were raincoats and uniforms. Over the years the tailor's workshop grew into a small factory.

When Germany—led by Adolf Hitler's National Socialist regime—went to war again in 1939, uniforms were in high demand. One year before the company's 75th anniversary, in August 1997, the Austrian current affairs magazine *Profil* reported that Hugo Boss's name appeared on a list of dormant Swiss bank accounts, revealing that the company produced uniforms for the Nazis, using forced laborers from France and Poland, during World War II. Two months after the article appeared, Hugo Boss's top management assigned a historian from a nearby university to research and document the company's history during the infamous Nazi era and in 1999 pledged to reimburse its former slave laborers.

### *1967–92: The Holy Era*

Nineteen years after the death of company founder Hugo Boss in 1948, two of his grandsons, in their mid-20s, Uwe and Jochen Holy, took over the firm. The business-savvy brothers turned the company around completely, steering it into a new, more promising direction: men's wear. While Jochen, the younger brother by two years, had a sense for the latest trends, his older brother Uwe developed the necessary marketing strategies. When Hugo Boss entered the market in the second half of the 1960s, Germany's men's wear manufacturers were trying to price one another out of the market in order to get a bigger peace of a shrinking pie. They had modernized their production plants and increased their capacities to satisfy the exploding demand during Germany's postwar economic boom. However, the short recession of 1966 signaled the end of the German ''economic miracle.'' Under the Holy brothers, Hugo Boss started making brown, blue, green, and black suits for men. The good-quality, sturdy fabric they used was also made in Metzingen, by textile maker Gaenslen &

## Company Perspectives:

*HUGO BOSS stands for innovation, creativity, and progress. Its objective is to further consolidate its position as a leading international fashion group and grow with its brands. HUGO BOSS implements stringent design and quality standards to produce superior products that deliver value for money. All the brand collections adhere to a lifestyle philosophy featuring a distinctive brand signature.* BOSS. *The core brand BOSS stands for clear-cut, contemporary design and high-quality detail. A perfect fit and specially selected fabric qualities form the starting point for the BOSS collections—for men and women, for every occasion.* HUGO. *Unconventional yet high-quality. Progressive yet tastefully casual—HUGO embraces contradictions. The brand for modern, self-assured men and women with their own individual styles.* BALDESSARINI. *Character and profile, paired with a passion for the finest fabrics and superb tailoring: the BALDESSARINI luxury collection. For men of consummate sophistication.*

Voelter. Priced above average and cut in a more youthful way than the suits of the German men's wear establishment of the time, the suits and jackets of the Holy brothers outperformed all their competitors' within just a decade. Traditionally, German suits for men were made out of stiff and heavy fabrics. At the turn of the decade, however, Hugo Boss introduced new lines of suits made out of high-quality, extremely light Italian fabrics in fashionable colors and designs. In the 1970s, the company began to charge even higher prices for their attractive new product lines. At the same time, they pioneered the trend to manufacture abroad, a trend that would later move all but a fraction of the German apparel industry outside the country's borders. The Holy brothers also conquered foreign markets for Hugo Boss. The resulting stream of cash flow allowed the company to prosper at a previously unknown level.

The melange of high-quality men's fashion made from Italian wool, silk, linen, or cotton in cutting-edge designs, in connection with massive advertising campaigns and clever product placement, made Hugo Boss the trend setter for a new generation of young, ambitious businessmen. After the Boss suit had conquered Western Europe, the apparel maker made the crucial step across the Atlantic. While the unknown German label was met with skepticism when the first Boss suits hit the stores in the United States in 1976, its acceptance grew steadily. Popularized by the testimonials of physically fit and handsome men such as star actor Sylvester Stallone, top athletes such as the five-time Wimbledon tennis champion Bjorn Borg, and the "swaggering, stubble-cheeked cops of television's *Miami Vice* in its signature palette of Baskin-Robbins pastels"—as described in *Forbes* by Joshua Levine—the Hugo Boss look represented the image of the successful professional with a hint of macho. For the youngsters who could not yet afford the broad-shouldered $400 to $500 Boss power suits, the company started making more casual wear such as sweaters and sports jackets in the mid-1980s.

In 1980, Hugo Boss passed the DM 100 million sales mark for the first time. Five years later the company went public, and concentrated on expanding geographically. Only one year after its initial public offering (IPO), Hugo Boss was worth more than the rest of the German men's wear manufacturers combined. By 1987, Hugo Boss grossed DM 500 million annually, reaching almost DM 1 billion by the end of the decade. At the peak of the company's success, in 1989, the Holy brothers sold a big chunk of the Hugo Boss shares to the Japanese Leyton House Group but remained actively involved in the firm's management. In 1991, the Italian fashion giant Marzotto became Hugo Boss's new parent company. Two years later, the Holy brothers, who had made Hugo Boss into Germany's largest manufacturer of men's wear and a leading force in the global high-fashion industry, retired from Hugo Boss management but kept running a couple of Holy's upscale men's wear designer stores in Munich and Stuttgart which remained under the umbrella of the Hugo Boss group.

### *1993–97: The Littmann Era*

In 1993, Hugo Boss stock was traded at less than half the price that the Holy brothers cashed in when they sold a 64 percent share to Leyton House. The German fashion industry was struggling with the economic recession that started in 1992. Consumers cut back on expensive clothing and retail sales dropped significantly, especially in the men's wear segment. At the same time, personnel cost rose and a devaluation of the Italian Lira by 20 to 30 percent gave the Italian men's fashion designers a huge price advantage over Boss. On top of that, consumers changed their basic values at the onset of the 1990s. The "yuppie"-era of conspicuous consumption that characterized the 1980s was replaced by a "new modesty" accompanied by a higher emphasis on teamwork and family values. The signs were clear: the company needed to change in order to stop the trend of declining profits. Struggling with shrinking profit margins themselves, the Marzotto group took a bold step when they hired Peter Littmann as new CEO of Hugo Boss. The 46-year-old native Czech with a Ph.D. in business administration from the University of Cologne was experienced in marketing textiles internationally—of a different kind however, namely carpets. However, he turned out to be an excellent choice. The fashion novice managed to put the company back on the growth track in record time.

After renaming the company Hugo Boss to soften that "bossy" image, Littmann decided to launch two additional labels besides Boss under the umbrella brand Hugo Boss, enabling the company to take a more sophisticated marketing approach. The first new label, Hugo, was aimed at younger professionals interested in trendy fashion who made their own decisions about what to wear—unlike their elder counterparts who reportedly more often than not let their wives make their fashion choices. Hugo suits went for about 10 percent less than the traditional Boss suit, which then cost between $500 and $800. The second novelty brand was named Baldessarini after the company's chief designer of many years. The Italian appeal of the Austrian native's name was purposefully used to communicate the exclusivity of this new line of fashion, which was targeted at the financially independent top executive who could afford the luxury of a perfectly tailored $1,500 suit made from only the best Italian fabrics. The classical Boss suit was renamed Boss Hugo Boss and the big shoulders of the 1980s were rounded off.

## Key Dates:

**1923:** German tailor Hugo Boss sets up his workshop in Metzingen.
**1948:** Company founder Hugo Boss dies.
**1967:** The Holy brothers take over management and transform the company into a men's fashion manufacturer.
**1985:** The company goes public and is renamed Hugo Boss AG.
**1991:** Marzotto S.p.A. becomes majority shareholder.
**1993:** The Holy brothers resign from management and are succeeded by new CEO Peter Littmann.
**1998:** Long-time chief designer Werner Baldessarini becomes CEO.
**1998:** Hugo Boss launches its first collection for women.

The three-label strategy was carried out very thoroughly by three separate teams for product development and sales to separate distribution outlets. To clearly distinguish the three new labels, men's fashion retailers had to limit themselves to only the one of them with the highest appeal to the store's core group of customers—which in the beginning caused some raised eyebrows and even resistance among retailers. Other leading design houses, such as Armani, placed merchandise with one brand name but different price levels, in the same store to attract a larger group of buyers. Littmann, however, wanted to prevent the watering down of the perceived high-value brand recognition of the Hugo Boss labels.

After Littmann had introduced the three-brand idea at his first board meeting in March 1993, he challenged the company's ambitious young management team to pull off the project in just three months—a quarter of the time they said they needed. The three new lines of Hugo Boss men's fashion were first shown in Cologne to an audience of 3,000 in the summer of the same year. In the following years, the range of labels was further diversified, including Boss Golf, Boss Sport, and Boss Black Label.

To further cut production costs, Littmann moved abroad half of the manufacturing still done in Germany—mainly to eastern Europe, where costs were between 70 and 90 percent lower—leaving the share of domestic production at one-fifth of the total. However, sewing men's suits is a rather complicated task that requires some skill and experience. Though Hugo Boss did not own most of the production plants, the company trained the workers in the Czech Republic, Slovakia, and Romania to ensure its quality standards. Only a handful of highly skilled German workers carried out the most difficult jobs, such as sewing the sleeves onto the jackets, at the company's Metzingen plant.

Littmann's bold strategy was doubtfully watched by industry insiders, competitors, and men's clothing retailers. Ultimately, it was a huge success. While total sales declined, profits jumped by 74 percent in 1994, the year after the launch of the three-brand campaign. Besides his three-label strategy, Littmann focused on expanding the company's global reach. One of the new markets the company focused on was Southeast Asia, where a subsidiary was established in Hong Kong and a number of Hugo Boss stores were opened in urban centers such as Tokyo, Beijing, and Shanghai. By the end of 1996, about two thirds of Hugo Boss's sales originated outside of Germany. The United States accounted for about one-fifth of the total.

After this impressive accomplishment it was rather surprising that Littmann resigned as Hugo Boss CEO. When his contract expired at the end of 1997, Littmann did not renew. The company announced that there was some disagreement over Hugo Boss's strategic direction. However, industry insiders speculated that Littmann had a hard time getting along with Marzotto's new CEO Jean de Jaegher. Joachim Vogt, on Hugo Boss's executive board responsible for production and logistics since 1990, took over as CEO in February 1997. Two other top executives joined the company at about the same time. Massimo Suppancig, the former vice-president of global marketing and business development of Munich-based women's fashion house Escada was appointed executive director of the Hugo Boss women's wear division. In the United States, former president and CEO of men's apparel maker Calvin Klein, Marty Staff, was appointed as the new boss of Hugo Boss USA.

### *1998–2001: The Baldessarini Era*

Joachim Vogt's term as CEO of Hugo Boss lasted one and a half years. He focused on what he could do best: optimizing production processes and logistics. However, for a top-notch men's fashion house, that was not enough. In November 1998, Hugo Boss officially announced that the company's upper management disagreed with Vogt's strategic goals and that Werner Baldessarini would take his place. The 55-year-old chief designer and marketing manager, who had joined the company in 1975, did not have a formal education in business administration but had been a member of the Hugo Boss executive board since 1988.

Despite the fact that the company's sales and profits were growing, the value of Hugo Boss stock stagnated after Baldessarini took over as CEO. Only when the new CEO announced his strategy to transform the company from a men's tailor to a lifestyle empire did the stock market take notice. By that time, Hugo Boss's line of products had expanded to include men's sportswear, shirts, underwear, and licensed accessories such as ties and sunglasses. However, the classic Boss Hugo Boss suit collection still brought in 90 percent of the company's revenues. The company's new collection for spring and summer 2000 featured a look that Baldessarini described as soft and modern at the same time, a mixture of romance and technology. It was first presented in Florence, Italy, and not—as usually—in Cologne.

Baldessarini greatly expanded the company's network of outlets to get closer to the customer. Hugo Boss products were already sold in 92 countries around the world. In 1999 and 2000, 130 new Hugo Boss stores were opened, increasing the company's distribution outlets to 300. Hugo Boss's presence in the United States, the company's second biggest market after Germany, grossing about $100 million, consisted of thirteen freestanding Hugo Boss franchise stores and nine shops inside larger specialty stores. Within two years, 23 new stores were opened, not only in cultural centers on the east and west coasts but also in lower-profile locations such as Paramus, New Jersey, King of Prussia, Pennsylvania, and at the Mall of America in Bloomington, Minnesota. In April 2001, the company opened one of the country's biggest designer stores on New York's Fifth Avenue. On 23,000 square meters, the four-level flagship store presented everything Hugo Boss had to offer, with men's wear accounting for about two-thirds and women's wear for the other third of the merchandise on display.

Hugo Boss continued its product placement and sponsoring activities. The Hugo Boss label got exposure in the Hollywood movies *Weapon 4*, *Godzilla*, and *The Professionals*. Since 1984, the company sponsored a Formula One Mercedes team and several top golf professionals. However, the company's new promotional strategy included a new focus on arts and culture, sponsoring a tour of prominent hip-hop artists and hosting the premiere for the movie *Charlie's Angels* in 2000. The event at Mann's Chinese Theater was attended by such actresses as Cameron Diaz and Drew Barrymore wearing Boss Woman, the second line of women's wear after the launch of Hugo Woman in 1998. The company added new ways to attract more customers, including in-store events, image seminars, and deliveries to hotels and offices.

In December 2001, Baldessarini announced that he would step down as Hugo Boss CEO and member of the executive board when his five-year contract expired in mid-2002. He said that he would be available as creative consultant but wanted to retire from the day-to-day operation of the business. During his tenure the company's sales grew between 18 and 22 percent annually. The company's stock traded in Frankfurt/Main doubled in value during 2000. In his foreword to the company's *2001 Annual Report*, Baldessarini, one of the apparel world's creative master minds who had been one of the major driving forces behind Hugo Boss, described his philosophy: ''As fashion definers and designers, ours is the task of enriching our social order with creative impulses. We make dreams come true, and enhance reality with elegance and beauty. Design and style lend progress an attractive face, meeting needs that are less tangible but all the more essential.''

Dr. Bruno Salzer succeeded Werner Baldessarini in July 2001. He defined the company's major short-term tasks: to make Hugo Boss's lines for women—which had not been as successful as the company expected—profitable, to expand the company's production facilities and cut costs, and to add new stores to the Hugo Boss distribution network, especially in Scandinavia and Belgium. Looking out into the future beyond 2003, Salzer could see Hugo Boss growing through acquisitions if the company's own organic growth should slow down.

## *Principal Subsidiaries*

Hugo Boss Industries S.A. (Switzerland); Bentex Holding S.A. (Switzerland); Werner Baldessarini Design GmbH; Hugo Boss Textile Industry, Ltd. (Turkey); Eura 2000 S.A. (Luxembourg); Hugo Boss España, S.A. (Spain); Hugo Boss Outlet Magazacilik Limited Sirketi (Turkey); Holy's GmbH (Germany); Hugo Boss RETAIL SARL (France); Hugo Boss International B.V. (Netherlands); Hugo Boss (Schweitz) AG (Switzerland); Hugo Boss France SARL (France); Hugo Boss UK Ltd.; Hugo Boss Nederland B.V. (Netherlands); Hugo Boss S.p.A. (Italy); Hugo Boss Italia S.p.A. (Italy); Della Croce SRL (Italy); Hugo Boss USA, Inc.; Hugo Boss, Inc. (U.S.); AMBRA, Inc. (U.S.); Hugo Boss Fashions, Inc. (U.S.); Hugo Boss Outlet, Inc. (U.S.); Hugo Boss Licensing, Inc. (U.S.); Hugo Boss Cleveland, Inc. (U.S.); The Joseph & Feiss Company (U.S.); Hugo Boss Canada, Inc.; Hugo Boss do Brasil Ltda. (Brazil); Hugo Boss Australia Pty. Ltd.; Hugo Boss Hong Kong Ltd.; Hugo Boss K.K. (Japan); Hugo Boss Mexico S.A. de C.V.

## *Principal Competitors*

Giorgio Armani S.p.A.; Gianni Versace SpA; Gucci Group N.V.

## *Further Reading*

Alexander, Charles P., ''A Boss Look for the Boardroom: West Germany Becomes a Force in Men's Fashion,'' *Time*, September 10, 1984, p. 41.

Board, Laura, ''Boss Reaches for the Stars to Aid Sales,'' *European*, April 18, 1996, p. 21.

Borowski, Barbara, ''Hugo Boss kündigt eigene Damenkollektion an,'' *HORIZONT*, April 10, 1997, p. 17.

''Boss im neuen Markenkleid,'' *Werben und Verkaufen*, April 22, 1994, p. 62.

Brown, Audrey, ''Better Suited for Good Business,'' *International Management*, September 1994, p. 34.

Conti, Samantha, ''Boss Shows Its Softer, Sensitive Side,'' *Daily News Record*, June 16, 1999, p. 4.

D'Aulnay, Sophie, and Stan Gellers, ''Hugo Boss Buys Della Croce, Its Swiss-Based Shirt Licensee; Denies Joseph & Feiss Division for Sale,'' *Daily News Record*, October 23, 1996, p. 2.

''Erfolg der Marke,'' *TextilWirtschaft*, April 4, 1996, p. 68.

Gellers, Stan, ''Baldessarini: The Thoroughly Modern Boss,'' *Daily News Record*, March 1, 1999, p. 52.

Goldman, Lea, ''The Boss Is Back,'' *Forbes*, January 22, 2001, p. 114.

''Hugo Boss to Be Major Sponsor of the Guggenheim Foundation,'' *Daily News Record*, March 2, 1995, p. 5.

Lockwood, Lisa, ''Hugo Boss Seeking to Clear Up Concerns About WWII Activities,'' *WWD*, August 14, 1997, p. 13.

Lohrer, Robert, ''Hugo Boss Sets Store on Top of Fifth Avenue Site,'' *WWD*, July 17, 2000, p. 2.

''Peter Littmann Leaving Boss at End of the Year; Joachim Vogt Tapped to Take Over,'' *Daily News Record*, January 15, 1997, p. 1.

Sims, Joshua, ''Profit & Boss,'' *European*, November 30, 1998, p. 28.

—Evelyn Hauser

# Indian Oil Corporation Ltd.

**Core-2**
**Scope Complex, 7, Institutional Area Lodhi Road**
**New Delhi 1100 003**
**India**
**Telephone: (91) 11 436-2896**
**Fax: (91) 11 436-4602**
**Web site: http://www.iocl.com**

*Public Company*
*Incorporated:* 1964
*Employees:* 32,266
*Sales:* Rs 113.32 billion ($24.2 billion) (2001)
*Stock Exchanges:* Mumbai
*Ticker Symbol:* 530965
*NAIC:* 324110 Petroleum Refineries

The Indian Oil Corporation Ltd. operates as the largest company in India in terms of turnover and is the only Indian company to rank in the Fortune ''Global 500'' listing. The oil concern is administratively controlled by India's Ministry of Petroleum and Natural Gas, a government entity that owns just over 90 percent of the firm. Since 1959, this refining, marketing, and international trading company served the Indian state with the important task of reducing India's dependence on foreign oil and thus conserving valuable foreign exchange. That changed in April 2002, however, when the Indian government deregulated its petroleum industry and ended Indian Oil's monopoly on crude oil imports. The firm owns and operates seven of the 17 refineries in India, controlling nearly 40 percent of the country's refining capacity.

## *Origins*

Indian Oil owes its origins to the Indian government's conflicts with foreign-owned oil companies in the period immediately following India's independence in 1947. The leaders of the newly independent state found that much of the country's oil industry was effectively in the hands of a private monopoly led by a combination of British-owned oil companies Burmah and Shell and U.S. companies Standard-Vacuum and Caltex.

An indigenous Indian industry barely existed. During the 1930s, a small number of Indian oil traders had managed to trade outside the international cartel. They imported motor spirit, diesel, and kerosene, mainly from the Soviet Union, at less than world market prices. Supplies were irregular, and they lacked marketing networks that could effectively compete with the multinationals.

Burmah-Shell entered into price wars against these independents, causing protests in the national press, which demanded government-set minimum and maximum prices for kerosene—a basic cooking and lighting requirement for India's people—and motor spirit. No action was taken, but some of the independents managed to survive until World War II, when they were taken over by the colonial government for wartime purposes.

During the war, the supply of petroleum products in India was regulated by a committee in London. Within India, a committee under the chairmanship of the general manager of Burmah-Shell and composed of oil company representatives pooled the supply and worked out a set price. Prices were regulated by the government, and the government coordinated the supply of oil in accordance with defense policy.

## *The Indian Oil Industry Evolves: Late 1940s–60s*

Wartime rationing lasted until 1950, and a shortage of oil products continued until well after independence. The government's 1948 Industrial Policy Resolution declared the oil industry to be an area of the economy that should be reserved for state ownership and control, stipulating that all new units should be government-owned unless specifically authorized. India remained effectively tied to a colonial supply system, however. Oil could only be afforded if imported from a country in the sterling area rather than from countries where it had to be paid for in dollars. In 1949, India asked the oil companies of Britain and the United States to offer advice on a refinery project to make the country more self-sufficient in oil. The joint technical committee advised against the project and said it could only be run at a considerable loss.

The oil companies were prepared to consider building two refineries, but only if these refineries were allowed to sell products at a price ten percent above world parity price. The

**Company Perspectives:**

*We strive be a major diversified, transnational, integrated energy company, with national leadership and a strong environmental conscience, playing a national role in oil security and public distribution.*

government refused, but within two years an event in the Persian Gulf caused the companies to change their minds and build the refineries. The companies had lost their huge refinery at Abadan in Iran to Prime Minister Mussadegh's nationalization decree and were unable to supply India's petroleum needs from a sterling-area country. With the severe foreign exchange problems created, the foreign companies feared new Iranian competition within India. Even more important, the government began to discuss setting up a refinery by itself.

Between 1954 and 1957, two refineries were built by Burmah-Shell and Standard-Vacuum at Bombay, and another was built at Vizagapatnam by Caltex. During the same period the companies found themselves in increasing conflict with the government.

The government came into disagreement with Burmah Oil over the Nahorkatiya oil field shortly after its discovery in 1953. It refused Burmah the right to refine or market this oil and insisted on joint ownership in crude production. Burmah then temporarily suspended all exploration activities in India.

Shortly afterward, the government accused the companies of charging excessive prices for importing oil. The companies also refused to refine Soviet oil that the government had secured on very favorable terms. The government was impatient with the companies' reluctance to expand refining capacity or train sufficient Indian personnel. In 1958, the government formed its own refinery company, Indian Refineries Ltd. With Soviet and Romanian assistance, the company was able to build its own refineries at Noonmati, Barauni, and Koyali. Foreign companies were told that they would not be allowed to build any new refineries unless they agreed to a majority shareholding by the Indian government.

In 1959, the Indian Oil Company was founded as a statutory body. At first, its objective was to supply oil products to Indian state enterprise. Then it was made responsible for the sale of the products of state refineries. After a 1961 price war with the foreign companies, it emerged as the nation's major marketing body for the export and import of oil and gas.

Growing Soviet imports led the foreign companies to respond with a price war in August 1961. At this time, Indian Oil had no retail outlets and could sell only to bulk consumers. The oil companies undercut Indian Oil's prices and left it with storage problems. Indian Oil then offered even lower prices. The foreign companies were the ultimate losers because the government was persuaded that a policy of allowing Indian Oil dominance in the market was correct. This policy allowed Indian Oil the market share of the output of all refineries that were partly or wholly owned by the government. Foreign oil companies would only be allowed such market share as equaled their share of refinery capacity.

### *Indian Oil Corporation: 1964 to the 1990s*

In September 1964, Indian Refineries Ltd. and the Indian Oil Company were merged to form the Indian Oil Corporation. The government announced that all future refinery partnerships would be required to sell their products through Indian Oil.

It was widely expected that Indian Oil and India's Oil and Natural Gas Commission (ONGC) would eventually be merged into a single state monopoly company. Both companies grew vastly in size and sales volume but, despite close links, they remained separate. ONGC retained control of most of the country's exploration and production capacity. Indian Oil remained responsible for refining and marketing.

During this same decade, India found that rapid industrialization meant a large fuel bill, which was a steady drain on foreign exchange. To meet the crisis, the government prohibited imported petroleum and petroleum product imports by private companies. In effect, Indian Oil was given a monopoly on oil imports.

A policy of state control was reinforced by India's closer economic and political links with the Soviet Union and its isolation from the mainstream of western multinational capitalism. Although India identified its international political stance as non-aligned, the government became increasingly friendly with the Soviet Bloc, because the United States and China were seen as too closely linked to India's major rival, Pakistan. India and the USSR entered into a number of trade deals. One of the most important of these trade pacts allowed Indian Oil to import oil from the USSR and Romania at prices lower than those prevailing in world markets and to pay in local currency, rather than dollars or other convertible currencies.

For a time, no more foreign refineries were allowed. By the mid-1960s, government policy was modified to allow expansions of foreign-owned refinery capacity. The Indian Oil Corporation worked out barter agreements with major oil companies in order to facilitate distribution of refinery products.

In the 1970s, the Oil and Natural Gas Commission of India, with the help of Soviet and other foreign companies, made several important new finds off the west coast of India, but this increased domestic supply was unable to keep up with demand. When international prices rose steeply after the 1973 Arab oil boycott, India's foreign exchange problems mounted. Indian Oil's role as the country's monopoly buyer gave the company an increasingly important role in the economy. While the Soviet Union continued to be an important supplier, Indian Oil also bought Saudi, Iraqi, Kuwaiti, and United Arab Emirate oil. India became the largest single purchaser of crude on the Dubai spot market.

The government decided to nationalize the country's remaining refineries. The Burmah-Shell refinery at Bombay and the Caltex refinery at Vizagapatnam were taken over in 1976. The Burmah-Shell refinery became the main asset of a new state company, Bharat Petroleum Ltd. Caltex Oil Refining (India) Ltd. was amalgamated with another state company, Hindustan Petroleum Corporation Ltd., in March 1978. Hindustan had become fully Indian-owned on October 1, 1976, when Esso's 26 percent share was bought out. On October 14, 1981, Burmah Oil's remaining interests in the Assam Oil Company were

**Key Dates:**

**1948:** India's government passes the Industrial Policy Resolution, which states that its oil industry should be state-owned and operated.
**1958:** The government forms its own refinery company, Indian Refineries Ltd.
**1959:** Indian Oil Company is founded as a statutory body to supply oil products to Indian state enterprise.
**1964:** Indian Refineries and Indian Oil Company merge to form the Indian Oil Corporation.
**1976:** The Burmah-Shell and the Caltex refineries are nationalized.
**1981:** Half of India's 12 refineries are operated by Indian Oil.
**1998:** The company's seventh refinery is commissioned at Panipat.
**2002:** The Indian petroleum industry is deregulated.

nationalized, and Indian Oil took over its refining and marketing activities. Half of India's 12 refineries belonged to Indian Oil. The other half belonged to other state-owned companies.

By the end of the 1980s, India's oil consumption continued to grow at eight percent per year, and Indian Oil expanded its capacity to about 150 million barrels of crude per annum. In 1989, Indian Oil announced plans to build a new refinery at Pradip and modernize the Digboi refinery, India's oldest. However, the government's Public Investment Board refused to approve a 120,000 barrels-per-day refinery at Daitari in Orissa because it feared future over-capacity.

By the early 1990s, Indian Oil refined, produced, and transported petroleum products throughout India. Indian Oil produced crude oil, base oil, formula products, lubricants, greases, and other petroleum products. It was organized into three divisions. The refineries and pipelines division had six refineries, located at Gwahati, Barauni, Gujarat, Haldia, Mathura, and Digboi. Together, the six represented 45 percent of the country's refining capacity. The division also laid and managed oil pipelines. The marketing division was responsible for storage and distribution and controlled about 60 percent of the total oil industry sales. The Assam Oil division controlled the marketing and distribution activities of the formerly British-owned company.

Indian Oil also established its own research center at Faridabad near New Delhi for testing lubricants and other petroleum products. It developed lubricants under the brand names Servo and Servoprime. The center also designed fuel-efficient equipment.

## *Changes in the Oil Industry: Late 1990s and Beyond*

The oil industry in India changed dramatically throughout the 1990s and into the new millennium. Reform in the downstream hydrocarbon sector—the sector in which Indian Oil was the market leader—began as early in 1991 and continued throughout the decade. In 1997, the government announced that the Administered Pricing Mechanism (APM) would be dismantled by 2002.

To prepare for the increased competition that deregulation would bring, Indian Oil added a seventh refinery to its holdings in 1998 when the Panipat facility was commissioned. The company also looked to strengthen its industry position by forming joint ventures. In 1993, the firm teamed up with Balmer Lawrie & Co. and NYCO SA of France to create Avi-Oil India Ltd., a manufacturer of oil products used by defense and civil aviation firms. One year later, Indo Mobil Ltd. was formed in a 50–50 joint venture with Exxon Mobil. The new company imported and blended Mobil brand lubricants for marketing in India, Nepal, and Bhutan. In addition, Indian Oil was involved in the formation of ten major ventures from 1996 through 2000.

Indian Oil also entered the public arena as the government divested nearly 10 percent of the company. In 2000, Indian Oil and ONGC traded a 10 percent equity stake in each other in a strategic alliance that would better position the two after the APM dismantling, which was scheduled for 2002. According to a 1999 *Hindu* article, Indian Oil Corporation's strategy at this time was "to become a diversified, integrated global energy corporation." The article went on to claim that "while maintaining its leadership in oil refining, marketing and pipeline transportation, it aims for higher growth through integration and diversification. For this, it is harnessing new business opportunities in petrochemicals, power, lube marketing, exploration and production . . . and fuel management in this country and abroad."

In early 2002, Indian Oil acquired IBP, a state-owned petroleum marketing company. The firm also purchased a 26 percent stake in financially troubled Haldia Petrochemicals Ltd. In April of that year, Indian Oil's monopoly over crude imports ended as deregulation of the petroleum industry went into effect. As a result, the company faced increased competition from large international firms as well as new domestic entrants to the market. During the first 45 days of deregulation, Indian Oil lost Rs7.25 billion, a signal that the India's largest oil refiner would indeed face challenges as a result of the changes.

Nevertheless, Indian Oil management believed that the deregulation would bring lucrative opportunities to the company and would eventually allow it to become one of the top 100 companies on the Fortune 500—in 2001 the company was ranked 209. With demand for petroleum products in India projected to grow from 148 million metric tons in 2006 to 368 million metric tons by 2025, Indian Oil believed it was well positioned for future growth and prosperity.

### *Principal Subsidiaries*

Indo Mobil Ltd. (50%); Avi-Oil Ltd. (25%); Indian Oiltanking Ltd. (25%); Petronet India Ltd. (16%); Petronet VK Ltd. (26%); Petronet CTM Ltd. (26%); Petronet CIPL Ltd. (12.5%); IndianOil Petronas Ltd. (50%); IndianOil Panipat Power Consortium Ltd. (26%); IndianOil TCG Petrochem Ltd. (50%); Librizol India Pvt. Ltd. (50%).

### *Principal Competitors*

Bharat Petroleum Corporation Ltd.; Hindustand Petroleum Corporation Ltd.; Royal Dutch/Shell Group of Companies.

### *Further Reading*

''Business Line: Deregulation of Oil Sector: Is Government Prepared?,'' *Chemical Business Newsbase*, March 17, 2002.

''Business Line: IOC Monopoly Over Import Ends,'' *Chemical Business Newsbase*, March 11, 2002.

Dasgupta, Bipab, *The Petroleum Industry in India*, London: Frank Cass & Company, 1971.

''Further Divestment in Indian Corp. Withheld,'' *Hindu*, May 2, 2000.

''Indian Oil Corp. Harnessing New Business Opportunities,'' *Hindu*, April 2, 1999.

''Indian Oil Corp. in Talks for Lifting Entire Oil and Natural Gas Corp. Output,'' *Business Line*, July 12, 1999.

''Indian Oil Firms Lose US$327 Mln During April 1—May 15,'' *AsiaPulse News*, May 27, 2002.

''India's IOC Seeks to be Among World's Top 100 Companies,'' *AsiaPulse News*, March 27, 2002.

''IOC Acquisition of Haldia Petro: Biting Off More Than it Can Chew?,'' *Business Line*, March 31, 2002.

—Clark Siewert
—update: Christina M. Stansell

# Infinity Broadcasting Corporation

**40 West 57th Street**
**New York, New York 10019**
**U.S.A.**
**Telephone: (212) 314-9200**
**Fax: (212) 314-9228**
**Web site: http://www.infinityradio.com**

*Majority-Owned Subsidiary of Viacom Inc.*
*Incorporated:* 1972
*Employees:* 8,200
*Gross Billings:* $3.6 billion (2001)
*NAIC:* 513111 Radio Networks; 513112 Radio Stations

Infinity Broadcasting Corporation operates as one of the largest radio broadcasting companies in the United States with over 180 radio stations in 41 markets. The majority of the company's stations are found in the 50 largest U.S. radio markets. Through the Viacom Outdoor Group, Infinity also operates as the largest outdoor advertising company in North America, offering advertising space on billboards, mall posters, phone kiosks, buses, bus shelters, benches, trains, and train platforms, as well as in commuter rail terminals. The company expanded during the 1980s and early 1990s by acquiring existing stations and successfully cultivating high-profile radio personalities. Infinity came under CBS ownership in 1997 and became a subsidiary of Viacom Inc. as part of the $39.8 billion Viacom/CBS merger.

### *Beginnings*

Infinity was created by partners Michael Wiener and Gerald Carrus, who formed the company in order to purchase KOME, an FM radio station broadcasting in San Jose that also served the San Francisco area. KOME had just received its license to broadcast from the Federal Communications Commission (FCC) in 1971 before Wiener and Carrus assumed ownership in 1973. At the time, FM radio was a burgeoning medium, although one that was still struggling to catch up with the long-popular AM band. As FM gained in popularity during the 1970s, Wiener and Carrus achieved notable success with KOME, eventually expanding it into one of the most successful rock-and-roll stations in its geographic niche.

During the 1970s, Infinity embarked on an acquisition program informed by the strategy that had made KOME profitable; it purchased developing or underperforming radio stations in major markets and then turned them around with improved programming and management. Infinity eventually sold many of these concerns as a way of "trading up" to larger stations. In 1979, Wiener and Carrus brought another FM station under the Infinity umbrella that, like KOME, would stay with the company through the mid-1990s. They purchased WBCN, an underperforming station in Boston that the two believed had the potential to become a local ratings leader. Wiener and Carrus planned to shape WBCN in the image of KOME, making it an album-oriented rock station geared towards males between the ages of 18 and 30.

### *Mel Karmazin Named Infinity President: 1981*

In 1981, Wiener and Carrus brought in Mel Karmazin to serve as company president and to oversee day-to-day operations. The 38-year-old Karmazin, a young, aggressive radio executive, agreed to accept the position with New York-based Infinity for a $125,000 annual salary and an opportunity to own part of the company should he prove responsible for significant growth. His only condition was that he was given total control of its operations. "You can't have three people run a company," Karmazin explained in the November 30, 1992 issue of *Broadcasting*.

Under Karmazin's direction, Infinity experienced steady, rapid growth during the 1980s. During his first year, in fact, he managed buyouts of two New York stations, WXRK-FM and WZRC-AM. He also picked up WYSP-FM in Philadelphia. In 1983, moreover, Infinity absorbed KXYZ-AM in Houston and WJMK-FM and WJJD-AM in Chicago. Those purchases substantially boosted the company's revenues and made it a contender in the upper ranks of the national radio broadcasting industry. Adhering to the company's original strategy of seeking undervalued companies, Karmazin nevertheless changed

## Company Perspectives:

*Infinity seeks to maintain substantial diversity among its radio stations in many respects. The geographically wide-ranging stations serve diverse target demographics through a broad range of programming formats, such as rock, oldies, news/talk, adult contemporary, sports/talk, and country. This diversity provides advertisers with convenience to select stations to reach a targeted demographic group or to select groups of stations to reach broad groups of consumers within and across markets.*

Infinity's direction by accruing a large portfolio of stations, the value of which he intended to increase over the long term.

Although Karmazin had significantly increased Infinity's assets and revenues with the string of early 1980s acquisitions, the company was strapped for cash by mid-decade. In a bid to raise investment capital for continued growth, Karmazin took Infinity public in 1986. Within a year, he had purchased six more stations: KROQ-FM in Los Angeles, WJFK-FM in Washington, D.C., WQYK-FM and WQYK-AM in Tampa, and KVIL-FM and KVIL-AM in Dallas. Then, in 1988, Karmazin and three other company executives borrowed more money in order to repurchase Infinity's stock and take the enterprise private again, reasoning that the stock market had undervalued the company and that they could profit in the future by selling off the repurchased stock. Despite the company's surging debt, management borrowed funds to procure three more stations during the late 1980s: WOMC-FM in Detroit and both WLIF-FM and WFJK-AM in Baltimore.

Infinity's critics during the late 1980s cited the company's high debt load and weak profit performance as evidence of its lackluster potential. However, many analysts believed that the company was a better investment than it appeared. Indeed, by the end of the 1980s, Infinity had positioned itself as a market-niche leader in several major broadcasting regions, a status achieved largely through a formula of developing unique and popular programs aimed at specific demographic groups, which boosted the stations' potential ad revenues. Infinity had been successful in purchasing key sports broadcasting rights, for example, and had cultivated several popular radio personalities, such as New York station WXRK's Howard Stern. Moreover, all of Infinity's stations provided nonentertainment programming, such as news or public affairs broadcasts.

Under Karmazin, stations acquired by Infinity were subjected to a rigorous regimen of financial reporting requirements and cost controls designed to improve their profit margins. In addition, Karmazin's team would adjust a new station's promotional strategy, usually by emphasizing local, rather than national, advertising sales. The overall programming and promotional initiatives usually resulted in high listener loyalty and healthy cash flow for most of Infinity's member stations.

Karmazin became known during the 1980s for his disciplined, hands-on management style. He met several times each week with his management team and continued to personally check up on local advertising accounts as he had since his days as a salesman. He also kept a heavy hand on all of Infinity's larger deals, such as the negotiation of rights to sports broadcasts. Karmazin's penchant for efficiency started at the top; Infinity's entire corporate staff in the early 1990s consisted of six people: Karmazin, a chief financial officer, an administrative assistant, and a three-person accounting office.

Infinity's spartan corporate staff was made possible by the autonomy that Karmazin afforded his local radio affiliates as long as their ratings continued to rise. An important element of Karmazin's strategy was decentralized local management. Infinity relied on a system of performance-based financial incentives to motivate its workers and attract high-quality personnel, who were well-compensated by industry standards. General managers earned money for increasing cash flow, for example, and program directors were rewarded for higher ratings. Karmazin was particularly proud of Infinity's pay scale for advertising salespeople, which was a straight 6 percent commission with no limit on total earnings. Many salespeople earned more than $100,000 annually, with a few topping the $300,000 mark. "If a salesperson is going to get rich on a six percent commission," Karmazin stated in a *Broadcasting* article, "the company is going to get very rich on the other 94 percent."

Karmazin's management talents were perhaps most apparent in the example of Jim Hardy, whom Karmazin hired to serve as general manager of KOME, the first division acquired by Infinity in 1973. Raised in a Colorado goldmining town before the onset of television, Hardy became interested in radio at a young age. He got his start in the business in the 1960s working for his college radio station, one of the first FM stations in Colorado. In 1970, he went on to work for the first all-rock station in the United States, Denver's KLZ-FM. Hardy then served a long stint as a salesman at KWFM in Arizona until the infamous 1982 assassination of that station's disk jockey, Bob Cook, by a fanatic listener. Hardy then became manager of the station and soon thereafter was spotted by Karmazin as a capable candidate for the general management slot at KOME. After accepting the job, Hardy moved KOME to a new facility and began to reposition its programming and promotional operations. Citing consistent support from Infinity and the freedom afforded him in making critical decisions as contributing factors to his success, Hardy successfully increased the station's ratings and advertising revenue. By the late 1980s, KOME was rated the best medium-market radio station by readers of *Rolling Stone* magazine and was finishing tops in the important 25 to 54-year-old demographic ratings. "Gold mining is just like radio," Hardy noted in the April 2, 1990, issue of *Business Journal-San Jose*, in that "you dig a lot of dirt and hope you strike gold."

Despite the success of KOME and several other member stations, Infinity's performance lagged following the stock buyback of 1988. In addition to the company's huge debt load, which topped $450 million in 1989, poor advertising revenues during the U.S. recession damaged Infinity's bottom line. While sales increased slowly to $123 million in 1989 and then to $135 million in 1991, the company posted successive net losses totaling more than $100 million during that period. Nevertheless, Infinity retained its strength in core markets and managed to sustain a healthy cash flow, an important measure of health for radio stations.

**Key Dates:**

**1972:** Michael Wiener and Gerald Carrus form Infinity.
**1979:** Infinity purchases the FM station WBCN.
**1981:** Mel Karmazin is named company president.
**1986:** Infinity goes public.
**1988:** Believing the stock market has undervalued Infinity, Karmazin and three company executives take Infinity private.
**1992:** The company earns $100 million in a second public offering.
**1997:** Infinity merges with Westinghouse Electric Corp., the parent company of CBS Inc.
**1998:** CBS announces the spin off of its radio and outdoor advertising businesses as Infinity Broadcasting.
**1999:** Outdoor Systems Inc. is acquired for $8.3 billion.
**2000:** CBS and Viacom Inc. merge; Infinity becomes a subsidiary of Viacom.
**2001:** The Viacom Outdoor Group is created and operates as the largest outdoor advertiser in the United States.

### *Going Public Again: 1992*

In an effort to slash its debt and continue acquiring new stations, Infinity elected to go public again in 1992, earning $100 million in the offering, much of which was used to buy WFAN-AM in New York. Early in 1993, Infinity borrowed money to purchase three additional stations—WUSN-FM in Chicago, WZLX-FM in Boston, and WZGC-FM in Atlanta—for a total of $100 million. Of all its acquisitions, the WFAN purchase garnered the most criticism from industry analysts, who regarded Infinity's payout of $70 million as excessive for an AM station, particularly a station that was not ranked in the top ten in its locale. Nevertheless, Karmazin viewed the addition as complementary to his strategy of focusing on radio sports; WFAN was an all-sports station.

In 1992, Infinity began to rebound as sales increased about 29 percent and net losses were cut to about $9.4 million, largely the result of a general economic recovery. In mid-1993, the company initiated another stock offering in order to help pare its debt. Perhaps most importantly, many of Infinity's marketing strategies were beginning to pay off during this time. Having cultivated what was possibly the most impressive assemblage of high-profile talk and sport show talent in the business, Infinity was prepared when the popularity of talk and sports radio experienced a rebirth. Among its most notable local celebrities were: Don Imus (WFAN); Doug ''The Greaseman'' Tracht, whom Infinity had hired away from another station and planned to syndicate nationally; G. Gordon Liddy, attorney and talk show host on WJFK; and Mike Francesa (WFAN), who had become well-known on CBS-TV.

Foremost among Infinity's talk show staff was Howard Stern, an outspoken, controversial morning radio personality. After Stern had achieved a huge following on New York's station WXRG, Infinity began syndicating Stern's show to other stations for $300,000 per year during the early 1990s. Stern soon became one of Infinity's most coveted assets, generating an estimated $15 million annually in sales and capturing as much as $2,000 per 30 second advertising slot. Stern's key attribute was his appeal to white-collar men aged 18 to 34, the most difficult-to-reach and lucrative demographic group sought by advertisers. Of that group, in fact, Stern attained higher ratings in the massive New York market than the highest-rated prime-time television shows.

However, Infinity's success in the rapidly growing talk show market came at a price. Several of its stations' most popular hosts had drawn the attention of regulatory agencies, who cited them for crude and deviant behavior on the air. As a result, some premier advertisers had been scared away from those stations. Although the FCC had loosened restrictions on material it viewed as repulsive, Stern and several other hosts continued to push the boundaries. In 1992, ''The Greaseman'' was under investigation for indecencies allegedly committed before his move to Infinity, and Infinity's KROQ-FM in Los Angeles came under fire for broadcasting a controversial murder hoax. Howard Stern generated the most controversy, drawing criticism not only from the FCC but also from a wide range of special interest groups. Karmazin's emphatic defense of these talk show hosts earned him a reputation among some observers as a staunch advocate of First Amendment rights, although not all analysts were favorably impressed.

As the economy improved and Infinity's programming and management strategies began to pay off, the company's financial performance improved. Of importance to Infinity's bottom line was its move in 1992 to begin syndicating more of its talk shows nationally. Syndication allowed the company an entirely new means of profiting from its most popular programs. In addition, in 1992 the FCC amended its restrictions, increasing the total number of U.S. stations allowed per operator from 24 to 36 and boosting the number that an operator could own on each band (AM and FM) in one city from one to four. Late in 1993, Infinity added WIP-AM, an all-sports station in Philadelphia, bringing its total number of holdings to 22.

In 1993, with revenues up more than 35 percent to $234 million, Infinity posted its first positive net income—$14 million—since the mid-1980s. The company was also experiencing strong gains in the value of its stock and reported operating profit margins of 45 percent, a full ten percentage points higher than the industry average. Acquisitions that year cemented Infinity's position as the largest company solely engaged in radio broadcasting. From just a few rock-and-roll stations in the early 1980s, Infinity had grown into a diversified industry leader with stations providing sports, oldies, country music, talk show, and even Spanish-language programming. Karmazin picked up the company's 23rd station early in 1994, acquiring KRTH-FM, an oldies station in Los Angeles, for $110 million, the largest sum ever paid for a U.S. radio station at the time.

### *Changes in Ownership: Late 1990s*

Taking advantage of the FCC's new, more permissive ownership regulations, the company continued to grow during the mid- to late 1990s. The Telecommunications Act of 1996 afforded Infinity additional expansion opportunities, and by the end of that year the firm had nearly doubled its station count. It was at this time, however, that Karmazin set his sights on the radio stations and television network of CBS. Michael Jordan, CEO of CBS's parent company, Westinghouse Electric Corp., refused to sell the firm to Karmazin but instead agreed to buy Infinity. Karmazin jumped at the chance to become part of the largest radio group in the United States, and the $4.9 billion deal was completed on December 31, 1996. As a result of the Westinghouse purchase, Infinity was merged into the CBS Radio Group, which named Karmazin as president.

Karmazin soon became chairman and CEO of the CBS Radio Group and also took control of the firm's television network. During 1997, Westinghouse sold off its industrial arm and took on the name CBS Corp. In 1998, CBS decided to spin off a portion of its radio and outdoor advertising holdings as Infinity Broadcasting Corp., once again bringing the Infinity name back to the public. The stock offering was the largest in the media industry at the time and raised $2.87 billion.

Karmazin, now CEO of both Infinity and CBS Corp., set his sights even higher in 1999. During May of that year, he announced the $8.3 billion purchase of Outdoor Systems Inc., the largest U.S. outdoor advertising company, and merged it into the Infinity business. Karmazin's most significant move during 1999 however, was the deal he struck with Viacom Inc. in September. Just as the FCC began allowing companies to own more than one television station in one market, Karmazin met with Sumner M. Redstone, Viacom's infamous CEO, to discuss merger options.

Much like the 1996 Westinghouse deal, Redstone shot down Karmazin's offer to buy Viacom. Karmazin then offered CBS to Redstone, who eventually made a $37 billion proposal to merge the two companies together. Viacom completed the CBS purchase in May 2000 for a total price of $39.8 billion—one of the largest media deals in history. Infinity became a subsidiary of Viacom as a result of the deal. Karmazin was named Viacom's president and chief operating officer while remaining CEO of Infinity.

## *Infinity Prospers in the New Century*

Under new ownership, Infinity continued to grow in the early years of the new century. During 2000, it acquired 18 radio stations from competitor Clear Channel Communications Inc. The firm also purchased Giraudy SA, an outdoor advertising company based in France. During that year, Viacom announced that it would purchase the remaining shares of Infinity that it did not already own, taking the business private for the third time in its history.

According to an August 2000 *Electronic Media* article, industry analysts considered Infinity to be one of the "most powerful cash-flow machines in U.S. media." The article went on to state that "it's clear that the company is fixed on taking radio consolidation and cross-media expansion to the next level." Infinity's 2001 cash flow in fact, was projected at $2 billion—cash which Viacom could use to fund further expansion. The article also suggested that Viacom, CBS, and Infinity had yet to realize all of the benefits and synergies of the Viacom/CBS merger.

During 2001, Karmazin named Farid Suleman president and CEO of Infinity. One year later however, Suleman resigned and John Sykes, a former executive of Viacom's MTV Networks Group, took the helm. Karmazin, who had orchestrated Infinity's rise to the top of the industry, remained president and COO of Viacom. During 2002, Infinity's operations included that of the Viacom Outdoor Group, the largest outdoor advertiser in the U.S., and nearly 185 radio stations. With a media giant as its parent, Infinity stood positioned for continued growth well into the future.

## *Principal Competitors*

Clear Channel Communications Inc.; Cumulus Media Inc.; Lamar Advertising Company.

## *Further Reading*

Bachman, Katy, "Karmazin Ups Suleman to Infinity President/CEO," *Mediaweek*, February 26, 2001.

Barry, David, "Jim Hard: He Played a Part in How the West Was Won—By FM Radio," *Business Journal-San Jose*, April 2, 1990, p. 12.

Breznik, Alan, "In IPO, Infinity Pitching WFAN to Street," *Crain's New York Business*, January 6, 1992, p. 4.

"CBS Takes Radio Public," *Communications Daily*, August 28, 1998.

Farhi, Paul, "Bad Taste, Good Business: To His Employer, Howard Stern Easily Passes a Classic Cost-Benefit Test," *Washington Post*, March 27, 1994, p. H1.

Flint, Joe, "Infinity No Stranger to FCC Complaints," *Broadcasting*, November 30, 1992, p. 37.

Kamen, Robin, "To Infinity and Beyond: Mel Takes on CBS," *Crain's New York Business*, November 24, 1997, p. 1.

Higgins, John M., and Paige Albiniak, "CBS Radio Becomes Infinity," *Broadcasting & Cable*, August 31, 1998.

"The Infinite Possibilities of Radio," *Broadcasting & Cable*, September 6, 1993, pp. 32–3.

Kanter, Bruce, "Westwood One and Infinity Broadcasting Enter Into Letter of Intent for Westwood One to Acquire Unistar Radio Networks," *Business Wire*, October 11, 1993.

Lippman, John, "New Notch for Infinity: KRTH Acquisition Continues Radio Group Owner's Trend," *Los Angeles Times*, June 18, 1993, p. D1.

Mermigas, Diane, "Behind the Deal; Viacom/Infinity," *Electronic Media*, August 21, 2000, p. 18.

——, "Viacom: To Infinity and Beyond," *Electronic Media*, August 7, 2000, p. 27.

Mirabella, Alan, "Is Summit Kissing WRKS Goodbye?," *Crain's New York Business*, December 6, 1993, p. 1.

Petrozzello, Donna, "Westinghouse, Infinity Become One," *Broadcasting & Cable*, January 6, 1997, p. 108.

Siklos, Richard, "Viacom-CBS: They Have it All Now," *Business Week*, September 20, 1999.

Viles, Peter, "Infinity Unbowed," *Broadcasting*, November 30, 1992, pp. 4+.

—Dave Mote
—update: Christina M. Stansell

# International Lease Finance Corporation

1999 Avenue of the Stars, 39th Floor
Los Angeles, California 90067
U.S.A.
Telephone: (310) 788-1999
Fax: (310) 788-1990
Web site: http://www.ilfc.com

*Wholly Owned Subsidiary of American International Group Inc.*
*Incorporated:* 1973
*Employees:* 100
*Sales:* $2.44 billion (2000)
*NAIC:* 532411 Commercial Air, Rail, and Water Transportation Equipment Rental and Leasing

International Lease Finance Corporation (ILFC) is considered the world's second largest lessor of aircraft after General Electric Capital Aviation Services (GECAS). ILFC makes substantial profits by leasing and selling civil aircraft to airlines. In 2000, the company owned a fleet of 500 airliners worth about $18 billion. The purchasing power of ILFC and its chief rival, GECAS, has helped the pair survive against a massive influx of would-be competitors to the risky yet lucrative business.

## *Origins*

The aircraft leasing industry dates to 1965, when Boeing sold its first plane to a leasing company. International Lease Finance Corporation's origins date to not long after that. Two of ILFC's founders, Louis Gonda and Steven Udvar-Hazy, met while UCLA students working as aircraft brokers in the early 1970s, records the *Financial Times.* "We sensed a need for a financing vehicle to relieve airlines of the financial burdens of wide-bodied aircraft," recalled Gonda some years later. The pair's first deal involved leasing a DC-8 to a Mexican airline.

Gonda and Udvar-Hazy established International Lease Finance Corporation in 1973. Each contributed $50,000; more funds came from Gonda's father Leslie, a Hungarian who had made a fortune in Venezuelan real estate before moving to the United States some ten years earlier. Leslie Gonda became chairman, while Udvar-Hazy, also Hungarian, was made president and Louis Gonda executive vice-president. ILFC went public in 1983 on the over-the-counter market; its three founders retained 58 percent of its ownership after the transaction.

Tax law changes in the mid-1980s made short-term operating leases more attractive to airlines than long-term and direct purchase leases, which had formerly offered airlines investment tax credits and depreciation deductions. The price of new aircraft alone was a deterrent to ownership—the Boeing 747, the largest airliner, cost $125 million each, in quantity.

The civil aircraft leasing market continued to grow, lead by GPA Group (formerly Guinness Peat Aviation, later to become a part of General Electric Capital Aviation Services) and ILFC. Operating lease companies bought a tenth of all the airliners made by Boeing and McDonnell Douglas, the two U.S. manufacturers, in 1986.

ILFC's profits rose 55 percent to $51.2 million in 1987 on revenues of $179.6 million—mostly from lease payments. ILFC had just 16 employees. By this time, wrote the *Financial Times,* the company had leased 230 aircraft to 70 airlines, with only two bad deals, thanks to its detailed analysis of lessees. The company also had a policy of withdrawing aircraft from lessees at the first sign of trouble. ILFC then specialized in smaller airlines that had difficulty obtaining traditional financing.

In May 1988 ILFC announced orders for 100 Boeing and 30 Airbus airplanes worth $5.04 billion—the largest single purchase of commercial aircraft to that date. The firm also took options for another $1.6 billion worth of planes. The orders were part of an effort to diversify ILFC's fleet, although McDonnell Douglas was left out of this historic deal.

The large order ensured that ILFC would have planes available as world airlines were expected to replace their aging planes en masse in the 1990s. The company did not generally purchase planes on speculation, however; customers were already lined up.

Critics complained that the growing dominance of the leasing companies blocked airlines from purchasing direct from

## Company Perspectives:

*The inevitability of change creates a constant flow of upswings and downturns in air transportation. But one thing does not change—the continuous need for rapid, economical deployment of high performance aircraft. ILFC understood this reality as early as 1973 when we pioneered the world's first aircraft operating lease. Quickly, airlines across the globe discovered the benefits. Today, with more than one-third of the world fleet under lease, we see major carriers regularly turn to the operating lease as the right financial solution for building a competitive edge in the marketplace. Despite the success of leasing, there is no room for complacency in our business. We're challenged daily to adapt our lease products to the fast-paced world around us. New regulatory pressures. Heightened competition. Change in customer preferences. That is why we'll renew our vision, refine our products and recommit to the mission: to provide airlines worldwide with optimized aircraft fleets to grow and the flexibility to maximize profits and develop markets.*

the manufacturers. Popular models often had waiting lists of up to two years. In 1988, leased planes accounted for about 15 percent of the world fleet and a similar percentage of new aircraft orders. By 1994, however, leased planes were expected to account for half the world fleet.

ILFC reported net income of $43.4 million on revenues of $213.2 million in 1988. The company had about 75 planes in its portfolio, but expected to increase it to 350 planes by 1994.

ILFC bought a 15 percent stake in Alaska Air Group, owner of Alaska Airlines, in January 1990, making it one of the largest shareholders. Alaska Air placed a large aircraft order potentially worth $2.5 billion to support its bid to become a major independent carrier. Alaska planned to lease 24 Boeing 737s from ILFC, but order 20 MD-90s direct from McDonnell Douglas, as well as place options on another 20 MD-90s.

### *Sold in 1990*

American International Group Inc. (AIG), an insurance company, bought ILFC for $1.26 billion in June 1990. The purchase was part of a drive by AIG to obtain earnings from the financial services sector. At the time of the acquisition, ILFC had debts of $2.3 billion and needed to raise $10 billion to pay for aircraft due to be delivered in the next five years. ILFC posted pre-tax profits of $139.7 million in 1991.

To the surprise of some analysts, aircraft leasing companies survived during the recession of the early 1990s, which held some of the airline industry's worst years. Demand for leased fuel-efficient planes remained stable, as airlines were less willing than ever to commit large sums of capital to aircraft purchases. While airlines were cutting back deliveries, ILFC placed a $4.1 billion order for 82 aircraft in January 1993, betting the market would eventually turn around. Helping to increase demand was a federal mandate to replace older, noisier jets.

There were signs of an industrywide recovery in 1995, as Singapore Airlines and others placed large orders with the aircraft manufacturers. At this time, ILFC and General Electric Capital Aviation Services, formed from the effective merger of GPA and San Francisco-based Polaris Aircraft Leasing, controlled the bulk of the aircraft leasing market.

Airbus won a $4 billion order for 65 aircraft from ILFC, its largest customer, in September 1997. The deal brought ILFC's number of Airbus aircraft on order to 266.

In October 1999, ILFC CEO Steven Udvar-Hazy gave the Smithsonian Institution $60 million toward building an addition to the National Air and Space Museum called the Dulles Center. The donation reflected Udvar-Hazy's gratitude to the aviation industry and to the United States, to which he had emigrated from Communist Hungary as a young boy. Not content to simply finance flight, he learned how to fly corporate jets.

Although ILFC had been buying more aircraft from the European consortium Airbus Industrie, its favorite aircraft remained the Boeing 737. Economical and flexible to operate, the 737 was popular among numerous airlines, most notably Southwest Airlines, which had based its entire fleet on the type. ILFC ordered 50 of the 737s from Boeing in December 1999 in a deal worth $2.4 billion. The next May, ILFC ordered 50 aircraft worth up to $3.2 billion from Airbus.

### *More Competition in the 1990s*

The 1990s saw a proliferation in the number of companies entering the operating lease business—at least 60 companies were leasing aircraft. By the end of the decade, competition had driven down profits and forced consolidation among the smaller players, noted *Aircraft Value News.* These smaller lessors typically offered less older, less desirable planes.

Larger, more established lessors benefited from greater purchasing power and higher rental rates. ILFC posted pre-tax income of $703 million on revenues of $2.3 billion in 1999. Among the more serious new entrants, however, were the manufacturers themselves, willing to provide creative financial solutions to keep their assembly lines busy.

In March 2001, ILFC signed a 12-year lease for the top six floors of the new MGM Century City headquarters building. The company had fewer than 100 employees, but had outgrown its offices at the SunAmerica Center in Los Angeles. The lease was estimated to represent a $100 million commitment.

In another round of alternating precedent-setting deals by ILFC and GECAS, Airbus announced an ILFC order for 111 aircraft worth $8.7 billion in June 2001. The largest order in Airbus history, this included five of the new A380 superjumbos.

In June 2001, *Flight International* reported that ILFC had abandoned plans to enter the regional jet (RJ) market. Regional jets had become popular with airlines as an alternative to the noisy and uncomfortable turboprops that had traditionally plied short-haul routes. ILFC apparently felt that as the manpower to service an RJ lease was the same as that required for a large airliner, it had little to gain. Rival GECAS had ordered regional

**Key Dates:**

**1973:** ILFC is formed by Hungarian immigrants.
**1983:** ILFC begins trading shares over the counter.
**1990:** Insurer AIG buys ILFC for $1.3 billion.
**2001:** ILFC gives Airbus its largest order ever, worth $8.7 billion.

jets for its fleet, however (its sister company GE Aircraft Engines supplied the engines).

At the same time, Boeing announced plans to triple the size of its financial services division by 2006, noted the *Financial Times.* Boeing Capital Corporation (BCC), inherited through Boeing's 1997 acquisition of McDonnell Douglas, was now a stand-alone unit with assets of $7 billion. A spokesman played down the potential for conflict with ILFC and other lessors, Boeing's largest client base, by pointing out that BCC would not be making any speculative orders.

Debis AirFinance, the world's fourth largest aircraft lessor with annual revenues of $179 million, was then being offered for sale by DaimlerChrysler, which had acquired the unit through its purchase of Ireland's AerFi Group. Whatever happened among the market's other players, ILFC seemed assured of a leading role.

### *Principal Competitors*

Boeing Capital Corporation; Boullioun Aviation; Debis AirFinance; GATX Capital; General Electric Capital Aviation Services; Singapore Aircraft Leasing Enterprise.

### *Further Reading*

''Aircraft Leasing; Rent-a-Jet,'' *The Economist,* May 21, 1988.
''Airplane Leasing Growth Forecast,'' *Journal of Commerce,* May 23, 1989, p. 5B.
Almazan, Alec, ''US$2 Billion Boeing Order Points to Recovery for Plane Makers,'' *Business Times* (Singapore), Shipping Times, July 27, 1995, p. 14.
Armbruster, William, ''Aircraft Lessor Inks Agreements with Nine Carriers,'' *Journal of Commerce,* January 22, 1993, p. 7B.
''Boeing, ILFC Agree on Deal for 50 737s,'' *Los Angeles Times,* December 23, 1999, p. C2.
Cameron, Doug, ''Boeing Financial Services Division Set to Take Off,'' *Financial Times,* Companies & Finance International, July 2, 2001, p. 22.
''Chapter 3 Lease Rentals Suffer from Intense Competition,'' *Aircraft Value News,* June 19, 2000.
Chuter, Andy, ''Leasing: ILFC Halts RJ Market Plans,'' *Flight International,* June 12, 2001, p. 6.
Done, Kevin, ''Airbus Secures $8.7 Billion Contract; European Group Announces Its Biggest Ever Deal to Supply 111 Aircraft to ILFC,'' *Financial Times,* June 20, 2001, p. 21.
Dunphy, Stephen H., ''Why Buy Aircraft When Planes Can Be Leased?,'' *Seattle Times,* August 20, 2000, p. E1.
Fisher, Lawrence M., ''Lessors Thrive on Aircraft Boom,'' *New York Times,* April 11, 1989, p. D1.
Hall, Kevin G., ''ILFC May Be Able to Ride Out Storm,'' *Journal of Commerce,* Specials Sec., June 28, 1993, p. 7.
Iannello, Lorraine, and Ira Breskin, ''AIG Acquisition Reflects 'Financial Services' Push,'' *Journal of Commerce,* June 27, 1990, p. 9A.
''ILFC Jet Purchase Is Largest Ever; Boeing, Airbus Share,'' *Journal of Commerce,* May 17, 1988, p. 5B.
''ILFC Reportedly Weighing Purchase of Daimler Unit,'' *Los Angeles Times,* Bus. Sec., June 20, 2001, p. 2.
Lane, Polly, ''Alaska Air Gets Jets, Investor,'' *Seattle Times,* January 23, 1990, p. B1.
——, ''Recession Gives Lift to Aircraft Leasing,'' *Seattle Times,* February 14, 1992, p. E1.
North, David M., ''ILFC Chief's Gift to Museum Sets Fine Example,'' *Aviation Week & Space Technology,* October 18, 1999, p. 64.
Oram, Roderick, ''Californian Lease Company in $5 Billion Jet Deals,'' *Financial Times,* Sec. I, May 17, 1988, p. 6.
——, ''ILFC Big Spenders Take Up Airlines' Burden,'' *Financial Times,* May 18, 1988, p. I6.
Proctor, Paul, ''Market Changes Spur Leasing Trend,'' *Aviation Week & Space Technology,* October 20, 1986, p. 42.
Robison, Peter, ''Airbus Reportedly Wins 50-Jet Order,'' *Seattle Times,* May 6, 2000, p. B1.
Skapinker, Michael, ''Airbus Wins $4 Billion Leasing Order,'' *Financial Times,* World Trade Sec., September 3, 1997, p. 7.
Smith, Bruce A., ''Savvy Business Strategy Underlies Major ILFC Buy,'' *Aviation Week & Space Technology,* January 4, 1993, p. 32.
Strahler, Steven R., ''Following the Financing: Lending Unit Takes a Few Pages Out of GE's Loan-Making Playbook,'' *Crain's Chicago Business,* August 20, 2001, p. E10.
Tait, Nikki, ''An Unpromising Corporate Couple's Marriage Still Flies,'' *Financial Times,* International Company News, February 26, 1993, p. 28.
Unsworth, Edwin, ''US Leasing Company Big Aircraft Buyer,'' *Journal of Commerce,* June 15, 1987, p. 5B.
Vartabedian, Ralph, ''Insurer to Pay $1.3 Billion for ILFC Jet-Leasing Firm,'' *Los Angeles Times,* June 26, 1990, p. D1.

—Frederick C. Ingram

# Ipsos SA

**99, rue de l'Abbé Groult**
**75739 Paris cedex 15**
**Telephone: (+33) 1 53 68 28 28**
**Fax: (+ 33) 1 53 68 01 82**
**Web site: http://www.ipsos.com**

*Public Company*
*Incorporated:* 1975
*Employees:* 3,362
*Sales:* EUR 480.1 million ($476 million) (2001)
*Stock Exchanges:* Euronext Paris
*Ticker Symbol:* IPSO.7329
*NAIC:* 541910 Marketing Research and Public Opinion Polling

France's Ipsos SA has climbed to the top ranks of the worldwide market research industry, claiming the number nine position worldwide. In certain categories, the company ranks even higher—number two worldwide in the advertising segment and number four worldwide in market research. Since 2001, Ipsos has also edged out French rival Sofres, part of Taylor Nelson Sofres, to claim the number one spot in France. Marketing Research accounts for the main source of Ipsos annual revenues, at 50 percent; the company is also active in Advertising and Media Research, which combined to add 33 percent to sales; Quality and Consumer Satisfaction Research, which represents 9 percent of sales; and Public Opinion and Social Research, adding 6 percent to the company's 2001 revenues of EUR 480 million. Ipsos is an internationally operating company with a network of subsidiaries in North America, Latin America, and the Far East. The company's European revenues accounted for 46 percent of Ipsos' revenues; North America contributed 39 percent to the company's total sales, while Latin America, particularly Argentina, Brazil and Mexico, where the company is present through its Novaction holding, contributed 12 percent. Since the beginning of the new century, Ipsos has also begun to focus on building up its position in the Asian Pacific region through acquisitions in Hong Kong and Australia. Much of Ipsos growth has come through a steady stream of acquisitions through the 1990s in a bid to assure its international presence and become a major contender in the market research industry. Having broken into the top 10 at the turn of the century, Ipsos intends to slow down on its external growth activities. Nonetheless, the company expects to pass the EUR 1 billion mark in sales by 2005. Ipsos, listed on the EURonext Paris Nouveau Marché exchange, is led by founder and co-president Didier Truchot and longtime friend and co-president Jean-Marc Rech. Major clients include Daimler-Chrysler, Colgate-Palmolive, Ford, Danone, General Mills, Johnson & Johnson, Kraft, L'Oreal, Procter & Gamble and Unilever.

### *A Different Kind of Researcher in the 1970s*

In the late 1960s, Didier Truchot joined France's IFOP (L'Institute Français d'Opinion Publique), which at the time was one of France's oldest and largest research organizations, together with Sofres, which later formed part of the Tayler Nelson Sofres group. Truchot then became a director at the IRSEC Institute in the early 1970s. In 1975, Truchot left IRSEC to form his own market research company, Ipsos.

Truchot set out to build a different kind of research company, targeting the advertising and media fields. He began developing tools to enable advertising agencies and their clients, as well as print media and television and radio broadcasters, to measure the effectiveness of their advertisements—an approach to market research entirely new in France. In 1977, Ipsos released its first such tool, dubbed the Baramètre d'Affichage (BAF), an instrument for measuring the effectiveness of billboard advertisements. The first of the company's "post-tests," the BAF was soon followed by other post-campaign measurement instruments developed by Ipsos to target specific media categories. Such measurements quickly became standard practice in the French media industry.

In 1979, Ipsos launched another innovative product, the FCA, or France des Cadres Actifs ("The French Businessmen Survey"), a tool that measured readership among the country's executives. Ipsos convinced a consortium of the country's newspapers and news magazines to share the costs of conduct-

## Company Perspectives:

*Consumers, citizens, and clients—we can be all of these in turn and at the same time.*

*At Ipsos, our researchers . . . identify what unites and what differentiates us as individuals. We call this "Profiling People," which assures our clients that we understand the dynamics of their markets and provide reliable information that gives them a leading edge.*

ing the FCA. Ipsos had successfully recognized a trend in France, as the country began to see a growing number of financial and economic news and information magazines.

By 1981, Ipsos had established itself as a strong voice in the French research community, while its revenues remained relatively modest, at just FFr5 million that year. Yet Ipsos was set to see strong growth during the decade, with sales leaping to FFr100 million by 1989. Part of the company's success was the addition of a new member to its executive team, Jean-Marc Lech.

Lech had joined IFOP in 1970 and quickly became friends with Truchot. When Truchot left the company, Lech remained and by 1980 was named IFOP's president and CEO. In 1982, Lech left IFOP to join Truchot at Ipsos. The two men complemented each other. Whereas Truchot had studied economics and maintained an interest in market research, Lech came from a far different background. The son of a Polish immigrant steelworker, Lech had studied philosophy and social sociology, and this perspective was to prove a valuable asset in forging Ipsos' unique character through the next decade.

Lech was named co-chairman alongside Truchot, and the pair set out to launch Ipsos into a new direction, that of public opinion research. If this area was to remain relatively minor for the company—yielding just 6 percent of revenues in 2001—it garnered the young company a great deal of attention and recognition in an industry where reputation, especially one built up over a long period of time, played a large role in a market research company's success. A fairly new concept to the French market, public opinion polling quickly proved popular, to the extent where observers commented that France had grown to become one of the most heavily polled of the industrial nations.

By the end of the 1980s, Ipsos had become the fifth-largest media research company in France. The company's emphasis on advertising and media research helped it become one of the market leaders in those sectors, while its public opinion research—and particularly its work in political polling—helped it reinforce its reputation as an important resource for the countries political class. In this the company was helped by the dynamic atmosphere of French politics in the 1980s and 1990s, which saw a great deal of shifts in power among France's political parties. As a result, politicians became more conscious of their public image and turned more and more often to Ipsos to help them measure and understand the factors underlying their public appeal. Lech and Truchot were also forging their own personal reputations, becoming respected figures for their insights not only into the market research industry but in politics and society in general.

### *European Expansion in the 1990s*

In the mid-1980s, Ipsos began to adapt new technologies to its measurement instruments. In 1986, for example, the company began using computer technology for conducting surveys—debuting its CATI, or computer-assisted telephone interviews. Computer technology was later extended to personal interviews, with a new class of instruments called CAPI (computer-assisted personal interviews) put into use in 1992.

The shift toward the globalization of the world economy that began in earnest in the early 1990s led Ipsos to begin plotting its own international expansion. As its customers extended their reach into the international arena, Ipsos was determined to accompany them in order to offer a unified product across national lines. Ipsos' initial expansion target remained Europe, especially Spain, Italy, Germany, and the United Kingdom. The company also built up interests in Central Europe, especially Hungary.

Acquisitions formed the primary component of the company's expansion program, in part because of the need for an established reputation in order to compete successfully in a given market's research industry. Ipsos defined a strict set of criteria for its acquisitions, namely that all takeovers be friendly, with existing management generally left in place. Takeovers were to be 100 percent, enabling Ipsos to create a unified international growth network. Targeted companies were expected to operate in at least one of the company's three core markets—media, advertising, and social research—and had to hold a top five position in their domestic markets.

Between 1990 and 1995, Ipsos made a strong series of acquisitions. Spain was one of the company's first targeted markets, with the acquisition of Eco and Eco Consulting. In 1992, the company paid £4 million to purchase RSL-Research Services, bringing the French company into the United Kingdom and giving it one of the leading media and advertising market research firms in that country. That year the company also moved into Germany, acquiring GfM-Getas and WBA. After acquiring Makrotest, the company reinforced its Italian presence with the 1994 acquisition of Explorer.

The company also continued its French expansion, acquiring Insight, a leading French company offering qualitative research, in 1993. The company's sales grew strongly during this period, jumping from the equivalent of nearly EUR 18 million in 1990 to EUR 108 million in 1995. Aiding the company's expansion was the opening of its capital to outside investors, including Baring Private Equity, in 1992. Nonetheless, Truchot and Lech maintained control of two-thirds of the company's shares.

### *Global Market Research Leader in the 21st Century*

By 1997, Ipsos, with sales of EUR 144 million, had joined the top five in European market research companies and claimed the second-place position in France. With its European network largely in place—and 50 percent of revenues generated internationally—the company now turned to expansion across the Atlantic. In order to pursue its global expansion, Ipsos took on new investment partners, selling 40 percent of the company to Artemis Group, led by François Pinault, and the Amstar investment fund led by Walter Butler.

## Key Dates:

**1975:** Ipsos is founded by Didier Truchot.
**1977:** Ipsos launches its first media measurement instrument, the BAF.
**1979:** The company launches the FCA, a measurement survey targeting French businessmen.
**1982:** Jean-Marc Lech joins Ipsos as co-chairman.
**1990:** The company begins expanding throughout Europe.
**1992:** Ipsos sells one-third of its shares to outside investors in order to pursue its expansion plan; the company acquires NFL-Research in England and Eco Consulting in Spain.
**1997:** Ipsos sells 40 percent of its shares in order to fuel expansion into the United States.
**1999:** Ipsos goes public on the EURonext Paris exchange's Nouveau Marché.
**2000:** The company acquires Angus Reid and Tandemar of Canada.
**2002:** Ipsos acquires the U.S. firm of Vantis, formerly a division of AC Nielsen Bates.

In December 1997, Ipsos made two significant acquisitions. The first brought the company into the Latin American market, with the purchase of Novaction and its subsidiaries in Mexico, Brazil, and Argentina. Under terms of that purchase agreement, Ipsos immediately acquired 33 percent of Novaction, with the option of taking complete control of that company, a move Ipsos made in 2000.

Two weeks later, Ipsos announced its entry into the North American market with an agreement to acquire ASI Market Research. The leader in the advertising research sector, ASI not only enabled Ipsos to establish itself in North America, but it also made it the world's top advertising research company specializing in broadcast advertising copy-testing. That category had been growing particularly strongly as advertisers, faced with the rising costs of creating and deploying their advertising campaigns, sought to test a campaign's effectiveness before the actual campaign launch.

The ASI and Novaction acquisitions transformed Ipsos into a worldwide market research force. The company's international activity now represented more than 70 percent of its total sales, which neared EUR 200 million at the end of 1998.

In 1999, Ipsos moved to step up its expansion, going public with a listing on the Paris stock exchange's Nouveau Marché. The successful offering, oversubscribed by more than 12 times, enabled Artemis and Amstar to cash out on their investments and also gave Ipsos a strong war chest for pursuing further international growth. Among the company's expansion moves following its public offering was the creation of an Internet audience research joint-venture MMXI Europe, with the majority of shares held by partner Media Matrix and 20 percent by Ipsos. The company also took control of four subsidiaries of NFO Worldwide specializing in the formation of access panels—that is, sample audiences who have agreed to respond to questionnaires on a regular basis. At the end of 1999, Ipsos moved to establish itself in the Asia-Pacific region, opening a subsidiary office in Hong Kong.

At the beginning of 2000, Ipsos acquired Australian company Marketing for Change, which was renamed as Ipsos-MfC, strengthening its position in the Pacific region. In Europe, the company acquired Médiangles, a specialist in Internet market research.

Yet the North American market, headquarters for many of Ipsos major corporate customers, remained the company's primary expansion target at the turn of the century. In March 2000, Ipsos' North American presence took a major step forward with the CA68 million acquisition of Canada's Angus Reid. That company, which was founded in 1979, had built up its own internationally operating network, with offices in Canada, the United States, and England. Angus Reid specialized in pubic opinion research and not only had become a leader in the Canadian market but had also built up a strong share of the United States market, which contributed one third of its sales. Renamed Ipsos-Reid following its acquisition, the subsidiary became an Ipsos flagship and a worldwide brand.

A month after the Angus Reid acquisition, Ipsos returned to Canada, now acquiring Tandemar. That company held the lead in the Canadian market for its specialty, advertising effectiveness post-testing. Tandemar was joined to the company's American-based Ipsos-ASI Inc. subsidiary and renamed Ipsos-ASI Ltd. for the Canadian market.

Later in 2000, Ipsos looked south, acquiring BIMSA, the leading Mexican market research company. At the same time, the company increased its shares of Novaction, taking 100 percent control of that network. The company's agreement to acquire Search Marketing, a company active in Chile, Brazil, and Argentina; this move, completed in 2001, established Ipsos as the top survey research company in the Latin American market.

At the end of 2000, Didier Truchot and Jean-Marc Lech took a step back from the company's direction, naming Pierre Giacommetti and Stephane Truchi to head the company's day-to-day operations. Truchot and Lech nonetheless remained active in the company as co-chairmen of the board. By then, the pair had built Ipsos into one of the world's top ten market research companies, with sales of nearly EUR 330 million.

Ipsos international expansion continued through 2001, notably with the purchase of the research division of NPD Marketing in the United States. The company had also acquired half of the United Kingdom's Research in Focus, with an agreement to extend to full control by 2003. In Asia, Ipsos had purchased a 40 percent share in Link Survey, which was renamed Ipsos-Link. The company also added Riehle Research, complementing its European presence.

In 2002, Ipsos took a break from the rapid expansion that saw it top EUR 480 million in revenues in 2001. That figure enabled the company to pass its chief French rival, Taylor Nelson Sofres, for the first time. Slowing down its acquisition drive did not, however, mean stopping completely—in April 2002, the company moved to acquire Vantis, a division of AC Nielsen Bates, strengthening Ipsos' leading position in the marketing consulting segment. And Ipsos continued to aim high, targeting revenues of more than EUR 1 billion by 2005.

### *Principal Subsidiaries*

Ipsos SA; Ipsos Access Panel Holding; GIE Ipsos Europe; Ipsos France SA; Ipsos Médias SA; Ipsos Médiangles SA; Ipsos Opinion SA; Ipsos Régions SARL; Ipsos Interviews SA; Insight Marques SARL IMS SA; Popcorn SNC (49.99%); IMS Développement SA; Ipsos Access Panel GIE; Int res SA Z(82%; Belgium); Ipsos-RSL Ltd Co. (U.K.); Pricesearch Ltd Co (U.K.); CatiCentre Ltd. Co (U.K.); Ipsos-Insight Ltd. Co (U.K.); Ipsos Deutschland Gmbh (Germany); Ipsos-Explorer SRL (Italy); Ipsos-Szonda Sté hongroise (50.1%)(Hungary); Eco SA (Spain); Ipsos USA Inc.; Ipsos America Inc.; Ipsos-ASI Inc. (U.S.); Ipsos Canada Ltd; Ipsos-ASI Ltd Canada; Cantrack Research Ltd (Canada); Ipsos-Reid Corp. Inc (Canada); Ipsos Portugal LDA (Portugal); Ipsos Latin America BV (Netherlands); Publimetria SA (78.2%) (Argentina); Novaction Argentina SA; Novaction Brazil LDA; Novaction Mexico SA; Ipsos-Bimsa SA 50; Ipsos Far East Ltd (Hong-Kong); Ipsos Australia PTY Ltd; AGB Stat-Ipsos (37.47%; Lebanon).

### *Principal Competitors*

AC Nielsen Corporation; IMS Health Inc.; Kantar Group Ltd.; Taylor Nelson Sofres plc; Information Resources Inc.; NFO Worldwide Inc.; Nielsen Media Research; GfK Group A.G.; United Information Group Ltd.; Westat Inc.; The Arbitron Company; Maritz Marketing Research; Market Facts Inc.; Video Research; The NPD Group Inc.; Marketing Intelligence Corp.; Opinion Research Corp. International; J.D. Power and Associates; Roper Starch Worldwide Inc.

### *Further Reading*

Cocquidé, Patrick, ''Jean-Mark Lech,'' *L'Expansion*, November 22, 2001.

Hassoux, Didier, ''Portrait: Jean-Marc Lech,'' *Liberation*, March 26, 2002.

''Ipsos vise 1 milliard d'EURos de chiffre d'affaires en 2005,'' *Reuters*, March 28, 2002.

Porier, Jérome, '' 'Aucun signe de ralentissement en vue,' '' *Newsbourse*, May 27, 2001.

—M.L. Cohen

# The Island ECN, Inc.

**50 Broad Street**
**New York, New York 10004**
**U.S.A.**
**Telephone: (212) 231-5000**
**Web site: http://www.island.com**

*Private Company*
*Incorporated:* 1996
*Employees:* 160
*Sales:* $166 million (2001)
*NAIC:* 523999 Miscellaneous Financial Investment Activities

The Island ECN, Inc. is an Electronic Communications Network (ECN), a computerized marketplace that automatically matches buyers and sellers of stocks and other securities. Island executed trades in 53.7 in 2000, and in 2001 traded more than 350 million shares a day on average. Since December 2001 it has led all other ECNs in trades in Nasdaq shares. A fundamental principle of Island ECN is that trading information should not be the domain of a privileged few insiders. Consequently, all buy and sell limit orders as well as all trades executed on Island are displayed instantaneously in its online order book, which can be viewed by anyone with an Internet browser. Only member dealers are able to trade shares on Island, however. By early 2002, Island had more than 700 subscribers. Island's trading day, which extends from 7:00 am Eastern Time until 8:00 pm Eastern Time every business day, is one of the longest in the industry. Among the services Island offers are IslandNET, a complete Island connectivity package that includes hardware, order management software, and 24-hour-a-day connection monitoring in case of power outages. Inlet offers subscribers access to pricing data, order history, and other trade information. Island ECN is a private corporation owned by an investment group that includes Bain Capital and TA Associates.

### *Beginnings*

The founding of Island ECN was a direct result of the upheaval in the Nasdaq markets in the late 1980s. Following the stock market crash of 1987, two new systems—small order execution system (SOES) and SelectNet, an electronic network—were introduced in Nasdaq. One result of the system was that trades of 500 shares or less were to the Nasdaq market maker with the best price and then executed automatically. A group of traders, called SOES bandits, arose in response to the system's unequaled speed and took advantage of it to reap quick profits trading small amounts of stock. The founders of Island developed some of the first trading software for SOES bandits.

The most important early figure was Joshua Levine. A Carnegie Mellon University dropout with a penchant for turtles, Levine moved to New York in the early 1990s where he began working with Jeffrey Citron, one of the founders of Datek Online, an online trading firm. The Watcher, one of Levine's early systems for Datek, provided traders with a way to plug directly into SOES. Levine's next development grew out of his observation of a peculiar situation: Some electronic trades were not being made, trades in which the buy and sell prices did not match because one person wanted to buy a stock for more than another wanted to sell. Levine's new system resolved the anomalous situation by enabling customers to trade stock with each other without going through traditional Nasdaq market makers. The system became the backbone of The Island ECN, Inc., which was founded by Levine and Datek Online cofounder Jeffrey Citron in 1996.

### *A New Way to Trade in the Late 1990s*

The system Levine created for Island was a masterpiece of efficiency and simplicity. Unlike the New York Stock Exchange or Nasdaq, where brokers worked through human ''specialists'' or ''market makers'' to buy or sell stock, Island's system was completely electronic—there was no middleman. When a member broker wanted to buy shares, he entered the stock, the quantity, and the price into Island's online order book. If there was a matching order to sell in the book, the trade was automatically executed. The only restrictions were that Island handled only limit orders of 500 shares or less of stocks listed on Nasdaq. Further, only Island's member brokers could trade on the system; others had to make trades through a member broker. Levine also designed Island to be virtually fail-safe. He did not use a single mainframe that could freeze up in periods of extremely heavy trading. Instead he strung together row upon

**Company Perspectives:**

*Since its inception, Island has consistently identified and capitalized on emerging industry trends by offering market professionals greater access to the market, increased transparency, stronger technological services, and lower transaction costs. Island's proprietary technology is the centerpiece of its success in meeting these goals. Island's technology automates traditionally labor-intensive securities transactions, connects Island to its subscribers, and allows Island to monitor and analyze system performance and subscriber behavior on a real-time basis.*

row of off-the-shelf Dell PCs, each programmed to perform one particular function, for example, to receive orders, match orders, or cancel orders; if one computer shut down, there would be a backup waiting to take over its work.

The Achilles heel of ECNs is their liquidity, in other words, how likely a trade is to be executed on the system. Island was founded as a subsidiary of Datek and in the beginning was used by the parent to execute its own trades. The connection to Datek Online, then one of the most successful day-trading firms on Wall Street, gave Island a huge head start. Datek sent tens of thousands of orders to Island every day, providing the needed liquidity to attract other brokers and even Nasdaq market makers.

A turning point came in 1997 when the Securities and Exchange Commission (SEC) promulgated new order handling rules that required Nasdaq market makers to send on to ECNs any limit orders whose price fell between the market maker's best buy and sell prices. Those ECN prices were displayed on the Nasdaq ticker. "For me to be able to have my orders displayed over the Nasdaq system was an absolute seminal event," Matthew Andresen, the day-trader at Datek who was one of the first to understand the rule's import, told the *Dallas Morning News*. "It's the difference between trying to sell your house with a sign in the yard or without a sign." The new Securities and Exchange Commission (SEC) rules were so critical to the company's success that Island would later call January 20, 1997—the day the order handling rules went into effect—the firm's real birthday. Island was one of the first ECNs to register with the National Association of Securities Dealers after the new rules were in place. By August 1997 it could announce that it was the first ECN to represent orders for all Nasdaq stocks.

### *New Leadership in 1998*

In mid-1998, Jeffrey Citron and Joshua Levine stepped aside and named the canny Andresen as Island's president. When Andresen took over Island had four employees, a handful of customers, and no marketing. But soon, under Andresen's leadership, Island started to really thrive. By autumn 1999 the firm had 40 employees and had set a record, trading 6.6 billion shares in a single quarter. Around that time James Marks, an analyst at Credit Suisse First Boston, told *Future Banker* that he considered Island the only ECN with enough liquidity to be taken seriously. Andresen put a series of new plans in the works. The company began talking about inaugurating a 24-hour trading day. It also hoped to attract a larger share of institutional traders, such as mutual funds, although most observers thought that would be a difficult goal to achieve—the average deal on Island involved 300 shares, while institutions traded hundreds of thousands, or even millions of shares regularly.

### *Island in 1999: The First For-Profit Securities Exchange?*

In June 1999, Island made what was perhaps its most significant (if in February 2002, still unrealized) move: It was the first ECN to apply to the SEC to become a national securities exchange, under new rules released by the Commission. If approved, the application for exchange status would put Island on the same level as the New York Stock Exchange (NYSE) and Nasdaq. It would bring Island numerous advantages: The firm would be able to trade stock listed on the NYSE. It could earn millions in revenues every year from the sale of its market data, as the NYSE and Nasdaq do. Furthermore, as an exchange it would qualify for participation in national market systems, such as ITS, which would give a powerful boost to Island's liquidity.

Some believed Island was not up to the challenge of becoming an independent securities exchange. They maintained the firm would be required to regulate itself and its members, it would have to put rules in place to prevent fraudulent practices, and it would need a trained regulatory staff approved by the SEC to perform its duties, all of which would be complicated and expensive. Island countered that its completely electronic form would make regulatory oversight much easier than that of a traditional exchange—it was completely transparent with a permanent audit trail for regulators. In January 1999, to aid its exchange application, Island named Cameron Dovi Smith general counsel. Smith, a former attorney with the SEC's division of market regulation, was hired to manage the legal end of the firm's exchange application, which was formally made in April 1999. At the same time, the company retained two attorneys, who also had SEC experience, from a Washington, D.C. law firm. Not content to put all of its eggs in one basket, Island explored other paths to exchange status. In summer 1999 it negotiated buying into the Pacific Stock Exchange (PCX), a deal that came to naught. Ties with PCX would eventually be forged first by Archipelago, a competing ECN, which would also be the very first ECN to become a securities exchange.

In September 1999, Island introduced 12-hour trading, beginning at 8:00 am and running until 8:00 pm Eastern Time. Island, which previously opened its trading day at 9:00 am, had noticed that trading early in the day was strong, with 20 percent of its trades occurring between 9:00 and 10:15. By the year's end, the numbers were bearing out the decision. Trades early and late in the day grew from about a million a day in June 1999 to around 15 million a day in January 2000, with average order and execution size climbing as well.

### *Introduction of Decimalization in 2000*

In April 2000 Island announced that it would list prices in its online book in decimal form as well as the traditional fractions. The move was, in part, a reaction to the SEC's indefinite postponement of a July 3 deadline to switch the entire securities marketplace to decimal pricing. The National Association of

**Key Dates:**

**1996:** Island ECN is founded.
**1997:** Island prices are first posted at Nasdaq in January; in August Island becomes the first ECN to represent orders for all Nasdaq stocks.
**1998:** Matthew Andresen becomes president of Island.
**1999:** Island files with the Securities and Exchange Commission to become the nation's first for-profit exchange in June; in September Island inaugurates the industry's first 12-hour trading day.
**2000:** Island ECN is spun off from Datek Online Holdings in December.
**2001:** Island becomes a member of the Cincinnati Stock Exchange in December and on December 5th sets sets a record with 589,248,934 shares traded in a single day.
**2002:** Company reaches an agreement to be purchased by Instinet Group Inc.

Securities Dealers (NASD) announced a month earlier that it would be unable to meet the July deadline. Island hoped its move would catalyze the market. Indeed, it elicited reactions that ranged from praise to denunciation. Instinet, the oldest ECN, sent a letter to Congress demanding a rapid switchover to decimals. Some of Island's own customers, however, considered the change irresponsible and felt that it would lead to confusion and instability. Andresen defended the move, pointing out that Island already traded in increments smaller than one-sixteenth of a point and was required to round off quotation information before it was submitted to Nasdaq. Those trades never caused system problems or confusion among investors.

The move to decimals met with approval on Capitol Hill. Legislators, in general, favored a prompt change to decimals. Island's move won the company points in Congress and was expected to aid the firm's application to become an exchange. Andresen had already begun making regular trips to Washington to lobby Congress to encourage changes in the way securities markets were structured. For example, public pressure by Island helped encourage NYSE in October 1999 to rescind Rule 390, which prohibited members from trading significant quantities of stock off the trading floor. As a result, in April 2000 Island began dealing in NYSE issues.

In an October 2000 letter to the SEC, Island formally called for an end to the Commission's ''trade through disclosure'' rule. The rule required exchanges to execute orders at the best price available. In practice this meant orders had to be forwarded to the market with the best price—which might no longer have the stock by the time an order arrived. Island argued that investors should be informed of better prices but also allowed to buy at a higher price—at an ECN, for example—if they chose. ''Knowing in a millisecond whether or not you got your trade executed—and knowing with absolute certainty—can sometimes be the single most important thing for an investor to know,'' Andresen argued in *Securities Industry News.*

It was not easy for Congress and the SEC to brush off such calls. Island ECN's remarkable success indicated that it had its finger on the pulse of the future. By mid-1999 its had 256 subscribers. At a time when ECNs were accounting for some 40 percent of all Nasdaq trades, the two leading ECNs, Island and Instinet, accounted for 87 percent of ECN trades. In 1999 Island reportedly executed trades in about 26 billion shares. In 2000 it would double that execution rate and boast nearly 400 subscribers. Island forged a number of strategic agreements in mid-2000. Ixnet, Inc. agreed in April 2000 to provide the firm with global network connectivity. It signed a deal with the South Korean Uclick Co. to establish the first Korean ECN. It also agreed, first with Unicredito Italiano SpA's TradingLab unit and then with the Spanish ECN Access Europe, to open their electronic networks to each other.

In December 2000 Island was spun off from its parent Datek Online Holdings Corporation The spin-off was the result of a $700 million investment that gave an investment group that included Bain Capital, TA Associates, Silver Lake Partners, and Advent International a 90 percent interest in both Datek and Island. Earlier investments in the two companies had fallen through because of a Datek subsidiary's alleged involvement in trading violations. Observers believed the spin-off would only help Island by distancing it from Datek's legal problems at a time its application to become a securities exchange was still before the SEC.

By the beginning of 2001 Island boasted a 14.5 percent share of all Nasdaq volume. In January alone the firm traded 7.86 billion shares, a 123 percent increase over the previous January—and that despite the Internet stock crash of late 2000. Island was the second largest ECN behind Instinet and closing quickly on the leader. The SEC had not yet ruled on the firm's exchange application—the Commission was moving slowly on the first application. The downturn in the Nasdaq resulting from the Internet stock collapse was expected to have repercussions for many ECNs—including Island—which drew their strength from day-trading first fueled by Internet speculation. Island was already pursuing a new course, however, wooing Institutional Investors.

On January 3, 2001, Island's computer system proved its worth. The Federal Reserve Board cut its interest rates that day and Nasdaq was flooded with orders as a result. The extremely high volumes caused delays in Nasdaq order executions; Island's system, however, continued to function uninterrupted, handling more than 10,000 orders a minute at one point. Later in the year, Island was able to handle more than 11,000 orders per minute for three hours straight. In Island's history, its computers never experienced a capacity-related shutdown. Only the September 11, 2001 terrorist attacks on the World Trade Center, just blocks from Island's headquarters in lower Manhattan, could force them out of service, if only temporarily. Smoke and soot from the burning towers engulfed Island's building, abruptly clogging the building's air conditioning units. Before long, the company's 2000 computers were dangerously overheated and had to be shut down. A new Island backup data center in Secaucus, New Jersey was within months of completion at the time. Within two days, however, the company had patched together a makeshift network for its subscribers.

### *Island Becomes a Leader at the Start of the 21st Century*

The attacks seemed to have but minimal impact on Island. In the month following the attack, the firm enjoyed an 18.18

percent growth rate. In October 2001 Island passed the American Stock Exchange (AMEX) to become the nation's largest marketplace for trading QQQs, the top 100 shares on Nasdaq. During the third week of October, Island traded more than 129 million QQQ shares, more than 18 million shares more than the AMEX. AMEX had depended on QQQs for a large share of its income. In response, AMEX filed a complaint with the SEC charging Island with violating the SEC's trade-through rule requiring orders to be forwarded to the exchange with the best price. In its defense, Island maintained that 87 percent of its volume came from professional traders whom it would be difficult to cheat. It also reiterated its philosophical stance that the price of an order's execution should not be given more weight than the speed or certainty of its execution. The question was still before the SEC in 2002.

In November 2001 Island's share of Nasdaq trades grew to 23.6 percent, with a share volume of 11.3 percent and a dollar volume of 12.7 percent, enabling it to surpass its longtime rival Instinet as the leading ECN. The surge in Nasdaq volume was seen as a vital boost to Island's hope for exchange status. As Isabelle Clary wrote in *Securities Industry News,* "If the largest ECN cannot manage to become a stock exchange, the exchange provision in Regulation ATS might as well become mute." Island, meanwhile, forged ahead with the application process, with the hope that the SEC would render a decision by spring 2002.

Island ECN became a member of the Cincinnati Stock Exchange in December 2001. The step was the first in a plan to find an alternative to Nasdaq to publish Island's market data, as required by the SEC. Nasdaq charged Island a fee for every trade reported, whereas Island did not share any of the revenues from Nasdaq's sale of its compiled data. The firm and CSE entered negotiations over a plan under which CSE would rebate up to 75 percent of market data revenues to Island. Island opted not to pursue a merger with CSE of the sort that Archipelago consummated with the Pacific Stock Exchange earlier in the year, a marriage that in October resulted in Archipelago being granted exchange status by the SEC. Membership in the CSE would not interfere with Island's application to become an exchange itself.

In June 2002, Island reached an agreement to be purchased by its chief competitor, Instinet Group Inc. for a deal valued at $508 million in stock. Together, the two companies would represent a significant challenge to its competitors, including Nasdaq. In a press release, an Instinet spokesperson stated: "The acquisition brings together superior trading platforms with a common goal of improving customers' performance by applying innovative technology solutions to equity trading. The combination is complementary on several levels. It is expected to deliver significant synergies as a result of expanded liquidity and cost savings in clearing, technology, facilities and administration."

### *Principal Competitors*

Instinet Group Inc.; Archipelago-RediBook; Brut ECN, LLC; Btrade.Com Inc.

### *Further Reading*


Andresen, Matthew, "Financial Marketplace Needs," *Congressional Testimony, Federal Document Clearing House,* March 22, 2000.

——, "Getting the Point About Decimalization," *Securities Week,* July 3, 2000, p. 7.

——, "Island's Andresen: Give Two Cheers to the SEC's Plan," *Securities Industry News,* August 14, 2000.

"As Island Gains Landmass, Exchanges Lose Theirs," *Future Banker,* November 11, 1999, p. 38.

Barboza, David, "Datek Is Said to Be Near Agreement to Sell Majority Stake to Group," *New York Times,* November 1, 2000, p. C1.

Birger, Jon, "Matthew Andresen, 29; President, Island ECN," *Crain's New York Business,* January 31, 2000, p. 18.

Burger, Andrew, "Island Sees Payoff in Registering As Exchange," *Securities Industry News,* December 21, 1998, p. 1.

Clary, Isabelle, "Fast-Growing Island Closer to Exchange Filing," *Securities Industry News,* December 10, 2001.

——, "Island Scores Points: ECN Bolsters Case for Exchange Status As It Tops Instinet's Volumes," *Securities Industry News,* January 7, 2002.

Deener, Bill, "Maverick Restyling America's Market ECNs Leads Charge in Stock-Trading Revolution," *Dallas Morning News,* February 20, 2000, p. H1.

"ECN Ad Campaign Keeps Battle Over Supermontage Going," *Securities Week,* August 14, 2000, p. 1.

Ewing, Terzah, "How Electronic Networks Snag Trades," *Wall Street Journal,* March 1, 1999, p. C1.

Graham, Jed, "Island Building a Beachhead in After-Hours Stock Trading," *Investor's Business Daily,* January 26, 2000, p. A6.

Green, Leslie, and Jerry Minkoff, "Investor Group Inks Deal for Datek Online," *BuyOuts,* December 18, 2000.

Hansard, Sara, "Day Trading Is All About Choice, and Giving People Access Is a Very Healthy Thing," *Investment News,* May 1, 2000, p. 54.

Harmon, Amy, "A Test Like None Before for the Computer Wizards," *New York Times,* September 17, 2001, p. C12.

Hendrickson, Mark, "Can Island Succeed Trading Listed Stocks?," *Securities Industry News,* February 14, 2000.

——, "Island's Move on Decimals Receives Mixed Response," *Securities Industry News,* April 24, 2000.

Henriques, Diana B., "Testing an Emerging Market; Can Wall St.'s Old Guards Cope with the New Trading?," *New York Times,* May 12, 1999, p. C1.

——, "3 Venture Capital Firms Take Stake in Datek Online Holdings," *New York Times,* May 25, 1999, p. C6.

"Island ECN's Surprise Decimal Option Could Help Persuade Congress ECNs a Positive Influence," *Securities Week,* April 24, 2000.

"Island May Not Be Alone in Move to Decimals," *Securities Week,* May 1, 2000, p. 1.

Johnson, Laura, "Island Eyes Ownership Stake in the P-coast," *Wall Street Letter,* August 30, 1999, p. 1.

Kite, Shane, and Mary Shroeder, "Island ECN Continues International Expansion," *Securities Industry News,* September 4, 2000.

Lux, Hal, and Jack Willoughby, "May Day II," *Institutional Investor,* February 1, 1999, p. 45.

McEachern, Cristina, Ivy Schmerken, Robert Sales, Kerry Massaro, and Andrew Rafalaf, "The Top 10 Financial Technology Innovators of the Decade," *WS&T,* December 1, 1999, p. 24.

Moskowitz, Eric, "Matt Andresen vs. Wall Street," *Money,* July, 2000, p. 132.

Raynovich, R. Scott, "A Challenger on Wall Street," *Redherring.com,* March 4, 1999.

Santini, Laura, "Island Wants Trade-Through Rule Removed," *Investment Dealers Digest,* October 16, 2000.

——, "A Rebel's Gamble Island Wants to Join the System, But Will It Work?," *Investment Dealers Digest,* January 29, 2001.

Schroeder, Mary, ''An Insider's Guide,'' *Securities Industry News,* January 17, 2000.

——, ''Island Eyes Move to Cincinnati Exchange,'' *Securities Industry News,* January 7, 2002.

''SEC Goes Back to the Industry for New Direction on Decimalization While Island ECN Prepares to Go It Alone,'' *Securities Week,* April 24, 2000.

Sommar, Jessica, ''AMEX Is Fighting Off Island,'' *New York Post,* October 24, 2001, p. 36.

Stirland, Sarah, ''Island Sees Long Haul to Exchange Status,'' *Securities Industry News,* January 25, 1999, p. 1.

''Unicredito's Tradinglab, Island ECN to Open Networks to Each Other's Clients,'' *AFX European Focus,* July 31, 2000.

Vogelstein, Fred, ''A Virtual Stock Market: Are the Nation's Two Big Stock Exchanges Obsolete?,'' *U.S. News & World Report,* April 26, 1999, pp. 47–48.

Wexler, Sanford, ''Wall Street's Top Blade: En Garde! ECN Official Ready to Fence with Wall Street Big Shots,'' *Traders Magazine,* March 1, 2000.

—Gerald E. Brennan

# J. D'Addario & Company, Inc.

595 Smith Street
Farmingdale, New York 11735
U.S.A.
Telephone: (631) 439-3300
Fax: (631) 439-3333
Web site: http://www.daddario.com

*Private Company*
*Incorporated:* 1975
*Employees:* 600
*Sales:* $62.40 million (2001)
*NAIC:* 339992 Musical Instrument Manufacturing

J. D'Addario & Company, Inc. is the largest maker of strings for musical instruments in the world. J. D'Addario also designs and manufacturers a collection of music-related accessories, including guitar straps and accessories, marketed under the Planet Waves brand name, and drum heads through its ownership of Evans Drumhead Company. A vertically integrated enterprise, the company designs and builds its own automated manufacturing equipment, operates its own printing press, and maintains a large research and development department. J. D'Addario's products are marketed in the United States through 20 wholesale distributors and roughly 5,400 retail music stores. The company exports its products through 120 distributors in more than 100 countries. The company is owned and managed by the D'Addario family.

### *Italian Origins*

The legacy behind the world's largest string maker goes back to 1680, when the D'Addario family first began making musical instrument string. The D'Addarios lived in a small village named Salle, in the province of Pescara, which was a hotbed of string manufacture. Dating back to the era of Stradivarius and Amati, Salle served as the home for scores of string producers, who chose the area because the local sheep herds provided a bountiful supply of gut. The D'Addario family thrived in Salle for centuries, hand-winding string for lutes, harps, guitars, and other musical instruments.

In 1905, a massive earthquake delivered a devastating blow to the community of string makers in Salle. Two D'Addario family members, Charles and Rocco, left the ruins of Salle and boarded a ship that took them to New York City, where they intended to use the D'Addario trade of string-making to survive. The brothers established modest production operations in a garage behind their home in Astoria, New York City, and traveled by subway to lower Manhattan, where slaughterhouses provided their new supply of sheep gut.

Within a decade, C. D'Addario & Co. was firmly established as a commercial enterprise. The company enjoyed a steady supply of business, selling handmade strings to violin makers and distributors. Reportedly, the only obstacle keeping the company's growth in check was Charles D'Addario's desire to keep the business small. According to accounts, Charles D'Addario was fiercely devoted to his family and unwilling to sacrifice time with his wife and children for the sake of C. D'Addario & Co.'s growth. It was a personality trait that his son, John D'Addario, born in 1916, did not inherit.

### *A New Generation in the 1930s*

John D'Addario proved to a pivotal force in the development of the D'Addario family business. In the 1930s, he played double bass for a dance band popular in New York City, serving as its front man. It was during this period, before John D'Addario reached his mid-twenties, that he convinced his father to begin manufacturing guitar strings. Charles D'Addario collaborated with a well-known guitar maker, John D'Angelico, to develop the first rational system of gauging guitar strings. Having felt success with his first attempt at innovation, Charles D'Addario began experimenting with other novel ideas. After World War II, he began working with synthetic materials, hoping to replace the traditional gut core used in strings for classical guitar strings, concert harps, and ukuleles. D'Addario's exploration of synthetic materials led to two positive results: it proved to be lucrative, and it made the C. D'Addario & Co. name part of U.S. pop culture in the 1950s.

In the course of his investigation into the potential of plastics, Charles D'Addario was introduced to Mario Maccafieri

## Company Perspectives:

*We receive letters each week regarding the correct pronunciation of the D'Addario name. Some years back, we even ran an ad that illustrated an easy way to pronounce the D'Addario name. The name is pronounced phonetically as follows: Da-Dairy-O. A simple way to pronounce the most difficult name in musical accessories!*

and his company, Mastro Plastics. Maccafieri had developed a plastic ukulele that millions of Americans saw on Arthur Godfrey's television program. The exposure Maccafieri's ukulele received on Godfrey's show triggered widespread interest in the plastic instrument. During a ten-year period, Maccafieri sold nearly seven million plastic ukuleles. D'Addario, who had collaborated with Maccafieri before the ukulele craze was ignited, sold nearly 28 million ukulele strings to Mastro Plastics, giving his company an unexpected surge in business.

Although Charles D'Addario experienced the financial rewards of delving into areas apart from his company's involvement in strings for classical instruments, he did display a more conservative side to his personality. John D'Addario, who had convinced his father to begin making guitar strings in the 1930s, was unable to persuade his father to make steel guitar strings during the 1950s. Not to be deterred, John D'Addario struck out on his own after he learned his father was unwilling to make an investment in steel guitar strings. In 1954, he formed a separate company, Archaic Strings, and almost immediately was rewarded for his resolve. Less than a year after Archaic Strings' formation, the U.S. was introduced to Elvis Presley, touching off a another nationwide craze that benefited the D'Addario name. Electric guitar sales across the country mushroomed, giving Archaic Strings a massive boost to its business.

As demonstrated in his determination to exploit the budding interest in rock-and-roll, John D'Addario was driven by ambition. Not long after the explosive growth of guitar sales in the country confirmed the value of forming Archaic Strings, John D'Addario was given the chance to impart his more ambitious nature onto his father's company. In 1962, Charles D'Addario retired and ceded control of the company to his son. John D'Addario promptly merged C. D'Addario & Co. with his eight-year-old Archaic Strings to form Darco Music Strings, Inc.

In the wake of D'Addario's move to consolidate the family's string-making operations, the Beatles landed on U.S. shores and ignited the greatest surge of growth in the history of the music industry. The fortunes to be made in the industry attracted massive conglomerates, ushering in an era of mergers and acquisitions that made for several incongruous corporate marriages. Broadcaster CBS acquired Fender Musical Instruments, energy behemoth Gulf & Western purchased Unicord Music, and retailer Sears acquired the U.S. rights to Vox amplifiers. There were numerous other corporate combinations made during the mid- to late 1960s, including John D'Addario's Darco Music Strings. In 1969, he sold the family business to the accomplished guitar-making company, C.F. Martin & Co., Inc., ending nearly three centuries of his family's independence in the string-making business.

### *A New Beginning in the 1970s*

John D'Addario continued his involvement with Darco Music Strings after its merger with C.F. Martin, but the union between the two companies was troubled from the start. The merger had been consummated before C.F. Martin's proposed initial public offering (IPO), but the guitar maker quickly fell victim to anemic market conditions. Industry-wide, sales plunged during the first half of the 1970s, which scotched C.F. Martin's plans to convert to public ownership. Ultimately, the relationship between John D'Addario and C.F. Martin management soured, prompting D'Addario to resign as Darco Music String's leader in 1974.

D'Addario decided to start anew after the failed pairing with C.F. Martin. He enlisted the help of his two sons, John, Jr., and Jim, and formed J. D'Addario & Company, Inc., a start-up company with nine generations of experience behind it. The new version of the D'Addario family business began with fewer than 20 employees housed in a 10,000-square-foot facility located in Lindenhurst, New York. The company quickly shed any resemblance to a fledgling enterprise by registering remarkable growth. By 1979, bigger quarters were needed to accommodate the company, leading to the relocation of headquarters to a 25,000-square-foot facility in Farmingdale, New York. In 1981, the company revisited the days of Charles and Rocco in Astoria by acquiring Kaplan Musical String Company, a venerable manufacturer of gut violin strings. In 1986, J. D'Addario delved into its first non-string related business, acquiring the Vandoren-Paris line of reeds and mouthpieces for woodwind instruments.

Against the backdrop of acquisitions, growth, and diversification, leadership of the company gradually was passed from father to sons. John D'Addario retired from active management of his company in 1983, yet remained chairman well into the 1990s. John, Jr., and Jim, however, began playing influential roles at J. D'Addario before their father's retirement.

### *Innovation in the 1980s*

During the 1980s, J. D'Addario dramatically advanced string manufacturing technology by drawing upon much the same formula that fueled Charles D'Addario's innovative work during the first half of the 20th century. The company's engineers precisely identified which attributes would create a superior product and then designed automated machinery to produce the product. The approach gradually led the company toward vertically integrating its operations to handling every step of the production process. Toward this end, the company excelled thanks largely to the spirit of innovation and self-reliance instilled by the younger D'Addario generation, John, Jr., and Jim.

The commitment to continually improve upon existing manufacturing processes resided in Jim D'Addario perhaps more than in John D'Addario, Jr. "My nature is inquisitive," Jim D'Addario remarked in a August 31, 2001 interview with *LI Business News*. "I visit factories, see what they're doing and think I can do it better." Shortly after J. D'Addario was formed, Jim D'Addario hired engineers to modify manufacturing equipment to deliver the product specifications he desired. The retrofit cost $18,000 per machine, prompting him to take matters into

**Key Dates:**

**1680:** The D'Addario family begins making strings for musical instruments.
**1905:** Charles and Rocco D'Addario move to New York City.
**1954:** John D'Addario forms Archaic Strings, a manufacturer of strings for electric guitars.
**1962:** C. D'Addario & Co. and Archaic Strings are merged, forming Darco Music Strings.
**1969:** Darco Music Strings is sold to C.F. Martin & Co.
**1975:** John D'Addario and his two sons, John, Jr., and Jim, start J. D'Addario & Co.
**1981:** Kaplan Musical String Company is acquired.
**1986:** The Vandoren-Paris line of reeds and mouthpieces is acquired.
**1995:** Evans Drumhead Company is acquired.
**1998:** Planet Waves, a line of guitar straps, is acquired.

his own hands and begin to vertically integrate the company's manufacturing operations. He hired engineers to design and build D'Addario's own proprietary machinery, which reduced the capital outlay to a remarkable $4,000 per machine.

The financial and quality-control rewards gained by taking command over all aspects of production led to the establishment of a full machine shop capable of designing manufacturing machinery and products. By using its research and development department and its machine shop, J. D'Addario dramatically advanced string-manufacturing technology during the 1980s. Imprecise hand-wound methods were replaced with automated, microprocessor-controlled winding machines that improved both efficiency and quality. Evidence of the benefits of the J. D'Addario approach was clearly shown in the company's growth during the 1980s: manufacturing output nearly doubled during the decade, but thanks to the efficiency of the J. D'Addario-designed machinery, the number of factory employees increased only modestly.

By the beginning of the 1990s, J. D'Addario ranked as the largest string maker in the world, commanding, according to company estimates, approximately 30 percent of the market. Annual sales exceeded $20 million and promised to rise higher after expansion projects slated for completion during the early years of the decade were completed. One such project, announced in early 1991, called for the construction of an 18,000-square-foot building to house its printing operation (J. D'Addario printed its own guitar string packages, catalogues, and stationery), research and development staff, and warehouse. The $2 million project augmented the company's nearby 42,000-square-foot engineering and manufacturing facility in Farmingdale. John D'Addario, Jr., in an April 1992 interview with *Music Trades,* remarked, ''Our core guitar string business has been expanding steadily, and our Vandoren reed and mouthpiece business has more than doubled over the past few years. With this increased business, we simply ran out of space.''

In the early 1980s, the company created a direct sales organization to help market its lines of guitar strings to retailers. By adding the Vandoren line of products to the merchandise that company representatives were able to present to retailers, the odds of reaching a sales agreement with a retailer improved. Consequently, after the successful incorporation of the Vandoren product line, the D'Addario brothers were on the prowl for additional product lines to add to the company's portfolio. In 1995, through the intervention of a European distributor, the brothers found their next acquisition target.

At the Frankfurt Fair in 1995, the D'Addario brothers were introduced to Bob Beals, owner of the Evans Drumhead Company. Founded by drummer Chick Evans in 1956, Evans Drumhead was the first company to sell a synthetic drumhead on the market. Beals, an early investor in Chick Evans' innovation, was ready to retire when he met the D'Addario brothers, who were ready to buy. A purchase agreement was reached within several months, and before the end of 1995 J. D'Addario acquired Evans Drumhead.

Once in control of the company, Jim D'Addario applied the D'Addario formula for success on Evans Drumhead. Working with a team of D'Addario engineers, Jim D'Addario spent two years concentrating on every aspect of the company's production process and making changes. By 1998, the improvements were noticeable. A host of new models had been introduced, the number of artist endorsers had swelled substantially, and a high-profile marketing campaign was underway. Production, housed in a new 47,000-square-foot factory in Farmingdale, had more than tripled from the pre-D'Addario era, reaching 4,000 drumheads per day.

The company's success with Evans Drumhead underscored the unique D'Addario ability to introduce sophisticated, innovative manufacturing and design techniques to the music industry. The turnaround effected at Evans Drumhead also encouraged the D'Addario brothers to venture further afield. In early 1998, they did so, acquiring guitar strap manufacturer Planet Waves. In typical D'Addario fashion, manufacturing processes were revamped and pioneering design innovations were introduced, including a rotary-buckle strap-locking device that enabled a Planet Wave guitar strap to fit on any guitar.

J. D'Addario's impressive rise from a small start-up firm to market champion was achieved largely because of the company's commitment to improving manufacturing processes. As it completed its first quarter-century of business and prepared for continued growth in the 21st century, the company's relentless drive for perfection promised to keep the J. D'Addario name at the top of its industry in the years ahead. ''If you think it's already been done or perfected, you need to think again,'' Jim D'Addario told *Music Trades* in June 1999. ''Dozens of products that people think are state-of-the-art are really ripe for change,'' he added. ''The next few years are going to be ones of great innovation at our company.''

### *Principal Subsidiaries*

J. D'Addario & Co. (Canada) Ltd.

### *Principal Competitors*

Dean Markley Strings, Inc.; Gibson Musical Instruments; C.F. Martin & Company, Inc.

### *Further Reading*

Bruinooge, Joel, ''D'Addario Expanding, Adding Staff,'' *LI Business News,* January 7, 1991, p. 13.

''D'Addario,'' *Music Trades,* November 1998, p. 136.

''D'Addario Expands Japanese Presence; Pearl Now Distributing D'Addario,'' *Music Trades,* September 2001, p. 38.

''D'Addario Opens New Manufacturing Facility,'' *Music Trades,* April 1992, p. 26.

''D'Addario R&D in Overdrive,'' *Music Trades,* March 2001, p. 192.

''D'Addario's New State-of-the-Art Plant,'' *Music Trades,* p. 142.

''D'Addario, String Maker, Dead at 84,'' *LI Business News,* June 9, 2000, p. 16A.

Genn, Adina, ''Vertical Integration Keeps D'Addario in Tune,'' *LI Business News,* August 31, 2001, p. 31A.

''Groundbreaking,'' *LI Business News,* December 3, 1990, p. 30.

''Laser Technology Improves D'Addario Strings; Advance Lasers Eliminate Inconsistencies in all Nylon Strings,'' *Music Trades,* February 1990, p. 98.

''The 'New' Evans Drumhead Company,'' *Music Trades,* November 1998, p. 80.

''Re-Thinking the Guitar Strap,'' *Music Trades,* June 1999, p. 76.

—Jeffrey L. Covell

# Jackson Hewitt, Inc.

**339 Jefferson Road**
**Parsippany, New Jersey 07054**
**U.S.A.**
**Telephone: (973) 496-1040**
**Toll Free: (877) 829-6291**
**Fax: (973) 496-2785**
**Web site: http://www.jacksonhewitt.com**

*Wholly Owned Subsidiary of Cendant Corporation*
*Incorporated:* 1982
*Employees:* 3,549
*Sales:* $140 million (2001 est.)
*NAIC:* 541213 Tax Preparation Services

Jackson Hewitt, Inc. is the second largest tax preparation service in the United States. The company has more than 3,300 franchised outlets in 48 states and the District of Columbia and prepares more than 2.2 million tax returns annually. A quarter of its offices are located inside Wal-Mart and Kmart stores. The company also offers tax refund-anticipation loans, free electronic filing, tax-preparation training, and tax audit representation. Jackson Hewitt was acquired by Cendant Corporation in 1998.

### *Beginnings*

Jackson Hewitt was founded in 1982 by John Hewitt, a former employee of tax-service giant H&R Block. Hewitt, a college dropout, had worked his way up to the position of regional manager after starting with Block in 1969. Feeling that tax preparation could be improved by the use of computers, he worked with his father to create a program that would streamline the client interview process. When they were unable to sell it to Block or other tax services, Hewitt and his wife decided to go into business for themselves. They assembled a group of a dozen investors and purchased the six-location Mel Jackson's Tax Service of Norfolk, Virginia in 1982, later renaming it Jackson Hewitt. For the next several years the company grew slowly, adding a handful of additional outlets.

In 1986, the year the IRS began to experiment with computerized tax filing, Jackson Hewitt began selling franchises. By the following tax season there were 22 offices. In October of 1989 the company received its biggest break to date when the Montgomery Ward department store chain contracted with it to open offices in 169 stores around the country. Ward rival Sears had for years been host to H&R Block in its stores. Unfortunately, the sudden growth surge was too much for Jackson Hewitt to handle, and to avoid entering bankruptcy during the height of tax season the firm closed 67 offices. By the end of 1990 the company had made a return to profitability, however, and eventually opened more locations in Ward stores.

Jackson Hewitt's competitive edge was provided by its Hewtax Software (later known as ProFiler), which took a tax preparer through a series of questions. Each response generated additional queries depending on the answer, a so-called "decision tree" format. An affirmative response to a question about stock ownership, for example, would trigger more specific questions about the stock. The software could also transfer all of the appropriate information to the state tax form from the federal one, as well as yield a completed electronic return that could be filed instantly to expedite a client's refund. Hewitt claimed that use of the software saved it 10 percent in labor costs. It also required less training time for new employees than industry leader Block (which was still not fully computerized) and resulted in more consistent results for customers.

### *The Number Two Tax Return Preparation Service by 1992*

By the 1992 tax season the Jackson Hewitt chain had grown to 515 offices in close to 30 states, up from 299 locations the year before. The company itself owned less than 5 percent of the total. It prepared 311,000 returns for taxpayers during the year, which helped yield annual revenues of $7.4 million and net earnings of $182,000. Industry leader H&R Block was still far larger, with more than 7,000 locations and revenues of $699 million, but Jackson Hewitt had nonetheless become the country's second largest tax preparation chain. The following year saw the company raise $2.5 million in funds for expansion from a venture capital company and move into new headquarters in Virginia Beach, Virginia.

The company's franchisees often came from the ranks of its preparers, ten of which worked at an average outlet. Jackson

## Company Perspectives:

*When it comes to taxes, we all can use a little bit of help—someone to guide us and someone we can trust. With over 3,000 offices nationwide, Jackson Hewitt is committed to the millions of Americans who rely on us as their tax preparer.* Fast. *Jackson Hewitt will expedite your tax return. With the development of electronic filing as the IRS's preferred method of filing returns, Jackson Hewitt is leading the way with its state-of-the-art computer-based filing capabilities. Electronic filing significantly limits the time it will take for you to receive your return and refund.* Accurate. *Accuracy is critical. The winning combination of Jackson Hewitt's exclusive ProFiler tax software and more than 10,000 skilled tax professionals ensures we take advantage of all the recent tax law changes.* Professional. *Possibly in no other area is customer service more important than tax preparation. Jackson Hewitt prides itself on taking care of the customer from the tax interview process to providing timely refund.*

Hewitt put the seasonal workers through its own ''tax school'' to prepare them for the 13- to 15-week tax season in the winter and early spring of each year. The school also was offered to the general public for those who wished to learn more about doing their own taxes—and Jackson Hewitt actively recruited from such students to find its own employees. Work as a tax preparer meant long hours and occasional stress as taxpayers argued over the legitimacy of their deductions. The company put boxes of tissue around its offices for clients who became teary-eyed when they did not get the tax breaks they had hoped for. For a franchisee, the startup cost was between $35,000 and $50,000, which included a $20,000 franchise fee and the costs of renting office space and purchasing equipment. Jackson Hewitt took a 12 percent royalty out of the office's earnings, and also charged 6 percent for advertising costs.

The company, with 900 offices in 37 states by 1993, was beginning to get noticed by the media. Jackson Hewitt was ranked 18th best franchiser in *Success* magazine and was listed as one of *Inc.* magazine's 500 fastest-growing private companies. The firm soon began making plans to go public, which took place in January of 1994 on the NASDAQ exchange. No new stock was issued, however, with the company's 700 investors' private shares simply converted into public ones. The move was made in part because the firm's accounting requirements were already close to those of public firms, and also to boost its profile to spur more franchise sales. During 1994 Jackson Hewitt experimented with operating several locations as combined tax office/mail service firms, seeking to give the company's franchisees additional sources of revenue during the eight months of the year when there was little work. Most of the company's income came during the fourth quarter of the fiscal year, with losses generally reported for the first three.

In early 1994 Jackson Hewitt made a deal to set up offices in some Sam's Club stores on a trial basis. The company hoped that it would lead to a systemwide contract with sister chain Wal-Mart, which could mean as many as 400 additional locations. The test was a success, and in the fall Jackson Hewitt made plans to open 18 offices in Wal-Mart stores, leasing space for use as combined tax preparation and business/mail service sites. The company also filed suit against H&R Block during the year, alleging that the industry leader's ad slogan ''Nothing's Faster, Nothing's Easier'' was untrue, as Jackson Hewitt's service was both faster and easier than Block's. The suit was dropped after a federal judge refused to halt the $5.5 million ad campaign.

### *Problems Caused by Changes in Tax Rules in 1995*

Jackson Hewitt received more unwelcome news in 1995 when a change in federal tax rules eliminated an automated ''direct deposit indicator'' for refunds, which had been used by the firm and its associated lenders to pre-approve clients for the popular refund anticipation loans that were offered for a fee. Income from these loans, which had become a welcome service for many cash-strapped taxpayers, accounted for nearly a quarter of the company's $18.6 million in 1994 annual revenues. After the rule change, Jackson Hewitt was forced to raise its requirements for the loans, which reduced the number of applicants eligible for them. Although many taxpayers were able to switch to the firm's ''accelerated check'' refunds, this was less profitable for the company. The 1995 tax season proved a difficult one for all concerned, angering those taxpayers who found out they would not get instant tax refunds, as well as others whose checks were partially held back due to additional last-minute IRS rule changes. In some locations customers threatened company employees with violence, and a near-riot at a Florida office required police intervention.

At the end of the 1995 filing season, Jackson Hewitt, ''battered'' by the effect of the tax rule changes, according to CEO John Hewitt, was hanging on by a thread. The firm's franchisees reportedly had not paid $3.5 million in fees to the company, which soon was nearing default on several loans from NationsBank. During the remainder of the year, 96 offices were closed. There was a management shakeup as well, and the firm began seeking a new CEO, with John Hewitt shifting his focus to long-term strategy from day-to-day operations. In June of 1996 newcomer Keith Alessi, who had most recently served as vice-chairman of supermarket chain Farm Fresh, Inc., was appointed to the top post. Three months later John Hewitt resigned from the company. Vowing to remain in the tax business, Hewitt later announced plans to form tax preparation services in Canada, England, and Australia, with the United States to follow when a two-year noncompete period was over.

The 1996 and 1997 tax seasons saw the company's fortunes improve dramatically, with earnings figures up and franchise numbers jumping from less than 1,400 to about 1,900. The 1997 total included 300 new locations inside Wal-Mart stores, where there were now 500 Jackson Hewitt offices chainwide. Federal tax changes that made filing more complicated played into the company's hand, with more taxpayers feeling the need to seek professional assistance. The firm's stock price began to soar, and one million new shares were offered in the summer, raising more than $18 million. By October the share price had grown tenfold since the beginning of the year, reaching $50.

### *Acquisition by Cendant in 1997*

In December the company announced that it was being acquired by HFS Inc. for $480 million, which further boosted the share price. Before the sale was complete, HFS merged with another firm and changed its name to Cendant Corporation.

## Key Dates:

**1982:** John Hewitt and investor group buy six-location Mel Jackson's Tax Service.
**1986:** Franchising of Jackson Hewitt offices starts.
**1989:** The company begins to open sites in Montgomery Ward stores.
**1992:** The firm goes public on the NASDAQ exchange.
**1994:** Offices begin opening in Sam's Club and Wal-Mart stores.
**1996:** Keith Alessi is named CEO; John Hewitt leaves the firm.
**1998:** The company is purchased by Cendant Corporation.
**1999:** The rate of expansion increases; the company sells its remaining sites to franchisees.
**2000:** Offices begin opening in Kmart stores.

Cendant owned a number of well-known franchise operations, including Ramada Inn, Days Inn, Avis Rent-A-Car, and realty chains Coldwell Banker and Century 21. In March of 1998, following completion of the acquisition, CEO Keith Alessi left Jackson Hewitt to head financially troubled TeleSpectrum Worldwide Inc. of Pennsylvania. With his stock options and a number of shares purchased on the open market, Alessi reaped a $20 million payoff from his time with Jackson Hewitt.

Under Cendant the company instituted a strategy of aggressive expansion. A total of 1,000 new offices were added by the start of the 1999 tax season, bringing the company up to a total of nearly 3,000. Experiments with kiosk locations in shopping malls and offices at Century 21 real estate agencies also were being tried. A national advertising campaign was soon launched, using the theme "Because you work hard for the money, we're going to work hard for you." The ads were targeted at both general and Hispanic audiences, with several television spots shown during Super Bowl pre-game programs. The company's customer base was, in large part, middle- and low-income taxpayers, many of them Hispanic Americans, who found it worth the typical fee of $100 to $150 to avoid having to navigate the increasingly complicated tax codes, as well as to get an accelerated refund check.

Following the 1999 tax season Jackson Hewitt named Daniel Tarantin president and moved the company's headquarters to Cendant's home base of Parsippany, New Jersey. The company also earmarked $30 million for the acquisition of independent tax preparation offices through Tax Services of America, which was its largest franchisee and partly owned by the firm. The company was now actively selling all of its remaining centrally owned locations. Meanwhile, deposed founder John Hewitt's startup Liberty Tax Service had grown into the third largest tax preparation chain in the United States, and he soon leased the former headquarters site of Jackson Hewitt in Virginia Beach, Virginia, vowing to beat the company that had spurned him.

In 2001 the company began opening offices in Kmart stores around the United States, following a successful trial run in select cities. The year also saw several new initiatives, including the issuance of MasterCard cash cards so customers could draw on their accelerated refund accounts, and the creation of a Premier Tax Service to handle more complicated returns. Some Jackson Hewitt locations began to offer ATM machines where clients could cash their refund checks on-site, as well. Independent tax service acquisitions continued throughout the year, with more than 3,300 offices, owned by 600 franchisees, operational by year's end. The company reported that it had handled a record 2.2 million returns during the 2001 tax season.

With the backing of Cendant, Jackson Hewitt was aggressively nipping at the heels of industry giant H&R Block. The company's future growth would continue to be dependent on the whims of the IRS to some extent, but it appeared clear that increasing numbers of Americans were becoming accustomed to hiring a service to do their taxes and to expedite their refund.

### *Principal Competitors*

H&R Block, Inc.; Liberty Tax Service.

### *Further Reading*

DeKok, David, "Tax Firm Moves to Add More Franchises," *Sunday Patriot-News Harrisburg,* June 16, 1996, p. D1.
Gore, Mollie, "Although a Distant Second, Service Has Eye on Leader," *Richmond Times-Dispatch,* September 17, 1992, p. B10.
Hock, Sandy, "Jackson Hewitt Shops for Clients at 18 Wal-Marts," *Accounting Today,* October 10, 1994, p. 1.
Hoene, Nancy, "Tax Firms Brace for Rush," *Capital Times,* March 10, 1999, p. 1C.
"It's Taxing to Challenge H&R Block Expansion," *Los Angeles Times,* March 4, 1993, p. 7.
Klein, Melissa, "Jackson Hewitt Plans Franchise Rollups," *Accounting Today,* April 17, 2000, p. 1.
Knight, Jerry, "A New Tax Bill? Another Boost to Jackson Hewitt," *Washington Post,* July 14, 1997, p. F25.
Mayfield, Dave, "Jackson Hewitt Launches Program to Reduce its Costs," *Virginian-Pilot and The Ledger-Star* (Norfolk, Va.), September 20, 1995, p. D1.
——, "Jackson Hewitt Seeks New Chief Executive," *Virginian-Pilot and The Ledger-Star* (Norfolk, Va.), December 16, 1995, p. D1.
——, "Maturing of Founder and Firm," *Virginian-Pilot and The Ledger-Star* (Norfolk, Va.), November 14, 1993, p. E1.
——, "Tax Season Turns Tumultuous," *Virginian-Pilot and The Ledger-Star* (Norfolk, Va.), February 19, 1995, p. D1.
Miller, Tracy L., "Jackson Hewitt Sold to HFS for $480 Million," *Accounting Today,* December 15, 1997, p. 1.
Richman, Tom, "The Best of Intentions: It's Not Enough to Do Well, You've Got to Know How," *Inc.,* April 1, 1991, p. 109.
Russell, Roger, "Jackson Hewitt Expansion Adds Locations, New Services," *Accounting Today,* February 12, 2001, p. 10.
Shean, Tom, "HFS to Buy Jackson Hewitt," *Virginian-Pilot and The Ledger-Star* (Norfolk, Va.), November 20, 1997, p. D1.
——, "The Ins and Outs of Franchising," *Virginian-Pilot and The Ledger-Star* (Norfolk, Va.), May 19, 1997, p. D1.
——, "Jackson Hewitt to Sell Shares," *Virginian-Pilot and The Ledger-Star* (Norfolk, Va.), July 29, 1997, p. D1.
——, "New Chief Remaking Tax-Preparation Service," *Virginian-Pilot and The Ledger-Star* (Norfolk, Va.), January 19, 1997, p. D1.
——, "Preparing a National Strategy," *Virginian-Pilot and The Ledger-Star* (Norfolk, Va.), October 5, 1998, p. D1.
——, "Tax Service CEO Moves On," *Virginian-Pilot and The Ledger-Star* (Norfolk, Va.), March 25, 1998, p. D1.
Swardson, Anne, "Competitor Hewitt Hopes Computers Will Snare Bigger Block of Returns," *Washington Post,* April 3, 1998, p. H2.

—Frank Uhle

# John W. Danforth Company

1940 Fillmore Avenue
Buffalo, New York 14214
U.S.A.
Telephone: (716) 832-1940
Fax: (716) 832-2388
Web site: http://www.jwdanforth.com

*Private company*
*Incorporated:* 1884
*Employees:* 250
*Sales:* $61 million
*NAIC:* 235110 Plumbing, Heating and Air-Conditioning Contractors

John W. Danforth Company is a mechanical contractor specializing in large-scale industrial, institutional, and commercial projects. The company's many capabilities include heating, ventilation, and air conditioning; plumbing; waste and sewage treatment; environmental compliance and remediation; refrigeration; fire protection; and industrial process piping. Danforth is headquartered in Buffalo, New York, and has branch offices in Niagara Falls, Rochester, and Syracuse, New York. While most the company's work is in the northeastern United States, it has also completed projects on the west coast and in Florida.

## *Modest Beginnings*

John W. Danforth Co. was founded in Buffalo, New York, in 1884 by John Willison Danforth, an engineer who did contract steam-heating and ventilating work for local clients. For the first decade of its existence, the small company focused on residential projects. Near the end of the 19th century, however, it began installing heating equipment in larger buildings such as clubs and churches. Danforth was a strong believer in the unionization of the American workforce. In 1889, the company became a member of the Master Steam and Hot Water Fitters Association of the United States—the forerunner to the Heating Piping Contractors National Association of America.

In 1903, John Danforth's son, Loring, joined the family business. Loring, who had received an engineering degree from Massachusetts Institute of Technology, helped his father expand beyond the residential business he had built into industrial and institutional contract work. Danforth was well positioned geographically for such work. The city of Buffalo, situated on Lake Erie and serving as both a major port and railway hub, had become a manufacturing center for such industries as steel, automobiles, and locomotives. Danforth began serving as a general contractor to Buffalo-area manufacturers, taking on larger-scale projects.

The firm also began bidding on projects outside the Buffalo area. Soon, it was handling projects throughout the eastern United States. During World War I, it served as a general contractor for the U.S. Navy Bureau of Yards and Docks, overseeing projects on both the east and west coast.

When John Danforth died in 1911, Loring became the company's leader. For the 22 years that this second-generation Danforth served as president, the company worked on a broad array of projects that spanned the United States, including a power station in Missouri, a hotel in North Carolina, and a significant amount of work in the Washington, D.C., area. In the 1920s, Danforth became a full-service mechanical contractor specializing in systems work for the fast-growing chemical and steel industries.

## *1930s–1960s: A New Family in Power*

In 1936, Loring Danforth died unexpectedly, and the business passed out of the Danforth family. It was acquired by the company's former vice-president, Leo Hopkins, and a business partner, Albert Wood. The two new owners decided to keep the well-thought-of Danforth name, and Leo Hopkins became the company's president. Following John Danforth's precedent, he hired his son, L. Nelson Hopkins, Jr., to help run the business.

The Hopkinses expanded the range of Danforth's services. The company began specializing in the installation of process piping for chemical, rubber, and steel manufacturers. Its growing expertise in this area soon opened up doors in the heavily

## Company Perspectives:

*The John W. Danforth Company offers a combination of experience, skills, and expertise in mechanical systems and equipment erection that is unmatched. No project is too big, too small, or too complicated. A stable work force of skilled union craftsmen offers expertise in fabricating common or the most exotic materials for the most demanding applications, from food processing and pharmaceutical production to chemical and industrial plants. Regardless of the nature of the project, the John W. Danforth Company is committed to meeting and exceeding the quality requirements of the customer.*

industrialized Niagara Falls region, just north of Buffalo. Similar to Buffalo, the Falls area was home to many major manufacturers, who had located there to take advantage of its water power and its proximity to the Canadian border. In the first few decades of the 20th century, Danforth completed projects for several Falls-area clients, including the companies today known as Occidental Chemical, Goodyear, and Bell Aircraft.

In the 1940s, the company was again called upon to aid in the war effort. It built aircraft-manufacturing plants in New York and in Louisville, Kentucky, all the while continuing to further expand its business in the steel and chemical plants of western New York. By mid-century, Danforth was doing enough business around Niagara Falls to justify opening a branch office there. That office opened in 1946 under the direction of Clifford Carroll.

As the 1950s gave way to the 1960s, John W. Danforth's headquarters moved from its facility on Ellicott Street in Buffalo to 1940 Fillmore Avenue, which was several blocks north and east of the old location. The early sixties also brought a succession in leadership. In 1964, Leo Hopkins became chairman of the board, and his son, L. Nelson Hopkins, took over his position as the company's president. Like his predecessors, Nelson Hopkins expanded the breadth of Danforth's contracting experience. The company developed the ability to contract for the building of "clean rooms"—the dust free, controlled research labs used by such companies as Westinghouse and Bell Aerospace. It also began specializing in the installation of fire protection equipment.

### *1970s–90s: Danforth Under the Reilly Family*

In 1978, Wayne Reilly became John W. Danforth's newest president. Reilly was a long-time veteran of the company, having started as clerk in the mid-1950s and worked his way up through the ranks. Reilly's assumption of the presidency coincided with the Love Canal crisis in Niagara Falls, a situation that provided Danforth with the opportunity to enter still another area of specialization.

Love Canal was a section of Niagara Falls that had been used as a dumping ground for a chemical company in the 1940s and 1950s. It had later been filled in, and housing had been built on the site. In the 1970s, however, research into the area's unusually high rates of illnesses and birth defects discovered that toxic waste had leaked into and contaminated the soil. In 1978, residents were evacuated from the area, and two years later Love Canal was declared a national emergency. After Congress created the Superfund law, cleanup of the area began. Danforth was one of the many contractors employed in the remediation, and was one of the first to be licensed by the Atomic Energy Commission to use radioactive isotopes to find leaks.

## Key Dates:

**1884:** John Willison Danforth establishes J.W. Danforth Company.
**1903:** Loring Danforth joins the company.
**1911:** John Danforth dies, leaving Loring Danforth in charge.
**1936:** Loring Danforth dies, and the company is acquired by Leo Hopkins and Albert Wood.
**1946:** Danforth opens a Niagara Falls branch office.
**1964:** Leo Hopkins's son, L. Nelson Hopkins, becomes Danforth's president.
**1978:** Wayne Reilly becomes Danforth's president.
**1980:** Danforth acquires Dineen Mechanical Contractors.
**1985:** JWD Group is established as a parent company for John W. Danforth and John W. Danforth Service Companies.
**1988:** Danforth acquires Nova Mechanical Contractors.
**1993:** Emmett Reilly succeeds his father as Danforth's president.
**2000:** Danforth works as a subcontractor constructing facilities for the Goodwill Winter Games.
**2001:** The company begins planning to relocate its headquarters.

Reilly not only expanded the company's range of services, he also broadened its geographic reach and slightly altered its corporate structure. In 1980, Danforth acquired Dineen Mechanical Contractors, Inc., of Rochester, New York. In 1985, the company formed the JWD Group, Inc., which served as a parent company to the various branch offices of the John W. Danforth Company and to the newly formed John W. Danforth Service Company, a business specializing in nonresidential heating and air conditioning services. In 1988, the company stretched still a little further east, acquiring the Syracuse-based Nova Mechanical Contractors. Both Dineen and Nova eventually became branch offices, taking on the Danforth name, which had become quite well known throughout upstate New York.

The company's expansion led to a tremendous increase in revenues. Whereas Danforth had started the eighties with sales of around $10 million, by the latter part of the decade that number had more than tripled. The late 1980s also brought the company back to its old headquarters on Ellicott Street, albeit only to serve as a contractor for Pilot Field, the baseball park that the city of Buffalo was building there. Danforth served as contractor for the new ballpark's heating and air conditioning, plumbing, irrigation, and sprinkler systems.

In 1993, Wayne Reilly became Danforth's CEO and chairman, vacating the office of president. That post was filled by Reilly's son Emmett, who had previously worked at Danforth in the Estimating and Project Management Department and had also headed up the company' Rochester office for three years. Reilly's two other sons, Patrick and Kevin, both served as senior vice-presidents.

### *A 21st Century Danforth*

The first year of the new century brought both good and bad news for Danforth. Business was strong; for the first quarter, the company booked some $30 million in projects—a full half of what the company was accustomed to billing annually. Much of the new business came from area schools, which were upgrading their infrastructures. The company also got the chance to participate in constructing the facilities for the Goodwill Winter Games that were held at Lake Placid, New York. Working as a subcontractor for a New York-based general contractor, Danforth installed almost 50 miles of ammonia refrigeration piping for the bobsled and luge tracks.

The bad news came in November, when a heavy storm dumped 25 inches of snow on Danforth's Buffalo headquarters, causing serious damage. As a temporary measure, the company obtained space in various Buffalo office buildings and spread its headquarters functions among them while it evaluated potential sites for a new headquarters. By the end of 2001, Danforth was in lease negotiations with a development company that was proposing to build a 61,294-square-foot commercial facility in Tonawanda, New York. If the companies were able to reach an agreement, it was expected that Danforth would occupy most of the facility.

Other than the impending headquarters relocation, it appeared that no major changes were in the offing for Danforth. The company was, however, in the process of expanding its John W. Danforth Service Company business slightly. In June of 2001, it acquired Applied Mechanical Testing, Inc, which broadened its service offerings to include air balancing and duct cleaning.

### *Principal Subsidiaries*

John W. Danforth Service Company.

### *Principal Competitors*

Sauer Inc.; Joseph Davis, Inc.; John J. Kirlin Inc.; PPL Energy Services Holdings, LLC; Herman Goldner Co. Inc.; HEC/Denron Plumbing & Hvac Inc.; Joule Industrial Contractors; PSEG Energy Technologies; EMCOR Group Inc.

### *Further Reading*

Hartley, Tom, "John W. Danforth Looks after the Mechanics of a Project," *Business First of Buffalo, 1990 Top 100 Private Companies*, 1990.

Mader, Robert, "Danforth Co. Shows It Is Pretty Slick," *Contractor*, February 2000, p. 1.

—Shawna Brynildssen

Kettle Foods

HAND COOKED · ALL NATURAL

# Kettle Foods Inc.

**3125 Kettle Court**
**Salem, Oregon 97301**
**U.S.A.**
**Telephone: (503) 364-0399**
**Fax: (503) 371-1447**
**Web site: http://www.kettlefoods.com**

*Private Company*
*Incorporated:* 1981 as N.S. Khalsa Co.
*Employees:* 250
*Sales:* $60 million (2000 est.)
*NAIC:* 311919 Potato Chips and Corn Chips/Snacks Manufacturer; 311423 Dried/Dehydrated Fruits and Vegetables Manufacturer; 311911 Salted and Roasted Nuts and Seeds Manufacturer

Kettle Foods Inc. of Salem, Oregon, is a maker of healthful gourmet snack foods: Kettle Chips, Kettle Crisps Baked Potato Chips, Krinkle Cut Kettle Chips, Kettle Tortilla Chips, Kettle Roaster Fresh Nut Butters, and Kettle Quality Handcrafted Nuts. The company has facilities in Salem, Oregon; Springfield, Ohio; and Norwich, England. Its products are sold in all 50 states, Canada, the Pacific Rim, the United Kingdom, and Western Europe.

### *1978 Entry Into the New Natural Foods Market*

Cameron Healy founded Kettle Foods as the N.S. Khalsa Co. in Salem, Oregon, in 1978, wholesaler of nuts, cheese, and trail mixes. With a $10,000 bank loan and no working capital, Healy (who then went by the name of Nirbhao Singh Khalsa) sold his all-natural items from a dilapidated van to natural food stores along Interstate 5 in Oregon. According to the company's web site, he had no master plan, but knew that he ''wanted to develop products of natural integrity that could be flexible in both the natural food and mainstream markets'' since ''the priority for quality lifestyles and values would be growing into more mass markets as baby boomers matured.''

Healy first had entered the natural food industry in 1972 when he invested $1,000 to start the Golden Temple Bakery in Eugene, Oregon. Golden Temple, which grew out of the local yoga and Sikh communities, produced granola and whole grain breads, which it distributed to natural food stores throughout the Willamette Valley. Healy, a native of Bend, Oregon, and son of businessman Bill Healy, the driving force behind the Mt. Bachelor ski resort, had never intended to enter business, according to a 1989 *Statesman Journal* article. At the University of Oregon, he had majored in general social science while pursuing a spiritual path involving kundalini yoga; he had converted to Sikhism in 1971. His business was a way to earn a living that fit and promoted his values and, as it grew, a way to employ other members of the commune where he lived. A year and a half later, upon completing college, Healy donated the bakery to the commune and moved to Salem, Oregon, where he taught yoga and started the Golden Temple Natural Food Distributors. After five years in the distribution business, Healy decided to get back into manufacturing, concentrating on turning commodity products into minimally processed branded food products.

For the first year, N.S. Khalsa Co. sold nuts. Healy then expanded into roasting nuts and making nut butters. Nuts proved too limited, however, and so he turned to chips. ''People love potato chips,'' he was quoted as saying in a 1999 *Statesman* article. ''I knew if I could create a distinctive enough product, there would be a mystique about them.''

Healy began experimenting with frying Oregon potatoes in his nut roaster at night in 1982 after a trip to Hawaii to the Maui Potato Chip Co. to learn about the original Maui old-fashioned chip, which he discovered was made with Klamath Falls potatoes. In keeping with his all-natural philosophy, N.S. Khalsa Co.'s potato chips were made from premium Russet Burbank potatoes grown in the Hermiston area of hot eastern Oregon on small, family-owned farms. These were cut thick, with the potato skin left intact, seasoned with natural ingredients, and stirred by hand in large kettles of high-oleic safflower oil. At that time, they were the only hand-cooked potato chips in the western United States.

Potato chips, however, had a long and colorful history in the United States. According to food historians, potato chips originated in 1853 at the Moon's Lake House Hotel in Saratoga Springs, New York, when chef George Crumb fried thinly sliced potatoes for a particularly demanding patron, who kept

### Company Perspectives:

*Through the commitment of our people, we handcraft great tasting, all natural snack foods.*

### Key Dates:

**1978:** Cameron Healy founds N.S. Khalsa Co. in Salem, Oregon.
**1980:** The company begins making nut butters, its first branded products.
**1988:** The company changes its name to Kettle Foods Inc. and purchases five acres of vacant land; the company rents part of the Tuckers factory in Norwich, England.
**1993:** Kettle Foods Ltd. moves to a new, larger site in Bowthorpe.
**1997:** Kettle Foods acquires a second processing plant in Springfield, Ohio.
**2000:** The company moves into its new headquarters and production facilities.

sending his French-fried potatoes back to the kitchen, complaining that they were not sliced thin enough. What was sent back by the chef in revenge became known as the Saratoga chip. By the 1920s and 1930s, every town in the United States had its own potato chipper where the chip maker sliced up bunches of potatoes and fried them one batch at a time. In the 1940s and 1950s, most chip manufacturers switched to a continuous method of production—automated conveyor belts that met the growing demand for chips. Potato farmers started breeding the sugars out of potatoes to accommodate this process because the variable sugar content in potatoes such as the Russet Burbank demands a more individualized frying process.

Healy originally wanted to call his chips ''pot chips'' because that is what they were called in the 1920s and 1930s on the east coast, but friends and family dissuaded him from doing so. So the chips became Kettle Chips to evoke their traditional manufacturing method. They were packaged in paper sacks printed in earth tones with the company's logo, a man stirring chips in an old-fashioned kettle. The company's first two years of making old-fashioned chips were times of experimentation and lessons learned about the way sugars develop in potatoes. ''There were times,'' Healy said in the *Statesman* in 1999, ''We had to pull product off the shelves because the quality wasn't there.'' Still, with its potato chip line just a year old, N.S. Khalsa Co. reached $3 million in sales.

### *Rapid Expansion Throughout the 1980s–90s*

Throughout the early 1980s, Kettle Chips were a strong item in natural food stores, which then enjoyed a $1.9 billion market segment in the United States. They also spread slowly into independent grocery stores. With little money for marketing, the company could not afford to buy shelf space in the larger national grocery chains, which is the way in which other potato chips were marketed. At first, Kettle Chips were available in only two versions—salted and unsalted—but in time the company added flavored varieties, such as New York Cheddar with Herbs, Yogurt and Green Onion, and Red Chile. By 1986, the company had revenues of $4.5 million, and Fred Meyer, a regional food chain in the Northwest, named N.S. Khalsa its ''Vendor of the Year.''

In 1987, with company sales doubling annually and a 15 percent annual growth in business, Healy took a seven-week break to motorcycle around Europe with his 19-year-old son. During this trip, Healy met Tim Meyer, a Salem native turned London resident, and the two decided to begin Kettle Chips' expansion into England. In 1988, Meyer and Healy made contact with an English potato merchant and set up an agreement with Tuckers, a British chips company in Norwich, England, to rent part of their factory. Sales of Kettle Crisps soared almost immediately, and by 1989, Kettle Crisps (which is what they were called in the United Kingdom) were selling throughout England, Scotland, and Wales, and at a few locations in Sweden and Germany. Breaking into the English market was far easier than breaking into the market at home, according to a 1989 *Statesman Journal* article, because the market in the United Kingdom was nationwide, whereas in the United States, there were regional markets. After five years at the Tuckers plant, Kettle Foods Ltd. moved to a new, larger site in Bowthorpe, on the outskirts of the city.

N.S. Khalsa Co. changed its name to Kettle Foods in 1988. The company purchased new equipment at home and began to make gains in the Canadian market, where it set up a manufacturing and distributing agreement with Lifestream Natural Foods of Vancouver, British Columbia. Healy, who owned about 90 percent of the company's stock, oversaw his business turn revenues of $6.4 million in 35 states and several foreign counties, about half of it in chips. The company, still committed to making use mostly of local products, bought about 100,000 pounds of potatoes each week from Klamath County. It controlled, according to company estimates, somewhere between 6 and 10 percent of the potato chip market in Oregon and between 2 and 5 percent in Washington state.

By the late 1980s to early 1990s, the company was outgrowing its 25,000-square-foot domestic plant. In 1994, Kettle Foods fried more than 6.5 million pounds of potatoes a year and produced almost five million bags of potato chips, a 480,000 increase from 1993. In 1995, 50 percent of the company's overall sales came from chips, which it sold throughout Oregon, Washington, and northern California, as well as in Canada and Japan; 30 percent came from nuts and trail mixes sold in bulk to grocery stores in the western United States; and 20 percent from tortilla chips and soybean margarine. Overseas, Kettle Foods Ltd. exported chips to Ireland, Germany, France, Holland, and Belgium. Healy, who formally reclaimed his family-given name in the fall of 1995, spent about two days a week at the Salem plant. The rest of the time, he worked from his Portland home or assisted his son in developing a brewery in Kona, Hawaii.

By mid-1997, Kettle Foods had acquired a second processing plant in Springfield, Ohio and began expanding aggressively in the Midwest and in eastern markets. Still, about 60 percent of the potatoes the company purchased came from a half dozen growers in the Willamette Valley, the remainder from farms elsewhere in Oregon, Washington, and Idaho. The company as a whole employed 80 people at its Salem headquarters and more than 200 people at its Norwich subsidiary.

By the late 1990s, Kettle workers rotated among five different buildings, one each for potato chips, tortilla chips, baked chips, peanuts, and offices. Then in 2000, the company moved its headquarters and production to a five-acre site it had purchased earlier on Mill Creek in Salem. There it combined the production lines for its various chips under one 61,000-square-foot roof. The nut mixes and butters stayed behind at the original Salem site, still manufactured using the company's original nut fryer. With the move, Kettle's processor began to operate around the clock six days a week, more than doubling its chip production. The company retained a half-time employee to manage its wetland acreage and restore them to their original state.

### *Continuing Innovation at the Turn of the Century*

The company introduced its e-commerce service in 2000. Online customers became able to buy chips by the case. Overseas, Kettle expanded its factory in England as Kettle sales in that country reached almost twice what they were in the United States. Yet Kettle Foods continued to embrace the philosophy upon which the company was founded: Making good snacking foods by hand with attention to ingredients.

In the new Salem plant, large signs lined the corridor: ''Be passionate about quality'' and ''Create good will in every action.'' In 2001, Kettle Foods began to offer seasonal additions of chips and organic chips made from organic potatoes cooked in oil from organically grown safflower seeds. With sales of natural food products topping $32 billion in 2000—a 7 percent increase from 1999 totals—Kettle Foods' commitment to all-natural products and to making the theory of sustainable agriculture work in the real marketplace seemed likely to find many customers worldwide.

### *Principal Subsidiaries*

Kettle Foods Ltd.

### *Principal Competitors*

Frito-Lay, Inc.; Keebler Foods Company.

### *Further Reading*

Barton, Gene, ''Natural Foods Put N.S. Khalsa in the Chips,'' *Bulletin,* June, 5, 1988, p. C1.

Cheng, Allen, ''Salem Man Bets His Chips, Wins,'' *Statesman Journal,* December 26, 1989, p. D5.

Colby, Richard, ''Special Spuds Put Company in the Chips,'' *Oregonian,* March 10, 1988, E1.

Kramer, Matt, ''The Potato Chip As a Gastronomic Art Form,'' *Oregonian,* October 14, 1984, p. 20.

Marta, Suzanne, ''Kettle Expands to Meet Chip Demand,'' *Statesman,* August 15, 1999, p. E1.

Phillabaum, Lacey, ''Kettle Foods and America's Love Affair with the Potato Chip,'' *In Good Tilth,* May-June 2001, p. 10.

—Carrie Rothburd

# Kimball International, Inc.

**1600 Royal Street**
**Jasper, Indiana 47549**
**U.S.A.**
**Telephone: (812) 482-1600**
**Toll Free: (800) 482-1616**
**Fax: (812) 482-8300**
**Web site: http://www.kimball.com**

*Public Company*
*Incorporated:* 1950 as the Jasper Corporation
*Employees:* 9,000
*Sales:* $1.26 billion (2001)
*Stock Exchanges:* NASDAQ
*Ticker Symbol:* KBALB
*NAIC:* 334418 Printed Circuit Assembly (Electronic Assembly) Manufacturing; 337121 Upholstered Household Furniture Manufacturing; 337122 Nonupholstered Wood Household Furniture Manufacturing; 337127 Institutional Furniture Manufacturing; 337211 Wood Office Furniture Manufacturing; 337214 Office Furniture (Except Wood) Manufacturing; 337215 Showcase, Partition, Shelving, and Locker Manufacturing

Once a leading piano manufacturer, Kimball International, Inc. is now known for two products: furniture and electronic assemblies. Furniture accounts for about 70 percent of Kimball's revenues. Its metal and wood furniture and fixtures are used in the hospitality and health care industries; the company also produces a line of home furniture. Kimball's electronic assemblies business supplies the computer, automotive, defense, medical, and telecom industries. The company also maintains a sizeable trucking fleet, a throwback to days when it manufactured and shipped its own pianos.

## *Origins*

In 1950, a group of investors led by Arnold F. Habig took over the floundering Midwest Manufacturing Co. of Jasper, Indiana, an establishment with 30 employees and 25,000 square feet of production space. They soon realized that the company needed more than an infusion of capital. The group took charge of managing the small television and radio cabinet manufacturer, which they renamed the Jasper Corporation on May 23, 1950. With Habig acting as president and manager, the privately-owned company flourished, becoming a major supplier of television cabinets to electronics manufacturers. By 1955, the company's sales had grown to $4.6 million, and it was employing 436 people.

During the 1950s, the Jasper Corporation took advantage of the booming market in televisions to increase its production capacity and to attain control of several of the stages in the manufacturing process, a strategy known as vertical integration. The company's first acquisition came at the pressure of its customers, who asked Jasper to diversify its manufacturing sites to ensure a steady supply of cabinets in case of accident. With this in mind, the company purchased the Borden Cabinet Corporation in Borden, Indiana, in 1952. The wisdom of diversification was made evident several years later, in 1962, when the Borden plant burned to the ground. Nevertheless, the plant was rebuilt on the same location within six months.

Jasper took its first step toward vertical integration in 1953 when it formed the Jasper-American Manufacturing Co. in Henderson, Kentucky. This company supplied flakeboard for Jasper's cabinets at a lower price than could be obtained elsewhere. Striving for efficiency, Jasper moved further in the direction of vertical integration in the years to come. The company acquired the Evansville Veneer and Lumber Co. in 1955 and formed the Lafayette Manufacturing Co. in 1959. These companies supplied high quality veneer and hardwood lumber and dimension wood parts, respectively. Such acquisitions allowed Jasper to tailor its supply of raw materials to fit its requirements, although the subsidiary companies were also able to produce goods for sale to other manufacturers. This efficient and diverse use of productive capacity fueled Jasper's sales, which grew to $14.6 million by 1959, and prompted management to consider the benefits of decreasing the company's reliance on the demands of consumer products manufacturers and becoming a consumer products manufacturer itself.

## Company Perspectives:

*We Build Success. Kimball International is a pre-eminent manufacturer of furniture, furniture components, and electronic assemblies, serving customers around the world. Our customers, both large and small, receive our undivided attention, as we treat everyone as the only one. Our work with our customers is integrated into such an array of products and services our touch is felt throughout daily life in both the workplace and in the home. Kimball builds products, brands, and a reputation as an ideal place to entrust your livelihood, whether as a customer, supplier, employee, or share owner. Our vision is to advance a new industrial covenant: immediate access to world-class design and manufacturing. Our products will reach end users through many paths, whether as one of our own brand names that we market, as a brand that we agree to provide for a separate company, or as a component of another product. Regardless of the Kimball product or whether the customer is ourselves, a company, or a person, our covenant will stand firm. Our unifying bonds across our company will continue to be our unique culture and our shared skills in the development of efficient, high quality operations and services. By fulfilling our vision, we will emerge as an employer and supplier of choice. Our name will signal reliability and quality to the countless people who use our products and services, as well as to the inventors, designers, and marketers whose dreams take form in our factories and whose success we help build. Kimball International builds success.*

### *W.W. Kimball Acquired 1959*

The Jasper Corporation made several major changes in 1959. Most notably, it purchased the W.W. Kimball Company of Melrose Park, Illinois. Acquisition of the Kimball Company, which had been manufacturing pianos since 1857, gave Jasper an established brand in a prestigious industry. Not coincidentally, Jasper already had the capacity to manufacture many of the raw materials that went into the construction of vertical and grand pianos. In the years to come, they would acquire companies involved in other steps in the manufacturing process of pianos as well. Also in 1959, Jasper formed a traffic division that provided transportation for raw materials between the company's growing number of plants and delivered Kimball products to retail dealers. In 1987, this division was renamed Kimball International Transit, Inc.; the outfit operated a fleet of trucks that carried the company's products and was also licensed to carry goods for other companies.

After purchasing the W.W. Kimball Company, the Jasper Corporation took several steps to expand and diversify the production of musical instruments under the Kimball name. Kimball Piano, as the division was named, moved its manufacturing facilities to West Baden, Indiana, and grew to include 300,000 square feet of floor space. The company's machine and equipment division fashioned advanced manufacturing processes for the plant, and over the years the company added a retail store—the Kimball Music Center—that sold Kimball and other musical products and offered piano lessons in its teaching studios. In 1961, it formed the Jasper Electronics Manufacturing Co. to produce Kimball electronic organs. Production facilities grew to 200,000 square feet in size, an expansion that made Kimball a leading manufacturer of electronic organs and allowed it to develop expertise in the production of electronic components.

Jasper also expanded piano and organ production into European markets with the acquisition of the English company Herrburger Brooks P.L.C. in 1965. Merged in 1991 into Kimball Europe P.L.C., the unit makes and markets Herrburger Brooks brand piano components and office furniture for sale in the United Kingdom. Further expansion occurred in 1966, when Jasper purchased L. Bosendorfer Klavierfabrik, A.G., of Vienna, Austria, makers of fine concert grand pianos since 1828. With two facilities in Austria, the company produces a limited number of high-quality Bosendorfer brand pianos, some of which sell for as much as $100,000.

### *Changing Tune in the 1960s*

As sales of pianos and organs declined beginning in the 1960s, Jasper (and later Kimball International) changed the nature of its involvement in this business segment. The company phased out organ operations in 1983, though it retained and expanded its electronic assembly business in the renamed Kimball Electronics-Jasper manufacturing facilities. Both U.S. and European piano manufacturing plants were made more efficient; U.S. facilities, for example, were converted to allow for the manufacture of products such as pool tables and jukebox cabinets for other companies. In addition, in 1988 the company expanded Kimco, S.A. de C.V., its Reynosa, Mexico, plant (established in 1973) to allow for lower-cost, up-to-date piano manufacturing. While the market for pianos continued to decrease into the 1990s, the company expected that gains in efficiency would allow this division to return to profitability after several years of losses.

By the late 1960s, Jasper Corporation had become highly efficient at manufacturing cabinetry and pianos, thanks in large part to Habig's efforts to achieve vertical integration and his ability to avoid debt by purchasing new companies outright. The company was capable of growing trees on its tree farms, processing lumber in its various sawmills, producing finished wood products in its veneer, laminate, and dimension lumber divisions, assembling a finished product in several assembly plants, and shipping its products via its own transport division. As the demand for television cabinets declined, the company took advantage of existing production capacity to manufacture office furniture out of its Borden, Indiana, plant beginning in 1970. Jasper also acquired an Alabama manufacturer of Victorian reproduction furniture in 1969; Jasper later renamed the company Kimball Furniture Reproductions, Inc. These new products became the center of the company's growth for the next two decades, propelling the company into the Fortune 500 and making it one of the largest employers in the state of Indiana.

### *Going Corporate in the 1970s and 1980s*

In 1974, stockholders, primarily members of the founding Habig and Thyen families, voted to change the name of the company to Kimball International, Inc., in order to reflect the

**Key Dates:**

**1950:** Investors take over Midwest Mfg. Co., a maker of cabinets for televisions, and rename it Jasper Corporation.
**1955:** Evansville Veneer and Lumber Co. is acquired.
**1959:** Piano manufacturer W.W. Kimball Co. acquired.
**1961:** Jasper Electronics Mfg. Co. formed to make electronic organs.
**1974:** Name changed to Kimball International, Inc.
**1976:** Kimball goes public.
**1979:** Kimball acquires Artec brand of office furniture.
**1980:** National Office Furniture division is created.
**1983:** Organ operations are phased out in favor of electronics.
**1992:** Metal office furniture maker Harpers, Inc. is acquired.
**2002:** Kimball exits music business.

increasing recognition that the Kimball brand pianos and office furniture enjoyed in the marketplace and to recognize the company's international scope. Just two years later, Kimball became a publicly held company by offering 500,000 shares of Class B common stock.

In the late 1970s and early 1980s, Kimball consolidated its position in the office furniture business through acquisition and reorganization. In November 1979, the company acquired design and manufacturing rights for a line of office furniture systems produced by Artec, which became a unit of Kimball International. The division, which operates a 200,000-square-foot plant in Jasper, Indiana, began producing the Cetra line of office furniture in 1988. This versatile system was designed for all levels of office use and became part of the Kimball Office Furniture line. In 1980, Kimball created the National Office Furniture division to manufacture economy-to-medium-priced furniture. This furniture was manufactured in two plants in Kentucky and Indiana. With two complete furniture lines—Kimball and National—Kimball International was able to manufacture and market to all segments of the wood office furniture market.

Kimball International grew quickly as a result of its strength in manufacturing and marketing office furniture: sales rose from $104.2 million in 1975 to $319.9 million in 1984. In 1988, net sales of $529.8 million placed the company on the Fortune 500 list of top companies in America. The company's organization came to reflect this vast growth as manufacturing and marketing facilities were relocated and consolidated. Kimball's Jasper, Indiana, corporate headquarters were enlarged in 1985 and 1989, and a lavish corporate showroom was created in 1983 to display the entire line of office, hospitality, and health care furniture. Kimball restructured its corporate divisions as well in the early 1990s, grouping its many divisions and plants under office, lodging, home furniture, and, for European products, international groupings.

### *New Lines in the 1990s*

The Lodging Group was created in a 1992 merger of Kimball Healthcare Co., a manufacturer of beds, casegoods, and seating for long-term care facilities, and Kimball Hospitality Furniture, Inc., which produced beds, seating, tables, dressers, and other furniture for the lodging industry. The Lodging Group achieved particular success in the early 1990s. In recognition of the company's growing commitment to producing products for the hospitality industry, the company expanded its showroom in 1991. Kimball sales administrator Mike Paar told *Lodging Hospitality* magazine, ''The mock-up rooms in the showroom provide one-source shopping and enable the lodging operator or designer to take care of his or her entire furnishings needs under one roof.'' Kimball achieved more tangible recognition for its success in this business unit in 1993 when it was chosen to furnish the guest rooms—all 10,500 of them—for four new hotels in Las Vegas, Nevada.

While Kimball has earned its name and garnered the majority of its sales from furniture and cabinets, it also developed a strong presence with its electronic contract assemblies. Sales of electronic assemblies grew from three percent of Kimball's total sales in 1984 to 25 percent of sales in 1994, a leap from $9.3 million to $204.1 million in sales. Kimball supplies electronic components and assemblies to corporate customers in the computer, automotive, telecommunications, and home appliance industries. What had begun as a spin-off business from manufacturing organs had matured into a major income producer. The company stated in its 1994 annual report that it had manufactured over 11 million computer keyboards, while it expected its share of the anti-lock brake subassembly market to grow through its continued connection supplying control modules for the Kelsey-Hayes Company.

In addition to its electronic components business, Kimball also continued to manufacture television cabinets and stands for television manufacturers such as Mitsubishi, Thomson, Sony, and Toshiba. It also manufactures speaker cabinets for Thomson and Definitive Technologies.

Through the 1980s and into the 1990s, Kimball also realized between 6 and 8 percent of total revenues from sales of processed wood products. Though the divisions producing such wood products as veneer, lumber, and plywood exist mainly to supply Kimball's furniture making plants, outside sales reached $54 million in 1994. Kimball also received a small portion of its sales from plastics and tooling operations, from its transport division, and from a transport repair division.

Kimball took a step toward further diversification in the production of furniture in 1992 when it acquired the Torrance, California-based Harpers, Inc., a manufacturer of metal office furniture. This acquisition gave Kimball an entrance into the largest segment of the office furniture market, estimated at $7.3 billion in 1992. Kimball immediately announced plans to move the company to Post Falls, Idaho, a small town just across the state line from Spokane, Washington. The Post Falls plant, at 461,000 square feet, is Kimball's largest and one of the largest in the inland Northwest. The plant began operations in 1994, manufacturing metal office furniture under the Harpers name.

Analysts have cited several factors in explaining the steady rise of Kimball International. Most notable is the stability that family control has given the company. The majority of the Class A stock and six of seven senior executive officer positions remained in the hands of the founding Habig and Thyen families in the mid-1990s. In 1994, founder Arnold F. Habig acted as assistant to the chief executive officer; his son Thomas L. Habig served as chairman of the board; and another son, Douglas A. Habig, acted as president and chief executive officer. ''Family control is a real asset,'' Indiana business expert Raymond H. Diggle, Jr., told *Indiana Business.* ''It allows them to run the enterprise for cash flow and long-term return on equity. They don't have to be as concerned about short-term swings.''

Another important component of the company's success, Kimball has contended, is a corporate ethic that reflects a sense of obligation to contribute to the communities—mostly small towns like that of Jasper, Indiana, where the company was founded—in which they base their operations. This community-minded ethic led Kimball to pursue sustainable timberland development on its acreage in Indiana, Ohio, and Kentucky; to sponsor the Habig Foundation to award scholarships to the children of company employees; and to allow its employees control over their jobs long before such a management philosophy became popular. With its sound financial base, its careful managerial philosophy, and its track record, Kimball seemed poised to grow well into the twenty-first century.

### *Furniture and Electronics: 1995–2001*

Kimball closed its sole piano store, Wilking Music Co., in September 1995. The Castleton, Indiana, store had been acquired in 1982 to use as a test market. Soon after, Kimball stopped making pianos in the United States. Japanese and Korean manufacturers dominated the lower and middle segments of the market. Kimball held on to its high-end Bosendorfer factory in Austria, but this too was sold in 2002.

Kimball Electronics acquired Elmo Semiconductor Corp., based in Burbank, California, in early 1996, as well as Elmo Semiconducteurs, located near Paris. Elmo was a $15 million business. This was the electronic unit's first acquisition; it had grown organically to revenues of $250 million a year.

Kimball entered the residential furniture business in 1997 under the Kimball Home brand. The first collections, Cherry Falls and Oak Meadow, debuted in April 1997 and were designed by Ron Stilwell of North Carolina. A string of acquisitions in the late 1990s gave Kimball several plants in Pennsylvania, California, Idaho, and the South. These included Southeast Millworks, a Boca Raton, Florida-based company specializing in customized store display fixtures.

Company founders Arnold F. Habig and Herb Thyen both died in 1999. Habig continued to assist his son, CEO and chairman Douglas A. Habig, until shortly before his death. James C. Thyen, son of the founder, was company president. The two families together owned about 13 percent of Kimball's stock.

Kimball had record sales of $1.1 billion in fiscal 1999, with 70 percent of revenues deriving from its furniture segment. Kimball Electronics Group, a contract maker of electronic assemblies, accounted for the remainder. Kimball International still maintained a large fleet, then numbering 35 tractors and 120 trailers, to carefully ship its wares. In 1995, the company began outsourcing maintenance for the trucks.

The electronics business was expanded with several acquisitions in 2000. In April 2000, a plant in Thailand opened. Construction of a 40,000-square-foot microelectronics plant in Valencia, California began in June. In September, the company entered Poland, buying an 80,000-square-foot plant in Poznan from Alcatel, which would be buying switching equipment made there from Kimball. The company also opened a plant in Jasper, Indiana.

In November 2001, Kimball Electronics took over another components plant. VDO North America LLC, a maker of automotive and aerospace instrumentation, sold Kimball its Auburn, Indiana, facility, which produced automotive sensors and circuit boards.

Kimball closed five plants in Indiana, North Carolina, Kentucky, and France in 2001, and cut 2,300 workers from its payroll, due to a slowdown in furniture demand. Consolidated sales rose slightly to $1.26 billion in 2001. Net income after restructuring charges was $16.6 million, down from fiscal 2000's net income of $48.5 million.

### *The Music Ends in 2002*

Kimball cut its remaining ties to the music industry when it sold Vienna-based L. Bösendorfer Klavierfabrik GmbH, the high-end piano maker, to BAWAG-Bank of Austria in early 2002. Around the same time, Kimball was temporarily closing its oldest plant (built in 1936), where subsidiary Jasper Corp. supplied it and other furniture makers on contract. Its 100-plus workers were transferred to the more modern Jasper Furniture Co. plant, which supplied the Kimball Lodging Group.

### *Principal Subsidiaries*

Elmo Semiconducteurs SARL (France); Jackson Furniture of Danville, LLC; Kepco, Inc.; Kimball de Juarez, S.A. de C.V. (Mexico); Kimball de Mexicali, S.A. de C.V. (Mexico); Kimball Electronics Design Services, Inc.; Kimball Electronics, Inc.; Kimball Electronics Manufacturing, Inc.; Kimball Electronics Poland, Sp.z.o.o. (Poland); Kimball Electronics (Thailand) Limited; Kimball Hospitality Furniture, Inc.; Kimball, Inc.; Kimball International Marketing, Inc.; Kimball International Manufacturing, Inc.; Kimball International Transit, Inc.; Kimball Microelectronics, Inc.; Kimball U.K., Inc.; Kimco, S.A. de C.V. (Mexico); McAllen-American Corporation.

### *Principal Operating Units*

Electronics Manufacturing Services; Office Furniture; Home Furniture; Hospitality Furniture; Health Care Furniture; Contract Manufacturing.

### *Principal Competitors*

Haworth Inc.; Herman Miller Inc.; HON Industries Inc.; Knoll Inc.; Steelcase Inc.

### *Further Reading*

Barlow, Saideh, ''Kimball Broadens Its International Presence,'' *Indianapolis Business Journal,* May 22, 2000, p. 17B.

Beck, Bill, ''Kimball International: Jasper-Based Company Nears 50 Years,'' *Indiana Business Magazine,* July 1998, p. 56.

Dinnen, S.P., ''Wilking Music Co. of Castleton, Ind. to Close,'' *Indianapolis Star,* July 21, 1995.

Garet, Barbara, ''Kimball Commits to Home Furniture,'' *Wood & Wood Products,* September 1997, pp. 27ff.

Hill, Sidney, Jr., ''Two Divisions, Same System,'' *Manufacturing Systems,* May 1998, pp. vii-viii.

Hoffman, Marilyn, ''Furniture Makers Target Multiplying Home Offices,'' *Christian Science Monitor,* April 5, 1994, p. 9.

Johnson, J. Douglas, ''Knock on Wood,'' *Indiana Business,* December 1992, p. 8.

Julian, Alan, ''Kimball Expands to Poland; Electronics Plant Marks Fourth Acquisition of Year,'' *Evansville Courier & Press,* September 23, 2000, p. B11.

Mabert, Vincent A., John F. Muth, and Roger W. Schmenner, ''Collapsing New Product Development Times: Six Case Studies,'' *Journal of Product Innovation Management,* Vol. 9, 1992, pp. 200–12.

McConville, Daniel, ''Fleet Owners and Proud of It,'' *Distribution,* April 1997, pp. 47ff.

Miller, Laura Novello, ''Manufacturers Contribute Most to Indiana Employment Scene,'' *Indianapolis Business Journal,* May 23, 1994, p. B24.

''Piano Industry Off-Key; Disappearing Commodity: Kimball's Exit from Manufacturing Reflects Social Changes,'' *Sun* (Baltimore), February 18, 1996, p. 2f.

Ripley, Richard, ''Kimball Buys Property near Big Harpers Plant,'' *Journal of Business—Spokane,* July 7, 1994, p. 3.

Sheerin, Matthew and Barry Greenberg, ''New Tune for Kimball,'' *Electronic Buyer's News,* February 26, 1996, pp. 4f.

''The Triple Lutz of Furniture,'' *Facilities Design & Management,* May 1998, pp. 30–1.

Weil, Marty, ''Moving More for Less,'' *Manufacturing Systems,* September 1998, pp. 90–4.

—Tom Pendergast
—update: Frederick C. Ingram

KYOWA

# Kyowa Hakko Kogyo Co., Ltd.

**6-1, Ohtemachi, Chiyoda-ku**
**Tokyo 100-8185**
**Japan**
**Telephone: (81) 3 3282-0007**
**Fax: (81) 3 3284-1968**
**Web site: http://www.kyowa.co.jp**

*Public Company*
*Incorporated:* 1949
*Employees:* 7,766
*Sales:* ¥375.6 billion ($2.97 billion) (2001)
*Stock Exchanges:* Tokyo
*Ticker Symbol:* 4151
*NAIC:* 325411 Medicinal and Botanical Manufacturing; 325412 Pharmaceutical Preparation Manufacturing; 325188 All Other Basic Inorganic Chemical Manufacturing; 312130 Wineries; 311942 Spice and Extract Manufacturing

Kyowa Hakko Kogyo Co., Ltd. is a research-based company that develops and manufacturers prescription medicines, amino acids, fine chemicals, and food additives and ingredients. The company has five main business segments including Pharmaceuticals, which made up approximately 34 percent of sales in 2001; Chemicals; Bio-Chemicals; Liquor and Food; and Other Business, a segment whose operations are related to transportation, warehousing, sales of equipment, and plant design. While the bulk of Kyowa Hakko's revenues are domestic, the company secures approximately 14 percent of sales from the Americas, Europe, and other Asian countries. In order to focus on its pharmaceutical related businesses, Kyowa Hakko announced the sale of its alcoholic beverage business in 2002.

## *Origins*

In June 1936, Takaro Shuzo, Godo Shusei, and Dainippon Shurui, three alcohol distillers, created a consortium. In November 1937 they further formalized their relationship by founding the Kyowa Chemical Research Laboratory. Benzaburo Kato became the first director of the Kyowa Laboratory and later served as chairman of Kyowa Hakko. Through extensive research, he discovered a fermentation process vital to the company's development. The company specialized in fermented products from the start. Its first commercially marketed products were ethyl alcohol, which is used in sake and other beverages; acetone; and butane.

A turning point for the newly formed research laboratory occurred when the Japanese government, noting Kyowa Laboratory's early ventures in chemical research, commissioned it to develop technology for the production of the chemical isooctane—used to determine octane levels in fuel.

During World War II, alcohols were much in demand. The extent of Kyowa's contribution to the war effort is difficult to gauge, but the company was forced by the occupation authorities to undergo some restructuring as a result of its wartime activities, as were many other Japanese businesses. Following restructuring, Kyowa Laboratory emerged as Kyowa Sangyo. The company did very well at this time by shifting some of its resources from research to production. Establishing a plant in Hofu, Kyowa Sangyo manufactured food items in high demand, including salt, gin, and *shochu*, a traditional grain-based liquor. In 1947, Kyowa Sangyo entered the pharmaceutical field for the first time, manufacturing penicillin.

## *Focusing on Pharmaceuticals and Food: 1950s–70s*

Kyowa Sangyo was incorporated on July 1, 1949, as Kyowa Hakko Kogyo Co., Ltd. Kyowa Hakko means "harmony fermentation." The goals of the company were to develop its own fermentation biotechnology while attracting foreign technology to Japan.

In 1951, Kyowa Hakko negotiated an agreement with Merck & Company, a U.S. pharmaceutical company, to produce and market the antibiotic streptomycin. This project engendered a separate pharmaceutical division of Kyowa Hakko. The company had also created the Allospas distiller in 1950, which helped to improve alcohol and wine production methods.

Kyowa Hakko gained international recognition in 1955 with the development of an anticancer drug called Mitomycin-C.

**Company Perspectives:**

*Kyowa Hakko will contribute to the health and well being of people worldwide by creating new value with the pursuit of advancements in life science and technology.*

Shigetoshi Wakaki of Kyowa Hakko, in conjunction with the Kitasato Research Institute, shared responsibility for this treatment for stomach, lung, breast, and other solid cancers. The drug was developed using Kyowa Hakko's fermentation expertise.

The year 1956 was significant for Kyowa Hakko in the food industry. Once again, the company's leadership in fermentation led to a notable achievement: Kyowa Hakko became the first company to control the internal metabolism of a microorganism in order to produce an amino acid. Prior to Kyowa Hakko's work, amino acid production had been expensive, because it required the use of protein-rich substances such as decomposed wheat and soybeans. Kyowa Hakko substituted inexpensive and readily available molasses. The discovery resulted in cheaper production of monosodium glutamate, an amino acid-based seasoning.

In 1958, Kyowa Hakko produced another amino acid, the feed-grade L-Lysine, a base for livestock feed. Kyowa Hakko's cost-effective production system has since become standard and is used internationally to develop amino and nucleic acids for medical treatment and as post-surgery nutrition supplements.

Steadily continuing chemical research and production, Kyowa Hakko also became a manufacturer of acetone, butanol, and other solvents and plasticizers. In 1961, the company decided to replace its fermentation method of producing solvents with petrochemical technology. Low oil prices instigated the change. Noting that the fermentation process resulted in large amounts of waste water, Kyowa Hakko studied various methods of water treatment and in 1964 began to market an organic compound fertilizer, a product popular in Japan and other nations.

Throughout the 1970s, Kyowa Hakko maintained its place as an innovator in antibiotic production. The company also moved into new arenas, including the production of cardiovascular agents, gastrointestinal drugs, hormones, dermatological medicines, vitamins, and advanced chemotherapeutics. Kyowa Hakko continued to apply biotechnology to create diagnostic reagents for cancer, the goal being to give accurate cancer diagnoses within minutes. In 1977, the company filed 45 drug-related patents in Japan, and in 1978 it formed the affiliate Janssen-Kyowa, dedicated to pharmaceutical research.

### *Forming Joint Ventures: 1980s*

Recognizing that the pharmaceutical industry was growing increasingly international in scope, Kyowa Hakko stepped up collaborative efforts in the early 1980s. The company jointly funded development of a thrombolytic agent with Genentech, a U.S. pharmaceutical company. In 1982, Kyowa Hakko formed Biokyowa in the United States as a fully-owned subsidiary. In a project with the Mexican government and Sumitomo Corporation, Fermentaciones Mexicanas (Fermex) was formed in Orizaba, Mexico. Both new ventures were organized to produce and market feed-grade L-Lysine.

The Japan Chemical Industry Association granted Kyowa Hakko its 1983 technology award for Sagamicin, another advance in chemotherapy. The same year, Kyowa Hakko developed a genetic-engineering technique involving DNA recombination that was expected to make amino acid production easier and less expensive.

By March 1984, Kyowa Hakko had launched another joint venture in association with Native Plants of the United States, Tata Enterprises of Switzerland, and the Sumitomo Corporation. The consortium's goal was to develop new strains of coffee and tea in Southeast Asia.

Demand for feed-grade L-Lysine increased significantly in the late 1980s. Kyowa Hakko responded with plans for a plant in Hungary that would be operated by Agroferm Hungarian Japanese Fermentation Industry and was scheduled to open in fall 1990. Kyowa Hakko also agreed to several joint projects in Japan, including ventures to produce and market frozen foods with Kitchenbell, develop cosmetic biotechnology with Shu Uemura, and introduce the frozen-food wholesaler Sun Kyowa. In 1989, Kyowa Hakko agreed to import Kane Foods products from the United States. The same year the company became the sole agent for the U.S. wine producer Alexis Lichine.

Kyowa Hakko entered the 1990s with representative offices in the United States, Mexico, China, Hungary, and Germany, and with ventures in progress in Southeast Asia. The company operated seven plants in Japan and two overseas, exporting goods to over 80 countries. Projects underway were international in scope, as Kyowa Hakko studied cloning and gene-mapping in order to develop new plant strains, researched amino acid application, and studied the safety of pharmaceuticals.

### *Restructuring: 1990s and Beyond*

This focus on pharmaceuticals and research and development strengthened throughout the 1990s. In 1991, the company launched Coniel, a drug that treated both hypertension and angina. Loracarbef, an antibiotic, was licensed to Eli Lilly & Company and made it to the U.S. market in 1992. The firm also licensed Olopatadine, an allergy medication, to Alcon Laboratories Inc. The drug was launched in eye drop form in the United States in 1997. In 1999, an anti-cancer drug, Navelbine, was also launched.

During this time period, the drug industry as whole was dealing with major changes due to rising development costs and new technological breakthroughs. Kyowa Hakko faced increased pressure in Japan, where the Ministry of Health and Welfare was passing new laws to reduce health care costs, particularly drug reimbursement prices. Meanwhile, the company's food and alcohol business had to deal with the rising taxes and decreasing demand brought on by a fall in consumer spending and a rapidly declining economy in Southeast Asia. These changes had a negative effect on Kyowa Hakko's sales figures, which remained stagnant in the late 1990s.

**Key Dates:**

**1936:** Three alcohol distillers—Takaro Shuzo, Godo Shusei, and Dainippon Shurui—create a consortium.
**1937:** The Kyowa Chemical Research Laboratory is created.
**1947:** Kyowa enters the pharmaceutical field.
**1949:** The company is incorporated as Kyowa Hakko Kogyo Co., Ltd.
**1955:** Kyowa Hakko develops an anticancer drug called Mitomycin-C.
**1956:** The firm becomes the first to control the internal metabolism of a microorganism in order to produce an amino acid.
**1964:** The company markets an organic compound fertilizer.
**1982:** Biokyowa Inc. is formed as a U.S. subsidiary.
**1989:** Kyowa begins to import Kane Foods products from the United States and is named the sole agent for U.S. wine producer Alexis Lichine.
**1997:** The company reports stagnant sales as the Japanese Ministry of Health and Welfare reduces drug reimbursement prices.
**2001:** The company creates a new vision for its pharmaceutical division.
**2002:** Kyowa sells its alcoholic beverage operations to Asahi Breweries Ltd.

At the same time, the company was named in a lysine price fixing cartel scandal. During 1996, the European Commission began an investigation into several firms involved in a global price fixing cartel. Kyowa Hakko, along with four other firms, were found guilty for operating the lysine cartel from 1990 to 1995. In 2000, Kyowa Hakko was fined $12 million for its involvement.

Challenging market conditions continued into the new millennium. In April 2000, the National Health Insurance drug price standard was lowered in Japan and the firm faced fierce competition in its pharmaceutical business segment. The company's bio-chemical and chemical operations also suffered and weak consumer spending continued to cause shortfalls in the Kyowa Hakko's liquor and food segment. As such, the firm began to restructure and streamline operations in order to remain competitive. With pharmaceuticals as its core concern, Kyowa Hakko launched a new strategy for this division entitled "Reform for Value Creation." The new plan, made up of two five-year stages, was designed to position the company as a leader in the pharmaceuticals industry. This plan stated that by 2011, Kyowa Hakko's pharmaceutical business would secure sales of ¥300 billion and be a leader in biopharmaceuticals and the treatment of cancer and allergies. The company hoped to achieve this goal by strengthening its domestic operations, developing new drug assets, and by expanding internationally.

In a move that signaled the firm's commitment to its drug and chemical related businesses, Kyowa Hakko announced the sale of its alcoholic beverage business to Asahi Breweries Ltd. in 2002. Its U.S. subsidiary BioKyowa Inc. also stopped production of feed-grade amino acid lysine in order to focus on various other high profit amino acids. During fiscal 2002, sales rose by .80 percent, while operating profit increased by 14.9 percent over the previous year. As Kyowa Hakko's business environment remained challenging as well as highly competitive, management continued to cut costs and restructure both its domestic and overseas operations.

### *Principal Subsidiaries*

Kyowa Yuka Co. Ltd. (94%); Kyowa Medex Co. Ltd.; Mohan Medicine Research Institute (98.9%); Shinwa Pharmaceutical Co. Ltd.; Kyowa Medical Promotion Co. Ltd.; Kyowa Nozai Co. Ltd.; Riken Kagaku Co. Ltd.; Asahi Foods Products Co. Ltd. (78%); Miyako Kagaku Co. Ltd. (52.9%); Kyowa Engineering Co. Ltd.; Kyowa Warehouse & Transportation Co. Ltd.; Seifu Co. Ltd.; Biokyowa Inc. (U.S.); Fermentaciones Mexicanas S.A. de C.V. (Mexico); Agroferm Hungarian-Japanese Fermentation Industry Ltd. (Hungary); Kyowa Hakko U.S.A. Inc.; Kyowa Hakko Europe GmbH (Germany).

### *Principal Competitors*

Meiji Seika Kaisha, Ltd.; Shionogi & Co. Ltd.; Yamanouchi Pharmaceutical Co. Ltd.

### *Further Reading*

"European Commission Fines Lysine Firms," *Feedstuffs*, June 12, 2000, p. 5.
*Formulating the Future*, Tokyo: Kyowa Hakko Kogyo Co., Ltd., 1986.
*Forty Years of Exciting Technological Development*, Tokyo: Kyowa Hakko Kogyo Co., Ltd., 1990.
"Kyowa Hakko Concentrates on Pharma," *SCRIP World Pharmaceutical News*, February 22, 2002, p. 9.
"Kyowa Hakko Sells Alcohol Stake," *Chemical Week*, February 27, 2002, p. 22.
"Kyowa Transfers Alcoholic Beverage Business to Asahi Breweries," *AsiaPulse News*, February 19, 2002.
Mirasol, Feliza, "Kyowa Hakko Expands and Targets Amino Acids," *Chemical Market Reporter*, September 14, 1998, p. 5.
Young, Ian, "Kyowa Hakko Appeals Against Cartel Fine," *Chemical Week*, September 6, 2000, p. 17.

—Frances E. Norton
—update: Christina M. Stansell

# L-3 Communications Holdings, Inc.

**600 3rd Avenue, 34th Floor**
**New York, New York 10016**
**U.S.A.**
**Telephone: (212) 697-1111**
**Fax: (212) 805-5353**
**Web site: http://www.L-3Com.com**

*Public Company*
*Incorporated:* 1997
*Employees:* 14,000
*Sales:* $1.91 billion (2000)
*Stock Exchanges:* New York
*Ticker Symbol:* LLL
*NAIC:* 334220 Radio and Television Broadcasting and Wireless Communications Equipment; 334290 Other Communications Equipment Manufacturing; 334512 Search, Detection, Navigation, Guidance, Aeronautical, and Nautical Systems and Instruments; 336412 Aircraft Engine and Engine Parts Manufacturing; 336413 Other Aircraft Parts and Auxiliary Equipment Manufacturing; 421610 Electrical Apparatus and Equipment, Wiring Supplies, and Construction Material Wholesalers; 551112 Offices of Other Holding Companies

L-3 Communications Holdings, Inc., through its L-3 Communications Corp. subsidiary, operates companies that produce secure communication systems, training systems, microwave components, avionics and ocean systems, telemetry, instrumentation, and space and wireless products. Its customers are mostly defense and intelligence agencies, as well as aircraft manufacturers and defense contractors. L-3 also supplies the commercial telecommunications industry. L-3 maintained a 60 percent defense, 40 percent commercial product mix. Like its predecessor Loral Corporation, L-3 Communications has undergone phenomenal growth, orchestrated by former Loral executives Frank Lanza and Robert LaPenta.

## *Origins*

Loral Corporation was an assemblage of defense units acquired from Fairchild, Ford, IBM, Unisys, and others between the mid-1970s and mid-1990s by Wall Street investor Bernard L. Schwartz. In April 1996, Lockheed Martin acquired most of these businesses for $9.1 billion. Two Loral executives, COO Frank Lanza and comptroller Robert LaPenta, joined Lockheed Martin as executive vice-president and vice-president, respectively. Loral's space businesses formed a separate firm, Loral Space & Communications Ltd., run by Schwartz.

Lockheed Martin, which had been formed in 1995 by the merger of Lockheed Corp. and Martin Marietta Corp., began to divest noncore units after the massive Loral acquisition. It sold its stake in the Martin Marietta construction materials business in 1996.

Lanza, described by the *Washington Post* as ''a taciturn New Yorker admired for his creativity and engineering genius,'' reportedly felt stifled by the bureaucratic corporate atmosphere at Lockheed Martin. An electrical engineer by training, Lanza had joined Loral in 1972 and was named president and chief operating officer in 1981. Along the way, he was instrumental in growing the company from modest origins to a $7 billion giant.

In 1997, as he approached traditional retirement age, Lanza convinced his new employer, Lockheed Chairman Norman R. Augustine, to spin off ten former Loral companies to form L-3 Communications. (''It took me less than half an hour to get a yes,'' Lanza later told *Business Week.*) Lanza finally got a chance to be CEO, and numbers whiz LaPenta was named president and chief financial officer.

The ten businesses spun off had annual revenues of $650 million and 4,900 employees. The largest of these were Wideband Systems in Salt Lake City and Communications Systems in Camden, New Jersey. Also included were two northern California companies, Randtron and Narda-Microwave, which manufactured microwave antennas for military applications. These two together had fewer than 400 employees.

## Company Perspectives:

*L-3 Communication's goal is to be the leading mezzanine supplier to prime contractors. The company will do so by investing in its core technologies and acquiring companies that enhance or complement its current technologies.*

Lockheed Martin received $503.8 million for selling 65 percent of its ownership in the ten companies. After the sale, a limited partnership led by Lehman Brothers owned half of L-3; Lockheed Martin retained a 35 percent interest and a management group accounted for another 15 percent. Lockheed agreed to invest $43.75 million in L-3, Lehman invested $62.5 million, and the management group provided $43.75 million. Another $375 million was financed with bank debt and high-yield bonds. The name of the new company came from Lanza, LaPenta, and either Lockheed or Lehman Brothers, according to varying reports.

In July 1997 L-3 found itself aggressively bidding against its part-owner, Lockheed Martin, for control of a Texas Instruments chip-making business that Raytheon was being forced to unload as part of a Justice Department settlement. The desired unit produced gallium arsenide high-power amplifier monolithic microwave integrated circuits, or MMICs, a proprietary product. L-3 was eager to expand its microwave components business, which accounted for a quarter of sales, and also sought out joint ventures with Sweden's Ericsson Microwave Systems AB and France's Thomson-CSF to bring new technologies into the U.S. military market.

L-3 had a well-developed commercial business as well. Its Advanced Recorders plant in Sarasota, Florida, which made ''black boxes'' for aircraft, landed a contract to supply American Airlines with solid-state flight data recorders for both its existing fleet and planes on order with Boeing. The deal had a potential value of $16 million.

### *1998 IPO*

L-3's first year revenues were $701 million. Plans for a $100 million initial public offering (IPO) were announced in February 1998. The IPO at $22 a share came on May 19; in the next six months the company's share price would rise to $46 a share, helped by strong earnings.

Lanza's acquisition strategy was to buy technology leaders, either struggling independent companies or black sheep divisions of major defense contractors, observed *Business Week*. Lanza focused on small to medium sized companies to avoid costly takeover battles with aerospace giants. ESSCO, a leading producer of ground-based radomes (protective shields for antennas) and precision millimeter wave antenna systems, acquired in September 1998, was a representative purchase.

By November 1998, L-3 had already acquired seven companies, including SPD Technologies, which supplied power equipment to the U.S. Navy, and Storm Control Systems, Inc., which made satellite control software. The company spent heavily—$40 to $50 million a year—on R&D to improve its existing products and to make them cheaper to produce.

In December 1998, L-3 agreed to acquire Microdyne Corp., based in Alexandria, Virginia, for $90 million. Microdyne made radio receivers used in tracking satellites and aircraft. L-3 companies already made the data hardware that used these antennas.

L-3 posted after-tax profits of $32 million on revenues of $1 billion in 1998. An additional stock offering was announced in early 1999, intending to raise $136 million to pay down debt and fund further acquisitions.

In December 1999, L-3 agreed to pay $55 million for two businesses Honeywell International Inc. was required to sell after its merger with Allied Signal Inc. One of these produced gyroscopes, controlled momentum devices, and sensors for weapons systems and satellites; the other made an inertial sensor product based on micromachined electro-mechanical systems (MEMS) technology used in advanced guidance systems. L-3 also bought Honeywell's Traffic-Alert Collision Avoidance System (TCAS) business for $255 million. L-3 incorporated the TCAS unit into a joint venture with Sextant, a Thomson-CSF affiliate. TCAS had recently been required on all European cargo aircraft and passenger planes with more than 30 seats.

Another important acquisition in 1999 was that of Satellite Transmission Systems. This brought L-3 into a $200 million a year business of fixed wireless communications systems, typically installed in developing countries that lacked traditional land lines. Meanwhile, new Federal Aviation Administration requirements were boosting L-3's cockpit voice recorder business.

In January 2000, L-3 agreed to buy Raytheon Company's flight simulation and training business for $160 million. Link Simulation and Training, based in Arlington, Virginia, became L-3's largest division, with $300 million a year in revenues. Link had pioneered the earliest mechanical flight simulators in the first decades of aviation, but had languished in later years as it was shuffled among a succession of corporate foster parents; Lanza declared L-3 was committed to help Link thrive in the growing training market. In March 2001, however, L-3 sued Raytheon to cancel its acquisition agreement, alleging that Raytheon failed to disclose liabilities in the business.

### *Bigger Game in the New Millennium*

When *Institutional Investor* asked Lanza L-3's next move in November 2000, he quipped, ''We're gonna go buy Lockheed.'' L-3's impressive growth made this a less than outrageous prospect. The company's share price reached $80 by the end of the year. A new stock offering announced in April 2001 was to raise $350 million.

In the spring of 2001, Lanza announced that he was changing his acquisition strategy to buy larger companies in a bid to become ''the Home Depot of the defense industry.'' He aimed for L-3 to have revenues of $6 or $7 billion within the next several years—a stretch for what was then a $2 billion company, but not a laughable one, especially given Lanza's reputation. Faster growth was deemed necessary to compete against Honeywell International Inc., which was being acquired by (the U.S.) General Electric Co., reported the *Wall Street Journal*.

At the 2001 Paris Air Show, Lanza told www.AviationNow.com that L-3 was a catalog company. It was more efficient, he

**Key Dates:**

**1997:** Lockheed Martin spins off ten Loral companies to form L-3.
**1998:** L-3 goes public in a very successful IPO.
**1999:** Another stock offering fuels continued expansion.
**2001:** L-3 begins setting sights on larger companies, offers more shares.

said, to approach the handful of major aerospace companies with a vast array of products, than to try to vie for their business as a small, $100 million supplier. L-3 also boasted considerable financial resources and R&D capabilities and offered administrative efficiencies to the companies it acquired.

### *Principal Subsidiaries*

L-3 Communications Corporation.

### *Principal Divisions*

Communication Systems & Wireless Products; Avionics & Ocean Products; Simulation & Training; Microwave Components; Telemetry, Instrumentation & Space; Commercial Products.

### *Principal Competitors*

CAE Inc.; The Carlyle Group; General Dynamics Corporation; General Electric Co. (U.K.); Global Technology Partners; Honeywell International Inc.; Lockheed Martin Corporation; Raytheon Company.

### *Further Reading*

Banks, Howard, ''Black-Box Man,'' *Forbes,* October 16, 2000, p. 69.
Byrnes, Nanette, ''Hey, If It Worked for Loral,'' *Business Week,* November 23, 1998, p. 123.
Cole, Jeff, ''New Firm Takes Over 10 Lockheed Martin Units,'' *Wall Street Journal,* April 4, 1997, p. A5.
Cox, Bob, ''A Fresh Start for Link; Flight Simulator Maker Flourishing Under New Ownership,'' *Fort Worth Star-Telegram,* August 8, 2001, p. 1.
——, ''No More Missing Link; New Owner Plans to Focus on Simulator Company,'' *Fort Worth Star-Telegram,* March 4, 2000, p. 1.
''Frank Lanza of L-3 Communications Holdings: Starting Over,'' *Institutional Investor,* August 1999, pp. 24–26.
Garrity, Brian, ''Lehman Lassos L-3 Lenders,'' *Bank Loan Report,* May 5, 1997, p. 14.
Hardies, Michael J., ''Partners in Health,'' *Occupational Health & Safety,* October 1998, pp. 140–41.
Klass, Philip J., ''Electronics Unit Restructuring,'' *Aviation Week & Space Technology,* May 26, 1997, p. 74.
Lanza, Frank, ''Life Lessons Among the Olives,'' *New York Times,* March 4, 2001.
''Lockheed Spinning Off Units: Deal Is Valued at $500 Million,'' *San Francisco Chronicle,* February 4, 1997.
McDonald, Michael, ''Bargain-Hunting L-3 Plays Aggressive Defense Game,'' *Crain's New York Business,* June 5, 2000, p. 20.
Mintz, John, ''Lockheed Martin Will Spin Off 10 Divisions; Partnership to Own Newly Created Company,'' *Washington Post,* February 4, 1997, p. C1.
Morris, John, ''On the Record with Frank Lanza, Chairman and CEO, L-3 Communications,'' *Aviation Week's www.AviationNow.com,* Paris Air Show 2001.
Muradian, Vago, ''L-3 Stock Drops Despite Solid Second Quarter, 50 Percent Net Income Rise,'' *Defense Daily International,* July 27, 2001, pp. 1f.
Pollick, Michael, ''Sarasota Company to Equip Jets; For the L-3 Advanced Recorders Manufacturing Plant, the American Airlines Deal Could Be Worth $16 Million,'' *Sarasota Herald Tribune,* January 28, 1998, p. 1D.
——, ''Sarasota's L-3 Firm Plans to Go Public,'' *Sarasota Herald Tribune,* February 28, 1993, p. 1D.
Prince, C.J., ''Rocket Man,'' *Chief Executive,* November 2000, pp. 24–26.
Smart, Tim, ''Growing by Small Leaps and Medium Bounds; L-3 Concentrates on Acquisitions of a Particular Size,'' *Washington Post,* December 14, 1998, p. F16.
Squeo, Anne Marie, ''Military Contractor L-3 Sets Its Sights on Bigger Targets—Ambitious Electronics Maker Wants to Offer 'One-Stop Shopping' to the Defense Industry,'' *Wall Street Journal,* May 10, 2001, p. B4.
Taverna, Michael A., ''Honeywell Sells TCAS Unit to L-3 Com, Thomson-SCF,'' *Aviation Week & Space Technology,* March 20, 2000, pp. 81–82.
Velocci, Jr., ''L-3 Targets TI Unit, Other Acquisitions,'' *Aviation Week & Space Technology,* July 28, 1997, p. 50.

—Frederick C. Ingram

# LabOne, Inc.

10101 Renner Boulevard
Lenexa, Kansas 66219
U.S.A.
Telephone: (913) 888-1770
Fax: (913)888-0771
Web site: http://www.labone.com

*Public Company*
*Incorporated:* 1987 as Home Office Reference Laboratory
*Employees:* 1,625
*Sales:* 233.9 million (2001)
*Stock Exchanges:* NASDAQ
*Ticker Symbol:* LABS
*NAIC:* 621511 Medical Laboratories

LabOne, Inc. is a laboratory testing and information services provider. The company operates in three main areas: risk-assessment testing for the insurance industry; clinical diagnostic testing for employers, HMOs, and physicians; and substance abuse testing for employers. LabOne receives blood, urine, and oral fluids samples from clients across the nation, conducts testing at its laboratory headquarters in Lenexa, Kansas, and sends results electronically to insurers, physicians, managed health care organizations, and employers. Through its subsidiaries, the company also underwrites requirements acquisition services, paramedical services, and claims investigation services to the insurance industry.

## *1970s: New Business, New Industry*

LabOne was founded in 1971 by Jim Osborn and Joe Jack Merriman, two Kansas City-area businessmen. Originally called Home Office Reference Laboratory, the business was formed to provide risk-assessment testing for insurance companies who wanted to screen policy applicants. Home Office's service was easy to use and effective. Insurance agencies sent their policy applicants to a local medical professional, who obtained a blood or urine sample. The medical professional then shipped the samples to the Home Office lab in Kansas City for testing. The lab ran tests that checked for specific disorders that might make the insurance applicant a high risk for the insurer. For example, a urine test might reveal kidney problems, or a blood test might indicate heart or liver disease. In addition, Home Office tested blood and urine for nicotine and illegal drugs—substances that would indicate health risk to the user—and for prescription drugs used to treat high blood pressure, heart disease, or diabetes—illnesses the policy applicant might have lied about having.

When Osborn and Merriman launched their business, most large insurers maintained their own labs for risk-assessment testing. Home Office Reference Laboratory essentially spawned a new industry, becoming one of the first independent testing labs in the United States. ''When I started the company, it was a niche market,'' Jim Osborn explained in a 1987 interview with *Barrons's* magazine. ''Highly specialized. . . . A very small, very sleepy market.''

The market did not stay small—or sleepy—for long. As large insurers recognized the value of outsourcing testing, they gradually began closing down their in-house labs and sending the work to outside labs. Within a dozen years of its inception, Home Office saw annual revenues grow to $7 million.

## *1980s: Changes in Ownership*

In 1983, Osborn and Merriman sold their company to Business Men's Assurance Company of America, a large and well-established insurance company headquartered in Kansas City. Business Men's Assurance (BMA) was itself a subsidiary of , a Kansas City-based holding company.

The timing of the acquisition proved highly fortunate for BMA. Within just a few years, the United States found itself in the grip of the AIDS epidemic. Insurers, already facing massive claims for AIDS-related illness and deaths, began scrambling to limit their exposure. Until that time, insurance companies had typically only called for blood or urine tests on those individuals who applied for sizable life insurance policies—for example, those in excess of $250,000. However, the rapid spread of the HIV virus—and the fact that it was detectable only through

**Company Perspectives:**

*At LabOne, we continually strive to offer solutions to our clients—the methods, processes, and results to improve their business. From the latest diagnostic and technical innovations to new products that meet ever-changing information needs, LabOne is always in the process of improving and exceeding clients' expectations.*

such testing—caused them to lower that threshold. This meant testing more applicants, which translated into more business for Home Office.

In October 1985, as insurance companies were tightening their screening processes, Home Office introduced a test that detected whether a person had been exposed to the AIDS virus. Called the Enzyme-Linked Immunosorbent Assay—or ELISA—the test screened not for the virus itself, but for antibodies present in the blood of a person who had been exposed to the virus. The company's sales skyrocketed, growing by more than 50 percent from year-end 1985 to year-end 1986. Revenues for the same period more than doubled.

In July 1987, Business Men's Assurance took Home Office public, selling 5.75 million shares, which totaled slightly less than 40 percent of the company. As revenues and earnings continued to mount during the remainder of the year, Home Office handily dominated the insurance lab-testing market, holding an 80 percent share.

### *Early 1990s: Responding to Challenges*

In 1990, Seafield Capital sold off its Business Men's Assurance subsidiary, but retained its stake in LabOne. It also began buying back stock in Home Office, increasing its ownership to more than 80 percent by 1993. The new decade ushered in some challenges for the testing company, however. Competition was growing in the once-tiny lab-testing market. Jim Osborn, who had founded and owned Home Office before selling it to Business Men's, reentered the testing business with a new venture called Osborn Laboratories. And by the early 1990s, Osborn was beginning to siphon revenues away from Home Office. In addition, intensifying competition from Osborn and other labs drove testing prices down, inflicting still more damage to Home Office's bottom line.

The threat to business was not only from other third-party labs. In early 1991, the company lost one of its largest clients—Metropolitan Life—when the mammoth insurance company moved all of its testing business in-house. MetLife had accounted for between 5 and 6 percent of Home Office's sales. Effects of the lost business were soon evident: sales dropped from $80.77 million in 1990 to $75.74 million in 1991 and continued to decrease over the ensuing three years to $69.38 in 1993. Earnings followed suit, sliding from $13.46 in 1990 to $10.57 in 1993.

In August 1993, Home Office got an infusion of fresh ideas when it appointed Bert Hood as its new chairman. Hood came from a background in the clinical laboratory industry, having served 14 years as senior vice-president for SmithKline/International Clinical Laboratories and two years as president and CEO of Unilab. He came to Home Office with the belief that the company needed to diversify into clinical testing. "The clinical laboratory testing market is over $30 billion with several niche markets that appear to fit HORL's structure as a centralized laboratory," he stated in an August 5, 1993 press release. "While further study needs to be completed before these markets are identified, HORL's core competency . . . could enable the company to be the low cost provider in defined markets. Moreover, the diversification opportunities reviewed to date can be adequately funded out of free cash flow."

Home Office wasted little time in pursuing Hood's suggested course of action. In December 1993, the company restructured into two divisions—one to continue focusing on insurance testing and another to market diagnostic lab services to the health care industry. Concurrent with this restructuring came a new name for the company—LabOne, Inc. The division of LabOne that retained its traditional, insurance-testing business also retained its former name, Home Office Reference Laboratory Division. The new, clinical testing division was named Center for Laboratory Services.

### *Mid-1990s: Ups and Downs*

LabOne's first big accomplishment in its new line of testing came in May 1994 when the company announced a partnership with PCS Health Systems, one of the nation's largest providers of managed pharmaceutical services. The partnership provided for LabOne and PCS to develop a managed lab program that would parallel PCS's existing managed pharmaceutical plan. The resulting program—called the "Lab Card" plan—used a point-of-service card system, similar to PCS's prescription card system. The system was designed to reduce the total expense of outpatient lab testing—thereby reducing the cost of health insurance.

The company also moved into the northern-California market, opening a series of clinical labs in the region. The labs were developed to collect specimens, which would then be shipped to LabOne's Kansas headquarters for testing. Results would be faxed or e-mailed to physicians and insurers the following day.

LabOne's foray into clinical testing was not enough to turn its finances around in 1994; the company posted year-end earnings of $5.7 million—down 46 percent from the previous year. The summer of 1995, however, brought some brighter news. The company announced that it had signed an agreement with Guardian Life Insurance Company of America and would soon be offering its Lab Card program to some 30,000 Guardian plan enrollees as a pilot. If all went well, there was huge potential for expanding the plan; Guardian had a customer base of more than 1.5 million.

In 1995, LabOne added a third division to focus on substance abuse screening. Although the company had offered drug screening for several years, it was only in the mid-1990s that it became certified by the Substance Abuse and Mental Health Services Administration (SAMHSA), a part of the U.S. Department of Health and Human Services. This certification allowed LabOne to offer drug screening services to federally regulated

**Key Dates:**

**1971:** Jim Osborn and Jack Merriman form Home Office Reference Laboratory.
**1983:** Business Men's Assurance Company, a company owned by Seafield Capital, acquires Home Office Reference Laboratory.
**1985:** Home Office introduces a test for exposure to the AIDS virus.
**1987:** Home Office goes public.
**1990:** Seafield Capital sells off Business Men's Assurance but retains its stake in Home Office.
**1993:** Home Office restructures in order to begin pursuing clinical diagnostic testing and changes its name to LabOne.
**1994:** LabOne introduces its Lab Card program.
**1998:** LabOne acquires Systematic Business Services Inc.
**1999:** LabOne acquires World Wide Health Services Inc.
**2001:** LabOne acquires Osborn Group Inc.

employers. It also gave the company access to a range of potential private-sector clients they had previously been unable to approach, since many major companies with drug-testing programs required their laboratories to be SAMHSA certified.

In October 1995, after just two years at the helm, LabOne's CEO Bert Hood left the company. He was replaced by Thomas Grant, the chairman and CEO of the company's parent, Seafield Capital. The news of Hood's departure was soon followed by news of yet another decline in sales and revenue. Year-end results for 1995 showed a 6 percent decrease in sales and, more significantly, a 51 percent decrease in earnings.

Despite his short tenure, Hood's efforts at LabOne ultimately proved effective; in 1996 and 1997, benefits from the company's restructuring began to accrue. The company signed agreements to provide its Lab Card to employees of a number of businesses, including Wal-Mart and Arvin Industries. It also was awarded an estimated $1 million contract with Principal Health Care of Kansas City, one of the area's largest managed health care organizations. Revenues began a steady increase. From year-end 1996 to year-end 1997, the company's clinical testing sales increased 91 percent, its insurance testing business increased 22 percent, and its substance abuse testing revenue increased 101 percent.

Having just struggled through a business slowdown, LabOne was, by late 1997, facing a new problem: how to accommodate its sudden growth. The company's solution was a new headquarters. In October, LabOne broke ground on a $32 million, 270,000-square-foot facility located on 54 acres in Lenexa, Kansas. The headquarters was completed in the spring of 1999.

### *Late 1990s: Full Steam Ahead*

In 1998, LabOne continued to expand. The company purchased Systematic Business Services Inc., a company that provided health insurers with various information services, including motor vehicle reports, claims investigations services, and physician statements. The acquisition, which added approximately $7 million in annual revenues, gave LabOne the ability to offer a broader range of underwriting services to the insurance industry. Additionally, all three of LabOne's divisions continued to experience excellent growth. At the end of 1998, the company reported record revenue of $102.2 million. Net earnings rose to $9.2 million—up from $2.2 million in 1997.

In 1999, LabOne merged with its parent company to form a single entity. The parent company, formerly called Seafield Capital, had changed its name in 1997 to Lab Holdings, Inc. to better reflect its focus on the lab testing industry. The newly merged company retained the LabOne name.

The remainder of 1999 was marked by a series of partnerships for LabOne. In May of that year, the company was chosen by Pennsylvania-based STC Technologies Inc. to be the exclusive testing facility for a new drug screening product that used oral fluids rather than blood or urine. The new product, named Intercept, was introduced in early 2000 and was marketed primarily to small and medium-sized businesses.

In June 1999, LabOne partnered with USA Managed Care Organization, a Kansas-based company, to market the Lab Card program to USA Managed Care's large client base. And in November of 1999, LabOne acquired World Wide Health Services Inc., a New Jersey company that provided exam and information services to the life and health insurance industry. The new subsidiary was renamed ExamOne World Wide.

### *2000 and Beyond*

LabOne suffered a bit of turbulence as the 20th century rolled into the 21st century. The company came under federal investigation as part of a dispute between Delta Airlines and some of its employees who had been fired due to questionable drug test results. The employees, who were terminated when LabOne reported that their urine tests had been tampered with, challenged the validity of the company's reports, launching a probe by the U.S. Department of Health and Human Services. Delta dropped LabOne as its testing agent in 2000, and, in 2001, one of the employees in question filed suit against the company. A jury found LabOne negligent in conducting validity testing and ordered it to pay the plaintiff $400,000 in damages.

The company also posted a net loss for 2000 of $524,000—down from earnings of $2.9 million the previous year. The company attributed the loss to write-downs of certain accounts receivable and to expenses incurred in efforts to develop its paramedical testing, risk-assessment testing, and substance abuse testing businesses.

Even with setbacks, however, LabOne continued to grow. Revenues increased steadily throughout 2000 and into 2001. In late 2001, the company launched a significant expansion by purchased its rival, Osborn Group Inc., for $49 million. With the acquisition, LabOne was expected to have annual revenues of $250 million and to perform lab testing for some ten million people each year. Once Osborn Group was fully integrated into LabOne, the company expected to realize up to $10 million in annual cost reductions by eliminating redundant operations.

### Principal Subsidiaries

ExamOne World Wide, Inc.; Intellisys; LabOne Canada Inc.; Systematic Business Services, Inc.

### Principal Divisions

Insurance; Drug Testing; Healthcare.

### Principal Competitors

Hooper Holmes, Inc.; Laboratory Corporation of America Holdings; Quest Diagnostics Inc.; American Bio Medica Corporation; ChoicePoint Inc.; Employee Information Services, Inc.; Kroll Laboratory Specialists, Inc.; Medtox Scientific, Inc.; PharmChem, Inc.; Psychemedics Corporation.

### Further Reading

Alpert, William, "The Acid Test—Home Office Reference Lab Faces Stiff Competition," *Barron's*, December 21, 1987.

Cronkleton, Robert, "Friendly Foes: Three Johnson County Laboratories Battle for the Insurance Testing Market," *Kansas City Star*, February 22, 1995, p. B3.

Moore, J.D., Jr., "A New Name and a New Role: Home Office to Do Diagnostic Testing," *Kansas City Star*, December 10, 1993, p. B1.

—Shawna Brynildssen

# Lauda Air Luftfahrt AG

**PO Box 56**
**1300 Airport Vienna**
**Austria**
**Telephone: (+43) 1 7000 79800**
**Fax: (+43) 1 7000 79015**
**Web site: http://www.laudaair.com**

*84%-Owned Subsidiary of Austrian Airlines Group*
*Incorporated:* 1979
*Employees:* 1,709
*Sales:* $393.1 million (2000)
*NAIC:* 488510 Freight Transportation Arrangement; 481111 Scheduled Passenger Air Transportation; 481112 Scheduled Freight Air Transportation; 481212 Nonscheduled Chartered Freight Air Transportation; 481211 Nonscheduled Chartered Passenger Air Transportation; 492110 Couriers

Lauda Air Luftfahrt AG is a unit of Austrian Airlines Group specializing in charters and Far East travel. Founded as a charter airline by Formula One racing legend Niki Lauda, the carrier grew quickly after obtaining the freedom to start long-haul scheduled services to Australia in the late 1980s. Lauda Air carried 1.7 million passengers to 38 destinations in 2000. Charter operations continued to account for a third of revenues.

### Born on the Track

Andreas Nikolaus ''Niki'' Lauda was born the son of a paper factory owner in Austria. At age 18, he began motor racing and won his first Formula One race at age 26. He was eventually named world champion three times. This made him a national hero in Austria, and his fame and hard-driving charisma no doubt helped inspire loyalty from his employees, from whom he was said to expect a ''150 percent effort.''

Lauda quit racing Ferraris (''driving around in circles'') to develop his own airline, which would be called Lauda Air Luftfahrt AG. In 1979, Lauda started flying passengers between Germany and Austria with two small Fokker F27 turboprop airliners.

The young airline quickly accumulated a mountain of debt, prompting Lauda to mortgage his house and return to the racing circuit; he won his third Formula One championship in 1984.

In 1985, the fleet was upgraded with two Boeing 737s, the plane of choice for low-cost start-up airlines. In the same year, Lauda forged a partnership with Greek financier Basile Varvaressos, owner of the ITAS travel agency.

Lauda earned a reputation as an involved manager with a focus on quality and cost control. While price was important, Lauda felt it equally important to differentiate the carrier with top-flight quality. ''Service is our success'' became the company's motto. The three keys were clean aircraft, good food (gourmet catering by Vienna-based DO & CO), and friendly cabin attendants. Business class service, in a nod to the company's Austrian origins as well as high expectations, was named Amadeus Class.

Lauda began flying from Vienna to Sydney via Bangkok in the late 1980s, its first scheduled long-haul route. This was also the fastest connection between Germany and Australia. Lauda Air obtained a license to operate limited scheduled flights in 1986; worldwide scheduled rights followed in August 1990. These were obtained against stiff opposition from government-controlled Austrian Airlines, then awash in red ink.

Twenty percent of the airline was floated on the Vienna stock market at Sch 210 a share in 1990, with proceeds earmarked to finance new aircraft. The company also started a cargo department in 1990.

In May 1991, Lauda Air lost a Boeing 767 airliner, which crashed in Thailand, killing all 213 passengers and ten crew members aboard. The puzzling accident was attributed to the inexplicable in-flight deployment of a thrust reverser rather than to pilot error.

### Partner of Lufthansa in 1993

Lauda Air held strategic partnership talks with Deutsche Lufthansa AG (LH) in the early 1990s. Lauda's Vienna hub and access to Eastern Europe made it strategically attractive to LH. The LH/Lauda pairing was initially seen as a move to counter

**Company Perspectives:**

*Lauda Air connects Austria to many paradises on earth with one of the world's most modern aircraft fleets. A rapid growth based on the fruitful, consequent realization of its slogan "Service is our success." But, as all airlines today basically fly equally far, equally quickly, using almost identical aircraft types, Lauda has always strove to make the time spent on board especially enjoyable for its passengers.*

the aborted Alcazar alliance, which would have linked Austrian Airlines, Swissair, SAS, and KLM.

In July 1992, Lufthansa acquired 26.47 percent of Lauda Air through its Condor charter unit (it bought a 26 percent stake in ITAS at the same time), and a strategic alliance agreement was officially announced in January 1993. The phrase "Partner of Lufthansa" was painted on the tails of Lauda aircraft.

By February 1993, the Lauda fleet numbered eight planes: four Boeing 737s and four long-range 767s. It served Munich, Miami, and Los Angeles using aircraft from Lufthansa's Condor unit. It was also flying cargo and passengers, on a weekly basis, as far as Sydney, Melbourne, Hong Kong, and Bangkok.

After-tax profits were Sch 43 million (U.S.$4.3 million) for the 1992–93 fiscal year. Though nearly 70 percent of passengers were on charter flights, earnings from scheduled and non-scheduled operations were equivalent. Lauda Air had about 700 employees. The founder was still logging 60 hours a month in the cockpit.

Lauda formed a Milan-based subsidiary, Lauda Air S.p.A., in early 1993 as the company launched a charter service linking Italy—with a population of 60 million, a market several times the size of Austria—with tourist destinations in the Caribbean.

In 1994, Lauda Air bought out the 25.9 percent stake held by Basile Varvaressos, the head of the Austrian ITAS travel conglomerate who had been Lauda's long-term partner. In July of that year, the 39.71 percent holding that Condor then held in Lauda Air shifted to its parent, Lufthansa. Niki Lauda personally held an equivalent number of shares, and the remaining 20.58 percent of shares were publicly traded.

By the fall of 1994, Lauda had added another three Boeing 767s, bringing its fleet to 11. Niki Lauda had reduced his own flying hours but was still certified to fly each of the types his namesake carrier operated. Lauda Air then served 42 charter destinations and 11 scheduled destinations.

Lauda Air carried 1.5 million passengers in 1995, half of them business travelers. In 1995, Lauda added four of Bombardier's Canadair Regional Jets (a long range derivative) to its fleet for regional routes, including a new route to Sofia, Bulgaria.

Staff grew to 1,200 employees in 1996. That year, Lauda began deploying its regional jets on unprecedented joint operations with Austrian Airlines to Rome, Nice, and Milan. After-tax profits rose 13 percent, to Sch 53.1 million (U.S.$3.8 million), in the fiscal year ending October 31, 1996.

**Key Dates:**

**1979:** Auto racing legend Niki Lauda launches his own charter airline.
**1985:** ITAS travel agency owner Basile Varvaressos taken on as a partner in the airline.
**1986:** Lauda Air begins limited scheduled operations to Australia.
**1990:** Lauda Air floats on the Vienna stock market.
**1992:** Lufthansa acquires a holding in Lauda Air.
**1994:** Niki Lauda buys out Varvaressos.
**1997:** Austrian Airlines acquires holding in Lauda Air.
**2000:** Niki Lauda steps down as chairman.

### *Austrian Cooperation in 1997*

Though it had a population of less than nine million, Austria's central location had 40 competitors flying into Vienna. Seeing a lack of growth potential in the home market, in the late 1990s Austria's three main airlines—Lauda, Austrian Airlines (AUA), and regional carrier Tyrolean Airways (42.8 percent owned by AUA)—began a strategy of cooperation. The three airlines hoped to save as much as $200 million a year through increased sales and combining maintenance, finance, and other operations. The influence of this tripartite grouping was extended through the alliance AUA had with Swissair, Sabena, and Delta, and Lauda's own codeshares, including a new one with Malaysian Airlines System. In March 2000, Lauda and AUA joined the Star Alliance global marketing affiliation led by United Airlines.

AUA was to focus on scheduled traffic on medium and long haul routes, while Tyrolean covered regional and domestic traffic and Lauda focused on charter operations and routes to Australia and Asia. Lauda Air began flying the advanced, long-range Boeing 777 in September 1997. The 777 was financed by AUA, which leased the plane to Lauda.

In the spring of 1997, AUA acquired a 19.7 percent stake in Lauda Air from Lufthansa. AUA also acquired shares from Niki Lauda and from another investor, giving it a 36 percent voting share altogether.

*Air Transport World* cataloged Lauda Air's style around this time. The planes were named after pop culture icons such as Marilyn Monroe, Elvis Presley, Freddie Mercury of Queen, Bob Marley, and, understandably, Enzo Ferrari. Flight attendants (who faced a mandatory retirement age of 38) wore blue jeans and signature red baseball caps like the one that had become Niki Lauda's trademark since a horrific Grand Prix accident in 1976.

### *Lauda Out in 2000*

In November 2000, AUA announced plans to reorganize Lauda Air following losses from high fuel prices and unfavorable foreign exchange transactions (essentially, failure to hedge against a strong U.S. dollar). Niki Lauda stepped down as chief executive, disputing the extent of the carrier's loss—its first since 1991. AUA officials calculated the loss at Sch 1 billion, about 50 percent higher than Lauda's reckoning.

AUA executive Ferdinand Schmidt succeeded Lauda while remaining CEO of Lauda Air Italy, in which he held a controlling stake. Soon after, AUA bought an additional 11 percent stake in Lauda Air from Lufthansa, raising its total holdings to 47 percent. (I Viaggi del Ventaglio Group, an Italian tour operator, acquired 40 percent of Lauda Air Italy in 2002.)

AUA continued to increased its shareholding in Lauda Air. The Vienna Stock Exchange delisted the stock in August 2001 due to the very low volume of free floating shares.

Lauda Air adopted a new symbol in the fall of 2001, the UFO. The spaceship represented high technology and the shape of things to come. At this time, AUA owned 67 percent of the airline's shares, with 30 percent owned by the Lauda Foundation.

AUA repositioned Lauda Air as a charter line. In April 2002, it was replaced by Rheintalflug, a regional subsidiary of AUA, on its route to the UK (Manchester). Scheduled service to Australia kept the Lauda brand.

### *Principal Competitors*

British Airways plc; Condor Flugdienst GmbH; Deutsche Lufthansa AG; Qantas Airways Limited; Société Air France.

### *Further Reading*

Boyes, Roger, ''Is This the Finishing Line for Fast-Track Lauda?,'' *Times* (Overseas News), December 9, 2000, p. 25.

Bright, Julia, ''The Driver Taking the Aerial Route,'' *Director,* August 1992, p. 74.

''Business as Usual for Lauda Air on 'Kangaroo Route','' *New Straits Times-Management Times* (Malaysia), September 18, 2001.

Cameron, Douglas, ''Waltzing Into Vienna,'' *Airline Business,* August 1992, p. 13.

De Wulf, Herman, ''Into the Unknown (Lauda Air's Joint Operations with Lufthansa),'' *Flight International,* April 20, 1994, p. 31.

Dib, Felisha, ''Lauda Air Offers Five-Star Dining in the Sky,'' *South Florida Business Journal,* June 15, 2001, p. 22.

Frey, Eric, ''Austrian Airlines Lifts Lauda Air Stake,'' *Financial Times,* November 27, 2000, p. 34.

——, ''Austrian Airlines Moves on Lauda,'' *Financial Times,* November 9, 2000, p. 40.

Hergesell, Alexandra, ''Niki Lauda Branded by Risk,'' *Europe,* September 2001, p. 45.

Hill, Leonard, ''Auspicious Austrian Upstart,'' *Air Transport World,* September 1994, p. 109.

——, '' 'Grand Prix' Airline,'' *Air Transport World,* July 1997, pp. 165–67.

——, ''A Lauda Trouble,'' *Air Transport World,* January 2001, pp. 42–6.

Jasper, Chris, ''Austrian Steps In as Strong Dollar Hits Lauda,'' *Flight International,* October 10, 2000, p. 6.

——, ''Austrian Takes Action to Stem Lauda's Decline,'' *Flight International,* December 19, 2000, p. 21.

——, ''Niki Lauda Quits the Driving Seat at Airline He Founded,'' *Flight International,* November 28, 2000, p. 26.

Johari, Shahriman, ''Building Up Small Firm a Challenge for Lenz,'' *Business Times* (Malaysia), April 21, 1999.

Kang Siew Li, ''Lauda Air Set to Soar Despite Asian Crisis,'' *Business Times,* November 21, 1998.

King, Sam, ''Austria Rivals Set for Battle,'' *Airline Business,* August 1995, p. 16.

Norris, Guy, ''Lauda Thrust-Reverser Under Suspicion,'' *Flight International,* June 12, 1991, pp. 16f.

O'Connor, Anthony, ''Austria's Airline Evolution,'' *Airfinance Journal,* October 1997, pp. 24–27.

Proctor, Paul, ''Italy's 60-Million Population Next Lauda Air Target,'' *Aviation Week & Space Technology,* July 22, 1996, p. 51.

''Profile: Lauda's Stormy Passage,'' *International Management,* July/August 1992, pp. 36ff.

Stone, Mark, ''Lauding Lauda,'' *Global Trade & Transportation,* November 1993, p. 43.

Theole, Peter, ''Control Is the Key to Expansion,'' *Airfinance Journal,* July/August 1994, p. 40.

''Volte-Face or Volte-Farce (FAA Admits Error Over Lauda Air Accident),'' *Flight International,* September 18, 1991, p. 3.

—Frederick C. Ingram

# The Legal Aid Society

**90 Church Street**
**New York, New York 10007**
**U.S.A.**
**Telephone: (212) 577-3300**
**Fax: (212) 577-7999**
**Web site: http://www.legal-aid.org**

*Non-Profit Corporation*
*Incorporated:* 1876 as Der Deutsche-Rechts-Schutz-Verein
*Employees:* 1,600
*Revenues:* $134.4 million (2001)
*NAIC:* 541110 Offices of Lawyers

The Legal Aid Society of New York City is the United States' oldest and largest provider of legal services to people unable to afford an attorney. With a roster of 900 lawyers, backed by a support staff of 800 and an annual budget of approximately $125 million, the Society is the largest legal employer in the New York metropolitan area. It handles some 300,000 cases each year that are divided into three areas: civil, criminal, and juvenile rights. The civil practice, the Society's oldest endeavor, is funded by private donations and government grants and concentrates on such areas as family law, consumer law, immigration issues, and the rights of the homeless. The Society's criminal practice is New York City's primary provider of indigent defense services. It is funded by a combination of city, state, and federal funds, as is the juvenile rights practice, which is involved in the representation of 90 percent of all children who appear before the city's family court. The Society, according to *Crain's New York Business,* is among the top 25 largest non-profit corporations in the city in terms of operating budget.

## *Legal Aid Society Established by German Immigrants*

The Legal Aid Society was organized by German immigrants who, because they had a limited facility with the English language and were unfamiliar with American customs, were easily exploited. The German Society in New York City was already providing some legal services when, on March 8, 1876, it incorporated the predecessor to the Legal Aid Society, Der Deutsche-Rechts-Schutz-Verein, in the offices of its first president, Edward Salomon, a practicing attorney who also served as counsel for the Prussian Government. His fellow incorporators included merchants and importers as well as lawyers, all devoted to providing legal protection for German immigrants. At the time, some 25 years before the creation of Greater New York, the city was limited to the million people who lived on the island of Manhattan. Most of the immigration to this point originated from Ireland, but the number of transplanted Germans was on the rise. They, like the influx of Italians and other nationalities to follow in the years to come, would face even greater difficulties assimilating into American society because, unlike the Irish, English was not their first language.

The Society's original charter limited aid to people of German birth, but Salomon had enough foresight to obtain the rights to the name "Legal Aid Society" well before non-Germans came within the organization's purview. Around 1885, a "New York Legal Aid Society" began advertising its "free" services in the city's German newspapers. Salomon investigated, concluded "that the affair was not in very clean hands," and took the necessary steps to enjoin the use of "Legal Aid Society." As a result, the use of "legal aid" would be reserved for the many non-profit organizations that would be established across the country in the years to come. America's second legal aid society was established in Chicago in 1888 as the Ethical Culture Society, the first to offer legal assistance regardless of nationality, race, or sex. In 1889, Salomon was succeeded by patent attorney Arthur von Briesen, who during the first year of his presidency oversaw a change in the Society's constitution that eliminated the restriction of clients to those of German heritage. In 1890, at his insistence, the organization cut its financial ties to The German Society, then in 1896 officially changed its name to The Legal Aid Society. Even with its previous subsidy, it had barely managed to scrape by and on several occasions came close to dissolving for lack of funds. In addition to small donations from individuals, the Society was supported by a 10 percent commission it charged on collecting money for clients, a practice begun in 1879. In 1896, a retainer fee of ten cents was initiated, subsequently raised to 25 cents in 1903, then 50 cents, although it was frequently waived. The Society also held fundraising events, in

## Company Perspectives:

*By providing counsel and assistance to those in need, the Society strives on a daily basis to honor its commitment to secure, through the law, the rights and the protection of the poor which should be afforded to all. In doing so, the Society helps to ensure that our civilization remains just in its treatment of all people.*

particular an annual opera benefit. Somehow it managed to hang on, but funding would remain a constant worry throughout the Society's history.

Initially the Society concentrated on civil matters, although the founders clearly intended to handle criminal cases as well. Again it was the lack of money, which translated into the lack of staff, that forced the Society to limit its activities. Criminal cases were only accepted after receiving special permission from the law committee, president, or the vice-president of the organization. In its early years, Society lawyers mostly handled cases involving wages or rent disputes and attempts to defraud. By the end of the century, neighborhood branch offices were opened, spreading the work of the Society to the other boroughs of Greater New York. In 1900, a Seaman's Branch was opened, which became instrumental in the elimination of the lucrative practice of shanghaiing sailors. Essentially, men in the waterfront areas were waylaid by the means of clubs or drugs and pressed into service on ships against their will. Society lawyers assigned to the Seaman's Branch spent many nights on launches in New York harbor running down the ''crimps'' involved in this trade. As a result of these efforts, the Society was able to secure a conviction that set a precedent for law enforcement around the country and helped to make shanghaiing a Federal offense.

Just as its Seamen's Branch championed the rights of sailors, the Society also began to support domestic workers, producing a pamphlet called ''Domestic Employment'' that laid out reasonable terms of employment for both servants and employers. Nevertheless, the Society was so deluged with cases involving the recovery of wages that by 1910 it was forced to limit its services to those servants who left their employment after giving reasonable notice. It was also during this period that the Society began to take on personal loan companies and furniture installment sellers. Many recent immigrants fell victim to the so-called installment game, buying goods on terms so restrictive that as soon as they missed a payment they were removed to the notorious Ludlow jail by complicit city marshals and held until family members were able to raise the necessary ransom. During this ''War on the Sharks,'' the Society also played an influential role in the passage of legislation to regulate interest rates that could be charged on small loans. Press recognition of the Society, which began with a 1906 article in the *Ladies Home Journal,* helped to spread the legal aid concept to other cities and led to the establishment of the National Alliance of Legal Aid Societies in 1912. Moreover, the Society was in the vanguard of promoting progressive ideals. In 1901, at a time when few women were members of the Bar, Rosalie Loew, after serving six years as a staff attorney, was named Attorney-in-Chief.

### *The Society During World War I*

With Europe involved in the bloody conflict of World War I, Von Briesen, who retained sympathies to his native Germany, found it necessary to step down as the president of the Society. He was replaced in 1917 by the most distinguished man to ever hold the office: Charles Evans Hughes, a man who had already been elected to two terms as governor of New York, served as an associate justice of the United States Supreme Court, and ran for the presidency in 1916. After five years as president of the Society, Hughes resigned to become Secretary of State, then returned to the Supreme Court where he was named Chief Justice. His connection to the Society was instrumental in raising the profile of the organization, which led to significant growth during the 1920s. The Bar as well as the general public increased their contributions, which allowed the Society to expand its work on criminal cases. By the end of the decade it received its millionth application for aid.

The advent of the Depression brought a number of changes to the Society in the 1930s, although some were simply a tribute to its successes. The Seaman's Branch lessened in importance, due in large part to legislation that the Society had championed. Caseloads were also reduced with the advent of the Workmen's Compensation Bureau, the Small Claims Court, and the Age Claims Division of the State Labor Department. Nevertheless, financial constraints forced the Society to close the Brooklyn and Harlem branches in 1932, and the retainer was increased from 25 cents to 50 cents. The Depression also led to complaints from practicing attorneys who felt that the Society was depriving them of potential business. In better times, of course, they would never take on such small matters, but now the Society had to be more scrupulous about turning away clients who had even the slightest ability to pay.

During World War II, the workload of the Society was inflated by the influx of military-related cases. Not only draft matters were handled but also issues involving expeditious marriages during furloughs for servicemen as well as allowances, allotments, and insurance for relatives. After the war, the Society offered legal assistance to any veterans, regardless of their ability to pay, for 90 days after their discharge. Following the war, there was renewed interest in legal aid in America, with the number of organizations growing from 64 to 90 by the end of the decade. Much of the Society's work now dealt with landlord and tenant cases due to a tight housing situation that resulted from building restrictions imposed during the war. Because the Society could only help the indigent, in 1948 it established Legal Referral Services, which connected clients with a marginal ability to pay, or those with unusual cases, to a list of volunteer lawyers who had been recruited by the bar association.

Because contributions from both lawyers and the general public increased significantly after the war, by 1950 the Society was able to start reopening the branch offices closed during the Depression. Services in the civil practice were increased, but the Society was still unable to represent many criminal cases. This situation changed in the 1960s when the Society received a contract from the city of New York to provide legal representation to poor defendants, the result of the landmark 1963 Supreme Court decision, *Gideon v. Wainwright*, which required

**Key Dates:**

**1876:** Der Deutsche-Rechts-Schutz-Verein incorporated to provide legal aid for German immigrants
**1896:** The organization officially changes its name to The Legal Aid Society.
**1901:** Rosalie Loew is named Attorney-in-Chief.
**1917:** Charles Evans Hughes is named president.
**1920:** Criminal practice added to the Society's services.
**1965:** The Society is awarded a contract to represent indigent criminal defendants in New York City.
**1975:** Archibald Murray is named Attorney-in-Chief and executive director.
**1994:** The Society's staff lawyers go on strike but return when Mayor Giuliani intervenes.

states and municipalities to provide counsel to indigents involved in criminal prosecution. Before this change, such legal work for the indigent had been used by politicians as patronage, with the result that all too often defendants were actually deprived of representation. Fueled by city and state funding of its criminal practice, the Society grew in size. It was also during this period that the Juvenile Rights Division and the Prisoners Rights Project were added. To supplement the Society's staff of lawyers, a formal internship program was established in 1967.

In 1975, Archibald Murray became attorney in chief and executive director of the Society, a post he held for 20 years. Born in Barbados he was the first black president of the New York State Bar Association and made a point of hiring more minority lawyers to the Society's staff, increasing the level from three percent to 19 percent. To augment the civil practice, which lacked public financing, he turned to city law firms, convincing them to not only contribute money but also to perform free legal work for Society clients. In 1978, the Volunteer Division was created to facilitate a partnership with members of the private bar. At the end of his term, however, Murray saw the Society's relationship with the city's mayor, Rudolph Giuliani, turn contentious and seriously jeopardize the future of the organization.

### *Society Attorneys Strike in 1994*

In October 1994, 919 staff attorneys, whose annual average salary was $45,000, went on strike against the Society, seeking a 4.5 percent raise in salary as well as parity in caseload with the district attorney's office. After Rudolph Giuliani had taken office at the beginning of the year, the number of misdemeanor arrests increased by almost 30 percent over a similar period the year before. Most of these arrests were the result of his administration's effort to attack ''quality of life crimes'' such as traffic-light squeegee men, subway panhandlers, graffiti artists, and street-corner prostitutes. The reasoning behind this effort was that by tolerating relatively petty transgressions, over the years the city had created an atmosphere in which more major crimes flourished. Although the strike was against the Society and not the city, and other work stoppages had recently occurred with legal aid workers making similar complaints in other municipalities, Mayor Giuliani responded with surprising ferocity. He not only gave 90 days notice that the city would cancel its contract with the Society, he also threatened to have the strikers fired and blacklisted from future city business if the Society did not accept an 18 percent cut in funding, increased workloads, and a no-strike agreement from the union. Because the city provided $79 million of the its $140 million budget, the Society faced immediate ruin. Ironically, just two weeks earlier, the mayor, displeased with the high costs of the Assigned Counsel Plan, had begun to shift some 13,000 cases to the Society.

After a four-day walkout, the attorneys, who agreed to a two percent annual bonus and arbitration over health care costs, returned to work, albeit somewhat shaken and demoralized. They had originally argued that their salary demands could be met by the Society making internal budget cuts and were clearly caught off guard by the mayor's intervention. Norman Siegel, head of the New York affiliate of the American Civil Liberties Union, commented at the time, ''My sense is that the lawyers became pawns in a much larger political and labor management scenario.'' Some of the strikers maintained that Giuliani saw the lawyers as an easy target, a useful foil to intimidate city unions in future negotiations.

Whatever may have been Mayor Giuliani's short-term goal, he continued to maintain an antagonistic attitude regarding the Society throughout the remainder of his time in office. He vowed to break the Society's ''monopoly'' on indigent legal work by awarding some of it to other groups, such as bar associations. With its budget slashed, the Society hired a management consultant to streamline its operation, which according to critics had become top heavy. As a result, about half of the 212 supervising attorneys were eliminated, with some demoted and others simply laid off. The Society was also forced to change the way it handled arraignments. Instead of maintaining continuity of representation, with the same attorney working with a client throughout the court system, the Society now assigned a lawyer to screen out lesser matters at the arraignment stage in order to concentrate on more serious charges. Despite the cuts in city funding, however, the Society established a Capital Division in 1995 in order to address cases affected by the state's new death penalty law.

In September 2001, Mayor Giuliani, who was set to leave office at the end of the year because of term limits, prepared a parting shot in his feud with the Society. He terminated the automatic renewal of its city contract, forcing the Society to bid on contracts with each borough. The terrorist attacks of September 11, however, intervened, leaving the matter to be resolved by a new mayor. With its main office located near the World Trade Center, the Society was adversely affected by the events, cut off from its headquarters for several weeks, and forced to work out of temporary accommodations. Even as it recovered from these extraordinary circumstances, the Society added programs to deal with the effects of the terrorists attacks. Budget cuts and an increased caseload began to take its toll on the organization, so that by the time Michael Bloomberg took office as New York's new mayor in 2002, the future of the Society was very much uncertain. Because the city, strapped for money after economic difficulties caused by September 11, would likely save money by investing in the Society, and a new administration presented a fresh start, circumstances seemed promising for a return to an atmosphere less hostile to legal aid in New York City.

### *Principal Divisions*

Criminal Defense Division; Federal Defender Division; Juvenile Rights Division; Civil Division; Volunteer Division.

### *Further Reading*

Hoffman, Jan, ''A New Round for Legal Aid and Giuliani,'' *New York Times,* October 20, 1994, p. 41.

——, ''For Legal Aid and the City, Peace at Last,'' *New York Times,* January 29, 1995, p. 33.

Rohde, David, ''Legal Aid's Last Challenge From an Old Adversary, Giuliani,'' *New York Times,* September 9, 2001, p. 41.

Tweed, Harrison, *The Legal Aid Society, New York City, 1987–1951,* New York: The Legal Aid Society, 1954, 122 p.

—Ed Dinger

# Leggett & Platt, Inc.

**One Leggett Road**
**Carthage, Missouri 64836**
**U.S.A.**
**Telephone: (417) 358-8131**
**Fax: (417) 358-5840**
**Web site: http://www.leggett.com**

*Public Company*
*Incorporated:* 1901 as Leggett & Platt Spring Bed & Manufacturing Co.
*Employees:* 31,000
*Sales:* $4.1 billion (2001)
*Stock Exchanges:* New York
*Ticker Symbol:* LEG
*NAIC:* 337910 Mattress Manufacturing; 337215 Showcase, Partition, Shelving, and Locker Manufacturing

Credited with launching the U.S. bedspring industry, Leggett & Platt, Inc., one of the nation's largest manufacturers of bedding and furnishing products, began operating in the late 19th century as the sole manufacturer of the coiled bedspring. From this single product, invented and patented by one of the company's founders, Leggett & Platt slowly expanded its product line to embrace an assortment of products primarily related to the furnishings industry. As the company's product line evolved, the company grew as a component supplier for other manufacturers rather than a marketer and distributor its own products at the retail level. Entering the new millennium, Leggett & Platt's product line comprised five categories: residential furnishings, commercial furnishings, aluminum products, industrial materials, and specialized products. In North America, the company held a leading market position in the following product lines: components for residential furniture and bedding, retail store fixtures and point-of-purchase displays, components for office furniture, non-automotive aluminum die castings, drawn steel wire, automotive seat support and lumbar systems, and bedding industry machinery for wire forming, sewing, and quilting. Since its initial public offering in 1967, Leggett & Platt has recorded an average growth rate of 15 percent per year.

## *Early History: Late 1800s*

In the late 19th century, two men living in Carthage, Missouri, joined their distinct skills to create a company that would outlive both them and their children and continue to flourish more than a century later. One of these men was J.P. Leggett, an inventor who had achieved modest success with several patented inventions, and the other was C.B. Platt, a businessman and manufacturer, whose family owned a factory in Carthage. By 1883, Leggett had developed an idea for a new product and turned to Platt, his brother-in-law, to solicit his manufacturing expertise and resources. Leggett's idea was innovative and had already garnered him a patent for his invention—the coiled bedspring.

Platt agreed to assist Leggett in manufacturing this new product, and the two formed a partnership in 1883, using the Platt Plow Works in Carthage as the production site for the first Leggett bedsprings. Until Leggett had developed the coiled bedspring, bedding in the United States generally consisted of cotton, feather, or horsehair mattresses, with no added cushion beyond that provided by the mattress material itself. Leggett's bedsprings were designed to be used as a foundation for these mattresses, with the coils fabricated separately, then sold to retail merchants and assembled in the backs of stores or on the walkways in front.

For 12 years, the Leggett and Platt partnership operated out of the Platt Plow Works, forming the coils with belt-driven machinery and selling them to retail merchants. By 1895, the partnership had its own factory and offices, a two-story building that housed both sides of the young company's operations and contained its entire work force, which at that point totaled seven people, including the two founders. Before the decade was over, another manufacturing plant was added in Louisville, Kentucky. The partnership incorporated in 1901 under the name Leggett & Platt Spring Bed & Manufacturing Co., with Leggett serving as its first president.

The waning years of the century marked a rush of activity for Leggett and Platt. The construction of two factories in five years, after 12 years of production at Platt Plow Works, and the incorporation of the growing concern appeared to foreshadow further expansion; however, in the 60 years that followed, the

### Company Perspectives:

*We pride ourselves on leadership in the areas of ethics and values. We have established, and seek to expand, our reputation for integrity and honesty. We believe that long-term relationships are strengthened, and the company's performance enhanced, by the following set of Leggett's cultural characteristics. We value honesty. We care about people. We are customer service zealots. We strive to outwork the competition. We continuously seek improvement and are not content with the status quo. We value innovation, creativity, and an entrepreneurial spirit. We value candor and constructive dissent. We encourage all employee partners to become shareholders of Leggett stock. And finally, we like to laugh, have fun, and enjoy good times with one another.*

company would barely exceed the pace of growth established between 1895 and 1900. Moreover, the first half century of Leggett's and Platt's business, from 1883 to 1933, would be almost entirely devoted to the production of a single product—Leggett's coiled bedsprings. From 1901 forward, the Leggett & Platt Spring Bed & Manufacturing Co. seemed resigned to fulfilling one need with one product, with little effort made toward expanding the company's scope. Leggett remained president until 1921, when Platt assumed the company's leadership and oversaw the construction of a new factory in Carthage in 1925 to replace the now outdated original factory.

## *Finding New Opportunities: 1930s*

Platt's stewardship of Leggett & Platt devolved in 1929 to Leggett's son, J.P. Leggett, Jr., who held the position for three years. In that time, he initiated the introduction of the company's first new product in 50 years and its first diversification into another market. In 1933, Leggett & Platt began manufacturing springs for innerspring mattresses that year, a product that would become integral to the company's operation. By this time, Leggett & Platt had effected an important and defining change in the way the company operated: it now sold its products to other manufacturers rather than to retailers, as the company had originally done. With a growing market for innerspring mattresses, the company found greater success and greater profits selling springs to mattress manufacturers, who then assembled a finished innerspring mattress with the springs provided by Leggett & Platt. Perhaps equally important to the evolution of Leggett & Platt into a diversified component specialist was its expansion into peripheral markets, specifically the manufacturing of coiled springs for the producers of upholstered furniture.

With these important changes behind it, and a rapidly growing market for springs waiting ahead, Leggett & Platt steadily developed as a business throughout the 1930s and into the 1940s. A new factory, built in Winchester, Kentucky, was established in 1942 to replace the Louisville facility. Five years later, another new plant went into operation, this time in Ennis, Texas.

The addition of the Ennis plant concluded Leggett & Platt's physical growth until 1960, a pivotal year that would inaugurate for the company a new era of expansion and diversification, a new corporate strategy, and new leadership, transforming the modestly sized company into a formidable force in the furnishings industry. Chiefly responsible for this dramatic change in course was Harry M. Cornell, Jr., J.P. Leggett's grandson, who joined the company in 1950 and then became manager of the Ennis, Texas, plant in 1953. When he was appointed as the company's president in 1960, Cornell inherited from his father, who was Leggett & Platt's president from 1953 to 1960, a company with three production plants and $7 million in annual sales.

## *Expansion Begins: 1960s*

The younger Cornell's plans for Leggett & Platt were entirely different from those actualized by each of the company's six previous presidents, who had limited Leggett & Platt to a regional business. What Cornell saw after an examination of the U.S. furnishings industry was the opportunity for a company such as Leggett & Platt to capitalize on a highly fragmented market for finished furnishings products. This could be done, he speculated, by broadening Leggett & Platt's scope to a national level and by manufacturing and distributing components of furnishings products to manufacturers at a lower production cost than they could attain on their own. The first step in this direction was achieved in October 1960, when the company acquired a small wood-working plant in Springfield, Missouri. Though the acquisition was small, it represented a move toward diversification, enabling Leggett & Platt to fabricate wooden bed frames.

Additional acquisitions would follow, seven throughout the decade, as Leggett & Platt strategically added more facilities for manufacturing an increasing variety of bedding and furniture components. By the early 1970s, roughly a decade after the implementation of the company's new business philosophy, Leggett & Platt's growing network of manufacturing and distribution facilities comprised 17 manufacturing plants and five warehouses. Annual revenues hovered around $50 million, reflecting a sales volume more than seven times greater than that recorded less than 15 years earlier.

The company continued its growth and diversification. By bolstering its presence in the bedding and furnishings market, the firm increased its economies of scale, which proved to be Leggett & Platt's point of leverage in a fragmented industry. The company had also begun to vertically integrate, establishing production facilities that would supply its raw material needs. Through a joint venture with Armco Steel Corporation, Leggett & Platt constructed a wire mill in Carthage in 1970, enabling the company to satisfy virtually all of its wire needs. Similarly, a wood saw mill was constructed in Naples, Texas, that same year, to assure a steady source of lumber for the company's wood frame business.

## *Product Development and Continued Growth: 1970s–80s*

Aside from Leggett & Platt's physical growth, progress was also being achieved in other areas, such as in the development of the company's products and in the machinery utilized to manufacture those products. At this point, in the early 1970s, the company had high hopes for a new and promising inner-

## Key Dates:

**1883:** J.P. Leggett and C.B. Platt form a partnership.
**1901:** The two partners establish Leggett & Platt Spring Bed & Manufacturing Co.
**1925:** A new factory is built in Carthage.
**1933:** Leggett & Platt begins to manufacture springs for innerspring mattresses.
**1942:** The company opens a plant in Kentucky.
**1960:** Harry M. Cornell, Jr., is named president and begins expansion efforts.
**1970:** The firm partners with Armco Steel Corp. to construct a wire mill in Carthage.
**1984:** Michigan-based Gordon Manufacturing Co. is acquired.
**1993:** The company purchases Hanes Holding Company and VWR Textiles & Supplies Inc.
**1994:** Fashion Bed Group, the largest metal bed manufacturer in the United States, is acquired.
**1999:** The company's net earnings climb to $290.5 million.
**2001:** Revenues decline for the second time in company history.

spring coil unit, the continuous coil spring, which required substantially less wire and less labor than the conventional coil assembly process. Also, new machinery for producing box-spring units was under development that would automate several manufacturing steps currently being performed by hand. All of these developments—the additional production facilities, the new products, the more sophisticated machinery—combined to increase and solidify Leggett & Platt's presence in the home-furnishings market, which was valued at $11 billion at the retail level, was growing at a rate of 6 percent annually, and offered a potential $900 million worth of business for a company with Leggett & Platt's interests.

Concurrent with this growth, Leggett & Platt became a more diversified company, a change evinced by the proportional representation of the company's products in terms of the sales each product category generated. This shift was particularly evident in the early 1970s, when the production of bedding components began to contribute less to Leggett & Platt's sales volume. In 1970, bedding components accounted for 70 percent of the company's $40 million in sales; in 1974 the production of bedding components represented 43 percent of the company's $94 million in sales. This decline indicated significant diversification engendered by a greater focus on the company's finished furniture and upholstered furniture components product lines.

Entering the 1980s, Leggett & Platt's annual sales exceeded $250 million, having increased 18 percent annually from 1975 to 1980 despite a lackluster 1979. The company now had 60 manufacturing plants throughout the United States that provided products for more than 10,000 large and small manufacturers. With 20 years of exponential growth behind it, the nation's largest independent supplier of components in the bedding industry continued to grow, doubling its sales volume by the mid-1980s to reach $500 million. This sales growth was even more remarkable considering that the rest of the industry had suffered through three years of stagnant growth between 1980 and 1983. Leggett & Platt's continuous coil innerspring unit was partly responsible for this growth. The product had inspired much confidence during the early 1970s but had remained in a developmental stage for ten years and was not put on the market until the mid-1980s.

Also contributing to the company's growth was a series of acquisitions, ten in the period between 1983 and 1986, that, combined, had generated $164 million in sales before being acquired by Leggett & Platt. Two of these acquisitions in particular brought the company into the office furniture market, an arena in which the company wanted to increase its presence. Gordon Manufacturing Co., a Grand Rapids, Michigan, manufacturer of chair controls and steel bases for office furniture, was acquired in 1984, followed by the purchase a year later of Northfield Metal Products, a leading manufacturer of similar products.

### *Acquisition Strategy Continues: 1990s and Beyond*

As part of a nationwide recession, Leggett & Platt experienced several years of less than robust growth in the early 1990s, posting a decline in sales between 1990 and 1991. Then the company began to show signs of recovery, recording a relatively small gain in 1992 of nearly $90 million to reach $1.17 billion in revenues. The company regained its momentum of prodigious sales growth in 1993, registering $1.52 billion in sales. That same year, it concluded two strategic acquisitions, adding to its network of 135 manufacturing facilities located throughout the United States and Canada. One of these was Hanes Holding Company, a converter and distributor of woven and non-woven industrial fabrics used in the construction of furniture and bedding. The other, Hickory, North Carolina-based VWR Textiles & Supplies, Inc., gave Leggett & Platt additional furniture and bedding fabric manufacturing resources, strengthening its position in another market related to the furnishings industry. In 1994, the firm made another significant purchased when it snatched up Fashion Bed Group, the largest metal bed manufacturer in the United States. By this time, Leggett & Platt held 22 percent of the furniture and bedding components market.

The company's prosperity continued during the latter half of the decade. A large portion of the firm's growth stemmed from its rigorous acquisition strategy. In fact, Leggett & Platt completed over 150 purchases during the 1990s alone. The company looked for certain characteristics in a firm before it set plans in motion to purchase it—a strategy that paid off handsomely for the manufacturer. Most of the acquired companies were small, with less than $20 million in annual revenues. The firms were private, had between one and five owners, and had management teams that were most often left intact. Nearly two-thirds of the companies that Leggett & Platt acquired were competitors. These distinct characteristics left the firm in a advantageous position as the deals involved little risk and gave the firm access to the acquired company's facilities. Through acquisition, Leggett & Platt grew externally, which proved to be more cost effective than either internal growth or funding the construction of a new facility.

Some of the firm's more notable purchases included Hoover Wire Products Inc., a wire and steel component manufacturer;

WBSCO, a bedding machinery concern; Steadley Co.; Les Bois Blanchet Inc.; and Pace Industries Inc. In 1997, Leggett & Platt acquired a total of 29 companies, including Cambridge Tool & Mfg. Co., the most prominent die caster on the East Coast; Amco Corp. and Rodgers-Wade Manufacturing Co., both custom store fixture manufacturers; and Spuhl Holding AG, a Swiss machinery company. That year, sales reached $2.9 billion. In 1999, net profit grew by over 17 percent to a record $290.5 million while sales continued to climb to $3.78 billion.

Overall, Leggett & Platt acquired 79 companies that were integrated into the company's residential furnishing segment by 2000. Thirty-seven firms had been purchased for the company's commercial furnishings business line, nine were related to the company's aluminum products segment, ten were part of the industrial materials line, and 21 purchases were made in the specialized products division, which manufactured automotive seating support and lumbar systems and control and power train cables systems.

With nearly 120 years of business experience under its belt, Leggett & Platt continued to experience success in the early years of the new millennium while battling a faltering economy. In response to weakening demand in several of its product segments, the company made a series of job cuts, restructured and sold off 20 of its manufacturing facilities, and reduced capital spending. For only the second time in its history as a public entity, the firm recorded a drop in sales—3.8 percent—during 2001. Cash flow from operations, however, increased by 21 percent to $534.5 million in 2001.

Under the leadership of Cornell—named chairman emeritus in May 2002—Leggett & Platt had evolved from a small, regional manufacturer into an international *Fortune* 500 company that operated as a leader in many of its market segments. A company executive commented on Leggett & Platt's 30-year history with customer Sears, Roebuck and Co. and its broad product reach in a May 2000 *Chain Store Age* article, stating that "retailers know us for our fixturing, display merchandising, and backroom storage systems. But our products are used everyday by people sleeping, driving, sitting, working, and shopping in practically any defined space of human activity. We're a behind-the-scene foundation for Sears, manufacturers, and ultimately consumers." With its long-standing record of success and a February 2002 five-star rating by Standard & Poor's, Leggett & Platt promised to remain a prosperous business entity for years to come.

### *Principal Subsidiaries*

ARC Specialties; IncAdvantage Technologies, Inc.; Beeline Group, Inc.; Cambridge Tool & Mfg. Co., Inc.; Collier-Keyworth, Inc.; Crest-Foam Corp.; Davidson Plyforms, Inc.; Design Fabricators, Inc.; Genesis Fixtures, Inc.; Genesis Seating, Inc.; Hanes CNC Services Co.; Hanes Companies-New Jersey, Inc.; Hanes Companies, Inc.; Hanes Fabrics, Inc.; KLM Industries, Inc.; KelMax Equipment Co.; L&P Central Asia Trading Company; L&P Financial Services Co.; L&P International Holdings Company; L&P Manufacturing, Inc.; L&P Products Company, Inc.; MPI (A Leggett & Platt Company), Inc.; Met Displays, Inc.; Metal Bed Rail Company, Inc.; Pace Industries, Inc.; Pace Industries of Mexico, LLC (51%); Product Technologies, Inc.; Shaped Wire, Inc.; Tallbot Industries, Inc.

### *Principal Competitors*

Foamex International Inc.; Hickory Springs Manufacturing Company; RHC/Spacemaster Corporation.

### *Further Reading*

"Efforts to Integrate Operations Paying Off for Leggett & Platt," *Barron's*, August 2, 1971, p. 28.

Eidelman, David R., "Leggett & Platt, Inc.," *Wall Street Transcript*, December 22, 1975.

*Fact Book*, Carthage: Leggett & Platt, Inc., September 2001.

Gordon, Mitchell, "Springing Ahead," *Barron's*, January 4, 1982, p. 41.

Langenberg, Oliver M., "Leggett & Platt," *Wall Street Transcript*, August 14, 1972.

"Leggett & Platt Buys Four Companies," *HFN The Weekly Newspaper for the Home Furnishing Network*, January 20, 1997, p. 18.

"Leggett & Platt: Evolving Retail Space, With Style," *Chain Store Age Executive*, May 2000, p. 70.

"Leggett & Platt Wins Dismissal of U.S. Suit on Antitrust Charges," *Wall Street Journal*, March 17, 1975, p. 14.

Levy, Efraim, "A Comfortable Investment," *Business Week*, February 19, 2002.

*Our Hundredth Year, 1883–1983*, Carthage: Leggett & Platt, Inc., 1983.

"A Real Front-Runner: Leggett & Platt Outperforms Its Industry," *Barron's*, November 17, 1986, p. 58.

Rovito, Rich, "Leggett & Platt Will Keep Grafton Plant Open," *Business Journal-Milwaukee*, September 15, 2000, p. 5.

—Jeffrey L. Covell
—update: Christina M. Stansell

# LoJack Corporation

333 Elm Street
Dedham, Massachusetts 02026
U.S.A.
Telephone: (781) 326-4700
Toll Free: (800) 698-8022
Fax: (781) 326-7255
Web site: www.lojack.com

*Public Company*
*Incorporated:* 1978
*Employees:* 562
*Sales:* $95.85 million (2001)
*Stock Exchanges:* NASDAQ
*Ticker Symbol:* LOJN
*NAIC:* 33429 Other Communications Equipment Manufacturing; 53311 Lessors of Nonfinancial Intangible Assets (Except Copyrighted Works)

LoJack Corporation is the recognized world leader in vehicle-tracking technology. In the United States, the company's radio-frequency recovery system—known as the LoJack System—has maintained a higher than 90 percent successful recovery rate since it was offered to consumers some 15 years ago. The LoJack System helps law enforcement personnel to locate, track, and recover stolen vehicles. In 20 states and the District of Columbia, LoJack Corporation operates in areas having the greatest population density and the highest number of new car sales and motor vehicle thefts. In more than 20 countries in Europe, Africa, Asia and the Western Hemisphere, where it is not feasible to implement the full LoJack System, the corporation operates CarSearch, a patented LoJack product that functions independently of law enforcement networks. With more than two million LoJack Units installed worldwide and more than 40,000 retrieved vehicles, LoJack has recovered assets approaching nearly $1 billion in value. *Boston Magazine* picked LoJack as one of the best places to work in the Boston area; *Consumer Digest* awarded LoJack a ''Best Buy Award''; and *Forbes* magazine, for the third time, in 2001 named LoJack one of the 200 Best Small Companies in America, ranking LoJack as 96th.

## *1963–80: Nurturing an Early Morning Idea*

After completing five and a half years of active duty as a naval aviator with the rank of lieutenant and then holding various executive positions at AVCO Corporation, William R. Reagan (Bill) founded W.R. Reagan Associates, Inc., an investment banking firm. From 1976—81, he also served as part-time Police Commissioner of Medfield, a town in the greater Boston area. According to John Swanson, who became a consultant for the LoJack Corporation in 1987, Bill was preoccupied with the growth of car thefts throughout the nation in general and the greater Boston area in particular. His concern was well grounded in facts: a shrinking economy had fueled a nationwide increase of crime. The recession that gained ground in the early 1970s increased unemployment; the competition drove down wages; and interest rates and mortgage payments shot up.

Car thefts were ''big business,'' ranking second only to the sale of drugs. ''Organized crime entered the auto theft business: from 1974–83, the percentage of arrests of persons 18 years and over rose from 44.8 percent to 65.5 percent,'' wrote John Swanson in an unpublished essay titled *LoJack: A Study for the Financial Community.* In previous years ''most vehicle thefts were classified as 'joyriding' and stolen cars were recovered 95 percent of the time, little the worse for wear,'' noted Swanson.

Inflation was another reason for the increase of car thefts. ''The average value of stolen vehicles rose 400 percent from $1,246 in 1974 to $4,888 in 1986,'' Swanson wrote. Stealing cars was a ''lucrative business.'' Car thieves worked very quickly, as illustrated by what was known in the ''business'' as the ''40/40 equation: 40 seconds to steal a car and 40 minutes for a chop shop to cut it down into a pile of parts.'' The parts were more valuable than the whole car; for example, a 1984 compact costing $8,885 yielded $32,548 worth of parts. Furthermore, over and above being costly for the consumer and insurance companies and dangerous work for police officers, car thefts were often part of other crimes, such as armed robbery, rape, and murder. On a nationwide basis, theft was the largest single factor impacting the cost of insurance coverage.

Bill Reagan wanted to find a way of recovering stolen cars and doing away with chop shops. At 3:00 o'clock one morning,

**Company Perspectives:**

*LoJack's mission is to be the leading, premium-branded aftermarket provider of vehicle tracking and related products. The company's strategy is to strengthen its position in current markets and expand into new markets while extending the LoJack brand into other related products, such as Telematics. The company expects to continue its strategy of licensing the LoJack brand in international markets.*
*—Chairman/CEO C. Michael Daley*

as he was snacking on milk and cookies, "he hit on the idea of a small homing device that could be hidden in cars and tracked if the vehicle was stolen," reported Leslie M. Schultz in the February 1984 issue of *Inc.* magazine. Bill then gathered a group of engineers and technicians to work with him and the police to bring his 3:00 a.m. inspiration into reality.

By studying the Federal Bureau of Investigation's profiles of professional motor vehicle thieves, the research group identified the characteristics of car thieves and their way of operating: 1. Car thieves often were drug addicts; they could bypass any theft-preventive device and start a car in a matter of seconds. 2. To avoid being followed by the police, a thief drove the car a short distance for a few minutes and then parked it; if the car was still there after about eight hours, the thief drove the car to a chop shop. The chop shop then used or introduced the dismantled parts into the used-part stream. The best way to combat the thieves, the research group concluded, was to work with the police—the official law enforcement agents whose mission it was to recover stolen property.

For nine years Bill Reagan and his associates developed designs and performed tests to create a prototype system for rapid recovery of stolen vehicles. The product that emerged was called the LoJack System; Bill had a patent for it in 1978. The patent became the property of W.R. Reagan Associates, which, in turn, licensed it to the LoJack Corporation, a company Bill had formerly established. In 1981 a new LoJack Corporation was formed by the merger of W.R. Reagan Associates and the LoJack Corporation, which then became the surviving company.

## *1983–93: Fighting Crime, Developing and Testing a Prototype, Creating a Market*

What was the meaning of the name *LoJack*? According to John R. White's story in the 1984 issue of the *Boston Globe,* Reagan said that *LoJack* was the antithesis of *hijack.* The LoJack System was not an alarm to prevent theft; rather, it was meant to assist in the recovery of stolen vehicles. The only responsibility resting on the owner of a stolen car equipped with a LoJack Unit was to report the theft to the local police. There were no switches, buttons, or codes for the car operator to activate. The basic goal of the company was to make optimum use of professional law enforcement officers to recover stolen cars with as little damage as possible and to eliminate false alarms.

The LoJack System consisted of four components: 1. The LoJack Unit, (a high-frequency transmitter and receiver package about the size of a pack of cigarettes) randomly hidden in a car; 2. The Police Tracking Computer for police patrol cars and other tracking locations; 3. The Sector Activation System (SAS) used by law enforcement agencies to maintain vehicle codes; and 4. The Registration System, a proprietary method of assigning digital codes for transmission and reception by LoJack Units in a way that allowed unique activation codes to be permanently correlated with the unique vehicle identification number the manufacturer had assigned to the car in which the LoJack Unit was located.

When the owner of a stolen car equipped with a LoJack Unit reported the theft to the police, the law enforcement computer and communications network linked to LoJack's SAS broadcasted a radio-frequency signal to activate the LoJack Unit in the stolen car. Then, this unit broadcasted a silent, coded tracking signal to the LoJack Police Tracking Computer, which received the signal, homed in, and displayed the stolen vehicle's make, year, distance from the police cruiser, and other pertinent data, while flashing directional signals leading to the stolen car.

To raise funds for the further development of the LoJack System, LoJack Corporation completed an initial public offering in 1983 and was traded on NASDAQ under the symbol LOJN. Reagan, who billed himself to his friends as "Kojak from LoJack" and sported a Telly Savalas hairdo, requested his home state of Massachusetts to test a prototype of the LoJack System. At the time, this commonwealth had the highest rate of car thefts in the country: 864.8 motor vehicle thefts per 100,000 population, according to John Swanson's quotation from *Uniform Crime Reports for 1985.*

Massachusetts pledged substantial resources of police vehicles, helicopters, transmission facilities, and technical personnel for the four-month experiment. At the conclusion of the demonstration, all LoJack equipment was to be donated to the state and become the property of Massachusetts, thus constituting the basis for the first operational LoJack system in the country. For the demonstration, 20 vehicles outfitted with the LoJack Unit were reported as stolen, and then traced. After four months of demonstrations and more than 550 simulations, Massachusetts Governor Michael Dukakis said the state police had located each "stolen" car within 11 minutes of the report of its theft.

In October 1985 Motorola, Inc. was contracted as principal vendor for volume production of the LoJack System. Beginning in December 1985, the LoJack System was distributed to the Massachusetts police; next, this system was introduced statewide to automobile dealerships and to the public for installation by LoJack's two Massachusetts distribution centers opened in Danvers and in West Roxbury. The LoJack System cost $495, a price that included entering registration of the vehicle and information about the owner in both the LoJack computers and those of the police, as well as installation, warranty, and all hardware. In 1986, Massachusetts became the first state to adopt the LoJack System. Now that his invention was on the market, Bill Reagan resigned from presidency of the LoJack Corporation and was succeeded by C. Michael Daley, who had been a director of the company since 1981.

In December 1988, LoJack Corporation received federal clearance to sell its system outside Massachusetts. Fresh from the success of its pilot venture, the company expanded into

**Key Dates:**

**1978:** William R. Reagan obtains a patent for the LoJack System.
**1983:** LoJack Corporation is traded on NASDAQ.
**1985:** A prototype of the LoJack System is tested by Massachusetts State Police.
**1986:** The LoJack System becomes available statewide in Massachusetts.
**1988:** LoJack receives federal clearance to sell outside of Massachusetts; the company expands into Florida.
**1995:** LoJack licenses its technology to selected international markets and develops the CarSearch Stolen Vehicle Recovery System, which operates independently of law enforcement networks.
**1998:** LoJack penetrates the construction and the heavy-equipment industries.
**1999:** LoJack installs its one millionth LoJack Unit.
**2001:** Motorola ships its two millionth LoJack Unit to LoJack Corporation.

Florida, the number four state in the nation for stolen cars. In September 1989, in answer to a petition filed by the LoJack Corporation, the Federal Communications Commission allocated a police radio band of 173.075 MHz for the Stolen Vehicle Recovery Network. LoJack President Daley commented that the FCC action paved the way for LoJack's nationwide expansion. By year-end 1989, LoJack had "installed 35,000 systems in Massachusetts and south Florida . . . and recovered over 900 cars for clients, a 95 percent recovery rate," Jacalyn Carfagno reported in the July 9, 1990 issue of *Money* magazine. About 38 percent of the cars were recovered within an hour, and 75 percent within 12 hours. If the car was not recovered within 24 hours after the theft was reported, the company refunded the cost of the LoJack Unit. In March 1989 Los Angeles signed a contract to establish a Stolen Vehicle Recovery Network in Los Angeles; the states of Michigan, Illinois, and New Jersey soon followed suit. The company's strategy was to expand into areas where the combination of population density, new-car sales, and vehicle theft was high.

In spite of a 27 percent increase in revenues for 1991, LoJack Corporation's stock shrank from $100 million to less than $33 million. In a 1992 commentary printed in *Forbes,* analyst Norm Alster commented, "The company had not yet built a large enough installed base to cover its heavy capital and marketing expenses." For example, LoJack gained the cooperation of a police department by donating the $1,750 Tracking Units for the police cruisers. In Los Angeles alone, the bill for outfitting "450 cruisers was close to $1 million." LoJack also installed and serviced the police units. Moreover, the company invested heavily in advertising for new customers. Faced with a 1991 net income loss of $6.26 million, President Daley and Chief Financial Officer Joseph Abely "persuaded holders of convertible debentures to swap their bonds for a convertible preferred that would not pay a dividend until the company could afford it. . . . The swap succeeded because Michael Hobert, president of Benefit Capital Management Corp., an investment company with $10 million of the bonds, went along," Alster wrote.

### *1994–99: A Rapid Turnaround, Revenue Growth, International Expansion*

Charles McEwen hailed the coming of the LoJack system to New York State in his November 6, 1994 article in the *New York Times.* Over and above New York and the other states named above, the company had installed LoJack Systems in Georgia, Rhode Island, and Virginia; installation was scheduled for Washington, D.C. and Connecticut.

To expand beyond the United States, the company licensed the use of its LoJack technology to selected international markets and developed the CarSearch Stolen Vehicle Recovery System. Unlike the LoJack System operational in the United States, CarSearch had the flexibility of operating independently of existing law enforcement communication networks. By the end of 1996, the company had licensees using LoJack's technology in six European countries, four countries in South America, as well as in Hong Kong, Trinidad, and Tobago.

In 1994, revenues increased to $30.23 million, compared with $14.1 million in 1991; net income peaked at $1.23 million, the first positive income result posted since 1989. Each common share of stock earned $0.01. In January 1996, Joseph F. Abely was promoted to president and chief operating officer; Chairman Daley remained chief executive officer. "Profits surged 154 percent a year during 1995 and 1996," wrote Alex Pham in his *Boston Globe* story of May 20, 1997. "That impressive performance made LoJack the 13th fastest-growing company in Massachusetts." The company said that by late May 1997 LoJack was installed in more than 14 percent of all new cars in Massachusetts; more than 10 percent of new car owners in New York, California, and Florida also bought LoJack Units. The company estimated that stolen cars with installed LoJack Units were recovered more quickly and suffered less damage—about $500 per vehicle, compared with an average loss of several thousand dollars for cars with no LoJack Units. Furthermore, some insurance companies offered discounts of up to 35 percent to policyholders who had a LoJack Unit in their car.

By 1997 annual vehicle theft had escalated to an estimated cost of $8 billion. In a joint effort to stem the illegal export of stolen cars, an activity that contributed significantly to this escalated car theft, LoJack Corporation and Liberty Mutual Insurance Co. partnered to donate a LoJack Stolen Vehicle Recovery System to the U.S. Customs Service at the Port of Miami. According to Kevin Hall's story in the July 21, 1997 issue of *Journal of Commerce,* many of the cars stolen in Miami and Dade County were exported illegally through the Port of Miami to Haiti, as well as to Central and South America.

In 1998, the company offered a more rugged version of the LoJack Retrieval System specifically designed to meet the needs of the construction and heavy equipment industry. In June 1999, according to *Heavy Equipment News,* LoJack reported recoveries of a $300,000 Caterpillar front-end loader, a Cat combination front-end loader/backhoe and, for one company a 580L backhoe, trailer, and a flatbed truck. On the lighter side, the one millionth Unit of the LoJack System was installed in the "Batmobile," the television vehicle owned by George Barris, the legendary "Kustom Kar King," who designed the Batmobile for the 1980s' series of "Batman."

### *2000 and Beyond*

LoJack Corporation continued work on the redesign of its LoJack System and increased its nationwide and international presence. The company formed a Commercial Business Unit to tap opportunities in the construction equipment and tractor trailer business. United Rentals, Inc., the largest construction equipment rental company in North America, told LoJack Corporation that the LoJack System was making a positive difference to the rental company's bottom line and insurance premiums. United had begun to install LoJack units on its equipment in 1999 and had since installed the units in more than 4,000 pieces of equipment ranging from light towers to heavy-duty dump trucks. Recovery in fewer than 24 hours—with less damage—also meant that its equipments could be put back to work more quickly.

LoJack sales through new car dealers continued to be the major revenue producer for the company, although dealerships of used cars also sold LoJack Systems. In January 2001, Motorola shipped its two millionth LoJack unit to LoJack Corporation, according to the *Illinois Daily Herald* of January 2001. The first million LoJack units were shipped over a ten-year period; the second million were shipped over a three-year period. The corporation reorganized its sales and customer service organization to provide targeted coverage of large dealer groups, without putting individually owned dealerships aside. International sales, in large part fueled by collaboration with the insurance industry in foreign countries, increased by 93 percent, a growth due mostly to South African and South American licensees. At the end of fiscal 2001, the LoJack Corporation was doing business in 20 states and the District of Columbia in the United States and had licensees in 20 foreign countries.

At the end of 2001, Chairman/CEO Daley retired from the company. That year, LoJack Corporation reported revenues of $95.85 million, down from revenues of $500 million plus when he first assumed the presidency. Daley was succeeded by Ronald J. Rossi, who had held senior executive positions at Gillette for 35 years before retiring as president of Oral-B Worldwide; Rossi was held in high esteem for his success in marketing, sales, and corporate leadership.

At the beginning of fiscal 2002 (in 2001 LoJack changed the end of its fiscal year to December 31), Entercom, the nation's fifth largest radio operator and owner of four Boston radio stations, equipped its company vehicles with the LoJack Units. In answer to the U.S. Department of Transportation's call for increased security on trucks carrying hazardous materials on the nation's roadways, the company licensed the use of its LoJack technology to selected international markets and developed the CarSearch Stolen Vehicle Recovery System. Unlike the LoJack System operational in the United States, CarSearch had the flexibility of operating independently of existing law enforcement communication networks. LoJack units designed specifically for trailers (which were not connected to the truck's electrical supply) were concealed on the trailer itself, operated with a 12V or 24V battery source, and were equipped with a back-up battery.

The company began to develop an optional enhancement for cars equipped with the LoJack unit: a LoJack Early Warning System that could notify car owners that their car had been moved so that they could immediately report the theft. By reducing the time between theft and notification, this improvement also reduced the amount of time for recovery. The company planned to introduce this option in selected markets in 2002.

Furthermore, the company signed an agreement with CSI Wireless, Inc., AirIQ, Inc., and Aeris.net, Inc. to develop and manufacture a state-of-the-art LoJack-branded product for the consumer and commercial markets. LoJack Corporation's strategy, wrote Chairman/CEO Daley in his last *Annual Report,* was to strengthen "its position in current markets and expand into new markets . . . [by] extending the LoJack brand into other related products, such as Telematics." Telematics was an emerging technology that developed from the convergence of information and communications technologies. A new product addressing the safety and security needs of consumers and businesses was to complement the existing LoJack Unit by using Global Positioning System (GPS) technology to determine the location of a vehicle and to give a car Internet access as well as providing many services, such as automatic collision notification, roadside assistance, medical alert, door unlock, and starter disable.

As it continued to evolve toward an advantageous future, LoJack Corporation was a powerful deterrent to crime related to stolen vehicles; these thefts, estimated at $7.5 billion annually, were the costliest property crime in the United States. Undaunted, the company expanded into the construction and corporate fleet markets and searched for improvements that would reduce the size of LoJack products and create new opportunities, such as LoJack Units installed in containerized shipping, motorcycles, and rental cars. In short, the company was continually finding new ways to recover a theft.

### *Principal Subsidiaries*

LoJack Arizona, LLC; LoJack FSC, Ltd. (Barbados); LoJack International Corporation; LoJack of New Jersey Corporation; LoJack of Pennsylvania, Inc.; LoJack Recovery Systems Business Trust; Recovery Systems, Inc.

### *Principal Competitors*

Audiovox Corporation; Directed Electronics, Inc.; The Eastern Company; Strattec Security Corporation.

### *Further Reading*


Alster, Norm, "A Car Thief's Nemesis," *Forbes,* May 11, 1992, p. 124.

"Car Thefts Rise for First Time in Decade," *Denver Business Journal,* December 11, 2001.

Carfango, Jacalyn, "Auto-Recovery Firms Targeting Hot Wheels," *USA Today,* July 9, 1990, p. B5.

"Equipment Theft Finding Solutions to a Billion Dollar Problem," *Heavy Equipment News,* June 1999.

Greenwood, Tom, "LoJack Helps Police Recover Stolen Vehicles," *Detroit News,* November 17, 2000.

Hall, Kevin G., "Putting a Lock on Car Thefts," *Journal of Commerce,* July 21, 1997, p. A16.

Kirchofer, Tom, "LoJack Eyes Hazardous Cargo Trailers," *Boston Herald,* December 12, 2001, p. 37.

''LoJack & Entercom Broadcasting Team Up to Increase Security for Boston Radio Station Vehicles,'' *Financial Times,* January 3, 2002.

''LoJack Stolen Vehicle Tracking System at Milestone with TV 'Batmobile' the One Millionth Installation,'' *Insurance Advocate,* August 28, 1999, p. 24.

McEwen, Charles, ''Driving Smart,'' *New York Times,* November 6, 1994, Sec. 11, p. 1.

''Motorola Reaches LoJack Record,'' *Illinois Daily Herald,* January 2001.

Pham, Alex, ''LoJack Corp. Car-Theft Fighter Locks in Success,'' *Boston Globe,* May 20, 1997, p. C27.

Schultz, Leslie M., ''To Catch a Thief,'' *Inc.,* February 1984, p. 27.

Smith, Hilary, ''LoJack System Aims to Keep Car Thieves in Check,'' *RCR Wireless News,* November 13, 2000, p. 2.

Swanson, John, *LoJack Corp.: A Study for the Financial Community,* Dedham, Mass.: Lojack, pp. 3–5, 10–16.

White, John R., ''LoJack: That's a Technological Version of Kojak,'' *Boston Globe,* December 23, 1984, p. A57.

—Gloria A. Lemieux

# Magellan Aerospace Corporation

3160 Derry Road East
Mississauga, Ontario L4T 1A9
Canada
Telephone: (905) 677-1889
Fax: (905) 677-5658
Web site: http://www.magellanaerospace.com

*Public Company*
*Incorporated:* 1995
*Employees:* 3,260
*Sales:* C$625.39 million ($432.64 million)(2000)
*Stock Exchanges:* Toronto
*Ticker Symbol:* MAL
*NAIC:* 336411 Aircraft Manufacturing; 336412 Aircraft Engine and Engine Parts Manufacturing; 336413 Other Aircraft Parts and Auxiliary Equipment Manufacturing; 336414 Guided Missile and Space Vehicle Manufacturing; 336415 Guided Missile and Space Vehicle Propulsion Unit and Propulsion Unit Parts Manufacturing; 541710 Research and Development in the Physical, Engineering, and Life Sciences

Magellan Aerospace Corporation is Canada's largest dedicated manufacturer of aerospace components. The firm acquired a number of historically significant aerospace firms in the 1980s and 1990s, such as Aeronca, Inc. and Bristol Aerospace.

## *Origins*

The origins of Magellan Aerospace Corporation, known as Fleet Aerospace Corporation before 1996, can be traced back to the beginnings of several well-known aviation firms. Fleet Industries, an aircraft manufacturer formed in 1930, would give the holding company its name. Bristol Aerospace Limited was formed the same year in Winnipeg as MacDonald Brothers Aircraft Company. Bristol produced light bombers and attack aircraft for the Royal Air Force during World War II. It would be acquired by Magellan Aerospace in 1997. Aeronca, Inc., a famous maker of light planes in the 1930s and 1940s, was founded in 1928 and acquired by Magellan in 1986. Ellanef Manufacturing Corp., not acquired until 1999, was founded in 1945. Orenda Aerospace, established in 1946, was also acquired in the 1990s.

By the 1980s, Fleet was supplying a number of major North American aerospace programs, including Boeing airliners, de Havilland commuter planes, and Grumman, Sikorsky, and Lockheed aircraft. It also supplied components for the Challenger business jet produced by Canadair.

Canadair, a state-owned company based in Quebec, was put up for sale after a Conservative administration came to power in 1984. Fleet investigated the possibility of acquiring it with a group of other investors. Canadair boasted a large technical talent base. Its products included Challenger business jets, fire-fighting water-bomber aircraft, battlefield surveillance systems, and components for a variety of civil and military aircraft. It would have made an attractive and complementary acquisition, but the deal was not completed.

## *Growth by Acquisition in the Mid-1980s*

Fleet soon did acquire another famous aerospace manufacturer. The company reached an agreement to acquire control of Charlotte-based Aeronca Inc. in June 1986. Fleet's bid was worth $18.6 million. When it initiated bidding, Fleet challenged an Ohio state law that prevented suitors from acquiring more than 20 percent of a company's shares without the approval of shareholders.

Aeronca had pioneered the light plane business in the United States but had specialized in advanced aero structures since the 1950s. The buy doubled Fleet's size and boosted its U.S. defense business. Sales of the combined company were about C$120 million ($87 million). By the 1980s, Aeronca had added subsidiaries producing boats and computer software; both would be axed after the Fleet acquisition.

Another merger followed in the last half of 1988. Fleet acquired Langley Corporation, a San Diego-based aerospace manufacturer with 125 employees. After the merger, Langley Corp. was renamed Fleet Aerospace Inc.; it continued to trade on the NASDAQ exchange while its corporate parent Fleet Aerospace Corporation remained listed in Toronto.

Fleet Aerospace Corp. (FAC) also owned Engineered Magnetics Inc., whose products were used in military aircraft, mis-

## Company Perspectives:

*Magellan is a consolidator in the aerospace industry. Original Equipment Manufacturers (OEMs) are asking for integrated, high value-added suppliers capable of sharing risk and delivering value. Magellan is positioned to leverage its critical mass and core competencies to provide that value, delivering integrated design, development, and project management in Aeroengines, Aerostructures, Rockets and Space, and Specialty Products. Magellan's dedication to establishing enduring customer relationships has earned it a global reputation for integrity and stability. Professional and experienced, Magellan conducts business openly and honestly at every level of the organization. Magellan's commitment to meeting deadlines and schedules, to working to budgets and agreements, and to taking a partnership approach with its customers is its operating mandate and culture. Quality and value are the fundamentals of the aerospace industry. Magellan recognizes this and has the processes, experiences and expertise in place to lead the market in delivering value. The drive to deliver value is fundamental to its engineering, development, and production processes, and exemplifies Magellan's commitment to the highest quality product at the lowest cost.*

sile systems, and satellites. A unit of FAC's Aeronca Electronics unit, the Brooks Automation Division, was acquired by its managers in April 1989. Brooks Automation produced wafer-handling equipment for the semiconductor industry.

FAC faced a series of major difficulties in the last half of the 1980s. In early 1986, the U.S. Department of Defense began investigating allegations by a former Fleet employee that the company had sold defective components to U.S. military contractors. The company's top officers would later be sanctioned for violating securities laws and misleading investors during 1987.

### *Scaling Back in the Early 1990s*

By October 1989, the parent company was trying to sell its 88 percent holding in Fleet Aerospace Inc., which was losing money thanks to a series of unprofitable long term contracts. Long-term debt more than doubled to nearly $18 million as FAC itself posted a $5.4 million loss for 1989, prompting it to put other subsidiaries on the block. FAC recorded a $2.3 million gain on its sale of an 83 percent shareholding in Fathom Oceanology Ltd. in 1989. Its Saskatchewan-based SED Systems Inc. unit attracted several potential owners in early 1990.

FAC sold Engineered Magnetics to a group led by Los Angeles investors in August 1990 for an undisclosed price. The sell-offs extended to a division of Aeronca Inc., and Fleet considered putting Aeronca Inc. up for sale before it found financing for it. Fleet Aerospace Corp. announced a C$32 million loss for the fiscal year ending September 30, 1990 on sales of C$134 million. In early 1991, Fleet announced the sale of its Langley Division business, apart from real property, for about $4 million to a group of investors based in Pennsylvania.

FAC's poor financial performance during this time prompted an attempt led by a former vice-president to oust the firm's top management. Ultimately, the company's efforts in scaling back operations reduced losses for fiscal 1991 to $2.7 million on sales of $119.7 million. In spite of a downturn in its business with de Havilland, these losses were largely due to the cost of downsizing. George Dragone, FAC's president since 1983, along with another director, resigned in early 1991 as the Ontario Securities Commission investigated charges they misled stockholders and broke stock exchange rules in 1987. The two were fined for the incident and barred from trading for a year.

By 1992, FAC's losses had narrowed slightly but the company was seeking a partner to help it face vigorous foreign price competition. In spite of cutbacks, foreign competitors were still reportedly able to undercut fleet by as much as 30 percent. At the time, FAC employed 340 workers, 80 percent of them at Aeronca Inc. in Middletown, Ohio, which was then specializing in high temperature engine compartments. FAC's Fleet Industries unit, based in Fort Erie, did 40 percent of its business with de Havilland. Losses for fiscal 1993 were C$7.3 million on revenues of C$99.5 million.

### *Mid-1990s Restructuring*

FAC underwent a capital restructuring in the mid-1990s. In the first phase, completed in January 1995, Fleet eliminated $29 million in bank debt. Fleet Aerospace Corporation was renamed Magellan Aerospace Corporation in October 1996. The headquarters was moved from downtown Toronto to the main plant in suburban Mississauga, Ontario.

The man behind the deal making was Murray Edwards, a Calgary financier who was just 35 years old when he took over Fleet in November 1995. An article in *Canadian Business* stated that Edwards and partner Larry Moeller bought out the Canadian Imperial Bank of Commerce and the Ontario government for C$20 million. Institutional investors provided the company C$8.5 million in capital. Edwards, who owned 45 percent of Fleet's outstanding shares, became CEO and chairman. (He had first invested $2,200 in the company in 1987, when he was a practicing lawyer. The subsequent downturn in Fleet shares ultimately spurred him to become more involved with the company.)

Magellan—still called Fleet—had added three other subsidiaries, at a combined cost of C$27 million: Mississauga, Ontario-based Orenda Aerospace Corporation; A-R Technologies, based in Richmond, British Columbia; and Middleton Aerospace of Massachusetts.

By 1997, employment at Magellan's Fleet Industries unit had swelled to 480. A C$3 million federal technology investment helped the unit land a contract to produce MD-95 wing components for South Korea's Hyundai Space and Aircraft Co. Another C$18 million in government aid allowed Magellan's Orenda Aerospace division to build a C$32 million piston engine plant at a retired military base in Nova Scotia.

### *More Acquisitions in the Late 1990s*

The recapitalized company was again on the make in 1997. In July, Magellan bought Bristol Aerospace Ltd., a Canadian unit of Rolls-Royce PLC, for C$62.5 million. Bristol, a 70-year-

**Key Dates:**

**1930:** Aircraft manufacturer Fleet Industries is founded.
**1986:** Fleet Aerospace acquires Aeronca, Inc.
**1996:** Fleet is renamed Magellan Aerospace after restructuring.
**1997:** Magellan embraces the role of industry consolidator.
**2000:** Magellan ventures into space, biofuels, and tank parts.

old aviation pioneer, had jet, rocket, and missile engine repair and overhaul facilities. Bristol stood to benefit from a parts and labor shortage at Boeing, many of whose suppliers had not recovered fully from the previous recession. The unit won a C$99 million contact from Boeing Canada Technologies to supply composite panels for the Boeing 737. Magellan posted a profit of C$15.5 million for 1997.

Magellan acquired another aerospace parts manufacturer, Chicopee Manufacturing Ltd., in May 1998. Based in Kitchener, Ontario, the company had annual revenues of about $45 million. The string of acquisitions had turned Magellan into Canada's largest dedicated producer of aerospace parts. Ellanef Manufacturing Corp., a New York state specialty manufacturing firm with revenues of $88 million a year, was acquired in May 1999.

In 1999, Magellan's units won new contracts to supply engine exhaust nozzles and plugs (Aeronca) for a new extended range version of the Airbus A340; engine turbine shafts for Allied Signal Aerospace (Middleton Aerospace); turbine frames for GE Aircraft Engines (Bristol); and fuselage components for the Cormorant Helicopter (Fleet Industries).

In the last half of the 1990s, Magellan subsidiary Orenda Aerospace was developing a turbine engine to operate on biofuels. Bio-fuels, made from agricultural or forestry waste, were difficult to burn in traditional jet or combustion engines. The new technology suggested potential remedies to both energy and waste problems.

## *New Horizons Beyond 2000*

In early 2000, Bristol Aerospace won a $13 million government contract to build SCISAT-1, Canada's first science satellite since 1971. Bristol had produced many payloads for rocket and space shuttle missions and was developing a role in the commercial space business.

Aeronca's exhaust system contract for the Airbus A340 led the unit to expand its Ohio plant and increase its workforce of 220 by 30 percent. Aeronca was also supplying the new A318 small jetliner program. Ellanef won contracts to supply Northrop Grumman Corp.'s F/A-18 programs in October 2000.

Another small airliner program, Boeing's B717-200, gave Magellan one of its largest contracts ever. The $400 million deal, announced in February 2001, had Fleet Industries and Bristol Aerospace producing wing flaps and other components for the B717, formerly known as the MD-95. This added to another $600 million worth of contracts Magellan already had to supply other Boeing programs through 2006. Bristol won a C$4.6 million order to supply engine collector housings for the U.S. Army's M1 Abrams tank in October 2001.

## *Principal Subsidiaries*

Aeronca, Inc. (U.S.); Ambel Precision Manufacturing Corporation (U.S.); Bristol Aerospace Limited; Chicopee Manufacturing Limited; Ellanef Manufacturing Corporation (U.S.); Fleet Industries Ltd.; Langley Aerospace; Magellan Aerospace USA, Inc.; Middleton Aerospace Corporation; Orenda Aerospace Corporation; Orenda Recip Inc.

## *Principal Competitors*

Bombardier Inc.; Lockheed Martin Corporation; Raytheon Company; TRW Inc.

## *Further Reading*

''Aerospace Manufacturing Jobs Head to Nova Scotia,'' *Plant,* May 26, 1997, p. 1.
''Attempt to Oust 4 Fleet Directors Ruled Out of Order on Technicality,'' *Toronto Star,* March 15, 1991, p. B8.
Chamberlain, Art, ''Fleet Seeking Partner with Money, Opportunities,'' *Toronto Star,* March 18, 1994, p. B2.
Daw, James, ''Ex-Officers of Fleet Face Ban on Trading,'' *Toronto Star,* May 14, 1992, p. D3.
DeMont, Philip, ''Asset Sales, Cost Cuts Will Help Fleet Outlook, Shareholders Promised,'' *Toronto Star,* March 15, 1990, p. C4.
Edelson, Abbe, ''Magellan Sews Up the Market for Engine Exhaust Nozzles and Plugs,'' *Silicon Valley North,* March 1999, p. 5.
Halloran, Richard, ''U.S. Inquiry on Canadian Supplier,'' *New York Times,* March 6, 1986, p. D4.
Love, Myron, ''Bristol Cashes In on Boeing-Magellan Deal,'' *Canadian Machinery & Metalworking,* January/February 2001, p. 9.
Lowman, Ron, ''Fleet Aero and Group May Buy Canadair,'' *Toronto Star,* October 24, 1985, p. E3.
Magellan Aerospace Corporation, ''The Power of Integration,'' Mississauga, Ontario: Magellan Aerospace Corporation, February 11, 2002.
''Magellan Aerospace Execs Face Grumbling Shareholders,'' *Canadian Press,* May 18, 2000.
''Magellan and Bombardier Win Major Deals,'' *Plant,* November 10, 1997, p. 1.
''Magellan Lands Contracts for $42.8 Million,'' *Plant,* October 9, 2000, p. 2.
''Magellan Signs $400 Million Parts Deal,'' *Plant,* February 12, 2001, p. 2.
''Orenda Takes Flight with Energy Savings,'' *Plant,* October 23, 2000, p. 25.
Pletsch, Adam, ''Orenda Takes Flight in Nova Scotia: Manufacturer Builds New Aero-Engine Plant on Retired Military Base,'' *Plant,* October 5, 1998, pp. 1, 2.
Talbot, Chris, ''Bio-Fuel Power System Turns Agricultural Waste into Electricity,'' *Silicon Valley North,* November 1999, p. 28.
Verburg, Peter, ''A Midas Touch,'' *Canadian Business,* July 1998, p. 101.
Wichmann, Lisa, ''SME Tours Aerospace Plant,'' *Plant,* April 24, 2000, p. 5.

—Frederick C. Ingram

# Maus Frères SA

**6 rue Cornavin**
**Case postale 1880**
**CH-1211 Genève 1**
**Switzerland**
**Telephone: +41 022/908.66.00**
**Fax : +41 022/732.91.05**
**Web site: http://www.maus.ch**

*Private Company*
*Incorporated:* 1901
*Employees:* Not Available.
*Sales:* CHF 5.2 billion ($3.31 billion)(1999 est.)
*NAIC:* 452110 Department Stores

Maus Frères SA is one of Switzerland's largest retail groups. The privately owned Geneva-based holding company guides an empire of department stores, sporting goods stores, hypermarkets, furniture stores, and other stores in Switzerland, many of which are grouped under flagship subsidiary Manor AG, the country's leading department store chain. Owned by the founding Maus and Nordmann families, the company's operations include Manor; the Jumbo Do-It Deco chain of 34 hardware stores; the nine-store Athleticum sporting goods store—leader in that category in Switzerland; the Swiss franchise for French-based Fly furniture and furnishings stores; a chain of restaurants under Manora name, attached to Manor stores but independently run; and six large-scale shopping centers, ''Les Centres Magiques.'' In 2001, Maus Frères placed its Jumbo hypermarket chain into a 60–40 joint-venture with France's Carrefour SA, called Distribis. Plans call for the Jumbo stores to adopt the Carrefour name and for the chain to be run by Carrefour. After shutting down nearly all of its international operation, which at one time included PA Bergner, at the beginning of the 1990s, Maus Frères has begun a new, albeit cautious foreign expansion. The company controls 90 percent of Devanlay SA, which holds worldwide licensing and manufacturing rights to the LaCoste brand and is also the major shareholder in Parashop SA, a leading chain of para-pharmacy (selling beauty products and personal care items but not pharmaceuticals) stores in France and the United Kingdom. Maus Frères is led by Philippe Nordmann, chairman of the board, and Jean-Bernard Rondeau, managing director. The company's sales in 1999 reached CHF 5.2 billion.

### *Pioneer Retailer at the Turn of the 20th Century*

Maus Frères was established at the end of the 19th century by two brothers, Ernest and Henri Maus. The Maus brothers' initially went into business as wholesalers selling linens, hosiery, and other textiles to small shops in their area and elsewhere in Switzerland. The Maus's became friendly with one of their clients, Leon Nordmann, who owned a small store called Au Petit Benefice—French for ''low profits'' to emphasize the store's bargain-priced goods.

Nordmann had become interested in a new retail model, the department store, which had been gaining in popularity elsewhere in Europe at the end of the 19th century. Despite the small size of his shop in Willisau, Nordmann had already introduced the concept of various departments for goods there. The Maus brothers, who had incorporated their business as Maus Frères in Geneva in 1901, and Nordmann decided to go into business together and open up a true department store in Lucerne. That store opened in 1902, using the name Leon Nordmann.

The new store represented a revolution in a number of ways. Unlike stores throughout much of Europe at the time, the new Nordmann store gave free entry to customers—other stores obliged customers to make purchases in order to enter the store. The Nordmann store also placed price tags on all of its goods, eliminating the practice of haggling that had made it possible for prices to change from customer to customer.

The Lucerne store's success convinced Nordmann to convert his Willisau store to the new format and signage. The Maus brothers decided to take the concept on the road and began approaching some of their other clients with the idea of opening department stores in other Swiss cities as well. Maus Frères soon presided over an empire of department stores under a variety of store names, such as Au Louvre, Nouvelles Galeries Martin, Keller-Ullmann, Innovazione, Galeries du Jura, and especially the flagship stores Magazine zur Rheinbrucke in Basel and La Placette in Lausanne and Geneva.

The Maus and Nordmann families' ties tightened when Robert Nordmann, Leon's son, married Ernest Maus's daughter

## Company Perspectives:

Values. *Since the Group's first store opened in 1902, the company's management has been handed down through four generations. Today, the Group continues to be managed by the descendants of the two founding families and has succeeded in expanding while remaining true to its culture. Over the years MANOR stores have been established all over Switzerland, selling goods under the Group's diversified brand names. Maus Brothers has become the leading privately-owned distribution group in Switzerland and in its activities beyond the country's borders it remains true to its vocation as a store manager.* Satisfying customer needs. *The customer is always right and is at the heart of the Group's concern.* Recognizing that people come first. *Such as all those who, over the years, have made the Group what it is today and who will continue making it tomorrow.* Encouraging entrepreneurship. *The key to success is embodied in individual enthusiasm and the desire for undertaking. Encouraging initiatives and entrusting responsibility into the hands of those who are capable of assuming it is part and parcel of this.* Maintaining the "family spirit." *Inspiration borne from this very special motivating and reassuring ingredient is indeed a precious bonus.* Diversifying while upholding our tradition of innovation, customer service and quality. *The Group is made up of successful and dynamic companies, each with its own identity, who work hand in hand together.* Providing ourselves with the means prerequisite to being the best. *The Group's member companies all aim at being leaders in their respective branches and optimization of acquired skills continues unceasingly. Through being able to count on a well-trained team, adequate management tools and the necessary infrastructure the Group is ready to take on this challenge.*

Simone. The younger Nordmann joined with André Maus, son of Henri, to take over leadership of the Maus Frères company. The new generation continued to build on their predecessors' success, establishing the Maus Frères retail empire as the preeminent retail company in Switzerland. In 1965, Maus Frères decided to unite all of its department stores under a single banner, creating a new subsidiary, Manor—a contraction of the Maus and Nordmann names.

Manor was not the only focus for Maus Frères' retail interests. In 1974, the company, facing pressure from a rising new breed of retailers—the so-called hypermarkets, which combined traditional grocery stores with department store-type product ranges, while touting discounted prices, moved into the hypermarket sector itself, opening the first Jumbo hypermarket in Dietlikon, near Zurich. Maus Frères quickly extended the Jumbo concept into another fast-growing retail sector, the do-it-yourself channel, launching a new store format of Jumbo "brico-bati-centres," later renamed Jumbo Do-it Deco.

At the same time, Maus Frères had taken a leaf from a growing trend in the United States, that of the construction of large-scale, covered shopping malls. Maus Frères inaugurated its first shopping center in 1974, in Sierre. The company later went on to open five more shopping centers, grouping them under the name "Les Centers Magiques."

During the 1980s, Maus Frères continued to expand. At the beginning of the decade, the company launched a new chain of restaurants, Manora. Attached to the Manor department stores, the company's restaurants were nonetheless operated independently and featured different operating hours. In 1985, Maus Frères introduced another retail concept, a chain of music stores called City Disc.

Apart from building its retail empire in Switzerland, Maus Frères had been expanding its holdings elsewhere in the world. For many years, the group held a majority shareholding position in famed Parisian department store group Au Printemps.

Another of Maus Frères' major international holdings was that of the Bergner department store group in the United States, acquired by the Maus and Nordmann families in 1938. Bergner had been founded in Peoria, Illinois, in 1889 by Peter Bergner. Under Maus Frères, Bergner's began to expand, acquiring Charles V. Weise Company, also of Illinois, in 1954 to create a nine-store chain focused on smaller midwestern markets. Led by Alan Anderson since the beginning of the 1960s, Bergner's continued to grow throughout the region, and, after acquiring the eight-store Myers Brothers chain based in southern Illinois, changed its name to PA Bergner & Co in 1979. In the mid-1980s, Bergner acquired the Boston Store chain from Federated Department Stores, Inc.

Then, in 1989, Anderson attempted to leap into the big time by acquiring Chicago-based Carson Pirie Scott for $453 million. Maus Frères now itself the owner of one of the United States' largest regional department store groups with 69 stores producing more than $1 billion in sales. Unfortunately for Maus Frères, in Anderson's eagerness, the Carson Pirie Scott acquisition was made without the necessary due diligence—and the financial weakness of Carson Pirie Scott went overlooked. Maus Frères soon discovered that the Carson Pirie Scott acquisition had also saddled the company with nearly $800 million in debt.

By 1991, Bergner was sinking fast—Maus Frères attempted to keep Bergner afloat by pumping more than $150 million into its failing U.S. subsidiary. In mid-1991, however, Maus Frères turned off the tap, and Bergner was forced to file for bankruptcy. In 1993, in a settlement agreement, Bergner was sold off to an investment group for $300 million, and its name changed to Carson Pirie Scott before later becoming part of the Saks retail group.

The Bergner fiasco hurt Maus Frères in more ways than one. In order to pay for its problems at Bergner, Maus Frères was forced to sell off its holding in Au Printemps. Initially the group had hoped to find a buyer for just half of its stake, which amounted to more than 42 percent of Au Printemps' shares and more than 56 percent of the company's voting rights. When François Pinault approached Maus Frères with an offer to purchase all of its stake in Au Printemps, the Geneva retail group was unable to refuse. Pinault quickly parried Printemps into one of France's—and the world's—leading retail empires, Pinault Printemps Redoute.

### *Refocused for the New Century*

Somewhat chastened by the Bergner debacle, Maus Frères switched its focus wholly to its domestic operations in the early 1990s. The company reorganized its operations, setting up

## Key Dates:

**1901:** Maus Frères is established as a wholesale textiles and linen business in Geneva by Ernest and Henri Maus.
**1902:** The Maus's join with Leon Nordmann to found a department store in Lucerne.
**1938:** Maus Frères acquires the Bergner department store group in the United States.
**1965:** Various department stores operated by Maus Frères united under the Manor group.
**1974:** Maus Frères launches Jumbo hypermarket chain and opens first of company operated shopping centers.
**1985:** Maus Frères launches City Disc music store concept.
**1991:** Bergner files for bankruptcy; Maus Frères sells its holding in 1993.
**1994:** Maus Frères launches new retail store formats Jeans & Co and ElectroPlus; all German-speaking department stores take on the Manor name.
**1995:** Maus Frères launches Athleticum Sportsmarket retail sporting goods format and acquires a controlling stake in France's Parashop SA.
**2001:** The company sells ElectroPlus and City Disc; the first Jumbo store is rebranded as Carrefour.

Maus Frères as a holding company and decentralizing management decisions to a newly restructured Manor Department Store Group. At this point, all of the company's stores in German-speaking Switzerland were renamed as Manor department stores. The remaining stores that had not yet taken the Manor name in the French- and Italian-speaking regions were rebranded as Manor stores in 2000.

Toward the mid-1990s, Maus Frères turned its attention toward testing new retail concepts for the Swiss market. In 1994, the company opened two new retail chains, the clothing store Jeans & Co. and the home electronics and computer specialist ElectroPlus. Then, in 1995, the company launched a sporting goods store format, Athleticum Sportsmarket.

While Jeans & Co and ElectroPlus met with limited success—the company sold both chains in 2000 and 2001, along with City Disc—Athleticum proved a stronger contender. Starting with three stores—in Suhr, Bussigny, and Heimberg—in 1995, Athleticum added a new store in 1996, two more stores in 1997, and a new store each year through the beginning of the new century, making it the leading sporting goods store in Switzerland.

Despite its retreat from international retailing, Maus Frères had not abandoned foreign expansion entirely. In 1995, the company bought a majority stake in a young French company, Parashop. Founded in 1993, in order to take advantage of French laws liberalizing the sale of certain items (excluding medications) hitherto exclusively controlled by the country's network of pharmacies, Parashop had opened three stores by 1995 when it began looking for investors to help it grow into a nationally operating chain. With Maus Frères' deep pockets—and its founders at the helm—Parashop stepped up the pace of its store openings, and by 2002 had opened more than 40 stores not only in France but in the United Kingdom as well.

In 1998, Maus Frères gained a new international holding when it acquired a 90 percent share of France's Devanlay SA. That company had long been the manufacturing force behind the world famous LaCoste brand name. As part of the Maus Frères holding, Devanlay began a transition from being a clothing manufacturing company to guiding development of the LaCoste brand name. Maus Frères partner in the Devanlay acquisition was La Chemise Lacoste, the company that controlled the brand name; in 2000, Devanlay, which by then had acquired 35 percent of La Chemise Lacoste, was granted a worldwide license for the LaCoste brand.

By the beginning of the new decade, Maus Frères' Jumbo chain had succeeded in gaining the number two position in the country's hypermarket sector. Yet it faced increasing pressure—particularly on its margins—from competing retail groups, Migros and Coop, the leaders in the country's supermarket sector. Maus Frères began looking for a partner to help its Jumbo operations build new momentum, and in 2000 the company announced that it had to agreed to form a new joint venture with French retailing powerhouse Carrefour. Called Distribis and held at 60 percent by Maus Frères and at 40 percent by Carrefour, the joint venture took over control of the Jumbo hypermarkets and placed management of their operations under Carrefour. The companies also planned to convert all of the Jumbo stores to the Carrefour signage, a process begun in 2001.

As it celebrated its 100th anniversary, Maus Frères had grown into one of Switzerland's retailing powerhouses with diversified operations covering many of the major market sectors in Switzerland. The company's core holding remained the Manor department store group, which had grown into a string of 75 stores and more than 320,000 square meters of selling space, with sales of nearly CHF 3 billion representing nearly half of all of Switzerland's department store market. Yet Maus Frères remained decidedly a family affair, with the latest generation represented by Phillippe Nordmann as chairman of the board.

### *Principal Subsidiaries*

Manor AG; Athleticum Sportmarket; Devanlay SA; Parashop SA.

### *Principal Competitors*

Migros-Genossenschafts-Bund; Coop Schweiz Genossenschaftsverband; Metro Holding AG.

### *Further Reading*

"Carrefour Enters Switzerland," *Progressive Grocer*, December 2000, p. 16.

"Carrefour s'installe en Suisse en s'associant à Maus Frères," *La Tribune*, October 5, 2000.

"Jelmoli Buys Seven Electrical Shops from Maus Frères," *Reuters*, March 18, 2001.

Weisman, Katherine, "Swiss Retailer Maus to Buy Devanlay," *Daily News Record*, April 16, 1993, p. 10.

—M.L. Cohen

# McCarthy Building Companies, Inc.

**1341 North Rock Hill Road**
**St. Louis, Missouri 63124-1498**
**U.S.A.**
**Telephone: (314) 968-3037**
**Fax: (314) 968-4502**
**Web site: http://www.mccarthy.com**

*Private Company*
*Incorporated:* 1907 as the McCarthy Lumber and Construction Company
*Employees:* 2,000
*Sales:* $1.6 billion (2001 est.)
*NAIC:* 233320 Commercial and Institutional Building Construction; 233310 Manufacturing and Industrial Building Construction

McCarthy Building Companies, Inc. is one of the largest construction firms in the United States. The company operates out of seven full service offices that include its home base of St. Louis, Missouri and others in Phoenix, Dallas, Las Vegas, San Francisco, Sacramento, and Newport Beach, California. McCarthy handles a wide range of building projects, with specializations in hospital, parking structure, bridge, educational, biotech, and high-tech industrial construction. Majority ownership of the firm was transferred to its employees in 1991, with former CEO and chairman Michael McCarthy, a descendent of the company's founder, retaining an interest of more than 40 percent. That interest was sold in 2002, making McCarthy one of the oldest employee-owned companies in the country.

### *19th Century Origins*

McCarthy traces its roots to the year 1864, when Irish immigrant Timothy McCarthy founded a lumber company in Ann Arbor, Michigan. The small concern built farmhouses and barns around the Ann Arbor area for the next four decades, later also building some public and commercial structures. During this time McCarthy trained his sons John W. and Timothy, Jr., as carpenters, while their brother Charles became a skilled bricklayer.

In 1905 John W. McCarthy decided to move to Farmington, Missouri, to be near a woman he loved. Intent on carrying on the family line of business, he convinced his brothers to move down and join him. The siblings incorporated the transplanted company in 1907 under the name McCarthy Lumber and Construction Company, with John W. McCarthy named to the post of president. Following the incorporation, the firm began to branch out into a wider range of construction, including commercial projects and post offices.

Business grew beyond the Farmington area over the next decade, and in 1917 the company moved to the larger city of St. Louis, where it was renamed McCarthy Brothers Construction Co. The firm was now well established in its new home state, having been chosen to build the Missouri Building at the San Francisco World's fair in 1916, with the construction crew traveling there by train. Many other projects were built in St. Louis and throughout Missouri during the 1920s and 1930s, including the court house in Farmington, completed in 1926. In 1934 the growing company moved its operations to a larger headquarters in St. Louis. A major contract of the decade was the post office and courthouse built in far-off Anchorage, Alaska, one of many federally-generated projects that helped the company weather the Great Depression.

The years of World War II saw McCarthy's government work continue with construction of Army and Navy lock and canal projects in the Panama Canal Zone, as well as an air base at Coco Solo. Following the war the company continued to grow, taking on more out-of-state work in the 1950s. A major project of this decade was the Army Corps of Engineers' Publications Center in St. Louis. In 1952 McCarthy also bought the Rock Hill Quarries Company, which provided a lucrative sideline for the firm.

An unusual project in 1961 brought McCarthy notice as a builder that could handle difficult projects and come up with creative solutions to the challenges they presented. The Priory Chapel, in St. Louis, featured two levels of interlocking curved concrete half-ovals, arrayed like petals of a flower, a difficult design which the company successfully executed. Other important jobs of the 1960s included the Queeny Tower and Barnes Hospital.

### Company Perspectives:

*Truth. Integrity. Passion. Sure, they're old-fashioned words and old-fashioned concepts, but they are ones that our clients appreciate the most. McCarthy is a customer-focused, national, entrepreneurial and diversified business with broad regional construction capabilities. Using the latest information and management technology, we provide total project services from initial concepts through planning, financing, design, procurement, construction, maintenance, operation and ownership. But what sets us truly apart is that once we are selected, we make a binding commitment that runs far deeper than contractual obligations. It's a human commitment that goes above and beyond ordinary expectations. Tools, training and opportunity for growth. An environment that encourages innovation. Challenging career opportunities. Exceptional financial rewards. Sense of family. A zealous commitment to safety.*

## *New Projects in the 1970s–80s*

During this period the company was taking on considerably more work in the healthcare area, as well as beginning to design and build parking structures starting in 1969. In 1972 McCarthy formed a subsidiary called McBro to perform healthcare construction management. The firm was a pioneer in the development of the new concept of construction management, a team-based approach in which the builder served as an advocate for the owner when working with the architects and consultants, acting to ensure that a project was built to strict standards. The 1970s saw the firm become the national leader in healthcare and parking structure construction, with a separate parking structure design/build group formed to facilitate work in the latter category. McCarthy's Rock Hill Quarries business was successfully converted into a landfill operation during the decade as well.

After more than a century in operation, McCarthy remained in the hands of its founding family. Melvin McCarthy had served as president during many of the postwar years, with a number of other family members including Merryl McCarthy, Timothy R. McCarthy, John E. McCarthy, and Francis F. McCarthy having also taken roles at the firm during the period. When Melvin died in 1976, his son Michael M. McCarthy took over as president.

As work around the country became more a part of McCarthy's business, setting up offices in other cities became a necessity. The first of these was opened in Phoenix, Arizona, in 1979, and more followed in other major cities including Washington, D.C., Boston, Tampa, Houston, Seattle, San Francisco, Dallas, Houston, Las Vegas, and Kansas City. In the 1980s the company began to take on new areas of work, beginning with bridge and civil construction jobs, and then, starting in 1985, high-tech and industrial projects. A milestone was achieved in 1986 when McCarthy did a billion dollars worth of business for the fist time. The firm was now operating with its first non-McCarthy family president, Roger H. Burnet, who took over the job from Michael M. McCarthy in 1984, though the latter remained CEO and board chairman.

## *1990s: Employee Ownership*

The company's stock, which had been held by the McCarthy family since its founding, was opened to the firm's employees in 1996. Michael McCarthy, who was the only family member to retain a stake in the firm, held on to about 45 percent of the company. Commenting on his motivation for the move, McCarthy later told the *St. Louis Dispatch,* "When employees have a significant amount of stock, the business becomes much more fun for them and they get a much more visceral feeling about their participation and the possibility of their being able to make a real contribution . . . we set a goal to be the best builder in America, which is a very serious goal for us. If we have any chance (to accomplish that goal), we have to have all of our people staying with us and be well trained and all focused on the same goals. Ownership is a part of that."

By this time the company's out-of-state offices included several full-service divisions which themselves were growing into leading building companies in their states. These included McCarthy's Phoenix, Seattle, Dallas, and Irvine, California, locations. In 1991 the company bought SDL, a Bellevue, Washington, contracting firm which was later named SDL McCarthy. The late 1980s and early 1990s also saw McCarthy's areas of expertise growing again to include semiconductor, bio-pharmaceutical, educational, research and development, and general manufacturing construction projects. During this period the company merged its healthcare, parking, and bridge divisions with the full-service regional offices. Noteworthy projects of the era included the $24 million Salk Institute for Biological Studies in La Jolla, California, and the David Axelrod Laboratory, a $45 million research facility in Albany, New York.

Another change of leadership took place in 1995 when Roger Burnet retired and Michael D. Hurst was named president and chief operating officer. Hurst had worked for McCarthy for 24 years. In the late 1990s the company also began looking at other areas of building to develop specializations in. A study of current trends revealed that the demand for construction of kindergarten through 12th grade schools was almost triple the size of the healthcare market. In 1999 McCarthy executives decided to form a new division, the Educational Services Group, to seek work in this area. Initially accounting for only about 2 percent of McCarthy's revenues, the company projected that K-12 projects could reach one-fifth to one-quarter of its business in less than a decade.

The same year that this division was created Michael McCarthy turned over the CEO duties to Michael D. Bolen, retaining the role of board chairman. Bolen had started as a carpenter at the firm in 1978, later moving up to supervisory positions and then serving as vice-president of operations and president of the firm's Pacific Division. He had a degree in engineering from the U.S. Air Force Academy and a graduate degree in guidance and counseling from the University of Northern Colorado.

In 2000 the firm's Texas division acquired the assets and contracts of the Houston office of Concrete Pavers, Inc. of Evansville, Indiana. The move was expected to give McCarthy the ability to offer lower bids on civil transportation contracts, which had previously required subcontracting of the paving

## Key Dates:

**1864:** Timothy McCarthy founds a lumber business in Ann Arbor, Michigan.
**1905:** Firm moves to Farmington, Missouri.
**1907:** Company is incorporated as McCarthy Lumber and Construction Co.
**1917:** Company moves to St. Louis and name is changed to McCarthy Brothers Construction Co.
**1934:** Company moves to larger site in St. Louis.
**1940s:** McCarthy builds U.S. military facilities in Panama Canal Zone during World War II.
**1952:** Company acquires Rock Hill Quarries Company.
**1969:** Company begins performing parking structure construction jobs nationwide.
**1972:** McBro subsidiary is formed to provide healthcare construction management.
**1979:** The first McCarthy regional office is opened in Phoenix.
**1986:** Company realizes its first billion dollar year.
**1996:** McCarthy creates employee stock-ownership plan, giving employees partial ownership in the company.
**1999:** Education Services Group is formed to specialize in K-12 school construction.
**2002:** Chairman Michael McCarthy sells his remaining stake, making the company 100 percent employee-owned.

work. The shrinking U.S. economy was causing a drop in construction projects, and the company made the decision to close its money-losing Bellevue and Portland offices in late 2001.

McCarthy continued to work on many important projects as it celebrated its fifth year of employee ownership. Completed work included the $615 million Hollywood & Highland entertainment/retail complex in Hollywood, which incorporated a new theater that would house the Academy Awards; a $110 million correctional facility in Bonne Terre, Missouri; a $57 million corporate laboratory and learning center in St. Louis; a $44 million psychology center at the University of Texas; and numerous hospitals, parking structures, and building expansions in California, Arizona, New York, Illinois, and other states. The company also had many projects still on the drawing board including a $100 million office building and a $92 million jail in Phoenix; a $60 million biotechnology studies building at Rensselaer Polytechnic Institute in Troy, New York; an $80 million mixed-use development project in Beaverton, Oregon; a $132 million infectious diseases laboratory for the Centers for Disease Control and Prevention in Atlanta; a $90 million Hornet jet fighter manufacturing plant for the Boeing Company in St. Louis; and many others around the country. McCarthy did not focus solely on large projects; some were budgeted at less than $500,000, including a modernization of a K-12 school in Long Beach, California, expected to cost $350,000, and a $181,000 office tenant improvement in Kirkland, Washington.

With a proud history of more than 138 years behind it, McCarthy continued to grow and add to its legacy. The firm's reputation for quality and its multiple fields of specialization, including the latest high-tech, biotech, and education facilities, were keeping its schedule full with no end in sight. In 2002, the last remaining family interest in McCarthy, held by Chairman Michael McCarthy, was sold back to the company. Press releases proudly noted that ''At the conclusion of this ownership transition, McCarthy will become one of the nation's oldest, 100 percent employee-owned construction firms with majority ownership via an employee stock ownership plan (ESOP).'' Michael McCarthy would step into the role of chairman emeritus, while Mike Bolen, McCarthy's CEO, retained that position and took on the role of chairman of the board as well.

### *Principal Subsidiaries*

McCarthy Holdings, Inc.; McCarthy Building Companies, Inc.; McCarthy Properties, LLC.

### *Principal Operating Units*

Institutional; Commercial; Healthcare Facilities; Industrial/Clean Manufacturing; Heavy/Civil; Parking Structures.

### *Principal Competitors*

Bechtel Group, Inc.; Turner Corporation; Peter Kiewit Sons Inc.; Swinerton Inc.

### *Further Reading*

Curley, John, ''McCarthy Leaders See Future Nailed Down,'' *St. Louis Post-Dispatch,* June 17, 2001, P. E1.
Duryee, Tricia, ''St. Louis-Based Builder to Close Offices in Portland, Ore., Bellevue, Wash.,'' *Seattle Times,* December 1, 2001.
''McCarthy Building Military Project,'' *Northwest Construction,* January 2001, p. 10
''McCarthy Starts 2 Projects,'' *California Construction Link,* December 2000, p. 90.
Napolitano, Paul, ''McCarthy Adds Cedars-Sinai to Impressive Portfolio,'' *California Construction Link,* September 2001, p. 4.
——, ''Mynsberge to Lead McCarthy's Health-Care Division,'' *California Construction Link,* September 2001, p. 7.

—Frank Uhle

The Men's Wearhouse

# The Men's Wearhouse, Inc.

**6094 Stewart Avenue**
**Fremont, California 94538**
**U.S.A.**
**Telephone: (877) 986-9669**
**Toll Free: (800) 776-SUIT (7848); (877) 986-9669**
**Fax: (877) 586-9669**
**Web site: http://www.menswearhouse.com**

*Public Company*
*Incorporated:* 1974
*Employees:* 10,800
*Sales:* $1.27 billion (2001)
*Stock Exchanges:* New York
*Ticker Symbol:* MW
*NAIC:* 448110 Men's Clothing Stores; 448120 Women's Clothing Stores; 315222 Men's and Boys' Cut and Sew Suit, Coat, and Overcoat Manufacturing; 315224 Men's and Boys' Cut and Sew Trouser, Slack, and Jean Manufacturing

The Men's Wearhouse, Inc. is one of the most successful men's specialty store chains in the United States, dominating the men's tailored clothing field. It has accomplished this by offering men a comfortable environment in which to buy high quality suits, dress slacks, sport jackets, and sweaters at 20 to 30 percent below department store prices. To attract men, who notoriously dislike shopping, the stores were located in upscale strip shopping centers nearby customers' homes and workplaces, eliminating the need to hike through large malls. A well-trained, friendly staff provided exceptional customer service, with tailors in every store and free pressing for the life of a garment. The combination of these factors plus aggressive radio and television advertising led to consistently increasing sales and earnings in a highly fragmented industry. With the acquisition of Moores Clothing, Men's Wearhouse became the owner of Canada's second largest manufacturing facility of men's suits and sport coats. In February 2002, the company operated 563 stores in the United States (497 under the Men's Wearhouse brand) and 113 Moores stores in Canada.

### *Early Years*

In 1972, George Zimmer had been out of college for two years and was just back from a year in Hong Kong, where he had set up a factory for his father's raincoat manufacturing business. He became a manufacturer's representative for his father's company, living in Dallas and driving throughout Texas, Louisiana, and Oklahoma to sell boys' raincoats to stores.

When the buyer at Foley's in Houston, his biggest account, complained about racks of unsold raincoats, Zimmer talked his father into taking back $10,000 worth of merchandise. Despite this gesture, Foley's dropped the raincoat line, which angered Zimmer. In a 1993 *Forbes* article, he explained, "As Tom Peters says, you have to be a monomaniac to build a business. The fuel for my monomania came from that situation with Foley's."

Taking $7,000, Zimmer rented a small store in a strip shopping center on the west side of Houston and stocked up with name-brand suits. He opened Men's Wearhouse in August 1973, selling the suits well below the prices charged at Foley's and other department stores. At the opening of the store, Zimmer was joined by his father and Harry Levy, a good friend from college.

It took his father's firm more than six months to find a replacement for him, and from Monday through Thursday Zimmer continued to work as a traveling raincoat salesman. On Friday and Saturday he would be in Houston on the sales floor of Men's Wearhouse. In those days, blue laws kept stores closed on Sundays. Harry Levy, who eventually became senior vice-president of planning, covered the store during the week.

Once he was able to devote his full time to Men's Wearhouse, Zimmer quickly opened two more stores and incorporated the company. He promoted his three stores with small advertisements in the Saturday sports section of local newspapers. In the first year, he had sales of $1 million and lost $20,000. At a friend's suggestion, he switched to TV, filming inexpensive ads and buying unsold commercial space at a discount. Executive vice-president Richard Goldman, who joined the company in 1974 after selling Zimmer advertising

## Company Perspectives:

*The mission of Men's Wearhouse is to maximize sales, provide value to our customers and deliver top quality customer service while still having fun and maintaining our values. These values include nurturing creativity, growing together, admitting to mistakes, promoting a happy and healthy lifestyle, enhancing a sense of community and striving toward becoming self-actualized people.*

space, told *MR Magazine,* "*Mary Hartman Mary Hartman* becomes the #1 rated TV show in Houston at 10:30 p.m.; commercials cost $700 each, except for ours, which we bought before the series started at $18.25 per spot." By 1981, there were 12 Men's Wearhouses, and by the end of 1985 the chain had grown to 25.

During those early years, Zimmer, Levy, and Goldman established the conceptual basis of their business, which has not changed. Goldman explained to *MR Magazine,* "Our strategy is to be like the old time men's clothing store around the corner, except that we add price as a key ingredient. We realize that men hate to shop, so we actually try to make it fun!"

The company targeted the moderate-income professional and semi-professional male worker. It kept its stores relatively small, between 4,000 and 4,500 square feet, because, as Zimmer told the *Daily News Record* in 1996, "Men don't really like taking their pants off in places larger than 5,000 square feet." The stores were clustered in mid-sized cities to take advantage of advertising and distribution savings and to make them convenient to get to. This was important because a customer had to go to the store twice (once to buy and get measured and again to pick up and try on the suit after alteration). The company expanded the merchandise mix, adding to its line of suits other tailored clothing—sport coats, dress shirts, and dress slacks—and offering accessories such as ties and belts.

The company emphasized integrity and service. Employees, trained in customer service skills, were also treated as family, with everyone on a first-name basis, and most were hired full time. Zimmer began donating a percentage of pre-tax profits to charities, establishing a reputation for the company as being socially responsible. Vendors were also treated well, and the company never canceled an order. One of Men's Wearhouse's biggest customers told Jeffrey Arlen of *Discount Store News,* "They do what they say they are going to do. They are very focused and honorable."

Some of the company's competitors disagreed. In the mid-1980s, Men's Wearhouse moved into California. Following its successful Texas formula, the company would open a store, advertise heavily with Zimmer doing his own television ads, and then open several more stores in the area. In 1989, Nordstrom Department Store sued Men's Wearhouse for false advertising, disputing the company's claim that Men's Wearhouse suits were identical to those sold by Nordstrom. In 1990, C&R Clothiers also sued, complaining about false claims regarding pricing. Both lawsuits were settled when Men's Wearhouse agreed to stop running the ads.

### *1990–94: Explosive Growth*

The first half of the 1990s saw tremendous growth for the company. It opened 17 new stores in 1990 and 19 the following year. In April 1992, Zimmer took the company public, selling 2.25 million shares at $8.67 per share and raising $12.7 million. That year, new store openings jumped to 31, including the first Men's Wearhouse outlet center, in Houston. At over 7,000 square feet, this was much larger than the regular Men's Wearhouse stores. The outlet had limited services and carried greater quantities of merchandise.

In the fall of 1992, the company introduced Made by America (MBA), a sportswear catalog. The catalog contained only quality, U.S.-made sportswear. In keeping with its ecologically and socially responsible culture, the company avoided mass mailings by distributing the catalogs through its retail stores. When that proved unsuccessful, the company mailed catalogs to customers who had previously bought clothing through the mail. Although cleverly written (and with a percentage of sales going to reduce the national deficit), the catalog did not generate sufficient sales and was discontinued in 1993.

In 1993, most discount stores suffered a decline in business, with the Discount Stores News Stock Index of 86 stocks falling 5.9 percent. Except for its MBA catalog, however, Men's Wearhouse had a great year. The company's second public offering raised $10.4 million, with 1.3 million shares selling at $12 per share. This allowed Zimmer to pay off debts while opening 40 stores during the year, including two more outlet stores. The company ended the year with net sales of $240.4 million and earnings of $8.7 million. Between 1991 and 1993, Men's Wearhouse doubled its net earnings on a net sales increase of 80 percent.

In May 1994, the company completed its third public offering of one million shares at $29 per share, which generated net proceeds of $14.5 million. This provided the financing to open more stores and to acquire the licenses for tailored clothing produced for French designer Pierre Balmain and Italian designer Vito Rufolo. The company began manufacturing as well as selling the new lines, using its direct-sourcing capabilities in the United States and overseas. In addition to its private labels, the company offered brand name suits by Pierre Cardin, Geoffrey Beene, Calvin Klein, and Oscar De la Renta.

Men's Wearhouse purchased the Coach House in Pittsburgh, which gave the company a major presence in western Pennsylvania. In June, Men's Wearhouse hired Michael Batlin from Macy's West to expand its shoe business. The company had started selling shoes three years earlier, offering Rockport, Florsheim, and Bostonian; it began offering its own private-label brand in early 1994.

The company also decided to offer Big and Tall sizes. To provide the space for these expansions, it increased the floor space of its new stores an additional 500 square feet to 5,000 square feet. Company growth was aimed at the Southeast, and by the middle of the year there were ten stores in Florida, five in North Carolina, 11 in Georgia, and about a dozen in neighboring states. At the end of 1994, there were 230 stores, more than double the number existing when the company went public in 1992. Net sales for the year increased 32 percent, to $317.1 million.

## Key Dates:

**1973:** The first Men's Wearhouse store opens in Houston.
**1991:** The company goes public.
**1995:** A new office opens in California that also handles distribution and the training of employees.
**1996:** The brands of Kuppenheimer and Joseph & Feiss are acquired.
**1997:** Value Priced Clothing division formed from C&R Clothiers Inc. and NAL chains.
**1998:** The company opens its first store in New York City.
**1999:** Canada's Moores Retail Group and Atlanta's K&G Men's Center are acquired.
**2000:** The first K&G Women's Superstore opens.

### *1995: A Big Year*

The year 1995 saw the opening of a 35,500-square-foot office, training, and redistribution facility in California. Staff training had always been an important part of Men's Wearhouse's strategy, and all employees went through a three-day Suits University program conducted at the company's executive headquarters. Richard Goldman explained the company's thinking in a 1995 interview with *Discount Store News.* ''We want our people to feel they are being treated fairly, and it all starts at Suits U. First of all it's an all-expenses-paid trip to northern California, which can mean a lot to a new employee. Once we get them at Suits U. we don't teach people how to use the cash register; that they can learn in the store. What we do is inculcate them with the corporate culture.'' Sessions included selling techniques, product information, in-store training meetings, and social events. Employees were trained in helping customers select an entire wardrobe, not just a suit or a pair of slacks.

During the year the company executed a revolving loan agreement of $100 million to be used primarily to pay for the company's planned growth and, in July, filed a secondary offering of two million shares. In September, Men's Wearhouse acquired the North American rights for exclusive use of the Botany, Botany 500, and Botany Couture labels. These had been owned by the McGregor division of Samsonite Corporation, which sold the tuxedos, sport coats, and suits through its 500 Fashion Group. Botany 500 became a prominent label in the industry in the 1930's. When Botany went bankrupt in 1972, its labels were bought by Joseph H. Cohen (JHC) of Philadelphia. JHC became a division of Rapid-American, which, after numerous acquisitions and name changes, was the predecessor of Samsonite Corp.

Although the company had planned to expand its Big and Tall inventory into more stores, it found the line selling better than expected in the first 50 stores, which, paradoxically, limited its expansion. ''We weren't able to roll it out to as many stores as we wanted to. We had to go back and fill in at the stores where it was selling well,'' Richard Goldman told *Daily News Record* in a January 1996 interview.

The year 1995 also saw the company move into new markets, including Cincinnati, Milwaukee, and Chicago, which was one of the top five markets for men's tailored clothing. The company's biggest competitor in Chicago, Today's Man, was facing financial difficulties, and within a year had closed all its stores in that market. In the meantime, sales in the new Men's Wearhouse stores were higher than expected.

Industry consolidation and weak sales were taking their toll on department and menswear specialty stores. Traditionally, most suits were sold in department stores or small mom-and-pop operations with one or two stores. In the first half of the 1990s, according to Kernkraut and Abramowitz at Bear Sterns, approximately 4,000, or 23 percent, of the men's clothing boutiques closed, and department stores cut back their men's suit departments. This industry trend was especially pronounced during 1995. Brooks Brothers, a subsidiary of Mark & Spencer, lost $4 million during the first half of the year; the 114-store Britches of Georgetown was put up for sale; Hartmarx sold its Kuppenheimer stores division; and several regional chains declared bankruptcy.

A major factor in the decreasing sales of tailored clothing was the move toward more casual business dress. Men's Wearhouse responded to this trend by slightly increasing its stores' selection of sport coats and slacks, replacing about 60 suits with an equal number of sport coats. At the same time, the company increased the training employees received, stressing all aspects of a customer's business attire needs.

In late 1995, the company produced a video entitled ''How to Dress Casually and Still Mean Business,'' in which a sales associate led the viewer on a guided tour of what is needed for a complete office wardrobe. The video was distributed to each Men's Wearhouse store. While managers could show it in the store (it was only seven minutes long), the company had a larger objective: staging free ''how-to'' fashion shows at local businesses. Managers mailed free copies of the video to human resource directors or other company contacts, with an accompanying letter offering to conduct a live fashion show for male employees, either on-site or at the store.

The company used a similar approach in a 1996 advertisement about business casual wear on Houston Chronicle Interactive, the *Houston Chronicle*'s web site. That piece discussed textures and colors of jackets and sport coats, with tips such as ''the belt should match your shoes,'' and ''business casual socks are printed socks you can wear with a suit.''

George Zimmer received some free advertising on the Web courtesy of Steve Kubby, publisher of Alpine World, an on-line magazine. In a letter to readers, Kubby wrote, ''Several months ago we approached Men's Wearhouse about supporting a tree-free alternative to magazines printed on paper made from trees. . . . I learned that under George's leadership, Men's Wearhouse was actively involved in recycling, in using hemp paper, and in supporting environmental causes. So they agreed to 'advertise' with us—only they didn't want an ad!'' Kubby also wrote that Zimmer actively participated, with money and time, in making the Oakland Zoo ''one that is endorsed by animal rights activists around the world.''

During 1996, the company opened its first store in the Washington, D.C., market, marking its initial entry into the Northeast. It planned to open several more in the Washington-Baltimore area and to enter the Boston-Providence market before the end of the year. First quarter net earnings were 53 percent higher than in 1995, and comparable store sales rose 7.6 percent, compared to a 4.3 percent increase for the same period the previous year. As analysts at Robertson, Stephens & Company noted in their recommendation of April 30, 1996, "The Men's Wearhouse has never depended on strong industry growth but solely on the company's superior fundamentals and growth prospects."

## *Ending the 1990s with a Shopping Spree*

The last half of the 1990s was largely a tale of growth by acquisition, though the company did try out a couple of new concepts later in the decade. During this time, Men's Wearhouse would become a billion dollar business, with even more ambitious targets ahead.

In March 1996, the company joined a liquidator (Buxbaum, Ginsberg & Associates) in buying the assets of Atlanta-based Kuppenheimer Men's Clothiers, which had 43 stores. The unique arrangement allowed Men's Wearhouse to control Kuppenheimer's going out of business sales.

In December 1996, Men's Wearhouse acquired several men's clothing brands from Joseph & Feiss Co. Inc. (J&F), including Cricketeer, Country Britches, Joseph & Feiss, and Cox & Hawkins. J&F, a subsidiary of Hugo Boss AG, produced clothing at a Cincinnati plant that was not part of the deal. Men's Wearhouse ended 1996 with about 300 stores.

In 1997, Men's Wearhouse acquired 17 stores of southern California's C&R Clothiers Inc. and the six super-sized stores, up to 19,000 square feet each, of Walter Pye's NAL in Houston. These formed the basis of the new Value Priced Clothing Inc. division, created in January of the year following the C&R purchase.

Men's Wearhouse underwent an extensive corporate makeover in 1997. New, more subdued advertising emphasized service and expertise, in contrast to the brash, price-centered pitches of earlier years. Sales rose 30.5 percent to $631.1 million in the 1997–98 fiscal year, and earnings were up 36.6 percent to $28.9 million. The company had 396 stores, including 25 in the Value Priced Clothing division.

Men's Wearhouse unsuccessfully tried to buy Today's Man, then based in Philadelphia and in bankruptcy. The company did enter the New York City market in 1998, setting up a massive 7,600-square-foot store on Madison Avenue. The company then turned its sights northward.

Men's Wearhouse acquired the 107-store Moores Retail Group in February 1999. Men's Wearhouse had begun courting Moores the Suit People, Canada's largest retailer of men's tailored clothing, in 1995. Moores' CEO Martin Prosserman declined Men's Wearhouse's $100 million purchase offer. Men's Wearhouse did end up buying the company three years later for about $125 million in stock and assumption of debt. Moores, which had 2,000 employees and sales of $121 million (C$183 million) in fiscal 1997–98, had been founded in 1961 as Golden Brand Clothing. It entered the retail business in 1980. Moores had its own 200,000-square-foot factory in Montreal, giving Men's Wearhouse a formidable private label capacity.

In March 1999, the company merged with K&G Men's Center Inc., a publicly traded, lower-end men's clothing chain open only on weekends. K&G, based in Atlanta, had 34 stores and 1998 sales of $139 million. This bolstered the Value Price Clothing division, which then operated 20 stores under the SuitMax name. These were renamed K&G after the merger. Men's Wearhouse soon added the four-unit, Detroit-area Suit Warehouse to its holdings.

By this time, Zimmer was projecting sales of $10 billion within fifteen years. First, the company had to deal with the relaxed, "business casual" dress code of the late-1990s. The percentage of tailored clothing offered at Men's Wearhouse stores was 65 percent and slipping as Men's Wearhouse gradually added more casual clothes. It also provided more space for big and tall offerings and set out to revamp and expand its stores to take on a range of competitors.

A couple of new concepts were rolled out. Men's Wearhouse eyed the highly fragmented formal wear business, testing tuxedo rentals at a dozen Seattle stores in the spring of 1999. The formal wear market was younger than Men's Wearhouse's traditional customer base. By February 2002, tuxedo rentals were being offered at 373 Men's Wearhouse stores.

In 1998, Men's Wearhouse was testing a K&G Ladies concept in the Atlanta area. It bought its first women's shop there in May 2000, under the name K&G Women's Superstore. It had plans to expand K&G Women's nationally beginning in 2002, eventually opening 165 stores nationwide. Zimmer believed the ladies' side could equal the $1 billion in volume the men's side was then seeing.

In January 2000, Men's Wearhouse had 450 Men's Wearhouse stores in the United States and another 51 stores of other types. Men's Wearhouse stock migrated from the NASDAQ Stock Exchange to the Big Board in the fall of 2000. Zimmer persuaded the New York Stock Exchange to simultaneously announce a new dress policy.

Men's Wearhouse was reported to be bidding for Brooks Bros., marketer of upscale men's clothing, in the summer of 2001; instead, Retail Brand Alliance bought it from U.K. retailer Marks & Spencer. Men's Wearhouse's net sales slipped 4.5 percent to $1.27 billion in the fiscal year ending February 2, 2002. Net earnings of $43.3 million were half those of the previous year. Nevertheless, using past performance as a predictor, the future of Men's Wearhouse continued to hold promise.

## *Principal Subsidiaries*

Golden Moores Finance Company (Canada); K&G Men's Center, Inc.; The Men's Wearhouse of Michigan, Inc.; Renwick Technologies, Inc.; TMW Capital Inc.; TMW Marketing Company, Inc.; TMW Realty Inc.; Twin Hill Acquisition Company, Inc.

## *Principal Divisions*

Men's Wearhouse; Moores Clothing for Men; K&G.

### *Principal Competitors*

Brooks Brothers; Federated Department Stores, Inc.; Jos. A. Bank Clothiers, Inc.; Today's Man, Inc.

### *Further Reading*

Arlen, Jeffrey, "The Men's Wearhouse: Tailoring an Off-Price Mix," *Discount Store News*, February 20, 1995, p. A16.

Duff, Mike, "Men's Wearhouse Adds Additional Layers with Expanded Casual Line, New Formalwear," *Discount Store News*, April 3, 2000, p. 3.

Evenson, Laura, "Nordstrom, Men's Wearhouse Settle," San Francisco Chronicle, May 12, 1989, p. C2.

Gellers, Stan, and Jean Palmieri, "Men's Wearhouse Acquires License for Three Botany Clothing Labels," *Daily News Record*, September 21, 1995, p. 1.

Gellers, Stan, Jean Palmieri, and Thomas Ryan, "Bidding War Brewing for C&R Clothiers," *Daily News Record*, November 19, 1996, p. 4.

Goldfield, Robert, "The Men's Wearhouse Trying On Women's Apparel Market for Size," *Houston Business Journal*, June 30, 2000, p. 8A.

Houston Chronicle Interactive, "The Men's Wearhouse—How to Dress: Business Casual," Houston Chronicle Marketplace, http://www.chron.com, July 1996.

Karr, Arnold, "Jockeying for Position," *MR Magazine*, June 1995, p. 56.

Kloppenburg, Janet, and Carolyn Capaccio, *The Men's Wearhouse, Inc.*, San Francisco: Robertson, Stephens & Company, 1996.

Kubby, Steve, "The Men's Wearhouse: An Unsolicited Testimonial by the Publisher," Alpine World Publishing, July 1996.

Mui, Nelson, "No Longer Full of Sound and Fury, George Zimmer Now Has a Soft Touch," *Daily News Record*, March 12, 1999, p. 10.

O'Reilly, Charles III, and Jeffrey Pfeffer, "The Men's Wearhouse: Growth in a Declining Market," *Hidden Value: How Great Companies Achieve Extraordinary Results with Ordinary People*, Boston: Harvard Business School Press, 2000, pp. 79–98.

Palmieri, Jean, and Stan Gellers, "J&F Labels Acquired by Men's Wearhouse; Brands Include Cricketeer, Country Britches," *Daily News Record*, December 17, 1996, p. 1.

Palmieri, Jean, James Fallon, and Samantha Conti, "Men's Wearhouse May Be in Bid for Brooks Bros.," *WWD*, July 2, 2001, p. 2.

Poole, Claire, "Don't Get Mad, Get Rich," *Forbes*, May 24, 1993, p. 58.

Veverka, Mark, "Analysts Say Men's Wearhouse Is All Dressed Up and Ready to Go," *Wall Street Journal*, December 10, 1997.

Zimmer, George, and Ilan Mochari, "My Biggest Mistake," *Inc.*, June 2000, p. 123.

—Ellen D. Wernick
—update: Frederick C. Ingram

Desjardins Caisse populaire Desjardins de Notre-Dame-du-Sacré-Coeur de la montagne

# Mouvement des Caisses Desjardins

**100 des Commandeurs**
**Levis, Québec G6V 7N5**
**Canada**
**Telephone: (418) 835-2323**
**Toll Free: (800) 224-7737**
**Fax: (418)833-4769**
**Web site: http://www.desjardins.com**

*Cooperative*
*Incorporated:* 1900 as Caisse Populaire de Lévis
*Employees:* 38,816
*Total Assets:* C$80.49 billion ($128 billion)(2001)
*NAIC:* 522298 All Other Non-Depository Credit Intermediation

Quebec cooperative Mouvement des Caisses Desjardins is that region's leading bank and the sixth-largest financial institution in Canada. A restructuring in July 2001 created a single, united Federation des Caisses Desjardins (previously there had been 14 federations) with total assets of $80 billion. The cooperative is also present in French-speaking regions of Acadia, Manitoba, and Ontario, which are organized under separate federations. In all, Mouvement des Caisses Desjardins offers a full-range financial services to 5.1 million members through more than 1,000 branches or "caisses." Desjardins controls some 46 percent of Quebec's traditional deposits activity and claims a market share of 7 percent and 15 percent in the mutual funds and securities markets, respectively. Credit makes up some 60 percent of the group's activities—the group provides some 70 percent of Quebec's personal and home mortgage loans, and 22 percent and 41 percent of the province's commercial and industrial and agricultural loans, respectively. Founded at the beginning of the 20th century by Alphonse Desjardins, the Mouvement has successively diversified its product range beyond the consumer market and is now one of Quebec's leading financial services providers to the corporate and institutional market. The group's more than 20 subsidiaries include publicly listed Desjardins-Laurentian Financial Corporation, which groups Desjardins' insurance and investment and asset management operations; Desjardins Specialized Financial Management, the leading trust company for group savings plans in Quebec; Desjardins Securities, which offers both full-service and discount brokerage services; Elantis Investment Management, which, with $11.5 billion in assets, is one of Quebec's top five investment management firms; and Desjardins Business, which, with 100,000 member companies and 68 corporate financial centers, handles some $20 billion in business volume each year. Mouvement des Caisses Desjardins has been led by chairman, president, and CEO Alban D'Amours since 2000.

### *Banking with Compassion at the Turn of the 20th Century*

The French Canadian rural farmers and their urban working class counterparts of the late 19th century were more or less abandoned by Canada's generally English-speaking banking community, which focused on corporations and wealthy customers. The French-speaking poor and low-income population, already subjected to a series of economic reversals in the latter decades of the century, were preyed upon by unscrupulous banks and moneylenders that were reported to charge interest rates as high as 3000 percent. Quebec's largely rural population had little access to savings facilities; the high interest rates of the loans available to them most often resulted in foreclosures on their homes. As a result, a growing number of French Canadians were fleeing to the cities or leaving Canada altogether.

Alphonse Desjardins had been working as a French-language stenographer for the Canadian House of Commons when, during a debate on the banking industry, he learned of the unjust conditions facing much of Quebec's population. By then, the cooperative movement, which began in England at the mid-19th century, had spread around the world, extending from the dairy and grocery industries to the banking industry. Desjardins became determined to adapt the European model of cooperative banking to the Quebec population.

Desjardins and a group of fellow investors launched Quebec's first "caisse populaire" based on a cooperative savings and loan model. Located in Desjardins' own home, the Caisse Populaire de Lévis grouped together 12 people who together

**Company Perspectives:**

*Mouvement Desjardins, the subsidiaries and the caisses, have as their mission to contribute to the improved economic and social well-being of people and groups within the compatible limits of its field of activity by developing an integrated cooperative network of sound and profitable financial services, on an ongoing basis, that are owned and administered by the members, as well as a network of complementary financial enterprises, all performing well in their respective fields of activity, controlled by the members, and by teaching democracy, economics, solidarity, and individual and collective responsibility, especially to members, officers, and employees.*

purchased shares for a total of C$26.40. The first savings deposit was for ten cents, with Desjardins himself accepting the financial risk.

The caisse caught on quickly, and by the end of its first year already boasted more than 700 members. Part of the new society's appeal was its commitment, beyond providing savings and loans facilities, to encouraging the growth of the Quebec economy and improving the conditions of its working class and rural population. Desjardins himself proved to be the group's strongest promoter, who turned to the region's clergy—Desjardins has been described as deeply religious—to promote the new banking concept among parishioners. A number of priests started up their own cooperatives for their parishes, while Desjardins himself founded new caisses in the towns of Lauzon, Hull, and Saint-Malo between 1902 and 1906. By that time, the group boasted total assets of just under C$10,000. From the outset, the Mouvement des Caisses Desjardins, as the rapidly growing collection of banking cooperatives came to be called, became associated with Quebec's Roman Catholic Church.

Apart from promoting the growth of the caisse populaire movement, Desjardins also began lobbying for government legislation recognizing the new banking structure and codifying its organization. Unsuccessful at the national level, where a bill was narrowly rejected in 1908, Desjardins' appeal nonetheless found support in the Quebec government, which adopted legislation governing the cooperative movement in 1906. The new law provided the first boom for the movement: between 1907 and 1914, Desjardins had launched nearly 150 new caisses. At the end of that period, the new caisses began incorporating Desjardins' name. The first of these was the Caisse Desjardins de Saint-Saveur-des-Monts, established in 1913.

Most of the caisses were located in Quebec. However, the movement had already begun to spread to other areas with significant populations of French Canadians, including Ontario and, beginning in 1909, the United States, in particular the New England region, which had a large population of French Canadians. By the end of the following decade, the movement had grown to 220 branches, with 187 located in Quebec, 24 in Ontario, and nine in the United States. Quebec remained the group's base, with more than C$6 million in total assets and a membership topping 30,000. The many branches remained independent operations with no central control, however, a feature Desjardins had begun to put into place shortly before his death in 1920.

The first move toward centralizing control of the caisse movement came at the end of that same year when a regional union of caisses was formed in Trois-Rivières. In 1921, the caisses operating in the Lévis-Quebec City region formed their own union. Other regional unions were formed in Montreal and in Gaspésie by the middle of the decade. These unions remained largely local through the end of the decade; in 1932, however, the four original unions joined together to create the Fédération de Québec des Unions Régionales des Caisse Populaires Desjardins, which now grouped regional unions on a province-wide basis. The federation added technical support for the individual branches and also inspection and oversight services.

The onset of the Great Depression slowed down the movement's growth as membership shrank amid the economic turmoil. The return to growth in the build up to World War II soon restored the Desjardins movement to growth, and the number of caisses once again began to build, nearing 900 at the end of the war with total assets of C$88 million. By then, the Mouvement des Caisses Desjardins had extended operations throughout Quebec. The strong growth of the movement led to the adoption of more professional management, as well as the first permanent employees. (The caisses had originally been staffed by volunteers from among their members.)

### *Diversifying: 1960s–80s*

Desjardins had begun to extend beyond its core savings and loan mandate by the end of World War II. In 1944, the group began offering insurance products—at first for theft, fire, and fraud—through a newly created group, Société d'Assurance des Caisses Populaires. Then, in 1948, the group added a new operation, Desjardins Life Assurance, which provided life and family insurance as well as savings life insurance and loan insurance to members. This insurance component, later known as Groupe Desjardins, took on greater weight in 1962 when the movement acquired La Sauvegarde, a life insurance company based in Quebec that was threatened with a possible takeover from a non-French Canadian company.

In 1963, Desjardins acquired another Quebec concern, Société de Fiducie du Québec, a trust company that was later renamed Fiducie Desjardins. This acquisition enabled Desjardins to extend its range of services to its members to include asset management, investment, estate planning, and similar services. In 1965, Société de Fiducie du Québec launched its first group investment vehicle; three years later, the group added a range of other services, including real estate brokerage and pension plan supplements.

These new products helped the Desjardins movement attract a growing number of members. Total assets climbed past the C$1 billion mark in 1964. By the beginning of the 1970s, Desjardins had grown to hold a central place in the Quebec economy, with total assets of more than C$2.5 billion. This position was recognized by the Quebec government, which passed legislation in 1971 enabling Desjardins to form its own investment vehicle,

## Key Dates:

**1900:** Alphonse Desjardins founds the first cooperative credit union in North America, Caisse Populaire de Lévis.
**1913:** Establishment of the first caisse (''branch'') to incorporate Desjardins name into its own.
**1920:** The first regional union of caisses is formed in Trois-Rivières.
**1932:** The four existing regional unions join together to create the Fédération de Québec des Unions Régionales des Caisse Populaires Desjardins.
**1944:** Mouvement Desjardins enters the personal insurance market with the creation of Société d'Assurance des Caisses Populaires
**1962:** The group acquires the life insurance firm La Sauvegarde, and the following year acquires Société de Fiducie de Québec.
**1974:** The launch of the Société d'Investissement Desjardins after passage of special legislation by the Quebec government in 1971.
**1979:** The group absorbs the Credit Union Federation, then the Quebec Credit Union League.
**1988:** The Savings and Credit Union Act enables group to reorganize its operations into subsidiaries and holding companies.
**1994:** The Laurentian Group is acquired, creating the Desjardins-Laurentian group, which is listed on the Toronto stock exchange.
**1999:** Group members vote to unify 11 existing federations into a single, centrally operating federation.
**2001:** The group announces merger agreement between Imperial Life and Desjardins-Laurentian.

Société d'Investissement Desjardins. That group began operations in 1974; in 1975, Desjardins decided to separate its business investment program activities from its industrial and commercial loans operations, placing the latter into a new corporation, Crédit Industrial Desjardins, formed in 1976.

Throughout the 1980s, Desjardins continued to add new products and features such as automated teller machines and credit card facilities—VISA Desjardins was to grow to become Quebec's largest credit-card issuer. The group also added securities brokerage products and other support operations such as a ''caisse centrale.'' Desjardins was also moving toward a consolidation of the Canadian cooperative financial sector. In 1979, the group absorbed Credit Union Federation, then added the Quebec Credit Union League at the beginning of the 1980s. Later that decade, the Desjardins federations operating in the French-speaking regions of Ontario, Manitoba, and Arcadia also joined the main Quebec-based movement. The additions helped boost the group's total assets to more than C$40 billion by the beginning of the 1990s.

### *A Modern Banking Group for the 21st Century*

In 1988, the Quebec government passed new legislation governing the province's banking cooperative. The Savings and Credit Union Act of that year enabled Desjardins to restructure its operations, grouping together its growing number of subsidiaries under holding companies that could provide central direction to each specific area of operation. The reorganization gave Desjardins the possibility of extending its range of services and providing these services through an integrated format.

In 1994, Desjardins acquired Laurentian Group, vastly expanding its insurance operations and giving it a particularly strong presence in Quebec's personal insurance sector. Desjardins-Laurentian, as the new entity came to be called, became a publicly listed company on the Toronto exchange, with subsidiaries and products ranging from insurance to asset management.

The Laurentian acquisition also brought Desjardins a new investment advisor firm, Elantis, which then took over as manager of the Desjardins Funds subsidiary. Under Elantis, Desjardins stepped up its development of new investment funds products, such as the launch, in 1990, of its ''ethical fund'' Desjardins Environment Fund. After establishing two international funds in 1996, the Worldwide Balanced Fund and the American Market Fund, they launched the Quebec Fund, which featured only Quebec-based shares. Then, in 1999, the group added a ''funds of funds'' product family, called Desjardins Select Funds, which invested in third-party funds. A year later, Desjardins added three new ethical funds as part of its funds of funds family.

By then, Desjardins had already begun preparing an overhaul of its organization into a single, streamlined federation, a move that had been voted for in 1999. Faced with increasing competition in its home market, as the financial community was becoming more and more international in scope, with an emphasis on new generations of products, such as brokering and related services, Desjardins had decided to unify its decision-making process into a single, central office. Such a move was also to provide cost-savings as the group eliminated many of the redundancies of its previous structure.

The reorganization was completed in July 2001, when the 11 existing Desjardins federations were regrouped under the single Fédération des Caisses Desjardins de Québec. This new federation then provided oversight for 15 new regional offices, based on existing regional borders in Quebec. Meanwhile, Desjardins began responding to the increasingly competitive financial markets with a series of external growth moves, such as the acquisitions of two property and casualty insurance firms, bought from Canadian Imperial Bank for C$352 million, which not only added some 60 percent to Desjardins' insurance activity, but also enabled it to extend its customer base beyond Quebec and into such provinces as Alberta and Ontario. In a similar move, the company's Desjardins-Laurentian subsidiary agreed to merge with Imperial Life, creating the seventh-largest life insurer in Canada.

With assets topping C$80 billion at the end of 2001, Desjardins appeared to be just at the start of a new growth drive to celebrate the beginning of its next century of operations. Among the group's targets was a strengthening of its position in the brokerage market, as well as building a full-service investment and corporate underwriting wing. The group took a step toward that direction in mid-2001 when it acquired Groome Capital, Inc., based in Montreal, followed by the acquisition of nearly 7,500 client accounts from Rampart Securities Inc., which had been operating in Toronto until it was closed down by securities regulators. At the end of the year, Desjardins admitted that it had entered talks to acquire a position in another troubled firm, Yorkton Securities Inc., said to be the target of a possible securities investigation. The addition of Yorkton, however, was set to give Desjardins a boost in the high-technology sector. If Alphonse Desjardins would be surprised by the modern appearance of the movement he had founded more than 100 years before, he would no doubt approve of the Mouvement des Caisse Desjardins' ability to retain its commitment to its founder's principles.

## *Principal Subsidiaries*

Fédération des Caisses Desjardins du Québec; Caisse Centrale Desjardins; Capital Desjardins; Fonds de Sécurité Desjardins; Société Historique Alphonse-Desjardins; Desjardins Federal Savings Bank; Fondation Desjardins; Développement International Desjardins; Société Financière Desjardins-Laurentienne ; Desjardins Sécurité Financière, Compagnie d'Assurance Vie; Le Groupe Desjardins, Assurances Générales; Assurances Générales des Caisses Desjardins; La Personnelle; Certas Direct, Compagnie d'Assurances; Gestion de Services Financiers Spécialisés; Fiducie Desjardins; Placements Elantis; Opvest; Investissement Desjardins; Valeurs Mobilières Desjardins; Capital Régional et Coopératif Desjardins.

## *Principal Competitors*

Woolwich Plc; Mouvement Des Caisses Desjardins; Aid Association for Lutherans/Lutheran Brotherhood; North Carolina State Employees' Credit Union; Golden 1 Credit Union; Vancouver City Savings Credit Union; State Employee's Credit Union; Credit Union Central Of British Columbia; Patelco Credit Union; Space Coast Credit Union; Credit Union ONE; Credit Union Central Of Saskatchewan Regina; Surrey Metro Savings Credit Union.

## *Further Reading*

Auger, Michel C., ''The Power of the Caisse,'' *Ottawa Sun*, January 28, 2000, p. 15.

Belanger, Guy, and Claude Genest, *La Caisse populaire de Lévis: Là où tout a commencé*, Ste-Foy and Lévis: Editions Multimondes and Editions Dorimene, 2000.

Kalawsky, Keith, ''Desjardins Taps Markets for US$400 Million to Expand,'' *Financial Post*, June 13, 2001.

''The Populist: Alphonse Desjardins,'' *Macleans*, September 4, 2000, p. 46.

Poulin, Pierre, *Desjardins, 100 ans d'histoire*, Ste-Foy and Lévis: Editions Multimondes and Editions Dorimene, 2000.

Tedesco, Theresa, ''Desjardins Eyes Yorkton Securities,'' *Financial Post*, October 29, 2001.

—M.L. Cohen

# Nikon

# Nikon Corporation

**Fuji Building**
**2-3, Marunouchi 3-chome**
**Chiyoda-ku, Tokyo 100-8331**
**Japan**
**Telephone: (81) 3 3214-5311**
**Fax: (81) 3 3201-5856**
**Web site: http://www.nikon.co.jp**

*Public Company*
*Incorporated:* 1917 as Nippon Kogaku K.K.
*Employees:* 13,894
*Sales:* ¥483.9 billion ($3.8 billion) (2001)
*Stock Exchanges:* Tokyo Osaka
*Ticker Symbol:* 7731
*NAIC:* 333315 Photographic and Photocopying Equipment Manufacturing; 334413 Semiconductor and Related Device Manufacturing

While Nikon Corporation is well known in the consumer world for its cameras, the Japanese firm also produces film scanners, telescopes and binoculars, eyeglasses and ophthalmic equipment, microscopes, surveying equipment, precision equipment, and optical equipment. Nikon has also made a name for itself in the semiconductor industry by manufacturing integrated circuit exposure systems, or steppers, that etch circuitry onto wafers. This business segment secures nearly half of company sales, while the imaging products business provides approximately 36 percent of total sales. Operating as a member of the Mitsubishi *keiretsu*, or business group, Nikon spent 1999 and the early years of 2000 restructuring by adopting an in-house company system as well as an executive officer platform, spinning off various operations, and consolidating its holding companies in both the United States and Europe.

### *Origins*

In 1917, three of Japan's foremost makers of optical equipment merged in order to offer a full line of optical products. The German optical-glass industry was by far the most advanced at the time. The company was called Nippon Kogaku (''Japan Optics'') and began producing optical glass in 1918. The new company had negotiated for technical assistance with the German engineering firm Carl Zeiss, but the negotiations fell through. Nevertheless, by 1919 Nippon Kogaku numbered among its employees eight leading, independent German engineers.

World War I had little effect on the new company, and postwar government policies that promoted the importation of foreign technology to develop domestic industry served to assist Nippon Kogaku. In the 1920s, the company used German technical advice to develop a line of ultra-small prism binoculars and the precise JOICO microscope. By 1932, Nippon Kogaku had designed its own camera lenses, the Nikkor brand. Nippon Kogaku was listed on the Tokyo Stock Exchange in 1939.

Nippon Kogaku expanded during the 1920s and 1930s. Military leaders saw expansion as the best way to attack the domestic problems of overpopulation and shortages of raw materials. The country looked to Southeast Asia as its natural extension, and in September 1940 Japan joined Germany and Italy in the Tripartite Pact to secure its interests in this area. As the threat of a major war increased, Japanese government planners chose to concentrate on improving precision optics for navigation and bombing equipment rather than radar and sonar technology, which was used by the U.S. armed forces. The decision meant new business for Nippon Kogaku and its competitor Minolta, both of which were primarily optical-equipment producers at the time. It also increased German technical aid to Japanese firms that were involved in the war effort, and Nippon Kogaku gained expertise through this arrangement.

The company continued to prosper in the postwar years, shifting from optics with military applications to optics with consumer applications. The company produced microscopes, binoculars, eyeglasses, and surveying instruments, which were especially in demand as Japan rebuilt its shattered infrastructure.

### *Nippon Kogaku Introduces Its First Camera: 1946*

After World War II, Nippon Kogaku entered the area for which it would become best known, introducing its first camera in 1946 under the Nikon brand name. Other Japanese firms

**Company Perspectives:**

*We are striving to create businesses for the new century that capitalize on our core competencies. We are actively working to expand business by evolving the nanotechnology we have amassed in our experience with steppers and, at the same time, entering into alliances that exceed the framework of our business, establishing new businesses for the twenty-first century centered primarily on the fields of semiconductors, life sciences, and optical communications.*

already had begun selling cameras. Minolta had produced cameras since it was founded in 1928, and Canon produced Japan's first 35-millimeter camera in 1934. However, the standard remained the German Leica 35-millimeter camera, accepted by professional photographers as the top of the line since its introduction in 1925.

The war temporarily took German cameras out of the market place. Although Nippon Kogaku had the advantage of German lens technology and the support of U.S. occupation forces that wanted to rebuild Japanese industry as soon as possible, the company did not immediately take advantage of the lack of competition in international markets. Company management insisted on producing cameras for the Japanese market.

It was not long before Japanese cameras became better known internationally. U.S. occupation forces found Japanese 35-millimeter cameras in post exchanges and took them back to the United States. The simple sand-cast bodies, uncomplicated iris shutters, and high-quality lenses soon earned Japanese cameras an excellent reputation, despite the poor reputation other Japanese-made goods suffered.

Nippon Kogaku's Nikon-brand cameras earned special attention for their high quality. Demand increased further when U.S. combat photographers covering the Korean War favored Nikon lenses, and photojournalists began asking Nippon Kogaku to make special lenses to fit their Leica cameras. The company's reputation spread by word of mouth among professional photographers. By the mid-1960s photographers for *Life, National Geographic*, and *Stern*—Germany's largest-selling picture magazine—used Nikon 35-millimeter cameras. Nikon had been accepted as the professional standard, and advanced amateurs followed the example, helping Nikon cameras to make inroads into that market as well.

One reason for Nippon Kogaku's success was its development of a completely new type of camera, the single-lens reflex (SLR) camera. The SLR lets a photographer see exactly what the camera will record, using an angled mirror to reflect images from the camera lens to a viewing screen. The rangefinder camera produced by Leitz, maker of the Leica, used two lenses, one for the film and a separate one for the viewer. That method worked until interchangeable lenses were developed in the 1950s. If a photographer used a wide-angle or telephoto lens, the Leica's viewer lens still showed a standard image. There could be a considerable difference between what the eye saw and what the camera's film recorded.

Nippon Kogaku brought the Nikon F SLR to market in 1959 and improved it when other Japanese companies offered competing models. Leitz did not introduce its SLR until 1964. Leitz's SLR was judged by the professional community to be an amateur model, not advanced enough for professional use. By then, the Nikon camera had become the high-end 35-millimeter standard. Even so, it was cheaper than the competing Leicaflex; in 1965, the Nikon F with a coupled light meter and standard f2 lens sold for $413, while a similarly equipped Leicaflex sold for $549.

Another reason for Nippon Kogaku's success in the international market was its ties to the Mitsubishi *keiretsu*, its transfer agent. After World War II, the United States had broken up the *zaibatsu*—powerful Japanese business conglomerates, such as Mitsubishi—but the trading companies, banks, and industrial concerns that had composed the *zaibatsu* continued to cooperate. For Nippon Kogaku, its ties to Mitsubishi meant ready credit and exporting advantages. Nippon Kogaku also promoted its photographic equipment through what it called ''photography culture,'' sponsoring photo contests and photo exhibits as well as establishing clubs that gave advice to amateur photographers.

Nikon cameras were best-sellers, and Nippon Kogaku was profitable by the mid-1960s. When other major Japanese camera companies, such as Canon and Minolta, entered the office-equipment field by introducing copiers, calculators, and related equipment, Nippon Kogaku continued to emphasize cameras. The company introduced new SLR cameras and an eight-millimeter movie camera during the 1960s and 1970s, as well as a new all-weather camera. The U.S. National Aeronautics and Space Administration chose Nikon SLR cameras for use in the space shuttle program.

### *Diversification: 1980s*

Changing economic conditions in the 1980s forced Nippon Kogaku to reevaluate its reliance on cameras. By 1982, 80 percent of Japanese households owned at least one 35-millimeter camera with all the attachments. Markets in Europe and the United States also were saturated. At the same time, new production techniques—such as use of computers to design lenses—and new materials—such as lightweight, tough plastics for camera bodies—took some of the skill and much of the profit out of making cameras. Since Nippon Kogaku, unlike other Japanese camera makers, was not heavily involved in office equipment or the new video technology, two-thirds of its revenues still came from the mature camera market in 1982.

At the same time, other Japanese companies mounted a new threat to the 35-millimeter camera market. In 1976, Canon introduced a new camera, the impact of which rivaled the introduction of the SLR camera in the 1950s. Canon's AE-I used a semiconductor chip to change automatically some of the settings the photographer would change on traditional 35-millimeter SLR's. Casual photographers often were intimidated by the need to set shutter speed, lens aperture, and focus; thus, when Canon pushed the AE-l's ease of use in an advertising campaign, its sales took off. Encouraged by that success, Canon next brought non-SLR 35-millimeter cameras back into the picture with its simple Snappy. That camera was a threat to the ''snapshooter'' market firmly held by U.S. camera makers Kodak and Polaroid, not Nippon Kogaku's high end of the

**Key Dates:**

**1917:** Three of Japan's optical equipment manufacturers merge to form Nippon Kogaku.
**1932:** By now the firm has launched camera lenses under the brand name Nikkor.
**1939:** Nippon Kogaku lists on the Tokyo Stock Exchange.
**1946:** The company introduces its first Nikon brand camera.
**1959:** The Nikon F SLR camera is launched.
**1972:** The firm enters the semiconductor industry with a measuring instrument for integrated circuits.
**1988:** The company officially adopts the name Nikon Corporation.
**1992:** Nikon launches the world's first underwater SLR camera.
**1998:** As the semiconductor market falters, the firm reports a loss of ¥18.2 billion.
**2000:** Nikon management launches the "Vision Nikon 21" strategy.

market. Nippon Kogaku introduced the FG 35-millimeter SLR, a programmed, automatic model, in mid-1982 and promoted it with a major ad campaign aimed at men who tended to buy SLR's. Nevertheless, Canon was slipping ahead of Nippon Kogaku in overall camera sales. Nippon Kogaku still held its reputation for building better cameras, but its conservative business approach was causing it to lose ground, just as Leitz's had caused it to lose out to Nippon Kogaku 30 years earlier. To survive, Nippon Kogaku not only had to continue camera development but also to diversify.

In the camera field, the company moved into the simpler end of the market with its successful One-Touch camera in 1983. The next year the Nikon FA received the Camera Grand Prix, a Japanese award. The company followed the One-Touch with the Nikon F-501, a new autofocus SLR camera, which received the 1986 European Camera of the Year Award. In 1989, another new autofocus SLR, the Nikon F-801, received both the Camera Grand Prix in Japan and the European Camera of the Year Award. By the beginning of the 1990s, Nikon Corporation—the name Nippon Kogaku had adopted officially in 1988—could claim to have a complete lineup of cameras ranging from professional top-of-the-line models to compact autofocus models for less serious photographers.

Nippon Kogaku had also diversified into areas in which it already had a foothold, including ophthalmic technology. It also produced sunglasses, plastic eyeglass lenses, and eyeglass frames. In 1979, the company marketed its automatic eye refractive index measuring machine. The following year, Nippon Kogaku moved in a new direction, developing a dental root implant using bioactive glass, which bonds with living bone tissue.

In 1972, Nippon Kogaku entered an important new area, marketing its laser interferometric X-Y measuring system, a measuring instrument for integrated circuits. In the 1980s, the company put more effort into developing semiconductor-production machinery, and Nikon became a world leader in that area. Nippon Kogaku continued to develop microscopes, telescopes, and binoculars as well as more advanced equipment for surveying and measuring instruments. It also made its first forays into new types of electronic imaging equipment: a color film scanner, used for computer input of photos and a color printer for computer graphic production. The Still Video Camera System needed no film at all—it recorded images electronically on floppy discs, allowing images to be reproduced immediately or transmitted over telephone lines. Nikon lenses were also being used in new high-definition television.

Nippon Kogaku's 1988 name change to Nikon recognized that optical equipment was no longer the company's focus in the electronics-oriented environment. The company historically known for its advanced optical glass parlayed its reputation as a leading camera maker into success in other fields.

Diversification into various fields, especially the semiconductor market, continued during the 1990s. By the end of the decade, this business segment was securing nearly half of the company's sales. During this time period Nikon also expanded internationally by establishing new subsidiaries in Hungary, Italy, the Czech Republic, Singapore, Taiwan, Sweden, the United States, China, and the United Kingdom.

Some of the company's new product launches during the 1990s included the industry's first underwater autofocus SLR camera, which was introduced in 1992. The following year, the firm developed the world's first electrochromic sunglasses with changing color lenses. Nikon also created a new series of digital cameras, including the Coolpix line, which became available in 1997.

### *Weakening Market Conditions: Late 1990s and Beyond*

During 1998, the company's dependence on the semiconductor industry did not play in its favor. The semiconductor market as a whole weakened due in part to over saturation and falling prices. Nikon posted a net loss of ¥18.2 billion and revenues dropped by 18 percent over the previous year. The sale of steppers picked up in 1999, however, and the firm was able to secure a net profit of ¥7.8 billion ($72.8 million).

During 1999 and into the new century, Nikon restructured itself and adopted an in-house company system to align its group companies and make each one accountable for a certain level of sales and profits. The firm also adopted an executive officer management system, spun off various assets, reorganized its U.S. sales subsidiaries, and created holding company Nikon Holdings Europe B.V. in an effort to consolidate its European businesses. In March 2000, Nikon also launched "Vision Nikon 21," a series of strategic business goals that would extend into the first decade of 2000.

As Nikon streamlined its operations, it was faced with weakening global economies, fierce competition in the manufacturing industry, as well as continued sluggishness in the semiconductor market. Under the leadership of company president Teruo Shimamura, Nikon focused on original product creation along with technological advancements. As part of its new strategy, it entered the chemical mechanical planarization

(CMP) or wafer polishing segment of the semiconductor market by partnering with Okamoto Machine Tool Works Ltd. to create a CMP tool, the NPS2301. Nikon also began focusing on increasing its consumer base. As such, it began offering certain cameras to mass merchandisers for the first time. In 2002, the company also launched a television advertising campaign—the first in eight years—for its Coolpix 2500 digital camera.

Nikon's long-term goals included creating a business structure that could weather the changes in the semiconductor industry while increasing profits. Management believed that semiconductors would continue to play a significant role in the development of information technology, which in turn would create demand for its steppers. The company also looked to expand its digital camera product line, its measuring and inspection equipment for semiconductors, and its microscope technologies. Even as market conditions remained challenging, Nikon management felt confident that the company would prosper well into the future. With a long-standing history of success and a highly reputable brand name, Nikon appeared to be on track to meet its long term goals.

### *Principal Subsidiaries*

Mito Nikon Corporation; Zao Nikon Co., Ltd.; Nikon Tec Corporation; Sendai Nikon Corporation; Nikon Photo Products Inc.; Kurobane Nikon Co., Ltd.; Nikon Instech Co., Ltd.; Kogaku Co., Ltd.; Nikon Digital Technologies, Co., Ltd.; Tochigi Nikon Corporation; Sagami Optical Co., Ltd.; Setagaya Industry Co., Ltd.; Nikon Engineering Co., Ltd.; Nikon Geotecs Co., Ltd.; Nikon Eyewear Co., Ltd.; Nikon Optical Shop Co., Ltd.; Nikon Vision Co., Ltd.; Nikon Technologies, Inc.; Nikon Systems Inc.; Nikon Sales-Promotion Co., Ltd.; Nikon Logistics Corporation; Nikon Tsubasa Inc.; Nikon-Essilor Co., Ltd.; Nasu Nikon Co., Ltd.; Aichi Nikon Co., Ltd.; Nikon Americas Inc. (U.S.); Nikon Precision Inc. (U.S.); Nikon Research Corporation of America; Nikon Inc. (U.S.); Nikon Instruments Inc. (U.S.); Nikon Canada Inc.; Nikon Holdings Europe B.V. (Netherlands); Nikon Precision Taiwan Ltd.; Nikon Precision Singapore Pte Ltd.; Nikon (Malaysia) Sdn. Bhd.; Nikon Hong Kong Ltd.; Nikon (Thailand) Co., Ltd.; Nanjing Nikon Jiangnan Optical Instrument Co., Ltd. (China); Beijing Nikon Ophthalmic Products Co., Ltd. (China).

### *Principal Competitors*

ASML Holding N.V.; Canon Inc.; Fuji Photo Film Co. Ltd.

### *Further Reading*


Beardi, Cara, "Nikon Extends Brand to Mass Market," *Advertising Age*, April 3, 2000, p. 26.

Chappell, Jeff, "Polishing an Emerging Technology," *Electronic News*, August 13, 2001, p. 24.

*Focusing on the Future: 1989*, Tokyo: Nikon Corporation, 1989.

"Japan's Nikon Group Net Profit Rebounds to US$72.8 Mln," *AsiaPulse News*, May 23, 2000.

"Japan's Nikon Posts 18 Bln Yen Net Loss For FY98," *AsiaPulse News*, June 1, 1999.

"New Heads Tell Workers to Think Differently, Speak Out," *Daily Yomiuri*, July 19, 2001.

"Nikon," *Advanced Imaging*, August 2001, p. 69.

"Nikon to Set Up Second Thai Plant," *Bangkok Post*, May 14, 2001.

"Nikon Sharpens Its Focus on Local Mart Share," *New Straits Times*, January 18, 2002.

"Nikon Slashes Its Earnings Forecast on Tech Slump," *Wall Street Journal*, September 4, 2001, p. 16.

Wasserman, Todd, "Nikon Focuses on Mass Market with TV," *Brandweek*, April 22, 2002, p. 4.


—Ginger G. Rodriguez
—update: Christina M. Stansell

# Nordson Corporation

**28601 Clemens Road**
**Westlake, Ohio 44145**
**U.S.A.**
**Telephone: (440) 892-1580**
**Fax: (440) 892-9507**
**Web site: http://www.nordson.com**

*Public Company*
*Incorporated:* 1935 as U.S. Automatic Corporation
*Employees:* 3,902
*Sales:* $731.4 million (2001)
*Stock Exchanges:* NASDAQ
*Ticker Symbol:* NDSN
*NAIC:* 333999 All Other Miscellaneous General Purpose Machinery Manufacturing

Nordson Corporation is a leading manufacturer of precision dispensing equipment that apply liquid and powder coatings, adhesives, and sealants to a wide variety of consumer and industrial products during the manufacturing process. Nordson-built machines are used in the appliance, automotive, book-binding, construction, container, converting, electronics, food and beverage, furniture, medical, metal finishing, nonwovens, packaging, pharmaceutical, and various other industries. The company also manufactures systems that are used in curing and surface treatment processes. Nearly 50 percent of the company's annual sales stem from operations outside the United States, and Nordson products are found in 31 countries across the globe. The firm's manufacturing plants are located in Alabama, California, Florida, Georgia, New Jersey, Ohio, Rhode Island, Germany, The Netherlands, and the United Kingdom.

## *Origins*

The firm traces its history to 1909 and the founding of U.S. Automatic Company in Amherst, Ohio, near Cleveland. The predecessor firm manufactured high-volume, low-cost screw machine parts for the emerging automobile industry. When the company went bankrupt in 1929, Walter G. Nord acquired control and in 1935 reorganized it as U.S. Automatic Corporation, shifting production emphasis to lower-volume precision parts, which proved vital to the U.S. armed forces during World War II. In the years following the war, Walter and his sons, Eric Nord and Evan Nord, acquired patents for the ''hot airless'' method of applying paint, coatings, and adhesives whereby machines sprayed materials through tiny openings at high pressure.

Walter's sons—Eric, who joined the firm in 1939 after earning a degree in mechanical engineering from Case Institute of Technology, and Evan—formed the Nordson Division of U.S. Automatic in 1954 to produce and market airless spray equipment. Evan ran the operations of the businesses, while Eric searched for the proprietary technology of the airless spray equipment, which became the basis of the new Nordson Division.

## *Expansion: 1960s to Mid-1980s*

The Nordson Division expanded into thermoplastic adhesion in the early 1960s. Machines developed during this period applied hot glue for such packaging as cartons and boxes as well as product assembly. Nordson soon emerged as a leader in this industry, which eventually became one of its primary businesses. The subsidiary grew quickly during the early years of the decade, establishing European marketing branches and absorbing parent U.S. Automatic in 1966. Walter G. Nord died the following year, leaving a legacy of beneficence in the Nordson Foundation, which was endowed with 5 percent of the corporation's pretax earnings.

Eric Nord advanced to the company's presidency, a position he occupied for 20 years. He was later to be credited with guiding the company's growth and providing an example of innovative thinking; before he retired, Nord was granted more than 25 patents for inventions. One noteworthy Nordson innovation of the late 1960s was a device that recovered and recycled over-sprayed powder coatings, thereby eliminating solid waste and pollutants while simultaneously saving customers money.

Nordson established a foothold in the burgeoning Japanese manufacturing market with the founding of Nordson K.K. in 1969 to distribute American-made machinery. Over the course of the 1970s, the corporation also increased its domestic pack-

## Company Perspectives:

*Nordson Corporation strives to be a vital, self-renewing, worldwide organization which, within the framework of ethical behavior and enlightened citizenship, grows and produces wealth for our customers, employees, shareholders, and communities.*

aging operations through the purchase of Domain Industries Inc., a manufacturer of packaging machinery, and the acquisition of a controlling interest in American Packaging Corporation, producer of Ampak brand flexible film and die-cutting equipment. Technological advances in hot melt adhesives and other thermoplastic compounds expanded Nordson's client base during the late 1970s and early 1980s. Soon the company's devices were modified for many applications within the automotive, off-road equipment, appliance, and woodworking industries for joining, caulking, and sealing.

Not all of Nordson's ventures were successful, however. In 1978, the company began manufacturing industrial robots. These spray-painting machines, which were less costly than human labor and could work in hazardous environments, were expected to become a high-growth venture. However, after six years of intense marketing, including a 1982 agreement with two Japanese firms, the program was dropped due to the industry's high rate of obsolescence.

A shift in management in the early 1980s brought public speculation that Nordson was a candidate for takeover. In 1982, James E. Taylor advanced to the presidency and chief executive office, while Eric Nord retired from day-to-day operations, retaining his seat at the head of the board of directors. Taylor divested two non-core businesses to focus corporate energies on what had become Nordson's most significant and promising businesses—packaging and assembly equipment to apply adhesives, sealants, caulking, and other thermoplastic substances, and liquid and powder coating technology. By 1984, the company had over $30 million in cash and had reportedly been plied with several takeover and/or merger proposals. Although the majority of Nordson's stock was very closely held—the Nord family owned 40 percent, the Nordson Foundation retained 10 percent, and current and former managers held another 10 percent—shareholders instituted anti-takeover measures.

Speculation about the possibly of a takeover increased in 1985, when Taylor resigned, bringing Eric Nord back to the offices of president and CEO. Taylor and Nordson cited ''philosophical differences'' for the departure: while Taylor preferred a centralized management scheme, Nord and the board of directors feared that tight controls would stifle the creativity necessary for the company to maintain its technological lead. Sales flattened out at $140 million in 1984 and 1985, while profits declined during the last year of Taylor's tenure from $11.3 million to $9.7 million.

### *Restructuring: Mid-1980s to Early 1990s*

After a six-month search, Nordson offered the top positions to William P. Madar, a 47-year-old executive of Standard Oil Co. (later renamed B.P. America, Inc.). Leaving a 20-year career at Standard Oil to capitalize on Nordson's untapped potential, Madar brought a new management style to the company, which he characterized as ''professorial,'' that encouraged problem-solving through the Socratic method: Madar preferred not to give specific instructions but to ask questions that would allow employees to arrive at their own conclusions. This corporate culture gave employees—over half of whom lived outside North America—freedom to customize the company's systems to accommodate local clients' needs.

Madar also moved immediately to revitalize his new employer, commissioning a study of the 3R's: resource review and reallocation. The restructuring recommended in the review included decentralization through the creation of four geographical sales and service divisions for North America, Japan, Pacific/South America (including Brazil, China, and India), and Europe. A core manufacturing and product development division retained responsibility for product lines. Madar removed redundant management tiers and formed a business-opportunity group to seek out new applications for existing technologies.

In 1987, the company built a new, $9 million laboratory for product engineering and development near its Amherst headquarters and committed an average of 5 percent of sales annually to research and development. The investments kept Nordson ahead of its competition and marketplace needs through technology developments. Edward B. Keaney, an analyst with Newhard, Cook & Co. of St. Louis, told the *Cleveland Plain Dealer* in May 1988 that Nordson ''tends to be the technology leader.'' This edge proved critical to the company's financial survival; had Nordson rested on its laurels, it would have quickly lost business. An estimated 20 percent of annual sales came from three- to four-year-old products, and by the late 1980s Nordson employees held over 1,000 patents and patent applications worldwide.

In interviews, Madar often used ''leap frog'' analogy to describe Nordson's development of new products, likening the application of existing technologies to new but closely related markets to ''a frog leaping from one lily pad to the next.'' New markets, or lily pads, in turn, would become the foundation from which to make another technological leap. For example, the company adapted an electrostatic powder painting technique, commonly used on household appliances and other metal parts, to the strategic application of a superabsorbent polymer powder to gender-specific disposable diapers. Similarly, with different technology, Nordson applies high-speed liquid-paint spraying techniques, generally used to spray adhesives on food cans, to computer circuit boards. The precisely applied coatings protect hundreds of delicate circuits from moisture and dirt each minute. By making such incremental leaps, Nordson augments its knowledge and technology while keeping financial risks in check.

In 1987, the company introduced a new adhesive process that impregnated a standard adhesive with an inert gas to make a sealant that foamed as it was applied. The compound reduced the amount of glue needed and thereby lessened manufacturing costs. Nordson customers who purchased the new machines could expect to recover their costs within two years.

The results of Madar's restructuring were virtually immediate: his first annual report, in 1986, registered a new sales record

**Dates:**

**1909:** U.S. Automatic Company is established in Ohio.
**1935:** Walter G. Nord acquires control of the firm and renames it U.S. Automatic Corporation.
**1954:** Walter's sons, Eric and Evan, form the Nordson Division to produce and market airless spray equipment.
**1966:** Nordson absorbs U.S. Automatic.
**1969:** Nordson K.K. is established in Japan.
**1978:** The company begins manufacturing industrial robots.
**1998:** The firm acquires competitor J&M Laboratories Inc.
**1999:** Nordson launches its Action 2000 management plan.
**2001:** The company purchases EFD Inc.

of $168.7 million, a 20 percent increase from 1985. Operating profit increased 44 percent, and Nordson's average annual return on equity of 29 percent was double that of the overall capital goods industry. Exports increased even faster than domestic sales, contributing 66 percent of total sales by the early 1990s, with noteworthy growth in Australia, Canada, Europe, the Far East, and South America. Nordson's 1993 decision to obtain ISO 9000 certification from the International Organization of Standardization in Switzerland promised increased global competitiveness as well. By that time, the company had established a manufacturing facility in its European market to better serve that geographic region and had invested in an international communications network.

Value Line responded to the improved results by giving the company's stock its highest recommendation. Annual sales tripled from 1986 to 1993 under Madar's direction, from $140 million to $461 million. Profits jumped 79 percent in fiscal 1987 alone, to $24.7 million, and peaked at $46.6 million in 1994. Nordson recorded its 31st consecutive year of increases in the cash dividend, and noted that ''more than 70% of employees are shareholders'' in its 1994 annual report. Analyst Timothy P. Burns, of First Boston Corporation in Chicago, ascribed most of Nordson's success during the period to ''management's well-crafted strategy, long-term investments, and the ability to find new ways to apply new glues, adhesives and other advanced materials.'' External factors, including rising automobile and appliance sales, as well as a weak dollar, also contributed to Nordson's early 1990s earnings boom.

Nordson's corporate tagline encouraged prospective clients to ''Expect More.'' In 1994, company spokespersons indicated that they would expect more from themselves as well, predicting that earnings would more than double by the turn of the 21st century to over $1 billion. CEO Madar and Chairperson Nord prepared for this growth by setting up a ''logical succession of leadership'' and creating a new layer of management. Moreover, Nordson established the position of executive vice-president and chief operating officer, which was filled by Edward P. Campbell. Analyst Maureen P. Lentz, of Roulson Research Corporation in Cleveland, told the *Cleveland Plain Dealer* that Nordson's plans to double sales in five years were ''do-able . . . because of the recovery in overseas markets.'' The company also implemented a formal employee empowerment training program in an effort to maintain its innovative edge.

### *Strategic Acquisitions: Late 1990s*

While Nordson had certainly improved operations during the late 1980s and into the early 1990s, it faced distinct economic challenges during the latter half of the decade that kept its sales goal out of reach. Revenues, however, did increase each year from 1994 to 2000 but failed to hit the planned $1 billion mark. Under the leadership of Campbell—named president and CEO in 1997—Nordson grew during this time period through a series of strategic acquisitions. In 1998, the firm purchased competitor J&M Laboratories Inc., a manufacturer of melt-blowing systems used to produce synthetic nonwoven fabrics. The company also manufactured adhesive dispensing equipment for diaper assembly, medical products, and feminine hygiene products.

In order to expand its hot melt adhesive dispensing business segment, Nordson also acquired Meltex of Germany and California-based Slautterback Corporation The firm added cold adhesive dispensing equipment to its product arsenal with the purchase of Veritec Technologies. Nordson also looked for key acquisitions to strengthen its presence in emerging high technology markets. As such, Spectral Technology Group, a United Kingdom-based ultraviolet curing systems manufacturer, was acquired along with New Jersey-based Horizon Lamps Inc. By the end of the decade, the company had also purchased glass plasma technology from March Instruments Inc. and Advanced Plasma Systems and had acquired California-based Asymtek, a manufacturer of dispensing equipment used in the electronics industry. Then, in late 2000, the company completed its purchase of EFD Inc., a manufacturer of industrial dispensing equipment.

Nordson entered the new millennium recording its 14th year of consecutive sales growth. While sales had reached $740.5 million in 2000, the company's growth had fallen short of expectations due to weakening economies in both Europe and Japan. To make matters worse, the U.S. economy was also beginning to falter. In response to the financial uncertainty, management implemented Action 2000, a two-year plan launched in late 1999 that was aimed at boosting financial growth and included the BEST program—a corporate strategy focused on three main ideas: improve, innovate, and grow.

Financial hardships continued into fiscal 2001. During that year, the company reported a slight decrease in sales while net income fell to $24.6 million, down from $54.6 million in 2000. In September 2001, the company announced it would cut its workforce by 10 percent as part of its cost cutting effort. By now, Nordson had also restructured its operations into three main business segments that included adhesive dispensing and nonwoven fiber systems, advanced technology systems, and coating and finishing systems.

Despite the turbulent economic outlook, Nordson management was confident that the firm would prosper well into the future. As in the mid-1990s, the company's strategy included doubling its sales over a five-year period by capitalizing on opportunities, investing in systems to maximize productivity, and continuing its expansion into growth markets. As a leader in nearly every market segment in which it operated, Nordson stood well positioned to withstand changing economies. Whether or not it would reach its five-year goal, however, remained to be seen.

### *Principal Subsidiaries*

Nordson Australia Pty. Limited; Nordson GmbH (Austria); Nordson Benelux S.A./N.V. (Belgium); Nordson do Brasil Industria E.Comercio Ltda.; Nordson Canada Limited; Nordson (China) Co. Ltd.; Nordson Andina Limitada (Columbia); Nordson CS, spol.s.r.o. (Czech Republic); Nordson Finland Oy; Nordson France S.A.; Nordson Deutschland GmbH; Nordson Engineering GmbH (Germany); Nordson Application Equipment, Inc. (Hong Kong); Nordson India Private Limited; Nordson Italia SpA; Nordson K.K. (Japan); Nordson Asymtek K.K. (Japan); Nordson (Malaysia) Sdn. Bhd.; Nordson de Mexico, S.A. de C.V.; Nordson Benelux B.V. (The Netherlands); Nordson European Distribution B.V. (The Netherlands); Nordson B.V. (The Netherlands); Nordson Norge A/S (Norway); Nordson Polska Sp.z.o.o. (Poland); Nordson Portugal Equipamento Industrial, Lda.; Nordson S.E. Asia (Pte.) Ltd. (Singapore); Nordson Sang San Ltd. (South Korea); Nordson Iberica, S.A. (Spain); Nordson AB (Sweden); Nordson Finishing AB (Sweden); Nordson (Schweiz) A.G. (Switzerland); Nordson (Thailand) Limited; Nordson (United Kingdom) Limited; Spectral Technology Group Limited (United Kingdom); Nordson U.V. Limited. (United Kingdom); Nordson International de Venezuela, C.A.; Asymptotic Technologies, Inc.; Slautterback Corporation; March Plasma Systems, Inc.; Electrostatic Technology, Inc.; Advanced Plasma Systems, Inc.; J & M Laboratories; Horizon Lamps, Inc.; Veritec Technologies, Inc.; Nordson Pacific, Inc.; Nordson U.S. Trading Company; Nordson U.V. Inc.; EFD, Inc.

### *Principal Competitors*

3M Company; Graco Inc.; Sames Corporation.

### *Further Reading*


Banks, Howard, ''The World's Most Competitive Economy,'' *Forbes*, March 30, 1992, p. 84.

Benson, Tracy E., ''Empowered Employees Sharpen the Edge,'' *Industry Week*, February 19, 1990, pp. 12–20.

Fuller, John, ''Production of Robots Spells a New Future for Two Ohio Firms,'' *Cleveland Plain Dealer*, October 7, 1980, pp. D1, D7.

Gleisser, Marcus, ''Nordson Fires 95 in Restructuring,'' *Cleveland Plain Dealer*, November 13, 1986, p. 1C.

Gerdel, Thomas W., ''Nordson's Search Ends in Board Room,'' *Cleveland Plain Dealer*, February 11, 1986, p. 4D.

Henry, Fran, ''William Madar,'' *Cleveland Plain Dealer*, November 29, 1992, p. 30S.

Karle, Delinda, ''No Sale, Nordson Exec Says,'' *Cleveland Plain Dealer*, July 16, 1985, pp. 1E, 3E.

Levine, Bernard, ''Nordson Completes EFD Buy,'' *Electronic News*, December 4, 2000, p. 66.

Robinson, Duncan, ''Exporter Knows When to Hedge,'' *Journal of Commerce and Commercial*, April 26, 1991, p. 1A, 5A.

Teresko, John, ''Running His Own Show,'' *Industry Week*, May 4, 1987, pp. 47–48.


—April Dougal Gasbarre
—update: Christina M. Stansell

# JSC MMC Norilsk Nickel

**22 Voznesensky Pereulok**
**Moscow, 103009**
**Russia**
**Telephone: (+7) 095 787 7667**
**Fax: (+7) 095 915 8385**
**Web site: http://www.nornik.ru**

*Public Company*
*Incorporated:* 1935
*Employees:* 96,013
*Sales:* Ru 106.97 billion ($3.43 billion) (2001)
*Stock Exchanges:* Moscow (MICEX) Russian (RTS)
*Ticker Symbol:* R.GMK
*NAIC:* 212234 Copper Ore and Nickel Ore Mining; 212234 Copper Ore and Nickel Ore Mining; 212299 Other Metal Ore Mining; 213114 Support Activities for Metal Mining; 421510 Metals Service Centers and Offices

With headquarters in Moscow, holding company JSC MMC Norilsk Nickel (Norilsk Nickel Mining and Metallurgical Company) oversees the mining of nickel, copper, cobalt, platinum group metals (PGMs), and other metals in isolated arctic towns on Russia's Kola and Tamyr peninsulas. The company is the largest producer of nonferrous and precious metals in Russia, accounting for 20 percent of all nickel produced in the world. Nickel is used mainly in the production of stainless steel and in coinage. Norilsk claimed 70 percent of the world's supply of palladium, a PGM used in automotive catalytic converters. Among its producing subsidiaries are the Severonickel Combine, in the Murmansk region, and the Pechenganickel MMC in the Pechenga region. Half a million people in the remote region rely on an economy driven by Norilsk Nickel. The settlement or "company town" of Norilsk is separated from the Russian highway system by 700 miles (470 versts). As a legacy of its communist past, Norilsk maintains extensive social services for area residents, a burden its owners would like to lift by transferring these obligations to the regional government, which itself would prefer to spend any surplus on relocating up to one-third of the population. In late 2001, the Norilsk community was declared off-limits to foreigners, whom local authorities blamed for bringing drugs, crime, and AIDS to the city.

## *Origins*

According to Norilsk Nickel's official history, copper-nickel ore was discovered in the Taimyr Peninsula of northwestern Siberia in the 1600s. It lay undisturbed in the frozen earth for another 300 years. Though estimates vary, Russia consumption of nickel remained small through the 1920s. Most of Russia's industrial efforts were suspended during the Bolshevik Revolution and the following civil war, which lasted until 1921. By 1937, the country was using 9,750 metric tons a year, and much more would be needed to bolster its armed forces. Russia was rich in manganese and chromium, which could be used as substitutes in such wartime uses as electrical wire, armor plating, and armor-piercing ammunition.

Production of nickel was initiated in the Second Five Year Plan. On June 23, 1935, the Council of Peoples' Commissars of the U.S.S.R. passed a resolution to build what would become the Soviet Union's largest mining and metallurgical company (MMC), located 2,000 kilometers north of Krasnoyarsk. The NKVD, or Commissariat of Home Affairs (Soviet security services), was responsible for Stalin's Gulag project; possibly more than 100,000 prisoners died during its construction.

Norilsk was not Russia's first source of indigenous nickel production; in 1934, a plant was established at Verkhnii Ufalei in the Urals, where nickel had been discovered in the last half of the 19th century. The Norilsk combine produced its first copper-nickel matte on March 10, 1939; however, due to its remoteness, it did not truly have operations in force until 1942.

Two more copper and nickel mines, which would be combined with the Norilsk organization during the Gorbachev administration, were located further east, on the Kola Peninsula of European Russia. The Severonickel combine was constructed near Murmansk in 1935. Pechenganickel MMC (formerly Petsamo) was built in 1940 by The International Nickel Company, Inc. (Inco) on territory then held by Finland. Russia took over the land after World War II, paying International Nickel

## Company Perspectives:

*The main principle of the MMC Norilsk Nickel's social policy is to maintain reasonable balance between the interests of the shareholders, the employees, and the state, which would be capable to provide for steady and efficient functioning of the company. Social expenses are considered by the company as investments in its people, which are no less profitable than investments in the production development. In 2000, for example, expenses on the social sphere and the social programs amounted to over 15 billion rubles.*

$20 million for the Pechenganickel operation. Pechenganickel produced about 15,500 metric tons of nickel in 1947.

### *Self-Sufficient in the Cold War*

Russia did not become self-sufficient in nickel until after World War II, when a large copper-nickel area was discovered near Norilsk through extensive exploration. Russia became a major world producer overnight. By 1953, Norilsk accounted for 35 percent of the Soviet Union's nickel production, 12 percent of its copper, 30 percent of its cobalt, and 90 percent of its platinum group metals (PGM's). The Soviet Union as a whole produced an estimated 33,000 tons of nickel in 1950.

Western sources placed total Soviet nickel production at 64,000 tons in 1960. By 1970, the Soviet Union was producing an estimated 110,000 tons of nickel a year, making it second only to Canada. The Soviets were investing more than $1 billion in developing new mines and increasing production capacity. A pipeline was being built to bring natural gas across the Yenisei River from western Siberia.

Norilsk was also a rich source of platinum group metals, particularly palladium. According to one estimate, the region supplied 75 percent of Russia's total PGM output of 2.5 million ounces in 1972.

### *Reorganized 1989*

The Severonickel, Pechenganickel, and Norilsk combines were brought together during perestroika into the State Concern for Non-Ferrous Metals Production Norilsk Nickel, created on November 4, 1989 by a resolution of the Council of Ministers. Also included with the Norilsk, Pechenganickel, and Severonickel combines were the Olenegorsk mechanical works, the Krasnoyarsk nonferrous metal processing works, and the Gipronickel Institute in St. Petersburg (then Leningrad)—the Russian nickel industry's leading research center.

A few years later, the company was privatized. The Russian State Concern for Non-Ferrous Metals Production Norilsk Nickel became a Russian Joint Stock Company (RAO) by presidential decree on June 30, 1993. Its new English name: RAO Norilsk Nickel for the Production of Non-Ferrous and Precious Metals, or RAO Norilsk Nickel for short. Shares were distributed to employees and investors in 1994; the state retained control with 38 percent of equity and 51 percent of the voting shares. After a mortgaging auction, Uneximbank became the nominal holder of these shares.

Norilsk had annual sales of $2 billion a year in the mid-1990s, when it employed about 160,000 workers. A project was being planned to refurbish the Pechenga plant in cooperation with Scandinavian companies (Kvaemer A/S, Elkem A/S and Boliden AB), partly with the aim of reducing Pechenganickel's notorious sulfur dioxide emissions by 95 percent.

### *Privatized in the Late 1990s*

In the last half of the 1990s, Russian businessman Vladimir Potanin, president of the Interros holding company and Uneximbank, acquired control of Norilsk Nickel in what was called a ''loans for shares'' deal with the Russian government. Uneximbank became nominal (managing) holder of a 38 percent controlling interest in Norilsk Nickel in a government auction in November 1995.

The Swift investment group, representing Uneximbank, bought this controlling interest in August 1997, with a bid of more than $270 million. (It and associated companies built up a 42 percent interest within a few years.) The bank promptly installed a new set of managers at the company led by Uneximbank board member Alexander Khloponin. Swift also invested $300 million to develop the Pelyatka condensed gas field near Norilsk, and another Ru 400 billion for social costs.

Net profits fell 32 percent to Ru 826 billion in 1997, though production at the three combines was up 23 percent. Norilsk exported 214,000 tons of nickel that year. Nickel prices plummeted in 1998. This was attributed to the Asian financial crisis as well as Norilsk's own massive export drive. Norilsk Nickel posted a loss of Ru 3.5 billion in the fiscal year ending March 1, 1998. Norilsk faced new low-cost, high-tech competition from Australia in 1999.

Norilsk was considered a high cost producer due to its aging plant and huge 130,000-strong workforce—fewer than half of whom were directly involved in production. The company was paying for medical and social services, housing, and heating for the residents of the community. At the same time, Norilsk was considered Russia's largest tax debtor, owing $2 billion to the federal government. Financial observers and union representatives agreed that up to 80,000 area residents should ideally be relocated to warmer, more economically robust climes. The potential cost for such a relocation project was estimated at $1 billion.

### *2000 and Beyond*

The federal government filed a lawsuit to overturn Norilsk Nickel's privatization in June 2000. Supporters claimed it was rigged to exclude other bidders. Others criticized the efforts to undo the privatization as merely an attempt by politicians to cash in. Revenues were Ru 152.99 billion in 2000, producing a gross profit of Ru 84.4 billion; both figures were up roughly 50 percent from 1999.

During 2001, Norilsk acquired Interros-Prom, including its Norimet Limited metals marketing subsidiary, for shares of Norilsk worth 8.23 billion in indexed rubles. Norilsk reported

## Key Dates:

**1935:** Norilsk Nickel MMC is established.
**1970:** Russia is producing 110,000 metric tons of nickel a year.
**1989:** Severonickel and Pechenganickel combined into Norilsk organization.
**1994:** Uneximbank obtains nominal control of company.
**1997:** Uneximbank buys controlling interest in Norilsk.
**2001:** Norilsk corporate structure is streamlined; Norimet is acquired.

a net profit of Ru 32.9 billion ($1 billion) on revenues of Ru 106.97 billion ($3.4 billion) for 2001, based on Russian Accounting Standards. Around the turn of the millennium, Norilsk officials were developing a plan to use retired Typhoon-class nuclear submarines (called *Akula*—"Shark"—by the Russians) to ship 12,000 tons of nickel each under the arctic ice.

### *Principal Subsidiaries*

Monchebank (54.95%); Baikal Hotel (65.65%); Gornometallurgichesky Kombinat Pechenganickel; Institut Gipronickel; Kolskaya Gornaya Kompaniya; Kombinat Severonickel; Norilsky Kombinat (99.86%); NTPO (99.99%); Olengorsky Mekhanichesky Zavod; Torginvest (90.09%); Interros-Prom; Norilskinvest (Interrosprom); ZAO "Interrosimpex"; Renons.

### *Principal Operating Units*

Arkhangelsk; Intersectoral Industrial Association Zapoliarye; Kolsky; Krasnoyarsk; Sanatorium Complex Beloye Lake; Zapaliarny.

### *Principal Competitors*

Falconbridge Ltd.; Inco Ltd.

### *Further Reading*

Dixon, Robyn, "Arctic City Turning Cold Shoulder to All," *Seattle Times,* November 9, 2001, p. A14.
Fineberg, Seth, "New Managers Aid Norilsk," *American Metal Market,* August 6, 1996, p. 16.
——, "Normaco Wins Norilsk's Trust; Russian Nickel Giant to Give Sales Agent a Bigger Role," *American Metal Market,* August 27, 1996, p. 16.
Forster, Harriet, "Harsh Climate: Norilsk Confronts Nickel Bears," *American Metal Market,* September 1, 1998, p. 7A.
——, "Norilsk Nickel Makes Appeal to Government, Again," *American Metal Market,* February 8, 1999, p. 6.
Franchetti, Mark," *Red October* Subs Put to Work as Freighters," *Sunday Times,* September 10, 2000, p. 24.
Fung, Shirley, "The End of the Road," *Across the Board,* May 1999, p. 72.
Goodwin, Scott, "Investor Group Rattles Legal Saber Over Norilsk Reorg.," *Emerging Markets Week,* December 25, 2000, p. 1.
Kaiser, Robert G., "Norilsk, Stalin's Siberian Hell, Thrives in Spite of Hideous Legacy," *Washington Post,* August 29, 2001, p. C1.
Kaiser, Robert G., "Thriving Citizens Swear by Polluted Siberian Outpost," *Pittsburgh Post-Gazette,* September 10, 2001, p. A1.
Kotov, Vladimir, and Elena Nikitina, "Norilsk Nickel," *Environment,* November 1996, pp. 6ff.
Pala, Christopher, "And Now for the Really Big One," *Bulletin of the Atomic Scientists,* March/April 2001, pp. 20+.
"Putin Descends Into Mine in Siberia," *Daily News Bulletin* (Moscow), March 24, 2002, p. 1.
Shimkin, Demitri B., *Minerals: A Key to Soviet Power,* Cambridge, Mass.: Harvard University Press, 1953.
Smith, A.P., "Investors Get Norilsk Role as ADR Shares Go Public," *American Metal Market,* June 21, 2001, p. 1.
"Socialism in One Company," *Economist,* January 10, 1998, pp. 58–59.
Sutulov, Alexander, *Mineral Resources and the Economy of the USSR,* New York: *Engineering & Mining Journal,* McGraw-Hill, 1973.
——, *The Soviet Challenge in Base Metals,* Salt Lake City: University of Utah, 1971.
"Top Court Deals Blow to Norilsk," *Moscow Times,* April 30, 2002, p. 5.
White, Gregory, and Alan S. Cullison, "Norilsk Appears Frozen in Soviet Past; Russia Taps New Managers to Force Thaw," *Wall Street Journal Europe,* April 16, 1996, p. 4.
Whittell, Giles, "Mining Giant Digs in for Kremlin Battle," *Times* (London), July 14, 2000, p. 14.

—Frederick C. Ingram

# Northeast Utilities

**174 Brush Hill Avenue**
**Berlin, Connecticut 01090-2010**
**PO Box 270**
**Hartford, Connecticut 06141-0270**
**U.S.A.**
**Telephone: (860) 665-5000**
**Toll Free: (800) 286-2000; (800) 286-5000**
**Fax: (860) 665-5418**
**Web site: http://www.nu.com**

*Public Company*
*Incorporated:* 1927 as Western Massachusetts Companies
*Employees:* 7,520
*Sales:* $10.24 billion (2001)
*Stock Exchanges:* New York
*Ticker Symbol:* NU
*NAIC:* 221122 Electric Power Generation, Transmission and Distribution; 22121 Natural Gas Distribution; 551112 Offices of Other Holding Companies

Northeast Utilities (NU) is New England's largest utility company. NU serves 1.8 million electricity customers in Connecticut, Massachusetts, and New Hampshire. Its Yankee Energy System supplies nearly 200,000 customers in Connecticut with natural gas.

### *Origins*

In 1966, Northeast Utilities was formed by combining Western Massachusetts Electric Company with Connecticut Light and Power Company and Hartford Electric Light Company. Western Massachusetts Companies, a voluntary association, had been organized in 1927 to acquire 11 utility companies in western Massachusetts. These were subsequently consolidated into Western Massachusetts Electric Company (WMECO), based in Springfield, Massachusetts. The company added Huntington Electric Light Company to its holdings in 1959.

An early NU project, begun in 1968, was the construction of a million-kilowatt, $72 million pumped-storage hydroelectric power project on the Connecticut River in Franklin County, Massachusetts. In a pumped-storage system, power is produced from high-elevation lakes during high demand periods; during less busy times, the water is pumped back to the high elevation.

### *Energy Alternatives for the 1970s*

Lelan F. Sillin, Jr., became president of NU in April 1968. Sillin was committed to developing New England's use of nuclear power. The region's electricity prices were higher than the national average, and Sillin viewed nuclear power as the least expensive, most efficient, and cleanest energy option. In 1973, NU generated 24 percent of its energy from nuclear units. By 1974, it was 33 percent, and by 1980 nuclear energy supplied almost half the company's requirements. As of 1992 nuclear power accounted for 60 percent of NU's energy needs.

Before joining the holding company, the individual utilities had invested together in four nuclear plants in New England known as the Yankee Rowe, Vermont Yankee, Maine Yankee, and Connecticut Yankee plants. NU added its Millstone Point nuclear power station, whose first unit went into commercial operation in 1970. Its second unit was completed in 1975. Millstone Point Company was established to construct and operate these two units. In 1972, the company launched a new program for nuclear fuel financing in which the fuel itself served as security on long-term debt. Plans for a third Millstone unit were set in 1975, and two more installations were planned for Montague, Massachusetts.

During the 1970s, the Middle East oil embargo, escalating inflation, and rising construction cost and time requirements began eroding NU's financial viability. The Montague units, originally set for 1981 and 1983, were rescheduled to start up in 1988 and 1992, and the third Millstone unit's in-service date was first pushed up from 1978 to 1980, then to 1982, and finally to 1986 to reduce the company's financial burden. The delay in the Millstone unit, along with inflation and regulatory requirements, increased its cost from $400 million to $2.49 billion. The company decreased its overall building budget by $2.5 billion from 1974 to 1982.

The 1970s were punctuated by annual tussles with the regulatory boards in Connecticut and Massachusetts. In all, the

**Company Perspectives:**

*Our Vision is clear: we're focused on becoming the leading energy delivery and marketing company in the Northeast region. Our approach to growth is a balanced one—concentrating on what we do well, not trying to be all things to all markets. We're focused on the 11-state geographic region where 25 percent of the nation's energy is consumed. Our strategy is standing the test of time. Continuing to deliver on a path set several years ago is a testament to the strength of our vision and our team.*

company filed eight rate increase requests in Connecticut and six in Massachusetts. Never successful in obtaining its full request, NU averaged about 51 percent of the total amount applied for. In 1976, for instance, the Connecticut regulatory commission answered the company's request for a $56 million increase with a rate reduction of $22 million.

The company had borrowed all that it could under federal laws by 1976 but still did not have enough money to remain financially stable. NU stock fell from 120 percent of book value in 1970 to 65 percent in 1981, and bond ratings deteriorated from AA to BAA standing in the same period.

### *Recovery in the 1980s*

By the early 1980s, NU had revamped its demand outlook considerably. In 1970, it had anticipated a decade of growth at 9 percent per year, and intended to build 6,238 megawatts of capacity, but the company actually experienced cumulative growth of only 25 percent during the entire decade and added only 2,813 megawatts of capacity. By 1980, its projected annual growth rate was reduced to just 1.7 percent with a target zone of no more than 1.5 percent annually.

NU would change its direction during the 1980s, largely due to its new chief executive officer, William B. Ellis. At Sillin's behest, Ellis left the consulting firm of McKinsey & Co. in 1976 to become NU's chief financial officer. In that year, total income was $85 million on revenues of $830 million. Two years later he was named president, and in 1983 he became chief executive officer. By 1982, revenues were up to $1.8 billion, but income had risen to only $151 million; by 1986, however, margins had improved, with sales of $2 billion and income of $300.9 million.

Ellis was able to create a more friendly relationship with regulators, one of his most successful negotiations being the Connecticut rate case settlement of 1986, the year Millstone's third unit came into full production. NU initially requested a $155.5 million increase, $133 million of which would go toward the Millstone unit's expenses. The request was denied, and the state ordered NU to put $46.5 million in a fund to offset rate increases in 1987. NU sued to protest the state's demand for this fund; eventually, in an out-of-court settlement, the state agreed to restore this amount, as well as to allow a rate increase phased in over five years, beginning in 1988, to cover Millstone. NU's Connecticut Light and Power subsidiary agreed not to ask for any more rate increases until 1988.

NU's financial recovery strategy also included a massive conservation effort. The utility planned to reduce all energy consumption, especially oil-generated energy. Oil-based production, already reduced from 74 percent in 1973 to 47 percent in 1980, was to be 10 percent by 1987. The Massachusetts legislature and the regulatory commissions of both Connecticut and Massachusetts allowed the company to use two-thirds of the fuel-cost savings to fund the conversion of facilities from oil- to coal-burning. The other third was passed on to customers immediately. The Mt. Tom plant was converted to coal in 1981 at a cost of about $35 million, recovered through oil-cost savings in about three years. The company planned to convert seven more plants, which originally had been oil-burning units but were switched to coal in 1971 in order to meet more stringent air pollution-control standards.

Other conservation efforts included ongoing research on "fuel cells," modular plants that cleanly and efficiently converted various fuels directly into electricity without burning them. NU also gave conservation tips to customers and gave school districts rebates for switching to energy-efficient equipment, such as fluorescent rather than incandescent lighting.

Despite these efforts, Connecticut regulators ruled during a 1988 rate-increase hearing that NU must greatly expand its conservation efforts. The company subsequently put up $250,000 to fund a collaborative project between itself, on the one hand, and, on the other, the Conservation Law Foundation of New England and attorneys general, consumer counsels, and other agencies in Massachusetts and Connecticut. The first project began in Connecticut in February 1988, and a multi-utility process followed in Massachusetts, with WMECO as a participant. This effort identified new areas for conservation by bringing the company into closer contact with the communities it served; for example, a conservation program for public housing projects was a result of the process.

### *Changes and Crises in the 1990s*

In April 1990, NU took over management of Public Service Company of New Hampshire (PSNH), which had filed for bankruptcy in 1988, substantially because of its investment in the Seabrook nuclear power plant. NU offered to buy PSNH outright, and PSNH accepted pending regulatory approval. In late 1991, the companies were awaiting approval from the Nuclear Regulatory Commission, the Federal Energy Regulatory Commission, and the Connecticut Department of Public Utility Control. With NU's purchase of PSNH's stock, valued at $750 million, and assumption of its liabilities, the deal's total price was $2.36 billion. The company would have enough capacity to sell over $100 million worth of excess electricity to other utilities each year. NU projected $516 million in savings from its management and operation of PSNH and Seabrook. The addition of Seabrook would eliminate the need for significant construction during the next decade.

The NU/PSNH merger was approved in spite of anticompetitive concerns from other utilities in the region. In another sweeping change, the Energy Policy Act was passed in 1992, allowed utilities to compete for wholesale customers. NU's most difficult challenges were just around the corner.

## Key Dates:

**1927:** Western Massachusetts Companies is formed.
**1959:** Western Massachusetts Electric Company (WMECO) acquires Huntington Electric Light Co.
**1966:** WMECO and Connecticut Light and Power join to form Northeast Utilities (NU).
**1970:** Millstone Point nuclear power station goes into operation.
**1990:** NU takes over Public Service Company of New Hampshire (PSNH).
**1992:** The Energy Policy Act is passed.
**1996:** Three of NU's four Connecticut nuclear plants shut down.
**1999:** NU enters natural gas business through Yankee Energy System acquisition.
**2001:** Planned Con Ed acquisition of NU falls through.

In May 1992, one of NU's nuclear plants went offline for seven months, costing the company $190 million. This problem recurred in late 1995 and 1996, when the Nuclear Regulatory Commission shut down NU's Millstone and Connecticut Yankee plants. By March 1996, Connecticut Yankee was closed, never to reopen, and two of the three remaining Connecticut plants (one partially-owned) were offline, costing NU $30 million a month for replacement power.

In September 1996, NU hired former South Carolina Electric & Gas Co. chief Bruce D. Kenyon to head its nuclear operations. At the time, only one of NU's five nuclear plants, PSNH-run Seabrook, was operating. Deregulation and the huge costs associated with fixing its nuclear plants dropped net income to $1.8 million in 1996 from $282.4 million the previous year.

Bernard Fox, chairman since 1987 and CEO since 1993, retired in the summer of 1997. He was succeeded by Michael G. Morris, former president and chief executive officer of Consumers Energy, the principal subsidiary of CMS Energy. In the late 1990s, NU sold off most of its fossil fuel and hydroelectric power plants in Connecticut and Massachusetts. The Millstone plants were also divested; Dominion Nuclear Connecticut took over operations there in April 2001. NU's regulated business became a ''wire and pipe'' operation concerned with the transmission and distribution of energy.

NU was broadening its offerings in response to the new competitive environment. Its unregulated, or ''competitive,'' businesses included Select Energy, Inc., New England's largest energy marketer; Select Energy Services, Inc. (formerly HEC Inc.), an energy engineering firm; Northeast Generation Company; Northeast Generation Services Company; and high-speed telecom specialist Mode 1 Communications.

NU acquired Yankee Energy System in the summer of 1999. It paid $478 million in cash and stock and agreed to assume $201 million of its debt. Yankee Energy, though its Yankee Gas Services Company subsidiary, was a large, modern natural gas distributor serving 183,000 customers in Connecticut.

In the last half of 1999, Consolidated Edison Inc. was preparing to acquire NU in a bid to become a national reseller of electricity. Con Ed, a power company with 3 million customers, was paying $3.3 billion in cash and stock and assuming more than $4 billion of debt in the deal.

The merger dragged on through 2000 without being finalized. It ultimately disintegrated into a courtroom brawl. The two parties sued each other for breach of contract; NU sought $1 billion to compensate for the value lost by its shareholders.

In 2001 and 2002, NU was aiming to grow the unregulated side of its business as the potential for profits for regulated service dwindled. Select Energy, NU's marketing subsidiary, was the default electric provider for Connecticut Light & Power customers but was losing money on the contract. Nevertheless, the unit was able to post a $30 million profit in 2000. NU's telecom subsidiary, Mode 1 Communications, was investing in a 28-mile fiber optic ring in downtown Hartford, Connecticut.

### *Principal Subsidiaries*

The Connecticut Light and Power Company (CL&P); Mode 1 Communications, Inc.; NorConn Properties, Inc.; North Atlantic Energy Corporation (NAEC); North Atlantic Energy Service Corporation (NAESCO); Northeast Generation Company; Northeast Generation Services Company; Northeast Utilities Service Company (NUSCO); NU Enterprises, Inc.; Properties Inc.; Public Service Company of New Hampshire (PSNH); The Quinnehtuk Company; The Rocky River Realty Company; Select Energy, Inc.; Select Energy New York, Inc.; Select Energy Services, Inc.; Western Massachusetts Electric Company (WMECO); Yankee Gas Services Company.

### *Principal Divisions*

Regulated Businesses; Unregulated Businesses.

### *Principal Operating Units*

Transmission; Generation.

### *Principal Competitors*

Energy East Corporation; National Grid USA; NiSource Inc.

### *Further Reading*


Burkhart, Lori A., ''Northeast Utilities Fights Back,'' *Public Utilities Fortnightly* (Arlington), April 15, 1997, p. 43.

Campbell, Tricia, ''Get Plugged In: Service with a :-),'' *Sales and Marketing Management,* March 1999, pp. 62–8.

*Celebrating Our 35th Anniversary: Diversity Fuels Our Success,* Berlin, CT: Northeast Utilities, June 2001.

Choiniere, Paul, ''Another Familiar Face Returns to Waterford, Conn.-Area Utility,'' *The Day* (New London, Conn.), December 13, 2001.

Christie, Claudia M., ''Businessperson of the Year. William B. Ellis: An Expectation of Excellence,'' *New England Business*, December 7, 1987.

David, Gregory E., ''Power Player,'' *Financial World,* September 27, 1994, p. 26.

Fitts, Stuart, ''Creative Use of Technology at Northeast Utilities,'' *TMA Journal,* July/August 1996, p. 5.

Geehern, Christopher, ''Regional Power,'' *New England Business*, January 1991.

''Green Power?,'' *New Hampshire Business Review,* May 23, 1997.

Irwin, Patricia, ''Northeast Utilities: A Utility That's Not Ready for Competition,'' *Electrical World,* October 1996, p. 29.

Jackson, Susan, ''The Millstones Around NU's Neck,'' *Business Week,* December 2, 1996, p. 80.

Madden, Don, ''PSNH Would Change 'The Deal'—If Someone Would Talk,'' *New Hampshire Business Review,* March 1, 1996.

Murphy, John R., ''An RBD Case: Northeast Utilities,'' *Training,* May 1997, pp. 60–1.

Pooley, Eric, ''Nuclear Safety Fallout,'' *Time,* March 17, 1997, pp. 34–6.

——, ''Nuclear Warriors,'' *Time,* March 4, 1996, p. 46.

Salpukas, Agis, ''Con Edison Buying a Neighbor Utility for $3.29 Billion,'' *New York Times,* October 13, 1999, p. 1.

——, ''A Conservative Con Ed Makes a Bold Move,'' *New York Times,* October 14, 1999, p. 2.

Scarponi, Diane, ''Utility Challenged, Must Grow Deregulated Profits,'' *Marketing News,* November 19, 2001, p. 25.

Sillin, Lelan F., Jr., ''Managing Utilities in an Inflationary Economy,'' *Public Utilities Fortnightly,* April 1, 1982.

Troutman, Josh, ''Partnership Solves Power Shortage,'' *Power Engineering,* October 1997.

Waxler, Caroline, ''Power Outage,'' *Forbes,* December 30, 1996, p. 163.

Weil, Gordon L., ''Requiem for a Heavyweight,'' *Public Utilities Fortnightly* (Washington), July 15, 1993, p. 18.

Zielbauer, Paul, ''A Faltering Utility Deal's Effects Are Debated,'' *New York Times,* March 7, 2001, p. B8.

—Elaine Belsito
—update: Frederick C. Ingram

# optioncare®

# Option Care Inc.

**100 Corporate North, Suite 212**
**Bannockburn, Illinois 60015**
**U.S.A.**
**Telephone: (847) 615-1690**
**Toll Free: (800) 879-6137**
**Fax: (847) 615-1794**
**Web site: http://www.optioncare.com**

*Public Company*
*Incorporated:* 1984
*Employees:* 1,202
*Sales:* $141.3 million (2000)
*Stock Exchanges:* NASDAQ
*Ticker Symbol:* OPTN
*NAIC:* 621610 Home Health Care Services

Bannockburn, Illinois-based Option Care Inc. provides specialty pharmacy services and infusion (IV) therapy to people in their homes through contracts with managed care organizations, hospitals, physicians, and other healthcare providers. In the early 2000s, the firm operated a network of 130 pharmacies—27 of which were company-owned and 103 of which were franchises—and two specialty distribution centers. While Option Care is a national operation, most of the company's locations are situated in the eastern half of the United States. Option Care's wholly owned subsidiary, OptionMed, contracts with managed care companies and physicians to provide injectable drugs and consulting services. A second subsidiary, Management By Information Inc., develops software applications for the home infusion business that automate different functions, including clinical documentation, distribution, financing, and marketing.

## *Beginnings*

Although Option Care had become a large, public corporation by the early 2000s, the firm had humble beginnings. Michael Prime and Mitchell Hoggard, two California pharmacists, founded Option Care in 1979. At the time, Prime was part owner of the oldest retail pharmacy in Chico, California, and Hoggard was a pharmacist at a small community hospital 50 miles north of Chico.

The catalyst for Option Care's creation started with the needs of one patient—a young man who, because of injuries suffered in a car accident, required daily nutritional feedings by means of infusion through an intravenous catheter. At the time, the patient went to the hospital every day, seven days a week, to pick up sterilely prepared solutions that he administered at his home through a central line catheter to his heart. Via a pump, the solutions would take 12 hours to infuse. To improve the young man's quality of life, Hoggard proposed that his hospital prepare and deliver seven-day supplies of the solutions to the man's home. When the hospital's administration refused, Hoggard and Prime considered providing the service on their own.

Within two weeks, Hoggard and Prime had secured permission from the young man, his doctor at the UC Davis Medical Center in Sacramento, and the patient's insurance carrier to provide the service. After they found a pharmaceutical company that would sell them the necessary medications and solutions and purchased the equipment necessary for the aseptic (sterile) preparation of the solutions, the two pharmacists found a location for their new enterprise.

## *Clinical Development: 1980–84*

By February 1980, the new facility had obtained a license, and Hoggard and Prime had formed a legal partnership. Operating under the company name CliniCare, they began preparing their first solutions. After submitting their first bill to the insurance carrier in April, the progressive pharmacists soon received another referral from their initial patient's doctor. They were on their way to trail-blazing a new healthcare industry segment.

In 1981, after Hoggard and Prime became comfortable servicing their first two patients, they began marketing their services to Chico-area physicians, positioning themselves as a home care company with a cheaper alternative to hospital care. As a result, the company began receiving more referrals to provide patients with total parenteral nutrition (TPN), or sterile nutritional intravenous solutions administered through a central line into a patient's heart. After learning everything they could about the care of the

### Company Perspectives:

*Our clinically-focused trained staff works with the patient, the patient's physician, and the national, regional, or local managed care organization to provide a simple, single solution for patient care.*

catheters and the maintenance of the infusion pumps being used, the pharmacists began receiving referrals from area physicians to provide intravenous antibiotics, chemotherapy, hydration, pain control, and enteral feedings.

The scope and complexity of CliniCare's services continued to increase. Physicians expected the company to train patients or family members in the administration and care of different therapies. Accordingly, CliniCare began to hire staff, adding its first nurse by the end of 1981 and a second nurse midway through the following year. It also became necessary for policies and procedures to be developed for clinical operations and the various therapies the company was providing. Hoggard and Prime brought on a minority partner named Tom Vickery, a clinical hospital pharmacist who could help to bring the services of pharmacy and nursing together. By the end of 1981, Prime was concentrating on patient care while Hoggard concentrated on marketing and future growth. Vickery, who lived near Sacramento and continued to work at his hospital pharmacy job, mainly acted as a consultant. By the end of 1982, policy and procedure manuals were completed, and CliniCare had developed training manuals for every therapy it advertised.

The firm began to develop license agreements in 1983 and by year's end had four locations up and running. Three were in California (Sacramento, Fresno, and Auburn) and one in Vancouver, Washington. When it was discovered that the name CliniCare could not be registered, the company's name was changed and registered as O.P.T.I.O.N. (Outpatient Parenteral Therapy and Intravenous Ongoing Nutrition) Care.

Toward the end of 1983 Sutter Community Hospital of Sacramento approached Option Care about a potential joint venture. They argued that, with Sutter's capital and resources, Option Care could develop a national franchise document and implement a marketing/development strategy. In April 1984, Option Care sold two-thirds of the company to Sutter Community Hospital.

"My fondest memories of this era are the patient care," recalled Michael Prime in an interview with the author. "Without a doubt, the greatest accomplishment during this period was our consistency of high quality patient care. Our physicians and patients loved us. All of our referrals at this time came by word-of-mouth. With one of my nurses, I personally trained every patient we had. I compounded and delivered all the supplies and medications. More than once I spent with them their first night home from the hospital until they became comfortable with their therapy. I firmly believe our main attraction to new franchises was our philosophy toward patient care."

### *Franchises: 1984–90*

The majority of Option Care's franchise growth occurred from 1984 to 1990. An offering circular and franchise document was created and the firm converted its four license arrangements to franchises. Hoggard and Vickery began to market Option Care nationally and realized much success by speaking at state pharmacy association meetings. The franchise document required that the pharmacist owner and his or her primary nurse had to be trained by Option Care in Chico, California, prior to opening their business.

Option Care's franchises started to grow in numbers. In 1984, the firm opened six new franchises. In 1985, two full-time franchise salespeople were hired and Option Care started to advertise in national pharmaceutical and nursing magazines. That same year, the company added approximately 20 new franchises. In 1986, approximately 30 franchises joined the Option Care family, followed by about 60 in 1987. By 1989, Option Care had more than 215 franchises in 42 states. Training took place in Chico every other week. Staff grew from a mere handful in 1984 to more than 150 in 1989.

During the mid- to late 1980s, competition began to heat up as the home infusion market exploded. There was no limit on what a company could charge for a therapy, and more than 24 national companies and hundreds of independents appeared. According to Prime, Option Care always maintained a consistent and conservative pricing structure. This became important in the late 1980s, when Medicare and Medicaid began to ratchet down their allowances, and especially in the early 1990s, when managed care took hold. Although competition was fierce during this time, Option Care was the only firm with a franchise concept.

By 1988, Sutter had appointed Hoggard as president of Option Care. Prime hired a replacement for his Chico patient care responsibilities and became vice-president of pharmacy operations and franchise relations. Vickery was named vice-president of franchise operations. Prime continued franchise training in Chico and also traveled around the country to a growing number of franchise locations to develop a national network and professional relationships.

It was during the late 1980s that Dr. John N. Kapoor and his investment company, EJ Financial, began to display interest in Option Care as a network. With a background in the pharmaceutical manufacturing industry, Kapoor saw potential in Option Care's network as a distribution vehicle. A native of Amristar, India, Kapoor pursued undergraduate education at the University of Bombay and came to the United States in 1964 at the age of 21. In 1970, he received a doctorate degree in medicinal chemistry from the State University of New York. He started his career with a New York-based pharmaceutical company. By 1978, he had become vice-president and general manager of Lypho-Med Inc., a division of Chicago's Stone Container Corporation. He was named president of Lypho-Med in 1980. The following year, Kapoor spent $24,000 of his own money, along with venture capital, to purchase Lypho-Med for $2 million. Kapoor became chairman of the firm, which was re-named LyphoMed Inc. The firm's sales totaled $6 million in 1981. LyphoMed went public in 1983 and by 1989 had become the nation's largest generic drug company, with sales of $159 million. Kapoor sold LyphoMed to Fujisawa Pharmaceutical Co. Ltd. of Japan in 1990. According to *Crain's Chicago Business*, the value of Kapoor's investment had grown to $130

### Key Dates:

**1979:** Michael Prime and Mitchell Hoggard, two California pharmacists, found the company that will become Option Care.
**1980:** Hoggard and Prime form a legal partnership, operating under the company name CliniCare.
**1983:** CliniCare begins to develop license agreements and changes its name to O.P.T.I.O.N. (Outpatient Parenteral Therapy and Intravenous Ongoing Nutrition) Care.
**1984:** Option Care sells two-thirds of the company to Sutter Community Hospital.
**1985:** Option Care hires two full-time franchise salespeople and begins advertising in national pharmaceutical and nursing magazines.
**1987:** Option Care adds approximately 60 franchises.
**1989:** Option Care has more than 215 franchises in 42 states and staff grows to more than 150 employees.
**1992:** Company goes public.
**1996:** Option Care acquires home healthcare industry software company Management By Information Inc.
**2000:** Option Care launches OptionMed, its specialty pharmacy and distribution company.

million at the time of the sale. Kapoor used his windfall to form venture capital firm EJ Financial Enterprises Inc., which would develop interests in a wide variety of different healthcare ventures over the years.

In October 1990, Sutter sold its interest to Kapoor's EJ Financial. In the end, Kapoor had obtained an 80 percent stake in Option Care for $22.4 million and Hoggard, Prime, and Vickery remained as minority owner-operators. In the July 29, 1991 issue of *Crain's Chicago Business*, Kapoor called the purchase his "biggest investment to date."

## *A Time of Change: 1990–92*

A period of change would unfold between October 1990 and April 1992. Although the original partners remained for a time, Hoggard resigned in February 1991 and sold his stock to Kapoor. Prime unofficially became the man in charge in Chico. Since EJ Financial was located in Lake Forest, Illinois, Kapoor wanted Option Care's management team in northern Chicago. He brought a new chief financial officer on board, who relocated from EJ Financial, and in May 1991 hired Sheldon "Shelly" Asher as the new president and CEO of Option Care. When he joined Option Care, Asher gave up his role as executive vice-president of Caremark Homecare Inc., a subsidiary of Baxter International Inc. that was one of Option Care's major competitors. In the September 30, 1991 issue of *Crain's Chicago Business*, Asher indicated that Option Care's strategy would be to target rural regions with populations of less than 300,000 people, which bigger players like Caremark had not targeted. Supporting this strategy were 180 Option Care franchises in rural markets.

In July 1991, Asher leased new office space for Option Care in Bannockburn, Illinois. Around the same time, Vickery resigned. By October Asher began to transfer the company's departments from Chico to Bannockburn. By the year's end all departments were relocated to Illinois except for clinical services, franchise training, franchise sales, and Chico patient care. Prime remained in charge of what remained in Chico, along with his franchise relations role. In the 1990s, after managed care took hold, Option Care and many of its franchises began to explore relationships with home health care agencies, which was more cost effective than maintaining a nursing staff. The company went public in April 1992.

## *After the IPO: 1993–2000*

After Option Care went public, the following seven or eight years would bring many challenges. A leading challenge involved Option Care's franchise-based business model. Balancing the interests and opinions of management, franchise owners, and stockholders was not always easy. Things also were difficult on the financial front. In 1993, Option Care's revenues reached $50.2 million. However, heavy pricing pressure caused the firm's income to fall by 95 percent late in the year. Revenues reached $59.4 million in 1994, but the company posted a $2 million loss, most of which stemmed from failed ventures in the areas of computer software and women's healthcare.

The early 1990s were characterized by many management changes. Asher resigned as Option Care's CEO in the summer of 1993. In his place, Kapoor hired Dave Anderson as chief operating officer. However, Anderson resigned after holding the position for less than a year. Option Care's next president and CEO was Erick "Rick" Hanson, who had served as Option Care's senior vice-president and had spent time with competitor Caremark International Inc., as well as Blue Cross-Blue Shield of Indiana.

Option Care's focus on the rural market was still going strong in 1995. By that time, the wide profit margins infusion once enjoyed had disappeared. In 1996, Option Care started to buy back some of its franchises and later began acquiring other competing firms and forging strategic alliances. That year, it added ten new home infusion firms to the fold. It also was in 1996 that Option Care acquired a home healthcare industry software company called Management By Information Inc. and began to focus on contracts with large HMO's and self-insured companies.

Michael Rusnak became Option Care's president and CEO in 1998. Rusnak had joined the company in 1997 and was serving as chief operating officer before the promotion. During his tenure, Rusnak focused on making Option Care a more profitable firm by concentrating on its primary business. Subsequently, in 1999 Option Care turned a profit of $4.6 million on revenues of $119.8 million. This followed a net loss of $691,000 on revenues of $114.4 million in 1998. As *Crain's Chicago Business* explained, "The company's major turnaround strategy included exiting low-margin businesses, improving distribution channels, operating more efficiently, improving contracts with customers, collecting unpaid bills and reducing debt."

## *Poised for Success in the New Century*

In 2000, Option Care launched a specialty pharmacy and distribution subsidiary called OptionMed. According to Option

Care, the purpose of the new operation was to "contract with managed care organizations and physician groups to provide biotech injectable drugs and provide pharmacy consulting services directly to physicians and patients." At that time, Option Care was building an e-commerce strategy in both the business-to-consumer and business-to-business arenas. It also was in 2000 that Option Care secured an additional $15 million in credit, giving the firm a total of $40 million for future acquisitions. Option care ended 2000 on a high note, reporting record revenues of $141.3 million and record earnings of $7.5 million.

In spring of 2001, Raj Rai was named CEO of Option Care. Rai joined Option Care in 1992 and held various positions in the areas of corporate finance and operations, including senior vice-president and executive vice-president. He became COO in August 1999 and assumed the additional role of president in June of 2000 after Rusnak left the company. Prior to becoming CEO, Rai was largely responsible for "double-digit growth in revenue and profit for the company's owned locations," according to a company news release. During 2001, Option Care continued to expand. One major acquisition involved Healix Health Services Inc. in November, which strengthened the company's foothold in Texas and bolstered its respiratory therapy services.

Although Option Care and the healthcare industry changed significantly since the company was established in 1979, co-founder Mike Prime, who retired in 1998, felt that many of the basic principals upon which the Option Care was founded still existed in the early 2000s. At that time, the patients Option Care served remained a focal point and many of the clinical staff from the firm's earlier years remained on-board.

### *Principal Subsidiaries*

OptionMed; Management by Information Inc.

### *Principal Competitors*

Apria Healthcare Group Inc.; Home Health Corporation of America Inc.; Lincare Holdings Inc.

### *Further Reading*


Arndorfer, James B., "Not Just Tech Firms Seeing Shares Rise: Better Performance Drives Option Care, Focal Gains," *Crain's Chicago Business*, April 10, 2000, p. 68.

Littman, Margaret, "Veteran Entrepreneurs Share Their Secrets," *Crain's Chicago Business*, October 22, 2001.

Murphy, H. Lee., "Option Care Prescribes Big Dose of Expansion," *Crain's Chicago Business*, June 19, 1995.

Oloroso, Arsenio, Jr., "Comings and Goings; CEO to Boost Health Firm's Home Base," *Crain's Chicago Business*, May 6, 1996.

——, "Former Baxter Exec Takes Reins at New Home Health Care Firm," *Crain's Chicago Business*, September 30, 1991, p. 35.

——, "In Health Care, He's Everywhere," *Crain's Chicago Business*, February 20, 1995.

Shepherd, Gary, "AvMed Enlists Illinois Firm to Help With Care, Equipment," *Tampa Bay Business Journal*, October 1, 1999, p. 18.

"Small Health Care Firm Weighs IPO," *Crain's Chicago Business*, November 18, 1991, p. 50.

"Welcome Back, Mr. Kapoor," *Crain's Chicago Business*, July 29, 1991.


—Paul R. Greenland

# Pan-American Life Insurance Company

**601 Poydras Street**
**New Orleans, Louisiana 70130**
**U.S.A.**
**Telephone: (504) 566-1300**
**Fax: (504) 566-3950**
**Web sites: http://www.wewill4u.com;**
**http://www.401k4u.com**

*Mutual Company*
*Incorporated:* 1911
*Employees:* 1,100
*Sales:* $280.9 million (2001)
*NAIC:* 524113 Direct Life Insurance Carriers

Founded in 1911, Pan-American Life Insurance Company (PALIC) is a venerable mutual insurance company headquartered in New Orleans, where it owns the 29-story Pan-American building and the Hotel Inter-Continental. It is an international financial services company and one of the leading insurance underwriters in Latin America, with affiliates in Panama, Guatemala, and Columbia, and branch offices in Ecuador, El Salvador, and Honduras. In Puerto Rico and some Latin American countries, it is the oldest surviving provider of security products. In addition, ranked among the top 30 mutual life insurance companies in the United States, it is a major domestic firm and is licensed in 42 states plus the District of Columbia, Puerto Rico, and the Virgin Islands. It currently maintains 16 branch locations in nine states. PALIC has amassed $2.2 billion in assets and claims a surplus or net worth of $243 million, making it New Orleans' top ranked private business. Having recently withdrawn from the healthcare insurance market, the firm now concentrates on individual and group life insurance, retirement plans, and investment products. Through its wholly owned subsidiary, Pan-American Financial Advisers Inc., it offers all brokerage and investment counseling services under such program names as IRA4u and TopHat4u and also sponsors 401k4u.com, an Internet site offering retirement information. Because of its long history of underwriting insurance in Spanish-speaking countries and territories, PALIC has a distinct market advantage among the growing number of Hispanic Americans in California and the Gulf and eastern seaboard states, and in recent years it has worked energetically to make significant gains in that special sector of the insurance market. Celebrating its 90th anniversary in 2001, Pan-American also began new advertising and marketing initiatives designed to enhance the company's image in the domestic market and particularly in its home city of New Orleans.

### *Early 20th-Century Beginnings*

In 1910, Crawford Ellis, president of the New Orleans-based United Fruit Co., faced what seemed an insurmountable problem: how to provide insurance for his company's employees who worked and lived in Central America. For decades, United Fruit had been importing bananas and other fresh fruits from Caribbean countries, a lucrative enterprise and one that had put the company in the front rank in America's fledgling export-import trade with Latin America. In fact, by the beginning of the 20th century, United Fruit had established something of a dynasty. Its ships regularly crisscrossed the Caribbean, carrying bananas to the United States and returning to Central America with sundry export goods. In the process, United Fruit had invested millions in such countries as Honduras and Guatemala, where its overseers ran plantations and the company employed, not just U.S. citizens, but thousands of native workers.

From a later perspective, it might seem that United Fruit was engaged in a highly exploitive venture, but the truth is that it was doing many things to help the people of the countries with which it was trading. It built roads and bridges and helped fund banks and utility companies. Moreover, it brought thousands of Central American immigrants to the United States, paying for their formal education and helping them adjust to their new life. That the company's impact was lasting is attested to by the fact that by the late 1990s, an estimated 100,000 people of Honduran descent were living in the New Orleans region; most of them could acknowledge the role played by United Fruit in bringing their families to the United States.

Back in 1910, however, insuring its native and U.S. workers in Central America had become a major stumbling block for

**Company Perspectives:**

*We Will—It's the purest expression of what we do. It represents our commitment, our goals, and our vision. It is who we are. We will help people secure their financial futures. We will help companies find financial solutions for their employees. We will provide peace of mind through personal and financial performance. It's nothing new for a company to say that it will do what it says it will do. What's new is actually doing it, and doing it well. That's performance. And performance is contagious. Anyone can make empty promises. But, like you, we're not satisfied being just anyone. Performance just got better. We will.*

United Fruit. Given the political turmoil and revolutionary climate of the Caribbean nations, U.S. insurance companies were adamant in their unwillingness to underwrite policies for persons working there, and the widely scattered Latin American insurance carriers offered only very limited help. Such was the quandary facing United Fruit.

As it turned out, luck was with Ellis. Right at the time that United Fruit's problem reached a critical stage, he met E.G. Simmons, an itinerant physician who was visiting New Orleans on his sojourn through the South. A man with a vision, Simmons had been traveling across the region, making contacts in an effort to start up and fund insurance companies. He had already created one in Texas and was looking for new opportunities in Louisiana. After Ellis explained United Fruit's problem to Simmons, the two men set out to form a group of local investors willing to fund a new insurance company that had a core obligation to underwrite insurance policies for the employees of United Fruit no matter where they worked. The two men soon joined forces with Marion Souchon, a physician on the staff of the Tulane University School of Medicine, and Eugene McGivney, a New Orleans attorney. With some other investors, these men raised $1 million to start up Pan-American Life.

## *1910–90: Eighty Years of Progress*

The next year, the new company began writing policies in Central America, and within a couple of years was doing business in every Central American country except Costa Rica, where restrictive laws prohibited the underwriting of insurance by foreign-owned companies. When the Central American markets reached their maximum growth, Pan-American moved into South America, writing policies in Columbia and Ecuador. Then it ventured into the Caribbean basin, operating in Cuba, the Dominican Republic, Puerto Rico, and the Virgin Islands. When a relaxation of government restrictions permitted, the company circled back and began selling insurance in countries that formerly barred it from operating in them, including Mexico and Costa Rica.

Although from the outset Pan-American also sold insurance in the United States, for years the epicenter of its business was Latin America. As a result, it had to contend with a plethora of problems far less often faced by domestic insurance companies, including everything from bad weather and disease to government interference and insurgency. It even suffered the hostility of emboldened competitors in the home markets, companies that publicized Pan-American's alleged exploitation of the poor in countries governed by immoral and greedy dictators. Despite such exigencies, Pan-American remained committed to its initial mission of making insurance available to both American citizens and natives working for American companies in South and Central America. In 1949, the year in which future chairman G. Frank Purvis, Jr., joined the company, 66 percent of Pan-American's revenue was still generated through sales in Latin America.

Political unrest and natural disasters in Latin America took a toll on Pan-American Life throughout the 20th century. It was, for example, one of the first companies forced out of Cuba after Fidel Castro gained power there. According to PALIC chairman G. Frank Purvis, Jr., quoted in "Of Banana Boats and Republics" in *World Trade* in 1997, that expulsion cost the company "a substantial amount of our assets." The economic instability of many Latin American countries also eroded Pan-American's profits. Currency devaluation and rampant inflation at times reached 40 percent and even 50 percent in some countries, which had a major negative impact on the company's business.

These problems led to a necessary change in strategy. PALIC began more aggressive marketing of its products at home. It also finally abandoned some Latin American markets, convinced that hostile government policies, political upheaval, and natural disasters were too common to risk further investment in them. Where possible, however, it did remain in Latin America, selling individual and group life insurance to foreign nationals and managing retirement funds. It also remained headquartered in New Orleans, a principal gateway to Latin America. United Fruit, on the other hand, did not. After several changes in ownership, it ended up as United Brands, headquartered in Cincinnati and operating under the Chiquita label.

## *1991–2001: Evolving in a Modern World*

In 1995, Pan-American Life ranked second among the top 100 private companies in New Orleans. Its revenues for that year fell off somewhat, down to $547.7 million from $599.6 million in 1994. The company, lacking serious concern, attributed the decline to a 5 percent reduction in group premiums and a lower yield on its investments. New regulations in Florida, where the company sold policies, had softened that market and made it less attractive.

By 1997, Pan-American had nearly 47,000 policies in effect through the Latin American and Caribbean regions, but that represented only about one-sixteenth of the nearly 8,000,000 individual and group domestic policies in effect. It remained committed to its south-of-the-border business, however, despite the fact that competition for Latin American business by U.S. insurance underwriters had begun heating up, thanks in part to an increasing privatization, a growing middle class, and the newly opened economies in Latin America. Company officials remained convinced that Pan-American's longevity in the region and its reputation for surmounting various difficulties had won it the respect, trust, and loyalty of its Latin American customers and had left it in a commanding position to increase its business as market conditions continued to improve. The

## Key Dates:

**1911:** Crawford Ellis, E.G. Simmons, Marion Souchon, and other investors found Pan-American Life; company begins servicing Panama.
**1912:** Pan-American begins writing policies in other Central America countries.
**1920:** Company begins service in Puerto Rico.
**1949:** G. Frank Purvis joins the company.
**1998:** Company stops underwriting domestic health insurance.

company knew the ropes, after all, and, through the efforts of people like Purvis, over the years it had also established lasting friendships with Latin American associates. Moreover, through trial and error, it had learned to tailor its products and services to the local mores and traditions of its customers, and, rather than invade the market with paper-waving gringos, it had hired local people to conduct its business. It also had developed the lesser markets—the rural areas and small towns—that its competitors simply lacked the experience and cultural sensitivity to tap into successfully.

In 1998, Pan-American decided to withdraw altogether from the domestic health insurance sector to focus on life insurance and retirement planning. At the time, the company had about $1.9 billion in assets and $246 million in total adjusted surplus. It indicated that its decision was part of its overall strategic plan for its remaining underwriting and planning units. According to John Roberts, Pan-American's CEO and president, company executives realized that the mutual firm would not be able to attain sustainable growth in the domestic health insurance industry. Although the company's group accident and health insurance business had been profitable through 1994, thereafter that sector of its business had become a burden, producing losses of $6 million in 1996 and $6.3 million in 1997. Estimates were that without the financial drag that sector created, in 1997 the company would have posted an operating profit of about $16 million. While not divulging terms, Pan-American agreed to sell, in September 1998, almost all of its small group health insurance business to United Wisconsin Services of Milwaukee. It would, however, continue to offer health insurance in the eight Latin American countries in which it was still licensed.

In fact, Pan-American Life continued to provide a wide range of healthcare products to individuals and groups, including companies, throughout Latin America and the Caribbean. Included were indemnity products, preferred provider organization, and point-of-service plans. The company also had negotiated a fee schedule with more than 200 hospitals in Latin America and more than 7,000 healthcare providers.

Though perhaps in a very tentative way, in 2001, Pan-American seemed to be once again testing the domestic health insurance business. In May, L & A Services Inc. of Phoenix, Arizona began marketing a basic employee benefits plan for small businesses unable to afford costlier, more comprehensive plans. The indemnity offering was made through Pan-American and used the Galaxy Network of more than 2,500 Arizona physicians. The benefits plan was designed for people like hotel employees who normally were unable to get any coverage at all. Whether Pan-American will play a future role in similar indemnity offerings remains uncertain.

According to the company's web site, by the century's end Pan-American Life had become financially stronger than at any time in its long history. It had achieved a high, 11 percent ratio of surplus to assets—more than four times the minimum surplus level defined by the National Association of Insurance Commissioners—plus a solid diversification of those assets. It also was committed to shaping a new vision for the future, remolding itself from a financial services firm into a personal and financial performance company. As the new century began, the company also launched a new campaign, replete with a redesigned corporate logo and branding policy focused on what it designated its new ''We Will'' attitude. In March 2001, in part to publicize its ''We Will'' strategy and commitments, the company began a year-long celebration of its 90th anniversary.

### *Principal Subsidiaries*

National Insurance Services Inc.; Pan-American Financial Advisers Inc.

### *Principal Divisions*

Pan-American Retirement & Investment Services.

### *Principal Competitors*

Citizens, Inc.; Credicorp Ltd.; FleetBoston Financial Corporation; GenAmerica Financial Corporation; Standard Management Corporation.

### *Further Reading*

Gonzales, Angela, ''Benefits for Small Business,'' *Business Journal—Serving Phoenix & the Valley of the Sun,* May 11, 2001, p. 11.
Niedzieldski, Joe, ''Pan-American Life Exits Health Ins. Market,'' *National Underwriter Life & Health—Financial Services Edition,* April 13, 1998, p. 39.
''Serving Companies and Individuals,'' *Latin Trade,* October 1998, p. 82.
Welsh, James, ''Of Banana Boats and Republics,'' *World Trade,* January 1, 1997, p. 16.

—John W. Fiero

# Pierre & Vacances SA

**L'Artois**
**Espace Pont de Flandre**
**11 rue de Cambrai**
**75947 Paris Cedex 19**
**France**
**Telephone: (+33) 01 58 21 58 21**
**Fax: (+33) 01 58 21 58 22**
**Web site: www.pierre-vacances.fr**

*Public Company*
*Incorporated:* 1967 as Pierre & Vacances
*Employees:* 8,238
*Sales:* EUR 604.9 million ($483.9 million)(2001)
*Stock Exchanges:* Euronext Paris
*Ticker Symbol:* 7304
*NAIC:* 721110 Hotels (Except Casino Hotels) and Motels

Pierre & Vacances SA has joined the top ranks of the European tourism industry—the French company claims the number one European spot in the tourist residence segment—with nearly 250,000 beds located primarily in France, the Netherlands, Germany, and Belgium. While France accounts for the largest share of the company's business, at 58 percent of revenues in 2001, at the turn of the century Pierre & Vacances has been engaged in aggressive international expansion. The Netherlands, where the company's acquired Gran Dorado in 2000 and Center Parcs in 2001, now accounts for 25 percent of revenues, while Germany and Belgium account for 9 and 8 percent of revenues, respectively. Another important acquisition was that of Maeva, the number two French tourist residence company, at the end of 2001. The company is also developing partnerships for expansion into Spain and Italy. Led by founder Gerard Brémond, Pierre & Vacances has based its success on selling rental and vacation services for residences generally developed or acquired by the company but owned in large part by others. Owners of the company's more than 52,000 homes and apartments turn over rental activities to Pierre & Vacance, keeping six to eight weeks of use of the property—either the property itself or in exchange with others among the company's network—and receiving a percentage of around 4.5 percent of rental fees per year. The company markets its residences under the Pierre & Vacances, Maeva, Orion, and Center Parcs brand names. Pierre & Vacances has been quoted on the Euronext Paris stock exchange since 1999. In its 2000–2001 year, the company posted revenues of EUR 605 million, more than three-quarters of which came from its tourism operations.

### *New Vacation Village Concept in the 1970s*

Gerard Brémond, son and grandson of real estate developers, went into business on his own in the 1960s. A meeting with famed French Olympic ski champion Jean Vuarnet gave Brémond, an avid skier himself, an idea: developing a vacation village dedicated to skiing. Vuarnet and Brémond joined together to build the Avoriaz ski resort in the French Alps, which opened in 1967. A number of features set Avoriaz apart from competing ski resorts. In particular, Avoriaz was developed around a concept of a ''village.'' Cars were banned and children had access to their own village area. Brémond also took care to adapt the village's architecture to its surrounding environment. These features were all to be remain hallmarks of Pierre & Vacances' later tourist resorts.

Filling the resort, especially off-season, remained something of a problem until Brémond combined that activity with another passion, film (Brémond started a second successful career as a film producer in the 1980s). In 1973, Avoriaz inaugurated its annual film festival dedicated to science fiction films, enabling the site to achieve a certain notoriety in France and elsewhere.

Adopting the name Pierre & Vacances in 1975, the company began adding to its operations, developing other mountain resort villages, then extending development operations to the extensive French coastline. That move caused Pierre & Vacances to become stigmatized as a company that had filled up the French coast with cement, a reputation it found hard to shake in later decades despite its transition from real-estate developer to tourist services group.

That transition began at the end of the 1970s when Brémond hit upon a new idea for his company's tourist residence activity. In 1979, Pierre & Vacances launched what it dubbed its

## Key Dates:

**1967:** Gérard Brémond and Jean Vuarnet open a ski resort village at Avoriaz.
**1973:** Brémond launches a science fiction film festival at Avoriaz as a public relations move.
**1975:** The company adopts the name and brand Pierre et Vacances.
**1988:** Pierre & Vacances acquires Geer and Sogerva.
**1993:** The company begins a wave of acquisitions.
**1998:** Subsidiaries of the company are restructured under the holding company Pierre & Vacances SA.
**1999:** Pierre & Vacances goes public on Paris exchange.
**2000:** The company enters into a partnership agreement with Beni Stabili to acquire properties in Italy.
**2002:** Pierre & Vacances acquires Italy's Valtur for EUR 30 million.

''Nouvelle Propriété'' (New Property) formula. Instead of ''owning the walls'' of its resorts, the company now proposed to sell the apartments and bungalows located within its vacation villages, while taking over all rental services for the properties. Owners were able to purchase a vacation property at a reduced price and receive a modest yet guaranteed annual return on the property as a percentage of rental fees over a ten-year period. Owners were also given use of the property for six to eight weeks each year and, later, the possibility to exchange this use with owners of other properties in the Pierre & Vacances network.

The New Property idea enabled Pierre & Vacances to grow without taking on large amounts of debt, and the company stepped up development of its string of vacation villages. It also helped transform the company from a real-estate developer into a tourist services business. The first site to be transformed into a New Property was also the company's first site at Avoriaz.

Through the mid-1980s, Pierre & Vacances continued to grow organically. In 1988, however, the company made two acquisitions, starting with Geer, which owned developments in Cap Esterel, along the Mediterranean; Les Coches, located in the Alps; Port-Bourgenay, on the Atlantic coast in the northwest; and Porty du Crouesty, in the Morbihan region. Following that acquisition, the company acquired Sogerva, which owned a number of properties located along the Atlantic coast. The Sogerva purchase added more than 5,000 beds to Pierre & Vacances' growing total.

### *Acquiring Size in the 1990s*

The long economic crisis that affected France and much of Europe at the beginning of the 1990s deeply affected both the tourism and real-estate sectors. Yet Pierre & Vacance's policy of non-ownership of its properties helped protect it from the collapse in property values seen during the period, while it continued to boast healthy profit margins on its activities. This period also spelled opportunity for the company as it began to buy up a number of its struggling rivals.

The company's next round of acquisitions began in 1993 with the purchase of Société des Montagnes de l'Arc, which held a park of more than 4,000 beds in the Arc area. In 1996, Pierre & Vacances added sites at Val-D'Isère, l'Alpe-d'Huez, Fréjus, and Ile de Ré when it bought up Rocher Soleil. That purchased increased the company's portfolio by more than 2,000 beds. Pierre & Vacance added another 2,000 beds the following year when it acquired Sofap Loisirs, which operated sites at La Tania, Menton, and Cap-d'Agde, in 1997. That same year, the company purchased Pont-Royal SA, particularly attractive for Pierre & Vacances as it held construction permits for more than 20,000 square meters in the highly prized—and highly priced—Provence region.

For the majority of its acquisitions, Pierre & Vacances sought companies with profiles similar to its own, that is, companies operating exclusively within the tourist residence sector and preferably focused on tourism services rather than property ownership. The few properties acquired by Pierre & Vacances were quickly sold off again to investors, helping to pay for its acquisitions and leaving the group debt-free.

As the French and European economies once again took off after the mid-1990s, Pierre & Vacances initiated a new resort development program. A number of the company's acquisitions had brought it lower quality properties, as Brémond admitted to the *Nouvel Observateur*, commenting: ''It's often those acquisitions that gave us a reputation as a cement-layer.'' For its new developments, however, Pierre & Vacances aimed higher, building sites of three- and even four-star quality. The company also was quick to recognize the demand for a new flexibility in resort-style vacations. Customers now sought quick vacations—often for less than a week or simply for a weekend—and the freedom to choose their own activities during their stay. The Pierre & Vacances model was easily adapted to these new trends, helping the company increase its booking percentages.

In 1998, the company launched a new type of resort, a so-called ''eco-village'' located in the Picardy region. The company also opened two resort sites, in Martinique and Guadeloupe, marking its first moves outside of France. That year, the company adopted a new holding structure, grouping all of its subsidiaries under the name Pierre & Vacances SA. In June of the following year, the company went public with a listing on the Paris stock exchange.

### *European Leader for the 21st Century*

By the late 1990s, Pierre & Vacances had already begun a more aggressive expansion phase. In March 1999, the company acquired French resorts rival Orion from owners Whitehall et Westmont Hospitality. The purchase, which cost the company more than EUR 50 million, gave it control of a park of 24 resort properties for a total of 7,200 beds. The company also entered an agreement with Italy's Beni Stabili to set up a joint-venture to acquire resort properties in Italy, which were then to be managed by Pierre et Vacances.

In April 2000, Pierre & Vacances acquired Gran Dorado, one of the leaders in the Benelux markets and in Germany in vacation home rentals, with a portfolio of nearly 3,500 homes and apartments located in six sites in the Netherlands and Germany. The addition of Gran Dorado added more than EUR 135 million to Pierre & Vacance's annual revenues, which had topped EUR 342 million in 1999. The Gran Dorado acquisition cost Pierre & Vacances EUR 100 million.

The company's next expansion move came in March 2001 when, in a joint-venture with Deutsche Bank, Pierre & Vacances acquired control of Center Parcs Europe. That company, which posted sales of EUR 354 million in 2000, had its origins in the late 1960s, when it began developing resort parks featuring full-comfort bungalows constructed with enclosed swimming pools and set in wooded locations. By the time of its acquisition, Center Parcs had grown into a network of 10 villages, with over 6,600 bungalows and more than 34,000 beds, primarily in the Netherlands but also in France, Belgium, and Germany (as well as sites in the United Kingdom not included in the acquisition). The joint-venture cost more than EUR 600 million. Pierre & Vacances took over management of Center Parcs, while placing the entirety of its Gran Dorado property portfolio into the joint-venture in order to meet Deutsche Bank's financial contribution, which covered the cost of the acquisition itself. The company then announced its plans to upgrade and rename the Gran Dorado sites, subsuming them under the Center Parcs brand.

Pierre & Vacances continued its expansion drive through 2001 as it sought to solidify its position as the European leader in the tourist resort sector. In July 2001, the company acquired the ski resort operations of Groupe Washington at the Valmoral resort, which included three hotels as well as 900 residential apartments. That acquisition also gave the company a ski lift operation, which it sold off later that year in a move that helped pay off part of the acquisition costs.

Meanwhile, the company was preparing a new and still larger acquisition. In September 2001, Pierre & Vacances announced that it had reached agreement to acquire Maeva SA, the number two resort operator in France. Created in 1967 under the name Clubhotel, that company had started out as a time-share operator before being acquired by Club Méditerranée in 1978. Club Med placed Clubhotel under its brand Maeva, created in 1976, then added new acquisition Utoring, a company specializing in resorts management. Maeva continued to grow over the next two decades, building up a park of more than 20,000 vacation homes and apartments with more than 86,000 beds.

The addition of Maeva made Pierre & Vacances the undisputed leader in the French market and allowed it to claim leadership across Europe in the residential resorts sector. The company was also able to evade the sharp drop in business suffered by most of the tourism industry following the World Trade Center attack in September 2001: travelers were now choosing to remain closer to home, and Pierre & Vacances, which saw the majority of clientele coming from within driving distance, benefited from this trend.

At the beginning of 2002, the company paused to digest its recent acquisitions as it restructured its portfolio around four primary brands—Pierre & Vacances, Orion, Center Parks, and Maeva. The company also began a revitalization program, particularly of the Maeva properties, which had an average age of some 20 years. In 2002, the company planned to spend some EUR 130 million fixing up those properties.

Meanwhile, Pierre & Vacances set its sites on the southern European market. In Spain, the company entered a partnership with financier George Soros to develop or acquire resort properties in the near future. Meanwhile, in Italy, the company's partnership with Beni Stabili at last came to fruition when the company announced its agreement to acquire Italy's Valtur, paying EUR 30 million for management control of nearly 1,300 apartments. With more than 50 percent of the company remaining firmly under founder Brémond's control, Pierre & Vacances prepared to go head to head with the tourism world's giants, including Accor, Thomas Cook, and TUI. At the same time, the company admitted a possible future interest in linking up with fellow French resort company Club Med.

## *Principal Subsidiaries*

Group Maeva SA; Pont Royal SA; Pierre & Vacances Tourisme SA; Pierre & Vacances Conseil Immobilier SA; Pierre & Vacances Services SNC; Pierre & Vacances FI SNC; Orion Vacances SA; Pierre & Vacances International SA; Pierre & Vacances Transactions SARL; Pierre & Vacances Investissement.

## *Principal Competitors*

Accor SA; Preussag AG; Thomas Cook International; Club Méditerranée SA; Boca Resorts, Inc; Inventive Leisure plc; Sandals Resorts International.

## *Further Reading*

Dupuy, Helena, "De l'immobilier au tourisme, un virage reussi," *La Tribune*, April 15, 2002.

Hachache, Nora, "Pierre & Vacances a toujours le vent en poupe," *Le Moniteur*, January 18, 2002, p. 136.

Michel, Caroline, "Pierre et Vacances, le nouveau roi des loisirs," *Capital*, October 2001, p. 53.

Tatu, Natacha, "La revanche du monsieur gris," *Nouvel Observateur*, February 2002.

—M.L. Cohen

THE PORT AUTHORITY OF NY & NJ

# The Port Authority of New York and New Jersey

**225 Park Avenue South**
**New York, New York 10003**
**U.S.A.**
**Telephone: (212) 435-7000**
**Web site: http://www.panynj.gov**

*State-Owned Company*
*Incorporated:* 1921
*Employees:* 7,000 (est.)
*Sales:* $2.65 billion (2000)
*NAIC:* 921130 Public Finance Activities

The Port Authority of New York and New Jersey is a self-supporting public corporation that develops and operates trade and transportation facilities in an area of New York and New Jersey that falls within a 25-mile radius of the Statue of Liberty. Receiving no tax dollars, the Port Authority depends on tolls, fee, and rents, providing a consistent revenue stream that allows it to raise vast sums through the issuance of bonds. Overseeing the corporation are 12 nonsalaried commissioners, six appointed by each governor of New York and New Jersey. Some of its facilities include the George Washington Bridge; the Holland and Lincoln tunnels; Newark, LaGuardia, and John F. Kennedy airports; Manhattan's only bus terminal; and the PATH rapid transit system. Perhaps the best known Port Authority property, the twin towers of the World Trade Center, were destroyed in the terrorist attack of September 11, 2001, which cost the lives of approximately 3,000 people, including the Port Authority's executive director and 73 other employees.

## *Bickering Over New York Harbor into the 20th Century*

Because New York and New Jersey bordered the New York Harbor and the Hudson River, the two states invariably came into conflict over the use of the common waterway. The situation was only exacerbated with the completion of the Erie Canal in 1825. The canal stretched from Lake Erie to the Hudson River in Albany, New York, which then allowed New York Harbor to be connected to the great interior of the United States, an arrangement that transformed New York City into the unrivaled commercial center of the nation. New York and New Jersey finally settled their border dispute with the Treaty of 1834, which essentially split the Hudson River down the middle, but conflict continued to dog the two states well after the Erie Canal was superceded by railroads. In 1916 the situation came to a head when New Jersey interests filed a complaint with the Interstate Commerce Commission over rail rates, which they claimed were set artificially high to protect New York interests. If New Jersey was successful in forcing railroads to lower freight costs, its harbor facilities would gain a decisive economic advantage and draw commerce away from Manhattan. Rather than fight the suit, New York leaders, led by Progressive politicians and the New York State Chamber of Commerce, elected to take a broader view of the conflict. Rather than just adjusting rail rates, they concluded that the parties needed a way to mutually manage the Port of New York, to reduce inefficiencies and ease congestion. The situation was simply intolerable: A tangle of railroad lines converged on New Jersey towns that lay across from Manhattan, at which point freight had to be loaded onto ferries to be transported across the Hudson. Rail congestion became so bad at times that trains were backed up as far away as Pittsburgh.

The man most responsible for the creation of the Port Authority was Julius Henry Cohen, the counsel of the New York State Chamber of Commerce, who was charged with looking into the ICC suit. He firmly believed in the principle of cooperative planning, as well as keeping politics and potential corruption out of public programs. In early 1917 he was able to convince politicians in New York and New Jersey to form a bistate commission to find a way to resolve their differences over the port. Cohen was then named counsel to the commission. Two years later he submitted a draft proposal for a Port of New York Authority, patterned in large part on the Port of London Authority. According to lore, the English had no name for their organization until a proposed Act of Parliament had been written. Because so many of the provisions began with the phrase, "Authority is hereby given," the drafters decided to call the organization the Port of London Authority. With New York Harbor now appropriating the term, Authority would be widely adopted by harbors and other agencies.

**Company Perspectives:**

*The company's mission is to identify and meet the critical transportation infrastructure needs of the bistate region's businesses, residents, and visitors: providing the highest quality, most efficient transportation and port commerce facilities and services that move people and goods within the region, provide access to the rest of the nation and to the world, and strengthen the economic competitiveness of the New York-New Jersey metropolitan region.*

### *Establishing the Port Authority of New York in 1921*

According to Princeton professor Jameson W. Doig, Cohen's draft proposal was "a regional planner's dream." It granted the agency regulatory powers and made it self-supportive and, therefore, insulated from politics, by generating self-supporting revenues. Moreover, it had the ability to borrow money, backed by the credit of the states. Over the course of the next two years, however, much of the teeth was taken out of Cohen's proposal before the two states finally approved it in April 1921. The Port Authority of New York (it would be renamed the Port Authority of New York and New Jersey in 1972) came into existence with an abstract mandate to "purchase, construct, lease and/or operate any terminal or transportation facility" within New York Harbor, and a vague ability to "borrow money and secure the same by bonds."

The first objective of the Port Authority was to bring order to the rail and waterborne freight system. By December 1921 it released a comprehensive plan that called for a coordinated system of railroad tracks, tunnels, and marine terminals designed to eliminate inefficiencies and spur economic growth. It also required the cooperation of a dozen rail lines, which meant consultations with all the parties. The result was a decade of endless discussions before the proposal finally withered and died. In the meantime, the Port Authority made its name in the construction of bridges, in particular the George Washington Bridge.

For decades bridge designer Gustav Lindenthal had been promoting his own idea of improving the area's transportation problems. He proposed a 12-track railroad bridge, enough to accommodate all the rival lines that crossed the Hudson River into the heart of midtown Manhattan (the 1921 version included an additional 20 automobile lanes). After the Port Authority rejected the plan, Lindenthal's chief assistant, Othmar Ammann, tried to convince him to scale down the bridge and move it north. Lindenthal refused to compromise on his dream, and Ammann left his service to develop his own plans for a bridge spanning the Palisades of Fort Lee, New Jersey, and the upper tip of Manhattan, one intended for the new automobile age. It would serve only cars and light-rail transit, making it much cheaper to build and eliminating the cooperation of the railroads. He was able to enlist the support of New Jersey's new elected governor, George Silzer, who, according to Doig, "was interested in advancing his political career through a record of tangible accomplishments." Silzer, through his commissioners, was able to persuade the Port Authority that vehicular traffic congestion fell within its purview. Although the Port Authority was interested in Ammann's bridge, it still held out hope that it could convince the railroads to agree to its transportation plan. Finally in 1924 Silzer and Ammann were able to persuade the Port Authority to build two smaller automobile bridges joining New Jersey to Staten Island, which would become the Outerbridge Crossing and the Goethals Bridge. With momentum now on their side, Silzer and Ammann gained enough support in both New York and New Jersey for the construction of the Fort Lee bridge, which upon completion in 1931 would be named the George Washington Bridge. (Before then, the Port Authority also built the Bayonne Bridge.) Under Ammann's leadership all four of the Port Authority bridges came in ahead of schedule and under budget, and firmly established the reputation of the bistate agency.

The building of the George Washington Bridge allowed the Port Authority to argue successfully that it should be allowed to build a midtown tunnel to New Jersey and to take over the Holland Tunnel, which opened in 1927, years behind schedule and well over budget. The merger made sense, because, according to Doig, "the two trans-Hudson crossings in separate hands would risk the possibility of destructive competition, as each tried to attract traffic by lowering tolls below its competitor's level." The toll revenues derived from the Holland Tunnel also allowed the Port Authority to service its debts while its bridges finally came on line and began to generate revenues. The new midtown tunnel, named the Lincoln Tunnel, would open in 1937 and add even more cash flow to the agency.

Following World War II the Port Authority expanded its scope to include commercial aviation. Newark Airport, which opened in 1928, had been a pioneering facility, boasting the first paved runways and the first air traffic control tower. It soon became the busiest airport in the country, but was eclipsed in 1939 by a new airport built in the borough of Queens by Mayor Fiorello LaGuardia. By 1945 Newark was asking to Port Authority to take over the operations of its airport. As had been the case with railroads earlier in the century, aviation clearly required more effective coordination. New York City considered the creation of a city airport authority, but in the end it also turned to the Port Authority, which in 1947 took over LaGuardia Airport, as well as New York International Airport (later renamed John F. Kennedy Airport), which was under construction and opened a year later. Rather than simply give the airports away, however, the city chose to lease them to the Port Authority, provided the agency agreed to develop and operate the facilities on a self-supporting basis. In 1949 the Port Authority added to its aviation portfolio by purchasing the small Teterboro Airport in the New Jersey Meadowlands. It opened a Heliport in lower Manhattan in 1960.

The Port Authority also became involved with buses when in 1944 New York City requested that the Port Authority build a midtown bus terminal. Once again the agency was charged with bringing order to a chaotic situation. Interstate bus traffic to Manhattan had resulted in the establishment of eight separate bus terminals located in a one-square-mile area. Aside from traffic congestion cause by so many buses wending their way through the island, the cramped terminals offered little in the way of comfort for passengers. The Port Authority drew up a plan to build a large consolidated bus terminal on the west side of Manhattan, with a connection to the Lincoln Tunnel to ease

**Key Dates:**

**1921:** Port Authority of New York is established.
**1930:** Port Authority takes over the operation of Holland Tunnel.
**1931:** The George Washington Bridge opens.
**1937:** The Lincoln Tunnel opens.
**1947:** Port Authority takes over New York's two airports.
**1962:** Port Authority takes over Hudson & Manhattan Railroad, creating PATH.
**1970:** The World Trade Center opens.
**1993:** The World Trade Center is bombed by terrorists.
**2001:** The twin towers and other buildings of the World Trade Center are destroyed by terrorists.

street traffic. Although most of the bus companies agreed to move into the proposed facility (which eventually opened in 1950), Greyhound, the largest bus operator, refused to give up its 34th Street terminal. The Port Authority was willing to compromise and allow Greyhound to keep its terminal, as long as it did not allow other bus companies to use it, but Greyhound rejected the proposal. A 20-year battle ensued. Over the years, Greyhound attempted to gain permission to expand its terminal, but each time it was denied. Finally in 1963 Greyhound gave up its 34th Street facility, as well as one on 50th Street, and began using the Port Authority Bus Terminal.

Although the Port Authority was involved in bridges and tunnels, airports, and a bus terminal, it was also heavily engaged in the marine activities of the Port of New York. In 1952 it assumed responsibility for the Hoboken piers, and in 1956 took over the Brooklyn Piers. The Port Authority then became involved in the revolutionary practice of containerization, which was introduced at Port Newark in 1956. Steel containers of cargo were stacked on ships and then directly unloaded onto specially designed trucks or rail cars, resulting in a significant savings of time as well as providing inventory and quality control measures. In 1962 the Port Authority established a standard when it opened the world's first all-container port facility, the Elizabeth-Port Authority Marine Terminal. This early embrace of containerization provided the Port of New York with a competitive edge that lasted well into the 1980s, when less expensive ports began to lure away customers.

### *Conceiving the World Trade Center in the 1950s*

The Port Authority's entry into the management of commercial property came through the World Trade Center, which was first conceived in the 1950s by a group of businessmen led by David Rockefeller, CEO of Chase Manhattan Bank and brother of New York's Governor Nelson Rockefeller. The goal was to revitalize lower Manhattan, which had been losing financial firms to outlying areas, by building a new office complex that, it was hoped, would attract new tenants involved in international trade. The Rockefeller Group turned to the Port Authority for a number of reasons: The agency already owned some of the land, it had cash in hand, and it could float bonds. Moreover, half of its commissioners were appointed by David Rockefeller's brother. The idea was met with enthusiasm by the Port Authority's director, Austin Tobin, who was interested in expanding the power of the agency.

Critics charged that the World Trade Center project was more about ego and politics than it was about sound business considerations. To get New Jersey's backing, the Port Authority had to agree to take over the troubled Hudson & Manhattan Railroad, used by many New Jersey residents who commuted to Manhattan. The system would be renamed the Port Authority Trans-Hudson, or PATH. Originally, the World Trade Center complex was to be built on the East Side of Manhattan, but New Jersey insisted on a West Side location, so it could at least be seen from the New Jersey side of the Hudson. To gain public support for the World Trade Center, its developers grossly underestimated its final costs. Furthermore, according to critics, the idea of building a pair of 110-story office towers was more hubris on Tobin's part than it was a reflection of market conditions. Construction began in 1966 and by the time the first tower was completed and went onto the market in 1970 its introduction simply aggravated an already difficult situation. The economy was entering a recession and the tower only added to a glut of available office space, resulting in a drop in real estate values. Moreover, it failed to bring in new firms to the city, instead drawing tenants from surrounding buildings. Even then, to ease the high vacancy rates the Port Authority had to rely on the State of New York to relocate almost all of its New York City Offices into the towers, and move its own offices there as well. The towers, and the other buildings that made up the World Trade Center complex, did not come close to full occupancy until the economic boom of the 1990s. Political critics portray the World Trade Center as a "patronage bonanza," while architectural critics regarded the twin towers as sterile and old-fashioned even before they opened.

In the 1990s the World Trade Center, and the twin towers in particular, would gain new meaning because of the people who chose to destroy it. At 12:18 p.m. on February 26, 1993, terrorists detonated a truck bomb in the underground garage of one of the towers, resulting in the deaths of six people and leaving more than 1,000 injured. Ironically, when the explosion occurred, some people thought that a plane had hit the building. The Port Authority moved quickly to repair the damage and reopen the World Trade Center. In short order evidence also was uncovered that led to the arrest and conviction of the terrorists who planted the bomb.

In 1995 George Marlin became executive director of the Port Authority and began instituting cost-savings measures that included budget cuts and layoffs. A firm believer in privatization, he was also instrumental in selling the Vista Hotel, part of the World Trade Center, to Host Marriott, as well as unloading other nontransportation businesses. The governors of New York and New Jersey disagreed over the allocations of the Port Authority's resources and its proposed toll increases, resulting in an 18-month stalemate that prevented the agency from launching new spending initiatives that would benefit both states. Once the impasse was settled in June 2000, the Port Authority announced a $9.6 billion, five-year capital plan to improve existing port, airport, and transportation facilities, as well as to provide financial support for a Second Avenue subway line that had been promised to Manhattan residents for decades.

The Port Authority's embrace of privatization reached its culmination in the spring of 2001 when it agreed to lease the twin towers of the World Trade Center to Silverstein Properties for 99 years at a cost of $3.22 billion. It was a deal of a lifetime for Larry Silverstein, but his control of the skyscrapers would be shortlived. On the morning of September 11, 2001, terrorists hijacked two commercial jet airliners, loaded with enough fuel for a coast-to-coast flight, and intentionally flew them into the towers. To everyone's horror, both skyscrapers collapsed to the ground within an hour, taking the lives of some 3,000 people. Silverstein vowed to rebuild the towers, although it was unlikely that he would construct anything close to 110 stories high. The Port Authority, with its offices in the twin towers, suffered the loss of its new director, Neil Levin, and dozens of other employees. The economy of the area served by the agency also was dealt a severe blow by the attack. With a major capital plan ready to implement, however, the Port Authority was again poised to make a key contribution in the revitalization of the New York and New Jersey economy.

### *Principal Subsidiaries*

Port Authority Trans-Hudson (PATH).

### *Principal Operating Units*

Air Terminals; Interstate Transportation; World Trade Center; Port Commerce; Economic Development.

### *Principal Competitors*

National Railroad Passenger Corporation (Amtrak); Coach USA Inc.; Helmsley Enterprises, Inc.; Metropolitan Transit Authority; The Trump Organization.

### *Further Reading*

Anderson, Bruce C., ''The Twin Towers Project: A Cautionary Tale,'' *City Journal,* Autumn 2001.

Croghan, Lore, ''Booms to Busts to Top of World: After Five Decades, Larry Silverstein Grabs Real Estate's Golden Crown,'' *Crain's New York Business,* May 14, 2001, p. 1.

Doig, Jameson W., *Empire on the Hudson: Entrepreneurial Visions and Political Power at the Port of New York Authority,* New York: Columbia University Press, 2001.

——, ''Expertise, Politics, and Technological Changes: The Search for Mission at the Port of New York Authority,'' *Journal of American Planning Association,* Winter 1993, pp. 31–44.

Mysak, Joe, *Perpetual Motion: The Illustrated History of the Port Authority of New York and New Jersey,* Los Angeles: General Pub. Group, 1996.

Shankar, P., ''A Time to Rebuild,'' *Business News New Jersey,* November 27, 2001, p. 14.

Smothers, Ronald, ''Port Authority Outlines Plans for New Revenue,'' *New York Times,* November 17, 2000, p. B9.

—Ed Dinger

# Praxair, Inc.

**39 Old Ridgebury Road**
**Danbury, Connecticut 06810**
**U.S.A.**
**Telephone: (716) 879-4077**
**Toll Free: 1-800-PRAXAIR**
**Fax: (716) 879-2040**
**Web site: http://www.praxair.com/**

*Public Company*
*Incorporated:* 1907 as Linde Air Products Co.
*Employees:* 24,271
*Sales:* $5.16 billion (2001)
*Stock Exchanges:* New York
*Ticker Symbol:* PX
*NAIC:* 325120 Industrial Gas Manufacturing; 332812 Metal Coating, Engraving (Except Jewelry and Silverware) and Allied Services to Manufacturers

With operations in 40 countries around the world, Praxair, Inc. is one of the world's top suppliers of industrial gases. The company's Praxair Surface Technologies subsidiary applies high-performance metal coatings for a variety of industries.

Formerly the Linde Division of chemical giant Union Carbide Corporation, Praxair was spun off to shareholders in 1992 as an independent company. Over half of the firm's sales are generated outside the United States. The company's surface coatings business, developed in the 1950s, supplies wear-resistant and high-temperature corrosion-resistant metallic and ceramic coatings and powders to many industries. Industrial gases by far constitute the greatest portion of Praxair's operations, contributing 86 percent of 2001 sales. Industrial gas products include atmospheric gases like oxygen, nitrogen, and argon, and process gases such as helium, hydrogen, and acetylene. Many of Praxair's largest customers, and an increasing number of smaller volume customers, utilize on-site distribution, wherein a dedicated plant is built on or adjacent to the customer's site to supply the product directly. On-site delivery constituted about 24 percent of Praxair's 2001 sales. Merchant liquid delivery involves transportation of medium-sized volumes of gases by tanker truck or railroad tank car to on-site storage containers owned and maintained by Praxair. This segment contributed 30 percent of the company's 2001 sales. Customers requiring small volumes of industrial gases receive them in metal cylinders or tanks. This packaged gases business constituted one-third of sales.

## *Origins*

Praxair's origins may be traced back to 19th-century Germany, where a professor of mechanical engineering at the College of Technology in Munich started experiments in refrigeration. Karl von Linde's research came to fruition with the 1895 development of a cryogenic air liquefier. Von Linde built his first oxygen production plant in 1902. His continuing research led to the establishment of the first plant for the production of pure nitrogen two years later. The entrepreneur-scientist went on to build air separation plants throughout Germany and Europe during the first decade of the 20th century.

Karl von Linde's 1907 foundation of Linde Air Products Company in Cleveland, Ohio, established the first firm in the country to produce oxygen from air using a cryogenic process. Although oxygen distillation was relatively inexpensive—the raw material is, after all, free—the storage and transportation of gases in heavy containers was very costly. With its foundation in scientific inquiry, the Linde Air Products Company made research and development a priority. As a result, the industrial gas business evolved into a very capital-intensive enterprise; in 1992, *Chemical Week* estimated that every dollar of annual sales cost over a dollar in assets.

The Linde Company's relationship with Union Carbide started around 1911, when the two competitors undertook joint experiments regarding the production and application of acetylene. Union Carbide had been formed in 1898 to manufacture calcium carbide, a catalyst for the production of metal alloys. The partners had hoped that acetylene—a flammable, gaseous by-product of alloying calcium carbide with aluminum—could be marketed for street and household lighting. While acetylene gas lighting was extensively used especially in rural areas and was also used for auto lights, Thomas Edison's invention and

## Company Perspectives:

*For Praxair to be successful, our employees must work towards a single vision, possess shared values, and demonstrate behaviors that support both the vision and values. Praxair's Vision: To be the best performing industrial gases company in the world as determined by our customers, employees, shareholders, suppliers, and the communities in which we operate. Praxair's Values: Total customer satisfaction. Results driven. Integrity. People excellence. Safety and environmental excellence. Increasing shareholder wealth. Praxair's Behaviors. Personal Accountability. Teamwork Externally driven. Urgency of action. Winning—making money.*

commercialization of electric incandescent light bulbs distracted some emphasis away from acetylene gas lighting. Fortunately, a French researcher's discovery that acetylene could be burned in oxygen to produce a hot, metal-cutting flame launched a whole new market for the gas.

### *Company Joins Union Carbide 1917*

In 1917, Linde pooled its resources with National Carbon Co., Inc., Prest-O-Lite Co., Inc., Electro Metallurgical Co., and Union Carbide Co. to form Union Carbide and Carbon Corporation. The new entity was organized as a holding company, with its five members acting relatively autonomously and cooperating where their businesses converged. As a subsidiary of one of the United States' largest chemical companies, Linde soon became one of the world's largest producer of such industrial gases as acetylene, hydrogen, and nitrogen, which formed the foundation of the petrochemical industry. The companies' combined research efforts coincided with a national push for new technologies to help win World War I, and new applications for industrial gases came in rapid succession. Cooperative research and development among Union Carbide companies used Linde's gases to facilitate production of corrosion and heat-resistant ferroalloys used in skyscrapers, bridges, and automobiles.

Linde also earned a reputation as an innovator in the industrial gases industry by developing new applications for industrial gases, especially in conjunction with the growing chemicals operations of its parent. During the 1940s, for example, Linde participated in Union Carbide's contribution to the development of the atomic bomb. Linde scientists perfected a refining process for treating uranium concentrates through gaseous diffusion.

In the late 1940s, Union Carbide executives attempted to centralize the traditionally autonomous nature of the corporation through a reorganization. The holding company arrangement was dissolved, and subsidiaries were transformed into divisions. Each division, however, retained the word ''company'' in its name, suggesting that a decentralized corporate culture still endured at Union Carbide.

### *Postwar Ups and Downs*

The Linde Division benefited from Union Carbide's mid-1950s to mid-1960s globalization and retained its position as America's top producer of industrial gases through continuous innovation. The development of oxygen-fired furnaces for steel manufacture and application of nitrogen as a refrigerant increased Linde's markets during the 1960s. The industrial gas company was even able to benefit from the energy crisis of the 1970s, when the rapidly rising costs of traditional fuels made oxy-fuel an attractive alternative to air-fuel because one received maximum heat from fuel. Applications of industrial gases in the food industry during this period included the use of hydrogen in hydrogenated cooking oils and nitrogen to quick-freeze foods.

However, Linde's steady performance throughout the 1970s and 1980s was largely obscured by the succession of financial, environmental, and human disasters endured by parent company Union Carbide, including the infamous disaster at its pesticide plant in Bhopal, India, in December 1984. Union Carbide's market value plummeted 75 percent to less than $3 billion in the aftermath, and the chemical giant was compelled to take on massive debt to repulse a takeover threat. Divestments scaled the parent company back to its three primary businesses (industrial gases, chemicals and plastics, and carbon products) in the late 1980s, but its debt load curbed research and development, diversification, and international expansion.

By the early 1980s, Linde was a $1 billion contributor to Union Carbide's $9 billion annual sales. However, over the course of the decade, Linde began to lose U.S. market share, particularly to U.S. rival Air Products and Chemicals, Inc. By the late 1980s, Linde was ranked second in nitrogen and hydrogen production and distribution. Linde maintained its reputation for innovation, including a small, profitable business segment with the development of such coatings processes as acetylene detonation, which metallurgically bonded protective coatings to metal surfaces. High-tech acetylene detonation and diffusion processes were used in aircraft engines and rolled steel, while also having applications in the automotive industry, most notably in the production of Rolls Royce cars. In 1989, the industrial gas company introduced a technological breakthrough in its primary market, air separation. Robert Reitzes, then an analyst with New York's C.J. Lawrence, predicted that the economical, noncryogenic, vacuum pressure swing adsorption (VPSA) technology would consume 20 to 25 percent of the merchant market by the year 2000. In fact, by 2000 the company would estimate that more than 40 percent of the merchant liquid market is served by noncryogenic systems, of both the VSPA and Membrane variety.

### *Company Spun Off in 1992*

In 1988, the Linde division was renamed Union Carbide Industrial Gases, and in June 1992 its shares were distributed to Union Carbide shareholders on the basis of one share of the new Praxair, Inc. for each share of the parent. The new company maintained some ties to its former parent; Union Carbide was still one of its largest customers, and the two continued to share a common headquarters. The name Praxair was derived from the Greek praxis, or practical application, plus the name of the company's primary product.

Praxair emerged with over $2.5 billion in annual sales, more employees (18,600) than its former parent (16,000) and a debt-

**Key Dates:**

**1907:** Linde Air Products Company is founded.
**1917:** Linde joins Union Carbide.
**1988:** Linde Division is renamed Union Carbide Industrial Gases.
**1992:** Praxair is spun off.
**1996:** CBI/Liquid Carbonic is acquired.
**2000:** William Lichtenberger, CEO since 1992, retires.

to-capital ratio of over 60 percent. Debt reduction was a high priority for CEO H. William Lichtenberger, who devised several corporate goals in the early 1990s: reducing overhead, doubling profitability, effecting 15 percent annual net income growth, and expanding Praxair's global presence, especially in Asia and South Africa. Expense reduction commenced immediately under a ''work process improvement initiative,'' and the company's work force was reduced by 10 percent in Praxair's first year of independence. The establishment of joint ventures in Indonesia and China was expected to help Praxair catch up quickly with its competitors in the region. Two joint ventures in Beijing and Shanghai were expected, according to press releases, to ''give Praxair the largest representation in China among industrial-gases companies.''

In 1994, Praxair earned one of the most comprehensive quality system certifications issued by the International Organization for Standardization (ISO). Covered by the ISO 9002 certificate were all 54 bulk-gas operating sites; 12 customer service centers; distribution facilities, including the company's North American Logistics Center; plant operations center and two pipeline control centers; and more than 250 on-site air separation plants in the United States, Canada, and Puerto Rico.

### *Growth in the Mid-1990s*

By 1995, Lichtenberger had largely delivered on the ambitious goals he set after the company was spun off in 1992. Rejecting a new share offering or a sell-off of assets, Praxair raised its margins by focusing on productivity and cost reductions, which saved an estimated $50 to $60 million a year. Lichtenberger told the *Financial Times,* ''The only sustainable way to improve productivity is to grow your top line while containing the increases in your costs.''

One way Praxair did this is by installing new plants faster at customers' sites. In the mid-1990s, the company had a hundred on-site plants in the design or construction stages. It was also installing the world's largest oxygen plant for the Jindal Vijayanagar Steel Ltd.'s facility in Kamataka, India.

New or expanded uses for industrial gases contributed to Praxair's bottom line. Use of oxygen in the glass, steel, coal, and paper industries could improve quality while reducing toxic emissions. Demand for hydrogen was up from the petroleum refining industry and from NASA.

In early 1996, Praxair acquired CBI Industries, an Oak Brook, Illinois-based carbon dioxide provider, in a $2.2 billion hostile takeover. The buy helped Praxair expand its Gulf Coast operations. Oil refining there was a large market for hydrogen.

CBI subsidiary Liquid Carbonic was the world leader in carbon dioxide, with sales of $440 million a year and twice that figure in total gases revenues. CBI's product lines merged well with those of Praxair, then a stranger to the carbon dioxide business. The buy also extended Praxair's presence in South America, Poland, and Thailand. In addition, Praxair was now investing in China and India.

Praxair was also making smaller acquisitions of cylinder gas operations in the United States. The company had exited the packaged gas business under Union Carbide. North American cylinder sales in 1999 were $900 million—$250 million of this due to the Liquid Carbonic acquisition. To contain costs, the packaged gas business was established as a subsidiary, Praxair Distribution.

Praxair sales were $4.83 billion in 1998. However, two key problems surfaced the next year. The steel industry in North America was being pummeled by cheap competition abroad, and Brazil, another major market, devalued its currency.

Following an industry trend, Praxair and German chemicals giant Merck KGaA began shipping each other's products. Their geographic ranges were entirely complementary. In March 1999, Praxair and BOC Group plc of Great Britain announced plans to combine to create the world's largest industrial gas company. Praxair was outbid, however, and BOC's assets were divided between Air Liquide and Air Products in an $11 billion deal. In fact, Praxair would be one of the few industrial gases companies not involved in a merger at the turn of the millennium.

Praxair stopped using the Linde name in 1999. In a deal brokered three years earlier, Praxair agreed to sell North American rights to the name to Linde AG of Germany for $60 million. Linde AG and its predecessors had been using the name in Europe and elsewhere in the world since its incorporation in 1895.

### *Lichtenberger Retires in 2000*

After the retirement of President and Chief Operating Officer (COO) Edgar Hotard in early 1999, Lichtenberger set up a temporary three-person ''office of the chairman'' manned by himself, Chief Financial Officer John Clerico, and Executive Vice-President Paul Bilek. Lichtenberger himself retired as CEO and chairman in November 2000 upon turning 65. His replacement, Dennis H. Reilley, was formerly a COO at DuPont.

Under the new leadership, a restructuring at Praxair was announced in December 2000 that would see plants closed and 750 employees laid off (3 percent of the total Praxair work force). Hoping to exploit some specific growth markets beyond its traditional industrial gases business—semiconductor materials, health care, metals technologies, and electronic coatings—the company nevertheless met with unfavorable economic conditions as a global recession ensued in 2001. Another series of layoffs was announced in late 2001. Still, the company seemed to meet the challenges; sales continued to climb as did Praxair stock prices, which outperformed the Standard & Poor 500

Index in 2001. Early in 2002, Praxair began plans to build two new hydrogen plants to supply its Gulf Coast pipeline.

### *Principal Subsidiaries*

Praxair Asia, Inc. (Singapore); Praxair Canada, Inc.; Praxair Mexico S.A. de C.V.; Praxair Holding N.V. (Belgium); Praxair Surface Technologies, Inc.; S.A. White Martins (Brazil; 69%).

### *Principal Competitors*

Air Liquide S.A.; Air Products & Chemicals, Inc.; Airgas Inc.; The BOC Group plc.

### *Further Reading*

Brown, Robert, ''Industrial Gases Industry Becomes Stronger in the Wake of the BOC Deal,'' *Chemical Marketing Reporter,* August 9, 1999, pp. 5, 27.

Canning, Kathie, ''Oxygenator Reduces Air Pollution from Wastewater Treatment, Study Confirms,'' *Pollution Engineering,* January 1999, pp. 13–15.

Chapman, Peter, ''Praxair Is Entering Revived CO2 Market,'' *Chemical Marketing Reporter,* January 15, 1996.

Dennis, Anita, ''Becoming a Business Partner,'' *Journal of Accountancy,* March 1997, pp. 72+.

Freedman, William, ''Praxair Seeks CO2 Entry Through CBI,'' *Chemical Week,* November 8, 1995, p. 16.

Harris, Barbara R., and Mark A. Huselid, ''Strategic Human Resource Management at Praxair,'' *Human Resource Management,* Winter 1999, pp. 315ff.

Hunter, David, ''Industrial Gases: Focus on Costs, Mix, and Geography,'' *Chemical Week,* February 23, 1994, pp. 25–7.

Hunter, David, Debbie Jackson, and Marjorie Coeyman, ''Industrial Gases: Quickening Pace in the Americas,'' *Chemical Week,* April 7, 1993, pp. 21–3.

Jarvis, Lisa, ''Industrial Gas Prices Show Firmer Tone as Producers Face Runup,'' *Chemical Market Reporter,* August 14, 2000, pp. 5f.

Moore, Samuel K., ''DuPont's Reilley Takes Top Spot at Praxair,'' *Chemical Week,* March 1, 2000, p. 10.

——, ''From Cash Cow to Bull,'' *Chemical Week,* March 17, 1999, pp. 18–21.

——, ''Praxair Hikes Prices for Bulk Products,'' *Chemical Week,* February 2, 2000, p. 16.

Nielsen, Karol, ''Praxair Cut Jobs, Closes Plants; Takes a $150-Million Charge,'' *Chemical Week,* December 20, 2000, p. 12.

——, ''Praxair Shuffles Management,'' *Chemical Week,* January 5, 2000, p. 16.

Plishner, Emily S., ''Breaking Free at Carbide: Hydrogen Propels Growth of Industrial Gases Unit,'' *Chemical Week,* May 13, 1992, pp. 56–7.

——, ''ISO 9000—Praxair: Learning From International Experience,'' *Chemical Week,* November 10, 1993, p. 73.

——, ''Mergers and Acquisitions Become Demergers and Spinoffs,'' *Chemical Week,* October 7, 1992, pp. 24–5.

——, ''Praxair Promises More Profits,'' *Chemical Week,* March 16, 1994, p. 13.

——, ''Reconstructing Balance Sheets,'' *Chemical Week,* October 7, 1992, pp. 22–4.

——, ''Unchained Melody,'' *Financial World,* August 29, 1995, p. 32.

''Praxair Names Reilley of DuPont to Succeed CEO Lichtenberger,'' *Wall Street Journal,* February 23, 2000, p. A4.

Shapiro, Lynn, ''Checks and Balances in Executive Pay,'' *Chemical Business,* October 1993, pp. 11–12.

Warren, Susan, Matthew Rose, and Paul M. Sherer, ''Praxair, BOC Discuss Potential Merger to Form Largest Industrial-Gas Concern,'' *Wall Street Journal,* May 12, 1999, p. A19.

—April Dougal Gasbarre
—update: Frederick C. Ingram

PRUDENTIAL

# Prudential plc

**Laurence Pountney Hill**
**London EC4R 0HH**
**United Kingdom**
**Telephone: (44) 20 7220-7588**
**Fax: (44) 20 7548-3850**
**Web site: http://www.prudential.co.uk**

*Public Company*
*Incorporated:* 1848 as Prudential Mutual Assurance, Investment, and Loan Association
*Employees:* 21,942
*Total Assets:* £156.7 billion (2001)
*Stock Exchanges:* New York London Hong Kong Paris Frankfurt
Ticker Symbol: PUK
*NAIC:* 524113 Direct Life Insurance Carriers

Prudential plc (known as ''the Pru'') has a long-standing history as a dominant force in financial services in the United Kingdom. The company spent the majority of the late 1990s restructuring, eliminating its famed direct sales force, and building brand recognition. Through its U.K. and European insurance operations, Prudential operates as a leading life and pensions provider. M&G Investments acts as the group's U.K. and European fund manager. Egg plc, the firm's online banking service, was launched in 1998. Prudential also has a strong hold on the U.S. market through subsidiary Jackson National Life Insurance Company, one of the leading life insurance companies in the United States with over 1.5 million policies in place. Prudential also serves 2.2 million customers in Asia through its Prudential Corporation Asia operations.

## *The British Insurance Industry Evolves: Mid- to Late 1880s*

In 1848, political rebellion surged across Europe, while England contended with Chartist unrest. For a group of investors who gathered in London in May of 1848, however, revolution promised financial opportunity. Secure in the knowledge that crises create a desire for security, they pledged to raise £1O0,000 to organize the Prudential Investment, Loan, and Assurance Association which was ultimately registered as the Prudential Mutual Assurance, Investment, and Loan Association. The company soon was renamed Prudential Assurance Company Limited. The founders, led by Chairman George Harrison, included a doctor of divinity, a naval officer, a leather merchant, a surveyor, a surgeon, and an auctioneer. In this competitive industry mere survival was an achievement. Between 1844 and 1883, 1,186 insurance promotions were launched. While 612 companies were formed, only 93 were still in operation by 1883, and the failure rate of these insurance companies was sometimes as high as 100 per year.

Most of those companies echoed the Prudential's early determination to serve an established middle-class clientele. The Prudential hoped for a patronage from clergymen, barristers, and successful tradesmen seeking what was perceived as a profitable market segment. The poor had unhealthy occupations and inadequate housing and suffered most from the frequent epidemics of the period. Conventional wisdom in the insurance field also emphasized the inconvenience of managing a myriad of small policies. The anticipated high overhead of any collection system convinced most professionals to avoid this segment of the market. Following such conventional wisdom brought the Prudential to the edge of bankruptcy. In its first 18 months, the company generated a mere £1,500 in premium income. In 1851, the amount was still under £2,000. By 1852, the prospects for the company's survival were bleak.

New conditions in the insurance industry in the 1850s provided the Prudential with the opportunity to thrive. As late as 1845, insurance remained a prerogative of the upper classes of British society. Of a population of 25 million people, fewer than 100,000 held life assurance. This distribution changed with the emergence of industrial life assurance companies selling policies to members of the working class. H.A.L. Cockerell declared in *The British Insurance Business* that these companies ''revolutionized the social distribution of life assurance.'' Such a company offered policies worth £20 or less and established a regular collection system outside the registered office, its legally designated location for official correspondence.

## Company Perspectives:

*At Prudential our aim is lasting relationships with our customers and policyholders through products and services that offer value for money and security. We also seek to enhance our company's reputation, built over 150 years, for integrity and for acting responsibly within society.*

Two events in 1852 encouraged the Prudential to consider a change in policy. A select committee of the House of Commons called for an expansion of insurance to all classes of society. Perhaps more important, the operatives of the Prudential had become restive with the existing approach. A deputation called on the secretary of the Prudential and urged entrance into the industrial field. The agents wished to follow the example of "friendly societies," a form of benevolent association, which provided benefits to their members. These associations offered an example of close personal contact between agent and member. The response of company directors to this approach was a lukewarm. Only a few industrial policies were issued in 1854, but they proved to be the seed of future greatness.

Henry Harben, who succeeded Henry Charles Barfoot as secretary in 1856, recognized the possibilities of industrial assurance. The *Century of Service* recalled his shrewd observation that "it is far more prudent to take the pick of the small policies than to have the crumbs which fall from the rich man's table." Careful management and cautious expansion produced a more stable company. In 1864, Harben turned a potential disaster into a tremendous success for the company. William Gladstone, then chancellor of the exchequer, criticized the operations of insurance companies, including the Prudential. Harben counterattacked vigorously. Not content with a war of words in the press, he called in independent actuaries who confirmed his claim that the company was sound and well managed. As a result of those actions, the Prudential experienced a dramatic rise in business and began to establish its reputation for reliability.

Gladstone's attack inadvertently aided the Prudential by making many smaller companies vulnerable. Many went out of business. In 1860, the Prudential had acquired its first firm, British Industry, changing the corporate name to the British Prudential Assurance Company. That action had spurred growth in industrial policies. The Prudential acquired an additional five companies in the 1860s.

By 1880, the Prudential had become the leading company in industrial policies. By that time no other industrial insurance companies extant in 1854 still existed. The following decades witnessed steady growth for the company. By 1905, the Prudential had issued 25 million policies in a population of 43 million. As Barry Supple acknowledged in *The Royal Exchange Assurance*, a history of a rival company, the Prudential had become "virtually a universal habit."

Leadership of the company remained in the hands of its founders into the 20th century. Edgar Horne, a founding director, served as chairman between 1877 and 1905, when Henry Harben succeeded him. Two years later, Harben, 84 years of age, passed the chairmanship to his son, Henry Andrade Harben. When H.A. Harben died in 1910, Thomas Dewey—with the company for 53 years—became chairman. Founder Horne's son, William Edgar Horne, was chairman between 1929 and 1941.

### *"The Man From the Pru" Appears: 1920s–40s*

The Prudential succeeded because of a single-minded determination to meet the needs of its customers. Around the turn of the century, a post office official selling government insurance policies summed up the difficulties of competing with the Prudential. The commemorative volume, *Century of Service*, recalled with pride the competitor's complaint that the Pru "made a point of smoothing over difficulties, of waiving objections and carrying through the business very promptly." Good customer relations became the touchstone for evaluating company policy. Maintaining contact between company and customer became the first priority in times of economic difficulty. The company worked to keep on the books customers who had fallen in arrears. The company also initiated a policy of bonuses for industrial policyholders. Between 1905 and 1948, over £78 million had been paid. The block system of collections, established by the 1920s, became the hallmark of the company's operations. Each agent had an area on the map defined as his territory. He would make a set number of calls per week. The efficiency of the system allowed management to reduce staff and cut costs. By 1948, representatives visited five million homes. The "man from the Pru" had become a national institution celebrated in popular culture.

Never was the stature of the Prudential more evident than in its participation in the two world wars. Warfare poses a true crisis for insurance companies since no actuary can calculate the likely number of casualties. Certainly no actuary could have predicted the carnage of the Western Front in World War I. The Courts (Emergency Powers) Act of 1914 had protected many customers against forfeiture of coverage due to nonpayment of premiums. The Prudential volunteered to honor the policies of those who died as a result of the war, providing that the policy had been initiated before the war. The Pru's most dramatic contribution came in 1915. The country badly needed U.S. dollars. The Prudential placed its total dollar securities, valued at £8.75 million, at the government's disposal.

During the World War II, the Prudential invested £242 million, over 50 percent of corporate assets, in government and government-guaranteed securities. The Prudential paid £5.5 million in war claims. The company could have denied half of those claims, since the policies in question had restricted liability to a return of premiums already paid. The directors, however, chose to suspend that provision. The traditions of customer service and national service became indistinguishable in such actions.

The giant company had become a national institution. In the decades following World War II, the Prudential did not undertake initiatives in a changing economy but remained a dominant force in life assurance, emphasizing its traditional strengths. By the 1970s, some financial observers began to believe that the Pru owed its dominance to sheer inertia, as the company failed to create new service and delivery systems. Senior managers began to realize, in the words of Brian Corby, the lifelong

## Key Dates:

**1848:** A group of investors create the Prudential Mutual Assurance, Investment, and Loan Association.
**1860:** Prudential acquires its first firm, British Industry.
**1915:** The company allows the government to use its dollar securities during the war effort.
**1921:** Prudential begins to sell fire and accident insurance in the Netherlands and France.
**1948:** By now, ''the man from the Pru'' has visited over five million homes.
**1978:** Corporate holdings are reorganized and Prudential Corporation is established as a holding company.
**1984:** The British government abolishes the life assurance premium relief.
**1998:** Prudential launches Egg plc, an online banking subsidiary.
**1999:** The firm changes its name to Prudential plc and announces a series of job cuts.
**2001:** The company sells its general insurance business to Winterthur Insurance Co.

Prudential employee who became CEO in 1982, that ''the Pru has no God-given right to stay the biggest.'' This simple realization, which Corby expressed to the *Investors Chronicle* in March 1986, laid the foundations for the most significant change since the decision to sell industrial policies.

### *Reorganization and Expansion: 1970s–80s*

Searching for methods that would make it more responsive to market forces, the company chose a policy of decentralization. In 1978, the corporate holdings were reorganized. Prudential Corporation was established as a holding company. Prudential Assurance became a subsidiary. In 1984, a more thorough reorganization created seven operating divisions: U.K. individual, U.K. group pensions, international, Mercantile and General Reinsurance, Prudential Portfolio Managers, Prudential Property Services, and Prudential Holborn. A number of ancillary services remained outside this divisional structure. By 1986, the reorganization began to show signs of success. As the *Financial Times* of May 4, 1986 noted: ''The City finally woke up to the fact that a series of apparently unrelated corporate moves were in fact part of a strategy to bring the bulk of the iceberg out of the water.''

The new approach emphasized foreign expansion and acquisitions. Fiammetta Rocco in the August 1989 *Institutional Investor*, pointed out that the Pru had been unique among the great 19th-century insurance companies because it thrived as an English rather than an imperial institution. After World War I, the Prudential had expanded into general insurance, and the new general branch had engaged in modest overseas enterprises. In 1921, the Pru had begun to sell fire and accident insurance in the Netherlands and France. Other operations in Europe, the Commonwealth, and South America followed. However, these enterprises did not alter the character of the company. The attitude toward acquisitions began to alter slowly. Between 1968 and 1973, the Pru acquired the Mercantile and General Reinsurance Company from Swiss Reinsurance Company. This purchase established the Prudential's preeminence in the reinsurance field. Other major additions included the purchase of the Belgian firm L'Escaut in 1972—sold in 1990—the Canadian firm Constellation in 1978, and the Insurance Corporation of Ireland (Life), now Prudential Life of Ireland, in 1985.

Most important was the acquisition of the U.S. Jackson National Life Company in 1986. Approximately 2,000 companies were selling insurance in the United States at the time. Jackson National Life ranked 18th in new ordinary insurance sold, 60th in premium income, and 91st in assets. Purchase of one of the fastest-growing U.S. insurance companies did more than give the Pru an important share of the U.S. market. The purchase price of $608 million brought an innovative and technologically advanced firm into the Pru family. Jackson National Life had been a leader in developing term life and universal life policies. Its operations were computerized and more efficient than the Prudential's administration. Jackson National Life would become an in-house resource for the modernization of Prudential's management. This acquisition indicated the Prudential's determination to recast itself at the end of the 20th century.

The determination to reshape the company did not require abandoning the company's established principles. The company had thrived because of its care for customer needs, willingness to deal with small customers, and determination to judge success on the basis of long-term profitability. These principles guided new ventures such as entrance into estate agency. The Prudential sought access to the younger generation of consumers, a group not concerned with life insurance but interested in acquiring housing.

In 1985, the Prudential purchased an East Anglian real estate agency as an experiment. Success in the local operation inspired a national effort. Because most estate agencies were small and local, Prudential Property Services became a major force almost overnight. By 1989, the company had over 800 local offices. Due to the expense of this rapid expansion and the downturn in the property market, the company expected to lose as much as £35 million in 1989. The Prudential's plan, however, anticipated that this enterprise would encourage young adults to become customers for other Prudential products.

Circumstances forced some changes on the Prudential Corporation. The company's reorganization coincided with revolutionary changes in financial services in Great Britain. Prior to that decade, insurance companies, banks, and building societies had offered discrete services. New government policies under Prime Minister Margaret Thatcher spurred innovation. In 1984, the government abolished life assurance premium relief, a tax advantage which had attracted many customers. The move shocked insurance companies, who were forced to adjust to the new situation. As Brian Corby informed the *Financial Times*, reported March 4, 1984, ''We must recognize we are in competition for the savings pound with everyone else.''

Seeking opportunities to expand its services, the Prudential Corporation established Prudential Holborn as its unit trust investment branch in 1985. The move appeared natural. No company seemed better suited to deal with small, cautious investors. The venture did not meet with immediate success. Prudential Holborn was founded just in time to feel the effects of the stock market crash of 1987. The unit trust business remained depressed for the rest of the decade. Prudential Holborn lost £105 million in 1988 and made a profit of £1.7 million in 1989. Prudential Corporation, though, remained content that the company was well positioned for an inevitable rise in the market.

This rapid expansion into a number of new services created a novel problem for the Pru: lack of consumer recognition. The corporate name was famous but the general population could not keep pace with the rate of corporate change. In 1986, a company survey discovered that only 20 percent of those who knew the Pru realized that the company had recently entered the mortgage business. Clearly, the other 80 percent were not thinking of the Pru first for every financial need. The diversified Pru required a higher profile and more advertising. When the Thatcher government deregulated the State Earnings-related Pension Scheme in 1988, the Pru launched a massive campaign for new pension business. Ten million people were covered by the state plan. Those who chose to leave would receive a rebate which could be invested in a new plan. The Prudential spent £7 million on advertising. In the opening stages of deregulation, the company issued 220,000 new contracts worth £110 million.

After a decade of reorganization, the Prudential Corporation presented a blend of innovation and traditional practice. The famed sales force remained 12,000 strong, still visiting five million homes for pension contributions and life assurance premiums. In an age of computers, this labor-intensive approach appeared anachronistic, but the system produced £1.3 billion in premium income in 1988. Prudential needed to convert this sales force into specialists able to market an integrated package of financial services, and 4,000 had been retrained for this task by the end of 1989.

The leadership of the Prudential Corporation provided the best indicator of future development. Sir Brian Corby, who directed much of the reorganization, had been trained as an actuary. His successor, Michael Newmarch, who became CEO in April 1990, also was a lifelong Prudential employee. However, Newmarch had served as an investment manager not as an actuary. The new portfolio manager in 1989, Hugh Jenkins, had no previous experience with the Prudential Corporation. This highly regarded manager oversaw a portfolio valued at £35 billion. Asked to comment on the appointment of Newmarch, Jenkins observed discreetly that ''the investment function has come to the top.''

### *Changes Continue: 1990s and Beyond*

During the 1990s, Prudential's long term strategy became focused on its diversification efforts, especially in the financial and investment services sector. Toward this end, the company made several key moves to reestablish its brand and transform it into a cutting edge global financial products and services and fund management firm. As part of its global expansion efforts, Prudential Corporation Asia was created in 1994 to take advantage of new business opportunities in the region. Sir Peter Davis took over as CEO in 1995, and under his leadership the Pru made distinct changes that proved to be crucial to its successful entrance into the next century.

In 1997, the company purchased Scottish Amicable Life Assurance Society and renamed it Scottish Amicable plc. That year, the company also laid the groundwork for the launch of Egg plc, a branchless bank that originally operated by telephone and mail but moved into the online arena in 1998. The online banking subsidiary offered such services as savings accounts, mortgages, and personal loans. The venture proved to be an instant success—the web site had over 1.75 million hits in its first week of operation.

In 1999, Prudential strengthened its reach in the mutual funds industry with its £1.9 billion acquisition of M&G Group plc. During that year, Prudential began yet another restructuring effort that included a 20 percent reduction of its domestic workforce. The job cuts signaled a shift from the ''man from the Pru'' direct sales force to a more cost efficient online and telephone customer service system. The firm also adopted a new name, Prudential plc.

Changes continued in the new millennium. By this time, the company's Egg subsidiary was operating as the UK's most successful Internet bank with over one million customers and $11 billion in assets. In 2000, the company spun off approximately 20 percent of the online bank to the public. Prudential itself also listed on the New York Stock Exchange. The firm's management structure changed that year when Jonathan Bloomer took over as CEO and Sir Roger Hurn was named chairman. Hurn announced he would relinquish his post in April 2002 due to his connection with the financially troubled Marconi plc, a telecommunications firm that he chaired from 1998 to September 2001.

During this time period, Prudential's strategy included global expansion to offset weakening U.K. operations. The company was the first U.K. life insurer to become licensed in Vietnam and opened an office in Hanoi in March 2000. Asian expansion also continued in 2001 with the purchase of Orico Life Insurance Co. based in Japan. Prudential commented on its move into the Japanese market in a December 2001 *Daily Yomiuri* article, stating that the firm's ''Japanese entry was a significant part of the program to build our businesses right across the main markets in Asia to continue to be a global creator of financial services solutions for individuals and embark on retail financial services strategies through life insurance, mutual funds, pensions, and eventually banking.''

Prudential also tried to strengthen its position in the United States during 2001. Its attempts were thwarted, however, when its planned $26.5 billion merger with American General Corp. fell through after the United States-based company instead accepted an offer to merge with American International Group.

Prudential forged ahead with its domestic insurance operations restructuring, and in late 2001 the company announced the sale of its general insurance business to Winterthur Insurance Company. As part of the deal, Prudential partnered with Winterthur's U.K. subsidiary, Churchill, to provide Prudential-branded general insurance products in the region.

With the dramatic changes of the 1980s and 1990s behind it, Prudential now stood with five major business segments that included Prudential's U.K. and European insurance operations, M&G Investments, Egg plc, Jackson National Life, and Prudential Corporation Asia. Management's long term goals continued to be centered on building a global retail financial services business. With a longstanding history of success behind it, Prudential appeared to be well positioned to achieve future success.

## *Principal Divisions*

Jackson National Life Insurance Company (U.S.); M&G Group plc; Egg plc; Prudential Corporation Asia (PCA); Prudential UK Insurance Operations; Prudential Europe.

## *Principal Competitors*

CGNU plc; Legal & General Group plc; Royal & Sun Alliance Insurance Group plc.

## *Further Reading*

*A Century of Service: The Story of the Prudential 1848–1948*, London: Prudential Life Assurance Company, 1948.

Fairlamb, David, ''Why Egg Is On a Roll,'' *Business Week*, March 11, 2002.

Noonan, Brendan, ''U.K.'s Prudential Hopes Its Egg Is Golden,'' *Best's Review*, November 1998, p. 41.

''PCA Life Insurance Cracks Japanese Market,'' *Daily Yomiuri*, December 24, 2001.

Power, Carol, ''In Brief: U.K. Web Bank Starts Diminished IPO,'' *American Banker*, May 26, 2000, p. 24.

''Prudential 2000 Profit Up 8% Despite Weak UK Market,'' *Futures World News*, June 8, 2001.

Purves, Libby, ''Safe Not Sorry,'' *Assets*, spring 1989.

Rocco, Fiammetta, ''Remodeling Britain's Pru,'' *Institutional Investor*, August 1989.

Taylor, Catherine, ''Prudential's Exit From Merger Raises Strategic Questions,'' *Wall Street Journal Europe*, May 14, 2001, p. 12.

''U.K. Prudential Chairman Resigns Over Ties to Troubled Telecom Firm,'' *A.M. Best Newswire*, April 24, 2002.

''U.K. Prudential Cuts Jobs, Sell Business to Winterthur,'' *A.M. Best Newswire*, November 2, 2001.

—Joseph Bator
—update: Christina M. Stansell

# Pumpkin Masters, Inc.

**1905 Sherman Street**
**Denver, Colorado 80203**
**U.S.A.**
**Telephone: (303) 860-8006**
**Web site: http://www.pumpkinmasters.com**

*Private Company*
*Incorporated:* 1986
*Employees:* 25
*Sales:* $10 million (2001 est.)
*NAIC:* 339943 Marking Device Manufacturing; 339999 All Other Miscellaneous Manufacturing

Colorado-based Pumpkin Masters, Inc. is the nation's leading producer of pumpkin carving kits and Halloween decorating products. Its products, available largely through mass retailers such as Target and Wal-Mart, include patterns, saws, candles, and candleholders. The company is 80 percent-owned by the publicly traded, Connecticut-based Security Capital Corporation, which also owns Possible Dreams (a seasonal giftware manufacturer) and Primrose (a preschool franchiser). In the early 2000s, Pumpkin Masters was focusing on bringing the pumpkin carving concept to a wider audience, particularly in Europe.

### *1983 Origins Based on a Family Tradition*

Paul Bardeen was a safety engineer who loved Halloween, especially carving pumpkins. As Bardeen's family grew, he looked for even safer ways to involve his children in his favorite holiday and favorite part of that holiday, carving pumpkins. He wanted to develop both an easier and safer way of making elaborate designs. Bardeen began experimenting with pattern making and devising small carving tools. His system consisted of using small saws and drill bits and, after trial and error, poking holes into a pumpkin from a pattern to transfer the design. Each year the pumpkins became more elaborate and were the envy of the neighborhood. Local newspapers often ran stories, accompanied by pictures of the Bardeens' latest creations. In addition to his own children, Bardeen also taught the neighborhood children his techniques for carving pumpkins and eventually held demonstrations at schools and community centers.

John Bardeen fondly recalled carving pumpkins with his father, when he was growing up in Racine, Wisconsin. Bardeen graduated from the University of Wisconsin-Madison in 1968. He moved to Denver, Colorado, where he helped develop a building company, U.S. Tennis Court and Track Builders. Bardeen's father died in 1983, and Bardeen and his four sisters—Dione, Janice, Pat, and Kathie—decided that a marketable pumpkin carving kit would be a nice tribute to their father's enthusiasm and expertise.

The original Pumpkin Masters carving kit took three years to develop. During that time, Bardeen's wife, Kea, retired from her law practice to help Bardeen launch the new company, Pumpkin Ltd., with headquarters in the Bardeen home.

Test-marketed in local grocery and craft stores, the kits originally retailed for $10 each, but the Bardeens quickly decided to scale back the kit's contents and reduce its cost to around $5, a more reasonable price for a seasonal impulse item. Sales continued and even improved. The Bardeens were ready to serve a larger population.

### *Convincing the Public in the Mid-1980s*

In fact, the Bardeens had the kits in stores across the United States within four years of their company's inception. This was largely due to innovative marketing, as the company worked to convince people of the need for special pumpkin carving kits when they already had perfectly serviceable knives in their kitchen.

In their first year, 1986, Pumpkin Masters placed about 6,000 kits in a Denver grocery chain, some toy stores, and a few craft stores. That initial trial was successful, so the company hired a Chicago-based marketing firm, who had national sales representatives, and a large public relations firm to take the carving kits nationwide.

Based on the early success, the marketing firm predicted sales of 600,000 kits for 1987. Riding the enthusiasm, Pumpkin Mas-

### Company Perspectives:

*The company's mission is to make products that make celebrating Halloween easier, safer and more fun for all ages.*

ters obtained bank financing and letters of credit to have 235,000 kits made overseas. Unfortunately, the sales target was way off—only 50,000 kits were sold through the efforts of the marketing firm. The public relations firm also failed to produce excitement over the company. Thanks to the efforts of Pumpkin Masters, a total of 92,000 kits were sold in 1997, but the company owed the bank $250,000 and a Minnesota warehouse held 143,000 unsold kits, 10 percent of which were without saw blades.

## *Publicity Key to Success in the Late 1980s–90s*

Bardeen, taking 1987 as a lesson to learn from, fired his marketing and public relation firms, and asked for and received an extension from the bank. Bardeen arranged for each carving kit to be inspected and hired his own sales representatives. In 1988, Bardeen received a call from a satisfied customer, who was also a public relations professional. She volunteered her services and, pointing out that ''Monday Night Football'' would be broadcasting on Halloween night that year, suggested Bardeen carve the likeness of the show's announcers. The idea was sold to ABC, and Bardeen debuted his carvings on national television on October 31, 1988. The publicity resulting from the original ''Monday Night Football'' appearance led to other television appearances and the company carved pumpkins for shows such as ''Wheel of Fortune,'' ''Seinfeld,'' ''Dateline NBC,'' ''ER,'' ''Monday Night Football,'' ''Home Improvement,'' ''The Rosie O'Donnell Show,'' and the ''Today'' show. The promotions became a large part of the company's business. By 1991, the success of the company prompted a move to larger facilities. In 1994, the name Pumpkin Masters was introduced as the trade name for Pumpkin Ltd. products.

By 1997, Pumpkin Masters had sold more than two million carving kits and was reporting sales of more than $7 million. In fact, the popularity of carving kits resulted in higher demand for and sales of pumpkins. By this time, Kea Bardeen was ready to retire, and John too began to scale back his involvement. They partnered with Security Capital Corporation, which obtained an 80 percent interest in Pumpkin Masters. Bardeen commented to Amy Berger in *Income Opportunities:* ''Our partners don't run the company on a day-to-day basis, but we take their input very seriously. Now Kea has money off the table for her retirement and I can still have a hand in Pumpkin Masters by contributing to promotions, public relations, marketing, product development and sourcing.''

Because of the company's turnaround, Pumpkin Masters was a 1998 honoree in the Blue Chip Enterprise Initiative, which recognizes small businesses that overcome challenges to become successful. The company also was named a ''Champion of Industry'' in 1999 by MSNBC, for producing high-quality products that made pumpkin carving safer.

For Halloween 1998, Pumpkin Masters introduced new kits, with more intricate patterns and new carving tools. The kits retailed for $4.99 and also included an entry form for a national carving contest, with $10,000 in prizes. Children's kits were available with simpler patters, plus the company offered painting kits, safety candles, and books of carving patterns.

Bardeen, noting that Halloween had become a major holiday, launched the Halloween Association in April 1998. The purpose of the association was stated as being ''dedicated to promoting a positive image for Halloween and to protecting and enhancing the Halloween industry.'' Bardeen's main purpose for forming the Halloween Association was to build momentum and garner support for his pet idea, that of changing the celebration of Halloween from October 31 to the last Saturday of October. Bardeen's arguments for changing the day of celebration for Halloween included: it would be safer for children, who would be trick-or-treating before the change to standard time; it would be better for children and teachers, as the celebration would not be on a school day; it would result in higher sales because of adult parties; it would be better for businesses, as employees would not leave early to take their children trick or treating. Bardeen remained active in the Halloween Association and continued to publicize his idea for moving the traditional date for the Halloween celebration. By the beginning of the 21st century, however, the idea had failed to catch on.

By the late 1990s, Halloween was second only to Christmas in terms of holiday sales and holiday decorating, and third in terms of parties, after New Year's Eve and Super Bowl Sunday. In 1997, Halloween-related sales were $2.5 billion, with $1 billion in costumes sales, $950 million spent on candy, and $50 million worth of greeting cards sold. By 1999, Halloween was a $5 billion business. It was estimated that in 2000 more than 80 percent of U.S. children dressed up for Halloween and went trick or treating and/or to parties. About three-quarters of U.S. adults also took part in Halloween festivities.

Pumpkin Masters was aggressive in defending its patent rights, scrutinizing retail outlets for copycat products. In 1999, Pumpkin Masters filed a lawsuit against the Disney Store, claiming patent infringement. Specifically, Pumpkin Masters demanded that Disney stop selling the Pooh Halloween Carving Kit and Pooh and Pals Pumpkin Carving Kits. Prior to 1999, the company settled suits brought against Kmart Corporation and Kraft General Foods Inc.

## *Expanding Beyond the United States in the Late 1990s*

Pumpkin Masters had sold kits in Canada for years, and beginning in 1999, it began expanding its global focus to include Europe. The U.S. Halloween holiday was piquing interest in Europe (in France in particular), with adults celebrating by hosting masquerades or other dress-up festivities. (The concept of children's trick-or-treat had yet to gain popularity.) The carving kits Pumpkin Masters began marketing in Europe featured instructions in English, French, German, Dutch, Portuguese, and Spanish. In France, Halloween sales amounted to about $100,000 in 1996, $200,000 in 1997, $5 million in 1998, and Halloween-related sales amounted to about $10 million in 1999. Pumpkin Masters prepared to take advantage of that trend, hopefully introducing the concept of carving pumpkins to Europeans.

## Key Dates:

**1983:** Paul Bardeen, pumpkin carving innovator, dies; Pumpkin Ltd. is formed by his children.
**1986:** The first pumpkin carving kit is introduced in Denver.
**1987:** A patent is filed for the pumpkin carving kit.
**1988:** National exposure on "Monday Night Football" results in higher sales.
**1994:** Pumpkin, Ltd. forms the Pumpkin Masters trade name.
**1998:** The company is an honoree for the Blue Chip Enterprise Initiative.
**1997:** Gay Burke becomes president and CEO.
**1999:** The company is recognized as a Champion of Industry by MSNBC.
**1999:** Pumpkin Masters begins selling carving kits in Europe.
**2001:** The company offers free Lanterns of Liberty patterns on its web site.

### *The Future*

In 1997 Kea Bardeen retired as president of Pumpkin Masters. Gay Burke, a former consultant to Pumpkin Masters, became the company's new president and chief executive officer. Although divorced, both Kea and John Bardeen remained active in the company—she as a consultant and he in the public relations and marketing aspects of Pumpkin Masters.

After the terrorist attacks on the United States on September 11, 2001, Pumpkin Masters produced a line of patterns called "Lanterns of Liberty." To encourage people to carve patriotic pumpkins, the company offered free downloadable patterns on their web site. Patterns included those of President George W. Bush, the statue of Liberty, the Liberty Bell, and the Stars and Stripes. Pumpkin Masters was looking to reflect and add to U.S. patriotism and was hoping that ten million homes would have patriotic pumpkins displayed along with traditionally carved pumpkins. For those who felt carving was beyond them, Pumpkin Masters urged Americans to decorate their pumpkins with red, white, and blue paint, stickers, foil, ribbons, and construction paper.

Pumpkin Masters looked to develop even easier ways to carve and decorate pumpkins, as well as more elaborate ways. Promotions through television shows remained the company's main form of advertising and marketing. Looking to branch out beyond Halloween, Pumpkin Masters introduced Watermelon Carving Kits and Exceptional Easter Egg Decorating Kits. The company looked to expand the non-Halloween lines into even more kits for decorating.

In 2001 Pumpkin Masters products included: Pumpkin Carving Kit—the original kit, which includes a poker, two carving saws, a drill, ten patterns, and instructions; children's line—kits made for use by children, including Kids Carving & Activity Kit, Kids Fright Lights, Trick-Or-Treat Lighted Safety Bucket, Kids Pumpkin Punch Out, Kids Paint & Patterns, and Kids Safe Pumpkin Light; new pumpkin decorating kits, including the Sculpting Kit, Pumpkin Punch Out, and Sparkling Pumpkin Jewels; accessories—pattern books, saws for cutting pumpkin tops, scoops to clean the inside of pumpkins, and candles and holders.

### *Principal Competitors*

HMS Mfg Co.

### *Further Reading*


Berger, Amy, "Pumpkin Master Carves Out Big Profits," *Income Opportunities,* October 1, 1998, p. 66.

Berta, Dina, "Coming Soon: Jacques-O'-Lanterns; Pumpkin Masters Expands into European Markets," *Denver Rocky Mountain News,* October 15, 1999, p. 2B.

——, "Firm Sues Disney, Others Over Pumpkin-Carving Kits," *Denver Rocky Mountain News,* October 15, 1999, p. 2B.

Brown, Suzanne S., "Carving a Halloween Niche," *Denver Post,* October 29, 2001, p. F-01.

Hajewski, Doris, "Selling Points Column," *Milwaukee Journal Sentinel,* March 11, 1998, p. 3.

"Halloween Kits," *MMR,* March 9, 1998, p. 14.

Landwehr, Rebecca, "Scare Tactics That Work; Halloween Lasts All Year for Some Denver Business," *Denver Business Journal,* October 8, 1999, p. 3A.

Love, Thomas, "Creating a Demand for a New Product," *Nation's Business,* August 1998, p. 11.

"Move Afoot to Carve Out Saturday for Halloween," *Denver Post,* October 20, 1998, p. C-05.

Pollack, Judann, "From Toaster Strudel to McD's Costumes, Halloween Is Howling," *Advertising Age,* September 14, 1998, p. 4.

Proctor, Cathy, "Reaping Profits from Pumpkins," *Denver Business Journal,* October 27, 2000, p. 1


—Lisa Musolf Karl

# PW Eagle, Inc.

**222 South 9th Street, Suite 2880**
**Minneapolis, Minnesota 55402**
**U.S.A.**
**Telephone: (612) 305-0339**
**Fax: (612) 371-9651**
**Web site: http://www.pwpipe.com**

*Public Company*
*Incorporated:* 1993
*Employees:* 691
*Sales:* $246.1 million (2001)
*Stock Exchanges:* NASDAQ
*Ticker Symbol:* PWEI
*NAIC:* 326122 Plastic Pipe and Pipe Fitting Manufacturing

PW Eagle, Inc. is the second largest manufacturer of polyvinyl chloride (PVC) and polyethylene (PE) tubing products in the United States and sells its products under the brand PWPipe, the name of the West Coast plastic pipe manufacturer it acquired in the fall of 1999. As the largest merchant buyer of PVC resin in the country, the company can demand favorable prices for its raw materials and thus enjoys a small advantage in a highly competitive industry. PW Eagle's wide range of plastic pipe products, ranging in diameter from one-half inch to 24 inches, are used for potable and sewage water transmission, turf and agricultural irrigation, plumbing, natural gas transmission, and, more recently, as casings for fiber optic lines and telecommunications cables. The company's primary distribution area is west of the Ohio and Mississippi Rivers, where its nine manufacturing facilities are located. At each of the facilities, PVC compound is melted in an extrusion machine, pulled through a sizing apparatus that determines the diameter and wall thickness of the pipe, moved through a cooling water trough, cut into lengths, and shipped out to regional consumers. Company President Larry Fleming heads a management team made up of former PWPipe executives at PW Eagle's operating headquarters in Eugene, Oregon, while CEO William H. Spell oversees the company from its corporate headquarters in Minneapolis. The largest shareholder in the company is Spell Capital Partners, a small private equity firm that holds about 40 percent of PW Eagle's outstanding shares.

### *Blackhawk: Entering the PVC Pipe Business*

The origins of PW Eagle lay in the early 1990s, when several separate plastic pipe manufacturers were united in an empty public shell know as Blackhawk Holdings. Blackhawk came out of Rath Packing Company, which ceased operations and went bankrupt in 1984. In 1985, a group of investors acquired the empty shell, changed the name to Blackhawk Holdings, Inc., and began operating in the field of financial services. When this venture failed, the board decided to make a fresh start and in 1992 brought in four members of Spell Capital Partners as directors. William H. Spell, a former investment banker, became president of the company. His father, Harry W. Spell, also joined the board, along with Bruce Richard, who had worked with the younger Spell at the Minneapolis utility Northern States Power Company, and Richard W. Perkins, president of a private asset management firm in suburban Minneapolis. William Spell's task was to liquidate Blackhawk's financial services assets and find acquisitions in a more promising industry. Richard and Perkins both supported the idea of finding a low-tech, dependable industry that could be consolidated under Blackhawk. At the time, the plastic pipe industry was fragmented into many regional enterprises. Raw materials accounted for close to 70 percent of the cost of producing the pipe, so if Blackhawk could gain enough of a presence in the industry, it could profit from increased buying power with suppliers of PVC resin.

In December 1993, Blackhawk gained control of Eagle Plastics in Hastings, Nebraska, for about $11.5 million. Under the deal, Blackhawk would own 91 percent of Eagle and the pipe manufacturer's managers would own 9 percent. Eagle Plastics had 100 employees in 1993 and revenues of $24.2 million for the first 11 months of the year. Founded in 1984, the company produced PVC and PE pipes for the commercial and industrial markets in the Midwest. Larry Schnase was one of the founders of the company and continued serving as president until 1996. Now acting as Blackhawk's CEO, William Spell

## Company Perspectives:

*PW Eagle strives to maintain and enhance its status as a leading provider of high-quality plastic pipe and tubing products and a recognized industry leader in quality and service.*

was glad to have an ownership position in the manufacturing industry. The *Minneapolis Star Tribune* quoted him as saying, "We're just so happy about it. The shareholders and the partners. It's just happy days."

### *Further Acquisitions: 1995–98*

The manufacture of plastic pipes was a growing business because builders were drawn to a product that did not corrode or allow seepage. Through the 1990s, PVC pipes gradually gained market share from alternatives such as concrete, cast iron, and other metals. In addition, demand was up as the economy recovered from a downturn in 1991. Blackhawk reported revenues of $34.1 million for 1994 and a net income of $1.4 million. In 1995, the company gained two more manufacturing companies. The first was Pacific Plastics, Inc., of Hillsboro, Oregon, which Blackhawk bought for $6.7 million. The company then acquired Arrow Pacific Plastics of Midvale, Utah. Blackhawk changed its name to Eagle Pacific Industries, Inc. and was listed on the NASDAQ exchange under the symbol EPII. Revenues for 1995 were $51.3 million, much higher than the previous year due to the recent acquisitions, but the company reported a net loss of $865,000 due to fluctuating prices for raw materials in that year. Because the plastic pipe industry tended to pass the cost of raw materials on to its consumer, the business generated more profit when the price of PVC resin was rising, given that the price of finished materials usually rose at a faster rate than that of raw materials. However, PVC suppliers were producing more resin than could be consumed, and prices were at a six-year low.

Eagle Pacific's performance improved in 1996, helped by the stabilization of the plastic resin market. The company posted net earnings of $3.5 million on sales of $65.3 million. Over the course of the year, Eagle Pacific bought a distribution center in Baker City, Oregon, integrated Pacific Plastics and Arrow into its operations, and strengthened its financial position by repurchasing some $3 million in subordinated debt. The company now had three manufacturing facilities and began the process of upgrading them to make production more efficient. Production capacity expanded in 1997 at Hastings and Hillsboro and total pounds sold for the year rose 13 percent over 1996. Net sales in 1997 reached $71.7 million, showing 10 percent growth for the year. Nevertheless, net income was only $931,000, once again the result of irregularities in the price of PVC resin. In the first half of the year, operational problems at several resin producers drove up the price of resin, but Eagle Pacific could not pass on the costs since the increase was not due to a true rise in demand. Consequently, the selling price remained low all year long.

The company gained some working capital in the spring of 1997 when it issued $10 million in preferred stock to Massachusetts Mutual Life Insurance Company. The capital was used to complete a series of infrastructure improvements, reduce debt, and support further growth. The infrastructure improvements paid off in 1998, as total pounds sold rose 13 percent, compared to industry-wide growth of 1 percent. However, lower selling prices offset the increase in sales volume, and net income was a modest $1.79 million on net sales of $74 million. Eagle Pacific was still looking to make acquisitions, and in December 1998 it announced its intention to take over a PVC resin plant in Oklahoma City, Oklahoma. CONDEA Vista Company, which owned the plant, would get a 40 to 50 percent stake in Eagle Pacific in exchange for control of the resin plant. At the same time, Eagle Pacific planned to buy a PVC pipe business that was located next door to the resin plant, paying owner Lamson & Sessions $58 million. The deal would have quadrupled Eagle's annual revenue, but it was officially dropped in April 1999 as PVC prices recovered from low levels and Vista and Lamson wanted to find a better deal.

### *Joining Forces With PWPipe in 1999*

Luckily, there was a more successful acquisition on the horizon. The company in question was Pacific Western Extruded Plastics Company, better known as PWPipe. PWPipe's history went back to 1967, when Simpson Investment Company, a family-controlled holding company, bought a small factory in Eugene, Oregon. The plant made PVC pipes for sewers and water mains. Simpson also owned the successful Simpson Timber Company, but the firm wanted to diversify since plastic pipe was cutting into the market for competing wood products. Simpson's pipe manufacturing business expanded through acquisitions. The company acquired a plant in Sunnyside, Washington from Robintech in 1977; a plant in Visalia, California, from Gifford-Hill in 1982; and a plant in Tacoma, Washington, from Western Plastics in 1985. That year the company changed its name to Pacific Western Extruded Plastics, or PWPipe. Two more acquisitions brought the total number of manufacturing sites to six: a plant in Cameron Park, California, was bought in 1987 from Certain-Teed, and another in Perris, California, was bought in 1989 from Gamma.

In 1995, parent company Simpson Investment decided to concentrate on its paper and timber business and sold PWPipe to Mitsubishi Chemical for about $85 million. At the time, PWPipe had approximately 500 employees and was led by James K. Rash, who had been company president since 1982. As Rash told Tacoma's *News Tribune*, "Our future will be brighter because we'll be associated with a petro-chemical company—better aligned than a forest-products company owning us." Mitsubishi aimed to vertically integrate its North American chemical operations and was considering building a resin production facility. However, an economic contraction in Asia, starting in the fall of 1997, pushed Mitsubishi to seek a buyer for PWPipe. The timing was just right for a deal with Eagle Pacific.

Eagle Pacific bought PWPipe in September 1999 for $73.8 million, gaining control of the Oregon producer's six west coast plants. The combined companies became the largest producer of PVC pipe in the western part of the United States. PWPipe's 1998 revenues were $180 million, more than double Eagle Pacific's figures. Concomitant with the sale, Eagle Pacific re-

**Key Dates:**

**1967:** PWPipe begins making PVC pipe in Oregon.
**1984:** Eagle Plastics is formed in Hastings, Nebraska.
**1993:** Blackhawk Holdings, Inc. buys Eagle Plastics.
**1995:** Blackhawk acquires Pacific Plastics and Arrow Plastics and changes its name to Eagle Pacific Industries, Inc.
**1999:** Eagle Pacific acquires Pacific Western Extruded Plastics Company (PWPipe) from Mitsubishi Chemical.
**2000:** The company name is changed to PW Eagle, Inc.

deemed all $10 million of its preferred stock from Massachusetts Mutual and completely refinanced itself. Significant shares in the company's equity were given to management executives at PWPipe.

### *Integration Under the PW Eagle Name: 2000–02*

With the PWPipe's management experience now working for Eagle Pacific, the transaction strengthened the company in the area where it was weakest. The company's operating headquarters was immediately moved to Oregon, and the top management positions were given to a group of six executives who had worked together at PWPipe since 1990. James K. Rash continued in his position as president; Roger R. Robb, who had been with PWPipe since 1984, carried on in his role of chief financial officer; and Larry I. Fleming, a PWPipe executive since 1990, continued as senior vice-president. Meanwhile, William Spell remained CEO, his father Harry Spell stayed on as chairman of the board, and Bruce Richard continued as vice-chairman. All of the company's products would now use the PWPipe brand name, although the official corporate name was changed to PW Eagle, Inc. in 2000. The combined companies were ready to play a strong role in the plastic pipe industry. William Spell said of the PWPipe acquisition, "In the last five years the two companies have spent a total of approximately $45 million in capital improvements to become low-cost efficient producers and both are currently reaping the benefits of those expenditures. The addition of the PWPipe management group will add significant experience and depth to our management team."

The market for plastic pipe looked good at the end of 1999. Demand had grown from two billion feet in 1989 to four billion in 1998, outpacing more moderate growth for copper and steel pipe during that period. Moreover, the low-tech product was experiencing demand from a high-tech industry: about one quarter of PW Eagle's pipe was being used to protect fiber optic and telecommunications connections. The company's sales were $154 million in 1999; if the PWPipe acquisition had been completed on the first of the year, sales would have been $303 million. Sales were boosted by higher raw materials prices, as no new capacity for producing PVC resin had been added since late 1997. At the same time, demand was strong. Net income for 1999 was $14.6 million.

PW Eagle rode a wave of success well into 2000. First quarter earnings exceeded analysts' estimates, and the company's stock price was up 310 percent in the first six months of the year. Spell, describing himself as a "reformed investment banker," told the *Minneapolis Star Tribune* that the company's growth had exceeded his expectations. "At the end of the day, give me a company that has a product and cash flow," he said. "That's where I'd rather be any day." In August, PW Eagle, looking to fill in the gaps in its market coverage, bought a plant in Phoenix. The acquisition would allow the company to supply this area while enjoying lower transportation costs. The year end figures for 2000 showed continued growth: net sales were $344.0 million, with a net income of $18.2 million.

However, an economic downturn had already started late in 2000, causing a fourth-quarter loss of $7.5 million. In a "Dutch Auction" tender offer in May 2001, PW Eagle tried to stabilize its stock price by buying back 1.2 million shares, about 15 percent of its outstanding common stock. However, the share price continued to fall steadily. The company then moved to scale back its operations. The Hillsboro plant, with 100 employees, was closed permanently, and the Phoenix plant, with 21 employees, ceased operations temporarily. The company hoped to reopen the Phoenix plant when demand picked up. After the closings, eight plants remained operational. The 2001 economy remained weak, pushing down both prices and sales. PW Eagle's net sales for the year were down 28 percent to $246.1 million, and the company reported a net loss of $12.9 million. A leadership change also took place in 2001: Jim Rash retired in February from his position as president and was replaced by Larry Fleming.

In a further effort to improve its financial condition, PW Eagle entered into an agreement in March 2002 to sell and lease back several of its facilities. The real estate investment banking firm W.P. Carey & Co. LLC acquired the Tacoma, Washington, West Jordan, Utah, and Perris, California, plants, as well as the operating headquarters in Eugene, Oregon, for about $13.7 million. Separately, PW Eagle also sold its Hillsboro, Oregon, property with some equipment for $1.31 million. Proceeds from the transactions were used to reduce the company's considerable debt. The euphoria of the company's rapid gains following the PWPipe acquisition was over. Spell would have to keep the company going through leaner times, waiting for an economic recovery to fuel renewed demand for plastic pipes.

### *Principal Competitors*

Formosa Plastics Corporation; NACO Industries, Inc.; NIBCO Inc.; Royal Group Technologies Inc.

### *Further Reading*

Adams, Jarret, "Eagle Drops Vista PVC Deal," *Chemical Week*, April 28, 1999, p. 19.
DePass, Dee, "Black Hawk Acquires Part of Nebraska Plastics Firm," *Minneapolis Star Tribune*, December 21, 1993, p. 3D.
"Eagle Pacific Industries Completes Major Refinancing & Acquisition of PW Pipe," *Business Wire*, September 21, 1999.
Elliot, Alan R., "Pipe Maker Overcomes the Stigma of Plastic," *Investor's Business Daily*, May 19, 2000.
Groeneveld, Benno, "PW Eagle's Boss Finds Fun in Plastic Pipes," *Corporate Report*, July 2000.
Oslund, John J., and Patrick Kennedy, "ST100 Mid-year Update: Back to Basics," *Minneapolis Star Tribune*, July 3, 2000.

Sinks, James, ''Pacific Western Plastics Makes Recycled Pipes to Control Landfill Runoff,'' *Knight-Ridder/Tribune Business News,* August 24, 1994.

Tucker, Rob, ''Simpson Investment to Sell Plastic-Pipe Subsidiary to Mitsubishi Chemical,'' *News Tribune* (Tacoma, Wash.), July 5, 1995.

Waters, John Jr., ''Eugene, Ore.-Based Pipe, Tube Company to Reel in Expenses,'' *Knight-Ridder/Tribune Business News*, March 11, 2002.

Weinstein, Randi, ''PW Eagle to Temporarily Cease Operations at Chandler Pipe Manufacturing Plant,'' *Business Journal - Serving Phoenix & the Valley of the Sun*, August 3, 2001, p. 50.

—Sarah Ruth Lorenz

# Quality Chekd Dairies, Inc.

**1733 Park Street**
**Naperville, Illinois 60563**
**U.S.A.**
**Telephone (630) 717-1110**
**Fax: (630) 717-1126**
**Web site: http://www.qchekd.com**

*Cooperative*
*Incorporated:* 1944
*Employees:* 14
*Sales:* $2.5 billion (2001)
*NAIC:* 311500 Dairy Product Manufacturing

Based in Naperville, Illinois, Quality Chekd Dairies, Inc. is a non-profit cooperative owned by some 40 independent dairy processors located in the United States as well as Mexico, El Salvador, and Columbia. Most U.S. consumers are familiar with Quality Chekd's trademark logo, a red checkmark inside a blue Q, stamped on a wide range of dairy products found in the supermarket. In fact, according to internal studies, almost 90 percent of consumers are aware of the QC logo. The co-op's marketing efforts include the designing of packaging as well as the production of TV and radio commercials that can be adopted by its members. In addition, Quality Chekd offers a number of other valuable services to members. It provides quality assurance testing using an independent laboratory, Silliker Labs, to conduct two random tests in order to make sure that the products of its members surpass industry standards. In this way, not only are consumers confident that QC-stamped products are of the highest quality, but the reputation of the individual dairies is protected. Quality Chekd also assists member dairies with a purchasing program through which the independent operators take advantage of their combined size in order to realize the best possible prices for ingredients and packaging materials. As a result, members are able to lower prices on their dairy products and gain an edge in the market. The organization helps further by making business consultants available to assist members with the implementation of new computer technology and accounting systems. Moreover, Quality Chekd provides the staff of member dairies with training and education through its Cow Tech program, which offers a broad-based curriculum of subjects, from personnel issues to technical matters. In addition to classes taught in person, Cow Tech also informs through video tape, interactive CR-ROMs, and the Internet.

### *World War II Origins*

Quality Chekd was originally created to benefit ice cream makers in anticipation of increased competition after World War II. The first commercial ice cream plant in the United States dated back to the mid-1800s, but because of the difficulties in properly transporting frozen products, the industry initially developed along local lines. Americans' love of ice cream grew so rapidly that virtually every community boasted its own milk and ice cream operation. Three large ice cream makers emerged in the early decades of the 20th century: Sealtest, Borden, and Meadow Gold. World War II forced restrictions on many of the ingredients of ice cream, and manufacturers were limited to 65 percent of the amount produced during the period of December 1, 1941 to November 30, 1942. As a result, independent dairies were able to sell as much ice cream as they could make, but by 1944, when it became apparent that the war would soon be over, the big three as well as other large ice cream makers were gearing up aggressive marketing campaigns that would be implemented once the restrictions were lifted. Local independent dairies would be at a clear disadvantage in the postwar world, and it became apparent that in order to survive they would have to band together.

Quality Chekd grew out of a committee established by five member companies of the United Dairy Products Buying Association. Although member dairies felt comfortable joining forces to save money on the purchase of supplies, they remained competitors in many cases, and it was agreed that the committee should operate independent of the association. Representatives from the five ice cream makers, three of which were located in Iowa and two in Wisconsin, began to meet monthly in Chicago at their own expense to develop a mutual advertising and merchandising program. Ultimately the group turned to Chicago's L.W. Ramsey Advertising Agency to develop a professional program, including a trademark that could be used by all the participating companies, a carton design, and a year-long

**Company Perspectives:**

*At Quality Chekd, top quality is a must. When the government establishes standards for the dairy industry, we push them further to provide customers the freshest, best-tasting products possible.*

advertising-merchandising program. Quality Chekd's five founding members split the $10,000 cost of the project. During much of 1944, the committee met with the Ramsey Agency to develop the initial program, which was ready by October of that year. According to research conducted in the Midwest, the agency learned that the primary concern of homemakers buying ice cream after the war would be the quality of the product. As a result, the program focused on assuring the consumer that the ice cream of member dairies was of the highest quality, a pledge that would be backed by regular product checking at an independent laboratory. It was this commitment to testing that led to the coining of the phrase "Quality Chekd" and the use of a red check mark in the trademark created by the Ramsey Agency. Originally the elements symbolizing product approval were contained within a cartouche, a decorative scroll.

On October 25, 1944, 21 ice cream manufacturers, including the five founding companies, were invited to Chicago for a presentation of the Quality Chekd program created by the Ramsey Agency. It was so well received that all 21 candidates immediately signed on. A cooperative was then incorporated under the laws of Wisconsin and named Quality Chekd Ice Cream Association. One of the five original committee members, Irving B. Weber of Sidwell Dairy Company located in Iowa City, Iowa, was named president, a post he would hold for the next 25 years. The remaining four members of the committee formed the organization's first board of directors. It was determined that member companies were to be charged annual dues of $250 and .75 cents on each gallon of ice cream sold. At this stage, Quality Chekd was represented by companies in only five states: ten in Wisconsin, seven in Iowa, three in Minnesota, and one each in Michigan and South Dakota. The total sales volume of the 21 charter members was $15 million. By the time of the first general meeting held in Chicago on April 25, 1945, additional members also joined the cooperative.

## *Operational After World War II*

Once wartime restrictions were lifted and Quality Chekd became operational, a managing director was hired to run the organization, Charles T. Walker. Because he lived in Cincinnati, Ohio, Quality Chekd was initially located there. Walker was successful in adding new members, but due to health problems was forced to step down after just a year and a half. His replacement, Harlie F. Zimmerman, enjoyed a much longer tenure, serving some 33 years in the post. A graduate of Iowa State University, where he majored in the dairy industry, Zimmerman gained practical experience in the business working at Babcock Dairy Company in Toledo, Ohio, a Quality Chekd member. Moreover, he possessed innate political instincts that served him well over the decades. He maintained close relationships with each member, allowing him to preserve harmony by resolving complaints before they reached the board. Moreover, he was an excellent public speaker and well represented Quality Chekd within the dairy industry.

When Zimmerman took over in March 1949, Quality Chekd's headquarters were moved to Chicago, at first consisting of nothing more than a six-foot-square office. With the economy picking up after the war, and young baby boomers eating ice cream at an ever increasing pace—in 1920 the average American ate 6.43 quarts each year, a number that increased to 14.66 quarts by 1950—Quality Chekd added new members and hired two field representatives, requiring the procurement of larger accommodations. In 1950, the organization needed even more space to support its activities, which now included a milk program. To better reflect Quality Chekd's broader interests, which would ultimately include a wide range of dairy products, the co-op changed its name from Quality Chekd Ice Cream Association to Quality Chekd Dairies, Inc.

With the hope of increasing its membership, Quality Chekd decided in 1952 to try national advertising, which would be used to support the rollout of a new product. Without conducting any market research, the organization's overly aggressive board settled on root beer-flavored ice cream they dubbed "Jolly Root Beer." It appeared at first to be an inspired idea, given the appeal of root beer in the early 1950s. The drink was sold at roadside barrel-shaped stands, and root beer floats that featured a scoop of vanilla ice cream were popular across the country. Quality Chekd spent $8,000 on advertising and also created point of sales materials to promote its root beer ice cream. After some initial success, however, sales quickly tailed off. Although a disaster at the time, Jolly Root Beer would be long remembered by the chastened board, which now knew the value of market testing and was determined not to repeat its mistake.

Later in the 1950s, Quality Chekd changed its logo and carton design. A chance meeting on a train by one of the directors led to a connection with Walter F. Landor, a well known industrial designer. He invited the entire board to his design offices in San Francisco, which was the site of that year's International Milk and Ice Cream Association's convention. Landor introduced the men to a sophisticated method of designing and market testing cartons. They balked, however, at his price to redesign the co-op's logo and create a carton series: $35,000. The board subsequently met with five other industrial designers, who failed to excite them, and finally in 1958 decided to go with Landor, despite the fact that by now his bid had increased to $45,000. Landor's efforts were instrumental in the continued refinement of the Quality Chekd logo, as well as an ongoing commitment to top-notch carton design.

## *Membership Peaks in 1955*

In 1955, Quality Chekd moved its offices from downtown Chicago to the suburb of LaGrange, Illinois. Also in that year, the number of members peaked at 156 dairies located in 37 states. Because of consolidation in the industry, the membership began a steady decline, although total member sales volume continue to grow at a steady pace. The organization also spread to new states, and in 1959 the first dairies in Canada joined Quality Chekd, a development which paved the way for even-

**Key Dates:**

**1944:** Quality Chekd Ice Cream Association is formed.
**1949:** Harlie F. Zimmerman is named managing director of the cooperative.
**1950:** The cooperative add a milk program and changes its name to Quality Chekd Dairies, Inc.
**1960:** A purchasing program is introduced.
**1977:** Revenues reach $825 million.
**1981:** Zimmerman retires.
**2001:** Peter Horvath becomes the fourth managing director of the cooperative.

tual expansion into Latin America. A key to attracting new members, and retaining old ones, was the 1960 introduction of a purchasing program, which transformed Quality Chekd into a full-fledged cooperative. By pooling its purchasing power with other Quality Chekd members, individual companies were soon able to cover their annual dues and fees from the savings realized by participation in the program. In 1963, Quality Chekd again attempted national advertising, this time with much better results than the Jolly Root Beer experience of a decade earlier. Periodic campaigns to promote the Quality Chekd brand furthered enhanced the value of the organization to individual members.

Under Zimmerman's leadership, Quality Chekd thrived. By 1977, total sales had grown to $825 million, but Zimmerman was nearing retirement and, with board approval, he began a search for his replacement. He settled on Mel Rapp, an executive with considerable experience in the dairy industry, including Quality Chekd member companies. Rapp succeeded Zimmerman in December 1981 and was instrumental in taking the co-op to the next level. Total member sales volume grew at an even faster clip. After reaching the $1 billion mark in 1980, Quality Chekd topped $1.5 billion in 1985 and $2.5 billion in 1990. The organization was so successful that in 1987 it was able to build its own office building, a three-story, 36,000-square-foot structure located in Naperville, Illinois, some 30 miles outside of Chicago. In addition to gaining new office space, Quality Chekd was now able to house the independent laboratory that conducted testing on member products. It was also able to offset costs by leasing the top two floors. In honor of the co-op's first president, Irving B, Weber, and its long-time general manager, Harlie F. Zimmerman, the structure was named the Weber-Zimmerman Building.

Quality Chekd's national advertising program reached a new level of sophistication in the early 1990s. Television commercials promoting the Quality Chekd logo were run on such major cable television networks as CNN, WTBS, USA, Nick at Nite, Lifetime, and The Discovery Channel. This effort was also a key factor in persuading large companies like Flav-O-Rich to join the cooperative. Another major national advertising campaign to support milk and ice cream products was launched in 1997. By 1999, one-quarter of the organization's budget was devoted to marketing efforts.

The commitment to promoting the Quality Chekd logo was especially important because of the changing conditions in the dairy industry. Total member sales volume topped out in the mid-1990s at the $3 billion range, then began to recede somewhat. Because of further consolidation in the industry, Quality Chekd faced competition from even larger competitors. This trend, however, made joining Quality Chekd an even more attractive option for dairies that desired to remain independent. With less bureaucracy than multi-unit processors, Quality Chekd and its members were able to adjust more quickly to a changing marketplace. Nevertheless, the organization also needed to find ways to sustain growth if it was to thrive in a new century. In 2001, the first South American dairy joined the fold: Alqueria, the largest fluid milk processor in Bogota, Columbia.

After serving 20 years as Quality Chekd's managing director, Rapp stepped down in favor of Peter Horvath, effective January 1, 2001. With only four managing directors in its history, Quality Chekd enjoyed great stability for more than five decades. Although it was improbable that Horvath would stay as long at the helm as Zimmerman and Rapp, it was more likely that under his leadership Quality Chekd would continue to find a way to adjust to changing business conditions and continue to offer valuable services to its members. Perhaps the co-op's greatest asset, a legacy left by its founding members, remained the highly recognizable logo, which enjoyed the kind of brand recognition that was the envy of its corporate rivals.

### *Principal Operating Units*

Productions and Quality Assurance; Training and Education; Marketing; Purchasing; Accounting/MIS.

### *Principal Competitors*

Dairy Farmers of America; Prairie Farms Dairy Inc.; Foremost Farms USA Cooperative; Michigan Milk Producers Association.

### *Further Reading*

"All Aboard," *Dairy Field,* September 1, 1998, p. 8.
Behrendt, Cathy, "Bigger Business," *Dairy Field,* September 1, 1998, p. 3.
"Cow Tech," *Dairy Field,* July 1, 1999, p. 15.
"Quality Chekd Earns High Marks," *Dairy Field,* September 1, 1998, p. 1.
Weber, Irving B., *Quality Chekd: An Idea Whose Times Has Come,* Naperville, Ill.: Quality Chekd Dairies, 1994, 53 p.

—Ed Dinger

# Riverwood International Corporation

3350 Riverwood Parkway
Suite 1400
Atlanta, Georgia 30339
U.S.A.
Telephone: (770) 644-3000
Fax: (770) 644-2962
Web site: http:///www.riverwood.com

*Private Company*
*Incorporated:* 1989
*Employees:* 4,100
*Sales:* $1.24 billion
*NAIC:* 322121 Paper (Except Newsprint) Mills; 322130 Paperboard Mills; 322212 Folding Paperboard Box Manufacturing; 333993 Packaging Machinery Manufacturing

Riverwood International Corporation is a global paperboard, packaging, and packaging machinery firm that produces coated unbleached kraft (CUK) paperboard, packaging products (including beverage carriers and folding cartons), and packaging machinery systems. Riverwood is a leading supplier of CUK paperboard—the thick, glossy paperboard used in secondary packaging—with an annual capacity of over one million tons. In 2001, nearly 93 percent of sales stemmed from the firm's coated board business. Riverwood serves both the beverage and the consumer packaging markets and its major customers include Anheuser-Busch Companies Inc., Campbell's, Coca-Cola Enterprises Inc., Dr. Pepper/7-Up, M&M Mars, Miller Brewing Co., Pepsi-Cola Bottling Group, Proctor & Gamble, and Sara Lee Corp. Formerly owned by Manville Corporation, Riverwood was privatized in 1995 by a group of investment firms and was preparing to go public once again in mid-2002.

## *Origins*

The foundation for Riverwood's integrated paper and packaging operations was laid in 1952, when Olin Mathieson Chemical Corporation acquired Frost Industries, Inc. Frost had begun in 1884 as an Arkansas sawmill company and owned five sawmills and timberlands in Louisiana, Arkansas, and Texas, which Olin used to form a forest products division. Three years later, Olin Corporation acquired the Brown Paper Mill Company. Established in 1923, the Brown Paper Mill was the first American company to produce sheet brown kraft paper and Southern Pine kraft linerboard. During World War II, the mill also developed Victory Board, used in corrugated supply boxes that were dropped from Allied airplanes.

Olin consolidated Brown Paper Mill into its forest products division and moved the division's headquarters to West Monroe, Louisiana. Between 1956 and 1958, Olin acquired a Louisiana sawmill and a Brazil pulp and paper mill, while developing and producing the world's first on-machine, clay-coated beverage carrierboard. During the 1960s, Olin developed the trademarked Marksman Packaging System for cans and bottles, installed the world's first paper machine specifically designed to produce the trademarked beverage carrierboard Aqua-Kote, and entered the plywood business. In 1967, Olinkraft, Inc. was established as a wholly owned subsidiary of Olin Corporation and that same year introduced the world's first solid unbleached sulfate (SUS) natural kraft folding cartonboard. In 1971, Olinkraft entered the particle board business, and, by the time Olinkraft was spun off as a separate public entity in 1974, the company had a diversified and integrated paper and wood products business that, in addition to particle board, was producing kraft paper, paperboard, packaging products, and building materials.

## *Johns-Manville Purchases Olinkraft: 1979*

In September 1978, the Johns-Manville Corporation initiated a bidding war for Olinkraft, despite the fact that Olinkraft had recently signed a merger agreement with Texas Eastern Corporation. By October, Olinkraft had agreed to accept a higher offer from Johns-Manville. The following year, Olinkraft was merged into a Johns-Manville subsidiary, which was renamed Manville Forest Products Corporation shortly thereafter.

During this time, however, several lawsuits threatened to put Johns-Manville out of business. Specifically, the suits charged

## Company Perspectives:

*As a member company of the American Forest and Paper Association, Riverwood International is committed to the principals of the Sustainable Forestry Initiative (SFI) Program. Riverwood International has adopted the following policy in support of these principals: all wood procurement professionals will complete the Master Loggers Program; suppliers of gatewood will complete the Master Loggers Program; chip suppliers are expected to support the principles of the SFI; we will support regional landowner meetings coordinated by such groups as the Forestry Association; and we will develop and implement a winter inventory plan for wood and chips to reduce any impacts to the forest during the wet season.*

that asbestos building materials used in insulating fiber made by Manville had caused several serious illnesses, including lung disease, among employees and those who used the product. By 1981, around 400 lawsuits per month were being filed. That year, Johns-Manville was reorganized as a holding company, Manville Corporation, with Manville Forest Products serving as one of five wholly separate operating subsidiaries. The following year, Manville and its subsidiaries—even though still profitable at the time—filed petitions for reorganization under the Chapter 11 Federal Bankruptcy Code in a move to shield the company against losses it faced as a result of the lawsuits. By 1985, Manville had exited the asbestos-based product business entirely.

While the Manville Corporation was withdrawing from the asbestos business, it was also plunging money into equipment updates and capital improvements for other operations, including forest products, while absorbing and expanding upon former Olinkraft operations. Between 1983 and 1986, Manville Forest Products acquired a plywood and sawmill plant in Louisiana, a folding carton plant in Mississippi, and Eastex Packaging Inc., which brought three additional folding carton plants in Memphis.

In 1988, Manville emerged from bankruptcy under a landmark reorganization plan that established an independent trust, the Manville Personal Injury Settlement Trust, to which Manville would funnel as much as $3 billion to asbestos-injury victims over a 30-year period and which gave its victims majority control of Manville. In return for a shield against future asbestos-related litigation, Manville gave trust stockholders $2.5 billion in assets, mostly in the form of stock, and promised to pay its victims $75 million annually beginning in August 1991, plus 20 percent of Manville's annual income until all claims were settled.

### *Forestry Products Expansion: Late 1980s–Early 1990s*

In 1989, a holding company (later renamed Riverwood International Corporation) was created for Manville's forest products operations. The company then embarked on a plan to double its size over the next five to seven years. In September 1989, the company acquired Papelok S.A., a paper mill and corrugated container plant in Brazil. In November, Thomas H. Johnson, who had served as president of both the coated board and paperboard divisions of rival Mead Corp.—now called MeadWestvaco—became president of Manville Forest Products.

In the early 1990s, Manville Forest Products relocated its headquarters from West Monroe, Louisiana, to Atlanta and began plans to embark on an international expansion program. At the time, Manville Forest Products was still largely a domestic concern, with foreign operations limited to Brazil, where a new anti-inflation program was tightening profit margins. In 1990, Manville Forest Products began developing its international folding carton converting base by acquiring DRG Cartons Ltd. (renamed Riverwood International Cartons), Britain's third-largest folding carton concern serving the frozen food, confectionery, and detergent markets and reporting $60 million in annual sales. Manville Forest Products also acquired the assets of the Australian concern Visypack Pty. (renamed Riverwood Cartons Pty. Ltd.), a maker of lithographic folding cartons for the food, consumer products, and beverage industries, with five carton plants and annual sales of $140 million. Manville Forest Products also expanded its base of paperboard production operations with the purchase of Fiskeby Board AB of Sweden, a European producer/converter of recycled cartonboard.

In June 1991, the company's name was changed to Riverwood International Corporation after Manville became the holding company for two subsidiaries: Riverwood, which had grown into one of two major players in the beer and soft-drink cardboard packaging industry, and Manville Sales Corp. (renamed Schuller International, Inc. in 1992), an insulation, reinforcement, filtration, and building products concern.

In a move to strengthen the company's focus on the development of packaging machinery systems, Riverwood created a packaging machinery division in 1991. Around the same time, the company began signing customers to leases for high-speed proprietary packaging machinery and, in the process, became those customers' sole supplier of paperboard used to produce beverage cartons and cases. To further develop its machinery business, Riverwood made several acquisitions, including Minnesota Automation Inc., a global supplier of packaging machinery; the JAK-ET-PAK machinery system, which included machinery, technology, patents, trademarks, and trade names; the paperboard packaging and machinery systems manufacturing operations of Jorba, S.A. and Syspack, S.A. (Syspack was later merged into Jorba), two privately held corporations located in Barcelona, Spain, with annual sales of more than $300 million; and M.E.A.D. Ltd., a Brazil company specializing in beverage packaging machinery. The company also entered a joint venture agreement with Rengo Company, Japan's leading producer of corrugated products, to market machinery-based packaging systems in Japan.

Between 1989 and 1991, a period of consolidation in the paper and packaging industry, Riverwood spent $250 million in acquisitions, as sales climbed from $774 million to $993 million, while earnings inched upward from $75 million to $89 million. By 1991, Riverwood controlled 25 percent of the overseas beverage packaging market and 45 percent of the American beverage market. Moreover, the company was the leading supplier of printed paperboard packaging to the domes-

**Key Dates:**

**1952:** Olin Mathieson Chemical Corp. acquires Frost Industries Inc.
**1955:** Olin purchases Brown Paper Mill Company.
**1967:** Olinkraft Inc. is established as a subsidiary of Olin Corp.
**1971:** Olinkraft enters the particle board business.
**1979:** Olinkraft is merged into a Johns-Manville Corp. subsidiary and is renamed Manville Forest Products Corp.
**1981:** Manville and its subsidiaries file for bankruptcy to protect themselves against asbestos-related lawsuits.
**1991:** Manville Forest Products adopts the name Riverwood International Corp.
**1992:** Riverwood goes public.
**1995:** A group of investors take Riverwood private.
**1996:** The company's Perry, Georgia, converting plant opens.
**2000:** Riverwood sells Brazilian subsidiary Igaras Papeis e Embalagens S.A.

tic brewing industry and was second only to Mead Corp. in supplying packaging to the U.S. soft-drink industry.

After expanding its international and machinery-lease operations, the company turned its attention to increasing its production of coated unbleached kraft (CUK) paperboard, used increasingly in the packaging industry by food and drink companies. By this time, Riverwood had successfully whittled out a profitable niche in CUK paperboard sales and was serving such customers as Anheuser-Busch, Miller Brewing Company, Coca-Cola, PepsiCo, Procter & Gamble, and Unilever.

### *Riverwood Goes Public: 1992*

In the spring of 1992, Riverwood announced it would offer about 20 percent of its common stock in an initial public offering designed to help finance the acquisition of Macon Kraft, Inc., a 525,000-ton linerboard mill in Macon, Georgia. As recent government allowances had granted certain banking companies reentry to the stock underwriting business, for the first time since the Depression, a bank—J.P. Morgan Securities—took the lead position in a stock offering, heading a Wall Street underwriters team that took Riverwood public.

In June 1992, Riverwood completed an initial public offering of 19.5 percent of its common stock for $172 million and raised an additional $400 million through its public debt offering. In July, Riverwood acquired Macon Kraft (renamed Riverwood International Georgia, Inc.) for $219 million, including the assumption of $169 million of debt, and began a two-year program to convert one of the two Macon plant's linerboard machines to produce Riverwood's proprietary CUK paperboard.

During 1992, 69 percent of Riverwood's revenues and 76 percent of its profits were generated from sales of specialized paperboard and leases of packaging machinery to beverage and consumer goods companies in more than a dozen countries. Although Riverwood's earnings rose to a record $1.18 billion, costs associated with the Macon Kraft acquisition and conversion, as well as the sluggish economy, led to an earnings decline, and Riverwood's profits fell to just $43.7 million. Before closing out the year Riverwood secured a $50 million line of back-up credit from Morgan Guaranty Trust Company.

During this time, Riverwood established a product development center in Atlanta for machinery-based packaging systems. The company also debuted its Twin-Stack packaging system, becoming the first company to offer a packaging innovation that could accommodate two-tiered can multiples of 12, 18, 24, 30, and 36. Riverwood's Twin-Stack system had numerous advantages over traditional slab packaging, offering beverage manufacturers better package graphics and expanded promotional and merchandising opportunities via paperboard pads separating two layers of cans. The new system also provided retailers improved utilization of shelf space and offered consumers a more compact and portable beverage container with handles and improved weight distribution. Working with PepsiCo, Riverwood began test marketing its Twin-Stack packaging. Four months after the first Twin-Stack pack appeared on store shelves, Mead joined the race for two-tiered packaging sales with its DuoStack system.

Riverwood continued its international expansion drive in 1993, forming a joint venture with Danapak Holding Ltd., the leader in Scandinavian carton converting, to serve the Scandinavian beverage market with packing machinery systems for beverage and foods. The venture was designed to provide beverage customers—in Denmark, Finland, Norway, Sweden, Iceland, Greenland, and the Faroe Islands—with multiple packaging beverage systems that used Riverwood's proprietary CUK paperboard, converted by Danapak into paperboard beverage cartons through Riverwood's packaging machinery.

In 1993, Riverwood also made several moves to improve its short-term financial condition, which was strained by the Macon conversion project and weak containerboard prices and international demand. Those moves included rescheduling debt payments and selling 60,000 acres of U.S. timberland for about $17 million. With earnings continuing to slide in late-1993, Riverwood undertook a series of capital-generating steps: it sold Manville additional stock, which increased the parent company's stake in Riverwood from 80.5 to 81.5 percent and gave Riverwood a much-needed infusion of $50 million; it sold another $125 million in bonds in a public debt offering; it brought a former General Electric executive George F. Varga on board to assume the new position of chief financial officer; and it initiated a restructuring program aimed at cutting costs and streamlining and consolidating operations which had doubled in size since 1989. Nonetheless, a linerboard glut in the paper and pulp industry, coupled with conversion costs, squeezed Riverwood's profits; in 1993, profits plunged to $1.1 million on sales that remained essentially flat at $1.12 billion.

Riverwood completed its Macon conversion in the mid-1990s. The new concern promised reduced exposure to commodity price fluctuations and would expanded the company's ability to serve the growing and increasingly competitive beverage packaging industry. In 1994, the company's leases of proprietary machines and sales of twin-pack beverage-can packages were exceeding expectations, and the company's stock prices were climbing.

Moreover, five years of expansion efforts had left Riverwood well positioned to take advantage of three trends which began in the United States and began to develop in Europe in the 1990s: the increase in popularity of cans as the preferred form of primary beverage container packaging, the growth in popularity of CUK paperboard as a form of secondary packaging due to an increase in the size of container multipacks, and the rising popularity of CUK paperboard as a marketing and promotional tool. With packaging never before so important an element in beverage promotions, Riverwood expected to capitalize on the industry trend of using packaging as a marketing tool; industry insiders predicted that the soft drink industry would launch a promotion a week by 1995, up from six promotions a year in the late 1980s.

Riverwood's future proved to be increasingly dependent on dominating the niche market for beer and soft-drink packaging, both through machine leases and CUK paperboard production and sales. Future sales to the beverage industry were expected to be paced by growth of two-tiered packaging. Riverwood's Twin-Stack, which had become better known as Pepsi's Cube, 7-Up's Double Dozun, and Dr. Pepper's Double Decker, had so far realized the greatest profits. Future company earnings related to CUK paperboard also increased after the Macon plant conversion was completed.

Riverwood moved into the mid-1990s as one of a few companies in the world that had operations in all three coated paperboard packaging segments: coated paperboard production, conversion systems, and machinery systems. Internationally, the company had a strong presence in North America and Europe and a growing presence in Latin America and Asia that was expected to help international sales eventually outpace domestic sales.

Domestically, by 1994 the company was producing 50 to 60 percent of all paperboard beer containers used in the United States and 20 to 30 percent of soft-drink containers. MeadWestvaco produced most of the remaining containers and remained Riverwood's principal competitor, particularly in sales of two-tiered packaging, though another competitor, C.W. Zumbiel Company, began producing its version of double-tiered packaging in 1993. Riverwood, like others in the industry, expected two-tiered packaging systems to become the standard for packaging as beverage producers move away from slab packaging, giving the company reason to believe that its Twin Stack machines, which could also manufacture slab packaging, would be vital to the industry.

### *Riverwood Is Privatized: 1995*

Riverwood's future as a Manville unit remained uncertain in 1994. By this time, Manville's two subsidiaries had grown into highly marketable, autonomous operations, with potential for a profitable sale or breakup in the event that the Manville Personal Injury Settlement Trust needed to liquidate its holdings in order to pay $2 billion or more in asbestos victim claims. Indeed, in 1995, Manville sold its 81.5 percent interest in Riverwood to a group of investment firms who took the company private—in 2002, Clayton, Dubilier, & Rice and EXOR Group each owned nearly 30 percent of Riverwood.

Out from under its troubled parent, Riverwood spent the remainder of the 1990s with a continued focus on serving the beverage industry. In March 1996, the firm opened a converting plant in Perry, Georgia, just 30 miles from its Macon facility. The new plant had a reel-to-reel offset press—the only such press in the U.S. beverage market—that enabled the firm to handle the ever-changing packaging and promotional requirements of the soft drink industry. By now, the company had six converting plants in the United States, several in the United Kingdom and Spain, four in France, and five in Australia. Riverwood executive G. Phillips Jones commented on the beverage packaging industry in a 1997 *Pulp & Paper* magazine article, claiming that "there is very little regular printing copy on soft drink packaging these days. It's pretty much one promo after another from all of our customers." As such, Riverwood's new reel-to-reel press, which could handle extensive, custom graphics, as well as frequent graphic changes, was expected to give it a competitive edge over its competitors.

During 1997, Stephen M. Humphrey was named president and CEO of Riverwood. Under his leadership, the firm continued to develop its multipackaging systems. The company launched new systems related to its Quikflex machines, new technology that packed bottles or cans in fully enclosed cartons, a new model that packaged glass bottles in wrap cartons, and various new enhancements related to its Twin-Stack system. By the new millennium, Riverwood was producing over one million tons of CUK paperboard per year while sales topped $1 billion.

### *New Growth Opportunities for the New Century*

During the early years of the new century, Riverwood continued to launch new products catering to the beverage industry but also began to look beyond this market for new growth opportunities.

In 2000, Riverwood began to expand its consumer products packaging segment and eyed this market as a lucrative avenue for future gains. By this time, nearly 40 percent of the firm's production was coated board sold to non-beverage clients. The company's strategy was also centered on new demands—especially in the food industry—for multipackaging. As part of the firm's focus on coated board, it sold its interest in Brazil-based Igaras Papeis e Embalagens S.A., a containerboard manufacturer, in late 2000.

Being heavily dependent upon natural resources, the firm also was also involved in the Sustainable Forestry Initiative (SFI) Program. In response to environmentalist's concerns about the destruction and depletion of the world's forests, the company complied with SFI standards by purchasing its wood from private landowners that were recognized for their natural resource management plans. These landowners typically made sure that trees were managed, harvested, and replanted—for every tree harvested, six to eight seedlings were planted.

In late 2001, Riverwood launched the Fridge Vendor, a new packaging design for 12-packs that was longer, thinner, and fit into refrigerators easier than traditional 12-packs. Coca-Cola, the company's first Fridge Vendor client, claimed the newly designed packaging was responsible for double-digit sales increases in Coca-Cola 12-packs. As launching new products and expanding into new consumer product areas remained at the forefront of Riverwood's business strategy, the company filed to go public once again in 2002 in order to raise funds for expansion. As Riverwood prepared for listing on the New York Stock Exchange, the firm stood well positioned for future growth in both domestic and international markets.

### *Principal Subsidiaries*

Danapak Riverwood Multipack A/S (Denmark); Fiskeby Board AB (Sweden); Fiskeby Board A/S (Denmark); Fiskeby Board Ltd. (U.K.); Fiskeby Board SARL (France); IL Returpapper AB (Sweden); Industrikompetens i Ostergotland AB (Sweden); New Materials Ltd. (U.K.); Recywrap Recycling GmbH (Germany); Rengo Riverwood Packaging, Ltd. (Japan); RIC Holding, Inc.; Riverwood Argentina S.A.; Riverwood do Brasil Ltda. (Brazil); Riverwood Espana, S.A. (Spain); Riverwood International Asia Pacific, Ltd. (Hong Kong); Riverwood International Asia Pte. Ltd. (Singapore); Riverwood International Australia Pty. Ltd.; Riverwood International B.V. (Netherlands); Riverwood International Corporation Philanthropic Fund; Riverwood International (Cyprus) Limited; Riverwood International Enterprises, Inc.; Riverwood International (Europe) S.A. (Belgium); Riverwood International France S.A.; Riverwood International Japan, Ltd.; Riverwood International Limited (U.K.); Riverwood International Machinery, Inc.; Riverwood International Mexicana, S. de R.L. de C.V. (Mexico); Riverwood International Pension Trustee Company Ltd. (U.K.); Riverwood International, S.A. (France); Riverwood International S.p.A. (Italy); Riverwood Mehrstuckverpackung GmbH (Germany); Slevin South Company; Svensk Kartongatervinning A.B. (Sweden).

### *Principal Competitors*

MeadWestvaco Corporation; Smurfit-Stone Container Corporation; Sonoco Products Company.

### *Further Reading*


Billips, Mike, "Co-Managers Work to Renovate Mill, Rebuild Labor Relations," *Macon Telegraph*, September 28, 1992.

Bleakley, Fred R., and Howard Hoffman, "A Long Hiatus: Morgan, a Bank, to Handle IPO," *Wall Street Journal*, April 23, 1992, pp. C1, C17.

Charlier, Marj, "For Manville, a Sale or Breakup Appears Imminent," *Wall Street Journal*, March 23, 1992, p. B4.

——, "Life After Asbestos: Manville Tries to Build New Identity as a Firm Keen on Environment," *Wall Street Journal*, May 31, 1990, pp. 1, A16.

Demarco, Edward, "Riverwood International Hopes to Box Up Greater Profits," *Denver Business Journal*, March 18, 1994, p. A13.

Jabbonsky, Larry, "Doubled Up," *Beverage World*, March 1994, pp. 94–8.

"Johns-Manville, Olinkraft Agree On Merger Plan," *Wall Street Journal*, November 10, 1978.

"Johns-Manville Seeks 49% Stake in Olinkraft Inc.," *Wall Street Journal*, September 26, 1978, p. 8.

"Kick Back and Chill with the Fridge Vendor," *Paperboard Packaging*, November 2001, p. 12.

Lee, Peter, "US Capital Markets: No Run-Of-The-Mill Deal," *Euromoney*, July 1992, pp. 9–10.

Leib, Jeffrey, "Manville: A New Identity, *Denver Post*, November 3, 1991, p. G1.

McNaughton, David, "Riverwood International Corp.—Making a Case for Growth," *Atlanta Constitution*, February 3, 1993, p. D1.

"Riverwood to Ride the Wave," *Packaging Week*, September 11, 1997, p. 12.

"Riverwood Sells Igaras Papeis," *Paperboard Packaging*, November 2000, p. 24.

Shaw, Monica, "Riverwood International Integrates Supply for Better Customer Service," *Pulp & Paper*, September 1997, p. 81.

Torres, Craig, "Riverwood's Fans Say Investors Should Look Beyond the Trees to See Paper Firm's Potential," *Wall Street Journal*, May 28, 1993, p. B5C.

Zipser, Andy, "The Asbestos Curse: After Many Painful Years, Manville Is Exorcising It," *Barron's*, October 14, 1991, p. 12.


—Roger W. Rouland
—update: Christina M. Stansell

# Roularta Media Group NV

**33 Meiboomlaan**
**8800 Roeselare**
**Belgium**
**Telephone: (+32) 0 51-266-111**
**Fax: (+32) 0 51-266-593**
**Web site: http://www.roularta.be**

*Public Company*
*Incorporated:* 1954
*Employees:* 2,062
*Sales:* EUR 438.6 million ($350.9 million)(2001)
*Stock Exchanges:* Euronext Brussels
*Ticker Symbol:* ROU
*NAIC:* 511110 Newspaper Publishers; 511120 Periodical Publishers; 513112 Radio Stations; 513120 Television Broadcasting

Roularta Media Group NV is a Belgian-based media conglomerate. The company had its beginnings in 1953, when Flemish lawyer Willy de Nolf set up a printing shop with a single sheet-fed machine behind his house in Roeselare, Belgium. That year, De Nolf and his wife launched a new newspaper for the local community, the *Roeselaarse Weekbode*. The paper's focus on its local and regional market quickly attracted advertisers, which helped swell the paper from its original ten-page format. The success of the Roeselare paper led de Nolf to repeat the format elsewhere in Belgium, including the towns of Izegem, Tielt, Torhout, and De Leie. De Nolf later acquired other regional Flemish-language weeklies, including the *Brugsch Handelsblad*, *Kortrijks Handelsblad*, and *De Zeewacht*, grouping all of the titles as *De Krant van West-Vlaanderen* in 1989. The last addition to *De Krant van West-Vlaanderen* came with the takeover of *Het Wekelijks Nieuws* in 2000. With 11 editions printed under five titles, *De Krant van West-Vlaanderen* had enabled Roularta to become the sole publisher of paid weekly newspapers for the west Flanders region.

### *Origins and Early Growth: 1953 to Mid-1980s*

From the company's founding in 1954, Roularta aimed to become a large media group. That year it introduced the advertising-supported free weekly *De Streekkrant*. As with their first newspaper, *Roeselaarse Weekbode*, which began publishing in 1953, the De Nolfs started with a local Roeselare edition. Soon, however, the circulation of *De Streekkrant* went national as the company built up coverage across the country's Flemish-speaking markets through the launch of a number of locally oriented papers under the *De Streekkrant* banner. By the end of the century, Roularta had built up a network of 50 local papers. With readership levels topping 2.75 million, *De Streekkrant* also became Belgium's single-largest newspaper.

At the end of the 1960s, Roularta had become synonymous with its door-to-door newspapers. With the next generation of the De Nolf family, in the form of Rik De Nolf, who joined the company in 1972, Roularta began to eye other growth markets. At the time, there were no quality news magazines targeting the small Flemish-speaking population of Belgium, and certainly none that matched the quality of such news magazines as *The Observer* in England, *L'Express* in France, or even *Elsevier* in the Netherlands. De Nolf decided to take on the challenge of launching a quality news magazine with a Flemish orientation, and in 1971 the company debuted the monthly *Knack* (apparently named for the 1965 British film *The Knack and How to Get It*). The driving force behind *Knack* proved to be Rik de Nolf, who refused to bow to critics who judged the Flemish market too small to guarantee the magazine's success.

Meanwhile, the magazine found itself facing a number of new competitors, as three other regional news magazines launched in the same year. Yet one of these did not last out its first year, the second closed the following year, and the third, although holding on longer, shut down in 1984. *Knack*, on the other hand, went from strength to strength, stepping up its publishing schedule to become a weekly. In the early 1980s, *Knack* began to add new sections, such as a special Antwerp city edition added in 1981. In 1983, Roularta launched another title, *Weekendblad*; the following year, *Knack* was separated into two parts, the weekly *Knack* news magazine, and the

## Key Dates:

**1953:** Willy De Nolf sets up a printing shop and begins publishing *De Roeselaarse Weekbode*, forming the basis of the later *De Krant van West-Vlaanderen.*
**1954:** Roularta is incorporated and launches first Roeselare edition of *De Streekrant.*
**1971:** Roularta launches first Flemish-language news magazine, *Knack.*
**1975:** Launch of *Trends*, a Flemish-language business news magazine.
**1984:** The company launches *Steps*, a free monthly lifestyle magazine.
**1989:** Roularta takes a share in RTM radio and television group.
**1998:** Roularta Media Group goes public on Brussels Stock Exchange.
**1999:** *Bizz*, a new business magazine, and *Trends International*, an English-language version of *Trends*, are launched.

lifestyle magazine *Weekend Knack*. Other later additions to the Knack group of titles included the quarterly titles *Knack Gezondheid* (Health) and *Knack Multimedia.*

Rick De Nolf took over the company after his father's death in 1981. Yet the younger De Nolf had already begun transforming the company. In 1975, De Nolf led the company to launch a new magazine title, *Trends*, targeting the financial and corporate new markets. That magazine, which also began publishing a French-language edition, once again took on the competition, growing to become one of Belgium's most important business news magazines. Like *Knack*, *Trends* began publishing as a monthly before converting to a weekly magazine. Boosting the magazine's credibility were copyright agreements with such leading magazines as *Forbes*, *The Economist*, and the *Financial Times.*

### *Expansion: Mid-1980s–Early 2000s*

Roularta launched a number of other successful magazine titles, including the sports magazines *Foot* and *Sportsmagazine*, which were fused together in the late 1990s. Another title was *Steps* (called *Style* in the Netherlands) a free magazine launched in 1984 and dedicated to the lifestyle and tourism markets. The *Steps* series distinguished itself by providing regionally focused editorial content in a glossy magazine format.

In 1988, Roularta launched another successful magazine concept, targeting the over-50 market with the title *Onze Tijd*, as well as a French-language version called *Notre Temps*. In 1990, Roularta exported the concept to the Netherlands, where it was given the title *Plus* and became one of that country's best-selling magazines.

By the beginning of the 1990s, however, Roularta was preparing to branch out into new areas, including book publishing. One of these was commercial printing, an operation that culminated in the creation, in 2000, of the Mercator Printing Group, formed through the merger of Roularta's commercial printing operations with those of Concentra Grafische Groep and Mercator Press. Roularta's stake in the new company stood at 40 percent. Another new area of operation was the events management field, brought under subsidiary Roularta Events, which began organizing events for Roularta itself—such as its awards ceremonies "Manager of the Year" and the "Cash! Awards"—and also for third party events, such as the Volvo Golfer of the Year award.

Partnerships led the way to another media diversification move for Roularta at the beginning of the 1990s. In 1988, the Belgian government had agreed to allow the formation of the country's first commercial television networks (the two existing stations were government owned). As part of that agreement, the country's major newspaper groups were given first crack at forming a television group. However, that effort fell through in 1989, and afterward Roularta joined a consortium of magazine publishers, including rival De Persgroep, in setting up Vlaams Media Maatschappij, which in turn launched the VTM network. Roularta eventually increased its holding in VMM to 50 percent.

In the mid-1990s, Roularta extended itself into other new media categories, such as CD-ROM duplication and publishing (and later DVD publishing) and Internet activities. The company continued to build on its magazine portfolio, launching in 1996 the jobs ad insert *Vacatures*, which targeted primarily Flemish and Dutch-speaking job seekers with higher education. *Vacatures* was included not only in *Knack*, *Trends*, and other Roularta publications, but also in third-party newspapers and magazines such as *Het Laatste Nieuws*, *De Morgen*, and *De Financieel Economische Tijd*. *Vacatures* also went online in 1997, then began branching out into more targeted areas, adding a "Science and Technology" supplement and a French-language version, *Vacatures Emploi*. In 1999, *Vacatures* joined with other European career sites to form the Talent4Europe.com web site, a service providing coverage of 16 European countries scheduled to begin operation in 2002.

Roularta Media Group went public in 1998 on the Brussels Stock Exchange, selling some 25 percent of its shares (the De Nolf family retained ownership of 75 of the company). The following year, the group stepped up the pace of its magazine launches, debuting a new financial magazine, *Bizz*, geared toward the young entrepreneur and executive set, and the English-language *Trends International.*

International growth became the company's target at the turn of the century. For this, Roularta intended to follow a two-prong approach, built on the one hand around its *De Streekkrant* free newspaper format, and on the other on its magazine titles, particularly its *Plus* series. The company entered Portugal, launching local editions of *De Streekkrant* as *Jornal da Região*, which quickly become one of that country's highest-circulation newspaper titles. The company also joined in the partnership behind the launch of the free French-language daily *Metro* (but pulled out again at the end of 2001). Roularta meanwhile had found a more successful partnership with France's Bayard Presse Paris, which shared 50–50 ownership of the growing number of *Plus* editions, which had spread to Denmark under the name of *Vi over 60*. The success of the *Plus* title encouraged the company to adopt the name in Belgium as well, replacing the *Onze Tijd/Notre Temps* titles in 2001. In that year, Roularta and Bayard launched a new variation of *Plus*, now to the German market, where the format received the name *Lenz*.

The year 2000 saw the launch of another title in the Roularta fold, *Grande*, a glossy magazine presenting photographic essays of worldwide subjects. In that year, the company grouped all of its various Internet activities into a single portal, Easy.be, which quickly became one of the Flemish-speaking markets busiest portals.

In mid-2001, Roularta was the center of speculation that it was preparing to merge with its chief Flemish rival, De Persgroep. Such a merger faced mergers and monopolies hurdles, however, as the resulting group would gain a de facto monopoly on the Flemish-speaking press. Meanwhile, De Nolf acknowledged that the company was interested in seeking partnerships with other media groups in Europe in order to step up the company's international expansion. The company was also exploring possible acquisitions, including a possible bid for parts of rival VNU's magazine division. At the end of 2001, the company launched a new magazine title, *Nest*, which replaced two former Roularta titles, *Levend Land* and *Spijs & Drank*.

Start-up costs for its new titles, including its participation in *Metro*, coupled with a slump in the advertising sector, hit Roularta hard in 2001. As its revenues barely climbed over the previous year, nearing EUR 439 million, the company slipped into the red, posting a loss of more than EUR 6 million. However, after exiting the *Metro* partnership, and with no new titles planned for the coming year, Roularta expected to be back into profits in 2000. Roularta had successfully expanded beyond its newspaper origins to become a leading Belgian media group poised to take on its giant European rivals in the new century.

### *Principal Subsidiaries*

Roularta Media Group NV; Newsco NV; Regie De Weekkrant NV; Roularta Books NV; Roularta IT-Solutions NV; Sportmagazine NV; Style Magazine BV; Trends Magazine NV; Vlaamse Tijdschriften Uitgeverij NV; West-Vlaamse Media Groep NV; De Streekkrant-De Weekkrantgroep NV; Oost-Vlaamse Media Groep NV; Vogue Trading Video NV; De Vastgoedmakelaar NV; Hippos Vademecum NV.

### *Principal Competitors*

Berkshire Hathaway Inc; News Corporation Ltd.; Cox Enterprises Inc.; Bertelsmann AG; Cox Enterprises Inc.; ABC Inc.; Pearson plc; Advance Publications Inc.; Hearst Corporation; Vivendi Universal.

### *Further Reading*


Albers, Isabel, "Roularta groeit in nieuw en oud," *De Standaard*, March 21, 2000.

——, "Roularta op weg naar langzaam beterschap," *De Standaard*, September 25, 2001.

——, "Roularta zet poort open voor fusie," *De Standaard*, June 26, 2001.

Dendooven, Pascal, "Belastingen duwen Roularta in het rood," *De Standaard,* March 26, 2002.

"Easypress: Roularta Selects Atomik for Cross-Media Publishing," *M2 Communications,* February 4, 2002.

"Roularta laat Ring TV nog niet los," *De Standaard*, March 29, 2002.


—M.L. Cohen

# SABATÉ

## Sabaté Diosos SA

**Espace Tech Ulrich**
**BP 301**
**66403 Ceret Cedex**
**France**
**Telephone: (+33) 4-68-87-20-20**
**Fax: (+33) 4-68-87-35-36**
**Web site: http://www.sabate.com**

*Public Company*
*Incorporated:* 1939
*Employees:* 1,549
*Sales:* EUR 231.7 million ($185.36 million) (2001)
*Stock Exchanges:* Euronext Paris
*Ticker Symbol:* SBT
*NAIC:* 321999 All Other Miscellaneous Wood Product Manufacturing

Sabaté Diosos SA is the world's number two producer of natural and artificial corks for wine bottles and the world's leading producer of oak barrels for the wine industry. Formed from the 2000 merger of Sabaté SA and Diosos SA, the company expects to build on its expanded range of wine industry support products to follow the increasing internationalization of the worldwide wine industry. With growing amounts of quality wine being produced outside of France—not only in the United States' Napa Valley but in Chile, South America, Australia, and elsewhere—Sabaté Diosos has positioned itself to remain a premium supplier of closures and barrels. Sabaté produces corks for wine and sparkling wines and champagnes. More than half of its cork sales come from natural cork; an increasing share of the company's revenues comes from sales of its Altec natural-artificial hybrid corks. Sabaté has strengthened its position as a vertically integrated company, with subsidiaries involved throughout the cork supply chain, from growing and harvesting, to raw material preparation and production of the final product. The company also operates a small business in supplying winemaking ingredients and additives. The Diosos cooperage side, formerly a holding of Remy Martin, produces barrels from the famed French oak and other oaks. Cooperage operations accounted for slightly more than half of Sabaté Diosos' revenues in 2001 of EUR 237 million. The company is led by co-CEOs Marc Sabaté and Michel de Tapol and is quoted on the Euronext Stock Exchange.

### *Cork Maker in the 1930s*

Modeste Sabaté was a journalist in his native Catalan, Spain, who fled his country when Ferdinand Franco came to power after the Spanish Civil War. Sabaté settled in Roussillon, near the Spanish border and the French Mediterranean basin. In 1939, Sabaté founded a company and began producing corks. He was joined by sons Augustin, Alex, Bernard, and Georges in 1960.

Cork had been used as a bottle stopper since the 1600s, when Dom Perignon fashioned the first cork for his famous champagne. Cork was quickly adopted for the so-called "tranquil" wines as well and, before long, cork had become synonymous with bottled wine. At first centered in the south of France, the cork industry gradually moved south, following the richest areas of the cork-producing oak, Quercus Suber in the Catalan region of Spain and Portugal. One of the earliest of the industrial cork makers appeared in Spain in the 1750s.

Cork remained a fairly rare commodity, growing only in certain areas along the Mediterranean basin. The growth cycle of the cork oak was rather long—more than 30 years for the maturation of a tree. Harvesting cork was a delicate process as well. A first harvest, culling the so-called "male" bark from the 30-year-old tree, exposed the underlying "female" or "mother" bark, which then required a further 9 to 11 years of growth before the cork could be harvested. The production of finished cork itself required another year to two years of effort.

Yet cork's success among French and international wine makers came from the natural material's qualities, allowing just enough air to pass through to aid in the oxidation process of aging fine wines, while being flexible enough to provide a tight seal for the bottle. Nonetheless, cork was not without its shortcomings. Being rare, it was rather expensive for bottlers of cheaper wines. In addition, cork was long plagued by its vulnerability to 2,4,6-trichloroanisole, or TCA, a chemical compound capable of tainting wine—producing the musty, off-flavors of so-called "corked" wines. The wine industry began a search for means of eliminating TCA.

## Company Perspectives:

*The Sabaté Diosos Group's perspectives lie with a logic of long-term growth based on: putting in place commercial synergies between the networks of Sabaté and Diosos (Australia, South Africa, South America); improving operating margins by rationalizing production and refocusing the product mix in the cork division and creating an integrated supply chain for American oak in the barrel-making division; searching for innovation both in the production process and the final product in order to improve productivity and to anticipate the needs of an international clientele by producing value-creating products and services.*

Modeste and sons, especially Augustin Sabaté, began building the company into one of France's leading cork producers. The company also took a leading role in the search for means of reducing, if not eliminating entirely, TCA from their corks. In 1985, the company patented a new method for cleaning cork, using hydrogen peroxide and dubbed SBM by Sabaté. The invention represented somewhat of a breakthrough for the wine industry and helped Sabaté capture a leading position among the world's cork makers. Modeste Sabaté died in 1986, and Augustin Sabaté took over as head of the family-owned company.

### *Integrated Wine Products Provider in the 21st Century*

The French wine industry stimulated the creation of other industries aside from cork making. One of the most important of these, at least as far as the fame of French wines was concerned, was that of the production of the casks used for aging wines. Crafted (typically by hand until rather late in the 20th century) from a specific species of French oak, the casks became essential to the quality of French wines.

An early cooperage was that of Tonnellerie Moreau, based in Charente, a region of western France near the Bordeaux wine industry. Founded in 1838, that company enjoyed a degree of prominence up until World War I. Moreau was joined by other cooperages, including Sequin, founded in 1870. The two companies were later brought together under Remy Martin, which took a majority share in Moreau in 1958 and reoriented the company toward the production of casks for Remy Martin's core cognac and related spirits products. Remy Martin acquired full control of the company in 1972. By the late 1970s, more than 70 percent of the company's sales came from its parent company. By then, however, Sequin Moreau had decided to refocus itself as a producer of casks for the Bordeaux wine producers, then for other wine producer regions of France. After successfully imposing itself as a leading cooperage for the French market, Sequin Moreau began attacking the international market, opening an office in Australia in 1988 and an office in Napa, California in 1992. The company also diversified into producing casks from other species of oak, notably from Russia and North America.

Another fast-growing cooperage was that of Tonnellerie Radoux, founded in 1947 by Robert Radoux. That company crafted its cask after the traditional fashion until the arrival of Radoux's son, Christian, at the company's head. The younger Radoux converted the company to limited liability status in 1982 and began industrializing much of its production processes, while maintaining nonetheless traditional methods, materials, and designs. In the late 1980s and early 1990s, Radoux began to seek greater vertical integration, buying up Sciage de Berry in 1987 and France Merrain in 1991 to ensure its supply of cask components. The company also launched its own winemaking ingredients distribution subsidiary in 1991.

Radoux sold out to investor Michel de Tapol in 1997. Two years later, Tapol merged Radoux with Sequin Moreau, one of its primary competitors. The new company, dubbed Diosos, became the world's leading producer of oak casks for the wine market. Remy Martin, meanwhile, remained a major shareholder in the company.

During this time, Sabaté also had been growing strongly. The SBM patent had helped establish the quality of Sabaté's cork, and the company soon grew to become the main rival for industry leader Corticeira Amorim, of Portugal. A major step in Sabaté's development came with its acquisition of Spain's Corchos de Mérida, a company specialized in raw product purchasing and storage. This acquisition enabled the company to begin the process toward creating a vertically integrated production chain. The Mérida acquisition notably helped the company ensure the supply and quality of its raw cork requirements.

The company's requirements were growing steadily in the late 1980s. Under Augustin Sabaté, the company now turned toward industrializing its production process. In 1991, the company completed construction of a new 65,000-square-meter headquarters and production facility in the town of Ceret. The company then was able to begin converting its production processes to comply with ISO 9002 regulations, a certificate the company obtained in 1995. In 1994, Sabaté confirmed its intention to build its position, placing its stock on the Paris Stock exchange's unlisted market. One year later, however, the company transferred its listing to the Parisian exchange's Secondary Market.

Sabaté's public offering and new production facility also enabled it to pursue development of a new product—a new cork material that the company dubbed Altec. The introduction of Altec allowed Sabaté to straddle an ongoing argument among wine producers of the virtues of natural cork versus newer artificial corks then appearing on the market. Altec was in fact a hybrid of natural and artificial materials, using cork powder produced from a purified cork and combining that with a material developed for Sabaté by Akso Nobel. The new Altec presented a number of interesting properties, notably a greater elasticity than natural cork, as well as a greater resistance to TCA tainting, while retaining some of natural cork's porosity.

Launched in 1995, Altec made steady inroads among wine producers, particularly on the international scene. By 1997, the company was selling more than 200 million units per year, some 80 percent of which were sold to the United States. By then, Sabaté had opened an office in the United States, under subsidiary Sabaté USA, located near the heart of the California wine producing region, which began operations in 1995. Sabaté continued to seek means to ensure its vertical integration, and in 1996, the company created a new subsidiary, Sabaté Maroc, a company specialized in the purchasing and treatment of raw cork. A year

## Key Dates:

**1838:** Tonnellerie Moreau, later a founding member of Diosos, is founded.
**1870:** Seguin, another member of the later Diosos company, begins producing casks.
**1939:** Modeste Sabaté starts up a cork production company in Rousillon, France.
**1947:** Robert Radoux begins crafting casks.
**1958:** Moreau and Sequin merge and Remy Martin becomes a majority shareholder.
**1960:** Modeste Sabaté is joined by sons Augustin, Alex, Bernard, and Georges.
**1972:** Remy Martin acquires full control of Moreau Seguin, which produces casks for cognac and eau-de-vie.
**1977:** Christian Radoux takes over his father's business and introduces industrial production methods.
**1979:** Moreau Seguin begins producing casks for the French wine industry.
**1985:** Sabaté patents the SBM cork cleansing process.
**1986:** Sabaté acquires Corchos de Mérida of Spain.
**1990:** Seguin Moreau begins international expansion and begins producing casks using Russian and American oaks.
**1991:** Sabaté opens a new 65,000-square-meter headquarters and production facility in Ceret, France.
**1994:** Sabaté launches its first public offering on Parisian unlisted securities market.
**1995:** Sabaté joins Paris stock exchange's Secondary Market.
**1999:** Moreau Seguin and Radoux merge to form Diosos SA.
**2000:** Sabaté and Diosos merge to form Sabaté Diosos SA.

later, the company expanded horizontally, acquiring cork flooring and materials specialist Aplicork, based in Spain.

Augustin Sabaté died in 1998 and son Marc Sabaté took over as the company's president. By then, Sabaté had sold more than one billion Altec corks, confirming the product's success. That number was to double again just two years later. The company faced a slight setback, however. Sabaté initially had claimed that Altec was entirely TCA-free. A series of TCA taints among its customers, however, forced the company to admit that it was impossible to eliminate the possibility of TCA tainting entirely. Despite a range of bad publicity, the extent of the TCA tainting remained limited to a very small percentage of all bottles using Altec corks. The setback barely slowed down the rise of Altec sales in Sabaté's revenues; by 2001, Altec represented some 45 percent of Sabaté's cork sales.

Sabaté moved to expand its bottle-stopping range as it turned toward the new century. In 1999, the company acquired two other companies, including Switzerland's Suber, a producer of cork for high-quality wines, as well as screwtop caps. Sabaté's entry into this latter category represented its growing determination to follow the trend toward internationalization of the wine industry, which saw consumers turning away from France to embrace ''new'' wines from other parts of the world. Screwtop caps were widely considered the best means of closing a bottle of wine. Although French winemakers—and their customers—refused to consider abandoning natural corks, especially for high-quality wines meant to age for long periods of time, other markets, such as Australia, were proving more and more receptive to the idea of adopting screwtop caps. Among the notable advantages of this system was the virtual absence of TCA tainting. Later in 1999, Sabaté took a stake in Sibel, a maker of corks for champagne and sparkling wines. By 2000, the company had completed its takeover of Sibel, taking 100 percent control.

Sabaté's determination to place itself in line with developments in the worldwide wine industry led it to make a more dramatic move in 2000. In that year the company announced that it had reached an agreement to merge with Diosos SA, creating Sabaté Diosos SA. The merger doubled Sabaté in size, as both the cork division and the cooperage division produced more than EUR 100 million in revenues. Under terms of the agreement, Marc Sabaté and Michel de Tapol agreed to function as co-CEOs of the enlarged group, which sought to position itself as a provider of services and products to the wine industry. Although greeted with some skepticism by stock market observers—who criticized in particular the lack of production synergies between the two companies—Sabaté Diosos remained confident that the merger would enable both sides of the larger group to take advantage of its widened distribution network as it wooed the world's winemakers. In 2001, the company, which continued to enlarge its production facilities in Ceret, began investigating opening new production facilities to be closer to the growing wine markets in Greece, South Africa, California, and Argentina.

### *Principal Subsidiaries*

Corchos de Mérida S.A.; Sabaté Maroc SARL; Altec S.A.; Suber Suisse S.A.; SC Finance; Diosos S.A.

### *Principal Competitors*

Corticeira Amorim, Sociedade Gestora de Participaçoes Sociais, S.A.; Supreme Corq Inc.; Tonnellerie Francois Freres SA; Tonnellerie Vicard SA; Nadalie-Tonnellerie Ludonnaise SA; Tonnellerie Taransaud SA; Tonnellerie Saury SA; Tonnellerie Bouts SA.

### *Further Reading*

Cuny, Delphine, ''Scepticisme sur le regroupement Sabaté-Diosos,'' *La Tribune,* October 24, 2000.
Hiaring, Philip, ''Sabaté,'' *Wines & Vines,* August 1999.
Kinetz, Erika, ''Cork and Barrel Makers Face Risks Too,'' *International Herald Tribune,* June 23, 2001.
''Plastic Wine Stoppers: A Corking Row,'' *Economist,* June 5, 1999.
''Sabaté Diosos abaisse ses perspectives de croissance,'' *La Tribune,* July 25, 2001.

—M.L. Cohen

# St. Louis Music, Inc.

**1400 Ferguson Avenue**
**St. Louis, Missouri 63133**
**U.S.A.**
**Telephone: (314) 727-4512**
**Toll Free: (800) 727-4512**
**Fax: (314) 727-8929**
**Web site: http://www.stlouismusic.com**

*Private Company*
*Incorporated:* 1922
*Employees:* 350
*Sales:* $80 million (2001 est.)
*NAIC:* 334310 Audio and Video Equipment Manufacturing

St. Louis Music, Inc. has a more than 80-year history as a manufacturer and distributor of musical instruments and accessories. Originally founded as a distributor of violins and violas, the company now has a diverse product line that ranges from hand-carved violins to guitar amplifiers. St. Louis Music has outlasted the vast majority of its competitors by adapting to upheavals in the music industry. In 1922, when the company was founded, there were 71 exhibitors at the NAMM (National Association of Music Merchants) show. The vast majority of them were forced out of business as the music industry went through the Depression and the upheavals caused by the evolution of popular music from jazz to rock and roll. St. Louis Music survived by adapting its product line to take advantage of new musical trends. The company developed its own proprietary lines soon after the rise of rock and roll, including the respected Alvarez guitars and well-known Crate amplifiers. In addition, the company's Knilling String Instruments division carries on the traditional business of wholesale violin distribution, placing special emphasis on service and adjustments performed by skilled craftspeople. Other divisions at St. Louis Music include Ampeg amplifiers, sound reinforcement equipment under the Audio Centron brand name, and the SLM Omni Division, which focuses on importing and wholesaling musical accessories and instruments. The SLM Electronics division encompasses both a factory and a research and development center, while the company's International Division takes care of the technical adjustments necessary for supplying distributors in Europe, Australia, and Japan. All of the company's lines are represented by a single sales force and supported by a central administrative staff. The company is led by Gene Kornblum, whose father founded St. Louis Music.

### *Building an Import and Distribution Business: 1922–60*

St. Louis Music was founded in 1922 by Bernard Kornblum, an immigrant from Vienna, Austria. Kornblum had nourished a love for music ever since he began studying the violin at age ten. However, his family's financial limitations, and the realization that his talent might not be truly exceptional, led him to abandon the path toward a professional career in music. In 1920, at the age of 19, he emigrated to St. Louis, Missouri, where some of his relatives had already established themselves. After short stints at a clothing and a music store, he got a job as a necktie salesman. Kornblum stayed in the haberdashery business for a few years but still yearned to satisfy his love for music. His chance came when the German music wholesaler Seibenbrun put an add in a Missouri paper looking for an agent to export musical instruments to the United States. Kornblum contacted the company and agreed to buy several hundred dollars worth of instruments and accessories to be paid for in German marks. His financial calculations did not take into account the fast depreciation of the German mark during that period, and by the time the shipment arrived it cost him considerably less than he had anticipated. As a result, Kornblum was able to offer the products to St. Louis area retailers at exceptionally low prices. The shipment sold out quickly, and Kornblum worked on establishing relationships with other European manufacturers. Soon he was importing a range of violins and violas from Markneukirchen, Germany, as well as harmonicas from Klingenthal. In 1922, he was able to quit his job selling ties and move his import business into office space in downtown St. Louis.

Bernard's sister Erna took over administrative duties at the business in 1923, and their younger brother David joined the enterprise the following year. The company took the name

## Company Perspectives:

*St. Louis Music's Mission is to be a worldwide music products industry leader in the development, production, distribution, and marketing of quality instruments, equipment, accessories, and related services that satisfy the needs of music makers. We strive to understand and learn from our reseller, end-users, suppliers, and associates, and whenever possible, establish mutually beneficial ''partnering'' relationships. Integrity is the centerpiece of our culture, and our people conduct themselves in a direct, forthright manner that leaves no ambiguity as to where we stand in terms of our actions, expectations, and policies.*

Kornblum Brothers Music. When Erna got married in 1925, her husband Jack Schoenberg also joined the company as a salesman. Business was good in the exuberant climate of the Roaring Twenties, and as the company's offerings expanded, the business made two moves to larger facilities by the end of 1927. In 1929, the Kornblum brothers' annual buying trips to Europe enticed them into establishing a business in Belgium. Eventually settling in Brussels, they sold instruments wholesale and imported Dixieland records from the states, capitalizing on the fact that, while Dixieland's popularity was waning in the United States, it was new to Europe. Meanwhile, their sister Erna and her husband Jack were running the business in St. Louis. The U.S. enterprise was small enough that the 1929 stock market crash had little negative effect on the company. In fact, Erna turned the crash to her advantage when she bought St. Louis Music, a sheet music wholesaler that was on the verge of bankruptcy. Kornblum Brothers Music took on the name of the sheet music company.

In 1933, Erna announced that she was pregnant, so Bernard and David abandoned their European venture and came back to St. Louis. Erna's husband Jack continued to play a major role in running the company. His conservative approach, however, conflicted with that of the Kornblum brothers, who wanted to adapt their offerings to changes in the music industry. The conflict ended in 1938 when Jack and Erna moved to California. Now the Kornblums expanded beyond violins and cellos to begin selling band instruments, sheet music, and music accessories. The business had about 20 employees at this time.

In 1941, the Japanese attacked Pearl Harbor, and the ensuing war put a brake on the music business. Not only were European import sources cut off, but restrictions in the United States made it impossible to manufacture instruments. The company survived by turning to alternative enterprises, including the sale of paint, leather goods, and fine writing instruments. The music business became profitable once again in the postwar period. St. Louis Music became a distributor for dozens of manufacturers. The company represented Harmony and Kay guitars, Regal ukuleles, York Band Instruments, Zildjian cymbals, Turner microphones, Vibrator reeds, and many other brand name products in the music industry. Electronic organs became popular in the mid-1950s, and the company became a distributor for the Thomas Organ Company in 1954. A few years later, St. Louis Music found a cheaper, portable version of the large home organs: Harmophone portable electric reed organs, which were made in Germany. St. Louis Music formed a separate company, Musical Products Corporation, to distribute the organs. The business capitalized on a brief craze for the product around 1958, then crashed when the fad ended.

### *Proprietary Products for the Rock and Roll Era*

By the 1960s, both the national music scene and the people in charge of St. Louis Music were changing. David Kornblum had died in 1954, and three years later Bernard's son Gene agreed to try out the family business before committing himself to pursuing a law degree. The music industry drew him in: he became a full-time employee in 1961 and would be one of the major forces for change at St. Louis Music over the next several decades. Soon after Gene entered the business, the birth of rock and roll began challenging the music industry to adapt. At first, the development was a boon for the whole industry. ''After the Beatles rock 'n' roll boom, we could sell anything that resembled a guitar or drum set,'' Gene Kornblum reminisced in a booklet celebrating the company's 75th anniversary. Firms that previously had little interest in the music business now tried to get a piece of the profits. CBS Corporation, for example, bought Fender guitars, and many small firms went public or were acquired by conglomerates. Inexpensive imports were gobbled up by an eager public. Meanwhile, leading manufacturers such as the Ludwig Drum Company and the CF Martin Guitar Company established their own sales forces, leaving wholesalers out of the picture. By the early 1970s, consumer demand leveled off, profits went down across the industry, and many of the businesses that were coveted during the 1960s rock and roll boom went bankrupt or were sold back.

Gene Kornblum had the vision to put St. Louis Music ahead of its competition. When he joined the company, there was little to differentiate it from other distributors with similar product lines. He realized that had to change. ''A long time ago we decided that there wasn't much future in simply distributing other people's products,'' he told *Music Trades* in 1992, ''To survive and grow, we needed to invest in developing our own product lines.'' The first step toward this goal was taken in 1964, when St. Louis Music became the exclusive distributor for German-made Trixon drums. The drums, in addition to being well made, had distinctive elliptical and cone shapes that Gene believed would appeal to the counter-culture attitude of rock and roll. His hunch was validated: although the drums cost more than alternative brands, St. Louis Music sold 3,000 sets in 1964. The next year, the company introduced a more affordable line under the Apollo name.

In 1968, a fruitful partnership began that gave birth to the Alvarez line of guitars. Gene Kornblum met the gifted Japanese luthier Kazuo Yairi through a Japanese trading partner. Yairi's fine guitar craftsmanship joined forces with St. Louis Music's marketing ability to produce handmade acoustic guitars under the Alvarez-Yairi name. The high-quality instruments, backed up by elegant catalogues and proficient marketing, gained a following among musicians, winning endorsements from popular guitarists such as Roy Clark and Waylon Jennings. Eventually, electric guitars were also produced under the Alvarez name, and the Alvarez Artist series was developed for entry-level players.

## Key Dates:

**1922:** Bernard Kornblum starts a violin import business.
**1929:** The Kornblum brothers travel to Belgium to start a short-lived European venture.
**1941:** World War II interrupts the production of musical instruments.
**1957:** Gene Kornblum joins St. Louis Music.
**1964:** St. Louis Music becomes the exclusive distributor for Trixon Drums.
**1968:** Alvarez-Yairi acoustic guitars are introduced.
**1975:** SLM Electronics is established with the introduction of the Electra MPC Guitar.
**1980:** The Crate amp is introduced at the National Association of Music Merchants (NAMM) show.
**1986:** St. Louis Music acquires Ampeg, a maker of guitar amplifiers.
**1994:** A second manufacturing facility opens in Yellville, Arkansas.

St. Louis Music was also making efforts to keep its traditional stringed instruments a step above the competition. Kornblum traveled abroad to solidify relationships with quality manufacturers, and in the early 1970s he developed a system to customize the company's products: stringed instruments were shipped to St. Louis without any strings or fittings, then completed in the company's assembly shop. Similar care was given to guitars: before being shipped to retailers, each instrument was inspected for its workmanship and, when necessary, adjusted for intonation and playability.

The company moved to expanded facilities on Ferguson Avenue in 1971. A few years later, electronic string keyboards entered the music world, and St. Louis Music managed to capture part of the market by becoming the exclusive distributor for Elka String Rhapsody keyboards, made in Italy. Sales of the product were huge for about a year. Soon, however, electric guitars would eclipse the company's other electronics activities. In the early 1970s, St. Louis Music offered several different electric guitars but had no breakthrough product. Then, in 1975, company salesman Curt Trainer implored St. Louis Music to create "a guitar that could make any crazy sound you wanted it to," according to the company's 75th anniversary booklet. St. Louis Music turned to John Karpowicz, a local electronics technician with a service and repair shop. Karpowicz designed a specially outfitted guitar that could accommodate two small signal-processing modules inserted into a back compartment. The prototype impressed the people at St. Louis Music, and the company bought out Karpowicz' repair business and took him on full-time. The prototype was refined into the Electra MPC (Modular Powered Circuit) Guitar and unveiled at the 1976 NAMM show in Washington, D.C. St. Louis Music formed the SLM Electronics division to support Karpowicz' design activities.

### *Surging Electronics Sales After 1980*

Now that the company had its own electric guitar, the next step was to develop a proprietary line of amplifiers. However, there was so much competition in the amplifier market that only a product with distinctive appeal was likely to be successful. Inspiration hit when Gene Kornblum visited a Crate & Barrel store in Chicago, where merchandise was creatively displayed using packing crates. Kornblum believed the wooden casing could be adapted to house an amplifier. In 1978, the first Crate guitar amplifier was made: a 10-watt practice amp known as the CR1. St. Louis Music decided to establish its own manufacturing operation for the product rather then source overseas. With their competitively low price and novelty packaging, Crate amps sold well enough to strain the company's manufacturing capabilities. More employees were added as a full line of Crate amps was developed, including keyboard amps and a range of solid-state guitar and bass amps. The packing crate was soon replaced with a traditional Tolex-covered cabinet, but the Crate name and the recognition it had gained stuck with the product.

SLM Electronics was the engine behind rapid growth at St. Louis Music in the 1980s. The division moved into its own facility in 1980, and into an even larger space in 1986. It offerings were enhanced with the development of the Audio Centron line of sound reinforcement equipment, including PA systems and mixers designed for sound engineers. Another brand name was added to the St. Louis Music lineup in 1986 when the company acquired the Ampeg Company. Founded in the late 1940s, Ampeg had been a pioneer in the development of bass amplifiers. After changing hands a number of times, however, the company ended up in bankruptcy court. St. Louis Music was attracted by Ampeg's famous SVT all-tube bass amp, a product that was introduced in 1967 and still coveted by serious musicians. After buying Ampeg, St. Louis Music returned to the amp's original specifications, made some refinements, and reintroduced the product. Retro products were coming back into style, and many musicians were glad to see the classic amplifier back on the market.

St. Louis Music had moved far beyond the distribution business by the late 1980s. Manufacturing and design activities now held center stage. As a result, the company's official name was changed in 1987 from St. Louis Music Supply to St. Louis Music, Inc. Sales expanded at a 20 percent annual rate for the next few years, and the number of employees grew to 400. Continued development was ensured with the opening of a new research and development center in 1991. The 20,000-square-foot facility was located across the street from the company's manufacturing facility, so that engineers and manufacturers could work together to generate new products quickly. St. Louis Music characterized its production development philosophy as a "net gain" approach: in addition to an emphasis on reliability and quality, new products were designed to have useful features not available anywhere else. For example, the company developed a hybrid tube/solid state amp that had the warm sound of a tube amp combined with the lower price of a solid-state amp.

St. Louis Music now had six divisions: Ampeg, Crate, Knilling String Instruments, Alvarez guitars, Audio Centron, and Omni Accessories. The Omni division, which carried on the company's traditional import and distribution activities, was provided with a computer system that let salespeople instantly quote the price and availability of thousands of items. As growth continued, orders began piling up at the St. Louis manufacturing plant. Three shifts were not enough to keep up with production demand, so the company opened a second manufacturing plant in 1994. Located in the rural town of Yellville, Arkansas, the facility was designed to work more efficiently than the St. Louis plant, which had been renovated in fits and starts over many years. The company planned to manufacture high-volume entry level products in Yellville, while continuing to produce complex products like Crate Vintage Club amps and the Ampeg SVT bass head in St. Louis, close to the research and development center.

In 1997, St. Louis Music celebrated its 75th anniversary with a huge party at the NAMM show. The company singled out long-term, dedicated employees as the key to its success. One new employee was Ted Kornblum, the third generation of his family to enter the music business. Ted began promoting St. Louis Music as a high school student, when he would take Alvarez guitars to the stage door at a rock concert and offer them free to the artists. He joined the company officially in 1996 and eventually became the Director of Artist Relations. Gene Kornblum remained president, leading the company into the 21st century with a philosophy of quality products and knowledgeable service. St. Louis Music was still going strong in 2002, when it marked its 80th anniversary in the music business.

### *Principal Divisions*

Ampeg; Crate; Audio Centron; Omni Accessories; Knilling String Instruments; Alvarez-Yairi Guitars.

### *Principal Competitors*

Fender Musical Instruments Company; Gibson Guitar Corporation; Yamaha Musical Instruments.

### *Further Reading*

"New St. Louis Music Plant in Arkansas," *Music Trades*, October 1994, pp. 138–40.
"SLM's Investment in Future Growth," *Music Trades*, February 1991, pp. 110–13.
*St. Louis Music: 75 Years*, St. Louis: St. Louis Music, Inc., 1997.
"St. Louis Music Celebrates 70th," *Music Trades*, September 1992, pp. 90–4.
"St. Louis Music Marks 75th," *Music Trades*, February 1997, p. 45.

—Sarah Ruth Lorenz

# Segway LLC

**286 Commercial Street**
**Manchester, New Hampshire 03101**
**U.S.A.**
**Telephone: (603) 222-6000**
**Toll Free: 1-866-4SEGWAY**
**Fax: (603) 222-6001**
**Web site: http://www.segway.com**

*Private Company*
*Incorporated:* 2000
*Employees:* 130
*Sales:* Not Available.
*NAIC:* 541710 Research and Development in the Physical, Engineering, and Life Sciences; 336999 All Other Transportation Equipment Manufacturing

Segway LLC was created to market an upright, self-balancing people-mover called the Segway Human Transporter (HT). The inventor of the Segway HT, Dean Kamen, has made a career of developing technical solutions to some of the world's most challenging problems. For most of his professional life, Kamen developed advanced medical devices under contract through his DEKA Research & Development Corporation. The Segway HT, spun-off from the six-wheeled, stair-climbing IBOT wheelchair created at DEKA, is his product for a mass consumer audience. If the amount of publicity the HT has garnered and the financial backing Segway LLC has attracted are any indication, Kamen's invention will change the way cities move. Kamen's other business ventures have included industrial automation firm Enstrom Helicopter Corporation, Teletrol, and New Power Concepts.

## *Origins*

Born in 1951, Dean Kamen was raised in Rockville Centre, New York. His father was a commercial artist as well as a cartoonist for such publications as *Mad* magazine. His mother taught high school business education and would later help with Kamen's bookkeeping. By age 17, Kamen had his first patent, for an automated control system for audiovisual displays. It was eventually used by sites such as the Hayden Planetarium, the Museum of the City of New York, and Madison Square Garden.

Kamen attended college at Worchester Polytechnic Institute in the 1970s. He was there for five years but did not graduate. Nevertheless, Kamen was soon tackling some of the most serious technical challenges in the world of medicine.

While Kamen was at college, his oldest brother, pediatric oncologist Bart Kamen, lamented the problem of giving patients medication in steady doses. In the mid-1970s, Kamen invented his pocket-sized infusion pump. AutoSyringe Inc. was set up in 1976 to market this device. One of the company's its board members, Bob Tuttle, would join Kamen in several other ventures. After the infusion pumps began being used to administer insulin to diabetes patients, the company's staff grew to 100 employees. In 1982, Kamen agreed to sell AutoSyringe to Baxter International Inc., making him a multimillionaire at age 30.

## *Origins of DEKA Research*

The same year, Kamen founded DEKA Research & Development Corporation in Manchester, New Hampshire. The firm's name was a contraction of his own first and last names. It was originally called Advanced Medical Development, and most of its clients were medical device manufacturers.

Kamen would be amply rewarded for his contributions to medical technology, and he was wont to use his wealth in interesting ways. For example, he made his daily ten-mile commute to work in one of two helicopters manufactured by Enstrom Helicopter Corp., a company he was involved with. Kamen also owned North Dumpling Island, a two-acre getaway off the coast of Connecticut that he declared a sovereign nation with its own currency based on the mathematical value of *pi.*

Kamen claims the slogan ''Live Free or Die'' on New Hampshire's license plates prompted him to move to that state, where he established a 5,500-square-foot plant along the banks of the Merrimack River. Kamen's 30,000-square-foot, hexagonal home—equipped with its own machine shop—was also the site of much of the inventor's work. Usually dressed head to toe

## Company Perspectives:

*Dean Kamen's inventions start the same way—looking at a problem, ignoring the conventional thinking that surrounds it, and working tirelessly until it is solved—a formula he's used since high school. Like most of his innovations, Segway HT reflects Dean's belief that science and engineering can be harnessed to improve people's daily lives. Dean and his team saw a way for his balancing technology to be applied to human transportation, brought together a core team to perfect it, and formed a new company to bring Segway HT and its vision to market.*

in blue denim, Kamen professed not to take vacations and hated wasting time away from work.

Doug Field, an engineer at DEKA, described the company's philosophy to *Design News* by quoting Nobel prizewinner Linus Pauling: "The best way to a good idea is to have lots to choose from." In a nod to the tale of Prince Charming, the company gave a "Frog Award" to the engineer with the most spectacular failure. To keep teams on schedule, meetings were clearly defined as either in "ideation" or "generation" mode.

In 1989, Kamen established For Inspiration and Recognition of Science and Technology (FIRST), a nonprofit group devoted to inspiring high school students to learn about science and technology. FIRST's main project was a robotics competition.

DEKA continued to improve medical devices—and the lives of their users—throughout the 1990s. A portable dialysis pump, only the size of a telephone book, replaced others the size of a dishwasher. DEKA also helped develop a flexible heart stent.

The company did not market these products itself; it was usually hired by large medical device manufacturers such as Baxter to design or improve them in exchange for fees and royalties. About 200 engineers worked with Kamen at DEKA. The firm was able to pick and choose the most intriguing projects.

In 1990, Kamen was troubled by the sight of a man trying to get his wheelchair over the curb of a sidewalk. Kamen's interest in solving this problem led to the development of DEKA's IBOT Mobility System. This six-wheel, motorized wheelchair could climb stairs. The IBOT could balance two sets of wheels on top of each other, allowing its most dramatic feature: the ability to lift handicapped people to eye level with the rest of the world. The IBOT was in clinical trials in 2002. Its manufacturer, a unit of Johnson & Johnson, hoped to begin selling the devices by the summer of 2003 at a projected cost of $25,000 each.

### *Segway HT: New Wheels for the New Millennium*

DEKA began development of the Segway Human Transporter (HT) in the mid-1990s. As the IBOT's code name had been "Fred Upstairs" after Fred Astaire, the HT was initially known as "Ginger" in honor of Ginger Rogers, the other half of the legendary Astaire/Rogers dancing duo. (The Christian Science Church, which partially controlled rights to Ginger Rogers' estate, reportedly would not allow the company to market the device under this name.) Subsequent prototypes were dubbed Mary Ann and Mrs. Howell after characters on the television sit-com *Gilligan's Island*.

For the HT, DEKA borrowed from the balancing technology developed for the IBOT. The HT was a two-wheeled platform with handlebars on which the user was seated upright. It used microprocessors and solid-state gyroscopes to balance itself on two wheels. Kamen did not like the word "scooter" applied to the unique invention; in function, he said, the device was more akin to "magic sneakers." Its speed was electronically limited 12.5 mph, though a police version had a theoretical top speed of more than twice that. Conventional friction brakes would not work, since it needed to keep its wheels active to balance itself; in the HT's braking process, energy from stopping was transferred back into the batteries.

The HT would cost $100 million to develop. Backing its commercial launches were Credit Suisse First Boston and the Silicon Valley venture capital firm Kleiner Perkins Caufield & Byers, which had previously bet on Netscape and Amazon.com. Kleiner Perkins partner John Doerr predicated Segway LLC would reach $1 billion in sales faster than any other company, reported *Vanity Fair.* The firm was valued at a colossal $600 million; Kamen gave up less than 15 percent of the company to his financiers: Credit Suisse and Kleiner Perkins invested $38 million each for their respective 7 percent shareholdings. These investments were lined up in the spring of 2000.

A book proposal about the HT—then known only as Ginger or "IT,"—was leaked to the press in January 2001, prompting a whirlwind of media speculation about the nature of the new device. The HT had not actually been described in the proposal, but the document was filled with titillating testimonials about the value of the device from a few of the select technology figures who had actually seen it.

After months of speculation about the nature of "IT," the Segway Human Transporter (HT) was officially unveiled in December 2001. It generated a great deal of publicity as celebrities tried the devices out on a variety of national TV shows. The HT was even written into an episode of the sit-com *Frasier.*

Kamen immediately began lobbying governments in Europe and the U.S. to allow the HT—a motorized vehicle—to be driven on city sidewalks. Eighteen U.S. states had agreed by the spring of 2002. In fact, *Vanity Fair* reported Atlanta municipal planners were keenly interested in the HT as a way to relieve that city's notorious congestion.

In 2002, the industrial version of the HT was being tested by the likes of the U.S. Postal Service and GE Plastics. Other launch partners included Michelin North America (the maker of the Segway's custom tires), the National Park Service, the City of Atlanta, and Amazon.com. The Boston Police Department was another early trial user.

The consumer version of the HT was scheduled for its commercial debut in late 2002, priced at $3,000. Segway LLC, the company created to develop and market the HT, was a separate venture from DEKA and employed 130 workers.

## Key Dates:

**1976:** AutoSyringe Inc. is founded to market Dean Kamen-designed infusion pumps.
**1982:** Kamen sells AutoSyringe and founds DEKA Research & Development Corp.
**1989:** For Inspiration and Recognition of Science and Technology (FIRST) is founded.
**1990:** IBOT, a six-wheeled wheelchair, goes into development.
**1995:** The company begins development of the Segway HT.
**2000:** Financing is obtained for Segway LLC.
**2001:** The Segway HT is unveiled.
**2002:** Consumer versions of the HT are scheduled for launch late in the year; IBOT undergoes FDA testing.

### *A Motor for the Future?*

After the launch of the Segway HT, Kamen held more than 150 patents. His next project was to build a working Stirling engine. The Reverend Robert Stirling, a Scottish minister, had first suggested the concept in 1816. This engine, which Kamen likened to a refrigerator compressor, ran on waste or anything that could burn as fuel. As a bonus, the engine's heat would purify water at the same time. Kamen hoped to eventually produce Stirling-powered Segways, thereby solving the problems of transportation, energy, and clean drinking water in the same product. Another advantage of the proposed machine was its theoretical ability to go for years without maintenance.

### *Principal Competitors*

C. Rizzato & Co.; Sanyo Electric Co., Ltd.; TH!NK Group; ZAP.

### *Further Reading*

Deagon, Brian, ''Inventor Builds on Knowledge; Innovate to Succeed: Inspiration from Surroundings Keeps Dean Kamen Pumped,'' *Investor's Business Daily,* December 27, 2001, p. A6.

Heilemann, John, ''Machine of Dreams,'' *Vanity Fair,* May 2002, pp. 184–88, 222–30.

Joshi, Pradnya, ''Dean of Invention—A Wheelchair That Climbs Stairs? It's Just One Product of Kamen's Idea Factory,'' *Newsday,* April 29, 2002, p. D1.

Lewis, John, and Karen Auguston Field, ''Balancing Act; An Exclusive Look at the Engineering Behind the Segway HT, with Some Never-Before-Published Technical Details,'' *Design News,* March 25, 2002, p. 52.

—Frederick C. Ingram

# SLI, Inc.

**500 Chapman Street**
**Canton, Massachusetts 02021-2040**
**U.S.A.**
**Telephone: (781) 828-2948**
**Fax: (781) 828-2012**
**Web site: http://www.sli-lighting.com**

*Public Company*
*Incorporated:* 1985
*Employees:* 9,526
*Sales:* $874 million (2002)
*Stock Exchanges:* New York
*Ticker Symbol:* SLI
*NAIC:* 335110 Electric Lamp Bulb and Part Manufacturing; 442299 Other Home Furnishings Stores; 541690 All Other Scientific and Technical Consulting Services; 334515 Instrument Manufacturing for Measuring and Testing Electricity and Electrical Signals; 335931 Current-Carrying Wiring Device Manufacturing; 421610 Electrical Apparatus and Equipment, Wiring Supplies, and Construction Material Wholesalers; 335121 Residential Electric Lighting Fixture Manufacturing; 336321 Vehicular Lighting Equipment Manufacturing

For the past 29 years, SLI, Inc. has expanded through a series of acquisitions, changing from a small, specialized manufacturer and distributor of neon light bulbs to one of the six largest vertically integrated manufacturers, suppliers, and designers of lighting systems worldwide. Its products include incandescent, fluorescent, compact fluorescent, high intensity discharge, halogen, miniature incandescent, neon, light-emitting diodes (LED), and special lamp lighting systems. The company also sells a full line of lamps for decorative and residential usage, as well as industrial and commercial fixtures, advanced fiber optic lighting systems, and specialty products, which are sold under a variety of brand names. Its flagship brand is Sylvania. Others brand names include Concord, Lumiance, Linolite, and Le Dauphin. Miniature lighting assemblies are sold under the Chicago Miniature Lamp and SLI Miniature Lighting brand. With a wide variety of markets, SLI serves a diverse international customer base. As a result, about 70 percent of the company's sales come from outside the United States. SLI has major plants in 15 countries and operates worldwide.

## *1980s: From Specialized Firm to Industry Leader*

The founder and CEO of SLI, Inc., Frank Ward, grew up in a poor Boston neighborhood and graduated with an electrical engineering degree from Northeastern University. After graduation, he began working as a field engineer. Arriving in Canton, Massachusetts, several years later, he got a job at Instron Corporation, where he was laid off after three years. At this point, he decided he wanted to control his own destiny, so he started his own manufacturer's representative agency in Canton, specializing in selling products for lighting companies. During this time, Ward became involved with a small firm, Xenell Marketing Corporation, which focused on distributing neon light bulbs manufactured by Xenell Corporation for use as ''power on'' indicators in the appliance industry. A few years later, Ward bought Xenell Marketing Corporation, and the company began to grow, hitting it big financially. However, Ward knew that only a manufacturer could control its own margins, so he bought Xenell Corporation in 1985. When he purchased Xenell, annual sales were $6 million dollars.

For seven years, Ward continued to develop the business, increasing his company's sales four-fold, with significant cash flows. Then, in 1992, he made a strategic decision to branch out into the highly fragmented miniature lighting industry through buyouts. He purchased Chicago Miniature Lamp from an investment firm based in Great Britain—VCH International Ltd. Established in 1910 and located in Buffalo Grove, Illinois, Chicago Miniature was another fast-growing maker of tiny light bulbs used in household appliances. The company also made fiber-optic products, lamp-making equipment, and miniature bulb sockets, and served the automotive, aviation, and marine markets. That year, Ward merged Xenell with Chicago Miniature Lamp, renaming the company Chicago Miniature Lamp, Inc (CML). The combined companies supplied a wide variety of

## Company Perspectives:

*SLI, Inc. has an established, strong tradition of leadership in the art of making light, and we continue to build on this reputation. Our business is solely focused in lighting applications, so we can dedicate all of our resources to that mission. At SLI, innovation means achieving worthwhile results through the development of practical solutions that deliver increasing customer value. Whether the need is for functional lighting systems for commercial and industrial applications, or decorative and architectural systems for domestic and interior design lighting, customers throughout the world know that SLI has the capabilities, competencies, and solutions to deliver precisely the lighting results required.*

miniature lighting products to diverse markets. Besides supplying appliance lights, CML also sold night-lights to Johnson & Johnson, warning beacon lights put out by the U.S. Coast Guard in coastal areas, lights for aircraft wingtips, and indicator lights in airplane cockpits. Sales increased significantly, and Ward formed his intention of becoming a big player in the lighting industry.

In 1993, CML continued to expand, acquiring its only major rival in the neon business, Glowlite Corporation, a manufacturer of neon lamps with approximately $3 million in sales. Then, continuing on an aggressive path, Ward purchased Industrial Devices Inc. in 1994. Based in Hackensack, New Jersey, Industrial Devices was a fabricator of plastic indicators and light-emitting diodes (LED) arrays with significant expertise in design, tooling, and molding. It specialized in encapsulating lighting components into assemblies used in automotive displays. With annual sales of roughly $23 million when acquired, Industrial Devices operated as a subsidiary and transformed CML into one of the nation's largest makers of miniature lighting components.

### *Mid-1990s: From Expansion to Vertical Integration*

At this point, Ward continued to plan his company's expansion in the U.S. and European markets, eyeing further acquisitions that would emphasize CML's U.S. manufacturing thrust. To further this goal, in June 1995, CML made its initial public offering of 2.2 million shares at $12.50 each. With the additional capital, CML acquired Plastomer Inc., an Ontario, Canada-based company, for $3.56 million. Plastomer was a manufacturer of incandescent and LED socket assemblies and predominantly serviced the automotive industry. A fully automated company that used process efficiencies such as injection molding, with capacities ranging from 30 to 1,000 tons and extensive use of robotics, Plastomer was already vertically integrated and offered CML a great opportunity in the original equipment manufacturer (OEM) marketplace, allowing it to use other companies' product components to build its own branded products. CML's business began to accelerate at an incredible rate. Going public helped to propel the company's growth, while the acquisition of Plastomer's 70,000-square-foot facility gave CML an entry into the Canadian market. CML had now grown into a $60 million dollar company and had a customer list that included AT&T, General Motors, Ford, Chrysler, Honda, and Siemens.

The Plastomer acquisition proved a step toward CML's vision of complete self-sufficiency. In a June 1995 article in *Electronic Buyers News*, executive vice-president Paul Flynn said: ''Plastomer gives an added dimension, which falls in line with CML's corporate strategy to be self-reliant and not depend on outside suppliers. We want to control it all.'' CML continued on its path towards this goal in September of that year when its subsidiary, Industrial Devices, acquired Fredon Development Industries Inc.—a tool and dye maker that designed, tested, and fabricated injection and plastic insert molds. Industrial Devices had been using these molds to produce sockets and could now manufacture these pieces on its own.

Then, in a strategic move to enable CML to expand beyond its core miniature lighting business, the company purchased STT Badalax, Ltd., designer of automatic bulb manufacturing machinery in 1995. This acquisition provided CML with the equipment to manufacture a range of bulbs. By December, CML had acquired a second European company, Phoenix Lighting (UK) Limited of Leicestershire, England. This acquisition, in conjunction with the Baladex purchase, accelerated another of CML's strategic plans: to expand its sales and manufacturing presence in the European market. Phoenix's assets and business were transferred and began to operate as Chicago Miniature Lamp, Europe, Ltd., a wholly-owned subsidiary of CML, Inc. Manufacturing high technology halogen, metal halide, and high-end specialty lamps in a wide variety of industrial, commercial, and retail applications, its most innovative product was the MR 16 lamp—a half-inch in diameter halogen bulb typically used in ceilings to emit bright light.

These buyouts enabled the company to develop its position as a global leader in the vertically integrated miniature lighting market and to improve its management and operational efficiencies. CML also acquired new and larger customers along the way, such as Cabletron, U.S. Robotics, Sunbeam, and Mr. Coffee.

### *Late 1990s: Diversification into New Markets*

However, these new purchases were not the end of CML's acquisition spree. Before the Phoenix purchase was even complete, CML announced yet another acquisition in December 1995—Electro Fiberoptics Corporation in Marlborough, Massachusetts. Viewing the fiber-optic firm as its entry into the next generation of the lighting industry, CML renamed its new acquisition CML Fiberoptics. Manufacturing custom designing and marketing fiber-based products used to transmit light or images—products that are widely used in the medical, dental, science, industrial, military, and transportation fields—the company enabled CML to branch out into new, unexplored markets.

The aggressive diversification and acquisition strategy was paying off. More and more equipment manufacturers were relying on outside companies to make their customized miniature lighting assemblies, and CML was poised to become a prime beneficiary of this trend. In addition, CML had created for itself

## Key Dates:

**1973:** Xenell Corporation is formed.
**1985:** Frank Ward buys Xenell Corporation
**1992:** Chicago Miniature Lamp is purchased; Xenell becomes Chicago Miniature Lamp, Inc. (CML).
**1993:** Strategic acquisitions begin; Glolite is purchased.
**1994:** CML acquires Industrial Devices Inc.
**1995:** Initial public offering is successfully completed; the company acquires Plastomer Inc.
**1998:** CML adopts the name SLI, Inc. after acquiring Sylvania Lighting International B.V. (SLI B.V.).
**2001:** SLI opens North America's first LED manufacturing plant.

an unusually high level of vertical integration, producing quality products at a very low cost.

The following year, 1996, looking to help clinch its place as a key supplier to carmakers and consumer goods manufacturers, CML purchased an electronic and magnetic ballast manufacturing operation for $25 million—Valmont Industries of Valley, Nebraska. CML also acquired a firm that made machines for molding tiny lamps, Gustave Bruckner Gmbh, to secure additional equipment to expand its German capacity.

In 1997, CML bought Sylvania Lighting International B.V. (SLI, B.V.), the third largest lighting company in Europe, for about $165 million cash from Siemens A.G. of Germany. Specializing in a full line of lamps, industrial and commercial fixtures, and specialty products, and based in Geneva, Sylvania had generated revenue of about $600 million in 1996 in 30 countries outside of North America. With such a monumental acquisition and its own revenue reaching $94.2 million, CML became one of the world's top lighting companies. To signify its new status, in May 1998, CML changed its name to SLI, Inc.

To further enhance its position in the European market and increase its miniature lamp manufacturing capacity, that same month SLI acquired 71 percent of the outstanding shares of VCH International Ltd., which, over the years, had been both a supplier and one of its strongest miniature lamp competitors in Europe and the United States. By August 1998, SLI acquired SOCOP SA and its subsidiaries. Located in Besacon, France, SOCOP was both a customer and a competitor of SLI's miniature lighting division in Europe, and a highly regarded manufacturer and supplier of miniature lighting products and systems, with sales of approximately $40 million. The combination of SOCOP with the recently acquired VCH operation, along with other new acquisitions provided a strong vertically and horizontally integrated European miniature lighting presence with a broad product range that became known as SLI Miniature Lighting. With SOCOP, SLI also obtained quality customers, including Renault, VW, and Magneti Marelli. By the end of 1997, SLI was operating in 30 countries and had 13 manufacturing plants in nine.

In 1999, SLI further augmented its position in the European lighting fixture market and strengthened its European lighting presence with the purchase of Lighting Partner B.V. of the Netherlands, a rapidly growing presence in the European retail market. A year later, it purchased assets from a British light maker, Emess Plc, a deal that the company projected would put its revenue over the $1 billion dollar threshold.

### *2000 and Beyond: Continued Expansion, Consolidation, and Restructuring*

In 1998, SLI was also gaining momentum at home with the purchase of IllumElex Corporation, enabling the company to branch out into the lightning maintenance, lighting retrofit, and installation services, as well as lamps, fixtures, ballasts, and lighting components. The following year, SLI made several additional domestic acquisitions that dramatically strengthened its general lighting presence at home, such as Supreme Lighting Corporation and Strategic Resource Solutions Corporation's Parke Industries. Supreme was the largest independent general lighting, bulb manufacturer in the United States with sales of approximately $60 million; Parke was one of the largest lighting-management companies in the nation. At this point, more than 80 percent of SLI's sales came from Latin America, Europe, and Australia, and SLI wanted this figure to change.

In addition to using acquisitions for this purpose, SLI reached an agreement in 1999 with Stanley Electric Co., Ltd., a major Japanese LED manufacturer, for a joint venture to establish the first-of-its-kind manufacturing plant for the production of LED's in North America.

By 1999, SLI's efforts toward innovations in lighting technology, along with programs to increase product offerings, helped the company earn 75 percent of its net sales from lamps and fixtures. It proceeded with a second public offering that has been on hold since 1998. Yet, with all its growth, the company had also acquired a large amount of debt; pricing issues in Europe and the decline of the Euro, along with an economic slow-down in the United States, began to take their toll. Fiscal year 2000 was challenging for SLI with sales only reaching $913.3 million, falling below earning expectations. By the end of 2000, with falling profits, the company decided to direct its focus on its core miniature lighting business, emphasizing the optoelectronics market, which represented the highest-margin side of its lighting business, and the fixture market, which was less price sensitive than other lighting segments. With this reorganization, SLI hoped to return the company to profitability. SLI began selling some assets and service contracts. In November, it cut 313 jobs in Europe and the United States and in February 2001, laid off two-thirds of the workers in its ballast plant in Juarez, Mexico.

However, 2001 was also a year of new beginnings for SLI when it opened North America's first, full-line surface mount LED manufacturing plant in Barrie, Ontario, Canada. Fully automated with minimal labor costs, the plant allowed SLI to compete in a highly competitive marketplace. This plant had been only a dream for Ward in 1994, who had come a long way from his company's small beginnings.

### *Principal Subsidiaries*

CML Air; Power Lighting Products; SLI Lighting Products; SLI Lighting Solutions; Concord Lighting; Lumiance B.V.; SLI

Lighting Solutions; SLI Lichtsysteme; SLI France; SLI Sylvania S.A.; Sylvania D.O.; Iluminacao.

## *Principal Competitors*

General Electric Company; Philips Electronics North America Corporation; Philips Electronics N.V.; Siemens AG.

## *Further Reading*

Chandler, Douglas, "SLI Lighting to Buy Parke Industries," *Electrical Wholesaling*, June 1999, p. 32.

Gatlin, Greg, "Canton's SLI Buys British Light Firm," *Boston Herald*, May 31, 2000, p. 33.

Gresock, Sam, "Canton-Mass.-Based Light Bulb Maker to Close Mullins, S.C. Factory," *State*, November 10, 2000, p. 45.

Hara, Yoshiko, "SLI, Stanley Team Up for LED Venture," *Electronic Engineering Times*, July 3, 2000, p. 30.

Lamb, Robin, "SLI to Open North America's First LED Plant," *Electronic Buyers News*, June 25, 2001, p. 24.

Taylor, Robyn Parets, "Brightening," *Investor's Business Daily*, November 27, 1995, p. A4.

——, "Chicago Miniature Lamp's Ward," *Investor's Daily*, October 20, 1996, p. A1.

—Carrie Rothburd

SNOW BRAND MILK PRODUCTS CO.,LTD.

# Snow Brand Milk Products Company, Ltd.

**13, Honshio-cho**
**Shinjuku-ku**
**Tokyo 160-0003**
**Japan**
**Telephone: (03) 3226-2158**
**Fax: (03) 3226-2150**
**Web site: http://www.snowbrand.co.jp**

*Public Company*
*Incorporated:* 1950
*Employees:* 15,325
*Sales:* $9 billion (2001)
*Stock Exchanges:* Tokyo Osaka Sapporo
*NAIC:* 311512 Creamery Butter Manufacturing; 311513 Cheese Manufacturing; 311514 Dry, Condensed, and Evaporated Dairy Product Manufacturing; 311520 Ice Cream and Frozen Dessert Manufacturing; 311511 Fluid Milk Manufacturing; 311514 Dry, Condensed, and Evaporated Dairy Product Manufacturing

Snow Brand Milk Products Company, Ltd. once operated as the largest—and most respected—dairy concern in Japan. During 2000, however, several of the company's milk related products were responsible for widespread instances of food poisoning among Japanese consumers. Just as the firm began to restructure and slowly recover from the incident, subsidiary Snow Brand Foods Co. was named in a beef labeling scandal. As a result, the company announced in 2002 that it would spin off all of its businesses and transfer its milk and dairy drink business to the National Federation of Agricultural Cooperatives Associations and trading firm Itochu Corp.

## *Early History: 1920s–50s*

Vegetables, rice, and fish had been the traditional Japanese diet for centuries before the late 19th-century move to colonize Hokkaido, the northernmost of Japan's four main islands. Like the others, Hokkaido is bisected by a mountain range, with little flat, arable land. Unlike the rest of Japan, however, Hokkaido's climate is too cold to grow most vegetable crops or rice profitably. But its verdant slopes did offer ample pasture land. Hokkaido's pioneers brought dairy cattle with them and succeeded in producing a fine grade of milk. However, for decades the market was too limited for these farmers to do much more than supply their own needs from their herds and small gardens.

The winter of 1920 was particularly severe; storms damaged fodder and frigid weather diminished herds. To add to these troubles, the post-World War I recession reached Japan in the early 1920s. Hardships multiplied until the spring of 1925, when a group of Hokkaido's hard-hit dairy farmers formed a cooperative association and began to formulate a survival plan. On May 17, 1925, the Hokkaido Dairy Cooperative was formed with 629 members.

Torizo Kurosawa, the cooperative's managing director, had noticed the difference milk had made in the nutrition of the local farmers. He spearheaded what was then a daring plan: to produce two heretofore exclusively Western products—butter and cheese—and market them throughout the country. By July, butter was in production, and by October the butter-marketing program was in full swing. Due in part to the fact that the entire economy had improved and continued to flourish for most of the decade, the plan succeeded.

By the following September, sales were so brisk that a new factory was built in Sapporo, which later became the site of the company's registered office. The Snow Brand trademark was first used in December 1926.

Two years into butter production, the cooperative dared to introduce another Western product: ice cream. It, too, quickly achieved popularity. The cooperative finally got around to the production of cheese in 1933, and several varieties of the product were successfully introduced to the Japanese.

Representatives of the group studied dairy-farming methods in several countries and decided to use Danish dairy farming as a guide. They realized that to keep the cooperative's growing variety of milk products uniform in quality, basic milk production methods also had to be kept uniform. To ensure that all members used the same methods to produce top-quality milk,

## Company Perspectives:

*Snow Brand has refocused on its original corporate mission of contributing to consumer health by providing superior milk and dairy products. For delicious, worry-free products, we are carrying out integrated quality assurance activities from raw materials procurement and production to distribution and sales. Our strategy includes establishing a product safety inspection department; thorough implementation of Hazard Analysis and Critical Control Point (HACCP) Management; enhancing plant inspection systems; reinforcing the quality assurance system for the Snow Brand group; and establishing a new food hygiene research facility and contribute research results to society.*

the cooperative established a training program for young farmers, the Hokkaido Dairy Farming School, in 1934.

By 1935, the cooperative's products had achieved popularity throughout Japan, and a new marketing effort was launched to export them. It began with a butter shipment to London in November and eventually proved successful for all products.

Japan's government, too, was pursuing expansionist policies. Having created a puppet state in Manchuria in 1931, Japan invaded China in 1937, alienating the Western democracies recently opened as markets by organizations such as the dairy cooperative. With foreign markets limited, the group turned its attention to expanding the variety of its products and established the Dairy Science Research Institute in 1937.

The Hokkaido Dairy Cooperative had started several new businesses in the next few years: meat processing, margarine production, leather goods, and the manufacture of special farming equipment. The group also went into the land improvement business. Even with the privations and losses of World War II, the group, which was reorganized in June 1941 as Hokkaido Rakuno Kosha Company, continued to expand.

In the wake of Japan's defeat in World War II, the size of the conglomerate was considered detrimental to the recovery of other Japanese businesses, and in 1948 legal steps were taken to prevent the formation of an economically overpowering cartel. A major reorganization took place, and Snow Brand Milk Products Company, Ltd. was established to succeed the cooperative in June 1950. Each of the entities that had formerly made up the conglomerate became an independent subsidiary.

### *Expansion: 1950s–80s*

During the 1950s, Snow Brand established additional subsidiaries in Tokyo and Osaka to handle the fluid-milk business and took over the milk and milk-products business of local dairy cooperatives in several other locations. Another reorganization in 1958 rejoined Snow Brand with Clover Milk Products Company (formerly the Hokkaido Butter Company), from which it had separated in 1950. In 1966, Snow Brand's headquarters moved to a new building in Tokyo.

Snow Brand continued to expand, adding new products in the 1970s and 1980s—including frozen foods, seasonings, powdered milk for aquatic animals, and oat products—and establishing new subsidiaries to handle them. The company also began to enter into productive business relationships with other companies both in Japan and abroad. Snow Brand established a joint venture in 1972 with Murray Goulburn Snow in Australia and began to sell wine in 1974 under contract with companies in five European countries. In 1981, Snow Brand bought Chateau Grower Winery Company and started its own wine production. An additional facility, Snow Brand Belle Foret Winery, has been in operation since 1985. Through a tie-up with Stokely-Van Kamp, the company has been selling Gatorade, a popular sports drink, since 1980. A joint venture with the Pillsbury Company in 1981 resulted in the establishment of Snow Brand Pillsbury, Inc. in Japan. Snow Brand also has agreements with the Quaker Oats Company (U.S.), Melkunie-Holland (Netherlands), Molkerie-Zentrak Sud GmbH. (Germany), Valio-Finnish Co-operative Dairies' Association (Finland), and Industria Gelati Sammontana (Italy).

In 1983, Snow Brand established the Embryo Transplantation Laboratory, with facilities for cryogenic storage where bisected high-grade cattle embryos were transplanted and sex was determined through prenatal tests. Further steps to improve herds were made by veterinarians on the dairy farms, and advice on cattle breeding and milk production spread from Hokkaido to the northern portion of the neighboring island of Honshu. In addition, processing plants had become highly mechanized for quality control.

Biotechnology research concerned with gene control, cell fusion, and tissue culture was carried on in Snow Brand's Research Institute of Life Sciences, also established in 1983. Research helped to develop new foods, such as varieties of yogurt, as well as pharmaceutical products. A medicine for senile dementia was also under development during the 1980s in cooperation with an Israeli biochemical institute, and Snow Brand was also working on an anti-cancer drug. The pharmaceutical products planning department, started in 1981, examined technical studies in connection with analyses of market needs.

Snow Brand's health-food line expanded throughout the 1980s, responding to growing public concern with fitness and nutrition. The company's infant formulas and follow-up formulas, basic to the line, were popular not only throughout Japan but also in southeast Asia and the Middle East. In 1985, the company opened its Health and Nutrition Institute, which published dietary advice in a periodical called *Health Digest*.

The company's ongoing concern with nutrition and fitness was reflected in its encouragement and sponsorship of sports activities. In 1960, the first Snow Brand Cup All-Japan Ski-Jumping Competition was held, and this soon turned into an annual event. The Snow Brand ice hockey team was formed in 1979. A year later, the company opened an ice skating center. In 1983, the Snow Brand Field Athletic Cup was established. The company also began supporting the Snow Brand Cup National Invitational Little League Competition.

The 50th anniversary of the founding of the cooperative dairy group was celebrated with the opening of the Snow Brand

**Key Dates:**

**1925:** The Hokkaido Dairy Cooperative is formed.
**1926:** The Snow Brand trademark is launched.
**1933:** Cheese is added to the coop's product line.
**1941:** The group is reorganized as Hokkaido Rakuno Company.
**1950:** Snow Brand Milk Products Company Limited is established.
**1971:** The firm expands into frozen foods.
**1974:** Snow Brand begins to sell wine.
**1981:** Chateau Grower Winery Company is acquired; the company begins its own wine production.
**1985:** Snow Brand opens the Health and Nutritional Institute.
**1990:** The firm partners with Hershey Foods Corp.
**2000:** Snow Brand products cause food poisoning in over 14,000 people in Japan.
**2002:** The company is involved in a beef labeling scandal; the subsidiary Snow Brand Foods Co. is dissolved as the firm undergoes a major restructuring.

Historical Museum in Sapporo. The innovative and expansionary policies of the company's early developers were adhered to just as consistently during the late 1980s. Biotechnology and computerization provided new directions for product development and quality control. Snow Brand's General Institute for Dairy Farming, founded in 1976, and its Cheese Research Laboratory, opened in 1979, were just two groups working to provide improvements to future cuisine options.

### *Challenges Lead to Disaster: 1990s and Beyond*

Snow Brand continued as the largest dairy concern in Japan throughout the 1990s. However, because Japan had begun to allow imports into the country at this time, pressure was brought to bear on domestic firms. A 1992 *Nikkei Weekly* article commented on the changing policy, claiming that "Japanese firms are greatly concerned that their home market, long a well-protected environment, will be swamped with low-priced imports from agricultural producers. New Zealand, for example, could supply fresh milk at a cost only 20 percent that of domestic milk."

Given the changing business climate for the Japanese dairy industry, Snow Brand began to form partnerships and expand internationally to remain competitive. In 1990, the company teamed up with United States-based Hershey Foods Corp. in a deal that allowed Snow Brand to produce Hershey-branded chocolate milk and ice cream products. Snow Brand also formed a licensing partnership with Kataoka and Co., an importer of Twinings Imported Teas.

As part of its global expansion strategy, the company began to export powdered milk to the Soviet Union. Shipments were halted in 1991, however, due to lack of payment. Snow Brand then moved into the Australian market with the acquisition of cheese manufacturer Piam Pty. Ltd. and planned to set up a research laboratory in the Netherlands. The firm also expanded into Thailand. As the Asian economy began to falter into the late 1990s, Snow Brand responded by streamlining operations. High costs related to the weakening yen against the dollar forced the firm to post a slight drop in profits during 1997. Profits continued to fall into 1999 as the company experienced its fourth consecutive year of after-tax profit declines.

The 1990s proved to be a challenging period for Snow Brand, and the company faced even greater obstacles in the early years of the next century. Disaster struck in June 2000 when nearly 15,000 people became ill and one person died after consuming low fat milk or a yogurt drink produced by Snow Brand. The outbreak was one of the worst cases of food poisoning in Japan's history. Furthermore, it soon became apparent that company officials tried to cover up the firm's negligence.

Negative publicity besieged the company as news broke that the firm was slow to recall all of the products that were manufactured at the infected Osaka plant. It was then discovered that the firm did not shut down its plants for inspection until almost two weeks after the poisoning was reported. Before police could begin their investigation into the contamination, Snow Brand began a company-sponsored investigation, an action that went against industry guidelines. The company almost immediately fell victim to foul-play rumors, and Snow Brand workers came under suspicion for destroying evidence, specifically a mechanical part connecting to the contaminated production line valve. This valve, which had not been cleaned regularly, allowed bacteria to grow.

As a result of the food poisoning incident, Snow Brand's president resigned and several executives faced criminal charges. During 2000, Snow Brand posted losses for the first time since its public inception in 1950. With its brand image severely battered, Snow Brand announced a corporate restructuring effort designed to reorganize the company's culture, strengthen quality assurance, and return the business to profitability.

Huge losses continued in 2001, and the firm cut jobs and closed factories. Just as the company was beginning to regain some of its lost market share, it became involved in yet another scandal. In early 2002, subsidiary Snow Brand Foods Co. Ltd. intentionally mislabeled Australian beef as Japanese in order to receive government subsidies. The subsidiary was dissolved in April 2002, and the following month five company executives were arrested on fraud charges.

With consumer confidence at an all-time low, the company launched a restructuring scheme in which all of its business units would be spun off. Its main dairy business would in effect become a subsidiary of the National Federation of Agricultural Associations and trading firm Itochu Corp. By 2003, it was expected that the company would be operating at one-third its size during the 1990s. Despite the firm's restructuring efforts, many industry analysts believed that Snow Brand's image was damaged beyond repair. Indeed, the future of this once well-respected dairy concern appeared uncertain.

### *Principal Competitors*

Meiji Dairies Corporation; Morinaga & Co. Ltd.; Nippon Meat Packers Inc.

### *Further Reading*

"Analysis: Snow Brand Milk Revival Plan Dubious," *Daily Yomiuri*, March 30, 2002.

"Beef Labeling Scandal Forces Yoshida to Bow Out," *Grocer*, February 2, 2002, p. 15.

"The Final Straw for Snow Brand?," *Eurofood*, February 28, 2002, p. 9.

"Five Ex-Snow Brand Food Execs Arrested Over Fraud in Japan," *Xinhua News Agency*, May 13, 2002.

Ito, Koichi, "Milk Makers Eye Asian Market," *Nikkei Weekly*, November 16, 1992, p. 10.

"Lessons From Japan's Milk Crisis," *Dairy Foods*, August 2000, p. 7.

"Snow Brand Linked to Mass Poisoning," *Dairy Industries International*, July 2000, p. 7.

"Snow Brand Milk Products to Set Up Lab in Netherlands," *Japan Economic Newswire*, January 28, 1991.

"Snow Brand Milks Sees 1st Red Ink Since Stock Listings," *Jiji Press Ticker Service*, May 18, 2000.

"Snow Brand Milk Ties Up With Hershey Foods," *Japan Economic Newswire*, January 25 1990.

"Snow Brand Reports Huge Net Loss," *Eurofood*, June 21, 2002, p. 13.

—update: Christina M. Stansell

SOLECTRON®

# Solectron Corporation

**777 Gibraltar Drive**
**Milpitas, California 95035**
**U.S.A.**
**Telephone: (408) 957-8500**
**Fax: (408) 957-6056**
**Web site: http://www.solectron.com**

*Public Company*
*Incorporated:* 1977
*Employees:* 60,000
*Sales:* $18.7 billion (2001)
*Stock Exchanges:* New York
*Ticker Symbol:* SLR
*NAIC:* 334412 Bare Printed Circuit Board Manufacturing; 334413 Semiconductor and Related Device Manufacturing; 334419 Other Electronic Component Manufacturing

Solectron Corporation operates as the world's largest electronics manufacturing services company. The company serves high-tech customers including those in the computer, telecommunications, computer peripheral, networking, semiconductor, and consumer electronics industries. Its clients include the likes of Ericsson, Cisco Systems, and Nortel Networks. Solectron achieved stellar growth during the 1990s and in fiscal 2001, achieved a compound annual sales growth rate of 43 percent for the fourth year in a row. Recognized as a global leader in service and quality, Solectron has over 400 quality and service awards to its name, including two prestigious Malcolm Baldridge National Quality Awards.

## *Origins*

Roy Kusumoto started Solectron in 1977 and was joined about one year later by Dr. Winston Chen. Kusumoto and Chen formed the company to take advantage of an opportunity that they saw opening up in the burgeoning solid state electronics market. They noted that many manufacturers of electronic equipment were often burdened by temporary periods of work overflow, during which they had trouble making or acquiring enough circuit boards or other assemblies to complete their components. Through Solectron, Kusumoto and Chen hoped to provide manufacturing services to companies that were experiencing shortages.

Most of Solectron's growth and success during the 1980s has been credited to Chen. During Solectron's first full year of operation Kusumoto lost $150,000. Then a friend put him in touch with Chen. Chen, a manufacturing expert with doctorates from Harvard, was employed at International Business Machines (IBM) at the time. Kusumoto, also a former IBM employee, became interested in Chen's ideas and asked for his help. Chen joined the tiny Solectron as executive vice-president in 1978 and was named president 12 months later. The company generated a profit of $400,000 during the first year under his leadership. From that point forward Solectron's earnings grew steadily. In 1984, Chen succeeded Kusumoto as chief executive.

By the time Chen joined Solectron, the 36-year-old already had acquired a reputation within his industry peer group as a highly intelligent, hard-working innovator. Chen was born and raised in a middle-class family in Taiwan. His father owned and managed a construction firm and impressed a strong work ethic on his children. Influenced by his family's construction background, Chen studied civil engineering at National Chang Kung University in Taiwan. He finished first in his class of 130 and earned a fellowship to study at Harvard in 1965.

Chen's chance to travel to the United States came at an opportune time because he had become dissatisfied with the political climate in Taiwan. Specifically, Chen was frustrated by barriers to economic and social mobility that existed in the country. "We were one of the lucky families in Taiwan," Chen recalled in the *Business Journal-San Jose*, "but that just made me realize how unfair the political system could be. It was terribly self-perpetuating." Chen had become one of the more outspoken students at his college and had seen some of his friends arrested. After studying at Harvard Chen decided to remain in the United States while most of his family stayed in Taiwan.

## Company Perspectives:

*Our mission is to provide worldwide responsiveness to our customers by offering the high quality, lowest total cost, customized, integrated, design, supply-chain, and manufacturing solutions through long-term partnerships based on integrity and ethical business practices.*

Chen earned two doctorates, one in applied mechanics and the other in applied physics, in less than five years at Harvard. "There's no secret to success in school or business: Hard work," explained Chen in the *Business Journal-San Jose*. Chen's accomplishments are additionally impressive because of the hurdles posed by learning the English language. An amusing episode related to a thesis Chen wrote on the theories of the relative strengths of certain materials illustrates Chen's struggles. He titled the piece "Necking in a Bar" before a professor suggested changing the name to "Necking of a Bar." Despite Chen's difficulty with word choice, his paper became influential in his field of study; he had utilized a new computer program that was subsequently adopted by many other researchers. Also while at Harvard, Chen discovered billiards, which became his hobby and escape as a student, and he married another Taiwanese doctoral student.

IBM recruited the 27-year-old Chen upon his graduation in 1969. He worked in New York for three years before he was transferred to San Jose, California. During his nearly ten years at IBM, Chen was exposed to both the manufacturing and marketing sides of the computer business. He was involved in several major projects, including the development of IBM's ink-jet printers and creation of various tape-head technologies. Also, Chen had developed an intense interest in the teachings of W. Edwards Deming, whose ideologies and techniques related to manufacturing and quality were being widely embraced in Japan and other parts of Asia. He believed in Deming's methods but was frustrated by IBM's failure to recognize their validity. So Chen was already open to the idea of starting and running a new company before Kusumoto asked for his help in 1978.

### *Growth Under Chen's Leadership: 1980s*

During the early and mid-1980s, Solectron found a willing market for its manufacturing services. Because of the founder's ties to IBM, much of their work came from that company. However, Solectron slowly diversified and was able to parlay its experience serving IBM into manufacturing contracts with several other major electronics companies. Furthermore, as its clients became familiar with its service and style, Solectron began to shift away from its early emphasis on overflow, production-oriented jobs. Eventually, customers started coming to Solectron for help with entire manufacturing programs and development projects.

Solectron's quick success during the early and mid-1980s stemmed from Chen's management techniques, many of which were grounded in Deming's philosophies. Deming is generally credited with inspiring the Total Quality Management philosophy that was adopted after World War II in Japan and became popular in the United States during the 1980s. Deming, an American, was sent to Japan to help rebuild that economy after World War II. His ideas were generally ignored in the United States until Japan began to pose a serious threat to the U.S. manufacturing sector. In short, Deming developed a people-focused management strategy designed to achieve continual increases in customer satisfaction and quality at continually lower costs. He advocated the use of comprehensive quality management techniques that saturated an organization, involving all departments and employees and extending backward and forward to envelop both the supply and customer chains.

"Dr. Deming's philosophy is simple: improvement doesn't happen by itself," Chen told the *Business Journal-San Jose*. "It must be a well-thought-out process, with everyone participating." Indeed, Solectron was among the first U.S. companies to truly implement Deming's basic philosophies into its environment. Deming's works became required reading for all Solectron managers. In addition, the company set up an elaborate computerized quality control system that could track every stage of a project. Furthermore, when other companies later rejected some popular quality initiatives, such as quality circles, as unworkable trends, Solectron continued to tinker the programs until they produced measurable results.

Chen's quality focus permeated Solectron from the start. For example, Chen had rules about the number of times that a telephone could ring before it was answered. He even set the example by answering his own telephone. And he required all Solectron managers to wear beepers so that their customers could access them at all times. Most importantly, Solectron tried to hire only the best people, paying them the best wages and treating them with respect. Although he set strict standards, Chen allowed his managers to operate autonomously and to make key decisions on their own. That independence and autonomy was a welcome change for the many Solectron managers who had been hired away from IBM. "IBM hires the cream of the crop and trains people better than anybody else, but they underutilized their people and micro-managed them," Koichi Nishimura, a Solectron employee since 1988, noted in the *Los Angeles Times*. As a result of its personnel policies, Solectron enjoyed one of the lowest employee turnover rates in the industry throughout the 1980s and early 1990s.

In addition to its innovative management philosophy, Solectron benefited from Chen's and his fellow managers marketing strategies. Chen focused the firm's long-term efforts on the surface-mount style of circuit board manufacturing early in the mid-1980s before most of Solectron's peers recognized the importance of the technology. Surface-mount circuit boards represented an improvement over more conventional through-hole boards because they were eventually less expensive to produce, lighter in weight, smaller, and could be printed on both sides of the board, among other advantages. Solectron's decision to emphasize surface-mount technology would pay off handsomely in the early and mid-1990s, when demand for that technology exploded.

### *The Outsourcing Trend Takes Hold*

Solectron prospered as a result of its sound management and marketing initiatives during the 1980s. The company also bene-

**Key Dates:**

**1977:** Roy Kusumoto establishes Solectron.
**1978:** Dr. Winston Chen joins the firm as executive vice-president.
**1984:** Chen is named CEO.
**1989:** Solectron goes public; the company's profits reach $4.5 million.
**1991:** The company receives the Malcolm Baldridge National Quality Award.
**1993:** Solectron begins a buying spree and purchases several manufacturing facilities both at home and abroad.
**1995:** Revenue reaches $2 billion.

fited, however, from a strong trend toward outsourcing by major manufacturers. Indeed, many producers learned that they could benefit significantly by hiring outside manufacturers, like Solectron, to handle specialty manufacturing activities. The potential benefits were numerous. As electronics markets became increasingly competitive during the 1980s, original equipment manufacturers (OEM's) were faced with constantly shrinking product life cycles, which meant that they had to reduce the amount of time they took to bring a new product from the concept stage to market. Specialists like Solectron were able to drastically reduce that time span.

In addition to "reduced time to market," another benefit that Solectron offered to its customers was reduced capital investments. Rather than having to invest the large sums of money necessary to develop production facilities for a particular type of circuit board, a company could pay a much smaller fee to have Solectron build the board. The OEM could then invest its resources in other activities. Solectron's technological advantage allowed it to produce circuit boards and other electronic assemblies for its customers at a much lower cost and at a much higher level of quality than its customers could achieve themselves given their limited resources and technological know-how.

By the end of the 1980s, Solectron was generating more than $100 million in annual revenues—1989 profits topped $4.5 million from sales of about $130 million, up from sales of just $88 million in 1988. Although the company had realized momentous growth since its inception not much more than ten years earlier, it was about to experience a five-year growth spurt that would outstrip even Chen's expectations. The expansion started in late 1989 when Chen took Solectron public in an effort to generate capital for expansion. Solectron sold stock for $6 per share in November. By July 1990, the stock price had nearly doubled to $10. Chen considered his success at taking Solectron public the achievement of his life.

### *Strong Demand Leads to Explosive Growth: Late 1980s to Mid-1990s*

At the same time that Solectron went public, the company began to benefit from extremely strong demand for its services related to surface-mount technology. As orders and contracts poured in from manufacturers around the globe, Solectron began to leave its two major competitors, Flextronics Inc. and SCI Systems Inc., behind. Surface-mount work represented 22 percent of Solectron's billings in 1988 before rising to 36 percent during 1989. As surface-mount sales soared, Solectron's revenues passed $200 million in 1990 and then rose to $265 million in 1991. Solectron's growth was largely the result of more then five years worth of large capital investments in new surface-mount equipment.

Awards bolstered Solectron's public image as a quality manufacturer. In 1991, it received the coveted Malcolm Baldridge National Quality Award in recognition of its system of ensuring customer satisfaction and quality products. Solectron had won more than 35 other quality awards since the early 1980s, including ten in 1990. The Baldridge Award, however, which is awarded to a maximum of two companies annually in the manufacturing category, was a crowning achievement. It reflected Solectron's incredible quality and service advantage over its industry peers. By the early 1990s, Solectron had surpassed even its Japanese competitors in most award categories.

Solectron's quality of customer service could be seen when comparing its performance to a good Japanese outsourcing company. While a good Japanese outsourcing company typically took six weeks to create a prototype of a circuit board for a new disk drive in 1991, Solectron could handle the task in 13 days. Likewise, most Japanese companies would not permit any schedule changes 30 days prior to delivery. In contrast, Solectron would often accept changes the day before production. Furthermore, Solectron delivered the highest quality product available. Indeed, by the early 1990s Solectron had become a global model for manufacturing quality and service. Although the company was already an industry leader in quality by the mid-1980s, it had reduced it defects-per-shipment by more than 50 percent between 1987 and 1992, to less than 233 defects per million parts manufactured. And its on-time delivery rate was nearly 98 percent.

As Solectron's customers began to rely on its services, the company's sales rose. To keep up with increasing demand, Solectron drew on its large capital base and began acquiring other production facilities. Early in 1992, Solectron purchased a circuit board assembly operation in North Carolina from IBM. The acquisition fit neatly into Solectron's organization because Solectron's managers, many of whom had worked at or with IBM, were already familiar with the new company's existing labor and production environment. Solectron even retained the plant's president, Hank Ewert. Ewert was known as a hard driving, resourceful manager. He welcomed the chance to leave IBM's shrinking organization, and to participate in Solectron's plans to build the facility into one of its major production arms. Solectron nearly doubled the plant's work force in one year to about 300, and planned to eventually add as many as 2,500 more workers.

Encouraged by the success of its North Carolina plant acquisition, Solectron went on a buying spree between 1993 and 1994, acquiring facilities from Hewlett-Packard, Phillips, Apple, and other major electronics producers in locations ranging from Scotland and Malaysia to France and Washington. Although many of the plants incorporated leading edge technology, they had failed to generate profits in the increasingly competitive electronics market. Solectron, with its proven management and production techniques, was able to move into the facilities and return them to profitability. In addition, Solectron would usually benefit by getting contracts from the previous owners of the facilities to produce circuit boards and related assemblies for their televisions, computers, and other goods.

Solectron's sales rose to $406 million in 1992, $836 million in 1993, and then to a $1.46 billion in 1994, making Solectron one of the fastest growing companies in the nation. Profits paralleled sales growth as net income almost quadrupled from $14.5 million in 1992 to $55.5 million in 1994. All the while, Solectron's debt load remained sparse as cash poured into the manufacturer's coffers. Hopeful observers heralded the success as a example of America's renewed manufacturing prowess. Solectron's rise did reflect a general trend toward increased U.S. competitiveness in high-tech industries, but it also mirrored the efforts of a vastly diverse, multicultural, multilingual work force representing more than 20 foreign cultures.

Solectron entered the 1990s without the guidance of Chen. Since 1991, Chen had been gradually removed himself from command of the company, and, by 1994, he had ceded his chairmanship of Solectron's board to Charles A. Dickinson, who had served as director of the company since 1984. Prior to that, Chen had handed off his president and chief executive positions to Kiochi Nishimura, who had been hired away from IBM in 1988. Nishimura was also named chairman in 1996. The still-young Chen left the company to spend more time with his family and to pursue other interests. The management team he left in charge, however, was committed to the same initiatives that had built the company from a fledgling start-up with a few hundred thousand dollars in sales to a leading, billion-dollar-plus global contender.

### *Continued Success: Mid-1990s and Beyond*

Indeed, Solectron prospered under Nishimura's leadership. By 1995, the company's revenues had surpassed $2 billion and were climbing to nearly $4 billion in 1997. By this time, Solectron's share of the contract manufacturing market had grown to 6 percent, up from 2 percent in the early 1990s. During 1997, the company acquired the Brazil-based printed circuit board assembly operations of Ericsson Telecomunicacoes S.A. and Force Computers Inc., a designer of OEM computer platforms. That year, the company was awarded the Baldridge Award for the second time, becoming the first firm to lay claim to two such awards.

Nishimura was recognized for his role in Solectron's good fortunes when he was named ''CEO of the Year'' by *Electronic Business* magazine in 1999. Like the leader before him, Nishimura was well respected throughout the industry. By now, the company held the number one slot in the contract manufacturing market with revenues of over $8 billion. The company's long standing history of quality and its solid performance left it with a prestigious reputation and Nishimura was often credited for his role in building contract manufacturing into a $60 billion industry by 1998. Even competitors such as Flextronics International Ltd. looked to Solectron as a role model. In fact, Flextronics' CEO Michael Marks stated in a 1999 Electronic Business article that Solectron gave ''the whole industry a good name.''

During the late 1990s and into the new millennium, Solectron grew dramatically through a series of strategic acquisitions. In 1998, the manufacturing assets of NCR Corp.'s Computer Systems and Retail Solutions divisions, which were located in Georgia, South Carolina, and Dublin, were purchased. The firm also took control of IBM's Electronic Card Assembly and Test (ECAT) operations based in both Texas and South Carolina. Sequel Inc., a liquid crystal display service and support firm, was acquired the following year.

The firm's acquisition spree reached a fevered pitch in the early years of the new millennium. Solectron purchased four manufacturing facilities owned by Nortel Networks, including those located in Canada, Mexico, and Wales. During 2001, the company acquired Singapore-based NatSteel Electronics Ltd., the world's sixth-largest electronics manufacturing services firm, for $2.4 billion. The deal strengthened the firm's capacity to meet increasing demand and also gave the firm a stronger foothold in the Asian market. Solectron went on to purchase Centennial Technologies Inc., Singapore Shinei Sangyo Pte Ltd., Iphotonics Inc., Artesyn Solutions Inc., and Stream International Inc. The company then ended the year with the $2.3 billion acquisition of C-MAC Industries Inc. The company expected the purchase of the Canada-based integrated electronics manufacturer to enhance its product and service offerings.

While the firm experienced remarkable sales in the first half of fiscal 2001, an economic downturn and weakening demand in the electronic sector took their toll on Solectron's bottom line. The firm reported record sales growth of $18.7 billion that year but was forced to post a loss of $124 million due to a $411 million restructuring charge. The company cut jobs, shut down several facilities, and scaled back certain operations. Its stock fell from $42 in January 2001 to $18 in August to under $10 in December of that year.

Despite the challenging economy, Solectron remained positive that its success would continue into the future. The firm claimed that the demand from OEM customers would increase and that the electronics manufacturing services industry would grow to $203 billion by 2004. As the leading force in this industry, Solectron appeared to be well positioned to continue its history of success and good fortune. As analysts predicted a rebound in the economy, Solectron's prospects for future growth looked promising.

### *Principal Subsidiaries*

Solectron Australia Pty. Ltd.; Solectron Brasil Ltda.; NatSteel Electronics International Ltd. (British Virgin Islands); Apex Data Inc.; Fine Pitch Corp.; NatSteel Electronics Inc.; RISQ Modular Systems Inc.; Smart Modular Technologies Inc.; Solectron Global Services Inc.; Solectron Technology Inc.; Solectron Canada Limited Partnership; Solectron Cayman (Asia) Ltd.; Solectron Ireland Holdings; Solectron Technology Co. Ltd. (China); Force Computers Inc.; Solectron Acquisition Company LLC; US Robotics Corporation; Solectron France SAS; Solectron GmbH (Germany); NatSteel Electronics Holding Ltd. (Hong Kong); Solectron Israel Ltd.; Solectron Japan Inc.; Solectron de Mexico S.A. de C.V.; Solectron Singapore Pte. Ltd.; Solectron Sweden AB; Smart Modular Technologies

Europe Ltd. (U.K.); Solectron Taiwan Co. Ltd.; Shinei USA Inc.

## *Principal Competitors*

Celestica Inc.; Flextronics International Ltd.; Sanmina-SCI Corporation.

## *Further Reading*

''Acquisitions Drive Solectron: From Small Valley Start,'' *Electronic News*, February 22, 1999, p. 32.

Byrne, Joe, ''Solectron Reports Financial Reports,'' *Business Wire*, April 16, 1989.

Fasca, Chad, ''Diversification Keys Hot Numbers at Solectron,'' *Electronic News*, March 30, 1998, p. 54.

Fralix, David, ''The Guy at the Top,'' *Business Journal-Charlotte*, December 21, 1992, p. 12.

Helm, Leslie, ''Solectron's Mantra for Success,'' *Los Angeles Times*, April 26, 1994, Sec. 2, p. 13.

Krey, Michael, ''Winston Chen; He Believes in Lots of Hard Work and a Little Meditation,'' *Business Journal-San Jose*, July 2, 1990, p. 12.

Larson, Mark, ''Solectron Pays $33M for Artesyn,'' *Sacramento Business Journal*, December 14, 2001, p. 1.

Levine, Bernard, ''EMS Deal Zeal Still Hot,'' *Electronic News*, January 29, 2001, p. 4.

Marcial, Gene G., ''Solectron May Be Set to Hum Again,'' *Business Week*, January 28, 2002.

Roberts, Bill, ''CEO of the Year,'' *Electronic Business*, December 1999, p. 63.

Scott, Jonathan, ''Solectron: New Player on Two Fronts,'' *Memphis Business Journal*, May 28, 1999, p. 3.

''Solectron Completes Buy of Nortel Facilities,'' *Business Journal*, June 9, 2000, p. 18.

''Solectron Corp.,'' *Business America*, October 21, 1991, p. 5.

''WRAP: Solectron Offers $2.4 Billion for Singapore's NatSteel,'' *Futures World News*, November 1, 2000.

—Dave Mote
—update: Christina M. Stansell

Standard Chartered

# Standard Chartered plc

**1 Aldermanbury Square**
**London EC2V 7SB**
**United Kingdom**
**Telephone: (020) 7280 7500**
**Fax: (020) 7280 7791**
**Web site: http://www.standardchartered.com**

*Public Company*
*Incorporated:* 1969 as The Standard and Chartered Banking Group Ltd.
*Employees:* 30,500
*Total Assets:* £68.59 billion ($102.2 billion)
*Stock Exchanges:* London
*Ticker Symbol:* STAN
*NAIC:* 522110 Commercial Banking; 522210 Credit Card Issuing; 522293 International Trade Financing

Standard Chartered plc operates as the leading emerging markets bank in the world. The banking group, known by many in the banking industry as Stanchart, operates over 500 offices in 50 countries throughout the Asia Pacific region, South Asia, the Middle East, Africa, the United Kingdom, and North and South America. Its Consumer banking division—responsible for 58 percent of operating profit in 2000—provides customers with credit cards, personal loans, mortgages, and investment services. Its Wholesale banking unit caters to corporate clients in the trade finance, cash management, custody, lending, foreign exchange, interest rate management, and debt capital markets. In 2000, the majority of Standard Chartered's revenue stemmed from its Hong Kong and Asia Pacific region operations, while the Middle East accounted for 18 percent, North and South America and the United Kingdom secured 14 percent, and Africa claimed 9 percent of revenues.

## *Origins*

Standard Chartered was formed in 1969 as a merger between the Standard Bank, which did business throughout Africa, and the Chartered Bank, which operated branches throughout India, China, and southeastern Asia. Lacking a truly strong domestic network, the banking group's progress has been largely dependent upon Third World economic and political conditions and emerging markets—an unenviable position at times.

Both the Standard Bank and the Chartered Bank had been in operation for more than a century when they combined forces. The Chartered Bank, originally incorporated in 1853 as the Chartered Bank of India, Australia, and China under a charter from Queen Victoria, was influential in the development of British colonial trade throughout Asia. Up until World War II, British trade in Asia flourished, and the Chartered Bank prospered.

The Standard Bank was established in 1862 as the Standard Bank of British South Africa by a schoolmaster named John Paterson. Paterson had eclectic interests, including mining, railroad promotion, and real estate development. He set out to make Standard a large bank, and proceeded to acquire smaller banks throughout southern Africa. For the next century, the bank played a significant role in the banking of the region.

Since both banks were products of the colonial era, with similar structures and experience, they made an excellent match. Their complementary geographic coverage and similar historical backgrounds made for a relatively smooth transition.

## *Integration and Expansion into Euro-Currency Markets: 1970s*

The new Standard and Chartered Banking Group took its time integrating the management of the two banks. Throughout 1970 each former unit performed its operations more or less unchanged—indeed, bank branches continued to operate under their old names for a number of years. Each was able to expand independently in its own markets, and there was no need to immediately restructure either of the bank's operations. However, the company slowly began to develop long-term plans for the entire bank.

Standard Chartered's first chairman, Sir Cyril Hawker, came to the group from the Bank of England, where he had served since 1920. His sensitivity to the needs of developing nations made him an excellent choice to guide Standard Chartered in its early years. In 1970, Hawker brought Standard Chartered deeper into the euro-currency markets. Both the Standard Bank

## Company Perspectives:

*Our consumer and wholesale banking operations are focused on countries in Asia, Africa, the Middle East, South Asia, and Latin America. Our greatest asset is our unique knowledge, insight, and understanding of these markets and of our customers' needs. We are committed to excellence in customer service, to delivering consistently superior performance and to building shareholder value. We recognize our responsibilities to the countries and communities in which we operate. Our values are based on trust, teamwork, and commitment—and on our pride in this organization.*

and the Chartered Bank had entered these markets in the 1960s. By 1970, Standard Chartered was using funds generated in the Euro-markets to finance projects throughout the world.

Because of its Third World involvement Standard Chartered dealt with more problems than most banks. Unstable political and economic conditions posed a constant threat to the bank. During the 1960s, some branches were nationalized by the countries they operated in. In the 1970s, though conditions were generally calmer, Standard Chartered had to be prepared to adapt to the whims of sometimes irrational governments in Africa and Asia. Wars and rebellions were a constant threat. When new regimes came to power, Standard Chartered's branches were at times subject to new regulations, nationalization, or a transfer of ownership to native financiers. In 1970, for example, the African nation of Zambia partially nationalized the Standard Bank operating there. Nationalization was the greatest fear of any overseas bank operating in politically unstable countries. At the same time, however, these regions were often very profitable.

In 1971, the Eastern Bank, a Middle Eastern bank Chartered had acquired in 1957, became fully integrated with the Chartered Bank. The Standard Bank's Nigerian branches had a good first year in the reconstruction period after the civil war there ended in 1970. Operations in Hong Kong, Singapore, and Malaysia showed strong results in the early 1970s, although depressed economic conditions in South Africa resulted in a poor performance for the Standard Bank branches operating there. Nevertheless, the bank's dependence on the unreliable conditions of Third World nations induced it to seek a stronger foothold in industrialized nations to add stability to its international network. Throughout the early 1970s, the bank increased operations in European and U.S. capital markets and began to cooperate with other international banks.

In 1973, the banking group diversified heavily. The acquisition of Mocatta and Goldsmid Ltd. brought Standard Chartered into the gold and precious metals markets. The group's computer leasing company, Standard and Charted Leasing, expanded into European markets. The banking group also formed a partnership in a merchant bank.

### *Focus on Overseas Commercial Banking: Mid- to Late 1970s*

By 1974, Standard Chartered's gradual integration was complete and the managements of the Standard Bank and of the Chartered Bank came together under one roof. In August 1974, Sir Cyril Hawker retired and was replaced by Lord Barber. Barber oversaw the formulation of a long-term strategy for the bank. Standard Chartered would concentrate on what it did best: overseas commercial banking. Unlike a growing number of international banks during this period, Standard Chartered did not intend to branch into other areas of financial services. The bank would continue to strengthen its European position to offset fluctuations in Third World economies, but would not attempt to enter retail banking in Britain. The 17 British branches Standard Chartered already operated focused on import-export financing and banking support services.

In 1974, Standard Chartered's diversity was key in insulating it from a worldwide recession. In October 1975, the group changed its name to the Standard Chartered Bank Ltd., although subsidiaries throughout the world still operated under their old established names.

The bank grew throughout the late 1970s. Profits improved consistently, and assets continued to grow. In 1979, Standard Chartered made a major acquisition in the United States by purchasing the Union Bancorp of California.

As international banking competition became more intense, Standard Chartered's management began to see weaknesses in the bank's lack of a domestic base. In 1981, the group bid on the Royal Bank of Scotland Group. This bank had the domestic branch network that Standard Chartered wanted and was amenable to a takeover by Standard Chartered. However, a rival bid by the Hongkong and Shanghai Bank sent the issue to the British Monopolies Commission, which ruled against both bids. The banking group entered the 1980s heavily reliant on the financial success of underdeveloped nations.

### *Financial Woes: Mid- to Late 1980s*

The 1980s were difficult times for many of the countries where Standard Chartered operated. Singapore and Malaysia fell into a serious recession in the mid-1980s. As Hong Kong's shipping industry struggled to survive, a number of large loans went bad, putting Standard Chartered in serious financial straits. By 1986, the Standard Chartered Bank was in a financial mess. The bank's strategy of focusing on commercial banking proved to have been an error, as large customers were choosing international banks that could provide them with a complete line of financial services, including stockbroking and issuing commercial paper. Capital markets and money markets were deregulated in many countries in 1986, leading to increased competition for which Standard Chartered was unprepared.

Standard Chartered's affiliate in South Africa had performed inconsistently in the 1980s, but was for the most part a profitable venture. Growing political pressure to divest South African holdings caused the bank some unrest. Standard Chartered was reluctant to sell its 39 percent interest in the bank at the unfavorable exchange rate of the time and take a large loss. Finally, in 1987 the bank divested its South African holdings, ending its 125-year presence in that nation. It was the last foreign bank to leave South Africa.

In 1986, London saw an explosion of mergers and acquisitions among banks with the financial deregulation known as the

## Key Dates:

**1853:** The Chartered Bank incorporates under a charter from Queen Victoria.
**1862:** The Standard Bank is established in British South Africa.
**1957:** The Chartered Bank acquires the Eastern Bank of the Middle East region.
**1969:** The Chartered Bank and Standard Bank merge, forming The Standard and Chartered Banking Group Ltd.
**1973:** The group begins to diversify and acquires Mocatta and Goldsmid Ltd.
**1975:** The company changes its name to Standard Chartered Bank Ltd.
**1979:** The firm acquires Union Bancorp of California.
**1986:** Company wards off a hostile takeover attempt by Lloyds Bank.
**1987:** The company divests its South African holdings.
**1988:** Standard Chartered sells its United Bank of Arizona and Union Banking group.
**1999:** The global trade finance division of Union Bank of Switzerland and a 75 percent stake in Nakornthon Bank plc are purchased.
**2000:** Standard Chartered completes two of its largest acquisitions to date: AZN Grindlays Bank and Chase Manhattan's Hong Kong banking operations.

''Big Bang.'' Standard Chartered became the target of a takeover by Lloyds Bank, which Standard Chartered's chief executive, Michael McWilliam, was determined to prevent. The purchase of 35 percent of Standard Chartered's shares by three businessmen helped to thwart the Lloyds bid. Standard Chartered received a thrashing in the British press when it became known that one of its white knights, Tan Sri Khoo, had received a large loan from the bank just before he invested in its shares, but the bank called for an investigation to clear its name and was vindicated by the Bank of England a year later.

Although Standard Chartered was successful in warding off the hostile takeover by Lloyds, its troubles were not over. The banking community's dependence on the Third World caught up with it in 1987, when, due to larger loan-loss provisions, Standard Chartered showed a net loss of £274 million. McWilliam tried to restructure the bank's operations and replaced many high-ranking executives. Chairman Sir Peter Graham stated that the bank needed to inject new capital through a rights issue. In 1988, the bank reversed its position on divesting non-core assets to raise capital and sold the United Bank of Arizona to Citibank and later, its profitable Union Banking group to California First, a subsidiary of the Bank of Tokyo.

Standard Chartered's situation began to improve in 1988. A new rights issue in September of 1988 helped repair the bank's capital balance. Profits for the first half of 1988 were £154 million compared to a loss of £222 million during the same period a year before. McWilliam, who had directed the bank's operations during its stormiest year, resigned in early 1988 and Sir Peter Graham, who had been chairman for only two years, retired. Rodney Galpin took over as both chairman and chief executive. Galpin had spent most of his career at the Bank of England and intended to be a ''hands-on'' chairman.

### *Focus on Emerging Markets: 1990s and Beyond*

Upon entering the 1990s, Standard Chartered continued to restructure. It divested holdings in Europe, the United States, and Africa and made a series of job cuts. Unprofitable businesses were shut down and internal operations were streamlined. Management began a new strategy of focusing on consumer banking, along with corporate and institutional banking in Asia, Africa, and the Middle East.

Even as Standard Chartered pared back certain operations, it continued to delve into emerging markets. In 1990, it reentered the Vietnamese market, and then two years later began operating in Cambodia and Iran. Tanzania followed, along with Myanmar in 1995. By the mid-1990s, the company had offices in every country in the Asia Pacific region except for North Korea. While both the Asian and African markets proved tumultuous, the company's financial performance remained strong. In 1997, the bank secured pre-tax profits of £870 million.

The bank then began a series of acquisitions that would strengthen its position in the emerging markets industry. In 1998, it acquired a majority interest in Banco Exterior de Los Andes, which enabled the firm to offer its banking services as well as trade finance services in Columbia, Peru, and Venezuela. The following year, the global trade finance business of Union Bank of Switzerland was purchased. The bank also acquired a 75 percent stake in Thailand's Nakornthon Bank PLC. In the fall of 1999, Standard Chartered increased in presence in China by opening a Beijing branch office.

During 2000, the company made two of its largest acquisitions to date. The first was the $1.34 billion cash purchase of ANZ Grindlays Bank's South Asian and Middle Eastern banking operations. The deal added 116 branches to Standard Chartered growing arsenal. The next acquisition was that of Chase Manhattan Corp.'s Hong Kong consumer banking and credit card operations. The $1.32 billion purchase secured the bank's position as Hong Kong's largest credit card operator with a 25 percent market share. The company also sold its Chartered Trust unit to Lloyds TSB that year for £627 million.

*Forbes* magazine commented the bank's commitment to its Asian markets in an October 2000. The article claimed that while most financial institutions had been exiting the turbulent Asian scene, Standard Chartered ''took a strikingly different road. Rather than hit the brakes, its chairman Sir Patrick Gillam, and its CEO, Rana Talwar, accelerated their plans to become the international bank most focused on Asia, and to a lesser degree, the world's other emerging markets.'' In fact, while pretax earnings fell by 42 percent during 1997 and 1999, revenues continued to grow despite the Asian economic collapse. If and when the Asian economy recovered, the bank stood to gain significant revenue and earnings.

By 2001, speculation arose that Standard Chartered may be courting takeover offers. Talwar agreed to consider these offers if the price was right; however, Gillam pushed to keep Standard Chartered intact. Shareholders agreed with Gillam's approach and in December of that year, Talwar—named CEO in 1998—was ousted from the company. Mervyn Davies was tapped to assume Talwar's position as his focus proved to be on the company's independence. Whether Standard Chartered would continue to lead the emerging markets banking industry alone or with a partner however, remained to be seen.

### *Principal Subsidiaries*

Standard Chartered Bank Australia Ltd.; Standard Chartered Bank (Bahrain); Standard Chartered Bank (Bangladesh); Standard Chartered Bank Botswana Ltd.; Standard Chartered Bank (Brunei); Standard Chartered Bank (Cambodia); Standard Chartered Bank Cameroon S.A.; Standard Chartered Bank (China); Standard Chartered Bank (Hong Kong); Banco Standard Chartered Columbia; Standard Chartered Bank (Falkland Islands); Standard Chartered Bank Ghana Ltd.; Standard Chartered Grindlays Bank (India); Standard Chartered Bank (Indonesia); Standard Chartered Bank Côte d'lvoire SA (Ivory Coast); Standard Chartered Bank (Japan); Standard Chartered Bank C.I. Ltd. (Jersey); Standard Chartered Grindlays Bank Ltd. (Jordan); Standard Chartered Bank Kenya Ltd.; Standard Chartered Bank s.a.l. (Lebanon); Standard Chartered Bank (Macau); Standard Chartered Bank Malaysia Berhad; Standard Chartered Bank Nigeria Ltd.; Standard Chartered Bank (Oman); Standard Chartered Bank (Pakistan); Banco Standard Chartered (Peru); Standard Chartered Bank (Philippines); Standard Chartered Bank (Qatar); Standard Chartered Bank (South Korea); Standard Chartered Bank Sierra Leone Ltd.; Standard Chartered Bank (Singapore); Standard Chartered Bank (Sri Lanka); Standard Chartered Bank (Taiwan); Standard Chartered Bank (Tanzania); Standard Chartered Bank (Thailand); Standard Chartered Nakornthon Bank Public Company Ltd. (Thailand); Standard Chartered Bank Uganda Ltd.; Standard Chartered Bank (United Arab Emirates); Standard Chartered Bank (UK); Standard Chartered Bank (U.S.); Banco Standard Chartered (Venezuela); Standard Chartered Bank (Vietnam); Standard Chartered Bank Zambia Ltd.; Standard Chartered Bank Zimbabwe Ltd.

### *Principal Competitors*

Citigroup Inc.; HSBC Holdings plc; J.P. Morgan Chase & Co.

### *Further Reading*

"Davies Succeeds Talwar at Standard Chartered Bank," *Africa News Service*, December 10, 2001.

Heller, Richard, "Damn the Torpedoes! Full Speed Ahead!," *Forbes*, October 2, 2000.

Luhnow, David, and Carrie Lee, "UK's Standard Chartered Strengthens Hong Kong Hand," *National Post*, September 2, 2000, p. D9.

"Not One of Us; Standard Chartered Bank," *Economic Review*, December 8, 2001.

Robinson, Karina, "A Perfect Fit in an Exotic Bank," *Banker*, October 2001, p. 40.

"SC Lands Grindlays for $1.34bn," *Banker*, June 2000, p. 40.

"Standard Chartered—Another Good Year," *Economic Review*, April 1998, p. 53.

"Standard Chartered Bank Established Branch in Beijing," *Alestron*, September 27, 1999.

"Standard Chartered Digesting But Still Hungry," *Middle East Economic Digest*, March 9, 2001, p. 7.

"UK Bank's Thailand Deal Approved," *American Banker*, September 7, 1999, p. 37.

—update: Christina M. Stansell

# OAO Surgutneftegaz

**1 Ul. Kukuevitskogo**
**Surgut**
**Tyumen Region 628400**
**Russia**
**Telephone: (+7) 346 233 4863**
**Fax: (+7) 346 233 3235**
**Web site: http://www.surgutneftegas.ru**

*Public Company*
*Incorporated:* 1993
*Employees:* 84,466
*Sales:* $5.48 billion (2001)
*Stock Exchanges:* Moscow (MICEX) Russian (RTS) St. Petersburg Frankfurt OTC
*Ticker Symbols:* SNGS; SGTZY
*NAIC:* 211111 Crude Petroleum and Natural Gas Extraction; 213112 Support Activities for Oil and Gas Operations; 324110 Petroleum Refineries

OAO Surgutneftegaz is one of the top three integrated oil companies in Russia, with an estimated 2.5 billion metric tons of oil and gas reserves in its West Siberian fields. The company's production facilities are centered around Surgut, a city of about 300,000 in Tyumen Province. There the company extracts about 13 percent of all oil produced in Russia as well as approximately ten billion cubic meters of associated gas per year. Surgutneftegaz also owns a refinement facility in the city of Kirishi, near St. Petersburg. Although the refinery is far from the company's oil fields, its location facilitates exports to Germany, Finland, Denmark, the Ukraine, and the Baltic countries. The refinery is operated by the Kirishinefteorgsintez subsidiary and has a capacity of about 390,000 barrels per day. Retail operations comprise the third branch of Surgutneftegaz's activities. The company owns retail units in northwest Russia in proximity to the cities of Pskov, Kaliningrad, Tver, and Novgorod.

Surgutneftegaz is recognized as one of the best-managed companies in the Russian oil industry. The firm has consistently placed a high priority on capital investment, promoting stable and cost-efficient production through explorative drilling, well maintenance, and the application of new drilling technologies. Surgutneftegaz operates with a conservative, anti-debt philosophy, placing much less emphasis than its competitors on looking abroad for partners in joint ventures or for financial support. The company remains firmly rooted in Western Siberia, shielding its operations and ownership structure from outside scrutiny. Surgutneftegaz is led by President and Director General Vladimir Bogdanov.

## *The Development of Western Siberian Oil in the Soviet Era*

The separate entities that eventually became part of Surgutneftegaz's integrated structure began their operations as state-owned enterprises in the Soviet Union. The oil production authority "Surgutneft" was organized in the northern Tyumen region in March 1964, marking the oil industry's first foray into Western Siberia. At the time, the region was undeveloped, inhabited only by a few thousand members of the Khanty tribe who survived by fishing and collecting berries. The Siberian climate and the ruggedness of the landscape made it nearly impossible to construct roads, pipes, and wells according to the usual methods. In the first few years, oil was extracted only during the warm season and was sent by barge down the Ob River to the Omsk refinery.

In 1967, the Ust-Surgut-Omsk pipeline was constructed, and the oil industry began year-round operations. Conditions remained primitive: in the mid-1960s there was still no paved road in the area, and power was generated by means of diesel electric plants. Nevertheless, in 1968 the one millionth metric ton of oil was extracted from the West Siberian fields. Soon other oil production entities sprang up in the area and development began in earnest. By the late 1970s, Surgut was seen as the oil capital of West Siberia, boasting huge power installations, a construction industry, a railroad, highways, and an airport.

Meanwhile, the Kirishi refinery was making a name for itself thousands of miles away in Leningrad Province. Construction of the refinery had begun in 1961 in a city that was originally founded to hold a chemical factory. World War II foiled plans for

### Company Perspectives:

*Without question, we have achieved much in the past few years, but those achievements were merely the result of a battle for survival in difficult conditions. Today we are anticipating a whole new stage of development: the achievement of our goals and the creation of a fully-valued, vertically-integrated oil company of world stature, with a corresponding capitalization. I believe that this vision corresponds to the interests of all Surgutneftegaz shareholders, and in that we see the foundation of our unity and mutual understanding, while the corporate values of the company—professionalism, responsibility, profitability and transparency—will help us in the achievement of our shared goals.*

the chemical factory and left the area devastated by the effects of battle and littered with mines. After military engineers removed the mines, the area was designated as the location of a project of nationwide significance: Soviet youths and industry experts were brought in to aid with the construction of an oil refinery. The first oil reached the refinery in 1965. In 1972, the Kirishi refinery was one of the five largest in the USSR. The oil industry as a whole was nearing peak production in the late 1970s.

## *Privatizing Russian Oil: 1991–96*

When the USSR fell apart in 1991, the oil industry was in poor shape. Drilling volume and field development had fallen sharply under Secretary General Mikhail Gorbachev, and production was at its lowest level in more than 15 years. Technical assistance for the oil industry was needed to avert an economic collapse. The former Ministry of the Oil and Gas Industry advocated swift privatization and the introduction of competition. Privatization was no simple task, however. Thirty-two separate oil production associations were left over from the Soviet era, run by managers who were sometimes more concerned about meeting targets than investing in sustainable production. Price controls also distorted the business climate, as the crude price was held low by government regulation while equipment had to be bought at free market prices.

The oil industry moved closer to privatization in 1992. Prices were freed in increments early in the year, and various decrees laid the ground for the creation of joint stock companies. Meanwhile, the directors of Surgutneftegaz travelled to Washington, D.C., to learn about capitalist operating methods. Soon they had a chance to apply what they had learned. On March 19, 1993, a decree of the Council of Ministers of the Russian Federation provided for the establishment of a vertically-integrated, open-type joint stock oil company, OAO NK Surgutneftegaz. The newly formed holding company included the Surgutneftegaz production association, the Kirishi refinery, and several retail associations in northwest Russia. State decree and the company charter both stipulated that 40.1 percent of the company would be retained by the state for at least three years, while foreign investors could hold no more than 5 percent. The Surgutneftegaz production association, which had accounted for 10 percent of Russia's total crude output in 1992, formed the core of the new company. Vladimir Bogdanov, who had run the Surgutneftegaz oil fields since 1983, was appointed president. Two other oil companies of similar stature, YuKOS and LUKoil, were created alongside Surgutneftegaz.

The new company managed to gain control of a large portion of its equity by mid-1994. Forty percent of the company was sold to the Neftinvest oil company, which was controlled by Surgutneftegaz. Eight percent was sold to investors at cash and check auctions, while another 7 percent was acquired by the company for subsequent sale on a securities market. Meanwhile, President Boris Yeltsin made an effort to encourage oil production in the summer of 1993 when he abolished a series of punitive taxes on oil sold at high prices. Nevertheless, Russia's crude price remained at about one-ninth of the world price, and production in 1994 at Surgutneftegaz was at two-thirds of its 1990 level. Bogdanov saw oil exports as the key means to finance capital investment in his Siberian fields, but beyond courting Western crude buyers, he showed little interest in forming partnerships with or adopting the management style of Western companies. One of Surgutneftegaz's only foreign partnerships was with the French oil company Elf Aquitaine. Under an agreement approved in 1994, Surgutneftegaz, along with two other Russian companies, would take a 24 percent interest in the construction of a new refinery at Leuna in eastern Germany. The Russian companies would be the sole suppliers to the refinery. However, the project was slow to move ahead because of higher-than-expected construction costs.

In 1995, Surgutneftegaz became even more closely held as a result of the Russian government's "shares-for-loans" program. Strapped for cash, the government offered shares in major enterprises as pledges against loans from financial institutions. At a controversial auction in November, Surgutneftegaz's own pension fund received a 40.12 percent share in the Surgutneftegaz holding company in exchange for a Ru 400 billion loan to the state and the payment of a Ru 1 trillion overdue tax bill. The stake was generally agreed to be undervalued, but because the government looked favorably on the prospect of Surgutneftegaz gaining control of itself, the pension fund was able to edge out the competition. A rival oil company, Rosneft, had wanted to bid at the auction but measures were taken to strongly discourage it from doing so, including an attempt to close the airport in the town of Surgut just before the auction was to be held. As auction winner, the Surgutneftegaz pension fund technically was merely holding the stake in trust for the government, since the 40 percent share was required by law to remain under the control of the state until 1996. In reality, the state budgeted no money to repay the loans and the auction winner had de facto control of the company.

Oil production began to show signs of a turnaround in 1995. Surgutneftegaz was the nation's number three producer at 33 million tons, down only 2.4 percent from the previous year. In addition, the company won a tender to prospect for fields in the Khanty-Mansi autonomous area, a West Siberian region estimated to hold about 140.9 million tons in oil reserves. Surgutneftegaz exported about one quarter of its oil in 1995, which helped fund the construction of over 600 new wells and 500 kilometers of pipeline. Further capital investment projects followed in 1996. Work began on a technologically advanced system of horizontal wells, which could boost production by increasing the yield of hard-to-reach deposits. The company

## Key Dates:

**1961:** Construction of the Kirishi refinery begins.
**1964:** The oil production authority "Surgutneft" is organized in northern Tyumen province.
**1968:** The one-millionth metric ton of oil is extracted from the Surgut fields.
**1972:** The Kirishi refinery is one of the five largest in the U.S.S.R.
**1991:** Nationwide oil production is at low levels as the U.S.S.R. disintegrates.
**1993:** A government decree combines several separate Soviet-era enterprises into the Surgutneftegaz holding company.
**1995:** Surgutneftegaz's pension fund buys a large stake in the oil company from the government.
**1996:** The oil industry contraction levels off; Surgutneftegaz publishes its first financial statements.
**2000:** Surgutneftegaz consolidates the equity of the holding company and the production subsidiary into a single share.

also gained government approval to build a harbor facility in the Batareinaya Bay on the Gulf of Finland, as well as a 200-mile pipeline from the Kirishi refinery to the port. The project was projected to be finished in 2000 but was later put off until 2004.

### *Profitability and Capital Investment: 1996–2002*

In mid-1996, as production and revenues were improving, Surgutneftegaz loosened its self-sufficient stance slightly. The company published financial statements for the first time, showing a pre-tax profit of Ru 5.2 billion in 1995, and rescinded the regulation limiting foreign investment to 5 percent. An agreement to issue level one American Depository Receipts (ADR) was signed with the Bank of New York in November, facilitating foreign investment in the company. Still, Bogdanov emphasized that his management style remained conservative. As reported by the *Moscow Times*, Bogdanov stated, "We spend only what we have. We don't have any debts, and we don't want to take any loans. We rely on our own resources."

Surgutneftegaz's growing reputation for friendliness to investors faltered in October 1996 after a questionable stock deal. Specifically, the company acquired the entire 500 share issue of its production subsidiary AO Surgutneftegaz in a closed auction, at a price 30 percent below market level. Minority shareholders were alarmed at the prospect of an arbitrary dilution of their holdings. Russia's Federal Securities Commission intervened in support of shareholder rights, saying that Surgutneftegaz could keep the stake only if it paid market price for it. The decision cleared the way for the planned ADR issue, and Surgutneftegaz stock rose on the news.

By the end of 1996, the oil industry contraction had levelled off. Profits and production at Surgutneftegaz were about the same as in 1995, but exports had risen to one third of total output. All of the company's exporting was done through the company Nafta Moskva. In order to reduce the cost of the export middlemen, Surgutneftegaz acquired a 15 percent stake in the crude exporter in April 1997. Surgutneftegaz paid Ru 71 billion for the stake and was to invest Ru 35 billion in the company over the coming three years. In all, 1997 was a profitable year, with net profits according to Russian standards reaching Ru 1.99 billion.

Low oil prices put a squeeze on the company in early 1998. However, Surgutneftegaz had invested over $1 billion in its oil fields in the previous two years and production was consequently more efficient than at rival companies. Instead of cutting production, Bogdanov said Surgutneftegaz would reduce investment by about 10 percent. Bogdanov's cautious leadership paid off when the nationwide economic crisis hit in August 1998. At that time, the Rule was devalued 78 percent and the government defaulted on its debts. But since Surgutneftegaz had little foreign debt and low dollar-denominated costs, it was able to weather the crisis fairly easily. The company closed the year with a pre-tax profit of Ru 6.08 billion. Crude oil and gas output had risen 3.8 and 2.8 percent, respectively.

Gas production posed a problem for Surgutneftegaz. Associated gas was extracted along with oil, but there was no profitable market for the product. The only option was to sell it to the gas refining monopoly Sibur at low government-fixed prices. The huge gas concern Gazprom, with controlled Sibur, used its influence to keep prices from being set at a higher rate. The solution, announced in June 1999, was to build gas-fired power plants for the Tyanskoye and Konitlorskoye oil fields. The plants would make use of Surgutneftegaz's gas production while also reducing the company's dependence on the electric power monopoly. Capital investment in the usual areas of field development and well maintenance was also a priority in 1999. Total investment more than doubled from the previous year, and overall results for 1999 showed that steady investment paid off. Crude production was up 6.8 percent and pre-tax profit increased seven times to Ru 42.7 billion, thanks to a combination of high oil prices and low costs due to the crash of the Rule. Despite this success, industry analysts criticized the company for its regional focus. They suggested that Surgutneftegaz should seek to acquire fields outside Western Siberia if it was to remain a world-class firm. Bogdanov, however, appeared firm in his belief that cutting costs and increasing production was the best was to ensure profitability.

Bogdanov's cautious management had made Surgutneftegaz popular with investors in the Russian stock market. The company's equity was complicated, however, by the fact that shares in the holding company NK Surgutneftegaz and the Surgutneftegaz production subsidiary were traded separately. In January 2000, the company announced plans to consolidate its equity into the production subsidiary, thereby unifying control and creating a single share price for the firm. The specific proposal was to issue 12 billion additional shares in the production arm, which would be swapped for shares in the parent company. The plan made minority shareholders uneasy. A group of outside investors wrote a letter to Bogdanov expressing the fear that their share would be diluted from 31 to 24 percent, thus depriving them of a blocking stake in the company. Nevertheless, a February ballot on the plan won the support of 98 percent of votes cast. The results ignored the votes of holders of preferred shares and ADRs, but those groups said they would protest only if the terms of the deal were unfair. When a swap was announced at a rate of one holding company share for 1,000 shares in the subsidiary, Surgutneftegaz seemed to be carrying through on its promise not to cheat investors. After the Federal Securities Commission approved the plan in April, the consolidation moved forward.

Soon a new conflict arose with minority shareholders, this time related to low-dividend payments. In May 2001, a group of small investors prepared a suit charging that the dividend of 18 kopecks for the year 2000 violated the company charter, which stipulates that 10 percent of net income must be paid in dividends on preferred shares. Bogdanov asserted that he needed a cash reserve for a time when oil prices might fall. Extensive investment in refinery and well renovations also swallowed a large chunk of profits. Capital investment projects, including increased drilling and the introduction of new fields, led to an 8 percent rise in total crude and condensate output for 2000, totalling 13 percent of the oil produced in Russia. Both capital investment, at Ru 33.1 billion, and pre-tax profits, at Ru 86.26, were more than double 1999's figures.

Surgutneftegaz continued cautious expansion in 2001. Through the subsidiary Kaliningradnefteprodukt, the company planned to enhance its network of gas stations around Kaliningrad by building several new stations and upgrading existing ones to multi-fuel stations. Work was also proceeding on an extensive upgrade of the Kirishi refinery in conjunction with plans to install an export terminal at Batareinaya Bay. A plan to expand production into Eastern Siberia, however, fell through when the company was denied a tender for a field in the Sakha republic after conducting a year-long feasibility study. The incident served to solidify Surgutneftegaz's commitment to Western Siberia.

Results for the first half of 2000 showed a drop in revenues from the previous year due to lower crude prices and rising costs. But even if the stellar results of the past few years would not soon be repeated, Surgutneftegaz was still confident in its potential for growth. The company announced plans to raise output 6.8 percent in 2002 and increase refining by 7.3 percent. Capital investment would also rise 18.7 percent, the company reported, mainly to finance work on the Kirishi refinery and the Surgutneftegaz retail network. Although minority investors were still pushing for more dynamic expansion, Bogdanov was unlikely to change the management style that had kept Surgutneftegaz close to the top of its industry for nearly a decade.

## *Principal Subsidiaries*

Surgutmebel; Insurance Society Surgutneftegaz; Central Surgut Depositary; Novgorodnefteprodukt; Retail Association Pskovnefteprodukt; Retail Association Tvernefteprodukt; Kaliningradnefteprodukt; Sovkhoz Chervishevskii; Production Association Kirishinefteorgsintez; Oil-Consulting; Oil Company Surgutneftegaz; Surgutneftegazbank; Invest-Zashchita; Surgutneftestroi; Investsibirstroi; Surgutneftegazburenie.

## *Principal Competitors*

OAO Gazprom; OAO LUKoil; OAO NK; YuKOS; Sibneft.

## *Further Reading*


Arvedlund, Erin, "Surgut Ups Its Holding of Major Exporter," *Moscow Times*, April 12, 1997.

Barshay, Jill, "Russian Oil Shares up for Auction," *Financial Times* (London), December 29, 1993, p. 2.

Freeland, Chrystia, "Bidders Claim Exclusion from Russian Oil Sell-off," *Financial Times* (London), November 1, 1995, p. 3.

——, "Russian Sell-off Controversy," *Financial Times* (London), November 6, 1995.

Gismatullin, Eduard, "Surgut Tackles Issue of Associated Gas," *Moscow Times*, June 2, 1999.

Henderson, Peter, "Investors Cautious of Surgut Plan," *Russia Journal*, January 17, 2000, p. 15.

Korchagina, Valeria, "Surgut: Consolidation to Be Investor-Friendly," *Moscow Times*, April 25, 2000.

Kovski, Alan, "Russians Study the Ways of the West and Await More Changes," *Oil Daily*, March 13, 1992, pp. 2–3.

Kremer, Vladimir, "First Oil Companies Created," *Current Digest of the Post-Soviet Press*, June 23, 1993, p. 20.

Lane, David, and Iskander Seifulmulukov, "Company Profiles: Surgutneftegaz" and "Structure and Ownership," in *The Political Economy of Russian Oil*, ed. David Lane, Lanham, Md.: Rowman & Littlefield Publisher, 1999, pp. 32–3, 117–19.

Lukianov, Sergei, "Oil Giant Opens Books, May Sell Stock," *Moscow Times*, June 1, 1996.

——, "Surgut Share Issue Violations Cited," *Moscow Times*, December 11, 1996.

*OAO Surgutneftegaz: Istoriia Kompanii*, Surgut, Russia: OAO Surgutneftegaz.

"The Oil Giant of Surgut, Asleep in Siberia," *Moscow Times*, October 31, 1995.

"The Prize: Russian Oil," *Economist*, August 7, 1993, pp. 61–62.

Raff, Anna, "Surgutneftegaz Revenues Fall 2%," *Moscow Times*, August 13, 2001.

"Russia—NK SurgutNefteGaz," *APS Review Downstream Trends*, August 14, 2000.

"Refinery Upgrades to Yield Dividends," *NEFTE Compass*, August 30, 2001, p. 4.

"Soviet Flow Skids to Less Than 10 Million b/d," *Oil and Gas Journal*, December 30, 1991, p. 24.

Stoughton, Sheldon, "Decree to Change Shape of Russian Oil Industry," *Oil and Gas Journal*, December 14, 1992, pp. 20–21.

"Surgutneftegaz," *Russia Journal*, June 22, 2001, p. 22.

"Surgutneftegaz Is to Put up a New Oil Terminal," *RusData DiaLine – BizEkon News*, May 31, 1996.

"Surgutneftegaz President Takes a Rather Dim View of the Future," *RusData DiaLine – BizEkon News*, February 14, 1996.

"Surgutneftegaz Shrugs Off Criticism," *FSU Energy*, May 11, 2001, p. 11.

"Surgutneftegaz Signs ADR Deal Despite Share Inquiry," *FT Energy Newsletter – East European Energy Report*, November 18, 1996.

Thornhill, John, "Oil Group Urged to Rethink, Revamp Plan," *Financial Times* (London), January 27, 2000, p. 37.

——, "Profits, Output Stabilise at Russian Oil Group," *Financial Times* (London), June 3, 1997, p. 18.

Whalen, Jeanne, "Russian Oil Firm Thrives—and Investors Are Fed Up With It," *Wall Street Journal*, May 8, 2001, p. A21.

——, "Russia Oil Firm Posts Big Jump in Pretax Profit for Latest Year," *Wall Street Journal*, April 26, 2000, p. A18.

——, "Siberian Secret," *The Moscow Times*, June 9, 1998.

——, "Surgutneftegaz Combats Oil Crisis," *The Moscow Times*, March 20, 1998.


—Sarah Ruth Lorenz

# Swiss International Air Lines Ltd.

**Postfach**
**CH-4002 Basel**
**Switzerland**
**Telephone: +41 (0)61 582 00 00**
**Fax: +41 (0)61 582 33 33**
**Web site: http://www.swiss.com**

*Public Company*
*Incorporated:* 1975 as Business Flyers Basel
*Employees:* 10,000
*Sales:* $1.9 billion (2002 est.)
*Stock Exchanges:* Swiss
*Ticker Symbol:* CRON CROZn
*NAIC:* 481111 Scheduled Passenger Air Transportation; 481211 Nonscheduled Chartered Passenger Air Transportation

Swiss International Air Lines Ltd. (SWISS) is Switzerland's national airline. The Swissair Group's regional subsidiary, Crossair AG, was made the legal basis for this new airline following collapse of the Swissair (Swiss Air Transport Company, Ltd.) in late 2001. After taking over much of the operations of the former Swissair Group, the new SWISS connects 126 destinations in 59 countries.

## *Origins*

Swiss International Air Lines Ltd.'s legal predecessor, Crossair AG, was launched in February 1975 as Business Flyers Basel by Moritz Suter. The airline began with just three routes. Crossair was based in French territory at the ''Euro-Airport'' at Basel/Mulhouse. This unique bi-national location freed Crossair from having to obtain work permits for its non-Swiss employees.

Then a DC-9 captain for Swissair, Suter continued to fly for that company. He was not the only pilot doing double duty at the new airline: co-pilots served drinks and sandwiches. This in-flight service would soon evolve into hot meals service in business class to cater to Crossair's high percentage (80 percent) of business travelers.

Crossair practiced a policy of cooperating with large airlines, particularly Swissair, rather than competing directly, reported *Air Transport World.* An agreement with the Swiss flag carrier limited Crossair to aircraft of 50 seats, while Swissair agreed not to fly planes with less than 100 seats. Under a Swiss law dating back to 1948, Swissair had first pick of routes. Crossair was also listed on Swissair's computer reservation system and operated some routes for both Swissair and Lufthansa.

Crossair's original equipment consisted of Fairchild Metro regional airliners. In October 1980, Crossair placed an order for ten Saab-Fairchild SF-340s, becoming the launch customer for the 35-seat commuter airliner. Technical problems with the SF-340 plagued the type following its somewhat delayed introduction in September 1984. The first three planes were soon taken out of service due to problems with the General Electric CT7 engine. Crossair leased old Fokker F27s, Caravelles, and McDonnell Douglas MD-81s to fill out its fleet. These problems were worked out eventually, and Crossair became an enthusiastic Saab owner. In the mid-1980s, Crossair, seeking to diversify, became the world's first certified CT7 engine service center.

Turnover was CHF 82 million in 1985, up a third from the previous year, producing profit of CHF 3.1 million, up about 25 percent. Passenger traffic accounted for 82 percent of income, with charter flying accounting for most of the remainder. The route network then stretched beyond Switzerland to Austria, France, Luxembourg, Italy, West Germany, Belgium, Holland, and Albania. The company had 320 employees, including 105 pilots.

Net profits were CHF 9.8 million ($7.5 million) in 1989. In 1988, Swissair had taken a 38 percent stake in Crossair, which became the group's only low-cost component. The new ownership produced some changes in Crossair's fleet. While still devoted to the Saab 340, the company ordered a few Fokker 50 turboprops to cover a shortage of capacity. In May 1990, the airline stepped up to the 83-seat British Aerospace BAe 146 jet, which the carrier dubbed ''Jumbolino,'' for use on trunk routes.

Passenger count topped one million in 1990. The airline connected 31 points in ten countries. Crossair was considered among the top European regional airlines, known for its respon-

**Company Perspectives:**

*Our Swissness: The proud brand heritage of the new airline is also the key to the future. The intrinsic values of Switzerland—quality, prestige, tradition in care, service, efficiency, security, reliability, and cleanliness—are also essential to creating a superior travel experience. Our belief in these values differentiates us from other air carriers.*

sive and creative management (who had an average age of just 36). However, after a decade of profit growth, the carrier posted a CHF 2.9 million loss in 1990. During the year, Crossair built a new hanger/office building that included a Chez Moritz staff restaurant featuring a glass-bottom floor with a view of the hangar below.

### *Dealing with Deregulation in the 1990s*

Crossair met the challenge of European deregulation with expansion. This was sometimes complicated by the fact that Switzerland was not a member of the European Community (EC), and nearly all of Crossair's international destinations were EC cities. Service between Lugano and Florence was cancelled by Italian authorities due to Crossair's competition with airlines there. Crossair also suffered when Switzerland's ban on 40-ton tractor-trailers miffed EC transport officials, who saw it as a protectionist policy.

The carrier was quick to capitalize upon opportunities in Eastern Europe, taking a third share Bratislava-based Tatra Air in collaboration with Slov-Air of Czechoslovakia. Crossair also owned shares in Delta Air and Alsavia, registered in France and Germany, respectively. It took a 15 percent share of Scotland's Business Air in 1990.

Limited access to the Italian market, competition, higher financing fees, and increased airport fees conspired to produce Crossair's second annual loss in a row in 1991. Suter soon launched a cost-cutting program, and the company's one-third share in unprofitable Tatra Air was sold in July 1992.

By this time, Swissair had increased its share in Crossair to 51.9 percent. In 1993, Swissair joined KLM, SAS, and Austrian Airlines in the pan-European "Alcazar" alliance to compete against larger rivals British Airways, Air France, and Lufthansa. However, after less than a year of negotiations, the grouping fell apart over the choice of a U.S. partner.

Swissair then set out to expand by acquiring holdings in EC airlines, such as Sabena. In 1995, Swissair paid CHF 267 million for a 49.5 percent holding (EC law limited it to a minority interest) in the notoriously unprofitable Belgian carrier. The next year, after failing to win reductions in labor costs, Swissair wrote off its equity in the company as it posted a CHF 497 million loss. However, in 1998, when Swissair posted a CHF 361 million profit, the strategy seemed to be working.

In 1995, Swissair closed its unprofitable Balair/CTA charter unit, transferring responsibility for its short-haul flights to Crossair, which also received its eight MD-80 airliners. The parent company decided that Crossair would handle all flights involving aircraft of 100 seats or less; Crossair soon ordered a dozen Avro regional jets for CHF 350 million. At the same time, Swissair was increasing its holdings in Crossair from 60 percent to 67 percent.

These changes—dubbed "Project ZGB"—also increased Crossair's workforce from 1,500 to 2,000 as its annual revenues nearly doubled in two years from CHF 430 million ($375 million) in 1994. Profits continued to rise even as these changes were taking place.

In early 1996, a unique cross-branding experiment with the Hotelplan travel agency and McDonald's restaurants had the hamburger giant catering a specially painted "McPlane" on package tour operations. Crossair set up a French airline, Europe Continental Airways (ECA), in 1997, taking a 35 percent holding in the company (French travel agency owner Foch Finances Investissement held the remainder). Based near Crossair at the EuroAirport Basel-Mulhouse-Freiburg, the new company was registered in France, allowing for the benefits of membership in the European Union, which was liberalizing the air traffic markets of member countries. ECA was renamed EuroCross by the time it started flight operations in late March 1998.

Crossair posted record profits of CHF 63.5 million in 1998 as operating revenues passed CHF 1 billion ($1.46 billion). It had 2,800 employees at the end of the year. However, while Crossair was thriving, Swissair, saddled with several loss-making subsidiaries outside Switzerland, was on a course for bankruptcy. Besides Sabena, it had acquired 49 percent stakes in German charter carrier LTU International Airways and three French regional airlines: Air Littoral, AOM French Airlines, and Air Liberté. It also acquired smaller stakes in LOT Polish Airlines, South African Airways, and Italy's Volate Airlines and Air Europe. Swissair posted a colossal CHF 2.89 billion loss in 2000. In March 2001, the board brought in Nestlé veteran Mario Corti as CEO. Nevertheless, the debts continued to mount.

### *A New Flag Carrier in 2001*

In September 2001, Swissair sold its 70.35 percent stake in Crossair to a group of investors led by Credit Suisse and UBS (Union de Banques Suisses) for around CHF 1.5 billion ($850 million), which accounted for a little more than half of the total new capital raised from government, banks, and industry.

The September 11 attacks on the World Trade Center in New York City depressed the airline business worldwide and multiplied insurance premiums. This situation was aggravated for Crossair when one of its Avro regional jets crashed in late November 2001, killing 24 people.

Swissair's planes were grounded in October 2001, stranding 18,000 passengers worldwide, until emergency financing—CHF 450 million from the Swiss government—could be arranged to keep the airline flying for the rest of the month. Some of Swissair's routes were already being assigned to Crossair.

Project Phoenix, approved on October 22, outlined the financial structure of the new Swiss flag carrier. The federal government provided another CHF 1 billion to keep Swissair

**Key Dates:**

**1975:** Crossair AG is formed by a Swissair DC-9 captain.
**1988:** Swissair acquires a minority holding in Crossair.
**1990:** Crossair's passenger count exceeds one million.
**1995:** Swissair shifts more flights and planes to Crossair as it closes its Balair/CTA charter unit.
**2001:** Crossair takes over the operations of grounded Swissair.
**2002:** Crossair is renamed Swiss International Air Lines Ltd.

going through March. It also bought a 19.2 percent stake in Crossair for CHF 600 million. UBS and Credit Suisse together invested CHF 350 million for a 19.5 percent stake. Regional governments and business interests invested another CHF 2.1 billion.

Two-thirds of Swissair's routes, including 36 international destinations, were transferred to Crossair. Under the Phoenix Business Plan, Crossair was to add 52 planes to its fleet of 75 in the next two years. Utilizing its lower cost structure, Crossair was hoping to break even in 2003 with revenues of CHF 5 billion ($3 billion). The company now had about 10,000 employees, versus the 5,500 it employed before taking over Swissair's operations.

Crossair was restructured as Swissair's successor, but company founder Moritz Suter was not able to oversee the transition. He and the entire Crossair board resigned at an emotional, six-hour board meeting on December 6, 2001. The bankers and bureaucrats appointed former KLM chief Pieter Bouw chairman in Suter's place, while André Dose was named CEO. Crossair itself posted a loss of CHF 314 million ($188 million) on revenues of CHF 1.39 billion ($834 million) in 2001, mostly due to restructuring charges.

Sabena Belgian World Airlines, 49 percent owned by Swissair, itself collapsed in the wake of Swissair's bankruptcy. Lawsuits ensued over alleged broken aid agreements on behalf of Air Liberté and TAP Air Portugal. As *Air Transport World* reported, the transition was complex and contentious. None of the shareholders, creditors, employees, or government officials could be 100 percent satisfied after such a collapse, but Switzerland still had an intercontinental airline. One of the biggest challenges would certainly be cultural, mixing the staff at entrepreneurial Crossair with their more conservative Swissair counterparts, mostly based in the banking center of Zurich.

Crossair began using the SWISS brand name in April 2002. Swiss International Air Lines Ltd. became the company's official new name effective July 1, 2002. SWISS was updating its fleet with 13 Airbus 340 aircraft due for delivery in 2003 and was aiming to join the United States-led Oneworld global airline alliance.

### *Principal Subsidiaries*

EuroCross; Mindpearl.

### *Principal Competitors*

Société Air France; Austrian Airlines; British Airways plc; Deutsche Lufthansa AG; KLM Royal Dutch Airlines; SAS AB.

### *Further Reading*

Baker, Colin, "Out of the Ashes," *Airline Business,* March 2002, pp. 38+.
Baumer-Burton, Helen, "Quick Off the Mark," *SwissBusiness,* July/August 1991, pp. 7+.
Buerkle, Tom, and Rick Smith, "Who Lost Swissair?," *Institutional Investor,* February 2002, pp. 42+.
Fiorino, Frances, "Swiss Comeback," *Aviation Week & Space Technology,* February 18, 2002, p. 19.
Flottau, Jens, "Honing New Image, Swiss Eyes Global Link," *Aviation Week & Space Technology,* February 25, 2002, p. 48.
——, "Swissair Refines Recovery Strategy," *Aviation Week & Space Technology,* July 16, 2001, p. 56.
French, Trevor, "Swiss But Not Swiss," *Airline Business,* December 1990, pp. 54+.
Gerresheim, Helmut, "At the Crossroads," *Flight International,* October 17, 1990, pp. 44+.
Hill, Leonard, "Crossair at the Crossroads," *Air Transport World,* February 2002, pp. 53–54.
——, "Hubbing for Home," *Air Transport World,* April 1998, pp. 74–5.
——, "Suter Jumps Gun on 728JET," *Air Transport World,* May 1998, p. 97.
Ivey, Jamie, "Swiss Soars Into Crowded Skies," *Corporate Finance,* April 2002, pp. 20+.
Marray, Michael, "Small Is Beautiful," *Airfinance Journal,* April 1999, pp. 60–1.
Maxon, Terry, "American Airlines to Join Swiss Air Lines in Marketing Partnership," *Dallas Morning News,* March 27, 2002.
Moxon, Julian, "Crossair's Confidence," *Flight International,* January 8, 1992, pp. 33+.
Olson, Elizabeth, "Amid Financial Wrangling, Swissair Gets Half Its Flights into the Air," *New York Times,* October 9, 2001, p. W1.
——, "Crossair's Entire Board Quits, and the Founder Steps Down," *New York Times,* December 7, 2001, p. W1.
Reed, Arthur, "Buildup at Crossair," *Air Transport World,* June 1995, p. 202.
——, "Crossair Remains Successful Despite Tough Times," *Air Transport World,* June 1986, pp. 85+.
——, "Exploding Expansion," *Air Transport World,* June 1996, p. 165.
Shifrin, Carole A., "Crossair Faces Biggest Challenge," *Aviation Week & Space Technology,* May 15, 1995, pp. 64+.
Shifrin, Carole A., and Pierre Sparaco, "Crossair Gets Bigger Role in Swissair Strategy Shift," *Aviation Week & Space Technology,* March 13, 1995, p. 34.
Sparaco, Pierre, " 'New' Swiss Carrier Intent on Rapid Rebound," *Aviation Week & Space Technology,* April 1, 2002, pp. 40+.
Stanley, Bruce, "Swiss Aims to Soar as a Premium Airline, But Skeptics Say Baggage from Bankrupt Swissair Weighs It Down," *AP Worldstream,* March 25, 2002.
Warburton, Simon, "Swissair Woes Affect Other Airlines," *Flight International,* October 9, 2001, p. 6.

—Frederick C. Ingram

# TA Triumph-Adler AG

**Südwestpark 23**
**D-90449 Nuremberg**
**Germany**
**Telephone: (49) (911) 6898-0**
**Fax: (49) (911) 6898-200**
**Web site: http://www.triumph-adler.de**

*Public Company*
*Incorporated:* 1896 as Deutsche Triumph Fahrradwerke AG
*Employees:* 4,509
*Sales:* EUR 702.6 million ($528 million) (2001)
*Stock Exchanges:* Frankfurt
*Ticker Symbol:* TWN
*NAIC:* 421420 Office Equipment Wholesalers; 233310 Manufacturing and Industrial Building Construction; 335999 All Other Miscellaneous Electrical Equipment and Component Manufacturing; 339992 Musical Instrument Manufacturing; 339931 Doll and Stuffed Toy Manufacturing; 339932 Game, Toy, and Children's Vehicle Manufacturing

TA Triumph-Adler AG is Germany's leading supplier of distribution services for printing, copying and presentation equipment. The company's Experts@output division distributes and services laser printers and copiers for more than 22,000 clients at over 80 locations. Originally a maker of bicycles, the company views its future focus as on Internet-based output solutions for documents and data in electronic form. The company's other mainstay is the holding company, TA Beteiligung, which oversees several mid-sized companies in such diverse fields as toys and leisure, construction technology, and electronics. TA Beteiligung is expected to go public in 2003.

### *Making Bicycles, Motorcycles, and Typewriters: 1896–1913*

At the turn of the 19th century the world was swept by a flood of technical innovations that paved the way for industrialization. One of them was the bicycle. In the 1890s the new vehicle took the public by storm. The predecessor of the modern bicycle—the *Velocipede*—was equipped with a giant front wheel and proved suitable only for acrobats. In 1884, however, two Englishmen invented a version with much smaller wheels which became increasingly popular. At about the same time two German entrepreneurs—Siegfried Bettmann and M. Schulte—founded a bicycle firm in Coventry, England, the Triumph Cycle Company Ltd. In July 1896 they established a subsidiary in Nuremberg, Germany—the Deutsche Triumph Fahrradwerke AG.

Six months after it had been established, Deutsche Triumph opened the Velodrom, a driving school for bicyclists. The Velodrom consisted of an open-air practice lot and a roofed cycling track where Triumph customers could learn to master their new vehicles. On Sunday afternoons, a crowd of curious spectators watched the bicyclists-in-the-making demonstrating their progress, while sipping coffee and enjoying live music. The creative promotion effort bore fruit. Deutsche Triumph realized a 10 percent profit from one million Reichsmark in sales in the company's first full business year.

Selling bicycles was a seasonal trade, however, and the company looked for new business opportunities. When the demand for bicycles dried out in the cold season, Deutsche Triumph used its production capacities to manufacture cigarette-making machines, surgery tables, elevators, and box springs. At the beginning of the 20th century the automobile caught most of the public attention. However, intense public interest did not immediately translate into purchases, due to the immense cost. This was an opportunity for another new vehicle which offered the convenience of motor-power but at a much lower price: the motorcycle. After German engineer Gottlieb Daimler had invented the world's first motorcycle in 1885, a number of manufacturers jumped at the opportunity. One of them was Deutsche Triumph, which presented its first motorcycle model in 1903. The company soon realized that the German market was still very limited and in 1907 decided to abandon motorcycles and focus solely on bicycles.

Only two years later Deutsche Triumph ventured into another new field when they took over the production of a bankrupt typewriter manufacturer in Nuremberg. The Norica type-

## Company Perspectives:

*Printing, copying, faxing and presenting. Triumph-Adler: We are Experts@Output, profiting from the dynamic growth in digital communication markets. As the German market leader in sales and servicing of output solutions our aim is further growth in Germany and Europe—leveraging the additional opportunities offered by our strong Triumph-Adler brand.*

writer became the company's second key product, and in 1911 Deutsche Triumph was renamed Triumph-Werke Nürnberg AG Nürnberg. Two years later Triumph-Werke became independent from its English parent company.

### *Surviving Two World Wars*

During World War I, from 1914 until 1919, Triumph-Werke made supplies crucial for the war: beds and tables for field hospitals, fuses, and ammunition. After the war the company resumed the production of motorcycles and launched Knirps—the first German motorcycle with a two-stroke engine. The popularity of motorcycles grew during the 1920s, bolstering Triumph-Werke sales. In fiscal 1923–24 the company's output amounted to 1,600 motorcycles. Five years later it had grown to over 13,500. Triumph-Werke also continued making bicycles, almost reaching the prewar output of about 16,000 by 1921. However, the demand for bicycles started declining in 1927 and Triumph-Werke united both the bicycle and motorcycle divisions under one organizational roof. In 1928 the company launched a new motorcycle—K9 Supra—which was so small that a driver's license was not required to drive it. For a short time Triumph-Werke also made four-stroke motorcycles but abandoned them in the late 1930s.

In 1920 Triumph-Werke also started making typewriters again, continuing with the prewar model Triumph 2. In 1925 the company received an order for 600 typewriters from the telegraph service division of the German post office, the Deutsche Reichspost. Three years later a Triumph typewriter was shipped to the Vatican, and the company received an endorsement from the pope himself. Triumph's typewriters were continuously improved throughout the 1920s. In 1928 the company introduced three smaller typewriter models: Durabel, Norm 6, and Perfect. In the mid-1930s Triumph-Werke erected a brand-new building for large-series production of its standard typewriter. In addition, the company extended its product range in the office equipment sector and started making adding machines. By 1938 Triumph-Werke employed about 1,800 people and was grossing 15 million Reichsmark annually.

In 1939 Germany went to war again, and the country's economy was administered by the National Socialist government. Triumph-Werke's mainstay during this time was its BD 250 motorcycle, which the German army ordered by the thousands. By 1940 the production of typewriters for civilian use was restricted and ceased completely at the end of 1942.

World War II left the company's offices and production facilities mostly untouched. Triumph-Werke then received a production permit and started making typewriters, bicycles and bicycle trailers, wheelbarrows, and hand-drawn carts. In 1948 the company also resumed the manufacture of motorcycles and in 1953 launched a new line of mopeds and motor scooters. The mid-1950s also saw a new Triumph typewriter, called the Matura, equipped with a patented carriage return mechanism.

### *Losing Ground and Independence: 1956–93*

In 1953, the takeover of Triumph-Werke by German entrepreneur Max Grundig, whose core business was in consumer electronics, ended the company's independence. Grundig reorganized the company to focus on office machines and shut down the vehicle production. Research and development (R&D) efforts were directed towards better electric typewriters which were becoming increasingly popular for their more comfortable features. With electronic data processing on the rise, Triumph-Werke introduced a telex-type tape punch in 1956. Triumph's new Family Typewriter—a name inspired by Grundig's granddaughter Gabriele—followed a year later. Another novelty—the F3 automated invoicing machine, equipped with a connector for card punches—marked the beginning of the office computer era. The company's new electric typewriter Electric 20 became its standard model of the 1960s. It was used by the world typing champion in Vienna in 1961, who scored 647 strokes per minute, setting a new world record.

In 1957 Triumph-Werke acquired a minority share in Frankfurt/Main-based typewriter manufacturer Adler. Combined, the two companies controlled over 50 percent of the German market for typewriters. By 1968 Triumph-Werke had an 82 percent stake in Adler, and the latter was merged with Triumph and the company renamed Triumph-Adler. Just around the time that the integration of the two companies was completed, Grundig sold Triumph-Adler to Beverly Hills-based Litton Industries Inc.

Backed by the new parent company, Triumph-Adler set out to conquer the growing market for microcomputers. In 1969 the company introduced the new TA 100 computer series. Triumph-Adler's microcomputer division—including R&D, manufacturing, marketing, and distribution—was based at headquarters in Nuremberg. In 1971 the company launched the TA 10, which dubbed "the people's computer." It was the size of a suitcase and offered at a competitive price. Only two years later Triumph-Adler had sold over 10,000 of the computers. Still, typewriters accounted for more than 60 percent of the company's total sales. In 1977 Triumph-Adler acquired the U.S.-based Royal Group, using used the company's production plants and distribution network to enter the American market. Ten years after the Litton takeover, Triumph-Adler's sales had grown ten-fold. The company's professional microcomputers had a 19 percent market share in Germany, a share larger than that of any other competitor.

In March 1979 German auto maker Volkswagen AG bought 55 percent of Triumph-Adler's share capital, acquiring another 43 percent from Litton and German Diehl GmbH in 1980. The company, which by 1980 had over 17,000 employees on its payroll, was renamed Triumph-Adler AG für Büro- und Informationstechnik.

That year marked the beginning of a challenging era for Triumph-Adler, as the company reported a loss of DM 50

## Key Dates:

**1896:** Deutsche Triumph Fahrradwerke AG is founded in Nuremberg.
**1909:** Triumph starts manufacturing typewriters.
**1953:** Triumph is taken over by Max Grundig, merged with Adlerwerke, and renamed Triumph-Adler.
**1968:** Litton Industries Inc. becomes the company's new majority shareholder.
**1979:** Triumph-Adler is acquired by Volkswagen AG.
**1985:** The company is renamed TA Triumph-Adler AG.
**1986:** Italian Olivetti group takes over the company.
**1994:** Olivetti sells to a group of German investors; Triumph-Adler becomes a management holding company.
**1997:** The typewriter production in Frankfurt/Main is closed down.
**2000:** Triumph-Adler declares imaging and output solutions its core business.

million. In the following years, top management focused on downsizing and restructuring. The company's workforce was cut in half and distribution was extended to include department stores. None of these measures, however, stopped the company from falling behind the competition. By 1986 Triumph-Adler was only number five in the German market for professional microcomputers, with its market share having shrunk to 6.4 percent. In that year, Volkswagen sold most of its holdings in Triumph-Adler to the Italian Olivetti group, one of the company's main European competitors.

The new parent, however, was not able to rescue the company from its downfall, caused by the increasingly popular IBM personal computers which rapidly replaced the older microcomputer technology. By 1988 the number of employees as well as the company's revenues had shrunk to less than half the figures of 1984. Only the company's typewriter division turned up a profit.

In the early 1990s Triumph-Adler became Olivetti's headquarters for office machines and an original equipment manufacturer for other computer makers. In 1991 the company launched a self-developed laptop computer. However, the rapidly declining prices for computer hardware components and the development cost for the new TA portable computer pushed the company heavily into the red. Moreover, parent company Olivetti was struggling too, cutting down on orders for Triumph-Adler by one-third. All of the company's production facilities in Nuremberg, Fürth, and Schwandorf were shut down while production was moved out of the country. Most of the company's assets, such as real estate and machinery, were sold to cover some of the DM 160 million in losses that Olivetti incurred in 1992 alone.

By 1993 Triumph-Adler had shrunk to a quarter of its former size. It was, in fact, left only with the typewriter production business in Frankfurt/Main. In that year Olivetti decided to rid itself of the loss-making enterprise and canceled the agreement with Triumph-Adler that had guaranteed that the Italian parent would be responsible for making up Triumph-Adler's losses. Olivetti then integrated Triumph-Adler's office machine distribution subsidiary, Triumph-Adler Vertriebs GmbH, into its own business.

### *New Beginning as a Management Holding in 1994*

In 1994 a group of investors, including two banks, an insurance company, and private investors, bought what was left of the former international brand typewriter maker. Within a few months they transformed the former manufacturing company into a management holding for mid-sized businesses. Those businesses—the backbone of Germany's economy—were struggling with several problems, including the challenge of finding successors for their enterprise if their own children were not available for the family business; financing research and development efforts or larger investments; and organizing and managing their companies more efficiently in increasingly competitive markets. Triumph-Adler's new management offered an umbrella under which such mid-sized companies could better meet those challenges. The idea behind the management holding model was to realize higher profits through bundling the resources and know-how of several mid-sized companies within in the same industry or market, but keeping intact their flat, more flexible organization.

Equipped with several hundred million in cash from outstanding Olivetti payments, the new Triumph-Adler holding company went on a shopping spree. In addition to the already existing holding for office related products, Triumph-Adler acquired a broad variety of companies, from toy manufacturers to health related products, and organized them into four major business divisions: TA Office, TA Toys & Leisure, TA Health and TA BauTech. The latter included a number of manufacturers and service providers in the construction industry.

In 1997 Triumph-Adler closed down its typewriter plant in Frankfurt/Main. In the mid-1990s the market for typewriters had shrunk drastically, by about 30 percent in 1996 alone. Personal computers had won the race against the more limited capabilities of the typewriter. Although in 2001 the company still sold Triumph-Adler typewriters worth EUR 12.7 million, the business was not profitable anymore.

For the better part of the late 1990s Triumph-Adler seemed to randomly add or dispose of its various subsidiaries. In 1997 the company sold off its health division which it had acquired two years earlier. In 1998 the management holding added a new business division in the area of electronics after the acquisition of the Hueco Group, a manufacturer of electrical and electronic components for the auto industry. In 1999 Triumph-Adler organized a public stock offering for their subsidiary Zapf, a manufacturer of dolls based in Rödental near Coburg with a long-standing tradition. It premiered on the Frankfurt stock exchange as Zapf Creation AG. In the same year the company acquired the firms Bell-Hermetics, Concord, Migua, PPE, and UTAX, some of which were sold off again soon after.

However, the concept of the *Mittelstandsholding* did not seem to turn up the profits expected by management and investors. The company's portfolio had branched out into many areas which were not connected in any way. In 2000 Triumph-Adler's top management decided to streamline its holdings and focus on office-based printing, imaging, and presentation technology. The new core business division was renamed Triumph-Adler Experts @ Output. The company's new strategy included selling off subsidiaries not related to the core business and acquiring new holdings in the defined area. In May 2001 Triumph-Adler sold its remaining shares in Zapf Creation. The cash inflow of EUR 30 million prevented the company from having to report a loss in the business year 2001. Looking to the future, Triumph-Adler planned to dispose of its holdings in the areas toys and leisure, construction technology, and electronics by 2003.

### *Principal Subsidiaries*

Triumph-Adler Experts @ Output GmbH; Triumph-Adler Output Solutions GmbH; TA Leasing GmbH; Triumph-Adler Ost GmbH; Triumph-Adler NordWest GmbH; Triumph-Adler SüdOst GmbH; UTAX GmbH; UTAX (U.K.) Ltd.; Triumph-Adler A-Vi-Tec Präsentations- und Medientechnik GmbH (97%); Presentation Products Europe Holding B.V. (Netherlands; 85%); TA electronic Holding GmbH; TA BauTech Holding GmbH; Concord Kinderautositze GmbH & Co. KG; Tectro Spielwaren GmbH; Triumph-Adler SüdWest GmbH.

### *Principal Competitors*

Buhrmann NV; Guilbert S.A.; Staples, Inc.

### *Further Reading*

*100 Jahre Triumph-Adler,* Nuremberg, Germany: Triumph-Adler AG, 1996, 31 p.

"In wenigen Wochen das Unternehmensprogramm weit aufgefächert," *Frankfurter Allgemeine Zeitung*, September 26, 1994, p. 22.

"Kein Lichtblick für Triumph-Adler," *Süddeutsche Zeitung*, May 25, 1993.

"Olivetti kündigt Beherrschung mit Triumph-Adler," *Süddeutsche Zeitung*, October 13, 1993.

"TA will keine neuen Geschäftsfelder mehr," *Frankfurter Allgemeine Zeitung*, November 16, 1999, p. 25.

"Triumph-Adler gibt eigene Fertigung von Schreibmaschinen auf," *Frankfurter Allgemeine Zeitung,* September 25, 1997, p. 28.

"Triumph Adler kauft weiter Unternehmen," *Frankfurter Allgemeine Zeitung*, March 4, 1995, p. 20.

"Triumph-Adler will durch internetgesteuerte Drucksysteme wachsen," *dpa,* May 12, 2000.

"Unternehmensverkauf muss nicht völlige Trennung bedeuten," *Frankfurter Allgemeine Zeitung*, December 28, 1998, p. 22.

"Verkäufe verhindern Verlust bei Triumph-Adler," *Frankfurter Allgemeine Zeitung*, March 22, 2002, p. 21.

—Evelyn Hauser

# Taylor Guitars

**1980 Gillespie Way**
**El Cajon, California 92020-1096**
**U.S.A.**
**Telephone: (619) 258-1207**
**Toll Free: (800) 943-6782**
**Fax: (619) 258-3799**
**Web site: http://www.taylorguitars.com**

*Private Company*
*Incorporated:* 1974 as Westland Music Company
*Employees:* 400
*Sales:* $43.6 million (2001 est.)
*NAIC:* 339992 Musical Instrument Manufacturing

Taylor Guitars is a leading maker of acoustic guitars for the mid-price and high-end market. The company produces over 40,000 instruments a year that range from the three-quarter size "Baby Taylor," retailing for under $500, to more than 60 different full-size models that start at $1,200 and go up to $10,000 and beyond. Taylor also occasionally makes limited edition guitars like the Liberty Tree of 2002, constructed from wood salvaged from a 400-year old tulip poplar under which American colonists gathered to plot the revolution. The company's guitars, prized for their tone and ease of play, are owned by many celebrated musicians, including Paul McCartney, Eric Clapton, Neil Young, and Bonnie Raitt. The privately-held firm is run by co-founders Bob Taylor and Kurt Listug.

### *Beginnings*

The roots of Taylor Guitars go back to the summer of 1973, when two young men began working together at a music store called American Dream in Lemon Grove, California. Kurt Listug, 20, had been painting buildings at nearby San Diego State University when he convinced owner Sam Radding to hire him to work in his repair shop, though he had no prior experience. A week later he was joined by another new hire, 18-year-old Bob Taylor, who had impressed Radding with several homemade guitars he had brought into the store to show off. Both Listug and Taylor started out doing instrument repairs and then moved up to making guitars.

Just a year after the pair were hired, Radding decided to sell American Dream, and his staff split into two factions that both sought to buy the business. Taylor, Listug, and a third partner, Steve Schemmer, won out, and they took possession on October 15, 1974, renaming the store Westland Music Company. They continued in much the same vein as before, repairing instruments and making some guitars for sale at the shop. The young luthiers soon decided to put the name Taylor on the headstock of the company's instruments, as Bob Taylor was their chief builder, changing the company's name to Taylor Guitars.

In 1976, the company's guitars were sold to outside dealers for the first time when Kurt Listug visited music stores in Los Angeles with a selection of the firm's instruments. Among other features, the early Taylor guitars had bolt-on, low-profile necks, which allowed for easy repair, and were made in several different neck widths.

Though Taylor was taking steps toward growth, the market for acoustic guitars had virtually bottomed out by the mid-1970s, and the firm was often on the edge of financial insolubility. In 1977, a distributor was engaged to help sell the company's guitars, but the low wholesale price received (between $150 and $380) made it difficult to turn a profit. After two years the distribution contract was terminated.

### *Struggling in the Early 1980s*

At the dawn of the 1980s, the firm continued to trudge along, making about ten guitars a week but seldom earning more than enough to cover expenses. Taylor had hired additional employees to boost output but let them go so that the owners could write themselves paychecks rather than simply piling up more unsold guitars.

In 1981, Taylor took out a loan to purchase additional manufacturing equipment, which helped speed up the processing and tooling of raw materials. The following year, with a backlog of instruments piling up, Listug took to the road to market the firm's guitars. On a route that took him to dealers as

## Company Perspectives:

*Established in 1974, Taylor Guitars evolved from a small venture between cofounders Bob Taylor and Kurt Listug to its current status as one of the world's most successful and highly regarded acoustic guitar manufacturers. As a leader in the industry, Taylor continues to revolutionize the design and manufacture of high-end acoustic guitars with significant innovations that produce superior instruments.*

far away as Maine, he managed to sell all of the stock he had taken with him. Finally paying more attention to marketing, and with improved efficiency due to its new manufacturing equipment, Taylor Guitars began to turn a profit at last. In 1983, Listug and Taylor bought out third partner Steve Schemmer, who had been less involved with the firm.

In 1984, with the acoustic guitar market still soft, the company received an unanticipated promotional boost from pop musician Prince. The ''Purple Rain'' star needed a purple 12-string instrument made for recording and video use, and Taylor built him one of its 655 series models in that color. Though Prince specified that it could not feature Taylor's logo, the news got around among guitar connoisseurs, which led to more orders for the company's high-end Artists Series instruments. Custom Taylors were subsequently built for Bonnie Raitt and Billy Idol, among others. The company's guitars were owned by a growing list of famous performers, including Neil Young, James Burton, and John Fogerty. By 1985, Taylor was grossing an estimated $400,000 annually and had 11 employees. Its instruments were now sold at 130 retail outlets around the United States.

The company was building its guitars mainly for the high end of the market, with most instruments priced between $800 and $2000, and specially built custom models costing as much as $4,500. With production beginning to increase rapidly, the firm announced plans to add a $600 mid-price line as well. In 1986, the company also introduced its first Signature Model, named for flatpicking guitarist Dan Crary.

### *Move to Larger Quarters in 1987*

In 1987, Taylor's growing success led it to move to a new 5,000-square-foot facility in Santee, California. The company's staff now numbered 35 and was producing 50 guitars per week. The following year saw revenues top $1 million for the first time. In 1989, Taylor bought its first computer-assisted manufacturing equipment, which allowed for greater precision in milling wood and more consistent quality across the product line. The machines also reduced costs and increased output. At the same time, the firm began making cases for its guitars in-house. The arch-topped cases, priced at $200, were made of poplar that was covered with vinyl, and lined with velvet. They replaced the generic models Taylor had previously outsourced; they also fit the guitars better while providing more protection. In 1990, a second Signature model bearing the name of Leo Kottke was introduced, this time a 12-string instrument.

July 1992 saw Taylor move to larger quarters yet again, with a new 25,000-square-foot facility in El Cajon becoming a combined headquarters and manufacturing site. The company's growth continued to be strong, and in 1993 it had an estimated $5 million in revenues. Eighty workers were employed by the firm, which was nearing production of 10,000 guitars per year. 350 U.S. dealers and 20 foreign distributors carried the Taylor line. The company's legion of well-known owners now included Eric Clapton, Bruce Springsteen, and Paul McCartney.

By this time, interest in the acoustic guitar had rebounded dramatically, due in part to the ''Unplugged'' phenomenon launched by MTV, which had spawned a best-selling Clapton album of acoustic versions of his hits. Technology also played a role, with improved electronics enabling the amplification of acoustic guitars in live rock band settings while preserving much of their natural sound and significantly reducing the troublesome feedback and distortion that was previously unavoidable when a hollow-body guitar was amplified either by external microphones or pickups mounted on the instrument. Taylor continued to seek new manufacturing solutions and 1994 saw the purchase of a special fretboard sanding machine and an ultraviolet finishing system, which cut the time required to varnish a guitar from several weeks to a single day. Sales continued to soar, rising 52 percent during the year.

### *''Baby Taylor'' Introduced in 1996*

In 1996, the company brought out a scaled-down guitar, the Baby Taylor, which was priced at less than $500. The three-quarter sized instrument was aimed at guitarists who wanted portability, such as backpackers or frequent travelers, as well as beginning musicians. It sold over 1,000 units during the year. A new full-size guitar, the ''Grand Auditorium'' model, was also added to the company's regular line, and it was pronounced by Bob Taylor ''the best we've ever made.'' Many customers and critics agreed. Taylor began offering branded clothing and accessories during 1996 as well. Sales for the year hit a record total of $20 million.

In January 1997, a custom Taylor guitar was presented to President Bill Clinton at the Arkansas Inaugural Ball in Washington. The so-called ''Presidential Guitar'' featured extensive mother-of-pearl inlays that depicted the Inaugural Seal and Inaugural Ceremonial Ribbon, as well as the names of Clinton and his home town of Hope. It was presented to him for Taylor by guitarist David Pack, who had been a featured performer at the event and had gotten the idea of making it for him.

In October 1997, the company built a special limited edition ''Cujo'' guitar in conjunction with author and semi-professional guitarist Stephen King, whose novel of the same name inspired the instrument. Wood for the guitar came from a black walnut tree that had been featured in the 1983 movie version of the book. A run of 250 of the instruments was produced, each of them with ''dog tag'' labels hand-signed by King. The guitars sold out in five days. By this time, Taylor had 190 employees and was shipping 100 guitars per day to more than 600 U.S. dealers and international distributors. The firm had an order backlog of one year.

In 1998 Taylor's guitars were celebrated on an album called ''Sounds of Wood and Steel,'' which featured celebrity guitarists—including Clint Black, Amy Grant, Vince Gill, Michael

## Key Dates:

**1974:** Bob Taylor and two partners buy a music store and begin making guitars.
**1977:** The firm begins distributing through an outside firm, but profits are small.
**1981:** New manufacturing equipment is purchased to increase production.
**1983:** Bob Taylor and cofounder/CEO Kurt Listug buy out their third partner's stake in the firm.
**1987:** The growing firm moves to a new 5,000-square-foot factory.
**1989:** Company buys its first computer-assisted manufacturing equipment.
**1992:** The company moves to a larger site in El Cajon, California.
**1996:** New three-quarter size "Baby Taylor" debuts.
**1999:** "New-Tech" neck design is introduced and wins accolades for innovation.
**2002:** A run of 400 Liberty Tree guitars, made from a historic tree, sells out on release.

Hedges, and Leo Kottke—all playing their favorite Taylor instruments. The CD sold well and was later followed by a second volume. The albums were great publicity, and the company itself produced a quarterly newsletter and sponsored guitar clinics at shops around the country which were conducted by respected musicians like Doyle Dykes, Chris Proctor, and Artie Traum. Tours of the company's factory were offered as well.

During 1998, the company constructed a new 44,000-square-foot factory adjacent to its existing plant in El Cajon, which would house most manufacturing operations as well as the offices of its administrative, advertising, and financial departments. The older facility would be used for final assembly and finishing as well as hosting the firm's research and development and sales offices.

### *"NT Neck" Debuts in 1999*

In 1999, Taylor introduced another technical innovation, a new neck design that was made possible by the greater cutting precision of computerized manufacturing equipment. The joint where the guitar neck was attached to the body had always presented problems for musicians wanting to adjust it to a different tension setting for playability, since the frets on the part of the neck away from the guitar's body and those that extended onto the body would go out of alignment, which adversely affected the fingering on each part of the fretboard. Taylor's NT ("New Tech") neck system united the previously separate elements so that string tension remained consistent on both. The NT design was a hit with guitarists and was later named "Product of the Year" by Music Trades magazine. Bob Taylor subsequently received a patent for the technology.

A survey of Taylor owners at this time found the majority to be married homeowners between the ages of 35 and 49 with household income of nearly $70,000. Ninety-seven percent were male, and most played the guitar daily for an hour or more. Many owned more than one instrument, including both acoustic and electric models. A typical Taylor guitar buyer was a "baby boomer" who had become interested in music during his formative years in the 1960s, then gotten away from playing until financial success allowed him the luxury of purchasing a high-end instrument.

In 2000, Taylor laid plans for another limited edition guitar, the Liberty Tree model. Much of its wood came from a 400-year-old tulip poplar, the last remaining "Liberty Tree" from the 13 original U.S. colonies. One tree in each colony had been given this name through its use as a gathering place where patriots plotted the American Revolution. Over the years all save the one in Maryland had been lost, but in September of 1999 Hurricane Floyd fatally damaged that tree as well. Some of the wood was cut up and distributed as mementos to the staff at St. John's College in Annapolis, where the tree had stood, but most was trucked to landfills. Mark Mehnert, a local landscaper, spent $70,000 to acquire the wood after discovering its fate by accident. A Taylor dealer in Baltimore who heard the story contacted the company, which was able to acquire the remnants of the tree, paying $78,000 for it and shipping it cross-country in a refrigerated truck. In addition to using it in the guitars, 14 seedlings were generated for planting in each of the 13 founding colonies and at the United States Botanic Garden in Washington, D.C.

The year 2000 also saw Taylor adding to its Signature line with new models signed by Clint Black, Kenny Loggins, Doyle Dykes, Jewel, and several others, and launching its first mass-market advertising campaign with an ad in *Rolling Stone* magazine. Taylor guitars remained popular, with 40,000 now made per year by the firm's 325 employees, up from annual production of 6,000 just seven years earlier. A new model introduced during the year was the "Big Baby," a 15/16 size model that was priced to appeal to guitar students. By now Taylor was offering more than 60 different models of acoustic guitars ranging in price from $1,248 to $10,494, with the Baby Taylor just $348. They were sold by more than 800 dealers in the United States and Canada and by 13 foreign distributors internationally. The year 2000 also saw the company start a program called Taylor Guitars for Schools to donate Baby Taylors to San Diego area elementary schools. During the first year the company gave away 240 instruments.

In 2001, Taylor installed an "acoustic room" at its factory, a specially-designed space that was used to analyze the sound of its guitars in a live performance setting. The room was also used for concerts and special events. In April 2002, Taylor's Liberty Tree guitars went on sale. The limited edition run of 400 instruments, priced at more than $6,000 each, sold out immediately.

After more than a quarter-century in business, Taylor Guitars had become one of the best-known makers of acoustic guitars in the world. Esteemed for their quality and technical innovation, the company's instruments were played by many famous musicians, as well as thousands of others who prized their clear tone and ease of use.

### *Principal Competitors*

C.F. Martin & Co., Inc.; Gibson Musical Instruments; Jean Larrivee Guitars Ltd.; Takamine Company; Alvarez Guitars.

### *Further Reading*

''CAM Inspires Guitar Innovation,'' *Wood & Wood Products*, November 1, 2000, p. 47.

Green, Frank, ''Taylor's Acoustic Guitars Find Hollow Praised,'' *The San Diego Union-Tribune*, June 27, 2000, p. C1.

Johnson, Greg, ''Taylor-Made Guitars,'' *Los Angeles Times*, June 16, 1985, p. 4.

Listug, Kurt, ''Why Acoustic Sales Will Continue to Grow,'' *Music Trades*, October 1, 1999, p. 98.

Mizejewski, Gerald, ''Liberty Tree Set to Make Music,'' *Washington Times*, June 13, 2000, p. C1.

''Pres. Clinton Raves About New Taylor Guitar,'' *Music Trades*, April 1, 1997, p. 26.

''Taylor Guitars Buys Wood From Last 'Liberty Tree','' *Music Trades*, September 1, 2000, p. 40.

''Taylor Opens the Perfect Acoustic Room,'' *Music Trades*, January 1, 2002, p. 74.

Whitley, Sharon, ''Taylor-Made,'' *Los Angeles Times*, June 13, 1993, p. 8.

Zuniga, Janine, ''Guitar Gift Boosts School Music,'' *San Diego Union-Tribune*, November 10, 2001, p. B5.

—Frank Uhle

# The Terlato Wine Group

**900 Armour Drive**
**Lake Bluff, Illinois 60044**
**U.S.A.**
**Telephone: (847) 604-8900**
**Fax: (847) 604-5829**
**Web site: http://www.terlatowinegroup.com**

*Private Company*
*Incorporated:* 1981 as International Products Corporation
*Employees:* 631
*Sales:* $260 million (2000)
*NAIC:* 422820 Wine and Distilled Alcoholic Beverage Wholesalers

The Terlato Wine Group, operating out of the Chicago suburb of Lake Bluff, Illinois, is a privately-owned holding company for 13 independent companies that are vertically integrated in the premium wine business. Terlato is owned and operated by the Terlato family, headed by its chairman and CEO Anthony J. Terlato, who is joined by his sons, William, president and chief operating officer, and John, senior vice-president. For decades, the family concentrated on importing and marketing quality wines, primarily catering to restaurants and upscale wine shops. The company developed an international presence, and in recent years has expanded its reach to include wine production and international marketing.

## *Origins of the Group in the 1940s*

Anthony Terlato formed the International Products Corporation in 1981, but the original parent company of what would become the Terlato Wine Group was Pacific Wine Company, originally owned by the founder's future father-in-law, Anthony Paterno. In 1946, Paterno was an importer of olive oil and other Italian food products when he acquired Pacific Wine Company, a Chicago bottler of California wines under a number of labels, one of which was Pacific Wine. Terlato's father, Salvatore, was a friend of Paterno and owned a northside Chicago wine shop. At the age of 20, Terlato already had considerable retail experience in the wine business when Paterno persuaded him in 1955 to take a job as a sales rep at Pacific Wine. The company, one of 35 area bottlers of wine, imported bulk wines from Gallo and the Charles Krug Winery for sale in local stores but faced a formidable challenge after Italian Swiss Colony began bottling and marketing its Roma wines. Terlato was instrumental in Pacific Wine changing its business from bottling to the distribution of premium wines, primarily to the restaurant market. He established Charles Krug Mondavi despite the price disadvantage of the wine being bottled in California. In the process, Terlato showed an innovative spirit, convincing restaurants to carry just one Charles Krug wine in exchange for free wine list printing and staff training. CK Mondavi also became the most expensive gallon wine in Chicago wine stores. Pacific Wine then introduced imported wines. Bolla Veronese Wines, Lancers, Blue Nun, and Mateus all became major successes that firmly established the company's restaurant trade.

In 1959, it was Terlato's chance meeting of Alexis Lichine, a major importer of French wines, that resulted in Pacific Wine distributing his products. The bottle operations were closed down and the company added Roederer Champagne to its portfolio, as well as premium burgundies and classified French Bordeaux. Pacific Wine was still very much an Illinois distributor, but that situation would begin to change in 1961 after Terlato discovered a dessert wine with an almond flavor, forerunner to Amaretto, which he named Sicilian Gold. In order to nationally distribute the product, he and his father-in-law created Paterno Imports. While his father-in-law assumed responsibility for Paterno, Terlato acted as president of Pacific Wine, although he was clearly destined to inherit control of the growing family empire.

Paterno's success with Sicilian Gold opened the door to other major imported wines, including Vittorio Gancia's famous Asti Spumante. One of the company's greatest successes was a personal discovery on the part of Terlato. In 1972, he was dining in a Rome restaurant, seated near a door leading to a terrace, and noticed that waiters were passing by with a large number of bottles bearing a distinctive green labels. Learning that the wine in question was named Corvo, he ordered a bottle. In a 1990 profile in *The Wine Spectator,* Terlato recalled, "We

## Company Perspectives:

*For more than 40 years, The Terlato Wine Group has dedicated itself to a simple philosophy—"place quality first." Adhering to this principle has helped Terlato Wine Group achieve a scope unmatched in the wine industry.*

lingered, and the glasses emptied, and he [the waiter] filled them up. Before I knew it, we had drunk three bottles. I went straight to Sicily and arranged to import it to America." Before being represented by Paterno Imports, Corvo's U.S. sales were less than 1,000 cases a year. Within seven years the number grew to more than 250,000 cases.

### *Anthony Terlato Becomes Head of Paterno Imports in 1977*

With the death of Anthony Paterno in 1977, Terlato succeeded his father-in-law as the head of Paterno Imports. Two years later it would be another one of his discoveries that became a turning point in the fortunes of the family wine interests. On a trip to Italy in search of a product that could replace the popular white wines of the day, Terlato visited a neighborhood restaurant in the small town of Portogruaro. He ordered every kind of Pinot Grigio on the establishment's wine list, some 18 bottles in all, with the wine of Santa Margherita proving exceptional. He visited the winery the next day and arranged to introduce its Pinot Grigio to America. A marketing campaign for Santa Margherita was launched in 1980, ultimately making it the most successful imported wine in history priced over $15.

In 1981, Terlato created International Products as a holding company for the family burgeoning wine businesses. During the next decade, several Illinois wine distributing companies would be added to the fold, which resulted in complete statewide coverage. At the same time, Paterno Imports grew into a full-service marketing company with an international reach. Beginning to help Terlato during this period were his sons. After graduating from Loyola University in 1981, William Terlato joined the family business, becoming Paterno's national sales manager in 1985, vice-president of the company in 1988, and president in 1994 at the age of 35. John Terlato also attended Loyola University, then went to John Marshall Law School and Harvard Business School, and worked for Caldwell Banker for two years before going to work for Pacific Wine. He became president of the company in 1995, also at the age of 35.

Despite continued success in the 1980s, International Products also faced challenges. Some Italian wines were discovered to be tainted with glycol, prompting Terlato to turn to California for new sources of premium wines. Moreover, economic conditions led to a significant decrease in the U.S. consumption of Italian wines. Early in the decade, Italian wines increased in price as a result of strong vintages but never receded after the results were not as strong. Moreover, due to the declining value of the dollar against European currencies, many of the Italian wines in the company's portfolio became even more expensive. As a result, demand for Italian wines plummeted. Despite maintaining a profitable business, International Products was too dependent on European imports, which accounted for over 92 percent of its business, and began an effort to diversify.

While competitors were looking for a California Cabernet to promote, Terlato opted for Pinot Noit and discovered a Sonoma Valley boutique winery named Rochioli, which became the first U.S. marketing client for Paterno Imports. Deals then followed with Napa Valley's Markham Winery and Freemark Abbey, both troubled brands that Terlato successfully turned around. As a result of these domestic marketing efforts, International Products was beginning to position itself as a beverage company, albeit one that concentrated on quality products. In 1992, it added two companies to better realize this expansive vision. Vintage Wine Co. was created to provide marketing support for premium wines with yearly sales of less than 25,000 cases. In addition to California wines Rochioli and Jaeger Inglewood, the Vintage family of wines included offerings from Italy, France, Germany, Mexico, and Chile.

### *New Corporate Headquarters in 1995*

International Products became one of the most profitable and influential importers and marketers of premier wines, due in large part to Anthony Terlato's commitment to quality. Accordingly, the company's motto, "Quality is a way of life," was more than just a phrase. With the launch of a new wine, customers would be picked up in limousines and brought to International Products headquarters for a sampling. When the standard cheese and bread accompanying the wine became too predictable, Terlato began to offer meals, many of which he cooked himself. Ultimately the company created some 300 recipes, and a chance to dine at International Products became a coveted invitation. To provide a more luxurious setting for these meals and further enhance the spirit of quality, in 1995 International Products purchased Tangley Oaks, a Tudor Gothic mansion to serve as it corporate headquarters. It was originally commissioned in 1916 by meat packing heir Philip D. Armour and his wife, and took 16 years to design, build, detail, and furnish. Tangley Oaks served as Armour's home from 1932 until 1953, when it was sold and became the headquarters of United Educators, Inc., a publishing house. Terlato commissioned a two-year restoration of the core of the manor, as well as the addition of a state-of-the-art gourmet kitchen to provide the kind of meals that the company's guests had come to expect from International Products.

In the same year it purchased a new corporate home, International Products took a significant step in achieving vertical integration in the premium wine business by becoming directly involved in the production side. It entered into a joint venture with Japan's Mercian Corporation, owners of Markham Vineyards. International Products had successfully sold Markham wine and was instrumental in convincing the winery to drop the Vinmark label, a conventional name it applied to some excess wine, in favor of developing a new wine, Glass Mountain. The two parties agreed to create a joint venture, with International Products providing the financial resources and marketing expertise and Markham producing the wine, in order to create a high-quality brand in the $14 per bottle range. In 1996, International Products acquired Napa Valley's Rutherford Hill Winery, another brand it already represented and famed as the first winery

## Key Dates:

**1946:** Anthony Paterno acquires Pacific Wine Company, a Chicago wine bottler.
**1955:** Paterno's son-in-law Anthony J. Terlato joins the business and is instrumental in changing its focus to distribution of quality wines.
**1961:** Paterno Imports is established.
**1977:** Paterno dies, and Terlato assumes control of the businesses.
**1981:** International Products Corporation is formed as a holding company for the family's wine interests.
**1995:** Tangley Oaks mansion is acquired to be used as corporate headquarters.
**1996:** Rutherford Hill winery is acquired.
**2000:** International Products changes name to The Terlato Wine Group.

to focus on Merlot. Terlato quickly took steps to make quality the top priority of Rutherford Hill. Inferior lots were cut, reducing overall production by 14,000, and production facilities were greatly improved, as were the public areas for tourists.

In 2000, International Products officially changed its name to Terlato Wine Group. The business had grown consistently under Anthony Terlato's leadership, doubling annual sales every five years for the past three decades until it was now estimated to total $250 million. Although Terlato and his sons, who were increasingly more responsible for expansion, were confident that they could continue the pace, the family business faced some obstacles. The California wine industry was undergoing a period of consolidation and prime vineyard land was becoming extremely expensive, in some cases priced in excess of $100,000 an acre. In March 2000, Terlato turned to Australia, where prime growing land could be purchased at less than a tenth the price. It entered into a joint venture with Michel Chapoutier of the Rhone Valley and Trevor Mast of Mount Langi Ghiran to purchase 475 acres in Western Victoria in Australia. The venture also held an option to purchase an additional 500 acres on a neighboring property. Initial results from the Australia plantings were not expected until 2006.

Terlato also became involved in the heated California market in 2000, acquiring a 50 percent stake in Chimney Rock Winery with an option to purchase the remaining half. The deal also included a nine-hole golf course owned by the vineyard, which would be closed and converted to vineyards. To some observers, Chimney Rock, with just $3.5 million in annual sales, was a surprising choice, but Anthony Terlato believed that the winery produced the best ''undermarketed'' Cabernets. He was also impressed with Chimney Rock's winemaker, Doug Fletcher, who boasted 25 years of experience after receiving a biology degree from the University of Oregon and had been with Chimney Rock since 1987. Not only did he possess technical sophistication, he shared the Terlato commitment to producing wines of global quality. In December 2001, Fletcher was named to the new position of Director of Winemaking for Terlato.

In 2001, Terlato was active on a number of fronts. To support both Chimney Rock and Rutherford Hill it purchased an additional 60 vineyard acres in Rutherford. Terlato also purchased a majority interest in Alderbrook Vineyards and Winery in Sonoma County, California. In November 2001, the company announced the formation of what it called a ''super-premium wine distribution company,'' aptly named Cream Wine Company, an Illinois distribution business. The focus of the venture was to discover, launch, and hand-sell distinctive, high quality wines from artisan wine producers in Australia, Spain, Portugal, New Zealand, Germany, South American, as well as California, the Pacific Northwest and other emerging wine growing areas around the world.

Although there was some speculation that Terlato might go public, the Terlato family seemed well positioned to continue to finance the company's growth and were clearly reluctant to take on pressure from shareholders with short-term goals. In addition, talk of selling the business appear unfounded. The family seemed content to run its diverse wine interests, answering to no one and following only their personal vision of quality.

### *Principal Subsidiaries*

Paterno Wines International; Pacific/Southern Wine & Spirits; Rutherford Hill Winery; Chimney Rock Winery; Cream Wine Company.

### *Principal Competitors*

Beringer Blass Wine Estates; Kendall-Jackson Wine Estates Ltd.; National Distributing Company Inc.; Southern Wine & Spirits of America, Inc.; Robert Mondavi Corporation; E. & J. Gallo Winery.

### *Further Reading*


Crown, Judith, ''Paterno Imports Uncorks U.S. Wine Deal,'' *Crain's Chicago Business,* December 7, 1992, p. 3.

Franson, Paul, ''Tony Terlato Jumps the Fence,'' *Wine Business Monthly,* September 2001.

Levandoski, Robert C., ''Paterno Reinvents the Role of the Importer,'' *Beverage Industry,* May 1993, p. 42.

Matthews, Thomas, ''Making a Business of Wine-and-Food Pleasure,'' *Wine Spectator,* May 15, 1990.

Morse, Julie, ''Business NOT as Usual,'' *Chicago Tribune,* October 8, 1995, Section 17, p. 1.

Murphy, H. Lee, ''Wine Firm Uncorks a Vintage Strategy,'' *Crain's Chicago Business,* September 18, 2000.


—Ed Dinger

# Terumo Corporation

44-1, 2-chome Hatagaya, Shibuya-ku
Tokyo 151-0072
Japan
Telephone: (+81) 3-3374-8111
Fax: (+81) 3-3374-8399
Web site: http://www.terumo.co.jp

*Public Company*
*Incorporated:* 1921
*Employees:* 7,412
*Sales:* ¥176.05 billion ($1.39 billion)(2001)
*Stock Exchanges:* Tokyo
*Ticker Symbol:* 4543
*NAIC:* 339112 Surgical and Medical Instrument Manufacturing; 339113 Surgical Appliance and Supplies Manufacturing; 339113 Surgical Appliance and Supplies Manufacturing; 334510 Electromedical and Electrotherapeutic Apparatus Manufacturing

Based in Tokyo, Terumo Corporation is Japan's largest manufacturer of medical supplies. The company is also active worldwide, with subsidiaries and manufacturing facilities in the United States, Belgium, Germany, the United Kingdom, India, the Philippines, and China and nearly 70 sales offices worldwide, including 38 office in Japan and 28 sales offices internationally. Terumo manufacturers and distributes a wide range of medical products, equipment, and supplies: drip-feed and enteral nutriment supplements and delivery systems; disposable medical equipment, including syringes, drainage tubes, and dressings; blood collection and processing equipment; angiography and other catheters; dialysis equipment and supplies; cardiopulmonary equipment; blood glucose monitors; hospital-grade medical electronic products; and home medical supplies and instruments such as thermometers, the company's first product. Terumo also acts as a Japanese distributor for third-party products. Pharmaceutical products account for 23 percent and the largest share of Terumo's sales, which topped ¥176 billion ($1.39 billion) in 2001. Catheter systems represented 20.5 percent of sales. Terumo targeted the cardiovascular systems segment as its main growth segment at the beginning of the new century. In 1999, the company acquired the CardioVascular Systems division of the 3M Co., a move that helped it strengthen its position in that worldwide market. Terumo is listed on the Tokyo Stock Exchange and is led by chairman and CEO Takashi Wachi.

## *Founding and Growth: 1920s–60s*

In 1921, a group of physicians and medical scientists joined together to form the Sekisen Ken-onki Corporation in order to develop a newer and more reliable clinical thermometer. Leading the group was famed Japanese medical researcher Dr. Shibasaburo Kitazato, who had graduated from the University of Tokyo's medical school before continuing his studies in Germany under researcher Robert Koch. Kitazato also collaborated with Emil von Behring, and in 1890 the two men became credited with discovering antitoxins for tetanus and diphtheria. Their work led to the development of antitoxin treatments for a variety of diseases. After returning to Japan, Kitazato was named director of the country's Institute of Infectious Diseases. In 1894, Kitazato succeeded in identifying the bacteria causing bubonic plague, and at the end of the decade identified the dysentery virus. In 1914, Kitazato was named dean of the Keio University medical school in Tokyo.

Kitazato's presence among the founding members of the Sekisen Ken-onki Corporation helped the young company quickly gain credibility in the Japanese medical market. In 1922, the company released its first thermometer, the Jintan Taionkei, the first in a line of Jintan-branded thermometers. The success of that product led the company to change its name in 1936 to Jintan Taionkei Co., which became the leading manufacturer and distributor of clinical thermometers to the Japanese market.

Following World War II, Jintan Taionkei continued developing its core thermometer line. In 1954, the company developed a new method of producing its thermometers using a vacuum filling technique. The resulting thermometer helped the company further strengthen its leadership position in Japan. Jintan Taionkei had also begun to diversify its product line,

**Company Perspectives:**

*TERUMO Values*—Contributing to Society Through Healthcare: *We contribute to society by providing valued products and services in the healthcare market and by responding to the needs of healthcare providers and the people they serve.* Open Management: *We maintain a fundamental policy of open management, work to secure and return to our benefactors a suitable profit, and strive to develop our business on a global basis as befits a leading company in the industry.* Enhanced Value: *We emphasize the importance of scientific thinking, creativity, and time appropriation, and respond in depth to customer needs by creating valued products and services.* Safety and Reliability: *We pride ourselves on our commitment to the development of technologies and quality assurance systems that ensure safe, reliable products.* Respect for our Associates: *We emphasize respect for the individual, promote intercultural understanding, and encourage openness in the workplace in accordance with our slogan ''Associate Spirit'' as we prepare to meet the challenges of the future.* Corporate Citizenship: *We conduct our business activities in a fair and equitable manner and act responsibly toward the environment as we fulfill our responsibilities as good corporate citizens.*

entering the broader clinical medical supplies market. In 1963, the company launched a new product—a disposable syringe, the first to become available in Japan—and soon after was making a number of disposable medical instruments.

At the end of 1963, the company change its name again and became Jintan Terumo Co. Ltd. The following year, Jintan Terumo scored another first in Japan when it introduced disposable hypodermic needles to the domestic market. During the same year, the company began selling a line of vacuum blood tubes for use in blood sampling. At the end of the 1960s, Jintan Terumo added another branch to its clinical supplies operations when in 1969 it launched a line of blood bags, once again a new product for the Japanese market and one that helped strengthen the country's blood supply network.

### *Diversified International Medical Supplier: 1970s–80s*

Jintan Terumo turned to the international market in the early 1970s. In 1971, the company launched two new subsidiaries, Terumo America (later renamed Terumo Medical Corporation) in New Jersey and Terumo Europe in Belgium. Terumo Corporation, as the company was renamed in 1974, supported its international and domestic expansion with the release of new products and the entry into new product categories. Such was the case in 1973, when the company began manufacturing and distributing its own line of catheters and urine bags. That same year, Terumo began producing intravenous solutions in soft plastic bags, another first for the Japanese market, enabling the company to take a leading share of the country's intravenous medicinal solutions market. The company continued to develop its soft bag delivery business, and in 1980 released the first soft-bag nutrient solutions line for the Japanese market.

During the 1970s, Terumo had begun developing hollow fiber technologies that were to help it impose itself on the international market. In 1977, the company released its first generation of hollow fiber dialyzers, a product that enabled it to enter the market for the manufacturing of artificial organs. In 1982, the company's continued development of its hollow fiber technology enabled it to present another breakthrough, a hollow-fiber oxygenator. Called the Capiox II, the new product was the world's first available hollow-fiber oxygenator and helped establish Terumo as a major medical products innovator.

The company's innovations continued through the 1980s. In 1983, the company released a ''predictive'' digital clinical thermometer. The following year, Terumo ended production of its mercury-based thermometers as it shifted to using other materials and technologies, such as the development of infrared-based thermometers. Then, in 1985, Terumo entered a new product category, unveiling the first of its diagnostic and surgical intervention catheter products, the Radifocus guidewire for angiography. The company's catheter operations were to grow into one of its key revenue producers.

While much of the company's product development remained targeted at the clinical medical market, Terumo entered the home medical products market toward the end of the 1980s. In 1988, the company released two such home medical products, an automated peritoneal dialysis system and a digital blood-pressure monitor. The following year, the company boosted its research and development operations with the opening of a new facility, the Shonan Center, in Nakai-machi, Kanagawa.

### *Medical Products Leader: 1990s and Beyond*

Terumo remained Japan's leading supplier of medical products in the 1990s, with four production facilities in addition to its new research and development center. The company was also making inroads into the international markets, opening 28 branch offices in addition to its foreign subsidiaries and extending its product reach to some 150 countries by the end of the decade. Terumo's growing business in other Asian markets led it to move closer to these markets in the mid-1990s.

In 1995, Terumo opened its first Chinese subsidiary, in Hangzhou City, which took over manufacturing of a number of Terumo's products for the Japanese market. A second Chinese subsidiary was created the following year, in Changchun City, as the company stepped up its exports to the broader Asian market. Meanwhile, in 1997, Terumo launched a new subsidiary and manufacturing facility in the United Kingdom which began production of blood lines for the company's oxygenator products. At the same time, the company began targeting the central and eastern European market for further growth, opening a branch office in Vienna, Austria, that took over responsibility for the company's marketing and sales in that country as well as in Hungary, Slovakia, the Czech Republic, and Switzerland.

In the second half of the 1990s, Terumo continued moving closer to its international markets. In 1997, the company began exporting its manufacturing processes, bringing its oxygenator manufacturing technology over to its Terumo Medical Corporation subsidiary in the United States. That same year, Terumo's

## Key Dates:

**1921:** Dr. Shibasaburo Kitazato leads a group of physicians and medical scientists who form the Sekisen Ken-onki Corporation in order to develop a newer and more reliable clinical thermometer.
**1922:** The company's first clinical thermometer, the Jintan Taionkei, is launched.
**1936:** The company changes its name to Jintan Taionkei Co.
**1954:** The company develops vacuum mercury filling technology for its clinical thermometers.
**1963:** The first disposable syringes are launched; the company changes its name to Jintan Terumo.
**1971:** Subsidiaries Terumo America (later Terumo Medical Corporation) and Terumo Europe are established.
**1974:** The company changes its name to Terumo Corporation.
**1982:** The first hollow-fiber oxygenator is launched.
**1999:** Terumo acquires CardioVascular Systems operations from the 3M Co.
**2001:** The company forms a marketing agreement for a new line of prefilled syringes with Tanabe Pharmaceuticals.
**2002:** Terumo reaches a distribution agreement for portable dialysis pump with Switzerland's Disetronic Group.

European operations were boosted with new technology, leading to the creation in Belgium of both a new facility for production of the Radifocus catheter systems range and, in 1998, the launch of production capacity for the company's sterile tubing products. In the United States, Terumo's Elkton, Maryland, plant had become a state-of-the-art, $100 million facility with nearly 500,00 square feet of production space on an 88-acre site.

In Japan, the company's manufacturing park was also evolving, including the combining of its production operations from two plants into a single, new 200,000-square-feet facility in Nakakoma-gun, where such products as syringes and syringe needles, urinary test paper, and topical medications were produced. That facility began operations in 1998. The following year, Terumo stepped into the Indian market, acquiring 74 percent of that country's Peninsula Polymerts Ltd., which was then renamed Terumo Penpol. That company produced blood bags for India and other markets.

A major step forward in Terumo's international ambitions took place in 1999 when it acquired the CardioVascular Systems operations from the 3M Co. The purchase gave Terumo operations amounting to $100 million per year and strengthened the company's interests in the cardiovascular products market, which became a key company target area at the turn of the century. The 3M operations were combined with Terumo's existing business to created a new subsidiary, Terumo Cardiovascular Systems Corporation. The company also launched two new products lines in 1999: coronary stents, the first to be manufactured in Japan, and two lines of prefilled syringes, a market that appeared certain to grow strongly in the coming years.

Terumo continued to expand its operations as it celebrated its 80th anniversary. In 2000, Terumo opened its newest production facility, in the Philippines, in order to produce syringes and other products to meet the surge in demand in the southeast Asian market. The company also doubled the size of its Hangzhou, China, facility. In 2001, the company reached an agreement with fellow Japanese company Tanabe Pharmaceuticals to launch and market a line of prefilled atropine sulfate syringes. Later that year, the company reached an agreement with Switzerland's Disetronic group to act as exclusive Japanese distributor for Diesetronic's portable insulin pump products. Terumo continued to take steps to increase its position in the worldwide market, including the establishment in May 2002 of a dedicated sales and marketing subsidiary for its South and Central American operations. Terumo had earned itself a place as an important player in the worldwide medical supplies market.

### *Principal Subsidiaries*

Terumo Europe N.V. (Belgium); Laboratoires Terumo France S.A.; Terumo (Deutschland) Gmbh (Germany); Terumo Cardiovascular Systems Europe Gmbh (Germany); Terumo Medical Corporation (U.S.); Terumo Latin America Corporation; Terumo Medical De Mexico S.A. de C.V.; Terumo Medical Do Brasil Ltda (Brazil); Terumo Cardiovascular Systems Corporation (U.S.); Terumo (Thailand) Co., Ltd.; Terumo Marketing Philippines, Inc.; Terumo Medical Products(Hangzhou) Co. Ltd. (China); Changchun Terumo Medical Products Co. Ltd. (China); Terumo (Philippines) Corporation; Terumo Penpol Ltd. (India).

### *Principal Competitors*

Eli Lilly and Co.; Siemens AG; RWE AG; Royal Philips Electronics NV; Abbott Laboratories; Wyeth; Asahi Kasai Corporation; Baxter International Inc.; Smiths Group plc (SHIN); GE Medical Systems; Medtronic Inc.; Fresenius AG; BOC Group plc; Allegiance Corporation; Baxter International Inc.; DAIICHI PHARMACEUTICAL CO., LTD.; Eisai Company, Ltd.; Johnson & Johnson; Owens & Minor, Inc.; Takeda Chemical Industries, Ltd.

### *Further Reading*

Feyder, Susan, "3M to Sell Heart Unit to Firm in Japan," *Minneapolis StarTribune*, April 16, 1999, p. 1D.
Fitzpatrick, Michael, "Japanese Micro Lifesaver Travels Down Blood Vessels," *Daily Telegraph*, December 11, 1999.
"Japanese Medical Suppliers: Under the Knife," *Economist*, September 13, 1997.
"Japan's Terumo to Make Syringes in the Philippines," *AsiaPulse News*, June 8, 2000, p. 56.

—M.L. Cohen

# Tiscali SpA

Viale Trento 39
Cagliari I-09123
Italy
Telephone: (+39) 07046011
Fax: (+39) 0704601400
Web site: http://www.tiscali.it

*Public Company*
*Incorporated:* 1997 as Telefonica della Sardegna
*Employees:* 3,082
*Sales:* EUR 635.7 million ($508.5 million)(2001)
*Stock Exchanges:* Italian
*Ticker Symbol:* TIS
*NAIC:* 51331 Wired Telecommunications Carriers

Italy's Tiscali SpA is leading the race for dominance of the European Internet access market. Founded in 1997, Tiscali has propelled itself to the top ranks, battling it out with Deutsche Telecom subsidiary T-Online for the top spot. At the beginning of 2002, Tiscali claimed the lead, boasting more than 16 million subscribers, including more than seven million active subscribers in 13 countries across Europe. Tiscali claimed a 16 percent share of the total market in 2001. In the major individual European markets, Tiscali ranks third in Italy, second in France and the Benelux markets, and fourth in Germany and the United Kingdom. Some 64 percent of the company's annual sales of EUR 635 million in 2001 were access revenues, that is, kickbacks from telephone companies from subscriber telephone charges (in most European countries, local telephone access is metered). In some markets, such as Italy, Tiscali receives as much as 50 percent of a subscriber's Internet access phone charges. Business-to-business services represents the next largest chunk of Tiscali's revenues, at 13 percent; portal revenues, generated through e-commerce and online advertising, accounts for 10 percent of the company's sales. Voice services—including Internet-based long-distance calls—reached 37 percent of sales in 2000, then dropped to just 9 percent of sales in 2001. After a long series of acquisitions, including the 2000 purchase of the Netherlands' World Online and the 2001 acquisition of France's Libertysurf, Tiscali is taking a break in its external growth to restructure its holdings and rebrand its entire network under the Tiscali name. The company, which trades on the Italian Stock Exchange, is led by founder, chairman, and CEO Renato Soru, whose 37 percent stake in the company, at times valued at more than EUR 14 billion, has made him one of Italy's richest individuals.

## *Internet Visionary in the 1990s*

Few people would have bet that the future of Europe's Internet business was to come from the economic backwater of Italy's Sardinia. Yet there was some precedent: the island boasted the CRS4 institute, set up in 1990 to study the Internet and the computer industry, which became the first web site registered with the ".it" (signifying Italy) suffix. Sardinian newspaper *Union Sarda* went online in 1994, making it one of the first newspapers in Europe to launch its own web site. Yet Sardinia, where unemployment rates doubled the mainland average, remained, as Renato Soru told *Newsweek,* "closer to Africa than Milan."

A native of Sanluri, Sardinia, Soru's mother had run a grocery store while his father worked as a school administrator. Soru went to study at Milan's Bocconi University and planned to become an economics professor. When his father died when Soru was 20 years old, however, Soru began shuttling back and forth between school and home in order to help out at the family store. He brought to the business a concept that had not yet reached the island—that of the supermarket, converting the family's store to this format and renaming it GS (after his mother's initials). The store took off, and the family soon was running a string of supermarkets around the island. At one point, however, the company ran into trouble, having underestimated its purchasing costs, and ended up in debt.

After graduating in 1980, Soru remained in Milan and began working as a bonds trader for a merchant bank. It was there that Soru encountered the Bloomberg machine, which provided financial information, and first discovered the possibilities of the Internet. Soru was also intrigued by Michael Bloomberg's success story, telling *Newsweek* "It's the first time I saw that a start-up really could compete with older companies."

## Company Perspectives:

*Having consolidated its position in Italy, Tiscali continues to develop its business on a pan-European scale. Its goal is to establish itself as the leading ISP and portal in Europe, and to achieve ''critical mass'' it has a target of being one of top three ISPs in each major European country. Tiscali's strategy involves utilizing Internet technologies to build a successful business model based on a new concept of a proprietary, IP-based, interconnected network. The company will provide customers throughout Europe with a full range of services—voice, Internet, and audio/video streaming—to compete effectively with traditional telecoms and cable players. The company is convinced that communications-related services should be available to customers regardless of the access means: fixed or mobile telephones, PC or television. Being an independent player represents a key factor in successfully developing and providing the best and most innovative services to customers.*

By the early 1990s, Soru had entered the real estate world as a shopping mall developer traveling about Europe, especially in the Czech Republic. In 1995, at the age of 32, Soru decided to return to Sardinia to continue his real estate career there. Instead, Soru encountered Nicola Grauso, who had set up one of Italy's earliest ISPs in Caligari, called Voice Online. Soru convinced Grauso to give him a franchise to set up a branch of Voice Online in the Czech Republic. Putting up some $200,000 of his own money, Soru launched the VOL Czech operation.

Unlike Italy, where the Internet was slow to take hold, the Czech Republic proved a fertile ground for VOL and the company was quickly profitable. Soru soon built VOL into the country's leading Internet provider, grabbing a 70 percent market share. He now decided to return to Italy to try his luck in the newly deregulating telephony marketplace. However, when he arrived back in Italy, he discovered that the VOL operation there had already been taken over by Telecom Italia, then in the process of extending its telephone dominance to the Internet market. Soru decided to take on Telecom Italia.

In 1997, Soru sold his house and, together with two friends, set up Telefonica della Sardegna in Caligari, Sardinia. (Soru sold the VOL Czech company to Deutsche Bank for $10 million in 1998). The new company acquired a license to lease telephone lines from Telecom Italia for a capacity of up to ten million customers. Because Sardinia itself had only 1.5 million potential customers, Soru targeted the new company at the Rome and Milan markets as well.

However, Soru quickly took the company national, rolling out the country's first telephone debit cards. Whereas credit cards had never caught on with the Italian consumer, the new type of debit-based phone cards were a success, and pioneer Telefonica della Sardegna's share of that market soared to nearly 30 percent.

Despite his position as head of a growing fixed-line telephone provider, Soru had not forgotten his earlier Internet success. Then Soru read about Freeserve, an Internet provider in the United Kingdom that had become the first ISP in Europe to offer free Internet access (that is, with no subscription fee—European consumers still paid metered rates for their online access to their local telephone companies). Soru decided to adapt the Freeserve model to the Italian market and created a new Internet service, which was called Tiscali.

Soru approached Telecom Italia, which agreed to kick back 50 percent of subscribers' phone charges to Tiscali, and in March 1999 he launched the first free Internet access service on the European continent. Tiscali was an instant success and became in turn a motor for Italy's Internet and computer market in general, as the Italian consumer, who had long shunned computers and the Internet, now began buying up PCs and going online. At the same time, the presence of Tiscali forced other providers, including Telecom Italia itself, to adopt the free subscription model.

### *European Domination in the 21st Century*

The instant success of Tiscali, which now became the company's name, encouraged Soru to enlarge his own vision of the company's future. By the middle of 1999, Soru became determined to expand Tiscali across Europe and build a market leader. In order to accomplish this, Soru took the company public in October 1999, listing it on the Italian stock exchange in Milan.

The initial public offering was a huge success, oversubscribed by some 40 times, and valuing Tiscali as high as EUR 14 billion—making it the country's highest-valued company, ahead of even automaker Fiat. Soru, who had retained two-thirds of Tiscali's stock, became the country's wealthiest person, at least on paper. Despite the company's success, and its international ambitions, Tiscali remained firmly rooted in Caligari.

Tiscali set out a multi-pronged growth plan based on international expansion through acquisition; development of Internet-based voice communications, e-commerce activities, and both pay and free content, as well as advertising revenues and the winning of a next-generation mobile-telephony UTMS license.

Tiscali had already begun its acquisition drive prior to its public offering when it acquired Italian company Infomedia Srl in June 1999 for EUR 400,000 in a move to form the basis of its e-commerce and online payment platform. In December 1999, Tiscali reached an agreement to acquire fiber-optic network developer Nets SA., in France, which was in process of building a high-speed network between Paris and London. Under Tiscali, Nets operations expanded to include the creation of fiber optic loops enabling Tiscali to operate a single European-wide network. An important feature of Soru's acquisition program was an insistence on acquiring only company's with significant cash reserves.

The year 2000 saw the company's acquisition drive take off in earnest. Among the first of its new acquisitions was that of Switzerland's DataComm SA, one of that market's leading independent ISPs, in January 2000. Next came Marseilles, France-based A Telecom SA, a telephone services provider which held an important interconnection agreement with France Telecom. Tiscali next targeted the Germany market, acquiring Nikoma Beteilgungs GmbH, an ISP and telephone services

**Key Dates:**

**1995:** Renato Soru starts up Czech Republic franchise of Italian ISP Voice Online and builds it into dominant Czech ISP.
**1997:** Soru founds Telefonica della Sardegna in Caligari, Sardinia, a regional telephone services provider that goes national.
**1998:** The company sells VOL Czech Republic for $10 million to Deutsche Bank.
**1999:** The company is renamed Tiscali and launches a free subscription Internet service in Italy; Tiscali goes public in October.
**2000:** Tiscali caps the year with the EUR 5.9 billion purchase of World Online, propelling it into the top ranks of European ISPs.

group in Hamburg, for EUR 370 million in Tiscali shares. Like Tiscali, Nikoma—which changed its name to Tiscali Germany—had been operating as a free Internet access provider with a subscriber base of 180,000.

After acquiring majority control of search engine developer Ideare in February 2000, Tiscali took a 60 percent share in the Motorcity SpA automotive portal joint-venture startup in March 2000. Similarly, Tiscali formed a travel and tourism portal joint venture with UVET SpA, called FreeTravel SpA. In June 2000, Tiscali acquired Quinary SpA, a software and hardware integration specialist in Italy. Another acquisition came in July of that year, when Tiscali bought Best Engineering SpA for EUR 5.6 million, giving it that company's online road mapping service.

Tiscali's Internet operation grew into a new market when the company acquired Belgium's Link Line SA, an ISP with more than 110,000 subscribers, in February 2000. In April, the company acquired another leading Belgium ISP, Interweb SA, with more than 85,000 subscribers. Later that year, Tiscali bundled both services under the brand TiscaliNet. At the same time, the company extended its fiber optic network to Brussels, as well as to the major urban markets in Germany. The company also moved into the Czech Republic, acquiring CD Telekomunikace sro, which not only held a telecommunications license but also the exclusive rights to lay a fiber optic network along the country's railroad system. In December 2000, the company acquired another German Internet provider, AddCom, formerly part of the Ebner Media Group. By the end of 2000, Tiscali had rebranded most of its Internet acquisitions under the TiscaliNet brand.

Tiscali's breakthrough came in December 2000 when it acquired Netherlands' troubled ISP World Online in an all-share deal worth EUR 5.9 billion. That company had already blazed the trail in creating a pan-European Internet group, amassing more than 3.5 million subscribers in 15 countries. Founded by Nina Brink in 1996, World Online had stumbled over a scandal surrounding its initial public offering in 2000—shortly before the IPO, Brink had sold off more than two-thirds of her own shares for just $6 per share, far lower than opening stock price. The resulting scandal forced Brink's resignation and torpedoed World Online's share price.

The World Online acquisition instantly catapulted Tiscali to the top ranks of European Internet access providers. The Dutch company also brought with it a war chest of some EUR 1.6 billion, enough to fuel Tiscali's continuing acquisition program.

By February 2001, Tiscali had made another significant acquisition, that of France's Freesurf, that country's second-largest ISP, in a cash and stock transaction worth $615 million. Then, in April, Tiscali expanded its German presence with the purchase of Guglielmo GmbH, which operated the ISP Planet-Interkom, from VIAG Interkom for a cash and share deal worth EUR 77 million, followed by the acquisition of SurfEU.com—an ISP and portal operator active in Germany, Austria, Switzerland, and Finland—for a total cash and share price of EUR 70 million. These two acquisitions added more than 1.3 million active subscribers to Tiscali's subscriber base.

In the United Kingdom, Tiscali acquired Springboard Internet Services Ltd in April 2001, which included the LineOne ISP and portal service, with more than 400,000 subscribers, for EUR 100 million. In July of that year, the company moved into Spain with the purchase of Inicia Comunicaciones SA, an ISP provider with 82,000 active subscribers, for EUR 8.2 million. Other acquisitions through the year included that of Tiny Online Ltd in the United Kingdom, Planetone Internet Service GmbH in Austria, Yucom and Infosources in Belgium, and WishNokNok in the Netherlands. By the end of the year, the company counted more than 16 million subscribers, including more than 7.3 million active subscribers.

At the beginning of 2002, Tiscali was forced to take a break in its acquisition plan as its losses mounted against slumping revenues. The poor climate of the Internet market had forced the company to write down the value of many of its acquisitions, which resulted in exceptional charges of more than EUR 1 billion that pushed the company's losses for the year to more than EUR 1.6 billion. While pointing out that most of its losses had been occurred by its subsidiaries before Tiscali had acquired them, Soru pledged to control the company's losses by the end of the year, cutting back on spending while simplifying its organization into a smaller number of Tiscali-branded subsidiaries. Soru also forecasted a rise in revenues to EUR 1 billion by the end of 2002.

While some observers had begun to question the company's business model—unlike many of its competitors, Tiscali remained committed to its free subscription model, meaning its revenues depended highly—64 percent of sales in 2001—on kickbacks from telephone companies. Although Tiscali had been slow to launch ADSL broadband service, a market that began to build in 2002, by the end of the first quarter of that year the company could point to its success in reducing losses and even claimed to be the first European ISP to turn a profit. As the European Internet market slowly consolidated—many analysts expected the market to shrink to just a handful of major, internationally operating groups—Tiscali appeared certain to fight hard to keep its place in the ISP winners circle.

### *Principal Subsidiaries*

Nacamar Internet Services; Tiscali Belgium; World Online s.r.o. (Czech Rep.); Denmark Tiscali A/S; World Online France

SA; Tiscali GmbH; B2B Tiscali Business GmbH (Germany); World Online BV (Netherlands); World Online AS (Norway); Tiscali Luxembourg S.A.; Tiscali Telecomunicaciones (Spain); World Online AB (Sweden); Tiscali DataComm AG (Switzerland); Vodacom World Online Ltd (South Africa); Tiscali UK Ltd; NETs S.A. (France); Liberty Surf UK.

### *Principal Competitors*

T-Online International AG; France Telecom SA; AOL-Time Warner; BT Group Ltd; Telecom Italia SpA; Terra Lycos, S.A.; Swisscom AG.

### *Further Reading*


Barker, Thorold, ''Italy's Upstart Empire-Builder,'' *Financial Times*, January 30, 2001.

Di Lillo, Claudia, ''Tiscali Losses Above Forecasts,'' *Reuters*, August 30, 2001.

Edmondson, Gail, ''An Italian Underdog Develops a Bite,'' *Business Week International*, February 26, 2001, p. 27.

Holmes, Mark, ''With Cash to Burn, Tiscali Buys Up Competitors,'' *Broadband Networking News*, May 22, 2001.

Kellner, Tomas, ''Expand or Die,'' *Forbes*, July 3, 2000.

Lowry Miller, Karen, ''The Man Who Would Be King,'' *Newsweek International*, February 19, 2001, p. 38.

Wall, Barbara, ''Buying Spree Grows Tiscali But Makes ISP Vulnerable,'' *International Herald Tribune*, April 28, 2001.


—M.L. Cohen

# Transiciel SA

**59/60, quai Alphonse le Gallo**
**92513 Boulogne Billancourt Cedex**
**France**
**Telephone: (+33) 1 41 22 41 22**
**Fax: (+33) 1 41 22 41 00**
**Web site: http://www.transiciel.fr**

*Public Company*
*Incorporated:* 1990
*Employees:* 9,000
*Sales:* EUR 505 million ($404 million)(2001)
*Stock Exchanges:* Euronext Paris
*Ticker Symbol:* TRA
*NAIC:* 541510 Computer Systems Design and Related Services; 541511 Custom Computer Programming Services

Transiciel SA in one of France's fastest-growing information technology consulting groups, claiming the number three position in that country's high-technology consulting sector behind Altran Technology and Alten SA. Transiciel's performance, boasting an average annual growth rate of more than 50 percent since its founding in 1990, was recognized in 2001 with the prestigious "Trophy of the Decade" given by French financial magazine *L'Expansion*. Transiciel operates in three distinct areas: Systems Integration, which generates nearly half of the company's annual sales of EUR 500 million; Facilities Management, generating one-third of sales; and Software Consulting, including development of in-house software sales and production scheduling solutions as well as support for third-party applications. Transiciel attributes much of its success and its business model: that of a network of more than 100 agencies operating independently and organized according to their geographic location, operational sector, or industry focus (and often a combination of these factors). The company features a number of large corporate clients such as Eurotunnel, Renault, France Telecom, Bouygues Telecom, Rhodia, Dassault, and Tenneco. While continuing to build on its presence in France, Transiciel has targeted international growth—the company expects to double its annual sales by 2004 while at the same time reducing the weight of domestic sales from 80 percent in 2001 to just 30 percent. The company has targeted Spain and the Benelux markets for its initial international growth, with acquisition including the Netherlands' UCC at the end of 2001 and Belgium's Ariane at the beginning of 2002. From these markets, the company expects to pursue a Europe-wide expansion in order to serve its larger, globally operating clients. Transiciel is led by founder and chairman Georges Cohen and has traded on the Euronext Paris stock exchange since 1998.

## *Best French Company of the 1990s*

Georges Cohen, the force behind Transiciel, already had more than 16 years of experience as an information technology (IT) consultant before forming what was to become one of France's fastest-growing IT consultant firms. In 1974, at the age of 19 and with no diploma, Cohen had been hired by Cap Gemini Sogeti as a technician. That company, founded as Sogeti in the mid-1960s by Serge Kampf when he was 33 years old, was itself in the process of formation after a bitterly fought hostile takeover of CAP by Sogeti earlier in the year, which itself was followed by the acquisition of Gemini Computer Systems. Sogeti had already distinguished itself by its willingness to move close to its customers, establishing a network of locally focused and largely autonomous agencies throughout France, before beginning a steady international expansion. Already France's largest IT consultants at the time of the Cap and Gemini acquisitions, with sales of more than FFr225 million in 1974, Cap Gemini Sogeti's expansion program of internal growth and targeted acquisitions helped it pass the FFr1 billion mark at the beginning of the 1980s. Another important feature of the company's growth was its insistence on targeting the nascent software market rather than attempt to gain a foothold on the hardware side. By the end of the 1980s, Cap Gemini Sogeti had become one of the world's top five IT consultants.

Meanwhile, Georges Cohen become part of Cap Gemini's success story, stepping up from the technical department to become one of the group's best salesmen. Cohen's drive quickly caught the attention of Serge Kampf, who boosted Cohen into the company's top management—Cohen was to be

## Company Perspectives:

*The Success Angels: Since Information control is the key to success, and since you cannot control Information alone, the TRANSICIEL Success Angels are there to help you. With their support, you will fly from success to success. There are 7000 of them. They are computer experts and cover all the requirements of the information systems operated by the major groups. They are recognized specialists, experienced in new technologies. They propose the technologies, the software, and the architectures to provide a solution that meets the requirements of the big accounts. With nearly 120 agencies, these Success Angels, aware of the stakes in your business, offer you a proximity service. To optimize their support, they are specialized by business activity. The Group's growth, one of the highest in the sector, is backed up by a sustained recruitment strategy. TRANSICIEL has a strong human relations policy, which ensures that staff are motivated and new talent attracted. With 1,500 people at the beginning of 1998, TRANSICIEL now has more than 9,000 employees.*

the youngest member of Cap Gemini's management team and later became considered as Kampf's right-hand man. Yet, as Cap Gemini's sales topped FFr9 billion at the beginning of the 1990s, Cohen was preparing to strike out on his own.

Cohen had long nourished the ambition to start up his own company during his years at Kampf's side. In 1990, Cohen, then 36 years old, decided it was time to try, reportedly telling Kampf, who tried to convince Cohen to remain with Cap Gemini: ''You started your business at 33 years, I'm three years late.'' Cohen took his FFr3 million in savings, and, with his wife serving as the firm's accountant, started up his own business in 1990. Cohen called his company Transiciel, a contraction of the French words for ''transforming'' and ''software,'' to highlight the company's targeted market.

Cohen made no secret of his ambition—becoming rich—and, using the lessons gained from his career at Cap Gemini, set about building Transiciel. Rather than take on the broad IT consultants market, the company quickly defined its core market, targeting at first the newly developing systems management sector as the computer industry made the transition to open client/server systems. Transiciel began by providing total information systems infrastructure engineering, management, and administration services. Despite the awkward timing—Transiciel was created during a worldwide IT industry slump that was soon exacerbated by a general recession and the effects of the Persian Gulf War—Cohen quickly proved an able student of Kampf.

Cohen's background in sales served the company well. Before the end of its first year, Transiciel had already gained a strong client list and had built up a workforce of more than 100. As a new company, Transiciel was able to turn directly to the deployment of open client/server systems, leaving it free of its competitors' baggage of supporting out-of-date legacy systems. The company was also in a position to target the market for major corporate accounts as larger companies began a growing trend for subcontracting their IT needs in the early 1990s. Transiciel quickly developed a second specialty, the integration of management systems, including consultancy services, client-specific software development, and software and systems integration services.

Cohen was joined by a number of former Cap Gemini colleagues in 1991, including Pierre Dalmaz, who would later become CEO of Transiciel. Once again, Cohen took a page from Cap Gemini's book, building a strong, independent management team while he ''managed the managers'' and guided the company's overall development. Not content merely with pursuing organic growth, Transiciel quickly began making acquisitions as well. In 1991, the company took its first external growth step, buying up competing group Excel. Two years later, the company made two more significant purchases—PBA and Axor. By the end of that year, Transiciel's revenues had topped FFr 200 million (EUR 30 million).

A drop-off in growth in the mid-1990s—during a deep crisis affecting much of the IT industry—led the company to restructure its operations in 1995, leading to the adoption of a new business model that the company claimed made it unique among its competitors. Cohen now developed a more decentralized approach, reorganizing the company's operations into a network of branch offices, each staffed by 40 to 100 employees in order to maintain a ''human scale'' for each branch. These branch offices were created according to various criteria—activity, geography, industry (or a combination of one or more of these)—with an emphasis placed on sales and marketing efforts. Each of the branch offices was then given a great deal of autonomy, yet at the same time they were all carefully monitored by means of a sophisticated data tracking system. Transiciel also gave its employees the opportunity to acquire shares in the company—a move which was to provide a strong incentive to its workforce.

By the 1996, the reorganization was already proving to be a success, as the company's sales topped EUR 56 million, while profits reached EUR 1.7 million. Transiciel was to post average annual growth rates of 50 percent and more through the second half of the decade, compared to an industry average of 16 percent, a record which was to earn it an award in 2001 as the best new company of the decade. Transiciel now began the march toward achieving critical mass, matching its organic growth with a new series of acquisitions.

### *Building Toward the EUR 1 Billion Mark in the 21st Century*

The first of Transiciel's new acquisitions came in 1997, when the company purchased two French companies, Odos and Sigle Informatique. These were followed up in 1998 with the acquisitions of Diaf, Progitec, and Vitamines. The acquisitions had left Georges Cohen—who made no secret of his fondness for gambling—personally in debt for more than EUR 150 million. Yet Cohen took the risk nonetheless, as he prepared his company for a public offering.

Transiciel went public in March 1998, initially taking a listing on the Paris Stock Exchange's secondary market. By February

## Key Dates:

**1990:** Georges Cohen sets up his own IT business under the name Transiciel.
**1991:** Transiciel acquires French company Excel.
**1995:** Transiciel restructures its operations.
**1997:** The company acquires Odos and Sigle Informatique to build its position in French IT sector.
**1998:** Transiciel goes public on the Paris stock exchange.
**1999:** The company acquires CR2A-DI to move into the high-technology consulting sector and begins international expansion with the acquisition of Spain's Seinto and Sysdata.
**2000:** Transiciel enters the Benelux market with the purchase of IT-Software Belgium and IT-Software Luxembourg.
**2002:** Ariane in Belgium is acquired.

1999, Transiciel had already been promoted to the IT CAC 50 board of leading technology stocks, and at the end of 1999 the company transferred to the Paris main board on the Monthly Settlements Market before joining the Deferred Settlements Market in 2000. The company's sales were evolving strongly as well, topping EUR 88 million in 1997, jumping to EUR 153 million in 1998, then nearing EUR 255 million in 1999.

The public offering enabled the company to step up its expansion as well as move into new territories. As Transiciel continued to impose itself on the French market—pushing its way into that country's IT consultants market top ten—Transiciel also began preparing to grow internationally. The company's international expansion came as much as a result of recognizing that it needed to follow the international growth of its major clients. Transiciel immediately targeted two markets—Spain and the Benelux countries—and began its expansion through a number of new acquisitions.

In Spain, the company acquired Seinto and Sysdata in 1999, then boosted its position into that country's top ten IT services and engineering companies with the acquisitions of Sysma and especially of Madrid-based Level Data in 2000. The acquisition of Bee Way in 2000 enabled the company to consolidate its systems management operation, adding a staff of 400 and annual sales of nearly EUR 40 million in the process. At the same time, Transiciel began its moves into the Benelux markets—seen as a key entry point into the larger northern European market—by acquiring IT-Software Belgium and IT-Software Luxembourg.

While pursuing its international growth, Transiciel was also diversifying into new market areas, adding e-business and net economy components as it entered a new market sector, high-technology consulting, a move achieved with the acquisition of French group CR2A-DI. Transiciel quickly moved to consolidate its position in the high-technology sector, acquiring French company Sinfor. With these acquisitions, Transiciel asserted itself quickly in the French market, capturing the number three position in the high-technology segment, behind Altran Technology and Alten, by 2001. Transiciel continued to build up that area, acquiring Gencom, a company specializing in the fields of telecommunications and digital television, and Retec Group, which focused on the research and development field.

Transiciel's sales continued to build, growing to EUR 377 million in 2000. Contributing to that increase was another important acquisition, that of the Netherlands' UCC (Universe Computer Consultants), for which Transiciel paid EUR 62 million. The company deepened its holdings in the Benelux markets with a takeover offer in 2000 for Belgium's Ariane; by the beginning of 2002, it had succeeded in acquiring 96 percent of that company. The addition of this company helped boost Transiciel's payroll to more than 9,000. By then, too, Transiciel's revenues had topped the EUR 500 million mark, while Georges Cohen had already defined a new goal—doubling the company's sales to top the EUR 1 billion mark by 2004. Yet Cohen, who continued to hold more than two-thirds of the company's stock, with a majority of its voting rights, had already succeeded in his original goal—making himself and his co-workers rich.

### *Principal Subsidiaries*

Transiciel Ingenerie; Transiciel Regions; Transiciel I.S.R.; Transiciel CISA; Transiciel International Ltd.; Transiciel Benelux; CR2A Holding; Sinfor Holding; Has.net.

### *Principal Competitors*

Altran Technology SA; Alten SA.

### *Further Reading*


Emmanuel, William, "Transiciel Studying Acquisitions," *Reuters*, March 6, 2000.

Sanders, Rik, "Interview with Pierre Dalmaz," *Computable*, December 21, 2001, p. 13.

"Transiciel a nouveau bien oriente," *La Tribune*, March 20, 2002.

"Transiciel, formate pour un marche en explosion," *L'Expansion*, March 5, 1998.

"Transiciel, le succes au culot," *L'Expansion*, October 25, 2001.


—M.L. Cohen

Universal Corporation

# Universal Corporation

1501 North Hamilton Street
Richmond, Virginia 23230
U.S.A.
Telephone: (804) 359-9311
Fax: (804) 254-3584
Web site: http://www.universalcorp.com

*Public Company*
*Incorporated:* 1918 as Universal Leaf Tobacco Company, Inc.
*Employees:* 26,000
*Sales:* $3 billion (2001)
*Stock Exchanges:* New York
*Ticker Symbol:* UVV
*NAIC:* 422590 Other Farm Product Raw Material Wholesalers; 325998 All Other Miscellaneous Chemical Product Manufacturing; 42131 Lumber, Plywood, Millwork and Wood Panel Wholesalers; 42245 Confectionery Wholesalers; 422490 Other Grocery and Related Product Wholesalers; 422990 Other Miscellaneous Nondurable Goods

Universal Corporation, known until 1987 as Universal Leaf Tobacco Company Inc., operates as the world's largest buyer and processor of leaf tobacco in nearly 40 countries across the globe. Universal selects, buys, ships, processes, packs, stores, and finances leaf tobacco in tobacco growing regions. The company sells this tobacco to tobacco product manufacturers. Sales from the company's largest customer, Philip Morris Companies Inc., accounted for just over 10 percent of consolidated revenues in 2001. The firm's tobacco operations account for over 65 percent of company revenues. Universal also buys, ships, processes, and distributes agri-products including tea, rubber, sunflower seeds, nuts, dried fruit, and canned and frozen foods. It distributes lumber and building products in the Netherlands and Belgium.

Historically, tobacco buying in the United States was conducted at auctions held throughout the prime growing areas in North Carolina, Kentucky, Virginia, and other states—during 2001, this was changed to a contract leaf purchasing system. As intermediaries between growers and manufacturers of tobacco products, leaf dealers achieved a position of some power prior to the formation in 1889 of The American Tobacco Company, the so-called tobacco trust of James B. Duke. Duke's trust controlled all of the large U.S. tobacco manufacturers, and it was not long before American Tobacco took steps to circumvent the tobacco leaf dealers by buying its product directly from farmers at auction. Under the pressure of American Tobacco's overwhelming presence in the market, the number of independent leaf dealers dwindled until the dissolution of the trust in 1911. By that time, what dealers remained had combined into larger and more effective organizations that were able to capitalize on the sharp rise in demand for tobacco then beginning. Although the successor companies to the tobacco trust—R.J. Reynolds, Liggett & Myers, Lorillard, and a smaller American Tobacco Company—continued to dominate the leaf markets, the overall growth in tobacco consumption in the United States left room for a limited number of independent dealers to prosper throughout the 1910s.

## *Foundation of Universal Leaf: 1916–20s*

The renewed vigor among the leaf dealers culminated in the 1916 establishment of the International Planters Corporation, a nationwide organization of dealers that was apparently powerful enough to maintain somewhat firmer prices to its large manufacturing customers. One of International Planters' largest clients was the new American Tobacco, whose president, Percival S. Hill, was instrumental in the creation of a second, competing organization of leaf dealers, Universal Leaf Tobacco Company. The company's nucleus had been formed in 1916, when Hill's vice-president of leaf purchasing, Thomas B. Yuille, resigned from American Tobacco and gained control of J.P. Taylor Company, a prosperous dealer in the rich tobacco lands of Virginia and North Carolina formed by Jaquelin Plummer Taylor. To this foundation, Yuille and Hill added 13 other local dealers, six from other states, and storage and shipping facilities in New York City. Together, Universal Leaf's subsidiaries and affiliates bought 100 million pounds of tobacco in the company's first year of existence, or nearly 10 percent of national production—an extraordinary figure for any industrial newcomer. Within eight years,

## Company Perspectives:

*Universal strives to be the leading supplier to each of the major tobacco product manufacturers worldwide by operating as one company worldwide with strong local management in key operating areas; by developing and maintaining mutually beneficial long-term strategic alliances with major manufacturers; by optimizing uncommitted inventory levels to reduce risk of loss during market declines; by increasing market share in traditional areas for both high quality flavor tobaccos and filler styles; by developing sources of low-cost tobacco; by maintaining diversified sources of supply to limit reliance on any one area and to meet customers' requirements for all major types and growths of leaf tobacco; and by maintaining financial strength to provide for manufacturers' worldwide tobacco needs and to provide the resources to expand into new areas with them.*

Universal became the largest independent tobacco dealer in the world, a status it has maintained.

Percival Hill died in 1925, and by 1930 American Tobacco was again doing all of its own leaf purchasing, while Universal Leaf had forged a new alliance with Philip Morris that would prove to be of long duration. Philip Morris was late in joining the ranks of the major tobacco manufacturers, and as its business expanded dramatically in the middle decades of the 20th century the company found it simpler to leave most of its leaf buying in the hands of Universal rather than take the time to create its own staff of buyers and warehousers. The relationship thus established between the two companies was intimate and durable, even including the financing by Universal of some of Philip Morris's tobacco purchases in the 1930s. In effect, Universal served as Philip Morris's tobacco purchasing department for many years. Philip Morris grew into the world's leading maker of cigarettes, and its leaf requirements increased, strengthening the relationship between Philip Morris and Universal Leaf.

A second important customer for Universal during its early years was Export Leaf Tobacco Company, the purchasing arm of British tobacco giant, British American Tobacco (BAT). Export Leaf did not buy its burley tobacco directly, relying instead on Universal Leaf's network of experienced burley dealers for its requirements. Leaf tobacco may broadly be divided between burley and flue-cured varieties; burley became a key ingredient of the increasingly popular ''American blend'' cigarette. Export Leaf shipped its burley purchases to BAT, which in turn used the bulk of it for the manufacture of Brown & Williamson brands, such as Raleigh and Viceroy. Universal bought all of its burley via a subsidiary of its own called Southwestern Tobacco Company, which by the end of the 1930s was buying about 20 percent of the entire U.S. crop. Some 60 percent of Southwestern's burley went to Export Leaf, making that company one of the two pillars, with Philip Morris, of Universal Leaf's prosperity at that time. Universal Leaf was able to carve out a place for itself in the international markets by offering large manufacturers the expertise they could not otherwise obtain. In the case of Export Leaf, it was probably helpful that the presidents of Export and of Universal were brothers.

### *International Growth Begins: 1930s*

Universal's numerous foreign affiliates and offices were important to its growth. As early as the 1930s, the company was both exporting and importing large quantities of tobacco leaf. In addition to its sales to Export Leaf, destined for markets in the British Commonwealth, Universal shipped U.S. cigarette tobacco to manufacturers around the world, including those in Scandinavia, Turkey, and Japan. Universal Leaf not only established trading offices around the world but also built processing plants for local threshing and storage and in some cases provided training and financial help to individual farmers. Its international business eventually included plants in Brazil, Italy, Korea, and the African nations of Malawi and Zimbabwe, as well as a network of dealers and brokers who slowly began to handle other commodities such as cocoa, tea, peanuts, and rubber. The trade in commodities was a natural outgrowth of Universal Leaf's foreign tobacco business; it developed slowly and was dispersed among a large number of non-consolidated subsidiaries and affiliates whose contribution to Universal Leaf's growth was rarely noted by financial analysts. Similarly, Universal Leaf quietly put together a large timber and building supplies distribution business in Europe, primarily in the Netherlands, which along with the commodities business grew to provide approximately 33 percent of the company's revenue.

In 1940, Universal Leaf was one of eight tobacco companies charged with violations of the Sherman Antitrust Act. The federal government brought suit in a Kentucky court, charging the industry leaders with price manipulation in both the purchasing and sales aspects of the business, including an alleged conspiracy to limit prices paid for leaf tobacco at auction. The three largest defendants—American Tobacco, R.J. Reynolds, and Liggett & Myers—stood trial on behalf of all eight, with Universal Leaf and the other four companies agreeing to abide by the court's decision. Like most antitrust cases, the outcome of this struggle was less than definitive. After years of argument, the eight defendants were found guilty as charged, although no evidence of actual collusion was found or even asserted. After paying the insignificant sum of $255,000, the eight companies returned to business as usual, the court offering no suggestions as to how the market might be made more competitive. The trial's message seemed to be that the tobacco market's domination by three or four manufacturers rendered it inherently monopolistic—or at least not ideally competitive—regardless of whether the parties involved were engaged in deliberate collusion. Nevertheless, no changes in the market were effected or recommended by the court. Universal Leaf was barely affected by the case, as its costs were largely borne by the three lead defendants.

The post-World War II decade saw a remarkable surge in the popularity of cigarette smoking in the United States, and in particular the rise of Philip Morris to national leadership. As Morris's unofficial leaf buyer, Universal Leaf benefited from the growing international success of such Philip Morris brands as Marlboro, which rose from obscurity to become the world's leading seller in the 1980s. Universal Leaf's sales reached $215 million in 1961, on which the company earned a low but very steady 2 percent to 3 percent profit. With commission work representing the bulk of Universal Leaf's business, its revenue was fixed to a cost-plus-fee basis, limiting net income but

**Key Dates:**

**1918:** Universal Leaf Tobacco Company Inc. incorporates.
**1940:** The firm is charged with violating the Sherman Antitrust Act.
**1968:** Universal acquires Inta Roto Company and Overton Container Corporation.
**1976:** The company fends off a hostile takeover bid made by Congoleum Corporation.
**1984:** Lawyers Title Insurance Company and Continental Land Title are purchased.
**1987:** The firm changes its name to Universal Corporation.
**1990:** Germany-based Gebrueder Kulenkampff AG is acquired.
**1991:** Universal spins off its insurance companies as Lawyers Title Corporation.
**1993:** The Casalee Group is purchased.
**1998:** Universal launches a share purchase program.
**2000:** The company reports its 30th consecutive year of annual dividend increases.

offering exceptionally stable growth from year to year. Still, the gradually accumulating evidence of tobacco's health hazards prompted Universal Leaf to diversify its asset base. The company's first significant acquisition outside the tobacco leaf business was its 1968 purchase of Inta Roto Company, makers of packaging equipment, and of Overton Container Corporation, suppliers of boxes to the tobacco industry. This was followed closely by the purchase of Unitized Systems Company, the beginning of Universal's interest in the building supplies industry, and the creation of a land development subsidiary called Universal Land Use Corporation. None of these early efforts at diversification was of great importance, however, when compared to Universal's holdings in the early 1990s in commodities and European building materials.

## *Fending Off Takeover Attempts: 1976*

By the mid-1970s, Universal Leaf's steady growth and valuable ties with Philip Morris attracted the attention of Congoleum Corporation, a Milwaukee-based maker of linoleum and furniture that was looking for acquisitions. In October 1976, Congoleum made an unsolicited bid of $32.50 per share for all of Universal's common stock, surprising Wall Street and enraging the directors of Universal. Universal's chairman and chief executive officer, Gordon Crenshaw, led a complex strategy of resistance to the takeover, filing suits in Virginia and Chicago and amending the corporate charter. When Crenshaw and other top Universal officials made it clear that if the company were bought they would take their customers with them to some new and competing venture, Congoleum withdrew its offer.

In 1984, with sales at around $1.3 billion, Universal made a second and more serious attempt at diversification when it purchased two of the leading title insurance companies in the United States, Lawyers Title Insurance Company and Continental Land Title. At first the insurers produced an excellent return on their $200 million in sales. The late 1980s saw a severe recession in real estate, however, which coincided with an increase in claims. In September 1991, with no end in sight for the real estate downturn, Universal spun off its title insurance companies as an independent corporation called Lawyers Title Corporation, with Universal shareholders becoming the initial owners of Lawyers Title's stock.

## *Continued Growth and Expansion: 1990s and Beyond*

During the late 1980s and into the 1990s, Universal Corporation—the company's name was changed in 1987 following the adoption of a holding company structure—was sailing on much as it had for the past 60 years, the core of its business generated by tobacco. In 1988, the firm acquired Thorpe & Ricks in order to expand its U.S. operations and also purchase the German firm Gebrueder Kulenkampff AG, which increased its hold in the Brazilian and Turkish markets. As a result of further diversification moves in the 1980s and early 1990s, its overseas subsidiaries in commodities and housing supplies flourished to such an extent that they supplied a significant amount of revenues and earnings.

Universal operated in the early 1990s and into the new millennium under the guidance of new chief executive Henry Harrell, who replaced Gordon Crenshaw in October 1988 after the latter had served nearly 25 years in that position. Expansion continued under his leadership, and in 1993 competitor Casalee Group was acquired. International growth continued even though market conditions forced Universal to shutter its tobacco operations in both Korea and Thailand. The company instead focused on Tanzania and Eastern Europe. In 1995, Holland-based Heuvelman, a softwood product processor and distributor, was purchased. Two years later, it acquired a tobacco leaf plant from the Tanzanian government along with the Polish tobacco operations of Reemtsma Cigarettenfabriken GmbH. During 1997, net income reached $100.8 million.

In 1998, the company launched a significant stock repurchase program that would eventually reach $300 million in repurchased shares. That year, Universal also joined with Socotab LLC in a venture that created the largest oriental tobacco leaf merchant across the globe.

As Universal entered the new millennium, it recorded its 30th year of annual dividend increases despite facing challenges. The tobacco industry as a whole continued to suffer due to declining demand and negative publicity related to the harmful effects of smoking. In the United States, the industry experienced smaller crop sizes and a change from the traditional auction-style selling platform to a direct contract purchasing system. The firm's Zimbabwe-based operations also suffered due to political unrest and economic challenges in the region. In Europe, Universal's Dutch lumber business was plagued by the weak Euro, which caused earnings in that sector to decline.

While Universal expected the difficult conditions to continue well into 2002, management felt confident that the firm was well positioned for continued success. With a long-standing history of good fortune and a solid business strategy in place,

Universal would in all probability remain a leader in the tobacco industry in the years to come.

## *Principal Subsidiaries*

B.V. European Tobacco Company (Netherlands); B.V. Deli-HTL Tabak Maatschappij (Netherlands); Beleggings-en Beheermaatschappij "DE Amstel" B.V. (Netherlands); Casa Exported Ltd.; Casalee (UK) Ltd.; Casalee Transtobac (PVT) Ltd. (Zimbabwe); Casalee Transtobac Lieferanten A.G. (Switzerland); Casalee, Inc.; Companhia Panamericana de Tabacos "Copata" (Dominican Republic); Continental Tobacco, S.A. (Switzerland); Corrie, MacColl & Son Ltd. (U.K.); Deli Maatschappij B.V. (Netherlands); Deli Universal, Inc.; Deltafina, S.p.A. (Italy); Gebruder Kulenkampff AG (Germany); Gebruder Kulenkampff, Inc.; Handelmatschappij Steffex B.V. (Netherlands); Industria AG (Switzerland); Itofina, S.A. (Switzerland); J.P. Taylor Company, Inc.; L'Agricola, S.p.A. (Italy); Lancaster Leaf Tobacco Company of Pennsylvania, Inc.; Latin America Tobacco Company; Limbe Leaf Tobacco Company, Ltd. (Malawi); Lytton Tobacco Company (Malawi) Ltd.; Lytton Tobacco Company (Private) Ltd. (Zimbabwe); Maclin-Zimmer-McGill Tobacco Company, Inc.; Red River Foods, Inc.; Simcoe Leaf Tobacco Company, Ltd. (Canada); Southern Processors, Inc.; Southwestern Tobacco Company, Inc.; Steffex Beheer B.V. Netherlands); Tabacos Argentinos S.A. (Argentina); Tabacos Del Pacifico Norte, S.A. De C.V. (Mexico); Tanzania Leaf Tobacco Co., Ltd. (Tanzania); Tobacco Processors, Inc.; Tobacco Trading International, Inc. Toutiana, S.A. (Switzerland); Universal Leaf (UK) Ltd.; Universal Leaf Tobacco Company, Inc.; Zimbabwe Leaf Tobacco Company (Private) Ltd.

## *Principal Competitors*

DIMON Inc.; Standard Commercial Corporation; British American Tobacco plc.

## *Further Reading*

"Giant Tobacco Firm Edgy About Zim Chaos," *Africa News Service*, February 14, 2002.

Nicholls, William H., *Price Policies in the Cigarette Industry*, Nashville, Tenn.: Vanderbilt University Press, 1951.

"Tobacco Industry," *The Value Line Investment Survey*, February 8, 2002.

—Jonathan Martin
—update: Christina M. Stansell

VARIAN

# Varian, Inc.

**3120 Hansen Way**
**Palo Alto, California 94304**
**U.S.A.**
**Telephone: (650) 213-8000**
**Fax: (650) 213-8200**
**Web site: http://www.varianinc.com**

*Public Company*
*Incorporated:* 1948
*Employees:* 4,300
*Sales:* $749 million (2001)
*Stock Exchanges:* NASDAQ
*Ticker Symbol:* VARI
*NAIC:* 334516 Analytical Laboratory Instrument Manufacturing

Varian, Inc. was formed in 1999 when Varian Associates Inc.—a pioneer of the renowned high-tech hotbed of Silicon Valley, California—reorganized into three independent public companies: Varian Medical Systems Inc.; Varian Semiconductor Equipment Associates Inc.; and Varian, Inc. Varian, Inc. operates as a leading supplier in scientific instruments, vacuum technologies, and contract manufacturing and has 14 locations in North America, Europe, and the Pacific Rim. The company caters to the life science, health care, semiconductor processing, and industrial industries and has over 20,000 customers. Varian's three main business segments include Scientific Instruments, Electronics Manufacturing, and Vacuum Technologies.

### *Klystron Development: 1930s–40s*

Varian was started in 1948 by brothers Russell and Sigurd Varian. Although they started with only $22,000 and a handful of employees, the Varian team was brimming with technical know-how. In fact, the Varian story dates back to at least the late 1930s, when the Varian brothers put their heads together to develop the famed klystron tube. The United States was faced with the need for improved navigational aids for its fledgling aviation industry as well as the possibility of war. The Varians' idea won them $100 for materials and part-time use of a laboratory at Stanford University. The goal of the project was to create the electron tube, a device that is capable of directing a beam of electrons and could, therefore, be utilized in a number of new applications.

The klystron was invented in the summer of 1937 and formally introduced in 1939 in the Journal of Applied Physics. European scientists were feverishly trying to develop similar technology at the time, so the announcement was welcomed in England. In fact, the United Kingdom wasted no time in adapting klystron technology to provide a lightweight source of microwaves for their radar receivers. By 1940, the Royal Air Force had equipped its night fighters with klystron radar receivers, which helped England defend its shores and claim victory in the Battle of Britain.

The Klystron Project team continued to advance its new technology during World War II. Later, team members would recall not only the Project's scientific achievements but also its contribution to technology management. Because of the war, team members were forced to couple their discoveries with real social needs rather than simply advancing technology for its own sake. Besides playing a role during World War II, the klystron was credited with initiating the microwave industry. Among other distinctions, microwave technology made commercial air navigation safe, allowed the development of worldwide communications satellites, and spawned numerous breakthrough devices, such as high-energy particle accelerators, that were integral to the advancement of medicine and nuclear physics.

After the war, the Varians and some of their Klystron Project peers decided to start their own company in California. They suspected that klystron technology was too expensive for them to get into on their own, but they felt that other emerging technologies, such as nuclear magnetic resonance, offered potential. So, with $22,000 and no real plan for exactly what they were going to do, the group started Varian Associates. The original company consisted of the Varians, Fred Salisbury, Myrl Stearns, and Russell's wife, Dorothy.

### *Postwar Opportunity*

Although they were dwarfed in terms of size and capital by their competitors, smallness turned out to be their greatest

### Company Perspectives:

*Varian, Inc. intends to capitalize on the burgeoning life sciences market with enabling tools that meet key customers needs for: accurate, reproducible results; simple, reliable analyses; improved sample throughput (productivity); and conformance to Good Laboratory Practices requirements as required by regulatory agencies. These are drivers that Varian, Inc. has repeatedly satisfied in its more traditional chemical analysis markets. In fact, the company has built over 40 years of institutional core competency in developing products that achieve these goals.*

advantage. When the government solicited bids for a klystron development project after the war, few manufacturers were interested because the project offered an unrealistically low allowance for overhead. Varian, however, with negligible overhead, decided to take on the project and soon developed the R-1 klystron. Its success with that project helped it earn several other government and private sector jobs and attract top scientific talent. During the following ten years, in fact, the Varian think tank produced a string of major breakthroughs related to various electronic technologies.

Among Varians' most recognized early achievements was its development of nuclear induction, or nuclear magnetic resonance (NMR), technology. NMR revolutionized chemistry by allowing chemists to quickly determine the structure of molecules. Russ Varian had tracked the development of NMR at Stanford and Harvard during World War II, and he hired Martin Packard, a key NMR researcher, to head Varian's project. ''Prior to the use of NMR . . . you could spend literally months and years trying to determine the structure of a molecule,'' Packard has explained. ''With NMR, infrared, mass spectrometry, and other such tools, the same problems can often be solved in hours, and the whole field of chemistry has been able to undergo a much more rapid advance and expansion.'' Varian and Packard applied for a U.S. patent on their ideas related to NMR in 1948.

Varian soon built upon its successful development of klystron and NMR technologies. The company eventually integrated klystron technology into a range of new applications for the telephone, radio, television broadcast, satellite, radar, and related communications industries. Likewise, Varian used NMR technology to develop a line of scientific instruments used in chemistry, physics, biology, medicine, and other fields. Varian opened its Palo Alto Microwave Tube Division in 1953 in Building 1 of the Stanford Industrial Park. The facility became known as the first high-tech industrial park in the United States and signaled the beginning of Silicon Valley.

Another major technological breakthrough ascribed to Varian in the 1950s was the medical linear accelerator. A linear accelerator is a machine used to produce x-rays, electrons, and other high-energy particles. It was invented by Bill Hansen and Ed Ginzton, both of whom had worked on the Klystron Project, joined Varian early on as directors, and served as consultants to the company. Varian's goal for its medical linear accelerator project was to take the large, clumsy linear accelerator, or linac, and shape it into a compact, agile device that doctors could use to accurately distribute dosages of particles to the human body.

In collaboration with Stanford Medical Center, Ginzton led the evolution of klystron technology to create the Varian Linac accelerator, the first practicable medical accelerator. The device soon became an important tool in the research of cancer treatment with radiation. Although implementation of the device in the private sector took several years, Varian used technology developed in the Linac project in other ventures and was eventually able to parlay the breakthrough into a marketable line of medical apparatuses. Considered one of Varian's crowning achievements, the resulting Varian Linac line of radiotherapy systems would become Varian's most successful product line.

Besides the klystron, NMR, and linear accelerator, a fourth major breakthrough for Varian was its electronic vacuum pump. Until the mid-1950s a major hurdle to the manufacturing of vacuum tubes was contaminants that attached themselves to the tubes' innards and shortened tube life. Part of the problem was debris from oil diffusion pumps that were used to create the vacuum in the tubes. Varian began experimenting with gas discharge ''sputtering,'' which lead to the sputter-ion pump. It turned out that, in addition to creating cleaner vacuum tubes, the pump was more portable, required no cooling water, and had a number of other beneficial attributes.

Varian developed a marketable pump called the VacIon Pump in 1958, and in 1959 launched an entire business division based on the new technology. Varian delivered some of its first pumps to RCA, the Atomic Energy Commission, and NASA. The division flourished during the 1960s as the VacIon Pump spawned several product lines for a variety of different applications. Most importantly, Varian's vacuum pump technology later provided ingress into the burgeoning semiconductor industry. Varian gradually honed important technology related to ion implantation and thin-film coating that became integral to the semiconductor fabrication process.

Because of its technological prowess, Varian earned a reputation as a leading technological innovator during the 1950s and 1960s. The same praise could not be applied to its business accomplishments, however. Despite a flurry of highly marketable product introductions, Varian's financial performance was spotty. Indeed, the company was so intently focused on the exciting science and engineering game that it sometimes ignored the bottom line. That resulted in part from the fact that most of the company's workers and managers had formerly been (and often continued to be) associated with academia. One well-known story within the company is of an engineer who invented a computer printer capable of printing enough data to cover a football field. When asked who in the world would want such a device, the engineer replied, ''Lawrence Livermore Laboratory. They'll buy one of everything.''

### *Restructuring Efforts: Late 1960s–80s*

While the academic environment at Varian had allowed its scientists a good deal of latitude for innovation, the company suffered from erratic profit performance because of its lack of business savvy. Business boomed in the late 1950s. In the early

## Key Dates:

**1937:** Brothers Russell and Sigurd Varian work to develop the klystron.
**1948:** The Varians along with several Klystron Project peers establish Varian Associates with $22,000 in start-up capital.
**1953:** Varian opens its Palo Alto Microwave Tube Division in Stanford Industrial Park.
**1959:** The firm creates an electronic vacuum pumps business division.
**1982:** Thomas Sege is named president and begins restructuring the company.
**1989:** While sales reach $1.3 billion, Varian is plagued with integration problems and spotty profits.
**1990:** Tracy O'Rourke takes the helm and launches a three-phase restructuring program.
**1994:** Varian posts record sales and earnings.
**1999:** The company is reorganized into three distinct businesses: Varian Medical Systems Inc., Varian Semiconductor Equipment Associates Inc., and Varian, Inc.
**2001:** Varian, Inc. grows through acquisition and remains committed to developing its life sciences business.

1960s, though, its government contracting business dried up and the company nearly went bust. The company staged a comeback in the mid-1960s by emphasizing nonmilitary markets. By the late 1960s, however, Varian was in financial trouble again. Varian brought in a new, business-oriented manager in 1971 who made several seemingly smart moves. Varian purchased a minicomputer company, for example, and eventually grabbed about 10 percent of that growing market. Indicative of the overall company performance, however, Varian scientists had trouble adapting to fast-changing markets, and the company was unable to control manufacturing costs. The computer division languished and was jettisoned in 1977.

Varian had about $640 million in sales in 1981 from its growing and diversified high-tech product lines. Unfortunately, it also lost $3.6 million. In another bid to bring its balance sheet in line with its technological ability, Varian brought in a new president in 1982, Thomas Sege. Sege was a 55-year-old former Yugoslavian who had escaped from that country in 1940, shortly before Hitler invaded. Sege believed that Varian's problems stemmed from its loose, splintered environment. "The name 'Varian Associates' is significant," he noted in *Forbes*. "It means a loose association of people doing their own thing. . . . We had a number of small shops with small objectives."

In an effort to rectify the situation, Sege quickly established tight controls over inventories and receivables and tied manager pay and incentives to financial performance. He also started selling or closing marginal operations that were losing money and diversifying into new businesses that promised to complement existing technologies. Although some researchers and managers resisted the change in the working environment, others welcomed the new direction and the feeling of an overall corporate focus. The changes seemed to work. In 1982, Varian announced the first of what would be three years of consecutively improved results, ending with record sales ($973 million) and earnings ($69.7 million) in 1984. During the mid-1980s, moreover, recovering defense markets boosted revenues over $800 million.

Although Varian's financial performance improved during the early and mid-1980s, its successes were short-lived. Varian's sales continued to surge, but profits were spotty and the company failed to become integrated. Under Sege's direction, Varian made a number of acquisitions, many of which it later dumped. By the late 1980s, Varian was generating more than $1 billion in sales from its diversified, global operations. However, it had also become an unwieldy, barely profitable techno-behemoth with 20 decentralized divisions. "They are not very well managed and have a history of problems," noted industry analyst Carolyn A. Rogers in the *Los Angeles Times*.

Despite Varian's business shortcomings, the company continued to be recognized as a leader in electronic-related technology. For example, Varian had introduced several major innovations in the semiconductor industry and had become a major player in specific segments of the health care industry, particularly those related to cancer treatment. In fact, by the early 1990s Varian had captured more than half the global market for radiation therapy equipment. Varian also retained a leadership role in instrument and electron device markets.

However, Varian had been criticized for being too focused on technology and for offering only ultra-high-end, premium products and ignoring the sometimes larger middle market. Likewise, the company had acquired a reputation for investing heavily in questionable new technologies. For example, Varian developed a system that could be used to irradiate produce, thus killing bugs and extending shelf life. The product never made it to market, though, because of glitches related to federal approval. "You just can't experiment without thinking about the bottom line," analyst Stephen Balog told *Fortune*.

### *A Turnaround in the Early 1990s*

In an effort to capitalize on its strong product and market position, Varian called Tracy O'Rourke to the helm in 1990 while Sege stepped aside and became vice-chairman. The 54-year-old O'Rourke boasted a track record of management successes. Most notably, he was credited with turning around the Allen-Bradley division of Rockwell International, a major high-tech defense contractor. He had taken that company from $450 million to $1.4 billion in sales, all the while improving profits and margins. O'Rourke was known as a visionary with a knack for international expansion. At the time of his arrival, Varian was similar to Allen-Bradley in both size and markets served, with $1.3 billion in 1989 sales and an international work force of 12,000.

Immediately after his arrival O'Rourke designed and began to implement a three-phase restructuring program aimed at whipping the technological giant into financial health. "Like a hummingbird, we were going from opportunity to opportunity, only to abandon them when the competition got too hot. We were simply spreading ourselves too thin," O'Rourke explained in *Industry Week*. During the first phase of O'Rourke's program, which Varian completed during the early 1990s, Varian sold 11 languishing divisions and product lines for $60 million, closed nonperforming units, and initiated a massive labor reduction designed to eventually pare about one-third of Varian's 12,400-member work force.

That effort alone allowed Varian to post a record profit of $58 million in 1991 following a depressing loss in 1990. Phase two of the process, which was started in 1992, was a long-term goal of significantly improved quality and service. O'Rourke wanted to consolidate and streamline the entire organization, reduce the amount of time required to take new ideas to market, and develop a customer-oriented culture. "People had fallen into the habit that it was o.k. to be late," O'Rourke recalled in *Industry Week*. "As a result, customer shipments from some of our core businesses would lag, sometimes by several months." Finally, O'Rourke's third phase entailed the development of a long-term profit and growth strategy designed to take Varian into the 21st century.

By 1994, the effects of O'Rourke's efforts were already apparent. Although sales hovered around the $1.3 billion mark, sales per employee jumped more than 50 percent and earnings ranged between $45 million and $60 million during 1991, 1992, and 1993. Order backlogs were reduced significantly, and quality control improved. Furthermore, Varian slashed its total corporate debt from about $110 million in 1989 to almost zero in 1993. Importantly, Varian boosted research and development spending, reflecting O'Rourke's intent to sustain Varian's legacy of technological leadership.

In 1993, Varian operated its subsidiaries through four core businesses: health care systems (30 percent); instruments (27 percent); semiconductor equipment (22 percent); and electron devices (21 percent). In 1994, Varian was the world's leading supplier of cancer radiation equipment, the top developer and producer (by sales volume) of analytical instrumentation for studying chemical composition of matter, one of the largest manufacturers of semiconductor fabrication equipment, and a leading U.S. supplier of microwave-related equipment, particularly for satellite communications. The company operated more than 50 sales offices outside of the United States (and about 40 domestically), with approximately 43 percent of revenues coming from foreign shipments. Varian's stock price rose steadily in the first half of the 1990s: the company's share price climbed to an all-time high ($46 per share), and it posted record sales and earnings in 1994 and 1995, suggesting market confidence in Varian's long-term potential.

The success of O'Rourke's three-phase program, however, appeared to be short-lived when Varian again became plagued with problems in the late 1990s. The prosperity it had experienced from 1993 to 1995 was due in part to the strong demand in the semiconductor market. That industry was becoming highly competitive and oversaturated in the late 1990s, which affected Varian's sales and profits. This business segment was also highly exposed to the Asian market, where an economic crisis had weakened overseas demand. Overall, sales were down nearly 11 percent in 1998 because of the slump in the market.

## *Varian Splits: 1999*

By this time, Varian had been restructuring for nearly seven years. It had jettisoned its electronic devices segment, leaving semiconductor equipment, healthcare systems, and analytical instruments as its core businesses. An August 1998, an *Electronic News* article stated that Varian management felt that there was "no longer a material synergy" among its three core operating units. As such, Varian Associates announced that it would reorganize into three separate and independent publicly held companies. In 1999, the break up was completed. Varian Associates' analytical instruments segment—the most solid segment of the company—took on the name Varian, Inc. The health care segment became Varian Medical Systems Inc., and Varian Semiconductor Equipment Associates Inc. was created to oversee the semiconductor manufacturing unit.

The new Varian, Inc. entered 2000 focused on three main businesses, including its scientific instruments business, which supplied equipment and laboratory products and services that were used for studying the chemical and molecular composition of compounds and substances; its vacuum technologies business that provided solutions for creating, maintaining, and controlling vacuum environments; and its electronics manufacturing businesses through which the company provided contract manufacturing services for original equipment manufacturers in the life science, health care, and telecommunications markets. A major portion of the firm's strategy, however, was centered on the life sciences sector. Through its scientific instruments segment, Varian, Inc. wanted to expand the sales of its products related to life science and health care research. The firm's long term goal was to secure 50 percent of its scientific instruments segment's sales from life science and health care research applications.

During the first several years of operating as a self-reliant company, Varian grew through acquisitions that included Imagine Manufacturing Solutions Inc., R&S Technology Inc., Bear Instruments Inc., and the VanKel Technology Group Inc. In early 2002, the firm completed its $45 million purchase of ANSYS Technologies Inc. Sales in 2001 reached $749 million, an increase of 6.4 percent over 2000 figures. While net income fell by 14 percent for the year, Varian management felt that the company was well positioned for future growth. With all three of its business segments operating in high growth markets, the new Varian appeared to be on track to prosper as an independent firm.

## *Principal Subsidiaries*

Chrompack, Inc.; Intralab Instrumentacao Analitica Limitada (Brazil); JMBS, Inc.; JEM'SY (France); Varian (Shanghai) International Trading Co. Ltd. (China); Varian A.G. (Switzerland); Varian AB (Sweden); Varian Argentina, Ltd.; Varian Australia Pty. Ltd.; Varian Australia, LLC; Varian B.V. (Netherlands); Varian Belgium N.V.; Varian Canada Inc.; Varian Deutschland GmbH (Germany); Varian FSC, Inc. (Barbados); Varian Gessellschaft (Austria); Varian Holdings (Australia) Pty. Limited; Varian Iberica S.L. (Spain); Varian India Pvt. Ltd.; Varian Industria E. Comercio Limitada (Brazil); Varian Instruments of Puerto Rico, Inc.; Varian Inter-American Corp.; Varian J.M.B.S., S.A.S. (France); Varian Limited (U.K.); Varian S.A. (France); Varian S.A. (Mexico); Varian S.p.A. (Italy); Varian Technologies Asia, Ltd.; Varian Technologies China, Ltd.; Varian Technologies Japan, Ltd.; Varian Technologies Korea, Ltd.; Varian Technologies, C.A. (Venezuela).

### *Principal Operating Units*

Scientific Instruments; Vacuum Technologies; Electronics Manufacturing.

### *Principal Competitors*

Agilent Technologies Inc.; PerkinElmer Inc.; Waters Corporation.

### *Further Reading*

Bates, James, ''Varian Finds Itself Tangled in Pentagon Scandal,'' *Los Angeles Times*, July 2, 1988, Sec. 4, p. 1.

''Company Expands Through Acquisitions,'' *R&D*, March 2002, p. 15.

Goldman, James S., ''Intevac Arises from Varian's Restructuring,'' *Business Journal-San Jose*, April 13, 1992, p. 1.

Krey, Michael, ''Varian's Laying It on the (Bottom) Line,'' *Business Journal-San Jose*, December 4, 1989, p. 1.

Nickel, Karen, ''Will a Disciplinarian Shake up Varian?,'' *Fortune*, May 7, 1990, p. 26.

Privett, Cyndi, ''Mired in Slump, Varian Struggles to Snap Free,'' *Business Journal-San Jose*, July 28, 1986, p. 1.

Simpson, Gary, ''Varian Associates Inc. Named O'Rourke Chairman, Chief Executive Officer,'' *Business Wire*, February 28, 1990.

Takahashi, Dean, ''Seven Years . . . And Counting,'' *Electronic Business*, February 1998, p. 62.

Teresko, John, ''Varian,'' *Industry Week*, October 19, 1992, p. 55.

''Vacuum Technology,'' *R&D*, April 2001, p. 27.

*Varian Associates: An Early History*, Palo Alto, Calif.: Varian Associates, Inc.

''Varian Balancing Focus,'' *Business Journal*, September 8, 2000, p. 34.

''Varian to Spin Off Businesses,'' *Electronic News*, August 24, 1998.

Weigner, Kathleen K., ''It's About Time,'' *Forbes*, April 25, 1983, p. 41.

—Dave Mote
—update: Christina M. Stansell

VICORP
RESTAURANTS, INC.

# VICORP Restaurants, Inc.

**400 West 48th Avenue**
**Denver, Colorado 80216**
**U.S.A.**
**Telephone: (303) 296-2121**
**Fax: (303) 672-2668**
**Web site: http:///www.vicorpinc.com**

*Private Company*
*Incorporated:* 1959 as Village Inn Pancake House, Inc.
*Employees:* 13,000
*Sales:* $350 million (2001 est.)
*NAIC:* 722110 Full-Service Restaurants

VICORP Restaurants, Inc., is a U.S. operator and franchiser of approximately 370 Village Inn and Bakers Square family restaurants. The Village Inn chain consists of both corporate-operated and franchised restaurants that are located primarily in the Rocky Mountain region, the upper Midwest, Arizona, and Florida. The smaller Bakers Square chain, concentrated in California and the upper Midwest, is entirely operated by the corporation. The two chains are known for their pies and other fresh-baked products as well as in-restaurant home-style meals. The company also operates VICOM, a bakery division that manufactures 34 varieties of pies for the two restaurant chains, and J. Horner's, a food service provider. VICORP is owned by investment firms Goldner Hawn Johnson & Morrison Inc. and BancBoston Capital.

### *Origins*

The origins of VICORP lie with two Coloradans, James Mola and Mertin Anderson, who in the late 1950s opened the first Village Inn restaurant in Colorado Springs. In 1959, the partners sold this original location and moved north to Denver, where they opened a new Village Inn at the corner of East Colfax Avenue and Yosemite Street. In December of that year, Mola and Anderson incorporated under the name Village Inn Pancake House, Inc. New buildings and acquisitions in the 1960s and 1970s allowed the corporation to grow steadily, with several Village Inn locations added in the Midwest and Mountain regions.

During the 1980s, VICORP acquired restaurants from competitors and expanded its business into new sectors. After going public in 1982, the May 1983 buyout of Poppin' Fresh Pies, Inc., a subsidiary of the Pillsbury Corporation, provided VICORP with 59 new restaurant locations in the Midwest and a baking facility outside Chicago. These restaurants were to become the nucleus of a new VICORP chain, Bakers Square. Emerson B. Kendall, who had served as president of Poppin' Fresh Pies since 1975, was kept on as president of the new Bakers Square division, which was operated out of an existing office in Matteson, Illinois.

### *Mid-1980s Expansion*

The year 1984 was a time of significant growth for VICORP in terms of restaurant acquisition, but rapid expansion also saddled the company with many unforeseen problems. In February, the company acquired 71 restaurants from the Continental Restaurant Systems division of Ralston Purina and incorporated them into its growing specialty restaurant group. In October, the corporation made another large acquisition, this time of 175 restaurant locations in California, Florida, and Arizona operated under the name Sambo's. The restaurants, which were slated for conversion either to Village Inn or Bakers Square establishments, proved to be a huge headache for the company. Long-range plans called for a relatively smooth conversion process to be completed within two years of the buyout.

Instead, the process dragged on for almost four years and resulted in an overall decline in management quality as mid-level managers were relocated to far flung and struggling establishments that were already experiencing falling levels of food and service quality. Management also cited the smaller size of many Sambo's locations—some as much as 20 percent smaller than the average Village Inn, which seats approximately 150 and covers 5,000 square feet—as another roadblock to quick conversion. The net effect for VICORP was a serious drop in profits that extended well into the 1980s.

VICORP experienced its greatest problems in Florida, where the acquisition and conversion of several Sambo's locations seriously depleted the company's resources in that region. In 1989,

**Company Perspectives:**

*VICORP Restaurants strive to provide good food and unbelievable pie. For four decades, Village Inn has been serving great tasting, home-style meals that are made to order with only the finest ingredients. And our customers come to Bakers Square knowing they'll enjoy the Best Pie in America. Uncompromising quality and consistency have made our pies famous for over 25 years.*

after closing 15 of the converted restaurants and threatening to do the same to the remaining ones, President and Chief Operating Officer Robert S. Benson summed up the situation in the *Nation's Restaurant News:* "We shot ourselves in the foot in 1985, pushing too many people into outlying Sambo's locations, which proved non-viable. . . . Then we compounded this judgment error by papering over these problems, sometimes recycling failed units to new franchises." Benson had joined the company in the fall of 1987 and hoped to slow its rapid expansion by instead focusing resources on existing units, as well as more clearly defining a market strategy to combat sluggish sales.

In 1988, Benson named James Carter president of Village Inn, hoping to provide renewed leadership for the foundering company. With one-third of its Florida establishments closed and put up for sale, VICORP cut its operating losses in that division to $1.3 million in 1989 (down from $2 million the previous year) and also tightened the reins on franchises, with the corporation taking at least temporary control of nearly 20 restaurants in the same period. Elsewhere, Village Inn West, which included all of the Village Inn locations outside of Florida, demonstrated sales gains of 5.6 percent in 1988 and continued strength into 1990.

The other side of VICORP's holdings, the still-young Bakers Square restaurant group, proved to be a mirror image of its sibling, Village Inn. Like Village Inn-Florida, the Bakers Square-West division, consisting of approximately 80 former Sambo's establishments spread throughout California, suffered in the late 1980s, particularly feeling the effects of labor shortages and high operating costs in that region. Under the leadership of Benson, VICORP reacted with a new emphasis on personnel and management training in an effort to stem high employee turnover. The initiative showed some tangible success, but California, like Florida, continued to be carried by the company's strongest division, Bakers Square-Midwest. In the late 1980s, the 62 restaurants of the Great Lakes region provided the company with an average annual gross of $1.9 million, nearly double the volume of similar units in California. At the same time, VICORP also drew profits from its six Taste of Bakers Square establishments, which provided the same fresh pies and baked goods as Bakers Square restaurants but for carry-out only.

Financial turnaround for VICORP was also promoted in the 1980s with the help of a long-term plan to cut company debt and spending. Operating margins for the corporation had peaked in 1984 at 14.5 percent, and, after a low in 1986 of 4.8 percent, hovered around 9.8 percent for 1988. The sale of 15 Village Inn restaurants in Florida also provided VICORP with a substantial write-off for 1988. Capital expenditures were curtailed by 62 percent between 1986 and 1988, reflecting VICORP's initiative to control growth and focus on better management. This allowed the company to cut its long-term debt from $110.5 million in 1986 to $40.6 million at the end of 1988.

In 1990, VICORP was the object of a class-action suit. On November 1, 1990, the company became aware of what it called accounting "irregularities" and disclosed a statement reassessing its earnings for the year at a value $4 million less than had been expected. The resulting plunge in VICORP stock, a dive from $13.5 to $6.75 per share, led to a shareholder outcry spearheaded by Florida stockholder Martin Kaplan. Kaplan had spoken with VICORP treasurer Peter Doane on October 30 and was assured by him that the company's financial position was sound. Soon after, Kaplan filed a lawsuit in the U.S. District Court of Denver. The case was settled in the spring of 1992, with Kaplan and approximately 3,500 other investors receiving a total of $6.5 million in damages from the company. VICORP, however, denied that it had intentionally mislead its shareholders. Doane stated that he was unaware of the problem at the time he spoke with Kaplan, and had revealed the information as soon as it was made available to him. The accounting problem itself was traced to two accountants, both of whom were fired. As Doane explained in *Restaurant Business*, "They were hiding costs in inventory accounts, and yes, the effect was to make the company appear to be doing better than it was. There was no theft involved." Doane also argued that "the market overreacted to the news." He added, "It took our net income down a total of $4 million over two fiscal years, but we were still a very healthy and profitable company in those years, and the market quickly came around to that. The stock was back up to $9 the next day, and within two months it was back to where it was."

### *Restructuring, Marketing, and Training: Early to Mid-1990s*

Despite the brief setback of the Kaplan suit, and with the financial outlook looking brighter after the mid-1980s slump, VICORP moved aggressively into the 1990s. The company carried on with, and improved, many of its capital and employee investment plans and devised several inventive renovation and advertising strategies for the new decade. Perhaps the single most important individual in overseeing these plans was James Caruso, named president of Village Inn in 1991. Caruso had brought 15 years of experience with Denny's restaurants to VICORP in 1990, when he was hired as vice-president of company operations. In an interview with the *Nation's Restaurant News*, Caruso explained his outlook on the company after his first year: "We have some very talented people here. . . . We've demonstrably improved operations over the past year and are now concentrating our efforts into our management programs and maintaining consistent levels of service." Caruso solidified these management training efforts in the new Village Inn Training and Leadership Program, or VITAL, which put each management trainee through an eight-week, hands-on rotation of every employee station in the restaurant. In addition, the program was designed to focus on individual career paths for restaurant managers in hopes of keeping employees at the management level with the company over the long term.

**Key Dates:**

**1959:** James Mola and Mertin Anderson open a Village Inn restaurant in Denver, Colorado.
**1982:** VICORP goes public.
**1983:** The company purchases Poppin' Fresh Pies Inc., which eventually becomes the Bakers Square chain.
**1984:** The firm acquires 246 restaurant locations.
**1990:** VICORP becomes involved in a class action lawsuit.
**1994:** The Angel's Diner & Bakery concept is launched.
**1996:** VICORP discontinues the Angel's concept and closes 11 unprofitable restaurants.
**1998:** Profits increase by 32 percent over the previous year.
**2001:** VICORP is acquired by the investment firms of Goldner Hawn Johnson & Morrison Inc. and BancBoston Capital.

Caruso also had his hand in another change undertaken in the early 1990s—the large-scale renovation of the Village Inn chain, including interior and exterior remodeling. Outside upgrades were designed to make each unit more visible and visually appealing, and included neon lighting and signage, as well as the construction of green mansard roofs. Inside, decorators provided each restaurant with a lighter color scheme and new carpeting. The cost for the remodeling ranged between $200,000 and $300,000 per restaurant but showed some positive effects in terms of sales and served to project a new and more vital image for Village Inn.

In terms of marketing and advertising, the early 1990s proved an exciting period of experimentation and change for VICORP. Village Inn, attempting to strengthen its lunch and dinner business, offered several new salad and sandwich choices on its menu and tested other dinner possibilities such as lasagna and pot roast. In 1994, the chain also expanded its line of hamburgers, hoping to take a portion of the lunch market from fast-food competitors. With the tagline ''Open Wide,'' Village Inn launched its All-World Double Cheeseburger and an assortment of other specialty burgers. The slogan was devised by the Denver-based Henry Gill Silverman advertising agency, which took the Village Inn account from the Minneapolis firm of McElligott Wright Morrison and White in mid-1992.

In the ensuing years, Silverman was allowed to break Village Inn out of its purely traditional image. The firm produced ads promoting the restaurant's line of healthy foods. Spandex-clad chickens on treadmills in one television ad, for instance, demonstrated a new and humorous approach for the chain. Silverman also wrote the jingle ''Drop on In. How Ya Been? Village Inn,'' which won an International Broadcast Award in 1992. He summed up his agency's contributions to Village Inn in the *Nation's Restaurant News* as follows: ''We've managed to capture the kind of neighborly, folksy image they already have in the eye of the consumer. . . . We've contrasted this warm, sincere music,'' he continued, ''against some wacko humor and great food photography. Those three things add up to a very human, memorable kind of place.'' The results of this approach continued to be positive, with the campaign increasing sales by an estimated $20 million between the years 1991 and 1993 to a level of approximately $240 million.

Bakers Square, likewise, made some advertising and marketing adjustments in the 1990s. In 1992, the chain launched its ''Square Deal Meals'' as a response to relatively lower prices among competitors in the mid-range lunch and dinner market. The company also hoped to muster more broad-based appeal and create a marketing edge with a new slogan, ''Nobody goes further than fresh,'' devised by CME KHBB Advertising of Chicago in 1993. The chain continued to struggle, however, in the 1990s. Declining sales—not only in California, but also in the Midwest division—culminated in the firing of president Emerson B. Kendall and executive vice-president of marketing, J.D. ''Jim'' Fisher, in November 1993. Kendall was replaced with James Caruso, whose success with Village Inn had put the chain back on the expansion track by mid-1993, with plans to open 30 new stores over the next two years.

Placing Caruso at the head of the struggling Bakers Square, however, had little effect over the short term. Continued declines in profits for the division, which fell an estimated $1 million over the course of 1993, brought about the resignation of VICORP president Robert Benson in July 1994. Benson, who had been with the company for seven years, explained to the *Nation's Restaurant News* soon after his departure, ''Our results have been disappointing, and in an organization where we stress accountability, I'll live up to those principles.'' Meanwhile, the company as a whole undertook a reassessment of its position, with its board of directors authorizing the repurchase of 500,000 shares of common stock, bringing the number of outstanding shares of VICORP stock to approximately 9.5 million. Then, in 1994, the firm announced that it planned to close 50 of its unprofitable locations.

### *Reorganizing: Mid-1990s and Beyond*

Despite these problems, 1994 also saw a new innovation for VICORP, a concept called Angel's Diner & Bakery. Essentially a converted Village Inn restaurant decorated with neon and stainless steel to resemble a postwar diner, the first Angel's location saw a near tripling of weekly sales in its first few months of operation. The Angel's Diner appeared to be a promising investment for the company, especially as an alternative to sluggish sales in the Bakers Square-West division. Still, VICORP remained cautious about the Diner, opening only a handful in 1994 and waiting to see if the conversion paid off in the long-term. The company saw modest overall growth in the early 1990s and, though still plagued with financial troubles in Florida and California, continued to focus its attention on innovation, renewal, and—with the help of Angel's Diner—growth.

It took several years before the company began to realize that growth, however, and it happened without the help of the Angel's concept, which was scrapped during 1996. VICORP did not open any new locations from 1995 to 1996 and instead focused on reorganizing and rebuilding the Baker's Square and Village Inn brands. While the company reported a loss of $929,000 in 1996, management felt that VICORP was better positioned to capture future profits as a result of its renewed focus and operational changes.

Indeed, the firm's financial position began to improve, and in 1998 the company opened three new restaurants. That year, profits increased by 32 percent to $9.12 million and VICORP announced that it would once again resume growth in its company-owned restaurants, especially in its Village Inn chain. In 1999, Joseph F. Trungale was named company president—he was eventually named CEO as well—and under his leadership VICORP stepped up the pace of its expansion program.

Success followed VICORP into the new millennium. In 2000, the company opened ten new Village Inn restaurants and a new Baker's Square location, the first expansion effort by this chain since 1993. Trungale commented on the firm's strategy in a December 2000 press release, stating, ''Our objective with Village Inn is to continue to fill in our existing company-operated markets while pursuing new growth of our franchise system.'' Trungale also commented, ''We have successfully built our Bakers Square concept to a level of profitability that now warrants unit expansion.''

With its finances back on track, VICORP began to receive unsolicited acquisitions offers. In an attempt to fend off takeover attempts, the company hired Salomon Smith Barney to evaluate its strategic alternatives. In December 2000, a stock repurchase program was launched that would take more than half of its common stock off the market. While revenues rose during 2000, earnings fell by 15 percent over the previous year, due in part to the expense related to hiring Salomon Smith Barney.

In 2001, VICORP announced that it would merge with a newly formed affiliate of investment firms Goldner Hawn Johnson & Morrison Inc. and BancBoston Capital. The deal, which would take VICORP out of the public arena, was met by opposition from company shareholders, who felt the purchase price of $173 million was too low. Two class action law suits were filed and eventually settled, and in May 2001 VICORP went private after offering its shareholders $25.65 per share. While VICORP had successfully overcome the problems of the 1990s and appeared to be back on track, its future success as a private firm remained to be seen.

### *Principal Operating Units*

Village Inn; Bakers Square; VICOM; J. Horner's.

### *Principal Competitors*

Advantica Restaurant Group Inc.; Brinker International Inc.; Marie Callender Pie Shops Inc.

### *Further Reading*

''Bakers Square Corners 'Fresh' in New Ads,'' *Nation's Restaurant News*, July 5, 1993, p. 12.

Carlino, Bill, ''Bakers Square, Village Inn on the Prowl for New Ad Agencies,'' *Nation's Restaurant News*, May 4, 1992, p. 12.

——, ''New Prexy Caruso Steers Village Inn Back to Value Track,'' *Nation's Restaurant News*, December 16, 1991, p. 3.

——, ''VICORP Fires Bakers Square President, Marketing Head: Headquarters to be Consolidated as Parent Plans 'Fresh Start' for Struggling Chain,'' *Nation's Restaurant News*, November 29, 1993, p. 1.

——, ''VICORP Ponders Future of Angel's Diner,'' *Nation's Restaurant News*, March 21, 1994, p. 3.

——, ''VICORP President, COO Benson Resigns Post,'' *Nation's Restaurant News*, July 11, 1994, p. 1.

Chaudhry, Rajan, ''VICORP Gives Florida Units Last Chance,'' *Nation's Restaurant News*, January 23, 1989, p. 1, 82.

——, ''VICORP Looks to Prosperous '89: Cuts Debt, Raises Earnings, and Trims Spending,'' Nation's Restaurant News, January 30, 1989, p. 64.

Howard, Theresa, ''Village Inn Joins Fast-Food Fray with Hamburger Line,'' *Nation's Restaurant News*, April 11, 1994, p. 12.

Papiernik, Richard, ''VICORP Studies Alternatives as Income Increases,'' *Nation's Restaurant News*, May 22, 2000, p. 18.

Ruggless, Ron, ''Trungale Named VICORP's New Prexy, Plans Village Inn Expansion,'' *Nation's Restaurant News*, November 8, 1999, p. 72.

Sokolove, Michael, ''Phone Call Costs VICORP $6.5 Million: Angry Florida Shareholder Spurs Call-Action Suit,'' *Restaurant Business*, July 1, 1992, p. 22.

Van Warner, Rick, ''VICORP Hitting Comeback Trail: ''Samboless' Company Getting Back to Basics,'' *Nation's Restaurant News*, April 24, 1988, p. 87.

Walkup, Carolyn, ''VICORP Boosts Profits, Targets Same-Store Sales,'' *Nation's Restaurant News*, November 3, 1997, p. 11.

—S. Thomas McCready
—update: Christina M. Stansell

# AO VimpelCom

**10-12, ul. 8 Marta**
**125083 Moscow**
**Russia**
**Telephone: (+7) 095-974-5888**
**Fax: (+7) 095-721-0017**
**Web site: http://www.vimpelcom.ru**

*Public Company*
*Incorporated:* 1992
*Employees:* 1,700
*Sales:* $274.1 million (2000)
*Stock Exchanges:* New York
*Ticker Symbol:* VIP
*NAIC:* 513322 Cellular and Other Wireless Telecommunications

AO VimpelCom keeps people connected in Russia, providing cellular phone services under the BeeLine brand name on either a U.S. or a European standard. The company's network covers all of Moscow, where the large majority of its subscribers are located. VimpelCom also holds licenses for nearly 70 percent of the territory of Russia, including Siberia, the Volga, Southern Russia, Central Russia, and the North Caucasus. A small but growing number of subscribers come from the regions as a result of the company's efforts extend its network into less densely populated territory. More than 1.3 million people subscribe to VimpelCom's services, making it one of the top cellular phone companies in Russia. Subscribers can take advantage of technologically advanced features that allow the user to send instant messages, access the Internet, or send e-mail through a mobile phone. In a country that has little experience with the Western style of capitalism, VimpelCom has been recognized for its high standards of corporate governance and transparency. The firm's adherence to international business standards helped it become the first modern Russian company to be listed on the New York Stock Exchange in 1996.

### *Fast Growth in a Boom Market: 1992–96*

Shortly after the demise of the Soviet Union in 1991, VimpelCom was organized by Dmitri Zimin, an entrepreneur with a background developing missile defense bases for a military radio institute in Moscow. Zimin's vision and determination won the confidence of Chicago businessman Augie Fabela. In mid-1992, the two set up a pilot cellular system in Moscow with a capacity of 200 subscribers. When that initial venture showed promise, AO VimpelCom was organized in September 1992. Zimin became president and CEO while Fabela served as board chairman.

Early in 1993, the company received a license to provide cellular services in Moscow on the AMPS (Advanced Mobile Phone Service) standard, which was widely used in North America. Using equipment acquired from the telecommunications equipment company Ericsson, VimpelCom built a new network capable of supporting 10,000 subscribers. In June 1994, commercial operations began under the Bee Line brand name.

A few months later, VimpelCom began modifying its network to a digital version of the American standard, known as D-AMPS. BeeLine 800 became the name for the service offered on this standard. The company also received licenses for regions of the Russian Federation that bordered Moscow, including Tver, Vladimir, and Ryazan. The company was now authorized to operate in an area that held about 24 million people, 16 percent of Russia's population. At the end of the first year of operation, VimpelCom had earned $27.97 million in sales revenue. With 5,358 subscribers, it had a 26 percent market share.

The cellular phone business was a boom market in the early 1990s. Mobile phones had been unknown under communism, and now the service provided an attractive alternative to often unreliable conventional telecommunications. VimpelCom courted customers with billboards all over Moscow and advertisements on television. The so-called "New Russians"– those who had profited most in the whirlwind transition to capitalism—made the new technology a status symbol. In the early years, they were willing to pay high prices for relatively ungainly handsets and even ordered phones decorated in diamonds

**Company Perspectives:**

*We strive to become the leading company in Russia providing mobile phone and other telecommunication services. We strive to operate efficiently and flexibly, working to anticipate the demands of tomorrow, attain the highest quality in the services we offer, and provide for growth in the value of the company. We strive to help people solve problems, experience the joy of personal interaction, and feel unrestrained by time and space. We strive to fuse all divisions of the company into a unified team that values competence, responsibility, and a willingness to give of oneself. We strive to maintain a company image that inspires trust and respect not only in our clients and business partners, but in society as a whole.*

and gold. Sales in 1995 nearly quadrupled from the year before. In addition to 22,553 subscribers in Moscow, VimpelCom had 435 subscribers in regions surrounding Russia's capital city.

After two years of profitable operation and sound accounting practices, VimpelCom was ready to enter the U.S. financial market. In November 1996, the company celebrated a successful entry into the New York Stock Exchange (NYSE), trading under the name ''Open Joint Stock Company Vimpel-Communications.'' VimpelCom became the first Russian company to be traded on the Big Board since the shares of the Trans-Siberian Railway were listed before the 1917 revolution. The offering garnered $66 million for the development of VimpelCom's network. The company's rapid growth continued after its NYSE debut. Revenue reached $213 million in 1996, and market share peaked at 56 percent with 59,214 total subscribers. Shares went up about 75 percent in the first six months of trading.

### *Reorientation to the GSM Standard: 1997–99*

Despite rapid growth in the early years of business, technological concerns threatened to weaken VimpelCom's ability to compete in the long term. The company's network operated on a U.S. standard, the D-AMPS system, which was gradually becoming outdated. VimpelCom's primary competitor, Mobile Telesystems (MTS) operated on the European GSM (Global Standard for Mobile) standard, having received the first GSM license granted by the Russian government. As a result, MTS was able to win customers away from VimpelCom with better quality, more advanced services, and wider reach when traveling outside Russia. VimpelCom would have to develop a GSM capability if it wanted to remain in the mobile phone market.

Since 1995, VimpelCom subsidiary AO KB Impuls had been investigating the possibility of implementing a GSM standard at an 1800 MHz frequency. MTS, in contrast, operated on a 900 MHz format. Impuls won a license to test the higher frequency, and soon VimpelCom began construction of a new GSM network. In a $135 million contract, equipment from Alcatel was used to construct 160 base stations on the GSM-1800 standard, enough to cover all of Moscow. The network became operational in June 1997, when VimpelCom introduced the ''BeeLine 1800'' service package.

VimpelCom more than doubled its subscriber base in 1997, and net profit was $61.1 million with total revenues reaching $305.9 million. VimpelCom's primary task now was to build a reputation as a GSM service provider, breaking the near-monopoly that its competitor had on the technologically advanced standard. With the acquisition of additional licenses in 1998, VimpelCom expanded its GSM capability. A license granted in April of that year allowed the company to use the GSM-1800 standard in vast regions of the Russian Federation outside Moscow. A further breakthrough came in August, when the Ministry of Communications granted the necessary licenses to convert to a dual band system, which offered better quality and greater flexibility by using both the 900 and 1800 MHz frequencies.

Unfortunately, implementation of the new network was delayed by the August 1998 economic crisis, when the ruble was severely devalued and the Russian government defaulted on its debts. VimpelCom's shares fell more than 80 percent in New York and the company lost $43.9 million in the third quarter. Still, the company moved ahead in October with the construction of its GSM-900 network. That fall VimpelCom also introduced a form of payment that was new to Moscow: GSM subscribers were able to buy time on pre-paid phone cards. The option was extended to D-AMPS subscribers a few months later.

Despite the financial crisis, VimpelCom was able to continue expanding its network because of a new partnership with a foreign investor. In December 1998, the Norwegian telecommunications company Telenor received a 25 percent stake in VimpelCom in exchange for $160 million in cash. The funds supported a significant widening of the zone of coverage, bringing the number of base stations to 500. VimpelCom also began working on providing its subscribers with automatic roaming services. An agreement with an operator in Krasnodar was the first step toward automatic national roaming.

Net loss for 1998 was $4.72 million, but VimpelCom nevertheless pushed ahead with the expansion of its GSM infrastructure. In May 1999, the company bought $10 million in equipment from the Finnish company Nokia. Nokia planned to assist VimpelCom with an expansion program called ''Big Beeline.'' The program would extend VimpelCom's reach, allowing GSM customers to call in an expanded area without incurring roaming charges. By July, construction had progressed far enough to begin operation of the dual-band GSM-900/1800 network. Roaming services were also expanding: customers were able to use their Moscow phone number in 50 countries in Europe, North America, Southeast Asia, the Near East, and Africa.

### *Courting the Mass Market: 1999–2000*

Despite energetic development efforts, VimpelCom still lagged behind MTS in the range of advanced services it offered. After the 1998 crisis, many users had switched to MTS's GSM-900 network, lured by price cuts at the competitor company. VimpelCom's market share in 1998 and 1999 was falling toward 40 percent. Telenor advised focusing on volume. In an aggressive move to capture the mass market, VimpelCom an-

**Key Dates:**

**1992:** AO VimpelCom is organized by Dmitri Zimin and Augie Fabela.
**1994:** Commercial operations start under the Bee Line brand name.
**1996:** VimpelCom becomes the first modern Russian company to list on the NYSE.
**1998:** VimpelCom receives licenses to operate a dual-band GSM network; Telenor becomes partner.
**2001:** The Alfa Group becomes a partner in the company's regional expansion effort.

nounced its ''phone in a box'' package in October 1999. For only $49, the consumer received a mobile telephone and a $10 calling card. The campaign was aimed at young people or those frustrated with the options available for fixed-line telephone installation: either pay high prices for a private company or endure a long wait before getting installation through the city. VimpelCom was actually selling its cell phones for less than they were worth, and ordinary Russians jumped at the offer. The initial production of 10,000 handsets sold out within days. In November, 50,000 new subscribers were drawn in. MTS joined the price war when it lowered its prices in December.

By the end of 1999, VimpelCom had 372,300 subscribers, which amounted to 47 percent of the mobile phone market. The combination of aggressive marketing and a lingering financial crisis took its toll on financial results, however. Total revenue in 1999 was $238.6 million, down $120 million from the year before, while net loss totaled $39.6 million. The company had spent $60 million on the development of its GSM network alone in 1999. The number of subscribers continued to grow into 2000, but stock price fell as investors became impatient with the strategy of sacrificing profit for market share.

Activities in 2000 centered on expanding the capabilities of cell phone service. Short messaging service (SMS), a capability that had been introduced in 1999, allowed subscribers to exchange short text messages through their handsets. SMS was promoted throughout 2000 until, by the end of the year, one million SMS messages were being transmitted daily. Another new technology was Wireless Application Protocol, or WAP, a standard for the wireless transmission of Web pages. VimpelCom introduced WAP services in mid-2000, allowing subscribers to access Internet sites that were specially adapted for small screens. At the new BeeOnline Internet portal, customers could tap into over 200 channels of news, entertainment, and financial information. An even newer technology, the Global Package Radio System (GPRS), offered the capability of transmitting large volumes of data to cell phones. Early in 2000, VimpelCom made an agreement under which Nokia would eventually provide GPRS to the BeeLine network. A security offering in July 2000 raised $225.4 million to finance the technological advances.

In the fall of 2000, a government move fueled worries about the stability of Russia's business environment. The Communications Ministry announced that it was taking back certain frequencies that had been granted to VimpelCom and its competitor MTS. The frequencies had originally been granted free of charge; the cell phone companies protested that regulatory policy needed to become more transparent and standardized. Observers suggested that the government would grant the frequencies to Sonic Duo, a new cell phone company that was majority owned by a state holding company. VimpelCom stock fell in reaction to the government's action.

A more positive development came in October, when VimpelCom acquired the Moscow cell phone dealer network MCC-Start, which operated under the Mobile-Center brand name. The acquisition would give VimpelCom more control over the retail end of the mobile phone sector, even as the company continued to use independent dealers.

### *Looking Toward the Regions Under New Leadership: 2000 and Beyond*

Near the end of 2000, a new president took over duties from founder Dmitri Zimin, who stayed on as CEO. Jo Lunder, a Norwegian national, had worked for VimpelCom's partner Telenor before becoming the Russian company's chief operating officer in fall of 1999. Now president of VimpelCom, he outlined his vision for the company in a December 2000 interview with *The Russia Journal*. ''What we're trying to do now is reposition VimpelCom to be seen as a GSM company,'' Lunder said. He noted that the company's GSM network had caught up with the competition in terms of quality and coverage after steady expansion in 2000. Over half of the company's subscribers now operated on the GSM standard, up from 35 percent at the beginning of 2000. With a reliable GSM infrastructure, Lunder expected to attract heavy mobile phone users in the corporate segment, while still offering services appropriate for the mass market.

Profitability was a sensitive issue at the end of 2000 as the company reported its third consecutive net loss, at $77.8 million higher than the two previous years. The subscriber base had doubled over the past year to 780,100, but VimpelCom's market share was at a modest 39 percent. Lunder hoped that sound business practices would eventually bring the company back to profitability. ''What is important for VimpelCom is that we build a strong, healthy company with high quality services and loyal subscribers and customers,'' he said.

Lunder believed that a key to long-term survival was expansion into Russia's regions outside of Moscow. These regions posed a particular challenge because of low population density and a more dismal economic situation than was found in the capital. Establishing a presence there would require a considerable investment that would only pay off after several years. VimpelCom began searching for a partner in the regional enterprise. In May 2001, an agreement was signed with Eco Telecom Ltd., part of the respected Alfa Group of companies in Russia. In a complicated arrangement, separately-managed subsidiary AO VimpelCom-Region would raise up to $337 million for regional expansion in contributions from Alfa, Telenor, and parent company VimpelCom. Telenor planned to purchase a package of treasury shares in order to maintain its 25 percent stake in VimpelCom; Alfa's $103 million contribution would gain it a 25 percent stake. VimpelCom founder Dmitri Zimin and his affiliates retained just over 10 percent. Zimin expressed satisfaction with the deal, saying, ''Combining Telenor's expertise in telecommunications and Alfa's knowledge of, and infrastructure in, the Russian regions, we have assembled an extremely powerful team that will lead VimpelCom to become Russia's premier national operator.''

The first tranche of the deal was concluded in November 2001. In the preceding months, VimpelCom-Region had launched five affiliates in Tver, Vladimir, Ryazan, Kaluga, and Lipetsk. Meanwhile, VimpelCom introduced its latest package for Moscow subscribers. The BeePlus GSM package offered automatic roaming, WAP Internet capabilities, and automatic caller ID. VimpelCom now had roaming agreements in over 100 countries, more than its competitor MTS.

Late in 2001, a new cell phone carrier, Sonic Duo, began operations. The new competitor's prices were similar to VimpelCom and MTS, and it offered coverage only in the Moscow area. Analysts noted that the Russian mobile phone market was close to saturation and suggested the new company might win a 15 percent market share. VimpelCom did not feel significantly threatened by the new entrant into the cell phone market. The company hoped to meet the challenges of competition, price wars, and regional expansion with a particular focus on customer service. Third quarter 2001 results showed a net income of $13.9 million, rasing hopes that VimpelCom was back in a period of profitability.

## *Principal Subsidiaries*

AO KB Impuls; ZAO BeeOnLine-Portal; ZAO VimpelCom-Region.

## *Principal Competitors*

Mobile Telesystems (MTS), Sonic Duo.

## *Further Reading*


Bogatyreva, Oksana, ''VimpelCom: 'Our regional expansion estimated to cost $337 million,' '' *Russia Journal*, October 26, 2001.

Chazan, Guy, ''Russia Reclaims Phone Channels in Blow Curbing Property Rights,'' *Wall Street Journal*, September 13, 2000, p. A21.

''In Moscow, Phone Wars Can Get Nasty,'' *Business Week*, May 31, 1999, p. 23.

''Is VimpelCom Racing to the Bottom?,'' *Business Week*, May 8, 2000, p. 19.

Kozlov, Vladimir, ''Third GSM Operator Unlikely to Change Sector,'' *Russia Journal*, November 23, 2001, p. 9.

——, ''VimpelCom sets eye on corporate, mass markets,'' *Russia Journal*, December 2, 2000, p. T2.

Merkushev, Vladimir, ''Russians Connect as Mobile Rates Fall,'' *Russia Journal*, December 13, 1999, p. 9.

Musatov, Andrei, ''VimpelCom 'Pulls Through' Despite Crisis Setbacks,'' *Russia Journal*, October 18, 1999, p. 13.

''Phone Farce in Russia,'' *Economist* (U.S.), September 16, 2000, p. 68.

''Russian Cellular Concern Seeks a Big Board Listing,'' *Wall Street Journal*, October 2, 1996, p. A15.

''Russian Telephones—Ivan the Talkative,'' *Economist* (U.S.), January 22, 2000, p. 64.

''VimpelCom Closes First Tranche of Investment from Alfa Group and Telenor to Accelerate Expansion,'' *Russian Telecom*, November 2001, pp. 6–7.

''VimpelCom Launches Expansion Program,'' *Russia Online & Wireless*, May 31, 1999, p. 4.

''VimpelCom, Telenor, and Alfa Group Form Strategic Partnership,'' *Russian Telecom*, June 2001, p. 5.

''VimpelCom: Upwardly Mobile,'' *Euromoney*, April 1997, p. 94.


—Sarah Ruth Lorenz

# Wella AG

**Berliner Allee 65**
**D-64274 Darmstadt**
**Germany**
**Telephone: (49) 6151 34 0**
**Fax: (49) 6151 34 27 48**
**Web site: http://www.wella.de**

*Public Company*
*Incorporated:* 1880 as Franz Ströher-Rothenkirchen
*Employees:* 17,210
*Sales:* EUR 3.1 billion ($2.8 billion) (2001)
*Stock Exchanges:* Munich Berlin Frankfurt Hamburg Dusseldorf Hannover
*Ticker Symbol:* 776560
*NAIC:* 325620 Toilet Preparation Manufacturing; 325998 All Other Miscellaneous Chemical Product and Preparation Manufacturing

Wella AG operates as one of the world's top cosmetic suppliers with brands found in over 150 countries. The company has three main divisions: Professional Hair Cosmetics, Consumer Hair Cosmetics, and Cosmetics and Fragrances. Its Professional unit accounts for nearly 50 percent of group sales and offers professional hairdressers hair care products under the brand names Wella, Sebastian, Graham Webb, Kadus, Londa, Welonda, Belvedere, and Tondeo. The Consumer division secures just over 30 percent of total sales and focuses on hair coloring products along with care and styling products. Holding company Cosmopolitan Cosmetics GmbH oversees the operations of the Cosmetics and Fragrances segment, which supplies fragrances in 120 countries through a network of 30 subsidiaries. This division accounts for 20 percent of Wella's total sales. Wella's logo remains one of the most familiar in Germany.

## *Early History: 1880s–Early 1900s*

In 1880, at the age of 26, the hairdresser Franz Ströher, the grand- and great-grandfather of today's generations of owners, founded a company for the production and distribution of artificial hair in the Saxon Vogtland. His company was registered on July 1 at the Auerbach district court. The region in which he chose to operate was a traditional stronghold of the textile industry, with a well-established local manufacturing base. Here, the people were skilled, diligent, and poor—an ideal workforce for the labor-intensive production of hairpieces and wigs, which were made out of natural and artificial hair. During his years spent traveling as an apprentice hairdresser in Germany, Holland, Switzerland, and France, Ströher learned about new hair fashions and acquired the necessary hairdressing techniques. In 1872, undulation waving was invented by the Frenchman François Marcel. This became a popular method for waving women's hair and was supplemented with the addition of natural or artificial hairpieces. In 1880, Ströher set up his own private firm, Franz Ströher-Rothenkirchen, for the manufacture and distribution of artificial hair. After initial difficulties with the development of new production methods, he eventually found a material in England that, with the aid of a waterproof finish that he had developed himself, could be used to make wigs. This product, ''Tullemoid waterproof,'' became a considerable success at the turn of the century, and in 1904 a larger manufacturing plant was built in Rothenkirchen. This plant still exists, although it has been modified extensively.

In 1908, Ströher's two older sons, Karl Ströher, a merchant, and Georg Ströher, a hairdresser, joined the business. They were to shape the company's history over the following 60 years. As early as 1931, sales extended to the United States, and in Rothenkirchen a staff of 30 was employed in addition to family members. They manufactured many kinds of wigs and hairpieces. The permanent wave had not yet become widely popular. Promising experiments were carried out in the United Kingdom and their results impressed the Continent, but World War I broke out before the hot-wave technique for women could be offered at a reasonable price. The war had a significant impact in more than one respect upon the history of the family business. Franz Ströher's three younger sons were killed, and Franz Ströher himself, almost broken by the events, left the management increasingly to his sons Karl and Georg, taking the less active role of senior partner until he died in 1936. To compound these problems, international hair fashions suddenly changed; the popularity of bobbed hair caused a rapid decline in the demand for hairpieces. This change led to a difficult period

### Company Perspectives:

*Create, experience, and scent are three terms with which all three group divisions—Professional, Consumer, and Cosmetics and Fragrances—identify. They are the embodiment of our activities, products, and services.*

of readjustment for the company. There was a brief episode of production of wigs for dolls, clothing for workers, mannequins for hairdressers, and sales of hairbrushes, washing brushes, toothbrushes, face towels, and shaving towels. The war also cut contacts abroad that were difficult to reestablish.

However, one new development after the mid-1920s led to a phase of relative prosperity for Franz Ströher OHG, as the company had been called since 1918. The permanent waving process was at last proving successful and gave a much wider scope to the hairdressing trade. François Marcel's waving technique was developed further in Germany by Karl Nessler and Josef Mayer. At this point, the Ströher brothers took the opportunity to acquire a license for the manufacture of a new generation of permanent wave machines that used 16 to 24 volts and were easy to operate.

## *The Wella Brand Is Launched: 1927*

In the meantime, the brand name "Wella" had been registered at the German patent office as a hairdressing trademark. Since 1927, the production and distribution of perm machines, hair driers, hairdressers' equipment, and salon furniture have been carried out under this name. Soon cosmetic hair products appeared as part of the production program alongside professional hairdressing equipment. These took into account the demands of hairdressers. A well-known product at this time was the hair treatment Kolestral, based on recent biological discoveries.

The year 1930 was the 50th anniversary of the company and marked the beginning of a new phase of expansion. The business adopted the legal status of a public limited company, Franz Ströher AG, with an original capital of 250,000 marks, and employed 150 staff members. From this time, the licensed Wella emblem, with a woman's head and stylized waves of hair, became an international symbol. The *Wella News*, a new trade magazine, was published by the company. This journal had a widespread distribution and, combined with the regular training courses offered to hairdressers, helped to establish a strong connection between the company and the hairdressing trade. The factory at Rothenkirchen was by this time manufacturing hair driers, hydraulic chairs, and electric hair-cutting equipment. The program also incorporated the production of furnishings for hairdressing salons and cosmetic products. These were partly produced by the company itself and partly supplied by others.

In the years before 1938, the company established many subsidiaries, and a manufacturing plant was set up in Plauen, Vogtland. International branches and subsidiary companies all over the world promoted the growth of the family business. It was no longer restricted by the unfavorable location of the Saxon Vogtland. In the course of an allocation policy pursued in the Thüringen region, the head offices of the corporation, together with the manufacturing and export divisions, were transferred to the town of Apolda, although the production of hair cosmetics continued at the parent plant at Rothenkirchen. When the factory at Apolda was dismantled at the end of World War II, in 1945, the firm had well over 800 employees.

This period of expansion also brought about important welfare innovations within the company, such as subsidies for children of employees and allowances for marriage, childbirth, death, and accidents. Provision for the retirement of former staff and their dependents was secured by regular benefit payments, and advanced training within the establishment was extended. Typical of the family business was the strong, almost patriarchal relationship between management and staff. Documents from the Wella archive in Darmstadt demonstrate that employees at the end of the 1930s were on average fairly young. Many surnames occur several times, which points to the recruitment of employees' relatives, and a major proportion of staff moved with the management from Sachsen to Thüringen.

As early as the 1930s, Wella laboratories were developing and constantly improving numerous hair cosmetic products that became best sellers, such as the bleaching compound Blondor, a non-alkaline washing agent concentrate called Wellapon, and the liquid foaming hair tint Wellaton, which came in an wide range of colors. Whereas bleaching and tinting agents were relatively well developed, it took longer to find an effective dyeing compound. Wella Percol Liquid was the best known product. Koleston, a gentle, conditioning cream dye available in a tube, had been developed but could not be produced during wartime, when the raw materials it required were unobtainable.

## *Postwar Reorganization*

The economic policy of the National Socialists and wartime conditions were not favorable to Wella. The Ströher brothers were active Freemasons and were opposed to National Socialism. In the course of time, important products could no longer be manufactured due to restrictions on raw-material supplies. The factory in Apolda built new ventilation systems and equipment for submarines and could no longer make permanent wave machines and hair driers. At the end of World War II, the Ströher's had to face the dismantling of the plant in Apolda and expropriation by the government of the plant in Rothenkirchen, still intact with more than 300 working staff, as communal state property.

The Ströher's, supported by a few tireless colleagues, began to look for a new sphere of influence and orientation. In September 1945, at the Hotel Krone, the reconstruction of the business began on a very small scale in Huenfeld, Osthessen, under the new name of Ondal GmbH. The brothers stayed for the time being in Rothenkirchen. It was only in 1946 that the production of cosmetic products resumed there, followed by the production of hairdressing equipment in May of that year. At the same time, Wella Hairdressing Requirements GmbH was founded in Berlin. After the expropriation of Rothenkirchen, a large-scale manufacturing plant was set up in Huenfeld, which has since been extended several times and represents the center of the company's production. After the division of Germany, Wella's former plant in Rothenkirchen continued to operate. As VEB Londa it became part of a larger chemical concern, which had very limited development potential due to the strict principles of

**Key Dates:**

**1880:** Franz Ströher establishes his private firm, Franz Ströher-Rothenkirchen, for the production and distribution of artificial hair in the Saxon Vogtland.
**1918:** The company is renamed Franz Ströher OHG.
**1927:** The Wella brand name is launched.
**1931:** The firm's sales extend into the United States.
**1945:** The company restructures as a result of World War II.
**1950:** The business is registered as Wella AG; hair conditioning cream tint Koleston is introduced.
**1973:** Day-to-day operations are entrusted to non-family directors for the first time.
**1983:** Wella goes public.
**1987:** The company expands into fragrances with the purchase of Parfum Rochas S.A.
**1994:** Fragrance manufacturer Muehlens KG is acquired.
**2000:** Vivality, a global hair care product, is launched.

East German economic planning. Nevertheless, it came to hold a significant position in the market before the reunification of Germany and had established a considerable number of outlets for the export of goods, mainly to Eastern Europe. However, the profile of the enterprise and the quality of its products were not compatible with western standards. In February 1990, political changes in East Germany brought about the reintegration of the Rothenkirchen plant into Wella in the form of a joint venture which was to produce and market hairdressing products and equipment in Germany and other European markets. Without the strong bond resulting from their shared origins in the family business the reintegration of the factory at Rothenkirchen with Wella would not have been possible.

From 1950, the business was registered as Wella AG. The central management of the company operated from Darmstadt, Hessen, where the head offices were based. The reintroduction of the successful Wella logo proved highly advantageous. Wella, having had a modest turnover of DM10 million in 1950, then attempted to retrieve international rights for trademarks which had been expropriated and business connections which had been lost after 1945.

Wella's international reputation grew due to its early and aggressive penetration of international markets. As early as the 1950s, Wella had included Third World countries in its trading policies and had met with strong opposition. Production started in 1952 in Chile, Italy, and the Netherlands, in 1953 in Africa, and in 1954 in Australia and Brazil. In the 1960s, the Asian and Pacific territories were entered in stages. An international distribution network was set up and larger manufacturing plants all over the world helped protect the firm from world trade friction and set the prototype for Germany's international business relations after World War II.

In 1950, Koleston, the first hair-conditioning cream tint, was introduced, initiating a new generation of hair products that conquered the markets. Koleston continued to be produced into the new century. During the 1980s, Wella's high research-and-development costs were reflected in a high price for both hairdressers and consumers. Wella also had a large range of successful products by this time, including such well-known brands as Wella Balsam, Shock Waves, Bellady, and System Professional. A change in consumer attitudes and a stronger awareness of the environment caused increasing recourse to natural ingredients, the abolition or reduction of propellant gas in sprays, and the increasing use of biodegradable packaging made of raw materials that break down naturally. In most cases, it was costly to develop new environmentally friendly products, as well as to market them effectively, since there was often a discrepancy between ecological requirements and consumer demand.

## *Growth as a Public Company: 1980s–1990s,*

As late as the 1980s, Wella continued to tout itself as an independent family business in which the founder's influence could still be felt, and members of the Ströher family's third generation had been brought into the management of the company since the early 1950s. However, Wella's considerable growth and diversification were indicative of a company far beyond the scope of a family business. In 1973, the day-to-day running of the group was entrusted to directors who were not members of the founding family. The actual family members themselves functioned in strictly supervisory and advisory roles. It was due to these changes that in 1978 Wella's worldwide sales passed DM1 billion for the first time and have continued to rise ever since. In 1983, Wella turned to the stock market in a move to adjust its capital structure to cope with its rapid growth.

As part of this growth strategy, Wella entered the fragrance market with the 1987 purchase of Parfum Rochas S.A., a French luxury goods manufacturer. It continued to beef up holdings in this segment with the 1994 purchase of Muehlens KG, the fragrance manufacturer of the 4711 product line. The deal was the largest in Wella history. Along with its fragrance business, Wella also began to aggressively pursue expansion in the retail hair care market. In 1993, it acquired United States-based Sebastian International.

During 1995, Wella's chairman, Peter Zuhlsdorff, resigned suddenly after disagreeing with family shareholders about Wella's future direction. Jorg von Craushaar took the helm and immediately set out to position the firm as a leader in both the hair care and fragrance markets. With new leadership in place, the group made a number of divestitures that included the Payot skin care and cosmetics brand, the Restoria line, the company's Chilean Laboratorio Arensburg S.A.I.C., Rene Garraud SA, and Anton Hubner KG.

As part of its realignment, Wella consolidated all of its cosmetics and fragrances businesses under holding company Cosmopolitan Cosmetics GmbH in 1997. While the group had been unable to secure the number one position overall in the industry, its financial results moved in a positive direction despite challenging economies in many of its major markets, including Asia and Latin America.

## *Success in the New Millennium*

By the time Wella entered the new millennium, the company stood as the largest German cosmetics supplier. During 2000, the company formed three distinct divisions—Professional, Consumer, and Cosmetics and Fragrances. In order to strengthen its Consumer segment, Wella focused on positioning it in the higher-priced segment of the market and also made several strategic acquisitions, including United States-based Johnson Products and Graham Webb International, the hair care line of Nicky Clarke, the brand rights to Yardley of London U.S. LLC, and the Daniel Galvin brand. Wella also launched Vivality, its first-ever globally marketed hair care product in 2000.

That year Wella achieved record results—the best it had seen in 30 years. Sales increased from EUR 2.3 billion recorded in 1999, to EUR 2.8 billion in 2000. The upward climb continued into 2001, as sales jumped to EUR 3.1 billion. Net profit also increased from EUR 80.2 million in 1999 and EUR 100.9 million in 2000 to EUR 123.6 million in 2001.

Wella's long-term goals continue to revolve around building each business segment into a market leader through acquisition and development of high-value, high-profile brands. In early 2002, Wella acquired Escada Beaute Group SA and formed a licensing agreement with Escada AG in which Wella would develop the Escada brand of perfumes. Heiner Gurtler, who took over for von Craushaar upon his retirement, commented on how the purchase related to the group's strategy in a March 2002 *Cosmetics International* article. "With the acquisition and the integration of the business into Cosmopolitan Cosmetics, two strategical targets of our cosmetics and fragrances business will be achieved: extending the brand portfolio and at the same time focusing on the segment of higher priced international prestige fragrances." Gurtler also claimed that "the strong position of Cosmopolitan Cosmetics in the global fragrance market will be expanded."

From its earliest days in the 1880s, Wella has preserved its character as an successful family business, and nearly 80 percent of company shares are still owned by members of the Ströher family. With its longstanding history of success, Wella's position among industry leaders would no doubt continue well into the future.

## *Principal Subsidiaries*

Ondal Industrietechnik GmbH; Cosmopolitan Cosmetics GmbH; Percol Beteiligungen GmbH; Kadabell GmbH & Co.KG; Emil Kiessling GmbH; Londa Rothenkirchen Produktions GmbH; Londa GmbH; Tondeo-Werk GmbH; Muelhens GmbH & Co. KG; Intercosmetic S.A., Groot-Bijgaarden (Belgium); Ondal-France E.u.r.l.; Wella France S.A.; Parfums Rochas S.A. (France); Wella (United Kingdom) Holdings Ltd.; Wella Italia Labocos s.p.a. (Italy); N.V. Handelsmaatschappij van Ravensberg (Netherlands); Wella International Finance B.V. (Netherlands); Herman Lepsøe A/S (Norway); Interkosmetik Ges.m.b.H. (Austria); Wella AB (Sweden); Wella Beteiligungen AG (Switzerland); Productos Cosméticos S.A. (Spain); Wella Polska sp.z.o.o. (Poland); Wella Magyarország Kft.(Wella Hungary Ltd.); Ondabel S.A. (Argentina); Cosmetic Products Pty. Ltd. (Australia); Belcosa Distribuidora de Cosmeticos Ltda. (Brazil); Wella Cosmetics China Ltd.; Wella Japan Co. Ltd.(83.9%); Productora de Cosméticos S.A.de C.V. (Mexico); Sonata Laboratories Ltd. (New Zealand); Wella Korea Co.Ltd.; The Wella Corporation (U.S.); Graham Webb International (U.S.).

## *Principal Divisions*

Professional; Consumer; Cosmetics and Fragrances.

## *Principal Competitors*

Alberto-Culver Company; Beiersdorf AG; L'Oréal SA; Johnson & Johnson; Procter & Gamble Co.

## *Further Reading*

"The Future Starts on a Good Footing for Wella," *Cosmetics International*, April 25, 2002, p. 5.

"Greater Focus Boosts Wella," *European Cosmetics Markets*, June 1999, p. 218.

"Not for Three Decades Has Wella Been so Dynamically Successful," *Cosmetics International*, April 25, 2001, p. 5.

"The Story So Far," *Grocer*, April 13, 2002, p. 70.

"Wella AG Acquires Yardley U.S.," *Drug Store News*, December 17, 2001, p. 73.

"Wella: Back on Track," *European Cosmetics Markets*, June 1998.

"Wella's Expansion Plans Into Perfumery Have Begun," *Cosmetics International*, March 25, 2002, p. 1.

"Wella's Global Developments," *Cosmetics International*, August 15, 2000, p. 7.

"Wella's on the Way to Another Prestige Success," *Cosmetics International*, June 10, 2001, p. 6.

"We're Alive and Wella," *Cosmetics International*, June 10, 2000, p. 5.

—Wieland Sachse English translation by Karin Potisk
—update: Christina M. Stansell

# Westpac Banking Corporation

**60 Martin Place**
**Sydney, New South Wales 2000**
**Australia**
**Telephone: (02) 9226 3311**
**Fax: (02) 9226 4128**
**Web site: http://www.westpac.com.au**

*Public Company*
*Incorporated:* 1850 as the Bank of New South Wales
*Employees:* 28,534
*Total Assets:* A$189.8 billion ($93.89 billion)
*Stock Exchanges:* Australia New Zealand Tokyo New York
*Ticker Symbol:* WBK
*NAIC:* 52211 Commercial Banking

Westpac Banking Corporation is one of the four main banks in Australia along with competitors National Australia Bank, Commonwealth Bank of Australia, and Australia and New Zealand Banking Group. The bank was founded in 1817 and was incorporated in 1850 as the Bank of New South Wales. In 1982, the bank merged with the Commercial Bank of Australia Limited, founded in the state of Victoria in 1866, and changed its name to Westpac Banking Corporation. Westpac's name is derived from the area which it has historically served—the western Pacific. The company caters to over eight million customers—both retail and commercial—and provides banking, investment, insurance, and various other financial services. Operations in Australia account for 68 percent of profits, while New Zealand secures 18 percent, and other regions shore up the remaining 14 percent.

## *Banking Background*

When Australia was settled, in the late 18th century, the colony's economy was based on a system of barter. A variety of foreign coins also circulated, but these usually found their way back overseas in exchange for the many imported goods the colony needed, so Australia had trouble keeping any form of currency in the colony. Governor Laughlan Macquarie was determined to solve his country's monetary problems. To help prevent currency from disappearing overseas, Macquarie had the center cut out of coins, creating a donut-shaped ''holey dollar.'' The center piece, known as a ''dump,'' was worth one quarter of a holey dollar. Still, currency and exchange problems continued to plague the Australian colonies.

In 1816, Governor Macquarie began to push for the establishment of a colonial bank, and a group of 46 subscribers formed a committee to organize the bank's operations. On April 8, 1817, the Bank of New South Wales opened for business in a house in Macquarie Place. Edward Smith Hall was the cashier/secretary, and Robert Campbell Junior was the head accountant. The bank's first depositor was Sergeant Jeremiah Murphy, who entrusted £50 to the new bank.

The bank of New South Wales operated for five years under its original charter, granted by Governor Macquarie, and then for another five under a renewal issued by Governor Brisbane. In 1828, however, the British authorities declared the Bank's charter invalid, claiming that colonial governors had no authority to issue such charters. The Bank of New South Wales was then reorganized as a joint-stock company.

As trade expanded throughout the Australian colonies, the Bank of New South Wales grew. In 1847, it employed the London Joint Stock Bank as its overseas agent in London. Foreign exchange was a growing area of the bank's activities. In 1850, the bank was incorporated by an act of the New South Wales Parliament and was allowed to establish branches. The first branch opened in the Moreton Bay area of what was soon to become the colony of Queensland. A year later gold fever struck Australia, and the bank soon sent its agents directly to the mining regions. Some branches were no more than a tent; others were built with furnaces to smelt gold right on the premises. In 1853, the bank established an office to handle the colony's growing export trade.

The mid- to late 1800s saw widespread development of the country's resources. Bank branches were established at scattered points across the continent. Travel was difficult and often dangerous, as the story of Robert White, the ''terror of the

## Company Perspectives:

*A good business should be both financially successful and a good corporate citizen. At Westpac, we know that to produce sound results for shareholders we must not only constantly deliver for our customers, but must meet our responsibilities to staff and the community. We fully accept our responsibility to fulfill our wider corporate social responsibilities and we see it as fundamental to our long-term sustainability and growth. Our vision is to be a great Australian company, judged in the eyes of our stakeholders. Our values are teamwork, integrity, and performance, and they represent the essential spirit of our company. Our strategy aims to provide a superior customer experience in delivering practical financial and banking solutions.*

bushrangers'' illustrates. In 1863, Robert White, an accountant at the Deniliquin branch of the Bank of New South Wales was held up. After putting up a fight, he found himself bound and gagged, and the bank robbers headed out of town with £3,000 in gold and notes. The accountant managed to free himself, however, and was soon on the bandits' trail. He successfully recovered the £3,000 and the bushrangers landed in jail. On another occasion, White was ambushed in Gympie while carrying a great deal of money. He drew his pistol and charged his adversaries, wounding two of them. After his banking career, White was elected to the New South Wales legislative assembly.

### *The Commercial Bank of Australia Is Created: 1866*

In 1866, the Commercial Bank of Australia opened in Melbourne. CBA focused on suburban and rural areas. In 1870, Henry Gyles Turner became general manager of CBA; Turner directed the bank for the next 30 years. By 1876, the bank was operating 34 offices and agencies throughout the Victoria territory. CBA expanded steadily across the rest of the continent and had offices in Sydney, Perth, Adelaide, and Brisbane by 1890.

In 1893, Australian banks faced a major crisis. Overvaluation of urban real estate and a sharp drop in wool prices precipitated a depression. Depositors panicked and scrambled to withdraw their funds. Fewer than half of the 28 conventional banks were able to continue operations without some interruption, but the Bank of New South Wales was able to. Not until after the turn of the century did the economy fully recover. At that time, both the Bank of New South Wales and the Commercial Bank of Australia branched out further. CBA soon moved to Tasmania and New Zealand; ''the Wales,'' as the Bank of New South Wales had come to be known, ventured to Fiji, Papua New Guinea, and Samurai Island. Increased trade with the neighboring islands paralleled a general increase in foreign trade.

In 1914, World War I broke out. Many employees of both the Bank of New South Wales and the CBA enlisted in the Australian Imperial Force. Of the 1,112 men from the two banks who volunteered, 186 were killed in action. In 1918, John Russell French, general manager of the Bank of New South Wales, was knighted for his service in helping Australia finance the war effort.

Australia experienced the economic boom of the 1920s along with the rest of the world. In 1929, on the eve of the Depression, the Bank of New South Wales appointed a new general manager. Alfred Charles Davidson took the helm at a time when Australian banking was undergoing many changes. Davidson introduced a travel department, which later became the largest in the southern hemisphere, and established the British and Foreign Department. The bank stepped up overseas operations in the early 1930s. In 1931, Alfred Davidson was instrumental in the Australian government's decision to devaluate its currency, a move that improved trade conditions for exporters. By the mid-1930s the economy was recovering from the Depression.

World War II brought about strict controls on Australian banking. Bank branches were closed to release manpower for the war effort. The Japanese invasion of the Pacific threatened some of the branches of the CBA and ''the Wales.'' Branches in New Guinea and elsewhere were closed. An air raid on the northern Queensland town of Darwin caused extensive damage to the Bank of New South Wales branch there, and lesser damage to CBA's branch. During the war, the Bank of New South Wales saw 3,330 (65%) of its male staff enlist.

### *Fighting Nationalization: Late 1940s*

After the war, private Australian trading banks were soon entrenched in another conflict. On August 16, 1947 Prime Minister Ben Chifley announced that the banks would be nationalized. According to Chifley's plan, the Commonwealth Bank (Australia's central bank) would acquire the shares of the private banks and then appoint directors to run them as arms of the central bank. The private banks immediately challenged the constitutionality of nationalization and waged a political war to have the Labour Party ousted and eliminate the threat of other obnoxious legislation. The bankers were successful on both counts. The Australian High Court declared the Bank Act of 1947 unconstitutional because it interfered with the freedom of trade and commerce among the states guaranteed in section 92 of the Australian constitution. In 1949, the Labour Party was overwhelmingly defeated in the general election. It was a major victory for the Bank of New South Wales, the Commercial Bank of Australia, and Australia's other private banks.

Throughout the 1950s, the Australian economy was in an upswing. Savings bank deposits were growing in popularity at this time. Before 1956, savings bank operations were conducted exclusively by the government-owned Commonwealth Bank. The Bank of New South Wales entered the savings bank field in the late 1950s and competed aggressively for savings accounts. In compliance with government regulations, the bank earmarked a certain percentage of its savings bank deposits for housing construction loans. Demand for housing and durable goods was high in the 1950s and 1960s. In 1957, the Bank of New South Wales purchased 40 percent of Australia's largest finance company, the Australian Guarantee Corporation Ltd. (AGC). AGC made loans to businesses as well as consumers and was active in investment and merchant banking as well as insurance.

In 1966, Australia switched from pounds to dollars. For the next two years, the public traded in its imperial currency—

## Key Dates:

**1817:** The Bank of New South Wales opens for business.
**1828:** The bank is reorganized as a joint-stock company.
**1850:** The company begins to establish branch offices.
**1866:** The Commercial Bank of Australia (CBA) is established.
**1893:** Australian banks face a major crisis during an economic depression.
**1949:** The Labour party, which introduced the failed Bank Act of 1947, is defeated in the general election.
**1957:** The Bank of New South Wales purchases 40 percent of the Australian Guarantee Corporation Ltd. (AGC).
**1974:** Australian banks enter the credit card field.
**1982:** Westpac is formed from the merger of the Bank of New South Wales and CBA.
**1988:** The company acquires the remaining shares of AGC.
**1995:** Westpac purchases Challenge Bank.
**1996:** The firm merges with Trust Bank New Zealand Limited.
**1997:** Westpac merges with Bank of Melbourne.
**1999:** Merger talks with National Australia Bank Ltd. are called off.

pounds, shillings, and pence—for new Australian dollars and cents. Banks had the difficult task of converting to the new decimal currency. Machinery had to be changed, staffs had to be retrained, and accounting had to be translated.

In the 1970s, the Bank of New South Wales and the Commercial Bank of Australia diversified both their services and their areas of operation. Both banks opened more branches overseas. At the same time each was busy acquiring different financial companies at home to expand upon the services they provided. The Bank of New South Wales's holding in the Australian Guarantee Corporation increased to 54 percent by the early 1970s, while the Commercial Bank of Australia operated a finance company, General Credit Ltd., as a wholly owned subsidiary. Both banks also became involved in merchant banking. The Bank of New South Wales, for instance, owned a substantial number of shares in Partnership Pacific Ltd., Schroder Darling & Company, and Australian United Corporation. CBA held significant interests in the merchant banks Euro-Pacific Finance and International Pacific Corporation. In 1974, Australian banks entered the credit card field with Bankcard. Banks also got involved in insurance activities in the 1970s.

### *The Formation of Westpac: Late 1970s–Early 1980s*

The mid-1970s saw the Australian continent in a severe recession. During these years the large amount of foreign investment in Australia's raw-commodities industries became a political hot potato. Australians felt that foreign investors had too much say in the allocation and development of their resources, particularly in petroleum and mining operations. The fact remained, however, that Australia lacked the capital to develop industry on its own. A debate over capital market regulations grew louder in the late 1970s. In 1979, growing pressure to deregulate the financial markets led to the appointment of a government committee to investigate the effects deregulation would have on the economy.

The committee, headed by Australian businessman Keith Campbell, reported its findings two years later, and deregulation soon followed. Foreign banks were allowed to set up shop in Australia, and many of the restrictions on the trading banks were removed. By 1982, it had become clear that competition from abroad and at home would be fierce in the future. Anticipating this inevitability, the Bank of New South Wales and the Commercial Bank of Australia decided to join forces to protect their position in the domestic market and strengthen their position overseas. Westpac was formed in October 1982, with Robert White as general manager. The merger was the largest in Australian history.

Robert White began his banking career at the age of 16 at the Bank of New South Wales. He rose through the ranks, becoming general manager in 1978. White was determined to strengthen Westpac's position in world banking. The bank was a leader in the implementation of technology. Westpac's "handybank" automated teller machine network gave customers instant access to their accounts as early as 1980, and had developed substantially after 1982. In 1984, Westpac began work on its CS90 computerized banking system. Employing an IBM mainframe and computer-aided software engineering designed by the Canadian firm Netron, the bank revolutionized computerized banking. By 1988, Westpac officials were boasting the most advanced system in the world.

### *Diversification and Expansion: Mid- to Late 1980s*

Technological innovation was one of Westpac's key goals throughout the 1980s, and diversification was another. The bank stepped up operations in the euro-currency markets. It also opened new offices or branches in Jersey, Los Angeles, Seoul, Kuala Lumpur, and Taipei. Westpac's thrust was rewarded quickly: between 1982 and 1986, assets more than doubled.

In the late 1980s, Westpac took advantage of the deregulated financial markets around the world. In 1986, it took a greater stake in the gold-bullion markets when it purchased part of the London dealer Johnson Matthey Bankers Ltd. In 1987, the bank acquired U.S. bond dealer William E. Pollock Government Securities. Westpac also continued to improve its branch network throughout the Pacific in the face of growing competition from Japanese banks.

Westpac's aggressive moves in the euromarkets and in technological development and application focused a great deal of attention on the bank. Its low exposure to Third World debt helped keep earnings healthy at a time when bad debt provisions were getting the best of many international banks.

On January 1, 1988, Stuart A. Fowler replaced Robert White as Westpac's managing director and CEO. Fowler continued the aggressive campaign begun by White. In 1988, the bank purchased the remaining shares of the Australian Guarantee Corporation, making it a wholly owned subsidiary. As the 1980s closed, Westpac focused on bringing operating costs down through automation and elimination of redundant branch services. The bank's domestic footing was solid; Westpac controlled 25 percent of Australia's bank deposits.

### *Growth Continues: 1990s and Beyond*

During the early 1990s, Australian banks saw profits dwindle as a result of increased exposure to bad loans. Westpac's expansion efforts were put on hold during this time period. By 1995, however, the industry recovered, and while Westpac was financially back on track, it had lost its leading position in the Australian banking industry.

In order to remain competitive, the company once again launched a growth program. It purchased Challenge Bank of Western Australia in 1995 in an A$684 million deal that enabled the bank to gain leading position in the Western region. The Challenge purchased was followed by a merger with Trust Bank New Zealand Limited in 1996. That year, the company secured profits of A$1.5 billion, an increase of 32 percent over the previous year. Then in 1997, Westpac acquired the Bank of Melbourne. During 1998, the company began to offer online banking to its customers.

In 1999, CEO Robert Joss planned to increase Westpac's holdings even further and proposed a merger with National Australia Bank Ltd. (NAB). At the time, Australia had a ''four pillar'' policy, which discouraged mergers between the region's largest banks. NAB however, wished to challenge the policy and announced the deal. Westpac's board—believing that it was a poor value for shareholders—turned down the deal. Joss resigned after the board's refusal and was replaced by David Morgan.

The new CEO immediately began a restructuring effort designed to reduce Westpac's cost-to-income ratio, which hovered at 58 percent due to its merger activity over the past three years. The ratio was the highest of the four leading banks. As part of the reorganization, the company announced that it would cut up to 3,000 jobs and focus on organic growth.

During the early years of the new century, Australian banks faced new problems. Consumer sentiment was falling rapidly as a result of the introduction of the Goods and Service Tax (GST) and rising interest rates. As Westpac reported its ninth consecutive year of profit growth in 2001, it became a target for angry consumers. In Westpac's 2001 Annual Report the company claimed that anti-bank sentiment was ''running red hot.'' Consumers, the report stated, were unhappy that there were fewer bank branches and felt that banks provided poor problem resolution; they also believed the bank's profits stemmed from consumers being overcharged for services that were once free and that banks cared only about those with large financial portfolios. The annual report also claimed that many consumers approached banks with skepticism, distrust, and impatience.

As such, Westpac's long-term strategy was heavily focused on improving customer satisfaction and creating new environmental and social awareness programs, along with exploring opportunities in Australia, New Zealand, and the Pacific region. While competition remained fierce among the four leading banks in Australia, Westpac's management believed the company was well positioned for future growth.

### *Principal Subsidiaries*

Westpac Banking Corporation; Australian Guarantee Corporation Ltd.; Bank of Tonga (Tonga; 60%); Beach Hill Investments Pty Ltd.; Bill Acceptance Corporation Ltd.; Biralo Pty Ltd.; Brenmar Holding Pty Ltd.; BLE Capital Ltd.; CBA Ltd.; Carseldine Pty Ltd.; Huben Holdings Pty Ltd.; MFS Services Pty Ltd.; Maracorp Financial Services Ltd.; Partnership Pacific Ltd.; Pitco Pty Ltd.; RESI Statewide Corporation Ltd.; Sallmoor Pty Ltd.; Sixty Martin Place Holdings Pty Ltd.; The Mortgage Company Pty Ltd.; Westpac Bank PNG Ltd. (Papua New Guinea; 89.9%); Westpac Bank Samoa Ltd. (Western Samoa; 93.5%); Westpac Capital Corporation (U.S.); Westpac Equity Holdings Pty Ltd.; Westpac Finance Pty Ltd.; Westpac Funding Holdings Pty Ltd.; Westpac Investment Holdings Pty Ltd.; Westpac Leasing Pty Ltd.; Westpac Properties Ltd.

### *Principal Competitors*

Australia and New Zealand Banking Group Ltd.; Commonwealth Bank of Australia; National Australia Bank Ltd.

### *Further Reading*

''Australian Banks Flex Their Muscles,'' *Banker*, January 1997, p. 13.

''Australian Consumer Sentiment Falls,'' *AsiaPulse News*, March 15, 2000.

''Australia's Westpac Restructuring to Involve 200 Job Cuts,'' *AsiaPulse News*, January 31, 2002.

*From Holey Dollars to Plastic Cards: The Westpac Story*, Sydney: Westpac Banking Corporation, 1987.

Westfield, Mark, ''Win Some, Lose Some,'' *Banker*, December 1999, p. 56.

''Westpac Banking Eyes Asia for Future Growth,'' *Bernama*, December 18, 2000.

—update: Christina M. Stansell

# White Mountains Insurance Group, Ltd.

**Crawford House**
**23 Church Street**
**Hamilton HM 11**
**Bermuda**
**Telephone: (441) 296-6011**
**Fax: (441) 296-9904**
**Web site: http://www.white mountains.com**

*Public Company*
*Incorporated:* 1980 as a Delaware corporation; 1999 as a Bermuda limited liability company
*Employees:* 6,983
*Total Assets:* $3.4 billion (2001)
*Stock Exchanges:* New York
*Ticker Symbol:* WTM
*NAIC:* 524130 Reinsurance Carriers, Fire, Marine, and Casualty

With U.S. offices in White River Junction, Vermont, White Mountains Insurance Group, Ltd. is an international financial services company based in Bermuda. Through its consolidated and unconsolidated subsidiaries and affiliates, the company conducts its principal businesses in property and casualty insurance and reinsurance. The company was formed in 1980 as a Delaware corporation and—after many name changes, acquisitions, mergers, and divestitures—resituated as a Bermuda corporation in 1999. White Mountains' major subsidiaries and affiliates include: Massachusetts-based OneBeacon Insurance Group LLC, which owns several property and casualty insurance and reinsurance companies throughout the United States; Folksamerica Holding Company, Inc., a New-York based, multi-line broker-market reinsurer; Fund American Reinsurance Company, Ltd, organized under the laws of Bermuda; Maryland-based Peninsula Insurance Company, a property and casualty insurer; White Mountains Underwriting Limited, an Ireland-based provider of reinsurance advisory and risk evaluation; Bermuda-based Montpelier Re Holdings Ltd, a reinsurance company; and New Hampshire-based Main Street America Holdings, Inc.

### *1980–97: The Early Career of John J. Byrne*

John J. Byrne, the driving force among the founders of White Mountains Insurance Group, entered the insurance business at an early age. According "See Jack Run," an article by John Gorham in the July 24, 2000 issue of *Forbes* magazine, young Byrne's after-school chores included working for his father, who owned a small insurance business in Wildwood, New Jersey. Later, while matriculating for a master's degree in mathematics at Rutgers University, Byrne spent his summers as an actuarial assistant for Travelers Group Inc. After serving in the Air Force, Byrne landed a job as a reinsurance salesman for Lincoln National Life Insurance. Then he returned to Travelers and drew an annual salary of $30,000 as "a consultant to the company's variable sales team. Within ten years he had worked himself up to executive vice-president in charge of Travelers' entire life insurance operation," wrote Gorham. By 1975, Byrne had developed two major phases of the company's more profitable operations. Yet, despite his other accomplishments, he was not chosen to replace Travelers' president. "He quit in a huff to become chief executive of a troubled Washington, D.C.-based auto insurer called GEICO," Gorham commented.

The new position tapped Byrne's special ability to direct his energy to rescuing companies on the brink of insolvency. Since its founding in 1936, GEICO (Government Employees Insurance Company) specialized in direct-mail sales of insurance to low-risk drivers. When GEICO began to insure riskier drivers and to underprice its policies, the company's shares dropped from $42 in 1974 to $5 in early 1976, and regulators threatened to close the company. Then Byrne came on board, reduced the work force, closed offices, raised prices, and cut out unprofitable business. It was at GEICO that Byrne identified Tom Kemp as an outstanding general manager; the two worked together for the next twenty years. Warren Buffett, who later played an important role in the development of White Mountains Insurance, paid over $4 million for a stake in GEICO. Byrne worked his magic: by 1981, GEICO shares were worth $15. Buffett referred to Byrne as the "Babe Ruth of Insurance," according to Gorham.

## Company Perspectives:

*White Mountains' mission is to be an intelligent owner of a premier group of regional or niche property/casualty and specialty underwriters which, with prudent operating and financial leverage, produces for its owners a long-term return of at least 700 basis points over ten-year treasuries after all applicable corporate tax. Each member of the group will be well managed in its own right and each underwriting-driven, using its own strategy. White Mountains will function as owner, capital provider, and allocator.*

### *1980–96: Transformation of Passive Investments Into Dynamic Companies*

Byrne dealt successfully with the vicissitudes of the insurance industry, including government regulations, damaging floods and storms, and brutal competition for insurance premiums. Then he accepted American Express chairman James Robinson's challenge to revive the profitability of Fireman's Fund Insurance Co. (an Amexco division). During 1983–84, Fireman's had chalked up pretax losses of about $356 million. Byrne greatly improved Fireman's underwriting ratios, and in 1985 he took the company public with an IPO that, at $25.75 a share, was the best offering in the history of IPO's.

The Babe Ruth of Insurance got results, he once said, by not paying much attention to advice from Wall Street or to its slavish attachment to accounting standards. As Gorham pointed out, Byrne knew that "standard accounting, especially in insurance, allowed companies to hide losses and inflate earnings." Instead of considering only a company's share price, Byrne focused on what he called its "intrinsic business value," that is, the fact that assets could appreciate even while they were still listed at cost on the books. Byrne followed his hunches; as Gorham noted, "When the industry was hurting, he was ready to buy."

In 1991, Byrne sold Fireman's insurance operations to Germany-based Allianz AG for $2.91 billion in cash. He retained the holding company, renamed it Fund American Enterprises, Inc. (based in Norwich, Vermont), and exchanged the cash for its equity investment portfolio. Soon after, he liquidated much of the portfolio and returned almost $3 billion to shareholders through stock buybacks. Byrne also held on to a substantial portion of investment securities and Michigan-based Source One Mortgage Services Corporation, one of the nation's largest mortgage banking companies.

Byrne was soon on the prowl for greater challenges. In 1994, Fund American began to invest in other insurance companies and conceptualized White Mountains Holdings to serve as the direct holding company for these investments. Byrne headed an investment group that wanted to inject $630 million into then-struggling Home Holdings Inc. but lost the battle to Zurich Financial Group. By the end of fiscal 1996, White Mountains' principal holdings included Financial Security Assurance Holdings Ltd. (FSA), a leading writer of financial guarantee insurance; Folksamerica Holding Company, Inc., a multi-line broker-market reinsurer; and Main Street America Holdings, an affiliate of National Grange Mutual Insurance Company, a New Hampshire-based property and casualty insurer.

Wholly-owned subsidiaries included White Mountains Insurance Co., which opened its New Hampshire-based commercial property and casualty operation in September 1995. White Mountains Holdings acquired Valley Group, Inc., which wrote personal and commercial lines in the Pacific Northwest, and Charter Group, Inc. Subsidiary Charter Indemnity Company wrote non-standard automobile insurance in Texas.

In his 1996 *Annual Report*, Byrne reported what he considered "modest results indeed." However, book value per share had grown 10 percent and 60 cents in earnings. Stock price had climbed 30 percent to over $100. Claiming that leaping over regulatory hurdles was "all too complicated" for him, Byrne emphasized that Fund American had emerged as "a collection of operating companies led by an energetic team of younger managers" and relinquished his active role as chairman, president, and CEO. The board of directors respected Byrne's decision to forsake his active role in the company and showed its appreciation for his pioneering efforts by electing him as non-executive chairman.

### *1997–99: Evolution Toward a Single Corporate Entity*

K. Thomas Kemp, Fund American's new president and chief executive officer, reported that 1997 was a solid year for the financial services holding company which operated through its principal subsidiary—White Mountains Holdings, Inc. The company ended fiscal 1997 with a book value per share of $102.19, a growth of 13.5 percent, and market value that peaked at 27.3 percent growth.

Fund American still owned a considerable passive investment portfolio primarily made up of common equity securities and other investments. Initially, the company's primary goal was either to place remaining investments and other assets into operating businesses compatible with management's knowledge and experience or to return excess capital to debt holders and shareholders. When no opportunities came for big transaction hits in the early 1990s, Byrne and Kemp were struck by the idea that "smaller regional or specialty insurance investments might be a more workable strategy than archeological work on dinosaurs caught in tar pits." They opted to have White Mountains Holdings keep and build a new insurance portfolio and gain substantial positions in their first operating investments: Main Street America (MSA) and Financial Security Assurance (FSA).

Therefore, in 1997 Fund American increased its ownership of MSA from 33 percent to 50 percent. Phil Koerner, MSA's chairman and president, kept the company and its independent agency partners at the forefront of a highly competitive marketplace. Committed to independent agents as MSA's sole distribution source, Koerner introduced use of the Internet as an agency processing platform. In 1998, when the warming temperatures and moisture brought by El Niño covered the northern portion of MSA's market with ice, the company spent more than $13 million to help clients put their lives back in place after the power lines and trees came down and pipes froze. However,

## Key Dates:

**1991:** John J. Byrne and other investors organize Fund American Enterprises Inc.
**1994:** White Mountains Holdings, Inc. is organized.
**1996:** K. Thomas Kemp replaces Byrne as president and chief operating officer.
**1999:** Fund American changes its name to White Mountains Insurance Group, Ltd. and relocates to Bermuda.
**2000:** Byrne returns to White Mountains as chairman and chief operating officer.
**2002:** White Mountains establishes itself as an internationally based reinsurance company.

despite this misfortune, MSA posted 11.2 percent returns on equity for 1998—and continued to grow. In 1998, 125 agents transferred entire books of business worth $18 million to MSA and another 123 new agents began to represent the company. With 100,000 new policies, MSA set a record for the second consecutive year. In 1999, Koerner continued to develop an Internet-based system for MSA, which was one of nine insurance companies to receive the IIAA Award of Excellence for participation in the national Communications Program.

FSA, one of the four major bond insurers, in 1997 enjoyed a breakthrough year in the municipal bond and asset-backed markets. With a full-service San Francisco office and a marketing office in Dallas, FSA provided the industry's strongest regional coverage. The company continued to be active in Europe and made a substantial investment in marketing its knowledge and expertise in the Pacific Rim markets, as well as in Australia, New Zealand, and Japan and other Asian markets. FSA insured securities in three sectors: consumer finance, residential mortgage finance, and structured finance. FSA produced $200 million U.S. asset-based premiums during 1999—an increase of 36 percent—and reached a record $133 million in international premiums.

In May 1999, Fund American Enterprises Holdings, Inc. divested itself of substantially all the mortgage banking assets of White Mountains Services Corporation (formerly Source One) for $181 million and exited the mortgage business. The sale was completed in July 2000. In June 1999, Fund American changed its name to White Mountains Insurance Group, Ltd. and sold Valley Group, Inc. to Unitrim for roughly twice its book value, that is, $139 million in cash, after receiving a special dividend of $77 million consisting of cash, investment securities, and the common stock of Valley National Insurance Company.

During October 1999, White Mountains completed a corporate reorganization that brought about the relocation of its domicile from Delaware to Bermuda. The redomestication was undertaken primarily to create a corporate structure more favorable to foreign-based insurance and reinsurance operations and to increase the company's ability to pursue business combinations with companies not based in the United States. White Mountains also acquired Consolidated International Group, Inc., parent of Peninsula Insurance Company. Maryland-based PIC was a property and casualty insurer that wrote both personal and commercial lines, primarily homeowners, private passenger auto, commercial auto, and commercial multiple peril.

### *2000 and Beyond*

In January 2000, after a three-year retirement, John J. Byrne claimed that he no longer was "getting any respect" and returned to White Mountains as chairman and chief executive officer. On May 5, 2000, Folksamerica acquired Risk Capital Reinsurance Company in a transaction that broadened its product offerings in marine, accident, and health insurance. New York-based Folksamerica Reinsurance Company provided reinsurance to insurers of property, casualty, accident, and health risks in the United States, Canada, Latin America, and the Caribbean. In July, management completed the sale of White Mountains Holdings Inc.—and a substantial amount of FSA stock—to Dexia Credit Local de France S.A. for proceeds of $620.4 million, thereby effecting a pretax gain of $391.4 million.

Much of 2000 was given to negotiating the purchase and financing of Boston-based CGU USA Insurance Company—for sale at $2.1 billion plus $470 million in assumed debt—and ranked as the 16th largest property and casualty insurer in the United States. Byrne contacted billionaire Warren Buffett, his longtime friend from GEICO days, and used that personal connection to out-duel competitors. White Mountains secured $1 billion in debt financing from Lehman Brothers, $300 million from private investors and management, and $300 million from billionaire Buffett, chairman of Berkshire Hathaway. Buffett accepted close to 30 percent of White Mountains stock for his investment. CGU was renamed OneBeacon Insurance Group; the acquisition was completed June 1, 2001.

During the fourth quarter of 2001, Folksamerica completed the acquisition of Esurance, a new distribution channel for property/casualty insurance and one of the leading Internet-based marketers of personal auto insurance. Esurance leveraged Internet technology to remove excess costs from the marketing, sales, and servicing of personal lines insurance products; its customer service center operated on a 24/7 basis. Through a partnership with Liberty Mutual Insurance Group, in November 2001 OneBeacon transferred its regional agency business, agents, and operations in 42 states and the District of Columbia to Liberty Mutual Insurance Group. It was also OneBeacon's goal to use new technology to replace the traditional way of marketing insurance in order to become the premier independent agency of property/casualty insurance in the Northeast.

The year 2001 was a one of unprecedented upheaval in the U.S. property and casualty insurance marketplace. The September 11, 2001, terrorist attacks caused more turmoil in insurance markets than did 1980's Hurricane Andrew. Prior to the attacks, most insurance companies had not explicitly faced the risk of substantive damages as a result of terrorist actions when underwriting their policies and had not paid much attention to the intricacies of reinsurance. White Mountains moved quickly to fix its balance sheet, restructure its investment portfolio, and improve underwriting. Despite some losses, the company emerged from September 11 in good health and invested large amounts of capital in the reinsurance business through a capital contribution to its Folksamerica Reinsurance Company. White Mountains also played a lead role with the Benfield Group to establish Montpelier Re Holdings, Ltd. in Bermuda to take advantage of the favorable underwriting and pricing environment in the reinsurance industry.

Furthermore, Folksamerica negotiated a quota-share retrocessional arrangement with Olympus Reinsurance Ltd. to capitalize on enhanced reinsurance fundamentals during 2002 and beyond. The company formed White Mountains Underwriting Limited (WMU) as an underwriting management company headquartered in Ireland. WMU expanded Folksamerica's access to international property excess of loss reinsurance business and provided professional insurance services to both Folksamerica and Olympus Re. White Mountains subsidiary Fund American Reinsurance Company Ltd. acquired substantially all the international reinsurance operations of the Folksam Group of Stockholm, Sweden. This acquisition began the formation and growth of White Mountains' internationally based reinsurance operations. Fund American was commercially domiciled in Bermuda but had an executive office and an operating branch in Stockholm as well as an additional branch in Singapore.

For the fiscal year ended December 31, 2001, White Mountains revenues totaled $3.23 billion, up from $848.2 million in 2000. By the end of first quarter 2002, the company stock was valued between a low of about $330 and a high of approximately $370 a share. The course for continuing success was set. As stated in its four operating principles, White Mountains gave priority to underwriting, invested for total return, maintained a disciplined balance sheet, and functioned as a low-cost operator. John J. Byrne was named 2001 insurance Leader of the Year by the School of Risk Management, Insurance and Actuarial Science at New York's St. John's University.

### *Principal Subsidiaries*

Folksamerica Holding Company, Inc.; Fund American Enterprises Holdings, Inc.; Fund American Reinsurance Company, Ltd. (Bermuda); OneBeacon Insurance Group LLC; Pennsylvania General Insurance Company; White Mountains Holdings SRL (Barbados); White Mountains Underwriting Ltd. (Ireland).

### *Principal Competitors*

The Allstate Corporation; GEICO Corporation; GeneralCologne Re; Munich Re; Reinsurance Group of America, Inc.

### *Further Reading*

Board, Laura, ''Britain's CGNU Is Paying Off,'' *Daily Deal* (London), August 12, 2001.

Gorham, John, ''See Jack Run,'' *Forbes*, July 24, 2000, p. 98.

Holman, Kelly, and Josh Kosman, ''PE Reinsurance Deals Net $1.1B,'' *Daily Deal*, December 10, 2001.

Howard, Lisa S., ''Capital Pouring Into Insurance Ventures,'' *National Underwriter: Property & Casualty/Risk & Benefits Management Edition*, November 12, 2001, p. 6.

Johnston, David Cay, ''A Big Tax Loophole for Insurers Prompts a Review on Capitol Hill,'' *New York Times*, October 5, 2000, p. C1.

McLeod, Douglas, ''White Mountains Heads to Pink Sands: Plans to Form New $1 Billion Reinsurer in Bermuda,'' *Business Insurance*, November 5, 2001, p. 2.

''White Mountains Set to Form New $1B Reinsurer,'' *Insurance Day*, November 6, 2001.

Wilkinson, Claire, ''Beacon to Transfer Operations to Liberty,'' *Insurance Day*, September 11, 2001, p. 1.

—Gloria A. Lemieux

# WHITTAKER CONTROLS

# Whittaker Corporation

**1955 North Surveyor Avenue**
**Simi Valley, California 93063-3369**
**U.S.A.**
**Telephone: (805) 526-5700**
**Fax: (805) 526-4369**
**Web site: http://www.whittakercontrols.com**

*Wholly Owned Subsidiary of Meggitt plc*
*Incorporated:* 1947
*Employees:* 175
*Sales:* $26.7 million (2001)
*NAIC:* 332912 Fluid Power Valve and Hose Fitting Manufacturing; 333995 Fluid Power Cylinder and Actuator Manufacturing; 335314 Relay and Industrial Control Manufacturing

Whittaker Corporation, once a $2 billion conglomerate, operates as the parent company of Whittaker Controls Inc. and is a subsidiary of Meggitt plc. As part of the U.K.-based aerospace concern, Whittaker stands as a leading designer and manufacturer of fluid control devices and systems for commercial and military aircraft. Its products are also used in a variety of industrial applications. Whittaker's major customers include Boeing, Airbus, General Electric, Rolls Royce, and Pratt & Whitney.

## *Origins*

In 1947, engineer William R. Whittaker borrowed $4,800 to begin the manufacture of aircraft valves. Later he broadened the product line through an acquisition to include the production of guidance instruments. In 1956, the company merged with one of the first computer software companies and the newly formed company assumed the name of one partner—the Telecomputing Corporation. Despite the reorganization, William R. Whittaker remained the top executive and principal shareholder of the company.

The further acquisitions of Monrovia Aviation Corporation and Narmco Industries allowed the company to enter into the manufacture of metal and non-metal materials. This shift in product orientation is attributed to Whittaker's desire to diversify away from its dependence on U.S. military contracts. Although the company had grown into a $60 million manufacturer of aerospace components, it remained vulnerable to trends in defense industry expenditures. In addition to the acquisitions, Whittaker's growth strategy included implementing cost control measures and performance records. The company now adopted the name of its founder and became the Whittaker Corporation.

## *Growth Through Acquisition: 1960s*

To guide the company through this period of reorientation and growth, William Whittaker looked for a new president. He found his ideal executive in 1964 in the person of William Meng Duke, a Ph.D. in engineering from UCLA. Duke's previous management positions included serving as senior vice-president at Los Angeles' Space Technology Laboratories and as head of International Telephone & Telegraph Corporation's U.S. Defense Group. Duke possessed both an impressive amount of scientific knowledge as well as a talent for business, and his leadership potential seemed well matched to Whittaker's goals. As the company founder moved up to the position of chairman, Duke attempted to prove his business acumen.

In the next five years, through an aggressive and expansive program of acquisition, Whittaker grew from an obscure Los Angeles-based company to a complex of 80 diverse companies with a total annual sales of $753.4 million in 1969. Although Whittaker's business ranged from manufacturing pleasure boats to industrial chemicals, Duke did not consider his company a conglomerate. According to Duke, 70 percent of Whittaker's products remained related to some aspect of the integrated manufacture of metal and non-metal materials. Whether in processing alloys, chemicals, or ceramics, Duke claimed his company could produce not only a variety of materials but also could construct a product tailored to a customer's particular needs.

Wall Street analysts observed the spectacular rise in Whittaker's stock price. From less than $1 a share in 1964, the stock price rose to $46 a share in 1967. Despite such growth, however, a number of problems began to surface. As late as 1967

## Company Perspectives:

*Through subsidiary Whittaker, Meggitt strives to consistently increase shareholder value by providing technically superior products in its Aerospace Equipment business segment.*

nearly one-third of Whittaker's business remained tied to military contracts. In particular, $30 million in volume was generated from products, such as helicopter blades, used in Vietnam. Moreover, the management of such a wide variety of businesses became troublesome. At the Columbus-Milpar subsidiary, for example, an undetected problem in inventory build-up and quality control caused a major profit loss. Finally, the number of acquisitions made by the company had put tremendous financial strain on Whittaker's resources.

### *Restructuring Under the Leadership of Alibrandi: 1970s*

By 1970, the company was operating on a $332 million debt. Stock prices dropped to $6 a share. To remedy the situation, Joseph F. Alibrandi, a 41-year-old executive from the missile's systems divisions at the Raytheon Company, assumed the position of president. Alibrandi took immediate action by selling nearly a quarter of the 135 acquisitions. The company's net income rose and long-term debt was significantly reduced. While these improvements brought tangible results, a number of surprise setbacks illustrated the types of difficulties facing the new top executive. One setback involved the attempted sale of the Crown Aluminum subsidiary. A $6 million inventory shortage canceled the sale and forced Whittaker into the embarrassing situation of regaining control of the subsidiary. Another problem surfaced when Whittaker's housing subsidiaries falsely anticipated a $2.8 million profit.

Despite these setbacks, Alibrandi continued his five-year program to restructure the company. Strict financial and organization guidelines were mandated to all levels of operation. The assiduous young executive was soon promoted to chief executive officer. The son of Italian immigrants, Alibrandi exhibited shrewd leadership skills while refusing the many perks associated with his high-level position. Of the 50 remaining businesses at Whittaker, Alibrandi planned to concentrate on five areas of growth, including technology, industrial chemicals, recreational products, transportation, and metals. These distinct areas were eventually absorbed into wholly-owned divisions.

By 1976, Wall Street analysts once again looked favorably on Whittaker's performance record. A welcomed increase to Whittaker's business came with a $100 million contract from Saudi Arabia to establish a health care program. Alibrandi had made prior contacts with the Saudis during his employment at Raytheon, and he had also managed the Hawk missile installation project. Using these former contacts, Alibrandi proposed the health care management contract to the Saudi Arabian ministry of defense.

In the marine division, the company constructed a line of recreational yachts. The Columbia division manufactured luxury sailing yachts requiring costly hand labor. Although these boats were sold at high prices, the division reported a $5.6 million loss. While many criticized Alibrandi for investing in an area of business that did not fit well with Whittaker's other operations, the president defended the division as a future profit maker.

Although the original five-year plan actually required seven, by 1977 the company reported two consecutive years of earnings growth. This achievement occurred despite major obstacles in two areas of business. A hydraulic device plant in France experienced difficult labor problems, and a freight-car manufacturing operation depleted its order backlog. Whittaker's greatest source of profits emerged from the life sciences group. The renewed Saudi Arabian contract contributed $150 million over the next two years, and products developed out of cancer research generated approximately $1 million.

As Whittaker's product lines continued to strengthen their performance, the metal division emerged as the company's largest operation. Moving into a highly diversified business of metal products, the group generated 42 percent of total sales in 1978. Included in this division was the manufacture of railroad freights, which now held a backlog of orders worth $200 million. The technology division volume, comprised of the hydraulic equipment business and the aerospace component operation, increased due to a growing demand for products. In the marine division, Whittaker became one of the largest producers of commercial fishing vessels and recreational boats.

Despite these gains, Alibrandi's major business thrust remained in the life sciences and chemical groups. Through the Saudi contract Whittaker was now the United States' largest healthcare service supplier to a foreign country. A $10 million contract to build a hospital in Abu Dhabi increased Whittaker's overseas presence. To augment growth, Alibrandi planned future expansion in the areas of biomedical testing, healthcare management consulting, and specialty chemicals. By 1980, five new chemical companies joined the division. In addition, Alibrandi sold the less profitable chemical operations and hired a new group of executives.

### *Focusing on Health Care: Early 1980s*

In 1981, Alibrandi announced a strengthened commitment to health care. In an effort to alleviate the company's dependence on the cyclical markets of chemicals, metals, and marine vessels, Alibrandi planned to make health care Whittaker's major line of business. Through a number of acquisitions the president and chief executive officer hoped to construct an integrated hospital supply and management company.

Even as the company experienced disappointments over the next several years, Alibrandi continued to expand the company's orientation toward health care. Several successful acquisitions reported less impressive performance records than was anticipated, and two attempted acquisitions failed. Even more disturbing was the fact that the Saudi Arabian contract was awarded to a competitor. Despite these setbacks, Alibrandi invested $100 million in building a nation-wide network of Health Maintenance Organizations (HMO's), an investment, it is said, that he hoped would become the foundation of Whittaker's business. The first of these HMO's was purchased in

## Key Dates:

**1947:** William R. Whittaker begins the manufacture of aircraft valves.
**1956:** Whittaker's firm merges with a computer software company and adopts the name Telecomputing Corporation.
**1969:** By now, the firm is operating under the name Whittaker Corporation and sales have reached $753.4 million.
**1970:** Joseph F. Alibrandi is named president and begins restructuring the firm.
**1989:** After a brief stint in the healthcare industry, Whittaker reorganizes and is focused on chemicals and its aerospace operations.
**1991:** The company sells its biotechnology business.
**1995:** Hughes LAN Systems Inc. is acquired and renamed Whittaker Communications Inc.
**1996:** Xyplex Inc. is purchased and merged with Whittaker Communications.
**1997:** In a major restructuring, Whittaker sells its communications interests and its defense electronics division.
**1999:** Meggitt Plc acquires Whittaker.

Norfolk, Virginia, and Alibrandi hoped to acquire ten similar organizations by the end of 1985.

Although Health Maintenance Organizations represented Whittaker's new market strategy, the pursuit of growth through specialty chemicals and aerospace equipment was not abandoned: between 1985 and 1986, Whittaker acquired five additional chemical subsidiaries and five defense electronic and aerospace subsidiaries. Ranging from manufacturers of enamel stripping to producers of coil coating, these new businesses attempted to strengthen Whittaker's diversified technologies

### *Shifting Market Direction: Late 1980s–90s*

A surprising turn of events in the late 1980s significantly changed Whittaker's business orientation. The company suddenly announced it was selling its HMO businesses to the Travelers Corporation. Although Alibrandi claimed he never planned to remain in the health maintenance field on his own, analysts attributed the abrupt shift to cost overruns. Critics accused the company of lacking a stable product line. Furthermore, the hospital supply business reported disappointing figures, the chemical division continued to suffer from cyclical markets, and the aerospace operations remained subject to trends in defense spending.

Whittaker continued shifting market orientations, and the company decided to sell all of its health care and metal production businesses and concentrate on chemicals. Wall Street analysts applauded this decision as an attempt to regain a company focus. The purchase of Du Pont's adhesive business, for example, increased Whittaker's sale of adhesives to 25 percent of total sales in chemicals. The company also announced it would buy back 6 million of its 12.8 million outstanding shares. While some analysts viewed this action as a protective move by management to defend against a possible takeover attempt, other analysts interpreted the stock repurchase as indicative of an attempt to attract a potential suitor. While Whittaker maintained it was not a takeover target, the company's precise business orientation still remained in question.

Indeed, Whittaker made further changes in its focus as a company throughout the 1990s. Continuing with its divestiture program of 1989, the company spun off its biotechnology business and also sold off a slew of chemical-related companies, proving that its emphasis on this segment was short-lived. By the time Alibrandi retired in 1994, Whittaker had been whittled down to a $126 million-per-year aerospace and defense electronics company.

Thomas Brancati, the company's president and chief operating officer, took over the helm and once again began expansion efforts. Eyeing the burgeoning communications industry as Whittaker's next target, Brancati acquired Hughes LAN Systems Inc. in 1995 and renamed it Whittaker Communications Inc., creating a new subsidiary focused on data networking and communications. Then, in 1996, the firm created Xyplex Networks by purchasing network access firm Xyplex Inc. and merging it with Whittaker Communications.

A 1997 *Forbes* article commented on Brancati's strategy, claiming that his idea "was to give Whittaker exposure to two booming markets—aerospace parts and high-tech communications networks—with the latter cushioning the company against defense spending cutbacks." The strategy however, proved unsuccessful as the firm posted significant losses. Brancati was replaced in September 1996 by Alibrandi, who came out of retirement to get the firm back on track.

Alibrandi began trimming Whittaker's holdings once again and in 1997, the firm sold its defense electronics division to Condor Systems Inc. The company also divested its communications business along with its integration services unit. With 1998 sales of $131.5 million, Whittaker's operations had been pared back to focus solely on aerospace related products and applications.

### *Whittaker Is Acquired: 1999*

In 1999, Whittaker became involved in merger discussions with Meggitt Plc, a UK-based company involved in the aerospace and defense industries. In June 1999, Whittaker announced that it would be acquired by Meggitt for $28 per share, or $380 million. Alibrandi commented in a June 1999 press release that the company believed "that this combination is in the best interests of Whittaker's stockholders and creates an excellent opportunity to leverage the significant aerospace strengths of both companies."

Whittaker entered the new millennium as part of Meggitt's aerospace equipment division. Meggitt, which had been restructuring over the past several years to position itself as a leading aerospace and defense company, felt confident that Whittaker's aircraft-related components and its fire and smoke detection systems would enhance the firm's division and give it greater leverage in the market. In 2000, Meggitt's aerospace equipment division recorded turnover of £161 million, a hefty increase over

1999 figures. In 2001, turnover increased to £178.8 million. Having experienced several decades of change and financial uncertainty, Whittaker appeared well positioned to advance into the future as a key component in Meggitt's aerospace operations.

### *Principal Subsidiaries*

Whittaker Controls Inc.

### *Principal Competitors*

Goodrich Corporation; Parker Hannifin Corporation; United Technologies Corporation.

### *Further Reading*

Darlin, Damon, ''What Did the Sellers Know That the Buyers Didn't?,'' *Forbes*, May 5, 1997, p. 113.

Jasper, Chris, ''Meggitt Acquires Whittaker for $380m,'' *Flight International*, June 23, 1999, p. 51.

Taub, Daniel, New Wave for Buyers; L.A. Aerospace Subcontractors, *Los Angeles Business Journal*, August 2, 1999, p. 6.

''Whittaker Sells Electronics Unit to Condor Systems,'' *Defense Daily*, September 8, 1997, p. 396.

—update: Christina M. Stansell

# OJSC Wimm-Bill-Dann Foods

**16 Yauzsky Boulevard**
**Moscow 10928**
**Russia**
**Telephone: (+7) 095 733-97-26**
**Fax: (+7) 095 733-97-25**
**Web site: http://www.wbd.ru; http://www.wbd.com**

*Public Company*
*Founded:* 1992
*Employees:* 10,900
*Sales:* $465.4 million (2000)
*Stock Exchanges:* New York
*Ticker Symbol:* WBD
*NAIC:* 311512 Creamery Butter Manufacturing; 311411 Frozen Fruit, Juice and Vegetable Processing; 311421 Fruit and Vegetable Canning; 311511 Fluid Milk Manufacturing; 311513 Cheese Manufacturing; 311520 Ice Cream and Frozen Dessert Manufacturing; 42243 Dairy Products (Except Dried or Canned) Wholesalers; 422490 Other Grocery and Related Product Wholesalers

Founded shortly after the 1991 breakup of the Soviet Union, OJSC Wimm-Bill-Dann Foods has become a market leader in the production of juices and dairy products in Russia. The company's J-7 line of juices is a nearly universally recognized brand name in Moscow, and the company's dairy brands, including Domik v Derevne (Little House in the Country) and Milaya Mila (Darling Mila) are also well known. In all, Wimm-Bill-Dann promotes over a dozen brand names for hundreds of dairy products ranging from traditional Russian berry drinks and fermented milk drinks made with kefir grains to flavored yogurt drinks and puddings to exotic fruit cocktails. Dairy products account for about 70 percent of the company's revenues and juice products for the remaining 30 percent. An emphasis on quality, close attention to market research and effective advertising have won Wimm-Bill-Dann its leading position. The company has expanded from a few plants in Moscow to include 14 food-processing enterprises in ten locations in Russia and neighboring countries, while its distribution network stretches into the Netherlands, Israel, the United Kingdom, Germany, Canada, and the United States. Wimm-Bill-Dann is regarded as one of the more well-run companies in Moscow, a reputation that helped win investor confidence during the company's 2002 initial public offering on the New York Stock Exchange.

### *Beginning Production in Moscow: 1992–95*

After the fall of the Soviet Union in 1991, Russia represented a vast untapped market for consumer goods that were scarce under communism. Yet the lack of developed business traditions and infrastructures forced any new enterprise to blaze its own trail. In this climate of uncertainty and opportunity, Pavel Dudnikov, Vladimir Tambov, and several other individuals teamed up to lease a production line at the Lianozovo Dairy Plant in Moscow. Their aim was to introduce a new product to Russia: juice in a carton. On November 25, 1992, the first carton of Wimm-Bill-Dann juice, bearing the trademark image of a mouse in a chef's hat, was produced at Lianozovo. The company's odd name was deliberately chosen to give the product the image of a western import, as Russians were drawn to the novelty of western products and did not yet trust the quality of domestically manufactured goods. The name's phonetic similarity to the famous Wimbledon tennis tournament was due to the fact that one of the founders was a fan of the sport.

In 1994, a series of seven fruit juices was launched at Lianozovo under the brand name J-7, a name with exotic western overtones, since there is no ''j'' in the Cyrillic alphabet. The juices came in basic flavors such as orange, apple, tomato, and grape. Their convenient packaging was supplied by Tetra Pak of Sweden, the company that patented the widely-used small rectangular beverage carton. Wimm-Bill-Dann's juice could be retained for up to 12 months in Tetra Pak's aseptically sealed packages. The Swedish company became a long-term partner of Wimm-Bill-Dann, offering the company credit and providing packaging for many of its best-selling brands. Wimm-Bill-Dann sold six million liters of the J-7 brand of juices in its first year of production, 50 million liters in 1995, and 90 million in 1996. The company eventually supplemented the original natural fruit

## Company Perspectives:

*Our goal is to offer our consumers quality food products through the use of carefully selected raw materials, modern production technology, and strict quality control. All of our products are made according with our own recipes and designed to address the desires and needs of our customers.*

juices with a line of ''nectars,'' including banana, mango, peach, and cherry. By the late 1990s, there were 22 different juices and nectars in the J-7 series.

Profits from juice sales allowed Wimm-Bill-Dann to lease production lines at other Moscow plants, and soon the company entered into dairy production under the brand name Domik v Derevne (Little House in the Country). By this time, Russia's infatuation with western goods was fading, and the more Slavic-sounding product was promoted with the slogan ''Russian goods are natural.'' The foodstuffs business was proving to be a good choice for Russia's new entrepreneurs. Nearly everyone was a potential consumer of juice and dairy products, and there was little in the way of domestic competition to challenge Wimm-Bill-Dann. The food sector was also fairly low-profile, flying under the radar of opportunists who were more interested in gaining control of Russia's lucrative oil and metal commodities. So Wimm-Bill Dann's sales grew, buoyed by the Russian consumer's newfound preference for domestic goods.

Nevertheless, Russia's volatile business climate challenged even the most well-managed and deftly promoted enterprises. There were few laws or standard procedures guiding businessmen, and long-term planning was difficult since the government was unpredictable. Wimm-Bill-Dann's managers had to learn as they went, watching the moves of western companies and building a distribution infrastructure and an advertising campaign from the ground up. Most of the company's growth was self-financed, although Moscow's Sberbank and the Moscow city administration provided some loans.

### *Acquiring Assets and Developing Products: 1995–98*

By 1995, the privatization of state-owned assets was widespread, and Wimm-Bill-Dann acquired a majority stake in the Lianozovo plant. Over the next two years, the company also gained control of the Tsaritsino and Ramenskii dairy plants in Moscow, along with the Moscow Baby Food Plant. The Lianozovo plant, however, remained the dominant enterprise. The plant consumed most of the milk produced by dairy farms in the Moscow area and accounted for about 70 percent of Wimm-Bill-Dann's 1996 production. At that time, the company was making yogurt on a small scale, about 20 tons per day, and the French firm Danone offered Wimm-Bill-Dann a licensing agreement to abandon Russian brands and produce Danone yogurt. The Russian company refused, however, and by the beginning of 1999 Wimm-Bill-Dann yogurt was being produced at a rate of 150 tons per day. The company's canned vegetables were produced in a partnership with Hungary's Globus and were sold under the brand name Iz Babushkinogo Pogrebka (From Grandma's Cellar).

With production taking place at numerous sites, Wimm-Bill-Dann developed into a holding company, leaving day-to-day management in the hands of individual plants. Most of firm's equity was held by the group of entrepreneurs that cooperated to found the company. However, a conflict broke out among company leadership in March 1997 and stopped production for ten days at the Lianozovo plant. Plant manager Vladimir Tambov wanted to remove the Wimm-Bill-Dann logo from the plant's products, even though Wimm-Bill-Dann owned 52 percent of Lianozovo and had invested billions of rubles in promoting the plant's products. The Moscow government, which owned 20 percent of the plant, set up a special commission to investigate the dispute. In the end, Tambov was dismissed and the plant's management structure and board of directors were restructured.

Toward the end of 1997, Wimm-Bill-Dann introduced a new juice product that was to be of the highest quality. Unlike the J-7 juice, which was made from concentrate, Rio Grande juices were pressed from fresh-picked fruits, with fruit pulp remaining in the final product. The juice was packaged in a distinctive elongated box produced by SIG Combibloc of Austria and included such varieties as orange, apple, pomegranate, and pear. Total juice production for 1997 was 141 million liters, in addition to 368,000 tons of dairy products.

Another product launch followed early in 1998, when Wimm-Bill-Dann introduced its version of a traditional Russian refreshment known as ''mors.'' The company's Chudo-Yagoda (Wonderberry) Mors was meant to duplicate a drink that had been prepared for centuries from berries gathered in Russia's forests and fields. Mors, once a homemade staple on the table of the Russian peasant, could now be purchased by the liter in varieties such as cranberry, raspberry, and red currant. Later in 1998, Wimm-Bill-Dann introduced the Chudo (Wonder) brand name for its line of yogurts. The product became the most popular yogurt in Russia and was followed by puddings, flavored milk cocktails, and dessert products under the Chudo brand name.

### *Expanding Production Beyond Moscow: 1998–2002*

Wimm-Bill-Dann made its first acquisitions outside Moscow in 1998. Although Russia's capital city was the company's most lucrative market, competition from western suppliers was more intense there. Also, the acquisition of production sites across the country would make it easier to develop a strong nationwide distribution network. Accordingly, Wimm-Bill-Dann purchased a controlling stake in a Vladivostok plant, located in the easternmost region of the country. By the end of 1999, the company also owned dairy plants in Novosibirsk and Nizhny Novgorod.

The Russian financial crisis of August 1998 had only a relatively mild effect on Wimm-Bill-Dann. In fact, the sharp devaluation of the ruble that provoked the crisis served to reduce competition from Wimm-Bill-Dann's western-based competitors. The French firm Danone postponed plans to open a plant in Moscow, and other foreign companies abandoned similar plans that would increase competition for milk products in Russia. Wimm-Bill-Dann's three Moscow plants continued to gobble up the lion's share of the region's milk production, as the company's market share grew due to the increased cost of

## Key Dates:

**1992:** Several Russian entrepreneurs lease a production line at a Moscow dairy plant.
**1994:** The J-7 line of natural fruit juices is launched.
**1996:** Wimm-Bill-Dann gains control of two more Moscow dairy plants.
**1998:** The company acquires dairy plants outside Moscow.
**2000:** Wimm-Bill-Dann begins exporting its products to the Netherlands and Israel.
**2002:** The company makes an initial public offering on the New York Stock Exchange.

western imports. The company claimed that sales had returned to pre-crisis levels by the beginning of 1999.

The Bio Max line of sour milk products was launched in May 1999. The series included traditional Russian dairy products such as kefir (a liquid yogurt drink) and tvorog (curdled cheese), which were enriched with bacteria and vitamins. Wimm-Bill-Dann claimed that its Bio Max kefir could reduce stress, improve the digestive tract, and strengthen the immune system. The company's products got a boost later that year when Russian pop star Alla Pugacheva endorsed Wimm-Bill-Dann. Pugacheva was a longtime cultural icon with immense influence on the country's tastes, and Wimm-Bill-Dann planned to have her star in commercials for the company.

Wimm-Bill-Dann also established its first overseas presence in 1999 with the opening of an office in Amsterdam. The company believed that its Wonderberry juices would do well in the European market. The juices began selling in the Netherlands in the fall of 2000 and soon were also sold in Germany through a distribution office in Berlin. In early 2000, an office opened in Tel Aviv to sell the Wonderberry juices. Wimm-Bill-Dann also cultivated a network of independent dealers in the Baltic countries, Canada, Mongolia, China, and the United States. Export sales were $724,000 in 2000 and reached $1.3 million in the first nine months of 2001. Explaining the company's outlook in the January 2001 issue of *Euromoney*, chairman David Iakobachvili stated, ''First we want to look at developing the domestic market, as it has huge potential. However, moving into western Europe is a challenge for us. It is all about quality: the quality of our goods is good or else we would never have gotten all the certificates and licenses to be able to sell in western Europe.''

Net profits were up 37 percent in 2000 to $48 million, according to chief executive Sergei Plastinin. The company continued to move ahead with domestic expansion, acquiring majority stakes in plants in Krasnodar and Bishkek, Kyrgyzstan, in 2000. The following year, Wimm-Bill-Dann moved into the Ukraine with the acquisition of a plant in Kiev and also opened plants in Ufa (Bashkortostan region), Rubtsovsk (Altaisky region), and Anna (Voronezh region). With expansion occurring at such a fast pace, Wimm-Bill-Dann felt the need for an outside source of capital. The company therefore began making preparations for an initial public offering (IPO) on the New York Stock Exchange. Wimm-Bill-Dann was organized in a fairly loose fashion, with a small group of individuals holding stock in the Lianozovo Dairy and in a holding company, RAG Rodnik, that was the parent for most other Wimm-Bill-Dann enterprises. In April 2001, the company's shareholders merged their holdings into Wimm-Bill-Dann Foods LLC. The following month the company was restructured into an open joint stock company.

Finally, in February 2002, Wimm-Bill-Dann became the fourth Russian company to make its IPO in the United States. The company raised $200 million in a successful offering of one quarter of its stock. Issued at $19.50, the shares traded up to $22.60 by the end of the first day. Investors were not scared away by certain disclosures made in Wimm-Bill-Dann's IPO prospectus, including the fact that the company's largest shareholder, Gavriil Yushvayev, had served nine years in a Soviet labor camp after being convicted of a violent crime, or the fact that some of the company's shareholders were owners of the Trinity Group, a conglomerate suspected to have ties to organized crime. In making such information public, Wimm-Bill-Dann wanted to demonstrate that it was a serious company that valued transparency and trusted that investors would forgive certain ''skeletons in the closet'' in the light of the unorthodox nature of Russia's business tradition.

Wimm-Bill-Dann planned to use the proceeds from its stock offering to finance further geographic expansion, as well as the renovation of existing plants to improve their efficiency. While concentrating on the its core juice and dairy business, the company also hoped to begin producing mineral water in 2002, building on a small bottling site it had in Novgorod. Despite its debut on an American exchange, Wimm-Bill-Dann did not want to slight domestic investors. In the spring of 2002, the company announced that it would soon be listed on the Russian Trading System. The listing would be largely symbolic at first, but the company felt that it made sense for a Russian company to be represented on a Russian exchange. Wimm-Bill-Dann had exploited a pseudo-Western image to win the attention of consumers in its first years of operation, but the company no longer felt any need to hide its Russian identity. The quality of its products, as well as its consumer-oriented approach, gave it a good chance of keeping a strong market share alongside both foreign and domestic competitors.

### *Principal Divisions*

Production; Advertising; Research; Protocol; Service; Scientific Centre; Supply.

### *Principal Subsidiaries*

Lianozovo Dairy (96%); Tsaritsino Dairy (86%); Baby Dairy Products (52%); Siberian Moloko (75%); Nizhny Novgorod Dairy (90%); Vladivostok Dairy (88%); Ramenski Dairy (91%); Karasuk Moloko (85%); Molochny Kombinat (92%); Bishkeksut (84%); Moloko (42%); Lianozovo-Samara (95%); Trade Company Wimm-Bill-Dann; Wimm-Bill-Dann Priobretatel; Wimm-Bill-Dann Netherlands B.V.; Podmoskovnoe Moloko (99%); Ramenskie Soki; Ramenskoye Moloko (75%); Wimm Bill Dann (Israel) Limited; Wimm-Bill-Dann Agro (80%); Nevsky Dairy Trade House (95%); Fruit Rivers; Nectarin; Kiev Dairy KMMZ

No. 3 (58%); Ufamolagroprom (46%); Rubtsovsky Dairy (95%); WBD Milk; WBD Asia; WBD Central Asia; WBD Ukraine; WBD Europe; WBD Netherlands, WBD Israel; WBD Germany; WBD Juice; WBD Mineral Water.

### *Principal Competitors*

Danone Group; The Coca-Cola Company; Petmol; Ostankino Dairy Plant; Parmalat; Multon.

### *Further Reading*


Aris, Ben, "Stars of the New Russian Consumer Sector," *Euromoney*, January 2001, pp. 62–4.

——, "Wimm-Bill-Dann Serves an Ace in Juice Game," *Euromoney*, March 2002, p. 20.

"Essential Guide," *Financial Times* (London), May 31, 1999, p. 10.

Helmer, John, "Russian Dairy Producer Survives Crash of the Ruble," *Journal of Commerce*, January 27, 1999, p. 12A.

Jack, Andrew, "If Wimm-Bill-Dann Can Make It There . . . ," *Financial Times* (London), February 8, 2002, p. 28.

Kozhakhmetova, Almira, "Wimm-Bill-Dann Is Through With Being Weaned," *RusData DiaLine-BizEkon News*, November 22, 1996.

Thornhill, John, "The Cream on the Top of Russian Capitalism," *Financial Times (London)*, May 31, 1999, p. 10.

——, "Russia Regains Patriotic Taste," *Financial Times* (London), August 5, 1999, p. 2.

Ulyanova, Yuliya, "Dairy Giant Plagued By Scandals," *RusData DiaLine-BizEkon News*, March 21, 1997.

"Wimm-Bill-Dann Boosts Profits By 37%," *Eurofood*, April 12, 2001, p. 12.

"Wimm-Bill-Dann Milks Thirst for Russian Equity Issuance," *Euroweek*, February 8, 2002, p. 25.

"Wimm-Bill-Dann to Trade Its Shares in RTS," *Vedomosti*, April 1, 2002.


—Sarah Ruth Lorenz

# WPP Group plc

**27 Farm Street**
**London WlJ 6RJ**
**United Kingdom**
**Telephone: (20) 7408-2204**
**Fax: (20) 7493-6819**
**Web site: http://www.wpp.com**

*Public Company*
*Incorporated:* 1971 as Wire & Plastic Products Ltd.
*Employees:* 65,000
*Gross Billings:* £20.8 billion (2001)
*Stock Exchanges:* London NASDAQ
*Ticker Symbol:* WPP
*NAIC:* 541810 Advertising Agencies

WPP Group plc operates as one of the largest communications services groups in the world, owning some of the most famous names in the advertising industry. These include the international media advertising giants JWT Group Inc., Ogilvy & Mather, and Young & Rubicam, the public relations firm Hill and Knowlton Inc., and information and consultancy firm The Kantar Group. WPP's clients include over 300 of the Fortune Global 500 and over half of the NASDAQ 100. The group has 1,400 locations in over 100 countries and its companies provide services in advertising, media investment management, information and consultancy, public relations and public affairs, branding and identity, and specialist communications.

## *The Birth of an Advertising Empire: Mid- to Late 1980s*

WPP is largely the creation of English businessman Martin Sorrell. Armed with an economics degree from Cambridge and an M.B.A. from Harvard, he made his name as financial director of the advertising giant Saatchi & Saatchi plc, joining the firm in 1977 and playing a key role in its growth through acquisitions. In 1986, Sorrell set out to build his own advertising empire. In need of a quoted company as a nucleus for acquisitions, he and a stockbroker friend had already bought a 27 percent stake in Wire and Plastics Products PLC in 1985. Having gone public in 1971, it was the holding company for a group of wire and plastic manufacturing businesses whose main products were shopping baskets and other domestic wire products. Sorrell became chief executive, changed the name of the company to WPP Group plc, and with the support of the other directors began adding marketing services to its activities.

In 1986, WPP made 11 acquisitions in this field, including design houses, incentive specialists, sales promotion consultants, and an audio-visual company. Sorrell's experience with Saatchi & Saatchi plc had taught him to be adept at publicizing his firm in the business press. He also followed their acquisition technique, buying companies on a five-year ''earn-out'' basis. In this way, the cost of the buyout is spread over a period of years, and the price finally paid for the company depends on the management increasing its pre-takeover profits.

The Saatchi brothers, with whom Sorrell was in close association, had taken a 10 percent stake in WPP. The price of WPP's shares was boosted, increasing their attractiveness as takeover currency. Investment bankers subsequently began suggesting takeover candidates to Sorrell.

In the first half of 1987, WPP turned its attention to the United States and acquired several companies there. Still purchasing marketing services companies, Sorrell professed to be uninterested in buying conventional advertising agencies at that time. In June 1987, however, WPP launched a bid for the JWT Group Inc., a media advertising agency in financial trouble in the mid-1980s. Although it had posted a loss in the first quarter of 1987 and takeover rumors were rife, some analysts were surprised to find the JWT Group bought out by a British company that had never owned a mainstream advertising agency. The two companies agreed to terms within two weeks and the whole JWT Group, including the public relations giant Hill & Knowlton Inc. and several satellite companies, became part of WPP.

WPP had to borrow part of the $566 million cost of this purchase. JWT's profit margin had dropped to 4 percent; however, with a few management changes and tough new profit targets, and with overstaffing and extravagant spending curbed, within three years both the JWT Group Inc. and Hill & Knowlton Inc. had raised their profit margins to 10 percent. In addition to increasing

## Company Perspectives:

*WPP operates with six strategic objectives. They are: to continue to raise operating margins to the levels of the best performing competition; to continue to increase the flexibility in our cost structure; to improve share owner value by optimizing the investment of the company's cash flow across the alternatives of capital expenditure; to continue to develop the role of the company as a parent company beyond that of a financial holding or investment company; to place greater emphasis on revenue growth; and to improve still further the quality of our creative output.*

revenue, a large property windfall helped to cover the purchase cost. A sale and lease back arrangement was organized with JWT's Tokyo office, which, when found to be worth over £100 million, was promptly sold along with other valuable properties.

### *The Ogilvy Purchase: 1989*

Despite its borrowings, WPP's profits rose steeply, from £1.7 million pre-tax in 1986 to £40.3 million in 1988. Sorrell's reputation as a financial wizard grew as well, and he continued to make other acquisitions. His biggest coup came in 1989, when he added the Ogilvy Group to his empire. Like the JWT Group, it was at the time an international network of agencies and satellite companies about equal in size to the WPP Group. Interpublic Group Inc. also put in a bid for Ogilvy, but after a brief tussle it fell to WPP for $864 million. David Ogilvy, the Ogilvy Group's founder, was persuaded to become chairman of WPP to help reassure Ogilvy clients.

WPP was now larger than Saatchi & Saatchi, the biggest advertising group of the time. However, the financing of its new purchases involved the company in preference shares and further large borrowings. Sorrell was convinced that he could pay these debts from increasing profits, but the task proved harder than it had with JWT because the Ogilvy group's margins were already averaging 8 percent.

WPP eventually overtook the Saatchis in worldwide billings, however, and its pre-tax profits hit new peaks in 1989 (£75 million) and 1990 (£90 million). Its earnings per share also rose in both years. It was only in the recession of the last quarter of 1990 that the company was forced to issue a warning of lower profits in 1991. Investors suddenly scrambled to get out and within a week WPP's shares lost two-thirds of their value.

In 1991, the company suspended all dividend payments and was forced to renegotiate its debts. Not helped by the effects of the Persian Gulf War and the continuing economic recession, the group's billings fell for the first time, and by the end of the year its profits had fallen by 38 percent before taxes. In 1992, a further refinancing became necessary, and in return the banks took more of the equity but had limited voting rights. While Martin Sorrell remained chief executive of the firm, a new chairman was appointed.

After spending a few years restructuring, WWP began to slowly expand its operations. In 1992, the firm launched CommonHealth, a virtual healthcare marketing communications network. Three years later, The Kantar Group was created to act as a holding company for the company's research businesses. Then, in 1996, WPP purchased a stake in Media Technology Ventures, a venture capital partnership designed to invest in emerging technology firms.

### *Expansion: Late 1990s and Beyond*

Because of its financial troubles of the early 1990s, WPP had put its growth strategy on the back burner. The group's financial position improved, however, and beginning in the late 1990s the group made a series of key purchases, launched new start-ups, and invested in media ventures. In 1997, WPP purchased a stake in Peapod, an online shopping service based in the United States; Syzygy, a digital media firm based in London; and HyperParallel, a San Francisco-based data mining firm. The company also invested in media firms in Latin America, Singapore, and Germany. In 1998, the firm acquired three high technology marketing consulting concerns along with United States-based Management Ventures Inc.; the Canada-based marketing research firm Goldfarb Consultants; Conway/Milliken, a research company based in Chicago; United States-based Alexander Communications, a technology public relations concern; and Asatsu-DK Inc., the third-largest advertising agency in Japan.

By this time, WPP had also launched MindShare, a new company involved in media planning, buying, and research in Europe and Asia. The firm also created Savatar, a start-up focused on new technology marketing in the United States. During 1998, profits rose by nearly 20 percent and non-media advertising—including Internet and Internet-related billings—accounted for 50 percent of the group's revenue for the first time in its history. WPP's frantic expansion pace continued in 1999 as the group made further investments in advertising communications-related firms and also acquired several companies, including Steve Perry Consultants, Shire Hall Group, Perspectives, The Brand Union, Blanc and Otus, Dazai Advertising, and P. Four.

WPP entered the new millennium focused on growth. While the group made a slew of acquisitions during 2000, its most publicized purchase of the year was that of Young & Rubicam Inc., a U.S. marketing concern. Sorrell made the firm's initial offer in January, which was followed by several months of hostile negotiations. The $4.7 billion transaction was finally completed in September. It stood as the largest such deal in the advertising industry at the time and created the world's leading marketing services group. That year, operating profits grew by 43 percent over the previous year to $631 million.

Sir Martin Sorrell—he was knighted in 2000—found himself involved in yet another attention-grabbing deal in 2001 when he made a bid for the Tempus Group plc, a media buying concern. By this time, WPP had amassed a 22 percent stake in the firm. Tempus, however, was not keen on a WPP takeover—its chairman, Chris Ingram, had made public the fact that he would never work for Sorrell—and looked to advertising conglomerate Havas to make a white knight bid. When Havas made its offer, WPP responded with a higher bid of $630 million.

## Key Dates:

**1971:** Wire & Plastics Products is incorporated and goes public.
**1985:** Martin Sorrell and a stockbroker friend purchase a 27 percent stake in Wire and Plastics.
**1986:** Sorrell is named chief executive and changes the name of the company to WPP Group plc.
**1987:** WPP acquires the JWT Group.
**1989:** The company purchases the Ogilvy Group and becomes the largest advertising group in the world.
**1992:** CommonHealth, a virtual healthcare marketing network, is launched.
**1995:** The Kantar Group is created to act as a holding company for the firm's research businesses.
**1997:** The group begins a major expansion effort.
**2000:** WPP acquires Young & Rubicam Inc.
**2001:** Tempus Group plc is purchased.

The advertising industry as a whole suffered as the tragic events of September 11, 2001, sent the U.S. economy into a deeper decline. As a result of the weakening market conditions, Havas allowed its bid to expire, leaving WPP the sole bidder. Sorrell tried to back out of the deal, but his efforts were denied by the UK Takeover Panel. The deal was completed in late 2001.

WPP characterized 2001 as a brutal year in its annual report. Nevertheless, the group continued to report significant profits despite the downturn in the industry. Turnover increased by nearly 50 percent over 2000 figures and pre-tax profits climbed by 12 percent. By this time, marketing services accounted for just over half of the group's revenues while countries outside of the United States secured 56 percent of turnover.

WPP's long term goal was to become the world's most successful and preferred provider of communications services to multinational and local companies. With Sorrell at the helm, the group was focused on overcoming hardships related to economic challenges, integrating both its Young & Rubicam and Tempus purchases, and increasing its marketing services business to 65 percent of total revenues.

### *Principal Subsidiaries*

J. Walter Thompson Company, Inc. (U.S.); The Ogilvy Group, Inc. (U.S.); Young & Rubicam Inc. (U.S.); The Kantar Group; Hill and Knowlton Inc. (U.S.); Tempus Group plc.

### *Principal Competitors*

Havas S.A.; The Interpublic Group of Companies Inc.; Omincom Group Inc.

### *Further Reading*

Brady, Diane, ''Now, WPP and Y&R Have to Kiss, Make Up—and Get to Work,'' *Business Week*, May 12, 2000.
Kapner, Suzanne, ''A Master Deal Maker Got More Than He Bargained For,'' *New York Times*, November 20, 2001, p. C8.
Katz, Richard, ''WPP Group Merges For Clout,'' *MediaWeek*, April 7, 1997, p. 6.
McCarthy, Michael, ''WPP Is in a Deal-Making Mood,'' *AdWeek*, September 15, 1997, p. 3.
McMains, Andrew, ''WPP Takes Reins of Y&R,'' *AdWeek*, October 9, 2000, p. 5.
O'Leary, Noreen, ''WPP's Martin Sorrell,'' *AdWeek*, May 22, 2000, p. 26.
Piggott, Stanley, *OBM, A Celebration: 125 Years in Advertising*, London: Ogilvy Benson & Mather, 1975.
''Uneasy Lies the Head,'' *The Economist*, February 24, 2001, p. 9.
Wentz, Laurel, and Richard Linnett, ''Tempus Tempest,'' *Advertising Age*, November 5, 2001, p. 3.
''WPP Group's Pre-Tax Profit Jump 20 Percent,'' *Campaign*, February 19 1999, p. 2.

—John Swan
—update: Christina M. Stansell

# X-Rite, Inc.

**3100 44th Street Southwest**
**Grandville, Michigan 49418-2582**
**U.S.A.**
**Telephone: (616) 534-7663**
**Fax: (616) 534-0723**
**Web site: http://www.x-rite.com**

*Public Company*
*Incorporated:* 1958
*Employees:* 687
*Sales:* $103.50 million
*Stock Exchanges:* NASDAQ
*Ticker Symbol:* XRIT
*NAIC:* 334514 Totalizing Fluid Meter and Counting Device Manufacturing; 334516 Analytical Laboratory Instrument Manufacturing

X-Rite, Inc. is a leader in the development and manufacturing of equipment that measures the composition and brightness of colors. The company's products are used for purposes that include making matching paint colors and regulating quality in the processing of film and x-rays. X-Rite also makes a device that helps match the colors of replacement teeth to a patient's own and a non-invasive cholesterol level tester that works by analyzing the color change of a chemical solution on the skin, as well as other specialty medical products. The Michigan-based, publicly traded firm, which has branches in Europe and Asia, distributes its products around the world.

### *Beginnings*

X-Rite was founded by a group of seven engineers at aircraft instrument maker Lear Siegler, Inc. who wanted to form a new company as a sideline. The seven founders, led by D. Ted Thompson, incorporated their new business on Christmas Eve 1958. Initially unsure of what they would make, they found inspiration for the company's first product when the wife of one engineer, a nurse, commented on the difficulty she had in making labels for x-rays. Thompson came up with the idea of a light-opaque silver tape that could be used in place of the standard metal letters that were photographed along with the patient. The tape was first marketed in 1961, but the firm remained small and had no full-time employees for several years.

By 1967, business had grown to the point that one of the company's founders was needed to dedicate his full attention to X-Rite, and Ted Thompson was chosen for the role. In addition to running the company, Thompson continued to look after new product development. One of his inventions, a silver recovery system for x-ray equipment, became the company's second major product when it was introduced in 1968. X-Rite would also later add a shrink-wrapping device to its offerings. In 1975, the company introduced another new product called a densitometer. The device measured the density of a film image for the printing of negatives and in other applications. After several years, X-Rite's densitometer was improved to allow it to feed data into a computer.

This newest product became popular with the photographic printing industry, in particular for use in monitoring print quality in ''one-hour photo'' mini-labs, and this led to a period of strong growth, with revenues increasing an average of 30 percent during each of the next ten years. Though X-Rite had entered a field already dominated by several larger competitors, by the mid-1980s the company controlled half of the $50 million densitometer market. By 1986, with annual sales topping $10 million, X-Rite was ready to go public. It did so early in the year and was subsequently added to the NASDAQ National Market System. During the first two years of X-Rite's listing, its share value tripled. In June 1987, the firm moved into its new corporate headquarters and manufacturing site in Grandville, Michigan.

### *Color Measurement Devices Prove Popular*

The year 1989 saw X-Rite introduce another color-analysis product, a spectrocolorimeter. Similar to the densitometer, the spectrocolorimeter could analyze colors of textiles, plastics, or paints and create a match that was essentially as good as the human eye was able to. Though there were several larger competitors, X-Rite's technological innovations and efficient manufac-

**Company Perspectives:**

*X-Rite is on an evolutionary track. By strengthening our technology and broadening our markets, we believe we are assuring our future. Rapid advances in technology over the past few years have revolutionized the global economy and created new opportunities. Amid all the changes, the factors that drive our company's success remain the same: First-mover leadership in markets served; Skilled development of knowledge-based systems; Products that offer great value; Strategic collaboration with key industry leaders; Global marketing and selling. As X-Rite's family of companies continues to grow, we are sharing ideas and embracing new technologies, new markets, and new possibilities. Our objective is to increase your return on the investment you have in X-Rite's future as a customer, employee, or shareholder.*

turing techniques allowed it to price its new product considerably lower than the industry average, at $3,500 as opposed to the $6,000 to $10,000 prices of models made by other companies. The battery-powered, portable X-Rite product was also more user friendly than those previously available. Users of spectrocolorimeters included graphic arts firms (to whom they were initially introduced), paint stores, and other customers who needed accurate color measurement. As its densitometer had done, X-Rite's spectrocolorimeter soon became one of the leaders in the market. The company had spent 18 months and more than $1.5 million to develop the product. At this time, X-Rite typically dedicated between 6 and 12 percent of its earnings to creating new products or upgrading old ones, with 47 of the firm's 203 employees working as engineers. Soon after the spectrocolorimeter's introduction, X-Rite signed a $1 million deal to sell densitometers and sensitometers, a similar product, to Kodak's medical division for use in controlling the quality of films used in mammography. In early 1990, the company announced another new variation on its spectrocolorimeter, X-Scan, which measured the color values of inks on a printed page with a portable unit that was interfaced with a computer. The $15,000 device cost less than half of what its competitors' versions did. A 30,000-square-foot expansion of the company's Grandville facility was completed in late fall to help fulfill orders for X-Scans and the company's successful line of spectrocolorimeters.

In 1991, another big order was signed to deliver $2.5 million worth of densitometers to a large photo company in Japan. At this time, X-Rite's overseas sales accounted for 30 percent of its revenues, an amount that was increasing every year. That same year also saw introduction of a multi-angle spectrophotometer, which could measure the color of metallic paint for customers such as auto manufacturers and body shops. The device took readings from several angles to arrive at a final value, which could then be used to create a paint match or to assure consistency in paint from batch to batch. Sales for fiscal 1991 were a record $29.1 million, with earnings of $4.3 million. The firm placed 95th on Forbes' annual list of the 200 best small companies in the United States during the year.

X-Rite introduced another new product in 1992, MiX-Rite, a $10,000 machine for use in paint stores that could formulate precisely blended paints to match the colors of wallpaper or fabrics in a home. The machine would analyze a color sample and then calculate the color formula for the tint, which would be mixed and then inserted into a can of paint base with an automated hole-punch and resealing mechanism. The process took a total of 90 seconds. As with other X-Rite products, the device was based on an existing idea but delivered it in a smaller and cheaper form. The first sales were made in 1993, a year which also saw the company open its first foreign office, in Cologne, Germany. Though X-Rite products were already sold and serviced internationally by a network of dealers, the new office gave the firm a better platform for the increased growth it was seeking abroad. A new subsidiary, X-Rite GmbH, was formed to run its German operations. In the early fall, X-Rite also signed a two-year, $10 million deal with DuPont to supply it with spectrophotometry instruments.

### *Expansion Through Acquisitions*

The spring of 1994 saw the expansion-minded X-Rite make its first purchase, H. Miller Graphics Arts of Congleton, England. H. Miller, an X-Rite distributor, was another link in the company's chain of overseas growth. It was subsequently renamed X-Rite, Ltd. The Miller acquisition was followed in September by the purchase of the assets of Colorgen, Inc., a bankrupt maker of color matching equipment. The fall of 1994 also saw Ted Thompson cede some of his duties to company newcomer Bruce Jorgensen, who took the title of president. Jorgensen had grown up in the Grand Rapids, Michigan, area and later worked around the world during a 27-year stint with Exxon Corp. The 65-year old Thompson remained in his long-held posts of CEO and board chairman.

The company's growth, despite a national recession, had swelled the ranks of its employees to more than 400 in Grandville and nearly 100 at the former Colorgen facility near Boston, Massachusetts, and its German and newly opened Hong Kong offices. X-Rite was continuing to introduce new products, such as the Digital Swatchbook, which could analyze a color in the real world and then transfer it to a computer screen. The $1,000 product, one of 11 new items introduced during the year, included a color sampling tool and software. During 1994 the debt-free company's stock value rose 80 percent.

The start of 1995 saw X-Rite's acquisition spree continue with the purchase of light measurement device maker Labsphere, Inc. of North Sutton, New Hampshire. The company also bought a second manufacturing site in Grandville, across the street from its main facility. A slowdown in the automotive and graphics arts markets, and a decline in orders from major customer DuPont, precipitated a restructuring that took place in January of 1996 and involved the layoff of 55 workers (about 10 percent of the company's workforce), and the elimination of all non-necessary expenditures. Company president Bruce Jorgensen also announced his resignation, with former Perrigo executive C. Mathew Peabody named as his replacement in the fall, though his own tenure ended abruptly the following summer.

Another acquisition was announced in June 1997 when X-Rite bought California-based Light Source Computer Images, Inc., a maker of color measuring equipment and computer scanner software. The following year another foreign branch

## Key Dates:

**1958:** X-Rite is incorporated by seven Lear Siegler engineers. 1961: The company's first product, x-ray marking tape, is introduced.
**1968:** Silver recovery equipment for x-rays debuts.
**1975:** X-Rite introduces its first densitometer for photographic printing use.
**1986:** X-Rite goes public.
**1987:** The company moves into new headquarters and production facility in Grandville, Michigan.
**1990:** X-Rite begins to shift its emphasis to the field of color-measurement.
**1994:** A round of acquisitions starts with purchase of H. Miller Graphic Arts of England.
**2001:** Co-founder Ted Thompson retires; Dental color matching system are unveiled.

was added when X-Rite formed X-Rite Méditerranée SARL to acquire an existing distributorship near Paris. In June 1998, former Cascade Engineering president Richard Cook took over as the firm's president from Ted Thompson, who had been wearing both CEO and president caps since Mathew Peabody's departure. Cook had earned physics, management, and divinity degrees from various Michigan schools.

### *A New President Faces Challenges*

In a reversal from 1997's record-setting $97 million in revenues and $18 million in profits, 1998 saw the company suffering its worst year ever, with a first-time quarterly loss reported during the third bookkeeping period. The red ink was attributed to a $4.4 million asset write-off related to X-Rite's underachieving digital imaging business, plus $400,000 in legal fees spent on a lawsuit for a patent infringement, as well as an overall drop in revenues and sales for the year. As a result, in September Cook effected a reorganization of X-Rite into four business units. These would consist of imaging; printing; coating, plastics, and textiles; and new business development. Cook stated that the goal of the restructuring was to put the firm back on track for 20 percent annual sales growth, with the realignment expected to facilitate finding new markets for X-Rite products.

At the end of 1998, X-Rite signed an agreement with retail chain Ace Hardware to put the company's current generation of paint matching devices, called MatchRite, into 5,000 Ace stores worldwide. The company also reached an agreement with Heidelberg Color Publishing Solutions to include X-Rite's Digital Swatchbook as part of Heidelberg's color management package for the printing industry. January 1999 saw X-Rite open a new office in Tokyo, Japan, while at the same time ramping up spending on research and development to create more new products.

In the summer of 1999, company patriarch Ted Thompson announced he was giving up the position of CEO, though he would remain on duty as board chairman. President Richard Cook was named to the top post the following February. The fiscal year was an improvement over 1998, with earnings of $13.6 million on sales of $100.2 million, and the sagging value of X-Rite stock began to shoot back up in early 2000. Shortly afterwards the firm brought in investment bank Broadview International LLC as a consultant on acquisitions and investments. The company formed a new subsidiary, XR Ventures, to facilitate this activity.

One of the first investments the new unit made was in Trident Technology, a Grand Rapids-area firm that developed networking and database software for corporations. The XR Ventures money would help Trident expand its network of sales offices in the Midwest and on the east coast. X-Rite also bought 90 percent of the rights to a tunable laser technology developed by Virginia-based Veridian, which it formed a new subsidiary, Coherix, to develop. The laser system was capable of precisely measuring three-dimensional objects for use in a variety of industrial processes. Another acquisition, that of the German firm Optronik GmbH, took place in September. Optronik, with $2.5 million in sales, was a maker of Web-based color and light measurement instruments and software.

In early 2001, X-Rite subsidiary Labsphere signed a major agreement with Cleveland-based Keithley Instruments, Inc. to sell it light measurement devices for use in the telecommunications industry. The firm also invested in two additional companies, MedPanel, Inc. of Cambridge, Massachusetts, an online medical research and marketing firm, and HandyLab, Inc. of Ann Arbor, Michigan, which became part of the Coherix operation. HandyLab was a developer of laser-based measuring devices.

In the spring of 2001, X-Rite announced the availability of its new Shade-Rite Dental Vision System, which utilized the company's color matching technology to produce accurately tinted replacement teeth. In June, XR Ventures invested in UrbanPixel, Inc. of San Francisco, which developed software for Web site development. Shortly after this, Richard Cook relinquished his president duties to newcomer Michael Ferrara, former CEO of Marine Optical Group, an eyewear maker. The company's new Cholesterol 1,2,3 System, which had been developed in 2000, was also undergoing testing by the U.S. Food and Drug Administration, having already been given the green light in Canada. Cholesterol 1,2,3, which had been developed in conjunction with Toronto, Canada-based International Medical Innovations, Inc., measured the amount of cholesterol in the bloodstream by checking the color of a chemical after it was placed on a patient's skin. The new device offered a quick, non-invasive test that also generated no medical wastes.

In late 2001, X-Rite chairman Ted Thompson announced his retirement from the firm he had helped found more than 40 years earlier. The 72-year-old's position would be taken by board member John Utley. Shortly afterward, the company announced another restructuring and layoffs of almost 10 percent of its workforce, which was expected to generate a savings of $3.5 million annually. With the transition of leadership from patriarch Ted Thompson successfully completed, the company was streamlining operations while simultaneously investing in new possibilities and seeking new markets around the world. X-Rite, Inc. remained a leader in the field of color measurement, while it looked to the future with its new medical and three-dimensional measurement technologies.

### *Principal Subsidiaries*

X-Rite International, Inc. (Barbados); X-Rite Holdings, Inc.; XR Ventures LLC; X-Rite GmbH (Germany); X-Rite Asia Pacific Limited (Hong Kong); X-Rite Ltd. (U.K.); X-Rite MA, Incorporated; OTP, Incorporated; Labsphere, Inc.; X-Rite Mediterranee SARL (France); X-Rite Global, Inc.; Coherix Corporation.

### *Principal Competitors*

Gretag MacBeth LLC; Excel Technology, Inc.; HunterLab Associates, Inc.; Minolta Co., Ltd.

### *Further Reading*


Couretas, John, ''Product Innovation Is Key to X-Rite Inc.'s Phenomenal Growth,'' *Grand Rapids Press*, December 27, 1992, p. H1.

Harger, Jim, ''X-Rite Buys Factory for Expansion, Will Stay in Grandville,'' *Grand Rapids Press*, May 16, 1995, p. B7.

Rivers, Anne, ''X-Rite Foresees Continued Growth,'' *Grand Rapids Business Journal*, July 21, 1986, p. 1.

Sabo, Mary Ann, ''Expenses Drag Down X-Rite's Bottom Line,'' *Grand Rapids Press*, May 21, 1996, p. C8.

——, ''President's Departure Could Make Search Much Tougher,'' *Grand Rapids Press*, July 24, 1997, p. A13.

——, ''X-Rite Announces Reorganization Plan,'' *Grand Rapids Press*, September 17, 1998, p. B5.

——, ''X-Rite Chief Steps Down,'' *Grand Rapids Press*, July 22, 1999, p. E1.

——, ''X-Rite-Firm's Strategy Includes a Better Job at Marketing Itself,'' *Grand Rapids Press*, September 27, 1998, p. F11.

——, ''X-Rite Looks for Brighter Colors as Markets Turn Gray,''

Sanchez, Mark, ''X-Rite Returning to Its Medical Roots,'' *Grand Rapids Business Journal*, September 10, 2001, p. 1.

Turner, Mike, ''Grandville's X-Rite Aims to Capture New Markets,'' *Grand Rapids Business Journal*, April 3, 1989, p. 3.

VanderVeen, Don, ''Inside Track: Bruce Jorgensen,'' *Grand Rapids Business Journal*, October 3, 1994, p. 5.

Vann, Sonya, ''X-Rite Shareholders Hear More Good News at the Annual Meeting,'' *Grand Rapids Press*, May 11, 1993, p. B7.

Whisenhunt, Eric, ''The X-Rite Stuff: True Colors Are Shining Through in Grandville,'' *Michigan Business*, October 1, 1989, p. 38.

Wieland, Barbara, ''Co-Founder's Retirement Ends Era at X-Rite,'' *Grand Rapids Press*, October 2, 2001, p. A15.


—Frank Uhle

# ZF Friedrichshafen AG

**Allmannsweilerstrasse 25**
**D-88038 Friedrichshafen**
**Germany**
**Telephone: (49) (7541) 77 0**
**Fax: (49) (7541) 77 90 80 00**
**Web site: http://www.zf-group.com**

*Private Company*
*Incorporated:* 1915 as Zahnradfabrik Friedrichshafen GmbH
*Employees:* 35,608
*Sales:* EUR 6.96 billion ($5.98 billion) (2001)
*NAIC:* 336350 Motor Vehicle Transmission and Power Train Parts Manufacturing; 336330 Motor Vehicle Steering and Suspension Components (Except Spring) Manufacturing

ZF Friedrichshafen AG—one of the world's largest vendors to the global auto industry—translates power into motion with its transmissions for motor vehicles for road, railroad, air, and water. The company also makes automotive steering and rear-axle systems and chassis components, and industrial drives and transmissions for heavy machinery. Headquartered in Friedrichshafen, Germany, ZF maintains a global presence though 25 production plants and 26 sales and service subsidiaries around the world. Roughly on-quarter of ZF's total sales is generated in the United States. The acquisition of four business divisions of Mannesmann Sachs AG from the German Siemens Group in 2001 made ZF Germany's third-largest vendor. The city of Friedrichshafen controls ZF through Zeppelin Stiftung, a nonprofit foundation that dates back to the early 20th century.

## *Zeppelin Spurs Company Foundation in 1915*

The beginning of the 20th century was a time that belonged to innovators and visionaries who paved the way for a new world driven by new technologies. One of them was Ferdinand Graf von Zeppelin, a 52-year-old retired army general whose passion it was to conquer the airways for human travel and transportation. His vision inspired many gifted inventors and engineers and transformed the small town of Friedrichshafen, located near picturesque Bodensee Lake, into one of the first centers of worldwide air travel.

After many years of pioneering construction work, the first airship "LZ1," launched from a raft, rose into the air over Bodensee Lake on July 2, 1900. One year later, the German-American aviation pioneer Gustave Whitehead undertook the first successful air trip with his motor-powered airplane. After Zeppelin had secured the funding for his second airship, it rose into the air in January 1906. "LZ 2" made 40 kilometers per hour but turned out to be hard to steer. When on August 1908 "LZ 4" burst into flames after gusty winds had pushed the Zeppelin against a tree after a forced landing in Echterdingen near Stuttgart, everyone, including "The Graf," was deeply shocked. The tragedy, however, was immediately followed by an unexpected event that was nothing short of a miracle. Zeppelin was overwhelmed by a spontaneous wave of sympathy by the masses of curious observers which set in motion an unprecedented flow of donations. By the end of the year, the donations for the construction of a new airship exceeded six million German marks.

The funds were used to set up the Zeppelin Foundation in Friedrichshafen, which in turn established a private company for the construction of Zeppelin airships: the Luftschiffbau-Zeppelin Ges.m.b.H.—in short LZ. The company's CEO, Alfred Colsman, gained the interest of a number of municipalities, banks, and private investors in the idea of Zeppelin-based air transportation, resulting in the foundation of Deutsche Luftschiffahrt AG (Delag), a public stock company that funded and promoted further development of the Zeppelin technology. After a series of failures which ended with the destruction of several airships, Delag's "LZ 10 Schwaben" became a success.

While Germany went to war in 1914 and the military reigned over the country, Graf Zeppelin envisioned the first Zeppelin crossing the Atlantic Ocean, and his engineers worked on refining the technology. To improve the transmission of the motor power to the propellers, Zeppelin's airships needed high-precision cogwheels which were not available at the market. Zeppelin's lead engineers turned for help to Max Maag, a Swiss engineer who had

## Company Perspectives:

*ZF is the world's largest independent specialist for transmission and chassis technology.* ZF products contribute worldwide to mobility. *ZF develops and produces transmissions, steering systems, and axles and chassis components, as well as complete systems for passenger cars, commercial vehicles, and off-road machinery. ZF is a major transmission specialist also for marine craft, rail-bound vehicles, and helicopters.* Technological leadership is ZF's key to a strong market position. *Consistent expansion of our technological position is a prerequisite for the development of innovative and successful products.* The decentralized company structure of ZF permits a high degree of market and customer proximity. *This flexibility and the worldwide cooperation of our development and production locations allow ZF customers to be provided with optimum products and service.* ZF intends to further expand its market position. *The objective is to continue to win customers on the basis of competence and excellent performance.*

invented a revolutionary technology for the manufacture of cog-wheels and owned a machine tool factory in Zurich.

On August 20, 1915, Zahnradfabrik Friedrichshafen—in short ZF—was founded as a private company, owned by LZ and Max Maag Zahnräderfabrik. The firm's purpose was to build cog-wheels and transmissions for airships, airplanes, automobiles, and motor boats. Zeppelin's research and development director, Alfred von Soden-Fraunhofen, a distinguished engineer who had earned his wings at Germany's automobile manufacturer Daimler, became the company's first CEO thanks to Graf Zeppelin. It was Zeppelin who managed to convince German authorities that the man he had chosen for this position was more seriously needed in the homeland than in the battlefield. Equipped with 40 planing and grinding machines from Max Maag, ZF started making cog-wheels and transmissions for airships and airplanes. The new company's staff was dedicated and prolific: by 1916, ZF had already registered ten patents. The following year brought a great loss for the company when on March 12, 1917, Graf Zeppelin died four days after major surgery.

### *1918–45: Vendor to the German Auto and War Industry*

World War I ended in the fall of 1918, resulting in the abdication of the German Kaiser and the establishment of the Weimar Republic in January 1919 as a result of democratic elections. The defeated Germany was not allowed to rebuild its own air force and ZF was forbidden to make transmissions for air vehicles.

The death of the company's founder and the postwar situation in Germany caused numerous difficulties for ZF. Led by CEO Soden and drawing on his experience in the auto industry, the company started building auto transmissions. The military authorities imposed a production limit of 75 transmissions per day on the company. On top of that, qualified workers, machinery, and raw material were hard to come by.

Despite these challenges, ZF managed to set a foundation for growth. The company's machine stock had grown to 190 grinding and planing machines, drills, and lathes—enough to get started with the serial production of the Soden pre-selector gearbox, a semi-automatic transmission invented by the company's CEO. The postwar economic recession, with its staggering rates of inflation, threatened the company's very existence. To secure a sufficient capital base for the financially struggling company, it was transformed into the joint stock corporation ZF Aktiengesellschaft. LZ owned four out of the company's five million marks of capital. The other 20 percent were owned by Maag Zahnräder- und Maschinen AG.

While the Soden gearbox proved to be a technological revolution, the German market was not ready for it. Automakers and consumers were not willing to pay the higher cost for a transmission that allowed gears to be pre-selected by means of a lever on the dashboard. ZF responded by developing and launching the Einheitsgetriebe, a standardized gearbox that allowed mass production at low cost, in 1925. With over 300,000 units sold, it became the company's hoped-for success. In the following year, ZF established a second production plant in Berlin. Three years later, the company launched its low-noise ''Aphon'' gearbox, which was first presented in an eight-cylinder sports convertible made by German automaker Autounion Horch.

The 1930s hit the German economy with another serious recession, caused by the onset of the Great Depression in the United States. While a regular Zeppelin service was resumed between Germany and South America, the number of people without a job skyrocketed. National Socialist leader Adolf Hitler came to power in 1933 and funded a highway construction program to create jobs. In a time of advancing motorization, ZF worked on refining its technologies. In 1932, the company ventured into steering systems, starting out with a license production of American ''Ross-Steering.'' Two years later, the company launched its first completely synchronized four-gear transmission for automobiles—a technological milestone which also became an economic success. By 1937, ZF had evolved as one of Europe's leading manufacturers of vehicle transmissions with 3,500 employees. The company was reaching its capacity limits and, consequently, a third production plant was set up in Schwäbisch Gmünd near Stuttgart in June 1937. One year later, the Schwäbische Zahnradwerke GmbH was founded. In the same year, a pension plan was launched for all employees of the Zeppelin Foundation firms.

The tragic explosion of the Zeppelin ''LZ 129 Hindenburg,'' in which 35 of the 96 passengers lost their lives on May 7, 1937 in Lakehurst, New Jersey, brought the ''Zeppelin-Era'' to a sudden end. Afterwards, ZF's development engineers started working on transmissions for tractors and motor ships. On September 1, 1939, German soldiers marched into Poland, marking the beginning of another devastating world war. Under tight government control, ZF started making transmissions for tanks and military trucks. Due to high demand from the German military, the company established new production facilities for steering mechanisms in Alsace and for tank gearboxes in Passau in 1943 and 1944. However, in 1944 the Allied Forces bombed Friedrichshafen, a center of the German war industry, and took over the Schlettstatt plant. In April 1945, Friedrichshafen was occupied by French troops.

**Key Dates:**

**1915:** Zahnradfabrik Friedrichshafen (ZF) is founded to make precision cog-wheels for Zeppelin airships.
**1918:** The company starts making transmissions for automobiles.
**1921:** ZF is transformed into a joint stock corporation.
**1932:** The company commences the licensed production of steering systems.
**1944:** The company premises in Friedrichshafen are destroyed almost completely during World War II.
**1950:** The city of Friedrichshafen becomes ZF's majority owner.
**1959:** A production plant is established in São Paulo, Brazil.
**1973:** The manufacture of automatic transmissions for passenger cars begins in Saarbrücken.
**1979:** ZF of North America is founded.
**1981:** The electronic ZF-Servotronic steering system is launched.
**1986:** ZF starts making transmissions for pick-up trucks in the United States.
**1992:** The company is renamed ZF Friedrichshafen AG.
**1998:** ZF ventures into China.
**1999:** The Steering Systems Division is integrated into a joint venture with Robert Bosch GmbH.
**2001:** ZF acquires four business divisions of Mannesmann Sachs AG.

## *1946–50: Reconstruction and Growth*

With the death of CEO Alfred Graf von Soden-Fraunhofen, the company had lost another visionary leader to the war. A legacy from the last year of his life was the prediction of a high demand in agricultural machinery for the postwar market. However, before ZF was able to take on this new direction, it had once more to fight for its existence. The Berlin plant was dismantled as a part of reparation payments, while the French military administration was determined to destroy the industrial power in Friedrichshafen. According to Delag's vice-president, Dr. Eckener, the Zeppelin group of companies was a dead enterprise. At the end of 1946, the French military government decided to shut down LZ, ZF's majority shareholder. The future of the Zeppelin companies was now in doubt.

Nonetheless, failure was not an option for ZF's management. After long and difficult negotiations, the company was granted permission to resume operations. A group of 650 workers began to clear away the rubble and rebuild the company facilities in Friedrichshafen. Soon the machinery was up and running again, making transmissions for tractors and trucks. The plant in Schwäbisch Gmünd recommenced the production of steering mechanisms. The Passau plant began to make engines for tractors.

In 1947, the Zeppelin Foundation as a private entity was dissolved. The founder had determined in the company charter that if the foundations purpose—the promotion of airship transportation—fell through, its assets would have to be turned over to Friedrichshafen's city government, which was obliged to administrate it under the name "Zeppelin Foundation" and to use its revenues for charitable and social purposes. The city of Friedrichshafen became the new majority owner of ZF. In times of food scarcity and a sluggish economy, the company grew vegetables on its grounds and developed and temporarily produced the low-cost, lightweight, one-man car "Champion." In August 1948, the good news reached the company that it was taken off the "to-be-dismantled" list. In 1950, the Berlin plant started operations.

## *1951–70: Expanding Reach and Range*

In the next 20 years, ZF evolved to become Europe's largest manufacturer of transmissions, steerings, and drives. One of the reasons for this successful development was diversification. Besides the auto and truck industry, the company targeted manufacturers of water and—once again—air vehicles, as well as the machine tool makers. In 1958, the company started developing transmissions for helicopters and machine tools. Three years later, ZF launched its first products. The plant in Passau started making axles for trucks and tractors in 1960. By 1966, the company also made motor breaks for trucks, drives for vehicles used in agriculture, transmissions for boats, electrical clutches, oil pumps, steerings and driven axles for machines used in agriculture and construction, and cog-wheels of all kinds. In 1968, the company commenced the production of transmissions for the air industry.

Another reason for the company's success was a constant flow of innovation and high production quality in its core market—the auto industry. In 1954, ZF acquired a production license for steering mechanisms from the U.S. firm Gemmer while its own hydraulic steering gained market acceptance. Soon the company became Europe's number one steering manufacturer. In 1961, ZF introduced a new automatic transmission for mid-sized cars. Four years later, the company started making automatic transmissions for BMW and Peugeot. In 1970, a subsidiary for the manufacturing of automatic transmissions for passenger cars was established in Saarbrücken, together with Chicago-based Borg-Warner Corporation. After the U.S. partner opted out of the business in 1972, the company was renamed ZF-Getriebe GmbH. To keep the stream of refined and new technologies flowing, ZF employed more than 800 engineers and technicians.

A third reason for ZF's success was the company's effort to explore new markets abroad. By 1951, exports accounted for 6.5 percent of total sales. This number was doubled within a year. By 1959, the number had climbed to 17 percent. In that year, the company also established a production subsidiary in São Paulo, Brazil. To get a foot in the door, many foreign automakers worked together with ZF do Brazil since they were required by law to use a high percentage of domestic vendors. The new facility started out with 200 workers, making the whole ZF product range.

Ever-increasing use of motor vehicles contributed to ZF's impressive performance at the end of the 1960s. Between 1967 and 1969 the company's revenues increased by 50 percent. More than every third commercial vehicle in Germany now carried a ZF-transmission or ZF-steering in 1968. In the early 1970s, for the first time, the company's annual sales passed the

DM1 billion mark. The number of ZF-employees had almost quadrupled in twenty years.

## *1973–2002: Partner of the Global Auto Industry*

In the 1970s, the company greatly expanded into all parts of the globe. Subsidiaries and sales offices were established in Austria, France, the United Kingdom, Denmark, Norway, Argentina, South Africa, and the United States. In the 1980s, ZF established a presence in Japan, Spain, India, South Korea, Singapore, Australia, Switzerland, and Turkey. The company also grew through acquisitions, including a 50 percent share in Henschel Flugzeug-Werke, a German manufacturer of parts for air vehicles; the share majority of the Lemförder group, based in northern Germany, a producer of parts from metal, plastic, and rubber used in transmissions, axles, and steerings; the Italian firm Pai Demin; and minority shares in a Spanish and a Malaysian company. An attempt in the early 1990s to take over General Motor's transmission manufacturer for buses and trucks, Allison Transmissions, was stopped by the German and U.S. antitrust authorities. Another project with Volkswagen AG to integrate the company's steering production into ZF—the so-called ''steering union''—encountered too much resistance and was finally given up. In mid-1995, the company took over a transmissions factory from Mercedes-Benz. In addition, ZF continued to venture into new markets and set up production plants in Russia and China.

Over the years, ZF became an indispensable partner for the global auto industry. Its broadened international reach enabled the company to attract more and more of the global automakers as customers. In 1974, French automaker Peugeot ordered 400,000 automatic 3 HP 22 transmissions over the course of seven years—a milestone that created a basis for further growth. In 1986, ZF founded ZF Transmissions Inc. and ZF Steering Gear Inc. (U.S.) and started making its new ''ECOLITE'' S 5-42 transmission for Ford Motor Company. In the late 1980s, the company also received orders from Chrysler and American Motors. The company's new electronic transmission 4 HP 24 for the German four-wheel-drive Audi V8 was later also installed in top auto brands, including BMW, Jaguar, Lotus, Maserati, Peugeot, Volvo, Alfa Romeo, Rover, Citroën, Fiat, Lancia, Saab, and Chrysler. In 1988, the company received awards for high product quality from Ford and Jaguar. In 1990, ZF teamed up with two Japanese companies and started making pumps and other components for steering systems in the United States. ZF's new ''Ecotronic'' transmission, which cut down the fuel used by 15 percent, attracted new big-name customers, including Volkswagen. In the late 1990s, automakers focused more and more on their core competencies and cut the number of vendors down to a few which were confronted with new demands. Instead of certain auto parts, they requested whole components and systems which had to be delivered just-in-time to their assembly lines. For example, for the production of the brand-new ''M-Class'' from Mercedes Benz, a new production plant was set up at a new location in Tuscaloosa, Alabama. ZF set up its own new factory just 26 miles away, where it started making complete axle-systems. Only the motor and the transmissions for the new ''M-Class'' were actually made by Daimler-Benz. This new trend also transferred more responsibility for developing new technologies for certain components, as well as the coordination of a bigger number of vendors worldwide, from the automaker to the vendor, or ''system partner.'' In 1998, ZF entered a joint venture with the German auto electronics maker Robert Bosch GmbH to develop and produce new steering systems with advanced electronic components. To help coordinate the new system-partner approach, ZF participated in the establishment of an electronic marketplace, Supplyon AG, together with other leading suppliers of vehicle components, in 2000.

However, despite its strong position as a preferred vendor for many automakers, ZF's success totally depended on ever-changing market conditions—the ups and downs to which automakers were forced to respond and adapt. The two oil crises in the 1970s, when oil prices at times increased 20-fold, set off a wave of research and development activities for automobiles that used significantly less fuel, while the German economy went through a recession. ZF came up with ''Ecosplit,'' a new transmission for heavy trucks, and an electronically controlled ''Servo'' steering. After a short-lived boom of auto sales due to the reunification of Germany in 1990, another recession caused automakers to drop their output by up to 30 percent. ZF slipped into the red. The company laid off 5,000 employees—one-fifth of its workforce. New regulations in Brazil and a sudden dry-up of demand in Argentina in 1996, the growing value of the German mark, a move to low-price steerings among automakers, and the Asian financial crisis in 1997 made things worse. In 1996, losses amounted to two-digit million figures, and for the first time in 48 years ZF did not pay any dividends to its stockholders. However, after implementing a rigorous cost-cutting program, the company recovered in the late 1990s. In October 2001, in the biggest acquisition of the company's history, ZF bought four business divisions of its second largest supplier, Mannesmann Sachs AG, from the German Siemens group in an estimated EUR 1.3 billion deal. The former Fichtel & Sachs group, founded in 1895, came under the dominance of the German Mannesmann group in 1987 and was sold to Siemens AG in 1999 after Mannesmann's plans to take it public fell through. The Sachs takeover made ZF Germany's third-largest vendor to the automotive industry, behind Robert Bosch GmbH and tire maker Continental AG. In the late 1990s, ZF turned back to its roots and started making airships again—this time for aviation research and tourism.

## *Principal Subsidiaries*

ZF Getriebe GmbH; ZF Lenksysteme GmbH; ZF Achsgetriebe GmbH (Germany); ZF Passau GmbH; Zeppelin Luftschiftechnik GmbH; ZF Bahntechnik GmbH; ZF Gotha GmbH; ZF Lehmförder Metallwaren AG (76%); ZF Maschinenantriebe GmbH; ZF Marine GmbH; ZF Luftfahrttechnik GmbH; ZF AG Holding Inc. (U.S.); ZF Industries Inc. (U.S.); ZF Hurth Marine S.p.A. (Italy); ZF Drivetech Japan Co. Ltd.; ZF Hungaria Kft. (Hungary); ZF Padova S.p.A. (Italy); ZF Argentina S.A.; ZF do Brasil S.A.; ZF Mathers LLC (U.S.); ZF Batavia LLC (U.S.; 51%); Bharat Gears Ltd. (India; 26%); ZF Korea Co. Ltd.; ZF of South Africa (Pty.) Ltd.; ZF Türk Sanayi ve Ticaret A.S. (Turkey); Beijing ZF North Drive Systems Technical Co. Ltd. (China; 70%); ZF Iran S.S.K. (49%); ZF Thailand Co. Ltd. (49%); Supplyon AG (18%).

## *Principal Competitors*

CARRARO S.p.A.; Eaton Corporation; GKN plc; Delphi Corporation; TRW Inc.

## *Further Reading*

"Berichte von der internationalen Automobilausstellung in Frankfurt; ZF Friedrichshafen will sich mit den Amerikanern bald einigen," *Frankfurter Allgemeine Zeitung*, September 10, 1993, p. 18.

"Bosch und ZF gemeinsam bei Lenkungen," *Frankfurter Allgemeine Zeitung*, April 24, 1998, p. 24.

"Brasilien verursacht überraschend Ertragseinbruch im ZF-Konzern," *Frankfurter Allgemeine Zeitung*, April 26, 1996, p. 22.

Brezonick, Mike, "ZF Unveils Newest WG Transmissions," *Diesel Progress*, August 1, 1997, p. 40.

"Damit der Schraubenhersteller Bescheid weiss," *Frankfurter Allgemeine Zeitung*, January 4, 2001, p. 20.

David, Fred, "Zeppelin's Erben," *Die Woche*, April 16, 1999, p. 20.

"Erstmals seit 48 Jahren keine Dividende," *Frankfurter Allgemeine Zeitung*, December 12, 1996, p. 22.

Feth, Gerd Gregor, "Vorbehalte gegen die Automatik," *Frankfurter Allgemeine Zeitung*, September 10, 1996, p. 6.

"Hohe Verluste beim Automobilzulieferer ZF Friedrichshafen," *Frankfurter Allgemeine Zeitung*, April 25, 1997, p. 27.

"Kartellamt streitet gegen ZF Friedrichshafen," *Frankfurter Allgemeine Zeitung*, November 18, 1993, p. 21.

"Renk und ZF arbeiten bei Wehrtechnik gemeinsam," *Frankfurter Allgemeine Zeitung*, June 4, 1998, p. 23.

Wildhage, Hans-Jürgen, "Vom Zulieferer zum 'Systempartner': Das Beispiel ZF," *Frankfurter Allgemeine Zeitung*, November 4, 1997, p. 6.

Wright, Chris, "After Sachs Deal, ZF Looks for New Acquisitions," *Automotive News Europe*, January 28, 2002, p. 12.

"ZF Backs Merger Trend," *Automotive News Europe*, April 24, 2000, 33.

"ZF baut in Russland ein Getriebewerk," *Süddeutsche Zeitung*, October 15, 1994.

"ZF Friedrichshafen ist in Südamerika über den Berg," *Süddeutsche Zeitung*, February 25, 1998.

"ZF hat den Einbruch in Asien ausgeglichen," *Frankfurter Allgemeine Zeitung*, November 4, 2000, p. 22.

"ZF Friedrichshafen rechnet mit deutlich niedrigerem Gewinn," *Frankfurter Allgemeine Zeitung*, December 20, 2001, p. 20.

"ZF Looks to a Modular Future," *Automotive News Europe*, May 6, 2002, p. 6.

"ZF startet Großserienfertigung in China," *Süddeutsche Zeitung*, September 3, 1996.

"ZF verzahnt sich mit MB do Brasil," *Süddeutsche Zeitung*, May 5, 1995.

"ZF will Teile von Sachs mit dem eigenen Geschäft zusammenführen," *Frankfurter Allgemeine Zeitung*, August 7, 2001, p. 17.

—Evelyn Hauser

# *INDEX TO COMPANIES*

# Index to Companies

Listings in this index are arranged in alphabetical order under the company name. Company names beginning with a letter or proper name such as Eli Lilly & Co. will be found under the first letter of the company name. Definite articles (The, Le, La) are ignored for alphabetical purposes as are forms of incorporation that precede the company name (AB, NV). Company names printed in bold type have full, historical essays on the page numbers appearing in bold. Updates to entries that appeared in earlier volumes are signified by the notation **(upd.)**. Company names in light type are references within an essay to that company, not full historical essays. This index is cumulative with volume numbers printed in bold type.


A & A Die Casting Company, **25** 312
A and A Limousine Renting, Inc., **26** 62
A & C Black Ltd., **7** 165
A&E Plastics, **12** 377
**A&E Television Networks, IV** 627; **19** 204; **32 3–7**; **46** 232
A. & J. McKenna, **13** 295
A&K Petroleum Company. *See* Kerr-McGee Corporation.
A & M Instrument Co., **9** 323
A&M Records, **23** 389
A&N Foods Co., **II** 553
A&P. *See* Great Atlantic & Pacific Tea Company, Inc.
A&P Water and Sewer Supplies, Inc., **6** 487
A. and T. McKenna Brass and Copper Works, **13** 295
**A & W Brands, Inc., II** 595; **25 3–5**
A-1 Supply. *See* International Game Technology.
A-R Technologies, **48** 275
A.A. Housman & Co., **II** 424; **13** 340
A.A. Mathews. *See* CRSS Inc.
A. Ahlström Oy, **IV** 276–77
A.B. Chance Industries Co., Inc., **II** 20; **31** 259
**A.B.Dick Company, II** 25; **28 6–8**
A.B. Hemmings, Ltd., **13** 51
A.B. Leasing Corp., **13** 111–12
A-B Nippondenso, **III** 593
**A.B. Watley Group Inc., 45 3–5**
A-BEC Mobility, **11** 487
A.C. Delco, **26** 347, 349
**A.C. Moore Arts & Crafts, Inc., 30 3–5**
**A.C. Nielsen Company, IV** 605; **13 3–5**. *See also* ACNielsen Corporation.
A.C. Wickman, **13** 296
A.D. International (Australia) Pty. Ltd., **10** 272
A. Dager & Co., **I** 404
A. Dunkelsbuhler & Co., **IV** 20–21, 65; **7** 122
A/E/C/ Systems International, **27** 362
A.E. Fitkin & Company, **6** 592–93
A.E. Gutman, **16** 486
A.E. LePage, **II** 457
A.E. Lottes, **29** 86
A.G. Becker, **II** 259–60; **11** 318; **20** 260
**A.G. Edwards, Inc., 8 3–5**; **19** 502; **32 17–21 (upd.)**
A.G. Industries, Inc., **7** 24
A.G. Morris, **12** 427
A.G. Spalding & Bros., Inc., **I** 428–29; **24** 402–03
A.G. Stanley Ltd., **V** 17, 19; **24** 75
A. Gettelman, Co., **I** 269
A. Goertz and Co., **IV** 91
**A.H. Belo Corporation, IV** 605; **10 3–5**; **28** 367, 369; **30 13–17 (upd.)**
A.H. Robins Co., **10** 70; **12** 188; **16** 438
A. Hirsh & Son, **30** 408
A.I. Credit Corp., **III** 196
A.J. Caley and Son. Ltd., **II** 569
A.J. Oster Co., **III** 681
A. Johnson & Co. *See* Axel Johnson Group.
A.L. Laboratories Inc., **12** 3
**A.L. Pharma Inc., 12 3–5**. *See also* Alpharma Inc.
A.L. Van Houtte Inc. *See* Van Houtte Inc.
A. Lambert International Inc., **16** 80
A. Leon Capel and Sons, Inc. *See* Capel Incorporated.
**A.M. Castle & Co., 25 6–8**
A.M. Collins Manufacturing Co., **IV** 286
**A.O. Smith Corporation, 7** 139; **22** 181, **11 3–6**; **24** 499; **40 3–8 (upd.)**
A-1 Steak Sauce Co., **I** 259
A-1 Supply, **10** 375
A.P. Green Refractories, **22** 285
A.R. Pechiney, **IV** 173
A. Roger Perretti, **II** 484
A.S. Abell Co., **IV** 678
A.S. Aloe, **III** 443
A.S. Cameron Steam Pump Works, **III** 525
A/S Titan, **III** 418
A.S. Watson & Company, **18** 254
**A.S. Yakovlev Design Bureau, 15 3–6**
A. Schilling & Company. *See* McCormick & Company, Incorporated.
**A. Schulman, Inc., 8 6–8**
A. Sulka & Co., **29** 457
**A.T. Cross Company, 17 3–5**
A.T. Massey Coal Company, **34** 164
A-T-O Inc. *See* Figgie International, Inc.
A.V. Roe & Co., **I** 50, 81; **III** 508; **24** 85
A.W. Bain Holdings, **III** 523
A.W. Shaw Co., **IV** 635
A.W. Sijthoff, **14** 555
A-Z International Companies, **III** 569; **20** 361
AA Development Corp., **I** 91
AA Distributors, **22** 14
AA Energy Corp., **I** 91
AAA Development Corp., **17** 238
Aardman Animations, **43** 143
Aachener und Münchener Feuer-Versicherungs-Gesellschaft, **III** 376
Aachener und Münchener Gruppe, **III** 349–50
Aachener Union, **II** 385
AAE Ahaus Alstatter Eisenbahn Holding AG, **25** 171
**AAF-McQuay Incorporated, 26 3–5**
AAI Corporation, **37** 399
Aalborg, **6** 367
Aansworth Shirt Makers, **8** 406
**AAON, Inc., 22 3–6**
**AAR Corp., III** 687; **IV** 60; **28 3–5**
Aargauische Portlandcement-Fabrik Holderbank-Wildegg, **III** 701
Aaron Brothers, Inc., **17** 320, 322
**Aaron Rents, Inc., 14 3–5**; **33** 368; **35 3–6 (upd.)**
**AARP, 27 3–5**
Aasche Transportation, **27** 404
Aastrom Biosciences, Inc., **13** 161
AAV Cos., **13** 48; **41** 22
Aavant Health Management Group, Inc., **11** 394
**Aavid Thermal Technologies, Inc., 29 3–6**

AB Capital & Investment Corporation, **23** 381
AB Ingredients Limited, **41** 32
AB-PT. *See* American Broadcasting-Paramount Theatres, Inc.
ABA. *See* Aktiebolaget Aerotransport.
Abacus Direct Corporation, **46** 156
Abacus Fund, Inc., **II** 445; **22** 405
ABACUS International Holdings Ltd., **26** 429
Abana Pharmaceuticals, **24** 257
Abar Staffing, **25** 434
**ABB Asea Brown Boveri Ltd., II 1–4,** 13; **III** 427, 466, 631–32; **IV** 66, 109, 204, 300; **15** 483; **22 7–12 (upd.)**, 64, 288; **28** 39; **34** 132
ABB Hafo AB. *See* Mitel Corp.
ABB RDM Service, **41** 326
Abba Seafood AB, **18** 396
Abbatoir St.-Valerien Inc., **II** 652
Abbey Business Consultants, **14** 36
Abbey Home Entertainment, **23** 391
Abbey Life Group PLC, **II** 309
Abbey Medical, Inc., **11** 486; **13** 366–67
**Abbey National plc, 10 6–8**; **39 3–6 (upd.)**
Abbey Rents, **II** 572
Abbey Road Building Society, **10** 6–7
**Abbott Laboratories, I 619–21**, 686, 690, 705; **II** 539; **10** 70, 78, 126; **11 7–9 (upd.)**, 91, 494; **12** 4; **14** 98, 389; **22** 75; **25** 55; **36** 38–39; **40 9–13 (upd.)**; **46** 394–95
Abbott, Proctor & Paine, **II** 445; **22** 405
**ABC Appliance, Inc., 10 9–11**
**ABC Carpet & Home Co. Inc., 26 6–8**
ABC, Inc., **I** 463–64; **II** 89, 129–33, 151, 156, 170, 173; **III** 188, 214, 251–52; **6** 157–59, 164; **11** 197–98; **17** 150; XVIII 65; **19** 201; **21** 25; **24** 516–17; **32** 3. *See also* Capital Cities/ABC Inc.
ABC Markets, **17** 558
**ABC Rail Products Corporation, 18 3–5**
ABC Records, **II** 144
**ABC Supply Co., Inc., 22 13–16**
ABC Treadco, **19** 455
ABD Securities Corp., **II** 239, 283
ABECOR. *See* Associated Banks of Europe Corp.
Abell-Howe Construction Inc., **42** 434
Abercom Holdings, **IV** 92
**Abercrombie & Fitch Co., V** 116; **15 7–9**; **17** 369; **25** 90; **35 7–10 (upd.)**
Aberthaw Cement, **III** 671
Abex Aerospace, **III** 512
Abex Corp., **I** 456; **10** 553; **18** 3
Abex Friction Products, **III** 512
ABF. *See* Associated British Foods PLC.
ABF Freight System, Inc., **16** 39–41
ABI. *See* American Furniture Company, Inc.
**Abigail Adams National Bancorp, Inc., 23 3–5**
Abington Shoe Company. *See* The Timberland Company.
**Abiomed, Inc., 47 3–6**
Abitec Corporation, **41** 32–33
**Abitibi-Consolidated, Inc., 25 9–13 (upd.)**; **26** 445
**Abitibi-Price Inc., IV 245–47**, 721; **9** 391
Abko Realty Inc., **IV** 449
**ABM Industries Incorporated, 25 14–16 (upd.)**
ABN. *See* Algemene Bank Nederland N.V.
ABN AMRO Rothschild, **39** 295
Above The Belt, Inc., **16** 37
ABR Foods, **II** 466
Abraham & Straus, **V** 168; **8** 443; **9** 209; **31** 192
Abraham Schaaffhausenscher Bankverein, **IV** 104
**Abrams Industries Inc., 23 6–8**
Abri Bank Bern, **II** 378
Absolut Company, **31** 458, 460
**Abu Dhabi National Oil Company, IV 363–64**, 476; **45 6–9 (upd.)**
Abu Qir Fertilizer and Chemical Industries Co., **IV** 413
AC Design Inc., **22** 196
AC Humko Corporation, **41** 32–33
AC Roma SpA, **44** 388
ACA Corporation, **25** 368
Academic Press, **IV** 622–23
**Academy Sports & Outdoors, 27 6–8**
Acadia Entities, **24** 456
Acadia Investors, **23** 99
Acadia Partners, **21** 92
**Acadian Ambulance & Air Med Services, Inc., 39 7–10**
Access Dynamics Inc., **17** 255
Access Graphics Technology Inc., **13** 128
Access Technology, **6** 225
Accessory Network Group, Inc., **8** 219
Accident and Casualty Insurance Co., **III** 230–31
**Acclaim Entertainment Inc., 13** 115; **24 3–8**, 538
**ACCO World Corporation, 7 3–5**; **12** 264
Accolade Inc., **35** 227
**Accor SA, 10 12–14**; **13** 364; **27 9–12 (upd.)**; **48** 199
Accord Energy, **18** 367
Accountants on Call, **6** 10
Accounting and Tabulating Corporation of Great Britain, **6** 240
Acctex Information Systems, **17** 468
Accuralite Company, **10** 492
Accurate Forming Co., **III** 643
AccuRead Limited, **42** 165, 167
Accuride Corp., **IV** 179
Accuscan, Inc., **14** 380
**ACE Cash Express, Inc., 33 3–6**
Ace Comb Company, **12** 216
Ace Electric Co., **I** 156
**Ace Hardware Corporation, 12 6–8**; **35 11–14 (upd.)**
ACE Limited, **45** 109
Ace Medical Company, **30** 164
Ace Novelty Company, **26** 374
Ace Refrigeration Ltd., **I** 315; **25** 81
**Acer Inc., 6** 244; **10** 257; **16 3–6**; **47** 385
Acer Sertek, **24** 31
Aceralia, **42** 414
Aceros Fortuna S.A. de C.V., **13** 141
**Aceto Corp., 38 3–5**
ACF Industries, **30** 282
Acheson Graphite Corp, **I** 399; **9** 517
ACI Holdings Inc., **I** 91; **28** 24
ACI Ltd., **29** 478
Aciéries de Ploërmel, **16** 514
Aciéries et Minières de la Sambre, **IV** 52
Aciéries Réunies de Burbach-Eich-Dudelange S.A. *See* ARBED S.A.
Acker Drill Company, **26** 70
**Ackerley Communications, Inc., 9 3–5**
Acklin Stamping Company, **8** 515
ACLC. *See* Allegheny County Light Company.
ACLI Government Securities Inc., **II** 422
ACM. *See* Advanced Custom Molders, Inc.
Acme Boot, **I** 440–41
Acme Brick Company, **19** 231–32
Acme Can Co., **I** 601; **13** 188
Acme Carton Co., **IV** 333
**Acme-Cleveland Corp., I** 531; **13 6–8**
Acme Corrugated Cases, **IV** 258
Acme Cotton Products, **13** 366
Acme-Delta Company, **11** 411
Acme Fast Freight Inc., **27** 473
Acme Market. *See* American Stores Company.
Acme Newspictures, **25** 507
Acme Quality Paint Co., **III** 744
Acme Quilting Co., Inc., **19** 304
Acme Road Machinery, **21** 502
Acme Screw Products, **14** 181
ACMI, **21** 118–19
**ACNielsen Corporation, 38 6–9 (upd.)**
Acordis, **41** 10
Acorn Computer, **III** 145
Acorn Financial Corp., **15** 328
Acoustics Development Corporation, **6** 313
Acova S.A., **26** 4
Acquired Systems Enhancement Corporation, **24** 31
ACR. *See* American Capital and Research Corp.
AcroMed Corporation, **30** 164
**Acsys, Inc., 44 3–5**
ACT Group, **45** 280
Act III Theatres, **25** 453
Actava Group, **14** 332
Action, **6** 393
Action Furniture by Lane, **17** 183
Action Gaming Inc., **44** 337
Action Labs Inc., **37** 285
**Action Performance Companies, Inc., 27 13–15**; **32** 344; **37** 319
Action Temporary Services, **29** 273
Active Apparel Group. *See* Everlast Worldwide Inc.
Activenture Corporation, **16** 253; **43** 209
**Activision, Inc., 24** 3; **32 8–11**
Acton Bolt Ltd., **IV** 658
Acumos, **11** 57
**Acuson Corporation, 10 15–17**; **36 3–6 (upd.)**
ACX Technologies, **13** 11; **36** 15
**Acxiom Corporation, 35 15–18**
Ad Astra Aero, **I** 121
AD-AM Gas Company, **11** 28
Adage Systems International, Inc., **19** 438
Adam, Meldrum & Anderson Company (AM&A), **16** 61–62
**Adam Opel AG, 7 6–8**; **11** 549; **18** 125; **21 3–7 (upd.)**
Adams Childrenswear, **V** 177
Adams Express Co., **II** 380–81, 395–96; **10** 59–60; **12** 533
**Adams Golf, Inc., 37 3–5**; **45** 76
Adams Industries, **19** 414
Adams/Cates Company, **21** 257
Adanac General Insurance Company, **13** 63
**Adaptec, Inc., 11** 56; **31 3–6**
Adaptive Data Systems, **25** 531
Adar Associates, Inc. *See* Scientific-Atlanta, Inc.
ADC of Greater Kansas City, Inc., **22** 443
**ADC Telecommunications, Inc., 10 18–21**; **30 6–9 (upd.)**; **44** 69

Adco Products, **I** 374
Addison Communications Plc, **45** 272
Addison Corporation, **31** 399
Addison Structural Services, Inc., **26** 433
Addison Wesley, **IV** 659
Addressograph-Multigraph, **11** 494
**Adecco S.A.**, **26** 240; **35** 441–42; **36 7–11 (upd.)**
Adelphi Pharmaceutical Manufacturing Co., **I** 496
**Adelphia Communications Corp.**, **17 6–8**
Ademco. *See* Alarm Device Manufacturing Company.
Adero Inc., **45** 202
ADESA Corporation, **34** 286
Adesso-Madden, Inc., **37** 372
Adger Assuranceselskab, **III** 310
Adhere Paper Co., **IV** 252; **17** 29
ADI Group Limited. *See* AHL Services, Inc.
**Adia S.A.**, **6 9–11**; **9** 327. *See also* Adecco S.A.
Adiainvest S.A., **6** 9, 11
**adidas AG**, **8** 392–93; **13** 513; **14 6–9**; **17** 244; **22** 202; **23** 472, 474; **25** 205, 207; **36** 344, 346
**adidas-Salomon AG**, **33 7–11 (upd.)**
Adirondack Industries, **24** 403
Adjusters Auto Rental Inc. **16** 380
Adler, **23** 219
Adler and Shaykin, **III** 56; **11** 556–57
Adler Line. *See* Transatlantische Dampfschiffahrts Gesellschaft.
Adley Express, **14** 567
ADM. *See* Archer-Daniels-Midland Co.
Administracion Corporativa y Mercantil, S.A. de C.V., **37** 178
Admiral Co., **II** 86; **III** 573
Admiral Cruise Lines, **6** 368; **27** 91
Adnan Dabbagh, **6** 115
ADNOC. *See* Abu Dhabi National Oil Company.
**Adobe Systems Incorporated**, **10 22–24**; **15** 149; **20** 46, 237; **33 12–16 (upd.)**; **43** 151
**Adolph Coors Company**, **I 236–38**, 255, 273; **13 9–11 (upd.)**; **18** 72; **26** 303, 306; **34** 37; **36 12–16 (upd.)**; **44** 198
Adolphe Lafont, **17** 210
Adonis Radio Corp., **9** 320
Adorence, **16** 482
ADP. *See* Automatic Data Processing, Inc.
Adria Produtos Alimenticos, Ltd., **12** 411
Adria Steamship Company, **6** 425
Adrian Hope and Company, **14** 46
Adriatico Banco d'Assicurazione, **III** 206, 345–46
Adrienne Vittadini, **15** 291
ADS. *See* Aerospace Display Systems.
Adsega, **II** 677
Adstaff Associates, Ltd., **26** 240
ADT Ltd., **26** 410; **28** 486
**ADT Security Services, Inc.**, **44 6–9 (upd.)**
**ADT Security Systems, Inc.**, **12 9–11**
Adtel, Inc., **10** 358
**Adtran Inc.**, **22 17–20**
Adtranz **34** 128, 132–33, 136; **42** 45. *See also* ABB ASEA Brown Boveri Ltd.
Advacel, **18** 20; **43** 17
Advance Chemical Company, **25** 15
Advance Foundry, **14** 42
Advance Publications Inc., **IV 581–84**; **13** 178, 180, 429; **19 3–7 (upd.)**; **31** 376, 378
Advance-Rumely Thresher Co., **13** 16
Advance Transformer Co., **13** 397
Advance/Newhouse Communications, **42** 114
Advanced Casino Systems Corporation, **21** 277
Advanced Communications Engineering. *See* Scientific-Atlanta, Inc.
Advanced Communications Inc. *See* Metrocall, Inc.
Advanced Custom Molders, Inc., **17** 533
Advanced Data Management Group S.A., **23** 212
Advanced Entertainment Group, **10** 286
Advanced Fiberoptic Technologies, **30** 267
Advanced Gravis, **28** 244
Advanced Logic Research, Inc., **27** 169
Advanced Marine Enterprises, Inc., **18** 370
**Advanced Marketing Services, Inc.**, **24** 354; **34 3–6**
Advanced Medical Technologies, **III** 512
Advanced Metal Technologies Inc., **17** 234
Advanced Metallurgy, Inc., **29** 460
**Advanced Micro Devices, Inc.**, **6 215–17**; **9** 115; **10** 367; **11** 308; **16** 316; **18** 18–19, 382; **19** 312; **20** 175; **30 10–12 (upd.)**; **32** 498; **43** 15–16; **47** 384
Advanced MobilComm, **10** 432
Advanced Plasma Systems, Inc., **48** 299
Advanced Structures, Inc., **18** 163
Advanced System Applications, **11** 395
**Advanced Technology Laboratories, Inc.**, **9 6–8**
Advanced Telecommunications Corporation, **8** 311
Advanced Tissue Sciences Inc., **41** 377
Advanced Web Technologies, **22** 357
AdvanceMed LLC, **45** 146
Advanstar Communications, **27** 361
**Advanta Corporation**, **8 9–11**; **11** 123; **38 10–14 (upd.)**
Advanta Partners, LP, **42** 322
Advantage Company, **8** 311; **27** 306
The Advantage Group, Inc., **25** 185–86
Advantage Health Plans, Inc., **11** 379
Advantage Health Systems, Inc., **25** 383
Advantage Insurers, Inc., **25** 185, 187
Advantage Publishers Group, **34** 5
Advantest Corporation, **39** 350, 353
**Advantica Restaurant Group, Inc.**, **27 16–19 (upd.)**; **29** 150
Advent Corporation, **22** 97
Advertising Unlimited, Inc., **10** 461
**Advo, Inc.**, **6 12–14**
**Advocat Inc.**, **46 3–5**
AEA. *See* United Kingdom Atomic Energy Authority.
AEA Investors Inc., **II** 628; **13** 97; **22** 169, 171; **28** 380; **30** 328
**AEG A.G.**, **I** 151, 193, **409–11**; **II** 12, 119, 279; **III** 466, 479; **IV** 167; **6** 489; **IX** 11; **14** 169; **15** 142; **22** 28; **23** 495; **34** 131–32
**Aegis Group plc**, **6 15–16**
Aegis Insurance Co., **III** 273
**AEGON N.V.**, **III 177–79**, 201, 273; **33** 418–20. *See also* Transamerica–An AEGON Company
**AEI Music Network Inc.**, **35 19–21**
AEL Ventures Ltd., **9** 512
Aeneas Venture Corp., **26** 502
AEON Group, **V** 96–99; **11** 498–99; **31** 430–31; **37** 227
AEP. *See* American Electric Power Company.
**AEP Industries, Inc.**, **36 17–19**
AEP-Span, **8** 546
**Aer Lingus Group plc**, **6** 59; **12** 367–68; **34 7–10**; **35** 382–84; **36** 230–31
Aera Energy LLC, **41** 359
Aérazur, **36** 529
Aerial Communications Inc., **31** 452
Aeritalia, **I** 51, 74–75, 467; **24** 86
Aero-Coupling Corp., **III** 641
Aero Engines, **9** 418
Aero International (Regional) SAS, **24** 88
Aero International Inc., **14** 43
Aero Mayflower Transit Company. *See* Mayflower Group Inc.
Aero O/Y, **6** 87–88
Aero-Portuguesa, **6** 125
**Aeroflot—Russian International Airlines**, **29 7–10 (upd.)**
**Aeroflot Soviet Airlines**, **I** 105, 110, 118; **6 57–59**; **14** 73; **27** 475
Aerojet, **8** 206, 208
Aerojet-General Corp., **9** 266
**Aerolíneas Argentinas S.A.**, **I** 107; **6** 97; **33 17–19**; **36** 281
Aeroméxico, **20** 168
Aeronautics Leasing, Inc., **39** 33
**Aeronca Inc.**, **46 6–8**; **48** 274
**Aéroports de Paris**, **33 20–22**
**Aeroquip Corporation**, **III** 640–42; **V** 255; **16 7–9**; **19** 508
Aerospace Avionics, **III** 509
Aerospace Display Systems, **36** 158
Aerospace International Services, **41** 38
**The Aérospatiale Group**, **I** 41–42, 46, 50, 74, 94; **7 9–12**; **12** 190–91; **14** 72; **21 8–11 (upd.)**; **24** 84–86, 88–89; **26** 179
Aerostar, **33** 359–61
**The AES Corporation**, **10 25–27**; **13 12–15 (upd.)**; **24** 359
**Aetna, Inc.**, **20** 59; **21 12–16 (upd.)**, 95; **22** 139, 142–43; **30** 364
**Aetna Life and Casualty Company**, **II** 170–71, 319; **III** 78, **180–82**, 209, 223, 226, 236, 254, 296, 298, 305, 313, 329, 389; **IV** 123, 703; **10** 75–76; **12** 367; **15** 26; **17** 324; **23** 135; **40** 199
Aetna National Bank, **13** 466
Aetna Oil Co., **IV** 373
AF Insurance Agency, **44** 33
**AFC Enterprises, Inc.**, **32 12–16 (upd.)**; **36** 517, 520
AFCO Industries, Inc., **III** 241; **IV** 341
Afcol, **I** 289; **24** 449–50
AFE Ltd., **IV** 241
Affiliated Enterprises Inc., **I** 114
Affiliated Hospital Products Inc., **37** 400
Affiliated Music Publishing, **22** 193
Affiliated Paper Companies, Inc., **31** 359, 361
Affiliated Physicians Network, Inc., **45** 194
Affiliated Products Inc., **I** 622
**Affiliated Publications, Inc.**, **6** 323; **7 13–16**; **19** 285
Affordable Inns, **13** 364
AFG Industries Inc., **I** 483; **9** 248; **48** 42
AFIA, **22** 143; **45** 104, 108
Afianzadora Insurgentes Serfin, **19** 190
AFL. *See* American Football League.
**AFLAC Incorporated**, **10 28–30 (upd.)**; **38 15–19 (upd.)**

AFP. *See* Australian Forest Products.
AFRA Enterprises Inc., **26** 102
African and European Investment, **IV** 96
African Coasters, **IV** 91
African Explosive and Chemical Industries, **IV** 22
AFT. *See* Advanced Fiberoptic Technologies.
AFW Fabric Corp., **16** 124
AG&E. *See* American Electric Power Company.
**Ag-Chem Equipment Company, Inc., 17 9–11**
AG Communication Systems Corporation, **15** 194; **43** 446
AGA, **I** 358
Agan Chemical Manufacturers Ltd., **25** 266–67
Agar Manufacturing Company, **8** 2
Agatha Christie Ltd., **31** 63 67
**AGCO Corp., 13 16–18**
Agefi, **34** 13
AGEL&P. *See* Albuquerque Gas, Electric Light and Power Company.
**Agence France-Presse, IV** 670; **34 11–14**
Agency, **6** 393
Agency Rent-A-Car, **16** 379
AGF, **III** 185; **27** 515
AGFA, **I** 310–11
Agfa-Ansco Corporation, **I** 337–38; **22** 225–27
Agfa-Gevaert, **III** 487; **18** 50, 184–86; **26** 540–41
**Aggregate Industries plc, 36 20–22**
**Aggreko Plc, 45 10–13**
Agiba Petroleum, **IV** 414
**Agilent Technologies Inc., 38 20–23**
Agip SpA, **IV** 419–21, 454, 466, 472–74, 498; **12** 153
Agiv AG, **39** 40–41
AGLP, **IV** 618
AGO, **III** 177, 179, 273, 310
Agor Manufacturing Co., **IV** 286
Agouron Pharmaceuticals, Inc., **38** 365
AGRAN, **IV** 505
AGRANA, **27** 436, 439
AgriBank FCB, **8** 489
Agribrands International, Inc., **40** 89
Agrico Chemical Company, **IV** 82, 84, 576; **7** 188; **31** 470
Agricole de Roquefort et Maria Grimal, **23** 219
Agricultural Insurance Co., **III** 191
Agricultural Minerals and Chemicals Inc., **IV** 84; **13** 504
Agrifan, **II** 355
Agrifull, **22** 380
Agrigenetics, Inc., **I** 361. *See also* Mycogen Corporation.
Agrippina Versicherungs AG, **III** 403, 412
Agrobios S.A., **23** 172
Agroferm Hungarian Japanese Fermentation Industry, **III** 43
Agromán S.A., **40** 218
AGTL. *See* Alberta Gas Trunk Line Company, Ltd.
Agua de la Falda S.A., **38** 231
Agua Pura Water Company, **24** 467
Aguila (Mexican Eagle) Oil Co. Ltd., **IV** 657
Agusta S.p.A., **46** 66
**Agway, Inc., 7 17–18; 21 17–19 (upd.); 36** 440
**AHL Services, Inc., 26** 149; **27 20–23; 45** 379
Ahmanson. *See* H.F. Ahmanson & Company.
AHMSA. *See* Altos Hornos de México, S.A. de C.V.
Ahold. *See* Koninklijke Ahold NV.
AHP. *See* American Home Products Corporation.
AHS. *See* American Hospital Supply Corporation.
AHSC Holdings Corp., **III** 9–10
Ahtna AGA Security, Inc., **14** 541
AI Automotive, **24** 204
AIC. *See* Allied Import Company.
AICA, **16** 421; **43** 308
Aichi Bank, **II** 373
Aichi Kogyo Co., **III** 415
Aichi Steel Works, **III** 637
AICPA. *See* The American Institute of Certified Public Accountants.
Aid Auto, **18** 144
Aida Corporation, **11** 504
AIG. *See* American International Group, Inc.
AIGlobal, **III** 197
Aiken Stores, Inc., **14** 92
Aikenhead's Home Improvement Warehouse, **18** 240; **26** 306
Aikoku Sekiyu, **IV** 554
AIL Technologies, **46** 160
AIM Create Co., Ltd., **V** 127
Ainsworth National, **14** 528
AIP. *See* Amorim Investimentos e Participaço.
**Air & Water Technologies Corporation, 6 441–42.** *See also* Aqua Alliance Inc.
Air BP, **7** 141
Air Brasil, **6** 134; **29** 496
**Air Canada, 6 60–62; 23 9–12 (upd.); 29** 302; **36** 230
**Air China, 46 9–11**
Air Compak, **12** 182
Air de Cologne, **27** 474
**Air Express International Corporation, 13 19–20; 40** 138; **46** 71
Air France, **I** 93–94, 104, 110, 120; **II** 163; **6** 69, 373; **8** 313; **12** 190; **24** 86; **27** 26; **33** 21, 50, 377. *See also* Groupe Air France *and* Societe Air France.
**Air-India Limited, 6 63–64; 27 24–26 (upd.); 41** 336–37
Air Inter. *See* Groupe Air France.
Air La Carte Inc., **13** 48
Air Lanka Catering Services Ltd., **6** 123–24; **27** 464
Air Liberté, **6** 208
Air Liquide. *See* L'Air Liquide SA.
Air London International, **36** 190
Air Micronesia, **I** 97; **21** 142
Air Midwest, Inc., **11** 299
**Air New Zealand Limited, 14 10–12; 24** 399–400; **27** 475; **38 24–27 (upd.)**
Air Nippon Co., Ltd., **6** 70
Air Pacific, **24** 396, 400
**Air Products and Chemicals, Inc., I 297–99**, 315, 358, 674; **10 31–33 (upd.); 11** 403; **14** 125
Air Russia, **24** 400
Air Sea Broker AG, **47** 286–87
Air Southwest Co. *See* Southwest Airlines Co.
Air Spec, Inc., **III** 643
Airborne Accessories, **II** 81
**Airborne Freight Corporation, 6 345–47** 345; **13** 19; **14** 517; **18** 177; **34 15–18 (upd.); 46** 72
Airbus Industrie, **6** 74; **7** 9–11, 504; **9** 418; **10** 164; **13** 356; **21** 8; **24** 84–89; **34** 128, 135; **48** 219. *See also* G.I.E. Airbus Industrie.
AirCal, **I** 91
Airco, **25** 81–82; **26** 94
Aircraft Marine Products, **II** 7; **14** 26
Aircraft Modular Products, **30** 73
Aircraft Services International, **I** 449
Aircraft Transport & Travel Ltd., **I** 92
Aircraft Turbine Center, Inc., **28** 3
Airex Corporation, **16** 337
Airguard Industries, Inc., **17** 104, 106
Airlease International, **II** 422
Airline Interiors Inc., **41** 368–69
Airlines of Britain Holdings, **34** 398; **38** 105–06
Airlink, **24** 396
Airmark Plastics Corp., **18** 497–98
Airmec-AEI Ltd., **II** 81
Airpax Electronics, Inc., **13** 398
Airport Ground Service Co., **I** 104, 106
Airshop Ltd., **25** 246
Airstream. *See* Thor Industries, Inc.
Airtel, **IV** 640
**AirTouch Communications, 11 10–12.** *See also* Vodafone Group PLC.
**Airtours Plc, II** 164; **27 27–29,** 90, 92
**AirTran Holdings, Inc., 22 21–23; 28** 266; **33** 302; **34** 32
AirWair Ltd., **23** 399, 401–02
AirWays Corporation. *See* AirTran Holdings, Inc.
Airways Housing Trust Ltd., **I** 95
Airwick Industries, **II** 567
**Aisin Seiki Co., Ltd., III 415–16; 14** 64; **48 3–5 (upd.)**
AIT Worldwide, **47** 286–87
Aitken, Inc., **26** 433
AITS. *See* American International Travel Service.
Aiuruoca, **25** 85
**Aiwa Co., Ltd., 28** 360; **30 18–20**
Ajax, **6** 349
Ajax Iron Works, **II** 16
**Ajinomoto Co., Inc., II 463–64**, 475; **III** 705; **28 9–11 (upd.)**
Ajman Cement, **III** 760
AJS Auto Parts Inc., **15** 246
**AK Steel Holding Corporation, 19 8–9; 41 3–6 (upd.)**
Akane Securities Co. Ltd., **II** 443
Akashic Memories, **11** 234
Akemi, **17** 310; **24** 160
Aker RGI, **32** 99
AKH Co. Inc., **20** 63
**Akin, Gump, Strauss, Hauer & Feld, L.L.P., 18** 366; **33 23–25; 47** 140
AKO Bank, **II** 378
**Akorn, Inc., 32 22–24**
Akro-Mills Inc., **19** 277–78
Akron Brass Manufacturing Co., **9** 419
Akron Corp., **IV** 290
Akroyd & Smithers, **14** 419
Akseli Gallen-Kallela, **IV** 314
Aktiebolaget Aerotransport, **I** 119
**Aktiebolaget Electrolux, 22 24–28 (upd.)**
**Aktiebolaget SKF, III 622–25; IV** 203; **38 28–33 (upd.)**
Aktiengesellschaft für Berg- und Hüttenbetriebe, **IV** 201

Aktiengesellschaft für Maschinenpapier-Zellstoff-Fabrikation, **IV** 323
Aktiv Placering A.B., **II** 352
**Akzo Nobel N.V., I** 674; **II** 572; **III** 44; **13 21–23**, 545; **14** 27; **15** 436; **16** 69, 462; **21** 466; **41 7–10 (upd.)**
Al Copeland Enterprises, Inc., **7** 26–28; **32** 13–15
Alaadin Middle East-Ersan, **IV** 564
Alabama Bancorp., **17** 152
Alabama Gas Corporation, **21** 207–08
Alabama Power Company, **38** 445, 447–48
Alabama Shipyards Inc., **21** 39–40
Alabaster Co., **III** 762
Aladdin Industries, **16** 487
Aladdin Mills Inc., **19** 276
Aladdin's Castle, **III** 430, 431
Alagasco, **21** 207–08
Alagroup, **45** 337
Alais et Camargue, **IV** 173
Alamac Knit Fabrics, Inc., **16** 533–34; **21** 192
Alamito Company, **6** 590
Alamo Engine Company, **8** 514
**Alamo Group Inc., 32 25–28**
**Alamo Rent A Car, Inc., 6 348–50**; **24 9–12 (upd.)**; **25** 93; **26** 409
Alania, **24** 88
ALANTEC Corporation, **25** 162
Alarm Device Manufacturing Company, **9** 413–15
Alaron Inc., **16** 357
Alascom, **6** 325–28; **26** 358
**Alaska Air Group, Inc., 6 65–67**; **11** 50; **29 11–14 (upd.)**; **48** 219
Alaska Co., **III** 439
Alaska Commercial Company, **12** 363
Alaska Hydro-Train, **6** 382; **9** 510
Alaska Junk Co., **19** 380
Alaska Natural Gas Transportation System, **V** 673, 683
Alaska Pulp Co., **IV** 284, 297, 321
Alaska Steel Co., **19** 381
Alatas Mammoet, **26** 279
Alba Foods, **III** 619–20; **27** 197; **43** 218
**Alba-Waldensian, Inc., 30 21–23**
Albany and Susquehanna Railroad, **II** 329
Albany Assurance Co., Ltd., **III** 293
Albany Cheese, **23** 219
Albany Felt Company. *See* Albany International Corp.
**Albany International Corp., 8 12–14**
Albemarle Paper Co., **I** 334–35; **10** 289
Albers Brothers Milling Co., **II** 487
Albert E. Reed & Co. Ltd. *See* Reed International PLC.
**The Albert Fisher Group plc, 41 11–13**
Albert Heijn NV, **II** 641–42; **38** 200, 202
Albert Nipon, Inc., **8** 323
Albert Willcox & Co., **14** 278
Alberta Distillers, **I** 377
**Alberta Energy Company Ltd., 16 10–12**; **43 3–6 (upd.)**
Alberta Gas Trunk Line Company, Ltd., **V** 673–74
Alberta Sulphate Ltd., **IV** 165
**Alberto-Culver Company, II** 641–42; **8 15–17**; **36 23–27 (upd.)**
**Albertson's Inc., II 601–03**, 604–05, 637; **7 19–22 (upd.)**; **8** 474; **15** 178, 480; **16** 249; **18** 8; **22** 38; **27** 247, 290, 292; **30 24–28 (upd.)**; **33** 306; **40** 366
Albi Enterprises, **III** 24
Albion Industries, Inc., **16** 357
Albion Reid Proprietary, **III** 673
Albright & Friel, **I** 313; **10** 154
Albright & Wilson Ltd., **I** 527; **IV** 165; **12** 351; **16** 461; **38** 378, 380
Albuquerque Gas & Electric Company. *See* Public Service Company of New Mexico.
Albuquerque Gas, Electric Light and Power Company, **6** 561–62
Albury Brickworks, **III** 673
**Alcan Aluminium Limited, II** 415; **IV 9–13**, 14, 59, 154–55; **9** 512; **14** 35; **31 7–12 (upd.)**; **45** 337
Alcantara and Sores, **II** 582
**Alcatel Alsthom Compagnie Générale d'Electricité, II** 13, 69, 117; **6** 304; **7** 9; **9 9–11**, 32; **11** 59, 198; **15** 125; **17** 353; **18** 155; **19** 164, 166; **21** 233
**Alcatel S.A., 36 28–31 (upd.)**; **42** 375–76
Alchem Capital Corp., **8** 141, 143
Alchem Plastics, **19** 414
Alco Capital Group, Inc., **27** 288
**Alco Health Services Corporation, III 9–10**. *See also* AmeriSource Health Corporation.
Alco Hydro-Aeroplane, **I** 64
Alco Office Products Inc., **24** 362
**Alco Standard Corporation, I 412–13**; **III** 9; **9** 261; **16** 473–74
ALCO Trade Show Services, **26** 102
Alcoa. *See* Aluminum Company of America.
Alcon Laboratories, **II** 547; **7** 382; **10** 46, 48; **30** 30–31
Alcudia, **IV** 528
Alden Merrell Corporation, **23** 169
Aldermac Mines Ltd., **IV** 164
**Aldi Group, 11** 240; **13 24–26**; **17** 125
**Aldila Inc., 46 12–14**
Aldine Press, **10** 34
Aldiscon, **37** 232
Aldrich Chemical Co., **I** 690
**Aldus Corporation, 10 34–36**
Aldwarke Main & Car House Collieries, **I** 573
Alenia, **7** 9, 11
Alert Centre Inc., **32** 373
Alert Management Systems Inc., **12** 380
Alessio Tubi, **IV** 228
Alestra, **19** 12
Alex & Ivy, **10** 166–68
**Alex Lee Inc., 18 6–9**; **44 10–14 (upd.)**
**Alexander & Alexander Services Inc., III** 280; **10 37–39**; **13** 476; **22** 318
**Alexander & Baldwin, Inc., I** 417; **10 40–42**; **24** 32; **29** 307; **40 14–19 (upd.)**
Alexander and Lord, **13** 482
Alexander Grant & Co., **I** 481, 656
Alexander Hamilton Life Insurance Co., **II** 420; **29** 256
Alexander Howden Group, **III** 280; **10** 38–39; **22** 318
Alexander Martin Co., **I** 374
Alexander-Schroder Lumber Company, **18** 514
Alexander Smith, Inc., **19** 275
**Alexander's, Inc., 10** 282; **12** 221; **26** 111; **45 14–16**
Alexis Lichine, **III** 43
**Alfa-Laval AB, III 417–21**; **IV** 203; **8** 376
**Alfa Romeo, I** 163, 167; **11** 102, 104, 139, 205; **13 27–29**, 218–19; **36 32–35 (upd.)**, 196–97
**Alfa, S.A. de C.V., II** 262; **11** 386; **19 10–12**; **37** 176
Alfa Trading Company, **23** 358
Alfalfa's Markets, **19** 500–02
Alfinal, **III** 420
Alfred A. Knopf, Inc., **13** 428, 429; **31** 376–79
Alfred Bullows & Sons, Ltd., **21** 64
Alfred Dunhill Limited, **19** 369; **27** 487–89
Alfred Hickman Ltd., **III** 751
Alfred Marks Bureau, Ltd., **6** 9–10
Alfred Nobel & Co., **III** 693
Alfred Teves, **I** 193
Alfried Krupp von Bohlen und Halbach Foundation, **IV** 89
ALG. *See* Arkla, Inc.
Alga, **24** 83
Algemeen Burgerlijk Pensioenfonds, **26** 421
Algemeene Bankvereeniging en Volksbank van Leuven, **II** 304
Algemeene Friesche, **III** 177–79
N.V. Algemeene Maatschappij tot Exploitatie van Verzekeringsmaatschappijen, **III** 199
Algemeene Maatschappij van Levensverzekering en Lijfrente, **III** 178
Algemeene Maatschappij voor Nijverheidskrediet, **II** 304–05
Algemeene Nederlandsche Maatschappij ter begunstiging van de Volksvlijt, **II** 294
**Algemene Bank Nederland N.V., II 183–84**, 185, 239, 527; **III** 200
**Algo Group Inc., 24 13–15**
Algoma Steel Corp., **IV** 74; **8** 544–45; **24** 143
Algonquin Energy, Inc., **6** 487
Algonquin Gas Transmission Company, **6** 486; **14** 124–26
ALI. *See* Aeronautics Leasing, Inc.
Alidata, **6** 69
Aligro Inc., **II** 664
Alimenta (USA), Inc., **17** 207
Alimentana S.A., **II** 547
Alimondo, **17** 505
**Alitalia–Linee Aeree Italiana, S.p.A., I** 110, 466–67; **6** 96, **68–69**; **24** 311; **29 15–17 (upd.)**
Alken, **II** 474
Oy Alkoholiliike Ab, **IV** 469
Alkor-Oerlikon Plastic GmbH, **7** 141
All American Airways. *See* USAir Group, Inc.
**All American Communications Inc., 20 3–7**; **25** 138
All American Gourmet Co., **12** 178, 199
All American Sports Co., **22** 458–59
All British Escarpment Company LTD, **25** 430
All-Clad Metalcrafters Inc., **34** 493, 496–97
**All Nippon Airways Co., Ltd., I** 106, 493; **6 70–71** 118, 427; **16** 168; **24** 326; **33** 50–51; **38 34–37 (upd.)**
All Seasons Vehicles, Inc. *See* ASV, Inc.
All Woods, Inc., **18** 514
Allami Biztosito, **III** 209; **15** 30
Allcom, **16** 392
**Allders plc, 37 6–8**
Alleanza & Unione Mediterranea, **III** 208
Alleanza-Securitas-Esperia, **III** 208
**Alleghany Corporation, II** 398; **IV** 180–81; **10 43–45**; **19** 319; **22** 494

Allegheny Airlines. *See* USAir Group, Inc. *and* US Airways Group, Inc.
Allegheny Beverage Corp., **7** 472–73
Allegheny County Light Company, **6** 483–84
**Allegheny Energy, Inc., 38 38–41 (upd.)**
Allegheny International, Inc., **III** 732; **8** 545; **9** 484; **22** 3, 436
**Allegheny Ludlum Corporation, I** 307; **II** 402; **8 18–20**; **9** 484; **21** 489
**Allegheny Power System, Inc., V 543–45**
Allegheny Steel and Iron Company, **9** 484
Allegiance Life Insurance Company, **22** 268
Allegis, Inc. *See* United Airlines.
Allegmeine Transpotmittel Aktiengesellschaft, **6** 394; **25** 169
Allegretti & Co., **22** 26
Allen & Co., **I** 512, 701; **II** 136; **12** 496; **13** 366; **25** 270
Allen & Ginter, **12** 108
Allen & Hanbury's, **I** 640
Allen-Bradley Co., **I** 80; **II** 110; **III** 593; **11** 429–30; **17** 478; **22** 373; **23** 211
Allen-Liversidge Ltd., **I** 315; **25** 80
**Allen Organ Company, 33 26–29**
Allen Tank Ltd., **21** 499
Allen's Convenience Stores, Inc., **17** 170
**Allergan, Inc., 10 46–49**; **23** 196; **30 29–33 (upd.)**
Allforms Packaging Corp., **13** 442
Allgemeine Deutsche Creditanstalt, **II** 211, 238, 383; **12** 536
Allgemeine Eisenbahn-Versicherungs-Gesellschaft, **III** 399
Allgemeine Elektricitäts-Gesellschaft. *See* AEG A.G.
Allgemeine Handelsgesellschaft der Verbraucher AG. *See* AVA AG.
Allgemeine Rentenstalt Lebens- und Rentenversicherung, **II** 258
Allgemeine Schweizerische Uhrenindustrie, **26** 480
Allgemeine Versicherungs-Gesellschaft Helvetia, **III** 375
Alliance Agro-Alimentaires S.A., **II** 577
Alliance Amusement Company, **10** 319
Alliance Assurance Co., **III** 369–73
**Alliance Atlantis Communications Inc.**, **35** 69; **39 11–14**
Alliance Brothers, **V** 356
Alliance Capital Management Corp., **22** 189
**Alliance Entertainment Corp.**, **17 12–14**; **35** 430
Alliance Gaming Corp., **15** 539; **24** 36
Alliance Insurance Co., **III** 224
Alliance Manufacturing Co., **13** 397
Alliance Marine, **III** 373
Alliance Mortgage Co., **I** 610
Alliance Packaging, **13** 443
Alliance Paper Group, **IV** 316
Alliance Tire and Rubber Co., **II** 47; **25** 267
AllianceWare, Inc., **16** 321
Alliant Energy Corp., **39** 261
**Alliant Techsystems Inc., 8 21–23**; **30 34–37 (upd.)**
**Allianz AG Holding, I** 411, 426; **II** 239, 257, 279–80; **III 183–86**, 200, 250, 252, 299–301, 347–48, 373, 377, 393; **IV** 222; **14** 169–70; **15 10–14 (upd.)**
Allibert, **III** 614
Allied Bakeries Ltd., **II** 465–66; **13** 52–53
Allied Breweries Ltd., **I** 215; **III** 105; **IV** 712
Allied Chemical, **I** 310, 332, 351–52; **8** 526; **9** 521–22; **13** 76; **22** 5. *See also* General Chemical Corp.
Allied Chemical & Dye Corp., **I** 414; **7** 262; **9** 154; **22** 29
Allied Color Industries, **8** 347
Allied Communications Group, **18** 77; **22** 297
Allied Construction Products, **17** 384
Allied Container Corp., **IV** 345
Allied Corporation, **I** 68, 141, 143, 414, 534; **III** 118, 511; **6** 599; **7** 356; **9** 134; **11** 435; **24** 164; **25** 224; **31** 135. *See also* AlliedSignal Inc.
Allied Crude Vegetable Oil Refining Co., **II** 398; **10** 62
Allied Distributing Co., **12** 106
**Allied Domecq PLC**, **24** 220; **29 18–20**, 85
Allied Dunbar, **I** 427
Allied Engineering Co., **8** 177
Allied Fibers, **19** 275
Allied Food Markets, **II** 662
Allied Gas Company, **6** 529
Allied Grape Growers, **I** 261
Allied Health and Scientific Products Company, **8** 215
**Allied Healthcare Products, Inc.**, **24 16–19**
Allied Holdings, Inc., **24** 411
Allied Import Company, **V** 96
**Allied Irish Banks, plc, 16 13–15**; **43 7–10 (upd.)**
Allied Leisure, **40** 296–98
**Allied-Lyons plc, I 215–16**, 258, 264, 438; **IV** 721; **9** 100, 391; **10** 170; **13** 258; **21** 228, 323; **29** 18, 84
Allied Maintenance Corp., **I** 514
Allied Mills, Inc., **10** 249; **13** 186; **43** 121
Allied Oil Co., **IV** 373
Allied Overseas Trading Ltd., **I** 216
Allied Plywood Corporation, **12** 397
Allied Polymer Group, **I** 429
**Allied Products Corporation**, **21 20–22**
Allied Radio, **19** 310
Allied Safety, Inc., **V** 215
Allied Shoe Corp., **22** 213
**Allied-Signal Corp.**, **I** 85, 141, 143, **414–16**; **III** 511–12; **V** 605; **6** 599–600; **9** 519; **11** 435, 444; **13** 227; **16** 436; **17** 20; **21** 200, 396–97; **40** 35; **43** 320
**Allied Signal Engines**, **9 12–15**
Allied Steel and Conveyors, **18** 493
Allied Steel and Wire Ltd., **III** 495
Allied Stores Corporation, **II** 350, 611–12; **V** 25–28; **9** 211; **10** 282; **13** 43; **15** 94, 274; **16** 60; **22** 110; **23** 59–60; **25** 249; **31** 192; **37**
Allied Structural Steel Company, **10** 44
Allied Supermarkets, Inc., **7** 570; **28** 511
Allied Suppliers, **II** 609
Allied Telephone Company. *See* Alltel Corporation.
Allied Tin Box Makers Ltd., **I** 604
Allied Towers Merchants Ltd., **II** 649
Allied Van Lines Inc., **6** 412, 414; **14** 37
Allied Vintners, **I** 215
**AlliedSignal Inc.**, **22 29–32 (upd.)**; **29** 408; **31** 154; **37** 158
Allis Chalmers Corporation, **I** 163; **II** 98, 121; **III** 543–44; **9** 17; **11** 104; **12** 545; **13** 16–17, 563; **14** 446; **21** 502–03; **22** 380
Allis-Gleaner Corp. *See* AGCO Corp.
Allison Engine Company, **21** 436
Allison Engineering Company. *See* Rolls-Royce Allison.
**Allison Gas Turbine Division**, **9 16–19**, 417; **10** 537; **11** 473
Allmanna Svenska Elektriska Aktiebolaget. *See* ABB ASEA Brown Boveri Ltd.
Allmänna Telefonaktiebolaget L.M. Ericsson, **V** 334
Allnatt London & Guildhall Properties, **IV** 724
Allnet, **10** 19
Allo Pro, **III** 633
Allor Leasing Corp., **9** 323
**Allou Health & Beauty Care, Inc.**, **28 12–14**
Alloy & Stainless, Inc., **IV** 228
Alloys Unlimited, **II** 82
Allserve Inc., **25** 367
Allsport plc., **31** 216, 218
**The Allstate Corporation**, **I** 23; **III** 231–32, 259, 294; **V** 180, 182; **6** 12; **10 50–52**; **13** 539; **18** 475; **21** 96–97; **22** 495; **23** 286–87; **25** 155; **27 30–33 (upd.)**; **29** 397
**ALLTEL Corporation**, **6 299–301**; **16** 318; **20** 440; **46 15–19 (upd.)**
Alltrans Group, **27** 472
**Alltrista Corporation**, **30 38–41**
**Allwaste, Inc.**, **18 10–13**
Almac Electronics Corporation, **10** 113
Almac's Inc., **17** 558–59
Almacenes de Baja y Media, **39** 201, 204
Almaden Vineyards, **I** 377–78; **13** 134; **34** 89
**Almanij NV**, **44 15–18**. *See also* Algemeene Maatschappij voor Nijverheidskrediet.
Almay, Inc., **III** 54
Almeida Banking House. *See* Banco Bradesco S.A.
Almours Security Co., **IV** 311; **19** 266
Almys, **24** 461
Aloe Vera of America, **17** 187
**Aloha Airlines, Incorporated**, **I** 97; **9** 271–72; **21** 142; **22** 251; **24 20–22**
Alp Sport Sandals, **22** 173
Alpen-Elektrowerke Aktiengesellschaft, **IV** 230
Alpex Computer Corp., **III** 157
Alpex, S.A. de C.V., **19** 12
Alpha Beta Co., **II** 605, 625, 653; **17** 559
Alpha Engineering Group, Inc., **16** 259–60
Alpha Healthcare Ltd., **25** 455
Alpha Processor Inc., **41** 349
Alpha Technical Systems, **19** 279
Alphaform, **40** 214–15
Alphanumeric Publication Systems, Inc., **26** 518
**Alpharma Inc.**, **35 22–26 (upd.)**
Alphonse Allard Inc., **II** 652
Alpina Versicherungs-Aktiengesellschaft, **III** 412
Alpine, **IV** 234
**Alpine Electronics, Inc.**, **II** 5; **13 30–31**
**Alpine Lace Brands, Inc.**, **18 14–16**
Alpine Securities Corporation, **22** 5
Alpre, **19** 192
**Alps Electric Co., Ltd.**, **II** 5–6; **13** 30; **44 19–21 (upd.)**
Alric Packing, **II** 466

Alsen-Breitenbury, **III** 702
ALSO Holding AG, **29** 419, 422
Alsons Corp., **III** 571; **20** 362
Alsthom, **II** 12
Alsthom-Atlantique, **9** 9
Alta Dena, **25** 83, 85
Alta Electric Company, **25** 15
Alta Gold Co., **IV** 76
ALTA Health Strategies, Inc., **11** 113
Alta Holidays Ltd., **I** 95
Altamil Corp., **IV** 137
Altana AG, **23** 498
**AltaVista Company, 43 11–13**
Alte Leipziger, **III** 242
Altec Electronics, **I** 489–90
ALTEC International, **21** 107–09
Altenburg & Gooding, **22** 428
**Altera Corporation, 18 17–20; 43 14–18 (upd.); 47** 384
Alternate Postal Delivery, **6** 14
Alternative Living Services. *See* Alterra Healthcare Corporation.
Alternative Youth Services, Inc., **29** 399–400
**Alterra Healthcare Corporation, 42 3–5**
Altex, **19** 192–93
Althoff KG, **V** 101
Althouse Chemical Company, **9** 153
Althus Corp, **I** 361
Altman Weil Pensa, **29** 237
Alton & Eastern Railroad Company, **6** 504
Alton Box Board Co., **IV** 295; **19** 225
Altos Computer Systems, **6** 279; **10** 362
**Altos Hornos de México, S.A. de C.V., 13** 144; **19** 220; **39** 188; **42 6–8**
**Altron Incorporated, 20 8–10**
Altura Energy Ltd., **41** 359
Aluar. *See* Aluminios Argentinos.
Aluma Systems Corp., **9** 512; **22** 14
Alumax Inc., **I** 508; **III** 758; **IV** 18–19; **8** 505–06; **22** 286
Alumina Partners of Jamaica, **IV** 123
Aluminate Sales Corp, **I** 373
Aluminio de Galicia, **IV** 174
Aluminios Argentinos, **26** 433
Aluminium Co. of London, **IV** 69
L'Aluminium Francais, **IV** 173
Aluminium Ltd., **IV** 9–11, 14, 153
Aluminium-Oxid Stade GmbH, **IV** 231
Aluminium Plant and Vessel Co., **III** 419
Aluminum Can Co., **I** 607
**Aluminum Company of America, I** 373, 599; **II** 315, 402, 422; **III** 490–91, 613; **IV** 9–12, **14–16**, 56, 59, 121–22, 131, 173, 703; **6** 39; **12** 346; **19** 240, 292; **20 11–14 (upd.)**; **22** 455; **42** 438
Aluminum Company of Canada Ltd., **II** 345; **IV** 10–12, 154
Aluminum Cooking Utensil Co., **IV** 14
Aluminum Forge Co., **IV** 137
Aluminum Norf GmbH, **IV** 231
Aluminum of Korea, **III** 516
Aluminum Rolling Mills, **17** 280
Aluminum Sales Corporation, **12** 346
Aluminum Seating Corp., **I** 201
Alun Cathcart, **6** 357
Alup-Kompressoren Pressorun, **III** 570; **20** 361
Alupak, A.G., **12** 377
Alusaf, **IV** 92
Alusuisse Lonza Group Ltd., **IV** 12; **31** 11
Alva Jams Pty., **I** 437
Alvic Group, **20** 363
**Alvis Plc, 47 7–9**
Alyeska Pipeline Service Co., **IV** 522, 571; **14** 542; **24** 521; **40** 356
Alyeska Seafoods Co., **II** 578
**ALZA Corporation, 10 53–55; 36 36–39 (upd.); 40** 11; **41** 200–01
Alzwerke GmbH, **IV** 230
AM Acquisition Inc., **8** 559–60
AM Cosmetics, Inc., **31** 89
Am-Par Records, **II** 129
Am-Safe, Inc., **16** 357
AM-TEX Corp., Inc., **12** 443
Amagasaki Co., **I** 492; **24** 325
Amagasaki Spinners Ltd., **V** 387
Amagasaki Steel Co., Ltd., **IV** 130
Amalgamaize Co., **14** 18
Amalgamated Chemicals, Ltd., **IV** 401
Amalgamated Dental International, **10** 271–72
Amalgamated Distilled Products, **II** 609
Amalgamated Press, **IV** 666; **7** 244, 342; **17** 397
Amalgamated Roadstone Corp., **III** 752; **28** 449
Amalgamated Sugar Co., **14** 18; **19** 467–68
Amalgamated Weatherware, **IV** 696
Amana Refrigeration Company, **II** 86; **11** 413; **18** 226; **38** 374; **42** 159
Amaray International Corporation, **12** 264
Amarillo Gas Company. *See* Atmos Energy Corporation.
Amarillo Railcar Services, **6** 580
Amarin Plastics, **IV** 290
Amax Gold, **36** 316
**AMAX Inc., I** 508; **III** 687; **IV 17–19**, 46, 139, 171, 239, 387; **6** 148; **12** 244; **22** 106, 286
**Amazon.com, Inc., 25 17–19**
Amazôna Mineracao SA, **IV** 56
Ambac Industries, **I** 85
AmBase Corp., **III** 264
Amber's Stores, Inc., **17** 360
**Amblin Entertainment, 21 23–27**; **33** 431
AMBRA, Inc., **48** 209
Ambrose Shardlow, **III** 494
**AMC Entertainment Inc., 12 12–14; 14** 87; **21** 362; **23** 126; **35 27–29 (upd.)**
AMCA International Corporation, **7** 513; **8** 545; **10** 329; **23** 299
AMCC. *See* Applied Micro Circuits Corporation.
Amcell. *See* American Cellular Network.
Amchem Products Inc., **I** 666
AMCO, Inc., **13** 159
**Amcor Limited, IV 248–50; 19 13–16 (upd.)**
**AMCORE Financial Inc., 44 22–26**
Amcraft Building Products Co., Inc., **22** 15
AMD. *See* Advanced Micro Devices, Inc.
**Amdahl Corporation, III 109–11**, 140; **6** 272; **12** 238; **13** 202; **14 13–16 (upd.)**; **16** 194, 225–26; **22** 293; **25** 87; **40 20–25 (upd.)**; **42** 147. *See also* Fujitsu Limited.
**Amdocs Ltd., 47 10–12**
AME Finanziaria, **IV** 587; **19** 19
AMEC plc, **I** 568; **36** 322
Amedco, **6** 295
**Amer Group plc, 24** 530; **41 14–16**
Amer Sport, **22** 202
**Amerada Hess Corporation, IV 365–67**, 400, 454, 522, 571, 658; **11** 353; **21 28–31 (upd.)**; **24** 521
**Amerco, 6 351–52**
Ameri-Kart Corp., **19** 277, 279
America Japan Sheet Glass Co., **III** 714
America Latina Companhia de Seguros, **III** 289
**America Online, Inc., 10 56–58**, 237; **13** 147; **15** 54, 265, 321; **18** 24; **19** 41; **22** 52, 519, 522; **26 16–20 (upd.)**; **27** 20, 106, 301, 430, 517–18; **29** 143, 227; **32** 163; **33** 254; **34** 361; **35** 304, 306; **38** 269–71. *See also* CompuServe Interactive Services, Inc.
America Publishing Company, **18** 213
America Today, **13** 545
America Unplugged, **18** 77
**America West Airlines, 6 72–74**, 121
America West Express, **32** 334
**America West Holdings Corporation, 34 22–26 (upd.)**
**America's Favorite Chicken Company, Inc., 7 26–28**. *See also* AFC Enterprises, Inc.
American & Efird, Inc., **12** 501; **23** 260
American Agricultural Chemical Co., **IV** 401
American Air Conditioning, **25** 15
American Air Filter, **26** 3–4
**American Airlines, I** 30–31, 48, 71, **89–91**, 97, 106, 115, 118, 124–26, 130, 132, 512, 530; **III** 102; **6** 60, 81, **75–77 (upd.)**, 121, 129–31; **9** 271–72; **10** 163; **11** 279; **12** 190, 192, 379, 381, 487, **13** 173; **14** 73; **16** 146; **18** 73; **21** 141, 143; **24** 21, 399–400; **25** 90–91, 403, 421–22; **26** 427–28, 441; **31** 103, 306; **33** 270, 302; **34** 118; **38** 105. *See also* AMR Corporation.
American Alliance Co., **III** 191
American Allsafe Co., **8** 386
American Amusements, Inc., **III** 430
American Appliance Co., **II** 85; **11** 411
American Arithmometer Company. *See* Burroughs Corporation.
American Asiatic Underwriters, **III** 195
American Association of Retired Persons, **9** 348. *See also* AARP.
American Austin Quality Foods Inc., **44** 40
American Automar Inc., **12** 29
American Automated, **11** 111
American Automobile Insurance Co., **III** 251
American Aviation and General Insurance Co., **III** 230
American Aviation Manufacturing Corp., **15** 246
American Avitron Inc, **I** 481
American Bakeries Company, **12** 275–76
American Bancorp, **11** 295
American Bancshares, Inc., **11** 457
American Bank, **9** 474–75
American Bank Note, **IV** 599
American Bank of Vicksburg, **14** 41
American Bankcorp, Inc., **8** 188
American Banker/Bond Buyer, **8** 526
**American Banknote Corporation, 30 42–45**
**American Bar Association, 35 30–33**
American Barge and Towing Company, **11** 194
American Beauty Cover Company, **12** 472
American Beef Packers, Inc., **16** 473
American Beet Sugar Company, **11** 13–14
American Bell Telephone Company, **V** 259; **14** 336
American Beryllium Co., Inc., **9** 323

American Beverage Corp., **II** 528
**American Biltrite Inc., 16 16–18; 18** 116, 118; **43 19–22 (upd.)**
American Biodyne Inc., **9** 348
American Biomedical Corporation, **11** 333
American Biscuit Co., **II** 542
American Box Board Company, **12** 376
American Box Co., **IV** 137
American Brake Shoe and Foundry Company, **I** 456. *See also* ABC Rail Products Corporation.
**American Brands, Inc., II** 468, 477; **IV** 251; **V 395–97**, 398–99, 405; **7** 3–4; **9** 408; **12** 87, 344; **14** 95, 271–72; **16** 108, 110, 242; **19** 168–69; **38** 169. *See also* Fortune Brands, Inc.
American Bridge Co., **II** 330; **IV** 572; **7** 549
American Broadcasting Co., **25** 418. *See also* ABC, Inc. *and* Capital Cities/ABC Inc.
American Builders & Contractors Supply Co. *See* ABC Supply Co., Inc.
American Builders, Inc., **8** 436
**American Building Maintenance Industries, Inc., 6 17–19**. *See also* ABM Industries Incorporated.
American Bus Lines Inc., **24** 118
**American Business Information, Inc., 18 21–25**
American Business Interiors. *See* American Furniture Company, Inc.
**American Business Products, Inc., 20 15–17**
American Cable Systems, Inc. *See* Comcast Corporation.
American Cablesystems, **7** 99
American Cafe, **I** 547
American Can Co., **IV** 36, 290; **8** 476; **10** 130; **11** 29, 197; **12** 408; **13** 255; **15** 127–28; **17** 106; **22** 210; **23** 98. *See also* Primerica Corp.
**The American Cancer Society, 24 23–25**
American Capital and Research Corp., **28** 201
American Car & Foundry Inc., **21** 503
American Carbide Corporation, **7** 584
American Cash Register Co., **III** 150; **6** 264
American Casualty Co., **III** 230–31, 404
American Casualty Co. of Dallas, **III** 203
American Cellular Network, **7** 91; **24** 122
American Cellulose and Chemical Manufacturing Co., **I** 317
American Cement Co. *See* Giant Cement Holding, Inc.
American Central Insurance Co., **III** 241
American Cereal Co., **II** 558; **12** 409
American Chicle Co., **I** 711; **21** 54; **38** 363–64
American Chocolate & Citrus Co., **IV** 409
American Chrome, **III** 699
**American Classic Voyages Company, 22** 340, **27 34–37**
American Clay Forming Company, **8** 178
American Clip Company, **7** 3
**American Coin Merchandising, Inc., 28 15–17**
**American Colloid Co., 13 32–35**
American Colonial Insurance Company, **44** 356
American Commercial Bank, **II** 336
American Commercial Lines Inc., **22** 164, 166–67
American Commonwealths Power Corporation, **6** 579
American Community Grocers, **II** 670
American Computer Systems. *See* American Software Inc.
American Construction Lending Services, Inc., **39** 380, 382
American Continental Insurance Co., **III** 191–92
American Cotton Cooperative Association, **17** 207; **33** 85
American Cotton Oil Co., **II** 497
American Council on Education, **12** 141
American Courier Express, Inc., **24** 126
American Crayon Company, **12** 115
American Credit Corporation, **II** 236; **20** 59
**American Crystal Sugar Company, 7** 377; **11 13–15; 32 29–33 (upd.)**
**American Cyanamid, I 300–02**, 619; **III** 22; **IV** 345, 552; **8 24–26 (upd.)**; **10** 269; **11** 494; **13** 231–32; **14** 254, 256; **16** 68; **22** 147; **27** 115–16
American Dairy Queen Corporation, **10** 373
American Data Technology, Inc., **11** 111
American Digital Communications, Inc., **33** 329
American Distilling Co., **I** 226; **10** 180–81
American District Telegraph Co., **III** 644; **12** 9
American Diversified Foods, Inc., **14** 351
American Drew, Inc., **12** 301
American Drug Company, **13** 367
American Eagle Airlines, Inc., **28** 22
American Eagle Fire Insurance Co., **III** 240–41
**American Eagle Outfitters, Inc., 14** 427; **24 26–28; 25** 121
American Education Press, **10** 479
American Electric Company, **II** 27; **12** 193; **22** 10
**American Electric Power Company, II** 3; **IV** 181; **V 546–49**; **6** 449, 524; **11** 516; **45 17–21 (upd.)**
American Empire Insurance Co., **III** 191
American Emulsions Co., **8** 455
American Encaustic Tiling Co., **22** 170
American Energy Management Inc., **39** 261
American Envelope Co., **III** 40; **16** 303; **28** 251; **43** 257
American Equipment Co., **I** 571
American Export Steamship Lines, **I** 89
**American Express Company, I** 26–27, 480, 614; **II** 108, 176, 309, 380–82, **395–99**, 450–52, 544; **III** 251–52, 319, 340, 389; **IV** 637, 721; **6** 206–07, 409; **8** 118; **9** 335, 343, 391, 468–69, 538; **10** 44–45, **59–64 (upd.)**; **11** 41, 416–17, 532; **12** 533; **14** 106; **15** 50; **18** 60, 112, 516, 543; **21** 97, 127; **23** 229; **26** 516; **33** 394–96; **38 42–48 (upd.)**
American Factors, Ltd. *See* Amfac/JMB Hawaii L.L.C.
**American Family Corporation, III 187–89**. *See also* AFLAC Inc.
American Family Life Insurance Company, **33** 407
American Family Publishers, **23** 393–94
American Feldmühle Corp., **II** 51; **21** 330
American Filtrona Corp., **IV** 260–61
American Finance Systems, **II** 349
**American Financial Corporation, II** 596; **III 190–92**, 221; **8** 537; **9** 452; **18** 549
**American Financial Group Inc., 48 6–10 (upd.)**
American Fine Wire, Inc., **33** 248
American First National Supermarkets, **16** 313
American Fitness Centers, **25** 40
American Fitness Products, Inc., **47** 128
American Flange, **30** 397
American Flavor & Fragrance Company, **9** 154
American Flyer Trains, **16** 336–37
American Food Management, **6** 45
**American Foods Group, 43 23–27**
American Football League, **29** 346
American Fore Group, **III** 241–42
American Foreign Insurance Association, **III** 223, 226. *See also* AFIA.
American Forest Products Co., **IV** 282; **9** 260
American Freightways Corporation, **42** 141
American Fructose Corp., **14** 18–19
American Fur Company, **25** 220
**American Furniture Company, Inc., 12** 300; **21 32–34**
American Gage Co., **I** 472
American Gaming and Electronics, Inc., **43** 461
American Gas & Electric. *See* American Electric Power Company.
American Gasoline Co., **IV** 540
American General Capital Corp., **I** 614
**American General Corporation, III 193–94; 10 65–67 (upd.)**; **11** 16; **46 20–23 (upd.)**; **47** 15
**American General Finance Corp., 11 16–17**
American General Life Insurance Company, **6** 294
**American Golf Corporation, 45 22–24**
American Graphics, **23** 100
**American Greetings Corporation, 7 23–25**; **12** 207–08; **15** 507; **16** 256; **21** 426–28; **22 33–36 (upd.)**
American Grinder and Manufacturing Company, **9** 26
American Hardware & Supply Company. *See* TruServ Corporation.
American Harvester, **II** 262
American Hawaii Cruises, **27** 34
American Health & Life Insurance Company, **27** 47
American Healthcorp Inc., **48** 25
American Heritage Savings, **II** 420
American Hoechst Corporation. *See* Hoechst Celanese Corporation.
American Hoist & Derrick Co., **8** 544
American Home Assurance Co., **III** 196–97
American Home Assurance Co. of New York, **III** 203
**American Home Mortgage Holdings, Inc., 46 24–26**
American Home Patients Centers Inc., **46** 4
**American Home Products, I** 527, **622–24**, 631, 676–77, 696, 700; **III** 18, 36, 444; **8** 282–83; **10 68–70 (upd.)**, 528; **11** 35; **15** 64–65; **16** 191, 438; **21** 466; **24** 288; **25** 477; **36** 87; **38** 365
American Home Publishing Co., Inc., **14** 460
American Home Shield, **6** 46; **23** 428, 430
American Home Video, **9** 186

**American Homestar Corporation, 18 26–29; 41 17–20 (upd.)**
American Homeware Inc., **15** 501
American Honda Motor Co., **I** 174; **10** 352
American Hospital Association, **10** 159
American Hospital Supply Co., **I** 627, 629; **III** 80; **10** 141–43; **11** 459, 486; **19** 103; **21** 118; **30** 496
American Hydron, **13** 366; **25** 55
American I.G. Chemical Corporation. *See* GAF Corporation.
American Impacts Corporation, **8** 464
American Improved Cements. *See* Giant Cement Holding, Inc.
American Independent Oil Co., **IV** 522, 537. *See also* Aminoil, Inc.
American Industrial Manufacturing Co., **I** 481
American Information Services, Inc., **11** 111
**American Institute of Certified Public Accountants (AICPA), 44 27–30**
American Institutional Products, Inc., **18** 246
American Instrument Co., **I** 628; **13** 233
American Insurance Agency, **III** 191, 352
American Insurance Co., **III** 251
American International Airways, Inc., **17** 318; **22** 311
**American International Group, Inc., II** 422; **III 195–98**, 200; **6** 349; **10** 39; **11** 532–33; **15 15–19 (upd.)**; **18** 159; **45** 109; **46** 20; **47 13–19 (upd.)**; **48** 219
American International Travel Service, **6** 367; **27** 90
American Iron and Steel Manufacturing Co., **IV** 35; **7** 48
American Isuzu Motors, Inc. *See* Isuzu Motors, Ltd.
**American Italian Pasta Company, 27 38–40**
American Janitor Service, **25** 15
American Jet Industries, **7** 205
American Ka-Ro, **8** 476
American Knitting Mills of Miami, Inc., **22** 213
American La-France, **10** 296
American Laboratories, **III** 73
American Land Cruiser Company. *See* Cruise America Inc.
**American Lawyer Media Holdings, Inc., 32 34–37**
American Learning Corporation, **7** 168
American Life Insurance Co., **III** 195–96
American Light and Traction. *See* MCN Corporation.
American Lightwave Systems, Inc., **10** 19
American Limestone Co., **IV** 33
American Limousine Corp., **26** 62
American Linseed Co, **II** 497
**American Locker Group Incorporated, 34 19–21**
**American Lung Association, 48 11–14**
American Machine and Foundry Co., **II** 7; **III** 443; **7** 211–13; **11** 397; **25** 197
American Machine and Metals, **9** 23
American Machinist Press, **IV** 634
American Magnesium Products Co., **I** 404
**American Maize-Products Co., 14 17–20**; **23** 464
**American Management Systems, Inc., 11 18–20**
American Manufacturers Mutual Insurance Co., **III** 269, 271; **15** 257
American-Marietta Corp., **I** 68, 405
American Materials & Technologies Corporation, **27** 117
**American Media, Inc., 27 41–44**
**American Medical Association, 39 15–18**
**American Medical International, Inc., III 73–75**, 79; **14** 232
American Medical Optics, **25** 55
**American Medical Response, Inc., 39 19–22**
American Medical Services, **II** 679–80; **14** 209
American Medicorp, Inc., **III** 81; **6** 191; **14** 432; **24** 230
American Melamine, **27** 317
American Merchandising Associates Inc., **14** 411
American Merchants Union Express Co., **II** 396
American Metal Climax, Inc. *See* AMAX.
American Metal Co. Ltd. *See* AMAX.
American Metal Products Company. *See* Lear Seating Corporation.
American Metal Products Corp., **I** 481
American Metals and Alloys, Inc., **19** 432
American Metals Corp., **III** 569; **20** 361
American Micro Devices, Inc., **16** 549
American Microsystems, **I** 193
American Milk Products Corp., **II** 487
The American Mineral Spirits Company, **8** 99–100
American Motorists Insurance Co., **III** 269, 271; **15** 257
**American Motors Corp., I 135–37**, 145, 152, 190; **II** 60, 313; **III** 543; **6** 27, 50; **8** 373; **10** 262, 264; **18** 493; **26** 403
American Movie Classics Co., **II** 161
American Multi-Cinema. *See* AMC Entertainment Inc.
American National Bank, **13** 221–22
American National Bank and Trust Co., **II** 286
American National Can Co., **III** 536; **IV** 173, 175; **26** 230; **45** 336
American National Corp., **II** 286
American National Fire Insurance Co., **III** 191
American National General Agencies Inc., **III** 221; **14** 109; **37** 85
**American National Insurance Company, 8 27–29; 27 45–48 (upd.)**; **39** 158
American Natural Resources Co., **I** 678; **IV** 395; **13** 416
American Natural Snacks Inc., **29** 480
American Newspaper Publishers Association, **6** 13
American of Philadelphia, **III** 234
American Oil Co., **IV** 369–70; **7** 101; **14** 22
American Olean Tile Company, **III** 424; **22** 48, 170
American Optical Co., **I** 711–12; **III** 607; **7** 436; **38** 363–64
American Overseas Airlines, **12** 380
American Overseas Holdings, **III** 350
**American Pad & Paper Company, 20 18–21**
American Paging, **9** 494–96
American-Palestine Trading Corp., **II** 205–06
American Paper Box Company, **12** 376
American Patriot Insurance, **22** 15
American Payment Systems, Inc., **21** 514
American Petrofina, Inc., **IV** 498; **7** 179–80; **19** 11
American Pfauter, **24** 186
American Phone Centers, Inc., **21** 135
American Photographic Group, **III** 475; **7** 161
American Physicians Service Group, Inc., **6** 45; **23** 430
American Platinum Works, **IV** 78
American Port Services (Amports), **45** 29
American Postage Meter Co., **III** 156
American Potash and Chemical Corporation, **IV** 95, 446; **22** 302
American Power & Light Co., **6** 545, 596–97; **12** 542
**American Power Conversion Corporation, 24 29–31**
**American Premier Underwriters, Inc., 10 71–74**; **48** 9
American Prepaid Professional Services, Inc. *See* CompDent Corporation.
**American President Companies Ltd., III** 512; **6 353–55**
**American Printing House for the Blind, 26 13–15**
American Protective Mutual Insurance Co. Against Burglary, **III** 230
American Public Automotive Group, **37** 115
American Publishing Co., **IV** 597; **24** 222
American Pure Oil Co., **IV** 497
American Radiator & Standard Sanitary Corp., **III** 663–64
American Railway Express Co., **II** 382, 397; **10** 61
American Railway Publishing Co., **IV** 634
**American Re Corporation, III** 182; **10 75–77**; **35 34–37 (upd.)**; **46** 303
American Record Corp., **II** 132
American Recreation Company Holdings, Inc., **16** 53; **44** 53–54
**American Red Cross, 40 26–29**
American Ref-Fuel, **V** 751
American Refrigeration Products S.A, **7** 429
American Republic Assurance Co., **III** 332
American Research and Development Corp., **II** 85; **III** 132; **6** 233; **19** 103
**American Residential Mortgage Corporation, 8 30–31**
American Residential Services, **33** 141
American Resorts Group, **III** 103
**American Retirement Corporation, 42 9–12**; **43** 46
**American Rice, Inc., 17** 161–62; **33 30–33**
American River Transportation Co., **I** 421; **11** 23
American Robot Corp., **III** 461
American Rolling Mill Co., **IV** 28; **8** 176–77
American Royalty Trust Co., **IV** 84; **7** 188
American Rug Craftsmen, **19** 275
American RX Pharmacy, **III** 73
American Safety Equipment Corp., **IV** 136
**American Safety Razor Company, III** 27–29; **20 22–24**
American Saint-Gobain, **16** 121
American Sales Book Co., Ltd., **IV** 644
American Salt Co., **12** 199
American Satellite Co., **6** 279; **15** 195
American Savings & Loan, **10** 117
American Savings Bank, **9** 276; **17** 528, 531

American Sealants Company. *See* Loctite Corporation.
American Seating Co., **I** 447; **21** 33
American Seaway Foods, Inc, **9** 451
American Service Corporation, **19** 223
American Sheet Steel Co., **IV** 572; **7** 549
American Shipbuilding, **18** 318
**American Skiing Company, 28 18–21; 31** 67, 229
American Sky Broadcasting, **27** 305; **35** 156
American Smelting and Refining Co., **IV** 31–33. *See also* ASARCO.
**The American Society of Composers, Authors and Publishers (ASCAP), 29 21–24**
**American Software Inc., 22** 214; **25 20–22**
American-South African Investment Co. Ltd., **IV** 79
American Southern Insurance Co., **17** 196
**American Standard Companies Inc., 30 46–50 (upd.)**
**American Standard Inc., III** 437, **663–65; 19** 455; **22** 4, 6; **28** 486; **40** 452
American States Insurance Co., **III** 276
**American States Water Company, 46 27–30**
American Steamship Company, **6** 394–95; **25** 168, 170
American Steel & Wire Co., **I** 355; **IV** 572; **7** 549; **13** 97–98; **40** 70, 72
American Steel Foundries, **7** 29–30
American Stock Exchange, **10** 416–17
**American Stores Company, II 604–06; 12** 63, 333; **13** 395; **17** 559; **18** 89; **22 37–40 (upd.)**; **25** 297; **27** 290–92; **30** 24, 26–27
American Sugar Refining Company. *See* Domino Sugar Corporation.
American Sumatra Tobacco Corp., **15** 138
American Superconductor Corporation, **41** 141
American Surety Co., **26** 486
American Systems Technologies, Inc., **18** 5
American Teaching Aids Inc., **19** 405
American Technical Services Company. *See* American Building Maintenance Industries, Inc. *and* ABM Industries Incorporated.
American Telephone and Telegraph Company. *See* AT&T.
American Television and Communications Corp., **I** 534–35; **II** 161; **IV** 596, 675; **7** 528–30; **18** 65
American Textile Co., **III** 571; **20** 362
American Thermos Bottle Company. *See* Thermos Company.
American Tile Supply Company, **19** 233
American Tin Plate Co., **IV** 572; **7** 549
American Tissue Company, **29** 136
American Title Insurance, **III** 242
American Tobacco Co., **I** 12–14, 28, 37, 425; **V** 395–97, 399, 408–09, 417–18, 600; **14** 77, 79; **15** 137–38; **16** 242; **18** 416; **27** 128–29; **33** 82; **43** 126. *See also* American Brands Inc., B.A.T. Industries PLC., *and* Fortune Brands, Inc.
American Tool & Machinery, **III** 420
American Tool Company, **13** 563
American Totalisator Corporation, **10** 319–20
**American Tourister, Inc., 10** 350; **13** 451, 453; **16 19–21**. *See also* Samsonite Corporation.
**American Tower Corporation, 33 34–38**
American Tractor Corporation, **10** 379
American Trading and Production Corporation, **7** 101
American Trans Air, **34** 31
American Transport Lines, **6** 384
American Trust and Savings Bank, **II** 261
American Trust Co., **II** 336, 382; **12** 535
American Twist Drill Co., **23** 82
American Ultramar Ltd., **IV** 567
**American Vanguard Corporation, 47 20–22**
American VIP Limousine, Inc., **26** 62
American Viscose Corp. *See* Avisco.
**American Water Works Company, Inc., V** 543–44; **6 443–45**; **26** 451; **38 49–52 (upd.)**
American Window Glass, **16** 120
American Wood Reduction Company, **14** 174
**American Woodmark Corporation, 31 13–16**
American Woolen, **I** 529
American Yard Products, **22** 26, 28
American Yearbook Company, **7** 255; **25** 252
American-Strevell Inc., **II** 625
Americana Entertainment Group, Inc., **19** 435
Americana Foods, Inc., **17** 474–75
Americana Healthcare Corp., **15** 522
Americana Hotel, **12** 316
AmeriFirst Bank, **11** 258
Amerifirst Federal Savings, **10** 340
AmeriGas Partners, L.P., **12** 498
AmeriGas Propane, Inc., **12** 500
**Amerihost Properties, Inc., 30 51–53**
AmeriKing Corp., **36** 309
Amerimark Inc., **II** 682
Amerin Corporation. *See* Radian Group Inc.
AmeriServe Food Distribution. *See* Holberg Industries, Inc.
**AmeriSource Health Corporation, 37 9–11 (upd.)**
**Ameristar Casinos, Inc., 33 39–42**
Amerisystems, **8** 328
**Ameritech Corporation, V 265–68; 6** 248; **7** 118; **10** 431; **11** 382; **12** 137; **14** 252–53, 257, 259–61, 364; **15** 197; **18 30–34 (upd.)**; **25** 499; **41** 288–90; **43** 447; **44** 49
Ameritech Illinois. *See* Illinois Bell Telephone Company.
**Ameritrade Holding Corporation, 34 27–30**
Ameritrust Corporation, **9** 476
**Ameriwood Industries International Corp., 17 15–17**
Amerock Corp., **13** 41
Amerotron, **I** 529
Amersil Co., **IV** 78
**Ames Department Stores, Inc., V** 197–98; **9 20–22**; **10** 497; **15** 88; **19** 449; **30 54–57 (upd.)**
Ametek Inc., **9 23–25**; **12** 88; **38** 169
**N.V. Amev, III 199–202**
**Amey Plc, 47 23–25**
**AMF Bowling, Inc., 19** 312; **23** 450; **40 30–33**
**Amfac Inc., I 417–18**, 566; **IV** 703; **10** 42; **23** 320
**Amfac/JMB Hawaii L.L.C., 24 32–35 (upd.)**
Amfas, **III** 310
AMFM Inc., **35** 221, 245, 248; **37** 104; bf]XLI 384
**Amgen, Inc., I** 266; **8** 216–17; **10 78–81**; **13** 240; **14** 255; **21** 320; **30 58–61 (upd.)**; **38** 204
Amherst Coal Co., **IV** 410; **7** 309
AMI. *See* Advanced Metallurgy, Inc.
Amiga Corporation, **7** 96
Aminoil, Inc., **IV** 523. *See also* American Independent Oil Co.
AMISA, **IV** 136
Amisys Managed Care Information Systems, **16** 94
Amitron S.A., **10** 113
Amity Leather Products Company. *See* AR Accessories Group, Inc.
AMK Corporation, **II** 595; **7** 85; **21** 111
Amkor, **23** 17
AMLI Realty Company, **33** 418, 420
Amling Co., **25** 89
Ammirati Puris Lintas, **14** 316; **22** 294
Ammo-Phos, **I** 300; **8** 24
L'Ammoniac Sarro-Lorrain S.a.r.l., **IV** 197
**Amoco Corporation, I** 516, 202; **II** 376; **III** 611; **IV 368–71**, 412, 424–25, 453, 525; **7** 107, 443; **10** 83–84; **11** 441; **12** 18; **14 21–25 (upd.)**, 494; **18** 365; **19** 297; **26** 369. *See also* BP p.l.c.
Amorim Investimentos e Participaço, **48** 117, 119
Amorim Revestimentos, **48** 118
Amoseas, **IV** 453–54
**Amoskeag Company, 6** 356; **8 32–33**; **9** 213–14, 217; **22** 54; **31** 199
Amot Controls Corporation, **15** 404
**AMP, Inc., II 7–8**; **11** 319; **13** 344; **14 26–28 (upd.)**; **17** 274; **22** 542; **28** 486; **36** 158
Ampad Holding Corporation. *See* American Pad & Paper Company.
AMPAL. *See* American-Palestine Trading Corp.
AMPCO Auto Parks, Inc. *See* American Building Maintenance Industries, Inc. *and* ABM Industries Incorporated.
Ampeg Company, **48** 353
AMPEP, **III** 625
**Ampex Corporation, III** 549; **6** 272; **17 18–20**
**Amphenol Corporation, 40 34–37**
Ampol Petroleum Ltd., **III** 729; **27** 473
Ampro, **25** 504–05
AMR. *See* American Medical Response, Inc.
AMR Combs Inc., **36** 190
**AMR Corporation, I** 90–91; **6** 76; **8** 315; **22** 252; **26** 427–28; **28 22–26 (upd.)**; **29** 409; **33** 19; **34** 119
AMR Information Services, **9** 95
Amram's Distributing Limited, **12** 425
AMRE, **III** 211
**AMREP Corporation, I** 563; **21 35–37**; **24** 78
Amro. *See* Amsterdam-Rotterdam Bank N.V.
Amrop International Australasia, **34** 249
AMS. *See* Advanced Marketing Services, Inc.
AMS Trading Co., **III** 112

Amsco International, **29** 450
Amserve Ltd., **48** 23
**AmSouth Bancorporation, 12 15–17; 48 15–18 (upd.)**
Amstar Corp., **14** 18
Amstar Sugar Corporation, **II** 582; **7** 466–67; **26** 122
**Amsted Industries Incorporated, 7 29–31**
Amstel Brewery, **I** 257; **34** 201
**Amsterdam-Rotterdam Bank N.V., II** 184, **185–86**, 279, 295, 319; **III** 200; **14** 169; **17** 324
**Amstrad plc, III 112–14; 48 19–23 (upd.)**
**AmSurg Corporation, 48 24–27**
AMT. *See* American Materials & Technologies Corporation.
Amtech. *See* American Building Maintenance Industries, Inc. *and* ABM Industries Incorporated.
Amtech Systems Corporation, **11** 65; **27** 405
Amtel, Inc., **8** 545; **10** 136
Amtliches Bayerisches Reisebüro, **II** 163
Amtorg, **13** 365
Amtrak, **II** 2; **10** 73; **19** 141; **26** 440. *See also* National Railroad Passenger Corporation.
**Amtran, Inc., 34 31–33**
AmTrans. *See* American Transport Lines.
Amvac Chemical Corporation, **47** 20
Amvent Inc., **25** 120
**Amway Corporation, III 11–14; 13 36–39 (upd.); 17** 186; **18** 67, 164; **20** 435; **23** 509; **29** 493; **30 62–66 (upd.); 31** 327
Amylum, **II** 582
ANA. *See* All Nippon Airways Co., Ltd.
Anacomp, Inc., **11** 19
Anaconda Aluminum, **11** 38
Anaconda Co., **III** 644; **IV** 33, 376; **7** 261–63
Anaconda-Jurden Associates, **8** 415
**Anadarko Petroleum Corporation, 10 82–84**
Anadex, Inc., **18** 435–36
Anaheim Imaging, **19** 336
**Analog Devices, Inc., 10 85–87; 18** 20; **19** 67; **38** 54; **43** 17, 311; **47** 384
**Analogic Corporation, 23 13–16**
**Analysts International Corporation, 36 40–42**
**Analytic Sciences Corporation, 10 88–90; 13** 417
**Analytical Surveys, Inc., 33 43–45**
**Anam Group, 21** 239; **23 17–19**
Anamax Mining Co., **IV** 33
AnAmo Co., **IV** 458
Anarad, Inc., **18** 515
**Anaren Microwave, Inc., 33 46–48**
ANB Bank, **I** 55
**Anchor Bancorp, Inc., 10 91–93**
Anchor Brake Shoe, **18** 5
**Anchor Brewing Company, 47 26–28**
Anchor Corporation, **12** 525
**Anchor Gaming, 24 36–39; 41** 216
**Anchor Hocking Glassware, I** 609–10; **13 40–42; 14** 483; **26** 353
Anchor Motor Freight, Inc., **12** 309–10
Anchor National Financial Services, Inc., **11** 482
Anchor National Life Insurance Company, **11** 482
Anchor Oil and Gas Co., **IV** 521
Anchor Records, **II** 130
Ancienne Mutuelle, **III** 210
Anders Wilhelmsen & Co., **22** 471
Andersen Consulting, **38** 430
**Andersen Corporation, 9** 344; **10 94–95; 11** 305; **22** 346; **39** 324
**Andersen Worldwide, 29 25–28 (upd.)**
Anderson & Kerr Drilling Co., **IV** 445
Anderson and Campbell, **II** 479
Anderson Box Co., **IV** 342; **8** 267
Anderson Clayton & Co., **II** 560; **12** 411
Anderson, Greenwood & Co., **11** 225–26
Anderson Testing Company, Inc., **6** 441
**The Andersons, Inc., 31 17–21**
Anderton, **III** 624
Andes Candies, **II** 520–21
Andian National Corp. Ltd., **IV** 415–16
André Courrèges, **III** 47; **8** 342–43
Andreas Christ, **26** 243
**Andreas Stihl, 16 22–24**
**Andrew Corporation, 10 96–98; 32 38–41 (upd.)**
Andrew Jergens Co., **III** 38; **25** 56
Andrew Weir & Co., **III** 273
Andrews, Clark & Company, **IV** 426; **7** 169
Andrews Group, Inc., **10** 402
**Andrews McMeel Universal, 40 38–41**
Andrews Office Supply and Equipment Co., **25** 500
Andritz AG, **27** 269
Anfor, **IV** 249–50
Angele Ghigi, **II** 475
**Angelica Corporation, 15 20–22; 43 28–31 (upd.)**
Angelo's Supermarkets, Inc., **II** 674
ANGI Ltd., **11** 28
Angle Steel, **25** 261
Anglian Water Plc, **38** 51
Anglo-American Chewing Gum Ltd., **II** 569
Anglo-American Clays Corp., **III** 691; **IV** 346
**Anglo American Corporation of South Africa Limited, I** 289, 423; **IV 20–23**, 56–57, 64–68, 79–80, 90, 92, 94–96, 118–20, 191, 239–40; **7** 121–23, 125; **16 25–30 (upd.)**, 292; **21** 211, 354; **22** 233; **28** 88, 93
Anglo-American Oil Company Limited, **IV** 427; **7** 170
Anglo American Paper Co., **IV** 286
Anglo-American Telegraph Company Ltd., **IV** 668; **25** 98
Anglo-Belge, **II** 474
Anglo-Canadian, **III** 704
Anglo-Canadian Mining & Refining, **IV** 110
Anglo-Canadian Telephone Company of Montreal. *See* British Columbia Telephone Company.
Anglo-Celtic Watch Company, **25** 430
Anglo Company, Ltd., **9** 363
Anglo-Dutch Unilever group, **9** 317
Anglo-Egyptian D.C.O., **II** 236
Anglo-Egyptian Oilfields, **IV** 412, 414
Anglo-Elementar-Versicherungs-AG, **III** 185
Anglo Energy, Ltd., **9** 364
Anglo-Huronian Ltd., **IV** 164
Anglo-Iranian Oil Co., **IV** 379, 419, 435, 450, 466, 559; **7** 57, 141; **21** 81
Anglo-Lautaro Nitrate Corporation, **9** 363
Anglo Mexican Petroleum Co. Ltd., **IV** 657
Anglo-Palestine Co., **II** 204
Anglo-Persian Oil Co., **IV** 363, 378–79, 381, 429, 450, 466, 515, 524, 531, 557–59; **7** 56–57, 140; **21** 80–81; **45** 47
Anglo-Swiss Condensed Milk Co., **II** 545
Anglo-Thai Corp., **III** 523
Anglo-Transvaal Consolidated, **IV** 534
Anglovaal Industries Ltd., **20** 263
Angus Hill Holdings, **IV** 249
**Anheuser-Busch Companies, Inc., 34 34–37 (upd.); 36** 12–15, 163
**Anheuser-Busch Company, Inc., I** 32, **217–19**, 236–37, 254–55, 258, 265, 269–70, 290–91, 598; **IV** 624; **6** 20–21, 48; **9** 100; **10 99–101 (upd.)**, 130; **11** 421; **12** 337–38; **13** 5, 10, 258, 366; **15** 429; **17** 256; **18** 65, 70, 72–73, 499, 501; **19** 221, 223; **21** 229, 319–20; **22** 421; **23** 403; **25** 281–82, 368; **26** 432; **29** 84–85; **29** 218; **31** 381, 383
ANIC Gela, **IV** 421
Anikem, **I** 374
Anitec Image Technology Corp., **IV** 287; **15** 229
Annabelle's, **II** 480–81; **26** 57
Anne Klein & Co., **15** 145–46; **24** 299; **40** 277–78
Anneplas, **25** 464
**AnnTaylor Stores Corporation, V** 26–27; **13 43–45; 15** 9; **25** 120–22; **37 12–15 (upd.)**
Annuaries Marcotte Ltd., **10** 461
Anocout Engineering Co., **23** 82
Anonima Infortunia, **III** 208
**ANR Pipeline Co., 17 21–23; 31** 119
Ansa Software, **9** 81
Ansaldo, **II** 191
Ansbacher-Siegle Corp., **13** 460
Anschütz & Co. GmbH, **III** 446
**The Anschutz Corporation, 12 18–20; 36 43–47 (upd.); 37** 312
Anschütz-Kaempfe, **III** 446
Ansell, **I** 215
Ansell Rubber Company, **10** 445
Anselmo L. Morvillo S.A., **19** 336
Ansett Airlines, **6** 73; **14** 11; **27** 475
Ansett Australia, **24** 398, 400; **26** 113
Ansett Transport Industries Limited, **V** 523–25; **27** 473
Ansonia Brass and Battery Co., **IV** 176–77
Ansonia Manufacturing Co., **IV** 176
ANSYS Technologies Inc., **48** 410
Ant Nachrichtentechnik GmbH., **I** 411
Anta Corporation, **6** 188; **25** 308
Antalis, **34** 38, 40
Antar group, **IV** 544, 546
Antares Alliance Group, **14** 15
Antares Electronics, Inc., **10** 257
Ante Corp., **22** 222
Antenna Company, **32** 40
ANTEX. *See* American National Life Insurance Company of Texas.
**Anthem Electronics, Inc., 13 46–47; 17** 276
Anthem P&C Holdings, **15** 257
Anthes Imperial Ltd., **I** 274; **26** 304
Anthes Industries Inc., **9** 512
Anthony Industries Inc. *See* K2 Inc.
Anthony Stumpf Publishing Company, **10** 460
Anthropologie, **14** 524–25
Antillaase Bank-Unie N.V., **II** 184

Antinori. *See* Marchesi Antinori SRL.
**The Antioch Company, 40 42–45**
Antique Street Lamps, **19** 212
ANTK Tupolev. *See* Aviacionny Nauchno-Tehnicheskii Komplex im. A.N. Tupoleva.
Antoine Saladin, **III** 675
Antwerp Co., **IV** 497
ANZ. *See* Australia and New Zealand Banking Group Ltd.
ANZ Securities, **24** 400
Anzon Limited, **III** 681; **44** 118–19
AO Sidanco, **45** 50
AOE Plastic GmbH, **7** 141
Aoki Corporation, **9** 547, 549; **29** 508
AOL. *See* America Online, Inc.
AOL Time Warner Inc., **45** 201; **47** 271
**Aon Corporation, III 203–05**; **22** 495; **45 25–28 (upd.)**
AP. *See* The Associated Press.
AP Bank, Ltd., **13** 439
AP Support Services, **25** 13
AP&L. *See* American Power & Light Co.
AP-Dow Jones/Telerate Company, **10** 277
APAC, Inc., **IV** 374
**Apache Corporation, 10 102–04**; **11** 28; **18** 366; **32 42–46 (upd.)**
Apache Energy Ltd., **25** 471
APACHE Medical Systems, Inc., **16** 94
Apartment Furniture Rental, **26** 102
APCOA/Standard Parking. *See* Holberg Industries, Inc.
Apex, **17** 363
Apex Financial Corp., **8** 10
Apex Oil, **37** 310–11
Apex One Inc., **31** 137
Apex Smelting Co., **IV** 18
APH. *See* American Printing House for the Blind.
Apita, **V** 210
APL. *See* American President Companies Ltd.
APL Corporation, **9** 346
APL Ltd., **41** 399
Aplex Industries, Inc., **26** 363
Apline Guild, **12** 173
Aplix, **19** 477
APM Ltd., **IV** 248–49
APN. *See* Affiliated Physicians Network, Inc.
**Apogee Enterprises, Inc., 8 34–36**; **22** 347
Apollo Advisors L.P., **16** 37; **26** 500, 502; **43** 438
Apollo Apparel Partners, L.P., **12** 431
Apollo Computer, **III** 143; **6** 238; **9** 471; **11** 284
**Apollo Group, Inc., 24 40–42**
Apollo Heating & Air Conditioning Inc., **15** 411
Apollo Investment Fund Ltd., **31** 211; **39** 174
Apollo Ski Partners LP of New York, **11** 543, 545
Apollo Technologies, **I** 332
Apotekarnes Droghandel A.B., **I** 664–65
Apothekernes Laboratorium A.S., **12** 3–5
Appalachian Computer Services, **11** 112
Appalachian Travel Services, Inc., **25** 185, 187
**Applause Inc.**, **17** 461; **24 43–46**
**Apple Computer, Inc., II** 6, 62, 103, 107, 124; **III** 114, **115–16**, 121, 125, 149, 172; **6 218–20 (upd.)**, 222, 225, 231, 244, 248, 254–58, 260, 289; **8** 138; **9** 166, 170–71, 368, 464; **10** 22–23, 34, 57, 233, 235, 404, 458–59, 518–19; **11** 45, 50, 57, 62, 490; **12** 139, 183, 335, 449, 455, 470; **13** 90, 388, 482; **16** 195, 367–68, 372, 417–18; **18** 93, 511, 521; **20** 31; **21** 391; **23** 209; **24** 370; **25** 299–300, 348, 530–31; **28** 244–45; **33** 12–14; **34** 512; **36 48–51 (upd.)**, 168; **38** 69
Apple Container Corp., **III** 536; **26** 230
Apple Orthodontix, Inc., **35** 325
Apple South, Inc., **21** 362; **35** 39. *See also* Avado Brands, Inc.
**Applebee's International Inc., 14 29–31**; **19** 258; **20** 159; **21** 362; **31** 40; **35 38–41 (upd.)**
Appleton & Cox, **III** 242
Appleton Papers, **I** 426
Appleton Wire Works Corp., **8** 13
Appliance Buyers Credit Corp., **III** 653
**Appliance Recycling Centers of America, Inc., 42 13–16**
**Applica Incorporated, 43 32–36 (upd.)**
Les Applications du Roulement, **III** 623
Applied Beverage Systems Ltd., **21** 339
Applied Biomedical Corp., **47** 4
**Applied Bioscience International, Inc., 10 105–07**
Applied Color Systems, **III** 424
Applied Communications, Inc., **6** 280; **11** 151; **25** 496; **29** 477–79
Applied Data Research, Inc., **6** 225; **18** 31–32
Applied Digital Data Systems Inc., **II** 83; **9** 514
Applied Engineering Services, Inc. *See* The AES Corporation.
**Applied Films Corporation**, **12** 121; **35** 148; **48 28–31**
Applied Industrial Materials Corporation, **22** 544, 547
Applied Komatsu Technology, Inc., **10** 109
Applied Laser Systems, **31** 124
Applied Learning International, **IV** 680
**Applied Materials, Inc., 10 108–09**; **18** 382–84; **46 31–34 (upd.)**
**Applied Micro Circuits Corporation, 38 53–55**
Applied Network Technology, Inc., **25** 162
**Applied Power Inc., 9 26–28**; **32 47–51 (upd.)**
Applied Programming Technologies, Inc., **12** 61
Applied Solar Energy, **8** 26
Applied Technology Corp., **11** 87
Applied Thermal Technologies, Inc., **29** 5
Approvisionnement Atlantique, **II** 652
Appryl, **I** 303
Apria Healthcare Inc., **43** 266
**Aprilia SpA, 17 24–26**
APS. *See* Arizona Public Service Company.
APS Healthcare, **17** 166, 168
Apura GmbH, **IV** 325
APUTCO, **6** 383
**Aqua Alliance Inc., 32 52–54 (upd.)**
Aqua-Chem, Inc., **I** 234; **10** 227
Aqua Glass, **III** 570; **20** 362
Aqua Pure Water Co., **III** 21
Aquafin N.V., **12** 443; **38** 427
Aquarium Supply Co., **12** 230
Aquarius Group, **6** 207
Aquila, **IV** 486
Aquila Energy Corp., **6** 593
Aquitaine. *See* Société Nationale des Petroles d'Aquitaine.
**AR Accessories Group, Inc., 23 20–22**
AR-TIK Systems, Inc., **10** 372
**ARA Services, II 607–08**; **21** 507; **25** 181
Arab Contractors, **III** 753
Arab Japanese Insurance Co., **III** 296
Arab Petroleum Pipeline Co., **IV** 412
Arabian American Oil Co., **I** 570; **IV** 386, 429, 464–65, 512, 536–39, 552, 553, 559; **7** 172, 352; **14** 492–93; **41** 392. *See also* Saudi Arabian Oil Co.
Arabian Gulf Oil Co., **IV** 454
Arabian Investment Banking Corp., **15** 94; **26** 53; **47** 361
Arabian Oil Co., **IV** 451
Aral, **IV** 487
**ARAMARK Corporation, 13 48–50**; **16** 228; **21** 114–15; **35** 415; **41 21–24**
Aramco. *See* Arabian American Oil Co. *and* Saudi Arabian Oil Company.
Aramis Inc., **30** 191
**Arandell Corporation, 37 16–18**
Arapuã. *See* Lojas Arapuã S.A.
Aratex Inc., **13** 49
Aratsu Sekiyu, **IV** 554
**ARBED S.A., IV 24–27**, 53; **22 41–45 (upd.)**; **26** 83; **42** 414
Arbeitsgemeinschaft der öffentlich-rechtlichen Rundfunkanstalten der Bundesrepublick. *See* ARD.
**The Arbitron Company, III** 128; **10** 255, 359; **13** 5; **38 56–61**
Arbor Acres, **13** 103
**Arbor Drugs Inc., 12 21–23**. *See also* CVS Corporation.
Arbor International, **18** 542
Arbor Living Centers Inc., **6** 478
Arbuthnot & Co., **III** 522
**Arby's Inc., II** 614; **8** 536–37; **14 32–34**, 351
ARC. *See* American Rug Craftsmen.
ARC International Corporation, **27** 57
ARC Ltd., **III** 501
ARC Materials Corp., **III** 688
ARC Propulsion, **13** 462
ARCA. *See* Appliance Recycling Centers of America, Inc.
Arcadia Company, **14** 138
**Arcadia Group plc, 28 27–30 (upd.)**, 95–96
Arcadia Partners, **17** 321
Arcadian Corporation, **18** 433; **27** 317–18
Arcadian Marine Service, Inc., **6** 530
**Arcadis NV, 26 21–24**
Arcata Corporation, **12** 413
Arcata National Corp., **9** 305
Arcelik, **I** 478
**Arch Mineral Corporation, IV** 374; **7 32–34**
Arch Petroleum Inc., **39** 331
**Arch Wireless, Inc., 39 23–26**; **41** 265, 267
Archbold Container Co., **35** 390
Archbold Ladder Co., **12** 433
**Archer-Daniels-Midland Co., I 419–21**; **IV** 373; **7** 432–33, 241 **8** 53; **11 21–23 (upd.)**; **17** 207; **22** 85, 426; **23** 384; **25** 241; **31** 234; **32 55–59 (upd.)**
Archer Drug, **III** 10
Archer Management Services Inc., **24** 360
Archers Gilles & Co., **II** 187
Archibald Candy Corporation, **36** 309

Archipelago RediBook, **48** 226, 228
**Archway Cookies, Inc.**, **29 29–31**
ARCO. *See* Atlantic Richfield Company.
**ARCO Chemical Company**, **IV** 376–77, 456–57; **10 110–11**
ARCO Comfort Products Co., **26** 4
Arco Electronics, **9** 323
Arco Pharmaceuticals, Inc., **31** 346
Arco Societa Per L'Industria Elettrotecnica, **II** 82
Arcon Corporation, **26** 287
**Arctco, Inc.**, **12** 400–01; **16 31–34**; **35** 349, 351
Arctic, **III** 479
Arctic Alaska Fisheries Corporation, **14** 515
**Arctic Cat Inc.**, **40 46–50 (upd.)**
Arctic Enterprises, **34** 44
**Arctic Slope Regional Corporation**, **38 62–65**
**ARD**, **41 25–29**
Ardal og Sunndal Verk AS, **10** 439
**Arden Group, Inc.**, **29 32–35**
Ardent Computer Corp., **III** 553
Ardent Risk Services, Inc. *See* General Re Corporation.
Areal Technologies, **III** 715
Argbeit-Gemeinschaft Lurgi und Ruhrchemie, **IV** 534; **47** 342
Argenbright Security Inc. *See* Securicor Plc.
Argentaria Caja Postal y Banco Hipotecario S.A. *See* Banco Bilbao Vizcaya Argentaria S.A.
Argentine National Bank, **14** 46
Argo Communications Corporation, **6** 300
Argon Medical, **12** 327
Argonaut, **I** 523–24; **10** 520–22
Argos, **I** 426; **22** 72
Argos Retail Group, **47** 165, 169
Argos Soditic, **43** 147, 149
**Argosy Gaming Company**, **21 38–41**
Argosy Group LP, **27** 197
Argus Chemical Co., **I** 405
Argus Corp., **IV** 22, 272, 611
Argus Energy, **7** 538
Argus Motor Company, **16** 7
Argyle Television Inc., **19** 204
**Argyll Group PLC**, **I** 241; **II 609–10**, 656; **12** 152–53; **24** 418
Aria Communications, Inc. *See* Ascend Communications, Inc.
Ariba Inc., **38** 432
Ariel Capital Management, **28** 421
**Ariens Company**, **48 32–34**
Aries Technology, **25** 305
**Aris Industries, Inc.**, **15** 275; **16 35–38**
Aristech Chemical Corp., **12** 342
Arizona Airways, **22** 219
Arizona Copper Co., **IV** 177
Arizona Edison Co., **6** 545
Arizona Growth Capital, Inc., **18** 513
AriZona Iced Tea. *See* Ferolito, Vultaggio & Sons.
Arizona One, **24** 455
Arizona Public Service Company, **6** 545–47; **19** 376, 412; **26** 359; **28** 425–26
Arizona Refrigeration Supplies, **14** 297–98
**Arjo Wiggins Appleton p.l.c.**, **13** 458; **27** 513; **34 38–40**
**Ark Restaurants Corp.**, **20 25–27**
Ark Securities Co., **II** 233
Arkady Co., Ltd., **I** 421; **11** 23
**Arkansas Best Corporation**, **16 39–41**; **19** 455; **42** 410
Arkansas Breeders, **II** 585
Arkansas Chemicals Inc., **I** 341
Arkansas Louisiana Gas Company. *See* Arkla, Inc.
Arkansas Power & Light, **V** 618
Arkay Computer, **6** 224
ARKE, **II** 164
Arkia, **23** 184, 186–87
**Arkla, Inc.**, **V 550–51**; **11** 441
**Arla Foods amba**, **48 35–38**
Arlesey Lime and Portland Cement Co., **III** 669
Arlington Corporation, **6** 295
Arlington Motor Holdings, **II** 587
Arlington Securities plc, **24** 84, 87–89
Arlon, Inc., **28** 42, 45
Armani. *See* Giorgio Armani S.p.A.
Armaturindistri, **III** 569
**Armco Inc.**, **III** 259, 721; **IV 28–30**, 125, 171; **10** 448; **11** 5, 255; **12** 353; **19** 8; **26** 407; **30** 282–83; **41** 3, 5
Armin Corp., **III** 645
Armin Poly Film Corp., **III** 645
Armitage Shanks, **III** 671
**Armor All Products Corp.**, **12** 333; **15** 507; **16 42–44**; **22** 148; **26** 349; **47** 235
Armor Elevator, **11** 5
**Armor Holdings, Inc.**, **27 49–51**
Armour. *See* Tommy Armour Golf Co.
Armour & Company, **8** 144; **12** 198; **13** 21, 506; **23** 173
Armour-Dial, **I** 14; **8** 144; **23** 173–74
Armour Food Co., **I** 449–50, 452; **II** 494, 518; **12** 81, 370; **13** 270; **42** 92
Armour Pharmaceutical Co., **III** 56
Armstrong Advertising Co., **I** 36
Armstrong Air Conditioning Inc. *See* Lennox International Inc.
Armstrong Autoparts, **III** 495
Armstrong Communications, **IV** 640
Armstrong Cork Co., **18** 118
Armstrong Nurseries, **I** 272
Armstrong Rees Ederer Inc., **IV** 290
Armstrong-Siddeley Co., **III** 508
Armstrong Tire Co., **15** 355
Armstrong, Whitworth & Co. Ltd., **I** 50; **III** 508; **IV** 257; **24** 85
**Armstrong World Industries, Inc.**, **III 422–24**; **9** 466; **12** 474–75; **22 46–50 (upd.)**, 170–71; **26** 507
Armtek, **7** 297
**Army and Air Force Exchange Service**, **39 27–29**
Army Cooperative Fire Insurance Company, **10** 541
Army Ordnance, **19** 430
Army Signal Corps Laboratories, **10** 96
Arndale, **IV** 696
Arno Press, **IV** 648; **19** 285
**Arnold & Porter**, **35 42–44**
Arnold Communications, **25** 381
Arnold Electric Company, **17** 213
Arnold Foods Co., **II** 498
Arnold Industries Inc., **35** 297
Arnold, Schwinn & Company. *See* Schwinn Cycle and Fitness L.P.
Arnold Thomas Co., **9** 411
**Arnoldo Mondadori Editore S.p.A.**, **IV 585–88**, 675; **19 17–21 (upd.)**
Arnotts Ltd., **II** 481; **26** 57–59
Aro Corp., **III** 527; **14** 477, 508; **15** 225
Aromat Corporation, **III** 710; **7** 303
Aromatic Industries, **18** 69
Arpet Petroleum, **III** 740; **IV** 550
Arpic, **III** 426
Arrosto Coffee Company, **25** 263
**Arrow Electronics, Inc.**, **10 112–14**; **13** 47; **19** 310–11, 313; **29** 414; **30** 175
Arrow Food Distributor, **II** 675
Arrow Furniture Co., **21** 32
Arrow Oil Co., **IV** 401
Arrow Oil Tools, **III** 570; **20** 360
Arrow Pacific Plastics, **48** 334
Arrow Pump Co., **I** 185
Arrow Shirt Co., **24** 384
Arrow Specialty Company, **III** 570; **20** 360
Arrowhead Mills Inc., **27** 197–98; **43** 218–19
Arrowsmith & Silver, **I** 428
Arsam Investment Co., **26** 261
A.B. Arsenalen, **II** 352
Arsynco, Inc., **38** 4
**The Art Institute of Chicago**, **29 36–38**
**Art Van Furniture, Inc.**, **28 31–33**
Artal Luxembourg SA, **33** 446, 449
Artal NV, **40** 51
Artec, **III** 420; **12** 297
Artech Digital Entertainments, Inc., **15** 133
Artek Systems Corporation, **13** 194
Artémis Group, **27** 513
Artesian Manufacturing and Bottling Company, **9** 177
Artesian Resources Corporation, **45** 277
Artesyn Solutions Inc., **48** 369
**Artesyn Technologies Inc.**, **46 35–38 (upd.)**
Artex Enterprises, **7** 256; **25** 167, 253
**Arthur Andersen & Company, Société Coopérative**, **III** 143; **6** 244; **10 115–17**, 174; **16** 92; **25** 358; **29** 392; **46** 186. *See also* Andersen Worldwide.
**Arthur D. Little, Inc.**, **35 45–48**
Arthur H. Fulton, Inc., **42** 363
**Arthur Murray International, Inc.**, **32 60–62**
Arthur Ovens Motor Freight Co., **6** 371
Arthur Rank Organisation, **25** 328
Arthur Tappan & Co., **IV** 604
Arthur Young & Company, **IV** 119; **10** 386; **19** 311; **33** 235. *See also* Ernst & Young.
**Artisan Entertainment Inc.**, **32 63–66 (upd.)**
Artisan Life Insurance Cooperative, **24** 104
Artisoft, Inc., **18** 143
Artistic Direct, Inc., **37** 108
Artists & Writers Press, Inc., **13** 560
Artists Management Group, **38** 164
ArtMold Products Corporation, **26** 342
Artra Group Inc., **40** 119–20
Arts and Entertainment Network. *See* A&E Television Networks.
Arundel Corp, **46** 196
Arvey Corp., **IV** 287
Arvida Corp., **IV** 703
**Arvin Industries, Inc.**, **8 37–40**
ASA Holdings, **47** 30
ASAB, **III** 480
**Asahi Breweries, Ltd.**, **I 220–21**, 282, 520; **13** 454; **20 28–30 (upd.)**; **21** 230, 319–20; **26** 456; **36** 404–05
Asahi Chemical Industry Co., **I** 221; **III** 760; **IV** 326
Asahi Corporation, **16** 84; **40** 93
**Asahi Glass Company, Ltd.**, **I** 363; **III 666–68**; **11** 234–35; **48 39–42 (upd.)**

Asahi Kasei Industry Co. Ltd., **IV** 476
Asahi Komag Co., Ltd., **11** 234
Asahi Kyoei Co., **I** 221
Asahi Manufacturing, **III** 592
Asahi Medix Co., Ltd., **36** 420
Asahi Milk Products, **II** 538
**Asahi National Broadcasting Company, Ltd., 9 29–31**
Asahi Oil, **IV** 542
Asahi Real Estate Facilities Co., Ltd., **6** 427
Asahi Seiko, **III** 595
*Asahi Shimbun*, **9** 29–30
Asahi Trust & Banking, **II** 323
Asano Group, **III** 718
**Asanté Technologies, Inc., 20 31–33**
**ASARCO Incorporated, I** 142; **IV 31–34**; **40** 220–22, 411
ASB Agency, Inc., **10** 92
ASB Air, **47** 286–87
Asbury Associates Inc., **22** 354–55
Asbury Group, **26** 501
ASCAP. *See* The American Society of Composers, Authors and Publishers.
**Ascend Communications, Inc., 24 47–51**; **34** 258
Aschaffenburger Zellstoffwerke AG, **IV** 323–24
ASCO Healthcare, Inc., **18** 195–97
Asco Products, Inc., **22** 413
**Ascom AG, 9 32–34**; **15** 125
Ascometal, **IV** 227
Ascotts, **19** 122
ASD, **IV** 228
**ASDA Group plc, II 611–12**, 513, 629; **11** 240; **28 34–36 (upd.)**
ASEA AB. *See* ABB ASEA Brown Boveri Ltd.
Asean Bintulu Fertilizer, **IV** 518
Asepak Corp., **16** 339
A.B. Asesores Bursatiles, **III** 197–98; **15** 18
ASF. *See* American Steel Foundries.
Asgrow Florida Company, **13** 503
Asgrow Seed Co., **29** 435; **41** 306
Ash Company, **10** 271
Ash Resources Ltd., **31** 398–99
**Ashanti Goldfields Company Limited, 43 37–40**
Ashbourne PLC, **25** 455
Ashitaka Rinsan Kogyo, **IV** 269
**Ashland Inc., 19 22–25**; **27** 316, 318
Ashland Iron and Mining Co., **IV** 28
**Ashland Oil, Inc., I** 420; **IV** 71, 198, 366, **372–74**, 472, 658; **7** 32–33; **8** 99; **9** 108; **11** 22; **18** 279
**Ashley Furniture Industries, Inc., 35 49–51**
**Ashtead Group plc, 34 41–43**
Ashton Joint Venture, **IV** 60, 67
Ashton Mining, **IV** 60
Ashton-Tate Corporation, **9** 81–82; **10** 504–05
**Ashworth, Inc., 26 25–28**
Asia Life Insurance Co., **III** 195–96
Asia Oil Co., Ltd., **IV** 404, 476
Asia Pulp & Paper, **38** 227
Asia Television, **IV** 718; **38** 320
Asia Terminals Ltd., **IV** 718; **38** 319
**AsiaInfo Holdings, Inc., 43 41–44**
Asian Football Confederation, **27** 150
**Asiana Airlines, Inc., 24** 400; **46 39–42**
Asiatic Petroleum Co., **IV** 434, 530
ASICS Corp., **24** 404
Asil çelik, **I** 479
**ASK Group, Inc., 9 35–37**; **25** 34
Ask Mr. Foster Agency, **22** 127; **26** 308
Asland SA, **III** 705, 740
ASMI. *See* Acer Semiconductor Manufacturing Inc.
Aso Cement, **III** 705
**Aspect Telecommunications Corporation, 16** 392–93; **22 51–53**
Aspen Imaging International, Inc., **17** 384
Aspen Mountain Gas Co., **6** 568
**Aspen Skiing Company, II** 170; **15 23–26**, 234; **43** 438
Aspen Systems, **14** 555
**Asplundh Tree Expert Co., 20 34–36**
Assam Co. Ltd., **III** 522–23
Assam Oil Co., **IV** 441, 483–84
Asset Management Company, **25** 86
Asset Marketing Inc. *See* Commercial Financial Services, Inc.
L'Assicuratrice Italiana, **III** 346–47
**Assicurazioni Generali SpA, II** 192; **III 206–09**, 211, 296, 298; **14** 85; **15 27–31 (upd.)**
**Assisted Living Concepts, Inc., 43 45–47**
Associate Venture Investors, **16** 418
Associated Anglo-Atlantic Corp., **III** 670
Associated Aviation Underwriters, **III** 220
Associated Banks of Europe Corp., **II** 184, 239
Associated Biscuit Co., **II** 631
Associated Book Publishers, **8** 527
Associated Bowater Industries, **IV** 258
Associated Brewing Co., **I** 254
**Associated British Foods plc, II 465–66**, 565, 609; **11** 526; **13 51–53 (upd.)**; **24** 475; **41 30–33 (upd.)**
Associated British Maltsters, **II** 500
Associated British Picture Corporation, **I** 531; **II** 157; **22** 193
**Associated British Ports Holdings Plc, 45 29–32**
Associated Bulk Carriers Ltd., **38** 345
Associated City Investment Trust, **IV** 696
Associated Communications Companies, **7** 78; **23** 479
Associated Container Transportation, **23** 161
Associated Cooperative Investment Trust Ltd., **IV** 696
Associated Dairies Ltd., **II** 611
Associated Dry Goods Corp., **V** 134; **12** 54–55; **24** 298
Associated Electrical Industries, Ltd., **II** 25; **III** 502
Associated Employers General Agency, **III** 248
**Associated Estates Realty Corporation, 25 23–25**
Associated Fire Marine Insurance Co., **26** 486
Associated Food Holdings Ltd., **II** 628
Associated Fresh Foods, **II** 611–12; **48** 37
Associated Fuel Pump Systems Corp., **III** 593
Associated Gas & Electric Company, **V** 621, 629–30; **6** 534; **14** 124
Associated Gas Services, Inc., **11** 28
**Associated Grocers, Incorporated, 9 38–40**; **19** 301; **31 22–26 (upd.)**
Associated Grocers of Arizona, **II** 625
Associated Grocers of Colorado, **II** 670
The Associated Group, **10** 45
Associated Hospital Service of New York, **III** 245–46
Associated Iliffe Press, **IV** 666; **17** 397
Associated Indemnity Co., **III** 251
Associated Inns and Restaurants Company of America, **14** 106; **25** 309; **26** 459
Associated Insurance Cos., **III** 194
Associated International Insurance Co. *See* Gryphon Holdings, Inc.
Associated Lead Manufacturers Ltd., **III** 679, 680–81
Associated London Properties, **IV** 705
Associated Madison Insurance, **I** 614
Associated Merchandisers, Inc., **27** 246
Associated Merchandising Corp., **16** 215
**Associated Milk Producers, Inc., 11 24–26**; **48 43–46 (upd.)**
Associated National Insurance of Australia, **III** 309
**Associated Natural Gas Corporation, 11 27–28**
Associated Newspapers Holdings P.L.C., **IV** 686; **19** 118, 120; **37** 121
Associated Octel Company Limited, **10** 290
Associated Oil Co., **IV** 460
Associated Pipeline Contractors, **III** 559
Associated Piping & Engineering Corp., **III** 535
Associated Portland Cement Manufacturers (1900) Ltd., **III** 669–71
**The Associated Press, IV** 629, 669–70; **7** 158; **10** 277; **13 54–56**; **25** 506; **31 27–30 (upd.)**; **34** 11
Associated Publishing Company, **19** 201
Associated Pulp & Paper Mills, **IV** 328
Associated Sales Agency, **16** 389
Associated Spring Co., **III** 581; **13** 73
Associated Stationers, **14** 521, 523
Associated Television, **7** 78
Associated Timber Exporters of British Columbia Ltd., **IV** 307
Associated TV, **IV** 666; **17** 397
Associates First Capital Corporation, **22** 207
Associates Investment Co., **I** 452
**Association des Centres Distributeurs E. Leclerc, 37 19–21**
Assubel, **III** 273
Assurances du Groupe de Paris, **III** 211
Assurances Générales de France, **III** 351; **27** 513; **42** 151
AST Holding Corp., **III** 663, 665
**AST Research, Inc., 9 41–43**; **10** 459, 518–19; **12** 470; **18** 260
Asta Pharma AG, **IV** 71
Asta Werke AG, **IV** 71
Astech, **18** 370
Asteroid, **IV** 97
Astley & Pearce, **10** 277
Aston Brooke Software, **14** 392
**Aston Villa plc, 41 34–36**
Astor Holdings Inc., **22** 32
Astor Trust Co., **II** 229
**Astoria Financial Corporation, 44 31–34**; **46** 316
**Astra AB, I 625–26**, 635, 651; **11** 290; **20 37–40 (upd.)**; **34** 282, 284
Astra Resources, **12** 543
Astrolac, **IV** 498
**Astronics Corporation, 35 52–54**
Astrotech Space Operations, L.P., **11** 429; **37** 365

Astrum International Corp., **12** 88; **13** 453; **16** 20–21; **43** 355
Asur. *See* Grupo Aeropuerto del Sureste, S.A. de C.V.
**ASV, Inc., 34 44–47**
ASW. *See* American Steel & Wire Corp.
Asylum Life Assurance Co., **III** 371
Asylum Records, **23** 33; **26** 150
Asymetrix, **6** 259
AT&E Corp., **17** 430
**AT&T Bell Laboratories, Inc., 13 57–59; 22** 17
**AT&T Corp., I** 462; **II** 13, 54, 61, 66, 80, 88, 120, 125, 252, 403, 430–31, 448; **III** 99, 110–11, 130, 145, 149, 160, 162, 167, 246, 282; **IV** 95, 287; **V 259–64**, 265–68, 269, 272–75, 302–04, 308–12, 318–19, 326–30, 334–36, 339, 341–342, 344–346; **6** 267, 299, 306–07, 326–27, 338–40; **7** 88, 118–19, 146, 288–89, 333; **8** 310–11; **9** 32, 43, 106–07, 138, 320, 321, 344, 478–80, 495, 514; **10** 19, 58, 87, 97, 175, 202–03, 277–78, 286, 431, 433, 455–57; **11** 10, 59, 91, 183, 185, 196, 198, 302, 395, 500–01; **12** 9, 135–36, 162, 544; **13** 212–13, 326, 402, 448; **14** 15, 95, 251–53, 257–61, 318, 336–37, 345, 347, 354, 363–64; **15** 125–26, 228, 455; **16** 223, 318, 368, 467; **18** 30, 32, 74, 76, 111–12, 155, 164–65, 368, 516–18, 569–70; **19** 12, 41; **20** 34, 313; **21** 70, 200–01, 514; **22** 51; **23** 135; **25** 100, 256, 301, 495–99; **26** 187, 225, 431, 520; **27** 363; **28** 242; **29** 59, **39–45 (upd.)**; **30** 99, 339; **33** 34–35, 37, 91, 93–94; **34** 257–59; **38** 269–70, 416; **42** 224; **43** 50, 222, 443; **44** 47; **46** 373; **47** 319–20
**AT&T Istel Ltd., 14 35–36**
**At Home Corporation, 43 48–51**
Ataka & Co., **I** 433; **II** 361
**Atari Corporation, II** 176; **III** 587; **IV** 676; **6** 244; **7** 395–96; **9 44–47**; **10** 284, 482, 485; **13** 472; **23 23–26 (upd.)**; **28** 319; **32** 8
ATAS International, **26** 527, 530
ATC, **III** 760; **13** 280
**Atchison Casting Corporation, 24** 144; **39 30–32**
Atchison, Topeka and Santa Fe Railroad, **V** 507–08; **12** 19–20; **27** 86
ATCO Ltd., **13** 132
ATD Group, **10** 113
ATE Investment, **6** 449
Atelier de Construction Electrique de Delle, **9** 9
ATEQ Corp., **III** 533
Atex, Inc., **III** 476; **7** 162; **10** 34; **36** 172, 174
ATH AG, **IV** 221
Atha Tool Co., **III** 627
Athalon Products, Ltd., **10** 181; **12** 313
Athena Assurances, **27** 513, 515
Athenia Steel Co., **13** 369
Athens National Bank, **III** 190
Athens Piraeus Electricity Co., **IV** 658
Athern, **16** 337
Athlete's Foot, **29** 186
Athletic Attic, **19** 230
Athletic Shoe Company, **17** 243
Athletic Textile Company, Inc., **13** 532
Athletic X-Press, **14** 293
Athleticum Sportmarket, **48** 279
Athol Machine Co., **13** 301
ATI, **IV** 651; **7** 390
Atlalait, **19** 50
**Atlanta Gas Light Company, 6 446–48; 23 27–30 (upd.)**
Atlanta-LaSalle Corporation, **43** 54
Atlanta National Bank, **16** 521
**Atlanta National League Baseball Club, Inc., 43 52–55**
Atlanta Paper Co., **IV** 311; **19** 267
Atlantic & Pacific Tea Company (A&P). *See* Great Atlantic & Pacific Tea Company, Inc.
Atlantic Acceptance Corporation, **7** 95
Atlantic Aircraft Corp., **I** 34; **17** 197
**Atlantic American Corporation, 23** 413; **44 35–37**
Atlantic Auto Finance Corp. *See* United Auto Group, Inc.
Atlantic Cellular, **43** 341
Atlantic Cement Co., **III** 671
Atlantic Coast Carton Company, **19** 77
Atlantic Coast Line Railroad Company. *See* CSX Corporation.
Atlantic Computers, **14** 35
Atlantic Container Lines Ltd., **23** 161
**Atlantic Energy, Inc., 6 449–50**
**The Atlantic Group, 23 31–33**
Atlantic Gulf and Caribbean Airways, **I** 115
Atlantic Import, **I** 285
Atlantic Mills, **27** 188
Atlantic Mutual, **41** 65
Atlantic Precision Instrument Company, **13** 234
Atlantic Precision Works, **9** 72
Atlantic Records, **II** 176; **18** 458; **26** 150
Atlantic Refining Co., **III** 497; **III** 498; **IV** 375–76, 456, 504, 566, 570; **24** 520–21
Atlantic Research Corp., **13** 462
**Atlantic Richfield Company, I** 452; **II** 90, 425; **III** 740; **IV 375–77**, 379, 435, 454, 456–57, 467, 494, 522, 536, 571; **7** 57, 108, 537–38, 558–59; **8** 184, 416; **10** 110; **13** 13, 341; **19** 175; **24** 521, 524; **26** 4, 372; **31 31–34 (upd.)**; **40** 358; **45** 49, 55, 252
Atlantic Sea Products, **13** 103
The Atlantic Seaboard Dispatch. *See* GATX.
Atlantic Securities Ltd., **II** 223; **III** 98
**Atlantic Southeast Airlines, Inc., 26** 439; **47 29–31**
Atlantic Southern Properties, Inc., **6** 449–50
Atlantic Surety Co., **III** 396
Atlantic Transport Company, **19** 198
Atlantic-Union Oil, **IV** 570; **24** 520
Atlantic Wholesalers, **II** 631
Atlantis Energy Inc., **44** 182
Atlantis Group, Inc., **17** 16; **19** 50, 390
Atlantis Ltd., **II** 566
Atlantis Resort and Casino. *See* Sun International Hotels Limited.
**Atlas Air, Inc., 39 33–35**
Atlas America, Inc., **42** 311
Atlas Assurance Co., **III** 370
Atlas Cement Company, **31** 252
Atlas Chemical Industries, **I** 353
**Atlas Copco AB, III 425–27**, 480; **IV** 203; **28 37–41 (upd.)**
Atlas Corp., **I** 58, 512; **10** 316
Atlas Eléctrica S.A., **22** 27
Atlas Hotels, Inc., **V** 164
Atlas Petroleum Ltd., **IV** 449
Atlas Plastics, **19** 414
Atlas Powder Company, **I** 343–44; **22** 260
Atlas Securities, **47** 160
Atlas Shipping, **I** 285
Atlas Steel Works, **I** 572
Atlas Steels, **IV** 191
Atlas Supply Co., **IV** 369
Atlas Tag & Label, **9** 72
**Atlas Van Lines, Inc., 14 37–39**
Atlas Ventures, **25** 96
Atlas-Werke AG, **IV** 88
Atlas Works, **I** 531
Atlatec SA de CV, **39** 192
Atle Byrnestad, **6** 368; **27** 92
**Atmel Corporation, 17 32–34; 19** 313
**Atmos Energy Corporation, 43 56–58**
Atmos Lebensmitteltechnik, **III** 420
Atmospherix Ltd. *See* Blyth Industries, Inc.
ATO Chimie, **I** 303; **IV** 560
**Atochem S.A., I 303–04**, 676; **IV** 525, 547; **7** 484–85
AtoHaas Americas, **26** 425
Atom-Energi, **II** 2; **22** 9
Atomic Austria GmbH, **41** 14–16
ATR, **7** 9, 11
ATS. *See* Magasins Armand Thiéry et Sigrand.
ATT Microelectrica España, **V** 339
Attachmate Corp., **11** 520
ATTC Manufacturing Inc., **48** 5
Atvidabergs Industrier, **25** 463
Atwater McMillian. *See* St. Paul Companies, Inc.
Atwood Resources Inc., **17** 372
ATX Technologies, Inc., **32** 374
ATx Telecom Systems Inc., **31** 124
Au Bon Marché, **26** 160
**Au Bon Pain Co., Inc., 18 35–38; 44** 327
**Au Printemps S.A., V 9–11; 17** 124; **41** 114. *See also* Pinault-Printemps-Redoute S.A.
Aubrey G. Lanston Co., **II** 301
**Auchan, 10** 205; **23** 230; **27** 94; **37 22–24**; **39** 183–85
AUDI AG, **I** 202; **IV** 570; **34** 55
Audio Accessories, Inc., **37** 301
Audio Development Company, **10** 18
Audio International Inc., **36** 159
**Audio King Corporation, 24 52–54**
Audio/Video Affiliates, Inc., **10** 468–69
Audiofina, **44** 377
Audiotronic Holdings, **III** 112
**Audiovox Corporation, 34 48–50**
Audits & Surveys Worldwide Inc., **28** 501, 504
Aufina Bank, **II** 378
Aug. Stenman A.B., **III** 493
Aughton Group, **II** 466
Augsburger Aktienbank, **III** 377
Auguri Mondadori S.p.A., **IV** 586
August Max Woman, **V** 207–08
August Schell's Brewing Co., **22** 421
August Thyssen-Hütte AG, **IV** 221–22
Auguste Metz et Cie, **IV** 24
**Ault Incorporated, 34 51–54**
Aunor Gold Mines, Ltd., **IV** 164
Aunt Fanny's Bakery, **7** 429
**Auntie Anne's, Inc., 35 55–57**
Aura Books plc, **34** 5
Aurec Information and Directory Systems. *See* Amdocs Ltd.
Aurora Dairy Corporation, **37** 195, 198
**Aurora Foods Inc., 26** 384; **32 67–69**

Aurora Products, **II** 543
Aurora Systems, Inc., **21** 135
Aurrera S.A., **35** 459
Aurum Corp., **38** 431
Ausilio Generale di Sicurezza, **III** 206
Ausimont N.V., **8** 271
Ausplay, **13** 319
AUSSAT Ltd., **6** 341
Aussedat-Rey, **IV** 288; **23** 366, 368
**The Austin Company, 8 41–44**
Austin Industries, **25** 402
Austin-Morris, **III** 494
Austin Motor Company, **I** 183; **III** 554; **7** 458
Austin Nichols, **I** 248, 261, 280–81
Austin Quality Foods, **36** 313
Austin Rover, **14** 321
Austral Waste Products, **IV** 248
Australasian Paper and Pulp Co. Ltd., **IV** 248
Australasian Sugar Co., **III** 686
Australasian United Steam Navigation Co., **III** 522
**Australia and New Zealand Banking Group Ltd., II 187–90**
Australia Gilt Co. Group, **II** 422
Australia National Bank, Limited, **10** 170
Australian Airlines, **6** 91, 112; **24** 399–400; **27** 475
Australian and Kandos Cement (Holdings) Ltd., **III** 687, 728; **28** 83
Australian and Overseas Telecommunications Corporation, **6** 341–42
Australian Associated Press, **IV** 669
Australian Automotive Air, Pty. Ltd., **III** 593
Australian Blue Asbestos, **III** 687
Australian Consolidated Investments, Limited, **10** 170
Australian Consolidated Press, **27** 42
Australian Forest Products, **I** 438–39
Australian Guarantee Corporation Ltd., **II** 389–90; **48** 427
Australian Gypsum Industries, **III** 673
Australian Iron & Steel Company, **IV** 45; **22** 105
Australian Metal Co., **IV** 139
Australian Mutual Provident Society, **IV** 61, 697
Australian Paper Co., **IV** 248
Australian Petroleum Pty. Ltd., **25** 471
Australian Tankerships Pty. Ltd., **25** 471
Australian Telecommunications Corporation, **6** 342
Australian United Corp., **II** 389
Australian Window Glass, **III** 726
**Austrian Airlines AG (Österreichische Luftverkehrs AG)**, **27** 26; **33 49–52**; **34** 398; **48** 258, 259
Austrian Industries, **IV** 485, 486
Austrian National Bank, **IV** 230
Austrian Star Gastronomie GmbH, **48** 63
Austro-Americana, **6** 425
Austro-Daimler, **I** 138, 206; **11** 31
**Authentic Fitness Corp.**, **16** 511; **20 41–43**; **46** 450
Auto Avio Costruzione, **13** 219
Auto Coil Springs, **III** 581
Auto-Flo Corp., **III** 569; **20** 360
Auto Ordnance Corporation, **19** 430–31
Auto Parts Wholesale, **26** 348
Auto Shack. *See* AutoZone, Inc.
Auto Strop Safety Razor Co., **III** 27–28
Auto-Trol Technology, **14** 15
Auto Union, **I** 150
**Auto Value Associates, Inc.**, **25 26–28**
**Autobytel Inc.**, **47 32–34**
**Autodesk, Inc.**, **10 118–20**
Autogrill, **24** 195
Autolite, **I** 29, 142; **III** 555
Autoliv AB, **41** 369
**Autologic Information International, Inc.**, **20 44–46**; **26** 518–20
Automat, **II** 614
Automated Building Components, **III** 735
Automated Communications, Inc., **8** 311
Automated Design Systems, **25** 348
Automated Loss Prevention Systems, **11** 445
Automated Security (Holdings) PLC, **11** 444
Automated Wagering Systems, **III** 128
Automatic Coil Corp., **33** 359, 361
**Automatic Data Processing, Inc.**, **III 117–19**; **9 48–51 (upd.)**, 125, 173; **21** 69; **46** 333; **47 35–39 (upd.)**
Automatic Fire Alarm Co., **III** 644
Automatic Manufacturing Corporation, **10** 319
Automatic Payrolls, Inc., **III** 117
Automatic Retailers of America, Inc., **II** 607; **13** 48
Automatic Sprinkler Corp. of America. *See* Figgie International, Inc.
Automatic Telephone & Electric, **II** 81
Automatic Toll Systems, **19** 111
Automatic Vaudeville Arcades Co., **II** 154
Automatic Voting Machine Corporation. *See* American Locker Group Incorporated.
Automobile Insurance Co., **III** 181–82
**Automobiles Citroen**, **I** 162, 188; **III** 676; **IV** 722; **V** 237; **7 35–38**; **11** 103; **16** 121, 420
**Automobili Lamborghini Holding S.p.A.**, **34 55–58 (upd.)**
**Automobili Lamborghini S.p.A.**, **13 60–62**, 219
Automotive Components Group Worldwide, **10** 325
Automotive Diagnostics, **10** 492
Automotive Group. *See* Lear Seating Corporation.
Automotive Industries Holding Inc., **16** 323
AutoNation USA, **41** 239. *See also* Republic Industries, Inc.
Autonet, **6** 435
Autonom Computer, **47** 36
Autophon AG, **9** 32
Autosite.com, **47** 34
**Autotote Corporation**, **20 47–49**
AutoTrol Technology, **III** 111
Autoweb.com, **47** 34
AUTOWORKS Holdings, Inc., **24** 205
**AutoZone, Inc.**, **9 52–54**; **26** 348; **31 35–38 (upd.)**; **36** 364
**AVA AG (Allgemeine Handelsgesellschaft der Verbraucher AG)**, **33 53–56**
**Avado Brands, Inc.**, **31 39–42**; **46** 234
Avalon Publishing Group. *See* Publishers Group, Inc.
Avana Group, **II** 565
Avantel, **27** 304
Avaya Inc., **41** 287, 289–90
Avco. *See* Aviation Corp. of the Americas.
Avco Corp., **34** 433
**Avco Financial Services Inc.**, **13 63–65**
Avco National Bank, **II** 420
Avdel, **34** 433
Avecor Cardiovascular Inc., **8** 347; **22** 360
**Aveda Corporation**, **24 55–57**
**Avedis Zildjian Co.**, **38 66–68**
Avendt Group, Inc., **IV** 137
Avenir, **III** 393
Avenor Inc., **25** 13
Aventis, **34** 280, 283–84; **38** 378, 380
**Avery Dennison Corporation**, **IV 251–54**; **15** 229, 401; **17 27–31 (upd.)**, 445
Avesta Steel Works Co., **I** 553–54
Avex Electronics Inc., **40** 68
Avfuel, **11** 538
Avgain Marine A/S, **7** 40; **41** 42
Avia Group International, Inc., **V** 376–77; **26** 397–99
Aviacion y Comercio, **6** 95–96
**Aviacionny Nauchno-Tehnicheskii Komplex im. A.N. Tupoleva**, **24 58–60**
AVIACO. *See* Aviacion y Comercio.
**Avianca Aerovías Nacionales de Colombia SA**, **36 52–55**
Aviation Corp. of the Americas, **I** 48, 78, 89, 115, 530; **III** 66; **6** 75; **9** 497–99; **10** 163; **11** 261, 427; **12** 379, 383; **13** 64
Aviation Inventory Management Co., **28** 5
Aviation Power Supply, **II** 16
**Aviation Sales Company**, **41 37–39**
Aviation Services West, Inc. *See* Scenic Airlines, Inc.
**Avid Technology Inc.**, **38 69–73**
Avimo, **47** 7–8
Avion Coach Corporation, **I** 76; **III** 484; **11** 363; **22** 206
**Avions Marcel Dassault-Breguet Aviation**, **I 44–46**; **7** 11; **7** 205; **8** 314. *See also* Groupe Dassault Aviation SA.
**Avis, Inc.**, **I** 30, 446, 463; **II** 468; **III** 502; **IV** 370; **6** 348–49, **356–58**, 392–93; **8** 33; **9** 284; **10** 419; **11** 198; **16** 379–80; **22** 524
**Avis Rent A Car, Inc.**, **22 54–57 (upd.)**; **24** 9; **25** 93, 143, 420–22
Avisco, **I** 317, 365, 442–43; **V** 359; **17** 117
Avisun Corp., **IV** 371
Avnet Electronics Supply Co., **19** 311, 313
**Avnet Inc.**, **9 55–57**; **10** 112–13; **13** 47
**Avon Products, Inc.**, **III** 13, **15–16**, 62; **8** 329; **9** 331; **11** 282, 366; **12** 314, 435; **13** 38; **14** 501–02; **17** 186; **19 26–29 (upd.)**, 253; **21** 49, 51; **25** 292; 456; **27** 429; **30** 64, 308–09; **46 43–46 (upd.)**
Avon Publications, Inc., **IV** 627; **19** 201, 204
Avon Rubber plc, **23** 146
Avoncraft Construction Co., **I** 512
**Avondale Industries, Inc.**, **I** 512–14; **7 39–41**; **41 40–43 (upd.)**
Avondale Mills, Inc., **8** 558–60; **9** 466
Avondown Properties Ltd., **IV** 711
Avro. *See* A.V. Roe & Company.
AVS, **III** 200
Avstar, **38** 72
Avtech Corp., **36** 159
Avtex Fibers Inc., **I** 443; **11** 134
AVX Corporation, **21** 329, 331
AW North Carolina Inc., **48** 5
AWA. *See* America West Holdings Corporation.

AWA Defence Industries (AWADI). *See* British Aerospace Defence Industries.
Award Foods, **II** 528
Awesome Transportation, Inc., **22** 549
**AXA Colonia Konzern AG, III** 209, **210–12**; **15** 30; **21** 147; **27 52–55**
Axe-Houghton Associates Inc., **41** 208
**Axel Johnson Group, I 553–55**
**Axel Springer Verlag AG, IV 589–91**; **20 50–53 (upd.)**; **23** 86; **35** 452
Axelrod Foods, **II** 528
Axon Systems Inc., **7** 336
Ayco Corp., **II** 398; **10** 62
**Aydin Corp., 19 30–32**
Ayerst, **I** 623
Ayr-Way Stores, **27** 452
AYS. *See* Alternative Youth Services, Inc.
Ayshire Collieries, **IV** 18
**Azcon Corporation, 23 34–36**
Azerty, **25** 13
Azienda Generale Italiana Petroli. *See* Agip SpA.
Azienda Nazionale Idrogenazione Combustibili, **IV** 419–22
AZL Resources, **7** 538
Aznar International, **14** 225
Azon Limited, **22** 282
AZP Group Inc., **6** 546
**Aztar Corporation, 13 66–68**
Azteca, **18** 211, 213
Azuma Leather Co. Ltd., **V** 380
Azuma Shiki Manufacturing, **IV** 326
Azusa Valley Savings Bank, **II** 382

B&D. *See* Barker & Dobson.
**B&G Foods, Inc., 40 51–54**
B & K Steel Fabrications, Inc., **26** 432
B&M Baked Beans, **40** 53
B & O. *See* Baltimore and Ohio Railroad.
B&Q plc, **V** 106, 108; **24** 266, 269–70
B&S. *See* Binney & Smith Inc.
B&W Diesel, **III** 513
**B.A.T. Industries PLC, 14** 77; **16** 242; **22 70–73 (upd.)**; **25** 154–56; **29** 196. *See also* Brown & Williamson Tobacco Corporation
B. B. & R. Knight Brothers, **8** 200; **25** 164
B.B. Foods, **13** 244
B-Bar-B Corp., **16** 340
B.C. Rail Telecommunications, **6** 311
B.C. Sugar, **II** 664
B.C. Ziegler and Co. *See* The Ziegler Companies, Inc.
**B. Dalton Bookseller Inc., 10** 136; **13** 545; **16** 160; **18** 136; **25 29–31**; **30** 68
B-E Holdings, **17** 60
**B/E Aerospace, Inc., 30 72–74**
B.F. Ehlers, **I** 417; **24** 32
B.F. Goodrich Co. *See* The BFGoodrich Company.
B.F. Walker, Inc., **11** 354
B.I.C. America, **17** 15, 17
B.J.'s Wholesale, **12** 335
**The B. Manischewitz Company, LLC, 31 43–46**
B. Perini & Sons, Inc., **8** 418
B.R. Simmons, **III** 527
B.S. Bull & Company. *See* Supervalu Inc.
B. Stroh Brewing Co., **I** 290
B.T.I. Chemicals Ltd., **I** 313; **10** 154
B Ticino, **21** 350
B.V. Tabak Export & Import Compagnie, **12** 109
BA. *See* British Airways.
**BAA plc, 10 121–23**; **29** 509, 511; **33 57–61 (upd.)**; **37** 8
Bålforsens Kraft AB, **28** 444
**Baan Company, 25 32–34**; **26** 496, 498
**Babbage's, Inc., 10 124–25**
Babcock & Wilcox Co., **III** 465–66, 516, 559–60; **V** 621; **23** 199; **37** 242–45
BABE. *See* British Aerospace plc.
Baby Dairy Products, **48** 438
Baby Furniture and Toy Supermarket, **V** 203
**Baby Superstore, Inc., 15 32–34**
Babybird Co., Ltd., **V** 150
BabyCenter.com, **37** 130
Babyliss, S.A., **17** 110
BAC. *See* Barclays American Corp. *and* British Aircraft Corporation.
**Bacardi Limited, 18 39–42**
**Baccarat, 23** 241; **24 61–63**; **27** 421, 423
Bache & Company, **III** 340; **8** 349
Bachman Foods, **15** 139
Bachman Holdings, Inc., **14** 165; **34** 144–45
**Bachman's Inc., 22 58–60**; **24** 513
Bachoco. *See* Industrias Bacholo, S.A. de C.V.
Bachrach Advertising, **6** 40
**Back Bay Restaurant Group, Inc., 20 54–56**
**Back Yard Burgers, Inc., 45 33–36**
Backer & Spielvogel, **I** 33; **12** 168; **14** 48–49; **22** 296
Backer Spielvogel Bates Worldwide **42** 329. *See also* Bates Worldwide, Inc.
Backroom Systems Group, **II** 317
Bacon & Matheson Drop Forge Co., **I** 185
Bacova Guild, Ltd., **17** 76
Bad Boy Entertainment, **31** 269
Baddour, Inc. *See* Fred's, Inc.
Badger Co., **II** 86
Badger Illuminating Company, **6** 601
**Badger Meter, Inc., 22 61–65**
Badger Paint and Hardware Stores, **II** 419
**Badger Paper Mills, Inc., 15 35–37**
Badin-Defforey, **27** 93
Badische Analin & Soda Fabrik A.G., **I** 305
BAe. *See* British Aerospace plc.
BAE Systems, **41** 412
BAFS. *See* Bangkok Aviation Fuel Services Ltd.
Bahia de San Francisco Television, **IV** 621
**Bahlsen GmbH & Co. KG, 44 38–41**
Bailey, Banks & Biddle, **16** 559
Bailey Controls, **III** 560
Bailey's Pub and Grille. *See* Total Entertainment Restaurant Corporation.
Bain & Co., **III** 429; **9** 343; **21** 143
Bain Capital, Inc., **14** 244–45; **16** 466; **20** 18; **24** 456, 482; **25** 254; **26** 184; **38** 107–09
Baird, **7** 235, 237
**Bairnco Corporation, 28 42–45**
**Bajaj Auto Limited, 39 36–38**
BÅKAB. *See* Bålforsens Kraft AB.
Bakelite Corp., **I** 399; **9** 517; **13** 231
**Baker and Botts, L.L.P., 28 46–49**
Baker & Co., **IV** 78
Baker & Crane, **II** 318; **17** 323
**Baker & Hostetler LLP, 40 55–58**
**Baker & McKenzie, 10 126–28**; **42 17–20 (upd.)**
**Baker & Taylor Corporation, I** 548; **16 45–47**; **43 59–62 (upd.)**
Baker Casing Shoe Co., **III** 429
Baker Cummins Pharmaceuticals Inc., **11** 208
Baker Extract Co., **27** 299
**Baker Hughes Incorporated, III 428–29**; **11** 513; **22 66–69 (upd.)**; **25** 74
Baker Industries, Inc., **III** 440; **8** 476; **13** 124
Baker International Corp., **III** 428–29
Baker Oil Tools. *See* Baker Hughes Incorporated.
Baker-Raulang Co., **13** 385
Bakers Best Snack Food Corporation, **24** 241
Bakers Square. *See* VICORP Restaurants, Inc.
Bakersfield Savings and Loan, **10** 339
Bakery Products Inc., **IV** 410
Balair Ltd., **I** 122
**Balance Bar Company, 32 70–72**
**Balchem Corporation, 42 21–23**
Balco, Inc., **7** 479–80; **27** 415
Balcor Co., **II** 398; **IV** 703
Balcor, Inc., **10** 62
Bald Eagle Corporation, **45** 126
**Baldor Electric Company, 21 42–44**
Baldwin-Ehret-Hill Inc., **28** 42
Baldwin Filters, Inc., **17** 104
Baldwin Hardware Manufacturing Co., **III** 570; **20** 361
Baldwin-Montrose Chemical Co., Inc., **31** 110
**Baldwin Piano & Organ Company, 16** 201; **18 43–46**
Baldwin Rubber Industries, **13** 79
**Baldwin Technology Company, Inc., 25 35–39**
Baldwin-United Corp., **III** 254, 293
Baldwins Ltd., **III** 494
Bålforsens Kraft AB, **IV** 339–40; **28** 444
**Balfour Beatty Construction Ltd., III** 433–34; **36 56–60 (upd.)**
Balfour Company, L.G., **19** 451–52
Balikpapan Forest Industries, **I** 504
Ball & Young Adhesives, **9** 92
Ball-Bartoe Aircraft Corp., **I** 598; **10** 130
**Ball Corporation, I 597–98**; **10 129–31 (upd.)**; **13** 254, 256; **15** 129; **16** 123; **30** 38
The Ball Ground Reps, Inc., **26** 257
Ball Industries, Inc., **26** 539
Ball Stalker Inc., **14** 4
Ballantine & Sons Ltd., **I** 263
Ballantine Beer, **6** 27
Ballantine Books, **13** 429; **31** 376–77, 379
**Ballantyne of Omaha, Inc., 27 56–58**
Ballard & Ballard Co., **II** 555
**Ballard Medical Products, 21 45–48**
Ballast Nedam Group, **24** 87–88
Balli Group plc, **26** 527, 530
Bally Entertainment Corp., **19** 205, 207
Bally Gaming International, **15** 539
**Bally Manufacturing Corporation, III 430–32**; **6** 210; **10** 375, 482; **12** 107; **15** 538–39; **17** 316–17, 443; **41** 214–15
**Bally Total Fitness Holding Corp., 25 40–42**
**Bâloise-Holding, 40 59–62**
**Baltek Corporation, 34 59–61**
AB Baltic, **III** 418–19
Baltic Cable, **15** 521
Baltica, **27** 54
Baltimar Overseas Limited, **25** 469

Baltimore & Ohio Railroad, **I** 584; **II** 329. *See also* CSX Corporation.
Baltimore Aircoil Company, **7** 30–31
**Baltimore Gas and Electric Company, V 552–54; 11** 388; **25 43–46 (upd.)**
Baltimore Paper Box Company, **8** 102
**Baltimore Technologies Plc, 42 24–26**
Baltino Foods, **13** 383
Balzaretti-Modigliani, **III** 676; **16** 121
Balzers Process Systems GmbH, **48** 30
Bamberger's of New Jersey, **V** 169; **8** 443
Banamex, **22** 285; **23** 170; **34** 81. *See also* Banco Nacional de Mexico.
Banana Boat Holding Corp., **15** 359
Banana Brothers, **31** 229
Banana Importers of Ireland, **38** 197
**Banana Republic Inc., V** 61–62; **18** 193–94; **25 47–49; 31** 51–52
Banc Internacional d'Andorra-Banca Mora, **48** 51
**Banc One Corporation, 9** 475; **10 132–34; 11** 181. *See also* Bank One Corporation.
Banca Brasiliana Italo-Belga, **II** 270
Banca Coloniale di Credito, **II** 271
**Banca Commerciale Italiana SpA, I** 368, 465, 467; **II 191–93**, 242, 271, 278, 295, 319; **III** 207–08, 347; **17** 324
BancA Corp., **11** 305
Banca d'America e d'Italia, **II** 280
Banca Dalmata di Sconto, **II** 271
Banca de Gottardo, **II** 361
Banca di Genova, **II** 270
Banca Internazionale Lombarda, **II** 192
Banca Italiana di Sconto, **II** 191
Banca Italo-Cinese, **II** 270
Banca Italo-Viennese, **II** 270
Banca Jacquet e Hijos, **II** 196
Banca Luis Roy Sobrino, **II** 196
Banca Nazionale de Lavoro, **II** 239
Banca Nazionale dell'Agricoltura, **II** 272
Banca Nazionale di Credito, **II** 271
Banca Serfin. *See* Grupo Financiero Serfin, S.A.
Banca Unione di Credito, **II** 270
Bancard Systems, **24** 395
BancBoston Capital, **48** 412
BancFinancial Services Corporation, **25** 187
BancItaly Corp., **II** 226–27, 288, 536; **13** 528
BancMortgage Financial Corp., **25** 185, 187
Banco Aleman-Panameno, **II** 521
Banco Aliança S.A., **19** 34
Banco Azteca, **19** 189
**Banco Bilbao Vizcaya Argentaria S.A., 48 47–51 (upd.)**
**Banco Bilbao Vizcaya, S.A., II 194–96**
**Banco Bradesco S.A., 13 69–71; 19** 33
Banco Capitalizador de Monterrey, **19** 189
**Banco Central, II 197–98**. *See also* Banco Santander Central Hispano S.A.
Banco Central de Crédito. *See* Banco Itaú.
Banco Chemical (Portugal) S.A. *See* Chemical Banking Corp.
Banco Comercial, **19** 188
Banco Comercial de Puerto Rico, **41** 311
Banco Credito y Ahorro Ponceno, **41** 312
Banco da América, **19** 34
Banco de Credito Local, **48** 51
Banco de Londres, Mexico y Sudamerica. *See* Grupo Financiero Serfin, S.A.
Banco de Madrid, **40** 147
Banco de Mexico, **19** 189
Banco de Ponce, **41** 313
Banco del Norte, **19** 189
Banco di Roma, **I** 465, 467; **II** 191, 257, 271
Banco di Santo Spirito, **I** 467
**Banco do Brasil S.A., II 199–200**
Banco Español de Credito, **II** 195, 198; **IV** 160
**Banco Espírito Santo e Comercial de Lisboa S.A., 15 38–40**
Banco Federal de Crédito. *See* Banco Itaú.
Banco Frances y Brasiliero, **19** 34
Banco Industrial de Bilbao, **II** 195
Banco Industrial de Monterrey, **19** 189
Banco Italo-Belga, **II** 270, 271
Banco Italo-Egiziano, **II** 271
**Banco Itaú S.A., 19 33–35**
Banco Nacional de Cuba, **II** 345
Banco Nacional de Mexico, **9** 333; **19** 188, 193
Banco Pinto de Mahalhães, **19** 34
Banco Popolar, **III** 348; **6** 97. *See also* Popular, Inc.
Banco Português do Brasil S.A., **19** 34
**Banco Santander Central Hispano S.A., 36 61–64 (upd.); 42** 349
Banco Serfin, **34** 82
Banco Sul Americano S.A., **19** 34
Banco Trento & Bolanzo, **II** 240
Banco União Comercial, **19** 34
Banco Vascongado, **II** 196
BancOhio National Bank in Columbus, **9** 475
Bancomer S.A., **19** 12; **48** 47
Bancorp Leasing, Inc., **14** 529
BancorpSouth, Inc., **14** 40–41
Bancroft Racket Co., **III** 24
BancSystems Association Inc., **9** 475, 476
**Bandag, Inc., 19 36–38**, 454–56
Bandai America Inc., **23** 388; **25** 488
Bandai Co., Ltd., **38** 415
Banesto. *See* Banco Español de Credito.
Banexi, **II** 233
**Banfi Products Corp., 36 65–67**
**Bang & Olufsen Holding A/S, 37 25–28**
Bangkok Airport Hotel, **6** 123–24
Bangkok Aviation Fuel Services Ltd., **6** 123–24
Bangladesh Krishi Bank, **31** 220
Bangor and Aroostook Railroad Company, **8** 33
Bangor Mills, **13** 169
Bangor Punta Alegre Sugar Corp., **30** 425
Bangor Punta Corp., **I** 452, 482; **II** 403
Banister Continental Corp. *See* BFC Construction Corporation.
**Bank Austria AG, 23 37–39**
**Bank Brussels Lambert, II 201–03**, 295, 407
Bank Bumiputra, **IV** 519
Bank Central Asia, **18** 181
Bank CIC-Union Européenne A.G., **II** 272
Bank du Louvre, **27** 423
Bank Européene de Credità Moyen Terme, **II** 319; **17** 324
Bank for International Settlements, **II** 368
Bank für Elektrische Unternehmungen. *See* Elektrowatt AG.
Bank für Gemeinwirtschaft, **II** 239
**Bank Hapoalim B.M., II 204–06; 25** 266, 268
Bank Hofmann, **21** 146–47
Bank Leu, **I** 252; **21** 146–47
Bank Leumi Le-Israel, **25** 268
Bank of Adelaide, **II** 189
**Bank of America Corporation, I** 536–37; **II** 252–55, 280, 288–89, 347, 382; **III** 218; **6** 385; **9** 50, 123–24, 333, 536; **12** 106, 466; **14** 170; **18** 516; **22** 542; **25** 432; **26** 486; **46 47–54 (upd.)**; **47** 37
Bank of Antwerp, **IV** 497
Bank of Asheville, **II** 336
Bank of Australasia, **II** 187–89
The Bank of Bishop and Co., Ltd., **11** 114
**Bank of Boston Corporation, II 207–09; 7** 114; **12** 31; **13** 467; **14** 90
Bank of Brandywine Valley, **25** 542
Bank of Britain, **14** 46–47
Bank of British Columbia, **II** 244, 298
Bank of British Honduras, **II** 344
Bank of British North America, **II** 220
Bank of California, **II** 322, 490. *See also* Union Bank of California.
Bank of Canada, **II** 210, 376
Bank of Central and South America, **II** 344
Bank of Chicago, **III** 270
Bank of China, **II** 298
Bank of Chosen, **II** 338
Bank of Commerce, **II** 331
Bank of Delaware, **25** 542
Bank of England, **II** 217, 235–36, 306–07, 318–19, 333–34, 357, 421–22, 427–28; **III** 234, 280; **IV** 119, 366, 382, 705, 711; **10** 8, 336; **14** 45–46; **17** 324–25; **47** 227
Bank of Finland, **III** 648
Bank of France, **II** 232, 264–65, 354; **III** 391
Bank of Hamilton, **II** 244
Bank of Hindustan, **IV** 699
Bank of Ireland, **16** 13–14; **19** 198
Bank of Israel, **II** 206
Bank of Italy, **I** 536; **II** 192, 226, 271–72, 288; **III** 209, 347; **8** 45
The Bank of Jacksonville, **9** 58
Bank of Japan, **I** 519; **II** 291, 325
Bank of Kobe, **II** 371
Bank of Lee County, **14** 40
Bank of Liverpool, **II** 236
Bank of London and South America, **II** 308
Bank of Manhattan Co., **II** 247–48
Bank of Mexico Ltd., **19** 188
The Bank of Milwaukee, **14** 529
**Bank of Mississippi, Inc., 14 40–41**
**Bank of Montreal, II 210–12**, 231, 375; **26** 304; **46 55–58 (upd.)**
Bank of Nettleton, **14** 40
Bank of New Brunswick, **II** 221
**Bank of New England Corporation, II 213–15; 9** 229
Bank of New Orleans, **11** 106
Bank of New Queensland, **II** 188
Bank of New South Wales, **II** 188–89. *See also* Westpac Banking Corporation.
**Bank of New York Company, Inc., II** 192, **216–19**, 247; **34** 82; **46 59–63 (upd.)**
Bank of North Mississippi, **14** 41
**Bank of Nova Scotia, II 220–23**, 345; **IV** 644
Bank of Oklahoma, **22** 4
Bank of Ontario, **II** 210
Bank of Osaka, **II** 360
Bank of Ottawa, **II** 221
Bank of Pasadena, **II** 382
Bank of Queensland, **II** 188

The Bank of Scotland. *See* The Governor and Company of the Bank of Scotland.
Bank of Sherman, **14** 40
Bank of Spain, **II** 194, 197
Bank of the Ohio Valley, **13** 221
Bank of the People, **II** 210
Bank of the United States, **II** 207, 216, 247
Bank of the West, **II** 233
**Bank of Tokyo, Ltd., II 224–25**, 276, 301, 341, 358; **IV** 151; **12** 138; **16** 496, 498; **24** 358
**Bank of Tokyo-Mitsubishi Ltd., 15 41–43 (upd.)**, 431; **26** 454, 457; **38** 387
Bank of Toronto, **II** 375–76
Bank of Tupelo, **14** 40
Bank of Upper Canada, **II** 210
Bank of Wales, **10** 336, 338
Bank of Western Australia, **II** 187
Bank of Winterthur, **II** 378
**Bank One Corporation, 36 68–75 (upd.)**
Bank Powszechny Depozytowy, **IV** 119
Bank-R Systems Inc., **18** 517
Bank voor Handel en Nijverheid, **II** 304
**BankAmerica Corporation, II 226–28**, 436; **8 45–48 (upd.)**, 295, 469, 471; **13** 69; **17** 546; **18** 518; **25** 187; **26** 65; **47** 401. *See also* Bank of America
BankBoston. *See* FleetBoston Financial Corporation.
BankCard America, Inc., **24** 394
Bankers and Shippers Insurance Co., **III** 389
Bankers Co., **II** 230
Bankers Corporation, **14** 473
Bankers Investment, **II** 349
Bankers Life and Casualty Co., **10** 247; **16** 207; **33** 110
Bankers Life Co., **III** 328–30
Bankers National Bank, **II** 261
Bankers National Life Insurance Co., **II** 182; **10** 246
Bankers Trust Co., **38** 411
**Bankers Trust New York Corporation, I** 601; **II** 211, **229–31**, 330, 339; **III** 84–86; **10** 425; **11** 416; **12** 165, 209; **13** 188, 466; **17** 559; **19** 34; **22** 102; **25** 268; 317
Bankhaus IG Herstatt, **II** 242
BankVermont Corp., **II** 208
BankWatch, **37** 143, 145
**Banner Aerospace, Inc., 14 42–44; 37 29–32 (upd.)**
Banner International, **13** 20
Banner Life Insurance Company, **III** 273; **24** 284
BanPonce Corporation, **41** 312
Banque Belge et Internationale en Egypte, **II** 295
Banque Belge pour l'Etranger, **II** 294
Banque Belgo-Zairoise, **II** 294
Banque Bruxelles Lambert. *See* Bank Brussels Lambert.
Banque Commerciale du Maroc, **II** 272
Banque Commerciale-Basle, **II** 270
Banque d'Anvers/Bank van Antwerpen, **II** 294–95
Banque de Bruxelles, **II** 201–02, 239
Banque de Credit et de Depot des Pays Bas, **II** 259
Banque de France, **14** 45–46
Banque de l'Indochine et de Suez, **II** 259
Banque de l'Union Européenne, **II** 94
Banque de l'Union Parisienne, **II** 270; **IV** 497, 557
Banque de la Construction et les Travaux Public, **II** 319; **17** 324
Banque de la Société Générale de Belgique, **II** 294–95
Banque de Louvain, **II** 202
Banque de Paris et des Pays-Bas, **II** 136, 259; **10** 346; **19** 188–89; **33** 179
Banque de Reports et de Depots, **II** 201
Banque du Congo Belge, **II** 294
Banque Européenne pour l'Amerique Latine, **II** 294
Banque Française et Espagnol en Paris, **II** 196
Banque Francaise pour le Commerce et l'Industrie, **II** 232, 270
Banque Génerale des Pays Roumains, **II** 270
Banque Générale du Luxembourg, **II** 294
Banque Indosuez, **II** 429
Banque Internationale de Bruxelles, **II** 201–02
Banque Internationale de Luxembourg, **II** 239; **42** 111
Banque Italo-Belge, **II** 294
Banque Italo-Francaise de Credit, **II** 271
Banque Lambert, **II** 201–02
**Banque Nationale de Paris S.A., II 232–34**, 239; **III** 201, 392–94; **9** 148; **13** 203; **15** 309; **19** 51; **33** 119. *See also* BNP Paribas Group.
Banque Nationale Pour le Commerce et l'Industrie, **II** 232–33
Banque Nordique du Commerce, **II** 366
Banque Orea, **II** 378
Banque Paribas, **II** 192, 260; **IV** 295; **19** 225. *See* BNP Paribas Group.
Banque Rothschild, **IV** 107
Banque Sino-Belge, **II** 294
Banque Stern, **II** 369
La Banque Suisse et Française. *See* Crédit Commercial de France.
Banque Transatlantique, **II** 271
Banque Worms, **III** 393; **27** 514
Banquet Foods Corp., **II** 90, 494; **12** 81; **42** 91
**Banta Corporation, 12 24–26; 19** 333; **32 73–77 (upd.)**
Bantam Ball Bearing Company, **13** 522
Bantam Books, Inc., **III** 190–91
Bantam Doubleday Dell Publishing Group, **IV** 594; **13** 429; **15** 51; **27** 222; **31** 375–76, 378
**Banyan Systems Inc., 25 50–52**
Banyu Pharmaceutical Co., **I** 651; **11** 290; **34** 283
Baoshan Iron and Steel, **19** 220
BAP of New York, Inc., **15** 246
BAPCO, **III** 745
Bar Technologies, Inc., **26** 408
Barat. *See* Barclays PLC.
Barber Dental Supply Inc., **19** 291
Barber-Greene, **21** 502
Barberet & Blanc, **I** 677
Barcel, **19** 192
Barclay Furniture Co., **12** 300
Barclay Group, **I** 335; **10** 290
Barclay White Inc., **38** 436
Barclays Business Credit, **13** 468
**Barclays PLC, I** 604–05; **II** 202, 204, **235–37**, 239, 244, 308, 319, 333, 383, 422, 429; **III** 516; **IV** 23, 722; **7** 332–33; **8** 118; **11** 29–30; **17** 324–25; **20 57–60 (upd.)**; **25** 101; **28** 167; **47** 227
**BarclaysAmerican Mortgage Corporation, 11 29–30**
Barco Manufacturing Co., **16** 8; **26** 541
**Barco NV, 44 42–45**
Barcolo Manufacturing, **15** 103; **26** 100
Barden Cablevision, **IV** 640; **26** 273
Bardon Group. *See* Aggregate Industries plc.
Bareco Products, **15** 352
Barefoot Inc., **23** 428, 431
Bari Shoes, Inc., **22** 213
**Barilla G. e R. Fratelli S.p.A., 17 35–37**
Baring Brothers & Co., Ltd., **39** 5
**Barings PLC, III** 699; **14 45–47**
Barker & Dobson, **II** 629; **47** 367
Barker and Company, Ltd., **13** 286
**Barlow Rand Ltd., I** 288–89, **422–24**; **IV** 22, 96
Barlow Specialty Advertising, Inc., **26** 341
**Barmag AG, 39 39–42**
Barmer Bankverein, **II** 238, 241
Barnato Brothers, **IV** 21, 65; **7** 122
Barneda Carton SA, **41** 326
**Barnes & Noble, Inc., 10 135–37; 12** 172; **13** 494, 545; **14** 61–62; **15** 62; **16** 160; **17** 524; **23** 370; **25** 17, 29–30; **30 67–71 (upd.)**; **41** 61; **43** 78, 408
Barnes Group, **III** 581
Barnes-Hind, **III** 56, 727
**Barnett Banks, Inc., 9 58–60**
Barnett Brass & Copper Inc., **9** 543
**Barnett Inc., 28 50–52**
Barnetts, Hoares, Hanbury and Lloyds, **II** 306
**Barney's, Inc., 28 53–55**; **36** 290, 292
Barnstead/Thermolyne Corporation, **14** 479–80
Baroid, **19** 467–68
**Baron Philippe de Rothschild S.A., 39 43–46**
Barr & Stroud Ltd., **III** 727
**Barr Laboratories, Inc., 26 29–31**
Barracuda Technologies, **47** 7, 9
Barranquilla Investments, **II** 138; **24** 193
**Barratt Developments plc, I 556–57**
Barret Fitch North, **II** 445; **22** 405
Barrett Burston, **I** 437
**Barrett Business Services, Inc., 16 48–50**
The Barrett Co., **I** 414–15; **18** 116; **22** 29
Barricini Foods Inc., **27** 197
**Barrick Gold Corporation, 34 62–65; 38** 232
Barris Industries, Inc., **23** 225
Barry & Co., **III** 522
**Barry Callebaut AG, 29 46–48**
Barry Wright Corporation, **9** 27; **32** 49
Barry's Jewelers. *See* Samuels Jewelers Incorporated.
Barsab Investment Trust. *See* South African Breweries Ltd.
Barsotti's, Inc., **6** 146
Bart Starr, **12** 284
Barth Smelting Corp., **I** 513
Bartlett & Co., **33** 261
Barton & Ludwig, Inc., **21** 96
Barton Beers, Ltd., **29** 219
Barton Brands, **I** 227; **II** 609; **10** 181
Barton, Duer & Koch, **IV** 282; **9** 261
Barton Incorporated, **13** 134; **24** 140; **34** 89
Bartow Food Company, **25** 332
Barwig Medizinische Systeme. *See* OEC Medical Systems, Inc.
Basel AG, **39** 304

**BASF Aktiengesellschaft**, **I** 275, **305–08**, 309, 319, 346–47, 632, 638; **II** 554; **IV** 70–71; **13** 75; **14** 308; **16** 462; **18** **47–51 (upd.)**, 186, 234; **21** 544; **24** 75; **26** 305, 368; **27** 22; **28** 194; **41** 45
**Bashas' Inc.**, **33** **62–64**
Basic American Retirement Communities, **III** 103
Basic Resources, Inc., **V** 725
Basics, **14** 295
BASIS Information Technologies, Inc., **11** 112–13, 132
Baskin-Robbins Ice Cream Co., **I** 215; **7** 128, 372; **17** 474–75; **25** 366; **29** 18
Basle A.G., **I** 632–33, 671–72; **8** 108–09
Basle Air Transport, **I** 121
Basler Bankverein, **II** 368
Bass & Co., **I** 142
Bass Brewers Ltd., **15** 441; **29** 85
Bass Brothers Enterprises Inc., **28** 107; **36** 472
Bass Charington, **29** 84
**Bass PLC**, **I** **222–24**; **III** 94–95; **9** 99, 425–26; **15** **44–47 (upd.)**; **16** 263; **23** 482; **24** 194; **33** 127; **35** 396; **38** **74–78 (upd.)**; **43** 226
**Bass Pro Shops, Inc.**, **42** **27–30**
Bassett Boat Company, **30** 303
Bassett Foods, **II** 478
**Bassett Furniture Industries, Inc.**, **18** **52–55**; **19** 275
Bassett-Walker Inc., **V** 390–91; **17** 512
Bassins Food Chain, **II** 649
BAT. *See* British-American Tobacco Co., Ltd.
**BAT Industries plc**, **I** **425–27**, 605; **II** 628; **III** 66, 185, 522; **9** 312; **23** 427; **30** 273
Bataafsche Petroleum Maatschappij, **V** 658
Batavia Wine Company, **13** 134
Batchelors Ltd., **I** 315; **25** 81
Bateaux Parisiens, **29** 442
Bateman Eichler Hill Richards, **III** 270
Bates, **16** 545
Bates & Robins, **II** 318; **17** 323
Bates Chemical Company, **9** 154
Bates Manufacturing Company, **10** 314
**Bates Worldwide, Inc.**, **14** **48–51**; **26** 500; **33** **65–69 (upd.)**
Batesville Casket Company, **10** 349–50
Bath & Body Works, **11** 41; **24** 237
Bath Industries Inc., **18** 117–18
**Bath Iron Works Corporation**, **12** **27–29**; **36** **76–79 (upd.)**
Bathurst Bank, **II** 187
Baton Rouge Gas Light Company. *See* Gulf States Utilities Company.
Battelle Laboratories, **25** 260
**Battelle Memorial Institute, Inc.**, **6** 288; **10** **138–40**
Batten Barton Durstine & Osborn, **I** 25, 28–31, 33; **16** 70; **41** 88
Battle Creek Food Company, **14** 557–58
Battle Creek Toasted Corn Flake Co., **II** 523; **13** 291
**Battle Mountain Gold Company**, **IV** 490; **23** **40–42**
Battlefield Equipment Rentals, **21** 499, 501
BATUS Inc., **9** 312; **18** 136; **30** 273
Bauborg, **I** 560–61
Baudhuin-Anderson Company, **8** 553
Bauer Audio Visual, Inc., **24** 96
Bauer Nike Hockey Inc., **36** 347
**Bauer Publishing Group**, **7** **42–43**; **20** 53
Baume & Mercier, **27** 487, 489
**Bausch & Lomb Inc.**, **III** 446; **7** **44–47**; **10** 46–47; **13** 365–66; **25** 22, **53–57 (upd.)**, 183; **30** 30; **42** 66
Bavaria SA, **36** 52
Bavarian Brewing Limited, **25** 280
Bavarian Railway, **II** 241
Bavarian Specialty Foods, **13** 383
Baxter Estates, **II** 649
Baxter Healthcare, **36** 497–98
**Baxter International Inc.**, **I** **627–29**; **9** 346; **10** **141–43 (upd.)**, 198–99; **11** 459–60; **12** 325; **18** 469; **22** 361; **25** 82; **26** 433; **36** 92
Baxter Travenol, **21** 119; **24** 75
The Bay, **16** 216
Bay Area Review Course, Inc., **IV** 623
Bay Cities Transportation Company, **6** 382
Bay City, **21** 502
Bay City Cash Way Company, **V** 222; **25** 534
Bay Colony Life Insurance Co., **III** 254
Bay Harbour Management L.C., **28** 55
Bay Networks, Inc., **20** 33, 69; **26** 276; **36** 352
Bay Petroleum, **I** 526
Bay Ridge Savings Bank, **10** 91
Bay Shipbuilding Corporation, **18** 320
**Bay State Gas Company**, **38** **79–82**
Bay State Glass Co., **III** 683
Bay State Iron Manufacturing Co., **13** 16
Bay State Tap and Die Company, **13** 7
Bay West Paper Corporation. *See* Mosinee Paper Corporation.
**BayBanks, Inc.**, **12** **30–32**
**Bayer A.G.**, **I** 305–06, **309–11**, 319, 346–47, 350; **II** 279; **12** 364; **13** **75–77 (upd.)**; **14** 169; **16** 439; **18** 47, 49, 51, 234; **21** 544; **22** 225; **41** **44–48 (upd.)**; **45** 255
Bayer S.p.A., **8** 179
Bayerische Aluminium AG, **IV** 230
**Bayerische Hypotheken- und Wechsel-Bank AG**, **II** **238–40**, 241–42; **IV** 323
Bayerische Kraftwerke AG, **IV** 229–30
Bayerische Landesbank, **II** 257–58, 280; **14** 170; **47** 83
**Bayerische Motoren Werke A.G.**, **I** 73, 75, **138–40**, 198; **II** 5; **III** 543, 556, 591; **11** **31–33 (upd.)**; **13** 30; **17** 25; **21** 441; **27** 20, 203; **38** **83–87 (upd.)**
Bayerische Rückversicherung AG, **III** 377
Bayerische Rumpler Werke, **I** 73
Bayerische Stickstoff-Werke AG, **IV** 229–30
**Bayerische Vereinsbank A.G.**, **II** 239–40, **241–43**; **III** 401
Bayerische Versicherungsbank, **II** 238; **III** 377
Bayerische Wagnisbeteiligung GmbH, **27** 192
Bayerische Wasserkraftwerke Aktiengesellschaft, **IV** 231
Bayerische Zellstoff, **IV** 325
**Bayernwerk AG**, **IV** 231–32, 323; **V** **555–58**, 698–700; **23** **43–47 (upd.)**; **39** 57
Bayliner Marine Corporation, **22** 116
Bayou Boeuf Fabricators, **III** 559
**Bayou Steel Corporation**, **IV** 234; **31** **47–49**
Bayside National Bank, **II** 230
Baystate Corporation, **12** 30
Baytree Investors Inc., **15** 87
Bayview, **III** 673
Bayview Water Company, **45** 277
Bazaar & Novelty. *See* Stuart Entertainment Inc.
Bazar de l'Hotel de Ville, **19** 308
BBA. *See* Bush Boake Allen Inc.
**BBAG Osterreichische Brau-Beteiligungs-AG**, **38** **88–90**
BBC. *See* British Broadcasting Corp.
BBC Brown, Boveri Ltd. *See* ABB ASEA Brown Boveri Ltd.
BBDO. *See* Batten Barton Durstine & Osborn.
BBDO Worldwide Network, **22** 394
BBME. *See* British Bank of the Middle East.
**BBN Corp.**, **19** **39–42**
BBO & Co., **14** 433
BBVA. *See* Banco Bilbao Vizcaya Argentaria S.A.
BC Development, **16** 481
BC TEL. *See* British Columbia Telephone Company.
BCal. *See* British Caledonian Airways.
BCC, **24** 266, 270
**BCE, Inc.**, **V** **269–71**; **6** 307; **7** 333; **12** 413; **18** 32; **36** 351; **44** **46–50 (upd.)**
BCI. *See* Banca Commerciale Italiana SpA.
Bcom3 Group, Inc., **40** 142
BCOP. *See* Boise Cascade Office Products.
BCP Corporation, **16** 228–29
BCPA. *See* British Commonwealth Pacific Airways.
BDB. *See* British Digital Broadcasting plc.
BDB Corp., **10** 136
BDDP. *See* Wells Rich Greene BDDP.
**BEA Systems, Inc.**, **36** **80–83**
Beach Hill Investments Pty Ltd., **48** 427
Beach Patrol Inc., **29** 181
BeachviLime Ltd., **IV** 74; **24** 143, 144
Beacon Communications Group, **23** 135
Beacon Manufacturing Company, **I** 377; **19** 304–05
Beacon Oil, **IV** 566
Beacon Participations, **III** 98
Beacon Publishing Co., **IV** 629
Beall-Ladymon, Inc., **24** 458
Bealls, **24** 456
Beamach Group Ltd., **17** 182–83
Beaman Corporation, **16** 96; **25** 390
Bean Fiberglass Inc., **15** 247
Bear Automotive Service Equipment Company, **10** 494
**Bear Creek Corporation**, **12** 444–45; **38** **91–94**; **39** 361
Bear Instruments Inc., **48** 410
**Bear Stearns Companies, Inc.**, **II** **400–01**, 450; **10** **144–45 (upd.)**, 382; **20** 313; **24** 272
Beard & Stone Electric Co., **I** 451
**Bearings, Inc.**, **I** 158–59; **13** **78–80**
Beasley Industries, Inc., **19** 125–26
**Beatrice Company**, **I** 353; 440–41; **II** **467–69**, 475; **III** 118, 437; **6** 357; **9** 318; **12** 82, 87, 93; **13** 162–63, 452; **14** 149–50; **15** 213–14, 358; **16** 160, 396; **19** 290; **24** 273; **26** 476, 494; **28** 475; **42** 92. *See also* TLC Beatrice International Holdings, Inc.
Beatrice Foods, **21** 322–24, 507, 545; **25** 277–78; **38** 169; **43** 355
Beauharnois Power Company, **6** 502
Beaulieu of America, **19** 276
Beaulieu Winery, **I** 260

Beaumont-Bennett Group, **6** 27
Beauté Prestige International S.A. *See* Shiseido Company Limited.
**BeautiControl Cosmetics, Inc., 21 49–52**
Beauty Biz Inc., **18** 230
Beaver Lumber Company Limited, **I** 274; **26** 303, 305–06
**Beazer Homes USA, Inc., 17 38–41**
Beazer Plc., **7** 209
**bebe stores, inc., 31 50–52**
BEC Group Inc., **22** 35
**Bechtel Group, Inc., I 558–59,** 563; **III** 248; **IV** 171, 576; **6** 148–49, 556; **13** 13; **24 64–67 (upd.)**; **25** 402; **26** 220
Beck & Gregg Hardware Co., **9** 253
Beck's North America, Inc. *See* Brauerei Beck & Co.
Becker Drill, Inc., **19** 247
Becker Group of Germany, **26** 231
Becker Paribas Futures, **II** 445; **22** 406
Becker Warburg Paribas, **II** 259
**Beckett Papers, 23 48–50**
Beckley-Cardy Co., **IV** 623–24
**Beckman Coulter, Inc., 22 74–77**
**Beckman Instruments, Inc., I** 694; **14 52–54**; **16** 94
BECOL. *See* Belize Electric Company Limited.
**Becton, Dickinson & Company, I 630–31**; **11 34–36 (upd.)**; **36 84–89 (upd.)**; **42** 182–83
**Bed Bath & Beyond Inc., 13 81–83**; **14** 61; **18** 239; **24** 292; **33** 384; **41 49–52 (upd.)**
Bedcovers, Inc., **19** 304
Beddor Companies, **12** 25
Bedford Chemical, **8** 177
Bedford-Stuyvesant Restoration Corp., **II** 673
Bee Chemicals, **I** 372
Bee Discount, **26** 476
Bee Gee Shoe Corporation, **10** 281
Bee Gee Shrimp, **I** 473
**Beech Aircraft Corporation, II** 87; **8 49–52,** 313; **11** 411, 413; **27** 98; **38** 375; **46** 354
Beech Holdings Corp., **9** 94
**Beech-Nut Nutrition Corporation, I** 695; **II** 489; **21 53–56**; **46** 290
Beecham Group PLC, **I** 626, 640, 668; **II** 331, 543; **III** 18, 65–66; **9** 264; **14** 53; **16** 438
Beechwood Insurance Agency, Inc., **14** 472
Beeck-Feinkost GmbH, **26** 59
ZAO BeeOnLine-Portal, **48** 419
Beerman Stores, Inc., **10** 281
Beers Construction Company, **38** 437
Beghin Say S.A., **II** 540
Behr-Manning Company, **8** 396
Behringwerke AG, **14** 255
**Beiersdorf AG, 29 49–53**; **41** 374–77
Beijerinvest Group, **I** 210
Beijing Contact Lens Ltd., **25** 56
Beijing Dentsu, **16** 168
Beijing Liyuan Co., **22** 487
Beijing Machinery and Equipment Corp., **II** 442
Beijing Yanshan Petrochemical Company, **22** 263
Beijing ZF North Drive Systems Technical Co. Ltd., **48** 450
Beirao, Pinto, Silva and Co. *See* Banco Espírito Santo e Comercial de Lisboa S.A.
Bejam Group PLC, **II** 678; **33** 206–07
Beker Industries, **IV** 84
**Bekins Company, 15 48–50**; **26** 197
Bel. *See* Fromageries Bel.
Bel Air Markets, **14** 397
Belairbus, **I** 42; **12** 191
Belcher New England, Inc., **IV** 394
Belcher Oil Co., **IV** 394
**Belco Oil & Gas Corp., 23** 219; **40 63–65**
**Belden Inc., II** 16; **19 43–45**
Beldis, **23** 219
Beldoch Industries Corp., **17** 137–38
Belfast Banking Co., **II** 318; **17** 323
**Belgacom, 6 302–04**
Belgian De Vaderlandsche, **III** 309
Belgian Rapid Access to Information Network Services, **6** 304
Belgian Société Internationale Forestière et Minière, **IV** 65
Belglas, **16** 420; **43** 307
Belgo Group plc, **31** 41
Belgochim, **IV** 499
Belize Electric Company Limited, **47** 137
Belize Sugar Industries, **II** 582
**Belk Stores Services, Inc., V 12–13**; **19 46–48 (upd.)**
Bell (Quarry and Concrete), **III** 674
Bell Aerospace, **I** 530; **24** 442; **34** 432–33
Bell Aircraft Company, **I** 529; **11** 267; **13** 267; **34** 431
**Bell and Howell Company, I** 463; **IV** 642; **9** 33, **61–64**; **11** 197; **14** 569; **15** 71; **29 54–58 (upd.),** 159
**Bell Atlantic Corporation, V 272–74**; **9** 171; **10** 232, 456; **11** 59, 87, 274; **12** 137; **13** 399; **18** 33; **25 58–62 (upd.),** 91, 497; **27** 22, 365. *See also* Verizon Communications.
Bell Canada Enterprises Inc. *See* BCE, Inc.
**Bell Canada International, Inc., V** 269, 308–09; **6 305–08**; **12** 413; **21** 308; **25** 102
Bell Communications Research, **13** 58; **25** 496
Bell Fibre Products, **12** 377
**Bell Helicopter Textron Inc., 46 64–67**
Bell Helmets Inc., **22** 458
**Bell Industries, Inc., 13** 47; **18** 498; **19** 311; **47 40–43**
Bell Laboratories, **II** 33, 60–61, 101, 112; **V** 259–64; **8** 157; **9** 171; **10** 108; **11** 327, 500–01; **12** 61; **14** 52, 281–82; **23** 181; **29** 41, 44; **34** 257–58. *See also* AT&T Bell Labroatories, Inc.
Bell Mountain Partnership, Ltd., **15** 26
Bell-Northern Research, Ltd., **V** 269–71; **15** 131
Bell Pharmacal Labs, **12** 387
Bell Resources, **I** 437–38; **III** 729; **10** 170; **27** 473
**Bell Sports Corporation, 16 51–53**; **44 51–54 (upd.)**
Bell System, **II** 72, 230; **6** 338–40; **7** 99, 333; **11** 500; **16** 392–93
Bell Telephone Company, **I** 409; **6** 332, 334
Bell Telephone Company of Pennsylvania, **I** 585
Bell Telephone Manufacturing, **II** 13
Bell's Asbestos and Engineering, **I** 428
Bellcore. *See* Bell Communications Research.
Belle Alkali Co., **IV** 409; **7** 308
Belledune Fertilizer Ltd., **IV** 165
Bellefonte Insurance Co., **IV** 29
Bellemead Development Corp., **III** 220; **14** 108; **37** 84
Bellofram Corp., **14** 43
**BellSouth Corporation, V 276–78**; **9** 171, 321; **10** 431, 501; **15** 197; **18** 23, 74, 76; **19** 254–55; **22** 19; **27** 20; **29 59–62 (upd.)**; **43** 447; **45** 390
**Bellway Plc, 45 37–39**
Belmin Systems, **14** 36
Belmont Electronics, **II** 85–86; **11** 412
Belmont Plaza, **12** 316
Belmont Savings and Loan, **10** 339
Belmont Springs Water Company, Inc., **I** 234; **10** 227
Belo Corporation. *See* A.H. Belo Corporation
**Beloit Corporation, 8** 243; **14 55–57**; **34** 358; **38** 224, 226–28
Beloit Tool Company. *See* Regal-Beloit Corporation.
Beloit Woodlands, **10** 380
Belridge Oil Co., **IV** 541
Belzer Group, **IV** 198–99
**Bemis Company, Inc., 8 53–55**; **26** 43
Bemrose group, **IV** 650
**Ben & Jerry's Homemade, Inc., 10 146–48**; **35 58–62**
Ben Franklin Retail Stores, Inc. *See* FoxMeyer Health Corporation.
Ben Franklin Savings & Trust, **10** 117
Ben Hill Griffin, **III** 53
Ben Johnson & Co. Ltd., **IV** 661
Ben Line, **6** 398
Ben Myerson Candy Co., Inc., **26** 468
Ben Venue Laboratories Inc., **16** 439; **39** 73
**Benchmark Electronics, Inc., 40 66–69**
Benckiser Group, **37** 269
Benckiser N.V. *See* Reckitt Benckiser plc.
Bendicks, **I** 592
**Bendix Corporation, I** 68, **141–43,** 154, 166, 192, 416; **II** 33; **III** 166, 555; **7** 356; **8** 545; **9** 16–17; **10** 260, 279; **11** 138; **13** 356–57; **15** 284; **17** 564; **21** 416; **22** 31
**Beneficial Corporation, II** 236; **8 56–58,** 117; **10** 490
Beneficial Finance Company, **27** 428–29
Beneficial National Bank USA, **II** 286
Beneficial Standard Life, **10** 247
Benefit Consultants, Inc., **16** 145
Benelli Arms S.p.A., **39** 151
Benesse Corporation, **13** 91, 93; **39** 49
**Benetton Group S.p.A., 8** 171; **10 149–52**; **15** 369; **18** 193; **25** 56
Bengal Iron and Steel Co., **IV** 205–06
**Benihana, Inc., 18 56–59**
Benjamin Allen & Co., **IV** 660
**Benjamin Moore and Co., 13 84–87**; **38 95–99 (upd.)**
Benlox Holdings PLC, **16** 465
Benn Bros. plc, **IV** 687
Bennett Biscuit Co., **II** 543
Bennett Industries, Inc., **17** 371–73
Bennett's Smokehouse and Saloon, **19** 122; **29** 201
Bennigan's, **II** 556–57; **7** 336; **12** 373; **13** 408; **19** 286; **25** 181
Bensdorp, **29** 47
Benson & Hedges, Ltd., **V** 398–99; **15** 137; **19** 171
Benson Wholesale Co., **II** 624

Bentalls, **37** 6, 8
Bentex Holding S.A., **48** 209
Bentley Laboratories, **22** 360
Bentley Mills, Inc., **8** 272
Bentley Motor Ltd., **I** 194; **21** 435
Bentley Systems, **6** 247
Benton & Bowles, **I** 33; **6** 20, 22
Benton International, Inc., **29** 376
**Benton Oil and Gas Company, 47 44–46**
Benwood Iron Works, **17** 355
Benxi Iron and Steel Corp., **IV** 167
Benzina, **IV** 487
Benzinol, **IV** 487
N.V. Benzit. *See* N.V. Gemeenschappelijk Benzit van Aandeelen Philips Gloeilampenfabriken.
Berec Group, **III** 502; **7** 208
Beresford International plc, **24** 335; **27** 159
Beretta. *See* Fabbrica D' Armi Pietro Beretta S.p.A.
Berg Manufacturing Sales Co., **I** 156
Berg- und Metallbank, **IV** 139–40
Bergdorf Goodman, **I** 246; **V** 30–31; **25** 177
Bergedorfer Eisenwerk, **III** 417–20
Bergen Bank, **II** 352
**Bergen Brunswig Corporation, I** 413; **V 14–16**, 152; **13 88–90 (upd.)**; **18** 97
Berger Associates, Inc., **26** 233
Berger, Jenson and Nicholson, **I** 347; **18** 236
Berger Manufacturing Company, **26** 405
Bergische-Markische Bank, **II** 278
Berglen, **III** 570; **20** 362
Bergmann & Co., **II** 27
Bergstrom Paper Company, **8** 413
Bergswerksgesellschaft Hibernia, **I** 349; **IV** 194
Bergvik & Ala, **IV** 336, 338–39
**Beringer Wine Estates Holdings, Inc., 22 78–81**; **36** 472
Berisford International plc, **19** 492, 494
Berjaya Group, **22** 464–65
Berkeley Computers, **III** 109; **14** 13
**Berkeley Farms, Inc., 46 68–70**
Berkey Photo Inc., **I** 447; **III** 475; **36** 171
Berkley Dean & Co., **15** 525
Berkline Corp., **17** 183; **20** 363; **39** 267
**Berkshire Hathaway Inc., III 213–15; 18 60–63 (upd.)**; **29** 191; **30** 411; **36** 191; **38** 98; **40** 196, 199, 398; **39** 232, 235; **42 31–36 (upd.)**
Berkshire International, **V** 390–91; **17** 512
Berkshire Partners, **10** 393
Berleca Ltd., **9** 395; **42** 269
Berlex Laboratories, **I** 682; **10** 214
Berli Jucker, **18** 180–82
Berlin Exchange, **I** 409
Berlin Göring-Werke, **IV** 233
BerlinDat Gesellschaft für Informationsverarbeitung und Systemtechnik GmbH, **39** 57
Berliner Bank, **II** 256
Berliner Bankverein, **II** 278
Berliner Handels- und Frankfurter Bank, **II** 242
Berliner Union, **I** 409
Berlinische Bodengesellschaft, **I** 560
**Berlitz International, Inc., IV** 643; **7** 286, 312; **13 91–93**; **39 47–50 (upd.)**
Berman Brothers Fur Co., **21** 525
Berman Buckskin, **21** 525
**Bernard C. Harris Publishing Company, Inc., 39 51–53**
**Bernard Chaus, Inc., 27 59–61**
Bernardin Ltd., **30** 39
Berndorf Austria, **44** 206
Berndorf Switzerland, **44** 206
Bernheim-Meyer: A l'Innovation. *See* GIB Group.
Berni Inns, **I** 247
Bernie Schulman's, **12** 132
**Bernina Holding AG, 47 47–50**
Bernstein Macauley, Inc., **II** 450
Berrios Enterprises, **14** 236
Berry Bearing Company, **9** 254
Berry Industries, **III** 628
**Berry Petroleum Company, 47 51–53**
**Berry Plastics Corporation, 21 57–59**
Bert L. Smokler & Company, **11** 257
Bertea Corp., **III** 603
**Bertelsmann A.G., IV 592–94**, 614–15; **10** 196; **15 51–54 (upd.)**; **17** 399; **19** 285; **22** 194; **26** 19, 43; **30** 67, 70; **31** 375, 378; **43 63–67 (upd.)**, 422; **44** 377
Bertolini's Authentic Trattorias, **30** 329
Bertram & Graf Gmbh, **28** 45
Bertron Griscom & Company, **V** 641
**Bertucci's Inc., 16 54–56**, 447
Berwick Industries, Inc., **35** 130–31
Berwind Corp., **14** 18
Beryl Corp., **26** 149
Beryllium Resources, **14** 80
Berzelius Metallhütten Gesellschaft, **IV** 141
Berzelius Umwelt-Service, **III** 625; **IV** 141
Besi, **26** 498
**Besnier SA, 19 49–51**; **23** 217, 219; **24** 444–45; **25** 83, 85
Bess Mfg., **8** 510
Bessemer Capital Partners L.P., **15** 505
Bessemer Gas Engine Co., **II** 15; **20** 163
Bessemer Limestone & Cement Co., **IV** 409; **31** 454
Bessemer Steamship, **IV** 572; **7** 549
Besser Vibrapac, **III** 673
Best Apparel, **V** 156
**Best Buy Co., Inc., 9 65–66**; **10** 305; **17** 489; **18** 532–33; **19** 362; **23 51–53 (upd.)**; **24** 52, 502; **29** 120, 123; **30** 464, 466; **38** 315
best energy GmbH, **39** 54, 57
Best Fabric Outlets, **16** 198
Best Holding Corporation. *See* Arkansas Best Corporation.
Best Manufacturing, **15** 490
Best Power, **24** 29
Best Products Inc., **19** 396–97
Best Read Guides Franchise Corp., **36** 341
Best Western, **14** 106; **25** 308
**Bestfoods, II** 496–97; **22 82–86 (upd.)**
Bestline Products, **17** 227
Bestop Inc., **16** 184
Bestwall Gypsum Co., **IV** 281; **9** 259
Bestway Distribution Services, Inc., **24** 126
Bestway Transportation, **14** 505
Beswick, **II** 17
**BET Holdings, Inc., 18 64–66**; **22** 224; **25** 213; **34** 43
Beta West Properties, **25** 496–97
Bethesda Research Laboratories, Inc., **I** 321; **17** 287, 289
**Bethlehem Steel Corporation, IV 35–37**, 228, 572–73; **6** 540; **7 48–51 (upd.)**, 447, 549–50; **11** 65; **12** 354; **13** 97, 157; **18** 378; **22** 285; **23** 305; **25** 45; **26** 405; **27 62–66 (upd.)**
Beton Union, **III** 738
Better Brands Ltd., **32** 518–19
Better Communications, **IV** 597
**Betz Laboratories, Inc., I 312–13; 10 153–55 (upd.)**; **15** 536
Bevan and Wedd Durlacher Morduant & Co., **II** 237
Beveridge-Marvellum Company, **8** 483
**Beverly Enterprises, Inc., III 76–77**, 80; **14** 242; **16 57–59 (upd.)**; **25** 309
Beverly Hills Savings, **II** 420
Beverly Pest Control, **25** 15
Bevis Custom Furniture, Inc., **12** 263
Bevrachtingskantoor, **26** 280
**Bewag AG, 38** 449; **39 54–57**
Bezeq, **25** 266
**BFC Construction Corporation, 25 63–65**
**The BFGoodrich Company, I** 28, 428, 440; **II** 414; **III** 118, 443; **V 231–33**; **8** 80–81, 290; **9** 12, 96, 133; **10** 438; **11** 158; **19 52–55 (upd.)**; **20** 260, 262; **21** 260; **22** 114; **23** 170; **25** 70; **30** 158; **31** 135. *See also* Goodrich Corporation.
BFI. *See* Browning-Ferris Industries, Inc.
BFP Holdings Corp. *See* Big Flower Press Holdings, Inc.
BG Freight Line Holding B.V., **30** 318
BG plc, **29** 104
BG&E. *See* Baltimore Gas and Electric Company.
BGC Finance, **II** 420
BGJ Enterprises, Inc. *See* Brown Printing Company.
BH Acquisition Corporation, **22** 439
Bharat Coking Coal Ltd., **IV** 48–49
Bharat Petroleum Ltd., **IV** 441
Bharti Telecom, **16** 84
**BHC Communications, Inc., 9** 119; **26 32–34**; **31** 109
BHP. *See* Broken Hill Proprietary Company Ltd.
BHP Steel of Australia, **18** 380
BHPC Marketing, Inc., **45** 41
**Bhs plc, 16** 466; **17 42–44**, 334–35
BHV. *See* Bazar de l'Hotel de Ville.
Bi-Lo Inc., **II** 641; **V** 35; **16** 313
Biacore International AB, **25** 377
Bianchi, **13** 27
Bibb Co., **31** 199
**BIC Corporation, III** 29; **8 59–61**; **20** 23; **23 54–57 (upd.)**
**BICC PLC, III 433–34**; **11** 520. *See also* Balfour Beatty plc.
BICE Med Grille, **16** 447
**Bicoastal Corporation, II 9–11**
Bidermann Industries, **22** 122; **41** 129
Biederman & Company, **14** 160
Biedermann Motech, **37** 112
Bieffe, **16** 52
Bienfaisance, **III** 391
Bierbrauerei Wilhelm Remmer, **9** 86
Biesemeyer Manufacturing Corporation, **26** 363
Biffa Waste Services Ltd. *See* Severn Trent PLC.
**Big B, Inc., 17 45–47**
**Big Bear Stores Co., 13 94–96**
Big Boy, **III** 102–03
Big D Construction Corporation, **42** 432
**Big Dog Holdings, Inc., 45 40–42**
Big 5 Sporting Goods, **12** 477
**Big Flower Press Holdings, Inc., 21 60–62**; **32** 465–66
Big Foot Cattle Co., **14** 537

Big Horn Mining Co., **8** 423
Big M, **8** 409–10
**Big O Tires, Inc., 20 61–63**
**Big Rivers Electric Corporation, 11 37–39**
Big Sky Western Bank, **35** 197, 199
Big Three Industries, **I** 358
**Big V Supermarkets, Inc., 25 66–68**
Big Y Foods, Inc., **23** 169
Bigelow-Sanford, Inc., **31** 199
BII. *See* Banana Importers of Ireland.
Bike Athletics, **23** 449
BIL. *See* Brierley Investments.
Bilbao Insurance Group, **III** 200
**Bilfinger & Berger Bau A.G., I 560–61**
**Bill & Melinda Gates Foundation, 41 53–55**, 119
Bill Acceptance Corporation Ltd., **48** 427
**Bill Blass Ltd., 32 78–80**
Bill France Racing, **19** 222
**Billabong International Ltd., 44 55–58**
Billboard Publications, Inc., **7** 15
Billerud, **IV** 336
**Billing Concepts Corp., 26 35–38**
Billiton International, **IV** 56, 532; **22** 237
Bill's Casino, **9** 426
Bilsom, **40** 96–97
Bilt-Rite Chase-Pitkin, Inc., **41** 416
Biltwell Company, **8** 249
Bimar Foods Inc., **19** 192
Bimbo Bakeries USA, **29** 341
Bimbo, S.A., **36** 162, 164
Binder Hamlyn, **IV** 685
Binderline Development, Inc., **22** 175
**Bindley Western Industries, Inc., 9 67–69**
Bing Crosby Productions, **IV** 595
**Bingham Dana LLP, 43 68–71**
Binghamton Container Company, **8** 102
Bingo King. *See* Stuart Entertainment Inc.
**Binks Sames Corporation, 21 63–66**
**Binney & Smith Inc., II** 525; **IV** 621; **13** 293; **25 69–72**
Binnie & Partners, **22** 89
Binny & Co. Ltd., **III** 522
Binter Canarias, **6** 97
Bio-Clinic, **11** 486–87
Bio-Dental Technologies Corporation, **46** 466
Bio-Dynamics, Inc., **10** 105, 107; **37** 111
Bio Foods Inc. *See* Balance Bar Company.
Bio Synthetics, Inc., **21** 386
Bio-Toxicological Research Laboratories, **IV** 409
Biodevelopment Laboratories, Inc., **35** 47
Biofermin Pharmaceutical, **I** 704
**Biogen Inc., I** 638, 685; **8** 210; **14 58–60**; **36 90–93 (upd.)**
Bioindustrias, **19** 475
Biokyowa, **III** 43; **48** 250
Biological Research, **III** 443
Biological Technology Corp., **IV** 252; **17** 29
Biomedical Reference Laboratories of North Carolina, **11** 424
Biomega Corp., **18** 422
**Biomet, Inc., 10 156–58**
Bionaire, Inc., **19** 360
BioSensor A.B., **I** 665
Biotechnica International, **I** 286
Bioteknik-Gruppen, **I** 665
Bioter-Biona, S.A., **II** 493
Bioter S.A., **III** 420
Biotherm, **III** 47
**Biovail Corporation, 47 54–56**
Biralo Pty Ltd., **48** 427
Bird & Sons, **22** 14
**Bird Corporation, 19 56–58**
Birdair, Inc., **35** 99–100
Birds Eye, **32** 474
Birdsall, Inc., **6** 529, 531
Bireley's, **22** 515
Birfield Ltd., **III** 494
Birkbeck, **10** 6
**Birkenstock Footprint Sandals, Inc., 12 33–35; 42 37–40 (upd.)**
Birmingham & Midland Bank. *See* Midland Bank plc.
Birmingham Joint Stock Bank, **II** 307
Birmingham Screw Co., **III** 493
Birmingham Slag Company, **7** 572–73, 575
**Birmingham Steel Corporation, 13 97–98**; **18** 379–80; **19** 380; **40 70–73 (upd.)**
Birra Moretti, **25** 281–82
Birtman Electric Co., **III** 653; **12** 548
Biscayne Bank. *See* Banco Espírito Santo e Comercial de Lisboa S.A.
Biscayne Federal Savings and Loan Association, **11** 481
Biscuiterie Nantaise, **II** 502; **10** 323
Biscuits Belin, **II** 543
Biscuits Delacre, **II** 480; **26** 56
Biscuits Gondolo, **II** 543
Bishop & Babcock Manufacturing Co., **II** 41
Bishop & Co. Savings Bank, **11** 114
Bishop National Bank of Hawaii, **11** 114
Bishopsgate Insurance, **III** 200
**BISSELL, Inc., 9 70–72; 30 75–78 (upd.)**
Bit Software, Inc., **12** 62
Bits & Pieces, **26** 439
Bitumax Proprietary, **III** 672
Bitumen & Oil Refineries (Australia) Ltd., **III** 672–73
BIW. *See* Bath Iron Works.
BIZ Enterprises, **23** 390
BizBuyer.com, **39** 25
Bizmark, **13** 176
BizMart, **6** 244–45; **8** 404–05
**BJ Services Company, 15** 534, 536; **25 73–75**
BJ's Pizza & Grill, **44** 85
BJ's Restaurant & Brewhouse, **44** 85
BJ's Wholesale Club, **12** 221; **13** 547–49; **33** 198
BJK&E. *See* Bozell Worldwide Inc.
Björknäs Nya Sågverks, **IV** 338
BK Tag, **28** 157
BKW, **IV** 229
BL Ltd., **I** 175; **10** 354
BL Systems. *See* AT&T Istel Ltd.
BL Universal PLC, **47** 168
**The Black & Decker Corporation, I** 667; **III 435–37**, 628, 665; **8** 332, 349; **15** 417–18; **16** 384; **17** 215; **20 64–68 (upd.)**; **22** 334; **43** 101, 289
**Black & Veatch LLP, 22 87–90**
Black Arrow Leasing, **II** 138; **24** 193
**Black Box Corporation, 20 69–71**
Black Clawson Company, **24** 478
Black Entertainment Television. *See* BET Holdings, Inc.
Black Flag Co., **I** 622
Black Hawk Broadcasting Group, **III** 188; **10** 29; **38** 17
**Black Hills Corporation, 20 72–74**
Black Pearl Software, Inc., **39** 396
Black Spread Eagle, **II** 235
Blackburn Group, **III** 508; **24** 85
Blackhawk Holdings, Inc. *See* PW Eagle Inc.
Blackhorse Agencies, **II** 309; **47** 227
Blackmer Pump Co., **III** 468
**Blacks Leisure Group plc, 39 58–60**
Blackstone Capital Partners L.P., **V** 223; **6** 378; **17** 366
The Blackstone Group, **II** 434, 444; **IV** 718; **11** 177, 179; **13** 170; **17** 238, 443; **22** 404, 416; **26** 408; **37** 309, 311
Blackstone Hotel Acquisition Co., **24** 195
Blaine Construction Company, **8** 546
Blair and Co., **II** 227
**Blair Corporation, 25 76–78; 31 53–55**
Blair Paving, **III** 674
Blair Radio, **6** 33
Blakiston Co., **IV** 636
Blane Products, **I** 403
Blanes, S.A. de C.V., **34** 197
Blatz Breweries, **I** 254
Blaupunkt-Werke, **I** 192–93
BLC Insurance Co., **III** 330
BLD Europe, **16** 168
Bleichröder, **II** 191
Blendax, **III** 53; **8** 434; **26** 384
**Blessings Corp., 14** 550; **19 59–61**
**Blimpie International, Inc., 15 55–57**; **17** 501; **32** 444
Bliss Manufacturing Co., **17** 234–35
Blitz-Weinhart Brewing, **18** 71–72
Bloch & Guggenheimer, Inc., **40** 51–52
Blochman Lawrence Goldfree, **I** 697
**Block Drug Company, Inc., 6** 26; **8 62–64**; **27 67–70 (upd.)**
Block Financial Corporation, **17** 265; **29** 227
Block Management, **29** 226
Block Medical, Inc., **10** 351
**Blockbuster Entertainment Corporation, II** 161; **IV** 597; **9 73–75**, 361; **11** 556–58; **12** 43, 515; **13** 494; **18** 64, 66; **19** 417; **22** 161–62; **23** 88, 503; **25** 208–10, 222; **26** 409; **28** 296; **29** 504
**Blockbuster Inc., 31 56–60 (upd.)**, 339–40
Blockson Chemical, **I** 380; **13** 379
Bloedel, Stewart & Welch, **IV** 306–07
Blohm & Voss, **I** 74
**Blonder Tongue Laboratories, Inc., 48 52–55**
**Bloomberg L.P., 18** 24; **21 67–71**
**Bloomingdale's Inc., I** 90; **III** 63; **IV** 651, 703; **9** 209, 393; **10** 487; **12 36–38**, 307, 403–04; **16** 328; **23** 210; **25** 257; **31** 190
**Blount International, Inc., I** 563; **12 39–41**; **24** 78; **26** 117, 119, 363; **48 56–60 (upd.)**
BLP Group Companies. *See* Boron, LePore & Associates, Inc.
BLT Ventures, **25** 270
Blue Arrow PLC, **II** 334–35; **9** 327; **30** 300
**Blue Bell Creameries L.P., 30 79–81**
Blue Bell, Inc., **V** 390–91; **12** 205; **17** 512
**Blue Bird Corporation, 35 63–66**
Blue Bunny Ice Cream. *See* Wells' Dairy, Inc.
Blue Byte, **41** 409
Blue Chip Stamps, **III** 213–14; **30** 412
**Blue Circle Industries PLC, III 669–71**, 702

**Blue Cross and Blue Shield Association, 10 159–61**; **14** 84
Blue Cross and Blue Shield Mutual of Northern Ohio, **12** 176
Blue Cross and Blue Shield of Colorado, **11** 175
Blue Cross and Blue Shield of Greater New York, **III** 245, 246
Blue Cross and Blue Shield of Ohio, **15** 114
Blue Cross Blue Shield of Michigan, **12** 22
Blue Cross of California, **25** 525
Blue Cross of Northeastern New York, **III** 245–46
**Blue Diamond Growers, 28 56–58**
Blue Dot Services, **37** 280, 283
Blue Funnel Line, **I** 521; **6** 415–17
Blue Line Distributing, **7** 278–79
Blue Metal Industries, **III** 687; **28** 82
**Blue Mountain Arts, Inc.**, **IV** 621; **29 63–66**
Blue Mountain Springs Ltd., **48** 97
Blue Ribbon Beef Pack, Inc., **II** 515–16
Blue Ribbon Sports. *See* Nike, Inc.
Blue Ridge Grocery Co., **II** 625
Blue Ridge Lumber Ltd., **16** 11
Blue Shield of California, **25** 527
**Blue Square Israel Ltd., 41 56–58**
Blue Tee Corporation, **23** 34, 36
Blue Water Food Service, **13** 244
Bluebird Inc., **10** 443
Bluffton Grocery Co., **II** 668
Blumberg Communications Inc., **24** 96
Blunt Ellis & Loewi, **III** 270
Blyth and Co., **I** 537; **13** 448, 529
Blyth Eastman Dillon & Company, **II** 445; **22** 405–06
**Blyth Industries, Inc., 18 67–69**
Blyth Merrill Lynch, **II** 448
Blythe Colours BV, **IV** 119
**BMC Industries, Inc.**, **6** 275; **17 48–51**
BMC Software Inc., **14** 391
BMG/Music, **IV** 594; **15** 51; **37** 192–93
BMI. *See* Broadcast Music Inc.
BMI Ltd., **III** 673
BMI Systems Inc., **12** 174
BMO Corp., **III** 209
BMO Nesbitt Burns, **46** 55
BMW. *See* Bayerische Motoren Werke.
BNA. *See* Banca Nazionale dell'Agricoltura *or* Bureau of National Affairs, Inc.
BNCI. *See* Banque Nationale Pour le Commerce et l'Industrie.
BNE. *See* Bank of New England Corp.
BNG, Inc., **19** 487
**BNP Paribas Group, 36 94–97 (upd.)**; **42** 349
BNS Acquisitions, **26** 247
Boa Shoe Company, **42** 325
BOAC. *See* British Overseas Airways Corp.
Boardwalk Regency, **6** 201
Boart and Hard Metals, **IV** 22
**Boart Longyear Company, 26 39–42**, 69
Boase Massimi Pollitt, **6** 48
**Boatmen's Bancshares Inc., 15 58–60**
BoatsDirect.com, **37** 398
**Bob Evans Farms, Inc., 9 76–79**; **10** 259; **35** 83–84
Bobbie Brooks Inc., **17** 384
Bobbs-Merrill, **11** 198
Bobingen A.G., **I** 347
Bobro Products. *See* BWP Distributors.
**BOC Group plc, I 314–16**, 358; **11** 402; **12** 500; **25 79–82 (upd.)**
**Boca Resorts, Inc., 37 33–36**
BOCAP Corp., **37** 372
Bochumer Verein für Gusstahlfabrikation, **IV** 88
Bock Bearing Co., **8** 530
Bodcaw Co., **IV** 287; **15** 228
Boddington, **21** 247
Bodegas, **8** 556
Bodeker Drug Company, **16** 399
**Bodum Design Group AG, 47 57–59**
**The Body Shop International PLC, 11 40–42**
Boehringer Ingelheim GmbH. *See* C.H. Boehringer Sohn.
Boehringer Mannheim Companies, **37** 111–12
**The Boeing Company**, **I** 41–43, **47–49**, 50, 55–56, 58, 61, 67–68, 70–72, 74, 77, 82, 84–85, 90, 92–93, 96–97, 100, 102, 104–05, 108, 111–13, 116, 121–22, 126, 128, 130, 195, 489–90, 511, 530; **II** 7, 32–33, 62, 442; **III** 512, 539; **IV** 171, 576; **6** 68, 96, 130, 327; **7** 11, 456, 504; **8** 81, 313, 315; **9** 12, 18, 128, 194, 206, 232, 396, 416–17, 458–60, 498; **10 162–65 (upd.)**, 262, 316, 369, 536; **11** 164, 267, 277–79, 363, 427; **12** 180, 190–91, 380; **13** 356–58; **21** 140, 143, 436; **24** 21, 84, 85–86, 88–89, 442; **25** 34, 224, 430–31; **26** 117; **28** 195, 225; **32 81–87 (upd.)**; **36** 122, 190; **38** 372; **48** 218–20
Boeke & Huidekooper, **III** 417
Boerenbond, **II** 304
Boettcher & Co., **III** 271
Bofors Nobel Inc., **9** 380–81; **13** 22
Bogen Company, **15** 213
**Bohemia, Inc., 13 99–101**; **31** 467
Bohm-Allen Jewelry, **12** 112
Böhme-Fettchemie, Chenmitz, **III** 32
Bohn Aluminum & Brass, **10** 439
**Boise Cascade Corporation**, **I** 142; **III** 499, 648, 664; **IV 255–56**, 333; **6** 577; **7** 356; **8 65–67 (upd.)**, 477; **15** 229; **16** 510; **19** 269, 445–46; **22** 154; **31** 13; **32 88–92 (upd.)**; **36** 509; **37** 140
Bokaro Steel Ltd., **IV** 206
Bolands Ltd., **II** 649
Bolar Pharmaceutical Co., **16** 529
Boley G.m.b.H., **21** 123
Boliden Mining, **II** 366
Bolinder-Munktell, **I** 209; **II** 366
Bolitho Bank, **II** 235
Bölkow GmbH, **I** 74
Bolles & Houghton, **10** 355
The Bolsa Chica Company, **8** 300
Bolt, Beranek & Newman Inc., **26** 520
Bolt Security, **32** 373
BOMAG, **8** 544, 546
Bombadier Defence Services UK, **41** 412
Bombardier Aerospace Group, **36** 190–91
Bombardier, Inc., **12** 400–01; **16** 78; **25** 423; **27** 281, 284; **34** 118–19; **35** 350–51; **42 41–46 (upd.)**
**The Bombay Company, Inc.**, **III** 581; **10 166–68**; **27** 429
**Bon Appetit Holding AG**, **II** 656; **48 61–63**
Bon Dente International Inc., **39** 320
**The Bon Marché, Inc.**, **V** 25; **9** 209; **19** 88, 306, 309; **23 58–60**; **26** 158, 160
**Bon Secours Health System, Inc., 24 68–71**
**The Bon-Ton Stores, Inc., 16 60–62**
Bonanza, **7** 336; **10** 331; **15** 361–63
Bonanza Steakhouse, **17** 320
Bonaventura, **IV** 611
Bonaventure Liquor Store Co., **I** 284
Bond Brewing International, **23** 405
**Bond Corporation Holdings Limited**, **I** 253, 255; **10 169–71**
Bondex International, **8** 456
Bonduel Pickling Co. Inc., **25** 517
**Bongrain SA**, **19** 50; **23** 217, 219; **25 83–85**
Boni & Liveright, **13** 428
Bonifiche Siele, **II** 272
Bonimart, **II** 649
**Bonneville International Corporation, 29 67–70**; **30** 15
Bontrager Bicycles, **16** 495
Bonwit Teller, **13** 43; **17** 43
Book-Mart Press, Inc., **41** 111
**Book-of-the-Month Club, Inc.**, **IV** 661, 675; **7** 529; **13 105–07**
**Booker plc, 13 102–04**; **31 61–64 (upd.)**
Booker Tate, **13** 102
Booklink Technologies, **26** 19
Bookmasters, **10** 136
**Books-A-Million, Inc., 14 61–62**; **16** 161; **41 59–62 (upd.)**
Bookstop, **10** 136
**Boole & Babbage, Inc., 25 86–88**
Booth Bay, Ltd., **16** 37
**Booth Creek Ski Holdings, Inc., 31 65–67**
Booth Fisheries, **II** 571
Booth, Inc., **II** 420
Booth-Kelly Lumber Co., **IV** 281; **9** 259
Booth Leasing, **I** 449
Bootprint Entertainment, **31** 240
**The Boots Company PLC**, **I** 640, 668, 708; **II** 650; **V 17–19**; **8** 548; **19** 122; **24 72–76 (upd.)**
Boots Pharmaceuticals, **18** 51
**Booz Allen & Hamilton Inc., 10 172–75**
**Boral Limited**, **III 672–74**; **43 72–76 (upd.)**
Borax Holdings, **IV** 191
Bordas, **IV** 615
Borden Cabinet Corporation, **12** 296
**Borden, Inc.**, **II 470–73**, 486, 498, 538, 545; **IV** 569; **7** 127, 129, 380; **11** 173; **15** 490; **16** 43; **17** 56; **22** 84, **91–96 (upd.)**; **24** 273, 288, 520; **27** 38, 40, 316, 318
Border Fine Arts, **11** 95
Border Television, **41** 352
**Borders Group, Inc.**, **9** 361; **10** 137; **15 61–62**; **17** 522; **18** 286; **25** 17; **30** 69; **43 77–79 (upd.)**, 408; **47** 211
Borders, Perrin and Norrander, **23** 480
Borealis A/S, **30** 205; **45** 8
Borg Instruments, **23** 494
Borg-Warner Australia, **47** 280
**Borg-Warner Automotive, Inc., 14 63–66**; **23** 171; **32 93–97 (upd.)**
**Borg-Warner Corporation**, **I** 193, 339, 393; **III** 428, **438–41**; **14** 63, 357; **22** 228; **25** 74, 253
Borg-Warner Security Corporation, **13** 123–25; **14** 63, 65, 541; **41** 79
**Borland International, Inc.**, **6** 255–56; **9 80–82**; **10** 237, 509, 519, 558; **15** 492; **25** 300–01, 349; **38** 417

Borman's, Inc., **II** 638; **16** 249
Borneo Airways. *See* Malaysian Airlines System BHD.
Borneo Co., **III** 523
**Boron, LePore & Associates, Inc., 45 43–45**
Borregaard Osterreich AG, **18** 395
Borror Corporation. *See* Dominion Homes, Inc.
Borsheim's, **III** 215; **18** 60
Borun Bros., **12** 477
Bosanquet, Salt and Co., **II** 306
Bosch. *See* Robert Bosch GmbH.
Boschert, **III** 434
**Boscov's Department Store, Inc., 31 68–70**
**Bose Corporation, 13 108–10; 36 98–101 (upd.)**
Bosendorfer, L., Klavierfabrik, A.G., **12** 297
Bosert Industrial Supply, Inc., **V** 215
Boso Condensed Milk, **II** 538
Bost Sports Clubs. *See* Town Sports International, Inc.
Bostich, **III** 628
**Boston Acoustics, Inc., 22 97–99**
Boston and Maine Corporation, **16** 350
**Boston Beer Company, 18 70–73; 22** 422; **31** 383
Boston Brewing Company, **18** 502
Boston Casualty Co., **III** 203
**Boston Celtics Limited Partnership, 14 67–69**
**Boston Chicken, Inc., 12 42–44; 23** 266; **29** 170, 172. *See also* Boston Market Corporation.
Boston Co., **II** 451–52
Boston Consulting Group, **I** 532; **9** 343; **18** 70; **22** 193
Boston Corp., **25** 66
Boston Distributors, **9** 453
**Boston Edison Company, 12 45–47**
Boston Educational Research, **27** 373
Boston Fruit Co., **II** 595
Boston Garden Arena Corporation, **14** 67
Boston Gas Company, **6** 486–88
Boston Globe, **7** 13–16
Boston Herald, **7** 15
Boston Industries Corp., **III** 735
Boston Marine Insurance Co., **III** 242
**Boston Market Corporation, 48 64–67 (upd.)**
Boston National Bank, **13** 465
Boston News Bureau, **IV** 601
Boston Overseas Financial Corp., **II** 208
Boston Popcorn Co., **27** 197–98; **43** 218
**Boston Professional Hockey Association Inc., 39 61–63**
**Boston Properties, Inc., 22 100–02**
**Boston Scientific Corporation, 37 37–40**
Boston Technology, **43** 117
Boston Ventures Limited Partnership, **17** 444; **27** 41, 393
Boston Whaler, Inc., **V** 376–77; **10** 215–16; **26** 398
Bostrom Seating, Inc., **23** 306
BOTAS, **IV** 563
Botsford Ketchum, Inc., **6** 40
Botswana General Insurance Company, **22** 495
Botto, Rossner, Horne & Messinger, **6** 40
Bottu, **II** 475
BOTWEB, Inc., **39** 95
Bougainville Copper Pty., **IV** 60–61
Boulanger, **37** 22
Boulder Creek Steaks & Saloon, **16** 447
Boulder Natural Gas Company, **19** 411
Boulet Dru DuPuy Petit Group. *See* Wells Rich Greene BDDP.
Boulevard Bancorp, **12** 165
Boulton & Paul Ltd., **31** 398–400
Boundary Gas, **6** 457
Boundary Healthcare, **12** 327
Bouquet, **V** 114
Bourdon, **19** 49
Bourjois, **12** 57
Boussois Souchon Neuvesel, **II** 474; **III** 677; **16** 121–22
**Bouygues S.A., I 562–64; 13** 206; **23** 475–76; **24 77–80 (upd.)**; **31** 126, 128; **48** 204
Bouzan Mines Ltd., **IV** 164
Bovaird Seyfang Manufacturing Co., **III** 471
Bovis Construction, **38** 344–45
Bovis Ltd., **I** 588
Bow Bangles, **17** 101, 103
Bow Flex of America, Inc. *See* Direct Focus, Inc.
Bow Valley Energy Inc., **47** 397
**Bowater PLC, III** 501–02; **IV 257–59; 7** 208; **8** 483–84; **25** 13; **30** 229
Bower Roller Bearing Company. *See* Federal-Mogul Corporation.
Bowers and Merena Galleries Inc., **48** 99
Bowery and East River National Bank, **II** 226
Bowery Savings Bank, **II** 182; **9** 173
Bowes Co., **II** 631
Bowman Gum, Inc., **13** 520
Bowmar Instruments, **II** 113; **11** 506
**Bowne & Co., Inc., 18** 331–32; **23 61–64**
**Bowthorpe plc, 33 70–72**
Box Innards Inc., **13** 442
Box Office Attraction Co., **II** 169
BoxCrow Cement Company, **8** 259
**The Boy Scouts of America, 34 66–69**
**Boyd Bros. Transportation Inc., 39 64–66**
**Boyd Gaming Corporation, 43 80–82**
**The Boyds Collection, Ltd., 29 71–73**
Boyer Brothers, Inc., **14** 17–18
Boyer's International, Inc., **20** 83
Boykin Enterprises, **IV** 136
Boyles Bros. Drilling Company. *See* Christensen Boyles Corporation.
Boys Market, **17** 558–59
Boz, **IV** 697–98
Bozel Électrométallurgie, **IV** 174
Bozell, Jacobs, Kenyon, and Eckhardt Inc. *See* True North Communications Inc.
**Bozell Worldwide Inc., 25 89–91**
Bozkurt, **27** 188
**Bozzuto's, Inc., 13 111–12**
BP. *See* British Petroleum Company PLC.
BP Amoco plc, **31** 31, 34; **40** 358
BP Canada. *See* Talisman Energy Inc.
**BP p.l.c., 45 46–56 (upd.)**, 409, 412
BPB, **III** 736
BPD, **13** 356
BPI Communications, Inc., **7** 15; **19** 285; **27** 500
BR. *See* British Rail.
Braas, **III** 734, 736
**Braathens ASA, 47 60–62**
Brabant, **III** 199, 201
Brabazon, **III** 555
**Brach and Brock Confections, Inc., 15 63–65; 29** 47
Brad Foote Gear Works, **18** 453
Bradbury Agnew and Co., **IV** 686
Braden Manufacturing, **23** 299–301
Bradford District Bank, **II** 333
Bradford Exchange Ltd. Inc., **21** 269
Bradford Insulation Group, **III** 687
Bradford Pennine, **III** 373
**Bradlees Discount Department Store Company, II** 666–67; **12 48–50; 24** 461
Bradley Lumber Company, **8** 430
Bradley Producing Corp., **IV** 459
Bradstreet Co., **IV** 604–05; **19** 133
Braegen Corp., **13** 127
Bragussa, **IV** 71
BRAINS. *See* Belgian Rapid Access to Information Network Services.
**Brake Bros plc, 45 57–59**
**Bramalea Ltd., 9 83–85; 10** 530–31
**Brambles Industries Limited, III** 494–95; **24** 400; **42 47–50**
Bramco, **III** 600
Bramwell Gates, **II** 586
Bran & Lübbe, **III** 420
Brand Companies, Inc., **9** 110; **11** 436
Branded Restaurant Group, Inc., **12** 372
Brandeis & Sons, **19** 511
Brandenburgische Motorenwerke, **I** 138
Brandt Zwieback-Biskuits GmbH, **44** 40
Brandywine Asset Management, Inc., **33** 261
Brandywine Holdings Ltd., **45** 109
Brandywine Insurance Agency, Inc., **25** 540
Brandywine Iron Works and Nail Factory, **14** 323
Brandywine Valley Railroad Co., **14** 324
Braniff Airlines, **I** 97, 489, 548; **II** 445; **6** 50, 119–20; **16** 274; **17** 504; **21** 142; **22** 406; **36** 231
Branigar Organization, Inc., **IV** 345
**Brannock Device Company, 48 68–70**
Brascade Resources, **IV** 308
Brascan Ltd., **II** 456; **IV** 165, 330; **25** 281
Braspetro, **IV** 454, 501–02
Brass Craft Manufacturing Co., **III** 570; **20** 361
**Brass Eagle Inc., 34 70–72**
Brasseries Kronenbourg, **II** 474–75
Braswell Motor Freight, **14** 567
Braud & Faucheux. *See* Manitou BF S.A.
**Brauerei Beck & Co., 9 86–87; 33 73–76 (upd.)**
Braun, **III** 29; **17** 214–15; **26** 335
Braunkohlenwerk Golpa-Jessnitz AG, **IV** 230
Brauns Fashions Corporation. *See* Christopher & Banks Corporation.
Brazilian Central Bank, **IV** 56
Brazos Gas Compressing, **7** 345
**Brazos Sportswear, Inc., 23 65–67**
Breakstone Bros., Inc., **II** 533
Breakthrough Software, **10** 507
Breckenridge-Remy, **18** 216
Breco Holding Company, **17** 558, 561
Bredel Exploitatie B.V., **8** 546
Bredell Paint Co., **III** 745
Bredero's Bouwbedrijf of Utrecht, **IV** 707–08, 724
BREED Technologies, Inc., **22** 31
Breedband NV, **IV** 133

Brega Petroleum Marketing Co., **IV** 453, 455
Breguet Aviation, **I** 44; **24** 86
Breitenburger Cementfabrik, **III** 701
**Bremer Financial Corp., 45 60–63**
Bremner Biscuit Co., **II** 562; **13** 426
Brenco Inc., **16** 514
Brenda Mines Ltd., **7** 399
Brennan College Services, **12** 173
**Brenntag AG, 8 68–69**, 496; **23 68–70 (upd.)**, **23** 453–54
Brentwood Associates Buyout Fund II LP, **44** 54
Bresler's Industries, Inc., **35** 121
Breslube Enterprises, **8** 464
Bresser Optik, **41** 264
Brewster Lines, **6** 410
Breyers Ice Cream Co. *See* Good Humor-Breyers.
BRI Bar Review Institute, Inc., **IV** 623; **12** 224
BRI International, **21** 425
Brian Mills, **V** 118
Briarpatch, Inc., **12** 109
Brickwood Breweries, **I** 294
Bricorama, **23** 231
Bricotruc, **37** 259
Bridas S.A., **24** 522
Bridel, **19** 49–50; **25** 85
Bridge Communications Inc., **34** 442–43
Bridge Oil Ltd., **I** 438
Bridge Technology, Inc., **10** 395
Bridgeman Creameries, **II** 536
Bridgeport Brass, **I** 377
**Bridgeport Machines, Inc., 17 52–54**
**Bridgestone Corporation, V 234–35**; **15** 355; **20** 262; **21 72–75 (upd.)**
Bridgestone Liquefied Gas, **IV** 364
Bridgestone/Firestone, **19** 454, 456
Bridgeway Plan for Health, **6** 186
Bridgford Company, **13** 382
**Bridgford Foods Corporation, 27 71–73**
Brier Hill, **IV** 114
Brierly Investment Limited, **19** 156; **24** 399
**Briggs & Stratton Corporation, III** 597; **8 70–73**; **27 74–78 (upd.)**
Briggs and Lundy Lumber Cos., **14** 18
Brigham's Inc., **15** 71
**Bright Horizons Family Solutions, Inc., 31 71–73**
Bright of America Inc., **12** 426
Bright Star Technologies, **13** 92; **15** 455; **41** 362
Brighter Vision Learning Adventures, **29** 470, 472
Brighton & Hove Bus and Coach Company, **28** 155–56
Brighton Federal Savings and Loan Assoc., **II** 420
**Brightpoint, Inc., 18 74–77**
Brightwork Development Inc., **25** 348
Briker, **23** 231
Brillion Iron Works Inc., **23** 306
Brimsdown Lead Co., **III** 680
Brin's Oxygen Company Limited. *See* BOC Group plc.
Brinco Ltd., **II** 211
Brink's, Inc., **IV** 180–82; **19** 319
**Brinker International, Inc., 10 176–78**; **18** 438; **38 100–03 (upd.)**
Brinson Partners Inc., **41** 198
BRIntec, **III** 434
Brinton Carpets, **III** 423
**BRIO AB, 24 81–83**
Brio Technology, **25** 97
Briones Alonso y Martin, **42** 19
Brisbane Gas Co., **III** 673
Brisco Engineering, **41** 412
Bristol Aeroplane, **I** 50, 197; **10** 261; **24** 85
Bristol-BTR, **I** 429
Bristol-Erickson, **13** 297
Bristol Gaming Corporation, **21** 298
**Bristol Hotel Company, 23 71–73**; **38** 77
**Bristol-Myers Squibb Company, I** 26, 30, 37, 301, 696, 700, 703; **III 17–19**, 36, 67; **IV** 272; **6** 27; **7** 255; **8** 210, 282–83; **9 88–91 (upd.)**; **10** 70; **11** 289; **12** 126–27; **16** 438; **21** 546; **25** 91, 253, 365; **32** 213; **34** 280, 282, 284; **37 41–45 (upd.)**
Bristol PLC, **IV** 83
Bristol-Siddeley, Ltd., **I** 50; **24** 85
Britannia Airways, **8** 525–26
Britannia Security Group PLC, **12** 10
Britannia Soft Drinks Limited, **38** 77
Britannica Software, **7** 168
Britannica.com, **39** 140, 144
Britches of Georgetowne, **10** 215–16
BRITE. *See* Granada Group PLC.
**Brite Voice Systems, Inc., 20 75–78**
BriteSmile, Inc., **35** 325
British & Commonwealth Shipping Company, **10** 277
British Aerospace plc, **48** 81, 274
**British Aerospace plc, I** 42, 46, **50–53**, 55, 74, 83, 132, 532; **III** 458, 507; **V** 339; **7** 9, 11, 458–59; **8** 315; **9** 499; **11** 413; **12** 191; **14** 36; **18** 125; **21** 8, 443; **24 84–90 (upd.)**; **27** 474
**British Airways plc, I** 34, 83, **92–95**, 109; **IV** 658; **6** 60, 78–79, 118, 132; **14 70–74 (upd.)**; **18** 80; **22** 52; **24** 86, 311, 396, 399–400; **26** 115; **27** 20–21, 466; **28** 25, 508; **31** 103; **33** 270; **34** 398; **37** 232; **38** 104–05; **39** 137–38; **43 83–88 (upd.)**
British Aluminium, Ltd., **II** 422; **IV** 15
British American Cosmetics, **I** 427
British American Financial Services, **42** 450
British American Insurance Co., **III** 350
British American Nickel, **IV** 110
British-American Tobacco Co., Ltd., **V** 396, 401–02, 417; **9** 312; **29** 194–95; **34** 39
British and Dominion Film Corp., **II** 157
British and Foreign Marine, **III** 350
British and Foreign Steam Navigation Company, **23** 160
British and French Bank, **II** 232–33
British and North American Royal Mail Steam Packet Company. *See* Cunard Line Ltd.
British Bank of North America, **II** 210
British Bank of the Middle East, **II** 298
**British-Borneo Oil & Gas PLC, 34 73–75**
British Borneo Timber Co., **III** 699
**British Broadcasting Corporation Ltd., III** 163; **IV** 651; **7 52–55**; **21 76–79 (upd.)**; **24** 192; **39** 198; **42** 114, 116
British Caledonian Airways, **I** 94–95; **6** 79
British Can Co., **I** 604
British Car Auctions, **14** 321
British Celanese Ltd., **I** 317
British Cellulose and Chemical Manufacturing Co., **I** 317
British Chrome, **III** 699
**British Coal Corporation, IV 38–40**
British Columbia Forest Products Ltd., **IV** 279; **19** 155
British Columbia Packers, **II** 631–32
British Columbia Resources Investment Corp., **IV** 308
**British Columbia Telephone Company, IV** 308; **6 309–11**
British Commonwealth Insurance, **III** 273
British Commonwealth Pacific Airways, **6** 110; **24** 398
British Continental Airlines, **I** 92
British Credit Trust, **10** 443
British Data Management, Ltd., **33** 212, 214
British Digital Broadcasting plc, **24** 192, 194
British Dyestuffs Corp., **I** 351
British Dynamite Co., **I** 351
British Electric Traction Company. *See* Rentokil Initial Plc.
British Energy Group, **19** 391
British Engine, **III** 350
British European Airways, **I** 93, 466
British Executive and General Aviation, **I** 50; **24** 85
British Fuels, **III** 735
**British Gas plc, II** 260; **V 559–63**; **6** 478–79; **11** 97; **18** 365–67; **38** 408. *See also* Centrica plc.
British Gauge and Instrument Company, **13** 234
British General, **III** 234
British General Post Office, **25** 99–100
British Goodrich Tyre Co., **I** 428
British Home Stores PLC. *See* Storehouse PLC.
British Hovercraft Corp., **I** 120
British Independent Television Enterprises Ltd. *See* Granada Group PLC.
British India and Queensland Agency Co. Ltd., **III** 522
British India Steam Navigation Co., **III** 521–22
British Industrial Solvents Ltd., **IV** 70
British Industry, **III** 335
British Insulated and Helsby Cables Ltd., **III** 433–34
British Interactive Broadcasting Ltd., **20** 79
British Isles Transport Co. Ltd., **II** 564
British Land Company PLC, **10** 6; **47** 168
British Leyland Motor Corporation, **I** 175, 186; **III** 516, 523; **13** 286–87; **14** 35–36; **47** 8
British Linen Bank, **10** 336
British Marine Air Navigation, **I** 92
British Metal Corp., **IV** 140, 164
**British Midland plc, 34** 398; **38 104–06**
British Motor Corporation, **III** 555; **7** 459; **13** 286
British Motor Holdings, **7** 459
British National Films Ltd., **II** 157
British National Oil Corp., **IV** 40
British Newfoundland Corporation, **6** 502
**British Nuclear Fuels PLC, I** 573; **6 451–54**; **13** 458
British Nylon Spinners (BNS), **17** 118
British Overseas Airways Corp., **I** 51, 93, 120–21; **III** 522; **6** 78–79, 100, 110, 112, 117; **14** 71; **24** 86, 397
British Oxygen Co. *See* BOC Group.
**The British Petroleum Company plc, I** 241, 303; **II** 449, 563; **IV** 61, 280,

BSN Medical, **41** 374, 377
BSR, **II** 82
BT. *See* British Telecommunications, plc.
**BTG, Inc., 45 68–70**
BTI Services, **9** 59
BTM. *See* British Tabulating Machine Company.
BTR Dunlop Holdings, Inc., **21** 432
**BTR plc, I 428–30; III** 185, 727; **8** 397; **24** 88
**BTR Siebe plc, 27 79–81**
**Buca, Inc., 38 115–17**
Buchanan, **I** 239–40
Buchanan Electric Steel Company, **8** 114
Buck Consultants Inc., **32** 459
**Buck Knives Inc., 48 71–74**
Buckaroo International. *See* Bugle Boy Industries, Inc.
Buckeye Business Products Inc., **17** 384
**Buckeye Technologies, Inc., 42 51–54**
Buckeye Tractor Ditcher, **21** 502
Buckeye Union Casualty Co., **III** 242
Buckhorn, Inc., **19** 277–78
Buckingham Corp., **I** 440, 468
**The Buckle, Inc., 18 84–86**
Buckler Broadcast Group, **IV** 597
Buckley/DeCerchio New York, **25** 180
Bucyrus Blades, Inc., **14** 81
Bucyrus-Erie Company, **7** 513
**Bucyrus International, Inc., 17 58–61**
Bud Bailey Construction, **43** 400
Budapest Bank, **16** 14
**The Budd Company, III** 568; **IV** 222; **8 74–76**; **20** 359
**Buderus AG, III** 692, 694–95; **37 46–49**
**Budget Group, Inc., 25 92–94**
**Budget Rent a Car Corporation, I** 537; **6** 348–49, 393; **9 94–95**; **13** 529; **22** 524; **24** 12, 409; **25** 143; **39** 370; **41** 402
Budgetel Inn. *See* Marcus Corporation.
Budweiser, **18** 70
Budweiser Japan Co., **21** 320
Buena Vista Distribution, **II** 172; **6** 174; **30** 487
Buena Vista Music Group, **44** 164
**Bufete Industrial, S.A. de C.V., 34 80–82**
Buffalo Forge Company, **7** 70–71
Buffalo Insurance Co., **III** 208
Buffalo Mining Co., **IV** 181
*Buffalo News*, **18** 60
Buffalo Paperboard, **19** 78
Buffalo-Springfield, **21** 502
**Buffets, Inc., 10 186–87**; **22** 465; **32 102–04 (upd.)**
Buffett Partnership, Ltd., **III** 213
Bugaboo Creek Steak House Inc., **19** 342
Bugatti Industries, **14** 321
**Bugle Boy Industries, Inc., 18 87–88**
**Buhrmann NV, 41 67–69**; **47** 90–91
Buick Motor Co., **I** 171; **III** 438; **8** 74; **10** 325
Builders Emporium, **13** 169; **25** 535
Builders Square, **V** 112; **9** 400; **12** 345, 385; **14** 61; **16** 210; **31** 20; **35** 11, 13; **47** 209
Building One Services Corporation. *See* Encompass Services Corporation.
Building Products of Canada Limited, **25** 232
Buitoni SpA, **II** 548; **17** 36
**Bulgari S.p.A., 20 94–97**
Bulgarian Oil Co., **IV** 454
Bulgheroni SpA, **27** 105
Bulkships, **27** 473
Bull. *See* Compagnie des Machines Bull S.A.
Bull-GE, **III** 123
Bull HN Information Systems, **III** 122–23
Bull Motors, **11** 5
Bull Run Corp., **24** 404
Bull S.A., **III** 122–23; **43 89–91 (upd.)**
Bull Tractor Company, **7** 534; **16** 178; **26** 492
Bull-Zenith, **25** 531
Bulldog Computer Products, **10** 519
Bullock's, **III** 63; **31** 191
Bulolo Gold Dredging, **IV** 95
**Bulova Corporation, I** 488; **II** 101; **III** 454–55; **12** 316–17, 453; **13 120–22**; **14** 501; **21** 121–22; **36** 325; **41 70–73 (upd.)**
Bumble Bee Seafoods, Inc., **II** 491, 508, 557; **24** 114
Bumkor-Ramo Corp., **I** 539
Bunawerke Hüls GmbH., **I** 350
**Bundy Corporation, 17 62–65**, 480
Bunker Ramo Info Systems, **III** 118
Bunte Candy, **12** 427
**Bunzl plc, IV 260–62**; **12** 264; **31 77–80 (upd.)**
Buquet, **19** 49
Burbank Aircraft Supply, Inc., **14** 42–43; **37** 29, 31
**Burberry Ltd., 41 74–76 (upd.)**; **47** 167, 169
**Burberrys Ltd., V** 68; **10** 122; **17 66–68**; **19** 181
**Burda Holding GmbH. & Co., 20** 53; **23 85–89**
Burdines, **9** 209; **31** 192
Bureau de Recherches de Pétrole, **IV** 544–46, 559–60; **7** 481–83; **21** 203–04
**The Bureau of National Affairs, Inc., 23 90–93**
**Burelle S.A., 23 94–96**
Burger and Aschenbrenner, **16** 486
Burger Boy Food-A-Rama, **8** 564
Burger Chef, **II** 532
**Burger King Corporation, I** 21, 278; **II** 556–57, **613–15**, 647; **7** 316; **8** 564; **9** 178; **10** 122; **12** 43, 553; **13** 408–09; **14** 25, 32, 212, 214, 452; **16** 95–97, 396; **17 69–72 (upd.)**, 501; **18** 437; **21** 25, 362; **23** 505; **24** 140–41; **25** 228; **26** 284; **33** 240–41; **36** 517, 519
Burgess, Anderson & Tate Inc., **25** 500
Bürhle, **17** 36
Burhmann-Tetterode, **22** 154
Burke Scaffolding Co., **9** 512
BURLE Industries Inc., **11** 444
Burlesdon Brick Co., **III** 734
**Burlington Coat Factory Warehouse Corporation, 10 188–89**
Burlington Homes of New England, **14** 138
**Burlington Industries, Inc., V** 118, **354–55**; **8** 234; **9** 231; **12** 501; **17 73–76 (upd.)**, 304–05; **19** 275
Burlington Mills Corporation, **12** 117–18
Burlington Motor Holdings, **30** 114
**Burlington Northern, Inc., IV** 182; **V 425–28**; **10** 190–91; **11** 315; **12** 145, 278
**Burlington Northern Santa Fe Corporation, 27 82–89 (upd.)**; **28** 495
**Burlington Resources Inc., 10 190–92**; **11** 135; **12** 144; **47** 238
**Burmah Castrol PLC, IV** 378, **381–84**, 440–41, 483–84, 531; **7** 56; **15** 246; **21** 80; **30 86–91 (upd.)**; **45** 55
Burmeister & Wain, **III** 417–18
Burn & Co., **IV** 205
Burn Standard Co. Ltd., **IV** 484
Burnards, **II** 677
Burndy, **19** 166
Burnham and Co., **II** 407–08; **6** 599; **8** 388
Burns & Ricker, Inc., **40** 51, 53
Burns & Wilcox Ltd., **6** 290
Burns-Alton Corp., **21** 154–55
Burns Companies, **III** 569; **20** 360
Burns Fry Ltd., **II** 349
**Burns International Security Services, III** 440; **13 123–25**; **42** 338. *See also* Securitas AB.
**Burns International Services Corporation, 41 77–80 (upd.)**
Burns Philp & Company Limited, **21** 496–98
Burnup & Sims, Inc., **19** 254; **26** 324
Burpee & Co. *See* W. Atlee Burpee & Co.
Burr & Co., **II** 424; **13** 340
**Burr-Brown Corporation, 19 66–68**
Burrill & Housman, **II** 424; **13** 340
Burris Industries, **14** 303
Burroughs Corp., **I** 142, 478; **III** 132, 148–49, 152, 165–66; **6** 233, 266, 281–83; **18** 386, 542. *See also* Unisys Corporation.
Burroughs Mfg. Co., **16** 321
Burroughs Wellcome & Co., **I** 713; **8** 216
Burrows, Marsh & McLennan, **III** 282
Burrups Ltd., **18** 331, 333; **47** 243
Burry, **II** 560; **12** 410
Bursley & Co., **II** 668
Burt Claster Enterprises, **III** 505
Burthy China Clays, **III** 690
Burton-Furber Co., **IV** 180
**Burton Group plc, V 20–22**. *See also* Arcadia Group plc.
Burton J. Vincent, Chesley & Co., **III** 271
Burton, Parsons and Co. Inc., **II** 547
Burton Retail, **V** 21
Burton Rubber Processing, **8** 347
**Burton Snowboards Inc., 22 118–20**, 460
Burtons Gold Medal Biscuits Limited, **II** 466; **13** 53
Burwell Brick, **14** 248
Bury Group, **II** 581
Busch Entertainment Corporation, **34** 36
**Bush Boake Allen Inc., IV** 346; **30 92–94**; **38** 247
**Bush Brothers & Company, 45 71–73**
Bush Hog, **21** 20–22
**Bush Industries, Inc., 20 98–100**
Bush Terminal Company, **15** 138
Business Communications Group, Inc. *See* Caribiner International, Inc.
Business Depot, Limited, **10** 498
Business Expansion Capital Corp., **12** 42
Business Express Airlines, Inc., **28** 22
Business Information Technology, Inc., **18** 112
**Business Men's Assurance Company of America, III** 209; **13** 476; **14 83–85**; **15** 30
**Business Objects S.A., 25 95–97**
**Business Post Group plc, 46 71–73**
Business Resources Corp., **23** 489, 491
Business Science Computing, **14** 36
Business Software Association, **10** 35
Business Software Technology, **10** 394

Business Wire, **25** 240
Businessland Inc., **III** 153; **6** 267; **10** 235; **13** 175–76, 277, 482
Busse Broadcasting Corporation, **7** 200; **24** 199
Büssing Automobilwerke AG, **IV** 201
Buster Brown, **V** 351–52
BUT S.A., **24** 266, 270
Butano, **IV** 528
Butler Bros., **21** 96
Butler Cox PLC, **6** 229
Butler Group, Inc., **30** 310–11
**Butler Manufacturing Co., 12 51–53; 43** 130
Butler Shoes, **16** 560
Butterfield & Butterfield, **32** 162
Butterfield & Swire. *See* Swire Pacific Ltd.
Butterfield, Wasson & Co., **II** 380, 395; **10** 59; **12** 533
**Butterick Co., Inc., 23 97–99**
Butterley Company, **III** 501; **7** 207
Butterworth & Co. (Publishers) Ltd., **IV** 641; **7** 311; **17** 398
**Buttrey Food & Drug Stores Co., 18 89–91**
Butz Thermo-Electric Regulator Co., **II** 40; **12** 246
Buxton, **III** 28; **23** 21
**buy.com, Inc., 46 74–77**
Buzzard Electrical & Plumbing Supply, **9** 399; **16** 186
BVA Investment Corp., **11** 446–47
BVD, **25** 166
**BWAY Corporation, 24 91–93**
BWP Distributors, **29** 86, 88
Byerly's, Inc. *See* Lund Food Holdings, Inc.
Byers Machines, **21** 502
Byrnes Long Island Motor Cargo, Inc., **6** 370
Byron Jackson, **III** 428, 439. *See also* BJ Services Company.
Byron Weston Company, **26** 105
Bytrex, Inc., **III** 643

**C&A, 40 74–77 (upd.)**
**C&A Brenninkmeyer KG, V 23–24**
C&E Software, **10** 507
C.&E. Cooper Co., **II** 14
C & G Systems, **19** 442
C.&G. Cooper Company, **II** 14; **20** 162
C & H Distributors, Inc., **27** 177
C & O. *See* Chesapeake and Ohio Railway.
C&R Clothiers, **17** 313
C&S Bank, **10** 425–26
C&S/Sovran Corporation, **10** 425–27; **18** 518; **26** 453; **46** 52
**C-COR.net Corp., 38 118–21**
**C-Cube Microsystems, Inc., 37 50–54; 43** 221–22
C.A. Delaney Capital Management Ltd., **32** 437
C.A. Pillsbury and Co., **II** 555
C.A. Reed Co., **IV** 353; **19** 498
C.A.S. Sports Agency Inc., **22** 460, 462
C.A. Swanson & Sons. *See* Vlasic Foods International Inc.
C. Bechstein, **III** 657
C. Brewer, **I** 417; **24** 32
C.D. Haupt, **IV** 296; **19** 226
C.D. Kenny Co., **II** 571
C.D. Magirus AG, **III** 541
C.E. Chappell & Sons, Inc., **16** 61–62
C.E.T. *See* Club Européen du Tourisme.
C.F. Burns and Son, Inc., **21** 154
C.F. Hathaway Company, **12** 522
**C.F. Martin & Co., Inc., 42 55–58; 48** 231
C.F. Mueller Co., **I** 497–98; **12** 332; **47** 234
C.F. Orvis Company. *See* The Orvis Company, Inc.
C. Francis, Son and Co., **III** 669
C.G. Conn, **7** 286
**C.H. Boehringer Sohn, 39 70–73**
C.H. Dexter & Co., **I** 320
**C.H. Heist Corporation, 24 111–13**
C.H. Knorr Company, **II** 497; **22** 83
C.H. Masland & Sons. *See* Masland Corporation.
C.H. Musselman Co., **7** 429
**C.H. Robinson, Inc., 8** 379–80; **11 43–44; 23** 357
**C.H. Robinson Worldwide, Inc., 40 78–81 (upd.)**
C-I-L, Inc., **III** 745; **13** 470
**C. Itoh & Co., I 431–33**, 492, 510; **II** 273, 292, 361, 442, 679; **IV** 269, 326, 516, 543; **7** 529; **10** 500; **17** 124; **24** 324–25; **26** 456. *See also* ITOCHU Corporation.
C.J. Devine, **II** 425
C.J. Lawrence, Morgan Grenfell Inc., **II** 429
C.J. Smith and Sons, **11** 3
C.L. Bencard, **III** 66
C. Lee Cook Co., **III** 467
C.M. Aikman & Co., **13** 168
C.M. Armstrong, Inc., **14** 17
C.M. Barnes Company, **10** 135
C.M. Page, **14** 112
C-MAC Industries Inc., **48** 369
C.O. Lovette Company, **6** 370
C.O.M.B. Company, **18** 131–33
C/P Utility Services Company, **14** 138
C.P.U., Inc., **18** 111–12
C.R. Anthony Company, **24** 458
**C.R. Bard Inc., IV** 287; **9 96–98; 22** 360–61
C.R. Eggs, Inc., **25** 332
C. Reichenbach'sche Maschinenfabrik, **III** 561
C. Rowbotham & Sons, **III** 740
C.S. Rolls & Co., **I** 194
C.T. Bowring, **III** 280, 283; **22** 318
C-Tec Corp. *See* Commonwealth Telephone Enterprises, Inc.
C.V. Buchan & Co., **I** 567
C.V. Gebroeders Pel, **7** 429
C.V. Mosby Co., **IV** 677–78
C.W. Acquisitions, **27** 288
C.W. Costello & Associates Inc., **31** 131
C.W. Holt & Co., **III** 450
C.W. Zumbiel Company, **11** 422
C. Wuppesahl & Co. Assekuranzmakler, **25** 538
CAA. *See* Creative Artists Agency LLC.
Cabana (Holdings) Ltd., **44** 318
**Cabela's Inc., 26 49–51**
**Cable & Wireless HKT, 30 95–98 (upd.)**. *See also* Hong Kong Telecomminications Ltd.
**Cable and Wireless plc, IV** 695; **V 283–86; 7** 332–33; **11** 547; **15** 69, 521; **17** 419; **18** 253; **25 98–102 (upd.); 26** 332; **27** 307
Cable Communications Operations, Inc., **6** 313
Cable London, **25** 497
Cable Management Advertising Control System, **25** 497
Cable News Network, **II** 166–68; **6** 171–73; **9** 30; **12** 546
Cablec Corp., **III** 433–34
Cableform, **I** 592
**Cabletron Systems, Inc., 10 193–94; 10** 511; **20** 8; **24** 183; **26** 276
**Cablevision Electronic Instruments, Inc., 32 105–07**
**Cablevision Systems Corporation, 7 63–65; 18** 211; **30 99–103 (upd.)**106; **47** 421. *See also* Cablevision Electronic Instruments, Inc.
Cabot, Cabot & Forbes, **22** 100
**Cabot Corporation, 8 77–79; 29 79–82 (upd.)**
Cabot Medical Corporation, **21** 117, 119
Cabot-Morgan Real Estate Co., **16** 159
Cabot Noble Inc., **18** 503, 507
Cabrera Vulcan Shoe Corp., **22** 213
**Cache Incorporated, 30 104–06**
**CACI International Inc., 21 85–87**
Cacique, **24** 237
Cadadia, **II** 641–42
**Cadbury Schweppes PLC, I** 25–26, 220, 288; **II 476–78**, 510, 512, 592; **III** 554; **6** 51–52; **9** 178; **15** 221; **22** 513; **25** 3, 5; **39** 383, 385
CADCAM Technology Inc., **22** 196
Caddell Construction Company, **12** 41
Cademartori, **23** 219
**Cadence Design Systems, Inc., 6** 247; **10** 118; **11 45–48**, 285, 490–91; **24** 235; **35** 346; **38** 188; **48 75–79 (upd.)**
Cadence Industries Corporation, **10** 401–02
Cadet Uniform Services Ltd., **21** 116
Cadillac Automobile Co., **I** 171; **10** 325
Cadillac Fairview Corp., **IV** 703
Cadillac Plastic, **8** 347
Cadisys Corporation, **10** 119
**Cadmus Communications Corporation, 16** 531; **23 100–03**
Cadoricin, **III** 47
**CAE USA Inc., 8** 519; **48 80–82**
**Caere Corporation, 20 101–03**
Caesar-Wollheim-Gruppe, **IV** 197
**Caesars World, Inc., 6 199–202; 17** 318
Caf'Casino, **12** 152
Café Express, **47** 443
Café Grand Mère, **II** 520
Caffarel, **27** 105
CAFO, **III** 241
Cagiva Group, **17** 24; **30** 172; **39** 37
**Cagle's, Inc., 20 104–07**
**Cahners Business Information, 43 92–95**
Cahners Publishing, **IV** 667; **12** 561; **17** 398; **22** 442
CAI Corp., **12** 79
Cailler, **II** 546
Cain Chemical, **IV** 481
Cains Marcelle Potato Chips Inc., **15** 139
Caisse Commericale de Bruxelles, **II** 270
Caisse de dépôt et placement du Quebec, **II** 664
Caisse des Dépôts, **6** 206
Caisse des Dépôts—Développement (C3D), **48** 107
Caisse National de Crédit Agricole, **II** 264–66
Caisse Nationale de Crédit Agricole, **15** 38–39
Caithness Glass Limited, **38** 402

Caja General de Depositos, **II** 194
Cajun Bayou Distributors and Management, Inc., **19** 301
Cajun Electric Power Cooperative, Inc., **21** 470
CAK Universal Credit Corp., **32** 80
CAL. *See* China Airlines.
Cal Circuit Abco Inc., **13** 387
CAL Corporation, **21** 199, 201
Cal-Dive International Inc., **25** 104–05
Cal-Van Tools. *See* Chemi-Trol Chemical Co.
Cal/Ink, **13** 228
Cala, **17** 558
Calais Railroad Company, **16** 348
**Calavo Growers, Inc., 47 63–66**
Calcined Coke Corp., **IV** 402
Calcitherm Group, **24** 144
Calco, **I** 300–01
**CalComp Inc., 13 126–29**
**Calcot Ltd., 33 84–87**
Calculating-Tabulating-Recording Company. *See* International Business Machines Corporation.
Calcutta & Burmah Steam Navigation Co., **III** 521
Caldbeck Macgregor & Co., **III** 523
Calder Race Course, Inc., **29** 118
Caldera Systems Inc., **38** 416, 420
**Caldor Inc., 12 54–56**, 508; **30** 57
Caledonian Airways. *See* British Caledonian Airways.
Caledonian Bank, **10** 337
Caledonian Paper plc, **IV** 302
Calédonickel, **IV** 107
Calgary Power Company. *See* TransAlta Utilities Corporation.
Calgene, Inc., **29** 330; **41** 155
Calgon Corporation, **6** 27; **16** 387; **34** 281
Calgon Vestal Laboratories, **37** 44
Calgon Water Management, **15** 154; **40** 176
Cali Realty. *See* Mack-Cali Realty Corporation.
California Arabian Standard Oil Co., **IV** 536, 552
California Automated Design, Inc., **11** 284
California Bank, **II** 289
California Charter Inc., **24** 118
California Cheese, **24** 444
California Computer Products, Inc. *See* CalComp Inc.
California Cooler Inc., **I** 227, 244; **10** 181
California Dental Supply Co., **19** 289
California Design Studio, **31** 52
California Federal Bank, **22** 275
California First, **II** 358
California Fruit Growers Exchange. *See* Sunkist Growers, Inc.
California Ink Company, **13** 227
California Institute of Technology, **9** 367
California Insurance Co., **III** 234
California Oilfields, Ltd., **IV** 531, 540
California Pacific, **22** 172
California Perfume Co., **III** 15
California Petroleum Co., **IV** 551–52
**California Pizza Kitchen Inc., 15 74–76**
California Plant Protection, **9** 408
California Portland Cement Co., **III** 718; **19** 69
California Pro Sports Inc., **24** 404
California Slim, **27** 197
California Steel Industries, **IV** 125
California Telephone and Light, **II** 490
California Test Bureau, **IV** 636
California Texas Oil Co., **III** 672
California Tile, **III** 673
California-Western States Life Insurance Co., **III** 193–94
California Woodfiber Corp., **IV** 266
Caligen, **9** 92
Caligor. *See* Henry Schein Medical.
Call-Chronicle Newspapers, Inc., **IV** 678
Callaghan & Company, **8** 526
Callard and Bowser, **II** 594
**Callaway Golf Company, 15 77–79; 16** 109; **19** 430, 432; **23** 267, 474; **37** 4; **45 74–77 (upd.); 46** 13
Callaway Wines, **I** 264
Callebaut, **II** 520–21
Callender's Cable and Construction Co. Ltd., **III** 433–34
**Callon Petroleum Company, 47 67–69**
Calloway's Nursery Inc., **12** 200
Calma, **II** 30; **12** 196
Calmar Co., **12** 127
**CalMat Co., III** 718; **19 69–72**
Calmic Ltd., **I** 715
Calor Group, **IV** 383
Caloric Corp., **II** 86
**Calpine Corporation, 36 102–04**
Calsil Ltd., **III** 674
**Caltex Petroleum Corporation, II** 53; **III** 672; **IV** 397, 434, 440–41, 479, 484, 492, 519, 527, 536, 545–46, 552, 560, 562, 718; **7** 483; **19 73–75; 21** 204; **25** 471; **38** 320; **41** 392–93
Calumatic Group, **25** 82
Calumet & Arizona Mining Co., **IV** 177
Calumet Electric Company, **6** 532
Calvert & Co., **I** 293
Calvert Insurance Co. *See* Gryphon Holdings, Inc.
Calvin Bullock Ltd., **I** 472
**Calvin Klein, Inc., 9** 203; **22 121–24; 25** 258; **27** 329; **32** 476
Calyx & Corolla Inc., **37** 162–63
Camargo Foods, **12** 531
Camas. *See* Aggregate Industries plc.
CamBar. *See* Cameron & Barkley Company.
Camber Corporation, **25** 405
Cambex, **46** 164
**Cambrex Corporation, 12** 147–48; **16 67–69; 44 59–62 (upd.)**
Cambria Steel Company, **IV** 35; **7** 48
Cambrian Wagon Works Ltd., **31** 369
Cambridge Applied Nutrition Toxicology and Biosciences Ltd., **10** 105
Cambridge Biotech Corp., **13** 241
Cambridge Electric Co., **14** 124, 126
Cambridge Gas Co., **14** 124
The Cambridge Instrument Company, **35** 272
Cambridge Interactive Systems Ltd., **10** 241
**Cambridge SoundWorks, 36** 101; **Inc., 48 83–86**
Cambridge Steam Corp., **14** 124
**Cambridge Technology Partners, Inc., 36 105–08**
Cambridge Tool & Mfg. Co. Inc., **48** 268
Camco Inc., **IV** 658
Camden Wire Co., Inc., **7** 408; **31** 354–55
CAMECO, **IV** 436
Camelot Barthropp Ltd., **26** 62
Camelot Group plc, **34** 140
**Camelot Music, Inc., 26 52–54**
**Cameron & Barkley Company, 13** 79; **28 59–61**
Cameron Ashley Inc., **19** 57
Cameron-Brown Company, **10** 298
Cameron Iron Works, **II** 17
Cameron Oil Co., **IV** 365
CAMI Automotive, **III** 581
Camintonn, **9** 41–42
Camp Manufacturing Co., **IV** 345; **8** 102
Campbell Box & Tag Co., **IV** 333
Campbell Cereal Company. *See* Malt-O-Meal Company.
Campbell, Cowperthwait & Co., **17** 498
Campbell-Ewald Co., **I** 16–17
Campbell Hausfeld. *See* Scott Fetzer Company.
Campbell Industries, Inc., **11** 534
**Campbell-Mithun-Esty, Inc., 13** 516; **16 70–72**
**Campbell Soup Company, I** 21, 26, 31, 599, 601; **II 479–81**, 508, 684; **7 66–69 (upd.)**, 340; **10** 382; **11** 172; **18** 58; **25** 516; **26 55–59 (upd.); 33** 32; **43** 121; **44** 295
Campbell Taggart, Inc., **I** 219; **19** 135–36, 191; **34** 36
**Campeau Corporation, IV** 721; **V 25–28; 9** 209, 211, 391; **12** 36–37; **13** 43; **15** 94; **17** 560; **22** 110; **23** 60; **31** 192; **37** 13
**Campo Electronics, Appliances & Computers, Inc., 16 73–75**
Campo Lindo, **25** 85
Campofrio Alimentacion, S.A., **18** 247
CAMPSA. *See* Compañia Arrendataria del Monopolio de Petróleos Sociedad Anónima.
Campus Services, Inc., **12** 173
Canada & Dominion Sugar Co., **II** 581
Canada Cable & Wire Company, **9** 11
Canada Cement, **III** 704–05
Canada Cup, **IV** 290
Canada Development Corp., **IV** 252; **17** 29
Canada Dry, **I** 281
Canada, Limited, **24** 143
**Canada Packers Inc., II 482–85; 41** 249
Canada Safeway Ltd., **II** 650, 654
Canada Surety Co., **26** 486
Canada Trust. *See* CT Financial Services Inc.
Canada Tungsten Mining Corp., Ltd., **IV** 18
Canada Wire & Cable Company, Ltd., **IV** 164–65; **7** 397–99
**Canadair, Inc., I** 58; **7** 205; **13** 358; **16 76–78**
Canadian Ad-Check Services Inc., **26** 270
Canadian Airlines International Ltd., **6** 61–62, 101; **12** 192; **23** 10; **24** 400
Canadian Bank of Commerce, **II** 244–45
Canadian British Aluminum, **IV** 11
**The Canadian Broadcasting Corporation (CBC), 37 55–58**
Canadian Cellucotton Products Ltd., **III** 40; **16** 302; **43** 256
Canadian Copper, **IV** 110
Canadian Copper Refiners, Ltd., **IV** 164
Canadian Dominion Steel and Coal Corp., **III** 508
Canadian Eastern Finance, **IV** 693
Canadian Fina Oil, **IV** 498
Canadian Football League, **12** 457
Canadian Forest Products, **IV** 270. *See also* Canfor Corporation.

Canadian Freightways, Ltd., **48** 113
Canadian Fuel Marketers, **IV** 566
Canadian General Electric Co., **8** 544–45
Canadian Government Merchant Marine, **6** 360–61
Canadian Gridoil Ltd., **IV** 373
**Canadian Imperial Bank of Commerce, II 244–46**; **IV** 693; **7** 26–28; **10** 8; **32** 12, 14
Canadian Industrial Alcohol Company Limited, **14** 141
Canadian International Paper Co., **IV** 286–87; **15** 228
Canadian Keyes Fibre Company, Limited of Nova Scotia, **9** 305
**Canadian National Railway System, I** 284; **6 359–62**; **12** 278–79; **22** 444; **23** 10
Canadian Niagara Power Company, **47** 137
Canadian Odeon Theatres, **6** 161; **23** 123
Canadian Overseas Telecommunications Corporation, **25** 100
Canadian Pacific Enterprises, **III** 611
**Canadian Pacific Limited, V 429–31**; **8** 544–46
**Canadian Pacific Railway Limited, I** 573; **II** 210, 220, 344; **III** 260; **IV** 272, 308, 437; **6** 359–60; **25** 230; **45 78–83 (upd.)**
Canadian Packing Co. Ltd., **II** 482
Canadian Petrofina, **IV** 498
Canadian Radio-Television and Telecommunications Commission, **6** 309
Canadian Steel Foundries, Ltd., **39** 31
Canadian Telephones and Supplies, **6** 310
Canadian Tire Corporation, Limited, **25** 144
Canadian Transport Co., **IV** 308
**Canadian Utilities Limited, 13 130–32**
Canadian Vickers, **16** 76
Canal Bank, **11** 105
Canal Electric Co., **14** 125–26
**Canal Plus, III** 48; **7** 392; **10 195–97**, 345, 347; **23** 476; **29** 369, 371; **31** 330; **33** 181; **34 83–86 (upd.)**
CanalSatellite, **29** 369, 371
CanAmera Foods, **7** 82
**Canandaigua Brands, Inc., 34 87–91 (upd.)**
**Canandaigua Wine Company, Inc., 13 133–35**
Cananwill, **III** 344
**Canary Wharf Group Plc, 30 107–09**
**Candela Corporation, 48 87–89**
**Candie's, Inc., 31 81–84**
Candle Corporation of America. *See* Blyth Industries, Inc.
**Candlewood Hotel Company, Inc., 41 81–83**
Candy SpA, **22** 350
**Canfor Corporation, IV** 321; **17** 540; **42 59–61**
Cannell Communications, **25** 418
Cannon Assurance Ltd., **III** 276
Cannon Mills, Co., **9** 214–16
**Cannondale Corporation, 16** 494; **21 88–90**; **26** 183, 412
**Canon Inc., I** 494; **II** 103, 292; **III 120–21**, 143, 172, 575, 583–84; **6** 238, 289; **9** 251; **10** 23; **13** 482; **15** 150; **18 92–95 (upd.)**, 186, 341–42, 383, 386–87; **24** 324; **26** 213; **33** 13; **43** 152, 283–84
Canpet Exploration Ltd., **IV** 566
Canpotex Ltd., **18** 432
Canrad-Hanovia, **27** 57
Cans Inc., **I** 607
**Canstar Sports Inc., 15** 396–97; **16 79–81**
Canteen Corp., **I** 127; **II** 679–80; **12** 489; **13** 321
Cantel Corp., **11** 184; **18** 32; **20** 76; **30** 388
**Canterbury Park Holding Corporation, 42 62–65**
Canterra Energy Ltd., **47** 180
Canton Chemical, **I** 323; **8** 147
Canton Railway Corp., **IV** 718; **38** 320
Cantor Fitzgerald Securities Corporation, **10** 276–78
**CanWest Global Communications Corporation, 35 67–70**; **39** 13
Canyon Cafes, **31** 41
**Cap Gemini Ernst & Young, 37 59–61**
**Cap Rock Energy Corporation, 6** 580; **46 78–81**
Capacity of Texas, Inc., **33** 105–06
CAPCO. *See* Central Area Power Coordination Group *or* Custom Academic Publishing Company.
Capco Energy, Inc., **33** 296
Capcom Co., **7** 396
Cape and Vineyard Electric Co., **14** 124–25
Cape Cod-Cricket Lane, Inc., **8** 289
Cape Cod Potato Chip Company, Inc., **41** 233
Cape Horn Methanol, **III** 512
Cape May Light and Power Company, **6** 449
Cape PLC, **22** 49
Cape Wine and Distillers, **I** 289
Capehart-Farnsworth, **I** 463; **11** 197
**Capel Incorporated, 45 84–86**
Capex, **6** 224
AB Capital & Investment Corporation, **6** 108; **23** 381
Capital Advisors, Inc., **22** 4
Capital Airlines, **I** 128; **III** 102; **6** 128
Capital and Counties Bank, **II** 307; **IV** 91
Capital Bank N.A., **16** 162
**Capital Cities/ABC Inc., II 129–31**; **III** 214; **IV** 608–09, 613, 652; **11** 331; **15** 464; **18** 60, 62–63, 329; **30** 490; **42** 31, 33–34. *See also* ABC, Inc.
Capital Concrete Pipe Company, **14** 250
Capital Controls Co., Inc. *See* Severn Trent PLC.
Capital Distributing Co., **21** 37
Capital Financial Services, **III** 242
Capital-Gazette Communications, Inc., **12** 302
Capital Grille, **19** 342
Capital Group, **26** 187
**Capital Holding Corporation, III 216–19**
Capital Life Insurance Company, **11** 482–83
Capital Management Services. *See* CB Commercial Real Estate Services Group, Inc.
Capital One, **18** 535
**Capital Radio plc, 35 71–73**; **39** 199
Capital Trust Corp., **17** 498
Capitol-EMI, **I** 531–32; **11** 557
Capitol Film + TV International, **IV** 591
Capitol Films, **25** 270
Capitol Pack, Inc., **13** 350
Capitol Printing Ink Company, **13** 227–28
Capitol Publishing, **13** 560
Capitol Radio Engineering Institute, **IV** 636
Capitol Records, **22** 192–93
Capper Pass, **IV** 191
Capseals, Ltd., **8** 476
**CapStar Hotel Company, 21 91–93**
Capsugel, **I** 712
Car-lac Electronic Industrial Sales Inc., **9** 420
Car-X, **10** 415
Caracas Petroleum Sociedad Anónima, **IV** 565–66
Caradco, Inc., **45** 216
**Caradon plc, 18** 561; **20 108–12 (upd.)**
Carando Foods, **7** 174–75
Carat Group, **6** 15–16
Caratti Sports, Ltd., **26** 184
**Caraustar Industries, Inc., 19 76–78**; **44 63–67 (upd.)**
Caravali, **13** 493–94
Caravelle Foods, **21** 500
**The Carbide/Graphite Group, Inc., 40 82–84**
Carbide Router Co., **III** 436
Carbis China Clay & Brick Co., **III** 690
Carbocol, **IV** 417
Carboline Co., **8** 455
CarboMedics, **11** 458–60
Carbon Research Laboratories, **9** 517
**Carbone Lorraine S.A., 33 88–90**
La Carbonique, **23** 217, 219
**Carborundum Company, III** 610; **15 80–82**
Cardàpio, **29** 444
Cardboard Containers, **IV** 249
Cardem Insurance Co., **III** 767; **22** 546
Cardiac Pacemakers, Inc., **I** 646; **11** 90; **11** 458; **22** 361
Cardinal Distributors Ltd., **II** 663
Cardinal Freight Carriers, Inc., **42** 365
**Cardinal Health, Inc., 18 96–98**
Cardiotronics Systems, Inc., **21** 47
Cardon-Phonocraft Company, **18** 492
Care Advantage, Inc., **25** 383
Care Group, **22** 276
**Career Education Corporation, 45 87–89**
CareerCom Corp., **25** 253
CareerStaff Unlimited Inc., **25** 455
**Caremark International Inc., 10** 143, **198–200**; **33** 185
Carenes, SA, **12** 377
CarePlus, **6** 42
CareUnit, Inc., **15** 123
CareWise, Inc., **36** 365, 367–68
Carey Canada Inc., **III** 766; **22** 546
**Carey International, Inc., 26 60–63**
Carey-McFall Corp., **V** 379; **19** 421
Carey Straw Mill, **12** 376
S.A. CARFUEL, **12** 152
**Cargill, Incorporated, II** 494, 517, **616–18**; **11** 92; **13 136–38 (upd.)**, 186, 351; **18** 378, 380; **21** 290, 500; **22** 85, 426; **25** 332; **31** 17, 20; **40 85–90 (upd.)**; **41** 306
Cargill Trust Co., **13** 467
Cargo Express, **16** 198
Cargo Furniture, **31** 436
Cargolux Airlines International S.A., **47** 287
CARGOSUR, **6** 96
**Carhartt, Inc., 30 110–12**
Cariani Sausage Co., **II** 518
Caribair, **I** 102

Caribbean Chemicals S.A., **I** 512
Caribe Co., **II** 493
Caribe Shoe Corp., **III** 529
**Caribiner International, Inc., 24 94–97**
Cariboo Pulp & Paper Co., **IV** 269
**Caribou Coffee Company, Inc., 28 62–65**
Carintusa Inc., **8** 271
CARIPLO, **III** 347
Carisam International Corp., **29** 511
Carita S.A., **III** 63; **22** 487
Caritas Foundation, **22** 411, 413
Carl Byoir & Associates, **I** 14
Carl Ed. Meyer GmbH, **48** 119
Carl I. Brown and Company, **48** 178
Carl Karcher Enterprises, Inc., **19** 435; **46** 94
Carl Marks & Co., **11** 260–61
**Carl-Zeiss-Stiftung, III 445–47**, 583; **33** 218; **34 92–97 (upd.)**
Carl's Jr. *See* CKE Restaurants, Inc.
Carl's Superstores, **9** 452
Carlan, **III** 614
Carless Lubricants, **IV** 451
Carleton Financial Computations Inc., **II** 317
Carlin Gold Mining Company, **7** 386–87
Carling O'Keefe Ltd., **I** 218, 229, 254, 269, 438–39; **7** 183; **12** 337; **26** 305
Carlingford, **II** 298
**Carlisle Companies Incorporated, 8 80–82**
Carlisle Memory Products, **14** 535
Carlo Erba S.p.A., **I** 635
Carlon, **13** 304–06
Carlova, Inc., **21** 54
**Carlsberg A/S, I** 247; **9 99–101; 29 83–85 (upd.)**
**Carlson Companies, Inc., 6 363–66; 22 125–29 (upd.); 26** 147, 439–40; **27** 9, 11; **29** 200; **38** 387
**Carlton and United Breweries Ltd., I 228–29**, 437–39; **7** 182–83
Carlton Cards, **39** 87
**Carlton Communications plc, 15 83–85; 23** 111, 113; **24** 194
Carlton Investments L.P., **22** 514
The Carlyle Group, **11** 364; **14** 43; **16** 47; **21** 97; **30** 472; **43** 60
CarMax, **26** 410; **29** 120, 123
Carmeda AB, **10** 439
**Carmichael Lynch Inc., 28 66–68**
**Carmike Cinemas, Inc., 14 86–88; 21** 362; **37 62–65 (upd.)**
Carmine's Prime Meats, Inc., **35** 84
**Carnation Company, I** 269; **II 486–89**, 518, 548; **7** 339, 383, 429; **10** 382; **12** 337; **28** 311
Carnaud Basse-Indre, **IV** 228
Carnaud Metalbox, **13** 190; **20** 111; **32** 125–26
Carnegie Brothers & Co., Ltd., **9** 407
**Carnegie Corporation of New York, 35 74–77; 45** 403–05
Carnegie Foundation for the Advancement of Teaching, **12** 141
Carnegie Group, **41** 371–72
Carnegie Steel Co., **II** 330; **IV** 572; **7** 549; **35** 74
**Carnival Corporation, 27 90–92 (upd.); 36** 194
**Carnival Cruise Lines, Inc., 6 367–68; 21** 106; **22** 444–46, 470; **27** 27
Caro Produce and Institutional Foods, **31** 359–61
Carol-Braugh-Robinson Co., **II** 624
Carol Moberg, Inc., **6** 40
Carol's Shoe Corp., **22** 213
Carolco Pictures Inc., **III** 48; **10** 196
Carolina Biological Supply, **11** 424
Carolina Coach Co., **13** 397–98
Carolina Coin Caterers Corporation, **10** 222
Carolina Energies, Inc., **6** 576
**Carolina First Corporation, 31 85–87**
Carolina First National, **II** 336
**Carolina Freight Corporation, 6 369–72**
Carolina Paper Board Corporation. *See* Caraustar Industries, Inc.
**Carolina Power & Light Company, V 564–66; 23 104–07 (upd.)**
**Carolina Telephone and Telegraph Company, 10 201–03**
Carolinas Capital Funds Group, **29** 132
Carolinas-Virginia Nuclear Power Association, **27** 130
Carpenter Investment and Development Corporation, **31** 279
Carpenter Paper Co., **IV** 282; **9** 261
**Carpenter Technology Corporation, 13 139–41**
CarpetMAX, **25** 320
Carpets International Plc., **8** 270–71
**CARQUEST Corporation, 26** 348; **29 86–89**
Carr Fowler, **III** 673
**Carr-Gottstein Foods Co., 17 77–80**
Carr-Lowrey Glass Co., **13** 40
Carr-Union Line, **6** 397
Carr's of Carlisle, **I** 604; **II** 594
Carrabba's Italian Grill, **12** 373–75
Carre Orban International, **34** 248
**Carrefour SA, II** 628; **8** 404–05; **10 204–06; 12** 153; **19** 98, 309; **21** 225; **23** 230–32; 246–47, 364; **24** 475; **27** 207, **93–96 (upd.); 34** 198; **37** 21, 23
Carreras, Limited, **V** 411–12; **19** 367–69
**Carriage Services, Inc., 37 66–68**
**Carrier Access Corporation, 44 68–73**
**Carrier Corporation, I** 85; **III** 329; **7 70–73; 13** 507; **22** 6; **26** 4; **29** 216
Carrington Laboratories, **33** 282
Carrington Viyella, **44** 105
Carroll County Electric Company, **6** 511
Carroll Reed Ski Shops, Inc., **10** 215
**Carroll's Foods, Inc., 7** 477; **22** 368; **43** 382; **46 82–85**
Carrows, **27** 16, 19
Carry Machine Supply, Inc., **18** 513
**The Carsey-Werner Company, L.L.C., 37 69–72**
Carsmart.com, **47** 34
Carso Global Telecom S.A. de C.V., **34** 362
**Carson, Inc., 31 88–90; 46** 278
**Carson Pirie Scott & Company, II** 669; **9** 142; **15 86–88; 19** 324, 511–12; **41** 343–44
Carson Water Company, **19** 411
CART. *See* Championship Auto Racing Teams, Inc.
Carte Blanche, **9** 335
CarTemps USA. *See* Republic Industries, Inc.
Carter & Co., **IV** 644
Carter Automotive Co., **I** 159
Carter, Berlind, Potoma & Weill, **II** 450
**Carter Hawley Hale Stores, I** 246; **V 29–32; 8** 160; **12** 356; **15** 88; **16** 466; **17** 43, 523; **18** 488; **25** 177
Carter Holt Harvey Ltd., **IV** 280; **15** 229; **19** 155
**Carter Lumber Company, 45 90–92**
Carter Oil Company, **IV** 171; **11** 353
**Carter-Wallace, Inc., 6** 27; **8 83–86; 38 122–26 (upd.)**
Carteret Savings Bank, **III** 263–64; **10** 340
Carterphone, **22** 17
Cartier, **27** 329, 487–89
**Cartier Monde, IV** 93; **V** 411, 413; **29 90–92**
Cartier Refined Sugars Ltd., **II** 662–63
Cartiera F.A. Marsoni, **IV** 587
Cartiere Ascoli Piceno, **IV** 586
Cartiers Superfoods, **II** 678
Cartillon Importers, Ltd., **6** 48
Carton Titan S.A. de C.V., **37** 176–77
Cartotech, Inc., **33** 44
**Carvel Corporation, 35 78–81**
Carver Pump Co., **19** 36
Carworth Inc., **I** 630; **11** 34
Cary-Davis Tug and Barge Company. *See* Puget Sound Tug and Barge Company.
CASA. *See* Construcciones Aeronautics S.A.
Casa Bancária Almeida e Companhia. *See* Banco Bradesco S.A.
Casa Bonita, **II** 587
**Casa Cuervo, S.A. de C.V., 31 91–93**
Casa Ley, S.A. de C.V., **24** 416
Casa Saba. *See* Grupo Casa Saba, S.A. de C.V.
Casablanca Records, **23** 390
Casalee, Inc., **48** 406
Casarotto Security, **24** 510
Cascade Communications Corp., **16** 468; **20** 8; **24** 50
Cascade Fertilizers Ltd., **25** 232
Cascade Fiber, **13** 99
Cascade Lumber Co., **IV** 255; **8** 65
**Cascade Natural Gas Corporation, 6** 568; **9 102–04**
Cascade Steel Rolling Mills, Inc., **19** 380–81
CasChem, Inc. *See* Cambrex Corporation.
**Casco Northern Bank, 14 89–91**
Case Corporation. *See* CNH Global N.V.
Case Manufacturing Corp., **I** 512
Case, Pomeroy & Co., Inc., **IV** 76
Case Technologies, Inc., **11** 504
Casein Co. of America, **II** 471
**Casey's General Stores, Inc., 19 79–81**
**Cash America International, Inc., 20 113–15; 33** 4
Cash Wise Foods and Liquor, **30** 133
Casino, **10** 205; **23** 231; **26** 160; **27** 93–94
Casino. *See* Etablissements Economiques de Casino Guichard, Perrachon et Cie, S.C.A.
Casino America, Inc. *See* Isle of Capri Casinos, Inc., **41** 218
Casino Frozen Foods, Inc., **16** 453
Casino Guichard S.A., **37** 23
Casino S.A., **22** 515
Casino USA, **16** 452
Casinos International Inc., **21** 300
**CASIO Computer Co., Ltd., III 448–49**, 455; **IV** 599; **10** 57; **16 82–84 (upd.); 21** 123; **26** 18; **40 91–95 (upd.)**
Caspian Pipeline Consortium, **47** 75

Cassa Generale Ungherese di Risparmio, **III** 207
Cassady Broiler Co., **II** 585
Cassandra Group, **42** 272
Cassatt, **II** 424
Cassco Ice & Cold Storage, Inc., **21** 534–35
CAST Inc., **18** 20; **43** 17
Cast-Matic Corporation, **16** 475
Castex, **13** 501
Castings, Inc., **29** 98
**Castle & Cooke, Inc., I** 417; **II 490–92**; **9** 175–76; **10** 40; **20 116–19 (upd.)**; **24** 32, 115. *See also* Dole Food Company, Inc.
Castle Brewery, **I** 287
Castle Cement, **31** 400
Castle Communications plc, **17** 13
Castle Harlan Investment Partners III, **36** 468, 471
Castle Rock Pictures, **23** 392
Castle Rubber Co., **17** 371
Castle Tretheway Mines Ltd., **IV** 164
Castlemaine Tooheys, **10** 169–70
Castorama S.A., **37** 258–60. *See also* Groupe Castorama-Dubois Investissements.
Castro Convertibles. *See* Krause's Furniture, Inc.
Castrol Ltd., **IV** 382–83
Castrorama, **10** 205; **27** 95
**Casual Corner Group, Inc., V** 207–08; **25** 121; **43 96–98**
**Catalina Lighting, Inc., 43 99–102 (upd.)**
**Catalina Marketing Corporation, 18 99–102**
Catalogue Marketing, Inc., **17** 232
Catalyst Telecom, **29** 414–15
**Catalytica Energy Systems, Inc., 44 74–77**
Catamaran Cruisers, **29** 442
Catamount Petroleum Corp., **17** 121
Cataract, Inc., **34** 373
CATCO. *See* Crowley All Terrain Corporation.
**Catellus Development Corporation, 24 98–101**; **27** 88
Caterair International Corporation, **16** 396
**Caterpillar Inc., I** 147, 181, 186, 422; **III 450–53**, 458, 463, 545–46; **9** 310; **10** 274, 377, 381, 429; **11** 473; **12** 90; **13** 513; **15 89–93 (upd.)**, 225; **16** 180, 309–10; **18** 125; **19** 293; **21** 173, 499–501, 503; **22** 542; **34** 44, 46–47
Cathay Insurance Co., **III** 221; **14** 109
**Cathay Pacific Airways Limited, I** 522; **II** 298; **6** 71, **78–80**; **16** 480–81; **18** 114–15; **34 98–102 (upd.)**
**Catherines Stores Corporation, 15 94–97**; **38** 129
Cathodic Protection Services Co., **14** 325
**Catholic Order of Foresters, 24 102–05**
CatiCentre Ltd. Co, **48** 224
**Cato Corporation, 14 92–94**
Cato Oil and Grease Company, **IV** 446; **22** 302
Catteau S.A., **24** 475
**Cattleman's, Inc., 20 120–22**
Cattybrook Brick Company, **14** 249
CATV, **10** 319
Caudill Rowlett Scott. *See* CRSS Inc.
Caudle Engraving, **12** 471
CAV, **III** 554–55
Cavallo Pipeline Company, **11** 441
Cavedon Chemical Co., **I** 341
Cavendish International Holdings, **IV** 695
Cavendish Land, **III** 273
Cavenham Ltd., **7** 202–03; **28** 163
Caves Altovisto, **22** 344
Caves de Roquefort, **19** 51; **24** 445
Cawoods Holdings, **III** 735
Caxton Holdings, **IV** 641
**CB Commercial Real Estate Services Group, Inc., 21 94–98**
CB&I, **7** 76–77
CB&Q. *See* Chicago, Burlington and Quincy Railroad Company.
CB&T. *See* Synovus Financial Corp.
CBC Film Sales Co., **II** 135
CBE Technologies Inc., **39** 346
**CBI Industries, Inc., 7 74–77**; **22** 228; **48** 323
CBM Realty Corp., **III** 643
CBN Cable Network, **13** 279–81
CBN Satellite Services, **13** 279
CBOT. *See* Chicago Board of Trade.
CBR-HCI Construction Materials Corp., **31** 253
**CBRL Group, Inc., 35 82–85 (upd.)**
**CBS Corporation, 28 69–73 (upd.)**; **30** 269, 272
**CBS Inc., I** 29, 488; **II** 61, 89, 102–03, 129–31, **132–34**, 136, 152, 166–67; **III** 55, 188; **IV** 605, 623, 652, 675, 703; **6 157–60 (upd.)**; **11** 327; **12** 75, 561; **16** 201–02; **17** 150, 182; **19** 210, 426, 428; **21** 24; **24** 516–17; **25** 330, 418; **26** 102; **36** 326; **43** 170–71
CBS Musical Instruments, **16** 201–02; **43** 170–71
CBS Radio Group, **37** 192; **48** 217
CBS Records, **II** 103, 134, 177; **6** 159; **22** 194; **23** 33; **28** 419; **40** 406
CBSI. *See* Complete Business Solutions, Inc.
CBT Corp., **II** 213–14
CBW Inc., **42** 129
CBWL-Hayden Stone, **II** 450
CC Beverage Corporation, **48** 97
CC Soft Drinks Ltd., **I** 248
cc:Mail, Inc., **25** 300
CCA. *See* Container Corporation of America *and* Corrections Corporation of America.
CCAir Inc., **11** 300
CCB Financial Corp., **33** 293
CCC Franchising Corporation. *See* Primedex Health Systems, Inc.
CCG. *See* The Clark Construction Group, Inc.
CCH Computax, **7** 93–94
**CCH Inc., 7** 93; **14 95–97**; **33** 461
CCI Asia-Pacific Ltd., **27** 362
CCI Electronique, **10** 113
CCL Industries, Ltd., **15** 129
CCM Inc. *See* The Hockey Company.
CCM Sport Maska, Inc., **15** 396
CCN Group Ltd., **45** 154
CCP Insurance, Inc., **10** 248
CCR, Inc. *See* Rica Foods, Inc.
CCS Automation Systems Inc., **I** 124
CCT. *See* Crowley Caribbean Transport.
CD Titles, Inc., **22** 409
CDC. *See* Canada Development Corporation *or* Control Data Corporation.
CdF-Chimie, **I** 303; **IV** 174, 198, 525
CDG Books Canada Inc., **27** 224
CDI. *See* Centre de Dechets Industriels Group.
**CDI Corporation, 6 139–41**
CDMS. *See* Credit and Data Marketing Services.
CDR. *See* Consortium de Realisation.
CDR International, **13** 228
CDS Holding Corp., **22** 475
**CDW Computer Centers, Inc., 16 85–87**
CDX Audio Development, Inc., **18** 208
CE-Minerals, **IV** 109
CEAG AG, **23** 498
Ceat Ltd., **III** 434; **20** 263
**CEC Entertainment, Inc., 31 94–98 (upd.)**
Ceco Doors, **8** 544–46
Ceco Industries, Inc. *See* Robertson-Ceco Corporation.
CeCorr Inc., **47** 149
CECOS International, Inc., **V** 750
Cedar Engineering, **III** 126
**Cedar Fair, L.P., 22 130–32**
Cedarapids, Inc., **11** 413; **38** 374, 376; **40** 432
Cedec S.A., **14** 43
Cederroth International AB, **8** 17; **36** 25–26
CEDIS, **12** 153
Cedric Chivers, **35** 243–44
Cegedur, **IV** 174
Cegetel SA, **38** 300
CEIR, **10** 255
**Celadon Group Inc., 30 113–16**
**Celanese Corp., I 317–19**, 347; **19** 192. *See also* Hoechst Celanese Corporation.
Celebrity Entertainment, Inc., **27** 43
**Celebrity, Inc., 22 133–35**, 472
Celeron Corporation, **20** 258, 262–63
Celestial Farms, **13** 383
**Celestial Seasonings, Inc., II** 534; **16 88–91**. *See also* The Hain Celestial Group, Inc.
Celestron International, **41** 262–63
Celfor Tool Company. *See* Clark Equipment Company.
Celite Corporation, **III** 706; **7** 291; **10** 43, 45
Cell-Tel Monitoring, Inc., **46** 386
Cella Italian Wines, **10** 181
CellAccess Technology, Inc., **25** 162
Cellnet Data Systems, **11** 547; **22** 65
Cellonit-Gesellschaft Dreyfus & Cie., **I** 317
Cellstar Corporation, **18** 74
Cellu-Products Co., **14** 430
Cellular America, **6** 300
Cellular One, **9** 321
Cellular 2000. *See* Rural Cellular Corporation.
CellularOne. *See* Rural Cellular Corporation.
CellularVision, **13** 399
Cellulosa d'Italia, **IV** 272
Cellulose & Chemical Manufacturing Co., **I** 317
Cellulose & Specialties, **8** 434
Cellulose du Pin, **III** 677, 704; **16** 121–22; **19** 226–27
Celotex Corporation, **III** 766–67; **22** 545
Celsius Energy Company, **6** 569
Celtex **I** 388–89. *See also* Pricel.
Cement Products, **46** 196
Cementia, **III** 705
Cementos Portland Moctezuma, **21** 261
Cementownia Chelm, **31** 398, 400

**Cemex SA de CV, 20 123–26**
Cemij, **IV** 132
Cemp Investments Ltd., **16** 79–80
Cemsto, **13** 545
CenCall Communications, **10** 433
Cenco, Inc., **6** 188; **10** 262–63; **25** 308; **35** 135
Cencor, **25** 432
Cendant Corporation, **48** 234–35
**Cendant Corporation, 41** 363; **44 78–84 (upd.)**
Cenex Cooperative, **21** 342
Cenex Inc., **II** 536; **19** 160
Cengas, **6** 313
Centaur Communications, **43** 204, 206
**Centel Corporation, 6 312–15**, 593; **9** 106, 480; **10** 203; **14** 258; **16** 318; **17** 7
**Centennial Communications Corporation, 39 74–76**
Centennial Technologies Inc., **48** 369
Center Co., Ltd., **48** 182
Center Rental & Sales Inc., **28** 387
**Centerior Energy Corporation, V 567–68**
Centerra Corporation, **24** 79
Centertel, **18** 33
**Centex Corporation, 8 87–89**, 461; **11** 302; **23** 327; **29 93–96 (upd.)**
**Centocor Inc., 14 98–100**; **36** 306
CentraBank, **II** 337; **10** 426
Central Alloy Steel Corporation. *See* Republic Engineered Steels, Inc.
**Central and South West Corporation, V 569–70**; **21** 197–98; **45** 21
Central Area Power Coordination Group, **V** 677
Central Arizona Light & Power Company, **6** 545
Central Asia Gas Pipeline Ltd, **24** 522
Central Bancorp of Cincinnati, **II** 342
Central Bank for Railway Securities, **II** 281
Central Bank of Italy, **II** 403
Central Bank of London, **II** 318; **17** 323
Central Bank of Oman, **IV** 516
Central Bank of Scotland, **10** 337
Central Coalfields Ltd., **IV** 48–49
Central Computer Systems Inc., **11** 65
Central Covenants, **II** 222
Central Detallista, S.A. de C.V., **12** 154; **16** 453
Central Electric & Gas Company. *See* Centel Corporation.
Central Electric and Telephone Company, Inc. *See* Centel Corporation.
Central Elevator Co., **19** 111
Central Fiber Products Company, **12** 376
Central Finance Corporation of Canada, **II** 418; **21** 282
Central Florida Press, **23** 101
Central Foam Corp., **I** 481, 563; **16** 322
**Central Garden & Pet Company, 23 108–10**
Central Hankyu Ltd., **V** 71
Central Hardware, **III** 530
**Central Hudson Gas And Electricity Corporation, 6 458–60**
Central Illinois Public Service Company. *See* CIPSCO Inc.
**Central Independent Television, 7 78–80**; **15** 84; **23 111–14 (upd.)**
Central India Spinning, Weaving and Manufacturing Co., **IV** 217
Central Indiana Power Company, **6** 556
Central Investment Corp., **12** 184
Central Japan Heavy Industries, **III** 578–79; **7** 348
**Central Japan Railway Company, 43 103–06**
**Central Maine Power, 6 461–64**; **14** 126
Central Maloney Transformer, **I** 434
Central Mining and Investment Corp., **IV** 23, 79, 95–96, 524, 565
Central National Bank, **9** 475
Central National Bank & Trust Co., **13** 467
Central National Life Insurance Co., **III** 463; **21** 174
Central Nebraska Packing, **10** 250
**Central Newspapers, Inc., 10 207–09**
Central Pacific Railroad, **II** 381; **13** 372
Central Park Bank of Buffalo, **11** 108
**Central Parking Corporation, 18 103–05**
Central Penn National Corp., **11** 295
Central Planning & Design Institute, **IV** 48
Central Point Software, **10** 509
Central Public Service Corporation, **6** 447; **23** 28
Central Public Utility Corp., **13** 397
Central Research Laboratories, **22** 194
Central Savings and Loan, **10** 339
Central Solvents & Chemicals Company, **8** 100
Central Songs, **22** 193
**Central Soya Company, Inc., 7 81–83**; **31** 20; **36** 185, 187
**Central Sprinkler Corporation, 29 97–99**
Central States Indemnity, **18** 62
Central Supply Company. *See* Granite Rock Company.
Central Telephone & Utilities Corporation. *See* Centel Corporation.
Central Terminal Company, **6** 504
Central Textile, **16** 36
Central Transformer, **I** 434
Central Trust Co., **II** 313; **11** 110
Central Union Telephone Company, **14** 251, 257
Central Union Trust Co. of New York, **II** 313
Central West Public Service Company. *See* Centel Corporation.
Centralab Inc., **13** 398
Centrale Verzorgingsdienst Cotrans N.V., **12** 443
Centran Corp., **9** 475
Centre de Dechets Industriels Group, **IV** 296; **19** 226
Centre Investissements et Loisirs, **48** 107
Centre Lait, **II** 577
Centre Partners Management LLC, **18** 355; **24** 482
**Centrica plc, 29 100–05 (upd.)**
Centron DPL Company, Inc., **25** 171
Centronics Corp., **16** 192
Centros Commerciales Pryca, **23** 246, 248
Centrum Communications Inc., **11** 520
CenTrust Federal Savings, **10** 340
Centura Software, **10** 244
Centurion Brick, **14** 250
Century Bakery. *See* Dawn Food Products, Inc.
Century Bank, **II** 312
Century Brewing Company. *See* Rainier Brewing Company.
Century Cellular Network, Inc., **18** 74
**Century Communications Corp., 10 210–12**
Century Data Systems, Inc., **13** 127
Century Electric Company, **13** 273
Century Finance, **25** 432
Century Hutchinson, Ltd., **13** 429
Century Manufacturing Company, **26** 363
Century Papers, Inc., **16** 387
Century Savings Assoc. of Kansas, **II** 420
Century Supply Corporation, **39** 346
**Century Telephone Enterprises, Inc., 9 105–07**
**Century Theatres, Inc., 31 99–101**
Century Tool Co., **III** 569; **20** 360
Century 21 Real Estate, **I** 127; **II** 679; **III** 293; **11** 292; **12** 489; **21** 97; **25** 444
CEPA. *See* Consolidated Electric Power Asia.
CEPAM, **21** 438
CEPCO. *See* Chugoku Electric Power Company Inc.
**Cephalon, Inc., 45 93–96**
CEPSA. *See* Compañia Española de Petroleos S.A.
Cera Trading Co., **III** 756
Ceramesh, **11** 361
Ceramic Art Company, **12** 312
Ceramic Supply Company, **8** 177
Cerberus Limited, **6** 490
Cereal and Fruit Products, **32** 519
Cereal Industries, **II** 466
Cereal Packaging, Ltd., **13** 294
Cereal Partners Worldwide, **10** 324; **13** 294; **36** 234, 237
Cerebos, **II** 565
Cereol, **36** 185
Cerestar, **36** 185, 187
Ceresucre, **36** 185
Cerex, **IV** 290
Ceridian Corporation, **10** 257; **38** 58
Cermalloy, **IV** 100
**Cerner Corporation, 16 92–94**
Cerro Corp., **IV** 11, 136
Cerro de Pasco Corp., **IV** 33; **40** 411
Cerro Metal Products Company, **16** 357
**CertainTeed Corporation, III** 621, 677–78, 762; **16** 8, 121–22; **19** 58; **35 86–89**
Certanium Alloys and Research Co., **9** 419
Certified Grocers of Florida, Inc., **15** 139
Certified Laboratories, **8** 385
Certified TV and Appliance Company, **9** 120
Certus International Corp., **10** 509
Cerus, **23** 492
Cerveceria Cuahtémoc Moctezuma, **25** 281
Cerveceria Cuauhtemoc, **19** 10
Cerveceria Moctezuma, **23** 170
**Cerveceria Polar, I 230–31**
**Cessna Aircraft Company, III** 512; **8** 49–51, **90–93**, 313–14; **26** 117; **27 97–101 (upd.)**; **34** 431, 433; **36** 190; **44** 309
CET. *See* Compagnie Européenne de Télésecurité.
**Cetelem S.A., 21 99–102**
Cetus Corp., **I** 637; **III** 53; **7** 427; **10** 78, 214; **41** 201
CF AirFreight, **6** 390; **25** 149
CF Braun, **13** 119
CF Holding Corporation, **12** 71
CF Industries, **IV** 576
CF&I Steel Corporation, **8** 135
CFC Investment Company, **16** 104
CFM. *See* Compagnie Française du Méthane.

CFP. *See* Compagnie Française des Pétroles.
CFS Continental, Inc., **II** 675; **26** 504
CG&E. *See* Cincinnati Gas & Electric Company.
CGCT, **I** 563
CGE. *See* Alcatel Alsthom.
CGM. *See* Compagnie Générale Maritime.
CGR-MeV, **III** 635
Chace Precision Metals, Inc., **29** 460–61
Chaco Energy Corporation, **V** 724–25
**Chadbourne & Parke, 36 109–12**
**Chadwick's of Boston, Ltd.**, **V** 197–98; **27** 348; **29 106–08**
Chalet Suisse International, Inc., **13** 362
Chalk's International Airlines, **12** 420
Challenge Corp. Ltd. *See* Fletcher Challenge Ltd.
Challenger Airlines, **22** 219
Challenger Minerals Inc., **9** 267
**The Chalone Wine Group, Ltd.**, **36 113–16**
Chamberlain Group, Ltd., **23** 82
Chambers Corporation, **8** 298; **17** 548–49
Chambosse Brokerage Co., **29** 33
Champ Industries, Inc., **22** 15
Champalimaud, **36** 63
Champcork-Rolhas de Champanhe SA, **48** 118
Champion Engineering Co., **III** 582
**Champion Enterprises, Inc.**, **17 81–84**; **22** 207
Champion Forge Co., **41** 366
Champion, Inc., **8** 459; **12** 457
**Champion Industries, Inc.**, **28 74–76**
**Champion International Corporation**, **III** 215; **IV 263–65**, 334; **12** 130; **15** 229; **18** 62; **20 127–30 (upd.)**; **22** 352; **26** 444; **47** 189, 191
Champion Modular Restaurant Company, Inc. *See* Checkers Drive-Up Restaurants Inc.
Champion Products Inc., **27** 194
Champion Spark Plug Co., **II** 17; **III** 593
Champion Valley Farms, **II** 480; **26** 56
**Championship Auto Racing Teams, Inc.**, **37 73–75**
Champlin Petroleum Company, **10** 83
Champps Americana, **27** 480–82
Champs Sports, **14** 293, 295. *See also* Venator Group Inc.
Chance Bros., **III** 724–27
Chance Vought Aircraft Co., **I** 67–68, 84–85, 489–91
**Chancellor Media Corporation**, **24 106–10**; **35** 247
Chancery Law Publishing Ltd., **17** 272
Chanco Medical Industries, **III** 73
Chandeleur Homes, Inc., **17** 83
The Chandris Group, **11** 377
**Chanel**, **12 57–59**; **23** 241
Changchun Terumo Medical Products Co. Ltd., **48** 395
Channel Master Corporation, **II** 91; **15** 134
Channel One Communications Corp., **22** 442
Channel Tunnel Group, **13** 206
Chansam Investments, **23** 388
Chantex Inc., **18** 519
Chantiers de l'Atlantique, **9** 9
**Chaparral Steel Co.**, **8** 522–24; **13 142–44**; **18** 379; **19** 380
Chapman Printing Company. *See* Champion Industries, Inc.
Chapman Valve Manufacturing Company, **8** 135
Chappel Music, **23** 389
Charan Industries Inc., **18** 519
Charan Toy Co., Inc., **18** 519
**Chargeurs International**, **6 373–75**, 379; **20** 79; **21 103–06 (upd.)**; **29** 369, 371
Charise Charles Ltd., **9** 68
Charisma Communications, **6** 323
Charles A. Eaton Co., **III** 24
Charles B. Perkins Co., **II** 667; **24** 461
Charles Barker, plc, **25** 91
Charles D. Burnes Co., Inc. *See* The Holson Burnes Group, Inc.
Charles Hobson, **6** 27
Charles Huston & Sons, **14** 323
Charles Luckman Assoc., **I** 513
Charles M. Schulz Creative Associates, **39** 95
Charles of the Ritz Group Ltd., **I** 695–97; **III** 56; **23** 237
Charles Pfizer Co., **I** 96
Charles Phillips & Co. Ltd., **II** 677
Charles R. McCormick Lumber Company, **12** 407
**Charles River Laboratories International, Inc.**, **25** 55; **42 66–69**
**The Charles Schwab Corporation**, **II** 228; **8 94–96**; **18** 552; **22** 52; **26 64–67 (upd.)**; **34** 407; **38** 430
Charles Scribner's Sons, **7** 166
**The Charles Stark Draper Laboratory, Inc.**, **35 90–92**
Charlesbank Capital Partners LLC, **44** 54
Charleston Consolidated Railway, Gas and Electric Company, **6** 574
Charlestown Foundry, **III** 690
Charley Brothers, **II** 669
Charley's Eating & Drinking Saloon, **20** 54
Charlie Browns, **24** 269–70
**Charlotte Russe Holding, Inc.**, **35 93–96**
Charmin Paper Co., **III** 52; **IV** 329; **8** 433; **26** 383
**Charming Shoppes, Inc.**, **8 97–98**; **38 127–29**; **39** 287, 289
Charrington & Co., **I** 223
Charrington United Breweries, **38** 76
**Chart House Enterprises, Inc.**, **II** 556, 613–14; **17** 70, 71, **85–88**
**Chart Industries, Inc.**, **21 107–09**
Charter Bank, **II** 348
Charter Club, **9** 315
**Charter Communications, Inc.**, **33 91–94**
Charter Consolidated, **IV** 23, 119–20; **16** 293
Charter Corp., **III** 254; **14** 460
Charter Golf, Inc. *See* Ashworth, Inc.
Charter Medical Corporation, **31** 356
Charter National Life Insurance Company, **11** 261
Charter Oil Co., **II** 620; **12** 240
Charter Security Life Insurance Cos., **III** 293
Chartered Bank, **II** 357
Chartered Co. of British New Guinea, **III** 698
Chartered Mercantile Bank of India, London and China, **II** 298
Charterhouse Japhet, **24** 269
Charterhouse Petroleum, **IV** 499
Chartwell Associates, **III** 16; **9** 331
Chartwell Investments, **44** 54
Chartwell Land plc, **V 106**; **24** 266, 269
Chas. A. Stevens & Co., **IV** 660
Chas. H. Tompkins Co., **16** 285–86
Chase & Sanborn, **II** 544
Chase Corp., **II** 402
Chase Drier & Chemical Co., **8** 177
Chase, Harris, Forbes, **II** 402
**The Chase Manhattan Corporation**, **I** 123, 334, 451; **II** 202, 227, **247–49**, 256–57, 262, 286, 317, 385, 397, 402; **III** 104, 248; **IV** 33; **6** 52; **9** 124; **10** 61; **13 145–48 (upd.)**, 476; **14** 48, 103; **15** 38–39; **16** 460; **17** 498; **23** 482; **36** 358; **46** 316. *See* J.P. Morgan Chase & Co.
Chase National Bank, **25** 114
Chastain-Roberts Company, **II** 669; **18** 504
Chaston Medical & Surgical Products, **13** 366
Chateau Cheese Co. Ltd., **II** 471
**Chateau Communities, Inc.**, **37 76–79**
Chateau Grower Winery Co., **II** 575
Chateau St. Jean, **22** 80
Chateau Souverain, **22** 80
Chateau Ste. Michelle Winery, **42** 245, 247
Chateaux St. Jacques, **24** 307
Chatfield & Woods Co., **IV** 311; **19** 267
Chatfield Paper Co., **IV** 282; **9** 261
Chatham and Phenix National Bank of New York, **II** 312
Chatham Bank, **II** 312
Chatham Technologies Inc., **38** 189
Chatillon. *See* John Chatillon & Sons Inc.
Chattanooga Gas Company, Inc., **6** 577
Chattanooga Gas Light Company, **6** 448; **23** 30
Chattanooga Medicine Company. *See* Chattem, Inc.
**Chattem, Inc.**, **17 89–92**
Chatto, Virago, Bodley Head & Jonathan Cape, Ltd., **13** 429; **31** 376
**Chautauqua Airlines, Inc.**, **38 130–32**
Chaux et Ciments de Lafarge et du Teil, **III** 703–04
Chaux et Ciments du Maroc, **III** 703
Check Express, **33** 4–5
Check Point Software Technologies Ltd., **20** 238
Checker Auto Parts. *See* CSK Auto Corporation.
Checker Holding, **10** 370
Checker Motors Corp., **10** 369
**Checkers Drive-Up Restaurants Inc.**, **14** 452; **16 95–98**; **46** 98
CheckFree Corporation, **22** 522
**Checkpoint Systems, Inc.**, **39 77–80**
**The Cheesecake Factory Inc.**, **17 93–96**
Chef-Boy-Ar-Dee Quality Foods Inc., **I** 622
Chef Boyardee, **10** 70
Chef Francisco, **13** 383
Chef Pierre, **II** 572
Chef's Orchard Airline Caterers Inc., **I** 513
Cheil Sugar Co., **I** 515
Cheil Wool Textile Co., **I** 515
Chelan Power Company, **6** 596
Chelsea GCA Realty, Inc., **27** 401
**Chelsea Milling Company**, **29 109–11**
Chem-Nuclear Systems, Inc., **9** 109–10
Chemap, **III** 420
**Chemcentral Corporation**, **8 99–101**
Chemcut, **I** 682
Chemdal Corp., **13** 34
**Chemed Corporation**, **13 149–50**; **15** 409–11; **16** 386–87
Chemetron Process Equipment, Inc., **8** 545
Chemex Pharmaceuticals, Inc., **8** 63; **27** 69

**Chemfab Corporation, 35 97–101**
ChemFirst, Inc., **27** 316
Chemgas Holding BV, **41** 340
Chemgrout, **26** 42
**Chemi-Trol Chemical Co., 16 99–101**
**Chemical Banking Corporation, II** 234, **250–52**, 254; **9** 124, 361; **12** 15, 31; **13** 49, 147, 411; **14 101–04 (upd.)**; **15** 39; **21** 138; **26** 453; **38** 253
Chemical Coatings Co., **I** 321
Chemical Process Co., **IV** 409; **7** 308
Chemical Products Company, **13** 295
Chemical Specialties Inc., **I** 512
**Chemical Waste Management, Inc., V** 753; **9 108–10**; **11** 435–36
Chemie Linz, **16** 439
Chemins de fer de Paris à Lyon et à la Méditerranée, **6** 424
Chemins de fer du Midi, **6** 425
Chemins de Fer Fédéraux, **V** 519
Chemisch-Pharmazeutische AG, **IV** 70
Chemische Fabrik auf Actien, **I** 681
Chemische Fabrik Friesheim Elektron AG, **IV** 229
Chemische Fabrik vormals Sandoz, **I** 671
Chemische Fabrik Wesseling AG, **IV** 70–71
Chemische Werke Hüls GmbH. *See* Hüls A.G.
Chemise Lacoste, **9** 157
ChemLawn, **13** 199; **23** 428, 431; **34** 153
Chemmar Associates, Inc., **8** 271
Chemonics Industries–Fire-Trol, **17** 161–62
Chemonics International–Consulting, **17** 161–62
Chempump, **8** 135
Chemurgic Corporation, **6** 148
Chemway Corp., **III** 423
Cheney Bigelow Wire Works, **13** 370
CHEP Pty Ltd., **42** 50
Cheplin Laboratories, **III** 17
**Cherokee Inc., 18 106–09**
Cherokee Insurance Co., **I** 153; **10** 265
Cherry-Burrell Process Equipment, **8** 544–45
Cherry Company Ltd., **I** 266; **21** 319
Cherry Hill Cheese, **7** 429
Cherry-Levis Co., **26** 172
Chesapeake and Ohio Railroad, **II** 329; **V** 438–40; **10** 43; **13** 372. *See also* CSX Corporation.
**Chesapeake Corporation, 8 102–04**; **10** 540; **25** 44; **30 117–20 (upd.)**
Chesapeake Microwave Technologies, Inc., **32** 41
Chesapeake Paperboard Company, **44** 66
**Chesebrough-Pond's USA, Inc., II** 590; **7** 544; **8 105–07**; **9** 319; **17** 224–25; **22** 123; **32** 475
Cheshire Wholefoods, **II** 528
Chester Engineers, **10** 412
Chester G. Luby, **I** 183
Chester Oil Co., **IV** 368
**Cheung Kong (Holdings) Limited, I** 470; **IV 693–95**; **18** 252; **20 131–34 (upd.)**; **23** 278, 280. *See also* Hutchison Whampoa Ltd.
Chevignon, **44** 296
Chevrolet, **V** 494; **9** 17; **19** 221, 223; **21** 153; **26** 500
**Chevron Corporation, II** 143; **IV** 367, **385–87**, 452, 464, 466, 479, 484, 490, 523, 531, 536, 539, 563, 721; **9** 391; **10** 119; **12** 20; **17** 121–22; **18** 365, 367; **19** 73, 75, **82–85 (upd.)**; **25** 444; **29** 385; **40** 354, 357–58; **41** 391, 394–95. *See also* ChevronTexaco Corporation.
Chevron U.K. Ltd., **15** 352
**ChevronTexaco Corporation, 47 70–76 (upd.)**, 343
Chevy Chase Savings Bank, **13** 439
Chevy's, Inc., **33** 140
Chevy's Mexican Restaurants, **27** 226
ChexSystems, **22** 181
**Cheyenne Software, Inc., 12 60–62**; **25** 348–49
CHF. *See* Chase, Harris, Forbes.
**Chi-Chi's Inc., 13 151–53**; **14** 195; **25** 181
**Chiat/Day Inc. Advertising, 9** 438; **11 49–52**. *See also* TBWA/Chiat/Day.
Chiba Riverment and Cement, **III** 760
**Chibu Electric Power Company, Incorporated, V 571–73**
**Chic by H.I.S, Inc., 20 135–37**
Chicago & Calumet Terminal Railroad, **IV** 368
Chicago and Alton Railroad, **I** 456
**Chicago and North Western Holdings Corporation, I** 440; **6 376–78**
Chicago and Southern Airlines Inc., **I** 100; **6** 81
**Chicago Bears Football Club, Inc., IV** 703 **33 95–97**
**Chicago Board of Trade, 41 84–87**
Chicago Bridge & Iron Company, **7** 74–77
Chicago Burlington and Quincy Railroad, **III** 282; **V** 425–28
Chicago Chemical Co., **I** 373; **12** 346
Chicago Corp., **I** 526
Chicago Cubs, **IV** 682–83
Chicago Cutlery, **16** 234
Chicago Directory Co., **IV** 660–61
Chicago Edison, **IV** 169
Chicago Flexible Shaft Company, **9** 484
Chicago Heater Company, Inc., **8** 135
Chicago Magnet Wire Corp., **13** 397
Chicago Medical Equipment Co., **31** 255
Chicago Motor Club, **10** 126
Chicago Musical Instrument Company, **16** 238
Chicago Pacific Corp., **I** 530; **III** 573; **12** 251; **22** 349; **23** 244; **34** 432
**Chicago Pizza & Brewery, Inc., 44 85–88**
Chicago Pneumatic Tool Co., **III** 427, 452; **7** 480; **21** 502; **26** 41; **28** 40
Chicago Radio Laboratory, **II** 123
Chicago Rawhide Manufacturing Company, **8** 462–63
Chicago Rock Island and Peoria Railway Co., **I** 558
Chicago Rollerskate, **15** 395
Chicago Screw Co., **12** 344
Chicago Shipbuilding Company, **18** 318
Chicago Steel Works, **IV** 113
Chicago Sun-Times Distribution Systems, **6** 14
Chicago Times, **11** 251
Chicago Title and Trust Co., **III** 276; **10** 43–45
Chicago Tribune. *See* Tribune Company.
**Chick-fil-A Inc., 23 115–18**
**Chicken of the Sea International, 24 114–16 (upd.)**
**Chico's FAS, Inc., 45 97–99**
Chicopee Manufacturing Corp., **III** 35
Chief Auto Parts, **II** 661; **32** 416
Chieftain Development Company, Ltd., **16** 11
Chiers-Chatillon-Neuves Maisons, **IV** 227
Chilcott Laboratories Inc., **I** 710–11
Child World Inc., **13** 166; **18** 524
Childers Products Co., **21** 108
Children's Book-of-the-Month Club, **13** 105
**Children's Comprehensive Services, Inc., 42 70–72**
**The Children's Place Retail Stores, Inc., 37 80–82**
Children's Record Guild, **13** 105
Children's Television Workshop, **12** 495; **13** 560; **35** 75
Children's World Learning Centers, **II** 608; **V** 17, 19; **13** 48; **24** 75
**Childtime Learning Centers, Inc., 34 103–06**
**Chiles Offshore Corporation, 9 111–13**
Chili's Grill & Bar, **10** 331; **12** 373–74; **19** 258; **20** 159
Chillicothe Co., **IV** 310; **19** 266
Chilton Corp., **III** 440; **25** 239; **27** 361
Chilton Publications. *See* Cahners Business Information.
Chiminter, **III** 48
Chimio, **I** 669–70; **8** 451–52
Chimney Rock Winery, **48** 392
**China Airlines, 6** 71; **34 107–10**; **39** 33–34
China Borneo Co., **III** 698
China Canada Investment and Development Co., **II** 457
China Coast, **10** 322, 324; **16** 156, 158
China Communications System Company, Inc. (Chinacom), **18** 34
China Development Corporation, **16** 4
**China Eastern Airlines Co. Ltd., 31 102–04**; **46** 10
China Electric, **II** 67
China Foreign Transportation Corporation, **6** 386
China Industries Co., **II** 325
China International Capital Corp., **16** 377
China International Trade and Investment Corporation, **II** 442; **IV** 695; **6** 80; **18** 113, 253; **19** 156; **25** 101; **34** 100. *See also* CITIC Pacific Ltd.
China Light & Power, **6** 499; **23** 278–80
China Mutual Steam Navigation Company Ltd., **6** 416
China National Automotive Industry Import and Export Corp., **III** 581
China National Aviation Corp., **I** 96; **18** 115; **21** 140
China National Cereals, Oils & Foodstuffs Import and Export Corporation, **24** 359
China National Chemicals Import and Export Corp., **IV** 395; **31** 120
China National Heavy Duty Truck Corporation, **21** 274
China National Machinery Import and Export Corporation, **8** 279
**China National Petroleum Corporation, 18** 483; **46 86–89**
China Navigation Co., **I** 521; **16** 479–80
China Orient Leasing Co., **II** 442
China Resources (Shenyang) Snowflake Brewery Co., **21** 320
**China Southern Airlines Company Ltd., 31** 102; **33 98–100**; **46** 10
China Unicom, **47** 320–21

China Zhouyang Fishery Co. Ltd., **II** 578
Chinese Electronics Import and Export Corp., **I** 535
Chinese Metallurgical Import and Export Corp., **IV** 61
**Chinese Petroleum Corporation, IV 388–90**, 493, 519; **31 105–108 (upd.)**
Chinese Steel Corp., **IV** 184
The Chinet Company, **30** 397
Chino Mines Co., **IV** 179
Chinon Industries, **III** 477; **7** 163
Chipcom, **16** 392
Chippewa Shoe, **19** 232
**CHIPS and Technologies, Inc., 6** 217; **9 114–17**
**Chiquita Brands International, Inc., II** 595–96; **III** 28; **7 84–86**; **21 110–13 (upd.)**; **38** 197
ChiRex, **38** 380
Chiro Tool Manufacturing Corp., **III** 629
**Chiron Corporation, 7** 427; **10 213–14**; **36 117–20 (upd.)**; **45** 94
**Chisholm-Mingo Group, Inc., 41 88–90**
Chisso Chemical, **II** 301
Chiswick Products, **II** 566
Chita Oil Co., **IV** 476
Chitaka Foods International, **24** 365
Chivers, **II** 477
Chiyoda Bank, **I** 503; **II** 321
Chiyoda Chemical, **I** 433
Chiyoda Fire and Marine, **III** 404
Chiyoda Kogaku Seiko Kabushiki Kaisha, **III** 574–75; **43** 282
Chiyoda Konpo Kogyo Co. Ltd., **V** 536
Chiyoda Mutual, **II** 374
Chloé Chimie, **I** 303
Chloride S.A., **I** 423
Choay, **I** 676–77
**Chock Full o'Nuts Corp., 17 97–100**; **20** 83
**Chocoladefabriken Lindt & Sprüngli AG, 27 102–05**; **30** 220
Chocolat Ibled S.A., **II** 569
Chocolat-Menier S.A., **II** 569
Chocolat Poulait, **II** 478
Chogoku Kogyo, **II** 325
**Choice Hotels International Inc., 6** 187, 189; **14 105–07**; **25** 309–10; **26** 460
ChoiceCare Corporation, **24** 231
ChoicePoint Services, Inc., **31** 358
Chorlton Metal Co., **I** 531
**Chorus Line Corporation, 25** 247; **30 121–23**
Chosen Sekiyu, **IV** 554
Chotin Transportation Co., **6** 487
Chouinard Equipment. *See* Lost Arrow Inc.
Chow Tai Fook Jewellery Co., **IV** 717
**Chris-Craft Industries, Inc., II** 176, 403; **III** 599–600; **9 118–19**; **26** 32; **31 109–112 (upd.)**; **46** 313
Christal Radio, **6** 33
**Christensen Boyles Corporation, 19** 247; **26 68–71**
Christensen Company, **8** 397
Christiaensen, **26** 160
Christian Bourgois, **IV** 614–15
Christian Broadcasting Network, **13** 279
**Christian Dalloz SA, 40 96–98**
**Christian Dior S.A., I** 272; **19 86–88**; **23** 237, 242
**Christian Salvesen Plc, 45** 10, **100–03**
Christian Supply Centers, Inc., **45** 352
Christiana Bank og Kredietklasse, **40** 336
Christie, Mitchell & Mitchell, **7** 344
**Christie's International plc, 15 98–101**; **39 81–85 (upd.)**
Christofle Orfevrerie, **44** 206
**Christofle SA, 40 99–102**
**Christopher & Banks Corporation, 42 73–75**
Christopher Charters, Inc. *See* Kitty Hawk, Inc.
Chromalloy American Corp., **13** 461
Chromalloy Gas Turbine Corp., **13** 462
Chromatic Color, **13** 227–28
**Chromcraft Revington, Inc., 15 102–05**; **26** 100
Chrompack, Inc., **48** 410
**The Chronicle Publishing Company, Inc., 23 119–22**
**Chronimed Inc., 26 72–75**
Chronoservice, **27** 475
**Chrysalis Group plc, 22** 194; **40 103–06**
**Chrysler Corporation, I** 10, 17, 28, 38, 59, 79, 136, **144–45**, 152, 162–63, 172, 178, 182, 188, 190, 207, 420, 504, 516, 525, 540; **II** 5, 313, 403, 448; **III** 439, 517, 544, 568, 591, 607, 637–38; **IV** 22, 449, 676, 703; **7** 205, 233, 461; **8** 74–75, 315, 505–07; **9** 118, 349–51, 472; **10** 174, 198, 264–65, 290, 317, 353, 430; **11 53–55 (upd.)**, 103–04, 429; **13** 28–29, 61, 448, 501, 555; **14** 321, 367, 457; **16** 184, 322, 484; **17** 184; **18** 173–74, 308, 493; **20** 359–60; **22** 52, 55, 175, 330; **23** 352–54; **25** 89–91, 93, 142–44, 329; **26** 403, 501; **31** 130; **36** 34, 242; **38** 480–81; **43** 163–64; **47** 436. *See also* DaimlerChrysler AG
Chrysler Financial Company, LLC, **45** 262
**CH2M Hill Ltd., 22 136–38**
Chu Ito & Co., **IV** 476
**Chubb Corporation, II** 84; **III** 190, **220–22**, 368; **11** 481; **14 108–10 (upd.)**; **29** 256; **37 83–87 (upd.)**; **45** 109
Chubb Security plc, **44** 258
**Chubu Electric Power Company, Inc., 46 90–93 (upd.)**
Chuck E. Cheese, **13** 472–74; **31** 94
Chugai Boyeki Co. Ltd., **44** 441
Chugai Pharmaceutical Company, **8** 215–16; **10** 79
Chugai Shogyo Shimposha, **IV** 654–55
**Chugoku Electric Power Company Inc., V 574–76**
Chunghwa Picture Tubes, **23** 469
Chuo Trust & Banking Co. *See* Yasuda Trust and Banking Company, Limited.
**Chupa Chups S.A., 38 133–35**
Church & Company, **45** 342, 344
**Church & Dwight Co., Inc., 29 112–15**
Church and Tower Group, **19** 254
Church, Goodman, and Donnelley, **IV** 660
Church's Fried Chicken, Inc., **I** 260; **7** 26–28; **15** 345; **23** 468; **32** 13–14
**Churchill Downs Incorporated, 29 116–19**
Churchill Insurance Co. Ltd., **III** 404
Churny Co. Inc., **II** 534
**Cianbro Corporation, 14 111–13**
Cianchette Brothers, Inc. *See* Cianbro Corporation.
**Ciba-Geigy Ltd., I** 625, **632–34**, 671, 690, 701; **III** 55; **IV** 288; **8** 63, **108–11 (upd.)**, 376–77; **9** 153, 441; **10** 53–54, 213; **15** 229; **18** 51; **21** 386; **23** 195–96; **25** 55; **27** 69; **28** 193, 195; **30** 327; **36** 36, 119. *See also* Novartis AG.
CIBC. *See* Canadian Imperial Bank of Commerce.
CIBC Wood Gundy Securities Corp., **24** 482
**Ciber, Inc., 18 110–12**
Ciby 2000, **24** 79
CICI, **11** 184
CIDLA, **IV** 504–06
Cie Continental d'Importation, **10** 249
Cie des Lampes, **9** 9
Cie Générale d'Electro-Ceramique, **9** 9
Cie. Generale des Eaux S.A., **24** 327
**Cifra, S.A. de C.V., 8** 556; **12 63–65**; **26** 524; **34** 197–98; **35** 320. *See also* Wal-Mart de Mexico, S.A. de C.V.
Cigarrera La Moderna, **21** 260; **22** 73
Cigarros la Tabacelera Mexicana (Cigatam), **21** 259
**CIGNA Corporation, III** 197, **223–27**, 389; **10** 30; **11** 243; **22 139–44 (upd.)**, 269; **38** 18; **45 104–10 (upd.)**
CIGWELD, **19** 442
Cii-HB, **III** 123, 678; **16** 122
Cilag-Chemie, **III** 35–36; **8** 282
Cilbarco, **II** 25
Cilva Holdings PLC, **6** 358
Cima, **14** 224–25
Cimaron Communications Corp., **38** 54
Cimarron Utilities Company, **6** 580
CIMCO Ltd., **21** 499–501
Cimenteries CBR S.A., **23** 325, 327
Ciments d'Obourg, **III** 701
Ciments de Chalkis Portland Artificiels, **III** 701
Ciments de Champagnole, **III** 702
Ciments de l'Adour, **III** 702
**Ciments Français, 40 107–10**
Ciments Lafarge France, **III** 704
Ciments Lafarge Quebec, **III** 704
Cimos, **7** 37
**Cinar Corporation, 40 111–14**
**Cincinnati Bell, Inc., 6 316–18**; **29** 250, 252
Cincinnati Chemical Works, **I** 633
Cincinnati Electronics Corp., **II** 25
**Cincinnati Financial Corporation, 16 102–04**; **44 89–92 (upd.)**
**Cincinnati Gas & Electric Company, 6 465–68**, 481–82
**Cincinnati Milacron Inc., 12 66–69**
**Cincom Systems Inc., 15 106–08**
Cine-Groupe, **35** 279
Cineamerica, **IV** 676
Cinecentrum, **IV** 591
Cinema International Corp., **II** 149
Cinemark, **21** 362; **23** 125
Cinemax, **IV** 675; **7** 222–24, 528–29; **23** 276
**Cineplex Odeon Corporation, II** 145, **6 161–63**; **14** 87; **23 123–26 (upd.)**; **33** 432
**Cinnabon Inc., 13** 435–37; **23 127–29**; **32** 12, 15
Cinquième Saison, **38** 200, 202
**Cinram International, Inc., 43 107–10**
**Cintas Corporation, 16** 228; **21 114–16**, 507; **30** 455
Cintel, **II** 158
Cintra. *See* Concesiones de Infraestructuras de Transportes, S.A. *or* Corporacion Internacional de Aviacion, S.A. de C.V.
Cipal-Parc Astérix, **27** 10

Ciprial S.A., **27** 260
**CIPSCO Inc.**, **6 469–72**, 505–06
Circa Pharmaceuticals, **16** 529
Circle A Ginger Ale Company, **9** 177
Circle International, Inc., **17** 216
**The Circle K Company**, **II 619–20**; **V** 210; **7** 113–14, 372, 374; **20 138–40 (upd.)**; **25** 125; **26** 447
Circle Plastics, **9** 323
**Circon Corporation**, **21 117–20**
**Circuit City Stores, Inc.**, **9** 65–66, **120–22**; **10** 235, 305–06, 334–35, 468–69; **12** 335; **14** 61; **15** 215; **16** 73, 75; **17** 489; **18** 533; **19** 362; **23** 51–53, 363; **24** 52, 502; **26** 410; **29 120–24 (upd.)**; **30** 464–65
**Circus Circus Enterprises, Inc.**, **6** 201, **203–05**; **19** 377, 379
Circus Knie, **29** 126
Circus World, **16** 389–90
**Cirque du Soleil Inc.**, **29 125–28**
**Cirrus Design Corporation**, **44 93–95**
**Cirrus Logic, Inc.**, **9** 334; **11 56–57**; **25** 117; **48 90–93 (upd.)**
**Cisco Systems, Inc.**, **11 58–60**, 520; **13** 482; **16** 468; **19** 310; **20** 8, 33, 69, 237; **25** 499; **26** 276–77; **34 111–15 (upd.)**, 441, 444; **36** 300; **38** 430; **43** 251
Cise, **24** 79
Cisneros Group, **47** 312
CIT Alcatel, **9** 9–10
CIT Financial Corp., **II** 90, 313; **8** 117; **12** 207
CIT Group/Business Credit, Inc., **13** 446
CIT Group/Commercial Services, **13** 536
**Citadel Communications Corporation**, **35 102–05**
Citadel General, **III** 404
Citadel, Inc., **27** 46
**CitFed Bancorp, Inc.**, **16 105–07**
**CITGO Petroleum Corporation**, **II** 660–61; **IV 391–93**, 508; **7** 491; **31 113–117 (upd.)**; **32** 414, 416–17; **45** 252, 254
Citibanc Group, Inc., **11** 456
Citibank, **II** 227, 230, 248, 250–51, 253–55, 331, 350, 358, 415; **III** 243, 340; **6** 51; **9** 124; **10** 150; **11** 418; **13** 146; **14** 101; **23** 3–4, 482; **25** 180, 542. *See also* Citigroup Inc
Citibank of Mexico, **34** 82
**CITIC Pacific Ltd.**, **16** 481; **18 113–15**; **20** 134. *See also* China International Trade and Investment Corporation.
Citicasters Inc., **23** 293–94
**Citicorp**, **II** 214, **253–55**, 268, 275, 319, 331, 361, 398, 411, 445; **III** 10, 220, 397; **7** 212–13; **8** 196; **9 123–26 (upd.)**, 441; **10** 463, 469; **11** 140; **12** 30, 310, 334; **13** 535; **14** 103, 108, 235; **15** 94, 146, 281; **17** 324, 559; **21** 69, 145; **22** 169, 406; **25** 198, 542
Cities Service Company, **IV** 376, 391–92, 481, 575; **12** 542; **22** 172
Citifor, **19** 156
**Citigroup Inc.**, **30 124–28 (upd.)**; **42** 332; **46** 316
Citinet. *See* Hongkong Telecommunications Ltd.
Citivision PLC, **9** 75
**Citizen Watch Co., Ltd.**, **III 454–56**, 549; **13** 121–22; **21 121–24 (upd.)**; **23** 212; **41** 71–82
Citizen's Electric Light & Power Company, **V** 641
Citizen's Federal Savings Bank, **10** 93
Citizen's Fidelity Corp., **II** 342
Citizen's Industrial Bank, **14** 529
Citizens and Southern Bank, **II** 337; **10** 426
Citizens Bank, **11** 105
Citizens Bank of Hamilton, **9** 475
Citizens Bank of Savannah, **10** 426
Citizens Building & Loan Association, **14** 191
Citizens Federal Savings and Loan Association, **9** 476
**Citizens Financial Group, Inc.**, **12** 422; **42 76–80**
Citizens Gas Co., **6** 529
Citizens Gas Fuel Company. *See* MCN Corporation.
Citizens Gas Light Co., **6** 455
Citizens Gas Supply Corporation, **6** 527
Citizens Mutual Savings Bank, **17** 529–30
Citizens National Bank, **II** 251; **13** 466; **25** 114; **41** 312
Citizens National Gas Company, **6** 527
Citizens Saving and Trust Company, **17** 356
Citizens Savings & Loan Association, **9** 173
Citizens Savings and Loan Society. *See* Citizens Mutual Savings Bank.
Citizens State Bank, **41** 178, 180
Citizens Telephone Company, **14** 257–58
Citizens Trust Co., **II** 312
**Citizens Utilities Company**, **7 87–89**; **37** 124–27
Citizens' Savings and Loan, **10** 339
**Citrix Systems, Inc.**, **44 96–99**
Citroën. *See* Automobiles Citroen *and* PSA Peugeot Citroen S.A.
City and St. James, **III** 501
City and Suburban Telegraph Association and Telephonic Exchange, **6** 316–17
City and Village Automobile Insurance Co., **III** 363
City Auto Stamping Co., **I** 201
City Bank Farmers' Trust Co., **II** 254; **9** 124
City Bank of New York, **II** 250, 253
City Brewery, **I** 253
City Capital Associates, **31** 211
City Centre Properties Ltd., **IV** 705–06
City Finance Company, **10** 340; **11** 261
City Ice Delivery, Ltd., **II** 660
City Investing Co., **III** 263; **IV** 721; **9** 391; **13** 363
City Light and Traction Company, **6** 593
City Light and Water Company, **6** 579
City Market Inc., **12** 112
City Mutual Life Assurance Society, **III** 672–73
City National Bank of Baton Rouge, **11** 107
City National Leasing, **II** 457
City of London Real Property Co. Ltd., **IV** 706
City of Seattle Water Department, **12** 443
The City Post Publishing Corp., **12** 359
City Products Corp., **II** 419
**City Public Service**, **6 473–75**
City Savings, **10** 340
City Stores Company, **16** 207
Cityhome Corp., **III** 263
Civic Drugs, **12** 21
Civic Parking LLC, **18** 105
Civil & Civic Pty. Ltd., **IV** 707–08; **17** 286
Civil Aviation Administration of China, **31** 102; **33** 98
Civil Service Employees Insurance Co., **III** 214
CJ Banks. *See* Christopher & Banks Corporation.
**CKE Restaurants, Inc.**, **19 89–93**, 433, 435; **25** 389; **27** 19; **29** 203; **37** 349–51; **46 94–99 (upd.)**
CKS Group Inc. *See* marchFIRST, Inc.
CKS Inc., **23** 479
Clabir Corp., **12** 199
Claeys, **22** 379–80
**Claire's Stores, Inc.**, **17 101–03**; **18** 411
Clairol, **III** 17–18; **17** 110
Clairton Steel Co., **IV** 572; **7** 550
Clal Electronic Industries Ltd., **24** 429
Clal Group, **18** 154
CLAM Petroleum, **7** 282
Clancy Paul Inc., **13** 276
Clapp-Eastham Company. *See* GenRad, Inc.
Clara Candy, **15** 65
**Clarcor Inc.**, **17 104–07**
Claremont Technology Group Inc., **31** 131
Clares Equipment Co., **I** 252
Clariden Bank, **21** 146–47
Claridge Group, **25** 266, 268
Clarify Corp., **38** 431
Clarion Hotels and Resorts, **25** 309
Clark & Co., **IV** 301
Clark & McKenney Hardware Co. *See* Clarcor Inc.
Clark & Rockefeller, **IV** 426
Clark Bros. Co., **III** 471
**The Clark Construction Group, Inc.**, **8 112–13**
Clark, Dietz & Associates-Engineers. *See* CRSS Inc.
**Clark Equipment Company**, **I** 153; **7** 513–14; **8 114–16**; **10** 265; **13** 500; **15** 226
Clark Estates Inc., **8** 13
Clark Filter, Inc., **17** 104
Clark Materials Handling Company, **7** 514
Clark Motor Co., **I** 158; **10** 292
Clark Retail Enterprises Inc., **37** 311
Clark-Schwebel, Inc., **28** 195
Clarkins, Inc., **16** 35–36
Clarkson International Tools, **I** 531
CLASSA. *See* Compañia de Líneas Aéreas Subvencionadas S.A.
Classic FM plc, **39** 198–200
**Classic Vacation Group, Inc.**, **46 100–03**
Claudel Roustand Galac, **19** 50
Claussen Pickle Co., **12** 371
Clayco Construction Company, **41** 225–26
Clayton & Dubilier, **III** 25
Clayton Brown Holding Company, **15** 232
Clayton Dubilier & Rice Inc., **25** 501; **29** 408; **40** 370
**Clayton Homes Incorporated**, **13 154–55**; **37** 77
Clayton-Marcus Co., **12** 300
Clayton/National Courier Systems, Inc., **24** 126
CLE. *See* Compagnie Laitière Européenne.
Clean Window Remodelings Co., **III** 757
Cleanaway Ltd., **III** 495
Cleancoal Terminal, **7** 582, 584

**Clear Channel Communications, Inc.**, **23** **130–32**, 294; **25** 418; **27** 278; **33** 322, 324; **35** 219–21, 233; **36** 422, 424; **37** 104–05
Clear Shield Inc., **17** 157, 159
Clearing Inc., **III** 514
**Clearly Canadian Beverage Corporation**, **48** **94–97**
Clearwater Tissue Mills, Inc., **8** 430
**Cleary, Gottlieb, Steen & Hamilton**, **35** **106–09**
**Cleco Corporation**, **37** **88–91**
Clef, **IV** 125
Clemente Capital Inc., **25** 542
Clements Energy, Inc., **7** 376
Cleo Inc., **12** 207–09; **35** 131
Le Clerc, **21** 225–26
Cletrac Corp., **IV** 366
Cleve-Co Jig Boring Co., **23** 82
Cleveland and Western Coal Company, **7** 369
**Cleveland-Cliffs Inc.**, **13** **156–58**; **17** 355
Cleveland Cotton Products Co., **37** 393
Cleveland Electric Illuminating Company. *See* Centerior Energy Theodor.
Cleveland Fabric Centers, Inc. *See* Fabri-Centers of America Inc.
Cleveland Grinding Machine Co., **23** 82
**Cleveland Indians Baseball Company, Inc.**, **37** **92–94**
Cleveland Iron Mining Company. *See* Cleveland-Cliffs Inc.
Cleveland Oil Co., **I** 341
Cleveland Paper Co., **IV** 311; **19** 267
Cleveland Pneumatic Co., **I** 457; **III** 512
Cleveland Precision Instruments, Inc., **23** 82
Cleveland Twist Drill Company. *See* Acme-Cleveland Corp.
Clevepak Corporation, **8** 229; **13** 442
Clevite Corporation, **14** 207
CLF Research, **16** 202; **43** 170
Click Messenger Service, Inc., **24** 126
Clifford & Wills, **12** 280–81
**Clifford Chance LLP**, **38** **136–39**
Cliffs Corporation, **13** 157; **27** 224
Climax Molybdenum Co., **IV** 17–19
Clinchfield Coal Corp., **IV** 180–81; **19** 320
Clinical Assays, **I** 628
Clinical Partners, Inc., **26** 74
Clinical Pathology Facility, Inc., **26** 391
Clinical Science Research Ltd., **10** 106
Clinique Laboratories, Inc., **30** 191
**Clinton Cards plc**, **39** **86–88**
Clinton Pharmaceutical Co., **III** 17; **37** 41
Clipper Group, **12** 439
Clipper, Inc., **IV** 597
Clipper Manufacturing Company, **7** 3
Clipper Seafoods, **II** 587
La Cloche d'Or, **25** 85
Clopay Corp., **34** 195
**The Clorox Company**, **III** **20–22**, 52; **8** 433; **22** **145–48 (upd.)**, 436; **26** 383
**Close Brothers Group plc**, **39** **89–92**
**The Clothestime, Inc.**, **20** **141–44**
Clouterie et Tréfilerie des Flandres, **IV** 25–26
Clover Club, **44** 348
Clover Leaf Creamery, **II** 528
Clover Milk Products Co., **II** 575
Clovis Water Co., **6** 580
CLSI Inc., **15** 372; **43** 182
Club Aurrera, **8** 556
Club Corporation of America, **26** 27
Club de Hockey Canadien Inc., **26** 305
Club Européen du Tourisme, **6** 207
**Club Méditerranée S.A.**, **I** 286; **6** **206–08**; **21** **125–28 (upd.)**; **27** 10
**ClubCorp, Inc.**, **33** **101–04**
Clubhôtel, **6** 207
Cluett Corporation, **22** 133
Cluett, Peabody & Co., Inc., **II** 414; **8** 567–68
Clyde Iron Works, **8** 545
Clydebank Engineering & Shipbuilding Co., **I** 573
Clydesdale Group, **19** 390
Clyne Maxon Agency, **I** 29
CM&M Equilease, **7** 344
CM&P. *See* Cresap, McCormick and Paget.
CM Industries, **I** 676
CMAC Investment Corporation. *See* Radian Group Inc.
CMB Acier, **IV** 228
CMB Packaging, **8** 477
CMC. *See* Commercial Metals Company.
CME. *See* Campbell-Mithun-Esty, Inc.
CMGI, Inc., **43** 11, 13, 420, 422
CMI International, Inc., **27** 202, 204
**CML Group, Inc.**, **10** **215–18**; **22** 382, 536; **38** 238
**CMP Media Inc.**, **26** **76–80**; **28** 504
CMP Properties Inc., **15** 122
**CMS Energy Corporation**, **IV** 23; **V** **577–79**; **8** 466; **14** **114–16 (upd.)**
CMS Healthcare, **29** 412
CMT Enterprises, Inc., **22** 249
CN. *See* Canadian National Railway System.
**CNA Financial Corporation**, **I** 488; **III** **228–32**, 339; **12** 317; **36** 325, 327; **38** **140–46 (upd.)**
CNA Health Plans, **III** 84
CNB Bancshares Inc., **31** 207
CNBC, Inc., **28** 298
CNC Holding Corp., **13** 166
CNCA. *See* Caisse National de Crédit Agricole.
CNEP. *See* Comptoir National d'Escompte de Paris.
**CNET Networks, Inc.**, **47** **77–80**
CNF Transportation. *See* Consolidated Freightways, Inc.
CNG. *See* Consolidated Natural Gas Company.
**CNH Global N.V.**, **38** **147–56 (upd.)**
CNI. *See* Community Networks Inc.
CNN. *See* Cable News Network.
CNP. *See* Compagnie Nationale à Portefeuille.
CNPC. *See* China National Petroleum Corporation.
**CNS, Inc.**, **20** **145–47**
Co-Axial Systems Engineering Co., **IV** 677
Co-Counsel, Inc., **29** 364
Co. Luxemburgeoise de Banque S.A., **II** 282
Co. of London Insurers, **III** 369
Co-Op Blue Square Consumer Cooperative Society, **41** 56–58
Co-Steel International Ltd., **8** 523–24; **13** 142–43; **24** 144
Coach and Car Equipment Corp., **41** 369
**Coach, Inc.**, **45** **111–15 (upd.)**
**Coach Leatherware**, **10** **219–21**; **12** 559
Coach Specialties Co. *See* Fleetwood Enterprises, Inc.
**Coach USA, Inc.**, **24** **117–19**; **30** 431, 433
Coachmen Industries Inc., **21** 153; **39** 393
**Coal India Ltd.**, **IV** **48–50**; **44** **100–03 (upd.)**
Coalport, **12** 528
Coast American Corporation, **13** 216
Coast Consolidators, Inc., **14** 505
Coast to Coast Hardware. *See* TruServ Corporation.
Coast-to-Coast Stores, **II** 419; **12** 8
Coastal Coca-Cola Bottling Co., **10** 223
Coastal Container Line Inc., **30** 318
**Coastal Corporation**, **IV** 366, **394–95**; **7** 553–54; **31** **118–121 (upd.)**
Coastal Lumber, S.A., **18** 514
Coastal States Corporation, **11** 481
Coastal States Life Insurance Company, **11** 482
Coastal Valley Canning Co., **I** 260
CoastAmerica Corp., **13** 176
Coates/Lorilleux, **14** 308
Coating Products, Inc., **III** 643
**Coats plc**, **44** **104–07 (upd.)**
**Coats Viyella Plc**, **V** **356–58**. *See also* Coats plc.
CoBank. *See* National Bank for Cooperatives.
Cobb & Branham, **14** 257
Cobb, Inc., **II** 585; **14** 515
**COBE Laboratories, Inc.**, **13** **159–61**; **22** 360
**Cobham plc**, **30** **129–32**
**Coborn's, Inc.**, **30** **133–35**
**Cobra Electronics Corporation**, **14** **117–19**
**Cobra Golf Inc.**, **16** **108–10**; **23** 474
Cobra Ventilation Products, **22** 229
Coburn Optical Industries, **III** 56
Coburn Vision Care, **III** 727
**Coca-Cola Bottling Co. Consolidated**, **II** 170, 468; **10** **222–24**; **15** 299
Coca-Cola Bottling Company of Northern New England, Inc., **21** 319
**The Coca-Cola Company**, **I** 17, **232–35**, 244, 248, 278–79, 286, 289, 440, 457; **II** 103, 136–37, 477–78; **III** 215; **IV** 297; **6** 20–21, 30; **7** 155, 383, 466; **8** 399; **9** 86, 177; **10** 130, 222–23, **225–28 (upd.)**; **11** 421, 450–51; **12** 74; **13** 284; **14** 18, 453; **15** 428; **16** 480–81; **17** 207; **18** 60, 62–63, 68, 467–68; **19** 391; **21** 337–39, 401; **23** 418–20; **24** 516; **25** 183; **27** 21, 150; **28** 271, 473; **29** 85; **31** 243; **32** 59, **111–16 (upd.)**; **40** 350–52; **42** 31, 34–35; **47** 289, 291
**Coca-Cola Enterprises, Inc.**, **10** 223; **13** **162–64**; **23** 455–57; **32** 115
Cochrane Corporation, **8** 135
Cochrane Foil Co., **15** 128
Cockburn & Campbell Ltd., **38** 501
Cockburn-Adelaide Cement, **31** 398, 400
**Cockerill Sambre Group**, **IV** 26–27, **51–53**; **22** 44; **26** **81–84 (upd.)**; **42** 416
Coco's, **I** 547; **27** 16, 19
Code Hennessey & Simmons Limited, **39** 358
Codec, **19** 328
Codelco. *See* Corporacion Nacional del Cobre de Chile.
Codex Corp., **II** 61
Codville Distributors Ltd., **II** 649
**Coeur d'Alene Mines Corporation**, **20** **148–51**
Coffee People, Inc., **40** 152–54
Cofica, **21** 99

COFINA, **III** 347
COFIRED, **IV** 108
Cofitel SA, **25** 466
**Coflexip S.A., 25 103–05**
Cofroma, **23** 219
Cogéma, **IV** 108
COGEMA Canada, **IV** 436
Cogeneracion Prat SA, **41** 325, 327
Cogeneration Development Corp., **42** 387–88
Cogent Data Technologies, Inc., **31** 5
**Cogentrix Energy, Inc., 10 229–31**
Cogetex, **14** 225
Cogifer, S.A., **18** 4; **31** 156, 158
Cognex Corp., **22** 373
CogniSeis Development, Inc., **18** 513, 515
Cognitive Solutions, Inc., **18** 140
**Cognos Inc., 11** 78; **25** 97; **44 108–11**
Cohasset Savings Bank, **13** 468
**Coherent, Inc., 31 122–25**
Coherix Corporation, **48** 446
Cohn-Hall-Marx Co. *See* United Merchants & Manufacturers, Inc.
Cohoes Bancorp Inc., **41** 212
**Cohu, Inc., 32 117–19**
Coils Plus, Inc., **22** 4
Coinamatic Laundry Equipment, **II** 650
**Coinmach Laundry Corporation, 20 152–54**
**Coinstar, Inc., 44 112–14**
Coktel Vision, **15** 455
**Colas S.A., 31 126–29**
Colbert Television Sales, **9** 306
Colchester Car Auctions, **II** 587
**Cold Spring Granite Company, 16 111–14**
**Coldwater Creek Inc., 21 129–31**
Coldwell Banker, **IV** 715, 727; **V** 180, 182; **11** 292; **12** 97; **18** 475, 478; **27** 32. *See also* CB Commercial Real Estate Services Group, Inc.
Cole & Weber Inc., **I** 27
Cole Haan Holdings Incorporated, **36** 346
**Cole National Corporation, 13 165–67,** 391
Cole Sewell Corporation, **39** 322, 324
Cole's Craft Showcase, **13** 166
Coleco Industries, Inc., **III** 506; **18** 520; **21** 375; **43** 229, 232
Coleman & Co., **II** 230
**The Coleman Company, Inc., III** 485; **9 127–29**; **22** 207; **26** 119; **28** 135, 247; **30 136–39 (upd.)**
Coleman Outdoor Products Inc., **21** 293
Colemans Ltd., **11** 241
Coles Book Stores Ltd., **7** 486, 488–89
**Coles Express Inc., 15 109–11**
**Coles Myer Ltd., V 33–35**; **18** 286; **20 155–58 (upd.)**
Colex Data, **14** 556
**Colgate-Palmolive Company, I** 260; **II** 672; **III 23–26**; **IV** 285; **9** 291; **11** 219, 317; **14 120–23 (upd.),** 279; **17** 106; **25** 365; **27** 212–13, 390; **35 110–15 (upd.)**
Colgens, **22** 193
Collabra Software Inc., **15** 322
**Collectors Universe, Inc., 48 98–100**
College Construction Loan Insurance Assoc., **II** 455; **25** 427
College Entrance Examination Board, **12** 141
College Survival, Inc., **10** 357
Collegiate Arlington Sports Inc., **II** 652
Collett Dickinson Pearce International Group, **I** 33; **16** 168
**Collins & Aikman Corporation, I** 483; **13 168–70**; **25** 535; **41 91–95 (upd.)**
**Collins Industries, Inc., 33 105–07**
Collins Radio Co., **III** 136; **11** 429
Collins Stewart, **41** 371–72
Colo-Macco. *See* CRSS Inc.
Cologne Re. *See* General Re Corporation *or* Kölnische Rückversicherungs-Gesellschaft AG.
Cologne Reinsurance Co., **III** 273, 299
Colombia Graphophone Company, **22** 192
Colombo, **25** 84
Colonia, **III** 273, 394
Colonia Versicherung Aktiengesellschaft. *See* AXA Colonia Konzern AG.
Colonial & General, **III** 359–60
Colonial Air Transport, **I** 89, 115; **12** 379
Colonial Airlines, **I** 102
Colonial Bancorp, **II** 208
Colonial Bank, **II** 236
Colonial Candle of Cape Cod, **18** 69
Colonial Container, **8** 359
Colonial Food Stores, **7** 373
Colonial Healthcare Supply Co., **13** 90
Colonial Insurance Co., **IV** 575–76
Colonial Life Assurance Co., **III** 359
Colonial Life Insurance Co. of America, **III** 220–21; **14** 108–09
Colonial Life Insurance Company, **11** 481
Colonial National Bank, **8** 9; **38** 10–12
Colonial National Leasing, Inc., **8** 9
Colonial Packaging Corporation, **12** 150
Colonial Penn Group Insurance Co., **11** 262; **27** 4
Colonial Penn Life Insurance Co., **V** 624
Colonial Rubber Works, **8** 347
Colonial Stores, **II** 397
Colonial Sugar Refining Co. Ltd. *See* CSR Limited.
Colony Capital, Inc., **27** 201
Colony Communications, **7** 99
Colony Gift Corporation, Ltd., **18** 67, 69
Color-Box, Inc., **8** 103
Color Corporation of America, **8** 553
Color Me Mine, **25** 263
Color Tile, **31** 435
Colorado Belle Casino, **6** 204
Colorado Cooler Co., **I** 292
Colorado Electric Company. *See* Public Service Company of Colorado.
Colorado Fuel & Iron (CF&I), **14** 369
Colorado Gaming & Entertainment Co., **21** 335
Colorado Gathering & Processing Corporation, **11** 27
Colorado Interstate Gas Co., **IV** 394
**Colorado MEDtech, Inc., 48 101–05**
Colorado National Bank, **12** 165
Colorado Technical University, Inc., **41** 419
Colorcraft, **I** 447
Colorfoto Inc., **I** 447
Coloroll, **44** 148
Colortree. *See* National Envelope Corporation.
ColorTyme, Inc., **45** 367
Colossal Pictures, **10** 286
Colson Co., **III** 96; **IV** 135–36
Colt, **19** 430–31
**Colt Industries Inc., I 434–36,** 482, 524; **III** 435
Colt Pistol Factory, **9** 416
**COLT Telecom Group plc, 41 96–99**
**Colt's Manufacturing Company, Inc., 12 70–72**
Coltec Industries Inc., **30** 158; **32** 96; **46** 213
Columbia Brewery, **25** 281
Columbia Broadcasting System. *See* CBS Corporation.
Columbia Chemical Co. *See* PPG Industries, Inc.
Columbia Electric Street Railway, Light and Power Company, **6** 575
Columbia Forest Products, **IV** 358
Columbia Gas & Electric Company, **6** 466. *See also* Columbia Gas System, Inc.
Columbia Gas Light Company, **6** 574
Columbia Gas of New York, Inc., **6** 536
**The Columbia Gas System, Inc., V 580–82**; **16 115–18 (upd.)**
Columbia Gas Transmission Corporation, **6** 467
Columbia General Life Insurance Company of Indiana, **11** 378
Columbia Hat Company, **19** 94
Columbia House, **IV** 676
Columbia Insurance Co., **III** 214
Columbia News Service, **II** 132
Columbia Paper Co., **IV** 311; **19** 266
**Columbia Pictures Entertainment, Inc., II** 103, 134, **135–37,** 170, 234, 619; **IV** 675; **10** 227; **12** 73, 455; **21** 360; **22** 193; **25** 139; **28** 71. *See also* Columbia TriStar Motion Pictures Companies.
Columbia Railroad, Gas and Electric Company, **6** 575
Columbia Records, **II** 132; **16** 201; **26** 150
Columbia Records Distribution Corp., **43** 170
Columbia River Packers, **II** 491
Columbia Savings & Loan, **II** 144
**Columbia Sportswear Company, 19 94–96**; **41 100–03 (upd.)**
Columbia Steamship Company, **17** 356
Columbia Steel Co., **IV** 28, 573; **7** 550
Columbia Transportation Co., **17** 357
**Columbia TriStar Motion Pictures Companies, 12 73–76 (upd.)**; **28** 71
Columbia TriStar Television Distribution, **17** 149
**Columbia/HCA Healthcare Corporation, 13** 90; **15 112–14**; **22** 409–10; **27** 356
Columbian Carbon Company, **25** 70–71
Columbian Chemicals Co., **IV** 179; **28** 352, 356
Columbian Peanut Co., **I** 421; **11** 23
Columbus & Southern Ohio Electric Company (CSO), **6** 467, 481–82
Columbus Bank & Trust. *See* Synovus Financial Corp.
**Columbus McKinnon Corporation, 37 95–98**
Columbus-Milpar, **I** 544
Columbus Realty Trust, **26** 378
Columbus Savings and Loan Society, **I** 536; **13** 528
Colwell Systems, **19** 291; **22** 181
Com Dev, Inc., **32** 435
Com Ed. *See* Commonwealth Edison.
Com-Link 21, Inc., **8** 310
**Comair Holdings Inc., 13 171–73**; **31** 420; **34 116–20 (upd.)**
Comalco Fabricators (Hong Kong) Ltd., **III** 758
Comalco Ltd., **IV** 59–61, 122, 191

Comark, **24** 316; **25** 417–18
Comat Services Pte. Ltd., **10** 514
Comau, **I** 163
Combibloc Inc., **16** 339
Combined American Insurance Co. of Dallas, **III** 203
Combined Casualty Co. of Philadelphia, **III** 203
Combined Communications Corp., **II** 619; **IV** 612; **7** 191
Combined Insurance Company of America, **III** 203–04; **45** 25–26
Combined International Corp., **III** 203–04
Combined Mutual Casualty Co. of Chicago, **III** 203
Combined Properties, Inc., **16** 160
Combined Registry Co., **III** 203
Combustion Engineering Group, **22** 11; **25** 534
Combustiveis Industriais e Domésticos. *See* CIDLA.
**Comcast Corporation**, **7 90–92**; **9** 428; **10** 432–33; **17** 148; **22** 162; **24 120–24 (upd.)**; **27** 342, 344
ComCore Semiconductor, Inc., **26** 330
Comdata, **19** 160
**Comdial Corporation**, **21 132–35**
**Comdisco, Inc.**, **9 130–32**; **11** 47, 86, 484, 490
Comdor Flugdienst GmbH., **I** 111
Comer Motor Express, **6** 370
Comerci. *See* Controladora Comercial Mexicana, S.A. de C.V.
Comercial Mexicana, S.A. *See* Controladora Comercial Mexicana, S.A. de C.V.
Comerco, **III** 21; **22** 147
**Comerica Incorporated**, **40 115–17**
Comet, **II** 139; **V** 106–09; **24** 194, 266, 269–70
Comet American Marketing, **33** 31
Comet Rice, Inc., **33** 31
Cometra Oil, **IV** 576
ComFed Bancorp, **11** 29
**COMFORCE Corporation**, **40 118–20**
Comfort Inns, **21** 362
Comforto GmbH, **8** 252; **39** 206
**Cominco Ltd.**, **37 99–102** 55
Comision Federal de Electricidad de Mexico (CFE), **21** 196–97
Comitato Interministrale per la Ricostruzione, **I** 465
Comm-Quip, **6** 313
CommAir. *See* American Building Maintenance Industries, Inc.
Commander Foods, **8** 409
Commander-Larabee Co., **I** 419; **25** 242
Commemorative Brands Inc., **19** 453
Commentry, **III** 676; **16** 120
Commerce and Industry Insurance Co., **III** 196, 203
**Commerce Clearing House, Inc.**, **7 93–94**. *See also* CCH Inc.
Commerce Group, **III** 393
Commerce.TV, **42** 323
Commerce Union, **10** 426
Commercial & General Life Assurance Co., **III** 371
Commercial Air Conditioning of Northern California, **25** 15
Commercial Air Lines, Inc., **23** 380
Commercial Alliance Corp. of New York, **II** 289
Commercial Aseguradora Suizo Americana, S.A., **III** 243
Commercial Assurance, **III** 359
Commercial Bank of Australia Ltd., **II** 189, 319, 388–89; **17** 324; **48** 425
Commercial Bank of London, **II** 334
Commercial Bank of Tasmania, **II** 188
Commercial Banking Co. of Sydney, **II** 187–89
Commercial Bureau (Australia) Pty., **I** 438
Commercial Chemical Company, **16** 99
**Commercial Credit Company**, **III** 127–28; **8 117–19**; **10** 255–56; **15** 464
Commercial Exchange Bank, **II** 254; **9** 124
**Commercial Federal Corporation**, **12 77–79**
Commercial Filters Corp., **I** 512
**Commercial Financial Services, Inc.**, **26 85–89**
Commercial Insurance Co. of Newark, **III** 242
Commercial Life, **III** 243
Commercial Life Assurance Co. of Canada, **III** 309
**Commercial Metals Company**, **15 115–17**; **42 81–84 (upd.)**
Commercial Motor Freight, Inc., **14** 42
Commercial National Bank, **II** 261; **10** 425
Commercial National Bank & Trust Co., **II** 230
Commercial National Bank of Charlotte, **II** 336
Commercial Realty Services Group, **21** 257
Commercial Ship Repair Co., **I** 185
**Commercial Union plc**, **II** 272, 308; **III** 185, **233–35**, 350, 373; **IV** 711
**Commerzbank A.G.**, **II** 239, 242, **256–58**, 280, 282, 385; **IV** 222; **9** 283; **14** 170; **47 81–84 (upd.)**
Commerzfilm, **IV** 591
CommLink Corp., **17** 264
Commodity Credit Corp., **11** 24
Commodore Corporation, **8** 229
**Commodore International, Ltd.**, **II** 6; **III** 112; **6** 243–44; **7 95–97**, 532; **9** 46; **10** 56, 284; **23** 25; **26** 16
Commonwealth & Southern Corporation, **V** 676
Commonwealth Aluminium Corp., Ltd. *See* Comalco Ltd.
Commonwealth Bank, **II** 188, 389
Commonwealth Board Mills, **IV** 248
**Commonwealth Edison**, **II** 28, 425; **III** 653; **IV** 169; **V 583–85**; **6** 505, 529, 531; **12** 548; **13** 341; **15** 422; **48** 163
**Commonwealth Energy System**, **14 124–26**
Commonwealth Hospitality Ltd., **III** 95
Commonwealth Industrial Gases, **25** 82
Commonwealth Industries, **III** 569; **11** 536; **20** 360
Commonwealth Insurance Co., **III** 264
Commonwealth Land Title Insurance Co., **III** 343
Commonwealth Life and Accident Insurance Company, **27** 46–47
Commonwealth Life Insurance Co., **III** 216–19
Commonwealth Limousine Services, Ltd., **26** 62
Commonwealth Mortgage Assurance Co., **III** 344
Commonwealth National Financial Corp., **II** 316; **44** 280
Commonwealth Oil Refining Company, **II** 402; **7** 517; **45** 410
Commonwealth Power Railway and Light Company, **14** 134
Commonwealth Southern Corporation, **14** 134
**Commonwealth Telephone Enterprises, Inc.**, **25 106–08**
Commtron, Inc., **V** 14, 16; **11** 195; **13** 90
Communication Services Ltd. *See* Hongkong Telecommunications Ltd.
Communications and Systems Specialists, **18** 370
Communications Consultants, Inc., **16** 393
Communications Corp. of America, **25** 418
Communications Data Services, Inc., **IV** 627; **19** 204
Communications Industries Inc., **25** 496
Communications Network Consultants, **29** 400
Communications Properties, Inc., **IV** 677
Communications Solutions Inc., **11** 520
Communications Technology Corp. (CTC), **13** 7–8
Communicorp, **III** 188; **10** 29; **38** 17
Community Direct, Inc., **7** 16
Community HealthCare Services, **6** 182
Community Hospital of San Gabriel, **6** 149
Community Medical Care, Inc., **III** 245
Community National Bank, **9** 474
Community Networks Inc., **45** 69
Community Newspapers, Inc., **45** 352
Community Power & Light Company, **6** 579–80
**Community Psychiatric Centers**, **15 118–20**
Community Public Service Company, **6** 514
Community Savings and Loan, **II** 317
Comnet Corporation, **9** 347
Comp-U-Card of America, Inc. *See* CUC International Inc.
Compac Corp., **11** 535
Compactom, **I** 588
Compagnia di Assicurazioni, **III** 345
Compagnia di Genova, **III** 347
Compagnia di Participazioni Assicurative ed Industriali S.p.A., **24** 341
Compagnie Auxilaire de Navigation, **IV** 558
Compagnie Bancaire, **II** 259; **21** 99–100
Compagnie Belge pour l'industrie, **II** 202
Compagnie Continentale, **I** 409–10
Compagnie d'Assurances Générales, **III** 391
Compagnie d'assurances Mutuelles contre l'incendie dans les départements de la Seine Inférieure et de l'Eure, **III** 210
Compagnie d'Investissements de Paris, **II** 233
Compagnie de Compteurs, **III** 617; **17** 418
Compagnie de Five-Lille, **IV** 469
Compagnie de Mokta, **IV** 107–08
Compagnie de Navigation Mixte, **III** 185
Compagnie de Reassurance Nord-Atlantique, **III** 276
Compagnie de Recherche et d'Exploitation du Pétrole du Sahara, **IV** 545; **21** 203
**Compagnie de Saint-Gobain S.A.**, **II** 117, 474–75; **III 675–78**, 704; **8** 395, 397; **15** 80; **16 119–23 (upd.)**; **19** 58, 226; **21** 222; **26** 446; **33** 338, 340; **35** 86, 88
Compagnie de Transport Aerien, **I** 122
**Compagnie des Alpes**, **48 106–08**

Compagnie des Cristalleries de Baccarat. *See* Baccarat.
**Compagnie des Machines Bull S.A.**, **II** 40, 42, 70, 125; **III 122–23**, 154; **IV** 600; **12** 139; **13** 574; **25** 33. *See also* Bull S.A. *and* Groupe Bull.
Compagnie des Messageries Maritimes, **6** 379
Compagnie des Produits Chimiques et Électrométallurgiques d'Alais, Froges et Camargue, **IV** 173–74
Compagnie du Midi, **III** 209, 211
Compagnie du Nord, **IV** 108
Compagnie Européenne de Publication, **IV** 614–15
Compagnie Européenne de Télésecurité, **32** 374
Compagnie Financier Richemont AG, **19** 367, 369–70
Compagnie Financiere Alcatel, **9** 10
Compagnie Financière Belge des Pétroles. *See* PetroFina S.A.
**Compagnie Financière de Paribas, II** 192, **259–60**; **III** 185; **21** 99; **27** 138; **33** 339. *See also* BNP Paribas Group.
Compagnie Financière de Richemont AG, **29** 90
Compagnie Financière de Suez. *See* Suez Lyonnaise des Eaux.
Compagnie Financiere du Groupe Victoire, **27** 54
Compagnie Financière Richemont AG, **27** 487; **29** 91–92
Compagnie Française Chaufour Investissement, **27** 100
Compagnie Française de Distribution en Afrique, **IV** 559
Compagnie Française de Manutention, **27** 295
Compagnie Française de Raffinage, **IV** 558–60
Compagnie Française des Lubricants, **I** 341
Compagnie Française des Minerais d'Uranium, **IV** 108
Compagnie Française des Mines de Diamants du Cap, **IV** 64; **7** 121
Compagnie Française des Pétroles. *See* TOTAL S.A.
Compagnie Française des Produits d'Orangina, **I** 281
Compagnie Française du Méthane, **V** 626
Compagnie Française Thomson-Houston, **I** 357; **II** 116. *See also* Thales S.A.
Compagnie Fromagère de la Vallée de l'Ance, **25** 84
**Compagnie Générale d'Électricité**, **I** 193; **II 12–13**, 25; **IV** 174, 615; **9** 9–10
Compagnie Generale de Cartons Ondules, **IV** 296; **19** 226
Compagnie Generale de Radiologie, **II** 117
Compagnie Generale de Telegraphie Sans Fils, **II** 116
Compagnie Générale des Eaux, **V** 632–33; **6** 441. *See also* Vivendi SA.
**Compagnie Générale des Établissements Michelin, V 236–39**; **19** 508; **42 85–89 (upd.)**
**Compagnie Générale Maritime et Financière, 6 379–81**
Compagnie Industriali Riunite S.p.A., **IV** 587–88
Compagnie Industrielle de Matérials de Manutention, **27** 296
Compagnie Industrielle des Fillers. *See* L'Entreprise Jean Lefebvre.
Compagnie Internationale de l'Informatique, **III** 123
Compagnie Internationale Express, **25** 120
Compagnie Internationale Pirelli S.A., **V** 249
Compagnie Laitière Européenne, **25** 83, 85
Compagnie Luxembourgeoise de Télédiffusion, **15** 54
Compagnie Nationale à Portefeuille, **29** 48
Compagnie Nationale de Navigation, **27** 515
Compagnie Navale Des Pétroles, **IV** 558
Compagnie Parisienne de Garantie, **III** 211
Compagnie Pneumatique Commerciale, **III** 426
Compagnie Tunisienne de Ressorts a Lames, **III** 581
Compal, **47** 152–53
Companhia Brasileira de Aluminio, **IV** 55
Companhia Brasileira de Mineracão e Siderugica, **IV** 54
Companhia de Celulose do Caima, **14** 250
Companhia de Diamantes de Angola, **IV** 21
Companhia de Minerales y Metales, **IV** 139
Companhia de Pesquisas Mineras de Angola, **IV** 65; **7** 122
Companhia de Seguros Argos Fluminense, **III** 221
Companhia de Seguros Tranquilidade Vida, S.A. *See* Banco Espírito Santo e Comercial de Lisboa S.A.
Companhia Siderúrgica de Tubarao, **IV** 125
Companhia Siderúrgica Mannesmann S.A., **III** 565–66
Companhia Siderúrgica Nacional, **II** 199; **43** 112
Companhia Uniao Fabril, **IV** 505
**Companhia Vale do Rio Doce, IV 54–57**; **43 111–14 (upd.)**
Compañia Arrendataria del Monopolio de Petróleos Sociedad Anónima, **IV** 396–97, 527–29
Compañia de Investigacion y Exploitaciones Petrolifera, **IV** 397
Compañia de Líneas Aéreas Subvencionadas S.A., **6** 95
**Compañia Española de Petroleos S.A., IV 396–98**, 527
Compania Fresnillo, **22** 286
Compania General de Aceptaciones. *See* Financiera Aceptaciones.
Compania Hulera Euzkadi, **21** 260; **23** 170
Compañia Mexicana de Transportación Aérea, **20** 167
Compania Minera de Penoles. *See* Industrias Penoles, S.A. de C.V.
Compañia Minera La India, **IV** 164
Compania Minera Las Torres, **22** 286
Compañia Nacional Minera Petrólia del Táchira, **IV** 507
Compania Siderurgica Huachipato, **24** 209
Compañía Telefónica Nacional de España S.A., **V** 337
**Compaq Computer Corporation, II** 45; **III** 114, **124–25**; **6** 217, **221–23 (upd.)**, 230–31, 235, 243–44; **9** 42–43, 166, 170–71, 472; **10** 87, 232–33, 366, 459, 518–19; **12** 61, 183, 335, 470; **13** 388, 483; **16** 4, 196, 367–68; **17** 274; **21** 123, 391; **22** 288; **25** 184, 239, 498, 531; **26 90–93 (upd.)**; **27** 365; **28** 191; **29** 439; **30** 12; **36** 384; **43** 13; **47** 153
Compart, **24** 341
Compass Airlines, **27** 475
Compass Design Automation, **16** 520
**Compass Group PLC**, **6** 193; **24** 194; **27** 482; **34 121–24**
**CompDent Corporation, 22 149–51**
Compeda, Ltd., **10** 240
Competence ApS, **26** 240
Competition Tire East/West, **V** 494; **19** 292
Competrol Ltd., **22** 189
Compex, **II** 233
**CompHealth Inc., 25 109–12**
**Complete Business Solutions, Inc., 31 130–33**
Completion Bond Co., **26** 487
Components Agents Ltd., **10** 113
Composite Craft Inc., **I** 387
Composite Research & Management Co., **17** 528, 530
**Comprehensive Care Corporation, 15 121–23**
Comprehensive Resources Corp., **IV** 83
Compressed Industrial Gases, **I** 297
Compression Labs Inc., **10** 456; **16** 392, 394; **27** 365
Compressor Controls Corporation, **15** 404
Comptoir d'Escompte de Mulhouse, **II** 232
Comptoir des Textiles Artificielles, **I** 122, 388–89
Comptoir Général de la Photographie. *See* Gaumont SA.
Comptoir Métallurgique Luxembourgeois, **IV** 25
Comptoir National d'Escompte de Paris, **II** 232–33, 270
**Comptoirs Modernes S.A., 19 97–99**
Compton Communications, **I** 33
Compton Foods, **II** 675
Compton's MultiMedia Publishing Group, Inc., **7** 165
Compton's New Media, Inc., **7** 168
Compu-Notes, Inc., **22** 413
**CompuAdd Computer Corporation, 11 61–63**
CompuChem Corporation, **11** 425
**CompuCom Systems, Inc., 10 232–34**, 474; **13** 176
Compugraphic, **III** 168; **6** 284
Compumech Technologies, **19** 312
Compumotor, **III** 603
CompuPharm, Inc., **14** 210
**CompUSA, Inc., 10 235–36**; **35 116–18 (upd.)**
**CompuServe Incorporated**, **9** 268–70; **10 237–39**; **12** 562; **13** 147; **15** 265; **16** 467, 508; **26** 16; **29** 224, 226–27; **34** 361. *See also* America Online, Inc.
**CompuServe Interactive Services, Inc., 27** 106, **106–08 (upd.)**, 301, 307. *See also* America Online, Inc.
Computax, **6** 227–28
**Computer Associates International, Inc., 6 224–26**; **10** 394; **12** 62; **14** 392; **27** 492
Computer City, **12** 470; **36** 387
The Computer Company, **11** 112
Computer Consoles Inc., **III** 164
**Computer Data Systems, Inc., 14 127–29**
The Computer Department, Ltd., **10** 89
Computer Depot, **6** 243

Computer Discount Corporation. *See* Comdisco, Inc.
Computer Dynamics, Inc., **6** 10
Computer Engineering Associates, **25** 303
Computer Factory, Inc., **13** 176
**Computer Learning Centers, Inc., 26 94–96**
Computer Network, **20** 237
Computer Peripheral Manufacturers Association, **13** 127
Computer Plaza K.K., **IV** 542–43
Computer Power, **6** 301
Computer Renaissance, Inc., **18** 207–8
Computer Research Corp., **III** 151; **6** 265
Computer Resources Management, Inc., **26** 36
**Computer Sciences Corporation, 6** 25, **227–29**; **13** 462; **15** 474; **18** 370
Computer Shoppe, **V** 191–92
Computer Systems and Applications, **12** 442
Computer Systems Division (CDS), **13** 201
Computer Terminal Corporation, **11** 67–68
ComputerCity, **10** 235
ComputerCraft, **27** 163
Computerized Lodging Systems, Inc., **11** 275
Computerized Waste Systems, **46** 248
**ComputerLand Corp., 6** 243; **9** 116; **10** 233, 563; **12** 335; **13 174–76**, 277; **33** 341–42
**Computervision Corporation, 6** 246–47; **7** 498; **10 240–42**; **11** 275; **13** 201; **24** 234
Computing Scale Company of America. *See* International Business Machines Corporation.
Computing-Tabulating-Recording Co., **III** 147
**Compuware Corporation, 10 243–45**; **30 140–43 (upd.)**; **38** 482
CompX International, Inc., **19** 466, 468
**Comsat Corporation, II** 425; **12** 19; **13** 341; **23 133–36**; **28** 241; **29** 42
**Comshare Inc., 23 137–39**
Comstock Canada, **9** 301
**Comstock Resources, Inc., 47 85–87**
Comtel Electronics, Inc., **22** 409
Comunicaciones Avanzados, S.A. de C.V., **39** 195
**Comverse Technology, Inc., 15 124–26**; **43 115–18 (upd.)**
Comviq GSM AB, **26** 331–33
Con Ed. *See* Consolidated Edison, Inc.
Con-Ferro Paint and Varnish Company, **8** 553
**ConAgra, Inc., II 493–95**, 517, 585; **7** 432, 525; **8** 53, 499–500; **12 80–82 (upd.)**; **13** 138, 294, 350, 352; **14** 515; **17** 56, 240–41; **18** 247, 290; **21** 290; **23** 320; **25** 243, 278; **26** 172, 174; **36** 416; **42 90–94 (upd.)**
Conahay & Lyon, **6** 27
**Conair Corp., 16** 539; **17 108–10**; **24** 131; **25** 56
Concept, Inc., **23** 154
**Concepts Direct, Inc., 39 93–96**
Concepts in Community Living, Inc., **43** 46
Concert Communications Company, **15** 69; **27** 304–05
Concesiones de Infraestructuras de Transportes, S.A., **40** 217
Concession Air, **16** 446
Concha y Toro. *See* Viña Concha y Toro S.A.
**Concord Camera Corporation, 41 104–07**
**Concord Fabrics, Inc., 16 124–26**
Concord International, **II** 298
Concord Watch Company, S.A., **28** 291
Concorde Hotels, **27** 421
Concordia, **IV** 497
Concrete Industries (Monier) Ltd., **III** 735
Concurrent Logic, **17** 34
**The Condé Nast Publications Inc., IV** 583–84; **13 177–81**; **19** 5; **23** 98
Condor Systems Inc., **15** 530
Cone Communications, **25** 258
**Cone Mills Corporation, 8 120–22**
Conelectron, **13** 398
Conestoga National Bank, **II** 316
**Conexant Systems, Inc., 36 121–25**; **43** 328
Confectionaire, **25** 283
Confederacion Norte-Centromericana y del Caribe de Futbol, **27** 150
Confederacion Sudamericana de Futbol, **27** 150
Confederation Africaine de Football, **27** 150
Confederation Freezers, **21** 501
Confederation of Engineering Industry, **IV** 484
Confidata Corporation, **11** 111
Confindustria, **I** 162
Confiserie-Group Hofbauer, **27** 105
Congas Engineering Canada Ltd., **6** 478
**Congoleum Corp., 12** 28; **16** 18; **18 116–19**; **36** 77–78; **43** 19, 21
Congress Financial Corp., **13** 305–06; **19** 108; **27** 276
Congressional Information Services, **IV** 610
Conic, **9** 324
Conifer Group, **II** 214
Conill Corp., **II** 261
Coniston Partners, **I** 130; **II** 680; **III** 29; **6** 130; **10** 302
CONNA Corp., **7** 113; **25** 125
Connect Group Corporation, **28** 242
Connecticut Bank and Trust Co., **II** 213–14
Connecticut General Corporation. *See* CIGNA Corporation.
Connecticut Health Enterprises Network, **22** 425
**Connecticut Light and Power Co., 13 182–84**; **21** 514; **48** 305
**Connecticut Mutual Life Insurance Company, III** 225, **236–38**, 254, 285
Connecticut National Bank, **13** 467
Connecticut River Banking Company, **13** 467
Connecticut Telephone Company. *See* Southern New England Telecommunications Corporation.
Connecticut Trust and Safe Deposit Co., **II** 213
Connecticut Yankee Atomic Power Company, **21** 513
Connecting Point of America, **6** 244
The Connection Group, Inc., **26** 257
Connectix Corporation, **28** 245
**The Connell Company, 29 129–31**
Conner Corp., **15** 327
**Conner Peripherals, Inc., 6 230–32**; **10** 403, 459, 463–64, 519; **11** 56, 234; **18** 260
Connie Lee. *See* College Construction Loan Insurance Assoc.
Connoisseur Communications, **37** 104
Connolly Data Systems, **11** 66
Connolly Tool and Machine Company, **21** 215
Connors Brothers, **II** 631–32
Connors Steel Co., **15** 116
**Conoco Inc., I** 286, 329, 346, 402–04; **II** 376; **IV** 365, 382, 389, **399–402**, 413, 429, 454, 476; **6** 539; **7** 346, 559; **8** 152, 154, 556; **11** 97, 400; **16 127–32 (upd.)**; **18** 366; **21** 29; **26** 125, 127
Conorada Petroleum Corp., **IV** 365, 400
Conover Furniture Company, **10** 183
ConQuest Telecommunication Services Inc., **16** 319
Conquistador Films, **25** 270
Conrad International Hotels, **III** 91–93
Conrail Inc., **22** 167, 376. *See also* Consolidated Rail Corporation.
Conran Associates, **17** 43
Conrock Co., **19** 70
**Conseco Inc., 10 246–48**; **15** 257; **33 108–12 (upd.)**
Consgold. *See* Consolidated Gold Fields of South Africa Ltd. *and* Consolidated Gold Fields PLC.
Conshu Holdings, **24** 450
**Conso International Corporation, 29 132–34**
Consodata S.A., **47** 345, 347
Consolidated Aircraft Corporation, **9** 16, 497
Consolidated Aluminum Corp., **IV** 178
Consolidated Asset Management Company, Inc., **25** 204
Consolidated-Bathurst Inc., **IV** 246–47, 334; **25** 11; **26** 445
Consolidated Brands Inc., **14** 18
Consolidated Cable Utilities, **6** 313
Consolidated Cement Corp., **III** 704
Consolidated Cigar Holdings, Inc., **I** 452–53; **15** 137–38; **27** 139–40; **28** 247
Consolidated Coal Co., **IV** 82, 170–71
Consolidated Coin Caterers Corporation, **10** 222
Consolidated Controls, **I** 155
Consolidated Converting Co., **19** 109
Consolidated Copper Corp., **13** 503
**Consolidated Delivery & Logistics, Inc., 24 125–28**
Consolidated Denison Mines Ltd., **8** 418
Consolidated Diamond Mines of South-West Africa Ltd., **IV** 21, 65–67; **7** 122–25; **16** 26
Consolidated Distillers Ltd., **I** 263
**Consolidated Edison Company of New York, Inc., I** 28; **V 586–89**; **6** 456; **35** 479
**Consolidated Edison, Inc., 45 116–20 (upd.)**
Consolidated Electric & Gas, **6** 447; **23** 28
Consolidated Electric Power Asia, **38** 448
Consolidated Electric Supply Inc., **15** 385
Consolidated Electronics Industries Corp. (Conelco), **13** 397–98
Consolidated Foods Corp., **II** 571–73, 584; **III** 480; **12** 159, 494; **22** 27; **29** 132
**Consolidated Freightways Corporation, V 432–34**; **6** 280, 388; **12** 278, 309; **13**

19; **14** 567; **21 136–39 (upd.)**; **25** 148–50; **48 109–13 (upd.)**
Consolidated Gas Company. *See* Baltimore Gas and Electric Company.
Consolidated Gold Fields of South Africa Ltd., **IV** 94, 96, 118, 565, 566
Consolidated Gold Fields PLC, **II** 422; **III** 501, 503; **IV** 23, 67, 94, 97, 171; **7** 125, 209, 387
Consolidated Grocers Corp., **II** 571
Consolidated Insurances of Australia, **III** 347
Consolidated Marketing, Inc., **IV** 282; **9** 261
Consolidated Mines Selection Co., **IV** 20, 23
Consolidated Mining and Smelting Co., **IV** 75
Consolidated National Life Insurance Co., **10** 246
**Consolidated Natural Gas Company**, **V 590–91**; **19 100–02 (upd.)**
Consolidated Oatmeal Co., **II** 558
**Consolidated Papers, Inc.**, **8 123–25**; **36 126–30 (upd.)**
Consolidated Plantations Berhad, **36** 434–35
Consolidated Power & Light Company, **6** 580
Consolidated Power & Telephone Company, **11** 342
Consolidated Press Holdings, **8** 551; **37** 408–09
**Consolidated Products, Inc.**, **14 130–32**, 352
**Consolidated Rail Corporation**, **II** 449; **V 435–37**, 485; **10** 44; **12** 278; **13** 449; **14** 324; **29** 360; **35** 291. *See also* Conrail Inc.
Consolidated Rand-Transvaal Mining Group, **IV** 90; **22** 233
Consolidated Rock Products Co., **19** 69
Consolidated Specialty Restaurants, Inc., **14** 131–32
Consolidated Steel, **I** 558; **IV** 570; **24** 520
Consolidated Stores Corp., **13** 543; **29** 311; **35** 254
Consolidated Temperature Controlling Co., **II** 40; **12** 246
Consolidated Theaters, Inc., **14** 87
Consolidated Tire Company, **20** 258
Consolidated Trust Inc., **22** 540
Consolidated Tyre Services Ltd., **IV** 241
Consolidated Vultee, **II** 7, 32
Consolidated Zinc Corp., **IV** 58–59, 122, 189, 191
Consolidation Coal Co., **IV** 401; **8** 154, 346–47
Consolidation Services, **44** 10, 13
**Consorcio G Grupo Dina, S.A. de C.V.**, **36 131–33**
Consortium, **34** 373
Consortium de Realisation, **25** 329
Consortium De Realization SAS, **23** 392
Consoweld Corporation, **8** 124
Constar International Inc., **8** 562; **13** 190; **32** 125
Constellation, **III** 335
Constellation Energy Corporation, **24** 29
Constellation Enterprises Inc., **25** 46
Constellation Insurance Co., **III** 191–92
Constinsouza, **25** 174
Construcciones Aeronauticas S.A., **I** 41–42; **7** 9; **12** 190; **24** 88
Construcciones y Contratas, **II** 198
Construction DJL Inc., **23** 332–33
Construtora Moderna SARL, **IV** 505
Consul Restaurant Corp., **13** 152
Consumer Access Limited, **24** 95
Consumer Products Company, **30** 39
Consumer Value Stores, **V** 136–37; **9** 67; **18** 199; **24** 290
Consumer's Gas Co., **I** 264
Consumers Cooperative Association, **7** 174. *See also* Farmland Industries, Inc.
Consumers Distributing Co. Ltd., **II** 649, 652–53
Consumers Electric Light and Power, **6** 582
**The Consumers Gas Company Ltd.**, **6 476–79**; **43** 154. *See also* Enbridge Inc.
Consumers Mutual Gas Light Company. *See* Baltimore Gas and Electric Company.
**Consumers Power Co.**, **V** 577–79, 593–94; **14** 114–15, **133–36**
Consumers Public Power District, **29** 352
**Consumers Union**, **26 97–99**
**Consumers Water Company**, **14 137–39**; **39** 329
Contact Software International Inc., **10** 509
Contadina, **II** 488–89
Container Corporation of America, **IV** 295, 465; **V** 147; **7** 353; **8** 476; **19** 225; **26** 446
**The Container Store**, **36 134–36**
Container Transport International, **III** 344
Containers Packaging, **IV** 249
Contaminant Recovery Systems, Inc., **18** 162
CONTAQ Microsystems Inc., **48** 127
Conte S.A., **12** 262
Contech, **10** 493
Contel Corporation, **II** 117; **V** 294–98; **6** 323; **13** 212; **14** 259; **15** 192; **43** 447
Contempo Associates, **14** 105; **25** 307
Contempo Casuals, Inc. *See* The Wet Seal, Inc.
Contemporary Books, **22** 522
Content Technologies Inc., **42** 24–25
Contex Graphics Systems Inc., **24** 428
Contherm Corp., **III** 420
Conti-Carriers & Terminals Inc., **22** 167
ContiCommodity Services, Inc., **10** 250–51
**ContiGroup Companies, Inc.**, **43 119–22 (upd.)**
Continental AG, **9** 248; **15** 355
**Continental Airlines, Inc.**, **I 96–98**, 103, 118, 123–24, 129–30; **6** 52, 61, 105, 120–21, 129–30; **12** 381; **20** 84, 262; **21 140–43 (upd.)**; **22** 80, 220; **25** 420, 423; **26** 439–40; **34** 398
**Continental Aktiengesellschaft**, **V 240–43**, 250–51, 256; **8** 212–14; **19** 508
Continental American Life Insurance Company, **7** 102
Continental Assurance Co., **III** 228–30
Continental Baking Co., **I** 463–64; **II** 562–63; **7** 320–21; **11** 198; **12** 276; **13** 427; **19** 192; **27** 309–10; **38** 252
Continental Bancor, **II** 248
Continental Bank and Trust Co., **II** 251; **14** 102
**Continental Bank Corporation**, **I** 526; **II 261–63**, 285, 289, 348; **IV** 702; **47** 231
Continental Bio-Clinical Laboratories, **26** 391
Continental Blacks Inc., **I** 403
**Continental Cablevision, Inc.**, **7 98–100**; **17** 148; **19** 201
**Continental Can Co., Inc.**, **I** 597; **II** 34, 414; **III** 471; **10** 130; **13** 255; **15 127–30**; **24** 428; **26** 117, 449; **32** 125
Continental-Caoutchouc und Gutta-Percha Compagnie, **V** 240
Continental Carbon Co., **I** 403–05; **II** 53; **IV** 401; **36** 146–48
Continental Care Group, **10** 252–53
Continental Casualty Co., **III** 196, 228–32; **16** 204
Continental Cities Corp., **III** 344
**Continental Corporation**, **III** 230, **239–44**, 273; **10** 561; **12** 318; **15** 30; **38** 142
Continental Cos., **III** 248
Continental Divide Insurance Co., **III** 214
Continental Electronics Corporation, **18** 513–14
Continental Emsco, **I** 490–91; **24** 305
Continental Equipment Company, **13** 225
Continental Express, **11** 299
Continental Fiber Drum, **8** 476
Continental Gas & Electric Corporation, **6** 511
**Continental General Tire Corp.**, **23 140–42**
**Continental Grain Company**, **10 249–51**; **13 185–87 (upd.)**; **30** 353, 355; **40** 87. *See also* ContiGroup Companies, Inc.
**Continental Group Co.**, **I 599–600**, 601–02, 604–05, 607–09, 612–13, 615; **IV** 334; **8** 175, 424; **17** 106
Continental Gummi-Werke Aktiengesellschaft, **V** 241; **9** 248
Continental Hair Products, Inc. *See* Conair Corp.
Continental Health Affiliates, **17** 307
Continental Homes, **26** 291
Continental Illinois Corp. *See* Continental Bank Corporation.
Continental Illinois Venture Co., **IV** 702
Continental Insurance Co., **III** 239–42, 372–73, 386
Continental Insurance Cos. of New York, **III** 230
Continental Investment Corporation, **9** 507; **12** 463; **22** 541; **33** 407
Continental Life Insurance Co., **III** 225
**Continental Medical Systems, Inc.**, **10 252–54**; **11** 282; **14** 233; **25** 111; **33** 185
Continental Milling Company, **10** 250
Continental Modules, Inc., **45** 328
Continental Motors Corp., **I** 199, 524–25; **10** 521–22
Continental Mutual Savings Bank, **17** 529
Continental National American Group, **III** 230, 404
Continental National Bank, **II** 261; **11** 119
Continental-National Group, **III** 230
Continental Oil Co., **IV** 39, 365, 382, 399–401, 476, 517, 575–76
Continental Packaging Inc., **13** 255
Continental Plastic Containers, Inc., **25** 512
Continental Radio, **IV** 607
Continental Reinsurance, **11** 533
Continental Research Corporation, **22** 541
Continental Restaurant Systems, **12** 510
Continental Risk Services, **III** 243
Continental Savouries, **II** 500
Continental Scale Works, **14** 229–30
Continental Securities Corporation, **II** 444; **22** 404

Continental Telephone Company, **V** 296–97; **9** 494–95; **11** 500; **15** 195
Continental Wood Preservers, Inc., **12** 397
Continentale Allgemeine, **III** 347
ContinueCare Corporation, **25** 41
Contran Corporation, **19** 467
Contrans Acquisitions, Inc., **14** 38
Contred Ltd., **20** 263
Control Data Corporation, **17** 49; **19** 110, 513–15; **25** 496; **30** 338; **38** 58; **46** 35
**Control Data Systems, Inc., III** 118, **126–28**, 129, 131, 149, 152, 165; **6** 228, 252, 266; **8** 117–18, 467; **10 255–57**, 359, 458–59; **11** 469; **16** 137
**Controladora Comercial Mexicana, S.A. de C.V., 36 137–39**
Controladora PROSA, **18** 516, 518
Controlled Materials and Equipment Transportation, **29** 354
Controlonics Corporation, **13** 195
Controls Company of America, **9** 67
Controlware GmbH, **22** 53
Convair, **I** 82, 121, 123, 126, 131; **II** 33; **9** 18, 498; **13** 357
Convenient Food Mart Inc., **7** 114; **25** 125
Convergent Technologies, **III** 166; **6** 283; **11** 519
**Converse Inc., III** 528–29; **V** 376; **9 133–36**, 234; **12** 308; **31 134–138 (upd.)**, 211; **39** 170, 172–74
Conway Computer Group, **18** 370
Conwest Exploration Company Ltd., **16** 10, 12; **43** 3
Conycon. *See* Construcciones y Contratas.
Conzinc Riotinto of Australia. *See* CRA Limited.
Cook Bates Inc., **40** 347–48
Cook Data Services, Inc., **9** 73
Cook Industrial Coatings, **I** 307
Cook Standard Tool Co., **13** 369
Cook United, **V** 172
Cooke Engineering Company, **13** 194
**The Cooker Restaurant Corporation, 20 159–61**
Cooking and Crafts Club, **13** 106
**Cookson Group plc, III 679–82**; **16** 290; **44 115–20 (upd.)**
**CoolBrands International Inc., 35 119–22**
Coolerator, **I** 463
Coolidge Mutual Savings Bank, **17** 529
**Coop Schweiz Genossenschaftsverband, 48 114–16**
**Cooper Cameron Corporation, 20 162–66 (upd.)**
Cooper Canada Ltd., **16** 80
**The Cooper Companies, Inc., 39 97–100**
**Cooper Industries, Inc., II 14–17**; **14** 564; **19** 43, 45, 140; **30** 266; **44 121–25 (upd.)**
Cooper Laboratories, **I** 667, 682
Cooper LaserSonics Inc., **IV** 100
Cooper McDougall & Robertson Ltd., **I** 715
**Cooper Tire & Rubber Company, 8 126–28**; **23 143–46 (upd.)**
Cooper-Weymouth, **10** 412
Cooper's, Inc., **12** 283
Cooperative Grange League Federation Exchange, **7** 17
**Coopers & Lybrand, 9 137–38**; **12** 391; **25** 383. *See also* PricewaterhouseCoopers.
CooperVision, **7** 46; **25** 55
Coordinated Caribbean Transport. *See* Crowley Caribbean Transport.
Coors Company. *See* Adolph Coors Company.
Coorsh and Bittner, **7** 430
Coos Bay Lumber Co., **IV** 281; **9** 259
Coosa River Newsprint Co., **III** 40; **16** 303; **43** 257
Coote & Jurgenson, **14** 64
Cooymans, **I** 281
**Copart Inc., 23 147–49**, 285, 287
Copeland Corp., **II** 20
Copeman Ridley, **13** 103
Copico, **44** 273
Copland Brewing Co., **I** 268; **25** 280
Copley Pharmaceuticals Inc., **13** 264
**The Copley Press, Inc., 23 150–52**
Copley Real Estate Advisors, **III** 313
Copolymer Corporation, **9** 242
Copper Queen Consolidated Mining Co., **IV** 176–77
Copper Range Company, **IV** 76; **7** 281–82
Copperweld Steel Co., **IV** 108–09, 237
**The Copps Corporation, 32 120–22**
Copycat Ltd., **8** 383
Cor Therapeutics, **47** 251
Cora Verlag, **IV** 590
Coral Drilling, **I** 570
Coral Energy, **41** 359
Coral Leisure Group, **I** 248
Coral Petroleum, **IV** 395
Corange, Ltd., **37** 111–13
Corbett Canyon. *See* The Wine Group, Inc.
Corbett Enterprises Inc., **13** 270
**Corbis Corporation, 31 139–42**
**Corby Distilleries Limited, 14 140–42**
Corchos de Mérida S.A., **48** 349
Corco. *See* Commonwealth Oil Refining Company.
Corco, Inc. *See* Liqui-Box Corporation.
Corcoran & Riggs. *See* Riggs National Corporation.
Cordiant plc. *See* Saatchi & Saatchi plc.
**Cordis Corporation, 19 103–05**; **36** 306; **46 104–07 (upd.)**
Cordon & Gotch, **IV** 619
Le Cordon Bleu, **II** 609; **45** 88; **45** 88
Cordovan Corp., **IV** 608
Core Laboratories Inc., **I** 486; **11** 265
**Corel Corporation, 15 131–33**; **33 113–16 (upd.)**
**CoreStates Financial Corp, 17 111–15**
CoreTek, Inc., **36** 353
Corfuerte S.A. de C.V., **23** 171
Corimon, **12** 218
Corinthian Broadcast Corporation, **IV** 605; **10** 4
**Corinthian Colleges, Inc., 39 101–04**
Corio Inc., **38** 188, 432
Cormetech, **III** 685
Corn Exchange Bank, **II** 316
Corn Exchange Bank Trust Co., **II** 251; **14** 102
Corn Exchange National Bank, **II** 261
Corn Products Company. *See* Bestfoods.
Corn Sweetners Inc., **I** 421; **11** 23
Cornelia Insurance Agency. *See* Advantage Insurers, Inc.
Cornell Corrections, **28** 255
Cornerstone Direct Marketing, **8** 385–86
Cornerstone Propane Partners, L.P., **37** 280, 283
Cornerstone Title Company, **8** 461
Cornhill Insurance Co., **I** 429; **III** 185, 385
Cornhusker Casualty Co., **III** 213
Corning Asahi Video Products Co., **III** 667
Corning Clinical Laboratories, **26** 390–92
Corning Consumer Products Company, **27** 288
**Corning Inc., I** 609; **III** 434, 667, **683–85**, 720–21; **8** 468; **11** 334; **13** 398; **22** 454; **25** 254; **30** 151–52; **44 126–30 (upd.)**
Coro International A.V.V., **39** 346
Coronado Corp., **II** 112
Coronet Industries, Inc., **II** 90; **14** 436
Corporacion Durango, S.A. de C.V., **37** 178
Corporacion Estatal Petrolera Ecuatoriana, **IV** 510–11
**Corporación Internacional de Aviación, S.A. de C.V. (Cintra), 20 167–69**
Corporación Moctezuma, **21** 261
**Corporacion Nacional del Cobre de Chile, 38** 231; **40 121–23**
Corporacion Siderurgica Integral, **22** 44
Corporación Venezolana de Petroleo, **IV** 507
Corporate Childcare Development, Inc. *See* Bright Horizons Family Solutions, Inc.
**Corporate Express, Inc., 22 152–55**, 531; **41** 67–69; **47 88–92 (upd.)**
Corporate Microsystems, Inc., **10** 395
Corporate Partners, **12** 391
**Corporate Software Inc., 9 139–41**
CorporateFamily Solutions. *See* Bright Horizons Family Solutions, Inc.
**Corporation for Public Broadcasting, 14 143–45**; **47** 259
Corporation of Lloyd's, **III** 278–79
Corporation Trust Co. *See* CCH Inc.
Corpoven, **IV** 508
Corrado Passera, **IV** 588
Corral Midwest, Inc., **10** 333
**Correctional Services Corporation, 30 144–46**
**Corrections Corporation of America, 23 153–55**; **28** 255
Corrigan-McKinney Steel Company, **13** 157
Corrigan's, **16** 559
Corroon & Black. *See* Willis Corroon Group Plc.
**Corrpro Companies, Inc., 20 170–73**
Corrugated Paper, **IV** 249
**CORT Business Services Corporation, 26 100–02**
**El Corte Inglés Group, 26 128–31 (upd.)**
Cortec Corporation, **14** 430
**Corticeira Amorim, Sociedade Gestora de Participaço es Sociais, S.A., 48 117–20**, 349
Corvallis Lumber Co., **IV** 358
Cory Bros & Co. Ltd., **31** 367, 369
Cory Components, **36** 158
Cory Corp., **II** 511
Cory Food Services, Inc., **II** 608
Cory Orchard and Turf. *See* Chemi-Trol Chemical Co.
Cosco Pacific, **20** 313
Cosden Petroleum Corp., **IV** 498; **26** 367
Cosgrove & Co., **III** 283
**Cosmair Inc., III** 47–48; **8 129–32**, 342–44; **12** 404; **31** 418; **46** 278
Cosmar Corp., **37** 269–71
**The Cosmetic Center, Inc., 22 156–58**
Cosmetic Technology International, Inc., **22** 409

**Cosmo Oil Co., Ltd., IV 403–04**
Cosmopolitan Cosmetics GmbH, **48** 420, 422
Cosmopolitan Productions, **IV** 626; **19** 203
Cosmotel, **46** 401
Cosorzio Interprovinciale Vini, **10** 181
**Cost Plus, Inc.**, **12** 393; **27 109–11**; **34** 337, 340
Costa Apple Products, **II** 480; **26** 57
Costa Cruise Lines, **27** 29, 90, 92
Costa e Ribeiro Ltd., **IV** 504
Costa Rica International, Inc., **41** 329
Costain Civil Engineering Ltd., **III** 495; **13** 206
Costain Homes, **31** 386
**Costco Wholesale Corporation**, **V 36**; **10** 206; **11** 240; **14** 393–95; **15** 470; **25** 235; **27** 95; **43 123–25 (upd.)**
Costruzioni Meccaniche Nazionalia, **13** 218
Côte d'Or, **II** 521
Cott Beverage Corporation, **9** 291
Cottees General Foods, **II** 477
**Cotter & Company**, **V 37–38**; **12** 8. *See also* TruServ Corporation.
Cotter Corporation, **29** 488
**Cotton Incorporated**, **46 108–11**
Cotton Producers Association. *See* Gold Kist Inc.
**Coty, Inc.**, **36 140–42**; **37** 270
**Coudert Brothers**, **30 147–50**
Coulter Corporation. *See* Beckman Coulter, Inc.
Counsel Corp., **46** 3
Counselor Co., **14** 230
Country Fresh, Inc., **26** 449
Country Kitchen Foods, **III** 21
Country Kitchen International, **22** 127
Country Music Television, **11** 153
Country Poultry, Inc., **II** 494
Country Seat Stores, Inc., **15** 87
Country Store of Concord, Inc., **10** 216
**Countrywide Credit Industries, Inc.**, **16 133–36**
County Bank, **II** 333
County Catering Co., **13** 103
County Data Corporation, **18** 24
County Fire Insurance Co., **III** 191
County Market, **II** 670
County NatWest, **II** 334–35
County Perfumery, **III** 65
**County Seat Stores Inc.**, **II** 669; **9 142–43**
County Trust Co., **II** 230
Cour des Comptes, **II** 233
Courage Brewing Group., **I** 229, 438–39; **III** 503
Courcoux-Bouvet, **II** 260
**Courier Corporation**, **41 108–12**
Courir S.A., **39** 183–85
Courrèges Parfums, **III** 48; **8** 343
The Courseware Developers, **11** 19
Court Courier Systems, Inc., **24** 126
Court House Square, **10** 44
**Courtaulds plc**, **I** 321; **IV** 261, 670; **V** 356–57, **359–61**; **12** 103; **17 116–19 (upd.)**; **33** 134; **41** 9
Courtney Wines International, **II** 477
Courtot Investments, **II** 222
**Courts Plc**, **45 121–24**
Courtyard by Marriott, **9** 427
Cousins Mortgage and Equity Investments, **12** 393
Coutts & Co., **II** 333–34
Couvrette & Provost Ltd., **II** 651
**Covance Inc.**, **30 151–53**
Covantage, **11** 379
Covenant Life Insurance, **III** 314
Coventry Climax Engines, Ltd., **13** 286
Coventry Co., **III** 213
Coventry Corporation, **17** 166, 168
Coventry Machinists Company, **7** 458
Coventry Ordnance Works, **I** 573
Coventry Union Banking Co., **II** 318; **17** 323
Covidea, **II** 252
Coville Inc., **16** 353
**Covington & Burling**, **40 124–27**
Cow & Gate Ltd., **II** 586–87
Cowham Engineering, **III** 704
**Cowles Media Company**, **IV** 613, 648; **7** 191; **19** 285; **23 156–58**; 344
Cox & Co., **II** 236, 307–08
Cox Cable Communications, Inc., **42** 114
**Cox Enterprises, Inc.**, **IV** 246, **595–97**; **6** 32; **7** 327; **9** 74; **17** 148; **22 159–63 (upd.)**; **24** 120; **30** 217; **38** 307–08
Cox Medical Enterprises, Inc., **21** 47
Cox Newsprint, Inc., **25** 11
Cox Pharmaceuticals, **35** 25
Cox Woodlands Company, **25** 11
Coz Chemical Co., **21** 20, 22
CP. *See* Canadian Pacific Limited.
CP/AAON. *See* AAON, Inc.
CP Air, **6** 60–61
CP National, **6** 300; **19** 412
CP Ships, **45** 80
**CPC International Inc.**, **II** 463, **496–98**; **27** 40. *See also* Bestfoods.
CP8, **43** 89
**CPI Corp.**, **38 157–60**
CPL. *See* Carolina Power & Light Company.
CR2A Holding, **48** 402
**CRA Limited**, **IV 58–61**, 67, 192; **7** 124. *See also* Rio Tinto plc.
Crabtree Electricals, **III** 503; **7** 210
**Cracker Barrel Old Country Store, Inc.**, **10 258–59**. *See also* CBRL Group, Inc.
Craft House Corp., **8** 456
Craftique, Inc., **33** 350–51
**Craftmade International, Inc.**, **44 131–33**
Craig Bit Company, **13** 297
**Crain Communications, Inc.**, **12 83–86**; **35 123–27 (upd.)**
**Cramer, Berkowitz & Co.**, **34 125–27**
Cramer Electronics, **10** 112
Cranberry Canners, Inc. *See* Ocean Spray Cranberries, Inc.
**Crane & Co., Inc.**, **26 103–06**; **30** 42
Crane Carton Co., **44** 66
**Crane Co.**, **8 133–36**, 179; **24** 332; **30 154–58 (upd.)**
Crane Packing Company, **19** 311
Crane Supply Company, **8** 135
Cranston Mills, **13** 168
**Cranswick plc**, **40 128–30**
**Crate and Barrel**, **9 144–46**; **27** 429; **36** 135. *See also* Euromarket Designs Inc.
**Cravath, Swaine & Moore**, **27** 325; **43 126–28**
Craven Tasker Ltd., **I** 573–74
Crawford and Watson, **IV** 278
Crawford Gosho Co., Ltd., **IV** 442
Crawford Group, Inc., **17** 372
Crawford Supply Company, **6** 392
**Cray Research, Inc.**, **III** 126, 128, **129–31**; **10** 256; **16 137–40 (upd.)**; **21** 391; **22** 428; **29** 440
Crayfish Company, Ltd., **36** 153
Crazy Eddie Inc., **23** 373
Crazy Shirts, Inc., **45** 42
CRD Total France, **IV** 560
Cream City Railway Company, **6** 601
Cream of Wheat Corp., **II** 543; **22** 427
Cream Wine Company, **48** 392
Creamola Food Products, **II** 569
Creasy Co., **II** 682
**Creative Artists Agency LLC**, **10** 228; **22** 297; **23** 512, 514; **32** 115; **38 161–64**
Creative Artists Associates, **43** 235
Creative BioMolecules, Inc., **29** 454
Creative Business Concepts, Inc., **39** 346
Creative Concepts in Advertising, **27** 194
Creative Displays, Inc., **27** 279
Creative Engineering Inc., **13** 472
Creative Food 'N Fun Co., **14** 29
Creative Forming, Inc., **8** 562
Creative Homes, Inc., **IV** 341
Creative Integration and Design Inc., **20** 146
Creative Memories, **40** 44
Creative Technologies Corp., **15** 401
Creative Technology, Inc., **48** 83
Credit & Risk Management Associates, Inc., **18** 170
**Credit Acceptance Corporation**, **18 120–22**
**Crédit Agricole**, **II 264–66**, 355; **19** 51
Credit and Data Marketing Services, **V** 118
Credit Clearing House, **IV** 605
Crédit Commercial de France, **25** 173
Crédit Communal de Belgique, **42** 111
Credit du Nord, **II** 260
Crédit Foncier, **II** 264
Crédit Général de Belgique, **II** 304
Credit Immobilier, **7** 538
Crédit Liégiois, **II** 270
Crédit Local de France, **42** 111
**Crédit Lyonnais**, **II** 242, 257, 354; **6** 396; **7** 12; **9 147–49**; **19** 34, 51, 166; **21** 226; **25** 170, 329; **33 117–21 (upd.)**
Credit Mobilier, **II** 294
**Crédit National S.A.**, **9 150–52**
Credit Service Exchange, **6** 24
Credit Suisse First Boston. *See* Financière Crédit Suisse-First Boston.
**Crédit Suisse Group**, **II 267–69**, 369–70, 378–79, 402–04; **21 144–47 (upd.)**. *See also* Schweizerische Kreditanstalt.
Credit Union Federation, **48** 290
Creditanstalt-Bankverein, **II** 242, 295
CrediThrift Financial, **11** 16
Credithrift Financial of Indiana, **III** 194
Credito de la Union Minera, **II** 194
**Credito Italiano**, **I** 368, 465, 567; **II** 191, **270–72**; **III** 347
Credito Minero y Mercantil, S.A., **22** 285
Credito Provincial Hipotecario, **19** 189
Creditrust Corp., **42** 259
Cree Research, Inc., **13** 399
Crellin Holding, Inc., **8** 477
Crellin Plastics, **8** 13
Crenlo Corp., **16** 180
**Creo Inc.**, **48 121–24**
Creole Petroleum Corporation, **IV** 428; **7** 171
Cresap, McCormick and Paget, **32** 458
Crescendo Productions, **6** 27
Crescent Box & Printing Co., **13** 442
Crescent Capital, **44** 95
Crescent Chemical, **I** 374
Crescent Niagara Corp., **II** 16

Crescent Real Estate Equities Company, **25** 454
Crescent Software Inc., **15** 373
Crescent Vert Company, Ltd., **II** 51; **21** 330
Crescent Washing Machine Company, **8** 298
Crescott, Inc., **15** 501
Cressbrook Dairy Co., **II** 546
Cressey Dockham & Co., **II** 682
Crest Fruit Co., **17** 458
Crest Ridge Homes, Inc., **17** 83
Crest Service Company, **9** 364
Crestbrook Forest Industries Ltd., **IV** 285
Crestmont Financial Corporation, **14** 472
Creusot-Loire, **II** 93–94; **19** 166
Crevettes du Cameroun, **13** 244
CRH plc, **37** 203, 206
Crimson Associates L.P., **26** 48
Crist Partners, **34** 249
Criterion Casualty Company, **10** 312
Criterion Life Insurance Company, **10** 311
Critikon, Inc., **III** 36
Crocker National Bank, **II** 226, 317, 319, 383; **13** 535; **17** 324–25
Crocker National Corporation, **12** 536
Crockett Container Corporation, **8** 268
**Croda International Plc**, **IV** 383; **45 125–28**
Croitex S.A., **26** 374
**Crompton & Knowles Corp.**, **I** 633; **9 153–55**
**Crompton Corporation**, **36 143–50 (upd.)**
Crop Production Services, Inc., **IV** 576
Crosby Enterprises, **17** 19
Croscill Home Fashions, **8** 510
**Croscill, Inc.**, **42 95–97**
Crosfield, Lampard & Co., **III** 696
Cross & Trecker Corporation, **10** 330
Cross-Continent Auto Retailers, **26** 501
Cross Country Group, **25** 358
Cross Creek Apparel, Inc., **30** 400
Cross Pointe Paper Corporation, **26** 363
Cross/Tessitore & Associates, **16** 259
Crossair AG. *See* Swiss International Air Lines Ltd.
Crosse and Blackwell, **II** 547
Crossett Lumber Co., **IV** 281; **9** 259
Crossland Capital Corp., **III** 293
Crossley Motors, Ltd., **13** 285
Crothall, **6** 44
Crothers Properties, Ltd., **21** 500
Crouse-Hinds Co., **II** 16; **19** 45
Crow Catchpole, **III** 752; **28** 448
Crowell-Collier Publishing Company, **IV** 310; **7** 286
Crowell Publishing Company, **19** 266
Crowley Foods, Inc., **II** 528
**Crowley Maritime Corporation**, **6 382–84**; **9** 510–11; **28 77–80 (upd.)**
**Crowley, Milner & Company**, **19 106–08**
Crown Advertising Agency. *See* King Kullen Grocery Co., Inc.
Crown Aluminum, **I** 544
Crown America Corp., **13** 393
**Crown Books Corporation**, **14** 61; **16 159–61**; **21 148–50**; **41** 61
Crown Can Co., **I** 601
Crown Center Redevelopment Corp., **IV** 621
**Crown Central Petroleum Corporation**, **7 101–03**
**Crown, Cork & Seal Company, Inc.**, **I 601–03**; **13 188–90 (upd.)**; **15** 129; **17** 106; **24** 264; **30** 475; **32 123–27 (upd.)**
Crown Courier Systems, Inc., **24** 126
**Crown Crafts, Inc.**, **16 141–43**
Crown Drugs, **II** 673
**Crown Equipment Corporation**, **15 134–36**
Crown Forest Industries, **IV** 279; **19** 155
Crown House Engineering, **44** 148
Crown Life Insurance Company, **III** 261; **6** 181–82
**Crown Media Holdings, Inc.**, **45 129–32**
Crown Oil and Refining Company, **7** 101
Crown Packaging, **19** 155
Crown Pet Foods Ltd., **39** 356
Crown Publishing Group, **IV** 584; **13** 429; **31** 376, 379
Crown Radio, **17** 123–24; **41** 114
Crown Technical Systems, Inc., **37** 215
**Crown Vantage Inc.**, **29 135–37**
Crown Zellerbach Corporation, **IV** 290, 345; **8** 261; **22** 210; **24** 247
Crownx Inc., **6** 181–82
Crowson and Son Ltd., **23** 219
**CRSS Inc.**, **6 142–44**; **23** 491
CRTC. *See* Canadian Radio-Television and Telecommunications Commission.
Crucible Steel, **I** 434–35
Crude Oil Pipe Line Co., **IV** 400
Cruden Investments Pty Ltd., **IV** 651; **7** 390
**Cruise America Inc.**, **21 151–53**
Cruise Associates, **22** 471
Crum & Forster Holdings, Inc., **II** 448; **III** 172; **6** 290; **13** 448; **26** 546
Crump E & S, **6** 290
Crump Inc., **I** 584
Crush International, **II** 478; **III** 53
Crushed Stone Sales Ltd., **IV** 241
Cruzan Rum Distillery, Ltd., **27** 478
Cruzcampo, **18** 501
Cruzeiro do Sul Airlines, **6** 133
Cryenco Sciences Inc., **21** 109
**CryoLife, Inc.**, **46 112–14**
Cryomedics Inc., **I** 667
**Crystal Brands, Inc.**, **9 156–58**; **12** 431
Crystal Market, **41** 174
Crystal Oil Co., **IV** 180, 548
CS Crable Sportswear Inc., **23** 66
**CS First Boston Inc.**, **II** 269, **402–04**; **III** 289; **12** 209; **21** 146. *See also* Credit Suisse Group.
CS Holding. *See* Credit Suisse Group.
CS Life, **21** 146–47
CSA. *See* China Southern Airlines Company Ltd.
CSA Press, **IV** 661
CSC. *See* Computer Sciences Corporation.
CSC Holdings, Inc., **32** 105
CSC Industries, Inc., **IV** 63
CSE Corp., **III** 214
CSFB. *See* Financière Crédit Suisse-First Boston *and* Credit Suisse Group.
CSFBdirect Inc., **46** 55
CSI Computer Systems, **47** 36
CSK, **10** 482
**CSK Auto Corporation**, **38 165–67**
CSO. *See* Columbus & Southern Ohio Electric Company.
**CSR Limited**, **III 686–88**, 728, 735–36; **IV** 46; **22** 106; **28 81–84 (upd.)**
CSR Rinker Materials Corp., **46** 197
**CSS Industries, Inc.**, **35 128–31**
CST Office Products, **15** 36; **42** 416
**CSX Corporation**, **V 438–40**, 485; **6** 340; **9** 59; **13** 462; **22 164–68 (upd.)**; **29** 360–61
CSY Agri-Processing, **7** 81–82
CT Financial Services Inc., **V** 401–02
CT&T. *See* Carolina Telephone and Telegraph Company.
CTA. *See* Comptoir des Textiles Artificielles.
**CTB International Corporation**, **43 129–31 (upd.)**
**CTG, Inc.**, **11 64–66**
CTI. *See* Cosmetic Technology International, Inc.
CTNE, **I** 462
CTR. *See* International Business Machines Corporation.
**CTS Corporation**, **19** 104; **39 105–08**
CTV Network, **35** 69
C2B Technologies, **45** 201
CTX Mortgage Company, **8** 88
Cub Foods, **II** 669–70; **14** 411; **17** 302; **18** 505; **22** 327
Cuban-American Manganese Corp., **IV** 81; **7** 186
Cuban American Nickel Co., **IV** 82; **7** 186
Cuban American Oil Company, **8** 348
Cuban Telephone Co., **I** 462–63
**Cubic Corporation**, **19 109–11**
Cubitts Nigeria, **III** 753
**CUC International Inc.**, **16 144–46**. *See also* Cendant Corporation.
Cuckler Steel Span Co., **I** 481
Cudahy Corp., **12** 199
**Cuisinart Corporation**, **17** 110; **24 129–32**
**Culbro Corporation**, **14** 19; **15 137–39**
Culinary Foods, Inc., **14** 516
**Cullen/Frost Bankers, Inc.**, **25 113–16**
**Culligan International Company**, **I** 373; **II** 468; **12 87–88**, 346; **16** 20
**Culligan Water Technologies, Inc.**, **38 168–70 (upd.)**
Cullinet Software Corporation, **6** 225; **14** 390; **15** 108
Cullman Bros. *See* Culbro Corporation.
Cullum Companies, **II** 670
**Culp, Inc.**, **29 138–40**
Culter Industries, Inc., **22** 353
**Cumberland Farms, Inc.**, **17 120–22**; **26** 450
Cumberland Federal Bancorporation, **13** 223; **31** 206
Cumberland Newspapers, **IV** 650; **7** 389
**Cumberland Packing Corporation**, **26 107–09**
Cumberland Paper Board Mills Ltd., **IV** 248
Cumberland Pipeline Co., **IV** 372
Cumberland Property Investment Trust Ltd., **IV** 711
Cummins Cogeneration Co. *See* Cogeneration Development Corp.
**Cummins Engine Co., Inc.**, **I 146–48**, 186; **III** 545; **IV** 252; **10** 273–74; **12 89–92 (upd.)**; **16** 297; **17** 29; **19** 293; **21** 503; **26** 256; **40 131–35 (upd.)**; **42** 387
Cumo Sports, **16** 109
**Cumulus Media Inc.**, **37 103–05**
CUNA Mutual Insurance Group, **11** 495
**Cunard Line Ltd.**, **I** 573; **23 159–62**; **27** 90, 92; **36** 323; **38** 341, 344

Cuno Kourten, **13** 353
Cupples Products Co., **IV** 15
**Current, Inc., 37 106–09**
Currys Group PLC, **V** 49; **19** 123
Cursenir, **I** 280
**Curtice-Burns Foods, Inc., 7** 17–18, **104–06; 21** 18, **154–57 (upd.)**
Curtin & Pease/Peneco, **27** 361
Curtis Circulation Co., **IV** 619
Curtis Homes, **22** 127
Curtis Industries, **13** 165
Curtis 1000 Inc. *See* American Business Products, Inc.
Curtis Squire Inc., **18** 455
Curtiss Candy Co., **II** 544
**Curtiss-Wright Corporation, I** 524; **III** 464; **7** 263; **8** 49; **9** 14, 244, 341, 417; **10 260–63; 11** 427; **21** 174; **23** 340; **35 132–37 (upd.)**
Curver Group, **III** 614
Curver-Rubbermaid, **III** 615
Cushman Motor Works, **III** 598
Custom Academic Publishing Company, **12** 174
**Custom Chrome, Inc., 16 147–49**
Custom Electronics, Inc., **9** 120
Custom Expressions, Inc., **7** 24; **22** 35
Custom Hoists, Inc., **17** 458
Custom, Ltd, **46** 197
Custom Metal Products, Inc., **III** 643
Custom Organics, **8** 464
Custom Primers, **17** 288
Custom Products Inc., **III** 643
Custom Publishing Group, **27** 361
Custom Technologies Corp., **19** 152
Custom Thermoform, **24** 512
Custom Tool and Manufacturing Company, **41** 366
Custom Transportation Services, Inc., **26** 62
Custom Woodwork & Plastics Inc., **36** 159
Customized Transportation Inc., **22** 164, 167
AB Custos, **25** 464
Cutler-Hammer Inc., **I** 155; **III** 644–45
**Cutter & Buck Inc., 27 112–14**
Cutter Laboratories, **I** 310
Cutter Precision Metals, Inc., **25** 7
CVE Corporation, Inc., **24** 395
CVG Aviation, **34** 118
CVI Incorporated, **21** 108
CVL Inc., **II** 457
CVN Companies, **9** 218
**CVS Corporation, 32** 166, 170; **34** 285; **45 133–38 (upd.)**
CWM. *See* Chemical Waste Management, Inc.
CWP. *See* Custom Woodwork & Plastics Inc.
CWT Farms International Inc., **13** 103
CXT Inc., **33** 257
Cyber Communications Inc., **16** 168
CyberCash Inc., **18** 541, 543
**Cybermedia, Inc., 25 117–19,** 349
Cybernet Electronics Corp., **II** 51; **21** 330
Cybernex, **10** 463
CyberSource Corp., **26** 441
CYBERTEK Corporation, **11** 395
CyberTel, **IV** 596–97
CyberTrust Solutions Inc., **42** 24–25
Cycle & Carriage Ltd., **20** 313
Cycle Video Inc., **7** 590
Cyclo Chemical Corp., **I** 627
Cyclo Getriebebau Lorenz Braren GmbH, **III** 634
Cyclone Co. of Australia, **III** 673
Cyclops Corporation, **10** 45; **13** 157
Cydsa. *See* Grupo Cydsa, S.A. de C.V.
Cygna Energy Services, **13** 367
**Cygne Designs, Inc., 25 120–23; 37** 14
Cymbal Co., Ltd., **V** 150
Cynosure Inc., **11** 88
Cyphernetics Corp., **III** 118
Cypress Amax Minerals Co., **13** 158; **22** 285–86
Cypress Insurance Co., **III** 214
**Cypress Semiconductor Corporation, 6** 216; **18** 17, 383; **20 174–76; 43** 14; **48 125–29 (upd.)**
Cyprus Amax Coal Company, **35** 367
**Cyprus Amax Minerals Company, 21 158–61**
**Cyprus Minerals Company, 7 107–09**
Cyrix Corp., **10** 367; **26** 329
**Cyrk Inc., 19 112–14; 21** 516; **33** 416
**Cytec Industries Inc., 27 115–17**
**Czarnikow-Rionda Company, Inc., 32 128–30**

D&D Enterprises, Inc., **24** 96
D&F Industries, Inc., **17** 227; **41** 204
**D&K Wholesale Drug, Inc., 14 146–48**
D&N Systems, Inc., **10** 505
D&O Inc., **17** 363
D & P Studios, **II** 157
D&W Computer Stores, **13** 176
D & W Food Stores, Inc., **8** 482; **27** 314
D.B. Kaplan's, **26** 263
D.B. Marron & Company, **II** 445; **22** 406
D.C. Heath & Co., **II** 86; **11** 413; **36** 273; **38** 374
D.C. National Bancorp, **10** 426
D. Connelly Boiler Company, **6** 145
D. de Ricci-G. Selnet et Associes, **28** 141
d.e.m.o., **28** 345
D.E. Makepeace Co., **IV** 78
D.E. Shaw & Co., **25** 17; **38** 269
D.E. Winebrenner Co., **7** 429
D.G. Calhoun, **12** 112
**D.G. Yuengling & Son, Inc., 38 171–73**
D. Hald & Co., **III** 417
D.I. Manufacturing Inc., **37** 351
D.K. Gold, **17** 138
D.L. Rogers Group, **37** 363
D.L. Saslow Co., **19** 290
D.M. Nacional, **23** 170
D.M. Osborne Co., **III** 650
D.R. Horton Inc., **25** 217; **26** 291
D.W. Mikesell Co. *See* Mike-Sell's Inc.
Da Gama Textiles Company, **24** 450
Dabney, Morgan & Co., **II** 329
D'Addario & Company, Inc. *See* J. D'Addario & Company, Inc.
Dade Reagents Inc., **19** 103
Dade Wholesale Products, **6** 199
DADG. *See* Deutsch-Australische Dampfschiffs-Gesellschaft.
Dae Won Kang Up Co., **III** 581
Daejin Shipping Company, **6** 98; **27** 271
Daesung Heavy Industries, **I** 516
**Daewoo Group, I** 516; **II** 53; **III 457–59,** 749; **12** 211; **18 123–27 (upd.); 30** 185
DAF, **I** 186; **III** 543; **7** 566–67
**Daffy's Inc., 26 110–12**
NV Dagblad De Telegraaf. *See* N.V. Holdingmaatschappij De Telegraaf.
Dage-Bell, **II** 86
Dagincourt. *See* Compagnie de Saint-Gobain S.A.
**D'Agostino Supermarkets Inc., 19 115–17**
Dagsbladunie, **IV** 611
DAH. *See* DeCrane Aircraft Holdings Inc.
Dahl Manufacturing, Inc., **17** 106
Dahlberg, Inc., **18** 207–08
Dahlgren, **I** 677
Dahlonega Equipment and Supply Company, **12** 377
Dai-Ichi. *See also listings under* Daiichi.
Dai-Ichi Bank, **I** 507, 511; **IV** 148
**Dai-Ichi Kangyo Bank Ltd., II 273–75,** 325–26, 360–61, 374; **III** 188
Dai-Ichi Mokko Co., **III** 758
Dai-Ichi Mutual Life Insurance Co., **II** 118; **III** 277, 401; **25** 289; **26** 511; **38** 18
Dai Nippon. *See also listings under* Dainippon.
Dai Nippon Brewery Co., **I** 220, 282; **21** 319
Dai Nippon Ink and Chemicals, **I** 303
Dai Nippon Mujin, **II** 371
**Dai Nippon Printing Co., Ltd., IV 598–600,** 631, 679–80
Dai Nippon X-ray Inc., **II** 75
Dai Nippon Yuben Kai, **IV** 631–32
Daido Boeki, **24** 325
Daido Spring Co., **III** 580
**Daido Steel Co., Ltd., IV 62–63**
Daido Trading, **I** 432, 492; **24** 324
**The Daiei, Inc., V** 11, **39–40; 17 123–25 (upd.); 18** 186, 285; **19** 308; **36** 418–19; **41 113–16 (upd.)**
Daig Corporation, **43** 349–50
Daignault Rolland, **24** 404
**Daihatsu Motor Company, Ltd., 7 110–12; 21 162–64 (upd.); 38** 415
Daiichi. *See also listings under* Dai-Ichi.
Daiichi Atomic Power Industry Group, **II** 22
Daiichi Bussan Kaisha Ltd., **I** 505, 507
Daiichi Fire, **III** 405
Daijugo Bank, **I** 507
Daiken Company. *See* Marubeni Corporation.
**Daikin Industries, Ltd., III 460–61**
Daikyo Oil Co., Ltd., **IV** 403–04, 476
Dailey & Associates, **I** 16
Daily Chronicle Investment Group, **IV** 685
**Daily Mail and General Trust plc, 19 118–20; 39** 198–99
Daily Mirror, **IV** 665–66; **17** 397
Daily Press Inc., **IV** 684; **22** 522
**The Daimaru, Inc., V 41–42,** 130; **42 98–100 (upd.)**
Daimler Airway, **I** 92
**Daimler-Benz Aerospace AG, 16 150–52; 24** 84
**Daimler-Benz AG, I** 27, 138, **149–51,** 186–87, 192, 194, 198, 411, 549; **II** 257, 279–80, 283; **III** 495, 523, 562, 563, 695, 750; **7** 219; **10** 261, 274; **11** 31; **12** 192, 342; **13** 30, 286, 414; **14** 169; **15 140–44 (upd.); 20** 312–13; **22** 11; **26** 481, 498
**DaimlerChrysler AG, 34 128–37 (upd.),** 306
Dain Bosworth Inc., **15** 231–33, 486
**Dain Rauscher Corporation, 35 138–41 (upd.)**
Daina Seikosha, **III** 620

Daini-Denden Incorporated, **12** 136–37
Daini-Denden Kikaku Company, Ltd., **II** 51. *See also* DDI Corporation.
Dainippon. *See also listings under* Dai-Nippon.
Dainippon Celluloid Company, **I** 509; **III** 486; **18** 183
Dainippon Ink & Chemicals, Inc., **IV** 397; **10** 466–67; **13** 308, 461; **17** 363; **28** 194
Dainippon Shurui, **III** 42
Dainippon Spinning Company, **V** 387
**Daio Paper Corporation, IV 266–67**, 269
**Dairy Crest Group plc, 32 131–33**
Dairy Farm Ice and Cold Storage Co., **IV** 700; **47** 176
Dairy Farm Management Services Ltd., **I** 471; **20** 312
Dairy Farmers of America Inc., **48** 45
Dairy Fresh, Inc., **26** 449
Dairy Maid Products Cooperative, **II** 536
**Dairy Mart Convenience Stores, Inc., 7 113–15**; **17** 501; **25 124–27 (upd.)**
Dairy Queen. *See* International Dairy Queen, Inc.
Dairy Queen National Development Company, **10** 372
Dairy Supply Co., **II** 586; **III** 418, 420
Dairyland Food Laboratories, **I** 677
Dairymen, Inc., **11** 24
**Daishowa Paper Manufacturing Co., Ltd. II** 361; **IV 268–70**, 326, 667; **17** 398
Daisy Manufacturing Company, Inc., **34** 72
Daisy Systems Corp., **11** 46, 284–85, 489
Daisy/Cadnetix Inc., **6** 248; **24** 235
**Daisytek International Corporation, 18 128–30**
**Daiwa Bank, Ltd., II 276–77**, 347, 438; **26** 457; **39 109–11 (upd.)**
**Daiwa Securities Company, Limited, II** 276, 300, **405–06**, 434; **9** 377
Daka, Inc. *See* Unique Casual Restaurants, Inc.
Dakin Inc., **24** 44; **33** 415
Dakota Power Company, **6** 580; **20** 73
Dakotah Mills, **8** 558–59; **16** 353
Daksoft, Inc., **20** 74
**Daktronics, Inc., 32 134–37**
**Dal-Tile International Inc., 22** 46, 49, **169–71**
Dalberg Co., **II** 61
**Dale Carnegie Training, Inc., 28 85–87**
Dale Electronics, **21** 519
Daleville & Middletown Telephone Company, **14** 258
Dalfort Corp., **15** 281
**Dalgety PLC, II 499–500**; **III** 21; **12** 411; **22** 147; **27** 258, 260. *See also* PIC International Group PLC
Dalian, **14** 556
Dalian Cement Factory, **III** 718
Dalian International Nordic Tire Co., **20** 263
D'Allaird's, **24** 315–16
Dallas Airmotive, **II** 16
Dallas Ceramic Co. *See* Dal-Tile International Inc.
**Dallas Cowboys Football Club, Ltd., 33 122–25**
Dallas-Fort Worth Suburban Newspapers, Inc., **10** 3
Dallas Lumber and Supply Co., **IV** 358
Dallas Power & Light Company, **V** 724
**Dallas Semiconductor Corporation, 13 191–93**; **31 143–46 (upd.)**
Dallas Southland Ice Co., **II** 660
Daltex General Agency, Inc., **25** 115
Damar, **IV** 610
**Damark International, Inc., 18 131–34**
Damart, **25** 523
Dameron-Pierson Co., **25** 500
**Dames & Moore, Inc., 25 128–31**. *See also* URS Corporation.
Dammann Asphalt, **III** 673
Damodar Valley Corp., **IV** 49
Damon, **21** 153
Damon Clinical Laboratories Inc., **26** 392
Damon Corporation, **11** 334
**Dan River Inc., 35 142–46**
Dan's Supreme, **24** 528
Dana Alexander Inc., **27** 197; **43** 218
**Dana Corporation, I 152–53**; **10 264–66 (upd.)**; **23** 170–71; **47** 376
Dana Design Ltd., **16** 297
**Danaher Corporation, 7 116–17**
Danair A/S, **I** 120
Danapak Holding Ltd., **11** 422
Danapak Riverwood Multipack A/S, **48** 344
Danat-Bank, **I** 138
Danbury Mint, **34** 370
Danbury Phamacal Inc., **31** 254
Dancer Fitzgerald Sample, **I** 33; **23** 505
**Daniel Industries, Inc., 16 153–55**
Daniel International Corp., **I** 570–71; **8** 192
Daniel James Insurance Group, **41** 64
Daniel P. Creed Co., Inc., **8** 386
Daniel's Jewelers, **16** 559
Danieli & C. Officine Meccaniche, **13** 98
Daniels Linseed Co., **I** 419
Daniels Packaging, **12** 25
Daniels Pharmaceuticals, Inc., **24** 257
**Danisco A/S, 44 134–37**
Danish Aalborg, **27** 91
Danish Almindelinge Brand-Assurance-Compagni, **III** 299
Danley Machine Corp., **I** 514
Danner Shoe Manufacturing Co., **18** 300
**Dannon Co., Inc., II** 468, 474–75; **14 149–51**
Danone Group, **25** 85; **35** 394, 397
Danray, **12** 135
Dansk Bioprotein, **IV** 406–07
Dansk International Designs Ltd., **10** 179, 181; **12** 313
Dansk Metal and Armaturindistri, **III** 569; **20** 361
Dansk Rejsebureau, **I** 120
**Danskin, Inc., 12 93–95**; **15** 358
Danville Resources, Inc., **13** 502
**Danzas Group, V 441–43**; **40 136–39 (upd.)**
DAP, Inc., **III** 66; **12** 7; **18** 549
DAP Products Inc., **36** 396
Dara Michelle, **17** 101–03
**D'Arcy Masius Benton & Bowles, Inc., I 233–34**; **6 20–22**; **10** 226–27; **26** 187; **28** 137; **32 138–43 (upd.)**
**Darden Restaurants, Inc., 16 156–58**; **36** 238; **44 138–42 (upd.)**
**Darigold, Inc., 9 159–61**
Darling and Hodgson, **IV** 91
Darling, Brown & Sharpe. *See* Brown & Sharpe Manufacturing Co.
Darmstadter, **II** 282
Darracq, **7** 6
Darrell J. Sekin Transport Co., **17** 218
Dart & Kraft Financial Corp., **II** 534; **III** 610–11; **7** 276; **12** 310; **14** 547
**Dart Group Corporation, II** 645, 656, 667, 674; **12** 49; **15** 270; **16 159–62**; **21** 148; **23** 370; **24** 418; **27** 158; **32** 168
Dart Industries, **II** 533–34; **III** 610; **9** 179–80. *See also* Premark International Inc.
Dart Transit Co., **13** 550
Dart Truck Co., **I** 185
Dartex, **18** 434
**Darty S.A., 27 118–20**
Darvel Realty Trust, **14** 126
Darya-Varia Laboratoria, **18** 182
DASA. *See* Daimler-Benz Aerospace AG *or* Deutsche Aerospace Airbus.
Dashwood Industries, **19** 446
Dassault Aviation SA, **21** 11
Dassault-Breguet. *See* Avions Marcel Dassault-Breguet Aviation.
**Dassault Systèmes S.A., 25 132–34**; **26** 179. *See also* Groupe Dassault Aviation SA.
Dassler, **14** 6
Dastek Inc., **10** 464; **11** 234–35
DAT GmbH, **10** 514
Dat Jidosha Seizo Co., **I** 183
Data Acquisition Systems, Inc., **16** 300
Data Architects, **14** 318
Data Base Management Inc., **11** 19
Data-Beam Corp., **25** 301
**Data Broadcasting Corporation, 31 147–50**
Data Business Forms, **IV** 640
Data Card Corp., **IV** 680
Data Corp., **IV** 311; **19** 267
Data Documents, **III** 157
Data Force Inc., **11** 65
**Data General Corporation, II** 208; **III** 124, 133; **6** 221, 234; **8 137–40**; **9** 297; **10** 499; **12** 162; **13** 201; **16** 418; **20** 8
Data One Corporation, **11** 111
Data Preparation, Inc., **11** 112
Data Printer, Inc., **18** 435
Data Resources, Inc., **IV** 637
Data Specialties Inc. *See* Zebra Technologies Corporation.
Data Structures Inc., **11** 65
Data Systems Technology, **11** 57; **38** 375
Data Technology Corp., **18** 510
Data 3 Systems, **9** 36
Datac plc, **18** 140
Datachecker Systems, **II** 64–65; **III** 164; **11** 150
Datacraft Corp., **II** 38
DataFocus, Inc., **18** 112
Datamatic Corp., **II** 41, 86; **12** 247
**Datapoint Corporation, 11 67–70**
Datapro Research Corp., **IV** 637
Dataquest Inc., **10** 558; **21** 235, 237; **22** 51; **25** 347
Datas Incorporated, **I** 99; **6** 81
**Datascope Corporation, 39 112–14**
Dataset Communications Inc., **23** 100
Datastream International Ltd., **IV** 605; **10** 89; **13** 417
DataTimes Corporation, **29** 58
Datavision Inc., **11** 444
Datec, **22** 17
**Datek Online Holdings Corp., 32 144–46**; **48** 225–27
Datext, **IV** 596–97
Datran, **11** 468

Datsun. *See* Nissan Motor Company, Ltd.
Datteln, **IV** 141
Datura Corp., **14** 391
**Dauphin Deposit Corporation, 14 152–54**
Dauphin Distribution Services. *See* Exel Logistics Ltd.
Daut + Rietz and Connectors Pontarlier, **19** 166
**Dave & Buster's, Inc., 33 126–29**
Davenport & Walter, **III** 765
Davenport Mammoet Heavy Transport Inc., **26** 280
**The Davey Tree Expert Company, 11 71–73**
**The David and Lucile Packard Foundation, 41 117–19**
David B. Smith & Company, **13** 243
David Berg & Co., **14** 537
David Brown & Son. *See* Brown & Sharpe Manufacturing Co.
David Brown, Ltd., **10** 380
David Clark, **30** 357
David Crystal, Inc., **II** 502; **9** 156; **10** 323
David Hafler Company, **43** 323
**The David J. Joseph Company, 14 155–56**; **19** 380
David Sandeman Group, **I** 592
David Sassoon & Co., **II** 296
David Williams and Partners, **6** 40
David Wilson Homes Ltd., **45** 442–43
**David's Bridal, Inc., 33 130–32**; **46** 288
David's Supermarkets, **17** 180
Davidson & Associates, **16** 146
Davidson & Leigh, **21** 94
Davidson Automatic Merchandising Co. Inc., **II** 607
Davidson Brothers Co., **19** 510
Davies, William Ltd., **II** 482
Davis & Geck, **I** 301; **27** 115
Davis & Henderson Ltd., **IV** 640
Davis Coal & Coke Co., **IV** 180
Davis Estates, **I** 592
Davis Manufacturing Company, **10** 380
**Davis Polk & Wardwell, 36 151–54**
**Davis Service Group PLC, 45 139–41**
Davis-Standard Company, **9** 154; **36** 144
Davis Vision, Inc., **27** 209
Davis Wholesale Company, **9** 20
Davison Chemical Corp., **IV** 190
Davlyn Industries, Inc., **22** 487
Davox Corporation, **18** 31
Davy Bamag GmbH, **IV** 142
Davy McKee AG, **IV** 142
**DAW Technologies, Inc., 25 135–37**
Dawe's Laboratories, Inc., **12** 3
**Dawn Food Products, Inc., 17 126–28**
Dawnay Day, **III** 501
**Dawson Holdings PLC, 43 132–34**
Dawson Mills, **II** 536
**Day & Zimmermann Inc.**, **6** 579; **9 162–64**; **31 151–155 (upd.)**
Day Brite Lighting, **II** 19
Day-Glo Color Corp., **8** 456
Day International, **8** 347
Day-Lee Meats, **II** 550
Day-N-Nite, **II** 620
**Day Runner, Inc., 14 157–58**; **41 120–23 (upd.)**
Daybridge Learning Centers, **13** 49, 299
Dayco Products, **7** 297
Daylin Corporation, **46** 271
Days Inns of America, Inc., **III** 344; **11** 178; **13** 362, 364; **21** 362
Daystar International Inc., **11** 44
Daystrom, **III** 617; **17** 418
Daytex, Inc., **II** 669; **18** 505
Dayton Engineering Laboratories, **I** 171; **9** 416; **10** 325
Dayton Flexible Products Co., **I** 627
**Dayton Hudson Corporation**, **V 43–44**; **8** 35; **9** 360; **10** 136, 391–93, 409–10, 515–16; **13** 330; **14** 376; **16** 176, 559; **18** 108, **135–37 (upd.)**; **22** 59
Dayton Power & Light Company, **6** 467, 480–82
Dayton Walther Corp., **III** 650, 652
Daytron Mortgage Systems, **11** 485
Dazey Corp., **16** 384; **43** 289
DB. *See* Deutsche Bundesbahn.
DB Reise & Touristik AG, **37** 250
DBA Holdings, Inc., **18** 24
DBMS Inc., **14** 390
**DC Comics Inc., 25 138–41**
DCA Advertising, **16** 168
DCA Food Industries, **II** 554; **27** 258–60, 299
DCL BioMedical, Inc., **11** 333
DCMS Holdings Inc., **7** 114; **25** 125
**DDB Needham Worldwide, 14 159–61**; **22** 394
DDD Energy, Inc., **47** 348, 350
**DDI Corporation, 7 118–20**; **13** 482; **21** 330–31
NV De Beer and Partners, **45** 386
**De Beers Consolidated Mines Limited / De Beers Centenary AG**, **I** 107; **IV** 20–21, 23, 60, **64–68**, 79, 94; **7 121–26 (upd.)**; **16** 25–26, 29; **21** 345–46; **28 88–94 (upd.)**
De Bono Industries, **24** 443
**De Dietrich & Cie., 31 156–59**
De Grenswisselkantoren NV, **III** 201
De Groote Bossche, **III** 200
de Havilland Aircraft Co., **I** 82, 92–93, 104, 195; **III** 507–08; **7** 11. *See also* Bombardier Inc.
de Havilland Holdings, Ltd., **24** 85–86
**De La Rue plc, 10 267–69**; **34 138–43 (upd.)**; **46** 251
De Laurentiis Entertainment Group, **III** 84; **25** 317
De Laval Turbine Company, **III** 418–20; **7** 236–37
De Leuw, Cather & Company, **8** 416
De Nederlandse Bank, **IV** 132
De Paepe, **45** 386
De-sta-Co., **III** 468
De Ster 1905 NV, **III** 200
De Streekkrant-De Weekkrantgroep NV, **48** 347
De Tomaso Industries, **11** 104
De Trey Gesellchaft, **10** 271
De Vito/Verdi, **26** 111
De Walt, **III** 436
de Wendel, **IV** 226–27
DEA Group, **23** 83
Dealer Equipment and Services, **10** 492
Dean & Barry Co., **8** 455
**Dean & DeLuca, Inc., 36 155–57**
Dean-Dempsy Corp., **IV** 334
**Dean Foods Company, 7 127–29**; **17** 56; **21** 157, **165–68 (upd.)**; **26** 447; **29** 434; **46** 70
**Dean Witter, Discover & Co.**, **II** 445; **IV** 186; **V** 180, 182; **7** 213; **12 96–98**; **18** 475; **21** 97; **22** 405–07. *See also* Morgan Stanley Dean Witter & Company.
Dearborn Publishing Group, **42** 211
**Death Row Records, 27 121–23**
**Deb Shops, Inc., 16 163–65**
DeBartolo Realty Corp., **27** 401
**Debenhams Plc, V 20–22**; **28** 29–30, **95–97**; **39** 88
**Debevoise & Plimpton, 39 115–17**
Debis, **26** 498
DeBoles Nutritional Foods Inc., **27** 197–98; **43** 218–19
Debron Investments Plc., **8** 271
DEC. *See* Digital Equipment Corp.
Decafin SpA, **26** 278, 280
Decathlon S.A., **39** 183–84
Decca Record Company Ltd., **II** 81, 83, 144; **23** 389
**Dechert, 43 135–38**
Decision Base Resources, **6** 14
Decision Systems Israel Ltd. (DSI), **21** 239
DecisionQuest, Inc., **25** 130
Decker, Howell & Co., **26** 451
**Deckers Outdoor Corporation, 22 172–74**
Deco Industries, Inc., **18** 5
Deco Purchasing Company, **39** 211
Decoflex Ltd., **IV** 645
Decolletage S.A. St.-Maurice, **14** 27
**Decora Industries, Inc., 31 160–62**
**DeCrane Aircraft Holdings Inc., 36 158–60**
Dee and Cee Toy Co., **25** 312
Dee Corporation plc, **I** 549; **II** 628–29, 642; **24** 269
Deeks McBride, **III** 704
Deep Ocean Services, L.L.C., **44** 203
Deep Oil Technology, **I** 570
Deep Rock Oil Company. *See* Kerr-McGee Corporation.
Deep Rock Water Co., **III** 21
DeepFlex Production Partners, L.P., **21** 171
Deepsea Ventures, Inc., **IV** 152; **24** 358
**DeepTech International Inc., 21 169–71**
Deepwater Light and Power Company, **6** 449
Deer Park Spring Water Co., **III** 21
**Deere & Company**, **I** 181, 527; **III 462–64**, 651; **10** 377–78, 380, 429; **11** 472; **13** 16–17, 267; **16** 179; **17** 533; **21 172–76 (upd.)**; **22** 542; **26** 492; **42 101–06 (upd.)**
Deering Harvesting Machinery Company. *See* Navistar.
Deering Milliken & Co. *See* Milliken & Co.
Def Jam Records, Inc., **23** 389, 391; **31** 269; **33** 373–75
Defense Plant Corp., **IV** 10, 408
Defense Technology Corporation of America, **27** 50
**Defiance, Inc., 22 175–78**
Deflecta-Shield Corporation, **40** 299–300
Deft Software, Inc., **10** 505
DEG. *See* Deutsche Edison Gesellschaft.
**Degussa Group**, **I** 303; **IV 69–72**, 118
**Degussa-Hüls AG, 32 147–53 (upd.)**; **34** 209
Deinhard, **I** 281
DEKA Research & Development Corporation. *See* Segway LLC.
DeKalb AgResearch Inc., **9** 411; **41** 304–06
Dekalb Energy Company, **18** 366

DeKalb Farmers Market, **23** 263–64
**DeKalb Genetics Corporation, 17 129–31**; **29** 330
DeKalb Office Supply, **25** 500
**Del Laboratories, Inc., 28 98–100**
Del Mar Avionics, **26** 491
**Del Monte Corporation, II** 595; **7 130–32**; **12** 439; **14** 287; **25** 234
**Del Monte Foods Company, 23 163–66 (upd.)**; **36** 472; **38** 198
Del-Rey Petroleum, **I** 526
**Del Webb Corporation, 14 162–64**; **17** 186–87; **19** 377–78; **26** 291
Delafield, Harvey, Tabrell, Inc., **17** 498
Delafield Industries, **12** 418
Delagrange, **I** 635
Delaware and Hudson Railway Company, Inc., **16** 350; **45** 78
Delaware Charter Guarantee & Trust Co., **III** 330
Delaware Guarantee and Trust Co. *See* Wilmington Trust Company.
Delaware Lackawanna & Western, **I** 584
Delaware Management Holdings, **III** 386
**Delaware North Companies Incorporated, 7 133–36**
Delbard, **I** 272
Delchamps, Inc., **II** 638; **27** 247
Delco Electronics Corporation, **II** 32–35; **III** 151; **6** 265; **25** 223–24; **45** 142–43
Delek Investment & Properties Ltd., **45** 170
**Delhaize "Le Lion" S.A., II** 626; **15** 176; **27** 94; **44 143–46**
Delhi Gas Pipeline Corporation, **7** 551
Delhi International Oil Corp., **III** 687; **28** 83
Deli Universal, **13** 545
**dELiA*s Inc., 29 141–44**
Delicious Foods, **13** 383
Delimaatschappij, **13** 545
**Dell Computer Corporation, 9 165–66**; **10** 309, 459; **11** 62; **16** 5, 196; **24** 31; **25** 254; **27** 168; **31 163–166 (upd.)**; **47** 323
Dell Distributing, **25** 483
Dell Publishing Co., **13** 560
Dellwood Elevator Co., **I** 419
Delmar Chemicals Ltd., **II** 484
Delmar Paper Box Co., **IV** 333
Delmarva Properties, Inc., **8** 103; **30** 118
Delmonico Foods Inc., **II** 511
Delmonico International, **II** 101
**Deloitte & Touche, 9 167–69**, 423; **24** 29
**Deloitte Touche Tohmatsu International, 29 145–48 (upd.)**
DeLong Engineering Co., **III** 558
DeLorean Motor Co., **10** 117; **14** 321
Delphax, **IV** 252; **17** 29
**Delphi Automotive Systems Corporation, 22** 52; **36** 243; **25** 223; **37** 429; **45 142–44**
Delprat, **IV** 58
Delta and Pine Land Company, **21** 386; **33 133–37**
Delta Acceptance Corporation Limited, **13** 63
**Delta Air Lines, Inc., I** 29, 91, 97, **99–100**, 102, 106, 120, 132; **6** 61, **81–83 (upd.)**, 117, 131–32, 383; **12** 149, 381; **13** 171–72; **14** 73; **21** 141, 143; **22** 22; **25** 420, 422–23; **26** 439; **27** 20, 409; **33** 50–51, 377; **34** 116–17, 119; **39 118–21 (upd.)**; **47** 29
Delta Biologicals S.r.l., **11** 208
Delta Biotechnology Ltd., **25** 82
Delta Campground Management Corp., **33** 399
Delta Communications, **IV** 610
Delta Education, **29** 470, 472
Delta Faucet Co., **III** 568–69; **39** 263
Delta International Machinery Corp., **26** 361–63
Delta Lloyd, **III** 235
Delta Manufacturing, **II** 85
Delta Motors, **III** 580
Delta Play, Ltd., **44** 261
Delta Pride Catfish Inc., **18** 247
Delta Queen Steamboat Company, **27** 34–35
Delta Resources Inc., **26** 519
Delta Savings Assoc. of Texas, **IV** 343
Delta Steamship Lines, **9** 425–26
Delta V Technologies, Inc., **33** 348
**Delta Woodside Industries, Inc., 8 141–43**; **17** 329; **30 159–61 (upd.)**; **42** 118
Deltak Corp., **23** 300
**Deltic Timber Corporation, 32** 339, 341; **46 115–17**
**Deluxe Corporation, 7 137–39**; **19** 291; **22 179–82 (upd.)**; **37** 107–08
Deluxe Data, **18** 518
DeLuxe Laboratories, **IV** 652
Deluxe Upholstering Ltd., **14** 303
Delvag Luftürsicherungs A.G., **I** 111
Demag AG, **II** 22; **III** 566; **IV** 206
Demerara Company, **13** 102
Deminex, **IV** 413, 424
Deming Company, **8** 135
Demka, **IV** 132–33
Demko, **30** 469
**DeMoulas / Market Basket Inc., 23 167–69**
Dempsey & Siders Agency, **III** 190
Den Fujita, **9** 74
Den Norske Bank, **22** 275
Den norske Creditbank, **II** 366
**Den Norske Stats Oljeselskap AS, IV 405–07**, 486
Den-Tal-Ez, **I** 702
Denain-Nord-Est-Longwy, **IV** 227
**DenAmerica Corporation, 29 149–51**
Denault Ltd., **II** 651
**Denby Group plc, 44 147–50**
**Denison International plc, 46 118–20**
Denison Mines, Ltd., **12** 198
Denker & Goodwin, **17** 498
Denki Seikosho, **IV** 62
Denmark Tiscali A/S, **48** 398
Denney-Reyburn, **8** 360
Dennison Manufacturing Company. *See* Avery Dennison Corporation.
Denny's Restaurants Inc., **II** 680; **III** 103; **V** 88–89; **12** 511; **13** 526; **27** 16–18
Denshi Media Services, **IV** 680
**DENSO Corporation, 46 121–26 (upd.)**
Dent & Co., **II** 296
Dental Capital Corp., **19** 290
Dental Research, **25** 56
DentiCare, Inc., **22** 149
Dentons Green Brewery, **21** 246
**Dentsply International Inc., 10 270–72**
**Dentsu Inc., I 9–11**, 36, 38; **6** 29; **9** 30; **13** 204; **16 166–69 (upd.)**; **25** 91; **40 140–44 (upd.)**
Denver & Rio Grande Railroad, **12** 18–19
Denver Chemical Company, **8** 84; **38** 124
Denver Gas & Electric Company. *See* Public Service Company of Colorado.
**DEP Corporation, 20 177–80**; **34** 209
**Department 56, Inc., 14 165–67**; **22** 59; **34 144–47 (upd.)**
Department Stores International, **I** 426; **22** 72
**Deposit Guaranty Corporation, 17 132–35**
Deposito and Administratie Bank, **II** 185
Depositors National Bank of Durham, **II** 336
DePree Company, **17** 90–91
**DePuy, Inc., 10** 156–57; **30 162–65**; **36** 306; **37 110–13 (upd.)**
Der Anker, **III** 177
Derby Commercial Bank, **II** 318; **17** 323
Derby Outdoor, **27** 280
Derbyshire Stone and William Briggs, **III** 752
Deritend Computers, **14** 36
Dermablend, Inc., **31** 89
Deruluft, **6** 57
Derwent Publications, **8** 526
Des Moines Electric Light Company, **6** 504
DESA Industries, **8** 545
**Desc, S.A. de C.V., 23 170–72**
Deseret Management Corporation, **29** 67
Deseret National Bank, **11** 118
Deseret Pharmaceutical Company, **21** 45
Desert Partners, **III** 763
Design-Center Southwest, **19** 411
Design Craft Ltd., **IV** 640
Design Trend, Inc., **37** 394
Designcraft Inc. *See* Sloan's Supermarkets Inc.
**Designer Holdings Ltd., 20 181–84**; **22** 123
Desmarais Frères, **IV** 557, 559
DeSoto, Inc., **8** 553; **13** 471
Desoutter Brothers plc, **III** 427; **28** 40
**Destec Energy, Inc., 12 99–101**
Det Danske/Norske Luftartselskab, **I** 119
Detroit Aircraft Corp., **I** 64; **11** 266
Detroit Automobile Co., **I** 164
Detroit Ball Bearing Co., **13** 78
Detroit Chemical Coatings, **8** 553
Detroit City Gas Company. *See* MCN Corporation.
Detroit Copper Co., **IV** 176–77
**Detroit Diesel Corporation, V** 494–95; **9** 18; **10 273–75**; **11** 471; **12** 90–91; **18** 308; **19** 292–94; **21** 503
**The Detroit Edison Company, I** 164; **V 592–95**; **7** 377–78; **11** 136; **14** 135; **18** 320. *See also* DTE Energy Co.
Detroit Fire & Marine Insurance Co., **III** 191
Detroit Gear and Machine Co., **III** 439
Detroit-Graphite Company, **8** 553
**The Detroit Pistons Basketball Company, 41 124–27**
Detroit Radiator Co., **III** 663
Detroit Red Wings, **7** 278–79; **24** 293; **37** 207; **46** 127
Detroit Steel Products Co., Inc., **IV** 136; **13** 157; **16** 357
Detroit Stoker Company, **37** 399–401
**Detroit Tigers Baseball Club, Inc., 24** 293; **37** 207; **46 127–30**
Detroit Toledo & Ironton Railroad, **I** 165
Detroit Vapor Stove Co., **III** 439
Detrola, **II** 60
Dettmers Industries Inc., **36** 159–60

Deutsch-Australische Dampfschiffs-Gesellschaft, **6** 398
Deutsch Erdol A.G., **IV** 552
**Deutsch, Inc., 42 107–10**
Deutsch-Luxembergische Bergwerks und Hütten AG, **I** 542; **IV** 105
Deutsch-Österreichische Mannesmannröhren-Werke Aktiengesellschaft, **III** 564–65
Deutsch Shea & Evans Inc., **I** 15
Deutsch-Skandinavische Bank, **II** 352
Deutsche Aerospace Airbus, **I** 41–42; **7** 9, 11; **12** 190–91; **21** 8
Deutsche Allgemeine Versicherungs-Aktiengesellschaft, **III** 412
Deutsche Anlagen Leasing GmbH, **II** 386
Deutsche-Asiatische Bank, **II** 238, 256
Deutsche BA, **14** 73; **24** 400; **26** 115
**Deutsche Babcock AG, II** 386; **III 465–66**
**Deutsche Bahn AG, 37** 250, 253; **46 131–35 (upd.)**
**Deutsche Bank AG, I** 151, 409, 549; **II** 98, 191, 239, 241–42, 256–58, **278–80**, 281–82, 295, 319, 385, 427, 429; **III** 154–55, 692, 695; **IV** 91, 141, 229, 232, 378, 557; **V** 241–42; **14 168–71 (upd.)**; **15** 13; **16** 364–65; **17** 324; **21** 147, **34** 29; **40 145–51 (upd.)**; **47** 81–84
Deutsche Börse, **37** 131–32
**Deutsche BP Aktiengesellschaft, 7 140–43**
**Deutsche Bundepost Telekom, V 287–90**; **18** 155
**Deutsche Bundesbahn, V 444–47**; **6** 424–26
Deutsche Edelstahlwerke AG, **IV** 222
Deutsche Edison Gesellschaft, **I** 409–10
Deutsche Erdol Aktiengesellschaft, **7** 140
Deutsche Gold-und Silber-Scheideanstalt vormals Roessler, **IV** 69, 118, 139
Deutsche Grammophon Gesellschaft, **23** 389
Deutsche Hydrierwerke, **III** 32
Deutsche Industriewerke AG, **IV** 230
Deutsche Kreditbank, **14** 170
Deutsche Länderbank, **II** 379
**Deutsche Lufthansa Aktiengesellschaft, I** 94, **110–11**, 120; **6** 59–60, 69, 95–96, 386; **12** 191; **25** 159; **26 113–16 (upd.)**; **27** 465; **33** 49; **36** 426; **48** 258
Deutsche Marathon Petroleum, **IV** 487
Deutsche Mineralöl-Explorationsgesellschaft mbH, **IV** 197
Deutsche-Nalco-Chemie GmbH., **I** 373
Deutsche Nippon Seiko, **III** 589
Deutsche Petroleum-Verkaufsgesellschaft mbH, **7** 140
**Deutsche Post AG, 29 152–58**; **40** 138
Deutsche Reichsbahn. *See* Deutsche Bundesbahn.
Deutsche Schiff-und Maschinenbau Aktiengesellschaft "Deschimag," **IV** 87
Deutsche Shell, **7** 140
Deutsche Spezialglas AG, **III** 446
Deutsche Strassen und Lokalbahn A.G., **I** 410
**Deutsche Telekom AG, 18** 155; **25** 102; **38** 296; **48 130–35 (upd.)**
Deutsche Texaco, **V** 709
Deutsche Union, **III** 693–94
Deutsche Union-Bank, **II** 278
Deutsche Wagnisfinanzierung, **II** 258; **47** 83
Deutsche Werke AG, **IV** 230
Deutscher Aero Lloyd, **I** 110
Deutscher Automobil Schutz Allgemeine Rechtsschutz-Versicherung AG, **III** 400
Deutscher Kommunal-Verlag Dr. Naujoks & Behrendt, **14** 556
Deutscher Ring, **40** 61
Deutsches Reisebüro DeR, **II** 163
**Deutz AG, III** 541; **39 122–26**
Deutz-Allis, **III** 544. *See also* AGCO Corp.
Deutz Farm Equipment, **13** 17
Devanlay SA, **48** 279
Devcon Corporation, **III** 519; **22** 282
**Deveaux S.A., 41 128–30**
Developer's Mortgage Corp., **16** 347
Development Finance Corp., **II** 189
Devenish, **21** 247
DeVilbiss Company, **8** 230
DeVilbiss Health Care, Inc., **11** 488
Deville, **27** 421
Devoe & Raynolds Co., **12** 217
Devoke Company, **18** 362
Devon Energy Corporation, **22** 304
**DeVry Incorporated, 9** 63; **29** 56, **159–61**
Dewars Brothers, **I** 239–40
Dewey & Almy Chemical Co., **I** 548
**Dewey Ballantine LLP, 48 136–39**
Dexer Corporation, **41** 10
**Dexia Group, 42 111–13**
**The Dexter Corporation, I 320–22**; **12 102–04 (upd.)**; **17** 287
Dexter Lock Company, **45** 269
Dexter Shoe, **18** 60, 63
DFS Dorland Worldwide, **I** 35
DFS Group Ltd., **33** 276
DFW Printing Company, **10** 3
DG Bank, **33** 358
DG&E. *See* Denver Gas & Electric Company.
DH Compounding, **8** 347
**DH Technology, Inc., 18 138–40**
Dharma Juice, **31** 350
DHI Corp., **II** 680
DHJ Industries, Inc., **12** 118
**DHL Worldwide Express, 6 385–87**; **18** 177, 316; **24 133–36 (upd.)**; **26** 441; **27** 471, 475; **29** 152
**Di Giorgio Corp., II** 602; **12 105–07**; **24** 528–29
Di-Rite Company, **11** 534
Dia Prosim, S.A., **IV** 409
**Diageo plc, 24 137–41 (upd.)**; **25** 411; **29** 19; **31** 92; **34** 89; **36** 404; **42** 223
Diagnostic Health Corporation, **14** 233
Diagnostic Imaging Services, Inc., **25** 384
Diagnostics Pasteur, **I** 677
**Dial-A-Mattress Operating Corporation, 32** 427; **46 136–39**
**The Dial Corporation, 8 144–46**; **23 173–75 (upd.)**; **29** 114; **32** 230; **34** 209
Dial Home Shopping Ltd., **28** 30
Dial-Net Inc., **27** 306
Dialight Corp., **13** 397–98
Dialog Information Services, Inc., **IV** 630
**Dialogic Corporation, 18 141–43**
Diamandis Communications Inc., **IV** 619, 678
Diamang, **IV** 65, 67
Diamedix, **11** 207
Diamond Animal Health, Inc., **39** 216
Diamond Communications, **10** 288
Diamond Corporation Ltd., **IV** 21, 66–67; **7** 123
Diamond Crystal Brands, Inc., **32** 274, 277
Diamond Electronics, **24** 510
Diamond Fields Resources Inc., **27** 457
Diamond Head Resources, Inc. *See* AAON, Inc.
Diamond International Corp., **IV** 290, 295; **13** 254–55; **19** 225; **26** 446
Diamond M Offshore Inc., **12** 318
Diamond Match Company, **14** 163
Diamond Offshore Drilling, Inc., **36** 325; **43** 202
Diamond Oil Co., **IV** 548
Diamond Park Fine Jewelers, **16** 559
Diamond Rug & Carpet Mills, **19** 276
Diamond Savings & Loan, **II** 420
**Diamond Shamrock Corporation, IV 408–11**, 481; **7** 34, 308–099, 345; **13** 118; **19** 177; **45** 411. *See also* Ultramar Diamond Shamrock Corporation.
Diamond-Star Motors Corporation, **9** 349–51
Diamond Trading Company, **IV** 66–67; **7** 123
Diamond Walnut Growers, **7** 496–97
Dianatel, **18** 143
Diapositive, **44** 296
Diasonics Ultrasound, Inc., **27** 355
**Dibrell Brothers, Incorporated, 12 108–10**; **13** 492
**dick clark productions, inc., 16 170–73**
Dick Simon Trucking, Inc. *See* Simon Transporation Services Inc.
Dickerman, **8** 366
Dickson Forest Products, Inc., **15** 305
Dickstein Partners, L.P., **13** 261
Dictaphone Corp., **III** 157
Didier Lamarthe, **17** 210
Didier Werke AG, **IV** 232
**Diebold, Incorporated, 7 144–46**; **22 183–87 (upd.)**
**Diedrich Coffee, Inc., 40 152–54**
Diehl Manufacturing Co., **II** 9
Diemakers Inc., **IV** 443
Diesel Nacional, S.A. *See* Consorcio G Grupo Dina, S.A. de C.V.
**Diesel SpA, 40 155–57**
Diesel United Co., **III** 533
AB Diesels Motorer, **III** 425–26
Diet Center, **10** 383
Dieter Hein Co., **14** 537
Dieterich Standard Corp., **III** 468
Dietrich & Cie. *See* De Dietrich & Cie.
Dietrich Corp., **II** 512; **15** 221
Dietrich's Bakeries, **II** 631
DiFeo Automotive Group, **26** 500–01
DiFranza Williamson, **6** 40
DIG Acquisition Corp., **12** 107
**Digex, Inc., 45** 201; **46 140–43**
**Digi International Inc., 9 170–72**; **20** 237
Digicom, **22** 17
Digidesign Inc., **38** 70, 72
DiGiorgio Corporation, **25** 421
Digital Audio Disk Corp., **II** 103
Digital City, Inc., **22** 522
Digital Data Systems Company, **11** 408
Digital Devices, Inc., **III** 643
Digital Directory Assistance, **18** 24
Digital Entertainment Network, **42** 272
**Digital Equipment Corporation, II** 8, 62, 108; **III** 118, 128, **132–35**, 142, 149, 166; **6** 225, **233–36 (upd.)**, 237–38, 242, 246–47, 279, 287; **8** 137–39, 519; **9** 35, 43, 57, 166, 170–71, 514; **10** 22–23, 34, 86, 242, 361, 463, 477; **11** 46, 86–88, 274, 491, 518–19; **12** 147,

162, 470; **13** 127, 202, 482; **14** 318; **15** 108; **16** 394, 418; **18** 143, 345; **19** 310; **21** 123; **25** 499; **26** 90, 93; **34** 441–43; **36** 81, 287; **43** 13; **45** 201
Digital Marketing, Inc., **22** 357
Digital Research in Electronic Acoustics and Music S.A., **17** 34
Digitech, **19** 414
Dii Group Inc., **38** 188–89
Diligent Engine Co., **III** 342
Dill & Collins, **IV** 311; **19** 266
Dill Enterprises, Inc., **14** 18
**Dillard Department Stores, Inc.**, **V 45–47**; **10** 488; **11** 349; **12** 64; **13** 544–45; **16 174–77 (upd.)**, 559; **19** 48, 324; **27** 61
**Dillard Paper Company**, **11 74–76**
**Dillingham Construction Corporation**, **44 151–54 (upd.)**
**Dillingham Corp.**, **I 565–66**
Dillingham Holdings Inc., **9** 511
**Dillon Companies Inc.**, **II** 645; **12 111–13**; **15** 267; **22** 194
Dillon Paper, **IV** 288
Dillon, Read, and Co., Inc., **I** 144, 559; **III** 151, 389; **6** 265; **11** 53; **20** 259; **24** 66
Dime Bancorp, **44** 32–33; **46** 316
Dime Banking and Loan Association of Rochester, **10** 91
**Dime Savings Bank of New York, F.S.B.**, **9 173–74**
Dimeling, Schrieber & Park, **11** 63; **44** 309
Dimensions in Sport, Ltd., **37** 5
Dimeric Development Corporation, **14** 392
**DIMON Inc.**, **12** 110; **27 124–27**
Dina. *See* Consorcio G Grupo Dina, S.A. de C.V.
Dinamica, S.A., **19** 12
Dine S.A., **23** 170–72
Dineen Mechanical Contractors, Inc., **48** 238
Diners Club, **II** 397; **6** 62; **9** 335; **10** 61
Dinner Bell Foods, Inc., **11** 93
de Dion, **III** 523
**Dionex Corporation**, **46 144–46**
Dirección General de Correos y Telecomunicaciónes, **V** 337
Dirección Nacional de los Yacimientos Petrolíferos Fiscales, **IV** 577–78
Direct Container Lines, **14** 505
**Direct Focus, Inc.**, **47 93–95**
Direct Friends, **25** 91
Direct Line, **12** 422
Direct Mail Services Pty. Ltd., **10** 461
Direct Marketing Technology Inc., **19** 184
Direct Spanish Telegraph Co., **I** 428
Direct Transit, Inc., **42** 364
Direction Générale des Télécommunications, **V** 471
DirectLine Insurance, **22** 52
**Directorate General of Telecommunications**, **7 147–49**
**DIRECTV, Inc.**, **21** 70; **35** 156, 158–59; **38 174–77**
Dirr's Gold Seal Meats, **6** 199
Disc Go Round, **18** 207, 209
Disc Manufacturing, Inc., **15** 378
Disclosure, Inc., **18** 24
Disco SA, **V** 11; **19** 308–09
Disconto-Gesellschaft, **II** 238, 279
**Discount Auto Parts, Inc.**, **18 144–46**; **26** 348
Discount Bank, **II** 205
Discount Corporation, **12** 565
**Discount Drug Mart, Inc.**, **14 172–73**
Discount Investment Corporation Ltd., **24** 429
Discount Labels, Inc., **20** 15
Discount Tire Co., **19** 294; **20** 263
Discover, **9** 335; **12** 97
**Discovery Communications, Inc.**, **42 114–17**
Discovery Toys, Inc., **19** 28
Discovery Zone, **31** 97
DiscoVision Associates, **III** 605
**Discreet Logic Inc.**, **20 185–87**
Disctronics, Ltd., **15** 380
Disney Channel, **6** 174–75; **13** 280
Disney Co. *See* The Walt Disney Company.
Disney Studios, **II** 408; **6** 174, 176; **43** 229–30, 233
Disneyland, **6** 175
Disneyland Paris. *See* Euro Disneyland SCA.
Dispatch Communications, **10** 432
Display Components Inc., **II** 110; **17** 479
Displayco Midwest Inc., **8** 103
Disposable Hospital Products, **I** 627
Distillers and Cattle Feeders Trust, **I** 376
**Distillers Co. plc**, **I 239–41**, 252, 263, 284–85; **II** 429, 609–10; **IV** 70; **43** 214
Distillers Securities, **I** 376
Distinctive Printing and Packaging Co., **8** 103
Distinctive Software Inc., **10** 285
Distribuidora Bega, S.A. de C.V., **31** 92
Distribution Centers Incorporated. *See* Exel Logistics Ltd.
Distribution Services, Inc., **10** 287
Distribution Solutions International, Inc., **24** 126
District Bank, **II** 333
District Cablevision, **II** 160
District News Co., **II** 607
Distrigas, **IV** 425
DITAS, **IV** 563
Ditzler Color Co., **III** 732
DIVAL, **III** 347
Divani & Divani. *See* Industrie Natuzzi S.p.A.
Divco-Wayne Corp., **17** 82
DIVE!, **26** 264
Diversey Corp., **I** 275, 333; **13** 150, 199; **26** 305–06; **32** 476
Diversified Agency Services, **I** 32
Diversified Foods Inc., **25** 179
Diversified Retailing Co., **III** 214
Diversified Services, **9** 95
Diversifoods Inc., **II** 556; **13** 408
Diversity Consultants Inc., **32** 459
DiviCom, **43** 221–22
Dixie Airline, **25** 420
Dixie Bearings, Inc., **13** 78
Dixie Carriers, Inc., **18** 277
Dixie Container Corporation, **12** 377
Dixie Crystals Brands, Inc., **32** 277
**The Dixie Group, Inc.**, **20 188–90**
Dixie Hi-Fi, **9** 120–21
Dixie Home Stores, **II** 683
Dixie-Narco Inc., **III** 573; **22** 349
Dixie Paper, **I** 612–14
Dixie Power & Light Company, **6** 514
Dixie Yarns, Inc., **9** 466; **19** 305
Dixieland Food Stores, **II** 624
**Dixon Industries, Inc.**, **26 117–19**; **48** 59
**Dixon Ticonderoga Company**, **12 114–16**
**Dixons Group plc**, **II** 139; **V 48–50**; **9** 65; **10** 45, 306; **19 121–24 (upd.)**; **23** 52; **24** 194, 269–70
DIY Home Warehouse, **16** 210
DJ Moldings Corp., **18** 276
DJ Pharma, Inc., **47** 56
Djedi Holding SA, **23** 242
DKB. *See* Dai-Ichi Kangyo Bank Ltd.
DLC. *See* Duquesne Light Company.
DLJ. *See* Donaldson, Lufkin & Jenrette.
DLJ Merchant Banking Partners II, **21** 188; **36** 158–59
DM Associates Limited Partnership, **25** 127
DMA, **18** 510
DMB&B. *See* D'Arcy Masius Benton & Bowles.
DMGT. *See* Daily Mail and General Trust.
**DMI Furniture, Inc.**, **44** 132; **46 147–50**
DMP Mineralöl Petrochemie GmbH, **IV** 487
DNATA, **39** 137, 139
DNAX Research Institute, **I** 685; **14** 424
DNEL-Usinor, **IV** 227
DNN Galvanizing Limited Partnership, **24** 144
DNP DENMARK A/S, **IV** 600
Do It All, **24** 75
**Do it Best Corporation**, **30 166–70**
Dobbs House, **21** 54
Dobbs Houses Inc., **I** 696–97; **15** 87
Dobrolet, **6** 57
Dobson Park Industries, **38** 227
Docks de France, **37** 23; **39** 183–84
Doctors' Hospital, **6** 191
Documentation Resources, **11** 65
**Documentum, Inc.**, **46 151–53**
DOD Electronics Corp., **15** 215
Dodd, Mead & Co., **14** 498
Dodge & Day. *See* Day & Zimmermann, Inc.
Dodge Corp., **I** 144; **8** 74; **11** 53
The Dodge Group, **11** 78
Dodge Manufacturing Company, **9** 440
Dodge Motor Company, **20** 259
Doduco Corporation, **29** 460–61
Dodwell & Co., **III** 523
Doe Run Company, **12** 244
Doeflex PLC, **33** 79
**Dofasco Inc.**, **IV 73–74**; **24 142–44 (upd.)**
Doherty Clifford Steers & Sherfield Inc., **I** 31
Doherty, Mann & Olshan. *See* Wells Rich Greene BDDP.
Dolan Design, Inc., **44** 133
**Dolby Laboratories Inc.**, **20 191–93**
Dole Corporation, **44** 152
**Dole Food Company, Inc.**, **I** 565; **II** 491–92; **9 175–76**; **20** 116; **31 167–170 (upd.)**
Dolland & Aitchison Group, **V** 399
Dollar Bills, Inc. *See* Dollar Tree Stores, Inc.
Dollar General, **26** 533
Dollar Rent A Car, **6** 349; **24** 10
Dollar Steamship Lines, **6** 353
**Dollar Thrifty Automotive Group, Inc.**, **25** 92, **142–45**
**Dollar Tree Stores, Inc.**, **16** 161; **23 176–78**
Dollfus Mieg & Cie. *See* Groupe DMC.
Dolphin Book Club, **13** 106
Dolphin Services, Inc., **44** 203

Dom Perignon, **25** 258
Domain Technology, **6** 231
Domaine Carneros, **43** 401
Domaine Chandon, **I** 272
Domaines Barons de Rothschild, **36** 113, 115
Dombrico, Inc., **8** 545
Domco Industries, **19** 407
Dome Laboratories, **I** 654
Dome Petroleum, Ltd., **II** 222, 245, 262, 376; **IV** 371, 401, 494; **12** 364
Domestic Electric Co., **III** 435
Domestic Operating Co., **III** 36
Dominick International Corp., **12** 131
Dominick's Finer Foods, **9** 451; **13** 25, 516; **17** 558, 560–61
Dominion Bank, **II** 375–76
Dominion Bridge Company, Limited, **8** 544
Dominion Cellular, **6** 322
Dominion Dairies, **7** 429
Dominion Engineering Works Ltd., **8** 544
Dominion Far East Line, **I** 469; **20** 311
Dominion Foils Ltd., **17** 280
Dominion Foundries and Steel, Ltd., **IV** 73–74
Dominion Hoist & Shovel Co., **8** 544
**Dominion Homes, Inc.**, **19 125–27**
Dominion Industries Ltd., **15** 229
Dominion Life Assurance Co., **III** 276
Dominion Mushroom Co., **II** 649–50
Dominion Ornamental, **III** 641
Dominion Paper Box Co. Ltd., **IV** 645
**Dominion Resources, Inc.**, **V** 591, **596–99**
Dominion Securities, **II** 345; **21** 447
Dominion Steel Castings Company, Ltd. *See* Dofasco Inc.
Dominion Stores Ltd., **II** 650, 652
Dominion Tar & Chemical Co. Ltd., **IV** 271–72
Dominion Terminal Associates, **IV** 171; **7** 582, 584
**Dominion Textile Inc.**, **V** 355; **8** 559–60; **12 117–19**
**Domino Sugar Corporation**, **26 120–22**; **42** 370
Domino Supermarkets, **24** 528
**Domino's Pizza, Inc.**, **7 150–53**; **9** 74; **12** 123; **15** 344, 346; **16** 447; **21 177–81 (upd.)**; **22** 353; **24** 295; **25** 179–80, 227–28; **26** 177; **33** 388; **37** 208
**Domtar Inc.**, **IV 271–73**, 308
Don Baxter Intravenous Products Co., **I** 627
**Don Massey Cadillac, Inc.**, **37 114–16**
Don's Foods, Inc., **26** 164
Donac Company, **V** 681
Donald L. Bren Co., **IV** 287
**Donaldson Co. Inc.**, **16 178–81**
**Donaldson, Lufkin & Jenrette, Inc.**, **II** 422, 451; **III** 247–48; **9** 115, 142, 360–61; **18** 68; **22 188–91**; **26** 348; **35** 247; **41** 197
Donaldson's Department Stores, **15** 274
Doncaster Newspapers Ltd., **IV** 686
Dong-A Motor, **III** 749
Dong-Myung Industrial Co. Ltd., **II** 540
Dongbang Life Insurance Co., **I** 515
Dongguan Shilong Kyocera Optics Co., Ltd., **21** 331
Dongil Frozen Foods Co., **II** 553
Dongsu Industrial Company, **III** 516; **7** 232
Donn, Inc., **18** 162
**Donna Karan Company**, **15 145–47**; **24** 299; **25** 294, 523
Donnelley, Gassette & Loyd, **IV** 660
Donnellon McCarthy Inc., **12** 184
Donnelly Coated Corporation, **48** 28
**Donnelly Corporation**, **12 120–22**; **35 147–50 (upd.)**
**Donnkenny, Inc.**, **17 136–38**
Donohue Inc., **12** 412
Donohue Meehan Publishing Co., **27** 362
Donruss Leaf Inc., **19** 386
Donzi Marine Corp., **III** 600
Dooner Laboratories, **I** 667
Door-to-Door, **6** 14
Dorado Beach Development Inc., **I** 103
Dordrecht, **III** 177–78
Dorenbecher Properties, **19** 381
Doric Corp., **19** 290
**Dorling Kindersley Holdings plc**, **20 194–96**
Dorman Long & Co. Ltd., **IV** 658
Dorman's, Inc., **27** 291
Dorney Park, **22** 130
Dornier, **I** 46, 74, 151; **15** 142; **34** 131
Dorothy Hamill International, **13** 279, 281
Dorothy Perkins, **V** 21
Dorr-Oliver Inc., **35** 134–35
**Dorsey & Whitney LLP**, **47 96–99**
Dortmunder Union, **II** 240; **IV** 103, 105
**Doskocil Companies, Inc.**, **12 123–25**. *See also* Foodbrands America, Inc.
Dot Wireless Inc., **46** 422
Doty Agency, Inc., **41** 178, 180
Double A Products Co., **23** 82–83
**DoubleClick Inc.**, **46 154–57**
Doubleday Book Shops, Inc., **10** 136; **25** 31; **30** 68
Doubleday-Dell, **IV** 594, 636
**Doubletree Corporation**, **21 182–85**; **41** 81–82
**Douglas & Lomason Company**, **16 182–85**
Douglas Aircraft Co., **I** 48, 70, 76, 96, 104, 195; **II** 32, 425; **III** 601; **9** 12, 18, 206; **10** 163; **13** 48, 341; **16** 77; **21** 141; **24** 375
Douglas-Dahlin Co., **I** 158–59
Douglas Dynamics L.L.C., **41** 3
Douglas Oil Co., **IV** 401
Doulton Glass Industries Ltd., **IV** 659
Douwe Egberts, **II** 572
Dove International, **7** 299–300
**Dover Corporation**, **III 467–69**; **28 101–05 (upd.)**
**Dover Downs Entertainment, Inc.**, **43 139–41**
**Dover Publications Inc.**, **34 148–50**; **41** 111
Dovrat Shrem, **15** 470
**Dow Chemical Co.**, **I 323–25**, 334, 341–42, 360, 370–71, 708; **II** 440, 457; **III** 617, 760; **IV** 83, 417; **8 147–50 (upd.)**, 153, 261–62, 548; **9** 328–29, 500–1; **10** 289; **11** 271; **12** 99–100, 254, 364; **14** 114, 217; **16** 99; **17** 418; **18** 279; **21** 387; **28** 411; **38** 187
Dow Corning, **II** 54; **III** 683, 685; **44** 129
**Dow Jones & Company, Inc.**, **IV 601–03**, 654, 656, 670, 678; **7** 99; **10** 276–78, 407; **13** 55; **15** 335–36; **19 128–31 (upd.)**, 204; **21** 68–70; **23** 157; **47 100–04 (upd.)**
**Dow Jones Telerate, Inc.**, **10 276–78**
DOW Stereo/Video Inc., **30** 466
Dowdings Ltd., **IV** 349
DowElanco, **21** 385, 387
Dowell Australia Ltd., **III** 674
Dowell Schlumberger. *See* Schlumberger Limited.
Dowidat GmbH, **IV** 197
Dowlais Iron Co., **III** 493
Down River International, Inc., **15** 188
Downe Communications, Inc., **14** 460
Downingtown Paper Company, **8** 476
Downyflake Foods, **7** 429
Dowty Aerospace, **17** 480
Doyle Dane Bernbach, **I** 9, 20, 28, 30–31, 33, 37, 206; **11** 549; **14** 159; **22** 396
DP&L. *See* Dayton Power & Light Company.
DPCE, **II** 139; **24** 194
DPF, Inc., **12** 275; **38** 250–51
**DPL Inc.**, **6 480–82**
**DQE**, **6 483–85**; **38** 40
Dr. Gerhard Mann Pharma, **25** 56
DR Holdings, Inc., **10** 242
Dr. Ing he F. Porsche GmbH, **13** 413–14
Dr. Karl Thomae GmbH, **39** 72–73
Dr. Martens, **23** 399, 401
Dr. Miles' Medical Co., **I** 653
**Dr Pepper/7Up Companies, Inc.**, **I** 245; **II** 477; **9 177–78**
**Dr Pepper/Seven Up, Inc.**, **32 154–57 (upd.)**
Dr. Richter & Co., **IV** 70
Dr. Solomon's Software Ltd., **25** 349
Dr. Tigges-Fahrten, **II** 163–64; **44** 432
**Drackett Professional Products**, **III** 17; **12 126–28**
DraftDirect Worldwide, **22** 297
Draftline Engineering Co., **22** 175
Dragados y Construcciones S.A., **II** 198
Dragon, **III** 391
Dragon International, **18** 87
Dragonair, **16** 481; **18** 114. *See also* Hong Kong Dragon Airlines.
The Drake, **12** 316
Drake Bakeries, **II** 562
**Drake Beam Morin, Inc.**, **IV** 623; **44 155–57**
Drake Steel Supply Co., **19** 343
Drallos Potato Company, **25** 332
Draper & Kramer, **IV** 724
Draper Corporation, **14** 219; **15** 384
Drathen Co., **I** 220
Dravo Corp., **6** 143
Draw-Tite, Inc., **11** 535
Drayton Corp., **II** 319; **17** 324
**DreamWorks SKG**, **17** 72; **21** 23, 26; **26** 150, 188; **43 142–46**
**The Drees Company, Inc.**, **41 131–33**
Dreher Breweries, **24** 450
**Dresdner Bank A.G.**, **I** 411; **II** 191, 238–39, 241–42, 256–57, 279–80, **281–83**, 385; **III** 201, 289, 401; **IV** 141; **14** 169–70; **15** 13; **47** 81–84
Dresdner Feuer-Versicherungs-Gesellschaft, **III** 376
Dresdner RCM Global Investors, **33** 128
**The Dress Barn, Inc.**, **24 145–46**
**Dresser Industries, Inc.**, **I** 486; **III** 429, **470–73**; 499, 527, 545–46; **12** 539; **14** 325; **15** 225–26, 468; **16** 310; **18** 219; **24** 208; **25** 188, 191
Dresser Power, **6** 555
Drew Graphics, Inc., **13** 227–28
**Drew Industries Inc.**, **28 106–08**
Drewry Photocolor, **I** 447

**Drexel Burnham Lambert Incorporated**, **II** 167, 329–30, **407–09**, 482; **III** 10, 253, 254–55, 531, 721; **IV** 334; **6** 210–11; **7** 305; **8** 327, 349, 388–90, 568; **9** 346; **12** 229; **13** 169, 299, 449; **14** 43; **15** 71, 281, 464; **16** 535, 561; **20** 415; **22** 55, 189; **24** 273; **25** 313; **33** 253. *See also* New Street Capital Inc.
**Drexel Heritage Furnishings Inc.**, **III** 571; **11** 534; **12 129–31**; **20** 362; **39** 266
**Dreyer's Grand Ice Cream, Inc.**, **10** 147–48; **17 139–41**; **30** 81; **35** 59–61
Dreyfus Interstate Development Corp., **11** 257
DRI. *See* Dominion Resources, Inc.
Dribeck Importers Inc., **9** 87
Drip In Irrigation, **26** 494
Drogueros S.A., **39** 188
Drott Manufacturing Company, **10** 379
Drouot Group, **III** 211
DRS Investment Group, **27** 370
Drug City, **II** 649
**Drug Emporium, Inc.**, **12 132–34**, 477
Drug House, **III** 9
Drug, Inc., **III** 17; **37** 42
Drummond Lighterage. *See* Puget Sound Tug and Barge Company.
Drummonds' Bank, **12** 422
Druout, **I** 563; **24** 78
Dry Milks Inc., **I** 248
DryClean U.S.A., **14** 25
Dryden and Co., **III** 340
**Drypers Corporation**, **18 147–49**
Drysdale Government Securities, **10** 117
**DSC Communications Corporation**, **9** 170; **12 135–37**
DSL Group Ltd., **27** 49
DSM Melamine America, **27** 316–18
**DSM N.V.**, **I 326–27**; **III** 614; **15** 229
DST Systems Inc., **6** 400–02; **26** 233
DTAG. *See* Dollar Thrifty Automotive Group, Inc.
**DTE Energy Company**, **20 197–201 (upd.)**
Du Bouzet, **II** 233
Du Mont Company, **8** 517
**Du Pareil au Même**, **43 147–49**
Du Pont. *See* E.I. du Pont de Nemours & Co.
Du Pont Fabricators, **III** 559
Du Pont Glore Forgan, Inc., **III** 137
Du Pont Photomask, **IV** 600
**Duane Reade Holding Corp.**, **21 186–88**
Dublin and London Steam Packet Company, **V** 490
DuBois Chemicals Division, **13** 149–50; **22** 188; **26** 306
Ducatel-Duval, **II** 369
**Ducati Motor Holding S.p.A.**, **17** 24; **30 171–73**; **36** 472
**Duck Head Apparel Company, Inc.**, **8** 141–43; **30** 159; **42 118–21**
Ducks Unlimited, **28** 306
**Duckwall-ALCO Stores, Inc.**, **24 147–49**
Duco Ltd., **25** 104–05
**Ducommun Incorporated**, **30 174–76**
Ducon Group, **II** 81
Ducros, **36** 185, 187–88
Dudley Stationery Ltd., **25** 501
Duff & Phelps Credit Rating, **37** 143, 145
Duff Bros., **III** 9–10
Duffy Meats, **27** 259
Duffy-Mott, **II** 477
**Duke Energy Corporation**, **27 128–31 (upd.)**; **40** 354, 358
Duke Energy Field Services, Inc., **24** 379; **40** 354, 358
**Duke Power Company**, **V 600–02**
Dumes SA, **13** 206
Dumez, **V** 655–57
Dumont Broadcasting Corporation, **7** 335
**The Dun & Bradstreet Corporation**, **I** 540; **IV 604–05**, 643, 661; **8** 526; **9** 505; **10** 4, 358; **13** 3–4; **19 132–34 (upd.)**; **38** 6
**Dun & Bradstreet Software Services Inc.**, **11 77–79**; **43** 183
Dunbar-Stark Drillings, Inc., **19** 247
Duncan Foods Corp., **I** 234; **10** 227
Duncan, Sherman & Co., **II** 329
Duncanson & Holt, Inc., **13** 539
Dundee Acquisition Corp., **19** 421
Dundee Bancorp, **36** 314
Dundee Cement Co., **III** 702; **8** 258–59
Dunfey Brothers Capital Group, **12** 368
Dunfey Hotels Corporation, **12** 367
Dunhams Stores Corporation, **V** 111
Dunhill Holdings, **IV** 93; **V** 411
Dunkin' Donuts, **II** 619; **21** 323; **29** 18–19
Dunlop Coflexip Umbilicals Ltd. *See* Duco Ltd.
Dunlop Holdings, **I** 429; **III** 697; **V** 250, 252–53
Dunlop Ltd., **25** 104
Dunn Bennett, **38** 401
Dunn Bros., **28** 63
Dunn Manufacturing Company, **25** 74
Dunn Paper Co., **IV** 290
Dunning Industries, **12** 109
Dunoyer. *See* Compagnie de Saint-Gobain S.A.
Dunwoodie Manufacturing Co., **17** 136
Duo-Bed Corp., **14** 435
Dupey Enterprises, Inc., **17** 320
Dupil-Color, Inc., **III** 745
Duplainville Transport, **19** 333–34
**Duplex Products, Inc.**, **17 142–44**, 445
Dupol, **III** 614
Dupont. *See* E.I. du Pont de Nemours & Company.
Dupont Chamber Works, **6** 449
Duquesne Light Company, **6** 483–84
Duquesne Systems, **10** 394
Dura Convertible Systems, **13** 170
Dura Corp., **I** 476
Dura-Vent, **III** 468
**Duracell International Inc.**, **9 179–81**; **12** 559; **13** 433; **17** 31; **24** 274; **39** 336, 339
**Durametallic**, **17** 147; **21 189–91**
Durand & Huguenin, **I** 672
Durango-Mapimi Mining Co., **22** 284
Duray, Inc., **12** 215
Durban Breweries and Distillers, **I** 287
D'Urban, Inc., **41** 169
Durham Chemicals Distributors Ltd., **III** 699
Durham Raw Materials Ltd., **III** 699
**Duriron Company Inc.**, **17 145–47**; **21** 189, 191
Durkee Famous Foods, **II** 567; **7** 314; **8** 222; **17** 106; **27** 297
**Dürr AG**, **44 158–61**
Durr-Fillauer Medical Inc., **13** 90; **18** 97
Dutch Boy, **II** 649; **III** 745; **10** 434–35
Dutch Crude Oil Company. *See* Nederlandse Aardolie Maatschappij.
Dutch East Indies Post, Telegraph and Telephone Service, **II** 67
Dutch Nuts Chocoladefabriek B.V., **II** 569
Dutch Pantry, **II** 497
Dutch State Mines. *See* DSM N.V.
Dutchland Farms, **25** 124
Dutton Brewery, **I** 294
Duttons Ltd., **24** 267
**Duty Free International, Inc.**, **11 80–82**. *See also* World Duty Free Americas, Inc.
Duval Corp., **IV** 489–90; **7** 280; **25** 461
DWG Corporation. *See* Triarc Companies, Inc.
**Dyckerhoff AG**, **35 151–54**
**Dyersburg Corporation**, **21 192–95**
Dyke and Dryden, Ltd., **31** 417
**Dylex Limited**, **29 162–65**
Dymed Corporation. *See* Palomar Medical Technologies, Inc.
Dynaco Corporation, **III** 643; **22** 409
Dynalectric Co., **45** 146
DynaMark, Inc., **18** 168, 170, 516, 518
Dynamatic Corp., **I** 154
Dynamem Corporation, **22** 409
Dynamic Capital Corp., **16** 80
Dynamic Controls, **11** 202
Dynamic Microprocessor Associated Inc., **10** 508
Dynamics Corporation of America, **39** 106
Dynamit Nobel AG, **III** 692–95; **16** 364; **18** 559
Dynamix, **15** 455
Dynapar, **7** 116–17
Dynaplast, **40** 214–15
Dynascan AK, **14** 118
Dynasty Footwear, Ltd., **18** 88
**Dynatech Corporation**, **13 194–96**
Dynatron/Bondo Corporation, **8** 456
**DynCorp**, **45 145–47**
Dynegy, Inc., **47** 70
Dynell Electronics, **I** 85
Dyno Industrier AS, **13** 555
Dyonics Inc., **I** 667
DYR, **I** 38; **16** 167
Dystrybucja, **41** 340

E. & B. Carpet Mills, **III** 423
E&B Company, **9** 72
E&B Marine, Inc., **17** 542–43
E & H Utility Sales Inc., **6** 487
**E. & J. Gallo Winery**, **I** 27, **242–44**, 260; **7 154–56 (upd.)**; **15** 391; **28 109–11 (upd.)**, 223
E&M Laboratories, **18** 514
E & S Retail Ltd. *See* Powerhouse.
**E! Entertainment Television Inc.**, **17 148–50**; **24** 120, 123; **47** 78
E-Stamp Corporation, **34** 474
**E-Systems, Inc.**, **I** 490; **9 182–85**
**E*Trade Group, Inc.**, **20 206–08**; **38** 439; **45** 4
E-II Holdings Inc., **II** 468; **9** 449; **12** 87; **43** 355. *See also* Astrum International Corp.
E-Z Haul, **24** 409
**E-Z Serve Corporation**, **15** 270; **17 169–71**
E.A. Miller, Inc., **II** 494
E.A. Pierce & Co., **II** 424; **13** 340
E.A. Stearns & Co., **III** 627
E.B. Badger Co., **11** 413
E.B. Eddy Forest Products, **II** 631
E.C. Snodgrass Company, **14** 112

E.C. Steed, **13** 103
E. de Trey & Sons, **10** 270–71
E.F. Hutton Group, **I** 402; **II** 399, 450–51; **8** 139; **9** 469; **10** 63
E.F. Hutton LBO, **24** 148
E. Gluck Trading Co., **III** 645
E.H. Bindley & Company, **9** 67
**E.I. du Pont de Nemours & Company**, **I** 21, 28, 305, 317–19, 323, **328–30**, 334, 337–38, 343–44, 346–48, 351–53, 365, 377, 379, 383, 402–03, 545, 548, 675; **III** 21; **IV** 69, 78, 263, 371, 399, 401–02, 409, 481, 599; **V** 360; **7** 546; **8** **151–54 (upd.)**, 485; **9** 154, 216, 352, 466; **10** 289; **11** 432; **12** 68, 365, 416–17; **13** 21, 124; **16** 127, 130, 201, 439, 461–62; **19** 11, 223; **21** 544; **22** 147, 260, 405; **24** 111, 388; **25** 152, 540; **26** **123–27 (upd.)**; **34** 80, 283–84; **37** 111; **40** 370; **45** 246
E.J. Brach & Sons, **II** 521. *See also* Brach and Brock Confections, Inc.
E.J. Longyear Company. *See* Boart Longyear Company.
E. Katz Special Advertising Agency. *See* Katz Communications, Inc.
E.L. Phillips and Company, **V** 652–53
E.M. Warburg Pincus & Co., **7** 305; **13** 176; **16** 319; **25** 313; **29** 262
E. Missel GmbH, **20** 363
E.N.V. Engineering, **I** 154
E.R.R. Enterprises, **44** 227
E.R. Squibb, **I** 695; **21** 54–55
E. Rabinowe & Co., Inc., **13** 367
E.S. Friedman & Co., **II** 241
E.S. International Holding S.A. *See* Banco Espírito Santo e Comercial de Lisboa S.A.
E.W. Bliss, **I** 452
E.W. Oakes & Co. Ltd., **IV** 118
**The E.W. Scripps Company**, **IV** **606–09**; **7** **157–59 (upd.)**; **24** 122; **25** 507; **28** **122–26 (upd.)**
E.W.T. Mayer Ltd., **III** 681
EADS. *See* European Aeronautic Defence and Space Company.
Eagle Airways Ltd., **23** 161
Eagle Credit Corp., **10** 248
Eagle Distributing Co., **37** 351
Eagle Family Foods, Inc., **22** 95
Eagle Floor Care, Inc., **13** 501; **33** 392
Eagle Gaming, L.P., **16** 263; **43** 226
**Eagle Hardware & Garden, Inc.**, **9** 399; **16** **186–89**; **17** 539–40
Eagle Industries Inc., **8** 230; **22** 282; **25** 536
Eagle-Lion Films, **II** 147; **25** 328
Eagle Managed Care Corp., **19** 354, 357
Eagle Oil Transport Co. Ltd., **IV** 657
**Eagle-Picher Industries, Inc.**, **8** **155–58**; **23** **179–83 (upd.)**
Eagle Plastics, **19** 414
Eagle Printing Co. Ltd., **IV** 295; **19** 225
Eagle Sentry Inc., **32** 373
Eagle Snacks Inc., **I** 219; **34** 36–37
Eagle Square Manufacturing Co., **III** 627
Eagle Star Insurance Co., **I** 426–27; **III** 185, 200
Eagle Supermarket, **II** 571
Eagle Thrifty Drug, **14** 397
Eagle Travel Ltd., **IV** 241
**Earl Scheib, Inc.**, **32** **158–61**
Early American Insurance Co., **22** 230
Early Learning Centre, **39** 240, 242
Earth Resources Company, **IV** 459; **17** 320
Earth Wise, Inc., **16** 90
Earth's Best, Inc., **21** 56; **36** 256
**The Earthgrains Company**, **36** **161–65**
**EarthLink, Inc.**, **33** 92; **36** **166–68**; **38** 269
EAS. *See* Executive Aircraft Services.
Easco Hand Tools, Inc., **7** 117
Eason Oil Company, **6** 578; **11** 198
East African External Communications Limited, **25** 100
East Chicago Iron and Forge Co., **IV** 113
East Hartford Trust Co., **13** 467
East India Co., **I** 468; **III** 521, 696; **IV** 48; **20** 309
East Japan Heavy Industries, **III** 578–79; **7** 348
**East Japan Railway Company**, **V** **448–50**
East Midlands Electricity, **V** 605
The East New York Savings Bank, **11** 108–09
East of Scotland, **III** 359
East Texas Pulp and Paper Co., **IV** 342, 674; **7** 528
East-West Airlines, **27** 475
East-West Federal Bank, **16** 484
East West Motor Express, Inc., **39** 377
Easter Enterprises, **8** 380; **23** 358
Easterday Supply Company, **25** 15
Eastern Air Group Co., **31** 102
**Eastern Airlines**, **I** 41, 66, 78, 90, 98–99, **101–03**, 116, 118, 123–25; **III** 102; **6** 73, 81–82, 104–05; **8** 416; **9** 17–18, 80; **11** 268, 427; **12** 191, 487; **21** 142, 143; **23** 483; **26** 339, 439; **39** 120
Eastern Associated Coal Corp., **6** 487
Eastern Australia Airlines, **24** 396
Eastern Aviation Group, **23** 408
Eastern Bank, **II** 357
Eastern Carolina Bottling Company, **10** 223
Eastern Coal Corp., **IV** 181
Eastern Coalfields Ltd., **IV** 48–49
**The Eastern Company**, **48** **140–43**
Eastern Corp., **IV** 703
Eastern Electricity, **13** 485
**Eastern Enterprises**, **IV** 171; **6** **486–88**
Eastern Gas and Fuel Associates, **I** 354; **IV** 171
Eastern Indiana Gas Corporation, **6** 466
Eastern Kansas Utilities, **6** 511
Eastern Machine Screw Products Co., **13** 7
Eastern Market Beef Processing Corp., **20** 120
Eastern Operating Co., **III** 23
Eastern Pine Sales Corporation, **13** 249
Eastern Software Distributors, Inc., **16** 125
Eastern States Farmers Exchange, **7** 17
Eastern Telegraph Company, **V** 283–84; **25** 99–100
Eastern Texas Electric. *See* Gulf States Utilities Company.
Eastern Tool Co., **IV** 249
Eastern Torpedo Company, **25** 74
Eastern Wisconsin Power, **6** 604
Eastern Wisconsin Railway and Light Company, **6** 601
Eastex Pulp and Paper Co., **IV** 341–42
**Eastman Chemical Company**, **14** **174–75**; **25** 22; **38** **178–81 (upd.)**
Eastman Christensen Company, **22** 68
**Eastman Kodak Company**, **I** 19, 30, 90, 323, 337–38, 690; **II** 103; **III** 171–72, **474–77**, 486–88, 547–48, 550, 584, 607–09; **IV** 260–61; **6** 288–89; **7** **160–64 (upd.)**, 436–38; **8** 376–77; **9** 62, 231; **10** 24; **12** 342; **14** 174–75, 534; **16** 168, 449; **18** 184–86, 342, 510; **25** 153; **29** 370; **36** **169–76 (upd.)**; **38** 178–79; **41** 104, 106; **43** 284; **45** 284
Eastman Radio, **6** 33
Eastmaque Gold Mines, Ltd., **7** 356
Eastover Mining, **27** 130
Eastpak, Inc., **30** 138
Eastwynn Theatres, Inc., **37** 63
**easyJet Airline Company Limited**, **39** **127–29**
Eatco, Inc., **15** 246
**Eateries, Inc.**, **33** **138–40**
Eaton Axle Co., **I** 154
Eaton, Cole & Burnham Company, **8** 134
**Eaton Corporation**, **I** **154–55**, 186; **III** 645; **10** **279–80 (upd.)**; **12** 547; **27** 100
**Eaton Vance Corporation**, **18** **150–53**
EAudio, Inc., **48** 92
Eavey Co., **II** 668
Ebamsa, **II** 474
EBASCO. *See* Electric Bond and Share Company.
Ebasco Services, **III** 499; **V** 612; **IV** 255–56
**eBay Inc.**, **32** **162–65**
EBC Amro Ltd., **II** 186
Eberhard Faber, **12** 115
Eberhard Foods, **8** 482
Eberhard Manufacturing Company, **48** 141
EBIC. *See* European Banks' International Co.
Ebiex S.A., **25** 312
EBS. *See* Electric Bond & Share Company *or* Electronic Bookshelf.
**EBSCO Industries, Inc.**, **17** **151–53**; **40** **158–61 (upd.)**
EC Comics, **25** 139
EC Erdolchemie GmbH, **7** 141
ECAD Inc., **48** 75
ECC. *See* Educational Credit Corporation.
**ECC Group plc**, **III** **689–91**. *See also* English China Clays plc.
**ECC International Corp.**, **42** **122–24**
Ecce, **41** 129
ECCO. *See* Adecco S.A.
Echigoya Saburobei Shoten, **IV** 292
**Echlin Inc.**, **I** **156–57**; **11** **83–85 (upd.)**; **15** 310
**Echo Bay Mines Ltd.**, **IV** **75–77**; **23** 40; **38** **182–85 (upd.)**
Les Echos, **IV** 659
**EchoStar Communications Corporation**, **35** **155–59**
EchoStar Satellite Corp., **39** 400
**ECI Telecom Ltd.**, **18** **154–56**
**Eckerd Corporation**, **9** **186–87**; **18** 272; **24** 263; **43** 247. *See also* J.C. Penney Company, Inc.
Eckert-Mauchly Corp., **III** 166
Ecko-Ensign Design, **I** 531
Ecko Products, **I** 527
ECL, **16** 238
Eclipse Candles, Ltd., **18** 67, 69
Eclipse Machine Co., **I** 141
Eclipse Telecommunications, Inc., **29** 252
Eco Hotels, **14** 107
Eco SA, **48** 224
**Ecolab Inc.**, **I** **331–33**; **13** **197–200 (upd.)**; **26** 306; **34** **151–56 (upd.)**, 205, 208

**Ecology and Environment, Inc., 39 130–33**
Econo Lodges of America, **25** 309
Econo-Travel Corporation, **13** 362
Economist Group, **15** 265
Economy Book Store, **10** 135
Economy Fire & Casualty, **22** 495
Economy Grocery Stores Company. *See* The Stop & Shop Companies, Inc.
Ecopetrol. *See* Empresa Colombiana de Petróleos.
EcoSystems Software, Inc., **10** 245; **30** 142
EcoWater Systems, Inc., **16** 357
**ECS S.A, 12 138–40**
Ecton, Inc., **36** 5
Ecusta Corporation, **8** 414
ed bazinet international, inc., **34** 144–45
Edah, **13** 544–45
**Eddie Bauer, Inc.**, **II** 503; **V** 160; **9 188–90**; **9** 316; **10** 324, 489, 491; **11** 498; **15** 339; **25** 48; **27** 427, 429–30; **29** 278; **36 177–81 (upd.)**
Eddy Bakeries, Inc., **12** 198
Eddy Paper Co., **II** 631
**Edeka Zentrale A.G.**, **II 621–23**; **33** 56; **47 105–07 (upd.)**
**edel music AG, 44 162–65**
**Edelbrock Corporation, 37 117–19**
Edelhoff AG & Co., **39** 415
Edelstahlwerke Buderus AG, **III** 695
Edenhall Group, **III** 673
Edenton Cotton Mills, **12** 503
EDF. *See* Electricité de France.
Edgars, **I** 289
Edgcomb Metals, **IV** 575–76; **31** 470–71
Edge Research, **25** 301
Edgell Communications Inc., **IV** 624
Edgewater Hotel and Casino, **6** 204–05
EDI, **26** 441
Edina Realty Inc., **13** 348
**Edison Brothers Stores, Inc.**, **9 191–93**; **17** 369, 409; **33** 126–28
Edison Electric Appliance Co., **II** 28; **12** 194
Edison Electric Co., **I** 368; **II** 330; **III** 433; **6** 572
Edison Electric Illuminating Co., **II** 402; **6** 595, 601; **14** 124
Edison Electric Illuminating Company of Boston, **12** 45
Edison Electric Light & Power, **6** 510
Edison Electric Light Co., **II** 27; **6** 565, 595; **11** 387; **12** 193
Edison General Electric Co., **II** 27, 120, 278; **12** 193; **14** 168; **26** 451
Edison Machine Works, **II** 27
Edison Phonograph, **III** 443
**Edison Schools Inc., 37 120–23**
Editions Albert Premier, **IV** 614
Editions Bernard Grasset, **IV** 618
Editions Dalloz, **IV** 615
Editions Jean-Baptiste Baillière, **25** 285
Editions Nathan, **IV** 615
Editions Ramsay, **25** 174
Editorial Centro de Estudios Ramón Areces, S.A., **V** 52; **26** 130
Editorial Televisa, **18** 211, 213; **23** 417
Editoriale L'Espresso, **IV** 586–87
Editoriale Le Gazzette, **IV** 587
EdK. *See* Edeka Zentrale A.G.
**Edmark Corporation**, **14 176–78**; **41 134–37 (upd.)**
Edmonton City Bakery, **II** 631
**EDO Corporation, 46 158–61**
Edogawa Oil Co., **IV** 403
EdoWater Systems, Inc., **IV** 137
EDP Group. *See* Electricidade de Portugal, S.A.
Edper Equities, **II** 456
EDS. *See* Electronic Data Systems Corporation.
Education Association Mutual Assurance Company. *See* Horace Mann Educators Corporation.
The Education Finance Group, **33** 418, 420
Education Funds, Inc., **II** 419
**Education Management Corporation, 35 160–63**
Education Systems Corporation, **7** 256; **25** 253
Educational & Recreational Services, Inc., **II** 607
**Educational Broadcasting Corporation, 48 144–47**
Educational Computer International, Inc. *See* ECC International Corp.
Educational Credit Corporation, **8** 10; **38** 12
Educational Loan Administration Group, Inc., **33** 420
Educational Publishing Corporation, **22** 519, 522
Educational Supply Company, **7** 255; **25** 252
**Educational Testing Service**, **12 141–43**; **42** 209–10, 290
Educorp, Inc., **39** 103
EduQuest, **6** 245
EduServ Technologies, Inc., **33** 420
Edusoft Ltd., **40** 113
EduTrek International, Inc., **45** 88
**Edw. C. Levy Co., 42 125–27**
Edward Ford Plate Glass Co., **III** 640–41, 731
**Edward J. DeBartolo Corporation**, **V** 116; **8 159–62**
**Edward Jones, 30 177–79**
Edward Lloyd Ltd., **IV** 258
Edward P. Allis Company, **13** 16
Edward Smith & Company, **8** 553
Edwards & Jones, **11** 360
Edwards Dunlop & Co. Ltd., **IV** 249
Edwards Food Warehouse, **II** 642
Edwards George and Co., **III** 283
Edwards Industries, **IV** 256
**Edwards Theatres Circuit, Inc., 31 171–73**
Edwardstone Partners, **14** 377
EEC Environmental, Inc., **16** 259
Eerste Nederlandsche, **III** 177–79
Eff Laboratories, **I** 622
Effectenbank, **II** 268; **21** 145
EFM Media Management, **23** 294
Efnadruck GmbH, **IV** 325
Efrat Future Technology Ltd. *See* Comverse Technology, Inc.
EFTEC, **32** 257
**EG&G Incorporated**, **8 163–65**; **18** 219; **22** 410; **29 166–69 (upd.)**
EGAM, **IV** 422
Egerton Hubbard & Co., **IV** 274
Egg plc, **48** 328
**Egghead Inc.**, **9 194–95**; **10** 284
**Egghead.com, Inc., 31 174–177 (upd.)**
EGPC. *See* Egyptian General Petroleum Corporation.
EGUZKIA-NHK, **III** 581
**EgyptAir**, **I** 107; **6 84–86**; **27 132–35 (upd.)**
**Egyptian General Petroleum Corporation**, **IV 412–14**; **32** 45
EHAPE Einheitspreis Handels Gesellschaft mbH. *See* Kaufhalle AG.
Ehrlich-Rominger, **48** 204
Eidgenössische Bank, **II** 378
Eidgenössische Versicherungs- Aktien-Gesellschaft, **III** 403
**Eiffage, 27 136–38**
Eiffel Construction Metallique, **27** 138
**800-JR Cigar, Inc., 27 139–41**
**84 Lumber Company**, **9 196–97**; **39 134–36 (upd.)**
Eildon Electronics Ltd., **15** 385
EIMCO, **I** 512
**Einstein/Noah Bagel Corporation**, **29 170–73**; **44** 313
**eircom plc, 31 178–181 (upd.)**
EIS Automotive Corp., **III** 603
EIS, Inc., **45** 176, 179
Eisai Company, **13** 77
Eisen-und Stahlwerk Haspe AG, **IV** 126
Eisen-und Stahlwerk Hoesch, **IV** 103
Eisenhower Mining Co., **IV** 33
EJ Financial Enterprises Inc., **48** 308–09
EKA AB, **I** 330; **8** 153
Eka Nobel AB, **9** 380
**Ekco Group, Inc.**, **12** 377; **16 190–93**
EKT, Inc., **44** 4
**El Al Israel Airlines Ltd.**, **I** 30; **23 184–87**
**El Camino Resources International, Inc., 11 86–88**
**El Chico Restaurants, Inc.**, **19 135–38**; **36** 162–63
**El Corte Inglés, S.A.**, **V 51–53**; **26 128–31 (upd.)**
El Dorado Investment Company, **6** 546–47
El-Mel-Parts Ltd., **21** 499
El Paso & Southwestern Railroad, **IV** 177
**El Paso Electric Company, 21 196–98**
El Paso Healthcare System, Ltd., **15** 112; **35** 215
**El Paso Natural Gas Company**, **10** 190; **11** 28; **12 144–46**; **19** 411; **27** 86
El Pollo Loco, **II** 680; **27** 16–18
El Taco, **7** 505
ELAN, **IV** 486
Elan Corp. plc, **10** 54
Elan Ski Company, **22** 483
Elanco Animal Health, **47** 112
**Elano Corporation, 14 179–81**
Elantis, **48** 290
Elastic Reality Inc., **38** 70
Elcat Company, **17** 91
Elco Corporation, **21** 329, 331
Elco Industries Inc., **22** 282
Elco Motor Yacht, **I** 57
Elda Trading Co., **II** 48; **25** 267
**Elder-Beerman Stores Corporation**, **10 281–83**; **19** 362
Elder Dempster Line, **6** 416–17
Elder Smith Goldsbrough Mort Ltd., **21** 227
Elder's Insurance Co., **III** 370
**Elders IXL Ltd.**, **I** 216, 228–29, 264, **437–39**, 592–93; **7** 182–83; **21** 227; **26** 305; **28** 201
Elders Keep, **13** 440
Eldorado Gold Corporation, **22** 237
ele Corporation, **23** 251
Electra Corp., **III** 569; **20** 361–62

Electra/Midland Corp., **13** 398
Electralab Electronics Corp., **III** 643
Electric Boat Co., **I** 57–59, 527; **II** 7; **10** 315
Electric Bond & Share Company, **V** 564–65; **6** 596
Electric Clearinghouse, Inc., **18** 365, 367
Electric Energy, Inc., **6** 470, 505
Electric Fuels Corp., **V** 621; **23** 200
Electric Heat Regulator Co., **II** 40; **12** 246
Electric Iron and Steel, **IV** 162
Electric Light and Power Company, **6** 483
Electric Light Company of Atlantic City. *See* Atlantic Energy, Inc.
**Electric Lightwave, Inc., 37 124–27**
Electric Storage Battery Co., **39** 338
Electric Thermostat Co., **II** 40; **12** 246
Electric Transit, Inc., **37** 399–400
Electrical Lamp Service Co. *See* EMI Group plc.
**Electricidade de Portugal, S.A., 47 108–11**
**Electricité de France**, **I** 303; **V 603–05**, 626–28; **41 138–41 (upd.)**
Electro-Alkaline Company. *See* The Clorox Company.
Electro-Chemische Fabrik Natrium GmbH, **IV** 69–70
Electro Dynamics Corp., **I** 57, 484; **11** 263
Electro-Flo, Inc., **9** 27
Electro-Mechanical Research, **III** 617; **17** 417
Electro Metallurgical Co., **I** 400; **9** 517; **11** 402
Electro-Motive Engineering Company, **10** 273
Electro-Nite International N.V., **IV** 100
Electro-Optical Systems, **III** 172; **6** 289
Electro Refractories and Abrasives Company, **8** 178
Electro String Instrument Corporation, **16** 201; **43** 169
Electrobel, **II** 202
ElectroData Corp., **III** 165; **6** 281
**Electrolux Group**, **II** 69, 572; **III** 420, **478–81**; **IV** 338; **6** 69; **11** 439; **12** 158–59, 250; **13** 562, 564; **17** 353; **21** 383. *See also* Aktiebolaget Electrolux.
**Electromagnetic Sciences Inc., 21 199–201**
Electromedics, **11** 460
**Electronic Arts Inc.**, **10 284–86**; **13** 115; **29** 76; **35** 227
Electronic Banking Systems, **9** 173
Electronic Book Technologies, Inc., **26** 216 **29** 427
**Electronic Data Systems Corporation**, **I** 172; **II** 65; **III 136–38**, 326; **6** 226; **9** 36; **10** 325, 327; **11** 62, 123, 131; **13** 482; **14** 15, 318; **22** 266; **27** 380; **28 112–16 (upd.)**; **241**; **XXIX** 375; **36** 242. *See also* Perot Systems Corporation.
Electronic Engineering Co., **16** 393
Electronic Hair Styling, Inc., **41** 228
Electronic Rentals Group PLC, **II** 139; **24** 194
Electronic Tool Company, **16** 100
Electronics Corp. of Israel Ltd. *See* ECI Telecom Ltd.
**Electronics for Imaging, Inc.**, **15 148–50**; **43 150–53 (upd.)**
Electrorail, **II** 93; **18** 472
Electrowatt Ltd., **21** 146–47
Electrowerke AG, **IV** 230
Elekom, **31** 176
Elektra. *See* Grupo Elektra, S.A. de C.V.
Elektra Records, **III** 480; **23** 33
Elektriska Aktiebolaget. *See* ABB Asea Brown Boveri Ltd.
Elektrizitäts-Gesellschaft Laufenburg, **6** 490
Elektrizitätswerk Wesertal GmbH, **30** 206
Elektrizitätswerk Westfalen AG, **V** 744
ElektroHelios, **III** 479; **22** 26
Elektromekaniska AB, **III** 478
Elektromekano, **II** 1
**Elektrowatt AG, 6 489–91**
Eleme Petrochemicals Co., **IV** 473
**Elementis plc, 40 162–68 (upd.)**
Eletson Corp., **13** 374
Elettra Broadcasting Corporation, **14** 509
Elettrofinanziaria Spa, **9** 152
Eleventh National Bank, **II** 373
**Elf Aquitaine SA, 21 202–06 (upd.)**; **23** 236, 238; **24** 494; **25** 104; **26** 369, 425. *See also* Société Nationale Elf Aquitaine.
Elfa International, **36** 134–35
Elgin Blenders, Inc., **7** 128
Elgin Exploration, Inc., **19** 247; **26** 70
**Eli Lilly and Company**, **I** 637, **645–47**, 666, 679, 687, 701; **III** 18–19, 60–61; **8** 168, 209; **9** 89–90; **10** 535; **11** 9, **89–91 (upd.)**, 458, 460; **12** 187, 278, 333; **14** 99–100, 259; **17** 437; **18** 420, 422; **19** 105; **21** 387; **26** 31; **32** 212; **44** 175; **45** 382; **47 112–16 (upd.)**, 221, 236
Eli Witt Company, **15** 137, 139; **43** 205
Elias Brothers Restaurants, **III** 103
Elit Circuits Inc., **I** 330; **8** 153
Elite Microelectronics, **9** 116
Elite Sewing Machine Mfg. Co. Ltd., **III** 415; **48** 5
**Elizabeth Arden, Inc.**, **I** 646, **III** 48; **8 166–68**, 344; **9** 201–02, 428, 449; **11** 90; **12** 314; **30** 188; **32** 476; **40 169–72 (upd.)**; **47** 113
**Eljer Industries, Inc.**, **II** 420; **24 150–52**
Elk River Resources, Inc., **IV** 550
Elka, **III** 54
Elke Corporation, **10** 514
Elko-Lamoille Power Company, **11** 343
Ellanef Manufacturing Corp., **48** 274
Ellenville Electric Company, **6** 459
**Ellerbe Becket, 41 142–45**
Ellesse International S.p.A., **V** 376; **26** 397–98
**Ellett Brothers, Inc., 17 154–56**
Ellington Recycling Center, **12** 377
Elliot Group Limited, **45** 139–40
Elliott Automation, **II** 25; **6** 241; **13** 225
Elliott Bay Design Group, **22** 276
Elliott Paint and Varnish, **8** 553
Ellipse Programmes, **48** 164–65
Ellis & Everard, **41** 341
Ellis Adding-Typewriter Co., **III** 151; **6** 265
Ellis Banks, **II** 336
Ellis, Chafflin & Co. *See* Mead Corporation.
Ellis-Don Ltd., **38** 481
Ellis Paperboard Products Inc., **13** 442
Ellis Park Race Course, **29** 118
Ellisco Co., **35** 130
Ellos A.B., **II** 640
ELMA Electronic, **III** 632
Elmendorf Board, **IV** 343
Elmer's Products, Inc. *See* Borden, Inc.
**Elmer's Restaurants, Inc., 42 128–30**
Elmo Semiconductor Corp., **48** 246
Elphinstone, **21** 501
Elrick & Lavidge, **6** 24
Elrick Industries, Inc., **19** 278
**Elscint Ltd., 20 202–05**
**Elsevier NV**, **IV 610–11**, 643, 659; **7** 244; **14** 555–56; **17** 396, 399. *See also* Reed Elsevier.
Elsi, **II** 86
**Elsinore Corporation**, **36** 158; **48 148–51**
ELTO Outboard Motor Co., **III** 597
Eltra Corporation, **I** 416, 524; **22** 31; **31** 135
Elwerath, **IV** 485
ELYO, **42** 387–88
Elyria Telephone Company, **6** 299
Email Ltd., **III** 672–73
**EMAP plc**, **35** 71–72, **164–66**, 242–44
Emballage, **III** 704
Embankment Trust Ltd., **IV** 659
Embassy Book Co., Ltd., **IV** 635
Embassy Hotel Group, **I** 216; **9** 426
Embassy Suites, **9** 425; **24** 253
Embedded Support Tools Corporation, **37** 419, 421
**Embers America Restaurants, 30 180–82**
Embotelladora Central, S.A., **47** 291
Embraer. *See* Empresa Brasileira de Aeronáutica S.A.
Embry-Riddle, **I** 89
**EMC Corporation**, **12 147–49**; **20** 8; **46 162–66 (upd.)**
EMC Technology Services, Inc., **30** 469
Emco, **III** 569; **20** 361
EMD Technologies, **27** 21; **40** 67
Emerald Coast Water Co., **III** 21
Emerald Technology, Inc., **10** 97
**Emerson, 46 167–71 (upd.)**
Emerson-Brantingham Company, **10** 378
Emerson Drug, **I** 711
**Emerson Electric Co.**, **II 18–21**, 92; **III** 625; **8** 298; **12** 248; **13** 225; **14** 357; **15** 405–06; **21** 43; **22** 64; **25** 530; **36** 400
Emerson Foote, Inc., **25** 90
**Emerson Radio Corp., 30 183–86**
**Emery Air Freight Corporation**, **6** 345–46, 386, **388–91**; **18** 177. *See also* Emery Worldwide Airlines, Inc.
Emery Group, **I** 377; **III** 33
**Emery Worldwide Airlines, Inc.**, **21** 139; **25 146–50 (upd.)**
Emeryville Chemical Co., **IV** 408
**Emge Packing Co., Inc., 11 92–93**
Emhart Corp., **III** 437; **8** 332; **20** 67
**EMI Group plc**, **I** 531; **6** 240; **22 192–95 (upd.)**; **24** 485; **26** 188, 314. *See also* Thorne EMI plc.
**The Emirates Group**, **24** 400; **39 137–39**
**Emmis Communications Corporation, 47 117–21**
Empain, **18** 472; **19** 165
Empain-Schneider, **II** 93
Empaques de Carton Titan, **19** 10–11
Empex Hose, **19** 37
**Empi, Inc., 27 132–35**
**Empire Blue Cross and Blue Shield, III 245–46**; **6** 195
Empire Brewery, **I** 253
Empire Co., **II** 653
Empire Cos., **IV** 391
Empire District Electric, **IV** 391
Empire Family Restaurants Inc., **15** 362
Empire Gas & Fuel, **IV** 391
Empire Hanna Coal Co., Ltd., **8** 346

Empire Inc., **II** 682
Empire Life and Accident Insurance Co., **III** 217
Empire National Bank, **II** 218
Empire of America, **11** 110
Empire Pencil, **III** 505; **43** 230
Empire Savings, Building & Loan Association, **8** 424
Empire State Group, **IV** 612
Empire State Petroleum, **IV** 374
Empire State Pickling Company, **21** 155
Empire Steel Castings, Inc., **39** 31–32
Empire Stores, **19** 309
Empire Trust Co., **II** 218
**Employee Solutions, Inc., 18 157–60**
employeesavings.com, **39** 25
Employers' Liability Assurance, **III** 235
Employer's Overload, **25** 432
Employers Reinsurance Corp., **II** 31; **12** 197
**Empresa Brasileira de Aeronáutica S.A. (Embraer), 36 182–84**
**Empresa Colombiana de Petróleos, IV 415–18**
Empresa de Obras y Montajes Ovalle Moore, S.A., **34** 81
Empresa Nacional de Electridad, **I** 459
Empresa Nacional del Petroleo, **IV** 528
Empresa Nacional Electrica de Cordoba, **V** 607
Empresa Nacional Hidro-Electrica del Ribagorzana, **I** 459; **V** 607
Empresa Nacional Hulleras del Norte, **I** 460
Empresas Emel S.A., **41** 316
Empresas Frisco, **21** 259
Empresas ICA, **34** 82
**Empresas ICA Sociedad Controladora, S.A. de C.V., 41 146–49**
Empresas La Moderna, **21** 413; **29** 435
Empresas Tolteca, **20** 123
Emprise Corporation, **7** 134–35
EMS-Chemie Holding AG, **III** 760; **32** 257
EMS Technologies, Inc., **21** 199, 201; **22** 173
Enagas, **IV** 528
**Enbridge Inc., 43 154–58**
**ENCAD, Incorporated, 25 151–53**
ENCASO, **IV** 528
ENCI, **IV** 132
**Encompass Services Corporation, 33 141–44**
Encon Safety Products, Inc., **45** 424
Encor Inc., **47** 396
**Encore Computer Corporation, 13 201–02**
Encore Distributors Inc., **17** 12–13
Encryption Technology Corporation, **23** 102
**Encyclopedia Britannica, Inc., 7 165–68; 12** 435, 554–55; **16** 252; **39 140–44 (upd.)**; **43** 208
Endata, Inc., **11** 112
**Endemol Entertainment Holding NV, 46 172–74**
**ENDESA S.A., V 606–08; 46 175–79 (upd.)**
Endevco Inc., **11** 28
Endiama, **IV** 67
Endicott Trust Company, **11** 110
Endo Vascular Technologies, Inc., **11** 460
Endovations, Inc., **21** 47
ENECO. *See* Empresa Nacional Electrica de Cordoba.
ENEL. *See* Ente Nazionale per l'Energia Elettrica.
Enerchange LLC, **18** 366
Enercon, Inc., **6** 25
Energas Company, **43** 56–57
**Energen Corporation, 6** 583; **21 207–09**
Energie-Verwaltungs-Gesellschaft, **V** 746
Energieversorgung Ostbayern AG, **23** 47
**Energis plc, 44** 363; **47 122–25**
**Energizer Holdings, Inc., 9** 180; **32 171–74**; **39** 336, 339
Energy & Minerals, Inc., **42** 354
Energy Absorption Systems, Inc., **15** 378
Energy Biosystems Corp., **15** 352
Energy Coatings Co., **14** 325
Energy Corp. of Louisiana, **V** 619
Energy Film Library, **31** 216, 218
Energy Foundation, **34** 386
The Energy Group, **26** 359
Energy Increments Inc., **19** 411
Energy National, Inc., **27** 485
Energy Resources, **27** 216
Energy Steel Corporation, **19** 472
Energy Systems Group, Inc., **13** 489
Energy Transportation Systems, Inc., **27** 88
Energyline Systems, **26** 5
EnergyOne, **19** 487
Enerplus Resources, **21** 500
**Enesco Corporation, 11 94–96**; **15** 475, 477–78
**Engelhard Corporation, II** 54; **IV** 23, **78–80**; **16** 28; **21 210–14 (upd.)**
Engen, **IV** 93; **22** 236
Engineered Polymers Co., **I** 202
Engineering Co. of Nigeria, **IV** 473
Engineering Company, **9** 16
Engineering for the Petroleum and Process Industries, **IV** 414
Engineering Plastics, Ltd., **8** 377
Engineering Research Associates, **III** 126, 129
Engineers & Fabricators, Inc., **18** 513
England Corsair Furniture, **14** 302
Englander Co., **I** 400
**Engle Homes, Inc., 46 180–82**
Engles Management Corp., **26** 448
**English China Clays Ltd., III** 689–91; **15 151–54 (upd.)**; **36** 20; **40 173–77 (upd.)**
English Condensed Milk Co., **II** 545
English Electric Co., **I** 50; **II** 25, 81; **6** 241; **24** 85
English Mercantile & General Insurance Co., **III** 376
English Property Corp., **IV** 712
English, Scottish and Australian Bank Ltd., **II** 187–89
**Engraph, Inc., 12 150–51**
Enhanced Services Billing, Inc. *See* Billing Concepts Corp.
ENHER. *See* Empresa Nacional Hidro-Electrica del Ribagorzana.
ENI. *See* Ente Nazionale Idrocarburi.
ENI S.p.A., **34** 75
ENIEPSA, **IV** 528
Enimont, **IV** 422, 525
Ennia, **III** 177, 179, 310
**Ennis Business Forms, Inc., 21 215–17**
Eno Proprietaries, **III** 65
Enocell Oy, **IV** 277
The Enoch F. Bills Co., **25** 365
Enogex, Inc., **6** 539–40
Enova Corporation. *See* Sempra Energy.
ENPAC Corporation, **18** 162
Enpetrol, **IV** 528
**Enquirer/Star Group, Inc., 10 287–88; 12** 358. *See also* American Media, Inc.
**Enrich International, Inc., 33 145–48**; **37** 340, 342
**Enron Corporation, III** 197; **V** 609–10; **6** 457, 593; **18** 365; **19 139–41**, 162, 487; **27** 266; **34** 82; **46 183–86 (upd.)**
Enseco, **III** 684
**Enserch Corp., V 611–13**
Ensidesa, **I** 460
Ensign Oil Company, **9** 490
Enskilda S.A., **II** 352–53
**Enso-Gutzeit Oy, IV 274–77**; **17** 539. *See also* Stora Enso Oyj
ENSTAR Corporation, **IV** 567; **11** 441
Enstar Group Inc., **13** 299
Ensys Environmental Products, Inc., **10** 107
ENTASA, **IV** 528
Ente Gestione Aziende Minerarie, **I** 466
Ente Nazionale di Energia Elettrica, **I** 466
**Ente Nazionale Idrocarburi, I** 369; **IV** 412, **419–22**, 424, 453, 466, 470, 486, 546; **V** 614–17
**Ente Nazionale per l'Energia Elettrica, V 614–17**
Entenmann's Bakery, **I** 246, 712; **10** 551; **35** 415; **38** 364
Entercom, **48** 272
**Entergy Corporation, V 618–20**; **6** 496–97; **45 148–51 (upd.)**
Enterprise Development Company, **15** 413
Enterprise Electronics Corporation, **18** 513–15
Enterprise Federal Savings & Loan, **21** 524
Enterprise Integration Technologies, **18** 541
**Enterprise Leasing, 6 392–93**
Enterprise Metals Pty. Ltd., **IV** 61
**Enterprise Oil plc, 11 97–99**
Enterprise Rent-A-Car, Inc., **16** 380; **33** 192
Enterra Corp., **25** 546
Entertainment Publications, **16** 146
Entertainment UK, **24** 266, 269
Entertainment Zone, Inc., **15** 212
Entex Information Services, **24** 29
Entity Software, **11** 469
Entrada Industries Incorporated, **6** 568–69; **26** 387
**Entravision Communications Corporation, 41 150–52**
Entré Computer Centers, **6** 243–44; **13** 175
Entremont, **I** 676
Entreprise de Recherches et d'Activités Pétrolières, **IV** 453, 467, 544, 560; **7** 481, 483–84
**Entreprise Nationale Sonatrach, IV 423–25**; **V** 626, 692; **10** 83–84; **12** 145
Entrex, Inc., **III** 154
Entrust Financial Corp., **16** 347
Envergure, **27** 421
Envirex, **11** 361
Envirodrill Services, Inc., **19** 247
**Envirodyne Industries, Inc., 17 157–60**
EnviroLease, Inc., **25** 171
ENVIRON International Corporation, **10** 106
Environmental Defense Fund, **9** 305
**Environmental Industries, Inc., 31 182–85**
Environmental Mediation, Inc., **47** 20
Environmental Planning & Research. *See* CRSS Inc.

Environmental Research and Technology, Inc., **23** 135
Environmental Systems Corporation, **9** 109
Environmental Testing and Certification Corporation, **10** 106–07
Environmentals Incorporated. *See* Angelica Corporation.
Envirosciences Pty. Ltd., **16** 260
Envision Corporation, **24** 96
Enwright Environmental Consulting Laboratories, **9** 110
Enzafruit Worldwide, **38** 202
**Enzo Biochem, Inc., 41 153–55**
Enzyme Bio-Systems, Ltd., **21** 386
Enzyme Technologies Corp., **I** 342; **14** 217
Eon Productions, **II** 147; **25** 328
Eon Systems, **III** 143; **6** 238; **38** 409
l'Epargne, **12** 152
EPE Technologies, **18** 473
EPI Group Limited, **26** 137
Epic Express, **48** 113
Les Epiceries Presto Limitée, **II** 651
Epiphone, **16** 238–39
Epoch Systems Inc., **9** 140; **12** 149
ePOWER International, **33** 3, 6
Eppler, Guerin & Turner, Inc., **III** 330
Eppley, **III** 99
Epsilon Trading Corporation, **6** 81
Epson, **18** 386–87, 435
Equator Bank, **II** 298
EQUICOR-Equitable HCA Corp., **III** 80, 226; **45** 104, 109
Equicor Group Ltd., **29** 343
**Equifax, Inc., 6 23–25**; **25** 182, 358; **28 117–21 (upd.)**
Equilink Licensing Group, **22** 458
Equilon Enterprises LLC, **41** 359, 395
Equistar Chemicals, LP, **45** 252, 254
EquiStar Hotel Investors L.P. *See* CapStar Hotel Co.
Equitable Bancorporation, **12** 329
Equitable Equipment Company, **7** 540
**Equitable Life Assurance Society of the United States, II** 330; **III** 80, 229, 237, **247–49**, 274, 289, 291, 305–06, 316, 329, 359; **IV** 171, 576, 711; **6** 23; **13** 539; **19** 324, 511; **22** 188–90; **23** 370, 482; **27** 46
**Equitable Resources, Inc., 6 492–94**
Equitable Trust Co., **II** 247, 397; **10** 61
Equitas, **22** 315
Equitec Financial Group, **11** 483
Equitex Inc., **16** 431
Equity & Law, **III** 211
Equity Corp. Tasman, **III** 735
Equity Corporation, **6** 599; **37** 67–68
Equity Group Investment, Inc., **22** 339
**Equity Marketing, Inc., 26 136–38**
Equity Title Services Company, **13** 348
Equivalent Company, **12** 421
Equus Capital Corp., **23** 65
Equus II Inc., **18** 11
Eramet, **IV** 108
ERAP. *See* Entreprise de Recherches et d'Activités Pétrolières.
Erasco Group, **II** 556; **26** 58
EraSoft Technologies, **27** 492
Ercea, **41** 128–29
ERCO Systems Group, **16** 461–63
ERDA Inc., **36** 160
Erdal, **II** 572
Erdölsproduktions-Gesellschaft AG, **IV** 485
Erftwerk AG, **IV** 229
**ERGO Versicherungsgruppe AG, 44 166–69**, 443
Ericson Yachts, **10** 215
Ericssan, AB, **11** 501
Ericsson, **9** 32–33; **11** 196; **17** 33, 353; **18** 74; **47** 321. *See also* Telefonaktiebolaget LM Ericsson.
**Eridania Béghin-Say S.A., 14** 17, 19; **36 185–88**
Erie and Pennyslvania, **I** 584
Erie County Bank, **9** 474
**Erie Indemnity Company, 35 167–69**
Erie Railroad, **I** 584; **II** 329; **IV** 180
Erie Scientific Company, **14** 479–80
Eritsusha, **IV** 326
erizon, **36** 264
ERKA. *See* Reichs Kredit-Gesellschaft mbH.
**ERLY Industries Inc., 17 161–62**; **33** 30–31
Ernest Oppenheimer and Sons, **IV** 21, 79
**Ernst & Young, I** 412; **9 198–200**, 309, 311; **10** 115; **25** 358; **29 174–77 (upd.)**, 236, 392
Ernst Göhner Foundation, **47** 286–87
Ernst, Homans, Ware & Keelips, **37** 224
Erol's, **9** 74; **11** 556
ERPI, **7** 167
Ersco Corporation, **17** 310; **24** 160
Erste Allgemeine, **III** 207–08
The Ertl Company, **37** 318
Erving Distributor Products Co., **IV** 282; **9** 260
Erving Healthcare, **13** 150
Erwin Wasey & Co., **I** 17, 22
Erzbergbau Salzgitter AG, **IV** 201
ES&A. *See* English, Scottish and Australian Bank Ltd.
Esanda, **II** 189
Esaote Biomedica, **29** 298
ESB Inc., **IV** 112; **18** 488
Esbjerg Thermoplast, **9** 92
Escada AG, **14** 467
**Escalade, Incorporated, 19 142–44**
Escambia Chemicals, **I** 298
Escan, **22** 354
Escanaba Paper Co., **IV** 311; **19** 266
Escaut et Meuse, **IV** 227
Escher Wyss, **III** 539, 632
Eschweiler Bergwerks-Verein AG, **IV** 25–26, 193
ESCO Electronics Corporation, **17** 246, 248; **24** 425
Esco Trading, **10** 482
Escoffier Ltd., **I** 259
Escotel Mobile Communications, **18** 180
Esdon de Castro, **8** 137
ESE Sports Co. Ltd., **V** 376; **26** 397
ESGM. *See* Elder Smith Goldsbrough Mort.
ESI Energy, Inc., **V** 623–24
Eskay Screw Corporation, **11** 536
Eskilstuna Separator, **III** 419
**Eskimo Pie Corporation, 21 218–20**; **35** 119, 121
Esmark, Inc., **I** 441; **II** 448, 468–69; **6** 357; **12** 93; **13** 448; **15** 357; **19** 290; **22** 55, 513
Esperance-Longdoz, **IV** 51–52
Espírito Santo. *See* Banco Espírito Santo e Comercial de Lisboa S.A.
ESPN Inc., **II** 131; **IV** 627; **19** 201, 204; **24** 516; **46** 232
**Esporta plc, 35 170–72**
**Esprit de Corp., 8 169–72**; **29 178–82 (upd.)**
La Espuela Oil Company, Ltd., **IV** 81–82; **7** 186
Esquire Education Group, **12** 173
Esquire Inc., **I** 453; **IV** 672; **13** 178; **19** 405
**ESS Technology, Inc., 22 196–98**
Essanelle Salon Co., **18** 455
Essantee Theatres, Inc., **14** 86
**Essef Corporation, 18 161–63**
**Esselte Leitz GmbH & Co. KG, 48 152–55**
**Esselte Pendaflex Corporation, 11 100–01**
**Essence Communications, Inc., 24 153–55**
Essener Reisebüro, **II** 164
Essex International Ltd., **19** 452
Essex Outfitters Inc., **9** 394; **42** 268–69
**Essilor International, 18** 392; **21 221–23**; **40** 96–98
Esso Petroleum, **I** 52; **II** 628; **III** 673; **IV** 46, 276, 397, 421, 423, 432–33, 439, 441, 454, 470, 484, 486, 517–19, 531, 555, 563; **7** 140, 171; **11** 97; **13** 558; **22** 106; **24** 86; **25** 229, 231–32. *See also* Imperial Oil Limited *and* Standard Oil Company of New Jersey.
Essroc Corporation, **40** 108
Estat Telecom Group plc, **31** 180
Estech, Inc., **19** 290
Estee Corp., **27** 197; **43** 218
**The Estée Lauder Companies Inc., 30 187–91 (upd.)**
**Estée Lauder Inc., I** 696; **III** 56; **8** 131; **9 201–04**; **11** 41; **24** 55
Estel N.V., **IV** 105, 133
**Esterline Technologies Corp., 15 155–57**
Eston Chemical, **6** 148
Estronicks, Inc., **19** 290
ETA Systems, Inc., **10** 256–57
Etablissement Mesnel, **I** 202
Etablissement Poulenc-Frères, **I** 388
Etablissements Badin-Defforey, **19** 98
Etablissements Braud. *See* Manitou BF S.A.
**Etablissements Economiques du Casino Guichard, Perrachon et ie, S.C.A., 12 152–54**; **16** 452
Etablissements Pierre Lemonnier S.A., **II** 532
Etablissements Robert Ouvrie S.A., **22** 436
**Etam Developpement SA, 35** 308; **44 170–72**
Eteq Microsystems, **9** 116
**Ethan Allen Interiors, Inc., III** 530–31; **10** 184; **12** 307; **12 155–57**; **39 145–48 (upd.)**, **39** 173–74
Ethical Personal Care Products, Ltd., **17** 108
**Ethicon, Inc., III** 35; **8** 281; **10** 213; **23 188–90**
**Ethyl Corp., I 334–36**, 342; **IV** 289; **10 289–91 (upd.)**; **14** 217
Etienne Aigner, **14** 224
Etimex Kunstoffwerke GmbH, **7** 141
Etkin Skanska, **38** 437
L'Etoile, **II** 139
Etos, **II** 641
**EToys, Inc., 37 128–30**
ETPM Entrêpose, **IV** 468
ETS. *See* Educational Testing Service.
Euclid, **I** 147; **12** 90

Euclid Chemical Co., **8** 455–56
Euclid Crane & Hoist Co., **13** 385
Euralux, **III** 209
Eurasbank, **II** 279–80; **14** 169
**The Eureka Company**, **III** 478, 480; **12 158–60**; **15** 416; **22** 26. *See also* White Consolidated Industries Inc.
Eureka Insurance Co., **III** 343
Eureka Specialty Printing, **IV** 253; **17** 30
Eureka Technology, **18** 20; **43** 17
Eureka Tent & Awning Co., **III** 59
Eureka X-Ray Tube, Inc., **10** 272
Eurex, **41** 84, 87
Euris, **22** 365
**Euro Disneyland SCA**, **6** 174, 176; **20 209–12**
Euro-Pacific Finance, **II** 389
**Euro RSCG Worldwide S.A.**, **10** 345, 347; **13 203–05**; **16** 168; **33** 181
Eurobel, **II** 139; **III** 200; **24** 193
Eurobrokers Investment Corp., **II** 457
Eurocan Pulp & Paper Co. Ltd., **III** 648; **IV** 276, 300
Eurocard France, **II** 265
Eurocom S.A. *See* Euro RSCG Worldwide S.A.
Eurocopter SA, **7** 9, 11; **21** 8
EuroCross, **48** 381
Eurodis, **46** 71
EuroDollar Rent A Car. *See* Republic Industries, Inc.
Eurofighter Jagdflugzeug GmbH, **24** 84
Eurofilter Airfilters Ltd., **17** 106
Eurogroup, **V** 65
Euroimpex, **18** 163
Euromarché SA, **10** 205; **19** 308–09; **23** 231; **27** 94–95
**Euromarket Designs Inc.**, **9** 144; **31 186–189 (upd.)**; **34** 324, 327
Euromissile Dynamics Group, **7** 9; **24** 84
Euromoney Publications, **19** 118, 120
Euronda, **IV** 296; **19** 226
**Euronext Paris S.A.**, **37 131–33**
Euronova S.R.L., **15** 340
Europa Discount Sud-Ouest, **23** 248
Europa Metalli, **IV** 174
Europaischen Tanklager- und Transport AG, **7** 141
Europate, S.A., **36** 162–63
Europcar Chauffeur Drive U.K. International, **26** 62
Europcar International Corporation, Limited, **25** 142, 144, **27** 9, 11
Europcar Interrent, **10** 419
Europe Computer Systems. *See* ECS S.A.
Europe Craft Imports, Inc., **16** 37
Europe Publications, **44** 416
European Aeronautic Defence and Space Company, **34** 128, 135
European-American Bank & Trust Company, **14** 169
European-American Banking Corp., **II** 279, 295
European and African Investments Ltd., **IV** 21
European Banking Co., **II** 186
European Banks' International Co., **II** 184–86, 295
European Coal and Steel, **II** 402
European Gas Turbines, **13** 356
European Health Spa, **46** 431
European Investment Bank, **6** 97
European Periodicals, Publicity and Advertising Corp., **IV** 641; **7** 311
European Petroleum Co., **IV** 562
European Retail Alliance (ERA), **12** 152–53
European Silicon Structures, **17** 34
European Software Company, **25** 87
Europeia, **III** 403
Europemballage, **I** 600
Europene du Zirconium (Cezus), **21** 491
Europensiones, **III** 348
Europoligrafico SpA, **41** 326
Eurosar S.A., **25** 455
Eurotec, **IV** 128
Eurotech BV, **25** 101
Eurotechnique, **III** 678; **16** 122
**Eurotunnel Group**, **37 134–38 (upd.)**
**Eurotunnel PLC**, **13 206–08**
Eurovida, **III** 348
Euthenics Systems Corp., **14** 334
EVA Airways Corporation, **13** 211
Evaluation Associates, Inc., **III** 306
Evan Picone, **III** 55
Evans, **V** 21
**Evans & Sutherland Computer Corporation**, **19 145–49**
Evans-Aristocrat Industries, **III** 570; **20** 361
Evans Drumhead Company, **48** 232
**Evans, Inc.**, **30 192–94**
Evans Products Co., **13** 249–50, 550
Evans Rents, **26** 101
Evansville Veneer and Lumber Co., **12** 296
Eve of Roma, **III** 28
Evelyn Haddon, **IV** 91
Evelyn Wood, Inc., **7** 165, 168
Evence Coppée, **III** 704–05
Evenflo Companies, Inc., **19** 144
Evening News Association, **IV** 612; **7** 191
Ever Ready Label Corp., **IV** 253; **17** 30
Ever Ready Ltd., **7** 209; **9** 179–80; **30** 231
Everan Capital Corp., **15** 257
Everest & Jennings, **11** 200
Everett Pulp & Paper Company, **17** 440
**Everex Systems, Inc.**, **12** 162; **16 194–96**
Everfresh Beverages Inc., **26** 326
Evergenius, **13** 210
Evergreen Healthcare, Inc., **14** 210
**Evergreen Marine Corporation Taiwan Ltd.**, **13 209–11**
Evergreen Media Corporation, **24** 106
Evergreen Resources, Inc., **11** 28
**Everlast Worldwide Inc.**, **47 126–29**
Everlaurel, **13** 210
Everready Battery Co., **13** 433; **39** 338
Eversharp, **III** 28
Everyday Learning Corporation, **22** 519, 522
Everything for the Office, **22** 154
Everything Yogurt, **25** 180
Everything's A Dollar Inc. (EAD), **13** 541–43
EVI, Inc., **39** 416
Evian, **6** 47, 49
Evinrude-ELTO, **III** 597
Evinrude Motor Co., **III** 597–99
Evinrude Outboard Motor Company, **27** 75
Ewell Industries, **III** 739
Ewo Breweries, **I** 469; **20** 311
Ex-Cell-O Corp., **IV** 297
Ex-Lax Inc., **15** 138–39
**Exabyte Corporation**, **12 161–63**; **26** 256; **40 178–81 (upd.)**
Exacta, **III** 122
ExamOne World Wide, **48** 256
**Exar Corp.**, **14 182–84**
Exatec A/S, **10** 113
Exbud, **38** 437
Excaliber, **6** 205
**EXCEL Communications Inc.**, **18 164–67**
Excel Corporation, **11** 92–93; **13** 138, 351
Excel Mining Systems, Inc., **13** 98
Excelsior Life Insurance Co., **III** 182; **21** 14
Excelsior Printing Company, **26** 105
Excerpta Medica International, **IV** 610
Exchange & Discount Bank, **II** 318; **17** 323
Exchange Bank of Yarmouth, **II** 210
Exchange Oil & Gas Corp., **IV** 282; **9** 260
Excite, Inc., **22** 519; **27** 517. *See also* At Home Corporation.
Exco International, **10** 277
Execu-Fit Health Programs, **11** 379
Executive Aircraft Services, **27** 21
Executive Airlines, Inc., **28** 22
Executive Fund Life Insurance Company, **27** 47
Executive Gallery, Inc., **12** 264
Executive Income Life Insurance Co., **10** 246
**Executive Jet, Inc.**, **36 189–91**; **42** 35
Executive Life Insurance Co., **III** 253–55; **11** 483
Executive Risk Inc., **37** 86
Executive Systems, Inc., **11** 18
**Executone Information Systems, Inc.**, **13 212–14**; **15** 195
ExecuTrain. *See* International Data Group, Inc.
Executrans, Inc., **21** 96
Exel Logistics Ltd., **6** 412, 414
Exel Ltd., **13** 150
**Exelon Corporation**, **48 156–63 (upd.)**
Exeter & Hampton Electric Company, **37** 406
Exeter Oil Co., **IV** 550
**Exide Electronics Group, Inc.**, **9** 10; **20 213–15**; **24** 29
Exmark Manufacturing Company, Inc., **26** 494
Exors. of James Mills, **III** 493
Exp@nets, **37** 280, 283
**Expand SA**, **48 164–66**
Expedia Inc., **46** 101, 103; **47** 421
**Expeditors International of Washington Inc.**, **17 163–65**
Expercom, **6** 303
**Experian Information Solutions Inc.**, **28** 120; **45 152–55**
Experian Ltd., **47** 165, 168–69
Experience, **III** 359
Exploitasi Tambang Minyak Sumatra Utara, **IV** 492
Explorer Motor Home Corp., **16** 296
Explosive Fabricators Corp., **III** 643
Export & Domestic Can Co., **15** 127
Export-Import Bank, **IV** 33, 184
Express Airlines, Inc., **28** 266
Express Baggage Reclaim Services Limited, **27** 21
Express Foods Inc, **I** 247–48
Express Newspapers plc, **IV** 687; **28** 503
Express Rent-a-Tire, Ltd., **20** 113
**Express Scripts Inc.**, **17 166–68**; **44 173–76 (upd.)**
Expression Homes, **22** 205, 207
Extel Corp., **II** 142; **III** 269–70
Extel Financial Ltd., **IV** 687

**Extended Stay America, Inc., 41 156–58**
**Extendicare Health Services, Inc., III** 81; **6 181–83**
Extracorporeal Medical Specialties, **III** 36
Extron International Inc., **16** 538; **43** 33
Exx Inc., **40** 334
**Exxon Corporation, I** 16–17, 360, 364; **II** 16, 62, 431, 451; **IV** 171, 363, 365, 403, 406, **426–30**, 431–33, 437–38, 454, 466, 506, 508, 512, 515, 522, 537–39, 554; **V** 605; **7 169–73 (upd.)**, 230, 538, 559; **9** 440–41; **11** 353; **14** 24–25, 291, 494; **12** 348; **16** 489, 548; **20** 262; **23** 317; **25** 229–30; **26** 102, 369; **27** 217; **32 175–82 (upd.)**; **45** 54
Exxon Mobil Corporation, **40** 358
Eye Masters Ltd., **23** 329
Eyeful Home Co., **III** 758
Eyelab, **II** 560; **12** 411
EZ Paintr Corporation, **9** 374
**EZCORP Inc., 43 159–61**
EZPor Corporation, **12** 377

F. & F. Koenigkramer Company, **10** 272
F&G International Insurance, **III** 397
F. & J. Heinz, **II** 507
F & J Meat Packers, Inc., **22** 548–49
F & M Distributors, **12** 132
F. & M. Schaefer Brewing Corporation, **I** 253, 291, **III** 137; **18** 500
F & M Scientific Corp., **III** 142; **6** 237
F & R Builders, Inc., **11** 257
F.A. Computer Technologies, Inc., **12** 60
F.A. Ensign Company, **6** 38
F.A.I. Insurances, **III** 729
F.A.O. Schwarz, **I** 548
F. Atkins & Co., **I** 604
F.B. McFarren, Ltd., **21** 499–500
F.C. Internazionale Milano SpA, **44** 387
F.E. Compton Company, **7** 167
F. Egger Co., **22** 49
F.F. Dalley Co., **II** 497
F.F. Publishing and Broadsystem Ltd., **IV** 652; **7** 392
F.H. Tomkins Buckle Company Ltd., **11** 525
**F. Hoffmann-La Roche & Co. A.G., I** 637, 640, **642–44**, 657, 685, 693, 710; **7** 427; **9** 264; **10** 80, 549; **11** 424–25; **14** 406; **32** 211–12
F.J. Walker Ltd., **I** 438
F.K.I. Babcock, **III** 466
F. Kanematsu & Co., Ltd. *See* Kanematsu Corporation.
F.L. Industries Inc., **I** 481, 483
F.L. Moseley Co., **III** 142; **6** 237
F.N. Burt Co., **IV** 644
F. Perkins, **III** 651–52
F.S. Smithers, **II** 445; **22** 405
F.W. Dodge Corp., **IV** 636–37
F.W. Means & Company, **11** 337
F.W. Sickles Company, **10** 319
F.W. Williams Holdings, **III** 728
F.W. Woolworth & Co. Ltd. *See* Kingfisher plc.
F.W. Woolworth Co. *See* Woolworth Corporation.
F.X. Matt Brewing Co., **18** 72
Fab-Asia, Inc., **22** 354–55
**Fab Industries, Inc., 27 142–44**
Fab 9, **26** 431
**Fabbrica D' Armi Pietro Beretta S.p.A., 39 149–51**
Fabco Automotive Corp., **23** 306; **27** 203
Fabergé, Inc., **II** 590; **III** 48; **8** 168, 344; **11** 90; **32** 475; **47** 114
**Fabri-Centers of America Inc., 15** 329; **16 197–99**; **18** 223; **43** 291
Fabrica de Cemento El Melan, **III** 671
Fabtek Inc., **48** 59
Facchin Foods Co., **I** 457
Facit, **III** 480; **22** 26
**Facom S.A., 32 183–85**; **37** 143, 145
Facts on File, Inc., **14** 96–97; **22** 443
Fafnir Bearing Company, **13** 523
FAG Kugelfischer Georg Schafer AG, **11** 84; **47** 280
Fagersta, **II** 366; **IV** 203
Fahr AG, **III** 543
Fahrzeugwerke Eisenach, **I** 138
FAI, **III** 545–46
Failsafe, **14** 35
**Fair Grounds Corporation, 44 177–80**
**Fair, Isaac and Company, 18 168–71**, 516, 518
Fairbanks Morse Co., **I** 158, 434–35; **10** 292; **12** 71
**Fairchild Aircraft, Inc., 9 205–08**, 460; **11** 278
Fairchild Camera and Instrument Corp., **II** 50, 63; **III** 110, 141, 455, 618; **6** 261–62; **7** 531; **10** 108; **11** 503; **13** 323–24; **14** 14; **17** 418; **21** 122, 330; **26** 327
Fairchild Communications Service, **8** 328
The Fairchild Corporation, **37** 30
**Fairchild Dornier GmbH, 48 167–71 (upd.)**
Fairchild Industries, **I** 71, 198; **11** 438; **14** 43; **15** 195; **34** 117
Fairchild Semiconductor Corporation, **II** 44–45, 63–65; **III** 115; **6** 215, 247; **10** 365–66; **16** 332; **24** 235; **41** 201
**Fairclough Construction Group plc, I 567–68**
Fairey Industries Ltd., **IV** 659
Fairfax, **IV** 650
**Fairfield Communities, Inc., 36 192–95**
The Fairfield Group, **33** 259–60
Fairfield Manufacturing Co., **14** 43
Fairfield Publishing, **13** 165
Fairmont Foods Co., **7** 430; **15** 139
Fairmont Hotels and Resorts Inc., **45** 80
Fairmont Insurance Co., **26** 487
Fairmount Glass Company, **8** 267
Fairport Machine Shop, Inc., **17** 357
Fairway Marketing Group, Inc., **24** 394
Fairway Outdoor Advertising, Inc., **36** 340, 342
**Faiveley S.A., 39 152–54**
Falcon Drilling Co. *See* Transocean Sedco Forex Inc.
Falcon Oil Co., **IV** 396
**Falcon Products, Inc., 33 149–51**
Falcon Seaboard Inc., **II** 86; **IV** 410; **7** 309
Falconbridge, Ltd., **IV** 165–66
Falconbridge Nickel Mines Ltd., **IV** 111
Falconet Corp., **I** 45
Falley's, Inc., **17** 558, 560–61
**Fallon McElligott Inc., 22 199–201**
Falls Financial Inc., **13** 223; **31** 206
Falls National Bank of Niagara Falls, **11** 108
Falls Rubber Company, **8** 126
FAME Plastics, Inc., **18** 162
Family Bookstores, **24** 548
Family Channel. *See* International Family Entertainment Inc.
**Family Dollar Stores, Inc., 13 215–17**
**Family Golf Centers, Inc., 29 183–85**
Family Health Program, **6** 184
Family Life Insurance Co., **II** 425; **13** 341
Family Mart Group, **V** 188; **36** 418, 420
Family Restaurants, Inc., **14** 194
Family Steak Houses of Florida, Inc., **15** 420
Famosa Bakery, **II** 543
Famous Amos Chocolate Chip Cookie Corporation, **27** 332
Famous Atlantic Fish Company, **20** 5
Famous-Barr, **46** 288
**Famous Dave's of America, Inc., 40 182–84** 4
Famous Players-Lasky Corp., **I** 451; **II** 154; **6** 161–62; **23** 123
Famous Restaurants Inc., **33** 139–40
FAN, **13** 370
Fancom Holding B.V., **43** 130
**Fannie Mae, 45 156–59 (upd.)**
Fannie May Candy Shops Inc., **36** 309
**Fansteel Inc., 19 150–52**
Fantastic Sam's, **26** 476
Fanthing Electrical Corp., **44** 132
Fantle's Drug Stores, **16** 160
Fantus Co., **IV** 605
**Fanuc Ltd., III 482–83**; **17 172–74 (upd.)**
Fanzz, **29** 282
**FAO Schwarz, 46 187–90**
Faprena, **25** 85
Far East Airlines, **6** 70
Far East Machinery Co., **III** 581
Far Eastern Air Transport, Inc., **23** 380
Far West Restaurants, **I** 547
Faraday National Corporation, **10** 269
**Farah Incorporated, 24 156–58**
Farben. *See* I.G. Farbenindustrie AG.
Farbenfabriken Bayer A.G., **I** 309
Farberware, Inc., **27** 287–88
Farbro Corp., **45** 15
Farbwerke Hoechst A.G., **I** 346–47; **IV** 486; **13** 262
Farine Lactée Henri Nestlé, **II** 545
Farinon Corp., **II** 38
Farley Candy Co., **15** 190
Farley Industries, **25** 166
**Farley Northwest Industries Inc., I 440–41**
Farm Credit Bank of St. Louis, **8** 489
Farm Credit Bank of St. Paul, **8** 489–90
Farm Electric Services Ltd., **6** 586
**Farm Family Holdings, Inc., 39 155–58**
Farm Fresh Foods, **25** 332
**Farm Journal Corporation, 42 131–34**
Farm Power Laboratory, **6** 565
Farmer Jack, **16** 247; **44** 145
Farmers and Mechanics Bank of Georgetown, **13** 439
Farmers and Merchants Bank, **II** 349
Farmers Bank of Delaware, **II** 315–16
**Farmers Insurance Group of Companies, 23** 286; **25 154–56**; **29** 397
Farmers' Loan and Trust Co., **II** 254; **9** 124
Farmers National Bank & Trust Co., **9** 474
Farmers Petroleum, Inc., **48** 175
Farmers Regional Cooperative, **II** 536
**Farmland Foods, Inc., IV** 474; **7** 17, **7 174–75**
**Farmland Industries, Inc., 39** 282; **48 172–75**
Farnam Cheshire Lime Co., **III** 763

**Farrar, Straus and Giroux Inc., 15 158–60**; **35** 451
FASC. *See* First Analysis Securities Corporation.
Fasco Consumer Products, **19** 360
Fasco Industries, **III** 509; **13** 369
Faserwerke Hüls GmbH., **I** 350
Fashion Bar, Inc., **24** 457
Fashion Bug, **8** 97
Fashion Co., **II** 503; **10** 324
Fasquelle, **IV** 618
Fasson. *See* Avery Dennison Corporation.
Fast Air, **31** 305
Fast Fare, **7** 102
**Fastenal Company, 14 185–87**; **42 135–38 (upd.)**
Fata European Group, **IV** 187; **19** 348
Fateco Förlag, **14** 556
FATS, Inc., **27** 156, 158
Fatum, **III** 308
Faugere et Jutheau, **III** 283
Faulkner, Dawkins & Sullivan, **II** 450
Fauquet, **25** 85
Favorite Plastics, **19** 414
Fawcett Books, **13** 429
**Fay's Inc., 17 175–77**
Fayette Tubular Products, **7** 116–17
Fayva, **13** 359–61
**Fazoli's Systems, Inc., 13** 321; **27 145–47**
FB&T Corporation, **14** 154
FBC. *See* First Boston Corp.
FBO. *See* Film Booking Office of America.
FC Holdings, Inc., **26** 363
FCBC, **IV** 174
FCC. *See* Federal Communications Commission.
FCC National Bank, **II** 286
FCI. *See* Framatome SA.
FDIC. *See* Federal Deposit Insurance Corp.
Fearn International, **II** 525; **13** 293
Feather Fine, **27** 361
**Featherlite Inc., 28 127–29**
Feature Enterprises Inc., **19** 452
Fechheimer Bros. Co., **III** 215; **18** 60, 62
**Fedders Corporation, 18 172–75**; **43 162–67 (upd.)**
Federal Barge Lines, **6** 487
Federal Bearing and Bushing, **I** 158–59
Federal Bicycle Corporation of America, **11** 3
Federal Cartridge, **26** 363
Federal Coca-Cola Bottling Co., **10** 222
Federal Communications Commission, **6** 164–65; **9** 321
Federal Deposit Insurance Corp., **II** 261–62, 285, 337; **12** 30, 79
Federal Electric, **I** 463; **III** 653
**Federal Express Corporation, II** 620; **V 451–53**; **6** 345–46, 385–86, 389; **12** 180, 192; **13** 19; **14** 517; **17** 504–05; **18** 315–17, 368, 370; **24** 22, 133; **25** 148; **26** 441; **27** 20, 22, 471, 475; **34** 15, 17; **39** 33, 35; **41** 245–47. *See also* FedEx Corporation.
Federal Home Life Insurance Co., **III** 263; **IV** 623
Federal Home Loan Bank, **II** 182
Federal Home Loan Mortgage Corp., **18** 168; **25** 427
Federal Insurance Co., **III** 220–21; **14** 108–109; **37** 83–85
Federal Lead Co., **IV** 32
Federal Light and Traction Company, **6** 561–62
Federal Mining and Smelting Co., **IV** 32
**Federal-Mogul Corporation, I 158–60**; **III** 596; **10 292–94 (upd.)**; **26 139–43 (upd.)**; **47** 279
**Federal National Mortgage Association, II 410–11**; **18** 168; **25** 427. *See also* Fannie Mae.
Federal Pacific Electric, **II** 121; **9** 440
Federal Packaging and Partition Co., **8** 476
Federal Packaging Corp., **19** 78
**Federal Paper Board Company, Inc., I** 524; **8 173–75**; **15** 229; **47** 189
Federal Paper Mills, **IV** 248
Federal Power, **18** 473
**Federal Prison Industries, Inc., 34 157–60**
Federal Reserve Bank of New York, **21** 68
Federal Savings and Loan Insurance Corp., **16** 346
**Federal Signal Corp., 10 295–97**
Federal Steel Co., **II** 330; **IV** 572; **7** 549
Federal Trade Commission, **6** 260; **9** 370
Federal Yeast Corp., **IV** 410
Federale Mynbou, **IV** 90–93
**Federated Department Stores Inc., IV** 703; **V** 25–28; **9 209–12**; **10** 282; **11** 349; **12** 37, 523; **13** 43, 260; **15** 88; **16** 61, 206; **17** 560; **18** 523; **22** 406; **23** 60; **27** 346–48; **30** 379; **31 190–194 (upd.)**; **35** 368; **36** 201, 204; **37** 13
Federated Development Company, **8** 349
Federated Metals Corp., **IV** 32
Federated Publications, **IV** 612; **7** 191
Federated Timbers, **I** 422
**Fédération Internationale de Football Association, 27 148–51**
Federation Nationale d'Achats des Cadres. *See* FNAC.
**FedEx Corporation, 18** 128, **176–79 (upd.)**, 535; **33** 20, 22; **34** 474; **42 139–44 (upd.)**; **46** 71
Fedmart, **V** 162
FEE Technology, **29** 461–62
Feed-Rite Controls, Inc., **16** 270
Feffer & Simons, **16** 46
Feikes & Sohn KG, **IV** 325
Feinblech-Contiglühe, **IV** 103
Felco. *See* Farmers Regional Cooperative.
**Feld Entertainment, Inc., 32 186–89 (upd.)**
**Feldmühle Nobel AG, II** 50–51; **III 692–95**; **IV** 142, 325, 337; **21** 330; **36** 449
Felixstowe Ltd., **18** 254
**Fellowes Manufacturing Company, 28 130–32**
Felten & Guilleaume, **IV** 25
Femsa, **19** 473. *See also* Formento Económico Mexicano, S.A. de C.V.
Femtech, **8** 513
Fendall Company, **40** 96, 98
Fendel Schiffahrts-Aktiengesellschaft, **6** 426
**Fender Musical Instruments Company, 16 200–02**; **43 168–72 (upd.)**
Fendi S.p.A., **45** 344
Fenestra Inc., **IV** 136
Fenicia Group, **22** 320
Fenn, Wright & Manson, **25** 121–22
Fenner & Beane, **II** 424
Fenton Hill American Limited, **29** 510
Fenwal Laboratories, **I** 627; **10** 141
Fenway Partners, **47** 361
**Fenwick & West LLP, 34 161–63**, 512
Ferembal S.A., **25** 512
Ferfin, **24** 341
Fergus Brush Electric Company, **18** 402
Ferguson Machine Co., **8** 135
Ferguson Manufacturing Company, **25** 164
Ferguson Radio Corp., **I** 531–32
Ferienreise GmbH., **II** 164
Fermec Manufacturing Limited, **40** 432
Fermentaciones Mexicanas S.A. de C.V., **III** 43; **48** 250
Fernando Roqué, **6** 404; **26** 243
Ferngas, **IV** 486
**Ferolito, Vultaggio & Sons, 27 152–55**
Ferranti Business Communications, **20** 75
Ferranti Ltd., **II** 81; **6** 240
**Ferrari S.p.A., I** 162; **11** 103; **13 218–20**; **36 196–200 (upd.)**
**Ferrellgas Partners, L.P., 35 173–75**
Ferrier Hodgson, **10** 170
**Ferro Corporation, III** 536; **8 176–79**; **9** 10; **26** 230
Ferro Engineering Co., **17** 357
Ferrocarril del Noreste, S.A. de C.V. *See* Grupo Transportación Ferroviaria Mexicana, S.A. de C.V.
Ferrovial. *See* Grupo Ferrovail
Ferroxcube Corp. of America, **13** 397
Ferrum Inc., **24** 144
Ferruzzi Agricola Finanziario, **I** 369; **7** 81–83
Ferruzzi Finanziaria S.p.A., **24** 341; **36** 186
Fesca, **III** 417–18
Fetzer Vineyards, **10** 182
FFI Fragrances. *See* Elizabeth Arden, Inc.
**FHP International Corporation, 6 184–86**; **17** 166, 168; **44** 174
Fianzas Monterrey, **19** 189
**Fiat S.p.A., I** 154, 157, **161–63**, 459–60, 466, 479; **II** 280; **III** 206, 543, 591; **IV** 420; **9** 10; **11 102–04 (upd.)**, 139; **13** 17, 27–29, 218–20; **16** 322; **17** 24; **22** 379–81; **36** 32–34, 196–97, 199, 240, 243
Fibamex, **17** 106
Fibar, **44** 261
Fiber Chemical Corporation, **7** 308
Fiberglas Canada, **III** 722
Fiberite, Inc., **27** 117; **28** 195
**FiberMark, Inc., 37 139–42**
Fibermux Corporation, **10** 19; **30** 7
Fibic Corp., **18** 118
Fibre Containers, **IV** 249
**Fibreboard Corporation, IV** 304; **12** 318; **14** 110; **16 203–05**
FibreChem, Inc., **8** 347
Fibro Tambor, S.A. de C.V., **8** 476
Fichtel & Sachs AG, **III** 566; **14** 328; **38** 299
Fidata Corp., **II** 317
Fidelco Capital Group, **10** 420
Fidelio Software GmbH, **18** 335, 337
Fidelity and Casualty Co. of New York, **III** 242
Fidelity and Guaranty Life Insurance Co., **III** 396–97
Fidelity Exploration & Production Company, **42** 249, 253
Fidelity Federal Savings and Loan, **II** 420
Fidelity Fire Insurance Co., **III** 240
Fidelity Insurance of Canada, **III** 396–97
**Fidelity Investments Inc., II 412–13**; **III** 588; **8** 194; **9** 239; **14 188–90 (upd.)**; **18** 552; **19** 113; **21** 147; **22** 52. *See also* FMR Corp.

Fidelity Leasing Corporation, **42** 312–13
Fidelity Life Association, **III** 269
Fidelity Mutual Insurance Co., **III** 231
Fidelity National Life Insurance Co., **III** 191
Fidelity National Title, **19** 92
Fidelity Oil Group, **7** 324
Fidelity-Phenix Fire Insurance Co., **III** 240–42
Fidelity Title and Trust Co., **II** 315
Fidelity Trust Co., **II** 230; **33** 293
Fidelity Union Life Insurance Co., **III** 185
Fidenas Investment Ltd., **30** 185
Fides Holding, **21** 146
Field Corporation, **18** 355
Field Enterprises Educational Corporation, **16** 252; **26** 15; **43** 208
Field Enterprises, Inc., **IV** 672; **12** 554; **19** 404
Field Group plc, **30** 120
Field Limited Partnership, **22** 441
Field Oy, **10** 113
**Fieldale Farms Corporation**, **23 191–93**; **25** 185–86
Fieldco Guide Dog Foundation, **42** 207
**Fieldcrest Cannon, Inc.**, **8** 32–33; **9 213–17**; **16** 535; **19** 276, 305; **31 195–200 (upd.)**; **41** 299–301
Fieldstone Cabinetry, **III** 571; **20** 362
**Fielmann AG**, **31 201–03**
Fiesta Restaurants Inc., **33** 139–40
FIFA. *See* Fédération Internationale de Football Association.
Fifa International, **39** 58
Fifteen Oil, **I** 526
Fifth Generation Systems Inc., **10** 509
**Fifth Third Bancorp**, **II** 291; **9** 475; **11** 466; **13 221–23**; **31 204–208 (upd.)**
50-Off Stores, **23** 177. *See also* LOT$OFF Corporation.
**Figgie International Inc.**, **7 176–78**; **24** 403–04
Figi's Inc., **9** 218, 220
FII Limited, **38** 197
Fil-Mag Group, **29** 461
**Fila Holding S.p.A.**, **20 216–18**; **39** 60
Filene's, **V** 132, 134
Filene's Basement. *See* Value City Department Stores, Inc.
Filergie S.A., **15** 355
Filipacchi Medias S.A. *See* Hachette Filipacchi Medias S.A.
Filiz Lastex, S.A., **15** 386
Filles S.A. de C.V., **7** 115; **25** 126
Film Booking Office of America, **II** 88
Films for the Humanities, Inc., **22** 441
Filofax Inc., **41** 120, 123
Filter Queen-Canada, **17** 234
Filterfresh Corporation, **39** 409
Filtertek, Inc., **24** 425
Filtrol Corp., **IV** 123
Filtrona International Ltd., **31** 77
Filtros Baldwin de Mexico, **17** 106
Filtros Continental, **17** 106
**Fimalac S.A.**, **37 143–45**
Fimaser, **21** 101
Fimestic, **21** 101
Fin. Comit SpA, **II** 192
**FINA, Inc.**, **7 179–81**; **26** 368
Finalrealm Limited, **42** 404
Financial Computer Services, Inc., **11** 111
Financial Corp. of Indonesia, **II** 257
Financial Data Services, Inc., **11** 111
Financial Investment Corp. of Asia, **III** 197
Financial Network Marketing Company, **11** 482
Financial News Ltd., **IV** 658
Financial News Network, Inc., **25** 507; **31** 147
Financial Security Assurance Inc., **III** 765; **25** 497
Financial Services Corp., **III** 306–07
Financial Services Corporation of Michigan, **11** 163
Financial Systems, Inc., **11** 111
Financial Technologies International, **17** 497
The Financial Times Group, **46** 337
Financiera Aceptaciones, **19** 189
Financière Crédit Suisse-First Boston, **II** 268, 402–04
Financiere de Suez, **II** 295
Financière Saint Dominique, **9** 151–52
FinansSkandic A.B., **II** 352–53
Finast. *See* First National Supermarkets, Inc.
Fincantieri, **I** 466–67
Find-A-Home Service, Inc., **21** 96
Findomestic, **21** 101
Findus, **II** 547; **25** 85
Fine Art Developments Ltd., **15** 340
Fine Fare, **II** 465, 609, 628–29
Fine Fragrances, **22** 213
Finelettrica, **I** 465–66
Finesco, LLC, **37** 200–01
Finevest Services Inc., **15** 526
**Fingerhut Companies, Inc.**, **I** 613; **V** 148; **9 218–20**; **15** 401; **18** 133; **31** 190; **34** 232; **36 201–05 (upd.)**; **37** 130
Fininvest Group, **IV** 587–88
**The Finish Line, Inc.**, **29 186–88**
**FinishMaster, Inc.**, **17** 310–11; **24 159–61**
Finland Wood Co., **IV** 275
**Finlay Enterprises, Inc.**, **16 206–08**
Finlay Forest Industries, **IV** 297
Finmare, **I** 465, 467
Finmeccanica S.p.A., **II** 86; **13** 28; **23** 83; **36** 34
**Finnair Oy**, **I** 120; **6 87–89**; **25 157–60 (upd.)**; **33** 50; **34** 398
Finnforest Oy, **IV** 316
Finnigan Corporation, **11** 513
Finnish Cable Works, **II** 69; **17** 352
Finnish Fiberboard Ltd., **IV** 302
Oy Finnish Peroxides Ab, **IV** 300
Finnish Rubber Works, **II** 69; **17** 352
Oy Finnlines Ltd., **IV** 276
Finsa, **II** 196
FinSer Capital Corporation, **17** 262
Finservizi SpA, **II** 192
Finsider, **I** 465–66; **IV** 125
Firan Motor Coach, Inc., **17** 83
Fire Association of Philadelphia, **III** 342–43
**Firearms Training Systems, Inc.**, **27 156–58**
**Fireman's Fund Insurance Company**, **I** 418; **II** 398, 457; **III** 214, **250–52**, 263; **10** 62
Firemen's Insurance Co. of Newark, **III** 241–42
Firestone Tire and Rubber Co., **III** 440, 697; **V** 234–35; **8** 80; **9** 247; **15** 355; **17** 182; **18** 320; **20** 259–62; **21** 73–74
Firma Hamburger Kaffee-Import- Geschäft Emil Tengelmann. *See* Tengelmann Group.
The First, **10** 340
First Acadiana National Bank, **11** 107
**First Albany Companies Inc.**, **37 146–48**
**First Alert, Inc.**, **28 133–35**
First American. *See* Bremer Financial Corp.
First American Bank Corporation, **8** 188; **41** 178
First American Media, Inc., **24** 199
First American National Bank, **19** 378
First American National Bank-Eastern, **11** 111
First Analysis Securities Corporation, **22** 5
First and Merchants, **10** 426
First Atlanta Corporation, **16** 523
First Atlantic Capital, Ltd., **28** 340, 342
First Bancard, Inc., **11** 106
First BanCorporation, **13** 467
First Bank and Trust of Mechanicsburg, **II** 342
First Bank of Savannah, **16** 522
First Bank of the United States, **II** 213, 253
**First Bank System Inc.**, **11** 130; **12 164–66**; **13** 347–48; **24** 393. *See also* U.S. Bancorp
First Boston Corp., **II** 208, 257, 267–69, 402–04, 406–07, 426, 434, 441; **9** 378, 386; **12** 439; **13** 152, 342; **21** 145–46. *See also* CSFB.
**First Brands Corporation**, **8 180–82**; **16** 44
First Capital Financial, **8** 229
First Carolina Investors Inc., **17** 357
**First Chicago Corporation**, **II 284–87**. *See also* Bank One Corporation.
First Chicago Venture Capital, **24** 516
**First Choice Holidays PLC**, **40 185–87**, 284–85
First Cincinnati, Inc., **41** 133
First City Bank of Rosemead, **II** 348
First Colony Farms, **II** 584
First Colony Life Insurance, **I** 334–35; **10** 290
**First Commerce Bancshares, Inc.**, **15 161–63**
**First Commerce Corporation**, **11 105–07**
First Commercial Savings and Loan, **10** 340
First Consumers National Bank, **10** 491; **27** 429
First Dallas, Ltd., **II** 415
**First Data Corporation**, **10** 63; **18** 516–18, 537; **24** 393 **30 195–98 (upd.)**; **46** 250
First Data Management Company of Oklahoma City, **11** 112
First Delaware Life Insurance Co., **III** 254
First Deposit Corp., **III** 218–19
**First Empire State Corporation**, **11 108–10**
First Engine and Boiler Insurance Co. Ltd., **III** 406
**First Executive Corporation**, **III 253–55**
First Express, **48** 177
First Federal Savings & Loan Assoc., **IV** 343; **9** 173
First Federal Savings and Loan Association of Crisp County, **10** 92
First Federal Savings and Loan Association of Hamburg, **10** 91

First Federal Savings and Loan Association of Fort Myers, **9** 476
First Federal Savings and Loan Association of Kalamazoo, **9** 482
First Federal Savings Bank of Brunswick, **10** 92
**First Fidelity Bank, N.A., New Jersey, 9 221–23**
First Fidelity Bank of Rockville, **13** 440
First Financial Insurance, **41** 178
**First Financial Management Corporation, 11 111–13**; **18** 542; **25** 183; **30** 195
First Florida Banks, **9** 59
**First Hawaiian, Inc., 11 114–16**
First Health, **III** 373
FIRST HEALTH Strategies, **11** 113
First Healthcare, **14** 242
First Heights, fsa, **8** 437
First Hospital Corp., **15** 122
First Industrial Corp., **II** 41
First Insurance Agency, Inc., **17** 527
First Insurance Co. of Hawaii, **III** 191, 242
First International Trust, **IV** 91
**First Interstate Bancorp, II** 228, **288–90**; **8** 295; **9** 334; **17** 546
First Investment Advisors, **11** 106
First Investors Management Corp., **11** 106
First Jersey National Bank, **II** 334
First Leisure Corporation plc. *See* Esporta plc.
First Liberty Financial Corporation, **11** 457
First Line Insurance Services, Inc., **8** 436
First Madison Bank, **14** 192
First Maryland Bancorp, **16** 14
First Mid America, **II** 445; **22** 406
**First Mississippi Corporation, 8 183–86.** *See also* ChemFirst, Inc.
First Mississippi National, **14** 41
First National Bank, **10** 298; **13** 467
First National Bank (Revere), **II** 208
First National Bank and Trust Company, **22** 4
First National Bank and Trust Company of Kalamazoo, **8** 187–88
First National Bank and Trust of Oklahoma City, **II** 289
First National Bank in Albuquerque, **11** 119
First National Bank of Akron, **9** 475
First National Bank of Allentown, **11** 296
First National Bank of Atlanta, **16** 522
First National Bank of Azusa, **II** 382
First National Bank of Boston, **II** 207–08, 402; **12** 310; **13** 446
First National Bank of Carrollton, **9** 475
First National Bank of Chicago, **II** 242, 257, 284–87; **III** 96–97; **IV** 135–36
First National Bank of Commerce, **11** 106
First National Bank of Harrington, Delaware. *See* J.C. Penny National Bank.
First National Bank of Hartford, **13** 466
First National Bank of Hawaii, **11** 114
First National Bank of Highland, **11** 109
First National Bank of Houma, **21** 522
The First National Bank of Lafayette, **11** 107
The First National Bank of Lake Charles, **11** 107
First National Bank of Lake City, **II** 336; **10** 425
First National Bank of Mexico, New York, **II** 231
First National Bank of Minneapolis, **22** 426–27
First National Bank of New York, **II** 254, 330
First National Bank of Raleigh, **II** 336
First National Bank of Salt Lake, **11** 118
First National Bank of Seattle, **8** 469–70
First National Bank of York, **II** 317
First National Bankshares, Inc., **21** 524
First National Boston Corp., **II** 208
First National Casualty Co., **III** 203
First National City Bank, **9** 124; **16** 13
First National City Bank of New York, **II** 254; **9** 124
First National City Corp., **III** 220–21
First National Holding Corporation, **16** 522
First National Insurance Co., **III** 352
First National Life Insurance Co., **III** 218
First National Supermarkets, Inc., **II** 641–42; **9** 452
First Nations Gaming, Ltd., **44** 334
**First Nationwide Bank, 8** 30; **14 191–93**
First Nationwide Financial Corp., **I** 167; **11** 139
First Nationwide Holdings Inc., **28** 246
First New England Bankshares Corp., **13** 467
First Nitrogen, Inc., **8** 184
**First of America Bank Corporation, 8 187–89**
First of America Bank-Monroe, **9** 476
First of Boston, **II** 402–03
First Omni Bank NA, **16** 14; **18** 518; **43** 8
**First Pacific Company Limited, 18 180–82**
First Penn-Pacific Life Insurance Co., **III** 276
First Physician Care, Inc., **36** 367
First Pick Stores, **12** 458
First Railroad and Banking Company, **11** 111
First Republic Bank of Texas, **II** 336
First Republic Corp., **III** 383; **14** 483
First RepublicBank Corporation, **II** 337; **10** 425–26
First Savings and Loan, **10** 339
First Seattle Dexter Horton National Bank, **8** 470
First Security Bank of Missoula, **35** 197–99
**First Security Corporation, 11 117–19**; **38** 491
First Signature Bank and Trust Co., **III** 268
First Sport Ltd., **39** 60
1st State Bank & Trust, **9** 474
First State Bank Southwest Indiana, **41** 178–79
First SunAmerican Life Insurance Company, **11** 482
**First Team Sports, Inc., 15** 396–97; **22 202–04**
**First Tennessee National Corporation, 11 120–21**; **48 176–79 (upd.)**
First Texas Pharmaceuticals, **I** 678
First Trust and Savings Bank, **II** 284
First Trust Bank, **16** 14
**First Union Corporation, 10 298–300**; **24** 482; **37** 148. *See also* Wachovia Corporation.
First Union Trust and Savings Bank, **II** 284–85; **11** 126; **22** 52
First United Financial Services Inc., **II** 286
**First USA, Inc., 11 122–24**
First USA Paymentech, **24** 393
**First Virginia Banks, Inc., 11 125–26**
First Westchester National Bank of New Rochelle, **II** 236
First Western Bank and Trust Co., **II** 289
First Women's Bank of New York, **23** 3
First Worth Corporation, **19** 232
**The First Years Inc., 46 191–94**
FirstAir Inc., **48** 113
Firstamerica Bancorporation, **II** 288–89
**Firstar Corporation, 11 127–29**; **33 152–55 (upd.)**
FirstBancorp., **13** 467
FirstGroup plc, **38** 321
FirstMiss, Inc., **8** 185
FirstPage USA Inc., **41** 265
Firth Carpet, **19** 275
Fischbach & Moore, **III** 535
Fischbach Corp., **III** 198; **8** 536–37
FISCOT, **10** 337
**Fiserv Inc., 11 130–32**; **33 156–60 (upd.)**
Fisher & Company, **9** 16
Fisher Body Company, **I** 171; **10** 325
Fisher Broadcasting Co., **15** 164
Fisher-Camuto Corp., **14** 441
**Fisher Companies, Inc., 15 164–66**
**Fisher Controls International, Inc., 13 224–26**; **15** 405, 407; **29** 330; **46** 171
Fisher Foods, Inc., **II** 602; **9** 451, 452; **13** 237; **41** 11, 13
Fisher Marine, **III** 444; **22** 116
Fisher Nut, **14** 275
**Fisher-Price Inc., II** 559–60; **12 167–69**, 410–11; **13** 317; **25** 314, 380; **32 190–94 (upd.)**; **34** 365
**Fisher Scientific International Inc., III** 511–12; **24 162–66**; **25** 260
Fishers Agricultural Holdings, **II** 466
Fishers Nutrition, **II** 466
Fishers Seed and Grain, **II** 466
Fishery Department of Tamura Kisen Co., **II** 552
Fisk Telephone Systems, **6** 313
**Fiskars Corporation, 33 161–64**
Fiskeby Board AB, **48** 344
**Fisons plc, 9 224–27**; **23 194–97 (upd.)**
Fitch IBCA Inc., **37** 143, 145
Fitch Lovell PLC, **13** 103
Fitchburg Daily News Co., **IV** 581
Fitchburg Gas and Electric Light, **37** 406
Fitchell and Sachs, **III** 495
Fitel, **III** 491
Fitzsimmons Stores Inc., **16** 452
Fitzwilton Public Limited Company, **12** 529; **34** 496
Five Bros. Inc., **19** 456
Five Star Entertainment Inc., **28** 241
546274 Alberta Ltd., **48** 97
FKM Advertising, **27** 280
FL Industries Holdings, Inc., **11** 516
Flachglass A.G., **II** 474
Flagship Resources, **22** 495
**Flagstar Companies, Inc., 10 301–03**; **29** 150. *See also* Advantica Restaurant Group, Inc.
Flair Corporation, **18** 467
Flair Fold, **25** 11
Flanagan McAdam Resources Inc., **IV** 76
Flapdoodles, **15** 291
Flashes Publishers, Inc., **36** 341
Flatbush Gas Co., **6** 455–56
Flatiron Mandolin Company, **16** 239
Flatow, Moore, Bryan, and Fairburn, **21** 33
Flavors Holdings Inc., **38** 294

Fleck Controls, Inc., **26** 361, 363
**Fleer Corporation**, **10** 402; **13** 519; **15 167–69**; **19** 386; **34** 447; **37** 295
Fleet Aerospace Corporation. *See* Magellan Aerospace Corporation.
Fleet Call, Inc., **10** 431–32
**Fleet Financial Group, Inc.**, **IV** 687; **9 228–30**; **12** 31; **13** 468; **18** 535; **38** 13, 393
Fleet Holdings, **28** 503
**FleetBoston Financial Corporation**, **36 206–14 (upd.)**
Fleetway, **7** 244
**Fleetwood Enterprises, Inc.**, **III 484–85**; **13** 155; **17** 83; **21** 153; **22 205–08 (upd.)**; **33** 399
Fleischmann Co., **II** 544; **7** 367
Fleischmann Malting Co., **I** 420–21; **11** 22
Fleming Chinese Restaurants Inc., **37** 297
**Fleming Companies, Inc.**, **II 624–25**, 671; **7** 450; **12** 107, 125; **13** 335–37; **17 178–81 (upd.)**; **18** 506–07; **23** 407; **24** 529; **26** 449; **28** 152, 154; **31** 25; **34** 198
Fleming Foodservice, **26** 504
Fleming Machine Co., **III** 435
Fleming-Wilson Co., **II** 624
**Fletcher Challenge Ltd.**, **III** 687; **IV** 250, **278–80**; **19 153–57 (upd.)**; **25** 12
**Fleury Michon S.A.**, **39 159–61**
Fleuve Noir, **IV** 614
Flex Elektrowerkzeuge GmbH, **26** 363
Flex Interim, **16** 421; **43** 308
Flex-O-Lite, **14** 325
Flexi-Van Corporations, **II** 492; **20** 118
Flexible Packaging, **I** 605
**Flexsteel Industries Inc.**, **15 170–72**; **41 159–62 (upd.)**
**Flextronics International Ltd.**, **12** 451; **38 186–89**
Flexys, **16** 462
FLGI Holding Company, **10** 321
Flick Industrial Group, **II** 280, 283; **III** 692–95
Flight One Logistics, Inc., **22** 311
Flight Refuelling Limited. *See* Cobham plc.
Flight Transportation Co., **II** 408
**FlightSafety International, Inc.**, **9 231–33**; **29 189–92 (upd.)**
Flint and Walling Water Systems, **III** 570; **20** 362
Flint Eaton & Co., **I** 627
**Flint Ink Corporation**, **13 227–29**; **41 163–66 (upd.)**
Flip Chip Technologies, LLC, **33** 248
Florafax International, Inc., **37** 162
Floral City Furniture Company, **14** 302–03
Flori Roberts, Inc., **11** 208
**Florida Crystals Inc.**, **35 176–78**
Florida Cypress Gardens, Inc., **IV** 623
Florida Distillers Company, **27** 479
Florida East Coast Railway Company, **8** 486–87; **12** 278
Florida Flavors, **44** 137
Florida Frozen Foods, **13** 244
**Florida Gaming Corporation**, **47 130–33**
Florida Gas Co., **15** 129
Florida Gas Transmission Company, **6** 578
Florida National Banks of Florida, Inc., **II** 252
Florida Panthers Hockey Club, Ltd., **37** 33, 35
Florida Presbyterian College, **9** 187
**Florida Progress Corp.**, **V 621–22**; **23 198–200 (upd.)**
**Florida Rock Industries, Inc.**, **23** 326; **46 195–97**
Florida Steel Corp., **14** 156
Florida Telephone Company, **6** 323
**Florida's Natural Growers**, **45 160–62**
FloridaGulf Airlines, **11** 300
Florimex Verwaltungsgesellschaft mbH, **12** 109
**Florists' Transworld Delivery, Inc.**, **28 136–38**
**Florsheim Shoe Group Inc.**, **III** 528–29; **9** 135, **234–36**; **12** 308; **16** 546; **31 209–212 (upd.)**; **39** 170, 172, 174
**Flour City International, Inc.**, **44 181–83**
Flow Laboratories, **14** 98
Flow Measurement, **26** 293
Flower Gate Inc., **I** 266; **21** 320
Flower Time, Inc., **12** 179, 200
**Flowers Industries, Inc.**, **12 170–71**; **35 179–82 (upd.)**. *See also* Keebler Foods Company.
**Flowserve Corporation**, **33 165–68**
Floyd West & Co., **6** 290
Fluent, Inc., **29** 4–6
Fluf N'Stuf, Inc., **12** 425
**Fluke Corporation**, **15 173–75**
Flunch, **37** 22
**Fluor Corporation**, **I 569–71**, 586; **III** 248; **IV** 171, 533, 535, 576; **6** 148–49; **8 190–93 (upd.)**; **12** 244; **26** 220, 433; **34 164–69 (upd.)**; **47** 340
Fluor Daniel Inc., **41** 148
The Fluorocarbon Company. *See* Furon Company.
Flushing Federal Savings & Loan Association, **16** 346
Flushing National Bank, **II** 230
**Flying J Inc.**, **19 158–60**
Flying Tiger Line, **V** 452; **6** 388; **25** 146; **39** 33
Flymo, **III** 478, 480; **22** 26
**FMC Corp.**, **I 442–44**, 679; **II** 513; **11 133–35 (upd.)**; **14** 457; **22** 415; **30** 471; **47** 238
**FMR Corp.**, **II** 412; **8 194–96**; **14** 188; **22** 413; **30** 331; **32 195–200 (upd.)**
FMXI, Inc. *See* Foamex International Inc.
FN Life Insurance Co., **III** 192
FN Manufacturing Co., **12** 71
**FNAC**, **21 224–26**; **26** 160
FNC Comercio, **III** 221
FNCB. *See* First National City Bank of New York.
FNMA. *See* Federal National Mortgage Association.
FNN. *See* Financial News Network.
**Foamex International Inc.**, **17 182–85**; **26** 500
Focal Surgery, Inc., **27** 355
Focke-Wulf, **III** 641; **16** 7
*FOCUS*, **44** 402
Fodens Ltd., **I** 186
Fodor's Travel Guides, **13** 429
Fogdog Inc., **36** 347
Fokker. *See* N.V. Koninklijke Nederlandse Vliegtuigenfabriek Fokker.
Fokker Aircraft Corporation of America, **9** 16
Fokker-VFW, **I** 41–42; **12** 191
**Foley & Lardner**, **28 139–42**
Folgers, **III** 52
Folksamerica Holding Company, Inc., **48** 431
Folland Aircraft, **I** 50; **III** 508; **24** 85
**Follett Corporation**, **12 172–74**; **16** 47; **39 162–65 (upd.)**; **43** 61
Follis DeVito Verdi. *See* De Vito/Verdi.
Fomento de Valores, S.A. de C.V., **23** 170
Fomento Economico Mexicano, S.A. de C.V. *See* Femsa.
Fonda Group, **36** 462
Fondiaria Group, **III** 351
Fonditalia Management, **III** 347
Font & Vaamonde, **6** 27
Font Vella, **II** 474
FONTAC, **II** 73
Fontana Asphalt, **III** 674
Food City, **II** 649–50
Food Fair, **19** 480
Food 4 Less Supermarkets, Inc., **II** 624; **17** 558–61
Food Giant, **II** 670
Food Ingredients Technologies, **25** 367
Food Investments Ltd., **II** 465
Food King, **20** 306
**Food Lion, Inc.**, **II 626–27**; **7** 450; **15 176–78 (upd.)**, 270; **18** 8; **21** 508; **33** 306; **44** 145
Food Machinery Corp. *See* FMC Corp.
Food Marketing Corp., **II** 668; **18** 504
Food Town Inc., **II** 626–27
Food World, **26** 46; **31** 372
**Foodarama Supermarkets, Inc.**, **28 143–45**
**FoodBrands America, Inc.**, **21** 290; **22** 510; **23 201–04**. *See also* Doskocil Companies, Inc.
FoodLand Distributors, **II** 625, 645, 682
**Foodmaker, Inc.**, **II** 562; **13** 152, 426; **14 194–96**
Foodstuffs, **9** 144
Foodtown, **II** 626; **V** 35; **15** 177; **24** 528
FoodUSA.com, **43** 24
Foodways National, Inc., **12** 531; **13** 383
Foot Locker, **V** 226; **14** 293–95. *See also* Venator Group Inc.
Footaction. *See* Footstar, Incorporated.
**Foote Cone & Belding Communications Inc.**, **I 12–15**, 28, 34; **11** 51; **13** 517; **22** 395; **25** 90–91. *See also* True North Communications Inc.
Foote Mineral Company, **7** 386–87
Footquarters, **14** 293, 295
**Footstar, Incorporated**, **24 167–69**
Forages et Exploitations Pétrolières. *See* Forex.
**Forbes Inc.**, **30 199–201**
**The Ford Foundation**, **34 170–72**
**Ford Motor Company**, **I** 10, 14, 20–21, 136, 142, 145, 152, 154–55, 162–63, **164–68**, 172, 183, 186, 201, 203–04, 280, 297, 337, 354, 423, 478, 484, 540, 693; **II** 7–8, 33, 60, 86, 143, 415; **III** 58, 259, 283, 439, 452, 495, 515, 555, 568, 591, 603, 637–38, 651, 725; **IV** 22, 187, 597, 722; **6** 27, 51; **7** 377, 461, 520–21; **8** 70, 74–75, 117, 372–73, 375, 505–06; **9** 94, 118, 126, 190, 283–84, 325, 341–43; **10** 32, 241, 260, 264–65, 279–80, 290, 353, 407, 430, 460, 465; **11** 53–54, 103–04, **136–40 (upd.)**, 263, 326, 339, 350, 528–29; **12** 68, 91, 294, 311; **13** 28, 219, 285, 287, 345, 555; **14** 191–92; **15** 91, 171, 513, 515; **16** 321–22; **17** 183, 303–04; **18** 112, 308, 319; **19** 11, 125, 221, 223, 482, 484; **20** 359; **21** 153, 200, 503; **22** 175, 380–81; **23** 143, 339–41, 434; **24** 12; **25** 90, 93,

142–43, 224, 226, 358; **26** 176, 452, 501; **27** 20, 202; **29** 265; **34** 133–34, 136, 303, 305; **36** 34, 180, 198, **215–21 (upd.)**, 242–43; **38** 86, 458–59; **40** 134; **41** 280–81
**Ford Motor Company, S.A. de C.V.**, **20 219–21**
Ford New Holland, Inc. *See* New Holland N.V.
Ford Transport Co., **I** 112; **6** 103
Fording Inc., **45** 80
Fordyce Lumber Co., **IV** 281; **9** 259
**FORE Systems, Inc.**, **25 161–63**; **33** 289
Forefront Communications, **22** 194
Foreman State Banks, **II** 285
Foremost Dairies, **47** 234–35
Foremost Dairy of California, **I** 496–97
Foremost-McKesson Inc., **I** 496–97, **III** 10; **11** 211; **12** 332
Foremost Warehouse Corp., **14** 372
Forenza, **V** 116
Forest City Auto Parts, **23** 491
**Forest City Enterprises, Inc.**, **16 209–11**
Forest City Ratner Companies, **17** 318
Forest E. Olson, Inc., **21** 96
**Forest Laboratories, Inc.**, **11 141–43**; **47** 55
**Forest Oil Corporation**, **19 161–63**
Forest Products, **III** 645
Forestry Corporation of New Zealand, **19** 156
Företagsfinans, **25** 464
Forethought Group, Inc., **10** 350
**Forever Living Products International Inc.**, **17 186–88**
Forex Chemical Corp., **I** 341; **14** 216; **17** 418
Forex-Neptune, **III** 617
Forge Books. *See* Tom Doherty Associates Inc.
Forges d'Eich–Le Gallais, Metz et Cie, **IV** 24; **22** 42
Forges de la Providence, **IV** 52
Forjas Metalicas, S.A. de C.V. (Formet), **44** 193
Formento Económico Mexicano, S.A. de C.V., **25** 279, 281
**Formica Corporation**, **10** 269; **13 230–32**
Forming Technology Co., **III** 569; **20** 361
Formonix, **20** 101
**Formosa Plastics Corporation**, **11** 159; **14 197–99**; **16** 194, 196
Formosa Plastics Group, **31** 108
Formosa Springs, **I** 269; **12** 337
Formularios y Procedimientos Moore, **IV** 645
Formule 1, **13** 364; **27** 10
Forney Fiber Company, **8** 475
Forsakrings A.B. Volvia, **I** 20
**Forstmann Little & Co.**, **I** 446, 483; **II** 478, 544; **III** 56; **7** 206; **10** 321; **12** 344, 562; **14** 166; **16** 322; **19** 372–73, 432; **22** 32, 60; **30** 426; **34** 145, 448; **36** 523; **38 190–92**
Fort Associates, **I** 418
Fort Bend Utilities Company, **12** 269
Fort Dummer Mills, **III** 213
Fort Garry Brewery, **26** 304
**Fort Howard Corporation**, **8 197–99**; **15** 305; **22** 209. *See also* Fort James Corporation.
**Fort James Corporation**, **22 209–12 (upd.)**; **29** 136
Fort Mill Manufacturing Co., **V** 378
Fort William Power Co., **IV** 246; **25** 10
Forte Plc, **15** 46; **16** 446; **24** 195; **29** 443
Forte's Holdings Ltd., **III** 104–05
**Fortis, Inc.**, **15 179–82**; **47 134–37 (upd.)**
**Fortum Corporation**, **30 202–07 (upd.)**
Fortun Foods, **26** 59
Fortuna Coffee Co., **I** 451
**Fortune Brands, Inc.**, **19** 168; **29 193–97 (upd.)**; **45** 269
Fortune Enterprises, **12** 60
**Fortunoff Fine Jewelry and Silverware Inc.**, **26 144–46**
Forum Cafeterias, **19** 299–300
Forum Hotels, **I** 248
Foseco plc, **IV** 383
Fosgate Electronics, **43** 322
Foss Maritime Co., **9** 509, 511
**Fossil, Inc.**, **17 189–91**
Foster & Kleiser, **7** 335; **14** 331
Foster & Marshall, **II** 398; **10** 62
Foster and Braithwaite, **III** 697
Foster Forbes, **16** 123
Foster Grant, **I** 670; **II** 595–96; **12** 214
Foster Management Co., **11** 366–67
Foster Medical Corp., **III** 16; **11** 282
**Foster Poultry Farms**, **32 201–04**
Foster-Probyn Ltd., **38** 501
Foster Sand & Gravel, **14** 112
**Foster Wheeler Corporation**, **I** 82; **6 145–47**; **23 205–08 (upd.)**; **25** 82
**Foster's Brewing Group Ltd.**, **7 182–84**; **21 227–30 (upd.)**; **26** 303, 305–06; **36** 15
Fotomat Corp., **III** 549
Fougerolle, **27** 136, 138
Foundation Computer Systems, Inc., **13** 201
Foundation Fieldbus, **22** 373
**Foundation Health Corporation**, **11** 174; **12 175–77**
Founders Equity Inc., **14** 235
Founders of American Investment Corp., **15** 247
**Fountain Powerboats Industries, Inc.**, **28 146–48**
Four Media Co., **33** 403
Four-Phase Systems, Inc., **II** 61; **11** 327
Four Queens Hotel and Casino. *See* The Elsinore Corporation.
**Four Seasons Hotels Inc.**, **II** 531; **9 237–38**; **29 198–200 (upd.)**
Four Seasons Nursing Centers, Inc., **6** 188; **25** 308
Four Winds, **21** 153
Four Winns, **III** 600
Fournier Furniture, Inc., **12** 301
4P, **30** 396–98
**Fourth Financial Corporation**, **11 144–46**; **15** 60
Foussard Associates, **I** 333
Fowler Road Construction Proprietary, **III** 672
Fowler, Roenau & Geary, LLC, **37** 224
Fowler-Waring Cables Co., **III** 162
Fox and Hound English Pub and Grille. *See* Total Entertainment Restaurant Corporation.
Fox & Jacobs, **8** 87
Fox Broadcasting Company, **II** 156; **IV** 608, 652; **7** 391–92; **9** 428; **21** 25, 360; **24** 517; **25** 174, 417–18; **46** 311
Fox Children's Network, **21** 26
**Fox Entertainment Group, Inc.**, **43 173–76**
**Fox Family Worldwide, Inc.**, **24 170–72**
Fox Film Corp., **II** 146–47, 154–55, 169; **25** 327–28
Fox, Fowler & Co., **II** 307
Fox Glacier Mints Ltd., **II** 569
Fox Grocery Co., **II** 682
Fox, Inc., **12** 359; **25** 490
Fox Network, **29** 426
Fox Paper Company, **8** 102
Fox Photo, **III** 475; **7** 161
Fox-Vliet Drug Company, **16** 212
**Foxboro Company**, **13 233–35**; **27** 81
**FoxMeyer Health Corporation**, **V** 152–53; **8** 55; **16 212–14**
Foxmoor, **29** 163
Foxx Hy-Reach, **28** 387
FP&L. *See* Florida Power & Light Co.
FPK LLC, **26** 343
**FPL Group, Inc.**, **V 623–25**; **45** 150
FR Corp., **18** 340; **43** 282
Fragrance Express Inc., **37** 271
Fram Corp., **I** 142, 567
**Framatome SA**, **9** 10; **19 164–67**
Framingham Electric Company, **12** 45
Franc-Or Resources, **38** 231–32
France Cables et Radio, **6** 303
France 5, **6** 374; **21** 105
France-Loisirs, **IV** 615–16, 619
France Quick, **12** 152; **26** 160–61; **27** 10
**France Telecom Group**, **V 291–93**, 471; **9** 32; **14** 489; **18** 33; **21 231–34 (upd.)**; **25** 96, 102; **34** 13; **47** 214
Franchise Associates, Inc., **17** 238
Franchise Business Systems, Inc., **18** 207
Franchise Finance Corp. of America, **19** 159; **37** 351
Francis H. Leggett & Co., **24** 527
Franciscan Vineyards, Inc., **34** 89
Franco-Américaine de Constructions Atomiques, **19** 165
Franco-American Food Co., **I** 428; **II** 479
Frank & Hirsch, **III** 608
Frank & Schulte GmbH, **8** 496
Frank Dry Goods Company, **9** 121
Frank H. Nott Inc., **14** 156
Frank J. Rooney, Inc., **8** 87
**Frank J. Zamboni & Co., Inc.**, **34 173–76**
**Frank Russell Company**, **45** 316; **46 198–200**
Frank Schaffer Publications, **19** 405; **29** 470, 472
Frank W. Horner, Ltd., **38** 123
**Frank's Nursery & Crafts, Inc.**, **12 178–79**, 198–200
**Frankel & Co.**, **39 166–69**
Fränkel & Selz, **II** 239
Frankenberry, Laughlin & Constable, **9** 393
Frankford-Quaker Grocery Co., **II** 625
Frankfort Oil Co., **I** 285
Frankfurter Allgemeine Versicherungs-AG, **III** 184
Franklin Assurances, **III** 211
Franklin Baker's Coconut, **II** 531
Franklin Brass Manufacturing Company, **20** 363
Franklin Container Corp., **IV** 312; **19** 267
Franklin Corp., **14** 130; **41** 388
**Franklin Covey Company**, **37 149–52 (upd.)**
**Franklin Electric Company, Inc.**, **43 177–80**
**Franklin Electronic Publishers, Inc.**, **23 209–13**

Franklin Life Insurance Co., **III** 242–43; **V** 397; **29** 195
Franklin Mint, **IV** 676; **9** 428; **37** 337–38
Franklin National Bank, **9** 536
Franklin Plastics, **19** 414
**Franklin Quest Co., 11 147–49; 41** 121. *See also* Franklin Covey Company.
Franklin Rayon Yarn Dyeing Corp., **I** 529
Franklin Research & Development, **11** 41
**Franklin Resources, Inc., 9 239–40**
Franklin Sports, Inc., **17** 243
Franklin Steamship Corp., **8** 346
Franks Chemical Products Inc., **I** 405
Frans Maas Beheer BV, **14** 568
Franz and Frieder Burda, **IV** 661
Franz Foods, Inc., **II** 584
Franz Ströher AG, **III** 68–69
Franzia. *See* The Wine Group, Inc.
Fraser & Chalmers, **13** 16
Fraser Cos. Ltd., **IV** 165
Fratelli Manzoli, **IV** 585
Fratelli Treves, **IV** 585
Fraternal Assurance Society of America, **III** 274
Fray Data International, **14** 319
Frazer & Jones, **48** 141
Fre Kote Inc., **I** 321
Frears, **II** 543
Fred Campbell Auto Supply, **26** 347
Fred Harvey Hotels, **I** 417
**Fred Meyer, Inc., II** 669; **V 54–56; 18** 505; **20 222–25 (upd.); 35** 370
Fred S. James and Co., **III** 280; **I** 537; **22** 318
Fred Sammons Co., **9** 72
Fred Sammons Company of Chicago, **30** 77
Fred Sands Realtors, **IV** 727
Fred Schmid Appliance & T.V. Co., Inc., **10** 305; **18** 532
**The Fred W. Albrecht Grocery Co., 13 236–38**
**Fred's, Inc., 23 214–16**
Freddie Mac. *See* Federal Home Loan Mortgage Corporation.
Fredelle, **14** 295
Frederick & Nelson, **17** 462
**Frederick Atkins Inc., 16 215–17**
Frederick Bayer & Company, **22** 225
Frederick Gas Company, **19** 487
Frederick Manufacturing Corporation, **26** 119; **48** 59
Frederick Miller Brewing Co., **I** 269
**Frederick's of Hollywood Inc., 16 218–20; 25** 521
Free-lance Uitzendburo, **26** 240
Freeborn Farms, **13** 244
**Freedom Communications, Inc., 36 222–25**
Freedom Group Inc., **42** 10–11
Freedom Technology, **11** 486
Freedom-Valvoline Oil Co., **IV** 373; **19** 23
Freeman, Spogli & Co., **17** 366; **18** 90; **32** 12, 15; **35** 276; **36** 358–59; **47** 142–43
Freemans, **V** 177
FreeMark Communications, **38** 269
**Freeport-McMoran Inc., IV 81–84; 7 185–89 (upd.); 16** 29; **23** 40
Freeport Power, **38** 448
Freezer House, **II** 398; **10** 62
Freezer Queen Foods, Inc., **21** 509
Freezer Shirt Corporation, **8** 406
Freiberger Papierfabrik, **IV** 323
Freight Car Services, Inc., **23** 306
Freight Outlet, **17** 297
Freightliner, **I** 150; **6** 413
FreightMaster, **III** 498
Frejlack Ice Cream Co., **II** 646; **7** 317
Fremlin Breweries, **I** 294
Fremont Butter and Egg Co., **II** 467
Fremont Canning Company, **7** 196
Fremont Group, **21** 97
Fremont Investors, **30** 268
Fremont Partners, **24** 265
Fremont Savings Bank, **9** 474–75
French and Richards & Co., **I** 692
French Bank of California, **II** 233
**French Connection Group plc, 41 167–69**
**French Fragrances, Inc., 22 213–15; 40** 170. *See also* Elizabeth Arden, Inc.
French Kier, **I** 568
French Petrofina, **IV** 497
French Quarter Coffee Co., **27** 480–81
Frequency Sources Inc., **9** 324
Fresenius Ag, **22** 360
**Fresh America Corporation, 20 226–28**
**Fresh Choice, Inc., 20 229–32**
Fresh Fields, **19** 501
**Fresh Foods, Inc., 25** 391; **29 201–03**
Fresh Start Bakeries, **26** 58
Freshbake Foods Group PLC, **II** 481; **7** 68; **25** 518; **26** 57
**Fretter, Inc., 9** 65; **10** 9–10, **304–06**, 502; **19** 124; **23** 52
**Freudenberg & Co., 41 170–73**
Frialco, **IV** 165
Frictiontech Inc., **11** 84
Friday's Front Row Sports Grill, **22** 128
Friden, Inc., **II** 10; **30** 418
Fridy-Gauker & Fridy, **I** 313; **10** 154
**Fried, Frank, Harris, Shriver & Jacobson, 35 183–86**
Fried. Krupp AG Hoesch- Krupp. *See* Thyssen Krupp AG.
**Fried. Krupp GmbH, II** 257; **IV** 60, **85–89**, 104, 128, 203, 206, 222, 234
**Friedman's Inc., 29 204–06**
Friedrich Flick Industrial Corp., **I** 548; **III** 692
Friedrich Roessler Söhne, **IV** 69
Friedrichshütte, **III** 694
Friendly Hotels PLC, **14** 107
**Friendly Ice Cream Corp., II** 511–12; **15** 221; **30 208–10**
Friesch-Groningsche Hypotheekbank, **III** 179
**Frigidaire Home Products, III** 572; **13** 564; **19** 361; **22** 28, **216–18**, 349
Frigo, **II** 587
Friguia, **IV** 165
Frisby P.M.C. Incorporated, **16** 475
**Frisch's Restaurants, Inc., 35 187–89**
Frisdranken Industries Winters B.V., **22** 515
Frisia Group, **IV** 197–98
**Frito-Lay Company, I** 219, 278–79; **III** 136; **22** 95; **32 205–10; 38** 347; **44** 348
**Fritz Companies, Inc., 12 180–82**
Fritz Gegauf AG. *See* Bernina Holding AG.
Fritz Thyssen Stiftung, **IV** 222
Fritz W. Glitsch and Sons, Inc. *See* Glitsch International, Inc.
Fritzsche Dodge and Ollcott, **I** 307
Froebel-Kan, **IV** 679
Frolic, **16** 545
Fromagerie d'Illoud. *See* Bongrain SA.
La Fromagerie du Velay, **25** 85
Fromagerie Paul Renard, **25** 85
**Fromageries Bel, II** 518; **6** 47; **19** 51; **23 217–19; 25 83–84**
Fromageries des Chaumes, **25** 84
Fromarsac, **25** 84
Frome Broken Hill Co., **IV** 59
Fromm & Sichel, **I** 285
Frontec, **13** 132
Frontenac Co., **24** 45
**Frontier Airlines, Inc., I** 97–98, 103, 118, 124, 129–30; **6** 129; **11** 298; **21** 141–42; **22 219–21; 25** 421; **26** 439–40; **39** 33
Frontier Communications, **32** 216, 218
**Frontier Corp., 16 221–23; 18** 164
Frontier Electronics, **19** 311
Frontier Expeditors, Inc., **12** 363
Frontier Oil Co., **IV** 373
Frontier Pacific Insurance Company, **21** 263
FrontLine Capital Group, **47** 330–31
**Frontline Ltd., 45 163–65**
Frosch Touristik, **27** 29
Frost National Bank. *See* Cullen/Frost Bankers, Inc.
**Frozen Food Express Industries, Inc., 20 233–35; 27** 404
Fru-Con Corp., **I** 561
**Fruehauf Corp., I 169–70**, 480; **II** 425; **III** 652; **7** 259–60, 513–14; **13** 341; **27** 202–03, 251; **40** 432
**Fruit of the Loom, Inc., 8 200–02; 16** 535; **25 164–67 (upd.)**
The Frustum Group Inc., **45** 280
Fry's Diecastings, **III** 681
Fry's Food Stores, **12** 112
Fry's Metal Foundries, **III** 681
Frye Copy Systems, **6** 599
**Frymaster Corporation, 27 159–62**
FSA Corporation, **25** 349
**FSI International, Inc., 17 192–94**. *See also* FlightSafety International, Inc.
FSP. *See* Frank Schaffer Publications.
FTD, **26** 344. *See also* Florists Transworld Delivery, Inc.
F3 Software Corp., **15** 474
**FTP Software, Inc., 20 236–38**
**Fubu, 29 207–09**
Fuddruckers, **27** 480–82
Fuel Pipeline Transportation Ltd., **6** 123–24; **27** 464
Fuel Resources Development Co., **6** 558–59
Fuel Resources Inc., **6** 457
FuelMaker Corporation, **6** 569
**Fuji Bank, Ltd., I** 494; **II 291–93**, 360–61, 391, 422, 459, 554; **III** 405, 408–09; **17** 556–57; **24** 324; **26** 455
**Fuji Electric Co., Ltd., II 22–23**, 98, 103; **III** 139; **13** 356; **18** 511; **22** 373; **42** 145; **48 180–82 (upd.)**
Fuji Gen-Gakki, **16** 202; **43** 171
Fuji Heavy Industries, **I** 207; **III** 581; **9** 294; **12** 400; **13** 499–501; **23** 290; **36** 240, 243
Fuji Iron & Steel Co., Ltd., **I** 493; **II** 300; **IV** 130, 157, 212; **17** 349–50; **24** 325
Fuji Kaolin Co., **III** 691
Fuji Paper, **IV** 320
**Fuji Photo Film Co., Ltd., III** 172, 476, **486–89**, 549–50; **6** 289; **7** 162; **18** 94, **183–87 (upd.)**, 341–42; **36** 172, 174; **43** 284
Fuji Photo Film USA, Inc., **45** 284

Fuji Seito, **I** 511
Fuji Television, **7** 249; **9** 29
Fuji Xerox. *See* Xerox Corporation.
Fuji Yoshiten Co., **IV** 292
Fujian Hualong Carburetor, **13** 555
Fujikoshi Kozai, **III** 595
Fujimoto Bill Broker & Securities Co., **II** 405
**Fujisawa Pharmaceutical Co.**, **I 635–36**; **III** 47; **8** 343
Fujita Airways, **6** 70
**Fujitsu-ICL Systems Inc.**, **11 150–51**
**Fujitsu Limited**, **I** 455, 541; **II** 22–23, 56, 68, 73, 274; **III** 109–11, 130, **139–41**, 164, 482; **V** 339; **6** 217, 240–42; **10** 238; **11** 308, 542; **13** 482; **14** 13–15, 512; **16** 139, **224–27 (upd.)**; **17** 172; **21** 390; **27** 107; **40** 20; **145–50 (upd.)**; **43** 285
Fujitsu Takamisawa, **28** 131
Fujiyi Confectionery Co., **II** 569
Fukuin Electric Works, Ltd., **III** 604
Fukuin Shokai Denki Seisakusho, **III** 604
Fukuju Fire, **III** 384
Fukuoka Paper Co., Ltd., **IV** 285
Fukutake Publishing Co., Ltd., **13** 91, 93
Ful-O-Pep, **10** 250
**Fulbright & Jaworski L.L.P.**, **22** 4; **47 138–41**
Fulcrum Communications, **10** 19
The Fulfillment Corporation of America, **21** 37
Fulham Brothers, **13** 244
Fullbright & Jaworski, **28** 48
Fuller Brush Co., **II** 572; **15** 475–76, 78
Fuller Co., **6** 395–96; **25** 169–70
Fuller Manufacturing Company **I** 154. *See also* H.B. Fuller Company.
**Fuller Smith & Turner P.L.C.**, **38 193–95**
Fulton Bank, **14** 40
Fulton Co., **III** 569; **20** 361
Fulton Insurance Co., **III** 463; **21** 173
Fulton Manufacturing Co., **11** 535
Fulton Municipal Gas Company, **6** 455
Fulton Performance Products, Inc., **11** 535
Funai-Amstrad, **III** 113
**Funco, Inc.**, **20 239–41**
Fund American Companies. *See* White Mountains Insurance Group, Ltd.
Fundimensions, **16** 337
Funk & Wagnalls, **IV** 605; **22** 441
Funk Software Inc., **6** 255; **25** 299
Funnel Cake Factory, **24** 241
**Fuqua Enterprises, Inc.**, **17 195–98**
**Fuqua Industries Inc.**, **I 445–47**, 452; **8** 545; **12** 251; **14** 86; **37** 62
Furalco, **IV** 15
Furnishings International Inc., **20** 359, 363; **39** 267
**Furniture Brands International, Inc.**, **31** 246, 248; **39 170–75 (upd.)**
The Furniture Center, Inc., **14** 236
**Furon Company**, **28 149–51**
**Furr's Supermarkets, Inc.**, **II** 601; **28 152–54**
Furst Group, **17** 106
**Furukawa Electric Co., Ltd.**, **II** 22; **III** 139, **490–92**; **IV** 15, 26, 153; **15** 514; **22** 44
Fusi Denki, **II** 98
Fuso Marine Insurance Co., **III** 367
Fuso Metal Industries, **IV** 212
Futagi Co., Ltd., **V** 96
Futronix Corporation, **17** 276
Future Diagnostics, Inc., **25** 384
Future Graphics, **18** 387
**Future Now, Inc.**, **6** 245; **12 183–85**
Futurestep, Inc., **34** 247, 249
Fuyo Group, **II** 274, 291–93, 391–92, 554
FWD Corporation, **7** 513
**Fyffes Plc**, **38 196–99**, 201

G&G Shops, Inc., **8** 425–26
G & H Products, **III** 419
**G&K Services, Inc.**, **16 228–30**; **21** 115
G&L Albu, **IV** 90
G&L Inc., **16** 202; **43** 170
G&R Pasta Co., Inc., **II** 512
G. and T. Earle, **III** 669, 670
G.A. Serlachius Oy, **IV** 314–15
G.B. Lewis Company, **8** 359
G. Bruss GmbH and Co. KG, **26** 141
G.C.E. International Inc., **III** 96–97
G.C. Murphy Company, **9** 21
G.C. Smith, **I** 423
**G.D. Searle & Co.**, **I** 365–66, **686–89**; **III** 47, 53; **8** 343, 398, 434; **9** 356–57; **10** 54; **12 186–89 (upd.)**; **16** 527; **26** 108, 383; **29** 331; **29** 331; **34 177–82 (upd.)**
G. Felsenthal & Sons, **17** 106
G.H. Bass & Co., **15** 406; **24** 383
G.H. Besselaar Associates, **30** 151
G.H. Rinck NV, **V** 49; **19** 122–23
G.H. Wetterau & Sons Grocery Co., **II** 681
**G. Heileman Brewing Co.**, **I 253–55**, 270; **10** 169–70; **12** 338; **18** 501; **23** 403, 405
**G.I.E. Airbus Industrie**, **I**
**G.I. Joe's, Inc.**, **30 221–23 41–43**, 49–52, 55–56, 70, 72, 74–76, 107, 111, 116, 121; **9** 458, 460; **11** 279, 363; **12 190–92 (upd.)**
**G-III Apparel Group, Ltd.**, **22 222–24**
G.J. Coles & Coy. Ltd., **20** 155
G.L. Kelty & Co., **13** 168
G.L. Rexroth GmbH, **III** 566; **38** 298, 300
G.M. Pfaff AG, **30** 419–20
G.P. Group, **12** 358
G.P. Putnam's Sons, **II** 144
G.R. Foods, Inc. *See* Ground Round, Inc.
G.R. Herberger's Department Stores, **19** 324–25; **41** 343–44
G.R. Kinney Corporation, **V** 226, 352; **14** 293; **20** 88
G. Riedel Kälte- und Klimatechnik, **III** 420
**G.S. Blodgett Corporation**, **15 183–85**; **22** 350
G.S. Capital Partners II L.P. *See* Goldman, Sachs & Company.
G. Washington Coffee Refining Co., **I** 622
**Gabelli Asset Management Inc.**, **13** 561; **30 211–14**. *See also* Lynch Corporation.
Gable House Properties, **II** 141
Gabriel Industries, **II** 532
GAC. *See* The Goodyear Tire & Rubber Company.
GAC Corp., **II** 182; **III** 592
GAC Holdings L.P., **7** 204; **28** 164
**Gadzooks, Inc.**, **18 188–90**; **33** 203
**GAF**, **I 337–40**, 524–25, 549; **II** 378; **III** 440; **8** 180; **9** 518; **18** 215; **22** 14, **225–29 (upd.)**; **25** 464
**Gage Marketing Group**, **26 147–49**; **27** 21
Gagliardi Brothers, **13** 383
**Gaiam, Inc.**, **41 174–77**
Gail Borden, Jr., and Company. *See* Borden, Inc.
Gain Technology, Inc., **10** 505
Gaines Dog Food Co., **II** 531
Gaines Furniture Manufacturing, Inc., **43** 315
Gainsborough Craftsmen Ltd., **II** 569
**Gainsco, Inc.**, **22 230–32**
Gair Paper Co., **I** 599
Galas Harland, S.A., **17** 266, 268
Galavision, Inc., **24** 515–17
Galaxy Carpet Mills Inc., **19** 276
Galaxy Energies Inc., **11** 28
Galbreath Escott, **16** 474
The Gale Group, Inc., **34** 437
Gale Research Inc., **8** 526; **23** 440
Galen Health Care, **15** 112; **35** 215–16
Galen Laboratories, **13** 160
Galerías Preciados, **26** 130
**Galeries Lafayette S.A.**, **V 57–59**; **23 220–23 (upd.)**
Galesburg Coulter Disc Co., **III** 439–40
**Galey & Lord, Inc.**, **20 242–45**
**Gallaher Limited**, **IV** 260; **V 398–400**; **19 168–71 (upd.)**; **29** 195
Gallatin Bank, **II** 312
Gallatin Steel Company, **18** 380; **24** 144
Galletas, **II** 543
Gallimard, **IV** 618
Gallo Winery. *See* E. & J. Gallo Winery.
Gallop Johnson & Neuman, L.C., **26** 348
**The Gallup Organization**, **37 153–56**; **41** 196–97
Galoob Toys. *See* Lewis Galoob Toys Inc.
Galor, **I** 676
GALP, **IV** 505; **48** 117, 119
Galvanizing Co., **IV** 159
Galveston *Daily News*, **10** 3
Galvin Manufacturing Corp., **II** 60; **11** 326
GALVSTAR, L.P., **26** 530
**Galyan's Trading Company, Inc.**, **47 142–44**s
Gamble-Skogmo Inc., **13** 169; **25** 535
**The Gambrinus Company**, **29** 219; **40 188–90**
Gambro Engstrom AB, **13** 159–61, 327–28
Gamebusters, **41** 409
Gamesa, **II** 544; **19** 192
GameTime, Inc., **19** 387; **27** 370–71
GAMI. *See* Great American Management and Investment, Inc.
Gamlestaden, **9** 381–82
Gamlestadens Fabriker, **III** 622
Gamma Capital Corp., **24** 3
Gammalink, **18** 143
**Gander Mountain, Inc.**, **20 246–48**
Gang-Nail Systems, **III** 735
**Gannett Co., Inc.**, **III** 159; **IV 612–13**, 629–30; **7 190–92 (upd.)**; **9** 3; **18** 63; **23** 157–58, 293; **24** 224; **25** 371; **30 215–17 (upd.)**; **32** 354–55; **41** 197–98
Gannett Supply, **17** 282
**Gantos, Inc.**, **17 199–201**
**The Gap, Inc.**, **V 60–62**; **9** 142, 360; **11** 499; **18 191–94 (upd.)**; **24** 27; **25** 47–48; **31** 51–52
GAR Holdings, **19** 78
Garamond Press, **23** 100
**Garan, Inc.**, **16 231–33**
Garantie Mutuelle des Fonctionnaires, **21** 225
Garden Botanika, **11** 41
Garden City Newspapers Inc., **38** 308
Garden Escape, **26** 441

**Garden Fresh Restaurant Corporation, 31 213–15**
Garden of Eatin' Inc., **27** 198; **43** 218–19
**Garden Ridge Corporation, 27 163–65**
Garden State BancShares, Inc., **14** 472
Garden State Life Insurance Company, **10** 312; **27** 47–48
Garden State Paper, **38** 307–08
**Gardenburger, Inc., 33 169–71**
Gardener's Eden, **17** 548–49
Gardenia, **II** 587
Gardner & Harvey Container Corporation, **8** 267
Gardner Advertising. *See* Wells Rich Green BDDP.
Gardner Cryogenics, **13** 140
Gardner-Denver Co., **II** 16
Gardner Merchant Ltd., **III** 104; **11** 325; **29** 442–44
Gardner Rubber Co. *See* Tillotson Corp.
Garelick Farms, Inc., **26** 449
Garfield Weston, **13** 51
Garfinckel, Brooks Brothers, Miller & Rhodes, Inc., **15** 94; **22** 110
Garfinckels, **37** 12
Garland Publishing, **44** 416
Garland-Compton, **42** 328
Garlock, **I** 435
Garnier, **III** 47
A.B. Garnisonen, **II** 352
Garrard Engineering, **II** 82
Garrett, **9** 18; **11** 472
Garrett & Company, **27** 326
Garrett AiResearch, **9** 18
Garrett-Buchanan, **I** 412
Garrett Poultry Co., **II** 584; **14** 514
Garrick Investment Holdings Ltd., **16** 293
Garrido y Compania, Inc., **26** 448
**Gart Sports Company, 24 173–75**
**Gartner Group, Inc., 21 235–37**; **25** 22
Gartrell White, **II** 465
**Garuda Indonesia, I** 107; **6 90–91**
Gary Fisher Mountain Bike Company, **16** 494
Gary Industries, **7** 4
Gary-Wheaton Corp., **II** 286
Gary-Williams Energy Corporation, **19** 177
Gas Authority of India Ltd., **IV** 484
Gas Corp. of Queensland, **III** 673
Gas Energy Inc., **6** 457
Gas Group, **III** 673
Gas Light and Coke Company. *See* British Gas plc.
Gas Light Company. *See* Baltimore Gas and Electric Company.
Gas Machinery Co., **I** 412
Gas Service Company, **6** 593; **12** 542
Gas Supply Co., **III** 672
Gas Tech, Inc., **11** 513
Gas Utilities Company, **6** 471
Gaston Paper Stock Co., Inc., **8** 476
Gasunie. *See* N.V. Nederlandse Gasunie.
GATC. *See* General American Tank Car Company.
Gate City Company, **6** 446
**The Gates Corporation, 9 241–43**
Gates Distribution Company, **12** 60
Gates Radio Co., **II** 37
Gates Rubber, **26** 349
Gates/FA Distributing Inc., **29** 413–14
Gateway Books, **14** 61
**Gateway Corporation Ltd., II** 612, **628–30**, 638, 642; **10** 442; **16** 249; **25** 119. *See also* Somerfield plc.
Gateway Foodmarkets Ltd., **II** 628; **13** 26
**Gateway, Inc., 27 166–69 (upd.)**
Gateway International Motorsports Corporation, Inc., **43** 139–40
Gateway State Bank, **39** 381–82
Gateway Technologies, Inc., **46** 387
**Gateway 2000, Inc., 10 307–09**; **11** 240; **22** 99; **24** 31; **25** 531
Gatliff Coal Co., **6** 583
Gattini, **40** 215
Gatwick Handling, **28** 157
**GATX, 6 394–96**; **25 168–71 (upd.)**; **47** 298
Gaultier. *See* Groupe Jean-Paul Gaultier.
**Gaumont SA, II** 157–58; **25 172–75**; **29** 369–71
Gauntlet Developments, **IV** 724
Gavilan Computer Corp., **III** 124; **6** 221
Gaya Motor, P.T. **23** 290
**Gaylord Container Corporation, 8 203–05**; **24** 92
**Gaylord Entertainment Company, 11 152–54**; **36 226–29 (upd.)**; **38** 456
Gaymer Group, **25** 82
**Gaz de France, IV** 425; **V 626–28**; **38** 407; **40 191–95 (upd.)**
Gazelle Graphics Systems, **28** 244
Gazprom, **18** 50; **30** 205. *See also* OAO Gazprom.
GB Foods Inc., **19** 92
GB-Inno-BM, **II** 658; **V** 63
GB Papers, **IV** 290
GB s.a. *See* GIB Group.
GB Stores, Inc., **14** 427
GBL, **IV** 499
**GC Companies, Inc., 25 176–78**
GCFC. *See* General Cinema Finance Co.
GD Express Worldwide, **27** 472, 475; **30** 463
GDE Systems, Inc., **17** 492
GDF. *See* Gaz de France.
GDS, **29** 412
GE. *See* General Electric Company.
**GE Aircraft Engines, 9 244–46**
**GE Capital Aviation Services, 36 230–33**
GE Capital Corporation, **29** 428, 430
GE Capital Services, **27** 276
GE SeaCo SRL, **29** 428, 431
**GEA AG, 27 170–74**
**GEAC Computer Corporation Ltd., 43 181–85**
Geant Casino, **12** 152
Gear Products, Inc., **48** 59
Gearhart Industries Inc., **III** 499; **15** 467
Gearmatic, **I** 185
Gebrüder Kiessel GmbH, **IV** 197
Gebrüder Sulzer Aktiengesellschaft. *See* Sulzer Brothers Limited.
Gebrüder Volkart, **III** 402
Gebrueder Ahle GmbH, **III** 581
GEC. *See* General Electric Company.
GECAS. *See* GE Capital Aviation Services.
**Gecina SA, 42 151–53**
GECO, **III** 618; **17** 419
Geco Mines Ltd., **IV** 165; **7** 398
Geer Drug, **III** 9–10
**Geerlings & Wade, Inc., 45 166–68**
**Geest Plc, 38** 198, **200–02**
**Geffen Records Inc., 21** 26; **23** 33; **26 150–52**; **43** 143
GEGC, **III** 434
**GEHE AG, 27 175–78**
**Gehl Company, 19 172–74**
**GEICO Corporation, III** 214, 248, 252, 273, 448; **10 310–12**; **18** 60, 61, 63; **40 196–99 (upd.)**; **42** 31–34
Gelatin Products Co., **I** 678
Gelco Express, **18** 177
Gelco Truck Services, **19** 293
Gellatly, Hankey and Sewell, **III** 521
Gelsenberg AG, **IV** 454; **7** 141
Gelsenkirchener Bergwerks AG, **I** 542; **IV** 194
Gelson's, **29** 32
Gem State Utilities, **6** 325, 328
GEMA Gesellschaft für Maschinen- und Apparatebau mbH, **IV** 198
GemChem, Inc., **47** 20
Gemco, **17** 366
Gemcolite Company, **8** 178
N.V. Gemeenschappelijk Benzit van Aandeelen Philips Gloeilampenfabriken, **II** 79; **13** 396
Gemeinhardt Co., **16** 201; **43** 170
Gemey, **III** 47
Gemina, **I** 369
Gemini Computer Systems, **III** 109; **14** 13; **37** 59–60
Gemini Group Limited Partnership, **23** 10
Gemini Industries, **17** 215
GemPlus, **18** 543
Gemstar-TV Guide International, **43** 431
Genbel Investments Ltd., **IV** 92
GenCare Health Systems, **17** 166–67
**Gencor Ltd., I** 423; **IV 90–93**, 95; **22 233–37 (upd.)**
**GenCorp Inc., 8** 206–08; **9 247–49**; **13** 381
Gendex Corp., **10** 270, 272
Gene Reid Drilling, **IV** 480
Gene Upton Co., **13** 166
Genencor International Inc., **44** 134, 136
Genender International Incorporated, **31** 52
**Genentech Inc., I** 628, **637–38**; **III** 43; **8 209–11 (upd.)**, 216–17; **10** 78, 80, 142, 199; **17** 289; **29** 386; **30** 164; **32 211–15 (upd.)**; **37** 112; **38** 204, 206; **41** 153, 155
**General Accident plc, III 256–57**, 350
General America Corp., **III** 352–53
General American Oil Co., **IV** 523
General American Tank Car Company. *See* GATX Corporation.
General Aniline and Film Corporation. *See* GAF Corporation.
General Aquatics, Inc., **16** 297
General Artificial Silk Co., **IV** 310; **19** 265
General Atlantic Partners, **25** 34; **26** 94
General Automotive Parts Corp., **I** 62; **9** 254
General Aviation Corp., **I** 54; **9** 16
General Battery Corp., **I** 440–41
**General Bearing Corporation, 45 169–71**
**General Binding Corporation, 10 313–14**
General Box Corp., **IV** 342
General Brewing Corp, **I** 269
General Bussan Kaisha, Ltd., **IV** 431–32, 555
**General Cable Corporation, IV** 32; **7** 288; **8** 367; **18** 549; **40 200–03**
General Casualty Co., **III** 258, 343, 352, 404
**The General Chemical Group Inc., I** 414; **22** 29, 115, 193, 349, 541; **29** 114; **37 157–60**
General Chocolate, **II** 521

General Cigar Company, **43** 204–05. *See also* Culbro Corporation.
General Cigar Holdings, Inc., **27** 139–40
**General Cinema Corporation, I 245–46;** **II** 478; **IV** 624; **12** 12–13, 226, 356; **14** 87; **19** 362; **26** 468; **27** 481
General Cinema Finance Co., **II** 157–58
General Cinema Theaters. *See* GC Companies, Inc.
General Co. for Life Insurance and Superannuation, **III** 309
General Corporation, **9** 173
General Credit Ltd., **II** 389
General Crude Oil Co., **II** 403; **IV** 287; **15** 228
**General DataComm Industries, Inc., 14 200–02**
General Diaper Corporation, **14** 550
**General Dynamics Corporation, I** 55, **57–60**, 62, 71, 74, 77, 482, 525, 527, 597; **6** 79, 229; **7** 520; **8** 51, 92, 315, 338; **9** 206, 323, 417–18, 498; **10 315–18 (upd.)**, 522, 527; **11** 67, 165, 269, 278, 364; **13** 374; **16** 77–78; **18** 62, 554; **27** 100; **30** 471; **36** 76, 78–79; **40 204–10 (upd.)**
General Electric Capital Aviation Services, **48** 218–19
General Electric Capital Corp., **15** 257, 282; **19** 190
**General Electric Company, I** 41, 52, 82–85, 195, 321, 454, 478, 532, 534, 537; **II** 2, 16, 19, 22, 24, **27–31**, 38–39, 41, 56, 58–59, 66, 82, 86, 88–90, 98–99, 116–17, 119–21, 143, 151–52, 330, 349, 431, 604; **III** 16, 110, 122–23, 132, 149, 152, 154, 170–71, 340, 437, 440, 443, 475, 483, 502, 526, 572–73, 614, 655; **IV** 66, 203, 287, 596, 675; **V** 564; **6** 13, 27, 32, 164–66, 240, 261, 266, 288, 452, 517; **7** 123, 125, 161, 456, 520, 532; **8** 157, 262, 332, 377; **9** 14–18, 27, 128, 162, 244, 246, 352–53, 417–18, 439, 514; **10** 16, 241, 536–37; **11** 46, 313, 318, 422, 472, 490; **12** 68, 190, **193–97 (upd.)**, 237, 247, 250, 252, 484, 544–45, 550; **13** 30, 124, 326, 396, 398, 501, 529, 554, 563–64; **15** 196, 228, 285, 380, 403, 467; **17** 149, 173, 272; **18** 228, 369; **19** 110, 164–66, 210, 335; **20** 8, 152; **22** 37, 218, 406; **23** 104–05, 181; **26** 371; **28** 4–5, 8, 298; **30** 490; **31** 123; **34 183–90 (upd.)**; **41** 366; **43** 447, 466; **45** 17, 19, 117; **47** 351
**General Electric Company, PLC, I** 411, 423; **II** 3, 12, **24–26**, 31, 58, 72, 80–83; **III** 509; **9** 9–10; **13** 356; **20** 290; **24** 87; **42** 373, 377. *See also* Marconi plc.
General Electric Credit Corporation, **19** 293; **20** 42
General Electric Railcar Wheel and Parts Services Corporation, **18** 4
General Electric Venture Capital Corporation, **9** 140; **10** 108
General Electronics Co., **III** 160
General Elevator Corporation, **25** 15
General Europea S.A., **V** 607
General Export Iron and Metals Company, **15** 116
General Felt Industries Inc., **I** 202; **14** 300; **17** 182–83
General Film Distributors Ltd., **II** 157
General Finance Corp., **II** 419; **III** 194, 232; **11** 16
General Finance Service Corp., **11** 447
General Fire and Casualty, **I** 449
General Fire Extinguisher Co. *See* Grinnell Corp.
General Foods Corp., **I** 26, 36, 608, 712; **II** 414, 463, 477, 497, 502, 525, 530–34, 557, 569; **III** 66; **V** 407; **7** 272–74; **10** 323, 551; **12** 167, 372; **13** 293; **18** 416, 419; **25** 517; **26** 251; **36** 236; **44** 341
General Foods, Ltd., **7** 577
General Furniture Leasing. *See* CORT Business Services Corporation.
General Gas Co., **IV** 432
General Glass Corporation, **13** 40
General Growth Properties, **III** 248
General Health Services, **III** 79
**General Host Corporation, 7** 372; **12** 178–79, **198–200**, 275; **15** 362; **17** 230–31
**General Housewares Corporation, 16 234–36; 18** 69
**General Instrument Corporation, II** 5, 112, 160; **10 319–21**; **17** 33; **34** 298
General Insurance Co. of America, **III** 352–53
General Jones Processed Food, **I** 438
General Learning Corp., **IV** 675; **7** 528
General Leisure, **16** 33
General Life Insurance Co. of America, **III** 353
General Medical Corp., **18** 469
General Merchandise Company, **V** 91
General Merchandise Services, Inc., **15** 480
General Milk Co., **II** 487; **7** 429
General Milk Products of Canada Ltd., **II** 586
**General Mills, Inc., II** 493, **501–03**, 525, 556, 576, 684; **III** 505; **7** 547; **8** 53–54; **9** 156, 189–90, 291; **10** 177, **322–24 (upd.)**; **11** 15, 497–98; **12** 80, 167–68, 275; **13** 244, 293–94, 408, 516; **15** 189; **16** 71, 156–58, 337; **18** 225, 523; **22** 337–38; **25** 90, 241, 243, 253; **30** 286; **31** 429–31; **33** 359; **36** 179–80, **234–39 (upd.)**; **44** 138–40
General Mining and Finance Corporation. *See* Gencor Ltd.
General Mortgage and Credit Corp., **II** 256
General Motors Acceptance Corporation, **21** 146; **22** 55
**General Motors Corporation, I** 10, 14, 16–17, 54, 58, 78–80, 85, 101–02, 125, 136, 141, 144–45, 147, 154–55, 162–63, 165–67, **171–73**, 181, 183, 186–87, 203, 205–06, 280, 328–29, 334–35, 360, 448, 464, 481–82, 529, 540; **II** 2, 5, 15, 32–35, 268, 431, 608; **III** 55, 136–38, 292, 442, 458, 482–83, 536, 555, 563, 581, 590–91, 637–38, 640–42, 760; **6** 140, 256, 336, 356, 358; **7** 6–8, 427, 461–64, 513, 565, 567, 599; **8** 151–52, 505–07; **9** 16–18, 36, 283, 293–95, 341, 343, 344, 439, 487–89; **10** 198, 232, 262, 264, 273–74, 279–80, 288–89, **325–27 (upd.)**, 419–20, 429, 460, 537; **11** 5, 29, 53, 103–04, 137–39, 339, 350, 427–29, 437–39, 471–72, 528, 530; **12** 90, 160, 309, 311, 487; **13** 109, 124, 179, 344–45, 357; **16** 321–22, 436, 484; **17** 173, 184, 304; **18** 125–26, 168, 308; **19** 293–94, 482, 484; **21** 3, 6, 444; **22** 13, 169, 175, 216; **23** 267–69, 288–91, 340, 459–61; **25** 142–43, 149, 223–24, 300; **29** 375, 407–08; **34** 133–35, 303; **36** 32, **240–44 (upd.)**, 298; **38** 86, 458, 461; **43** 319; **45** 142, 170
General Nucleonics Corp., **III** 643
**General Nutrition Companies, Inc., 11 155–57**; **24** 480; **29 210–14 (upd.)**; **31** 347; **37** 340, 342; **45** 210
General Office Products Co., **25** 500
General Packing Service, Inc., **19** 78
General Parts Inc., **29** 86
General Petroleum and Mineral Organization of Saudi Arabia, **IV** 537–39
General Petroleum Corp., **IV** 412, 431, 464; **7** 352
General Physics Corporation, **13** 367
General Portland Cement Co., **III** 704–05; **17** 497
General Portland Inc., **28** 229
General Precision Equipment Corp., **II** 10; **30** 418
General Printing and Paper, **II** 624–25
General Printing Ink Corp. *See* Sequa Corp.
General Property Trust, **IV** 708
**General Public Utilities Corporation, V 629–31**; **6** 484, 534, 579–80; **11** 388; **20** 73
General Radio Company. *See* GenRad, Inc.
General Railway Signal Company. *See* General Signal Corporation.
**General Re Corporation, III 258–59**, 276; **24 176–78 (upd.)**; **42** 31, 35
General Rent A Car, **6** 349; **25** 142–43
General Research Corp., **14** 98
General Seafoods Corp., **II** 531
**General Sekiyu K.K., IV 431–33**, 555; **16** 490
**General Signal Corporation, III** 645; **9 250–52**; **11** 232
General Spring Products, **16** 321
General Steel Industries Inc., **14** 324
General Supermarkets, **II** 673
General Telephone and Electronics Corp., **II** 47; **V** 295, 345–46; **13** 398; **19** 40; **25** 267
General Telephone Corporation, **V** 294–95; **9** 478, 494
General Time Corporation, **16** 483
**General Tire, Inc., 8** 206–08, **212–14**; **9** 247–48; **20** 260, 262; **22** 219
General Transistor Corporation, **10** 319
General Utilities Company, **6** 555
General Waterworks Corporation, **40** 449
**Generale Bank, II 294–95**
Genérale Biscuit S.A., **II** 475
Générale de Banque, **36** 458
Générale de Mécanique Aéronautique, **I** 46
**Générale des Eaux Group, V 632–34**; **21** 226. *See* Vivendi Universal S.A.
Generale du Jouet, **16** 428
Générale Occidentale, **II** 475; **IV** 614–15
Générale Restauration S.A., **34** 123
Generali. *See* Assicurazioni Generali.
Génération Y2K, **35** 204, 207
GenerComit Gestione SpA, **II** 192
**Genesco Inc., 14** 501; **17 202–06**; **27** 59
**Genesee & Wyoming Inc., 27 179–81**
Genesee Brewing Co., **18** 72
Genesee Iron Works. *See* Wickes Inc.
Genesis, **II** 176–77

**Genesis Health Ventures, Inc., 18 195–97**; **25** 310
Genetic Anomalies, Inc., **39** 395
Genetic Systems Corp., **I** 654; **III** 18; **37** 43
**Genetics Institute, Inc., 8 215–18**; **10** 70, 78–80
Geneva Metal Wheel Company, **20** 261
Geneva Pharmaceuticals, Inc., **8** 549; **22** 37, 40
Geneva Rubber Co., **17** 373
**Geneva Steel, 7 193–95**
Genex Corp., **I** 355–56; **26** 246
GENIX, **V** 152
Genix Group. *See* MCN Corporation.
**Genmar Holdings, Inc., 45 172–75**
Genossenschaftsbank Edeka, **II** 621–22
Genosys Biotechnologies, Inc., **36** 431
**Genovese Drug Stores, Inc., 18 198–200**; **21** 187; **32** 170; **43** 249
Genpack Corporation, **21** 58
**GenRad, Inc., 24 179–83**
GenSet, **19** 442
Genstar, **22** 14; **23** 327
Genstar Gypsum Products Co., **IV** 273
Genstar Stone Products Co., **III** 735; **15** 154; **40** 176
GenTek Inc., **37** 157; **41** 236
**Gentex Corporation, 26 153–57**; **35** 148–49
Gentex Optics, **17** 50; **18** 392
GenTrac, **24** 257
Gentry Associates, Inc., **14** 378
Gentry International, **I** 497; **47** 234
Genty-Cathiard, **39** 183–84
**Genuardi's Family Markets, Inc., 35 190–92**
Genuin Golf & Dress of America, Inc., **32** 447
**Genuine Parts Company, 9 253–55**; **45 176–79 (upd.)**
Genung's, **II** 673
Genus, **18** 382–83
**Genzyme Corporation, 13 239–42**; **38 203–07 (upd.)**; **47** 4
Genzyme Transgenics Corp., **37** 44
Geo Space Corporation, **18** 513
GEO Specialty Chemicals, Inc., **27** 117
Geo. W. Wheelwright Co., **IV** 311; **19** 266
**geobra Brandstätter GmbH & Co. KG, 48 183–86**
Geodynamics Oil & Gas Inc., **IV** 83
Geographics, Inc., **25** 183
Geomarine Systems, **11** 202
**The Geon Company, 11 158–61**
Geon Industries, Inc. *See* Johnston Industries, Inc.
Geophysical Service, Inc., **II** 112; **III** 499–500; **IV** 365
GeoQuest Systems Inc., **17** 419
Georesources, Inc., **19** 247
Georg Fischer Foundries Group, **38** 214
**George A. Hormel and Company, II 504–06**; **7** 547; **12** 123–24; **18** 244. *See also* Hormel Foods Corporation.
George A. Touche & Co., **9** 167
George Batten Co., **I** 28
George Booker & Co., **13** 102
George Buckton & Sons Limited, **40** 129
George Fischer, Ltd., **III** 638
George H. Dentler & Sons, **7** 429
The George Hyman Construction Company, **8** 112–13; **25** 403
George J. Ball, Inc., **27** 507
George K. Baum & Company, **25** 433
George K. Smith & Co., **I** 692
George Kent, **II** 3; **22** 10
George Newnes Company, **IV** 641; **7** 244
George Peabody & Co., **II** 329, 427
George R. Newell Company. *See* Supervalu Inc.
George R. Rich Manufacturing Company. *See* Clark Equipment Company.
George Smith Financial Corporation, **21** 257
George W. Neare & Co., **III** 224
**George Weston Limited, II 631–32**; **36 245–48 (upd.)**; **41** 30, 33
**George Wimpey PLC, 12 201–03**; **28** 450
Georges Renault SA, **III** 427; **28** 40
Georgetown Group, Inc., **26** 187
Georgetown Steel Corp., **IV** 228
Georgia Carpet Outlets, **25** 320
Georgia Cotton Producers Association. *See* Gold Kist Inc.
Georgia Credit Exchange, **6** 24
Georgia Federal Bank, **I** 447; **11** 112–13; **30** 196
**Georgia Gulf Corporation, IV** 282; **9 256–58**, 260
Georgia Hardwood Lumber Co., **IV** 281; **9** 259
Georgia International Life Insurance Co., **III** 218
Georgia Kraft Co., **IV** 312, 342–43; **8** 267–68; **19** 268
Georgia Natural Gas Corporation, **6** 447–48
**Georgia-Pacific Corporation, IV 281–83**, 288, 304, 345, 358; **9** 256–58, **259–62 (upd.)**; **12** 19, 377; **15** 229; **22** 415, 489; **31** 314; **44** 66; **47 145–51 (upd.)**
Georgia Power & Light Co., **V** 621; **6** 447, 537; **23** 28; **27** 20
Georgia Power Company, **38** 446–48
Georgia Railway and Electric Company, **6** 446–47; **23** 28
Georgie Pie, **V** 35
GeoScience Corporation, **18** 515; **44** 422
Geosource Inc., **III** 182; **21** 14; **22** 189
Geotec Boyles Brothers, S.A., **19** 247
**Geotek Communications Inc., 21 238–40**
GeoTel Communications Corp., **34** 114
Geothermal Resources International, **11** 271
GeoVideo Networks, **34** 259
Geoworks Corporation, **25** 509
Geraghty & Miller Inc., **26** 23
**Gerald Stevens, Inc., 37 161–63**
Gérard, **25** 84
**Gerber Products Company, II** 481; **III** 19; **7 196–98**, 547; **9** 90; **11** 173; **21** 53–55, **241–44 (upd)**; **25** 366; **34** 103; **36** 256
**Gerber Scientific, Inc., 12 204–06**
Gerbes Super Markets, Inc., **12** 112
Gerbo Telecommunicacoes e Servicos Ltda., **32** 40
Geren Associates. *See* CRSS Inc.
Geriatrics Inc., **13** 49
**Gericom AG, 47 152–54**
Gerling of Cologne, **III** 695
Germaine Monteil Cosmetiques Corp., **I** 426; **III** 56
**German American Bancorp, 41 178–80**
German-American Car Company. *See* GATX.
German-American Securities, **II** 283
German Cargo Service GmbH., **I** 111
German Mills American Oatmeal Factory, **II** 558; **12** 409
The German Society. *See* The Legal Aid Society.
Germania Refining Co., **IV** 488–89
Germplasm Resource Management, **III** 740
**Gerresheimer Glas AG, II** 386; **IV** 232; **43 186–89**
Gerrity Oil & Gas Corporation, **11** 28; **24** 379–80
Gervais Danone, **II** 474
GESA. *See* General Europea S.A.
Gesbancaya, **II** 196
Gesellschaft für Chemische Industrie im Basel, **I** 632
Gesellschaft für den Bau von Untergrundbahnen, **I** 410
Gesellschaft für Linde's Eisenmachinen, **I** 581
Gesellschaft für Markt- und Kühlhallen, **I** 581
Gesparal, **III** 47; **8** 342
Gestettner, **II** 159
Gestione Pubblicitaria Editoriale, **IV** 586
GET Manufacturing Inc., **36** 300
**Getronics NV, 39 176–78**
**Getty Images, Inc., 31 216–18**
Getty Oil Co., **II** 448; **IV** 367, 423, 429, 461, 479, 488, 490, 551, 553; **6** 457; **8** 526; **11** 27; **13** 448; **17** 501; **18** 488; **27** 216; **41** 391, 394–95; bf]XLVII 436
Getz Corp., **IV** 137
Geyser Peak Winery, **I** 291
Geysers Geothermal Co., **IV** 84, 523; **7** 188
GFS. *See* Gordon Food Service Inc.
GFS Realty Inc., **II** 633
GGT Group, **44** 198
GHH, **II** 257
GHI, **28** 155, 157
**Ghirardelli Chocolate Company, 24** 480; **27** 105; **30 218–20**
GI Communications, **10** 321
GI Export Corp. *See* Johnston Industries, Inc.
GIAG, **16** 122
**Gianni Versace SpA, 22 238–40**
Giant Bicycle Inc., **19** 384
**Giant Cement Holding, Inc., 23 224–26**
Giant Eagle, Inc., **12** 390–91; **13** 237
**Giant Food Inc., II 633–35**, 656; **13** 282, 284; **15** 532; **16** 313; **22 241–44 (upd.)**; **24** 462
**Giant Industries, Inc., 19 175–77**
Giant Resources, **III** 729
Giant Stores, Inc., **7** 113; **25** 124
Giant TC, Inc. *See* Campo Electronics, Appliances & Computers, Inc.
Giant Tire & Rubber Company, **8** 126
Giant Video Corporation, **29** 503
Giant Wholesale, **II** 625
**GIB Group, V 63–66**; **22** 478; **23** 231; **26 158–62 (upd.)**
Gibbons, Green, van Amerongen Ltd., **II** 605; **9** 94; **12** 28; **19** 360
Gibbs Automatic Molding Co., **III** 569; **20** 360
Gibbs Construction, **25** 404
GIBCO Corp., **I** 321; **17** 287, 289
Gibraltar Casualty Co., **III** 340
Gibraltar Financial Corp., **III** 270–71
**Gibraltar Steel Corporation, 37 164–67**

**Gibson, Dunn & Crutcher LLP, 36 249–52; 37** 292
**Gibson Greetings, Inc.**, 7 24; **12 207–10; 16** 256; **21** 426–28; **22** 34–35
**Gibson Guitar Corp., 16 237–40**
Gibson McDonald Furniture Co., **14** 236
GIC. *See* The Goodyear Tire & Rubber Company.
**Giddings & Lewis, Inc., 8** 545–46; **10 328–30; 23** 299; **28** 455
Giftmaster Inc., **26** 439–40
Gil-Wel Manufacturing Company, **17** 440
**Gilbane, Inc., 34 191–93**
Gilbert & John Greenall Limited, **21** 246
Gilbert-Ash Ltd., **I** 588
Gilbert Lane Personnel, Inc., **9** 326
Gilde-Verlag, **IV** 590
Gilde-Versicherung AG, **III** 400
Gildon Metal Enterprises, **7** 96
Gilkey Bros. *See* Puget Sound Tug and Barge Company.
Gill and Duffus, **II** 500
Gill Industries, **II** 161
Gill Interprovincial Lines, **27** 473
**Gillett Holdings, Inc., 7 199–201; 11** 543, 545; **43** 437–38
**The Gillette Company, III 27–30**, 114, 215; **IV** 722; **8** 59–60; **9** 381, 413; **17** 104–05; **18** 60, 62, 215, 228; **20 249–53 (upd.)**; **23** 54–57; **26** 334; **28** 247; **39** 336
Gilliam Furniture Inc., **12** 475
Gilliam Manufacturing Co., **8** 530
Gilman & Co., **III** 523
Gilman Fanfold Corp., Ltd., **IV** 644
Gilman Paper Co., **37** 178
Gilmore Brother's, **I** 707
Gilmore Steel Corporation. *See* Oregon Steel Mills, Inc.
Gilroy Foods, **27** 299
Giltspur, **II** 587
Gimbel Brothers, Inc. *See* Saks Holdings, Inc.
Gimbel's Department Store, **I** 426–27; **8** 59; **22** 72
Gindick Productions, **6** 28
Ginn & Co., **IV** 672; **19** 405
Ginnie Mae. *See* Government National Mortgage Association.
Gino's, **III** 103
Gino's East, **21** 362
Ginsber Beer Group, **15** 47; **38** 77
**Giorgio Armani S.p.A., 45 180–83**
Giorgio Beverly Hills, Inc., **26** 384
Giorgio, Inc., **III** 16; **19** 28
Girard Bank, **II** 315–16; **44** 280
Girbaud, **17** 513; **31** 261
**Girl Scouts of the USA, 35 193–96**
Girling, **III** 556
Giro Sport Designs International Inc., **16** 53; **44** 53–54
Girod, **19** 50
Girsa S.A., **23** 170
Girvin, Inc., **16** 297
Gist-Brocades Co., **III** 53; **26** 384
**The Gitano Group, Inc., 8 219–21; 20** 136 **25** 167; **37** 81
**Givaudan SA, 43 190–93**
GJM International Ltd., **25** 121–22
GK Technologies Incorporated, **10** 547
GKH Partners, **29** 295
**GKN plc, III 493–96**, 554, 556; **38 208–13 (upd.)**; **42** 47; **47** 7, 9, 279–80
Glaceries de Saint-Roch, **III** 677; **16** 121
Glaces de Boussois, **II** 474–75
**Glacier Bancorp, Inc., 35 197–200**
Glacier Park Co., **10** 191
**Glacier Water Services, Inc., 47 155–58**
Gladieux Corp., **III** 103
Glamar Group plc, **14** 224
Glamor Shops, Inc., **14** 93
Glanbia Group, **38** 196, 198
Glasrock Home Health Care, **I** 316; **25** 81
Glass Containers Corp., **I** 609–10
Glass Fibres Ltd., **III** 726
Glasstite, Inc., **33** 360–61
GlasTec, **II** 420
Glastron. *See* Genmar Holdings, Inc.
Glatfelter Wood Pulp Company, **8** 413
Glaverbel, **III** 667
**Glaxo Holdings plc, I 639–41**, 643, 668, 675, 693; **III** 66; **6** 346; **9 263–65 (upd.)**; **10** 551; **11** 173; **20** 39; **26** 31; **34** 284; **38** 365
**GlaxoSmithKline plc, 46 201–08 (upd.)**
**Gleason Corporation, 24 184–87**
Glen & Co, **I** 453
Glen Alden Corp., **15** 247
Glen Cove Mutual Insurance Co., **III** 269
Glen-Gery Corporation, **14** 249
Glen Iris Bricks, **III** 673
Glen Line, **6** 416
Glencairn Ltd., **25** 418
Glendale Federal Savings, **IV** 29
The Glenlyte Group, **29** 469
Glenlyte Thomas Group LLC, **29** 466
Glenn Advertising Agency, **25** 90
Glenn Pleass Holdings Pty. Ltd., **21** 339
Glens Falls Insurance Co., **III** 242
GLF-Eastern States Association, **7** 17
**The Glidden Company, I** 353; **8 222–24; 21** 545
Glimcher Co., **26** 262
Glitsch International, Inc., **6** 146; **23** 206, 208
Global Access, **31** 469
Global Apparel Sourcing Ltd., **22** 223
Global Communications of New York, Inc., **45** 261
**Global Crossing Ltd., 32 216–19**
Global Energy Group, **II** 345
Global Engineering Company, **9** 266
Global Health Care Partners, **42** 68
**Global Industries, Ltd., 37 168–72**
Global Information Solutions, **34** 257
Global Interactive Communications Corporation, **28** 242
**Global Marine Inc., 9 266–67; 11** 87
Global Natural Resources, **II** 401; **10** 145
Global Telesystems Ltd. *See* Global Crossing Ltd.
Global Transport Organization, **6** 383
Global Vacations Group. *See* Classic Vacation Group, Inc.
GlobalCom Telecommunications, Inc., **24** 122
GlobaLex, **28** 141
**GlobalSantaFe Corporation, 48 187–92 (upd.)**
Globe & Rutgers Insurance Co., **III** 195–96
Globe Business Furniture, **39** 207
Globe Co. **I** 201
Globe Electric Co., **III** 536
Globe Feather & Down, **19** 304
Globe Files Co., **I** 201
Globe Grain and Milling Co., **II** 555
Globe Industries, **I** 540
Globe Insurance Co., **III** 350
Globe Life Insurance Co., **III** 187; **10** 28; **38** 15
Globe National Bank, **II** 261
Globe Newspaper Co., **7** 15
Globe Pequot Press, **36** 339, 341
Globe Petroleum Ltd., **IV** 401
Globe Steel Abrasive Co., **17** 371
Globe Telegraph and Trust Company, **25** 99
Globe-Union, **III** 536; **26** 229
Globe-Wernicke Co., **I** 201
Globelle Corp., **43** 368
Globetrotter Communications, **7** 199
Globo, **18** 211
**Glock Ges.m.b.H., 42 154–56**
Gloria Jean's Gourmet Coffees, **20** 83
La Gloria Oil and Gas Company, **7** 102
Gloria Separator GmbH Berlin, **III** 418
Glosser Brothers, **13** 394
Gloster Aircraft, **I** 50; **III** 508; **24** 85
Gloucester Cold Storage and Warehouse Company, **13** 243
Glovatorium, **III** 152; **6** 266; **30** 339
Glowlite Corporation, **48** 359
Glycomed Inc., **13** 241; **47** 222
Glyn, Mills and Co., **II** 308; **12** 422
GM. *See* General Motors Corp.
**GM Hughes Electronics Corporation, II 32–36; 10** 325. *See also* Hughes Electronics Corporation.
GMARA, **II** 608
GMFanuc Robotics, **III** 482–83
GMR Properties, **21** 257
GNB International Battery Group, **10** 445
GND Holdings Corp., **7** 204; **28** 164
GNMA. *See* Government National Mortgage Association.
Gnôme & Rhône, **46** 369
**The Go-Ahead Group Plc, 28 155–57**
Go Fly Ltd., **39** 128
Go-Gro Industries, Ltd., **43** 99
Go Sport. *See* Groupe Go Sport S.A.
Go-Video, Inc. *See* Sensory Science Corporation.
Goal Systems International Inc., **10** 394
**Godfather's Pizza Incorporated, II** 556–57; **11** 50; **12** 123; **14** 351; **17** 86; **25 179–81**
Godfrey Co., **II** 625
Godfrey L. Cabot, Inc., **8** 77
Godiva Chocolatier, **II** 480; **26** 56
Godo Shusei, **III** 42
Godsell, **10** 277
Godtfred Kristiansen, **13** 310–11
Goebel & Wetterau Grocery Co., **II** 681
Goelitz Confectionary. *See* Herman Goelitz, Inc.
Goering Werke, **II** 282
Göhner AG, **6** 491
Gokey Company, **10** 216; **28** 339
Gold Bond Stamp Company, **6** 363–64; **22** 125
Gold Crust Bakeries, **II** 465
Gold Dust Corp., **II** 497
Gold Exploration and Mining Co. Limited Partnership, **13** 503
**Gold Fields of South Africa Ltd., I** 423; **IV** 91, **94–97**
**Gold Kist Inc.**, **7** 432; **17 207–09; 26 166–68**
Gold Lance Inc., **19** 451–52
Gold Lion, **20** 263
Gold Seal, **II** 567

Gold Star Foods Co., **IV** 410
Gold's Gym Enterprises, **25** 450
Goldblatt Bros., **IV** 135
Goldblatt's Department Stores, **15** 240–42
Golden Bear International, **33** 103; **42** 433; **45** 300
**Golden Belt Manufacturing Co., 16 241–43**
**Golden Books Family Entertainment, Inc., 28 158–61**
Golden Circle Financial Services, **15** 328
**Golden Corral Corporation, 10 331–33**
Golden Eagle Exploration, **IV** 566–67
**Golden Enterprises, Inc., 26 163–65**
Golden Gate Airlines, **25** 421
Golden Grain Macaroni Co., **II** 560; **12** 411; **30** 219; **34** 366
Golden Hope Rubber Estate, **III** 697, 699
Golden Moores Finance Company, **48** 286
Golden Nugget, Inc. *See* Mirage Resorts, Incorporated.
Golden Ocean Group, **45** 164
Golden Partners, **10** 333
Golden Peanut Company, **17** 207
Golden Poultry Company, **26** 168
Golden Press, Inc., **13** 559–61
Golden Sea Produce, **10** 439
Golden Skillet, **10** 373
Golden State Bank, **II** 348
**Golden State Foods Corporation, 32 220–22**
Golden State Newsprint Co. Inc., **IV** 296; **19** 226; **23** 225
Golden State Sanwa Bank, **II** 348
**Golden State Vintners, Inc., 33 172–74**
Golden Tulip International, **I** 109
**Golden West Financial Corporation, 47 159–61**
Golden West Homes, **15** 328
Golden West Publishing Corp., **38** 307–08
Golden Wonder, **II** 500; **III** 503
Golden Youth, **17** 227
Goldenberg Group, Inc., **12** 396
Goldenlay Eggs, **II** 500
Goldfield Corp., **12** 198
Goldfine's Inc., **16** 36
Goldkuhl & Broström, **III** 419
Goldline Laboratories Inc., **11** 208
**Goldman, Sachs & Co., II** 11, 268, 326, 361, **414–16**, 432, 434, 448; **III** 80, 531; **IV** 611; **9** 378, 441; **10** 423; **12** 405; **13** 95, 448, 554; **15** 397; **16** 195; **20 254–57 (upd.)**, 258; **21** 146; **22** 427–28; **26** 456; **27** 317; **29** 508; **36** 190–91; **38** 289, 291
Goldner Hawn Johnson & Morrison Inc., **48** 412
Goldome Savings Bank, **11** 110; **17** 488
Goldsbrough Mort & Co., **I** 437
Goldsmith's, **9** 209
**Goldstar Co., Ltd., II** 5, 53–54; **III** 517; **7** 233; **12 211–13**; **13** 213; **30** 184; **43** 428
Goldwell, **III** 38
Goldwin Golf, **45** 76
Goldwyn Films. *See* Metro-Goldwyn-Mayer Inc.
Goleta National Bank, **33** 5
Golf Day, **22** 517
**The Golub Corporation, 26 169–71**
Gomoljak, **14** 250
**Gonnella Baking Company, 40 211–13**
Good Foods, Inc., **II** 497
**The Good Guys!, Inc., 10 334–35**; **30 224–27 (upd.)**
**The Good Humor-Breyers Ice Cream Company, II** 533; **14 203–05**; **15** 222; **17** 140–41; **32** 474, 476
Good Natural Café, **27** 481
Good Times, Inc., **8** 303
Good Vibrations, Inc., **28** 345
Good Weather International Inc., **III** 221; **14** 109
Goodbody & Company, **II** 425; **13** 341; **22** 428
Goodbody James Capel, **16** 14
Goodby, Berlin & Silverstein, **10** 484
Goodebodies, **11** 41
Gooderham and Worts, **I** 216, 263–64
Goodlass, Wall & Co., **III** 680–81
Goodman Bros. Mfg. Co., **14** 436
Goodman Fielder, **44** 137
Goodman Fielder, Wattie's, Ltd., **II** 565; **7** 577
**Goodman Holding Company, 42 157–60**
**GoodMark Foods, Inc., 26 172–74**
**Goodrich Corporation, 46 209–13 (upd.)**
Goodrich Oil Co., **IV** 365
Goodrich, Tew and Company, **V** 231
Goodrich Tire Company, **V** 240–41; **6** 27
Goodson Newspaper Group, **29** 262
**GoodTimes Entertainment Ltd., 31** 238; **48 193–95**
**Goodwill Industries International, Inc., 15** 511; **16 244–46**
Goodwin & Co., **12** 108
Goodwin, Dannenbaum, Littman & Wingfield, **16** 72
**Goody Products, Inc., 12 214–16**
**Goody's Family Clothing, Inc., 20 265–67**
**The Goodyear Tire & Rubber Company, I** 21; **II** 304; **III** 452; **V 244–48**; **8** 81, 291–92, 339; **9** 324; **10** 445; **15** 91; **16** 474; **19** 221, 223, 455; **20 259–64 (upd.)**; **21** 72–74
Gordon A. Freisen, International, **III** 73
Gordon B. Miller & Co., **7** 256; **25** 254
Gordon Capital Corp., **II** 245
**Gordon Food Service Inc., 8 225–27**; **39 179–82 (upd.)**
Gordon Investment Corp., **II** 245
Gordon Jewelry Corporation, **16** 559, 561; **40** 472
Gordon Manufacturing Co., **11** 256
Gordon Publications, **IV** 610
Gordon S. Black Corporation, **41** 197–98
Gordon-Van Cheese Company, **8** 225
Gordy Company, **26** 314
Gore Newspapers Company, **IV** 683; **22** 521
Gorges Foodservice, Inc., **14** 516
Gorham Silver, **12** 313
Gorilla Sports Club, **25** 42
Gorman Eckert & Co., **27** 299
**The Gorman-Rupp Company, 18 201–03**
Gormully & Jeffrey, **IV** 660
**Gorton's, II** 502; **10** 323; **13 243–44**
The Gosho Co. *See* Kanematsu Corporation.
**Goss Holdings, Inc., 43 194–97**
Gotaas-Larsen Shipping Corp., **6** 368; **27** 91
Götabanken, **II** 303, 353
Göteborgs Handelsbank, **II** 351
Göteborgs Handelskompani, **III** 425
Gothenburg Light & Power Company, **6** 580
Gothenburg Tramways Co., **II** 1
Gott Corp., **III** 614; **21** 293
Gottleib Group, **38** 437
**Gottschalks, Inc., 18 204–06**; **26** 130
Goulard and Olena, **I** 412
**Gould Electronics, Inc., III** 745; **11** 45; **13** 127, 201; **14 206–08**; **21** 43
Goulding Industries Ltd., **IV** 295; **19** 225
**Goulds Pumps Inc., 24 188–91**
Gourmet Award Foods, **29** 480–81
Gourmet Foods, **II** 528
Government Bond Department, **9** 369
Government Employees Insurance Company. *See* GEICO Corporation.
Government National Mortgage Assoc., **II** 410
Government Technology Services Inc., **45** 69
Governor and Company of Adventurers of England. *See* Hudson's Bay Company.
**The Governor and Company of the Bank of Scotland, II** 422; **III** 360; **V** 166; **10 336–38**
**Goya Foods Inc., 22 245–47**; **24** 516
GP Group Acquisition Limited Partnership, **10** 288; **27** 41–42
GPE. *See* General Precision Equipment Corporation.
GPI. *See* General Parts Inc.
GPM Gas Corporation, **40** 357–58
GPS Pool Supply, **29** 34
GPT, **15** 125
GPU. *See* General Public Utilities Corporation.
**GPU, Inc., 27 182–85 (upd.)**
Graber Industries, Inc., **V** 379; **19** 421
Grace. *See* W.R. Grace & Co.
Grace Drilling Company, **9** 365
Grace-Sierra Horticultural Products Co., **22** 475
**Graco Inc., 19 178–80**
Gradco Systems, Inc., **6** 290
Gradiaz, Annis & Co., **15** 138
Gradmann & Holler, **III** 283
Graef & Schmidt, **III** 54
Graf, **23** 219
Graf Bertel Dominique/New York, **6** 48
Graficas e Instrumentos S.A., **13** 234
Graficas Monte Alban S.A., **47** 326
Graftek Press, Inc., **26** 44
Graham Brothers, **27** 267, 269
Graham Container Corp., **8** 477
Graham Page, **III** 568; **20** 359
Grahams Builders Merchants, **I** 429
Gralla, **IV** 687
**Grameen Bank, 31 219–22**
Gramercy Pictures, **23** 391
Gramophone Company, **22** 192
Grampian Electricity Supply Company, **13** 457
Gran Central Corporation, **8** 487
Gran Dorado, **48** 315
**Granada Group PLC, II** 70, **138–40**; **17** 353; **24 192–95 (upd.)**, 269; **25** 270; **32** 404
Granada Royale Hometels, **9** 426
Granaria Holdings B.V., **23** 183
**GranCare, Inc., 14 209–11**; **25** 310
Grand Bazaar Innovations Bon Marché, **13** 284; **26** 159–60
**Grand Casinos, Inc., 20 268–70**; **21** 526; **25** 386

Grand Department Store, **19** 510
**Grand Hotel Krasnapolsky N.V., 23 227–29**
Grand Magasin de Nouveautés Fournier d'Annecy, **27** 93
**Grand Metropolitan plc, I 247–49**, 259, 261; **II** 555–57, 565, 608, 613–15; **9** 99; **13** 391, 407, 409; **14 212–15 (upd.)**; **15** 72; **17** 69, 71; **20** 452; **21** 401; **26** 58; **33** 276; **34** 121; **35** 438; **42** 223; **43** 215. *See also* Diageo plc.
Grand Ole Opry. *See* Gaylord Entertainment Company.
Grand Prix Association of Long Beach, Inc., **43** 139–40
Grand Rapids Carpet Sweeper Company, **9** 70
Grand Rapids Gas Light Company. *See* MCN Corporation.
Grand Rapids Wholesale Grocery Company, **8** 481
Grand Trunk Corp., **6** 359–61
**Grand Union Company, II** 637, 662; **7 202–04**; **8** 410; **13** 394; **16** 249; **28 162–65 (upd.)**
Grand Valley Gas Company, **11** 28
Grand-Perret, **39** 152–53
Grandes Superficies S.A., **23** 247
Grandmet USA, **I** 248
Les Grands Magasins Au Bon Marché, **26** 159–60
Grands Magasins L. Tietz, **V** 103
**GrandVision S.A., 43 198–200**
Grandy's, **15** 345
Granger Associates, **12** 136
Gränges, **III** 480; **22** 27
**Granite Broadcasting Corporation, 42 161–64**
Granite City Steel Company, **12** 353
Granite Furniture Co., **14** 235
**Granite Rock Company, 26 175–78**
**Granite State Bankshares, Inc., 37 173–75**
Grant Oil Tool Co., **III** 569; **20** 361
Grant Street National Bank, **II** 317; **44** 280
Grantham, Mayo, Van Otterloo & Co. LLC, **24** 407
Grantree Corp., **14** 4; **33** 398
Graphic Controls Corp., **IV** 678
**Graphic Industries Inc., 25 182–84**; **36** 508
Graphic Research, Inc., **13** 344–45
Graphic Services, **III** 166; **6** 282
Graphics Systems Software, **III** 169; **6** 285; **8** 519
Graphite Oil Product Co., **I** 360
Graphix Zone, **31** 238
Grass Valley Group, **8** 518, 520
Grasselli Chemical Company, **22** 225
Grasselli Dyestuffs Corp., **I** 337
Grasset, **IV** 617–18
Grasso Production Management Inc., **37** 289
Grattan Plc, **V** 160; **29** 356
The Graver Company, **16** 357
**Gray Communications Systems, Inc., 24 196–200**
Gray Dawes & Co., **III** 522–23
Gray Drug Stores, **III** 745
Gray Dunn and Co., **II** 569
Gray Line, **24** 118
Gray, Siefert & Co., Inc., **10** 44; **33** 259–60
Grayarc, **III** 157
Grayrock Capital, **I** 275
Grays Harbor Mutual Savings Bank, **17** 530
Greaseater, Ltd., **8** 463–64
Great Alaska Tobacco Co., **17** 80
Great American Bagel and Coffee Co., **27** 482
Great American Broadcasting Inc., **18** 65–66; **22** 131; **23** 257–58
Great American Cookie Company. *See* Mrs. Fields' Original Cookies, Inc.
Great American Entertainment Company, **13** 279; **48** 194
Great American First Savings Bank of San Diego, **II** 420
Great American Insurance Company, **48** 9
Great American Life Insurance Co., **III** 190–92
Great American Lines Inc., **12** 29
**Great American Management and Investment, Inc., 8 228–31**
Great American Reserve Insurance Co., **IV** 343; **10** 247
Great American Restaurants, **13** 321
**The Great Atlantic & Pacific Tea Company, Inc., II 636–38**, 629, 655–56, 666; **13** 25, 127, 237; **15** 259; **16** 63–64, **247–50 (upd.)**; **17** 106; **18** 6; **19** 479–80; **24** 417; **26** 463; **33** 434
Great Bagel and Coffee Co., **27** 480–81
Great Beam Co., **III** 690
Great Eastern Railway, **6** 424
Great 5¢ Store, **V** 224
Great Halviggan, **III** 690
**Great Harvest Bread Company, 44 184–86**
**Great Lakes Bancorp, 8 232–33**
Great Lakes Bankgroup, **II** 457
Great Lakes Carbon Corporation, **12** 99
**Great Lakes Chemical Corp., I 341–42**; **8** 262; **14 216–18 (upd.)**
Great Lakes Corp., **IV** 136
Great Lakes Energy Corp., **39** 261
Great Lakes Pipe Line Co., **IV** 400, 575; **31** 470
Great Lakes Steel Corp., **IV** 236; **8** 346; **12** 352; **26** 528
Great Lakes Window, Inc., **12** 397
Great Land Seafoods, Inc., **II** 553
Great Northern, **III** 282
Great Northern Import Co., **I** 292
Great Northern Nekoosa Corp., **IV** 282–83, 300; **9** 260–61; **47** 148
Great Northern Railway Company, **6** 596
Great Plains Software Inc., **38** 432
Great Plains Transportation, **18** 226
Great Shoshone & Twin Falls Water Power Company, **12** 265
**The Great Universal Stores plc, V 67–69**; **15** 83; **17** 66, 68; **19 181–84 (upd.)**; **41** 74, 76; **45** 152. *See also* GUS plc.
**Great-West Lifeco Inc., III 260–61**; **21** 447. *See also* Power Corporation of Canada.
The Great Western Auction House & Clothing Store, **19** 261
Great Western Bank, **47** 160
Great Western Billiard Manufactory, **III** 442
**Great Western Financial Corporation, 10 339–41**
Great Western Foam Co., **17** 182
Great Western Railway, **III** 272
Great World Foods, Inc., **17** 93
Greatamerica Corp., **I** 489; **10** 419; **24** 303
Greater All American Markets, **II** 601; **7** 19
Greater New York Film Rental Co., **II** 169
Greater Washington Investments, Inc., **15** 248
Greb Industries Ltd., **16** 79, 545
Grebner GmbH, **26** 21
**Grede Foundries, Inc., 38 214–17**
Greeley Beef Plant, **13** 350
Greeley Gas Company, **43** 56–57
Green Acquisition Co., **18** 107
Green Bay Food Company, **7** 127
**The Green Bay Packers, Inc., 32 223–26**
Green Capital Investors L.P., **23** 413–14
Green Cross K.K., **I** 665
Green Giant, **II** 556; **13** 408; **14** 212, 214; **24** 140–41
Green Island Cement (Holdings) Ltd. Group, **IV** 694–95
Green Line Investor Services, **18** 553
**Green Mountain Coffee, Inc., 31 227–30**
Green Power & Light Company. *See* UtiliCorp United Inc.
Green River Electric Corporation, **11** 37
Green Thumb, **II** 562
**Green Tree Financial Corporation, 11 162–63**. *See also* Conseco, Inc.
**The Greenalls Group PLC, 21 245–47**
**The Greenbrier Companies, 19 185–87**
**Greene King plc, 31 223–26**
Greenfield Healthy Foods, **26** 58
Greenfield Industries Inc., **13** 8
Greenham Construction Materials, **38** 451–52
Greenleaf Corp., **IV** 203
Greenman Brothers Inc. *See* Noodle Kidoodle.
**GreenPoint Financial Corp., 28 166–68**
Greensboro Life Insurance Company, **11** 213
Greenville Insulating Board Corp., **III** 763
Greenville Tube Corporation, **21** 108
Greenwell Montagu Gilt-Edged, **II** 319; **17** 325
Greenwich Associates, **19** 117
Greenwich Capital Markets, **II** 311
**Greenwood Mills, Inc., 14 219–21**
Greenwood Publishing Group, **IV** 610
Greenwood Trust Company, **18** 478
Gregg Publishing Co., **IV** 636
**Greif Bros. Corporation, 15 186–88**
Greiner Engineering Inc., **45** 421
Grenfell and Colegrave Ltd., **II** 245
Gresham Insurance Company Limited, **24** 285
Gresham Life Assurance, **III** 200, 272–73
GretagMacbeth Holdings AG, **18** 291
Gretel's Pretzels, **35** 56
**Grey Advertising, Inc., I** 175, 623; **6 26–28**; **10** 69; **14** 150; **22** 396; **25** 166, 381
Grey United Stores, **II** 666
**Grey Wolf, Inc., 43 201–03**
**Greyhound Corp., I 448–50**; **II** 445; **6** 27; **8** 144–45; **10** 72; **12** 199; **16** 349; **22** 406, 427; **23** 173–74; **27** 480; **42** 394
**Greyhound Lines, Inc., 32 227–31 (upd.)**; **48** 319
Greyhound Temporary Services, **25** 432
Greylock Mills, **III** 213
GRiD Systems Corp., **II** 107
Griesheim Elektron, **IV** 140

Grieveson, Grant and Co., **II** 422–23
Griffin and Sons, **II** 543
Griffin Bacal, **25** 381
**Griffin Land & Nurseries, Inc.**, **43 204–06**
Griffin Pipe Products Co., **7** 30–31
Griffin Wheel Company, **7** 29–30
**Griffon Corporation**, **34 194–96**
Griffon Cutlery Corp., **13** 166
Grigg, Elliot & Co., **14** 555
Grimes Aerospace, **22** 32
Grindlays Bank, **II** 189
Gringoir/Broussard, **II** 556
**Grinnell Corp.**, **III** 643–45; **11** 198; **13 245–47**
Grip Printing & Publishing Co., **IV** 644
Grisewood & Dempsey, **IV** 616
**Grist Mill Company**, **15 189–91**; **22** 338
Gristede Brothers, **23** 407; **24** 528–29
**Gristede's Sloan's, Inc.**, **31 231–33**
GRM Industries Inc., **15** 247–48
Grocer Publishing Co., **IV** 638
Grocery Store Products Co., **III** 21
Grocery Warehouse, **II** 602
Groen Manufacturing, **III** 468
Grogan-Cochran Land Company, **7** 345
**Grolier Inc.**, **IV** 619; **16 251–54**; **43 207–11 (upd.)**
Grolier Interactive, **41** 409
Groot-Noordhollandsche, **III** 177–79
Groovy Beverages, **II** 477
Gross Brothers Laundry. *See* G&K Services, Inc.
Gross Townsend Frank Hoffman, **6** 28
Grosset & Dunlap, Inc., **II** 144; **III** 190–91
Grosskraftwerk Franken AG, **23** 47
**Grossman's Inc.**, **13 248–50**
Grossmith Agricultural Industries, **II** 500
Grosvenor Marketing Co., **II** 465
Groton Victory Yard, **I** 661
**Ground Round, Inc.**, **21 248–51**
Ground Services Inc., **13** 49
Group Arnault, **32** 146
**Group 4 Falck A/S**, **42 165–68**, 338
**Group Health Cooperative**, **41 181–84**
Group Hospitalization and Medical Services, **10** 161
Group Lotus, **13** 357
Group Maeva SA, **48** 316
Group Maintenance America Corp. *See* Encompass Services Corporation.
Group Schneider S.A., **20** 214
Groupe AB, **19** 204
Groupe AG, **III** 201–02
**Groupe Air France**, **6 92–94**. *See also* Air France *and* Societe Air France.
Groupe Ancienne Mutuelle, **III** 210–11
**Groupe André**, **17 210–12**
Groupe Axime, **37** 232
Groupe Barrière SA, **48** 199
Groupe Barthelmey, **III** 373
Groupe Bisset, **24** 510
Groupe Bollore, **37** 21
Groupe Bruxelles Lambert, **26** 368
Groupe Bull, **10** 563–64; **12** 246; **21** 391; **34** 517. *See also* Compagnie des Machines Bull.
Groupe Casino. *See* Etablissements Economiques de Casino Guichard, Perrachon et Cie, S.C.A.
**Groupe Castorama-Dubois Investissements**, **23 230–32**
**Groupe Danone**, **14** 150; **32 232–36 (upd.)**
Le Groupe Darty, **24** 266, 270
**Groupe Dassault Aviation SA**, **26 179–82 (upd.)**; **42** 373, 376
**Groupe de la Cité**, **IV 614–16**, 617
Groupe de la Financière d'Angers, **IV** 108
**Groupe DMC (Dollfus Mieg & Cie)**, **27 186–88**
**Groupe Fournier SA**, **44 187–89**
**Groupe Go Sport S.A.**, **39 183–85**
**Groupe Guillin SA**, **40 214–16**
**Groupe Jean-Claude Darmon**, **44 190–92**
Groupe Jean Didier, **12** 413
Groupe Jean-Paul Gaultier, **34** 214
Groupe Lagardère S.A., **15** 293; **21** 265, 267
**Groupe Lapeyre S.A.**, **33 175–77**
**Groupe Legris Industries**, **23 233–35**
**Groupe Les Echos**, **25 283–85**
**Groupe Partouche SA**, **48 196–99**
Groupe Pechiney, **33** 89
Groupe Pinault-Printemps-Redoute, **19** 306, 309; **21** 224, 226
Groupe Poron, **35** 206
**Groupe Promodès S.A.**, **19 326–28**
Groupe Rallye, **39** 183–85
Groupe Rothschild, **22** 365
**Groupe Rougier SA**, **21 438–40**
Groupe Roussin, **34** 13
Groupe Salvat, **IV** 619
**Groupe SEB**, **35 201–03**
**Groupe Sidel S.A.**, **21 252–55**
Groupe Victoire, **III** 394
**Groupe Vidéotron Ltée.**, **20 271–73**
**Groupe Yves Saint Laurent**, **23 236–39**
**Groupe Zannier S.A.**, **35 204–07**
Groupement des Exploitants Pétroliers, **IV** 545
Groupement des Mousquetaires. *See* ITM Entreprises SA.
Groupement Français pour l'Investissement Immobilier, **42** 153
Groupement Laitier du Perche, **19** 50
Groupement pour le Financement de la Construction. *See* Gecina SA.
GroupMAC. *See* Encompass Services Corporation.
Groux Beverage Corporation, **11** 451
Grove Manufacturing Co., **I** 476–77; **9** 393
**Grow Biz International, Inc.**, **18 207–10**
**Grow Group Inc.**, **12 217–19**, 387–88
Growing Healthy Inc., **27** 197; **43** 218
Growmark, **I** 421; **11** 23
Growth International, Inc., **17** 371
**Grubb & Ellis Company**, **21 256–58**
Gruene Apotheke, **I** 681
**Gruma, S.A. de C.V.**, **19** 192; **31 234–36**
**Grumman Corp.**, **I** 58–59, **61–63**, 67–68, 78, 84, 490, 511; **7** 205; **8** 51; **9** 17, 206–07, 417, 460; **10** 316–17, 536; **11 164–67 (upd.)**, 363–65, 428; **15** 285; **28** 169
Grün & Bilfinger A.G., **I** 560–61
**Grundig AG**, **I** 411; **II** 80, 117; **12** 162; **13** 402–03; **15** 514; **27 189–92**; **48** 383
Grunenthal, **I** 240
Gruner + Jahr AG & Co., **IV** 590, 593; **7** 245; **15** 51; **20** 53; **22** 442; **23** 85
**Gruntal & Co., L.L.C.**, **III** 263; **20 274–76**
Gruntal Financial Corp., **III** 264
Grupo Acerero del Norte,
Grupo Acerero del Norte, S.A. de C.V., **22** 286; **42** 6
**Grupo Aeropuerto del Sureste, S.A. de C.V.**, **48 200–02**
Grupo Bimbo, S.A. de C.V., **31** 236
Grupo Bufete. *See* Bufete Industrial, S.A. de C.V.
Grupo Cabal S.A., **23** 166
Grupo Campi, S.A. de C.V., **39** 230
**Grupo Carso, S.A. de C.V.**, **14** 489; **21 259–61**
**Grupo Casa Saba, S.A. de C.V.**, **39 186–89**
Grupo Corvi S.A. de C.V., **7** 115; **25** 126
Grupo Cruzcampo S.A., **34** 202
Grupo Cuervo, S.A. de C.V., **31** 91–92
**Grupo Cydsa, S.A. de C.V.**, **39 190–93**
Grupo de Ingenieria Ecologica, **16** 260
Grupo Dina. *See* Consorcio G Grupo Dina, S.A. de C.V.
Grupo DST, **41** 405–06
**Grupo Elektra, S.A. de C.V.**, **39 194–97**
**Grupo Ferrovial, S.A.**, **40 217–19**
Grupo Financiero Banamex-Accival, **27** 304
Grupo Financiero Inbursa, **21** 259
Grupo Financiero Inverlat, S.A., **39** 188
**Grupo Financiero Serfin, S.A.**, **19 188–90**, 474; **36** 63
**Grupo Gigante, S.A. de C.V.**, **34 197–99**
Grupo Hecali, S.A., **39** 196
**Grupo Herdez, S.A. de C.V.**, **35 208–10**
Grupo Hermes, **24** 359
**Grupo IMSA, S.A. de C.V.**, **44 193–96**
Grupo Industrial Alfa, S.A. de C.V., **44** 332. *See also* Alfa, S.A. de C.V.
Grupo Industrial Atenquique, S.A. de C.V., **37** 176
**Grupo Industrial Bimbo**, **19 191–93**; **29** 338
**Grupo Industrial Durango, S.A. de C.V.**, **37 176–78**
Grupo Industrial Maseca S.A. de C.V. (Gimsa). *See* Gruma, S.A. de C.V.
Grupo Irsa, **23** 171
**Grupo Mexico, S.A. de C.V.**, **40 220–23**, 413
**Grupo Modelo, S.A. de C.V.**, **29 218–20**
Grupo Nacional Provincial, **22** 285
Grupo Pipsamex S.A., **37** 178
Grupo Protexa, **16** 210
Grupo Pulsar. *See* Pulsar Internacional S.A.
Grupo Quan, **19** 192–93
Grupo Salinas, **39** 196
Grupo Sanborns S.A. de C.V., **35** 118
**Grupo TACA**, **38 218–20**
**Grupo Televisa, S.A.**, **9** 429; **18 211–14**; **19** 10; **24** 515–17; **39** 188, 398
**Grupo Transportación Ferroviaria Mexicana, S.A. de C.V.**, **47 162–64**
Grupo Tribasa, **34** 82
Grupo Tudor, **IV** 471
Grupo Xtra, **39** 186, 188
Grupo Zeta, **IV** 652–53; **7** 392
Gruppo Buffetti S.p.A., **47** 345–46
**Gruppo Coin S.p.A.**, **41 185–87**
Gruppo GFT, **22** 123
Gruppo IRI, **V** 325–27
Gryphon Development, **24** 237
**Gryphon Holdings, Inc.**, **21 262–64**
**GSD&M Advertising**, **44 197–200**
GSG&T, **6** 495
GSG Holdings Ltd., **39** 87
GSI. *See* Geophysical Service, Inc.

GSI Acquisition Co. L.P., **17** 488
GSR, Inc., **17** 338
GSU. *See* Gulf States Utilities Company.
**GT Bicycles**, **26 183–85**, 412
**GT Interactive Software**, **19** 405; **31 237–41**. *See also* Infogrames Entertainment S.A.
**GTE Corporation**, **II** 38, 47, 80; **III** 475; **V 294–98**; **9** 49, 171, 478–80; **10** 19, 97, 431; **11** 500; **14** 259, 433; **15 192–97 (upd.)**; **18** 74, 111, 543; **22** 19; **25** 20–21, 91; **26** 520; **27** 302, 305; **46** 373. *See also* British Columbia Telephone Company *and* Verizon Communications.
GTE Northwest Inc., **37** 124–26
GTECH Holdings, Inc., **27** 381
GTI Corporation, **29** 461–62
GTM-Entrepose, **23** 332
GTM Group, **43** 450, 452
GTO. *See* Global Transport Organization.
GTS Duratek, Inc., **13** 367–68
GTSI. *See* Government Technology Services Inc.
Guangzhou M. C. Packaging, **10** 130
Guaranty Bank & Trust Company, **13** 440
Guaranty Federal Bank, F.S.B., **31** 441
Guaranty Federal Savings & Loan Assoc., **IV** 343
Guaranty Properties Ltd., **11** 258
Guaranty Savings and Loan, **10** 339
Guaranty Trust Co., **II** 329–32, 428; **IV** 20; **16** 25; **22** 110; **36** 152
Guardforce Limited, **45** 378
Guardian, **III** 721
Guardian Bank, **13** 468
Guardian Federal Savings and Loan Association, **10** 91
Guardian Mortgage Company, **8** 460
Guardian National Bank, **I** 165; **11** 137
Guardian Refrigerator Company. *See* Frigidaire Home Products.
**Guardian Royal Exchange Plc**, **III** 350; **11 168–70**; **33** 319
Gubor Schokoladen, **15** 221
Gucci Group N.V., **45** 343–44
**Guccio Gucci, S.p.A.**, **12** 281; **15 198–200**; **27** 329
GUD Holdings, Ltd., **17** 106
Guelph Dolime, **IV** 74
**Guerbet Group**, **46 214–16**
Guerdon Homes, Inc., **41** 19
**Guerlain**, **23 240–42**; **33** 272
Guernsey Banking Co., **II** 333
**Guess, Inc.**, **15 201–03**; **17** 466; **23** 309; **24** 157; **27** 329
Guest, Keen and Nettlefolds plc. *See* GKN plc.
**Guest Supply, Inc.**, **18 215–17**
Gueyraud et Fils Cadet, **III** 703
Guidant Corp., **30** 316; **37** 39; **43** 351
Guideoutdoors.com Inc., **36** 446
**Guilbert S.A.**, **42 169–71**
Guild Press, Inc., **13** 559
Guild Wineries, **13** 134; **34** 89
Guilford Industries, **8** 270–72
**Guilford Mills Inc.**, **8 234–36**; **40 224–27 (upd.)**
Guilford of Maine, Inc., **29** 246
Guilford Transportation Industries, Inc., **16** 348, 350
**Guillemot Corporation**, **41 188–91**, 407, 409
Guillin. *See* Groupe Guillin SA
Guinness Mahon, **36** 231
Guinness Overseas Ltd., **25** 281
Guinness Peat Aviation, **10** 277; **36** 426
**Guinness plc**, **I** 239, 241, **250–52**, 268, 272, 282; **II** 428–29, 610; **9** 100, 449; **10** 399; **13** 454; **18** 62, 501; **29** 84; **33** 276; **36** 405–06. *See also* Diageo plc.
**Guinness/UDV**, **43 212–16 (upd.)**
**Guitar Center, Inc.**, **29 221–23**
Gujarat State Fertilizer Co., **III** 513
Gulco Industries, Inc., **11** 194
Güldner Aschaffenburg, **I** 582
**Gulf + Western Inc.**, **I** 418, **451–53**, 540; **II** 147, 154–56, 177; **III** 642, 745; **IV** 289, 672; **7** 64; **10** 482; **13** 121, 169, 470; **22** 210; **24** 33; **25** 328, 535; **33** 3; **41** 71
Gulf + Western Industries, **22** 122. *See also* Paramount Communications.
Gulf Air, **6** 63; **27** 25; **39** 137–38
Gulf Canada Ltd., **I** 216, 262, 264; **IV** 495, 721; **6** 478; **9** 391; **13** 557–58
Gulf Caribbean Marine Lines, **6** 383
Gulf Coast Sportswear Inc., **23** 65
Gulf Energy Development, **22** 107
Gulf Engineering Co. Ltd., **IV** 131
Gulf Exploration Co., **IV** 454
**Gulf Island Fabrication, Inc.**, **44 201–03**
Gulf Marine & Maintenance Offshore Service Company, **22** 276
Gulf Mobile and Northern Railroad, **I** 456
Gulf Mobile and Ohio Railroad, **I** 456; **11** 187
Gulf of Suez Petroleum Co., **IV** 412–14
Gulf Oil Chemical Co., **13** 502
Gulf Oil Corp., **I** 37, 584; **II** 315, 402, 408, 448; **III** 225, 231, 259, 497; **IV** 198, 287, 385–87, 392, 421, 450–51, 466, 470, 472–73, 476, 484, 508, 510, 512, 531, 538, 565, 570, 576; **17** 121–22; **21** 494; **24** 521; **25** 444; **33** 253
Gulf Plains Corp., **III** 471
Gulf Power Company, **38** 446, 448
Gulf Public Service Company, Inc, **6** 580; **37** 89
Gulf Resources & Chemical Corp., **15** 464
Gulf States Paper, **IV** 345
Gulf States Steel, **I** 491
**Gulf States Utilities Company**, **6 495–97**; **12** 99
Gulf United Corp., **III** 194
**Gulfstream Aerospace Corporation**, **7 205–06**; **13** 358; **24** 465; **28 169–72 (upd.)**; **36** 190–91
Gulfstream Banks, **II** 336
Gulfwind Marine USA, **30** 303
Gulistan Holdings Inc., **28** 219
Gulton Industries Inc., **7** 297; **19** 31
Gummi Werke, **I** 208; **44** 218
Gump's, **7** 286
Gunder & Associates, **12** 553
Gunderson, Inc. *See* The Greenbrier Companies.
Gunfred Group, **I** 387
Gunite Corporation, **23** 306
**The Gunlocke Company**, **12** 299; **13** 269; **23 243–45**
Gunnite, **27** 203
Gunns Ltd., **II** 482
Gunpowder Trust, **I** 379; **13** 379
Gunter Wulff Automaten, **III** 430
Gunther, S.A., **8** 477
Gupta, **15** 492
Gurneys, Birkbeck, Barclay & Buxton, **II** 235
**GUS plc**, **47 165–70 (upd.)**
Gusswerk Paul Saalmann & Sohne, **I** 582
Gustav Schickendanz KG, **V** 165
Gustavus A. Pfeiffer & Co., **I** 710
Gustin-Bacon Group, **16** 8
Gutehoffnungshütte Aktienverein AG, **III** 561, 563; **IV** 104, 201
Guthrie Balfour, **II** 499–500
**Guthy-Renker Corporation**, **32 237–40**
Gutta Percha Co., **I** 428
Gutteridge, Haskins & Davey, **22** 138
Gutzeit. *See* W. Gutzeit & Co.
Guy Carpenter & Co., **III** 282
**Guy Degrenne SA**, **44 204–07**
Guy Motors, **13** 286
Guy Pease Associates, **34** 248
Guy Salmon Service, Ltd., **6** 349
**Guyenne et Gascogne**, **23 246–48**
Guyomarc'h, **39** 356
GW Utilities Ltd., **I** 264; **6** 478
**Gwathmey Siegel & Associates Architects LLC**, **II** 424; **13** 340; **26 186–88**
GWC. *See* General Waterworks Corporation.
GWK GmbH, **45** 378
**GWR Group plc**, **39 198–200**
**Gymboree Corporation**, **15 204–06**
Gynecare Inc., **23** 190
Gynetics, Inc., **26** 31
Gypsum, Lime, & Alabastine Canada Ltd., **IV** 271

H&D. *See* Hinde & Dauch Paper Company.
H&H Craft & Floral, **17** 322
H & H Plastics Co., **25** 312
**H & R Block, Incorporated**, **9 268–70**; **25** 434; **27** 106, 307; **29 224–28 (upd.)**; **48** 234, 236
H.A. Job, **II** 587
H.B. Claflin Company, **V** 139
H.B. Fenn and Company Ltd., **25** 485
**H.B. Fuller Company**, **8 237–40**; **32 254–58 (upd.)**
H.B. Nickerson & Sons Ltd., **14** 339
H.B. Reese Candy Co., **II** 511
H.B. Tuttle and Company, **17** 355
H.B. Viney Company, Inc., **11** 211
H. Berlind Inc., **16** 388
H.C. Christians Co., **II** 536
H.C. Frick Coke Co., **IV** 573; **7** 550
H.C. Petersen & Co., **III** 417
H.C. Prange Co., **19** 511–12
H Curry & Sons. *See* Currys Group PLC.
H.D. Lee Company, Inc. *See* Lee Apparel Company, Inc.
H.D. Pochin & Co., **III** 690
**H.D. Vest, Inc.**, **46 217–19**
H. Douglas Barclay, **8** 296
**H.E. Butt Grocery Company**, **13 251–53**; **32 259–62 (upd.)**; **33** 307
H.E. Moss and Company Tankers Ltd., **23** 161
**H.F. Ahmanson & Company**, **II 181–82**; **10 342–44 (upd.)**; **28** 167; **47** 160
H. Fairweather and Co., **I** 592
H.G. Anderson Equipment Corporation, **6** 441
H.H. Brown Shoe Company, **18** 60, **18** 62
H.H. Cutler Company, **17** 513
H.H. Robertson, Inc., **19** 366

H.H. West Co., **25** 501
H. Hackfeld & Co., **I** 417
H. Hamilton Pty, Ltd., **III** 420
H.I.G. Capital L.L.C., **30** 235
H.I. Rowntree and Co., **II** 568
H.J. Green, **II** 556
**H.J. Heinz Company**, **I** 30–31, 605, 612; **II** 414, 480, 450, **507–09**, 547; **III** 21; **7** 382, 448, 576, 578; **8** 499; **10** 151; **11** **171–73 (upd.)**; **12** 411, 529, 531–32; **13** 383; **21** 55, 500–01; **22** 147; **25** 517; **27** 197–98; **33** 446–49; **36** **253–57 (upd.)**; **43** 217–18
H.J. Justin & Sons. *See* Justin Industries, Inc.
H.K. Ferguson Company, **7** 355
H.K. Porter Company, Inc., **19** 152
H.L. Green Company, Inc., **9** 448
H.L. Judd Co., **III** 628
H.L. Yoh Company. *See* Day & Zimmerman, Inc.
H. Lewis and Sons, **14** 294
**H. Lundbeck A/S**, **44** **208–11**
H.M. Byllesby & Company, Inc., **6** 539
H.M. Goush Co., **IV** 677–78
H.M. Spalding Electric Light Plant, **6** 592
H. Miller & Sons, Inc., **11** 258
H N Norton Co., **11** 208
H.O. Houghton & Company, **10** 355
H.O. Systems, Inc., **47** 430
H-P. *See* Hewlett-Packard Co.
H.P. Foods, **II** 475
H.P. Hood, **7** 17–18
H.P. Smith Paper Co., **IV** 290
H.R. MacMillan Export Co., **IV** 306–08
H. Reeve Angel & Co., **IV** 300
H. Salt Fish and Chips, **13** 320
H.T. Cherry Company, **12** 376
H.V. McKay Proprietary, **III** 651
H.W. Heidmann, **I** 542
H.W. Johns Manufacturing Co., **III** 663, 706–08; **7** 291
H.W. Madison Co., **11** 211
H.W.S. Solutions, **21** 37
H.W. Wilson Company, **17** 152; **23** 440
H. Williams and Co., Ltd., **II** 678
**Ha-Lo Industries, Inc.**, **27** **193–95**
Häagen-Dazs, **II** 556–57, 631; **10** 147; **14** 212, 214; **19** 116; **24** 140, 141
Haake-Beck Brauerei AG, **9** 86
Haas, Baruch & Co. *See* Smart & Final, Inc.
Haas Corp., **I** 481
Haas Publishing Companies, Inc., **22** 442
Haas Wheat & Partners, **15** 357
**Habersham Bancorp**, **25** **185–87**
Habirshaw Cable and Wire Corp., **IV** 177
**Habitat for Humanity International**, **36** **258–61**
Habitat/Mothercare PLC. *See* Storehouse PLC.
**Hach Co.**, **14** 309; **18** **218–21**
**Hachette Filipacchi Medias S.A.**, **21** **265–67**; **33** 310
**Hachette S.A.**, **IV** 614–15, **617–19**, 675; **10** 288; **11** 293; **12** 359; **16** 253–54; **17** 399; **21** 266; **22** 441–42; **23** 476; **43** 210. *See also* Matra-Hachette S.A.
Hachmeister, Inc., **II** 508; **11** 172
Hacker-Pschorr Brau, **II** 242; **35** 331
**Hackman Oyj Adp**, **44** 204, **212–15**
**Hadco Corporation**, **24** **201–03**
Hadleigh-Crowther, **I** 715
Haemocell, **11** 476
**Haemonetics Corporation**, **20** **277–79**
Hafez Insurance Co., **III** 242
**Hagemeyer N.V.**, **18** 180–82; **39** **201–04**; **45** 426
**Haggar Corporation**, **19** **194–96**; **24** 158
**Haggen Inc.**, **38** **221–23**
Haggie, **IV** 91
Hägglunds Vehicle AB, **47** 7, 9
**Hahn Automotive Warehouse, Inc.**, **24** **204–06**
Hahn Department Stores. *See* Allied Stores Corp.
Hahn, Inc., **17** 9
Haile Mines, Inc., **12** 253
**The Hain Celestial Group, Inc.**, **43** **217–20 (upd.)**
**Hain Food Group, Inc.**, **I** 514; **27** **196–98**; **36** 256
Hainaut-Sambre, **IV** 52
A.B. Hakon Swenson, **II** 639
**Hakuhodo, Inc.**, **6** **29–31**, 48–49; **16** 167; **42** **172–75 (upd.)**
Hakunetsusha & Company, **12** 483
**HAL Inc.**, **6** 104; **9** **271–73**. *See also* Hawaiian Airlines, Inc.
Halcon International, **IV** 456
Hale and Dorr, **31** 75
Haleko Hanseatisches Lebensmittel Kontor GmbH, **29** 500
Halewood, **21** 246
**Half Price Books, Records, Magazines Inc.**, **37** **179–82**
Halfords Ltd., **IV** 17, 19, 382–83; **24** 75
Halifax Banking Co., **II** 220
Halifax Timber, **I** 335
Hall & Levine Agency, **I** 14
Hall and Co., **III** 737
Hall and Ham River, **III** 739
Hall Bros. Co., **IV** 620–21; **7** 23
Hall Containers, **III** 739
Hall Laboratories, Inc., **45** 209
Hall-Mark Electronics, **23** 490
Hallamore Manufacturing Co., **I** 481
La Halle aux Chaussures, **17** 210
Haller, Raymond & Brown, Inc., **II** 10
**Halliburton Company**, **II** 112; **III** 473, **497–500**, 617; **11** 505; **13** 118–19; **17** 417; **25** **188–92 (upd.)**
Hallivet China Clay Co., **III** 690
**Hallmark Cards, Inc.**, **IV** **620–21**; **7** 23–25; **12** 207, 209; **16** **255–57 (upd.)**, 427; **18** 67, 69, 213; **21** 426–28; **22** 33, 36; **24** 44, 516–17; **25** 69, 71, 368; **28** 160; **29** 64; **39** 87; **40** **228–32 (upd.)**; **45** 131
Hallmark Chemical Corp., **8** 386
Hallmark Investment Corp., **21** 92
Hallmark Residential Group, Inc., **45** 221
Halo Lighting, **30** 266
Haloid Company. *See* Xerox Corporation.
Halsam Company, **25** 380
Halsey, Stuart & Co., **II** 431; **III** 276
Halstead Industries, **26** 4
Halter Marine, **22** 276
Hamada Printing Press, **IV** 326
Hamashbir Lata'asiya, **II** 47; **25** 267
Hambrecht & Quist Group, **10** 463, 504; **26** 66; **27** 447; **31** 349
Hambro American Bank & Trust Co., **11** 109
Hambro Countrywide Security, **32** 374
Hambro Life Assurance Ltd., **I** 426; **III** 339
Hambros Bank, **II** 422; **16** 14; **27** 474; **43** 7
Hamburg-Amerikanische-Packetfahrt-Actien-Gesellschaft, **6** 397–98
Hamburg Banco, **II** 351
Hamburg-Amerika, **I** 542
Hamburger Flugzeubau GmbH., **I** 74
Hamelin Group, Inc., **19** 415
Hamer Hammer Service, Inc., **11** 523
Hamersley Holdings, **IV** 59–61
Hamil Textiles Ltd. *See* Algo Group Inc.
Hamilton Aero Manufacturing, **I** 47, 84; **10** 162
**Hamilton Beach/Proctor-Silex Inc.**, **7** 369–70; **16** 384; **17** **213–15**; **24** 435; **43** 289
Hamilton Blast Furnace Co., **IV** 208
Hamilton Brown Shoe Co., **III** 528
Hamilton Group Limited, **15** 478
Hamilton Industries, Inc., **25** 261
Hamilton Malleable Iron Co., **IV** 73; **24** 142
Hamilton National Bank, **13** 465
Hamilton Oil Corp., **IV** 47; **22** 107
Hamilton Standard, **9** 417
Hamilton Steel and Iron Co., **IV** 208
Hamilton/Hall-Mark, **19** 313
Hamish Hamilton, **IV** 659; **8** 526
**Hammacher Schlemmer & Company**, **21** **268–70**; **26** 439–40
Hammamatsu Commerce Bank, **II** 291
Hammarplast, **13** 493
Hammarsforsens Kraft, **IV** 339
Hammerich & Lesser, **IV** 589
Hammermill Paper Co., **IV** 287; **15** 229; **23** 48–49; **47** 189
Hammers Plastic Recycling, **6** 441
**Hammerson plc**, **40** **233–35**
**Hammerson Property Investment and Development Corporation PLC**, **IV** **696–98**; **26** 420
Hammery Furniture Company, **14** 302–03
Hammes Co., **38** 482
Hamming-Whitman Publishing Co., **13** 559
Hammond Corp., **IV** 136
Hammond Lumber Co., **IV** 281; **9** 259
Hammond's, **II** 556
Hammonton Electric Light Company, **6** 449
Hamomag AG, **III** 546
**Hampton Industries, Inc.**, **20** **280–82**
Hampton Inns, **9** 425–26
Hampton Roads Food, Inc., **25** 389
Hamworthy Engineering Ltd., **31** 367, 369
Han Kook Fertilizer Co., **I** 516
Hanbury, Taylor, Lloyd and Bowman, **II** 306
**Hancock Fabrics, Inc.**, **16** 197–99; **18** **222–24**
**Hancock Holding Company**, **15** **207–09**
Hancock Jaffe Laboratories, **11** 460
Hancock Park Associates. *See* Leslie's Poolmart, Inc.
Hancock Textile Co., Inc., **27** 291
Hand in Hand, **III** 234
Handelsbank of Basel, **III** 375
Handelsfinanz Bank of Geneva, **II** 319; **17** 324
Handelsmaatschappij Montan N.V., **IV** 127
Handelsunion AG, **IV** 222
**Handleman Company**, **15** **210–12**
Handley Page Transport Ltd., **I** 50, 92–93; **24** 85
**Handy & Harman**, **23** **249–52**

Handy Andy Home Improvement Centers, Inc., **16** 210; **26** 160–61
Handy Dan, **V** 75
Hanes Corp., **II** 572–73; **8** 202, 288; **15** 436; **25** 166
Hanes Holding Company, **11** 256; **48** 267
Hang Chong, **18** 114
Hang Seng Bank, **II** 298; **IV** 717
**Hanger Orthopedic Group, Inc.**, **41** **192–95**
Haniel & Cie. GmbH, **27** 175
Hanil Development Company, **6** 98
Hanjin Group, **6** 98; **27** 271–72
Hankook Tyre Manufacturing Company, **V** 255–56; **19** 508
Hankuk Glass Industry Co., **III** 715
**Hankyu Corporation**, **V** **454–56**; **23** **253–56 (upd.)**
**Hankyu Department Stores, Inc.**, **V** **70–71**
Hanley Brick, **14** 250
Hanmi Citizen Precision Industry, **III** 455
**Hanna-Barbera Cartoons Inc.**, **7** 306; **18** 65; **23** **257–59**, 387; **25** 313; **33** 432
Hanna Iron Ore Co., **IV** 236; **26** 528
Hanna Mining Co., **8** 346–47
Hanna Ore Mining Company, **12** 352
**Hannaford Bros. Co.**, **12** **220–22**
Hannen Brauerei GmbH, **9** 100
Hannifin Corp., **III** 602
Hannoversche Bank, **II** 278
Hanover Bank, **II** 312–13
**Hanover Direct, Inc.**, **36** **262–65**
**Hanover Foods Corporation**, **35** **211–14**
Hanover House, Inc., **24** 154
Hanovia Co., **IV** 78
Hanrstoffe-und Düngemittelwerk Saar-Lothringen GmbH, **IV** 197
Hans Grohe, **III** 570; **20** 362
Hansa Linie, **26** 279–80
Hanseco Reinsurance Co., **III** 343
**Hansen Natural Corporation**, **31** **242–45**
Hanson Industries, **44** 257
**Hanson PLC**, **I** 438, 475, 477; **III** **501–03**, 506; **IV** 23, 94, 97, 169, 171, 173, 290; **7** **207–10 (upd.)**; **13** 478–79; **17** 39–40, 325; **23** 296–97; **27** 287–88; **30** **228–32 (upd.)**, 441; **37** 6–7, 205; **39** 345; **45** 332
Hansvedt Industries Inc., **25** 195
**Hapag-Lloyd Ag**, **6** **397–99**; **42** 283
Happy Air Exchangers Ltd., **21** 499
Happy Eater Ltd., **III** 106
**Happy Kids Inc.**, **30** **233–35**
Haralambos Beverage Corporation, **11** 451
Harald Quant Group, **III** 377
**Harbert Corporation**, **13** 98; **14** **222–23**
**Harbison-Walker Refractories Company**, **III** 472; **24** **207–09**
Harbor Group, **41** 262–63
Harbor Tug and Barge Co., **6** 382
Harborlite Corporation, **10** 45
Harbour Group, **24** 16
Harco, Inc., **37** 31
**Harcourt Brace and Co.**, **IV** 622; **12** **223–26**
**Harcourt Brace Jovanovich, Inc.**, **II** 133–34; **III** 118; **IV** **622–24**, 642, 672; **7** 312; **12** 224; **13** 106; **14** 177; **19** 404; **25** 177
**Harcourt General, Inc.**, **12** 226; **20** **283–87 (upd.)**; **25** 178
Harcros Chemical Group, **III** 699
Harcros Investment Trust Ltd., **III** 698–99
**Hard Rock Cafe International, Inc.**, **12** **227–29**; **25** 387; **27** 201; **32** **241–45 (upd.)**; **37** 191; **41** 308
Hardee's Food Systems Inc., **II** 679; **7** 430; **8** 564; **9** 178; **15** 345; **16** 95; **19** 93; **23** 505; **27** 16–18; **46** 98
Hardin Stockton, **21** 96
**Harding Lawson Associates Group, Inc.**, **16** **258–60**
**Hardinge Inc.**, **25** **193–95**
Hardison & Stewart Oil, **IV** 569; **24** 519
Hardman Inc., **III** 699
Hardware Wholesalers Inc., **12** 8. *See also* Do it Best Corporation.
Hardwick Stove Company, **III** 573; **22** 349
Hardy Oil & Gas, **34** 75
Hardy Spicer, **III** 595
**HARIBO GmbH & Co. KG**, **44** **216–19**
Harima Shipbuilding & Engineering Co., Ltd., **I** 511, 534; **III** 513, 533; **12** 484
Harima Zosenjo, Ltd., **IV** 129
Harken Energy Corporation, **17** 169–70
**Harland and Wolff Holdings plc**, **19** **197–200**
Harlem Globetrotters, **7** 199, 335
Harlequin Enterprises Ltd., **IV** 587, 590, 617, 619, 672; **19** 405; **29** 470–71, 473
**Harley-Davidson, Inc.**, **III** 658; **7** **211–14**; **13** 513; **16** 147–49; **21** 153; **23** 299–301; **25** 22, **196–200 (upd.)**; **40** 31
**Harleysville Group Inc.**, **37** **183–86**
Harlow Metal Co. Ltd., **IV** 119
**Harman International Industries Inc.**, **15** **213–15**; **36** 101
**Harmon Industries, Inc.**, **25** **201–04**
Harmon Publishing Company, **12** 231
**Harmonic Inc.**, **43** **221–23**
Harmsworth Brothers, **17** 396
Harmsworth Publishing, **19** 118, 120
**Harnischfeger Industries, Inc.**, **I** 186; **8** **241–44**; **14** 56; **26** 355; **38** **224–28 (upd.)**
Harold A. Wilson & Co., **I** 405
**Harold's Stores, Inc.**, **22** **248–50**
Harp Lager Ltd., **15** 442; **35** 395, 397
**Harper Group Inc.**, **12** 180; **13** 20; **17** **216–19**
Harper House, Inc. *See* Day Runner, Inc.
Harper Robinson and Company, **17** 163
**HarperCollins Publishers**, **IV** 652; **7** 389, 391; **14** 555–56; **15** **216–18**; **23** 156, 210; **24** 546; **46** 196, 311
Harpers, Inc., **12** 298; **48** 245
**Harpo Entertainment Group**, **28** **173–75**; **30** 270
**Harrah's Entertainment, Inc.**, **9** 425–27; **16** **261–63**; **27** 200; **43** **224–28 (upd.)**
Harrell International, **III** 21; **22** 146
Harriman Co., **IV** 310; **19** 266
Harriman, Ripley and Co., **II** 407
Harris Abattoir Co., **II** 482
Harris Adacom Corporation B.V., **21** 239
Harris Bankcorp, **II** 211; **46** 55
**Harris Corporation**, **II** **37–39**; **11** 46, 286, 490; **20** **288–92 (upd.)**; **27** 364
Harris Daishowa (Australia) Pty., Ltd., **IV** 268
Harris-Emery Co., **19** 510
Harris Financial, Inc., **11** 482
**Harris Interactive Inc.**, **41** **196–99**
Harris Laboratories, **II** 483; **14** 549
Harris Manufacturing Company, **25** 464
Harris Microwave Semiconductors, **14** 417
Harris Oil Company, **17** 170
Harris Pharmaceuticals Ltd., **11** 208
Harris Publications, **13** 179
Harris Publishing. *See* Bernard C. Harris Publishing Company, Inc.
Harris Queensway, **24** 269
**Harris Teeter Inc.**, **23** **260–62**
Harris Transducer Corporation, **10** 319
Harrisburg National Bank and Trust Co., **II** 315–16
Harrison & Sons (Hanley) Ltd., **III** 681
**Harrisons & Crosfield plc**, **III** **696–700**. *See also* Elementis plc.
**Harrods Holdings**, , **21** 353; **45** 188; **47** **171–74**
Harrow Stores Ltd., **II** 677
Harry and David. *See* Bear Creek Corporation.
Harry F. Allsman Co., **III** 558
Harry Ferguson Co., **III** 651
Harry N. Abrams, Inc., **IV** 677; **17** 486
**Harry Winston Inc.**, **45** **184–87**
**Harry's Farmers Market Inc.**, **23** **263–66**
Harry's Premium Snacks, **27** 197; **43** 218
Harsah Ceramics, **25** 267
**Harsco Corporation**, **8** **245–47**; **11** 135; **30** 471
Harshaw Chemical Company, **9** 154; **17** 363
Harshaw/Filtrol Partnership, **IV** 80
Hart Glass Manufacturing, **III** 423
Hart Press, **12** 25
Hart Schaffner & Marx. *See* Hartmarx Corporation.
Hart Son and Co., **I** 592
Harte & Co., **IV** 409; **7** 308
**Harte-Hanks Communications, Inc.**, **17** **220–22**
Harter Bank & Trust, **9** 474–75
Hartford Container Company, **8** 359
Hartford Electric Light Co., **13** 183
Hartford Financial Services Group, **41** 64
Hartford Fire Insurance, **11** 198
Hartford Insurance Group, **I** 463–64; **22** 428
Hartford Machine Screw Co., **12** 344
Hartford National Bank and Trust Co., **13** 396
Hartford National Corporation, **13** 464, 466–67
Hartford Trust Co., **II** 213
Hartley's, **II** 477
Hartmann & Braun, **III** 566; **38** 299
Hartmann Fibre, **12** 377
Hartmann Luggage, **12** 313
**Hartmarx Corporation**, **8** **248–50**; **25** 258; **32** **246–50 (upd.)**
**The Hartstone Group plc**, **14** **224–26**
**The Hartz Mountain Corporation**, **12** **230–32**; **46** **220–23 (upd.)**
Harvard Private Capital Group Inc., **26** 500, 502
Harvard Sports, Inc., **19** 144
Harvard Table Tennis, Inc., **19** 143–44
Harvard Ventures, **25** 358
Harvest Day, **27** 291
Harvest International, **III** 201
Harvest Partners, Inc., **40** 300
Harvestore, **11** 5
Harvey Aluminum Inc., **I** 68; **22** 188
Harvey Benjamin Fuller, **8** 237–38
Harvey Group, **19** 312
Harvey Hotel Corporation, **23** 71, 73
Harvey Lumber and Supply Co., **III** 559
**Harveys Casino Resorts**, **27** **199–201**

Harwood Homes, **31** 386
**Harza Engineering Company**, **14 227–28**
Has.net, **48** 402
**Hasbro, Inc.**, **III 504–06**; **IV** 676; **7** 305, 529; **12** 168–69, 495; **13** 561; **16 264–68 (upd.)**; **17** 243; **18** 520–21; **21** 375; **25** 313, 380–81, 487–89; **28** 159; **34** 369; **43 229–34 (upd.)**
Haslemere Estates, **26** 420
Hasler Holding AG, **9** 32
Hassenfeld Brothers Inc., **III** 504
Hasten Bancorp, **11** 371
**Hastings Entertainment, Inc.**, **29 229–31**
Hastings Filters, Inc., **17** 104
Hastings Manufacturing Company, **17** 106
Hatch Grinding, **29** 86, 88
Hatersley & Davidson, **16** 80
Hatfield Jewelers, **30** 408
Hathaway Manfacturing Co., **III** 213
Hathaway Shirt Co., **I** 25–26
Hatteras Yachts Inc., **45** 175
Hattori Seiko Co., Ltd. *See* Seiko Corporation.
**Hauser, Inc.**, **46 224–27**
Hausted, Inc., **29** 451
**Havas, SA**, **IV** 616; **10** 195–96, **345–48**; **13** 203–04; **33 178–82 (upd.)**; **34** 83. *See also* Vivendi Universal Publishing
Haven Automation International, **III** 420
**Haverty Furniture Companies, Inc.**, **31 246–49**
Havertys, **39** 174
Haviland Candy Co., **15** 325
Hawaii National Bank, **11** 114
**Hawaiian Airlines Inc.**, **9** 271–73; **22 251–53 (upd.)**; **24** 20–22; **26** 339. *See also* HAL Inc.
Hawaiian Dredging & Construction Co., **I** 565–66
**Hawaiian Electric Industries, Inc.**, **9 274–77**
Hawaiian Fertilizer Co., **II** 490
Hawaiian Pineapple Co., **II** 491
Hawaiian Tug & Barge, **9** 276
Hawaiian Tuna Packers, **II** 491
**Hawker Siddeley Group Public Limited Company**, **I** 41–42, 50, 71, 470; **III 507–10**; **8** 51; **12** 190; **20** 311; **24** 85–86
Hawkeye Cablevision, **II** 161
**Hawkins Chemical, Inc.**, **16 269–72**
Hawley & Hazel Chemical Co., **III** 25
Hawley Group Limited, **12** 10
Hawley Products, **16** 20
**Haworth Inc.**, **8 251–52**; **27** 434; **39 205–08 (upd.)**
Hawthorn Company, **8** 287
Hawthorn-Mellody, **I** 446; **11** 25
Hawthorne Appliance and Electronics, **10** 9–11
Haxton Foods Inc., **21** 155
Hay Group, **I** 33; **42** 329–30
Hayakawa Electrical Industries, **II** 95–96
Hayakawa Metal Industrial Laboratory, **II** 95; **12** 447
Hayaku Zenjiro, **III** 408
Hayama Oil, **IV** 542
Hayashi Kane Shoten, **II** 578
Hayashikane Shoten K.K., **II** 578
Hayden Clinton National Bank, **11** 180
Hayden Publications, **27** 499
Hayden Stone, **II** 450; **9** 468
Hayes Conyngham & Robinson, **24** 75
**Hayes Corporation**, **24 210–14**
Hayes Industries Inc., **16** 7
**Hayes Lemmerz International, Inc.**, **27 202–04**
Hayes Microcomputer Products, **9** 515
Hayes Wheel Company, **7** 258
Hayne, Miller & Swearingen, Inc., **22** 202
Hays Petroleum Services, **IV** 451
**Hays Plc**, **27 205–07**
Hazard, **I** 328
HAZCO International, Inc., **9** 110
Hazel-Atlas Glass Co., **I** 599; **15** 128
Hazel Bishop, **III** 55
**Hazelden Foundation**, **28 176–79**
Hazell Sun Ltd., **IV** 642; **7** 312
Hazeltine, Inc., **II** 20
Hazlenut Growers of Oregon, **7** 496–97
Hazleton Laboratories Corp., **30** 151
**Hazlewood Foods plc**, **32 251–53**
Hazzard and Associates, **34** 248
HBO. *See* Home Box Office Inc.
**HCA - The Healthcare Company**, **35 215–18 (upd.)**
HCI Holdings, **I** 264
HCL America, **10** 505
HCL Sybase, **10** 505
HCR Manor Care, **25** 306, 310
HCS Technology, **26** 496–97
HDM Worldwide Direct, **13** 204; **16** 168
**HDR Inc.**, **I** 563; **48 203–05**
HDS. *See* Heartland Express, Inc.
Head Sportswear International, **15** 368; **16** 296–97; **43** 374
Headrick Outdoor, **27** 280
Heads and Threads, **10** 43
**Headway Corporate Resources, Inc.**, **40 236–38**
Heal's, **13** 307
Heald Machine Co., **12** 67
Healey & Baker, **IV** 705
Healing Arts Publishing, Inc., **41** 177
Healix Health Services Inc., **48** 310
Health & Tennis Corp., **III** 431; **25** 40
Health and Diet Group, **29** 212
**Health Care & Retirement Corporation**, **III** 79; **22 254–56**; **25** 306, 310
Health Care International, **13** 328
Health Development Corp., **46** 432
Health Maintenance Organization of Pennsylvania. *See* U.S. Healthcare, Inc.
Health Maintenance Organizations, **I** 545
Health Management Center West, **17** 559
Health-Mor Inc. *See* HMI Industries.
**Health O Meter Products Inc.**, **14 229–31**; **15** 307
Health Plan of America, **11** 379
Health Plan of Virginia, **III** 389
Health Products Inc., **I** 387
**Health Risk Management, Inc.**, **24 215–17**
Health Services, Inc., **10** 160
**Health Systems International, Inc.**, **11 174–76**; **25** 527
Health Way, Inc., **II** 538
HealthAmerica Corp., **III** 84
Healthcare, L.L.C., **29** 412
HealthCare USA, **III** 84, 86
HealthCo International, Inc., **19** 290
Healthdyne, Inc., **17** 306–09; **25** 82
Healthmagic, Inc., **29** 412
HealthRider Corporation, **38** 238
HealthRite, Inc., **45** 209
Healthshares L.L.C, **18** 370
Healthsource Inc., **22** 143; **45** 104, 109
**HealthSouth Corporation**, **33 183–86 (upd.)**
**HealthSouth Rehabilitation Corporation**, **14 232–34**; **25** 111
**Healthtex, Inc.**, **17 223–25**, 513
HealthTrust, **III** 80; **15** 112; **35** 215, 217
Healthy Choice, **12** 531
**The Hearst Corporation**, **IV** 582, 596, 608, **625–27**; **12** 358–59; **19 201–204 (upd.)**; **21** 404; **22** 161; **32** 3; **46 228–32 (upd.)**
Hearthstone Insurance Co. of Massachusetts, **III** 203
Heartland Building Products, **II** 582
Heartland Components, **III** 519; **22** 282
**Heartland Express, Inc.**, **13** 550–51; **18 225–27**
Heartland Homes, Inc., **41** 19
Heartland Industrial Partners L.P., **41** 94
Heartland Securities Corp., **32** 145
Heartstream Inc., **18** 423
Heat Transfer Pty. Ltd., **III** 420
Heatcraft Inc., **8** 320–22
Heath Co., **II** 124; **13** 573; **34** 516
Heath Steele Mines Ltd., **IV** 18
Heatilator Inc., **13** 269
Heavy Duty Parts, Inc., **19** 37
Hebrew National Kosher Foods, **III** 24
**Hechinger Company**, **12 233–36**; **28** 51
Hecker-H-O Co., **II** 497
Heckett Technology Services Inc., **8** 246–47
Heckler & Koch GmbH, **24** 88
**Hecla Mining Company**, **17** 363; **20** 149, **293–96**
Heco Envelope Co., **IV** 282; **9** 261
Hede Nielsen A/S, **47** 219
**Heekin Can Inc.**, **10** 130; **13 254–56**
HEFCO, **17** 106
Hefei Rongshida Group Corporation, **22** 350
HEI Investment Corp., **9** 276
**HEICO Corporation**, **15** 380; **30 236–38**
**Heidelberger Druckmaschinen AG**, **III** 701; **33** 346; **40 239–41**
**Heidelberger Zement AG**, **23** 325–26; **31 250–53**
Heidelburger Drueck, **III** 301
Heidemij. *See* Arcadis NV.
Heidi Bakery, **II** 633
**Heidrick & Struggles International, Inc.**, **14** 464; **28 180–82**
Heights of Texas, fsb, **8** 437
Heil Company, **28** 103
Heil-Quaker Corp., **III** 654
Heileman Brewing Co. *See* G. Heileman Brewing Co.
**Heilig-Meyers Company**, **14 235–37**; **23** 412, 414; **40 242–46 (upd.)**
Heim-Plan Unternehmensgruppe, **25** 455
Heimstatt Bauspar AG, **III** 401
**Heineken N.V.**, **I** 219, **256–58**, 266, 288; **II** 642; **13 257–59 (upd.)**; **14** 35; **17** 256; **18** 72; **21** 319; **25** 21–22; **26** 305; **34 200–04 (upd.)**
Heinkel Co., **I** 74
Heinrich Bauer North America, **7** 42–43
Heinrich Bauer Verlag, **23** 85–86
Heinrich Koppers GmbH, **IV** 89
Heinrich Lanz, **III** 463; **21** 173
Heinz Co. *See* H.J. Heinz Company.
Heinz Deichert KG, **11** 95
Heinz Italia S.p.A., **15** 221
Heisers Inc., **I** 185

Heisey Glasswork Company, **19** 210
Heiwa Sogo Bank, **II** 326, 361
Heizer Corp., **III** 109–11; **14** 13–15
HEL&P. *See* Houston Electric Light & Power Company.
Helados La Menorquina S.A., **22** 515
Helemano Co., **II** 491
**Helen of Troy Corporation**, **18 228–30**
Helen's Arts & Crafts, **17** 321
Helena Rubenstein, Inc., **III** 24, 48; **8** 343–44; **9** 201–02; **14** 121; **30** 188; **35** 111; **46** 277
**Helene Curtis Industries, Inc.**, **I** 403; **8 253–54**; **18** 217; **22** 487; **28 183–85 (upd.)**; **32** 476
Heliotrope Studios, Inc., **39** 396
Helix Biocore, **11** 458
Hellefors Jernverk, **III** 623
**Heller, Ehrman, White & McAuliffe**, **41 200–02**
Heller Financial, Inc., **7** 213; **16** 37; **25** 198
Hellman, Haas & Co. *See* Smart & Final, Inc.
Hellschreiber, **IV** 669
**Helly Hansen ASA**, **18** 396; **25 205–07**
Helme Products, Inc., **15** 139
**Helmerich & Payne, Inc.**, **18 231–33**
**Helmsley Enterprises, Inc.**, **9 278–80**; **39 209–12 (upd.)**
Helmut Delhey, **6** 428
Helmuth Hardekopf Bunker GmbH, **7** 141
Help-U-Sell, Inc., **III** 304
Helvetia General, **III** 376
Helvetia Milk Condensing Co., **II** 486; **7** 428
Helvetia Schweizerische Feuerversicherungs-Gesellschaft St. Gallen, **III** 375
Hely Group, **IV** 294; **19** 225
**Helzberg Diamonds**, **18** 60, 63; **40 247–49**
Hemelinger Aktienbrauerei, **9** 86
Hemex, **11** 458
**Hemlo Gold Mines Inc.**, **9 281–82**; **23** 40, 42
Hemma, **IV** 616
A.B. Hemmings, Ltd., **II** 465
Henderson Brothers Holdings, Inc., **37** 225
Henderson-Union Electric Cooperative, **11** 37
Henderson's Industries, **III** 581
Henijean & Cie, **III** 283
**Henkel KGaA**, **III** 21, **31–34**, 45; **IV** 70; **9** 382; **13** 197, 199; **22** 145, 257; **30** 291; **34** 153, **205–10 (upd.)**
**Henkel Manco Inc.**, **22 257–59**
Henley Drilling Company, **9** 364
**The Henley Group, Inc.**, **I** 416; **III 511–12**; **6** 599–600; **9** 298; **11** 435; **12** 325; **17** 20; **37** 158
Henlys Group plc, **35** 63, 65
**Hennes & Mauritz AB**, **29 232–34**
Hennessy Company, **19** 272
Henney Motor Company, **12** 159
Henredon Furniture Industries, **III** 571; **11** 534; **20** 362; **39** 266
Henri Bendel Inc., **17** 203–04
Henry Broderick, Inc., **21** 96
Henry Denny & Sons, **27** 259
Henry Grant & Co., **I** 604
Henry Holt & Co., **IV** 622–23; **13** 105; **27** 223; **35** 451
Henry I. Siegel Co., **20** 136
Henry J. Kaiser Company, Ltd., **28** 200
Henry J. Tully Corporation, **13** 531
The Henry Jones Co-op Ltd., **7** 577
Henry Jones Foods, **I** 437–38, 592; **7** 182; **11** 212
Henry L. Doherty & Company, **IV** 391; **12** 542
Henry Lee Company, **16** 451, 453
Henry, Leonard & Thomas Inc., **9** 533
Henry Meadows, Ltd., **13** 286
**Henry Modell & Company Inc.**, **32 263–65**
Henry Pratt Company, **7** 30–31
Henry S. King & Co., **II** 307
Henry S. Miller Companies, **21** 257
**Henry Schein, Inc.**, **29** 298; **31 254–56**
Henry Tate & Sons, **II** 580
Henry Telfer, **II** 513
Henry Waugh Ltd., **I** 469; **20** 311
Henry Willis & Co. *See* Willis Corroon Group Plc.
Henthy Realty Co., **III** 190
HEPCO. *See* Hokkaido Electric Power Company Inc.
Hepworth plc, **44** 438
**Her Majesty's Stationery Office**, **7 215–18**
**Heraeus Holding GmbH**, **IV 98–100**, 118
Herald and Weekly Times, **IV** 650, 652; **7** 389, 391
Herald Publishing Company, **12** 150
Heralds of Liberty, **9** 506
**Herbalife International, Inc.**, **17 226–29**; **18** 164; **41 203–06 (upd.)**
Herbert Clough Inc., **24** 176
Herbert W. Davis & Co., **III** 344
Herby's Foods, **36** 163
Herco Technology, **IV** 680
Hercofina, **IV** 499
Hercules Filter, **III** 419
**Hercules Inc.**, **I 343–45**, 347; **III** 241; **19** 11; **22 260–63 (upd.)**; **28** 195; **30** 36
Hercules Nut Corp., **II** 593
Hercules Offshore Drilling, **28** 347–48
Hereford Paper and Allied Products Ltd., **14** 430
Herff Jones, **II** 488; **25** 254
Heritage Bankcorp, **9** 482
Heritage Communications, **II** 160–61
Heritage Federal Savings and Loan Association of Huntington, **10** 92
Heritage House of America Inc., **III** 81
Heritage Life Assurance, **III** 248
Heritage Media Group, **25** 418
Heritage National Health Plan, **III** 464
Heritage Springfield $$Heritage Springfield, **14** 245
**Herley Industries, Inc.**, **33 187–89**
**Herman Goelitz, Inc.**, **28 186–88**
**Herman Miller, Inc.**, **8** 251–52, **255–57**; **39** 205–07
Herman's World of Sports, **I** 548; **II** 628–29; **15** 470; **16** 457; **43** 385
Hermann Pfauter Group, **24** 186
Hermannshütte, **IV** 103, 105
**Hermès International S.A.**, **34 211–14 (upd.)**
Hermes Kreditversicherungsbank, **III** 300
**Hermès S.A.**, **14 238–40**
Herrburger Brooks P.L.C., **12** 297
Herrick, Waddell & Reed. *See* Waddell & Reed, Inc.
Herring-Hall-Marvin Safe Co. of Hamilton, Ohio, **7** 145
Hersey Products, Inc., **III** 645
Hershey Bank, **II** 342
**Hershey Foods Corporation**, **I** 26–27; **II** 478, 508, **510–12**, 569; **7** 300; **11** 15; **12** 480–81; **15** 63–64, **219–22 (upd.)**, 323; **27** 38–40; **30** 208–09
Hertel AG, **13** 297
Hertford Industrial Estates, **IV** 724
**Hertie Waren- und Kaufhaus GmbH**, **V 72–74**; **19** 234, 237
Herts & Beds Petroleum Co., **IV** 566
Herts Pharmaceuticals, **17** 450; **41** 375–76
**The Hertz Corporation**, **I** 130; **II** 90; **6** 52, 129, 348–50, 356–57, 392–93; **V** 494; **9 283–85**; **10** 419; **11** 494; **16** 379; **21** 151; **22** 54, 56, 524; **24** 9, 409; **25** 143; **33 190–93 (upd.)**; **36** 215
Hertz-Penske Leasing. *See* Penske Corporation.
Hervillier, **27** 188
**Heska Corporation**, **39 213–16**
Hespeler Hockey Inc., **22** 204
Hess Department Stores Inc., **16** 61–62; **19** 323–24; **41** 343
Hess Oil & Chemical Corp., **IV** 366
Hessische Berg- und Hüttenwerke AG, **III** 695
Hessische Landesbank, **II** 385–86
Hessische Ludwigs-Eisenbahn-Gesellschaft, **6** 424
Hesston Corporation, **13** 17; **22** 380
Hetteen Hoist & Derrick. *See* Polaris Industries Inc.
**Heublein Inc.**, **I** 226, 246, 249, **259–61**, 281; **7** 266–67; **10** 180; **14** 214; **21** 314–15; **24** 140; **25** 177; **31** 92; **34** 89
Heuer. *See* TAG Heuer International SA.
Heuga Holdings B.V., **8** 271
Hewitt & Tuttle, **IV** 426; **17** 355–56
Hewitt Motor Company, **I** 177; **22** 329
**Hewlett-Packard Company**, **II** 62; **III** 116, **142–43**; **6** 219–20, 225, **237–39 (upd.)**, 244, 248, 278–79, 304; **8** 139, 467; **9** 7, 35–36, 57, 115, 471; **10** 15, 34, 86, 232, 257, 363, 404, 459, 464, 499, 501; **11** 46, 234, 274, 284, 382, 491, 518; **12** 61, 147, 162, 183, 470; **13** 128, 326, 501; **14** 354; **15** 125; **16** 5, 139–40, 299, 301, 367, 394, 550; **18** 386–87, 434, 436, 571; **19** 515; **20** 8; **25** 96, 118, 151–53, 499, 531; **26** 177, 520; **27** 221; **28 189–92 (upd.)**; **33** 15; **36** 3, 81–82, 299–300; **38** 20, 187, 417–19; **41** 117, 288; **43** 294
Hexalon, **26** 420
Hexatec Polymers, **III** 742
**Hexcel Corporation**, **11** 475; **27** 50; **28 193–95**
Heyden Newport Chemical Corp., **I** 526
Heyer-Schulte, **26** 286
Heytesbury Party Ltd., **34** 422
HFC. *See* Household Finance Corporation.
HFS Inc., **21** 97; **22** 54, 56
HG Hawker Engineering Co. Ltd., **III** 508
HGCC. *See* Hysol Grafil Composite Components Co.
HH Finch Ltd., **38** 501
HI. *See* Houston Industries Incorporated.
Hi-Bred Corn Company, **9** 410
Hi-Lo Automotive, Inc., **26** 348–49
Hi-Mirror Co., **III** 715
Hi Tech Consignments, **18** 208
Hi-Tek Polymers, Inc., **8** 554
**Hibbett Sporting Goods, Inc.**, **26 189–91**
Hibbing Transportation, **I** 448

Hibernia & Shamrock-Bergwerksgesellschaft zu Berlin, **I** 542–43
Hibernia Bank, **18** 181
**Hibernia Corporation**, **37 187–90**
Hibernian Banking Assoc., **II** 261
Hickman Coward & Wattles, **24** 444
**Hickory Farms, Inc.**, **12** 178, 199; **17 230–32**
Hickorycraft, **III** 571; **20** 362
Hicks & Greist, **6** 40
Hicks & Haas, **II** 478
Hicks, Muse, Tate & Furst, Inc., **24** 106; **30** 220; **36** 423
Hicksgas Gifford, Inc., **6** 529
Hidden Creek Industries, Inc., **16** 397; **24** 498
HiFi Buys, **30** 465
Higginson et Hanckar, **IV** 107
Higgs & Young Inc., **I** 412
High Point Chemical Corp., **III** 38
High Retail System Co., Ltd., **V** 195; **47** 391
Highgate Hotels, Inc., **21** 93
Highland Container Co., **IV** 345
Highland Superstores, **9** 65–66; **10** 9–10, 304–05, 468; **23** 51–52
Highland Telephone Company, **6** 334
Highlander Publications, **38** 307–08
Highlands Insurance Co., **III** 498
**Highmark Inc.**, **I** 109; **27 208–11**
Highveld Steel and Vanadium Corp., **IV** 22
Higo Bank, **II** 291
Hilbun Poultry, **10** 250
Hilco Technologies, **III** 143; **6** 238
**Hildebrandt International**, **29 235–38**
Hilex Poly Co., Inc., **8** 477
Hill & Knowlton Inc. *See* WPP Group PLC.
Hill Publishing Co., **IV** 634
Hill-Rom Company, **10** 349–50
Hill Stores, **II** 683
**Hill's Pet Nutrition, Inc.**, **14** 123; **26** 207; **27 212–14**, 390. *See also* Colgate-Palmolive Company.
Hillard Oil and Gas Company, Inc., **11** 523
Hillards, PLC, **II** 678
**Hillenbrand Industries, Inc.**, **6** 295; **10 349–51**; **16** 20
Hiller Aircraft Company, **9** 205; **48** 167
Hiller Group, **14** 286
Hillerich & Bradsby Co., **24** 403
**The Hillhaven Corporation**, **III** 76, 87–88; **6** 188; **14 241–43**; **16** 57, 515, 517; **25** 307, 456
Hillin Oil, **IV** 658
Hillman, **I** 183
Hills & Dales Railway Co. *See* Dayton Power & Light Company.
Hills Brothers Inc., **II** 548; **7** 383; **28** 311
Hills Pet Products, **III** 25
**Hills Stores Company**, **11** 228; **13 260–61**; **21** 459; **30** 57
Hillsborough Holdings Corporation. *See* Walter Industries, Inc.
Hillsdale Machine & Tool Company, **8** 514
**Hillsdown Holdings, PLC**, **II 513–14**; **24 218–21 (upd.)**; **28** 490; **41** 252
Hillshire Farm, **II** 572
Hillside Industries Inc., **18** 118
Hilo Electric Light Company, **9** 276
Hilton, Anderson and Co., **III** 669
Hilton Athletic Apparel, **16** 296–97
Hilton Gravel, **III** 670
**Hilton Hotels Corporation**, **II** 208; **III 91–93**, 98–99, 102; **IV** 703; **6** 201, 210; **9** 95, 426; **19 205–08 (upd.)**; **21** 91, 93, 182, 333, 363; **23** 482; **27** 10
Hilton International Co., **6** 385; **12** 489
Himley Brick, **14** 248
Himolene, Inc., **8** 181
Hinde & Dauch Ltd., **IV** 272
Hinde & Dauch Paper Company, **19** 496
Hindell's Dairy Farmers Ltd., **II** 611–12
Hinds, Hayden & Eldredge, **10** 135
Hindustan Petroleum Corp. Ltd., **IV** 441
Hindustan Shipyard, **IV** 484
Hindustan Steel Ltd., **IV** 205–07
**Hino Motors, Ltd.**, **7 219–21**; **21** 163, **271–74 (upd.)**; **23** 288
Hinode Life Insurance Co., Ltd., **II** 360; **III** 365
Hinomaru Truck Co., **6** 428
HIP Health Plan, **22** 425
Hip Hing Construction Company Limited, **IV** 717; **38** 319
Hipercor, S.A., **V** 52; **26** 129
**Hiram Walker Resources Ltd.**, **I** 216, **262–64**; **IV** 721; **6** 478; **9** 391; **18** 41
Hiram Walker-Consumers' Home Ltd. *See* Consumers' Gas Company Ltd.
Hiram Walker-Gooderham & Worts Ltd., **29** 18
Hire-Purchase Company of Ireland, **16** 13; **43** 7
Hiroshima Yakult Co., **25** 449
The Hirsh Company, **17** 279
Hirth-Krause Company. *See* Wolverine World Wide Inc.
Hirz, **25** 85
**Hispanic Broadcasting Corporation**, **35 219–22**; **41** 383, 385
Hispanica de Petroleos, **IV** 424, 527, 546
Hispano Aviacion, **I** 74
HISPANOBRAS, **IV** 55
Hispanoil. *See* Hispanica de Petroleos.
Hispeed Tools, **I** 573
Hisshin-DCA foods, **II** 554
History Book Club, **13** 105–06
**HIT Entertainment PLC**, **40 250–52**
Hit or Miss, **V** 197–98
**Hitachi, Ltd.**, **I 454–55**, 494, 534; **II** 5, 30, 59, 64–65, 68, 70, 73, 75, 114, 273–74, 292–91; **III** 130, 140, 143, 464, 482; **IV** 101; **6** 238, 262; **7** 425; **9** 297; **11** 45, 308, 507; **12 237–39 (upd.)**, 484; **14** 201; **16** 139; **17** 353, 556; **18** 383; **19** 11; **21** 174–75, 390; **23** 53; **24** 324; **40 253–57 (upd.)**
**Hitachi Metals, Ltd.**, **IV 101–02**
**Hitachi Zosen Corporation**, **III 513–14**; **8** 449
**Hitchiner Manufacturing Co., Inc.**, **23 267–70**
Hitco, **III** 721–22
Hjalmar Blomqvist A.B., **II** 639
HL&P. *See* Houston Lighting and Power Company.
HLH Products, **7** 229
**HMI Industries, Inc.**, **17 233–35**
HMO-PA. *See* U.S. Healthcare, Inc.
HMT Technology Corp., **IV** 102
HMV, **I** 531
Hoan Products Ltd. *See* Lifetime Hoan Corporation.
Hoare Govett Ltd., **II** 349
**HOB Entertainment, Inc.**, **37 191–94**
Hobart Corporation, **II** 534; **III** 610–11, 654; **7** 276; **12** 549; **22** 282, 353
Hobart Manufacturing Company, **8** 298
Hobbes Manufacturing, **I** 169–70
Hobby Lobby Stores Inc., **17** 360
Hobson, Bates & Partners, Ltd., **14** 48
Hochschild, Kohn Department Stores, **II** 673
**Hochtief AG**, **14** 298; **17** 376; **24** 88; **33 194–97**
**The Hockey Company**, **34 215–18**
Hocking Glass Company, **13** 40
Hoden Oil, **IV** 478
Hodenpyl-Walbridge & Company, **14** 134
Hodgart Consulting. *See* Hildebrandt International.
Hodgkin, Barnett, Pease, Spence & Co., **II** 307
**Hoechst AG**, **I** 305–06, 309, 317, **346–48**, 605, 632, 669–70; **IV** 451; **8** 262, 451–53; **13** 75, 262–64; **18** 47, 49, 51, **234–37 (upd.)**, 401; **21** 544; **22** 32; **25** 376; **34** 284; **35** 455–57; **38** 380
**Hoechst Celanese Corporation**, **8** 562; **11** 436; **12** 118; **13** 118, **262–65**; **22** 278; **24** 151; **26** 108
Hoeganaes Corporation, **8** 274–75
**Hoenig Group Inc.**, **41 207–09**
Hoerner Waldorf Corp., **IV** 264; **20** 129
**Hoesch AG**, **IV 103–06**, 128, 133, 195, 228, 232, 323
Hofbräubierzentrale GmbH Saarbrücken, **41** 222
Hoffman Enclosures Inc., **26** 361, 363
Hoffmann-La Roche & Co. *See* F. Hoffmann- La Roche & Co.
Hoffritz, **27** 288
Hofmann Herbold & Partner, **34** 249
**Hogan & Hartson L.L.P.**, **44 220–23**; **47** 445–46
Högbo Stål & Jernwerks, **IV** 202
Högforsin Tehdas Osakeyhtiö, **IV** 300
Hojalata y Laminas S.A., **19** 10
Hojgaard & Schultz, **38** 436
Hokkaido Butter Co., **II** 575
Hokkaido Colonial Bank, **II** 310
Hokkaido Dairy Cooperative, **II** 574
Hokkaido Dairy Farm Assoc., **II** 538
**Hokkaido Electric Power Company Inc.**, **V 635–37**
Hokkaido Forwarding, **6** 428
Hokkaido Rakuno Kosha Co., **II** 574
Hokkaido Takushoku Bank, **II** 300
Hokoku Cement, **III** 713
Hokoku Fire, **III** 384
Hokuetsu Paper Manufacturing, **IV** 327
**Hokuriku Electric Power Company**, **V 638–40**
Hokusin Kai, **IV** 475
Hokuyo Sangyo Co., Ltd., **IV** 285
**Holberg Industries, Inc.**, **36 266–69**
Holbrook Grocery Co., **II** 682
Holco BV, **41** 12
Holcroft & Company, **7** 521
Hold Everything, **17** 548–50
Holden Group, **II** 457
**Holderbank Financière Glaris Ltd.**, **III 701–02**; **8** 258–59, 456; **39** 217. *See also* Holnam Inc
**N.V. Holdingmaatschappij De Telegraaf**, **23 271–73**
Holec Control Systems, **26** 496
Holes-Webway Company, **40** 44
Holga, Inc., **13** 269

Holgate Toys, **25** 379–80
Holiday Corp., **16** 263; **22** 418; **38** 76; **43** 226
**Holiday Inns, Inc.**, **I** 224; **III 94–95**, 99–100; **6** 383; **9** 425–26; **10** 12; **11** 178, 242; **13** 362; **14** 106; **15** 44, 46; **16** 262; **18** 216; **21** 361–62; **23** 71; **24** 253; **25** 386; **27** 21. *See also* The Promus Cos., Inc.
Holiday Magic, Inc., **17** 227
Holiday Mart, **17** 124; **41** 114–15
Holiday Rambler Corporation, **7** 213; **25** 198
**Holiday RV Superstores, Incorporated**, **26 192–95**
Holland & Barrett, **13** 103; **31** 346, 348
Holland America Line, **6** 367–68; **26** 279; **27** 90–91
**Holland Burgerville USA**, **44 224–26**
Holland Casino, **23** 229
Holland Electro B.V., **17** 234
Holland Hannen and Cubitts, **III** 753
Holland House, **I** 377–78
Holland Motor Express, **14** 505
Holland Studio Craft, **38** 402
Holland van 1859, **III** 200
Hollandsche Bank-Unie, **II** 184–85
Hollandse Signaalapparaten, **13** 402
Holley Carburetor, **I** 434
**Hollinger International Inc.**, **24 222–25**; **32** 358
Hollingsead International, Inc., **36** 158–60
Hollingsworth & Whitney Co., **IV** 329
Hollostone, **III** 673
**Holly Corporation**, **12 240–42**
Holly Farms Corp., **II** 585; **7** 422–24; **14** 515; **23** 376–77
Holly Sugar Company. *See* Imperial Holly Corporation.
**Hollywood Casino Corporation**, **21 275–77**
**Hollywood Entertainment Corporation**, **25 208–10**; **29** 504; **31** 339
**Hollywood Park, Inc.**, **20 297–300**
Hollywood Park Race Track, **29** 118
Hollywood Pictures, **II** 174; **30** 487
Hollywood Records, **6** 176
**Holme Roberts & Owen LLP**, **28 196–99**
Holmen Hygiene, **IV** 315
Holmen S.A., **IV** 325
Holmens Bruk, **IV** 317–18
Holmes Electric Protective Co., **III** 644
Holmes International. *See* Miller Industries, Inc.
Holmsund & Kramfors, **IV** 338
**Holnam Inc.**, **III** 702; **8 258–60**; **39 217–20 (upd.)**
**Holophane Corporation**, **19 209–12**
**Holson Burnes Group, Inc.**, **14 244–45**
Holsten Brauerei AG, **35** 256, 258
Holt Manufacturing Co., **III** 450–51
Holt, Rinehart and Winston, Inc., **IV** 623–24; **12** 224
**Holt's Cigar Holdings, Inc.**, **42 176–78**
Holthouse Furniture Corp., **14** 236
Holtzbrinck. *See* Verlagsgruppe Georg von Holtzbrinck.
Holvick Corp., **11** 65
Holvis AG, **15** 229
Holyman Sally Ltd., **29** 431
Holyoke Food Mart Inc., **19** 480
Holzer and Co., **III** 569; **20** 361
Holzverkohlungs-Industrie AG, **IV** 70
Homart Development, **V** 182
Home & Automobile Insurance Co., **III** 214
Home and Community Care, Inc., **43** 46
**Home Box Office Inc.**, **II** 134, 136, 166–67, 176–77; **IV** 675; **7 222–24**, 528–29; **10** 196; **12** 75; **18** 65; **23 274–77 (upd.)**, 500; **25** 498; **28** 71
Home Builders Supply, Inc. *See* Scotty's, Inc.
Home Centers of America, Inc., **18** 286
Home Charm Group PLC, **II** 141
Home Choice Holdings, Inc., **33** 366–67
**The Home Depot, Inc.**, **V 75–76**; **9** 400; **10** 235; **11** 384–86; **12** 7, 235, 345, 385; **13** 250, 548; **16** 187–88, 457; **17** 366; **18 238–40 (upd.)**; **19** 248, 250; **21** 356, 358; **22** 477; **23** 232; **26** 306; **27** 416, 481; **31** 20; **35** 11–13; **39** 134; **43** 385; **44** 332–33
Home Entertainment of Texas, Inc., **30** 466
Home Furnace Co., **I** 481
**Home Insurance Company**, **I** 440; **III 262–64**
Home Interiors, **15** 475, 477
Home Nutritional Services, **17** 308
Home Office Reference Laboratory, Inc., **22** 266
Home Oil Company Ltd., **I** 264; **6** 477–78
Home Products Corp., **18** 492
Home Properties Co., Inc., **21** 95
**Home Properties of New York, Inc.**, **42 179–81**
Home Quarters Warehouse, Inc., **12** 233, 235
Home Savings of America, **II** 181–82; **10** 342–43; **16** 346; **28** 167; **47** 160
The Home School, Inc., **41** 111
**Home Shopping Network, Inc.**, **V 77–78**; **9** 428; **18** 76; **24** 517; **25 211–15 (upd.)**; **26** 441; **33** 322
Home Telephone and Telegraph Company, **10** 201
Home Telephone Company. *See* Rochester Telephone Corporation.
Home Vision Entertainment Inc., **31** 339–40
**HomeBase, Inc.**, **II** 658; **13** 547–48; **33 198–201 (upd.)**
HomeClub Inc., **13** 547–48; **16** 187; **17** 366. *See also* HomeBase, Inc.
Homécourt, **IV** 226
HomeFed Bank, **10** 340
Homegrocer.com Inc., **38** 223
Homelite, **21** 175
Homemade Ice Cream Company, **10** 371
Homemakers Furniture. *See* John M. Smyth Co.
HomeMax, Inc., **41** 20
Homer McKee Advertising, **I** 22
Homes By Oakwood, Inc., **15** 328
Homeserve.net Ltd., **46** 72
**Homestake Mining Company**, **IV** 18, 76; **12 243–45**; **20** 72; **27** 456; **38 229–32 (upd.)**
**Hometown Auto Retailers, Inc.**, **44 227–29**
HomeTown Buffet, Inc., **19** 435; **22** 465. *See also* Buffets, Inc
Homette Corporation, **30** 423
Homewood Stores Co., **IV** 573; **7** 550
Homewood Suites, **9** 425–26
Hominal Developments Inc., **9** 512
**Hon Industries Inc.**, **13 266–69**; **23** 243–45
Honam Oil Refinery, **II** 53
Honcho Real Estate, **IV** 225; **24** 489
Honda Giken Kogyo Kabushiki Kaisha. *See* Honda Motor Company Limited.
**Honda Motor Company Limited**, **I** 9–10, 32, **174–76**, 184, 193; **II** 5; **III** 495, 517, 536, 603, 657–58, 667; **IV** 443; **7** 212–13, 459; **8** 71–72; **9** 294, 340–42; **10 352–54 (upd.)**; **11** 33, 49–50, 352; **12** 122, 401; **13** 30; **16** 167; **17** 25; **21** 153; **23** 289–90, 338, 340; **25** 197–99; **27** 76; **29 239–42 (upd.)**; **34** 305–06; **36** 243
Hondo Oil & Gas Co., **IV** 375–76
**Honeywell Inc.**, **I** 63; **II** 30, **40–43**, 54, 68; **III** 122–23, 149, 152, 165, 535, 548–49, 732; **6** 266, 281, 283, 314; **8** 21; **9** 171, 324; **11** 198, 265; **12 246–49 (upd.)**; **13** 234, 499; **17** 33; **18** 341; **22** 373, 436; **23** 471; **29** 464; **30** 34; **33** 334, 337; **43** 284
Hong Kong Aircraft Engineering Co., **I** 522; **6** 79; **16** 480
Hong Kong Airways, **6** 78–79; **16** 480
Hong Kong and Kowloon Wharf and Godown Co., **I** 470; **IV** 699
Hong Kong Dragon Airlines, **18** 114
Hong Kong Industrial Co., Ltd., **25** 312
Hong Kong Island Line Co., **IV** 718
Hong Kong Mass Transit Railway Corp., **19** 111
Hong Kong Resort Co., **IV** 718; **38** 320
**Hong Kong Telecommunications Ltd.**, **IV** 700; **V** 285–86; **6 319–21**; **18** 114; **25** 101–02. *See also* Cable & Wireless HKT.
Hong Kong Telephone Company, **47** 177
Hong Leong Corp., **III** 718
Hong Leong Group Malaysia, **26** 3, 5
Hongkong & Kowloon Wharf & Godown Company, **20** 312
**Hongkong and Shanghai Banking Corporation Limited**, **II** 257, **296–99**, 320, 358; **III** 289; **17** 325; **18** 253; **25** 12. *See also* HSBC Holdings plc.
**Hongkong Electric Company Ltd.**, **6 498–500**; **20** 134
**Hongkong Electric Holdings Ltd.**, **23 278–81 (upd.)**; **47** 177
**Hongkong Land Holdings Ltd.**, **I** 470–71; **IV 699–701**; **6** 498–99; **20** 312–13; **23** 280; **47 175–78 (upd.)**
Honig-Copper & Harrington, **I** 14
Honjo Copper Smeltery, **III** 490
Honolua Plantation Land Company, Inc., **29** 308
Honolulu Oil, **II** 491
Honolulu Sugar Refining Co., **II** 490
**Honshu Paper Co., Ltd.**, **IV** 268, **284–85**, 292, 297, 321, 326
Hood Rubber Company, **15** 488–89
Hood Sailmakers, Inc., **10** 215
Hoogovens. *See* Koninklijke Nederlandsche Hoogovens en Staalfabricken NV.
Hooiberg, **I** 256
Hook's Drug Stores, **9** 67
Hooker Chemical, **IV** 481
Hooker Corp., **19** 324
Hooker Furniture Corp. *See* Bassett Furniture Industries, Inc.
Hooker Petroleum, **IV** 264
**Hooper Holmes, Inc.**, **22 264–67**
Hoosier Park L.P., **29** 118
**Hooters of America, Inc.**, **18 241–43**

Hoover Ball and Bearing Co., **III** 589
**The Hoover Company**, **II** 7; **III** 478; **12** 158, **250–52**; **15** 416, 418; **21** 383; **30** 75, 78; **40 258–62 (upd.)**
Hoover Group Inc., **18** 11
Hoover Industrial, **III** 536; **26** 230
Hoover-NSK Bearings, **III** 589
Hoover Treated Wood Products, Inc., **12** 396
Hopkinton LNG Corp., **14** 126
Hopper Soliday and Co. Inc., **14** 154
**Hops Restaurant Bar and Brewery**, **31** 41; **46 233–36**
Hopwood & Company, **22** 427
**Horace Mann Educators Corporation**, **22 268–70**
Horizon Air Industries, Inc. *See* Alaska Air Group, Inc.
Horizon Bancorp, **II** 252; **14** 103
Horizon Corporation, **8** 348
Horizon Group Inc., **27** 221
Horizon Healthcare Corporation, **25** 456
Horizon Holidays, **14** 36
Horizon Industries, **19** 275
Horizon Lamps, Inc., **48** 299
**Horizon Organic Holding Corporation**, **37 195–99**
Horizon Travel Group, **8** 527
Horizon/CMS Healthcare Corp., **25** 111, 457; **33** 185
Horizons Laitiers, **25** 85
**Hormel Foods Corporation**, **18 244–47 (upd.)**
Horn & Hardart, **II** 614
Horn Silver Mines Co., **IV** 83; **7** 187
Horn Venture Partners, **22** 464
Hornblower & Co., **II** 450
Hornbrook, Inc., **14** 112
Horne's, **I** 449; **16** 62
Hornsberg Land Co., **I** 553
Horsham Corp. *See* TrizecHahn.
Horst Breuer GmbH, **20** 363
Horst Salons Inc., **24** 56
Horten, **II** 622; **47** 107
**Horton Homes, Inc.**, **25 216–18**
**Hospital Corporation of America**, **II** 331; **III 78–80**; **15** 112; **23** 153; **27** 237. *See also* HCA - The Healthcare Company.
Hospital Cost Consultants, **11** 113
Hospital Products, Inc., **10** 534
Hospital Service Association of Pittsburgh, **III** 325
Hospital Specialty Co., **37** 392
**Hospitality Franchise Systems, Inc.**, **11 177–79**; **14** 106; **17** 236. *See also* Cendant Corporation.
**Hospitality Worldwide Services, Inc.**, **26 196–98**
Hosposable Products, Inc. *See* Wyant Corporation.
Host Communications Inc., **24** 404
Host Marriott Corporation, **21** 366
Host Marriott Services Corp., **III** 103; **16** 446; **17** 95
Hot 'n Now, **16** 96–97
Hot Dog Construction Co., **12** 372
Hot Sam Co., **12** 179, 199. *See also* Mrs. Fields' Original Cookies, Inc.
Hot Shoppes Inc., **III** 102
**Hot Topic, Inc.**, **33 202–04**
Hotchkiss-Brandt, **II** 116; **42** 378
Hoteiya, **V** 209–10
Hotel Corporation of America, **16** 337
Hotel Corporation of India, **27** 26
Hotel Properties Ltd., **30** 107
Hotel Reservations Network, Inc., **47** 420
Hotel Scandinavia K/S, **I** 120
HotRail Inc., **36** 124
HotWired, **45** 200
Houbigant, **37** 270
Houdry Chemicals, **I** 298
**Houghton Mifflin Company**, **10 355–57**; **26** 215; **36 270–74 (upd.)**; **46** 441
Houlihan's Restaurant Group, **25** 546
Housatonic Power Co., **13** 182
House and Land Syndicate, **IV** 710
House of Blues, **32** 241, 244
**House of Fabrics, Inc.**, **16** 197–98; **18** 223; **21 278–80**
**House of Fraser PLC**, **21** 353; **37** 6, 8; **45 188–91**; **47** 173. *See also* Harrods Holdings.
House of Miniatures, **12** 264
House of Windsor, Inc., **9** 533
**Household International, Inc.**, **I** 31; **II 417–20**, 605; **7** 569–70; **8** 117; **10** 419; **16** 487–88; **21 281–86 (upd.)**; **22** 38, 542; **24** 152
Household Products Inc., **I** 622; **10** 68
Household Rental Systems, **17** 234
Housing Development Finance Corporation, **20** 313
Housmex Inc., **23** 171
Houston, Effler & Partners Inc., **9** 135
Houston Electric Light & Power Company, **44** 368
Houston General Insurance, **III** 248
**Houston Industries Incorporated**, **V 641–44**; **7** 376. *See also* Reliant Energy Inc.
Houston International Teleport, Inc., **11** 184
Houston Natural Gas Corp., **IV** 395; **V** 610
Houston Oil & Minerals Corp., **11** 440–41
Houston Oil Co., **IV** 342, 674
Houston Pipe Line Company, **45** 21
Hoveringham Group, **III** 753; **28** 450
Hoving Corp., **14** 501
Hovis-McDougall Co., **II** 565
**Hovnanian Enterprises, Inc.**, **29 243–45**
Howaldtswerke-Deutsche Werft AG, **IV** 201
Howard B. Stark Candy Co., **15** 325
Howard Flint Ink Company, **13** 227
Howard H. Sweet & Son, Inc., **14** 502
**Howard Hughes Medical Institute**, **II** 33, 35; **39 221–24**
Howard Hughes Properties, Ltd., **17** 317
Howard Humphreys, **13** 119
**Howard Johnson International, Inc.**, **III** 94, 102–03; **6** 27; **7** 266; **11** 177–78; **15** 36; **16** 156; **17 236–39**; **25** 309
Howard Printing Co., **III** 188; **10** 29
Howard Research and Development Corporation, **15** 412, 414
Howard, Smith & Levin, **40** 126
Howard Smith Paper Mills Ltd., **IV** 271–72
Howden. *See* Alexander Howden Group.
Howdy Company, **9** 177
Howe & Fant, Inc., **23** 82
Howe and Brainbridge Inc., **I** 321
Howe Sound Co., **12** 253
Howe Sound Inc., **IV** 174
Howe Sound Pulp and Paper Ltd., **IV** 321
Howmedica, **29** 455
**Howmet Corporation**, **12 IV** 174; **253–55**; **22** 506
Hoya Corp., **III** 715
Hoyt Archery Company, **10** 216
HQ Global Workplaces, Inc., **47** 331
HQ Office International, **8** 405; **23** 364
HRB Business Services, **29** 227
Hrubitz Oil Company, **12** 244
**HSBC Holdings plc**, **12 256–58**; **17** 323, 325–26; **26 199–204 (upd.)**
HSN Inc., **25** 411
HSS Hire Service Group PLC, **45** 139–41
HTH, **12** 464
HTM Goedkoop, **26** 278–79
H2O Plus, **11** 41
Hua Bei Oxygen, **25** 82
Huaneng Raw Material Corp., **III** 718
**Hub Group, Inc.**, **26** 533; **38 233–35**
Hub Services, Inc., **18** 366
Hubbard Air Transport, **10** 162
Hubbard, Baker & Rice, **10** 126
**Hubbard Broadcasting Inc.**, **24 226–28**
Hubbard Construction Co., **23** 332
Hubbard, Westervelt & Motteley, **II** 425; **13** 341
**Hubbell Incorporated**, **9 286–87**; **31 257–259 (upd.)**
Hubinger Co., **II** 508; **11** 172; **36** 254
Huck Manufacturing Company, **22** 506
Huddart Parker, **III** 672
Hudepohl-Schoenling Brewing Co., **18** 72
Hudnut, **I** 710
Hudson Automobile Company, **18** 492
**The Hudson Bay Mining and Smelting Company, Limited**, **12 259–61**; **13** 502–03; **16** 29
Hudson Engineering Corp., **III** 559
**Hudson Foods Inc.**, **13 270–72**
Hudson Housewares Corp., **16** 389
Hudson Motor Car Co., **I** 135, 158; **III** 568; **10** 292; **20** 359
Hudson Packaging & Paper Co., **IV** 257
Hudson Pharmaceutical Corp., **31** 347
**Hudson River Bancorp, Inc.**, **41 210–13**
Hudson River Railroad, **II** 396
Hudson River Rubber Company, **V** 231
Hudson Scott & Sons, **I** 604
Hudson Software, **13** 481
Hudson Underground Telephone Company, **6** 299
Hudson's. *See* Dayton Hudson Corporation.
**Hudson's Bay Company**, **I** 284; **IV** 400–01, 437; **V 79–81**; **6** 359; **8** 525; **12** 361; **25 219–22 (upd.)**, 230
Hue International, **8** 324
Hueppe Duscha, **III** 571; **20** 362
Huff Daland Dusters, **I** 99; **6** 81
Huffco, **IV** 492
Huffman Manufacturing Company, **7** 225–26
Huffy Bicycles Co., **19** 383
**Huffy Corporation**, **7 225–27**; **26** 184, 412; **30 239–42 (upd.)**
Hugerot, **19** 50
Hugh O'Neill Auto Co., **12** 309
Hughes Air West, **25** 421
Hughes Aircraft Corporation, **I** 172, 484, 539; **III** 428, 539; **7** 426–27; **9** 409; **10** 327; **11** 263, 540; **13** 356, 398; **15** 528, 530; **21** 201; **23** 134; **24** 442; **25** 86, 223; **30** 175. *See also* GM Hughes Electronics Corporation.
Hughes Communications, Inc., **13** 398; **18** 211
Hughes Corp., **18** 535
Hughes Electric Heating Co., **II** 28; **12** 194

**Hughes Electronics Corporation**, **25** **223–25**; **36** 240, 243; **38** 175, 375; **46** 327
Hughes Helicopter, **26** 431; **46** 65
**Hughes Hubbard & Reed LLP**, **44** **230–32**
**Hughes Markets, Inc.**, **22** **271–73**
Hughes Network Systems Inc., **21** 239
Hughes Properties, Inc., **17** 317
Hughes Space and Communications Company, **33** 47–48
**Hughes Supply, Inc.**, **14** **246–47**; **39** 360
Hughes Television Network, **11** 184
Hughes Tool Co., **I** 126; **II** 32; **12** 488; **15** 467; **25** 74; **35** 425. *See also* Baker Hughes Incorporated.
**Hugo Boss AG**, **48** **206–09**
Hugo Neu Corporation, **19** 381–82
Hugo Stinnes GmbH, **I** 542; **8** 69, 494–95
Huguenot Fenal, **IV** 108
Huhtamaki, **30** 396, 398
**Hulman & Company**, **44** **233–36**; **46** 245
**Hüls A.G.**, **I** **349–50**; **25** 82. *See also* Degussa-Hüls AG.
Hulton, **17** 397
Hulton Getty, **31** 216–17
**Humana Inc.**, **III** 79, **81–83**; **6** 28, 191–92, 279; **15** 113; **24** **229–32 (upd.)**; **35** 215–16
Humanetics Corporation, **29** 213
Humanities Software, **39** 341
Humason Manufacturing Co., **III** 628
Humber, **I** 197
Humberside Sea & Land Services, **31** 367
Humble Oil & Refining Company, **III** 497; **IV** 373, 428; **7** 171; **13** 118; **14** 291. *See also* Exxon.
Humboldt-Deutz-Motoren AG, **III** 541–42, 543; **IV** 126
Hummel, **II** 163–64
Hummel Lanolin Corporation, **45** 126
Hummel-Reise, **44** 432
Hummer, Winblad Venture Partners, **36** 157
Hummingbird, **18** 313
Humongous Entertainment, Inc., **31** 238–40
Humphrey Instruments, **I** 693
Humphrey's Estate and Finance, **IV** 700
Humphreys & Glasgow Ltd., **V** 612
Hunco Ltd., **IV** 640; **26** 273
Hungária Biztositó, **III** 185
Hungarian-Soviet Civil Air Transport Joint Stock Company. *See* Malæv Plc.
Hungarotex, **V** 166
**Hungry Howie's Pizza and Subs, Inc.**, **25** **226–28**
**Hunt Consolidated, Inc.**, **27** **215–18 (upd.)**
Hunt Lumber Co., **IV** 358
**Hunt Manufacturing Company**, **12** **262–64**
**Hunt Oil Company**, **IV** 367, 453–54; **7** **228–30**, 378. *See also* Hunt Consolidated, Inc.
**Hunt-Wesson, Inc.**, **17** **240–42**; **25** 278
Hunter-Douglas, **8** 235
Hunter Engineering Co., **IV** 18
**Hunter Fan Company**, **13** **273–75**
Hunter-Hayes Elevator Co., **III** 467
Hunters' Foods, **II** 500
Hunting Aircraft, **I** 50; **24** 85
**Huntingdon Life Sciences Group plc**, **42** **182–85**
**Huntington Bancshares Inc.**, **11** **180–82**
Huntley and Palmer Foods, **II** 544
Huntley Boorne & Stevens, **I** 604
**Hunton & Williams**, **35** **223–26**
**Huntsman Chemical Corporation**, **8** **261–63**; **9** 305
Hupp Motor Car Company, **III** 601; **8** 74; **10** 261
Hurd & Houghton, **10** 355
Hurlburt Paper Co., **IV** 311; **19** 267
Huron Steel Company, Inc., **16** 357
Huse Food Group, **14** 352
**Husky Energy Inc.**, **47** **179–82**
Husky Oil Ltd., **IV** 454, 695; **V** 673–75; **18** 253–54; **19** 159
Husqvarna Forest & Garden Company, **III** 480; **13** 564; **22** 26–27
Hussmann Corporation, **I** 457–58; **7** 429–30; **10** 554; **13** 268; **22** 353–54
Hutcheson & Grundy, **29** 286
Hutchinson-Mapa, **IV** 560
**Hutchinson Technology Incorporated**, **18** **248–51**
Hutchinson Wholesale Grocery Co., **II** 624
Hutchison Microtel, **11** 548
**Hutchison Whampoa Ltd.**, **I** 470; **IV** 694–95; **18** 114, **252–55**; **20** 131, 312–13; **25** 101; **47** 181
Huth Manufacturing Corporation, **10** 414
Hüttenwerk Oberhausen AG, **IV** 222
Hüttenwerk Salzgitter AG, **IV** 201
Huttig Building Products, **31** 398, 400
Huttig Sash & Door Company, **8** 135
Hutton, E.F. *See* E.F. Hutton.
Huyck Corp., **I** 429
**Hvide Marine Incorporated**, **22** **274–76**
HWI. *See* Hardware Wholesalers, Inc.
Hy-Form Products, Inc., **22** 175
**Hy-Vee, Inc.**, **36** **275–78**; **42** 432
Hyatt-Clark Industries Inc., **45** 170
**Hyatt Corporation**, **II** 442; **III** 92, **96–97**; **9** 426; **16** **273–75 (upd.)**; **22** 101; **23** 482; **48** 148
Hyatt Legal Services, **20** 435; **29** 226
Hyatt Medical Enterprises, **III** 73
Hyatt Roller Bearing Co., **I** 171–72; **9** 17; **10** 326
Hybridtech, **III** 18
**Hyde Athletic Industries, Inc.**, **17** **243–45**. *See* Saucony Inc.
Hyde Company, A.L., **7** 116–17
**Hyder plc**, **34** **219–21**
Hydra Computer Systems, Inc., **13** 201
Hydrac GmbH, **38** 300
Hydraulic Brake Co., **I** 141
**Hydril Company**, **46** **237–39**
Hydro-Aire Incorporated, **8** 135
Hydro Carbide Corp., **19** 152
Hydro-Carbon Light Company, **9** 127
Hydro Electric, **19** 389–90
Hydro-Electric Power Commission of Ontario, **6** 541; **9** 461
Hydro Med Sciences, **13** 367
**Hydro-Quebéc**, **6** **501–03**; **32** **266–69 (upd.)**
Hydrocarbon Services of Nigeria Co., **IV** 473
Hydroponic Chemical Co., **III** 28
Hydrox Corp., **II** 533
Hyer Boot, **19** 232
Hygeia Sciences, Inc., **8** 85, 512
Hygienic Ice Co., **IV** 722
Hygrade Containers Ltd., **IV** 286
Hygrade Foods, **III** 502; **7** 208; **14** 536
Hyland Laboratories, **I** 627
Hylsa. *See* Hojalata y Laminas S.A.
**Hylsamex, S.A. de C.V.**, **39** **225–27**
Hyosung Group, **III** 749
Hyper Shoppes, Inc., **II** 670; **18** 507
**Hypercom Corporation**, **27** **219–21**
Hyperion Press, **6** 176
**Hyperion Software Corporation**, **22** **277–79**
Hypermart USA, **8** 555–56
Hyplains Beef, **7** 175
Hypo-Bank. *See* Bayerische Hypotheken- und Wechsel-Bank AG.
Hypobaruk, **III** 348
Hyponex Corp., **22** 475
Hypro Engineering Inc., **I** 481
Hysol Corp., **I** 321; **12** 103
**Hyster Company**, **17** **246–48**; **33** 364
Hyster-Yale Materials Handling, Inc., **I** 424; **7** 369–71
Hystron Fibers Inc., **I** 347
**Hyundai Group**, **I** 207, 516; **II** 53–54, 122; **III** 457–59, **515–17**; **7** **231–34 (upd.)**; **9** 350; **10** 404; **12** 211, 546; **13** 280, 293–94; **18** 124; **23** 353; **25** 469; **29** 264, 266
Hyundai Motors, **47** 279

I Can't Believe It's Yogurt, Inc., **17** 474; **35** 121
I Pellettieri d'Italia S.p.A., **45** 342
I. Appel, **30** 23
I.B. Kleinert Rubber Company, **37** 399
I.C.H. Corp., **I** 528
**I.C. Isaacs & Company**, **31** **260–62**
I.C. Johnson and Co., **III** 669
I.D. Systems, Inc., **11** 444
I-DIKA Milan SRL, **12** 182
I. Feldman Co., **31** 359
I.G. Farbenindustrie AG, **I** 305–06, 309–11, 337, 346–53, 619, 632–33, 698–99; **II** 257; **III** 677, 694; **IV** 111, 485; **8** 108–09; **11** 7; **13** 75–76, 262; **16** 121; **18** 47; **21** 544; **22** 225–26; **26** 452. *See also* BASF A.G. *and* Bayer A.G. *and* Hoechst A.G.
I.J. Stokes Corp., **I** 383
I.M. Pei & Associates, **I** 580; **III** 267; **41** 143
I.M. Singer and Co., **II** 9
I. Magnin Inc., **8** 444; **15** 86; **24** 422; **30** 383; **31** 191, 193
I.N. Kote, **IV** 116; **19** 219
I.N. Tek, **IV** 116; **19** 219
I.R. Maxwell & Co. Ltd., **IV** 641; **7** 311
I-T-E Circuit Breaker, **II** 121
I-X Corp., **22** 416
IAL. *See* International Aeradio Limited.
IAM/Environmental, **18** 11
**Iams Company**, **26** **205–07**; **27** 213
IAWS Group plc, **46** 405
IBANCO, **26** 515
IBC Holdings Corporation, **12** 276
IBCA. *See* International Banking and Credit Analysis.
Iberdrola, **V** 608; **47** 110
**Iberia Líneas Aéreas De España S.A.**, **I** 110; **6** **95–97**; **33** 18; **36** **279–83 (upd.)**
**IBERIABANK Corporation**, **37** **200–02**
Ibero-Amerika Bank, **II** 521
Iberswiss Catering, **6** 96
Ibex Engineering Co., **III** 420
IBH Holding AG, **7** 513
IBJ. *See* The Industrial Bank of Japan Ltd.

IBM. *See* International Business Machines Corporation.
**IBP, Inc., II 515–17**; 7 525; **21 287–90 (upd.)**; **23** 201
IBS Conversions Inc., **27** 492
**Ibstock Brick Ltd., 37 203–06 (upd.)**
**Ibstock plc, III** 735; **14 248–50**
IC Designs, Inc., **48** 127
**IC Industries Inc., I 456–58**; **III** 512; **7** 430; **10** 414, 553; **18** 3; **22** 197; **43** 217. *See also* Whitman Corporation.
**ICA AB, II 639–40**
ICA Fluor Daniel, S. de R.L. de C.V., **41** 148
ICA Mortgage Corporation, **8** 30
ICA Technologies, Ltd., **III** 533
Icahn Capital Corp., **35** 143
Icarus Consulting AG, **29** 376
ICE, **I** 333
ICEE-USA, **24** 240
**Iceland Group plc, 33 205–07**
**ICF Kaiser International, Inc., 28 200–04**
ICH Corporation, **19** 468
Ichikoh Industries Ltd., **26** 154
ICI. *See* Imperial Chemical Industries plc.
ICI Canada, **22** 436
**ICL plc, II** 65, 81; **III** 141, 164; **6 240–42**; **11** 150; **16** 226
ICM Mortgage Corporation, **8** 436
ICOA Life Insurance, **III** 253
**Icon Health & Fitness, Inc., 38 236–39**
Icon International, **24** 445
iConcepts, Inc., **39** 95
Icot Corp., **18** 543
ICS. *See* International Care Services.
ICS, **26** 119
ICX, **IV** 136
ID, Inc., **9** 193
id Software, **31** 237–38; **32** 9
Idaho Frozen Foods, **II** 572–73
**Idaho Power Company, 12 265–67**
**IDB Communications Group, Inc., 11 183–85**; **20** 48; **27** 301, 307
IDC, **25** 101
Ide Megumi, **III** 549
Ideal Basic Industries, **III** 701–02; **8** 258–59; **12** 18
Ideal Corp., **III** 602; **23** 335
Ideal Loisirs Group, **23** 388
IDEC Pharmaceuticals Corporation, **32** 214
Idemitso Petrochemicals, **8** 153
**Idemitsu Kosan K.K., II** 361; **IV 434–36**, 476, 519
Identification Business, Inc., **18** 140
**Identix Inc., 44 237–40**
**IDEXX Laboratories, Inc., 23 282–84**
**IDG Books Worldwide, Inc., 27 222–24**. *See also* International Data Group, Inc.
IDG Communications, Inc, **7** 238
IDG World Expo Corporation, **7** 239
IDI, **22** 365
IDI Temps, **34** 372
IDO. *See* Nippon Idou Tsushin.
IDS Ltd., **22** 76
**IDT Corporation, 34 222–24**
**IEC Electronics Corp., 42 186–88**
IEL. *See* Industrial Equity Ltd.
IFC Disposables, Inc., **30** 496–98
IFF. *See* International Flavors & Fragrances Inc.
IFI, **I** 161–62; **III** 347
Ifil, **27** 515
IFM, **25** 85
IFS Industries, **6** 294
IG. *See* Integrated Genetics.
IG Farben. *See* I.G. Farbenindustrie AG.
IG Holdings, **27** 430
IGA, **II** 624, 649, 668, 681–82; **7** 451; **15** 479; **18** 6, 9; **25** 234
Iggesund Bruk, **IV** 317–18
**Igloo Products Corp., 21 291–93**; **22** 116
IGT-International, **10** 375–76
IGT-North America, **10** 375
IHI. *See* Ishikawajima Harima Heavy Industries.
IHI Granitech Corp., **III** 533
**IHOP Corporation, 17 249–51**; **19** 435, 455
Iida & Co., **I** 493; **24** 325
IinteCom, **III** 169
IIS, **26** 441
IISCO-Ujjain Pipe and Foundry Co. Ltd., **IV** 206
IJ Holdings Corp., **45** 173
IK Coach, Ltd., **23** 290
**IKEA Group, V 82–84**
**IKEA International A/S, 26** 161, **208–11 (upd.)**
**Il Fornaio (America) Corporation, 27 225–28**
Il Giornale, **13** 493
Ilaco, **26** 22
ILFC. *See* International Lease Finance Corporation.
**Ilitch Holdings Inc., 37 207–210**; **46** 130
Illco Toy Co. USA, **12** 496
**Illinois Bell Telephone Company, IV** 660; **14 251–53**; **18** 30
**Illinois Central Corporation, I** 456, 584; **8** 410; **10** 553; **11 186–89**
Illinois Glass Co., **I** 609
Illinois Lock Company, **48** 142
Illinois Merchants Trust Co., **II** 261
Illinois National Bank & Trust Co., **III** 213–14
**Illinois Power Company, 6** 470, **504–07**
Illinois Steel Co., **IV** 572; **7** 549; **8** 114
Illinois Terminal Company, **6** 504
**Illinois Tool Works Inc., III 518–20**; **22 280–83 (upd.)**; **44** 193
Illinois Traction Company, **6** 504
Illinois Trust and Savings Bank, **II** 261
Illinova Energy Partners, **27** 247
Illuminet Holdings Inc., **47** 430
Ilmor Engineering of Great Britain, **V** 494
Ilse-Bergbau AG, **IV** 229–30
Ilselder Hütte, **IV** 201
Ilwaco Telephone and Telegraph Company. *See* Pacific Telecom, Inc.
Ilyushin, **24** 60
IMA Bancard, Inc., **24** 395
IMA Holdings Corp., **III** 73–74
Imabari, **25** 469
Image Business Systems Corp., **11** 66
Image Industries, Inc., **25** 320–21
Image Technologies Corporation, **12** 264
Imageline Inc., **25** 348
Imagine Entertainment, **43** 144
Imagine Manufacturing Solutions Inc., **48** 410
ImagiNet, **41** 97
Imaging Technologies, **25** 183
Imaje, S.A., **28** 104
IMall Inc., **26** 441
Imasa Group, **IV** 34
**Imasco Limited, I** 514; **II** 605; **V 401–02**
**Imation Corporation, 20 301–04**; **33** 348. *See also* Minnesota Mining & Manufacturing Company.
Imatran Voima Oy, **IV** 469. *See also* Fortum Corporation
**Imax Corporation, 21** 362; **28 205–08**; **46** 422
IMC. *See* Intertec Marine Corporation.
IMC Drilling Mud, **III** 499
**IMC Fertilizer Group, Inc., 8 264–66**
Imcera Group, Inc., **8** 264, 266
**IMCO Recycling, Incorporated, 32 270–73**
IMED Corp., **I** 712; **III** 511–12; **10** 551; **38** 364
**Imerys S.A., 40** 176, **263–66 (upd.)**
**Imetal S.A., IV 107–09**
IMG. *See* International Management Group.
**IMI plc, III** 593; **9 288–89**; **29** 364
Imigest Fondo Imicapital, **III** 347
Imlo, **26** 22
Immersion Corporation, **28** 245
Immobilier Batibail, **42** 152
**Immunex Corporation, 8** 26; **14 254–56**
Immuno Serums, Inc., **V** 174–75
Immuno Therapeutics, Inc., **25** 382
**Imo Industries Inc., 7 235–37**; **27 229–32 (upd.)**
IMO Ltd., **III** 539
Impala Platinum Holdings, **IV** 91–93
Impark Limited, **42** 433
**IMPATH Inc., 45 192–94**
Imperial Airways. *See* British Overseas Airways Corporation.
Imperial and International Communications Limited, **25** 100
Imperial Bank of Canada, **II** 244–45
Imperial Bank of Persia, **II** 298
Imperial British East Africa Co., **III** 522
Imperial Business Forms, **9** 72
**Imperial Chemical Industries plc, I** 303, **351–53**, 374, 605, 633; **II** 448, 565; **III** 522, 667, 677, 680, 745; **IV** 38, 110, 698; **7** 209; **8** 179, 222, 224; **9** 154, 288; **10** 436; **11** 97, 361; **12** 347; **13** 448, 470; **16** 121; **17** 118; **18** 50; **21** 544; **44** 116–17
Imperial Feather Company, **19** 304
Imperial Fire Co., **III** 373
Imperial Goonbarrow, **III** 690
Imperial Group Ltd., **II** 513; **III** 503; **7** 209; **17** 238
**Imperial Holly Corporation, 12 268–70**. *See also* Imperial Sugar Company.
Imperial Japanese Government Steel Works, **17** 349–50
Imperial Life Co., **III** 288, 373
Imperial Marine Insurance Co., **III** 384, 405–06
Imperial Metal Industries Ltd. *See* IMI plc.
**Imperial Oil Limited, IV** 428, **437–39**, 494; **25 229–33 (upd.)**; **32** 179–80
Imperial Outdoor, **27** 280
Imperial Packing Co. *See* Beech-Nut Nutrition Corp.
Imperial Paper, **13** 169
Imperial Pneumatic Tool Co., **III** 525
Imperial Premium Finance, **III** 264
Imperial Savings Association, **8** 30–31
Imperial Smelting Corp., **IV** 58
Imperial Sports, **19** 230
**Imperial Sugar Company, 32 274–78 (upd.)**

Imperial Tobacco Company, **I** 425–26, 605; **IV** 260; **V** 401. *See also* B.A.T. Industries PLC.
IMPO Import Parfumerien, **48** 116
Imported Auto Parts, Inc., **15** 246
Impressions Software, **15** 455
Imprimis, **8** 467
Impulse, **9** 122
Impulse Designs, **31** 435–36
IMRA America Inc., **48** 5
Imreg, **10** 473–74
IMRS. *See* Hyperion Software Corporation.
IMS International, Inc., **10** 105
**In Focus Systems, Inc.**, **22 287–90**
In Home Health, Inc., **25** 306, 309–10
**In-N-Out Burger**, **19 213–15**
In-Sink-Erator, **II** 19
INA Corporation, **II** 403; **III** 79, 208, 223–25, 226; **11** 481; **22** 269. *See also* CIGNA Corporation.
INA-Naftaplin, **IV** 454
INA Wälzlager Schaeffler, **III** 595; **47** 278
Inabata & Co., **I** 398
**InaCom Corporation**, **13** 176, **276–78**; **19** 471
Incasso Bank, **II** 185
Incentive Group, **27** 269
**Inchcape PLC**, **II** 233; **III 521–24**; **16 276–80 (upd.)**
Incheon Iron & Steel Co., **III** 516
Inchon Heavy Industrial Corp., **IV** 183
INCO-Banco Indústria e Comércio de Santa Catarina, **13** 70
**Inco Limited**, **IV** 75, 78, **110–12**; **39** 338; **45 195–99 (upd.)**
Incola, S.A., **II** 471; **22** 93
Incon Research Inc., **41** 198
InControl Inc., **11** 460
Incredible Universe, **12** 470; **17** 489; **36** 387
Ind Coope, **I** 215
Indemnité, **III** 391
Indemnity Insurance Company. *See* CIGNA Corporation.
Indentimat Corp., **14** 542
Independent Breweries Company, **9** 178
Independent Delivery Services, Inc., **37** 409
Independent Election Corp. of America, **47** 37
Independent Exhibitions Ltd., **27** 362
Independent Grocers Alliance. *See* IGA.
Independent Lock Co., **13** 166
Independent Metal Products Co., **I** 169
Independent Oil & Gas Co., **IV** 521
Independent Petrochemical, **14** 461
Independent Power Generators, **V** 605
Independent Stave Company, **28** 223
Independent Torpedo Company, **25** 73
Independent Warehouses, Inc., **IV** 180
India Exotics, Inc., **22** 133
India General Steam Navigation and Railway Co., **III** 522
India Life Assurance Co., **III** 359
India Rubber, Gutta Percha & Telegraph Works Co., **I** 428
Indian Airlines Corporation. *See* Air-India.
**Indian Airlines Ltd.**, **46 240–42**
Indian Archery and Toy Corp., **19** 142–43
Indian Iron & Steel Co. Ltd., **IV** 49, 205–07
**Indian Oil Corporation Ltd.**, **IV 440–41**, 483; **48 210–13 (upd.)**
Indian Point Farm Supply, Inc., **IV** 458–59
Indiana Bearings, Inc., **13** 78
**Indiana Bell Telephone Company, Incorporated**, **14 257–61**; **18** 30
Indiana Board and Filler Company, **12** 376
Indiana Electric Corporation, **6** 555
**Indiana Energy, Inc.**, **27 233–36**
Indiana Gaming Company, **21** 40
Indiana Gas & Water Company, **6** 556
Indiana Group, **I** 378
Indiana Oil Purchasing Co., **IV** 370
Indiana Parts and Warehouse, **29** 86, 88
Indiana Power Company, **6** 555
Indiana Refining Co., **IV** 552
Indiana Tube Co., **23** 250
Indianapolis Air Pump Company, **8** 37
Indianapolis Brush Electric Light & Power Company, **6** 508
Indianapolis Cablevision, **6** 508–09
Indianapolis Light and Power Company, **6** 508
**Indianapolis Motor Speedway Corporation**, **9** 16; **46 243–46**
Indianapolis Power & Light Company, **6** 508–09
Indianapolis Pump and Tube Company, **8** 37
Indianhead Truck Lines, **6** 371
IndianOil Companies. *See* Indian Oil Corporation Ltd.
**Indigo NV**, **26 212–14**, 540–41
Indo-Asahi Glass Co., Ltd., **III** 667
Indo-China Steam Navigation Co., **I** 469; **20** 311
Indo Mobil Ltd., **48** 212
Indola Cosmetics B.V., **8** 16
Indonesia Petroleum Co., **IV** 516
Indresco, Inc., **22** 285
Induba, S.A. de C.V., **39** 230
Induban, **II** 196
Indura SA Industria Y Commercio, **25** 82
Industri Kapital, **27** 269
Industria Gelati Sammontana, **II** 575
Industria Metalgrafica, **I** 231
Industria Raffinazione Oli Minerali, **IV** 419
Industrial & Trade Shows of Canada, **IV** 639
Industrial Acceptance Bank, **I** 337
Industrial Air Products, **19** 380–81
Industrial Air Tool, **28** 387
Industrial Bancorp, **9** 229
**Industrial Bank of Japan, Ltd.**, **II 300–01**, 310–11, 338, 369, 433, 459; **17** 121
Industrial Bank of Scotland, **10** 337
Industrial Bio-Test Laboratories, **I** 374, 702
Industrial Cartonera, **IV** 295; **19** 226
Industrial Chemical and Equipment, **16** 271
Industrial Circuits, **IV** 680
Industrial Computer Corp., **11** 78
Industrial Development Corp., **IV** 22, 92, 534
Industrial Development Corp. of Zambia Ltd., **IV** 239–41
Industrial Devices Inc., **48** 359
Industrial Engineering, **III** 598
Industrial Engineering Associates, Inc., **II** 112
Industrial Equity Ltd., **I** 438; **17** 357
Industrial Fuel Supply Co., **I** 569
Industrial Gas Equipment Co., **I** 297
Industrial Gases Lagos, **25** 82
Industrial Instrument Company. *See* Foxboro Company.
Industrial Light & Magic, **12** 322
Industrial Mutual Insurance, **III** 264
Industrial National Bank, **9** 229
Industrial Powder Coatings, Inc., **16** 475
Industrial Publishing Company, **9** 413; **27** 361
Industrial Reorganization Corp., **III** 502, 556
Industrial Resources, **6** 144
**Industrial Services of America, Inc.**, **46 247–49**
Industrial Shows of America, **27** 362
Industrial Tectonics Corp., **18** 276
Industrial Trade & Consumer Shows Inc., **IV** 639; **26** 272
Industrial Trust Co. of Wilmington, **25** 540
Industrial Trust Company, **9** 228
Industrial Vehicles Corp. B.V., **III** 543–44
**Industrias Bachoco, S.A. de C.V.**, **39 228–31**
Industrias del Atlantico SA, **47** 291
Industrias Nacobre, **21** 259
Industrias Negromex, **23** 170
**Industrias Penoles, S.A. de C.V.**, **22 284–86**
Industrias Resistol S.A., **23** 170–71
Industrias y Confecciones, S.A. **V** 51; **26** 129
Industrie-Aktiengesellschaft, **IV** 201
**Industrie Natuzzi S.p.A.**, **18 256–58**
Industrie Regionale du Bâtiment, **IV** 108
Industriegas GmbH., **I** 581
Les Industries Ling, **13** 443
Industriförvaltnings AB Kinnevik, **26** 331–33; **36** 335
Industrionics Control, Inc., **III** 643
AB Industrivärden, **II** 366; **32** 397
Induyco. *See* Industrias y Confecciones, S.A.
Indy Lighting, **30** 266
Indy Racing League, **37** 74
Inelco Peripheriques, **10** 459
Inespo, **16** 322
Inexco Oil Co., **7** 282
**Infinity Broadcasting Corporation**, **11 190–92**; **22** 97; **23** 510; **28** 72; **35** 232; **48 214–17 (upd.)**
Infinity Enterprises, Inc., **44** 4
Infinity Partners, **36** 160
INFLEX, S.A., **8** 247
Inflight Sales Group Limited, **11** 82; **29** 511
InfoAsia, **28** 241
Infobase Services, **6** 14
Infocom, **32** 8
**Infogrames Entertainment S.A.**, **35 227–30**; **41** 407
Infonet Services Corporation, **6** 303; **27** 304
Infoplan, **14** 36
Informatics General Corporation, **III** 248; **11** 468; **25** 86
Informatics Legal Systems, **III** 169; **6** 285
**Information Access Company**, **12** 560–62; **17 252–55**; **34** 438. *See also* The Thomson Corporation.
Information and Communication Group, **14** 555
Information Associates Inc., **11** 78
**Information Builders, Inc.**, **14** 16; **22 291–93**
Information Consulting Group, **9** 345
Information, Dissemination and Retrieval Inc., **IV** 670
**Information Holdings Inc.**, **47 183–86**

Information International. *See* Autologic Information International, Inc.
Information Management Reporting Services. *See* Hyperion Software Corporation.
Information Management Science Associates, Inc., **13** 174
Information Please LLC, **26** 216
**Information Resources, Inc.**, **10 358–60**; **13** 4; **25** 366
Information Unlimited Software, **6** 224
**Informix Corporation**, **10 361–64**, 505; **30 243–46 (upd.)**
Infoseek Corporation, **27** 517; **30** 490
InfoSoft International, Inc. *See* Inso Corporation.
Infostrada S.p.A., **38** 300
**Infosys Technologies Ltd.**, **38 240–43**
Infotech Enterprises, Ltd., **33** 45
Infotechnology Inc., **25** 507–08
Infrasud, **I** 466
Infun, S.A., **23** 269
ING, B.V., **14** 45, 47
**Ing. C. Olivetti & C., S.p.A.**, **III** 122, **144–46**, 549, 678; **10** 499; **16** 122; **25** 33. *See also* Olivetti S.p.A
Ingalls Quinn and Johnson, **9** 135
**Ingalls Shipbuilding, Inc.**, **I** 485; **11** 264–65; **12** 28, **271–73**; **36** 78–79; **41** 42
Ingear, **10** 216
**Ingenico—Compagnie Industrielle et Financière d'Ingénierie**, **46 250–52**
Ingenious Designs Inc., **47** 420
**Ingersoll-Rand Company**, **III** 473, **525–27**; **10** 262; **13** 27, 523; **15** 187, **223–26 (upd.)**; **22** 542; **33** 168; **34** 46
Ingka Holding B.V. *See* IKEA International A/S.
Ingleby Enterprises Inc. *See* Caribiner International, Inc.
Inglenook Vineyards, **13** 134; **34** 89
**Ingles Markets, Inc.**, **20 305–08**
Inglis Ltd., **III** 654; **12** 549
Ingram Book Group, **30** 70
Ingram Corp. Ltd., **III** 559; **IV** 249
**Ingram Industries, Inc.**, **10** 518–19; **11 193–95**; **13** 90, 482
Ingram Micro Corporation, **24** 29
AB Ingredients, **II** 466
Ingredients Technology Corp., **9** 154
Ingres Corporation, **9** 36–37; **25** 87
Ingwerson and Co., **II** 356
INH. *See* Instituto Nacional de Hidrocarboros.
Inha Works Ltd., **33** 164
Inhalation Therapy Services, **III** 73
INI. *See* Instituto Nacional de Industria.
Initial Towel Supply. *See* Rentokil Initial Plc.
**Inktomi Corporation**, **41** 98; **45 200–04**
**Inland Container Corporation**, **IV** 311, 341–42, 675; **7** 528; **8 267–69**; **19** 267
Inland Motors Corporation, **18** 291
Inland Paperboard and Packaging, Inc., **31** 438
Inland Pollution Control, **9** 110
Inland Specialty Chemical Corp., **I** 342; **14** 217
**Inland Steel Industries, Inc.**, **II** 403; **IV 113–16**, 158, 703; **7** 447; **13** 157; **15** 249–50; **17** 351; **19** 9, **216–20 (upd.)**, 311, 381; **23** 35; **30** 254; **40** 269, 381; **41** 4
Inland Valley, **23** 321
Inmac, Inc., **16** 373
Inmos Ltd., **I** 532; **11** 307; **29** 323
InnCOGEN Limited, **35** 480
InnerCity Foods Joint Venture Company, **16** 97
Inno-BM, **26** 158, 161
Inno-France. *See* Societe des Grandes Entreprises de Distribution, Inno-France.
Innova International Corporation, **26** 333
Innovacom, **25** 96
Innovation, **26** 158
Innovative Marketing Systems. *See* Bloomberg L.P.
Innovative Pork Concepts, **7** 82
Innovative Products & Peripherals Corporation, **14** 379
Innovative Software Inc., **10** 362
Innovative Sports Systems, Inc., **15** 396
Innovative Valve Technologies Inc., **33** 167
Innovex Ltd., **21** 425
Inns and Co., **III** 734
Innwerk AG, **IV** 229
Inoue Electric Manufacturing Co., **II** 75–76
Inpaco, **16** 340
Inpacsa, **19** 226
Inprise/Borland Corporation, **33** 115
Input/Output, Inc., **11** 538
INS. *See* International News Service.
Insalaco Markets Inc., **13** 394
INSCO, **III** 242
**Inserra Supermarkets**, **25 234–36**
**Insight Enterprises, Inc.**, **18 259–61**
Insight Marques SARL IMS SA, **48** 224
**Insilco Corporation**, **I** 473; **12** 472; **16 281–83**; **23** 212; **36** 469–70
Insley Manufacturing Co., **8** 545
**Inso Corporation**, **26 215–19**; **36** 273
Inspiration Resources Corporation, **12** 260; **13** 502–03
Inspirations PLC, **22** 129
Insta-Care Holdings Inc., **16** 59
Insta-Care Pharmacy Services, **9** 186
Instant Auto Insurance, **33** 3, 5
Instant Interiors Corporation, **26** 102
Instant Milk Co., **II** 488
Instapak Corporation, **14** 429
**Instinet Corporation**, **34 225–27**; **48** 227–28
Institut de Sérothérapie Hémopoiétique, **I** 669
Institut für Gemeinwohl, **IV** 139
Institut Merieux, **I** 389
Institut Ronchese, **I** 676
Institute de Development Industriel, **19** 87
Institute for Professional Development, **24** 40
Institute for Scientific Information, **8** 525, 528
Institution Food House. *See* Alex Lee Inc.
Institutional Financing Services, **23** 491
Instituto Nacional de Hidrocarboros, **IV** 528
**Instituto Nacional de Industria**, **I 459–61**; **V** 606–07; **6** 95–96
Instituto per la Ricostruzione Industriale, **V** 614
Instone Airline, **I** 92
Instromet International, **22** 65
Instrument Systems Corp. *See* Griffon Corporation.
Instrumentarium Corp., **13** 328; **25** 82
Instrumentation Laboratory Inc., **III** 511–12; **22** 75
Instrumentation Scientifique de Laboratoire, S.A., **15** 404
Insulite Co. of Finland, **IV** 275
**Insurance Auto Auctions, Inc.**, **23** 148, **285–87**
Insurance Co. against Fire Damage, **III** 308
Insurance Co. of Scotland, **III** 358
Insurance Co. of the State of Pennsylvania, **III** 196
Insurance Company of North America. *See* CIGNA Corporation.
Insurance Corp. of Ireland (Life), **III** 335
Insurance Partners L.P., **15** 257
InSync Communications, **42** 425
Intabex Holdings Worldwide, S.A., **27** 126
Intalco Aluminum Corp., **12** 254
Intamin, **17** 443
Intarsia Corp., **38** 187
Intat Precision Inc., **48** 5
INTEC, **6** 428
InteCom Inc., **6** 285
Integon Corp., **IV** 374
Integra-A Hotel and Restaurant Company, **13** 473
Integral Corporation, **14** 381; **23** 446; **33** 331
Integrated Business Information Services, **13** 5
Integrated Computer Systems. *See* Learning Tree International Inc.
Integrated Data Services Co., **IV** 473
Integrated Defense Technologies, **44** 423
Integrated Genetics, **I** 638; **8** 210; **13** 239; **38** 204, 206
Integrated Health Services, Inc., **11** 282
Integrated Medical Systems Inc., **12** 333; **47** 236
Integrated Resources, Inc., **11** 483; **16** 54; **19** 393
Integrated Silicon Solutions, Inc., **18** 20; **43** 17; **47** 384
Integrated Software Systems Corporation, **6** 224; **11** 469
Integrated Systems Operations. *See* Xerox Corporation.
Integrated Systems Solutions Corp., **9** 284; **11** 395; **17** 264
Integrated Technology, Inc., **6** 279
Integrated Telecom Technologies, **14** 417
**Integrity Inc.**, **44 241–43**
Integrity Life Insurance, **III** 249
**Intel Corporation**, **II 44–46**, 62, 64; **III** 115, 125, 455; **6** 215–17, 222, 231, 233, 235, 257; **9** 42–43, 57, 114–15, 165–66; **10 365–67 (upd.)**, 477; **11** 62, 308, 328, 490, 503, 518, 520; **12** 61, 449; **13** 47; **16** 139–40, 146, 394; **17** 32–33; **18** 18, 260; **19** 310, 312; **20** 69, 175; **21** 36, 122; **22** 542; **24** 233, 236, 371; **25** 418, 498; **26** 91, 432; **27** 365–66; **30** 10; **34** 441; **36** 123, **284–88 (upd.)**; **38** 71, 416; **41** 408; **43** 14–16; **47** 153
Intelcom Support Services, Inc., **14** 334
Intelicom Solutions Corp., **6** 229
**IntelliCorp, Inc.**, **9** 310; **31** 298; **45 205–07**
**Intelligent Electronics, Inc.**, **6 243–45**; **12** 184; **13** 176, 277
Intelligent Software Ltd., **26** 275
Intelligraphics Inc., **33** 44

Intellimetrics Instrument Corporation, **16** 93
Intellisys, **48** 257
Inter American Aviation, Inc. *See* SkyWest, Inc.
Inter-American Development Bank, **IV** 55
Inter-American Satellite Television Network, **7** 391
Inter-City Gas Ltd., **III** 654; **19** 159
Inter-City Western Bakeries Ltd., **II** 631
Inter-City Wholesale Electric Inc., **15** 385
Inter-Comm Telephone, Inc., **8** 310
Inter-Continental Hotels and Resorts, **38** 77
Inter IKEA Systems B.V., **V** 82
Inter-Island Airways, Ltd., **22** 251; **24** 20
Inter-Island Steam Navigation Co. *See* Hawaiian Airlines.
Inter Island Telephone, **6** 326, 328
Inter-Mountain Telephone Co., **V** 344
Inter-Ocean Corporation, **16** 103; **44** 90
**Inter Parfums Inc., 35 235–38**
**Inter-Regional Financial Group, Inc., 15 231–33**. *See also* Dain Rauscher Corporation.
Inter State Telephone, **6** 338
Inter Techniek, **16** 421
Interactive Computer Design, Inc., **23** 489, 491
Interactive Systems, **7** 500
Interamericana de Talleras SA de CV, **10** 415
Interbake Foods, **II** 631
InterBold, **7** 146; **11** 151
Interbrás, **IV** 503
**Interbrew S.A., 16** 397; **17 256–58**; **25** 279, 282; **26** 306; **34** 202; **38** 74, 78
Interchemical Corp., **13** 460
Intercity Food Services, Inc., **II** 663
**Interco Incorporated, III 528–31**; **9** 133, 135, 192, 234–35; **10** 184; **12** 156, 306–08; **22** 49; **29** 294; **31** 136–37, 210; **39** 146. *See also* Furniture Brands International, Inc.
Intercolonial, **6** 360
Intercomi, **II** 233
Intercontessa AG, **35** 401; **36** 294
Intercontinental Apparel, **8** 249
Intercontinental Breweries, **I** 289
Intercontinental Electronics Corp. *See* IEC Electronics Corp.
Intercontinental Hotels, **I** 248–49
Intercontinental Mortgage Company, **8** 436
Intercontinental Rubber Co., **II** 112
Intercontinentale, **III** 404
Intercord, **22** 194
Intercostal Steel Corp., **13** 97
Interdesign, **16** 421
Interdiscount/Radio TV Steiner AG, **48** 116
Interealty Corp., **43** 184
Interedi-Cosmopolitan, **III** 47
**Interep National Radio Sales Inc., 35 231–34**
Interessen Gemeinschaft Farbenwerke. *See* I.G. Farbenindustrie AG.
Interface Group, **13** 483
**Interface, Inc., 8 270–72**; **18** 112; **29 246–49 (upd.)**
Interferon Sciences, Inc., **13** 366–67
Interfinancial, **III** 200
InterFirst Bankcorp, Inc., **9** 482
Interfood Ltd., **II** 520–21, 540
Interglas S.A., **22** 515
Intergram, Inc., **27** 21
**Intergraph Corporation, 6 246–49**; **10** 257; **24 233–36 (upd.)**
Interhandel, **I** 337–38; **II** 378; **22** 226
INTERIM Services, Inc., **9** 268, 270; **25** 434; **29** 224, 227
Interinvest S.A., **33** 19
Interlabor, **16** 420–21
Interlabor Interim, **43** 308
**The Interlake Corporation, 8 273–75**; **38** 210
Interlake Steamship Company, **15** 302
Intermaco S.R.L., **43** 368
Intermagnetics General Corp., **9** 10
Intermarché, **35** 398, 401. *See also* ITM Entreprises SA.
Intermark, Inc., **12** 394; **34** 338–39
Intermec Corporation, **29** 414
Intermed, **I** 429
Intermedia, **25** 499
Intermedics, **III** 633; **11** 458–59; **12** 325–26; **40** 66–67
Intermedics Intraocular Inc., **I** 665
**Intermet Corporation, 32 279–82**
Intermoda, **V** 166
Intermountain Broadcasting and Television Corp., **IV** 674
**Intermountain Health Care, Inc., 27 237–40**
ITM International, **IV** 239
International Aeradio Limited, **47** 352
International Aero Engines, **9** 418
International Agricultural Corporation, **8** 264–65
International Air Service Co., **24** 21
International Assurance Co., **III** 195
International Bank, **II** 261
International Bank of Japan, **17** 122
International Bank of Moscow, **II** 242
International Banking and Credit Analysis (IBCA), **37** 144
International Banking Corp., **II** 253; **9** 123
International Banking Technologies, Inc., **11** 113
International Basic Economy Corporation, **13** 103
International Beauty Supply, Ltd. *See* L.L. Knickerbocker Co., Inc.
International Beverage Corporation. *See* Clearly Canadian Beverage Corporation.
International Brewing Holdings Pty., **21** 229
**International Brotherhood of Teamsters, 37 211–14**
International Business Directories, Inc., **26** 484
**International Business Machines Corporation, I** 26, 455, 523, 534, 541; **II** 6, 8, 10, 42, 44–45, 56, 62, 68, 70, 73, 86, 99, 107, 113, 134, 159, 211, 274, 326, 379, 397, 432, 440; **III** 9, 109–11, 113–18, 121–28, 130, 132–34, 136, 139–43, 145, **147–49**, 151–52, 154–55, 157, 165–72, 200, 246, 313, 319, 326, 458, 475, 549, 618, 685; **IV** 443, 711; **6** 51, 218–25, 233–35, 237, 240–42, 244–48, **250–53 (upd.)**, 254–60, 262, 265, 269–71, 275–77, 279, 281–89, 320, 324, 346, 390, 428; **7** 145–46, 161; **8** 138–39, 466–67; **9** 36, 41–42, 48, 50, 114–15, 131, 139, 165–66, 170–71, 184, 194, 284, 296–97, 310, 327, 463–64; **10** 19, 22–24, 58, 119, 125, 161, 194, 232, 237, 243–44, 255–56, 309, 361–62, 366–67, 394, 456, 463, 474, 500–01, 505, 510, 512–13, 518–19, 542; **11** 19, 45, 50, 59, 61–62, 64–65, 68, 86–88, 150, 273–74, 285, 364, 395, 469, 485, 491, 494, 506, 519; **12** 61, 138–39, 147–49, 161–62, 183, 204, 238, 278, 335, 442, 450, 469–70, 484; **13** 47, 127, 174, 214, 326, 345, 387–88, 403, 482; **14** 13–15, 106, 268–69, 318, 354, 391, 401, 432–33, 446, 533; **15** 106, 440, 454–55, 491–92; **16** 4, 94, 140, 224–26, 301, 367–68, 372; **17** 353, 418, 532–34; **18** 94, 110, 112, 162, 250, 292, 305–07, 344, 434–36; **19** 41, 110, 310, 312, 437; **20** 237, 313; **21** 86, 391; **23** 135, 138, 209, 470; **24** 234; **25** 20–21, 34, 86–87, 96, 133–34, 149, 298–301, 356, 358, 530–32; **26** 90, 187, 275–76, 427, 429, 441, 540, 542; **28** 112, 189; **29** 375, 414; **30 247–51 (upd.)**, 140, 300, 337–38; **34** 442–43; **36** 81–82, 171, 480–81; **38** 54–55, 250, 417; **43** 126–27; **46** 165; **47** 153
International Care Services, **6** 182
International Cellucotton Products Co., **III** 40; **16** 302–03; **43** 256–57
International Cementers Inc., **25** 74
International Commercial Bank, **II** 257
International Communication Materials, Inc., **18** 387
International Computers. *See* ICL plc.
**International Controls Corporation, 10 368–70**
International Corona Corporation, **12** 244
**International Creative Management, Inc., 38** 161; **43 235–37**
International Credit Card Business Assoc., **II** 436
**International Dairy Queen, Inc., 7** 266; **10 371–74**; **39 232–36 (upd.)**
**International Data Group, Inc., 7 238–40**; **12** 561; **25 237–40 (upd.)**; **27** 222
International Development Bank, **IV** 417
International Digital Communications, Inc., **6** 327
International Distillers & Vintners Ltd., **31** 92
International Egyptian Oil Co., **IV** 412
International Engineering Company, Inc., **7** 355
International Epicure, **12** 280
International Equities Corp., **III** 98
International Factoring Corp., **II** 436
International Factors, Limited, **II** 208
**International Family Entertainment Inc., 13 279–81**
International Finance Corp., **19** 192
**International Flavors & Fragrances Inc., 9 290–92**; **38 244–48 (upd.)**
International Foods, **II** 468
International Fuel Cells Inc., **39** 394
**International Game Technology, 10 375–76**; **24** 37 **25** 313; **41 214–16 (upd.)**
International Graphics Corp., **IV** 645
International Group, **13** 277
International Harvester Co., **III** 473, 650, 651; **10** 264, 280, 378, 380, 528; **13** 16; **17** 158; **22** 380. *See also* Navistar International Corporation.
International Healthcare, **III** 197
International Home Foods, Inc., **42** 94

International House of Pancakes. *See* IHOP Corporation.
International Hydron, **10** 47; **13** 367
International Imaging Limited, **29** 58
International Income Property, **IV** 708
International Industries, **17** 249
International Learning Systems Corp. Ltd., **IV** 641–42; **7** 311
**International Lease Finance Corporation**, **III** 198; **6** 67; **36** 231; **48 218–20**
International Light Metals Corp., **IV** 163
International MacGregor, **27** 269
**International Management Group**, **18 262–65**
International Marine Oil Co., **IV** 363
International Marine Services, **22** 276
International Match, **12** 463
International Mercantile Marine Co., **II** 330
International Milling. *See* International Multifoods Corporation.
International Mineral & Chemical, Inc., **8** 265–66
International Minerals and Chemical Corporation, **19** 253
**International Multifoods Corporation**, **II** 493; **7 241–43**; **12** 80, 125; **14** 515; **21** 289; **23** 203; **25 241–44 (upd.)**; **28** 238
International Music Co., **16** 202; **43** 171
International News Service, **IV** 626–27; **19** 203; **25** 507
International Nickel Co. of Canada, Ltd. *See* Inco Limited.
International Nutrition Laboratories, **14** 558
**International Olympic Committee**, **44 244–47**
International Organization of Consumers Unions, **26** 98
International Pacific Corp., **II** 389
**International Paper Company**, **I** 27; **II** 208, 403; **III** 693, 764; **IV** 16, 245, **286–88**, 289, 326; **8** 267; **11** 76, 311; **15 227–30 (upd.)**; **16** 349; **17** 446; **23** 48–49, 366, 368; **25** 9; **26** 444; **30** 92, 94; **32** 91, 346; **47 187–92 (upd.)**
International Parts Corporation, **10** 414
International Periodical Distributors, **34** 5
International Permalite, **22** 229
International Petroleum Co., Ltd., **IV** 415–16, 438, 478; **25** 230
International Petroleum Corp., **IV** 454, 484
International Playtex, Inc., **12** 93
International Products Corporation. *See* The Terlato Wine Group.
International Proteins Corporation, **21** 248
International Publishing Corp., **IV** 641, 666–67; **7** 343; **17** 397; **23** 350
International Raw Materials, Ltd., **31** 20
**International Rectifier Corporation**, **31 263–66**
International Roofing Company, **22** 13–14
International Sealants Corporation, **8** 333
**International Shipholding Corporation, Inc.**, **27 241–44**
International Shoe Co., **III** 528–30
International Silver Company, **I** 30; **12** 472; **14** 482–83
International Specialty Products, Inc., **22** 225, 228–29
**International Speedway Corporation**, **19 221–23**; **32** 439
International Standard Electric, **II** 66–68
International Stores, **I** 427
International Supply Consortium, **13** 79
International Talent Group, **25** 281
International Talent Management, Inc. *See* Motown Records Company L.P.
International Telcell Group, **7** 336
International Telecommunications Satellite Organization, **46** 328
**International Telephone & Telegraph Corporation**, **I** 434, 446, **462–64**, 544; **II** 13, 66, 68, 86, 130, 331; **III** 98–99, 162–64, 166, 644–45, 684; **V** 334–35, 337–38; **6** 356; **8** 157; **9** 10–11, 324; **10** 19, 44, 301; **11 196–99 (upd.)**, 337, 516; **12** 18; **13** 246; **14** 332, 488; **19** 131, 205, 208; **22** 55; **25** 100, 432; **46** 412
International Television Corporation Entertainment Group, **23** 391
International Thomson Organisation Ltd. *See* The Thomson Corporation.
International Thomson Organization Ltd., **23** 92
International Time Recording Company. *See* International Business Machines Corporation.
**International Total Services, Inc.**, **37 215–18**
International Trust and Investment Corp., **II** 577
International Trust Co., **II** 207
International Utilities Corp., **IV** 75–76; **6** 444
International Western Electric Co., **I** 462; **II** 66; **III** 162; **11** 196
International Wind Systems, **6** 581
International Wine & Spirits Ltd., **9** 533
International Wire Works Corp., **8** 13
International Wireless Inc., **21** 261
Internationale Industriële Beleggung Maatschappij Amsterdam BV, **IV** 128
Internationale Nederlanden Group, **24** 88
Internet Shopping Network, **26** 441
InterNorth, Inc., **II** 16; **V** 610
Interocean Management Corp., **9** 509–11
Interpac Belgium, **6** 303
Interprovincial Pipe Line Ltd., **I** 264; **IV** 439; **25** 231. *See also* Enbridge Inc.
**The Interpublic Group of Companies, Inc.**, **I 16–18**, 31, 36; **6** 53; **14** 315; **16** 70, 72, 167; **20** 5; **22 294–97 (upd.)**; **23** 478; **28** 66–67; **32** 142; **42** 107
Interra Financial. *See* Dain Rauscher Corporation.
InterRedec, Inc., **17** 196
Interscience, **17** 271
Interscope Communications, Inc., **23** 389, 391; **27** 121
**Interscope Music Group**, **31 267–69**
Intersec, Inc., **27** 21
Intersil Inc., **II** 30; **12** 196; **16** 358
Interstate & Ocean Transport, **6** 577
Interstate Bag, **I** 335
**Interstate Bakeries Corporation**, **7** 320; **12 274–76**; **27** 310; **38 249–52 (upd.)**
Interstate Brick Company, **6** 568–69
Interstate Electric Manufacturing Company. *See* McGraw Electric Company.
Interstate Finance Corp., **11** 16
Interstate Financial Corporation, **9** 475
Interstate Iron and Steel Company. *See* Republic Engineered Steels, Inc.
Interstate Logos, Inc., **27** 278
Interstate Paint Distributors, Inc., **13** 367
Interstate Power Company, **6** 555, 605; **18** 404
Interstate Properties Inc., **45** 15–16
Interstate Public Service Company, **6** 555
Interstate Stores Inc., **V** 203; **15** 469; **18** 522
Interstate Supply Company. *See* McGraw Electric Company.
Interstate United Corporation, **II** 679; **III** 502; **13** 435
Intertec Design, Inc., **34** 371–72
Intertec Publishing Corp., **22** 441
Intertechnique SA, **36** 530
Interturbine Holland, **19** 150
Intertype Corp., **II** 37
Interunfall, **III** 346
Intervideo TV Productions-A.B., **II** 640
Intervision Express, **24** 510
Interweb, **IV** 661
InterWest Partners, **16** 418
**Intimate Brands, Inc.**, **24 237–39**' **29** 357
InTouch Systems, Inc., **43** 118
Intrac Handelsgesellschaft mbH, **7** 142
Intradal, **II** 572
Intraph South Africa Ltd., **6** 247
IntraWest Bank, **II** 289
**The Intrawest Corporation**, **15 234–36**; **31** 67; **43** 438
Intrepid Corporation, **16** 493
IntroGene B.V., **13** 241
**Intuit Inc.**, **13** 147; **14 262–64**; **23** 457; **33 208–11 (upd.)**
**Invacare Corporation**, **11 200–02**, 486; **47 193–98 (upd.)**
Invenex Laboratories, **17** 287
Invento Products Corporation, **21** 269
Invep S.p.A., **10** 150
Inveresk Paper Co., **III** 693; **IV** 685
Invergordon Distillers, **III** 509
Inverness Medical Innovations, Inc., **45** 208
Inverness Medical Technology, Inc., **45** 210
Inversale, **9** 92
INVESCO MIM Management Limited, **21** 397
Invesgen S.A., **26** 129
InvestCorp International, **15** 200; **24** 195, 420; **25** 205, 207
Investcorp S.A. *See* Arabian Investment Banking Corp.
Investimentos Itaú S.A., **19** 33
Investors Bank and Trust Company, **18** 152
Investors Diversified Services, Inc., **II** 398; **6** 199; **8** 348–49; **10** 43–45, 59, 62; **21** 305; **25** 248; **38** 42
Investors Group, **III** 261. *See also* Power Corporation of Canada.
Investors Management Corp., **10** 331
Investors Overseas Services, **10** 368–69
Investrónica S.A., **26** 129
Invista Capital Management, **III** 330
The Invus Group, Ltd., **33** 449
Iolab Corp., **III** 36
**Iomega Corporation**, **18** 509–10; **21 294–97**
**IONA Technologies plc**, **43 238–41**
Ionpure Technologies Corporation, **6** 486–88
Iowa Beef Packers, **21** 287
Iowa Beef Processors, **II** 516–17; **IV** 481–82; **13** 351
Iowa Manufacturing, **II** 86
Iowa Mold Tooling Co., Inc., **16** 475
Iowa Public Service Company, **6** 524–25
IP Gas Supply Company, **6** 506

IP Services, Inc., **IV** 597
IP Timberlands Ltd., **IV** 288
IP&L. *See* Illinois Power & Light Corporation.
**Ipalco Enterprises, Inc., 6 508–09**
IPC. *See* International Publishing Corp.
IPC Communications, Inc., **15** 196
**IPC Magazines Limited, IV** 650; **7 244–47**
IPD. *See* International Periodical Distributors.
IPEC Holdings Ltd., **27** 474–75
Iphotonics Inc., **48** 369
Ipko-Amcor, **14** 225
IPL Energy Inc. *See* Enbridge Inc.
IPS Praha a.s., **38** 437
IPS Publishing, **39** 341–42
IPSOA Editore, **14** 555
**Ipsos SA, 24** 355; **48 221–24**
IQUE, Inc., **21** 194
Iran Air, **6** 101
Iran Pan American Oil Co., **IV** 466
Iranian Oil Exploration and Producing Co., **IV** 466–67
Iraq Petroleum Co., **IV** 363, 386, 429, 450, 464, 558–60
Irby-Gilliland Company, **9** 127
Irdeto, **31** 330
IRI. *See* Instituto per la Ricostruzione Industriale.
Irideon, Inc., **35** 435
Iris Associates, Inc., **25** 299, 301
IRIS Holding Co., **III** 347
Irish Air. *See* Aer Lingus Group plc.
Irish Life Assurance Company, **16** 14; **43** 7
Irish Paper Sacks Ltd., **IV** 295; **19** 225
Irish Sugar Co., **II** 508
Iron and Steel Corp., **IV** 22, 41, 92, 533–34
Iron and Steel Press Company, **27** 360
Iron Cliffs Mining Company, **13** 156
Iron Mountain Forge, **13** 319
**Iron Mountain, Inc., 33 212–14**
Iron Ore Company of Canada, **8** 347
Iroquois Gas Corporation, **6** 526
**Irvin Feld & Kenneth Feld Productions, Inc., 15 237–39**. *See also* Feld Entertainment, Inc.
Irving Bank Corp., **II** 192
Irving Tanning Company, **17** 195
Irving Trust Coompany, **II** 257; **22** 55
Irvington Smelting, **IV** 78
Irwin Lehrhoff Associates, **11** 366
**Irwin Toy Limited, 14 265–67**
Isabela Shoe Corporation, **13** 360
Isagro S.p.A., **26** 425
Iscor. *See* Iron and Steel Corporation.
**Isetan Company Limited, V 85–87**; **36 289–93 (upd.)**
Iseya Tanji Drapery, **V** 85
**Ishikawajima-Harima Heavy Industries Co., Ltd., I** 508, 511, 534; **II** 274; **III 532–33**; **9** 293; **12** 484; **41** 41
Ishizaki Honten, **III** 715
Isis Distributed Systems, Inc., **10** 501
Island Air, **24** 22
**The Island ECN, Inc., 48 225–29**
Island Equipment Co., **19** 381
Island Holiday, **I** 417
Island Pictures Corp., **23** 389
Island Records, **23** 389
Islands Restaurants, **17** 85–87
**Isle of Capri Casinos, Inc., 33** 41; **41 217–19**
Isolite Insulating Products Co., **III** 714
Isosceles PLC, **II** 628–29; **24** 270; **47** 367–68
Isotec Communications Incorporated, **13** 213
Isover, **III** 676; **16** 121
**Ispat Inland Inc., 40 267–72 (upd.)**, 381
**Ispat International N.V., 30 252–54**
ISS International Service System, Inc., **8** 271
ISS Securitas, **42** 165, 167
ISSI. *See* Integrated Silicon Solutions Inc.
Istanbul Fertilizer Industry, **IV** 563
Istante Vesa s.r.l., **22** 239
Istituto Farmacologico Serono S.p.A. *See* Serono S.A.
**Istituto per la Ricostruzione Industriale S.p.A., I** 207, 459, **465–67**; **II** 191–92, 270–71; **IV** 419; **11 203–06**; **13** 28, 218
**Isuzu Motors, Ltd., II** 274; **III** 581, 593; **7** 8, 219; **9 293–95**; **10** 354; **23 288–91 (upd.)**; **36** 240, 243
Isuzu Motors of Japan, **21** 6
IT Group, **28** 203
IT International, **V** 255
IT-Software Companies, **48** 402
Itabira Iron Ore Co. Ltd., **IV** 54; **43** 111
ITABRASCO, **IV** 55
Italcarta, **IV** 339
Italcementi, **IV** 420
Italcimenti Group, **40** 107–08
Italianni's, **22** 128
Italiatour, **6** 69
Italmobiliare, **III** 347
Italstate. *See* Societa per la Infrastrutture e l'Assetto del Territoria.
Italtel, **V** 326–27
Italware, **27** 94
Itaú. *See* Banco Itaú S.A.
Itaú Winterthur Seguradura S.A., **III** 404
Itaúsa. *See* Investimentos Itaú S.A.
Itek Corp., **I** 486; **11** 265
**Itel Corporation, II** 64; **III** 512; **6** 262, 354; **9** 49, **296–99**; **15** 107; **22** 339; **26** 328, 519; **47** 37
**Items International Airwalk Inc., 17 259–61**
Ithaca Gas & Electric. *See* New York State Electric and Gas.
ITI Education Corporation, **29** 472
**ITM Entreprises SA, 36 294–97**
Ito Carnation Co., **II** 518
Ito Food Processing Co., **II** 518
Ito Gofuku Co. Ltd., **V** 129
Ito Meat Processing Co., **II** 518
Ito Processed Food Co., **II** 518
**Ito-Yokado Co., Ltd., II** 661; **V 88–89**; **32** 414, 416–17; **42 189–92 (upd.)**
Itochu and Renown, Inc., **12** 281
**ITOCHU Corporation, 19** 9; **32 283–87 (upd.)**; **34** 231; **42** 342
Itochu Housing, **38** 415
Itochu of Japan, **14** 550
Itoh. *See* C. Itoh & Co.
**Itoham Foods Inc., II 518–19**
Itokin, **III** 48
Itoman & Co., **26** 456
ITT, **21** 200; **24** 188, 405; **30** 101; **47** 103. *See also* International Telephone and Telegraph Corporation.
ITT Aerospace, **33** 48
**ITT Educational Services, Inc., 33 215–17**
**ITT Sheraton Corporation, III 98–101**; **23** 484
ITT World Directories, **27** 498, 500
iTurf Inc., **29** 142–43
ITW. *See* Illinois Tool Works Inc.
ITW Devcon, **12** 7
IU International, **23** 40
IURA Edition, **14** 556
IV Therapy Associates, **16** 440
IVAC Corp., **I** 646; **11** 90
IVACO Industries Inc., **11** 207
Ivanhoe, Inc., **II** 662, 664
**IVAX Corporation, 11 207–09**; **41** 420–21
**IVC Industries, Inc., 45 208–11**
Iveco, **I** 148; **12** 91
Ives Trains, **16** 336
**iVillage Inc., 46** 232, **253–56**
Ivy Mortgage Corp., **39** 380, 382
Iwai & Co., **I** 492, 509–10; **IV** 151; **24** 325, 358
Iwata Air Compressor, **III** 427
**Iwerks Entertainment, Inc., 33** 127; **34 228–30**
**IXC Communications, Inc., 29 250–52**; **37** 127
IXI Ltd., **38** 418–19
IYG Holding Company of Japan, **7** 492; **32** 414, 417
The IZOD Gant Corporation, **24** 385
Izod Lacoste, **II** 502–03; **9** 156–57; **10** 324
Izukyu Corporation, **47** 408
Izumi Fudosan, **IV** 726
Izumiya, **V** 477; **36** 418

J&E Davy, **16** 14
J&G Meakin, **12** 529
J&J Colman, **II** 566
J&J Corrugated Box Corp., **IV** 282; **9** 261
**J & J Snack Foods Corporation, 24 240–42**
J&L Industrial Supply, **13** 297
J&L Steel. *See* Jones & Laughlin Steel Corp.
J & M Laboratories, **48** 299
**J&R Electronics Inc., 26 224–26**
J. & W. Seligman and Co., **17** 498
J.A. Baldwin Manufacturing Company, **17** 106
**J.A. Jones, Inc., 16 284–86**; **17** 377
J. Aron & Co., **II** 415
J.B. Hudson & Son, **18** 136
**J.B. Hunt Transport Services Inc., 12 277–79**; **15** 440; **26** 533
J.B. Lippincott & Company, **IV** 652; **14** 554–56; **33** 460
J.B. McLean Publishing Co., Ltd., **IV** 638
J.B. Williams Company, **III** 66; **8** 63
J.B. Wolters Publishing Company, **14** 554
**J. Baker, Inc., 13** 361; **31 270–73**
J. Beres & Son, **24** 444–45
J Bibby & Sons, **I** 424
J Bibby Agriculture Limited, **13** 53
J. Bulova Company. *See* Bulova Corporation.
J. Byrons, **9** 186
J.C. Baxter Co., **15** 501
J.C. Hillary's, **20** 54
**J.C. Penney Company, Inc., I** 516; **V 90–92**; **6** 336; **8** 288, 555; **9** 156, 210, 213, 219, 346–94; **10** 409, 490; **11** 349; **12** 111, 431, 522; **14** 62; **16** 37, 327–28; **17** 124, 175, 177, 366, 460; **18** 108, 136,

168, 200, **269–73 (upd.)**, 373, 478; **19** 300; **21** 24, 527; **25** 91, 254, 368; **26** 161; **27** 346, 429; **31** 260–61; **32** 166, 168–70; **39** 270; **41** 114–15; **43 245–50 (upd.)**
**J. Crew Group Inc.**, **12 280–82**; **25** 48; **34 231–34 (upd.)**; **36** 472
J.D. Bassett Manufacturing Co. *See* Bassett Furniture Industries, Inc.
**J.D. Edwards & Company**, **14 268–70**; **38** 431
**J.D. Power and Associates**, **9** 166; **32 297–301**
**J. D'Addario & Company, Inc.**, **48 230–33**
J.E. Baxter Co., **I** 429
J.E. Nolan, **11** 486
J.E. Sirrine. *See* CRSS Inc.
J.E. Smith Box & Printing Co., **13** 441
J. Edward Connelly Associates, Inc., **22** 438
J. Evershed & Son, **13** 103
J.F. Corporation, **V** 87
J.F. Lauman and Co., **II** 681
J. Fielding & Co., **IV** 249
J.G. McMullen Dredging Co., **III** 558
J. Gadsden Paper Products, **IV** 249
J. George Leyner Engineering Works Co., **III** 525–26
J.H. Heafner Co., **20** 263
J.H. Stone & Sons, **IV** 332
J.H. Whitney & Company, **9** 250; **32** 100
J. Homestock. *See* R.H. Macy & Co.
J. Horner's, **48** 415
**J.I. Case Company**, **I** 148, 527; **III** 651; **10 377–81**; **13** 17; **22** 380. *See also* CNH Global N.V.
**The J. Jill Group, Inc.**, **35 239–41**
J.K. Armsby Co., **7** 130–31
J.K. Starley and Company Ltd, **7** 458
J.L. Clark, Inc. *See* Clarcor Inc.
J.L. Hudson Company. *See* Dayton Hudson Corporation.
J.L. Kraft & Bros. Co., **II** 532
J.L. Shiely Co., **III** 691
J.L. Wright Company, **25** 379
J. Levin & Co., Inc., **13** 367
J. Lyons & Co., **I** 215
J.M. Brunswick & Brothers, **III** 442
J.M. Douglas & Company Limited, **14** 141
J.M. Horton Ice Cream Co., **II** 471
J.M. Huber Corporation, **40** 68
J.M. Jones Co., **II** 668; **18** 504
J.M. Kohler Sons Company, **7** 269
**The J.M. Smucker Company**, **11 210–12**
J.M. Tull Metals Co., Inc., **IV** 116; **15** 250; **19** 219
**J.M. Voith AG**, **33 222–25**
J. Mandelbaum & Sons, **19** 510
J-Mar Associates, **31** 435–36
J-Mass, **IV** 289
J. Muirhead Ltd., **I** 315; **25** 81
J.P. Heilwell Industries, **II** 420
**J.P. Morgan & Co. Incorporated**, **II** 281, **329–32**, 407, 419, 427–28, 430–31, 441; **III** 237, 245, 380; **IV** 20, 180, 400; **9** 386; **11** 421; **12** 165; **13** 13; **16** 25, 375; **19** 190; **26** 66, 500; **30 261–65 (upd.)**; **33** 464; **35** 74; **36** 151–53
**J.P. Morgan Chase & Co.**, **38 253–59 (upd.)**
J.P. Stevens Inc., **8** 234; **12** 404; **16** 533–35; **17** 75; **19** 420; **27** 468–69; **28** 218
J.P. Wood, **II** 587
J.R. Brown & Sharpe. *See* Brown & Sharpe Manufacturing Co.
J.R. Geigy S.A., **I** 632–33, 635, 671; **8** 108–10; **39** 72
J.R. Parkington Co., **I** 280
**J.R. Simplot Company**, **16 287–89**; **21** 508; **26** 309
J.R. Wyllie & Sons, **I** 437
J. Ray McDermott & Co., **III** 558–59
J.S. Fry & Sons, **II** 476
J.S. Morgan & Co., **II** 329, 427
**J Sainsbury plc**, **II 657–59**, 677–78; **10** 442; **11** 239, 241; **13 282–84 (upd.)**; **17** 42; **21** 335; **22** 241; **32** 253; **38 260–65 (upd.)**
J. Sanders & Sons, **IV** 711
J. Sears & Company, **V** 177
J. Spiegel and Company. *See* Spiegel, Inc.
J.T. Wing and Co., **I** 158
J.U. Dickson Sawmill Inc. *See* Dickson Forest Products, Inc.
J.W. Bateson, **8** 87
J.W. Buderus and Sons, **III** 694
J.W. Charles Financial Services Inc., **25** 542
J.W. Childs Associates, L.P., **46** 220
J.W. Childs Equity Partners LP, **40** 274
J.W. Foster and Sons, Inc. *See* Reebok International Ltd.
J.W. Higman & Co., **III** 690
J.W. Spear, **25** 314
J.W. Wassall Ltd. *See* Wassall PLC.
J. Walter Thompson Co., **I** 9, 17, 25, 37, 251, 354, 623; **10** 69; **11** 51; **12** 168; **16** 167; **48** 442
J. Weingarten Inc., **7** 203; **28** 163
J. Wiss & Sons Co., **II** 16
J.Z. Sales Corp., **16** 36
J. Zinmeister Co., **II** 682
**Jabil Circuit, Inc.**, **36 298–301**
Jacintoport Corporation, **7** 281
Jack Daniel Distillery, **10** 180
Jack Daniel's. *See* Brown-Forman Corporation.
Jack Eckerd Corp., **16** 160; **19** 467
Jack Frain Enterprises, **16** 471
**Jack Henry and Associates, Inc.**, **17 262–65**
Jack Houston Exploration Company, **7** 345
Jack in the Box, Inc. *See* Foodmaster, Inc.
**Jack Schwartz Shoes, Inc.**, **18 266–68**
**Jackpot Enterprises Inc.**, **21 298–300**; **24** 36
Jackson & Curtis, **II** 444; **22** 405
Jackson & Perkins. *See* Bear Creek Corporation.
Jackson Box Co., **IV** 311; **19** 267
Jackson Cushion Spring Co., **13** 397
Jackson Furniture of Danville, LLC, **48** 246
**Jackson Hewitt, Inc.**, **48 234–36**
Jackson Ice Cream Co., **12** 112
Jackson Marine Corp., **III** 499
Jackson Mercantile Co. *See* Jitney-Jungle Stores of America, Inc.
**Jackson National Life Insurance Company**, **III** 335–36; **8 276–77**; **48** 327
Jackson Purchase Electric Cooperative Corporation, **11** 37
Jacksonville Shipyards, **I** 170
**Jaco Electronics, Inc.**, **19** 311; **30 255–57**
Jacob Holm & Sons A/S, **22** 263
**Jacob Leinenkugel Brewing Company**, **12** 338; **28 209–11**
Jacobs Brake Manufacturing Company, **7** 116–17
**Jacobs Engineering Group Inc.**, **6 148–50**; **26 220–23 (upd.)**
**Jacobs Suchard (AG)**, **II 520–22**, 540, 569; **15** 64; **29** 46–47. *See also* Kraft Jacobs Suchard AG.
**Jacobson Stores Inc.**, **21 301–03**
Jacoby & Meyers, **20** 435
**Jacor Communications, Inc.**, **6** 33; **23 292–95**; **24** 108; **27** 339; **35** 220
Jacques Borel International, **II** 641; **10** 12
Jacques Fath Perfumes, **III** 47
**Jacuzzi Inc.**, **7** 207, 209; **23 296–98**
Jade Accessories, **14** 224
Jade KK, **25** 349
Jadepoint, **18** 79–80
JAF Pampryl, **I** 281
Jafra Cosmetics, **15** 475, 477
Jagenberg AG, **9** 445–46; **14** 57
**Jaguar Cars, Ltd.**, **III** 439, 495; **11** 140; **13** 28, 219, **285–87**, 414; **36** 198, 217. *See also* Ford Motor Company.
JAI Parabolic Spring Ltd., **III** 582
JAIX Leasing Company, **23** 306
Ab Jakobstads Cellulosa-Pietarsaaren Selluloosa Oy, **IV** 302
JAL. *See* Japan Air Lines.
**Jalate Inc.**, **25 245–47**
Jaluzot & Cie. *See* Pinault-Printemps-Redoute S.A.
Jamaica Gas Light Co., **6** 455
Jamaica Plain Trust Co., **II** 207
Jamaica Water Supply Company. *See* JWP Inc.
**Jamba Juice Company**, **47 199–202**
JAMCO, **III** 589
James A. Ryder Transportation (Jartran), **V** 505
James Bay Development Corporation, **6** 502
James Beam Distilling Co., **I** 226; **10** 180
**James Beattie plc**, **43 242–44**
James Burn/American, Inc., **17** 458
James C. Heintz Company, **19** 278
James Ericson, **III** 324
James Felt Realty, Inc., **21** 257
James Fison and Sons. *See* Fisons plc.
James Fleming, **II** 500
James G. Fast Company. *See* Angelica Corporation.
James Gulliver Associates, **II** 609
James Hardie Industries Limited, **IV** 249; **26** 494
James Hartley & Son, **III** 724
James Heekin and Company, **13** 254
James Lyne Hancock Ltd., **I** 428
James Magee & Sons Ltd., **IV** 294; **19** 224
James McNaughton Ltd., **IV** 325
James O. Welch Co., **II** 543
James Publishing Group, **17** 272
James R. Osgood & Company, **10** 356
**James River Corporation of Virginia**, **IV 289–91**; **8** 483; **22** 209; **29** 136. *See also* Fort James Corporation.
James Stedman Ltd., **II** 569
James Talcott, Inc., **11** 260–61
James Thompson, **IV** 22
James Wellbeloved, **39** 354, 356
James Wholesale Company, **18** 7
James Wrigley & Sons, **IV** 257
Jamestown Publishers, **22** 522

Jamesway Corporation, **IV** 136; **13** 261; **23** 177
Jamie Scott, Inc., **27** 348
Jamieson & Co., **22** 428
Jamna Auto Industries Pvt. Ltd., **III** 581
Jämsänkoski Oy, **IV** 347
Jan Bell Marketing Inc., **24** 335. *See also* Mayor's Jewelers, Inc.
Janata Bank, **31** 219
Jane Jones Enterprises, **16** 422; **43** 309
Jane's Information Group, **8** 525
Janesville Electric, **6** 604
Janet Frazer, **V** 118
Janin, S.A., **36** 163
Janna Systems Inc., **38** 433
Janson Publications, **22** 522
Janssen-Kyowa, **III** 43
N.V. Janssen M&L, **17** 147
Janssen Pharmaceutica, **III** 36; **8** 282
JANT Pty. Ltd., **IV** 285
Jantzen Inc., **V** 391; **17** 513
Janus Capital Corporation, **6** 401–02; **26** 233
Japan Acoustics, **II** 118
Japan Advertising Ltd., **16** 166
Japan Air Filter Co., Ltd., **III** 634
**Japan Airlines Company, Ltd.**, **I 104–06**; **6** 70–71, 118, 123, 386, 427; **24** 399–400; **27** 464; **32 288–92 (upd.)**
Japan Brewery. *See* Kirin Brewery Company, Limited.
**Japan Broadcasting Corporation**, **I** 586; **II** 66, 101, 118; **7 248–50**; **9** 31
Japan-California Bank, **II** 274
Japan Commerce Bank, **II** 291
Japan Copper Manufacturing Co., **II** 104; **IV** 211
Japan Cotton Co., **IV** 150; **24** 357
Japan Creative Tours Co., **I** 106
Japan Credit Bureau, **II** 348
Japan Dairy Products, **II** 538
Japan Day & Night Bank, **II** 292
Japan Development Bank, **II** 300, 403
Japan Dyestuff Manufacturing Co., **I** 397
Japan Elanco Company, Ltd., **17** 437
Japan Electricity Generation and Transmission Company (JEGTCO), **V** 574
Japan Energy Corporation, **13** 202; **14** 206, 208
Japan Food Corporation, **14** 288
Japan International Bank, **II** 292
Japan International Liquor, **I** 220
Japan Iron & Steel Co., Ltd., **IV** 157; **17** 349–50
**Japan Leasing Corporation**, **8 278–80**; **11** 87
Japan Medico, **25** 431
Japan National Oil Corp., **IV** 516
Japan National Railway, **V** 448–50; **6** 70
Japan Oil Development Co., **IV** 364
Japan Petroleum Development Corp., **IV** 461
Japan Petroleum Exploration Co., **IV** 516
**Japan Pulp and Paper Company Limited**, **IV 292–93**, 680
Japan Reconstruction Finance Bank, **II** 300
Japan Special Steel Co., Ltd., **IV** 63
Japan Steel Manufacturing Co., **IV** 211
Japan Steel Works, **I** 508
Japan Telecom, **7** 118; **13** 482
Japan Telegraphic Communication Company (Nihon Denpo-Tsushin Sha), **16** 166
**Japan Tobacco Inc.**, **V 403–04**; **30** 387; **46 257–60 (upd.)**
Japan Trust Bank, **II** 292
Japan Try Co., **III** 758
Japan Vilene Company Ltd., **41** 170–72
Japanese and Asian Development Bank, **IV** 518
Japanese Electronic Computer Co., **III** 140
Japanese Enterprise Co., **IV** 728
Japanese National Railway, **I** 579; **III** 491; **43** 103
Japanese Victor Co., **II** 118
Japex Oman Co., **IV** 516
Japonica Partners, **9** 485
Jara Enterprises, Inc., **31** 276
Jarcho Brothers Inc., **I** 513
Jardinay Manufacturing Corp., **24** 335
**Jardine Matheson Holdings Limited**, **I 468–71**, 521–22, 577, 592; **II** 296; **IV** 189, 699–700; **16** 479–80; **18** 114; **20 309–14 (upd.)**; **47** 175–78
Jartran Inc., **V** 505; **24** 410
Järvenpään Kotelo Oy, **IV** 315
**Jarvis plc**, **39 237–39**
Jas, Hennessy & Co., **I** 272
Jas. I. Miller Co., **13** 491
JASCO Products, **III** 581
**Jason Incorporated**, **23 299–301**
Jasper Corporation, **III** 767; **22** 546. *See also* Kimball International, Inc.
JAT, **27** 475
Jato, **II** 652
Jauch & Hübener, **14** 279
Java-China-Japan Line, **6** 403–04; **26** 242
Java Software, **30** 453
Javelin Software Corporation, **10** 359
Javex Co., **IV** 272
Jax, **9** 452
Jay Cooke and Co., **III** 237; **9** 370
**Jay Jacobs, Inc.**, **15 243–45**
Jay-Ro Services, **III** 419
Jay's Washateria, Inc., **7** 372
**Jayco Inc.**, **13 288–90**
Jaywoth Industries, **III** 673
**Jazzercise, Inc.**, **45 212–14**
**JB Oxford Holdings, Inc.**, **32 293–96**
JBA Holdings PLC, **43** 184
JBL, **22** 97
JCB, **14** 321
JCJL. *See* Java-China-Japan Line.
**JD Wetherspoon plc**, **30 258–60**
**JDS Uniphase Corporation**, **34 235–37**
**The Jean Coutu Group (PJC) Inc.**, **46 261–65**
Jean-Jacques, **19** 50
Jean Lassale, **III** 619–20; **17** 430
Jean Lincet, **19** 50
Jean Nate, **I** 695
Jean Pagées et Fils, **III** 420
Jean-Philippe Fragrances, Inc. *See* Inter Parfums, Inc.
Jean Prouvost, **IV** 618
Jeanmarie Creations, Inc., **18** 67, 69
Jeanne Piaubert, **III** 47
**Jefferies Group, Inc.**, **25 248–51**
Jefferson Bancorp, Inc., **37** 201
Jefferson Chemical Co., **IV** 552
Jefferson Fire Insurance Co., **III** 239
Jefferson National Life Group, **10** 247
**Jefferson-Pilot Corporation**, **11 213–15**; **29 253–56 (upd.)**
**Jefferson Smurfit Group plc**, **IV 294–96**; **16** 122; **19 224–27 (upd.)**. *See also* Smurfit-Stone Container Corporation.
Jefferson Standard Life Insurance, **11** 213–14
Jefferson Ward, **12** 48–49
Jefferson Warrior Railroad Company, **III** 767; **22** 546
Jeffery Sons & Co. Ltd., **IV** 711
Jeffrey Galion, **III** 472
JEGTCO. *See* Japan Electricity Generation and Transmission Company (JEGTCO).
**Jeld-Wen, Inc.**, **33** 409; **45 215–17**
Jell-O Co., **II** 531
Jem Development, **17** 233
Jenaer Glaswerk Schott & Genossen, **III** 445, 447
Jenn-Air Corporation, **III** 573; **22** 349
Jennie-O Foods, **II** 506
**Jennifer Convertibles, Inc.**, **31 274–76**
**Jenny Craig, Inc.**, **10 382–84**; **12** 531; **29 257–60 (upd.)**
Jeno's, **13** 516; **26** 436
**Jenoptik AG**, **33 218–21**
Jensen Salsbery, **I** 715
Jenson, Woodward & Lozier, Inc., **21** 96
JEORA Co., **IV** 564
Jeppesen Sanderson, Inc., **IV** 677; **17** 486
Jepson Corporation, **8** 230
Jeri-Jo Knitwear, Inc., **27** 346, 348
Jerome Increase Case Machinery Company. *See* J.I. Case Company.
Jerrico Inc., **27** 145
Jerrold Corporation, **10** 319–20
Jerry Bassin Inc., **17** 12–14
**Jerry's Famous Deli Inc.**, **24 243–45**
Jerry's Restaurants, **13** 320
Jersey Central Power & Light Company, **27** 182
Jersey Paper, **IV** 261
Jersey Standard. *See* Standard Oil Co. of New Jersey.
**Jervis B. Webb Company**, **24 246–49**
Jesse Jones Sausage Co. *See* GoodMark Foods, Inc.
Jesse L. Lasky Feature Play Co., **II** 154
Jessup & Moore Paper Co., **IV** 351; **19** 495
Jet America Airlines, **I** 100; **6** 67, 82
Jet Capital Corp., **I** 123
Jet Petroleum, Ltd., **IV** 401
Jet Research Center, **III** 498
Jet Set Corporation, **18** 513
**JetBlue Airways Corporation**, **44 248–50**
**Jetro Cash & Carry Enterprises Inc.**, **38 266–68**
Jetway Systems, **III** 512
Jeumont-Industrie, **II** 93
Jeumont-Schneider Industries, **II** 93–94; **9** 10; **18** 473
Jevic Transportation, Inc., **45** 448
Jewel Companies, Inc., **II** 605; **6** 531; **12** 63; **18** 89; **22** 38; **26** 476; **27** 291
Jewel Food Stores, **7** 127–28; **13** 25
Jewell Ridge Coal Corp., **IV** 181
JFD-Encino, **24** 243
**JG Industries, Inc.**, **15 240–42**
Jheri Redding Products, Inc., **17** 108
JHT, Inc., **39** 377
Jiamusi Combine Harvester Factory, **21** 175
Jiangsu General Ball & Roller Co., Ltd., **45** 170
JIB Group plc, **20** 313
Jiffee Chemical Corporation, **III** 21; **22** 146
Jiffy Auto Rental, **16** 380

Jiffy Convenience Stores, **II** 627
Jiffy Lube International, Inc., **IV** 490; **21** 541; **24** 339; **25** 443–45
Jiffy Mixes, **29** 109–10
Jiffy Packaging, **14** 430
Jiji, **16** 166
Jil Sander A.G., **45** 342, 344
**Jillian's Entertainment Holdings, Inc., 40 273–75**
**Jim Beam Brands Co., 14 271–73; 29** 196
Jim Cole Enterprises, Inc., **19** 247
**The Jim Henson Company, 23 302–04; 45** 130
**The Jim Pattison Group, 37 219–22**
Jim Walter Corporation. *See* Walter Industries, Inc.
Jim Walter Papers, **IV** 282; **9** 261
Jimmy Carter Work Project. *See* Habitat for Humanity International.
Jintan Taionkei Co. *See* Terumo Corporation.
**Jitney-Jungle Stores of America, Inc., 27 245–48**
Jitsugyo no Nihon-sha, **IV** 631
Jitsuyo Jidosha Seizo Co., **I** 183
**JJB Sports plc, 32 302–04**
JLA Credit, **8** 279
JMB Internacionale S.A., **25** 121
**JMB Realty Corporation, IV 702–03.** *See also* Amfac/JMB Hawaii L.L.C.
Jno. H. Swisher & Son. *See* Swisher International Group Inc.
JNR. *See* Japan National Railway.
Jo-Ann Fabrics and Crafts, **16** 197
Jo-Gal Shoe Company, Inc., **13** 360
Joanna Cotton Mills, **14** 220
Joannes Brothers, **II** 668
Jobete Music. *See* Motown Records Company L.P.
JobWorks Agency, Inc., **16** 50
**Jockey International, Inc., 12 283–85; 34 238–42 (upd.)**
Joe Alexander Press, **12** 472; **36** 469
Joe B. Hughes, **III** 498
Joe's American Bar & Grill, **20** 54
Joe's Crab Shack, **15** 279
Joh. A. Benckiser GmbH, **36** 140
Joh. Parviaisen Tehtaat Oy, **IV** 276
Johann Jakob Rieter & Co., **III** 402
Johannesburg Consolidated Investment Co. Ltd., **IV** 21–22, 118; **16** 293
John A. Frye Shoe Company, **V** 376; **8** 16; **26** 397–98; **36** 24
John A. Pratt and Associates, **22** 181
John Alden Life Insurance, **10** 340
**John B. Sanfilippo & Son, Inc., 14 274–76**
John Bean Spray Pump Co., **I** 442
John Blair & Company, **6** 13
**John Brown plc, I 572–74**
John Bull, **II** 550
John Carr Group, **31** 398–400
John Chatillon & Sons Inc., **29** 460
John Crane International, **17** 480
John Crosland Company, **8** 88
**The John D. and Catherine T. MacArthur Foundation, 34 243–46**
John de Kuyper and Son, **I** 377
John Deere. *See* Deere & Company.
John F. Jelke Company, **9** 318
John F. Murray Co., **I** 623; **10** 69
**John Fairfax Holdings Limited, 7 251–54**
John Gardner Catering, **III** 104
John Govett & Co., **II** 349
John Gund Brewing Co., **I** 253
**John H. Harland Company, 17 266–69**
John H.R. Molson & Bros. *See* The Molson Companies Limited.
**John Hancock Financial Services, Inc., 42 193–98 (upd.)**
**John Hancock Mutual Life Insurance Company, III 265–68,** 291, 313, 332, 400; **IV** 283; **13** 530; **25** 528
John Hill and Son, **II** 569
John Holroyd & Co. of Great Britain, **7** 236
John L. Wortham & Son Agency, **III** 193
John Labatt Ltd., **I** 267; **II** 582; **8** 399; **16** 397; **17** 256–57. *See also* Labatt Brewing Company Limited.
**John Laing plc, I 575–76,** 588
**John Lewis Partnership plc, V 93–95; 13** 307; **42 199–203 (upd.)**
John Lucas Co., **III** 745
John Lysaght, **III** 493–95
John M. Hart Company, **9** 304
John M. Smyth Co., **15** 282
John Macfarlane and Sons, **II** 593
John Mackintosh and Sons, **II** 568–69
John McConnell & Co., **13** 102
John McLean and Sons Ltd., **III** 753
**John Menzies plc, 39 240–43**
John Morrell and Co., **II** 595–96; **21** 111
John Nicholls & Co., **III** 690
**The John Nuveen Company, III** 356; **21 304–06; 22** 492, 494–95
John Oster Manufacturing Company. *See* Sunbeam-Oster.
**John Paul Mitchell Systems, 24 250–52**
John Pew & Company, **13** 243
**John Q. Hammons Hotels, Inc., 24 253–55**
John R. Figg, Inc., **II** 681
John Rogers Co., **9** 253
John Sands, **22** 35
John Schroeder Lumber Company, **25** 379
John Sexton & Co., **26** 503
John Strange Paper Company, **8** 358
John Swire & Sons Ltd. *See* Swire Pacific Ltd.
**John W. Danforth Company, 48 237–39**
John Walker & Sons, **I** 239–40
John Wanamaker, **22** 110
**John Wiley & Sons, Inc., 17 270–72**
John Williams, **III** 691
John Wyeth & Bro., **I** 713
John Yokley Company, **11** 194
John Zink Company, **22** 3–4; **25** 403
**Johnny Rockets Group, Inc., 31 277–81**
Johns Manville Corporation, **III** 708; **7** 293; **11** 420; **19** 211–12
Johns Perry, **III** 673
Johnsen, Jorgensen and Wettre, **14** 249
Johnson. *See* Axel Johnson Group.
**Johnson & Higgins, 14 277–80**
Johnson and Howe Furniture Corporation, **33** 151
**Johnson & Johnson, III** 18, **35–37; IV** 285, 722; **7** 45–46; **8 281–83 (upd.),** 399, 511–12; **9** 89–90; **10** 47, 69, 78, 80, 534–35; **15** 357–58, 360; **16** 168, 440; **17** 104–05, 340, 342–43, 533; **19** 103, 105; **25** 55–56; **34** 280, 283–84; **36 302–07 (upd.); 37** 110–11, 113; **41** 154–55; **46** 104
Johnson and Patan, **III** 671
Johnson and Sons Smelting Works Ltd., **IV** 119
Johnson Brothers, **12** 528
Johnson, Carruthers & Rand Shoe Co., **III** 528
**Johnson Controls, Inc., III 534–37; 13** 398; **16** 184, 322; **26 227–32 (upd.)**
Johnson Diversified, Inc., **III** 59
Johnson Engineering Corporation, **37** 365
**Johnson Matthey PLC, II** 390; **IV** 23, **117–20; 16** 28, **290–94 (upd.),** 439
Johnson Motor Co., **III** 597–99
Johnson Products Co., Inc., **11** 208; **31** 89
**Johnson Publishing Company, Inc., 27** 361; **28 212–14**
Johnson Systems, **6** 224
Johnson Wax. *See* S.C. Johnson & Son, Inc.
**Johnson Worldwide Associates, Inc., 24** 530; **28 215–17,** 412
Johnston Coca-Cola Bottling Company of Chattanooga, **13** 163–64
Johnston Evans & Co., **IV** 704
Johnston Foil Co., **IV** 18
Johnston Harvester Co., **III** 650
**Johnston Industries, Inc., 15 246–48**
**Johnston Press plc, 35 242–44**
**Johnstown America Industries, Inc., 23 305–07**
Johnstown Sanitary Dairy, **13** 393
Jointless Rim Ltd., **I** 428
Jokisch, **II** 556
Jonathan Backhouse & Co., **II** 235
Jonathan Logan Inc., **13** 536
Jonell Shoe Manufacturing Corporation, **13** 360
Jones & Babson, Inc., **14** 85
Jones & Johnson, **14** 277
Jones & Laughlin Steel Corp., **I** 463, 489–91; **IV** 228; **11** 197
**Jones Apparel Group, Inc., 11 216–18; 27** 60; **30** 310–11; **39 244–47 (upd.),** 301, 303
Jones Brothers Tea Co., **7** 202
**Jones, Day, Reavis & Pogue, 33 226–29**
Jones Environmental, **11** 361
Jones Financial Companies, L.P. *See* Edward Jones.
**Jones Intercable, Inc., 14** 260; **17** 7; **21 307–09; 24** 123; **25** 212
Jones Janitor Service, **25** 15
**Jones Medical Industries, Inc., 24 256–58; 34** 460
Jones Motor Co., **10** 44
Jones-Rodolfo Corp. *See* Cutter & Buck, Inc.
Jonker Fris, **II** 571
Jonkoping & Vulcan, **12** 462
**Jordache Enterprises, Inc., 15** 201–02; **23 308–10**
The Jordan Co., **11** 261; **16** 149
**Jordan Industries, Inc., 36 308–10**
Jordan Marsh, **III** 608; **V** 26; **9** 209
Jordan Valley Electric Cooperative, **12** 265
**Jos. A. Bank Clothiers, Inc., II** 560; **12** 411; **31 282–85**
Josef Meys, **III** 418
The Joseph & Feiss Company, **48** 209
Joseph Bellamy and Sons Ltd., **II** 569
Joseph Campbell Company. *See* Campbell Soup Company.
Joseph Crosfield, **III** 31
Joseph E. Seagram & Sons Inc., **I** 266, 285; **21** 319

Joseph Garneau Co., **I** 226; **10** 180
Joseph Leavitt Corporation, **9** 20
Joseph Littlejohn & Levy, **27** 204
Joseph Lucas & Son, **III** 554–56
Joseph Lumber Company, **25** 379
Joseph Magnin, **I** 417–18; **17** 124; **41** 114
Joseph Malecki Corp., **24** 444–45
Joseph Nathan & Co., **I** 629–40
Joseph Rank Limited, **II** 564
Joseph Schlitz Brewing Company, **25** 281
**Joseph T. Ryerson & Son, Inc.**, **IV** 114; **15 249–51**; **19** 217, 381. *See also* Ryerson Tull, Inc.
Josephson International, **27** 392; **43** 235
Joshin Denki, **13** 481
Joshu Railway Company, **6** 431
Joshua's Christian Bookstores, **31** 435–36
Josiah Wedgwood and Sons Limited. *See* Waterford Wedgewood plc..
**Jostens, Inc.**, **7 255–57**; **25 252–55 (upd.)**; **36** 470
**Journal Register Company**, **29 261–63**
Journey's End Corporation, **14** 107
Jovan, **III** 66
Jove Publications, Inc., **II** 144; **IV** 623; **12** 224
Jovi, **II** 652
Joy Manufacturing, **III** 526
Joy Planning Co., **III** 533
Joy Technologies Inc., **II** 17; **26** 70; **38** 227
Joyce International, Inc., **16** 68
JP Foodservice Inc., **24** 445
JP Household Supply Co. Ltd., **IV** 293
JP Information Center Co., Ltd., **IV** 293
JP Planning Co. Ltd., **IV** 293
JPC Co., **IV** 155
JPF Holdings, Inc. *See* U.S. Foodservice.
JPS Automotive L.P., **17** 182–84
**JPS Textile Group, Inc.**, **28 218–20**
JPT Publishing, **8** 528
JR Central, **43** 103
JR Tokai, **43** 103
**JSC MMC Norilsk Nickel**, **48 300–02**
JT Aquisitions, **II** 661
JTL Corporation, **13** 162–63
JTN Acquisition Corp., **19** 233
JTS Corporation, **23** 23, 26
Jude Hanbury, **I** 294
Judel Glassware Co., Inc., **14** 502
Judson Dunaway Corp., **12** 127
Judson Steel Corp., **13** 97
Jugend & Volk, **14** 556
Jugo Bank, **II** 325
Juice Bowl Products, **II** 480–81; **26** 57
Juice Works, **26** 57
Jujamycn, **24** 439
**Jujo Paper Co., Ltd.**, **IV** 268, 284–85, 292–93, **297–98**, 321, 326, 328, 356
JuJu Media, Inc., **41** 385
Julius Berger-Bauboag A.G., **I** 560–61
Julius Garfinckel & Co., Inc., **22** 110
Jumping-Jacks Shoes, Inc., **17** 390
Jung-Pumpen, **III** 570; **20** 361
Junghans Uhren, **10** 152
**Juniper Networks, Inc.**, **43 251–55**
Junkers Luftverkehr, **I** 110, 197; **6** 87–88
**Juno Lighting, Inc.**, **30 266–68**
**Juno Online Services, Inc.**, **38 269–72**; **39** 25–26
Juovo Pignone, **13** 356
Jupiter National, **15** 247–48; **19** 166
Jupiter Tyndall, **47** 84
Jurgens, **II** 588–89
Jurgensen's, **17** 558
Jurgovan & Blair, **III** 197
Juristförlaget, **14** 556
Jusco Car Life Company, **23** 290
**JUSCO Co., Ltd.**, **V 96–99**; **11** 498; **36** 419; **43** 386
Jusco Group, **31** 430
**Just Born, Inc.**, **32 305–07**
**Just For Feet, Inc.**, **19 228–30**
Just Squeezed, **31** 350
Just Toys, Inc., **29** 476
**Justin Industries, Inc.**, **19 231–33**
Juventus F.C. S.p.A., **44** 387–88
JVC. *See* Victor Company of Japan, Ltd.
JW Aluminum Company, **22** 544
JW Bernard & Zn., **39** 203
JWD Group, Inc., **48** 238
**JWP Inc.**, **9 300–02**; **13** 176
**JWT Group Inc.**, **I** 9, **19–21**, 23; **6** 53. *See also* WPP Group plc.
Jylhävaara, **IV** 348
JZC. *See* John Zink Company.

**K&B Inc.**, **12 286–88**; **17** 244
K&F Manufacturing. *See* Fender Musical Instruments.
**K & G Men's Center, Inc.**, **21 310–12**; **48** 286
K&K Insurance Group, **26** 487
K&K Toys, Inc., **23** 176
K&L, **6** 48
K&M Associates L.P., **16** 18; **43** 19
K & R Warehouse Corporation, **9** 20
K-C Aviation, **III** 41; **16** 304; **43** 258
K-Graphics Inc., **16** 306; **43** 261
K-Group, **27** 261
K-H Corporation, **7** 260
**K-Swiss, Inc.**, **33 243–45**
**K-tel International, Inc.**, **21 325–28**
K-III Holdings. *See* Primedia Inc.
K.C.C. Holding Co., **III** 192
K.F. Kline Co., **7** 145; **22** 184
K.H. Wheel Company, **27** 202
K. Hattori & Co., Ltd., **III** 454–55, 619–20. *See also* Seiko Corporation.
k.k. Staatsbahnen, **6** 419
K Line. *See* Kawasaki Kisen Kaisha, Ltd.
K.O. Lester Co., **31** 359, 361
K.W. Muth Company, **17** 305
KA Teletech, **27** 365
Ka Wah AMEV Insurance, **III** 200–01
Kabelvision AB, **26** 331–33
Kable News Company. *See* AMREP Corporation.
Kable Printing Co., **13** 559
Kaduna Refining and Petrochemicals Co., **IV** 473
Kaepa, **16** 546
Kaestner & Hecht Co., **II** 120
Kafte Inc., **28** 63
Kaga Forwarding Co., **6** 428
Kagami Crystal Works, **III** 714
Kagle Home Health Care, **11** 282
Kagoshima Central Research Laboratory, **21** 330
Kahan and Lessin, **II** 624–25
Kahn's Meats, **II** 572
Kai Tak Land Investment Co., **IV** 717
Kaiser + Kraft GmbH, **27** 175
**Kaiser Aluminum & Chemical Corporation**, **IV** 11–12, 15, 59–60, **121–23**, 191; **6** 148; **12** 377; **8** 348, 350; **22** 455. *See also* ICF Kaiser International, Inc.
Kaiser Cement, **III** 501, 760; **IV** 272
Kaiser Company, **6** 184
Kaiser Engineering, **IV** 218
Kaiser Industries, **III** 760
Kaiser Packaging, **12** 377
Kaiser Permanente Corp., **6** 279; **12** 175; **24** 231; **25** 434, 527; **41** 183
Kaiser Steel, **IV** 59
Kaiser's Kaffee Geschäft AG, **27** 461
Kaizosha, **IV** 632
Kajaani Oy, **II** 302; **IV** 350
**Kajima Corp.**, **I 577–78**
**Kal Kan Foods, Inc.**, **22 298–300**
Kalamazoo Paper Co., **IV** 281; **9** 259
Kalbfleish, **I** 300
Kaldveer & Associates, **14** 228
Kaliningradnefteprodukt, **48** 378
Kalitta Group, **22** 311
Kalua Koi Corporation, **7** 281
Kalumburu Joint Venture, **IV** 67
Kamaishi, **IV** 157; **17** 349
**Kaman Corporation**, **12 289–92**; **16** 202; **42 204–08 (upd.)**; **43** 171
Kamewa Group, **27** 494, 496
Kaminski/Engles Capital Corp. *See* Suiza Foods Corporation.
Kamioka Mining & Smelting Co., Ltd., **IV** 145, 148
Kammer Valves, A.G., **17** 147
**Kampgrounds of America, Inc.**, **33 230–33**
**Kamps AG**, **44 251–54**
Kanagawa Bank, **II** 291
Kanda Shokai, **16** 202; **43** 171
Kanders Florida Holdings, Inc., **27** 50
Kane Financial Corp., **III** 231
Kane Foods, **III** 43
Kane Freight Lines, **6** 370
Kane-Miller Corp., **12** 106
Kanebo Spinning Inc., **IV** 442
Kanegafuchi Shoji, **IV** 225
**Kanematsu Corporation**, **IV 442–44**; **24 259–62 (upd.)**
Kangaroo. *See* Seino Transportation Company, Ltd.
Kangol Ltd., **IV** 136
Kangyo Bank, **II** 300, 310, 361
Kanhym, **IV** 91–92
Kanoldt, **24** 75
**Kansai Electric Power Co., Inc.**, **IV** 492; **V 645–48**
Kansai Seiyu Ltd., **V** 188
Kansai Sogo Bank, **II** 361
**Kansallis-Osake-Pankki**, **II** 242, **302–03**, 366; **IV** 349
**Kansas City Power & Light Company**, **6 510–12**, 592; **12** 541–42
Kansas City Securities Corporation, **22** 541
**Kansas City Southern Industries, Inc.**, **6 400–02**; **26 233–36 (upd.)**; **29** 333; **47** 162
Kansas City White Goods Company. *See* Angelica Corporation.
Kansas Fire & Casualty Co., **III** 214
Kansas Power Company, **6** 312
Kansas Public Service Company, **12** 541
Kansas Utilities Company, **6** 580
The Kantar Group, **48** 442
Kanto Steel Co., Ltd., **IV** 63
Kanzaki Paper Manufacturing Co., **IV** 285, 293
**Kao Corporation**, **III 38–39**, 48; **16** 168; **20 315–17 (upd.)**
Kaohsiung Refinery, **IV** 388

Kaolin Australia Pty Ltd., **III** 691
Kapalua Land Company, Ltd., **29** 307–08
Kaplan Educational Centers, **12** 143
**Kaplan, Inc., 42 209–12**, 290
Kaplan Musical String Company, **48** 231
Kapok Computers, **47** 153
Kapy, **II** 139; **24** 194
Karafuto Industry, **IV** 320
Karan Co. *See* Donna Karan Company.
Karastan Bigelow, **19** 276
Karg'sche Familienstiftung, **V** 73
**Karlsberg Brauerei GmbH & Co KG, 41 220–23**
Karmelkorn Shoppes, Inc., **10** 371, 373; **39** 232, 235
**Karstadt Aktiengesellschaft, V 100–02; 19 234–37 (upd.)**
Kasado Dockyard, **III** 760
Kasai Securities, **II** 434
Kasco Corporation, **28** 42, 45
Kaset Rojananil, **6** 123
**Kash n' Karry Food Stores, Inc., 20 318–20**; **44** 145
Kasmarov, **9** 18
Kaspare Cohn Commercial & Savings Bank. *See* Union Bank of California.
**Kasper A.S.L., Ltd., 40 276–79**
Kast Metals, **III** 452; **15** 92
Kasuga Radio Company. *See* Kenwood Corporation.
Kat-Em International Inc., **16** 125
Katalco, **I** 374
Kataoka Electric Co., **II** 5
Katelise Group, **III** 739–40
Katharine Gibbs Schools Inc., **22** 442
Kathleen Investment (Australia) Ltd., **III** 729
Kathy's Ranch Markets, **19** 500–01
Katies, **V** 35
Kativo Chemical Industries Ltd., **8** 239; **32** 256
**Katy Industries Inc., I 472–74**; **14** 483–84; **16** 282
**Katz Communications, Inc., 6 32–34**
Katz Drug, **II** 604
**Katz Media Group, Inc., 35** 232, **245–48**
Kauffman-Lattimer, **III** 9–10
Kaufhalle AG, **V** 104; **23** 311; **41** 186–87
**Kaufhof Holding AG, II** 257; **V 103–05**
**Kaufhof Warenhaus AG, 23 311–14 (upd.)**
**Kaufman and Broad Home Corporation, 8 284–86**; **11** 481–83. *See also* KB Home.
Kaufmann Department Stores, Inc., **V** 132–33; **6** 243; **19** 262
**Kaufring AG, 35 249–52**
Kaukaan Tehdas Osakeyhtiö, **IV** 301
Oy Kaukas Ab, **IV** 300–02; **19** 462
Kaukauna Cheese Inc., **23** 217, 219
Kauppaosakeyhtiö Kymmene Aktiebolag, **IV** 299
Kauppiaitten Oy, **8** 293
Kautex-Bayern GmbH, **IV** 128
Kautex-Ostfriedland GmbH, **IV** 128
Kautex Werke Reinold Hagen AG, **IV** 128
Kawachi Bank, **II** 361; **26** 455
Kawamata, **11** 350
Kawasaki Denki Seizo, **II** 22
**Kawasaki Heavy Industries, Ltd., I** 75; **II** 273–74; **III** 482, 513, 516, **538–40**, 756; **IV** 124; **7** 232; **8** 72; **23** 290
**Kawasaki Kisen Kaisha, Ltd., V 457–60**
**Kawasaki Steel Corporation, I** 432; **II** 274; **III** 539, 760; **IV** 30, **124–25**, 154, 212–13; **13** 324; **19** 8
Kawashimaya Shoten Inc. Ltd., **II** 433
Kawecki Berylco Industries, **8** 78
Kawneer GmbH., **IV** 18
Kawsmouth Electric Light Company. *See* Kansas City Power & Light Company.
**Kay-Bee Toy Stores, V** 137; **15 252–53**; **16** 389–90. *See also* KB Toys.
Kay County Gas Co., **IV** 399
Kay Home Products, **17** 372
Kay's Drive-In Food Service, **II** 619
**Kaydon Corporation, 18 274–76**
Kaye, Scholer, Fierman, Hays & Handler, **47** 436
Kayex, **9** 251
Kaynar Manufacturing Company, **8** 366
Kayser Aluminum & Chemicals, **8** 229
Kayser Roth Corp., **8** 288; **22** 122
Kaysersberg, S.A., **IV** 290
**KB Home, 45 218–22 (upd.)**
AO KB Impuls, **48** 419
**KB Toys, 35 253–55 (upd.)**
KBLCOM Incorporated, **V** 644
KC. *See* Kenneth Cole Productions, Inc.
KC Holdings, Inc., **11** 229–30
KCI Konecranes International, **27** 269
KCPL. *See* Kansas City Power & Light Company.
KCS Industries, **12** 25–26
KCSI. *See* Kansas City Southern Industries, Inc.
KCSR. *See* Kansas City Southern Railway.
KD Acquisition Corporation, **34** 103–04
KD Manitou, Inc. *See* Manitou BF S.A.
KDT Industries, Inc., **9** 20
Keane Inc., **38** 431
The Keds Corp., **37** 377, 379
**Keebler Foods Company, II** 594; **35** 181; **36 311–13**
Keefe Manufacturing Courtesy Coffee Company, **6** 392
Keegan Management Co., **27** 274
Keen, Robinson and Co., **II** 566
Keene Packaging Co., **28** 43
KEG Productions Ltd., **IV** 640; **26** 272
Keihan JUSCO, **V** 96
Keil Chemical Company, **8** 178
**Keio Teito Electric Railway Company, V 461–62**
Keisei Electric Railway, **II** 301
Keith-Albee-Orpheum, **II** 88
Keith Prowse Music Publishing, **22** 193
**Keithley Instruments Inc., 16 299–301**; **48** 445
Kelco, **34** 281
**Kelda Group plc, 45 223–26**
Keller Builders, **43** 400
Keller-Dorian Graveurs, S.A., **17** 458
Kelley & Partners, Ltd., **14** 130
**Kelley Drye & Warren LLP, 40 280–83**
Kellock, **10** 336
**Kellogg Company, I** 22–23; **II** 463, 502–03, **523–26**, 530, 560; **10** 323–24; **12** 411; **13** 3, **291–94 (upd.)**; **15** 189; **18** 65, 225–26; **22** 336, 338; **25** 90; **27** 39; **29** 30, 110; **36** 236–38
Kellogg Foundation, **41** 118
**Kellwood Company, V** 181–82; **8 287–89**
Kelly & Associates, **III** 306
Kelly & Cohen, **10** 468
Kelly, Douglas and Co., **II** 631
Kelly Nason, Inc., **13** 203
**Kelly Services, Inc., 6 35–37**, 140; **9** 326; **16** 48; **25** 356, 432; **26 237–40 (upd.)**; **40** 236, 238
**The Kelly-Springfield Tire Company, 8 290–92**; **20** 260, 263
**Kelsey-Hayes Group of Companies, I** 170; **III** 650, 652; **7 258–60**; **27 249–52 (upd.)**
Kelso & Co., **III** 663, 665; **12** 436; **19** 455; **21** 490; **30** 48–49; **33** 92
Kelty Pack, Inc., **10** 215
Kelvinator Inc., **17** 487
KemaNobel, **9** 380–81; **13** 22
**Kemet Corp., 14 281–83**
Kemi Oy, **IV** 316
Kemira, Inc., **III** 760; **6** 152
Kemp's Biscuits Limited, **II** 594
**Kemper Corporation, III 269–71**, 339; **15 254–58 (upd.)**; **22** 495; **33** 111; **42** 451
Kemper Financial Services, **26** 234
Kemper Motorenfabrik, **I** 197
Kemper Snowboards, **22** 460
Kemperco Inc., **III** 269–70
Kempinski Group, **II** 258
Kemps Biscuits, **II** 594
Ken-L-Ration, **II** 559
**Kendall International, Inc., I** 529; **III** 24–25; **IV** 288; **11 219–21**; **14** 121; **15** 229; **28** 486
**Kendall-Jackson Winery, Ltd., 28** 111, **221–23**
**Kenetech Corporation, 11 222–24**
**Kennametal, Inc., IV** 203; **13 295–97**
**Kennecott Corporation, III** 248; **IV** 33–34, 79, 170–71, 179, 192, 288, 576; **7 261–64**; **10** 262, 448; **12** 244; **27 253–57 (upd.)**; **35** 135; **38** 231; **45** 332
Kennedy Automatic Products Co., **16** 8
Kenner, **II** 502; **10** 323; **12** 168
Kenner Parker Toys, Inc., **II** 503; **9** 156; **10** 324; **14** 266; **16** 337; **25** 488–89
**Kenneth Cole Productions, Inc., 22** 223; **25 256–58**
Kenneth O. Lester, Inc., **21** 508
Kenny Rogers' Roasters, **22** 464; **29** 342, 344
Kenroy International, Inc., **13** 274
Kent Drugs Ltd., **II** 640, 650
**Kent Electronics Corporation, 17 273–76**
Kent Fire, **III** 350
Kent-Moore Corp., **I** 200; **10** 492–93
Kentland-Elkhorn Coal Corp., **IV** 181
Kentrox Industries, **30** 7
Kentucky Bonded Funeral Co., **III** 217
**Kentucky Electric Steel, Inc., 31 286–88**
Kentucky Fried Chicken, **I** 260–61; **II** 533; **III** 78, 104, 106; **6** 200; **7** 26–28, 433; **8** 563; **12** 42; **13** 336; **16** 97; **18** 8, 538; **19** 92; **21** 361; **22** 464; **23** 384, 504. *See also* KFC Corporation.
Kentucky Institution for the Education of the Blind. *See* American Printing House for the Blind.
**Kentucky Utilities Company, 6 513–15**; **11** 37, 236–38
Kenway, **I** 155
**Kenwood Corporation, I** 532; **19** 360; **23** 53; **31 289–91**
Kenwood Silver Company, Inc., **31** 352
Kenworth Motor Truck Corp., **I** 185–86; **26** 354
Kenyon & Eckhardt Advertising Agency, **25** 89–91

Kenyon Corp., **18** 276
Kenyon Sons and Craven Ltd., **II** 593–94
Kenzo, **25** 122
Keo Cutters, Inc., **III** 569; **20** 360
KEPCO. *See* Kyushu Electric Power Company Inc.
Kerlick, Switzer & Johnson, **6** 48
Kerlyn Oil Co., **IV** 445–46
Kern County Land Co., **I** 527; **10** 379, 527
Kernite SA, **8** 386
Kernkraftwerke Lippe-Ems, **V** 747
Kernridge Oil Co., **IV** 541
Kerr-Addison Mines Ltd., **IV** 165
Kerr Concrete Pipe Company, **14** 250
Kerr Corporation, **14** 481
Kerr Drug Stores, **32** 170
**Kerr Group Inc.**, **III** 423; **10** 130; **22** 48; **24 263–65**; **30** 39
**Kerr-McGee Corporation**, **IV 445–47**; **13** 118; **22 301–04 (upd.)**
**Kerry Group plc**, **27 258–60**
**Kerry Properties Limited**, **22 305–08**; **24** 388
Keski-Suomen Tukkukauppa Oy, **8** 293
**Kesko Ltd (Kesko Oy)**, **8 293–94**; **27 261–63 (upd.)**
Ketchikan International Sales Co., **IV** 304
Ketchikan Paper Company, **31** 316
Ketchikan Pulp Co., **IV** 304
**Ketchum Communications Inc.**, **6 38–40**
Ketner and Milner Stores, **II** 683
**Kettle Foods Inc.**, **26** 58; **48 240–42**
Kettle Restaurants, Inc., **29** 149
Keumkang Co., **III** 515; **7** 231
Kewanee Public Service Company, **6** 505
**Kewaunee Scientific Corporation**, **25 259–62**
Key Computer Laboratories, Inc., **14** 15
Key Industries, Inc., **26** 342
Key Markets, **II** 628
Key Pharmaceuticals, Inc., **11** 207; **41** 419
**Key Tronic Corporation**, **14 284–86**
**KeyCorp**, **8 295–97**; **11** 110; **14** 90
**Keyes Fibre Company**, **9 303–05**
Keypage. *See* Rural Cellular Corporation.
**KeySpan Energy Co.**, **27 264–66**
Keystone Aircraft, **I** 61; **11** 164
Keystone Consolidated Industries, Inc., **19** 467
Keystone Custodian Fund, **IV** 458
Keystone Foods Corporation, **10** 443
Keystone Franklin, Inc., **III** 570; **9** 543; **20** 362
Keystone Frozen Foods, **17** 536
Keystone Gas Co., **IV** 548
Keystone Health Plan West, Inc., **27** 211
Keystone Insurance and Investment Co., **12** 564
**Keystone International, Inc.**, **11 225–27**; **28** 486
Keystone Life Insurance Co., **III** 389; **33** 419
Keystone Paint and Varnish, **8** 553
Keystone Pipe and Supply Co., **IV** 136
Keystone Portland Cement Co., **23** 225
Keystone Savings and Loan, **II** 420
Keystone Tube Inc., **25** 8
Keytronics, **18** 541
**KFC Corporation**, **7 265–68**; **10** 450; **21 313–17 (upd.)**; **23** 115, 117, 153; **32** 12–14
KFF Management, **37** 350
Khalda Petroleum Co., **IV** 413
KHBB, **16** 72
KHD AG. *See* Klöckner-Humboldt-Deutz AG.
**KHD Konzern**, **III 541–44**
KHL. *See* Koninklijke Hollandsche Lloyd.
**Kia Motors Corporation**, **I** 167; **12 293–95**; **29 264–67 (upd.)**
Kiabi, **37** 22–23
Kickers Worldwide, **35** 204, 207
Kidd, Kamm & Co., **21** 482
**Kidde Inc.**, **I 475–76**; **III** 503; **7** 209; **23** 297; **39** 344–46
**Kidde plc**, **44 255–59 (upd.)**
Kidder, Peabody & Co., **II** 31, 207, 430; **IV** 84; **7** 310; **12** 197; **13** 465–67, 534; **16** 322; **22** 406
Kidder Press Co., **IV** 644
Kiddie Products, Inc. *See* The First Years Inc.
Kids "R" Us, **V** 203–05; **9** 394; **37** 81
Kids Foot Locker, **14** 293, 295
Kidston Mines, **I** 438
Kiekhaefer Corporation, **III** 443; **22** 115
Kien, **13** 545
Kienzle Apparate GmbH, **III** 566; **38** 299
Kierulff Electronics, **10** 113
Kieser Verlag, **14** 555
Kiewit Diversified Group Inc., **11** 301
Kiewit-Murdock Investment Corp., **15** 129
Kijkshop/Best-Sellers, **13** 545
**Kikkoman Corporation**, **I** 9; **14 287–89**; **47 203–06 (upd.)**
Kilburn & Co., **III** 522
Kilgo Motor Express, **6** 370
Kilgore Ceramics, **III** 671
Kilgore Federal Savings and Loan Assoc., **IV** 343
Killington, Ltd., **28** 21
Kilpatrick's Department Store, **19** 511
Kilsby Tubesupply, **I** 570
**Kimball International, Inc.**, **12 296–98**; **48 243–47 (upd.)**
Kimbell Inc., **II** 684
Kimberley Central Mining Co., **IV** 64; **7** 121
**Kimberly-Clark Corporation**, **I** 14, 413; **III** 36, **40–41**; **IV** 249, 254, 297–98, 329, 648, 665; **8** 282; **15** 357; **16 302–05 (upd.)**; **17** 30, 397; **18** 147–49; **19** 14, 284, 478; **22** 209; **43 256–60 (upd.)**
**Kimco Realty Corporation**, **11 228–30**
Kimowelt Medien, **39** 13
Kincaid Furniture Company, **14** 302–03
Kindai Golf Company, **32** 447
Kinden Corporation, **7** 303
**Kinder Morgan, Inc.**, **45 227–30**
**KinderCare Learning Centers, Inc.**, **13 298–300**; **34** 105; **35** 408
Kinear Moodie, **III** 753
Kineret Acquisition Corp. *See* The Hain Celestial Group, Inc.
**Kinetic Concepts, Inc.**, **20 321–23**
**King & Spalding**, **23 315–18**
**The King Arthur Flour Company**, **31 292–95**
King Bearing, Inc., **13** 79
King Cullen, **II** 644
King Features Syndicate, **IV** 626; **19** 201, 203–04; **46** 232
King Folding Box Co., **13** 441
King Fook Gold and Jewellery Co., **IV** 717
King Hickory, **17** 183
**King Kullen Grocery Co., Inc.**, **15 259–61**; **19** 481; **24** 528
**King Ranch, Inc.**, **14 290–92**
King-Seeley, **II** 419; **16** 487
King Soopers Inc., **12** 112–13
**King World Productions, Inc.**, **9 306–08**; **28** 174; **30 269–72 (upd.)**
King's Lynn Glass, **12** 528
Kingbird Media Group LLC, **26** 80
**Kingfisher plc**, **V 106–09**; **10** 498; **19** 123; **24 266–71 (upd.)**; **27** 118, 120; **28** 34, 36
Kings, **24** 528
Kings County Lighting Company, **6** 456
Kings County Research Laboratories, **11** 424
Kings Mills, Inc., **13** 532
Kings Super Markets, **24** 313, 316
Kingsford Corporation, **III** 21; **22** 146
Kingsin Line, **6** 397
Kingsport Pulp Corp., **IV** 310; **19** 266
**Kingston Technology Corporation**, **20 324–26**; **38** 441
**Kinki Nippon Railway Company Ltd.**, **V 463–65**
**Kinko's Inc.**, **12** 174; **16 306–08**; **18** 363–64; **43 261–64 (upd.)**
Kinnevik. *See* Industriförvaltnings AB Kinnevik.
Kinney Corporation, **23** 32; **24** 373
Kinney National Service Inc., **II** 176; **IV** 672; **19** 404; **25** 140
Kinney Services, **6** 293
**Kinney Shoe Corp.**, **V** 226; **11** 349; **14 293–95**
Kinney Tobacco Co., **12** 108
Kinoshita Sansho Steel Co., **I** 508
Kinpo Electronic, **23** 212
**Kinross Gold Corporation**, **36 314–16**
Kinson Resources Inc., **27** 38
Kintec Corp., **10** 97
Kirby. *See* Scott Fetzer Company.
**Kirby Corporation**, **18 277–79**; **22** 275
Kirby Forest Industries, **IV** 305
Kirch Gruppe, **10** 196; **35** 452
Kirchner, Moore, and Co., **II** 408
KirchPayTV, **46** 402
**Kirin Brewery Company, Limited**, **I** 220, 258, **265–66**, 282; **10** 78, 80; **13** 258, 454; **20** 28; **21 318–21 (upd.)**; **36** 404–05
Kirk Stieff Company, **10** 181; **12** 313
Kirkland Messina, Inc., **19** 392, 394
Kirkstall Forge Engineering, **III** 494
Kirsch Co., **II** 16
Kirschner Manufacturing Co., **16** 296
Kishimoto & Co., **I** 432, 492; **24** 325
Kishimoto Shoten Co., Ltd., **IV** 168
Kistler, Lesh & Co., **III** 528
**Kit Manufacturing Co.**, **18 280–82**
Kita Consolidated, Ltd., **16** 142
Kita Karafunto Oil Co., **IV** 475
Kita Nippon Paper Co., **IV** 321
Kitagawa & Co. Ltd., **IV** 442
**Kitchell Corporation**, **14 296–98**
**KitchenAid**, **III** 611, 653–54; **8 298–99**
Kitchenbell, **III** 43
Kitchens of Sara Lee, **II** 571–73
Kittery Electric Light Co., **14** 124
Kittinger, **10** 324
**Kitty Hawk, Inc.**, **22 309–11**
**Kiwi International Airlines Inc.**, **20 327–29**
Kiwi Packaging, **IV** 250
Kiwi Polish Co., **15** 507
KJJ. *See* Klaus J. Jacobs Holdings.

Kjøbenhavns Bandelsbank, **II** 366
KJPCL. *See* Royal Interocean Lines.
KKK Shipping, **II** 274
KKR. *See* Kohlberg Kravis Roberts & Co.
**KLA Instruments Corporation, 11 231–33**; **20** 8
**KLA-Tencor Corporation, 45 231–34 (upd.)**
Klaus J. Jacobs Holdings, **29** 46–47
KLC/New City Televentures, **25** 269
Klein Bicycles, **16** 495
Klein Sleep Products Inc., **32** 426
Kleiner, Perkins, Caufield & Byers, **I** 637; **6** 278; **10** 15, 504; **14** 263; **16** 418; **27** 447
**Kleinwort Benson Group PLC, II** 379, **421–23**; **IV** 191; **22** 55
Kline Manufacturing, **II** 16
KLLM Transport Services, **27** 404
KLM Royal Dutch Airlines, **26** 33924 311, 396–97; **27** 474; **29** 15, 17; **33** 49, 51; **34** 397; **47** 60–61. *See also* Koninklijke Luftvaart Maatschappij N.V.
Klöckner-Humboldt-Deutz AG, **I** 542; **III** 541–44; **IV** 126–27; **13** 16–17
**Klöckner-Werke AG, IV** 43, 60, **126–28**, 201; **19** 64; **39** 125
Klondike, **14** 205
Klopman International, **12** 118
Kloth-Senking, **IV** 201
Klüber Lubrication München KG, **41** 170
Kluwer Publishers, **IV** 611; **14** 555
Klynveld Main Goerdeler, **10** 387
Klynveld Peat Marwick Goerdeler. *See* KPMG Worldwide.
KM&G. *See* Ketchum Communications Inc.
Kmart Canada Co., **25** 222
**Kmart Corporation, I** 516; **V** 35, **110–12**; **6** 13; **7** 61, 444; **9** 361, 400, 482; **10** 137, 410, 490, 497, 515–16; **12** 48, 54–55, 430, 477–78, 507–08; **13** 42, 260–61, 274, 317–18, 444, 446; **14** 192, 394; **15** 61–62, 210–11, 330–31, 470; **16** 35–37, 61, 187, 210, 447, 457; **17** 297, 460–61, 523–24; **18** 137, **283–87 (upd.)**, 477; **19** 511; **20** 155–56; **21** 73; **22** 258, 328; **23** 210, 329; **24** 322–23; **25** 121; **26** 348, 524; **27** 313, 429, 451, 481; **32** 169; **43** 77–78, 293, 385; **47 207–12 (upd.)**; **48** 331
Kmart Mexico, **36** 139
KMC Enterprises, Inc., **27** 274
KMP Holdings, **I** 531
KN. *See* Kühne & Nagel Group.
KN Energy. *See* Kinder Morgan, Inc.
Kna-Shoe Manufacturing Company, **14** 302
**Knape & Vogt Manufacturing Company, 17 277–79**
Knapp & Tubbs, **III** 423
Knapp Communications Corporation, **II** 656; **13** 180; **24** 418
Knapp-Monarch, **12** 251
Knauf, **III** 721, 736
KNI Retail A/S, **12** 363
Knickerbocker Toy Co., **III** 505
Knickerbocker Trust Company, **13** 465
Knife River Coal Mining Company, **7** 322–25
Knife River Corporation, **42** 249, 253
Knight Paper Co., **III** 766; **22** 545
**Knight-Ridder, Inc., III** 190; **IV** 597, 613, **628–30**, 670; **6** 323; **7** 191, 327; **10** 407; **15 262–66 (upd.)**; **18** 323; **30** 216; **38** 307
Knightsbridge Partners, **26** 476
KNILM, **24** 397
Knoff-Bremse, **I** 138
Knogo Corp., **11** 444; **39** 78
**Knoll Group Inc., I** 202; **14 299–301**
Knoll Pharmaceutical, **I** 682
Knomark, **III** 55
Knorr-Bremse, **11** 31
Knorr Co. *See* C.H. Knorr Co.
Knorr Foods Co., Ltd., **28** 10
Knott, **III** 98
**Knott's Berry Farm, 18 288–90**; **22** 130
Knowledge Systems Concepts, **11** 469
**KnowledgeWare Inc., 9 309–11**; **27** 491; **31 296–298 (upd.)**; **45** 206
Knox County Insurance, **41** 178
Knox Reeves Advertising Agency, **25** 90
Knoxville Glove Co., **34** 159
Knoxville Paper Box Co., Inc., **13** 442
KNP BT. *See* Buhrmann NV.
KNSM. *See* Koninklijke Nederlandsche Stoomboot Maatschappij.
Knudsen & Sons, Inc., **11** 211
Knudsen Foods, **27** 330
Knutange, **IV** 226
Knutson Construction, **25** 331
KOA. *See* Kampgrounds of America, Inc.
**Koala Corporation, 44 260–62**
Kobacker Co., **18** 414–15
Kobayashi Tomijiro Shoten, **III** 44
Kobe Shipbuilding & Engine Works, **II** 57
**Kobe Steel, Ltd., I** 511; **II** 274; **IV** 16, **129–31**, 212–13; **8** 242; **11** 234–35; **13** 297; **19 238–41 (upd.)**; **38** 225–26
Kobelco America Inc., **19** 241
Kobelco Middle East, **IV** 131
Kobold. *See* Vorwerk & Co.
Kobrand Corporation, **24** 308; **43** 402
**Koç Holdings A.S., I** 167, **478–80**; **11** 139; **27** 188
**Koch Enterprises, Inc., 29 215–17**
**Koch Industries, Inc., IV 448–49**; **20 330–32 (upd.)**; **21** 108; **22** 3
Koch-Light Laboratories, **13** 239; **38** 203–04
Kockos Brothers, Inc., **II** 624
Kodak. *See* Eastman Kodak Company.
**Kodansha Ltd., IV 631–33**; **38 273–76 (upd.)**
Ködel & Böhn GmbH, **III** 543
Koehring Company, **8** 545; **23** 299
Koehring Cranes & Excavators, **7** 513
Koei Real Estate Ltd., **V** 195; **47** 390
Koenig Plastics Co., **19** 414
Kogaku Co., Ltd., **48** 295
**Kohl's Corporation, 9 312–13**; **22** 72; **30 273–75 (upd.)**
Kohl's Food Stores, Inc., **I** 426–27; **16** 247, 249
**Kohlberg Kravis Roberts & Co., I** 566, 609–11; **II** 370, 452, 468, 544, 645, 654, 656, 667; **III** 263, 765–67; **IV** 642–43; **V** 55–56, 408, 410, 415; **6** 357; **7** 130, 132, 200; **9** 53, 180, 230, 469, 522; **10** 75–77, 302; **12** 559; **13** 163, 166, 363, 453; **14** 42; **15** 270; **17** 471; **18** 3; **19** 493; **22** 55, 91, 441, 513, 544; **23** 163; **24** 92, **272–74**, 416, 418; **25** 11, 278; **26** 46, 48, 352; **27** 11; **28** 389, 475; **30** 386; **32** 408; **33** 255; **35** 35; **38** 190; **40** 34, 36, 366; **43** 355; **44** 153; **45** 243
Kohler Bros., **IV** 91
**Kohler Company, 7 269–71**; **10** 119; **24** 150; **32 308–12 (upd.)**
Kohler Mix Specialties, Inc., **25** 333
Kohner Brothers, **II** 531
Koholyt AG, **III** 693
Koike Shoten, **II** 458
Kojiro Matsukata, **V** 457–58
Kokkola Chemicals Oy, **17** 362–63
Kokomo Gas and Fuel Company, **6** 533
Kokuei Paper Co., Ltd., **IV** 327
Kokura Sekiyu Co. Ltd., **IV** 554
Kokura Steel Manufacturing Co., Ltd., **IV** 212
Kokusai Kisen, **V** 457–58
Kokusaku Kiko Co., Ltd., **IV** 327
Kokusaku Pulp Co., **IV** 327
Kolb-Lena, **25** 85
Kolbenschmidt, **IV** 141
Kolker Chemical Works, Inc., **IV** 409; **7** 308
**The Koll Company, 8 300–02**; **21** 97; **25** 449
**Kollmorgen Corporation, 18 291–94**
Kölnische Rückversicherungs- Gesellschaft AG, **24** 178
**Komag, Inc., 11 234–35**
**Komatsu Ltd., III** 453, 473, **545–46**; **15** 92; **16 309–11 (upd.)**
Kommanditgesellschaft S. Elkan & Co., **IV** 140
Kommunale Energie-Beteiligungsgesellschaft, **V** 746
Kompro Computer Leasing, **II** 457
Konan Camera Institute, **III** 487
**Kone Corporation, 27 267–70**
Kongl. Elektriska Telegraf-Verket, **V** 331
Kongo Bearing Co., **III** 595
**Konica Corporation, III 547–50**; **30 276–81 (upd.)**; **43** 284
**König Brauerei GmbH & Co. KG, 35 256–58 (upd.)**
**Koninklijke Ahold N.V., II 641–42**; **12** 152–53; **16 312–14 (upd.)**
Koninklijke Bols Wessanen, N.V., **29** 480–81
Koninklijke Distilleerderijen der Erven Lucas Böls, **I** 226
Koninklijke Hoogovens NV, **26** 527, 530
Koninklijke Java-China Paketvaart Lijnen. *See* Royal Interocean Lines.
NV Koninklijke KNP BT. *See* Buhrmann NV.
Koninklijke KPN N.V. *See* Royal KPN N.V.
**Koninklijke Luchtvaart Maatschappij N.V., I** 55, **107–09**, 119, 121; **6** 95, 105, 109–10; **14** 73; **28 224–27 (upd.)**
**Koninklijke Nederlandsche Hoogovens en Staalfabrieken NV, IV** 105, 123, **132–34**
Koninklijke Nederlandsche Maatschappig Tot Exploitatie van Petroleumbronnen in Nederlandsch-indie, **IV** 530
Koninklijke Nederlandsche Petroleum Maatschappij, **IV** 491
Koninklijke Nederlandsche Stoomboot Maatschappij, **26** 241
**N.V. Koninklijke Nederlandse Vliegtuigenfabriek Fokker, I** 46, **54–56**, 75, 82, 107, 115, 121–22; **28 327–30 (upd.)**
**Koninklijke Nedlloyd Groep N.V., 6 403–05**

**Koninklijke Nedlloyd N.V., 26 241–44 (upd.)**
Koninklijke Numico N.V. *See* Royal Numico N.V.
Koninklijke Paketvaart Maatschappij, **26** 242
**Koninklijke PTT Nederland NV, V 299–301**; **27** 471–72, 475. *See also* Royal KPN NV.
Koninklijke Van Ommeren, **22** 275
**Koninklijke Wessanen N.V., II 527–29**
Koninklijke West-Indische Maildienst, **26** 242
Koniphoto Corp., **III** 548
Konishi Honten, **III** 547
Konishi Pharmaceutical, **I** 704
Konishiroku Honten Co., Ltd., **III** 487, 547–49
Konoike Bank, **II** 347
Konrad Hornschuch AG, **31** 161–62
**Koo Koo Roo, Inc., 25 263–65**
Koop Nautic Holland, **41** 412
Koopman & Co., **III** 419
**Koor Industries Ltd., II 47–49**; **22** 501; **25 266–68 (upd.)**
Koors Perry & Associates, Inc., **24** 95
Koortrade, **II** 48
Kop-Coat, Inc., **8** 456
Kopin Corp., **13** 399
Köpings Mekaniska Verkstad, **26** 10
Koppel Steel, **26** 407
Koppens Machinenfabriek, **III** 420
Kopper United, **I** 354
**Koppers Inc., I** 199, **354–56**; **III** 645, 735; **6** 486; **17** 38–39
**Koppers Industries, Inc., 26 245–48 (upd.)**
Koracorp Industries Inc., **16** 327
Korbel, **I** 226
Korea Automotive Fuel Systems Ltd., **13** 555
Korea Automotive Motor Corp., **16** 436; **43** 319
Korea Development Leasing Corp., **II** 442
Korea Steel Co., **III** 459
Korea Telecommunications Co, **I** 516
**Korean Air Lines Co. Ltd., II** 442; **6 98–99**; **24** 443; **27 271–73 (upd.)**; **46** 40
Korean Development Bank, **III** 459
Korean Tungsten Mining Co., **IV** 183
Kori Kollo Corp., **23** 41
**Korn/Ferry International, 34 247–49**
Koro Corp., **19** 414
Korrekt Gebäudereinigung, **16** 420; **43** 307
KorrVu, **14** 430
Kortbetalning Servo A.B., **II** 353
Kortgruppen Eurocard-Köpkort A.B., **II** 353
Korvettes, E.J., **14** 426
Koryeo Industrial Development Co., **III** 516; **7** 232
Koryo Fire and Marine Insurance Co., **III** 747
**Koss Corporation, 38 277–79**
Kosset Carpets, Ltd., **9** 467
**Kotobukiya Co., Ltd., V 113–14**
Kowa Metal Manufacturing Co., **III** 758
Koyo Seiko, **III** 595–96, 623–24
KPM. *See* Koninklijke Paketvaart Maatschappij.
**KPMG International, 29** 176; **33 234–38 (upd.)**
**KPMG Worldwide, 7** 266; **10** 115, **385–87**
KPN. *See* Koninklijke PTT Nederland N.V.
KPR Holdings Inc., **23** 203
**Kraft Foods Inc., II** 129, **530–34**, 556; **V** 407; **III** 610; **7 272–77 (upd.)**, 339, 433, 547; **8** 399, 499; **9** 180, 290, 318; **11** 15; **12** 372, 532; **13** 408, 515, 517; **14** 204; **16** 88, 90; **17** 56; **18** 67, 246, 416, 419; **19** 51; **22** 82, 85; **23** 219, 384; **25** 366, 517; **26** 249, 251; **28** 479; **44** 342; **45 235–44 (upd.)**; **48** 331
Kraft Foodservice, **26** 504; **31** 359–60
**Kraft Jacobs Suchard AG, 26 249–52 (upd.)**
Kraft-Versicherungs-AG, **III** 183
Kraftco Corporation, **II** 533; **14** 204
KraftMaid Cabinetry, Inc., **20** 363; **39** 267
Kraftwerk Union, **I** 411; **III** 466
Kragen Auto Supply Co., **27** 291. *See also* CSK Auto Corporation.
Kramer, **III** 48
Krämer & Grebe, **III** 420
Kramer Guitar, **29** 222
Kramer Machine and Engineering Company, **26** 117
Krames Communications Co., **22** 441, 443
Kransco, **25** 314
Krasnapolsky Restaurant and Wintergarden Company Ltd., **23** 228
**Kraus-Anderson, Incorporated, 36 317–20**
**Krause Publications, Inc., 35 259–61**
**Krause's Furniture, Inc., 27 274–77**
Krauss-Maffei AG, **I** 75; **II** 242; **III** 566, 695; **14** 328; **38** 299
Kravco, **III** 248
**Kredietbank N.V., II** 295, **304–05**
**Kreditanstalt für Wiederaufbau, IV** 231–32; **29 268–72**
Kreft, **III** 480; **22** 26
Kreher Steel Co., **25** 8
Krelitz Industries, Inc., **14** 147
Krema Hollywood Chewing Gum Co. S.A., **II** 532
Kremers-Urban, **I** 667
Kresge Foundation, **V** 110
Kreuger & Toll, **IV** 338; **12** 462–63
Kreymborg, **13** 544–45
Kriegschemikalien AG, **IV** 229
Kriegsmetall AG, **IV** 229
Kriegswollbedarfs AG, **IV** 229
Krislex Knits, Inc., **8** 235
Krispy Kitchens, Inc., **II** 584
**Krispy Kreme Doughnut Corporation, 21 322–24**
Kroeze, **25** 82
**The Kroger Company, II** 605, 632, **643–45**, 682; **III** 218; **6** 364; **7** 61; **12** 111–13; **13** 25, 237, 395; **15** 259, **267–70 (upd.)**, 449; **16** 63–64; **18** 6; **21** 323, 508; **22** 37, 126; **24** 416; **25** 234; **28** 512; **30** 24, 27; **40** 366
Krohn-Fechheimer Shoe Company, **V** 207
Krone AG, **33** 220
Krones A.G., **I** 266; **21** 319
**Kronos, Inc., 18 295–97**; **19** 468
Krovtex, **8** 80
Kroy Tanning Company, **17** 195
Krueger Insurance Company, **21** 257
**Kruger Inc., 17 280–82**
Krumbhaar Chemical Inc., **14** 308
Krupp, **17** 214; **22** 364. *See also* Fried. Krupp GmbH *and* Thyssen Krupp AG.
Krupp Widia GmbH, **12** 66
Kruse International, **32** 162
**The Krystal Company, 33 239–42**
KSSU Group, **I** 107–08, 120–21
KT Contract Services, **24** 118
KTR. *See* Keio Teito Electric Railway Company.
**K2 Inc., 16 295–98**; **22** 481, 483; **23** 474; **43** 389
**KU Energy Corporation, 6** 513, 515; **11 236–38**
**Kubota Corporation, I** 494; **III 551–53**; **10** 404; **12** 91, 161; **21** 385–86; **24** 324; **39** 37; **40** 134
Kubota, Gonshiro. *See* Gonshiro Oode.
**Kudelski Group SA, 44 263–66**
Kuhara Mining Co., **IV** 475
**Kuhlman Corporation, 20 333–35**
Kuhlmann, **III** 677; **IV** 174; **16** 121
Kühn + Bayer, **24** 165
Kuhn Loeb, **II** 402–03
**Kühne & Nagel International AG, V 466–69**
Kuitu Oy, **IV** 348
KUK, **III** 577, 712
Kukje Group, **III** 458
**Kulicke and Soffa Industries, Inc., 33 246–48**
Kulka Smith Inc., **13** 398
Kulmobelwerk G.H. Walb and Co., **I** 581
Kum-Kleen Products, **IV** 252; **17** 29
**Kumagai Gumi Co., I 579–80**
Kumsung Companies, **III** 747–48
Kunkel Industries, **19** 143
Kunst und Technik Verlag, **IV** 590
Kuo International Ltd., **I** 566; **44** 153
Kuok Group, **28** 84
**Kuoni Travel Holding Ltd., 40 284–86**
The Kuppenheimer Company, **8** 248–50; **32** 247
Kureha Chemical Industry, **I** 675
Kureha Spinning, **24** 325
Kureha Textiles, **I** 432, 492
Kurosawa Construction Co., Ltd., **IV** 155
Kurose, **III** 420
Kurt Möller Verlag, **7** 42
Kurushima Dockyard, **II** 339
**The Kushner-Locke Company, 25 269–71**
Kuusankoski Aktiebolag, **IV** 299
Kuwait Airways, **27** 135
Kuwait Investment Office, **II** 198; **IV** 380, 452; **27** 206
**Kuwait Petroleum Corporation, IV** 364, **450–52**, 567; **18** 234; **38** 424
**Kvaerner ASA, 20** 313; **31** 367, 370; **36 321–23**
KW, Inc. *See* Coca-Cola Bottling Company of Northern New England, Inc.
Kwaishinsha Motor Car Works, **I** 183
**Kwik Save Group plc, 11 239–41**; **13** 26; **47** 368
Kwik Shop, Inc., **12** 112
Kwikasair Ltd., **27** 473
KWIM. *See* Koninklijke West-Indische Maildienst.
KWV, **I** 289
Kygnus Sekiyu K.K., **IV** 555
Kymi Paper Mills Ltd., **IV** 302
**Kymmene Corporation, IV** 276–77, **299–303**, 337. *See also* UPM-Kymmene Corporation.
**Kyocera Corporation, II 50–52**; **III** 693; **7** 118; **21 329–32 (upd.)**

Kyodo, **16** 166
Kyodo Dieworks Thailand Co., **III** 758
Kyodo Gyogyo Kaisha, Limited, **II** 552
Kyodo Kako, **IV** 680
Kyodo Kokusan K.K., **21** 271
Kyodo Oil Co. Ltd., **IV** 476
Kyodo Securities Co., Ltd., **II** 433
Kyodo Unyu Kaisha, **I** 502–03, 506; **IV** 713; **V** 481
Kyoei Mutual Fire and Marine Insurance Co., **III** 273
Kyoritsu Pharmaceutical Industry Co., **I** 667
Kyosai Trust Co. *See* Yasuda Trust and Banking Company, Limited.
Kyoto Bank, **II** 291
Kyoto Ceramic Co., Ltd. *See* Kyocera Corporation.
Kyoto Ouchi Bank, **II** 292
**Kyowa Hakko Kogyo Co., Ltd., III 42–43**; **45** 94; **48 248–50 (upd.)**
Kyusha Refining Co., **IV** 403
**Kyushu Electric Power Company Inc.**, **IV** 492; **V 649–51**; **17** 349
Kyushu Oil Refinery Co. Ltd., **IV** 434
Kywan Petroleum Ltd., **13** 556
KYZ International, **9** 427
KZO, **13** 21

L & G, **27** 291
L. & H. Sales Co., **16** 389
L&W Supply Corp., **III** 764
**L-3 Communications Holdings, Inc., 48 251–53**
L.A. Darling Co., **IV** 135–36; **16** 357
**L.A. Gear, Inc., 8 303–06**; **11** 349; **31** 413; **32 313–17 (upd.)**
L.A. Mex. *See* Checkers Drive-Up Restaurants Inc.
**L.A. T Sportswear, Inc., 26 257–59**
L.B. DeLong, **III** 558
**L.B. Foster Company, 33 255–58**
L. Bamberger & Co., **V** 169; **8** 443
L. Bosendorfer Klavierfabrik, A.G., **12** 297
L.C. Bassford, **III** 653
L.D. Canocéan, **25** 104
The L.D. Caulk Company, **10** 271
L. Fish, **14** 236
L.G. Balfour Company, **12** 472; **19** 451–52; **36** 469
L. Greif & Bro. Inc., **17** 203–05
L. Grossman and Sons. *See* Grossman's Inc.
L.H. Parke Co., **II** 571
L.J. Knowles & Bros., **9** 153
L.J. Melody & Co., **21** 97
L.K. Liggett Company, **24** 74
L. Kellenberger & Co. AG, **25** 194
**L.L. Bean, Inc.**, **9** 190, 316; **10 388–90**; **12** 280; **19** 333; **21** 131; **22** 173; **25** 48, 206; **29** 278; **36** 180, 420; **38 280–83 (upd.)**
**The L.L. Knickerbocker Co., Inc., 25 272–75**
**L. Luria & Son, Inc., 19 242–44**
L.M. Electronics, **I** 489
L.M. Ericsson, **I** 462; **II** 1, 70, 81–82, 365; **III** 479–80; **11** 46, 439; **14** 488. *See also* Telefonaktiebolaget LM Ericsson.
L-N Glass Co., **III** 715
L-N Safety Glass, **III** 715
L-O-F Glass Co. *See* Libbey-Owens-Ford Glass Co.
L. Prang & Co., **12** 207
L.S. DuBois Son and Co., **III** 10
**L.S. Starrett Co., 13 301–03**
L. Straus and Sons, **V** 168
L.W. Hammerson & Co., **IV** 696
L.W. Pierce Co., Inc. *See* Pierce Leahy Corporation.
L.W. Singer, **13** 429
La Banque Suisse et Française. *See* Crédit Commercial de France.
La Barge Mirrors, **III** 571; **20** 362
La Cerus, **IV** 615
**La Choy Food Products Inc.**, **II** 467–68; **17** 241; **25 276–78**
La Cinq, **IV** 619
La Cloche d'Or, **25** 85
La Concorde, **III** 208
La Crosse Telephone Corporation, **9** 106
La Cruz del Campo S.A., **9** 100
La Favorita Bakery, **II** 543
La Fromagerie du Velay, **25** 85
La Grange Foundry, Inc., **39** 31
La Halle aux Chaussures, **17** 210
La India Co., **II** 532
**La Madeleine French Bakery & Café, 33 249–51**
La Oroya, **22** 286
La Petite Academy, **13** 299
La Pizza Loca Inc., **44** 86
**La Poste, V 270–72**; ], **47 213–16 (upd.)**
**The La Quinta Companies, 42 213–16 (upd.)**
**La Quinta Inns, Inc., 11 242–44**; **21** 362
La Redoute S.A., **19** 306, 309
La Rinascente, **12** 153
La-Ru Truck Rental Company, Inc., **16** 386
La Ruche Meridionale, **12** 153
La 7, **47** 345, 347
La Societe Anonyme Francaise Holophane, **19** 211
La Vie Claire, **13** 103
**La-Z-Boy Chair Company, 14 302–04**; **31** 248
Laakirchen, **IV** 339–40; **28** 445
LAB. *See* Lloyd Aereo de Bolivia.
The Lab, Inc., **37** 263
LaB Investing Co. L.L.C, **37** 224
LaBakelite S.A., **I** 387
**LaBarge Inc., 41 224–26**
**Labatt Brewing Company Limited, I 267–68**; **18** 72; **25 279–82 (upd.)**; **26** 303, 306
Labaz, **I** 676; **IV** 546
Labelcraft, Inc., **8** 360
LaBelle Iron Works, **7** 586
**LabOne, Inc., 48 254–57**
Labor für Impulstechnik, **III** 154
**Labor Ready, Inc., 29 273–75**
Laboratoire L. Lafon, **45** 94
Laboratoire Michel Robilliard, **IV** 546
Laboratoire Roger Bellon, **I** 389
Laboratoires d'Anglas, **III** 47
**Laboratoires de Biologie Végétale Yves Rocher, 35 262–65**
Laboratoires Goupil, **III** 48
Laboratoires Roche Posay, **III** 48
Laboratoires Ruby d'Anglas, **III** 48
Laboratorios Grossman, **III** 55
Laboratorios Liade S.A., **24** 75
**Laboratory Corporation of America Holdings, 42 217–20 (upd.)**
Laboratory for Electronics, **III** 168; **6** 284
LaBour Pump, **I** 473
LaBow, Haynes Co., **III** 270
**LaBranche & Co. Inc., 37 223–25**
Labsphere, Inc., **48** 446
Lachine Rapids Hydraulic and Land Company, **6** 501
Lackawanna Steel & Ordnance Co., **IV** 35, 114; **7** 48
**Laclede Steel Company, 15 271–73**
Lacombe Electric. *See* Public Service Company of Colorado.
Lacquer Products Co., **I** 321
**LaCrosse Footwear, Inc., 18 298–301**
Lacto Ibérica, **23** 219
Lactos, **25** 85
Lacy Diversified Industries, Ltd., **24** 159–61
**Ladbroke Group PLC**, **II** 139, **141–42**; **19** 208; **21 333–36 (upd.)**; **24** 194; **42** 64
Ladd and Tilton, **14** 527–28
**LADD Furniture, Inc., 12 299–301**; **23** 244
Ladd Petroleum Corp., **II** 30
LADECO, **6** 97; **31** 304; **36** 281
Ladenburg, Thalmann & Co. Inc., **17** 346
Ladenso, **IV** 277
**Ladish Co., Inc., 30 282–84**
Lady Foot Locker, **V** 226; **14** 293, 295
Lady Lee, **27** 291
Laerdal Medical, **18** 423
**Lafarge Coppée S.A.**, **III** 702, **703–05**, 736; **8** 258; **10** 422–23; **23** 333
**Lafarge Corporation**, **24** 332; **28 228–31**
Lafayette Manufacturing Co., **12** 296
Lafayette Radio Electronics Corporation, **9** 121–22
Laflin & Rand Powder Co., **I** 328; **III** 525
**Lafuma S.A., 39 248–50**
LAG&E. *See* Los Angeles Gas and Electric Company.
LaGard Inc., **20** 363
Lagardère Groupe SCA, **16** 254; **24** 84, 88; **34** 83
Lagoven, **IV** 508
Laidlaw Inc., **39** 19, 21
Laidlaw Transportation, Inc., **6** 410; **32** 227, 231
Laing, **IV** 696
Laing's Properties Ltd., **I** 575
**L'Air Liquide SA**, **I** 303, **357–59**; **11** 402; **47 217–20 (upd.)**
Laitaatsillan Konepaja, **IV** 275
Laiterie Centrale Krompholtz, **25** 84
Laiterie de la Vallée du Dropt, **25** 84
Laiterie Ekabe, **19** 50
SA Laiterie Walhorn Molkerel, **19** 50
Laiteries Prairies de l'Orne, **19** 50
Lake Arrowhead Development Co., **IV** 255
Lake Central Airlines, **I** 131; **6** 131
Lake Erie Screw Corp., **11** 534, 536
Lake Odessa Machine Products, **18** 494
Lake Superior Consolidated Mines Company, **IV** 572; **7** 549; **17** 355–56
Lake Superior Paper Industries, **26** 363
Lakehead Pipe Line Partners, L.P., **43** 155
Lakeland Fire and Casualty Co., **III** 213
**Lakeland Industries, Inc., 45 245–48**
Läkemedels-Industri Föreningen, **I** 664
Laker Airways, **I** 94; **6** 79; **24** 399
Lakeside Laboratories, **III** 24
The Lakeside Publishing and Printing Co., **IV** 660
Lakestone Systems, Inc., **11** 469
**Lam Research Corporation**, **IV** 213; **11 245–47**; **18** 383; **31 299–302 (upd.)**
**Lamar Advertising Company, 27 278–80**

**The Lamaur Corporation**, **41 227–29**
Lamb Technicon Corp., **I** 486
**Lamb Weston, Inc.**, **I** 417; **23 319–21**; **24** 33–34
Lambda Electronics Inc., **32** 411
Lambert Brothers, Inc., **7** 573
Lambert Brussels Financial Corporation, **II** 407; **11** 532
Lambert Frères, **33** 339
Lambert Kay Company, **8** 84
Lambert Pharmacal Co., **I** 710–11; **III** 28
Lambert Rivière, **41** 340
Lamborghini. *See* Automobili Lamborghini S.p.A.
Lamkin Brothers, Inc., **8** 386
Lamons Metal Gasket Co., **III** 570; **11** 535; **20** 361
Lamontagne Ltd., **II** 651
**Lamonts Apparel, Inc.**, **15 274–76**
Lampadaires Feralux, Inc., **19** 472
**Lamson & Sessions Co.**, **13 304–06**
Lamson Bros., **II** 451
Lamson Corporation, **7** 145
Lamson Industries Ltd., **IV** 645
Lamson Store Service Co., **IV** 644
**Lan Chile S.A.**, **31 303–06**; **33**
Lanca, **14** 224
Lancashire, **III** 350
Lancaster Caramel Co., **II** 510
**Lancaster Colony Corporation**, **8 307–09**
Lancaster Cork Works, **III** 422
Lancaster Financial Ltd., **14** 472
Lancaster National Bank, **9** 475
Lancaster Press, **23** 102
**Lance, Inc.**, **14 305–07**; **41 230–33 (upd.)**
Lancel, **27** 487, 489
**Lancer Corporation**, **21 337–39**
Lanchester Motor Company, Ltd., **13** 286
Lancia, **I** 162; **11** 102
Lancôme, **III** 46–48; **8** 342
**Land O'Lakes, Inc.**, **II 535–37**; **7** 339; **13** 351; **21 340–43 (upd.)**
Land-O-Sun Dairies, L.L.C., **26** 449
**Land Securities PLC**, **IV 704–06**
Land-Wheelwright Laboratories, **III** 607; **7** 436
Lander Alarm Co., **III** 740
Lander Company, **21** 54
Länderbank, **II** 282
Landesbank für Westfalen Girozentrale, Münster, **II** 385
Landis International, Inc., **10** 105–06
Landmark Banks, **10** 426
**Landmark Communications, Inc.**, **12 302–05**; **22** 442
Landmark Financial Services Inc., **11** 447
Landmark Target Media, **IV** 597
Landmark Union Trust, **18** 517
Landoll, Inc., **22** 522
Landor Associates, **I** 94
**Landry's Seafood Restaurants, Inc.**, **15 277–79**
**Lands' End, Inc.**, **9 314–16**; **12** 280; **16** 37; **19** 333; **26** 439; **27** 374, 429; **29 276–79 (upd.)**
Landstar, **26** 533
Lane Bryant, **V** 115–16
**The Lane Co., Inc.**, **III** 528, 530; **12 306–08**; **39** 170, 173–74
Lane Drug Company, **12** 132
Lane, Piper, and Jaffray, Inc. *See* Piper Jaffray Companies.
Lane Processing Inc., **II** 585
Lane Publishing Co., **IV** 676; **7** 529
Lane Rossi, **IV** 421
Laneco, Inc., **II** 682
Lang Exploratory Drilling, **26** 42
Langdon Rieder Corp., **21** 97
Lange International S.A., **15** 462; **43** 375–76
Lange, Maxwell & Springer, **IV** 641; **7** 311
Langford Labs, **8** 25
Lanier Business Products, Inc., **II** 39; **8** 407; **20** 290
Lanman Companies, Inc., **23** 101
Lannet Data Communications Ltd., **18** 345–46; **26** 275–77
Lano Corp., **I** 446
Lansi-Suomen Osake-Pankki, **II** 303
Lanson Pere et Fils, **II** 475
Lantic Industries, Inc., **II** 664
Lanvin, **I** 696; **III** 48; **8** 343
LAPE. *See* Líneas Aéreas Postales Españolas.
Lapeyre S.A. *See* Groupe Lapeyre S.A.
LaPine Technology, **II** 51; **21** 331
Laporte Industries Ltd., **I** 303; **IV** 300
Lapp, **8** 229
Lara, **19** 192
Larami Corp., **14** 486
Lareco, **26** 22
Largardère Groupe, **43** 210
Largo Entertainment, **25** 329
Laroche Navarron, **I** 703
Larousse Group, **IV** 614–15
Larrowe Milling Co., **II** 501; **10** 322
**Larry Flynt Publishing Inc.**, **31 307–10**
**Larry H. Miller Group**, **29 280–83**
Larry's Food Products, **36** 163
Larsen & Toubro, **IV** 484
Larsen Company, **7** 128
Larson Boats. *See* Genmar Holdings, Inc.
Larson Lumber Co., **IV** 306
Larwin Group, **III** 231
Las Vegas Gas Company, **19** 411
LaSalle Machine Tool, Inc., **13** 7–8
LaSalle National Bank, **II** 184
LaSalle Steel Corporation, **28** 314
LaSalles & Koch Co., **8** 443
Lasco Shipping Co., **19** 380
Laser Tech Color, **21** 60
Lasercharge Pty Ltd, **18** 130
LaserSoft, **24** 349
Oy Läskelä Ab, **IV** 300
Lasky's, **II** 141; **24** 269
Lasmo, **IV** 455, 499
**Lason, Inc.**, **31 311–13**
**Latham & Watkins**, **33 252–54**; **37** 292
Latin Communications Group Inc., **41** 151
Latitude Communications, **22** 52
Latrobe Brewing Co., **25** 281
Latrobe Steel Company, **8** 529–31
**Lattice Semiconductor Corp.**, **16 315–17**; **43** 17
**Lauda Air Luftfahrt AG**, **48 258–60**
Lauder Chemical, **17** 363
**Laura Ashley Holdings plc**, **13 307–09**; **37 226–29 (upd.)**
Laura Scudders, **7** 429; **44** 348
Laurel Glen, **34** 3, 5
**Laurent-Perrier SA**, **42 221–23**
Laurentian Group, **48** 290
Laurentien Hotel Co., **III** 99
Lauson Engine Company, **8** 515
LaVista Equipment Supply Co., **14** 545
Lavold, **16** 421; **43** 308
Law Life Assurance Society, **III** 372
Lawn Boy Inc., **7** 535–36; **8** 72; **26** 494
Lawrence Manufacturing Co., **III** 526
Lawrence Warehouse Co., **II** 397–98; **10** 62
Lawrenceburg Gas Company, **6** 466
The Lawson Co., **7** 113; **25** 125
Lawson Inc., **41** 113, 115
Lawson Milk, **II** 572
**Lawson Software**, **38 284–88**
**Lawter International Inc.**, **14 308–10**; **18** 220
Lawyers Cooperative, **8** 527–28
Lawyers Trust Co., **II** 230
Layer Five, **43** 252
Layne & Bowler Pump, **11** 5
**Layne Christensen Company**, **19 245–47**; **26** 71
Layton Homes Corporation, **30** 423
Lazard Freres & Co., **II** 268, 402, 422; **IV** 23, 79, 658–59; **6** 356; **7** 287, 446; **10** 399; **12** 165, 391, 547, 562; **21** 145
**Lazard LLC**, **38 289–92**
**Lazare Kaplan International Inc.**, **21 344–47**
Lazio. *See* Societá Sportiva Lazio SpA.
LBO Holdings, **15** 459
LBS Communications, **6** 28
**LCI International, Inc.**, **16 318–20**
LCP Hotels. *See* CapStar Hotel Co.
**LDDS-Metro Communications, Inc.**, **8 310–12**
LDDS WorldCom, Inc., **16** 467–68
LDI. *See* Lacy Diversified Industries, Ltd.
LDS Health Services Corporation, **27** 237
LDX NET, Inc., **IV** 576
Le Bon Marché. *See* Bon Marché.
Le Brun and Sons, **III** 291
Le Buffet System-Gastronomie, **V** 74
Le Chameau, **39** 250
Le Clerc, **21** 225–26
Le Courviour S.A., **10** 351
**Le Monde S.A.**, **33 308–10**
Le Rocher, Compagnie de Reassurance, **III** 340
Le Touquet's, SA, **48** 197
Lea & Perrins, **II** 475
Lea County Gas Co., **6** 580
Lea Lumber & Plywood Co., **12** 300
Lea Manufacturing, **23** 299
Leach McMicking, **13** 274
Lead Industries Group Ltd., **III** 681; **IV** 108
Leadership Housing Inc., **IV** 136
Leaf River Forest Products Inc., **IV** 282, 300; **9** 261
Leahy & Co. *See* Pierce Leahy Corporation.
Leamington Priors & Warwickshire Banking Co., **II** 318; **17** 323
Lean Cuisine, **12** 531
Lear Corporation, **17** 303, 305
Lear Inc., **II** 61; **8** 49, 51
Lear Romec Corp., **8** 135
**Lear Seating Corporation**, **16 321–23**
Lear Siegler Holdings Corporation, **25** 431
**Lear Siegler Inc.**, **I 481–83**; **III** 581; **8** 313; **13** 169, 358, 398; **19** 371–72; **30** 426; **44** 308
**Learjet Inc.**, **8 313–16**; **9** 242; **27 281–85 (upd.)**
**The Learning Company Inc.**, **24 275–78**, 480; **29** 74, 77; **41** 409
**Learning Tree International Inc.**, **24 279–82**

**LeaRonal, Inc., 23 322–24**
Leasco Data Processing Equipment Corp., **III** 342–44; **IV** 641–42; **7** 311
Lease International SA, **6** 358
Leaseway Personnel Corp., **18** 159
**Leaseway Transportation Corp.**, **V** 494; **12 309–11**; **19** 293
Leatherback Industries, **22** 229
**LeBoeuf, Lamb, Greene & MacRae, L.L.P., 29 284–86**
Lebr Associates Inc., **25** 246
Lech Brewery, **24** 450
**Lechmere Inc., 10 391–93**
**Lechters, Inc., 11 248–50; 39 251–54 (upd.)**
Leclerc. *See* Association des Centres Distributeurs E. Leclerc.
**LeCroy Corporation, 41 234–37**
Lectorum Publications, **29** 426
**Ledcor Industries Limited, 46 266–69**
Lederle Laboratories, **I** 300–02, 657, 684; **8** 24–25; **14** 254, 256, 423; **27** 115
Lederle Standard Products, **26** 29
Lee Ackerman Investment Company, **18** 513
**Lee Apparel Company, Inc., 8 317–19**; **17** 512, 514
Lee Brands, **II** 500
Lee Company, **V** 390–92
**Lee Enterprises, Incorporated, 11 251–53**; **47** 120
Lee Hecht Harrison, **6** 10
Lee International, **24** 373
Lee National Corporation, **26** 234
Lee Optical, **13** 390
Lee Rubber and Tire Corp., **16** 8
Lee Telephone Company, **6** 313
Lee Way Holding Co., **14** 42
Lee Way Motor Freight, **I** 278
**Leeann Chin, Inc., 30 285–88**
Leeds & County Bank, **II** 318; **17** 323
Leeds & Northrup Co., **III** 644–45; **28** 484
Lees Carpets, **17** 76
Leewards Creative Crafts Inc., **17** 322
Lefeldt, **III** 417, 418
**Lefrak Organization Inc., 8** 357; **26 260–62**
Legacy Homes Ltd., **26** 290
**Legal & General Group plc, III 272–73**; **IV** 705, 712; **24 283–85 (upd.)**; **30** 494; **33** 319
**The Legal Aid Society, 48 261–64**
Legal Technologies, Inc., **15** 378
Legault and Masse, **II** 664
**Legent Corporation, 10 394–96**; **14** 392
Legetojsfabrikken LEGO Billund A/S. *See* Lego A/S.
**Legg Mason, Inc., 11** 493; **33 259–62**
**Leggett & Platt, Inc., 9** 93; **11 254–56**; **48 265–68 (upd.)**
Leggett Stores Inc., **19** 48
**Lego A/S, 12** 495; **13 310–13**; **40 287–91 (upd.)**
**Legrand SA, 21 348–50**
Lehigh Acquisition Corp., **34** 286
**Lehigh Portland Cement Company, 23 325–27**; **31** 252
Lehigh Railroad, **III** 258
Lehman Brothers, **I** 78, 125, 484; **II** 192, 259, 398, 448, 450–51; **6** 199; **10** 62–63; **11** 263–64; **13** 448; **14** 145; **22** 445; **25** 301; **38** 411; **48** 59
Lehman Merchant Bank Partners, **19** 324
Lehmer Company. *See* Centel Corporation.
Lehn & Fink, **I** 699
Lehnkering AG, **IV** 140
Lehrman Bros., **III** 419
Lehser Communications, Inc., **15** 265
**Leica Camera AG, 35 266–69**
**Leica Microsystems Holdings GmbH, 35 270–73**
Leigh-Mardon Security Group, **30** 44
Leighton Holdings Ltd., **19** 402
Leinenkugel Brewing Company. *See* Jacob Leinenkugel Brewing Company.
**Leiner Health Products Inc., 34 250–52**
The Leisure Company, **34** 22
Leisure Lodges, **III** 76
Leisure System Inc., **12** 359
Leitz, **III** 583–84
LeMaster Litho Supply, **13** 228
Lemmerz Holding GmbH, **27** 202, 204
Lempereur, **13** 297
Lena Goldfields Ltd., **IV** 94
Lenc-Smith, **III** 430
**Lend Lease Corporation Limited, IV 707–09**; **17 283–86 (upd.)**; **47** 410
Lender's Bagel, **32** 69
Lending Textiles, **29** 132
Lenel Systems International Inc., **24** 510
**Lennar Corporation, 11 257–59**
Lennon's, **II** 628
Lennox Industries, Inc., **22** 6
**Lennox International Inc., 8 320–22**; **28 232–36 (upd.)**
Lenoir Furniture Corporation, **10** 183
**Lenox, Inc., I** 227; **10** 179, 181; **12 312–13**; **18** 69; **38** 113
Lens, Inc., **30** 267–68
**LensCrafters Inc., V** 207–08; **13** 391; **17** 294; **23 328–30**; **43** 199
Lentheric, **I** 426
**L'Entreprise Jean Lefebvre, 23 331–33**
**Leo Burnett Company, Inc., I 22–24**, 25, 31, 37; **11** 51, 212; **12** 439; **20 336–39 (upd.)**
The Leo Group, **32** 140; **40** 140
Léon Gaumont et Cie. *See* Gaumont SA.
Leonard Bernstein Music Publishing Company, **23** 391
Leonard Development Group, **10** 508
Leonard Express, Inc., **6** 371
Leonard Green & Partners LP, **12** 477–78; **24** 173
Leonard Machinery Corp., **16** 124
Leonard Parker Company, **26** 196
Leonard Silver, **14** 482
Leonardi Manufacturing, **48** 70
Leonardo Editore, **IV** 587
Leonberger Bausparkasse, **II** 258
Lepco Co., **III** 596
**Leprino Foods Company, 28 237–39**
Lern, Inc., **II** 420
Lerner Plastics, **9** 323
Lerner Stores, **V** 116
Leroy-Merlin, **23** 230; **37** 24
Les Chantiers de l'Atlantique, **II** 13
Les Echos. *See* Groupe Les Echos.
Les Grands Magasins Au Bon Marché: Etablissements Vaxelaire-Claes, **26** 159–60
Les Industries Ling, **13** 443
Les Papeteries du Limousin, **19** 227
L'Escaut, **III** 335
**Lesco Inc., 19 248–50**
**The Leslie Fay Companies, Inc., 8 323–25**
**The Leslie Fay Company, Inc., 39 255–58 (upd.)**; **40** 276–77
Leslie Paper, **IV** 288
**Leslie's Poolmart, Inc., 18 302–04**
Lesser-Goldman, **II** 18
Lester B. Knight & Associates, **II** 19
Lester Ink and Coatings Company, **13** 228
Lestrem Group, **IV** 296; **19** 226
Let op Uw Einde, **III** 199
Létang et Rémy, **44** 205
Lettuce Entertain You Enterprises, **38** 103
**Leucadia National Corporation, 6** 396; **11** ; **25** 170 **260–62**
Leuna-Werke AG, **7** 142
Level Five Research, Inc., **22** 292
N.V. Levensverzekering Maatschappji Utrecht, **III** 199–200
**Lever Brothers Company, I** 17, 21, 26, 30, 333; **II** 497, 588–89; **III** 31; **7** 542–43, 545; **9** 291, **317–19**; **13** 199; **14** 314. *See also* Unilever.
**Levi Strauss & Co., I** 15; **II** 634, 669; **V** 60–61, **362–65**; **9** 142; **12** 430; **16 324–28 (upd.)**, 509, 511; **17** 512; **18** 191–92; **19** 196; **23** 422; **24** 158; **25** 47
Leviathan Gas Pipeline Company, **21** 171
Levine, Huntley, Vick & Beaver, **6** 28
Levitt & Sons, **IV** 728
Levitt Corp., **21** 471
Levitt Homes, **I** 464; **11** 198
Levitt Industries, **17** 331
Levitt Investment Company, **26** 102
**Levitz Furniture Inc., 15 280–82**; **23** 412, 414
Levtex Hotel Ventures, **21** 363
Levy Bakery Goods, **I** 30
**Levy Restaurants L.P., 26 263–65**
Lew Liberbaum & Co., **27** 197
The Lewin Group, Inc., **21** 425
Lewis and Marks, **IV** 21–22, 96; **16** 27
Lewis Batting Company, **11** 219
Lewis Construction, **IV** 22
**Lewis Galoob Toys Inc., 16 329–31**
Lewis Grocer Co., **II** 669; **18** 504
Lewis Homes, **45** 221
Lewis-Howe Co., **III** 56
Lewis Refrigeration Company, **21** 500
Lewis's, **V** 178
Lewis's Bank, **II** 308
Lex Electronics, **10** 113
Lex Service plc, **19** 312
Lexecon, Inc., **26** 187
Lexington Broadcast Services, **6** 27
Lexington Furniture Industries, **III** 571; **20** 362
Lexington Ice Company, **6** 514
Lexington Insurance Co., **III** 197
Lexington Utilities Company, **6** 514; **11** 237
**LEXIS-NEXIS Group, 17** 399; **18** 542; **21** 70; **31** 388, 393; **33 263–67**
Lexitron, **II** 87
**Lexmark International, Inc., 9** 116; **10** 519; **18 305–07**; **30** 250
Leybold GmbH, **IV** 71; **48** 30
Leyland and Birmingham Rubber Co., **I** 429
Leyland Motor Corporation, **7** 459
LFC Financial, **10** 339
LFC Holdings Corp. *See* Levitz Furniture Inc.
LFE Corp., **7** 297
LG Chemical Ltd., **26** 425
LG Electronics Inc., **13** 572, 575; **43** 428

LG Group, **18** 124; **34** 514, 517–18
**LG&E Energy Corp., 6 516–18; 18** 366–67
Lhomme S.A., **8** 477
Liaison Agency, **31** 216–17
Lianozovo Dairy, **48** 438
Liaoyang Automotive Spring Factory, **III** 581
Libbey-Owens-Ford Company, **I** 609; **III** 640–42, 707, 714–15, 725–26, 731; **IV** 421; **7** 292; **16** 7–9; **22** 434; **23** 83; **26** 353; **31** 355
Libby, **II** 547; **7** 382
Libby McNeil & Libby Inc., **II** 489
Libeltex, **9** 92
Liber, **14** 556
Liberty Bank of Buffalo, **9** 229
Liberty Brokerage Investment Company, **10** 278
Liberty Can and Sign Company, **17** 105–06
**The Liberty Corporation, 22 312–14**
Liberty Gauge Company, **17** 213
Liberty Hardware Manufacturing Corporation, **20** 363
Liberty House, **I** 417–18
Liberty Life, **IV** 91, 97
**Liberty Livewire Corporation, 42 224–27**
Liberty Media Corporation, **18** 66; **19** 282; **25** 214; **34** 224; **42** 114, 224; **47** 414, 416, 418. *See also* Liberty Livewire Corporation.
Liberty Mexicana, **III** 415
Liberty Mutual Insurance Group, **I** 28; **11** 379; **48** 271
Liberty Mutual Savings Bank, **17** 530
Liberty National Bank, **II** 229
Liberty National Insurance Holding Company. *See* Torchmark Corporation.
Liberty National Life Insurance Co., **III** 217; **9** 506–07
Liberty Natural Gas Co., **11** 441
Liberty Software, Inc., **17** 264
Liberty Surf UK, **48** 399
Liberty Tax Service, **48** 236
Liberty's, **13** 307
Libra Bank Ltd., **II** 271
Librairie de Jacques-Francois Brétif, **IV** 617
Librairie Fayard, **IV** 618
Librairie Générale Francaise, **IV** 618
Librairie Larousse, **IV** 614–16
Librairie Louis Hachette, **IV** 617–18
Librairie Nathan, **IV** 614, 616
Librairie Victor Lecou, **IV** 617
Librizol India Pvt. Ltd., **48** 212
Libyan Arab Airline, **6** 85
Libyan Arab Foreign Bank, **IV** 454
**Libyan National Oil Corporation, IV 453–55**
Libyan-Turkish Engineering and Consultancy Corp., **IV** 563
Lidköpings Mekaniska Verkstad AB, **III** 623
Lieberman Enterprises, **24** 349
Liebert Corp., **II** 20
Life and Casualty Insurance Co. of Tennessee, **III** 193
Life Assoc. of Scotland, **III** 310
Life Fitness Inc., **III** 431
Life Insurance Co. of Georgia, **III** 310
Life Insurance Co. of Scotland, **III** 358
Life Insurance Co. of Virginia, **III** 204
Life Insurance Securities, Ltd., **III** 288
Life Investors International Ltd., **III** 179; **12** 199
Life of Eire, **III** 273
Life Partners Group, Inc., **33** 111
Life Retail Stores. *See* Angelica Corporation.
Life Savers Corp., **II** 129, 544; **7** 367; **21** 54
Life Science Research, Inc., **10** 105–07
**Life Technologies, Inc., I** 321; **12** 103; **17 287–89**
Life Uniform Shops. *See* Angelica Corporation.
Lifecycle, Inc., **III** 431; **25** 40
Lifeline Systems, Inc., **32** 374
LifeLink, **11** 378
Lifemark Corp., **III** 74; **14** 232; **33** 183
Lifestyle Fitness Clubs, **46** 432
LIFETIME, **IV** 627; **19** 204
Lifetime Corp., **29** 363–64
Lifetime Foam Products, Inc., **12** 439
**Lifetime Hoan Corporation, 27 286–89**
Lift Parts Manufacturing, **I** 157
**Ligand Pharmaceuticals Incorporated, 10** 48; **47 221–23**
Liggett & Meyers, **V** 396, 405, 417–18; **18** 416; **29** 195
Liggett Group Inc., **I** 248; **7** 105; **14** 213; **15** 71; **16** 242; **37** 295. *See also* Vector Group Inc.
Light & Power Company, **12** 265
Light Corrugated Box Co., **IV** 332
Light Savers U.S.A., Inc. *See* Hospitality Worldwide Services, Inc.
Light-Servicos de Eletricidade S.A., **II** 456
Lightel Inc., **6** 311
Lighthouse, Ltd., **24** 95
Lighting Corp. of America, **I** 476
LIGHTNET, **IV** 576
Lightwell Co., **III** 634
Lignum Oil Co., **IV** 658
Lil' Champ Food Stores, Inc., **36** 359
LILCO. *See* Long Island Lighting Company.
Lilia Limited, **17** 449
Lille Bonnières et Colombes, **37** 143–44
**Lillian Vernon Corporation, 12 314–15; 35 274–77 (upd.)**
Lillie Rubin, **30** 104–06
Lilliput Group plc, **11** 95; **15** 478
Lilly & Co. *See* Eli Lilly & Co.
Lilly Industries, **22** 437
Lillybrook Coal Co., **IV** 180
Lillywhites Ltd., **III** 105
Lily Tulip Co., **I** 609, 611; **8** 198
Limburger Fabrik und Hüttenverein, **IV** 103
Limhamns Golvindustri AB. *See* Tarkett Sommer AG.
**The Limited, Inc., V 115–16; 9** 142; **12** 280, 356; **15** 7, 9; **16** 219; **18** 193, 215, 217, 410; **20 340–43 (upd.); 24** 237; **25** 120–21, 123; **28** 344; **47** 142–43
Limmer and Trinidad Ltd., **III** 752
**LIN Broadcasting Corp., II** 331; **6** 323; **9 320–22; 11** 330
Lin Data Corp., **11** 234
**Linamar Corporation, 18 308–10**
**Lincare Holdings Inc., 43 265–67**
Lincoln American Life Insurance Co., **10** 246
Lincoln Automotive, **26** 363
Lincoln Benefit Life Company, **10** 51
**Lincoln Electric Co., II** 19; **13 314–16**
Lincoln Electric Motor Works, **9** 439
Lincoln Federal Savings, **16** 106
Lincoln First Bank, **II** 248
Lincoln Income Life Insurance Co., **10** 246
Lincoln Liberty Life Insurance Co., **III** 254
Lincoln Marketing, Inc., **18** 518
Lincoln Motor Co., **I** 165
**Lincoln National Corporation, III 274–77; 6** 195; **10** 44; **22** 144; **25 286–90 (upd.)**
**Lincoln Property Company, 8 326–28**
Lincoln Savings, **10** 340
Lincoln Savings & Loan, **9** 199
**Lincoln Snacks Company, 24 286–88**
**Lincoln Telephone & Telegraph Company, 14 311–13**
LinCom Corp., **8** 327
**Lindal Cedar Homes, Inc., 29 287–89**
**Linde A.G., I** 297–98, 315, **581–83; 9** 16, 516; **10** 31–32; **11** 402–03; **25** 81; **48** 323
Lindemann's, **I** 220
Lindex, **II** 640
**Lindsay Manufacturing Co., 20 344–46**
Lindsay Parkinson & Co., **I** 567
Lindt & Sprüngli. *See* Chocoladefabriken Lindt & Sprüngli AG.
Lindustries, **III** 502; **7** 208
Linear Corp., **III** 643
**Linear Technology, Inc., 16 332–34**
Líneas Aéreas Postales Españolas, **6** 95
**Linens 'n Things, Inc., 13** 81–82; **24 289–92; 33** 384; **41** 50
Linfood Cash & Carry, **13** 103
Linfood Holdings Ltd., **II** 628–29
Ling Products, **12** 25
Ling-Temco-Vought. *See* LTV Corporation.
Lingerie Time, **20** 143
Linguaphone Group, **43** 204, 206
Linjeflyg, **I** 120
Link-Belt Corp., **I** 443; **IV** 660
Link House Publications PLC, **IV** 687
Link Motor Supply Company, **26** 347
Linmark Westman International Limited, **25** 221–22
Linroz Manufacturing Company L.P., **25** 245
**Lintas: Worldwide, I** 18; **6** 30; **14 314–16**
Lintott Engineering, Ltd., **10** 108
Linz, **16** 559
**Lion Corporation, III 44–45**
Lion Manufacturing, **III** 430; **25** 40
Lion Match Company, **24** 450
Lion Oil, **I** 365
Lion's Head Brewery. *See* The Stroh Brewery Company.
**Lionel L.L.C., 12** 494; **16 335–38; 18** 524
Lionex Corporation, **13** 46
**Lions Gate Entertainment Corporation, 35 278–81**
Liontech, **16** 337–38
Lippincott & Margulies, **III** 283
Lippincott-Raven Publishers, **14** 556
Lipschutz Bros., Inc., **29** 511
Lipson Alport Glass & Associates, **27** 195
Lipton. *See* Thomas J. Lipton Company.
**Liqui-Box Corporation, 16 339–41**
Liquid Ag Systems Inc., **26** 494
Liquid Carbonic, **7** 74, 77
Liquid Holdings, Inc., **45** 168
Liquor Barn, **II** 656
Liquorland, **V** 35

Liquorsave, **II** 609–10
LIRCA, **III** 48
Liris, **23** 212
Lisbon Coal and Oil Fuel Co., **IV** 504
Liscaya, **II** 196
Listening Library Inc., **31** 379
Lister, **21** 503
Litco Bancorp., **II** 192
LiTel Communications, Inc., **16** 318
**Lithia Motors, Inc., 41 238–40**
Litho-Krome Corp., **IV** 621
LitleNet, **26** 441
Litronix, **III** 455; **21** 122
**Littelfuse, Inc., 26 266–69**
Little, Brown & Company, **IV** 675; **7** 528; **10** 355; **36** 270
**Little Caesar Enterprises, Inc., 24 293–96 (upd.)**; **27** 481. *See also* Ilitch Holdings Inc.
**Little Caesar International, Inc., 7 278–79**; **7** 278–79; **15** 344, 346; **16** 447; **25** 179, 227–28
Little Chef Ltd., **III** 105–06
Little General, **II** 620; **12** 179, 200
Little Giant Pump Company, **8** 515
Little League Baseball, Incorporated, **23** 450
Little Leather Library, **13** 105
Little, Royal, **I** 529–30; **8** 545; **13** 63
Little Switzerland, **19** 451
**Little Tikes Co., III** 614; **12** 169; **13 317–19**
Littlewoods Financial Services, **30** 494
**Littlewoods Organisation PLC, V 117–19**; **24** 316
**Littlewoods plc, 42 228–32 (upd.)**
**Litton Industries Inc., I** 85, 452, 476, **484–86**, 523–24; **II** 33; **III** 293, 473, 732; **IV** 253; **6** 599; **10** 520–21, 537; **11 263–65 (upd.)**, 435; **12** 248, 271–72, 538–40; **15** 287; **17** 30; **19** 31, 110, 290; **21** 86; **22** 436; **45** 306; **48** 383. *See also* Avondale Industries.
Litwin Engineers & Constructors, **8** 546
Livanos, **III** 516
**LIVE Entertainment Inc., 18** 64, 66; **20 347–49**; **24** 349
Liverpool and London and Globe Insurance Co., **III** 234, 350
Liverpool and London Fire and Life Insurance Co., **III** 349
Liverpool Fire and Life Insurance Co., **III** 350
Liverpool Mexico S.A., **16** 216
Livia, **I** 154; **10** 279
Living Arts, Inc., **41** 174
Living Centers of America, **13** 49
Living Videotext, **10** 508
Livingston Communications, **6** 313
Livingston, Fargo and Co., **II** 380, 395; **10** 59
LivingWell Inc., **12** 326
**Liz Claiborne, Inc., 8 329–31**; **16** 37, 61; **25** 258, **291–94 (upd.)**
LKB-Produkter AB, **I** 665
Lloyd A. Fry Roofing, **III** 721
Lloyd Adriatico S.p.A., **III** 377
Lloyd Aereo de Bolivia, **6** 97
Lloyd Creative Staffing, **27** 21
Lloyd George Management, **18** 152
Lloyd Instruments, Ltd., **29** 460–61
Lloyd Italico, **III** 351
Lloyd Thompson Group plc, **20** 313
Lloyd-Truax Ltd., **21** 499
Lloyd's Electronics, **14** 118
**Lloyd's of London, III** 234, **278–81**; **9** 297; **10** 38; **11** 533; **22 315–19 (upd.)**
**Lloyds Bank PLC, II 306–09** 319, 334, 358; **17** 324–25; **48** 373
Lloyds Chemists plc, **27** 177
Lloyds Life Assurance, **III** 351
**Lloyds TSB Group plc, 39** 6; **47 224–29 (upd.)**
LM Ericsson. *See* Telefonaktiebolaget LM Ericsson.
LMC Metals, **19** 380
LME. *See* Telefonaktiebolaget LM Ericsson.
LNG Co., **IV** 473–74
LNM Group, **30** 252
Lo-Cost, **II** 609
Lo-Vaca Gathering Co., **IV** 394; **7** 553
Loadometer Co., **III** 435
Lobitos Oilfields Ltd., **IV** 381–82
**Loblaw Companies Limited, II** 631–32; **19** 116; **43 268–72**. *See also* George Weston Limited.
Local Data, Inc., **10** 97
Locations, Inc., **IV** 727
Locke, Lancaster and W.W.&R. Johnson & Sons, **III** 680
Lockhart Catering, **III** 104
Lockhart Corporation, **12** 564
**Lockheed Corporation, I** 13, 41, 48, 50, 52, 54, 61, 63, **64–66**, 67–68, 71–72, 74, 76–77, 82, 84, 90, 92–94, 100, 102, 107, 110, 113, 121, 126, 195, 493–94, 529; **II** 19, 32–33; **III** 84, 539, 601; **IV** 15; **6** 71; **9** 12, 17–18, 272, 417, 458–60, 501; **10** 163, 262–63, 317, 536; **11** 164, 166, **266–69 (upd.)**, 278–79, 363–65; **12** 190; **13** 126, 128; **17** 306; **21** 140; **22** 506; **24** 84–85, 87, 311, 326, 375, 397; **25** 303, 316, 347; **34** 371
**Lockheed Martin Corporation, 15 283–86 (upd.)**; **21** 86; **24** 88; **29** 409; **32** 437; **33** 47–48; **38** 372, 376; **45** 306; **48** 251
Lockwood Banc Group, Inc., **11** 306
Lockwood Greene Engineers, Inc., **17** 377
Lockwood National Bank, **25** 114
Lockwood Technology, Inc., **19** 179
Lockwoods Foods Ltd., **II** 513
**Loctite Corporation, 8 332–34**; **30 289–91 (upd.)**; **34** 209
Lodding Engineering, **7** 521
Lodestar Group, **10** 19
Lodge-Cottrell, **III** 472
Lodge Plus, Ltd., **25** 430
**LodgeNet Entertainment Corporation, 26** 441; **28 240–42**
The Lodging Group, **12** 297; **48** 245
Loeb Rhoades, Hornblower & Co., **II** 450–51; **9** 469
**Loehmann's Inc., 24 297–99**
Loening Aeronautical, **I** 61; **11** 164
Loew's Consolidated Enterprises, **II** 154
Loew's, Inc., **31** 99
**The Loewen Group, Inc., 16 342–44**; **37** 67–68; **40 292–95 (upd.)**
Loewenstein Furniture Group, Inc., **21** 531–33
Loewi Financial Cos., **III** 270
Loews Cineplex Entertainment Corp., **37** 64
**Loews Corporation, I** 245, **487–88**; **II** 134, 148–49, 169; **III** 228, 231; **12 316–18 (upd.)**, 418; **13** 120–21; **19** 362; **22** 73; **25** 177, 326–28; **36 324–28 (upd.)**; **38** 142; **41** 70, 72
LOF Plastics, Inc. *See* Libbey-Owens-Ford.
Loffland Brothers Company, **9** 364
Loft Inc., **I** 276; **10** 451
**Logan's Roadhouse, Inc., 19** 287–88; **22** 464; **29 290–92**; **35** 84
Logged Off Land Co., **IV** 355–56
Logic Modeling, **11** 491
**Logica plc, 14 317–19**; **37 230–33 (upd.)**
**Logicon Inc., 20 350–52**; **45** 68, 310
Logility, **25** 20, 22
Logistics, **III** 431
Logistics Data Systems, **13** 4
Logistics Industries Corporation, **39** 77
Logistics Management Systems, Inc., **8** 33
**Logitech International SA, 9** 116; **28 243–45**
Logo Athletic, Inc., **35** 363
Logo 7, Inc., **13** 533
Logon, Inc., **14** 377
**LoJack Corporation, 48 269–73**
**Lojas Arapuã S.A., 22 320–22**
Loma Linda Foods, **14** 557–58
Lomak Petroleum, Inc., **24** 380
Lomas & Nettleton Financial Corporation, **III** 249; **11** 122
Lombard North Central, **II** 442
Lombard Orient Leasing Ltd., **II** 442
London and County Bank, **II** 334
London and Hanseatic Bank, **II** 256
London & Hull, **III** 211
London and Lancashire Insurance Co., **III** 350
London & Leeds Development Corp., **II** 141
London & Midland Bank. *See* Midland Bank plc.
London & Overseas Freighters plc. *See* Frontline Ltd.
London & Rhodesia Mining & Land Company. *See* Lonrho Plc.
London and Scottish Marine Oil, **11** 98
London & Western Trust, **39** 90
London and Westminster Bank, **II** 333–34
London Asiastic, **III** 699
London Assurance Corp., **III** 278, 369–71, 373
London Brick Co., **III** 502; **7** 208; **14** 249
London Brokers Ltd., **6** 290
London Buses Limited, **6** 406
London Cargo Group, **25** 82
London Central, **28** 155–56
London Chartered Bank of Australia, **II** 188
London Clermont Club, **III** 431
London County and Westminster Bank, **II** 334
London County Freehold & Leasehold Properties, **IV** 711
**London Drugs Ltd., 46 270–73**
London East India Company, **12** 421
London, Edinburgh and Dublin Insurance Co., **III** 350
London Electricity, **12** 443; **41** 141
London Film Productions Ltd., **II** 157; **14** 399
**London Fog Industries, Inc., 16** 61; **29 293–96**
London General Omnibus Company, **6** 406
London Guarantee and Accident Co., **III** 372
London Insurance Group, **III** 373; **36** 372

London Joint-Stock Bank, **II** 318, 388; **17** 324
London Life Assoc., **IV** 711
London Life Insurance Co., **II** 456–57
London Precision Machine & Tool, Ltd., **39** 32
London, Provincial and South Western Bank, **II** 235
London Records, **23** 390
**London Regional Transport, 6 406–08**
London South Partnership, **25** 497
**London Stock Exchange Limited, 34 253–56**; **37** 131–33
London Transport, **19** 111
London Weekend Television, **IV** 650–51; **7** 389
Londontown Manufacturing Company. *See* London Fog Industries, Inc.
Lone Star and Crescent Oil Co., **IV** 548
Lone Star Brewing Co., **I** 255
Lone Star Gas Corp., **V** 609, 611
Lone Star Industries, **III** 718, 729, 753; **IV** 304; **23** 326; **28** 450; **35** 154
Lone Star Steakhouse, **21** 250
Lone Star Steel, **I** 440–41
Lone Star Technologies, Inc., **22** 3
Long-Airdox Co., **IV** 136
Long Distance Discount Services, Inc., **8** 310; **27** 305
Long Distance/USA, **9** 479
Long Island Airways, **I** 115; **12** 379
**Long Island Bancorp, Inc., 16 345–47**; **44** 33
Long Island Cable Communication Development Company, **7** 63
Long Island Daily Press Publishing Co., **IV** 582–83
**Long Island Lighting Company, V 652–54**; **6** 456; **27** 264
Long Island Power Authority, **27** 265
Long Island Rail Road, **35** 290
Long Island Trust Co., **II** 192, 218
**Long John Silver's Restaurants Inc., 13 320–22**
Long Lac Mineral Exploration, **9** 282
Long Life Fish Food Products, **12** 230
Long Manufacturing Co., **III** 439; **14** 63
**Long-Term Credit Bank of Japan, Ltd., II** 301, **310–11**, 338, 369
Long Valley Power Cooperative, **12** 265
**The Longaberger Company, 12 319–21**; **44 267–70 (upd.)**
Longchamps, Inc., **38** 385; **41** 388
LongHorn Steaks Inc., **19** 341
Longines-Wittenauer Watch Co., **II** 121
Longman Group Ltd., **IV** 611, 658
Longmat Foods, **II** 494
**Longs Drug Stores Corporation, V 120**; **25 295–97 (upd.)**
**Longview Fibre Company, 8 335–37**; **37 234–37 (upd.)**
Longwy, **IV** 227
**Lonrho Plc, IV** 651–52; **10** 170; **21 351–55**; **43** 38
Lonsdale Investment Trust, **II** 421
Lonvest Corp., **II** 456–57
Loomis Armored Car Service Limited, **45** 378
Loomis Fargo Group, **42** 338
Loomis, Sayles & Co., **III** 313
Loose Leaf Metals Co., Inc., **10** 314
Lor-Al, Inc., **17** 10
**Loral Corporation, II** 38; **7** 9; **8 338–40**; **9 323–25**; **13** 356; **15** 283, 285; **20** 262; **47** 319
Lord & Taylor, **13** 44; **14** 376; **15** 86; **18** 137, 372; **21** 302
Lord & Thomas, **I** 12–14; **IV** 660
Lord Baltimore Press, Inc., **IV** 286
**L'Oréal, II** 547; **III 46–49**, 62; **7** 382–83; **8** 129–31; **341–44 (upd.)**; **11** 41; **23** 238, 242; **31** 418; **46 274–79 (upd.)**
Lorenz, **I** 463
Lorillard Industries, **I** 488; **V** 396, 407, 417; **12** 317; **18** 416; **22** 73; **29** 195; **36** 324, 327
Lorimar Telepictures, **II** 149, 177; **25** 90–91, 329
Loronix Inc., **24** 509
Lorraine-Escaut, **IV** 227
Lorvic Corp., **I** 679
Los Angeles Can Co., **I** 599
Los Angeles Drug Co., **12** 106
Los Angeles Gas and Electric Company, **V** 682; **25** 413
Los Angeles Steamship Co., **II** 490
Los Lagos Corp., **12** 175
Los Nietos Co., **IV** 570; **24** 520
Loss Prevention Inc., **24** 509
**Lost Arrow Inc., 22 323–25**
**LOT Polish Airlines (Polskie Linie Lotnicze S.A.), 33 268–71**
Lothringer Bergwerks- und Hüttenverein Aumetz-Friede AG, **IV** 126
**LOT$OFF Corporation, 24 300–01**
**Lotus Cars Ltd., 14 320–22**
**Lotus Development Corporation, IV** 597; **6** 224–25, 227, **254–56**, 258–60, 270–71, 273; **9** 81, 140; **10** 24, 505; **12** 335; **16** 392, 394; **20** 238; **21** 86; **22** 161; **25 298–302 (upd.)**; **30** 251; **38** 417
Lotus Publishing Corporation, **7** 239; **25** 239
Lotus Radio, **I** 531
Louart Corporation, **29** 33–34
Loucks, Hoffman & Company, **8** 412
Loughead Aircraft Manufacturing Co., **I** 64
Louis Allis, **15** 288
Louis B. Mayer Productions, **II** 148; **25** 326–27
Louis C. Edwards, **II** 609
Louis Dreyfus Energy Corp., **28** 471
Louis Harris & Associates, Inc., **22** 188
Louis Kemp Seafood Company, **14** 515
Louis Marx Toys, **II** 559; **12** 410
Louis Rich, Inc., **II** 532; **12** 372
**Louis Vuitton, I** 272; **III** 48; **8** 343; **10 397–99**. *See also* LVMH Moët Hennessy Louis Vuitton SA.
Louisiana & Southern Life Insurance Co., **14** 460
Louisiana Bank & Trust, **11** 106
Louisiana Corporation, **19** 301
Louisiana Energy Services, **27** 130
**The Louisiana Land and Exploration Company, IV** 76, 365, 367; **7 280–83**
**Louisiana-Pacific Corporation, IV** 282, **304–05**; **9** 260; **16** 203; **22** 491; **31 314–317 (upd.)**; **32** 91
Louisville Cement Co., **IV** 409
Louisville Gas and Electric Company. *See* LG&E Energy Corporation.
Louisville Home Telephone Company, **14** 258
Loup River Public Power District, **29** 352
Louthan Manufacturing Company, **8** 178
LoVaca Gathering Company. *See* The Coastal Corporation.
Lovelace Truck Service, Inc., **14** 42
Loveman's, Inc., **19** 323
Lovering China Clays, **III** 690
Lowe Bros. Co., **III** 745
Lowe Group, **22** 294
**Lowe's Companies, Inc., V 122–23**; **11** 384; **12** 234, 345; **18** 239; **21** 324, **356–58 (upd.)**; **27** 416; **44** 333
Lowell Bearing Co., **IV** 136
Lowell Shoe, Inc., **13** 360
Löwenbräu, **I** 220, 257; **II** 240
Lower Manhattan Development Corporation, **47** 360
Lowes Food Stores. *See* Alex Lee Inc.
Lowney/Moirs, **II** 512
**Lowrance Electronics, Inc., 18 311–14**
Lowrey's Meat Specialties, Inc., **21** 156
Loyalty Group, **III** 241–43
LPL Investment Group, **40** 35–36
LRL International, **II** 477
LSI. *See* Lear Siegler Inc.
**LSI Logic Corporation, 13 323–25**; **18** 382
LTA Ltd., **IV** 22
**LTU Group Holding GmbH, 37 238–41**
**The LTV Corporation, I** 62–63, **489–91**; **7** 107–08; **8** 157, 315; **10** 419; **11** 166, 364; **12** 124; **17** 357; **18** 110, 378; **19** 466; **24 302–06 (upd.)**; **26** 406; **45** 306
Luberef, **IV** 538
**The Lubrizol Corporation, 30 292–95 (upd.)**
**Lubrizol Enterprises, Inc., I 360–62**; **21** 385–87
**Luby's Cafeteria's, Inc., 17 290–93**; **19** 301
**Luby's, Inc., 42 233–38 (upd.)**
Lucas Bols, **II** 642
Lucas Digital Ltd., **12** 322
Lucas Girling, **I** 157
**Lucas Industries Plc, III** 509, **554–57**; **27** 251
Lucas Ingredients, **27** 258
Lucas-Milhaupt, Inc., **23** 250
LucasArts Entertainment Company, **32** 9
**Lucasfilm Ltd., 9** 368, 472; **12 322–24**; **22** 459; **34** 350; **38** 70
LucasVarity plc, **27** 249, 251
Lucchini, **IV** 228
**Lucent Technologies Inc., 18** 154, 180; **20** 8; **22** 19; **26** 275, 277; **29** 44, 414; **34 257–60**; **36** 122, 124; **41** 289–90; **44** 426; **48** 92
**Lucille Farms, Inc., 45 249–51**
Lucky Brand Dungarees, **18** 85
**Lucky-Goldstar, II 53–54**; **III** 457; **13** 574. *See also* Goldstar Co., Ltd.
Lucky Lager Brewing Co, **I** 268; **25** 280
Lucky Stores Inc., **II** 605, 653; **6** 355; **8** 474; **12** 48; **17** 369, 559; **22** 39; **27 290–93**
Lucky Strike, **II** 143
Ludi Wap S.A., **41** 409
Ludlow Corp., **III** 645
Ludovico, **25** 85
Lufkin Rule Co., **II** 16
Luftag, **I** 110
Lufthansa. *See* Deutsche Lufthansa Aktiengesellschaft.
The Luggage Company, **14** 224
**Lukens Inc., 14 323–25**; **27** 65
Lukey Mufflers, **IV** 249

LUKOIL. *See* OAO LUKOIL.
Lum's, **6** 199–200
Lumac B.V., **I** 387
Lumbermen's Investment Corp., **IV** 341
Lumbermens Mutual Casualty Co., **III** 269–71; **15** 257
Lumex, Inc., **17** 197
La Lumière Economique, **II** 79
**Luminar Plc**, **40 296–98**
Lummus Crest, **IV** 469; **26** 496
Lumonics Inc., **III** 635
**Lunar Corporation**, **29 297–99**
Luncheon Voucher, **27** 10
Lund Boat Co. *See* Genmar Holdings, Inc.
**Lund Food Holdings, Inc.**, **22 326–28**
**Lund International Holdings, Inc.**, **40 299–301**
Lundstrom Jewelers, **24** 319
Lunenburg Sea Products Limited, **14** 339
Lunevale Products Ltd., **I** 341
L'Unite Hermetique S.A., **8** 515
Lunn Poly, **8** 525–26
Luotto-Pankki Oy, **II** 303
Lurgei, **6** 599
LURGI. *See* Metallurgische Gesellschaft Aktiengesellschaft.
Luria Bros. and Co., **I** 512–13; **6** 151
Lutèce, **20** 26
Luther's Bar-B-Q, **II** 556
**Lutheran Brotherhood**, **31 318–21**
Lux, **III** 478
Lux Mercantile Co., **II** 624
Luxor, **II** 69; **6** 205; **17** 353
**Luxottica SpA**, **17 294–96**; **23** 328; **43** 96. *See also* Casual Corner Group, Inc.
LuxSonor Semiconductor Inc., **48** 92
Luxury Linens, **13** 81–82
**LVMH Moët Hennessy Louis Vuitton SA**, **I** 272; **19** 86; **24** 137, 140; **33 272–77 (upd.)**; **45** 344; **46** 277
LVO Cable Inc., **IV** 596
LXE Inc., **21** 199–201
Lycos, **27** 517; **37** 384; **47** 420. *See also* Terra Lycos, Inc.
Lydex, **I** 527
Lykes Corp., **I** 490–91; **24** 303
Lyn Knight Currency Auctions, Inc, **48** 100
**Lynch Corporation**, **43 273–76**; 301–02
Lynde Company, **16** 269–71
Lynx Express Delivery, **6** 412, 414
Lyon & Healy, **IV** 660
Lyon's Technological Products Ltd., **III** 745
**Lyondell Chemical Company**, **45 252–55 (upd.)**
**Lyondell Petrochemical Company**, **IV** 377, **456–57**; **10** 110
Lyonnaise Communications, **10** 196; **25** 497
**Lyonnaise des Eaux-Dumez**, **I** 576; **V 655–57**; **23** 332. *See also* Suez Lyonnaise des Eaux.
Lyons. *See* J. Lyons & Co. Ltd.
LyphoMed Inc., **IV** 333; **17** 287
Oy Lypsyniemen Konepaja, **IV** 275–76
Lysaght, **24** 143
Lysaght's Canada, Ltd., **IV** 73
Lystads, **I** 333
Lytag Ltd., **31** 398–99

M & C Saatchi, **42** 330
**M&F Worldwide Corp.**, **38 293–95**
M and G Fund Management, **III** 699
M&G Group plc, **48** 328
M&J Diesel Locomotive Filter Co., **17** 106
M&M Limited, **7** 299
M and M Manufacturing Company, **23** 143
M&M/Mars, **14** 48; **15** 63–64; **21** 219
M & S Computing. *See* Intergraph Corporation.
M&T Capital Corporation, **11** 109
M/A Com Inc., **6** 336; **14** 26–27
**M.A. Hanna Company**, **8 345–47**; **12** 352
M.A.N., **III** 561–63; **IV** 86
M.B. McGerry, **21** 94
M-Cell Ltd., **31** 329
M.D.C., **11** 258
M.E.P.C. Ltd., **IV** 711
M.F. Patterson Dental Supply Co. *See* Patterson Dental Co.
M.G. Waldbaum Company, **25** 332–33
M. Guggenheim's Sons, **IV** 31
M.H. McLean Wholesaler Grocery Company, **8** 380
**M.H. Meyerson & Co., Inc.**, **46 280–83**
M. Hensoldt & Söhne Wetzlar Optische Werke AG, **III** 446
M-I Drilling Fluids Co., **III** 473; **15** 468
M.I. Schottenstein Homes Inc., **19** 125–26
M.J. Brock Corporation, **8** 460
M.J. Designs, Inc., **17** 360
M.L.C. Partners Limited Partnership, **22** 459
M. Loeb Ltd., **II** 652
M. Lowenstein Corp., **V** 379
M.M. Warburg. *See* SBC Warburg.
M.P. Burke PLC, **13** 485–86
M.P. Pumps, Inc., **8** 515
M. Polaner Inc., **10** 70; **40** 51–52
M-R Group plc, **31** 312–13
M.S. Carriers, Inc., **42** 363, 365
M. Samuel & Co., **II** 208
M. Sobol, Inc., **28** 12
M Stores Inc., **II** 664
M.T.G.I. Textile Manufacturers Group, **25** 121
M.W. Carr, **14** 245
M.W. Kellogg Co., **III** 470; **IV** 408, 534; **34** 81
M-Web Holdings Ltd., **31** 329–30
Ma. Ma-Macaroni Co., **II** 554
Maakauppiaitten Oy, **8** 293–94
Maakuntain Keskus-Pankki, **II** 303
MaasGlas, **III** 667
Maatschappij tot Exploitatie van de Onderneming Krasnapolsky. *See* Grand Hotel Krasnapolsky N.V.
Maatschappij tot Exploitatie van Steenfabrieken Udenhout, voorheen Weyers, **14** 249
MABAG Maschinen- und Apparatebau GmbH, **IV** 198
Mabley & Carew, **10** 282
**Mac Frugal's Bargains - Closeouts Inc.**, **17 297–99**
**Mac-Gray Corporation**, **44 271–73**
Mac Publications LLC, **25** 240
Mac Tools, **III** 628
**MacAndrews & Forbes Holdings Inc.**, **II** 679; **III** 56; **9** 129; **11** 334; **28 246–49**; **30** 138; **38** 293–94
MacArthur Foundation. *See* The John D. and Catherine T. MacArthur Foundation.
Macau Telephone, **18** 114
Maccabees Life Insurance Co., **III** 350
MacCall Management, **19** 158
**MacDermid Incorporated**, **32 318–21**
MacDonald Companies, **15** 87
MacDonald Dettwiler and Associates, **32** 436
MacDonald, Halsted, and Laybourne, **10** 127
Macdonald Hamilton & Co., **III** 522–23
Macey Furniture Co., **7** 493
Macfarlane Lang & Co., **II** 592–93
Macfield Inc., **12** 502
MacFrugal's Bargains Close-Outs Inc., **29** 312
MacGregor Sporting Goods Inc., **III** 443; **22** 115, 458; **23** 449
Mach Performance, Inc., **28** 147
Machine Vision International Inc., **10** 232
Macintosh. *See* Apple Computer, Inc.
**Mack-Cali Realty Corporation**, **42 239–41**
**Mack Trucks, Inc.**, **I** 147, **177–79**; **9** 416; **12** 90; **22 329–32 (upd.)**
Mack-Wayne Plastics, **42** 439
**Mackay Envelope Corporation**, **45 256–59**
MacKay-Shields Financial Corp., **III** 316
MacKenzie & Co., **II** 361
Mackenzie Hill, **IV** 724
Mackenzie Mann & Co. Limited, **6** 360
Mackey Airways, **I** 102
**Mackie Designs Inc.**, **30** 406; **33 278–81**
Mackinnon Mackenzie & Co., **III** 521–22
Maclaren Power and Paper Co., **IV** 165
**Maclean Hunter Limited**, **III** 65; **IV 638–40**, **22** 442; **23** 98
**Maclean Hunter Publishing Limited**, **26 270–74 (upd.)**; **30** 388
Maclin Co., **12** 127
The MacManus Group, **32** 140; **40** 140
MacMark Corp., **22** 459
MacMarr Stores, **II** 654
Macmillan & Co. Ltd., **35** 452
**MacMillan Bloedel Limited**, **IV** 165, 272, **306–09**, 721; **9** 391; **19** 444, 446; **25** 12; **26** 445
**Macmillan, Inc.**, **IV** 637, 641–43; **7 284–86**, 311–12, 343; **9** 63; **12** 226; **13** 91, 93; **17** 399; **18** 329; **22** 441–42; **23** 350, 503; **25** 484; **27** 222–23
Macnaughton Blair, **III** 671
**The MacNeal-Schwendler Corporation**, **25 303–05**
Macneill & Co., **III** 522
Macon Gas Company, **6** 447; **23** 28
Macon Kraft Co., **IV** 311; **11** 421; **19** 267
Maconochie Bros., **II** 569
Macrodata, **18** 87
Macwhyte Company, **27** 415
Macy's. *See* R.H. Macy & Co., Inc.
Macy's California, **21** 129
Mad Dog Athletics, **19** 385
Maddingley Brown Coal Pty Ltd., **IV** 249
Maddux Air Lines, **I** 125; **12** 487
**Madge Networks N.V.**, **18** 346; **26 275–77**
Madison & Sullivan, Inc., **10** 215
Madison Dearborn Partners, **46** 289
Madison Financial Corp., **16** 145
Madison Foods, **14** 557
Madison Furniture Industries, **14** 436
**Madison Gas and Electric Company**, **6** 605–06; **39 259–62**
Madison Resources, Inc., **13** 502
Madison Square Garden, **I** 452
MAEFORT Hungarian Air Transport Joint Stock Company, **24** 310

Maersk Lines, **22** 167
Maes Group Breweries, **II** 475
Maeva Group, **6** 206
Mafco Holdings, Inc., **28** 248; **38** 293–95
Magasins Armand Thiéry et Sigrand, **V** 11; **19** 308
Magazine and Book Services, **13** 48
Magazins Réal Stores, **II** 651
Magcobar, **III** 472
MagCorp, **28** 198
Magdeburg Insurance Group, **III** 377
Magdeburger Versicherungsgruppe, **III** 377
Magee Company, **31** 435–36
**Magellan Aerospace Corporation**, **46** 8; **48 274–76**
Magellan Corporation, **22** 403
Magic Chef Co., **III** 573; **8** 298; **22** 349
Magic City Food Products Company. *See* Golden Enterprises, Inc.
Magic Marker, **29** 372
Magic Pan, **II** 559–60; **12** 410
Magic Pantry Foods, **10** 382
Magicsilk, Inc., **22** 133
MagicSoft Inc., **10** 557
Magirus, **IV** 126
Maglificio di Ponzano Veneto dei Fratelli Benetton. *See* Benetton.
**Magma Copper Company**, **7 287–90**, 385–87; **22** 107
**Magma Power Company**, **11 270–72**
Magna Computer Corporation, **12** 149; **13** 97
Magna Distribuidora Ltda., **43** 368
Magnaflux, **III** 519; **22** 282
Magnavox Co., **13** 398; **19** 393
Magne Corp., **IV** 160
Magnesium Metal Co., **IV** 118
Magnet Cove Barium Corp., **III** 472
**MagneTek, Inc.**, **15 287–89**; **41 241–44(upd.)**
Magnetic Controls Company, **10** 18
Magnetic Peripherals Inc., **19** 513–14
Magnivision, **22** 35
Magnolia Petroleum Co., **III** 497; **IV** 82, 464
Magnus Co., **I** 331; **13** 197
La Magona d'Italia, **IV** 228
Magor Railcar Co., **I** 170
Magro, **48** 63
MAGroup Inc., **11** 123
Magyar Viscosa, **37** 428
Mahalo Air, **22** 252; **24** 22
Maharam Fabric, **8** 455
Mahir, **I** 37
Mahir & Numan A.S., **48** 154
Mahou, **II** 474
Mai Nap Rt, **IV** 652; **7** 392
MAI PLC, **28** 504
**MAI Systems Corporation**, **10** 242; **11 273–76**; **26** 497, 499
**Maidenform Worldwide Inc.**, **20 352–55**
**Mail Boxes Etc.**, **18 315–17**; **25** 500; **41 245–48 (upd.)**. *See also* U.S. Office Products Company.
Mail.com Inc., **38** 271
**Mail-Well, Inc.**, **25** 184; **28 250–52**
Mailson Ferreira da Nobrega, **II** 200
Mailtek, Inc., **18** 518
MAIN. *See* Mid-American Interpool Network.
Main Event Management Corp., **III** 194
Main Plaza Corporation, **25** 115
Main Street Advertising USA, **IV** 597
**Maine Central Railroad Company**, **16 348–50**
Mainline Industrial Distributors, Inc., **13** 79
Mainline Travel, **I** 114
Maison Blanche Department Stores Group, **35** 129
Maison Bouygues, **I** 563
Maison de Schreiber and Aronson, **25** 283
Maison de Valérie, **19** 309
**Maison Louis Jadot**, **24 307–09**
Maizuru Heavy Industries, **III** 514
Majestic Contractors Ltd., **8** 419–20
Majestic Industries, Inc., **43** 459
Majestic Wine Warehouses Ltd., **II** 656
**The Major Automotive Companies, Inc.**, **45 260–62**
Major League Baseball, **12** 457
Major Video Concepts, **6** 410
Major Video, Inc., **9** 74
MaK Maschinenbau GmbH, **IV** 88
Mak van Waay, **11** 453
Makepeace Preserving Co., **25** 365
Makhteshim Chemical Works Ltd., **II** 47; **25** 266–67
**Makita Corporation**, **III** 436; **20** 66; **22 333–35**
Makiyama, **I** 363
Makovsky & Company, **12** 394
Makro Inc., **18** 286
Malama Pacific Corporation, **9** 276
Malapai Resources, **6** 546
Malayan Breweries, **I** 256
Malayan Motor and General Underwriters, **III** 201
Malaysia LNG, **IV** 518–19
**Malaysian Airlines System Berhad**, **6** 71, **100–02**, 117, 415; **29 300–03 (upd.)**
Malaysian International Shipping Co., **IV** 518
Malaysian Sheet Glass, **III** 715
Malbak Ltd., **IV** 92–93
**Malcolm Pirnie, Inc.**, **42 242–44**
Malcolm's Diary & Time-Table, **III** 256
Malcus Industri, **III** 624
**Malden Mills Industries, Inc.**, **16 351–53**
**Malév Plc**, **24 310–12**; **27** 474; **29** 17
Malheur Cooperative Electric Association, **12** 265
Malibu, **25** 141
Mall.com, **38** 271
Mallard Bay Drilling, Inc., **28** 347–48
Malleable Iron Works, **II** 34
**Mallinckrodt Group Inc.**, **III** 16; **IV** 146; **8** 85; **19** 28, **251–53**
Malmö Aviation, **47** 61
Malmö Flygindustri, **I** 198
Malmö Woodworking Factory. *See* Tarkett Sommer AG.
Malmsten & Bergvalls, **I** 664
Malone & Hyde, Inc., **II** 625, 670–71; **9** 52–53; **14** 147; **18** 506
Malrite Communications Group, **IV** 596
Malt-A-Milk Co., **II** 487
**Malt-O-Meal Company**, **15** 189; **22 336–38**
Mameco International, **8** 455
**Mammoet Transport B.V.**, **26** 241, **278–80**
**Man Aktiengesellschaft**, **III** 301, **561–63**
MAN Gutehoffnungshütte AG, **15** 226
**Management and Training Corporation**, **28 253–56**
Management By Information Inc., **48** 307
Management Decision Systems, Inc., **10** 358
Management Engineering and Development Co., **IV** 310; **19** 266
Management Recruiters International, **6** 140
Management Science America, Inc., **11** 77; **25** 20
Manbré and Garton, **II** 582
Manchester and Liverpool District Banking Co., **II** 307, 333
Manchester Board and Paper Co., **19** 77
Manchester Commercial Buildings Co., **IV** 711
**Manchester United Football Club plc**, **30 296–98**; **44** 388
Manco, Inc., **13** 166. *See also* Henkel Manco Inc.
Mancuso & Co., **22** 116
Mandabach & Simms, **6** 40
Mandalay Pictures, **35** 278–80
**Mandalay Resort Group**, **32 322–26 (upd.)**
Mandarin, Inc., **33** 128
Mandarin Oriental Hotel Group International Ltd., **I** 471; **IV** 700; **20** 312
Mandarin Oriental International Limited, **47** 177
Mandel Bros., **IV** 660
Manetta Mills, Inc., **19** 304
Manhattan Card Co., **18** 114
Manhattan Co., **II** 217, 247
Manhattan Construction Company. *See* Rooney Brothers Co.
Manhattan Electrical Supply Co., **9** 517
Manhattan Fund, **I** 614
Manhattan International Limousine Network Ltd., **26** 62
Manhattan Trust Co., **II** 229
Manheim Auctions, Inc. *See* Cox Enterprises, Inc.
Manifatture Cotoniere Meridionali, **I** 466
Manischewitz Company. *See* B. Manischewitz Company.
Manistique Papers Inc., **17** 282
Manistique Pulp and Paper Co., **IV** 311; **19** 266
Manitoba Bridge and Engineering Works Ltd., **8** 544
Manitoba Paper Co., **IV** 245–46; **25** 10
Manitoba Rolling Mill Ltd., **8** 544
**Manitou BF S.A.**, **27 294–96**
**Manitowoc Company, Inc.**, **18 318–21**
Mann Egerton & Co., **III** 523
Mann Theatres Chain, **I** 245; **25** 177
Mann's Wine Company, Ltd., **14** 288
Mann's Wine Pub Co., Ltd., **47** 206
**Mannatech Inc.**, **33 282–85**
Manne Tossbergs Eftr., **II** 639
**Mannesmann AG**, **I** 411; **III 564–67**; **IV** 222, 469; **14 326–29 (upd.)**; **34** 319; **38 296–301 (upd.)**. *See also* Vodafone Group PLC.
Mannheimer Bank, **IV** 558
Manning, Selvage & Lee, **6** 22
Mannstaedt, **IV** 128
Manor AG, **48** 279
**Manor Care, Inc.**, **6 187–90**; **14** 105–07; **15** 522; **25 306–10 (upd.)**
Manor Healthcare Corporation, **26** 459
Manorfield Investments, **II** 158
Manos Enterprises, **14** 87

**Manpower, Inc.**, **6** 10, 140; **9 326–27**; **16** 48; **25** 432; **30 299–302 (upd.)**; **40** 236, 238; **44** 157
Mantrec S.A., **27** 296
Mantua Metal Products. *See* Tyco Toys, Inc.
**Manufactured Home Communities, Inc.**, **22 339–41**; **46** 378
Manufacturers & Merchants Indemnity Co., **III** 191
Manufacturers and Traders Trust Company, **11** 108–09
Manufacturers Casualty Insurance Co., **26** 486
Manufacturers Fire Insurance Co., **26** 486
**Manufacturers Hanover Corporation**, **II** 230, 254, **312–14**, 403; **III** 194; **9** 124; **11** 16, 54, 415; **13** 536; **14** 103; **16** 207; **17** 559; **22** 406; **26** 453; **38** 253
Manufacturers National Bank of Brooklyn, **II** 312
Manufacturers National Bank of Detroit, **I** 165; **11** 137; **40** 116
Manufacturers Railway, **I** 219; **34** 36
Manufacturing Management Inc., **19** 381
Manus Nu-Pulse, **III** 420
**Manville Corporation**, **III 706–09**, 721; **7 291–95 (upd.)**; **10** 43, 45; **11** 420–22. *See also* Riverwood International Corporation.
Manweb plc, **19** 389–90
**MAPCO Inc.**, **IV 458–59**; **26** 234; **31** 469, 471
Mapelli Brothers Food Distribution Co., **13** 350
Maple Grove Farms of Vermont, Inc., **40** 51–52
**Maple Leaf Foods Inc.**, **41 249–53**
Maple Leaf Mills, **II** 513–14; **41** 252
MAPP. *See* Mid-Continent Area Power Planner.
Mapra Industria e Comercio Ltda., **32** 40
MAR Associates, **48** 54
Mar-O-Bar Company, **7** 299
A.B. Marabou, **II** 511
Marantha! Music, **14** 499
Marantz Co., **14** 118
Marathon Insurance Co., **26** 486
Marathon Oil Co., **IV** 365, 454, 487, 572, 574; **7** 549, 551; **13** 458
Marathon Paper Products, **I** 612, 614
Marauder Company, **26** 433
Maraven, **IV** 508
Marblehead Communications, Inc., **23** 101
Marbodal, **12** 464
Marboro Books, Inc., **10** 136
Marbro Lamp Co., **III** 571; **20** 362
Marc's Big Boy. *See* The Marcus Corporation.
Marcade Group. *See* Aris Industries, Inc.
Marceau Investments, **II** 356
March-Davis Bicycle Company, **19** 383
**March of Dimes**, **31 322–25**
March Plasma Systems, Inc., **48** 299
Marchand, **13** 27
**Marchesi Antinori SRL**, **42 245–48**
**marchFIRST, Inc.**, **34 261–64**
Marchland Holdings Ltd., **II** 649
Marchon Eyewear, **22** 123
Marciano Investments, Inc., **24** 157
Marcillat, **19** 49
Marcon Coating, Inc., **22** 347
**Marconi plc**, **33 286–90 (upd.)**
Marconi Wireless Telegraph Co. of America, **II** 25, 88
Marconiphone, **I** 531
**The Marcus Corporation**, **21 359–63**
Marcus Samuel & Co., **IV** 530
Marcy Fitness Products, Inc., **19** 142, 144
Mardon Packaging International, **I** 426–27
Mardorf, Peach and Co., **II** 466
Maremont Corporation, **8** 39–40
**Margarete Steiff GmbH**, **23 334–37**
Margarine Unie N.V. *See* Unilever PLC (Unilever N.V.).
Marge Carson, Inc., **III** 571; **20** 362
Margo's La Mode, **10** 281–82; **45** 15
Marico Acquisition Corporation, **8** 448, 450
**Marie Brizard & Roger International S.A.**, **22 342–44**
**Marie Callender's Restaurant & Bakery, Inc.**, **13** 66; **28 257–59**
Marie-Claire Album, **III** 47
Marigold Foods Inc., **II** 528
Marina Mortgage Company, **46** 25
Marinduque Mining & Industrial Corp., **IV** 146
Marine Bank and Trust Co., **11** 105
Marine Bank of Erie, **II** 342
Marine Computer Systems, **6** 242
Marine Diamond Corp., **IV** 66; **7** 123
Marine-Firminy, **IV** 227
Marine Group, **III** 444; **22** 116
Marine Harvest International, **13** 103
Marine Midland Corp., **I** 548; **II** 298; **9** 475–76; **11** 108; **17** 325
Marine Office of America, **III** 220, 241–42
Marine United Inc., **42** 361
Marinela, **19** 192–93
Marineland Amusements Corp., **IV** 623
**MarineMax, Inc.**, **30 303–05**; **37** 396
Marion Brick, **14** 249
Marion Foods, Inc., **17** 434
Marion Freight Lines, **6** 370
**Marion Laboratories Inc.**, **I 648–49**; **8** 149; **9** 328–29; **16** 438
Marion Manufacturing, **9** 72
**Marion Merrell Dow, Inc.**, **9 328–29 (upd.)**
Marionet Corp., **IV** 680–81
**Marisa Christina, Inc.**, **15 290–92**; **25** 245
Maritime Electric Company, Limited, **15** 182; **47** 136–37
**Maritz Inc.**, **38 302–05**
Mark Controls Corporation, **30** 157
Mark Cross, Inc., **17** 4–5
Mark Goldston, **8** 305
Mark Hopkins, **12** 316
**Mark IV Industries, Inc.**, **7 296–98**; **21** 418; **28 260–64 (upd.)**
Mark Travel Corporation, **30** 448
Mark Trouser, Inc., **17** 338
Markborough Properties, **II** 222; **V** 81; **8** 525; **25** 221
Market Growth Resources, **23** 480
Market Horizons, **6** 27
Market National Bank, **13** 465
Marketime, **V** 55
Marketing Data Systems, Inc., **18** 24
Marketing Equities International, **26** 136
Marketing Information Services, **6** 24
MarketSpan Corp. *See* KeySpan Energy Co.
Markham & Co., **I** 573–74
**Marks and Spencer p.l.c.**, **I** 588; **II** 513, 678; **V 124–26**; **10** 442; **17** 42, 124; **22** 109, 111; **24** 268, 270; **313–17 (upd.)**, 474; **28** 96; **35** 308, 310; **41** 114; **42** 231
Marks-Baer Inc., **11** 64
**Marks Brothers Jewelers, Inc.**, **24 318–20**
Marland Refining Co., **IV** 399–400
Marlene Industries Corp., **16** 36–37
MarLennan Corp., **III** 283
Marley Co., **19** 360
Marley Holdings, L.P., **19** 246
Marley Tile, **III** 735
Marlin-Rockwell Corp., **I** 539; **14** 510
Marlow Foods, **II** 565
Marman Products Company, **16** 8
**The Marmon Group**, **III** 97; **IV 135–38**; **16 354–57 (upd.)**
Marmon-Perry Light Company, **6** 508
Marolf Dakota Farms, Inc., **18** 14–15
Marotte, **21** 438
Marquam Commercial Brokerage Company, **21** 257
Marquardt Aircraft, **I** 380; **13** 379
**Marquette Electronics, Inc.**, **13 326–28**
Marquette Paper Corporation, **III** 766; **22** 545
Marquis Who's Who, **17** 398
Marriage Mailers, **6** 12
Marriner Group, **13** 175
Marriot Inc., **29** 442
Marriot Management Services, **29** 444
**Marriott Corporation**, **II** 173, 608; **III** 92, 94, 99–100, **102–03**, 248; **7** 474–75; **9** 95, 426; **15** 87; **17** 238; **18** 216; **19** 433–34; **21** 91, 364; **22** 131; **23** 436–38; **27** 334; **38** 386; **41** 82
**Marriott International, Inc.**, **21** 182, **364–67 (upd.)**; **29** 403, 406; **41** 156–58
**Mars, Incorporated**, **II** 510–11; **III** 114; **7 299–301**; **22** 298, 528; **40 302–05 (upd.)**
Marschke Manufacturing Co., **III** 435
Marsene Corp., **III** 440
**Marsh & McLennan Companies, Inc.**, **III** 280, **282–84**; **10** 39; **14** 279; **22** 318; **45** 28, **263–67 (upd.)**
**Marsh Supermarkets, Inc.**, **17 300–02**
Marshalk Company, **I** 16; **22** 294
Marshall Die Casting, **13** 225
Marshall Field & Co., **I** 13, 426; **III** 329; **IV** 660; **V** 43–44; **8** 33; **9** 213; **12** 283; **15** 86; **18** 136–37, 488; **22** 72
Marshall Industries, **19** 311
**Marshalls Incorporated**, **13 329–31**; **14** 62
Marsin Medical Supply Co., **III** 9
Marstellar, **13** 204
The Mart, **9** 120
Marten Transport, **27** 404
Martha, **IV** 486
Martha Lane Adams, **27** 428
**Martha Stewart Living Omnimedia, L.L.C.**, **24 321–23**; **47** 211
Martin & Pagenstecher GMBH, **24** 208
Martin Bros. Tobacco Co., **14** 19
Martin-Brower Corp., **II** 500; **III** 21; **17** 475
Martin Collet, **19** 50
Martin Dennis Co., **IV** 409
Martin Dunitz, **44** 416
Martin Electric Co., **III** 98
Martin Guitar Company. *See* C.F. Martin & Co., Inc.

**Martin Industries, Inc., 44 274–77**
**Martin Marietta Corporation**, I 47, **67–69**, 71, 102, 112, 142–43, 184, 416; II 32, 67; III 671; IV 60, 163; 7 356, 520; 8 315; 9 310; 10 162, 199, 484; 11 166, 277–78, 364; 12 127, 290; 13 327, 356; 15 283; 17 564; 18 369; 19 70; 22 400; 28 288. *See also* Lockheed Martin Corporation.
Martin Mathys, 8 456
Martin Rooks & Co., I 95
Martin-Senour Co., III 744
Martin Sorrell, 6 54
Martin Theaters, 14 86
Martin-Yale Industries, Inc., 19 142–44
Martin Zippel Co., 16 389
Martin's, 12 221
Martindale-Hubbell, 17 398
Martineau and Bland, I 293
Martini & Rossi, 18 41
Martins Bank, II 236, 308
Martinus Nijhoff, 14 555; 25 85
**Marubeni Corporation, 24 324–27 (upd.)**
**Marubeni K.K.**, I 432, **492–95**, 510; II 292, 391; III 760; IV 266, 525; 12 147; 17 556
Maruei & Co., IV 151; 24 358
Maruetsu, 17 124; 41 114
Marufuku Co., Ltd., III 586; 7 394
**Marui Co. Ltd., V 127**
Marukuni Kogyo Co., Ltd., IV 327
Marutaka Kinitsu Store Ltd., V 194; 47 389
**Maruzen Co., Limited**, II 348; IV 403–04, 476, 554; **18 322–24**
**Marvel Entertainment Group, Inc., 10 400–02**; 18 426, 520–21; 21 404; 25 141; 34 449
Marvel Metal Products, III 570; 20 361
Marvel-Schebler Carburetor Corp., III 438; 14 63–64
Marvin & Leonard Advertising, 13 511–12
Marvin H. Sugarman Productions Inc., 20 48
**Marvin Lumber & Cedar Company**, 10 95; **22 345–47**
Marwick, Mitchell & Company, 10 385
Marwitz & Hauser, III 446
Marx, 12 494
Mary Ann Co. Ltd., V 89
Mary Ann Restivo, Inc., 8 323
Mary Ellen's, Inc., 11 211
Mary Kathleen Uranium, IV 59–60
**Mary Kay Corporation**, III 16; **9 330–32**; 12 435; 15 475, 477; 18 67, 164; 21 49, 51; **30 306–09 (upd.)**
Maryland Casualty Co., III 193, 412
Maryland Cup Company, 8 197
Maryland Distillers, I 285
Maryland Medical Laboratory Inc., 26 391
Maryland National Corp., 11 287
Maryland National Mortgage Corporation, 11 121; 48 177
Maryland Shipbuilding and Drydock Co., I 170
Maryland Steel Co., IV 35; 7 48
**Marzotto S.p.A., 20 356–58**; 48 206–07
Masayoshi Son, 13 481–82
Mascan Corp., IV 697
Maschinenbauanstalt Humboldt AG, III 541
Maschinenfabrik Augsburg-Nürnberg. *See* M.A.N.
Maschinenfabrik Deutschland, IV 103
Maschinenfabrik für den Bergbau von Sievers & Co., III 541
Maschinenfabrik Gebr. Meer, III 565
Maschinenfabrik Sürth, I 581
**Masco Corporation, III 568–71**; 11 385, 534–35; 12 129, 131, 344; 13 338; 18 68; **20 359–63 (upd.)**; **39 263–68 (upd.)**
Masco Optical, 13 165
Mascon Toy Co., III 569; 20 360
MASCOR, 14 13
Mase Westpac Limited, 11 418
Maserati. *See* Officine Alfieri Maserati S.p.A.
**Mashantucket Pequot Gaming Enterprise Inc., 35 282–85**
Masinfabriks A.B. Scania, I 197
MASkargo Ltd., 6 101
**Masland Corporation, 17 303–05**; 19 408
Mason & Hamlin, III 656
Mason Best Co., IV 343
Masonite Corp., III 764; 47 189
Masonite Holdings, III 687
Mass Rapid Transit Corp., 19 111
Massachusetts Bank, II 207
Massachusetts Capital Resources Corp., III 314
**Massachusetts Mutual Life Insurance Company**, III 110, **285–87**, 305; 14 14; 25 528
Massachusetts Technology Development Corporation, 18 570
Massachusetts's General Electric Company, 32 267
Massey Burch Investment Grou Master Boot Polish Co., II 566
Master Builders, I 673
Master Electric Company, 15 134
Master Glass & Color, 24 159–60
**Master Lock Company, 45 268–71**
Master Pneumatic Tool Co., III 436
Master Processing, 19 37
Master Products, 14 162
Master Shield Inc., 7 116
Master Tank and Welding Company, 7 541
Master Tek International, Inc., 47 372
MasterBrand Industries Inc., 12 344–45
**MasterCard International, Inc., 9 333–35**; 18 337, 543; 25 41; 26 515; 41 201
Mastercraft Homes, Inc., 11 257
Mastercraft Industries Corp., III 654
Mastex Industries, 29 132
Maszovlet. *See* Malév Plc.
Matador Records, 22 194
Matairco, 9 27
Matane Pulp & Paper Company, 17 281
Matchbox Toys Ltd., 12 168
MatchLogic, Inc., 41 198
Matco Tools, 7 116
Material Management and Services Inc., 28 61
Materials Services Corp., I 58
Mathematica, Inc., 22 291
Mather & Crother Advertising Agency, I 25
Mather Co., I 159
Mather Metals, III 582
Matheson & Co., IV 189
Mathews Conveyor Co., 14 43
Mathieson Chemical Corp., I 379–80, 695; 13 379
Matra, II 38, 70; IV 617–19; 13 356; 17 354; 24 88
Matra Aerospace Inc., 22 402
**Matra-Hachette S.A., 15 293–97 (upd.)**; 21 267
**Matria Healthcare, Inc., 17 306–09**
Matrix Science Corp., II 8; 14 27
Matson Navigation Company, Inc., II 490–91; 10 40; 41 399
Matsumoto Medical Instruments, Inc., 11 476; 29 455
**Matsushita Electric Industrial Co., Ltd.**, II 5, **55–56**, 58, 61, 91–92, 102, 117–19, 361, 455; III 476, 710; 6 36; 7 163, 302; 10 286, 389, 403, 432; 11 487; 12 448; 13 398; 18 18; 20 81; 26 511; 33 432; 36 399–400, 420
**Matsushita Electric Works, Ltd., III 710–11**; **7 302–03 (upd.)**; 12 454; 16 167; 27 342
Matsushita Kotobuki Electronics Industries, Ltd., 10 458–59
Matsuura Trading Co., Ltd., IV 327
**Matsuzakaya Company, V 129–31**
Mattatuck Bank & Trust Co., 13 467
**Mattel, Inc.**, II 136; III 506; **7 304–07**; 12 74, 168–69, 495; 13 560–61; 15 238; 16 264, 428; 17 243; 18 520–21; **25 311–15 (upd.)**, 381, 488; 27 20, 373, 375; 28 159; 29 74, 78; 32 187; 34 369–70; 43 229, 232–33
Matthes & Weber, III 32
Matthew Bender & Company, Inc., IV 677; 7 94; 14 97; 17 486
**Matthews International Corporation, 29 304–06**
Matthews Paint Co., 22 437
Maud Foster Mill, II 566
Maui Electric Company, 9 276
**Maui Land & Pineapple Company, Inc., 29 307–09**
Mauna Kea Properties, 6 129
Maurice H. Needham Co., I 31
**Maus Frères SA**,19 307; **48 277–79**
Maus-Nordmann, V 10; 19 308
**Max & Erma's Restaurants Inc., 19 258–60**
Max Factor & Co., III 54, 56; 6 51; 12 314
Max-Grundig-Stiftung, 27 190–91
Max Klein, Inc., II 572
Max Media Properties LLC, 25 419
Max Television Co., 25 418
Maxcell Telecom Plus, 6 323
**Maxco Inc., 17 310–11**; 24 159, 160
Maxell Corp., I 500; 14 534
Maxi-Papier-Markt, 10 498; 24 270
Maxi Vac, Inc., 9 72
**Maxicare Health Plans, Inc., III 84–86**; **25 316–19 (upd.)**; 44 174
Maxie's of America, 25 389
**The Maxim Group, 25** 88, **320–22**
**Maxim Integrated Products, Inc., 16 358–60**
**MAXIMUS, Inc., 43 277–80**
Maxis Software, 13 115
Maxoptix Corporation, 10 404
Maxpro Sports Inc., 22 458
Maxpro Systems, 24 509–10
**Maxtor Corporation**, 6 230; **10 403–05**, 459, 463–64
**Maxus Energy Corporation**, IV 410; **7 308–10**; 10 191; 31 456
**Maxwell Communication Corporation plc**, IV 605, 611, **641–43**; 7 286, **311–13 (upd.)**, 343; 10 288; 13 91–93; 23 350; 39 49; 47 326

Maxwell Morton Corp, **I** 144, 414
**Maxwell Shoe Company, Inc.**, **30 310–12**
Maxwell Travel Inc., **33** 396
**MAXXAM Inc.**, **IV** 121, 123; **8 348–50**
**Maxxim Medical Inc.**, **12 325–27**
May and Baker, **I** 388
May & Speh Inc., **35** 17
**The May Department Stores Company**, **I** 540; **II** 414; **V 132–35**; **8** 288; **11** 349; **12** 55, 507–08; **13** 42, 361; **15** 275; **16** 62, 160, 206–07; **18** 414–15; **19 261–64 (upd.)**; **23** 345; **27** 61, 291, 346, 348; **33** 471, 473; **46 284–88 (upd.)**
Maybelline, **I** 684
Mayer & Schweitzer, **26** 66
**Mayer, Brown, Rowe & Maw**, **47 230–32**
Mayfair Foods, **I** 438; **16** 314
Mayfield Dairy Farms, Inc., **7** 128
**Mayflower Group Inc.**, **6 409–11**; **15** 50
Mayne Nickless Ltd., **IV** 248
**Mayo Foundation**, **9 336–39**; **13** 326; **34 265–69 (upd.)**
**Mayor's Jewelers, Inc.**, **41 254–57**
**Maytag Corporation**, **III 572–73**; **12** 252, 300; **21** 141; **22** 218, **348–51 (upd.)**; **23** 244; **42** 159; **43** 166
Mayville Metal Products Co., **I** 513
**Mazda Motor Corporation**, **I** 520; **II** 4, 361; **III** 603; **9 340–42**; **11** 86; **13** 414; **16** 322; **23 338–41 (upd.)**; **36** 215
**Mazel Stores, Inc.**, **29 310–12**
MB Group, **20** 108
MBB. *See* Messerschmitt-Bölkow-Blohm.
MBC. *See* Middle East Broadcasting Centre, Ltd.
**MBC Holding Company**, **40 306–09**
MBE. *See* Mail Boxes Etc.
**MBNA Corporation**, **11** 123; **12 328–30**; **33 291–94 (upd.)**
MBPXL Corp., **II** 494
MC Distribution Services, Inc., **35** 298
**MCA Inc.**, **II 143–45**; **6** 162–63; **10** 286; **11** 557; **17** 317; **21** 23, 25–26; **22** 131, 194; **23** 125; **25** 411; **26** 151, 314; **33** 431
McAfee Associates. *See* Network Associates, Inc.
The McAlpin Company, **19** 272
McAndrew & Forbes Holdings Inc., **23** 407; **26** 119
McArthur Glen Realty, **10** 122; **33** 59
MCC. *See* Morris Communications Corporation.
McCaffrey & McCall, **I** 33; **11** 496
McCain Feeds Ltd., **II** 484
McCain Foods, **41** 252
McCall Pattern Company, **22** 512; **23** 99
McCall Printing Co., **14** 460
McCall's Corp., **23** 393
McCann-Erickson Worldwide, **I** 10, 14, 16–17, 234; **6** 30; **10** 227; **14** 315; **16** 167; **18** 68; **22** 294; **32** 114
McCann-Erickson Hakuhodo, Ltd., **42** 174
**McCarthy Building Companies, Inc.**, **48 280–82**
McCarthy Milling, **II** 631; **27** 245–47
McCaughan Dyson and Co., **II** 189
**McCaw Cellular Communications, Inc.**, **II** 331; **6** 274, **322–24**; **7** 15; **9** 320–21; **10** 433; **15** 125, 196; **27** 341, 343–44; **29** 44, 61; **36** 514–15; **43** 447
McClanahan Oil Co., **I** 341; **14** 216
**McClatchy Newspapers, Inc.**, **23** 156, 158, **342–44**
McCleary, Wallin and Crouse, **19** 274
McClintic-Marshall, **IV** 36; **7** 49
The McCloskey Corporation, **8** 553
The McClure Syndicate, **25** 138
McColl-Frontenac Petroleum Inc., **IV** 439; **25** 232
McComb Manufacturing Co., **8** 287
McCormack & Dodge, **IV** 605; **11** 77
**McCormick & Company, Incorporated**, **7 314–16**; **17** 104, 106; **21** 497; **27 297–300 (upd.)**; **36** 185, 188
McCormick & Schmick's, **31** 41
McCormick Harvesting Machine Co., **I** 180; **II** 330
McCown De Leeuw & Co., **16** 510
McCracken Brooks, **23** 479; **25** 91
McCrory Stores, **II** 424; **9** 447–48; **13** 340
McCulloch Corp., **III** 436; **8** 348–49
McCullough Environmental Services, **12** 443
**McDermott International, Inc.**, **III 558–60**; **37 242–46 (upd.)**
McDonald Glass Grocery Co. Inc., **II** 669
McDonald's Company (Japan) Ltd., **V** 205
**McDonald's Corporation**, **I** 23, 31, 129; **II** 500, 613–15 **646–48**; **III** 63, 94, 103; **6** 13; **7** 128, 266–67, 316, **317–19 (upd.)**, 435, 505–06; **8** 261–62, 564; **9** 74, 178, 290, 292, 305; **10** 122; **11** 82, 308; **12** 43, 180, 553; **13** 494; **14** 25, 32, 106, 195, 452–53; **16** 95–97, 289; **17** 69–71; **19** 85, 192, 214; **21** 25, 315, 362; **23** 505; **25** 179, 309, 387; **26 281–85 (upd.)**; **31** 278; **32** 442–44; **33** 240; **36** 517, 519–20; **39** 166, 168; **48** 67
**McDonnell Douglas Corporation**, **I** 41–43, 45, 48, 50–52, 54–56, 58–59, 61–62, 67–68, **70–72**, 76–77, 82, 84–85, 90, 105, 108, 111, 121–22, 321, 364, 490, 511; **II** 442; **III** 512, 654; **6** 68; **7** 456, 504; **8** 49–51, 315; **9** 18, 183, 206, 231, 271–72, 418, 458, 460; **10** 163–64, 317, 536; **11** 164–65, 267, **277–80 (upd.)**, 285, 363–65; **12** 190–91, 549; **13** 356; **15** 283; **16** 78, 94; **18** 368; **24** 84–85, 87; **28** 225; **32** 81, 83, 85
McDonough Co., **II** 16; **III** 502
McDougal, Littell & Company, **10** 357
McDowell Energy Center, **6** 543
McDowell Furniture Company, **10** 183
McDuff, **10** 305
McElligott Wright Morrison and White, **12** 511
McFadden Holdings L.P., **27** 41
McFadden Industries, **III** 21
McFadden Publishing, **6** 13
McGaughy, Marsha 584, **634–37**, 643, 656, 674; **10** 62; **12** 359; **13** 417; **18 325–30 (upd.)**; **26** 79; **27** 360
McGaw Inc., **11** 208
McGill Manufacturing, **III** 625
McGraw-Edison Co., **II** 17, 87
McGraw Electric Company. *See* Centel Corporation.
**The McGraw-Hill Companies, Inc.**, **II** 398; **IV** 584, **634–37**, 643, 656, 674; **10** 62; **12** 359; **13** 417; **18 325–30 (upd.)**; **26** 79; **27** 360
McGregor Corporation, **6** 415; **26** 102
McGrew Color Graphics, **7** 430
MCI. *See* Manitou Costruzioni Industriali SRL. *or* Melamine Chemicals, Inc.
**MCI Communications Corporation**, **II** 408; **III** 13, 149, 684; **V 302–04**; **6** 51–52, 300, 322; **7** 118–19; **8** 310; **9** 171, 478–80; **10** 19, 80, 89, 97, 433, 500; **11** 59, 183, 185, 302, 409, 500; **12** 135–37; **13** 38; **14** 252–53, 260, 364; **15** 222; **16** 318; **18** 32, 112, 164–66, 569–70; **19** 255; **25** 358; **26** 102, 441; **27** 430; **29** 42; **46** 374
**MCI WorldCom, Inc.**, **27 301–08 (upd.)**
**McIlhenny Company**, **20 364–67**
McIlwraith McEachern Limited, **27** 474
McJunkin Corp., **13** 79; **28** 61
**McKechnie plc**, **34 270–72**
**McKee Foods Corporation**, **7 320–21**; **27 309–11 (upd.)**
McKenna Metals Company, **13** 295–96
**McKesson Corporation**, **I** 413, **496–98**, 713; **II** 652; **III** 10; **6** 279; **8** 464; **9** 532; **11** 91; **12 331–33 (upd.)**; **16** 43; **18** 97; **37** 10; **41** 340; **47 233–37 (upd.)**
McKesson General Medical, **29** 299
**McKinsey & Company, Inc.**, **I** 108, 144, 437, 497; **III** 47, 85, 670; **9 343–45**; **10** 175; **13** 138; **18** 68; **25** 34, 317; **26** 161
McLain Grocery, **II** 625
McLane America, Inc., **29** 481
**McLane Company, Inc.**, **V** 217; **8** 556; **13 332–34**; **36** 269
McLaren Consolidated Cone Corp., **II** 543; **7** 366
McLaughlin Motor Company of Canada, **I** 171; **10** 325
McLean Clinic, **11** 379
**McLeodUSA Incorporated**, **32 327–30**; **38** 192
McLouth Steel Products, **13** 158
MCM Electronics, **9** 420
McMahan's Furniture Co., **14** 236
McMan Oil and Gas Co., **IV** 369
McManus, John & Adams, Inc., **6** 21
McMoCo, **IV** 82–83; **7** 187
McMoRan, **IV** 81–83; **V** 739; **7** 185, 187
McMullen & Yee Publishing, **22** 442
McMurtry Manufacturing, **8** 553
**MCN Corporation**, **6 519–22**; **13** 416; **17** 21–23; **45** 254
McNeil Corporation, **26** 363
McNeil Laboratories, **III** 35–36; **8** 282–83
McNellan Resources Inc., **IV** 76
MCO Holdings Inc., **8** 348–49
MCorp, **10** 134; **11** 122
McPaper AG, **29** 152
McQuay International. *See* AAF-McQuay Incorporated.
McRae's, Inc., **19** 324–25; **41** 343–44
MCS, Inc., **10** 412
**MCSi, Inc.**, **41 258–60**
MCT Dairies, Inc., **18** 14–16
McTeigue & Co., **14** 502
McVitie & Price, **II** 592–93
McWhorter Inc., **8** 553; **27** 280
MD Distribution Inc., **15** 139
MD Foods (Mejeriselskabet Danmark Foods), **48** 35
MD Pharmaceuticals, **III** 10
MDC. *See* Mead Data Central, Inc.
MDI Co., Ltd., **IV** 327
MDS/Bankmark, **10** 247
**MDU Resources Group, Inc.**, **7 322–25**; **42 249–53 (upd.)**

**The Mead Corporation**, **IV 310–13**, 327, 329, 342–43; **8** 267; **9** 261; **10** 406; **11** 421–22; **17** 399; **19 265–69 (upd.)**; **20** 18; **33** 263, 265
Mead Cycle Co., **IV** 660
**Mead Data Central, Inc.**, **IV** 312; **7** 581; **10 406–08**; **19** 268. *See also* LEXIS-NEXIS Group.
Mead John & Co., **19** 103
Mead Johnson, **III** 17
Mead Packaging, **12** 151
Meade County Rural Electric Cooperative Corporation, **11** 37
**Meade Instruments Corporation**, **41 261–64**
Meadow Gold Dairies, Inc., **II** 473
**Meadowcraft, Inc.**, **29 313–15**
Means Services, Inc., **II** 607
Mears & Phillips, **II** 237
Measurex Corporation, **8** 243; **14** 56; **38** 227
Mebetoys, **25** 312
MEC - Hawaii, UK & USA, **IV** 714
MECA Software, Inc., **18** 363
Mecair, S.p.A., **17** 147
Mecca Leisure PLC, **I** 248; **12** 229; **32** 243
Mechanics Exchange Savings Bank, **9** 173
Mechanics Machine Co., **III** 438; **14** 63
**Mecklermedia Corporation**, **24 328–30**; **26** 441; **27** 360, 362
Medal Distributing Co., **9** 542
Medallion Pictures Corp., **9** 320
Medar, Inc., **17** 310–11
**Medco Containment Services Inc.**, **9 346–48**; **11** 291; **12** 333; **44** 175
Medcom Inc., **I** 628
Medeco Security Locks, Inc., **10** 350
Medfield Corp., **III** 87
Medford, Inc., **19** 467–68
Medi Mart Drug Store Company. *See* The Stop & Shop Companies, Inc.
**Media Arts Group, Inc.**, **42 254–57**
Media Exchange International, **25** 509
**Media General, Inc.**, **III** 214; **7 326–28**; **18** 61; **23** 225; **38 306–09 (upd.)**
Media Groep West B.V., **23** 271
Media News Corporation, **25** 507
Media Play. *See* Musicland Stores Corporation.
MediaBay, **41** 61
Mediacom Inc., **25** 373
Mediamark Research, **28** 501, 504
Mediamatics, Inc., **26** 329
MediaOne Group Inc. *See* U S West, Inc.
Medic Computer Systems LLC, **16** 94; **45** 279–80
Medical Care America, Inc., **15** 112, 114; **35** 215–17
Medical Development Corp. *See* Cordis Corp.
Medical Development Services, Inc., **25** 307
Medical Economics Data, **23** 211
Medical Expense Fund, **III** 245
Medical Indemnity of America, **10** 160
Medical Innovations Corporation, **21** 46
Medical Marketing Group Inc., **9** 348
Medical Service Assoc. of Pennsylvania, **III** 325–26
Medical Tribune Group, **IV** 591; **20** 53
Medicare-Glaser, **17** 167
Medicine Bow Coal Company, **7** 33–34
Medicine Shoppe International. *See* Cardinal Health, Inc.
Medicor, Inc., **36** 496
Medicus Intercon International, **6** 22
Medifinancial Solutions, Inc., **18** 370
**MedImmune, Inc.**, **35 286–89**
Medinol Ltd., **37** 39
Mediobanca Banca di Credito Finanziario SpA, **II** 191, 271; **III** 208–09; **11** 205
The Mediplex Group, Inc., **III** 16; **11** 282
Medis Health and Pharmaceuticals Services Inc., **II** 653
Medite Corporation, **19** 467–68
**Meditrust**, **11 281–83**
Medlabs Inc., **III** 73
MedPartners, **36** 367
Medtech, Ltd., **13** 60–62
**Medtronic, Inc.**, **8 351–54**; **11** 459; **18** 421; **19** 103; **22** 359–61; **26** 132; **30 313–17 (upd.)**; **37** 39; **43** 349
**Medusa Corporation**, **8** 135; **24 331–33**; **30** 156
Mees & Hope, **II** 184
The MEGA Life and Health Insurance Co., **33** 418–20
MEGA Natural Gas Company, **11** 28
MegaBingo, Inc., **41** 273, 275
**Megafoods Stores Inc.**, **13 335–37**; **17** 560
MegaKnowledge Inc., **45** 206
Megasong Publishing, **44** 164
Megasource, Inc., **16** 94
**Meggitt PLC**, **34 273–76**; **48** 432, 434
MEI Diversified Inc., **18** 455
Mei Foo Investments Ltd., **IV** 718; **38** 319
**Meier & Frank Co.**, **23 345–47**
**Meijer Incorporated**, **7 329–31**; **15** 449; **17** 302; **27 312–15 (upd.)**
Meiji Commerce Bank, **II** 291
Meiji Fire Insurance Co., **III** 384–85
**Meiji Milk Products Company, Limited**, **II 538–39**
**Meiji Mutual Life Insurance Company**, **II** 323; **III 288–89**
**Meiji Seika Kaisha, Ltd.**, **I** 676; **II 540–41**
Meikosha Co., **II** 72
Meinecke Muffler Company, **III** 495; **10** 415
Meineke Discount Muffler Shops, **38** 208
Meis of Illiana, **10** 282
Meisei Electric, **III** 742
Meisel. *See* Samuel Meisel & Co.
Meisenzahl Auto Parts, Inc., **24** 205
Meissner, Ackermann & Co., **IV** 463; **7** 351
Meister, Lucious and Company, **13** 262
Meiwa Manufacturing Co., **III** 758
N.V. Mekog, **IV** 531
**Mel Farr Automotive Group**, **20 368–70**
Mel Klein and Partners, **III** 74
**Melaleuca Inc.**, **31 326–28**
**Melamine Chemicals, Inc.**, **27 316–18**
Melbourne Engineering Co., **23** 83
Melbur China Clay Co., **III** 690
Melco, **II** 58; **44** 285
Meldisco. *See* Footstar, Incorporated.
Melkunie-Holland, **II** 575
Mellbank Security Co., **II** 316
Mello Smello. *See* The Miner Group International.
**Mellon Bank Corporation**, **I** 67–68, 584; **II 315–17**, 342, 402; **III** 275; **9** 470; **13** 410–11; **18** 112
**Mellon Financial Corporation**, **42** 76; **44 278–82 (upd.)**
Mellon Indemnity Corp., **III** 258–59; **24** 177
**Mellon-Stuart Co.**, **I 584–85**; **14** 334
Melmarkets, **24** 462
Mélotte, **III** 418
Meloy Laboratories, Inc., **11** 333
Melroe Company, **8** 115–16; **34** 46
**Melville Corporation**, **V 136–38**; **9** 192; **13** 82, 329–30; **14** 426; **15** 252–53;, **16** 390; **19** 449; **21** 526; **23** 176; **24** 167, 290; **35** 253. *See also* CVS Corporation.
**Melvin Simon and Associates, Inc.**, **8 355–57**; **26** 262
Melwire Group, **III** 673
MEM, **37** 270–71
Memco, **12** 48
Memorex Corp., **III** 110, 166; **6** 282–83
Memphis International Motorsports Corporation Inc., **43** 139–40
**The Men's Wearhouse, Inc.**, **17 312–15**; **21** 311; **48 283–87 (upd.)**
Menasco Manufacturing Co., **I** 435; **III** 415
**Menasha Corporation**, **8 358–61**
Menck, **8** 544
Mendelssohn & Co., **II** 241
Meneven, **IV** 508
Menka Gesellschaft, **IV** 150; **24** 357
The Mennen Company, **I** 19; **6** 26; **14** 122; **18** 69; **35** 113
Mental Health Programs Inc., **15** 122
**The Mentholatum Company Inc.**, **IV** 722; **32 331–33**
**Mentor Corporation**, **26 286–88**
**Mentor Graphics Corporation**, **III** 143; **8** 519; **11** 46–47, **284–86**, 490; **13** 128
**MEPC plc**, **IV 710–12**
Mepco/Electra Inc., **13** 398
MeraBank, **6** 546
MERBCO, Inc., **33** 456
Mercantile Agency, **IV** 604
Mercantile and General Reinsurance Co., **III** 335, 377
Mercantile Bancorporation Inc., **33** 155
Mercantile Bank, **II** 298
**Mercantile Bankshares Corp.**, **11 287–88**
Mercantile Credit Co., **16** 13
Mercantile Estate and Property Corp. Ltd., **IV** 710
Mercantile Fire Insurance, **III** 234
Mercantile Mutual, **III** 310
Mercantile Property Corp. Ltd., **IV** 710
Mercantile Security Life, **III** 136
**Mercantile Stores Company, Inc.**, **V** 139; **19 270–73 (upd.)**
Mercantile Trust Co., **II** 229, 247
Mercator & Noordstar N.V., **40** 61
Mercedes Benz. *See* Daimler-Benz A.G.
Mercedes Benz of North America, **22** 52
Merchant Bank Services, **18** 516, 518
Merchant Co., **III** 104
Merchant Distributors, Inc., **20** 306
Merchants & Farmers Bank of Ecru, **14** 40
Merchants Bank, **II** 213
Merchants Bank & Trust Co., **21** 524
Merchants Bank of Canada, **II** 210
Merchants Bank of Halifax, **II** 344
Merchants Dispatch, **II** 395–96; **10** 60
Merchants Distributors Inc. *See* Alex Lee Inc.
Merchants Fire Assurance Corp., **III** 396–97
Merchants Home Delivery Service, **6** 414
Merchants Indemnity Corp., **III** 396–97

Merchants Life Insurance Co., **III** 275
Merchants National Bank, **9** 228; **14** 528; **17** 135
Merchants National Bank of Boston, **II** 213
Merchants Union Express Co., **II** 396; **10** 60
Merchants' Assoc., **II** 261
Merchants' Loan and Trust, **II** 261; **III** 518
Merchants' Savings, Loan and Trust Co., **II** 261
Mercier, **I** 272
**Merck & Co., Inc.**, **I** 640, 646, **650–52**, 683–84, 708; **II** 414; **III** 42, 60, 66, 299; **8** 154, 548; **10** 213; **11** 9, 90, **289–91 (upd.)**; **12** 325, 333; **14** 58, 422; **15** 154; **16** 440; **20** 39, 59; **26** 126; **34 280–85 (upd.)**; **36** 91, 93, 305; **38** 380; **44** 175; **47** 236
**Mercury Air Group, Inc., 20 371–73**
Mercury Asset Management (MAM), **14** 420; **40** 313
**Mercury Communications, Ltd.**, **V** 280–82; **7 332–34**; **10** 456; **11** 547–48; **25** 101–02; **27** 365
**Mercury General Corporation, 25 323–25**
Mercury, Inc., **8** 311
Mercury Mail, Inc., **22** 519, 522
Mercury Records, **13** 397; **23** 389, 391
Mercury Telecommunications Limited, **15** 67, 69
Meredith and Drew, **II** 593
**Meredith Corporation**, **IV** 661–62; **11 292–94**; **17** 394; **18** 239; **23** 393; **29 316–19 (upd.)**
Merfin International, **42** 53
Merial, **34** 284
Merico, Inc., **36** 161–64
**Meridian Bancorp, Inc., 11 295–97**; **17** 111, 114
Meridian Emerging Markets Ltd., **25** 509
**Meridian Gold, Incorporated, 47 238–40**
Meridian Healthcare, **18** 197
Meridian Insurance Co., **III** 332
Meridian Investment and Development Corp., **22** 189
Meridian Oil Inc., **10** 190–91
Meridian Publishing, Inc., **28** 254
**Merillat Industries Inc.**, **III** 570; **13 338–39**; **20** 362; **39** 266, 268
**Merisel, Inc.**, **10** 518–19; **12 334–36**; **13** 174, 176, 482
Merit Distribution Services, **13** 333
**Merit Medical Systems, Inc., 29 320–22**; **36** 497
Merit Tank Testing, Inc., **IV** 411
Merita/Cotton's Bakeries, **38** 251
**Meritage Corporation, 26 289–92**
MeritaNordbanken, **40** 336
Meritor Automotive Inc., **43** 328
Merivienti Oy, **IV** 276
**Merix Corporation, 36 329–31**
Merkur Direktwerbegesellschaft, **29** 152
Merla Manufacturing, **I** 524
Merlin Gérin, **II** 93–94; **18** 473; **19** 165
Merpati Nusantara Airlines, **6** 90–91
Merrell, **22** 173
Merrell Dow, **16** 438
Merrell Drug, **I** 325
Merrell-Soule Co., **II** 471
Merriam and Morgan Paraffine Co., **IV** 548
Merriam-Webster, Inc., **7** 165, 167; **23** 209–10; **39** 140, 143
**Merrill Corporation, 18 331–34**; **47 241–44 (upd.)**
Merrill Gas Company, **9** 554
**Merrill Lynch & Co., Inc.**, **I** 26, 339, 681, 683, 697; **II** 149, 257, 260, 268, 403, 407–08, 412, **424–26**, 441, 445, 449, 451, 456, 654–55, 680; **III** 119, 253, 340, 440; **6** 244; **7** 130; **8** 94; **9** 125, 187, 239, 301, 386; **11** 29, 122, 348, 557; **13** 44, 125, **340–43 (upd.)**, 448–49, 512; **14** 65; **15** 463; **16** 195; **17** 137; **21** 68–70, 145; **22** 404–06, 542; **23** 370; **25** 89–90, 329; **29** 295; **32** 14, 168; **40 310–15 (upd.)**
Merrill Lynch Capital Partners, **47** 363
Merrill, Pickard, Anderson & Eyre IV, **11** 490
Merrill Publishing, **IV** 643; **7** 312; **9** 63; **29** 57
Merrimack Services Corp., **37** 303
**Merry-Go-Round Enterprises, Inc.**, **8 362–64**; **24** 27
Merry Group, **III** 673
Merry Maids, **6** 46; **23** 428, 430
Merryhill Schools, Inc., **37** 279
**The Mersey Docks and Harbour Company, 30 318–20**
Mersey Paper Co., **IV** 258
Mersey White Lead Co., **III** 680
Merv Griffin Enterprises, **II** 137; **12** 75; **22** 431
**Mervyn's**, **V** 43–44; **10 409–10**; **13** 526; **18** 136–37; **27** 452
**Mervyn's California, 39 269–71 (upd.)**
**Mesa Air Group, Inc., 32 334–37 (upd.)**
**Mesa Airlines, Inc., 11 298–300**
Mesa LP, **IV** 410, 523; **11** 441; **40** 357
Mesa Petroleum, **IV** 392, 571; **24** 521, 522; **27** 217
**Mesaba Holdings, Inc.**, **I** 448; **22** 21; **28 265–67**
Messageries du Livre, **IV** 614
**Messerschmitt-Bölkow-Blohm GmbH.**, **I** 41–42, 46, 51–52, 55, **73–75**, 111; **II** 242; **III** 539; **11** 267; **24** 86
Messner, Vetere, Berger, Carey, Schmetterer, **13** 204
Mesta Machine Co., **22** 415
**Mestek, Inc., 10 411–13**
Met Food Corp. *See* White Rose Food Corp.
Met-Mex Penoles. *See* Industrias Penoles, S.A. de C.V.
META Group, Inc., **37** 147
Metabio-Joullie, **III** 47
Metaframe Corp., **25** 312
**Metal Box plc, I 604–06**; **20** 108
Metal-Cal. *See* Avery Dennison Corporation.
Metal Casting Technology, Inc., **23** 267, 269
Metal Closures, **I** 615
Metal Industries, **I** 531–32
Metal Manufactures, **III** 433–34
Metal Office Furniture Company, **7** 493
Metales y Contactos, **29** 461–62
**Metaleurop S.A.**, **IV** 108–09; **21 368–71**
MetalExchange, **26** 530
Metall Mining Corp., **IV** 141; **27** 456
**Metallgesellschaft AG**, **IV** 17, **139–42**, 229; **16 361–66 (upd.)**
MetalOptics Inc., **19** 212
MetalPro, Inc., **IV** 168
Metals and Controls Corp., **II** 113
Metals Exploration, **IV** 82
Metalurgica Mexicana Penoles, S.A. *See* Industrias Penoles, S.A. de C.V.
Metaphase Technology, Inc., **10** 257
**Metatec International, Inc., 47 245–48**
Metcalf & Eddy Companies, Inc., **6** 143, 441; **32** 52
Meteor Film Productions, **23** 391
**Meteor Industries Inc., 33 295–97**
Methane Development Corporation, **6** 457
**Methanex Corporation, 12** 365; **19** 155–56; **40 316–19**
**Methode Electronics, Inc., 13 344–46**
Metinox Steel Ltd., **IV** 203
MetLife General Insurance Agency, **III** 293; **45** 294
MetLife HealthCare, **36** 366
MetMor Financial, Inc., **III** 293
Meto AG, **39** 79
MetPath, Inc., **III** 684; **26** 390
Metra Steel, **19** 381
Metrastock Ltd., **34** 5
Metric Constructors, Inc., **16** 286
Metric Systems Corporation, **18** 513; **44** 420
Metris Companies, **25** 41
Metro AG, **23** 311
Metro Distributors Inc., **14** 545
Metro Drug Corporation, **II** 649–50; **18** 181
Metro Glass, **II** 533
**Metro-Goldwyn-Mayer Inc.**, **25** 173, 253, **326–30 (upd.)**; **33**
Metro Holding AG, **38** 266
**Metro Information Services, Inc., 36 332–34**
Metro International SA, **36** 335
Metro-Mark Integrated Systems Inc., **11** 469
Metro-North Commuter Railroad Company, **35** 292
Metro Pacific, **18** 180, 182
Metro-Richelieu Inc., **II** 653
Metro Southwest Construction. *See* CRSS Inc.
Metro Support Services, Inc., **48** 171
Metro Vermögensverwaltung GmbH & Co. of Dusseldorf, **V** 104
Metro-Verwegensverwaltung, **II** 257
**Metrocall, Inc.**, **18** 77; **39** 25; **41 265–68**
Metrol Security Services, Inc., **32** 373
Metroland Printing, Publishing and Distributing Ltd., **29** 471
Metromail Corp., **IV** 661; **18** 170; **38** 370
**Metromedia Companies**, **II** 171; **6** 33, 168–69; **7** 91, **335–37**; **14 298–300**
Metropolitan Accident Co., **III** 228
Metropolitan Bank, **II** 221, 318; **III** 239; **IV** 644; **17** 323
**Metropolitan Baseball Club Inc., 39 272–75**
Metropolitan Broadcasting Corporation, **7** 335
Metropolitan Clothing Co., **19** 362
Metropolitan Distributors, **9** 283
Metropolitan District Railway Company, **6** 406
Metropolitan Edison Company, **27** 182
Metropolitan Estate and Property Corp. Ltd., **IV** 710–11
**Metropolitan Financial Corporation, 12** 165; **13 347–49**
Metropolitan Furniture Leasing, **14** 4
Metropolitan Gas Light Co., **6** 455

Metropolitan Housing Corp. Ltd., **IV** 710
**Metropolitan Life Insurance Company**, **II** 679; **III** 265–66, 272, **290–94**, 313, 329, 337, 339–40, 706; **IV** 283; **6** 256; **8** 326–27; **11** 482; **22** 266; **25** 300; **42** 194; **45** 411
Metropolitan National Bank, **II** 284
**Metropolitan Opera Association, Inc.**, **40** **320–23**
Metropolitan Petroleum Corp., **IV** 180–81; **19** 319
Metropolitan Railway, **6** 407
Metropolitan Railways Surplus Lands Co., **IV** 711
Metropolitan Reference Laboratories Inc., **26** 391
Metropolitan Tobacco Co., **15** 138
**Metropolitan Transportation Authority**, **35 290–92**
Metropolitan Vickers, **III** 670
METSA, Inc., **15** 363
**Metsä-Serla Oy**, **IV 314–16**, 318, 350
**Metso Corporation**, **30 321–25 (upd.)**
**Mettler-Toledo International Inc.**, **30** **326–28**
Mettler United States Inc., **9** 441
Metwest, **26** 391
Metz Baking Company, **36** 164
Metzdorf Advertising Agency, **30** 80
Metzeler Kautschuk, **15** 354
Mexican Eagle Oil Co., **IV** 365, 531
Mexican Metal Co. *See* Industrias Penoles, S.A. de C.V.
Mexican Original Products, Inc., **II** 585; **14** 515
**Mexican Restaurants, Inc.**, **41 269–71**
Mexofina, S.A. de C.V., **IV** 401
Meyer and Charlton, **IV** 90
Meyer Brothers Drug Company, **16** 212
Meyer Corporation, **27** 288
Meyerland Company, **19** 366
Meyers and Co., **III** 9
Meyers & Muldoon, **6** 40
Meyers Motor Supply, **26** 347
Meyers Parking, **18** 104
Meyr Melnhof Karton AG, **41** 325–27
Meyrin, **I** 122
MFI, **II** 612
**MFS Communications Company, Inc.**, **11 301–03**; **14** 253; **27** 301, 307
MG&E. *See* Madison Gas & Electric.
MG Holdings. *See* Mayflower Group Inc.
MG Ltd., **IV** 141
MGD Graphics Systems. *See* Goss Holdings, Inc.
MGIC Investment Corp., **45** 320
MGM. *See* McKesson General Medical.
**MGM Grand Inc.**, **III** 431; **6** 210; **17** **316–19**; **18** 336–37
MGM Mirage. *See* Mirage Resorts, Incorporated.
**MGM/UA Communications Company**, **I** 286, 487; **II** 103, 135, **146–50**, 155, 161, 167, 169, 174–75, 408; **IV** 676; **6** 172–73; **12** 73, 316, 323, 455; **15** 84; **17** 316. *See also* Metro-Goldwyn-Mayer Inc.
MH Alshaya Group, **28** 96
mh Bausparkasse AG, **III** 377
MH Media Monitoring Limited, **26** 270
MHI Group, Inc., **13** 356; **16** 344
MHS Holding Corp., **26** 101
MHT. *See* Manufacturers Hanover Trust Co.
MI. *See* Masco Corporation.
Miami Computer Supply Corporation. *See* MCSi, Inc.
Miami Power Corporation, **6** 466
Miami Subs Corp., **29** 342, 344
Micamold Electronics Manufacturing Corporation, **10** 319
Mich-Wis. *See* Michigan Wisconsin Pipe Line.
**Michael Anthony Jewelers, Inc.**, **24** **334–36**
**Michael Baker Corp.**, **14 333–35**
MICHAEL Business Systems Plc, **10** 257
**Michael Foods, Inc.**, **25 331–34**; **39** 319–321
Michael Joseph, **IV** 659
**Michael Page International plc**, **45** **272–74**
Michael Reese Health Plan Inc., **III** 82
Michael's Fair-Mart Food Stores, Inc., **19** 479
**Michaels Stores, Inc.**, **17 320–22**, 360; **25** 368
MichCon. *See* MCN Corporation.
Michelin, **III** 697; **7** 36–37; **8** 74; **11** 158, 473; **20** 261–62; **21** 72, 74; **28** 372. *See also* Compagnie Générale des Établissements Michelin.
Michelin et Compagnie, **V** 236
Michiana Merchandising, **III** 10
Michie Co., **IV** 312; **19** 268; **33** 264–65
Michigan Automotive Compressor, Inc., **III** 593, 638–39
Michigan Automotive Research Corporation, **23** 183
**Michigan Bell Telephone Co.**, **14** **336–38**; **18** 30
Michigan Carpet Sweeper Company, **9** 70
Michigan Consolidated Gas Company. *See* MCN Corporation.
Michigan Fruit Canners, **II** 571
Michigan General, **II** 408
Michigan International Speedway, **V** 494
Michigan Livestock Exchange, **36** 442
Michigan Motor Freight Lines, **14** 567
**Michigan National Corporation**, **11** **304–06**; **18** 517
Michigan Oil Company, **18** 494
Michigan Packaging Company, **15** 188
Michigan Plating and Stamping Co., **I** 451
Michigan Radiator & Iron Co., **III** 663
Michigan Shoe Makers. *See* Wolverine World Wide Inc.
Michigan Spring Company, **17** 106
Michigan State Life Insurance Co., **III** 274
Michigan Steel Corporation, **12** 352
Michigan Tag Company, **9** 72
Michigan Wisconsin Pipe Line, **39** 260
Mick's Inc., **30** 329
Mickey Shorr Mobile Electronics, **10** 9–11
Micro-Circuit, Inc., **III** 645
Micro Contract Manufacturing Inc., **44** 441
Micro D, Inc., **11** 194
Micro Decisionware, Inc., **10** 506
Micro Focus Inc., **27** 491
Micro Magic, Inc., **43** 254
Micro Peripherals, Inc., **18** 138
Micro-Power Corp., **III** 643
Micro Power Systems Inc., **14** 183
Micro Switch, **14** 284
Micro/Vest, **13** 175
**Micro Warehouse, Inc.**, **16 371–73**
**MicroAge, Inc.**, **16 367–70**; **29** 414
Microamerica, **12** 334
Microban Products Company, **27** 288
MicroBilt Corporation, **11** 112
Microcom, Inc., **26** 93
MicroComputer Accessories, **III** 614
Microcomputer Asset Management Services, **9** 168
Microcomputer Systems, **22** 389
**Microdot Inc.**, **I** 440; **8 365–68**, 545
Microfal, **I** 341
Microform International Marketing Corp., **IV** 642; **7** 312
Microfral, **14** 216
MicroFridge, **44** 273
Micromass Ltd., **43** 455
Micromedex, **19** 268
**Micron Technology, Inc.**, **III** 113; **11** **307–09**; **29 323–26 (upd.)**
Micropolis Corp., **10** 403, 458, 463
MicroPro International Corp., **10** 556. *See also* The Learning Company Inc.
Microprocessor Systems, **13** 235
Microprose Inc., **24** 538
**Micros Systems, Inc.**, **18 335–38**
Microseal Corp., **I** 341
Microsensor Systems Inc., **43** 366
**Microsoft Corporation**, **III** 116; **6** 219–20, 224, 227, 231, 235, 254–56, **257–60**, 269–71; **9** 81, 140, 171, 195, 472; **10** 22, 34, 57, 87, 119, 237–38, 362–63, 408, 477, 484, 504, 557–58; **11** 59, 77–78, 306, 519–20; **12** 180, 335; **13** 115, 128, 147, 482, 509; **14** 262–64, 318; **15** 132–33, 321, 371, 483, 492, 511; **16** 4, 94, 367, 392, 394, 444; **18** 24, 64, 66, 306–7, 345, 349, 367, 541, 543; **19** 310; **20** 237; **21** 86; **24** 120, 233, 236, 371; **25** 21, 32, 34, 96, 117, 119, 184, 298–301, 498–99, 509; **26** 17, 294–95, 441, 520; **27 319–23 (upd.)**, 448, 517; **28** 245, 301; **29** 65, 439; **30** 391, 450; **33** 115–16, 210; **34** 443, 445, 513; **36** 384; **37** 383; **38** 71, 416; **41** 53–54; **42** 424; **43** 240; **44** 97; **45** 200–02; **47** 419–21
Microsoft Network, **38** 270–71
Microtek, Inc., **22** 413
Microtel Limited, **6** 309–10
Microware Surgical Instruments Corp., **IV** 137
Microwave Communications, Inc., **V** 302; **27** 302
Mid-America Capital Resources, Inc., **6** 508
**Mid-America Dairymen, Inc.**, **II** 536; **7** **338–40**; **11** 24; **21** 342; **22** 95; **26** 448
Mid-America Industries, **III** 495
Mid-America Interpool Network, **6** 506, 602
Mid-America Packaging, Inc., **8** 203
Mid-America Tag & Label, **8** 360
Mid Bus Inc., **33** 107
Mid-Central Fish and Frozen Foods Inc., **II** 675
Mid-Continent Area Power Planner, **V** 672
Mid-Continent Computer Services, **11** 111
Mid-Continent Life Insurance Co., **23** 200
Mid-Continent Telephone Corporation. *See* Alltel Corporation.
Mid-Georgia Gas Company, **6** 448
Mid-Illinois Gas Co., **6** 529
Mid-Pacific Airlines, **9** 271; **24** 21–22
Mid-Packaging Group Inc., **19** 78
Mid-South Towing, **6** 583
Mid-States Development, Inc., **18** 405

Mid-Texas Communications Systems, **6** 313
Mid-Valley Dairy, **14** 397
Mid-West Drive-In Theatres Inc., **I** 245
Mid-West Paper Ltd., **IV** 286
MidAmerican Communications Corporation, **8** 311
**Midas International Corporation, I** 457–58; **10 414–15**, 554; **24** 337
MIDCO, **III** 340
MidCon, **IV** 481; **25** 363
Middle East Broadcasting Centre, Ltd., **25** 506, 508
Middle East Tube Co. Ltd., **25** 266
Middle South Utilities. *See* Entergy Corporation.
Middle West Corporation, **6** 469–70
Middle West Utilities Company, **V** 583–84; **6** 555–56, 604–05; **14** 227; **21** 468–69
Middle Wisconsin Power, **6** 604
Middleburg Steel and Alloys Group, **I** 423
**The Middleby Corporation, 22 352–55**
Middlesex Bank, **II** 334
**Middlesex Water Company, 45 275–78**
Middleton Aerospace, **48** 275
Middleton Packaging, **12** 377
Middleton's Starch Works, **II** 566
Middletown Manufacturing Co., Inc., **16** 321
Middletown National Bank, **13** 467
Midhurst Corp., **IV** 658
Midial, **II** 478
**Midland Bank plc, II** 208, 236, 279, 295, 298, **318–20**, 334, 383; **9** 505; **12** 257; **14** 169; **17 323–26 (upd.)**; **19** 198; **26** 202; **33** 395
Midland Brick, **14** 250
Midland Cooperative, **II** 536
Midland Counties Dairies, **II** 587
Midland Electric Coal Co., **IV** 170
Midland Enterprises Inc., **6** 486–88
Midland Gravel Co., **III** 670
Midland Independent Newspaper plc, **23** 351
Midland Industrial Finishes Co., **I** 321
Midland Insurance, **I** 473
Midland International, **8** 56–57
Midland Investment Co., **II** 7
Midland Linseed Products Co., **I** 419
Midland National Bank, **11** 130
Midland Railway Co., **II** 306
Midland-Ross Corporation, **14** 369
Midland Southwest Corp., **8** 347
Midland Steel Products Co., **13** 305–06
Midland United, **6** 556; **25** 89
Midland Utilities Company, **6** 532
Midlands Electricity, **13** 485
Midlands Energy Co., **IV** 83; **7** 188
Midlantic Corp., **13** 411
Midlantic Hotels Ltd., **41** 83
Midrange Performance Group, **12** 149
Midrex Corp., **IV** 130
Midvale Steel and Ordnance Co., **IV** 35, 114; **7** 48
**Midway Airlines Corporation, 6** 105, 120–21; **33 301–03**
**Midway Games, Inc., 25 335–38**
Midway Manufacturing Company, **III** 430; **15** 539
Midwest Agri-Commodities Company, **11** 15; **32** 29
Midwest Air Charter, **6** 345
Midwest Biscuit Company, **14** 306
Midwest Com of Indiana, Inc., **11** 112
Midwest Dairy Products, **II** 661
**Midwest Express Holdings, Inc., 35 293–95**; **43** 258
Midwest Federal Savings & Loan Association, **11** 162–63
Midwest Financial Group, Inc., **8** 188
Midwest Foundry Co., **IV** 137
Midwest Manufacturing Co., **12** 296
Midwest Realty Exchange, Inc., **21** 257
Midwest Refining Co., **IV** 368
**Midwest Resources Inc., 6 523–25**
Midwest Staffing Systems, **27** 21
Midwest Steel Corporation, **13** 157
Midwest Synthetics, **8** 553
Midwinter, **12** 529
Miele & Cie., **III** 418
MIG Realty Advisors, Inc., **25** 23, 25
Miguel Galas S.A., **17** 268
**MIH Limited, 31 329–32**
**Mikasa, Inc., 28 268–70**
**Mike-Sell's Inc., 15 298–300**
Mikemitch Realty Corp., **16** 36
Mikko, **II** 70
Mikko Kaloinen Oy, **IV** 349
**Mikohn Gaming Corporation, 39 276–79**
Mikon, Ltd., **13** 345
Milac, **27** 259
Milan A.C., S.p.A., **44** 387
Milani Foods, **II** 556; **36** 24
Milbank Insurance Co., **III** 350
**Milbank, Tweed, Hadley & McCloy, 27 324–27**
Milbank, Tweed, Hope & Webb, **II** 471
Milcor Steel Co., **IV** 114
Miles Druce & Co., **III** 494
Miles Inc., **22** 148
Miles Kimball Co., **9** 393
**Miles Laboratories, I** 310, **653–55**, 674, 678; **6** 50; **13** 76; **14** 558
Miles Redfern, **I** 429
Milgo Electronic Corp., **II** 83; **11** 408
Milgram Food Stores Inc., **II** 682
Milgray Electronics Inc., **19** 311; **47** 41
Milk Producers, Inc., **11** 24
Milk Specialties Co., **12** 199
Mill-Power Supply Company, **27** 129–30
Millbrook Press Inc., **IV** 616
Millennium Chemicals Inc., **30** 231; **45** 252, 254
**Millennium Pharmaceuticals, Inc., 47 249–52**
**Miller Brewing Company, I** 218–19, 236–37, 254–55, 257–58, **269–70**, 283, 290–91, 548; **10** 100; **11** 421; **12 337–39 (upd.)**, 372; **13** 10, 258; **15** 429; **17** 256; **18** 70, 72, 418, 499, 501; **21** 230; **22** 199, 422; **26** 303, 306; **27** 374; **28** 209–10; **34** 36–37; **36** 12–15; **44** 342
Miller Chemical & Fertilizer Corp., **I** 412
Miller Companies, **17** 182
Miller Container Corporation, **8** 102
Miller Freeman, Inc., **IV** 687; **27** 362; **28** 501, 504
Miller Group Ltd., **22** 282
**Miller Industries, Inc., 26 293–95**
Miller, Mason and Dickenson, **III** 204–05
Miller, Tabak, Hirsch & Co., **13** 394; **28** 164
Millet, **39** 250
Millet's Leisure, **V** 177–78
Millicom, **11** 547; **18** 254
**Milliken & Co., V 366–68**; **8** 270–71; **17 327–30 (upd.)**; **29** 246
Milliken, Tomlinson Co., **II** 682
**Millipore Corporation, 9** 396; **23** 284; **25 339–43**; **43** 454
Mills Clothing, Inc. *See* The Buckle, Inc.
Millstone Point Company, **V** 668–69
Millville Electric Light Company, **6** 449
Millway Foods, **25** 85
Milne & Craighead, **48** 113
Milne Fruit Products, Inc., **25** 366
Milner, **III** 98
**Milnot Company, 46 289–91**
Milsco Manufacturing Co., **23** 299, 300
**Milton Bradley Company, III** 504–06; **16** 267; **17** 105; **21 372–75**; **25** 380; **43** 229, 232
Milton Light & Power Company, **12** 45
Milton Roy Co., **8** 135
Milupa S.A., **37** 341
**Milwaukee Brewers Baseball Club, 37 247–49**
Milwaukee Cheese Co. Inc., **25** 517
Milwaukee Electric Manufacturing Co., **III** 534
Milwaukee Electric Railway and Light Company, **6** 601–02, 604–05
Milwaukee Electric Tool, **28** 40
Milwaukee Insurance Co., **III** 242
Milwaukee Mutual Fire Insurance Co., **III** 321
Minatome, **IV** 560
Mindpearl, **48** 381
Mindport, **31** 329
Mindset Corp., **42** 424–25
Mindspring Enterprises, Inc., **36** 168
**Mine Safety Appliances Company, 31 333–35**
Minemet Recherche, **IV** 108
**The Miner Group International, 22 356–58**
Mineral Point Public Service Company, **6** 604
Minerales y Metales, S.A. *See* Industrias Penoles, S.A. de C.V.
Minerals & Chemicals Philipp, **IV** 79–80
**Minerals & Metals Trading Corporation of India Ltd., IV 143–44**
Minerals and Resources Corporation Limited, **IV** 23; **13** 502. *See also* Minorco.
**Minerals Technologies Inc., 11 310–12**
Minerec Corporation, **9** 363
Minerva, **III** 359
Minerve, **6** 208
Mines et Usines du Nord et de l'Est, **IV** 226
Minet Group, **III** 357; **22** 494–95
Mini Stop, **V** 97
Mining and Technical Services, **IV** 67
Mining Corp. of Canada Ltd., **IV** 164
Mining Development Corp., **IV** 239–40
Mining Trust Ltd., **IV** 32
MiniScribe, Inc., **6** 230; **10** 404
Minister of Finance Inc., **IV** 519
Minitel, **21** 233
Minivator Ltd., **11** 486
Minneapolis General Electric of Minnesota, **V** 670
Minneapolis Heat Regulator Co., **II** 40–41; **12** 246
Minneapolis-Honeywell Regulator Co., **II** 40–41, 86; **8** 21; **12** 247; **22** 427
Minneapolis Millers Association, **10** 322

Minneapolis Steel and Machinery Company, **21** 502
Minnesota Brewing Company. *See* MBC Holding Company.
Minnesota Cooperative Creamery Association, Inc., **II** 535; **21** 340
Minnesota Linseed Oil Co., **8** 552
**Minnesota Mining & Manufacturing Company**, **I** 28, 387, **499–501**; **II** 39; **III** 476, 487, 549; **IV** 251, 253–54; **6** 231; **7** 162; **8** 35, **369–71 (upd.)**; **11** 494; **13** 326; **17** 29–30; **22** 427; **25** 96, 372; **26 296–99 (upd.)**
Minnesota Paints, **8** 552–53
**Minnesota Power & Light Company**, **11 313–16**
**Minnesota Power, Inc.**, **34 286–91 (upd.)**
Minnesota Sugar Company, **11** 13
Minnesota Valley Canning Co., **I** 22
Minnetonka Corp., **II** 590; **III** 25; **22** 122–23
**Minntech Corporation**, **22 359–61**
Minn-Dak Farmers Cooperative, **32** 29
**Minolta Camera Co., Ltd.**, **III 574–76**, 583–84
**Minolta Co., Ltd.**, **18** 93, 186, **339–42 (upd.)**; **43 281–85 (upd.)**
Minorco, **III** 503; **IV** 67–68, 84, 97; **16** 28, 293
Minstar Inc., **11** 397; **15** 49; **45** 174
Minton China, **38** 401
**The Minute Maid Company**, **I** 234; **10** 227; **28 271–74**, 473; **32** 116
Minute Tapioca, **II** 531
**Minuteman International Inc.**, **46 292–95**
**Minyard Food Stores, Inc.**, **33 304–07**
Mippon Paper, **21** 546
MIPS Computer Systems, **II** 45; **11** 491
Miracle Food Mart, **16** 247, 249–50
Miracle-Gro Products, Inc., **22** 474
Miraflores Designs Inc., **18** 216
**Mirage Resorts, Incorporated**, **6 209–12**; **15** 238; **28 275–79 (upd.)**; **29** 127; **43** 82
Miramar Hotel & Investment Co., **IV** 717; **38** 318
Mirant, **39** 54, 57
Mircali Asset Management, **III** 340
Mircor Inc., **12** 413
Mirrlees Blackstone, **III** 509
**Mirror Group Newspapers plc**, **IV** 641; **7** 244, 312, **341–43**; **23 348–51 (upd.)**
Mirror Printing and Binding House, **IV** 677
Misceramic Tile, Inc., **14** 42
Misr Airwork. *See* AirEgypt.
Misr Bank of Cairo, **27** 132
Misrair. *See* AirEgypt.
Miss Erika, Inc., **27** 346, 348
Miss Selfridge, **V** 177–78
Misset Publishers, **IV** 611
Mission Energy Company, **V** 715
Mission First Financial, **V** 715
Mission Group, **V** 715, 717
Mission Insurance Co., **III** 192
Mission Jewelers, **30** 408
**Mississippi Chemical Corporation**, **8** 183; **IV** 367; **27** 316; **39 280–83**
Mississippi Drug, **III** 10
Mississippi Gas Company, **6** 577
Mississippi Power & Light, **V** 619
Mississippi Power Company, **38** 446–47
Mississippi River Corporation, **10** 44
Mississippi River Recycling, **31** 47, 49
Missoula Bancshares, Inc., **35** 198–99
Missouri Book Co., **10** 136
Missouri Fur Company, **25** 220
Missouri Gaming Company, **21** 39
Missouri Gas & Electric Service Company, **6** 593
Missouri-Kansas-Texas Railroad, **I** 472; **IV** 458
Missouri Pacific Railroad, **10** 43–44
Missouri Public Service Company. *See* UtiliCorp United Inc.
Missouri Utilities Company, **6** 580
Mist Assist, Inc. *See* Ballard Medical Products.
Mistik Beverages, **18** 71
Mistral Plastics Pty Ltd., **IV** 295; **19** 225
**Misys PLC**, **45 279–81**; **46 296–99**
Mitchel & King Skates Ltd., **17** 244
Mitchell Construction, **III** 753
**Mitchell Energy and Development Corporation**, **7 344–46**
Mitchell Home Savings and Loan, **13** 347
Mitchell Hutchins, Inc., **II** 445; **22** 405–06
Mitchell International, **8** 526
Mitchells & Butler, **I** 223
Mitchum Co., **III** 55
Mitchum, Jones & Templeton, **II** 445; **22** 405
MiTek Industries Inc., **IV** 259
MiTek Wood Products, **IV** 305
**Mitel Corporation**, **15** 131–32; **18 343–46**
MitNer Group, **7** 377
**MITRE Corporation**, **26 300–02**
Mitre Sport U.K., **17** 204–05
**MITROPA AG**, **37 250–53**
Mitsubishi Aircraft Co., **III** 578; **7** 348; **9** 349; **11** 164
**Mitsubishi Bank, Ltd.**, **II** 57, 273–74, 276, **321–22**, 323, 392, 459; **III** 289, 577–78; **7** 348; **15** 41; **16** 496, 498. *See also* Bank of Tokyo-Mitsubishi Ltd.
**Mitsubishi Chemical Industries Ltd.**, **I** 319, **363–64**, 398; **II** 57; **III** 666, 760; **11** 207
**Mitsubishi Corporation**, **I** 261, 431–32, 492, **502–04**, 505–06, 510, 515, 519–20; **II** 57, 59, 101, 118, 224, 292, 321–25, 374; **III** 577–78; **IV** 285, 518, 713; **6** 499; **7** 82, 233, 590; **9** 294; **12 340–43 (upd.)**; **17** 349, 556; **24** 325, 359; **27** 511
**Mitsubishi Electric Corporation**, **II** 53, **57–59**, 68, 73, 94, 122; **III** 577, 586; **7** 347, 394; **18** 18; **23** 52–53; **43** 15; **44 283–87 (upd.)**
**Mitsubishi Estate Company, Limited**, **IV 713–14**
Mitsubishi Foods, **24** 114
Mitsubishi Group, **V** 481–82; **7** 377; **21** 390
**Mitsubishi Heavy Industries, Ltd.**, **II** 57, 75, 323, 440; **III** 452–53, 487, 532, 538, **577–79**, 685, 713; **IV** 184, 713; **7 347–50 (upd.)**; **8** 51; **9** 349–50; **10** 33; **13** 507; **15** 92; **24** 359; **40 324–28 (upd.)**
Mitsubishi International Corp., **16** 462
Mitsubishi Kasei Corp., **III** 47–48, 477; **8** 343; **14** 535
Mitsubishi Kasei Industry Co. Ltd., **IV** 476
Mitsubishi Marine, **III** 385
**Mitsubishi Materials Corporation**, **III 712–13**; **IV** 554; **38** 463
**Mitsubishi Motors Corporation**, **III** 516–17, 578–79; **6** 28; **7** 219, 348–49; **8** 72, 374; **9 349–51**; **23 352–55 (upd.)**; **34** 128, 136; **40** 326
**Mitsubishi Oil Co., Ltd.**, **IV 460–62**, 479, 492
Mitsubishi Paper Co., **III** 547
**Mitsubishi Rayon Co. Ltd.**, **I** 330; **V 369–71**; **8** 153
Mitsubishi Sha Holdings, **IV** 554
Mitsubishi Shipbuilding Co. Ltd., **II** 57; **III** 513, 577–78; **7** 348; **9** 349
Mitsubishi Shokai, **III** 577; **IV** 713; **7** 347
Mitsubishi Trading Co., **IV** 460
**Mitsubishi Trust & Banking Corporation**, **II 323–24**; **III** 289
**Mitsui & Co., Ltd.**, **I** 282; **IV** 18, 224, 432, 654–55; **V** 142; **6** 346; **7** 303; **13** 356; **24** 325, 488–89; **27** 337; **28 280–85 (upd.)**
**Mitsui Bank, Ltd.**, **II** 273–74, 291, **325–27**, 328, 372; **III** 295–97; **IV** 147, 320; **V** 142; **17** 556
**Mitsui Bussan K.K.**, **I** 363, 431–32, 469, 492, 502–04, **505–08**, 510, 515, 519, 533; **II** 57, 66, 101, 224, 292, 323, 325–28, 392; **III** 295–96, 717–18; **IV** 147, 431; **9** 352–53. *See also* Mitsui & Co., Ltd.
Mitsui Gomei Kaisha, **IV** 715
Mitsui Group, **9** 352; **16** 84; **20** 310; **21** 72
Mitsui House Code, **V** 142
Mitsui Light Metal Processing Co., **III** 758
**Mitsui Marine and Fire Insurance Company, Limited**, **III** 209, **295–96**, 297
**Mitsui Mining & Smelting Co., Ltd.**, **IV 145–46**, 147–48
**Mitsui Mining Company, Limited**, **IV** 145, **147–49**
**Mitsui Mutual Life Insurance Company**, **III 297–98**; **39 284–86 (upd.)**
Mitsui-no-Mori Co., Ltd., **IV** 716
**Mitsui O.S.K. Lines, Ltd.**, **I** 520; **IV** 383; **V 473–76**; **6** 398; **26** 278–80
**Mitsui Petrochemical Industries, Ltd.**, **I** 390, 516; **9 352–54**
**Mitsui Real Estate Development Co., Ltd.**, **IV 715–16**
Mitsui Shipbuilding and Engineering Co., **III** 295, 513
Mitsui Toatsu, **9** 353–54
Mitsui Trading, **III** 636
**Mitsui Trust & Banking Company, Ltd.**, **II 328**; **III** 297
**Mitsukoshi Ltd.**, **I** 508; **V 142–44**; **14** 502; **41** 114; **47** 391
Mitsuya Foods Co., **I** 221
Mitteldeutsche Creditbank, **II** 256
Mitteldeutsche Energieversorgung AG, **V** 747
Mitteldeutsche Privatbank, **II** 256
Mitteldeutsche Stickstoff-Werke Ag, **IV** 229–30
Mitteldeutsches Kraftwerk, **IV** 229
**Mity Enterprises, Inc.**, **38 310–12**
Mixconcrete (Holdings), **III** 729
Miyoshi Electrical Manufacturing Co., **II** 6
**Mizuno Corporation**, **25 344–46**
Mizushima Ethylene Co. Ltd., **IV** 476
MJB Coffee Co., **I** 28
MK-Ferguson Company, **7** 356
MLC Ltd., **IV** 709

MLH&P. *See* Montreal Light, Heat & Power Company.
MLT Vacations Inc., **30** 446
MMAR Group Inc., **19** 131
MMC Networks Inc., **38** 53, 55
MML Investors Services, **III** 286
MMS America Corp., **26** 317
MNC Financial. *See* MBNA Corporation.
MNC Financial Corp., **11** 447
MND Drilling, **7** 345
MNet, **11** 122
**Mo och Domsjö AB**, **IV** 315, **317–19**, 340
Moa Bay Mining Co., **IV** 82; **7** 186
Mobay, **I** 310–11; **13** 76
**Mobil Corporation**, **I** 30, 34, 403, 478; **II** 379; **IV** 93, 295, 363, 386, 401, 403, 406, 423, 428, 454, **463–65**, 466, 472–74, 486, 492, 504–05, 515, 517, 522, 531, 538–39, 545, 554–55, 564, 570–71; **V** 147–48; **6** 530; **7** 171, **351–54 (upd.)**; **8** 552–53; **9** 546; **10** 440; **12** 348; **16** 489; **17** 363, 415; **19** 140, 225, 297; **21 376–80 (upd.)**; **24** 496, 521; **25** 232, 445; **26** 369; **32** 175, 179, 181; **45** 50
Mobil Oil Australia, **24** 399
Mobile America Housing Corporation. *See* American Homestar Corporation.
Mobile and Ohio Railroad, **I** 456
Mobile Corporation, **25** 232
Mobile Mini, Inc., **21** 476
**Mobile Telecommunications Technologies Corp.**, **V** 277–78; **6** 323; **16** 74; **18 347–49**
Mobile Telesystems, **48** 419
Mobilefone, Inc., **25** 108
MobileMedia Corp., **39** 23, 24
MobileStar Network Corp., **26** 429
Mobira, **II** 69; **17** 353
Mobley Chemical, **I** 342
Mobu Company, **6** 431
Mobujidosha Bus Company, **6** 431
MOÇACOR, **IV** 505
Mocatta and Goldsmid Ltd., **II** 357
Mochida Pharaceutical Co. Ltd., **II** 553
Moctezuma Copper Co., **IV** 176–77
Modar, **17** 279
Mode 1 Communications, Inc., **48** 305
Modell's Shoppers World, **16** 35–36
Modell's Sporting Goods. *See* Henry Modell & Company Inc.
Modeluxe Linge Services SA, **45** 139–40
Modem Media, **23** 479
Modern Equipment Co., **I** 412
Modern Furniture Rentals Inc., **14** 4; **27** 163
Modern Handling Methods Ltd., **21** 499
Modern Maid Food Products, **II** 500
Modern Merchandising Inc., **19** 396
Modern Patterns and Plastics, **III** 641
**Modern Times Group AB**, **36 335–38**
Modernistic Industries Inc., **7** 589
**Modine Manufacturing Company**, **8 372–75**
MoDo. *See* Mo och Domsjö AB.
MoDo Paper AB, **28** 446
**Moen Incorporated**, **12 344–45**
**Moët-Hennessy**, **I 271–72**; **10** 397–98; **23** 238, 240, 242. *See also* LVMH Moët Hennessy Louis Vuitton SA.
Mogen David. *See* The Wine Group, Inc.
Mogul Corp., **I** 321; **17** 287
The Mogul Metal Company. *See* Federal-Mogul Corporation.
Mohasco Corporation, **15** 102; **26** 100–01
Mohawk & Hudson Railroad, **9** 369
Mohawk Airlines, **I** 131; **6** 131
Mohawk Carpet Corp., **26** 101
**Mohawk Industries, Inc.**, **19 274–76**; **31** 199
Mohawk Rubber Co. Ltd., **V** 256; **7** 116; **19** 508
**Mohegan Tribal Gaming Authority**, **37 254–57**
Mohr-Value Stores, **8** 555
Moilliet and Sons, **II** 306
Mojave Foods Corporation, **27** 299
Mojo MDA Group Ltd., **11** 50–51; **43** 412
Mokta. *See* Compagnie de Mokta.
MOL. *See* Mitsui O.S.K. Lines, Ltd.
Molecular Biosystems, **III** 61
**Molex Incorporated**, **II** 8; **11 317–19**; **14** 27
Moline National Bank, **III** 463; **21** 173
Molinera de México S.A. de C.V., **31** 236
Molinos de Puerto Rico, **II** 493
Molinos Nacionales C.A., **7** 242–43; **25** 241
Molins Co., **IV** 326
Molkerie-Zentrak Sud GmbH, **II** 575
Moll Plasticrafters, L.P., **17** 534
Molloy Manufacturing Co., **III** 569; **20** 360
Mölnlycke AB, **IV** 338–39; **28** 443–45; **36** 26
**The Molson Companies Limited**, **I 273–75**, 333; **II** 210; **7** 183–84; **12** 338; **13** 150, 199; **21** 320; **23** 404; **25** 279; **26 303–07 (upd.)**; **36** 15
Molycorp, **IV** 571; **24** 521
Mon-Dak Chemical Inc., **16** 270
Mon-Valley Transportation Company, **11** 194
Mona Meyer McGrath & Gavin, **47** 97
MONACA. *See* Molinos Nacionales C.A.
**Monaco Coach Corporation**, **31 336–38**
**Monadnock Paper Mills, Inc.**, **21 381–84**
Monarch Air Lines, **22** 219
Monarch Development Corporation, **38** 451–52
Monarch Food Ltd., **II** 571
Monarch Foods, **26** 503
Monarch Marking Systems, **III** 157
MonArk Boat, **III** 444; **22** 116
Mond Nickel Co., **IV** 110–11
Mondadori. *See* Arnoldo Monadori Editore S.p.A.
Mondex International, **18** 543
Mondi Foods BV, **41** 12
Mondi Paper Co., **IV** 22
Moneris Solutions Corp., **46** 55
Monet Jewelry, **II** 502–03; **9** 156–57; **10** 323–24
Money Access Service Corp., **11** 467
**Monfort, Inc.**, **13 350–52**
Monheim Group, **II** 521
Monier Roof Tile, **III** 687, 735
Monis Wineries, **I** 288
Monitor Dynamics Inc., **24** 510
Monitor Group Inc., **33** 257
Monk-Austin Inc., **12** 110
Monmouth Pharmaceuticals Ltd., **16** 439
Monochem, **II** 472; **22** 93
Monogram Aerospace Fasteners, Inc., **11** 536
Monogram Models, **25** 312
Monogramme Confections, **6** 392
Monolithic Memories Inc., **6** 216; **16** 316–17, 549
Monon Corp., **13** 550
Monon Railroad, **I** 472
Monongahela Power, **38** 40
Monoprix, **V** 57–59
**Monro Muffler Brake, Inc.**, **24 337–40**
Monroe Auto Equipment, **I** 527
Monroe Calculating Machine Co., **I** 476, 484
Monroe Cheese Co., **II** 471
Monroe Savings Bank, **11** 109
Monrovia Aviation Corp., **I** 544
**Monsanto Company**, **I** 310, 363, **365–67**, 402, 631, 666, 686, 688; **III** 741; **IV** 290, 367, 379, 401; **8** 398; **9** 318, **355–57 (upd.)**, 466; **12** 186; **13** 76, 225; **16** 460–62; **17** 131; **18** 112; **22** 107; **23** 170–71; **26** 108; **29 327–31 (upd.)**; **33** 135; **34** 179; **41** 306
Monsavon, **III** 46–47
**Monsoon plc**, **39 287–89**
Mont Blanc, **17** 5; **27** 487, 489
Montabert S.A., **15** 226
Montan TNT Pty Ltd., **27** 473
Montan Transport GmbH, **IV** 140
Montana-Dakota Utilities Co., **7** 322–23; **37** 281–82; **42** 249–50, 252
Montana Enterprises Inc., **I** 114
**The Montana Power Company**, **6** 566; **7** 322; **11 320–22**; **37** 280, 283; **44 288–92 (upd.)**
Montana Refining Company, **12** 240–41
Montana Resources, Inc., **IV** 34
Montaup Electric Co., **14** 125
MontBell America, Inc., **29** 279
Montecatini, **I** 368; **IV** 421, 470, 486
**Montedison S.p.A.**, **I 368–69**; **IV** 413, 421–22, 454, 499; **14** 17; **22** 262; **24 341–44 (upd.)**; **26** 367; **36** 185–86, 188
Montefibre, **I** 369
Montefina, **IV** 499; **26** 367
Montell N.V., **24** 343
Monterey Homes Corporation. *See* Meritage Corporation.
Monterey Mfg. Co., **12** 439
Monterey's Acquisition Corp., **41** 270
Monterey's Tex-Mex Cafes, **13** 473
Monterrey, Compania de Seguros sobre la Vida. *See* Seguros Monterrey.
Monterrey Group, **19** 10–11, 189
Montfort of Colorado, Inc., **II** 494
Montgomery Elevator Company, **27** 269
**Montgomery Ward & Co., Incorporated**, **III** 762; **IV** 465; **V 145–48**; **7** 353; **8** 509; **9** 210; **10** 10, 116, 172, 305, 391, 393, 490–91; **12** 48, 309, 315, 335, 430; **13** 165; **15** 330, 470; **17** 460; **18** 477; **20** 263, **374–79 (upd.)**, 433; **22** 535; **25** 144; **27** 428–30; **43** 292
Montiel Corporation, **17** 321
Montinex, **24** 270
Montreal Bank, **II** 210
Montreal Engineering Company, **6** 585
Montreal Light, Heat & Power Consolidated, **6** 501–02
Montreal Mining Co., **17** 357
**Montres Rolex S.A.**, **8** 477; **13 353–55**; **19** 452; **34 292–95 (upd.)**
Montrose Capital, **36** 358
Montrose Chemical Company, **9** 118, 119
Montrose Chrome, **IV** 92
Monument Property Trust Ltd., **IV** 710
Monumental Corp., **III** 179

MONYCo., **III** 306
Moody's Investment Service, **IV** 605; **16** 506; **19** 133; **22** 189
**Moog Inc., 13 356–58**
Moon-Hopkins Billing Machine, **III** 165
Mooney Chemicals, Inc. *See* OM Group, Inc.
Moonlight Mushrooms, Inc. *See* Sylvan, Inc.
Moonstone Mountaineering, Inc., **29** 181
Moore and McCormack Co. Inc., **19** 40
**Moore Corporation Limited, IV 644–46,** 679; **15** 473; **16** 450; **36** 508
Moore Gardner & Associates, **22** 88
The Moore Group Ltd., **20** 363
**Moore-Handley, Inc., IV** 345–46; **39 290–92**
Moore McCormack Resources Inc., **14** 455
**Moore Medical Corp., 17 331–33**
Moorhouse, **II** 477
Moran Group Inc., **II** 682
Moran Health Care Group Ltd., **25** 455
MoRan Oil & Gas Co., **IV** 82–83
**Moran Towing Corporation, Inc., 15 301–03**
Morana, Inc., **9** 290
Moreland and Watson, **IV** 208
Moretti-Harrah Marble Co., **III** 691
Morgan & Banks Limited, **30** 460
Morgan & Cie International S.A., **II** 431
Morgan Construction Company, **8** 448
Morgan Edwards, **II** 609
Morgan Engineering Co., **8** 545
Morgan Grampian Group, **IV** 687
**Morgan Grenfell Group PLC, II** 280, 329, **427–29**; **IV** 21, 712
**The Morgan Group, Inc., 46 300–02**
Morgan Guaranty International Banking Corp., **II** 331; **9** 124
Morgan Guaranty Trust Co. of New York, **I** 26; **II** 208, 254, 262, 329–32, 339, 428, 431, 448; **III** 80; **10** 150
Morgan Guaranty Trust Company, **11** 421; **13** 49, 448; **14** 297; **25** 541; **30** 261
Morgan, Harjes & Co., **II** 329
Morgan, J.P. & Co. Inc. *See* J.P. Morgan & Co. Incorporated.
**Morgan, Lewis & Bockius LLP, 29 332–34**
Morgan, Lewis, Githens & Ahn, Inc., **6** 410
Morgan Mitsubishi Development, **IV** 714
Morgan Schiff & Co., **29** 205
**Morgan Stanley Dean Witter & Company, 33 311–14 (upd.)**; **38** 289, 291, 411
**Morgan Stanley Group, Inc., I** 34; **II** 211, 330, 403, 406–08, 422, 428, **430–32**, 441; **IV** 295, 447, 714; **9** 386; **11** 258; **12** 529; **16 374–78 (upd.)**; **18** 448–49; **20** 60, 363; **22** 404, 407; **25** 542; **30** 353–55; **34** 496; **36** 153
Morgan Yacht Corp., **II** 468
Morgan's Brewery, **I** 287
Mori Bank, **II** 291
Moria Informatique, **6** 229
Morino Associates, **10** 394
Morita & Co., **II** 103
Mormac Marine Group, **15** 302
Morning Star Technologies Inc., **24** 49
Morning Sun, Inc., **23** 66
Morris Air, **24** 455
**Morris Communications Corporation, 36 339–42**
Morris Motors, **III** 256; **7** 459
**Morris Travel Services L.L.C., 26 308–11**
Morrison Industries Ltd., **IV** 278; **19** 153
**Morrison Knudsen Corporation, IV** 55; **7 355–58**; **11** 401, 553; **28 286–90 (upd.)**; **33** 442. *See also* The Washington Companies.
Morrison Machine Products Inc., **25** 193
**Morrison Restaurants Inc., 11 323–25**; **18** 464
Morse Chain Co., **III** 439; **14** 63
Morse Equalizing Spring Company, **14** 63
Morse Industrial, **14** 64
**Morse Shoe Inc., 13 359–61**
Morss and White, **III** 643
Morstan Development Co., Inc., **II** 432
Mortgage & Trust Co., **II** 251
Mortgage Associates, **9** 229
Mortgage Insurance Co. of Canada, **II** 222
Mortgage Resources, Inc., **10** 91
Morton Foods, Inc., **II** 502; **10** 323; **27** 258
**Morton International Inc., 9 358–59 (upd.)**, 500–01; **16** 436; **22** 505–06; **43** 319
**Morton Thiokol Inc., I** 325, **370–72**; **19** 508; **28** 253–54. *See also* Thiokol Corporation.
**Morton's Restaurant Group, Inc., 28** 401; **30 329–31**
Mos Magnetics, **18** 140
MOS Technology, **7** 95
Mosby-Year Book, Inc., **IV** 678; **17** 486
Moseley, Hallgarten, Estabrook, and Weeden, **III** 389
Mosher Steel Company, **7** 540
**Mosinee Paper Corporation, 15 304–06**
Moskatel's, Inc., **17** 321
Mosler Safe Co., **III** 664–65; **7** 144, 146; **22** 184
Moss-Rouse Company, **15** 412
Mossgas, **IV** 93
**Mossimo, Inc., 27 328–30**
Mostek Corp., **I** 85; **II** 64; **11** 307–08; **13** 191; **20** 175; **29** 323
Mostjet Ltd. *See* British World Airlines Ltd.
Móstoles Industrial S.A., **26** 129
Mostra Importaciones S.A., **34** 38, 40
**Motel 6 Corporation, 10** 13; **13 362–64.** *See also* Accor SA
Mother Karen's, **10** 216
Mother's Oats, **II** 558–59; **12** 409
Mothercare Stores, Inc., **16** 466
**Mothercare UK Ltd., 17** 42–43, **334–36**
**Mothers Work, Inc., 18 350–52**
Motif Inc., **22** 288
Motion Designs, **11** 486
Motion Factory, Inc., **38** 72
Motion Picture Association of America, **37** 353–54
Motion Picture Corporation of America, **25** 326, 329
Motiva Enterprises LLC, **41** 359, 395
MotivePower. *See* Wabtec Corporation.
**The Motley Fool, Inc., 40 329–31**
**Moto Photo, Inc., 45 282–84**
Moto-Truc Co., **13** 385
**Motor Cargo Industries, Inc., 35 296–99**
Motor Club of America Insurance Company, **44** 354
Motor Coaches Industries International Inc., **36** 132
Motor Haulage Co., **IV** 181
Motor Parts Industries, Inc., **9** 363
Motor Transit Corp., **I** 448; **10** 72
Motor Wheel Corporation, **20** 261; **27** 202–04
**Motorcar Parts & Accessories, Inc., 47 253–55**
Motoren-und-Turbinen-Union, **I** 151; **III** 563; **9** 418; **15** 142; **34** 128, 131, 133
Motoren-Werke Mannheim AG, **III** 544
Motorenfabrik Deutz AG, **III** 541
Motorenfabrik Oberursel, **III** 541
Motornetic Corp., **III** 590
**Motorola, Inc., I** 534; **II** 5, 34, 44–45, 56, **60–62**, 64; **III** 455; **6** 238; **7** 119, 494, 533; **8** 139; **9** 515; **10** 87, 365, 367, 431–33; **11** 45, 308, **326–29 (upd.)**, 381–82; **12** 136–37, 162; **13** 30, 356, 501; **17** 33, 193; **18** 18, 74, 76, 260, 382; **19** 391; **20** 8, 439; **21** 123; **22** 17, 19, 288, 542; **26** 431–32; **27** 20, 341–42, 344; **33** 47–48; **34 296–302 (upd.)**; **38** 188; **43** 15; **44** 97, 357, 359; **45** 346, 348; **47** 318, 320, 385; **48** 270, 272
**Motown Records Company L.P., II** 145; **22** 194; **23** 389, 391; **26 312–14**
**Moulinex S.A., 22 362–65**
Mound Metalcraft. *See* Tonka Corporation.
Mount. *See also* Mt.
Mount Hood Credit Life Insurance Agency, **14** 529
Mount Isa Mines, **IV** 61
Mount Vernon Group, **8** 14
Mountain Fuel Supply Company. *See* Questar Corporation.
Mountain Fuel Supply Company, **6** 568–69
Mountain Pass Canning Co., **7** 429
Mountain Safety Research, **18** 445–46
Mountain State Telephone Company, **6** 300
**Mountain States Mortgage Centers, Inc., 29 335–37**
Mountain States Power Company. *See* PacifiCorp.
Mountain States Telephone & Telegraph Co., **V** 341; **25** 495
Mountain States Wholesale, **II** 602; **30** 25
Mountain Valley Indemnity Co., **44** 356
Mountain West Bank, **35** 197
Mountleigh PLC, **16** 465
Mounts Wire Industries, **III** 673
Mountsorrel Granite Co., **III** 734
**Mouvement des Caisses Desjardins, 48 288–91**
**Movado Group, Inc., 28 291–94**
Movado-Zenith-Mondia Holding, **II** 124
**Movie Gallery, Inc., 31 339–41**
**Movie Star Inc., 17 337–39**
Movies To Go, Inc., **9** 74; **31** 57
Movil@ccess, S.A. de C.V., **39** 25, 194
Moving Co. Ltd., **V** 127
The Moving Picture Company, **15** 83
The Mowry Co., **23** 102
MPB Corporation, **8** 529, 531
MPI. *See* Michael Page International plc.
MPM, **III** 735
MP3.com, **43** 109
**Mr. Bricolage S.A., 37 258–60**
**Mr. Coffee, Inc., 14** 229–31; **15 307–09**; **17** 215; **27** 275; **39** 406
Mr. D's Food Centers, **12** 112
Mr. Donut, **21** 323
**Mr. Gasket Inc., 11** 84; **15 310–12**
Mr. Gatti's, **15** 345

Mr. Goodbuys, **13** 545
Mr. How, **V** 191–92
Mr. M Food Stores, **7** 373
Mr. Maintenance, **25** 15
Mr. Payroll Corp., **20** 113
MRC Bearings, **III** 624
MRN Radio Network, **19** 223
**Mrs. Baird's Bakeries, 29 338–41**
**Mrs. Fields' Original Cookies, Inc., 27 331–35**
Mrs. Paul's Kitchens, **II** 480; **26** 57–58
Mrs. Smith's Frozen Foods, **II** 525; **13** 293–94; **35** 181
MS-Relais GmbH, **III** 710; **7** 302–03
MSAS Cargo International, **6** 415, 417
MSE Corporation, **33** 44
MSI Data Corp., **10** 523; **15** 482
M6. *See* Métropole Télévision.
MSL Industries, **10** 44
MSNBC, **28** 301
MSR. *See* Mountain Safety Research.
MSU. *See* Middle South Utilities.
Mt. *See also* Mount.
Mt. Beacon Insurance Co., **26** 486
Mt. Carmel Public Utility Company, **6** 506
Mt. Goldsworthy Mining Associates, **IV** 47
Mt. Lyell Investments, **III** 672–73
**Mt. Olive Pickle Company, Inc., 44 293–95**
Mt. Summit Rural Telephone Company, **14** 258
Mt. Vernon Iron Works, **II** 14
MTC. *See* Management and Training Corporation.
MTC Pharmaceuticals, **II** 483
MTel. *See* Mobile Telecommunications Technologies Corp.
MTG. *See* Modern Times Group AB.
MTM Entertainment Inc., **13** 279, 281
**MTS Inc., 37 261–64**
MTV, **31** 239
MTV Asia, **23** 390
MTVi Group, **37** 194
Muehlens KG, **48** 422
Mueller Co., **III** 645; **28** 485
Mueller Furniture Company, **8** 252; **39** 206
**Mueller Industries, Inc., 7 359–61**
Mujirushi Ryohin, **V** 188
Mukluk Freight Lines, **6** 383
Mule Battery Manufacturing Co., **III** 643
Mule-Hide Products Co., **22** 15
Mülheimer Bergwerksvereins, **I** 542
Mullen Advertising, **13** 513
Mullens & Co., **14** 419
Multex Systems, **21** 70
Multi Restaurants, **II** 664
Multibank Inc., **11** 281
Multicom Publishing Inc., **11** 294
Multilink, Inc., **27** 364–65
MultiMed, **11** 379
**Multimedia Games, Inc., 41 272–76**
**Multimedia, Inc., IV** 591; **11 330–32**; **30** 217
Multimedia Security Services, Inc., **32** 374
Multiple Access Systems Corp., **III** 109
Multiple Properties, **I** 588
MultiScope Inc., **10** 508
Multitech International. *See* Acer Inc.
Multiview Cable, **24** 121
Münchener Rückversicherungs-Gesellschaft. *See* Munich Re.
Munford, Inc., **17** 499
Mungana Mines, **I** 438
**Munich Re (Münchener Rückversicherungs-Gesellschaft Aktiengesellschaft in München), II** 239; **III** 183–84, 202, **299–301**, 400–01, 747; **35** 34, 37; **46 303–07 (upd.)**
Municipal Assistance Corp., **II** 448
Munising Paper Co., **III** 40; **13** 156; **16** 303; **43** 257
Munising Woodenware Company, **13** 156
Munksjö, **19** 227
Munksund, **IV** 338
Munsingwear, Inc., **22** 427; **25** 90; **27** 443, 445; **41** 291. *See also* PremiumWear, Inc.
Munson Transportation Inc., **18** 227
Munster and Leinster Bank Ltd., **16** 13
Mura Corporation, **23** 209
Murata, **37** 347
**Murdock Madaus Schwabe, 26 315–19**, 470
Murfin Inc., **8** 360
Murmic, Inc., **9** 120
Murphey Favre, Inc., **17** 528, 530
**Murphy Family Farms Inc., 7** 477; **21** 503; **22 366–68**; **46** 84
**Murphy Oil Corporation, 7 362–64**; **32 338–41 (upd.)**
Murphy-Phoenix Company, **14** 122
Murray Bay Paper Co., **IV** 246; **25** 10
Murray Corp. of America, **III** 443
Murray Goulburn Snow, **II** 575
Murray Inc., **19** 383
Murrayfield, **IV** 696
Murtaugh Light & Power Company, **12** 265
Musashino Railway Company, **V** 510
Muscatine Journal, **11** 251
Muscocho Explorations Ltd., **IV** 76
Muse Air Corporation, **6** 120; **24** 454
Muse, Cordero, Chen, **41** 89
Music and Video Club, **24** 266, 270
Music-Appreciation Records, **13** 105
Music Corporation of America. *See* MCA Inc.
Music Go Round, **18** 207–09
Music Man, Inc., **16** 202; **43** 170
Music Plus, **9** 75
Musical America Publishing, Inc., **22** 441
Musician's Friend, **29** 221, 223
**Musicland Stores Corporation, 9 360–62**; **11** 558; **19** 417; **37** 263; **38 313–17 (upd.)**
Musitek, **16** 202; **43** 170
Muskegon Gas Company. *See* MCN Corporation.
Musotte & Girard, **I** 553
Mutoh Industries, Ltd., **6** 247; **24** 234
**Mutual Benefit Life Insurance Company, III** 243, **302–04**
Mutual Broadcasting System, **23** 509
Mutual Gaslight Company. *See* MCN Corporation.
Mutual Life Insurance Co. of the State of Wisconsin, **III** 321
**Mutual Life Insurance Company of New York, II** 331; **III** 247, 290, **305–07**, 316, 321, 380
Mutual Marine Office Inc., **41** 284
Mutual Medical Aid and Accident Insurance Co., **III** 331
Mutual of Omaha, **III** 365; **25** 89–90; **27** 47
Mutual Oil Co., **IV** 399
Mutual Papers Co., **14** 522
Mutual Safety Insurance Co., **III** 305
Mutual Savings & Loan Association, **III** 215; **18** 60
Mutualité Générale, **III** 210
Mutuelle d'Orléans, **III** 210
Mutuelle de l'Quest, **III** 211
Mutuelle Vie, **III** 210
Mutuelles Unies, **III** 211
**Muzak, Inc., 7** 90–91; **18 353–56**; **35** 19–20
Muzzy-Lyon Company. *See* Federal-Mogul Corporation.
MVC. *See* Music and Video Club.
MVR Products Pte Limited, **47** 255
Mwinilunga Canneries Ltd., **IV** 241
MXL Industries, **13** 367
MY Holdings, **IV** 92
Myanmar Oil and Gas Enterprise, **IV** 519
MYCAL Group, **V** 154
Myco-Sci, Inc. *See* Sylvan, Inc.
**Mycogen Corporation, 21 385–87**
Mycrom, **14** 36
Myer Emporium Ltd., **20** 156
**Myers Industries, Inc., 19 277–79**
Mygind International, **8** 477
**Mylan Laboratories Inc., I 656–57**; **20 380–82 (upd.)**
Myllykoski Träsliperi AB, **IV** 347–48
Myokenya, **III** 757
Myrna Knitwear, Inc., **16** 231
Myson Group PLC, **III** 671
Mysore State Iron Works, **IV** 205

N.A. Otto & Cie., **III** 541
N.A. Woodworth, **III** 519; **22** 282
N. Boynton & Co., **16** 534
N.C. Cameron & Sons, Ltd., **11** 95
N.C. Monroe Construction Company, **14** 112
N.E.M., **23** 228
N.H. Geotech. *See* New Holland N.V.
N.K. Fairbank Co., **II** 497
N.L. Industries, **19** 212
N M Electronics, **II** 44
**N M Rothschild & Sons Limited, IV** 64, 712; **24** 267; **39 293–95**
N.M.U. Transport Ltd., **II** 569
N.R.F. Gallimard, **IV** 618
N. Shure Company, **15** 477
N.V. *see under first word of company name*
N.W. Ayer & Son, **I** 36; **II** 542
N.W. Ayer and Partners, **32** 140
N.Y.P. Holdings Inc., **12** 360
Na Pali, S.A. *See* Quiksilver, Inc.
Naamloze Vennootschap tot Exploitatie van het Café Krasnapolsky. *See* Grand Hotel Krasnapolsky N.V.
Nabisco, **24** 358
**Nabisco Brands, Inc., II** 475, 512, **542–44**; **7** 128, 365–67; **12** 167; **25** 366. *See also* RJR Nabisco.
**Nabisco Foods Group, 7 365–68 (upd.)**; **9** 318; **14** 48. *See also* Kraft Foods Inc.
Nabisco Holdings Corporation, **25** 181; **42** 408; **44** 342
Nabisco Ltd., **24** 288
**Nabors Industries, Inc., 9 363–65**
Nacamar Internet Services, **48** 398
**NACCO Industries, Inc., 7 369–71**; **17** 213–15, 246, 248
Nacional de Drogas, S.A. de C.V., **39** 188
Nacional Financiera, **IV** 513

NACO Finance Corp., **33** 398
Nadler Sportswear. *See* Donnkenny, Inc.
Naegele Outdoor Advertising Inc., **36** 340
**Naf Naf SA, 44 296–98**
NAFI Corp. *See* Chris-Craft Industries, Inc.
Nagano Seiyu Ltd., **V** 188
Nagasaki Shipyard, **I** 502
**Nagasakiya Co., Ltd., V 149–51**
Nagasco, Inc., **18** 366
**Nagase & Company, Ltd., 8 376–78**
Nagase-Alfa, **III** 420
Nagel Meat Markets and Packing House, **II** 643
Nagoya Bank, **II** 373
Nagoya Electric Light Co., **IV** 62
NAI. *See* Network Associates, Inc.
Naigai Tsushin Hakuhodo, **6** 29
Naikoku Tsu-un Kabushiki Kaisha, **V** 477
Naiman Co., **25** 449
Nairn Linoleum Co., **18** 116
Nakai Shoten Ltd., **IV** 292
Nakano Vinegar Co. Ltd., **26** 58
**Nalco Chemical Corporation, I 373–75; 12 346–48 (upd.)**
Nalfloc, **I** 374
Nalge Co., **14** 479–80
NAM. *See* Nederlandse Aardolie Maatschappij.
Namco, **III** 431
Namibia Breweries Ltd., **33** 75
Namkwang Engineering & Construction Co. Ltd., **III** 749
NAMM. *See* North American Medical Management Company, Inc.
Nampack, **I** 423
Nan Ya Plastics Corp., **14** 197–98
NANA Regional Corporation, **7** 558
Nanfang South China Motor Corp., **34** 132
Nankai Kogyo, **IV** 225; **24** 489
Nansei Sekiyu, **IV** 432
**Nantucket Allserve, Inc., 22 369–71**
Nantucket Corporation, **6** 226
Nantucket Mills, **12** 285; **34** 240
Nanyo Bussan, **I** 493; **24** 326
NAPA. *See* National Automotive Parts Association.
NAPC. *See* North American Philips Corp.
Napier, **I** 194
NAPP Systems, Inc., **11** 253
Narmco Industries, **I** 544
NAS. *See* National Audubon Society.
NASA. *See* National Aeronautics and Space Administration.
NASCAR. *See* National Association for Stock Car Auto Racing.
NASDAQ, **37** 132
Nash DeCamp Company, **23** 356–57
**Nash Finch Company, 8 379–81**; **11** 43; **23 356–58 (upd.)**; **40** 80
Nash-Kelvinator Corp., **I** 135; **12** 158
Nash Motors Co., **I** 135; **8** 75
Nashaming Valley Information Processing, **III** 204
**Nashua Corporation, 8 382–84**
The Nashville Network, **11** 153
Nashville Speedway USA, Inc., **43** 139–41
Nassau Gas Light Co., **6** 455
Nassco Holdings Inc., **36** 79
NASTECH, **III** 590
Nasu Aluminium Manufacturing Co., **IV** 153
Nasu Nikon Co., Ltd., **48** 295
Nat Robbins, **37** 269–70
Natal Brewery Syndicate, **I** 287
Natco Corp., **I** 445
NaTec Ltd. *See* CRSS Inc.
**Nathan's Famous, Inc., 29 342–44**
National, **10** 419
National Acme Company. *See* Acme-Cleveland Corp.
National Advanced Systems, **II** 64–65
National Advertising Company, **27** 280
National Aeronautics and Space Administration, **II** 139; **6** 227–29, 327; **11** 201, 408; **12** 489; **37** 364–65
National Air Transport Co., **I** 128; **6** 128; **9** 416; **11** 427
National Airlines, **I** 97, 116; **6** 388; **21** 141; **25** 146
National Allied Publications. *See* DC Comics Inc.
National Aluminate Corp., **I** 373; **12** 346
National Aluminum Company, **11** 38
National American Corporation, **33** 399
National American Life Insurance Co. of California, **II** 181
National American Title Insurance Co., **II** 181
**National Amusements Inc., 28 295–97**
National Aniline & Chemical Coompany, **I** 414; **22** 29
**National Association for Stock Car Auto Racing, 32 342–44**
**National Association of Securities Dealers, Inc., 10 416–18**
**National Audubon Society, 26 320–23**
National Australia Bank, **III** 673
**National Auto Credit, Inc., 16 379–81**
National Automobile and Casualty Insurance Co., **III** 270
National Automotive Fibers, Inc. *See* Chris- Craft Industries, Inc.
National Automotive Parts Association, **26** 348
National Aviation, **I** 117
National Baby Shop, **V** 203
National Bancard Corporation, **11** 111–13
National Bancorp of Arizona, **12** 565
National Bank, **II** 312
National Bank for Cooperatives, **8** 489–90
National Bank für Deutschland, **II** 270
National Bank of Belgium, **II** 294
National Bank of Commerce, **II** 331; **9** 536; **11** 105–06; **13** 467
National Bank of Commerce Trust & Savings Association, **15** 161
National Bank of Detroit, **I** 165. *See also* NBD Bancorp, Inc.
National Bank of Egypt, **II** 355
**National Bank of Greece, 41 277–79**
The National Bank of Jacksonville, **9** 58
National Bank of New Zealand, **II** 308; **19** 155
National Bank of North America, **II** 334
National Bank of South Africa Ltd., **II** 236
National Bank of the City of New York, **II** 312
National Bank of Turkey, **IV** 557
National Bank of Washington, **13** 440
National BankAmericard Inc. *See* Visa International.
National Bankers Express Co., **II** 396; **10** 60
National Basketball Association, **12** 457
National Bell Telephone Company, **V** 259
National-Ben Franklin Insurance Co., **III** 242
National Benefit and Casualty Co., **III** 228
National Benefit Co., **III** 228
**National Beverage Corp., 26 324–26**
National Binding Company, **8** 382
National BioSystems, **47** 37
National Biscuit Co., **IV** 152; **22** 336. *See also* Nabisco.
National Bridge Company of Canada, Ltd., **8** 544
National Broach & Machine Co., **I** 481–82
**National Broadcasting Company, Inc., II** 30, 88–90, 129–33, **151–53**, 170, 173, 487, 543; **III** 188, 329; **IV** 596, 608, 652; **6** 157–59, **164–66 (upd.)**; **10** 173; **17** 149–50; **19** 201, 210; **21** 24; **23** 120; **28** 69, **298–301 (upd.)**; **30** 99; **32** 3; **33** 324; **34** 186; **42** 161, 163. *See also* General Electric Company.
National Building Society, **10** 6–7
National Cable & Manufacturing Co., **13** 369
National Cable Television Association, **18** 64
**National Can Corp.**, **I** 601–02, **607–08**; **IV** 154; **13** 255
**National Car Rental System, Inc.**, **I** 489; **II** 419–20, 445; **6** 348–49; **10** 373, **419–20**; **21** 284; **22** 406, 524; **24** 9; **25** 93, 143. *See also* Republic Industries, Inc.
National Carbon Co., Inc., **I** 400; **9** 516; **11** 402
National Carriers, **6** 413–14
National Cash Register Company. *See* NCR Corporation.
National Cement Co., **35** 419
National Cheerleaders Association, **15** 516–18
National Chemsearch Corp. *See* NCH Corporation.
National Child Care Centers, Inc., **II** 607
National City Bank, **9** 475
National City Bank of New York, **I** 337, 462; **II** 253–54; **III** 380; **IV** 81
National City Co., **II** 254; **9** 124
**National City Corp.**, **9** 475; **15 313–16**
National Cleaning Contractors, **II** 176
National Coal Board, **IV** 38–40
National Coal Development Corp., **IV** 48
National Comics Publications. *See* DC Comics Inc.
National Commercial Bank, **11** 108; **12** 422; **13** 476
National Components Industries, Inc., **13** 398
National Container Corp., **I** 609
**National Convenience Stores Incorporated, 7 372–75**; **20** 140
National Cranberry Association. *See* Ocean Spray Cranberries, Inc.
National Credit Office, **IV** 604
National CSS, **IV** 605
National Dairy Products Corp., **II** 533; **7** 275; **14** 204
National Data Corporation, **24** 393
National Demographics & Lifestyles Inc., **10** 461
National Development Bank, **IV** 56
**National Discount Brokers Group, Inc., 28 302–04**
National Disinfectant Company. *See* NCH Corporation.
**National Distillers and Chemical Corporation**, **I** 226, **376–78**; **IV** 11; **8** 439–41; **9** 231; **10** 181; **30** 441

National Drive-In Grocery Corporation, **7** 372
National Drug Ltd., **II** 652
National Economic Research Associates, **III** 283
National Education Association, **9** 367
National Educational Corporation, **26** 95
**National Educational Music Co. Ltd., 47 256–58**
National Electric Company, **11** 388
National Electric Instruments Co., **IV** 78
National Electric Products Corp., **IV** 177
National Employers Life Assurance Co. Ltd., **13** 539
*National Enquirer*, **10** 287–88
**National Envelope Corporation, 32 345–47**
National Executive Service. *See* Carey International, Inc.
National Express Laboratories, Inc., **10** 107
National Family Opinion. *See* NFO Worldwide, Inc.
National Fence Manufacturing Co., Inc., **45** 327
National Fidelity Life Insurance Co., **10** 246
National Fidelity Life Insurance Co. of Kansas, **III** 194; **IV** 343
National Finance Corp., **IV** 22–23
National Fire & Marine Insurance Co., **III** 213–14; **42** 32
National Fire Insurance Co., **III** 229–30
**National Football League, 12** 457; **29 345–47**; **37** 294
National Freight Corporation, **6** 412–13
**National Fuel Gas Company, 6 526–28**
National Gateway Telecom, **6** 326–27
National General Corp., **III** 190–91; **48** 7
**National Geographic Society, 9 366–68; 30 332–35 (upd.)**; **42** 115, 117
National Golf Properties, Inc. *See* American Golf Corporation
**National Grape Co-operative Association, Inc., 20 383–85**
National Greyhound Racing Club, **II** 142
National Grid Group plc, **11** 399–400; **12** 349; **13** 484; **45** 298–99; **47** 122
National Grocers of Ontario, **II** 631
National Guardian Corp., **18** 33
**National Gypsum Company, 8** 43; **10 421–24**; **13** 169; **22** 48, 170; **25** 535
National Health Enterprises, **III** 87
**National Health Laboratories Incorporated, 11 333–35.** *See also* Laboratory Corporation of America Holdings.
**National Hockey League, 35 300–03**
**National Home Centers, Inc., 44 299–301**
National Hotel Co., **III** 91
National Housing Systems, Inc., **18** 27
National Hydrocarbon Corp., **IV** 543
National ICEE Corporation, **24** 242
National Import and Export Corp. Ltd., **IV** 240
National Indemnity Co., **III** 213–14; **42** 32–33
National India Rubber Company, **9** 228
National Industries, **I** 446
National Inking Appliance Company, **14** 52
**National Instruments Corporation, 22 372–74**
National Integrity Life Insurance, **III** 249
**National Intergroup, Inc., IV** 237, 574; **V 152–53**; **12** 354; **16** 212; **26** 529. *See also* FoxMeyer Health Corporation.
**National Iranian Oil Company, III** 748; **IV** 370, 374, **466–68**, 484, 512, 535; **47** 342
National Key Company. *See* Cole National Corporation.
National Kinney Corp., **IV** 720; **9** 391
National Law Publishing Company, Inc., **32** 35
National Lead Co., **III** 681; **IV** 32; **21** 489
National Leisure Group, **47** 421
National Liability and Fire Insurance Co., **III** 214
National Liberty Corp., **III** 218–19
National Life and Accident Insurance Co., **III** 194
National Life Insurance Co., **III** 290
National Life Insurance Co. of Canada, **III** 243
National Living Centers, **13** 49
National Loss Control Service Corp., **III** 269
National Lumber Co. *See* National Home Centers, Inc.
National Magazine Company Limited, **19** 201
National Manufacturing Co., **III** 150; **6** 264; **13** 6
National Marine Service, **6** 530
National Market System, **9** 369
**National Media Corporation, 27 336–40**
National Medical Care, **22** 360
**National Medical Enterprises, Inc., III** 79, **87–88**; **6** 188; **10** 252; **14** 233; **25** 307–08; **33** 185
National Minerals Development Corp., **IV** 143–44
National Mobility Corp., **30** 436
National Mortgage Agency of New Zealand Ltd., **IV** 278; **19** 153
National Mortgage Assoc. of Washington, **II** 410
The National Motor Bearing Company. *See* Federal-Mogul Corporation.
The National Motor Club of America, Inc., **33** 418
National Mutual Life Assurance of Australasia, **III** 249
National Office Furniture, **12** 297
National Oil Corp. *See* Libyan National Oil Corporation.
National Oil Distribution Co., **IV** 524
National Old Line Insurance Co., **III** 179
National Packaging, **IV** 333
National Paper Co., **8** 476
National Parks Transportation Company, **25** 420–22
**National Patent Development Corporation, 7** 45; **13 365–68**; **25** 54
National Periodical Publications. *See* DC Comics Inc.
National Permanent Mutual Benefit Building Society, **10** 6
National Petrochemical Co., **IV** 467
National Petroleum Publishing Co., **IV** 636
National Petroleum Refiners of South Africa, **47** 340
National Pharmacies, **9** 346
**National Picture & Frame Company, 24 345–47**
National Pig Development Co., **46** 84
National Postal Meter Company, **14** 52
National Potash Co., **IV** 82; **7** 186
**National Power PLC, 11** 399–400; **12 349–51**; **13** 458, 484
**National Presto Industries, Inc., 16 382–85; 43 286–90 (upd.)**
National Processing, Inc., **24** 394
National Propane Corporation, **8** 535–37
National Provident Institution for Mutual Life Assurance, **IV** 711
National Provincial Bank, **II** 319–20, 333–34; **IV** 722; **17** 324
**National Public Radio, 19 280–82; 47 259–62 (upd.)**
National Publishing Company, **41** 110
National Quotation Bureau, Inc., **14** 96–97
**National R.V. Holdings, Inc., 32 348–51**
**National Railroad Passenger Corporation, 22 375–78**
National Railways of Mexico, **IV** 512
**National Record Mart, Inc., 29 348–50**
National Register Publishing Co., **17** 399; **23** 442
National Regulator Co., **II** 41
National Reinsurance Corporation. *See* General Re Corporation.
National Rent-A-Car, **6** 392–93
National Research Corporation, **8** 397
National Restaurants Management, Inc., **38** 385–87
National Revenue Corporation, **22** 181
**National Rifle Association of America, 37 265–68**
National Rubber Machinery Corporation, **8** 298
**National Sanitary Supply Co., 13** 149–50; **16 386–87**
National Satellite Paging, **18** 348
National School Studios, **7** 255; **25** 252
National Science Foundation, **9** 266
**National Sea Products Ltd., 14 339–41**
National Seal, **I** 158
**National Semiconductor Corporation, II 63–65**; **III** 455, 618, 678; **6** 215, **261–63**; **9** 297; **11** 45–46, 308, 463; **16** 122, 332; **17** 418; **18** 18; **19** 312; **21** 123; **26 327–30 (upd.)**; **43** 15
**National Service Industries, Inc., 11 336–38**
National Shoe Products Corp., **16** 17
National Slicing Machine Company, **19** 359
National-Southwire Aluminum Company, **11** 38; **12** 353
National Stamping & Electric Works, **12** 159
**National Standard Co., IV** 137; **13 369–71**
National Star Brick & Tile Co., **III** 501; **7** 207
National Starch and Chemical Corp., **IV** 253; **17** 30; **32** 256–57
National Starch Manufacturing Co., **II** 496
National Steel and Shipbuilding Company, **7** 356
National Steel Car Corp., **IV** 73; **24** 143–44
**National Steel Corporation, I** 491; **IV** 74, 163, 236–37, 572; **V** 152–53; **7** 549; **8** 346, 479–80; **11** 315; **12 352–54**; **14** 191; **16** 212; **23** 445; **24** 144; **26** 527–29; **28** 325. *See also* FoxMeyer Health Corporation.
National Student Marketing Corporation, **10** 385–86

National Supply Co., **IV** 29
National Surety Co. of New York, **III** 395
National System Company, **9** 41; **11** 469
National Tanker Fleet, **IV** 502
National Tea, **II** 631–32
National Technical Laboratories, **14** 52
**National TechTeam, Inc., 41 280–83**
National Telecommunications of Austin, **8** 311
National Telephone and Telegraph Corporation. *See* British Columbia Telephone Company.
National Telephone Co., **III** 162; **7** 332, 508
National Theatres, Inc., **III** 190
National Trading Manufacturing, Inc., **22** 213
National Transcontinental, **6** 360
National Travelers' Insurance Co., **III** 290
National Trust Life Insurance Co., **III** 218
National Tube Co., **II** 330; **IV** 572; **7** 549
National Union Electric Corporation, **12** 159
National Union Fire Insurance Co. of Pittsburgh, Pa., **III** 195–97
National Union Life and Limb Insurance Co., **III** 290
National Utilities & Industries Corporation, **9** 363
**National Westminster Bank PLC**, **II** 237, **333–35**; **IV** 642; **13** 206
Nationalbank, **I** 409
Nationale Bank Vereeniging, **II** 185
**Nationale-Nederlanden N.V.**, **III** 179, 200–01, **308–11**; **IV** 697
Nationar, **9** 174
**NationsBank Corporation**, **6** 357; **10** **425–27**; **11** 126; **13** 147; **18** 516, 518; **23** 455; **25** 91, 186; **26** 348, 453. *See also* Bank of America Corporation
NationsRent, **28** 388
Nationwide Cellular Service, Inc., **27** 305
Nationwide Credit, **11** 112
Nationwide Group, **25** 155
Nationwide Income Tax Service, **9** 326
Nationwide Logistics Corp., **14** 504
Nationwide Mutual Insurance Co., **26** 488
NATIOVIE, **II** 234
Native Plants, **III** 43
NATM Buying Corporation, **10** 9, 468
Natomas Co., **IV** 410; **6** 353–54; **7** 309; **11** 271
Natref. *See* National Petroleum Refiners of South Africa.
Natronag, **IV** 325
Natronzellstoff-und Papierfabriken AG, **IV** 324
NatSteel Electronics Ltd., **48** 369
NatTeknik, **26** 333
Natudryl Manufacturing Company, **10** 271
Natural Gas Clearinghouse, **11** 355. *See also* NGC Corporation.
Natural Gas Corp., **19** 155
Natural Gas Pipeline Company, **6** 530, 543; **7** 344–45
Natural Gas Service of Arizona, **19** 411
**Natural Wonders Inc.**, **14 342–44**
NaturaLife International, **26** 470
The Nature Company, **10** 215–16; **14** 343; **26** 439; **27** 429; **28** 306
**The Nature Conservancy**, **26** 323; **28** **305–07**, 422
**Nature's Sunshine Products, Inc.**, **15** **317–19**; **26** 470; **27** 353; **33** 145
Nature's Way Products Inc., **26** 315
Natuzzi Group. *See* Industrie Natuzzi S.p.A.
NatWest Bancorp, **38** 393
NatWest Bank, **22** 52. *See also* National Westminster Bank PLC.
Naugles, **7** 506
**Nautica Enterprises, Inc.**, **16** 61; **18** **357–60**; **25** 258; **27** 60; **44 302–06 (upd.)**
Nautilus International, Inc., **III** 315–16; **13** 532; **25** 40; **30** 161
Nautor Ab, **IV** 302
Navaho Freight Line, **16** 41
Navajo Refining Company, **12** 240
Navajo Shippers, Inc., **42** 364
Navale, **III** 209
Navan Resources, **38** 231
**Navarre Corporation**, **22** 536; **24 348–51**
Naviera Vizcaina, **IV** 528
**Navigant International, Inc.**, **47 263–66**
Navigation Mixte, **III** 348
Navire Cargo Gear, **27** 269
**Navistar International Corporation**, **I** 152, 155, **180–82**, 186, 525, 527; **II** 330; **10** 280, **428–30 (upd.)**; **17** 327; **33** 254. *See also* International Harvester Co.
**Navy Exchange Service Command**, **31** **342–45**
**Navy Federal Credit Union**, **33 315–17**
Naxon Utilities Corp., **19** 359
Naylor, Hutchinson, Vickers & Company. *See* Vickers PLC.
NBC **24** 516–17. *See also* National Broadcasting Company, Inc.
NBC Bankshares, Inc., **21** 524
NBC/Computer Services Corporation, **15** 163
**NBD Bancorp, Inc.**, **9** 476; **11 339–41**, 466. *See also* Bank One Corporation.
**NBTY, Inc.**, **31 346–48**
NCA Corporation, **9** 36, 57, 171
NCB. *See* National City Bank of New York.
NCB Brickworks, **III** 501; **7** 207
NCC L.P., **15** 139
**NCH Corporation**, **8 385–87**
Nchanga Consolidated Copper Mines, **IV** 239–40
nChip, **38** 187–88
**NCNB Corporation**, **II 336–37**; **12** 519; **26** 453
**NCO Group, Inc.**, **42 258–60**
**NCR Corporation**, **I** 540–41; **III** 147–52, **150–53**, 157, 165–66; **IV** 298; **V** 263; **6** 250, **264–68 (upd.)**, 281–82; **9** 416; **11** 62, 151, 542; **12** 162, 148, 246, 484; **16** 65; **29** 44; **30 336–41 (upd.)**; **36** 81
NCS. *See* Norstan, Inc.
NCTI (Noise Cancellation Technologies Inc.), **19** 483–84
nCube Corp., **14** 15; **22** 293
ND Marston, **III** 593
NDB. *See* National Discount Brokers Group, Inc.
NDL. *See* Norddeutscher Lloyd.
NEA. *See* Newspaper Enterprise Association.
NEAC Inc., **I** 201–02
Nearly Me, **25** 313
Neatherlin Homes Inc., **22** 547
Nebraska Bell Company, **14** 311
Nebraska Cellular Telephone Company, **14** 312
Nebraska Consolidated Mills Company, **II** 493; **III** 52; **8** 433; **26** 383
Nebraska Furniture Mart, **III** 214–15; **18** 60–61, 63
Nebraska Light & Power Company, **6** 580
Nebraska Power Company, **25** 89
**Nebraska Public Power District**, **29** **351–54**
NEBS. *See* New England Business Services, Inc.
**NEC Corporation**, **I** 455, 520; **II** 40, 42, 45, 56–57, **66–68**, 73, 82, 91, 104, 361; **III** 122–23, 130, 140, 715; **6** 101, 231, 244, 287; **9** 42, 115; **10** 257, 366, 463, 500; **11** 46, 308, 490; **13** 482; **16** 139; **18** 382–83; **19** 391; **21 388–91 (upd.)**; **25** 82, 531; **36** 286, 299–300; **47** 320
Neches Butane Products Co., **IV** 552
Neckermann Versand AG, **V** 100–02
Nedbank, **IV** 23
Nederland Line. *See* Stoomvaart Maatschappij Nederland.
Nederlander Organization, **24** 439
Nederlands Talen Institut, **13** 544
Nederlandsche Electriciteits Maatschappij. *See* N.E.M.
Nederlandsche Handel Maatschappij, **26** 242
Nederlandsche Heide Maatschappij, **III** 199
Nederlandsche Heidenmaatschappij. *See* Arcadis NV.
Nederlandsche Kunstzijdebariek, **13** 21
Nederlandsche Nieuw Guinea Petroleum Maatschappij, **IV** 491
Nederlandsche Stoomvart Maatschappij Oceaan, **6** 416
Nederlandse Cement Industrie, **III** 701
Nederlandse Credietbank N.V., **II** 248
Nederlandse Dagbladunie NV, **IV** 610
**N.V. Nederlandse Gasunie**, **I** 326; **V** 627, **658–61**; **38** 407
Nederlandse Handel Maatschappij, **II** 183, 527; **IV** 132–33
Nederlandse Vliegtuigenfabriek, **I** 54
Nedlloyd Group. *See* Koninklijke Nedlloyd N.V.
Nedsual, **IV** 23; **16** 28
Neeco, Inc., **9** 301
Needham Harper Worldwide, **I** 23, 28, 30–33; **13** 203; **14** 159
Needlecraft, **II** 560; **12** 410
Needleworks, Inc., **23** 66
Neenah Paper Co., **III** 40; **16** 303; **43** 257
Neenah Printing, **8** 360
NEES. *See* New England Electric System.
**Neff Corp.**, **32 352–53**
Negromex, **23** 171–72
Neighborhood Restaurants of America, **18** 241
Neilson/Cadbury, **II** 631
Neiman Bearings Co., **13** 78
**Neiman-Marcus Co.**, **I** 246; **II** 478; **V** 10, 31; **12 355–57**; **15** 50, 86, 291; **17** 43; **21** 302; **25** 177–78; **27** 429
Neisler Laboratories, **I** 400
Neisner Brothers, Inc., **9** 20
Nekoosa Edwards Paper Co., **IV** 282; **9** 261
NEL Equity Services Co., **III** 314
Nelio Chemicals, Inc., **IV** 345
Nelson Bros., **14** 236
Nelson Entertainment Group, **47** 272
Nelson Publications, **22** 442
Nemuro Bank, **II** 291

Nenuco, **II** 567
Neo Products Co., **37** 401
Neodata, **11** 293
Neos, **21** 438
Neoterics Inc., **11** 65
Neozyme I Corp., **13** 240
Nepera, Inc., **I** 682; **16** 69
Neptun Maritime Oyj, **29** 431
**Neptune Orient Lines Limited, 47 267–70**
NER Auction Group, **23** 148
**NERCO, Inc.**, **V** 689, **7 376–79**
Nesbitt Thomson, **II** 211
Nesco Inc., **28** 6, 8
Nescott, Inc., **16** 36
Nesher Israel Cement Enterprises Ltd., **II** 47; **25** 266
Nespak SpA, **40** 214–15
**Neste Oy**, **IV** 435, **469–71**, 519. *See also* Fortum Corporation
**Nestlé S.A.**, **I** 15, 17, 251–52, 369, 605; **II** 379, 456, 478, 486–89, 521, **545–49**, 568–70; **III** 47–48; **6** 16; **7 380–84 (upd.)**; **8** 131, 342–44, 498–500; **10** 47, 324; **11** 15, 205; **12** 480–81; **13** 294; **14** 214; **15** 63; **16** 168; **19** 50–51; **21** 55–56, 219; **22** 78, 80; **23** 219; **24** 388; **25** 21, 85, 366; **28 308–13 (upd.)**; **32** 115, 234; **36** 234, 237; **44** 351; **46** 274
**NetCom Systems AB, 26 331–33**
NetCreations, **47** 345, 347
Netherland Bank for Russian Trade, **II** 183
Netherlands Fire Insurance Co. of Tiel, **III** 308, 310
Netherlands India Steam Navigation Co., **III** 521
Netherlands Insurance Co., **III** 179, 308–10
Netherlands Trading Co. *See* Nederlandse Handel Maatschappij.
NetHold B.V., **31** 330
NetLabs, **25** 117
NetMarket Company, **16** 146
NetPlane Systems, **36** 124
Netron, **II** 390
**Netscape Communications Corporation, 15 320–22**; **35 304–07 (upd.)**; **44** 97
NetStar Communications Inc., **24** 49; **35** 69
NetStar Inc.,
Nettai Sangyo, **I** 507
Nettingsdorfer, **19** 227
Nettle Creek Corporation, **19** 304
Nettlefolds Ltd., **III** 493
Netto, **11** 240
Net2Phone Inc., **34** 224
NetWest Securities, **25** 450
**Network Associates, Inc.**, **25** 119, **347–49**
Network Communications Associates, Inc., **11** 409
Network Solutions, Inc., **47** 430
Network Ten, **35** 68–69
NetZero Inc., **38** 271
Neue Frankfurter Allgemeine Versicherungs-AG, **III** 184
Neue Holding AG, **III** 377
Neuenberger Versicherungs-Gruppe, **III** 404
Neuralgyline Co., **I** 698
Neuro Navigational Corporation, **21** 47
**Neutrogena Corporation, 17 340–44**; **36** 305
**Nevada Bell Telephone Company**, **V** 318–20; **14 345–47**
Nevada Community Bank, **11** 119
Nevada National Bank, **II** 381; **12** 534
Nevada Natural Gas Pipe Line Co., **19** 411
**Nevada Power Company, 11 342–44**; **12** 265
Nevada Savings and Loan Association, **19** 412
Nevada Southern Gas Company, **19** 411
Neversink Dyeing Company, **9** 153
Nevex Software Technologies, **42** 24, 26
New Access Communications, **43** 252
New America Publishing Inc., **10** 288
New Asahi Co., **I** 221
**New Balance Athletic Shoe, Inc.**, **17** 245; **25 350–52**; **35** 388
New Bedford Gas & Edison Light Co., **14** 124–25
New Broken Hill Consolidated, **IV** 58–61
**New Brunswick Scientific Co., Inc., 45 285–87**
New Century Network, **13** 180; **19** 204, 285
New City Releasing, Inc., **25** 269
New Consolidated Canadian Exploration Co., **IV** 96
New Consolidated Gold Fields, **IV** 21, 95–96
New CORT Holdings Corporation. *See* CORT Business Services Corporation.
New Daido Steel Co., Ltd., **IV** 62–63
**New Dana Perfumes Company, 37 269–71**
New Departure, **9** 17
New Departure Hyatt, **III** 590
New England Audio Company, Inc. *See* Tweeter Home Entertainment Group, Inc.
**New England Business Services, Inc., 18 361–64**
**New England Confectionery Co., 15 323–25**
New England CRInc, **8** 562
**New England Electric System, V 662–64**
New England Gas & Electric Association, **14** 124–25
New England Glass Co., **III** 640
New England Life Insurance Co., **III** 261
New England Merchants National Bank, **II** 213–14; **III** 313
**New England Mutual Life Insurance Co., III 312–14**
New England National Bank of Boston, **II** 213
New England Network, Inc., **12** 31
New England Nuclear Corporation, **I** 329; **8** 152
New England Power Association, **V** 662
New England Trust Co., **II** 213
New Fire Office, **III** 371
New Found Industries, Inc., **9** 465
New Galveston Company, Inc., **25** 116
New Guinea Goldfields, **IV** 95
New Halwyn China Clays, **III** 690
New Hampshire Gas & Electric Co., **14** 124
New Hampshire Insurance Co., **III** 196–97
New Hampshire Oak, **III** 512
New Hampton, Inc., **27** 429
New Haven District Telephone Company. *See* Southern New England Telecommunications Corporation.
New Haven Electric Co., **21** 512
New Hokkai Hotel Co., Ltd., **IV** 327
**New Holland N.V., 22 379–81**. *See also* CNH Global N.V.
New Horizon Manufactured Homes, Ltd., **17** 83
New Hotel Showboat, Inc. *See* Showboat, Inc.
New Ireland, **III** 393
New Jersey Bell, **9** 321
New Jersey Educational Music Company. *See* National Educational Music Co. Ltd.
New Jersey Hot Water Heating Company, **6** 449
New Jersey Shale, **14** 250
New Jersey Tobacco Co., **15** 138
New Jersey Zinc, **I** 451
**New Line Cinema, Inc., 47 271–74**
New London City National Bank, **13** 467
New London Ship & Engine, **I** 57
**New Look Group plc, 35 308–10**
New Materials Ltd., **48** 344
New Mather Metals, **III** 582
New Mitsui Bussan, **I** 507; **III** 296
New Nippon Electric Co., **II** 67
New Orleans Canal and Banking Company, **11** 105
New Orleans Refining Co., **IV** 540
**The New Piper Aircraft, Inc., 44 307–10**
**New Plan Realty Trust, 11 345–47**
New Process Company, **25** 76–77
New Process Cork Company Inc., **I** 601; **13** 188
New South Wales Health System, **16** 94
**New Street Capital Inc., 8 388–90 (upd.)**. *See also* Drexel Burnham Lambert Incorporated.
New Sulzer Diesel, **III** 633
**New Times, Inc., 45 288–90**
New Toyo Group, **19** 227
New Trading Company. *See* SBC Warburg.
New United Motor Manufacturing Inc., **I** 205; **38** 461
New UPI Inc., **25** 507
**New Valley Corporation, 17 345–47**
New Vanden Borre, **24** 266–70
New World Coffee-Manhattan Bagel, Inc., **32** 15
New World Communications Group, **22** 442; **28** 248
**New World Development Company Limited, IV 717–19**; **8** 500; **38 318–22 (upd.)**
New World Entertainment, **17** 149
New World Hotel (Holdings) Ltd., **IV** 717; **13** 66
**New World Restaurant Group, Inc., 44 311–14**
New York Air, **I** 90, 103, 118, 129; **6** 129
New York Airways, **I** 123–24
New York and Richmond Gas Company, **6** 456
New York and Suburban Savings and Loan Association, **10** 91
New York Biscuit Co., **II** 542
New York Capital Bank, **41** 312
New York Central Railroad Company, **II** 329, 369; **IV** 181; **9** 228; **10** 43–44, 71–73; **17** 496
New York Chemical Manufacturing Co., **II** 250
New York City Transit Authority, **8** 75
New York Condensed Milk Co., **II** 470
**New York Daily News, 32 357–60**
New York Electric Corporation. *See* New York State Electric and Gas.
New York Envelope Co., **32** 346
*New York Evening Enquirer*, **10** 287

New York Fabrics and Crafts, **16** 197
New York Gas Light Company. *See* Consolidated Edison Company of New York.
New York Glucose Co., **II** 496
New York Guaranty and Indemnity Co., **II** 331
New York Harlem Railroad Co., **II** 250
New York Improved Patents Corp., **I** 601; **13** 188
New York, Lake Erie & Western Railroad, **II** 395; **10** 59
**New York Life Insurance Company**, **II** 217–18, 330; **III** 291, 305, **315–17**, 332; **10** 382; **45 291–95 (upd.)**
New York Magazine Co., **IV** 651; **7** 390; **12** 359
New York Manufacturing Co., **II** 312
New York Marine and Gotham Insurance, **41** 284
New York Marine Underwriters, **III** 220
New York Quinine and Chemical Works, **I** 496
New York Quotation Company, **9** 370
**New York Restaurant Group, Inc.**, **32 361–63**
New York, Rio and Buenos Aires Airlines, **I** 115
New York Sports Clubs. *See* Town Sports International, Inc.
New York State Board of Tourism, **6** 51
**New York State Electric and Gas Corporation**, **6 534–36**
**New York Stock Exchange, Inc.**, **9 369–72**; **10** 416–17; **34** 254; **39 296–300 (upd.)**
New York Telephone Co., **9** 321
**The New York Times Company**, **III** 40; **IV 647–49**; **6** 13; **15** 54; **16** 302; **19 283–85 (upd.)**; **23** 158; **32** 508; **43** 256
New York Trust Co., **I** 378; **II** 251
New York, West Shore and Buffalo Railroad, **II** 329
New York Zoological Society. *See* Wildlife Conservation Society.
New York's Bankers Trust Co., **12** 107
New York-Newport Air Service Co., **I** 61
New Zealand Aluminum Smelters, **IV** 59
New Zealand Co., **II** 187
New Zealand Countrywide Banking Corporation, **10** 336
New Zealand Forest Products, **IV** 249–50
New Zealand Press Assoc., **IV** 669
New Zealand Sugar Co., **III** 686
New Zealand Wire Ltd., **IV** 279; **19** 154
Newark Electronics Co., **9** 420
Newco Waste Systems, **V** 750
**Newcor, Inc.**, **40 332–35**
Newcrest Mining Ltd., **IV** 47; **22** 107
Newell and Harrison Company. *See* Supervalu Inc.
**Newell Co.**, **9 373–76**; **12** 216; **13** 40–41; **22** 35; **25** 22
Newey and Eyre, **I** 429
Newfoundland Brewery, **26** 304
Newfoundland Energy, Ltd., **17** 121
Newfoundland Light & Power Co. *See* Fortis, Inc.
Newfoundland Processing Ltd. *See* Newfoundland Energy, Ltd.
Newgateway PLC, **II** 629
**Newhall Land and Farming Company**, **14 348–50**
Newhouse Broadcasting, **6** 33
**Newman's Own, Inc.**, **37 272–75**
Newmark & Lewis Inc., **23** 373
**Newmont Mining Corporation**, **III** 248; **IV** 17, 20, 33, 171, 576; **7** 287–89, **385–88**; **12** 244; **16** 25; **23** 40; **38** 231–32; **40** 411–12
Newnes, **17** 397
**Newport News Shipbuilding and Dry Dock Co.**, **I** 58, 527; **13 372–75**; **27** 36
**Newport News Shipbuilding Inc.**, **38 323–27 (upd.)**; **41** 42; **45** 306
News & Observer Publishing Company, **23** 343
**News America Publishing Inc.**, **12 358–60**; **27** 42; **37** 408
News and Westminster Ltd., **IV** 685
News Communications & Media Plc, **35** 242
**News Corporation Limited**, **II** 169; **IV 650–53**; **7 389–93 (upd.)**; **8** 551; **9** 429; **12** 358–60; **17** 398; **18** 211, 213, 254; **22** 194, 441; **23** 121; **24** 224; **25** 490; **26** 32; **27** 305, 473; **32** 239; **35** 157–58; **37** 408; **43** 174, 433; **46 308–13 (upd.)**
News International Corp., **20** 79
News of the World Organization (NOTW), **46** 309
Newsco NV, **48** 347
Newsfoto Publishing Company, **12** 472; **36** 469
Newspaper Co-op Couponing, **8** 551
Newspaper Enterprise Association, **7** 157–58
Newspaper Proprietors' Assoc., **IV** 669
Newspaper Supply Co., **IV** 607
**Newsquest plc**, **32 354–56**
Newsweek, Inc., **IV** 688
Newth-Morris Box Co. *See* Rock-Tenn Company.
Newtherm Oil Burners, Ltd., **13** 286
Newton Yarn Mills, **19** 305
Newtown Gas Co., **6** 455
Nexar Technologies, Inc., **22** 409
NEXCOM. *See* Navy Exchange Service Command.
NeXT Incorporated, **III** 116, 121; **6** 219; **18** 93; **34** 348; **36** 49
**Next plc**, **6** 25; **29 355–57**
**Nextel Communications, Inc.**, **10 431–33**; **21** 239; **26** 389; **27 341–45 (upd.)**
NEXTLINK Communications, Inc., **38** 192
Neyveli Lignite Corp. Ltd., **IV** 49
**NFC plc**, **6 412–14**; **14** 547
NFL Properties, Inc., **22** 223
**NFO Worldwide, Inc.**, **24 352–55**
**NGC Corporation**, **18 365–67**
NGI International Precious Metals, Ltd., **24** 335
NHK. *See* Japan Broadcasting Corporation.
**NHK Spring Co., Ltd.**, **III 580–82**
NI Industries, **20** 362
**Niagara Corporation**, **28 314–16**
Niagara Fire Insurance Co., **III** 241–42
Niagara First Savings and Loan Association, **10** 91
Niagara Insurance Co. (Bermuda) Ltd., **III** 242
**Niagara Mohawk Holdings Inc.**, **45 296–99 (upd.)**
**Niagara Mohawk Power Corporation**, **V 665–67**; **6** 535; **25** 130
Niagara of Wisconsin, **26** 362–63
Niagara Silver Co., **IV** 644
Niagara Sprayer and Chemical Co., **I** 442
NIBRASCO, **IV** 55
Nicaro Nickel Co., **IV** 82, 111; **7** 186
Nice Day, Inc., **II** 539
Nice Systems, **11** 520
NiceCom Ltd., **11** 520
Nichi-Doku Shashinki Shoten, **III** 574; **43** 281
Nichia Steel, **IV** 159
Nichibo, **V** 387
**Nichii Co., Ltd.**, **V 154–55**; **15** 470; **36** 418
**Nichimen Corporation**, **II** 442; **IV 150–52**, 154; **10** 439; **24 356–59 (upd.)**
Nichimo Sekiyu Co. Ltd., **IV** 555; **16** 490
Nicholas Kiwi Ltd., **II** 572; **15** 436
Nicholas Turkey Breeding Farms, **13** 103
Nicholas Ungar, **V** 156
Nichols & Company, **8** 561
Nichols Copper Co., **IV** 164, 177
Nichols-Homeshield, **22** 14
**Nichols plc**, **44 315–18**
**Nichols Research Corporation**, **18 368–70**
Nicholson File Co., **II** 16
Nicholson Graham & Jones, **28** 141
Le Nickel. *See* Société Le Nickel.
Nickelodeon, **25** 381
**Nicklaus Companies**, **45 300–03**
Nicolai Pavdinsky Co., **IV** 118
Nicolet Instrument Company, **11** 513
**NICOR Inc.**, **6 529–31**
Niederbayerische Celluloswerke, **IV** 324
Niederrheinische Hütte AG, **IV** 222
Niehler Maschinenfabrick, **III** 602
Nielsen, **10** 358
Nielsen & Petersen, **III** 417
Nielsen Marketing Research. *See* A.C. Nielsen Company.
Niemann Chemie, **8** 464
Niese & Coast Products Co., **II** 681
Niesmann & Bischoff, **22** 207
Nieuw Rotterdam, **27** 54
Nieuwe Eerste Nederlandsche, **III** 177–79
Nieuwe HAV-Bank of Schiedam, **III** 200
Nigeria Airways, **I** 107
**Nigerian National Petroleum Corporation**, **IV 472–74**
Nigerian Shipping Operations, **27** 473
Nihol Repol Corp., **III** 757
Nihon Denko, **II** 118
**Nihon Keizai Shimbun, Inc.**, **IV 654–56**
Nihon Kensetsu Sangyo Ltd., **I** 520
Nihon Kohden Corporation, **13** 328
Nihon Lumber Land Co., **III** 758
Nihon Sangyo Co., **I** 183; **II** 118
Nihon Sugar, **I** 511
Nihon Synopsis, **11** 491
Nihon Teppan, **IV** 159
Nihon Timken K.K., **8** 530
Nihon Waters K.K., **43** 456
Nihon Yusen Kaisha, **I** 503, 506; **III** 577, 712
Nihron Yupro Corp., **III** 756
NII. *See* National Intergroup, Inc.
Niitsu Oil, **IV** 542
**NIKE, Inc.**, **V 372–74**, 376; **8** 303–04, **391–94 (upd.)**; **9** 134–35, 437; **10** 525; **11** 50, 349; **13** 513; **14** 8; **15** 397; **16** 79, 81; **17** 244–45, 260–61; **18** 264, 266–67, 392; **22** 173; **25** 352; **27** 20; **29** 187–88; **31** 413–14; **36 343–48 (upd.)**
Nikka Oil Co., **IV** 150; **24** 357
Nikka Whisky Distilling Co., **I** 220

Nikkei. *See also* Nihon Keizai Shimbun, Inc.
Nikkei Aluminium Co., **IV** 153–55
Nikkei Shimbun Toei, **9** 29
**Nikken Global Inc., 32 364–67**
Nikken Stainless Fittings Co., Ltd., **IV** 160
Nikko Copper Electrolyzing Refinery, **III** 490
Nikko International Hotels, **I** 106
Nikko Kido Company, **6** 431
Nikko Petrochemical Co. Ltd., **IV** 476
**The Nikko Securities Company Limited**, **II** 300, 323, 383, **433–35**; **9 377–79 (upd.)**; **12** 536
Nikko Trading Co., **I** 106
Nikolaiev, **19** 49, 51
**Nikon Corporation**, **III** 120–21, 575, **583–85**; **9** 251; **12** 340; **18** 93, 186, 340, 342; **43** 282; **48 292–95 (upd.)**
Nile Faucet Corp., **III** 569; **20** 360
Nillmij, **III** 177–79
Nilpeter, **26** 540, 542
Nimas Corp., **III** 570; **20** 362
**Nimbus CD International, Inc.**, **20 386–90**
9 Telecom, **24** 79
**Nine West Group Inc.**, **11 348–49**; **14** 441; **23** 330; **39** 247, **301–03 (upd.)**
Nineteen Hundred Washer Co., **III** 653; **12** 548
**99¢ Only Stores**, **25 353–55**
Ningbo General Bearing Co., Ltd., **45** 170
**Nintendo Co., Ltd.**, **III 586–88**; **7 394–96 (upd.)**; **10** 124–25, 284–86, 483–84; **13** 403; **15** 539; **16** 168, 331; **18** 520; **23** 26; **28 317–21 (upd.)**; **31** 237; **38** 415
Nintendo of America, **24** 4
NIOC. *See* National Iranian Oil Company.
Nippon ARC Co., **III** 715
Nippon Breweries Ltd. *See* Sapporo Breweries Ltd.
Nippon Broilers Co., **II** 550
Nippon Cable Company, **15** 235
Nippon Cargo Airlines, **6** 71
Nippon Chemical Industries, **I** 363
**Nippon Credit Bank**, **II** 310, **338–39**; **38** 439
Nippon Del Monte Corporation, **47** 206
Nippon Educational Television (NET). *See* Asahi National Broadcasting Company, Ltd.
Nippon Electric Company, Limited. *See* NEC Corporation.
**Nippon Express Co., Ltd.**, **II** 273; **V 477–80**
Nippon-Fisher, **13** 225
Nippon Fruehauf Co., **IV** 154
Nippon Fukokin Kinyu Koku, **II** 300
Nippon Funtai Kogyo Co., **III** 714
Nippon Gakki Co., Ltd., **III** 656–58; **16** 554, 557
Nippon Ginko, **III** 408
Nippon Gyomo Sengu Co. Ltd., **IV** 555
Nippon Hatsujo Kabushikikaisha. *See* NHK Spring Co., Ltd.
Nippon Helicopter & Aeroplane Transport Co., Ltd., **6** 70
Nippon Hoso Kyokai. *See* Japan Broadcasting Corporation.
Nippon Idou Tsushin, **7** 119–20
Nippon International Container Services, **8** 278
Nippon Interrent, **10** 419–20
Nippon K.K. *See* Nikon Corporation.
Nippon Kairiku Insurance Co., **III** 384
Nippon Kakoh Seishi, **IV** 293
Nippon Kogaku K.K. *See* Nikon Corporation.
Nippon Kogyo Co. Ltd. *See* Nippon Mining Co. Ltd.
Nippon Kokan K.K., **IV** 161–63, 184, 212; **8** 449; **12** 354
**Nippon Life Insurance Company**, **II** 374, 451; **III** 273, 288, **318–20**; **IV** 727; **9** 469
**Nippon Light Metal Company, Ltd.**, **IV 153–55**
Nippon Machinery Trading, **I** 507
**Nippon Meat Packers, Inc.**, **II 550–51**
Nippon Menka Kaisha. *See* Nichimen Corporation.
Nippon Merck-Banyu, **I** 651; **11** 290
**Nippon Mining Co., Ltd.**, **III** 759; **IV 475–77**; **14** 207
Nippon Motorola Manufacturing Co., **II** 62
Nippon New Zealand Trading Co. Ltd., **IV** 327
**Nippon Oil Company, Limited**, **IV** 434, 475–76, **478–79**, 554; **19** 74
Nippon Onkyo, **II** 118
Nippon Paint Co., Ltd, **11** 252
Nippon Pelnox Corp., **III** 715
Nippon Phonogram, **23** 390
Nippon Polaroid Kabushiki Kaisha, **III** 608; **7** 437; **18** 570
Nippon Pulp Industries, **IV** 321
Nippon Rayon, **V** 387
Nippon Sangyo Co., Ltd., **IV** 475
Nippon Sanso Corp., **I** 359; **16** 486, 488
**Nippon Seiko K.K.**, **III 589–90**, 595; **47** 278
Nippon Sekiyu Co. *See* Nippon Oil Company, Limited.
**Nippon Sheet Glass Company, Limited**, **III 714–16**
**Nippon Shinpan Company, Ltd.**, **II 436–37**, 442; **8** 118
Nippon Silica Kogyo Co., **III** 715
Nippon Soda, **II** 301
Nippon Soken, **III** 592
Nippon Steel Chemical Co., **10** 439
**Nippon Steel Corporation**, **I** 466, 493–94, 509; **II** 300, 391; **IV** 116, 130, **156–58**, 184, 212, 228, 298; **6** 274; **14** 369; **17 348–51 (upd.)**, 556; **19** 219; **24** 324–25, 370
**Nippon Suisan Kaisha, Limited**, **II 552–53**
Nippon Tar, **I** 363
**Nippon Telegraph and Telephone Corporation**, **II** 51, 62; **III** 139–40; **V 305–07**; **7** 118–20; **10** 119; **13** 482; **16** 224; **21** 330; **25** 301; **27** 327, 365
Nippon Television, **7** 249; **9** 29
Nippon Tire Co., Ltd. *See* Bridgestone Corporation.
Nippon Trust Bank Ltd., **II** 405; **15** 42
Nippon Typewriter, **II** 459
Nippon Victor (Europe) GmbH, **II** 119
Nippon Wiper Blade Co., Ltd., **III** 592
**Nippon Yusen Kabushiki Kaisha**, **IV** 713; **V 481–83**; **6** 398
Nippon Yusoki Company, Ltd., **13** 501
**Nippondenso Co., Ltd.**, **III 591–94**, 637–38. *See also* DENSO Corporation.
**NIPSCO Industries, Inc.**, **6 532–33**
Nishi Taiyo Gyogyo Tosei K.K., **II** 578
Nishikawaya Co., Ltd., **V** 209
Nishimbo Industries Inc., **IV** 442
Nishizono Ironworks, **III** 595
NiSource, Inc., **38** 81
Nissan Construction, **V** 154
Nissan Motor Acceptance Corporation, **22** 207
**Nissan Motor Co., Ltd.**, **I** 9–10, **183–84**, 207, 494; **II** 118, 292–93, 391; **III** 485, 517, 536, 579, 591, 742, 750; **IV** 63; **7** 111, 120, 219; **9** 243, 340–42; **10** 353; **11** 50–51, **350–52 (upd.)**; **16** 167; **17** 556; **23** 338–40, 289; **24** 324; **27** 203; **34** 133, **303–07 (upd.)**
Nissan Trading Company, Ltd., **13** 533
Nisshin Chemical Industries, **I** 397
Nisshin Chemicals Co., **II** 554
**Nisshin Flour Milling Company, Ltd.**, **II 554**
Nisshin Pharaceutical Co., **II** 554
**Nisshin Steel Co., Ltd.**, **I** 432; **IV** 130, **159–60**; **7** 588
**Nissho Iwai K.K.**, **I** 432, **509–11**; **IV** 160, 383; **V** 373; **6** 386; **8** 75, 392; **15** 373; **25** 449; **27** 107; **36** 345
Nissho Kosan Co., **III** 715
Nissui. *See* Nippon Suisan Kaisha.
Nitratos de Portugal, **IV** 505
Nitroglycerin AB, **13** 22
Nitroglycerin Ltd., **9** 380
Nittetsu Curtainwall Corp., **III** 758
Nittetsu Sash Sales Corp., **III** 758
Nitto Warehousing Co., **I** 507
Nittoku Metal Industries, Ltd., **III** 635
Nittsu. *See* Nippon Express Co., Ltd.
Niugini Mining Ltd., **23** 42
**Nixdorf Computer AG**, **I** 193; **II** 279; **III** 109, **154–55**; **12** 162; **14** 13, 169; **26** 497
Nixdorf-Krein Industries Inc. *See* Laclede Steel Company.
Nizhny Novgorod Dairy, **48** 438
**NKK Corporation**, **IV** 74, **161–63**, 212–13; **V** 152; **24** 144; **28 322–26 (upd.)**
**NL Industries, Inc.**, **III** 681; **10 434–36**; **19** 466–68
NLG. *See* National Leisure Group.
NLM City-Hopper, **I** 109
NLM Dutch Airlines, **I** 108
NLT Corp., **II** 122; **III** 194; **10** 66; **12** 546
NM Acquisition Corp., **27** 346
NMC Laboratories Inc., **12** 4
NMH Stahlwerke GmbH, **IV** 128
NMT. *See* Nordic Mobile Telephone.
No-Leak-O Piston Ring Company, **10** 492
No-Sag Spring Co., **16** 321
Noah's New York Bagels, **13** 494. *See also* Einstein/Noah Bagel Corporation.
Nobel-Bozel, **I** 669
Nobel Drilling Corporation, **26** 243
Nobel-Hoechst Chimie, **I** 669
**Nobel Industries AB**, **I** 351; **9 380–82**; **16** 69. *See also* Akzo Nobel N.V.
**Nobel Learning Communities, Inc.**, **37 276–79**
**Noble Affiliates, Inc.**, **11 353–55**; **18** 366
Noble Broadcast Group, Inc., **23** 293
**Noble Roman's Inc.**, **14 351–53**
Nobles Industries, **13** 501
Noblesville Telephone Company, **14** 258
Noblitt-Sparks Industries, Inc., **8** 37–38
Nobody Beats the Wiz. *See* Cablevision Electronic Instruments, Inc.
Nocona Belt Company, **31** 435–36

Nocona Boot Co. *See* Justin Industries, Inc.
Noel Group, Inc., **24** 286–88
Noell, **IV** 201
NOK Corporation, **41** 170–72
**Nokia Corporation, II 69–71**; **IV** 296; **6** 242; **15** 125; **17** 33, **352–54 (upd.)**; **18** 74, 76; **19** 226; **20** 439; **38 328–31 (upd.)**; **47** 318–19
NOL Group. *See* Neptune Orient Lines Limited.
**Noland Company, 35 311–14**
Nolte Mastenfabriek B.V., **19** 472
Noma Industries, **11** 526
Nomai Inc., **18** 510
Nomura Bank of Japan, **34** 221
**Nomura Securities Company, Limited, II** 276, 326, 434, **438–41**; **9** 377, **383–86 (upd.)**; **39** 109
Nomura Toys Ltd., **16** 267; **43** 232
Non-Fiction Book Club, **13** 105
Non-Stop Fashions, Inc., **8** 323
Nonpareil Refining Co., **IV** 488
**Noodle Kidoodle, 16 388–91**
Noordwinning Group, **IV** 134
NOP Research Group, **28** 501, 504
Nopco Chemical Co., **IV** 409; **7** 308
Nopri, **V** 63–65
Nor-Am Agricultural Products, **I** 682
Nor-Cal Engineering Co. GmbH, **18** 162
Nora Industrier A/S, **18** 395
NORAND, **9** 411
**Noranda Inc., IV 164–66**; **7 397–99 (upd.)**; **9** 282; **26** 363
Norandex, **16** 204
Norbro Corporation. *See* Stuart Entertainment Inc.
Norcast Manufacturing Ltd., **IV** 165
Norcen Energy Resources, Ltd., **8** 347
Norcliff Thayer, **III** 66
Norco Plastics, **8** 553
Norcon, Inc., **7** 558–59
Norcore Plastics, Inc., **33** 361
Nord-Aviation, **I** 45, 74, 82, 195; **7** 10
Nordarmatur, **I** 198
Nordbanken, **9** 382
Norddeutsche Affinerie, **IV** 141
Norddeutsche Bank A.G., **II** 279
Norddeutscher-Lloyd, **I** 542; **6** 397–98
**Nordea AB, 40 336–39**
Nordfinanzbank, **II** 366
Nordic Baltic Holding. *See* Nordea AB.
Nordic Bank Ltd., **II** 366
Nordic Joint Stock Bank, **II** 302
Nordic Mobile Telephone, **II** 70
Nordica, **10** 151; **15** 396–97
**NordicTrack, 10** 215–17; **22 382–84**; **38** 238. *See also* Icon Health & Fitness, Inc.
Nordland Papier GmbH, **IV** 300, 302
**Nordson Corporation, 11 356–58**; **48 296–99 (upd.)**
Nordstahl AG, **IV** 201
Nordstjernan, **I** 553–54
**Nordstrom, Inc., V 156–58**; **11** 349; **13** 494; **14** 376; **17** 313; **18 371–74 (upd.)**; **21** 302; **22** 173
Nordwestdeutsche Kraftwerke AG, **III** 466; **V** 698–700
Norelco, **17** 110
**Norelco Consumer Products Co., 12** 439; **26 334–36**
Norelec, **27** 138
Norex Laboratories, **I** 699
Norex Leasing, Inc., **16** 397
Norfolk Carolina Telephone Company, **10** 202
**Norfolk Southern Corporation, V 484–86**; **6** 436, 487; **12** 278; **22** 167; **29 358–61 (upd.)**
Norfolk Steel, **13** 97
Norge Co., **III** 439–40; **18** 173–74; **43** 163–64
Noric Corporation, **39** 332
**Norinchukin Bank, II 340–41**
NORIS Bank GmbH, **V** 166
Norlin, **16** 238–39
**Norm Thompson Outfitters, Inc., 47 275–77**
Norma Cie., **III** 622
Norman BV, **9** 93; **33** 78
Norman J. Hurll Group, **III** 673
Normandy Mining Ltd., **23** 42
Normark Corporation. *See* Rapala-Normark Group, Ltd.
Normond/CMS, **7** 117
**Norrell Corporation, I** 696; **6** 46; **23** 431; **25 356–59**
Norris Cylinder Company, **11** 535
Norris Grain Co., **14** 537
Norris Oil Company, **47** 52
**Norsk Hydro ASA, 10 437–40**; **35 315–19 (upd.)**; **36** 322
**Norstan, Inc., 16 392–94**
Norstar Bancorp, **9** 229
**Nortek, Inc., I** 482; **14** 482; **22** 4; **26** 101; **34 308–12**; **37** 331
**Nortel Networks Corporation, 36 349–54 (upd.)**
Nortex International, **7** 96; **19** 338
North & South Wales Bank, **II** 318; **17** 323
North Advertising, Inc., **6** 27
North African Petroleum Ltd., **IV** 455
North American Aviation, **I** 48, 71, 78, 81, 101; **7** 520; **9** 16; **10** 163; **11** 278, 427
North American Bancorp, **II** 192
North American Carbon, **19** 499
North American Cellular Network, **9** 322
North American Coal Corporation, **7** 369–71
North American Company, **6** 443, 552–53, 601–02
North American Dräger, **13** 328
North American Energy Conservation, Inc., **35** 480
North American Insurance Co., **II** 181
North American InTeleCom, Inc., **IV** 411
North American Life and Casualty Co., **III** 185, 306
North American Light & Power Company, **V** 609; **6** 504–05; **12** 541
North American Managers, Inc., **III** 196
North American Medical Management Company, Inc., **36** 366
North American Mogul Products Co. *See* Mogul Corp.
North American Philips Corporation, **II** 79–80; **19** 393; **21** 520
North American Printed Circuit Corp., **III** 643
North American Printing Ink Company, **13** 228
North American Reinsurance Corp., **III** 377
North American Rockwell Corp., **10** 173
North American Systems, **14** 230
North American Training Corporation. *See* Rollerblade, Inc.
North American Van Lines, **I** 278; **14** 37
North American Watch Company. *See* Movado Group, Inc.
North Atlantic Energy Corporation, **21** 411
North Atlantic Packing, **13** 243
North British Insurance Co., **III** 234–35
North British Rubber Company, **20** 258
North Broken Hill Peko, **IV** 61
North Carolina Motor Speedway, Inc., **19** 294
North Carolina National Bank Corporation, **II** 336; **10** 425–27; **18** 518; **46** 52
North Carolina Natural Gas Corporation, **6** 578
North Carolina Shipbuilding Co., **13** 373
North Central Airlines, **I** 132
North Central Finance, **II** 333
North Central Financial Corp., **9** 475
North Central Utilities, Inc., **18** 405
North Cornwall China Clay Co., **III** 690
North East Insurance Company, **44** 356
North Eastern Bricks, **14** 249
North Eastern Coalfields Ltd., **IV** 48
**The North Face, Inc., 8** 169; **18 375–77**; **25** 206; **41** 103
**North Fork Bancorporation, Inc., 44** 33; **46 314–17**
North Goonbarrow, **III** 690
North Holland Publishing Co., **IV** 610
North New York Savings Bank, **10** 91
North of Scotland Bank, **II** 318; **17** 324
North of Scotland Hydro-Electric Board, **19** 389
North Pacific Paper Corp., **IV** 298
North Pacific Railroad, **II** 330
North Sea Ferries, **26** 241, 243
North Sea Oil and Gas, **10** 337
North Sea Sun Oil Co. Ltd., **IV** 550
North Shore Gas Company, **6** 543–44
North Shore Land Co., **17** 357
North Shore Medical Centre Pty, Ltd., **IV** 708
North Star Egg Case Company, **12** 376
North Star Marketing Cooperative, **7** 338
North Star Mill, **12** 376
**North Star Steel Company, 13** 138; **18 378–81**; **19** 380; **40** 87
North Star Universal, Inc., **25** 331, 333
North Supply, **27** 364
**The North West Company, Inc., 12 361–63**; **25** 219–20
North-West Telecommunications, **6** 327
**North West Water Group plc, 11 359–62**
Northamptonshire Union Bank, **II** 333
Northbrook Corporation, **24** 32
Northbrook Holdings, Inc., **22** 495
Northcliffe Newspapers, **IV** 685; **19** 118
Northeast Airlines Inc., **I** 99–100; **6** 81
Northeast Federal Corp., **13** 468
Northeast Petroleum Industries, Inc., **11** 194; **14** 461
Northeast Savings Bank, **12** 31; **13** 467–68
**Northeast Utilities, V 668–69**; **13** 182–84; **21** 408, 411; **48 303–06 (upd.)**
Northeastern Bancorp of Scranton, **II** 342
Northeastern New York Medical Service, Inc., **III** 246
Northern Aluminum Co. Ltd., **IV** 9–10
Northern and Employers Assurance, **III** 235
Northern Arizona Light & Power Co., **6** 545
Northern Border Pipeline Co., **V** 609–10
Northern California Savings, **10** 340

Northern Crown Bank, **II** 344
Northern Dairies, **10** 441
Northern Development Co., **IV** 282
Northern Drug Company, **14** 147
Northern Electric Company. *See* Northern Telecom Limited.
Northern Energy Resources Company. *See* NERCO, Inc.
Northern Engineering Industries Plc, **21** 436
Northern Fibre Products Co., **I** 202
**Northern Foods PLC**, **I** 248; **II** 587; **10** **441–43**
Northern Illinois Gas Co., **6** 529–31
Northern Indiana Power Company, **6** 556
Northern Indiana Public Service Company, **6** 532–33
Northern Infrastructure Maintenance Company, **39** 238
Northern Joint Stock Bank, **II** 303
Northern Leisure, **40** 296–98
Northern Light Electric Company, **18** 402–03
Northern National Bank, **14** 90
Northern Natural Gas Co., **V** 609–10
Northern Pacific Corp., **15** 274
Northern Pacific Railroad, **II** 278, 329; **III** 228, 282; **14** 168; **26** 451
Northern Paper, **I** 614
Northern Pipeline Construction Co., **19** 410, 412
**Northern Rock plc**, **33** **318–21**
Northern Star Co., **25** 332
Northern States Life Insurance Co., **III** 275
**Northern States Power Company**, **V** **670–72**; **18** 404; **20** **391–95 (upd.)**
Northern Stores, Inc., **12** 362
Northern Sugar Company, **11** 13
**Northern Telecom Limited**, **II** 70; **III** 143, 164; **V** 271; **V** **308–10**; **6** 242, 307, 310; **9** 479; **10** 19, 432; **11** 69; **12** 162; **14** 259; **16** 392, 468; **17** 353; **18** 111; **20** 439; **22** 51; **25** 34; **27** 342; **47** 318–20. *See also* Nortel Networks Corporation.
**Northern Trust Company**, **III** 518; **9** **387–89**; **22** 280
Northfield Metal Products, **11** 256
Northgate Computer Corp., **16** 196
Northland. *See* Scott Fetzer Company.
**Northland Cranberries, Inc.**, **38** **332–34**
Northland Publishing, **19** 231
NorthPrint International, **22** 356
**Northrop Corporation**, **I** 47, 49, 55, 59, **76–77**, 80, 84, 197, 525; **III** 84; **9** 416, 418; **10** 162; **11** 164, 166, 266, 269, **363–65 (upd.)**; **25** 316
**Northrop Grumman Corporation**, **41** 43; **45** **304–12 (upd.)**
Northrup King Co., **I** 672
NorthStar Computers, **10** 313
**Northwest Airlines Inc.**, **I** 42, 64, 91, 97, 100, 104, **112–14**, 125, 127; **6** 66, 74, 82 **103–05 (upd.)**, 123; **9** 273; **11** 266, 315; **12** 191, 487; **21** 141, 143; **22** 252; **26** **337–40 (upd.)**, 441; **27** 20; **28** 226, 265–66; **30** 447; **31** 419–20; **33** 50–51, 302. *See also* Mesaba Holdings, Inc.
Northwest Benefit Assoc., **III** 228
Northwest Engineering, **21** 502
Northwest Engineering Co. *See* Terex Corporation.
Northwest Express. *See* Bear Creek Corporation.
Northwest Industries, **I** 342; **II** 468 **8** 367; **25** 165–66. *See also* Chicago and North Western Holdings Corporation.
Northwest Instruments, **8** 519
Northwest Linen Co., **16** 228
**Northwest Natural Gas Company**, **45** **313–15**
Northwest Outdoor, **27** 280
Northwest Paper Company, **8** 430
Northwest Steel Rolling Mills Inc., **13** 97
Northwest Telecommunications Inc., **6** 598
Northwestern Bell Telephone Co., **V** 341; **25** 495
Northwestern Benevolent Society, **III** 228
**NorthWestern Corporation**, **37** **280–83**
Northwestern Engraving, **12** 25
Northwestern Expanded Metal Co., **III** 763
Northwestern Financial Corporation, **11** 29
Northwestern Industries, **III** 263
Northwestern Manufacturing Company, **8** 133
**Northwestern Mutual Life Insurance Company**, **III** **321–24**, 352; **IV** 333; **45** **316–21 (upd.)**; **46** 198
Northwestern National Bank, **16** 71
Northwestern National Insurance Co., **IV** 29
Northwestern National Life Insurance Co., **14** 233
Northwestern Public Service Company, **6** 524
Northwestern States Portland Cement Co., **III** 702
Northwestern Telephone Systems, **6** 325, 328
**Norton Company**, **III** 678; **8** **395–97**; **16** 122; **22** 68; **26** 70
Norton Healthcare Ltd., **11** 208
**Norton McNaughton, Inc.**, **25** 245; **27** **346–49**
Norton Opax PLC, **IV** 259; **34** 140
Norton Professional Books. *See* W.W. Norton & Company, Inc.
Norton Simon Industries, **I** 446; **IV** 672; **6** 356; **19** 404; **22** 513
Norwales Development Ltd., **11** 239
Norwalk Truck Lines, **14** 567
NORWEB plc, **13** 458; **24** 270
Norwegian Assurance, **III** 258
Norwegian Caribbean Line, **27** 90
Norwegian Globe, **III** 258
Norwegian Petroleum Consultants, **III** 499
Norweld Holding A.A., **13** 316
Norwest Bank, **19** 412
Norwest Corp., **16** 135
Norwest Mortgage Inc., **11** 29
Norwest Publishing, **IV** 661
Norwich-Eaton Pharmaceuticals, **III** 53; **8** 434; **26** 383
Norwich Pharmaceuticals, **I** 370–71; **9** 358
Norwich Union Fire Insurance Society, Ltd., **III** 242, 273, 404; **IV** 705
Norwich Winterthur Group, **III** 404
Norwood Company, **13** 168
**Norwood Promotional Products, Inc.**, **26** **341–43**
Nostell Brick & Tile, **14** 249
Notre Capital Ventures II, L.P., **24** 117
Nottingham Manufacturing Co., **V** 357
Nouvelle Compagnie Havraise Pénninsulaire, **27** 514
Nouvelles Galeries Réunies, **10** 205; **19** 308; **27** 95
Nouvelles Messageries de la Presse Parisienne, **IV** 618
Nova Corporation, **18** 365–67; **24** 395
**Nova Corporation of Alberta**, **V** **673–75**; **12** 364–66
Nova Information Systems, **24** 393
Nova Mechanical Contractors, **48** 238
Nova Pharmaceuticals, **14** 46
Nova Scotia Steel Company, **19** 186
**NovaCare, Inc.**, **11** **366–68**; **14** 233; **33** 185; **41** 194
**Novacor Chemicals Ltd.**, **12** **364–66**
Novaction Argentina SA, **48** 224
Novagas Clearinghouse Ltd., **18** 367
Novalta Resources Inc., **11** 441
Novamax Technologies Inc., **34** 209
Novanet Semiconductor, **36** 124
**Novartis AG**, **18** 51; **34** 284; **39** **304–10 (upd.)**
**Novell, Inc.**, **6** 255–56, 260, **269–71**; **9** 170–71; **10** 232, 363, 473–74, 558, 565; **11** 59, 519–20; **12** 335; **13** 482; **15** 131, 133, 373, 492; **16** 392, 394; **20** 237; **21** 133–34; **23** **359–62 (upd.)**; **25** 50–51, 117, 300, 499; **33** 113, 115; **34** 442–43; **36** 80; **38** 418–19
Novello and Co., **II** 139; **24** 193
**Novellus Systems, Inc.**, **18** **382–85**
Novgorodnefteprodukt, **48** 378
**Novo Industri A/S**, **I** **658–60**, 697
Novotel. *See* Accor SA.
NOVUM. *See* Industrie Natuzzi S.p.A.
NOVUS Financial Corporation, **33** 314
Nowell Wholesale Grocery Co., **II** 681
Nowsco Well Services Ltd., **25** 73
Nox Ltd., **I** 588
Noxell Corporation, **III** 53; **8** 434; **26** 384
**NPC International, Inc.**, **40** **340–42**
NPD Group, **13** 4
NPD Trading (USA), Inc., **13** 367
NPR. *See* National Public Radio, Inc.
NPS Waste Technologies, **13** 366
NRG Energy, Inc., **11** 401
NS. *See* Norfolk Southern Corporation.
NS Group, **31** 287
NS Petites Inc., **8** 323
NSG Information System Co., **III** 715
NSK. *See* Nippon Seiko K.K.
NSK Ltd., **42** 384
NSK-Warner, **14** 64
NSMO. *See* Nederlandsche Stoomvart Maatschappij Oceaan.
NSN Network Services, **23** 292, 294
NSP. *See* Northern States Power Company.
NSU Werke, **10** 261
NTC Publishing Group, **22** 519, 522
NTCL. *See* Northern Telecom Limited.
**NTN Corporation**, **III** **595–96**, 623; **28** 241; **47** **278–81 (upd.)**
NTRON, **11** 486
NTT. *See* Nippon Telegraph and Telephone Corp.
NTTPC. *See* Nippon Telegraph and Telephone Public Corporation.
NU. *See* Northeast Utilities.
Nu-Era Gear, **14** 64
**Nu-kote Holding, Inc.**, **18**
**Nu Skin Enterprises, Inc.**, **27** **350–53**; **31** 327 **386–89**
Nuclear Electric, **6** 453; **11** 399–401; **12** 349; **13** 484
Nuclear Power International, **19** 166
Nucoa Butter Co., **II** 497

**Nucor Corporation**, **7 400–02**; **13** 143, 423; **14** 156; **18** 378–80; **19** 380; **21 392–95 (upd.)**; **26** 407
Nucorp Energy, **II** 262, 620
NUG Optimus Lebensmittel-Einzelhandelgesellschaft mbH, **V** 74
Nugget Polish Co. Ltd., **II** 566
NUMAR Corporation, **25** 192
Numerax, Inc., **IV** 637
NUMMI. *See* New United Motor Manufacturing, Inc.
Nuovo Pignone, **IV** 420–22
NUR Touristic GmbH, **V** 100–02
Nurad, **III** 468
Nurotoco Inc. *See* Roto-Rooter Service Company.
Nursefinders, **6** 10
Nutmeg Industries, Inc., **17** 513
**Nutraceutical International Corporation, 37 284–86**
**NutraSweet Company**, **II** 463, 582; **8 398–400**; **26** 108; **29** 331
Nutrena, **II** 617; **13** 137
Nutri-Foods International, **18** 467–68
Nutri/System Inc., **29** 258
Nutrilite Co., **III** 11–12
NutriSystem, **10** 383; **12** 531
**Nutrition for Life International Inc., 22 385–88**
Nuveen. *See* John Nuveen Company.
NV Dagblad De Telegraaf. *See* N.V. Holdingmaatschappij De Telegraaf.
**NVR L.P., 8 401–03**
NWA, Inc. *See* Northwest Airlines Corporation.
NWK. *See* Nordwestdeutsche Kraftwerke AG.
NWL Control Systems, **III** 512
NWS BANK plc, **10** 336–37
Nya AB Atlas, **III** 425–26
Nydqvist & Holm, **III** 426
Nyhamms Cellulosa, **IV** 338
NYK. *See* Nihon Yusen Kaisha, Nippon Yusen Kabushiki Kaisha *and* Nippon Yusen Kaisha.
Nyland Mattor, **25** 464
NYLCare Health Plans, **45** 293–94
Nylex Corp., **I** 429
NYLife Care Health Plans, Inc., **17** 166
Nylon de Mexico, S.A., **19** 10, 12
**NYMAGIC, Inc., 41 284–86**
Nyman & Schultz Affarsresbyraer A.B., **I** 120
Nymofil, Ltd., **16** 297
**NYNEX Corporation**, **V 311–13**; **6** 340; **11** 19, 87; **13** 176; **25** 61–62, 102; **26** 520; **43** 445
NYRG. *See* New York Restaurant Group, Inc.
Nyrop, **I** 113
Nysco Laboratories, **III** 55
NYSEG. *See* New York State Electric and Gas Corporation.
NZI Corp., **III** 257

O&K Rolltreppen, **27** 269
O&Y. *See* Olympia & York Developments Ltd.
O.B. McClintock Co., **7** 144–45
O.G. Wilson, **16** 560
O. Kraft & Sons, **12** 363
O.N.E. Color Communications L.L.C., **29** 306
O-Pee-Chee, **34** 447–48
O.S. Designs Inc., **15** 396
O.Y.L. Industries Berhad, **26** 3, 5
Oahu Railway & Land Co., **I** 565–66
Oak Creek Homes Inc., **41** 18
Oak Farms Dairies, **II** 660
Oak Hill Investment Partners, **11** 490
Oak Hill Sportswear Corp., **17** 137–38
**Oak Industries Inc.**, **III** 512; **21 396–98**
**Oak Technology, Inc., 22 389–93**
OakBrook Investments, LLC, **48** 18
**Oakley, Inc., 18 390–93**
OakStone Financial Corporation, **11** 448
Oaktree Capital Management, **30** 185
OakTree Health Plan Inc., **16** 404
Oakville, **7** 518
**Oakwood Homes Corporation**, **13** 155; **15 326–28**
**OAO Gazprom, 42 261–65**
**OAO LUKOIL, 40 343–46**
**OAO NK YUKOS, 47 282–85**
**OAO Tatneft, 45 322–26**
OASIS, **IV** 454
Oasis Group P.L.C., **10** 506
OASYS, Inc., **18** 112
Obayashi Corp., **44** 154
ÖBB. *See* Österreichische Bundesbahnen GmbH.
Obbola Linerboard, **IV** 339
Oberheim Corporation, **16** 239
Oberland, **16** 122
Oberrheinische Bank, **II** 278
Oberschlesische Stickstoff-Werge AG, **IV** 229
Oberusel AG, **III** 541
Obi, **23** 231
Object Design, Inc., **15** 372
O'Boy Inc. *See* Happy Kids Inc.
O'Brien Kreitzberg, Inc., **25** 130
Obunsha, **9** 29
Occidental Bank, **16** 497
Occidental Chemical Corporation, **19** 414; **45** 254
Occidental Insurance Co., **III** 251
Occidental Life Insurance Company, **I** 536–37; **13** 529; **26** 486–87; **41** 401
Occidental Overseas Ltd., **11** 97
**Occidental Petroleum Corporation**, **I** 527; **II** 432, 516; **IV** 264, 312, 392, 410, 417, 453–54, 467, **480–82**, 486, 515–16; **7** 376; **8** 526; **12** 100; **19** 268; **25 360–63 (upd.)**; **29** 113; **31** 115, 456; **37** 309, 311; **45** 252, 254
Occidental Petroleum Great Britain Inc., **21** 206
**Océ N.V., 24 360–63**
Ocean, **III** 234
Ocean Combustion Services, **9** 109
Ocean Drilling and Exploration Company. *See* ODECO.
**Ocean Group plc, 6 415–17**
Ocean Reef Management, **19** 242, 244
Ocean Salvage and Towage Co., **I** 592
Ocean Scientific, Inc., **15** 380
Ocean Specialty Tankers Corporation, **22** 275
**Ocean Spray Cranberries, Inc.**, **7 403–05**; **10** 525; **19** 278; **25 364–67 (upd.)**; **38** 334
Ocean Steam Ship Company. *See* Malaysian Airlines System BHD.
Ocean Systems Inc., **I** 400
Ocean Transport & Trading Ltd., **6** 417
Oceania Football Confederation, **27** 150
Oceanic Contractors, **III** 559
Oceanic Properties, **II** 491–92
Oceanic Steam Navigation Company, **19** 197; **23** 160
Oceans of Fun, **22** 130
Ocelet Industries Ltd., **25** 232
**O'Charley's Inc., 19 286–88**
OCL. *See* Overseas Containers Ltd.
Ocoma Foods, **II** 584
Octek, **13** 235
**Octel Communications Corp.**, **III** 143; **14** 217, **354–56**; **16** 394
**Octel Messaging, 41 287–90 (upd.)**
Octopus Publishing, **IV** 667; **17** 398
Oculinum, Inc., **10** 48
**Odakyu Electric Railway Company Limited, V 487–89**
Odam's and Plaistow Wharves, **II** 580–81
Odd Job Trading Corp., **29** 311–12
Odd Lot Trading Company, **V** 172–73
Odda Smelteverk A/S, **25** 82
Odeco Drilling, Inc., **7** 362–64; **11** 522; **12** 318; **32** 338, 340
Odegard Outdoor Advertising, L.L.C., **27** 280
Odeon Theatres Ltd., **II** 157–59
**Odetics Inc., 14 357–59**
Odhams Press Ltd., **IV** 259, 666–67; **7** 244, 342; **17** 397–98
ODM, **26** 490
ODME. *See* Toolex International N.V.
O'Donnell-Usen Fisheries, **II** 494
**Odwalla, Inc., 31 349–51**
Odyssey Holdings, Inc., **18** 376
Odyssey Partners Group, **II** 679; **V** 135; **12** 55; **13** 94; **17** 137; **28** 218
Odyssey Press, **13** 560
Odyssey Publications Inc., **48** 99
**OEC Medical Systems, Inc., 27 354–56**
Oelwerken Julias Schindler GmbH, **7** 141
OEN Connectors, **19** 166
Oertel Brewing Co., **I** 226; **10** 180
Oësterreichischer Phönix in Wien, **III** 376
Oetker Group, **I** 219
Off the Rax, **II** 667; **24** 461
Off Wall Street Consulting Group, **42** 313
**Office Depot Incorporated**, **8 404–05**; **10** 235, 497; **12** 335; **13** 268; **15** 331; **18** 24, 388; **22** 154, 412–13; **23 363–65 (upd.)**; **27** 95; **34** 198; **43** 293
Office Mart Holdings Corporation, **10** 498
Office National du Crédit Agricole, **II** 264
Office Systems Inc., **15** 407
The Office Works, Inc., **13** 277; **25** 500
**OfficeMax Inc.**, **8** 404; **15 329–31**; **18** 286, 388; **20** 103; **22** 154; **23** 364–65; **43 291–95 (upd.)**
Official Airline Guides, Inc., **IV** 605, 643; **7** 312, 343; **17** 399
**Officine Alfieri Maserati S.p.A.**, **11** 104; **13** 28, **376–78**
Offset Gerhard Kaiser GmbH, **IV** 325
The Offshore Company, **III** 558; **6** 577; **37** 243
Offshore Food Services Inc., **I** 514
**Offshore Logistics, Inc., 37 287–89**
Offshore Transportation Corporation, **11** 523
**Ogden Corporation**, **I 512–14**, 701; **6 151–53**, 600; **7** 39; **25** 16; **27** 21, 196; **41** 40–41; **43** 217
Ogden Food Products, **7** 430
Ogden Gas Co., **6** 568
Ogden Ground Services, **39** 240, 242

Ogilvie Flour Mills Co., **I** 268; **IV** 245; **25** 9, 281
Ogilvy & Mather, **22** 200
**Ogilvy Group Inc.**, **I** 20, **25–27**, 31, 37, 244; **6** 53; **9** 180. *See also* WPP Group.
**Oglebay Norton Company**, **17 355–58**
**Oglethorpe Power Corporation**, **6 537–38**
O'Gorman and Cozens-Hardy, **III** 725
Ogura Oil, **IV** 479
Oh la la!, **14** 107
**Ohbayashi Corporation**, **I** 586–87
**The Ohio Art Company**, **14 360–62**
Ohio Ball Bearing. *See* Bearings Inc.
Ohio Barge Lines, Inc., **11** 194
**Ohio Bell Telephone Company**, **14 363–65**; **18** 30
Ohio Boxboard Company, **12** 376
Ohio Brass Co., **II** 2
**Ohio Casualty Corp.**, **III** 190; **11 369–70**
Ohio Crankshaft Co. *See* Park-Ohio Industries Inc.
**Ohio Edison Company**, **V 676–78**
Ohio Electric Railway Co., **III** 388
Ohio Mattress Co., **12** 438–39
Ohio Oil Co., **IV** 365, 400, 574; **6** 568; **7** 551
Ohio Pizza Enterprises, Inc., **7** 152
Ohio Power Shovel, **21** 502
Ohio Pure Foods Group, **II** 528
Ohio River Company, **6** 487
Ohio-Sealy Mattress Mfg. Co., **12** 438–39
Ohio Valley Electric Corporation, **6** 517
Ohio Ware Basket Company, **12** 319
Ohlmeyer Communications, **I** 275; **26** 305
Ohlsson's Cape Breweries, **I** 287–88; **24** 449
OHM Corp., **17** 553
Ohmeda. *See* BOC Group plc.
Ohmite Manufacturing Co., **13** 397
Ohrbach's Department Store, **I** 30
Ohta Keibin Railway Company, **6** 430
ÖIAG, **IV** 234
Oil Acquisition Corp., **I** 611
**Oil and Natural Gas Commission**, **IV** 440–41, **483–84**
Oil and Solvent Process Company, **9** 109
Oil City Oil and Grease Co., **IV** 489
Oil Co. of Australia, **III** 673
Oil Distribution Public Corp., **IV** 434
**Oil-Dri Corporation of America**, **20 396–99**
Oil Drilling, Incorporated, **7** 344
Oil Dynamics Inc., **43** 178
Oil Equipment Manufacturing Company, **16** 8
Oil India Ltd., **IV** 440, 483–84
Oil Shale Corp., **IV** 522; **7** 537
Oilfield Industrial Lines Inc., **I** 477
Oilfield Service Corp. of America, **I** 342
Oita Co., **III** 718
**Oji Paper Co., Ltd.**, **I** 506, 508; **II** 326; **IV** 268, 284–85, 292–93, 297–98, **320–22**, 326–27
**OJSC Wimm-Bill-Dann Foods**, **48 436–39**
OK Bazaars, **I** 289; **24** 450
OK Turbines, Inc., **22** 311
Okadaya Co. Ltd., **V** 96
O'Keefe Marketing, **23** 102
**Oki Electric Industry Company, Limited**, **II** 68, **72–74**; **15** 125; **21** 390
Okidata, **9** 57; **18** 435
Okinoyama Coal Mine, **III** 759
Oklahoma Airmotive, **8** 349
Oklahoma Entertainment, Inc., **9** 74
**Oklahoma Gas and Electric Company**, **6 539–40**; **7** 409–11
Oklahoma Oil Co., **I** 31
Oklahoma Publishing Company, **11** 152–53; **30** 84
Okonite, **I** 489
**Okura & Co., Ltd.**, **I** 282; **IV 167–68**
Oland & Sons Limited, **25** 281
Olathe Manufacturing, **26** 494
OLC. *See* Orient Leasing Co., Ltd.
Olcott & McKesson, **I** 496
**Old America Stores, Inc.**, **17 359–61**
Old Colony Envelope Co., **32** 345–46
Old Colony Trust Co., **II** 207; **12** 30
Old Country Buffet Restaurant Co. (OCB). *See* Buffets, Inc.
Old Dominion Power Company, **6** 513, 515
Old El Paso, **I** 457; **14** 212; **24** 140–41
Old Harbor Candles, **18** 68
**Old Kent Financial Corp.**, **11 371–72**
Old Line Life Insurance Co., **III** 275
Old Mutual, **IV** 23, 535
**Old National Bancorp**, **14** 529; **15 332–34**
Old Navy Clothing Company, **18** 193
Old Quaker Paint Company, **13** 471
**Old Republic International Corp.**, **11 373–75**
**Old Spaghetti Factory International Inc.**, **24 364–66**
Old Stone Trust Company, **13** 468
Oldach Window Corp., **19** 446
Oldham Estate, **IV** 712
Oldover Corp., **23** 225
Olds Motor Vehicle Co., **I** 171; **10** 325
Olds Oil Corp., **I** 341
Ole's Innovative Sports. *See* Rollerblade, Inc.
Olean Tile Co., **22** 170
Oleochim, **IV** 498–99
OLEX. *See* Deutsche BP Aktiengesellschaft.
Olex Cables Ltd., **10** 445
**Olin Corporation**, **I** 318, 330, **379–81**, 434, 695; **III** 667; **IV** 482; **8** 23, 153; **11** 420; **13 379–81 (upd.)**; **16** 68, 297; **32** 319
Olinkraft, Inc., **II** 432; **III** 708–09; **11** 420; **16** 376
Olins Rent-a-Car, **6** 348
Olinvest, **IV** 454
Olive Garden Italian Restaurants, **10** 322, 324; **16** 156–58; **19** 258; **35** 83
Oliver Rubber Company, **19** 454, 456
**Olivetti S.p.A.**, **34 316–20 (upd.)**; **38** 300
Olivine Industries, Inc., **II** 508; **11** 172; **36** 255
Olmstead Products Co., **23** 82
Olofsson, **I** 573
Olohana Corp., **I** 129; **6** 129
Olsen Dredging Co., **III** 558
Olson & Wright, **I** 120; **34** 398
Olsonite Corp., **I** 201
**Olsten Corporation**, **6 41–43**; **9** 327; **29 362–65 (upd.)**. *See also* Adecco S.A.
Olveh, **III** 177–79
**Olympia & York Developments Ltd.**, **IV** 245, 247, 712, **720–21**; **6** 478; **8** 327; **9 390–92 (upd.)**; **25** 11–12; **30** 108
Olympia Arenas, Inc., **7** 278–79; **24** 294
Olympia Brewing, **I** 260; **11** 50
Olympia Entertainment, **37** 207
Olympia Floor & Tile Co., **IV** 720
Olympiaki, **III** 401
Olympic Airways, **II** 442
Olympic Courier Systems, Inc., **24** 126
Olympic Fastening Systems, **III** 722
Olympic Insurance Co., **26** 486
Olympic Packaging, **13** 443
Olympus Communications L.P., **17** 7
Olympus Optical Company, Ltd., **15** 483
Olympus Sport, **V** 177–78
Olympus Symbol, Inc., **15** 483
**OM Group, Inc.**, **17 362–64**
Omaha Cold Store Co., **II** 571
Omaha Public Power District, **29** 353
Oman Oil Refinery Co., **IV** 516
Omega Gas Company, **8** 349
Omega Gold Mines, **IV** 164
Omega Protein Corporation, **25** 546
**O'Melveny & Myers**, **37 290–93**
Omex Corporation, **6** 272
OMI Corporation, **IV** 34; **9** 111–12; **22** 275
Omlon, **II** 75
Ommium Française de Pétroles, **IV** 559
Omnes, **17** 419
Omni Construction Company, Inc., **8** 112–13
Omni Hearing Aid Systems, **I** 667
**Omni Hotels Corp.**, **12 367–69**
Omni-Pac, **12** 377
Omni Products International, **II** 420
Omnibus Corporation, **9** 283
Omnicad Corporation, **48** 75
Omnicare, Inc., **13** 150
**Omnicom Group Inc.**, **I 28–32**, 33, 36; **14** 160; **22 394–99 (upd.)**; **23** 478; **43** 410. *See also* TBWA Worldwide.
Omnipoint Communications Inc., **18** 77
**OmniSource Corporation**, **14 366–67**
Omnitel Pronto Italia SpA, **38** 300
**Omron Corporation**, **28 331–35 (upd.)**
**Omron Tateisi Electronics Company**, **II 75–77**; **III** 549
**ÖMV Aktiengesellschaft**, **IV** 234, 454, **485–87**
**On Assignment, Inc.**, **20 400–02**
On Command Video Corp., **23** 135
On Cue, **9** 360
On-Line Software International Inc., **6** 225
On-Line Systems. *See* Sierra On-Line Inc.
Onan Corporation, **8** 72
Onbancorp Inc., **11** 110
Once Upon A Child, Inc., **18** 207–8
Oncogen, **III** 18
Ondal Industrietechnik GmbH, **III** 69; **48** 423
Ondulato Imolese, **IV** 296; **19** 226
**1-800-FLOWERS, Inc.**, **26 344–46**; **28** 137
1-800-Mattress. *See* Dial-A-Mattress Operating Corporation.
One For All, **39** 405
One Hundred Thirtieth National Bank, **II** 291
One Hundredth Bank, **II** 321
**One Price Clothing Stores, Inc.**, **20 403–05**
O'Neal, Jones & Feldman Inc., **11** 142
OneBeacon Insurance Group LLC, **48** 431
Oneida Bank & Trust Company, **9** 229
Oneida County Creameries Co., **7** 202
Oneida Gas Company, **9** 554

**Oneida Ltd.**, **7 406–08**; **31 352–355 (upd.)**
**ONEOK Inc.**, **7 409–12**
**Onex Corporation**, **16 395–97**; **22** 513; **24** 498; **25** 282
OneZero Media, Inc., **31** 240
Onitsuka Tiger Co., **V** 372; **8** 391; **36** 343–44
Online Distributed Processing Corporation, **6** 201
Online Financial Communication Systems, **11** 112
Only One Dollar, Inc. *See* Dollar Tree Stores, Inc.
**Onoda Cement Co., Ltd.**, **I** 508; **III 717–19**
Onomichi, **25** 469
Onsale Inc., **31** 177
Onstead Foods, **21** 501
OnTarget Inc., **38** 432
**Ontario Hydro Services Company**, **6 541–42**; **9** 461; **32 368–71 (upd.)**
Ontel Corporation, **6** 201
OnTrak Systems Inc., **31** 301
Oode Casting Iron Works, **III** 551
O'okiep Copper Company, Ltd., **7** 385–86
Opel. *See* Adam Opel AG.
Open Board of Brokers, **9** 369
Open Cellular Systems, Inc., **41** 225–26
Open Market, Inc., **22** 522
OpenTV, Inc., **31** 330–31
Operadora de Bolsa Serfin. *See* Grupo Financiero Serfin, S.A.
Operon Technologies Inc., **39** 335
**Opinion Research Corporation**, **35** 47; **46 318–22**
Opp and Micolas Mills, **15** 247–48
Oppenheimer. *See* Ernest Oppenheimer and Sons.
Oppenheimer & Co., **17** 137; **21** 235; **22** 405; **25** 450
Opryland USA, **11** 152–53; **25** 403; **36** 229
Optel Corp., **17** 331
OPTi Computer, **9** 116
Opti-Ray, Inc., **12** 215
Optical Radiation Corporation, **27** 57
Optilink Corporation, **12** 137
Optima Pharmacy Services, **17** 177
Optimum Financial Services Ltd., **II** 457
**Option Care Inc.**, **48 307–10**
**Optische Werke G. Rodenstock**, **44 319–23**
Opto-Electronics Corp., **15** 483
Optronics, Inc., **6** 247; **24** 234
Optus Communications, **25** 102
Optus Vision, **17** 150
**Opus Group**, **34 321–23**
OPW, **III** 467–68
**Oracle Corporation**, **24 367–71 (upd.)**; **25** 34, 96–97, 499
**Oracle Systems Corporation**, **6 272–74**; **10** 361, 363, 505; **11** 78; **13** 483; **14** 16; **15** 492; **18** 541, 543; **19** 310; **21** 86; **22** 154, 293
Orange and Rockland Utilities, Inc., **45** 116, 120
Orange Julius of America, **10** 371, 373; **39** 232, 235
Orange Line Bus Company, **6** 604
Orange PLC, **24** 89; **38** 300
Orb Books. *See* Tom Doherty Associates Inc.
Orbis Entertainment Co., **20** 6
Orbis Graphic Arts. *See* Anaheim Imaging.
Orbital Engine Corporation Ltd., **17** 24
**Orbital Sciences Corporation**, **22 400–03**
**Orchard Supply Hardware Stores Corporation**, **17 365–67**; **25** 535
Orcofi, **III** 48
OrderTrust LLP, **26** 440
Ore and Chemical Corp., **IV** 140
**Ore-Ida Foods Incorporated**, **II** 508; **11** 172; **12** 531; **13 382–83**; **36** 254, 256
Orebehoved Fanerfabrik, **25** 464
Oregon Ale and Beer Company, **18** 72
Oregon Craft & Floral Supply, **17** 322
Oregon Cutting Systems, **26** 119
**Oregon Metallurgical Corporation**, **20 406–08**
Oregon Pacific and Eastern Railway, **13** 100
**Oregon Steel Mills, Inc.**, **14 368–70**; **19** 380
**O'Reilly Automotive, Inc.**, **26 347–49**
Orenda Aerospace, **48** 274
Orford Copper Co., **IV** 110
**Organización Soriana, S.A. de C.V.**, **35 320–22**
Organon, **I** 665
Orico Life Insurance Co., **48** 328
Oriel Foods, **II** 609
Orient, **21** 122
Orient Express Hotels Inc., **29** 429–30
Orient Glass, **III** 715
Orient Leasing. *See* Orix Corporation.
Orient Overseas, **18** 254
Oriental Brewery Co., Ltd., **21** 320
Oriental Cotton Trading. *See* Tomen Corporation.
Oriental Land Co., Ltd., **IV** 715
Oriental Precision Company, **13** 213
Oriental Trading Corp., **22** 213
Oriental Yeast Co., **17** 288
Origin Energy Limited, **43** 75. *See also* Boral Limited.
Origin Systems Inc., **10** 285
Origin Technology, **14** 183
Original Arizona Jean Company. *See* J.C. Penney Company, Inc.
Original Cookie Co., **13** 166. *See also* Mrs. Fields' Original Cookies, Inc.
Original Musical Instrument Company (O.M.I.), **16** 239
Original Wassertragers Hummel, **II** 163
Origins Natural Resources Inc., **30** 190
Orinoco Oilfields, Ltd., **IV** 565
Orion, **III** 310
Orion Bank Ltd., **II** 271, 345, 385
Orion Healthcare Ltd., **11** 168
Orion Personal Insurances Ltd., **11** 168
**Orion Pictures Corporation**, **II** 147; **6 167–70**; **7** 336; **14** 330, 332; **25** 326, 328–29; **31** 100
Orit Corp., **8** 219–20
**ORIX Corporation**, **II 442–43**, 259, 348; **44 324–26 (upd.)**
Orkem, **IV** 547, 560; **21** 205
Orkin Pest Control, **11** 431–32, 434
**Orkla A/S**, **18 394–98**; **25** 205–07; **36** 266
Orlimar Golf Equipment Co., **45** 76
Orm Bergold Chemie, **8** 464
Ormco Corporation, **14** 481
ÖROP, **IV** 485–86
Orowheat Baking Company, **10** 250
La Oroya, **22** 286
ORSCO, Inc., **26** 363
Ortho Diagnostic Systems, Inc., **10** 213; **22** 75
Ortho Pharmaceutical Corporation, **III** 35; **8** 281; **10** 79–80; **30** 59–60
**Orthodontic Centers of America, Inc.**, **35 323–26**
Orthopedic Services, Inc., **11** 366
Orval Kent Food Company, Inc., **7** 430
Orville Redenbacher/Swiss Miss Foods Co., **17** 241
**The Orvis Company, Inc.**, **28 336–39**
**Oryx Energy Company**, **IV** 550; **7 413–15**
Osaka Aluminium Co., **IV** 153
Osaka Beer Brewing Co., **I** 220, 282; **20** 28
Osaka Electric Tramway, **V** 463
**Osaka Gas Co., Ltd.**, **V 679–81**
Osaka General Bussan, **IV** 431
Osaka Iron Works, **III** 513
Osaka Marine and Fire Insurance Co., **III** 367
Osaka Nomura Bank, **II** 276, 438–39
Osaka North Harbor Co. Ltd., **I** 518
Osaka Shinyo Kumiai, **15** 495
Osaka Shosen Kaisha, **I** 503; **V** 473–74, 481–82
Osaka Spinning Company, **V** 387
Osaka Sumitomo Marine and Fire Insurance Co., Ltd., **III** 367
Osaka Textile Co., **I** 506
Osakeyhtiö Gustaf Cederberg & Co., **IV** 301
Osakeyhtiö T. & J. Salvesen, **IV** 301
Osborn Group Inc., **48** 256
Osborne Books, **IV** 637
**Oscar Mayer Foods Corp.**, **II** 532; **7** 274, 276; **12** 123, **370–72**
Osco Drug, **II** 604–05
OSF Japan Ltd., **24** 365
**Oshawa Group Limited**, **II 649–50**
**OshKosh B'Gosh, Inc.**, **9 393–95**; **42 266–70 (upd.)**
Oshkosh Electric Power, **9** 553
Oshkosh Gas Light Company, **9** 553
**Oshkosh Truck Corporation**, **7 416–18**; **14** 458
**Oshman's Sporting Goods, Inc.**, **16** 560; **17 368–70**; **27** 7
OSi Specialties, Inc., **16** 543; **36** 148–49
Osiris Holding Company, **16** 344
OSK. *See* Osaka Shosen Kaisha.
**Osmonics, Inc.**, **18 399–401**
Oster. *See* Sunbeam-Oster.
Österreichische Brau-Beteiligungs AG. *See* BBAG Österreichische Brau-Beteiligungs AG.
**Österreichische Bundesbahnen GmbH**, **6 418–20**
Österreichische Creditanstalt-Wiener Bankverein, **IV** 230
Österreichische Elektrowerke, **IV** 230
Österreichische Industrieholding AG, **IV** 486–87
Österreichische Industriekredit AG, **IV** 230
Österreichische Länderbank, **II** 239; **23** 37
Österreichische Luftverkehrs AG. *See* Austrian Airlines AG.
Österreichische Mineralölverwaltung AG, **IV** 485
**Österreichische Post- und Telegraphenverwaltung**, **V 314–17**
Österreichische Stickstoffswerke, **IV** 486
Ostravar A.S., **38** 77

Ostschweizer Zementwerke, **III** 701
**O'Sullivan Industries Holdings, Inc., 34 313–15**
Osuuskunta Metsäliito, **IV** 316
Oswald Tillotson Ltd., **III** 501; **7** 207
Otagiri Mercantile Co., **11** 95
Otake Paper Manufacturing Co., **IV** 327
OTC, **10** 492
Other Options, **29** 400
Otis Company, **6** 579
**Otis Elevator Company, Inc., I** 85, **III** 467, 663; **13 384–86**; **27** 267, 268; **29** 422; **39 311–15 (upd.)**
Otis Engineering Corp., **III** 498
**Otis Spunkmeyer, Inc., 28 340–42**
Otosan, **I** 167, 479–80
OTP, Incorporated, **48** 446
**OTR Express, Inc., 25 368–70**
Otsego Falls Paper Company, **8** 358
Ott and Brewer Company, **12** 312
Ottawa Fruit Supply Ltd., **II** 662
**Ottaway Newspapers, Inc., 15 335–37**
**Otter Tail Power Company, 18 402–05**; **37** 282
Otter-Westelaken, **16** 420; **43** 308
Otto Bremer Foundation. *See* Bremer Financial Corp.
Otto-Epoka mbH, **15** 340
Otto Sumisho Inc., **V** 161
**Otto Versand GmbH & Co., V 159–61**; **10** 489–90; **15 338–40 (upd.)**; **27** 427, 429; **31** 188; **34 324–28 (upd.)**; **36** 177, 180
Ottumwa Daily Courier, **11** 251
Ourso Investment Corporation, **16** 344
**Outback Steakhouse, Inc., 12 373–75**; **34 329–32 (upd.)**
**Outboard Marine Corporation, III** 329, **597–600**; **8** 71; **16** 383; **20 409–12 (upd.)**; **26** 494; **42** 45; **43** 287; **45** 174
The Outdoor Group Limited, **39** 58, 60
**Outdoor Systems, Inc., 25 371–73**; **27** 278–80; **48** 217
Outdoor World. *See* Bass Pro Shops, Inc.
The Outdoorsman, Inc., **10** 216
Outlet, **6** 33
Outlet Retail Stores, Inc., **27** 286
**Outlook Group Corporation, 37 294–96**
Outlook Window Partnership, **19** 446
Outokumpu Metals Group. *See* OM Group, Inc.
**Outokumpu Oyj, IV** 276; **38 335–37**
Ovako Oy, **III** 624
Ovation, **19** 285
OVC, Inc., **6** 313
Overhill Farms, **10** 382
Overland Energy Company, **14** 567
Overland Mail Co., **II** 380–81, 395; **10** 60; **12** 533
Overland Western Ltd., **27** 473
**Overnite Transportation Co., 14 371–73**; **28** 492
Overseas Air Travel Ltd., **I** 95
Overseas Containers Ltd., **6** 398, 415–16
Overseas Petroleum and Investment Corp., **IV** 389
**Overseas Shipholding Group, Inc., 11 376–77**
Overseas Telecommunications Commission, **6** 341–42
Overseas Telecommunications, Inc., **27** 304
Ovox Fitness Clubs, **46** 432
Owatonna Tool Co., **I** 200; **10** 493
Owen Owen, **37** 8
Owen Steel Co. Inc., **15** 117
**Owens & Minor, Inc., 10** 143; **16 398–401**
**Owens Corning Corporation, I** 609; **III** 683, **720–23; 8** 177; **13** 169; **20 413–17 (upd.)**; **25** 535; **30** 283; **35** 98–99
Owens-Corning Fiberglas, **44** 127
**Owens-Illinois Inc., I 609–11**, 615; **II** 386; **III** 640, 720–21; **IV** 282, 343; **9** 261; **16** 123; **22** 254; **24** 92; **26 350–53 (upd.)**; **42** 438; **43** 188
Owens Yacht Company, **III** 443; **22** 115
Owensboro Municipal Utilities, **11** 37
**Owosso Corporation, 29 366–68**
Oxdon Investments, **II** 664
Oxfam America, **13** 13
Oxford-AnsCo Development Co., **12** 18
Oxford Biscuit Fabrik, **II** 543
Oxford Bus Company, **28** 155–56
Oxford Chemical Corp., **II** 572
Oxford Financial Group, **22** 456
**Oxford Health Plans, Inc., 16 402–04**
**Oxford Industries, Inc., 8 406–08**; **24** 158
Oxford Instruments, **III** 491
Oxford Learning Centres, **34** 105
Oxford Paper Co., **I** 334–35; **10** 289
Oxford University Press, **23** 211
Oxirane Chemical Co., **IV** 456
OXO International, **16** 234
Oxy Petrochemicals Inc., **IV** 481
Oxy Process Chemicals, **III** 33
Oxycal Laboratories Inc., **46** 466
OxyChem, **11** 160
Oxygen Media, **28** 175
Ozalid Corporation, **I** 337–38; **IV** 563; **22** 226
Ozark Airlines, **I** 127; **12** 489
Ozark Automotive Distributors, **26** 347–48
Ozark Pipe Line Corp., **IV** 540
Ozark Utility Company, **6** 593
OZM. *See* OneZero Media, Inc.

**P&C Foods Inc., 8 409–11**; **13** 95, 394
P&C Groep N.V., **46** 344
**P & F Industries, Inc., 45 327–29**
P&F Technologies Ltd., **26** 363
P&G. *See* Procter & Gamble Company.
P&L Coal Holdings Corporation, **45** 333
P & M Manufacturing Company, **8** 386
P & O. *See* Peninsular & Oriental Steam Navigation Company.
P&O Nedlloyd, **26** 241, 243
P.A. Bergner & Company, **9** 142; **15** 87–88
P.A. Geier Company. *See* Royal Appliance Manufacturing Company.
P.A.J.W. Corporation, **9** 111–12
P.A. Rentrop-Hubbert & Wagner Fahrzeugausstattungen GmbH, **III** 582
P.C. Hanford Oil Co., **IV** 368
**P.C. Richard & Son Corp., 23 372–74**
P. D'Aoust Ltd., **II** 651
P.D. Associated Collieries Ltd., **31** 369
P.D. Kadi International, **I** 580
P.D. Magnetics, **I** 330; **8** 153
P.E.C. Israel Economic Corporation, **24** 429
**P.F. Chang's China Bistro, Inc., 37 297–99**
P.G. Realty, **III** 340
**P.H. Glatfelter Company, 8 412–14**; **30 349–52 (upd.)**
P.Ink Press, **24** 430
P.L. Porter Co., **III** 580
P.R. Mallory, **9** 179
P.S.L. Food Market, Inc., **22** 549
P. Sharples, **III** 418
P.T. Bridgeport Perkasa Machine Tools, **17** 54
P.T. Dai Nippon Printing Indonesia, **IV** 599
P.T. Darya-Varia Laboratoria, **18** 180
P.T. Gaya Motor, **23** 290
P.T. Muaratewe Spring, **III** 581
P.T. Semen Nusantara, **III** 718
P.W. Huntington & Company, **11** 180
P.W.J. Surridge & Sons, Ltd., **43** 132
Pabst, **I** 217, 255; **10** 99; **18** 502
Pac-Am Food Concepts, **10** 178; **38** 102
Pac-Fab, Inc., **18** 161
PAC Insurance Services, **12** 175; **27** 258
**PACCAR Inc., I** 155, **185–86**; **10** 280; **26 354–56 (upd.)**; **40** 135
Pace-Arrow, Inc., **III** 484; **22** 206
Pace Companies, **6** 149; **26** 221
PACE Entertainment Corp., **36** 423–24
Pace Express Pty. Ltd., **13** 20
Pace Foods Ltd., **26** 58
Pace Management Service Corp., **21** 91
PACE Membership Warehouse, Inc., **V** 112; **10** 107; **12** 50; **18** 286; **40** 387; **47** 209
Pace Pharmaceuticals, **16** 439
Pacemaker Plastics, Inc., **7** 296
**Pacer Technology, 40 347–49**
Pacer Tool and Mold, **17** 310
Pachena Industries Ltd., **6** 310
Pacific Advantage, **43** 253
Pacific Aero Products Co., **I** 47; **10** 162
Pacific Air Freight, Incorporated, **6** 345
Pacific Air Transport, **I** 47, 128; **6** 128; **9** 416
Pacific Alaska Fuel Services, **6** 383
Pacific and European Telegraph Company, **25** 99
Pacific Bell, **V** 318–20; **11** 59; **12** 137; **21** 285; **22** 19; **37** 126
Pacific Brick Proprietary, **III** 673
Pacific-Burt Co., Ltd., **IV** 644
Pacific Car & Foundry Company. *See* PACCAR Inc.
Pacific Cascade Land Co., **IV** 255
Pacific Coast Co., **IV** 165
Pacific Coast Condensed Milk Co., **II** 486
Pacific Coast Oil Co., **IV** 385
Pacific Communication Sciences, **11** 57
Pacific Dry Dock and Repair Co., **6** 382
**Pacific Dunlop Limited, 10 444–46**
Pacific Electric Heating Co., **II** 28; **12** 194
Pacific Electric Light Company, **6** 565
**Pacific Enterprises, V 682–84**; **12** 477. *See also* Sempra Energy.
Pacific Express Co., **II** 381
Pacific Finance Corp., **I** 537; **9** 536; **13** 529; **26** 486
Pacific Fur Company, **25** 220
Pacific Gamble Robinson, **9** 39
**Pacific Gas and Electric Company, I** 96; **V 685–87**; **11** 270; **12** 100, 106; **19** 411; **25** 415. *See also* PG&E Corporation.
Pacific Glass Corp., **48** 42
Pacific Guardian Life Insurance Co., **III** 289
Pacific Health Beverage Co., **I** 292
Pacific Home Furnishings, **14** 436
Pacific Indemnity Corp., **III** 220; **14** 108, 110; **16** 204

Pacific Lighting Corp., **IV** 492; **V** 682–84; **12** 477; **16** 496. *See also* Sempra Energy.
Pacific Linens, **13** 81–82
Pacific Link Communication, **18** 180
Pacific Lumber Company, **III** 254; **8** 348–50
Pacific Magazines and Printing, **7** 392
Pacific Mail Steamship Company, **6** 353
Pacific Manifolding Book/Box Co., **IV** 644
Pacific Media K.K., **18** 101
Pacific Metal Bearing Co., **I** 159
Pacific Monolothics Inc., **11** 520
Pacific National Bank, **II** 349
Pacific National Insurance Co. *See* TIG Holdings, Inc.
Pacific Natural Gas Corp., **9** 102
Pacific Northern, **6** 66
Pacific Northwest Bell Telephone Co., **V** 341; **25** 495
Pacific Northwest Laboratories, **10** 139
Pacific Northwest Pipeline Corporation, **9** 102–104, 540; **12** 144
Pacific Northwest Power Company, **6** 597
Pacific Pearl, **I** 417
Pacific Petroleums Ltd., **IV** 494; **9** 102
Pacific Plastics, Inc., **48** 334
Pacific Platers Ltd., **IV** 100
Pacific Power & Light Company. *See* PacifiCorp.
Pacific Pride Bakeries, **19** 192
Pacific Recycling Co. Inc., **IV** 296; **19** 226; **23** 225
Pacific Refining Co., **IV** 394–95
Pacific Resources Inc., **IV** 47; **22** 107
Pacific Sentinel Gold Corp., **27** 456
Pacific-Sierra Research, **I** 155
Pacific Silver Corp., **IV** 76
Pacific/Southern Wine & Spirits, **48** 392
Pacific Southwest Airlines Inc., **I** 132; **6** 132
Pacific Steel Ltd., **IV** 279; **19** 154
Pacific Stock Exchange, **48** 226
**Pacific Sunwear of California, Inc.**, **28** **343–45**; **47** 425
**Pacific Telecom, Inc.**, **V** 689; **6** **325–28**; **25** 101
**Pacific Telesis Group**, **V** **318–20**; **6** 324; **9** 321; **11** 10–11; **14** 345, 347; **15** 125; **25** 499; **26** 520; **29** 387; **47** 318
Pacific Teletronics, Inc., **7** 15
Pacific Towboat. *See* Puget Sound Tug and Barge Company.
Pacific Trading Co., Ltd., **IV** 442
Pacific Trail Inc., **17** 462; **29** 293, 295–96
Pacific Western Extruded Plastics Company, **17** 441. *See also* PW Eagle Inc.
Pacific Western Oil Co., **IV** 537
Pacific Wine Co., **18** 71
**PacifiCare Health Systems, Inc.**, **III** 85; **11** **378–80**; **25** 318
**PacifiCorp, Inc.**, **V** **688–90**; **6** 325–26, 328; **7** 376–78; **26** **357–60 (upd.)**; **27** 327, 483, 485; **32** 372
Package Products Company, Inc., **12** 150
Packaged Ice, Inc., **21** 338; **26** 449
**Packaging Corporation of America**, **I** 526; **12** **376–78**, 397; **16** 191
**Packard Bell Electronics, Inc.**, **I** 524; **II** 86; **10** 521, 564; **11** 413; **13** **387–89**, 483; **21** 391; **23** 471
Packard Motor Co., **I** 81; **8** 74; **9** 17
Packer's Consolidated Press, **IV** 651
Packerland Packing Company, **7** 199, 201
Pacolet Manufacturing Company, **17** 327
PacTel. *See* Pacific Telesis Group.
Paddington Corp., **I** 248
PAFS. *See* Pacific Alaska Fuel Services.
Page, Bacon & Co., **II** 380; **12** 533
Page Boy Inc., **9** 320
PageAhead Software, **15** 492
Pageland Coca-Cola Bottling Works, **10** 222
PageMart Wireless, Inc., **18** 164, 166
**Paging Network Inc.**, **11** **381–83**; **39** 24–25; **41** 266–67
Pagoda Trading Company, Inc., **V** 351, 353; **20** 86
Paid Prescriptions, **9** 346
Paige Publications, **18** 66
**PaineWebber Group Inc.**, **I** 245; **II** **444–46**, 449; **III** 409; **13** 449; **22** 352, **404–07 (upd.)**, 542; **25** 433
Painter Carpet Mills, **13** 169
Painton Co., **II** 81
PairGain Technologies, **36** 299
Paisley Products, **32** 255
La Paix, **III** 273
Pak-a-Sak, **II** 661
Pak-All Products, Inc., **IV** 345
Pak Arab Fertilizers Ltd., **IV** 364
Pak Mail Centers, **18** 316
Pak-Paino, **IV** 315
Pak Sak Industries, **17** 310; **24** 160
Pak-Well, **IV** 282; **9** 261
Pakhoed Holding, N.V., **9** 532; **26** 420; **41** 339–40
**Pakistan International Airlines Corporation**, **46** **323–26**
Pakkasakku Oy, **IV** 471
Paknet, **11** 548
Pakway Container Corporation, **8** 268
PAL. *See* Philippine Airlines, Inc.
Pal Plywood Co., Ltd., **IV** 327
Palace Station Hotel & Casino. *See* Station Casinos Inc.
Palais Royal, Inc., **24** 456
Palatine Insurance Co., **III** 234
Palco Industries, **19** 440
Pale Ski & Sports GmbH, **22** 461
Palestine Coca-Cola Bottling Co., **13** 163
PALIC. *See* Pan-American Life Insurance Company.
**Pall Corporation**, **9** **396–98**
Palm Beach Holdings, **9** 157
**Palm Harbor Homes, Inc.**, **39** **316–18**
**Palm, Inc.**, **34** 441, 445; **36** **355–57**; **38** 433
Palm Shipping Inc., **25** 468–70
Palmafina, **IV** 498–99
Palmax, **47** 153
Palmer Communications, **25** 418
Palmer G. Lewis Co., **8** 135
Palmer Tyre Ltd., **I** 428–29
Palmolive Co. *See* Colgate-Palmolive Company.
Palo Alto Brewing, **22** 421
Palo Alto Products International, Inc., **29** 6
Palo Alto Research Center, **10** 510
**Palomar Medical Technologies, Inc.**, **22** **408–10**; **31** 124
PAM Group, **27** 462
**Pamida Holdings Corporation**, **15** **341–43**
Pamour Porcupine Mines, Ltd., **IV** 164
Pampa OTT, **27** 473
**The Pampered Chef, Ltd.**, **18** **406–08**
Pamplemousse, **14** 225
Pamplin Corp. *See* R.B. Pamplin Corp.
Pan-Alberta Gas Ltd., **16** 11
Pan American Banks, **II** 336
**Pan-American Life Insurance Company**, **48** **311–13**
Pan American Petroleum & Transport Co., **IV** 368–70
**Pan American World Airways, Inc.**, **I** 20, 31, 44, 64, 67, 89–90, 92, 99, 103–04, 112–13, **115–16**, 121, 124, 126, 129, 132, 248, 452, 530, 547–48; **III** 536; **6** 51, 65–66, 71, 74–76, 81–82, 103–05, 110–11, 123, 129–30; **9** 231, 417; **10** 561; **11** 266; **12** 191, **379–81 (upd.)**, 419; **13** 19; **14** 73; **24** 397; **29** 189; **36** 52–53; **39** 120
Pan European Publishing Co., **IV** 611
Pan Geo Atlas Corporation, **18** 513
Pan Ocean, **IV** 473
Pan Pacific Fisheries, **24** 114
Panacon Corporation, **III** 766; **22** 545
Panagra, **I** 547–48; **36** 53
**Panalpina World Transport (Holding) Ltd.**, **47** **286–88**
Panama Refining and Petrochemical Co., **IV** 566
**Panamerican Beverages, Inc.**, **47** **289–91**
**PanAmSat Corporation**, **18** 211, 213; **46** **327–29**
Panarctic Oils, **IV** 494
Panasonic, **9** 180; **10** 125; **12** 470; **43** 427
Panatech Research & Development Corp., **III** 160
Panavia Aircraft GmbH, **24** 84, 86–87
Panavia Consortium, **I** 74–75
**Panavision Inc.**, **24** **372–74**; **28** 249; **38** 295
PanCanadian Petroleum Ltd., **27** 217; **45** 80
**Pancho's Mexican Buffet, Inc.**, **46** **330–32**
**Panda Management Company, Inc.**, **35** **327–29**
Pandair, **13** 20
Pandel, Inc., **8** 271
Pandick Press Inc., **23** 63
PanEnergy Corporation, **27** 128, 131
**Panera Bread Company**, **44** 186, **327–29**
Panerai, **27** 489
**Panhandle Eastern Corporation**, **I** 377, 569; **IV** 425; **V** **691–92**; **10** 82–84; **11** 28; **14** 135; **17** 21
Panhandle Oil Corp., **IV** 498
Panhandle Power & Light Company, **6** 580
Panhard, **I** 194
Panhard-Levassor, **I** 149
Panificadora Bimbo, **19** 191
AB Pankakoski, **IV** 274
Panmure Gordon, **II** 337
Pannill Knitting Company, **13** 531
Panocean Storage & Transport, **6** 415, 417
Panola Pipeline Co., **7** 228
Panosh Place, **12** 168
Pansophic Systems Inc., **6** 225
Pantepec Oil Co., **IV** 559, 570; **24** 520
Pantera Energy Corporation, **11** 27
Pantheon Books, **13** 429; **31** 376
Panther, **III** 750
Panther Express International Company, **6** 346
**The Pantry, Inc.**, **36** **358–60**
Pantry Pride Inc., **I** 668; **II** 670, 674; **III** 56; **23** 407–08

Pants Corral, **II** 634
**Papa John's International, Inc.**, **15 344–46**; **16** 447; **24** 295
Pape and Co., Ltd., **10** 441
Papelera General, S.A. de C.V., **39** 188
Papelera Navarra, **IV** 295; **19** 226
Papeleria Calparsoro S.A., **IV** 325
Papeles Venezolanos C.A., **17** 281
Paper Direct, **37** 107–08
The Paper Factory of Wisconsin, Inc., **12** 209
Paper Magic Group, **35** 130–31
Paper Makers Chemical Corp., **I** 344
Paper Recycling International, **V** 754
Paper Software, Inc., **15** 322
Paper Stock Dealers, Inc., **8** 476
Paperituote Oy, **IV** 347–48
PaperMate, **III** 28; **23** 54
Paperwork Data-Comm Services Inc., **11** 64
Papeterie de Pont Sainte Maxence, **IV** 318
Papeteries Aussedat, **III** 122
Papeteries Boucher S.A., **IV** 300
Les Papeteries de la Chapelle-Darblay, **IV** 258–59, 302, 337
**Papeteries de Lancey**, **23 366–68**
Les Papeteries du Limousin, **19** 227
Papeteries Navarre, **III** 677; **16** 121
**Papetti's Hygrade Egg Products, Inc.**, **25** 332–33; **39 319–21**
Papierfabrik Salach, **IV** 324
Papierwaren Fleischer, **IV** 325
Papierwerke Waldhof-Aschaffenburg AG, **IV** 323–24
Papyrus Design Group, **IV** 336; **15** 455
Para-Med Health Services, **6** 181–82
Parachute Press, **29** 426
Parade Gasoline Co., **7** 228
Paradigm Entertainment, **35** 227
Paradise Creations, **29** 373
Paradise Island Resort and Casino. *See* Sun International Hotels Limited.
**Paradise Music & Entertainment, Inc.**, **42 271–74**
Paradyne, **22** 19
Paragon Communications, **44** 372
Paragon Corporate Holdings, Inc., **IV** 552; **28** 6, 8
Paragon Vineyard Company, **36** 114
Paragren Technologies Inc., **38** 432
Parallax Software Inc., **38** 70
Paramax, **6** 281–83
**Parametric Technology Corp.**, **16 405–07**
Parametrics Corp., **25** 134
Paramount Communications Inc., **16** 338; **19** 403–04; **28** 296
Paramount Fire Insurance Co., **26** 486
Paramount Oil Company, **18** 467
Paramount Paper Products, **8** 383
**Paramount Pictures Corporation**, **I** 451–52; **II** 129, 135, 146–47, **154–56**, 171, 173, 175, 177; **IV** 671–72, 675; **7** 528; **9** 119, 428–29; **10** 175; **12** 73, 323; **19** 404; **21** 23–25; **23** 503; **24** 327; **25** 88, 311, 327–29, 418; **31** 99; **35** 279
Parashop SA, **48** 279
Parasitix Corporation. *See* Mycogen Corporation.
Parasole Restaurant Holdings, Inc., **38** 117
Paravision International, **III** 48; **8** 343
Parcelforce, **V** 498
PARCO Co., Ltd., **V** 184–85; **42** 341
Parcor, **I** 676
ParentWatch, **34** 105
Parfums Chanel, **12** 57
Parfums Christian Dior, **I** 272
Parfums Rochas S.A., **I** 670; **III** 68; **8** 452; **48** 422
Parfums Stern, **III** 16
Pargas, **I** 378
Paribas. *See* Banque de Paris et des Pays-Bas, BNP Paribas Group *and* Compagnie Financiere de Paribas.
Paridoc and Giant, **12** 153
Paris Bourse, **34** 13
**Paris Corporation**, **22 411–13**
Paris Group, **17** 137
Paris Playground Equipment, **13** 319
**Parisian, Inc.**, **14 374–76**; **19** 324–25; **41** 343–44
Park Acquisitions, Inc., **38** 308
Park-Brannock Shoe Company, **48** 69
Park Consolidated Motels, Inc., **6** 187; **14** 105; **25** 306
**Park Corp.**, **22 414–16**
Park Drop Forge Co. *See* Park-Ohio Industries Inc.
Park Hall Leisure, **II** 140; **24** 194
Park Inn International, **11** 178
**Park-Ohio Industries Inc.**, **17 371–73**
Park Ridge Corporation, **9** 284
Park View Hospital, Inc., **III** 78
Parkdale State Bank, **25** 114
Parkdale Wines, **I** 268; **25** 281
Parke-Bernet, **11** 453
Parke, Davis & Co. *See* Warner-Lambert Co.
Parker, **III** 33
Parker Appliance Co., **III** 601–02
Parker Brothers, **II** 502; **III** 505; **10** 323; **16** 337; **21** 375; **25** 489; **43** 229, 232
**Parker Drilling Company**, **28 346–48**
Parker Drilling Company of Canada, **9** 363
**Parker-Hannifin Corporation**, **III 601–03**; **21** 108; **24 375–78 (upd.)**
Parker Pattern Works Co., **46** 293
Parker Pen Corp., **III** 218; **9** 326
Parker's Pharmacy, Inc., **15** 524
Parkinson Cowan, **I** 531
Parkmount Hospitality Corp., **II** 142
Parks-Belk Co., **19** 324
Parks Box & Printing Co., **13** 442
Parkway Distributors, **17** 331
Parr's Bank, **II** 334; **III** 724
Parson and Hyman Co., Inc., **8** 112
**Parsons Brinckerhoff, Inc.**, **34 333–36**
**The Parsons Corporation**, **III** 749; **8 415–17**
Parsons International Trading Business, **27** 195
Parsons Place Apparel Company, **8** 289
Partech, **28** 346, 348
Partek Corporation, **11** 312
Partex, **IV** 515
Parthénon, **27** 10
Parthenon Insurance Co., **III** 79
Participating Annuity Life Insurance Co., **III** 182; **21** 14
La Participation, **III** 210
Partlow Corporation, **7** 116
Partnership Pacific Ltd., **II** 389
Partouche SA. *See* Groupe Partouche SA.
Parts Industries Corp., **III** 494–95
Parts Plus, **26** 348
PartyLite Gifts, Inc., **18** 67, 69
Pascagoula Lumber Company, **28** 306
Pascale & Associates, **12** 476
Paschen Contractors Inc., **I** 585
Pasha Pillows, **12** 393
Pasminco, **IV** 61
Pasqua Inc., **28** 64
Pass & Seymour, **21** 348–49
Passive Power Products, Inc., **32** 41
Patagonia, **16** 352; **18** 376; **21** 193; **25** 206. *See also* Lost Arrow Inc.
Patak Spices Ltd., **18** 247
Pataling Rubber Estates Syndicate, **III** 697, 699
Patch Rubber Co., **19** 277–78
Patchoque-Plymouth Co., **IV** 371
PATCO. *See* Philippine Airlines, Inc.
Patent Arms Manufacturing Company, **12** 70
Patent Nut & Bolt Co., **III** 493
Patent Slip and Dock Co., **I** 592
La Paternelle, **III** 210
Paterno Wines International, **48** 392
Paternoster Stores plc, **V** 108; **24** 269
Paterson Candy Ltd., **22** 89
Paterson, Simons & Co., **I** 592
Path-Tek Laboratories, Inc., **6** 41
Pathé Cinéma, **6** 374
Pathe Communications Co., **IV** 676; **7** 529; **25** 329
Pathé Fréres, **IV** 626; **19** 203
**Pathé SA**, **29 369–71**. *See also* Chargeurs International.
**Pathmark Stores, Inc.**, **II** 672–74; **9** 173; **15** 260; **18** 6; **19** 479, 481; **23 369–71**; **33** 436
PathoGenesis Corporation, **36** 119
Patience & Nicholson, **III** 674
Patient Care, Inc., **13** 150
Patil Systems, **11** 56
**Patina Oil & Gas Corporation**, **24 379–81**
Patino N.V., **17** 380
**Patrick Industries, Inc.**, **30 342–45**
Patrick Raulet, S.A., **36** 164
Patricof & Company, **24** 45
Patriot American Hospitality, Inc., **21** 184
Patriot Co., **IV** 582
Patriot Life Insurance Co., **III** 193
PATS Inc., **36** 159
**Patterson Dental Co.**, **19 289–91**
Patterson Industries, Inc., **14** 42
Pattison & Bowns, Inc., **IV** 180
Patton Electric Company, Inc., **19** 360
Patton Paint Company. *See* PPG Industries, Inc.
Paul A. Brands, **11** 19
Paul Andra KG, **33** 393
Paul Boechat & Cie, **21** 515
Paul C. Dodge Company, **6** 579
Paul Davril, Inc., **25** 258
Paul H. Rose Corporation, **13** 445
**Paul Harris Stores, Inc.**, **15** 245; **18 409–12**
**Paul, Hastings, Janofsky & Walker LLP**, **27 357–59**
Paul Koss Supply Co., **16** 387
Paul Marshall Products Inc., **16** 36
Paul Masson, **I** 285
Paul Ramsay Group, **41** 323
**The Paul Revere Corporation**, **12 382–83**
Paul Revere Insurance, **34** 433
Paul Wahl & Co., **IV** 277
**Paul, Weiss, Rifkind, Wharton & Garrison**, **47 292–94**
Paul Williams Copier Corp., **IV** 252; **17** 28

Paul Wurth, **IV** 25
**Paulaner Brauerei GmbH & Co. KG, 35 330–33**
Pauls Plc, **III** 699
Pavallier, **18** 35
Pavex Construction Company. *See* Granite Rock Company.
Pawnee Industries, Inc., **19** 415
Paxall, Inc., **8** 545
**Paxson Communications Corporation, 33 322–26**
**Pay 'N Pak Stores, Inc., 9 399–401; 16** 186–88
Pay 'n Save Corp., **12** 477; **15** 274; **17** 366
Pay Less, **II** 601, 604
**Paychex, Inc., 15 347–49; 46 333–36 (upd.)**
PayConnect Solutions, **47** 39
**Payless Cashways, Inc., 11 384–86; 13** 274; **44 330–33 (upd.)**
Payless DIY, **V** 17, 19
PayLess Drug Stores, **12** 477–78; **18** 286; **22** 39
**Payless ShoeSource, Inc., V** 132, 135; **13** 361; **18 413–15; 26** 441
PBF Corp. *See* Paris Corporation.
PBL. *See* Publishing and Broadcasting Ltd.
PBS. *See* Public Broadcasting Stations.
**PC Connection, Inc., 37 300–04**
PC Globe, Inc., **13** 114
PC Realty, Canada Ltd., **III** 340
PCA-Budafok Paperboard Ltd., **12** 377
pcBoat.com, **37** 398
PCI Acquisition, **11** 385
PCI/Mac-Pak Group, **IV** 261
PCI NewCo Inc., **36** 159
PCI Services, Inc. *See* Cardinal Health, Inc.
PCL Industries Ltd., **IV** 296; **19** 226
PCO, **III** 685
PCS. *See* Potash Corp. of Saskatchewan Inc.
PCS Health Systems Inc., **12** 333; **47** 115, 235–36
PCX. *See* Pacific Stock Exchange.
PDA Engineering, **25** 305
PDA Inc., **19** 290
PDO. *See* Petroleum Development Oman.
PDQ Transportation Inc., **18** 226
**PDS Gaming Corporation, 44 334–37**
PDV America, Inc., **31** 113
PDVSA. *See* Petróleos de Venezuela S.A.
**Peabody Coal Company, I** 559; **III** 248; **IV** 47, 169–71, 576; **7** 387–88; **10 447–49**
**Peabody Energy Corporation, 45 330–33 (upd.)**
**Peabody Holding Company, Inc., IV** 19, **169–72; 6** 487; **7** 209
Peabody, Riggs & Co., **II** 427
Peaches Entertainment Corporation, **24** 502
Peachtree Doors, **10** 95
Peachtree Federal Savings and Loan Association of Atlanta, **10** 92
Peachtree Software Inc., **18** 364
Peak Audio Inc., **48** 92
Peak Oilfield Service Company, **9** 364
**The Peak Technologies Group, Inc., 14 377–80**
Peakstone, **III** 740
**Peapod, Inc., 22** 522; **30 346–48**
Pearce-Uible Co., **14** 460
Pearl Health Services, **I** 249
Pearl Package Co., Ltd., **IV** 327
**Pearle Vision, Inc., I** 688; **12** 188; **13 390–92; 14** 214; **23** 329; **24** 140; **34** 179
**Pearson plc, IV** 611, 652, **657–59; 14** 414; **25** 283, 285; **32** 355; **38** 402; **46 337–41 (upd.)**
Peasant Restaurants Inc., **30** 330
Pease Industries, **39** 322, 324
Peat Marwick. *See* KPMG Peat Marwick.
Peaudouce, **IV** 339
**Peavey Electronics Corporation, II** 494; **12** 81; **16 408–10**
Peavey Paper Mills, Inc., **26** 362
Pebble Beach Corp., **II** 170
PEC Plastics, **9** 92
Pechelbronn Oil Company, **III** 616; **17** 416–17
Pechenganickel MMC, **48** 300
**Pechiney S.A., I** 190, 341; **IV** 12, 59, 108, **173–75**, 560; **V** 605; **12** 253–54; **14** 216; **26** 403; **31** 11; **45 334–37 (upd.)**
Péchiney-Saint-Gobain, **I** 389; **III** 677; **16** 121
**PECO Energy Company, 11 387–90**. *See also* Exelon Corporation.
**Pediatric Services of America, Inc., 31 356–58**
Pedigree Petfoods, **22** 298
**Peebles Inc., 16 411–13; 43 296–99 (upd.)**
**Peek & Cloppenburg KG, 46 342–45**
Peekskill Chemical Works. *See* Binney & Smith Inc.
Peel-Conner Telephone Works, **II** 24
Peerless, **III** 467; **8** 74; **11** 534
Peerless Gear & Machine Company, **8** 515
Peerless Industries, Inc., **III** 569; **20** 360; **39** 264
Peerless Paper Co., **IV** 310; **19** 266
Peerless Pump Co., **I** 442
Peerless Spinning Corporation, **13** 532
Peerless Systems, Inc., **17** 263
**Peet's Coffee & Tea, Inc., 13** 493; **18** 37; **38 338–40**
Pegulan, **I** 426–27; **25** 464
PEI. *See* Process Engineering Inc.
Peine, **IV** 201
Pekema Oy, **IV** 470–71
Peko-Wallsend Ltd., **13** 97
Pel-Tex Oil Co., **IV** 84; **7** 188
Pelican and British Empire Life Office, **III** 372
Pelican Homestead and Savings, **11** 107
Pelican Insurance Co., **III** 349
Pelican Life Assurance, **III** 371–72
Pelikan Holding AG, **18** 388
**Pella Corporation, 10** 95; **12 384–86; 22** 346; **39 322–25 (upd.)**
Pelto Oil Corporation, **14** 455; **44** 362
PEM International Ltd., **28** 350
Pemex. *See* Petróleos Mexicanos.
Peñarroya, **IV** 107–08
Penda Corp., **19** 415
Pendexcare Ltd., **6** 181
Pendle Travel Services Ltd. *See* Airtours Plc.
**Pendleton Woolen Mills, Inc., 42 275–78**
Pengrowth Gas Corp., **25** 232
The Penguin Group, **46** 337
Penguin Publishing Co. Ltd., **IV** 585, 659
Penhaligon's, **24** 237
Peninsula Stores, Ltd. *See* Lucky Stores, Inc.
**The Peninsular and Oriental Steam Navigation Company, II** 296; **III** 521–22, 712; **V 490–93; 22** 444; **26** 241, 243; **37** 137; **38 341–46 (upd.)**
**Peninsular and Oriental Steam Navigation Company (Bovis Division), I 588–89**
Peninsular Portland Cement, **III** 704
Peninsular Power, **6** 602
Peninsular Railroad Company, **17** 440
Penn Advertising, **27** 280
Penn-American Refining Co., **IV** 489
Penn Central Corp., **I** 435; **II** 255; **IV** 576; **10** 71, 73, 547; **17** 443
Penn Champ Co., **9** 72
Penn Controls, **III** 535–36; **26** 229
Penn Corp., **13** 561
Penn Cress Ice Cream, **13** 393
**Penn Engineering & Manufacturing Corp., 28 349–51**
Penn Fuel Co., **IV** 548
Penn Health, **III** 85
**Penn National Gaming, Inc., 33 327–29**
Penn Square Bank, **II** 248, 262
Penn-Texas Corporation, **I** 434; **12** 71
**Penn Traffic Company, 8** 409–10; **13** 95, **393–95**
Penn-Western Gas and Electric, **6** 524
Pennaco Hosiery, Inc., **12** 93
Pennington Drug, **III** 10
**Pennon Group Plc, 45 338–41**
Pennroad Corp., **IV** 458
Pennsalt Chemical Corp., **I** 383
**Pennsylvania Blue Shield, III 325–27**
Pennsylvania Coal & Coke Corp., **I** 434
Pennsylvania Coal Co., **IV** 180
Pennsylvania Electric Company, **6** 535; **27** 182
Pennsylvania Farm Bureau Cooperative Association, **7** 17–18
Pennsylvania Gas and Water Company, **38** 51
Pennsylvania General Fire Insurance Assoc., **III** 257
Pennsylvania General Insurance Company, **48** 431
Pennsylvania Glass Sand Co., **I** 464; **11** 198
Pennsylvania House, Inc., **10** 324; **12** 301
Pennsylvania International Raceway, **V** 494
Pennsylvania Life Insurance Company, **27** 47
**Pennsylvania Power & Light Company, V** 676, **693–94; 11** 388
Pennsylvania Pump and Compressor Co., **II** 16
Pennsylvania Railroad, **I** 456, 472; **II** 329, 490; **6** 436; **10** 71–73; **26** 295
Pennsylvania Refining Co., **IV** 488–89
Pennsylvania Salt Manufacturing Co., **I** 383
Pennsylvania Steel Co., **IV** 35; **7** 48
Pennsylvania Steel Foundry and Machine Co., **39** 32
Pennsylvania Water & Power Company, **25** 44
**Pennwalt Corporation, I 382–84; IV** 547; **12** 18; **21** 205
Penny Curtiss Baking Co., Inc., **13** 395
**Pennzoil Company, IV 488–90**, 551, 553; **10** 190; **14** 491, 493; **20 418–22 (upd.); 23** 40–41; **25** 443, 445; **39** 330; **41** 391, 394; **47** 436
Penray, **I** 373
Penrod Drilling Corporation, **7** 228, 558

Pension Benefit Guaranty Corp., **III** 255; **12** 489
**Penske Corporation**, **V 494–95**; **19** 223, **292–94 (upd.)**; **20** 263
Penske Motorsports, **32** 440
Penske Truck Rental, **24** 445
**Pentair, Inc.**, **III** 715; **7 419–21**; **11** 315; **26 361–64 (upd.)**
Pental Insurance Company, Ltd., **11** 523
Pentane Partners, **7** 518
Pentastar Transportation Group, Inc. *See* Dollar Thrifty Automotive Group, Inc.
Pentaverken A.B., **I** 209
**Pentech International, Inc.**, **14** 217; **29 372–74**
Pentes Play, Inc., **27** 370, 372
**Pentland Group plc**, **20 423–25**; **35** 204, 206–07
Pentland Industries PLC, **V** 375; **26** 396–97
**Penton Media, Inc.**, **9** 414; **27 360–62**; **33** 335–36
**People Express Airlines Inc.**, **I** 90, 98, 103, **117–18**, 123–24, 129–30; **6** 129; **21** 142; **22** 220
People That Love (PTL) Television, **13** 279
People's Bank of Halifax, **II** 210
People's Bank of New Brunswick, **II** 210
People's Drug Store, **II** 604–05; **22** 37–38
People's Ice and Refrigeration Company, **9** 274
People's Insurance Co., **III** 368
People's Natural Gas, **IV** 548; **6** 593
People's Radio Network, **25** 508
People's Trust Co. of Brooklyn, **II** 254; **9** 124
Peoples, **24** 315–16
Peoples Bancorp, **14** 529
Peoples Bank, **13** 467; **17** 302
Peoples Bank & Trust Co., **31** 207
Peoples Bank of Youngstown, **9** 474
**Peoples Energy Corporation**, **6 543–44**
Peoples Finance Co., **II** 418
Peoples Gas Light & Coke Co., **IV** 169; **6** 529, 543–44
Peoples Gas Light Co., **6** 455; **25** 44
Peoples Jewelers of Canada, **16** 561; **40** 472
Peoples Life Insurance Co., **III** 218
Peoples National Bank, **41** 178–79
Peoples Natural Gas Company of South Carolina, **6** 576
Peoples Restaurants, Inc., **17** 320–21
Peoples Savings of Monroe, **9** 482
Peoples Security Insurance Co., **III** 219
PeopleServe, Inc., **29** 401
**PeopleSoft Inc.**, **11** 78; **14 381–83**; **33 330–33 (upd.)**; **38** 432
**The Pep Boys—Manny, Moe & Jack**, **11 391–93**; **16** 160; **26** 348; **36 361–64 (upd.)**
PEPCO. *See* Portland Electric Power Company *and* Potomac Electric Power Company.
Pepe Clothing Co., **18** 85
**Pepper Hamilton LLP**, **43 300–03**
Pepperell Manufacturing Company, **16** 533–34
Pepperidge Farm, **I** 29; **II** 480–81; **7** 67–68; **26** 56–57, 59
**The Pepsi Bottling Group, Inc.**, **40 350–53**
**PepsiCo, Inc.**, **I** 234, 244–46, 257, 269, **276–79**, 281, 291; **II** 103, 448, 477, 608; **III** 106, 116, 588; **7** 265, 267, 396, 404, 434–35, 466, 505–06; **8** 399; **9** 177, 343; **10** 130, 199, 227, 324, **450–54 (upd.)**; **11** 421, 450; **12** 337, 453; **13** 162, 284, 448, 494; **15** 72, 75, 380; **16** 96; **18** 65; **19** 114, 221; **21** 143, 313, 315–16, 362, 401, 405, 485–86; **22** 95, 353; **23** 418, 420; **25** 91, 177–78, 366, 411; **28** 271, 473, 476; **31** 243; **32** 59, 114, 205; **36** 234, 237; **38 347–54 (upd.)**; **40** 340–42, 350–52
Pepsodent Company, **I** 14; **9** 318
Perception Technology, **10** 500
Percy Bilton Investment Trust Ltd., **IV** 710
Percy Street Investments Ltd., **IV** 711
**Perdue Farms Inc.**, **7 422–24**, 432; **23 375–78 (upd.)**; **32** 203
Perfect Circle Corp., **I** 152
Perfect Fit Industries, **17** 182–84
Perfect-Ventil GmbH, **9** 413
Performance Contracting, Inc., **III** 722; **20** 415
**Performance Food Group Company**, **31 359–62**
Performance Technologies, Inc., **10** 395
Perfumania, Inc., **22** 157
Pergamon Holdings, **15** 83
Pergamon Press, **IV** 611, 641–43, 687; **7** 311–12
**Perini Corporation**, **8 418–21**; **38** 481
Perisem, **I** 281
**The Perkin-Elmer Corporation**, **III** 455, 727; **7 425–27**; **9** 514; **13** 326; **21** 123
Perkins, **I** 147; **12** 90
Perkins Bacon & Co., **10** 267
Perkins Cake & Steak, **9** 425
Perkins Engines Ltd., **III** 545, 652; **10** 274; **11** 472; **19** 294; **27** 203
**Perkins Family Restaurants, L.P.**, **22 417–19**
Perkins Oil Well Cementing Co., **III** 497
Perkins Products Co., **II** 531
Perl Pillow, **19** 304
Perland Environmental Technologies Inc., **8** 420
Permal Group, **27** 276, 513
Permaneer Corp., **IV** 281; **9** 259. *See also* Spartech Corporation.
Permanent General Companies, Inc., **11** 194
Permanent Pigments Inc., **25** 71
Permanente Cement Company, **I** 565; **44** 152
Permanente Metals Corp., **IV** 15, 121–22
Permian Corporation, **V** 152–53
PERMIGAN, **IV** 492
Permodalan, **III** 699
**Pernod Ricard S.A.**, **I** 248, **280–81**; **21 399–401 (upd.)**
Pernvo Inc., **I** 387
**Perot Systems Corporation**, **13** 482; **29 375–78**
Perret-Olivier, **III** 676; **16** 120
Perrier, **19** 50
Perrier Corporation of America, **16** 341
**Perrigo Company**, **12** 218, **387–89**
Perrin, **IV** 614
Perrot Brake Co., **I** 141
Perrow Motor Freight Lines, **6** 370
Perry Brothers, Inc., **24** 149
Perry Capital Corp., **28** 138
Perry Drug Stores Inc., **12** 21; **26** 476
**Perry Ellis International, Inc.**, **16** 37; **41 291–94**
Perry Manufacturing Co., **16** 37
Perry Sports, **13** 545; **13** 545
Perry Tritech, **25** 103–05
Perry's Shoes Inc., **16** 36
Perscombinatie, **IV** 611
Pershing & Co., **22** 189
Personal Care Corp., **17** 235
Personal Performance Consultants, **9** 348
Personal Products Company, **III** 35; **8** 281, 511
Personnel Pool of America, **29** 224, 26–27
**Perstorp A.B.**, **I 385–87**
**PERTAMINA**, **IV** 383, 461, **491–93**, 517, 567
Pertec Computer Corp., **17** 49; **18** 434
Pertech Computers Ltd., **18** 75
Perusahaan Minyak Republik Indonesia, **IV** 491
Peruvian Corp., **I** 547
Pet Food & Supply, **14** 385
Pet Foods Plus Inc., **39** 355
**Pet Incorporated**, **I** 457; **II** 486–87; **7 428–31**; **10** 554; **12** 124; **13** 409; **14** 214; **24** 140; **27** 196; **43** 217; **46** 290
**Petco Animal Supplies, Inc.**, **29 379–81**
**Pete's Brewing Company**, **18** 72, 502; **22 420–22**
Peter Bawden Drilling, **IV** 570; **24** 521
Peter, Cailler, Kohler, Chocolats Suisses S.A., **II** 546; **7** 381
Peter Cundill & Associates Ltd., **15** 504
Peter Gast Shipping GmbH, **7** 40; **41** 42
Peter J. Schmitt Co., **13** 394; **24** 444–45
Peter J. Schweitzer, Inc., **III** 40; **16** 303; **43** 257
Peter Jones, **V** 94
**Peter Kiewit Sons' Inc.**, **I** 599–600; **III** 198; **8 422–24**; **15** 18; **25** 512, 514
Peter Norton Computing Group, **10** 508–09
Peter Paul/Cadbury, **II** 477, 512; **15** 221
Peterbilt Motors Co., **I** 185–86; **26** 355
Peters-Revington Corporation, **26** 100. *See also* Chromcraft Revington, Inc.
Peters Shoe Co., **III** 528
**Petersen Publishing Company**, **21 402–04**
Peterson, Howell & Heather, **V** 496
Peterson Soybean Seed Co., **9** 411
Petit Bateau, **35** 263
La Petite Academy, **13** 299
Petite Sophisticate, **V** 207–08
Petoseed Co. Inc., **29** 435
**Petrie Stores Corporation**, **8 425–27**
Petrini's, **II** 653
**Petro-Canada Limited**, **IV** 367, **494–96**, 499; **13** 557
Petro/Chem Environmental Services, Inc., **IV** 411
Petro-Coke Co. Ltd., **IV** 476
Petro-Lewis Corp., **IV** 84; **7** 188
Petroamazonas, **IV** 511
Petrobas, **21** 31
Petrobel, **IV** 412
Petrobrás. *See* Petróleo Brasileiro S.A.
Petrocarbona GmbH, **IV** 197–98
Petrocel, S.A., **19** 12
Petrochemical Industries Co., **IV** 451
Petrochemicals Company, **17** 90–91
Petrochemie Danubia GmbH, **IV** 486–87
Petrochim, **IV** 498
PetroChina Company Ltd., **46** 86
Petrocomercial, **IV** 511

Petrocorp. *See* Petroleum Company of New Zealand.
Petroecuador. *See* Petróleos del Ecuador.
Petrofertil, **IV** 501
**PetroFina S.A.**, **IV** 455, 495, **497–500**, 576; **7** 179; **26 365–69 (upd.)**
Petrogal. *See* Petróleos de Portugal.
Petroindustria, **IV** 511
Petrol, **IV** 487
Petrol Ofisi Anonim Sirketi, **IV** 564
Petrolane Properties, **17** 558
**Petróleo Brasileiro S.A.**, **IV** 424, **501–03**
Petróleo Mecânica Alfa, **IV** 505
**Petróleos de Portugal S.A.**, **IV 504–06**
**Petróleos de Venezuela S.A.**, **II** 661; **IV** 391–93, **507–09**, 571; **24** 522; **31** 113
**Petróleos del Ecuador**, **IV 510–11**
**Petróleos Mexicanos**, **IV 512–14**, 528; **19** 10, **295–98 (upd.)**; **41** 147
Petroleum and Chemical Corp., **III** 672
Petroleum Authority of Thailand, **IV** 519
Petroleum Company of New Zealand, **IV** 279; **19** 155
Petroleum Development (Qatar) Ltd., **IV** 524
Petroleum Development (Trucial States) Ltd., **IV** 363
Petroleum Development Corp. of the Republic of Korea, **IV** 455
**Petroleum Development Oman LLC**, **IV 515–16**
**Petroleum Helicopters, Inc.**, **35 334–36**; **37** 288; **39** 8
Petroleum Projects Co., **IV** 414
Petroleum Research and Engineering Co. Ltd., **IV** 473
Petrolgroup, Inc., **6** 441
Petroliam Nasional Bhd. *See* Petronas.
**Petrolite Corporation**, **15 350–52**
Petrolube, **IV** 538
Petromex. *See* Petróleos de Mexico S.A.
Petromin Lubricating Oil Co., **17** 415
**Petronas**, **IV 517–20**; **21** 501
Petronor, **IV** 514, 528
Petropeninsula, **IV** 511
Petroproduccion, **IV** 511
Petroquímica de Venezuela SA, **IV** 508
Petroquimica Española, **I** 402
Petroquisa, **IV** 501
PETROSUL, **IV** 504, 506
Petrotransporte, **IV** 511
**PETsMART, Inc.**, **14 384–86**; **27** 95; **29** 379–80; **41 295–98 (upd.)**; **45** 42
Petstuff, Inc., **14** 386; **41** 297
Pettibone Corporation, **19** 365
Petzazz, **14** 386
**Peugeot S.A.**, **I** 163, **187–88**; **II** 13; **III** 508; **11** 104; **26** 11. *See also* PSA Peugeot Citroen S.A.
**The Pew Charitable Trusts**, **35 337–40**
**Pez Candy, Inc.**, **38 355–57**
Pfaff-Pegasus of U.S.A. Inc., **15** 385
Pfaltz & Bauer, Inc., **38** 3
The Pfaltzgraff Co. *See* Susquehanna Pfaltzgraff Company.
Pfaudler Vacuum Co., **I** 287
Pfauter-Maag Cutting Tools, **24** 186
PFCI. *See* Pulte Financial Companies, Inc.
PFD Supply, Inc., **47** 304
PFI Acquisition Corp., **17** 184
Pfizer, Hoechst Celanese Corp., **8** 399
**Pfizer Inc.**, **I** 301, 367, **661–63**, 668; **9** 356, **402–05 (upd.)**; **10** 53–54; **11** 207, 310–11, 459; **12** 4; **17** 131; **19** 105; **38 358–67 (upd.)**; **44** 175
Pflueger Corporation, **22** 483
**PG&E Corporation**, **26 370–73 (upd.)**; **27** 131. *See also* Portland General Electric.
PGA. *See* The Professional Golfers' Association.
PGH Bricks and Pipes, **III** 735
Phaostron Instruments and Electronic Co., **18** 497–98
**Phar-Mor Inc.**, **12** 209, **390–92**, 477; **18** 507; **21** 459; **22** 157
Pharma Plus Drugmarts, **II** 649–50
PharmaCare Management Services, Inc., **45** 136
**Pharmacia & Upjohn Inc.**, **25** 22, **374–78 (upd.)**; **34** 177, 179
**Pharmacia A.B.**, **I** 211, **664–65**
Pharmaco Dynamics Research, Inc., **10** 106–07
Pharmacom Systems Ltd., **II** 652
Pharmacy Corporation of America, **16** 57
PharmaKinetics Laboratories, Inc., **10** 106
Pharmanex, Inc., **27** 352
Pharmaprix Ltd., **II** 663
Pharmazell GmbH, **IV** 324
Pharmedix, **11** 207
Pharos, **9** 381
Phelan & Collender, **III** 442
Phelan Faust Paint, **8** 553
**Phelps Dodge Corporation**, **IV** 33, **176–79**, 216; **7** 261–63, 288; **19** 375; **28 352–57 (upd.)**; **40** 411
Phenix Bank, **II** 312
Phenix Cheese Corp., **II** 533
Phenix Insurance Co., **III** 240
Phenix Mills Ltd., **II** 662
PHF Life Insurance Co., **III** 263; **IV** 623
**PHH Corporation**, **V 496–97**; **6** 357; **22** 55
PHI. *See* Pizza Hut, Inc.
Phibro Corporation, **II** 447–48; **IV** 80; **13** 447–48; **21** 67
Philadelphia and Reading Corp., **I** 440; **II** 329; **6** 377; **25** 165
Philadelphia Carpet Company, **9** 465
Philadelphia Coke Company, **6** 487
Philadelphia Company, **6** 484, 493
Philadelphia Drug Exchange, **I** 692
**Philadelphia Eagles**, **37 305–08**
**Philadelphia Electric Company**, **V 695–97**; **6** 450
Philadelphia Life, **I** 527
Philadelphia Smelting and Refining Co., **IV** 31
Philadelphia Sports Clubs. *See* Town Sports International, Inc.
**Philadelphia Suburban Corporation**, **39 326–29**
Philco Corp., **I** 167, 531; **II** 86; **III** 604; **13** 402
Phildar, **37** 22
Phildrew Ventures, **44** 147
**Philip Environmental Inc.**, **16 414–16**
**Philip Morris Companies Inc.**, **I** 23, 269; **II** 530–34; **V** 397, 404, **405–07**, 409, 417; **6** 52; **7** 272, 274, 276, 548; **8** 53; **9** 180; **12** 337, 372; **13** 138, 517; **15** 64, 72–73, 137; **18** 72, **416–19 (upd.)**; **19** 112, 369; **20** 23; **22** 73, 338; **23** 427; **26** 249, 251; **29** 46–47; **32** 472, 476; **44 338–43 (upd.)**. *See also* Kraft Foods Inc.
Philip Smith Theatrical Enterprises. *See* GC Companies, Inc.
Philipp Abm. Cohen, **IV** 139
Philipp Brothers Chemicals, Inc., **II** 447; **IV** 79–0; **25** 82
**Philipp Holzmann AG**, **II** 279, 386; **14** 169; **16** 284, 286; **17 374–77**
Philippine Aerospace Development Corporation, **27** 475
**Philippine Airlines, Inc.**, **I** 107; **6 106–08**, 122–23; **23 379–82 (upd.)**; **27** 464
Philippine American Life Insurance Co., **III** 195
Philippine Sinter Corp., **IV** 125
Philips, **V** 339; **6** 101; **10** 269; **22** 194
**Philips Electronics N.V.**, **8** 153; **9** 75; **10** 16; **12** 475, 549; **13** 396, **400–03 (upd.)**; **14** 446; **23** 389; **26** 334; **27** 190–92; **32** 373; **34** 258; **37** 121; **47** 383–86
**Philips Electronics North America Corp.**, **13 396–99**; **26** 334
N.V. Philips Gloeilampenfabriken, **I** 107, 330; **II** 25, 56, 58, **78–80**, 99, 102, 117, 119; **III** 479, 654–55; **IV** 680; **12** 454. *See also* Philips Electronics N.V.
Philips Medical Systems, **29** 299
Phillip Hawkins, **III** 169; **6** 285
Phillip Securities, **16** 14; **43** 8
Phillippe of California, **8** 16; **36** 24
Phillips & Drew, **II** 379
Phillips & Jacobs, Inc., **14** 486
Phillips Cables, **III** 433
Phillips Carbon Black, **IV** 421
Phillips Colleges Inc., **22** 442; **39** 102
Phillips Manufacturing Company, **8** 464
**Phillips Petroleum Company**, **I** 377; **II** 15, 408; **III** 752; **IV** 71, 290, 366, 405, 412, 414, 445, 453, 498, **521–23**, 567, 570–71, 575; **10** 84, 440; **11** 522; **13** 356, 485; **17** 422; **19** 176; **24** 521; **31** 457; **38** 407; **40 354–59 (upd.)**; **47** 70
Phillips Sheet and Tin Plate Co., **IV** 236
**Phillips-Van Heusen Corporation**, **24 382–85**
PHLCorp., **11** 261
PHM Corp., **8** 461
Phoenicia Glass, **25** 266–67
Phoenix Assurance Co., **III** 242, 257, 369, 370–74
Phoenix Financial Services, **11** 115
Phoenix Fire Office, **III** 234
Phoenix Insurance Co., **III** 389; **IV** 711
Phoenix Microsystems Inc., **13** 8
Phoenix Mutual Life Insurance, **16** 207
Phoenix Oil and Transport Co., **IV** 90
Phoenix-Rheinrohr AG, **IV** 222
Phoenix State Bank and Trust Co., **II** 213
Phoenix Technologies Ltd., **13** 482
Phone America of Carolina, **8** 311
Phonogram, **23** 389
PhotoChannel Networks, Inc., **45** 283
Photocircuits Corp., **18** 291–93
PhotoDisc Inc., **31** 216, 218
**PHP Healthcare Corporation**, **22 423–25**
Phuket Air Catering Company Ltd., **6** 123–24; **27** 464
**PhyCor, Inc.**, **36 365–69**
Physical Measurements Information, **31** 357
Physician Corporation of America, **24** 231
**Physician Sales & Service, Inc.**, **14 387–89**
Physician's Weight Loss Center, **10** 383
Physicians Formula Cosmetics, **8** 512

Physicians Placement, **13** 49
**Physio-Control International Corp., 18 420–23; 30** 316
Physiotherapy Associates Inc., **29** 453
Piaget, **27** 487, 489
**Piaggio & C. S.p.A., 17** 24; **20 426–29; 36** 472; **39** 36–37
Piam Pty. Ltd., **48** 364
**PIC International Group PLC, 24 386–88 (upd.)**
Pic 'N' Save, **17** 298–99
PIC Realty Corp., **III** 339
Picard Surgeles, **27** 93
Picault, **19** 50
**Piccadilly Cafeterias, Inc., 19 299–302**
Pick, **III** 98
Pick-N-Pay, **II** 642; **9** 452
Pick Pay, **48** 63
Pickands Mather, **13** 158
Picker International Corporation, **II** 25; **8** 352; **30** 314
Pickfords Ltd., **6** 412–14
Pickland Mather & Co., **IV** 409
PickOmatic Systems, **8** 135
Pickwick Dress Co., **III** 54
Pickwick International, **I** 613; **9** 360; **38** 315
Piclands Mather, **7** 308
Pico Ski Area Management Company, **28** 21
Picture Classified Network, **IV** 597
**PictureTel Corp., 10 455–57; 27 363–66 (upd.)**
Piece Goods Shops, **16** 198
Piedmont Airlines, Inc., **6** 132; **12** 490; **28** 507
Piedmont Coca-Cola Bottling Partnership, **10** 223
Piedmont Concrete, **III** 739
**Piedmont Natural Gas Company, Inc., 27 367–69**
Piedmont Pulp and Paper Co. *See* Westvaco Corporation.
**Pier 1 Imports, Inc., 12** 179, 200, **393–95; 34 337–41 (upd.)**
Pierburg GmbH, **9** 445–46
Pierce, **IV** 478
Pierce Brothers, **6** 295
**Pierce Leahy Corporation, 24 389–92.** *See also* Iron Mountain Inc.
Pierce National Life, **22** 314
Pierce Steam Heating Co., **III** 663
**Piercing Pagoda, Inc., 29 382–84; 40** 472
**Pierre & Vacances SA, 48 314–16**
Pierre Foods, **13** 270–72; **29** 203
Pierson, Heldring, and Pierson, **II** 185
Pietrafesa Corporation, **29** 208
Pietro's Pizza Parlors, **II** 480–81; **26** 56–57; **44** 85
Piezo Electric Product, Inc., **16** 239
Pig Improvement Co., **II** 500
**Piggly Wiggly Southern, Inc., II** 571, 624; **13** 251–52, **404–06; 18** 6, 8; **21** 455; **22** 127; **26** 47; **27** 245; **31** 406, 408; **32** 260
Pignone, **IV** 420
Pike Adding Machine, **III** 165
Pike Corporation of America, **I** 570; **8** 191
Pikrose and Co. Ltd., **IV** 136
Pilgrim Curtain Co., **III** 213
**Pilgrim's Pride Corporation, 7 432–33; 23 383–85 (upd.); 39** 229
**Pilkington plc, I** 429; **II** 475; **III** 56, 641–42, 676–77, 714–15, **724–27; 16** 7, 9, 120–21; **22** 434; **34 342–47 (upd.)**
Pillar Holdings, **IV** 191
Pilliod Furniture, Inc., **12** 300
**Pillowtex Corporation, 19 303–05; 31** 200; **41 299–302 (upd.)**
**Pillsbury Company, II** 133, 414, 493–94, 511, **555–57**, 575, 613–15; **7** 106, 128, 277, 469, 547; **8** 53–54; **10** 147, 176; **11** 23; **12** 80, 510; **13 407–09 (upd.)**, 516; **14** 212, 214; **15** 64; **16** 71; **17** 70–71, 434; **22** 59, 426; **24** 140–41; **25** 179, 241; **27** 196, 287; **29** 433; **32** 32, 67; **38** 100
**Pillsbury Madison & Sutro LLP, 29 385–88**
Pilot, **I** 531
Pilot Freight Carriers, **27** 474
Pilot Insurance Agency, **III** 204
Pinal-Dome Oil, **IV** 569; **24** 520
**Pinault-Printemps-Redoute S.A., 15** 386; **19 306–09 (upd.); 22** 362; **27** 513; **41** 185–86; **42** 171
Pincus & Co., **7** 305
Pine Tree Casting. *See* Sturm, Ruger & Company, Inc.
Pinecliff Publishing Company, **10** 357
Pinelands, Inc., **9** 119; **26** 33
Pinelands Water Company, **45** 275, 277
Pineville Kraft Corp., **IV** 276
Pinewood Studios, **II** 157
Pininfarina, **I** 188
**Pinkerton's Inc., 9 406–09; 13** 124–25; **14** 541; **16** 48; **41** 77, 79. *See also* Securitas AB.
Pinnacle Art and Frame, **31** 436
Pinnacle Books, **25** 483
Pinnacle Fitness, **25** 42
**Pinnacle West Capital Corporation, 6 545–47; 26** 359
Pinsetter Corp., **III** 443
Pinto Island Metals Company, **15** 116
Pioneer Airlines, **I** 96; **21** 141
Pioneer Asphalt Co., **I** 404; **36** 146–47
Pioneer Asphalts Pty. Ltd., **III** 728
Pioneer Bank, **41** 312
Pioneer Concrete Services Ltd., **III** 728–29
Pioneer Cotton Mill, **12** 503
**Pioneer Electronic Corporation, II** 103; **III 604–06; 28 358–61 (upd.)**
Pioneer Federal Savings Bank, **10** 340; **11** 115
Pioneer Financial Corp., **11** 447
Pioneer Food Stores Co-op, **24** 528
**Pioneer Hi-Bred International, Inc., 9 410–12; 17** 131; **21** 387; **41 303–06 (upd.)**
**Pioneer International Limited, III** 687, **728–30; 28** 83
Pioneer Life Insurance Co., **III** 274
Pioneer Natural Gas Company, **10** 82
Pioneer Outdoor, **27** 280
Pioneer Plastics Corporation, **31** 399–400
Pioneer Readymixed Concrete and Mortar Proprietary Ltd., **III** 728
Pioneer Saws Ltd., **III** 598
**Pioneer-Standard Electronics Inc., 13** 47; **19 310–14**
Pipasa, **41** 329
Pipe Line Service Company. *See* Plexco.
Pipeline and Products Marketing Co., **IV** 473
Piper Aircraft Corp., **I** 482; **II** 403; **8** 49–50
**Piper Jaffray Companies Inc., 22 426–30**, 465. *See also* U.S. Bancorp.
**Pirelli S.p.A., IV** 174, 420; **V 249–51; 10** 319; **15 353–56 (upd.); 16** 318; **21** 73; **28** 262
Piscataquis Canal and Railroad Company, **16** 348
Pisces Inc., **13** 321
Pispalan Werhoomo Oy, **I** 387
The Piston Ring Company, **I** 199; **10** 492
Pitcairn Aviation, **I** 101
**Pitney Bowes, Inc., III 156–58**, 159; **19 315–18 (upd.); 47 295–99 (upd.)**
Pittman Company, **28** 350
Pittsburgh & Lake Angeline Iron Company, **13** 156
Pittsburgh & Lake Erie Railroad, **I** 472
Pittsburgh Aluminum Alloys Inc., **12** 353
Pittsburgh Brewing Co., **10** 169–70; **18** 70, 72
Pittsburgh Chemical Co., **IV** 573; **7** 551
Pittsburgh Consolidation Coal Co., **8** 346
Pittsburgh Corning Corp., **III** 683
Pittsburgh Life, **III** 274
Pittsburgh National Bank, **II** 317, 342; **22** 55
Pittsburgh National Corp., **II** 342
Pittsburgh Paint & Glass. *See* PPG Industries, Inc.
Pittsburgh Plate Glass Co. *See* PPG Industries, Inc.
Pittsburgh Railway Company, **9** 413
Pittsburgh Reduction Co., **II** 315; **IV** 9, 14
Pittsburgh Steel Company, **7** 587
Pittsburgh Trust and Savings, **II** 342
**The Pittston Company, IV 180–82**, 566; **10** 44; **19 319–22 (upd.)**
**Pittway Corporation, 9 413–15; 27** 361–62; **28** 133–34; **33 334–37 (upd.)**
**Pixar Animation Studios, 34 348–51**
Pixel Semiconductor, **11** 57
Pizitz, Inc., **19** 324
Pizza Dispatch. *See* Dominos's Pizza, Inc.
**Pizza Hut Inc., I** 221, 278, 294; **II** 614; **7** 152–53, 267, **434–35**, 506; **10** 450; **11** 50; **12** 123; **13** 336, 516; **14** 107; **15** 344–46; **16** 446; **17** 71, 537; **21** 24–25, 315, **405–07 (upd.); 22** 353; **24** 295; **25** 179–80, 227; **28** 238; **33** 388; **40** 340
**Pizza Inn, Inc., 46 346–49; 16** 447; **25** 179
PizzaCo, Inc., **7** 152
Pizzeria Uno, **25** 178
PJS Publications, **22** 442
PKbanken, **II** 353
Place Two, **V** 156
Placer Cego Petroleum Ltd., **IV** 367
Placer Development Ltd., **IV** 19
**Placer Dome Inc., IV** 571; **20 430–33; 24** 522; **36** 314
Placid Oil Co., **7** 228
Plaid Holdings Corp., **9** 157
Plain Jane Dress Company, **8** 169
Plainwell Paper Co., Inc., **8** 103
**Planet Hollywood International, Inc., 18 424–26; 25** 387–88; **32** 241, 243–44; **41 307–10 (upd.)**
Planet Insurance Co., **III** 343
Planet Waves, **48** 232
Plank Road Brewery, **I** 269; **12** 337
Plankinton Packing Co., **III** 534
Plant Genetics Inc., **I** 266; **21** 320

Planters Company, **24** 287
Planters Lifesavers, **14** 274–75
Planters Nut & Chocolate Co., **I** 219; **II** 544
Plas-Techs, Inc., **15** 35
Plastic Coating Corporation, **IV** 330; **8** 483
Plastic Containers, Inc., **15** 129; **25** 512
Plastic Engineered Products Company. *See* Ballard Medical Products.
Plastic Parts, Inc., **19** 277
Plasticos Metalgrafica, **I** 231
Plastics, Inc., **13** 41
Plasto Bambola. *See* BRIO AB.
Plastrier. *See* Compagnie de Saint-Gobain S.A.
Plate Glass Group, **24** 450
Plateau Holdings, Inc., **12** 260; **13** 502
**Platinum Entertainment, Inc., 35 341–44**
**PLATINUM Technology, Inc., 14 390–92**
**Plato Learning, Inc., 44 344–47**
Platt & Co., **I** 506
Platt Bros., **III** 636
Platt's Price Service, Inc., **IV** 636–37
**Play by Play Toys & Novelties, Inc., 26 374–76**
Play It Again Sam (PIAS), **44** 164
Play It Again Sports, **18** 207–08
**Playboy Enterprises, Inc., 18 427–30; 48** 148
**PlayCore, Inc., 27 370–72**
**Players International, Inc., 16** 263, 275; **19** 402; **22 431–33**; **33** 41; **43** 226–27
Playland, **16** 389
**Playmates Toys, 23 386–88**
Playmobil. *See* geobra Brandstätter GmbH & Co. KG.
**Playskool, Inc., III** 504, 506; **12** 169; **13** 317; **16** 267; **25 379–81**; **43** 229, 232
**Playtex Products, Inc., II** 448, 468; **8** 511; **13** 448; **15 357–60**; **24** 480
Playworld, **16** 389–90
Plaza Coloso S.A. de C.V., **10** 189
Plaza Medical Group, **6** 184
Plaza Securities, **I** 170
PLC. *See* Prescription Learning Corporation.
**Pleasant Company, 25** 314; **27 373–75**
Pleasurama PLC, **I** 248; **12** 228; **32** 243
**Plessey Company, PLC, II** 25, 39, **81–82**; **IV** 100; **6** 241; **33** 287–88
Plews Manufacturing Co., **III** 602
Plexco, **7** 30–31
**Plexus Corporation, 35 345–47**
Plezall Wipers, Inc., **15** 502
Plitt Theatres, Inc., **6** 162; **23** 126
Plon et Juillard, **IV** 614
Plough Inc., **I** 684
Plum Associates, **12** 270
**Plum Creek Timber Company, Inc., 43 304–06**
**Pluma, Inc., 27 376–78**
Plumb Tool, **II** 16
Plus Development Corporation, **10** 458–59
Plus Mark, Inc., **7** 24
Plus System Inc., **9** 537
Plus-Ultra, **II** 196
Plus Vita, **36** 162
Pluto Technologies International Inc., **38** 72
**Ply Gem Industries Inc., 12 396–98; 23** 225
Plymouth County Electric Co., **14** 124
Plymouth Mills Inc., **23** 66
PMC Contract Research AB, **21** 425
PMC Specialties Group, **III** 745
PMI Corporation, **6** 140. *See also* Physical Measurements Information
PMI Mortgage Insurance Company, **10** 50
PMS Consolidated, **8** 347
**PMT Services, Inc., 24 393–95**
PN Pertambangan Minyak Dan Gas Bumi Negara, **IV** 492
**PNC Bank Corp., 13 410–12 (upd.); 14** 103; **18** 63
**PNC Financial Corporation, II** 317, **342–43**; **9** 476; **17** 114
**The PNC Financial Services Group Inc., 46 350–53 (upd.)**
Pneumo Abex Corp., **I** 456–58; **III** 512; **10** 553–54; **38** 293–94
Pneumo Dynamics Corporation, **8** 409
PNL. *See* Pacific Northwest Laboratories.
PNM. *See* Public Service Company of New Mexico.
PNP. *See* Pacific Northwest Power Company.
POAS, **IV** 563
POB Polyolefine Burghausen GmbH, **IV** 487
Pocahontas Foods USA, **31** 359, 361
Pocket Books, Inc., **10** 480; **13** 559–60
Poclain Company, **10** 380
Poe & Associates, Inc., **41** 63–64
**Pogo Producing Company, I** 441; **39 330–32**
**Pohang Iron and Steel Company Ltd., IV 183–85**; **17** 351
Pohjan Sellu Oy, **IV** 316
Pohjoismainen Osakepankki, **II** 302
Pohjola Voima Oy, **IV** 348
Pohjolan Osakepankki, **II** 303
Point Chehalis Packers, **13** 244
Polak & Schwarz Essencefabricken, **9** 290
Poland Spring Natural Spring Water Co., **31** 229
Polar Manufacturing Company, **16** 32
Polar Star Milling Company, **7** 241
**Polaris Industries Inc., 12 399–402; 35 348–53 (upd.)**; **40** 47, 50
**Polaroid Corporation, I** 30–31; **II** 412; **III** 475–77, 549, 584, **607–09**; **IV** 330; **7** 161–62, **436–39 (upd.)**; **12** 180; **28 362–66 (upd.)**; **36** 171–73; **41** 104, 106
Polbeth Packaging Limited, **12** 377
Polenghi, **25** 84
**Policy Management Systems Corporation, 11 394–95**
**Poliet S.A., 33** 175–77, **338–40**; **40** 108
Polioles, S.A. de C.V., **19** 10, 12
Politos, S.A. de C.V., **23** 171
**Polk Audio, Inc., 34 352–54**
Pollenex Corp., **19** 360
Polo Food Corporation, **10** 250
**Polo/Ralph Lauren Corporation, 9** 157; **12 403–05**; **16** 61; **25** 48
Polser, **19** 49, 51
Polskie Linie Lotnicze S.A. *See* LOT Polish Airlines.
Poly-Glas Systems, Inc., **21** 65
Poly-Hi Corporation, **8** 359
Poly P, Inc., **IV** 458
Poly Version, Inc., **III** 645
Polyblend Corporation, **7** 4
Polycell Holdings, **IV** 666; **17** 397
Polydesign België, **16** 421
Polydesign Nederland, **16** 421
Polydor B.V., **23** 389
Polydor KK, **23** 390
Polydress Plastic GmbH, **7** 141
Polygon Networks Inc., **41** 73
**PolyGram N.V., 13** 402; **22** 194; **23 389–92**; **25** 411; **26** 152, 314, 394; **31** 269
Polyken Technologies, **11** 220
Polymer Technologies Corporation, **26** 287
Polysar Energy & Chemical Corporation of Toronto, **V** 674
Polysius AG, **IV** 89
**Pomeroy Computer Resources, Inc., 33 341–44**
Pomeroy's, **16** 61
Pommersche Papierfabrik Hohenkrug, **III** 692
Pommery et Greno, **II** 475
**Ponderosa Steakhouse, 7** 336; **12** 373; **14** 331; **15 361–64**
Ponderosa System Inc., **12** 199
Pont-à-Mousson S.A., **III** 675, 677–78, 704; **16** 119, 121–22; **21** 253
Pont Royal SA, **48** 316
Pontiac, **III** 458; **10** 353
Pontificia, **III** 207
Ponto Frio Bonzao, **22** 321
Pony Express, **II** 380–81, 395
**Poore Brothers, Inc., 44 348–50**
Poorman-Douglas Corporation, **13** 468
Pop.com, **43** 144
**Pope and Talbot, Inc., 12 406–08**
Pope Cable and Wire B.V., **19** 45
Pope Tin Plate Co., **IV** 236; **26** 527
Popeye's/Church's, **23** 115, 117
Popeyes Famous Fried Chicken and Biscuits, Inc., **7** 26–28; **32** 13
Pophitt Cereals, Inc., **22** 337
Poppe Tyson Inc., **23** 479; **25** 91
Poppin' Fresh Pies, Inc., **12** 510
Popsicle, **II** 573; **14** 205
Popular Aviation Company, **12** 560
Popular Club Plan, **12** 280; **34** 232
**Popular, Inc., 41 311–13**
Popular Merchandise, Inc., **12** 280
Pori, **IV** 350
Poron Diffusion, **9** 394
Poron, S.A., **42** 268–69
**Porsche AG, 13** 28, 219, **413–15**; **31 363–366 (upd.)**; **36** 198
Port Arthur Finance Corp., **37** 309
**The Port Authority of New York and New Jersey, 47** 359; **48 317–20**
Port Blakely Mill Company, **17** 438
Port Dickson Power Sdn. Bhd., **36** 435–36
Port Harcourt Refining Co., **IV** 473
Port of London Authority, **48** 317
Port Stockton Food Distributors, Inc., **16** 451, 453
Portage Industries Corp., **19** 415
**Portal Software, Inc., 47 300–03**
Portals Water Treatment, **11** 510
Porter-Cable Corporation, **26** 361–63
Porter Chadburn plc, **28** 252
Porter Shoe Manufacturing Company, **13** 360
Portex, **25** 431
Portia Management Services Ltd., **30** 318
**Portland General Corporation, 6 548–51**
Portland General Electric, **45** 313
Portland Heavy Industries, **10** 369
Portland Plastics, **25** 430–31
Portland-Zementwerke Heidelberg A.G., **23** 326
Portnet, **6** 435
Portsmouth & Sunderland, **35** 242, 244

Portugalia, **46** 398
Portways, **9** 92
Poseidon Exploration Ltd., **IV** 84; **7** 188
Posey, Quest, Genova, **6** 48
Positive Response Television, Inc., **27** 337–38
Post Office Counters, **V** 496
**Post Office Group, V 498–501**
**Post Properties, Inc., 26 377–79**
PostBank, **II** 189
**La Poste, V 470–72**
**Posti- Ja Telelaitos, 6 329–31**
PostScript, **17** 177
Postum Cereal Company, **II** 497, 523, 530–31; **7** 272–73; **13** 291
**Potash Corporation of Saskatchewan Inc.**, **18** 51, **431–33**; **27** 318
**Potlatch Corporation**, **IV** 282; **8 428–30**; **9** 260; **19** 445; **34 355–59 (upd.)**
Potomac Edison Company, **38** 39–40
**Potomac Electric Power Company**, **6 552–54**; **25** 46
Potomac Insurance Co., **III** 257
Potomac Leasing, **III** 137
**Potter & Brumfield Inc., 11 396–98**
Pottery Barn, **13** 42; **17** 548–50
Potts, **IV** 58
Poulan/Weed Eater. *See* White Consolidated Industries Inc.
Poulsen Wireless, **II** 490
PowCon, Inc., **17** 534
**Powell Duffryn plc**, **III** 502; **IV** 38; **31 367–70**
Powell Energy Products, **8** 321
Powell Group, **33** 32
Powell River Co. Ltd., **IV** 306–07
**Powell's Books, Inc.**, **37** 181; **40 360–63**
Power Applications & Manufacturing Company, Inc., **6** 441
**Power Corporation of Canada**, **36 370–74 (upd.)**
Power Financial Corp., **III** 260–61
Power Jets Ltd., **I** 81
Power Parts Co., **7** 358
Power Products, **8** 515
Power Specialty Company, **6** 145
Power Team, **10** 492
**PowerBar Inc., 44 351–53**
Powercor. *See* PacifiCorp.
PowerFone Holdings, **10** 433
**PowerGen PLC**, **11 399–401**; **12** 349; **13** 458, 484
**Powerhouse Technologies, Inc.**, **13** 485; **27 379–81**
Powers Accounting Machine Company, **6** 240
Powers Regulator, **III** 535
Powers-Samas, **6** 240
PowerSoft Corp., **11** 77; **15** 374
Powertel Inc., **48** 130
Pozzi-Renati Millwork Products, Inc., **8** 135
PP&L. *See* Pennsylvania Power & Light Company.
PP&L Global, Inc., **44** 291
**PPG Industries, Inc.**, **I** 330, 341–42; **III** 21, 641, 667, 676, 722, 725, **731–33**; **8** 153, 222, 224; **16** 120–21; **20** 415; **21** 221, 223; **22** 147, **434–37 (upd.)**; **37** 73; **39** 292
PPI. *See* Precision Pattern Inc.
**PPL Corporation**, **41 314–17 (upd.)**
PR Holdings, **23** 382
**PR Newswire, 35 354–56**
Prac, **I** 281
Practical and Educational Books, **13** 105
Practical Business Solutions, Inc., **18** 112
**Prada Holding B.V., 45 342–45**
Pragma Bio-Tech, Inc., **11** 424
Prairie Farmer Publishing Co., **II** 129
**Prairie Farms Dairy, Inc., 47 304–07**
Prairie Holding Co., **IV** 571; **24** 522
Prairie Oil and Gas Co., **IV** 368
Prairielands Energy Marketing, Inc., **7** 322, 325
Prakla Seismos, **17** 419
**Pratt & Whitney**, **I** 47, 78, 82–85, 128, 434; **II** 48; **III** 482; **6** 128; **7** 456; **9** 14, 16–18, 244–46, **416–18**; **10** 162; **11** 299, 427; **12** 71; **13** 386; **14** 564; **24** 312; **25** 267; **39** 313
Pratt Holding, Ltd., **IV** 312; **19** 268
Pratt Hotel Corporation, **21** 275; **22** 438
Pratt Properties Inc., **8** 349
Pratta Electronic Materials, Inc., **26** 425
**Praxair, Inc.**, **11 402–04**; **16** 462; **43** 265; **48 321–24 (upd.)**
Praxis Biologics, **8** 26; **27** 115
Praxis Corporation, **30** 499
Pre-Fab Cushioning, **9** 93
**Pre-Paid Legal Services, Inc., 20 434–37**
PreAnalytiX, **39** 335
Precious Metals Development, **IV** 79
Precise Fabrication Corporation, **33** 257
Precise Imports Corp., **21** 516
**Precision Castparts Corp., 15 365–67**
Precision Games, **16** 471
Precision Husky Corporation, **26** 494
Precision Interconnect Corporation, **14** 27
Precision LensCrafters, **13** 391
Precision Moulds, Ltd., **25** 312
Precision Optical Co., **III** 120, 575
Precision Optical Industry Company, Ltd. *See* Canon Inc.
Precision Pattern Inc., **36** 159
Precision Power, Inc., **21** 514
Precision Response Corporation, **47** 420
Precision Software Corp., **14** 319
Precision Studios, **12** 529
Precision Tube Formers, Inc., **17** 234
Precor, **III** 610–11
Predica, **II** 266
Predicasts Inc., **12** 562; **17** 254
Preferred Medical Products. *See* Ballard Medical Products.
Preferred Products, Inc., **II** 669; **18** 504
PREINCO Holdings, Inc., **11** 532
PREL&P. *See* Portland Railway Electric Light & Power Company.
Prelude Corp., **III** 643
**Premark International, Inc.**, **II** 534; **III 610–12**; **14** 548; **28** 479–80
**Premcor Inc., 37 309–11**
Premex A.G., **II** 369
Premier (Transvaal) Diamond Mining Co., **IV** 65–66
Premier & Potter Printing Press Co., Inc., **II** 37
Premier Brands Foods, **II** 514
Premier Consolidated Oilfields PLC, **IV** 383
Premier Cruise Lines, **6** 368; **27** 92
Premier Diamond Mining Company, **7** 122
Premier Health Alliance Inc., **10** 143
**Premier Industrial Corporation**, **9 419–21**; **19** 311
Premier Insurance Co., **26** 487
Premier Medical Services, **31** 357
Premier Milling Co., **II** 465
Premier One Products, Inc., **37** 285
**Premier Parks, Inc., 27 382–84**
Premier Radio Networks, Inc., **23** 292, 294
Premier Rehabilitation Centers, **29** 400
Premier Sport Group Inc., **23** 66
Premiere Products, **I** 403
Premisteres S.A., **II** 663
**Premium Standard Farms, Inc., 30 353–55**
**PremiumWear, Inc., 30 356–59**
Prémontré, **III** 676; **16** 120
Prentice Hall Computer Publishing, **10** 24
Prentice Hall Inc., **I** 453; **IV** 672; **19** 405; **23** 503
Prescott Ball & Turben, **III** 271; **12** 60
Prescott Investors, **14** 303
Prescription Learning Corporation, **7** 256; **25** 253
Présence, **III** 211
La Preservatrice, **III** 242
**Preserver Group, Inc., 44 354–56**
Preserves and Honey, Inc., **II** 497
President Baking Co., **36** 313
**President Casinos, Inc., 22 438–40**
President Riverboat Casino-Mississippi Inc., **21** 300
Presidential Airlines, **I** 117
Presidents Island Steel & Wire Company. *See* Laclede Steel Company.
Presidio Oil Co., **III** 197; **IV** 123
Press Associates, **IV** 669; **19** 334
Press Trust of India, **IV** 669
Presse Pocket, **IV** 614
Pressed Steel Car Co., **6** 395; **25** 169
Presses de la Cité, **IV** 614–15
Presstar Printing, **25** 183
**Presstek, Inc., 33 345–48**
Pressware International, **12** 377
Prest-O-Lite Co., Inc., **I** 399; **9** 16, 516; **11** 402
Prestage Farms, **46** 83
Prestige et Collections, **III** 48
Prestige Fragrance & Cosmetics, Inc., **22** 158
The Prestige Group plc., **19** 171
Prestige International, **33** 284
Prestige Leather Creations, **31** 435–36
Prestige Properties, **23** 388
Presto Products, Inc., **II** 609–10; **IV** 187; **19** 348
**Preston Corporation**, **6 421–23**; **14** 566, 568
Prestone Products Corp., **22** 32; **26** 349
Prestwick Mortgage Group, **25** 187
Pretty Good Privacy, Inc., **25** 349
Pretty Neat Corp., **12** 216
Pretty Paper Inc., **14** 499
Pretty Polly, **I** 429
Pretzel Time. *See* Mrs. Fields' Original Cookies, Inc.
Pretzelmaker. *See* Mrs. Fields' Original Cookies, Inc.
Pretzels Incorporated, **24** 241
**Preussag AG**, **I** 542–43; **II** 386; **IV** 109, 201, 231; **17 378–82**; **21** 370; **28** 454; **42 279–83 (upd.)**; **44** 432
**Preussenelektra Aktiengesellschaft**, **I** 542; **V 698–700**; **39** 57
Preval, **19** 49–50
Previews, Inc., **21** 96
PreVision Marketing, Inc., **37** 409
Priam Corporation, **10** 458
Priba, **26** 158, 160

Pribina, **25** 85
Price Chopper Supermarkets. *See* The Golub Corporation.
Price Club, **V** 162–64
Price Co., **34** 198
**Price Communications Corporation, 42 284–86**
**Price Company Ltd, II** 664; **IV** 246–47; **V 162–64**; **14** 393–94; **25** 11
Price Enterprises, Inc., **14** 395
Price, McCormick & Co., **26** 451
Price Rite, **25** 67
**Price Waterhouse LLP, III** 84, 420, 527; **9 422–24**; **14** 245; **26** 439. *See also* PricewaterhouseCoopers
**PriceCostco, Inc., 14 393–95**
Pricel, **6** 373; **21** 103
Pricesearch Ltd Co, **48** 224
**PricewaterhouseCoopers, 29 389–94 (upd.)**
Prichard and Constance, **III** 65
Pride & Clarke, **III** 523
Pride Petroleum Services. *See* DeKalb Genetics Corporation.
Priggen Steel Building Co., **8** 545
Primadonna Resorts Inc., **17** 318
**Primark Corp., 10** 89–90; **13 416–18**
Prime Care International, Inc., **36** 367
Prime Computer, Inc. *See* Computervision Corporation.
Prime Motor Inns Inc., **III** 103; **IV** 718; **11** 177; **17** 238
The Prime-Mover Co., **13** 267
Prime Service, Inc., **28** 40
Prime Telecommunications Corporation, **8** 311
PrimeAmerica, **III** 340
**Primedex Health Systems, Inc., 25 382–85**
**Primedia Inc., 7** 286; **12** 306; **21** 403–04; **22 441–43**; **23** 156, 158, 344, 417; **24** 274
Primergy Corp., **39** 261
**Primerica Corporation, I** 597, 599–602, 604, 607–09, **612–14**, 615; **II** 422; **III** 283 **8** 118; **9** 218–19, 360–61; **11** 29; **15** 464; **27** 47; **36** 202. *See also* American Can Co.
Primerica Financial Services, **30** 124
PriMerit Bank, **19** 412
Primes Régal Inc., **II** 651
PrimeSource, **26** 542
Primestar, **38** 176
PRIMESTAR Partners L.P., **28** 241
Primex Fibre Ltd., **IV** 328
Primo Foods Ltd., **I** 457; **7** 430
Prince Co., **II** 473
Prince Gardner Company, **17** 465; **23** 21
Prince Golf International, Ltd., **23** 450
Prince Holding Corporation, **26** 231
Prince Motor Co. Ltd., **I** 184
Prince of Wales Hotels, PLC, **14** 106; **25** 308
**Prince Sports Group, Inc., 15 368–70**
Prince Street Technologies, Ltd., **8** 271
Prince William Bank, **II** 337; **10** 425
**Princess Cruise Lines, IV** 256; **22 444–46**
Princess Dorothy Coal Co., **IV** 29
Princess Hotel Group, **21** 353
Princess Hotels International Inc., **45** 82
Princess Metropole, **21** 354
Princeton Gas Service Company, **6** 529
Princeton Laboratories Products Company, **8** 84; **38** 124
**The Princeton Review, Inc., 12** 142; **42** 210, **287–90**
Princeton Telecommunications Corporation, **26** 38
Princeville Airlines, **24** 22
**Principal Mutual Life Insurance Company, III 328–30**
Principles, **V** 21–22
Princor Financial Services Corp., **III** 329
Pringle Barge Line Co., **17** 357
Print Technologies, Inc., **22** 357
Printex Corporation, **9** 363
**Printrak, A Motorola Company, 44 357–59**
**Printronix, Inc., 14** 377–78; **18 434–36**
Priority Records, **22** 194
Pripps Ringnes, **18** 394, 396–97
Prism Systems Inc., **6** 310
Prismo Universal, **III** 735
Prisunic SA, **V** 9–11; **19** 307–09
Prisunic-Uniprix, **26** 160
Pritchard Corporation. *See* Black & Veatch, Inc.
Pritzker & Pritzker, **III** 96–97
Privatbanken, **II** 352
Pro-Fac Cooperative, Inc., **7** 104–06; **21** 154–55, 157
Pro-Lawn, **19** 250
Pro-Line Corporation, **36** 26
Pro-optik AG, **31** 203
Probe Exploration Inc., **25** 232
Process Engineering Inc., **21** 108
Process Systems International, **21** 108
Processing Technologies International. *See* Food Ingredients Technologies.
Procino-Rossi Corp., **II** 511
Procor Limited, **16** 357
Procordia Foods, **II** 478; **18** 396
**Procter & Gamble Company, I** 34, 129, 290, 331, 366; **II** 478, 493, 544, 590, 684, 616; **III** 20–25, 36–38, 40–41, 44, **50–53**; **IV** 282, 290, 329–30; **6** 26–27, 50–52, 129, 363; **7** 277, 300, 419; **8** 63, 106–07, 253, 282, 344, 399, **431–35 (upd.)**, 477, 511–12; **9** 260, 291, 317–19, 552; **10** 54, 288; **11** 41, 421; **12** 80, 126–27, 439; **13** 39, 197, 199, 215; **14** 121–22, 262, 275; **15** 357; **16** 302–04, 440; **18** 68, 147–49, 217, 229; **22** 146–47, 210; **26 380–85 (upd.)**; **32** 208, 474–77; **35** 111, 113; **37** 270; **38** 365; **42** 51; **43** 257–58
Proctor & Collier, **I** 19
Proctor & Schwartz, **17** 213
Proctor-Silex. *See* Hamilton Beach/Proctor-Silex Inc.
Prodega Ltd. *See* Bon Appetit Holding AG.
**Prodigy Communications Corporation, 10** 237–38; **12** 562; **13** 92; **27** 517; **34 360–62**
Product Components, Inc., **19** 415
Production Association Kirishinefteorgsintez, **48** 378
Productos Ortiz, **II** 594
Produits Chimiques Ugine Kuhlmann, **I** 303; **IV** 547
Produits Jaeger, **27** 258
Profarmaco Nobel S.r.l., **16** 69
Professional Care Service, **6** 42
Professional Computer Resources, Inc., **10** 513
Professional Education Systems, Inc., **17** 272
**The Professional Golfers' Association of America, 41 318–21**
Professional Health Care Management Inc., **14** 209
Professional Research, **III** 73
**Proffitt's, Inc., 19 323–25**, 510, 512. *See also* Saks Holdings, Inc.
Profile Extrusion Company, **22** 337
Profimatics, Inc., **11** 66
PROFITCo., **II** 231
Progenx, Inc., **47** 221
Progil, **I** 389
Progress Development Organisation, **10** 169
**Progress Software Corporation, 15 371–74**
Progressive Bagel Concepts, Inc. *See* Einstein/Noah Bagel Corporation.
**Progressive Corporation, 11 405–07**; **29 395–98 (upd.)**
Progressive Distributions Systems, **44** 334
Progressive Distributors, **12** 220
Progressive Grocery Stores, **7** 202
Progressive Networks, **37** 193
Progresso, **I** 514; **14** 212
Project Carriers. *See* Hansa Linie.
Projexions Video Supply, Inc., **24** 96
Projiis, **II** 356
Prolabo, **I** 388
Proland, **12** 139
Proler International Corp., **13** 98; **19** 380–81
Promarkt Holding GmbH, **24** 266, 270
Promigas, **IV** 418
Promodès Group, **24** 475; **26** 158, 161; **37** 21
Promotional Graphics, **15** 474
Promstroybank, **II** 242
**Promus Companies, Inc., III** 95; **9 425–27**; **15** 46; **16** 263; **22** 537; **38** 76–77; **43** 225–26
Pronto Pacific, **II** 488
Prontophot Holding Limited, **6** 490
Prontor-Werk Alfred Gauthier GmbH, **III** 446
Propaganda Films, Inc., **23** 389, 391
Prophet Foods, **I** 449
Propwix, **IV** 605
ProSiebenSat.1 Media AG, **46** 403
Prosim, S.A., **IV** 409
**Proskauer Rose LLP, 47 308–10**
ProSource Distribution Services, Inc., **16** 397; **17** 475
Prospect Farms, Inc., **II** 584; **14** 514
The Prospect Group, Inc., **11** 188
Prospect Provisions, Inc. *See* King Kullen Grocery Co., Inc.
Prospectors Airways, **IV** 165
Protan & Fagertun, **25** 464
**Protection One, Inc., 32 372–75**
Protective Closures, **7** 296–97
La Protectrice, **III** 346–47
Protek, **III** 633
Proto Industrial Tools, **III** 628
Protogene Laboratories Inc., **17** 288
Proveedora de Seguridad del Golfo, S.A. de C.V., **45** 425–26
Proventus A.B., **II** 303
Proventus Handels AB, **35** 362
Provi-Soir, **II** 652
Provi-Viande, **II** 652
Provibec, **II** 652

**The Providence Journal Company**, **28 367–69**; **30** 15
La Providence, **III** 210–11
Providence National Bank, **9** 228
Providence Steam and Gas Pipe Co. *See* Grinnell Corp.
Providencia, **III** 208
Provident Bank, **III** 190
Provident Institution for Savings, **13** 467
**Provident Life and Accident Insurance Company of America**, **III 331–33**, 404
Provident National Bank, **II** 342
Provident Services, Inc., **6** 295
Provident Travelers Mortgage Securities Corp., **III** 389
**Provigo Inc.**, **II 651–53**; **12** 413
Provimi, **36** 185
Les Provinces Réunies, **III** 235
Provincetown-Boston Airlines, **I** 118
Provincial Bank of Ireland Ltd., **16** 13
Provincial Engineering Ltd, **8** 544
Provincial Gas Company, **6** 526
Provincial Insurance Co., **III** 373
Provincial Newspapers Ltd., **IV** 685–86; **28** 502
Provincial Traders Holding Ltd., **I** 437
Provinzial-Hülfskasse, **II** 385
Provost & Provost, **II** 651
PROWA, **22** 89
Proximity Technology, **23** 210
Prudential Assurance Company, **24** 314
Prudential Bache Securities, **9** 441
Prudential-Bache Trade Corporation, **II** 51; **21** 331
**Prudential Corporation plc**, **II** 319; **III 334–36**; **IV** 711; **8** 276–77. *See also* Prudential plc.
**Prudential Insurance Company of America**, **I** 19, 334, 402; **II** 103, 456; **III** 79, 92, 249, 259, 265–67, 273, 291–93, 313, 329, **337–41**; **IV** 410, 458; **10** 199; **11** 243; **12** 28, 453, 500; **13** 561; **14** 95, 561; **16** 135, 497; **17** 325; **22** 266; **23** 226; **25** 399; **30 360–64 (upd.)**; **36** 77–78; **42** 193, 196; **45** 294
Prudential Oil & Gas, Inc., **6** 495–96
**Prudential plc**, **48 325–29 (upd.)**
Prudential Refining Co., **IV** 400
Prudential Steel, **IV** 74; **24** 143–44
PSA. *See* Pacific Southwest Airlines.
**PSA Peugeot Citroen S.A.**, **7** 35; **28 370–74 (upd.)**
PSB Company, **36** 517
PSCCo. *See* Public Service Company of Colorado.
PSE, Inc., **12** 100
PSF. *See* Premium Standard Farms, Inc.
PSI. *See* Process Systems International.
**PSI Resources**, **6 555–57**
**Psion PLC**, **45 346–49**
Psychiatric Institutes of America, **III** 87–88
Psychological Corp., **IV** 623; **12** 223
PT Components, **14** 43
PT PERMINA, **IV** 492, 517
PTI Communications, Inc. *See* Pacific Telecom, Inc.
PTT Nederland N.V., **27** 472; **30** 393–94
PTT Telecom BV, **V** 299–301; **6** 303
PTV. *See* Österreichische Post- und Telegraphenverwaltung.
**Pubco Corporation**, **17 383–85**
Publi-Graphics, **16** 168
Public Broadcasting Stations, **29** 426
Public Home Trust Co., **III** 104
Public National Bank, **II** 230
Public Savings Insurance Co., **III** 219
Public Service Co., **14** 124
**Public Service Company of Colorado**, **6 558–60**
Public Service Company of Indiana. *See* PSI Energy.
**Public Service Company of New Hampshire**, **21 408–12**
**Public Service Company of New Mexico**, **6 561–64**; **27** 486
Public Service Corporation of New Jersey, **44** 360
Public Service Electric and Gas Company, **IV** 366; **V** 701–03; **11** 388
**Public Service Enterprise Group Inc.**, **V 701–03**; **44 360–63 (upd.)**
Public Service Market. *See* The Golub Corporation.
Public Storage, Inc., **21** 476
Public/Hacienda Resorts, Inc. *See* Santa Fe Gaming Corporation.
Publicaciones Citem, S.A. de C.V., **39** 188
**Publicis S.A.**, **13** 204; **19 329–32**; **21** 265–66; **23** 478, 480; **25** 91; **33** 180; **39** 166, 168; **42** 328, 331
Publicker Industries Inc., **I** 226; **10** 180
**Publishers Clearing House**, **23 393–95**; **27** 20
**Publishers Group, Inc.**, **35 357–59**
Publishers Paper Co., **IV** 295, 677–78; **19** 225
Publishers Press Assoc., **IV** 607; **25** 506
Publishing and Broadcasting Ltd., **19** 400–01
**Publix Super Markets Inc.**, **II** 155, 627; **7 440–42**; **9** 186; **20** 84, 306; **23** 261; **31 371–374 (upd.)**
Puck Holdings, **35** 474, 476
Puck Lazaroff Inc. *See* The Wolfgang Puck Food Company, Inc.
**Pueblo Xtra International, Inc.**, **47 311–13**
Puente Oil, **IV** 385
Puerto Rican Aqueduct and Sewer Authority, **6** 441
Puerto Rican-American Insurance Co., **III** 242
**Puerto Rico Electric Power Authority**, **47 314–16**
Puget Mill Company, **12** 406–07
Puget Sound Alaska Van Lines. *See* Alaska Hydro-Train.
Puget Sound National Bank, **8** 469–70
**Puget Sound Power And Light Company**, **6 565–67**
Puget Sound Pulp and Timber Co., **IV** 281; **9** 259
Puget Sound Tug and Barge Company, **6** 382
**Pulaski Furniture Corporation**, **33 349–52**
**Pulitzer Publishing Company**, **15 375–77**
Pullman Co., **II** 403; **III** 94, 744
Pullman Savings and Loan Association, **17** 529
Pullman Standard, **7** 540
**Pulsar Internacional S.A.**, **21 413–15**
Pulse Engineering, Inc., **29** 461
**Pulte Corporation**, **8 436–38**; **22** 205, 207
**Pulte Homes, Inc.**, **42 291–94 (upd.)**
**Puma AG Rudolf Dassler Sport**, **35 360–63**; **36** 344, 346
AB Pump-Separator, **III** 418–19
**Pumpkin Masters, Inc.**, **48 330–32**
Punchcraft, Inc., **III** 569; **20** 360
Purdue Fredrick Company, **13** 367
Pure Milk Products Cooperative, **11** 24
Pure Oil Co., **III** 497; **IV** 570; **24** 521
Pure Packed Foods, **II** 525; **13** 293
Purex Corporation, **I** 450; **III** 21; **22** 146
Purex Pool Systems, **I** 13, 342; **18** 163
Purfina, **IV** 497
**Purina Mills, Inc.**, **32 376–79**
Puris Inc., **14** 316
**Puritan-Bennett Corporation**, **13 419–21**
Puritan Chemical Co., **I** 321
Puritan Fashions Corp., **22** 122
Purity Stores, **I** 146
Purity Supreme, Inc., **II** 674; **24** 462
Purle Bros., **III** 735
Purnell & Sons Ltd., **IV** 642; **7** 312
Purodenso Co., **III** 593
Purolator Courier, Inc., **6** 345–46, 390; **16** 397; **18** 177; **25** 148
**Purolator Products Company**, **III** 593; **21 416–18**; **28** 263
Puros de Villa Gonzales, **23** 465
Purup-Eskofot, **44** 44
Push Records, Inc., **42** 271
Puss 'n Boots, **II** 559
Putnam Investments Inc., **25** 387; **30** 355. *See also* Marsh & McLennan Companies, Inc.
Putnam Management Co., **III** 283
Putnam Reinsurance Co., **III** 198
**Putt-Putt Golf Courses of America, Inc.**, **23 396–98**
**PW Eagle, Inc.**, **48 333–36**
**PWA Group**, **IV 323–25**; **28** 446
PWS Holding Corporation, **13** 406; **26** 47
PWT Projects Ltd., **22** 89
PWT Worldwide, **11** 510
PYA/Monarch, **II** 675; **26** 504
**Pyramid Breweries Inc.**, **33 353–55**
Pyramid Communications, Inc., **IV** 623
Pyramid Electric Company, **10** 319
Pyramid Electronics Supply, Inc., **17** 275
Pyramid Technology Corporation, **10** 504; **27** 448
Pytchley Autocar Co. Ltd., **IV** 722
Pyxis. *See* Cardinal Health, Inc.
Pyxis Resources Co., **IV** 182

Q Lube, Inc., **18** 145; **24** 339
**Qantas Airways Limited**, **I** 92–93; **6** 79, 91, 100, 105, **109–13**, 117; **14** 70, 73; **24 396–401 (upd.)**; **27** 466; **31** 104; **38** 24
**Qatar General Petroleum Corporation**, **IV 524–26**
**Qiagen N.V.**, **39 333–35**
Qintex Australia Ltd., **II** 150; **25** 329
QMS Ltd., **43** 284
QO Chemicals, Inc., **14** 217
QSP, Inc., **IV** 664
Qtera Corporation, **36** 352
**Quad/Graphics, Inc.**, **19 333–36**
Quail Oil Tools, **28** 347–48
Quaker Alloy, Inc., **39** 31–32
**Quaker Fabric Corp.**, **19 337–39**
**Quaker Oats Company**, **I** 30; **II 558–60**, 575, 684; **12** 167, 169, **409–12 (upd.)**; **13** 186; **22** 131, 337–38; **25** 90, 314; **27**

197; **30** 219; **31** 282; **34 363–67 (upd.)**; **38** 349; **43** 121, 218
**Quaker State Corporation, 7 443–45; 21 419–22 (upd.)**; **25** 90; **26** 349
**QUALCOMM Incorporated, 20 438–41**; **26** 532; **38** 271; **39** 64; **41** 289; **43** 312–13; **46** 410, 422; **47 317–21 (upd.)**
Qualicare, Inc., **6** 192
QualiTROL Corporation, **7** 116–17
Quality Bakers of America, **12** 170
Quality Care Inc., **I** 249
**Quality Chekd Dairies, Inc., 48 337–39**
Quality Courts Motels, Inc., **14** 105. *See also* Choice Hotels International, Inc.
**Quality Dining, Inc., 18 437–40**
**Quality Food Centers, Inc., 17 386–88**; **22** 271, 273
Quality Importers, **I** 226; **10** 180
Quality Inns International, **13** 363; **14** 105. *See also* Choice Hotels International, Inc.
Quality Markets, Inc., **13** 393
Quality Oil Co., **II** 624–25
Quality Paperback Book Club (QPB), **13** 105–07
Quality Products, Inc., **18** 162
Qualtec, Inc., **V** 623
**Quanex Corporation, 13 422–24**
**Quanta Computer Inc., 47 322–24**
Quantex Microsystems Inc., **24** 31
**Quantum Chemical Corporation, 8 439–41**; **11** 441; **30** 231, 441
Quantum Computer Services, Inc. *See* America Online, Inc.
**Quantum Corporation, 6** 230–31; **10** 56, 403, **458–59**, 463; **25** 530; **36** 299–300
Quantum Health Resources, **29** 364
Quantum Marketing International, Inc., **27** 336
Quantum Offshore Contractors, **25** 104
Quantum Overseas N.V., **7** 360
Quantum Restaurant Group, Inc., **30** 330
Quarex Industries, Inc. *See* Western Beef, Inc.
**Quark, Inc., 36 375–79**
Quarrie Corporation, **12** 554
Quasi-Arc Co., **I** 315; **25** 80
Quebec Bank, **II** 344
Quebec Credit Union League, **48** 290
Quebéc Hydro-Electric Commission. *See* Hydro-Quebéc.
**Quebecor Inc., 12 412–14**; **19** 333; **26** 44; **29** 471; **47 325–28 (upd.)**
Queen Casuals, **III** 530
Queen City Broadcasting, **42** 162
Queen Insurance Co., **III** 350
Queens Isetan Co., Ltd., **V** 87
Queensborough Holdings PLC, **38** 103
Queensland Alumina, **IV** 59
Queensland and Northern Territories Air Service. *See* Qantas Airways Limited.
Queensland Mines Ltd., **III** 729
Queensland Oil Refineries, **III** 672
Queiroz Pereira, **IV** 504
**Quelle Group, V 165–67**
Quennessen, **IV** 118
Quesarias Ibéricas, **23** 219
Quesnel River Pulp Co., **IV** 269
Quest Aerospace Education, Inc., **18** 521
**Quest Diagnostics Inc., 26 390–92**
Quest Education Corporation, **42** 212
Quest Pharmacies Inc., **25** 504–05
**Questar Corporation, 6 568–70**; **10** 432; **26 386–89 (upd.)**
Questor Partners, **I** 332; **26** 185
**The Quick & Reilly Group, Inc., 18** 552; **20 442–44**; **26** 65
QUICK Corp., **IV** 656
Quick-Shop, **II** 619
Quicken.com. *See* Intuit Inc.
Quickie Designs, **11** 202, 487–88
Quik Stop Markets, Inc., **12** 112
**Quiksilver, Inc., 18 441–43**; **27** 329
**QuikTrip Corporation, 36 380–83**
QuikWok Inc., **II** 556; **13** 408
**Quill Corporation, 28 375–77**
Quillery, **27** 138
Quilter Goodison, **II** 260
Quimica Industrial Huels Do Brasil Ltda., **I** 350
Quimicos Industriales Penoles. *See* Industrias Penoles, S.A. de C.V.
Quincy Compressor Co., **I** 434–35
Quincy Family Steak House, **II** 679; **10** 331; **19** 287; **27** 17, 19
Quintana Roo, Inc., **17** 243, 245; **25** 42
Quintex Australia Limited, **25** 329
**Quintiles Transnational Corporation, 21 423–25**
Quinton Hazell Automotive, **III** 495; **IV** 382–83
Quintron, Inc., **11** 475
Quintus Computer Systems, **6** 248
**Quixote Corporation, 15 378–80**
Quixtar Inc., **30** 62
Quixx Corporation, **6** 580
**The Quizno's Corporation, 32** 444; **42 295–98**
Quoddy Products Inc., **17** 389, 390
Quotron Systems, Inc., **III** 119; **IV** 670; **9** 49, 125; **30** 127; **47** 37
**QVC Network Inc., 9 428–29**; **10** 175; **12** 315; **18** 132; **20** 75; **24** 120, 123
**Qwest Communications International, Inc., 25** 499; **26** 36; **32** 218; **36** 43–44; **37** 126, **312–17**
QwikSilver II, Inc., **37** 119

R&B Falcon Corp. *See* Transocean Sedco Forex Inc.
R & B Manufacturing Co., **III** 569; **20** 361
R&O Software-Technik GmbH, **27** 492
R&S Technology Inc., **48** 410
R. and W. Hawaii Wholesale, Inc., **22** 15
R-Anell Custom Homes Inc., **41** 19
R-B. *See* Arby's, Inc.
R-Byte, **12** 162
R-C Holding Inc. *See* Air & Water Technologies Corporation.
R.A. Waller & Co., **III** 282
**R.B. Pamplin Corp., 45 350–52**
R. Buckland & Son Ltd., **IV** 119
R.C. Bigelow, **16** 90
R.C. Willey Home Furnishings, **18** 60
R. Cubed Composites Inc., **I** 387
R.E. Funsten Co., **7** 429
**R.G. Barry Corp., 17 389–91**; **44 364–67 (upd.)**
R.G. Dun-Bradstreet Corp., **IV** 604–05
**R. Griggs Group Limited, 23 399–402**; **31** 413–14
**R.H. Macy & Co., Inc., I** 30; **V 168–70**; **8 442–45 (upd.)**; **10** 282; **11** 349; **13** 42; **15** 281; **16** 206–07, 328, 388, 561; **23** 60; **27** 60, 481; **30 379–83 (upd.)**; **31** 190, 192–93; **45** 15
R.H. Squire, **III** 283
R.H. Stengel & Company, **13** 479
R. Hoe & Co., **I** 602; **13** 189
R. Hornibrook (NSW), **I** 592
R.J. Brown Co., **IV** 373
R.J. Reynolds, **I** 259, 261, 363; **II** 542, 544; **III** 16; **IV** 523; **V** 396, 404–05, 407–10, 413, 415, 417–18; **7** 130, 132, 267, 365, 367; **9** 533; **13** 490; **14** 78; **15** 72–73; **16** 242; **18** 416; **19** 369; **21** 315; **27** 125; **29** 195; **32** 344. *See also* RJR Nabisco.
**R.J. Reynolds Tobacco Holdings, Inc., 30 384–87 (upd.)**
R.J. Tower Corporation. *See* Tower Automotive, Inc.
R.K. Brown, **14** 112
R.L. Crain Limited, **15** 473
R.L. Manning Company, **9** 363–64
**R.L. Polk & Co., 10 460–62**
R.N. Coate, **I** 216
R-O Realty, Inc., **43** 314
R.O. Hull Co., **I** 361
R.P.M., Inc., **25** 228
**R.P. Scherer Corporation, I 678–80**; **33** 145
R.R. Bowker Co., **17** 398; **23** 440
**R.R. Donnelley & Sons Company, IV 660–62**, 673; **9 430–32 (upd.)**; **11** 293; **12** 414, 557, 559; **18** 331; **19** 333; **38 368–71 (upd.)**
R.S.R. Corporation, **31** 48
R.S. Stokvis Company, **13** 499
R. Scott Associates, **11** 57
R. Stock AG, **IV** 198
R-T Investors LC, **42** 323–24
R.T. French USA, **II** 567
R.T. Securities, **II** 457
R.W. Beck, **29** 353
R.W. Harmon & Sons, Inc., **6** 410
R.W. Sears Watch Company, **V** 180
RABA PLC, **10** 274
Rabbit Software Corp., **10** 474
**Rabobank Group, 26** 419; **33 356–58**
**Racal-Datacom Inc., 11 408–10**
**Racal Electronics PLC, II 83–84**; **11** 408, 547; **42** 373, 376
Race Z, Inc. *See* Action Peformance Companies, Inc.
Rachel's Dairy Ltd., **37** 197–98
Racine Hardware Co., **III** 58
Racine Hidraulica, **21** 430
Racine Threshing Machine Works, **10** 377
Racing Champions. *See* Action Performance Companies, Inc.
**Racing Champions Corporation, 37 318–20**
Racing Collectables Club of America, Inc. *See* Action Performance Companies, Inc.
Rack Rite Distributors, **V** 174
Racket Store. *See* Duckwall-ALCO Stores, Inc.
Rada Corp., **IV** 250
**Radian Group Inc., 42 299–301**
Radiant Lamp Corp., **13** 398
Radiation Dynamics, **III** 634–35
Radiation, Inc., **II** 37–38
Radiation-Medical Products Corp., **I** 202
Radiator Specialty Co., **III** 570; **20** 362
Radio & Allied Industries, **II** 25
Radio & Television Equipment Company (Radio-Tel), **16** 200–01; **43** 168–69
Radio Austria A.G., **V** 314–16
Radio Cap Company. *See* Norwood Promotional Products, Inc.
Radio City Productions, **30** 102

Radio Corporation of America. *See* RCA Corporation.
**Radio Flyer Inc., 34 368–70**
Radio-Keith-Orpheum, **II** 32, 88, 135, 146–48, 175; **III** 428; **9** 247; **12** 73; **31** 99
Radio Receptor Company, Inc., **10** 319
Radio Shack, **II** 106–08; **12** 470; **13** 174
Radio Vertrieb Fürth. *See* Grundig AG.
Radiocel, **39** 194
Radiometer A/S, **17** 287
Radiometrics, Inc., **18** 369
RadioShack Canada Inc., **30** 391
**RadioShack Corporation, 36 384–88 (upd.)**
Radiotelevision Española, **7** 511
Radisson Hotels Worldwide, **22** 126–27
Radium Pharmacy, **I** 704
**Radius Inc., 16 417–19**
Radix Group, Inc., **13** 20
RadNet Managed Imaging Services, Inc., **25** 382–84
Radnor Venture Partners, LP, **10** 474
Raet, **39** 177
Raf, Haarla Oy, **IV** 349
Raffinerie Tirlemontoise S.A., **27** 436
Raffineriegesellschaft Vohburg/Ingolstadt mbH, **7** 141
**RAG AG, 35 364–67**
**Rag Shops, Inc., 30 365–67**
Ragan Outdoor, **27** 280
Ragazzi's, **10** 331
Ragnar Benson Inc., **8** 43–43
RAI, **I** 466
Rail Link, Inc., **27** 181
Railroad Enterprises, Inc., **27** 347
**RailTex, Inc., 20 445–47**
Railtrack, **39** 238
Railway Express Agency, **I** 456; **II** 382; **6** 388–89; **25** 146–48
Railway Maintenance Equipment Co., **14** 43
Railway Officials and Employees Accident Assoc., **III** 228
Railway Passengers Assurance Co., **III** 178, 410
Rainbow Crafts, **II** 502; **10** 323
Rainbow Home Shopping Ltd., **V** 160
Rainbow Media, **47** 421
Rainbow Production Corp., **I** 412
Rainbow Programming Holdings, **7** 63–64
Rainbow Resources, **IV** 576
RainbowBridge Communications, Inc., **25** 162
Raincoast Book Distribution, **34** 5
Rainer Pulp & Paper Company, **17** 439
Rainfair, Inc., **18** 298, 300
**Rainforest Café, Inc., 25 386–88**; **32** 241, 244
**Rainier Brewing Company, 23 403–05**
Rainier Pulp and Paper Company. *See* Rayonier Inc.
Rainy River Forest Products, Inc., **26** 445
Rajastan Breweries, Ltd., **18** 502
Raky-Danubia, **IV** 485
Ralcorp Holdings, Inc., **13** 293, 425, 427; **15** 189, 235; **21** 53, 56; **22** 337; **36** 238; **43** 438. *See also* Ralston Purina Company.
**Raley's Inc., 14 396–98**
Ralli International, **III** 502; **IV** 259
**Rally's Hamburgers, Inc., 25 389–91**; **46** 97
Rally's Inc., **14** 452; **15** 345; **16** 96–97; **23** 225
Rallye S.A., **12** 154. *See also* Casino.
Ralph & Kacoo's. *See* Piccadilly Cafeterias, Inc.
Ralph Lauren. *See* Polo/Ralph Lauren Corportion.
The Ralph M. Parsons Company. *See* The Parsons Corporation.
Ralph Wilson Plastics, **III** 610–11
Ralph's Industries, **31** 191
**Ralphs Grocery Company, 35 368–70**
**Ralston Purina Company, I** 608, **II** 544, 560, **561–63**, 617; **III** 588; **6** 50–52; **7** 209, 396, 547, 556; **8** 180; **9** 180; **12** 276, 411, 510; **13** 137, 270, 293, **425–27 (upd.)**; **14** 194–95, 558; **18** 312; **21** 56; **23** 191. *See also* Ralcorp Holdings, Inc.
Ram dis Ticaret, **I** 479
Ram Golf Corp., **III** 24; **32** 447
Ram's Insurance, **III** 370
Ramada International Hotels & Resorts, **II** 142; **III** 99; **IV** 718; **9** 426; **11** 177; **13** 66; **21** 366; **25** 309; **28** 258; **38** 320
Ramazotti, **I** 281
Rambol, **25** 84
Ramo-Woolridge Corp., **I** 539; **14** 510
Ramón Areces Foundation, **V** 52
Rampage Clothing Co., **35** 94
**Ramsay Youth Services, Inc., 41 322–24**
Ranbar Packing, Inc. *See* Western Beef, Inc.
Ranchers Packing Corp. *See* Western Beef, Inc.
Rand American Investments Limited, **IV** 79; **21** 211
Rand Capital Corp., **35** 52–53
Rand Drill Co., **III** 525
Rand Group, Inc., **6** 247; **24** 234
**Rand McNally & Company, 28 378–81**
Rand Mines Ltd., **I** 422; **IV** 22, 79, 94
Rand Selection Corp. Ltd., **IV** 79
**Randall's Food Markets, Inc., 40 364–67**
**Random House, Inc., II** 90; **IV** 583–84, 637, 648; **13** 113, 115, 178, **428–30**; **14** 260; **18** 329; **19** 6, 285; **31 375–380 (upd.)**; **42** 287
Randon Meldkamer, **43** 307
**Randstad Holding n.v., 16 420–22**; **43 307–10 (upd.)**
Randsworth Trust P.L.C., **IV** 703
**Range Resources Corporation, 45 353–55**
**Rank Organisation PLC, II** 139, 147, **157–59**; **III** 171; **IV** 698; **6** 288; **12** 229; **14 399–402 (upd.)**; **24** 194; **26** 543, 546; **32** 241, 243–44; **34** 140; **40** 296, 298
**Ranks Hovis McDougall Limited, II** 157, **564–65**; **28 382–85 (upd.)**
Ransburg Corporation, **22** 282
Ransom and Randolph Company, **10** 271
Ransomes America Corp., **III** 600
**RAO Unified Energy System of Russia, 45 356–60**
**Rapala-Normark Group, Ltd., 30 368–71**
Rapicom, **III** 159
Rapid American, **I** 440
Rapides Bank & Trust Company, **11** 107
Rapidforms, Inc., **35** 130–31
Rapifax of Canada, **III** 160
**Rare Hospitality International Inc., 19 340–42**
RAS. *See* Riunione Adriatica di Sicurtà SpA.
Rascal House, **24** 243
Rassini Rheem, **III** 581
Rational GmbH, **22** 354
Rational Systems Inc., **6** 255; **25** 299
Ratti Vallensasca, **25** 312
Raufast et Fils, **35** 205
Rauland Corp., **II** 124; **13** 573
Rauma-Repola Oy, **II** 302; **IV** 316, 340, 349–50. *See also* Metso Corporation
Rauscher Pierce Refsnes, Inc., **15** 233
**Raven Industries, Inc., 33 359–61**
Raven Press, **14** 555
Ravenhead, **16** 120
Ravenna Metal Products Corp., **12** 344
Ravenseft Properties Ltd., **IV** 696, 704–05
RAVIcad, **18** 20; **43** 17
**Rawlings Sporting Goods Co., Inc., 7** 177; **23** 449; **24 402–04**
Rawlplug Co. Ltd., **IV** 382–83
Rawls Brothers Co., **13** 369
Rawson, Holdsworth & Co., **I** 464
Ray Industries, **22** 116
Ray Simon, **24** 94
Ray Strauss Unlimited, **22** 123
Ray's Printing of Topeka, **II** 624
**Raychem Corporation, III** 492; **8 446–47**
Raycom Sports, **6** 33
Raymar Book Corporation, **11** 194
Raymond International Inc., **28** 201
Raymond, Jones & Co., **IV** 647
Raymond, Trice & Company, **14** 40
Raynet Corporation, **8** 447
Rayonese Textile, Inc., **29** 140
**Rayonier Inc., 24 405–07**
**Rayovac Corporation, 13 431–34**; **17** 105; **23** 497; **24** 480; **39 336–40 (upd.)**
**Raytheon Aircraft Holdings Inc., 46 354–57**
**Raytheon Company, I** 463, 485, 544; **II** 41, 73, **85–87**; **III** 643; **8** 51, 157; **11** 197, **411–14 (upd.)**; **12** 46, 247; **14** 223; **17** 419, 553, 564; **21** 200; **23** 181; **24** 88; **25** 223; **36** 190–91; **38 372–77 (upd.)**; **42** 373, 376; **48** 252
Razorback Acquisitions, **19** 455
**Razorfish, Inc., 37 321–24**
RB&W Corp., **17** 372
RBC Dominion Securities, **25** 12
**RCA Corporation, I** 142, 454, 463; **II** 29–31, 34, 38, 56, 61, 85–86, **88–90**, 96, 102, 117–18, 120, 124, 129, 132–33, 151–52, 313, 609, 645; **III** 118, 122, 132, 149, 152, 165, 171, 569, 653–54; **IV** 252, 583, 594; **6** 164–66, 240, 266, 281, 288, 334; **7** 520; **8** 157; **9** 283; **10** 173; **11** 197, 318, 411; **12** 204, 208, 237, 454, 544, 548; **13** 106, 398, 429, 506, 573; **14** 357, 436; **16** 549; **17** 29; **20** 361; **21** 151; **22** 541; **23** 181; **26** 358, 511; **28** 349; **31** 376; **34** 186, 516; **38** 373
RCA Global Communications, Inc., **27** 304
RCG International, Inc., **III** 344
**RCM Technologies, Inc., 34 371–74**
RCN Corp., **25** 107
**RDO Equipment Company, 33 362–65**
REA. *See* Railway Express Agency.
Rea & Derick, **II** 605
Rea Construction Company, **17** 377
Rea Magnet Wire Co., **IV** 15
React-Rite, Inc., **8** 271
Read, R.L., **II** 417

**Read-Rite Corp.**, **10** 403–04, **463–64**; **18** 250
**The Reader's Digest Association, Inc.**, **IV 663–64**; **17 392–95 (upd.)**
Reader's Garden Inc., **22** 441
Reading & Bates Corp. *See* Transocean Sedco Forex Inc.
Reading Railroad, **9** 407
Ready Mixed Concrete, **III** 687, 737–40; **28** 82
Real Decisions, **21** 236
Real Estate Maintenance, **25** 15
Real Fresh, **25** 85
Real Goods Trading Company, **41** 177
Real-Share, Inc., **18** 542
RealCom Communications Corporation, **15** 196
Reale Mutuale, **III** 273
Reality Group Limited, **47** 165, 169
**The Really Useful Group**, **23** 390; **26 393–95**; **34** 422
Realty Development Co. *See* King Kullen Grocery Co., Inc.
Realty Investment Group, **25** 127
Realty Parking Properties II L.P., **18** 104
Réassurances, **III** 392
Reavis & McGrath, **47** 139
Recaro North America Inc., **26** 231
**Reckitt & Colman plc**, **II 566–67**; **15** 46, 360; **18** 556; **22** 148; **27** 69
**Reckitt Benckiser plc**, **42 302–06 (upd.)**
**Reckson Associates Realty Corp.**, **47 329–31**
Reconstruction Bank of Holland, **IV** 707
Reconstruction Finance Bank, **II** 292
Reconstruction Finance Corp., **I** 67, 203; **II** 261; **IV** 10, 333
Record Bar / Licorice Pizza, **9** 361
Record Merchandisers. *See* Entertainment UK.
Record World Inc., **9** 361
**Recoton Corp.**, **15 381–83**
Recoupe Recycling Technologies, **8** 104
Recovery Centers of America, **III** 88
**Recovery Engineering, Inc.**, **25 392–94**
**Recreational Equipment, Inc.**, **18 444–47**; **22** 173
Recticel S.A., **III** 581; **17** 182–84
Rectigraph Co., **III** 171
**Recycled Paper Greetings, Inc.**, **21 426–28**
RED, **44** 164
Red & White, **II** 682
The Red Adair Company, **37** 171
Red Ant Entertainment, **17** 14
**Red Apple Group, Inc.**, **23 406–08**; **24** 528–29; **31** 231
Red Arrow, **II** 138
Red Ball, Inc., **18** 300
Red Brick Systems Inc., **30** 246
Red Bull, **31** 244
Red Carpet Food Systems, **39** 409
Red Food Stores, Inc., **19** 327–28
**Red Hat, Inc.**, **45 361–64**
Red House Books Ltd., **29** 426
Red Kap, **V** 390–91
Red L Foods, **13** 244
Red Line HealthCare Corporation, **47** 236
Red Lion Entertainment, **29** 503
Red Lobster Inns of America, **16** 156–58
Red Lobster Restaurants, **II** 502–03; **6** 28; **10** 322–24; **19** 258
Red Oak Consulting, **42** 244
Red Owl Stores, Inc., **II** 670; **18** 506
**Red Roof Inns, Inc.**, **13** 363; **18 448–49**; **21** 362
Red Rooster, **V** 35
Red Sea Insurance Co., **III** 251
Red Star Express, **14** 505
Red Star Milling Co., **II** 501; **6** 397; **10** 322
Red Storm, **41** 409
The Red Wing Co., Inc., **28** 382
**Red Wing Shoe Company, Inc.**, **9 433–35**; **30 372–75 (upd.)**
Redactron, **III** 166; **6** 282
Redbook Florists Service, **28** 138
Redbook Publishing Co., **14** 460
Reddy Elevator Co., **III** 467
Reddy Ice, **II** 661
Redentza, **IV** 504
Redgate Communications, **26** 19
Redhill Tile Co., **III** 734
**Redhook Ale Brewery, Inc.**, **31 381–84**
Redi, **IV** 610
Rediffusion, **II** 139; **24** 194
Reditab S.p.A., **12** 109
Redken Laboratories, **8** 131; **24** 251
Redland Plasterboard, **28** 83
**Redland plc**, **III** 495, 688, **734–36**; **14** 249, 739; **15** 154; **37** 205
Redlaw Industries Inc., **15** 247
Redman Industries, Inc., **17** 81, 83
Redmond & Co., **I** 376
La Redoute, S.A., **V** 11; **19** 306, 309
Redpath Industries, **II** 581–82
**Redrow Group plc**, **31 385–87**
Redwood Design Automation, **11** 47; **16** 520
Redwood Fire & Casualty Insurance Co., **III** 214
Redwood Systems, **48** 112
**Reebok International Ltd.**, **V 375–77**; **8** 171, 303–04, 393; **9** 134–35, **436–38 (upd.)**; **11** 50–51, 349; **13** 513; **14** 8; **17** 244–45, 260; **18** 266; **19** 112; **22** 173; **25** 258, 352, 450; **26 396–400 (upd.)**; **36** 346
Reed & Ellis, **17** 439
Reed & Gamage, **13** 243
Reed Corrugated Containers, **IV** 249
**Reed Elsevier plc**, **19** 268; **23** 271, 273; **31 388–394 (upd.)**; **32** 354; **33** 263, 265–66, 458; **34** 438; **43** 92–93
**Reed International PLC**, **I** 423; **IV** 270, 642, **665–67**, 711; **7** 244–45, 343; **10** 407; **12** 359; **17 396–99 (upd.)**; **23** 350
Reed Tool Coompany, **III** 429; **22** 68
Reeder Light, Ice & Fuel Company, **6** 592
Reedpack, **IV** 339–40, 667; **28** 445
**Reeds Jewelers, Inc.**, **22 447–49**
Reese Finer Foods, Inc., **7** 429
Reese Products, **III** 569; **11** 535; **20** 361
Reeves Banking and Trust Company, **11** 181
Reeves Brothers, **17** 182
Reeves Pulley Company, **9** 440
Refco, Inc., **10** 251; **22** 189
Reference Software International, **10** 558
Refined Sugars, **II** 582
Reflectone Inc. *See* CAE USA Inc.
Reflex Winkelmann & Pannhoff GmbH, **18** 163
Reform Rt, **IV** 652; **7** 392
Refractarios Mexicanos, S.A. de C.V., **22** 285
Refrigeração Paraná S.A., **22** 27
Refrigerantes do Oeste, SA, **47** 291
**Regal-Beloit Corporation**, **18 450–53**
Regal Drugs, **V** 171
Regal Inns, **13** 364
Regal Manufacturing Co., **15** 385
Regency, **12** 316
Regency Electronics, **II** 101
Regency Health Services Inc., **25** 457
Regency International, **10** 196
Regenerative Environmental Equipment Company, Inc., **6** 441
Regeneron Pharmaceuticals Inc., **10** 80
Regent Canal Co., **III** 272
Regent Carolina Corporation, **37** 226
Regent Communications Inc., **23** 294
Regent Insurance Co., **III** 343
Regent International Hotels Limited, **9** 238; **29** 200
Régie Autonome des Pétroles, **IV** 544–46; **21** 202–04
Régie des Mines de la Sarre, **IV** 196
Régie des Télégraphes et Téléphones. *See* Belgacom.
**Régie Nationale des Usines Renault**, **I** 136, 145, 148, 178–79, 183, **189–91**, 207, 210; **II** 13; **III** 392, 523; **7** 566–67; **11** 104; **12** 91; **15** 514; **19** 50; **22** 331. *See also* Renault SA.
Regina Verwaltungsgesellschaft, **II** 257
Regional Bell Operating Companies, **15** 125; **18** 111–12, 373
**Regis Corporation**, **18 454–56**; **22** 157; **26** 475, 477
Register & Tribune Co. *See* Cowles Media Company.
Registered Vitamin Company, **V** 171
Regnecentralen AS, **III** 164
Rego Supermarkets and American Seaway Foods, Inc., **9** 451; **13** 237
Rehab Hospital Services Corp., **III** 88; **10** 252
RehabClinics Inc., **11** 367
REI. *See* Recreational Equipment, Inc.
Reich, Landman and Berry, **18** 263
Reichart Furniture Corp., **14** 236
**Reichhold Chemicals, Inc.**, **I** 386, 524; **8** 554; **10 465–67**
Reichs-Kredit-Gesellschaft mbH, **IV** 230
Reichs-Kredit- und Krontrollstelle GmbH, **IV** 230
Reichswerke AG für Berg- und Hüttenbetriebe Hermann Göring, **IV** 200
Reichswerke AG für Erzbergbau und Eisenhütten, **IV** 200
Reichswerke Hermann Göring, **IV** 233
Reid Bros. & Carr Proprietary, **III** 672–73
Reid Dominion Packaging Ltd., **IV** 645
Reid Ice Cream Corp., **II** 471
Reid, Murdoch and Co., **II** 571
Reid Press Ltd., **IV** 645
Reidman Corporation, **41** 65
Reidsville Fashions, Inc., **13** 532
Reigel Products Corp., **IV** 289
Reimersholms, **31** 458–60
Reims Aviation, **8** 92; **27** 100
Rein Elektronik, **10** 459
Reinsurance Agency, **III** 204–05
Reisebüro Bangemann, **II** 164
Reisholz AG, **III** 693
Reisland GmbH, **15** 340
Reiue Nationale des Usines Renault, **7** 220
Rekkof Restart NV, **28** 327
Relational Courseware, Inc., **21** 235–36
Relational Database Systems Inc., **10** 361–62

Relational Technology Inc., **10** 361
Relationship Marketing Group, Inc., **37** 409
Release Technologies, **8** 484
Reliable Stores Inc., **14** 236
Reliable Tool, **II** 488
**Reliance Electric Company**, **IV** 429; **9** **439–42**
**Reliance Group Holdings, Inc.**, **II** 173; **III** **342–44**; **IV** 642
Reliance Life Insurance Co., **III** 275–76
Reliance National Indemnity Company, **18** 159
**Reliance Steel & Aluminum Co.**, **19** **343–45**
**Reliant Energy Inc.**, **44** **368–73 (upd.)**
ReLife Inc., **14** 233; **33** 185
Relocation Central. *See* CORT Business Services Corporation.
Rembrandt Group, **I** 289; **IV** 91, 93, 97; **V** 411–13; **19** 367–69; **24** 449
**RemedyTemp, Inc.**, **20** **448–50**
Remgro, **IV** 97
**Remington Arms Company, Inc.**, **I** 329; **8** 152; **12** **415–17**; **26** 125; **40** **368–71 (upd.)**
**Remington Products Company, L.L.C.**, **42** **307–10**
Remington Rand, **III** 122, 126, 148, 151, 165–66, 642; **6** 251, 265, 281–82; **10** 255; **12** 416; **19** 430; **30** 337
Remmele Engineering, Inc., **17** 534
**Rémy Cointreau S.A.**, **20** **451–53**
Remy Martin, **48** 348–49
REN Corp. USA, Inc., **13** 161
Renaissance Communications Corp., **22** 522
Renaissance Connects, **16** 394
Renaissance Cosmetics Inc. *See* New Dana Perfumes Co.
Renaissance Energy Ltd., **47** 181
Renaissance Hotel Group N.V., **38** 321
**Renaissance Learning Systems, Inc.**, **39** **341–43**
Renal Systems, Inc. *See* Minntech Corporation.
Renault. *See* Régie Nationale des Usines Renault.
**Renault S.A.**, **26** 11, **401–04 (upd.)**; **34** 303, 306
Rendeck International, **11** 66
Rendic International, **13** 228
René Garraud, **III** 68
Renfro Corp., **25** 167
**Rengo Co., Ltd.**, **IV** **326**
**Renishaw plc**, **46** **358–60**
**RENK AG**, **37** **325–28**
Rennies Consolidated Holdings, **I** 470; **20** 312
**Reno Air Inc.**, **23** **409–11**; **24** 400; **28** 25
**Reno de Medici S.p.A.**, **41** **325–27**
Réno-Dépôt Inc., **26** 306
Reno Technologies, **12** 124
**Rent-A-Center, Inc.**, **22** 194; **24** 485; **33** 366, 368; **45** **365–67**
**Rent-Way, Inc.**, **33** **366–68**
**Rental Service Corporation**, **28** **386–88**
Renters Choice Inc. *See* Rent-A-Center, Inc.
**Rentokil Initial Plc**, **34** 43; **47** **332–35**
**Rentrak Corporation**, **35** **371–74**
Rentz, **23** 219
Renwick Technologies, Inc., **48** 286
Reo Products. *See* Lifetime Hoan Corporation.
Repco Ltd., **15** 246
REPESA, **IV** 528
Replacement Enterprises Inc., **16** 380
Repligen Inc., **13** 241
Repola Ltd., **19** 465; **30** 325
Repola Oy, **IV** 316, 347, 350
**Repsol S.A.**, **IV** 396–97, 506, 514, **527–29**; **16** **423–26 (upd.)**
**Repsol-YPF S.A.**, **40** **372–76 (upd.)**
Repubblica, **IV** 587
Republic Aircraft Co., **I** 89
Republic Airlines, **I** 113, 132; **6** 104; **25** 421; **28** 265
Republic Aviation Corporation, **I** 55; **9** 205–07; **48** 167
Republic Broadcasting Corp., **23** 292
Republic Corp., **I** 447
**Republic Engineered Steels, Inc.**, **7** **446–47** **26** **405–08 (upd.)**
Republic Freight Systems, **14** 567
Republic Indemnity Co. of America, **III** 191
**Republic Industries, Inc.**, **24** 12; **26** **409–11**, 501
Republic Insurance, **III** 404
Republic National Bank, **19** 466
**Republic New York Corporation**, **11** **415–19**
Republic Pictures, **9** 75
Republic Powdered Metals, Inc., **8** 454
Republic Realty Mortgage Corp., **II** 289
Republic Rubber, **III** 641
Republic Steel Corp., **I** 491; **IV** 114; **7** 446; **12** 353; **13** 169, 157; **14** 155; **24** 304. *See also* Republic Engineered Steels, Inc.
Republic Supply Co. of California, **I** 570
**Res-Care, Inc.**, **29** **399–402**
Research Analysis Corporation, **7** 15
Research Cottrell, Inc., **6** 441
Research Polymers International, **I** 321; **12** 103
Research Publications, **8** 526
Resem SpA, **I** 387
Reserve Mining Co., **17** 356
Reservoir Productions, **17** 150
Residence Inns, **III** 103; **9** 426
Residential Funding Corporation, **10** 92–93
Resin Exchange, **19** 414
Resinous Products, **I** 392
ResNet Communications Inc., **28** 241
Resolution Systems, Inc., **13** 201
Resolution Trust Corp., **10** 117, 134; **11** 371; **12** 368
**Resorts International, Inc.**, **I** 452; **12** **418–20**; **19** 402; **26** 462
**Resource America, Inc.**, **42** **311–14**
Resource Associates of Alaska, Inc., **7** 376
The Resource Club, **32** 80
Resource Electronics, **8** 385
Resource Group International, **25** 207
ReSource NE, Inc., **17** 553
reSOURCE PARTNER, INC., **22** 95
**Response Oncology, Inc.**, **27** **385–87**
Rest Assured, **I** 429
The Restaurant Company, **22** 417
Restaurant Enterprises Group Inc., **14** 195
Restaurant Franchise Industries, **6** 200
Restaurant Property Master, **19** 468
Restaurants Les Pres Limitée, **II** 652
Restaurants Universal Espana S.A., **26** 374
**Restaurants Unlimited, Inc.**, **13** **435–37**; **23** 127–29
**Restoration Hardware, Inc.**, **30** **376–78**
Resurgens Communications Group, **7** 336; **8** 311; **27** 306
Retail Association Pskovnefteprodukt, **48** 378
Retail Credit Company. *See* Equifax.
Retail Systems Consulting, Inc., **24** 395
Retail Ventures Inc., **14** 427; **24** 26
Retailers Commercial Agency, Inc., **6** 24
Retequattro, **19** 19
Retirement Care Associates Inc., **25** 457
Retirement Inns of America, Inc., **III** 16; **11** 282
Reuben H. Donnelley Corp., **IV** 605, 661; **19** 133
Reunion Properties, **I** 470; **20** 311–12
**Reuters Holdings PLC**, **IV** 259, 652, 654, 656, **668–70**; **10** 277, 407; **21** 68–70; **22** **450–53 (upd.)**; **34** 11, 227
**Revco D.S., Inc.**, **II** 449; **III** 10; **V** **171–73**; **9** 67, 187; **12** 4; **13** 449; **16** 560; **19** 357; **32** 169–70; **45** 136
**Revell-Monogram Inc.**, **16** **427–29**; **25** 71; **27** 14
Revere Copper and Brass Co., **IV** 32. *See also* The Paul Revere Corporation.
Revere Foil Containers, Inc., **12** 377
Revere Furniture and Equipment Company, **14** 105; **25** 307
**Revere Ware Corporation**, **22** **454–56**
**Revlon Inc.**, **I** 29, 449, 620, 633, 668, 677, 693, 696; **II** 498, 679; **III** 29, 46, **54–57**, 727; **6** 27; **8** 131, 341; **9** 202–03, 291; **11** 8, 333–34; **12** 314; **16** 439; **17** 110, **400–04 (upd.)**; **18** 229; **22** 157; **25** 55; **26** 384; **28** 246–47; **30** 188–89
Revson Bros., **III** 54
Rewe Group, **37** 241
Rewe-Liebbrand, **28** 152
Rex Pulp Products Company, **9** 304
**REX Stores Corp.**, **10** **468–69**; **19** 362
Rexall Drug & Chemical Co., **II** 533–34; **III** 610; **13** 525; **14** 547
Rexall Sundown, Inc., **37** 340, 342
**Rexam PLC**, **32** **380–85 (upd.)**; **45** 337
**Rexel, Inc.**, **15** **384–87**
Rexene Products Co., **III** 760; **IV** 457
Rexham Inc., **IV** 259; **8** 483–84
**Rexnord Corporation**, **I** 524; **14** 43; **21** **429–32**; **37** 30
Reydel Industries, **23** 95–96
Reyes Holdings, Inc., **24** 388
Reymer & Bros., Inc., **II** 508; **11** 172
Reymersholm, **II** 366
Reynolds and Reynolds Company, **17** 142, 144
Reynolds Electric Co., **22** 353
**Reynolds Metals Company**, **II** 421–22; **IV** 11–12, 15, 59, **186–88**; **IV** 122; **12** 278; **19** **346–48 (upd.)**; **21** 218; **22** 455; **25** 22
RF Communications, **II** 38
**RF Micro Devices, Inc.**, **43** **311–13**
RF Monolithics Inc., **13** 193
RHC Holding Corp., **10** 13; **13** 364; **27** 11
RHD Holdings, **23** 413
Rhee Syngman, **I** 516; **12** 293
Rheem Manufacturing, **25** 368
Rhein-Elbe Gelsenkirchener Bergwerks A.G., **IV** 25
Rheinelbe Union, **I** 542
Rheinisch Kalksteinwerke Wulfrath, **III** 738
Rheinisch Oelfinwerke, **I** 306

Rheinisch-Westfalische Bank A.G., **II** 279
Rheinisch-Westfälischer Sprengstoff AG, **III** 694
Rheinisch-Westfälisches Elektrizatätswerke AG, **I** 542–43; **III** 154; **IV** 231; **V** 744; **25** 102
Rheinische Aktiengesellschaft für Braunkohlenbergbau, **V** 708
Rheinische Creditbank, **II** 278
Rheinische Metallwaaren- und Maschinenfabrik AG, **9** 443–44
Rheinische Wasserglasfabrik, **III** 31
Rheinische Zuckerwarenfabrik GmbH, **27** 460
**Rheinmetall Berlin AG, 9 443–46**
Rheinsche Girozentrale und Provinzialbank, Düsseldorf, **II** 385
Rheinstahl AG, **IV** 222
Rheinstahl Union Brueckenbau, **8** 242
Rheintalische Zementfabrik, **III** 701
Rhenus-Weichelt AG, **6** 424, 426
RHI Entertainment Inc., **16** 257
**Rhino Entertainment Company, 18 457–60**; **21** 326
RHM. *See* Ranks Hovis McDougall.
Rhodes & Co., **8** 345
**Rhodes Inc., 23 412–14**
Rhodesian Anglo American Ltd., **IV** 21, 23; **16** 26
Rhodesian Development Corp., **I** 422
Rhodesian Selection Trust, Ltd., **IV** 17–18, 21
Rhodesian Sugar Refineries, **II** 581
**Rhodia SA, 38 378–80**
Rhodiaceta, **I** 388–89
Rhokana Corp., **IV** 191
Rhône Moulage Industrie, **39** 152, 154
**Rhône-Poulenc S.A., I** 303–04, 371, **388–90**, 670, 672, 692; **III** 677; **IV** 174, 487, 547; **8** 153, 452; **9** 358; **10 470–72 (upd.)**; **16** 121, 438; **21** 466; **23** 194, 197; **34** 284; **38** 379
Rhymey Breweries, **I** 294
Rhymney Iron Company, **31** 369
Rhythm Watch Co., Ltd., **III** 454; **21** 121
La Riassicuratrice, **III** 346
**Rica Foods, Inc., 41 328–30**
Ricard, **I** 280
Riccar, **17** 124; **41** 114
Riccardo's Restaurant, **18** 538
Rice Broadcasting Co., Inc., **II** 166
Rice-Stix Dry Goods, **II** 414
Riceland Foods, Inc., **27** 390
**Rich Products Corporation, 7 448–49**; **38 381–84 (upd.)**
Rich's Inc., **9** 209; **10** 515; **31** 191
Richard A. Shaw, Inc., **7** 128
Richard D. Irwin Inc., **IV** 602–03, 678; **47** 102
Richard Hellman Co., **II** 497
Richard Manufacturing Co., **I** 667
Richard P. Simmons, **8** 19
Richard Shops, **III** 502
Richard Thomas & Baldwins, **IV** 42
Richards & O'Neil LLP, **43** 70
Richards Bay Minerals, **IV** 91
Richardson Company, **36** 147
**Richardson Electronics, Ltd., 17 405–07**
Richardson-Vicks Company, **III** 53; **8** 434; **26** 383
Richardson's, **21** 246
Richfield Oil Corp., **IV** 375–76, 456
**Richfood Holdings, Inc., 7 450–51**
Richland Co-op Creamery Company, **7** 592
Richland Gas Company, **8** 349
Richmon Hill & Queens County Gas Light Companies, **6** 455
Richmond American Homes of Florida, Inc., **11** 258
Richmond Carousel Corporation, **9** 120
Richmond Cedar Works Manufacturing Co., **12** 109; **19** 360
Richmond Corp., **I** 600; **15** 129
Richmond Paperboard Corp., **19** 78
Richmond Pulp and Paper Company, **17** 281
**Richton International Corporation, 39 344–46**
Richway, **10** 515
Richwood Building Products, Inc., **12** 397
Richwood Sewell Coal Co., **17** 357
Ricils, **III** 47
Rickards, Roloson & Company, **22** 427
Rickel Home Centers, **II** 673
Ricky Shaw's Oriental Express, **25** 181
**Ricoh Company, Ltd., III** 121, 157, **159–61**, 172, 454; **6** 289; **8** 278; **18** 386, 527; **19** 317; **21** 122; **24** 429; **36 389–93 (upd.)**
Ricolino, **19** 192
Riddell Inc., **33** 467
**Riddell Sports Inc., 22 457–59**; **23** 449
Ridder Publications, **IV** 612–13, 629; **7** 191
**Ride, Inc., 22 460–63**
Ridge Tool Co., **II** 19
Ridgewell's Inc., **15** 87
Ridgewood Properties Inc., **12** 394
Ridgway Co., **23** 98
Ridgway Color, **13** 227–28
Rieck-McJunkin Dairy Co., **II** 533
Riedel-de Haën AG, **22** 32; **36** 431
Riegel Bag & Paper Co., **IV** 344
Rieke Corp., **III** 569; **11** 535; **20** 361
**The Riese Organization, 38 385–88**
**Rieter Holding AG, 42 315–17**
Rieter Machine Works, **III** 638
Rig Tenders Company, **6** 383
Riggin & Robbins, **13** 244
**Riggs National Corporation, 13 438–40**
Right Associates, **27** 21; **44** 156
**Right Management Consultants, Inc., 42 318–21**
Right Source, Inc., **24** 96
RightSide Up, Inc., **27** 21
Rijnhaave Information Systems, **25** 21
Rike's, **10** 282
Riken Corp., **IV** 160; **10** 493
Riken Kagaku Co. Ltd., **48** 250
Riken Kankoshi Co. Ltd., **III** 159
Riken Optical Co., **III** 159
**Riklis Family Corp., 9 447–50**; **12** 87; **13** 453; **38** 169; **43** 355
Riku-un Moto Kaisha, **V** 477
La Rinascente, **12** 153
Ring King Visibles, Inc., **13** 269
Ring Ltd., **43** 99
Ringier America, **19** 333
Ringköpkedjan, **II** 640
Ringling Bros., Barnum & Bailey Circus, **25** 312–13
Ringnes Bryggeri, **18** 396
Rini-Rego Supermarkets Inc., **13** 238
Rini Supermarkets, **9** 451; **13** 237
Rinker Materials Corp., **III** 688
Rio Grande Industries, Inc., **12** 18–19
Rio Grande Oil Co., **IV** 375, 456
Rio Grande Servaas, S.A. de C.V., **23** 145
Rio Grande Valley Gas Co., **IV** 394
Rio Sportswear Inc., **42** 269
Rio Sul Airlines, **6** 133
**Rio Tinto plc, 19 349–53 (upd.)**; **27** 253; **42** 395
Rio Tinto-Zinc Corp., **II** 628; **IV** 56, 58–61, 189–91, 380; **21** 352
Rioblanco, **II** 477
Riordan Freeman & Spogli, **13** 406
Riordan Holdings Ltd., **I** 457; **10** 554
**Riser Foods, Inc., 9 451–54**; **13** 237–38
Rising Sun Petroleum Co., **IV** 431, 460, 542
Risk Management Partners Ltd., **35** 36
Risk Planners, **II** 669
Rit Dye Co., **II** 497
**Ritchie Bros. Auctioneers Inc., 41 331–34**
**Rite Aid Corporation, V 174–76**; **9** 187, 346; **12** 221, 333; **16** 389; **18** 199, 286; **19 354–57 (upd.)**; **23** 407; **29** 213; **31** 232; **32** 166, 169–70
Rite-Way Department Store, **II** 649
Riteway Distributor, **26** 183
Rittenhouse and Embree, **III** 269
Rittenhouse Financial Services, **22** 495
Ritter Co. *See* Sybron Corp.
**Ritz Camera Centers, 18** 186; **34 375–77**
**Ritz-Carlton Hotel Company L.L.C., 9 455–57**; **21** 366; **29 403–06 (upd.)**
Ritz Firma, **13** 512
**Riunione Adriatica di Sicurtà SpA, III** 185, 206, **345–48**
**The Rival Company, 17** 215; **19 358–60**
Rivarossi, **16** 337
Rivaud Group, **29** 370
River Boat Casino, **9** 425–26
River City Broadcasting, **25** 418
River North Studios. *See* Platinum Entertainment, Inc.
**River Oaks Furniture, Inc., 43 314–16**
River-Raisin Paper Co., **IV** 345
River Ranch Fresh Foods—Salinas, Inc., **41** 11
River Steam Navigation Co., **III** 522
River Thames Insurance Co., Ltd., **26** 487
Riverdeep Group plc, **41** 137
Riverside Chemical Company, **13** 502
Riverside Furniture, **19** 455
Riverside Insurance Co. of America, **26** 487
Riverside Iron Works, Ltd., **8** 544
Riverside National Bank of Buffalo, **11** 108
Riverside Press, **10** 355–56
Riverside Publishing Company, **36** 272
**Riverwood International Corporation, 7** 294; **11 420–23**; **48 340–44 (upd.)**
Riviana Foods, **III** 24, 25; **27 388–91**
Riyadh Armed Forces Hospital, **16** 94
Rizzoli Publishing, **IV** 586, 588; **19** 19; **23** 88
RJMJ, Inc., **16** 37
**RJR Nabisco Holdings Corp., I** 249, 259, 261; **II** 370, 426, 477–78, 542–44; **V 408–10, 415; 7** 130, 132, 277, 596; **9** 469; **12** 82, 559; **13** 342; **14** 214, 274; **17** 471; **22** 73, 95, 441; **23** 163; **24** 273; **30** 384; **32** 234; **33** 228; **36** 151, 153; **46** 259. *See also* R.J Reynolds Tobacco Holdings Inc., Nabisco Brands, Inc. *and* R.J. Reynolds Industries, Inc.
RKO. *See* Radio-Keith-Orpheum.
RKO-General, Inc., **8** 207

RKO Radio Sales, **6** 33
RLA Polymers, **9** 92
RM Marketing, **6** 14
**RMC Group p.l.c., III** 734, **737–40**; **34 378–83 (upd.)**
RMF Inc., **I** 412
**RMH Teleservices, Inc., 42 322–24**
RMP International, Limited, **8** 417
**Roadhouse Grill, Inc., 22 464–66**
Roadline, **6** 413–14
**Roadmaster Industries, Inc., 16 430–33**; **22** 116
Roadmaster Transport Company, **18** 27; **41** 18
RoadOne. *See* Miller Industries, Inc.
**Roadway Express, Inc., 25 395–98 (upd.)**
**Roadway Services, Inc., V 502–03**; **12** 278, 309; **14** 567; **15** 111
Roaman's, **V** 115
Roan Selection Trust Ltd., **IV** 18, 239–40
Roanoke Capital Ltd., **27** 113–14
**Roanoke Electric Steel Corporation, 45 368–70**
Roanoke Fashions Group, **13** 532
Robb Engineering Works, **8** 544
**Robbins & Myers Inc., 13** 273; **15 388–90**
Robbins Co., **III** 546
Robeco Group, **IV** 193; **26** 419–20
**Roberds Inc., 19 361–63**
Roberk Co., **III** 603
Robert Allen Companies, **III** 571; **20** 362
Robert Benson, Lonsdale & Co. Ltd., **II** 232, 421–22; **IV** 191
**Robert Bosch GmbH, I 392–93**, 411; **III** 554, 555, 591, 593; **13** 398; **16 434–37 (upd.)**; **22** 31; **43 317–21 (upd.)**
Robert E. McKee Corporation, **6** 150
Robert Fleming Holdings Ltd., **I** 471; **IV** 79; **11** 495
Robert Gair Co., **15** 128
Robert Garrett & Sons, Inc., **9** 363
Robert Grace Contracting Co., **I** 584
**Robert Half International Inc., 18 461–63**
Robert Hall Clothes, Inc., **13** 535
Robert Johnson, **8** 281–82
Robert McLane Company. *See* McLane Company, Inc.
Robert McNish & Company Limited, **14** 141
**Robert Mondavi Corporation, 15 391–94**; **39** 45
Robert R. Mullen & Co., **I** 20
Robert Skeels & Company, **33** 467
Robert Stigwood Organization Ltd., **23** 390
Robert W. Baird & Co., **III** 324; **7** 495
Robert Warschauer and Co., **II** 270
Robert Watson & Co. Ltd., **I** 568
**Robert Wood Johnson Foundation, 35 375–78**
**Robertet SA, 39 347–49**
Roberts Express, **V** 503
Roberts, Johnson & Rand Shoe Co., **III** 528–29
**Roberts Pharmaceutical Corporation, 16 438–40**
Robertson Building Products, **8** 546
**Robertson-Ceco Corporation, 8** 546; **19 364–66**
Robertson, Stephens & Co., **22** 465
Robin Hood Flour Mills, Ltd., **7** 241–43; **25** 241
Robin International Inc., **24** 14
Robinair, **10** 492, 494
Robinson & Clark Hardware. *See* Clarcor Inc.
Robinson Clubs, **II** 163–64
Robinson-Danforth Commission Co., **II** 561
Robinson-Humphrey, **II** 398; **10** 62
Robinson Industries, **24** 425
Robinson Radio Rentals, **I** 531
Robinson Smith & Robert Haas, Inc., **13** 428
Robinson's Japan Co. Ltd., **V** 89; **42** 191
Robinsons Soft Drinks Limited, **38** 77
Robot Manufacturing Co., **16** 8
Robotic Vision Systems, Inc., **16** 68
ROC Communities, Inc., **I** 272; **22** 341
Roccade, **39** 177
Roch, S.A., **23** 83
**Roche Biomedical Laboratories, Inc., 8** 209–10; **11 424–26**. *See also* Laboratory Corporation of America Holdings.
**Roche Bioscience, 14 403–06 (upd.)**
Roche Holding AG, **30** 164; **32** 211, 213–14; **37** 113
Roche Products Ltd., **I** 643
Rocher Soleil, **48** 315
Rochester American Insurance Co., **III** 191
**Rochester Gas And Electric Corporation, 6 571–73**
Rochester German Insurance Co., **III** 191
Rochester Instrument Systems, Inc., **16** 357
**Rochester Telephone Corporation, 6 332–34**; **12** 136; **16** 221
Röchling Industrie Verwaltung GmbH, **9** 443
**Rock Bottom Restaurants, Inc., 25 399–401**
Rock Island Oil & Refining Co., **IV** 448–49
Rock Island Plow Company, **10** 378
**Rock of Ages Corporation, 37 329–32**
Rock Systems Inc., **18** 337
**Rock-Tenn Company, IV** 312; **13 441–43**; **19** 268
Rockcor Inc., **I** 381; **13** 380
Rockcote Paint Company, **8** 552–53
Rockefeller & Andrews, **IV** 426; **7** 169
**The Rockefeller Foundation, 34 384–87**
Rockefeller Group, **IV** 714
Rocket Chemical Company. *See* WD-40 Company.
**Rockford Corporation, 43 322–25**
Rockford Drilling Co., **III** 439
Rockhaven Asset Management, LLC, **48** 18
Rocking Horse Child Care Centers of America Inc. *See* Nobel Learning Communities, Inc.
Rockland Corp., **8** 271
Rockland React-Rite, Inc., **8** 270
Rockmoor Grocery, **II** 683
Rockower of Canada Ltd., **II** 649
Rockport Company, **V** 376–77; **26** 397
Rockresorts, Inc., **22** 166
**RockShox, Inc., 26 412–14**
**Rockwell Automation, 43 326–31 (upd.)**
**Rockwell International Corporation, I** 71, **78–80**, 154–55, 186; **II** 3, 94, 379; **6** 263; **7** 420; **8** 165; **9** 10; **10** 279–80; **11** 268, 278, **427–30 (upd.)**, 473; **12** 135, 248, 506; **13** 228; **18** 369, 571; **22** 51, 53, 63–64; **32** 81, 84–85; **33** 27; **35** 91; **36** 121–22; **39** 30; **44** 357
Rocky Mountain Bankcard, **24** 393
Rocky Mountain Financial Corporation, **13** 348
Rocky Mountain Pipe Line Co., **IV** 400
Rocky River Power Co. *See* Connecticut Light and Power Co.
**Rocky Shoes & Boots, Inc., 26 415–18**
Rod's Food Products, **36** 163
**Rodale, Inc., 47 336–39 (upd.)**
**Rodale Press, Inc., 22** 443; **23 415–17**
**Rodamco N.V., IV** 698; **26 419–21**
Rodel, Inc., **26** 425
Röder & Co., **34** 38, 40
Rodeway Inns of America, **II** 142; **III** 94; **11** 242; **25** 309
Rodgers Instrument Corporation, **38** 391
Rodney Square Management Corp., **25** 542
Rodven Records, **23** 391
Roederstein GmbH, **21** 520
Roegelein Co., **13** 271
Roehr Products Co., **III** 443
Roermond, **IV** 276
Roessler & Hasslacher Chemical Co., **IV** 69
Roger Cleveland Golf Company, **15** 462; **43** 375–76
Roger Williams Foods, **II** 682
Rogers & Oling, Inc., **17** 533
Rogers Bros., **I** 672
Rogers CanGuard, Inc., **32** 374
**Rogers Communications Inc., 30 388–92 (upd.)**. *See also* Maclean Hunter Publishing Limited.
**Rohde & Schwarz GmbH & Co. KG, 39 350–53**
Rohe Scientific Corp., **13** 398
**Röhm and Haas Company, I 391–93**; **14** 182–83; **26 422–26 (upd.)**
**ROHN Industries, Inc., 22 467–69**
Rohölgewinnungs AG, **IV** 485
Rohr Gruppe, **20** 100
**Rohr Incorporated, I** 62; **9 458–60**; **11** 165
Roja, **III** 47
The Rokke Group, **16** 546; **32** 100
Rokuosha, **III** 547
Rol Oil, **IV** 451
Rola Group, **II** 81
**Roland Berger & Partner GmbH, 37 333–36**
**Roland Corporation, 38 389–91**
**Roland Murten A.G., 7 452–53**
Roland NV, **41** 340
Rolex. *See* Montres Rolex S.A.
**Roll International Corporation, 37 337–39**
Rollalong, **III** 502; **7** 208
**Rollerblade, Inc., 15 395–98**; **22** 202–03; **34 388–92 (upd.)**
Rolling Stones Records, **23** 33
Rollins Burdick Hunter Company, **III** 204; **45** 27
Rollins Communications, **II** 161
**Rollins, Inc., 11 431–34**
Rollins Specialty Group, **III** 204
Rollo's, **16** 95
**Rolls-Royce Allison, 29 407–09 (upd.)**
**Rolls-Royce Motors Ltd., I** 25–26, 81–82, 166, **194–96**; **III** 652; **9** 16–18, 417–18; **11** 138, 403; **21** 435
**Rolls-Royce plc, I** 41, 55, 65, **81–83**, 481; **III** 507, 556; **7 454–57 (upd.)**; **9** 244; **11** 268; **12** 190; **13** 414; **21 433–37 (upd.)**; **24** 85; **27** 495–96; **46** 358–59; **47** 7, 9

Rolm Corp., **II** 99; **III** 149; **18** 344; **22** 51; **34** 512
Rolodex Electronics, **23** 209, 212
Rolscreen. *See* Pella Corporation.
Rombas, **IV** 226
Rome Cable and Wire Co., **IV** 15
Rome Network, Inc., **24** 95
Romper Room Enterprises, Inc., **16** 267
Rompetrol, **IV** 454
Ron Nagle, **I** 247
**Ronco, Inc.**, **15 399–401**; **21** 327
Rondel's, Inc., **8** 135
Ronel, **13** 274
Roni-Linda Productions, Inc., **27** 347
Ronnebyredds Trävaru, **25** 463
Ronningen-Petter, **III** 468
Ronzoni Foods Corp., **15** 221
Roombar S.A., **28** 241
**Rooms To Go Inc.**, **28 389–92**
**Rooney Brothers Co.**, **25 402–04**
**Roots Canada Ltd.**, **27** 194; **42 325–27**
Roots-Connersville Blower Corp., **III** 472
**Roper Industries Inc.**, **III** 655; **12** 550; **15 402–04**; **25** 89
Ropert Group, **18** 67
**Ropes & Gray**, **40 377–80**
RoProperty Services BV. *See* Rodamco N.V.
**Rorer Group**, **I 666–68**; **12** 4; **16** 438; **24** 257
Rosaen Co., **23** 82
Rosarita Food Company, **25** 278
Rose & Co., **26** 65
Rose Exterminator Company, **25** 15
Rose Foundation, **9** 348
**Rose's Stores, Inc.**, **13** 261, **444–46**; **23** 215
Rosebud Dolls Ltd., **25** 312
Rosefield Packing Co., **II** 497
Rosehaugh, **24** 269
RoseJohnson Incorporated, **14** 303
**Rosemount Inc.**, **II** 20; **13** 226; **15 405–08**; **46** 171
Rosen Enterprises, Ltd., **10** 482
Rosenblads Patenter, **III** 419
**Rosenbluth International Inc.**, **14 407–09**
Rosenfeld Hat Company. *See* Columbia Hat Company.
Rosenmund-Guèdu, **31** 158
Rosenthal A.G., **I** 347; **18** 236; **34** 493, 496
Rosevear, **III** 690
Rosewood Financial, Inc., **24** 383
Roshco, Inc., **27** 288
Roslyn Bancorp, **46** 316
Ross Carrier Company, **8** 115
Ross Clouston, **13** 244
Ross Gear & Tool Co., **I** 539; **14** 510
Ross Hall Corp., **I** 417
**Ross Stores, Inc.**, **17 408–10**; **43 332–35 (upd.)**
Rossendale Combining Company, **9** 92
Rossignol Ski Company, Inc. *See* Skis Rossignol S.A.
Rössing Uranium Ltd., **IV** 191
Rossville Union Distillery, **I** 285
Rostocker Brauerei VEB, **9** 87
Roswell Public Service Company, **6** 579
Rota Bolt Ltd., **III** 581
Rotadisk, **16** 7
Rotan Mosle Financial Corporation, **II** 445; **22** 406
**Rotary International**, **31 395–97**
Rotary Lift, **III** 467–68
Rotax, **III** 555–56. *See also* Orbital Engine Corporation Ltd.
Rote. *See* Avery Dennison Corporation.
Rotelcom Data Inc., **6** 334; **16** 222
Rotex, **IV** 253
Roth Co., **16** 493
Roth Freres SA, **26** 231
Rothmans International BV, **33** 82
**Rothmans International p.l.c.**, **I** 438; **IV** 93; **V 411–13**; **27** 488
**Rothmans UK Holdings Limited**, **19 367–70 (upd.)**
Rothschild Financial Corporation, **13** 347
Rothschild Group, **6** 206
Rothschild Investment Trust, **I** 248; **III** 699
**Roto-Rooter Corp.**, **13** 149–50; **15 409–11**; **16** 387
Rotodiesel, **III** 556
Rotor Tool Co., **II** 16
**Rotork plc**, **46 361–64**
Rotterdam Bank, **II** 183–85
Rotterdam Beleggings (Investment) Consortium. *See* Robeco.
Rotterdam Lloyd, **6** 403–04; **26** 241–42
**The Rottlund Company, Inc.**, **28 393–95**
Rouge et Or, **IV** 614
**Rouge Steel Company**, **8 448–50**
Roughdales Brickworks, **14** 249
Rougier. *See* Groupe Rougier, SA.
**Roularta Media Group NV**, **48 345–47**
Round Hill Foods, **21** 535
Round Table, **16** 447
Roundup Wholesale Grocery Company, **V** 55
**Roundy's Inc.**, **14 410–12**
**The Rouse Company**, **II** 445; **15 412–15**; **22** 406
**Roussel Uclaf**, **I 669–70**; **8 451–53 (upd.)**; **18** 236; **19** 51; **25** 285; **38** 379
Rousselot, **I** 677
Routh Robbins Companies, **21** 96
Roux Séguéla Cayzac & Goudard. *See* Euro RSCG Worldwide S.A.
**Rover Group Ltd.**, **I** 186; **7 458–60**; **11** 31, 33; **14** 36; **21 441–44 (upd.)**; **24** 87–88; **38** 83, 85–86
**Rowan Companies, Inc.**, **43 336–39**
Rowe & Pitman, **14** 419
Rowe Bros. & Co., **III** 680
Rowe Price-Fleming International, Inc., **11** 495
Rowell Welding Works, **26** 433
Rowenta. *See* Groupe SEB.
Rowland Communications Worldwide, **42** 328, 331
Rowntree and Co., **27** 104
**Rowntree Mackintosh PLC**, **II** 476, 511, 521, 548, **568–70**; **7** 383; **28** 311
Roxana Petroleum Co., **IV** 531, 540
Roxell, N.V., **43** 129
Roxoil Drilling, **7** 344
Roy and Charles Moore Crane Company, **18** 319
**Roy F. Weston, Inc.**, **33 369–72**
Roy Farrell Import-Export Company, **6** 78
Roy Rogers, **III** 102
Royal Ahold. *See* Koninklijke Ahold N.V.
Royal Aluminium Ltd., **IV** 9
**Royal Appliance Manufacturing Company**, **15 416–18**; **17** 233
Royal Baking Powder Co., **II** 544; **14** 17
Royal Bank of Australia, **II** 188
**The Royal Bank of Canada**, **II 344–46**; **21 445–48 (upd.)**
Royal Bank of Ireland Ltd., **16** 13
Royal Bank of Queensland, **II** 188
**The Royal Bank of Scotland Group plc**, **II** 298, 358; **10** 336–37; **12 421–23**; **38** 13, **392–99 (upd.)**; **42** 76
Royal Bankgroup of Acadiana, Inc., **37** 201
Royal Brewing Co., **I** 269; **12** 337
Royal Business Machines, **I** 207, 485; **III** 549
Royal Canada, **III** 349
**Royal Canin S.A.**, **39 354–57**
**Royal Caribbean Cruises Ltd.**, **6** 368; **22** 444–46; **470–73**; **27** 29, 91
Royal Copenhagen A/S, **9** 99
**Royal Crown Company, Inc.**, **II** 468; **6** 21, 50; **8** 536–37; **14** 32–33; **23 418–20**
Royal Data, Inc. *See* King Kullen Grocery Co., Inc.
**Royal Doulton plc**, **IV** 659; **14 413–15**; **34** 497; **38 400–04 (upd.)**
Royal Dutch Harbour Co., **IV** 707
Royal Dutch Paper Co., **IV** 307
**Royal Dutch Petroleum Company**, **IV 530–32**, 657; **24** 496. *See also* Shell Transport and Trading Company p.l.c.
Royal Dutch/Shell Group, **I** 368, 504; **III** 616; **IV** 132–33, 378, 406, 413, 429, 434, 453–54, 460, 491–92, 512, 515, 517–18, 530–32, 540–45, 557–58, 569; **7** 56–57, 172–73, 481–82; **17** 417; **19** 73, 75; **21** 203; **22** 237; **24** 520; **32** 175, 180; **41** 356–57, 359; **45** 47
Royal Electric Company, **6** 501
Royal Exchange Assurance Corp., **III** 233–34, 278, 349, 369–71, 373
Royal Farms, **24** 528
Royal Food Distributors, **II** 625
Royal Food Products, **24** 528–29; **36** 163
Royal General Insurance Co., **III** 242
Royal Hawaiian Macadamia Nut Co., **II** 491
Royal Industries, Inc., **19** 371
**Royal Insurance Holdings plc**, **III 349–51**
Royal International, **II** 457; **III** 349
Royal Interocean Lines, **6** 404; **26** 243
Royal Jackson, **14** 236
Royal Jordanian, **6** 101
**Royal KPN N.V.**, **30 393–95**, 461, 463
Royal London Mutual Insurance, **IV** 697
Royal Mail Group, **V** 498; **6** 416; **19** 198
Royal Nedlloyd. *See* Koninglijke Nedlloyd N.V.
**Royal Nepal Airline Corporation**, **41 335–38**
Royal Netherlands Steamship Company. *See* KNSM.
**Royal Numico N.V.**, **33** 145, 147; **37 340–42**
Royal Orchid Holidays, **6** 122–23
Royal Ordnance plc, **13** 356; **24** 87–88
**Royal Packaging Industries Van Leer N.V.**, **9** 305; **30 396–98**
Royal Pakhoed N.V., **9** 532
Royal PTT Post, **30** 463
Royal Re, **III** 349
Royal Sash Manufacturing Co., **III** 757
Royal Securities Company, **6** 585
Royal Securities Corp. of Canada, **II** 425
Royal Sporting House Pte. Ltd., **21** 483
Royal Trust Co., **II** 456–57; **V** 25
Royal Union Life Insurance Co., **III** 275
Royal USA, **III** 349
**Royal Vopak NV**, **41 339–41**

Royal Wessanen, **II** 527
Royale Belge, **III** 177, 200, 394
Royale Inns of America, **25** 307
Royalite, **I** 285
Royce Electronics, **III** 569; **18** 68; **20** 361
Royce Ltd., **I** 194
Royster-Clark, Inc., **13** 504
Rozes, **I** 272
RPC Industries, **III** 635
RPI. *See* Research Polymers International.
**RPM Inc., 8 III** 598; **454–57; 36 394–98 (upd.)**
**RSA Security Inc., 46 365–68; 47** 430
RSC. *See* Rental Service Corporation.
RSI Corp., **8** 141–42; **30** 160
RSO Records, **23** 390
RSV, **26** 496
RTE Corp., **II** 17
**RTL Group SA, 41** 29; **44 374–78**
RTL-Véeronique, **IV** 611
**RTZ Corporation PLC, IV 189–92; 7** 261, 263; **27** 256
RTZ-CRA Group. *See* Rio Tinto plc.
Rubber Latex Limited, **9** 92
**Rubbermaid Incorporated, III 613–15; 12** 168–69; **13** 317–18; **19** 407; **20** 262, **454–57 (upd.)**; **21** 293; **28** 479; **31** 160–61; **34** 369
Ruberoid Corporation, **I** 339; **22** 227
Rubicon Group plc, **32** 50
**Rubio's Restaurants, Inc., 35 379–81**
Rubloff Inc., **II** 442
Rubo Lederwaren, **14** 225
Rubry Owen, **I** 154
Ruby, **III** 47
**Ruby Tuesday, Inc., 18 464–66**
Rubyco, Inc., **15** 386
La Ruche Meridionale, **12** 153
Ruddick Corporation, **23** 260
Rudisill Printing Co., **IV** 661
Rudolf Wolff & Co., **IV** 165
Rudolph Fluor & Brother, **I** 569
Ruel Smith Transportation Services, Inc., **39** 66
Ruff Hewn, **25** 48
Rug Corporation of America, **12** 393
**The Rugby Group plc, 31 398–400; 34** 380
Ruger Corporation, **19** 431
Ruhr-Zink, **IV** 141
**Ruhrgas AG, V 704–06; 7** 141; **18** 50; **38 405–09 (upd.)**; **42** 263
**Ruhrkohle AG, IV 193–95**. *See also* RAG AG.
Ruinart Père et Fils, **I** 272
Rumbelows, **I** 532
Runcorn White Lead Co., **III** 680
Runnymede Construction Co., **8** 544
Runo-Everth Treibstoff und Ol AG, **7** 141
Rural Bank, **IV** 279; **19** 155
**Rural Cellular Corporation, 43 340–42**
**Rural/Metro Corporation, 28 396–98; 39** 22
Rurhkohle AG, **V** 747
**Rush Communications, 33 373–75**
Rush Laboratories, Inc., **6** 41
**Russ Berrie and Company, Inc., 12 424–26**
Russell & Co., **II** 296
**Russell Corporation, 8 458–59; 12** 458; **30 399–401 (upd.)**
Russell Electric, **11** 412
Russell Electronics, **II** 85
Russell Kelly Office Services, Inc. *See* Kelly Services Inc.
Russell, Majors & Waddell, **II** 381
**Russell Reynolds Associates Inc., 38 410–12**
**Russell Stover Candies Inc., 12 427–29**
Russwerke Dortmund GmbH, **IV** 70
Rust Craft Greeting Cards Incorporated, **12** 561
**Rust International Inc., V** 754; **6** 599–600; **11 435–36**
Rust-Oleum Corporation, **36** 396
Rustenburg Platinum Co., **IV** 96, 118, 120
Rütgerswerke AG, **IV** 193; **8** 81
**Ruth's Chris Steak House, 28 399–401; 37** 297
Rutherford Hill Winery, **48** 392
Ruti Machinery Works, **III** 638
Rutland Plastics, **I** 321; **12** 103
**RWE Group, V 707–10; 33** 194, 196
RxAmerica, **22** 40; **25** 297
Ryan Aeronautical, **I** 525; **10** 522; **11** 428
Ryan Aircraft Company, **9** 458
Ryan Homes, Inc., **8** 401–02
Ryan Insurance Company, **III** 204; **45** 26
Ryan Milk Company of Kentucky, **7** 128
**Ryan's Family Steak Houses, Inc., 15 419–21; 19** 287; **22** 464
**Ryanair Holdings plc, 35 382–85**
Rycade Corp., **IV** 365, 658
Rydelle-Lion, **III** 45
**Ryder System, Inc., V 504–06; 13** 192; **19** 293; **24 408–11 (upd.)**; **25** 93, 144; **28** 3; **41** 37
**Ryerson Tull, Inc., 19** 216; **40** 269, **381–84 (upd.)**
Rykoff-Sexton, Inc., **21** 497; **26** 503, 505
**The Ryland Group, Inc., 8 460–61; 19** 126; **37 343–45 (upd.)**
Ryobi Ltd., **I** 202
Ryohin Keikaku Co., Ltd., **36** 420
Rypper Corp., **16** 43
Rysher Entertainment, **22** 162; **25** 329
Ryukyu Cement, **III** 760
The Ryvita Company Limited, **II** 466; **13** 52; **41** 31

S&A Restaurant Corp., **7** 336; **10** 176; **14** 331; **15** 363; **38** 100–01
**S&C Electric Company, 15 422–24**
S&H. *See* Sperry and Hutchinson Co.
S&H Diving Corporation, **6** 578
**S&K Famous Brands, Inc., 23 421–23**
S&V Screen Inks, **13** 227–28
S. & W. Berisford, **II** 514, 528
S&W Fine Foods, **12** 105
S+T Gesellschaft fur Reprotechnik mbH, **29** 306
S.A. CARFUEL, **12** 152
S.A. Cockerill Sambre. *See* Cockerill Sambre Group.
S.A. de C.V., **29** 461
S.A. des Ateliers d'Aviation Louis Breguet. *See* Groupe Dassault Aviation SA.
s.a. GB-Inno-BM. *See* GIB Group.
S.A. Greetings Corporation, **22** 35
S.A. Innovation—Bon Marché N.V., **26** 160
S.A. Schonbrunn & Co., **14** 18
S.B. Irving Trust Bank Corp., **II** 218
S.B. Penick & Co., **I** 708; **8** 548
**S.C. Johnson & Son, Inc., I** 14; **III** 45, **58–59; 8** 130; **10** 173; **12** 126–28; **17** 215; **21** 386; **28** 215, **409–12 (upd.)**
S-C-S Box Company, **8** 173
S.D. Cohn & Company, **10** 455; **27** 364
S.D. Warren Co., **IV** 329–30
S-E Bank Group, **II** 351–53
S.E. Massengill, **III** 66
S.E. Rykoff & Co., **26** 503
S.F. Braun, **IV** 451
S.G. Warburg and Co., **II** 232, 259–60, 422, 629; **14** 419; **16** 377. *See also* SBC Warburg.
S. Grumbacher & Son. *See* The Bon-Ton Stores, Inc.
S.H. Benson Ltd., **I** 25–26
S.H. Kress & Co., **17** 203–04
S.I.P., Co., **8** 416
**S-K-I Limited, 15 457–59**
S.K. Wellman, **14** 81
S. Kuhn & Sons, **13** 221
S.M.A. Corp., **I** 622
S.P. Richards Co., **45** 177–79
S Pearson & Son Ltd., **IV** 657–59; **38** 290
S.R. Dresser Manufacturing Co., **III** 470–71
S.S. Kresge Company. *See* Kmart Corporation.
S.S.V. Inc., **36** 420
S.S. White Dental Manufacturing Co., **I** 383
S. Smith & Sons. *See* Smiths Industries PLC.
S.T. Cooper & Sons, **12** 283
S.T. Dupont Company, **III** 28; **23** 55
S.W.M. Chard, **27** 259
SA Alliance Air, **28** 404
SA Express, **28** 404
Sa SFC NA, **18** 163
Sa SFC NV, **18** 162
SAA. *See* South African Airways.
**SAA (Pty) Ltd., 28 402–04**
SAAB. *See* Svenska Aeroplan Aktiebolaget.
**Saab Automobile AB, 32 386–89 (upd.)**; **36** 242–43
**Saab-Scania A.B., I 197–98**, 210; **III** 556; **V** 339; **10** 86; **11 437–39 (upd.)**; **16** 322; **34** 117
**Saarberg-Konzern, IV 196–99**
Saarstahl AG, **IV** 228
**Saatchi & Saatchi plc, I** 21, 28, **33–35**, 36; **6** 53, 229; **14** 49–50; **16** 72; **21** 236; **22** 296; **33** 65, 67; **328–31 (upd.)**
SAB. *See* South African Breweries Ltd.
Sabah Timber Co., **III** 699
Saban Entertainment, **24** 171
**Sabaté Diosos SA, 48 348–50**
**Sabena S.A./N.V., 6** 96; **18** 80; **33** 49, 51, **376–79; 34** 398
Saber Energy, Inc., **7** 553–54
Saber Software Corp., **25** 348
Sabi International Ltd., **22** 464
Sabian Ltd., **38** 68
SABIM Sable, **12** 152
Sabine Corporation, **7** 229
Sabine Investment Co. of Texas, Inc., **IV** 341
SABO Maschinenfabrik AG, **21** 175
**Sabratek Corporation, 29 410–12**
**SABRE Group Holdings, Inc., 25** 144; **26 427–30; 28** 22
Sabre Interactive, **46** 434
Sacer, **31** 127–28
Sachs-Dolmer G.m.b.H., **22** 334
Sachsgruppe, **IV** 201
Sacilor, **IV** 174, 226–27

Sackett Plasterboard Co., **III** 762
Sacks Industries, **8** 561
OY Saco AB, **23** 268
SACOR, **IV** 250, 504–06
Sacramento Savings & Loan Association, **10** 43, 45
SADE Ingenieria y Construcciones S.A., **38** 435, 437
SAE Magnetics Ltd., **18** 250
Saeger Carbide Corp., **IV** 203
Saes, **III** 347
**SAFECO Corporation, III 352–54**; **10** 44
**Safeguard Scientifics, Inc.**, **10** 232–34, **473–75**; **27** 338
**Safelite Glass Corp., 19 371–73**
Safer, Inc., **21** 385–86
**Safeskin Corporation, 18 467–70**
**Safety 1st, Inc., 24 412–15**; **46** 192
Safety Fund Bank, **II** 207
**Safety-Kleen Corp., 8 462–65**
Safety Rehab, **11** 486
Safety Savings and Loan, **10** 339
**Safeway Inc.**, **II** 424, 601, 604–05, 609–10, 628, 632, 637, **654–56**; **6** 364; **7** 61, 569; **9** 39; **10** 442; **11** 239, 241; **12** 113, 209, 559; **13** 90, 336, 340; **16** 64, 160, 249, 452; **22** 37, 126; **24** 273, **416–19 (upd.)**; **25** 296; **27** 292; **28** 510; **30** 24, 27; **33** 305; **40** 366
Saffa SpA, **41** 325–26
Safilo, **40** 155–56
Safmarine, **IV** 22
SAFR. *See* Société Anonyme des Fermiers Reúnis.
Safrap, **IV** 472
**Saga Communications, Inc.**, **II** 608; **III** 103; **IV** 406; **27** 226, **392–94**
Saga Petroleum ASA, **35** 318
Sagami Optical Co., Ltd., **48** 295
**The Sage Group, 43 343–46**
Sagebrush Sales, Inc., **12** 397
Sagebrush Steakhouse, **29** 201
**SAGEM S.A., 37 346–48**
Saginaw Dock & Terminal Co., **17** 357
Sagitta Arzneimittel, **18** 51
Sagittarius Productions Inc., **I** 286
Sahara Casino Partners L.P., **19** 379
Sahara Resorts. *See* Santa Fe Gaming Corporation.
SAI. *See* Stamos Associates Inc.
Sai Baba, **12** 228
Saia Motor Freight Line, Inc., **6** 421–23; **45** 448
Saibu Gas, **IV** 518–19
SAIC Velcorex, **12** 153; **27** 188
Saiccor, **IV** 92
Sainrapt et Brice, **9** 9
Sainsbury's. *See* J Sainsbury PLC.
St. Alban Boissons S.A., **22** 515
St. Alban's Sand and Gravel, **III** 739
St. Andrews Insurance, **III** 397
St. Charles Manufacturing Co., **III** 654
St. Clair Industries Inc., **I** 482
St. Clair Press, **IV** 570
St. Croix Paper Co., **IV** 281; **9** 259
St. George Reinsurance, **III** 397
Saint-Gobain. *See* Compagnie de Saint Gobain S.A.
St. Helens Crown Glass Co., **III** 724
St. Ives Laboratories Inc., **36** 26
**St Ives plc, 34 393–95**
St. James Associates, **32** 362–63
**The St. Joe Company, 31 422–25**
St. Joe Gold, **23** 40
St. Joe Minerals Corp., **I** 569, 571; **8** 192
**St. Joe Paper Company, 8 485–88**
**St. John Knits, Inc., 14 466–68**
St. John's Wood Railway Company, **6** 406
St. Joseph Co., **I** 286, 684
**St. Jude Medical, Inc.**, **6** 345; **11 458–61**; **43 347–52 (upd.)**
St. Laurent Paperboard Inc., **30** 119
St. Lawrence Cement Inc., **III** 702; **8** 258–59
St. Lawrence Corp. Ltd., **IV** 272
St. Lawrence Steamboat Co., **I** 273; **26** 303
St. Louis and Illinois Belt Railway, **6** 504
Saint Louis Bread Company, **18** 35, 37; **44** 327
St. Louis Concessions Inc., **21** 39
**St. Louis Music, Inc., 48 351–54**
St. Louis Refrigerator Car Co., **I** 219; **34** 36
St. Louis Troy and Eastern Railroad Company, **6** 504
St. Martin's Press, **25** 484–85; **35** 452
St. Michel-Grellier S.A., **44** 40
**St. Paul Bank for Cooperatives, 8 489–90**
St. Paul Book and Stationery, Inc., **47** 90
**The St. Paul Companies, III 355–57**; **15** 257; **21** 305; **22** 154, **492–95 (upd.)**
St. Paul Fire and Marine Insurance Co., **III** 355–56
St. Paul Venture Capital Inc., **34** 405–06
Saint-Quirin, **III** 676; **16** 120
St. Regis Corp., **I** 153; **IV** 264, 282; **9** 260; **10** 265; **20** 129
St. Regis Paper Co., **IV** 289, 339; **12** 377; **22** 209
Sainte Anne Paper Co., **IV** 245–46; **25** 10
Saipem, **IV** 420–22, 453
SAirGroup, **29** 376; **33** 268, 271; **37** 241; **46** 398; **47** 287
Saison Group, **V** 184–85, 187–89; **36** 417–18, 420; **42** 340–41
Saito Ltd., **IV** 268
Saiwa, **II** 543
Sako Ltd., **39** 151
Saks Fifth Avenue, **I** 426; **15** 291; **18** 372; **21** 302; **22** 72; **25** 205; **27** 329
**Saks Holdings, Inc., 24 420–23**
**Saks Inc., 41 342–45 (upd.)**
Sakura Bank, **39** 286
Sakurai Co., **IV** 327
Salada Foods, **II** 525; **13** 293
**Salant Corporation, 12 430–32**; **27** 445
Sale Knitting Company, **12** 501. *See also* Tultex Corporation.
Salem Broadcasting, **25** 508
Salem Carpet Mills, Inc., **9** 467
Salem Sportswear, **25** 167
Salen Energy A.B., **IV** 563
Salick Health Care, Inc., **21** 544, 546
Salim Group, **18** 180–81
Salinas Equipment Distributors, Inc., **33** 364
Sallie Mae. *See* SLM Holding Corp. *and* Student Loan Marketing Association.
Sally Beauty Company, Inc., **8** 15–17; **36** 23–26
Salmon Carriers, **6** 383
Salmon River Power & Light Company, **12** 265
Salomon Brothers Inc., **28** 164
**Salomon Inc.**, **I** 630–31; **II** 268, 400, 403, 406, 426, 432, 434, 441, **447–49**; **III** 221, 215, 721; **IV** 80, 137; **7** 114; **9** 378–79, 386; **11** 35, 371; **13** 331, **447–50 (upd.)** Inc.; **18** 60, 62; **19** 293; **21** 67, 146; **22** 102; **23** 472–74; **25** 12, 125; **42** 34
Salomon Smith Barney, **30** 124
**Salomon Worldwide, 20 458–60**; **33** 7. *See also* adidas-Salomon AG.
Salora, **II** 69; **17** 353
Salsåkers Ångsågs, **IV** 338
**Salt River Project, 19 374–76**
**Salton, Inc., 30 402–04**
Saltos del Sil, **II** 197
Salvagnini Company, **22** 6
**The Salvation Army USA**, **15** 510–11; **32 390–93**
**Salzgitter AG**, **IV** 128, 198, **200–01**; **17** 381
SAM. *See* Sociedad Aeronáutica de Medellín, S.A.
Sam & Libby Inc., **30** 311
**Sam Ash Music Corporation, 30 405–07**
Sam Goody, **I** 613; **9** 360–61
**Sam's Club**, **V** 216–17; **8** 555–57; **12** 221, 335; **13** 548; **14** 393; **15** 470; **16** 64; **25** 235; **40 385–87**; **41** 254–56
Samancor Ltd., **IV** 92–93
Samaritan Senior Services Inc., **25** 503
Samas-Groep N.V., **47** 91
Sambo's, **12** 510
Sambre-et-Moselle, **IV** 52
Samcor Glass, **III** 685
Samedan Oil Corporation, **11** 353
Sames, S.A., **21** 65–66
Samim, **IV** 422
Samkong Fat Ltd. Co., **III** 747
Samna Corp., **6** 256; **25** 300
Sampson's, **12** 220–21
Samson Technologies Corp., **30** 406
**Samsonite Corporation**, **6** 50; **13** 311, **451–53**; **16** 20–21; **38** 169; **43 353–57 (upd.)**
Samsung-Calex, **17** 483
**Samsung Electronics Co., Ltd., 14 416–18**; **18** 139, 260; **41 346–49 (upd.)**
**Samsung Group, I 515–17**; **II** 53–54; **III** 143, 457–58, 517, 749; **IV** 519; **7** 233; **12** 211–12; **13** 387; **18** 124; **29** 207–08
Samuel Austin & Son Company, **8** 41
Samuel Meisel & Company, Inc., **11** 80–81; **29** 509, 511
Samuel Montagu & Co., **II** 319; **17** 324–25
Samuel Moore & Co., **I** 155
Samuel Samuel & Co., **IV** 530, 542
Samuel, Son & Co. Ltd., **24** 144
**Samuels Jewelers Incorporated, 30 408–10**
Samwha Paper Co., **III** 748
San Antonio Public Service Company, **6** 473
**San Diego Gas & Electric Company, V 711–14**; **6** 590; **11** 272; **25** 416
San Francisco Mines of Mexico Ltd., **22** 285
San Gabriel Light & Power Company, **16** 496
San Giorgio Macaroni Inc., **II** 511
SAN-MIC Trading Co., **IV** 327
**San Miguel Corporation**, **I** 221; **15 428–30**; **23** 379
Sanborn Co., **III** 142; **6** 237
**Sanborn Hermanos, S.A., 20 461–63**; **21** 259
Sanborn Manufacturing Company, **30** 138

Sandcastle 5 Productions, **25** 269–70
Sanders Associates, Inc., **9** 324; **13** 127–28
Sanderson & Porter, **I** 376
Sanderson Computers, **10** 500
**Sanderson Farms, Inc., 15 425–27**
**Sandoz Ltd.**, **I** 632–33, **671–73**, 675; **7** 315, 452; **8** 108–09, 215; **10** 48, 199; **11** 173; **12** 388; **15** 139; **18** 51; **22** 475; **27** 299. *See also* Novartis AG.
Sandoz Nutrition Corp., **24** 286
SandPoint Corp., **12** 562; **17** 254
Sandusky Plastics, Inc., **17** 157
Sandusky Portland Cement Company, **24** 331
**Sandvik AB**, **III** 426–27; **IV 202–04**; **32 394–98 (upd.)**
Sandwell, Inc., **6** 491
Sandwich Chef, Inc. *See* Wall Street Deli, Inc.
Sandy's Pool Supply, Inc. *See* Leslie's Poolmart, Inc.
SANFLO Co., Ltd., **IV** 327
Sanford-Brown College, Inc., **41** 419–20
Sangu Express Company, **V** 463
Sanichem Manufacturing Company, **16** 386
Sanitary Farm Dairies, Inc., **7** 372
Sanitas Food Co., **II** 523
Sanitation Systems, Inc. *See* HMI Industries.
Sanjushi Bank, **II** 347
Sanka Coffee Corp., **II** 531
Sankin Kai Group, **II** 274
Sanko Kabushiki Kaisha. *See* Marubeni Corporation.
**Sankyo Company Ltd.**, **I** 330, **674–75**; **III** 760; **8** 153
Sanlam, **IV** 91, 93, 535
Sano Railway Company, **6** 430
**Sanofi Group**, **I** 304, **676–77**; **III** 18; **IV** 546; **7** 484–85; **21** 205; **23** 236, 238, 242; **35** 262–63, 265
**Sanrio Company, Ltd., 38 413–15**
Sanseisha Co., **IV** 326
Santa Ana Savings and Loan, **10** 339
Santa Ana Wholesale Company, **16** 451
**Santa Barbara Restaurant Group, Inc., 37 349–52**
**The Santa Cruz Operation, Inc.**, **6** 244; **38 416–21**
Santa Cruz Portland Cement, **II** 490
**Santa Fe Gaming Corporation, 19 377–79**
Santa Fe Gold Corporation, **38** 232
Santa Fe Industries, **II** 448; **12** 19; **13** 448; **28** 498
**Santa Fe International Corporation**, **IV** 451–52; **38 422–24**
**Santa Fe Pacific Corporation**, **V 507–09**; **24** 98. *See also* Burlington Northern Santa Fe Corporation.
Santa Fe Railway, **12** 278; **18** 4
Santa Fe Southern Pacific Corp., **III** 512; **IV** 721; **6** 150, 599; **9** 391; **22** 491
Santa Rosa Savings and Loan, **10** 339
Santal, **26** 160
Santiam Lumber Co., **IV** 358
Santone Industries Inc., **16** 327
Sanus Corp. Health Systems, **III** 317
**Sanwa Bank, Ltd.**, **II** 276, 326, **347–48**, 442, 511; **III** 188, 759; **IV** 150–51; **7** 119; **15** 43, **431–33 (upd.)**; **24** 356, 358
Sanyo Chemical Manufacturing Co., **III** 758
**Sanyo Electric Co., Ltd.**, **I** 516; **II** 55–56, **91–92**; **III** 569, 654; **6** 101; **14** 535; **20** 361; **36 399–403 (upd.)**
Sanyo Ethylene Co. Ltd., **IV** 476
**Sanyo-Kokusaku Pulp Co., Ltd.**, **IV** 326, **327–28**
Sanyo Petrochemical Co. Ltd., **IV** 476
Sanyo Railway Co., **I** 506; **II** 325
Sanyo Semiconductor, **17** 33
**SAP AG**, **11** 78; **16 441–44**; **25** 34; **26** 496, 498; **43 358–63 (upd.)**
SAP America Inc., **38** 431–32
SAPAC. *See* Société Parisienne d'Achats en Commun.
Sapirstein Greeting Card Company. *See* American Greetings Corporation.
Sappi Ltd., **IV** 91–93
**Sapporo Breweries Limited**, **I 282–83**; **13 454–56 (upd.)**; **20** 28–29; **21** 319–20; **36 404–07 (upd.)**
**Sara Lee Corporation**, **I** 15, 30; **II 571–73**, 675; **7** 113 **8** 262; **10** 219–20; **11** 15, 486; **12** 494, 502, 531; **15** 359, **434–37 (upd.)**, 507; **19** 192; **25** 91, 125, 166, 523; **26** 325, 503; **29** 132; **38** 381; **45** 111–12, 114
Saracen's Head Brewery, **21** 245
Saratoga Partners, **24** 436
Sarawak Trading, **14** 448
Sargent & Lundy, **6** 556
Sarget S.A., **IV** 71
SARL, **12** 152
Sarma, **III** 623–24; **26** 159–61
Sarmag, **26** 161
Saros Corp., **15** 474
Sarotti A.G., **II** 546
Sarpe, **IV** 591
Sarriò S.A., **41** 325–26
Sartek Industries Inc., **44** 441
**The SAS Group, 34 396–99 (upd.)**
**SAS Institute Inc.**, **10 476–78**; **38** 432
Saseba Heavy Industries, **II** 274
Saskatchewan Oil and Gas Corporation, **13** 556–57
**Sasol Limited**, **IV 533–35**; **47 340–44 (upd.)**
Sason Corporation, **V** 187
SAT. *See* Stockholms Allmänna Telefonaktiebolag.
Satcom Group of Companies, **32** 40
Satellite Business Systems, **III** 182; **21** 14; **23** 135; **27** 304
Satellite Information Services, **II** 141
Satellite Software International, **10** 556
Satellite Television PLC, **IV** 652; **7** 391; **23** 135
Satellite Transmission and Reception Specialist Company, **11** 184
Säteri Oy, **IV** 349
Sato Yasusaburo, **I** 266
Saturday Evening Post Co., **II** 208; **9** 320
**Saturn Corporation**, **III** 593, 760; **7 461–64**; **21 449–53 (upd.)**; **22** 154; **36** 242
Saturn Industries, Inc., **23** 489
SATV. *See* Satellite Television PLC.
Saucona Iron Co., **IV** 35; **7** 48
**Saucony Inc., 35 386–89**
**Sauder Woodworking Co.**, **12 433–34**; **35 390–93 (upd.)**
**Saudi Arabian Airlines**, **6** 84, **114–16**; **27** 132, **395–98 (upd.)**
**Saudi Arabian Oil Company**, **IV 536–39**; **17 411–15 (upd.)**. *See also* Arabian American Oil Co.
Saudi Arabian Parsons Limited, **8** 416
Saudi British Bank, **II** 298
Saudi Consolidated Electric Co., **IV** 538; **17** 414
Saudi Refining Inc., **IV** 539; **17** 414
Saudia. *See* Saudi Arabian Airlines.
Sauer Motor Company, **I** 177; **22** 329
Saul Lerner & Co., **II** 450
Saunders Karp & Co., **26** 190
Saunders, Karp, and Megrue, LP, **28** 258
Saunders-Roe Ltd., **IV** 658
Sauza, **31** 92
Sav-on Drug, **II** 605; **12** 477
Sav-X, **9** 186
Sava Group, **20** 263
Savacentre Ltd., **II** 658; **13** 284
Savage, **19** 430
Savage Shoes, Ltd., **III** 529
Savannah Electric & Power Company, **38** 448
**Savannah Foods & Industries, Inc.**, **7 465–67**; **32** 274, 277; **35** 178
Savannah Gas Company, **6** 448; **23** 29
Save & Prosper Group, **10** 277
Save-A-Lot, **II** 682; **11** 228
Save Mart, **14** 397; **27** 292
Save.com, **37** 409
Savia S.A. de C.V., **29** 435
Saviem, **III** 543
Savin, **III** 159; **26** 497
Savings of America, **II** 182
Savio, **IV** 422
Oy Savo-Karjalan Tukkuliike, **8** 293
Savon Sellu Mills, **IV** 315
Savory Milln, **II** 369
Savoy Group, **I** 248; **IV** 705; **24** 195
Savoy Industries, **12** 495
Savoy Pictures Entertainment Inc., **25** 214
Sawdust Pencil Company, **29** 372
Sawgrass Asset Management, LLC, **48** 18
Sawhill Tubular Products, **41** 3
**Sawtek Inc., 43 364–66 (upd.)**
Sawyer Electrical Manufacturing Company, **11** 4
Sawyer Industries, Inc., **13** 532
Sawyer Research Products, Inc., **14** 81
Saxby, S.A., **13** 385
Saxon and Norman Cement Co., **III** 670
Saxon Oil, **11** 97
Saxon Petroleum, Inc., **19** 162
Sayama Sekiyu, **IV** 554
SB Acquisitions, Inc., **46** 74
SBAR, Inc., **30** 4
**Sbarro, Inc.**, **16 445–47**; **19** 435; **27** 146
**SBC Communications Inc.**, **25** 498–99; **29** 62; **32 399–403 (upd.)**; **34** 362; **43** 447; **47** 10
**SBC Warburg**, **II** 369; **14 419–21**; **15** 197
Sberbank, **II** 242
SBK Entertainment World, Inc., **22** 194; **24** 485; **26** 187
**SBS Technologies, Inc., 25 405–07**
SCA. *See* Svenska Cellulosa Aktiebolaget.
SCA Services, Inc., **V** 754; **9** 109
Scaldia Paper BV, **15** 229
Scali, McCabe & Sloves, **I** 27; **22** 200
Scan Screen, **IV** 600
**Scana Corporation**, **6 574–76**; **19** 499
Scanair, **34** 397–98
Scancem, **38** 437

**Scandinavian Airlines System**, **I** 107, **119–20**, 121; **6** 96, 122; **25** 159; **26** 113; **27** 26, 463, 474; **31** 305; **33** 50; **38** 105. *See also* The SAS Group.
Scandinavian Bank, **II** 352
Scandinavian Trading Co., **I** 210
ScanDust, **III** 625
Scania-Vabis. *See* Saab-Scania AB.
**ScanSource, Inc.**, **29 413–15**
Scantron Corporation, **17** 266–68
**Scarborough Public Utilities Commission**, **9 461–62**
Scaturro Supermarkets, **24** 528
**SCB Computer Technology, Inc.**, **29 416–18**
**SCEcorp**, **V** 713–14, **715–17**; **6** 590
Scenic Airlines, Inc., **25** 420, 423
Scenographic Designs, **21** 277
Schäfer, **31** 158
Schaffhausenschor Bankverein, **II** 281
Schaper Mfg. Co., **12** 168
Scharff-Koken Manufacturing Co., **IV** 286
Scharnow-Reisen, **II** 163–64; **44** 432
Schaum Publishing Co., **IV** 636
Schauman Wood Oy, **IV** 277, 302
**Schawk, Inc.**, **24 424–26**
Schein Pharmaceutical Inc., **13** 77
**Schenker-Rhenus Ag**, **6 424–26**
Schenley Industries Inc., **I** 226, 285; **9** 449; **10** 181; **24** 140
Scherer. *See* R.P. Scherer.
**Schering A.G.**, **I 681–82**, 684, 701; **10** 214; **14** 60; **16** 543; **36** 92, 148
**Schering-Plough Corporation**, **I** 682, **683–85**; **II** 590; **III** 45, 61; **11** 142, 207; **14** 58, 60, **422–25 (upd.)**; **36** 91–92; **45** 382
Schiavi Homes, Inc., **14** 138
**Schibsted ASA**, **31 401–05**
Schicht Co., **II** 588
Schick Products, **41** 366
Schick Shaving, **I** 711; **III** 55; **38** 363, 365
Schieffelin & Co., **I** 272
**Schindler Holding AG**, **II** 122; **12** 546; **27** 267; **29 419–22**
Schlage Lock Co., **III** 526
Schleppschiffahrtsgesellschaft Unterweser, **IV** 140
Schlesischer Bankverein, **II** 278
Schlitz Brewing Co., **I** 218, 255, 268, 270, 291, 600; **10** 100; **12** 338; **18** 500; **23** 403
**Schlotzsky's, Inc.**, **36 408–10**
**Schlumberger Limited**, **III** 429, 499, **616–18**; **13** 323; **17 416–19 (upd.)**; **22** 64, 68; **25** 191; **43** 91, 338; **45** 418
Schmalbach-Lubeca-Werke A.G., **15** 128
Schmid, **19** 166
Schmidt, **I** 255
**Schmitt Music Company**, **40 388–90**
Schneider Co., **III** 113
Schneider et Cie, **IV** 25; **22** 42
**Schneider National, Inc.**, **36 411–13**; **47** 318–19
**Schneider S.A.**, **II 93–94**; **18 471–74 (upd.)**; **19** 165–66; **37** 39
**Schneiderman's Furniture Inc.**, **28 405–08**
**Schnitzer Steel Industries, Inc.**, **19 380–82**
Schnoll Foods, **24** 528
Schober Direktmarketing, **18** 170
Schocken Books, **13** 429
Schoeller & Hoesch Group, **30** 349, 352
Schoenfeld Industries, **16** 511
**Scholastic Corporation**, **10 479–81**; **29** 143, **423–27 (upd.)**
Scholl Inc., **I** 685; **14** 424
Schöller, **27** 436, 439
Scholz Homes Inc., **IV** 115
Schott Glass Technologies Inc., **34** 94
Schott Glaswerke, **III** 445–47
Schott-Zwiesel-Glaswerke AG, **34** 94
**Schottenstein Stores Corp.**, **14 426–28**; **19** 108; **24** 26; **38** 475. *See also* American Eagle Outfitters, Inc.
Schrader Bellows, **III** 603
Schreiber Foods, **26** 432
Schreiber Frères. *See* Groupe Les Echos.
Schrock Cabinet Company, **13** 564
Schroder Darling & Co., **II** 389
**Schroders plc**, **42 332–35**
Schroders Ventures, **18** 345
Schroeter, White and Johnson, **III** 204
Schroff Inc., **26** 361, 363
Schubach, **30** 408
Schubert & Salzer GmbH, **42** 316
Schuck's Auto Supply. *See* CSK Auto Corporation.
**Schuff Steel Company**, **26 431–34**
Schuitema, **II** 642; **16** 312–13
Schuler Chocolates, **15** 65
Schuller International, Inc., **11** 421
**Schultz Sav-O Stores, Inc.**, **21 454–56**; **31 406–08**
Schumacher Co., **II** 624
Schuykill Energy Resources, **12** 41
Schwabe-Verlag, **7** 42
Schwabel Corporation, **19** 453
**Schwan's Sales Enterprises, Inc.**, **7 468–70**; **26 435–38 (upd.)**
Schwartz Iron & Metal Co., **13** 142
Schwarze Pumpe, **38** 408
Schweitzer-Maudit International Inc., **16** 304; **43** 258
Schweiz Allgemeine, **III** 377
Schweiz Transport-Vericherungs-Gesellschaft, **III** 410
Schweizer Rück Holding AG, **III** 377
Schweizerische Bankgesellschaft AG, **II** 379; **V** 104
Schweizerische Kreditanstalt, **III** 375, 410; **6** 489
Schweizerische Nordostbahn, **6** 424
**Schweizerische Post-, Telefon- und Telegrafen-Betriebe**, **V 321–24**
Schweizerische Ruckversicherungs-Gesellschaft. *See* Swiss Reinsurance Company.
Schweizerische Unfallversicherungs-Actiengesellschaft in Winterthur, **III** 402
Schweizerische Unionbank, **II** 368
Schweizerischer Bankverein, **II** 368
Schweppe, Paul & Gosse, **II** 476
Schweppes Ltd. *See* Cadbury Schweppes PLC.
**Schwinn Cycle and Fitness L.P.**, **16** 494; **19 383–85**; **26** 412; **47** 95
The Schwinn GT Co., **26** 185
Schwitzer, **II** 420
SCI. *See* Service Corporation International *or* Société Centrale d'Investissement.
**SCI Systems, Inc.**, **9 463–64**; **12** 451
Scicon, **14** 317
SciCor Inc., **30** 152
**Science Applications International Corporation**, **15 438–40**
**Scientific-Atlanta, Inc.**, **6 335–37**; **45 371–75 (upd.)**
Scientific Communications, Inc., **10** 97
Scientific Data Systems, **II** 44; **III** 172; **6** 289; **10** 365
Scientific Games Holding Corp., **III** 431; **20** 48
Scientific Materials Company, **24** 162
SciMed Life Systems, **III** 18–19; **37** 43
Scioto Bank, **9** 475
**Scitex Corporation Ltd.**, **15** 148, 229; **24 427–32**; **26** 212; **43** 150; **48** 123
SCM Corp., **I** 29; **III** 502; **IV** 330; **7** 208; **8** 223–24; **17** 213
SCO. *See* Santa Cruz Operation, Inc.
SCOA Industries, Inc., **13** 260
Scopus Technology Inc., **38** 431
**SCOR S.A.**, **III** 394; **20 464–66**
**The Score Board, Inc.**, **19 386–88**
Score! Learning, Inc., **42** 211
Scot Bowyers, **II** 587
Scot Lad Foods, **14** 411
Scotch House Ltd., **19** 181
Scotia Securities, **II** 223
Scotiabank. *See* The Bank of Nova Scotia.
**Scotsman Industries, Inc.**, **II** 420; **16** 397; **20 467–69**
Scott-Ballantyne Company. *See* Ballantyne of Omaha, Inc.
Scott Communications, Inc., **10** 97
**Scott Fetzer Company**, **III** 214; **12 435–37**, 554–55; **17** 233; **18** 60, 62–63; **42** 33
Scott, Foresman, **IV** 675
Scott Graphics, **IV** 289; **8** 483
Scott Health Care, **28** 445
Scott Holdings, **19** 384
Scott Lithgow, **III** 516; **7** 232
Scott-McDuff, **II** 107
**Scott Paper Company**, **III** 749; **IV** 258, 289–90, 311, 325, 327, **329–31**; **8** 483; **16** 302, 304; **17** 182; **18** 181; **19** 266; **22** 210; **29** 333; **31 409–412 (upd.)**; **43** 258
Scott Transport, **27** 473
Scotti Brothers, **20** 3
**Scottish & Newcastle plc**, **15 441–44**; **35 394–97 (upd.)**
Scottish Amicable plc, **48** 328
Scottish Aviation, **I** 50; **24** 85–86
Scottish Brick, **14** 250
Scottish Electric, **6** 453
Scottish General Fire Assurance Corp., **III** 256
**Scottish Hydro-Electric PLC**, **13 457–59**
Scottish Inns of America, Inc., **13** 362
Scottish Land Development, **III** 501; **7** 207
Scottish Malt Distillers, **I** 240
**Scottish Media Group plc**, **32 404–06**; **41** 350–52
Scottish Mutual plc, **39** 5–6
Scottish Nuclear, Ltd., **19** 389
**Scottish Radio Holding plc**, **41 350–52**
Scottish Sealand Oil Services Ltd., **25** 171
Scottish Union Co., **III** 358
Scottish Universal Investments, **45** 189
**ScottishPower plc**, **19 389–91**; **27** 483, 486
ScottishTelecom plc, **19** 389
**The Scotts Company**, **22 474–76**
Scotts Stores, **I** 289
**Scotty's, Inc.**, **12** 234; **22 477–80**; **26** 160–61
**Scovill Fasteners Inc.**, **IV** 11; **22** 364; **24 433–36**

**SCP Pool Corporation, 39 358–60**
Scranton Corrugated Box Company, Inc., **8** 102
Scranton Plastics Laminating Corporation, **8** 359
Screen Gems, **II** 135–36; **12** 74; **22** 193
Screg Group, **I** 563; **24** 79; **31** 128
Scribbans-Kemp Ltd., **II** 594
Scriha & Deyhle, **10** 196
Scripps-Howard, Inc., **IV** 607–09, 628; **7** 64, 157–59. *See also* The E.W. Scripps Company.
Scrivner Inc., **17** 180
SCS Interactive, **44** 261
Scudder Kemper Investments. *See* Zurich Financial Services.
Scudder, Stevens & Clark, **II** 448; **13** 448
Scurlock Oil Co., **IV** 374
SD-Scicon plc, **24** 87
SDA Systems Inc., **48** 75
SDC Coatings, **III** 715
SDGE. *See* San Diego Gas & Electric Company.
SDK Health Care Information Systems, **16** 94
SDK Parks, **IV** 724
Sea-Alaska Products, **II** 494
**Sea Containers Ltd., 29 428–31**
Sea Diamonds Ltd., **IV** 66; **7** 123
Sea Far of Norway, **II** 484
Sea Insurance Co. Ltd., **III** 220
Sea-Land Service Inc., **I** 476; **9** 510–11; **22** 164, 166
Sea Life Centre Aquariums, **10** 439
Sea Ray, **III** 444
Sea Star Line, **41** 399
Sea World, Inc., **IV** 623–24; **12** 224
Seabee Corp., **18** 276
Seaboard Air Line Railroad. *See* CSX Corporation.
**Seaboard Corporation, 36 414–16**
Seaboard Finance Company, **13** 63
Seaboard Fire and Marine Insurance Co., **III** 242
Seaboard Life Insurance Co., **III** 193
Seaboard Lumber Sales, **IV** 307
Seaboard Oil Co., **IV** 552
Seaboard Surety Company, **III** 357; **22** 494
Seabourn Cruise Lines, **6** 368; **27** 90, 92
Seabrook Farms Co., **24** 527–28
Seabulk Offshore International. *See* Hvide Marine Incorporated.
Seabury & Smith, **III** 283
Seacat-Zapata Off-Shore Company, **18** 513
Seacoast Products, **III** 502
Seafield Capital Corporation, **27** 385, 387. *See also* LabOne, Inc.
Seafield Estate and Consolidated Plantations Berhad, **14** 448
Seafirst. *See* Seattle First National Bank, Inc.
SeaFirst Corp., **II** 228; **17** 462
**Seagate Technology, Inc.,** **6** 230–31; **8 466–68**; **9** 57; **10** 257, 403–04, 459; **11** 56, 234; **13** 483; **18** 250; **25** 530; **34 400–04 (upd.)**; **45** 429
**The Seagram Company Ltd.,** **I** 26, 240, 244, **284–86**, 329, 403; **II** 456, 468; **IV** 401; **7** 155; **18** 72; **21** 26, 401; **22** 194; **23** 125; **25** 266, 268, 366, **408–12 (upd.)**; **26** 125, 127, 152; **28** 475; **29** 196; **31** 269; **33** 375, 424, 432; **46** 438; **47** 418–20
**Seagull Energy Corporation, 11 440–42**
Seahawk Services Ltd., **37** 289
Seal Products, Inc., **12** 264
Seal Sands Chemicals, **16** 69
Sealand Petroleum Co., **IV** 400
Sealectro, **III** 434
**Sealed Air Corporation, 14 429–31**
**Sealed Power Corporation, I 199–200; 10** 492–94. *See also* SPX Corporation.
**Sealright Co., Inc., 17 420–23**
SealRite Windows, **19** 446
Sealtest, **14** 205
**Sealy Inc., 12 438–40**; **28** 416; **34** 407
**Seaman Furniture Company, Inc., 28** 389; **32 407–09**
Seamless Rubber Co., **III** 613
Seaquist Manufacturing Corporation, **9** 413–14; **33** 335–36
Searle & Co. *See* G.D. Searle & Co.
Sears Canada Inc., **25** 221
Sears Logistics Services, **18** 225–26
**Sears plc, V 177–79**
**Sears, Roebuck and Co.,** **I** 26, 146, 516, 556; **II** 18, 60, 134, 331, 411, 414; **III** 259, 265, 340, 536, 598, 653–55; **V 180–83**; **6** 12–13; **7** 166, 479; **8** 224, 287–89; **9** 44, 65–66 156, 210, 213, 219, 235–36, 430–31, 538; **10** 10, 50–52, 199, 236–37, 288, 304–05, 490–91; **11** 62, 349, 393, 498; **12** 54, 96–98, 309, 311, 315, 430–31, 439, 522, 548, 557; **13** 165, 260, 268, 277, 411, 545, 550, 562–63; **14** 62; **15** 402, 470; **16** 73, 75, 160, 327–28, 560; **17** 366, 460, 487; **18** 65, 168, 283, 445, **475–79 (upd.)**; **19** 143, 221, 309, 490; **20** 259, 263; **21** 73, 94, 96–97; **23** 23, 52, 210; **25** 221, 357, 535; **27** 30, 32, 163, 347–48, 416, 428–30; **33** 311–12; **36** 418
**Sears Roebuck de México, S.A. de C.V., 20 470–72**; **21** 259; **34** 340
Seashore Transportation Co., **13** 398
Season-all Industries, **III** 735
SEAT. *See* Sociedad Española de Automoviles de Turismo.
**Seat Pagine Gialle S.p.A., 47 345–47**
Seatrain International, **27** 474
Seattle Brewing and Malting Company. *See* Rainier Brewing Company.
Seattle Coffee Company, **32** 12, 15
Seattle Electric Company, **6** 565
**Seattle FilmWorks, Inc., 20 473–75**
**Seattle First National Bank Inc., 8 469–71**
**Seattle Times Company, 15 445–47**
Seaview Oil Co., **IV** 393
Seaway Express, **9** 510
**Seaway Food Town, Inc., 9** 452; **15 448–50**
SeaWest, **19** 390
SEB-Fastigheter A.B., **II** 352
SEB S.A. *See* Groupe SEB.
Sebastian International, **48** 422
**Sebastiani Vineyards, Inc., 28 413–15**; **39** 421
SECA, **IV** 401
SECDO, **III** 618
SECO Industries, **III** 614
Seco Products Corporation, **22** 354
Secon GmbH, **13** 160
Second Bank of the United States, **II** 213; **9** 369
**Second Harvest, 29 432–34**
Second National Bank, **II** 254
Second National Bank of Bucyrus, **9** 474
Second National Bank of Ravenna, **9** 474
Secoroc, **III** 427
Le Secours, **III** 211
SecPac. *See* Security Pacific Corporation.
Secure Horizons, **11** 378–79
Secure Networks, Inc., **25** 349
**Securicor Plc, 11** 547; **45 376–79**
**Securitas AB, 41** 77, 80; **42** 165–66, **336–39**
Securitas Esperia, **III** 208
Securities Industry Automation Corporation, **9** 370
Securities International, Inc., **II** 440–41
Securities Management & Research, Inc., **27** 46
Security Bancorp, **25** 186–87
**Security Capital Corporation, 17 424–27**; **21** 476; **48** 330–31
Security Connecticut Life Insurance Co., **III** 276
Security Data Group, **32** 373
Security Dynamics Technologies, Inc., **46** 367
Security Engineering, **III** 472
Security Express, **10** 269
Security First National Bank of Los Angeles, **II** 349
Security Life and Annuity Company, **11** 213
Security Management Company, **8** 535–36
Security National Bank, **II** 251, 336
Security National Corp., **10** 246
**Security Pacific Corporation, II 349–50,** 422; **III** 366; **8** 45, 48; **11** 447; **17** 137
Security Trust Company, **9** 229, 388
Security Union Title Insurance Co., **10** 43–44
**SED International Holdings, Inc., 43 367–69**
Sedat Eldem, **13** 475
SEDCO, **17** 418
Sedgwick Group PLC, **I** 427; **III** 280, 366; **10** 38; **22** 318
Sedgwick Sales, Inc., **29** 384
SEDTCO Pty., **13** 61
**See's Candies, Inc., III** 213; **18** 60–61; **30 411–13**
Seeburg Corporation, **II** 22; **III** 430; **15** 538
Seed Restaurant Group Inc., **13** 321; **27** 145
Seed Solutions, Inc., **11** 491
Seeger-Orbis, **III** 624
Seeger Refrigerator Co., **III** 653; **12** 548
Seeman Brothers. *See* White Rose, Inc.
SEEQ Technology, Inc., **9** 114; **13** 47; **17** 32, 34
SEG, **I** 463
Sega Enterprises, Ltd., **28** 320
**Sega of America, Inc., 7** 396; **10** 124–25, 284–86, **482–85**; **18** 520
Sega of Japan, **24** 4
Segespar, **II** 265
Sego Milk Products Company, **7** 428
Seguros Comercial America, **21** 413
Seguros El Corte Inglés, **V** 52
Seguros Monterrey Aetna, **19** 189; **45** 294
Seguros Serfin S.A., **25** 290
**Segway LLC, 48 355–57**
Seibels, Bruce & Co., **11** 394–95
Seiberling Rubber Company, **V** 244; **20** 259

Seibu Allstate Life Insurance Company, Ltd., **27** 31
**Seibu Department Stores, Ltd., II** 273; **V 184–86**; **42 340–43 (upd.)**
Seibu Group, **36** 417–18; **47** 408–09
**Seibu Railway Co. Ltd., V** 187, **510–11**, 526
Seibu Saison, **6** 207
Seifu Co. Ltd., **48** 250
**Seigle's Home and Building Centers, Inc., 41 353–55**
Seijo Green Plaza Co., **I** 283
Seikatsu-Soko, **V** 210
**Seiko Corporation, I** 488; **III** 445, **619–21**; **11** 46; **12** 317; **13** 122; **16** 168, 549; **17 428–31 (upd.)**; **21** 122–23; **22** 413; **41** 72
Seiko Instruments USA Inc., **23** 210
Seimi Chemical Co. Ltd., **48** 41
Seine, **III** 391
**Seino Transportation Company, Ltd., 6 427–29**
Seismograph Service Limited, **II** 86; **11** 413; **17** 419
**Seita, 23 424–27**
**Seitel, Inc., 47 348–50**
Seiwa Fudosan Co., **I** 283
**The Seiyu, Ltd., V 187–89**; **36 417–21 (upd.)**
Seizo-sha, **12** 483
**Sekisui Chemical Co., Ltd., III 741–43**
SEL, **I** 193, 463
Selat Marine Services, **22** 276
Selby Shoe Company, **48** 69
Selden, **I** 164, 300
**Select Comfort Corporation, 34 405–08**
Select Energy, Inc., **48** 305
Select-Line Industries, **9** 543
Select Theatres Corp. *See* Shubert Organization Inc.
Selection Trust, **IV** 67, 380, 565
Selective Auto and Fire Insurance Co. of America, **III** 353
Selective Insurance Co., **III** 191
Selectronics Inc., **23** 210
Selectrons Ltd., **41** 367
Selena Coffee Inc., **39** 409
Selenia, **I** 467; **II** 86; **38** 374
Self Auto, **23** 232
The Self-Locking Carton Company, **14** 163
Self-Service Drive Thru, Inc., **25** 389
Self Service Restaurants, **II** 613
**Selfridges Plc, V** 94, 177–78; **34 409–11**
Seligman & Latz, **18** 455
Selkirk Communications Ltd., **26** 273
Selleck Nicholls, **III** 691
Sells-Floto, **32** 186
**The Selmer Company, Inc., 19 392–94**, 426, 428
Seltel International Inc., **6** 33; **35** 246
Semarca, **11** 523
Sematech, **18** 384, 481
Sembler Company, **11** 346
**SEMCO Energy, Inc., 44 379–82**
Semet-Solvay, **22** 29
Semi-Tech Global, **30** 419–20
**Seminis, Inc., 21** 413; **29 435–37**
Seminole Electric Cooperative, **6** 583
Seminole Fertilizer, **7** 537–38
Seminole National Bank, **41** 312
Semitic, Inc., **33** 248
**Semitool, Inc., 18 480–82**
**Sempra Energy, 25 413–16 (upd.)**
Semrau and Sons, **II** 601
**Semtech Corporation, 32 410–13**
SEN AG, **IV** 128
Sencel Aero Engineering Corporation, **16** 483
**Seneca Foods Corporation, 17 432–34**
Senelle-Maubeuge, **IV** 227
Senior Corp., **11** 261
Senshusha, **I** 506
Sensi, Inc., **22** 173
**Sensormatic Electronics Corp., 11 443–45**; **39** 77–79
**Sensory Science Corporation, 37 353–56**
Sentinel Foam & Envelope Corporation, **14** 430
Sentinel Group, **6** 295
Sentinel Savings and Loan, **10** 339
Sentinel-Star Company, **IV** 683; **22** 521
Sentinel Technologies, **III** 38
Sentrust, **IV** 92
Sentry, **II** 624
Sentry Insurance Company, **10** 210
Senyo Kosakuki Kenkyujo, **III** 595
Seohan Development Co., **III** 516; **7** 232
Sepa, **II** 594
Sepal, Ltd., **39** 152, 154
AB Separator, **III** 417–19
SEPECAT, **24** 86
SEPIC, **I** 330
**Sepracor Inc., 45 380–83**
Sept, **IV** 325
**Sequa Corp., 13 460–63**
Séquanaise, **III** 391–92
Sequel Corporation, **41** 193
Sequent Computer Systems Inc., **10** 363
Sequoia Athletic Company, **25** 450
Sequoia Insurance, **III** 270
Sequoia Pharmacy Group, **13** 150
Sera-Tec Biologicals, Inc., **V** 175–76; **19** 355
Seraco Group, **V** 182
Seragen Inc., **47** 223
Serck Group, **I** 429
**Serco Group plc, 47 351–53**
SEREB, **I** 45; **7** 10
Sereg Valves, S.A., **17** 147
Serewatt AG, **6** 491
Sergeant Drill Co., **III** 525
Sero-Genics, Inc., **V** 174–75
**Serono S.A., 47 354–57**
**Serta, Inc., 28 416–18**
Serval Marketing, **18** 393
Servam Corp., **7** 471–73
Servel Inc., **III** 479; **22** 25
**Service America Corp., 7 471–73**; **27** 480–81
Service Bureau Corp., **III** 127
Service Co., Ltd., **48** 182
Service Control Corp. *See* Angelica Corporation.
**Service Corporation International, 6 293–95**; **16** 343–44; **37** 66–68
Service Corporation of America, **17** 552
Service Games Company, **10** 482
Service Master L.P., **34** 153
**Service Merchandise Company, Inc., V 190–92**; **6** 287; **9** 400; **19 395–99 (upd.)**
Service Partner, **I** 120
Service Pipe Line Co., **IV** 370
Service Q. General Service Co., **I** 109
Service Systems, **III** 103
**ServiceMaster Inc., 23 428–31 (upd.)**
**Servicemaster Limited Partnership, 6 44–46**; **13** 199
Services Maritimes des Messageries Impériales. *See* Compagnie des Messageries Maritimes.
ServiceWare, Inc., **25** 118
Servicios Financieros Quadrum S.A., **14** 156
Servisco, **II** 608
ServiStar Coast to Coast Corporation. *See* TruServ Corporation.
ServoChem A.B., **I** 387
Servomation Corporation, **7** 472–73
Servomation Wilbur. *See* Service America Corp.
Servoplan, S.A., **8** 272
SES Staffing Solutions, **27** 21
Sesame Street Book Club, **13** 560
Sesamee Mexicana, **48** 142
Sespe Oil, **IV** 569; **24** 519
Sessler Inc., **19** 381
SET, **I** 466
Setagaya Industry Co., Ltd., **48** 295
SETCAR, **14** 458
Settsu Marine and Fire Insurance Co., **III** 367
Seven Arts Limited, **25** 328
Seven Arts Productions, Ltd., **II** 147, 176
**7-Eleven, Inc., 32 414–18 (upd.)**; **36** 358
Seven-Eleven Japan Co., **41** 115. *See also* Ito-Yokado Co., Ltd.
Seven Generation, Inc., **41** 177
Seven Network Limited, **25** 329
Seven-Up Bottling Co. of Los Angeles, **II** 121
Seven-Up Co., **I** 245, 257; **II** 468, 477; **18** 418
**Sevenson Environmental Services, Inc., 42 344–46**
**Severn Trent PLC, 12 441–43**; **38 425–29 (upd.)**
Severonickel Combine, **48** 300
Seversky Aircraft Corporation, **9** 205
Sevin-Rosen Partners, **III** 124; **6** 221
Sewell Coal Co., **IV** 181
Sewell Plastics, Inc., **10** 222
Sextant In-Flight Systems, LLC, **30** 74
Seybold Machine Co., **II** 37; **6** 602
Seymour Electric Light Co., **13** 182
Seymour International Press Distributor Ltd., **IV** 619
Seymour Press, **IV** 619
Seymour Trust Co., **13** 467
SFIC Holdings (Cayman) Inc., **38** 422
SFIM Industries, **37** 348
SFNGR. *See* Nouvelles Galeries Réunies.
SFS Bancorp Inc., **41** 212
SFX Broadcasting Inc., **24** 107
**SFX Entertainment, Inc., 36 422–25**; **37** 383–84
SGC. *See* Supermarkets General Corporation.
SGE. *See* Vinci.
**SGI, 29 438–41 (upd.)**
SGL Carbon Group, **40** 83; **46** 14
SGLG, Inc., **13** 367
SGS Corp., **II** 117; **11** 46
Shaffer Clarke, **II** 594
**Shakespeare Company, 16** 296; **22 481–84**
Shakey's Pizza, **16** 447
**Shaklee Corporation, 12 444–46**; **17** 186; **38** 93; **39 361–64 (upd.)**
Shalco Systems, **13** 7
Shampaine Industries, Inc., **37** 399
Shamrock Advisors, Inc., **8** 305

Shamrock Broadcasting Inc., **24** 107
Shamrock Capital L.P., **7** 81–82
Shamrock Holdings, **III** 609; **7** 438; **9** 75; **11** 556; **25** 268
Shamrock Oil & Gas Co., **I** 403–04; **IV** 409; **7** 308
Shan-Chih Business Association, **23** 469
Shandwick International, **47** 97
Shanghai Crown Maling Packaging Co. Ltd., **13** 190
Shanghai General Bearing Co., Ltd., **45** 170
Shanghai Hotels Co., **IV** 717
Shanghai International Finance Company Limited, **15** 433
Shanghai Kyocera Electronics Co., Ltd., **21** 331
**Shanghai Petrochemical Co., Ltd.**, **18** **483–85**; **21** 83; **45** 50
Shangri-La Asia Ltd., **22** 305
**Shanks Group plc**, **45** **384–87**
**Shannon Aerospace Ltd.**, **36** **426–28**
Shannon Group, Inc., **18** 318, 320
Shansby Group, **27** 197; **43** 218
Share Drug plc, **24** 269
Shared Financial Systems, Inc., **10** 501
**Shared Medical Systems Corporation**, **14** **432–34**
Shared Technologies Inc., **12** 71
Shared Use Network Systems, Inc., **8** 311
ShareWave Inc., **48** 92
Shari Lewis Enterprises, Inc., **28** 160
Sharon Steel Corp., **I** 497; **7** 360–61; **8** 536; **13** 158, 249; **47** 234
Sharon Tank Car Corporation, **6** 394; **25** 169
Sharp & Dohme, Incorporated, **I** 650; **11** 289, 494
**Sharp Corporation**, **I** 476; **II** **95–96**; **III** 14, 428, 455, 480; **6** 217, 231; **11** 45; **12** **447–49 (upd.)**; **13** 481; **16** 83; **21** 123; **22** 197; **40** **391–95 (upd.)**
**The Sharper Image Corporation**, **10** **486–88**; **23** 210; **26** 439; **27** 429
Sharples Co., **I** 383
Sharples Separator Co., **III** 418–20
Shasta Beverages. *See* National Beverage Corp.
Shaw Communications Inc., **26** 274; **35** 69
**Shaw Industries, Inc.**, **9** **465–67**; **19** 274, 276; **25** 320; **40** **396–99 (upd.)**
Shaw's Supermarkets, Inc., **II** 658–59; **23** 169
Shawell Precast Products, **14** 248
Shawinigan Water and Power Company, **6** 501–02
**Shawmut National Corporation**, **II** 207; **12** 31; **13** **464–68**
Shea's Winnipeg Brewery Ltd., **I** 268; **25** 280
Sheaffer Group, **23** 54, 57
**Shearman & Sterling**, **32** **419–22**; **35** 467
Shearson Hammill & Company, **22** 405–06
**Shearson Lehman Brothers Holdings Inc.**, **I** 202; **II** 398–99, 450, 478; **III** 319; **8** 118; **9** **468–70 (upd.)**; **10** 62–63; **11** 418; **12** 459; **15** 124, 463–64
**Shearson Lehman Hutton Holdings Inc.**, **II** 339, 445, **450–52**; **III** 119; **9** 125; **10** 59, 63; **17** 38–39
Shedd's Food Products Company, **9** 318
Sheepbridge Engineering, **III** 495
Sheffield Banking Co., **II** 333
Sheffield Exploration Company, **28** 470
Sheffield Forgemasters Group Ltd., **39** 32
Sheffield Motor Co., **I** 158; **10** 292
Sheffield Twist Drill & Steel Co., **III** 624
Shekou Container Terminal, **16** 481; **38** 345
Shelby Insurance Company, **10** 44–45
Shelby Steel Tube Co., **IV** 572; **7** 550
**Shelby Williams Industries, Inc.**, **14** **435–37**
Shelco, **22** 146
**Sheldahl Inc.**, **23** **432–35**
Shelf Life Inc. *See* King Kullen Grocery Co., Inc.
Shell. *See* Shell Transport and Trading Company p.l.c. *and* Shell Oil Company.
Shell Australia Ltd., **III** 728
Shell BV, **IV** 518
Shell Canada Limited, **32** 45
Shell Chemical Corporation, **IV** 410, 481, 531–32, 540; **8** 415; **24** 151
Shell Coal International, **IV** 532
Shell Forestry, **21** 546
Shell France, **12** 153
Shell Nederland BV, **V** 658–59
**Shell Oil Company**, **I** 20, 26, 569; **III** 559; **IV** 392, 400, 531, **540–41**; **6** 382, 457; **8** 261–62; **11** 522; **14** 25, **438–40 (upd.)**; **17** 417; **19** 175–76; **21** 546; **22** 274; **24** 520; **25** 96, 232, 469; **26** 496; **41** **356–60 (upd.)**, 395; **45** 54
**Shell Transport and Trading Company p.l.c.**, **I** 605; **II** 436, 459; **III** 522, 735; **IV** 363, 378–79, 381–82, 403, 412, 423, 425, 429, 440, 454, 466, 470, 472, 474, 484–86, 491, 505, 508, **530–32**, 564; **31** 127–28. *See also* Royal Dutch Petroleum Company *and* Royal Dutch/Shell.
Shell Western E & P, **7** 323
Shell Winning, **IV** 413–14
**Sheller-Globe Corporation**, **I** **201–02**; **17** 182
**Shells Seafood Restaurants, Inc.**, **43** **370–72**
Shelly Brothers, Inc., **15** 65
Shenley Laboratories, **I** 699
Shepard Warner Elevator Co., **III** 467
Shepard's Citations, Inc., **IV** 636–37
Shepherd Hardware Products Ltd., **16** 357
**Shepherd Neame Limited**, **30** **414–16**
Shepherd Plating and Finishing Company, **13** 233
Shepler Equipment Co., **9** 512
Sheraton Corp. of America, **I** 463–64, 487; **III** 98–99; **11** 198; **13** 362–63; **21** 91
Sherborne Group Inc./NH Holding Inc., **17** 20
Sherbrooke Paper Products Ltd., **17** 281
Sheridan Bakery, **II** 633
Sheridan Catheter & Instrument Corp., **III** 443
Sherix Chemical, **I** 682
Sherr-Gold, **23** 40
Sherritt Gordon Mines, **7** 386–87; **12** 260
**The Sherwin-Williams Company**, **III** **744–46**; **8** 222, 224; **11** 384; **12** 7; **13** **469–71 (upd.)**; **19** 180; **24** 323; **30** 474
Sherwood Equity Group Ltd. *See* National Discount Brokers Group, Inc.
Sherwood Medical Group, **I** 624; **III** 443–44; **10** 70
SHI Resort Development Co., **III** 635
ShianFu Optical Fiber, **III** 491
Shibaura Seisakusho Works, **I** 533; **12** 483
Shieh Chi Industrial Co., **19** 508
Shields & Co., **9** 118
Shikoku Drinks Co., **IV** 297
**Shikoku Electric Power Company, Inc.**, **V** **718–20**
Shikoku Machinery Co., **III** 634
Shiley, Inc., **38** 361
Shillito's, **31** 192
Shimizu Construction Company Ltd., **44** 153
Shimotsuke Electric Railway Company, **6** 431
Shimura Kako, **IV** 63
Shin-Nihon Glass Co., **I** 221
Shin Nippon Machine Manufacturing, **III** 634
Shinano Bank, **II** 291
Shinko Electric Co., Ltd., **IV** 129
Shinko Rayon Ltd., **I** 363; **V** 369–70
Shinriken Kogyo, **IV** 63
Shintech, **11** 159–60
Shinwa Pharmaceutical Co. Ltd., **48** 250
Shinwa Tsushinki Co., **III** 593
Shiomi Casting, **III** 551
**Shionogi & Co., Ltd.**, **I** 646, 651; **III** **60–61**; **11** 90, 290; **17** **435–37 (upd.)**
Ship 'n Shore, **II** 503; **9** 156–57; **10** 324
Shipley Co. Inc., **26** 425
Shipowners and Merchants Tugboat Company, **6** 382
Shipper Group, **16** 344
Shipstad & Johnson's Ice Follies, **25** 313
Shiro Co., Ltd., **V** 96
Shirokiya Co., Ltd., **V** 199
**Shiseido Company, Limited**, **II** 273–74, 436; **III** 46, 48, **62–64**; **8** 341, 343; **22** **485–88 (upd.)**
SHL Systemhouse Inc., **27** 305
Shochiku Company Ltd., **28** 461
Shockley Electronics, **20** 174
**Shoe Carnival Inc.**, **14** **441–43**
Shoe Corp., **I** 289
Shoe Supply, Inc., **22** 213
Shoe-Town Inc., **23** 310
Shoe Works Inc., **18** 415
Shohin Kaihatsu Kenkyusho, **III** 595
Shoman Milk Co., **II** 538
Shonac Corp., **14** 427
Shonco, Inc., **18** 438
**Shoney's, Inc.**, **7** **474–76**; **14** 453; **19** 286; **23** **436–39 (upd.)**; **29** 290–91
Shop & Go, **II** 620
Shop 'n Bag, **II** 624
Shop 'n Save, **II** 669, 682; **12** 220–21
Shop Rite Foods Inc., **II** 672–74; **7** 105; **19** 479. *See also* Big V Supermarkets, Inc.
**ShopKo Stores Inc.**, **II** 669–70; **18** 505–07; **21** **457–59**
Shoppers Food Warehouse Corporation, **16** 159, 161
Shoppers World Stores, Inc. *See* LOT$OFF Corporation.
ShopRite, **24** 528. *See also* Foodarama Supermarkets, Inc.
Shopwell/Food Emporium, **II** 638; **16** 247, 249
Shore Manufacturing, **13** 165
**Shorewood Packaging Corporation**, **28** **419–21**; **47** 189
Short Aircraft Co., **I** 50, 55, 92
Short Brothers, **24** 85
Shoseido Co., **17** 110
Shoshi-Gaisha, **IV** 320

Shotton Paper Co. Ltd., **IV** 350
Showa Aircraft Industry Co., **I** 507–08
Showa Aluminum Corporation, **8** 374
Showa Bank, **II** 291–92
Showa Bearing Manufacturing Co., **III** 595
Showa Cotton Co., Ltd., **IV** 442
Showa Denko, **I** 493–94; **II** 292; **IV** 61; **24** 324–25
Showa Marutsutsu Co. Ltd., **8** 477
Showa Paper Co., **IV** 268
Showa Photo Industry, **III** 548
Showa Products Company, **8** 476
**Showa Shell Sekiyu K.K.**, **II** 459; **IV 542–43**
**ShowBiz Pizza Time, Inc.**, **12** 123; **13 472–74**; **15** 73; **16** 447. *See also* CEC Entertainment, Inc.
**Showboat, Inc.**, **19 400–02**; **43** 227
Showcase of Fine Fabrics, **16** 197
Showco, Inc., **35** 436
Showerings, **I** 215
Showscan Entertainment Inc., **34** 230
Showscan Film Corporation, **28** 206
Showtime, **II** 173; **7** 222–23; **9** 74; **23** 274–75, 391, 503; **25** 329–30
Shredded Wheat Co., **II** 543; **7** 366
Shreve and Company, **12** 312
Shreveport Refrigeration, **16** 74
Shrewsbury and Welshpool Old Bank, **II** 307
Shu Uemura, **III** 43
**Shubert Organization Inc.**, **24 437–39**
Shubrooks International Ltd., **11** 65
Shueisha, **IV** 598
Shuford Mills, Inc., **14** 430
Shugart Associates, **6** 230; **8** 466; **22** 189
Shull Lumber & Shingle Co., **IV** 306
Shulman Transport Enterprises Inc., **27** 473
Shun Fung Ironworks, **IV** 717
Shunan Shigyo Co., Ltd., **IV** 160
Shurgard Storage Centers of Seattle, **21** 476
Shuttleworth Brothers Company. *See* Mohawk Industries, Inc.
Shuwa Corp., **22** 101; **36** 292
SHV Holdings N.V., **IV** 383; **14** 156
SI Holdings Inc., **10** 481; **29** 425
SIAS, **19** 192
SIAS-MPA, **I** 281
SIATA S.p.A., **26** 363
SIB Financial Services, **39** 382
Sibco Universal, S.A., **14** 429
Sibel, **48** 350
Siberian Moloko, **48** 438
Siboney Shoe Corp., **22** 213
SIBV/MS Holdings, **IV** 295; **19** 226
Sicard Inc., **I** 185
SICC. *See* Univision Communications Inc.
Sichuan Station Wagon Factory, **38** 462
Sick's Brewery, **26** 304
Siclet, **25** 84
Sicma Aero Seat, **36** 529
Siddeley Autocar Co., **III** 508
Sidel. *See* Groupe Sidel S.A.
Sidélor, **IV** 226
Siderbrás, **IV** 125
Siderca S.A.I.C., **41** 405–06
Sidermex, **III** 581
Sidérurgie Maritime, **IV** 26
**Sidley Austin Brown & Wood**, **40 400–03**
SIDMAR NV, **IV** 128
Siebe plc, **13** 235. *See also* BTR Siebe plc.
Siebel Group, **13** 544–45
Siebel Marketing Group, **27** 195
**Siebel Systems, Inc.**, **38 430–34**
**Siebert Financial Corp.**, **32 423–25**
Siegas, **III** 480; **22** 26
Siegler Heater Corp., **I** 481
**Siemens AG**, **I** 74, 192, 409–11, 462, 478, 542; **II** 22, 25, 38, 80–82, **97–100**, 122, 257, 279; **III** 139, 154–55, 466, 482, 516, 724; **6** 215–16; **7** 232; **9** 11, 32, 44; **10** 16, 363; **11** 59, 196, 235, 397–98, 460; **12** 546; **13** 402; **14** 169, **444–47 (upd.)**; **15** 125; **16** 392; **18** 32; **19** 166, 313; **20** 290; **22** 19, 373–74; **23** 389, 452, 494–95; **24** 88; **30** 11; **33** 225, 288
Siemens Solar Industries L.P., **44** 182
**The Sierra Club**, **28 422–24**
Sierra Designs, Inc., **10** 215–16
**Sierra Health Services, Inc.**, **15 451–53**
Sierra Leone External Telegraph Limited, **25** 100
Sierra Leone Selection Trust, **IV** 66
**Sierra On-Line, Inc.**, **13** 92, 114; **14** 263; **15 454–56**; **16** 146; **29** 75; **41 361–64 (upd.)**
**Sierra Pacific Industries**, **22 489–91**
Sierrita Resources, Inc., **6** 590
**SIFCO Industries, Inc.**, **41**
Sight & Sound Entertainment, **35** 21
**Sigma-Aldrich Corporation**, **I 690–91**; **36 429–32 (upd.)**
Sigma Alimentos, S.A. de C.V., **19** 11–12
Sigma Coatings, **IV** 499
Sigma Network Systems, **11** 464
Sigmor Corp., **IV** 410; **31** 455
Signal Companies, Inc. *See* AlliedSignal Inc.
Signal Galaxies, **13** 127
Signal Oil & Gas Inc., **I** 71, 178; **IV** 382; **7** 537; **11** 278; **19** 175; **22** 331
Signalite, Inc., **10** 319
Signature Brands USA Inc., **28** 135; **30** 139
Signature Corporation, **22** 412–13
Signature Flight Support Services Corporation, **47** 450
Signature Group, **V** 145
Signature Health Care Corp., **25** 504
**Signet Banking Corporation**, **11 446–48**
Signet Communications Corp., **16** 195
Signetics Co., **III** 684; **11** 56; **18** 383; **44** 127
Signode Industries, **III** 519; **22** 282
Sika Finanz AG, **28** 195
SIKEL NV, **IV** 128
Sikes Corporation, **III** 612
**Sikorsky Aircraft Corporation**, **I** 47, 84, 115, 530; **III** 458, 602; **9** 416; **10** 162; **18** 125; **24 440–43**; **41** 368; **46** 65
SIL&P. *See* Southern Illinois Light & Power Company.
SILA. *See* Swedish Intercontinental Airlines.
Silband Sports Corp., **33** 102
Silenka B.V., **III** 733; **22** 436
Silex. *See* Hamilton Beach/Proctor-Silex Inc.
Silgan Holdings Inc., **26** 59
Silicon Beach Software, **10** 35
Silicon Compiler Systems, **11** 285
Silicon Engineering, **18** 20; **43** 17
**Silicon Graphics Inc.**, **9 471–73**; **10** 119, 257; **12** 323; **15** 149, 320; **16** 137, 140; **20** 8; **25** 96; **28** 320; **38** 69; **43** 151. *See also* SGI.
Silicon Light Machines Corporation, **48** 128
Silicon Magnetic Systems, **48** 128
Silicon Microstructures, Inc., **14** 183
Silicon Systems Inc., **II** 110
Silo Electronics, **16** 73, 75
Silo Holdings, **9** 65; **23** 52
Silo Inc., **V** 50; **10** 306, 468; **19** 123
Silver & Co., **I** 428
Silver Burdett Co., **IV** 672, 675; **7** 528; **19** 405
Silver City Airways. *See* British World Airlines Ltd.
Silver City Casino, **6** 204
Silver Dollar Mining Company, **20** 149
Silver Dolphin, **34** 3, 5
Silver Furniture Co., Inc., **15** 102, 104
Silver King Communications, **25** 213
Silver King Mines, **IV** 76
Silver Screen Partners, **II** 174
Silver's India Rubber Works & Telegraph Cable Co., **I** 428
Silverado Banking, **9** 199
Silverado Partners Acquisition Corp., **22** 80
Silverline, Inc., **16** 33
Silvermans Menswear, Inc., **24** 26
**SilverPlatter Information Inc.**, **23 440–43**
Silvershoe Partners, **17** 245
Silverstar Ltd. S.p.A., **10** 113
**Silverstein Properties, Inc.**, **47 358–60**; **48** 320
Silvertown Rubber Co., **I** 428
Silvey Corp., **III** 350
Simca, **I** 154, 162; **11** 103
**Simco S.A.**, **37 357–59**
**Sime Darby Berhad**, **14 448–50**; **36 433–36 (upd.)**
Simeira Comercio e Industria Ltda., **22** 320
SIMEL S.A., **14** 27
Simer Pump Company, **19** 360
SIMEST, **24** 311
Simi Winery, Inc., **34** 89
Simicon Co., **26** 153
Simkins Industries, Inc., **8** 174–75
**Simmons Company**, **34** 407; **47 361–64**
Simms, **III** 556
**Simon & Schuster Inc.**, **II** 155; **IV 671–72**; **13** 559; **19 403–05 (upd.)**; **23** 503; **28** 158
Simon Adhesive Products, **IV** 253; **17** 30
Simon de Wit, **II** 641
Simon DeBartolo Group Inc., **26** 146; **27** 401
Simon Engineering, **11** 510
Simon Marketing, Inc., **19** 112, 114
**Simon Property Group, Inc.**, **27 399–402**
**Simon Transportation Services Inc.**, **27 403–06**
Simonius'sche Cellulosefabriken AG, **IV** 324
Simonize, **I** 371
Simons Inc., **26** 412
AB Simpele, **IV** 347
Simple Shoes, Inc., **22** 173
Simplex Industries, Inc., **16** 296
**Simplex Technologies Inc.**, **21 460–63**
Simplex Wire and Cable Co., **III** 643–45
Simplicity Pattern Company, **I** 447; **8** 349; **23** 98; **29** 134
**Simpson Investment Company**, **17 438–41**

Simpson Marketing, **12** 553
**Simpson Thacher & Bartlett, 27** 327; **39 365–68**
Simpson Timber Company. *See* PW Eagle Inc.
Simpsons, **V** 80; **25** 221
Sims Telephone Company, **14** 258
Simsmetal USA Corporation, **19** 380
SimuFlite, **II** 10
**Simula, Inc., 41 368–70**
Sinai Kosher Foods, **14** 537
Sincat, **IV** 453
**Sinclair Broadcast Group, Inc., 25 417–19; 47** 120
Sinclair Coal Co., **IV** 170; **10** 447–48
Sinclair Crude Oil Purchasing Co., **IV** 369
Sinclair Oil Corp., **I** 355, 569; **IV** 376, 394, 456–57, 512, 575
Sinclair Paint Company, **12** 219
Sinclair Petrochemicals Inc., **IV** 456
Sinclair Pipe Line Co., **IV** 368–69
Sinclair Research Ltd., **III** 113
Sindo Ricoh Co., **III** 160
Sinfor Holding, **48** 402
Sing Tao Holdings Ltd., **29** 470–71
**Singapore Airlines Ltd., 6** 100, **117–18,** 123; **12** 192; **20** 313; **24** 399; **26** 115; **27** 26, **407–09 (upd.)**, 464, 466; **29** 301; **38** 26
Singapore Alpine Electronics Asia Pte. Ltd., **13** 31
Singapore Candle Company, **12** 393
Singapore Cement, **III** 718
Singapore Petroleum Co., **IV** 452
Singapore Shinei Sangyo Pte Ltd., **48** 369
Singapore Straits Steamship Company, **6** 117
Singapore Telecom, **18** 348
Singapour, **II** 556
Singareni Collieries Ltd., **IV** 48–49
**Singer & Friedlander Group plc, I** 592; **41 371–73**
Singer Company, **I** 540; **II** 9–11; **6** 27, 241; **9** 232; **11** 150; **13** 521–22; **19** 211; **22** 4; **26** 3; **29** 190. *See also* Bicoastal Corp.
**The Singer Company N.V., 30 417–20 (upd.)**
Singer Controls, **I** 155
Singer Hardware & Supply Co., **9** 542
Singer Sewing Machine Co., **12** 46
Singer Supermarkets, **25** 235
Single Service Containers Inc., **IV** 286
Singleton Seafood, **II** 494
Singular Software, **9** 80
Sinister Games, **41** 409
Sinkers Inc., **21** 68
Sinochem. *See* China National Chemicals Import and Export Corp.
Sinopec. *See* China National Petroleum Corporation.
Sintel, S.A., **19** 256
Sioux City Gas and Electric Company, **6** 523–24
SIP. *See* Società Italiana per L'Esercizio delle Telecommunicazioni p.A.
Siporex, S.A., **31** 253
**Sir Speedy, Inc., 16 448–50; 33** 231
SIRCOMA, **10** 375
SIREM, **23** 95
The Sirena Apparel Group Inc., **25** 245
Sirloin Stockade, **10** 331
Sirrine. *See* CRSS Inc.
Sirrine Environmental Consultants, **9** 110
Sirte Oil Co., **IV** 454
Sisters Chicken & Biscuits, **8** 564
Sisters of Bon Secours USA. *See* Bon Secours Health System, Inc.
SIT-Siemens. *See* Italtel.
Sitca Corporation, **16** 297
Sithe Energies, Inc., **24** 327
Sitmar Cruises, **22** 445
Sitzmann & Heinlein GmbH, **IV** 198–99
Six Companies, Inc., **IV** 121; **7** 355
**Six Flags Theme Parks, Inc., III** 431; **IV** 676; **17 442–44**
600 Fanuc Robotics, **III** 482–83
Six Industries, Inc., **26** 433
61 Going to the Game!, **14** 293
**Sixt AG, 39 369–72**
Sizes Unlimited, **V** 115
Sizzler International Inc., **15** 361–62. *See also* Worldwide Restaurant Concepts, Inc.
SJB Equities, Inc., **30** 53
The SK Equity Fund, L.P., **23** 177
Skånes Enskilda Bank, **II** 351
Skånska Ättiksfabriken, **I** 385
**Skadden, Arps, Slate, Meagher & Flom, 10** 126–27; **18 486–88; 27** 325, 327
Skaggs-Albertson's Properties, **II** 604
Skaggs Companies, **22** 37
Skaggs Drug Centers, Inc., **II** 602–04; **7** 20; **27** 291; **30** 25–27
Skagit Nuclear Power Plant, **6** 566
Skandia, **25** 85
**Skandinaviska Enskilda Banken, II 351–53**, 365–66; **IV** 203
**Skanska AB, IV** 204; **25** 463; **32** 396; **38 435–38**
Skanza Mammoet Transport Sdn Bhd, **26** 280
**Skechers U.S.A. Inc., 31 413–15**
Skelly Oil Co., **IV** 575
Sketchley plc, **19** 124
SKF. *See* Aktiebolaget SKF.
SKF Industries Inc. *See* AB Volvo.
Ski-Doo. *See* Bombardier Inc.
**Skidmore, Owings & Merrill, 13 475–76**
Skil-Craft Playthings, Inc., **13** 560
Skillern, **16** 560
Skillware, **9** 326
Skinner Macaroni Co., **II** 511
**Skis Rossignol S.A., 15 460–62; 43 373–76 (upd.)**
**Skoda Auto a.s., 39 373–75**
SKODA Group, **37** 399–400
Skönvik, **IV** 338
SKS Group, **20** 363
SKW Nature's Products, Inc., **25** 332
SKW-Trostberg AG, **IV** 232
Sky Channel, **IV** 652
Sky Chefs, Inc., **16** 397
Sky Climber Inc., **11** 436
Sky Courier, **6** 345
Sky Merchant, Inc., **V** 78
Sky Television, **IV** 652–53; **7** 391–92
Skyband, Inc., **IV** 652; **7** 391; **12** 359
SkyBox International Inc., **15** 72–73
Skylight, **25** 508
**Skyline Corporation, 30 421–23**
Skyline Homes, **17** 82
**SkyMall, Inc., 26 439–41; 28** 241
Skypak, **27** 474
Skyservice Airlines Inc., **42** 327
SkyTel Corp., **18** 349; **23** 212
Skywalker Sound, **12** 322
Skyway Airlines, **6** 78; **11** 299; **32** 335; **35** 293–94
**SkyWest, Inc., 25 420–24**
**SL Green Realty Corporation, 44 383–85**
SL Holdings. *See* Finlay Enterprises, Inc.
Slade Gorton & Company, **13** 243
Slater Co. Foods, **II** 607
Slater Electric, **21** 349
Slater Systems, Inc., **13** 48
Slautterback Corporation, **48** 299
**Sleepy's Inc., 32 426–28**
**SLI, Inc., 48 358–61**
Slick Airways, **6** 388; **25** 146
**Slim-Fast Nutritional Foods International, Inc., 12** 531; **18 489–91; 27** 196
Slim Jim, Inc. *See* GoodMark Foods, Inc.
Slingerland Drum Company, **16** 239
Slip-X Safety Treads, **9** 72
SLJFB Vedrenne, **22** 344
**SLM Holding Corp., 25 425–28 (upd.)**
SLM International Inc. *See* The Hockey Company.
SLN-Peñarroya, **IV** 108
Sloan's Supermarkets Inc. *See* Gristede's Sloan's, Inc.
Sloman Neptun Schiffahrts, **26** 279
Slope Indicator Company, **26** 42
Sloss Industries Corporation, **22** 544
Slots-A-Fun, **6** 204
**Slough Estates plc, IV 722–25**
AB Small Business Investment Co., Inc., **13** 111–12
Small Tube Products, Inc., **23** 517
SMALLCO, **III** 340
Smalley Transportation Company, **6** 421–23
SMAN. *See* Societe Mecanique Automobile du Nord.
**Smart & Final, Inc., 12** 153–54; **16 451–53**
Smart Communications, **18** 180, 182
Smart Products, **44** 261
Smart Shirts Ltd., **8** 288–89
Smart Talk Network, Inc., **16** 319
SmartCash, **18** 543
**SmartForce PLC, 43 377–80**
SmarTTarget Marketing, **36** 342
**Smead Manufacturing Co., 17 445–48**
Smed International, **39** 207
Smedley's, **II** 513
Smethwick Drop Forgings, **III** 494
SMH. *See* The Swatch Group SA.
SMI Industries, **25** 15
Smiles Holdings Ltd., **38** 501
Smirnoff, **14** 212; **18** 41
Smit International, **26** 241
Smith and Bell Insurance, **41** 178, 180
Smith & Butterfield Co., Inc., **28** 74
Smith & Hawken, **10** 215, 217
**Smith & Nephew plc, 17 449–52; 41 374–78 (upd.)**
**Smith & Wesson Corporation, 30 424–27**
Smith & Weston, **19** 430
Smith & Wollensky Operating Corp., **32** 362
**Smith Barney Inc., I** 614; **III** 569; **6** 410; **10** 63; **13** 328; **15 463–65; 19** 385; **20** 360; **22** 406
Smith Bros., **I** 711
**Smith Corona Corp., III** 502; **7** 209; **13 477–80; 14** 76; **23** 210

Smith-Higgins, **III** 9–10
**Smith International, Inc.**, **III** 429; **15 466–68**
Smith Mackenzie & Co., **III** 522
Smith McDonell Stone and Co., **14** 97
Smith Meter Co., **11** 4
Smith New Court PLC, **13** 342; **40** 313
Smith Packaging Ltd., **14** 429
Smith Parts Co., **11** 3
Smith Transfer Corp., **II** 607–08; **13** 49
Smith Wall Associates, **32** 145
**Smith's Food & Drug Centers, Inc.**, **8 472–74**; **17** 558, 561; **24** 36; **26** 432
Smith's Stampings, **III** 494
**Smithfield Foods, Inc.**, **7 477–78**, 524–25; **22** 509, 511; **43** 25, **381–84 (upd.)**; **46** 83
**SmithKline Beckman Corporation**, **I** 389, 636, 640, 644, 646, 657, **692–94**, 696; **II** 331; **III** 65–66; **14** 46, 53; **26** 391; **30** 29–31. *See also* GlaxoSmithKline plc.
**SmithKline Beecham plc**, **III 65–67**; **8** 210; **9** 347; **10** 47, 471; **11** 9, 90, 337; **13** 77; **14** 58; **16** 438; **17** 287; **24** 88; **25** 82; **32** 212–13, **429–34 (upd.)**; **36** 91; **38** 362. *See also* GlaxoSmithKline plc.
Smiths Bank, **II** 333
Smiths Food Group, Ltd., **II** 502; **10** 323
**Smiths Industries PLC**, **III** 555; **25 429–31**
**Smithsonian Institution**, **27 410–13**
**Smithway Motor Xpress Corporation**, **39 376–79**
Smitty's Super Valu Inc., **II** 663–64; **12** 391; **17** 560–61
Smittybilt, Incorporated, **40** 299–300
SMP Clothing, Inc., **22** 462
SMS, **IV** 226; **7** 401
Smucker. *See* The J.M. Smucker Company.
Smurfit Companies. *See* Jefferson Smurfit Group plc.
**Smurfit-Stone Container Corporation**, **26 442–46 (upd.)**
SN Repal. *See* Société Nationale de Recherche de Pétrole en Algérie.
Snack Ventures Europe, **10** 324; **36** 234, 237
Snake River Sugar Company, **19** 468
Snam Montaggi, **IV** 420
Snam Progetti, **IV** 420, 422
**Snap-On, Incorporated**, **27 414–16 (upd.)**; **32** 397
**Snap-on Tools Corporation**, **III** 628; **7 479–80**; **25** 34
Snapper, **I** 447
**Snapple Beverage Corporation**, **11 449–51**; **12** 411; **24** 480; **27** 153; **31** 243; **34** 366; **39** 383, 386
Snapps Drive-Thru, **25** 389
Snappy Car Rental, Inc., **6** 393; **25** 142–43. *See also* Republic Industries, Inc.
SNE Enterprises, Inc., **12** 397
SNEA. *See* Société Nationale Elf Aquitaine.
**Snecma Group**, **17** 482; **46 369–72**
**Snell & Wilmer L.L.P.**, **28 425–28**
Snell Acoustics, **22** 99
SNET. *See* Southern New England Telecommunications Corporation.
SNMC Management Corporation, **11** 121; **48** 177
Snoqualmie Falls Plant, **6** 565
**Snow Brand Milk Products Company, Ltd.**, **II 574–75**; **48 362–65 (upd.)**
Snow King Frozen Foods, **II** 480; **26** 57
Snow White Dairies Inc. *See* Dairy Mart Convenience Stores, Inc.
Snowy Mountains Hydroelectric Authority, **IV** 707; **13** 118
SNPA, **IV** 453
Snyder Communications, **35** 462, 465
Snyder Oil Company, **24** 379–81; **45** 354
Snyder's of Hanover, **35** 213
SnyderGeneral Corp., **8** 321. *See also* AAF-McQuay Incorporated.
*Soap Opera Magazine*, **10** 287
Sobrom, **I** 341
Sobu Railway Company, **6** 431
Socal. *See* Standard Oil Company (California).
Socamel-Rescaset, **40** 214, 216
Socar, Incorporated, **IV** 505; **45** 370
Sochiku, **9** 30
Sociade Intercontinental de Compressores Hermeticos SICOM, S.A., **8** 515
La Sociale di A. Mondadori & C., **IV** 585
La Sociale, **IV** 585
Sociedad Aeronáutica de Medellín, S.A., **36** 53
Sociedad Alfa-Laval, **III** 419
Sociedad Bilbaina General de Credito, **II** 194
Sociedad Española de Automobiles del Turismo S.A. (SEAT), **I** 207, 459–60; **6** 47–48; **11** 550
Sociedad Financiera Mexicana, **19** 189
Sociedade Anónima Concessionária de Refinacao em Portugal. *See* SACOR.
Sociedade de Lubrificantes e Combustiveis, **IV** 505
Sociedade Nacional de Petróleos, **IV** 504
Sociedade Portuguesa de Petroquimica, **IV** 505
Società Anonima Fabbrica Italiana di Automobili, **I** 161
Società Anonima Lombarda Fabbrica Automobili, **13** 27
Società Azionaria Imprese Perforazioni, **IV** 419–20
Società Concessioni e Costruzioni Autostrade, **I** 466
Società Edison, **II** 86
Societa Esercizio Fabbriche Automobili e Corse Ferrari, **13** 219
Società Finanziaria Idrocarburi, **IV** 421
**Società Finanziaria Telefonica per Azioni**, **I** 465–66; **V 325–27**
Società Generale di Credito Mobiliare, **II** 191
Società Idrolettrica Piemonte, **I** 465–66
Societa Industria Meccanica Stampaggio S.p.A., **24** 500
Societa Italiana Gestione Sistemi Multi Accesso, **6** 69
Società Italiana per L'Esercizio delle Telecommunicazioni p.A., **I** 466–67; **V** 325–27
Società Italiana per la Infrastrutture e l'Assetto del Territoria, **I** 466
Società Italiana Pirelli, **V** 249
Società Italiana Vetro, **IV** 421
Società Nazionale Metanodotti, **IV** 419–21
Società Ravennate Metano, **IV** 420
Società Reale Mutua, **III** 207
**Società Sportiva Lazio SpA**, **44 386–88**
Société Africaine de Déroulage des Ets Rougier, **21** 439
**Société Air France**, **27 417–20 (upd.)**. *See also* Groupe Air France.
Société Alsacienne de Magasins SA, **19** 308
Societe Anonima Italiana Ing. Nicola Romeo & Company, **13** 27
Societe Anonomie Alfa Romeo, **13** 28
Societe Anonyme Automobiles Citroen, **7** 35–36. *See also* PSA Peugeot Citroen S.A.
Société Anonyme Belge des Magasins Prisunic-Uniprix, **26** 159
Société Anonyme de la Manufactures des Glaces et Produits Chimiques de Saint-Gobain, Chauny et Cirey. *See* Compagnie de Saint-Gobain S.A.
Société Anonyme des Ciments Luxembourgeois, **IV** 25
Société Anonyme des Fermiers Reúnis, **23** 219
Société Anonyme des Hauts Fourneaux et Aciéries de Differdange-St. Ingbert-Rumelange, **IV** 26
Société Anonyme des Hauts Fourneaux et Forges de Dudelange, **22** 42
Société Anonyme des Mines du Luxembourg et des Forges de Sarrebruck, **IV** 24; **22** 42
La Societe Anonyme Francaise Holophane, **19** 211
Societe Anonyme Francaise Timken, **8** 530
Société Anonyme Telecommunications, **III** 164
Société, Auxiliaire d'Entrepreses SA, **13** 206
Société Belge de Banque, **II** 294–95
Société BIC, S.A., **III** 29; **8** 60–61; **23** 55–57
Société Calédonia, **IV** 107
Société Centrale d'Investissement, **29** 48
Société Centrale Union des Assurances de Paris, **III** 391, 393
Société Chimiques des Usines du Rhône, **I** 388
Société Civil des Mousquetaires. *See* ITM Entreprises SA.
Société Civile Valoptec, **21** 222
Societe Commerciale Citroen, **7** 36
Société Congolaise des Grands Magasins Au Bon Marché, **26** 159
Société d'Emboutissage de Bourgogne. *See* Groupe SEB.
Société d'Investissement de Travaux Publics, **31** 128
Société d'Ougrée-Marihaye, **IV** 51
Société de Collecte des Prodicteirs de Preval, **19** 50
Societe de Construction des Batignolles, **II** 93
Société de Crédit Agricole, **II** 264
Société de Développements et d'Innovations des Marchés Agricoles et Alimentaires, **II** 576
Société de Diffusion de Marques, **II** 576
Société de Diffusion Internationale Agro-Alimentaire, **II** 577
Société de Fiducie du Québec, **48** 289
Societé de garantie des Crédits à court terme, **II** 233
Société de l'Oléoduc de la Sarre a.r.l., **IV** 197

Société de Prospection Électrique, **III** 616; **17** 416
La Société de Traitement des Minerais de Nickel, Cobalt et Autres, **IV** 107
Société des Caves de Roquefort, **24** 444
Société des Caves et des Producteurs Reunis de Roquefort, **19** 49
Société des Ciments Français, **33** 339
Societé des Eaux d'Evian, **II** 474
Société des Etablissements Gaumont. *See* Gaumont SA.
Société des Forges d'Eich–Metz et Cie, **IV** 24
Société des Forges et Aciéries du Nord-Est, **IV** 226
Société des Forges et Fonderies de Montataire, **IV** 226
Société des Grandes Entreprises de Distribution, Inno-France, **V** 58
Société des Hauts Fourneaux et Forges de Denain-Anzin, **IV** 226
Société des Immeubles de France, **37** 357, 359
Société des Mines du Luxembourg et de Sarrebruck, **IV** 25
Société des Moteurs Gnôme, **46** 369
Société des Pétroles d'Afrique Equatoriale, **IV** 545; **7** 482
Société des Usines Chimiques des Laboratoires Français, **I** 669
Société des Vins de France, **I** 281
**Société du Louvre, 27 421–23**
Société Economique de Rennes, **19** 98
Société Électrométallurgique Francaise, **IV** 173
Société European de Semi-Remorques, **7** 513
Societé Européenne de Brasseries, **II** 474–75
Société Européenne de Production de L'avion E.C.A.T. *See* SEPECAT.
Société Financiére Européenne, **II** 202–03, 233
Societe Financiere pour l caise pour l'Exploitation du Pétrole, **IV** 557
Société Française de Casinos, **48** 198
Société Gélis-Poudenx-Sans, **IV** 108
Société General de Banque, **17** 324
**Société Générale, II** 233, 266, 295, **354–56**; **9** 148; **13** 203, 206; **19** 51; **33** 118–19; **42 347–51 (upd.)**; **47** 411–12
Société Générale de Banque, **II** 279, 295, 319; **14** 169
Société Générale de Belgique S.A., **II** 270, 294–95; **IV** 26; **10** 13; **22** 44; **26** 368; **27** 11; **36** 456
Société Générale des Entreprises. *See* Vinci.
Société Générale du Telephones, **21** 231
Société Générale pour favoriser l'Industrie nationale, **II** 294
Societe-Hydro-Air S.a.r.L., **9** 27
Société Industrielle Belge des Pétroles, **IV** 498–99
Société Internationale Pirelli S.A., **V** 250
Société Irano-Italienne des Pétroles, **IV** 466
Société Laitière Vendômoise, **23** 219
Société Le Nickel, **IV** 107–08, 110
Societe Mecanique Automobile de l'Est/du Nord, **7** 37
Société Métallurgique, **IV** 25–26, 227
Société Minière de Bakwanga, **IV** 67
Société Minière des Terres Rouges, **IV** 25–26
Société Nationale de Programmes de Télévision Française 1. *See* Télévision Française 1.
Société Nationale de Recherche de Pétrole en Algérie, **IV** 545, 559; **7** 482
Société Nationale de Transport et de Commercialisation des Hydrocarbures, **IV** 423
**Société Nationale des Chemins de Fer Français, V 512–15**
Société Nationale des Pétroles d'Aquitaine, **21** 203–05
**Société Nationale Elf Aquitaine, I** 303–04, 670, 676–77; **II** 260; **IV** 174, 397–98, 424, 451, 453–54, 472–74, 499, 506, 515–16, 518, 525, 535, **544–47**, 559–60; **V** 628; **7 481–85 (upd.)**; **8** 452; **11** 97; **12** 153
Société Nationale pour la Recherche, la Production, le Transport, la Transformation et la Commercialisation des Hydrocarbures, **IV** 423–24
Société Nord Africaine des Ciments Lafarge, **III** 703
Société Nouvelle d'Achat de Bijouterie, **16** 207
Société Nouvelle des Etablissements Gaumont. *See* Gaumont SA.
Société Parisienne d'Achats en Commun, **19** 307
Societe Parisienne pour l'Industrie Electrique, **II** 93
Société Parisienne Raveau-Cartier, **31** 128
Société pour l'Eportation de Grandes Marques, **I** 281
Société pour l'Étude et la Realisation d'Engins Balistiques. *See* SEREB.
Société pour L'Exploitation de la Cinquième Chaîne, **6** 374
Société pour le Financement de l'Industrie Laitière, **19** 51
Société Samos, **23** 219
Société Savoyarde des Fromagers du Reblochon, **25** 84
Société Succursaliste S.A. d'Approvisonnements Guyenne et Gascogne. *See* Guyenne et Gascogne.
Société Suisse de Microelectronique & d'Horlogerie. *See* The Swatch Group SA.
Société Tefal. *See* Groupe SEB.
Societe Vendeenne des Embalages, **9** 305
**Society Corporation, 9 474–77**
Society of Lloyd's, **III** 278–79
SOCO Chemical Inc., **8** 69
Socombel, **IV** 497
Socony. *See* Standard Oil Co. (New York).
Socony Mobil Oil Co., Inc., **IV** 465; **7** 353
Socony-Vacuum Oil Company. *See* Mobil Corporation.
Sodak Gaming, Inc., **9** 427; **41** 216
Sodastream Holdings, **II** 477
**Sodexho Alliance SA**, **23** 154; **29 442–44**; **47** 201
**Sodiaal S.A.**, **II** 577; **19** 50; **36 437–39 (upd.)**
SODIMA. *See* Sodiaal S.A.
Sodiso, **23** 247
Sodyeco, **I** 673
Soekor, **IV** 93
Soffo, **22** 365
Soficom, **27** 136
SOFIL. *See* Société pour le Financement de l'Industrie Laitière.
Sofimex. *See* Sociedad Financiera Mexicana.
Sofiran, **IV** 467
Sofitam, S.A., **21** 493, 495
Sofitels. *See* Accor SA.
Sofrem, **IV** 174
Soft Lenses Inc., **25** 55
**Soft Sheen Products, Inc.**, **31 416–18**; **46** 278
Soft*Switch, **25** 301
**Softbank Corp.**, **12** 562; **13 481–83**; **16** 168; **27** 516, 518; **36** 523; **38 439–44 (upd.)**
Softimage Inc., **38** 71–72
SoftKat. *See* Baker & Taylor, Inc.
SoftKey Software Products Inc., **24** 276
Softsel Computer Products, **12** 334–35
SoftSolutions Technology Corporation, **10** 558
Software AG, **11** 18
Software Arts, **6** 254; **25** 299
Software Development Pty., Ltd., **15** 107
Software Dimensions, Inc. *See* ASK Group, Inc.
Software, Etc., **13** 545
The Software Group Inc., **23** 489, 491
Software International, **6** 224
Software Plus, Inc., **10** 514
Software Publishing Corp., **14** 262
Softwood Holdings Ltd., **III** 688
Sogara S.A., **23** 246–48
Sogebra S.A., **I** 257
Sogedis, **23** 219
Sogen International Corp., **II** 355
Sogexport, **II** 355
Soginnove, **II** 355–56
Sogo Co., **42** 342
Sohio Chemical Company, **13** 502
Sohken Kako Co., Ltd., **IV** 327
Soil Teq, Inc., **17** 10
Soilserv, Inc. *See* Mycogen Corporation.
Soinlahti Sawmill and Brick Works, **IV** 300
Sola Holdings, **III** 727
Solair Inc., **14** 43; **37** 30–31
La Solana Corp., **IV** 726
Solar, **IV** 614
Solar Electric Corp., **13** 398
Solaray, Inc., **37** 284–85
Solect Technology Group, **47** 12
**Solectron Corporation**, **12** 161–62, **450–52**; **38** 186, 189; **46** 38; **48 366–70 (upd.)**
Solel Boneh Construction, **II** 47; **25** 266–67
Soletanche Co., **I** 586
Solid Beheer B.V., **10** 514
Solid State Dielectrics, **I** 329; **8** 152
Solite Corp., **23** 224–25
Söll, **40** 96, 98
Sollac, **IV** 226–27; **24** 144; **25** 96
Solley's Delicatessen and Bakery, **24** 243
Solmer, **IV** 227
**Solo Serve Corporation**, **23** 177; **28 429–31**
Soloman Brothers, **17** 561
Solomon Smith Barney Inc., **22** 404
Solomon Valley Milling Company, **6** 592
Solon Automated Services, **II** 607
Solsound Industries, **16** 393
Soltam, **25** 266
Solutia Inc., **29** 330

**Solvay & Cie S.A., I** 303, **394–96**, 414–15; **III** 677; **IV** 300; **16** 121; **21** 254, **464–67 (upd.)**
Solvay Animal Health Inc., **12** 5
Solvent Resource Recovery, Inc., **9** 109
Solvents Recovery Service of New Jersey, Inc., **8** 464
SOMABRI, **12** 152
SOMACA, **12** 152
Somali Bank, **31** 220
Someal, **27** 513, 515
**Somerfield plc, 47 365–69 (upd.)**
Somerville Electric Light Company, **12** 45
Somerville Packaging Group, **28** 420
**Sommer-Allibert S.A., 19 406–09**; **22** 49; **25** 462, 464
Sommers Drug Stores, **9** 186
SONAP, **IV** 504–06
**Sonat, Inc., 6 577–78**; **22** 68
Sonatrach. *See* Entreprise Nationale Sonatrach.
Sonecor Systems, **6** 340
Sonesson, **I** 211
**Sonesta International Hotels Corporation, 44 389–91**
Sonet Media AB, **23** 390
**Sonic Corp., 37 14 451–53**; **16** 387; **360–63 (upd.)**
Sonic Duo, **48** 419
Sonic Restaurants, **31** 279
Sonneborn Chemical and Refinery Co., **I** 405
Sonnen Basserman, **II** 475
SonnenBraune, **22** 460
**Sonoco Products Company, 8 475–77**; **12** 150–51; **16** 340
The Sonoma Group, **25** 246
Sonoma Mortgage Corp., **II** 382
Sonometrics Inc., **I** 667
**Sony Corporation, I** 30, 534; **II** 56, 58, 91–92, **101–03**, 117–19, 124, 134, 137, 440; **III** 141, 143, 340, 658; **6** 30; **7** 118; **9** 385; **10** 86, 119, 403; **11** 46, 490–91, 557; **12** 75, 161, 448, **453–56 (upd.)**; **13** 399, 403, 482, 573; **14** 534; **16** 94; **17** 533; **18** 18; **19** 67; **20** 439; **21** 129; **22** 194; **24** 4; **25** 22; **26** 188, 433, 489, 511; **28** 241; **30** 18; **31** 239; **40 404–10 (upd.)**; **43** 15; **47** 318–20, 410
Sonzogno, **IV** 585
Soo Line Corporation, **V** 429–30; **24** 533; **45** 80
Soo Line Mills, **II** 631
Sooner Trailer Manufacturing Co., **29** 367
Soparind, **25** 83–85
Sope Creek, **30** 457
SOPEAL, **III** 738
Sophia Jocoba GmbH, **IV** 193
SOPI, **IV** 401
SOPORCEL, **34** 38–39
Sopwith Aviation Co., **III** 507–08
Soravie, **II** 265
Sorbents Products Co. Inc., **31** 20
Sorbus, **6** 242
Sorcim, **6** 224
Soreal, **8** 344
Sorenson Research Company, **36** 496
Sorg Paper Company. *See* Mosinee Paper Corporation.
Soriana. *See* Organización Soriana, S.A. de C.V.
**Soros Fund Management LLC, 27** 198; **28 432–34**; **43** 218
**Sorrento, Inc., 19** 51; **24 444–46**; **26** 505
SOS Co., **II** 531
**SOS Staffing Services, 25 432–35**
Sosa, Bromley, Aguilar & Associates, **6** 22
Soterra, Inc., **15** 188
**Sotheby's Holdings, Inc., 11 452–54**; **15** 98–100; **29 445–48 (upd.)**; **32** 164; **39** 81–84
**Sound Advice, Inc., 41 379–82**
Sound of Music Inc. *See* Best Buy Co., Inc.
Sound Trek, **16** 74
Sound Video Unlimited, **16** 46; **43** 60
Sound Warehouse, **9** 75
Souplantation Incorporated. *See* Garden Fresh Restaurant Corporation.
Source One Mortgage Services Corp., **12** 79
Source Perrier, **7** 383; **24** 444
Souriau, **19** 166
South African Airways Ltd., **6** 84, 433, 435; **27** 132
**The South African Breweries Limited, I 287–89**, 422; **24 447–51 (upd.)**; **26** 462
South African Coal, Oil and Gas Corp., **IV** 533
South African Railways, **6** 434–35
South African Torbanite Mining and Refining Co., **IV** 534
South African Transport Services, **6** 433, 435
South American Cable Co., **I** 428
South Asia Tyres, **20** 263
South Bend Toy Manufacturing Company, **25** 380
South Carolina Electric & Gas Company, **6** 574–76
South Carolina Industries, **IV** 333
South Carolina National Corporation, **16** 523, 526
South Carolina Power Company, **38** 446–47
South Central Bell Telephone Co. **V** 276–78
South Central Railroad Co., **14** 325
South China Morning Post (Holdings) Ltd., **II** 298; **IV** 652; **7** 392
South Coast Gas Compression Company, Inc., **11** 523
South Coast Terminals, Inc., **16** 475
South Dakota Public Service Company, **6** 524
South Fulton Light & Power Company, **6** 514
South Improvement Co., **IV** 427
**South Jersey Industries, Inc., 42 352–55**
South Manchuria Railroad Co. Ltd., **IV** 434
South of Scotland Electricity Board, **19** 389–90
South Penn Oil Co., **IV** 488–89
South Puerto Rico Sugar Co., **I** 452
South Puerto Rico Telephone Co., **I** 462
South Sea Textile, **III** 705
South Texas Stevedore Co., **IV** 81
South Wales Electric Company, **34** 219
South West Water Plc. *See* Pennon Group Plc.
South Western Electricity plc, **38** 448; **41** 316
South-Western Publishing Co., **8** 526–28
**Southam Inc., 7 486–89**; **15** 265; **24** 223; **36** 374
Southco, **II** 602–03; **7** 20–21; **30** 26
Southcorp Holdings Ltd., **17** 373; **22** 350
**Southdown, Inc., 14 454–56**
Southeast Bank of Florida, **11** 112
Southeast Banking Corp., **II** 252; **14** 103
Southeast Public Service Company, **8** 536
Southeastern Personnel. *See* Norrell Corporation.
Southeastern Power and Light Company, **6** 447; **23** 28
Southeastern Telephone Company, **6** 312
Southern and Phillips Gas Ltd., **13** 485
Southern Australia Airlines, **24** 396
Southern Bank, **10** 426
Southern Bearings Co., **13** 78
Southern Bell, **10** 202
Southern Biscuit Co., **II** 631
Southern Blvd. Supermarkets, Inc., **22** 549
Southern Box Corp., **13** 441
Southern California Edison Co., **II** 402; **V** 711, 713–15, 717; **11** 272; **12** 106; **35** 479
Southern California Financial Corporation, **27** 46
Southern California Fruit Growers Exchange. *See* Sunkist Growers, Inc.
Southern California Gas Co., **I** 569; **25** 413–14, 416
Southern Casualty Insurance Co., **III** 214
Southern Clay Products, **III** 691
Southern Clays Inc., **IV** 82
Southern Co., **24** 525
Southern Colorado Power Company, **6** 312
Southern Comfort Corp., **I** 227
**The Southern Company, 38 445–49 (upd.)**
Southern Connecticut Newspapers Inc., **IV** 677
Southern Cotton Co., **IV** 224; **24** 488
Southern Cotton Oil Co., **I** 421; **11** 23
Southern Cross Paints, **38** 98
Southern Discount Company of Atlanta, **9** 229
**Southern Electric PLC, 13 484–86**
Southern Electric Supply Co., **15** 386
Southern Electronics Corp. *See* SED International Holdings, Inc.
Southern Equipment & Supply Co., **19** 344
Southern Extract Co., **IV** 310; **19** 266
Southern Forest Products, Inc., **6** 577
Southern Gage, **III** 519; **22** 282
Southern Graphic Arts, **13** 405
Southern Guaranty Cos., **III** 404
Southern Idaho Water Power Company, **12** 265
Southern Illinois Light & Power Company, **6** 504
**Southern Indiana Gas and Electric Company, 13 487–89**
Southern Japan Trust Bank, **V** 114
Southern Kraft Corp., **IV** 286
Southern Lumber Company, **8** 430
Southern Manufacturing Company, **8** 458
Southern Minnesota Beet Sugar Cooperative, **32** 29
Southern National Bankshares of Atlanta, **II** 337; **10** 425
Southern Natural Gas Co., **III** 558; **6** 447–48, 577
Southern Nevada Power Company, **11** 343
Southern Nevada Telephone Company, **6** 313; **11** 343
**Southern New England Telecommunications Corporation, 6 338–40**
Southern Nitrogen Co., **IV** 123

Southern Oregon Broadcasting Co., **7** 15
Southern Pacific Communications Corporation, **9** 478–79
Southern Pacific Rail Corp., **12** 18–20. *See also* Union Pacific Corporation.
Southern Pacific Railroad, **I** 13; **II** 329, 381, 448; **IV** 625; **19** 202
**Southern Pacific Transportation Company, V 516–18; 12** 278; **26** 235; **37** 312
Southern Peru Copper Corp.,
**Southern Peru Copper Corporation, IV** 3; **40** 220, 222, **411–13**
Southern Phenix Textiles Inc., **15** 247–48
Southern Pine Lumber Co., **IV** 341
Southern Power Company. *See* Duke Energy Corporation.
Southern Railway Company, **V** 484–85; **29** 359
Southern Science Applications, Inc., **22** 88
**Southern States Cooperative Incorporated, 36 440–42**
Southern States Trust Co., **II** 336
Southern Sun Hotel Corporation. *See* South African Breweries Ltd. and *Sun International Hotels Limited.*
Southern Surety Co., **III** 332
Southern Telephone Company, **14** 257
Southern Television Corp., **II** 158; **IV** 650; **7** 389
**Southern Union Company, 12** 542; **27 424–26**
Southern Utah Fuel Co., **IV** 394
Southern Video Partnership, **9** 74
Southern Water plc, **19** 389–91
Southgate Medical Laboratory System, **26** 391
**The Southland Corporation, II** 449, 620, **660–61**; **IV** 392, 508; **V** 89; **7** 114, 374, **490–92 (upd.)**; **9** 178; **13** 333, 449, 525; **23** 406–07; **25** 125; **26** 447; **31** 115, 231; **42** 191. *See also* 7- Eleven, Inc.
Southland Mobilcom Inc., **15** 196
Southland Paper, **13** 118
Southland Royal Company, **27** 86
Southland Royalty Co., **10** 190
Southlife Holding Co., **III** 218
Southmark Corp., **11** 483; **33** 398
Southport, Inc., **44** 203
**Southtrust Corporation, 11 455–57**
Southview Pulp Co., **IV** 329
**Southwest Airlines Co., I** 106; **6** 72–74, **119–21**; **21** 143; **22** 22; **24 452–55 (upd.)**; **25** 404; **26** 308, 439–40; **33** 301–02; **35** 383; **44** 197, 248
Southwest Airmotive Co., **II** 16
Southwest Convenience Stores, LLC, **26** 368
Southwest Converting, **19** 414
Southwest Enterprise Associates, **13** 191
Southwest Forest Industries, **IV** 287, 289, 334
**Southwest Gas Corporation, 19 410–12**
Southwest Hide Co., **16** 546
Southwest Potash Corp., **IV** 18; **6** 148–49
**Southwest Water Company, 47 370–73**
**Southwestern Bell Corporation, V 328–30**; **6** 324; **10** 431, 500; **14** 489; **17** 110; **18** 22. *See also* SBC Communications Inc.
Southwestern Bell Publications, **26** 520
**Southwestern Electric Power Co., 21 468–70**
Southwestern Gas Pipeline, **7** 344
Southwestern Illinois Coal Company, **7** 33
Southwestern Life Insurance, **I** 527; **III** 136
Southwestern Pipe, **III** 498
**Southwestern Public Service Company, 6 579–81**
Southwestern Refining Company, Inc., **IV** 446; **22** 303
Southwestern Textile Company, **12** 393
**Southwire Company, Inc., 8 478–80; 12** 353; **23 444–47 (upd.)**
Souvall Brothers, **8** 473
Sovereign Corp., **III** 221; **14** 109; **37** 84
Sovran Financial, **10** 425–26
SovTransavto, **6** 410
Soyland Power Cooperative, **6** 506
SP Reifenwerke, **V** 253
SP Tyres, **V** 253
Space Control GmbH, **28** 243–44
Space Craft Inc., **9** 463
Space Data Corporation, **22** 401
Space Systems Corporation. *See* Orbital Sciences Corporation.
Space Systems/Loral, **9** 325
**Spacehab, Inc., 37 364–66**
Spacemakers Inc., **IV** 287
**Spaghetti Warehouse, Inc., 25 436–38**
Spagnesi, **18** 258
Spago. *See* The Wolfgang Puck Food Company, Inc.
Spalding & Evenflo, **24** 530
Spalding, Inc., **17** 243; **23** 449
**Spangler Candy Company, 44 392–95**
**Spanish Broadcasting System, Inc., 41 383–86**
Spanish International Communications Corp. *See* Univision Communications Inc.
Spanish River Pulp and Paper Mills, **IV** 246; **25** 10
SPAO, **39** 184
**Spar Aerospace Limited, 32 435–37**
**SPAR Handels AG, 35 398–401; 36** 296
Sparbanken Bank, **18** 543
SPARC International, **7** 499
Spare Change, **10** 282
Sparklets Ltd., **I** 315; **25** 80
Sparks Computerized Car Care Centers, **25** 445
Sparks Family Hospital, **6** 191
Sparks-Withington Company. *See* Sparton Corporation.
Sparrow Records, **22** 194
Sparta, Inc., **18** 369
Sparta Surgical Corporation, **33** 456
Spartan Communications, **38** 308–09
Spartan Industries, Inc., **45** 15
Spartan Insurance Co., **26** 486
**Spartan Motors Inc., 14 457–59**
**Spartan Stores Inc., I** 127; **II** 679–80; **8 481–82**; **10** 302; **12** 489; **14** 412
**Spartech Corporation, 9** 92; **19 413–15**; **33** 78–79
**Sparton Corporation, 18 492–95**
SPCM, Inc., **14** 477
**Spec's Music, Inc., 19 416–18**
Spécia, **I** 388
Special Agent Investigators, Inc., **14** 541
Special Foods, **14** 557
Special Light Alloy Co., **IV** 153
Special Zone Limited, **26** 491
Specialized Bicycle Components Inc., **19** 384
Specialty Brands Inc., **25** 518
**Specialty Coatings Inc., 8 483–84**
**Specialty Equipment Companies, Inc., 25 439–42**
Specialty Foods Corporation, **29** 29, 31
Specialty Papers Co., **IV** 290
Specialty Products Co., **8** 386
Specialty Retailers, Inc., **24** 456
Spectra-Physics AB, **9** 380–81
Spectra Star, Inc., **18** 521
Spectradyne, **28** 241
Spectral Dynamics Corporation. *See* Scientific- Atlanta, Inc.
Spectron MicroSystems, **18** 143
Spectrum Club, **25** 448–50
Spectrum Communications Holdings International Limited, **24** 95
Spectrum Concepts, **10** 394–95
Spectrum Data Systems, Inc., **24** 96
Spectrum Dyed Yarns of New York, **8** 559
Spectrum Health Care Services, **13** 48
Spectrum Medical Technologies, Inc., **22** 409
Spectrum Technology Group, Inc., **7** 378; **18** 112
Spectrumedia, **21** 361
Speed-O-Lac Chemical, **8** 553
SpeeDee Marts, **II** 661
**SpeeDee Oil Change and Tune-Up, 25 443–47**
**Speedway Motorsports, Inc., 32 438–41**
Speedy Auto Glass, **30** 501
Speedy Muffler King, **10** 415; **24** 337, 339
Speidel Newspaper Group, **IV** 612; **7** 191
**Speizman Industries, Inc., 44 396–98**
**Spelling Entertainment, 14 460–62; 35 402–04 (upd.)**
Spencer & Spencer Systems, Inc., **18** 112
Spencer Beef, **II** 536
Spencer Gifts, Inc., **II** 144; **15** 464
**Spencer Stuart and Associates, Inc., 14 463–65**
Spenco Medical Corp., **III** 41; **16** 303; **43** 257
Sperry & Hutchinson Co., **12** 299; **23** 243–44
Sperry Aerospace Group, **II** 40, 86; **6** 283; **12** 246, 248
Sperry Corporation, **I** 101, 167; **III** 165, 642; **6** 281–82; **8** 92; **11** 139; **12** 39; **13** 511; **18** 386, 542; **22** 379; **36** 481. *See also* Unisys Corporation.
Sperry Milling Co., **II** 501; **10** 322
Sperry New Holland. *See* New Holland N.V.
Sperry Rand Corp., **II** 63, 73; **III** 126, 129, 149, 166, 329, 642; **6** 241, 261, 281–82; **16** 137
Sperry Top-Sider, Inc., **37** 377, 379
Sphere Inc., **8** 526; **13** 92
Sphere SA, **27** 9
Spherion Corporation, **45** 272, 274
Spicer Manufacturing Co., **I** 152; **III** 568; **20** 359; **23** 170–71
Spider Software, Inc., **46** 38
Spie Batignolles SA, **I** 563; **II** 93–94; **13** 206; **18** 471–73; **24** 79
**Spiegel, Inc., III** 598; **V** 160; **8** 56–58; **10** 168, **489–91**; **11** 498; **9** 190, 219; **13** 179; **15** 339; **27 427–31 (upd.)**; **34** 232, 324, 326; **36** 177, 180
**SPIEGEL-Verlag Rudolf Augstein GmbH & Co. KG, 44 399–402**
Spillers, **II** 500
Spin Physics, **III** 475–76; **7** 163

SpinCircuit Inc., **38** 188
Spinnaker Industries, Inc., **43** 276
Spinnaker Software Corp., **24** 276
SPIRE Corporation, **14** 477
Spire, Inc., **25** 183
Spirella Company of Great Britain Ltd., **V** 356; **44** 105
**Spirit Airlines, Inc., 31 419–21**
Spirit Cruises, **29** 442–43
Spliethoff, **26** 280
Spoerle Electronic, **10** 113
Spokane Falls Electric Light and Power Company. *See* Edison Electric Illuminating Company.
Spokane Falls Water Power Company, **6** 595
Spokane Gas and Fuel, **IV** 391
Spokane Natural Gas Company, **6** 597
Spokane Street Railway Company, **6** 595
Spokane Traction Company, **6** 596
Spom Japan, **IV** 600
Spon Press, **44** 416
Spoor Behrins Campbell and Young, **II** 289
Spoornet, **6** 435
Sporis, **27** 151
Sporloisirs S.A., **9** 157
**Sport Chalet, Inc., 16 454–56**
Sport Developpement SCA, **33** 10
**Sport Supply Group, Inc., 22** 458–59; **23 448–50**; **30** 185
Sporting Dog Specialties, Inc., **14** 386
Sporting News Publishing Co., **IV** 677–78
Sportland, **26** 160
Sportmagazine NV, **48** 347
**Sportmart, Inc., 15 469–71**. *See also* Gart Sports Company.
Sports & Co. *See* Hibbett Sporting Goods, Inc.
**Sports & Recreation, Inc., 15** 470; **17 453–55**
**The Sports Authority, Inc., 15** 470; **16 457–59**; **17** 453; **18** 286; **24** 173; **43 385–88 (upd.)**
**The Sports Club Company, 25 448–51**
Sports Experts Inc., **II** 652
Sports Holdings Corp., **34** 217
Sports Inc., **14** 8; **33** 10
Sports Plus, **44** 192
Sports-Tech Inc., **21** 300
Sports Traders, Inc., **18** 208
Sportservice Corporation, **7** 133–35
**The Sportsman's Guide, Inc., 36 443–46**
Sportstown, Inc., **15** 470
Sportsystems Corporation, **7** 133, 135
Sprague Co., **I** 410
Sprague Devices, Inc., **11** 84
Sprague Electric Company, **6** 261
Sprague Electric Railway and Motor Co., **II** 27; **12** 193
Sprague Technologies, **21** 520
Sprague, Warner & Co., **II** 571
Spray-Rite, **I** 366
Sprayon Products, **III** 745
Spraysafe, **29** 98
Sprecher & Schub, **9** 10
Spreckels Sugar Company, Inc., **32** 274, 277
Spring Co., **21** 96, 246
Spring Forge Mill, **8** 412
Spring Grove Services, **45** 139–40
**Spring Industries, Inc., V 378–79**
Spring Valley Brewery. *See* Kirin Brewery Company, Limited.
Springbok Editions, **IV** 621
Springer Verlag GmbH & Co., **IV** 611, 641
Springfield Bank, **9** 474
Springfield Gas Light Company, **38** 81
Springhouse Corp., **IV** 610
Springhouse Financial Corp., **III** 204
Springmaid International, Inc., **19** 421
**Springs Industries, Inc., 19 419–22 (upd.)**; **29** 132; **31** 199
Sprint Canada Inc., **44** 49
**Sprint Communications Company, L.P., 9 478–80**; **10** 19, 57, 97, 201–03; **11** 183, 185, 500–01; **18** 32, 164–65, 569–70; **22** 19, 162; **24** 120, 122; **25** 102; **26** 17; **27** 365; **36** 167. *See also* Sprint Corporation and *US Sprint Communications.*
**Sprint Corporation, 46 373–76 (upd.)**
Sprint PCS, **33** 34, 36–37; **38** 433
Sprout Group, **37** 121
Spruce Falls Power and Paper Co., **III** 40; **IV** 648; **16** 302, 304; **19** 284; **43** 256
**SPS Technologies, Inc., 30 428–30**
Spun Yarns, Inc., **12** 503
Spur Oil Co., **7** 362
**SPX Corporation, 10 492–95**; **47 374–79 (upd.)**
SPZ, Inc., **26** 257
SQ Software, Inc., **10** 505
SQL Solutions, Inc., **10** 505
Square D Company, **18** 473
Square Industries, **18** 103, 105
Squibb Beech-Nut. *See* Beech-Nut Nutrition Corp.
**Squibb Corporation, I** 380–81, 631, 651, 659, 675, **695–97**; **III** 17, 19, 67; **8** 166; **9** 6–7; **13** 379–80; **16** 438–39[see_ aslo]Bristol-Myers Squibb Company.
Squire Fashions Inc. *See* Norton McNaughton of Squire, Inc.
SR. *See* Southern Railway.
SR Beteilgungen Aktiengesellschaft, **III** 377
SRI International, **10** 139
SRI Strategic Resources Inc., **6** 310
SS Cars, Ltd. *See* Jaguar Cars, Ltd.
SS Lazio. *See* Societá Sportiva Lazio SpA.
SSA. *See* Stevedoring Services of America Inc.
**Ssangyong Cement Industrial Co., Ltd., III 747–50**; **IV** 536–37, 539
Ssangyong Motor Company, **34** 132
SSC&B-Lintas, **I** 16–17; **14** 315
SSDS, Inc., **18** 537; **43** 433
SSI Medical Services, Inc., **10** 350
SSMC Inc., **II** 10
SSP Company, Inc., **17** 434
St. *See under* Saint
Staal Bankiers, **13** 544
Stackpole Fibers, **37** 427
Stadia Colorado Corporation, **18** 140
Stadt Corporation, **26** 109
Städtische Elecktricitäts-Werke A.G., **I** 410
Staefa Control System Limited, **6** 490
Staff International, **40** 157
StaffAmerica, Inc., **16** 50
Stafford-Lowdon, **31** 435
Stafford Old Bank, **II** 307
Stag Cañon Fuel Co., **IV** 177
**Stage Stores, Inc., 24 456–59**
**Stagecoach Holdings plc, 30 431–33**
Stags' Leap Winery, **22** 80
Stahl-Urban Company, **8** 287–88
Stahlwerke Peine-Salzgitter AG, **IV** 201
Stahlwerke Röchling AG, **III** 694–95
Stahlwerke Südwestfalen AG, **IV** 89
Stal-Astra GmbH, **III** 420
Staley Continental, **II** 582
Stamford Drug Group, **9** 68
Stamford FHI Acquisition Corp., **27** 117
Stamos Associates Inc., **29** 377
Stamps.com Inc., **34** 474
**Stanadyne Automotive Corporation, 37 367–70**
Stanadyne, Inc., **7** 336; **12** 344
Standard & Poor's Corp., **IV** 29, 482, 636–37; **12** 310; **25** 542
Standard Accident Co., **III** 332
Standard Aero, **III** 509
Standard Aircraft Equipment, **II** 16
Standard Alaska, **7** 559
Standard Bank, **17** 324
Standard Bank of Canada, **II** 244
Standard Box Co., **17** 357
Standard Brands, **I** 248; **II** 542, 544; **7** 365, 367; **18** 538
Standard Car Truck, **18** 5
**Standard Chartered plc, II** 298, 309, 319, **357–59**, 386; **10** 170; **47** 227; **48 371–74 (upd.)**
Standard Chemical Products, **III** 33
**Standard Commercial Corporation, 12** 110; **13 490–92**; **27** 126
Standard Drug Co., **V** 171
Standard Electric Time Company, **13** 233
Standard Electrica, **II** 13
Standard Elektrik Lorenz A.G., **II** 13, 70; **17** 353
Standard Equities Corp., **III** 98
**Standard Federal Bank, 9 481–83**
Standard Fire Insurance Co., **III** 181–82
Standard Fruit and Steamship Co. of New Orleans, **II** 491; **31** 168
Standard Gauge Manufacturing Company, **13** 233
Standard General Insurance, **III** 208
Standard Gypsum Corp., **19** 77
Standard Industrial Group Ltd., **IV** 658
Standard Insert Co., **28** 350
Standard Insulation Co., **I** 321
Standard Insurance Co. of New York, **III** 385
Standard Investing Corp., **III** 98
Standard Kollsman Industries Inc., **13** 461
Standard Life & Accident Insurance Company, **27** 47–48
**Standard Life Assurance Company, III 358–61**; **IV** 696–98
Standard Life Insurance Company, **11** 481
Standard Magnesium & Chemical Co., **IV** 123
Standard Metals Corp., **IV** 76
**Standard Microsystems Corporation, 11 462–64**
Standard Milling Co., **II** 497
Standard Motor Co., **III** 651
**Standard Motor Products, Inc., 40 414–17**
Standard of America Life Insurance Co., **III** 324
Standard of Georgia Insurance Agency, Inc., **10** 92
Standard Oil Co., **III** 470, 513; **IV** 46, 372, 399, 426–29, 434, 463, 478, 488–89, 530–31, 540, 542, 551, 574, 577–78, 657; **V** 590, 601; **6** 455; **7** 169–72, 263, 351, 414, 551; **8** 415; **10** 110, 289; **14**

21, 491–92; **25** 230; **27** 129. *See also* Exxon Corporation.
Standard Oil Co. (California), **II** 448; **IV** 18–19, 385–87, 403, 429, 464, 536–37, 545, 552, 560, 578; **6** 353; **7** 172, 352, 483; **13** 448
Standard Oil Co. (Illinois), **IV** 368
Standard Oil Co. (Indiana), **II** 262; **IV** 366, 368–71, 466–67; **7** 443; **10** 86; **14** 222
Standard Oil Co. (Minnesota), **IV** 368
Standard Oil Co. (New York), **IV** 428–29, 431, 460, 463–65, 485, 504, 537, 549, 558; **7** 171, 351–52
Standard Oil Co. of Iowa, **IV** 385
Standard Oil Co. of Kentucky, **IV** 387
Standard Oil Co. of New Jersey, **I** 334, 337, 370; **II** 16, 496; **IV** 378–79, 385–86, 400, 415–16, 419, 426–29, 431–33, 438, 460, 463–64, 488, 522, 531, 537–38, 544, 558, 565, 571; **V** 658–59; **7** 170–72, 253, 351; **13** 124; **17** 412–13; **24** 521
Standard Oil Co. of Ohio, **IV** 373, 379, 427, 452, 463, 522, 571; **7** 57, 171, 263; **12** 309; **21** 82; **24** 521
Standard Oil Development Co., **IV** 554
Standard Oil Trust, **IV** 31, 368, 375, 385–86, 427, 463
Standard Plastics, **25** 312
Standard Printing Company, **19** 333
Standard Process & Engraving, Inc., **26** 105
Standard Products Company, **19** 454
Standard Rate & Data Service, **IV** 639; **7** 286
**Standard Register Co., 15 472–74**
Standard Sanitary, **III** 663–64
Standard Screw Co., **12** 344
Standard Shares, **9** 413–14
Standard Steel Propeller, **I** 47, 84; **9** 416; **10** 162
Standard Telephone and Radio, **II** 13
Standard Telephones and Cables, Ltd., **III** 162–63; **6** 242
Standard Tin Plate Co., **15** 127
Standard-Vacuum Oil Co., **IV** 431–32, 440, 460, 464, 491–92, 554–55; **7** 352
**Standex International Corporation, 16 470–71; 17 456–59; 44 403–06 (upd.)**
**Stanhome Inc., 9** 330; **11** 94–96; **15 475–78**
Stanhome Worldwide Direct Selling, **35** 262, 264
STANIC, **IV** 419, 421
Stanko Fanuc Service, **III** 483
Stanley Electric Manufacturing Co., **II** 28; **12** 194
**Stanley Furniture Company, Inc., 34 412–14**
Stanley Home Products, Incorporated. *See* Stanhome Inc.
Stanley Mining Services, Ltd., **19** 247
**The Stanley Works, III 626–29; 7** 480; **9** 543; **13** 41; **20 476–80 (upd.)**
StanMont, Inc., **24** 425
Stanolind Oil & Gas Co., **III** 498; **IV** 365, 369–70
Stant Corporation, **15** 503, 505
**Staples, Inc., 8** 404–05; **10 496–98; 18** 24, 388; **20** 99; **22** 154; **23** 363, 365; **24** 270
*Star*, **10** 287–88
Star Air Service. *See* Alaska Air Group, Inc.
Star Alliance, **26** 113; **33** 51; **38** 36
**Star Banc Corporation, 11 465–67; 13** 222; **31** 206. *See also* Firstar Corporation.
Star Building Systems, Inc., **19** 366
Star Engraving, **12** 471
Star Enterprise, **IV** 536, 539, 553
Star Enterprises, Inc., **6** 457
Star Finishing Co., **9** 465
Star Laboratories Inc., **24** 251
Star Markets Company, Inc., **23** 169
Star Medical Technologies, Inc., **22** 409; **31** 124
Star Paper Ltd., **IV** 300
Star Paper Tube, Inc., **19** 76–78
Star Sportwear Manufacturing Corp., **29** 294
Star Video, Inc., **6** 313
Starber International, **12** 181
**Starbucks Corporation, 13 493–94; 18** 37; **22** 370; **25** 178, 501; **28** 63; **34 415–19 (upd.); 36** 156–57; **37** 181; **38** 340; **40** 152–53; **44** 313
**Starcraft Corporation, III** 444; **13** 113; **22** 116; **30 434–36**
Stardent Computer Inc., **III** 553; **26** 256
Starfish Software, **23** 212
Stark Record and Tape Service. *See* Camelot Music, Inc.
StarKist Foods, **II** 508; **11** 172; **36** 254–55
Starlawerken, **I** 527
Starlen Labs, Ltd., **31** 346
Starlight Networks, Inc., **27** 366
Starline Optical Corp., **22** 123
StarMed Staffing Corporation, **6** 10
Starpointe Savings Bank, **9** 173
**Starrett Corporation, 21 471–74**
Star's Discount Department Stores, **16** 36
Startech Semiconductor Inc., **14** 183
Startel Corp., **15** 125
**Starter Corp., 12 457–458**
Starwood Capital, **29** 508
Starwood Hotels and Resorts Worldwide Inc., **33** 217
State Bank of Albany, **9** 228
State Farm Insurance Companies, **27** 30; **29** 397; **39** 155
**State Farm Mutual Automobile Insurance Company, III 362–64; 10** 50; **22** 266; **23** 286; **25** 155; **41** 313
State Finance and Thrift Company, **14** 529
State Leed, **13** 367
State Metal Works, **III** 647
State-o-Maine, **18** 357–59
State-Record Co., **IV** 630
State Savings Bank and Trust Co., **11** 180; **42** 429
**State Street Boston Corporation, 8 491–93**
State Trading Corp. of India Ltd., **IV** 143
Staten Island Advance Corp., **IV** 581–82; **19** 4
**Staten Island Bancorp, Inc., 39 380–82**
Stater Brothers, **17** 558
Statex Petroleum, Inc., **19** 70
Static, Inc., **14** 430
**Station Casinos Inc., 25 452–54**
Stationers Distributing Company, **14** 523
Stationers, Inc., **28** 74
Statler Hotel Co., **III** 92, 98; **19** 206
Statoil. *See* Den Norske Stats Oljeselskap AS.
StatScript Management Services, **26** 73
Statter, Inc., **6** 27
Staubli International, **II** 122; **12** 546
Stauffer Chemical Company, **8** 105–07; **21** 545
Stauffer Communications, Inc., **36** 339–41
Stauffer-Meiji, **II** 540
Stax Records, **23** 32
**STC PLC, III** 141, **162–64**; **25** 497; **36** 351
Stead & Miller, **13** 169
Steag AG, **IV** 193
Steak & Ale, **II** 556–57; **7** 336; **12** 373; **13** 408–09
**The Steak n Shake Company, 14** 130–31; **41 387–90**
Steam and Gas Pipe Co., **III** 644
Steam Boiler Works, **18** 318
Steamboat Ski and Resort Corporation, **28** 21
Stearman, **I** 47, 84; **9** 416; **10** 162
Stearns & Foster, **12** 439
Stearns Catalytic World Corp., **II** 87; **11** 413
Stearns Coal & Lumber, **6** 514
**Stearns, Inc., 43 389–91**
Stearns Manufacturing Co., **16** 297
Steaua-Romana, **IV** 557
Steego Auto Paints, **24** 160
Steel and Tube Co. of America, **IV** 114
**Steel Authority of India Ltd., IV 205–07**
Steel Ceilings and Aluminum Works, **IV** 22
Steel Co. of Canada Ltd., **IV** 208
Steel Dynamics, Inc., **18** 380; **26** 530
Steel Mills Ltd., **III** 673
Steel Products Engineering Co., **I** 169
Steel Stamping Co., **III** 569; **20** 360
**Steelcase Inc., 7 493–95; 8** 251–52, 255, 405; **25** 500; **27 432–35 (upd.); 39** 205–07
Steelmade Inc., **I** 513
Steely, **IV** 109
Steenfabriek De Ruiterwaard, **14** 249
Steenkolen Handelsvereniging, **IV** 132; **39** 176
Steering Aluminum, **I** 159
Stefany, **12** 152
Stegbar Pty Ltd., **31** 398–400
Steger Furniture Manufacturing Co., **18** 493
Steiff. *See* Margarete Steiff GmbH.
Steil, Inc., **8** 271
**Stein Mart Inc., 19 423–25**
Stein Printing Company, **25** 183
Stein Robaire Helm, **22** 173
Steinbach Inc., **IV** 226; **14** 427
Steinbach Stores, Inc., **19** 108
**Steinberg Incorporated, II** 652–53, **662–65**; **V** 163
Steinberger, **16** 239
Steinheil Optronik GmbH, **24** 87
Steinman & Grey, **6** 27
Steinmüller Verwaltungsgesellschaft, **V** 747
Steinway & Sons, **16** 201; **43** 170
**Steinway Musical Properties, Inc., 19** 392, 394, **426–29**
**Stelco Inc., IV 208–10; 24** 144
Stella Bella Corporation, **19** 436
Stella D'Oro Company, **7** 367
Stellar Systems, Inc., **III** 553; **14** 542
Stellenbosch Farmers Winery, **I** 288
Stelux Manufacturing Company, **13** 121; **41** 71
Stena AB, **25** 105; **29** 429–30
Stena Line AB, **38** 345

Stena-Sealink, **37** 137
Stens Corporation, **48** 34
Stensmölla Kemiska Tekniska Industri, **I** 385
Stentor Canadian Network Management, **6** 310
Stenval Sud, **19** 50
**Stepan Company**, **30 437–39**
Stephen F. Whitman & Son, Inc., **7** 429
Stephens Inc., **III** 76; **16** 59; **18** 223
Stephenson Clarke and Company, **31** 368–69
Sterchi Bros. Co., **14** 236
**Stericycle Inc.**, **33 380–82**
**STERIS Corporation**, **29 449–52**
**Sterling Chemicals, Inc.**, **16 460–63**; **27** 117
**Sterling Drug Inc.**, **I** 309–10, **698–700**; **III** 477; **7** 163; **13** 76–77; **36** 173; **41** 45
**Sterling Electronics Corp.**, **18 496–98**; **19** 311
Sterling Engineered Products, **III** 640, 642; **16** 9
Sterling Forest Corp., **III** 264
Sterling House Corp., **42** 4
Sterling Industries, **13** 166
Sterling Information Services, Ltd., **IV** 675; **7** 528
Sterling Manhattan, **7** 63
Sterling Oil, **I** 526
Sterling Oil & Development, **II** 490
Sterling Organics Ltd., **12** 351
Sterling Plastics, **III** 642
Sterling Plastics Inc., **16** 9
Sterling Products Inc., **I** 622; **10** 68
Sterling Remedy Co., **I** 698
**Sterling Software, Inc.**, **11 468–70**; **31** 296
Sterling Stores Co. Inc., **24** 148
Sterling Winthrop, **7** 164; **36** 174
Stern & Stern Textiles, **11** 261
Stern-Auer Shoe Company, **V** 207
Stern Bros. Investment Bank, **V** 362–65; **19** 359
Stern Bros., LLC, **37** 224
Stern Publishing, **38** 478
Stern's, **9** 209
Sternco Industries, **12** 230–31
STET. *See* Società Finanziaria Telefonica per Azioni.
Steuben Glass, **III** 683
Stevcoknit Fabrics Company, **8** 141–43
**Stevedoring Services of America Inc.**, **28 435–37**
**Steven Madden, Ltd.**, **37 371–73**
Stevens Linen Associates, Inc., **8** 272
Stevens Park Osteopathic Hospital, **6** 192
Stevens Sound Proofing Co., **III** 706; **7** 291
Stevens, Thompson & Runyan, Inc. *See* CRSS Inc.
Steve's Ice Cream, **16** 54–55
Steward Esplen and Greenhough, **II** 569
Stewards Foundation, **6** 191
**Stewart & Stevenson Services Inc.**, **11 471–73**
Stewart Bolling Co., **IV** 130
Stewart Cash Stores, **II** 465
**Stewart Enterprises, Inc.**, **16** 344; **20 481–83**; **37** 67
Stewart P. Orr Associates, **6** 224
Stewart Systems, Inc., **22** 352–53
**Stewart's Beverages**, **39 383–86**
Steyr Walzlager, **III** 625
Stichting Continuiteit AMEV, **III** 202
Stieber Rollkupplung GmbH, **14** 63
Stihl Inc. *See* Andreas Stihl.
Stilecraft, **24** 16
**Stillwater Mining Company**, **47 380–82**
Stimson & Valentine, **8** 552
**Stinnes AG**, **6** 424, 426; **8** 68–69, **494–97**; **23** 68–70, **451–54 (upd.)**; **33** 195
Stirling Readymix Concrete, **III** 737–38
STM Systems Corp., **11** 485
Stock, **IV** 617–18
Stock Clearing Corporation, **9** 370
**Stock Yards Packing Co., Inc.**, **37 374–76**
Stockholder Systems Inc., **11** 485
Stockholm Southern Transportation Co., **I** 553
Stockholms Allmänna Telefonaktiebolag, **V** 334
Stockholms Enskilda Bank, **II** 1, 351, 365–66; **III** 419, 425–26
Stockholms Intecknings Garanti, **II** 366
Stockpack Ltd., **44** 318
Stockton and Hartlepool Railway, **III** 272
Stockton Wheel Co., **III** 450
Stoelting Brothers Company, **10** 371
Stokely Van Camp, **II** 560, 575; **12** 411; **22** 338
Stokvis/De Nederlandsche Kroon Rijwiefabrieken, **13** 499
**Stoll-Moss Theatres Ltd.**, **34 420–22**
**Stolt-Nielsen S.A.**, **42 356–59**
**Stone & Webster, Inc.**, **13 495–98**
Stone and Kimball, **IV** 660
Stone-Consolidated Corporation, **25** 9, 12
**Stone Container Corporation**, **IV 332–34**; **8** 203–04; **15** 129; **17** 106; **25** 12. *See also* Smurfit-Stone Container Corporation.
Stone Exploration Corp., **IV** 83; **7** 187
**Stone Manufacturing Company**, **14 469–71**; **43 392–96 (upd.)**
Stonega Coke & Coal Co. *See* Westmoreland Coal Company.
Stoner Associates. *See* Severn Trent PLC.
Stonewall Insurance Co., **III** 192
Stonington Partners, **19** 318
StonyBrook Services Inc., **24** 49
Stoody Co., **19** 440
Stoof, **26** 278–79
Stoomvaart Maatschappij Nederland, **6** 403–04; **26** 241
**The Stop & Shop Companies, Inc.**, **II 666–67**; **9** 451, 453; **12** 48–49; **16** 160, 314; **23** 169; **24 460–62 (upd.)**
Stop N Go, **7** 373; **25** 126
Stoppenbauch Inc., **23** 202
**Stora Enso Oyj**, **36** 128, **447–55 (upd.)**
**Stora Kopparbergs Bergslags AB**, **III** 693, 695; **IV 335–37**, 340; **12** 464; **28** 445–46
Storage Dimensions Inc., **10** 404
**Storage Technology Corporation**, **III** 110; **6 275–77**; **12** 148, 161; **16** 194; **28** 198
**Storage USA, Inc.**, **21 475–77**
Storebrand Insurance Co., **III** 122
**Storehouse PLC**, **II** 658; **13** 284; **16 464–66**; **17** 42–43, 335; **24** 75
Storer Communications, **II** 161; **IV** 596; **7** 91–92, 200–1; **24** 122
Storer Leasing Inc., **I** 99; **6** 81
Storm Technology, **28** 245
Storz Instruments Co., **I** 678; **25** 56; **27** 115
**Stouffer Corp.**, **I** 485; **II** 489, 547; **6** 40; **7** 382; **8 498–501**
Stouffer Foods Corporation, **28** 238
Stout Air Services, **I** 128; **6** 128
Stout Airlines, **I** 47, 84; **9** 416; **10** 162
Stout Metal Airplane Co., **I** 165
Stowe Machine Co., Inc., **30** 283
Stowe Woodward, **I** 428–29
STP, **19** 223; **26** 349
STRAAM Engineers. *See* CRSS Inc.
Straits Steamship Co. *See* Malaysian Airlines System.
Stran, **8** 546
Strata Energy, Inc., **IV** 29
**StrataCom, Inc.**, **11** 59; **16 467–69**; **34** 113
Strategic Implications International, Inc., **45** 44
Strategix Solutions, **43** 309
Stratford Corporation, **15** 103; **26** 100
Strathmore Consolidated Investments, **IV** 90
Stratos Boat Co., Ltd., **III** 600
Stratton Oakmont Inc., **37** 372–73; **46** 282
Stratton Ski Corporation, **15** 235
**Stratus Computer, Inc.**, **6** 279; **10 499–501**
Straus-Frank Company, **29** 86, 88
Strauss Turnbull and Co., **II** 355
Strawberries, **30** 465
Strawbridge & Clothier's, **6** 243
Stream International Inc., **48** 369
Stream Machine Co., **48** 92
Streamline Holdings, **39** 237–38
De Streekkrant-De Weekkrantgroep NV, **48** 347
Street & Smith Publications, Inc., **IV** 583; **13** 178
**The Stride Rite Corporation**, **8 502–04**; **9** 437; **33** 244; **37 377–80 (upd.)**
Stroehmann Bakeries, **II** 631
Stroh and Co., **IV** 486
**The Stroh Brewery Company**, **I** 32, 255, **290–92**; **13** 10–11, 455; **18** 72, **499–502 (upd.)**; **22** 422; **23** 403, 405; **36** 14–15
Strömberg, **IV** 300; **27** 267, 268
Stromberg Carburetor Co., **I** 141
Stromberg-Carlson, **II** 82
Stromeyer GmbH, **7** 141
Strong Brewery, **I** 294
Strong Electric Corporation, **19** 211
Strong International, **27** 57
**Stroock & Stroock & Lavan LLP**, **40 418–21**
Strother Drug, **III** 9–10
**Strouds, Inc.**, **33 383–86**
Structural Dynamics Research Corporation, **10** 257
Structural Fibers, Inc. *See* Essef Corporation.
Structural Iberica S.A., **18** 163
Struebel Group, **18** 170
Strydel, Inc., **14** 361
**Stryker Corporation**, **10** 351; **11 474–76**; **29 453–55 (upd.)**
Stuart & Sons Ltd., **34** 493, 496
Stuart Co., **I** 584
**Stuart Entertainment Inc.**, **16 470–72**
Stuart Hall Co., **17** 445
Stuart Medical, Inc., **10** 143; **16** 400
Stuart Perlman, **6** 200
Stuckey's, Inc., **7** 429

Studebaker Co., **I** 141–42, 451; **8** 74; **9** 27
Studebaker-Packard, **9** 118; **10** 261
Studebaker Wagon Co., **IV** 660
**Student Loan Marketing Association, II 453–55.** *See also* SLM Holding Corp.
Studiengesellschaft, **I** 409
StudioCanal, **48** 164–65
Studley Products Inc., **12** 396
Stuffit Co., **IV** 597
**Stuller Settings, Inc., 35 405–07**
Sturbridge Yankee Workshop, Inc., **10** 216
Sturgeon Bay Shipbuilding and DryDock Company, **18** 320
**Sturm, Ruger & Company, Inc., 19 430–32**
Stuttgart Gas Works, **I** 391
Stuttgarter Verein Versicherungs-AG, **III** 184
Stuyvesant Insurance Group, **II** 182
Style Magazine BV, **48** 347
Styleclick.com, Inc., **47** 420
Stylus Writing Instruments, **27** 416
Stymer Oy, **IV** 470–71
SU214, **28** 27, 30
Suave Shoe Corporation. *See* French Fragrances, Inc.
**Sub-Zero Freezer Co., Inc., 31 426–28**
Subaru, **6** 28; **23** 290
Suber Suisse S.A., **48** 350
SubLogic, **15** 455
Submarine Boat Co., **I** 57
Submarine Signal Co., **II** 85–86; **11** 412
Suburban Cablevision, **IV** 640
Suburban Coastal Corporation, **10** 92
Suburban Cos., **IV** 575–76
Suburban Light and Power Company, **12** 45
**Suburban Propane Partners, L.P., I** 378; **30 440–42[ro**
Suburban Savings and Loan Association, **10** 92
**Subway, 15** 56–57; **32 442–44**
**Successories, Inc., 30 443–45[ro**
Suchard Co., **II** 520
Sud-Aviation, **I** 44–45; **7** 10; **8** 313
**Sudbury Inc., 16 473–75; 17** 373
Sudbury River Consulting Group, **31** 131
Suddeutsche Bank A.G., **II** 279
Süddeutsche Donau- Dampfschiffahrts-Gesellschaft, **6** 425
Süddeutsche Kalkstickstoffwerke AG, **IV** 229, 232
Sudler & Hennessey, **I** 37
Südpetrol, **IV** 421
**Südzucker AG, 27 436–39**
Suez Bank, **IV** 108
Suez Canal Co., **IV** 530
**Suez Lyonnaise des Eaux, 36 456–59 (upd.); 38** 321; **40** 447, 449; **42** 386, 388; **45** 277; **47** 219
Suez Oil Co., **IV** 413–14
Suffolk County Federal Savings and Loan Association, **16** 346
Sugar Land State Bank, **25** 114
Sugar Mount Capital, LLC, **33** 355
Sugarland Industries. *See* Imperial Holly Corporation.
SugarLoaf Creations, Inc. *See* American Coin Merchandising, Inc.
Sugarloaf Mountain Corporation, **28** 21
Suita Brewery, **I** 220
Suito Sangyo Co., Ltd. *See* Seino Transportation Company, Ltd.
SUITS. *See* Scottish Universal Investments.
**Suiza Foods Corporation, 25** 512, 514; **26 447–50; 37** 197; **38** 381
**Sukhoi Design Bureau Aviation Scientific-Industrial Complex, 24 463–65**
Sullair Co., **I** 435
**Sullivan & Cromwell, 26 451–53; 27** 327; **47** 437
Sullivan-Schein Dental Products Inc., **31** 256
Sullivan, Stauffer, Colwell & Bayles, **14** 314
Sullivan Systems, **III** 420
Sulpetro Limited, **25** 232
Sulphide Corp., **IV** 58
Sulzbach, **I** 409
**Sulzer Brothers Limited, III** 402, 516, **630–33**, 638
Sumergrade Corporation, **19** 304; **41** 300
Suminoe Textile Co., **8** 235
Sumisei Secpac Investment Advisors, **III** 366
Sumisho Electronics Co. Ltd., **18** 170
**Sumitomo Bank, Limited, I** 587; **II** 104, 224, 273–74, 347, **360–62**, 363, 392, 415; **IV** 269, 726; **9** 341–42; **18** 170; **23** 340; **26 454–57 (upd.)**
**Sumitomo Chemical Company Ltd., I** 363, **397–98; II** 361; **III** 715; **IV** 432
**Sumitomo Corporation, I** 431–32, 492, 502, 504–05, 510–11, 515, **518–20; III** 43, 365; **V** 161; **7** 357; **11 477–80 (upd.)**, 490; **15** 340; **17** 556; **18** 170; **24** 325; **28** 288; **36** 420; **45** 115
**Sumitomo Electric Industries, I** 105; **II 104–05; III** 490, 684; **IV** 179; **V** 252
**Sumitomo Heavy Industries, Ltd., III** 533, **634–35; 10** 381; **42 360–62 (upd.)**
**Sumitomo Life Insurance Co., II** 104, 360, 422; **III** 288, **365–66**
**Sumitomo Marine and Fire Insurance Company, Limited, III 367–68**
**Sumitomo Metal Industries, Ltd., I** 390; **II** 104, 361; **IV** 130, **211–13**, 216; **10** 463–64; **11** 246; **24** 302
**Sumitomo Metal Mining Co., Ltd., IV 214–16; 9** 340; **23** 338
**Sumitomo Realty & Development Co., Ltd., IV 726–27**
**Sumitomo Rubber Industries, Ltd., V 252–53; 20** 263
Sumitomo Trading, **45** 8
**Sumitomo Trust & Banking Company, Ltd., II** 104, **363–64; IV** 726
Sumitomo Wire Company, **16** 555
Summa Corporation, **9** 266; **17** 317
Summer Paper Tube, **19** 78
SummerGate Inc., **48** 148
Summers Group Inc., **15** 386
**The Summit Bancorporation, 14 472–74**
Summit Constructors. *See* CRSS Inc.
Summit Engineering Corp., **I** 153
**Summit Family Restaurants Inc., 19** 89, 92, **433–36**
Summit Gear Company, **16** 392–93
Summit Management Co., Inc., **17** 498
Summit Screen Inks, **13** 228
Summit Systems Inc., **45** 280
Summit Technology Inc., **30** 485
Sun Aire, **25** 421–22
**Sun Alliance Group PLC, III** 296, **369–74**, 400; **37** 86
Sun Apparel Inc., **39** 247
Sun Chemical Corp. *See* Sequa Corp.
**Sun Communities Inc., 46 377–79**
**Sun Company, Inc., I** 286, 631; **IV** 449, **548–50; 7** 114, 414; **11** 484; **12** 459; **17** 537; **25** 126
**Sun Country Airlines, I** 114; **30 446–49**
**Sun-Diamond Growers of California, 7 496–97**
**Sun Distributors L.P., 12 459–461**
Sun Electric, **15** 288
Sun Electronics, **9** 116
Sun Equities Corporation, **15** 449
Sun-Fast Color, **13** 227
Sun Federal, **7** 498
Sun Federal Savings and Loan Association of Tallahassee, **10** 92
Sun Financial Group, Inc., **25** 171
Sun Fire Coal Company, **7** 281
Sun Fire Office, **III** 349, 369–71
Sun Foods, **12** 220–21
**Sun Healthcare Group Inc., 25 455–58**
**Sun International Hotels Limited, 12** 420; **26 462–65; 37** 254–55
Sun Kyowa, **III** 43
Sun Life Assurance Co. of Canada, **IV** 165
Sun Life Group of America, **11** 482
Sun-Maid Growers of California, **7** 496–97
Sun Mark, Inc., **21** 483
Sun Media, **27** 280; **29** 471–72; **47** 327
Sun Men's Shop Co., Ltd., **V** 150
**Sun Microsystems, Inc., II** 45, 62; **III** 125; **6** 222, 235, 238, 244; **7 498–501; 9** 36, 471; **10** 118, 242, 257, 504; **11** 45–46, 490–91, 507; **12** 162; **14** 15–16, 268; **15** 321; **16** 140, 195, 418–19; **18** 537; **20** 175, 237; **21** 86; **22** 154; **23** 471; **25** 348, 499; **26** 19; **27** 448; **30 450–54 (upd.); 36** 80–81; **38** 416, 418; **43** 238–40; **44** 97; **45** 200
Sun Newspapers, **III** 213–14
Sun Oil Co., **III** 497; **IV** 371, 424, 548–50; **7** 413–14; **11** 35; **18** 233; **19** 162; **36** 86–87. *See also* Sunoco, Inc.
Sun Optical Co., Ltd., **V** 150
Sun Pac Foods, **45** 161
Sun-Pat Products, **II** 569
Sun Pharmaceuticals, **24** 480
Sun Shades 501 Ltd., **21** 483
Sun Ship, **IV** 549
**Sun Sportswear, Inc., 17 460–63; 23** 65–66
Sun State Marine Services, Inc. *See* Hvide Marine Incorporated.
Sun Techno Services Co., Ltd., **V** 150
Sun Technology Enterprises, **7** 500
**Sun Television & Appliances Inc., 10 502–03; 19** 362
Sun Valley Equipment Corp., **33** 363
SunAir, **11** 300
**SunAmerica Inc., 11 481–83**
**Sunbeam-Oster Co., Inc., 9 484–86; 14** 230; **16** 488; **17** 215; **19** 305; **22** 3; **28** 135, 246; **30** 136; **42** 309
Sunbelt Beverage Corporation, **32** 520
Sunbelt Coca-Cola, **10** 223
Sunbelt Nursery Group, Inc., **12** 179, 200, 394
Sunbelt Rentals Inc., **34** 42
Sunbird, **III** 600; **V** 150
**Sunburst Hospitality Corporation, 26 458–61**
Sunburst Technology Corporation, **36** 273
Sunburst Yarns, Inc., **13** 532
Sunciti Manufacturers Ltd., **III** 454; **21** 122

Sunclipse Inc., **IV** 250
Sunco N.V., **22** 515
Suncoast Motion Picture Company, **9** 360
SunCor Development Company, **6** 546–47
Suncor Energy, **33** 167
Sundance Publishing, **IV** 609; **12** 559
Sunday Pictorial, **IV** 665–66; **17** 397
Sundheim & Doetsch, **IV** 189
Sunds Defibrator AG, **IV** 338–40, 350; **28** 444
**Sundstrand Corporation, 7 502–04; 21 478–81 (upd.)**
**Sundt Corp., 24 466–69**
**SunGard Data Systems Inc., 11 484–85**
**Sunglass Hut International, Inc., 18** 393; **21 482–84**
Sunglee Electronics Co. Ltd., **III** 748–49
Sunila Oy, **IV** 348–49
Sunkiss Thermoreactors, **21** 65
**Sunkist Growers, Inc., 7** 496; **25** 366; **26 466–69**; **47** 63
Sunkist Soft Drinks Inc., **I** 13
Sunkus Co. Ltd., **V** 150
Sunlight Services Group Limited, **45** 139
Sunlit Industries, **44** 132
Sunnybrook Farms, **25** 124
**Sunoco, Inc., 28 438–42 (upd.)**
SunQuest HealthCare Corp. *See* Unison HealthCare Corporation.
Sunquest Information Systems Inc., **45** 279, 281
Sunray DX Oil Co., **IV** 550, 575; **7** 414
**The Sunrider Corporation, 26** 316, **470–74**; **27** 353
SunRise Imaging, **44** 358
**Sunrise Medical Inc., 11** 202, **486–88**
Sunrise Test Systems, **11** 491
Sunsations Sunglass Company, **21** 483
Sunshine Biscuit Co., **35** 181; **36** 313
Sunshine Bullion Co., **25** 542
Sunshine Jr. Stores, Inc., **17** 170
Sunshine Mining Company, **20** 149
SunSoft Inc., **7** 500; **43** 238
Sunstate, **24** 396
Sunsweet Growers, **7** 496
Suntory Ltd., **13** 454; **21** 320; **36** 404
**SunTrust Banks Inc., 23 455–58**; **33** 293
Sunward Technologies, Inc., **10** 464
Supasnaps, **V** 50
Supelco, Inc., **36** 431
Super Bazars, **26** 159
Super D Drugs, **9** 52
Super Dart. *See* Dart Group Corporation.
Super 8 Motels, Inc., **11** 178
**Super Food Services, Inc., 15 479–81**; **18** 8
Super Oil Seals & Gaskets Ltd., **16** 8
Super 1 Stores. *See* Brookshire Grocery Company.
Super-Power Company, **6** 505
Super Quick, Inc., **7** 372
Super Rite Foods, Inc., **V** 176; **19** 356
Super Sagless Spring Corp., **15** 103
Super Sol Ltd., **41** 56–57
Super Store Industries, **14** 397
**Super Valu Stores, Inc., II** 632, **668–71**; **6** 364; **7** 450; **8** 380; **14** 411; **17** 180; **22** 126; **23** 357–58. *See also* Supervalu Inc.
SuperAmerica Group, Inc., **IV** 374
Superbrix, **14** 248
Supercomputer Systems, Inc., **III** 130; **16** 138
**Supercuts Inc., 26 475–78**
Superdrug plc, **V** 175; **24** 266, 269–70
Superenvases Envalic, **I** 231
Superior Bearings Company. *See* Federal-Mogul Corporation.
Superior Foam and Polymers, Inc., **44** 261
Superior Healthcare Group, Inc., **11** 221
**Superior Industries International, Inc., 8 505–07**
Superior Oil Co., **III** 558; **IV** 400, 465, 524; **7** 353
Superior Recycled Fiber Industries, **26** 363
Superior Transfer, **12** 309
**Superior Uniform Group, Inc., 30 455–57**
SuperMac Technology Inc., **16** 419
Supermarchés GB, **26** 159
Supermarchés Montréal, **II** 662–63
**Supermarkets General Holdings Corporation, II 672–74**; **16** 160; **23** 369–70
Supermart Books, **10** 136
Supersaver Wholesale Clubs, **8** 555
Supersnaps, **19** 124
SuperStation WTBS, **6** 171
Supertest Petroleum Corporation, **9** 490
**Supervalu Inc., 18 503–08 (upd.)**; **21** 457–57; **22** 327. *See also* Super Valu Stores, Inc.
Supervalue Corp., **13** 393
Supervised Investors Services, **III** 270
SupeRx, **II** 644
Supplyon AG, **48** 450
**Suprema Specialties, Inc., 27 440–42**
**Supreme International Corporation, 27 443–46**; **30** 358; **41** 291
Supreme Life Insurance Company of America, **28** 212
Supreme Sugar Co., **I** 421; **11** 23
Supron Energy Corp., **15** 129
Surety Life Insurance Company, **10** 51
SureWay Air Traffic Corporation, **24** 126
Surgical Health Corporation, **14** 233
Surgical Mechanical Research Inc., **I** 678
Surgical Plastics, **25** 430–31
Surgikos, Inc., **III** 35
Surgitool, **I** 628
**OAO Surgutneftegaz, 48 375–78**
Suroflex GmbH, **23** 300
Surpass Software Systems, Inc., **9** 81
Surplus Software, **31** 176
Surridge Dawson Ltd. *See* Dawson Holdings PLC.
Survey Research Group, **10** 360
SurVivaLink, **18** 423
Susan Bristol, **16** 61
Susan Kay Cosmetics. *See* The Cosmetic Center, Inc.
SuSE Linux AG, **45** 363
Susie's Casuals, **14** 294
**Susquehanna Pfaltzgraff Company, 8 508–10**
Sussex Group, **15** 449
Sussex Trust Company, **25** 541
Sutherland Lumber Co., **19** 233
Sutter Corp., **15** 113
Sutter Health, **12** 175–76
**Sutter Home Winery Inc., 16 476–78**
Sutton & Towne, Inc., **21** 96
Sutton Laboratories, **22** 228
Suunto Oy, **41** 14, 16
Suwa Seikosha, **III** 620
Suzaki Hajime, **V** 113–14
Suzannah Farms, **7** 524
Suze, **I** 280
Suzhou Elevator Company, **29** 420
Suzuki & Co., **I** 509–10; **IV** 129; **9** 341–42; **23** 340
**Suzuki Motor Corporation, III** 581, 657; **7** 110; **8** 72; **9 487–89**; **23** 290, **459–62 (upd.)**; **36** 240, 243; **39** 38
Suzuki Shoten Co., **V** 380, 457–58
Suzy Shier, **18** 562
Svea Choklad A.G., **II** 640
Svensk Fastighetskredit A.B., **II** 352
Svensk Golvindustri, **25** 463
Svenska A.B. Humber & Co., **I** 197
Svenska Aeroplan Aktiebolaget. *See* Saab-Scania AB.
**Svenska Cellulosa Aktiebolaget SCA, II** 365–66; **IV** 295–96, 325, 336, **338–40**, 667; **17** 398; **19** 225–26; **28 443–46 (upd.)**
Svenska Centrifug AB, **III** 418
Svenska Elektron, **III** 478
A.B. Svenska Flaktfabriken, **II** 2; **22** 8
Svenska Flygmotor A.B., **I** 209; **26** 10
**Svenska Handelsbanken, II** 353, **365–67**; **IV** 338–39; **28** 443–44
Svenska Järnvagsverkstäderna A.B., **I** 197
Svenska Kullagerfabriken A.B., **I** 209; **III** 622; **7** 565; **26** 9. *See also* AB Volvo.
Svenska Oljeslageri AB, **IV** 318
Svenska Stålpressnings AB, **26** 11
Svenska Varv, **6** 367
Svenska Varv, **27** 91
Svenskt Stål AB, **IV** 336
**Sverdrup Corporation, 14 475–78**
Sverker Martin-Löf, **IV** 339
SVF. *See* Société des Vins de France.
SVIDO, **17** 250
Sviluppo Iniziative Stradali Italiene, **IV** 420
SVPW, **I** 215
Swallow Airplane Company, **8** 49; **27** 98
Swallow Sidecar and Coach Building Company, **13** 285
Swan, **10** 170
Swan Electric Light Co., **I** 410
Swan's Down Cake Flour, **II** 531
**Swank Inc., 17 464–66**
Swann Corp., **I** 366
**Swarovski International Holding AG, 40 422–25**
**The Swatch Group SA, 7** 532–33; **25** 481; **26 479–81**
Swearingen Aircraft Company, **9** 207; **48** 169
SwedeChrome, **III** 625
Swedish Ericsson Group, **17** 353
Swedish Furniture Research Institute, **V** 82
Swedish Intercontinental Airlines, **I** 119; **34** 396
**Swedish Match AB, 39 387–90 (upd.)**
**Swedish Match S.A., IV** 336–37; **9** 381; **12 462–64**; **23** 55; **25** 464
Swedish Ordnance-FFV/Bofors AB, **9** 381–82
**Swedish Telecom, V 331–33**
Sweedor, **12** 464
Sweeney Specialty Restaurants, **14** 131
Sweeney's, **16** 559
Sweet & Maxwell, **8** 527
Sweet Life Foods Inc., **18** 507
Sweet Traditions LLC, **21** 323
**Sweetheart Cup Company, Inc., 36 460–64**
Swenson Granite Company, Inc., **37** 331
Swett & Crawford Group, **III** 357; **22** 494

Swift & Co., **II** 447, 550; **13** 351, 448; **17** 124; **41** 114
Swift Adhesives, **10** 467
Swift-Armour S.A., **II** 480
Swift-Armour S.A. Argentina, **25** 517; **26** 57
Swift-Eckrich, **II** 467
Swift Independent Packing Co., **II** 494; **13** 350, 352; **42** 92
Swift Textiles, Inc., **12** 118; **15** 247
**Swift Transportation Co., Inc.**, **26** 533; **33** 468; **42 363–66**
**Swinerton Inc.**, **43 397–400**
Swing-N-Slide, Inc. *See* PlayCore, Inc.
Swingline, Inc., **7** 3–5
Swire Group, **34** 100
**Swire Pacific Ltd.**, **I** 469–70, **521–22**; **6** 78; **16 479–81 (upd.)**; **18** 114; **20** 310, 312
**Swisher International Group Inc.**, **14** 17–19; **23 463–65**; **27** 139
**Swiss Air Transport Company Ltd.**, **I** 107, 119, **121–22**; **24** 312; **27** 409; **33** 49, 51, 271
Swiss-American Corporation, **II** 267; **21** 145
Swiss Banca de Gottardo, **26** 456
Swiss Banca della Svizzera Italiano, **II** 192
**Swiss Bank Corporation**, **II** 267, **368–70**, 378–79; **14** 419–20; **21** 145–46
Swiss Cement-Industrie-Gesellschaft, **III** 701
Swiss Colony Wines, **I** 377
Swiss Drilling Co., **IV** 372; **19** 22
**Swiss Federal Railways (Schweizerische Bundesbahnen)**, **V 519–22**
Swiss General Chocolate Co., **II** 545–46; **7** 380–81
**Swiss International Air Lines Ltd.**, **48 379–81**
Swiss Locomotive and Machine Works, **III** 631–32
Swiss Oil Co., **IV** 372–73
**Swiss Reinsurance Company (Schweizerische Rückversicherungs-Gesellschaft)**, **III** 299, 301, 335, **375–78**; **15** 13; **21** 146; **45** 110; **46 380–84 (upd.)**
Swiss Saurer AG, **39** 39, 41
Swiss Time Australia Pty Ltd, **25** 461
Swiss Volksbank, **21** 146–47
Swissair Associated Co., **I** 122; **6** 60, 96, 117; **34** 397–98; **36** 426
Swissair Group, **47** 286–87
Switchboard Inc., **25** 52
SXI Limited, **17** 458
**Sybase, Inc.**, **6** 255, 279; **10** 361, **504–06**; **11** 77–78; **15** 492; **25** 96, 299; **27 447–50 (upd.)**
SyberVision, **10** 216
Sybra, Inc., **19** 466–68
**Sybron International Corp.**, **14 479–81**; **19** 289–90
**Sycamore Networks, Inc.**, **45 388–91**
SYCOM, Inc., **18** 363
Sydney Electricity, **12** 443
Sydney Paper Mills Ltd., **IV** 248
Sydney Ross Co., **I** 698–99
Syfrets Trust Co., **IV** 23
**Sykes Enterprises, Inc.**, **45 392–95**
Sylacauga Calcium Products, **III** 691
Syllogic B.V., **29** 376
**Sylvan, Inc.**, **22 496–99**
Sylvan Lake Telephone Company, **6** 334
**Sylvan Learning Systems, Inc.**, **35 408–11**
Sylvan Learning Systems Inc., **13** 299; **34** 439
Sylvania Companies, **I** 463; **II** 63; **III** 165, 475; **V** 295; **7** 161; **8** 157; **11** 197; **13** 402; **23** 181
Sylvia Paperboard Co., **IV** 310; **19** 266
**Symantec Corporation**, **10 507–09**; **25** 348–49
Symbian Ltd., **45** 346, 348
Symbios Logic Inc., **19** 312; **31** 5
Symbiosis Corp., **10** 70
**Symbol Technologies, Inc.**, **10** 363, 523–24; **15 482–84**
Symington-Wayne, **III** 472
Symphony International, **14** 224
**Syms Corporation**, **29 456–58**
Symtron Systems Inc., **37** 399–400
Symtronix Corporation, **18** 515
Syn-Optics, Inc., **29** 454
Synbiotics Corporation, **23** 284
Syncordia Corp., **15** 69
Syncrocom, Inc., **10** 513
Syncrude Canada Limited, **25** 232
Synercom Technology Inc., **14** 319
Synercon Corporation, **25** 538
Synergen Inc., **13** 241
Synergy Dataworks, Inc., **11** 285
Synergy Software Inc., **31** 131
Synetic, Inc., **16** 59
Synfloor SA, **25** 464
**Synopsis, Inc.**, **11 489–92**; **18** 20; **43** 17
**SynOptics Communications, Inc.**, **10** 194, **510–12**; **11** 475; **16** 392; **22** 52
**Synovus Financial Corp.**, **12 465–67**; **18** 516–17
Syntax Ophthalmic Inc., **III** 727
**Syntex Corporation**, **I** 512, **701–03**; **III** 18, 53; **8** 216–17, 434, 548; **10** 53; **12** 322; **26** 384
Syntex Pharmaceuticals Ltd., **21** 425
Synthecolor S.A., **8** 347
Synthélabo, **III** 47–48
Synthetic Blood Corp., **15** 380
Synthetic Pillows, Inc., **19** 304
Syntron, Inc., **18** 513–15
**SyQuest Technology, Inc.**, **18 509–12**
Syracuse China, **8** 510
**Syratech Corp.**, **14 482–84**; **27** 288
Syrian Airways, **6** 85; **27** 133
Syroco, **14** 483–84
**SYSCO Corporation**, **II 675–76**; **9** 453; **16** 387; **18** 67; **24 470–72 (upd.)**, 528; **26** 504; **47** 457
Syscon Corporation, **38** 227
Sysorex Information Systems, **11** 62
SysScan, **V** 339
Systech Environmental Corporation, **28** 228–29
System Designers plc. *See* SD-Scicon plc.
System Development Co., **III** 166; **6** 282
System Fuels, Inc., **11** 194
System Integrators, Inc., **6** 279
System Parking West, **25** 16
**System Software Associates, Inc.**, **10 513–14**
Systematic Business Services, Inc., **48** 256–57
Systematics Inc., **6** 301; **11** 131
Systembolaget, **31** 459–60
**Systems & Computer Technology Corp.**, **19 437–39**
Systems and Services Company. *See* SYSCO Corporation.
Systems Center, Inc., **6** 279; **11** 469
Systems Construction Ltd., **II** 649
Systems Development Corp., **25** 117
Systems Engineering and Manufacturing Company, **11** 225
Systems Engineering Labs (SEL), **11** 45; **13** 201
Systems Exploration Inc., **10** 547
Systems Magnetic Co., **IV** 101
Systems Marketing Inc., **12** 78
Systronics, **13** 235
**Sytner Group plc**, **45 396–98**
Syufy Enterprises. *See* Century Theatres, Inc.
Szabo, **II** 608

T. and J. Brocklebank Ltd., **23** 160
T&N PLC, **26** 141
T-Fal. *See* Groupe SEB.
**T-Netix, Inc.**, **46 385–88**
T.G.I. Friday's, **10** 331; **19** 258; **20** 159; **21** 250; **22** 127; **44** 349
T.J. Falgout, **11** 523
T.J. Maxx, **V** 197–98; **13** 329–30; **14** 62
T. Kobayashi & Co., Ltd., **III** 44
T.L. Smith & Company, **21** 502
T/Maker, **9** 81
T. Mellon & Sons, **II** 315
**T. Rowe Price Associates, Inc.**, **10** 89; **11 493–96**; **34 423–27 (upd.)**
T.S. Farley, Limited, **10** 319
T-Shirt Brokerage Services, Inc., **26** 257
T-Tech Industries, **26** 363
T. Wear Company S.r.l., **25** 121
TA Associates Inc., **10** 382; **32** 146
TA Media AG, **15** 31
**TA Triumph-Adler AG**, **48 382–85**
**TAB Products Co.**, **17 467–69**
**Tabacalera, S.A.**, **V 414–16**; **15** 139; **17 470–73 (upd.)**
**TABCORP Holdings Limited**, **44 407–10**
Table Supply Stores, **II** 683
Tabulating Machine Company. *See* International Business Machines Corporation.
TACA. *See* Grupo TACA.
**Taco Bell Corp.**, **I** 278; **7** 267, **505–07**; **9** 178; **10** 450; **13** 336, 494; **14** 453; **15** 486; **16** 96–97; **17** 537; **21** 315, **485–88 (upd.)**; **25** 178; **37** 349, 351
**Taco Cabana, Inc.**, **23 466–68**
**Taco John's International Inc.**, **15 485–87**
Taco Kid, **7** 506
Tadiran Telecommunications Ltd., **II** 47; **25** 266–67
Taehan Cement, **III** 748
Taft Broadcasting Co. *See* Great American Broadcasting Inc.
**TAG Heuer International SA**, **7** 554; **25 459–61**
TAG Pharmaceuticals, **22** 501
Taguchi Automobile. *See* Seino Transportation Company, Ltd.
Tahoe Joe's, Inc., **32** 102 **32** 249
TAI, Ltd., **34** 397
Taiba Corporation, **8** 250
Taiheiyo Bank, **15** 495
Taikoo Dockyard Co., **I** 521; **16** 480
Taikoo Sugar Refinery, **I** 521; **16** 480
Taio Paper Mfg. Co., Ltd. *See* Daio Paper Co., Ltd.

Taisho America, **III** 295
Taisho Marine and Fire Insurance Co., Ltd., **III** 209, 295–96
Taisho Pharmaceutical, **I** 676; **II** 361
**Taittinger S.A.**, **27** 421; **43 401–05**
Taiwan Aerospace Corp., **11** 279; **24** 88
Taiwan Auto Glass, **III** 715
Taiwan Power Company, **22** 89
**Taiwan Semiconductor Manufacturing Company Ltd.**, **18** 20; **22** 197; **43** 17; **47 383–87**
Taiway, **III** 596
Taiyo Bussan, **IV** 225; **24** 489
**Taiyo Fishery Company, Limited**, **II 578–79**
**Taiyo Kobe Bank, Ltd.**, **II** 326, **371–72**
Taiyo Kogyo Corporation, **35** 98, 100
Taiyo Metal Manufacturing Co., **III** 757
Takada & Co., **IV** 151; **24** 358
Takanashi Milk Products Ltd., **37** 197
Takara, **25** 488
Takaro Shuzo, **III** 42
**Takashimaya Company, Limited**, **V 193–96**; **41** 114; **47 388–92 (upd.)**
**Take-Two Interactive Software, Inc.**, **46 389–91**
**Takeda Chemical Industries, Ltd.**, **I 704–06**; **III** 760; **46 392–95 (upd.)**
Takeda Riken, **11** 504
Takeuchi Mining Co., **III** 545
Takihyo, **15** 145
Takkyubin, **V** 537
Tako Oy, **IV** 314
**The Talbots, Inc.**, **II** 503; **10** 324; **11 497–99**; **12** 280; **31 429–432 (upd.)**
Talcott National Corporation, **11** 260–61
Talegen Holdings Inc., **26** 546
Talent Net Inc., **44** 164
Taliq Corp., **III** 715
**Talisman Energy Inc.**, **9 490–93**; **47 393–98 (upd.)**
TALK Corporation, **34** 48
Talk Radio Network, Inc., **23** 294
**Talley Industries, Inc.**, **10** 386; **16 482–85**
Tally Corp., **18** 434
Talmadge Farms, Inc., **20** 105
TAM Ceramics Inc., **III** 681; **44** 118–19
Tamar Bank, **II** 187
Tamarkin Co., **12** 390
**Tambrands Inc.**, **III** 40; **8 511–13**; **12** 439; **15** 359–60, 501; **16** 303; **26** 384; **37** 394
Tamco, **12** 390; **19** 380
TAMET, **IV** 25
Tamglass Automotive OY, **22** 436
Tampa Electric Company, **6** 582–83
Tampax Inc. *See* Tambrands Inc.
Oy Tampella Ab, **II** 47; **III** 648; **IV** 276; **25** 266
Tampere Paper Board and Roofing Felt Mill, **IV** 314
Tampereen Osake-Pankki, **II** 303
Tampimex Oil, **11** 194
TAMSA. *See* Tubos de Acero de Mexico, S.A.
Tamura Kisan Co., **II** 552
Tanaka, **6** 71
Tanaka Kikinzoku Kogyo KK, **IV** 119
Tanaka Matthey KK, **IV** 119
**Tandem Computers, Inc.**, **6 278–80**; **10** 499; **11** 18; **14** 318; **26** 93; **29** 477–79
Tandon, **25** 531
**Tandy Corporation**, **II** 70, **106–08**; **6** 257–58; **9** 43, 115, 165; **10** 56–57, 166–67, 236; **12 468–70 (upd.)**; **13** 174; **14** 117; **16** 84; **17** 353–54; **24** 502; **25** 531; **26** 18; **34** 198. *See also* RadioShack Corporation.
**Tandycrafts, Inc.**, **31 433–37**
Tangent Industries, **15** 83
Tangent Systems, **6** 247–48
Tangiers International. *See* Algo Group Inc.
Tangram Rehabilitation Network, Inc., **29** 401
Tanjong Pagar Dock Co., **I** 592
Tanks Oil and Gas, **11** 97
Tanne-Arden, Inc., **27** 291
Tanner-Brice Company, **13** 404
Tantalum Mining Corporation, **29** 81
**TAP—Air Portugal Transportes Aéreos Portugueses S.A.**, **46 396–99 (upd.)**
Tapiola Insurance, **IV** 316
Tapis-St. Maclou, **37** 22
Tappan. *See* White Consolidated Industries Inc.
Tara Exploration and Development Ltd., **IV** 165
Tara Foods, **II** 645
Target Rock Corporation, **35** 134–36
**Target Stores**, **V** 35, 43–44; **10** 284, **515–17**; **12** 508; **13** 261, 274, 446; **14** 398; **15** 275; **16** 390; **17** 460–61; **18** 108, 137, 283, 286; **20** 155; **22** 328; **27** 315, **451–54 (upd.)**; **39** 269, 271
**Tarkett Sommer AG**, **12** 464; **25 462–64**
**Tarmac plc**, **III** 734, **751–54**; **14** 250; **28 447–51 (upd.)**; **36** 21
TarMacadam (Purnell Hooley's Patent) Syndicate Ltd., **III** 751
Tarragon Oil and Gas Ltd., **24** 522
**Tarragon Realty Investors, Inc.**, **45 399–402**
Tarslag, **III** 752
TASC. *See* Analytical Sciences Corp.
Tashima Shoten, **III** 574
Tasman Pulp and Paper Co. Ltd. *See* Fletcher Challenge Ltd.
Tasman U.E.B., **IV** 249
Tasmanian Fibre Containers, **IV** 249
Tastee Freeze, **39** 234
**Tasty Baking Company**, **14 485–87**; **35 412–16 (upd.)**
TAT European Airlines, **14** 70, 73; **24** 400
Tata Airlines. *See* Air-India Limited.
Tata Enterprises, **III** 43
Tata Industries, **20** 313; **21** 74
**Tata Iron & Steel Co. Ltd.**, **IV** 48, 205–07, **217–19**; **44 411–15 (upd.)**
**Tate & Lyle PLC**, **II** 514, **580–83**; **7** 466–67; **13** 102; **26** 120; **42 367–72 (upd.)**
Tatebayashi Flour Milling Co., **II** 554
Tateisi Electric Manufacturing, **II** 75
Tateisi Medical Electronics Manufacturing Co., **II** 75
Tatham Corporation, **21** 169, 171
Tatham/RSCG, **13** 204
**Tati SA**, **25 465–67**
Tatneft. *See* OAO Tatneft.
**Tattered Cover Book Store**, **43 406–09**
**Tatung Co.**, **III** 482; **13** 387; **23 469–71**
Taurus Exploration, **21** 208
Taurus Programming Services, **10** 196
**TaurusHolding GmbH & Co. KG**, **46 400–03**
Tax Management, Inc., **23** 92
**Taylor & Francis Group plc**, **44 416–19**
Taylor Aircraft Corporation, **44** 307
**Taylor Corporation**, **36 465–67**; **37** 108
Taylor Diving and Salvage Co., **III** 499
Taylor-Evans Seed Co., **IV** 409
**Taylor Guitars**, **48 386–89**
**Taylor Made Golf Co.**, **23** 270, **472–74**; **33** 7
Taylor Material Handling, **13** 499
Taylor Medical, **14** 388
**Taylor Nelson Sofres plc**, **34 428–30**; **37** 144
Taylor Petroleum, Inc., **17** 170
**Taylor Publishing Company**, **12 471–73**; **25** 254; **36 468–71 (upd.)**
Taylor Rental Corp., **III** 628
Taylor Wines Co., **I** 234; **10** 227
**Taylor Woodrow plc**, **I 590–91**; **III** 739; **13** 206; **38 450–53 (upd.)**
Taylors and Lloyds, **II** 306
Tayto Ltd., **22** 515
Tazuke & Co., **IV** 151; **24** 358
TBC Corp., **20** 63
TBS. *See* Turner Broadcasting System, Inc.
**TBWA Advertising, Inc.**, **6 47–49**; **22** 394
TBWA Worldwide, **42** 175; **43** 412
**TBWA\Chiat\Day**, **43 410–14 (upd.)**
TC Advertising. *See* Treasure Chest Advertising, Inc.
TC Debica, **20** 264
TCA. *See* Air Canada.
TCBC. *See* Todays Computers Business Centers.
**TCBY Enterprises Inc.**, **17 474–76**
TCF. *See* Tokyo City Finance.
**TCF Financial Corporation**, **47 399–402**
TCF Holdings, Inc., **II** 170–71
TCH Corporation, **12** 477
TCI. *See* Tele-Communications, Inc.
TCI Communications, **29** 39
TCI Inc., **33** 92–93
TCI International Inc., **43** 48
TCPL. *See* TransCanada PipeLines Ltd.
TCS Management Group, Inc., **22** 53
TCW Capital, **19** 414–15
**TDK Corporation**, **I** 500; **II 109–11**; **IV** 680; **17 477–79 (upd.)**
**TDL Group Ltd.**, **46 404–06**
TDL Infomedia Ltd., **47** 347
TDS. *See* Telephone and Data Systems, Inc.
Teaberry Electronics Corp., **III** 569; **20** 361
**Teachers Insurance and Annuity Association**, **III 379–82**; **22** 268; **35** 75; **47** 331
**Teachers Insurance and Annuity Association-College Retirement Equities Fund**, **45 403–07 (upd.)**
Teachers Service Organization, Inc., **8** 9–10
Team America, **9** 435
Team Penske, **V** 494
Team Rental Group. *See* Budget Group, Inc.
Teams, Inc., **37** 247
Teamsters Central States Pension Fund, **19** 378
Teamsters Union, **13** 19
**TearDrop Golf Company**, **32 445–48**
Tebel Maschinefabrieken, **III** 420
Tebel Pneumatiek, **III** 420

**Tech Data Corporation**, **10 518–19**
Tech Pacific International, **18** 180; **39** 201, 203
**Tech-Sym Corporation**, **18 513–15**; **44 420–23 (upd.)**
Tech Textiles, USA, **15** 247–48
Techalloy Co., **IV** 228
Technair Packaging Laboratories, **18** 216
Technical Ceramics Laboratories, Inc., **13** 141
Technical Coatings Co., **13** 85; **38** 96–97
Technical Materials, Inc., **14** 81
Technical Olympic USA, **46** 180
Technical Publishing, **IV** 605
Technicare, **11** 200
Technicolor Inc., **28** 246
Technicon Instruments Corporation, **III** 56; **11** 333–34; **22** 75
Technifax, **8** 483
Techniques d'Avant-Garde. *See* TAG Heuer International SA.
Technisch Bureau Visser, **16** 421
**Technitrol, Inc.**, **29 459–62**
Techno-Success Company, **V** 719
AB Technology, **II** 466
Technology Management Group, Inc., **18** 112
Technology Resources International Ltd., **18** 76
Technology Venture Investors, **11** 490; **14** 263
Technophone Ltd., **17** 354
TechTeam Europe, Ltd., **41** 281
**Teck Corporation**, **9** 282; **27 455–58**
Tecnamotor S.p.A., **8** 72, 515
Tecneco, **IV** 422
Tecnifax Corp., **IV** 330
Tecnipublicaciones, **14** 555
Tecnost S.p.A., **34** 319
**TECO Energy, Inc.**, **6 582–84**
Tecom Industries, Inc., **18** 513–14
Tecstar, Inc., **30** 436
**Tecumseh Products Company**, **8** 72, **514–16**
Ted Bates, Inc., **I** 33, 623; **10** 69; **16** 71–72
Teddy's Shoe Store. *See* Morse Shoe Inc.
Tedelex, **IV** 91–92
**Teekay Shipping Corporation**, **25 468–71**
Tees and Hartlepool, **31** 367, 369
Tefal. *See* Groupe SEB.
TEFSA, **17** 182
TEIC. *See* B.V. Tabak Export & Import Compagnie.
**Teijin Limited**, **I** 511; **V 380–82**
Teikoku Bank, **I** 507; **II** 273, 325–26
Teikoku Hormone, **I** 704
Teikoku Jinken. *See* Teijin Limited.
Teikoku Sekiyu Co. Ltd., **IV** 475
Teikoku Shiki, **IV** 326
Teito Electric Railway, **V** 461
Teito Transport Co. Ltd., **V** 536
Tejas Gas Co., **41** 359
Tejas Snacks LP, **44** 349
**Tejon Ranch Company**, **35 417–20**
Teklogix International, **45** 346, 348
Tekmunc A/S, **17** 288
Teknekron Infoswitch Corporation, **22** 51
Teknika Electronics Corporation, **43** 459
Tekrad, Inc. *See* Tektronix, Inc.
Tekton Corp., **IV** 346
**Tektronix, Inc.**, **II** 101; **8 517–21**; **10** 24; **11** 284–86; **12** 454; **36** 331; **38** 71; **39** 350, 353; **41** 235
Tel-A-Data Limited, **11** 111
TelAutograph Corporation, **29** 33–34
Telcon. *See* Telegraph Construction and Maintenance Company.
**Tele-Communications, Inc.**, **II 160–62**, 167; **10** 484, 506; **11** 479; **13** 280; **15** 264–65; **17** 148; **18** 64–66, 211, 213, 535; **19** 282; **21** 307, 309; **23** 121, 502; **24** 6, 120; **25** 213–14; **26** 33; **28** 241; **38** 120; **42** 114–15; **43** 433
Tele Consulte, **14** 555
Télé Luxembourg, **44** 376
Telebook, **25** 19
Telec Centre S.A., **19** 472
TeleCheck Services, **18** 542
TeleCheck Services, Inc., **11** 113
TeleChef, **33** 387, 389
Teleclub, **IV** 590
Teleco Oilfield Services Inc., **6** 578; **22** 68
TeleColumbus, **11** 184
**Telecom Australia**, **6 341–42**
Telecom Canada. *See* Stentor Canadian Network Management.
**Telecom Eireann**, **7 508–10**. *See also* eircom plc.
**Telecom Italia S.p.A.**, **15** 355; **24** 79; **34** 316, 319; **43 415–19**; **47** 345–46
Telecom New Zealand, **18** 33
Telecom One, Inc., **29** 252
Telecom*USA, **27** 304
Telecommunications of Jamaica Ltd., **25** 101
Telecomputing Corp., **I** 544
Telecredit, Inc., **6** 25
Telectronic Pacing Systems, **10** 445
**Teledyne Inc.**, **I** 486, **523–25**; **II** 33, 44; **10** 262–63, 365, **520–22 (upd.)**; **11** 265; **13** 387; **17** 109; **18** 369; **29** 400; **35** 136
Teleflora Inc., **28** 1 8–90; **19** 12; **21** 259
Teleflora LLC, **37** 337
**Telefonaktiebolaget LM Ericsson**, **V 334–36**; **46 407–11 (upd.)**
**Telefónica de España, S.A.**, **V 337–40**; **43** 422
**Telefónica S.A.**, **46** 172, **412–17 (upd.)**
**Telefonos de Mexico S.A. de C.V.**, **14 488–90**
Téléfrance, **25** 174
Telefunken Fernseh & Rundfunk GmbH., **I** 411; **II** 117
telegate AG, **18** 155; **47** 345, 347
Teleglobe Inc., **14** 512
Telegraph Condenser Co., **II** 81
Telegraph Construction and Maintenance Company, **25** 98–100
Telegraph Manufacturing Co., **III** 433
Telegraph Works, **III** 433
Telegraphic Service Company, **16** 166
Telekomunikacja S.A., **18** 33
Telelistas Editors Ltda., **26** 520
TeleMarketing Corporation of Louisiana, **8** 311
Telemarketing Investments, Ltd., **8** 311
Telematics International Inc., **18** 154, 156
Télémécanique, **II** 94; **18** 473; **19** 166
Telemundo Group, Inc., **III** 344; **24** 516
Telenet Communications, **18** 32
Telenet Information Services, **47** 37
Telenor, **31** 221
Telenorma, **I** 193
Telenova, **III** 169; **6** 285
Teleos Communications Inc., **26** 277
**Telephone and Data Systems, Inc.**, **9 494–96**, 527–529; **31** 449
Telephone Company of Ireland, **7** 508
Telephone Exchange Company of Indianapolis, **14** 257
Telephone Management Corporation, **8** 310
Telephone Utilities, Inc. *See* Pacific Telecom, Inc.
Telephone Utilities of Washington, **6** 325, 328
Telepictures, **II** 177
**TelePizza S.A.**, **33 387–89**
Teleport Communications Group, **14** 253; **24** 122
Teleprompter Corp., **II** 122; **7** 222; **10** 210; **18** 355
Telerate Systems Inc., **IV** 603, 670; **10** 276–78; **21** 68; **47** 102–03
Teleregister Corp., **I** 512
Telerent Europe. *See* Granada Group PLC.
TeleRep, **IV** 596
Telesat Cable TV, Inc., **23** 293
Telesis Oil and Gas, **6** 478
Telesistema, **18** 212
Telesistema Mexico. *See* Grupo Televisa.
TeleSite, U.S.A., Inc., **44** 442
Telesphere Network, Inc., **8** 310
Telesystems SLW Inc., **10** 524
Telettra S.p.A., **V** 326; **9** 10; **11** 205
Tele2 AB, **26** 331–33
Teletype Corp., **14** 569
Televimex, S.A., **18** 212
Television de Mexico, S.A., **18** 212
**Television Española, S.A.**, **7 511–12**; **18** 211
**Télévision Française 1**, **23 475–77**
Television Sales and Marketing Services Ltd., **7** 79–80
Teleway Japan, **7** 118–19; **13** 482
Telex Corporation, **II** 87; **13** 127
Telfin, **V** 339
Telia Mobitel, **11** 19; **26** 332
Telihoras Corporation, **10** 319
Telinfo, **6** 303
Telinq Inc., **10** 19
Telios Pharmaceuticals, Inc., **11** 460; **17** 288
**Tellabs, Inc.**, **11 500–01**; **40 426–29 (upd.)**; **45** 390
Telmex. *See* Teléfonos de México S.A. de C.V.
Telpar, Inc., **14** 377
Telport, **14** 260
Telrad Telecommunications Ltd., **II** 48; **25** 266–67
**Telxon Corporation**, **10 523–25**
Tembec, Inc., **IV** 296; **19** 226
Temco Electronics and Missile Co., **I** 489
Temenggong of Jahore, **I** 592
Temerlin McClain, **23** 479; **25** 91
TEMIC TELEFUNKEN, **34** 128, 133, 135
Temp Force, **16** 421–22; **43** 308
Temp World, Inc., **6** 10
Temple, Barker & Sloan/Strategic Planning Associates, **III** 283
Temple Frosted Foods, **25** 278
Temple Inks Company, **13** 227
**Temple-Inland Inc.**, **IV** 312, **341–43**, 675; **8** 267–69; **19** 268; **31 438–442 (upd.)**
Temple Press Ltd., **IV** 294–95; **19** 225
Templeton, **II** 609
TEMPO Enterprises, **II** 162
Tempo-Team, **16** 420; **43** 307

Thermal Energies, Inc., **21** 514
Thermal Power Company, **11** 270
Thermal Snowboards, Inc., **22** 462
Thermal Transfer Ltd., **13** 485
ThermaStor Technologies, Ltd., **44** 366
**Thermo BioAnalysis Corp.**, **25 475–78**
**Thermo Electron Corporation**, **7 520–22**; **11** 512–13; **13** 421; **24** 477; **25** 475–76
**Thermo Fibertek, Inc.**, **24 477–79**
**Thermo Instrument Systems Inc.**, **11 512–14**; **25** 475–77
**Thermo King Corporation**, **13 505–07**
Thermodynamics Corp., **III** 645
Thermoforming USA, **16** 339
Thermogas Co., **IV** 458–59; **35** 175
Thermolase Corporation, **22** 410
Thermoplast und Apparatebau GmbH, **IV** 198
**Thermos Company**, **16 486–88**
TheStreet.com, **34** 125
Thies Companies, **13** 270
Thiess, **III** 687
Thiess Dampier Mitsui, **IV** 47
Things Remembered, **13** 165–66
Think Entertainment, **II** 161
Think Technologies, **10** 508
**Thiokol Corporation**, **I** 370; **8** 472; **9** 358–59, **500–02 (upd.)**; **12** 68; **22 504–07 (upd.)**
Third National Bank. *See* Fifth Third Bancorp.
Third National Bank of Dayton, **9** 475
Third National Bank of New York, **II** 253
Third Wave Publishing Corp. *See* Acer Inc.
Thirteen/WNET. *See* Educational Broadcasting Corporation.
Thistle Group, **9** 365
Thom McAn, **V** 136–37; **11** 349
**Thomas & Betts Corp.**, **II** 8; **11 515–17**; **14** 27
Thomas and Hochwalt, **I** 365
Thomas & Howard Co., **II** 682; **18** 8
Thomas and Judith Pyle, **13** 433
Thomas Barlow & Sons Ltd., **I** 288, 422; **IV** 22
Thomas Bros. Maps, **28** 380
Thomas Cook Group Ltd., **17** 325
**Thomas Cook Travel Inc.**, **6** 84; **9 503–05**; **27** 133; **33 394–96 (upd.)**; **42** 282
Thomas De La Rue and Company, Ltd., **44** 357–58
Thomas Firth & Sons, **I** 573
**Thomas H. Lee Co.**, **11** 156, 450; **14** 230–31; **15** 309; **19** 371, 373; **24 480–83**; **25** 67; **28** 134; **30** 219; **32** 362
**Thomas Industries Inc.**, **29 466–69**
**Thomas J. Lipton Company**, **II** 609, 657; **11** 450; **14 495–97**; **16** 90; **32** 474
Thomas Jefferson Life Insurance Co., **III** 397
Thomas Kinkade Galleries. *See* Media Arts Group, Inc.
Thomas Linnell & Co. Ltd., **II** 628
Thomas Nationwide Transport. *See* TNT.
Thomas Nationwide Transport Limited. *See* TNT Post Group N.V.
**Thomas Nelson Inc.**, **8** 526; **14 498–99**; **24** 548; **38 454–57 (upd.)**
**Thomas Publishing Company**, **26 482–85**
Thomas Tilling plc, **I** 429
Thomas Y. Crowell, **IV** 605
**Thomaston Mills, Inc.**, **27 467–70**
**Thomasville Furniture Industries, Inc.**, **III** 423; **12 474–76**; **22** 48; **28** 406; **31** 248; **39** 170, 174
Thompson and Formby, **16** 44
Thompson Aircraft Tire Corp., **14** 42
Thompson-Hayward Chemical Co., **13** 397
Thompson Medical Company. *See* Slim-Fast Nutritional Foods International Inc.
Thompson Nutritional Products, **37** 286
Thompson PBE Inc., **24** 160–61
Thompson Products Co., **I** 539
Thompson-Ramo-Woolridge, **I** 539
Thompson-Werke, **III** 32
Thomson BankWatch Inc., **19** 34
Thomson-Bennett, **III** 554
Thomson-Brandt, **I** 411; **II** 13, 116–17; **9** 9
**The Thomson Corporation**, **IV** 651, 686; **7** 390; **8 525–28**; **10** 407; **12** 361, 562; **17** 255; **22** 441; **34 435–40 (upd.)**; **44** 155
Thomson-CSF, **II** 116–17; **III** 556. *See also* Thales S.A.
Thomson-Houston Electric Co., **II** 27, 116, 330; **12** 193
Thomson International, **37** 143
Thomson-Jenson Energy Limited, **13** 558
Thomson-Lucas, **III** 556
**THOMSON multimedia S.A.**, **18** 126; **36** 384; **42 377–80 (upd.)**
Thomson-Ramo-Woolridge. *See* TRW Inc.
**Thomson S.A.**, **I** 411; **II** 31, **116–17**; **7** 9; **13** 402. *See also* THOMSON multimedia S.A.
Thomson T-Line, **II** 142
Thomson Travel Group, **27** 27
Thonet Industries Inc., **14** 435–36
**Thor Industries, Inc.**, **39 391–94**
**Thorn Apple Valley, Inc.**, **7 523–25**; **12** 125; **22 508–11 (upd.)**; **23** 203
**Thorn EMI plc**, **I** 52, 411, **531–32**; **II** 117, 119; **III** 480; **19** 390; **22** 27, 192–94; **24** 87, 484–85; **26** 151; **40** 105
**Thorn plc**, **24 484–87**
Thorncraft Inc., **25** 379
Thorndike, Doran, Paine and Lewis, Inc., **14** 530
Thornton, **III** 547
Thornton & Co., **II** 283
Thornton Stores, **14** 235
**Thorntons plc**, **46 424–26**
Thoroughgood, **II** 658
Thorsen Realtors, **21** 96
Thos. & Wm. Molson & Company. *See* The Molson Companies Limited.
**Thousand Trails, Inc.**, **13** 494; **33 397–99**
Thousands Springs Power Company, **12** 265
**THQ, Inc.**, **39 395–97**
Threadz, **25** 300
Three-Diamond Company. *See* Mitsubishi Shokai.
**The 3DO Company**, **10** 286; **43 426–30**
3 Guys, **II** 678, **V** 35
3-in-One Oil Co., **I** 622
3 Maj, **25** 469
Three Rivers Pulp and Paper Company, **17** 281
Three Score, **23** 100
3 Suisses International, **12** 281
**3Com Corporation**, **III** 143; **6** 238, 269; **10** 237; **11 518–21**; **20** 8, 33; **26** 276; **34 441–45 (upd.)**; **36** 122, 300, 357. *See also* Palm, Inc.
3D Planet SpA, **41** 409
3M. *See* Minnesota Mining & Manufacturing Co.
3S Systems Support Services Ltd., **6** 310
360networks inc., **46** 268
Threlfall Breweries, **I** 294
Threshold Entertainment, **25** 270
Thrif D Discount Center, **V** 174
Thrift Drug, **V** 92
Thrift Mart, **16** 65
ThriftiCheck Service Corporation, **7** 145
Thriftimart Inc., **12** 153; **16** 452
Thriftway Food Drug, **21** 530
Thriftway Foods, **II** 624
Thrifty Corporation, **25** 413, 415–16
**Thrifty PayLess, Inc.**, **V** 682, 684; ; **12 477–79**; **18** 286; **19** 357; **25** 297
Thrifty Rent-A-Car, **6** 349; **24** 10; **44** 355. *See also* Dollar Thrifty Automotive Group, Inc.
Throwing Corporation of America, **12** 501
Thrustmaster S.A., **41** 190
Thummel Schutze & Partner, **28** 141
Thunder Bay Press, **34** 3–5
Thuringia Insurance Co., **III** 299
Thurmond Chemicals, Inc., **27** 291
Thurston Motor Lines Inc., **12** 310
Thy-Marcinelle, **IV** 52
**Thyssen AG**, **II** 279; **III** 566; **IV** 195, **221–23**, 228; **8** 75–76; **14** 169, 328
**Thyssen Krupp AG**, **28** 104, **452–60 (upd.)**; **42** 417
Thyssen-Krupp Stahl AG, **26** 83
Thyssengas, **38** 406–07
TI. *See* Texas Instruments.
TI Corporation, **10** 44
**TI Group plc**, **17 480–83**
TIAA-CREF. *See* Teachers Insurance and Annuity Association-College Retirement Equities Fund.
Tianjin Agricultural Industry and Commerce Corp., **II** 577
Tianjin Automobile Industry Group, **21** 164
Tianjin Bohai Brewing Company, **21** 230
Tibbals Floring Co., **III** 611
**Tibbett & Britten Group plc**, **32 449–52**
Tiber Construction Company, **16** 286
Tichenor Media System Inc., **35** 220
Ticino Societa d'Assicurazioni Sulla Vita, **III** 197
**Ticketmaster Corp.**, **13 508–10**; **25** 214; **36** 423–24
**Ticketmaster Group, Inc.**, **37 381–84 (upd.)**; **47** 419, 421
Ticketron, **13** 508–09; **24** 438; **37** 381–82
Tichnor & Fields, **10** 356
Tickometer Co., **III** 157
Ticor Title Insurance Co., **10** 45
Tidel Systems, **II** 661; **32** 416
**Tidewater Inc.**, **11 522–24**; **37 385–88 (upd.)**
Tidewater Oil Co., **IV** 434, 460, 489, 522
Tidewater Utilities, Inc., **45** 275, 277
Tidi Wholesale, **13** 150
Tidy House Products Co., **II** 556
Tiel Utrecht Fire Insurance Co., **III** 309–10
Tien Wah Press (Pte.) Ltd., **IV** 600
Le Tierce S.A., **II** 141
Tierco Group, Inc., **27** 382
Tierney & Partners, **23** 480
**Tiffany & Co.**, **III** 16; **12** 312; **14 500–03**; **15** 95; **19** 27; **26** 145; **27** 329; **41** 256

**TIG Holdings, Inc., 26 486–88**
Tiger Accessories, **18** 88
Tiger International, Inc., **17** 505; **18** 178; **42** 141
Tiger Management Associates, **13** 158, 256
Tiger Oats, **I** 424
Tigon Corporation, **V** 265–68; **41** 288
Tilcon, **I** 429
Tilden Interrent, **10** 419
Tile & Coal Company, **14** 248
Tilgate Pallets, **I** 592
Tillie Lewis Foods Inc., **I** 513–14
Tillinghast, Nelson & Warren Inc., **32** 459
**Tillotson Corp., 14** 64; **15 488–90**
Tim-Bar Corp., **IV** 312; **19** 267
Tim Horton's Restaurants, **23** 507; **47** 443. *See also* TDL Group Ltd.
Timber Lodge Steakhouse, Inc., **37** 351–52
Timber Realization Co., **IV** 305
**The Timberland Company, 11** 349; **13 511–14**; **17** 245; **19** 112; **22** 173; **25** 206
**Timberline Software Corporation, 15 491–93**
TIMCO. *See* Triad International Maintenance Corp.
Time Distribution Services, **13** 179
Time Electronics, **19** 311
Time Industries, **IV** 294; **19** 225; **26** 445
Time-Life Books, Inc. **44** 447, 449. *See also* Time Warner Inc.
Time Life Music, **44** 242
Time-O-Stat Controls Corp., **II** 41; **12** 247
Time Saver Stores, Inc., **12** 112; **17** 170
Time-Sharing Information, **10** 357
**Time Warner Inc., II** 155, 161, 168, 175–177, 252, 452; **III** 245; **IV** 341–42, 636, **673–76**; **6** 293; **7** 63, 222–24, 396, **526–30 (upd.)**; **8** 267–68, 527; **9** 119, 469, 472; **10** 168, 286, 484, 488, 491; **12** 531; **13** 105–06, 399; **14** 260; **15** 51, 54; **16** 146, 223; **17** 148, 442–44; **18** 66, 535; **19** 6, 336; **22** 52, 194, 522; **23** 31, 33, 257, 274, 276, 393; **24** 321–22; **25** 141, 498–99; **26** 33, 151, 441; **27** 121, 429–30; **43** 55
Timely Brands, **I** 259
Timeplex, **III** 166; **6** 283; **9** 32
Times Fiber Communications, Inc., **40** 35–36
Times Media Ltd., **IV** 22
**The Times Mirror Company, I** 90; **IV** 583, 630, **677–78**; **14** 97; **17 484–86 (upd.)**; **21** 404; **22** 162, 443; **26** 446; **35** 419
Times Newspapers, **8** 527
Times-Picayune Publishing Co., **IV** 583
TIMET. *See* Titanium Metals Corporation.
**Timex Corporation, 25 479–82 (upd.)**
**Timex Enterprises Inc., III** 455; **7 531–33**; **10** 152; **12** 317; **21** 123; **25** 22
**The Timken Company, III** 596; **7** 447; **8 529–31**; **15** 225; **42 381–85 (upd.)**
Timothy Whites, **24** 74
Timpte Industries, **II** 488
Tioxide Group plc, **III** 680; **44** 117, 119
Tip Corp., **I** 278
Tip Top Drugstores plc, **24** 269
Tip Top Tailors, **29** 162
TIPC Network. *See* Gateway 2000.
Tiphook PLC, **13** 530
Tipton Centers Inc., **V** 50; **19** 123
Tiroler Hauptbank, **II** 270
**Tiscali SpA, 48 396–99**
TISCO. *See* Tata Iron & Steel Company Ltd.
Tishman Realty and Construction, **III** 248
**Tishman Speyer Properties, L.P., 47 403–06**
Tissue Papers Ltd., **IV** 260
Tissue Technologies, Inc., **22** 409
**The Titan Corporation, 36 475–78**; **45** 68, 70
Titan Manufacturing Company, **19** 359
**Titanium Metals Corporation, 10** 434; **21 489–92**
Titanium Technology Corporation, **13** 140
Titianium Enterprises, **IV** 345
TITISA, **9** 109
Title Guarantee & Trust Co., **II** 230
Titmus Optical Inc., **III** 446
Titmuss Sainer Dechert. *See* Dechert.
Tivoli Audio, **48** 85
Tivoli Systems, Inc., **14** 392
**TJ International, Inc., 19 444–47**
**The TJX Companies, Inc., V 197–98**; **13** 548; **14** 426; **19 448–50 (upd.)**; **29** 106
TKD Electronics Corp., **II** 109
TKM Foods, **II** 513
TKR Cable Co., **15** 264
TLC Associates, **11** 261
**TLC Beatrice International Holdings, Inc., 22 512–15**
TLC Gift Company, **26** 375
TLC Group, **II** 468
TLO, **25** 82
TMB Industries, **24** 144
TMC Industries Ltd., **22** 352
TML Information Services Inc., **9** 95
**TMP Worldwide Inc., 30 458–60**
TMS, Inc., **7** 358
TMS Marketing, **26** 440
TMS Systems, Inc., **10** 18
TMT. *See* Trailer Marine Transport.
TMW Capital Inc., **48** 286
TN Technologies Inc., **23** 479
TNT Crust, Inc., **23** 203
**TNT Freightways Corporation, IV** 651; **14 504–06**
**TNT Limited, V 523–25**; **6** 346
**TNT Post Group N.V., 27 471–76 (upd.)**; **30** 393, **461–63 (upd.)**
Toa Airlines, **I** 106; **6** 427
Toa Fire & Marine Reinsurance Co., **III** 385
Toa Kyoseki Co. Ltd., **IV** 476
Toa Medical Electronics Ltd., **22** 75
Toa Nenryo Kogyo, **IV** 432
Toa Oil Co. Ltd., **IV** 476, 543
Toa Tanker Co. Ltd., **IV** 555
Toasted Corn Flake Co., **II** 523; **13** 291
Toastmaster, **17** 215; **22** 353
Tobacco Group PLC, **30** 231
Tobacco Products Corporation, **18** 416
Tobata Imaon Co., **I** 183
Tobias, **16** 239
Tobler Co., **II** 520–21
**Tobu Railway Co Ltd, 6 430–32**
TOC Retail Inc., **17** 170
Tocom, Inc., **10** 320
**Today's Man, Inc., 20 484–87**; **21** 311
Todays Computers Business Centers, **6** 243–44
Todays Temporary, **6** 140
**The Todd-AO Corporation, 33 400–04.** *See also* Liberty Livewire Corporation.
**Todd Shipyards Corporation, IV** 121; **7** 138; **14 507–09**
**Todhunter International, Inc., 27 477–79**
Todito.com, S.A. de C.V., **39** 194, 196
Todorovich Agency, **III** 204
Toei Co. Ltd., **9** 29–30; **28** 462
Tofas, **I** 479–80
Toggenburger Bank, **II** 378
Togo's Eatery, **29** 19
**Toho Co., Ltd., I** 363; **IV** 403; **24** 327; **28 461–63**
Tohoku Alps, **II** 5
Tohoku Pulp Co., **IV** 297
Tohokushinsha Film Corporation, **18** 429
**Tohuku Electric Power Company, Inc., V** 724, 732
Tojo Railway Company, **6** 430
Tokai Aircraft Co., Ltd., **III** 415
**The Tokai Bank, Limited, II 373–74**; **15 494–96 (upd.)**
Tokai Kogyo Co. Ltd., **I** 615; **48** 42
Tokai Paper Industries, **IV** 679
**Tokheim Corporation, 21 493–95**
**Tokio Marine and Fire Insurance Co., Ltd., II** 323; **III** 248, 289, 295, **383–86**
Tokos Medical Corporation, **17** 306, 308–09
Tokushima Ham Co., **II** 550
Tokushima Meat Processing Factory, **II** 550
Tokushu Seiko, Ltd., **IV** 63
Tokuyama Soda, **I** 509
Tokuyama Teppan Kabushikigaisha, **IV** 159
Tokyo Broadcasting System, **7** 249; **9** 29; **16** 167
Tokyo Car Manufacturing Co., **I** 105
Tokyo City Finance, **36** 419–20
Tokyo Confectionery Co., **II** 538
Tokyo Corporation, **V** 199
Tokyo Dairy Industry, **II** 538
Tokyo Denki Kogaku Kogyo, **II** 109
Tokyo Dento Company, **6** 430
Tokyo Disneyland, **IV** 715; **6** 123, 176
Tokyo Electric Company, Ltd., **I** 533; **12** 483
Tokyo Electric Express Railway Co., **IV** 728
Tokyo Electric Light Co., **IV** 153
**Tokyo Electric Power Company, IV** 167, 518; **V 729–33**
Tokyo Electronic Corp., **11** 232
Tokyo Express Highway Co., Ltd., **IV** 713–14
Tokyo Express Railway Company, **V** 510, 526
Tokyo Fire Insurance Co. Ltd., **III** 405–06, 408
Tokyo Food Products, **I** 507
Tokyo Fuhansen Co., **I** 502, 506
Tokyo Gas and Electric Industrial Company, **9** 293
**Tokyo Gas Co., Ltd., IV** 518; **V 734–36**
Tokyo Ishikawajima Shipbuilding and Engineering Company, **III** 532; **9** 293
Tokyo Maritime Insurance Co., **III** 288
Tokyo Motors. *See* Isuzu Motors, Ltd.
Tokyo Sanyo Electric, **II** 91–92
Tokyo Shibaura Electric Company, Ltd., **I** 507, 533; **12** 483
Tokyo Steel Works Co., Ltd., **IV** 63
Tokyo Stock Exchange, **34** 254
Tokyo Tanker Co., Ltd., **IV** 479
Tokyo Telecommunications Engineering Corp. *See* Tokyo Tsushin Kogyo K.K.
Tokyo Trust & Banking Co., **II** 328

Tokyo Tsushin Kogyo K.K., **II** 101, 103
Tokyo Yokohama Electric Railways Co., Ltd., **V** 199
**Tokyu Corporation**, **IV** 728; **V** 199, **526–28**; **47 407–10 (upd.)**
**Tokyu Department Store Co., Ltd.**, **V 199–202**; **32 453–57 (upd.)**
Toledo Edison Company. *See* Centerior Energy Corporation.
Toledo Milk Processing, Inc., **15** 449
Toledo Scale Corp., **9** 441; **30** 327
Toledo Seed & Oil Co., **I** 419
**Toll Brothers Inc.**, **15 497–99**
**Tollgrade Communications, Inc.**, **44 424–27**
Tom Bowling Lamp Works, **III** 554
**Tom Brown, Inc.**, **37 389–91**
**Tom Doherty Associates Inc.**, **25 483–86**
Tom Huston Peanut Co., **II** 502; **10** 323
Tom Piper Ltd., **I** 437
Tom Snyder Productions, **29** 470, 472
Tom Thumb, **40** 365–66
Tom Thumb-Page, **16** 64
**Tom's of Maine, Inc.**, **45 414–16**
Tomakomai Paper Co., Ltd., **IV** 321
Toman Corporation, **19** 390
**Tombstone Pizza Corporation**, **13 515–17**
Tomei Fire and Marine Insurance Co., **III** 384–85
**Tomen Corporation**, **IV 224–25**; **19** 256; **24 488–91 (upd.)**
Tomen Transportgerate, **III** 638
Tomkins-Johnson Company, **16** 8
**Tomkins plc**, **11 525–27**; **28** 382, 384; **30** 424, 426; **44 428–31 (upd.)**
Tomlee Tool Company, **7** 535; **26** 493
Tommy Armour Golf Co., **32** 446–47
**Tommy Hilfiger Corporation**, **16** 61; **20 488–90**; **25** 258
Tomoe Trading Co., **III** 595
Tonami Transportation Company, **6** 346
**Tone Brothers, Inc.**, **21 496–98**
Tone Coca-Cola Bottling Company, Ltd., **14** 288; **47** 206
**Tonen Corporation**, **IV 554–56**; **16 489–92 (upd.)**
Tong Yang Group, **III** 304
Toni Co., **III** 28; **9** 413
**Tonka Corporation**, **12** 169; **14** 266; **16** 267; **25** 380, **487–89**; **43** 229, 232
Tonkin, Inc., **19** 114
Tony Lama Company Inc., **19** 233
Tony Roma's, A Place for Ribs Inc., **40** 340–41
Tony Stone Images, **31** 216–17
Toohey, **10** 170
**Toolex International N.V.**, **26 489–91**
Tootal Group, **V** 356–57
**Tootsie Roll Industries Inc.**, **12 480–82**; **15** 323
Top End Wheelchair Sports, **11** 202
Top Green International, **17** 475
Top Man, **V** 21
Top Shop, **V** 21
Top Tool Company, Inc., **25** 75
Top Value Stamp Co., **II** 644–45; **6** 364; **22** 126
Topco Associates, **17** 78
Topkapi, **17** 101–03
**Toppan Printing Co., Ltd.**, **IV** 598–99, **679–81**
**Topps Company, Inc.**, **13 518–20**; **19** 386; **34 446–49 (upd.)**
Topps Markets, **16** 314
**Tops Appliance City, Inc.**, **17 487–89**
TopTip, **48** 116
Topy Industries, Limited, **8** 506–07
Tor Books. *See* Tom Doherty Associates Inc.
**Toray Industries, Inc.**, **V** 380, **383; 17** 287
Torbensen Gear & Axle Co., **I** 154
**Torchmark Corporation**, **III** 194; **9 506–08**; **10** 66; **11** 17; **22** 540–43; **33 405–08 (upd.)**
Torfeaco Industries Limited, **19** 304
Torise Ham Co., **II** 550
Tornator Osakeyhtiö, **IV** 275–76
Toro Assicurazioni, **III** 347
**The Toro Company**, **III** 600; **7 534–36**; **26 492–95 (upd.)**
**Toromont Industries, Ltd.**, **21 499–501**
Toronto and Scarborough Electric Railway, **9** 461
**Toronto-Dominion Bank**, **II** 319, **375–77**, 456; **16** 13–14; **17** 324; **18** 551–53; **21** 447; **43** 7
Toronto Electric Light Company, **9** 461
Toronto Sun Publishing Company. *See* Sun Media.
Torpshammars, **IV** 338
Torrey Canyon Oil, **IV** 569; **24** 519
**The Torrington Company**, **III** 526, 589–90; **13 521–24**
Torrington National Bank & Trust Co., **13** 467
**Torstar Corporation**, **IV** 672; **7** 488–89; **19** 405; **29 470–73**
Tosa Electric Railway Co., **II** 458
Toscany Co., **13** 42
**Tosco Corporation**, **7 537–39**; **12** 240; **20** 138; **24** 522; **36** 359; **40** 358
**Toshiba Corporation**, **I** 221, 507–08, **533–35**; **II** 5, 56, 59, 62, 68, 73, 99, 102, 118, 122, 326, 440; **III** 298, 461, 533, 604; **6** 101, 231, 244, 287; **7** 529; **9** 7, 181; **10** 518–19; **11** 46, 328; **12** 454, **483–86 (upd.)**, 546; **13** 324, 399, 482; **14** 117, 446; **16** 5, 167; **17** 533; **18** 18, 260; **21** 390; **22** 193, 373; **23** 471; **40 435–40 (upd.)**; **43** 15;
Toshiba Corporation, **47** 153–54
Toshin Kaihatsu Ltd., **V** 195; **47** 390
Toshin Paper Co., Ltd., **IV** 285
Tostem. *See* Toyo Sash Co., Ltd.
Total Audio Visual Services, **24** 95
Total Beverage Corporation, **16** 159, 161
**Total Compagnie Française des Pétroles S.A.**, **I** 303; **II** 259; **III** 673; **IV** 363–64, 423–25, 466, 486, 498, 504, 515, 525, 544–47, **557–61**; **V** 628; **7** 481–84; **13** 557; **21** 203
**Total Entertainment Restaurant Corporation**, **46 427–29**
Total Exploration S.A., **11** 537
Total Fina Elf S.A., **47** 342, 365, 368
Total Global Sourcing, Inc., **10** 498
Total Home Entertainment (THE), **39** 240, 242
Total Petroleum Corporation, **21** 500
**TOTAL S.A.**, **24 492–97 (upd.)**, 522; **25** 104; **26** 369
**Total System Services, Inc.**, **12** 465–66; **18** 168, 170, **516–18**
**Totem Resources Corporation**, **9 509–11**
Totino's Finer Foods, **II** 556; **13** 516; **26** 436
Toto Bank, **II** 326
**TOTO LTD.**, **III 755–56**; **28 464–66 (upd.)**
Totsu Co., **I** 493; **24** 325
Touch America Inc., **37** 127; **44** 288
Touch-It Corp., **22** 413
Touche Remnant Holdings Ltd., **II** 356
Touche Ross. *See* Deloitte Touche Tohmatsu International.
Touchstone Films, **II** 172–74; **6** 174–76; **30** 487
Le Touquet's, SA, **48** 197
Tour d'Argent, **II** 518
Tourang Limited, **7** 253
**Touristik Union International GmbH. and Company K.G.**, **II 163–65**; **46** 460
Touron y Cia, **III** 419
Touropa, **II** 163–64; **44** 432
Toval Japon, **IV** 680
Towa Nenryo Kogyo Co. Ltd., **IV** 554–55
Towa Optical Manufacturing Company, **41** 261–63
**Tower Air, Inc.**, **28 467–69**
**Tower Automotive, Inc.**, **24 498–500**
Tower Records, **9** 361; **10** 335; **11** 558; **30** 224. *See also* MTS Inc.
Towers, **II** 649
**Towers Perrin**, **32 458–60**
Towle Manufacturing Co., **14** 482–83; **18** 69
Town & City, **IV** 696
**Town & Country Corporation**, **7** 372; **16** 546; **19 451–53**; **25** 254
Town Investments, **IV** 711
**Town Sports International, Inc.**, **46 430–33**
Townsend Hook, **IV** 296, 650, 652; **19** 226
Toxicol Laboratories, Ltd., **21** 424
**Toy Biz, Inc.**, **10** 402; **18 519–21**
Toy Liquidators, **13** 541–43
Toy Park, **16** 390
Toyad Corp., **7** 296
**Toymax International, Inc.**, **29 474–76**
Toyo Bearing Manufacturing, **III** 595
Toyo Cotton Co., **IV** 224–25
Toyo Ink Manufacturing, **26** 213
Toyo Kogyo, **I** 167; **II** 361; **11** 139
Toyo Marine and Fire, **III** 385
Toyo Menka Kaisha Ltd. *See* Tomen Corporation.
Toyo Microsystems Corporation, **11** 464
Toyo Oil Co., **IV** 403
Toyo Pulp Co., **IV** 322
Toyo Rayon, **V** 381, 383
**Toyo Sash Co., Ltd.**, **III 757–58**
**Toyo Seikan Kaisha Ltd.**, **I 615–16**
Toyo Soda, **II** 301
Toyo Tire & Rubber Co., **V** 255–56; **9** 248
Toyo Toki Co., Ltd., **III** 755
Toyo Tozo Co., **I** 265; **21** 319
Toyo Trust and Banking Co., **II** 347, 371; **17** 349
**Toyoda Automatic Loom Works, Ltd.**, **I** 203; **III** 591, 593, 632, **636–39**
Toyokawa Works, **I** 579
Toyoko Co., Ltd., **V** 199
Toyoko Kogyo, **V** 199
Toyomenka (America) Inc., **IV** 224
Toyomenka (Australia) Pty., Ltd., **IV** 224
Toyota Gossei, **I** 321
Toyota Industrial Equipment, **27** 294, 296
**Toyota Motor Corporation**, **I** 9–10, 174, 184, **203–05**, 507–08, 587; **II** 373; **III** 415, 495, 521, 523, 536, 579, 581,

591–93, 624, 636–38, 667, 715, 742; **IV** 702; **6** 514; **7** 111, 118, 212, 219–21; **8** 315; **9** 294, 340–42; **10** 353, 407; **11** 351, 377, 487, **528–31 (upd.)**; **14** 321; **15** 495; **21** 162, 273; **23** 289–90, 338–40; **25** 198; **34** 303, 305–06; **38** **458–62 (upd.)**
Toyota Tsusho America, Inc., **13** 371
**Toys 'R' Us, Inc.**, **III** 588; **V 203–06**; **7** 396; **10** 235, 284, 484; **12** 178; **13** 166; **14** 61; **15** 469; **16** 389–90, 457; **18** **522–25 (upd.)**; **24** 412; **25** 314; **31** 477–78; **37** 129; **43** 385
Tozer Kemsley & Milbourn, **II** 208
TP Transportation, **39** 377
TPA. *See* Aloha Airlines Incorporated.
TPCR Corporation, **V** 163; **14** 394
TPG. *See* TNT Post Group N.V.
Trac Inc., **44** 355
Trace International Holdings, Inc., **17** 182–83; **26** 502
Tracey Bros., **IV** 416
Tracey-Locke, **II** 660
Tracinda Corporation, **25** 329–30
Tracker Marine. *See* Bass Pro Shops, Inc.
Tracker Services, Inc., **9** 110
Traco International N.V., **8** 250; **32** 249
**Tracor Inc.**, **10** 547; **17 490–92**; **26** 267
**Tractebel S.A.**, **20 491–93**. *See also* Suez Lyonnaise des Eaux.
Tractor Supply Corp., **I** 446
Tradax, **II** 617; **13** 137
Trade Assoc. of Bilbao, **II** 194
Trade Development Bank, **11** 415–17
Trade Source International, **44** 132
Trade Waste Incineration, Inc., **9** 109
Trade Winds Campers, **III** 599
TradeARBED, **IV** 25
**Trader Joe's Co.**, **13 525–27**; **41** 422
Trader Publications, Inc., **IV** 597
Trader Publishing Company, **12** 302
Traders & General Insurance, **III** 248
Traders Bank of Canada, **II** 344
Traders Group Ltd., **11** 258
Tradesmens National Bank of Philadelphia, **II** 342
The Trading Service, **10** 278
Traex Corporation, **8** 359
Trafalgar House Investments Ltd., **I** 248–49, 572–74; **IV** 259, 711; **20** 313; **23** 161; **24** 88; **36** 322
Trafalgar House PLC, **47** 178
Trafiroad NV, **39** 239
**Trailer Bridge, Inc.**, **41 397–99**
Trailer Marine Transport, **6** 383
Trailways Lines, Inc., **I** 450; **9** 425; **32** 230
Trak Auto Corporation, **16** 159–62
TRAK Communications Inc., **44** 420
TRAK Microwave Corporation, **18** 497, 513
**Trammell Crow Company**, **IV** 343; **8** 326–28, **532–34**
Tran Telecommunications Corp., **III** 110; **14** 14
Trane Company, **III** 663, 665; **10** 525; **21** 107; **22** 6; **26** 4; **30** 46, 48–49
Trans Air System, **6** 367; **27** 90
Trans-Arabian Pipe Line Co., **IV** 537, 552
Trans-Australia Airlines, **6** 110–12
Trans-Canada Air Lines. *See* Air Canada.
Trans Colorado, **11** 299
Trans-Continental Leaf Tobacco Company, (TCLTC), **13** 491
Trans Freight Lines, **27** 473–74
Trans International Airlines, **I** 537; **13** 529; **41** 402
Trans Louisiana Gas Company, **43** 56–57
Trans-Mex, Inc. S.A. de C.V., **42** 365
Trans-Natal Coal Corp., **IV** 93
Trans Ocean Products, **II** 578; **8** 510
Trans-Pacific Airlines, **22** 251. *See also* Aloha Airlines Incorporated.
Trans Rent-A-Car, **6** 348
Trans-Resources Inc., **13** 299
Trans Union Corp., **IV** 137; **6** 25; **28** 119
Trans Western Publishing, **25** 496
**Trans World Airlines, Inc.**, **I** 58, 70, 90, 97, 99–100, 102, 113, 121, 123–24, **125–27**, 132, 466; **II** 32–33, 142, 425, 679; **III** 92, 428; **6** 50, 68, 71, 74, 76–77, 81–82, 114, 130; **9** 17, 232; **10** 301–03, 316; **11** 277, 427; **12** 381, **487–90 (upd.)**; **13** 341; **14** 73; **15** 419; **21** 141–42; **22** 22, 219; **26** 439; **29** 190; **35 424–29 (upd.)**
Trans-World Corp., **19** 456; **47** 231
**Trans World Entertainment Corporation**, **24 501–03**
Trans World International, **18** 262–63
Trans World Life Insurance Company, **27** 46–47
Trans World Music, **9** 361
Trans World Seafood, Inc., **13** 244
**Transaction Systems Architects, Inc.**, **29 477–79**
Transaction Technology, **12** 334
**TransAlta Utilities Corporation**, **6 585–87**
**Transamerica—An AEGON Company**, **41 400–03 (upd.)**
**Transamerica Corporation**, **I 536–38**; **II** 147–48, 227, 288–89, 422; **III** 332, 344; **7** 236–37; **8** 46; **11** 273, 533; **13** **528–30 (upd.)**; **21** 285; **25** 328; **27** 230; **46** 48. *See also* TIG Holdings, Inc.
Transamerica Pawn Holdings. *See* EZCORP Inc.
TransAmerican Waste Industries Inc., **41** 414
Transat. *See* Compagnie Générale Transatlantique (Transat).
**Transatlantic Holdings, Inc.**, **III** 198; **11** **532–33**; **15** 18
Transatlantische Dampfschiffahrts Gesellschaft, **6** 397
Transatlantische Gruppe, **III** 404
**TransBrasil S/A Linhas Aéreas**, **6** 134; **29** 495; **31 443–45**; **46** 398
**TransCanada PipeLines Limited**, **I** 264; **V** 270–71, **737–38**; **17** 22–23
**Transco Energy Company**, **IV** 367; **V** 739–40; **6** 143; **18** 366
Transcontinental Air Transport, **I** 125; **9** 17; **11** 427; **12** 487
Transcontinental and Western Air Lines, **9** 416; **12** 487
Transcontinental Gas Pipe Line Corporation, **V** 739; **6** 447
Transcontinental Pipeline Company, **6** 456–57
Transcontinental Services Group N.V., **16** 207
TransCor America, Inc., **23** 154
Transelco, Inc., **8** 178
TransEuropa, **II** 164
Transfer Drivers, Inc., **46** 301
Transflash, **6** 404; **26** 243
Transfracht, **6** 426
**Transiciel SA**, **48 400–02**
Transinternational Life, **II** 422
Transit Homes of America, Inc., **46** 301
Transit Mix Concrete and Materials Company, **7** 541
Transitions Optical Inc., **21** 221, 223
Transitron, **16** 332
Transking Inc. *See* King Kullen Grocery Co., Inc.
Transkrit Corp., **IV** 640; **26** 273
Translite, **III** 495
Transmanche-Link, **13** 206–08; **37** 135
**Transmedia Network Inc.**, **20 494–97**
Transmedica International, Inc., **41** 225
Transmisiones y Equipos Mecanicos, S.A. de C.V., **23** 171
Transmitter Equipment Manufacturing Co., **13** 385
**TransMontaigne Inc.**, **28 470–72**
Transmontane Rod and Gun Club, **43** 435–36
**Transnet Ltd.**, **6 433–35**
TransOcean Oil, **III** 559
**Transocean Sedco Forex Inc.**, **45 417–19**
Transpac, **IV** 325
Transport Management Co., **III** 192
Transport- und Unfall-Versicherungs-Aktiengesellschaft Zürich, **III** 411
Transportacion Maritima Mexicana S.A. de C.V., **12** 279; **26** 236; **47** 162
Transportation Insurance Co., **III** 229
Transportation.com, **45** 451
Transportes Aéreas Centro-Americanos. *See* Grupo TACA.
**Transportes Aereos Portugueses, S.A.**, **6** **125–27**. *See also* TAP—Air Portugal Transportes Aéreos Portugueses S.A.
Transportes Aeromar, **39** 188
Transrack S.A., **26** 363
Transtar, **6** 120–21; **24** 454
Transue & Williams Steel Forging Corp., **13** 302
Transvaal Silver and Base Metals, **IV** 90
Transway International Corp., **10** 369
Transworld Communications, **35** 165
Transworld Corp., **14** 209
Transworld Drilling Company Limited. *See* Kerr-McGee Corporation.
**The Tranzonic Companies**, **8** 512; **15** **500–02**; **37 392–95**
Trapper's, **19** 286
Trasgo, S.A. de C.V., **14** 516
Trausch Baking Co., **I** 255
Trävaru Svartvik, **IV** 338
Travel Air Manufacturing Company, **8** 49; **27** 97
Travel Automation Services Ltd., **I** 95
Travel Inc., **26** 309
Travel Information Group, **17** 398
**Travel Ports of America, Inc.**, **17 493–95**
Travelers Bank & Trust Company, **13** 467
Travelers Book Club, **13** 105
**Travelers Corporation**, **I** 37, 545; **III** 313, 329, **387–90**, 707–08; **6** 12; **15** 463 124. *See also* Citigroup Inc.
Travelers/Aetna Property Casualty Corp., **21** 15
Traveller's Express, **I** 449
**Travelocity.com, Inc.**, **46 434–37**
TraveLodge, **III** 94, 104–06
Travenol Laboratories, **I** 627–28; **10** 141–43
Travers Morgan Ltd., **42** 183
**Travis Boats & Motors, Inc.**, **37 396–98**

**Travis Perkins plc, 34 450–52**
Travocéan, **25** 104
Trayco, **III** 570; **20** 362
Traylor Engineering & Manufacturing Company, **6** 395; **25** 169
TRC. *See* Tennessee Restaurant Company.
**TRC Companies, Inc., 32 461–64**
TRE Corp., **23** 225
**Treadco, Inc., 16** 39; **19** 38, **454–56**
**Treasure Chest Advertising Company, Inc., 21** 60; **32 465–67**
Treasure House Stores, Inc., **17** 322
Treatment Centers of America, **11** 379
Trebuhs Realty Co., **24** 438
Trechmann, Weekes and Co., **III** 669
Tredegar Industries, Inc., **10** 291
**Tree of Life, Inc., II** 528; **29 480–82**
Tree Sweet Products Corp., **12** 105; **26** 325
Tree Tavern, Inc., **27** 197
TrefilARBED, **IV** 26
Tréfimétaux, **IV** 174
Trefoil Capital Investors, L.P., **8** 305
Trek, **IV** 90, 92–93
**Trek Bicycle Corporation, 16 493–95; 19** 384–85
Trelleborg A.B., **III** 625; **IV** 166
Tremec. *See* Transmisiones y Equipos Mecanicos, S.A. de C.V.
Tremletts Ltd., **IV** 294; **19** 225
Tremont Corporation, **21** 490
Trencherwood Plc, **45** 443
Trend International Ltd., **13** 502
**Trend-Lines, Inc., 22 516–18**
Trends Magazine NV, **48** 347
**Trendwest Resorts, Inc., 12** 439; **33 409–11**. *See also* Jeld-Wen, Inc.
Trent Tube, **I** 435
Trenton Foods, **II** 488
TrentonWorks Limited. *See* The Greenbrier Companies.
Tresco, **8** 514
Trethowal China Clay Co., **III** 690
Tri-City Federal Savings and Loan Association, **10** 92
Tri-City Utilities Company, **6** 514
Tri-County National Bank, **9** 474
Tri-Marine International Inc., **24** 116
Tri-Miller Packing Company, **7** 524
Tri-Sonics, Inc., **16** 202; **43** 170
Tri-State Improvement Company, **6** 465–66
Tri-State Publishing & Communications, Inc., **22** 442
Tri-State Recycling Corporation, **15** 117
Tri-State Refining Co., **IV** 372
Tri-Union Seafoods LLC, **24** 116
**Tri Valley Growers, 32 468–71**
Triad, **14** 224
Triad Artists Inc., **23** 514
Triad International Maintenance Corp., **13** 417
Triad Nitrogen, Inc., **27** 316, 318
Triad Systems Corp., **38** 96
Triangle Auto Springs Co., **IV** 136
The Triangle Group, **16** 357
Triangle Industries Inc., **I** 602, 607–08, 614; **II** 480–81; **14** 43
Triangle Manufacturing, **26** 57
Triangle Portfolio Associates, **II** 317
Triangle Publications, Inc., **IV** 652; **7** 391; **12** 359–60
Triangle Refineries, **IV** 446; **22** 302
Triangle Sheet Metal Works, Inc., **45** 327
**Triarc Companies, Inc., 8 535–37; 13** 322; **14** 32–33; **34 453–57 (upd.)**; **39** 383, 385
Triathlon Leasing, **II** 457
Tribe Computer Works. *See* Zoom Telephonics.
**Tribune Company, III** 329; **IV 682–84**; **10** 56; **11** 331; **22 519–23 (upd.)**; **26** 17; **32** 358–59; **38** 306; **42** 133
Trical Resources, **IV** 84
Tricity Cookers, **I** 531–32
Trick & Murray, **22** 153
**Trico Products Corporation, I** 186; **15 503–05**
Tricon Global Restaurants, Inc., **21** 313, 317, 405, 407, 485; **40** 342
**Tridel Enterprises Inc., 9 512–13**
Trident NGL Holdings Inc., **18** 365, 367
Trident Seafoods, **II** 494
Trifari, Krussman & Fishel, Inc., **9** 157
**Trigen Energy Corporation, 6** 512; **42 386–89**
Trigon Industries, **13** 195; **14** 431
Trilan Developments Ltd., **9** 512
Trilogy Fabrics, Inc., **16** 125
**Trilon Financial Corporation, II 456–57**; **IV** 721; **9** 391
Trimac Ltd., **25** 64
**TriMas Corp., III** 571; **11 534–36**; **20** 359, 362; **39** 266
**Trimble Navigation Limited, 40 441–43**
Trimel Corp., **47** 54
Trinidad and Tobago External Telecommunications Company, **25** 100
Trinidad Oil Co., **IV** 95, 552
Trinidad-Tesoro Petroleum Company Limited, **7** 516, 518
Trinity Beverage Corporation, **11** 451
Trinity Broadcasting, **13** 279
Trinity Capital Opportunity Corp., **17** 13
Trinity Distributors, **15** 139
**Trinity Industries, Incorporated, 7 540–41**
Trinkaus und Burkhardt, **II** 319; **17** 324
**TRINOVA Corporation, III 640–42**, 731; **13** 8; **16** 7, 9
Trintex, **6** 158
Triology Corp., **III** 110
**Triple P N.V., 26 496–99**
Triplex, **6** 279
Triplex (Northern) Ltd., **III** 725
Trippe Manufacturing Co., **10** 474; **24** 29
Triquet Paper Co., **IV** 282; **9** 261
TriStar Pictures, **I** 234; **II** 134, 136–37; **6** 158; **10** 227; **12** 75, 455; **23** 275; **28** 462; **32** 114. *See also* Columbia TriStar Motion Pictures Companies.
Triton Bioscience, **III** 53; **26** 384
Triton Cellular Partners, L.P., **43** 341
**Triton Energy Corporation, 11 537–39**
Triton Group Ltd., **I** 447; **31** 287; **34** 339
Triton Oil, **IV** 519
Triton Systems Corp., **22** 186
Triumph-Adler, **I** 485; **III** 145; **11** 265. *See also* TA Triumph-Adler AG.
Triumph American, Inc., **12** 199
Triumph Films, **25** 174
Triumph, Finlay, and Philips Petroleum, **11** 28
**Triumph Group, Inc., 21** 153; **31 446–48**
Trivest, Inc., **II** 457; **21** 531–32
**Trizec Corporation Ltd., 9** 84–85; **10 529–32**
TrizecHahn, **37** 311
**TRM Copy Centers Corporation, 18 526–28**
Trojan, **III** 674
Troll, **13** 561
Trolley Barn Brewery Inc., **25** 401
Trona Corp., **IV** 95
Tropical Marine Centre, **40** 128–29
Tropical Oil Co., **IV** 415–16
Tropical Shipping, Inc., **6** 529, 531
Tropical Sportswear Int'l Corporation, **42** 120
**Tropicana Products, Inc., II** 468, 525; **13** 293; **25** 366; **28** 271, **473–77**; **38** 349; **45** 160–62
Trotter-Yoder & Associates, **22** 88
Troxel Cycling, **16** 53
Troy & Nichols, Inc., **13** 147
Troy Metal Products. *See* KitchenAid.
Troyfel Ltd., **III** 699
TRT Communications, Inc., **6** 327; **11** 185
Tru-Run Inc., **16** 207
Tru-Stitch, **16** 545
Tru-Trac Therapy Products, **11** 486
Truck Components Inc., **23** 306
Trudeau Marketing Group, Inc., **22** 386
True Form Boot Co., **V** 177
**True North Communications Inc., 23 478–80**; **25** 91
True Temper Hardware Co., **30** 241–42
True Value Hardware Stores, **V** 37–38; **30** 168. *See also* TruServ Corporation.
Trugg-Hansa Holding AB, **III** 264
TruGreen, **23** 428, 430
Truitt Bros., **10** 382
Truman Dunham Co., **III** 744
Truman Hanburg, **I** 247
Trumball Asphalt, **III** 721
Trümmer-Verwertungs-Gesellschaft, **IV** 140
**Trump Organization, 16** 262; **23 481–84**; **43** 225
Trunkline Gas Company, **6** 544; **14** 135
Trunkline LNG Co., **IV** 425
Trus Joist Corporation. *See* TJ International, Inc.
**TruServ Corporation, 24 504–07**
Trussdeck Corporation. *See* TJ International, Inc.
Trust Company of the West, **19** 414; **42** 347
Trustcorp, Inc., **9** 475–76
Trusted Information Systems, Inc., **25** 349
Trustees, Executors and Agency Co. Ltd., **II** 189
**Trusthouse Forte PLC, I** 215; **III 104–06**; **16** 446
**TRW Inc., I 539–41**; **II** 33; **6** 25; **8** 416; **9** 18, 359; **10** 293; **11** 68, **540–42 (upd.)**; **12** 238; **14 510–13 (upd.)**; **16** 484; **17** 372; **18** 275; **19** 184; **23** 134; **24** 480; **26** 141; **28** 119; **32** 437; **33** 47; **34** 76; **43** 311, 313; **45** 152
TRW Vehicle Safety Systems Inc., **41** 369
Tryart Pty. Limited, **7** 253
TSA. *See* Transaction Systems Architects, Inc.
Tsai Management & Research Corp., **III** 230–31
**TSB Group plc, 12 491–93**; **16** 14
TSI Inc., **38** 206
TSI Soccer Corporation, **29** 142–43
TSMC. *See* Taiwan Semiconductor Manufacturing Company Ltd.

TSO. *See* Teacher's Service Organization, Inc.
TSO Financial Corp., **II** 420; **8** 10
Tsogo Sun Gaming & Entertainment, **17** 318
TSP. *See* Tom Snyder Productions.
TSR Inc., **24** 538
Tsuang Hine Co., **III** 582
Tsubakimoto-Morse, **14** 64
Tsukumo Shokai, **I** 502; **III** 712
Tsumeb Corp., **IV** 17–18
Tsurumi Steelmaking and Shipbuilding Co., **IV** 162
Tsurusaki Pulp Co., Ltd., **IV** 285
Tsutsunaka Plastic Industry Co., **III** 714; **8** 359
TSYS. *See* Total System Services, Inc.
TTK. *See* Tokyo Tsushin Kogyo K.K.
**TTX Company**, **6 436–37**
Tube Fab Ltd., **17** 234
Tube Forming, Inc., **23** 517
Tube Investments, **II** 422; **IV** 15
Tube Reducing Corp., **16** 321
Tube Service Co., **19** 344
Tubed Chemicals Corporation, **27** 299
Tuborg, **9** 99
**Tubos de Acero de Mexico, S.A. (TAMSA)**, **41 404–06**
Tuboscope, **42** 420
Tucker, Lynch & Coldwell. *See* CB Commercial Real Estate Services Group, Inc.
TUCO, Inc., **8** 78
**Tucson Electric Power Company**, **V** 713; **6 588–91**; **42** 388
Tucson Gas & Electric, **19** 411–12
**Tuesday Morning Corporation**, **18 529–31**
Tuff Stuff Publications, **23** 101
TUI. *See* Touristik Union International GmbH. and Company K.G.
**TUI Group GmbH**, **42** 283; **44 432–35**
Tuileries et Briqueteries d'Hennuyeres et de Wanlin, **14** 249
TUJA, **27** 21
**Tultex Corporation**, **13 531–33**
**Tumbleweed, Inc.**, **33 412–14**
Tunhems Industri A.B., **I** 387
**Tupolev Aviation and Scientific Technical Complex**, **24 58–60**
**Tupperware Corporation**, **I** 29; **II** 534; **III** 610–12;, **15** 475, 477; **17** 186; **18** 67; **28 478–81**
Turbinbolaget, **III** 419
Turbine Engine Asset Management LLC, **28** 5
TurboLinux Inc., **45** 363
Turcot Paperboard Mills Ltd., **17** 281
Turkish Engineering, Consultancy and Contracting Corp., **IV** 563
Turkish Petroleum Co. *See* Türkiye Petrolleri Anonim Ortakliği.
Türkiye Garanti Bankasi, **I** 479
**Türkiye Petrolleri Anonim Ortakliği**, **IV** 464, 557–58, **562–64**; **7** 352
Turnbull, **III** 468
**Turner Broadcasting System, Inc.**, **II** 134, 149, 161 **166–68**; **IV** 676; **6 171–73 (upd.)**; **7** 64, 99, 306, 529; **23** 33, 257; **25** 313, 329, 498; **28** 71; **30** 100; **47** 272
**The Turner Corporation**, **8 538–40**; **23 485–88 (upd.)**; **25** 402; **33** 197
Turner Entertainment Co., **18** 459
Turner Glass Company, **13** 40
Turner Network Television, **21** 24
Turner's Turkeys, **II** 587
Turnstone Systems, **44** 426
TURPAS, **IV** 563
**Turtle Wax, Inc.**, **15 506–09**; **16** 43; **26** 349
**Tuscarora Inc.**, **17** 155; **29 483–85**
Tussauds Group Ltd., **IV** 659
Tutt Bryant Industries PLY Ltd., **26** 231
Tuttle, Oglebay and Company. *See* Oglebay Norton Company.
TV & Stereo Town, **10** 468
TV Asahi, **7** 249
**TV Azteca, S.A. de C.V.**, **39** 194–95, **398–401**
TV Food Network, **22** 522
**TV Guide, Inc.**, **43 431–34 (upd.)**
TVA. *See* Tennessee Valley Authority.
TVE. *See* Television Española, S.A.
TVE Holdings, **22** 307
TVH Acquisition Corp., **III** 262, 264
**TVI, Inc.**, **15 510–12**
TVN Entertainment Corporation, **32** 239
TVS Entertainment PLC, **13** 281
TVW Enterprises, **7** 78
TVX, **II** 449; **13** 449
TW Kutter, **III** 420
**TW Services, Inc.**, **II 679–80**; **10** 301–03
TWA. *See* Trans World Airlines *and* Transcontinental & Western Airways.
Tweco Co., **19** 441
Tweeds, **12** 280
**Tweeter Home Entertainment Group, Inc.**, **30 464–66**; **41** 379, 381
Twen-Tours International, **II** 164
**Twentieth Century Fox Film Corporation**, **II** 133, 135, 146, 155–56, **169–71**, 175; **IV** 652; **7** 391–92; **12** 73, 322, 359; **15** 23, 25, 234; **25** 327, **490–94 (upd.)**; **43** 173; **46** 311
Twentsche Bank, **II** 183
"21" International Holdings, **17** 182
21 Invest International Holdings Ltd., **14** 322
21st Century Food Products. *See* Hain Food Group, Inc.
21st Century Mortgage, **18** 28
Twenty-Second National Bank, **II** 291
TWI. *See* Trans World International.
Twin City Wholesale Drug Company, **14** 147
**Twin Disc, Inc.**, **21 502–04**
Twin Hill Acquisition Company, Inc., **48** 286
Twining Crosfield Group, **II** 465; **13** 52
Twinings' Foods International, **II** 465–66; **III** 696
Twinings Tea, **41** 31
**Twinlab Corporation**, **34 458–61**
Twinpak, **IV** 250
Two Guys, **12** 49
2-in-1 Shinola Bixby Corp., **II** 497
21st Century Mortgage, **41** 18, 20
TWW Plc, **26** 62
TXEN, Inc., **18** 370
TXL Oil Corp., **IV** 552
TXP Operation Co., **IV** 367
TxPort Inc., **13** 8
Ty-D-Bol, **III** 55
**Ty Inc.**, **33 415–17**
**Tyco International Ltd.**, **21** 462; **28 482–87 (upd.)**; **30** 157; **44** 6
**Tyco Laboratories, Inc.**, **III 643–46**; **13** 245–47
Tyco Submarine Systems Ltd., **32** 217
**Tyco Toys, Inc.**, **12 494–97**; **13** 312, 319; **18** 520–21; **25** 314
**Tyler Corporation**, **23 489–91**
Tymnet, **18** 542
Tyndall Fund-Unit Assurance Co., **III** 273
Typhoo Tea, **II** 477
Typpi Oy, **IV** 469
Tyrolean Airways, **9** 233; **33** 50
Tyrvään Oy, **IV** 348
Tyskie Brewery, **24** 450
**Tyson Foods, Inc.**, **II 584–85**; **7** 422–23, 432; **14 514–16 (upd.)**; **21** 535; **23** 376, 384; **26** 168; **39** 229

U.C.L.A.F. *See* Roussel-Uclaf.
U-Haul International Inc. *See* Amerco.
U.K. Corrugated, **IV** 296; **19** 226
**U.S. Aggregates, Inc.**, **42 390–92**
U.S. Appliances, **26** 336
**U.S. Bancorp**, **12** 165; **14 527–29**; **36 489–95 (upd.)**
U.S. Bank of Washington, **14** 527
U.S. Banknote Company, **30** 43
U.S. Bearings Company. *See* Federal-Mogul Corporation.
U.S. Billing, Inc. *See* Billing Concepts Corp.
U.S. Biomedicals Corporation, **27** 69
U.S. Bioscience, Inc., **35** 286, 288
**U.S. Borax, Inc.**, **42 393–96**
U.S. Brass., **24** 151
**U.S. Can Corporation**, **30 474–76**
**U.S. Cellular Corporation**, **31 449–452 (upd.)**
U.S. Computer of North America Inc., **43** 368
**U.S. Delivery Systems, Inc.**, **22** 153, **531–33**; **47** 90
U.S. Electrical Motors, **II** 19
U.S. Elevator Corporation, **19** 109–11
U.S. Envelope, **19** 498
U.S. Food Products Co., **I** 376
**U.S. Foodservice**, **26 503–06**; **37** 374, 376
U.S.G. Co., **III** 762
U.S. Generating Company, **26** 373
U.S. Geological Survey, **9** 367
U.S. Graphite. *See* Wickes Inc.
U.S. Guarantee Co., **III** 220; **14** 108
**U.S. Healthcare, Inc.**, **6 194–96**; **21** 16
**U.S. Home Corporation**, **8 541–43**
U.S. Industries, Inc., **7** 208; **18** 467; **23** 296; **24** 150; **27** 288
U.S. Intec, **22** 229
U.S. International Reinsurance, **III** 264
U.S. Investigations Services Inc., **35** 44
U.S. Land Co., **IV** 255
U.S. Lawns, **31** 182, 184
U.S. Life Insurance, **III** 194
U.S. Lines, **I** 476; **III** 459; **11** 194
U.S. Lock Corporation, **9** 543; **28** 50–52
U.S. Long Distance Corp. *See* Billing Concepts Corp.
U.S. Marine Corp., **III** 444
**U.S. News and World Report Inc.**, **30 477–80**
**U.S. Office Products Company**, **25 500–02**; **41** 69, 247; **47** 91
U.S. Overall Company, **14** 549
U.S. Plywood Corp. *See* United States Plywood Corp.
U.S. Realty and Improvement Co., **III** 98

U.S. RingBinder Corp., **10** 313–14
**U.S. Robotics Inc.**, **9 514–15**; **20** 8, 69; **22** 17; **24** 212; **34** 444; **36** 122, 357; **48** 369
U.S. Rubber Company, **I** 478; **10** 388
**U.S. Satellite Broadcasting Company, Inc.**, **20 505–07**
U.S. Satellite Systems, **III** 169; **6** 285
U.S. Shoe Corporation, **43** 98; **44** 365
U.S. Smelting Refining and Mining, **7** 360
U.S. Software Inc., **29** 479
U.S. Steel Corp. *See* United States Steel Corp.
U.S. Telephone Communications, **9** 478
U.S. Tile Co., **III** 674
**U.S. Timberlands Company, L.P.**, **42 397–400**
U.S. Time Corporation, **13** 120
U.S. Trust Co. of New York, **II** 274
**U.S. Trust Corp.**, **17 496–98**
U.S. Vanadium Co., **9** 517
U.S. Venture Partners, **15** 204–05
U.S. Vitamin & Pharmaceutical Corp., **III** 55
**U S West, Inc.**, **V 341–43**; **11** 12, 59, 547; **25** 101, **495–99 (upd.)**; **32** 218; **36** 43; **37** 124–27
U.S. Windpower, **11** 222–23
U.S. Xpress Enterprises, Inc., **18** 159
U-Tote'M, **II** 620; **7** 372
UA. *See* Metro- Goldwyn-Mayer Inc., MGM/UA Communications Company, *and* United Artists Corp.
UAA. *See* EgyptAir.
**UAL Corporation**, **34 462–65 (upd.)**
UAL, Inc. *See* United Airlines.
UAP. *See* Union des Assurances de Paris.
UAP Inc., **45** 179
UARCO Inc., **15** 473–74
UAT. *See* UTA.
Ub Iwerks, **6** 174
**Ube Industries, Ltd.**, **III 759–61**; **38 463–67 (upd.)**
Uberseebank A.G., **III** 197
**Ubi Soft Entertainment S.A.**, **41** 188–89, **407–09**
Ubique Ltd, **25** 301
UBL Educational Loan Center, **42** 211
UBS. *See* Union Bank of Switzerland.
Ucabail, **II** 265
UCAR International, Inc., **40** 83
UCC-Communications Systems, Inc., **II** 38
Uccel, **6** 224
Uchiyama, **V** 727
UCI, **IV** 92; **25** 173
UCPMI, **IV** 226
Uddeholm and Bohler, **IV** 234
Udet Flugzeugwerke, **I** 73
Udo Fischer Co., **8** 477
UE Automotive Manufacturing, **III** 580
Ueda Kotsu Company, **47** 408
UETA Inc., **29** 510–11
Ufa Sports, **44** 190
Ugg Holdings, Inc., **22** 173
UGI. *See* United Gas Improvement.
**UGI Corporation**, **12 498–500**
Ugine-Kuhlmann, **IV** 108, 174
**Ugine S.A.**, **IV** 174; **20 498–500**
Ugine Steels, **IV** 227
**Ugly Duckling Corporation**, **22 524–27**
Uhlmans Inc., **24** 458
UI International, **6** 444
UIB. *See* United Independent Broadcasters, Inc.
**UICI**, **33 418–21**
Uinta Co., **6** 568
Uintah National Corp., **11** 260
UIS Co., **13** 554–55; **15** 324
Uitgeversmaatschappij Elsevier, **IV** 610
Uitzendbureau Amstelveen. *See* Randstad Holding n.v.
UJB Financial Corp., **14** 473
UK Paper, **IV** 279; **19** 155
UKF. *See* Unie van Kunstmestfabrieken.
**Ukrop's Super Market's, Inc.**, **39 402–04**
UL. *See* Underwriters Laboratories, Inc.
Ullrich Copper, Inc., **6** 146
Ullstein AV Produktions-und Vertriebsgesellschaft, **IV** 590
Ullstein Langen Müller, **IV** 591
Ullstein Tele Video, **IV** 590
ULN. *See* Union Laitière Normande.
ULPAC, **II** 576
Ulstein Holding ASA, **27** 494
Ulster Bank, **II** 334
**Ultimate Electronics, Inc.**, **18 532–34**; **21** 33; **24** 52, 269
Ultra Bancorp, **II** 334
Ultra High Pressure Units Ltd., **IV** 66; **7** 123
Ultra Mart, **16** 250
**Ultra Pac, Inc.**, **24 512–14**
Ultra Radio & Television, **I** 531
UltraCam. *See* Ultrak Inc.
UltraCare Products, **18** 148
**Ultrak Inc.**, **24 508–11**
Ultralar, **13** 544
**Ultramar Diamond Shamrock Corporation**, **31 453–457 (upd.)**
**Ultramar PLC**, **IV 565–68**
Ultrametl Mfg. Co., **17** 234
Ultronic Systems Corp., **IV** 669
UM Technopolymer, **III** 760
Umacs of Canada Inc., **9** 513
Umberto's of New Hyde Park Pizzeria, **16** 447
Umbro Holdings Ltd., **43** 392. *See also* Stone Manufacturing Company.
UMC. *See* United Microelectronics Corp.
UMG. *See* Universal Music Group.
UMI Company, **29** 58
**NV Umicore SA**, **47 411–13**
Umm-al-Jawabi Oil Co., **IV** 454
Umpqua River Navigation Company, **13** 100
Unadulterated Food Products, Inc., **11** 449
UNAT, **III** 197–98
Unbrako Socket Screw Company Ltd., **30** 429
Uncas-Merchants National Bank, **13** 467
**Uncle Ben's Inc.**, **22 528–30**
Under Sea Industries, **III** 59
Underground Group, **6** 407
Underwood, **III** 145; **24** 269
Underwriters Adjusting Co., **III** 242
**Underwriters Laboratories, Inc.**, **30 467–70**
Underwriters Reinsurance Co., **10** 45
Unefon, S.A., **39** 194, 196
UNELCO. *See* Union Electrica de Canarias S.A.
Unelec, Inc., **13** 398
Unfall, **III** 207
Ungermann-Bass, Inc., **6** 279
Uni-Cardan AG, **III** 494
Uni-Cast. *See* Sturm, Ruger & Company, Inc.
Uni-Charm, **III** 749
Uni Europe, **III** 211
**Uni-Marts, Inc.**, **17 499–502**
Uni-Sankyo, **I** 675
**Unibail SA**, **40 444–46**
Unibank, **40** 336
Unic, **V** 63
Unicapital, Inc., **15** 281
Unicare Health Facilities, **6** 182; **25** 525
Unicco Security Services, **27** 22
Unicel. *See* Rural Cellular Corporation.
Unicer, **9** 100
Unichem, **25** 73
Unichema International, **13** 228
Unicoa, **I** 524
**Unicom Corporation**, **29 486–90 (upd.)**. *See also* Exelon Corporation.
Unicomi, **II** 265
Unicon Producing Co., **10** 191
Unicoolait, **19** 51
UNICOR. *See* Federal Prison Industries, Inc.
Unicord, **24** 115
Unicorn Shipping Lines, **IV** 91
UniCorp, **8** 228
Unicorp Financial, **III** 248
Unicredit, **II** 265
Uniden, **14** 117
Unidrive, **47** 280
UniDynamics Corporation, **8** 135
Unie van Kunstmestfabrieken, **I** 326
Uniface Holding B.V., **10** 245; **30** 142
**Unifi, Inc.**, **12 501–03**
Unified Energy System of Russia. *See* RAO Unified Energy System of Russia.
Unified Management Corp., **III** 306
Unified Western Grocers, **31** 25
**UniFirst Corporation**, **16** 228; **21** 115, **505–07**
Uniforce Services Inc., **40** 119
**Unigate PLC**, **II 586–87**; **28 488–91 (upd.)**; **29** 150
Unigep Group, **III** 495
Unigesco Inc., **II** 653
Uniglory, **13** 211
Unigroup, **15** 50
UniHealth America, **11** 378–79
Unijoh Sdn, Bhd, **47** 255
Unik S.A., **23** 170–171
Unilab Corp., **26** 391
Unilac Inc., **II** 547
**Unilever PLC/Unilever N.V.**, **I** 369, 590, 605; **II** 547, **588–91**; **III** 31–32, 46, 52, 495; **IV** 532; **7** 382, **542–45 (upd.)**, 577; **8** 105–07, 166, 168, 341, 344; **9** 449; **11** 205, 421; **13** 243–44; **14** 204–05; **18** 395, 397; **19** 193; **21** 219; **22** 123; **23** 242; **26** 306; **28** 183, 185; **30** 396–97; **32 472–78 (upd.)**; **36** 237
Unilife Assurance Group, **III** 273
UniLife Insurance Co., **22** 149
**Unilog SA**, **42 401–03**
UniMac Companies, **11** 413
Unimat, **II** 265
Unimation, **II** 122
Unimetal, **IV** 227; **30** 252
Uninsa, **I** 460
Union, **III** 391–93
Union & NHK Auto Parts, **III** 580
Union Acceptances Ltd., **IV** 23
Unión Aérea Española, **6** 95
Union Aéromaritime de Transport. *See* UTA.
Union Assurance, **III** 234
Union Bag-Camp Paper Corp., **IV** 344–45

Union Bancorp of California, **II** 358
Union Bank. *See* State Street Boston Corporation.
Union Bank of Australia, **II** 187–89
Union Bank of Birmingham, **II** 318; **17** 323
**Union Bank of California**, **16 496–98**
Union Bank of Canada, **II** 344
Union Bank of England, **II** 188
Union Bank of Finland, **II** 302, 352
Union Bank of Halifax, **II** 344
Union Bank of London, **II** 235
Union Bank of New London, **II** 213
Union Bank of New York, **9** 229
Union Bank of Prince Edward Island, **II** 220
Union Bank of Scotland, **10** 337
**Union Bank of Switzerland**, **II** 257, 267, 334, 369, 370, **378–79**; **21** 146
Union Battery Co., **III** 536
Union Bay Sportswear, **17** 460
**Union Camp Corporation**, **IV 344–46**; **8** 102; **39** 291; **47** 189
Union-Capitalisation, **III** 392
**Union Carbide Corporation**, **I** 334, 339, 347, 374, 390, **399–401**, 582, 666; **II** 103, 313, 562; **III** 742, 760; **IV** 92, 374, 379, 521; **7** 376; **8** 180, 182, 376; **9** 16, **516–20 (upd.)**; **10** 289, 472; **11** 402–03; **12** 46, 347; **13** 118; **14** 281–82; **16** 461; **17** 159; **18** 235; **22** 228, 235; **43** 265–66; **48** 321
Union Cervecera, **9** 100
Union Colliery Company, **V** 741
Union Commerce Corporation, **11** 181
Union Commerciale, **19** 98
Union Corporation. *See* Gencor Ltd.
Union d'Etudes et d'Investissements, **II** 265
**Union des Assurances de Paris**, **II** 234; **III** 201, **391–94**
Union des Coopératives Bressor, **25** 85
Union des Cooperatives Laitières. *See* Unicoolait.
Union des Transports Aériens. *See* UTA.
**Union Electric Company**, **V** 741–43; **6** 505–06; **26** 451
Union Electrica de Canarias S.A., **V** 607
Union Equity Co-Operative Exchange, **7** 175
Union et Prévoyance, **III** 403
Union Fertilizer, **I** 412
Union Fidelity Corporation, **III** 204; **45** 26
Union Financiera, **19** 189
Union Gas & Electric Co., **6** 529
Union Générale de Savonnerie, **III** 33
l'Union Générale des Pétroles, **IV** 545–46, 560; **7** 482–83
Union Glass Co., **III** 683
Union Hardware, **III** 443; **22** 115
Union Hop Growers, **I** 287
Union Laitière Normande, **19** 50. *See also* Compagnie Laitière Européenne.
Union Levantina de Seguros, **III** 179
Union Light, Heat & Power Company, **6** 466
Union Marine, **III** 372
Union Minière. *See* NV Umicore SA.
Union Mutual Life Insurance Company. *See* UNUM Corp.
Union National Bank, **II** 284; **10** 298
Union National Bank of Wilmington, **25** 540
Union of European Football Association, **27** 150
Union of Food Co-ops, **II** 622
Union of London, **II** 333
Union Oil Associates, **IV** 569
Union Oil Co., **9** 266
Union Oil Co. of California, **I** 13; **IV** 385, 400, 403, 434, 522, 531, 540, 569, 575; **11** 271. *See also* Unocal Corporation.
**Union Pacific Corporation**, **I** 473; **II** 381; **III** 229; **V 529–32**; **12** 18–20, 278; **14** 371–72; **28 492–500 (upd.)**; **36** 43–44
Union Pacific Tea Co., **7** 202
Union Paper Bag Machine Co., **IV** 344
Union Petroleum Corp., **IV** 394
L'Union pour le Developement Régional, **II** 265
Union Power Company, **12** 541
Union Rückversicherungs-Gesellschaft, **III** 377
Union Savings, **II** 316
Union Savings and Loan Association of Phoenix, **19** 412
Union Savings Bank, **9** 173
Union Savings Bank and Trust Company, **13** 221
Union Steam Ship Co., **IV** 279; **19** 154
Union Steamship Co. of New Zealand Ltd., **27** 473
Union Steel Co., **IV** 22, 572; **7** 550
Union Sugar, **II** 573
Union Suisse des Coopératives de Consommation. *See* Coop Schweiz.
Union Sulphur Co., **IV** 81; **7** 185
Union Supply Co., **IV** 573; **7** 550
Union Tank Car Co., **IV** 137
Union Telecard Alliance, LLC, **34** 223
Union Telephone Company, **14** 258
**Union Texas Petroleum Holdings, Inc.**, **I** 415; **7** 379; **9 521–23**; **22** 31
Union-Transport, **6** 404; **26** 243
Union Trust Co., **II** 284, 313, 315–16, 382; **9** 228; **13** 222
The Union Underwear Company, **I** 440–41; **8** 200–01; **25** 164–66
Union Wine, **I** 289
Unionamerica, Inc., **16** 497
Unionamerica Insurance Group, **III** 243
UnionBay Sportswear Co., **27** 112
Unione Manifatture, S.p.A., **19** 338
Uniphase Corporation. *See* JDS Uniphase Corporation.
Uniplex Business Software, **41** 281
**Unique Casual Restaurants, Inc.**, **27 480–82**
Uniroy of Hempstead, Inc. *See* Aris Industries, Inc.
Uniroyal Chemical Corporation, **36** 145
Uniroyal Corp., **I** 30–31; **II** 472; **V** 242; **8** 503; **11** 159; **20** 262
Uniroyal Goodrich, **42** 88
Uniroyal Holdings Ltd., **21** 73
Unishops, Inc. *See* Aris Industries, Inc.
**Unison HealthCare Corporation**, **25 503–05**
Unisource Worldwide, Inc., **I** 413, **47** 149
Unistar Radio Networks, **23** 510
**Unisys Corporation**, **II** 42; **III 165–67**; **6 281–83 (upd.)**; **8** 92; **9** 32, 59; **12** 149, 162; **17** 11, 262; **18** 345, 386, 434, 542; **21** 86; **36 479–84 (upd.)**
The Unit Companies, Inc., **6** 394, 396; **25** 170
Unit Group plc, **8** 477
Unitech plc, **27** 81
United Acquisitions, **7** 114; **25** 125
United Advertising Periodicals, **12** 231
United Agri Products, **II** 494
United AgriSeeds, Inc., **21** 387
United Air Express. *See* United Parcel Service of America Inc.
United Air Fleet, **23** 408
United Aircraft and Transportation Co., **I** 48, 76, 78, 85–86, 96, 441, 489; **9** 416, 418; **10** 162, 260; **12** 289; **21** 140
**United Airlines**, **I** 23, 47, 71, 84, 90, 97, 113, 116, 118, 124, **128–30**; **II** 142, 419, 680; **III** 225; **6** 71, 75–77, 104, 121, 123, **128–30 (upd.)**, 131, 388–89; **9** 271–72, 283, 416, 549; **10** 162, 199, 301, 561; **11** 299; **12** 192, 381; **14** 73; **21** 141; **22** 199, 220; **24** 21, 22; **25** 146, 148, 421–23; **26** 113, 338–39, 440; **27** 20; **29** 507; **38** 105. *See also* UAL Corporation.
United Alaska Drilling, Inc., **7** 558
United Alkalai Co., **I** 351
United Alloy Steel Company, **26** 405
United-American Car, **13** 305
United American Insurance Company of Dallas, **9** 508; **33** 407
United American Lines, **6** 398
United Arab Airlines. *See* EgyptAir.
United Artists Corp., **I** 537; **II** 135, 146–48, 149, 157–58, 160, 167, 169; **III** 721; **IV** 676; **6** 167; **9** 74; **12** 13, 73; **13** 529; **14** 87, 399; **21** 362; **23** 389; **26** 487; **36** 47; **41** 402. *See also* MGM/UA Communications Company *and* Metro-Goldwyn-Mayer Inc.
United Artists Theatre Circuit, Inc., **37** 63–64
United Auto Group, Inc., **45** 261
**United Auto Group, Inc.**, **26 500–02**
United Bank of Arizona, **II** 358
**United Biscuits (Holdings) plc**, **II** 466, 540, **592–94**; **III** 503; **26** 59; **36** 313; **42 404–09 (upd.)**
**United Brands Company**, **II 595–97**; **III** 28; **7** 84–85; **12** 215; **21** 110, 112; **25** 4
United Breweries Ltd. **I** 221, 223, 288; **24** 449. *See also* Carlsberg A/S.
United Broadcasting Corporation Public Company Ltd., **31** 330
United Cable Television Corporation, **II** 160; **9** 74; **18** 65; **43** 431
United California Bank, **II** 289
United Car, **I** 540; **14** 511
United Carbon Co., **IV** 373
United Central Oil Corporation, **7** 101
United Cigar Manufacturers Company, **II** 414. *See also* Culbro Corporation.
United Cities Gas Company, **43** 56, 58
United City Property Trust, **IV** 705
United Co., **I** 70
United Communications Systems, Inc. **V** 346
United Computer Services, Inc., **11** 111
United Consolidated Industries, **24** 204
United Corp., **10** 44
United County Banks, **II** 235
United Dairies, **II** 586–87
United Dairy Farmers, **III** 190
**United Defense, L.P.**, **30 471–73**
United Distiller & Vintners, **43** 215. *See also* Diageo plc.
United Distillers Glenmore, Inc., **34** 89
United Dominion Corp., **III** 200

**United Dominion Industries Limited**, **IV** 288; **8 544–46**; **16 499–502 (upd.)**; **47** 378
United Drapery Stores, **III** 502; **7** 208
United Drug Co., **II** 533
United Electric Light and Water Co., **13** 182
United Engineering Steels, **III** 495
United Engineers & Constructors, **II** 86; **11** 413
United Express, **11** 299
United Factors Corp., **13** 534–35
United Features Syndicate, Inc., **IV** 607–08
United Federal Savings and Loan of Waycross, **10** 92
United Financial Corporation, **12** 353
United Financial Group, Inc., **8** 349
United 5 and 10 Cent Stores, **13** 444
**United Foods, Inc.**, **21 508–11**
United Fruit Co., **I** 529, 566; **II** 120, 595; **IV** 308; **7** 84–85; **21** 110–11; **44** 152
United Funds, Inc., **22** 540–41
United Gas and Electric Company of New Albany, **6** 555
United Gas and Improvement Co., **13** 182
United Gas Corp., **IV** 488–90
United Gas Improvement Co., **IV** 549; **V** 696; **6** 446, 523; **11** 388
United Gas Industries, **III** 502; **7** 208
United Gas Pipe Line Co., **IV** 489–90
United Geophysical Corp., **I** 142
United Graphics, **12** 25
United Grocers, **II** 625
United Guaranty Corp., **III** 197
United Health Maintenance, Inc., **6** 181–82
**United HealthCare Corporation**, **9 524–26**; **24** 229, 231. *See also* Humana Inc.
**The United Illuminating Company**, **21 512–14**
United Image Entertainment, **18** 64, 66
United Independent Broadcasters, Inc., **II** 132
**United Industrial Corporation**, **37 399–402**
United Industrial Syndicate, **8** 545
United Information Systems, Inc., **V** 346
United Insurance Co., **I** 523
Oy United International, **IV** 349
United International Holdings Inc., **28** 198
United International Pictures, **II** 155
United Investors Life Insurance Company, **22** 540; **33** 407
United Iron & Metal Co., **14** 156
**United Jewish Communities**, **33 422–25**
United Kent Fire, **III** 350
United Kingdom Atomic Energy Authority, **6** 451–52
United Knitting, Inc., **21** 192, 194
United Liberty Life Insurance Co., **III** 190–92
United Life & Accident Insurance Co., **III** 220–21; **14** 109
United Life Insurance Company, **12** 541
United Light & Railway Co., **V** 609
United Light and Power, **6** 511
United Machinery Co., **15** 127
United Match Factories, **12** 462
United Media, **22** 442
United Medical Service, Inc., **III** 245–46
United Merchandising Corp., **12** 477
**United Merchants & Manufacturers, Inc.**, **13 534–37**; **31** 160
United Meridian Corporation, **8** 350
United Metals Selling Co., **IV** 31
United Microelectronics Corporation, **22** 197; **47** 384, 386
United Micronesian, **I** 97; **21** 142
United Molasses, **II** 582
United Mortgage Servicing, **16** 133
**United Natural Foods, Inc.**, **32 479–82**
United Natural Gas Company, **6** 526
United Netherlands Navigation Company. *See* Vereenigde Nederlandsche Scheepvaartmaatschappij.
**United News & Media plc**, **28 501–05 (upd.)**; **35** 354
**United Newspapers plc**, **IV 685–87**
United of Omaha, **III** 365
United Office Products, **11** 64
United Oil Co., **IV** 399
United Optical, **10** 151
United Pacific Financial Services, **III** 344
United Pacific Insurance Co., **III** 343
United Pacific Life Insurance Co., **III** 343–44
United Pacific Reliance Life Insurance Co. of New York, **III** 343
United Packages, **IV** 249
**United Pan-Europe Communications NV**, **47 414–17**
**United Paper Mills Ltd.**, **II** 302; **IV** 316, **347–50**
United Paramount Network, **25** 418–19; **26** 32; **31** 109
United Paramount Theatres, **II** 129
**United Parcel Service of America Inc.**, **V 533–35**; **6** 345–46, 385–86, 390; **11** 11; **12** 309, 334; **13** 19, 416; **14** 517; **17 503–06 (upd.)**; **18** 82, 177, 315–17; **24** 22, 133; **25** 148, 150, 356; **27** 471, 475; **34** 15, 17, 473; **39** 33; **41** 245; **42** 140
United Pipeline Co., **IV** 394
United Power and Light Corporation, **6** 473; **12** 541
United Presidential Life Insurance Company, **12** 524, 526
**United Press International, Inc.**, **IV** 607, 627, 669–70; **7** 158–59; **16** 166; **19** 203; **22** 453; **25 506–09**
United Railways & Electric Company, **25** 44
United Refining Co., **23** 406, 408
**United Rentals, Inc.**, **28** 386, 388; **34 466–69**; **48** 272
United Resources, Inc., **21** 514
**United Retail Group Inc.**, **33 426–28**
United Retail Merchants Stores Inc., **9** 39
United Roasters, **III** 24; **14** 121
United Satellite Television, **10** 320
United Savings of Texas, **8** 349
United Scientific Holdings, **47** 8
United Servomation, **7** 471–72
United Shirt Shops, Inc. *See* Aris Industries, Inc.
United Skates of America, **8** 303
United Software Consultants Inc., **11** 65
United States Aluminum Co., **17** 213
United States Aviation Underwriters, Inc., **24** 176
United States Baking Co., **II** 542
United States Can Co., **15** 127, 129
**United States Cellular Corporation**, **9** 494–96, **527–29**. *See also* U.S. Cellular Corporation.
United States Department of Defense, **6** 327
United States Distributing Corp., **IV** 180–82
United States Electric and Gas Company, **6** 447
United States Electric Light and Power Company, **25** 44
The United States Electric Lighting Company, **11** 387
United States Export-Import Bank, **IV** 55
United States Express Co., **II** 381, 395–96; **10** 59–60; **12** 534
United States Fidelity and Guaranty Co., **III** 395
**United States Filter Corporation**, **I** 429; **IV** 374; **20 501–04**; **38** 168, 170
United States Foil Co., **IV** 186; **19** 346
United States Football League, **29** 347
United States Glucose Co., **II** 496
United States Graphite Company, **V** 221–22
United States Gypsum Co., **III** 762–64
United States Health Care Systems, Inc. *See* U.S. Healthcare, Inc.
United States Independent Telephone Company, **6** 332
United States Leasing Corp., **II** 442
United States Mail Steamship Co., **23** 160
United States Medical Finance Corp., **18** 516, 518
United States Mortgage & Trust Company, **II** 251; **14** 102
United States National Bancshares, **25** 114
United States National Bank of Galveston. *See* Cullen/Frost Bankers, Inc.
United States National Bank of Oregon, **14** 527
The United States National Bank of Portland, **14** 527–28
United States National Bank of San Diego, **II** 355
United States Pipe and Foundry Co., **III** 766; **22** 544–45
United States Plywood Corp., **IV** 264, 282, 341; **9** 260; **13** 100; **20** 128
**United States Postal Service**, **10** 60; **14 517–20**; **34 470–75 (upd.)**; **42** 140
United States Realty-Sheraton Corp., **III** 98
United States Satellite Broadcasting Company Inc., **24** 226; **38** 176
United States Security Trust Co., **13** 466
**United States Shoe Corporation**, **V 207–08**; **17** 296, 390; **23** 328; **39** 301
United States Steel Corp., **I** 298, 491; **II** 129, 330; **III** 282, 326, 379; **IV** 35, 56, 110, 158, 572–74; **6** 514; **7** 48, 70–73, 401–02, 549–51; **10** 32; **11** 194; **12** 353–54; **17** 350, 356; **18** 378; **26** 405, 451. *See also* USX Corporation.
United States Sugar Refining Co., **II** 496
**United States Surgical Corporation**, **10 533–35**; **13** 365; **21** 119–20; **28** 486; **34 476–80 (upd.)**
United States Tobacco Company, **9** 533
United States Trucking Corp., **IV** 180–81
United States Trust Co. of New York. *See* U.S. Trust Corp.
United States Underseas Cable Corp., **IV** 178
United States Zinc Co., **IV** 32
**United Stationers Inc.**, **14 521–23**; **25** 13; **36** 508
United Steel, **III** 494
United Steel Mills Ltd., **25** 266
United Supers, **II** 624

**United Technologies Automotive Inc., 15 513–15**
**United Technologies Corporation, I** 68, **84–86**, 143, 411, 530, 559; **II** 64, 82; **III** 74; **9** 18, 418; **10 536–38 (upd.)**; **11** 308; **12** 289; **13** 191, 384–86; **22** 6; **34** 371–72, 432, **481–85 (upd.)**; **39** 311, 313
**United Telecommunications, Inc., V 344–47**; **8** 310; **9** 478–80; **10** 202; **12** 541
United Telephone Company, **7** 508; **14** 257
United Telephone Company of the Carolinas, **10** 202
United Telephone of Indiana, **14** 259
United Telephone System, Inc., **V** 346
United Telespectrum, **6** 314
United Television, Inc., **9** 119; **26** 32
United Television Programs, **II** 143
United Thermal Corp., **42** 388
United Transportation Co., **6** 382
United Truck Lines, **14** 505
United Utilities, Inc., **V** 344; **10** 202
United Van Lines, **14** 37; **15** 50
United Verde Copper Co., **IV** 178
**United Video Satellite Group, 18 535–37**. *See also* TV Guide, Inc.
United Vintners, **I** 243, 260–61
**United Water Resources, Inc., 40 447–50**; **45** 277
**United Way of America, 36 485–88**
United Westburne Inc., **19** 313
United Westphalia Electricity Co., **IV** 127
Unitek Corp., **III** 18
Unitel Communications Inc., **6** 311; **44** 49; **46** 401; **47** 136
**Unitika Ltd., V 387–89**
**Unitil Corporation, 37 403–06**
**Unitog Co., 16** 228; **19 457–60**; **21** 115
Unitransa, **27** 474
**Unitrin Inc., 16 503–05**
Unitron Medical Communications, **29** 412
Unity Cellular Systems, Inc. *See* Rural Cellular Corporation.
Unity Financial Corp., **19** 411
Unity Joint-Stock Bank, **II** 334
UNIVAC, **III** 133, 152, 313; **6** 233, 240, 266
**Univar Corporation, 8** 99; **9 530–32**; **12** 333; **41** 340
Univas, **13** 203 **23** 171
Univasa, **39** 229
Univel Inc., **38** 418
Universal Adding Machine, **III** 165
Universal American, **I** 452
Universal Atlas Cement Co., **IV** 573–74; **7** 550–51
Universal Belo Productions, **10** 5
Universal Cheerleaders Association. *See* Varsity Spirit Corp.
Universal Cigar Corp., **14** 19
Universal Consumer Products Group, **30** 123
Universal Containers, **IV** 249
Universal Controls, Inc., **10** 319
Universal Cooler Corp., **8** 515
**Universal Corporation, V 417–18**; **48 403–06 (upd.)**
Universal Data Systems, **II** 61; **22** 17
**Universal Electronics Inc., 39 405–08**
**Universal Foods Corporation, 7 546–48**; **21** 498
Universal Footcare Products Inc., **31** 255
**Universal Forest Products Inc., 10 539–40**
Universal Frozen Foods, **23** 321
Universal Furniture, **III** 571; **20** 362
Universal Genève, **13** 121
Universal Guaranty Life Insurance Company, **11** 482
**Universal Health Services, Inc., 6 191–93**
Universal Highways, **III** 735
Universal Industries, Inc., **10** 380; **13** 533
Universal Instruments Corp., **III** 468
**Universal International, Inc., 25** 353, 355, **510–11**
Universal Juice Co., **21** 55
Universal Leaf Tobacco Company. *See* Universal Corporation.
Universal Manufacturing, **I** 440–41; **25** 167
Universal Marking Systems, **25** 331
Universal Match, **12** 464
Universal Matchbox Group, **12** 495
Universal Matthey Products Ltd., **IV** 119
Universal Music Group, **22** 194; **26** 152; **37** 193
Universal Paper Bag Co., **IV** 345
Universal Pictures, **II** 102, 135, 144, 154–55, 157; **10** 196; **14** 399; **25** 271. *See also* Universal Studios, Inc.
Universal Press Syndicate, **10** 4; **40** 38
Universal Records, **27** 123
Universal Resources Corporation, **6** 569; **26** 388
Universal Shoes, Inc., **22** 213
Universal Stamping Machine Co., **III** 156
Universal Studios Florida, **14** 399
**Universal Studios, Inc., II** 143–44; **12** 73; **21** 23–26; **25** 411; **33 429–33**; **47** 419–21
Universal Telephone, **9** 106
Universal Television, **II** 144
Universal Textured Yarns, **12** 501
Universal Transfers Co. Ltd., **IV** 119
University Computing Corp., **II** 38; **11** 468; **17** 320; **25** 87
University Microfilms, **III** 172; **6** 289
University of Phoenix, **24** 40
Univisa, **24** 516
**Univision Communications Inc., IV** 621; **18** 213; **24 515–18**; **41** 150–52
Unix System Laboratories Inc., **6** 225; **25** 20–21; **38** 418
UNM. *See* United News & Media plc.
Uno-e Bank, **48** 51
**Uno Restaurant Corporation, 16** 447; **18** 465, **538–40**
Uno-Ven, **IV** 571; **24** 522
**Unocal Corporation, IV** 508, **569–71**; **24 519–23 (upd.)**
UNR Industries, Inc. *See* ROHN Industries, Inc.
Unterberg Harris, **25** 433
**UNUM Corp., III** 236; **13 538–40**
**Uny Co., Ltd., II** 619; **V 209–10**, 154; **13** 545; **36** 419
UPC. *See* United Pan-Europe Communications NV.
UPI. *See* United Press International.
**Upjohn Company, I** 675, 684, 686, 700, **707–09**; **III** 18, 53; **6** 42; **8 547–49 (upd.)**; **10** 79; **12** 186; **13** 503; **14** 423; **16** 440; **29** 363. *See also* Pharmacia & Upjohn Inc.
**UPM-Kymmene Corporation, 19 461–65**; **25** 12; **30** 325
UPN. *See* United Paramount Network.
Upper Deck Company, LLC, **34** 448; **37** 295
UPS. *See* United Parcel Service of America Inc.
UPSHOT, **27** 195
Upton Machine Company, **12** 548
Uraga Dock Co., **II** 361; **III** 634
Uraga Heavy Industries, **III** 634
Urbaine, **III** 391–92
Urban Investment and Development Co., **IV** 703
**Urban Outfitters, Inc., 14 524–26**
Urban Systems Development Corp., **II** 121
Urenco, **6** 452
**URS Corporation, 45 420–23**
Urwick Orr, **II** 609
US Airways Express, **32** 334; **38** 130
**US Airways Group, Inc., 28 506–09 (upd.)**; **33** 303
US Industrial Chemicals, Inc., **I** 377; **8** 440
US Industries Inc., **30** 231
US 1 Industries, **27** 404
US Order, Inc., **10** 560, 562
US Sprint Communications Company, **V** 295–96, 346–47; **6** 314; **8** 310; **9** 32; **10** 543; **11** 302; **12** 136, 541; **14** 252–53; **15** 196; **16** 318, 392; **25** 101; **29** 44; **43** 447. *See also* Sprint Communications Company, L.P.
US Telecom, **9** 478–79
US West Communications Services, Inc., **19** 255; **21** 285; **29** 39, 45, 478; **37** 312, 315–16. *See also* Regional Bell Operating Companies.
USA Cafes, **14** 331
USA Floral Products Inc., **27** 126
**USA Interactive, Inc., 47 418–22 (upd.)**
USA Networks Inc., **25** 330, 411; **33** 432; **37** 381, 383–84; **43** 422
USA Security Systems, Inc., **27** 21
**USA Truck, Inc., 42 410–13**
**USAA, 10 541–43**
**USAir Group, Inc., I** 55, **131–32**; **III** 215; **6** 121, **131–32 (upd.)**; **11** 300; **14** 70, 73; **18** 62; **21** 143; **24** 400; **26** 429; **42** 34. *See also* US Airways Group, Inc.
**USANA, Inc., 27** 353; **29 491–93**
USCC. *See* United States Cellular Corporation.
USCP-WESCO Inc., **II** 682
Usego AG., **48** 63
**USF&G Corporation, III 395–98**; **11** 494–95; **19** 190
USFL. *See* United States Football League.
USFreightways, **27** 475
**USG Corporation, III 762–64**; **26 507–10 (upd.)**
USH. *See* United Scientific Holdings.
Usines de l'Espérance, **IV** 226
Usines Métallurgiques de Hainaut, **IV** 52
**Usinor SA, 42 414–17 (upd.)**
**Usinor Sacilor, IV 226–28**; **22** 44; **24** 144; **26** 81, 84
USLD Communications Corp. *See* Billing Concepts Corp.
USLIFE, **III** 194
USM, **10** 44
Usource LLC, **37** 406
USPS. *See* United States Postal Service.
USSC. *See* United States Surgical Corporation.
USSI. *See* U.S. Software Inc.
**UST Inc., 9 533–35**; **42** 79

UST Wilderness Management Corporation, **33** 399
USV Pharmaceutical Corporation, **11** 333
USWeb/CKS. *See* marchFIRST, Inc.
**USX Corporation**, **I** 466; **IV** 130, 228, **572–74**; **7** 193–94, **549–52 (upd.)**
UT Starcom, **44** 426
UTA, **I** 119, 121; **6** 373–74, 93; **34** 397
Utag, **11** 510
Utah Construction & Mining Co., **I** 570; **IV** 146; **14** 296
Utah Federal Savings Bank, **17** 530
Utah Gas and Coke Company, **6** 568
Utah Group Health Plan, **6** 184
Utah International, **II** 30; **12** 196
**Utah Medical Products, Inc.**, **36 496–99**
Utah Mines Ltd., **IV** 47; **22** 107
Utah Oil Refining Co., **IV** 370
**Utah Power and Light Company**, **9** 536; **12** 266; **27 483–86**. *See also* PacifiCorp.
UTI Energy Corp., **12** 500
Utilicom, **6** 572
**Utilicorp United Inc.**, **6 592–94**
UtiliTech Solutions, **37** 88
Utilities Power & Light Corporation, **I** 512; **6** 508
Utility Constructors Incorporated, **6** 527
Utility Engineering Corporation, **6** 580
Utility Fuels, **7** 377
Utility Service Affiliates, Inc., **45** 277
Utility Services, Inc., **42** 249, 253
Utility Supply Co. *See* United Stationers Inc.
AB Utra Wood Co., **IV** 274
Utrecht Allerlei Risico's, **III** 200
**UUNET**, **38 468–72**
UV Industries, Inc., **7** 360; **9** 440

V & V Cos., **I** 412
V&S Variety Stores, **V** 37
V.A.W. of America Inc., **IV** 231
V.L. Churchill Group, **10** 493
VA Linux Systems, **45** 363
Vabis, **I** 197
Vacheron Constantin, **27** 487, 489
Vaco, **38** 200, 202
Vaculator Division. *See* Lancer Corporation.
Vacuum Metallurgical Company, **11** 234
Vacuum Oil Co., **IV** 463–64, 504, 549; **7** 351–52
Vadic Corp., **II** 83
Vadoise Vie, **III** 273
Vagnfabriks A.B., **I** 197
**Vail Associates, Inc.**, **11 543–46**; **31** 65, 67
**Vail Resorts, Inc.**, **43 435–39 (upd.)**
**Vaillant GmbH**, **44 436–39**
Val Corp., **24** 149
Val-Pak Direct Marketing Systems, Inc., **22** 162
Val Royal LaSalle, **II** 652
**Valassis Communications, Inc.**, **8 550–51**; **37 407–10 (upd.)**
Valcambi S.A., **II** 268; **21** 145
Valcom, **13** 176
ValCom Inc. *See* InaCom Corporation.
Valdi Foods Inc., **II** 663–64
Valdosta Drug Co., **III** 9–10
Vale do Rio Doce Navegacao SA—Docenave, **43** 112
Vale Harmon Enterprises, Ltd., **25** 204
Vale Power Company, **12** 265
Valentine & Company, **8** 552–53
**Valeo**, **III** 593; **23 492–94**
**Valero Energy Corporation**, **IV** 394; **7 553–55**; **19** 140; **31** 119
**Valhi, Inc.**, **10** 435–36; **19 466–68**
Valid Logic Systems Inc., **11** 46, 284; **48** 77
Valio-Finnish Co-operative Dairies' Assoc., **II** 575
Valke Oy, **IV** 348
**Vallen Corporation**, **45 424–26**
Valley Bank of Helena, **35** 197, 199
Valley Bank of Maryland, **46** 25
Valley Bank of Nevada, **19** 378
Valley Crest Tree Company, **31** 182–83
Valley Deli Inc., **24** 243
Valley East Medical Center, **6** 185
Valley Falls Co., **III** 213
Valley Fashions Corp., **16** 535
Valley Federal of California, **11** 163
Valley Fig Growers, **7** 496–97
Valley Forge Life Insurance Co., **III** 230
**Valley Media Inc.**, **35 430–33**
Valley National Bank, **II** 420
Valley-Todeco, Inc., **13** 305–06
Valley Transport Co., **II** 569
Valleyfair, **22** 130
Vallourec, **IV** 227
Valmac Industries, **II** 585
**Valmet Corporation**, **I** 198; **III 647–49**; **IV** 276, 350, 471
Valmet Oy. *See* Metso Corporation.
**Valmont Industries, Inc.**, **13** 276; **19** 50, **469–72**
**Valores Industriales S.A.**, **19** 10, 12, 189, **473–75**; **29** 219
**The Valspar Corporation**, **8 552–54**; **32 483–86 (upd.)**
Valtec Industries, **III** 684
Valtek International, Inc., **17** 147
Valtur, **6** 207; **48** 316
Value America, **29** 312
Value City Department Stores,
**Value City Department Stores, Inc.**, **29** 311; **38 473–75**
Value Foods Ltd., **11** 239
Value Giant Stores, **12** 478
Value House, **II** 673
Value Investors, **III** 330
**Value Line, Inc.**, **16 506–08**
**Value Merchants Inc.**, **13 541–43**
Value Rent-A-Car, **9** 350; **23** 354
Valueland, **8** 482
**ValueVision International, Inc.**, **22 534–36**; **27** 337
ValuJet, Inc. *See* AirTran Holdings, Inc.
Valvoline, Inc., **I** 291; **IV** 374
Valvtron, **11** 226
Van Ameringen-Haebler, Inc., **9** 290
Van Brunt Manufacturing Co., **III** 462; **21** 173
**Van Camp Seafood Company, Inc.**, **II** 562–63; **7 556–57**; **13** 426. *See also* Chicken of the Sea International.
Van Cleef & Arpels Inc., **26** 145
Van de Kamp's, Inc., **II** 556–57; **7** 430; **32** 67
Van den Bergh Foods, **II** 588; **9** 319
Van der Horst Corp. of America, **III** 471
Van der Moolen Holding NV, **37** 224
Van Dorn Company, **13** 190
Van Dorn Electric Tool Co., **III** 435
Van Gend and Loos, **6** 404; **26** 241, 243
Van Houton, **II** 521
**Van Houtte Inc.**, **39 409–11**
Van Kirk Chocolate, **7** 429
Van Kok-Ede, **II** 642
Van Leer Containers Inc., **30** 397
Van Leer Holding, Inc., **9** 303, 305
Van Leer N.V. *See* Royal Packaging Industries Van Leer N.V.
Van Mar, Inc., **18** 88
Van Munching & Company, Inc., **I** 256; **13** 257, 259; **34** 202
Van Nostrand Reinhold, **8** 526
Van Ommeren, **41** 339–40
Van Ryn Gold Mines Estate, **IV** 90
Van Schaardenburg, **II** 528
Van Sickle, **IV** 485
Van Waters & Rogers, **8** 99; **41** 340
Van Wezel, **26** 278–79
Van Wijcks Waalsteenfabrieken, **14** 249
Vanadium Alloys Steel Company (VASCO), **13** 295–96
Vanant Packaging Corporation, **8** 359
Vance International Airways, **8** 349
Vancouver Pacific Paper Co., **IV** 286
Vanderbilt Mortgage and Finance, **13** 154
Vanderlip-Swenson-Tilghman Syndicate, **IV** 81; **7** 185
Vanessa and Biffi, **11** 226
**The Vanguard Group, Inc.**, **34 486–89 (upd.)**
**The Vanguard Group of Investment Companies**, **9** 239; **14 530–32**
Vanguard International Semiconductor Corp., **47** 385
Vanity Fair Mills, Inc., **V** 390–91
Vanity Fair Paper Mills, **IV** 281; **9** 259
**Vans, Inc.**, **16 509–11**; **17** 259–61; **47 423–26 (upd.)**
Vansickle Industries, **III** 603
Vanstar, **13** 176
Vantage Analysis Systems, Inc., **11** 490
Vantive Corporation, **33** 333; **38** 431–32
Vantona Group Ltd., **V** 356; **44** 105
Vantress Pedigree, Inc., **II** 585
Vapor Corp., **III** 444
**Varco International, Inc.**, **42 418–20**
Varco-Pruden, Inc., **8** 544–46
Vare Corporation, **8** 366
**Vari-Lite International, Inc.**, **35 434–36**
Variable Annuity Life Insurance Co., **III** 193–94
**Varian Associates Inc.**, **12 504–06**
**Varian, Inc.**, **48 407–11 (upd.)**
Varibus Corporation, **6** 495
Variform, Inc., **12** 397
**VARIG S.A. (Viação Aérea Rio-Grandense)**, **6 133–35**; **26** 113; **29 494–97 (upd.)**; **31** 443–45; **33** 19
**Varity Corporation**, **III 650–52**; **7** 258, 260; **19** 294; **27** 203, 251
**Varlen Corporation**, **16 512–14**
Varney Air Lines, **I** 47, 128; **6** 128; **9** 416
Varney Speed Lines. *See* Continental Airlines, Inc.
Varo, **7** 235, 237
**Varsity Spirit Corp.**, **15 516–18**; **22** 459
**Varta AG**, **III** 536; **9** 180–81; **23 495–99**; **26** 230
Vasco Metals Corp., **I** 523; **10** 520, 522
Vascoloy-Ramet, **13** 295
VASP (Viaçao Aérea de Sao Paulo), **6** 134; **29** 495; **31** 444–45
Vasset, S.A., **17** 362–63
Vast Solutions, **39** 24
**Vastar Resources, Inc.**, **24 524–26**; **38** 445, 448

Vaughan Harmon Systems Ltd., **25** 204
Vaughan Printers Inc., **23** 100
Vaungarde, Inc., **22** 175
Vauxhall, **19** 391
VAW Leichtmetall GmbH, **IV** 231
VBB Viag-Bayernwerk-Beteiligungs-Gesellschaft mbH, **IV** 232
VDM Nickel-Technologie AG, **IV** 89
VEB Londa, **III** 69
**Veba A.G., I** 349–50, **542–43; III** 695; **IV** 194–95, 199, 455, 508; **8** 69, 494–495; **15 519–21 (upd.); 23** 69, 451, 453–54; **24** 79; **25** 102; **26** 423; **32** 147
**VECO International, Inc., 7 558–59**
Vector Automotive Corporation, **13** 61
Vector Casa de Bolsa, **21** 413
Vector Gas Ltd., **13** 458
**Vector Group Ltd., 35 437–40 (upd.)**
Vector Video, Inc., **9** 74
Vedelectric, **13** 544
**Vedior NV, 35 441–43; 44** 5
**Veeco Instruments Inc., 32 487–90**
Veeder-Root Company, **7** 116–17
**Veit Companies, 43 440–42**
Vel-Tex Chemical, **16** 270
Velcarta S.p.A., **17** 281
**Velcro Industries N.V., 19 476–78**
Velda Farms, Inc., **26** 448
Vellumoid Co., **I** 159
VeloBind, Inc., **10** 314
Velsicol, **I** 342, 440
Velva-Sheen Manufacturing Co., **23** 66
Vemar, **7** 558
**Venator Group Inc., 35 444–49 (upd.)**
Vencemos, **20** 124
**Vencor, Inc., IV** 402; **14** 243; **16 515–17; 25** 456
**Vendex International N.V., 10** 136–37; **13 544–46; 26** 160; **46** 187, 189
**Vendôme Luxury Group plc, 27 487–89; 29** 90, 92
Vendors Supply of America, Inc., **7** 241–42; **25** 241
**Venetian Casino Resort, LLC, 47 427–29**
Venevision, **24** 516, 517
Vennootschap Nederland, **III** 177–78
Ventshade Company, **40** 299–300
Ventura, **29** 356–57
Venture Out RV, **26** 193
**Venture Stores Inc., V** 134; **12 507–09**
Venturi, Inc., **9** 72
Vepco. *See* Virginia Electric and Power Company.
Vera Cruz Electric Light, Power and Traction Co. Ltd., **IV** 658
Vera Imported Parts, **11** 84
Verafumos Ltd., **12** 109
Veragon Corporation. *See* Drypers Corporation.
Veratex Group, **13** 149–50
Veravision, **24** 510
**Verbatim Corporation, III** 477; **7** 163; **14 533–35; 36** 173
Verbundnetz Gas AG, **38** 408
Verd-A-Fay, **13** 398
Vereenigde Nederlandsche Scheepvaartmaatschappij, **6** 404; **26** 242
Vereeniging Refractories, **IV** 22
Vereeniging Tiles, **III** 734
Verein für Chemische Industrie, **IV** 70
Vereinigte Aluminium Werke AG, **IV** 229–30, 232
Vereinigte Deutsche Metallwerke AG, **IV** 140
Vereinigte Elektrizitäts und Bergwerke A.G., **I** 542
**Vereinigte Elektrizitätswerke Westfalen AG, IV** 195; **V 744–47**
Vereinigte Energiewerke AG, **V** 709
Vereinigte Flugtechnische Werke GmbH., **I** 42, 55, 74–75
Vereinigte Glanzstoff-Fabriken, **13** 21
Vereinigte Industrie-Unternehmungen Aktiengesellschaft, **IV** 229–30
Vereinigte Leichmetall-Werke GmbH, **IV** 231
Vereinigte Papierwarenfabriken GmbH, **IV** 323
Vereinigte Papierwerke Schickedanz AG, **26** 384
Vereinigte Stahlwerke AG, **III** 565; **IV** 87, 104–05, 132, 221; **14** 327
Vereinigte Versicherungsgruppe, **III** 377
Vereinigten Westdeutsche Waggonfabriken AG, **III** 542–43
Vereinsbank Wismar, **II** 256
Vereinte Versicherungen, **III** 377
Verenigde Bedrijven Bredero, **26** 280
N.V. Verenigde Fabrieken Wessanen and Laan, **II** 527
Verenigde Nederlandse Uitgeverijen. *See* VNU N.V.
Verenigde Spaarbank Groep. *See* VSB Groep.
Verienigte Schweizerbahnen, **6** 424
Verifact Inc. (IVI), **46** 251
**VeriFone, Inc., 15** 321; **18 541–44; 27** 219–21; **28** 191
Verilyte Gold, Inc., **19** 452
**VeriSign, Inc., 47 430–34**
Veritas Capital Fund L.P., **44** 420, 423
Veritas Capital Partners, **26** 408
**Veritas Software Corporation, 45 427–31**
Veritec Technologies, Inc., **48** 299
Veritus Inc., **27** 208–09
**Verizon Communications, 43 443–49 (upd.)**
Verizon Wireless, Inc., **42** 284
Verlagsgruppe Georg von Holtzbrinck GmbH, **15** 158, 160; **25** 485; **35 450–53**
**Vermeer Manufacturing Company, 17 507–10**
**The Vermont Teddy Bear Co., Inc., 36 500–02**
Verneuil Holding Co, **21** 387
Vernitron Corporation, **18** 293
Vernon and Nelson Telephone Company. *See* British Columbia Telephone Company.
Vernon Graphics, **III** 499
Vernon Paving, **III** 674
Vernon Savings & Loan, **9** 199
Vernons, **IV** 651
Vernors, Inc., **25** 4
Vero, **III** 434
La Verrerie Souchon-Neuvesel, **II** 474
Verreries Champenoises, **II** 475
Versace. *See* Gianni Versace SpA.
Versatec Inc., **13** 128
Versatile Farm and Equipment Co., **22** 380
Versax, S.A. de C.V., **19** 12
Versicherungs-Verein, **III** 402, 410–11
Verson Allsteel Press Co., **21** 20, 22
Vert Baudet, **19** 309
Vertical Technology Industries, **14** 571
Verticom, **25** 531
Verve Records, **23** 389
Vessel Management Services, Inc., **28** 80
Vestar Capital Partners, **42** 309
Vestek Systems, Inc., **13** 417
Vestro, **19** 309
Vesuvius Crucible Co., **III** 681
Vesuvius USA Corporation, **8** 179
Veszpremtej, **25** 85
Veterinary Cos. of America, **III** 25
**VEW AG, IV** 234; **39 412–15**
Vexlar, **18** 313
**VF Corporation, V 390–92; 12** 205; **13** 512; **17** 223, 225, **511–14 (upd.); 25** 22; **31** 261
VFW-Fokker B.V., **I** 41, 55, 74–75
VHA Long Term Care, **23** 431
VH1 Inc., **23** 503
VI-Jon Laboratories, Inc., **12** 388
VIA/Rhin et Moselle, **III** 185
Via-Générale de Transport et d'Industrie SA, **28** 155
Viacao Aerea Rio Grandense of South America. *See* VARIG, SA.
Viacom Enterprises, **6** 33; **7** 336
**Viacom Inc., 23** 274–76, **500–03 (upd.); 24** 106, 327; **26** 32; **28** 295; **30** 101; **31** 59, 109; **35** 402; **48** 214. *See also* National Amusements Inc.
**Viacom International Inc., 7** 222–24, 530, **560–62; 9** 429; **10** 175; **19** 403
**Viag AG, IV 229–32**, 323; **25** 332; **32** 153; **43** 188–89
Viajes El Corte Inglés, S.A., **26** 129
VIASA, **I** 107; **6** 97; **36** 281
**Viasoft Inc., 27 490–93**
**Viatech Continental Can Company, Inc., 25 512–15 (upd.)**
Vichy, **III** 46
Vickers-Armstrong Ltd., **I** 50, 57, 82; **24** 85
Vickers Inc., **III** 640, 642; **13** 8; **23** 83
**Vickers plc, I** 194–95; **II** 3; **III** 555, 652, 725; **16** 9; **21** 435; **27 494–97; 47** 9
VICOM, **48** 415
**Vicon Industries, Inc., 44 440–42**
Vicoreen Instrument Co., **I** 202
**VICORP Restaurants, Inc., 12 510–12; 48 412–15 (upd.)**
Vicra Sterile Products, **I** 628
Vicsodrive Japan, **III** 495
Victor Company, **10** 483
**Victor Company of Japan, Ltd., I** 411; **II** 55–56, 91, 102, **118–19; III** 605; **IV** 599; **12** 454; **26 511–13 (upd.)**
Victor Comptometer, **I** 676; **III** 154
Victor Equipment Co., **19** 440
Victor Manufacturing and Gasket Co., **I** 152
Victor Musical Industries Inc., **II** 119; **10** 285
Victor Talking Machine Co., **II** 88, 118
Victor Value, **II** 678
Victoria, **III** 308
Victoria & Co., **39** 247
Victoria & Legal & General, **III** 359
Victoria Coach Station, **6** 406
Victoria Creations Inc., **13** 536
**Victoria Group, 44 443–46 (upd.)**
**VICTORIA Holding AG, III 399–401**. *See also* Victoria Group.
Victoria Paper Co., **IV** 286
Victoria Sugar Co., **III** 686
Victoria Wine Co., **I** 216

Victoria's Secret, **V** 115–16; **11** 498; **12** 557, 559; **16** 219; **18** 215; **24** 237; **25** 120–22, 521
**Victorinox AG, 21 515–17**
Victory Fire Insurance Co., **III** 343
Victory Insurance, **III** 273
Victory Oil Co., **IV** 550
Victory Refrigeration Company, **22** 355
Victory Savings and Loan, **10** 339
Victory Supermarket. *See* Big V Supermarkets, Inc.
Vidal Sassoon, **17** 110
Video Concepts, **9** 186
Video Independent Theatres, Inc., **14** 86
Video Library, Inc., **9** 74
Video News International, **19** 285
Video Superstores Master Limited Partnership, **9** 74
Videoconcepts, **II** 107
VideoFusion, Inc., **16** 419
Videotex Network Japan, **IV** 680
Videotron, **25** 102
VideV, **24** 509
La Vie Claire, **13** 103
Vielle Montaign, **22** 285
**Vienna Sausage Manufacturing Co., 14 536–37**
**Viessmann Werke GmbH & Co., 37 411–14**
View-Master/Ideal Group, **12** 496
Viewdata Corp., **IV** 630; **15** 264
Viewer's Edge, **27** 429
Viewlogic, **11** 490
ViewStar Corp., **20** 103
Viewtel, **14** 36
ViewTrade Holding Corp., **46** 282
Vigilance-Vie, **III** 393
Vigilant Insurance Co., **III** 220; **14** 108; **37** 83
Vigoro, **22** 340
Vigortone, **II** 582
Viiala Oy, **IV** 302
Viking, **II** 10; **IV** 659
Viking Brush, **III** 614
Viking Building Products, **22** 15
Viking Computer Services, Inc., **14** 147
Viking Consolidated Shipping Corp, **25** 470
Viking Direct Limited, **10** 545
Viking Foods, Inc., **8** 482; **14** 411
Viking Industries, **39** 322, 324
**Viking Office Products, Inc., 10 544–46**
Viking Penguin, **IV** 611
Viking Press, **12** 25
Viking Pump Company, **21** 499–500
Viking Star Shipping, Inc. *See* Teekay Shipping Corporation.
Viktor Achter, **9** 92
Village Inn. *See* VICORP Restaurants, Inc.
**Village Super Market, Inc., 7 563–64**
**Village Voice Media, Inc., 38 476–79**
Villager, Inc., **11** 216; **39** 244
Villazon & Co., **27** 139
**Villeroy & Boch AG, 37 415–18**
VILPAC, S.A., **26** 356
**AO VimpelCom, 48 416–19**
Vimto. *See* Nichols plc.
**Vin & Spirit AB, 31 458–61**
**Viña Concha y Toro S.A., 45 432–34**
**Vinci, 27** 54; **43 450–52**
Vine Products Ltd., **I** 215
Viner Bros., **16** 546
Vingaarden A/S, **9** 100
Vingresor A.B., **I** 120
Vining Industries, **12** 128
Viniprix SA, **10** 205; **19** 309; **27** 95
Vinland Web-Print, **8** 360
**Vinson & Elkins L.L.P., 28** 48; **30 481–83**; **47** 139–40, 447
**Vintage Petroleum, Inc., 42 421–23**
Vintners International, **34** 89
Vinyl Maid, Inc., **IV** 401
Vipont Pharmaceutical, **III** 25; **14** 122
VIPS, **11** 113
Viratec Thin Films, Inc., **22** 347
**Virco Manufacturing Corporation, 17 515–17**
Virgin Atlantic Airlines. *See* Virgin Group PLC.
Virgin Express, **35** 384
**Virgin Group PLC, 12 513–15**; **14** 73; **18** 80; **22** 194; **24** 486; **29** 302; **32 491–96 (upd.)**
The Virgin Islands Telephone Co., **19** 256
Virgin Retail Group Ltd., **9** 75, 361; **37** 262
Virginia Eastern Shore Sustainable Development Corporation, **28** 307
Virginia Electric and Power Company, **V** 596–98
Virginia Fibre Corporation, **15** 188
Virginia Folding Box Company, **IV** 352; **19** 497
Virginia Laminating, **10** 313
Virginia Mason Medical Center, **41** 183
Virginia National Bankshares, **10** 426
Virginia Railway and Power Company (VR&P), **V** 596
Virginia Trading Corp., **II** 422
Viridor Waste Limited, **45** 338
Viromedics, **25** 382
Visa. *See* Valores Industriales S.A.
**Visa International, II** 200; **9** 333–35, **536–38**; **18** 543; **20** 59; **26 514–17 (upd.)**; **41** 200–01
Visco Products Co., **I** 373; **12** 346
Viscodrive GmbH, **III** 495
Viscount Industries Limited, **6** 310
**Vishay Intertechnology, Inc., 11** 516; **21 518–21**
VisiCorp, **6** 254; **25** 298
Vision Centers, **I** 688; **12** 188
Vision Technology Group Ltd., **19** 124
Visionware Ltd., **38** 419
Visionworks, **9** 186
Viskase Corporation, **17** 157, 159
Visking Co., **I** 400
Visnews Ltd., **IV** 668, 670
VisQueen, **I** 334
Vista Bakery Inc., **14** 306
**Vista Chemical Company, I 402–03**; **V** 709
Vista Concepts, Inc., **11** 19
Vista Resources, Inc., **17** 195
Vista 2000, Inc., **36** 444
**Vistana, Inc., 22 537–39**; **26** 464
Visual Action Holdings plc, **24** 96, 374
Visual Information Technologies, **11** 57
Visual Technology, **6** 201
**VISX, Incorporated, 30 484–86**
Vita-Achter, **9** 92
Vita Lebensversicherungs-Gesellschaft, **III** 412
Vita Liquid Polymers, **9** 92
Vitafoam Incorporated, **9** 93; **33** 78
Vital Health Corporation, **13** 150
Vital Processing Services LLC, **18** 516, 518
Vitalink Communications Corp., **11** 520; **34** 444
**Vitalink Pharmacy Services, Inc., 15 522–24**; **25** 309–10
Vitalscheme, **38** 426
Vitamin World, **31** 346–48
**Vitesse Semiconductor Corporation, 32 497–500**
Vitex Foods, **10** 382
Vitoria-Minas Railroad, **43** 111
**Vitro Corp., 8** 178; **10 547–48**; **17** 492
**Vitro Corporativo S.A. de C.V., 34 490–92**
Vitro S.A., **19** 189
VIVA, **23** 390
Viva Home Co., **III** 757
**Vivendi Universal S.A., 29** 369, 371; **32** 52, 54; **33** 178, 181; **34** 83, 85; **38** 168, 170; **40** 408; **41** 361; **43** 450, 452; **44** 190; **46 438–41 (upd.)**; **47** 420–21; **48** 164–65
Vivendia, **40** 449
Vivesvata Iron and Steel Ltd., **IV** 207
Viviane Woodard Cosmetic Corp., **II** 531
**Vivra, Inc., 15** 119; **18 545–47**
VK Mason Construction Ltd., **II** 222
VKI Technologies Inc., **39** 409
Vladivostok Dairy, **48** 438
**Vlasic Foods International Inc., II** 480–81; **7** 67–68; **25 516–19**; **26** 56, 59
VLN Corp., **I** 201
**VLSI Technology, Inc., 11** 246; **16 518–20**; **31** 300
VMG Products. *See* Drypers Corporation.
VMX Inc., **14** 355; **41** 289
VND, **III** 593
Vnesheconobank, **II** 242
VNG. *See* Verbundnetz Gas AG.
VNS. *See* Vereenigde Nederlandsche Scheepvaartmaatschappij.
**VNU N.V., 27** 361, **498–501**; **38** 8
VNU/Claritas, **6** 14
Vobis Microcomputer, **20** 103; **23** 311
VocalTec, Inc., **18** 143
Vodac, **11** 548
Vodacom World Online Ltd, **48** 399
**Vodafone Group Plc, II** 84; **11 547–48**; **34** 85; **36 503–06 (upd.)**; **38** 296, 300
Vodapage, **11** 548
Vodata, **11** 548
Vodavi Technology Corporation, **13** 213
**Voest-Alpine Stahl AG, IV 233–35**; **31** 47–48
Vogel Peterson Furniture Company, **7** 4–5
Vogoro Corp., **13** 503
Voice Data Systems, **15** 125
Voice Powered Technology International, Inc., **23** 212
Voice Response, Inc., **11** 253
VoiceStream Wireless Corporation, **48** 130
Voith Sulzer Papiermaschinen GmbH. *See* J.M. Voith AG.
Vokes, **I** 429
Volition, Inc., **39** 395
Volkert Stampings, **III** 628
**Volkswagen Aktiengesellschaft, I** 30, 32, 186, 192, **206–08**, 460; **II** 279; **IV** 231; **7** 8; **10** 14; **11** 104, **549–51 (upd.)**; **13** 413; **14** 169; **16** 322; **19** 484; **26** 12; **27** 11, 496; **31** 363–65; **32 501–05 (upd.)**; **34** 55, 130; **39** 373–74
**Volt Information Sciences Inc., 26 518–21**
Volta Aluminium Co., Ltd., **IV** 122

Volume Distributors. *See* Payless ShoeSource, Inc.
Volume Service Company. *See* Restaurants Unlimited, Inc.
Volume Shoe Corporation. *See* Payless ShoeSource,Inc.
Voluntary Hospitals of America, **6** 45
Volunteer Leather Company, **17** 202, 205
Volunteer State Life Insurance Co., **III** 221; **37** 84
**AB Volvo, I** 186, 192, 198, **209–11; II** 5, 366; **III** 543, 591, 623, 648; **IV** 336; **7 565–68 (upd.)**; **9** 283–84, 350, 381; **10** 274; **12** 68, 342; **13** 30, 356; **14** 321; **15** 226; **16** 322; **18** 394; **23** 354; **26 9–12 (upd.)**, 401, 403; **33** 191, 364; **39** 126. *See also* Ford Motor Company.
Volvo-Penta, **21** 503
von Roll, **6** 599
Von Ruden Manufacturing Co., **17** 532
von Weise Gear Co., **III** 509
Von's Grocery Co., **II** 419; **8** 474; **17** 559
**The Vons Companies, Incorporated, II** 655; **7 569–71**; **12** 209; **24** 418; **28 510–13 (upd.)**; **35** 328
VOP Acquisition Corporation, **10** 544
**Vornado Realty Trust, 20 508–10**; **39** 211; **45** 14–16; **47** 360
Voroba Hearing Systems, **25** 56
Vortex Management, Inc., **41** 207
**Vorwerk & Co., 27 502–04**
**Vosper Thornycroft Holding plc, 41 410–12**
Votainer International, **13** 20
Vought Aircraft Company, **11** 364; **45** 309
Voxson, **I** 531; **22** 193
Voyage Conseil, **II** 265
Voyager Communications Inc., **24** 5
Voyager Energy, **IV** 84
Voyager Ltd., **12** 514
Voyager Petroleum Ltd., **IV** 83; **7** 188
Voyageur Travel Insurance Ltd., **21** 447
VR&P. *See* Virginia Railway and Power Company.
Vratislavice A.S., **38** 77
VRG International. *See* Roberts Pharmaceutical Corporation.
Vroom & Dreesmann, **13** 544–46
Vrumona B.V., **I** 257
VS Services, **13** 49
VSA. *See* Vendors Supply of America, Inc.
VSB Groep, **III** 199, 201
VSD Communications, Inc., **22** 443
VSEL, **24** 88
VSM. *See* Village Super Market, Inc.
VST. *See* Vision Technology Group Ltd.
Vtel Corporation, **10** 456; **27** 365
VTR Incorporated, **16** 46; **43** 60
Vu-Tech Communications, Inc., **48** 54
**Vulcan Materials Company, 7 572–75**; **12** 39; **25** 266; **41** 147, 149
Vulcan Ventures Inc., **32** 145; **43** 144
Vulcraft, **7** 400–02
VVM, **III** 200
VW&R. *See* Van Waters & Rogers.
VWR Textiles & Supplies, Inc., **11** 256
VWR United Company, **9** 531
Vycor Corporation, **25** 349
Vyvx, **31** 469

W&A Manufacturing Co., LLC, **26** 530
W&F Fish Products, **13** 103
W. & G. Turnbull & Co., **IV** 278; **19** 153
W & J Sloane Home Furnishings Group, **35** 129
W. & M. Duncan, **II** 569
W.A. Bechtel Co., **I** 558
W.A. Harriman & Co., **III** 471
W.A. Krueger Co., **19** 333–35
**W. Atlee Burpee & Co., II** 532; **11** 198; **27 505–08**
W.B. Constructions, **III** 672
W.B. Doner & Company, **10** 420; **12** 208; **28** 138
W.B. Saunders Co., **IV** 623–24
W.C. Bradley Company, **18** 516
W.C.G. Sports Industries Ltd. *See* Canstar Sports Inc.
W.C. Heraeus GmbH, **IV** 100
W.C. Norris, **III** 467
W.C. Platt Co., **IV** 636
W.C. Ritchie & Co., **IV** 333
W.C. Smith & Company Limited, **14** 339
W. Duke & Sons, **V** 395, 600
W. Duke Sons & Company, **27** 128
W.E. Andrews Co., Inc., **25** 182
W.E. Dillon Company, Ltd., **21** 499
W.F. Linton Company, **9** 373
W. Gunson & Co., **IV** 278; **19** 153
W. Gutzeit & Co., **IV** 274–77
**W.H. Brady Co., 17 518–21**
W.H. Gunlocke Chair Co. *See* Gunlocke Company.
W.H. McElwain Co., **III** 528
W.H. Morton & Co., **II** 398; **10** 62
W.H. Smith & Son (Alacra) Ltd., **15** 473
**W H Smith Group PLC, V 211–13**
W.J. Noble and Sons, **IV** 294; **19** 225
**W.L. Gore & Associates, Inc., 14 538–40**; **26** 417
W.M. Bassett Furniture Co. *See* Bassett Furniture Industries, Inc.
W.M. Ritter Lumber Co., **IV** 281; **9** 259
W.O. Daley & Company, **10** 387
W.R. Bean & Son, **19** 335
**W.R. Berkley Corp., III** 248; **15 525–27**
W.R. Breen Company, **11** 486
W.R. Case & Sons Cutlery Company, **18** 567
**W.R. Grace & Company, I 547–50; III** 525, 695; **IV** 454; **11** 216; **12** 337; **13** 149, 502, 544; **14** 29; **16** 45–47; **17** 308, 365–66; **21** 213, 507, 526; **22** 188, 501; **25** 535; **35** 38, 40; **43** 59–60
W. Rosenlew, **IV** 350
W.S. Barstow & Company, **6** 575
W.T. Grant Co., **16** 487
W.T. Rawleigh, **17** 105
W.T. Young Foods, **III** 52; **8** 433; **26** 383
W. Ullberg & Co., **I** 553
W.V. Bowater & Sons, Ltd., **IV** 257–58
W.W. Cargill and Brother, **II** 616; **13** 136
**W.W. Grainger, Inc., V 214–15**; **13** 297; **26 537–39 (upd.)**
W.W. Kimball Company, **12** 296; **18** 44
**W.W. Norton & Company, Inc., 28 518–20**
**Waban Inc., V** 198; **13 547–49**; **19** 449. *See also* HomeBase, Inc.
**Wabash National Corp., 13 550–52**
Wabash Valley Power Association, **6** 556
**Wabtec Corporation, 40 451–54**
Wabush Iron Co., **IV** 73; **24** 143
Wachbrit Insurance Agency, **21** 96
**Wachovia Bank of Georgia, N.A., 16 521–23**
**Wachovia Bank of South Carolina, N.A., 16 524–26**
**Wachovia Corporation, II** 336; **10** 425; **12** 16, **516–20**; **16** 521, 524, 526; **23** 455; **46 442–49 (upd.)**
**Wachtell, Lipton, Rosen & Katz, 47 435–38**
**The Wackenhut Corporation, 13** 124–25; **14 541–43**; **28** 255; **41** 80
**Wacker-Chemie GmbH, 35 454–58**
Wacker Oil Inc., **11** 441
Waco Aircraft Company, **27** 98
**Wacoal Corp., 25 520–24**
**Waddell & Reed, Inc., 22 540–43**; **33** 405, 407
Wade Smith, **28** 27, 30
Wadsworth Inc., **8** 526
WaferTech, **18** 20; **43** 17; **47** 385
**Waffle House Inc., 14 544–45**
Wagenseller & Durst, **25** 249
**Waggener Edstrom, 42 424–26**
The Wagner & Brown Investment Group, **9** 248
Wagner Castings Company, **16** 474–75
Wagner Litho Machinery Co., **13** 369–70
Wagner Spray Tech, **18** 555
Wagonlit Travel, **22** 128
Wagons-Lits, **27** 11; **29** 443; **37** 250–52
Wah Chang Corp., **I** 523–24; **10** 520–21
AB Wahlbecks, **25** 464
Wahlstrom & Co., **23** 480
Waialua Agricultural Co., **II** 491
Waitaki International Biosciences Co., **17** 288
Waite Amulet Mines Ltd., **IV** 164
Waitrose Ltd. *See* John Lewis Partnership plc.
**Wakefern Food Corporation, II** 672; **7** 563–64; **18** 6; **25** 66, 234–35; **28** 143; **33 434–37**
Wako Shoji Co. Ltd. *See* Wacoal Corp.
Wakodo Co., **I** 674
**Wal-Mart de Mexico, S.A. de C.V., 35** 322, **459–61 (upd.)**
**Wal-Mart Stores, Inc., II** 108; **V 216–17**; **6** 287; **7** 61, 331; **8** 33, 295, **555–57 (upd.)**; **9** 187, 361; **10** 236, 284, 515–16, 524; **11** 292; **12** 48, 53–55, 63–64, 97, 208–09, 221, 277, 333, 477, 507–08; **13** 42, 215–17, 260–61, 274, 332–33, 444, 446; **14** 235; **15** 139, 275; **16** 61–62, 65, 390; **17** 297, 321, 460–61; **18** 108, 137, 186, 283, 286; **19** 511; **20** 263; **21** 457–58; **22** 224, 257, 328; **23** 214; **24** 148, 149, 334; **25** 221–22, 254, 314; **26 522–26 (upd.)**, 549; **27** 286, 313, 315, 416, 451; **29** 230, 314, 318; **32** 169, 338, 341; **33** 307; **34** 198; **37** 64; **41** 61, 115; **45** 408, 412
**Walbridge Aldinger Co., 38 480–82**
**Walbro Corporation, 13 553–55**
Walchenseewerk AG, **23** 44
**Waldbaum, Inc., II** 638; **15** 260; **16** 247, 249; **19 479–81**; **24** 528
**Walden Book Company Inc., V** 112; **10** 136–37; **16** 160; **17 522–24**; **25** 30; **47** 209
Waldes Truarc Inc., **III** 624
Oy Waldhof AB, **IV** 324
Wales & Company, **14** 257
**Walgreen Co., V 218–20**; **9** 346; **18** 199; **20 511–13 (upd.)**; **21** 186; **24** 263; **32** 166, 170; **45** 133, 137

Walk Haydel & Associates, Inc., **25** 130
Walk Softly, Inc., **25** 118
Walker & Lee, **10** 340
Walker Cain, **I** 215
Walker Dickson Group Limited, **26** 363
Walker Interactive Systems, **11** 78; **25** 86
**Walker Manufacturing Company**, **I** 527; **19 482–84**
Walker McDonald Manufacturing Co., **III** 569; **20** 361
Walkers Parker and Co., **III** 679–80
Walki GmbH, **IV** 349
AB Walkiakoski, **IV** 347
Walkins Manufacturing Corp., **III** 571; **20** 362
Walkup's Merchant Express Inc., **27** 473
**Wall Drug Store, Inc.**, **40 455–57**
Wall Paper Manufacturers, **IV** 666; **17** 397
**Wall Street Deli, Inc.**, **33 438–41**
Wall Street Leasing, **III** 137
Wallace and Tiernan, **I** 383; **11** 361
The Wallace Berrie Company. *See* Applause Inc.
**Wallace Computer Services, Inc.**, **36 507–10**
Wallace International Silversmiths, **I** 473; **14** 482–83
Wallace Murray Corp., **II** 420
Wallbergs Fabriks A.B., **8** 14
Wallens Dairy Co., **II** 586
Wallin & Nordstrom, **V** 156
Wallingford Bank and Trust Co., **II** 213
Wallis, **V** 177
Wallis Arnold Enterprises, Inc., **21** 483
Wallis Tin Stamping Co., **I** 605
Wallis Tractor Company, **21** 502
Walrus, Inc., **18** 446
Walsin-Lihwa, **13** 141
Walston & Co., **II** 450; **III** 137
**Walt Disney Company**, **II** 102, 122, 129, 156, **172–74**; **III** 142, 504, 586; **IV** 585, 675, 703; **6** 15, **174–77 (upd.)**, 368; **7** 305; **8** 160; **10** 420; **12** 168, 208, 229, 323, 495–96; **13** 551; **14** 260; **15** 197; **16** 143, 336; **17** 243, 317, 442–43; **21** 23–26, 360–61; **23** 257–58, 303, 335, 476, 514; **25** 172, 268, 312–13; **27** 92, 287; **30 487–91 (upd.)**; **34** 348; **43** 142, 447
Walt Disney World, **6** 82, 175–76; **18** 290
Walter Baker's Chocolate, **II** 531
Walter Bau, **27** 136, 138
Walter E. Heller, **17** 324
Walter Herzog GmbH, **16** 514
**Walter Industries, Inc.**, **III 765–67**; **22 544–47 (upd.)**
Walter Kidde & Co., **I** 475, 524; **27** 287
Walter Pierce Oil Co., **IV** 657
Walter Wright Mammoet, **26** 280
Walton Manufacturing, **11** 486
**Walton Monroe Mills, Inc.**, **8 558–60**
Wander Ltd., **I** 672
Wanderer Werke, **III** 154
Wang Global, **39** 176–78
**Wang Laboratories, Inc.**, **II** 208; **III 168–70**; **6 284–87 (upd.)**; **8** 139; **9** 171; **10** 34; **11** 68, 274; **12** 183; **18** 138; **19** 40; **20** 237
Wanishi, **IV** 157; **17** 349
WAP, **26** 420
Waples-Platter Co., **II** 625
War Damage Corp., **III** 353, 356; **22** 493
War Emergency Tankers Inc., **IV** 552
Warbasse-Cogeneration Technologies Partnership, **35** 479
Warburg, Pincus Capital Corp., **6** 13; **9** 524; **14** 42; **24** 373
Warburg USB, **38** 291
Warburtons Bakery Cafe, Inc., **18** 37
Ward Manufacturing Inc., **IV** 101
Ward's Communications, **22** 441
Wardley Ltd., **II** 298
Wards. *See* Circuit City Stores, Inc.
Waring and LaRosa, **12** 167
**The Warnaco Group Inc.**, **9** 156; **12 521–23**; **22** 123; **25** 122, 523; **46 450–54 (upd.)**. *See also* Authentic Fitness Corp.
Warner & Swasey Co., **III** 168; **6** 284; **8** 545
Warner Brothers, **25** 327–28; **26** 102
**Warner Communications Inc.**, **II** 88, 129, 135, 146–47, 154–55, 169–70, **175–77**, 208, 452; **III** 443, 505; **IV** 623, 673, 675–76; **7** 526, 528–30 **8** 527; **9** 44–45, 119, 469; **10** 196; **11** 557; **12** 73, 495–96; **17** 65, 149, 442–43; **21** 23–25, 360; **22** 519, 522; **23** 23–24, 390, 501; **24** 373; **25** 418–19, 498; **26** 151. *See also* Time Warner Inc.
Warner Cosmetics, **III** 48; **8** 129
Warner Gear Co., **III** 438–39; **14** 63–64
**Warner-Lambert Co.**, **I** 643, 674, 679, 696, **710–12**; **7** 596; **8** 62–63; **10 549–52 (upd.)**; **12** 480, 482; **13** 366; **16** 439; **20** 23; **25** 55, 366; **34** 284; **38** 366
Warner Records, **II** 177
Warner Sugar Refining Co., **II** 496
Warren Apparel Group Ltd., **39** 257
Warren Bank, **13** 464
Warren, Gorham & Lamont, **8** 526
Warren Oilfield Services, **9** 363
Warren Petroleum Company, **18** 365, 367
Warri Refining and Petrochemicals Co., **IV** 473
Warrick Industries, **31** 338
Warringah Brick, **III** 673
Warrington Products Ltd. *See* Canstar Sports Inc.
Warrior River Coal Company, **7** 281
Wartsila Marine Industries Inc., **III** 649
Warwick Chemicals, **13** 461
Warwick Electronics, **III** 654
Warwick International Ltd., **13** 462
Wasa, **I** 672–73
Wasag-Chemie AG, **III** 694
Wasatch Gas Co., **6** 568
**Wascana Energy Inc.**, **13 556–58**
Washburn Crosby Co., **II** 501, 555; **10** 322
Washburn Graphics Inc., **23** 100
**The Washington Companies**, **33 442–45**
Washington Duke Sons & Co., **12** 108
**Washington Federal, Inc.**, **17 525–27**
**Washington Football, Inc.**, **35 462–65**
**Washington Gas Light Company**, **19 485–88**
Washington Inventory Service, **30** 239
Washington Mills Company, **13** 532
**Washington Mutual, Inc.**, **17 528–31**
**Washington National Corporation**, **11** 482; **12 524–26**
**Washington Natural Gas Company**, **9 539–41**
**The Washington Post Company**, **III** 214; **IV 688–90**; **6** 323; **11** 331; **18** 60, 61, 63; **20 515–18 (upd.)**; **23** 157–58; **42** 31, 33–34, 209–10
Washington Railway and Electric Company, **6** 552–53
**Washington Scientific Industries, Inc.**, **17 532–34**
Washington Specialty Metals Corp., **14** 323, 325
Washington Sports Clubs. *See* Town Sports International, Inc.
Washington Steel Corp., **14** 323, 325
**Washington Water Power Company**, **6** 566, **595–98**
Washtenaw Gas Company. *See* MCN Corporation.
**Wassall Plc**, **18 548–50**
Wasserstein Perella Partners, **II** 629; **III** 512, 530–31; **V** 223; **17** 366
**Waste Connections, Inc.**, **46 455–57**
Waste Control Specialists LLC, **19** 466, 468
**Waste Holdings, Inc.**, **41 413–15**
**Waste Management, Inc.**, **V** 749–51, **752–54**; **6** 46, 600; **9** 73, 108–09; **11** 435–36; **18** 10; **20** 90; **23** 430
Water Engineering, **11** 360
**Water Pik Technologies, Inc.**, **I** 524–25; **34 498–501**
Water Products Group, **6** 487–88
Water Street Corporate Recovery Fund, **10** 423
The Waterbury Companies, **16** 482
**Waterford Wedgwood Holdings PLC**, **IV** 296; **12 527–29**
**Waterford Wedgwood plc**, **34 493–97 (upd.)**; **38** 403
**Waterhouse Investor Services, Inc.**, **18 551–53**
Waterloo Gasoline Engine Co., **III** 462; **21** 173
Waterlow and Sons, **10** 269
Waterman Marine Corporation, **27** 242
The Waterman Pen Company. *See* BIC Corporation.
WaterPro Supplies Corporation, **6** 486, 488
**Waters Corporation**, **43 453–57**
Waterstone's, **42** 444
Waterstreet Inc., **17** 293
Watertown Insurance Co., **III** 370
**Watkins-Johnson Company**, **15 528–30**
Watkins Manufacturing Co., **I** 159
Watkins-Strathmore Co., **13** 560
Watmough and Son Ltd., **II** 594
Watney Mann and Truman Brewers, **I** 228, 247; **9** 99
Watson-Haas Lumber Company, **33** 257
**Watson Pharmaceuticals Inc.**, **16 527–29**
Watson-Triangle, **16** 388, 390
Watson-Wilson Transportation System, **V** 540; **14** 567
**Watson Wyatt Worldwide**, **42 427–30**
Watt & Shand, **16** 61
Watt AG, **6** 491
Watt Electronic Products, Limited, **10** 319
The Watt Stopper, **21** 348, 350
Wattie Pict Ltd., **I** 437
**Wattie's Ltd.**, **7 576–78**; **11** 173
**Watts Industries, Inc.**, **19 489–91**
Watts/Silverstein, Inc., **24** 96
Waukesha Engine Servicenter, **6** 441
Waukesha Foundry Company, **11** 187
Waukesha Motor Co., **III** 472
Wausau Paper Mills, **15** 305
Wausau Sulphate Fibre Co. *See* Mosinee Paper Corporation.

Wavelength Corporate Communications Pty Limited, **24** 95
**Waverly, Inc.**, **10** 135; **16 530–32**; **19** 358
Waverly Oil Works, **I** 405
Waverly Pharmaceutical Limited, **11** 208
**Wawa Inc.**, **17 535–37**
**Waxman Industries, Inc.**, **III** 570; **9 542–44**; **20** 362; **28** 50–51
Wayco Foods, **14** 411
Waycross-Douglas Coca-Cola Bottling, **10** 222
Wayne Home Equipment. *See* Scott Fetzer Company.
Wayne Oakland Bank, **8** 188
WB. *See* Warner Communications Inc.
WBI Holdings, Inc., **42** 249, 253
WCI Holdings Corporation, **V** 223; **13** 170; **41** 94
WCK, Inc., **14** 236
WCRS Group plc, **6** 15
WCT Live Communication Limited, **24** 95
**WD-40 Company**, **18 554–57**
Wear-Ever, **17** 213
WearGuard, **13** 48
Wearne Brothers, **6** 117
The Weather Department, Ltd., **10** 89
Weather Guard, **IV** 305
**Weatherford International, Inc.**, **39 416–18**
Weathers-Lowin, Leeam, **11** 408
Weaver, **III** 468
Webb & Knapp, **10** 43
Webb Corbett and Beswick, **38** 402
Webber Gage Co., **13** 302
WeBco International LLC, **26** 530
Webco Securities, Inc., **37** 225
Weber, **16** 488
Weber Aircraft Inc., **41** 369
Weber Metal, **30** 283–84
**Weber-Stephen Products Co.**, **40 458–60**
Webers, **I** 409
Weblock, **I** 109
WebLogic Inc., **36** 81
Webster Publishing Co., **IV** 636
Webtron Corp., **10** 313
Webvan Group Inc., **38** 223
Wedgwood. *See* Waterford Wedgewood Holdings PLC.
Week's Dairy, **II** 528
Wegert Verwaltungs-GmbH and Co. Beteiligungs-KG, **24** 270
**Wegmans Food Markets, Inc.**, **9 545–46**; **24** 445; **41 416–18 (upd.)**
Weidemann Brewing Co., **I** 254
Weider Health and Fitness, Inc., **38** 238
**Weider Nutrition International, Inc.**, **29 498–501**; **33** 146–47; **34** 459
Weider Sporting Goods, **16** 80
Weifang Power Machine Fittings Ltd., **17** 106
Weight Watchers Gourmet Food Co., **43** 218
**Weight Watchers International Inc.**, **II** 508; **10** 383; **11** 172; **12 530–32**; **13** 383; **27** 197; **33 446–49 (upd.)**; **36** 255–56
**Weiner's Stores, Inc.**, **33 450–53**
**Weirton Steel Corporation**, **I** 297; **IV 236–38**; **7** 447, 598; **8** 346, 450; **10** 31–32; **12** 352, 354; **26** 407, **527–30 (upd.)**
**Weis Markets, Inc.**, **15 531–33**
**The Weitz Company, Inc.**, **42 431–34**
Welbecson, **III** 501
**Welbilt Corp.**, **19 492–94**; **27** 159
Welborn Transport Co., **39** 64, 65
Welch's, **25** 366
Welcome Wagon International Inc., **III** 28; **16** 146
Weldless Steel Company, **8** 530
Welex Jet Services, **III** 498–99
**Wella AG**, **48 420–23 (upd.)**
**Wella Group**, **III 68–70**
Wellby Super Drug Stores, **12** 220
**Wellcome Foundation Ltd.**, **I** 638, **713–15**; **8** 210, 452; **9** 265; **10** 551; **32** 212
Wellcome Trust, **41** 119
Weller Electric Corp., **II** 16
Wellington, **II** 457
Wellington Management Company, **14** 530–31; **23** 226
Wellington Sears Co., **15** 247–48
**Wellman, Inc.**, **8 561–62**; **21** 193
Wellmark, Inc., **10** 89
Wellness Co., Ltd., **IV** 716
**WellPoint Health Networks Inc.**, **25 525–29**
Wells Aircraft, **12** 112
**Wells Fargo & Company**, **II 380–84**, 319, 395; **III** 440; **10** 59–60; **12** 165, **533–37 (upd.)**; **17** 325; **18** 60, 543; **19** 411; **22** 542; **25** 434; **27** 292; **32** 373; **38** 44, **483–92 (upd.)**; **41** 200–01; **46** 217. *See also* American Express Company.
Wells Fargo HSBC Trade Bank, **26** 203
**Wells-Gardner Electronics Corporation**, **43 458–61**
Wells Lamont, **IV** 136
**Wells Rich Greene BDDP**, **6** 48, **50–52**
**Wells' Dairy, Inc.**, **36 511–13**
Wellspring Associates L.L.C., **16** 338
Wellspring Resources LLC, **42** 429
Welsbach Mantle, **6** 446
Welsh Associated Collieries Ltd., **31** 369
Welsh Water. *See* Hyder plc.
Weltkunst Verlag GmbH, **IV** 590
**Wendy's International, Inc.**, **II** 614–15, 647; **7** 433; **8 563–65**; **9** 178; **12** 553; **13** 494; **14** 453; **16** 95, 97; **17** 71, 124; **19** 215; **23** 384, **504–07 (upd.)**; **26** 284; **33** 240; **36** 517, 519; **41** 114; **46** 404–05; **47 439–44 (upd.)**
Wenger S.A., **III** 419; **21** 515
Wenlock Brewery Co., **I** 223
**Wenner Media, Inc.**, **32 506–09**
Wenstroms & Granstoms Electriska Kraftbolag, **II** 1
Werkhof GmbH, **13** 491
Werknet, **16** 420; **43** 308
Werner Baldessarini Design GmbH, **48** 209
**Werner Enterprises, Inc.**, **26 531–33**
Werner International, **III** 344; **14** 225
Wernicke Co., **I** 201
Wertheim Schroder & Company, **17** 443
**Weru Aktiengesellschaft**, **18 558–61**
Wesco Financial Corp., **III** 213, 215; **18** 62; **42** 32–34
Wesco Food Co., **II** 644
Wescot Decisison Systems, **6** 25
Weserflug, **I** 74
Wesper Co., **26** 4
Wesray and Management, **17** 213
Wesray Capital Corporation, **6** 357; **13** 41; **17** 443; **47** 363
Wesray Corporation, **22** 55
Wesray Holdings Corp., **13** 255
Wesray Transportation, Inc., **14** 38
Wessanen. *See* Koninklijke Wessanen N.V.
Wessanen and Laan, **II** 527
Wessanen Cacao, **II** 528
Wessanen USA, **II** 528; **29** 480
Wessanen's Koninklijke Fabrieken N.V., **II** 527
Wesson/Peter Pan Foods Co., **17** 241
West Australia Land Holdings, Limited, **10** 169
**West Bend Co.**, **III** 610–11; **14 546–48**; **16** 384; **43** 289
**West Coast Entertainment Corporation**, **29 502–04**
West Coast Grocery Co., **II** 670; **18** 506
West Coast Machinery, **13** 385
West Coast of America Telegraph, **I** 428
West Coast Power Company, **12** 265
West Coast Restaurant Enterprises, **25** 390
West Coast Savings and Loan, **10** 339
West Coast Telecom, **III** 38
**West Corporation**, **42 435–37**
West End Family Pharmacy, Inc., **15** 523
**West Fraser Timber Co. Ltd.**, **IV** 276; **17 538–40**
West Georgia Coca-Cola Bottlers, Inc., **13** 163
**West Group**, **34** 438, **502–06 (upd.)**
West Ham Gutta Percha Co., **I** 428
West Harrison Gas & Electric Company, **6** 466
West India Oil Co., **IV** 416, 428
West Japan Heavy Industries, **III** 578–79; **7** 348
West Jersey Electric Company, **6** 449
West Lynn Creamery, Inc., **26** 450
**West Marine, Inc.**, **17 541–43**; **37** 398
West Missouri Power Company. *See* UtiliCorp United Inc.
West Newton Savings Bank, **13** 468
West Newton Telephone Company, **14** 258
West of England, **III** 690
West of England Sack Holdings, **III** 501; **7** 207
**West One Bancorp**, **11 552–55**; **36** 491
West Penn Electric. *See* Allegheny Power System, Inc.
West Penn Power Company, **38** 38–40
**West Pharmaceutical Services, Inc.**, **42 438–41**
**West Point-Pepperell, Inc.**, **8 566–69**; **9** 466; **15** 247; **25** 20; **28** 218. *See also* WestPoint Stevens Inc. *and* JPS Textile Group, Inc.
**West Publishing Co.**, **IV** 312; **7 579–81**; **10** 407; **19** 268; **33** 264–65. *See also* The West Group.
West Rand Consolidated Mines, **IV** 90
West Rand Investment Trust, **IV** 21; **16** 27
West Richfield Telephone Company, **6** 299
West Side Bank, **II** 312
West Side Printing Co., **13** 559
West Surrey Central Dairy Co. Ltd., **II** 586
West TeleServices Corporation. *See* West Corporation.
West Texas Utilities Company, **6** 580
West Union Corporation, **22** 517
West Virginia Bearings, Inc., **13** 78
West Virginia Pulp and Paper Co. *See* Westvaco Corporation.
West Witwatersrand Areas Ltd., **IV** 94–96
West Yorkshire Bank, **II** 307
West's Holderness Corn Mill, **II** 564
**Westaff Inc.**, **33 454–57**

WestAir Holding Inc., **11** 300; **25** 423; **32** 336
**Westamerica Bancorporation, 17 544–47**
Westbrae Natural, Inc., **27** 197–98; **43** 218
Westburne Group of Companies, **9** 364
Westchester County Savings & Loan, **9** 173
Westchester Specialty Group, Inc., **26** 546
Westclox Seth Thomas, **16** 483
Westcott Communications Inc., **22** 442
**Westdeutsche Landesbank Girozentrale, II** 257–58, **385–87**; **33** 395; **46 458–61 (upd.)**; **47** 83
Westec Corporation. *See* Tech-Sym Corporation.
Western Aerospace Ltd., **14** 564
Western Air Express, **I** 125; **III** 225; **9** 17
Western Air Lines, **I** 98, 100, 106; **6** 82; **21** 142; **25** 421–23
Western Alaska Fisheries, **II** 578
Western American Bank, **II** 383
Western Assurance Co., **III** 350
**Western Atlas Inc., III** 473; **12 538–40**; **17** 419
Western Australian Specialty Alloys Proprietary Ltd., **14** 564
Western Auto, **19** 223
Western Auto Supply Co., **8** 56; **11** 392
Western Automatic Machine Screw Co., **12** 344
Western Bancorporation, **I** 536; **II** 288–89; **13** 529
Western Bank, **17** 530
**Western Beef, Inc., 22 548–50**
Western Bingo, **16** 471
Western California Canners Inc., **I** 513
Western Canada Airways, **II** 376
Western Coalfields Ltd., **IV** 48–49
**Western Company of North America, 15 534–36**; **25** 73, 75
Western Condensing Co., **II** 488
Western Copper Mills Ltd., **IV** 164
Western Corrugated Box Co., **IV** 358
Western Crude, **11** 27
Western Dairy Products, **I** 248
Western Data Products, Inc., **19** 110
**Western Digital Corp., 10** 403, 463; **11** 56, 463; **25 530–32**
Western Edison, **6** 601
Western Electric Co., **II** 57, 66, 88, 101, 112; **III** 162–63, 440; **IV** 181, 660; **V** 259–64; **VII** 288; **11** 500–01; **12** 136; **13** 57
Western Empire Construction. *See* CRSS Inc.
Western Equities, Inc. *See* Tech-Sym Corporation.
Western Family Foods, **47** 457
Western Federal Savings & Loan, **9** 199
Western Fire Equipment Co., **9** 420
**Western Gas Resources, Inc., 45 435–37**
Western Geophysical, **I** 485; **11** 265; **12** 538–39
Western Glucose Co., **14** 17
Western Grocers, Inc., **II** 631, 670
Western Hotels Inc. *See* Westin Hotels and Resorts Worldwide.
Western Illinois Power Cooperative, **6** 506
Western Inland Lock Navigation Company, **9** 228
Western International Communications, **35** 68
Western International Hotels, **I** 129; **6** 129
Western International Media, **22** 294
Western International University, **24** 40
Western Kentucky Gas Company, **43** 56–57
Western Kraft Corp., **IV** 358; **8** 476
Western Life Insurance Co., **III** 356; **22** 494
Western Light & Telephone Company. *See* Western Power & Gas Company.
Western Light and Power. *See* Public Service Company of Colorado.
Western Massachusetts Co., **13** 183
Western Medical Services, **33** 456
Western Merchandise, Inc., **8** 556
Western Merchandisers, Inc., **29** 229–30
Western Mining Corp., **IV** 61, 95
Western-Mobile, **III** 735
Western Mortgage Corporation, **16** 497
Western National Life Company, **10** 246; **14** 473
Western Natural Gas Company, **7** 362
Western New York State Lines, Inc., **6** 370
Western Newell Manufacturing Company. *See* Newell Co.
Western Nuclear, Inc., **IV** 179
Western Offset Publishing, **6** 13
Western Offshore Drilling and Exploration Co., **I** 570
Western Pacific, **22** 220
Western Pacific Industries, **10** 357
Western Paper Box Co., **IV** 333
Western Pioneer, Inc., **18** 279
Western Piping and Engineering Co., **III** 535
Western Platinum, **21** 353
Western Playing Card Co., **13** 559
Western Powder Co., **I** 379; **13** 379
Western Power & Gas Company. *See* Centel Corporation.
Western Printing and Lithographing Company, **19** 404
Western Public Service Corporation, **6** 568
**Western Publishing Group, Inc., IV** 671; **13** 114, **559–61**; **15** 455; **25** 254, 313; **28** 159; **29** 76
Western Reserve Bank of Lake County, **9** 474
Western Reserve Telephone Company. *See* Alltel Corporation.
Western Reserves, **12** 442
**Western Resources, Inc., 12 541–43**; **27** 425; **32** 372–75
Western Rosin Company, **8** 99
Western Sizzlin', **10** 331; **19** 288
Western Slope Gas, **6** 559
Western Steel Group, **26** 407
Western Steer Family Restaurant, **10** 331; **18** 8
Western Sugar Co., **II** 582; **42** 371
Western Telegraph Company, **25** 99
Western Telephone Company, **14** 257
Western Union Corporation, **I** 512; **III** 644; **6** 227–28, 338, 386; **9** 536; **10** 263; **12** 9; **14** 363; **15** 72; **17** 345–46; **21** 25; **24** 515
Western Union Insurance Co., **III** 310
Western Vending, **13** 48; **41** 22
Western Veneer and Plywood Co., **IV** 358
**Western Wireless Corporation, 36 514–16**
Westfair Foods Ltd., **II** 649
Westfalenbank of Bochum, **II** 239
Westfalia AG, **III** 418–19
Westfalia Dinnendahl Gröppel AG, **III** 543
Westfälische Transport AG, **6** 426
Westfälische Verbands- Elektrizitätswerk, **V** 744
Westgate House Investments Ltd., **IV** 711
Westimex, **II** 594
**Westin Hotel Co., I** 129–30; **6** 129; **9** 283, **547–49**; **21** 91
**Westin Hotels and Resorts Worldwide, 29 505–08 (upd.)**
Westinghouse Air Brake Company. *See* Wabtec Corporation.
Westinghouse Brake & Signal, **III** 509
Westinghouse Cubic Ltd., **19** 111
**Westinghouse Electric Corporation, I** 4, 7, 19, 22, 28, 33, 82, 84–85, 524; **II** 57–58, 59, 80, 86, 88, 94, 98–99, **120–22**, 151; **III** 440, 467, 641; **IV** 59, 401; **6** 39, 164, 261, 452, 483, 556; **9** 12, 17, 128, 162, 245, 417, 439–40, 553; **10** 280, 536; **11** 318; **12** 194, **544–47 (upd.)**; **13** 230, 398, 402, 506–07; **14** 300–01; **16** 8; **17** 488; **18** 320, 335–37, 355; **19** 164–66, 210; **21** 43; **26** 102; **27** 269; **28** 69; **33** 253; **36** 327; **41** 366; **45** 306; **48** 217. *See also* CBS Radio Group.
**WestJet Airlines Ltd., 38 493–95**
Westland Aircraft Ltd., **I** 50, 573; **IV** 658; **24** 85
WestLB. *See* Westdeutsche Landesbank Girozentrale.
Westmark Mortgage Corp., **13** 417
Westmark Realty Advisors, **21** 97
Westmark Systems, Inc., **26** 268
Westmill Foods, **II** 466
Westminster Bank Ltd., **II** 257, 319, 320, 333–34; **17** 324
Westminster Press Ltd., **IV** 658
Westminster Trust Ltd., **IV** 706
**Westmoreland Coal Company, 7 582–85**
Westmount Enterprises, **I** 286
Weston and Mead, **IV** 310
Weston Bakeries, **II** 631
Weston Foods Inc. *See* George Weston Limited.
Weston Pharmaceuticals, **V** 49; **19** 122–23
Weston Resources, **II** 631–32
**Westpac Banking Corporation, II 388–90**; **17** 285; **48 424–27 (upd.)**
Westphalian Provinzialbank-Hülfskasse, **II** 385
**WestPoint Stevens Inc., 16 533–36**; **21** 194; **28** 219. *See also* JPS Textile Group, Inc.
Westport Woman, **24** 145
**Westvaco Corporation, I** 442; **IV 351–54**; **19 495–99 (upd.)**
The Westwood Group, **20** 54
**Westwood One, Inc., 17** 150; **23 508–11**
Westwood Pharmaceuticals, **III** 19
Westwools Holdings, **I** 438
Westworld Resources Inc., **23** 41
Westwynn Theatres, **14** 87
**The Wet Seal, Inc., 18 562–64**
**Wetterau Incorporated, II** 645, **681–82**; **7** 450; **18** 507; **32** 222
Wexpro Company, **6** 568–69
**Weyco Group, Incorporated, 32 510–13**
**Weyerhaeuser Company, I** 26; **IV** 266, 289, 298, 304, 308, **355–56**, 358; **8** 428, 434; **9 550–52 (upd.)**; **19** 445–46, 499; **22** 489; **26** 384; **28 514–17 (upd.)**; **31** 468; **32** 91; **42** 397
Weyman-Burton Co., **9** 533

WFSC. *See* World Fuel Services Corporation.
WGM Safety Corp., **40** 96–97
**WH Smith PLC, 42 442–47 (upd.)**
Whalstrom & Co., **I** 14
Wharf Holdings Limited, **12** 367–68; **18** 114
**Whatman plc, 46 462–65**
Wheat, First Securities, **19** 304–05
**Wheaton Industries, 8 570–73**
Wheatsheaf Investment, **27** 94
Wheel Horse, **7** 535
Wheel Restaurants Inc., **14** 131
**Wheelabrator Technologies, Inc., I** 298; **II** 403; **III** 511–12; **V** 754; **6 599–600**; **10** 32; **11** 435
Wheeled Coach Industries, Inc., **33** 105–06
Wheeler Condenser & Engineering Company, **6** 145
Wheeler, Fisher & Co., **IV** 344
**Wheeling-Pittsburgh Corp., 7 586–88**
Wheelock Marden, **I** 470; **20** 312
Whemco, **22** 415
Whemo Denko, **I** 359
**Wherehouse Entertainment Incorporated, 9** 361; **11 556–58**; **29** 350; **35** 431–32
WHI Inc., **14** 545
Whippet Motor Lines Corporation, **6** 370
Whippoorwill Associates Inc., **28** 55
Whirl-A-Way Motors, **11** 4
**Whirlpool Corporation, I** 30; **II** 80; **III** 572, 573, **653–55**; **8** 298–99; **11** 318; **12** 252, 309, **548–50 (upd.)**; **13** 402–03, 563; **15** 403; **18** 225–26; **22** 218, 349; **23** 53; **25** 261
Whirlwind, Inc., **6** 233; **7** 535
Whiskey Trust, **I** 376
Whistler Corporation, **13** 195
Whitaker-Glessner Company, **7** 586
Whitaker Health Services, **III** 389
Whitall Tatum, **III** 423
**Whitbread PLC, I** 288, **293–94**; **18** 73; **20 519–22 (upd.)**; **29** 19; **35** 395; **42** 247
Whitby Pharmaceuticals, Inc., **10** 289
**White & Case LLP, 35 466–69**
White Automotive, **10** 9, 11
White Brand, **V** 97
White Brothers, **39** 83, 84
White Bus Line, **I** 448
**White Castle System, Inc., 12 551–53**; **33** 239; **36 517–20 (upd.)**
**White Consolidated Industries Inc., II** 122; **III** 480, 654, 573; **8** 298; **12** 252, 546; **13 562–64**; **22** 26–28, 216–17, 349
White Discount Department Stores, **16** 36
White Eagle Oil & Refining Co., **IV** 464; **7** 352
White Fuel Corp., **IV** 552
White Industrial Power, **II** 25
White Miller Construction Company, **14** 162
White Motor Co., **II** 16
White Mountain Freezers, **19** 360
**White Mountains Insurance Group, Ltd., 48 428–31**
White-New Idea, **13** 18
White Oil Corporation, **7** 101
White Rock Corp., **I** 377; **27** 198; **43** 218
White-Rodgers, **II** 19
**White Rose, Inc., 12** 106; **24 527–29**
White Star Line, **23** 161
White Stores, **II** 419–20
White Swan Foodservice, **II** 625
White Tractor, **13** 17
**White Wave, 43 462–64**
White Weld, **II** 268; **21** 145
White-Westinghouse. *See* White Consolidated Industries Inc.
Whiteaway Laidlaw, **V** 68
Whitehall Canadian Oils Ltd., **IV** 658
Whitehall Company Jewellers, **24** 319
Whitehall Electric Investments Ltd., **IV** 658
Whitehall Labs, **8** 63
Whitehall Petroleum Corp. Ltd., **IV** 657–58
Whitehall Securities Corp., **IV** 658
Whitehall Trust Ltd., **IV** 658
Whitewater Group, **10** 508
Whitewear Manufacturing Company. *See* Angelica Corporation.
**Whitman Corporation, 7** 430; **10** 414–15, **553–55 (upd.)**; **11** 188; **22** 353–54; **27** 196; **43** 217
**Whitman Education Group, Inc., 41 419–21**
Whitman Publishing Co., **13** 559–60
Whitman's Chocolates, **I** 457; **7** 431; **12** 429
Whitmire Distribution. *See* Cardinal Health, Inc.
Whitney Communications Corp., **IV** 608
Whitney Group, **40** 236–38
**Whitney Holding Corporation, 21 522–24**
Whitney National Bank, **12** 16
Whitney Partners, L.L.C., **40** 237
**Whittaker Corporation, I 544–46**; **III** 389, 444; **34** 275; **48 432–35 (upd.)**
Whittar Steel Strip Co., **IV** 74; **24** 143
Whitteways, **I** 215
Whittle Communications L.P., **IV** 675; **7** 528; **13** 403; **22** 442
Whittman-Hart Inc. *See* marchFIRST, Inc.
Whitworth Brothers Company, **27** 360
**Whole Foods Market, Inc., 19** 501–02; **20 523–27**; **41** 422–23; **47** 200
Wholesale Cellular USA. *See* Brightpoint, Inc.
The Wholesale Club, Inc., **8** 556
Wholesale Depot, **13** 547
Wholesale Food Supply, Inc., **13** 333
Wholesome Foods, L.L.C., **32** 274, 277
Wholly Harvest, **19** 502
Whyte & Mackay Distillers Ltd., **V** 399; **19** 171
Wicanders Group, **48** 119
Wicat Systems, **7** 255–56; **25** 254
Wichita Industries, **11** 27
**Wickes Companies, Inc., I** 453, 483; **II** 262; **III** 580, 721; **V 221–23**; **10** 423; **13** 169–70; **15** 281; **17** 365–66; **19** 503–04; **20** 415; **41** 93
**Wickes Inc., 25 533–36 (upd.)**
Wickman-Wimet, **IV** 203
Widows and Orphans Friendly Society, **III** 337
Wielkopolski Bank Kredytowy, **16** 14
Wien Air Alaska, **II** 420
Wienerwald Holding, **17** 249
Wiesner, Inc., **22** 442
Wifstavarfs, **IV** 325
Wiggins Teape Ltd., **I** 426; **IV** 290
Wild by Nature. *See* King Cullen Grocery Co., Inc.
Wild Leitz G.m.b.H., **23** 83
**Wild Oats Markets, Inc., 19 500–02**; **29** 213; **41 422–25 (upd.)**
**Wildlife Conservation Society, 31 462–64**
Wildwater Kingdom, **22** 130
Wiles Group Ltd., **III** 501; **7** 207
Wiley Manufacturing Co., **8** 545
Oy Wilh. Schauman AB, **IV** 300–02; **19** 463
Wilhelm Fette GmbH, **IV** 198–99
Wilhelm Weber GmbH, **22** 95
Wilhelm Wilhelmsen Ltd., **7** 40; **41** 42
Wilkins Department Store, **19** 510
Wilkinson, Gaddis & Co., **24** 527
Wilkinson Sword Co., **III** 23, 28–29; **12** 464; **38** 365
Willamette Falls Electric Company. *See* Portland General Corporation.
**Willamette Industries, Inc., IV 357–59**; **13** 99, 101; **16** 340; **28** 517; **31 465–468 (upd.)**
Willcox & Gibbs Sewing Machine Co., **15** 384
Willetts Manufacturing Company, **12** 312
William A. Rogers Ltd., **IV** 644
William B. Tanner Co., **7** 327
William Barnet and Son, Inc., **III** 246
William Barry Co., **II** 566
William Benton Foundation, **7** 165, 167
William Bonnel Co., **I** 334; **10** 289
The William Brooks Shoe Company. *See* Rocky Shoes & Boots, Inc.
William Burdon, **III** 626
William Byrd Press Inc., **23** 100
William Carter Company, **17** 224
William Colgate and Co., **III** 23
William Collins & Sons, **II** 138; **IV** 651–52; **7** 390–91; **24** 193
William Cory & Son Ltd., **6** 417
William Crawford and Sons, **II** 593
William Douglas McAdams Inc., **I** 662; **9** 403
William Duff & Sons, **I** 509
William E. Pollack Government Securities, **II** 390
William E. Wright Company, **9** 375
William Esty Company, **16** 72
William Gaymer and Son Ltd., **I** 216
William George Company, **32** 519
William Grant Company, **22** 343
William H. Rorer Inc., **I** 666
William Hancock & Co., **I** 223
William Hewlett, **41** 117
William Hodges & Company, **33** 150
William Hollins & Company Ltd., **44** 105
William J. Hough Co., **8** 99–100
William Lyon Homes, **III** 664
William M. Mercer Cos. Inc., **III** 283; **32** 459
William Mackinnon & Co., **III** 522
William McDonald & Sons, **II** 593
**William Morris Agency, Inc., III** 554; **23 512–14**; **43** 235–36
William Morrow & Company, **19** 201
William Neilson, **II** 631
William Odhams Ltd., **7** 244
William P. Young Contruction, **43** 400
William Penn Cos., **III** 243, 273
William Penn Life Insurance Company of New York, **24** 285
William Press, **I** 568
William R. Warner & Co., **I** 710
William S. Kimball & Co., **12** 108
William Southam and Sons, **7** 487
William T. Blackwell & Company, **V** 395

William Underwood Co., **I** 246, 457; **7** 430
William Varcoe & Sons, **III** 690
William Zinsser & Co., **8** 456
**Williams & Connolly LLP, 47 445–48**
Williams & Glyn's Bank Ltd., **12** 422
Williams & Wilkins. *See* Waverly, Inc.
Williams Brother Offshore Ltd., **I** 429
**Williams Communications Group, Inc., 6** 340; **25** 499; **34 507–10**
**The Williams Companies, Inc., III** 248; **IV** 84, 171, **575–76**; **27** 307; **31 469–472 (upd.)**
Williams Deacon's Bank, **12** 422
Williams, Donnelley and Co., **IV** 660
Williams Electronics, **III** 431; **12** 419
Williams Electronics Games, Inc., **15** 539
Williams Gold Refining Co., **14** 81
The Williams Manufacturing Company, **19** 142–43
Williams/Nintendo Inc., **15** 537
Williams Oil-O-Matic Heating Corporation, **12** 158; **21** 42
Williams plc, **44** 255
Williams Printing Company. *See* Graphic Industries Inc.
**Williams-Sonoma, Inc., 13** 42; **15** 50; **17 548–50**; **27** 225, 429; **44 447–50 (upd.)**
Williamsburg Gas Light Co., **6** 455
**Williamson-Dickie Manufacturing Company, 14 549–50**; **45 438–41 (upd.)**
Willie G's, **15** 279
**Willis Corroon Group plc, III** 280, 747; **22** 318; **25 537–39**
Willis Stein & Partners, **21** 404
Williston Basin Interstate Pipeline Company, **7** 322, 324. *See also* WBI Holdings, Inc.
Willor Manufacturing Corp., **9** 323
Willys-Overland, **I** 183; **8** 74
Wilmington Coca-Cola Bottling Works, Inc., **10** 223
**Wilmington Trust Corporation, 25 540–43**
Wilsdorf & Davis, **13** 353–54
Wilshire Real Estate Investment Trust Inc., **30** 223
Wilshire Restaurant Group Inc., **13** 66; **28** 258
Wilson & Co., **I** 490
**Wilson Bowden Plc, 45 442–44**
Wilson Brothers, **8** 536
Wilson Foods Corp., **I** 489, 513; **II** 584–85; **12** 124; **14** 515; **22** 510
Wilson, H.W., Company. *See* H.W. Wilson Company.
Wilson Jones Company, **7** 4–5
Wilson Learning Group, **17** 272
Wilson-Maeulen Company, **13** 234
Wilson Pharmaceuticals & Chemical, **I** 489
**Wilson Sonsini Goodrich & Rosati, 34 511–13**
**Wilson Sporting Goods Company, I** 278, 489; **13** 317; **16** 52; **23** 449; **24** 403, **530–32**; **25** 167; **41** 14–16
Wilson's Motor Transit, **6** 370
Wilson's Supermarkets, **12** 220–21
**Wilsons The Leather Experts Inc., 21 525–27**
WilTel Network Services, **27** 301, 307
Wilts and Dorset Banking Co., **II** 307
Wiltshire United Dairies, **II** 586
Wimpey International Ltd., **13** 206
Wimpey's plc, **I** 315, 556
Win-Chance Foods, **II** 508; **36** 255
Win Schuler Foods, **II** 480; **25** 517; **26** 57
Wincanton Group, **II** 586–87
Winchell's Donut Shops, **II** 680
Winchester Arms, **I** 379–81, 434; **13** 379
**Wind River Systems, Inc., 37 419–22**
**Windmere Corporation, 16 537–39**. *See also* Applica Incorporated.
Windmere-Durable Holdings, Inc., **30** 404
WindowVisions, Inc., **29** 288
Windsor Forestry Tools, Inc., **48** 59
Windsor Manufacturing Company, **13** 6
Windsor Trust Co., **13** 467
Windstar Sail Cruises, **6** 368; **27** 90–91
Windsurfing International, **23** 55
Windward Capital Partners, **28** 152, 154
**The Wine Group, Inc., 39 419–21**
Wine World, Inc., **22** 78, 80
Winfire, Inc., **37** 194
Wingate Partners, **14** 521, 523
Wings & Wheels, **13** 19
Wings Luggage, Inc., **10** 181
WingspanBank.com, **38** 270
Winkelman Stores, Inc., **8** 425–26
Winkler-Grimm Wagon Co., **I** 141
Winlet Fashions, **22** 223
Winmar Co., **III** 353
**Winn-Dixie Stores, Inc., II** 626–27, 670, **683–84**; **7** 61; **11** 228; **15** 178; **16** 314; **18** 8; **21 528–30 (upd.)**; **34** 269
**Winnebago Industries Inc., 7 589–91**; **22** 207; **27 509–12 (upd.)**
Winners Apparel Ltd., **V** 197
Winning International, **21** 403
Winschermann group, **IV** 198
**WinsLoew Furniture, Inc., 21 531–33**
Winston & Newell Company. *See* Supervalu Inc.
**Winston & Strawn, 35 470–73**
Winston Furniture Company, Inc., **21** 531–33
Winston Group, **10** 333
Winston, Harper, Fisher Co., **II** 668
WinterBrook Corp., **26** 326
Winterflood Securities Limited, **39** 89, 91
Wintershall AG, **I** 306; **IV** 485; **18** 49; **38** 408
Winterthur Insurance, **21** 144, 146–47
**Winterthur Schweizerische Versicherungs-Gesellschaft, III** 343, **402–04**
Winthrop Laboratories, **I** 698–99
Winthrop Lawrence Corporation, **25** 541
Winton Engines, **10** 273
Winton Motor Car Company, **V** 231
**Wipro Limited, 43 465–68**
Wire and Cable Specialties Corporation, **17** 276
Wire and Plastic Products PLC. *See* WPP Group PLC.
Wireless Hong Kong. *See* Hong Kong Telecommunications Ltd.
Wireless LLC, **18** 77
Wireless Management Company, **11** 12
Wireless Speciality Co., **II** 120
Wirtz Productions Ltd., **15** 238
Wisaforest Oy AB, **IV** 302
**Wisconsin Bell, Inc., 14 551–53**; **18** 30
**Wisconsin Central Transportation Corporation, 12** 278; **24 533–36**
**Wisconsin Dairies, 7 592–93**
**Wisconsin Energy Corporation, 6 601–03**, 605
Wisconsin Gas Company, **17** 22–23
Wisconsin Knife Works, **III** 436
Wisconsin Power and Light, **22** 13; **39** 260
**Wisconsin Public Service Corporation, 6** 604–06; **9 553–54**
Wisconsin Steel, **10** 430; **17** 158–59
Wisconsin Tissue Mills Inc., **8** 103
Wisconsin Toy Company. *See* Value Merchants Inc.
Wisconsin Wire and Steel, **17** 310; **24** 160
Wise Foods, Inc., **22** 95
Wiser's De Luxe Whiskey, **14** 141
Wishnick-Tumpeer Chemical Co., **I** 403–05
Wispark Corporation, **6** 601, 603
Wisser Service Holdings AG, **18** 105
Wisvest Corporation, **6** 601, 603
**Witco Corporation, I** 403, **404–06**; **16 540–43 (upd.)**
Wite-Out Products, Inc., **23** 56–57
Witech Corporation, **6** 601, 603
Withington Company. *See* Sparton Corporation.
Wittington Investments Ltd., **13** 51
The Wiz. *See* Cablevision Electronic Instruments, Inc.
**Wizards of the Coast Inc., 24 537–40**; **43** 229, 233
WizardWorks Group, Inc., **31** 238–39
WLIW-TV. *See* Educational Broadcasting Corporation.
**WLR Foods, Inc., 14** 516; **21 534–36**
WM Investment Company, **34** 512
**Wm. Morrison Supermarkets PLC, 38 496–98**
Wm. Underwood Company, **40** 53
**Wm. Wrigley Jr. Company, 7 594–97**
**WMC, Limited, 43 469–72**
**WMS Industries, Inc., III** 431; **15 537–39**; **41** 215–16
**WMX Technologies Inc., 11** 435–36; **17 551–54**; **26** 409
Woermann and German East African Lines, **I** 542
Wöhlk, **III** 446
Wolf Furniture Enterprises, **14** 236
Wolfe & Associates, **25** 434
Wolfe Industries, Inc., **22** 255
Wolff Printing Co., **13** 559
**The Wolfgang Puck Food Company, Inc., 26 534–36**
**Wolohan Lumber Co., 19 503–05**; **25** 535
**Wolters Kluwer NV, IV** 611; **14 554–56**; **31** 389, 394; **33 458–61 (upd.)**
Wolvercote Paper Mill, **IV** 300
Wolverine Die Cast Group, **IV** 165
Wolverine Insurance Co., **26** 487
**Wolverine Tube Inc., 23 515–17**
**Wolverine World Wide Inc., 16 544–47**; **17** 390; **32** 99; **44** 365
Womack Development Company, **11** 257
Women's Specialty Retailing Group. *See* Casual Corner Group, Inc.
Women's World, **15** 96
Wometco Coca-Cola Bottling Co., **10** 222
Wometco Coffee Time, **I** 514
Wometco Enterprises, **I** 246, 514
Wonderware Corp., **22** 374
Wong International Holdings, **16** 195
Wood Fiberboard Co., **IV** 358
Wood Gundy, **II** 345; **21** 447
**Wood Hall Trust plc, I** 438, **592–93**
Wood-Metal Industries, Inc. *See* Wood-Mode, Inc.

**Wood-Mode, Inc., 23 518–20**
Wood River Oil and Refining Company, **11** 193
Wood Shovel and Tool Company, **9** 71
Wood, Struthers & Winthrop, Inc., **22** 189
Wood Wyant Inc., **30** 496–98
Woodall Industries, **III** 641; **14** 303
Woodard-Walker Lumber Co., **IV** 358
Woodbury Co., **19** 380
Woodcock, Hess & Co., **9** 370
Woodfab, **IV** 295; **19** 225
Woodhaven Gas Light Co., **6** 455
Woodhill Chemical Sales Company, **8** 333
Woodland Publishing, Inc., **37** 286
Woodlands, **7** 345–46
Woods and Co., **II** 235
Woods Equipment Company, **32** 28
Woodside Travel Trust, **26** 310
Woodville Appliances, Inc., **9** 121
Woodward-Clyde Group Inc., **45** 421
Woodward Corp., **IV** 311; **19** 267
**Woodward Governor Co., 13 565–68**
Woodworkers Warehouse, **22** 517
Woolco Department Stores, **II** 634; **7** 444; **V** 107, 225–26; **14** 294; **22** 242
Woolverton Motors, **I** 183
**The Woolwich plc, 30 492–95**
**Woolworth Corporation, II** 414; **6** 344; **V** 106–09, **224–27**; **8** 509; **14** 293–95; **17** 42, 335; **20 528–32 (upd.)**; **25** 22. *See also* Venator Group Inc.
Woolworth Holdings, **II** 139; **V** 108; **19** 123; **24** 194
Woolworth's Ltd., **II** 656. *See also* Kingfisher plc.
Wooster Preserving Company, **11** 211
Wooster Rubber Co., **III** 613
Worcester City and County Bank, **II** 307
Worcester Gas Light Co., **14** 124
Worcester Wire Works, **13** 369
Word, Inc., **14** 499; **38** 456
Word Processors Personnel Service, **6** 10
**WordPerfect Corporation, 6** 256; **10** 519, **556–59**; **12** 335; **25** 300; **41** 281. *See also* Corel Corporation.
WordStar International, **15** 149; **43** 151. *See also* The Learning Company Inc.
Work Wear Corp., **II** 607; **16** 229
**Working Assets Funding Service, 43 473–76**
Working Title Films, **23** 389
Workscape Inc., **42** 430
World Air Network, Ltd., **6** 71
World Airways, **10** 560–62; **28** 404
**World Bank Group, 33 462–65**
World Book Group. *See* Scott Fetzer Company.
**World Book, Inc., IV** 622; **12 554–56**
World Championship Wrestling (WCW), **32** 516
**World Color Press Inc., 12 557–59**; **19** 333; **21** 61
World Commerce Corporation, **25** 461
World Communications, Inc., **11** 184
**World Duty Free Americas, Inc., 29 509–12 (upd.)**
World Duty Free plc, **33** 59
World Film Studio, **24** 437
World Financial Network National Bank, **V** 116
World Flight Crew Services, **10** 560
World Foot Locker, **14** 293
**World Fuel Services Corporation, 47 449–51**
World Gift Company, **9** 330
World International Holdings Limited, **12** 368
World Journal Tribune Inc., **IV** 608
World Machinery Company, **45** 170–71
World Online, **48** 398–39
World Publishing Co., **8** 423
World Savings and Loan, **19** 412; **47** 159–60
World Service Life Insurance Company, **27** 47
World Trade Corporation. *See* International Business Machines Corporation.
World Trans, Inc., **33** 105
World-Wide Shipping Group, **II** 298; **III** 517
**World Wrestling Federation Entertainment, Inc., 32 514–17**
World Yacht Enterprises, **22** 438
**World's Finest Chocolate Inc., 39 422–24**
WorldCom, Inc., **14** 330, 332; **18** 33, 164, 166; **29** 227; **38** 269–70, 468; **46** 376. *See also* MCI WorldCom, Inc.
**WorldCorp, Inc., 10 560–62**
WorldGames, **10** 560
WorldMark, The Club, **33** 409
Worlds of Fun, **22** 130
Worlds of Wonder, Inc., **25** 381; **26** 548
Worldview Systems Corporation, **26** 428; **46** 434
WorldWay Corporation, **16** 41
Worldwide Fiber Inc., **46** 267
Worldwide Insurance Co., **48** 9
Worldwide Logistics, **17** 505
**Worldwide Restaurant Concepts, Inc., 47 452–55**
Worldwide Semiconductor Manufacturing Co., **47** 386
Worldwide Underwriters Insurance Co., **III** 218–19
Wormald International Ltd., **13** 245, 247
**Worms et Cie, 27** 275–76, **513–15**
Wormser, **III** 760
Worth Corp., **27** 274
Wortham, Gus Sessions, **III** 193; **10** 65
Worthen Banking Corporation, **15** 60
Worthington & Co., **I** 223
Worthington Corp., **I** 142
**Worthington Foods, Inc., I** 653; **14 557–59**; **33** 170
**Worthington Industries, Inc., 7 598–600**; **8** 450; **21 537–40 (upd.)**
Worthington Telephone Company, **6** 312
Woven Belting Co., **8** 13
**WPL Holdings, 6 604–06**
WPM. *See* Wall Paper Manufacturers.
**WPP Group plc, I** 21; **6 53–54**; **22** 201, 296; **23** 480; **48 440–42 (upd.)**. *See also* Ogilvy Group Inc.
Wrather Corporation, **18** 354
Wrenn Furniture Company, **10** 184
WRG. *See* Wells Rich Greene BDDP.
Wright & Company Realtors, **21** 257
Wright Aeronautical, **9** 16
Wright Airplane Co., **III** 151; **6** 265
Wright and Son, **II** 593
Wright Company, **9** 416
Wright Engine Company, **11** 427
Wright Group, **22** 519, 522
Wright Manufacturing Company, **8** 407
Wright Plastic Products, **17** 310; **24** 160
Wright, Robertson & Co. *See* Fletcher Challenge Ltd.
Wright Stephenson & Co., **IV** 278
Wrightson Limited, **19** 155
Write Right Manufacturing Co., **IV** 345
**WS Atkins Plc, 45 445–47**
WSGC Holdings, Inc., **24** 530
WSI Corporation, **10** 88–89
WSM Inc., **11** 152
WSMC. *See* Worldwide Semiconductor Manufacturing Co.
WSMP, Inc., **29** 202
WTC Airlines, Inc., **IV** 182
**WTD Industries, Inc., 20 533–36**
Wührer, **II** 474
Wunderlich Ltd., **III** 687
Wunderman, Ricotta & Kline, **I** 37
Wurlitzer Co., **17** 468; **18** 45
Württembergische Landes- Elektrizitäts AG, **IV** 230
WVPP. *See* Westvaco Corporation.
WWG Industries, Inc., **22** 352–53
WWTV, **18** 493
Wyandotte Chemicals Corporation, **18** 49
Wyandotte Corp., **I** 306
**Wyant Corporation, 30 496–98**
Wycombe Bus Company, **28** 155–56
Wyeth-Ayerst Laboratories, **25** 477; **27** 69
Wyeth Laboratories, **I** 623; **10** 69
**Wyle Electronics, 14 560–62**; **19** 311
Wyly Corporation, **11** 468
**Wyman-Gordon Company, 14 563–65**; **30** 282–83; **41** 367
Wymore Oil Co., **IV** 394
Wynkoop Brewing Company, **43** 407
**Wynn's International, Inc., 22** 458; **33 466–70**
Wynncor Ltd., **IV** 693
Wyoming Mineral Corp., **IV** 401
**Wyse Technology, Inc., 10** 362; **15 540–42**

X-Acto, **12** 263
X-Chem Oil Field Chemicals, **8** 385
**X-Rite, Inc., 48 443–46**
XA Systems Corporation, **10** 244
Xaos Tools, Inc., **10** 119
Xcelite, **II** 16
Xcor International, **III** 431; **15** 538
**Xeikon NV, 26 540–42**
Xenell Corporation, **48** 358
Xenia National Bank, **9** 474
Xenotech, **27** 58
**Xerox Corporation, I** 31–32, 338, 490, 693; **II** 10, 117, 157, 159, 412, 448; **III** 110, 116, 120–21, 157, 159, **171–73**, 475; **IV** 252, 703; **6** 244, **288–90 (upd.)**, 390; **7** 45, 161; **8** 164; **10** 22, 139, 430, 510–11; **11** 68, 494, 518; **13** 127, 448; **14** 399; **17** 28–29, 328–29; **18** 93, 111–12; **22** 411–12; **25** 54–55, 148, 152; **26** 213, 540, 542, **543–47 (upd.)**; **28** 115; **36** 171; **40** 394; **41** 197; **46** 151
Xiamen Airlines, **33** 99
**Xilinx, Inc., 16** 317, **548–50**; **18** 17, 19; **19** 405; **43** 15–16
XMR, Inc., **42** 361
XP, **27** 474
Xpert Recruitment, Ltd., **26** 240
Xpress Automotive Group, Inc., **24** 339
XR Ventures LLC, **48** 446
XRAL Storage and Terminaling Co., **IV** 411
Xros, Inc., **36** 353
XTRA Corp., **18** 67
XTX Corp., **13** 127

Xynetics, **9** 251
Xytek Corp., **13** 127

Y & S Candies Inc., **II** 511
Yacimientos Petrolíferos Fiscales Sociedad Anónima, **IV** 578
**Yageo Corporation, 16 551–53**
**Yahoo! Inc., 25** 18; **27 516–19; 38** 439; **45** 201
Yakovlev, **24** 60
Yale & Towne Manufacturing Co., **I** 154–55; **10** 279
Yamabun Oil Co., **IV** 403
Yamagata Enterprises, **26** 310
Yamaguchi Bank, **II** 347
**Yamaha Corporation, III** 366, 599, **656–59; 11** 50; **12** 401; **16** 410, **554–58 (upd.); 17** 25; **18** 250; **19** 428; **22** 196; **33** 28; **40 461–66 (upd.)**
Yamaha Musical Instruments, **16** 202; **43** 170
Yamaichi Capital Management, **42** 349
**Yamaichi Securities Company, Limited, II** 300, 323, 434, **458–59; 9** 377
Yamano Music, **16** 202; **43** 171
Yamanouchi Consumer Inc., **39** 361
Yamanouchi Pharmaceutical Co., Ltd., **12** 444–45; **38** 93
Yamatame Securities, **II** 326
**Yamato Transport Co. Ltd., V 536–38**
Yamazaki Baking Co., **II** 543; **IV** 152; **24** 358
Yanbian Industrial Technology Training Institute, **12** 294
Yangzhou Motor Coach Manufacturing Co., **34** 132
**The Yankee Candle Company, Inc., 37 423–26; 38** 192
Yankee Energy Gas System, Inc., **13** 184
Yankee Gas Services Company, **48** 305
**YankeeNets LLC, 35 474–77**
Yankton Gas Company, **6** 524
Yarmouth Group, Inc., **17** 285
Yaryan, **I** 343
Yashica Co., Ltd., **II** 50–51; **21** 330
**Yasuda Fire and Marine Insurance Company, Limited, II** 292, 391; **III 405–07**, 408; **45** 110
**Yasuda Mutual Life Insurance Company, II** 292, 391, 446; **III** 288, 405, **408–09; 22** 406–07; **39 425–28 (upd.)**
**The Yasuda Trust and Banking Company, Limited, II** 273, 291, **391–92; 17 555–57 (upd.)**
Yates-Barco Ltd., **16** 8
Yates Circuit Foil, **IV** 26
Yawata Iron & Steel Co., Ltd., **I** 493, 509; **II** 300; **IV** 130, 157, 212; **17** 350; **24** 325
Year Book Medical Publishers, **IV** 677–78
Yearbooks, Inc., **12** 472
Yeargin Construction Co., **II** 87; **11** 413
Yellow Cab Co., **I** 125; **V** 539; **10** 370; **12** 487; **24** 118
**Yellow Corporation, 14 566–68; 45 448–51 (upd.)**
**Yellow Freight System, Inc. of Deleware, V** 503, **539–41; 12** 278
Yeomans & Foote, **I** 13
Yeomans & Partners Ltd., **I** 588
**YES! Entertainment Corporation, 10** 306; **26 548–50**
Yesco Audio Environments, **18** 353, 355
Yeti Cycles Inc., **19** 385
Yeung Chi Shing Estates, **IV** 717
YGK Inc., **6** 465, 467
Yhtyneet Paperitehtaat Oy. *See* United Paper Mills Ltd.
Yili Food Co., **II** 544
YKK, **19** 477
**YMCA of the USA, 31 473–76**
Ymos A.G., **IV** 53; **26** 83
**YOCREAM International, Inc., 47 456–58**
Yogen Fruz World-Wide, Inc. *See* CoolBrands International Inc.
Yokado Clothing Store, **V** 88
Yokogawa Electric Corp., **III** 142–43, 536; **26** 230
Yokogawa Electric Works, Limited, **6** 237; **13** 234
Yokohama Bottle Plant, **21** 319
Yokohama Cooperative Wharf Co., **IV** 728
Yokohama Electric Cable Manufacturing Co., **III** 490
**The Yokohama Rubber Co., Ltd., V 254–56; 19 506–09 (upd.)**
Yokohama Specie Bank, **I** 431; **II** 224
Yokohama Tokyu Deppartment Store Co., Ltd., **32** 457
Yoosung Enterprise Co., Ltd., **23** 269
Yoplait S.A. *See* Sodiaal S.A.
York & London, **III** 359
The York Bank and Trust Company, **16** 14; **43** 8
York-Benimaru, **V** 88
York Corp., **III** 440
York Developments, **IV** 720
**York International Corp., 13 569–71; 22** 6
**York Research Corporation, 35 478–80**
York Manufacturing Co $$York Manufacturing Co., **13** 385
York Safe & Lock Company, **7** 144–45; **22** 184
York Steak House, **16** 157
York Wastewater Consultants, Inc., **6** 441
Yorkshire and Pacific Securities Ltd., **IV** 723
Yorkshire Energies, **45** 21
Yorkshire Insurance Co., **III** 241–42, 257
Yorkshire Paper Mills Ltd., **IV** 300
Yorkshire Post Newspapers, **IV** 686; **28** 503
Yorkshire Television Ltd., **IV** 659
Yorkshire-Tyne Tees Television, **24** 194
Yorkshire Water Services Ltd. *See* Kelda Group plc.
Yorkville Group, **IV** 640
Yosemite Park & Curry Co., **II** 144
Yoshikazu Taguchi, **6** 428
Yoshitomi Pharmaceutical, **I** 704
**Young & Co.'s Brewery, P.L.C., 38 499–502**
**Young & Rubicam Inc., I** 9–11, 25, **36–38; II** 129; **6** 14, 47; **9** 314; **13** 204; **16** 166–68; **22 551–54 (upd.); 41** 89–90, 198; **48** 442
Young & Selden, **7** 145
Young & Son, **II** 334
**Young Broadcasting Inc., 40 467–69; 42** 163
**Young Innovations, Inc., 44 451–53**
Young Readers of America, **13** 105
Young's Engineering Company Limited, **IV** 717; **38** 319
**Young's Market Company, LLC, 32 518–20**
Youngblood Truck Lines, **16** 40
Youngs Drug Products Corporation, **8** 85; **38** 124
Youngstown, **IV** 114
Youngstown Pressed Steel Co., **III** 763
Youngstown Sheet & Tube, **I** 490–91; **13** 157
**Younkers, Inc., 19** 324–25, **510–12; 41** 343–44
Yount-Lee Oil Co., **IV** 369
Youth Centre Inc., **16** 36
**Youth Services International, Inc., 21 541–43; 30** 146
Youthtrack, Inc., **29** 399–400
Yoxall Instrument Company, **13** 234
Yoyoteiki Cargo Co., Ltd., **6** 428
**YPF Sociedad Anónima, IV 577–78**. *See also* Repsol-YPF S.A.
Yside Investment Group, **16** 196
YTT. *See* Yorkshire-Tyne Tees Television.
Yuasa Battery Co., **III** 556
Yuba Heat Transfer Corp., **I** 514
**The Yucaipa Cos., 17 558–62; 22** 39; **32** 222; **35** 369
Yukon Pacific Corporation, **22** 164, 166
YUKOS. *See* OAO NK YUKOS.
Yurakucho Seibu Co., Ltd., **V** 185
Yutani Heavy Industries, Ltd., **IV** 130
Yves Rocher. *See* Laboratoires de Biologie Végétale Yves Rocher.
Yves Saint Laurent, **I** 697; **12** 37
Yves Soulié, **II** 266
**YWCA of the U.S.A., 45 452–54**

Z.C. Mines, **IV** 61
Z-Spanish Media Corp., **35** 220; **41** 151
Zaadunie B.V., **I** 672
Zagara's Inc., **35** 190–91
Zahnfabrik Weinand Sohne & Co. G.m.b.H., **10** 271
Zahnradfabrik Friedrichshafen, **III** 415
**Zale Corporation, 16** 206, **559–61; 17** 369; **19** 452; **23** 60; **40 470–74 (upd.)**
Zambezi Saw Mills (1968) Ltd., **IV** 241
Zambia Breweries, **25** 281
**Zambia Industrial and Mining Corporation Ltd., IV 239–41**
Zamboni. *See* Frank J. Zamboni & Co., Inc.
Zander & Ingeström, **III** 419
Zanders Feinpapiere AG, **IV** 288; **15** 229
Zanussi, **III** 480; **22** 27
**Zany Brainy, Inc., 31 477–79; 36** 502
Zap, Inc., **25** 546
**Zapata Corporation, 17** 157, 160; **25 544–46**
Zapata Drilling Co., **IV** 489
Zapata Gulf Marine Corporation, **11** 524
Zapata Offshore Co., **IV** 489
Zapata Petroleum Corp., **IV** 489
Zaring Premier Homes, **41** 133
Zausner, **25** 83
Zayre Corp., **V** 197–98; **9** 20–21; **13** 547–48; **19** 448; **29** 106; **30** 55–56; **33** 198
ZCMI. *See* Zion's Cooperative Mercantile Institution.
ZDF, **41** 28–29
ZDNet, **36** 523
Zealand Mines S.A., **23** 41
Zebco, **22** 115

**Zebra Technologies Corporation**, **14** 378, **569–71**
Zecco, Inc., **III** 443; **6** 441
Zee Medical, Inc., **47** 235
Zehrmart, **II** 631
Zeiss Ikon AG, **III** 446
Zell Bros., **16** 559
Zell/Chilmark Fund LP, **12** 439; **19** 384
Zellers, **V** 80; **25** 221
Zellstoff AG, **III** 400
Zellstoffabrik Waldhof AG, **IV** 323–24
Zellweger Telecommunications AG, **9** 32
**Zeneca Group PLC**, **21 544–46**
Zengine, Inc., **41** 258–59
Zenit Bank, **45** 322
**Zenith Data Systems, Inc.**, **II** 124–25; **III** 123; **6** 231; **10 563–65**; **36** 299
**Zenith Electronics Corporation**, **II** 102, **123–25**; **10** 563; **11** 62, 318; **12** 183, 454; **13** 109, 398, **572–75 (upd.)**; **18** 421; **34 514–19 (upd.)**
Zenith Media, **42** 330–31
Zentec Corp., **I** 482
Zentralsparkasse und Kommerzialbank Wien, **23** 37
Zentronics, **19** 313
Zeppelin Luftschifftechnik GmbH, **48** 450
Zergo Holdings, **42** 24–25
**Zero Corporation**, **17 563–65**
Zero Plus Dialing, Inc. *See* Billing Concepts Corp.
Zetor s.p., **21** 175
Zeus Components, Inc., **10** 113
Zewawell AG, **IV** 324
**ZF Friedrichshafen AG**, **48 447–51**
Zhongbei Building Material Products Company, **26** 510
**Ziebart International Corporation**, **30 499–501**
**The Ziegler Companies, Inc.**, **24 541–45**
**Ziff Communications Company**, **7** 239–40; **12** 359, **560–63**; **13** 483; **16** 371; **17** 152, 253; **25** 238, 240; **41** 12
**Ziff Davis Media Inc.**, **36 521–26 (upd.)**; **47** 77, 79. *See also* CNET Networks, Inc.
Ziff-Davis Publishing Co., **38** 441
Zijlker, **IV** 491
**Zila, Inc.**, **46 466–69**
Zilber Ltd., **13** 541
Zildjian. *See* Avedis Zildjian Co.
Zilkha & Company, **12** 72
**Zilog, Inc.**, **15 543–45**; **16** 548–49; **22** 390
Zimbabwe Sugar Refineries, **II** 581
Zimmer AG, **IV** 142
**Zimmer Holdings, Inc.**, **45 455–57**
Zimmer Inc., **10** 156–57; **11** 475
Zimmer Manufacturing Co., **III** 18; **37** 110, 113
Zinc Corp., **IV** 58–59, 61
Zinc Products Company, **30** 39
Zion Foods, **23** 408
**Zion's Cooperative Mercantile Institution**, **33 471–74**
**Zions Bancorporation**, **12 564–66**; **24** 395
**Zippo Manufacturing Company**, **18 565–68**
Zipps Drive-Thru, Inc., **25** 389
Zippy Mart, **7** 102
Zircotube, **IV** 174
Zivnostenska, **II** 282
**Zodiac S.A.**, **36 527–30**
Zody's Department Stores, **9** 120–22
Zoecon, **I** 673
Zoll Medical, **18** 423
Zoloto Mining Ltd., **38** 231
**Zoltek Companies, Inc.**, **37 427–30**
**Zondervan Publishing House**, **14** 499; **24 546–49**
**Zoom Telephonics, Inc.**, **18 569–71**
Zortech Inc., **10** 508
Zotos International, Inc., **III** 63; **17** 110; **22** 487; **41** 228
ZPT Radom, **23** 427
ZS Sun Limited Partnership, **10** 502
Zuari Cement, **40** 107, 109
Zuellig Group N.A., Inc., **46** 226
Zuid Nederlandsche Handelsbank, **II** 185
Zuka Juice, **47** 201
Zürcher Bankverein, **II** 368
**Zurich Financial Services**, **40** 59, 61; **42 448–53 (upd.)**
Zurich Insurance Group, **15** 257; **25** 154, 156
**Zürich Versicherungs-Gesellschaft**, **III** 194, 402–03, **410–12.** *See also* Zurich Financial Services
Zurn Industries, Inc., **24** 150
Zwarovski, **16** 561
Zycad Corp., **11** 489–91
Zycon Corporation, **24** 201
**Zygo Corporation**, **42 454–57**
Zymaise, **II** 582
ZyMOS Corp., **III** 458
**Zytec Corporation**, **19 513–15**. *See also* Artesyn Technologies Inc.

# *INDEX TO INDUSTRIES*

# Index to Industries


## ACCOUNTING

American Institute of Certified Public Accountants (AICPA), 44
Andersen Worldwide, 29 (upd.)
Automatic Data Processing, Inc., 47 (upd.)
Deloitte & Touche, 9
Deloitte Touche Tohmatsu International, 29 (upd.)
Ernst & Young, 9; 29 (upd.)
KPMG International, 33 (upd.)
L.S. Starrett Co., 13
McLane Company, Inc., 13
NCO Group, Inc., 42
Paychex, Inc., 46 (upd.)
Price Waterhouse, 9
PricewaterhouseCoopers, 29 (upd.)
Robert Wood Johnson Foundation, 35
Univision Communications Inc., 24

## ADVERTISING & OTHER BUSINESS SERVICES

A.C. Nielsen Company, 13
ABM Industries Incorporated, 25 (upd.)
Ackerley Communications, Inc., 9
ACNielsen Corporation, 38 (upd.)
Acsys, Inc., 44
Adecco S.A., 36 (upd.)
Adia S.A., 6
Advo, Inc., 6
Aegis Group plc, 6
AHL Services, Inc., 27
Amdocs Ltd., 47
American Building Maintenance Industries, Inc., 6
The American Society of Composers, Authors and Publishers (ASCAP), 29
Amey Plc, 47
Analysts International Corporation, 36
The Arbitron Company, 38
Armor Holdings, Inc., 27
Ashtead Group plc, 34
The Associated Press, 13
Barrett Business Services, Inc., 16
Bates Worldwide, Inc., 14; 33 (upd.)
Bearings, Inc., 13
Berlitz International, Inc., 13
Big Flower Press Holdings, Inc., 21
Boron, LePore & Associates, Inc., 45
Bozell Worldwide Inc., 25
Bright Horizons Family Solutions, Inc., 31
Broadcast Music Inc., 23
Burns International Services Corporation, 13; 41 (upd.)
Cambridge Technology Partners, Inc., 36
Campbell-Mithun-Esty, Inc., 16
Career Education Corporation, 45
Carmichael Lynch Inc., 28
Central Parking Corporation, 18
Chiat/Day Inc. Advertising, 11
Chicago Board of Trade, 41
Chisholm-Mingo Group, Inc., 41
Christie's International plc, 15; 39 (upd.)
Cintas Corporation, 21
COMFORCE Corporation, 40
Computer Learning Centers, Inc., 26
Corporate Express, Inc., 47 (upd.)
CORT Business Services Corporation, 26
Cox Enterprises, Inc., 22 (upd.)
Creative Artists Agency LLC, 38
Cyrk Inc., 19
Dale Carnegie Training, Inc., 28
D'Arcy Masius Benton & Bowles, Inc., 6; 32 (upd.)
Dawson Holdings PLC, 43
DDB Needham Worldwide, 14
Deluxe Corporation, 22 (upd.)
Dentsu Inc., I; 16 (upd.); 40 (upd.)
Deutsch, Inc., 42
Deutsche Post AG, 29
DoubleClick Inc., 46
Drake Beam Morin, Inc., 44
Earl Scheib, Inc., 32
EBSCO Industries, Inc., 17
Ecology and Environment, Inc., 39
Edison Schools Inc., 37
Education Management Corporation, 35
Employee Solutions, Inc., 18
Ennis Business Forms, Inc., 21
Equifax Inc., 6; 28 (upd.)
Equity Marketing, Inc., 26
ERLY Industries Inc., 17
Euro RSCG Worldwide S.A., 13
Fallon McElligott Inc., 22
Fiserv, Inc., 33 (upd.)
FlightSafety International, Inc., 29 (upd.)
Florists' Transworld Delivery, Inc., 28
Foote, Cone & Belding Communications, Inc., I
Frankel & Co., 39
Franklin Covey Company, 37 (upd.)
Gage Marketing Group, 26
The Gallup Organization, 37
Grey Advertising, Inc., 6
Group 4 Falck A/S, 42
Groupe Jean-Claude Darmon, 44
GSD&M Advertising, 44
Gwathmey Siegel & Associates Architects LLC, 26
Ha-Lo Industries, Inc., 27
Hakuhodo, Inc., 6; 42 (upd.)
Handleman Company, 15
Havas SA, 33 (upd.)
Hays Plc, 27
Headway Corporate Resources, Inc., 40
Heidrick & Struggles International, Inc., 28
Hildebrandt International, 29
Interep National Radio Sales Inc., 35
International Brotherhood of Teamsters, 37
International Management Group, 18
International Total Services, Inc., 37
The Interpublic Group of Companies, Inc., I; 22 (upd.)
Ipsos SA, 48
Iron Mountain, Inc., 33
ITT Educational Services, Inc., 33
J.D. Power and Associates, 32
Jackson Hewitt, Inc., 48
Japan Leasing Corporation, 8
Jostens, Inc., 25 (upd.)
JWT Group Inc., I
Katz Communications, Inc., 6
Katz Media Group, Inc., 35
Kelly Services Inc., 6; 26 (upd.)
Ketchum Communications Inc., 6
Kinko's Inc., 16; 43 (upd.)
Korn/Ferry International, 34
Labor Ready, Inc., 29
Lamar Advertising Company, 27
Learning Tree International Inc., 24
Leo Burnett Company Inc., I; 20 (upd.)
Lintas: Worldwide, 14
Mail Boxes Etc., 18; 41 (upd.)
Manpower, Inc., 30 (upd.)
marchFIRST, Inc., 34
Maritz Inc., 38
MAXIMUS, Inc., 43
National Media Corporation, 27
New England Business Services, Inc., 18
New Valley Corporation, 17
NFO Worldwide, Inc., 24
Nobel Learning Communities, Inc., 37
Norrell Corporation, 25
Norwood Promotional Products, Inc., 26
The Ogilvy Group, Inc., I
Olsten Corporation, 6; 29 (upd.)
Omnicom Group, I; 22 (upd.)
On Assignment, Inc., 20
1-800-FLOWERS, Inc., 26
Opinion Research Corporation, 46
Outdoor Systems, Inc., 25
Paris Corporation, 22
Paychex, Inc., 15
Pierce Leahy Corporation, 24
Pinkerton's Inc., 9
PMT Services, Inc., 24
Publicis S.A., 19
Publishers Clearing House, 23
Randstad Holding n.v., 16; 43 (upd.)
RemedyTemp, Inc., 20
Rental Service Corporation, 28
Rentokil Initial Plc, 47
Right Management Consultants, Inc., 42
Ritchie Bros. Auctioneers Inc., 41
Robert Half International Inc., 18
Roland Berger & Partner GmbH, 37
Ronco, Inc., 15
Russell Reynolds Associates Inc., 38
Saatchi & Saatchi, I; 42 (upd.)
Securitas AB, 42
ServiceMaster Limited Partnership, 6
Shared Medical Systems Corporation, 14
Sir Speedy, Inc., 16
Skidmore, Owings & Merrill, 13
SmartForce PLC, 43
SOS Staffing Services, 25
Sotheby's Holdings, Inc., 11; 29 (upd.)
Spencer Stuart and Associates, Inc., 14
Superior Uniform Group, Inc., 30
Sykes Enterprises, Inc., 45
Sylvan Learning Systems, Inc., 35
TA Triumph-Adler AG, 48
Taylor Nelson Sofres plc, 34
TBWA Advertising, Inc., 6
TBWA\Chiat\Day, 43 (upd.)

Thomas Cook Travel Inc., 33 (upd.)
Ticketmaster Group, Inc., 13; 37 (upd.)
TMP Worldwide Inc., 30
TNT Post Group N.V., 30
Towers Perrin, 32
Transmedia Network Inc., 20
Treasure Chest Advertising Company, Inc., 32
TRM Copy Centers Corporation, 18
True North Communications Inc., 23
Tyler Corporation, 23
U.S. Office Products Company, 25
UniFirst Corporation, 21
United News & Media plc, 28 (upd.)
Unitog Co., 19
Valassis Communications, Inc., 37 (upd.)
Vedior NV, 35
The Wackenhut Corporation, 14
Waggener Edstrom, 42
Wells Rich Greene BDDP, 6
Westaff Inc., 33
Whitman Education Group, Inc., 41
William Morris Agency, Inc., 23
WPP Group plc, 6; 48 (upd.)
Young & Rubicam, Inc., I; 22 (upd.)

## AEROSPACE

A.S. Yakovlev Design Bureau, 15
Aeronca Inc., 46
The Aerospatiale Group, 7; 21 (upd.)
Alliant Techsystems Inc., 30 (upd.)
Aviacionny Nauchno-Tehnicheskii Komplex im. A.N. Tupoleva, 24
Avions Marcel Dassault-Breguet Aviation, I
B/E Aerospace, Inc., 30
Banner Aerospace, Inc., 14
Beech Aircraft Corporation, 8
Bell Helicopter Textron Inc., 46
The Boeing Company, I; 10 (upd.); 32 (upd.)
Bombardier Inc., 42 (upd.)
British Aerospace plc, I; 24 (upd.)
CAE USA Inc., 48
Canadair, Inc., 16
Cessna Aircraft Company, 8
Cirrus Design Corporation, 44
Cobham plc, 30
Daimler-Benz Aerospace AG, 16
DeCrane Aircraft Holdings Inc., 36
Ducommun Incorporated, 30
Empresa Brasileira de Aeronáutica S.A. (Embraer), 36
Fairchild Aircraft, Inc., 9
Fairchild Dornier GmbH, 48 (upd.)
G.I.E. Airbus Industrie, I; 12 (upd.)
General Dynamics Corporation, I; 10 (upd.); 40 (upd.)
GKN plc, 38 (upd.)
Goodrich Corporation, 46 (upd.)
Groupe Dassault Aviation SA, 26 (upd.)
Grumman Corporation, I; 11 (upd.)
Grupo Aeropuerto del Sureste, S.A. de C.V., 48
Gulfstream Aerospace Corporation, 7; 28 (upd.)
HEICO Corporation, 30
International Lease Finance Corporation, 48
N.V. Koninklijke Nederlandse Vliegtuigenfabriek Fokker, I; 28 (upd.)
Learjet Inc., 8; 27 (upd.)
Lockheed Corporation, I; 11 (upd.)
Lockheed Martin Corporation, 15 (upd.)
Magellan Aerospace Corporation, 48
Martin Marietta Corporation, I
McDonnell Douglas Corporation, I; 11 (upd.)
Meggitt PLC, 34
Messerschmitt-Bölkow-Blohm GmbH., I
Moog Inc., 13
The New Piper Aircraft, Inc., 44
Northrop Corporation, I; 11 (upd.)
Northrop Grumman Corporation, 45 (upd.)
Orbital Sciences Corporation, 22
Pratt & Whitney, 9
Raytheon Aircraft Holdings Inc., 46
Rockwell International Corporation, I; 11 (upd.)
Rolls-Royce Allison, 29 (upd.)
Rolls-Royce plc, I; 7 (upd.); 21 (upd.)
Sequa Corp., 13
Shannon Aerospace Ltd., 36
Sikorsky Aircraft Corporation, 24
Smiths Industries PLC, 25
Snecma Group, 46
Société Air France, 27 (upd.)
Spacehab, Inc., 37
Spar Aerospace Limited, 32
Sukhoi Design Bureau Aviation Scientific-Industrial Complex, 24
Sundstrand Corporation, 7; 21 (upd.)
Textron Lycoming Turbine Engine, 9
Thales S.A., 42
Thiokol Corporation, 9; 22 (upd.)
United Technologies Corporation, I; 10 (upd.)
Whittaker Corporation, 48 (upd.)
Zodiac S.A., 36

## AIRLINES

Aer Lingus Group plc, 34
Aeroflot—Russian International Airlines, 6; 29 (upd.)
Aerolíneas Argentinas S.A., 33
Air Canada, 6; 23 (upd.)
Air China, 46
Air New Zealand Limited, 14; 38 (upd.)
Air-India Limited, 6; 27 (upd.)
AirTran Holdings, Inc., 22
Alaska Air Group, Inc., 6; 29 (upd.)
Alitalia-Linee Aeree Italiana, S.p.A., 6; 29 (upd.)
All Nippon Airways Company Limited, 6; 38 (upd.)
Aloha Airlines, Incorporated, 24
America West Holdings Corporation, 6; 34 (upd.)
American Airlines, I; 6 (upd.)
AMR Corporation, 28 (upd.)
Amtran, Inc., 34
Asiana Airlines, Inc., 46
Atlantic Southeast Airlines, Inc., 47
Atlas Air, Inc., 39
Austrian Airlines AG (Österreichische Luftverkehrs AG), 33
Aviacionny Nauchno-Tehnicheskii Komplex im. A.N. Tupoleva, 24
Avianca Aerovías Nacionales de Colombia SA, 36
Banner Aerospace, Inc., 37 (upd.)
Braathens ASA, 47
British Airways PLC, I; 14 (upd.); 43 (upd.)
British Midland plc, 38
British World Airlines Ltd., 18
Cathay Pacific Airways Limited, 6; 34 (upd.)
Chautauqua Airlines, Inc., 38
China Airlines, 34
China Eastern Airlines Co. Ltd., 31
China Southern Airlines Company Ltd., 33
Comair Holdings Inc., 13; 34 (upd.)
Continental Airlines, Inc., I; 21 (upd.)
Corporación Internacional de Aviación, S.A. de C.V. (Cintra), 20
Delta Air Lines, Inc., I; 6 (upd.); 39 (upd.)
Deutsche Lufthansa Aktiengesellschaft, I; 26 (upd.)
Eastern Airlines, I
easyJet Airline Company Limited, 39
EgyptAir, 6; 27 (upd.)
El Al Israel Airlines Ltd., 23
The Emirates Group, 39
Finnair Oy, 6; 25 (upd.)
Frontier Airlines, Inc., 22
Garuda Indonesia, 6
Groupe Air France, 6
Grupo TACA, 38
HAL Inc., 9
Hawaiian Airlines, Inc., 22 (upd.)
Iberia Líneas Aéreas de España S.A., 6; 36 (upd.)
Indian Airlines Ltd., 46
Japan Air Lines Company Ltd., I; 32 (upd.)
JetBlue Airways Corporation, 44
Kitty Hawk, Inc., 22
Kiwi International Airlines Inc., 20
Koninklijke Luchtvaart Maatschappij, N.V. (KLM Royal Dutch Airlines), I; 28 (upd.)
Korean Air Lines Co., Ltd., 6; 27 (upd.)
Lan Chile S.A., 31
Lauda Air Luftfahrt AG, 48
LOT Polish Airlines (Polskie Linie Lotnicze S.A.), 33
LTU Group Holding GmbH, 37
Malév Plc, 24
Malaysian Airlines System Berhad, 6; 29 (upd.)
Mesa Air Group, Inc., 32 (upd.)
Mesa Airlines, Inc., 11
Mesaba Holdings, Inc., 28
Midway Airlines Corporation, 33
Midwest Express Holdings, Inc., 35
Northwest Airlines Corporation, I; 6 (upd.); 26 (upd.)
Offshore Logistics, Inc., 37
Pakistan International Airlines Corporation, 46
Pan American World Airways, Inc., I; 12 (upd.)
Panalpina World Transport (Holding) Ltd., 47
People Express Airlines, Inc., I
Petroleum Helicopters, Inc., 35
Philippine Airlines, Inc., 6; 23 (upd.)
Preussag AG, 42 (upd.)
Qantas Airways Limited, 6; 24 (upd.)
Reno Air Inc., 23
Royal Nepal Airline Corporation, 41
Ryanair Holdings plc, 35
SAA (Pty) Ltd., 28
Sabena S.A./N.V., 33
The SAS Group, 34 (upd.)
Saudi Arabian Airlines, 6; 27 (upd.)
Scandinavian Airlines System, I
Singapore Airlines Ltd., 6; 27 (upd.)
SkyWest, Inc., 25
Southwest Airlines Co., 6; 24 (upd.)
Spirit Airlines, Inc., 31
Sun Country Airlines, 30
Swiss Air Transport Company, Ltd., I
Swiss International Air Lines Ltd., 48
TAP—Air Portugal Transportes Aéreos Portugueses S.A., 46
Texas Air Corporation, I
Thai Airways International Public Company Limited, 6; 27 (upd.)
Tower Air, Inc., 28
Trans World Airlines, Inc., I; 12 (upd.); 35 (upd.)
TransBrasil S/A Linhas Aéreas, 31

Transportes Aereos Portugueses, S.A., 6
TV Guide, Inc., 43 (upd.)
UAL Corporation, 34 (upd.)
United Airlines, I; 6 (upd.)
US Airways Group, Inc., 28 (upd.)
USAir Group, Inc., I; 6 (upd.)
VARIG S.A. (Viação Aérea Rio-Grandense), 6; 29 (upd.)
WestJet Airlines Ltd., 38

## AUTOMOTIVE

AB Volvo, I; 7 (upd.); 26 (upd.)
Adam Opel AG, 7; 21 (upd.)
Aisin Seiki Co., Ltd., 48 (upd.)
Alfa Romeo, 13; 36 (upd.)
Alvis Plc, 47
American Motors Corporation, I
Applied Power Inc., 32 (upd.)
Arvin Industries, Inc., 8
Automobiles Citroen, 7
Automobili Lamborghini Holding S.p.A., 13; 34 (upd.)
Bajaj Auto Limited, 39
Bayerische Motoren Werke AG, I; 11 (upd.); 38 (upd.)
Bendix Corporation, I
Blue Bird Corporation, 35
Bombardier Inc., 42 (upd.)
Borg-Warner Automotive, Inc., 14; 32 (upd.)
The Budd Company, 8
CARQUEST Corporation, 29
Chrysler Corporation, I; 11 (upd.)
CNH Global N.V., 38 (upd.)
Consorcio G Grupo Dina, S.A. de C.V., 36
CSK Auto Corporation, 38
Cummins Engine Company, Inc., I; 12 (upd.); 40 (upd.)
Custom Chrome, Inc., 16
Daihatsu Motor Company, Ltd., 7; 21 (upd.)
Daimler-Benz A.G., I; 15 (upd.)
DaimlerChrysler AG, 34 (upd.)
Dana Corporation, I; 10 (upd.)
Deere & Company, 42 (upd.)
Delphi Automotive Systems Corporation, 45
Don Massey Cadillac, Inc., 37
Douglas & Lomason Company, 16
Ducati Motor Holding S.p.A., 30
Eaton Corporation, I; 10 (upd.)
Echlin Inc., I; 11 (upd.)
Edelbrock Corporation, 37
Federal-Mogul Corporation, I; 10 (upd.); 26 (upd.)
Ferrari S.p.A., 13; 36 (upd.)
Fiat S.p.A, I; 11 (upd.)
FinishMaster, Inc., 24
Ford Motor Company, I; 11 (upd.); 36 (upd.)
Ford Motor Company, S.A. de C.V., 20
Fruehauf Corporation, I
General Motors Corporation, I; 10 (upd.); 36 (upd.)
Gentex Corporation, 26
Genuine Parts Company, 9; 45 (upd.)
GKN plc, 38 (upd.)
Harley-Davidson Inc., 7; 25 (upd.)
Hayes Lemmerz International, Inc., 27
The Hertz Corporation, 33 (upd.)
Hino Motors, Ltd., 7; 21 (upd.)
Hometown Auto Retailers, Inc., 44
Honda Motor Company Limited (Honda Giken Kogyo Kabushiki Kaisha), I; 10 (upd.); 29 (upd.)
Insurance Auto Auctions, Inc., 23
Isuzu Motors, Ltd., 9; 23 (upd.)
Kelsey-Hayes Group of Companies, 7; 27 (upd.)
Kia Motors Corporation, 12; 29 (upd.)
Lear Seating Corporation, 16
Lithia Motors, Inc., 41
Lotus Cars Ltd., 14
Lund International Holdings, Inc., 40
Mack Trucks, Inc., I; 22 (upd.)
The Major Automotive Companies, Inc., 45
Masland Corporation, 17
Mazda Motor Corporation, 9; 23 (upd.)
Mel Farr Automotive Group, 20
Metso Corporation, 30 (upd.)
Midas International Corporation, 10
Mitsubishi Motors Corporation, 9; 23 (upd.)
Monaco Coach Corporation, 31
Monro Muffler Brake, Inc., 24
National R.V. Holdings, Inc., 32
Navistar International Corporation, I; 10 (upd.)
Nissan Motor Co., Ltd., I; 11 (upd.); 34 (upd.)
O'Reilly Automotive, Inc., 26
Officine Alfieri Maserati S.p.A., 13
Oshkosh Truck Corporation, 7
Paccar Inc., I
PACCAR Inc., 26 (upd.)
Pennzoil Company, 20 (upd.)
Penske Corporation, 19 (upd.)
The Pep Boys—Manny, Moe & Jack, 11; 36 (upd.)
Peugeot S.A., I
Piaggio & C. S.p.A., 20
Porsche AG, 13; 31 (upd.)
PSA Peugeot Citroen S.A., 28 (upd.)
Regie Nationale des Usines Renault, I
Renault S.A., 26 (upd.)
Republic Industries, Inc., 26
Robert Bosch GmbH., I; 16 (upd.); 43 (upd.)
RockShox, Inc., 26
Rockwell Automation, 43 (upd.)
Rolls-Royce plc, I; 21 (upd.)
Rover Group Ltd., 7; 21 (upd.)
Saab Automobile AB, 32 (upd.)
Saab-Scania A.B., I; 11 (upd.)
Safelite Glass Corp., 19
Saturn Corporation, 7; 21 (upd.)
Sealed Power Corporation, I
Sheller-Globe Corporation, I
Sixt AG, 39
Skoda Auto a.s., 39
Spartan Motors Inc., 14
SpeeDee Oil Change and Tune-Up, 25
SPX Corporation, 10; 47 (upd.)
Standard Motor Products, Inc., 40
Superior Industries International, Inc., 8
Suzuki Motor Corporation, 9; 23 (upd.)
Sytner Group plc, 45
Tower Automotive, Inc., 24
Toyota Motor Corporation, I; 11 (upd.); 38 (upd.)
TRW Inc., 14 (upd.)
Ugly Duckling Corporation, 22
United Auto Group, Inc., 26
United Technologies Automotive Inc., 15
Valeo, 23
Volkswagen Aktiengesellschaft, I; 11 (upd.); 32 (upd.)
Walker Manufacturing Company, 19
Winnebago Industries Inc., 7; 27 (upd.)
ZF Friedrichshafen AG, 48
Ziebart International Corporation, 30

## BEVERAGES

A & W Brands, Inc., 25
Adolph Coors Company, I; 13 (upd.); 36 (upd.)
Allied Domecq PLC, 29
Allied-Lyons PLC, I
Anchor Brewing Company, 47
Anheuser-Busch Companies, Inc., I; 10 (upd.); 34 (upd.)
Asahi Breweries, Ltd., I; 20 (upd.)
Bacardi Limited, 18
Banfi Products Corp., 36
Baron Philippe de Rothschild S.A., 39
Bass PLC, I; 15 (upd.); 38 (upd.)
BBAG Osterreichische Brau-Beteiligungs-AG, 38
Beringer Wine Estates Holdings, Inc., 22
Boston Beer Company, 18
Brauerei Beck & Co., 9; 33 (upd.)
Brown-Forman Corporation, I; 10 (upd.); 38 (upd.)
Canandaigua Brands, Inc., 34 (upd.)
Canandaigua Wine Company, Inc., 13
Carlsberg A/S, 9; 29 (upd.)
Carlton and United Breweries Ltd., I
Casa Cuervo, S.A. de C.V., 31
Cerveceria Polar, I
The Chalone Wine Group, Ltd., 36
Clearly Canadian Beverage Corporation, 48
Coca Cola Bottling Co. Consolidated, 10
The Coca-Cola Company, I; 10 (upd.); 32 (upd.)
Corby Distilleries Limited, 14
D.G. Yuengling & Son, Inc., 38
Dean Foods Company, 21 (upd.)
Distillers Company PLC, I
Dr Pepper/Seven Up, Inc., 9; 32 (upd.)
E. & J. Gallo Winery, I; 7 (upd.); 28 (upd.)
Ferolito, Vultaggio & Sons, 27
Florida's Natural Growers, 45
Foster's Brewing Group Ltd., 7; 21 (upd.)
Fuller Smith & Turner P.L.C., 38
G. Heileman Brewing Company Inc., I
The Gambrinus Company, 40
Geerlings & Wade, Inc., 45
General Cinema Corporation, I
Golden State Vintners, Inc., 33
Grand Metropolitan PLC, I
Green Mountain Coffee, Inc., 31
The Greenalls Group PLC, 21
Greene King plc, 31
Grupo Modelo, S.A. de C.V., 29
Guinness/UDV, I; 43 (upd.)
The Hain Celestial Group, Inc., 43 (upd.)
Hansen Natural Corporation, 31
Heineken N.V, I; 13 (upd.); 34 (upd.)
Heublein, Inc., I
Hiram Walker Resources, Ltd., I
Interbrew S.A., 17
Jacob Leinenkugel Brewing Company, 28
JD Wetherspoon plc, 30
Karlsberg Brauerei GmbH & Co KG, 41
Kendall-Jackson Winery, Ltd., 28
Kikkoman Corporation, 14
Kirin Brewery Company, Limited, I; 21 (upd.)
König Brauerei GmbH & Co. KG, 35 (upd.)
Labatt Brewing Company Limited, I; 25 (upd.)
Laurent-Perrier SA, 42
Maison Louis Jadot, 24
Marchesi Antinori SRL, 42
Marie Brizard & Roger International S.A., 22
MBC Holding Company, 40
Miller Brewing Company, I; 12 (upd.)
The Minute Maid Company, 28
Moët-Hennessy, I

The Molson Companies Limited, I, 26 (upd.)
National Beverage Corp., 26
National Grape Cooperative Association, Inc., 20
Nichols plc, 44
Ocean Spray Cranberries, Inc., 25 (upd.)
Odwalla, Inc., 31
Panamerican Beverages, Inc., 47
Paulaner Brauerei GmbH & Co. KG, 35
Peet's Coffee & Tea, Inc., 38
The Pepsi Bottling Group, Inc., 40
Pepsico, Inc., I; 10 (upd.); 38 (upd.)
Pernod Ricard S.A., I; 21 (upd.)
Pete's Brewing Company, 22
Philip Morris Companies Inc., 18 (upd.)
Pyramid Breweries Inc., 33
Rainier Brewing Company, 23
Redhook Ale Brewery, Inc., 31
Rémy Cointreau S.A., 20
Robert Mondavi Corporation, 15
Royal Crown Company, Inc., 23
Sapporo Breweries Limited, I; 13 (upd.); 36 (upd.)
Scottish & Newcastle plc, 15; 35 (upd.)
The Seagram Company Ltd., I; 25 (upd.)
Sebastiani Vineyards, Inc., 28
Shepherd Neame Limited, 30
Snapple Beverage Corporation, 11
The South African Breweries Limited, I; 24 (upd.)
Starbucks Corporation, 13; 34 (upd.)
Stewart's Beverages, 39
The Stroh Brewery Company, I; 18 (upd.)
Sutter Home Winery Inc., 16
Taittinger S.A., 43
The Terlato Wine Group, 48
Todhunter International, Inc., 27
Triarc Companies, Inc., 34 (upd.)
Van Houtte Inc., 39
Vin & Spirit AB, 31
Viña Concha y Toro S.A., 45
Whitbread and Company PLC, I
The Wine Group, Inc., 39
Young & Co.'s Brewery, P.L.C., 38

## BIOTECHNOLOGY

Amgen, Inc., 10; 30 (upd.)
Biogen Inc., 14; 36 (upd.)
Cambrex Corporation, 44 (upd.)
Centocor Inc., 14
Charles River Laboratories International, Inc., 42
Chiron Corporation, 10; 36 (upd.)
Covance Inc., 30
CryoLife, Inc., 46
Delta and Pine Land Company, 33
Dionex Corporation, 46
Enzo Biochem, Inc., 41
Genentech, Inc., 32 (upd.)
Genzyme Corporation, 38 (upd.)
Howard Hughes Medical Institute, 39
Huntingdon Life Sciences Group plc, 42
IDEXX Laboratories, Inc., 23
Immunex Corporation, 14
IMPATH Inc., 45
Life Technologies, Inc., 17
Medtronic, Inc., 30 (upd.)
Millipore Corporation, 25
Minntech Corporation, 22
Mycogen Corporation, 21
New Brunswick Scientific Co., Inc., 45
Qiagen N.V., 39
Quintiles Transnational Corporation, 21
Seminis, Inc., 29
Sigma-Aldrich Corporation, 36 (upd.)
STERIS Corporation, 29
Waters Corporation, 43
Whatman plc, 46

## CHEMICALS

A. Schulman, Inc., 8
Aceto Corp., 38
Air Products and Chemicals, Inc., I; 10 (upd.)
Akzo Nobel N.V., 13
AlliedSignal Inc., 22 (upd.)
American Cyanamid, I; 8 (upd.)
American Vanguard Corporation, 47
ARCO Chemical Company, 10
Atochem S.A., I
Baker Hughes Incorporated, 22 (upd.)
Balchem Corporation, 42
BASF Aktiengesellschaft, I; 18 (upd.)
Bayer A.G., I; 13 (upd.); 41 (upd.)
Betz Laboratories, Inc., I; 10 (upd.)
The BFGoodrich Company, 19 (upd.)
BOC Group plc, I; 25 (upd.)
Brenntag AG, 8; 23 (upd.)
Burmah Castrol PLC, 30 (upd.)
Cabot Corporation, 8; 29 (upd.)
Cambrex Corporation, 16
Catalytica Energy Systems, Inc., 44
Celanese Corporation, I
Chemcentral Corporation, 8
Chemi-Trol Chemical Co., 16
Church & Dwight Co., Inc., 29
Ciba-Geigy Ltd., I; 8 (upd.)
The Clorox Company, 22 (upd.)
Croda International Plc, 45
Crompton & Knowles, 9
Crompton Corporation, 36 (upd.)
Cytec Industries Inc., 27
Degussa-Hüls AG, 32 (upd.)
DeKalb Genetics Corporation, 17
The Dexter Corporation, I; 12 (upd.)
Dionex Corporation, 46
The Dow Chemical Company, I; 8 (upd.)
DSM, N.V, I
E.I. du Pont de Nemours & Company, I; 8 (upd.); 26 (upd.)
Eastman Chemical Company, 14; 38 (upd.)
Ecolab Inc., I; 13 (upd.); 34 (upd.)
Elementis plc, 40 (upd.)
English China Clays Ltd., 15 (upd.); 40 (upd.)
ERLY Industries Inc., 17
Ethyl Corporation, I; 10 (upd.)
Ferro Corporation, 8
First Mississippi Corporation, 8
Formosa Plastics Corporation, 14
Fort James Corporation, 22 (upd.)
G.A.F., I
The General Chemical Group Inc., 37
Georgia Gulf Corporation, 9
Givaudan SA, 43
Great Lakes Chemical Corporation, I; 14 (upd.)
Guerbet Group, 46
H.B. Fuller Company, 32 (upd.)
Hauser, Inc., 46
Hawkins Chemical, Inc., 16
Henkel KGaA, 34 (upd.)
Hercules Inc., I; 22 (upd.)
Hoechst A.G., I; 18 (upd.)
Hoechst Celanese Corporation, 13
Huls A.G., I
Huntsman Chemical Corporation, 8
IMC Fertilizer Group, Inc., 8
Imperial Chemical Industries PLC, I
International Flavors & Fragrances Inc., 9; 38 (upd.)
Koppers Industries, Inc., I; 26 (upd.)
L'Air Liquide SA, I; 47 (upd.)
Lawter International Inc., 14
LeaRonal, Inc., 23
Loctite Corporation, 30 (upd.)
Lubrizol Corporation, I; 30 (upd.)
Lyondell Chemical Company, 45 (upd.)
M.A. Hanna Company, 8
MacDermid Incorporated, 32
Mallinckrodt Group Inc., 19
MBC Holding Company, 40
Melamine Chemicals, Inc., 27
Methanex Corporation, 40
Mississippi Chemical Corporation, 39
Mitsubishi Chemical Industries, Ltd., I
Mitsui Petrochemical Industries, Ltd., 9
Monsanto Company, I; 9 (upd.); 29 (upd.)
Montedison SpA, I
Morton International Inc., 9 (upd.)
Morton Thiokol, Inc., I
Nagase & Company, Ltd., 8
Nalco Chemical Corporation, I; 12 (upd.)
National Distillers and Chemical Corporation, I
National Sanitary Supply Co., 16
NCH Corporation, 8
NL Industries, Inc., 10
Nobel Industries AB, 9
Norsk Hydro ASA, 35 (upd.)
Novacor Chemicals Ltd., 12
NutraSweet Company, 8
Olin Corporation, I; 13 (upd.)
OM Group, Inc., 17
Pennwalt Corporation, I
Perstorp A.B., I
Petrolite Corporation, 15
Pioneer Hi-Bred International, Inc., 41 (upd.)
Praxair, Inc., 11
Quantum Chemical Corporation, 8
Reichhold Chemicals, Inc., 10
Rhodia SA, 38
Rhône-Poulenc S.A., I; 10 (upd.)
Robertet SA, 39
Rohm and Haas Company, I; 26 (upd.)
Roussel Uclaf, I; 8 (upd.)
RPM, Inc., 36 (upd.)
The Scotts Company, 22
SCP Pool Corporation, 39
Sequa Corp., 13
Shanghai Petrochemical Co., Ltd., 18
Sigma-Aldrich Corporation, 36 (upd.)
Solvay & Cie S.A., I; 21 (upd.)
Stepan Company, 30
Sterling Chemicals, Inc., 16
Sumitomo Chemical Company Ltd., I
Takeda Chemical Industries, Ltd., 46 (upd.)
Terra Industries, Inc., 13
Teva Pharmaceutical Industries Ltd., 22
TOTAL S.A., 24 (upd.)
Ube Industries, Ltd., 38 (upd.)
Union Carbide Corporation, I; 9 (upd.)
Univar Corporation, 9
The Valspar Corporation, 32 (upd.)
Vista Chemical Company, I
Witco Corporation, I; 16 (upd.)
Zeneca Group PLC, 21

## CONGLOMERATES

Accor SA, 10; 27 (upd.)
AEG A.G., I
Alcatel Alsthom Compagnie Générale d'Electricité, 9
Alco Standard Corporation, I
Alexander & Baldwin, Inc., 40 (upd.)
Alfa, S.A. de C.V., 19
Allied Domecq PLC, 29
Allied-Signal Inc., I
AMFAC Inc., I

The Anschutz Corporation, 36 (upd.)
Aramark Corporation, 13
ARAMARK Corporation, 41
Archer-Daniels-Midland Company, I; 11 (upd.)
Arkansas Best Corporation, 16
Associated British Ports Holdings Plc, 45
BAA plc, 33 (upd.)
Barlow Rand Ltd., I
Bat Industries PLC, I
Berkshire Hathaway Inc., 42 (upd.)
Bond Corporation Holdings Limited, 10
BTR PLC, I
Bunzl plc, 31 (upd.)
Burlington Northern Santa Fe Corporation, 27 (upd.)
Business Post Group plc, 46
C. Itoh & Company Ltd., I
Cargill, Incorporated, 13 (upd.); 40 (upd.)
CBI Industries, Inc., 7
Chemed Corporation, 13
Chesebrough-Pond's USA, Inc., 8
CITIC Pacific Ltd., 18
Colt Industries Inc., I
The Connell Company, 29
CSR Limited, 28 (upd.)
Daewoo Group, 18 (upd.)
De Dietrich & Cie., 31
Deere & Company, 21 (upd.)
Delaware North Companies Incorporated, 7
Desc, S.A. de C.V., 23
The Dial Corp., 8
EBSCO Industries, Inc., 40 (upd.)
El Corte Inglés Group, 26 (upd.)
Elders IXL Ltd., I
Engelhard Corporation, 21 (upd.)
Farley Northwest Industries, Inc., I
Fimalac S.A., 37
First Pacific Company Limited, 18
Fisher Companies, Inc., 15
Fletcher Challenge Ltd., 19 (upd.)
FMC Corporation, I; 11 (upd.)
Fortune Brands, Inc., 29 (upd.)
Fuqua Industries, Inc., I
General Electric Company, 34 (upd.)
GIB Group, 26 (upd.)
Gillett Holdings, Inc., 7
Grand Metropolitan PLC, 14 (upd.)
Great American Management and Investment, Inc., 8
Greyhound Corporation, I
Grupo Carso, S.A. de C.V., 21
Grupo Industrial Bimbo, 19
Gulf & Western Inc., I
Hagemeyer N.V., 39
Hankyu Corporation, 23 (upd.)
Hanson PLC, III; 7 (upd.)
Hitachi, Ltd., I; 12 (upd.); 40 (upd.)
Hutchison Whampoa Ltd., 18
IC Industries, Inc., I
Ilitch Holdings Inc., 37
Inchcape plc, 16 (upd.)
Ingram Industries, Inc., 11
Instituto Nacional de Industria, I
International Controls Corporation, 10
International Telephone & Telegraph Corporation, I; 11 (upd.)
Istituto per la Ricostruzione Industriale, I
ITOCHU Corporation, 32 (upd.)
Jardine Matheson Holdings Limited, I; 20 (upd.)
Jason Incorporated, 23
Jefferson Smurfit Group plc, 19 (upd.)
The Jim Pattison Group, 37
Jordan Industries, Inc., 36
Justin Industries, Inc., 19
Kanematsu Corporation, 24 (upd.)
Kao Corporation, 20 (upd.)
Katy Industries, Inc., I
Kesko Ltd. (Kesko Oy), 8; 27 (upd.)
Kidde plc, 44 (upd.)
Kidde, Inc., I
KOC Holding A.S., I
Koninklijke Nedlloyd N.V., 26 (upd.)
Koor Industries Ltd., 25 (upd.)
K2 Inc., 16
The L.L. Knickerbocker Co., Inc., 25
Lancaster Colony Corporation, 8
Larry H. Miller Group, 29
Lear Siegler, Inc., I
Lefrak Organization Inc., 26
Leucadia National Corporation, 11
Litton Industries, Inc., I; 11 (upd.)
Loews Corporation, I; 12 (upd.); 36 (upd.)
Loral Corporation, 8
LTV Corporation, I
LVMH Moët Hennessy Louis Vuitton SA, 33 (upd.)
Marubeni Corporation, 24 (upd.)
Marubeni K.K., I
MAXXAM Inc., 8
McKesson Corporation, I
Menasha Corporation, 8
Metallgesellschaft AG, 16 (upd.)
Metromedia Co., 7
Minnesota Mining & Manufacturing Company (3M), I; 8 (upd.); 26 (upd.)
Mitsubishi Corporation, I; 12 (upd.)
Mitsubishi Heavy Industries, Ltd., 40 (upd.)
Mitsui & Co., Ltd., 28 (upd.)
Mitsui Bussan K.K., I
The Molson Companies Limited, I; 26 (upd.)
Montedison S.p.A., 24 (upd.)
NACCO Industries, Inc., 7
National Service Industries, Inc., 11
New World Development Company Limited, 38 (upd.)
Nichimen Corporation, 24 (upd.)
Nissho Iwai K.K., I
Norsk Hydro A.S., 10
Ogden Corporation, I
Onex Corporation, 16
Orkla A/S, 18
Park-Ohio Industries Inc., 17
Pentair, Inc., 7
Philip Morris Companies Inc., 44 (upd.)
Poliet S.A., 33
Powell Duffryn plc, 31
Power Corporation of Canada, 36 (upd.)
Preussag AG, 17
Pubco Corporation, 17
Pulsar Internacional S.A., 21
R.B. Pamplin Corp., 45
The Rank Organisation Plc, 14 (upd.)
Red Apple Group, Inc., 23
Roll International Corporation, 37
Rubbermaid Incorporated, 20 (upd.)
Samsung Group, I
San Miguel Corporation, 15
Sara Lee Corporation, 15 (upd.)
Schindler Holding AG, 29
Sea Containers Ltd., 29
Seaboard Corporation, 36
ServiceMaster Inc., 23 (upd.)
Sime Darby Berhad, 14; 36 (upd.)
Société du Louvre, 27
Standex International Corporation, 17; 44 (upd.)
Stinnes AG, 23 (upd.)
Sudbury Inc., 16
Sumitomo Corporation, I; 11 (upd.)
Swire Pacific Ltd., I; 16 (upd.)
Talley Industries, Inc., 16
Tandycrafts, Inc., 31
TaurusHolding GmbH & Co. KG, 46
Teledyne, Inc., I; 10 (upd.)
Tenneco Inc., I; 10 (upd.)
Textron Inc., I; 34 (upd.)
Thomas H. Lee Co., 24
Thorn Emi PLC, I
Thorn plc, 24
TI Group plc, 17
Time Warner Inc., IV; 7 (upd.)
Tokyu Corporation, 47 (upd.)
Tomen Corporation, 24 (upd.)
Tomkins plc, 11; 44 (upd.)
Toshiba Corporation, I; 12 (upd.); 40 (upd.)
Tractebel S.A., 20
Transamerica–An AEGON Company, I; 13 (upd.); 41 (upd.)
The Tranzonic Cos., 15
Triarc Companies, Inc., 8
TRW Inc., I; 11 (upd.)
Unilever, II; 7 (upd.); 32 (upd.)
United Technologies Corporation, 34 (upd.)
Universal Studios, Inc., 33
Valhi, Inc., 19
Valores Industriales S.A., 19
Veba A.G., I; 15 (upd.)
Vendôme Luxury Group plc, 27
Viacom Inc., 23 (upd.)
Virgin Group, 12; 32 (upd.)
W.R. Grace & Company, I
The Washington Companies, 33
Wheaton Industries, 8
Whitbread PLC, 20 (upd.)
Whitman Corporation, 10 (upd.)
Whittaker Corporation, I
WorldCorp, Inc., 10
Worms et Cie, 27
Yamaha Corporation, 40 (upd.)

## CONSTRUCTION

A. Johnson & Company H.B., I
ABC Supply Co., Inc., 22
Abrams Industries Inc., 23
AMREP Corporation, 21
ASV, Inc., 34
The Austin Company, 8
Balfour Beatty plc, 36 (upd.)
Baratt Developments PLC, I
Beazer Homes USA, Inc., 17
Bechtel Group, Inc., I; 24 (upd.)
Bellway Plc, 45
BFC Construction Corporation, 25
Bilfinger & Berger Bau A.G., I
Bird Corporation, 19
Black & Veatch LLP, 22
Boral Limited, 43 (upd.)
Bouygues S.A., I; 24 (upd.)
Brown & Root, Inc., 13
Bufete Industrial, S.A. de C.V., 34
CalMat Co., 19
Centex Corporation, 8; 29 (upd.)
Cianbro Corporation, 14
The Clark Construction Group, Inc., 8
Colas S.A., 31
Day & Zimmermann, Inc., 31 (upd.)
Dillingham Construction Corporation, I; 44 (upd.)
Dominion Homes, Inc., 19
The Drees Company, Inc., 41
Edw. C. Levy Co., 42
Eiffage, 27
Ellerbe Becket, 41
Empresas ICA Sociedad Controladora, S.A. de C.V., 41
Encompass Services Corporation, 33
Engle Homes, Inc., 46
Environmental Industries, Inc., 31

Eurotunnel PLC, 13
Fairclough Construction Group PLC, I
Fleetwood Enterprises, Inc., 22 (upd.)
Fluor Corporation, I; 8 (upd.); 34 (upd.)
George Wimpey PLC, 12
Gilbane, Inc., 34
Granite Rock Company, 26
Grupo Ferrovial, S.A., 40
Habitat for Humanity International, 36
Hillsdown Holdings plc, 24 (upd.)
Hochtief AG, 33
Horton Homes, Inc., 25
Hospitality Worldwide Services, Inc., 26
Hovnanian Enterprises, Inc., 29
J.A. Jones, Inc., 16
Jarvis plc, 39
John Brown PLC, I
John Laing PLC, I
John W. Danforth Company, 48
Kajima Corporation, I
Kaufman and Broad Home Corporation, 8
KB Home, 45 (upd.)
Kitchell Corporation, 14
The Koll Company, 8
Komatsu Ltd., 16 (upd.)
Kraus-Anderson, Incorporated, 36
Kumagai Gumi Company, Ltd., I
L'Entreprise Jean Lefebvre, 23
Ledcor Industries Limited, 46
Lennar Corporation, 11
Lincoln Property Company, 8
Lindal Cedar Homes, Inc., 29
Linde A.G., I
McCarthy Building Companies, Inc., 48
Mellon-Stuart Company, I
Michael Baker Corp., 14
Morrison Knudsen Corporation, 7; 28 (upd.)
New Holland N.V., 22
NVR L.P., 8
Ohbayashi Corporation, I
Opus Group, 34
The Peninsular & Oriental Steam Navigation Company (Bovis Division), I
Perini Corporation, 8
Peter Kiewit Sons' Inc., 8
Philipp Holzmann AG, 17
Post Properties, Inc., 26
Pulte Homes, Inc., 8; 42 (upd.)
Redrow Group plc, 31
RMC Group p.l.c., 34 (upd.)
Rooney Brothers Co., 25
The Rottlund Company, Inc., 28
The Ryland Group, Inc., 8; 37 (upd.)
Sandvik AB, 32 (upd.)
Schuff Steel Company, 26
Shorewood Packaging Corporation, 28
Simon Property Group, Inc., 27
Skanska AB, 38
Sundt Corp., 24
Swinerton Inc., 43
Taylor Woodrow plc, I; 38 (upd.)
Thyssen Krupp AG, 28 (upd.)
Toll Brothers Inc., 15
Trammell Crow Company, 8
Tridel Enterprises Inc., 9
The Turner Corporation, 8; 23 (upd.)
U.S. Aggregates, Inc., 42
U.S. Home Corporation, 8
Veit Companies, 43
Walbridge Aldinger Co., 38
Walter Industries, Inc., 22 (upd.)
The Weitz Company, Inc., 42
Wilson Bowden Plc, 45
Wood Hall Trust PLC, I

## CONTAINERS

Ball Corporation, I; 10 (upd.)
BWAY Corporation, 24
Clarcor Inc., 17
Continental Can Co., Inc., 15
Continental Group Company, I
Crown Cork & Seal Company, Inc., I; 13 (upd.); 32 (upd.)
Gaylord Container Corporation, 8
Golden Belt Manufacturing Co., 16
Greif Bros. Corporation, 15
Grupo Industrial Durango, S.A. de C.V., 37
Inland Container Corporation, 8
Kerr Group Inc., 24
Keyes Fibre Company, 9
Liqui-Box Corporation, 16
The Longaberger Company, 12
Longview Fibre Company, 8
The Mead Corporation, 19 (upd.)
Metal Box PLC, I
National Can Corporation, I
Owens-Illinois, Inc., I; 26 (upd.)
Primerica Corporation, I
Reynolds Metals Company, 19 (upd.)
Royal Packaging Industries Van Leer N.V., 30
Sealright Co., Inc., 17
Smurfit-Stone Container Corporation, 26 (upd.)
Sonoco Products Company, 8
Thermos Company, 16
Toyo Seikan Kaisha, Ltd., I
U.S. Can Corporation, 30
Ultra Pac, Inc., 24
Viatech Continental Can Company, Inc., 25 (upd.)
Vitro Corporativo S.A. de C.V., 34

## DRUGS/PHARMACEUTICALS

A.L. Pharma Inc., 12
Abbott Laboratories, I; 11 (upd.); 40 (upd.)
Akorn, Inc., 32
Alpharma Inc., 35 (upd.)
ALZA Corporation, 10; 36 (upd.)
American Home Products, I; 10 (upd.)
Amgen, Inc., 10
Astra AB, I; 20 (upd.)
Barr Laboratories, Inc., 26
Bayer A.G., I; 13 (upd.)
Biovail Corporation, 47
Block Drug Company, Inc., 8
Bristol-Myers Squibb Company, III; 9 (upd.); 37 (upd.)
C.H. Boehringer Sohn, 39
Carter-Wallace, Inc., 8; 38 (upd.)
Cephalon, Inc., 45
Chiron Corporation, 10
Ciba-Geigy Ltd., I; 8 (upd.)
D&K Wholesale Drug, Inc., 14
Eli Lilly and Company, I; 11 (upd.); 47 (upd.)
Express Scripts Inc., 44 (upd.)
F. Hoffmann-Laroche & Company A.G., I
Fisons plc, 9; 23 (upd.)
FoxMeyer Health Corporation, 16
Fujisawa Pharmaceutical Company Ltd., I
G.D. Searle & Co., I; 12 (upd.); 34 (upd.)
GEHE AG, 27
Genentech, Inc., I; 8 (upd.)
Genetics Institute, Inc., 8
Genzyme Corporation, 13
Glaxo Holdings PLC, I; 9 (upd.)
GlaxoSmithKline plc, 46 (upd.)
Groupe Fournier SA, 44
H. Lundbeck A/S, 44
Hauser, Inc., 46
Heska Corporation, 39
Huntingdon Life Sciences Group plc, 42
Johnson & Johnson, III; 8 (upd.)
Jones Medical Industries, Inc., 24
Kyowa Hakko Kogyo Co., Ltd., 48 (upd.)
Leiner Health Products Inc., 34
Ligand Pharmaceuticals Incorporated, 47
Marion Merrell Dow, Inc., I; 9 (upd.)
McKesson Corporation, 12; 47 (upd.)
MedImmune, Inc., 35
Merck & Co., Inc., I; 11 (upd.)
Miles Laboratories, I
Millennium Pharmaceuticals, Inc., 47
Monsanto Company, 29 (upd.)
Moore Medical Corp., 17
Murdock Madaus Schwabe, 26
Mylan Laboratories Inc., I; 20 (upd.)
National Patent Development Corporation, 13
Novartis AG, 39 (upd.)
Novo Industri A/S, I
Pfizer Inc., I; 9 (upd.); 38 (upd.)
Pharmacia & Upjohn Inc., I; 25 (upd.)
Quintiles Transnational Corporation, 21
R.P. Scherer, I
Roberts Pharmaceutical Corporation, 16
Roche Bioscience, 14 (upd.)
Rorer Group, I
Roussel Uclaf, I; 8 (upd.)
Sandoz Ltd., I
Sankyo Company, Ltd., I
Sanofi Group, I
Schering A.G., I
Schering-Plough Corporation, I; 14 (upd.)
Sepracor Inc., 45
Serono S.A., 47
Shionogi & Co., Ltd., 17 (upd.)
Sigma-Aldrich Corporation, I; 36 (upd.)
SmithKline Beckman Corporation, I
SmithKline Beecham plc, 32 (upd.)
Squibb Corporation, I
Sterling Drug, Inc., I
The Sunrider Corporation, 26
Syntex Corporation, I
Takeda Chemical Industries, Ltd., I
Teva Pharmaceutical Industries Ltd., 22
The Upjohn Company, I; 8 (upd.)
Vitalink Pharmacy Services, Inc., 15
Warner-Lambert Co., I; 10 (upd.)
Watson Pharmaceuticals Inc., 16
The Wellcome Foundation Ltd., I
Zila, Inc., 46

## ELECTRICAL & ELECTRONICS

ABB ASEA Brown Boveri Ltd., II; 22 (upd.)
Acer Inc., 16
Acuson Corporation, 10; 36 (upd.)
ADC Telecommunications, Inc., 30 (upd.)
Adtran Inc., 22
Advanced Micro Devices, Inc., 30 (upd.)
Advanced Technology Laboratories, Inc., 9
Agilent Technologies Inc., 38
Aiwa Co., Ltd., 30
Akzo Nobel N.V., 41 (upd.)
Alliant Techsystems Inc., 30 (upd.)
AlliedSignal Inc., 22 (upd.)
Alpine Electronics, Inc., 13
Alps Electric Co., Ltd., II
Altera Corporation, 18; 43 (upd.)
Altron Incorporated, 20
Amdahl Corporation, 40 (upd.)
American Power Conversion Corporation, 24
AMP Incorporated, II; 14 (upd.)
Amphenol Corporation, 40
Amstrad plc, 48 (upd.)

Analog Devices, Inc., 10
Analogic Corporation, 23
Anam Group, 23
Anaren Microwave, Inc., 33
Andrew Corporation, 10; 32 (upd.)
Apple Computer, Inc., 36 (upd.)
Applied Power Inc., 32 (upd.)
Arrow Electronics, Inc., 10
Ascend Communications, Inc., 24
Astronics Corporation, 35
Atari Corporation, 9; 23 (upd.)
Atmel Corporation, 17
Audiovox Corporation, 34
Ault Incorporated, 34
Autodesk, Inc., 10
Avnet Inc., 9
Bang & Olufsen Holding A/S, 37
Barco NV, 44
Benchmark Electronics, Inc., 40
Bicoastal Corporation, II
Blonder Tongue Laboratories, Inc., 48
Bose Corporation, 13; 36 (upd.)
Boston Acoustics, Inc., 22
Bowthorpe plc, 33
Broadcom Corporation, 34
Bull S.A., 43 (upd.)
Burr-Brown Corporation, 19
C-COR.net Corp., 38
Cabletron Systems, Inc., 10
Cadence Design Systems, Inc., 48 (upd.)
Cambridge SoundWorks, Inc., 48
Canon Inc., 18 (upd.)
Carbone Lorraine S.A., 33
Carl-Zeiss-Stiftung, 34 (upd.)
CASIO Computer Co., Ltd., 16 (upd.); 40 (upd.)
Checkpoint Systems, Inc., 39
Cirrus Logic, Inc., 48 (upd.)
Cisco Systems, Inc., 34 (upd.)
Citizen Watch Co., Ltd., 21 (upd.)
Cobham plc, 30
Cobra Electronics Corporation, 14
Coherent, Inc., 31
Cohu, Inc., 32
Compagnie Générale d'Électricité, II
Conexant Systems, Inc., 36
Cooper Industries, Inc., II
Cray Research, Inc., 16 (upd.)
CTS Corporation, 39
Cubic Corporation, 19
Cypress Semiconductor Corporation, 20; 48 (upd.)
Daktronics, Inc., 32
Dallas Semiconductor Corporation, 13; 31 (upd.)
De La Rue plc, 34 (upd.)
Dell Computer Corporation, 31 (upd.)
DH Technology, Inc., 18
Digi International Inc., 9
Discreet Logic Inc., 20
Dixons Group plc, 19 (upd.)
Dolby Laboratories Inc., 20
Dynatech Corporation, 13
E-Systems, Inc., 9
Electronics for Imaging, Inc., 15; 43 (upd.)
Emerson, 46 (upd.)
Emerson Electric Co., II
Emerson Radio Corp., 30
ENCAD, Incorporated, 25
ESS Technology, Inc., 22
Everex Systems, Inc., 16
Exabyte Corporation, 40 (upd.)
Exar Corp., 14
Exide Electronics Group, Inc., 20
Flextronics International Ltd., 38
Fluke Corporation, 15
Foxboro Company, 13
Fuji Electric Co., Ltd., II; 48 (upd.)
Fujitsu Limited, 16 (upd.); 42 (upd.)
General Dynamics Corporation, 40 (upd.)
General Electric Company, II; 12 (upd.)
General Electric Company, PLC, II
General Instrument Corporation, 10
General Signal Corporation, 9
GenRad, Inc., 24
GM Hughes Electronics Corporation, II
Goldstar Co., Ltd., 12
Gould Electronics, Inc., 14
Grundig AG, 27
Guillemot Corporation, 41
Hadco Corporation, 24
Hamilton Beach/Proctor-Silex Inc., 17
Harman International Industries Inc., 15
Harris Corporation, II; 20 (upd.)
Hayes Corporation, 24
Herley Industries, Inc., 33
Hewlett-Packard Company, 28 (upd.)
Holophane Corporation, 19
Honeywell Inc., II; 12 (upd.)
Hubbell Incorporated, 9; 31 (upd.)
Hughes Supply, Inc., 14
Hutchinson Technology Incorporated, 18
Hypercom Corporation, 27
IEC Electronics Corp., 42
Imax Corporation, 28
In Focus Systems, Inc., 22
Indigo NV, 26
Intel Corporation, II; 10 (upd.)
International Business Machines Corporation, 30 (upd.)
International Rectifier Corporation, 31
Itel Corporation, 9
Jabil Circuit, Inc., 36
Jaco Electronics, Inc., 30
JDS Uniphase Corporation, 34
Juno Lighting, Inc., 30
Keithley Instruments Inc., 16
Kemet Corp., 14
Kent Electronics Corporation, 17
Kenwood Corporation, 31
Kimball International, Inc., 48 (upd.)
Kingston Technology Corporation, 20
KitchenAid, 8
KLA-Tencor Corporation, 45 (upd.)
KnowledgeWare Inc., 9
Kollmorgen Corporation, 18
Konica Corporation, 30 (upd.)
Koor Industries Ltd., II
Koss Corporation, 38
Kudelski Group SA, 44
Kulicke and Soffa Industries, Inc., 33
Kyocera Corporation, II
LaBarge Inc., 41
Lattice Semiconductor Corp., 16
LeCroy Corporation, 41
Legrand SA, 21
Linear Technology, Inc., 16
Littelfuse, Inc., 26
Loral Corporation, 9
Lowrance Electronics, Inc., 18
LSI Logic Corporation, 13
Lucent Technologies Inc., 34
Lucky-Goldstar, II
Lunar Corporation, 29
Mackie Designs Inc., 33
MagneTek, Inc., 15; 41 (upd.)
Marconi plc, 33 (upd.)
Marquette Electronics, Inc., 13
Matsushita Electric Industrial Co., Ltd., II
Maxim Integrated Products, Inc., 16
Merix Corporation, 36
Methode Electronics, Inc., 13
Mitel Corporation, 18
MITRE Corporation, 26
Mitsubishi Electric Corporation, II; 44 (upd.)
Motorola, Inc., II; 11 (upd.); 34 (upd.)
National Instruments Corporation, 22
National Presto Industries, Inc., 16; 43 (upd.)
National Semiconductor Corporation, II; 26 (upd.)
NEC Corporation, II; 21 (upd.)
Nintendo Co., Ltd., 28 (upd.)
Nokia Corporation, II; 17 (upd.); 38 (upd.)
Nortel Networks Corporation, 36 (upd.)
Northrop Grumman Corporation, 45 (upd.)
Oak Technology, Inc., 22
Oki Electric Industry Company, Limited, II
Omron Corporation, II; 28 (upd.)
Otter Tail Power Company, 18
Palm, Inc., 36
Palomar Medical Technologies, Inc., 22
The Peak Technologies Group, Inc., 14
Peavey Electronics Corporation, 16
Philips Electronics N.V., II; 13 (upd.)
Philips Electronics North America Corp., 13
Pioneer Electronic Corporation, 28 (upd.)
Pioneer-Standard Electronics Inc., 19
Pitney Bowes Inc., 47 (upd.)
Pittway Corporation, 9
The Plessey Company, PLC, II
Plexus Corporation, 35
Polk Audio, Inc., 34
Potter & Brumfield Inc., 11
Premier Industrial Corporation, 9
Protection One, Inc., 32
Quanta Computer Inc., 47
Racal Electronics PLC, II
RadioShack Corporation, 36 (upd.)
Radius Inc., 16
Raychem Corporation, 8
Rayovac Corporation, 13
Raytheon Company, II; 11 (upd.); 38 (upd.)
RCA Corporation, II
Read-Rite Corp., 10
Reliance Electric Company, 9
Rexel, Inc., 15
Richardson Electronics, Ltd., 17
Ricoh Company, Ltd., 36 (upd.)
The Rival Company, 19
Rockford Corporation, 43
S&C Electric Company, 15
SAGEM S.A., 37
St. Louis Music, Inc., 48
Sam Ash Music Corporation, 30
Samsung Electronics Co., Ltd., 14; 41 (upd.)
SANYO Electric Co., Ltd., II; 36 (upd.)
ScanSource, Inc., 29
Schneider S.A., II; 18 (upd.)
SCI Systems, Inc., 9
Scientific-Atlanta, Inc., 45 (upd.)
Scitex Corporation Ltd., 24
Seagate Technology, Inc., 34 (upd.)
Semtech Corporation, 32
Sensormatic Electronics Corp., 11
Sensory Science Corporation, 37
SGI, 29 (upd.)
Sharp Corporation, II; 12 (upd.); 40 (upd.)
Sheldahl Inc., 23
Siemens A.G., II; 14 (upd.)
Silicon Graphics Incorporated, 9
Smiths Industries PLC, 25
Solectron Corporation, 12; 48 (upd.)
Sony Corporation, II; 12 (upd.); 40 (upd.)
SPX Corporation, 47 (upd.)
Sterling Electronics Corp., 18
Sumitomo Electric Industries, Ltd., II
Sun Microsystems, Inc., 30 (upd.)
Sunbeam-Oster Co., Inc., 9
SyQuest Technology, Inc., 18

Tandy Corporation, II; 12 (upd.)
Tatung Co., 23
TDK Corporation, II; 17 (upd.)
Tech-Sym Corporation, 18
Technitrol, Inc., 29
Tektronix, Inc., 8
Telxon Corporation, 10
Teradyne, Inc., 11
Texas Instruments Inc., II; 11 (upd.); 46 (upd.)
Thales S.A., 42
THOMSON multimedia S.A., II; 42 (upd.)
The Titan Corporation, 36
Tops Appliance City, Inc., 17
Toromont Industries, Ltd., 21
Trimble Navigation Limited, 40
Tweeter Home Entertainment Group, Inc., 30
Ultrak Inc., 24
Universal Electronics Inc., 39
Varian Associates Inc., 12
Veeco Instruments Inc., 32
Vicon Industries, Inc., 44
Victor Company of Japan, Limited, II; 26 (upd.)
Vishay Intertechnology, Inc., 21
Vitesse Semiconductor Corporation, 32
Vitro Corp., 10
VLSI Technology, Inc., 16
Wells-Gardner Electronics Corporation, 43
Westinghouse Electric Corporation, II; 12 (upd.)
Wyle Electronics, 14
Yageo Corporation, 16
York Research Corporation, 35
Zenith Data Systems, Inc., 10
Zenith Electronics Corporation, II; 13 (upd.); 34 (upd.)
Zoom Telephonics, Inc., 18
Zytec Corporation, 19

## ENGINEERING & MANAGEMENT SERVICES

AAON, Inc., 22
Aavid Thermal Technologies, Inc., 29
Alliant Techsystems Inc., 30 (upd.)
Amey Plc, 47
Analytic Sciences Corporation, 10
Arcadis NV, 26
Arthur D. Little, Inc., 35
The Austin Company, 8
Balfour Beatty plc, 36 (upd.)
Brown & Root, Inc., 13
Bufete Industrial, S.A. de C.V., 34
C.H. Heist Corporation, 24
CDI Corporation, 6
CH2M Hill Ltd., 22
The Charles Stark Draper Laboratory, Inc., 35
Coflexip S.A., 25
Corrections Corporation of America, 23
CRSS Inc., 6
Dames & Moore, Inc., 25
DAW Technologies, Inc., 25
Day & Zimmermann Inc., 9; 31 (upd.)
Donaldson Co. Inc., 16
EG&G Incorporated, 8; 29 (upd.)
Eiffage, 27
Essef Corporation, 18
Fluor Corporation, 34 (upd.)
Foster Wheeler Corporation, 6; 23 (upd.)
Framatome SA, 19
Gilbane, Inc., 34
Halliburton Company, 25 (upd.)
Harding Lawson Associates Group, Inc., 16
Harza Engineering Company, 14
HDR Inc., 48
ICF Kaiser International, Inc., 28
Jacobs Engineering Group Inc., 6; 26 (upd.)
JWP Inc., 9
Kvaerner ASA, 36
Layne Christensen Company, 19
The MacNeal-Schwendler Corporation, 25
Malcolm Pirnie, Inc., 42
McDermott International, Inc., 37 (upd.)
McKinsey & Company, Inc., 9
Ogden Corporation, 6
Opus Group, 34
Parsons Brinckerhoff, Inc., 34
The Parsons Corporation, 8
RCM Technologies, Inc., 34
Renishaw plc, 46
Rosemount Inc., 15
Roy F. Weston, Inc., 33
Royal Vopak NV, 41
Rust International Inc., 11
Sandvik AB, 32 (upd.)
Science Applications International Corporation, 15
Serco Group plc, 47
Stone & Webster, Inc., 13
Susquehanna Pfaltzgraff Company, 8
Sverdrup Corporation, 14
Tech-Sym Corporation, 44 (upd.)
Tetra Tech, Inc., 29
Thyssen Krupp AG, 28 (upd.)
Towers Perrin, 32
Tracor Inc., 17
TRC Companies, Inc., 32
Underwriters Laboratories, Inc., 30
United Dominion Industries Limited, 8; 16 (upd.)
URS Corporation, 45
VECO International, Inc., 7
Vinci, 43
WS Atkins Plc, 45

## ENTERTAINMENT & LEISURE

A&E Television Networks, 32
Acclaim Entertainment Inc., 24
Activision, Inc., 32
AEI Music Network Inc., 35
Airtours Plc, 27
All American Communications Inc., 20
Alliance Entertainment Corp., 17
Amblin Entertainment, 21
AMC Entertainment Inc., 12; 35 (upd.)
American Golf Corporation, 45
American Skiing Company, 28
Ameristar Casinos, Inc., 33
AMF Bowling, Inc., 40
Anchor Gaming, 24
Applause Inc., 24
Aprilia SpA, 17
Argosy Gaming Company, 21
The Art Institute of Chicago, 29
Artisan Entertainment Inc., 32 (upd.)
Asahi National Broadcasting Company, Ltd., 9
Aspen Skiing Company, 15
Aston Villa plc, 41
Atlanta National League Baseball Club, Inc., 43
The Atlantic Group, 23
Autotote Corporation, 20
Aztar Corporation, 13
Baker & Taylor Corporation, 43 (upd.)
Baker & Taylor, Inc., 16
Bally Total Fitness Holding Corp., 25
Bertelsmann A.G., 15 (upd.); 43 (upd.)
Bertucci's Inc., 16
Blockbuster Inc., 9; 31 (upd.)
Boca Resorts, Inc., 37
Bonneville International Corporation, 29
Booth Creek Ski Holdings, Inc., 31
Boston Celtics Limited Partnership, 14
Boston Professional Hockey Association Inc., 39
The Boy Scouts of America, 34
British Broadcasting Corporation Ltd., 7; 21 (upd.)
British Sky Broadcasting Group Plc, 20
Cablevision Systems Corporation, 7
Callaway Golf Company, 45 (upd.)
Canterbury Park Holding Corporation, 42
Capital Cities/ABC Inc., II
Carlson Companies, Inc., 22 (upd.)
Carmike Cinemas, Inc., 14; 37 (upd.)
Carnival Corporation, 27 (upd.)
Carnival Cruise Lines, Inc., 6
The Carsey-Werner Company, L.L.C., 37
CBS Inc., II; 6 (upd.)
Cedar Fair, L.P., 22
Central Independent Television, 7; 23 (upd.)
Century Theatres, Inc., 31
Championship Auto Racing Teams, Inc., 37
Chicago Bears Football Club, Inc., 33
Chris-Craft Industries, Inc., 31 (upd.)
Chrysalis Group plc, 40
Churchill Downs Incorporated, 29
Cinar Corporation, 40
Cineplex Odeon Corporation, 6; 23 (upd.)
Cinram International, Inc., 43
Cirque du Soleil Inc., 29
Classic Vacation Group, Inc., 46
Cleveland Indians Baseball Company, Inc., 37
ClubCorp, Inc., 33
Columbia Pictures Entertainment, Inc., II
Columbia TriStar Motion Pictures Companies, 12 (upd.)
Comcast Corporation, 7
Compagnie des Alpes, 48
Continental Cablevision, Inc., 7
Corporation for Public Broadcasting, 14
Cox Enterprises, Inc., 22 (upd.)
Crown Media Holdings, Inc., 45
Cruise America Inc., 21
Cunard Line Ltd., 23
Dallas Cowboys Football Club, Ltd., 33
Dave & Buster's, Inc., 33
Death Row Records, 27
The Detroit Pistons Basketball Company, 41
Detroit Tigers Baseball Club, Inc., 46
dick clark productions, inc., 16
DIRECTV, Inc., 38
Dover Downs Entertainment, Inc., 43
DreamWorks SKG, 43
E! Entertainment Television Inc., 17
edel music AG, 44
Educational Broadcasting Corporation, 48
Edwards Theatres Circuit, Inc., 31
Elsinore Corporation, 48
Endemol Entertainment Holding NV, 46
Equity Marketing, Inc., 26
Esporta plc, 35
Euro Disneyland SCA, 20
Fair Grounds Corporation, 44
Family Golf Centers, Inc., 29
FAO Schwarz, 46
Fédération Internationale de Football Association, 27
Feld Entertainment, Inc., 32 (upd.)
First Choice Holidays PLC, 40
First Team Sports, Inc., 22
Fisher-Price Inc., 32 (upd.)
Florida Gaming Corporation, 47
Fox Entertainment Group, Inc., 43

Fox Family Worldwide, Inc., 24
Gaumont SA, 25
Gaylord Entertainment Company, 11; 36 (upd.)
GC Companies, Inc., 25
Geffen Records Inc., 26
Gibson Guitar Corp., 16
Girl Scouts of the USA, 35
GoodTimes Entertainment Ltd., 48
Granada Group PLC, II; 24 (upd.)
Grand Casinos, Inc., 20
The Green Bay Packers, Inc., 32
Groupe Partouche SA, 48
Hallmark Cards, Inc., 40 (upd.)
Hanna-Barbera Cartoons Inc., 23
Hard Rock Cafe International, Inc., 32 (upd.)
Harpo Entertainment Group, 28
Harrah's Entertainment, Inc., 16; 43 (upd.)
Harveys Casino Resorts, 27
Hasbro, Inc., 43 (upd.)
Hastings Entertainment, Inc., 29
The Hearst Corporation, 46 (upd.)
HIT Entertainment PLC, 40
HOB Entertainment, Inc., 37
Hollywood Casino Corporation, 21
Hollywood Entertainment Corporation, 25
Hollywood Park, Inc., 20
Home Box Office Inc., 7; 23 (upd.)
Imax Corporation, 28
Indianapolis Motor Speedway Corporation, 46
Infinity Broadcasting Corporation, 48 (upd.)
Infogrames Entertainment S.A., 35
Integrity Inc., 44
International Creative Management, Inc., 43
International Family Entertainment Inc., 13
International Game Technology, 41 (upd.)
International Olympic Committee, 44
International Speedway Corporation, 19
Interscope Music Group, 31
The Intrawest Corporation, 15
Irvin Feld & Kenneth Feld Productions, Inc., 15
Isle of Capri Casinos, Inc., 41
iVillage Inc., 46
Iwerks Entertainment, Inc., 34
Jackpot Enterprises Inc., 21
Japan Broadcasting Corporation, 7
Jazzercise, Inc., 45
Jillian's Entertainment Holdings, Inc., 40
The Jim Henson Company, 23
Kampgrounds of America, Inc. (KOA), 33
King World Productions, Inc., 9; 30 (upd.)
Knott's Berry Farm, 18
Kuoni Travel Holding Ltd., 40
The Kushner-Locke Company, 25
Ladbroke Group PLC, II; 21 (upd.)
Lego A/S, 13; 40 (upd.)
Liberty Livewire Corporation, 42
Lionel L.L.C., 16
Lions Gate Entertainment Corporation, 35
LIVE Entertainment Inc., 20
LodgeNet Entertainment Corporation, 28
Lucasfilm Ltd., 12
Luminar Plc, 40
Manchester United Football Club plc, 30
Mandalay Resort Group, 32 (upd.)
The Marcus Corporation, 21
Mashantucket Pequot Gaming Enterprise Inc., 35
MCA Inc., II
Media General, Inc., 7
Metro-Goldwyn-Mayer Inc., 25 (upd.)
Metromedia Companies, 14
Métropole Télévision, 33
Metropolitan Baseball Club Inc., 39
Metropolitan Opera Association, Inc., 40
MGM Grand Inc., 17
MGM/UA Communications Company, II
Midway Games, Inc., 25
Mikohn Gaming Corporation, 39
Milwaukee Brewers Baseball Club, 37
Mizuno Corporation, 25
Mohegan Tribal Gaming Authority, 37
Motown Records Company L.P., 26
Movie Gallery, Inc., 31
Multimedia Games, Inc., 41
Muzak, Inc., 18
National Amusements Inc., 28
National Association for Stock Car Auto Racing, 32
National Broadcasting Company, Inc., II; 6 (upd.)
National Football League, 29
National Hockey League, 35
National Public Radio, Inc., 19; 47 (upd.)
National Rifle Association of America, 37
Navarre Corporation, 24
Navigant International, Inc., 47
New Line Cinema, Inc., 47
News Corporation Limited, 46 (upd.)
Nicklaus Companies, 45
Nintendo Co., Ltd., 28 (upd.)
O'Charley's Inc., 19
Orion Pictures Corporation, 6
Paradise Music & Entertainment, Inc., 42
Paramount Pictures Corporation, II
Pathé SA, 29
PDS Gaming Corporation, 44
Penn National Gaming, Inc., 33
Philadelphia Eagles, 37
Pierre & Vacances SA, 48
Pixar Animation Studios, 34
Platinum Entertainment, Inc., 35
Play by Play Toys & Novelties, Inc., 26
Players International, Inc., 22
PolyGram N.V., 23
Powerhouse Technologies, Inc., 27
Premier Parks, Inc., 27
President Casinos, Inc., 22
Preussag AG, 42 (upd.)
Princess Cruise Lines, 22
The Professional Golfers' Association of America, 41
Promus Companies, Inc., 9
Putt-Putt Golf Courses of America, Inc., 23
Rainforest Cafe, Inc., 25
Rank Organisation PLC, II
Rawlings Sporting Goods Co., Inc., 24
The Really Useful Group, 26
Rentrak Corporation, 35
Rhino Entertainment Company, 18
Ride, Inc., 22
Rollerblade, Inc., 34 (upd.)
Roularta Media Group NV, 48
Royal Caribbean Cruises Ltd., 22
RTL Group SA, 44
Rush Communications, 33
S-K-I Limited, 15
Salomon Worldwide, 20
Santa Fe Gaming Corporation, 19
Schwinn Cycle and Fitness L.P., 19
Scottish Radio Holding plc, 41
Seattle FilmWorks, Inc., 20
Sega of America, Inc., 10
SFX Entertainment, Inc., 36
Showboat, Inc., 19
Shubert Organization Inc., 24
Six Flags Theme Parks, Inc., 17
Smithsonian Institution, 27
Società Sportiva Lazio SpA, 44
Sony Corporation, 40 (upd.)
Speedway Motorsports, Inc., 32
Spelling Entertainment Group, Inc., 14
The Sports Club Company, 25
Station Casinos Inc., 25
Stoll-Moss Theatres Ltd., 34
Stuart Entertainment Inc., 16
TABCORP Holdings Limited, 44
Take-Two Interactive Software, Inc., 46
Tele-Communications, Inc., II
Television Española, S.A., 7
Thomas Cook Travel Inc., 9
The Thomson Corporation, 8
Thousand Trails, Inc., 33
THQ, Inc., 39
Ticketmaster Corp., 13
The Todd-AO Corporation, 33
Toho Co., Ltd., 28
The Topps Company, Inc., 34 (upd.)
Touristik Union International GmbH. and Company K.G., II
Town Sports International, Inc., 46
Toy Biz, Inc., 18
Trans World Entertainment Corporation, 24
Travelocity.com, Inc., 46
TUI Group GmbH, 44
Turner Broadcasting System, Inc., II; 6 (upd.)
Twentieth Century Fox Film Corporation, II; 25 (upd.)
Ubi Soft Entertainment S.A., 41
United Pan-Europe Communications NV, 47
Universal Studios, Inc., 33
Univision Communications Inc., 24
USA Interactive, Inc., 47 (upd.)
Vail Resorts, Inc., 11; 43 (upd.)
Venetian Casino Resort, LLC, 47
Viacom Inc., 7; 23 (upd.)
Vivendi Universal S.A., 46 (upd.)
Walt Disney Company, II; 6 (upd.); 30 (upd.)
Warner Communications Inc., II
Washington Football, Inc., 35
West Coast Entertainment Corporation, 29
Wherehouse Entertainment Incorporated, 11
Wildlife Conservation Society, 31
Wilson Sporting Goods Company, 24
Wizards of the Coast Inc., 24
World Wrestling Federation Entertainment, Inc., 32
YankeeNets LLC, 35
YES! Entertainment Corporation, 26
YMCA of the USA, 31
Young Broadcasting Inc., 40

## FINANCIAL SERVICES: BANKS

Abbey National plc, 10; 39 (upd.)
Abigail Adams National Bancorp, Inc., 23
Algemene Bank Nederland N.V., II
Allied Irish Banks, plc, 16; 43 (upd.)
Almanij NV, 44
AMCORE Financial Inc., 44
American Residential Mortgage Corporation, 8
AmSouth Bancorporation,12; 48 (upd.)
Amsterdam-Rotterdam Bank N.V., II
Anchor Bancorp, Inc., 10
Astoria Financial Corporation, 44
Australia and New Zealand Banking Group Ltd., II
Banc One Corporation, 10
Banca Commerciale Italiana SpA, II
Banco Bilbao Vizcaya Argentaria S.A., 48 (upd.)
Banco Bilbao Vizcaya, S.A., II
Banco Bradesco S.A., 13
Banco Central, II

Banco do Brasil S.A., II
Banco Espírito Santo e Comercial de Lisboa S.A., 15
Banco Itaú S.A., 19
Banco Santander Central Hispano S.A., 36 (upd.)
Bank Austria AG, 23
Bank Brussels Lambert, II
Bank Hapoalim B.M., II
Bank of America Corporation, 46 (upd.)
Bank of Boston Corporation, II
Bank of Mississippi, Inc., 14
Bank of Montreal, II; 46 (upd.)
Bank of New England Corporation, II
The Bank of New York Company, Inc., II; 46 (upd.)
The Bank of Nova Scotia, II
Bank of Tokyo-Mitsubishi Ltd., II; 15 (upd.)
Bank One Corporation, 36 (upd.)
BankAmerica Corporation, II; 8 (upd.)
Bankers Trust New York Corporation, II
Banque Nationale de Paris S.A., II
Barclays PLC, II; 20 (upd.)
BarclaysAmerican Mortgage Corporation, 11
Barings PLC, 14
Barnett Banks, Inc., 9
BayBanks, Inc., 12
Bayerische Hypotheken- und Wechsel-Bank AG, II
Bayerische Vereinsbank A.G., II
Beneficial Corporation, 8
BNP Paribas Group, 36 (upd.)
Boatmen's Bancshares Inc., 15
Bremer Financial Corp., 45
Brown Brothers Harriman & Co., 45
Canadian Imperial Bank of Commerce, II
Carolina First Corporation, 31
Casco Northern Bank, 14
The Chase Manhattan Corporation, II; 13 (upd.)
Chemical Banking Corporation, II; 14 (upd.)
Citicorp, II; 9 (upd.)
Citigroup Inc., 30 (upd.)
Citizens Financial Group, Inc., 42
Close Brothers Group plc, 39
Commercial Credit Company, 8
Commercial Federal Corporation, 12
Commerzbank A.G., II; 47 (upd.)
Compagnie Financiere de Paribas, II
Continental Bank Corporation, II
CoreStates Financial Corp, 17
Countrywide Credit Industries, Inc., 16
Crédit Agricole, II
Crédit Lyonnais, 9; 33 (upd.)
Crédit National S.A., 9
Credit Suisse Group, II; 21 (upd.)
Credito Italiano, II
Cullen/Frost Bankers, Inc., 25
The Dai-Ichi Kangyo Bank Ltd., II
The Daiwa Bank, Ltd., II; 39 (upd.)
Dauphin Deposit Corporation, 14
Deposit Guaranty Corporation, 17
Deutsche Bank AG, II; 14 (upd.); 40 (upd.)
Dexia Group, 42
Dime Savings Bank of New York, F.S.B., 9
Donaldson, Lufkin & Jenrette, Inc., 22
Dresdner Bank A.G., II
Fifth Third Bancorp, 13; 31 (upd.)
First Bank System Inc., 12
First Chicago Corporation, II
First Commerce Bancshares, Inc., 15
First Commerce Corporation, 11
First Empire State Corporation, 11
First Fidelity Bank, N.A., New Jersey, 9
First Hawaiian, Inc., 11
First Interstate Bancorp, II
First Nationwide Bank, 14
First of America Bank Corporation, 8
First Security Corporation, 11
First Tennessee National Corporation, 11; 48 (upd.)
First Union Corporation, 10
First Virginia Banks, Inc., 11
Firstar Corporation, 11; 33 (upd.)
Fleet Financial Group, Inc., 9
FleetBoston Financial Corporation, 36 (upd.)
Fourth Financial Corporation, 11
The Fuji Bank, Ltd., II
Generale Bank, II
German American Bancorp, 41
Glacier Bancorp, Inc., 35
Golden West Financial Corporation, 47
The Governor and Company of the Bank of Scotland, 10
Grameen Bank, 31
Granite State Bankshares, Inc., 37
Great Lakes Bancorp, 8
Great Western Financial Corporation, 10
GreenPoint Financial Corp., 28
Grupo Financiero Serfin, S.A., 19
H.F. Ahmanson & Company, II; 10 (upd.)
Habersham Bancorp, 25
Hancock Holding Company, 15
Hibernia Corporation, 37
The Hongkong and Shanghai Banking Corporation Limited, II
HSBC Holdings plc, 12; 26 (upd.)
Hudson River Bancorp, Inc., 41
Huntington Bancshares Inc., 11
IBERIABANK Corporation, 37
The Industrial Bank of Japan, Ltd., II
J Sainsbury plc, 38 (upd.)
J.P. Morgan & Co. Incorporated, II; 30 (upd.)
J.P. Morgan Chase & Co., 38 (upd.)
Japan Leasing Corporation, 8
Kansallis-Osake-Pankki, II
KeyCorp, 8
Kredietbank N.V., II
Kreditanstalt für Wiederaufbau, 29
Lloyds Bank PLC, II
Lloyds TSB Group plc, 47 (upd.)
Long Island Bancorp, Inc., 16
Long-Term Credit Bank of Japan, Ltd., II
Manufacturers Hanover Corporation, II
MBNA Corporation, 12
Mellon Bank Corporation, II
Mellon Financial Corporation, 44 (upd.)
Mercantile Bankshares Corp., 11
Meridian Bancorp, Inc., 11
Metropolitan Financial Corporation, 13
Michigan National Corporation, 11
Midland Bank PLC, II; 17 (upd.)
The Mitsubishi Bank, Ltd., II
The Mitsubishi Trust & Banking Corporation, II
The Mitsui Bank, Ltd., II
The Mitsui Trust & Banking Company, Ltd., II
Mouvement des Caisses Desjardins, 48
N M Rothschild & Sons Limited, 39
National Bank of Greece, 41
National City Corp., 15
National Westminster Bank PLC, II
NationsBank Corporation, 10
NBD Bancorp, Inc., 11
NCNB Corporation, II
Nippon Credit Bank, II
Nordea AB, 40
Norinchukin Bank, II
North Fork Bancorporation, Inc., 46
Northern Rock plc, 33
Northern Trust Company, 9
NVR L.P., 8
Old Kent Financial Corp., 11
Old National Bancorp, 15
PNC Bank Corp., II; 13 (upd.)
The PNC Financial Services Group Inc., 46 (upd.)
Popular, Inc., 41
Pulte Corporation, 8
Rabobank Group, 33
Republic New York Corporation, 11
Riggs National Corporation, 13
The Royal Bank of Canada, II; 21 (upd.)
The Royal Bank of Scotland Group plc, 12; 38 (upd.)
The Ryland Group, Inc., 8
St. Paul Bank for Cooperatives, 8
The Sanwa Bank, Ltd., II; 15 (upd.)
SBC Warburg, 14
Seattle First National Bank Inc., 8
Security Capital Corporation, 17
Security Pacific Corporation, II
Shawmut National Corporation, 13
Signet Banking Corporation, 11
Singer & Friedlander Group plc, 41
Skandinaviska Enskilda Banken, II
Société Générale, II; 42 (upd.)
Society Corporation, 9
Southtrust Corporation, 11
Standard Chartered plc, II; 48 (upd.)
Standard Federal Bank, 9
Star Banc Corporation, 11
State Street Boston Corporation, 8
Staten Island Bancorp, Inc., 39
The Sumitomo Bank, Limited, II; 26 (upd.)
The Sumitomo Trust & Banking Company, Ltd., II
The Summit Bancorporation, 14
SunTrust Banks Inc., 23
Svenska Handelsbanken, II
Swiss Bank Corporation, II
Synovus Financial Corp., 12
The Taiyo Kobe Bank, Ltd., II
TCF Financial Corporation, 47
The Tokai Bank, Limited, II; 15 (upd.)
The Toronto-Dominion Bank, II
TSB Group plc, 12
U.S. Bancorp, 14; 36 (upd.)
U.S. Trust Corp., 17
Union Bank of California, 16
Union Bank of Switzerland, II
Wachovia Bank of Georgia, N.A., 16
Wachovia Bank of South Carolina, N.A., 16
Wachovia Corporation, 12
Washington Mutual, Inc., 17
Wells Fargo & Company, II; 12 (upd.); 38 (upd.)
West One Bancorp, 11
Westamerica Bancorporation, 17
Westdeutsche Landesbank Girozentrale, II; 46 (upd.)
Westpac Banking Corporation, II; 48 (upd.)
Whitney Holding Corporation, 21
Wilmington Trust Corporation, 25
The Woolwich plc, 30
World Bank Group, 33
The Yasuda Trust and Banking Company, Ltd., II; 17 (upd.)
Zions Bancorporation, 12


## FINANCIAL SERVICES: NON-BANKS


A.B. Watley Group Inc., 45
A.G. Edwards, Inc., 8; 32 (upd.)
ACE Cash Express, Inc., 33

ADVANTA Corp., 8
Advanta Corporation, 38 (upd.)
American Express Company, II; 10 (upd.); 38 (upd.)
American General Finance Corp., 11
American Home Mortgage Holdings, Inc., 46
Ameritrade Holding Corporation, 34
Arthur Andersen & Company, Société Coopérative, 10
Avco Financial Services Inc., 13
Bear Stearns Companies, Inc., II; 10 (upd.)
Bill & Melinda Gates Foundation, 41
Bozzuto's, Inc., 13
Carnegie Corporation of New York, 35
Cash America International, Inc., 20
Cendant Corporation, 44 (upd.)
Cetelem S.A., 21
The Charles Schwab Corporation, 8; 26 (upd.)
Citfed Bancorp, Inc., 16
Coinstar, Inc., 44
Comerica Incorporated, 40
Commercial Financial Services, Inc., 26
Coopers & Lybrand, 9
Cramer, Berkowitz & Co., 34
Credit Acceptance Corporation, 18
CS First Boston Inc., II
Dain Rauscher Corporation, 35 (upd.)
Daiwa Securities Company, Limited, II
Datek Online Holdings Corp., 32
The David and Lucile Packard Foundation, 41
Dean Witter, Discover & Co., 12
Dow Jones Telerate, Inc., 10
Drexel Burnham Lambert Incorporated, II
E*Trade Group, Inc., 20
Eaton Vance Corporation, 18
Edward Jones, 30
Euronext Paris S.A., 37
Experian Information Solutions Inc., 45
Fair, Isaac and Company, 18
Fannie Mae, 45 (upd.)
Federal National Mortgage Association, II
Fidelity Investments Inc., II; 14 (upd.)
First Albany Companies Inc., 37
First Data Corporation, 30 (upd.)
First USA, Inc., 11
FMR Corp., 8; 32 (upd.)
Forstmann Little & Co., 38
Fortis, Inc., 15
Frank Russell Company, 46
Franklin Resources, Inc., 9
Gabelli Asset Management Inc., 30
Goldman, Sachs & Co., II; 20 (upd.)
Grede Foundries, Inc., 38
Green Tree Financial Corporation, 11
Gruntal & Co., L.L.C., 20
H & R Block, Incorporated, 9; 29 (upd.)
H.D. Vest, Inc., 46
Hoenig Group Inc., 41
Household International, Inc., II; 21 (upd.)
Ingenico—Compagnie Industrielle et Financière d'Ingénierie, 46
Instinet Corporation, 34
Inter-Regional Financial Group, Inc., 15
The Island ECN, Inc., 48
Istituto per la Ricostruzione Industriale S.p.A., 11
JB Oxford Holdings, Inc., 32
Jefferies Group, Inc., 25
John Hancock Financial Services, Inc., 42 (upd.)
The John Nuveen Company, 21
Kansas City Southern Industries, Inc., 26 (upd.)
Kleinwort Benson Group PLC, II
Kohlberg Kravis Roberts & Co., 24
KPMG Worldwide, 10
La Poste, 47 (upd.)
LaBranche & Co. Inc., 37
Lazard LLC, 38
Legg Mason, Inc., 33
London Stock Exchange Limited, 34
M.H. Meyerson & Co., Inc., 46
MacAndrews & Forbes Holdings Inc., 28
MasterCard International, Inc., 9
MBNA Corporation, 33 (upd.)
Merrill Lynch & Co., Inc., II; 13 (upd.); 40 (upd.)
Morgan Grenfell Group PLC, II
Morgan Stanley Dean Witter & Company, II; 16 (upd.); 33 (upd.)
Mountain States Mortgage Centers, Inc., 29
National Association of Securities Dealers, Inc., 10
National Auto Credit, Inc., 16
National Discount Brokers Group, Inc., 28
Navy Federal Credit Union, 33
New Street Capital Inc., 8
New York Stock Exchange, Inc., 9; 39 (upd.)
The Nikko Securities Company Limited, II; 9 (upd.)
Nippon Shinpan Company, Ltd., II
Nomura Securities Company, Limited, II; 9 (upd.)
Orix Corporation, II
ORIX Corporation, 44 (upd.)
PaineWebber Group Inc., II; 22 (upd.)
The Pew Charitable Trusts, 35
Piper Jaffray Companies Inc., 22
Pitney Bowes Inc., 47 (upd.)
The Prudential Insurance Company of America, 30 (upd.)
The Quick & Reilly Group, Inc., 20
Resource America, Inc., 42
Safeguard Scientifics, Inc., 10
Salomon Inc., II; 13 (upd.)
SBC Warburg, 14
Schroders plc, 42
Shearson Lehman Brothers Holdings Inc., II; 9 (upd.)
Siebert Financial Corp., 32
SLM Holding Corp., 25 (upd.)
Smith Barney Inc., 15
Soros Fund Management LLC, 28
State Street Boston Corporation, 8
Student Loan Marketing Association, II
T. Rowe Price Associates, Inc., 11; 34 (upd.)
Teachers Insurance and Annuity Association-College Retirement Equities Fund, 45 (upd.)
Texas Pacific Group Inc., 36
Total System Services, Inc., 18
Trilon Financial Corporation, II
United Jewish Communities, 33
The Vanguard Group of Investment Companies, 14
The Vanguard Group, Inc., 34 (upd.)
VeriFone, Inc., 18
Visa International, 9; 26 (upd.)
Wachovia Corporation, 46 (upd.)
Waddell & Reed, Inc., 22
Washington Federal, Inc., 17
Waterhouse Investor Services, Inc., 18
Watson Wyatt Worldwide, 42
Working Assets Funding Service, 43
Yamaichi Securities Company, Limited, II
The Ziegler Companies, Inc., 24
Zurich Financial Services, 42 (upd.)

## FOOD PRODUCTS

Agway, Inc., 7
Ajinomoto Co., Inc., II; 28 (upd.)
The Albert Fisher Group plc, 41
Alberto-Culver Company, 8
Aldi Group, 13
Alpine Lace Brands, Inc., 18
American Crystal Sugar Company, 11; 32 (upd.)
American Foods Group, 43
American Italian Pasta Company, 27
American Maize-Products Co., 14
American Rice, Inc., 33
Amfac/JMB Hawaii L.L.C., 24 (upd.)
Archer-Daniels-Midland Company, 32 (upd.)
Archway Cookies, Inc., 29
Arla Foods amba, 48
Associated British Foods plc, II; 13 (upd.); 41 (upd.)
Associated Milk Producers, Inc., 11; 48 (upd.)
Aurora Foods Inc., 32
B&G Foods, Inc., 40
The B. Manischewitz Company, LLC, 31
Bahlsen GmbH & Co. KG, 44
Balance Bar Company, 32
Baltek Corporation, 34
Barilla G. e R. Fratelli S.p.A., 17
Bear Creek Corporation, 38
Beatrice Company, II
Beech-Nut Nutrition Corporation, 21
Ben & Jerry's Homemade, Inc., 10; 35
Berkeley Farms, Inc., 46
Besnier SA, 19
Bestfoods, 22 (upd.)
Blue Bell Creameries L.P., 30
Blue Diamond Growers, 28
Bongrain SA, 25
Booker PLC, 13; 31 (upd.)
Borden, Inc., II; 22 (upd.)
Brach and Brock Confections, Inc., 15
Brake Bros plc, 45
Bridgford Foods Corporation, 27
Brothers Gourmet Coffees, Inc., 20
Broughton Foods Co., 17
Brown & Haley, 23
Bruce Foods Corporation, 39
BSN Groupe S.A., II
Burger King Corporation, 17 (upd.)
Bush Boake Allen Inc., 30
Bush Brothers & Company, 45
C.H. Robinson Worldwide, Inc., 40 (upd.)
Cadbury Schweppes PLC, II
Cagle's, Inc., 20
Calavo Growers, Inc., 47
Calcot Ltd., 33
Campbell Soup Company, II; 7 (upd.); 26 (upd.)
Canada Packers Inc., II
Cargill Inc., 13 (upd.)
Carnation Company, II
Carroll's Foods, Inc., 46
Carvel Corporation, 35
Castle & Cooke, Inc., II; 20 (upd.)
Cattleman's, Inc., 20
Celestial Seasonings, Inc., 16
Central Soya Company, Inc., 7
Chelsea Milling Company, 29
Chicken of the Sea International, 24 (upd.)
Chiquita Brands International, Inc., 7; 21 (upd.)
Chock Full o'Nuts Corp., 17
Chocoladefabriken Lindt & Sprüngli AG, 27
Chupa Chups S.A., 38
The Clorox Company, 22 (upd.)
Coca-Cola Enterprises, Inc., 13
ConAgra Foods, Inc., 42 (upd.)
Conagra, Inc., II; 12 (upd.)

The Connell Company, 29
ContiGroup Companies, Inc., 43 (upd.)
Continental Grain Company, 10; 13 (upd.)
CoolBrands International Inc., 35
CPC International Inc., II
Cranswick plc, 40
Cumberland Packing Corporation, 26
Curtice-Burns Foods, Inc., 7; 21 (upd.)
Czarnikow-Rionda Company, Inc., 32
Dairy Crest Group plc, 32
Dalgery, PLC, II
Danisco A/S, 44
Dannon Co., Inc., 14
Darigold, Inc., 9
Dawn Food Products, Inc., 17
Dean Foods Company, 7; 21 (upd.)
DeKalb Genetics Corporation, 17
Del Monte Foods Company, 7; 23 (upd.)
Di Giorgio Corp., 12
Diageo plc, 24 (upd.)
Dole Food Company, Inc., 9; 31 (upd.)
Domino Sugar Corporation, 26
Doskocil Companies, Inc., 12
Dreyer's Grand Ice Cream, Inc., 17
The Earthgrains Company, 36
Emge Packing Co., Inc., 11
Eridania Béghin-Say S.A., 36
ERLY Industries Inc., 17
Eskimo Pie Corporation, 21
Farmland Foods, Inc., 7
Farmland Industries, Inc., 48
Fieldale Farms Corporation, 23
Fleer Corporation, 15
Fleury Michon S.A., 39
Florida Crystals Inc., 35
Flowers Industries, Inc., 12; 35 (upd.)
FoodBrands America, Inc., 23
Foster Poultry Farms, 32
Fresh America Corporation, 20
Fresh Foods, Inc., 29
Frito-Lay Company, 32
Fromageries Bel, 23
Fyffes Plc, 38
Gardenburger, Inc., 33
Geest Plc, 38
General Mills, Inc., II; 10 (upd.); 36 (upd.)
George A. Hormel and Company, II
George Weston Limited, 36 (upd.)
Gerber Products Company, 7; 21 (upd.)
Ghirardelli Chocolate Company, 30
Givaudan SA, 43
Gold Kist Inc., 17; 26 (upd.)
Golden Enterprises, Inc., 26
Gonnella Baking Company, 40
Good Humor-Breyers Ice Cream Company, 14
GoodMark Foods, Inc., 26
Gorton's, 13
Goya Foods Inc., 22
Great Harvest Bread Company, 44
Grist Mill Company, 15
Groupe Danone, 32 (upd.)
Gruma, S.A. de C.V., 31
Grupo Herdez, S.A. de C.V., 35
H.J. Heinz Company, II; 11 (upd.); 36 (upd.)
The Hain Celestial Group, Inc., 27; 43 (upd.)
Hanover Foods Corporation, 35
HARIBO GmbH & Co. KG, 44
The Hartz Mountain Corporation, 12
Hazlewood Foods plc, 32
Herman Goelitz, Inc., 28
Hershey Foods Corporation, II; 15 (upd.)
Hill's Pet Nutrition, Inc., 27
Hillsdown Holdings plc, II; 24 (upd.)
Horizon Organic Holding Corporation, 37
Hormel Foods Corporation, 18 (upd.)
Hudson Foods Inc., 13
Hulman & Company, 44
Hunt-Wesson, Inc., 17
Iams Company, 26
IBP, Inc., II; 21 (upd.)
Iceland Group plc, 33
Imperial Holly Corporation, 12
Imperial Sugar Company, 32 (upd.)
Industrias Bachoco, S.A. de C.V., 39
International Multifoods Corporation, 7; 25 (upd.)
Interstate Bakeries Corporation, 12; 38 (upd.)
Itoham Foods Inc., II
J & J Snack Foods Corporation, 24
The J.M. Smucker Company, 11
J.R. Simplot Company, 16
Jacobs Suchard A.G., II
Jim Beam Brands Co., 14
John B. Sanfilippo & Son, Inc., 14
Just Born, Inc., 32
Kal Kan Foods, Inc., 22
Kamps AG, 44
Keebler Foods Company, 36
Kellogg Company, II; 13 (upd.)
Kerry Group plc, 27
Kettle Foods Inc., 48
Kikkoman Corporation, 14; 47 (upd.)
The King Arthur Flour Company, 31
King Ranch, Inc., 14
Koninklijke Wessanen N.V., II
Kraft Foods Inc., 45 (upd.)
Kraft General Foods Inc., II; 7 (upd.)
Kraft Jacobs Suchard AG, 26 (upd.)
Krispy Kreme Doughnut Corporation, 21
La Choy Food Products Inc., 25
Lamb Weston, Inc., 23
Lance, Inc., 14; 41 (upd.)
Land O'Lakes, Inc., II; 21 (upd.)
Leprino Foods Company, 28
Lincoln Snacks Company, 24
Lucille Farms, Inc., 45
Malt-O-Meal Company, 22
Maple Leaf Foods Inc., 41
Mars, Incorporated, 7; 40 (upd.)
Maui Land & Pineapple Company, Inc., 29
McCormick & Company, Incorporated, 7; 27 (upd.)
McIlhenny Company, 20
McKee Foods Corporation, 7; 27 (upd.)
Meiji Milk Products Company, Limited, II
Meiji Seika Kaisha, Ltd., II
Michael Foods, Inc., 25
Mid-America Dairymen, Inc., 7
Mike-Sell's Inc., 15
Milnot Company, 46
Monfort, Inc., 13
Mrs. Baird's Bakeries, 29
Mt. Olive Pickle Company, Inc., 44
Murphy Family Farms Inc., 22
Nabisco Foods Group, II; 7 (upd.)
Nantucket Allserve, Inc., 22
Nathan's Famous, Inc., 29
National Presto Industries, Inc., 43 (upd.)
National Sea Products Ltd., 14
Nestlé S.A., II; 7 (upd.); 28 (upd.)
New England Confectionery Co., 15
Newhall Land and Farming Company, 14
Newman's Own, Inc., 37
Nippon Meat Packers, Inc., II
Nippon Suisan Kaisha, Limited, II
Nisshin Flour Milling Company, Ltd., II
Northern Foods PLC, 10
Northland Cranberries, Inc., 38
Nutraceutical International Corporation, 37
NutraSweet Company, 8
Ocean Spray Cranberries, Inc., 7; 25 (upd.)
OJSC Wimm-Bill-Dann Foods, 48
Ore-Ida Foods Incorporated, 13
Oscar Mayer Foods Corp., 12
Otis Spunkmeyer, Inc., 28
Papetti's Hygrade Egg Products, Inc., 39
PepsiCo, Inc., 38 (upd.)
Perdue Farms Inc., 7; 23 (upd.)
Pet Incorporated, 7
Pez Candy, Inc., 38
Philip Morris Companies Inc., 18 (upd.)
PIC International Group PLC, 24 (upd.)
Pilgrim's Pride Corporation, 7; 23 (upd.)
Pillsbury Company, II; 13 (upd.)
Pioneer Hi-Bred International, Inc., 9
Pizza Inn, Inc., 46
Poore Brothers, Inc., 44
PowerBar Inc., 44
Prairie Farms Dairy, Inc., 47
Premium Standard Farms, Inc., 30
The Procter & Gamble Company, III; 8 (upd.); 26 (upd.)
Purina Mills, Inc., 32
Quaker Oats Company, II; 12 (upd.); 34 (upd.)
Quality Chekd Dairies, Inc., 48
Ralston Purina Company, II; 13 (upd.)
Ranks Hovis McDougall Limited, II; 28 (upd.)
Reckitt & Colman PLC, II
Reckitt Benckiser plc, 42 (upd.)
Rica Foods, Inc., 41
Rich Products Corporation, 7; 38 (upd.)
Riviana Foods Inc., 27
Roland Murten A.G., 7
Rowntree Mackintosh, II
Royal Numico N.V., 37
Russell Stover Candies Inc., 12
Sanderson Farms, Inc., 15
Sara Lee Corporation, II; 15 (upd.)
Savannah Foods & Industries, Inc., 7
Schlotzsky's, Inc., 36
Schwan's Sales Enterprises, Inc., 7
See's Candies, Inc., 30
Seminis, Inc., 29
Smithfield Foods, Inc., 7; 43 (upd.)
Snow Brand Milk Products Company, Ltd., II; 48 (upd.)
Sodiaal S.A., 36 (upd.)
SODIMA, II
Sorrento, Inc., 24
Spangler Candy Company, 44
Stock Yards Packing Co., Inc., 37
Stolt-Nielsen S.A., 42
Stouffer Corp., 8
Südzucker AG, 27
Suiza Foods Corporation, 26
Sun-Diamond Growers of California, 7
Sunkist Growers, Inc., 26
Supervalu Inc., 18 (upd.)
Suprema Specialties, Inc., 27
Sylvan, Inc., 22
Taiyo Fishery Company, Limited, II
Tasty Baking Company, 14; 35 (upd.)
Tate & Lyle PLC, II; 42 (upd.)
TCBY Enterprises Inc., 17
TDL Group Ltd., 46
Thomas J. Lipton Company, 14
Thorn Apple Valley, Inc., 7; 22 (upd.)
Thorntons plc, 46
TLC Beatrice International Holdings, Inc., 22
Tombstone Pizza Corporation, 13
Tone Brothers, Inc., 21
Tootsie Roll Industries Inc., 12
Tri Valley Growers, 32
Tropicana Products, Inc., 28
Tyson Foods, Incorporated, II; 14 (upd.)
U.S. Foodservice, 26
Uncle Ben's Inc., 22

Unigate PLC, II; 28 (upd.)
United Biscuits (Holdings) plc, II; 42 (upd.)
United Brands Company, II
United Foods, Inc., 21
Universal Foods Corporation, 7
Van Camp Seafood Company, Inc., 7
Vienna Sausage Manufacturing Co., 14
Vlasic Foods International Inc., 25
Wattie's Ltd., 7
Wells' Dairy, Inc., 36
White Wave, 43
OJSC Wimm-Bill-Dann Foods, 48
Wisconsin Dairies, 7
WLR Foods, Inc., 21
Wm. Wrigley Jr. Company, 7
World's Finest Chocolate Inc., 39
Worthington Foods, Inc., 14
YOCREAM International, Inc., 47

## FOOD SERVICES & RETAILERS

Advantica Restaurant Group, Inc., 27 (upd.)
AFC Enterprises, Inc., 32 (upd.)
Albertson's Inc., II; 7 (upd.); 30 (upd.)
Aldi Group, 13
Alex Lee Inc., 18; 44 (upd.)
America's Favorite Chicken Company, Inc., 7
American Stores Company, II
Applebee's International, Inc., 14; 35 (upd.)
ARA Services, II
Arby's Inc., 14
Arden Group, Inc., 29
Argyll Group PLC, II
Ark Restaurants Corp., 20
Asahi Breweries, Ltd., 20 (upd.)
Asda Group PLC, II
ASDA Group plc, 28 (upd.)
Associated Grocers, Incorporated, 9; 31 (upd.)
Association des Centres Distributeurs E. Leclerc, 37
Au Bon Pain Co., Inc., 18
Auchan, 37
Auntie Anne's, Inc., 35
Avado Brands, Inc., 31
Back Bay Restaurant Group, Inc., 20
Back Yard Burgers, Inc., 45
Bashas' Inc., 33
Bear Creek Corporation, 38
Benihana, Inc., 18
Big Bear Stores Co., 13
Big V Supermarkets, Inc., 25
Blimpie International, Inc., 15
Bob Evans Farms, Inc., 9
Bon Appetit Holding AG, 48
Boston Chicken, Inc., 12
Boston Market Corporation, 48 (upd.)
Brinker International, Inc., 10; 38 (upd.)
Brookshire Grocery Company, 16
Bruno's, Inc., 7; 26 (upd.)
Buca, Inc., 38
Buffets, Inc., 10; 32 (upd.)
Burger King Corporation, II
C.H. Robinson, Inc., 11
California Pizza Kitchen Inc., 15
Cargill, Inc., II
Caribou Coffee Company, Inc., 28
Carlson Companies, Inc., 22 (upd.)
Carr-Gottstein Foods Co., 17
Casey's General Stores, Inc., 19
CBRL Group, Inc., 35 (upd.)
CEC Entertainment, Inc., 31 (upd.)
Chart House Enterprises, Inc., 17
Checkers Drive-Up Restaurants Inc., 16
The Cheesecake Factory Inc., 17
Chi-Chi's Inc., 13
Chicago Pizza & Brewery, Inc., 44
Chick-fil-A Inc., 23
Cinnabon Inc., 23
The Circle K Corporation, II
CKE Restaurants, Inc., 19; 46 (upd.)
Coborn's, Inc., 30
Compass Group PLC, 34
Comptoirs Modernes S.A., 19
Consolidated Products Inc., 14
Controladora Comercial Mexicana, S.A. de C.V., 36
The Cooker Restaurant Corporation, 20
The Copps Corporation, 32
Cracker Barrel Old Country Store, Inc., 10
D'Agostino Supermarkets Inc., 19
Dairy Mart Convenience Stores, Inc., 7; 25 (upd.)
Darden Restaurants, Inc., 16; 44 (upd.)
Dean & DeLuca, Inc., 36
Delhaize "Le Lion" S.A., 44
DeMoulas / Market Basket Inc., 23
DenAmerica Corporation, 29
Diedrich Coffee, Inc., 40
Domino's Pizza, Inc., 7; 21 (upd.)
Eateries, Inc., 33
Edeka Zentrale A.G., II; 47 (upd.)
Einstein/Noah Bagel Corporation, 29
El Chico Restaurants, Inc., 19
Elmer's Restaurants, Inc., 42
Embers America Restaurants, 30
Etablissements Economiques du Casino Guichard, Perrachon et Cie, S.C.A., 12
Famous Dave's of America, Inc., 40
Fazoli's Systems, Inc., 27
Flagstar Companies, Inc., 10
Fleming Companies, Inc., II
Food Lion, Inc., II; 15 (upd.)
Foodarama Supermarkets, Inc., 28
Foodmaker, Inc., 14
The Fred W. Albrecht Grocery Co., 13
Fresh Choice, Inc., 20
Fresh Foods, Inc., 29
Friendly Ice Cream Corp., 30
Frisch's Restaurants, Inc., 35
Fuller Smith & Turner P.L.C., 38
Furr's Supermarkets, Inc., 28
Garden Fresh Restaurant Corporation, 31
The Gateway Corporation Ltd., II
Genuardi's Family Markets, Inc., 35
George Weston Limited, II; 36 (upd.)
Ghirardelli Chocolate Company, 30
Giant Food Inc., II; 22 (upd.)
Godfather's Pizza Incorporated, 25
Golden Corral Corporation, 10
Golden State Foods Corporation, 32
The Golub Corporation, 26
Gordon Food Service Inc., 8; 39 (upd.)
The Grand Union Company, 7; 28 (upd.)
The Great Atlantic & Pacific Tea Company, Inc., II; 16 (upd.)
Gristede's Sloan's, Inc., 31
Ground Round, Inc., 21
Groupe Promodès S.A., 19
Guyenne et Gascogne, 23
H.E. Butt Grocery Co., 13; 32 (upd.)
Haggen Inc., 38
Hannaford Bros. Co., 12
Hard Rock Cafe International, Inc., 12
Harris Teeter Inc., 23
Harry's Farmers Market Inc., 23
Hickory Farms, Inc., 17
Holberg Industries, Inc., 36
Holland Burgerville USA, 44
Hooters of America, Inc., 18
Hops Restaurant Bar and Brewery, 46
Hughes Markets, Inc., 22
Hungry Howie's Pizza and Subs, Inc., 25
Hy-Vee, Inc., 36
ICA AB, II
Iceland Group plc, 33
IHOP Corporation, 17
Il Fornaio (America) Corporation, 27
In-N-Out Burger, 19
Ingles Markets, Inc., 20
Inserra Supermarkets, 25
International Dairy Queen, Inc., 10; 39 (upd.)
ITM Entreprises SA, 36
Ito-Yokado Co., Ltd., 42 (upd.)
J Sainsbury plc, II; 13 (upd.); 38 (upd.)
Jamba Juice Company, 47
JD Wetherspoon plc, 30
Jerry's Famous Deli Inc., 24
Jitney-Jungle Stores of America, Inc., 27
John Lewis Partnership plc, 42 (upd.)
Johnny Rockets Group, Inc., 31
KFC Corporation, 7; 21 (upd.)
King Kullen Grocery Co., Inc., 15
Koninklijke Ahold N.V. (Royal Ahold), II; 16 (upd.)
Koo Koo Roo, Inc., 25
The Kroger Company, II; 15 (upd.)
The Krystal Company, 33
Kwik Save Group plc, 11
La Madeleine French Bakery & Café, 33
Landry's Seafood Restaurants, Inc., 15
Leeann Chin, Inc., 30
Levy Restaurants L.P., 26
Little Caesar Enterprises, Inc., 7; 24 (upd.)
Loblaw Companies Limited, 43
Logan's Roadhouse, Inc., 29
Long John Silver's Restaurants Inc., 13
Luby's Cafeteria's, Inc., 17
Luby's, Inc., 42 (upd.)
Lucky Stores, Inc., 27
Lund Food Holdings, Inc., 22
Marie Callender's Restaurant & Bakery, Inc., 28
Marsh Supermarkets, Inc., 17
Max & Erma's Restaurants Inc., 19
McDonald's Corporation, II; 7 (upd.); 26 (upd.)
Megafoods Stores Inc., 13
Meijer Incorporated, 7
Metromedia Companies, 14
Mexican Restaurants, Inc., 41
The Middleby Corporation, 22
Minyard Food Stores, Inc., 33
MITROPA AG, 37
Morrison Restaurants Inc., 11
Morton's Restaurant Group, Inc., 30
Mrs. Fields' Original Cookies, Inc., 27
Nash Finch Company, 8; 23 (upd.)
Nathan's Famous, Inc., 29
National Convenience Stores Incorporated, 7
New World Restaurant Group, Inc., 44
New York Restaurant Group, Inc., 32
Noble Roman's Inc., 14
NPC International, Inc., 40
O'Charley's Inc., 19
Old Spaghetti Factory International Inc., 24
The Oshawa Group Limited, II
Outback Steakhouse, Inc., 12; 34 (upd.)
P&C Foods Inc., 8
P.F. Chang's China Bistro, Inc., 37
Pancho's Mexican Buffet, Inc., 46
Panda Management Company, Inc., 35
Panera Bread Company, 44
Papa John's International, Inc., 15
Pathmark Stores, Inc., 23
Peapod, Inc., 30
Penn Traffic Company, 13
Performance Food Group Company, 31

Perkins Family Restaurants, L.P., 22
Piccadilly Cafeterias, Inc., 19
Piggly Wiggly Southern, Inc., 13
Pizza Hut Inc., 7; 21 (upd.)
Planet Hollywood International, Inc., 18; 41 (upd.)
Players International, Inc., 22
Ponderosa Steakhouse, 15
Provigo Inc., II
Publix Super Markets Inc., 7; 31 (upd.)
Pueblo Xtra International, Inc., 47
Quality Dining, Inc., 18
Quality Food Centers, Inc., 17
The Quizno's Corporation, 42
Rally's Hamburgers, Inc., 25
Ralphs Grocery Company, 35
Randall's Food Markets, Inc., 40
Rare Hospitality International Inc., 19
Restaurants Unlimited, Inc., 13
Richfood Holdings, Inc., 7
The Riese Organization, 38
Riser Foods, Inc., 9
Roadhouse Grill, Inc., 22
Rock Bottom Restaurants, Inc., 25
Rubio's Restaurants, Inc., 35
Ruby Tuesday, Inc., 18
Ruth's Chris Steak House, 28
Ryan's Family Steak Houses, Inc., 15
Safeway Inc., II; 24 (upd.)
Santa Barbara Restaurant Group, Inc., 37
Sbarro, Inc., 16
Schlotzsky's, Inc., 36
Schultz Sav-O Stores, Inc., 21
Schwan's Sales Enterprises, Inc., 26 (upd.)
Seaway Food Town, Inc., 15
Second Harvest, 29
See's Candies, Inc., 30
Seneca Foods Corporation, 17
Service America Corp., 7
Shells Seafood Restaurants, Inc., 43
Shoney's, Inc., 7; 23 (upd.)
ShowBiz Pizza Time, Inc., 13
Smart & Final, Inc., 16
Smith's Food & Drug Centers, Inc., 8
Sodexho Alliance SA, 29
Somerfield plc, 47 (upd.)
Sonic Corporation, 14; 37 (upd.)
The Southland Corporation, II; 7 (upd.)
Spaghetti Warehouse, Inc., 25
SPAR Handels AG, 35
Spartan Stores Inc., 8
The Steak n Shake Company, 41
Steinberg Incorporated, II
The Stop & Shop Companies, Inc., II
Subway, 32
Super Food Services, Inc., 15
Super Valu Stores, Inc., II
Supermarkets General Holdings Corporation, II
Supervalu Inc., 18 (upd.)
SYSCO Corporation, II; 24 (upd.)
Taco Bell Corp., 7; 21 (upd.)
Taco Cabana, Inc., 23
Taco John's International Inc., 15
TelePizza S.A., 33
Tesco PLC, II
Total Entertainment Restaurant Corporation, 46
Trader Joe's Co., 13
Travel Ports of America, Inc., 17
Tree of Life, Inc., 29
Triarc Companies, Inc., 34 (upd.)
Tumbleweed, Inc., 33
TW Services, Inc., II
Ukrop's Super Market's, Inc., 39
Unique Casual Restaurants, Inc., 27
United Natural Foods, Inc., 32
Uno Restaurant Corporation, 18
Vail Resorts, Inc., 43 (upd.)
VICORP Restaurants, Inc., 12; 48 (upd.)
Village Super Market, Inc., 7
The Vons Companies, Incorporated, 7; 28 (upd.)
Waffle House Inc., 14
Wakefern Food Corporation, 33
Waldbaum, Inc., 19
Wall Street Deli, Inc., 33
Wawa Inc., 17
Wegmans Food Markets, Inc., 9; 41 (upd.)
Weis Markets, Inc., 15
Wendy's International, Inc., 8; 23 (upd.); 47 (upd.)
Wetterau Incorporated, II
White Castle System, Inc., 12; 36 (upd.)
White Rose, Inc., 24
Wild Oats Markets, Inc., 19; 41 (upd.)
Winn-Dixie Stores, Inc., II; 21 (upd.)
Wm. Morrison Supermarkets PLC, 38
The Wolfgang Puck Food Company, Inc., 26
Worldwide Restaurant Concepts, Inc., 47
Young & Co.'s Brewery, P.L.C., 38
Yucaipa Cos., 17

## HEALTH & PERSONAL CARE PRODUCTS

Akorn, Inc., 32
Alberto-Culver Company, 8
Alco Health Services Corporation, III
Allergan, Inc., 10; 30 (upd.)
American Safety Razor Company, 20
American Stores Company, 22 (upd.)
Amway Corporation, III; 13 (upd.)
Aveda Corporation, 24
Avon Products, Inc., III; 19 (upd.); 46 (upd.)
Bally Total Fitness Holding Corp., 25
Bausch & Lomb Inc., 7; 25 (upd.)
Baxter International Inc., I; 10 (upd.)
BeautiControl Cosmetics, Inc., 21
Becton, Dickinson & Company, I; 11 (upd.)
Beiersdorf AG, 29
Big B, Inc., 17
Bindley Western Industries, Inc., 9
Block Drug Company, Inc., 8; 27 (upd.)
The Boots Company PLC, 24 (upd.)
Bristol-Myers Squibb Company, III; 9 (upd.)
C.R. Bard Inc., 9
Candela Corporation, 48
Cardinal Health, Inc., 18
Carson, Inc., 31
Carter-Wallace, Inc., 8
Chattem, Inc., 17
Chesebrough-Pond's USA, Inc., 8
Chronimed Inc., 26
The Clorox Company, III
CNS, Inc., 20
Colgate-Palmolive Company, III; 14 (upd.); 35 (upd.)
Conair Corp., 17
Cordis Corp., 19
Cosmair, Inc., 8
Coty, Inc., 36
Datascope Corporation, 39
Del Laboratories, Inc., 28
Dentsply International Inc., 10
DEP Corporation, 20
DePuy, Inc., 30
The Dial Corp., 23 (upd.)
Direct Focus, Inc., 47
Drackett Professional Products, 12
Elizabeth Arden, Inc., 8; 40 (upd.)
Empi, Inc., 26
Enrich International, Inc., 33
The Estée Lauder Companies Inc., 9; 30 (upd.)
Ethicon, Inc., 23
Forest Laboratories, Inc., 11
Forever Living Products International Inc., 17
French Fragrances, Inc., 22
General Nutrition Companies, Inc., 11; 29 (upd.)
Genzyme Corporation, 13
The Gillette Company, III; 20 (upd.)
Groupe Yves Saint Laurent, 23
Guerlain, 23
Guest Supply, Inc., 18
Hanger Orthopedic Group, Inc., 41
Helen of Troy Corporation, 18
Helene Curtis Industries, Inc., 8; 28 (upd.)
Henkel KGaA, III
Henry Schein, Inc., 31
Herbalife International, Inc., 17; 41 (upd.)
Inter Parfums Inc., 35
Invacare Corporation, 11
IVAX Corporation, 11
IVC Industries, Inc., 45
The Jean Coutu Group (PJC) Inc., 46
John Paul Mitchell Systems, 24
Johnson & Johnson, III; 8 (upd.); 36 (upd.)
Kao Corporation, III
Kendall International, Inc., 11
Kimberly-Clark Corporation, III; 16 (upd.); 43 (upd.)
Kyowa Hakko Kogyo Co., Ltd., III
L'Oréal SA, III; 8 (upd.); 46 (upd.)
Laboratoires de Biologie Végétale Yves Rocher, 35
The Lamaur Corporation, 41
Lever Brothers Company, 9
Lion Corporation, III
Luxottica SpA, 17
Mannatech Inc., 33
Mary Kay Corporation, 9; 30 (upd.)
Maxxim Medical Inc., 12
Medco Containment Services Inc., 9
Medtronic, Inc., 8
Melaleuca Inc., 31
The Mentholatum Company Inc., 32
Mentor Corporation, 26
Merck & Co., Inc., 34 (upd.)
Merit Medical Systems, Inc., 29
Nature's Sunshine Products, Inc., 15
NBTY, Inc., 31
Neutrogena Corporation, 17
New Dana Perfumes Company, 37
Nikken Global Inc., 32
Nutrition for Life International Inc., 22
OEC Medical Systems, Inc., 27
Patterson Dental Co., 19
Perrigo Company, 12
Physician Sales & Service, Inc., 14
Playtex Products, Inc., 15
The Procter & Gamble Company, III; 8 (upd.); 26 (upd.)
Revlon Inc., III; 17 (upd.)
Roche Biomedical Laboratories, Inc., 11
S.C. Johnson & Son, Inc., III
Safety 1st, Inc., 24
Schering-Plough Corporation, 14 (upd.)
Shaklee Corporation, 39 (upd.)
Shionogi & Co., Ltd., III
Shiseido Company, Limited, III; 22 (upd.)
Slim-Fast Nutritional Foods International, Inc., 18
Smith & Nephew plc, 17
SmithKline Beecham PLC, III
Soft Sheen Products, Inc., 31
Sunrise Medical Inc., 11
Tambrands Inc., 8

Terumo Corporation, 48
Tom's of Maine, Inc., 45
The Tranzonic Companies, 37
Turtle Wax, Inc., 15
United States Surgical Corporation, 10; 34 (upd.)
USANA, Inc., 29
Utah Medical Products, Inc., 36
VISX, Incorporated, 30
Water Pik Technologies, Inc., 34
Weider Nutrition International, Inc., 29
Wella AG, 48 (upd.)
Wella Group, III
West Pharmaceutical Services, Inc., 42
Zila, Inc., 46
Zimmer Holdings, Inc., 45

## HEALTH CARE SERVICES

Acadian Ambulance & Air Med Services, Inc., 39
Advocat Inc., 46
Alterra Healthcare Corporation, 42
The American Cancer Society, 24
American Lung Association, 48
American Medical Association, 39
American Medical International, Inc., III
American Medical Response, Inc., 39
American Red Cross, 40
AmeriSource Health Corporation, 37 (upd.)
AmSurg Corporation, 48
Applied Bioscience International, Inc., 10
Assisted Living Concepts, Inc., 43
Beverly Enterprises, Inc., III; 16 (upd.)
Bon Secours Health System, Inc., 24
Caremark International Inc., 10
Children's Comprehensive Services, Inc., 42
Chronimed Inc., 26
COBE Laboratories, Inc., 13
Columbia/HCA Healthcare Corporation, 15
Community Psychiatric Centers, 15
CompDent Corporation, 22
CompHealth Inc., 25
Comprehensive Care Corporation, 15
Continental Medical Systems, Inc., 10
Express Scripts Incorporated, 17
Extendicare Health Services, Inc., 6
FHP International Corporation, 6
Genesis Health Ventures, Inc., 18
GranCare, Inc., 14
Group Health Cooperative, 41
Hazelden Foundation, 28
HCA - The Healthcare Company, 35 (upd.)
Health Care & Retirement Corporation, 22
Health Risk Management, Inc., 24
Health Systems International, Inc., 11
HealthSouth Corporation, 14; 33 (upd.)
Highmark Inc., 27
The Hillhaven Corporation, 14
Hooper Holmes, Inc., 22
Hospital Corporation of America, III
Howard Hughes Medical Institute, 39
Humana Inc., III; 24 (upd.)
Intermountain Health Care, Inc., 27
Jenny Craig, Inc., 10; 29 (upd.)
Kinetic Concepts, Inc. (KCI), 20
LabOne, Inc., 48
Laboratory Corporation of America Holdings, 42 (upd.)
Lincare Holdings Inc., 43
Manor Care, Inc., 6; 25 (upd.)
March of Dimes, 31
Matria Healthcare, Inc., 17
Maxicare Health Plans, Inc., III; 25 (upd.)
Mayo Foundation, 9; 34 (upd.)
Merit Medical Systems, Inc., 29
National Health Laboratories Incorporated, 11
National Medical Enterprises, Inc., III
NovaCare, Inc., 11
Option Care Inc., 48
Orthodontic Centers of America, Inc., 35
Oxford Health Plans, Inc., 16
PacifiCare Health Systems, Inc., 11
Palomar Medical Technologies, Inc., 22
Pediatric Services of America, Inc., 31
PHP Healthcare Corporation, 22
PhyCor, Inc., 36
Primedex Health Systems, Inc., 25
Quest Diagnostics Inc., 26
Ramsay Youth Services, Inc., 41
Res-Care, Inc., 29
Response Oncology, Inc., 27
Rural/Metro Corporation, 28
Sabratek Corporation, 29
St. Jude Medical, Inc., 11; 43 (upd.)
Sierra Health Services, Inc., 15
Smith & Nephew plc, 41 (upd.)
The Sports Club Company, 25
Stericycle Inc., 33
Sun Healthcare Group Inc., 25
Twinlab Corporation, 34
U.S. Healthcare, Inc., 6
Unison HealthCare Corporation, 25
United HealthCare Corporation, 9
United Way of America, 36
Universal Health Services, Inc., 6
Vencor, Inc., 16
VISX, Incorporated, 30
Vivra, Inc., 18
WellPoint Health Networks Inc., 25
YWCA of the U.S.A., 45

## HOTELS

Amerihost Properties, Inc., 30
Aztar Corporation, 13
Bass PLC, 38 (upd.)
Boca Resorts, Inc., 37
Boyd Gaming Corporation, 43
Bristol Hotel Company, 23
The Broadmoor Hotel, 30
Caesars World, Inc., 6
Candlewood Hotel Company, Inc., 41
Carlson Companies, Inc., 22 (upd.)
Castle & Cooke, Inc., 20 (upd.)
Cedar Fair, L.P., 22
Cendant Corporation, 44 (upd.)
Choice Hotels International Inc., 14
Circus Circus Enterprises, Inc., 6
Club Mediterranée S.A., 6; 21 (upd.)
Doubletree Corporation, 21
Extended Stay America, Inc., 41
Fibreboard Corporation, 16
Four Seasons Hotels Inc., 9; 29 (upd.)
Fuller Smith & Turner P.L.C., 38
Gaylord Entertainment Company, 36 (upd.)
Granada Group PLC, 24 (upd.)
Grand Casinos, Inc., 20
Grand Hotel Krasnapolsky N.V., 23
Helmsley Enterprises, Inc., 9
Hilton Hotels Corporation, III; 19 (upd.)
Holiday Inns, Inc., III
Hospitality Franchise Systems, Inc., 11
Howard Johnson International, Inc., 17
Hyatt Corporation, III; 16 (upd.)
ITT Sheraton Corporation, III
JD Wetherspoon plc, 30
John Q. Hammons Hotels, Inc., 24
The La Quinta Companies, 11; 42 (upd.)
Ladbroke Group PLC, 21 (upd.)
Mandalay Resort Group, 32 (upd.)
Manor Care, Inc., 25 (upd.)
The Marcus Corporation, 21
Marriott International, Inc., III; 21 (upd.)
Mirage Resorts, Incorporated, 6; 28 (upd.)
Motel 6 Corporation, 13
Omni Hotels Corp., 12
Park Corp., 22
Players International, Inc., 22
Preussag AG, 42 (upd.)
Promus Companies, Inc., 9
Red Roof Inns, Inc., 18
Resorts International, Inc., 12
Ritz-Carlton Hotel Company L.L.C., 9; 29 (upd.)
Santa Fe Gaming Corporation, 19
The SAS Group, 34 (upd.)
Showboat, Inc., 19
Sonesta International Hotels Corporation, 44
Sun International Hotels Limited, 26
Sunburst Hospitality Corporation, 26
Trusthouse Forte PLC, III
Vail Resorts, Inc., 43 (upd.)
The Walt Disney Company, 30 (upd.)
Westin Hotels and Resorts Worldwide, 9; 29 (upd.)
Young & Co.'s Brewery, P.L.C., 38

## INFORMATION TECHNOLOGY

A.B. Watley Group Inc., 45
Acxiom Corporation, 35
Adaptec, Inc., 31
Adobe Systems Incorporated, 10; 33 (upd.)
Advanced Micro Devices, Inc., 6
Agence France-Presse, 34
Agilent Technologies Inc., 38
Aldus Corporation, 10
AltaVista Company, 43
Amdahl Corporation, III; 14 (upd.); 40 (upd.)
Amdocs Ltd., 47
America Online, Inc., 10 ; 26 (upd.)
American Business Information, Inc., 18
American Management Systems, Inc., 11
American Software Inc., 25
Amstrad PLC, III
Analytic Sciences Corporation, 10
Analytical Surveys, Inc., 33
Apollo Group, Inc., 24
Apple Computer, Inc., III; 6 (upd.)
The Arbitron Company, 38
Asanté Technologies, Inc., 20
AsiaInfo Holdings, Inc., 43
ASK Group, Inc., 9
AST Research Inc., 9
At Home Corporation, 43
AT&T Bell Laboratories, Inc., 13
AT&T Corporation, 29 (upd.)
AT&T Istel Ltd., 14
Autologic Information International, Inc., 20
Automatic Data Processing, Inc., III; 9 (upd.)
Autotote Corporation, 20
Avid Technology Inc., 38
Aydin Corp., 19
Baan Company, 25
Baltimore Technologies Plc, 42
Banyan Systems Inc., 25
Battelle Memorial Institute, Inc., 10
BBN Corp., 19
BEA Systems, Inc., 36
Bell and Howell Company, 9; 29 (upd.)
Bell Industries, Inc., 47
Billing Concepts Corp., 26
Bloomberg L.P., 21
Boole & Babbage, Inc., 25
Booz Allen & Hamilton Inc., 10
Borland International, Inc., 9

Bowne & Co., Inc., 23
Brite Voice Systems, Inc., 20
Broderbund Software, 29 (upd.)
Broderbund Software, Inc., 13
BTG, Inc., 45
Bull S.A., 43 (upd.)
Business Objects S.A., 25
C-Cube Microsystems, Inc., 37
CACI International Inc., 21
Cadence Design Systems, Inc., 11
Caere Corporation, 20
Cahners Business Information, 43
CalComp Inc., 13
Cambridge Technology Partners, Inc., 36
Canon Inc., III
Cap Gemini Ernst & Young, 37
Caribiner International, Inc., 24
Catalina Marketing Corporation, 18
CDW Computer Centers, Inc., 16
Cerner Corporation, 16
Cheyenne Software, Inc., 12
CHIPS and Technologies, Inc., 9
Ciber, Inc., 18
Cincom Systems Inc., 15
Cirrus Logic, Incorporated, 11
Cisco Systems, Inc., 11
Citizen Watch Co., Ltd., 21 (upd.)
Citrix Systems, Inc., 44
CNET Networks, Inc., 47
Cognos Inc., 44
Commodore International Ltd., 7
Compagnie des Machines Bull S.A., III
Compaq Computer Corporation, III; 6 (upd.); 26 (upd.)
Complete Business Solutions, Inc., 31
CompuAdd Computer Corporation, 11
CompuCom Systems, Inc., 10
CompUSA, Inc., 35 (upd.)
CompuServe Incorporated, 10
CompuServe Interactive Services, Inc., 27 (upd.)
Computer Associates International, Inc., 6
Computer Data Systems, Inc., 14
Computer Sciences Corporation, 6
Computervision Corporation, 10
Compuware Corporation, 10; 30 (upd.)
Comshare Inc., 23
Conner Peripherals, Inc., 6
Control Data Corporation, III
Control Data Systems, Inc., 10
Corbis Corporation, 31
Corel Corporation, 15; 33 (upd.)
Corporate Software Inc., 9
Cray Research, Inc., III
CTG, Inc., 11
Cybermedia, Inc., 25
Dassault Systèmes S.A., 25
Data Broadcasting Corporation, 31
Data General Corporation, 8
Datapoint Corporation, 11
Dell Computer Corp., 9
Dialogic Corporation, 18
Digex, Inc., 46
Digital Equipment Corporation, III; 6 (upd.)
Documentum, Inc., 46
The Dun & Bradstreet Corporation, IV; 19 (upd.)
Dun & Bradstreet Software Services Inc., 11
DynCorp, 45
EarthLink, Inc., 36
ECS S.A, 12
Edmark Corporation, 14; 41 (upd.)
Egghead Inc., 9
El Camino Resources International, Inc., 11
Electronic Arts Inc., 10
Electronic Data Systems Corporation, III; 28 (upd.)
Electronics for Imaging, Inc., 43 (upd.)
EMC Corporation, 12; 46 (upd.)
Encore Computer Corporation, 13
Evans & Sutherland Computer Corporation, 19
Exabyte Corporation, 12
Experian Information Solutions Inc., 45
First Financial Management Corporation, 11
Fiserv Inc., 11
FlightSafety International, Inc., 9
FORE Systems, Inc., 25
Franklin Electronic Publishers, Inc., 23
FTP Software, Inc., 20
Fujitsu Limited, III; 42 (upd.)
Fujitsu-ICL Systems Inc., 11
Future Now, Inc., 12
Gartner Group, Inc., 21
Gateway 2000, Inc., 10
Gateway, Inc., 27 (upd.)
GEAC Computer Corporation Ltd., 43
Gericom AG, 47
Getronics NV, 39
GT Interactive Software, 31
Guthy-Renker Corporation, 32
Hewlett-Packard Company, III; 6 (upd.)
Hyperion Software Corporation, 22
ICL plc, 6
Identix Inc., 44
Imation Corporation, 20
Information Access Company, 17
Information Builders, Inc., 22
Information Resources, Inc., 10
Informix Corporation, 10; 30 (upd.)
Infosys Technologies Ltd., 38
Ing. C. Olivetti & C., S.p.a., III
Inktomi Corporation, 45
Inso Corporation, 26
Intel Corporation, 36 (upd.)
IntelliCorp, Inc., 45
Intelligent Electronics, Inc., 6
Intergraph Corporation, 6; 24 (upd.)
International Business Machines Corporation, III; 6 (upd.); 30 (upd.)
Intuit Inc., 14; 33 (upd.)
Iomega Corporation, 21
IONA Technologies plc, 43
J.D. Edwards & Company, 14
Jack Henry and Associates, Inc., 17
Juniper Networks, Inc., 43
Juno Online Services, Inc., 38
KLA Instruments Corporation, 11
KnowledgeWare Inc., 31 (upd.)
Komag, Inc., 11
Kronos, Inc., 18
Lam Research Corporation, 11
Lason, Inc., 31
Lawson Software, 38
The Learning Company Inc., 24
Learning Tree International Inc., 24
Legent Corporation, 10
LEXIS-NEXIS Group, 33
Logica plc, 14; 37 (upd.)
Logicon Inc., 20
Logitech International SA, 28
LoJack Corporation, 48
Lotus Development Corporation, 6; 25 (upd.)
The MacNeal-Schwendler Corporation, 25
Madge Networks N.V., 26
MAI Systems Corporation, 11
Maxtor Corporation, 10
Mead Data Central, Inc., 10
Mecklermedia Corporation, 24
Mentor Graphics Corporation, 11
Merisel, Inc., 12
Metatec International, Inc., 47
Metro Information Services, Inc., 36
Micro Warehouse, Inc., 16
Micron Technology, Inc., 11; 29 (upd.)
Micros Systems, Inc., 18
Microsoft Corporation, 6; 27 (upd.)
Misys plc, 45; 46
MITRE Corporation, 26
The Motley Fool, Inc., 40
National Semiconductor Corporation, 6
National TechTeam, Inc., 41
Navarre Corporation, 24
NCR Corporation, III; 6 (upd.); 30 (upd.)
Netscape Communications Corporation, 15; 35 (upd.)
Network Associates, Inc., 25
Nextel Communications, Inc., 10
NFO Worldwide, Inc., 24
Nichols Research Corporation, 18
Nimbus CD International, Inc., 20
Nixdorf Computer AG, III
Novell, Inc., 6; 23 (upd.)
Océ N.V., 24
Odetics Inc., 14
Oracle Corporation, 24 (upd.)
Oracle Systems Corporation, 6
Packard Bell Electronics, Inc., 13
Parametric Technology Corp., 16
PC Connection, Inc., 37
PeopleSoft Inc., 14; 33 (upd.)
Perot Systems Corporation, 29
Pitney Bowes Inc., III
PLATINUM Technology, Inc., 14
Policy Management Systems Corporation, 11
Portal Software, Inc., 47
Primark Corp., 13
The Princeton Review, Inc., 42
Printrak, A Motorola Company, 44
Printronix, Inc., 18
Prodigy Communications Corporation, 34
Progress Software Corporation, 15
Psion PLC, 45
Quantum Corporation, 10
Quark, Inc., 36
Racal-Datacom Inc., 11
Razorfish, Inc., 37
RCM Technologies, Inc., 34
Red Hat, Inc., 45
Renaissance Learning Systems, Inc., 39
Reuters Holdings PLC, 22 (upd.)
Ricoh Company, Ltd., III
RSA Security Inc., 46
SABRE Group Holdings, Inc., 26
The Sage Group, 43
The Santa Cruz Operation, Inc., 38
SAP AG, 16; 43 (upd.)
SAS Institute Inc., 10
SBS Technologies, Inc., 25
SCB Computer Technology, Inc., 29
Schawk, Inc., 24
Seagate Technology, Inc., 8
Siebel Systems, Inc., 38
Sierra On-Line, Inc., 15; 41 (upd.)
SilverPlatter Information Inc., 23
SmartForce PLC, 43
Softbank Corp., 13; 38 (upd.)
Standard Microsystems Corporation, 11
STC PLC, III
Sterling Software, Inc., 11
Storage Technology Corporation, 6
Stratus Computer, Inc., 10
Sun Microsystems, Inc., 7; 30 (upd.)
SunGard Data Systems Inc., 11
Sybase, Inc., 10; 27 (upd.)
Sykes Enterprises, Inc., 45
Symantec Corporation, 10
Symbol Technologies, Inc., 15

Synopsis, Inc., 11
System Software Associates, Inc., 10
Systems & Computer Technology Corp., 19
Tandem Computers, Inc., 6
TenFold Corporation, 35
Terra Lycos, Inc., 43
The Thomson Corporation, 34 (upd.)
3Com Corporation, 11; 34 (upd.)
The 3DO Company, 43
Timberline Software Corporation, 15
Transaction Systems Architects, Inc., 29
Transiciel SA, 48
Triple P N.V., 26
Ubi Soft Entertainment S.A., 41
Unilog SA, 42
Unisys Corporation, III; 6 (upd.); 36 (upd.)
UUNET, 38
Verbatim Corporation, 14
VeriFone, Inc., 18
VeriSign, Inc., 47
Veritas Software Corporation, 45
Viasoft Inc., 27
Volt Information Sciences Inc., 26
Wang Laboratories, Inc., III; 6 (upd.)
West Group, 34 (upd.)
Western Digital Corp., 25
Wind River Systems, Inc., 37
Wipro Limited, 43
Wolters Kluwer NV, 33 (upd.)
WordPerfect Corporation, 10
Wyse Technology, Inc., 15
Xerox Corporation, III; 6 (upd.); 26 (upd.)
Xilinx, Inc., 16
Yahoo! Inc., 27
Zapata Corporation, 25
Ziff Davis Media Inc., 36 (upd.)
Zilog, Inc., 15

## INSURANCE

AEGON N.V., III
Aetna, Inc., III; 21 (upd.)
AFLAC Incorporated, 10 (upd.); 38 (upd.)
Alexander & Alexander Services Inc., 10
Alleghany Corporation, 10
Allianz Aktiengesellschaft Holding, III; 15 (upd.)
The Allstate Corporation, 10; 27 (upd.)
American Family Corporation, III
American Financial Corporation, III
American Financial Group Inc., 48 (upd.)
American General Corporation, III; 10 (upd.); 46 (upd.)
American International Group, Inc., III; 15 (upd.); 47 (upd.)
American National Insurance Company, 8; 27 (upd.)
American Premier Underwriters, Inc., 10
American Re Corporation, 10; 35 (upd.)
N.V. AMEV, III
Aon Corporation, III; 45 (upd.)
Assicurazioni Generali SpA, III; 15 (upd.)
Atlantic American Corporation, 44
Axa, III
AXA Colonia Konzern AG, 27
B.A.T. Industries PLC, 22 (upd.)
Bâloise-Holding, 40
Berkshire Hathaway Inc., III; 18 (upd.)
Blue Cross and Blue Shield Association, 10
Brown & Brown, Inc., 41
Business Men's Assurance Company of America, 14
Capital Holding Corporation, III
Catholic Order of Foresters, 24
The Chubb Corporation, III; 14 (upd.); 37 (upd.)
CIGNA Corporation, III; 22 (upd.); 45 (upd.)
Cincinnati Financial Corporation, 16; 44 (upd.)
CNA Financial Corporation, III; 38 (upd.)
Commercial Union PLC, III
Connecticut Mutual Life Insurance Company, III
Conseco Inc., 10; 33 (upd.)
The Continental Corporation, III
Empire Blue Cross and Blue Shield, III
Enbridge Inc., 43
Engle Homes, Inc., 46
The Equitable Life Assurance Society of the United States Fireman's Fund Insurance Company, III
ERGO Versicherungsgruppe AG, 44
Erie Indemnity Company, 35
Farm Family Holdings, Inc., 39
Farmers Insurance Group of Companies, 25
First Executive Corporation, III
Foundation Health Corporation, 12
Gainsco, Inc., 22
GEICO Corporation, 10; 40 (upd.)
General Accident PLC, III
General Re Corporation, III; 24 (upd.)
Great-West Lifeco Inc., III
Gryphon Holdings, Inc., 21
Guardian Royal Exchange Plc, 11
Harleysville Group Inc., 37
The Home Insurance Company, III
Horace Mann Educators Corporation, 22
Household International, Inc., 21 (upd.)
Jackson National Life Insurance Company, 8
Jefferson-Pilot Corporation, 11; 29 (upd.)
John Hancock Financial Services, Inc., III; 42 (upd.)
Johnson & Higgins, 14
Kemper Corporation, III; 15 (upd.)
Legal & General Group plc, III; 24 (upd.)
The Liberty Corporation, 22
Lincoln National Corporation, III; 25 (upd.)
Lloyd's of London, III; 22 (upd.)
The Loewen Group Inc., 40 (upd.)
Lutheran Brotherhood, 31
Marsh & McLennan Companies, Inc., III; 45 (upd.)
Massachusetts Mutual Life Insurance Company, III
The Meiji Mutual Life Insurance Company, III
Mercury General Corporation, 25
Metropolitan Life Insurance Company, III
Mitsui Marine and Fire Insurance Company, Limited, III
Mitsui Mutual Life Insurance Company, III; 39 (upd.)
Munich Re (Münchener Rückversicherungs-Gesellschaft Aktiengesellschaft in München), III; 46 (upd.)
The Mutual Benefit Life Insurance Company, III
The Mutual Life Insurance Company of New York, III
Nationale-Nederlanden N.V., III
New England Mutual Life Insurance Company, III
New York Life Insurance Company, III; 45 (upd.)
Nippon Life Insurance Company, III
Northwestern Mutual Life Insurance Company, III; 45 (upd.)
NYMAGIC, Inc., 41
Ohio Casualty Corp., 11
Old Republic International Corp., 11
Pan-American Life Insurance Company, 48
The Paul Revere Corporation, 12
Pennsylvania Blue Shield, III
Preserver Group, Inc., 44
Principal Mutual Life Insurance Company, III
The Progressive Corporation, 11; 29 (upd.)
Provident Life and Accident Insurance Company of America, III
Prudential Corporation PLC, III
The Prudential Insurance Company of America, III; 30 (upd.)
Prudential plc, 48 (upd.)
Radian Group Inc., 42
Reliance Group Holdings, Inc., III
Riunione Adriatica di Sicurtà SpA, III
Royal Insurance Holdings PLC, III
SAFECO Corporaton, III
The St. Paul Companies, Inc., III; 22 (upd.)
SCOR S.A., 20
The Standard Life Assurance Company, III
State Farm Mutual Automobile Insurance Company, III
Sumitomo Life Insurance Company, III
The Sumitomo Marine and Fire Insurance Company, Limited, III
Sun Alliance Group PLC, III
SunAmerica Inc., 11
Swiss Reinsurance Company (Schweizerische Rückversicherungs-Gesellschaft), III; 46 (upd.)
Teachers Insurance and Annuity Association-College Retirement Equities Fund, III; 45 (upd.)
Texas Industries, Inc., 8
TIG Holdings, Inc., 26
The Tokio Marine and Fire Insurance Co., Ltd., III
Torchmark Corporation, 9; 33 (upd.)
Transatlantic Holdings, Inc., 11
The Travelers Corporation, III
UICI, 33
Union des Assurances de Pans, III
Unitrin Inc., 16
UNUM Corp., 13
USAA, 10
USF&G Corporation, III
Victoria Group, 44 (upd.)
VICTORIA Holding AG, III
W.R. Berkley Corp., 15
Washington National Corporation, 12
White Mountains Insurance Group, Ltd., 48
Willis Corroon Group plc, 25
"Winterthur" Schweizerische Versicherungs-Gesellschaft, III
The Yasuda Fire and Marine Insurance Company, Limited, III
The Yasuda Mutual Life Insurance Company, III; 39 (upd.)
"Zürich" Versicherungs-Gesellschaft, III

## LEGAL SERVICES

Akin, Gump, Strauss, Hauer & Feld, L.L.P., 33
American Bar Association, 35
American Lawyer Media Holdings, Inc., 32
Arnold & Porter, 35
Baker & Hostetler LLP, 40
Baker & McKenzie, 10; 42 (upd.)
Baker and Botts, L.L.P., 28
Bingham Dana LLP, 43
Brobeck, Phleger & Harrison, LLP, 31
Cadwalader, Wickersham & Taft, 32
Chadbourne & Parke, 36
Cleary, Gottlieb, Steen & Hamilton, 35
Clifford Chance LLP, 38
Coudert Brothers, 30

Covington & Burling, 40
Cravath, Swaine & Moore, 43
Davis Polk & Wardwell, 36
Debevoise & Plimpton, 39
Dechert, 43
Dewey Ballantine LLP, 48
Dorsey & Whitney LLP, 47
Fenwick & West LLP, 34
Foley & Lardner, 28
Fried, Frank, Harris, Shriver & Jacobson, 35
Fulbright & Jaworski L.L.P., 47
Gibson, Dunn & Crutcher LLP, 36
Heller, Ehrman, White & McAuliffe, 41
Hildebrandt International, 29
Hogan & Hartson L.L.P., 44
Holme Roberts & Owen LLP, 28
Hughes Hubbard & Reed LLP, 44
Hunton & Williams, 35
Jones, Day, Reavis & Pogue, 33
Kelley Drye & Warren LLP, 40
King & Spalding, 23
Latham & Watkins, 33
LeBoeuf, Lamb, Greene & MacRae, L.L.P., 29
The Legal Aid Society, 48
Mayer, Brown, Rowe & Maw, 47
Milbank, Tweed, Hadley & McCloy, 27
Morgan, Lewis & Bockius LLP, 29
O'Melveny & Myers, 37
Paul, Hastings, Janofsky & Walker LLP, 27
Paul, Weiss, Rifkind, Wharton & Garrison, 47
Pepper Hamilton LLP, 43
Pillsbury Madison & Sutro LLP, 29
Pre-Paid Legal Services, Inc., 20
Proskauer Rose LLP, 47
Ropes & Gray, 40
Shearman & Sterling, 32
Sidley Austin Brown & Wood, 40
Simpson Thacher & Bartlett, 39
Skadden, Arps, Slate, Meagher & Flom, 18
Snell & Wilmer L.L.P., 28
Stroock & Stroock & Lavan LLP, 40
Sullivan & Cromwell, 26
Vinson & Elkins L.L.P., 30
Wachtell, Lipton, Rosen & Katz, 47
White & Case LLP, 35
Williams & Connolly LLP, 47
Wilson Sonsini Goodrich & Rosati, 34
Winston & Strawn, 35

## MANUFACTURING

A.B.Dick Company, 28
A.O. Smith Corporation, 11; 40 (upd.)
A.T. Cross Company, 17
AAF-McQuay Incorporated, 26
AAON, Inc., 22
AAR Corp., 28
ABC Rail Products Corporation, 18
Abiomed, Inc., 47
ACCO World Corporation, 7
Acme-Cleveland Corp., 13
Acuson Corporation, 36 (upd.)
Adams Golf, Inc., 37
AEP Industries, Inc., 36
Ag-Chem Equipment Company, Inc., 17
AGCO Corp., 13
Aisin Seiki Co., Ltd., III
AK Steel Holding Corporation, 41 (upd.)
Aktiebolaget Electrolux, 22 (upd.)
Aktiebolaget SKF, III; 38 (upd.)
Alamo Group Inc., 32
Alberto-Culver Company, 36 (upd.)
Aldila Inc., 46
Alfa-Laval AB, III
Allen Organ Company, 33
Alliant Techsystems Inc., 8; 30 (upd.)
Allied Healthcare Products, Inc., 24
Allied Products Corporation, 21
Allied Signal Engines, 9
AlliedSignal Inc., 22 (upd.)
Allison Gas Turbine Division, 9
Alltrista Corporation, 30
Alps Electric Co., Ltd., 44 (upd.)
Alvis Plc, 47
Amer Group plc, 41
American Biltrite Inc., 43 (upd.)
American Business Products, Inc., 20
American Homestar Corporation, 18; 41 (upd.)
American Locker Group Incorporated, 34
American Standard Companies Inc., 30 (upd.)
American Tourister, Inc., 16
American Woodmark Corporation, 31
Ameriwood Industries International Corp., 17
AMETEK, Inc., 9
AMF Bowling, Inc., 40
Ampex Corporation, 17
Amway Corporation, 30 (upd.)
Analogic Corporation, 23
Anchor Hocking Glassware, 13
Andersen Corporation, 10
The Andersons, Inc., 31
Andreas Stihl, 16
Anthem Electronics, Inc., 13
Applica Incorporated, 43 (upd.)
Applied Films Corporation, 48
Applied Materials, Inc., 10; 46 (upd.)
Applied Micro Circuits Corporation, 38
Applied Power Inc., 9; 32 (upd.)
ARBED S.A., 22 (upd.)
Arctco, Inc., 16
Arctic Cat Inc., 40 (upd.)
Ariens Company, 48
Armor All Products Corp., 16
Armstrong World Industries, Inc., III; 22 (upd.)
Artesyn Technologies Inc., 46 (upd.)
Asahi Glass Company, Ltd., 48 (upd.)
Ashley Furniture Industries, Inc., 35
Astronics Corporation, 35
ASV, Inc., 34
Atlas Copco AB, III; 28 (upd.)
Avedis Zildjian Co., 38
Avery Dennison Corporation, 17 (upd.)
Avondale Industries, 7; 41 (upd.)
Badger Meter, Inc., 22
Baker Hughes Incorporated, III
Baldor Electric Company, 21
Baldwin Piano & Organ Company, 18
Baldwin Technology Company, Inc., 25
Balfour Beatty plc, 36 (upd.)
Ballantyne of Omaha, Inc., 27
Ballard Medical Products, 21
Bally Manufacturing Corporation, III
Baltek Corporation, 34
Barmag AG, 39
Barnes Group Inc., 13
Barry Callebaut AG, 29
Bassett Furniture Industries, Inc., 18
Bath Iron Works, 12; 36 (upd.)
Beckman Coulter, Inc., 22
Beckman Instruments, Inc., 14
Becton, Dickinson & Company, 36 (upd.)
Beiersdorf AG, 29
Belden Inc., 19
Bell Sports Corporation, 16; 44 (upd.)
Beloit Corporation, 14
Benjamin Moore & Co., 13; 38 (upd.)
Bernina Holding AG, 47
Berry Plastics Corporation, 21
BIC Corporation, 8; 23 (upd.)
BICC PLC, III
Billabong International Ltd., 44
Binks Sames Corporation, 21
Binney & Smith Inc., 25
Biomet, Inc., 10
BISSELL Inc., 9; 30 (upd.)
The Black & Decker Corporation, III; 20 (upd.)
Blount International, Inc., 48 (upd.)
Blount, Inc., 12
Blyth Industries, Inc., 18
BMC Industries, Inc., 17
Bodum Design Group AG, 47
Boral Limited, 43 (upd.)
Borden, Inc., 22 (upd.)
Borg-Warner Automotive, Inc., 14
Borg-Warner Corporation, III
Boston Scientific Corporation, 37
The Boyds Collection, Ltd., 29
Brannock Device Company, 48
Brass Eagle Inc., 34
Bridgeport Machines, Inc., 17
Briggs & Stratton Corporation, 8; 27 (upd.)
BRIO AB, 24
British Vita plc, 33 (upd.)
Brother Industries, Ltd., 14
Brown & Sharpe Manufacturing Co., 23
Brown-Forman Corporation, 38 (upd.)
Broyhill Furniture Industries, Inc., 10
Brunswick Corporation, III; 22 (upd.)
BTR Siebe plc, 27
Buck Knives Inc., 48
Buckeye Technologies, Inc., 42
Bucyrus International, Inc., 17
Bugle Boy Industries, Inc., 18
Bulgari S.p.A., 20
Bulova Corporation, 13; 41 (upd.)
Bundy Corporation, 17
Burelle S.A., 23
Burton Snowboards Inc., 22
Bush Boake Allen Inc., 30
Bush Industries, Inc., 20
Butler Manufacturing Co., 12
C.F. Martin & Co., Inc., 42
Callaway Golf Company, 15; 45 (upd.)
Cannondale Corporation, 21
Caradon plc, 20 (upd.)
The Carbide/Graphite Group, Inc., 40
Carbone Lorraine S.A., 33
Carl-Zeiss-Stiftung, III; 34 (upd.)
Carrier Corporation, 7
CASIO Computer Co., Ltd., III; 40 (upd.)
Catalina Lighting, Inc., 43 (upd.)
Caterpillar Inc., III; 15 (upd.)
Central Sprinkler Corporation, 29
Cessna Aircraft Company, 27 (upd.)
Champion Enterprises, Inc., 17
Chanel, 12
Chart Industries, Inc., 21
Chris-Craft Industries, Inc., 31 (upd.)
Christian Dalloz SA, 40
Christofle SA, 40
Chromcraft Revington, Inc., 15
Ciments Français, 40
Cincinnati Milacron Inc., 12
Cinram International, Inc., 43
Circon Corporation, 21
Cirrus Design Corporation, 44
Citizen Watch Co., Ltd., III
Clarcor Inc., 17
Clark Equipment Company, 8
Clayton Homes Incorporated, 13
The Clorox Company, 22 (upd.)
CNH Global N.V., 38 (upd.)
Coach, Inc., 45 (upd.)
Cobra Golf Inc., 16
Cockerill Sambre Group, 26 (upd.)

Cohu, Inc., 32
Colas S.A., 31
The Coleman Company, Inc., 30 (upd.)
Collins & Aikman Corporation, 41 (upd.)
Collins Industries, Inc., 33
Colorado MEDtech, Inc., 48
Colt's Manufacturing Company, Inc., 12
Columbia Sportswear Company, 19
Columbus McKinnon Corporation, 37
Concord Camera Corporation, 41
Congoleum Corp., 18
Conso International Corporation, 29
Consorcio G Grupo Dina, S.A. de C.V., 36
Converse Inc., 9
The Cooper Companies, Inc., 39
Cooper Industries, Inc., 44 (upd.)
Cordis Corporation, 46 (upd.)
Corning Inc., 44 (upd.)
Corrpro Companies, Inc., 20
Corticeira Amorim, Sociedade Gestora de Participaço es Sociais, S.A., 48
Crane Co., 8; 30 (upd.)
Creo Inc., 48
Crown Equipment Corporation, 15
CTB International Corporation, 43 (upd.)
Cuisinart Corporation, 24
Culligan Water Technologies, Inc., 12; 38 (upd.)
Cummins Engine Company, Inc., 40 (upd.)
Curtiss-Wright Corporation, 10; 35 (upd.)
Cutter & Buck Inc., 27
Daewoo Group, III
Daikin Industries, Ltd., III
Danaher Corporation, 7
Daniel Industries, Inc., 16
Danisco A/S, 44
Day Runner, Inc., 41 (upd.)
Decora Industries, Inc., 31
DeCrane Aircraft Holdings Inc., 36
Deere & Company, III; 42 (upd.)
Defiance, Inc., 22
Denby Group plc, 44
Denison International plc, 46
DENSO Corporation, 46 (upd.)
Department 56, Inc., 14
DePuy Inc., 37 (upd.)
Detroit Diesel Corporation, 10
Deutsche Babcock A.G., III
Deutz AG, 39
Dial-A-Mattress Operating Corporation, 46
Diebold, Incorporated, 7; 22 (upd.)
Diesel SpA, 40
Dixon Industries, Inc., 26
Dixon Ticonderoga Company, 12
DMI Furniture, Inc., 46
Donnelly Corporation, 12; 35 (upd.)
Douglas & Lomason Company, 16
Dover Corporation, III; 28 (upd.)
Dresser Industries, Inc., III
Drew Industries Inc., 28
Drexel Heritage Furnishings Inc., 12
Drypers Corporation, 18
Ducommun Incorporated, 30
Duracell International Inc., 9
Durametallic, 21
Duriron Company Inc., 17
Dürr AG, 44
Eagle-Picher Industries, Inc., 8; 23 (upd.)
The Eastern Company, 48
Eastman Kodak Company, III; 7 (upd.); 36 (upd.)
ECC International Corp., 42
Ecolab Inc., 34 (upd.)
Eddie Bauer Inc., 9
EDO Corporation, 46
EG&G Incorporated, 29 (upd.)
Ekco Group, Inc., 16
Elano Corporation, 14
Electrolux Group, III
Eljer Industries, Inc., 24
Elscint Ltd., 20
Encompass Services Corporation, 33
Energizer Holdings, Inc., 32
Enesco Corporation, 11
English China Clays Ltd., 40 (upd.)
Escalade, Incorporated, 19
Esselte Leitz GmbH & Co. KG, 48
Essilor International, 21
Esterline Technologies Corp., 15
Ethan Allen Interiors, Inc., 12; 39 (upd.)
The Eureka Company, 12
Everlast Worldwide Inc., 47
Fabbrica D' Armi Pietro Beretta S.p.A., 39
Facom S.A., 32
Faiveley S.A., 39
Falcon Products, Inc., 33
Fanuc Ltd., III; 17 (upd.)
Farah Incorporated, 24
Fastenal Company, 42 (upd.)
Featherlite Inc., 28
Fedders Corporation, 18; 43 (upd.)
Federal Prison Industries, Inc., 34
Federal Signal Corp., 10
Fellowes Manufacturing Company, 28
Fender Musical Instruments Company, 16; 43 (upd.)
Figgie International Inc., 7
Firearms Training Systems, Inc., 27
First Alert, Inc., 28
First Brands Corporation, 8
The First Years Inc., 46
Fisher Controls International, Inc., 13
Fisher Scientific International Inc., 24
Fisher-Price Inc., 12; 32 (upd.)
Fiskars Corporation, 33
Fisons plc, 9
Fleetwood Enterprises, Inc., III; 22 (upd.)
Flexsteel Industries Inc., 15; 41 (upd.)
Flextronics International Ltd., 38
Flint Ink Corporation, 41 (upd.)
Florsheim Shoe Company, 9
Flour City International, Inc., 44
Flowserve Corporation, 33
Fort James Corporation, 22 (upd.)
Fountain Powerboats Industries, Inc., 28
Foxboro Company, 13
Framatome SA, 19
Frank J. Zamboni & Co., Inc., 34
Franklin Electric Company, Inc., 43
Freudenberg & Co., 41
Frigidaire Home Products, 22
Frymaster Corporation, 27
FSI International, Inc., 17
Fuji Photo Film Co., Ltd., III; 18 (upd.)
Fuqua Enterprises, Inc., 17
Furniture Brands International, Inc., 39 (upd.)
Furon Company, 28
The Furukawa Electric Co., Ltd., III
G.S. Blodgett Corporation, 15
The Gates Corporation, 9
GE Aircraft Engines, 9
GEA AG, 27
Gehl Company, 19
GenCorp Inc., 8; 9 (upd.)
General Bearing Corporation, 45
General Cable Corporation, 40
General Dynamics Corporation, 40 (upd.)
General Housewares Corporation, 16
Genmar Holdings, Inc., 45
geobra Brandstätter GmbH & Co. KG, 48
Gerber Scientific, Inc., 12
Gerresheimer Glas AG, 43
Giddings & Lewis, Inc., 10
The Gillette Company, 20 (upd.)
GKN plc, III; 38 (upd.)
Gleason Corporation, 24
The Glidden Company, 8
Glock Ges.m.b.H., 42
Goodman Holding Company, 42
Goodrich Corporation, 46 (upd.)
Goody Products, Inc., 12
The Gorman-Rupp Company, 18
Goss Holdings, Inc., 43
Goulds Pumps Inc., 24
Graco Inc., 19
Griffon Corporation, 34
Grinnell Corp., 13
Groupe André, 17
Groupe Guillin SA, 40
Groupe Legis Industries, 23
Groupe SEB, 35
Grow Group Inc., 12
Grupo Cydsa, S.A. de C.V., 39
Grupo IMSA, S.A. de C.V., 44
Gulf Island Fabrication, Inc., 44
The Gunlocke Company, 23
Guy Degrenne SA, 44
H.B. Fuller Company, 8; 32 (upd.)
Hach Co., 18
Hackman Oyj Adp, 44
Haemonetics Corporation, 20
Halliburton Company, III
Hallmark Cards, Inc., 40 (upd.)
Hanson PLC, 30 (upd.)
Hardinge Inc., 25
Harland and Wolff Holdings plc, 19
Harmon Industries, Inc., 25
Harnischfeger Industries, Inc., 8; 38 (upd.)
Harsco Corporation, 8
Hartmarx Corporation, 32 (upd.)
The Hartz Mountain Corporation, 46 (upd.)
Hasbro, Inc., III; 16 (upd.)
Hawker Siddeley Group Public Limited Company, III
Haworth Inc., 8; 39 (upd.)
Health O Meter Products Inc., 14
Heekin Can Inc., 13
HEICO Corporation, 30
Heidelberger Druckmaschinen AG, 40
Henkel Manco Inc., 22
The Henley Group, Inc., III
Herman Miller, Inc., 8
Hermès International S.A., 34 (upd.)
Hillenbrand Industries, Inc., 10
Hillsdown Holdings plc, 24 (upd.)
Hitachi Zosen Corporation, III
Hitchiner Manufacturing Co., Inc., 23
HMI Industries, Inc., 17
Holnam Inc., 8
Holson Burnes Group, Inc., 14
HON INDUSTRIES Inc., 13
The Hoover Company, 12; 40 (upd.)
Huffy Corporation, 7; 30 (upd.)
Hunt Manufacturing Company, 12
Hunter Fan Company, 13
Hydril Company, 46
Hyster Company, 17
Hyundai Group, III; 7 (upd.)
Icon Health & Fitness, Inc., 38
Igloo Products Corp., 21
Illinois Tool Works Inc., III; 22 (upd.)
IMI plc, 9
Imo Industries Inc., 7; 27 (upd.)
Inchcape PLC, III; 16 (upd.)
Industrie Natuzzi S.p.A., 18
Ingalls Shipbuilding, Inc., 12
Ingersoll-Rand Company, III; 15 (upd.)
Insilco Corporation, 16
Interco Incorporated, III
Interface, Inc., 8
The Interlake Corporation, 8
International Controls Corporation, 10

International Flavors & Fragrances Inc., 38 (upd.)
International Game Technology, 10
Invacare Corporation, 47 (upd.)
Irwin Toy Limited, 14
Ishikawajima-Harima Heavy Industries Co., Ltd., III
J. D'Addario & Company, Inc., 48
J.I. Case Company, 10
J.M. Voith AG, 33
Jabil Circuit, Inc., 36
Jacuzzi Inc., 23
Japan Tobacco Inc., 46 (upd.)
Jayco Inc., 13
Jeld-Wen, Inc., 45
Jenoptik AG, 33
Jervis B. Webb Company, 24
Johnson Controls, Inc., III; 26 (upd.)
Johnson Worldwide Associates, Inc., 28
Johnstown America Industries, Inc., 23
Jones Apparel Group, Inc., 11
Jostens, Inc., 7; 25 (upd.)
Kaman Corporation, 12; 42 (upd.)
Kasper A.S.L., Ltd., 40
Kawasaki Heavy Industries, Ltd., III
Kaydon Corporation, 18
KB Toys, 35 (upd.)
Kerr Group Inc., 24
Kewaunee Scientific Corporation, 25
Key Tronic Corporation, 14
Keystone International, Inc., 11
KHD Konzern, III
Kimball International, Inc., 12; 48 (upd.)
Kit Manufacturing Co., 18
Knape & Vogt Manufacturing Company, 17
Knoll Group Inc., 14
Koala Corporation, 44
Kobe Steel, Ltd., IV; 19 (upd.)
Koch Enterprises, Inc., 29
Kohler Company, 7; 32 (upd.)
Komatsu Ltd., III; 16 (upd.)
Kone Corporation, 27
Konica Corporation, III
Kubota Corporation, III; 26 (upd.)
Kuhlman Corporation, 20
Kyocera Corporation, 21 (upd.)
L-3 Communications Holdings, Inc., 48
L.B. Foster Company, 33
LADD Furniture, Inc., 12
Ladish Co., Inc., 30
Lafarge Corporation, 28
Lafuma S.A., 39
Lakeland Industries, Inc., 45
Lam Research Corporation, 31 (upd.)
Lamson & Sessions Co., 13
Lancer Corporation, 21
The Lane Co., Inc., 12
Leggett & Platt, Inc., 11; 48 (upd.)
Leica Camera AG, 35
Leica Microsystems Holdings GmbH, 35
Lennox International Inc., 8; 28 (upd.)
Lenox, Inc., 12
Lexmark International, Inc., 18
Linamar Corporation, 18
Lincoln Electric Co., 13
Lindal Cedar Homes, Inc., 29
Lindsay Manufacturing Co., 20
Little Tikes Co., 13
Loctite Corporation, 8
Logitech International SA, 28
The Longaberger Company, 12; 44 (upd.)
Louis Vuitton, 10
Lucas Industries PLC, III
Lynch Corporation, 43
M&F Worldwide Corp., 38
MacAndrews & Forbes Holdings Inc., 28
Mackay Envelope Corporation, 45
Mail-Well, Inc., 28
Makita Corporation, 22
MAN Aktiengesellschaft, III
Manitou BF S.A., 27
Manitowoc Company, Inc., 18
Mannesmann AG, III; 14 (upd.)
Margarete Steiff GmbH, 23
Marisa Christina, Inc., 15
Mark IV Industries, Inc., 7; 28 (upd.)
The Marmon Group, 16 (upd.)
Martin Industries, Inc., 44
Marvin Lumber & Cedar Company, 22
Mary Kay, Inc., 30 (upd.)
Masco Corporation, III; 20 (upd.); 39 (upd.)
Master Lock Company, 45
Mattel, Inc., 7; 25 (upd.)
Matthews International Corporation, 29
Maxco Inc., 17
Maxwell Shoe Company, Inc., 30
Maytag Corporation, III; 22 (upd.)
McDermott International, Inc., III
McKechnie plc, 34
Meade Instruments Corporation, 41
Meadowcraft, Inc., 29
Meggitt PLC, 34
Merck & Co., Inc., 34 (upd.)
Merillat Industries Inc., 13
Mestek Inc., 10
Metso Corporation, 30 (upd.)
Mettler-Toledo International Inc., 30
Michael Anthony Jewelers, Inc., 24
Microdot Inc., 8
Mikasa, Inc., 28
Mikohn Gaming Corporation, 39
Miller Industries, Inc., 26
Milton Bradley Company, 21
Mine Safety Appliances Company, 31
Minolta Co., Ltd., III; 18 (upd.); 43 (upd.)
Minuteman International Inc., 46
Mitsubishi Heavy Industries, Ltd., III; 7 (upd.)
Mity Enterprises, Inc., 38
Modine Manufacturing Company, 8
Moen Incorporated, 12
Mohawk Industries, Inc., 19
Molex Incorporated, 11
Montres Rolex S.A., 13; 34 (upd.)
Motorcar Parts & Accessories, Inc., 47
Moulinex S.A., 22
Movado Group, Inc., 28
Mr. Coffee, Inc., 15
Mr. Gasket Inc., 15
Mueller Industries, Inc., 7
Nashua Corporation, 8
National Envelope Corporation, 32
National Gypsum Company, 10
National Picture & Frame Company, 24
National Standard Co., 13
NCR Corporation, 30 (upd.)
New Balance Athletic Shoe, Inc., 25
New Holland N.V., 22
Newcor, Inc., 40
Newell Co., 9
Newport News Shipbuilding Inc., 13; 38 (upd.)
NHK Spring Co., Ltd., III
NIKE, Inc., 36 (upd.)
Nikon Corporation, III; 48 (upd.)
Nintendo Co., Ltd., III; 7 (upd.)
Nippon Seiko K.K., III
Nippondenso Co., Ltd., III
NKK Corporation, 28 (upd.)
NordicTrack, 22
Nordson Corporation, 11; 48 (upd.)
Nortek, Inc., 34
Norton Company, 8
Norton McNaughton, Inc., 27
Novellus Systems, Inc., 18
NTN Corporation, III; 47 (upd.)
Nu-kote Holding, Inc., 18
O'Sullivan Industries Holdings, Inc., 34
Oak Industries Inc., 21
Oakwood Homes Corporation, 15
The Ohio Art Company, 14
Oil-Dri Corporation of America, 20
Oneida Ltd., 7; 31 (upd.)
Optische Werke G. Rodenstock, 44
Osmonics, Inc., 18
Otis Elevator Company, Inc., 13; 39 (upd.)
Outboard Marine Corporation, III; 20 (upd.)
Owens Corning Corporation, 20 (upd.)
Owosso Corporation, 29
P & F Industries, Inc., 45
Pacer Technology, 40
Pacific Dunlop Limited, 10
Pall Corporation, 9
Palm Harbor Homes, Inc., 39
Panavision Inc., 24
Park Corp., 22
Parker-Hannifin Corporation, III; 24 (upd.)
Patrick Industries, Inc., 30
Pechiney SA, 45 (upd.)
Pella Corporation, 12; 39 (upd.)
Penn Engineering & Manufacturing Corp., 28
Pentair, Inc., 26 (upd.)
Pentech International, Inc., 29
The Perkin-Elmer Corporation, 7
Phillips-Van Heusen Corporation, 24
Physio-Control International Corp., 18
Pilkington plc, 34 (upd.)
Pioneer Electronic Corporation, III
Pitney Bowes, Inc., 19
Pittway Corporation, 33 (upd.)
PlayCore, Inc., 27
Playmates Toys, 23
Playskool, Inc., 25
Pleasant Company, 27
Ply Gem Industries Inc., 12
Polaris Industries Inc., 12; 35 (upd.)
Polaroid Corporation, III; 7 (upd.); 28 (upd.)
PPG Industries, Inc., 22 (upd.)
Prada Holding B.V., 45
Praxair, Inc., 48 (upd.)
Precision Castparts Corp., 15
Premark International, Inc., III
Presstek, Inc., 33
Prince Sports Group, Inc., 15
Printronix, Inc., 18
Pulaski Furniture Corporation, 33
Pumpkin Masters, Inc., 48
Puritan-Bennett Corporation, 13
Purolator Products Company, 21
PW Eagle, Inc., 48
Quixote Corporation, 15
R. Griggs Group Limited, 23
Racing Champions Corporation, 37
Radio Flyer Inc., 34
Rapala-Normark Group, Ltd., 30
Raven Industries, Inc., 33
Raychem Corporation, 8
Rayovac Corporation, 39 (upd.)
Recovery Engineering, Inc., 25
Red Wing Shoe Company, Inc., 9
Regal-Beloit Corporation, 18
Reichhold Chemicals, Inc., 10
Remington Arms Company, Inc., 12; 40 (upd.)
Remington Products Company, L.L.C., 42
RENK AG, 37
Revell-Monogram Inc., 16
Revere Ware Corporation, 22
Rexam PLC, 32 (upd.)

Rexnord Corporation, 21
RF Micro Devices, Inc., 43
Rheinmetall Berlin AG, 9
Riddell Sports Inc., 22
Rieter Holding AG, 42
River Oaks Furniture, Inc., 43
RMC Group p.l.c., 34 (upd.)
Roadmaster Industries, Inc., 16
Robbins & Myers Inc., 15
Robertson-Ceco Corporation, 19
RockShox, Inc., 26
Rockwell Automation, 43 (upd.)
Rohde & Schwarz GmbH & Co. KG, 39
ROHN Industries, Inc., 22
Rohr Incorporated, 9
Roland Corporation, 38
Rollerblade, Inc., 15; 34 (upd.)
Roper Industries Inc., 15
Rotork plc, 46
Royal Appliance Manufacturing Company, 15
Royal Canin S.A., 39
Royal Doulton plc, 14; 38 (upd.)
RPM, Inc., 8; 36 (upd.)
Rubbermaid Incorporated, III
Russ Berrie and Company, Inc., 12
S.C. Johnson & Son, Inc., 28 (upd.)
Sabaté Diosos SA, 48
Safeskin Corporation, 18
Salant Corporation, 12
Salton, Inc., 30
Samsonite Corporation, 13; 43 (upd.)
Sandvik AB, 32 (upd.)
Sanrio Company, Ltd., 38
Sauder Woodworking Company, 12; 35 (upd.)
Sawtek Inc., 43 (upd.)
Schindler Holding AG, 29
Schlumberger Limited, III
Scotsman Industries, Inc., 20
Scott Fetzer Company, 12
The Scotts Company, 22
Scovill Fasteners Inc., 24
Sealed Air Corporation, 14
Sealy Inc., 12
Segway LLC, 48
Seiko Corporation, III; 17 (upd.)
Select Comfort Corporation, 34
The Selmer Company, Inc., 19
Semitool, Inc., 18
Sequa Corp., 13
Serta, Inc., 28
Shakespeare Company, 22
Shelby Williams Industries, Inc., 14
Shorewood Packaging Corporation, 28
SIFCO Industries, Inc., 41
Simmons Company, 47
Simula, Inc., 41
The Singer Company N.V., 30 (upd.)
Skis Rossignol S.A., 15; 43 (upd.)
Skyline Corporation, 30
SLI, Inc., 48
Smead Manufacturing Co., 17
Smith & Wesson Corporation, 30
Smith Corona Corp., 13
Smith International, Inc., 15
Smiths Industries PLC, 25
Snap-on Tools Corporation, 7
Snap-On, Incorporated, 27 (upd.)
Sparton Corporation, 18
Specialty Equipment Companies, Inc., 25
Speizman Industries, Inc., 44
SPS Technologies, Inc., 30
SPX Corporation, 47 (upd.)
Stanadyne Automotive Corporation, 37
Standex International Corporation, 17
Stanley Furniture Company, Inc., 34
The Stanley Works, III; 20 (upd.)
Stearns, Inc., 43
Steelcase, Inc., 7; 27 (upd.)
Steinway Musical Properties, Inc., 19
Stewart & Stevenson Services Inc., 11
Stryker Corporation, 11; 29 (upd.)
Sturm, Ruger & Company, Inc., 19
Sub-Zero Freezer Co., Inc., 31
Sudbury Inc., 16
Sulzer Brothers Limited (Gebruder Sulzer Aktiengesellschaft), III
Sumitomo Heavy Industries, Ltd., III; 42 (upd.)
Susquehanna Pfaltzgraff Company, 8
Swank Inc., 17
Swarovski International Holding AG, 40
The Swatch Group SA, 26
Swedish Match AB, 12; 39 (upd.)
Sweetheart Cup Company, Inc., 36
Sybron International Corp., 14
Syratech Corp., 14
TAB Products Co., 17
TAG Heuer International SA, 25
Taiwan Semiconductor Manufacturing Company Ltd., 47
Tarkett Sommer AG, 25
Taylor Guitars, 48
Taylor Made Golf Co., 23
TearDrop Golf Company, 32
Tecumseh Products Company, 8
Tektronix, Inc., 8
Tennant Company, 13; 33 (upd.)
Terex Corporation, 7; 40 (upd.)
Thales S.A., 42
Thermadyne Holding Corporation, 19
Thermo BioAnalysis Corp., 25
Thermo Electron Corporation, 7
Thermo Fibertek, Inc., 24
Thermo Instrument Systems Inc., 11
Thermo King Corporation, 13
Thiokol Corporation, 22 (upd.)
Thomas & Betts Corp., 11
Thomas Industries Inc., 29
Thomasville Furniture Industries, Inc., 12
Thor Industries, Inc., 39
Thyssen Krupp AG, 28 (upd.)
Timex Corporation, 7; 25 (upd.)
The Timken Company, 8; 42 (upd.)
TJ International, Inc., 19
Todd Shipyards Corporation, 14
Tokheim Corporation, 21
Tonka Corporation, 25
Toolex International N.V., 26
Topps Company, Inc., 13
The Toro Company, 7; 26 (upd.)
The Torrington Company, 13
TOTO LTD., 28 (upd.)
Town & Country Corporation, 19
Toymax International, Inc., 29
Toyoda Automatic Loom Works, Ltd., III
Trek Bicycle Corporation, 16
Trico Products Corporation, 15
TriMas Corp., 11
Trinity Industries, Incorporated, 7
TRINOVA Corporation, III
Triumph Group, Inc., 31
Tubos de Acero de Mexico, S.A. (TAMSA), 41
Tultex Corporation, 13
Tupperware Corporation, 28
Twin Disc, Inc., 21
Ty Inc., 33
Tyco International Ltd., III; 28 (upd.)
Tyco Toys, Inc., 12
U.S. Robotics Inc., 9
Ube Industries, Ltd., 38 (upd.)
United Defense, L.P., 30
United Dominion Industries Limited, 8; 16 (upd.)
United Industrial Corporation, 37
United States Filter Corporation, 20
Unitog Co., 19
Utah Medical Products, Inc., 36
Vaillant GmbH, 44
Valmet Corporation (Valmet Oy), III
Valmont Industries, Inc., 19
The Valspar Corporation, 8
Vari-Lite International, Inc., 35
Varian, Inc., 48 (upd.)
Varity Corporation, III
Varlen Corporation, 16
Varta AG, 23
Velcro Industries N.V., 19
Vermeer Manufacturing Company, 17
Vickers plc, 27
Victorinox AG, 21
Viessmann Werke GmbH & Co., 37
Villeroy & Boch AG, 37
Virco Manufacturing Corporation, 17
Vitro Corporativo S.A. de C.V., 34
Vorwerk & Co., 27
Vosper Thornycroft Holding plc, 41
W.H. Brady Co., 17
W.L. Gore & Associates, Inc., 14
W.W. Grainger, Inc., 26 (upd.)
Wabash National Corp., 13
Wabtec Corporation, 40
Walbro Corporation, 13
Washington Scientific Industries, Inc., 17
Wassall Plc, 18
Waterford Wedgwood plc, 12; 34 (upd.)
Waters Corporation, 43
Watts Industries, Inc., 19
WD-40 Company, 18
Weber-Stephen Products Co., 40
Welbilt Corp., 19
Wellman, Inc., 8
Weru Aktiengesellschaft, 18
West Bend Co., 14
Western Digital Corp., 25
Whirlpool Corporation, III; 12 (upd.)
White Consolidated Industries Inc., 13
Williamson-Dickie Manufacturing Company, 45 (upd.)
Wilson Sporting Goods Company, 24
Windmere Corporation, 16
WinsLoew Furniture, Inc., 21
WMS Industries, Inc., 15
Wolverine Tube Inc., 23
Wood-Mode, Inc., 23
Woodward Governor Co., 13
Wyant Corporation, 30
Wyman-Gordon Company, 14
Wynn's International, Inc., 33
X-Rite, Inc., 48
Yamaha Corporation, III; 16 (upd.)
York International Corp., 13
Young Innovations, Inc., 44
Zero Corporation, 17
Zippo Manufacturing Company, 18
Zodiac S.A., 36
Zygo Corporation, 42


## MATERIALS


AK Steel Holding Corporation, 19
American Biltrite Inc., 16
American Colloid Co., 13
American Standard Inc., III
Ameriwood Industries International Corp., 17
Apogee Enterprises, Inc., 8
Asahi Glass Company, Limited, III
Bairnco Corporation, 28
Bayou Steel Corporation, 31
Blessings Corp., 19
Blue Circle Industries PLC, III

Boral Limited, III
British Vita PLC, 9
Cameron & Barkley Company, 28
Carborundum Company, 15
Carl-Zeiss-Stiftung, 34 (upd.)
Carlisle Companies Incorporated, 8
Cemex SA de CV, 20
CertainTeed Corporation, 35
Chargeurs International, 21 (upd.)
Chemfab Corporation, 35
Compagnie de Saint-Gobain S.A., III; 16 (upd.)
Cookson Group plc, III; 44 (upd.)
Corning Incorporated, III
CSR Limited, III
Dal-Tile International Inc., 22
The David J. Joseph Company, 14
The Dexter Corporation, 12 (upd.)
Dyckerhoff AG, 35
ECC Group plc, III
Edw. C. Levy Co., 42
84 Lumber Company, 9; 39 (upd.)
English China Clays Ltd., 15 (upd.); 40 (upd.)
Envirodyne Industries, Inc., 17
Feldmuhle Nobel A.G., III
Fibreboard Corporation, 16
Florida Rock Industries, Inc., 46
Foamex International Inc., 17
Formica Corporation, 13
GAF Corporation, 22 (upd.)
The Geon Company, 11
Giant Cement Holding, Inc., 23
Gibraltar Steel Corporation, 37
Granite Rock Company, 26
Groupe Sidel S.A., 21
Harbison-Walker Refractories Company, 24
Harrisons & Crosfield plc, III
Heidelberger Zement AG, 31
Hexcel Corporation, 28
''Holderbank'' Financière Glaris Ltd., III
Holnam Inc., 39 (upd.)
Howmet Corp., 12
Ibstock Brick Ltd., 14; 37 (upd.)
Imerys S.A., 40 (upd.)
Joseph T. Ryerson & Son, Inc., 15
Lafarge Coppée S.A., III
Lafarge Corporation, 28
Lehigh Portland Cement Company, 23
Manville Corporation, III; 7 (upd.)
Matsushita Electric Works, Ltd., III; 7 (upd.)
Medusa Corporation, 24
Mitsubishi Materials Corporation, III
Nippon Sheet Glass Company, Limited, III
OmniSource Corporation, 14
Onoda Cement Co., Ltd., III
Owens-Corning Fiberglass Corporation, III
Pilkington plc, III; 34 (upd.)
Pioneer International Limited, III
PPG Industries, Inc., III
Redland plc, III
RMC Group p.l.c., III
Rock of Ages Corporation, 37
The Rugby Group plc, 31
Schuff Steel Company, 26
Sekisui Chemical Co., Ltd., III
Shaw Industries, 9
The Sherwin-Williams Company, III; 13 (upd.)
Simplex Technologies Inc., 21
Sommer-Allibert S.A., 19
Southdown, Inc., 14
Spartech Corporation, 19
Ssangyong Cement Industrial Co., Ltd., III
Sun Distributors L.P., 12
Tarmac PLC, III
Tarmac plc, 28 (upd.)
TOTO LTD., III; 28 (upd.)
Toyo Sash Co., Ltd., III
Tuscarora Inc., 29
U.S. Aggregates, Inc., 42
Ube Industries, Ltd., III
USG Corporation, III; 26 (upd.)
Vulcan Materials Company, 7
Wacker-Chemie GmbH, 35
Walter Industries, Inc., III
Waxman Industries, Inc., 9
Zoltek Companies, Inc., 37

## MINING & METALS

A.M. Castle & Co., 25
Aggregate Industries plc, 36
Aktiebolaget SKF, 38 (upd.)
Alcan Aluminium Limited, IV; 31 (upd.)
Alleghany Corporation, 10
Allegheny Ludlum Corporation, 8
Altos Hornos de México, S.A. de C.V., 42
Aluminum Company of America, IV; 20 (upd.)
AMAX Inc., IV
Amsted Industries Incorporated, 7
Anglo American Corporation of South Africa Limited, IV; 16 (upd.)
ARBED S.A., IV, 22 (upd.)
Arch Mineral Corporation, 7
Armco Inc., IV
ASARCO Incorporated, IV
Ashanti Goldfields Company Limited, 43
Atchison Casting Corporation, 39
Barrick Gold Corporation, 34
Battle Mountain Gold Company, 23
Bethlehem Steel Corporation, IV; 7 (upd.); 27 (upd.)
Birmingham Steel Corporation, 13; 40 (upd.)
Boart Longyear Company, 26
Boral Limited, 43 (upd.)
British Coal Corporation, IV
British Steel plc, IV; 19 (upd.)
Broken Hill Proprietary Company Ltd., IV, 22 (upd.)
Brush Wellman Inc., 14
Buderus AG, 37
Carpenter Technology Corporation, 13
Chaparral Steel Co., 13
Christensen Boyles Corporation, 26
Cleveland-Cliffs Inc., 13
Coal India Ltd., IV; 44 (upd.)
Cockerill Sambre Group, IV; 26 (upd.)
Coeur d'Alene Mines Corporation, 20
Cold Spring Granite Company, 16
Cominco Ltd., 37
Commercial Metals Company, 15; 42 (upd.)
Companhia Vale do Rio Doce, 43
Companhia Vale do Rio Duce, IV
Corporacion Nacional del Cobre de Chile, 40
CRA Limited, IV
Cyprus Amax Minerals Company, 21
Cyprus Minerals Company, 7
Daido Steel Co., Ltd., IV
De Beers Consolidated Mines Limited/De Beers Centenary AG, IV; 7 (upd.); 28 (upd.)
Degussa Group, IV
Dofasco Inc., IV; 24 (upd.)
Echo Bay Mines Ltd., IV; 38 (upd.)
Engelhard Corporation, IV
Fansteel Inc., 19
Fluor Corporation, 34 (upd.)
Freeport-McMoRan Inc., IV; 7 (upd.)
Fried. Krupp GmbH, IV
Gencor Ltd., IV, 22 (upd.)
Geneva Steel, 7
Gold Fields of South Africa Ltd., IV
Grupo Mexico, S.A. de C.V., 40
Handy & Harman, 23
Hanson PLC, 30 (upd.)
Hecla Mining Company, 20
Hemlo Gold Mines Inc., 9
Heraeus Holding GmbH, IV
Hitachi Metals, Ltd., IV
Hoesch AG, IV
Homestake Mining Company, 12; 38 (upd.)
The Hudson Bay Mining and Smelting Company, Limited, 12
Hylsamex, S.A. de C.V., 39
IMCO Recycling, Incorporated, 32
Imerys S.A., 40 (upd.)
Imetal S.A., IV
Inco Limited, IV; 45 (upd.)
Industrias Penoles, S.A. de C.V., 22
Inland Steel Industries, Inc., IV; 19 (upd.)
Intermet Corporation, 32
Ispat Inland Inc., 40 (upd.)
Ispat International N.V., 30
Johnson Matthey PLC, IV; 16 (upd.)
JSC MMC Norilsk Nickel, 48
Kaiser Aluminum & Chemical Corporation, IV
Kawasaki Steel Corporation, IV
Kennecott Corporation, 7; 27 (upd.)
Kentucky Electric Steel, Inc., 31
Kerr-McGee Corporation, 22 (upd.)
Kinross Gold Corporation, 36
Klockner-Werke AG, IV
Kobe Steel, Ltd., IV; 19 (upd.)
Koninklijke Nederlandsche Hoogovens en Staalfabrieken NV, IV
Laclede Steel Company, 15
Layne Christensen Company, 19
Lonrho Plc, 21
The LTV Corporation, 24 (upd.)
Lukens Inc., 14
Magma Copper Company, 7
The Marmon Group, IV; 16 (upd.)
MAXXAM Inc., 8
Meridian Gold, Incorporated, 47
Metaleurop S.A., 21
Metallgesellschaft AG, IV
Minerals and Metals Trading Corporation of India Ltd., IV
Minerals Technologies Inc., 11
Mitsui Mining & Smelting Co., Ltd., IV
Mitsui Mining Company, Limited, IV
National Steel Corporation, 12
NERCO, Inc., 7
Newmont Mining Corporation, 7
Niagara Corporation, 28
Nichimen Corporation, IV
Nippon Light Metal Company, Ltd., IV
Nippon Steel Corporation, IV; 17 (upd.)
Nisshin Steel Co., Ltd., IV
NKK Corporation, IV; 28 (upd.)
Noranda Inc., IV; 7 (upd.)
North Star Steel Company, 18
Nucor Corporation, 7; 21 (upd.)
Oglebay Norton Company, 17
Okura & Co., Ltd., IV
Oregon Metallurgical Corporation, 20
Oregon Steel Mills, Inc., 14
Outokumpu Oyj, 38
Park Corp., 22
Peabody Coal Company, 10
Peabody Energy Corporation, 45 (upd.)
Peabody Holding Company, Inc., IV
Pechiney, IV
Pechiney SA, 45 (upd.)
Peter Kiewit Sons' Inc., 8
Phelps Dodge Corporation, IV; 28 (upd.)
The Pittston Company, IV; 19 (upd.)

Placer Dome Inc., 20
Pohang Iron and Steel Company Ltd., IV
Potash Corporation of Saskatchewan Inc., 18
Quanex Corporation, 13
RAG AG, 35
Reliance Steel & Aluminum Co., 19
Republic Engineered Steels, Inc., 7; 26 (upd.)
Reynolds Metals Company, IV
Rio Tinto plc, 19 (upd.)
RMC Group p.l.c., 34 (upd.)
Roanoke Electric Steel Corporation, 45
Rouge Steel Company, 8
The RTZ Corporation PLC, IV
Ruhrkohle AG, IV
Ryerson Tull, Inc., 40 (upd.)
Saarberg-Konzern, IV
Salzgitter AG, IV
Sandvik AB, IV
Schnitzer Steel Industries, Inc., 19
Southern Peru Copper Corporation, 40
Southwire Company, Inc., 8; 23 (upd.)
Steel Authority of India Ltd., IV
Stelco Inc., IV
Stillwater Mining Company, 47
Sumitomo Metal Industries, Ltd., IV
Sumitomo Metal Mining Co., Ltd., IV
Tata Iron & Steel Co. Ltd., IV; 44 (upd.)
Teck Corporation, 27
Texas Industries, Inc., 8
Thyssen AG, IV
The Timken Company, 8; 42 (upd.)
Titanium Metals Corporation, 21
Tomen Corporation, IV
U.S. Borax, Inc., 42
Ugine S.A., 20
NV Umicore SA, 47
Usinor SA, IV; 42 (upd.)
Usinor Sacilor, IV
VIAG Aktiengesellschaft, IV
Voest-Alpine Stahl AG, IV
Walter Industries, Inc., 22 (upd.)
Weirton Steel Corporation, IV; 26 (upd.)
Westmoreland Coal Company, 7
Wheeling-Pittsburgh Corp., 7
WMC, Limited, 43
Worthington Industries, Inc., 7; 21 (upd.)
Zambia Industrial and Mining Corporation Ltd., IV

## PAPER & FORESTRY

Abitibi-Consolidated, Inc., 25 (upd.)
Abitibi-Price Inc., IV
Amcor Limited, IV; 19 (upd.)
American Pad & Paper Company, 20
Arjo Wiggins Appleton p.l.c., 34
Asplundh Tree Expert Co., 20
Avery Dennison Corporation, IV
Badger Paper Mills, Inc., 15
Beckett Papers, 23
Bemis Company, Inc., 8
Bohemia, Inc., 13
Boise Cascade Corporation, IV; 8 (upd.); 32 (upd.)
Bowater PLC, IV
Bunzl plc, IV
Canfor Corporation, 42
Caraustar Industries, Inc., 19; 44 (upd.)
Carter Lumber Company, 45
Champion International Corporation, IV; 20 (upd.)
Chesapeake Corporation, 8; 30 (upd.)
Consolidated Papers, Inc., 8; 36 (upd.)
Crane & Co., Inc., 26
Crown Vantage Inc., 29
CSS Industries, Inc., 35
Daio Paper Corporation, IV
Daishowa Paper Manufacturing Co., Ltd., IV
Deltic Timber Corporation, 46
Dillard Paper Company, 11
Domtar Inc., IV
Enso-Gutzeit Oy, IV
Esselte Pendaflex Corporation, 11
Federal Paper Board Company, Inc., 8
FiberMark, Inc., 37
Fletcher Challenge Ltd., IV
Fort Howard Corporation, 8
Fort James Corporation, 22 (upd.)
Georgia-Pacific Corporation, IV; 9 (upd.); 47 (upd.)
Groupe Rougier SA, 21
Guilbert S.A., 42
Honshu Paper Co., Ltd., IV
International Paper Company, IV; 15 (upd.); 47 (upd.)
James River Corporation of Virginia, IV
Japan Pulp and Paper Company Limited, IV
Jefferson Smurfit Group plc, IV
Jujo Paper Co., Ltd., IV
Kimberly-Clark Corporation, 16 (upd.); 43 (upd.)
Kruger Inc., 17
Kymmene Corporation, IV
Longview Fibre Company, 8; 37 (upd.)
Louisiana-Pacific Corporation, IV; 31 (upd.)
MacMillan Bloedel Limited, IV
The Mead Corporation, IV; 19 (upd.)
Metsa-Serla Oy, IV
Mo och Domsjö AB, IV
Monadnock Paper Mills, Inc., 21
Mosinee Paper Corporation, 15
Nashua Corporation, 8
National Envelope Corporation, 32
NCH Corporation, 8
Oji Paper Co., Ltd., IV
P.H. Glatfelter Company, 8; 30 (upd.)
Packaging Corporation of America, 12
Papeteries de Lancey, 23
Plum Creek Timber Company, Inc., 43
Pope and Talbot, Inc., 12
Potlatch Corporation, 8; 34 (upd.)
PWA Group, IV
Rayonier Inc., 24
Rengo Co., Ltd., IV
Reno de Medici S.p.A., 41
Rexam PLC, 32 (upd.)
Riverwood International Corporation, 11; 48 (upd.)
Rock-Tenn Company, 13
St. Joe Paper Company, 8
Sanyo-Kokusaku Pulp Co., Ltd., IV
Scott Paper Company, IV; 31 (upd.)
Sealed Air Corporation, 14
Sierra Pacific Industries, 22
Simpson Investment Company, 17
Specialty Coatings Inc., 8
Stone Container Corporation, IV
Stora Enso Oyj, 36 (upd.)
Stora Kopparbergs Bergslags AB, IV
Svenska Cellulosa Aktiebolaget SCA, IV; 28 (upd.)
Temple-Inland Inc., IV; 31 (upd.)
TJ International, Inc., 19
U.S. Timberlands Company, L.P., 42
Union Camp Corporation, IV
United Paper Mills Ltd. (Yhtyneet Paperitehtaat Oy), IV
Universal Forest Products Inc., 10
UPM-Kymmene Corporation, 19
West Fraser Timber Co. Ltd., 17
Westvaco Corporation, IV; 19 (upd.)
Weyerhaeuser Company, IV; 9 (upd.); 28 (upd.)
Wickes Inc., 25 (upd.)
Willamette Industries, Inc., IV; 31 (upd.)
WTD Industries, Inc., 20

## PERSONAL SERVICES

AARP, 27
ADT Security Services, Inc., 12; 44 (upd.)
American Retirement Corporation, 42
Arthur Murray International, Inc., 32
Berlitz International, Inc., 39 (upd.)
Carriage Services, Inc., 37
Childtime Learning Centers, Inc., 34
Corinthian Colleges, Inc., 39
Correctional Services Corporation, 30
CUC International Inc., 16
Davis Service Group PLC, 45
DeVry Incorporated, 29
Educational Testing Service, 12
The Ford Foundation, 34
Franklin Quest Co., 11
Goodwill Industries International, Inc., 16
Jazzercise, Inc., 45
The John D. and Catherine T. MacArthur Foundation, 34
Kaplan, Inc., 42
KinderCare Learning Centers, Inc., 13
The Loewen Group Inc., 16; 40 (upd.)
Management and Training Corporation, 28
Manpower, Inc., 9
Michael Page International plc, 45
Regis Corporation, 18
The Rockefeller Foundation, 34
Rollins, Inc., 11
Rosenbluth International Inc., 14
Rotary International, 31
The Salvation Army USA, 32
Service Corporation International, 6
SOS Staffing Services, 25
Stewart Enterprises, Inc., 20
Supercuts Inc., 26
Weight Watchers International Inc., 12; 33 (upd.)
Youth Services International, Inc., 21
YWCA of the U.S.A., 45

## PETROLEUM

Abu Dhabi National Oil Company, IV; 45 (upd.)
Agway, Inc., 21 (upd.)
Alberta Energy Company Ltd., 16; 43 (upd.)
Amerada Hess Corporation, IV; 21 (upd.)
Amoco Corporation, IV; 14 (upd.)
Anadarko Petroleum Corporation, 10
ANR Pipeline Co., 17
Anschutz Corp., 12
Apache Corporation, 10; 32 (upd.)
Arctic Slope Regional Corporation, 38
Ashland Inc., 19
Ashland Oil, Inc., IV
Atlantic Richfield Company, IV; 31 (upd.)
Baker Hughes Incorporated, 22 (upd.)
Belco Oil & Gas Corp., 40
Benton Oil and Gas Company, 47
Berry Petroleum Company, 47
BJ Services Company, 25
BP p.l.c., 45 (upd.)
The British Petroleum Company plc, IV; 7 (upd.); 21 (upd.)
British-Borneo Oil & Gas PLC, 34
Broken Hill Proprietary Company Ltd., 22 (upd.)
Burlington Resources Inc., 10
Burmah Castrol PLC, IV; 30 (upd.)
Callon Petroleum Company, 47

Caltex Petroleum Corporation, 19
Chevron Corporation, IV; 19 (upd.)
ChevronTexaco Corporation, 47 (upd.)
Chiles Offshore Corporation, 9
China National Petroleum Corporation, 46
Chinese Petroleum Corporation, IV; 31 (upd.)
CITGO Petroleum Corporation, IV; 31 (upd.)
The Coastal Corporation, IV; 31 (upd.)
Compañia Española de Petróleos S.A., IV
Comstock Resources, Inc., 47
Conoco Inc., IV; 16 (upd.)
Cooper Cameron Corporation, 20 (upd.)
Cosmo Oil Co., Ltd., IV
Crown Central Petroleum Corporation, 7
DeepTech International Inc., 21
Den Norse Stats Oljeselskap AS, IV
Deutsche BP Aktiengesellschaft, 7
Diamond Shamrock, Inc., IV
Egyptian General Petroluem Corporation, IV
Elf Aquitaine SA, 21 (upd.)
Empresa Colombiana de Petróleos, IV
Enbridge Inc., 43
Energen Corporation, 21
Enron Corporation, 19
Ente Nazionale Idrocarburi, IV
Enterprise Oil plc, 11
Entreprise Nationale Sonatrach, IV
Exxon Corporation, IV; 7 (upd.); 32 (upd.)
Ferrellgas Partners, L.P., 35
FINA, Inc., 7
Flying J Inc., 19
Forest Oil Corporation, 19
OAO Gazprom, 42
General Sekiyu K.K., IV
Giant Industries, Inc., 19
Global Industries, Ltd., 37
Global Marine Inc., 9
GlobalSantaFe Corporation, 48 (upd.)
Grey Wolf, Inc., 43
Halliburton Company, 25 (upd.)
Helmerich & Payne, Inc., 18
Holly Corporation, 12
Hunt Consolidated, Inc., 27 (upd.)
Hunt Oil Company, 7
Husky Energy Inc., 47
Idemitsu Kosan K.K., IV
Imperial Oil Limited, IV; 25 (upd.)
Indian Oil Corporation Ltd., IV; 48 (upd.)
Kanematsu Corporation, IV
Kerr-McGee Corporation, IV; 22 (upd.)
Kinder Morgan, Inc., 45
King Ranch, Inc., 14
Koch Industries, Inc., IV; 20 (upd.)
Koppers Industries, Inc., 26 (upd.)
Kuwait Petroleum Corporation, IV
Libyan National Oil Corporation, IV
The Louisiana Land and Exploration Company, 7
OAO LUKOIL, 40
Lyondell Petrochemical Company, IV
MAPCO Inc., IV
Maxus Energy Corporation, 7
McDermott International, Inc., 37 (upd.)
Meteor Industries Inc., 33
Mitchell Energy and Development Corporation, 7
Mitsubishi Oil Co., Ltd., IV
Mobil Corporation, IV; 7 (upd.); 21 (upd.)
Murphy Oil Corporation, 7; 32 (upd.)
Nabors Industries, Inc., 9
National Iranian Oil Company, IV
Neste Oy, IV
NGC Corporation, 18
Nigerian National Petroleum Corporation, IV
Nippon Oil Company, Limited, IV
OAO NK YUKOS, 47
Noble Affiliates, Inc., 11
OAO Gazprom, 42
OAO LUKOIL, 40
OAO NK YUKOS, 47
OAO Surgutneftegaz, 48
OAO Tatneft, 45
Occidental Petroleum Corporation, IV; 25 (upd.)
Oil and Natural Gas Commission, IV
ÖMV Aktiengesellschaft, IV
Oryx Energy Company, 7
Parker Drilling Company, 28
Patina Oil & Gas Corporation, 24
Pennzoil Company, IV; 20 (upd.)
PERTAMINA, IV
Petro-Canada Limited, IV
PetroFina S.A., IV; 26 (upd.)
Petróleo Brasileiro S.A., IV
Petróleos de Portugal S.A., IV
Petróleos de Venezuela S.A., IV
Petróleos del Ecuador, IV
Petróleos Mexicanos, IV; 19 (upd.)
Petroleum Development Oman LLC, IV
Petronas, IV
Phillips Petroleum Company, IV; 40 (upd.)
Pogo Producing Company, 39
Premcor Inc., 37
Qatar General Petroleum Corporation, IV
Quaker State Corporation, 7; 21 (upd.)
Range Resources Corporation, 45
Repsol S.A., IV; 16 (upd.)
Repsol-YPF S.A., 40 (upd.)
Resource America, Inc., 42
Rowan Companies, Inc., 43
Royal Dutch Petroleum Company/ The "Shell" Transport and Trading Company p.l.c., IV
Santa Fe International Corporation, 38
Sasol Limited, IV; 47 (upd.)
Saudi Arabian Oil Company, IV; 17 (upd.)
Schlumberger Limited, 17 (upd.)
Seagull Energy Corporation, 11
Seitel, Inc., 47
Shanghai Petrochemical Co., Ltd., 18
Shell Oil Company, IV; 14 (upd.); 41 (upd.)
Showa Shell Sekiyu K.K., IV
Société Nationale Elf Aquitaine, IV; 7 (upd.)
Suburban Propane Partners, L.P., 30
Sun Company, Inc., IV
Sunoco, Inc., 28 (upd.)
OAO Surgutneftegaz, 48
Talisman Energy Inc., 9; 47 (upd.)
OAO Tatneft, 45
Tesoro Petroleum Corporation, 7; 45 (upd.)
Texaco Inc., IV; 14 (upd.); 41 (upd.)
Tidewater Inc., 37 (upd.)
Tom Brown, Inc., 37
Tonen Corporation, IV; 16 (upd.)
Tosco Corporation, 7
TOTAL S.A., IV; 24 (upd.)
TransMontaigne Inc., 28
Transocean Sedco Forex Inc., 45
Travel Ports of America, Inc., 17
Triton Energy Corporation, 11
Türkiye Petrolleri Anonim Ortakliği, IV
Ultramar Diamond Shamrock Corporation, IV; 31 (upd.)
Union Texas Petroleum Holdings, Inc., 9
Unocal Corporation, IV; 24 (upd.)
USX Corporation, IV; 7 (upd.)
Valero Energy Corporation, 7
Varco International, Inc., 42
Vastar Resources, Inc., 24
Vintage Petroleum, Inc., 42
Wascana Energy Inc., 13
Weatherford International, Inc., 39
Western Atlas Inc., 12
Western Company of North America, 15
Western Gas Resources, Inc., 45
The Williams Companies, Inc., IV; 31 (upd.)
World Fuel Services Corporation, 47
YPF Sociedad Anonima, IV

## PUBLISHING & PRINTING

A.B.Dick Company, 28
A.H. Belo Corporation, 10; 30 (upd.)
Advance Publications Inc., IV; 19 (upd.)
Advanced Marketing Services, Inc., 34
Affiliated Publications, Inc., 7
Agence France-Presse, 34
American Banknote Corporation, 30
American Greetings Corporation, 7, 22 (upd.)
American Media, Inc., 27
American Printing House for the Blind, 26
Andrews McMeel Universal, 40
The Antioch Company, 40
Arandell Corporation, 37
Arnoldo Mondadori Editore S.p.A., IV; 19 (upd.)
The Associated Press, 31 (upd.)
The Atlantic Group, 23
Axel Springer Verlag AG, IV; 20 (upd.)
Banta Corporation, 12; 32 (upd.)
Bauer Publishing Group, 7
Berlitz International, Inc., 13
Bernard C. Harris Publishing Company, Inc., 39
Bertelsmann A.G., IV; 15 (upd.); 43 (upd.)
Big Flower Press Holdings, Inc., 21
Blue Mountain Arts, Inc., 29
Book-of-the-Month Club, Inc., 13
Bowne & Co., Inc., 23
Broderbund Software, 29 (upd.)
Brown Printing Company, 26
Burda Holding GmbH. & Co., 23
The Bureau of National Affairs, Inc., 23
Butterick Co., Inc., 23
Cadmus Communications Corporation, 23
Cahners Business Information, 43
CCH Inc., 14
Central Newspapers, Inc., 10
Champion Industries, Inc., 28
The Chronicle Publishing Company, Inc., 23
Chrysalis Group plc, 40
CMP Media Inc., 26
Commerce Clearing House, Inc., 7
Concepts Direct, Inc., 39
The Condé Nast Publications Inc., 13
Consumers Union, 26
The Copley Press, Inc., 23
Courier Corporation, 41
Cowles Media Company, 23
Cox Enterprises, Inc., IV; 22 (upd.)
Crain Communications, Inc., 12; 35 (upd.)
Current, Inc., 37
Dai Nippon Printing Co., Ltd., IV
Daily Mail and General Trust plc, 19
Dawson Holdings PLC, 43
Day Runner, Inc., 14
DC Comics Inc., 25
De La Rue plc, 10; 34 (upd.)
Deluxe Corporation, 7; 22 (upd.)
Dorling Kindersley Holdings plc, 20
Dover Publications Inc., 34
Dow Jones & Company, Inc., IV; 19 (upd.); 47 (upd.)
The Dun & Bradstreet Corporation, IV; 19 (upd.)

Duplex Products Inc., 17
The E.W. Scripps Company, IV; 7 (upd.); 28 (upd.)
Edmark Corporation, 14
Electronics for Imaging, Inc., 43 (upd.)
Elsevier N.V., IV
EMAP plc, 35
EMI Group plc, 22 (upd.)
Encyclopaedia Britannica, Inc., 7; 39 (upd.)
Engraph, Inc., 12
Enquirer/Star Group, Inc., 10
Entravision Communications Corporation, 41
Essence Communications, Inc., 24
Farm Journal Corporation, 42
Farrar, Straus and Giroux Inc., 15
Flint Ink Corporation, 13
Follett Corporation, 12; 39 (upd.)
Forbes Inc., 30
Franklin Electronic Publishers, Inc., 23
Freedom Communications, Inc., 36
Gannett Co., Inc., IV; 7 (upd.); 30 (upd.)
Gibson Greetings, Inc., 12
Golden Books Family Entertainment, Inc., 28
Goss Holdings, Inc., 43
Graphic Industries Inc., 25
Gray Communications Systems, Inc., 24
Grolier Incorporated, 16; 43 (upd.)
Groupe de la Cite, IV
Groupe Les Echos, 25
Hachette, IV
Hachette Filipacchi Medias S.A., 21
Hallmark Cards, Inc., IV; 16 (upd.); 40 (upd.)
Harcourt Brace and Co., 12
Harcourt Brace Jovanovich, Inc., IV
Harcourt General, Inc., 20 (upd.)
HarperCollins Publishers, 15
Harris Interactive Inc., 41
Harte-Hanks Communications, Inc., 17
Havas SA, 10; 33 (upd.)
Hazelden Foundation, 28
The Hearst Corporation, IV; 19 (upd.); 46 (upd.)
Her Majesty's Stationery Office, 7
N.V. Holdingmaatschappij De Telegraaf, 23
Hollinger International Inc., 24
Houghton Mifflin Company, 10; 36 (upd.)
IDG Books Worldwide, Inc., 27
Information Holdings Inc., 47
International Data Group, Inc., 7; 25 (upd.)
IPC Magazines Limited, 7
John Fairfax Holdings Limited, 7
John H. Harland Company, 17
John Wiley & Sons, Inc., 17
Johnson Publishing Company, Inc., 28
Johnston Press plc, 35
Jostens, Inc., 25 (upd.)
Journal Register Company, 29
Kaplan, Inc., 42
Kinko's, Inc., 43 (upd.)
Knight-Ridder, Inc., IV; 15 (upd.)
Kodansha Ltd., IV; 38 (upd.)
Krause Publications, Inc., 35
Landmark Communications, Inc., 12
Larry Flynt Publishing Inc., 31
Le Monde S.A., 33
Lee Enterprises, Incorporated, 11
LEXIS-NEXIS Group, 33
Maclean Hunter Publishing Limited, IV; 26 (upd.)
Macmillan, Inc., 7
Martha Stewart Living Omnimedia, L.L.C., 24
Marvel Entertainment Group, Inc., 10
Matra-Hachette S.A., 15 (upd.)
Maxwell Communication Corporation plc, IV; 7 (upd.)
McClatchy Newspapers, Inc., 23
The McGraw-Hill Companies, Inc., IV; 18 (upd.)
Mecklermedia Corporation, 24
Media General, Inc., 38 (upd.)
Meredith Corporation, 11; 29 (upd.)
Merrill Corporation, 18; 47 (upd.)
The Miner Group International, 22
Mirror Group Newspapers plc, 7; 23 (upd.)
Moore Corporation Limited, IV
Morris Communications Corporation, 36
Multimedia, Inc., 11
National Audubon Society, 26
National Geographic Society, 9; 30 (upd.)
New Times, Inc., 45
New York Daily News, 32
The New York Times Company, IV; 19 (upd.)
News America Publishing Inc., 12
News Corporation Limited, IV; 7 (upd.)
Newsquest plc, 32
Nihon Keizai Shimbun, Inc., IV
Ottaway Newspapers, Inc., 15
Outlook Group Corporation, 37
Pearson plc, IV; 46 (upd.)
Penton Media, Inc., 27
Petersen Publishing Company, 21
Plato Learning, Inc., 44
Playboy Enterprises, Inc., 18
Pleasant Company, 27
PR Newswire, 35
Primedia Inc., 22
The Providence Journal Company, 28
Publishers Group, Inc., 35
Pulitzer Publishing Company, 15
Quad/Graphics, Inc., 19
Quebecor Inc., 12; 47 (upd.)
R.L. Polk & Co., 10
R.R. Donnelley & Sons Company, IV; 9 (upd.); 38 (upd.)
Rand McNally & Company, 28
Random House Inc., 13; 31 (upd.)
The Reader's Digest Association, Inc., IV; 17 (upd.)
Recycled Paper Greetings, Inc., 21
Reed Elsevier plc, 31 (upd.)
Reed International PLC, IV; 17 (upd.)
Reuters Holdings PLC, IV; 22 (upd.)
Rodale Press, Inc., 23
Rodale, Inc., 47 (upd.)
Rogers Communications Inc., 30 (upd.)
St Ives plc, 34
Schawk, Inc., 24
Schibsted ASA, 31
Scholastic Corporation, 10; 29 (upd.)
Scott Fetzer Company, 12
Scottish Media Group plc, 32
Seat Pagine Gialle S.p.A., 47
Seattle Times Company, 15
The Sierra Club, 28
Simon & Schuster Inc., IV; 19 (upd.)
Sir Speedy, Inc., 16
SkyMall, Inc., 26
Softbank Corp., 13
Southam Inc., 7
SPIEGEL-Verlag Rudolf Augstein GmbH & Co. KG, 44
Standard Register Co., 15
Taylor & Francis Group plc, 44
Taylor Corporation, 36
Taylor Publishing Company, 12; 36 (upd.)
Thomas Nelson, Inc., 14; 38 (upd.)
Thomas Publishing Company, 26
The Thomson Corporation, 8; 34 (upd.)
The Times Mirror Company, IV; 17 (upd.)
Tom Doherty Associates Inc., 25
Toppan Printing Co., Ltd., IV
The Topps Company, Inc., 34 (upd.)
Torstar Corporation, 29
Tribune Company, IV, 22 (upd.)
U.S. News and World Report Inc., 30
United News & Media plc, 28 (upd.)
United Newspapers plc, IV
United Press International, Inc., 25
Valassis Communications, Inc., 8
Value Line, Inc., 16
Verlagsgruppe Georg von Holtzbrinck GmbH, 35
Village Voice Media, Inc., 38
VNU N.V., 27
Volt Information Sciences Inc., 26
W.W. Norton & Company, Inc., 28
Wallace Computer Services, Inc., 36
The Washington Post Company, IV; 20 (upd.)
Waverly, Inc., 16
Wenner Media, Inc., 32
West Group, 7; 34 (upd.)
Western Publishing Group, Inc., 13
WH Smith PLC, 42 (upd.)
Wolters Kluwer NV, 14; 33 (upd.)
World Book, Inc., 12
World Color Press Inc., 12
Xeikon NV, 26
Zebra Technologies Corporation, 14
Ziff Communications Company, 12
Ziff Davis Media Inc., 36 (upd.)
Zondervan Publishing House, 24

## REAL ESTATE

Alexander's, Inc., 45
Amfac/JMB Hawaii L.L.C., 24 (upd.)
Associated Estates Realty Corporation, 25
Boston Properties, Inc., 22
Bramalea Ltd., 9
Canary Wharf Group Plc, 30
CapStar Hotel Company, 21
Castle & Cooke, Inc., 20 (upd.)
Catellus Development Corporation, 24
CB Commercial Real Estate Services Group, Inc., 21
Chateau Communities, Inc., 37
Cheung Kong (Holdings) Limited, IV; 20 (upd.)
Del Webb Corporation, 14
The Edward J. DeBartolo Corporation, 8
Fairfield Communities, Inc., 36
Forest City Enterprises, Inc., 16
Gecina SA, 42
Griffin Land & Nurseries, Inc., 43
Grubb & Ellis Company, 21
The Haminerson Property Investment and Development Corporation plc, IV
Hammerson plc, 40
Harbert Corporation, 14
Helmsley Enterprises, Inc., 39 (upd.)
Home Properties of New York, Inc., 42
Hongkong Land Holdings Limited, IV; 47 (upd.)
Hyatt Corporation, 16 (upd.)
JMB Realty Corporation, IV
Kaufman and Broad Home Corporation, 8
Kerry Properties Limited, 22
Kimco Realty Corporation, 11
The Koll Company, 8
Land Securities PLC, IV
Lefrak Organization Inc., 26
Lend Lease Corporation Limited, IV; 17 (upd.)
Lincoln Property Company, 8
The Loewen Group Inc., 40 (upd.)
Mack-Cali Realty Corporation, 42
Manufactured Home Communities, Inc., 22

Maui Land & Pineapple Company, Inc., 29
Maxco Inc., 17
Meditrust, 11
Melvin Simon and Associates, Inc., 8
MEPC plc, IV
Meritage Corporation, 26
Mitsubishi Estate Company, Limited, IV
Mitsui Real Estate Development Co., Ltd., IV
The Nature Conservancy, 28
New Plan Realty Trust, 11
New World Development Company Ltd., IV
Newhall Land and Farming Company, 14
Olympia & York Developments Ltd., IV; 9 (upd.)
Park Corp., 22
Perini Corporation, 8
Post Properties, Inc., 26
Reckson Associates Realty Corp., 47
Rodamco N.V., 26
The Rouse Company, 15
Shubert Organization Inc., 24
The Sierra Club, 28
Silverstein Properties, Inc., 47
Simco S.A., 37
SL Green Realty Corporation, 44
Slough Estates PLC, IV
Starrett Corporation, 21
Storage USA, Inc., 21
Sumitomo Realty & Development Co., Ltd., IV
Sun Communities Inc., 46
Tarragon Realty Investors, Inc., 45
Taylor Woodrow plc, 38 (upd.)
Tejon Ranch Company, 35
Tishman Speyer Properties, L.P., 47
Tokyu Land Corporation, IV
Trammell Crow Company, 8
Trendwest Resorts, Inc., 33
Tridel Enterprises Inc., 9
Trizec Corporation Ltd., 10
Trump Organization, 23
Unibail SA, 40
Vistana, Inc., 22
Vornado Realty Trust, 20

## RETAIL & WHOLESALE

A.C. Moore Arts & Crafts, Inc., 30
Aaron Rents, Inc., 14; 35 (upd.)
ABC Appliance, Inc., 10
ABC Carpet & Home Co. Inc., 26
Abercrombie & Fitch Co., 15
Academy Sports & Outdoors, 27
Ace Hardware Corporation, 12; 35 (upd.)
Action Performance Companies, Inc., 27
Alba-Waldensian, Inc., 30
Alberto-Culver Company, 36 (upd.)
Allders plc, 37
Allou Health & Beauty Care, Inc., 28
Amazon.com, Inc., 25
American Coin Merchandising, Inc., 28
American Eagle Outfitters, Inc., 24
American Furniture Company, Inc., 21
American Stores Company, 22 (upd.)
AmeriSource Health Corporation, 37 (upd.)
Ames Department Stores, Inc., 9; 30 (upd.)
Amway Corporation, 13; 30 (upd.)
The Andersons, Inc., 31
AnnTaylor Stores Corporation, 13; 37 (upd.)
Appliance Recycling Centers of America, Inc., 42
Arbor Drugs Inc., 12
Arcadia Group plc, 28 (upd.)
Army and Air Force Exchange Service, 39
Art Van Furniture, Inc., 28
ASDA Group plc, 28 (upd.)
Ashworth, Inc., 26
Au Printemps S.A., V
Audio King Corporation, 24
Authentic Fitness Corp., 20
Auto Value Associates, Inc., 25
Autobytel Inc., 47
AutoZone, Inc., 9; 31 (upd.)
AVA AG (Allgemeine Handelsgesellschaft der Verbraucher AG), 33
Aveda Corporation, 24
Aviation Sales Company, 41
B. Dalton Bookseller Inc., 25
Babbage's, Inc., 10
Baby Superstore, Inc., 15
Baccarat, 24
Bachman's Inc., 22
Banana Republic Inc., 25
Barnes & Noble, Inc., 10; 30 (upd.)
Barnett Inc., 28
Barney's, Inc., 28
Bass Pro Shops, Inc., 42
Bear Creek Corporation, 38
Bearings, Inc., 13
bebe stores, inc., 31
Bed Bath & Beyond Inc., 13; 41 (upd.)
Belk Stores Services, Inc., V; 19 (upd.)
Bergen Brunswig Corporation, V; 13 (upd.)
Bernard Chaus, Inc., 27
Best Buy Co., Inc., 9; 23 (upd.)
Bhs plc, 17
Big Dog Holdings, Inc., 45
Big O Tires, Inc., 20
Birkenstock Footprint Sandals, Inc., 42 (upd.)
Black Box Corporation, 20
Blacks Leisure Group plc, 39
Blair Corporation, 25; 31 (upd.)
Bloomingdale's Inc., 12
Blue Square Israel Ltd., 41
Blyth Industries, Inc., 18
The Body Shop International PLC, 11
The Bombay Company, Inc., 10
The Bon Marché, Inc., 23
The Bon-Ton Stores, Inc., 16
Books-A-Million, Inc., 14; 41 (upd.)
The Boots Company PLC, V; 24 (upd.)
Borders Group, Inc., 15; 43 (upd.)
Boscov's Department Store, Inc., 31
Bozzuto's, Inc., 13
Bradlees Discount Department Store Company, 12
Brambles Industries Limited, 42
Broder Bros. Co., 38
Brooks Brothers Inc., 22
Brookstone, Inc., 18
The Buckle, Inc., 18
Buhrmann NV, 41
Burlington Coat Factory Warehouse Corporation, 10
The Burton Group plc, V
Buttrey Food & Drug Stores Co., 18
buy.com, Inc., 46
C&A, V; 40 (upd.)
Cabela's Inc., 26
Cablevision Electronic Instruments, Inc., 32
Cache Incorporated, 30
Caldor Inc., 12
Camelot Music, Inc., 26
Campeau Corporation, V
Campo Electronics, Appliances & Computers, Inc., 16
Carrefour SA, 10; 27 (upd.)
Carson Pirie Scott & Company, 15
Carter Hawley Hale Stores, Inc., V
Carter Lumber Company, 45
Cartier Monde, 29
Casual Corner Group, Inc., 43
Catherines Stores Corporation, 15
Cato Corporation, 14
CDW Computer Centers, Inc., 16
Celebrity, Inc., 22
Central Garden & Pet Company, 23
Chadwick's of Boston, Ltd., 29
Charlotte Russe Holding, Inc., 35
Charming Shoppes, Inc., 38
ChevronTexaco Corporation, 47 (upd.)
The Children's Place Retail Stores, Inc., 37
Christopher & Banks Corporation, 42
Cifra, S.A. de C.V., 12
The Circle K Company, 20 (upd.)
Circuit City Stores, Inc., 9; 29 (upd.)
Clinton Cards plc, 39
The Clothestime, Inc., 20
CML Group, Inc., 10
Coach, Inc., 45 (upd.)
Coborn's, Inc., 30
Coinmach Laundry Corporation, 20
Coldwater Creek Inc., 21
Cole National Corporation, 13
Coles Myer Ltd., V; 20 (upd.)
Collectors Universe, Inc., 48
Comdisco, Inc., 9
CompUSA, Inc., 10
Computerland Corp., 13
Concepts Direct, Inc., 39
The Container Store, 36
Controladora Comercial Mexicana, S.A. de C.V., 36
Coop Schweiz Genossenschaftsverband, 48
Corby Distilleries Limited, 14
Corporate Express, Inc., 22; 47 (upd.)
The Cosmetic Center, Inc., 22
Cost Plus, Inc., 27
Costco Wholesale Corporation, V; 43 (upd.)
Cotter & Company, V
County Seat Stores Inc., 9
Courts Plc, 45
CPI Corp., 38
Crate and Barrel, 9
Croscill, Inc., 42
Crowley, Milner & Company, 19
Crown Books Corporation, 21
Cumberland Farms, Inc., 17
CVS Corporation, 45 (upd.)
Daffy's Inc., 26
The Daiei, Inc., V; 17 (upd.); 41 (upd.)
The Daimaru, Inc., V; 42 (upd.)
Dairy Mart Convenience Stores, Inc., 25 (upd.)
Daisytek International Corporation, 18
Damark International, Inc., 18
Dart Group Corporation, 16
Darty S.A., 27
David's Bridal, Inc., 33
Dayton Hudson Corporation, V; 18 (upd.)
Deb Shops, Inc., 16
Debenhams Plc, 28
dELiA*s Inc., 29
Department 56, Inc., 34 (upd.)
Designer Holdings Ltd., 20
Deveaux S.A., 41
Diesel SpA, 40
Dillard Department Stores, Inc., V; 16 (upd.)
Dillon Companies Inc., 12
Discount Auto Parts, Inc., 18
Discount Drug Mart, Inc., 14
Dixons Group plc, V; 19 (upd.)
Do it Best Corporation, 30
Dollar Tree Stores, Inc., 23
The Dress Barn, Inc., 24
Drug Emporium, Inc., 12
Du Pareil au Même, 43
Duane Reade Holding Corp., 21

Duckwall-ALCO Stores, Inc., 24
Duty Free International, Inc., 11
Dylex Limited, 29
E-Z Serve Corporation, 17
Eagle Hardware & Garden, Inc., 16
eBay Inc., 32
Eckerd Corporation, 9; 32 (upd.)
Eddie Bauer, Inc., 36 (upd.)
Egghead.com, Inc., 31 (upd.)
El Corte Inglés Group, V
Elder-Beerman Stores Corporation, 10
Ellett Brothers, Inc., 17
EMI Group plc, 22 (upd.)
Ethan Allen Interiors, Inc., 39 (upd.)
EToys, Inc., 37
Euromarket Designs Inc., 31 (upd.)
Evans, Inc., 30
EZCORP Inc., 43
Family Dollar Stores, Inc., 13
Fastenal Company, 14; 42 (upd.)
Fay's Inc., 17
Federated Department Stores, Inc., 9; 31 (upd.)
Fielmann AG, 31
Fila Holding S.p.A., 20
Fingerhut Companies, Inc., 9; 36 (upd.)
The Finish Line, Inc., 29
Finlay Enterprises, Inc., 16
Fleming Companies, Inc., 17 (upd.)
Florsheim Shoe Group Inc., 9; 31 (upd.)
FNAC, 21
Follett Corporation, 12
Footstar, Incorporated, 24
Fortunoff Fine Jewelry and Silverware Inc., 26
Frank's Nursery & Crafts, Inc., 12
Fred Meyer, Inc., V; 20 (upd.)
Fred's, Inc., 23
Frederick Atkins Inc., 16
Fretter, Inc., 10
Friedman's Inc., 29
Funco, Inc., 20
G.I. Joe's, Inc., 30
Gadzooks, Inc., 18
Gaiam, Inc., 41
Galeries Lafayette S.A., V; 23 (upd.)
Galyan's Trading Company, Inc., 47
Gander Mountain, Inc., 20
Gantos, Inc., 17
The Gap, Inc., V; 18 (upd.)
Garden Ridge Corporation, 27
Gart Sports Company, 24
GEHE AG, 27
General Binding Corporation, 10
General Host Corporation, 12
Genesco Inc., 17
Genovese Drug Stores, Inc., 18
Genuine Parts Company, 45 (upd.)
Gerald Stevens, Inc., 37
Giant Food Inc., 22 (upd.)
GIB Group, V; 26 (upd.)
Glacier Water Services, Inc., 47
The Good Guys, Inc., 10; 30 (upd.)
Goodwill Industries International, Inc., 16
Goody's Family Clothing, Inc., 20
Gottschalks, Inc., 18
GrandVision S.A., 43
The Great Universal Stores plc, V; 19 (upd.)
Griffin Land & Nurseries, Inc., 43
Grossman's Inc., 13
Groupe Castorama-Dubois Investissements, 23
Groupe DMC (Dollfus Mieg & Cie), 27
Groupe Go Sport S.A., 39
Groupe Lapeyre S.A., 33
Groupe Zannier S.A., 35
Grow Biz International, Inc., 18
Grupo Casa Saba, S.A. de C.V., 39
Grupo Elektra, S.A. de C.V., 39
Grupo Gigante, S.A. de C.V., 34
Gruppo Coin S.p.A., 41
GT Bicycles, 26
Guccio Gucci, S.p.A., 15
Guilbert S.A., 42
Guitar Center, Inc., 29
GUS plc, 47 (upd.)
Hahn Automotive Warehouse, Inc., 24
Half Price Books, Records, Magazines Inc., 37
Hallmark Cards, Inc., 40 (upd.)
Hammacher Schlemmer & Company, 21
Hancock Fabrics, Inc., 18
Hankyu Department Stores, Inc., V
Hanover Direct, Inc., 36
Harold's Stores, Inc., 22
Harrods Holdings, 47
Harry Winston Inc., 45
Hasbro, Inc., 43 (upd.)
Haverty Furniture Companies, Inc., 31
Hechinger Company, 12
Heilig-Meyers Company, 14; 40 (upd.)
Helzberg Diamonds, 40
Hennes & Mauritz AB, 29
Henry Modell & Company Inc., 32
Hertie Waren- und Kaufhaus GmbH, V
Hibbett Sporting Goods, Inc., 26
Hills Stores Company, 13
The Hockey Company, 34
Holiday RV Superstores, Incorporated, 26
Holt's Cigar Holdings, Inc., 42
The Home Depot, Inc., V; 18 (upd.)
Home Shopping Network, Inc., V; 25 (upd.)
HomeBase, Inc., 33 (upd.)
Hot Topic, Inc., 33
House of Fabrics, Inc., 21
House of Fraser PLC, 45
Hudson's Bay Company, V; 25 (upd.)
IKEA International A/S, V; 26 (upd.)
InaCom Corporation, 13
Insight Enterprises, Inc., 18
Intimate Brands, Inc., 24
Isetan Company Limited, V; 36 (upd.)
Ito-Yokado Co., Ltd., V; 42 (upd.)
J&R Electronics Inc., 26
J. Baker, Inc., 31
The J. Jill Group, Inc., 35
J.C. Penney Company, Inc., V; 18 (upd.); 43 (upd.)
Jack Schwartz Shoes, Inc., 18
Jacobson Stores Inc., 21
Jalate Inc., 25
James Beattie plc, 43
Jay Jacobs, Inc., 15
Jennifer Convertibles, Inc., 31
Jetro Cash & Carry Enterprises Inc., 38
JG Industries, Inc., 15
JJB Sports plc, 32
John Lewis Partnership plc, V; 42 (upd.)
JUSCO Co., Ltd., V
Just For Feet, Inc., 19
K & B Inc., 12
K & G Men's Center, Inc., 21
K-tel International, Inc., 21
Karstadt Aktiengesellschaft, V; 19 (upd.)
Kash n' Karry Food Stores, Inc., 20
Kasper A.S.L., Ltd., 40
Kaufhof Warenhaus AG, V; 23 (upd.)
Kaufring AG, 35
Kay-Bee Toy Stores, 15
Kingfisher plc, V; 24 (upd.)
Kinney Shoe Corp., 14
Kmart Corporation, V; 18 (upd.); 47 (upd.)
Knoll Group Inc., 14
Kohl's Corporation, 9; 30 (upd.)
Kotobukiya Co., Ltd., V
Krause's Furniture, Inc., 27
L. Luria & Son, Inc., 19
L.A. T Sportswear, Inc., 26
L.L. Bean, Inc., 38 (upd.)
La-Z-Boy Chair Company, 14
Lamonts Apparel, Inc., 15
Lands' End, Inc., 9; 29 (upd.)
Laura Ashley Holdings plc, 37 (upd.)
Lazare Kaplan International Inc., 21
Lechmere Inc., 10
Lechters, Inc., 11; 39 (upd.)
LensCrafters Inc., 23
Lesco Inc., 19
Leslie's Poolmart, Inc., 18
Levitz Furniture Inc., 15
Lewis Galoob Toys Inc., 16
Lifetime Hoan Corporation, 27
Lillian Vernon Corporation, 12; 35
The Limited, Inc., V; 20 (upd.)
Linens 'n Things, Inc., 24
The Littlewoods Organisation PLC, V
Littlewoods plc, 42 (upd.)
Liz Claiborne, Inc., 25 (upd.)
Loehmann's Inc., 24
Lojas Arapuã S.A., 22
London Drugs Ltd., 46
Longs Drug Stores Corporation, V; 25 (upd.)
Lost Arrow Inc., 22
LOT$OFF Corporation, 24
Lowe's Companies, Inc., V; 21 (upd.)
Mac Frugal's Bargains - Closeouts Inc., 17
Mac-Gray Corporation, 44
MarineMax, Inc., 30
Marks and Spencer p.l.c., V; 24 (upd.)
Marks Brothers Jewelers, Inc., 24
Marshalls Incorporated, 13
Marui Co., Ltd., V
Maruzen Co., Limited, 18
Mary Kay, Inc., 30 (upd.)
Matsuzakaya Company Limited, V
Maus Frères SA, 48
The Maxim Group, 25
The May Department Stores Company, V; 19 (upd.); 46 (upd.)
Mayor's Jewelers, Inc., 41
Mazel Stores, Inc., 29
McKesson Corporation, 47 (upd.)
McLane Company, Inc., 13
MCSi, Inc., 41
Media Arts Group, Inc., 42
Meier & Frank Co., 23
Meijer Incorporated, 27 (upd.)
Melville Corporation, V
The Men's Wearhouse, Inc., 17; 48 (upd.)
Menard, Inc., 34
Mercantile Stores Company, Inc., V; 19 (upd.)
Merry-Go-Round Enterprises, Inc., 8
Mervyn's California, 10; 39 (upd.)
Michaels Stores, Inc., 17
Micro Warehouse, Inc., 16
MicroAge, Inc., 16
Mitsukoshi Ltd., V
Monsoon plc, 39
Montgomery Ward & Co., Incorporated, V; 20 (upd.)
Moore-Handley, Inc., 39
Morse Shoe Inc., 13
Mothers Work, Inc., 18
Moto Photo, Inc., 45
Mr. Bricolage S.A., 37
MTS Inc., 37
Musicland Stores Corporation, 9; 38 (upd.)
Nagasakiya Co., Ltd., V
National Educational Music Co. Ltd., 47
National Home Centers, Inc., 44

National Intergroup, Inc., V
National Record Mart, Inc., 29
Natural Wonders Inc., 14
Navy Exchange Service Command, 31
Neff Corp., 32
Neiman Marcus Co., 12
New Look Group plc, 35
Next plc, 29
Nichii Co., Ltd., V
NIKE, Inc., 36 (upd.)
Nine West Group Inc., 11
99¢ Only Stores, 25
Noland Company, 35
Noodle Kidoodle, 16
Nordstrom, Inc., V; 18 (upd.)
Norelco Consumer Products Co., 26
Norm Thompson Outfitters, Inc., 47
The North West Company, Inc., 12
Norton McNaughton, Inc., 27
Nu Skin Enterprises, Inc., 27
Office Depot Incorporated, 8; 23 (upd.)
OfficeMax, Inc., 15; 43 (upd.)
Old America Stores, Inc., 17
One Price Clothing Stores, Inc., 20
Orchard Supply Hardware Stores Corporation, 17
Organización Soriana, S.A. de C.V., 35
The Orvis Company, Inc., 28
OshKosh B'Gosh, Inc., 42 (upd.)
Oshman's Sporting Goods, Inc., 17
Otto Versand (GmbH & Co.), V; 15 (upd.); 34 (upd.)
Owens & Minor, Inc., 16
P.C. Richard & Son Corp., 23
Pamida Holdings Corporation, 15
The Pampered Chef, Ltd., 18
The Pantry, Inc., 36
Parisian, Inc., 14
Paul Harris Stores, Inc., 18
Pay 'N Pak Stores, Inc., 9
Payless Cashways, Inc., 11; 44 (upd.)
Payless ShoeSource, Inc., 18
Pearle Vision, Inc., 13
Peebles Inc., 16; 43 (upd.)
Peet's Coffee & Tea, Inc., 38
Petco Animal Supplies, Inc., 29
Petrie Stores Corporation, 8
PETsMART, Inc., 14; 41 (upd.)
Phar-Mor Inc., 12
Pier 1 Imports, Inc., 12; 34 (upd.)
Piercing Pagoda, Inc., 29
Pinault-Printemps Redoute S.A., 19 (upd.)
Pomeroy Computer Resources, Inc., 33
Powell's Books, Inc., 40
The Price Company, V
PriceCostco, Inc., 14
Proffitt's, Inc., 19
Purina Mills, Inc., 32
Quelle Group, V
QuikTrip Corporation, 36
Quill Corporation, 28
R.H. Macy & Co., Inc., V; 8 (upd.); 30 (upd.)
RadioShack Corporation, 36 (upd.)
Rag Shops, Inc., 30
Raley's Inc., 14
Rapala-Normark Group, Ltd., 30
RDO Equipment Company, 33
Reckitt Benckiser plc, 42 (upd.)
Recoton Corp., 15
Recreational Equipment, Inc., 18
Reeds Jewelers, Inc., 22
Rent-A-Center, Inc., 45
Rent-Way, Inc., 33
Restoration Hardware, Inc., 30
Revco D.S., Inc., V
REX Stores Corp., 10
Rhodes Inc., 23
Richton International Corporation, 39
Riklis Family Corp., 9
Rite Aid Corporation, V; 19 (upd.)
Ritz Camera Centers, 34
Roberds Inc., 19
Rocky Shoes & Boots, Inc., 26
Rogers Communications Inc., 30 (upd.)
Rooms To Go Inc., 28
Roots Canada Ltd., 42
Rose's Stores, Inc., 13
Ross Stores, Inc., 17; 43 (upd.)
Roundy's Inc., 14
S&K Famous Brands, Inc., 23
Saks Holdings, Inc., 24
Saks Inc., 41 (upd.)
Sam Ash Music Corporation, 30
Sam's Club, 40
Samuels Jewelers Incorporated, 30
Sanborn Hermanos, S.A., 20
Schmitt Music Company, 40
Schneiderman's Furniture Inc., 28
Schottenstein Stores Corp., 14
Schultz Sav-O Stores, Inc., 31
The Score Board, Inc., 19
Scotty's, Inc., 22
SCP Pool Corporation, 39
Seaman Furniture Company, Inc., 32
Sears plc, V
Sears Roebuck de México, S.A. de C.V., 20
Sears, Roebuck and Co., V; 18 (upd.)
SED International Holdings, Inc., 43
Seibu Department Stores, Ltd., V; 42 (upd.)
Seigle's Home and Building Centers, Inc., 41
The Seiyu, Ltd., V; 36 (upd.)
Selfridges Plc, 34
Service Merchandise Company, Inc., V; 19 (upd.)
7-Eleven, Inc., 32 (upd.)
Shaklee Corporation, 12
The Sharper Image Corporation, 10
Shoe Carnival Inc., 14
ShopKo Stores Inc., 21
SkyMall, Inc., 26
Sleepy's Inc., 32
Solo Serve Corporation, 28
Sound Advice, Inc., 41
Southern States Cooperative Incorporated, 36
Spec's Music, Inc., 19
Spiegel, Inc., 10; 27 (upd.)
Sport Chalet, Inc., 16
Sport Supply Group, Inc., 23
Sportmart, Inc., 15
Sports & Recreation, Inc., 17
The Sports Authority, Inc., 16; 43 (upd.)
The Sportsman's Guide, Inc., 36
Stage Stores, Inc., 24
Stanhome Inc., 15
Staples, Inc., 10
Starbucks Corporation, 34 (upd.)
Starcraft Corporation, 30
Stein Mart Inc., 19
Stinnes AG, 8
The Stop & Shop Companies, Inc., 24 (upd.)
Storehouse PLC, 16
Stride Rite Corporation, 8
Strouds, Inc., 33
Stuller Settings, Inc., 35
Successories, Inc., 30
Sun Television & Appliances Inc., 10
Sunglass Hut International, Inc., 21
Supreme International Corporation, 27
Swarovski International Holding AG, 40
Syms Corporation, 29
Takashimaya Company, Limited, V; 47 (upd.)
The Talbots, Inc., 11; 31 (upd.)
Target Stores, 10; 27 (upd.)
Tati SA, 25
Tattered Cover Book Store, 43
Tech Data Corporation, 10
Tengelmann Group, 27
Tesco PLC, 24 (upd.)
Thrifty PayLess, Inc., 12
Tiffany & Co., 14
The TJX Companies, Inc., V; 19 (upd.)
Today's Man, Inc., 20
Tokyu Department Store Co., Ltd., V; 32 (upd.)
Tops Appliance City, Inc., 17
Toys "R" Us, Inc., V; 18 (upd.)
Travis Boats & Motors, Inc., 37
Travis Perkins plc, 34
Trend-Lines, Inc., 22
TruServ Corporation, 24
Tuesday Morning Corporation, 18
Tupperware Corporation, 28
TVI, Inc., 15
Tweeter Home Entertainment Group, Inc., 30
Ultimate Electronics, Inc., 18
Ultramar Diamond Shamrock Corporation, 31 (upd.)
Uni-Marts, Inc., 17
United Rentals, Inc., 34
The United States Shoe Corporation, V
United Stationers Inc., 14
Universal International, Inc., 25
Uny Co., Ltd., V
Urban Outfitters, Inc., 14
Vallen Corporation, 45
Valley Media Inc., 35
Value City Department Stores, Inc., 38
Value Merchants Inc., 13
ValueVision International, Inc., 22
Vans, Inc., 47 (upd.)
Venator Group Inc., 35 (upd.)
Vendex International N.V., 13
Venture Stores Inc., 12
The Vermont Teddy Bear Co., Inc., 36
Viking Office Products, Inc., 10
Vorwerk & Co., 27
W. Atlee Burpee & Co., 27
W H Smith Group PLC, V
W.W. Grainger, Inc., V
Waban Inc., 13
Wacoal Corp., 25
Wal-Mart de Mexico, S.A. de C.V., 35 (upd.)
Wal-Mart Stores, Inc., V; 8 (upd.); 26 (upd.)
Walden Book Company Inc., 17
Walgreen Co., V; 20 (upd.)
Wall Drug Store, Inc., 40
Weiner's Stores, Inc., 33
West Marine, Inc., 17
Western Beef, Inc., 22
The Wet Seal, Inc., 18
Weyco Group, Incorporated, 32
WH Smith PLC, 42 (upd.)
Whole Foods Market, Inc., 20
Wickes Inc., V; 25 (upd.)
Williams-Sonoma, Inc., 17; 44 (upd.)
Wilsons The Leather Experts Inc., 21
Wolohan Lumber Co., 19
Woolworth Corporation, V; 20 (upd.)
World Duty Free Americas, Inc., 29 (upd.)
The Yankee Candle Company, Inc., 37
Young's Market Company, LLC, 32
Younkers, Inc., 19
Zale Corporation, 16; 40 (upd.)
Zany Brainy, Inc., 31

Ziebart International Corporation, 30
Zion's Cooperative Mercantile Institution, 33

## RUBBER & TIRE

Aeroquip Corporation, 16
Bandag, Inc., 19
The BFGoodrich Company, V
Bridgestone Corporation, V; 21 (upd.)
Carlisle Companies Incorporated, 8
Compagnie Générale des Établissements Michelin, V; 42 (upd.)
Continental Aktiengesellschaft, V
Continental General Tire Corp., 23
Cooper Tire & Rubber Company, 8; 23 (upd.)
Elementis plc, 40 (upd.)
General Tire, Inc., 8
The Goodyear Tire & Rubber Company, V; 20 (upd.)
The Kelly-Springfield Tire Company, 8
Myers Industries, Inc., 19
Pirelli S.p.A., V; 15 (upd.)
Safeskin Corporation, 18
Sumitomo Rubber Industries, Ltd., V
Tillotson Corp., 15
Treadco, Inc., 19
Ube Industries, Ltd., 38 (upd.)
The Yokohama Rubber Co., Ltd., V; 19 (upd.)

## TELECOMMUNICATIONS

A.H. Belo Corporation, 30 (upd.)
Acme-Cleveland Corp., 13
ADC Telecommunications, Inc., 10
Adelphia Communications Corp., 17
Adtran Inc., 22
AEI Music Network Inc., 35
AirTouch Communications, 11
Alcatel S.A., 36 (upd.)
Alliance Atlantis Communications Inc., 39
ALLTEL Corporation, 6; 46 (upd.)
American Telephone and Telegraph Company, V
American Tower Corporation, 33
Ameritech Corporation, V; 18 (upd.)
Amstrad plc, 48 (upd.)
AO VimpelCom, 48
Arch Wireless, Inc., 39
ARD, 41
Ascom AG, 9
Aspect Telecommunications Corporation, 22
AT&T Bell Laboratories, Inc., 13
AT&T Corporation, 29 (upd.)
BCE Inc., V; 44 (upd.)
Belgacom, 6
Bell Atlantic Corporation, V; 25 (upd.)
Bell Canada, 6
BellSouth Corporation, V; 29 (upd.)
BET Holdings, Inc., 18
BHC Communications, Inc., 26
Bonneville International Corporation, 29
Bouygues S.A., 24 (upd.)
Brightpoint, Inc., 18
Brite Voice Systems, Inc., 20
British Columbia Telephone Company, 6
British Telecommunications plc, V; 15 (upd.)
C-COR.net Corp., 38
Cable & Wireless HKT, 30 (upd.)
Cable and Wireless plc, V; 25 (upd.)
Cablevision Systems Corporation, 30 (upd.)
The Canadian Broadcasting Corporation (CBC), 37
Canal Plus, 10; 34 (upd.)
CanWest Global Communications Corporation, 35
Capital Radio plc, 35
Carlton Communications plc, 15
Carolina Telephone and Telegraph Company, 10
Carrier Access Corporation, 44
CBS Corporation, 28 (upd.)
Centel Corporation, 6
Centennial Communications Corporation, 39
Century Communications Corp., 10
Century Telephone Enterprises, Inc., 9
Chancellor Media Corporation, 24
Charter Communications, Inc., 33
Chris-Craft Industries, Inc., 9
Chrysalis Group plc, 40
Cincinnati Bell, Inc., 6
Citadel Communications Corporation, 35
Clear Channel Communications, Inc., 23
COLT Telecom Group plc, 41
Comcast Corporation, 24 (upd.)
Comdial Corporation, 21
Commonwealth Telephone Enterprises, Inc., 25
Comsat Corporation, 23
Comverse Technology, Inc., 15; 43 (upd.)
Corning Inc., 44 (upd.)
Craftmade International, Inc., 44
Cumulus Media Inc., 37
DDI Corporation, 7
Deutsche Bundespost TELEKOM, V
Deutsche Telekom AG, 48 (upd.)
Dialogic Corporation, 18
Directorate General of Telecommunications, 7
DIRECTV, Inc., 38
Discovery Communications, Inc., 42
DSC Communications Corporation, 12
EchoStar Communications Corporation, 35
ECI Telecom Ltd., 18
eircom plc, 31 (upd.)
Electric Lightwave, Inc., 37
Electromagnetic Sciences Inc., 21
Emmis Communications Corporation, 47
Energis plc, 47
Entravision Communications Corporation, 41
EXCEL Communications Inc., 18
Executone Information Systems, Inc., 13
Expand SA, 48
Fox Family Worldwide, Inc., 24
France Télécom Group, V; 21 (upd.)
Frontier Corp., 16
Gannett Co., Inc., 30 (upd.)
Gaylord Entertainment Company, 36 (upd.)
General DataComm Industries, Inc., 14
Geotek Communications Inc., 21
Getty Images, Inc., 31
Global Crossing Ltd., 32
Granite Broadcasting Corporation, 42
Gray Communications Systems, Inc., 24
Groupe Vidéotron Ltée., 20
Grupo Televisa, S.A., 18
GTE Corporation, V; 15 (upd.)
Guthy-Renker Corporation, 32
GWR Group plc, 39
Harmonic Inc., 43
Havas, SA, 10
Hispanic Broadcasting Corporation, 35
Hong Kong Telecommunications Ltd., 6
Hubbard Broadcasting Inc., 24
Hughes Electronics Corporation, 25
IDB Communications Group, Inc., 11
IDT Corporation, 34
Illinois Bell Telephone Company, 14
Indiana Bell Telephone Company, Incorporated, 14
Infinity Broadcasting Corporation, 11
IXC Communications, Inc., 29
Jacor Communications, Inc., 23
Jones Intercable, Inc., 21
Koninklijke PTT Nederland NV, V
LCI International, Inc., 16
LDDS-Metro Communications, Inc., 8
LIN Broadcasting Corp., 9
Lincoln Telephone & Telegraph Company, 14
LodgeNet Entertainment Corporation, 28
Mannesmann AG, 38 (upd.)
MasTec, Inc., 19
McCaw Cellular Communications, Inc., 6
MCI WorldCom, Inc., V; 27 (upd.)
McLeodUSA Incorporated, 32
Mercury Communications, Ltd., 7
Metrocall, Inc., 41
Metromedia Companies, 14
Métropole Télévision, 33
MFS Communications Company, Inc., 11
Michigan Bell Telephone Co., 14
MIH Limited, 31
MITRE Corporation, 26
Mobile Telecommunications Technologies Corp., 18
Modern Times Group AB, 36
The Montana Power Company, 44 (upd.)
Multimedia, Inc., 11
National Broadcasting Company, Inc., 28 (upd.)
NCR Corporation, 30 (upd.)
NetCom Systems AB, 26
Nevada Bell Telephone Company, 14
New Valley Corporation, 17
Nextel Communications, Inc., 27 (upd.)
Nippon Telegraph and Telephone Corporation, V
Norstan, Inc., 16
Nortel Networks Corporation, 36 (upd.)
Northern Telecom Limited, V
NYNEX Corporation, V
Octel Communications Corp., 14
Octel Messaging, 41 (upd.)
Ohio Bell Telephone Company, 14
Olivetti S.p.A., 34 (upd.)
Österreichische Post- und Telegraphenverwaltung, V
Pacific Telecom, Inc., 6
Pacific Telesis Group, V
Paging Network Inc., 11
PanAmSat Corporation, 46
Paxson Communications Corporation, 33
PictureTel Corp., 10; 27 (upd.)
Posti- ja Telelaitos, 6
Price Communications Corporation, 42
QUALCOMM Incorporated, 20; 47 (upd.)
QVC Network Inc., 9
Qwest Communications International, Inc., 37
RMH Teleservices, Inc., 42
Rochester Telephone Corporation, 6
Rogers Communications Inc., 30 (upd.)
Royal KPN N.V., 30
Rural Cellular Corporation, 43
Saga Communications, Inc., 27
Sawtek Inc., 43 (upd.)
SBC Communications Inc., 32 (upd.)
Schweizerische Post-, Telefon- und Telegrafen-Betriebe, V
Scientific-Atlanta, Inc., 6; 45 (upd.)
Seat Pagine Gialle S.p.A., 47
Securicor Plc, 45
Sinclair Broadcast Group, Inc., 25
Società Finanziaria Telefonica per Azioni, V
Southern New England Telecommunications Corporation, 6

Southwestern Bell Corporation, V
Spanish Broadcasting System, Inc., 41
Spelling Entertainment, 35 (upd.)
Sprint Communications Company, L.P., 9
Sprint Corporation, 46 (upd.)
StrataCom, Inc., 16
Swedish Telecom, V
Sycamore Networks, Inc., 45
SynOptics Communications, Inc., 10
T-Netix, Inc., 46
Telecom Australia, 6
Telecom Eireann, 7
Telecom Italia S.p.A., 43
Telefonaktiebolaget LM Ericsson, V; 46 (upd.)
Telefónica de España, S.A., V
Telefónica S.A., 46 (upd.)
Telefonos de Mexico S.A. de C.V., 14
Telephone and Data Systems, Inc., 9
Télévision Française 1, 23
Tellabs, Inc., 11; 40 (upd.)
Tiscali SpA, 48
The Titan Corporation, 36
Tollgrade Communications, Inc., 44
TV Azteca, S.A. de C.V., 39
U.S. Satellite Broadcasting Company, Inc., 20
U S West, Inc., V; 25 (upd.)
U.S. Cellular Corporation, 9; 31 (upd.)
United Pan-Europe Communications NV, 47
United Telecommunications, Inc., V
United Video Satellite Group, 18
USA Interactive, Inc., 47 (upd.)
Verizon Communications, 43 (upd.)
Vivendi Universal S.A., 46 (upd.)
Vodafone Group PLC, 11; 36 (upd.)
The Walt Disney Company, 30 (upd.)
Watkins-Johnson Company, 15
West Corporation, 42
Western Wireless Corporation, 36
Westwood One, Inc., 23
Williams Communications Group, Inc., 34
The Williams Companies, Inc., 31 (upd.)
Wipro Limited, 43
Wisconsin Bell, Inc., 14
Working Assets Funding Service, 43
Young Broadcasting Inc., 40

## TEXTILES & APPAREL

Abercrombie & Fitch Co., 35 (upd.)
Adidas AG, 14
adidas-Salomon AG, 33 (upd.)
Alba-Waldensian, Inc., 30
Albany International Corp., 8
Algo Group Inc., 24
American Safety Razor Company, 20
Amoskeag Company, 8
Angelica Corporation, 15; 43 (upd.)
AR Accessories Group, Inc., 23
Aris Industries, Inc., 16
Authentic Fitness Corp., 20
Banana Republic Inc., 25
Benetton Group S.p.A., 10
Bill Blass Ltd., 32
Birkenstock Footprint Sandals, Inc., 12
Blair Corporation, 25
Brazos Sportswear, Inc., 23
Brooks Brothers Inc., 22
Brooks Sports Inc., 32
Brown Group, Inc., V; 20 (upd.)
Bugle Boy Industries, Inc., 18
Burberry Ltd., 17; 41 (upd.)
Burlington Industries, Inc., V; 17 (upd.)
Calcot Ltd., 33
Calvin Klein, Inc., 22
Candie's, Inc., 31
Canstar Sports Inc., 16
Capel Incorporated, 45
Carhartt, Inc., 30
Cato Corporation, 14
Chargeurs International, 21 (upd.)
Charming Shoppes, Inc., 8
Cherokee Inc., 18
Chic by H.I.S, Inc., 20
Chico's FAS, Inc., 45
Chorus Line Corporation, 30
Christian Dior S.A., 19
Christopher & Banks Corporation, 42
Claire's Stores, Inc., 17
Coach Leatherware, 10
Coats plc, 44 (upd.)
Coats Viyella Plc, V
Collins & Aikman Corporation, 13
Columbia Sportswear Company, 19; 41 (upd.)
Concord Fabrics, Inc., 16
Cone Mills Corporation, 8
Converse Inc., 31 (upd.)
Cotton Incorporated, 46
Courtaulds plc, V; 17 (upd.)
Croscill, Inc., 42
Crown Crafts, Inc., 16
Crystal Brands, Inc., 9
Culp, Inc., 29
Cygne Designs, Inc., 25
Dan River Inc., 35
Danskin, Inc., 12
Deckers Outdoor Corporation, 22
Delta Woodside Industries, Inc., 8; 30 (upd.)
Designer Holdings Ltd., 20
The Dixie Group, Inc., 20
Dominion Textile Inc., 12
Donna Karan Company, 15
Donnkenny, Inc., 17
Duck Head Apparel Company, Inc., 42
Dyersburg Corporation, 21
Edison Brothers Stores, Inc., 9
Esprit de Corp., 8; 29 (upd.)
Etam Developpement SA, 44
Evans, Inc., 30
Fab Industries, Inc., 27
Fabri-Centers of America Inc., 16
Fieldcrest Cannon, Inc., 9; 31 (upd.)
Fila Holding S.p.A., 20
Florsheim Shoe Group Inc., 31 (upd.)
Fossil, Inc., 17
Frederick's of Hollywood Inc., 16
French Connection Group plc, 41
Fruit of the Loom, Inc., 8; 25 (upd.)
Fubu, 29
G&K Services, Inc., 16
G-III Apparel Group, Ltd., 22
Galey & Lord, Inc., 20
Garan, Inc., 16
Gianni Versace SpA, 22
Giorgio Armani S.p.A., 45
The Gitano Group, Inc. 8
Greenwood Mills, Inc., 14
Groupe DMC (Dollfus Mieg & Cie), 27
Groupe Yves Saint Laurent, 23
Guccio Gucci, S.p.A., 15
Guess, Inc., 15
Guilford Mills Inc., 8; 40 (upd.)
Gymboree Corporation, 15
Haggar Corporation, 19
Hampton Industries, Inc., 20
Happy Kids Inc., 30
Hartmarx Corporation, 8
The Hartstone Group plc, 14
Healthtex, Inc., 17
Helly Hansen ASA, 25
Hermès S.A., 14
The Hockey Company, 34
Hugo Boss AG, 48
Hyde Athletic Industries, Inc., 17
I.C. Isaacs & Company, 31
Interface, Inc., 8; 29 (upd.)
Irwin Toy Limited, 14
Items International Airwalk Inc., 17
J. Crew Group, Inc., 12; 34 (upd.)
Jockey International, Inc., 12; 34 (upd.)
Johnston Industries, Inc., 15
Jones Apparel Group, Inc., 39 (upd.)
Jordache Enterprises, Inc., 23
Jos. A. Bank Clothiers, Inc., 31
JPS Textile Group, Inc., 28
K-Swiss, Inc., 33
Kellwood Company, 8
Kenneth Cole Productions, Inc., 25
Kinney Shoe Corp., 14
L.A. Gear, Inc., 8; 32 (upd.)
L.L. Bean, Inc., 10; 38 (upd.)
LaCrosse Footwear, Inc., 18
Laura Ashley Holdings plc, 13
Lee Apparel Company, Inc., 8
The Leslie Fay Company, Inc., 8; 39 (upd.)
Levi Strauss & Co., V; 16 (upd.)
Liz Claiborne, Inc., 8
London Fog Industries, Inc., 29
Lost Arrow Inc., 22
Maidenform Worldwide Inc., 20
Malden Mills Industries, Inc., 16
Marzotto S.p.A., 20
Milliken & Co., V; 17 (upd.)
Mitsubishi Rayon Co., Ltd., V
Mossimo, Inc., 27
Mothercare UK Ltd., 17
Movie Star Inc., 17
Naf Naf SA, 44
Nautica Enterprises, Inc., 18; 44 (upd.)
New Balance Athletic Shoe, Inc., 25
Nike, Inc., V; 8 (upd.)
Nine West Group, Inc., 39 (upd.)
The North Face, Inc., 18
Oakley, Inc., 18
OshKosh B'Gosh, Inc., 9; 42 (upd.)
Oxford Industries, Inc., 8
Pacific Sunwear of California, Inc., 28
Peek & Cloppenburg KG, 46
Pendleton Woolen Mills, Inc., 42
Pentland Group plc, 20
Perry Ellis International, Inc., 41
Pillowtex Corporation, 19; 41 (upd.)
Pluma, Inc., 27
Polo/Ralph Lauren Corporation, 12
Prada Holding B.V., 45
PremiumWear, Inc., 30
Puma AG Rudolf Dassler Sport, 35
Quaker Fabric Corp., 19
Quiksilver, Inc., 18
R.G. Barry Corporation, 17; 44 (upd.)
Recreational Equipment, Inc., 18
Red Wing Shoe Company, Inc., 30 (upd.)
Reebok International Ltd., V; 9 (upd.); 26 (upd.)
Rieter Holding AG, 42
Rollerblade, Inc., 15
Russell Corporation, 8; 30 (upd.)
St. John Knits, Inc., 14
Saucony Inc., 35
Shaw Industries, Inc., 40 (upd.)
Shelby Williams Industries, Inc., 14
Skechers U.S.A. Inc., 31
Springs Industries, Inc., V; 19 (upd.)
Starter Corp., 12
Steven Madden, Ltd., 37
Stone Manufacturing Company, 14; 43 (upd.)
The Stride Rite Corporation, 8; 37 (upd.)
Sun Sportswear, Inc., 17
Superior Uniform Group, Inc., 30

Teijin Limited, V
Thomaston Mills, Inc., 27
The Timberland Company, 13
Tommy Hilfiger Corporation, 20
Toray Industries, Inc., V
Tultex Corporation, 13
Unifi, Inc., 12
United Merchants & Manufacturers, Inc., 13
United Retail Group Inc., 33
Unitika Ltd., V
Vans, Inc., 16; 47 (upd.)
Varsity Spirit Corp., 15
VF Corporation, V; 17 (upd.)
Walton Monroe Mills, Inc., 8
The Warnaco Group Inc., 12; 46 (upd.)
Wellman, Inc., 8
West Point-Pepperell, Inc., 8
WestPoint Stevens Inc., 16
Weyco Group, Incorporated, 32
Williamson-Dickie Manufacturing Company, 14
Wolverine World Wide Inc., 16

## TOBACCO

American Brands, Inc., V
B.A.T. Industries PLC, 22 (upd.)
Brooke Group Ltd., 15
Brown & Williamson Tobacco Corporation, 14; 33 (upd.)
Culbro Corporation, 15
Dibrell Brothers, Incorporated, 12
DIMON Inc., 27
800-JR Cigar, Inc., 27
Gallaher Limited, V; 19 (upd.)
Holt's Cigar Holdings, Inc., 42
Imasco Limited, V
Japan Tobacco Incorporated, V
Philip Morris Companies Inc., V; 18 (upd.)
R.J. Reynolds Tobacco Holdings, Inc., 30 (upd.)
RJR Nabisco Holdings Corp., V
Rothmans UK Holdings Limited, V; 19 (upd.)
Seita, 23
Standard Commercial Corporation, 13
Swisher International Group Inc., 23
Tabacalera, S.A., V; 17 (upd.)
Universal Corporation, V; 48 (upd.)
UST Inc., 9
Vector Group Ltd., 35 (upd.)

## TRANSPORT SERVICES

Aéroports de Paris, 33
Air Express International Corporation, 13
Airborne Freight Corporation, 6; 34 (upd.)
Alamo Rent A Car, Inc., 6; 24 (upd.)
Alexander & Baldwin, Inc., 10
Amerco, 6
American Classic Voyages Company, 27
American President Companies Ltd., 6
Anschutz Corp., 12
Aqua Alliance Inc., 32 (upd.)
Atlas Van Lines, Inc., 14
Avis Rent A Car, Inc., 6; 22 (upd.)
BAA plc, 10
Bekins Company, 15
Boyd Bros. Transportation Inc., 39
Brambles Industries Limited, 42
British Railways Board, V
Broken Hill Proprietary Company Ltd., 22 (upd.)
Budget Group, Inc., 25
Budget Rent a Car Corporation, 9
Burlington Northern Santa Fe Corporation, V; 27 (upd.)
C.H. Robinson Worldwide, Inc., 40 (upd.)
Canadian National Railway System, 6
Canadian Pacific Railway Limited, V; 45 (upd.)
Carey International, Inc., 26
Carlson Companies, Inc., 6
Carolina Freight Corporation, 6
Celadon Group Inc., 30
Central Japan Railway Company, 43
Chargeurs, 6
Chicago and North Western Holdings Corporation, 6
Christian Salvesen Plc, 45
Coach USA, Inc., 24
Coles Express Inc., 15
Compagnie Générale Maritime et Financière, 6
Consolidated Delivery & Logistics, Inc., 24
Consolidated Freightways Corporation, V; 21 (upd.); 48 (upd.)
Consolidated Rail Corporation, V
Crowley Maritime Corporation, 6; 28 (upd.)
CSX Corporation, V; 22 (upd.)
Danzas Group, V; 40 (upd.)
Deutsche Bahn AG, 46 (upd.)
Deutsche Bundesbahn, V
DHL Worldwide Express, 6; 24 (upd.)
Dollar Thrifty Automotive Group, Inc., 25
East Japan Railway Company, V
Emery Air Freight Corporation, 6
Emery Worldwide Airlines, Inc., 25 (upd.)
Enterprise Rent-A-Car Company, 6
Eurotunnel Group, 37 (upd.)
Evergreen Marine Corporation Taiwan Ltd., 13
Executive Jet, Inc., 36
Expeditors International of Washington Inc., 17
Federal Express Corporation, V
FedEx Corporation, 18 (upd.); 42 (upd.)
Fritz Companies, Inc., 12
Frontline Ltd., 45
Frozen Food Express Industries, Inc., 20
GATX Corporation, 6; 25 (upd.)
GE Capital Aviation Services, 36
Genesee & Wyoming Inc., 27
The Go-Ahead Group Plc, 28
The Greenbrier Companies, 19
Greyhound Lines, Inc., 32 (upd.)
Grupo Transportación Ferroviaria Mexicana, S.A. de C.V., 47
Hankyu Corporation, V; 23 (upd.)
Hapag-Lloyd AG, 6
Harland and Wolff Holdings plc, 19
Harper Group Inc., 17
Heartland Express, Inc., 18
The Hertz Corporation, 9
Holberg Industries, Inc., 36
Hospitality Worldwide Services, Inc., 26
Hub Group, Inc., 38
Hvide Marine Incorporated, 22
Illinois Central Corporation, 11
International Shipholding Corporation, Inc., 27
J.B. Hunt Transport Services Inc., 12
John Menzies plc, 39
Kansas City Southern Industries, Inc., 6; 26 (upd.)
Kawasaki Kisen Kaisha, Ltd., V
Keio Teito Electric Railway Company, V
Kinki Nippon Railway Company Ltd., V
Kirby Corporation, 18
Koninklijke Nedlloyd Groep N.V., 6
Kuhne & Nagel International A.G., V
La Poste, V; 47 (upd.)
Leaseway Transportation Corp., 12
London Regional Transport, 6
Maine Central Railroad Company, 16
Mammoet Transport B.V., 26
Mayflower Group Inc., 6
Mercury Air Group, Inc., 20
The Mersey Docks and Harbour Company, 30
Metropolitan Transportation Authority, 35
Miller Industries, Inc., 26
Mitsui O.S.K. Lines, Ltd., V
Moran Towing Corporation, Inc., 15
The Morgan Group, Inc., 46
Morris Travel Services L.L.C., 26
Motor Cargo Industries, Inc., 35
National Car Rental System, Inc., 10
National Railroad Passenger Corporation, 22
Neptune Orient Lines Limited, 47
NFC plc, 6
Nippon Express Co., Ltd., V
Nippon Yusen Kabushiki Kaisha, V
Norfolk Southern Corporation, V; 29 (upd.)
Ocean Group plc, 6
Odakyu Electric Railway Company Limited, V
Oglebay Norton Company, 17
Österreichische Bundesbahnen GmbH, 6
OTR Express, Inc., 25
Overnite Transportation Co., 14
Overseas Shipholding Group, Inc., 11
The Peninsular and Oriental Steam Navigation Company, V; 38 (upd.)
Penske Corporation, V
PHH Corporation, V
The Port Authority of New York and New Jersey, 48
Post Office Group, V
Preston Corporation, 6
RailTex, Inc., 20
Roadway Express, Inc., 25 (upd.)
Roadway Services, Inc., V
Royal Vopak NV, 41
Ryder System, Inc., V; 24 (upd.)
Santa Fe Pacific Corporation, V
Schenker-Rhenus AG, 6
Schneider National, Inc., 36
Securicor Plc, 45
Seibu Railway Co. Ltd., V
Seino Transportation Company, Ltd., 6
Simon Transportation Services Inc., 27
Smithway Motor Xpress Corporation, 39
Société Nationale des Chemins de Fer Français, V
Southern Pacific Transportation Company, V
Stagecoach Holdings plc, 30
Stevedoring Services of America Inc., 28
Stinnes AG, 8
Stolt-Nielsen S.A., 42
Sunoco, Inc., 28 (upd.)
Swift Transportation Co., Inc., 42
The Swiss Federal Railways (Schweizerische Bundesbahnen), V
Teekay Shipping Corporation, 25
Tibbett & Britten Group plc, 32
Tidewater Inc., 11; 37 (upd.)
TNT Freightways Corporation, 14
TNT Post Group N.V., V; 27 (upd.); 30 (upd.)
Tobu Railway Co Ltd, 6
Tokyu Corporation, V
Totem Resources Corporation, 9
Trailer Bridge, Inc., 41
Transnet Ltd., 6
TTX Company, 6
U.S. Delivery Systems, Inc., 22
Union Pacific Corporation, V; 28 (upd.)
United Parcel Service of America Inc., V; 17 (upd.)
United States Postal Service, 14; 34 (upd.)

USA Truck, Inc., 42
Werner Enterprises, Inc., 26
Wisconsin Central Transportation Corporation, 24
Yamato Transport Co. Ltd., V
Yellow Corporation, 14; 45 (upd.)
Yellow Freight System, Inc. of Delaware, V

## UTILITIES

The AES Corporation, 10; 13 (upd.)
Aggreko Plc, 45
Air & Water Technologies Corporation, 6
Alberta Energy Company Ltd., 16; 43 (upd.)
Allegheny Energy, Inc., 38 (upd.)
Allegheny Power System, Inc., V
American Electric Power Company, Inc., V; 45 (upd.)
American States Water Company, 46
American Water Works Company, Inc., 6; 38 (upd.)
Arkla, Inc., V
Associated Natural Gas Corporation, 11
Atlanta Gas Light Company, 6; 23 (upd.)
Atlantic Energy, Inc., 6
Atmos Energy Corporation, 43
Baltimore Gas and Electric Company, V; 25 (upd.)
Bay State Gas Company, 38
Bayernwerk AG, V; 23 (upd.)
Bewag AG, 39
Big Rivers Electric Corporation, 11
Black Hills Corporation, 20
Boston Edison Company, 12
Bouygues S.A., 24 (upd.)
British Gas plc, V
British Nuclear Fuels plc, 6
Brooklyn Union Gas, 6
Calpine Corporation, 36
Canadian Utilities Limited, 13
Cap Rock Energy Corporation, 46
Carolina Power & Light Company, V; 23 (upd.)
Cascade Natural Gas Corporation, 9
Centerior Energy Corporation, V
Central and South West Corporation, V
Central Hudson Gas and Electricity Corporation, 6
Central Maine Power, 6
Centrica plc, 29 (upd.)
Chubu Electric Power Company, Inc., V; 46 (upd.)
Chugoku Electric Power Company Inc., V
Cincinnati Gas & Electric Company, 6
CIPSCO Inc., 6
Citizens Utilities Company, 7
City Public Service, 6
Cleco Corporation, 37
CMS Energy Corporation, V, 14
The Coastal Corporation, 31 (upd.)
Cogentrix Energy, Inc., 10
The Coleman Company, Inc., 9
The Columbia Gas System, Inc., V; 16 (upd.)
Commonwealth Edison Company, V
Commonwealth Energy System, 14
Connecticut Light and Power Co., 13
Consolidated Edison, Inc., V; 45 (upd.)
Consolidated Natural Gas Company, V; 19 (upd.)
Consumers Power Co., 14
Consumers Water Company, 14
Consumers' Gas Company Ltd., 6
Destec Energy, Inc., 12
The Detroit Edison Company, V
Dominion Resources, Inc., V
DPL Inc., 6
DQE, Inc., 6
DTE Energy Company, 20 (upd.)
Duke Energy Corporation, V; 27 (upd.)
Eastern Enterprises, 6
El Paso Electric Company, 21
El Paso Natural Gas Company, 12
Electricidade de Portugal, S.A., 47
Electricité de France, V; 41 (upd.)
Elektrowatt AG, 6
Enbridge Inc., 43
ENDESA Group, V
ENDESA S.A., 46 (upd.)
Enron Corporation, V; 46 (upd.)
Enserch Corporation, V
Ente Nazionale per L'Energia Elettrica, V
Entergy Corporation, V; 45 (upd.)
Equitable Resources, Inc., 6
Exelon Corporation, 48 (upd.)
Florida Progress Corporation, V; 23 (upd.)
Fortis, Inc., 15; 47 (upd.)
Fortum Corporation, 30 (upd.)
FPL Group, Inc., V
Gaz de France, V; 40 (upd.)
General Public Utilities Corporation, V
Générale des Eaux Group, V
GPU, Inc., 27 (upd.)
Gulf States Utilities Company, 6
Hawaiian Electric Industries, Inc., 9
Hokkaido Electric Power Company Inc., V
Hokuriku Electric Power Company, V
Hongkong Electric Holdings Ltd., 6; 23 (upd.)
Houston Industries Incorporated, V
Hyder plc, 34
Hydro-Québec, 6; 32 (upd.)
Idaho Power Company, 12
Illinois Bell Telephone Company, 14
Illinois Power Company, 6
Indiana Energy, Inc., 27
IPALCO Enterprises, Inc., 6
The Kansai Electric Power Co., Inc., V
Kansas City Power & Light Company, 6
Kelda Group plc, 45
Kenetech Corporation, 11
Kentucky Utilities Company, 6
KeySpan Energy Co., 27
KU Energy Corporation, 11
Kyushu Electric Power Company Inc., V
LG&E Energy Corporation, 6
Long Island Lighting Company, V
Lyonnaise des Eaux-Dumez, V
Madison Gas and Electric Company, 39
Magma Power Company, 11
MCN Corporation, 6
MDU Resources Group, Inc., 7; 42 (upd.)
Middlesex Water Company, 45
Midwest Resources Inc., 6
Minnesota Power, Inc., 11; 34 (upd.)
The Montana Power Company, 11; 44 (upd.)
National Fuel Gas Company, 6
National Power PLC, 12
Nebraska Public Power District, 29
N.V. Nederlandse Gasunie, V
Nevada Power Company, 11
New England Electric System, V
New York State Electric and Gas, 6
Niagara Mohawk Holdings Inc., V; 45 (upd.)
NICOR Inc., 6
NIPSCO Industries, Inc., 6
North West Water Group plc, 11
Northeast Utilities, V; 48 (upd.)
Northern States Power Company, V; 20 (upd.)
Northwest Natural Gas Company, 45
NorthWestern Corporation, 37
Nova Corporation of Alberta, V
Oglethorpe Power Corporation, 6
Ohio Edison Company, V
Oklahoma Gas and Electric Company, 6
ONEOK Inc., 7
Ontario Hydro Services Company, 6; 32 (upd.)
Osaka Gas Co., Ltd., V
Otter Tail Power Company, 18
Pacific Enterprises, V
Pacific Gas and Electric Company, V
PacifiCorp, V; 26 (upd.)
Panhandle Eastern Corporation, V
PECO Energy Company, 11
Pennon Group Plc, 45
Pennsylvania Power & Light Company, V
Peoples Energy Corporation, 6
PG&E Corporation, 26 (upd.)
Philadelphia Electric Company, V
Philadelphia Suburban Corporation, 39
Piedmont Natural Gas Company, Inc., 27
Pinnacle West Capital Corporation, 6
Portland General Corporation, 6
Potomac Electric Power Company, 6
PowerGen PLC, 11
PPL Corporation, 41 (upd.)
PreussenElektra Aktiengesellschaft, V
PSI Resources, 6
Public Service Company of Colorado, 6
Public Service Company of New Hampshire, 21
Public Service Company of New Mexico, 6
Public Service Enterprise Group Inc., V; 44 (upd.)
Puerto Rico Electric Power Authority, 47
Puget Sound Power and Light Company, 6
Questar Corporation, 6; 26 (upd.)
RAO Unified Energy System of Russia, 45
Reliant Energy Inc., 44 (upd.)
Rochester Gas and Electric Corporation, 6
Ruhrgas AG, V; 38 (upd.)
RWE Group, V
Salt River Project, 19
San Diego Gas & Electric Company, V
SCANA Corporation, 6
Scarborough Public Utilities Commission, 9
SCEcorp, V
Scottish Hydro-Electric PLC, 13
ScottishPower plc, 19
SEMCO Energy, Inc., 44
Sempra Energy, 25 (upd.)
Severn Trent PLC, 12; 38 (upd.)
Shikoku Electric Power Company, Inc., V
Sonat, Inc., 6
South Jersey Industries, Inc., 42
The Southern Company, V; 38 (upd.)
Southern Electric PLC, 13
Southern Indiana Gas and Electric Company, 13
Southern Union Company, 27
Southwest Gas Corporation, 19
Southwest Water Company, 47
Southwestern Electric Power Co., 21
Southwestern Public Service Company, 6
Suez Lyonnaise des Eaux, 36 (upd.)
TECO Energy, Inc., 6
Texas Utilities Company, V; 25 (upd.)
Thames Water plc, 11
Tohoku Electric Power Company, Inc., V
The Tokyo Electric Power Company, Incorporated, V
Tokyo Gas Co., Ltd., V
TransAlta Utilities Corporation, 6
TransCanada PipeLines Limited, V
Transco Energy Company, V
Trigen Energy Corporation, 42
Tucson Electric Power Company, 6

UGI Corporation, 12
Unicom Corporation, 29 (upd.)
Union Electric Company, V
The United Illuminating Company, 21
United Water Resources, Inc., 40
Unitil Corporation, 37
Utah Power and Light Company, 27
UtiliCorp United Inc., 6
Vereinigte Elektrizitätswerke Westfalen AG, V
VEW AG, 39
Washington Gas Light Company, 19
Washington Natural Gas Company, 9
Washington Water Power Company, 6
Western Resources, Inc., 12
Wheelabrator Technologies, Inc., 6
Wisconsin Energy Corporation, 6
Wisconsin Public Service Corporation, 9
WPL Holdings, Inc., 6

## WASTE SERVICES

Allwaste, Inc., 18
Appliance Recycling Centers of America, Inc., 42
Azcon Corporation, 23
Brambles Industries Limited, 42
Browning-Ferris Industries, Inc., V; 20 (upd.)
Chemical Waste Management, Inc., 9
Copart Inc., 23
Ecology and Environment, Inc., 39
Industrial Services of America, Inc., 46
Kelda Group plc, 45
Pennon Group Plc, 45
Philip Environmental Inc., 16
Roto-Rooter Corp., 15
Safety-Kleen Corp., 8
Sevenson Environmental Services, Inc., 42
Severn Trent PLC, 38 (upd.)
Shanks Group plc, 45
Stericycle Inc., 33
TRC Companies, Inc., 32
Veit Companies, 43
Waste Connections, Inc., 46
Waste Holdings, Inc., 41
Waste Management, Inc., V
WMX Technologies Inc., 17

# *GEOGRAPHIC INDEX*

# Geographic Index


## Algeria

Entreprise Nationale Sonatrach, IV

## Argentina

Aerolíneas Argentinas S.A., 33
YPF Sociedad Anonima, IV

## Australia

Amcor Limited, IV; 19 (upd.)
Australia and New Zealand Banking Group Ltd., II
Billabong International Ltd., 44
Bond Corporation Holdings Limited, 10
Boral Limited, III; 43 (upd.)
Brambles Industries Limited, 42
Broken Hill Proprietary Company Ltd., IV; 22 (upd.)
Carlton and United Breweries Ltd., I
Coles Myer Ltd., V; 20 (upd.)
CRA Limited, IV
CSR Limited, III; 28 (upd.)
Elders IXL Ltd., I
Foster's Brewing Group Ltd., 7; 21 (upd.)
John Fairfax Holdings Limited, 7
Lend Lease Corporation Limited, IV; 17 (upd.)
News Corporation Limited, IV; 7 (upd.); 46 (upd.)
Pacific Dunlop Limited, 10
Pioneer International Limited, III
Qantas Airways Limited, 6; 24 (upd.)
TABCORP Holdings Limited, 44
Telecom Australia, 6
Westpac Banking Corporation, II; 48 (upd.)
WMC, Limited, 43

## Austria

Austrian Airlines AG (Österreichische Luftverkehrs AG), 33
Bank Austria AG, 23
BBAG Osterreichische Brau-Beteiligungs-AG, 38
Gericom AG, 47
Glock Ges.m.b.H., 42
Lauda Air Luftfahrt AG, 48
ÖMV Aktiengesellschaft, IV
Österreichische Bundesbahnen GmbH, 6
Österreichische Post- und Telegraphenverwaltung, V
Voest-Alpine Stahl AG, IV

## Bahamas

Sun International Hotels Limited, 26
Teekay Shipping Corporation, 25

## Bangladesh

Grameen Bank, 31

## Belgium

Almanij NV, 44
Bank Brussels Lambert, II
Barco NV, 44
Belgacom, 6
C&A, 40 (upd.)
Cockerill Sambre Group, IV; 26 (upd.)
Delhaize ''Le Lion'' S.A., 44
Generale Bank, II
GIB Group, V; 26 (upd.)
Interbrew S.A., 17
Kredietbank N.V., II
PetroFina S.A., IV; 26 (upd.)
Roularta Media Group NV, 48
Sabena S.A./N.V., 33
Solvay & Cie S.A., I; 21 (upd.)
Tractebel S.A., 20
NV Umicore SA, 47
Xeikon NV, 26

## Bermuda

Bacardi Limited, 18
Frontline Ltd., 45
Jardine Matheson Holdings Limited, I; 20 (upd.)
Sea Containers Ltd., 29
Tyco International Ltd., III; 28 (upd.)
White Mountains Insurance Group, Ltd., 48

## Brazil

Banco Bradesco S.A., 13
Banco Itaú S.A., 19
Companhia Vale do Rio Doce, IV; 43 (upd.)
Empresa Brasileira de Aeronáutica S.A. (Embraer), 36
Lojas Arapua S.A., 22
Petróleo Brasileiro S.A., IV
TransBrasil S/A Linhas Aéreas, 31
VARIG S.A. (Viaçâo Aérea Rio-Grandense), 6; 29 (upd.)

## Canada

Abitibi-Consolidated, Inc., V; 25 (upd.)
Abitibi-Price Inc., IV
Air Canada, 6; 23 (upd.)
Alberta Energy Company Ltd., 16; 43 (upd.)
Alcan Aluminium Limited, IV; 31 (upd.)
Algo Group Inc., 24
Alliance Atlantis Communications Inc., 39
Bank of Montreal, II; 46 (upd.)
Bank of Nova Scotia, The, II
Barrick Gold Corporation, 34
BCE Inc., V; 44 (upd.)
Bell Canada, 6
BFC Construction Corporation, 25
Biovail Corporation, 47
Bombardier Inc., 42 (upd.)
Bramalea Ltd., 9
British Columbia Telephone Company, 6
Campeau Corporation, V
Canada Packers Inc., II
Canadair, Inc., 16
Canadian Broadcasting Corporation (CBC), The, 37
Canadian Imperial Bank of Commerce, II
Canadian National Railway System, 6
Canadian Pacific Railway Limited, V; 45 (upd.)
Canadian Utilities Limited, 13
Canfor Corporation, 42
Canstar Sports Inc., 16
CanWest Global Communications Corporation, 35
Cinar Corporation, 40
Cineplex Odeon Corporation, 6; 23 (upd.)
Cinram International, Inc., 43
Cirque du Soleil Inc., 29
Clearly Canadian Beverage Corporation, 48
Cognos Inc., 44
Cominco Ltd., 37
Consumers' Gas Company Ltd., 6
CoolBrands International Inc., 35
Corby Distilleries Limited, 14
Corel Corporation, 15; 33 (upd.)
Creo Inc., 48
Discreet Logic Inc., 20
Dofasco Inc., IV; 24 (upd.)
Dominion Textile Inc., 12
Domtar Inc., IV
Dylex Limited, 29
Echo Bay Mines Ltd., IV; 38 (upd.)
Enbridge Inc., 43
Extendicare Health Services, Inc., 6
Fortis, Inc., 15; 47 (upd.)
Four Seasons Hotels Inc., 9; 29 (upd.)
GEAC Computer Corporation Ltd., 43
George Weston Limited, II; 36 (upd.)
Great-West Lifeco Inc., III
Groupe Vidéotron Ltée., 20
Hemlo Gold Mines Inc., 9
Hiram Walker Resources, Ltd., I
Hockey Company, The, 34
Hudson Bay Mining and Smelting Company, Limited, The, 12
Hudson's Bay Company, V; 25 (upd.)
Husky Energy Inc., 47
Hydro-Québec, 6; 32 (upd.)
Imasco Limited, V
Imax Corporation, 28
Imperial Oil Limited, IV; 25 (upd.)
Inco Limited, IV; 45 (upd.)
Intrawest Corporation, The, 15
Irwin Toy Limited, 14
Jean Coutu Group (PJC) Inc., The, 46
Jim Pattison Group, The, 37
Kinross Gold Corporation, 36
Kruger Inc., 17
Labatt Brewing Company Limited, I; 25 (upd.)
Ledcor Industries Limited, 46
Linamar Corporation, 18
Lions Gate Entertainment Corporation, 35
Loblaw Companies Limited, 43
Loewen Group, Inc., The, 16; 40 (upd.)
London Drugs Ltd., 46
Maclean Hunter Publishing Limited, IV; 26 (upd.)
MacMillan Bloedel Limited, IV
Magellan Aerospace Corporation, 48

**Canada** *(continued)*

Maple Leaf Foods Inc., 41
Methanex Corporation, 40
Mitel Corporation, 18
Molson Companies Limited, The, I; 26 (upd.)
Moore Corporation Limited, IV
Mouvement des Caisses Desjardins, 48
National Sea Products Ltd., 14
Noranda Inc., IV; 7 (upd.)
Nortel Networks Corporation, 36 (upd.)
North West Company, Inc., The, 12
Northern Telecom Limited, V
Nova Corporation of Alberta, V
Novacor Chemicals Ltd., 12
Olympia & York Developments Ltd., IV; 9 (upd.)
Onex Corporation, 16
Ontario Hydro Services Company, 6; 32 (upd.)
Oshawa Group Limited, The, II
Petro-Canada Limited, IV
Philip Environmental Inc., 16
Placer Dome Inc., 20
Potash Corporation of Saskatchewan Inc., 18
Power Corporation of Canada, 36 (upd.)
Provigo Inc., II
Quebecor Inc., 12; 47 (upd.)
Ritchie Bros. Auctioneers Inc., 41
Rogers Communications Inc., 30 (upd.)
Roots Canada Ltd., 42
Royal Bank of Canada, The, II; 21 (upd.)
Scarborough Public Utilities Commission, 9
Seagram Company Ltd., The, I; 25 (upd.)
Southam Inc., 7
Spar Aerospace Limited, 32
Steinberg Incorporated, II
Stelco Inc., IV
Talisman Energy Inc., 9; 47 (upd.)
TDL Group Ltd., 46
Teck Corporation, 27
Thomson Corporation, The, 8; 34 (upd.)
Toromont Industries, Ltd., 21
Toronto-Dominion Bank, The, II
Torstar Corporation, 29
TransAlta Utilities Corporation, 6
TransCanada PipeLines Limited, V
Tridel Enterprises Inc., 9
Trilon Financial Corporation, II
Trizec Corporation Ltd., 10
Van Houtte Inc., 39
Varity Corporation, III
Wascana Energy Inc., 13
West Fraser Timber Co. Ltd., 17
WestJet Airlines Ltd., 38

**Chile**

Corporacion Nacional del Cobre de Chile, 40
Lan Chile S.A., 31
Viña Concha y Toro S.A., 45

**China**

Air China, 46
Asia Info Holdings, Inc., 43
China Eastern Airlines Co. Ltd., 31
China National Petroleum Corporation, 46
China Southern Airlines Company Ltd., 33
Chinese Petroleum Corporation, IV; 31 (upd.)
Directorate General of Telecommunications, 7
Hongkong and Shanghai Banking Corporation Limited, The, II
Shanghai Petrochemical Co., Ltd., 18

**Colombia**

Avianca Aerovías Nacionales de Colombia SA, 36
Empresa Colombiana de Petróleos, IV

**Czech Republic**

Skoda Auto a.s., 39

**Denmark**

Arla Foods amba, 48
Bang & Olufsen Holding A/S, 37
Carlsberg A/S, 9; 29 (upd.)
Danisco A/S, 44
Group 4 Falck A/S, 42
H. Lundbeck A/S, 44
IKEA International A/S, V; 26 (upd.)
Lego A/S, 13; 40 (upd.)
Novo Industri A/S, I

**Ecuador**

Petróleos del Ecuador, IV

**Egypt**

EgyptAir, 6; 27 (upd.)
Egyptian General Petroluem Corporation, IV

**El Salvador**

Grupo TACA, 38

**Finland**

Amer Group plc, 41
Enso-Gutzeit Oy, IV
Finnair Oy, 6; 25 (upd.)
Fiskars Corporation, 33
Fortum Corporation, 30 (upd.)
Hackman Oyj Adp, 44
Kansallis-Osake-Pankki, II
Kesko Ltd. (Kesko Oy), 8; 27 (upd.)
Kone Corporation, 27
Kymmene Corporation, IV
Metsa-Serla Oy, IV
Metso Corporation, 30 (upd.)
Neste Oy, IV
Nokia Corporation, II; 17 (upd.); 38 (upd.)
Outokumpu Oyj, 38
Posti- ja Telelaitos, 6
Stora Enso Oyj, 36 (upd.)
United Paper Mills Ltd. (Yhtyneet Paperitehtaat Oy), IV
UPM-Kymmene Corporation, 19
Valmet Corporation (Valmet Oy), III

**France**

Accor SA, 10; 27 (upd.)
Aéroports de Paris, 33
Aerospatiale Group, The, 7; 21 (upd.)
Agence France-Presse, 34
Alcatel Alsthom Compagnie Générale d'Electricité, 9
Alcatel S.A., 36 (upd.)
Association des Centres Distributeurs E. Leclerc, 37
Atochem S.A., I
Au Printemps S.A., V
Auchan, 37
Automobiles Citroen, 7
Avions Marcel Dassault-Breguet Aviation, I
Axa, III
Baccarat, 24
Banque Nationale de Paris S.A., II
Baron Philippe de Rothschild S.A., 39
Besnier SA, 19
BNP Paribas Group, 36 (upd.)
Bongrain SA, 25
Bouygues S.A., I; 24 (upd.)
BSN Groupe S.A., II
Bull S.A., 43 (upd.)
Burelle S.A., 23
Business Objects S.A., 25
Canal Plus, 10; 34 (upd.)
Cap Gemini Ernst & Young, 37
Carbone Lorraine S.A., 33
Carrefour SA, 10; 27 (upd.)
Cetelem S.A., 21
Chanel, 12
Chargeurs International, 6; 21 (upd.)
Christian Dalloz SA, 40
Christian Dior S.A., 19
Christofle SA, 40
Ciments Français, 40
Club Mediterranée S.A., 6; 21 (upd.)
Coflexip S.A., 25
Colas S.A., 31
Compagnie de Saint-Gobain S.A., III; 16 (upd.)
Compagnie des Alpes, 48
Compagnie des Machines Bull S.A., III
Compagnie Financiere de Paribas, II
Compagnie Générale d'Électricité, II
Compagnie Générale des Établissements Michelin, V; 42 (upd.)
Compagnie Générale Maritime et Financière, 6
Comptoirs Modernes S.A., 19
Crédit Agricole, II
Crédit Lyonnais, 9; 33 (upd.)
Crédit National S.A., 9
Darty S.A., 27
Dassault Systèmes S.A., 25
De Dietrich & Cie., 31
Deveaux S.A., 41
Dexia Group, 42
Du Pareil au Même, 43
ECS S.A, 12
Eiffage, 27
Electricité de France, V; 41 (upd.)
Elf Aquitaine SA, 21 (upd.)
Eridania Béghin-Say S.A., 36
Essilor International, 21
Etablissements Economiques du Casino Guichard, Perrachon et Cie, S.C.A., 12
Etam Developpement SA, 44
Euro Disneyland SCA, 20
Euro RSCG Worldwide S.A., 13
Euronext Paris S.A., 37
Expand SA, 48
Facom S.A., 32
Faiveley S.A., 39
Fimalac S.A., 37
Fleury Michon S.A., 39
FNAC, 21
Framatome SA, 19
France Télécom Group, V; 21 (upd.)
Fromageries Bel, 23
G.I.E. Airbus Industrie, I; 12 (upd.)
Galeries Lafayette S.A., V; 23 (upd.)
Gaumont SA, 25
Gaz de France, V; 40 (upd.)
Gecina SA, 42
Générale des Eaux Group, V
GrandVision S.A., 43
Groupe Air France, 6
Groupe André, 17
Groupe Castorama-Dubois Investissements, 23
Groupe Danone, 32 (upd.)
Groupe Dassault Aviation SA, 26 (upd.)
Groupe de la Cite, IV

Groupe DMC (Dollfus Mieg & Cie), 27
Groupe Fournier SA, 44
Groupe Go Sport S.A., 39
Groupe Guillin SA, 40
Groupe Jean-Claude Darmon, 44
Groupe Lapeyre S.A., 33
Groupe Legris Industries, 23
Groupe Les Echos, 25
Groupe Partouche SA, 48
Groupe Promodès S.A., 19
Groupe Rougier SA, 21
Groupe SEB, 35
Groupe Sidel S.A., 21
Groupe Yves Saint Laurent, 23
Groupe Zannier S.A., 35
Guerbet Group, 46
Guerlain, 23
Guilbert S.A., 42
Guillemot Corporation, 41
Guy Degrenne SA, 44
Guyenne et Gascogne, 23
Hachette, IV
Hachette Filipacchi Medias S.A., 21
Havas, SA, 10; 33 (upd.)
Hermès International S.A., 14; 34 (upd.)
Imerys S.A., 40 (upd.)
Imetal S.A., IV
Infogrames Entertainment S.A., 35
Ingenico—Compagnie Industrielle et Financière d'Ingénierie, 46
ITM Entreprises SA, 36
L'Air Liquide SA, I; 47 (upd.)
L'Entreprise Jean Lefebvre, 23
L'Oreal, III; 8 (upd.)
L'Oréal SA, 46 (upd.)
La Poste, V; 47 (upd.)
Laboratoires de Biologie Végétale Yves Rocher, 35
Lafarge Coppée S.A., III
Lafuma S.A., 39
Laurent-Perrier SA, 42
Lazard LLC, 38
Le Monde S.A., 33
Legrand SA, 21
Louis Vuitton, 10
LVMH Möet Hennessy Louis Vuitton SA, 33 (upd.)
Lyonnaise des Eaux-Dumez, V
Maison Louis Jadot, 24
Manitou BF S.A., 27
Marie Brizard & Roger International S.A., 22
Matra-Hachette S.A., 15 (upd.)
Metaleurop S.A., 21
Métropole Télévision, 33
Moët-Hennessy, I
Moulinex S.A., 22
Mr. Bricolage S.A., 37
Naf Naf SA, 44
Papeteries de Lancey, 23
Pathé SA, 29
Pechiney SA, IV; 45 (upd.)
Pernod Ricard S.A., I; 21 (upd.)
Peugeot S.A., I
Pierre & Vacances SA, 48
Pinault-Printemps Redoute S.A., 19 (upd.)
Poliet S.A., 33
PSA Peugeot Citroen S.A., 28 (upd.)
Publicis S.A., 19
Regie Nationale des Usines Renault, I
Rémy Cointreau S.A., 20
Renault S.A., 26 (upd.)
Rhodia SA, 38
Rhône-Poulenc S.A., I; 10 (upd.)
Robertet SA, 39
Roussel Uclaf, I; 8 (upd.)
Royal Canin S.A., 39
Sabaté Diosos SA, 48
SAGEM S.A., 37
Salomon Worldwide, 20
Sanofi Group, I
Schneider S.A., II; 18 (upd.)
SCOR S.A., 20
Seita, 23
Simco S.A., 37
Skis Rossignol S.A., 15; 43 (upd.)
Snecma Group, 46
Société Air France, 27 (upd.)
Société du Louvre, 27
Société Générale, II; 42 (upd.)
Société Nationale des Chemins de Fer Français, V
Société Nationale Elf Aquitaine, IV; 7 (upd.)
Sodexho Alliance SA, 29
Sodiaal S.A., 36 (upd.)
SODIMA, II
Sommer-Allibert S.A., 19
Suez Lyonnaise des Eaux, 36 (upd.)
Taittinger S.A., 43
Tati SA, 25
Télévision Française 1, 23
Thales S.A., 42
THOMSON multimedia S.A., II; 42 (upd.)
TOTAL S.A., IV; 24 (upd.)
Transiciel SA, 48
Ubi Soft Entertainment S.A., 41
Ugine S.A., 20
Unibail SA, 40
Unilog SA, 42
Union des Assurances de Pans, III
Usinor SA, 42 (upd.)
Usinor Sacilor, IV
Valeo, 23
Vinci, 43
Vivendi Universal S.A., 46 (upd.)
Worms et Cie, 27
Zodiac S.A., 36

**Germany**

Adam Opel AG, 7; 21 (upd.)
Adidas AG, 14
adidas-Salomon AG, 33 (upd.)
AEG A.G., I
Aldi Group, 13
Allianz Aktiengesellschaft Holding, III; 15 (upd.)
Andreas Stihl, 16
ARD, 41
AVA AG (Allgemeine Handelsgesellschaft der Verbraucher AG), 33
AXA Colonia Konzern AG, 27
Axel Springer Verlag AG, IV; 20 (upd.)
Bahlsen GmbH & Co. KG, 44
Barmag AG, 39
BASF Aktiengesellschaft, I; 18 (upd.)
Bauer Publishing Group, 7
Bayer A.G., I; 13 (upd.); 41 (upd.)
Bayerische Hypotheken- und Wechsel-Bank AG, II
Bayerische Motoren Werke AG, I; 11 (upd.); 38 (upd.)
Bayerische Vereinsbank A.G., II
Bayernwerk AG, V; 23 (upd.)
Beiersdorf AG, 29
Bertelsmann A.G., IV; 15 (upd.); 43 (upd.)
Bewag AG, 39
Bilfinger & Berger Bau A.G., I
Brauerei Beck & Co., 9; 33 (upd.)
Brenntag AG, 8; 23 (upd.)
Buderus AG, 37
Burda Holding GmbH. & Co., 23
C&A Brenninkmeyer KG, V
C.H. Boehringer Sohn, 39
Carl-Zeiss-Stiftung, III; 34 (upd.)
Commerzbank A.G., II; 47 (upd.)
Continental Aktiengesellschaft, V
Daimler-Benz A.G., I; 15 (upd.)
Daimler-Benz Aerospace AG, 16
DaimlerChrysler AG, 34 (upd.)
Degussa Group, IV
Degussa-Huls AG, 32 (upd.)
Deutsche Babcock A.G., III
Deutsche Bahn AG, 46 (upd.)
Deutsche Bank AG, II; 14 (upd.); 40 (upd.)
Deutsche BP Aktiengesellschaft, 7
Deutsche Bundesbahn, V
Deutsche Bundespost TELEKOM, V
Deutsche Lufthansa Aktiengesellschaft, I; 26 (upd.)
Deutsche Post AG, 29
Deutsche Telekom AG, 48 (upd.)
Deutz AG, 39
Dresdner Bank A.G., II
Dürr AG, 44
Dyckerhoff AG, 35
Edeka Zentrale A.G., II; 47 (upd.)
edel music AG, 44
ERGO Versicherungsgruppe AG, 44
Esselte Leitz GmbH & Co. KG, 48
Fairchild Dornier GmbH, 48 (upd.)
Feldmuhle Nobel A.G., III
Fielmann AG, 31
Freudenberg & Co., 41
Fried. Krupp GmbH, IV
GEA AG, 27
GEHE AG, 27
geobra Brandstätter GmbH & Co. KG, 48
Gerresheimer Glas AG, 43
Grundig AG, 27
Hapag-Lloyd AG, 6
HARIBO GmbH & Co. KG, 44
Heidelberger Druckmaschinen AG, 40
Heidelberger Zement AG, 31
Henkel KGaA, III; 34 (upd.)
Heraeus Holding GmbH, IV
Hertie Waren- und Kaufhaus GmbH, V
Hochtief AG, 33
Hoechst A.G., I; 18 (upd.)
Hoesch AG, IV
Hugo Boss AG, 48
Huls A.G., I
J.M. Voith AG, 33
Jenoptik AG, 33
Kamps AG, 44
Karlsberg Brauerei GmbH & Co KG, 41
Karstadt Aktiengesellschaft, V; 19 (upd.)
Kaufhof Holding AG, V
Kaufhof Warenhaus AG, 23 (upd.)
Kaufring AG, 35
KHD Konzern, III
Klockner-Werke AG, IV
König Brauerei GmbH & Co. KG, 35 (upd.)
Kreditanstalt für Wiederaufbau, 29
Leica Camera AG, 35
Leica Microsystems Holdings GmbH, 35
Linde A.G., I
LTU Group Holding GmbH, 37
MAN Aktiengesellschaft, III
Mannesmann AG, III; 14 (upd.); 38 (upd.)
Margarete Steiff GmbH, 23
Messerschmitt-Bölkow-Blohm GmbH., I
Metallgesellschaft AG, IV; 16 (upd.)
MITROPA AG, 37
Munich Re (Münchener Rückversicherungs-Gesellschaft Aktiengesellschaft in München), III; 46 (upd.)
Nixdorf Computer AG, III
Optische Werke G. Rodenstock, 44
Otto Versand GmbH & Co., V; 15 (upd.); 34 (upd.)

**Germany** *(continued)*

Paulaner Brauerei GmbH & Co. KG, 35
Peek & Cloppenburg KG, 46
Philipp Holzmann AG, 17
Porsche AG, 13; 31 (upd.)
Preussag AG, 17; 42 (upd.)
PreussenElektra Aktiengesellschaft, V
Puma AG Rudolf Dassler Sport, 35
PWA Group, IV
Qiagen N.V., 39
Quelle Group, V
RAG AG, 35
RENK AG, 37
Rheinmetall Berlin AG, 9
Robert Bosch GmbH, I; 16 (upd.); 43 (upd.)
Rohde & Schwarz GmbH & Co. KG, 39
Roland Berger & Partner GmbH, 37
Ruhrgas AG, V; 38 (upd.)
Ruhrkohle AG, IV
RWE Group, V
Saarberg-Konzern, IV
Salzgitter AG, IV
SAP AG, 16; 43 (upd.)
Schenker-Rhenus AG, 6
Schering AG
Siemens A.G., II; 14 (upd.)
Sixt AG, 39
SPAR Handels AG, 35
SPIEGEL-Verlag Rudolf Augstein GmbH & Co. KG, 44
Stinnes AG, 8; 23 (upd.)
Südzucker AG, 27
TA Triumph-Adler AG, 48
Tarkett Sommer AG, 25
TaurusHolding GmbH & Co. KG, 46
Tengelmann Group, 27
Thyssen Krupp AG, IV; 28 (upd.)
Touristik Union International GmbH. and Company K.G., II
TUI Group GmbH, 44
Vaillant GmbH, 44
Varta AG, 23
Veba A.G., I; 15 (upd.)
Vereinigte Elektrizitätswerke Westfalen AG, V
Verlagsgruppe Georg von Holtzbrinck GmbH, 35
VEW AG, 39
VIAG Aktiengesellschaft, IV
Victoria Group, 44 (upd.)
VICTORIA Holding AG, III
Viessmann Werke GmbH & Co., 37
Villeroy & Boch AG, 37
Volkswagen Aktiengesellschaft, I; 11 (upd.); 32 (upd.)
Vorwerk & Co., 27
Wacker-Chemie GmbH, 35
Wella AG, 48 (upd.)
Wella Group, III
Weru Aktiengesellschaft, 18
Westdeutsche Landesbank Girozentrale, II; 46 (upd.)
ZF Friedrichshafen AG, 48

## Ghana

Ashanti Goldfields Company Limited, 43

## Greece

National Bank of Greece, 41

## Hong Kong

Cable & Wireless HKT, 30 (upd.)
Cathay Pacific Airways Limited, 6; 34 (upd.)
Cheung Kong (Holdings) Limited, IV; 20 (upd.)
CITIC Pacific Ltd., 18
First Pacific Company Limited, 18
Hong Kong Telecommunications Ltd., 6
Hongkong Electric Holdings Ltd., 6; 23 (upd.)
Hongkong Land Holdings Limited, IV; 47 (upd.)
Hutchison Whampoa Ltd., 18
Kerry Properties Limited, 22
New World Development Company Limited, IV; 38 (upd.)
Playmates Toys, 23
Singer Company N.V., The, 30 (upd.)
Swire Pacific Ltd., I; 16 (upd.)
Tommy Hilfiger Corporation, 20

## Hungary

Malév Plc, 24

## India

Air-India Limited, 6; 27 (upd.)
Bajaj Auto Limited, 39
Coal India Limited, IV; 44 (upd.)
Indian Airlines Ltd., 46
Indian Oil Corporation Ltd., IV; 48 (upd.)
Infosys Technologies Ltd., 38
Minerals and Metals Trading Corporation of India Ltd., IV
Oil and Natural Gas Commission, IV
Steel Authority of India Ltd., IV
Tata Iron & Steel Co. Ltd., IV; 44 (upd.)
Wipro Limited, 43

## Indonesia

Garuda Indonesia, 6
PERTAMINA, IV

## Iran

National Iranian Oil Company, IV

## Ireland

Aer Lingus Group plc, 34
Allied Irish Banks, plc, 16; 43 (upd.)
Baltimore Technologies Plc, 42
eircom plc, 31 (upd.)
Fyffes Plc, 38
Harland and Wolff Holdings plc, 19
IONA Technologies plc, 43
Jefferson Smurfit Group plc, IV; 19 (upd.)
Kerry Group plc, 27
Ryanair Holdings plc, 35
Shannon Aerospace Ltd., 36
Telecom Eireann, 7
Waterford Wedgwood plc, 34 (upd.)

## Israel

Amdocs Ltd., 47
Bank Hapoalim B.M., II
Blue Square Israel Ltd., 41
ECI Telecom Ltd., 18
El Al Israel Airlines Ltd., 23
Elscint Ltd., 20
Koor Industries Ltd., II; 25 (upd.)
Scitex Corporation Ltd., 24
Teva Pharmaceutical Industries Ltd., 22

## Italy

Alfa Romeo, 13; 36 (upd.)
Alitalia-Linee Aeree Italiana, S.p.A., 6; 29 (upd.)
Aprilia SpA, 17
Arnoldo Mondadori Editore S.p.A., IV; 19 (upd.)
Assicurazioni Generali SpA, III; 15 (upd.)
Automobili Lamborghini Holding S.p.A., 34 (upd.)
Automobili Lamborghini S.p.A., 13
Banca Commerciale Italiana SpA, II
Barilla G. e R. Fratelli S.p.A., 17
Benetton Group S.p.A., 10
Bulgari S.p.A., 20
Credito Italiano, II
Diesel SpA, 40
Ducati Motor Holding S.p.A., 30
Ente Nazionale Idrocarburi, IV
Ente Nazionale per L'Energia Elettrica, V
Fabbrica D' Armi Pietro Beretta S.p.A., 39
Ferrari S.p.A., 13; 36 (upd.)
Fiat S.p.A, I; 11 (upd.)
Fila Holding S.p.A., 20
Gianni Versace SpA, 22
Giorgio Armani S.p.A., 45
Gruppo Coin S.p.A., 41
Guccio Gucci, S.p.A., 15
Industrie Natuzzi S.p.A., 18
Ing. C. Olivetti & C., S.p.a., III
Istituto per la Ricostruzione Industriale S.p.A., I; 11
Luxottica SpA, 17
Marchesi Antinori SRL, 42
Marzotto S.p.A., 20
Montedison SpA, I; 24 (upd.)
Officine Alfieri Maserati S.p.A., 13
Olivetti S.p.A., 34 (upd.)
Piaggio & C. S.p.A., 20
Pirelli S.p.A., V; 15 (upd.)
Reno de Medici S.p.A., 41
Riunione Adriatica di Sicurtè SpA, III
Seat Pagine Gialle S.p.A., 47
Società Finanziaria Telefonica per Azioni, V
Società Sportiva Lazio SpA, 44
Telecom Italia S.p.A., 43
Tiscali SpA, 48

## Japan

Aisin Seiki Co., Ltd., III; 48 (upd.)
Aiwa Co., Ltd., 30
Ajinomoto Co., Inc., II; 28 (upd.)
All Nippon Airways Co., Ltd., 6; 38 (upd.)
Alpine Electronics, Inc., 13
Alps Electric Co., Ltd., II; 44 (upd.)
Asahi Breweries, Ltd., I; 20 (upd.)
Asahi Glass Company, Ltd., III; 48 (upd.)
Asahi National Broadcasting Company, Ltd., 9
Bank of Tokyo-Mitsubishi Ltd., II; 15 (upd.)
Bridgestone Corporation, V; 21 (upd.)
Brother Industries, Ltd., 14
C. Itoh & Company Ltd., I
Canon Inc., III; 18 (upd.)
CASIO Computer Co., Ltd., III; 16 (upd.); 40 (upd.)
Central Japan Railway Company, 43
Chubu Electric Power Company, Inc., V; 46 (upd.)
Chugoku Electric Power Company Inc., V
Citizen Watch Co., Ltd., III; 21 (upd.)
Cosmo Oil Co., Ltd., IV
Dai Nippon Printing Co., Ltd., IV
Dai-Ichi Kangyo Bank Ltd., The, II
Daido Steel Co., Ltd., IV
Daiei, Inc., The, V; 17 (upd.); 41 (upd.)
Daihatsu Motor Company, Ltd., 7; 21 (upd.)
Daikin Industries, Ltd., III
Daimaru, Inc., The, V; 42 (upd.)
Daio Paper Corporation, IV

Daishowa Paper Manufacturing Co., Ltd., IV
Daiwa Bank, Ltd., The, II; 39 (upd.)
Daiwa Securities Company, Limited, II
DDI Corporation, 7
DENSO Corporation, 46 (upd.)
Dentsu Inc., I; 16 (upd.); 40 (upd.)
East Japan Railway Company, V
Fanuc Ltd., III; 17 (upd.)
Fuji Bank, Ltd., The, II
Fuji Electric Co., Ltd., II; 48 (upd.)
Fuji Photo Film Co., Ltd., III; 18 (upd.)
Fujisawa Pharmaceutical Company Ltd., I
Fujitsu Limited, III; 16 (upd.); 42 (upd.)
Furukawa Electric Co., Ltd., The, III
General Sekiyu K.K., IV
Hakuhodo, Inc., 6; 42 (upd.)
Hankyu Corporation, V; 23 (upd.)
Hino Motors, Ltd., 7; 21 (upd.)
Hitachi Ltd., I; 12 (upd.)
Hitachi Metals, Ltd., IV
Hitachi Zosen Corporation, III
Hitachi, Ltd., 40 (upd.)
Hokkaido Electric Power Company Inc., V
Hokuriku Electric Power Company, V
Honda Motor Company Limited, I; 10 (upd.); 29 (upd.)
Honshu Paper Co., Ltd., IV
Idemitsu Kosan K.K., IV
Industrial Bank of Japan, Ltd., The, II
Isetan Company Limited, V; 36 (upd.)
Ishikawajima-Harima Heavy Industries Co., Ltd., III
Isuzu Motors, Ltd., 9; 23 (upd.)
Ito-Yokado Co., Ltd., V; 42 (upd.)
ITOCHU Corporation, 32 (upd.)
Itoham Foods Inc., II
Japan Airlines Company, Ltd., I; 32 (upd.)
Japan Broadcasting Corporation, 7
Japan Leasing Corporation, 8
Japan Pulp and Paper Company Limited, IV
Japan Tobacco Inc., V; 46 (upd.)
Jujo Paper Co., Ltd., IV
JUSCO Co., Ltd., V
Kajima Corporation, I
Kanematsu Corporation, IV; 24 (upd.)
Kansai Electric Power Co., Inc., The, V
Kao Corporation, III; 20 (upd.)
Kawasaki Heavy Industries, Ltd., III
Kawasaki Kisen Kaisha, Ltd., V
Kawasaki Steel Corporation, IV
Keio Teito Electric Railway Company, V
Kenwood Corporation, 31
Kikkoman Corporation, 14; 47 (upd.)
Kinki Nippon Railway Company Ltd., V
Kirin Brewery Company, Limited, I; 21 (upd.)
Kobe Steel, Ltd., IV; 19 (upd.)
Kodansha Ltd., IV; 38 (upd.)
Komatsu Ltd., III; 16 (upd.)
Konica Corporation, III; 30 (upd.)
Kotobukiya Co., Ltd., V
Kubota Corporation, III; 26 (upd.)
Kumagai Gumi Company, Ltd., I
Kyocera Corporation, II; 21 (upd.)
Kyowa Hakko Kogyo Co., Ltd., III; 48 (upd.)
Kyushu Electric Power Company Inc., V
Lion Corporation, III
Long-Term Credit Bank of Japan, Ltd., II
Makita Corporation, 22
Marubeni Corporation, I; 24 (upd.)
Marui Co., Ltd., V
Maruzen Co., Limited, 18
Matsushita Electric Industrial Co., Ltd., II
Matsushita Electric Works, Ltd., III; 7 (upd.)
Matsuzakaya Company Limited, V
Mazda Motor Corporation, 9; 23 (upd.)
Meiji Milk Products Company, Limited, II
Meiji Mutual Life Insurance Company, The, III
Meiji Seika Kaisha, Ltd., II
Minolta Co., Ltd., III; 18 (upd.); 43 (upd.)
Mitsubishi Bank, Ltd., The, II
Mitsubishi Chemical Industries, Ltd., I
Mitsubishi Corporation, I; 12 (upd.)
Mitsubishi Electric Corporation, II; 44 (upd.)
Mitsubishi Estate Company, Limited, IV
Mitsubishi Heavy Industries, Ltd., III; 7 (upd.); 40 (upd.)
Mitsubishi Materials Corporation, III
Mitsubishi Motors Corporation, 9; 23 (upd.)
Mitsubishi Oil Co., Ltd., IV
Mitsubishi Rayon Co., Ltd., V
Mitsubishi Trust & Banking Corporation, The, II
Mitsui & Co., Ltd., 28 (upd.)
Mitsui Bank, Ltd., The, II
Mitsui Bussan K.K., I
Mitsui Marine and Fire Insurance Company, Limited, III
Mitsui Mining & Smelting Co., Ltd., IV
Mitsui Mining Company, Limited, IV
Mitsui Mutual Life Insurance Company, III; 39 (upd.)
Mitsui O.S.K. Lines, Ltd., V
Mitsui Petrochemical Industries, Ltd., 9
Mitsui Real Estate Development Co., Ltd., IV
Mitsui Trust & Banking Company, Ltd., The, II
Mitsukoshi Ltd., V
Mizuno Corporation, 25
Nagasakiya Co., Ltd., V
Nagase & Company, Ltd., 8
NEC Corporation, II; 21 (upd.)
NHK Spring Co., Ltd., III
Nichii Co., Ltd., V
Nichimen Corporation, IV; 24 (upd.)
Nihon Keizai Shimbun, Inc., IV
Nikko Securities Company Limited, The, II; 9 (upd.)
Nikon Corporation, III; 48 (upd.)
Nintendo Co., Ltd., III; 7 (upd.); 28 (upd.)
Nippon Credit Bank, II
Nippon Express Co., Ltd., V
Nippon Life Insurance Company, III
Nippon Light Metal Company, Ltd., IV
Nippon Meat Packers, Inc., II
Nippon Oil Company, Limited, IV
Nippon Seiko K.K., III
Nippon Sheet Glass Company, Limited, III
Nippon Shinpan Company, Ltd., II
Nippon Steel Corporation, IV; 17 (upd.)
Nippon Suisan Kaisha, Limited, II
Nippon Telegraph and Telephone Corporation, V
Nippon Yusen Kabushiki Kaisha, V
Nippondenso Co., Ltd., III
Nissan Motor Company Ltd., I; 11 (upd.); 34 (upd.)
Nisshin Flour Milling Company, Ltd., II
Nisshin Steel Co., Ltd., IV
Nissho Iwai K.K., I
NKK Corporation, IV; 28 (upd.)
Nomura Securities Company, Limited, II; 9 (upd.)
Norinchukin Bank, II
NTN Corporation, III; 47 (upd.)
Odakyu Electric Railway Company Limited, V
Ohbayashi Corporation, I
Oji Paper Co., Ltd., IV
Oki Electric Industry Company, Limited, II
Okura & Co., Ltd., IV
Omron Corporation, II; 28 (upd.)
Onoda Cement Co., Ltd., III
Orix Corporation, II
ORIX Corporation, 44 (upd.)
Osaka Gas Co., Ltd., V
Pioneer Electronic Corporation, III; 28 (upd.)
Rengo Co., Ltd., IV
Ricoh Company, Ltd., III; 36 (upd.)
Roland Corporation, 38
Sankyo Company, Ltd., I
Sanrio Company, Ltd., 38
Sanwa Bank, Ltd., The, II; 15 (upd.)
SANYO Electric Company, Ltd., II; 36 (upd.)
Sanyo-Kokusaku Pulp Co., Ltd., IV
Sapporo Breweries, Ltd., I; 13 (upd.); 36 (upd.)
Seibu Department Stores, Ltd., V; 42 (upd.)
Seibu Railway Co. Ltd., V
Seiko Corporation, III; 17 (upd.)
Seino Transportation Company, Ltd., 6
Seiyu, Ltd., The, V; 36 (upd.)
Sekisui Chemical Co., Ltd., III
Sharp Corporation, II; 12 (upd.); 40 (upd.)
Shikoku Electric Power Company, Inc., V
Shionogi & Co., Ltd., III; 17 (upd.)
Shiseido Company, Limited, III; 22 (upd.)
Showa Shell Sekiyu K.K., IV
Snow Brand Milk Products Company, Ltd., II; 48 (upd.)
Softbank Corp., 13; 38 (upd.)
Sony Corporation, II; 12 (upd.); 40 (upd.)
Sumitomo Bank, Limited, The, II; 26 (upd.)
Sumitomo Chemical Company Ltd., I
Sumitomo Corporation, I; 11 (upd.)
Sumitomo Electric Industries, Ltd., II
Sumitomo Heavy Industries, Ltd., III; 42 (upd.)
Sumitomo Life Insurance Company, III
Sumitomo Marine and Fire Insurance Company, Limited, The, III
Sumitomo Metal Industries, Ltd., IV
Sumitomo Metal Mining Co., Ltd., IV
Sumitomo Realty & Development Co., Ltd., IV
Sumitomo Rubber Industries, Ltd., V
Sumitomo Trust & Banking Company, Ltd., The, II
Suzuki Motor Corporation, 9; 23 (upd.)
Taiyo Fishery Company, Limited, II
Taiyo Kobe Bank, Ltd., The, II
Takashimaya Company, Limited, V; 47 (upd.)
Takeda Chemical Industries, Ltd., I; 46 (upd.)
TDK Corporation, II; 17 (upd.)
Teijin Limited, V
Terumo Corporation, 48
Tobu Railway Co Ltd, 6
Toho Co., Ltd., 28
Tohoku Electric Power Company, Inc., V
Tokai Bank, Limited, The, II; 15 (upd.)
Tokio Marine and Fire Insurance Co., Ltd., The, III
Tokyo Electric Power Company, Incorporated, The, V
Tokyo Gas Co., Ltd., V
Tokyu Corporation, V; 47 (upd.)
Tokyu Department Store Co., Ltd., V; 32 (upd.)
Tokyu Land Corporation, IV
Tomen Corporation, IV; 24 (upd.)

**Japan** *(continued)*

Tonen Corporation, IV; 16 (upd.)
Toppan Printing Co., Ltd., IV
Toray Industries, Inc., V
Toshiba Corporation, I; 12 (upd.); 40 (upd.)
TOTO LTD., III; 28 (upd.)
Toyo Sash Co., Ltd., III
Toyo Seikan Kaisha, Ltd., I
Toyoda Automatic Loom Works, Ltd., III
Toyota Motor Corporation, I; 11 (upd.); 38 (upd.)
Ube Industries, Ltd., III; 38 (upd.)
Unitika Ltd., V
Uny Co., Ltd., V
Victor Company of Japan, Limited, II; 26 (upd.)
Wacoal Corp., 25
Yamaha Corporation, III; 16 (upd.); 40 (upd.)
Yamaichi Securities Company, Limited, II
Yamato Transport Co. Ltd., V
Yasuda Fire and Marine Insurance Company, Limited, The, III
Yasuda Mutual Life Insurance Company, The, III; 39 (upd.)
Yasuda Trust and Banking Company, Ltd., The, II; 17 (upd.)
Yokohama Rubber Co., Ltd., The, V; 19 (upd.)

## Korea

Anam Group, 23
Asiana Airlines, Inc., 46
Daewoo Group, III; 18 (upd.)
Electronics Co., Ltd., 14
Goldstar Co., Ltd., 12
Hyundai Group, III; 7 (upd.)
Kia Motors Corporation, 12; 29 (upd.)
Korean Air Lines Co., Ltd., 6; 27 (upd.)
Lucky-Goldstar, II
Pohang Iron and Steel Company Ltd., IV
Samsung Electronics Co., Ltd., 41 (upd.)
Samsung Group, I
Ssangyong Cement Industrial Co., Ltd., III

## Kuwait

Kuwait Petroleum Corporation, IV

## Luxembourg

ARBED S.A., IV; 22 (upd.)
RTL Group SA, 44

## Lybia

Libyan National Oil Corporation, IV

## Malaysia

Malaysian Airlines System Berhad, 6; 29 (upd.)
Petronas, IV
Sime Darby Berhad, 14; 36 (upd.)

## Mexico

Alfa, S.A. de C.V., 19
Altos Hornos de México, S.A. de C.V., 42
Bufete Industrial, S.A. de C.V., 34
Casa Cuervo, S.A. de C.V., 31
Cemex SA de CV, 20
Cifra, S.A. de C.V., 12
Consorcio G Grupo Dina, S.A. de C.V., 36
Controladora Comercial Mexicana, S.A. de C.V., 36
Corporación Internacional de Aviación, S.A. de C.V. (Cintra), 20
Desc, S.A. de C.V., 23
Empresas ICA Sociedad Controladora, S.A. de C.V., 41
Gruma, S.A. de C.V., 31
Grupo Aeropuerto del Sureste, S.A. de C.V., 48
Grupo Carso, S.A. de C.V., 21
Grupo Casa Saba, S.A. de C.V., 39
Grupo Cydsa, S.A. de C.V., 39
Grupo Elektra, S.A. de C.V., 39
Grupo Financiero Serfin, S.A., 19
Grupo Gigante, S.A. de C.V., 34
Grupo Herdez, S.A. de C.V., 35
Grupo IMSA, S.A. de C.V., 44
Grupo Industrial Bimbo, 19
Grupo Industrial Durango, S.A. de C.V., 37
Grupo Mexico, S.A. de C.V., 40
Grupo Modelo, S.A. de C.V., 29
Grupo Televisa, S.A., 18
Grupo Transportación Ferroviaria Mexicana, S.A. de C.V., 47
Hylsamex, S.A. de C.V., 39
Industrias Bachoco, S.A. de C.V., 39
Industrias Penoles, S.A. de C.V., 22
Organización Soriana, S.A. de C.V., 35
Petróleos Mexicanos, IV; 19 (upd.)
Pulsar Internacional S.A., 21
Sanborn Hermanos, S.A., 20
Sears Roebuck de México, S.A. de C.V., 20
Telefonos de Mexico S.A. de C.V., 14
Tubos de Acero de Mexico, S.A. (TAMSA), 41
TV Azteca, S.A. de C.V., 39
Valores Industriales S.A., 19
Vitro Corporativo S.A. de C.V., 34
Wal-Mart de Mexico, S.A. de C.V., 35 (upd.)

## Nepal

Royal Nepal Airline Corporation, 41

## New Zealand

Air New Zealand Limited, 14; 38 (upd.)
Fletcher Challenge Ltd., IV; 19 (upd.)
Wattie's Ltd., 7

## Nigeria

Nigerian National Petroleum Corporation, IV

## Norway

Braathens ASA, 47
Den Norse Stats Oljeselskap AS, IV
Helly Hansen ASA, 25
Kvaerner ASA, 36
Norsk Hydro ASA, 10; 35 (upd.)
Orkla A/S, 18
Schibsted ASA, 31

## Oman

Petroleum Development Oman LLC, IV

## Pakistan

Pakistan International Airlines Corporation, 46

## Panama

Panamerican Beverages, Inc., 47

## Peru

Southern Peru Copper Corporation, 40

## Philippines

Philippine Airlines, Inc., 6; 23 (upd.)
San Miguel Corporation, 15

## Poland

LOT Polish Airlines (Polskie Linie Lotnicze S.A.), 33

## Portugal

Banco Espírito Santo e Comercial de Lisboa S.A., 15
Corticeira Amorim, Sociedade Gestora de Participaço es Sociais, S.A., 48
Electricidade de Portugal, S.A., 47
Petróleos de Portugal S.A., IV
TAP—Air Portugal Transportes Aéreos Portugueses S.A., 46
Transportes Aereos Portugueses, S.A., 6

## Puerto Rico

Puerto Rico Electric Power Authority, 47

## Qatar

Qatar General Petroleum Corporation, IV

## Russia

A.S. Yakovlev Design Bureau, 15
Aeroflot—Russian International Airlines, 6; 29 (upd.)
AO VimpelCom, 48
Aviacionny Nauchno-Tehnicheskii Komplex im. A.N. Tupoleva, 24
JSC MMC Norilsk Nickel, 48
OAO Gazprom, 42
OAO LUKOIL, 40
OAO NK YUKOS, 47
OAO Surgutneftegaz, 48
OAO Tatneft, 45
OJSC Wimm-Bill-Dann Foods, 48
RAO Unified Energy System of Russia, 45
Sukhoi Design Bureau Aviation Scientific-Industrial Complex, 24
OAO Surgutneftegaz, 48
AO VimpelCom, 48
OJSC Wimm-Bill-Dann Foods, 48

## Saudi Arabia

Saudi Arabian Airlines, 6; 27 (upd.)
Saudi Arabian Oil Company, IV; 17 (upd.)

## Scotland

Distillers Company PLC, I
General Accident PLC, III
Governor and Company of the Bank of Scotland, The, 10
Royal Bank of Scotland Group plc, The, 12
Scottish & Newcastle plc, 15
Scottish Hydro-Electric PLC, 13
Scottish Media Group plc, 32
ScottishPower plc, 19
Stagecoach Holdings plc, 30
Standard Life Assurance Company, The, III

## Singapore

Flextronics International Ltd., 38
Neptune Orient Lines Limited, 47
Singapore Airlines Ltd., 6; 27 (upd.)

## South Africa

Anglo American Corporation of South Africa Limited, IV; 16 (upd.)

Barlow Rand Ltd., I
De Beers Consolidated Mines Limited/De Beers Centenary AG, IV; 7 (upd.); 28 (upd.)
Gencor Ltd., IV; 22 (upd.)
Gold Fields of South Africa Ltd., IV
SAA (Pty) Ltd., 28
Sasol Limited, IV; 47 (upd.)
South African Breweries Limited, The, I; 24 (upd.)
Transnet Ltd., 6

## Spain

Banco Bilbao Vizcaya Argentaria S.A., 48 (upd.)
Banco Bilbao Vizcaya, S.A., II
Banco Central, II
Banco do Brasil S.A., II
Banco Santander Central Hispano S.A., 36 (upd.)
Chupa Chups S.A., 38
Compañia Española de Petróleos S.A., IV
El Corte Inglés Group, V; 26 (upd.)
ENDESA Group, V
ENDESA S.A., 46 (upd.)
Grupo Ferrovial, S.A., 40
Iberia Líneas Aéreas de España S.A., 6; 36 (upd.)
Instituto Nacional de Industria, I
Repsol S.A., IV; 16 (upd.)
Repsol-YPF S.A., 40 (upd.)
Tabacalera, S.A., V; 17 (upd.)
Telefónica de España, S.A., V
Telefónica S.A., 46 (upd.)
TelePizza S.A., 33
Television Española, S.A., 7
Terra Lycos, Inc., 43

## Sweden

A. Johnson & Company H.B., I
AB Volvo, I; 7 (upd.); 26 (upd.)
Aktiebolaget Electrolux, 22 (upd.)
Aktiebolaget SKF, III; 38 (upd.)
Alfa-Laval AB, III
Astra AB, I; 20 (upd.)
Atlas Copco AB, III; 28 (upd.)
BRIO AB, 24
Electrolux Group, III
Hennes & Mauritz AB, 29
ICA AB, II
Mo och Domsjö AB, IV
Modern Times Group AB, 36
NetCom Systems AB, 26
Nobel Industries AB, 9
Nordea AB, 40
Perstorp A.B., I
Saab Automobile AB, 32 (upd.)
Saab-Scania A.B., I; 11 (upd.)
Sandvik AB, IV; 32 (upd.)
SAS Group, The, 34 (upd.)
Scandinavian Airlines System, I
Securitas AB, 42
Skandinaviska Enskilda Banken, II
Skanska AB, 38
Stora Kopparbergs Bergslags AB, IV
Svenska Cellulosa Aktiebolaget SCA, IV; 28 (upd.)
Svenska Handelsbanken, II
Swedish Match AB, 39 (upd.)
Swedish Telecom, V
Telefonaktiebolaget LM Ericsson, V; 46 (upd.)
Vin & Spirit AB, 31

## Switzerland

ABB ASEA Brown Boveri Ltd., II; 22 (upd.)
Adecco S.A., 36 (upd.)
Adia S.A., 6
Arthur Andersen & Company, Société Coopérative, 10
Ascom AG, 9
Bâloise-Holding, 40
Barry Callebaut AG, 29
Bernina Holding AG, 47
Bodum Design Group AG, 47
Bon Appetit Holding AG, 48
Chocoladefabriken Lindt & Sprüngli AG, 27
Ciba-Geigy Ltd., I; 8 (upd.)
Coop Schweiz Genossenschaftsverband, 48
Credit Suisse Group, II; 21 (upd.)
Danzas Group, V; 40 (upd.)
De Beers Consolidated Mines Limited/De Beers Centenary AG, IV; 7 (upd.); 28 (upd.)
Elektrowatt AG, 6
F. Hoffmann-Laroche & Company A.G., I
Fédération Internationale de Football Association, 27
Givaudan SA, 43
Holderbank Financière Glaris Ltd., III
International Olympic Committee, 44
Jacobs Suchard A.G., II
Kraft Jacobs Suchard AG, 26 (upd.)
Kudelski Group SA, 44
Kuhne & Nagel International A.G., V
Kuoni Travel Holding Ltd., 40
Logitech International SA, 28
Maus Frères SA, 48
Mettler-Toledo International Inc., 30
Montres Rolex S.A., 13; 34 (upd.)
Nestlé S.A., II; 7 (upd.); 28 (upd.)
Novartis AG, 39 (upd.)
Panalpina World Transport (Holding) Ltd., 47
Rieter Holding AG, 42
Roland Murten A.G., 7
Sandoz Ltd., I
Schindler Holding AG, 29
Schweizerische Post-, Telefon- und Telegrafen-Betriebe, V
Serono S.A., 47
Sulzer Brothers Limited (Gebruder Sulzer Aktiengesellschaft), III
Swarovski International Holding AG, 40
Swatch Group SA, The, 26
Swedish Match S.A., 12
Swiss Air Transport Company, Ltd., I
Swiss Bank Corporation, II
Swiss Federal Railways (Schweizerische Bundesbahnen), The, V
Swiss International Air Lines Ltd., 48
Swiss Reinsurance Company (Schweizerische Rückversicherungs-Gesellschaft), III; 46 (upd.)
TAG Heuer International SA, 25
Union Bank of Switzerland, II
Victorinox AG, 21
Winterthur Schweizerische Versicherungs-Gesellschaft, III
Zurich Financial Services, 42 (upd.)
Zürich Versicherungs-Gesellschaft, III

## Taiwan

Acer Inc., 16
China Airlines, 34
Evergreen Marine Corporation Taiwan Ltd., 13
Formosa Plastics Corporation, 14
Quanta Computer Inc., 47
Taiwan Semiconductor Manufacturing Company Ltd., 47
Tatung Co., 23
Yageo Corporation, 16

## Thailand

Thai Airways International Public Company Limited, 6; 27 (upd.)

## The Netherlands

AEGON N.V., III
Akzo Nobel N.V., 13; 41 (upd.)
Algemene Bank Nederland N.V., II
Amsterdam-Rotterdam Bank N.V., II
Arcadis NV, 26
Baan Company, 25
Buhrmann NV, 41
CNH Global N.V., 38 (upd.)
DSM, N.V, I
Elsevier N.V., IV
Endemol Entertainment Holding NV, 46
Getronics NV, 39
Grand Hotel Krasnapolsky N.V., 23
Hagemeyer N.V., 39
Heineken N.V., I; 13 (upd.); 34 (upd.)
Indigo NV, 26
Ispat International N.V., 30
Koninklijke Ahold N.V. (Royal Ahold), II; 16 (upd.)
Koninklijke Luchtvaart Maatschappij, N.V. (KLM Royal Dutch Airlines), I; 28 (upd.)
Koninklijke Nederlandsche Hoogovens en Staalfabrieken NV, IV
Koninklijke Nedlloyd N.V., 6; 26 (upd.)
Koninklijke PTT Nederland NV, V
Koninklijke Wessanen N.V., II
KPMG International, 10; 33 (upd.)
Mammoet Transport B.V., 26
MIH Limited, 31
N.V. AMEV, III
N.V. Holdingmaatschappij De Telegraaf, 23
N.V. Koninklijke Nederlandse Vliegtuigenfabriek Fokker, I; 28 (upd.)
N.V. Nederlandse Gasunie, V
Nationale-Nederlanden N.V., III
New Holland N.V., 22
Océ N.V., 24
Philips Electronics N.V., II; 13 (upd.)
PolyGram N.V., 23
Prada Holding B.V., 45
Qiagen N.V., 39
Rabobank Group, 33
Randstad Holding n.v., 16; 43 (upd.)
Rodamco N.V., 26
Royal Dutch Petroleum Company/ The Shell Transport and Trading Company p.l.c., IV
Royal KPN N.V., 30
Royal Numico N.V., 37
Royal Packaging Industries Van Leer N.V., 30
Royal Vopak NV, 41
TNT Post Group N.V., V, 27 (upd.); 30 (upd.)
Toolex International N.V., 26
Triple P N.V., 26
Unilever N.V., II; 7 (upd.); 32 (upd.)
United Pan-Europe Communications NV, 47
Vedior NV, 35
Velcro Industries N.V., 19
Vendex International N.V., 13
VNU N.V., 27
Wolters Kluwer NV, 14; 33 (upd.)

### Turkey

KOC Holding A.S., I
Türkiye Petrolleri Anonim Ortakliği, IV

### United Arab Emirates

Abu Dhabi National Oil Company, IV; 45 (upd.)
Emirates Group, The, 39

### United Kingdom

Abbey National plc, 10; 39 (upd.)
Aegis Group plc, 6
Aggregate Industries plc, 36
Aggreko Plc, 45
Airtours Plc, 27
Albert Fisher Group plc, The, 41
Allders plc, 37
Allied Domecq PLC, 29
Allied-Lyons PLC, I
Alvis Plc, 47
Amey Plc, 47
Amstrad plc, III; 48 (upd.)
Arcadia Group plc, 28 (upd.)
Argyll Group PLC, II
Arjo Wiggins Appleton p.l.c., 34
ASDA Group plc, II; 28 (upd.)
Ashtead Group plc, 34
Associated British Foods plc, II; 13 (upd.); 41 (upd.)
Associated British Ports Holdings Plc, 45
Aston Villa plc, 41
AT&T Istel Ltd., 14
B.A.T. Industries PLC, I; 22 (upd.)
BAA plc, 10; 33 (upd.)
Balfour Beatty plc, 36 (upd.)
Barclays PLC, II; 20 (upd.)
Barings PLC, 14
Barratt Developments PLC, I
Bass PLC, I; 15 (upd.); 38 (upd.)
Bat Industries PLC, I; 20 (upd.)
Bellway Plc, 45
Bhs plc, 17
BICC PLC, III
Blacks Leisure Group plc, 39
Blue Circle Industries PLC, III
BOC Group plc, I; 25 (upd.)
Body Shop International PLC, The, 11
Booker plc, 13; 31 (upd.)
Boots Company PLC, The, V; 24 (upd.)
Bowater PLC, IV
Bowthorpe plc, 33
BP p.l.c., 45 (upd.)
Brake Bros plc, 45
British Aerospace plc, I; 24 (upd.)
British Airways PLC, I; 14 (upd.); 43 (upd.)
British Broadcasting Corporation Ltd., 7; 21 (upd.)
British Coal Corporation, IV
British Gas plc, V
British Midland plc, 38
British Nuclear Fuels plc, 6
British Petroleum Company plc, The, IV; 7 (upd.); 21 (upd.)
British Railways Board, V
British Sky Broadcasting Group Plc, 20
British Steel plc, IV; 19 (upd.)
British Telecommunications plc, V; 15 (upd.)
British Vita plc, 9; 33 (upd.)
British World Airlines Ltd., 18
British-Borneo Oil & Gas PLC, 34
BTR PLC, I
BTR Siebe plc, 27
Bunzl plc, IV; 31 (upd.)
Burberry Ltd., 17; 41 (upd.)
Burmah Castrol PLC, IV; 30 (upd.)
Burton Group plc, The, V
Business Post Group plc, 46
Cable and Wireless plc, V; 25 (upd.)
Cadbury Schweppes PLC, II
Canary Wharf Group Plc, 30
Capital Radio plc, 35
Caradon plc, 20 (upd.)
Carlton Communications plc, 15
Cartier Monde, 29
Central Independent Television, 7; 23 (upd.)
Centrica plc, 29 (upd.)
Christian Salvesen Plc, 45
Christie's International plc, 15; 39 (upd.)
Chrysalis Group plc, 40
Clifford Chance LLP, 38
Clinton Cards plc, 39
Close Brothers Group plc, 39
Coats plc, 44 (upd.)
Coats Viyella Plc, V
Cobham plc, 30
COLT Telecom Group plc, 41
Commercial Union PLC, III
Compass Group PLC, 34
Cookson Group plc, III; 44 (upd.)
Courtaulds plc, V; 17 (upd.)
Courts Plc, 45
Cranswick plc, 40
Croda International Plc, 45
Daily Mail and General Trust plc, 19
Dairy Crest Group plc, 32
Dalgety, PLC, II
Davis Service Group PLC, 45
Dawson Holdings PLC, 43
De La Rue plc, 10; 34 (upd.)
Debenhams Plc, 28
Denby Group plc, 44
Denison International plc, 46
Diageo plc, 24 (upd.)
Dixons Group plc, V; 19 (upd.)
Dorling Kindersley Holdings plc, 20
easyJet Airline Company Limited, 39
ECC Group plc, III
Elementis plc, 40 (upd.)
EMAP plc, 35
EMI Group plc, 22 (upd.)
Energis plc, 47
English China Clays Ltd., 15 (upd.); 40 (upd.)
Enterprise Oil plc, 11
Esporta plc, 35
Eurotunnel Group, 37 (upd.)
Eurotunnel PLC, 13
Fairclough Construction Group PLC, I
First Choice Holidays PLC, 40
Fisons plc, 9; 23 (upd.)
French Connection Group plc, 41
Fuller Smith & Turner P.L.C., 38
Gallaher Limited, V; 19 (upd.)
Gateway Corporation Ltd., The, II
Geest Plc, 38
General Electric Company PLC, II
George Wimpey PLC, 12
GKN plc, III; 38 (upd.)
Glaxo Holdings PLC, I; 9 (upd.)
GlaxoSmithKline plc, 46 (upd.)
Go-Ahead Group Plc, The, 28
Granada Group PLC, II; 24 (upd.)
Grand Metropolitan PLC, I; 14 (upd.)
Great Universal Stores plc, The, V; 19 (upd.)
Greenalls Group PLC, The, 21
Greene King plc, 31
Guardian Royal Exchange Plc, 11
Guinness/UDV, I; 43 (upd.)
GUS plc, 47 (upd.)
GWR Group plc, 39
Hammerson plc, 40
Hammerson Property Investment and Development Corporation plc, The, IV
Hanson PLC, III; 7 (upd.); 30 (upd.)
Harrisons & Crosfield plc, III
Harrods Holdings, 47
Hartstone Group plc, The, 14
Hawker Siddeley Group Public Limited Company, III
Hays Plc, 27
Hazlewood Foods plc, 32
Her Majesty's Stationery Office, 7
Hillsdown Holdings plc, II; 24 (upd.)
HIT Entertainment PLC, 40
House of Fraser PLC, 45
HSBC Holdings plc, 12; 26 (upd.)
Huntingdon Life Sciences Group plc, 42
Ibstock Brick Ltd., 14; 37 (upd.)
ICL plc, 6
IMI plc, 9
Imperial Chemical Industries PLC, I
Inchcape PLC, III; 16 (upd.)
IPC Magazines Limited, 7
J Sainsbury plc, II; 13 (upd.); 38 (upd.)
James Beattie plc, 43
Jarvis plc, 39
JD Wetherspoon plc, 30
JJB Sports plc, 32
John Brown PLC, I
John Laing PLC, I
John Lewis Partnership plc, V; 42 (upd.)
John Menzies plc, 39
Johnson Matthey PLC, IV; 16 (upd.)
Johnston Press plc, 35
Kelda Group plc, 45
Kennecott Corporation, 7; 27 (upd.)
Kidde plc, 44 (upd.)
Kingfisher plc, V; 24 (upd.)
Kleinwort Benson Group PLC, II
Kvaerner ASA, 36
Ladbroke Group PLC, II; 21 (upd.)
Land Securities PLC, IV
Laura Ashley Holdings plc, 13; 37 (upd.)
Legal & General Group plc, III; 24 (upd.)
Littlewoods plc, V; 42 (upd.)
Lloyd's of London, III; 22 (upd.)
Lloyds Bank PLC, II
Lloyds TSB Group plc, 47 (upd.)
Logica plc, 14; 37 (upd.)
London Regional Transport, 6
London Stock Exchange Limited, 34
Lonrho Plc, 21
Lotus Cars Ltd., 14
Lucas Industries PLC, III
Luminar Plc, 40
Madge Networks N.V., 26
Manchester United Football Club plc, 30
Marconi plc, 33 (upd.)
Marks and Spencer p.l.c., V; 24 (upd.)
Maxwell Communication Corporation plc, IV; 7 (upd.)
McKechnie plc, 34
Meggitt PLC, 34
MEPC plc, IV
Mercury Communications, Ltd., 7
Mersey Docks and Harbour Company, The, 30
Metal Box PLC, I
Michael Page International plc, 45
Midland Bank PLC, II; 17 (upd.)
Mirror Group Newspapers plc, 7; 23 (upd.)
Misys plc, 45; 46
Monsoon plc, 39
Morgan Grenfell Group PLC, II
Mothercare UK Ltd., 17
N M Rothschild & Sons Limited, 39
National Power PLC, 12
National Westminster Bank PLC, II

New Look Group plc, 35
Newsquest plc, 32
Next plc, 29
NFC plc, 6
Nichols plc, 44
North West Water Group plc, 11
Northern Foods PLC, 10
Northern Rock plc, 33
Ocean Group plc, 6
Pearson plc, IV; 46 (upd.)
Peninsular & Oriental Steam Navigation Company (Bovis Division), The, I
Peninsular and Oriental Steam Navigation Company, The, V; 38 (upd.)
Pennon Group Plc, 45
Pentland Group plc, 20
PIC International Group PLC, 24 (upd.)
Pilkington plc, III; 34 (upd.)
Plessey Company, PLC, The, II
Post Office Group, V
Powell Duffryn plc, 31
PowerGen PLC, 11
Prudential plc, 48 (upd.)
Psion PLC, 45
R. Griggs Group Limited, 23
Racal Electronics PLC, II
Rank Organisation Plc, The, II; 14 (upd.)
Ranks Hovis McDougall Limited, II; 28 (upd.)
Really Useful Group, The, 26
Reckitt Benckiser plc, II; 42 (upd.)
Redland plc, III
Redrow Group plc, 31
Reed Elsevier plc, IV; 17 (upd.); 31 (upd.)
Renishaw plc, 46
Rentokil Initial Plc, 47
Reuters Holdings PLC, IV; 22 (upd.)
Rexam PLC, 32 (upd.)
Rio Tinto plc, 19 (upd.)
RMC Group p.l.c., III ; 34 (upd.)
Rolls-Royce Motors Ltd., I
Rolls-Royce plc, I; 7 (upd.); 21 (upd.)
Rothmans International p.l.c., V
Rothmans UK Holdings Limited, 19 (upd.)
Rotork plc, 46
Rover Group Ltd., 7; 21 (upd.)
Rowntree Mackintosh, II
Royal Bank of Scotland Group plc, The, 38 (upd.)
Royal Doulton plc, 14; 38 (upd.)
Royal Dutch Petroleum Company/ The Shell Transport and Trading Company p.l.c., IV
Royal Insurance Holdings PLC, III
RTZ Corporation PLC, The, IV
Rugby Group plc, The, 31
Saatchi & Saatchi PLC, I
Sage Group, The, 43
SBC Warburg, 14
Schroders plc, 42
Scottish & Newcastle plc, 35 (upd.)
Scottish Radio Holding plc, 41
Sea Containers Ltd., 29
Sears plc, V
Securicor Plc, 45
Selfridges Plc, 34
Serco Group plc, 47
Severn Trent PLC, 12; 38 (upd.)
Shanks Group plc, 45
Shepherd Neame Limited, 30
Singer & Friedlander Group plc, 41
Slough Estates PLC, IV
Smith & Nephew plc, 17;41 (upd.)
SmithKline Beecham plc, III; 32 (upd.)
Smiths Industries PLC, 25
Somerfield plc, 47 (upd.)
Southern Electric PLC, 13
St Ives plc, 34
Standard Chartered plc, II; 48 (upd.)
STC PLC, III
Stoll-Moss Theatres Ltd., 34
Stolt-Nielsen S.A., 42
Storehouse PLC, 16
Sun Alliance Group PLC, III
Sytner Group plc, 45
Tarmac plc, III; 28 (upd.)
Tate & Lyle PLC, II; 42 (upd.)
Taylor & Francis Group plc, 44
Taylor Nelson Sofres plc, 34
Taylor Woodrow plc, I; 38 (upd.)
Tesco PLC, II; 24 (upd.)
Thames Water plc, 11
Thorn Emi PLC, I
Thorn plc, 24
Thorntons plc, 46
TI Group plc, 17
Tibbett & Britten Group plc, 32
Tomkins plc, 11; 44 (upd.)
Travis Perkins plc, 34
Trusthouse Forte PLC, III
TSB Group plc, 12
Ultramar PLC, IV
Unigate PLC, II; 28 (upd.)
Unilever PLC, II; 7 (upd.); 32 (upd.)
United Biscuits (Holdings) plc, II; 42 (upd.)
United News & Media plc, 28 (upd.)
United Newspapers plc, IV
Vendôme Luxury Group plc, 27
Vickers plc, 27
Virgin Group, 12; 32 (upd.)
Vodafone Group PLC, 11; 36 (upd.)
Vosper Thornycroft Holding plc, 41
W H Smith Group PLC, V
Wassall Plc, 18
Waterford Wedgwood Holdings PLC, 12
Watson Wyatt Worldwide, 42
Wellcome Foundation Ltd., The, I
WH Smith PLC, 42 (upd.)
Whatman plc, 46
Whitbread PLC, I; 20 (upd.)
Willis Corroon Group plc, 25
Wilson Bowden Plc, 45
Wm. Morrison Supermarkets PLC, 38
Wood Hall Trust PLC, I
Woolwich plc, The, 30
WPP Group plc, 6; 48 (upd.)
WS Atkins Plc, 45
Young & Co.'s Brewery, P.L.C., 38
Zeneca Group PLC, 21

**United States**

A & E Television Networks, 32
A & W Brands, Inc., 25
A. Schulman, Inc., 8
A.B. Watley Group Inc., 45
A.B.Dick Company, 28
A.C. Moore Arts & Crafts, Inc., 30
A.C. Nielsen Company, 13
A.G. Edwards, Inc., 8; 32
A.H. Belo Corporation, 10; 30 (upd.)
A.L. Pharma Inc., 12
A.M. Castle & Co., 25
A.O. Smith Corporation, 11; 40 (upd.)
A.T. Cross Company, 17
AAF-McQuay Incorporated, 26
AAON, Inc., 22
AAR Corp., 28
Aaron Rents, Inc., 14; 35 (upd.)
AARP, 27
Aavid Thermal Technologies, Inc., 29
Abbott Laboratories, I; 11 (upd.); 40 (upd.)
ABC Appliance, Inc., 10
ABC Carpet & Home Co. Inc., 26
ABC Rail Products Corporation, 18
ABC Supply Co., Inc., 22
Abercrombie & Fitch Co., 15; 35 (upd.)
Abigail Adams National Bancorp, Inc., 23
Abiomed, Inc., 47
ABM Industries Incorporated, 25 (upd.)
Abrams Industries Inc., 23
Academy Sports & Outdoors, 27
Acadian Ambulance & Air Med Services, Inc., 39
Acclaim Entertainment Inc., 24
ACCO World Corporation, 7
ACE Cash Express, Inc., 33
Ace Hardware Corporation, 12; 35 (upd.)
Aceto Corp., 38
Ackerley Communications, Inc., 9
Acme-Cleveland Corp., 13
ACNielsen Corporation, 38 (upd.)
Acsys, Inc., 44
Action Performance Companies, Inc., 27
Activision, Inc., 32
Acuson Corporation, 10; 36 (upd.)
Acxiom Corporation, 35
Adams Golf, Inc., 37
Adaptec, Inc., 31
ADC Telecommunications, Inc., 10; 30 (upd.)
Adelphia Communications Corp., 17
Adobe Systems Inc., 10; 33 (upd.)
Adolph Coors Company, I; 13 (upd.); 36 (upd.)
ADT Security Services, Inc., 12; 44 (upd.)
Adtran Inc., 22
Advance Publications Inc., IV; 19 (upd.)
Advanced Marketing Services, Inc., 34
Advanced Micro Devices, Inc., 6; 30 (upd.)
Advanced Technology Laboratories, Inc., 9
Advanta Corporation, 8; 38 (upd.)
Advantica Restaurant Group, Inc., 27 (upd.)
Advo, Inc., 6
Advocat Inc., 46
AEI Music Network Inc., 35
AEP Industries, Inc., 36
Aeronca Inc., 46
Aeroquip Corporation, 16
AES Corporation, The, 10; 13 (upd.)
Aetna, Inc., III; 21 (upd.)
AFC Enterprises, Inc., 32
Affiliated Publications, Inc., 7
AFLAC Incorporated, 10 (upd.); 38 (upd.)
Ag-Chem Equipment Company, Inc., 17
AGCO Corp., 13
Agilent Technologies Inc., 38
Agway, Inc., 7; 21 (upd.)
AHL Services, Inc., 27
Air & Water Technologies Corporation, 6
Air Express International Corporation, 13
Air Products and Chemicals, Inc., I; 10 (upd.)
Airborne Freight Corporation, 6; 34 (upd.)
AirTouch Communications, 11
AirTran Holdings, Inc., 22
AK Steel Holding Corporation, 19; 41 (upd.)
Akin, Gump, Strauss, Hauer & Feld, L.L.P., 33
Akorn, Inc., 32
Alamo Group Inc., 32
Alamo Rent A Car, Inc., 6; 24 (upd.)
Alaska Air Group, Inc., 6; 29 (upd.)
Alba-Waldensian, Inc., 30
Albany International Corp., 8
Alberto-Culver Company, 8; 36 (upd.)
Albertson's Inc., II; 7 (upd.); 30 (upd.)
Alco Health Services Corporation, III
Alco Standard Corporation, I
Aldila Inc., 46
Aldus Corporation, 10

**United States** *(continued)*


Alex Lee Inc., 18; 44 (upd.)
Alexander & Alexander Services Inc., 10
Alexander & Baldwin, Inc., 10; 40 (upd.)
Alexander's, Inc., 45
All American Communications Inc., 20
Alleghany Corporation, 10
Allegheny Energy, Inc., 38 (upd.)
Allegheny Ludlum Corporation, 8
Allegheny Power System, Inc., V
Allen Organ Company, 33
Allergan, Inc., 10; 30 (upd.)
Alliance Entertainment Corp., 17
Alliant Techsystems Inc., 8; 30 (upd.)
Allied Healthcare Products, Inc., 24
Allied Products Corporation, 21
Allied Signal Engines, 9
AlliedSignal Inc., I; 22 (upd.)
Allison Gas Turbine Division, 9
Allou Health & Beauty Care, Inc., 28
Allstate Corporation, The, 10; 27 (upd.)
ALLTEL Corporation, 6; 46 (upd.)
Alltrista Corporation, 30
Allwaste, Inc., 18
Aloha Airlines, Incorporated, 24
Alpharma Inc., 35 (upd.)
Alpine Lace Brands, Inc., 18
AltaVista Company, 43
Altera Corporation, 18; 43 (upd.)
Alterra Healthcare Corporation, 42
Altron Incorporated, 20
Aluminum Company of America, IV; 20 (upd.)
ALZA Corporation, 10; 36 (upd.)
AMAX Inc., IV
Amazon.com, Inc., 25
Amblin Entertainment, 21
AMC Entertainment Inc., 12; 35 (upd.)
AMCORE Financial Inc., 44
Amdahl Corporation, III; 14 (upd.); 40 (upd.)
Amdocs Ltd., 47
Amerada Hess Corporation, IV; 21 (upd.)
Amerco, 6
America Online, Inc., 10 ; 26 (upd.)
America West Airlines, 6
America West Holdings Corporation, 34 (upd.)
America's Favorite Chicken Company, Inc., 7
American Airlines, I; 6 (upd.)
American Banknote Corporation, 30
American Bar Association, 35
American Biltrite Inc., 16; 43 (upd.)
American Brands, Inc., V
American Building Maintenance Industries, Inc., 6
American Business Information, Inc., 18
American Business Products, Inc., 20
American Cancer Society, The, 24
American Classic Voyages Company, 27
American Coin Merchandising, Inc., 28
American Colloid Co., 13
American Crystal Sugar Company, 9; 32 (upd.)
American Cyanamid, I; 8 (upd.)
American Eagle Outfitters, Inc., 24
American Electric Power Company, Inc., V; 45 (upd.)
American Express Company, II; 10 (upd.); 38 (upd.)
American Family Corporation, III
American Financial Corporation, III
American Financial Group Inc., 48 (upd.)
American Foods Group, 43
American Furniture Company, Inc., 21
American General Corporation, III; 10 (upd.); 46 (upd.)
American General Finance Corp., 11
American Golf Corporation, 45
American Greetings Corporation, 7; 22 (upd.)
American Home Mortgage Holdings, Inc., 46
American Home Products, I; 10 (upd.)
American Homestar Corporation, 18; 41 (upd.)
American Institute of Certified Public Accountants (AICPA), 44
American International Group, Inc., III; 15 (upd.); 47 (upd.)
American Italian Pasta Company, 27
American Lawyer Media Holdings, Inc., 32
American Locker Group Incorporated, 34
American Lung Association, 48
American Maize-Products Co., 14
American Management Systems, Inc., 11
American Media, Inc., 27
American Medical Association, 39
American Medical International, Inc., III
American Medical Response, Inc., 39
American Motors Corporation, I
American National Insurance Company, 8; 27 (upd.)
American Pad & Paper Company, 20
American Power Conversion Corporation, 24
American Premier Underwriters, Inc., 10
American President Companies Ltd., 6
American Printing House for the Blind, 26
American Re Corporation, 10; 35 (upd.)
American Red Cross, 40
American Residential Mortgage Corporation, 8
American Retirement Corporation, 42
American Rice, Inc., 33
American Safety Razor Company, 20
American Skiing Company, 28
American Society of Composers, Authors and Publishers (ASCAP), The, 29
American Software Inc., 25
American Standard Companies Inc., III; 30 (upd.)
American States Water Company, 46
American Stores Company, II; 22 (upd.)
American Telephone and Telegraph Company, V
American Tourister, Inc., 16
American Tower Corporation, 33
American Vanguard Corporation, 47
American Water Works Company, Inc., 6; 38 (upd.)
American Woodmark Corporation, 31
Amerihost Properties, Inc., 30
AmeriSource Health Corporation, 37 (upd.)
Ameristar Casinos, Inc., 33
Ameritech Corporation, V; 18 (upd.)
Ameritrade Holding Corporation, 34
Ameriwood Industries International Corp., 17
Ames Department Stores, Inc., 9; 30 (upd.)
AMETEK, Inc., 9
AMF Bowling, Inc., 40
Amfac/JMB Hawaii L.L.C., I; 24 (upd.)
Amgen, Inc., 10; 30 (upd.)
Amoco Corporation, IV; 14 (upd.)
Amoskeag Company, 8
AMP Incorporated, II; 14 (upd.)
Ampex Corporation, 17
Amphenol Corporation, 40
AMR Corporation, 28 (upd.)
AMREP Corporation, 21
AmSouth Bancorporation, 12; 48 (upd.)
Amsted Industries Incorporated, 7
AmSurg Corporation, 48
Amtran, Inc., 34
Amway Corporation, III; 13 (upd.); 30 (upd.)
Anadarko Petroleum Corporation, 10
Analog Devices, Inc., 10
Analogic Corporation, 23
Analysts International Corporation, 36
Analytic Sciences Corporation, 10
Analytical Surveys, Inc., 33
Anaren Microwave, Inc., 33
Anchor Bancorp, Inc., 10
Anchor Brewing Company, 47
Anchor Gaming, 24
Anchor Hocking Glassware, 13
Andersen Corporation, 10
Andersen Worldwide, 29 (upd.)
Andersons, Inc., The, 31
Andrew Corporation, 10; 32 (upd.)
Andrews McMeel Universal, 40
Angelica Corporation, 15; 43 (upd.)
Anheuser-Busch Companies, Inc., I; 10 (upd.); 34 (upd.)
AnnTaylor Stores Corporation, 13; 37 (upd.)
ANR Pipeline Co., 17
Anschutz Corporation, The, 12; 36 (upd.)
Anthem Electronics, Inc., 13
Antioch Company, The, 40
Aon Corporation, III; 45 (upd.)
Apache Corporation, 10; 32 (upd.)
Apogee Enterprises, Inc., 8
Apollo Group, Inc., 24
Applause Inc., 24
Apple Computer, Inc., III; 6 (upd.); 36 (upd.)
Applebee's International Inc., 14; 35 (upd.)
Appliance Recycling Centers of America, Inc., 42
Applica Incorporated, 43 (upd.)
Applied Bioscience International, Inc., 10
Applied Films Corporation, 48
Applied Materials, Inc., 10; 46 (upd.)
Applied Micro Circuits Corporation, 38
Applied Power, Inc., 9; 32 (upd.)
Aqua Alliance Inc., 32 (upd.)
AR Accessories Group, Inc., 23
ARA Services, II
ARAMARK Corporation, 13; 41 (upd.)
Arandell Corporation, 37
Arbitron Company, The, 38
Arbor Drugs Inc., 12
Arby's Inc., 14
Arch Mineral Corporation, 7
Arch Wireless, Inc., 39
Archer-Daniels-Midland Company, I; 11 (upd.); 32 (upd.)
Archway Cookies, Inc., 29
ARCO Chemical Company, 10
Arctco, Inc., 16
Arctic Cat Inc., 40 (upd.)
Arctic Slope Regional Corporation, 38
Arden Group, Inc., 29
Argosy Gaming Company, 21
Ariens Company, 48
Aris Industries, Inc., 16
Ark Restaurants Corp., 20
Arkansas Best Corporation, 16
Arkla, Inc., V
Armco Inc., IV
Armor All Products Corp., 16
Armor Holdings, Inc., 27
Armstrong World Industries, Inc., III; 22 (upd.)
Army and Air Force Exchange Service, 39
Arnold & Porter, 35
Arrow Electronics, Inc., 10
Art Institute of Chicago, The, 29

Art Van Furniture, Inc., 28
Artesyn Technologies Inc., 46 (upd.)
Arthur D. Little, Inc., 35
Arthur Murray International, Inc., 32
Artisan Entertainment Inc., 32 (upd.)
Arvin Industries, Inc., 8
Asanté Technologies, Inc., 20
ASARCO Incorporated, IV
Ascend Communications, Inc., 24
Ashland Inc., 19
Ashland Oil, Inc., IV
Ashley Furniture Industries, Inc., 35
Ashworth, Inc., 26
ASK Group, Inc., 9
Aspect Telecommunications Corporation, 22
Aspen Skiing Company, 15
Asplundh Tree Expert Co., 20
Assisted Living Concepts, Inc., 43
Associated Estates Realty Corporation, 25
Associated Grocers, Incorporated, 9; 31 (upd.)
Associated Milk Producers, Inc., 11; 48 (upd.)
Associated Natural Gas Corporation, 11
Associated Press, The, 13; 31 (upd.)
AST Research Inc., 9
Astoria Financial Corporation, 44
Astronics Corporation, 35
ASV, Inc., 34
At Home Corporation, 43
AT&T Bell Laboratories, Inc., 13
AT&T Corporation, 29 (upd.)
Atari Corporation, 9; 23 (upd.)
Atchison Casting Corporation, 39
Atlanta Gas Light Company, 6; 23 (upd.)
Atlanta National League Baseball Club, Inc., 43
Atlantic American Corporation, 44
Atlantic Energy, Inc., 6
Atlantic Group, The, 23
Atlantic Richfield Company, IV; 31 (upd.)
Atlantic Southeast Airlines, Inc., 47
Atlas Air, Inc., 39
Atlas Van Lines, Inc., 14
Atmel Corporation, 17
Atmos Energy Corporation, 43
Au Bon Pain Co., Inc., 18
Audio King Corporation, 24
Audiovox Corporation, 34
Ault Incorporated, 34
Auntie Anne's, Inc., 35
Aurora Foods Inc., 32
Austin Company, The, 8
Authentic Fitness Corp., 20
Auto Value Associates, Inc., 25
Autobytel Inc., 47
Autodesk, Inc., 10
Autologic Information International, Inc., 20
Automatic Data Processing, Inc., III; 9 (upd.); 47 (upd.)
Autotote Corporation, 20
AutoZone, Inc., 9; 31 (upd.)
Avado Brands, Inc., 31
Avco Financial Services Inc., 13
Aveda Corporation, 24
Avedis Zildjian Co., 38
Avery Dennison Corporation, IV; 17 (upd.)
Aviation Sales Company, 41
Avid Technology Inc., 38
Avis Rent A Car, Inc., 6; 22 (upd.)
Avnet Inc., 9
Avon Products, Inc., III; 19 (upd.); 46 (upd.)
Avondale Industries, 7; 41 (upd.)
Aydin Corp., 19
Azcon Corporation, 23
Aztar Corporation, 13
B&G Foods, Inc., 40
B. Dalton Bookseller Inc., 25
B. Manischewitz Company, LLC, The, 31
B/E Aerospace, Inc., 30
Babbage's, Inc., 10
Baby Superstore, Inc., 15
Bachman's Inc., 22
Back Bay Restaurant Group, Inc., 20
Back Yard Burgers, Inc., 45
Badger Meter, Inc., 22
Badger Paper Mills, Inc., 15
Bairnco Corporation, 28
Baker & Hostetler LLP, 40
Baker & McKenzie, 10; 42 (upd.)
Baker & Taylor Corporation, 16; 43 (upd.)
Baker and Botts, L.L.P., 28
Baker Hughes Incorporated, III; 22 (upd.)
Balance Bar Company, 32
Balchem Corporation, 42
Baldor Electric Company, 21
Baldwin Piano & Organ Company, 18
Baldwin Technology Company, Inc., 25
Ball Corporation, I; 10 (upd.)
Ballantyne of Omaha, Inc., 27
Ballard Medical Products, 21
Bally Manufacturing Corporation, III
Bally Total Fitness Holding Corp., 25
Baltek Corporation, 34
Baltimore Gas and Electric Company, V; 25 (upd.)
Banana Republic Inc., 25
Banc One Corporation, 10
Bandag, Inc., 19
Banfi Products Corp., 36
Bank of America Corporation, 46 (upd.)
Bank of Boston Corporation, II
Bank of Mississippi, Inc., 14
Bank of New England Corporation, II
Bank of New York Company, Inc., The, II; 46 (upd.)
Bank One Corporation, 36 (upd.)
BankAmerica Corporation, II; 8 (upd.)
Bankers Trust New York Corporation, II
Banner Aerospace, Inc., 14; 37 (upd.)
Banta Corporation, 12; 32 (upd.)
Banyan Systems Inc., 25
BarclaysAmerican Mortgage Corporation, 11
Barnes & Noble, Inc., 10; 30 (upd.)
Barnes Group Inc., 13
Barnett Banks, Inc., 9
Barnett Inc., 28
Barney's, Inc., 28
Barr Laboratories, Inc., 26
Barrett Business Services, Inc., 16
Bashas' Inc., 33
Bass Pro Shops, Inc., 42
Bassett Furniture Industries, Inc., 18
Bates Worldwide, Inc., 14; 33 (upd.)
Bath Iron Works, 12; 36 (upd.)
Battelle Memorial Institute, Inc., 10
Battle Mountain Gold Company, 23
Bausch & Lomb Inc., 7; 25 (upd.)
Baxter International Inc., I; 10 (upd.)
Bay State Gas Company, 38
BayBanks, Inc., 12
Bayou Steel Corporation, 31
BBN Corp., 19
BEA Systems, Inc., 36
Bear Creek Corporation, 38
Bear Stearns Companies, Inc., II; 10 (upd.)
Bearings, Inc., 13
Beatrice Company, II
BeautiControl Cosmetics, Inc., 21
Beazer Homes USA, Inc., 17
bebe stores, inc., 31
Bechtel Group, Inc., I; 24 (upd.)
Beckett Papers, 23
Beckman Coulter, Inc., 22
Beckman Instruments, Inc., 14
Becton, Dickinson & Company, I; 11 (upd.); 36 (upd.)
Bed Bath & Beyond Inc., 13; 41 (upd.)
Beech Aircraft Corporation, 8
Beech-Nut Nutrition Corporation, 21
Bekins Company, 15
Belco Oil & Gas Corp., 40
Belden Inc., 19
Belk Stores Services, Inc., V; 19 (upd.)
Bell and Howell Company, 9; 29 (upd.)
Bell Atlantic Corporation, V; 25 (upd.)
Bell Helicopter Textron Inc., 46
Bell Industries, Inc., 47
Bell Sports Corporation, 16; 44 (upd.)
BellSouth Corporation, V; 29 (upd.)
Beloit Corporation, 14
Bemis Company, Inc., 8
Ben & Jerry's Homemade, Inc., 10; 35 (upd.)
Benchmark Electronics, Inc., 40
Bendix Corporation, I
Beneficial Corporation, 8
Benihana, Inc., 18
Benjamin Moore & Co., 13; 38 (upd.)
Benton Oil and Gas Company, 47
Bergen Brunswig Corporation, V; 13 (upd.)
Beringer Wine Estates Holdings, Inc., 22
Berkeley Farms, Inc., 46
Berkshire Hathaway Inc., III; 18 (upd.); 42 (upd.)
Berlitz International, Inc., 13; 39 (upd.)
Bernard C. Harris Publishing Company, Inc., 39
Bernard Chaus, Inc., 27
Berry Petroleum Company, 47
Berry Plastics Corporation, 21
Bertucci's Inc., 16
Best Buy Co., Inc., 9; 23 (upd.)
Bestfoods, 22 (upd.)
BET Holdings, Inc., 18
Bethlehem Steel Corporation, IV; 7 (upd.); 27 (upd.)
Betz Laboratories, Inc., I; 10 (upd.)
Beverly Enterprises, Inc., III; 16 (upd.)
BFGoodrich Company, The, V; 19 (upd.)
BHC Communications, Inc., 26
BIC Corporation, 8; 23 (upd.)
Bicoastal Corporation, II
Big V Supermarkets, Inc., 25
Big B, Inc., 17
Big Bear Stores Co., 13
Big Dog Holdings, Inc., 45
Big Flower Press Holdings, Inc., 21
Big O Tires, Inc., 20
Big Rivers Electric Corporation, 11
Bill & Melinda Gates Foundation, 41
Bill Blass Ltd., 32
Billing Concepts Corp., 26
Bindley Western Industries, Inc., 9
Bingham Dana LLP, 43
Binks Sames Corporation, 21
Binney & Smith Inc., 25
Biogen Inc., 14; 36 (upd.)
Biomet, Inc., 10
Bird Corporation, 19
Birkenstock Footprint Sandals, Inc., 12; 42 (upd.)
Birmingham Steel Corporation, 13; 40 (upd.)
BISSELL Inc., 9; 30 (upd.)
BJ Services Company, 25
Black & Decker Corporation, The, III; 20 (upd.)
Black & Veatch LLP, 22
Black Box Corporation, 20

**United States** *(continued)*
Black Hills Corporation, 20
Blair Corporation, 25; 31
Blessings Corp., 19
Blimpie International, Inc., 15
Block Drug Company, Inc., 8; 27 (upd.)
Blockbuster Inc., 9; 31 (upd.)
Blonder Tongue Laboratories, Inc., 48
Bloomberg L.P., 21
Bloomingdale's Inc., 12
Blount International, Inc., 48 (upd.)
Blount, Inc., 12
Blue Bell Creameries L.P., 30
Blue Bird Corporation, 35
Blue Cross and Blue Shield Association, 10
Blue Diamond Growers, 28
Blue Mountain Arts, Inc., 29
Blyth Industries, Inc., 18
BMC Industries, Inc., 17
Boart Longyear Company, 26
Boatmen's Bancshares Inc., 15
Bob Evans Farms, Inc., 9
Boca Resorts, Inc., 37
Boeing Company, The, I; 10 (upd.); 32 (upd.)
Bohemia, Inc., 13
Boise Cascade Corporation, IV; 8 (upd.); 32 (upd.)
Bombay Company, Inc., The, 10
Bon Marché, Inc., The, 23
Bon Secours Health System, Inc., 24
Bon-Ton Stores, Inc., The, 16
Bonneville International Corporation, 29
Book-of-the-Month Club, Inc., 13
Books-A-Million, Inc., 14; 41 (upd.)
Boole & Babbage, Inc., 25
Booth Creek Ski Holdings, Inc., 31
Booz Allen & Hamilton Inc., 10
Borden, Inc., II; 22 (upd.)
Borders Group, Inc., 15; 43 (upd.)
Borg-Warner Automotive, Inc., 14; 32 (upd.)
Borg-Warner Corporation, III
Borland International, Inc., 9
Boron, LePore & Associates, Inc., 45
Boscov's Department Store, Inc., 31
Bose Corporation, 13; 36 (upd.)
Boston Acoustics, Inc., 22
Boston Beer Company, 18
Boston Celtics Limited Partnership, 14
Boston Chicken, Inc., 12
Boston Edison Company, 12
Boston Market Corporation, 48 (upd.)
Boston Professional Hockey Association Inc., 39
Boston Properties, Inc., 22
Boston Scientific Corporation, 37
Bowne & Co., Inc., 23
Boy Scouts of America, The, 34
Boyd Bros. Transportation Inc., 39
Boyd Gaming Corporation, 43
Boyds Collection, Ltd., The, 29
Bozell Worldwide Inc., 25
Bozzuto's, Inc., 13
Brach and Brock Confections, Inc., 15
Bradlees Discount Department Store Company, 12
Brannock Device Company, 48
Brass Eagle Inc., 34
Brazos Sportswear, Inc., 23
Bremer Financial Corp., 45
Bridgeport Machines, Inc., 17
Bridgford Foods Corporation, 27
Briggs & Stratton Corporation, 8; 27 (upd.)
Bright Horizons Family Solutions, Inc., 31
Brightpoint, Inc., 18
Brinker International, Inc., 10; 38 (upd.)
Bristol Hotel Company, 23
Bristol-Myers Squibb Company, III; 9 (upd.); 37 (upd.)
Brite Voice Systems, Inc., 20
Broadcast Music Inc., 23
Broadcom Corporation, 34
Broadmoor Hotel, The, 30
Brobeck, Phleger & Harrison, LLP, 31
Broder Bros. Co., 38
Broderbund Software, Inc., 13; 29 (upd.)
Brooke Group Ltd., 15
Brooklyn Union Gas, 6
Brooks Brothers Inc., 22
Brooks Sports Inc., 32
Brookshire Grocery Company, 16
Brookstone, Inc., 18
Brothers Gourmet Coffees, Inc., 20
Broughton Foods Co., 17
Brown & Brown, Inc., 41
Brown & Haley, 23
Brown & Root, Inc., 13
Brown & Sharpe Manufacturing Co., 23
Brown & Williamson Tobacco Corporation, 14; 33 (upd.)
Brown Brothers Harriman & Co., 45
Brown Group, Inc., V; 20 (upd.)
Brown Printing Company, 26
Brown-Forman Corporation, I; 10 (upd.); 38 (upd.)
Browning-Ferris Industries, Inc., V; 20 (upd.)
Broyhill Furniture Industries, Inc., 10
Bruce Foods Corporation, 39
Bruno's, Inc., 7; 26 (upd.)
Brunswick Corporation, III; 22 (upd.)
Brush Wellman Inc., 14
BTG, Inc., 45
Buca, Inc., 38
Buck Knives Inc., 48
Buckeye Technologies, Inc., 42
Buckle, Inc., The, 18
Bucyrus International, Inc., 17
Budd Company, The, 8
Budget Group, Inc., 25
Budget Rent a Car Corporation, 9
Buffets, Inc., 10; 32 (upd.)
Bugle Boy Industries, Inc., 18
Bulova Corporation, 13; 41 (upd.)
Bundy Corporation, 17
Bureau of National Affairs, Inc.,The 23
Burger King Corporation, II; 17 (upd.)
Burlington Coat Factory Warehouse Corporation, 10
Burlington Industries, Inc., V; 17 (upd.)
Burlington Northern Santa Fe Corporation, V; 27 (upd.)
Burlington Resources Inc., 10
Burns International Services Corporation, 13; 41 (upd.)
Burr-Brown Corporation, 19
Burton Snowboards Inc., 22
Bush Boake Allen Inc., 30
Bush Brothers & Company, 45
Bush Industries, Inc., 20
Business Men's Assurance Company of America, 14
Butler Manufacturing Co., 12
Butterick Co., Inc., 23
Buttrey Food & Drug Stores Co., 18
buy.com, Inc., 46
BWAY Corporation, 24
C-COR.net Corp., 38
C-Cube Microsystems, Inc., 37
C.F. Martin & Co., Inc., 42
C.H. Heist Corporation, 24
C.H. Robinson Worldwide, Inc., 11; 40 (upd.)
C.R. Bard Inc., 9
Cabela's Inc., 26
Cabletron Systems, Inc., 10
Cablevision Electronic Instruments, Inc., 32
Cablevision Systems Corporation, 7; 30 (upd.)
Cabot Corporation, 8; 29 (upd.)
Cache Incorporated, 30
CACI International Inc., 21
Cadence Design Systems, Inc., 11; 48 (upd.)
Cadmus Communications Corporation, 23
Cadwalader, Wickersham & Taft, 32
CAE USA Inc., 48
Caere Corporation, 20
Caesars World, Inc., 6
Cagle's, Inc., 20
Cahners Business Information, 43
Calavo Growers, Inc., 47
CalComp Inc., 13
Calcot Ltd., 33
Caldor Inc., 12
California Pizza Kitchen Inc., 15
Callaway Golf Company, 15; 45 (upd.)
Callon Petroleum Company, 47
CalMat Co., 19
Calpine Corporation, 36
Caltex Petroleum Corporation, 19
Calvin Klein, Inc., 22
Cambrex Corporation, 16; 44 (upd.)
Cambridge SoundWorks, Inc., 48
Cambridge Technology Partners, Inc., 36
Camelot Music, Inc., 26
Cameron & Barkley Company, 28
Campbell Soup Company, II; 7 (upd.); 26 (upd.)
Campbell-Mithun-Esty, Inc., 16
Campo Electronics, Appliances & Computers, Inc., 16
Canandaigua Brands, Inc., 34 (upd.)
Canandaigua Wine Company, Inc., 13
Candela Corporation, 48
Candie's, Inc., 31
Candlewood Hotel Company, Inc., 41
Cannondale Corporation, 21
Canterbury Park Holding Corporation, 42
Cap Rock Energy Corporation, 46
Capel Incorporated, 45
Capital Cities/ABC Inc., II
Capital Holding Corporation, III
CapStar Hotel Company, 21
Caraustar Industries, Inc., 19; 44 (upd.)
Carbide/Graphite Group, Inc., The, 40
Carborundum Company, 15
Cardinal Health, Inc., 18
Career Education Corporation, 45
Caremark International Inc., 10
Carey International, Inc., 26
Cargill, Incorporated, II; 13 (upd.); 40 (upd.)
Carhartt, Inc., 30
Caribiner International, Inc., 24
Caribou Coffee Company, Inc., 28
Carlisle Companies Incorporated, 8
Carlson Companies, Inc., 6; 22 (upd.)
Carmichael Lynch Inc., 28
Carmike Cinemas, Inc., 14; 37 (upd.)
Carnation Company, II
Carnegie Corporation of New York, 35
Carnival Corporation, 27 (upd.)
Carnival Cruise Lines, Inc., 6
Carolina First Corporation, 31
Carolina Freight Corporation, 6
Carolina Power & Light Company, V; 23 (upd.)
Carolina Telephone and Telegraph Company, 10
Carpenter Technology Corporation, 13

CARQUEST Corporation, 29
Carr-Gottstein Foods Co., 17
Carriage Services, Inc., 37
Carrier Access Corporation, 44
Carrier Corporation, 7
Carroll's Foods, Inc., 46
Carsey-Werner Company, L.L.C., The, 37
Carson Pirie Scott & Company, 15
Carson, Inc., 31
Carter Hawley Hale Stores, Inc., V
Carter Lumber Company, 45
Carter-Wallace, Inc., 8; 38 (upd.)
Carvel Corporation, 35
Cascade Natural Gas Corporation, 9
Casco Northern Bank, 14
Casey's General Stores, Inc., 19
Cash America International, Inc., 20
Castle & Cooke, Inc., II; 20 (upd.)
Casual Corner Group, Inc., 43
Catalina Lighting, Inc., 43 (upd.)
Catalina Marketing Corporation, 18
Catalytica Energy Systems, Inc., 44
Catellus Development Corporation, 24
Caterpillar Inc., III; 15 (upd.)
Catherines Stores Corporation, 15
Catholic Order of Foresters, 24
Cato Corporation, 14
Cattleman's, Inc., 20
CB Commercial Real Estate Services Group, Inc., 21
CBI Industries, Inc., 7
CBRL Group, Inc., 35 (upd.)
CBS Corporation, II; 6 (upd.); 28 (upd.)
CCH Inc., 14
CDI Corporation, 6
CDW Computer Centers, Inc., 16
CEC Entertainment, Inc., 31 (upd.)
Cedar Fair, L.P., 22
Celadon Group Inc., 30
Celanese Corporation, I
Celebrity, Inc., 22
Celestial Seasonings, Inc., 16
Cendant Corporation, 44 (upd.)
Centel Corporation, 6
Centennial Communications Corporation, 39
Centerior Energy Corporation, V
Centex Corporation, 8; 29 (upd.)
Centocor Inc., 14
Central and South West Corporation, V
Central Garden & Pet Company, 23
Central Hudson Gas and Electricity Corporation, 6
Central Maine Power, 6
Central Newspapers, Inc., 10
Central Parking Corporation, 18
Central Soya Company, Inc., 7
Central Sprinkler Corporation, 29
Century Communications Corp., 10
Century Telephone Enterprises, Inc., 9
Century Theatres, Inc., 31
Cephalon, Inc., 45
Cerner Corporation, 16
CertainTeed Corporation, 35
Cessna Aircraft Company, 8; 27 (upd.)
Chadbourne & Parke, 36
Chadwick's of Boston, Ltd., 29
Chalone Wine Group, Ltd., The, 36
Champion Enterprises, Inc., 17
Champion Industries, Inc., 28
Champion International Corporation, IV; 20 (upd.)
Championship Auto Racing Teams, Inc., 37
Chancellor Media Corporation, 24
Chaparral Steel Co., 13
Charles River Laboratories International, Inc., 42
Charles Schwab Corporation, The, 8; 26 (upd.)
Charles Stark Draper Laboratory, Inc., The, 35
Charlotte Russe Holding, Inc., 35
Charming Shoppes, Inc., 8; 38
Chart House Enterprises, Inc., 17
Chart Industries, Inc., 21
Charter Communications, Inc., 33
Chase Manhattan Corporation, The, II; 13 (upd.)
Chateau Communities, Inc., 37
Chattem, Inc., 17
Chautauqua Airlines, Inc., 38
Checkers Drive-Up Restaurants Inc., 16
Checkpoint Systems, Inc., 39
Cheesecake Factory Inc., The, 17
Chelsea Milling Company, 29
Chemcentral Corporation, 8
Chemed Corporation, 13
Chemfab Corporation, 35
Chemi-Trol Chemical Co., 16
Chemical Banking Corporation, II; 14 (upd.)
Chemical Waste Management, Inc., 9
Cherokee Inc., 18
Chesapeake Corporation, 8; 30 (upd.)
Chesebrough-Pond's USA, Inc., 8
Chevron Corporation, IV; 19 (upd.)
ChevronTexaco Corporation, 47 (upd.)
Cheyenne Software, Inc., 12
Chi-Chi's Inc., 13
Chiat/Day Inc. Advertising, 11
Chic by H.I.S, Inc., 20
Chicago and North Western Holdings Corporation, 6
Chicago Bears Football Club, Inc., 33
Chicago Board of Trade, 41
Chick-fil-A Inc., 23
Chicken of the Sea International, 24 (upd.)
Chico's FAS, Inc., 45
Children's Comprehensive Services, Inc., 42
Children's Place Retail Stores, Inc., The, 37
Childtime Learning Centers, Inc., 34
Chiles Offshore Corporation, 9
CHIPS and Technologies, Inc., 9
Chiquita Brands International, Inc., 7; 21 (upd.)
Chiron Corporation, 10; 36 (upd.)
Chisholm-Mingo Group, Inc., 41
Chock Full o' Nuts Corp., 17
Choice Hotels International Inc., 14
Chorus Line Corporation, 30
Chris-Craft Industries, Inc., 9; 31 (upd.)
Christensen Boyles Corporation, 26
Christopher & Banks Corporation, 42
Chromcraft Revington, Inc., 15
Chronicle Publishing Company, Inc., The, 23
Chronimed Inc., 26
Chrysler Corporation, I; 11 (upd.)
CH2M Hill Ltd., 22
Chubb Corporation, The, III; 14 (upd.); 37 (upd.)
Church & Dwight Co., Inc., 29
Churchill Downs Incorporated, 29
Cianbro Corporation, 14
Ciber, Inc., 18
CIGNA Corporation, III; 22 (upd.); 45 (upd.)
Cincinnati Bell, Inc., 6
Cincinnati Financial Corporation, 16; 44 (upd.)
Cincinnati Gas & Electric Company, 6
Cincinnati Milacron Inc., 12
Cincom Systems Inc., 15
Cinnabon Inc., 23
Cintas Corporation, 21
CIPSCO Inc., 6
Circle K Company, The, II; 20 (upd.)
Circon Corporation, 21
Circuit City Stores, Inc., 9; 29 (upd.)
Circus Circus Enterprises, Inc., 6
Cirrus Design Corporation, 44
Cirrus Logic, Inc., 11; 48 (upd.)
Cisco Systems, Inc., 11; 34 (upd.)
Citadel Communications Corporation, 35
Citfed Bancorp, Inc., 16
CITGO Petroleum Corporation, IV, 31 (upd.)
Citicorp, II; 9 (upd.)
Citigroup Inc., 30 (upd.)
Citizens Financial Group, Inc., 42
Citizens Utilities Company, 7
Citrix Systems, Inc., 44
City Public Service, 6
CKE Restaurants, Inc., 19; 46 (upd.)
Claire's Stores, Inc., 17
Clarcor Inc., 17
Clark Construction Group, Inc., The, 8
Clark Equipment Company, 8
Classic Vacation Group, Inc., 46
Clayton Homes Incorporated, 13
Clear Channel Communications, Inc., 23
Cleary, Gottlieb, Steen & Hamilton, 35
Cleco Corporation, 37
Cleveland Indians Baseball Company, Inc., 37
Cleveland-Cliffs Inc., 13
Clorox Company, The, III; 22 (upd.)
Clothestime, Inc., The, 20
ClubCorp, Inc., 33
CML Group, Inc., 10
CMP Media Inc., 26
CMS Energy Corporation, V, 14
CNA Financial Corporation, III; 38 (upd.)
CNET Networks, Inc., 47
CNS, Inc., 20
Coach Leatherware, 10
Coach USA, Inc., 24
Coach, Inc., 45 (upd.)
Coastal Corporation, The, IV, 31 (upd.)
COBE Laboratories, Inc., 13
Coborn's, Inc., 30
Cobra Electronics Corporation, 14
Cobra Golf Inc., 16
Coca Cola Bottling Co. Consolidated, 10
Coca-Cola Company, The, I; 10 (upd.); 32 (upd.)
Coca-Cola Enterprises, Inc., 13
Coeur d'Alene Mines Corporation, 20
Cogentrix Energy, Inc., 10
Coherent, Inc., 31
Cohu, Inc., 32
Coinmach Laundry Corporation, 20
Coinstar, Inc., 44
Cold Spring Granite Company, 16
Coldwater Creek Inc., 21
Cole National Corporation, 13
Coleman Company, Inc., The, 9; 30 (upd.)
Coles Express Inc., 15
Colgate-Palmolive Company, III; 14 (upd.); 35 (upd.)
Collectors Universe, Inc., 48
Collins & Aikman Corporation, 13; 41 (upd.)
Collins Industries, Inc., 33
Colorado MEDtech, Inc., 48
Colt Industries Inc., I
Colt's Manufacturing Company, Inc., 12
Columbia Gas System, Inc., The, V; 16 (upd.)
Columbia Pictures Entertainment, Inc., II

**United States** *(continued)*
Columbia Sportswear Company, 19; 41 (upd.)
Columbia TriStar Motion Pictures Companies, 12 (upd.)
Columbia/HCA Healthcare Corporation, 15
Columbus McKinnon Corporation, 37
Comair Holdings Inc., 13; 34 (upd.)
Comcast Corporation, 7; 24 (upd.)
Comdial Corporation, 21
Comdisco, Inc., 9
Comerica Incorporated, 40
COMFORCE Corporation, 40
Commerce Clearing House, Inc., 7
Commercial Credit Company, 8
Commercial Federal Corporation, 12
Commercial Financial Services, Inc., 26
Commercial Metals Company, 15; 42 (upd.)
Commodore International Ltd., 7
Commonwealth Edison Company, V
Commonwealth Energy System, 14
Commonwealth Telephone Enterprises, Inc., 25
Community Psychiatric Centers, 15
Compaq Computer Corporation, III; 6 (upd.); 26 (upd.)
CompDent Corporation, 22
CompHealth Inc., 25
Complete Business Solutions, Inc., 31
Comprehensive Care Corporation, 15
CompuAdd Computer Corporation, 11
CompuCom Systems, Inc., 10
CompUSA, Inc., 10; 35 (upd.)
CompuServe Interactive Services, Inc., 10; 27 (upd.)
Computer Associates International, Inc., 6
Computer Data Systems, Inc., 14
Computer Learning Centers, Inc., 26
Computer Sciences Corporation, 6
Computerland Corp., 13
Computervision Corporation, 10
Compuware Corporation, 10; 30 (upd.)
Comsat Corporation, 23
Comshare Inc., 23
Comstock Resources, Inc., 47
Comverse Technology, Inc., 15; 43 (upd.)
ConAgra Foods, Inc., II; 12 (upd.); 42 (upd.)
Conair Corp., 17
Concepts Direct, Inc., 39
Concord Camera Corporation, 41
Concord Fabrics, Inc., 16
Condé Nast Publications Inc., The, 13
Cone Mills Corporation, 8
Conexant Systems, Inc., 36
Congoleum Corp., 18
Connecticut Light and Power Co., 13
Connecticut Mutual Life Insurance Company, III
Connell Company, The, 29
Conner Peripherals, Inc., 6
Conoco Inc., IV; 16 (upd.)
Conseco, Inc., 10; 33 (upd.)
Conso International Corporation, 29
Consolidated Delivery & Logistics, Inc., 24
Consolidated Edison Company of New York, Inc., V
Consolidated Edison, Inc., 45 (upd.)
Consolidated Freightways Corporation, V; 21 (upd.); 48 (upd.)
Consolidated Natural Gas Company, V; 19 (upd.)
Consolidated Papers, Inc., 8; 36 (upd.)
Consolidated Products Inc., 14
Consolidated Rail Corporation, V
Consumers Power Co., 14
Consumers Union, 26
Consumers Water Company, 14
Container Store, The, 36
ContiGroup Companies, Inc., 43 (upd.)
Continental Airlines, Inc., I; 21 (upd.)
Continental Bank Corporation, II
Continental Cablevision, Inc., 7
Continental Can Co., Inc., 15
Continental Corporation, The, III
Continental General Tire Corp., 23
Continental Grain Company, 10; 13 (upd.)
Continental Group Company, I
Continental Medical Systems, Inc., 10
Control Data Corporation, III
Control Data Systems, Inc., 10
Converse Inc., 9; 31 (upd.)
Cooker Restaurant Corporation, The, 20
Cooper Cameron Corporation, 20 (upd.)
Cooper Companies, Inc., The, 39
Cooper Industries, Inc., II; 44 (upd.)
Cooper Tire & Rubber Company, 8; 23 (upd.)
Coopers & Lybrand, 9
Copart Inc., 23
Copley Press, Inc., The, 23
Copps Corporation, The, 32
Corbis Corporation, 31
Cordis Corporation, 19; 46 (upd.)
CoreStates Financial Corp, 17
Corinthian Colleges, Inc., 39
Corning Inc., III; 44 (upd.)
Corporate Express, Inc., 22; 47 (upd.)
Corporate Software Inc., 9
Corporation for Public Broadcasting, 14
Correctional Services Corporation, 30
Corrections Corporation of America, 23
Corrpro Companies, Inc., 20
CORT Business Services Corporation, 26
Cosmair, Inc., 8
Cosmetic Center, Inc., The, 22
Cost Plus, Inc., 27
Costco Wholesale Corporation, V; 43 (upd.)
Cotter & Company, V
Cotton Incorporated, 46
Coty, Inc., 36
Coudert Brothers, 30
Countrywide Credit Industries, Inc., 16
County Seat Stores Inc., 9
Courier Corporation, 41
Covance Inc., 30
Covington & Burling, 40
Cowles Media Company, 23
Cox Enterprises, Inc., IV; 22 (upd.)
CPC International Inc., II
CPI Corp., 38
Cracker Barrel Old Country Store, Inc., 10
Craftmade International, Inc., 44
Crain Communications, Inc., 12; 35 (upd.)
Cramer, Berkowitz & Co., 34
Crane & Co., Inc., 26
Crane Co., 8; 30 (upd.)
Crate and Barrel, 9
Cravath, Swaine & Moore, 43
Cray Research, Inc., III; 16 (upd.)
Creative Artists Agency LLC, 38
Credit Acceptance Corporation, 18
Crompton & Knowles, 9
Crompton Corporation, 36 (upd.)
Croscill, Inc., 42
Crowley Maritime Corporation, 6; 28 (upd.)
Crowley, Milner & Company, 19
Crown Books Corporation, 21
Crown Central Petroleum Corporation, 7
Crown Crafts, Inc., 16
Crown Equipment Corporation, 15
Crown Media Holdings, Inc., 45
Crown Vantage Inc., 29
Crown, Cork & Seal Company, Inc., I; 13; 32 (upd.)
CRSS Inc., 6
Cruise America Inc., 21
CryoLife, Inc., 46
Crystal Brands, Inc., 9
CS First Boston Inc., II
CSK Auto Corporation, 38
CSS Industries, Inc., 35
CSX Corporation, V; 22 (upd.)
CTB International Corporation, 43 (upd.)
CTG, Inc., 11
CTS Corporation, 39
Cubic Corporation, 19
CUC International Inc., 16
Cuisinart Corporation, 24
Culbro Corporation, 15
Cullen/Frost Bankers, Inc., 25
Culligan Water Technologies, Inc., 12; 38 (upd.)
Culp, Inc., 29
Cumberland Farms, Inc., 17
Cumberland Packing Corporation, 26
Cummins Engine Company, Inc., I; 12 (upd.); 40 (upd.)
Cumulus Media Inc., 37
Cunard Line Ltd., 23
Current, Inc., 37
Curtice-Burns Foods, Inc., 7; 21 (upd.)
Curtiss-Wright Corporation, 10; 35 (upd.)
Custom Chrome, Inc., 16
Cutter & Buck Inc., 27
CVS Corporation, 45 (upd.)
Cybermedia, Inc., 25
Cygne Designs, Inc., 25
Cypress Semiconductor Corporation, 20; 48 (upd.)
Cyprus Amax Minerals Company, 21
Cyprus Minerals Company, 7
Cyrk Inc., 19
Cytec Industries Inc., 27
Czarnikow-Rionda Company, Inc., 32
D&K Wholesale Drug, Inc., 14
D'Agostino Supermarkets Inc., 19
D'Arcy Masius Benton & Bowles, Inc., VI; 32 (upd.)
D.G. Yuengling & Son, Inc., 38
Daffy's Inc., 26
Dain Rauscher Corporation, 35 (upd.)
Dairy Mart Convenience Stores, Inc., 7; 25 (upd.)
Daisytek International Corporation, 18
Daktronics, Inc., 32
Dal-Tile International Inc., 22
Dale Carnegie Training, Inc., 28
Dallas Cowboys Football Club, Ltd., 33
Dallas Semiconductor Corporation, 13; 31 (upd.)
Damark International, Inc., 18
Dames & Moore, Inc., 25
Dan River Inc., 35
Dana Corporation, I; 10 (upd.)
Danaher Corporation, 7
Daniel Industries, Inc., 16
Dannon Co., Inc., 14
Danskin, Inc., 12
Darden Restaurants, Inc., 16; 44 (upd.)
Darigold, Inc., 9
Dart Group Corporation, 16
Data Broadcasting Corporation, 31
Data General Corporation, 8
Datapoint Corporation, 11
Datascope Corporation, 39
Datek Online Holdings Corp., 32
Dauphin Deposit Corporation, 14
Dave & Buster's, Inc., 33
Davey Tree Expert Company, The, 11

David and Lucile Packard Foundation, The, 41
David J. Joseph Company, The, 14
David's Bridal, Inc., 33
Davis Polk & Wardwell, 36
DAW Technologies, Inc., 25
Dawn Food Products, Inc., 17
Day & Zimmermann Inc., 9; 31 (upd.)
Day Runner, Inc., 14; 41 (upd.)
Dayton Hudson Corporation, V; 18 (upd.)
DC Comics Inc., 25
DDB Needham Worldwide, 14
Dean & DeLuca, Inc., 36
Dean Foods Company, 7; 21 (upd.)
Dean Witter, Discover & Co., 12
Death Row Records, 27
Deb Shops, Inc., 16
Debevoise & Plimpton, 39
Dechert, 43
Deckers Outdoor Corporation, 22
Decora Industries, Inc., 31
DeCrane Aircraft Holdings Inc., 36
DeepTech International Inc., 21
Deere & Company, III; 21 (upd.); 42 (upd.)
Defiance, Inc., 22
DeKalb Genetics Corporation, 17
Del Laboratories, Inc., 28
Del Monte Foods Company, 7; 23 (upd.)
Del Webb Corporation, 14
Delaware North Companies Incorporated, 7
dELiA*s Inc., 29
Dell Computer Corporation, 9; 31 (upd.)
Deloitte Touche Tohmatsu International, 9; 29 (upd.)
Delphi Automotive Systems Corporation, 45
Delta Air Lines, Inc., I; 6 (upd.); 39 (upd.)
Delta and Pine Land Company, 33
Delta Woodside Industries, Inc., 8; 30 (upd.)
Deltic Timber Corporation, 46
Deluxe Corporation, 7; 22 (upd.)
DeMoulas / Market Basket Inc., 23
DenAmerica Corporation, 29
Denison International plc, 46
Dentsply International Inc., 10
DEP Corporation, 20
Department VVI, Inc., 14; 34 (upd.)
Deposit Guaranty Corporation, 17
DePuy Inc., 30; 37 (upd.)
Designer Holdings Ltd., 20
Destec Energy, Inc., 12
Detroit Diesel Corporation, 10
Detroit Edison Company, The, V
Detroit Pistons Basketball Company, The, 41
Detroit Tigers Baseball Club, Inc., 46
Deutsch, Inc., 42
DeVry Incorporated, 29
Dewey Ballantine LLP, 48
Dexter Corporation, The, I; 12 (upd.)
DH Technology, Inc., 18
DHL Worldwide Express, 6; 24 (upd.)
Di Giorgio Corp., 12
Dial Corp., The, 8; 23 (upd.)
Dial-A-Mattress Operating Corporation, 46
Dialogic Corporation, 18
Diamond Shamrock, Inc., IV
Dibrell Brothers, Incorporated, 12
dick clark productions, inc., 16
Diebold, Incorporated, 7; 22 (upd.)
Diedrich Coffee, Inc., 40
Digex, Inc., 46
Digi International Inc., 9
Digital Equipment Corporation, III; 6 (upd.)
Dillard Department Stores, Inc., V; 16 (upd.)
Dillard Paper Company, 11
Dillingham Construction Corporation, I; 44 (upd.)
Dillon Companies Inc., 12
Dime Savings Bank of New York, F.S.B., 9
DIMON Inc., 27
Dionex Corporation, 46
Direct Focus, Inc., 47
DIRECTV, Inc., 38
Discount Auto Parts, Inc., 18
Discount Drug Mart, Inc., 14
Discovery Communications, Inc., 42
Dixie Group, Inc., The, 20
Dixon Industries, Inc., 26
Dixon Ticonderoga Company, 12
DMI Furniture, Inc., 46
Do it Best Corporation, 30
Documentum, Inc., 46
Dolby Laboratories Inc., 20
Dole Food Company, Inc., 9; 31 (upd.)
Dollar Thrifty Automotive Group, Inc., 25
Dollar Tree Stores, Inc., 23
Dominion Homes, Inc., 19
Dominion Resources, Inc., V
Domino Sugar Corporation, 26
Domino's Pizza, Inc., 7; 21 (upd.)
Don Massey Cadillac, Inc., 37
Donaldson Co. Inc., 16
Donaldson, Lufkin & Jenrette, Inc., 22
Donna Karan Company, 15
Donnelly Corporation, 12; 35 (upd.)
Donnkenny, Inc., 17
Dorsey & Whitney LLP, 47
Doskocil Companies, Inc., 12
DoubleClick Inc., 46
Doubletree Corporation, 21
Douglas & Lomason Company, 16
Dover Corporation, III; 28 (upd.)
Dover Downs Entertainment, Inc., 43
Dover Publications Inc., 34
Dow Chemical Company, The, I; 8 (upd.)
Dow Jones & Company, Inc., IV; 19 (upd.); 47 (upd.)
Dow Jones Telerate, Inc., 10
DPL Inc., 6
DQE, Inc., 6
Dr Pepper/Seven Up, Inc., 9; 32 (upd.)
Drackett Professional Products, 12
Drake Beam Morin, Inc., 44
DreamWorks SKG, 43
Drees Company, Inc., The, 41
Dress Barn, Inc., The, 24
Dresser Industries, Inc., III
Drew Industries Inc., 28
Drexel Burnham Lambert Incorporated, II
Drexel Heritage Furnishings Inc., 12
Dreyer's Grand Ice Cream, Inc., 17
Drug Emporium, Inc., 12
Drypers Corporation, 18
DSC Communications Corporation, 12
DTE Energy Company, 20 (upd.)
Duane Reade Holding Corp., 21
Duck Head Apparel Company, Inc., 42
Duckwall-ALCO Stores, Inc., 24
Ducommun Incorporated, 30
Duke Energy Corporation, V; 27 (upd.)
Dun & Bradstreet Corporation, The, IV; 19 (upd.)
Dun & Bradstreet Software Services Inc., 11
Duplex Products Inc., 17
Duracell International Inc., 9
Durametallic, 21
Duriron Company Inc., 17
Duty Free International, Inc., 11
Dyersburg Corporation, 21
Dynatech Corporation, 13
DynCorp, 45
E! Entertainment Television Inc., 17
E*Trade Group, Inc., 20
E. & J. Gallo Winery, I; 7 (upd.); 28 (upd.)
E.I. du Pont de Nemours & Company, I; 8 (upd.); 26 (upd.)
E.W. Scripps Company, The, IV; 7 (upd.); 28 (upd.)
Eagle Hardware & Garden, Inc., 16
Eagle-Picher Industries, Inc., 8; 23 (upd.)
Earl Scheib, Inc., 32
Earthgrains Company, The, 36
EarthLink, Inc., 36
Eastern Airlines, I
Eastern Company, The, 48
Eastern Enterprises, 6
Eastman Chemical Company, 14; 38 (upd.)
Eastman Kodak Company, III; 7 (upd.); 36 (upd.)
Eateries, Inc., 33
Eaton Corporation, I; 10 (upd.)
Eaton Vance Corporation, 18
eBay Inc., 32
EBSCO Industries, Inc., 17; 40 (upd.)
ECC International Corp., 42
Echlin Inc., I; 11 (upd.)
EchoStar Communications Corporation, 35
Eckerd Corporation, 9; 32 (upd.)
Ecolab, Inc., I; 13 (upd.); 34 (upd.)
Ecology and Environment, Inc., 39
Eddie Bauer, Inc., 9; 36 (upd.)
Edelbrock Corporation, 37
Edison Brothers Stores, Inc., 9
Edison Schools Inc., 37
Edmark Corporation, 14; 41 (upd.)
EDO Corporation, 46
Education Management Corporation, 35
Educational Broadcasting Corporation, 48
Educational Testing Service, 12
Edw. C. Levy Co., 42
Edward J. DeBartolo Corporation, The, 8
Edward Jones, 30
Edwards Theatres Circuit, Inc., 31
EG&G Incorporated, 8; 29 (upd.)
Egghead Inc., 9
Egghead.com, Inc., 31 (upd.)
84 Lumber Company, 9; 39 (upd.)
800-JR Cigar, Inc., 27
Einstein/Noah Bagel Corporation, 29
Ekco Group, Inc., 16
El Camino Resources International, Inc., 11
El Chico Restaurants, Inc., 19
El Paso Electric Company, 21
El Paso Natural Gas Company, 12
Elano Corporation, 14
Elder-Beerman Stores Corporation, 10
Electric Lightwave, Inc., 37
Electromagnetic Sciences Inc., 21
Electronic Arts Inc., 10
Electronic Data Systems Corporation, III; 28 (upd.)
Electronics for Imaging, Inc., 15; 43 (upd.)
Eli Lilly and Company, I; 11 (upd.); 47 (upd.)
Elizabeth Arden, Inc., 8; 40 (upd.)
Eljer Industries, Inc., 24
Ellerbe Becket, 41
Ellett Brothers, Inc., 17
Elmer's Restaurants, Inc., 42
Elsinore Corporation, 48
Embers America Restaurants, 30
EMC Corporation, 12; 46 (upd.)
Emerson, 46 (upd.)
Emerson Electric Co., II
Emerson Radio Corp., 30

**United States** *(continued)*
Emery Worldwide Airlines, Inc., 6; 25 (upd.)
Emge Packing Co., Inc., 11
Emmis Communications Corporation, 47
Empi, Inc., 26
Empire Blue Cross and Blue Shield, III
Employee Solutions, Inc., 18
ENCAD, Incorporated, 25
Encompass Services Corporation, 33
Encore Computer Corporation, 13
Encyclopaedia Britannica, Inc., 7; 39 (upd.)
Energen Corporation, 21
Energizer Holdings, Inc., 32
Enesco Corporation, 11
Engelhard Corporation, IV, 21 (upd.)
Engle Homes, Inc., 46
Engraph, Inc., 12
Ennis Business Forms, Inc., 21
Enquirer/Star Group, Inc., 10
Enrich International, Inc., 33
Enron Corporation, V, 19; 46 (upd.)
Enserch Corporation, V
Entergy Corporation, V; 45 (upd.)
Enterprise Rent-A-Car Company, 6
Entravision Communications Corporation, 41
Envirodyne Industries, Inc., 17
Environmental Industries, Inc., 31
Enzo Biochem, Inc., 41
Equifax Inc., 6; 28 (upd.)
Equitable Life Assurance Society of the United States, III
Equitable Resources, Inc., 6
Equity Marketing, Inc., 26
Erie Indemnity Company, 35
ERLY Industries Inc., 17
Ernst & Young, 9; 29 (upd.)
Escalade, Incorporated, 19
Eskimo Pie Corporation, 21
Esprit de Corp., 8; 29 (upd.)
ESS Technology, Inc., 22
Essef Corporation, 18
Esselte Pendaflex Corporation, 11
Essence Communications, Inc., 24
Estée Lauder Companies Inc., The, 9; 30 (upd.)
Esterline Technologies Corp., 15
Ethan Allen Interiors, Inc., 12; 39 (upd.)
Ethicon, Inc., 23
Ethyl Corporation, I; 10 (upd.)
EToys, Inc., 37
Eureka Company, The, 12
Euromarket Designs Inc., 31 (upd.)
Evans & Sutherland Computer Corporation, 19
Evans, Inc., 30
Everex Systems, Inc., 16
Everlast Worldwide Inc., 47
Exabyte Corporation, 12; 40 (upd.)
Exar Corp., 14
EXCEL Communications Inc., 18
Executive Jet, Inc., 36
Executone Information Systems, Inc., 13
Exelon Corporation, 48 (upd.)
Exide Electronics Group, Inc., 20
Expeditors International of Washington Inc., 17
Experian Information Solutions Inc., 45
Express Scripts Inc., 17; 44 (upd.)
Extended Stay America, Inc., 41
Exxon Corporation, IV; 7 (upd.); 32 (upd.)
EZCORP Inc., 43
E-Systems, Inc., 9
E-Z Serve Corporation, 17
Fab Industries, Inc., 27
Fabri-Centers of America Inc., 16
Fair Grounds Corporation, 44
Fair, Isaac and Company, 18
Fairchild Aircraft, Inc., 9
Fairfield Communities, Inc., 36
Falcon Products, Inc., 33
Fallon McElligott Inc., 22
Family Dollar Stores, Inc., 13
Family Golf Centers, Inc., 29
Famous Dave's of America, Inc., 40
Fannie Mae, 45 (upd.)
Fansteel Inc., 19
FAO Schwarz, 46
Farah Incorporated, 24
Farley Northwest Industries, Inc., I
Farm Family Holdings, Inc., 39
Farm Journal Corporation, 42
Farmers Insurance Group of Companies, 25
Farmland Foods, Inc., 7
Farmland Industries, Inc., 48
Farrar, Straus and Giroux Inc., 15
Fastenal Company, 14; 42 (upd.)
Fay's Inc., 17
Fazoli's Systems, Inc., 27
Featherlite Inc., 28
Fedders Corporation, 18; 43 (upd.)
Federal Express Corporation, V
Federal National Mortgage Association, II
Federal Paper Board Company, Inc., 8
Federal Prison Industries, Inc., 34
Federal Signal Corp., 10
Federal-Mogul Corporation, I; 10 (upd.); 26 (upd.)
Federated Department Stores Inc., 9; 31 (upd.)
FedEx Corporation, 18 (upd.); 42 (upd.)
Feld Entertainment, Inc., 32 (upd.)
Fellowes Manufacturing Company, 28
Fender Musical Instruments Company, 16; 43 (upd.)
Fenwick & West LLP, 34
Ferolito, Vultaggio & Sons, 27
Ferrellgas Partners, L.P., 35
Ferro Corporation, 8
FHP International Corporation, 6
FiberMark, Inc., 37
Fibreboard Corporation, 16
Fidelity Investments Inc., II; 14 (upd.)
Fieldale Farms Corporation, 23
Fieldcrest Cannon, Inc., 9; 31 (upd.)
Fifth Third Bancorp, 13; 31 (upd.)
Figgie International Inc., 7
FINA, Inc., 7
Fingerhut Companies, Inc., 9; 36 (upd.)
Finish Line, Inc., The, 29
FinishMaster, Inc., 24
Finlay Enterprises, Inc., 16
Firearms Training Systems, Inc., 27
Fireman's Fund Insurance Company, III
First Albany Companies Inc., 37
First Alert, Inc., 28
First Bank System Inc., 12
First Brands Corporation, 8
First Chicago Corporation, II
First Commerce Bancshares, Inc., 15
First Commerce Corporation, 11
First Data Corporation, 30 (upd.)
First Empire State Corporation, 11
First Executive Corporation, III
First Fidelity Bank, N.A., New Jersey, 9
First Financial Management Corporation, 11
First Hawaiian, Inc., 11
First Interstate Bancorp, II
First Mississippi Corporation, 8
First Nationwide Bank, 14
First of America Bank Corporation, 8
First Security Corporation, 11
First Team Sports, Inc., 22
First Tennessee National Corporation, 11; 48 (upd.)
First Union Corporation, 10
First USA, Inc., 11
First Virginia Banks, Inc., 11
First Years Inc., The, 46
Firstar Corporation, 11; 33 (upd.)
Fiserv Inc., 11; 33 (upd.)
Fisher Companies, Inc., 15
Fisher Controls International, Inc., 13
Fisher Scientific International Inc., 24
Fisher-Price Inc., 12; 32 (upd.)
Flagstar Companies, Inc., 10
Fleer Corporation, 15
Fleet Financial Group, Inc., 9
FleetBoston Financial Corporation, 36 (upd.)
Fleetwood Enterprises, Inc., III; 22 (upd.)
Fleming Companies, Inc., II; 17 (upd.)
Flexsteel Industries Inc., 15; 41 (upd.)
FlightSafety International, Inc., 9; 29 (upd.)
Flint Ink Corporation, 13; 41 (upd.)
Florida Crystals Inc., 35
Florida Gaming Corporation, 47
Florida Progress Corporation, V; 23 (upd.)
Florida Rock Industries, Inc., 46
Florida's Natural Growers, 45
Florists' Transworld Delivery, Inc., 28
Florsheim Shoe Group Inc., 9; 31 (upd.)
Flour City International, Inc., 44
Flowers Industries, Inc., 12; 35 (upd.)
Flowserve Corporation, 33
Fluke Corporation, 15
Fluor Corporation, I; 8 (upd.); 34 (upd.)
Flying J Inc., 19
FMC Corporation, I; 11 (upd.)
FMR Corp., 8; 32 (upd.)
Foamex International Inc., 17
Foley & Lardner, 28
Follett Corporation, 12; 39 (upd.)
Food Lion, Inc., II; 15 (upd.)
Foodarama Supermarkets, Inc., 28
FoodBrands America, Inc., 23
Foodmaker, Inc., 14
Foote, Cone & Belding Communications, Inc., I
Footstar, Incorporated, 24
Forbes Inc., 30
Ford Foundation, The, 34
Ford Motor Company, I; 11 (upd.); 36 (upd.)
Ford Motor Company, S.A. de C.V., 20
FORE Systems, Inc., 25
Forest City Enterprises, Inc., 16
Forest Laboratories, Inc., 11
Forest Oil Corporation, 19
Forever Living Products International Inc., 17
Formica Corporation, 13
Forstmann Little & Co., 38
Fort Howard Corporation, 8
Fort James Corporation, 22 (upd.)
Fortune Brands, Inc., 29 (upd.)
Fortunoff Fine Jewelry and Silverware Inc., 26
Fossil, Inc., 17
Foster Poultry Farms, 32
Foster Wheeler Corporation, 6; 23 (upd.)
Foundation Health Corporation, 12
Fountain Powerboats Industries, Inc., 28
Fourth Financial Corporation, 11
Fox Entertainment Group, Inc., 43
Fox Family Worldwide, Inc., 24
Foxboro Company, 13
FoxMeyer Health Corporation, 16
FPL Group, Inc., V
Frank J. Zamboni & Co., Inc., 34
Frank Russell Company, 46

Frank's Nursery & Crafts, Inc., 12
Frankel & Co., 39
Franklin Covey Company, 37 (upd.)
Franklin Electric Company, Inc., 43
Franklin Electronic Publishers, Inc., 23
Franklin Quest Co., 11
Franklin Resources, Inc., 9
Fred Meyer, Inc., V; 20 (upd.)
Fred W. Albrecht Grocery Co., The, 13
Fred's, Inc., 23
Frederick Atkins Inc., 16
Frederick's of Hollywood Inc., 16
Freedom Communications, Inc., 36
Freeport-McMoRan Inc., IV; 7 (upd.)
French Fragrances, Inc., 22
Fresh America Corporation, 20
Fresh Choice, Inc., 20
Fresh Foods, Inc., 29
Fretter, Inc., 10
Fried, Frank, Harris, Shriver & Jacobson, 35
Friedman's Inc., 29
Friendly Ice Cream Corp., 30
Frigidaire Home Products, 22
Frisch's Restaurants, Inc., 35
Frito-Lay Company, 32
Fritz Companies, Inc., 12
Frontier Airlines, Inc., 22
Frontier Corp., 16
Frozen Food Express Industries, Inc., 20
Fruehauf Corporation, I
Fruit of the Loom, Inc., 8; 25 (upd.)
Frymaster Corporation, 27
FSI International, Inc., 17
FTP Software, Inc., 20
Fubu, 29
Fujitsu-ICL Systems Inc., 11
Fulbright & Jaworski L.L.P., 47
Funco, Inc., 20
Fuqua Enterprises, Inc., 17
Fuqua Industries, Inc., I
Furniture Brands International, Inc., 39 (upd.)
Furon Company, 28
Furr's Supermarkets, Inc., 28
Future Now, Inc., 12
G&K Services, Inc., 16
G-III Apparel Group, Ltd., 22
G. Heileman Brewing Company Inc., I
G.A.F., I
G.D. Searle & Company, I; 12 (upd.); 34 (upd.)
G.I. Joe's, Inc., 30
G.S. Blodgett Corporation, 15
Gabelli Asset Management Inc., 30
Gadzooks, Inc., 18
GAF Corporation, 22 (upd.)
Gage Marketing Group, 26
Gaiam, Inc., 41
Gainsco, Inc., 22
Galey & Lord, Inc., 20
Gallup Organization, The, 37
Galyan's Trading Company, Inc., 47
Gambrinus Company, The, 40
Gander Mountain, Inc., 20
Gannett Co., Inc., IV; 7 (upd.); 30 (upd.)
Gantos, Inc., 17
Gap, Inc., The, V; 18 (upd.)
Garan, Inc., 16
Garden Fresh Restaurant Corporation, 31
Garden Ridge Corporation, 27
Gardenburger, Inc., 33
Gart Sports Company, 24
Gartner Group, Inc., 21
Gates Corporation, The, 9
Gateway, Inc., 10; 27 (upd.)
GATX Corporation, 6; 25 (upd.)
Gaylord Container Corporation, 8
Gaylord Entertainment Company, 11; 36 (upd.)
GC Companies, Inc., 25
GE Aircraft Engines, 9
GE Capital Aviation Services, 36
Geerlings & Wade, Inc., 45
Geffen Records Inc., 26
Gehl Company, 19
GEICO Corporation, 10; 40 (upd.)
GenCorp Inc., 8; 9
Genentech, Inc., I; 8 (upd.); 32 (upd.)
General Bearing Corporation, 45
General Binding Corporation, 10
General Cable Corporation, 40
General Chemical Group Inc., The, 37
General Cinema Corporation, I
General DataComm Industries, Inc., 14
General Dynamics Corporation, I; 10 (upd.); 40 (upd.)
General Electric Company, II; 12 (upd.); 34 (upd.)
General Host Corporation, 12
General Housewares Corporation, 16
General Instrument Corporation, 10
General Mills, Inc., II; 10 (upd.); 36 (upd.)
General Motors Corporation, I; 10 (upd.); 36 (upd.)
General Nutrition Companies, Inc., 11; 29 (upd.)
General Public Utilities Corporation, V
General Re Corporation, III; 24 (upd.)
General Signal Corporation, 9
General Tire, Inc., 8
Genesco Inc., 17
Genesee & Wyoming Inc., 27
Genesis Health Ventures, Inc., 18
Genetics Institute, Inc., 8
Geneva Steel, 7
Genmar Holdings, Inc., 45
Genovese Drug Stores, Inc., 18
GenRad, Inc., 24
Gentex Corporation, 26
Genuardi's Family Markets, Inc., 35
Genuine Parts Company, 9; 45 (upd.)
Genzyme Corporation, 13; 38 (upd.)
Geon Company, The, 11
George A. Hormel and Company, II
Georgia Gulf Corporation, 9
Georgia-Pacific Corporation, IV; 9 (upd.); 47 (upd.)
Geotek Communications Inc., 21
Gerald Stevens, Inc., 37
Gerber Products Company, 7; 21 (upd.)
Gerber Scientific, Inc., 12
German American Bancorp, 41
Getty Images, Inc., 31
Ghirardelli Chocolate Company, 30
Giant Cement Holding, Inc., 23
Giant Food Inc., II; 22 (upd.)
Giant Industries, Inc., 19
Gibraltar Steel Corporation, 37
Gibson Greetings, Inc., 12
Gibson Guitar Corp., 16
Gibson, Dunn & Crutcher LLP, 36
Giddings & Lewis, Inc., 10
Gilbane, Inc., 34
Gillett Holdings, Inc., 7
Gillette Company, The, III; 20 (upd.)
Girl Scouts of the USA, 35
Gitano Group, Inc., The, 8
Glacier Bancorp, Inc., 35
Glacier Water Services, Inc., 47
Gleason Corporation, 24
Glidden Company, The, 8
Global Crossing Ltd., 32
Global Industries, Ltd., 37
Global Marine Inc., 9
GlobalSantaFe Corporation, 48 (upd.)
GM Hughes Electronics Corporation, II
Godfather's Pizza Incorporated, 25
Gold Kist Inc., 17; 26 (upd.)
Golden Belt Manufacturing Co., 16
Golden Books Family Entertainment, Inc., 28
Golden Corral Corporation, 10
Golden Enterprises, Inc., 26
Golden State Foods Corporation, 32
Golden State Vintners, Inc., 33
Golden West Financial Corporation, 47
Goldman, Sachs & Co., II; 20 (upd.)
Golub Corporation, The, 26
Gonnella Baking Company, 40
Good Guys, Inc., The, 10; 30 (upd.)
Good Humor-Breyers Ice Cream Company, 14
Goodman Holding Company, 42
GoodMark Foods, Inc., 26
Goodrich Corporation, 46 (upd.)
GoodTimes Entertainment Ltd., 48
Goodwill Industries International, Inc., 16
Goody Products, Inc., 12
Goody's Family Clothing, Inc., 20
Goodyear Tire & Rubber Company, The, V; 20 (upd.)
Gordon Food Service Inc., 8; 39 (upd.)
Gorman-Rupp Company, The, 18
Gorton's, 13
Goss Holdings, Inc., 43
Gottschalks, Inc., 18
Gould Electronics, Inc., 14
Goulds Pumps Inc., 24
Goya Foods Inc., 22
GPU, Inc., 27 (upd.)
Graco Inc., 19
GranCare, Inc., 14
Grand Casinos, Inc., 20
Grand Union Company, The, 7; 28 (upd.)
Granite Broadcasting Corporation, 42
Granite Rock Company, 26
Granite State Bankshares, Inc., 37
Graphic Industries Inc., 25
Gray Communications Systems, Inc., 24
Great American Management and Investment, Inc., 8
Great Atlantic & Pacific Tea Company, Inc., The, II; 16 (upd.)
Great Harvest Bread Company, 44
Great Lakes Bancorp, 8
Great Lakes Chemical Corporation, I; 14 (upd.)
Great Western Financial Corporation, 10
Grede Foundries, Inc., 38
Green Bay Packers, Inc., The, 32
Green Mountain Coffee, Inc., 31
Green Tree Financial Corporation, 11
Greenbrier Companies, The, 19
GreenPoint Financial Corp., 28
Greenwood Mills, Inc., 14
Greif Bros. Corporation, 15
Grey Advertising, Inc., 6
Grey Wolf, Inc., 43
Greyhound Lines, Inc., I; 32 (upd.)
Griffin Land & Nurseries, Inc., 43
Griffon Corporation, 34
Grinnell Corp., 13
Grist Mill Company, 15
Gristede's Sloan's, Inc., 31
Grolier Incorporated, 16; 43 (upd.)
Grossman's Inc., 13
Ground Round, Inc., 21
Group Health Cooperative, 41
Grow Biz International, Inc., 18
Grow Group Inc., 12
Grubb & Ellis Company, 21
Grumman Corporation, I; 11 (upd.)
Gruntal & Co., L.L.C., 20

**United States** *(continued)*

Gryphon Holdings, Inc., 21
GSD&M Advertising, 44
GT Bicycles, 26
GT Interactive Software, 31
GTE Corporation, V; 15 (upd.)
Guccio Gucci, S.p.A., 15
Guess, Inc., 15
Guest Supply, Inc., 18
Guilford Mills Inc., 8; 40 (upd.)
Guitar Center, Inc., 29
Gulf & Western Inc., I
Gulf Island Fabrication, Inc., 44
Gulf States Utilities Company, 6
Gulfstream Aerospace Corporation, 7; 28 (upd.)
Gunlocke Company, The, 23
Guthy-Renker Corporation, 32
Gwathmey Siegel & Associates Architects LLC, 26
Gymboree Corporation, 15
H & R Block, Incorporated, 9; 29 (upd.)
H.B. Fuller Company, 8; 32 (upd.)
H.D. Vest, Inc., 46
H.E. Butt Grocery Company, 13; 32 (upd.)
H.F. Ahmanson & Company, II; 10 (upd.)
H.J. Heinz Company, II; 11 (upd.); 36 (upd.)
Ha-Lo Industries, Inc., 27
Habersham Bancorp, 25
Habitat for Humanity International, 36
Hach Co., 18
Hadco Corporation, 24
Haemonetics Corporation, 20
Haggar Corporation, 19
Haggen Inc., 38
Hahn Automotive Warehouse, Inc., 24
Hain Celestial Group, Inc., The, 27; 43 (upd.)
HAL Inc., 9
Half Price Books, Records, Magazines Inc., 37
Halliburton Company, III; 25 (upd.)
Hallmark Cards, Inc., IV; 16 (upd.); 40 (upd.)
Hamilton Beach/Proctor-Silex Inc., 17
Hammacher Schlemmer & Company, 21
Hampton Industries, Inc., 20
Hancock Fabrics, Inc., 18
Hancock Holding Company, 15
Handleman Company, 15
Handy & Harman, 23
Hanger Orthopedic Group, Inc., 41
Hanna-Barbera Cartoons Inc., 23
Hannaford Bros. Co., 12
Hanover Direct, Inc., 36
Hanover Foods Corporation, 35
Hansen Natural Corporation, 31
Happy Kids Inc., 30
Harbert Corporation, 14
Harbison-Walker Refractories Company, 24
Harcourt Brace and Co., 12
Harcourt Brace Jovanovich, Inc., IV
Harcourt General, Inc., 20 (upd.)
Hard Rock Cafe International, Inc., 12; 32 (upd.)
Harding Lawson Associates Group, Inc., 16
Hardinge Inc., 25
Harley-Davidson Inc., 7; 25 (upd.)
Harleysville Group Inc., 37
Harman International Industries Inc., 15
Harmon Industries, Inc., 25
Harmonic Inc., 43
Harnischfeger Industries, Inc., 8; 38 (upd.)
Harold's Stores, Inc., 22
Harper Group Inc., 17
HarperCollins Publishers, 15
Harpo Entertainment Group, 28
Harrah's Entertainment, Inc., 16; 43 (upd.)
Harris Corporation, II; 20 (upd.)
Harris Interactive Inc., 41
Harris Teeter Inc., 23
Harry Winston Inc., 45
Harry's Farmers Market Inc., 23
Harsco Corporation, 8
Harte-Hanks Communications, Inc., 17
Hartmarx Corporation, 8; 32 (upd.)
Hartz Mountain Corporation, The, 12; 46 (upd.)
Harveys Casino Resorts, 27
Harza Engineering Company, 14
Hasbro, Inc., III; 16 (upd.); 43 (upd.)
Hastings Entertainment, Inc., 29
Hauser, Inc., 46
Haverty Furniture Companies, Inc., 31
Hawaiian Airlines, Inc., 22 (upd.)
Hawaiian Electric Industries, Inc., 9
Hawkins Chemical, Inc., 16
Haworth Inc., 8; 39 (upd.)
Hayes Corporation, 24
Hayes Lemmerz International, Inc., 27
Hazelden Foundation, 28
HCA - The Healthcare Company, 35 (upd.)
HDR Inc., 48
Headway Corporate Resources, Inc., 40
Health Care & Retirement Corporation, 22
Health O Meter Products Inc., 14
Health Risk Management, Inc., 24
Health Systems International, Inc., 11
HealthSouth Corporation, 33 (upd.)
HealthSouth Rehabilitation Corporation, 14
Healthtex, Inc., 17
Hearst Corporation, The, IV; 19 (upd.); 46 (upd.)
Heartland Express, Inc., 18
Hechinger Company, 12
Hecla Mining Company, 20
Heekin Can Inc., 13
HEICO Corporation, 30
Heidrick & Struggles International, Inc., 28
Heilig-Meyers Company, 14; 40 (upd.)
Helen of Troy Corporation, 18
Helene Curtis Industries, Inc., 8; 28 (upd.)
Heller, Ehrman, White & McAuliffe, 41
Helmerich & Payne, Inc., 18
Helmsley Enterprises, Inc., 9; 39 (upd.)
Helzberg Diamonds, 40
Henkel Manco Inc., 22
Henley Group, Inc., The, III
Henry Modell & Company Inc., 32
Henry Schein, Inc., 31
Herbalife International, Inc., 17; 41 (upd.)
Hercules Inc., I; 22 (upd.)
Herley Industries, Inc., 33
Herman Goelitz, Inc., 28
Herman Miller, Inc., 8
Hershey Foods Corporation, II; 15 (upd.)
Hertz Corporation, The, 9; 33 (upd.)
Heska Corporation, 39
Heublein, Inc., I
Hewlett-Packard Company, III; 6 (upd.); 28 (upd.)
Hexcel Corporation, 28
Hibbett Sporting Goods, Inc., 26
Hibernia Corporation, 37
Hickory Farms, Inc., 17
Highmark Inc., 27
Hildebrandt International, 29
Hill's Pet Nutrition, Inc., 27
Hillenbrand Industries, Inc., 10
Hillhaven Corporation, The, 14
Hills Stores Company, 13
Hilton Hotels Corporation, III; 19 (upd.)
Hispanic Broadcasting Corporation, 35
Hitchiner Manufacturing Co., Inc., 23
HMI Industries, Inc., 17
HOB Entertainment, Inc., 37
Hoechst Celanese Corporation, 13
Hoenig Group Inc., 41
Hogan & Hartson L.L.P., 44
Holberg Industries, Inc., 36
Holiday Inns, Inc., III
Holiday RV Superstores, Incorporated, 26
Holland Burgerville USA, 44
Hollinger International Inc., 24
Holly Corporation, 12
Hollywood Casino Corporation, 21
Hollywood Entertainment Corporation, 25
Hollywood Park, Inc., 20
Holme Roberts & Owen LLP, 28
Holnam Inc., 8; 39 (upd.)
Holophane Corporation, 19
Holson Burnes Group, Inc., 14
Holt's Cigar Holdings, Inc., 42
Home Box Office Inc., 7; 23 (upd.)
Home Depot, Inc., The, V; 18 (upd.)
Home Insurance Company, The, III
Home Properties of New York, Inc., 42
Home Shopping Network, Inc., V; 25 (upd.)
HomeBase, Inc., 33 (upd.)
Homestake Mining Company, 12; 38 (upd.)
Hometown Auto Retailers, Inc., 44
HON INDUSTRIES Inc., 13
Honda Motor Company Limited, I; 10 (upd.); 29 (upd.)
Honeywell Inc., II; 12 (upd.)
Hooper Holmes, Inc., 22
Hooters of America, Inc., 18
Hoover Company, The, 12; 40 (upd.)
Hops Restaurant Bar and Brewery, 46
Horace Mann Educators Corporation, 22
Horizon Organic Holding Corporation, 37
Hormel Foods Corporation, 18 (upd.)
Horton Homes, Inc., 25
Hospital Corporation of America, III
Hospitality Franchise Systems, Inc., 11
Hospitality Worldwide Services, Inc., 26
Hot Topic, Inc., 33
Houghton Mifflin Company, 10; 36 (upd.)
House of Fabrics, Inc., 21
Household International, Inc., II; 21 (upd.)
Houston Industries Incorporated, V
Hovnanian Enterprises, Inc., 29
Howard Hughes Medical Institute, 39
Howard Johnson International, Inc., 17
Howmet Corp., 12
Hub Group, Inc., 38
Hubbard Broadcasting Inc., 24
Hubbell Incorporated, 9; 31 (upd.)
Hudson Foods Inc., 13
Hudson River Bancorp, Inc., 41
Huffy Corporation, 7; 30 (upd.)
Hughes Electronics Corporation, 25
Hughes Hubbard & Reed LLP, 44
Hughes Markets, Inc., 22
Hughes Supply, Inc., 14
Hulman & Company, 44
Humana Inc., III; 24 (upd.)
Hungry Howie's Pizza and Subs, Inc., 25
Hunt Consolidated, Inc., 27 (upd.)
Hunt Manufacturing Company, 12
Hunt Oil Company, 7
Hunt-Wesson, Inc., 17
Hunter Fan Company, 13
Huntington Bancshares Inc., 11
Hunton & Williams, 35
Huntsman Chemical Corporation, 8
Hutchinson Technology Incorporated, 18
Hvide Marine Incorporated, 22
Hy-Vee, Inc., 36
Hyatt Corporation, III; 16 (upd.)
Hyde Athletic Industries, Inc., 17

Hydril Company, 46
Hypercom Corporation, 27
Hyperion Software Corporation, 22
Hyster Company, 17
I.C. Isaacs & Company, 31
Iams Company, 26
IBERIABANK Corporation, 37
IBP, Inc., II; 21 (upd.)
IC Industries, Inc., I
ICF Kaiser International, Inc., 28
Icon Health & Fitness, Inc., 38
Idaho Power Company, 12
IDB Communications Group, Inc., 11
Identix Inc., 44
IDEXX Laboratories, Inc., 23
IDG Books Worldwide, Inc., 27
IDT Corporation, 34
IEC Electronics Corp., 42
Igloo Products Corp., 21
IHOP Corporation, 17
Il Fornaio (America) Corporation, 27
Ilitch Holdings Inc., 37
Illinois Bell Telephone Company, 14
Illinois Central Corporation, 11
Illinois Power Company, 6
Illinois Tool Works Inc., III; 22 (upd.)
Imation Corporation, 20
IMC Fertilizer Group, Inc., 8
IMCO Recycling, Incorporated, 32
Immunex Corporation, 14
Imo Industries Inc., 7; 27 (upd.)
IMPATH Inc., 45
Imperial Holly Corporation, 12
Imperial Sugar Company, 32 (upd.)
In Focus Systems, Inc., 22
In-N-Out Burger, 19
InaCom Corporation, 13
Indiana Bell Telephone Company, Incorporated, 14
Indiana Energy, Inc., 27
Indianapolis Motor Speedway Corporation, 46
Industrial Services of America, Inc., 46
Infinity Broadcasting Corporation, 11; 48 (upd.)
Information Access Company, 17
Information Builders, Inc., 22
Information Holdings Inc., 47
Information Resources, Inc., 10
Informix Corporation, 10; 30 (upd.)
Ingalls Shipbuilding, Inc., 12
Ingersoll-Rand Company, III; 15 (upd.)
Ingles Markets, Inc., 20
Ingram Industries, Inc., 11
Inktomi Corporation, 45
Inland Container Corporation, 8
Inland Steel Industries, Inc., IV; 19 (upd.)
Inserra Supermarkets, 25
Insight Enterprises, Inc., 18
Insilco Corporation, 16
Inso Corporation, 26
Instinet Corporation, 34
Insurance Auto Auctions, Inc., 23
Integrity Inc., 44
Intel Corporation, II; 10 (upd.); 36 (upd.)
IntelliCorp, Inc., 45
Intelligent Electronics, Inc., 6
Inter Parfums Inc., 35
Inter-Regional Financial Group, Inc., 15
Interco Incorporated, III
Interep National Radio Sales Inc., 35
Interface, Inc., 8; 29 (upd.)
Intergraph Corporation, 6; 24 (upd.)
Interlake Corporation, The, 8
Intermet Corporation, 32
Intermountain Health Care, Inc., 27
International Brotherhood of Teamsters, 37
International Business Machines Corporation, III; 6 (upd.); 30 (upd.)
International Controls Corporation, 10
International Creative Management, Inc., 43
International Dairy Queen, Inc., 10; 39 (upd.)
International Data Group, Inc., 7; 25 (upd.)
International Family Entertainment Inc., 13
International Flavors & Fragrances Inc., 9; 38 (upd.)
International Game Technology, 10; 41 (upd.)
International Lease Finance Corporation, 48
International Management Group, 18
International Multifoods Corporation, 7; 25 (upd.)
International Paper Company, IV; 15 (upd.); 47 (upd.)
International Rectifier Corporation, 31
International Shipholding Corporation, Inc., 27
International Speedway Corporation, 19
International Telephone & Telegraph Corporation, I; 11 (upd.)
International Total Services, Inc., 37
Interpublic Group of Companies, Inc., The, I; 22 (upd.)
Interscope Music Group, 31
Interstate Bakeries Corporation, 12; 38 (upd.)
Intimate Brands, Inc., 24
Intuit Inc., 14; 33 (upd.)
Invacare Corporation, 11; 47 (upd.)
Iomega Corporation, 21
IPALCO Enterprises, Inc., 6
Iron Mountain, Inc., 33
Irvin Feld & Kenneth Feld Productions, Inc., 15
Island ECN, Inc., The, 48
Isle of Capri Casinos, Inc., 41
Ispat Inland Inc., 40 (upd.)
Itel Corporation, 9
Items International Airwalk Inc., 17
ITT Educational Services, Inc., 33
ITT Sheraton Corporation, III
IVAX Corporation, 11
IVC Industries, Inc., 45
iVillage Inc., 46
Iwerks Entertainment, Inc., 34
IXC Communications, Inc., 29
J & J Snack Foods Corporation, 24
J&R Electronics Inc., 26
J. Baker, Inc., 31
J. Crew Group Inc., 12; 34 (upd.)
J. D'Addario & Company, Inc., 48
J. Jill Group, Inc., The, 35
J.A. Jones, Inc., 16
J.B. Hunt Transport Services Inc., 12
J.C. Penney Company, Inc., V; 18 (upd.); 43 (upd.)
J.D. Edwards & Company, 14
J.D. Power and Associates, 32
J.I. Case Company, 10
J.M. Smucker Company, The, 11
J.P. Morgan & Co. Incorporated, II; 30 (upd.)
J.P. Morgan Chase & Co., 38 (upd.)
J.R. Simplot Company, 16
Jabil Circuit, Inc., 36
Jack Henry and Associates, Inc., 17
Jack Schwartz Shoes, Inc., 18
Jackpot Enterprises Inc., 21
Jackson Hewitt, Inc., 48
Jackson National Life Insurance Company, 8
Jaco Electronics, Inc., 30
Jacob Leinenkugel Brewing Company, 28
Jacobs Engineering Group Inc., 6; 26 (upd.)
Jacobson Stores Inc., 21
Jacor Communications, Inc., 23
Jacuzzi Inc., 23
Jalate Inc., 25
Jamba Juice Company, 47
James River Corporation of Virginia, IV
Jason Incorporated, 23
Jay Jacobs, Inc., 15
Jayco Inc., 13
Jazzercise, Inc., 45
JB Oxford Holdings, Inc., 32
JDS Uniphase Corporation, 34
Jefferies Group, Inc., 25
Jefferson-Pilot Corporation, 11; 29 (upd.)
Jeld-Wen, Inc., 45
Jennifer Convertibles, Inc., 31
Jenny Craig, Inc., 10; 29 (upd.)
Jerry's Famous Deli Inc., 24
Jervis B. Webb Company, 24
JetBlue Airways Corporation, 44
Jetro Cash & Carry Enterprises Inc., 38
JG Industries, Inc., 15
Jillian's Entertainment Holdings, Inc., 40
Jim Beam Brands Co., 14
Jim Henson Company, The, 23
Jitney-Jungle Stores of America, Inc., 27
JMB Realty Corporation, IV
Jockey International, Inc., 12; 34 (upd.)
John B. Sanfilippo & Son, Inc., 14
John D. and Catherine T. MacArthur Foundation, The, 34
John H. Harland Company, 17
John Hancock Financial Services, Inc., III; 42 (upd.)
John Nuveen Company, The, 21
John Paul Mitchell Systems, 24
John Q. Hammons Hotels, Inc., 24
John W. Danforth Company, 48
John Wiley & Sons, Inc., 17
Johnny Rockets Group, Inc., 31
Johnson & Higgins, 14
Johnson & Johnson, III; 8 (upd.); 36 (upd.)
Johnson Controls, Inc., III; 26 (upd.)
Johnson Publishing Company, Inc., 28
Johnson Worldwide Associates, Inc., 28
Johnston Industries, Inc., 15
Johnstown America Industries, Inc., 23
Jones Apparel Group, Inc., 11; 39 (upd.)
Jones, Day, Reavis & Pogue, 33
Jones Intercable, Inc., 21
Jones Medical Industries, Inc., 24
Jordache Enterprises, Inc., 23
Jordan Industries, Inc., 36
Jos. A. Bank Clothiers, Inc., 31
Joseph T. Ryerson & Son, Inc., 15
Jostens, Inc., 7; 25 (upd.)
Journal Register Company, 29
JPS Textile Group, Inc., 28
Juniper Networks, Inc., 43
Juno Lighting, Inc., 30
Juno Online Services, Inc., 38
Just Born, Inc., 32
Just For Feet, Inc., 19
Justin Industries, Inc., 19
JWP Inc., 9
JWT Group Inc., I
K & B Inc., 12
K & G Men's Center, Inc., 21
K-Swiss, Inc., 33
K-tel International, Inc., 21
Kaiser Aluminum & Chemical Corporation, IV
Kal Kan Foods, Inc., 22
Kaman Corporation, 12; 42 (upd.)
Kampgrounds of America, Inc. 33

**United States** *(continued)*


Kansas City Power & Light Company, 6
Kansas City Southern Industries, Inc., 6; 26 (upd.)
Kaplan, Inc., 42
Kash n' Karry Food Stores, Inc., 20
Kasper A.S.L., Ltd., 40
Katy Industries, Inc., I
Katz Communications, Inc., 6
Katz Media Group, Inc., 35
Kaufman and Broad Home Corporation, 8
Kay-Bee Toy Stores, 15
Kaydon Corporation, 18
KB Home, 45 (upd.)
KB Toys, 35 (upd.)
Keebler Foods Company, 36
Keithley Instruments Inc., 16
Kelley Drye & Warren LLP, 40
Kellogg Company, II; 13 (upd.)
Kellwood Company, 8
Kelly Services Inc., 6; 26 (upd.)
Kelly-Springfield Tire Company, The, 8
Kelsey-Hayes Group of Companies, 7; 27 (upd.)
Kemet Corp., 14
Kemper Corporation, III; 15 (upd.)
Kendall International, Inc., 11
Kendall-Jackson Winery, Ltd., 28
Kenetech Corporation, 11
Kenneth Cole Productions, Inc., 25
Kent Electronics Corporation, 17
Kentucky Electric Steel, Inc., 31
Kentucky Utilities Company, 6
Kerr Group Inc., 24
Kerr-McGee Corporation, IV; 22 (upd.)
Ketchum Communications Inc., 6
Kettle Foods Inc., 48
Kewaunee Scientific Corporation, 25
Key Tronic Corporation, 14
KeyCorp, 8
Keyes Fibre Company, 9
KeySpan Energy Co., 27
Keystone International, Inc., 11
KFC Corporation, 7; 21 (upd.)
Kidde, Inc., I
Kikkoman Corporation, 47 (upd.)
Kimball International, Inc., 12; 48 (upd.)
Kimberly-Clark Corporation, III; 16 (upd.); 43 (upd.)
Kimco Realty Corporation, 11
Kinder Morgan, Inc., 45
KinderCare Learning Centers, Inc., 13
Kinetic Concepts, Inc. (KCI), 20
King & Spalding, 23
King Arthur Flour Company, The, 31
King Kullen Grocery Co., Inc., 15
King Ranch, Inc., 14
King World Productions, Inc., 9; 30 (upd.)
Kingston Technology Corporation, 20
Kinko's, Inc., 16; 43 (upd.)
Kinney Shoe Corp., 14
Kirby Corporation, 18
Kit Manufacturing Co., 18
Kitchell Corporation, 14
KitchenAid, 8
Kitty Hawk, Inc., 22
Kiwi International Airlines Inc., 20
KLA-Tencor Corporation, 11; 45 (upd.)
Kmart Corporation, V; 18 (upd.); 47 (upd.)
Knape & Vogt Manufacturing Company, 17
Knight-Ridder, Inc., IV; 15 (upd.)
Knoll Group Inc., 14
Knott's Berry Farm, 18
KnowledgeWare Inc., 9; 31 (upd.)
Koala Corporation, 44
Koch Enterprises, Inc., 29
Koch Industries, Inc., IV; 20 (upd.)
Kohl's Corporation, 9; 30 (upd.)
Kohlberg Kravis Roberts & Co., 24
Kohler Company, 7; 32 (upd.)
Koll Company, The, 8
Kollmorgen Corporation, 18
Komag, Inc., 11
Koo Koo Roo, Inc., 25
Koppers Industries, Inc., I; 26 (upd.)
Korn/Ferry International, 34
Koss Corporation, 38
Kraft Foods Inc., 45 (upd.)
Kraft General Foods Inc., II; 7 (upd.)
Kraus-Anderson, Incorporated, 36
Krause Publications, Inc., 35
Krause's Furniture, Inc., 27
Krispy Kreme Doughnut Corporation, 21
Kroger Company, The, II; 15 (upd.)
Kronos, Inc., 18
Krystal Company, The, 33
K2 Inc., 16
KU Energy Corporation, 11
Kuhlman Corporation, 20
Kulicke and Soffa Industries, Inc., 33
Kushner-Locke Company, The, 25
L-3 Communications Holdings, Inc., 48
L. Luria & Son, Inc., 19
L.A. Gear, Inc., 8; 32 (upd.)
L.A. T Sportswear, Inc., 26
L.B. Foster Company, 33
L.L. Bean, Inc., 10; 38 (upd.)
L.L. Knickerbocker Co., Inc., The, 25
L.S. Starrett Co., 13
La Choy Food Products Inc., 25
La Madeleine French Bakery & Café, 33
La Quinta Companies, The, 11; 42 (upd.)
La-Z-Boy Chair Company, 14
LaBarge Inc., 41
LabOne, Inc., 48
Labor Ready, Inc., 29
Laboratory Corporation of America Holdings, 42 (upd.)
LaBranche & Co. Inc., 37
Laclede Steel Company, 15
LaCrosse Footwear, Inc., 18
LADD Furniture, Inc., 12
Ladish Co., Inc., 30
Lafarge Corporation, 28
Lakeland Industries, Inc., 45
Lam Research Corporation, 11; 31 (upd.)
Lamar Advertising Company, 27
Lamaur Corporation, The, 41
Lamb Weston, Inc., 23
Lamonts Apparel, Inc., 15
Lamson & Sessions Co., 13
Lancaster Colony Corporation, 8
Lance, Inc., 14; 41 (upd.)
Lancer Corporation, 21
Land O'Lakes, Inc., II; 21 (upd.)
Landmark Communications, Inc., 12
Landry's Seafood Restaurants, Inc., 15
Lands' End, Inc., 9; 29 (upd.)
Lane Co., Inc., The, 12
Larry Flynt Publishing Inc., 31
Larry H. Miller Group, 29
Lason, Inc., 31
Latham & Watkins, 33
Lattice Semiconductor Corp., 16
Lawson Software, 38
Lawter International Inc., 14
Layne Christensen Company, 19
Lazare Kaplan International Inc., 21
LCI International, Inc., 16
LDDS-Metro Communications, Inc., 8
Lear Seating Corporation, 16
Lear Siegler, Inc., I
Learjet Inc., 8; 27 (upd.)
Learning Company Inc., The, 24
Learning Tree International Inc., 24
LeaRonal, Inc., 23
Leaseway Transportation Corp., 12
LeBoeuf, Lamb, Greene & MacRae, L.L.P., 29
Lechmere Inc., 10
Lechters, Inc., 11; 39 (upd.)
LeCroy Corporation, 41
Lee Apparel Company, Inc., 8
Lee Enterprises, Incorporated, 11
Leeann Chin, Inc., 30
Lefrak Organization Inc., 26
Legal Aid Society, The, 48
Legent Corporation, 10
Legg Mason, Inc., 33
Leggett & Platt, Inc., 11; 48 (upd.)
Lehigh Portland Cement Company, 23
Leiner Health Products Inc., 34
Lennar Corporation, 11
Lennox International Inc., 8; 28 (upd.)
Lenox, Inc., 12
LensCrafters Inc., 23
Leo Burnett Company Inc., I; 20 (upd.)
Leprino Foods Company, 28
Lesco Inc., 19
Leslie Fay Companies, Inc., The, 8; 39 (upd.)
Leslie's Poolmart, Inc., 18
Leucadia National Corporation, 11
Lever Brothers Company, 9
Levi Strauss & Co., V; 16 (upd.)
Levitz Furniture Inc., 15
Levy Restaurants L.P., 26
Lewis Galoob Toys Inc., 16
LEXIS-NEXIS Group, 33
Lexmark International, Inc., 18
LG&E Energy Corporation, 6
Liberty Corporation, The, 22
Liberty Livewire Corporation, 42
Life Technologies, Inc., 17
Lifetime Hoan Corporation, 27
Ligand Pharmaceuticals Incorporated, 47
Lillian Vernon Corporation, 12; 35 (upd.)
Limited, Inc., The, V; 20 (upd.)
LIN Broadcasting Corp., 9
Lincare Holdings Inc., 43
Lincoln Electric Co., 13
Lincoln National Corporation, III; 25 (upd.)
Lincoln Property Company, 8
Lincoln Snacks Company, 24
Lincoln Telephone & Telegraph Company, 14
Lindal Cedar Homes, Inc., 29
Lindsay Manufacturing Co., 20
Linear Technology, Inc., 16
Linens 'n Things, Inc., 24
Lintas: Worldwide, 14
Lionel L.L.C., 16
Liqui-Box Corporation, 16
Lithia Motors, Inc., 41
Littelfuse, Inc., 26
Little Caesar Enterprises, Inc., 7; 24 (upd.)
Little Tikes Co., 13
Litton Industries, Inc., I; 11 (upd.)
LIVE Entertainment Inc., 20
Liz Claiborne, Inc., 8; 25 (upd.)
Lockheed Corporation, I; 11 (upd.)
Lockheed Martin Corporation, 15 (upd.)
Loctite Corporation, 8; 30 (upd.)
LodgeNet Entertainment Corporation, 28
Loehmann's Inc., 24
Loews Corporation, I; 12 (upd.); 36 (upd.)
Logan's Roadhouse, Inc., 29
Logicon Inc., 20
LoJack Corporation, 48
London Fog Industries, Inc., 29
Long Island Bancorp, Inc., 16

Long Island Lighting Company, V
Long John Silver's Restaurants Inc., 13
Longaberger Company, The, 12; 44 (upd.)
Longs Drug Stores Corporation, V; 25 (upd.)
Longview Fibre Company, 8; 37 (upd.)
Loral Corporation, 8; 9
Lost Arrow Inc., 22
LOT$OFF Corporation, 24
Lotus Development Corporation, 6; 25 (upd.)
Louisiana Land and Exploration Company, The, 7
Louisiana-Pacific Corporation, IV; 31 (upd.)
Lowe's Companies, Inc., V; 21 (upd.)
Lowrance Electronics, Inc., 18
LSI Logic Corporation, 13
LTV Corporation, The, I; 24 (upd.)
Lubrizol Corporation, I; 30 (upd.)
Luby's, Inc., 17; 42 (upd.)
Lucasfilm Ltd., 12
Lucent Technologies Inc., 34
Lucille Farms, Inc., 45
Lucky Stores, Inc., 27
Lukens Inc., 14
Lunar Corporation, 29
Lund Food Holdings, Inc., 22
Lund International Holdings, Inc., 40
Lutheran Brotherhood, 31
Lynch Corporation, 43
Lyondell Chemical Company, IV; 45 (upd.)
M&F Worldwide Corp., 38
M.A. Hanna Company, 8
M.H. Meyerson & Co., Inc., 46
Mac Frugal's Bargains - Closeouts Inc., 17
Mac-Gray Corporation, 44
MacAndrews & Forbes Holdings Inc., 28
MacDermid Incorporated, 32
Mack Trucks, Inc., I; 22 (upd.)
Mack-Cali Realty Corporation, 42
Mackay Envelope Corporation, 45
Mackie Designs Inc., 33
Macmillan, Inc., 7
MacNeal-Schwendler Corporation, The, 25
Madison Gas and Electric Company, 39
Magma Copper Company, 7
Magma Power Company, 11
MagneTek, Inc., 15; 41 (upd.)
MAI Systems Corporation, 11
Maidenform Worldwide Inc., 20
Mail Boxes Etc., 18; 41 (upd.)
Mail-Well, Inc., 28
Maine Central Railroad Company, 16
Major Automotive Companies, Inc., The, 45
Malcolm Pirnie, Inc., 42
Malden Mills Industries, Inc., 16
Mallinckrodt Group Inc., 19
Malt-O-Meal Company, 22
Management and Training Corporation, 28
Mandalay Resort Group, 32 (upd.)
Manitowoc Company, Inc., 18
Mannatech Inc., 33
Manor Care, Inc., 6; 25 (upd.)
Manpower, Inc., 9; 30 (upd.)
Manufactured Home Communities, Inc., 22
Manufacturers Hanover Corporation, II
Manville Corporation, III; 7 (upd.)
MAPCO Inc., IV
March of Dimes, 31
marchFIRST, Inc., 34
Marcus Corporation, The, 21
Marie Callender's Restaurant & Bakery, Inc., 28
MarineMax, Inc., 30
Marion Laboratories, Inc., I
Marisa Christina, Inc., 15
Maritz Inc., 38
Mark IV Industries, Inc., 7; 28 (upd.)
Marks Brothers Jewelers, Inc., 24
Marmon Group, The, IV; 16 (upd.)
Marquette Electronics, Inc., 13
Marriott International, Inc., III; 21 (upd.)
Mars, Incorporated, 7; 40 (upd.)
Marsh & McLennan Companies, Inc., III; 45 (upd.)
Marsh Supermarkets, Inc., 17
Marshalls Incorporated, 13
Martha Stewart Living Omnimedia, L.L.C., 24
Martin Industries, Inc., 44
Martin Marietta Corporation, I
Marvel Entertainment Group, Inc., 10
Marvin Lumber & Cedar Company, 22
Mary Kay Corporation, 9; 30 (upd.)
Masco Corporation, III; 20 (upd.); 39 (upd.)
Mashantucket Pequot Gaming Enterprise Inc., 35
Masland Corporation, 17
Massachusetts Mutual Life Insurance Company, III
MasTec, Inc., 19
Master Lock Company, 45
MasterCard International, Inc., 9
Matria Healthcare, Inc., 17
Mattel, Inc., 7; 25 (upd.)
Matthews International Corporation, 29
Maui Land & Pineapple Company, Inc., 29
Max & Erma's Restaurants Inc., 19
Maxco Inc., 17
Maxicare Health Plans, Inc., III; 25 (upd.)
Maxim Group, The, 25
Maxim Integrated Products, Inc., 16
MAXIMUS, Inc., 43
Maxtor Corporation, 10
Maxus Energy Corporation, 7
Maxwell Shoe Company, Inc., 30
MAXXAM Inc., 8
Maxxim Medical Inc., 12
May Department Stores Company, The, V; 19 (upd.); 46 (upd.)
Mayer, Brown, Rowe & Maw, 47
Mayflower Group Inc., 6
Mayo Foundation, 9; 34 (upd.)
Mayor's Jewelers, Inc., 41
Maytag Corporation, III; 22 (upd.)
Mazel Stores, Inc., 29
MBC Holding Company, 40
MBNA Corporation, 12; 33 (upd.)
MCA Inc., II
McCarthy Building Companies, Inc., 48
McCaw Cellular Communications, Inc., 6
McClatchy Newspapers, Inc., 23
McCormick & Company, Incorporated, 7; 27 (upd.)
McDermott International, Inc., III; 37 (upd.)
McDonald's Corporation, II; 7 (upd.); 26 (upd.)
McDonnell Douglas Corporation, I; 11 (upd.)
McGraw-Hill Companies, Inc., The, IV; 18 (upd.)
MCI WorldCom, Inc., V; 27 (upd.)
McIlhenny Company, 20
McKee Foods Corporation, 7; 27 (upd.)
McKesson Corporation, I; 12; 47 (upd.)
McKinsey & Company, Inc., 9
McLane Company, Inc., 13
McLeodUSA Incorporated, 32
MCN Corporation, 6
MCSi, Inc., 41
MDU Resources Group, Inc., 7; 42 (upd.)
Mead Corporation, The, IV; 19 (upd.)
Mead Data Central, Inc., 10
Meade Instruments Corporation, 41
Meadowcraft, Inc., 29
Mecklermedia Corporation, 24
Medco Containment Services Inc., 9
Media Arts Group, Inc., 42
Media General, Inc., 7; 38 (upd.)
MedImmune, Inc., 35
Meditrust, 11
Medtronic, Inc., 8; 30 (upd.)
Medusa Corporation, 24
Megafoods Stores Inc., 13
Meier & Frank Co., 23
Meijer Incorporated, 7; 27 (upd.)
Mel Farr Automotive Group, 20
Melaleuca Inc., 31
Melamine Chemicals, Inc., 27
Mellon Bank Corporation, II
Mellon Financial Corporation, 44 (upd.)
Mellon-Stuart Company, I
Melville Corporation, V
Melvin Simon and Associates, Inc., 8
Men's Wearhouse, Inc., The, 17; 48 (upd.)
Menard, Inc., 34
Menasha Corporation, 8
Mentholatum Company Inc., The, 32
Mentor Corporation, 26
Mentor Graphics Corporation, 11
Mercantile Bankshares Corp., 11
Mercantile Stores Company, Inc., V; 19 (upd.)
Merck & Co., Inc., I; 11 (upd.); 34 (upd.)
Mercury Air Group, Inc., 20
Mercury General Corporation, 25
Meredith Corporation, 11; 29 (upd.)
Meridian Bancorp, Inc., 11
Meridian Gold, Incorporated, 47
Merillat Industries Inc., 13
Merisel, Inc., 12
Merit Medical Systems, Inc., 29
Meritage Corporation, 26
Merix Corporation, 36
Merrell Dow, Inc., I; 9 (upd.)
Merrill Corporation, 18; 47 (upd.)
Merrill Lynch & Co., Inc., II; 13 (upd.); 40 (upd.)
Merry-Go-Round Enterprises, Inc., 8
Mervyn's California, 10; 39 (upd.)
Mesa Air Group, Inc., 11; 32 (upd.)
Mesaba Holdings, Inc., 28
Mestek Inc., 10
Metatec International, Inc., 47
Meteor Industries Inc., 33
Methode Electronics, Inc., 13
Metro Information Services, Inc., 36
Metro-Goldwyn-Mayer Inc., 25 (upd.)
Metrocall, Inc., 41
Metromedia Co., 7; 14
Metropolitan Baseball Club Inc., 39
Metropolitan Financial Corporation, 13
Metropolitan Life Insurance Company, III
Metropolitan Opera Association, Inc., 40
Metropolitan Transportation Authority, 35
Mexican Restaurants, Inc., 41
MFS Communications Company, Inc., 11
MGM Grand Inc., 17
MGM/UA Communications Company, II
Michael Anthony Jewelers, Inc., 24
Michael Baker Corp., 14
Michael Foods, Inc., 25
Michaels Stores, Inc., 17
Michigan Bell Telephone Co., 14
Michigan National Corporation, 11
Micro Warehouse, Inc., 16
MicroAge, Inc., 16
Microdot Inc., 8
Micron Technology, Inc., 11; 29 (upd.)

**United States** *(continued)*

Micros Systems, Inc., 18
Microsoft Corporation, 6; 27 (upd.)
Mid-America Dairymen, Inc., 7
Midas International Corporation, 10
Middleby Corporation, The, 22
Middlesex Water Company, 45
Midway Airlines Corporation, 33
Midway Games, Inc., 25
Midwest Express Holdings, Inc., 35
Midwest Resources Inc., 6
Mikasa, Inc., 28
Mike-Sell's Inc., 15
Mikohn Gaming Corporation, 39
Milbank, Tweed, Hadley & McCloy, 27
Miles Laboratories, I
Millennium Pharmaceuticals, Inc., 47
Miller Brewing Company, I; 12 (upd.)
Miller Industries, Inc., 26
Milliken & Co., V; 17 (upd.)
Millipore Corporation, 25
Milnot Company, 46
Milton Bradley Company, 21
Milwaukee Brewers Baseball Club, 37
Mine Safety Appliances Company, 31
Miner Group International, The, 22
Minerals Technologies Inc., 11
Minnesota Mining & Manufacturing Company (3M), I; 8 (upd.); 26 (upd.)
Minnesota Power, Inc., 11; 34 (upd.)
Minntech Corporation, 22
Minute Maid Company, The, 28
Minuteman International Inc., 46
Minyard Food Stores, Inc., 33
Mirage Resorts, Incorporated, 6; 28 (upd.)
Mississippi Chemical Corporation, 39
Mitchell Energy and Development Corporation, 7
MITRE Corporation, 26
Mity Enterprises, Inc., 38
Mobil Corporation, IV; 7 (upd.); 21 (upd.)
Mobile Telecommunications Technologies Corp., 18
Modine Manufacturing Company, 8
Moen Incorporated, 12
Mohawk Industries, Inc., 19
Mohegan Tribal Gaming Authority, 37
Molex Incorporated, 11
Monaco Coach Corporation, 31
Monadnock Paper Mills, Inc., 21
Monfort, Inc., 13
Monro Muffler Brake, Inc., 24
Monsanto Company, I; 9 (upd.); 29 (upd.)
Montana Power Company, The, 11; 44 (upd.)
Montgomery Ward & Co., Incorporated, V; 20 (upd.)
Moog Inc., 13
Moore Medical Corp., 17
Moore-Handley, Inc., 39
Moran Towing Corporation, Inc., 15
Morgan Group, Inc., The, 46
Morgan Stanley Dean Witter & Company, 33 (upd.)
Morgan Stanley Group Inc., II; 16 (upd.)
Morgan, Lewis & Bockius LLP, 29
Morris Communications Corporation, 36
Morris Travel Services L.L.C., 26
Morrison Knudsen Corporation, 7; 28 (upd.)
Morrison Restaurants Inc., 11
Morse Shoe Inc., 13
Morton International Inc., 9 (upd.)
Morton Thiokol, Inc., I
Morton's Restaurant Group, Inc., 30
Mosinee Paper Corporation, 15
Mossimo, Inc., 27
Motel 6 Corporation, 13
Mothers Work, Inc., 18
Motley Fool, Inc., The, 40
Moto Photo, Inc., 45
Motor Cargo Industries, Inc., 35
Motorcar Parts & Accessories, Inc., 47
Motorola, Inc., II; 11 (upd.); 34 (upd.)
Motown Records Company L.P., 26
Mountain States Mortgage Centers, Inc., 29
Movado Group, Inc., 28
Movie Gallery, Inc., 31
Movie Star Inc., 17
Mr. Coffee, Inc., 15
Mr. Gasket Inc., 15
Mrs. Baird's Bakeries, 29
Mrs. Fields' Original Cookies, Inc., 27
Mt. Olive Pickle Company, Inc., 44
MTS Inc., 37
Mueller Industries, Inc., 7
Multimedia Games, Inc., 41
Multimedia, Inc., 11
Murdock Madaus Schwabe, 26
Murphy Family Farms Inc., 22
Murphy Oil Corporation, 7; 32 (upd.)
Musicland Stores Corporation, 9; 38 (upd.)
Mutual Benefit Life Insurance Company, The, III
Mutual Life Insurance Company of New York, The, III
Muzak, Inc., 18
Mycogen Corporation, 21
Myers Industries, Inc., 19
Mylan Laboratories Inc., I; 20 (upd.)
Nabisco Foods Group, II; 7 (upd.)
Nabors Industries, Inc., 9
NACCO Industries, Inc., 7
Nalco Chemical Corporation, I; 12 (upd.)
Nantucket Allserve, Inc., 22
Nash Finch Company, 8; 23 (upd.)
Nashua Corporation, 8
Nathan's Famous, Inc., 29
National Amusements Inc., 28
National Association for Stock Car Auto Racing, 32
National Association of Securities Dealers, Inc., 10
National Audubon Society, 26
National Auto Credit, Inc., 16
National Beverage Corp., 26
National Broadcasting Company, Inc., II; 6 (upd.); 28 (upd.)
National Can Corporation, I
National Car Rental System, Inc., 10
National City Corp., 15
National Convenience Stores Incorporated, 7
National Discount Brokers Group, Inc., 28
National Distillers and Chemical Corporation, I
National Educational Music Co. Ltd., 47
National Envelope Corporation, 32
National Football League, 29
National Fuel Gas Company, 6
National Geographic Society, 9; 30 (upd.)
National Grape Cooperative Association, Inc., 20
National Gypsum Company, 10
National Health Laboratories Incorporated, 11
National Hockey League, 35
National Home Centers, Inc., 44
National Instruments Corporation, 22
National Intergroup, Inc., V
National Media Corporation, 27
National Medical Enterprises, Inc., III
National Patent Development Corporation, 13
National Picture & Frame Company, 24
National Presto Industries, Inc., 16; 43 (upd.)
National Public Radio, Inc., 19; 47 (upd.)
National R.V. Holdings, Inc., 32
National Railroad Passenger Corporation, 22
National Record Mart, Inc., 29
National Rifle Association of America, 37
National Sanitary Supply Co., 16
National Semiconductor Corporation, II; VI, 26 (upd.)
National Service Industries, Inc., 11
National Standard Co., 13
National Steel Corporation, 12
National TechTeam, Inc., 41
NationsBank Corporation, 10
Natural Wonders Inc., 14
Nature Conservancy, The, 28
Nature's Sunshine Products, Inc., 15
Nautica Enterprises, Inc., 18; 44 (upd.)
Navarre Corporation, 24
Navigant International, Inc., 47
Navistar International Corporation, I; 10 (upd.)
Navy Exchange Service Command, 31
Navy Federal Credit Union, 33
NBD Bancorp, Inc., 11
NBTY, Inc., 31
NCH Corporation, 8
NCNB Corporation, II
NCO Group, Inc., 42
NCR Corporation, III; 6 (upd.); 30 (upd.)
Nebraska Public Power District, 29
Neff Corp., 32
Neiman Marcus Co., 12
NERCO, Inc., 7
Netscape Communications Corporation, 15; 35 (upd.)
Network Associates, Inc., 25
Neutrogena Corporation, 17
Nevada Bell Telephone Company, 14
Nevada Power Company, 11
New Balance Athletic Shoe, Inc., 25
New Brunswick Scientific Co., Inc., 45
New Dana Perfumes Company, 37
New Line Cinema, Inc., 47
New Piper Aircraft, Inc., The, 44
New Plan Realty Trust, 11
New Street Capital Inc., 8
New Times, Inc., 45
New UK Business Services, Inc., 18
New UK Confectionery Co., 15
New UK Electric System, V
New UK Mutual Life Insurance Company, III
New Valley Corporation, 17
New World Restaurant Group, Inc., 44
New York Daily News, 32
New York Life Insurance Company, III; 45 (upd.)
New York Restaurant Group, Inc., 32
New York State Electric and Gas, 6
New York Stock Exchange, Inc., 9; 39 (upd.)
New York Times Company, The, IV; 19 (upd.)
Newcor, Inc., 40
Newell Co., 9
Newhall Land and Farming Company, 14
Newman's Own, Inc., 37
Newmont Mining Corporation, 7
Newport News Shipbuilding Inc., 13; 38 (upd.)
News America Publishing Inc., 12
Nextel Communications, Inc., 10; 27 (upd.)
NFO Worldwide, Inc., 24
NGC Corporation, 18
Niagara Corporation, 28

Niagara Mohawk Holdings Inc., V; 45 (upd.)
Nichols Research Corporation, 18
Nicklaus Companies, 45
NICOR Inc., 6
NIKE, Inc., V; 8 (upd.); 36 (upd.)
Nikken Global Inc., 32
Nimbus CD International, Inc., 20
Nine West Group, Inc., 11; 39 (upd.)
99¢ Only Stores, 25
NIPSCO Industries, Inc., 6
NL Industries, Inc., 10
Nobel Learning Communities, Inc., 37
Noble Affiliates, Inc., 11
Noble Roman's Inc., 14
Noland Company, 35
Noodle Kidoodle, 16
NordicTrack, 22
Nordson Corporation, 11; 48 (upd.)
Nordstrom, Inc., V; 18 (upd.)
Norelco Consumer Products Co., 26
Norfolk Southern Corporation, V; 29 (upd.)
Norm Thompson Outfitters, Inc., 47
Norrell Corporation, 25
Norstan, Inc., 16
Nortek, Inc., 34
North Face, Inc., The, 18
North Fork Bancorporation, Inc., 46
North Star Steel Company, 18
Northeast Utilities, V; 48 (upd.)
Northern States Power Company, V; 20 (upd.)
Northern Trust Company, 9
Northland Cranberries, Inc., 38
Northrop Corporation, I; 11 (upd.)
Northrop Grumman Corporation, 45 (upd.)
Northwest Airlines Corporation, I; 6 (upd.); 26 (upd.)
Northwest Natural Gas Company, 45
NorthWestern Corporation, 37
Northwestern Mutual Life Insurance Company, III; 45 (upd.)
Norton Company, 8
Norton McNaughton, Inc., 27
Norwood Promotional Products, Inc., 26
NovaCare, Inc., 11
Novell, Inc., 6; 23 (upd.)
Novellus Systems, Inc., 18
NPC International, Inc., 40
Nu Skin Enterprises, Inc., 27
Nu-kote Holding, Inc., 18
Nucor Corporation, 7; 21 (upd.)
Nutraceutical International Corporation, 37
NutraSweet Company, 8
Nutrition for Life International Inc., 22
NVR L.P., 8
NYMAGIC, Inc., 41
NYNEX Corporation, V
O'Charley's Inc., 19
O'Melveny & Myers, 37
O'Reilly Automotive, Inc., 26
O'Sullivan Industries Holdings, Inc., 34
Oak Industries Inc., 21
Oak Technology, Inc., 22
Oakley, Inc., 18
Oakwood Homes Corporation, 15
Occidental Petroleum Corporation, IV; 25 (upd.)
Ocean Spray Cranberries, Inc., 7; 25 (upd.)
Octel Communications Corp., 14
Octel Messaging, 41 (upd.)
Odetics Inc., 14
Odwalla, Inc., 31
OEC Medical Systems, Inc., 27
Office Depot Incorporated, 8; 23 (upd.)
OfficeMax, Inc., 15; 43 (upd.)
Offshore Logistics, Inc., 37
Ogden Corporation, I; 6
Ogilvy Group, Inc., The, I
Oglebay Norton Company, 17
Oglethorpe Power Corporation, 6
Ohio Art Company, The, 14
Ohio Bell Telephone Company, 14
Ohio Casualty Corp., 11
Ohio Edison Company, V
Oil-Dri Corporation of America, 20
Oklahoma Gas and Electric Company, 6
Old America Stores, Inc., 17
Old Kent Financial Corp., 11
Old National Bancorp, 15
Old Republic International Corp., 11
Old Spaghetti Factory International Inc., 24
Olin Corporation, I; 13 (upd.)
Olsten Corporation, 6; 29 (upd.)
OM Group, Inc., 17
Omni Hotels Corp., 12
Omnicom Group, I; 22 (upd.)
OmniSource Corporation, 14
On Assignment, Inc., 20
One Price Clothing Stores, Inc., 20
1-800-FLOWERS, Inc., 26
Oneida Ltd., 7; 31 (upd.)
ONEOK Inc., 7
Opinion Research Corporation, 46
Option Care Inc., 48
Opus Group, 34
Oracle Corporation, 6; 24 (upd.)
Orbital Sciences Corporation, 22
Orchard Supply Hardware Stores Corporation, 17
Ore-Ida Foods Incorporated, 13
Oregon Metallurgical Corporation, 20
Oregon Steel Mills, Inc., 14
Orion Pictures Corporation, 6
Orthodontic Centers of America, Inc., 35
Orvis Company, Inc., The, 28
Oryx Energy Company, 7
Oscar Mayer Foods Corp., 12
OshKosh B'Gosh, Inc., 9; 42 (upd.)
Oshkosh Truck Corporation, 7
Oshman's Sporting Goods, Inc., 17
Osmonics, Inc., 18
Otis Elevator Company, Inc., 13; 39 (upd.)
Otis Spunkmeyer, Inc., 28
OTR Express, Inc., 25
Ottaway Newspapers, Inc., 15
Otter Tail Power Company, 18
Outback Steakhouse, Inc., 12; 34 (upd.)
Outboard Marine Corporation, III; 20 (upd.)
Outdoor Systems, Inc., 25
Outlook Group Corporation, 37
Overnite Transportation Co., 14
Overseas Shipholding Group, Inc., 11
Owens & Minor, Inc., 16
Owens Corning Corporation, III; 20 (upd.)
Owens-Illinois, Inc., I; 26 (upd.)
Owosso Corporation, 29
Oxford Health Plans, Inc., 16
Oxford Industries, Inc., 8
P&C Foods Inc., 8
P & F Industries, Inc., 45
P.C. Richard & Son Corp., 23
P.F. Chang's China Bistro, Inc., 37
P.H. Glatfelter Company, 8; 30 (upd.)
Paccar Inc., I; 26 (upd.)
Pacer Technology, 40
Pacific Enterprises, V
Pacific Gas and Electric Company, V
Pacific Sunwear of California, Inc., 28
Pacific Telecom, Inc., 6
Pacific Telesis Group, V
PacifiCare Health Systems, Inc., 11
PacifiCorp, V; 26 (upd.)
Packaging Corporation of America, 12
Packard Bell Electronics, Inc., 13
Paging Network Inc., 11
PaineWebber Group Inc., II; 22 (upd.)
Pall Corporation, 9
Palm Harbor Homes, Inc., 39
Palm, Inc., 36
Palomar Medical Technologies, Inc., 22
Pamida Holdings Corporation, 15
Pampered Chef, Ltd., The, 18
Pan American World Airways, Inc., I; 12 (upd.)
Pan-American Life Insurance Company, 48
Panamerican Beverages, Inc., 47
PanAmSat Corporation, 46
Panavision Inc., 24
Pancho's Mexican Buffet, Inc., 46
Panda Management Company, Inc., 35
Panera Bread Company, 44
Panhandle Eastern Corporation, V
Pantry, Inc., The, 36
Papa John's International, Inc., 15
Papetti's Hygrade Egg Products, Inc., 39
Paradise Music & Entertainment, Inc., 42
Parametric Technology Corp., 16
Paramount Pictures Corporation, II
Paris Corporation, 22
Parisian, Inc., 14
Park Corp., 22
Park-Ohio Industries Inc., 17
Parker Drilling Company, 28
Parker-Hannifin Corporation, III; 24 (upd.)
Parsons Brinckerhoff, Inc., 34
Parsons Corporation, The, 8
Pathmark Stores, Inc., 23
Patina Oil & Gas Corporation, 24
Patrick Industries, Inc., 30
Patterson Dental Co., 19
Paul Harris Stores, Inc., 18
Paul Revere Corporation, The, 12
Paul, Hastings, Janofsky & Walker LLP, 27
Paul, Weiss, Rifkind, Wharton & Garrison, 47
Paxson Communications Corporation, 33
Pay 'N Pak Stores, Inc., 9
Paychex, Inc., 15; 46 (upd.)
Payless Cashways, Inc., 11; 44 (upd.)
Payless ShoeSource, Inc., 18
PC Connection, Inc., 37
PDS Gaming Corporation, 44
Peabody Coal Company, 10
Peabody Energy Corporation, 45 (upd.)
Peabody Holding Company, Inc., IV
Peak Technologies Group, Inc., The, 14
Peapod, Inc., 30
Pearle Vision, Inc., 13
Peavey Electronics Corporation, 16
PECO Energy Company, 11
Pediatric Services of America, Inc., 31
Peebles Inc., 16; 43 (upd.)
Peet's Coffee & Tea, Inc., 38
Pella Corporation, 12; 39 (upd.)
Pendleton Woolen Mills, Inc., 42
Penn Engineering & Manufacturing Corp., 28
Penn National Gaming, Inc., 33
Penn Traffic Company, 13
Pennsylvania Blue Shield, III
Pennsylvania Power & Light Company, V
Pennwalt Corporation, I
Pennzoil Company, IV; 20 (upd.)
Penske Corporation, V; 19 (upd.)
Pentair, Inc., 7; 26 (upd.)
Pentech International, Inc., 29
Penton Media, Inc., 27
People Express Airlines, Inc., I
Peoples Energy Corporation, 6
PeopleSoft Inc., 14; 33 (upd.)

**United States** *(continued)*

Pep Boys—Manny, Moe & Jack, The, 11; 36 (upd.)
Pepper Hamilton LLP, 43
Pepsi Bottling Group, Inc., The, 40
Pepsico, Inc., I; 10 (upd.); 38 (upd.)
Perdue Farms Inc., 7; 23 (upd.)
Performance Food Group Company, 31
Perini Corporation, 8
Perkin-Elmer Corporation, The, 7
Perkins Family Restaurants, L.P., 22
Perot Systems Corporation, 29
Perrigo Company, 12
Perry Ellis International, Inc., 41
Pet Incorporated, 7
Petco Animal Supplies, Inc., 29
Pete's Brewing Company, 22
Peter Kiewit Sons' Inc., 8
Petersen Publishing Company, 21
Petrie Stores Corporation, 8
Petroleum Helicopters, Inc., 35
Petrolite Corporation, 15
PETsMART, Inc., 14; 41 (upd.)
Pew Charitable Trusts, The, 35
Pez Candy, Inc., 38
Pfizer Inc., I; 9 (upd.); 38 (upd.)
PG&E Corporation, 26 (upd.)
Phar-Mor Inc., 12
Pharmacia & Upjohn Inc., I; 25 (upd.)
Phelps Dodge Corporation, IV; 28 (upd.)
PHH Corporation, V
Philadelphia Eagles, 37
Philadelphia Electric Company, V
Philadelphia Suburban Corporation, 39
Philip Morris Companies Inc., V; 18 (upd.); 44 (upd.)
Philips Electronics North America Corp., 13
Phillips Petroleum Company, IV; 40 (upd.)
Phillips-Van Heusen Corporation, 24
PHP Healthcare Corporation, 22
PhyCor, Inc., 36
Physician Sales & Service, Inc., 14
Physio-Control International Corp., 18
Piccadilly Cafeterias, Inc., 19
PictureTel Corp., 10; 27 (upd.)
Piedmont Natural Gas Company, Inc., 27
Pier 1 Imports, Inc., 12; 34 (upd.)
Pierce Leahy Corporation, 24
Piercing Pagoda, Inc., 29
Piggly Wiggly Southern, Inc., 13
Pilgrim's Pride Corporation, 7; 23 (upd.)
Pillowtex Corporation, 19; 41 (upd.)
Pillsbury Company, II; 13 (upd.)
Pillsbury Madison & Sutro LLP, 29
Pinkerton's Inc., 9
Pinnacle West Capital Corporation, 6
Pioneer Hi-Bred International, Inc., 9; 41 (upd.)
Pioneer-Standard Electronics Inc., 19
Piper Jaffray Companies Inc., 22
Pitney Bowes Inc., III; 19; 47 (upd.)
Pittston Company, The, IV; 19 (upd.)
Pittway Corporation, 9; 33 (upd.)
Pixar Animation Studios, 34
Pizza Hut Inc., 7; 21 (upd.)
Pizza Inn, Inc., 46
Planet Hollywood International, Inc., 18; 41 (upd.)
Platinum Entertainment, Inc., 35
PLATINUM Technology, Inc., 14
Plato Learning, Inc., 44
Play by Play Toys & Novelties, Inc., 26
Playboy Enterprises, Inc., 18
PlayCore, Inc., 27
Players International, Inc., 22
Playskool, Inc., 25
Playtex Products, Inc., 15
Pleasant Company, 27
Plexus Corporation, 35
Plum Creek Timber Company, Inc., 43
Pluma, Inc., 27
Ply Gem Industries Inc., 12
PMT Services, Inc., 24
PNC Bank Corp., II; 13 (upd.)
PNC Financial Services Group Inc., The, 46 (upd.)
Pogo Producing Company, 39
Polaris Industries Inc., 12; 35 (upd.)
Polaroid Corporation, III; 7 (upd.); 28 (upd.)
Policy Management Systems Corporation, 11
Polk Audio, Inc., 34
Polo/Ralph Lauren Corporation, 12
PolyGram N.V., 23
Pomeroy Computer Resources, Inc., 33
Ponderosa Steakhouse, 15
Poore Brothers, Inc., 44
Pope and Talbot, Inc., 12
Popular, Inc., 41
Port Authority of New York and New Jersey, The, 48
Portal Software, Inc., 47
Portland General Corporation, 6
Post Properties, Inc., 26
Potlatch Corporation, 8; 34 (upd.)
Potomac Electric Power Company, 6
Potter & Brumfield Inc., 11
Powell's Books, Inc., 40
PowerBar Inc., 44
Powerhouse Technologies, Inc., 27
PPG Industries, Inc., III; 22 (upd.)
PPL Corporation, 41 (upd.)
PR Newswire, 35
Prairie Farms Dairy, Inc., 47
Pratt & Whitney, 9
Praxair, Inc., 11; 48 (upd.)
Pre-Paid Legal Services, Inc., 20
Precision Castparts Corp., 15
Premark International, Inc., III
Premcor Inc., 37
Premier Industrial Corporation, 9
Premier Parks, Inc., 27
Premium Standard Farms, Inc., 30
PremiumWear, Inc., 30
Preserver Group, Inc., 44
President Casinos, Inc., 22
Presstek, Inc., 33
Preston Corporation, 6
Price Communications Corporation, 42
Price Company, The, V
Price Waterhouse, 9
PriceCostco, Inc., 14
PricewaterhouseCoopers, 29 (upd.)
Primark Corp., 13
Primedex Health Systems, Inc., 25
Primedia Inc., 22
Primerica Corporation, I
Prince Sports Group, Inc., 15
Princess Cruise Lines, 22
Princeton Review, Inc., The, 42
Principal Mutual Life Insurance Company, III
Printrak, A Motorola Company, 44
Printronix, Inc., 18
Procter & Gamble Company, The, III; 8 (upd.); 26 (upd.)
Prodigy Communications Corporation, 34
Professional Golfers' Association of America, The, 41
Proffitt's, Inc., 19
Progress Software Corporation, 15
Progressive Corporation, The, 11; 29 (upd.)
Promus Companies, Inc., 9
Proskauer Rose LLP, 47
Protection One, Inc., 32
Providence Journal Company, The, 28
Provident Life and Accident Insurance Company of America, III
Prudential Insurance Company of America, The, III; 30 (upd.)
PSI Resources, 6
Pubco Corporation, 17
Public Service Company of Colorado, 6
Public Service Company of New Hampshire, 21
Public Service Company of New Mexico, 6
Public Service Enterprise Group Inc., V; 44 (upd.)
Publishers Clearing House, 23
Publishers Group, Inc., 35
Publix Supermarkets Inc., 7; 31 (upd.)
Pueblo Xtra International, Inc., 47
Puget Sound Power and Light Company, 6
Pulaski Furniture Corporation, 33
Pulitzer Publishing Company, 15
Pulte Corporation, 8
Pulte Homes, Inc., 42 (upd.)
Pumpkin Masters, Inc., 48
Purina Mills, Inc., 32
Puritan-Bennett Corporation, 13
Purolator Products Company, 21
Putt-Putt Golf Courses of America, Inc., 23
PW Eagle, Inc., 48
Pyramid Breweries Inc., 33
Quad/Graphics, Inc., 19
Quaker Fabric Corp., 19
Quaker Oats Company, The, II; 12 (upd.); 34 (upd.)
Quaker State Corporation, 7; 21 (upd.)
QUALCOMM Incorporated, 20; 47 (upd.)
Quality Chekd Dairies, Inc., 48
Quality Dining, Inc., 18
Quality Food Centers, Inc., 17
Quanex Corporation, 13
Quantum Chemical Corporation, 8
Quantum Corporation, 10
Quark, Inc., 36
Quest Diagnostics Inc., 26
Questar Corporation, 6; 26 (upd.)
Quick & Reilly Group, Inc., The, 20
Quiksilver, Inc., 18
QuikTrip Corporation, 36
Quill Corporation, 28
Quintiles Transnational Corporation, 21
Quixote Corporation, 15
Quizno's Corporation, The, 42
QVC Network Inc., 9
Qwest Communications International, Inc., 37
R.B. Pamplin Corp., 45
R.G. Barry Corporation, 17; 44 (upd.)
R.H. Macy & Co., Inc., V; 8 (upd.); 30 (upd.)
R.J. Reynolds Tobacco Holdings, Inc., 30 (upd.)
R.L. Polk & Co., 10
R.P. Scherer, I
R.R. Donnelley & Sons Company, IV; 9 (upd.); 38 (upd.)
Racal-Datacom Inc., 11
Racing Champions Corporation, 37
Radian Group Inc., 42
Radio Flyer Inc., 34
RadioShack Corporation, 36 (upd.)
Radius Inc., 16
Rag Shops, Inc., 30
RailTex, Inc., 20
Rainforest Cafe, Inc., 25
Rainier Brewing Company, 23
Raley's Inc., 14
Rally's Hamburgers, Inc., 25

Ralphs Grocery Company, 35
Ralston Purina Company, II; 13 (upd.)
Ramsay Youth Services, Inc., 41
Rand McNally & Company, 28
Randall's Food Markets, Inc., 40
Random House, Inc., 13; 31 (upd.)
Range Resources Corporation, 45
Rapala-Normark Group, Ltd., 30
Rare Hospitality International Inc., 19
Raven Industries, Inc., 33
Rawlings Sporting Goods Co., Inc., 24
Raychem Corporation, 8
Rayonier Inc., 24
Rayovac Corporation, 13; 39 (upd.)
Raytheon Aircraft Holdings Inc., 46
Raytheon Company, II; 11 (upd.); 38 (upd.)
Razorfish, Inc., 37
RCA Corporation, II
RCM Technologies, Inc., 34
RDO Equipment Company, 33
Read-Rite Corp., 10
Reader's Digest Association, Inc., The, IV; 17 (upd.)
Reckson Associates Realty Corp., 47
Recoton Corp., 15
Recovery Engineering, Inc., 25
Recreational Equipment, Inc., 18
Recycled Paper Greetings, Inc., 21
Red Apple Group, Inc., 23
Red Hat, Inc., 45
Red Roof Inns, Inc., 18
Red Wing Shoe Company, Inc., 9; 30 (upd.)
Redhook Ale Brewery, Inc., 31
Reebok International Ltd., V; 9 (upd.); 26 (upd.)
Reeds Jewelers, Inc., 22
Regal-Beloit Corporation, 18
Regis Corporation, 18
Reichhold Chemicals, Inc., 10
Reliance Electric Company, 9
Reliance Group Holdings, Inc., III
Reliance Steel & Aluminum Co., 19
Reliant Energy Inc., 44 (upd.)
RemedyTemp, Inc., 20
Remington Arms Company, Inc., 12; 40 (upd.)
Remington Products Company, L.L.C., 42
Renaissance Learning Systems, Inc., 39
Reno Air Inc., 23
Rent-A-Center, Inc., 45
Rent-Way, Inc., 33
Rental Service Corporation, 28
Rentrak Corporation, 35
Republic Engineered Steels, Inc., 7; 26 (upd.)
Republic Industries, Inc., 26
Republic New York Corporation, 11
Res-Care, Inc., 29
Resorts International, Inc., 12
Resource America, Inc., 42
Response Oncology, Inc., 27
Restaurants Unlimited, Inc., 13
Restoration Hardware, Inc., 30
Revco D.S., Inc., V
Revell-Monogram Inc., 16
Revere Ware Corporation, 22
Revlon Inc., III; 17 (upd.)
REX Stores Corp., 10
Rexel, Inc., 15
Rexnord Corporation, 21
Reynolds Metals Company, IV; 19 (upd.)
RF Micro Devices, Inc., 43
Rhino Entertainment Company, 18
Rhodes Inc., 23
Rica Foods, Inc., 41
Rich Products Corporation, 7; 38 (upd.)
Richardson Electronics, Ltd., 17
Richfood Holdings, Inc., 7
Richton International Corporation, 39
Riddell Sports Inc., 22
Ride, Inc., 22
Riese Organization, The, 38
Riggs National Corporation, 13
Right Management Consultants, Inc., 42
Riklis Family Corp., 9
Riser Foods, Inc., 9
Rite Aid Corporation, V; 19 (upd.)
Ritz Camera Centers, 34
Ritz-Carlton Hotel Company L.L.C., 9; 29 (upd.)
Rival Company, The, 19
River Oaks Furniture, Inc., 43
Riverwood International Corporation, 11; 48 (upd.)
Riviana Foods Inc., 27
RJR Nabisco Holdings Corp., V
RMH Teleservices, Inc., 42
Roadhouse Grill, Inc., 22
Roadmaster Industries, Inc., 16
Roadway Express, Inc., V; 25 (upd.)
Roanoke Electric Steel Corporation, 45
Robbins & Myers Inc., 15
Roberds Inc., 19
Robert Half International Inc., 18
Robert Mondavi Corporation, 15
Robert Wood Johnson Foundation, 35
Roberts Pharmaceutical Corporation, 16
Robertson-Ceco Corporation, 19
Roche Bioscience, 11; 14 (upd.)
Rochester Gas and Electric Corporation, 6
Rochester Telephone Corporation, 6
Rock Bottom Restaurants, Inc., 25
Rock of Ages Corporation, 37
Rock-Tenn Company, 13
Rockefeller Foundation, The, 34
Rockford Corporation, 43
RockShox, Inc., 26
Rockwell Automation, 43 (upd.)
Rockwell International Corporation, I; 11 (upd.)
Rocky Shoes & Boots, Inc., 26
Rodale Press, Inc., 23
Rodale, Inc., 47 (upd.)
Rohm and Haas Company, I; 26 (upd.)
ROHN Industries, Inc., 22
Rohr Incorporated, 9
Roll International Corporation, 37
Rollerblade, Inc., 15; 34 (upd.)
Rollins, Inc., 11
Rolls-Royce Allison, 29 (upd.)
Ronco, Inc., 15
Rooms To Go Inc., 28
Rooney Brothers Co., 25
Roper Industries Inc., 15
Ropes & Gray, 40
Rorer Group, I
Rose's Stores, Inc., 13
Rosemount Inc., 15
Rosenbluth International Inc., 14
Ross Stores, Inc., 17; 43 (upd.)
Rotary International, 31
Roto-Rooter Corp., 15
Rottlund Company, Inc., The, 28
Rouge Steel Company, 8
Roundy's Inc., 14
Rouse Company, The, 15
Rowan Companies, Inc., 43
Roy F. Weston, Inc., 33
Royal Appliance Manufacturing Company, 15
Royal Caribbean Cruises Ltd., 22
Royal Crown Company, Inc., 23
RPM, Inc., 8; 36 (upd.)
RSA Security Inc., 46
Rubbermaid Incorporated, III; 20 (upd.)
Rubio's Restaurants, Inc., 35
Ruby Tuesday, Inc., 18
Rural Cellular Corporation, 43
Rural/Metro Corporation, 28
Rush Communications, 33
Russ Berrie and Company, Inc., 12
Russell Corporation, 8; 30 (upd.)
Russell Reynolds Associates Inc., 38
Russell Stover Candies Inc., 12
Rust International Inc., 11
Ruth's Chris Steak House, 28
Ryan's Family Steak Houses, Inc., 15
Ryder System, Inc., V; 24 (upd.)
Ryerson Tull, Inc., 40 (upd.)
Ryland Group, Inc., The, 8; 37 (upd.)
S&C Electric Company, 15
S&K Famous Brands, Inc., 23
S-K-I Limited, 15
S.C. Johnson & Son, Inc., III; 28 (upd.)
Saatchi & Saatchi, 42 (upd.)
Sabratek Corporation, 29
SABRE Group Holdings, Inc., 26
SAFECO Corporaton, III
Safeguard Scientifics, Inc., 10
Safelite Glass Corp., 19
Safeskin Corporation, 18
Safety 1st, Inc., 24
Safety-Kleen Corp., 8
Safeway Inc., II; 24 (upd.)
Saga Communications, Inc., 27
St. Joe Company, The, 31
St. Joe Paper Company, 8
St. John Knits, Inc., 14
St. Jude Medical, Inc., 11; 43 (upd.)
St. Louis Music, Inc., 48
St. Paul Bank for Cooperatives, 8
St. Paul Companies, Inc., The, III; 22 (upd.)
Saks Holdings, Inc., 24
Saks Inc., 41 (upd.)
Salant Corporation, 12
Salomon Inc., II; 13 (upd.)
Salt River Project, 19
Salton, Inc., 30
Salvation Army USA, The, 32
Sam Ash Music Corporation, 30
Sam's Club, 40
Samsonite Corporation, 13; 43 (upd.)
Samuels Jewelers Incorporated, 30
San Diego Gas & Electric Company, V
Sanderson Farms, Inc., 15
Santa Barbara Restaurant Group, Inc., 37
Santa Cruz Operation, Inc., The, 38
Santa Fe Gaming Corporation, 19
Santa Fe International Corporation, 38
Santa Fe Pacific Corporation, V
Sara Lee Corporation, II; 15 (upd.)
SAS Institute Inc., 10
Saturn Corporation, 7; 21 (upd.)
Saucony Inc., 35
Sauder Woodworking Company, 12; 35 (upd.)
Savannah Foods & Industries, Inc., 7
Sawtek Inc., 43 (upd.)
Sbarro, Inc., 16
SBC Communications Inc., 32 (upd.)
SBS Technologies, Inc., 25
SCANA Corporation, 6
ScanSource, Inc., 29
SCB Computer Technology, Inc., 29
SCEcorp, V
Schawk, Inc., 24
Schering-Plough Corporation, I; 14 (upd.)
Schlotzsky's, Inc., 36
Schlumberger Limited, III; 17 (upd.)
Schmitt Music Company, 40
Schneider National, Inc., 36

**United States** *(continued)*


Schneiderman's Furniture Inc., 28
Schnitzer Steel Industries, Inc., 19
Scholastic Corporation, 10; 29 (upd.)
Schottenstein Stores Corp., 14
Schuff Steel Company, 26
Schultz Sav-O Stores, Inc., 21; 31 (upd.)
Schwan's Sales Enterprises, Inc., 7; 26 (upd.)
Schwinn Cycle and Fitness L.P., 19
SCI Systems, Inc., 9
Science Applications International Corporation, 15
Scientific-Atlanta, Inc., 6; 45 (upd.)
Score Board, Inc., The, 19
Scotsman Industries, Inc., 20
Scott Fetzer Company, 12
Scott Paper Company, IV, 31 (upd.)
Scotts Company, The, 22
Scotty's, Inc., 22
Scovill Fasteners Inc., 24
SCP Pool Corporation, 39
Seaboard Corporation, 36
Seagate Technology, Inc., 8; 34 (upd.)
Seagull Energy Corporation, 11
Sealed Air Corporation, 14
Sealed Power Corporation, I
Sealright Co., Inc., 17
Sealy Inc., 12
Seaman Furniture Company, Inc., 32
Sears, Roebuck and Co., V; 18 (upd.)
Seattle FilmWorks, Inc., 20
Seattle First National Bank Inc., 8
Seattle Times Company, 15
Seaway Food Town, Inc., 15
Sebastiani Vineyards, Inc., 28
Second Harvest, 29
Security Capital Corporation, 17
Security Pacific Corporation, II
SED International Holdings, Inc., 43
See's Candies, Inc., 30
Sega of America, Inc., 10
Segway LLC, 48
Seigle's Home and Building Centers, Inc., 41
Seitel, Inc., 47
Select Comfort Corporation, 34
Selmer Company, Inc., The, 19
SEMCO Energy, Inc., 44
Seminis, Inc., 29
Semitool, Inc., 18
Sempra Energy, 25 (upd.)
Semtech Corporation, 32
Seneca Foods Corporation, 17
Sensormatic Electronics Corp., 11
Sensory Science Corporation, 37
Sepracor Inc., 45
Sequa Corp., 13
Serta, Inc., 28
Service America Corp., 7
Service Corporation International, 6
Service Merchandise Company, Inc., V; 19 (upd.)
ServiceMaster Inc., 6; 23 (upd.)
7-11, Inc., 32 (upd.)
Sevenson Environmental Services, Inc., 42
SFX Entertainment, Inc., 36
SGI, 29 (upd.)
Shakespeare Company, 22
Shaklee Corporation, 12; 39 (upd.)
Shared Medical Systems Corporation, 14
Sharper Image Corporation, The, 10
Shaw Industries, Inc., 9; 40 (upd.)
Shawmut National Corporation, 13
Shearman & Sterling, 32
Shearson Lehman Brothers Holdings Inc., II; 9 (upd.)
Shelby Williams Industries, Inc., 14
Sheldahl Inc., 23
Shell Oil Company, IV; 14 (upd.); 41 (upd.)
Sheller-Globe Corporation, I
Shells Seafood Restaurants, Inc., 43
Sherwin-Williams Company, The, III; 13 (upd.)
Shoe Carnival Inc., 14
Shoney's, Inc., 7; 23 (upd.)
ShopKo Stores Inc., 21
Shorewood Packaging Corporation, 28
ShowBiz Pizza Time, Inc., 13
Showboat, Inc., 19
Shubert Organization Inc., 24
Sidley Austin Brown & Wood, 40
Siebel Systems, Inc., 38
Siebert Financial Corp., 32
Sierra Club, The, 28
Sierra Health Services, Inc., 15
Sierra On-Line, Inc., 15; 41 (upd.)
Sierra Pacific Industries, 22
SIFCO Industries, Inc., 41
Sigma-Aldrich Corporation, I; 36 (upd.)
Signet Banking Corporation, 11
Sikorsky Aircraft Corporation, 24
Silicon Graphics Incorporated, 9
SilverPlatter Information Inc., 23
Silverstein Properties, Inc., 47
Simmons Company, 47
Simon & Schuster Inc., IV; 19 (upd.)
Simon Property Group, Inc., 27
Simon Transportation Services Inc., 27
Simplex Technologies Inc., 21
Simpson Investment Company, 17
Simpson Thacher & Bartlett, 39
Simula, Inc., 41
Sinclair Broadcast Group, Inc., 25
Sir Speedy, Inc., 16
Six Flags Theme Parks, Inc., 17
Skadden, Arps, Slate, Meagher & Flom, 18
Skechers USA Inc., 31
Skidmore, Owings & Merrill, 13
Skyline Corporation, 30
SkyMall, Inc., 26
SkyWest, Inc., 25
SL Green Realty Corporation, 44
Sleepy's Inc., 32
SLI, Inc., 48
Slim-Fast Nutritional Foods International, Inc., 18
SLM Holding Corp., 25 (upd.)
Smart & Final, Inc., 16
SmartForce PLC, 43
Smead Manufacturing Co., 17
Smith & Wesson Corporation, 30
Smith Barney Inc., 15
Smith Corona Corp., 13
Smith International, Inc., 15
Smith's Food & Drug Centers, Inc., 8
Smithfield Foods, Inc., 7; 43 (upd.)
SmithKline Beckman Corporation, I
Smithsonian Institution, 27
Smithway Motor Xpress Corporation, 39
Smurfit-Stone Container Corporation, 26 (upd.)
Snap-On, Incorporated, 7; 27 (upd.)
Snapple Beverage Corporation, 11
Snell & Wilmer L.L.P., 28
Society Corporation, 9
Soft Sheen Products, Inc., 31
Solectron Corporation, 12; 48 (upd.)
Solo Serve Corporation, 28
Sonat, Inc., 6
Sonesta International Hotels Corporation, 44
Sonic Corp., 14; 37 (upd.)
Sonoco Products Company, 8
Soros Fund Management LLC, 28
Sorrento, Inc., 24
SOS Staffing Services, 25
Sotheby's Holdings, Inc., 11; 29 (upd.)
Sound Advice, Inc., 41
South Jersey Industries, Inc., 42
Southdown, Inc., 14
Southern Company, The, V; 38 (upd.)
Southern Indiana Gas and Electric Company, 13
Southern New UK Telecommunications Corporation, 6
Southern Pacific Transportation Company, V
Southern States Cooperative Incorporated, 36
Southern Union Company, 27
Southland Corporation, The, II; 7 (upd.)
Southtrust Corporation, 11
Southwest Airlines Co., 6; 24 (upd.)
Southwest Gas Corporation, 19
Southwest Water Company, 47
Southwestern Bell Corporation, V
Southwestern Electric Power Co., 21
Southwestern Public Service Company, 6
Southwire Company, Inc., 8; 23 (upd.)
Spacehab, Inc., 37
Spaghetti Warehouse, Inc., 25
Spangler Candy Company, 44
Spanish Broadcasting System, Inc., 41
Spartan Motors Inc., 14
Spartan Stores Inc., 8
Spartech Corporation, 19
Sparton Corporation, 18
Spec's Music, Inc., 19
Specialty Coatings Inc., 8
Specialty Equipment Companies, Inc., 25
SpeeDee Oil Change and Tune-Up, 25
Speedway Motorsports, Inc., 32
Speizman Industries, Inc., 44
Spelling Entertainment, 14; 35 (upd.)
Spencer Stuart and Associates, Inc., 14
Spiegel, Inc., 10; 27 (upd.)
Spirit Airlines, Inc., 31
Sport Chalet, Inc., 16
Sport Supply Group, Inc., 23
Sportmart, Inc., 15
Sports & Recreation, Inc., 17
Sports Authority, Inc., The, 16; 43 (upd.)
Sports Club Company, The, 25
Sportsman's Guide, Inc., The, 36
Springs Industries, Inc., V; 19 (upd.)
Sprint Communications Company, L.P., 9
Sprint Corporation, 46 (upd.)
SPS Technologies, Inc., 30
SPX Corporation, 10; 47 (upd.)
Squibb Corporation, I
Stage Stores, Inc., 24
Stanadyne Automotive Corporation, 37
Standard Commercial Corporation, 13
Standard Federal Bank, 9
Standard Microsystems Corporation, 11
Standard Motor Products, Inc., 40
Standard Register Co., 15
Standex International Corporation, 17; 44 (upd.)
Stanhome Inc., 15
Stanley Furniture Company, Inc., 34
Stanley Works, The, III; 20 (upd.)
Staples, Inc., 10
Star Banc Corporation, 11
Starbucks Corporation, 13; 34 (upd.)
Starcraft Corporation, 30
Starrett Corporation, 21
Starter Corp., 12
State Farm Mutual Automobile Insurance Company, III
State Street Boston Corporation, 8

Staten Island Bancorp, Inc., 39
Station Casinos Inc., 25
Steak n Shake Company, The, 41
Stearns, Inc., 43
Steelcase, Inc., 7; 27 (upd.)
Stein Mart Inc., 19
Steinway Musical Properties, Inc., 19
Stepan Company, 30
Stericycle Inc., 33
STERIS Corporation, 29
Sterling Chemicals, Inc., 16
Sterling Drug, Inc., I
Sterling Electronics Corp., 18
Sterling Software, Inc., 11
Stevedoring Services of America Inc., 28
Steven Madden, Ltd., 37
Stewart & Stevenson Services Inc., 11
Stewart Enterprises, Inc., 20
Stewart's Beverages, 39
Stillwater Mining Company, 47
Stock Yards Packing Co., Inc., 37
Stone & Webster, Inc., 13
Stone Container Corporation, IV
Stone Manufacturing Company, 14; 43 (upd.)
Stop & Shop Companies, Inc., The, II; 24 (upd.)
Storage Technology Corporation, 6
Storage USA, Inc., 21
Stouffer Corp., 8
StrataCom, Inc., 16
Stratus Computer, Inc., 10
Stride Rite Corporation, The, 8; 37 (upd.)
Stroh Brewery Company, The, I; 18 (upd.)
Stroock & Stroock & Lavan LLP, 40
Strouds, Inc., 33
Stryker Corporation, 11; 29 (upd.)
Stuart Entertainment Inc., 16
Student Loan Marketing Association, II
Stuller Settings, Inc., 35
Sturm, Ruger & Company, Inc., 19
Sub-Zero Freezer Co., Inc., 31
Suburban Propane Partners, L.P., 30
Subway, 32
Successories, Inc., 30
Sudbury Inc., 16
Suiza Foods Corporation, 26
Sullivan & Cromwell, 26
Summit Bancorporation, The, 14
Summit Family Restaurants, Inc. 19
Sun Communities Inc., 46
Sun Company, Inc., IV
Sun Country Airlines, 30
Sun Distributors L.P., 12
Sun Healthcare Group Inc., 25
Sun Microsystems, Inc., 7; 30 (upd.)
Sun Sportswear, Inc., 17
Sun Television & Appliances Inc., 10
Sun-Diamond Growers of California, 7
SunAmerica Inc., 11
Sunbeam-Oster Co., Inc., 9
Sunburst Hospitality Corporation, 26
Sundstrand Corporation, 7; 21 (upd.)
Sundt Corp., 24
SunGard Data Systems Inc., 11
Sunglass Hut International, Inc., 21
Sunkist Growers, Inc., 26
Sunoco, Inc., 28 (upd.)
Sunrider Corporation, The, 26
Sunrise Medical Inc., 11
SunTrust Banks Inc., 23
Super Food Services, Inc., 15
Super Valu Stores, Inc., II
Supercuts Inc., 26
Superior Industries International, Inc., 8
Superior Uniform Group, Inc., 30
Supermarkets General Holdings Corporation, II
Supervalu Inc., 18 (upd.)
Suprema Specialties, Inc., 27
Supreme International Corporation, 27
Susquehanna Pfaltzgraff Company, 8
Sutter Home Winery Inc., 16
Sverdrup Corporation, 14
Swank Inc., 17
Sweetheart Cup Company, Inc., 36
Swift Transportation Co., Inc., 42
Swinerton Inc., 43
Swisher International Group Inc., 23
Sybase, Inc., 10; 27 (upd.)
Sybron International Corp., 14
Sycamore Networks, Inc., 45
Sykes Enterprises, Inc., 45
Sylvan Learning Systems, Inc., 35
Sylvan, Inc., 22
Symantec Corporation, 10
Symbol Technologies, Inc., 15
Syms Corporation, 29
Synopsis, Inc., 11
SynOptics Communications, Inc., 10
Synovus Financial Corp., 12
Syntex Corporation, I
SyQuest Technology, Inc., 18
Syratech Corp., 14
SYSCO Corporation, II; 24 (upd.)
System Software Associates, Inc., 10
Systems & Computer Technology Corp., 19
T-Netix, Inc., 46
T. Rowe Price Associates, Inc., 11; 34 (upd.)
TAB Products Co., 17
Taco Bell Corp., 7; 21 (upd.)
Taco Cabana, Inc., 23
Taco John's International Inc., 15
Take-Two Interactive Software, Inc., 46
Talbots, Inc., The, 11; 31 (upd.)
Talley Industries, Inc., 16
Tambrands Inc., 8
Tandem Computers, Inc., 6
Tandy Corporation, II; 12 (upd.)
Tandycrafts, Inc., 31
Target Stores, 10; 27 (upd.)
Tarragon Realty Investors, Inc., 45
Tasty Baking Company, 14; 35 (upd.)
Tattered Cover Book Store, 43
Taylor Corporation, 36
Taylor Guitars, 48
Taylor Made Golf Co., 23
Taylor Publishing Company, 12; 36 (upd.)
TBWA Advertising, Inc., 6
TBWA\Chiat\Day, 43 (upd.)
TCBY Enterprises Inc., 17
TCF Financial Corporation, 47
Teachers Insurance and Annuity Association-College Retirement Equities Fund, III; 45 (upd.)
TearDrop Golf Company, 32
Tech Data Corporation, 10
Tech-Sym Corporation, 18; 44 (upd.)
Technitrol, Inc., 29
TECO Energy, Inc., 6
Tecumseh Products Company, 8
Tejon Ranch Company, 35
Tektronix, Inc., 8
Tele-Communications, Inc., II
Teledyne, Inc., I; 10 (upd.)
Telephone and Data Systems, Inc., 9
Tellabs, Inc., 11; 40 (upd.)
Telxon Corporation, 10
Temple-Inland Inc., IV; 31 (upd.)
TenFold Corporation, 35
Tennant Company, 13; 33 (upd.)
Tenneco Inc., I; 10 (upd.)
Teradyne, Inc., 11
Terex Corporation, 7; 40 (upd.)
Terlato Wine Group, The, 48
Terra Industries, Inc., 13
Tesoro Petroleum Corporation, 7; 45 (upd.)
Tetra Tech, Inc., 29
Texaco Inc., IV; 14 (upd.); 41 (upd.)
Texas Air Corporation, I
Texas Industries, Inc., 8
Texas Instruments Inc., II; 11 (upd.); 46 (upd.)
Texas Pacific Group Inc., 36
Texas Utilities Company, V; 25 (upd.)
Textron Inc., I , 34 (upd.)
Textron Lycoming Turbine Engine, 9
Thermadyne Holding Corporation, 19
Thermo BioAnalysis Corp., 25
Thermo Electron Corporation, 7
Thermo Fibertek, Inc., 24
Thermo Instrument Systems Inc., 11
Thermo King Corporation, 13
Thermos Company, 16
Thiokol Corporation, 9; 22 (upd.)
Thomas & Betts Corp., 11
Thomas Cook Travel Inc., 9; 33 (upd.)
Thomas H. Lee Co., 24
Thomas Industries Inc., 29
Thomas J. Lipton Company, 14
Thomas Nelson, Inc., 14; 38 (upd.)
Thomas Publishing Company, 26
Thomaston Mills, Inc., 27
Thomasville Furniture Industries, Inc., 12
Thor Industries, Inc., 39
Thorn Apple Valley, Inc., 7; 22 (upd.)
Thousand Trails, Inc., 33
THQ, Inc., 39
3Com Corporation, 11; 34 (upd.)
3DO Company, The, 43
Thrifty PayLess, Inc., 12
Ticketmaster Group, Inc., 13; 37 (upd.)
Tidewater Inc., 11; 37 (upd.)
Tiffany & Co., 14
TIG Holdings, Inc., 26
Tillotson Corp., 15
Timberland Company, The, 13
Timberline Software Corporation, 15
Time Warner Inc., IV; 7 (upd.)
Times Mirror Company, The, IV; 17 (upd.)
Timex Corporation, 7; 25 (upd.)
Timken Company, The, 8; 42 (upd.)
Tishman Speyer Properties, L.P., 47
Titan Corporation, The, 36
Titanium Metals Corporation, 21
TJ International, Inc., 19
TJX Companies, Inc., The, V; 19 (upd.)
TLC Beatrice International Holdings, Inc., 22
TMP Worldwide Inc., 30
TNT Freightways Corporation, 14
Today's Man, Inc., 20
Todd Shipyards Corporation, 14
Todd-AO Corporation, The, 33
Todhunter International, Inc., 27
Tokheim Corporation, 21
Toll Brothers Inc., 15
Tollgrade Communications, Inc., 44
Tom Brown, Inc., 37
Tom Doherty Associates Inc., 25
Tom's of Maine, Inc., 45
Tombstone Pizza Corporation, 13
Tone Brothers, Inc., 21
Tonka Corporation, 25
Tootsie Roll Industries Inc., 12
Topps Company, Inc., The, 13; 34 (upd.)
Tops Appliance City, Inc., 17
Torchmark Corporation, 9; 33 (upd.)
Toro Company, The, 7; 26 (upd.)
Torrington Company, The, 13
Tosco Corporation, 7

**United States** *(continued)*


Total Entertainment Restaurant Corporation, 46
Total System Services, Inc., 18
Totem Resources Corporation, 9
Tower Air, Inc., 28
Tower Automotive, Inc., 24
Towers Perrin, 32
Town & Country Corporation, 19
Town Sports International, Inc., 46
Toy Biz, Inc., 18
Toymax International, Inc., 29
Toys 'R'' Us, Inc., V; 18 (upd.)
Tracor Inc., 17
Trader Joe's Co., 13
Trailer Bridge, Inc., 41
Trammell Crow Company, 8
Trans World Airlines, Inc., I; 12 (upd.); 35 (upd.)
Trans World Entertainment Corporation, 24
Transaction Systems Architects, Inc., 29
Transamerica Corporation, I; 13 (upd.)
Transamerica–An AEGON Company, 41 (upd.)
Transatlantic Holdings, Inc., 11
Transco Energy Company, V
Transmedia Network Inc., 20
TransMontaigne Inc., 28
Transocean Sedco Forex Inc., 45
Tranzonic Companies, The, 37
Travel Ports of America, Inc., 17
Travelers Corporation, The, III
Travelocity.com, Inc., 46
Travis Boats & Motors, Inc., 37
TRC Companies, Inc., 32
Treadco, Inc., 19
Treasure Chest Advertising Company, Inc., 32
Tree of Life, Inc., 29
Trek Bicycle Corporation, 16
Trend-Lines, Inc., 22
Trendwest Resorts, Inc., 33
Tri Valley Growers, 32
Triarc Companies, Inc., 8; 34 (upd.)
Tribune Company, IV; 22 (upd.)
Trico Products Corporation, 15
Trigen Energy Corporation, 42
TriMas Corp., 11
Trimble Navigation Limited, 40
Trinity Industries, Incorporated, 7
TRINOVA Corporation, III
Triton Energy Corporation, 11
Triumph Group, Inc., 31
TRM Copy Centers Corporation, 18
Tropicana Products, Inc., 28
True North Communications Inc., 23
Trump Organization, 23
TruServ Corporation, 24
TRW Inc., I; 11 (upd.); 14 (upd.)
TTX Company, 6
Tucson Electric Power Company, 6
Tuesday Morning Corporation, 18
Tultex Corporation, 13
Tumbleweed, Inc., 33
Tupperware Corporation, 28
Turner Broadcasting System, Inc., II; 6 (upd.)
Turner Corporation, The, 8; 23 (upd.)
Turtle Wax, Inc., 15
Tuscarora Inc., 29
TV Guide, Inc., 43 (upd.)
TVI, Inc., 15
TW Services, Inc., II
Tweeter Home Entertainment Group, Inc., 30
Twentieth Century Fox Film Corporation, II; 25 (upd.)
Twin Disc, Inc., 21
Twinlab Corporation, 34
Ty Inc., 33
Tyco Toys, Inc., 12
Tyler Corporation, 23
Tyson Foods, Incorporated, II; 14 (upd.)
U S West, Inc., V; 25 (upd.)
U.S. Aggregates, Inc., 42
U.S. Bancorp, 14; 36 (upd.)
U.S. Borax, Inc., 42
U.S. Can Corporation, 30
U.S. Cellular Corporation, 31 (upd.)
U.S. Delivery Systems, Inc., 22
U.S. Foodservice, 26
U.S. Healthcare, Inc., 6
U.S. Home Corporation, 8
U.S. News and World Report Inc., 30
U.S. Office Products Company, 25
U.S. Robotics Inc., 9
U.S. Satellite Broadcasting Company, Inc., 20
U.S. Timberlands Company, L.P., 42
U.S. Trust Corp., 17
UAL Corporation, 34 (upd.)
UGI Corporation, 12
Ugly Duckling Corporation, 22
UICI, 33
Ukrop's Super Market's, Inc., 39
Ultimate Electronics, Inc., 18
Ultra Pac, Inc., 24
Ultrak Inc., 24
Ultramar Diamond Shamrock Corporation, 31 (upd.)
Uncle Ben's Inc., 22
Underwriters Laboratories, Inc., 30
Uni-Marts, Inc., 17
Unicom Corporation, 29 (upd.)
Unifi, Inc., 12
UniFirst Corporation, 21
Union Bank of California, 16
Union Camp Corporation, IV
Union Carbide Corporation, I; 9 (upd.)
Union Electric Company, V
Union Pacific Corporation, V; 28 (upd.)
Union Texas Petroleum Holdings, Inc., 9
Unique Casual Restaurants, Inc., 27
Unison HealthCare Corporation, 25
Unisys Corporation, III; 6 (upd.); 36 (upd.)
United Airlines, I; 6 (upd.)
United Auto Group, Inc., 26
United Brands Company, II
United Defense, L.P., 30
United Dominion Industries Limited, 8; 16 (upd.)
United Foods, Inc., 21
United HealthCare Corporation, 9
United Illuminating Company, The, 21
United Industrial Corporation, 37
United Jewish Communities, 33
United Merchants & Manufacturers, Inc., 13
United Natural Foods, Inc., 32
United Parcel Service of America Inc., V; 17 (upd.)
United Press International, Inc., 25
United Rentals, Inc., 34
United Retail Group Inc., 33
United States Cellular Corporation, 9
United States Filter Corporation, 20
United States Postal Service, 14; 34 (upd.)
United States Shoe Corporation, The, V
United States Surgical Corporation, 10; 34 (upd.)
United Stationers Inc., 14
United Technologies Automotive Inc., 15
United Technologies Corporation, I; 10 (upd.); 34 (upd.)
United Telecommunications, Inc., V
United Video Satellite Group, 18
United Water Resources, Inc., 40
United Way of America, 36
Unitil Corporation, 37
Unitog Co., 19
Unitrin Inc., 16
Univar Corporation, 9
Universal Corporation, V; 48 (upd.)
Universal Electronics Inc., 39
Universal Foods Corporation, 7
Universal Forest Products Inc., 10
Universal Health Services, Inc., 6
Universal International, Inc., 25
Universal Studios, Inc., 33
Univision Communications Inc., 24
Uno Restaurant Corporation, 18
Unocal Corporation, IV; 24 (upd.)
UNUM Corp., 13
Upjohn Company, The, I; 8 (upd.)
Urban Outfitters, Inc., 14
URS Corporation, 45
US Airways Group, Inc., 28 (upd.)
USA Interactive, Inc., 47 (upd.)
USA Truck, Inc., 42
USAA, 10
USAir Group, Inc., I; 6 (upd.)
USANA, Inc., 29
USF&G Corporation, III
USG Corporation, III; 26 (upd.)
UST Inc., 9
USX Corporation, IV; 7 (upd.)
Utah Medical Products, Inc., 36
Utah Power and Light Company, 27
UtiliCorp United Inc., 6
UUNET, 38
Vail Resorts, Inc., 11; 43 (upd.)
Valassis Communications, Inc., 8; 37 (upd.)
Valero Energy Corporation, 7
Valhi, Inc., 19
Vallen Corporation, 45
Valley Media Inc., 35
Valmont Industries, Inc., 19
Valspar Corporation, The, 8; 32 (upd.)
Value City Department Stores, Inc., 38
Value Line, Inc., 16
Value Merchants Inc., 13
ValueVision International, Inc., 22
Van Camp Seafood Company, Inc., 7
Vanguard Group, Inc., The, 14; 34 (upd.)
Vans, Inc., 16; 47 (upd.)
Varco International, Inc., 42
Vari-Lite International, Inc., 35
Varian Associates Inc., 12
Varian, Inc., 48 (upd.)
Varlen Corporation, 16
Varsity Spirit Corp., 15
Vastar Resources, Inc., 24
VECO International, Inc., 7
Vector Group Ltd., 35 (upd.)
Veeco Instruments Inc., 32
Veit Companies, 43
Venator Group Inc., 35 (upd.)
Vencor, Inc., 16
Venetian Casino Resort, LLC, 47
Venture Stores Inc., 12
Verbatim Corporation, 14
VeriFone, Inc., 18
VeriSign, Inc., 47
Veritas Software Corporation, 45
Verizon Communications, 43 (upd.)
Vermeer Manufacturing Company, 17
Vermont Teddy Bear Co., Inc., The, 36
VF Corporation, V; 17 (upd.)
Viacom Inc., 7; 23 (upd.)
Viasoft Inc., 27
Viatech Continental Can Company, Inc., 25 (upd.)

Vicon Industries, Inc., 44
VICORP Restaurants, Inc., 12; 48 (upd.)
Vienna Sausage Manufacturing Co., 14
Viking Office Products, Inc., 10
Village Super Market, Inc., 7
Village Voice Media, Inc., 38
Vinson & Elkins L.L.P., 30
Vintage Petroleum, Inc., 42
Virco Manufacturing Corporation, 17
Visa International, 9; 26 (upd.)
Vishay Intertechnology, Inc., 21
Vista Chemical Company, I
Vistana, Inc., 22
VISX, Incorporated, 30
Vitalink Pharmacy Services, Inc., 15
Vitesse Semiconductor Corporation, 32
Vitro Corp., 10
Vivra, Inc., 18
Vlasic Foods International Inc., 25
VLSI Technology, Inc., 16
Volt Information Sciences Inc., 26
Vons Companies, Incorporated, The, 7; 28 (upd.)
Vornado Realty Trust, 20
Vulcan Materials Company, 7
W. Atlee Burpee & Co., 27
W.H. Brady Co., 17
W.L. Gore & Associates, Inc., 14
W.R. Berkley Corp., 15
W.R. Grace & Company, I
W.W. Grainger, Inc., V; 26 (upd.)
W.W. Norton & Company, Inc., 28
Waban Inc., 13
Wabash National Corp., 13
Wabtec Corporation, 40
Wachovia Bank of Georgia, N.A., 16
Wachovia Bank of South Carolina, N.A., 16
Wachovia Corporation, 12; 46 (upd.)
Wachtell, Lipton, Rosen & Katz, 47
Wackenhut Corporation, The, 14
Waddell & Reed, Inc., 22
Waffle House Inc., 14
Waggener Edstrom, 42
Wakefern Food Corporation, 33
Wal-Mart Stores, Inc., V; 8 (upd.); 26 (upd.)
Walbridge Aldinger Co., 38
Walbro Corporation, 13
Waldbaum, Inc., 19
Walden Book Company Inc., 17
Walgreen Co., V; 20 (upd.)
Walker Manufacturing Company, 19
Wall Drug Store, Inc., 40
Wall Street Deli, Inc., 33
Wallace Computer Services, Inc., 36
Walt Disney Company, The, II; 6 (upd.); 30 (upd.)
Walter Industries, Inc., II; 22 (upd.)
Walton Monroe Mills, Inc., 8
Wang Laboratories, Inc., III; 6 (upd.)
Warnaco Group Inc., The, 12; 46 (upd.)
Warner Communications Inc., II
Warner-Lambert Co., I; 10 (upd.)
Washington Companies, The, 33
Washington Federal, Inc., 17
Washington Football, Inc., 35
Washington Gas Light Company, 19
Washington Mutual, Inc., 17
Washington National Corporation, 12
Washington Natural Gas Company, 9
Washington Post Company, The, IV; 20 (upd.)
Washington Scientific Industries, Inc., 17
Washington Water Power Company, 6
Waste Connections, Inc., 46
Waste Holdings, Inc., 41
Waste Management, Inc., V
Water Pik Technologies, Inc., 34
Waterhouse Investor Services, Inc., 18
Waters Corporation, 43
Watkins-Johnson Company, 15
Watson Pharmaceuticals Inc., 16
Watson Wyatt Worldwide, 42
Watts Industries, Inc., 19
Waverly, Inc., 16
Wawa Inc., 17
Waxman Industries, Inc., 9
WD-40 Company, 18
Weatherford International, Inc., 39
Weber-Stephen Products Co., 40
Wegmans Food Markets, Inc., 9; 41 (upd.)
Weider Nutrition International, Inc., 29
Weight Watchers International Inc., 12; 33 (upd.)
Weiner's Stores, Inc., 33
Weirton Steel Corporation, IV; 26 (upd.)
Weis Markets, Inc., 15
Weitz Company, Inc., The, 42
Welbilt Corp., 19
Wellman, Inc., 8
WellPoint Health Networks Inc., 25
Wells Fargo & Company, II; 12 (upd.); 38 (upd.)
Wells Rich Greene BDDP, 6
Wells' Dairy, Inc., 36
Wells-Gardner Electronics Corporation, 43
Wendy's International, Inc., 8; 23 (upd.); 47 (upd.)
Wenner Media, Inc., 32
Werner Enterprises, Inc., 26
West Bend Co., 14
West Coast Entertainment Corporation, 29
West Corporation, 42
West Group, 34 (upd.)
West Marine, Inc., 17
West One Bancorp, 11
West Pharmaceutical Services, Inc., 42
West Point-Pepperell, Inc., 8
West Publishing Co., 7
Westaff Inc., 33
Westamerica Bancorporation, 17
Western Atlas Inc., 12
Western Beef, Inc., 22
Western Company of North America, 15
Western Digital Corp., 25
Western Gas Resources, Inc., 45
Western Publishing Group, Inc., 13
Western Resources, Inc., 12
Western Wireless Corporation, 36
Westin Hotels and Resorts Worldwide, 9; 29 (upd.)
Westinghouse Electric Corporation, II; 12 (upd.)
Westmoreland Coal Company, 7
WestPoint Stevens Inc., 16
Westvaco Corporation, IV; 19 (upd.)
Westwood One, Inc., 23
Wet Seal, Inc., The, 18
Wetterau Incorporated, II
Weyco Group, Incorporated, 32
Weyerhaeuser Company, IV; 9 (upd.); 28 (upd.)
Wheaton Industries, 8
Wheelabrator Technologies, Inc., 6
Wheeling-Pittsburgh Corp., 7
Wherehouse Entertainment Incorporated, 11
Whirlpool Corporation, III; 12 (upd.)
White & Case LLP, 35
White Castle System, Inc., 12; 36 (upd.)
White Consolidated Industries Inc., 13
White Rose, Inc., 24
Whitman Corporation, 10 (upd.)
Whitman Education Group, Inc., 41
Whitney Holding Corporation, 21
Whittaker Corporation, I; 48 (upd.)
Whole Foods Market, Inc., 20
Wickes Inc., V; 25 (upd.)
Wild Oats Markets, Inc., 19; 41 (upd.)
Wildlife Conservation Society, 31
Willamette Industries, Inc., IV; 31 (upd.)
William Morris Agency, Inc., 23
Williams & Connolly LLP, 47
Williams Communications Group, Inc., 34
Williams Companies, Inc., The, IV; 31 (upd.)
Williams-Sonoma, Inc., 17; 44 (upd.)
Williamson-Dickie Manufacturing Company, 14; 45 (upd.)
Wilmington Trust Corporation, 25
Wilson Sonsini Goodrich & Rosati, 34
Wilson Sporting Goods Company, 24
Wilsons The Leather Experts Inc., 21
Wind River Systems, Inc., 37
Windmere Corporation, 16
Wine Group, Inc., The, 39
Winn-Dixie Stores, Inc., II; 21 (upd.)
Winnebago Industries Inc., 7; 27 (upd.)
WinsLoew Furniture, Inc., 21
Winston & Strawn, 35
Wisconsin Bell, Inc., 14
Wisconsin Central Transportation Corporation, 24
Wisconsin Dairies, 7
Wisconsin Energy Corporation, 6
Wisconsin Public Service Corporation, 9
Witco Corporation, I; 16 (upd.)
Wizards of the Coast Inc., 24
WLR Foods, Inc., 21
Wm. Wrigley Jr. Company, 7
WMS Industries, Inc., 15
WMX Technologies Inc., 17
Wolfgang Puck Food Company, Inc., The, 26
Wolohan Lumber Co., 19
Wolverine Tube Inc., 23
Wolverine World Wide Inc., 16
Wood-Mode, Inc., 23
Woodward Governor Co., 13
Woolworth Corporation, V; 20 (upd.)
WordPerfect Corporation, 10
Working Assets Funding Service, 43
World Bank Group, 33
World Book, Inc., 12
World Color Press Inc., 12
World Duty Free Americas, Inc., 29 (upd.)
World Fuel Services Corporation, 47
World Wrestling Federation Entertainment, Inc., 32
World's Finest Chocolate Inc., 39
WorldCorp, Inc., 10
Worldwide Restaurant Concepts, Inc., 47
Worthington Foods, Inc., 14
Worthington Industries, Inc., 7; 21 (upd.)
WPL Holdings, Inc., 6
WTD Industries, Inc., 20
Wyant Corporation, 30
Wyle Electronics, 14
Wyman-Gordon Company, 14
Wynn's International, Inc., 33
Wyse Technology, Inc., 15
X-Rite, Inc., 48
Xerox Corporation, III; 6 (upd.); 26 (upd.)
Xilinx, Inc., 16
Yahoo! Inc., 27
Yankee Candle Company, Inc., The, 37
YankeeNets LLC, 35
Yellow Corporation, 14; 45 (upd.)
Yellow Freight System, Inc. of Delaware, V
YES! Entertainment Corporation, 26
YMCA of the USA, 31
YOCREAM International, Inc., 47

**United States** *(continued)*

York International Corp., 13
York Research Corporation, 35
Young & Rubicam, Inc., I; 22 (upd.)
Young Broadcasting Inc., 40
Young Innovations, Inc., 44
Young's Market Company, LLC, 32
Younkers, Inc., 19
Youth Services International, Inc., 21
Yucaipa Cos., 17
YWCA of the United States, 45
Zale Corporation, 16; 40 (upd.)
Zany Brainy, Inc., 31
Zapata Corporation, 25
Zebra Technologies Corporation, 14
Zenith Data Systems, Inc., 10
Zenith Electronics Corporation, II; 13 (upd.); 34 (upd.)
Zero Corporation, 17
Ziebart International Corporation, 30
Ziegler Companies, Inc., The, 24
Ziff Communications Company, 12
Ziff Davis Media Inc., 36 (upd.)
Zila, Inc., 46
Zilog, Inc., 15
Zimmer Holdings, Inc., 45
Zion's Cooperative Mercantile Institution, 33
Zions Bancorporation, 12
Zippo Manufacturing Company, 18
Zoltek Companies, Inc., 37
Zondervan Publishing House, 24
Zoom Telephonics, Inc., 18
Zygo Corporation, 42
Zytec Corporation, 19

## Venezuela

Cerveceria Polar, I
Petróleos de Venezuela S.A., IV

## Wales

Hyder plc, 34
Iceland Group plc, 33
Kwik Save Group plc, 11

## Zambia

Zambia Industrial and Mining Corporation Ltd., IV

# *NOTES ON CONTRIBUTORS*

# Notes on Contributors

**AMOROSINO, Chris.** Connecticut-based freelance writer.

**BIANCO, David.** Freelance writer, editor, and publishing consultant.

**BRENNAN, Gerald E.** Freelance writer based in California.

**BRYNILDSSEN, Shawna.** Freelance writer and editor based in Bloomington, Indiana.

**CAMPBELL, June.** Freelance writer and Internet marketer living in Vancouver, Canada.

**COHEN, M. L.** Novelist and freelance writer living in Paris.

**COVELL, Jeffrey L.** Seattle-based freelance writer.

**DINGER, Ed.** Brooklyn-based freelance writer and editor.

**FIERO, John W.** Freelance writer, researcher, and consultant.

**GREENLAND, Paul R.** Illinois-based writer and researcher; author of two books and former senior editor of a national business magazine; contributor to *The Encyclopedia of Chicago History* (University of Chicago Press) and *Company Profiles for Students.*

**HALASZ, Robert.** Former editor in chief of *World Progress* and *Funk & Wagnalls New Encyclopedia Yearbook*; author, *The U.S. Marines* (Millbrook Press, 1993).

**HAUSER, Evelyn.** Researcher, writer and marketing specialist based in Arcata, California; expertise includes historical and trend research in such topics as globalization, emerging industries and lifestyles, future scenarios, biographies, and the history of organizations.

**INGRAM, Frederick C.** Utah-based business writer who has contributed to *GSA Business, Appalachian Trailway News,* the *Encyclopedia of Business,* the *Encyclopedia of Global Industries,* the *Encyclopedia of Consumer Brands,* and other regional and trade publications.

**KARL, Lisa Musolf.** Freelance editor, writer, and columnist living in the Chicago area.

**LEMIEUX, Gloria A.** Freelance writer and editor living in Nashua, New Hampshire.

**LORENZ, Sarah Ruth.** Minnesota-based freelance writer.

**MONTGOMERY, Bruce P.** Curator and director of historical collection, University of Colorado at Boulder.

**ROTHBURD, Carrie.** Freelance writer and editor specializing in corporate profiles, academic texts, and academic journal articles.

**STANSELL, Christina M.** Freelance writer and editor based in Farmington Hills, Michigan.

**TRADII, Mary.** Freelance writer based in Denver, Colorado.

**UHLE, Frank.** Ann Arbor-based freelance writer; movie projectionist, disc jockey, and staff member of *Psychotronic Video* magazine.

**WALDEN, David M.** Freelance writer and historian in Salt Lake City; adjunct history instructor at Salt Lake City Community College.

**WOODWARD, A.** Freelance writer.